2025 FAR/AIM

Federal Aviation Regulations / Aeronautical Information Manual

Rules and Procedures for Aviators
U.S. Department of Transportation
From Titles 14 and 49 of the Code of Federal Regulations

AVIATION SUPPLIES & ACADEMICS, INC.
NEWCASTLE, WASHINGTON

FAR/AIM
Federal Aviation Regulations and Aeronautical Information Manual
2025 Edition

Aviation Supplies & Academics, Inc.
7005 132nd Place SE
Newcastle, Washington 98059
asa@asa2fly.com | 425-235-1500 | asa2fly.com

This publication contains current regulations as of May 10, 2024.
The *Aeronautical Information Manual* is current through March 21, 2024.

Visit the FAA's website to review changes to the regulations:
www.faa.gov/regulations_policies/faa_regulations/

Visit **asa2fly.com/farupdate** for regulation and *AIM* changes released after this printing date. ASA provides a free Update service with email notification when rules and procedures change.

Front cover photo: © Ethan O'Rourke

ASA-25-FR-AM-BK
ISBN 978-1-64425-368-7

Additional formats available:
eBook EPUB ISBN 978-1-64425-370-0
eBook PDF ISBN 978-1-64425-371-7

Printed in the United States of America

2025 2024 9 8 7 6 5 4 3 2 1

Stay informed with ASA online resources.

Website

asa2fly.com

Updates

asa2fly.com/farupdate

Follow, like, share.

instagram.com/asa2fly
facebook.com/asa2fly
youtube.com/asa2fly
linkedin.com/company/asa2fly

2025 FAR/AIM

Federal Aviation Regulations / Aeronautical Information Manual

Contents

Additional Online Resources

Stay current on all regulation changes
that affect this book with ASA's free
Update service: **asa2fly.com/farupdate**

Access ASA's suggested study list
of AIM paragraphs and regulations
pertinent to specific pilot certificates
and ratings: **asa2fly.com/faraim**

Introduction

ASA 2025 FAR/AIM Series
FAR/AIM • FAR for Flight Crew • FAR for AMT

ASA has been supplying the standard reference of the industry, the FAR/AIM series, for nearly 80 years. The 2025 series continues to provide the Federal Aviation Regulations and the *Aeronautical Information Manual* along with these important features:

- All changes since the last edition are clearly identified.
- Access to online suggested study list of *AIM* paragraphs and regulations pertinent to specific pilot certificates and ratings (see asa2fly.com/faraim).
- Index includes both FAR and *AIM* terms to provide an alphabetized listing of subject matter for quick look-up.
- *AIM* produced with full-color graphics.

Each regulation Part is preceded by a table of contents. Changes since last year's printing are identified on page vii and in the table of contents for each regulation Part (in bold and marked with an asterisk), as well as within the text for quick reference (changed text is indicated with a bold line in the margin). In the *AIM*, changes are explained in a list at the beginning and with bold lines in the margins. It is recommended that you familiarize yourself with all the changes to identify those that affect your aviation activities.

Changes affecting the regulations can take place daily; the *AIM* changes every 6 months. ASA tracks all changes and offers you two options for free **Updates** at **asa2fly.com/farupdate**:

- You can download the latest Updates from the ASA website anytime.
- You may sign up for ASA's free service to have Update notices automatically emailed to you.

Visit the Federal Aviation Administration (FAA) website at www.faa.gov to review Advisory Circulars (AC), Notices of Proposed Rulemaking (NPRM), current regulations, FSDO contact details, and FAA Orders and publications. Pilots operating internationally should be familiar with Customs and Border Protection regulations, which can be found at cbp.gov.

Although ASA is not a government agency, and we do not write the regulations or the *AIM*, we do work closely with the FAA. Questions or concerns can be forwarded to our attention, and we will in turn pass the comments on to the responsible office within the agency. The FAA is interested in user feedback and your comments could foster improvements in the regulations that affect the entire industry.

FAR/AIM Comments
Aviation Supplies & Academics, Inc.
7005 132nd Place SE
Newcastle, Washington 98059

Website asa2fly.com
Email asa@asa2fly.com

Identifying Regulation Changes Since Last Year

Changes since last year's printing of the book are noted in the table of contents of each Part with an asterisk and bold title:

Example:

> ***61.5 Certificates and ratings issued
> under this part.**

The updated text within the context of the regulation is indicated by a bold line in the margin:

> **(a)** The following certificates are issued under this part to an applicant who satisfactorily accomplishes the training and certification requirements for the certificate sought:
> (1) Pilot certificates—
> (i) Student pilot.
> (ii) Sport pilot.
> (iii) Recreational pilot.
> (iv) Private pilot.
> (v) Commercial pilot.
> (vi) Airline transport pilot.
> (2) Flight instructor certificates.
> (3) Ground instructor certificates.

How to Identify the Currency of the Regulations

In each Part following the Table of Contents is a Source, with the date of origin for that regulation.

Example:

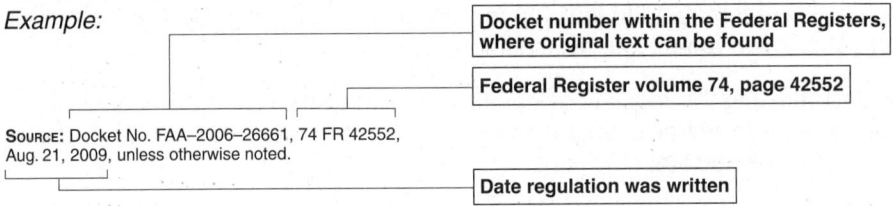

Docket number within the Federal Registers, where original text can be found

Federal Register volume 74, page 42552

Source: Docket No. FAA–2006–26661, 74 FR 42552, Aug. 21, 2009, unless otherwise noted.

Date regulation was written

If a change has taken place since the original Regulation was written, it is noted at the end of the regulation.

Example:

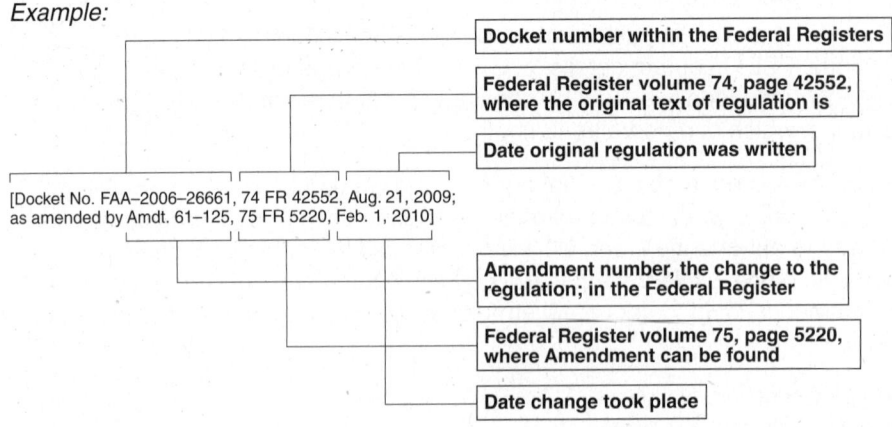

Docket number within the Federal Registers

Federal Register volume 74, page 42552, where the original text of regulation is

Date original regulation was written

[Docket No. FAA–2006–26661, 74 FR 42552, Aug. 21, 2009; as amended by Amdt. 61–125, 75 FR 5220, Feb. 1, 2010]

Amendment number, the change to the regulation; in the Federal Register

Federal Register volume 75, page 5220, where Amendment can be found

Date change took place

Summary of Major FAR Changes Since 2024 Book Was Published

All changes are identified in the table of contents of each Part with bold Section titles and asterisks and in the regulation text with bold lines in the margins.

These regulation changes from the *Federal Register* affect this book as follows:

14 CFR

Part 5:

- Updates requirements for safety management systems and requires certain certificate holders and commercial air tour operators to develop and implement a safety management system (SMS).

Part 43

- Amends the Automatic Dependent Surveillance–Broadcast (ADS-B) Out requirements to allow aircraft meeting the performance requirements in Technical Standard Order (TSO)-C166c or TSO-C154d to meet the regulations.

Part 61

- Revises certain regulations governing airman certification by incorporating by reference the FAA Airman Certification Standards and Practical Test Standards into the certification requirements for pilots and flight instructors.

Part 71

- Amends regulations relating to airspace designations to reflect the incorporation by reference of FAA Order JO 7400.11H, Airspace Designations and Reporting Points.

Part 91

- Amends the regulatory definitions of certain air carrier and commercial operations to add powered-lift to these definitions to ensure the appropriate sets of rules apply to air carriers' and certain commercial operators' operations of aircraft that FAA regulations define as powered-lift.
- Amends the Automatic Dependent Surveillance–Broadcast (ADS-B) Out requirements to allow aircraft meeting the performance requirements in Technical Standard Order (TSO)-C166c or TSO-C154d to meet the regulations.
- Updates certain basic requirements that apply to management specifications that persons who participate in a fractional ownership program under Part 91, Subpart K, must maintain.
- Updates requirements for safety management systems and requires certain certificate holders and commercial air tour operators to develop and implement a safety management system (SMS).
- Extends SFAR No. 79—Prohibition Against Certain Flights in the Pyongyang Flight Information Region (FIR) (ZKKP).
- Removes SFAR No. 113—Prohibition Against Certain Flights in Specified Areas of the Dnipro Flight Information Region (FIR) (UKDV).
- Extends SFAR No. 114—Prohibition Against Certain Flights in the Damascus Flight Information Region (FIR) (OSTT).

(continued)

- Amends SFAR No. 115—Prohibition Against Certain Flights in Specified Areas of the Sanaa Flight Information Region (FIR) (OYSC) to update the current waypoint names and locations.
- Adds SFAR No. 119—Prohibition Against Certain Flights in the Kabul Flight Information Region (FIR) (OAKX).

Part 110

- Amends the regulatory definitions of certain air carrier and commercial operations to add powered-lift to these definitions to ensure the appropriate sets of rules apply to air carriers' and certain commercial operators' operations of aircraft that FAA regulations define as powered-lift.

Part 119

- Amends the regulatory definitions of certain air carrier and commercial operations to add powered-lift to these definitions to ensure the appropriate sets of rules apply to air carriers' and certain commercial operators' operations of aircraft that FAA regulations define as powered-lift.
- Updates requirements for safety management systems and requires certain certificate holders and commercial air tour operators to develop and implement a safety management system (SMS).

Part 136

- Amends the regulatory definitions of certain air carrier and commercial operations to add powered-lift to these definitions to ensure the appropriate sets of rules apply to air carriers' and certain commercial operators' operations of aircraft that FAA regulations define as powered-lift.

49 CFR

Part 1552:

- Amends the Flight Training Security Program (FTSP) rule (formerly known as the Alien Flight Student Program) to prevent flight schools from providing flight training to any individuals who are not U.S. citizens or nationals, and who have not been vetted by the Federal Government to determine whether the flight training candidate is a security threat.

The *Aeronautical Information Manual* printed in this book is current through March 21, 2024. The major changes are summarized in the *AIM* introductory text.

Note: Changes affecting the regulations can take place daily. ASA tracks all changes and posts them on the ASA website so you always have the most current information. To view the rules currently in effect and to have Update notices automatically emailed to you, visit **asa2fly.com/farupdate**.

Pilot's Bill of Rights

The following legislative excerpt was signed into law by the U.S. Congress. It is law pertinent to the aviation industry that is outside the usual placement of Title 14 or 49 Code of Federal Regulations, but is included here since it has a direct effect on all pilots. Current congressional bills can be found at govtrack.us/congress/bills/.

Public Law 112–153
112th Congress

An Act

To amend title 49, United States Code, to provide rights for pilots, and for other purposes.

Be it enacted by the Senate and House of Representatives of the United States of America in Congress assembled,

SECTION 1. SHORT TITLE.

This Act may be cited as the "Pilot's Bill of Rights".

SEC. 2. FEDERAL AVIATION ADMINISTRATION ENFORCEMENT PROCEEDINGS AND ELIMINATION OF DEFERENCE.

(a) IN GENERAL.—Any proceeding conducted under subpart C, D, or F of part 821 of title 49, Code of Federal Regulations, relating to denial, amendment, modification, suspension, or revocation of an airman certificate, shall be conducted, to the extent practicable, in accordance with the Federal Rules of Civil Procedure and the Federal Rules of Evidence.

(b) ACCESS TO INFORMATION.—

(1) IN GENERAL.—Except as provided under paragraph (3), the Administrator of the Federal Aviation Administration (referred to in this section as the "Administrator") shall provide timely, written notification to an individual who is the subject of an investigation relating to the approval, denial, suspension, modification, or revocation of an airman certificate under chapter 447 of title 49, United States Code.

(2) INFORMATION REQUIRED.—The notification required under paragraph (1) shall inform the individual—
(A) of the nature of the investigation;
(B) that an oral or written response to a Letter of Investigation from the Administrator is not required;
(C) that no action or adverse inference can be taken against the individual for declining to respond to a Letter of Investigation from the Administrator;
(D) that any response to a Letter of Investigation from the Administrator or to an inquiry made by a representative of the Administrator by the individual may be used as evidence against the individual;
(E) that the releasable portions of the Administrator's investigative report will be available to the individual; and
(F) that the individual is entitled to access or otherwise obtain air traffic data described in paragraph (4).

(3) EXCEPTION.—The Administrator may delay timely notification under paragraph (1) if the Administrator determines that such notification may threaten the integrity of the investigation.

(4) ACCESS TO AIR TRAFFIC DATA.—

 (A) FAA AIR TRAFFIC DATA.—The Administrator shall provide an individual described in paragraph (1) with timely access to any air traffic data in the possession of the Federal Aviation Administration that would facilitate the individual's ability to productively participate in a proceeding relating to an investigation described in such paragraph.

 (B) AIR TRAFFIC DATA DEFINED.—As used in subparagraph (A), the term "air traffic data" includes—

 (i) relevant air traffic communication tapes;

 (ii) radar information;

 (iii) air traffic controller statements;

 (iv) flight data;

 (v) investigative reports; and

 (vi) any other air traffic or flight data in the Federal Aviation Administration's possession that would facilitate the individual's ability to productively participate in the proceeding.

 (C) GOVERNMENT CONTRACTOR AIR TRAFFIC DATA.—

 (i) IN GENERAL.—Any individual described in paragraph (1) is entitled to obtain any air traffic data that would facilitate the individual's ability to productively participate in a proceeding relating to an investigation described in such paragraph from a government contractor that provides operational services to the Federal Aviation Administration, including control towers and flight service stations.

 (ii) REQUIRED INFORMATION FROM INDIVIDUAL.—The individual may obtain the information described in clause (i) by submitting a request to the Administrator that—

 (I) describes the facility at which such information is located; and

 (II) identifies the date on which such information was generated.

 (iii) PROVISION OF INFORMATION TO INDIVIDUAL.—If the Administrator receives a request under this subparagraph, the Administrator shall—

 (I) request the contractor to provide the requested information; and

 (II) upon receiving such information, transmitting the information to the requesting individual in a timely manner.

(5) TIMING.—Except when the Administrator determines that an emergency exists under section 44709(c)(2) or 46105(c), the Administrator may not proceed against an individual that is the subject of an investigation described in paragraph (1) during the 30-day period beginning on the date on which the air traffic data required under paragraph (4) is made available to the individual.

(c) AMENDMENTS TO TITLE 49.—

(1) AIRMAN CERTIFICATES.—Section 44703(d)(2) of title 49, United States Code, is amended by striking "but is bound by all validly adopted interpretations of laws and regulations the Administrator carries out unless the Board finds an interpretation is arbitrary, capricious, or otherwise not according to law".

(2) AMENDMENTS, MODIFICATIONS, SUSPENSIONS, AND REVOCATIONS OF CERTIFICATES.—Section 44709(d)(3) of such title is amended by striking "but is bound by all validly adopted interpretations of laws and regulations the Administrator carries out and of written agency policy guidance available to the public related to sanctions to be imposed under this section unless the Board finds an interpretation is arbitrary, capricious, or otherwise not according to law".

(3) REVOCATION OF AIRMAN CERTIFICATES FOR CONTROLLED SUBSTANCE VIOLATIONS.—Section 44710(d)(1) of such title is amended by striking "but shall be bound by all validly adopted interpretations of laws and regulations the Administrator carries out and of written agency policy guidance available to the public related to sanctions to be imposed under this section unless the Board finds an interpretation is arbitrary, capricious, or otherwise not according to law".

(d) APPEAL FROM CERTIFICATE ACTIONS.—

(1) IN GENERAL.—Upon a decision by the National Transportation Safety Board upholding an order or a final decision by the Administrator denying an airman certificate under section 44703(d) of title 49, United States Code, or imposing a punitive civil action or an emergency order of revocation under subsections (d) and (e) of section 44709 of such title, an individual substantially affected by an order of the Board may, at the individual's election, file an appeal in the United States district court in which the individual resides or in which the action in question occurred, or in the United States District Court for the District of Columbia. If the individual substantially affected by an order of the Board elects not to file an appeal in a United States district court, the individual may file an appeal in an appropriate United States court of appeals.

(2) EMERGENCY ORDER PENDING JUDICIAL REVIEW.—Subsequent to a decision by the Board to uphold an Administrator's emergency order under section 44709(e)(2) of title 49, United States Code, and absent a stay of the enforcement of that order by the Board, the emergency order of amendment, modification, suspension, or revocation of a certificate shall remain in effect, pending the exhaustion of an appeal to a Federal district court as provided in this Act.

(e) STANDARD OF REVIEW.—

(1) IN GENERAL.—In an appeal filed under subsection (d) in a United States district court, the district court shall give full independent review of a denial, suspension, or revocation ordered by the Administrator, including substantive independent and expedited review of any decision by the Administrator to make such order effective immediately.

(2) EVIDENCE.—A United States district court's review under paragraph (1) shall include in evidence any record of the proceeding before the Administrator and any record of the proceeding before the National Transportation Safety Board, including hearing testimony, transcripts, exhibits, decisions, and briefs submitted by the parties.

SEC. 3. NOTICES TO AIRMEN.

(a) IN GENERAL.—

(1) DEFINITION.—In this section, the term "NOTAM" means Notices to Airmen.

(2) IMPROVEMENTS.—Not later than 180 days after the date of the enactment of this Act, the Administrator of the Federal Aviation Administration shall begin a Notice to Airmen Improvement Program (in this section referred to as the "NOTAM Improvement Program")—

(A) to improve the system of providing airmen with pertinent and timely information regarding the national airspace system;
(B) to archive, in a public central location, all NOTAMs, including the original content and form of the notices, the original date of publication, and any amendments to such notices with the date of each amendment; and
(C) to apply filters so that pilots can prioritize critical flight safety information from other airspace system information.

(b) GOALS OF PROGRAM.—The goals of the NOTAM Improvement Program are—

(1) to decrease the overwhelming volume of NOTAMs an airman receives when retrieving airman information prior to a flight in the national airspace system;

(2) make the NOTAMs more specific and relevant to the airman's route and in a format that is more useable to the airman;

(3) to provide a full set of NOTAM results in addition to specific information requested by airmen;

(4) to provide a document that is easily searchable; and

(5) to provide a filtering mechanism similar to that provided by the Department of Defense Notices to Airmen.

(c) ADVICE FROM PRIVATE SECTOR GROUPS.—The Administrator shall establish a NOTAM Improvement Panel, which shall be comprised of representatives of relevant nonprofit and not-for-profit general aviation pilot groups, to advise the Administrator in carrying out the goals of the NOTAM Improvement Program under this section.

(d) PHASE-IN AND COMPLETION.—The improvements required by this section shall be phased in as quickly as practicable and shall be completed not later than the date that is 1 year after the date of the enactment of this Act.

SEC. 4. MEDICAL CERTIFICATION.

(a) ASSESSMENT.—

(1) IN GENERAL.—Not later than 180 days after the date of the enactment of this Act, the Comptroller General of the United States shall initiate an assessment of the Federal Aviation Administration's medical certification process and the associated medical standards and forms.

(2) REPORT.—The Comptroller General shall submit a report to Congress based on the assessment required under paragraph (1) that examines—

(A) revisions to the medical application form that would provide greater clarity and guidance to applicants;

(B) the alignment of medical qualification policies with present-day qualified medical judgment and practices, as applied to an individual's medically relevant circumstances; and

(C) steps that could be taken to promote the public's understanding of the medical requirements that determine an airman's medical certificate eligibility.

(b) GOALS OF THE FEDERAL AVIATION ADMINISTRATION'S MEDICAL CERTIFICATION PROCESS.—The goals of the Federal Aviation Administration's medical certification process are—

(1) to provide questions in the medical application form that—

(A) are appropriate without being overly broad;

(B) are subject to a minimum amount of misinterpretation and mistaken responses;

(C) allow for consistent treatment and responses during the medical application process; and

(D) avoid unnecessary allegations that an individual has intentionally falsified answers on the form;

(2) to provide questions that elicit information that is relevant to making a determination of an individual's medical qualifications within the standards identified in the Administrator's regulations;

(3) to give medical standards greater meaning by ensuring the information requested aligns with present-day medical judgment and practices; and

(4) to ensure that—

 (A) the application of such medical standards provides an appropriate and fair evaluation of an individual's qualifications; and

 (B) the individual understands the basis for determining medical qualifications.

(c) ADVICE FROM PRIVATE SECTOR GROUPS.—The Administrator shall establish a panel, which shall be comprised of representatives of relevant nonprofit and not-for-profit general aviation pilot groups, aviation medical examiners, and other qualified medical experts, to advise the Administrator in carrying out the goals of the assessment required under this section.

(d) FEDERAL AVIATION ADMINISTRATION RESPONSE.—Not later than 1 year after the issuance of the report by the Comptroller General pursuant to subsection (a)(2), the Administrator shall take appropriate actions to respond to such report.

Approved August 3, 2012.

LEGISLATIVE HISTORY—S. 1335:
CONGRESSIONAL RECORD, Vol. 158 (2012):
June 29, considered and passed Senate.
July 23, considered and passed House.

FAR Parts Listed in Titles 14 and 49 of the Code of Federal Regulations

Regulations available from ASA and FAA.

Part	Title	FAR/AIM book	FAR-FC book	FAR-AMT book	FAR/AIM app	FAR-AMT app	www.faa.gov
14 CFR Aeronautics and Space							
Chapter I							
Subchapter A—Definitions and General Requirements							
1	Definitions and abbreviations	•	•	•	•	•	•
3	General requirements			•		•	•
5	Safety management systems	•	•	•	•	•	•
Subchapter B—Procedural Rules							
11	General rulemaking procedures						•
13	Investigative and enforcement procedures				•	•	•
14	Rules implementing the Equal Access to Justice Act of 1980						•
15	Administrative claims under Federal Tort Claims Act						•
16	Rules of practice for Federally-assisted airport enforcement proceedings						•
17	Procedures for protests and contract disputes						•
Subchapter C—Aircraft							
21	Certification procedures for products and articles			•	•	•	•
23	Airworthiness standards: Normal category airplanes			•	•	•	•
25	Airworthiness standards: Transport category airplanes				•	•	•
26	Continued airworthiness and safety improvements for transport category airplanes			•		•	•
27	Airworthiness standards: Normal category rotorcraft			•	•	•	•
29	Airworthiness standards: Transport category rotorcraft				•	•	•
31	Airworthiness standards: Manned free balloons						•
33	Airworthiness standards: Aircraft engines			•		•	•
34	Fuel venting and exhaust emission requirements for turbine engine powered airplanes			•		•	•
35	Airworthiness standards: Propellers			•		•	•
36	Noise standards: Aircraft type and airworthiness certification						•
38	Airplane fuel efficiency certification			•		•	•
39	Airworthiness directives			•	•	•	•
43	Maintenance, preventive maintenance, rebuilding, and alteration	•		•	•	•	•
45	Identification and registration marking			•		•	•
47	Aircraft registration			•		•	•
48	Registration and marking requirements for small unmanned aircraft	•		•	•	•	•
49	Recording of aircraft titles and security documents						•
50-59	*[Reserved]*						
Subchapter D—Airmen							
60	Flight simulation training device initial and continuing qualification and use						•
61	Certification: Pilots, flight instructors, and ground instructors	•			•		•
63	Certification: Flight crewmembers other than pilots		•		•		•
65	Certification: Airmen other than flight crewmembers			•	•	•	•
67	Medical standards and certification	•			•		•
68	Requirements for operating certain small aircraft without a medical certificate	•			•		•

Part	Title	FAR/AIM book	FAR-FC book	FAR-AMT book	FAR/AIM app	FAR-AMT app	www.faa.gov
Subchapter E—Airspace							
71	Designation of class A, B, C, D, and E airspace areas; air traffic service routes; and reporting points	•			•		•
73	Special use airspace	•			•		•
75	*[Reserved]*						
77	Safe, efficient use, and preservation of the navigable airspace						•
Subchapter F—Air Traffic and General Operating Rules							
89	Remote identification of unmanned aircraft	•			•		•
91	General operating and flight rules	•	•*	•	•	•	•
93	Special air traffic rules						•
95	IFR altitudes						•
97	Standard instrument procedures	•			•		•
99	Security control of air traffic						•
101	Moored balloons, kites, amateur rockets, and unmanned free balloons						•
103	Ultralight vehicles	•			•		•
105	Parachute operations	•			•		•
106	*[Reserved]*						
107	Small unmanned aircraft systems	•			•		•
108-109	*[Reserved]*						
Subchapter G—Air Carriers and Operators for Compensation or Hire: Certification and Operations							
110	General requirements	•	•	•	•	•	•
111	Pilot Records Database		•		•		•
112-116	*[Reserved]*						
117	Flight and duty limitations and rest requirements: Flightcrew members		•		•		•
118	*[Reserved]*						
119	Certification: Air carriers and commercial operators	•	•	•	•	•	•
120	Drug and alcohol testing program		•		•		•
121	Operating requirements: Domestic, flag, and supplemental operations		•	•**	•	•	•
125	Certification and operations: Airplanes having a seating capacity of 20 or more passengers or a maximum payload capacity of 6,000 pounds or more; and rules governing persons on board such aircraft			•	•	•	•
129	Operations: Foreign air carriers and foreign operators of U.S.-registered aircraft engaged in common carriage						•
133	Rotorcraft external-load operations					•	•
135	Operating requirements: Commuter and on-demand operations and rules governing persons on board such aircraft		•	•	•	•	•
136	Commercial air tours and national parks air tour management	•			•		•
137	Agricultural aircraft operations	•			•		•
139	Certification of airports						•
Subchapter H—Schools and Other Certificated Agencies							
140	*[Reserved]*						
141	Pilot schools	•			•		•
142	Training centers	•			•		•
143	*[Reserved]*						
145	Repair stations			•		•	•
147	Aviation maintenance technician schools			•		•	•

Part	Title	FAR/AIM book	FAR-FC book	FAR-AMT book	FAR/AIM app	FAR-AMT app	www.faa.gov
Subchapter I—Airports							
150	Airport noise compatibility planning						•
151	Federal aid to airports						•
152	Airport aid program						•
153	Airport operations						•
155	Release of airport property from surplus property disposal restrictions						•
156	State block grant pilot program						•
157	Notice of construction, alteration, activation, and deactivation of airports						•
158	Passenger facility charges (PFCs)						•
161	Notice and approval of airport noise and access restrictions						•
169	Expenditure of Federal funds for nonmilitary airports or air navigation facilities thereon						•
Subchapter J—Navigational Facilities							
170	Establishment and discontinuance criteria for air traffic control services and navigational facilities						•
171	Non-Federal navigation facilities						•
Subchapter K—Administrative Regulations							
183	Representatives of the Administrator			•		•	•
185	Testimony by employees and production of records in legal proceedings, and service of legal process and pleadings						•
187	Fees						•
189	Use of Federal Aviation Administration communications system						•
193	Protection of voluntarily submitted information						•
Subchapters L through M [Reserved]							
Subchapter N—War Risk Insurance							
198	Aviation insurance						•
199	[Reserved]						
Chapter II							
Subchapter D—Special Regulations							
375	Navigation of foreign civil aircraft within the United States						•
49 CFR Transportation							
Subtitle B—Other Regulations Pertaining to Transportation							
172	Hazardous materials table, special provisions, hazardous materials communications, emergency response information, training requirements, and security plans				•		•
175	Hazardous materials: Carriage by aircraft			•	•		•
830	Notification and reporting of aircraft accidents or incidents and overdue aircraft, and preservation of aircraft wreckage, mail, cargo, and records	•			•		•
1544	Aircraft operator security: Air carriers and commercial operators		•		•		•
1552	Flight schools	•			•		•

* ASA's FAR-FC book contains Part 91, Subpart K only.
** ASA's FAR-AMT book contains Part 121, Subparts J, L, Z, AA, and DD only

Pilots operating internationally should be familiar with Customs and Border Protection regulations, which can be found at cbp.gov.

FAR Contents

Federal Aviation Regulations (from Titles 14 and 49 Code of Federal Regulations)

Part tabs: 1 | 5 | 43 | 48 | 61 | 67 | 68 | 71 | 73 | 89 | 91 | 97 | 103 | 105 | 107 | 110 | 119 | 136 | 137 | 141 | 142 | 49 CFR

PART 1

DEFINITIONS AND ABBREVIATIONS

Sec.
1.1 General definitions.
1.2 Abbreviations and symbols.
1.3 Rules of construction.

Authority: 49 U.S.C. 106(f), 106(g), 40113, 44701.

§1.1 General definitions.

As used in Subchapters A through K of this chapter, unless the context requires otherwise:

Administrator means the Federal Aviation Administrator or any person to whom he has delegated his authority in the matter concerned.

Aerodynamic coefficients means nondimensional coefficients for aerodynamic forces and moments.

Air carrier means a person who undertakes directly by lease, or other arrangement, to engage in air transportation.

Air commerce means interstate, overseas, or foreign air commerce or the transportation of mail by aircraft or any operation or navigation of aircraft within the limits of any Federal airway or any operation or navigation of aircraft which directly affects, or which may endanger safety in, interstate, overseas, or foreign air commerce.

Aircraft means a device that is used or intended to be used for flight in the air.

Aircraft engine means an engine that is used or intended to be used for propelling aircraft. It includes turbosuperchargers, appurtenances, and accessories necessary for its functioning, but does not include propellers.

Airframe means the fuselage, booms, nacelles, cowlings, fairings, airfoil surfaces (including rotors but excluding propellers and rotating airfoils of engines), and landing gear of an aircraft and their accessories and controls.

Airplane means an engine-driven fixed-wing aircraft heavier than air, that is supported in flight by the dynamic reaction of the air against its wings.

Airport means an area of land or water that is used or intended to be used for the landing and takeoff of aircraft, and includes its buildings and facilities, if any.

Airship means an engine-driven lighter-than-air aircraft that can be steered.

Air traffic means aircraft operating in the air or on an airport surface, exclusive of loading ramps and parking areas.

Air traffic clearance means an authorization by air traffic control, for the purpose of preventing collision between known aircraft, for an aircraft to proceed under specified traffic conditions within controlled airspace.

Air traffic control means a service operated by appropriate authority to promote the safe, orderly, and expeditious flow of air traffic.

Air Traffic Service (ATS) route is a specified route designated for channeling the flow of traffic as necessary for the provision of air traffic services. The term "ATS route" refers to a variety of airways, including jet routes, area navigation (RNAV) routes, and arrival and departure routes. An ATS route is defined by route specifications, which may include:

(1) An ATS route designator;

(2) The path to or from significant points;

(3) Distance between significant points;

(4) Reporting requirements; and

(5) The lowest safe altitude determined by the appropriate authority.

Air transportation means interstate, overseas, or foreign air transportation or the transportation of mail by aircraft.

Alert Area. An alert area is established to inform pilots of a specific area wherein a high volume of pilot training or an unusual type of aeronautical activity is conducted.

Alternate airport means an airport at which an aircraft may land if a landing at the intended airport becomes inadvisable.

Altitude engine means a reciprocating aircraft engine having a rated takeoff power that is producible from sea level to an established higher altitude.

Amateur rocket means an unmanned rocket that:

(1) Is propelled by a motor or motors having a combined total impulse of 889,600 Newton-seconds (200,000 pound-seconds) or less; and

(2) Cannot reach an altitude greater than 150 kilometers (93.2 statute miles) above the earth's surface.

Appliance means any instrument, mechanism, equipment, part, apparatus, appurtenance, or accessory, including communications equipment, that is used or intended to be used in operating or controlling an aircraft in flight, is installed in or attached to the aircraft, and is not part of an airframe, engine, or propeller.

Approved, unless used with reference to another person, means approved by the FAA or any person to whom the FAA has delegated its authority in the matter concerned, or approved under the provisions of a bilateral agreement between the United States and a foreign country or jurisdiction.

Area navigation (RNAV) is a method of navigation that permits aircraft operations on any desired flight path.

Area navigation (RNAV) route is an ATS route based on RNAV that can be used by suitably equipped aircraft.

Armed Forces means the Army, Navy, Air Force, Marine Corps, and Coast Guard, including their regular and reserve components and members serving without component status.

Autorotation means a rotorcraft flight condition in which the lifting rotor is driven entirely by action of the air when the rotorcraft is in motion.

Auxiliary rotor means a rotor that serves either to counteract the effect of the main rotor torque on a rotorcraft or to maneuver the rotorcraft about one or more of its three principal axes.

Balloon means a lighter-than-air aircraft that is not engine driven, and that sustains flight through the use of either gas buoyancy or an airborne heater.

Brake horsepower means the power delivered at the propeller shaft (main drive or main output) of an aircraft engine.

Calibrated airspeed means the indicated airspeed of an aircraft, corrected for position and instrument error. Calibrated airspeed is equal to true airspeed in standard atmosphere at sea level.

Canard means the forward wing of a canard configuration and may be a fixed, movable, or variable geometry surface, with or without control surfaces.

Canard configuration means a configuration in which the span of the forward wing is substantially less than that of the main wing.

Category:

(1) As used with respect to the certification, ratings, privileges, and limitations of airmen, means a broad classification of aircraft. Examples include: airplane; rotorcraft; glider; and lighter-than-air; and

(2) As used with respect to the certification of aircraft, means a grouping of aircraft based upon intended use or operating limitations. Examples include: transport, normal, utility, acrobatic, limited, restricted, and provisional.

Category A, with respect to transport category rotorcraft, means multiengine rotorcraft designed with engine and system isolation features specified in Part 29 and utilizing scheduled takeoff and landing operations under a critical engine failure concept which assures adequate designated surface area and adequate performance capability for continued safe flight in the event of engine failure.

Category B, with respect to transport category rotorcraft, means single-engine or multiengine rotorcraft which do not fully meet all Category A standards. Category B rotorcraft have no guaranteed stay-up ability in the event of engine failure and unscheduled landing is assumed.

Category II operations, with respect to the operation of aircraft, means a straight-in ILS approach to the runway of an airport under a Category II ILS instrument approach procedure issued by the Administrator or other appropriate authority.

Category III operations, with respect to the operation of aircraft, means an ILS approach to, and landing on, the runway of an airport using a Category III ILS instrument approach procedure issued by the Administrator or other appropriate authority.

Ceiling means the height above the earth's surface of the lowest layer of clouds or obscuring phenomena that is reported as "broken," "overcast," or "obscuration," and not classified as "thin" or "partial."

Civil aircraft means aircraft other than public aircraft.

Class:

(1) As used with respect to the certification, ratings, privileges, and limitations of airmen, means a classification of aircraft within a category having similar operating characteristics. Examples include: single engine; multiengine; land; water; gyroplane; helicopter; airship; and free balloon; and

(2) As used with respect to the certification of aircraft, means a broad grouping of aircraft having similar characteristics of propulsion, flight, or landing. Examples include: airplane; rotorcraft; glider; balloon; landplane; and seaplane.

Clearway means:

(1) For turbine engine powered airplanes certificated after August 29, 1959, an area beyond the runway, not less than 500 feet wide, centrally located about the extended centerline of the runway, and under the control of the airport authorities. The clearway is expressed in terms of a clearway plane, extending from the end of the runway with an upward slope not exceeding 1.25 percent, above which no object nor any terrain protrudes. However, threshold lights may protrude above the plane if their height above the end of the runway is 26 inches or less and if they are located to each side of the runway.

(2) For turbine engine powered airplanes certificated after September 30, 1958, but before August 30, 1959, an area beyond the takeoff runway extending no less than 300 feet on either side of the extended centerline of the runway, at an elevation no higher than the elevation of the end of the runway, clear of all fixed obstacles, and under the control of the airport authorities.

Climbout speed, with respect to rotorcraft, means a referenced airspeed which results in a flight path clear of the height-velocity envelope during initial climbout.

Commercial operator means a person who, for compensation or hire, engages in the carriage by aircraft in air commerce of persons or property, other than as an air carrier or foreign air carrier or under the authority of Part 375 of this title. Where it is doubtful that an operation is for "compensation or hire", the test applied is whether the carriage by air is merely incidental to the person's other business or is, in itself, a major enterprise for profit.

Configuration, Maintenance, and Procedures (CMP) document means a document approved by the FAA that contains minimum configuration, operating, and maintenance requirements, hardware life-limits, and Master Minimum Equipment List (MMEL) constraints necessary for an airplane-engine combination to meet ETOPS type design approval requirements.

Consensus standard means, for the purpose of certificating light-sport aircraft, an industry-developed consensus standard that applies to aircraft design, production, and airworthiness. It includes, but is not limited to, standards for aircraft design and performance, required equipment, manufacturer quality assurance systems, production acceptance test procedures, operating instructions, maintenance and inspection procedures, identification and recording of major repairs and major alterations, and continued airworthiness.

Controlled airspace means an airspace of defined dimensions within which air traffic control service is provided to IFR flights and to VFR flights in accordance with the airspace classification.

NOTE—Controlled airspace is a generic term that covers Class A, Class B, Class C, Class D, and Class E airspace.

Controlled Firing Area. A controlled firing area is established to contain activities, which if not conducted in a controlled environment, would be hazardous to nonparticipating aircraft.

Crewmember means a person assigned to perform duty in an aircraft during flight time.

Critical altitude means the maximum altitude at which, in standard atmosphere, it is possible to maintain, at a specified rotational speed, a specified power or a specified manifold pressure. Unless otherwise stated, the critical altitude is the maximum altitude at which it is possible to maintain, at the maximum continuous rotational speed, one of the following:

(1) The maximum continuous power, in the case of engines for which this power rating is the same at sea level and at the rated altitude.

(2) The maximum continuous rated manifold pressure, in the case of engines, the maximum continuous power of which is governed by a constant manifold pressure.

Critical engine means the engine whose failure would most adversely affect the performance or handling qualities of an aircraft.

Decision altitude (DA) is a specified altitude in an instrument approach procedure at which the pilot must decide whether to initiate an immediate missed approach if the pilot does not see the required visual reference, or to continue the approach. Decision altitude is expressed in feet above mean sea level.

Decision height (DH) is a specified height above the ground in an instrument approach procedure at which the pilot must decide whether to initiate an immediate missed approach if the pilot does not see the required visual reference, or to continue the approach. Decision height is expressed in feet above ground level.

Early ETOPS means ETOPS type design approval obtained without gaining non-ETOPS service experience on the candidate airplane-engine combination certified for ETOPS.

EFVS operation means an operation in which visibility conditions require an EFVS to be used in lieu of natural vision to perform an approach or landing, determine enhanced flight visibility, identify required visual references, or conduct a rollout.

Enhanced flight visibility (EFV) means the average forward horizontal distance, from the cockpit of an aircraft in flight, at which prominent topographical objects may be clearly distinguished and identified by day or night by a pilot using an enhanced flight vision system.

Enhanced flight vision system (EFVS) means an installed aircraft system which uses an electronic means to provide a display of the forward external scene topography (the natural or man-made features of a place or region especially in a way to show their relative positions and elevation) through the use of imaging sensors, including but not limited to forward-looking infrared, millimeter wave radiometry, millimeter wave radar, or low-light level image intensification. An EFVS includes the display element, sensors, computers and power supplies, indications, and controls.

Equivalent airspeed means the calibrated airspeed of an aircraft corrected for adiabatic compressible flow for the particular altitude. Equivalent airspeed is equal to calibrated airspeed in standard atmosphere at sea level.

ETOPS Significant System means an airplane system, including the propulsion system, the failure or malfunctioning of which could adversely affect the safety of an ETOPS flight, or the continued safe flight and landing of an airplane during an ETOPS diversion. Each ETOPS significant system is either an ETOPS group 1 significant system or an ETOPS group 2 significant system.

(1) An ETOPS group 1 Significant System—

(i) Has fail-safe characteristics directly linked to the degree of redundancy provided by the number of engines on the airplane.

(ii) Is a system, the failure or malfunction of which could result in an IFSD, loss of thrust control, or other power loss.

(iii) Contributes significantly to the safety of an ETOPS diversion by providing additional redundancy for any system power source lost as a result of an inoperative engine.

(iv) Is essential for prolonged operation of an airplane at engine inoperative altitudes.

(2) An ETOPS group 2 significant system is an ETOPS significant system that is not an ETOPS group 1 significant system.

Extended Operations (ETOPS) means an airplane flight operation, other than an all-cargo operation in an airplane with more than two engines, during which a portion of the flight is conducted beyond a time threshold identified in part 121 or part 135 of this chapter that is determined using an approved one-engine-inoperative cruise speed under standard atmospheric conditions in still air.

Extended over-water operation means—

(1) With respect to aircraft other than helicopters, an operation over water at a horizontal distance of more than 50 nautical miles from the nearest shoreline; and

(2) With respect to helicopters, an operation over water at a horizontal distance of more than 50 nautical miles from the nearest shoreline and more than 50 nautical miles from an off-shore heliport structure.

External load means a load that is carried, or extends, outside of the aircraft fuselage.

External-load attaching means the structural components used to attach an external load to an aircraft, including external-load containers, the backup structure at the attachment points, and any quick-release device used to jettison the external load.

Final approach fix (FAF) defines the beginning of the final approach segment and the point where final segment descent may begin.

Final takeoff speed means the speed of the airplane that exists at the end of the takeoff path in the en route configuration with one engine inoperative.

Fireproof—

(1) With respect to materials and parts used to confine fire in a designated fire zone, means the capacity to withstand at least as well as steel in dimensions appropriate for the purpose for which they are used, the heat produced when there is a severe fire of extended duration in that zone; and

(2) With respect to other materials and parts, means the capacity to withstand the heat associated with fire at least as well as steel in dimensions appropriate for the purpose for which they are used.

Fire resistant—

(1) With respect to sheet or structural members means the capacity to withstand the heat associated with fire at least as well as aluminum alloy in dimensions appropriate for the purpose for which they are used; and

(2) With respect to fluid-carrying lines, fluid system parts, wiring, air ducts, fittings, and powerplant controls, means the capacity to perform the intended functions under the heat and other conditions likely to occur when there is a fire at the place concerned.

Flame resistant means not susceptible to combustion to the point of propagating a flame, beyond safe limits, after the ignition source is removed.

Flammable, with respect to a fluid or gas, means susceptible to igniting readily or to exploding.

Flap extended speed means the highest speed permissible with wing flaps in a prescribed extended position.

Flash resistant means not susceptible to burning violently when ignited.

Flightcrew member means a pilot, flight engineer, or flight navigator assigned to duty in an aircraft during flight time.

Flight level means a level of constant atmospheric pressure related to a reference datum of 29.92 inches of mercury. Each is stated in three digits that represent hundreds of feet. For example, flight level 250 represents a barometric altimeter indication of 25,000 feet; flight level 255, an indication of 25,500 feet.

Flight plan means specified information, relating to the intended flight of an aircraft, that is filed orally or in writing with air traffic control.

Flight simulation training device (FSTD) means a full flight simulator or a flight training device.

Flight time means:

(1) Pilot time that commences when an aircraft moves under its own power for the purpose of flight and ends when the aircraft comes to rest after landing; or

(2) For a glider without self-launch capability, pilot time that commences when the glider is towed for the purpose of flight and ends when the glider comes to rest after landing.

Flight training device (FTD) means a replica of aircraft instruments, equipment, panels, and controls in an open flight deck area or an enclosed aircraft cockpit replica. It includes the equipment and computer programs necessary to represent aircraft (or set of aircraft) operations in ground and flight conditions having the full range of capabilities of the systems installed in the device as described in part 60 of this chapter and the qualification performance standard (QPS) for a specific FTD qualification level.

Flight visibility means the average forward horizontal distance, from the cockpit of an aircraft in flight, at which prominent unlighted objects may be seen and identified by day and prominent lighted objects may be seen and identified by night.

Foreign air carrier means any person other than a citizen of the United States, who undertakes directly, by lease or other arrangement, to engage in air transportation.

Foreign air commerce means the carriage by aircraft of persons or property for compensation or hire, or the carriage of mail by aircraft, or the operation or navigation of aircraft in the conduct or furtherance of a business or vocation, in commerce between a place in the United States and any place outside thereof; whether such commerce moves wholly by aircraft or partly by aircraft and partly by other forms of transportation.

Foreign air transportation means the carriage by aircraft of persons or property as a common carrier for compensation or hire, or the carriage of mail by aircraft, in commerce between a place in the United States and any place outside of the United States, whether that commerce moves wholly by aircraft or partly by aircraft and partly by other forms of transportation.

Forward wing means a forward lifting surface of a canard configuration or tandem-wing configuration airplane. The surface may be a fixed, movable, or variable geometry surface, with or without control surfaces.

Full flight simulator (FFS) means a replica of a specific type; or make, model, and series aircraft cockpit. It includes the assemblage of equipment and computer programs necessary to represent aircraft operations in ground and flight conditions, a visual system providing an out-of-the-cockpit view, a system that provides cues at least equivalent to those of a three-degree-of-freedom motion system, and has the full range of capabilities of the systems installed in the device as described in part 60 of this chapter and the qualification performance standards (QPS) for a specific FFS qualification level.

Glider means a heavier-than-air aircraft, that is supported in flight by the dynamic reaction of the air against its lifting surfaces and whose free flight does not depend principally on an engine.

Go-around power or thrust setting means the maximum allowable in-flight power or thrust setting identified in the performance data.

Ground visibility means prevailing horizontal visibility near the earth's surface as reported by the United States National Weather Service or an accredited observer.

Gyrodyne means a rotorcraft whose rotors are normally engine-driven for takeoff, hovering, and landing, and for forward flight through part of its speed range, and whose means of propulsion, consisting usually of conventional propellers, is independent of the rotor system.

Gyroplane means a rotorcraft whose rotors are not engine-driven, except for initial starting, but are made to rotate by action of the air when the rotorcraft is moving; and whose means of propulsion, consisting usually of conventional propellers, is independent of the rotor system.

Helicopter means a rotorcraft that, for its horizontal motion, depends principally on its engine-driven rotors.

Heliport means an area of land, water, or structure used or intended to be used for the landing and takeoff of helicopters.

Idle thrust means the jet thrust obtained with the engine power control level set at the stop for the least thrust position at which it can be placed.

IFR conditions means weather conditions below the minimum for flight under visual flight rules.

IFR over-the-top, with respect to the operation of aircraft, means the operation of an aircraft over-the-top on an IFR flight plan when cleared by air traffic control to maintain "VFR conditions" or "VFR conditions on top".

Indicated airspeed means the speed of an aircraft as shown on its pitot static airspeed indicator calibrated to reflect standard atmosphere adiabatic compressible flow at sea level uncorrected for airspeed system errors.

In-flight shutdown (IFSD) means, for ETOPS only, when an engine ceases to function (when the airplane is airborne) and is shutdown, whether self induced, flightcrew initiated or caused by an external influence. The FAA considers IFSD for all causes: for example, flameout, internal failure, flightcrew initiated shutdown, foreign object ingestion, icing, inability to obtain or control desired thrust or power, and cycling of the start control, however briefly, even if the engine operates normally for the remainder of the flight. This definition excludes the airborne cessation of the functioning of an engine when immediately followed by an automatic engine relight and when an engine does not achieve desired thrust or power but is not shutdown.

Instrument means a device using an internal mechanism to show visually or aurally the attitude, altitude, or operation of an aircraft or aircraft part. It includes electronic devices for automatically controlling an aircraft in flight.

Instrument approach procedure (IAP) is a series of predetermined maneuvers by reference to flight instruments with specified protection from obstacles and assurance of navigation signal reception capability. It begins from the initial approach fix, or where applicable, from the beginning of a defined arrival route to a point:

(1) From which a landing can be completed; or

(2) If a landing is not completed, to a position at which holding or en route obstacle clearance criteria apply.

Interstate air commerce means the carriage by aircraft of persons or property for compensation or hire, or the carriage of mail by aircraft, or the operation or navigation of aircraft in the conduct or furtherance of a business or vocation, in commerce between a place in any State of the United States, or the District of Columbia, and a place in any other State of the United States, or the District of Columbia; or between places in the same State of the United States through the airspace over any place outside thereof; or between places in the same territory or possession of the United States, or the District of Columbia.

Interstate air transportation means the carriage by aircraft of persons or property as a common carrier for compensation or hire, or the carriage of mail by aircraft in commerce:

(1) Between a place in a State or the District of Columbia and another place in another State or the District of Columbia;

(2) Between places in the same State through the airspace over any place outside that State; or

(3) Between places in the same possession of the United States;

Whether that commerce moves wholly by aircraft or partly by aircraft and partly by other forms of transportation.

Intrastate air transportation means the carriage of persons or property as a common carrier for compensation or hire, by turbojet-powered aircraft capable of carrying thirty or more persons, wholly within the same State of the United States.

Kite means a framework, covered with paper, cloth, metal, or other material, intended to be flown at the end of a rope or cable, and having as its only support the force of the wind moving past its surfaces.

Landing gear extended speed means the maximum speed at which an aircraft can be safely flown with the landing gear extended.

Landing gear operating speed means the maximum speed at which the landing gear can be safely extended or retracted.

Large aircraft means aircraft of more than 12,500 pounds, maximum certificated takeoff weight.

Lighter-than-air aircraft means aircraft that can rise and remain suspended by using contained gas weighing less than the air that is displaced by the gas.

Light-sport aircraft means an aircraft, other than a helicopter or powered-lift that, since its original certification, has continued to meet the following:

(1) A maximum takeoff weight of not more than—

(i) 1,320 pounds (600 kilograms) for aircraft not intended for operation on water; or

(ii) 1,430 pounds (650 kilograms) for an aircraft intended for operation on water.

(2) A maximum airspeed in level flight with maximum continuous power (V_H) of not more than 120 knots CAS under standard atmospheric conditions at sea level.

(3) A maximum never-exceed speed (V_{NE}) of not more than 120 knots CAS for a glider.

(4) A maximum stalling speed or minimum steady flight speed without the use of lift-enhancing devices (V_{S1}) of not more than 45 knots CAS at the aircraft's maximum certificated takeoff weight and most critical center of gravity.

(5) A maximum seating capacity of no more than two persons, including the pilot.

(6) A single, reciprocating engine, if powered.

(7) A fixed or ground-adjustable propeller if a powered aircraft other than a powered glider.

(8) A fixed or feathering propeller system if a powered glider.

(9) A fixed-pitch, semi-rigid, teetering, two-blade rotor system, if a gyroplane.

(10) A nonpressurized cabin, if equipped with a cabin.

(11) Fixed landing gear, except for an aircraft intended for operation on water or a glider.

(12) Fixed or retractable landing gear, or a hull, for an aircraft intended for operation on water.

(13) Fixed or retractable landing gear for a glider.

Load factor means the ratio of a specified load to the total weight of the aircraft. The specified load is expressed in terms of any of the following: aerodynamic forces, inertia forces, or ground or water reactions.

Long-range communication system (LRCS). A system that uses satellite relay, data link, high frequency, or another approved communication system which extends beyond line of sight.

Long-range navigation system (LRNS). An electronic navigation unit that is approved for use under instrument flight rules as a primary means of navigation, and has at least one source of navigational input, such as inertial navigation system or global positioning system.

Mach number means the ratio of true airspeed to the speed of sound.

Main rotor means the rotor that supplies the principal lift to a rotorcraft.

Maintenance means inspection, overhaul, repair, preservation, and the replacement of parts, but excludes preventive maintenance.

Major alteration means an alteration not listed in the aircraft, aircraft engine, or propeller specifications—

(1) That might appreciably affect weight, balance, structural strength, performance, powerplant operation, flight characteristics, or other qualities affecting airworthiness; or

(2) That is not done according to accepted practices or cannot be done by elementary operations.

Major repair means a repair:

(1) That, if improperly done, might appreciably affect weight, balance, structural strength, performance, powerplant operation, flight characteristics, or other qualities affecting airworthiness; or

(2) That is not done according to accepted practices or cannot be done by elementary operations.

Manifold pressure means absolute pressure as measured at the appropriate point in the induction system and usually expressed in inches of mercury.

Maximum engine overtorque, as it applies to turbopropeller and turboshaft engines incorporating free power turbines for all ratings except one engine inoperative (OEI) ratings of two minutes or less, means the maximum torque of the free power turbine rotor assembly, the inadvertent occurrence of which, for periods of up to 20 seconds, will not require rejection of the engine from service, or any maintenance action other than to correct the cause.

Maximum speed for stability characteristics, V_{FC}/M_{FC} means a speed that may not be less than a speed midway between maximum operating limit speed (V_{MO}/M_{MO}) and demonstrated flight diving speed (V_{DF}/M_{DF}), except that, for altitudes where the Mach number is the limiting factor, M_{FC} need not exceed the Mach number at which effective speed warning occurs.

Medical certificate means acceptable evidence of physical fitness on a form prescribed by the Administrator.

Military operations area. A military operations area (MOA) is airspace established outside Class A airspace to separate or segregate certain non-hazardous military activities from IFR Traffic and to identify for VFR traffic where these activities are conducted.

Minimum descent altitude (MDA) is the lowest altitude specified in an instrument approach procedure, expressed in feet above mean sea level, to which descent is authorized on final approach or during circle-to-land maneuvering until the pilot sees the required visual references for the heliport or runway of intended landing.

Minor alteration means an alteration other than a major alteration.

Minor repair means a repair other than a major repair.

National defense airspace means airspace established by a regulation prescribed, or an order issued under, 49 U.S.C. 40103(b)(3).

Navigable airspace means airspace at and above the minimum flight altitudes prescribed by or under this chapter, including airspace needed for safe takeoff and landing.

Night means the time between the end of evening civil twilight and the beginning of morning civil twilight, as published in the Air Almanac, converted to local time.

Nonprecision approach procedure means a standard instrument approach procedure in which no electronic glide slope is provided.

Operate, with respect to aircraft, means use, cause to use or authorize to use aircraft, for the purpose (except as provided in §91.13 of this chapter) of air navigation including the piloting of aircraft, with or without the right of legal control (as owner, lessee, or otherwise).

Operational control, with respect to a flight, means the exercise of authority over initiating, conducting or terminating a flight.

Overseas air commerce means the carriage by aircraft of persons or property for compensation or hire, or the carriage of mail by aircraft, or the operation or navigation of aircraft in the conduct or furtherance of a business or vocation, in commerce between a place in any State of the United States, or the District of Columbia, and any place in a territory or possession of the United States; or between a place in a territory or possession of the United States, and a place in any other territory or possession of the United States.

Overseas air transportation means the carriage by aircraft of persons or property as a common carrier for compensation or hire, or the carriage of mail by aircraft, in commerce:

(1) Between a place in a State or the District of Columbia and a place in a possession of the United States; or

(2) Between a place in a possession of the United States and a place in another possession of the United States; whether that commerce moves wholly by aircraft or partly by aircraft and partly by other forms of transportation.

Over-the-top means above the layer of clouds or other obscuring phenomena forming the ceiling.

Parachute means a device used or intended to be used to retard the fall of a body or object through the air.

Person means an individual, firm, partnership, corporation, company, association, joint-stock association, or governmental entity. It includes a trustee, receiver, assignee, or similar representative of any of them.

Pilotage means navigation by visual reference to landmarks.

Pilot in command means the person who:

(1) Has final authority and responsibility for the operation and safety of the flight;

(2) Has been designated as pilot in command before or during the flight; and

(3) Holds the appropriate category, class, and type rating, if appropriate, for the conduct of the flight.

Pitch setting means the propeller blade setting as determined by the blade angle measured in a manner, and at a radius, specified by the instruction manual for the propeller.

Portable oxygen concentrator means a medical device that separates oxygen from other gasses in ambient air and dispenses this concentrated oxygen to the user.

Positive control means control of all air traffic, within designated airspace, by air traffic control.

Powered-lift means a heavier-than-air aircraft capable of vertical takeoff, vertical landing, and low speed flight that depends principally on engine-driven lift devices or engine thrust for lift during these flight regimes and on nonrotating airfoil(s) for lift during horizontal flight.

Powered parachute means a powered aircraft comprised of a flexible or semi-rigid wing connected to a fuselage so that the wing is not in position for flight until the aircraft is in motion. The fuselage of a powered parachute contains the aircraft engine, a seat for each occupant and is attached to the aircraft's landing gear.

Precision approach procedure means a standard instrument approach procedure in which an electronic glide slope is provided, such as ILS and PAR.

Preventive maintenance means simple or minor preservation operations and the replacement of small standard parts not involving complex assembly operations.

Prohibited area. A prohibited area is airspace designated under part 73 within which no person may operate an aircraft without the permission of the using agency.

Propeller means a device for propelling an aircraft that has blades on an engine-driven shaft and that, when rotated, produces by its action on the air, a thrust approximately perpendicular to its plane of rotation. It includes control components normally supplied by its manufacturer, but does not include main and auxiliary rotors or rotating airfoils of engines.

Public aircraft means any of the following aircraft when not being used for a commercial purpose or to carry an individual other than a crewmember or qualified non-crewmember:

(1) An aircraft used only for the United States Government; an aircraft owned by the Government and operated by any person for purposes related to crew training, equipment development, or demonstration; an aircraft owned and operated by the government of a State, the District of Columbia, or a territory or possession of the United States or a political subdivision of one of these governments; or an aircraft exclusively leased for at least 90 continuous days by the government of a State, the District of Columbia, or a territory or possession of the United States or a political subdivision of one of these governments.

(i) For the sole purpose of determining public aircraft status, commercial purposes means the transportation of persons or property for compensation or hire, but does not include the operation of an aircraft by the armed forces for reimbursement when that reimbursement is required by any Federal statute, regulation, or directive, in effect on November 1, 1999, or by one government on behalf of another government under a cost reimbursement agreement if the government on whose behalf the operation is conducted certifies to the Administrator of the Federal Aviation Administration that the operation is necessary to respond to a significant and imminent threat to life or property (including natural resources) and that no service by a private operator is reasonably available to meet the threat.

(ii) For the sole purpose of determining public aircraft status, governmental function means an activity undertaken by a government, such as national defense, intelligence missions, firefighting, search and rescue, law enforcement (including transport of prisoners, detainees, and illegal aliens), aeronautical research, or biological or geological resource management.

(iii) For the sole purpose of determining public aircraft status, qualified non-crewmember means an individual, other than a member of the crew, aboard an aircraft operated by the armed forces or an intelligence agency of the United States Government, or whose presence is required to perform, or is associated with the performance of, a governmental function.

(2) An aircraft owned or operated by the armed forces or chartered to provide transportation to the armed forces if—

(i) The aircraft is operated in accordance with title 10 of the United States Code;

(ii) The aircraft is operated in the performance of a governmental function under title 14, 31, 32, or 50 of the United States Code and the aircraft is not used for commercial purposes; or

(iii) The aircraft is chartered to provide transportation to the armed forces and the Secretary of Defense (or the Secretary of the department in which the Coast Guard is operating) designates the operation of the aircraft as being required in the national interest.

(3) An aircraft owned or operated by the National Guard of a State, the District of Columbia, or any territory or possession of the United States, and that meets the criteria of paragraph (2) of this definition, qualifies as a public aircraft only to the extent that it is operated under the direct control of the Department of Defense.

Rated continuous OEI power, with respect to rotorcraft turbine engines, means the approved brake horsepower developed under static conditions at specified altitudes and temperatures within the operating limitations established for the engine under part 33 of this chapter, and limited in use to the time required to complete the flight after the failure or shutdown of one engine of a multiengine rotorcraft.

Rated maximum continuous augmented thrust, with respect to turbojet engine type certification, means the approved jet thrust that is developed statically or in flight, in standard atmosphere at a specified altitude, with fluid injection or with the burning of fuel in a separate combustion chamber, within the engine operating limitations established under Part 33 of this chapter, and approved for unrestricted periods of use.

Rated maximum continuous power, with respect to reciprocating, turbopropeller, and turboshaft engines, means the approved brake horsepower that is developed statically or in flight, in standard atmosphere at a specified altitude, within the engine operating limitations established under Part 33, and approved for unrestricted periods of use.

Rated maximum continuous thrust, with respect to turbojet engine type certification, means the approved jet thrust that is developed statically or in flight, in standard atmosphere at a specified altitude, without fluid injection and without the burning of fuel in a separate combustion chamber, within the engine operating limitations established under Part 33 of this chapter, and approved for unrestricted periods of use.

Rated takeoff augmented thrust, with respect to turbojet engine type certification, means the approved jet thrust that is developed statically under standard sea level conditions, with fluid injection or with the burning of fuel in a separate combustion chamber, within the engine operating limitations established under Part 33 of this chapter, and limited in use to periods of not over 5 minutes for takeoff operation.

Rated takeoff power, with respect to reciprocating, turbopropeller, and turboshaft engine type certification, means the approved brake horsepower that is developed statically under standard sea level conditions, within the engine operating limitations established under Part 33, and limited in use to periods of not over 5 minutes for takeoff operation.

Rated takeoff thrust, with respect to turbojet engine type certification, means the approved jet thrust that is developed statically under standard sea level conditions, without fluid injection and without the burning of fuel in a separate combustion chamber, within the engine operating limitations established under Part 33 of this chapter, and limited in use to periods of not over 5 minutes for takeoff operation.

Rated 30-minute OEI power, with respect to rotorcraft turbine engines, means the approved brake horsepower developed under static conditions at specified altitudes and temperatures within the operating limitations established for the engine under part 33 of this chapter, and limited in use to one period of use no longer than 30 minutes after the failure or shutdown of one engine of a multiengine rotorcraft.

Rated 30-second OEI power, with respect to rotorcraft turbine engines, means the approved brake horsepower developed under static conditions at specified altitudes and temperatures within the operating limitations established for the engine under part 33 of this chapter, for continuation of one flight operation after the failure or shutdown of one engine in multiengine rotorcraft, for up to three periods of use no longer than 30 seconds each in any one flight, and followed by mandatory inspection and prescribed maintenance action.

Rated 2-minute OEI power, with respect to rotorcraft turbine engines, means the approved brake horsepower developed under static conditions at specified altitudes and temperatures within the operating limitations established for the engine under part 33 of this chapter, for continuation of one flight operation after the failure or shutdown of one engine in multiengine rotorcraft, for up to three periods of use no longer than 2 minutes each in any one flight, and followed by mandatory inspection and prescribed maintenance action.

Rated 2½-minute OEI power, with respect to rotorcraft turbine engines, means the approved brake horsepower developed under static conditions at specified altitudes and temperatures within the operating limitations established for the engine under part 33 of this chapter for periods of use no longer than 2-1/2 minutes each after the failure or shutdown of one engine of a multiengine rotorcraft.

Rating means a statement that, as a part of a certificate, sets forth special conditions, privileges, or limitations.

Reference landing speed means the speed of the airplane, in a specified landing configuration, at the point where it descends through the 50 foot height in the determination of the landing distance.

Reporting point means a geographical location in relation to which the position of an aircraft is reported.

Restricted area. A restricted area is airspace designated under Part 73 within which the flight of aircraft, while not wholly prohibited, is subject to restriction.

Rocket means an aircraft propelled by ejected expanding gases generated in the engine from self-contained propellants and not dependent on the intake of outside substances. It includes any part which becomes separated during the operation.

Rotorcraft means a heavier-than-air aircraft that depends principally for its support in flight on the lift generated by one or more rotors.

Rotorcraft-load combination means the combination of a rotorcraft and an external-load, including the external-load attaching means. Rotorcraft-load combinations are designated as Class A, Class B, Class C, and Class D, as follows:

(1) Class A rotorcraft-load combination means one in which the external load cannot move freely, cannot be jettisoned, and does not extend below the landing gear.

(2) Class B rotorcraft-load combination means one in which the external load is jettisonable and is lifted free of land or water during the rotorcraft operation.

(3) Class C rotorcraft-load combination means one in which the external load is jettisonable and remains in contact with land or water during the rotorcraft operation.

(4) Class D rotorcraft-load combination means one in which the external-load is other than a Class A, B, or C and has been specifically approved by the Administrator for that operation.

Route segment is a portion of a route bounded on each end by a fix or navigation aid (NAVAID).

Sea level engine means a reciprocating aircraft engine having a rated takeoff power that is producible only at sea level.

Second in command means a pilot who is designated to be second in command of an aircraft during flight time.

Show, unless the context otherwise requires, means to show to the satisfaction of the Administrator.

Small aircraft means aircraft of 12,500 pounds or less, maximum certificated takeoff weight.

Small unmanned aircraft means an unmanned aircraft weighing less than 55 pounds on takeoff, including everything that is on board or otherwise attached to the aircraft.

Small unmanned aircraft system (small UAS) means a small unmanned aircraft and its associated elements (including communication links and the components that control the small unmanned aircraft) that are required for the safe and efficient operation of the small unmanned aircraft in the national airspace system.

Special VFR conditions mean meteorological conditions that are less than those required for basic VFR flight in controlled airspace and in which some aircraft are permitted flight under visual flight rules.

Special VFR operations means aircraft operating in accordance with clearances within controlled airspace in meteorological conditions less than the basic VFR weather minima. Such operations must be requested by the pilot and approved by ATC.

Standard atmosphere means the atmosphere defined in U.S. Standard Atmosphere, 1962 (Geopotential altitude tables).

Stopway means an area beyond the takeoff runway, no less wide than the runway and centered upon the extended centerline of the runway, able to support the airplane during an aborted takeoff, without causing structural damage to the airplane, and designated by the airport authorities for use in decelerating the airplane during an aborted takeoff.

Suitable RNAV system is an RNAV system that meets the required performance established for a type of operation, e.g. IFR; and is suitable for operation over the route to be flown in terms of any performance criteria (including accuracy) established by the air navigation service provider for certain routes (e.g. oceanic, ATS routes, and IAPs). An RNAV system's suitability is dependent upon the availability of ground and/or satellite navigation aids that are needed to meet any route performance criteria that may be prescribed in route specifications to navigate the aircraft along the route to be flown. Information on suitable RNAV systems is published in FAA guidance material.

Synthetic vision means a computer-generated image of the external scene topography from the perspective of the flight deck that is derived from

aircraft attitude, high-precision navigation solution, and database of terrain, obstacles and relevant cultural features.

Synthetic vision system means an electronic means to display a synthetic vision image of the external scene topography to the flight crew.

Takeoff power:

(1) With respect to reciprocating engines, means the brake horsepower that is developed under standard sea level conditions, and under the maximum conditions of crankshaft rotational speed and engine manifold pressure approved for the normal takeoff, and limited in continuous use to the period of time shown in the approved engine specification; and

(2) With respect to turbine engines, means the brake horsepower that is developed under static conditions at a specified altitude and atmospheric temperature, and under the maximum conditions of rotor shaft rotational speed and gas temperature approved for the normal takeoff, and limited in continuous use to the period of time shown in the approved engine specification.

Takeoff safety speed means a referenced airspeed obtained after lift-off at which the required one-engine-inoperative climb performance can be achieved.

Takeoff thrust, with respect to turbine engines, means the jet thrust that is developed under static conditions at a specific altitude and atmospheric temperature under the maximum conditions of rotorshaft rotational speed and gas temperature approved for the normal takeoff, and limited in continuous use to the period of time shown in the approved engine specification.

Tandem wing configuration means a configuration having two wings of similar span, mounted in tandem.

TCAS I means a TCAS that utilizes interrogations of, and replies from, airborne radar beacon transponders and provides traffic advisories to the pilot.

TCAS II means a TCAS that utilizes interrogations of, and replies from airborne radar beacon transponders and provides traffic advisories and resolution advisories in the vertical plane.

TCAS III means a TCAS that utilizes interrogation of, and replies from, airborne radar beacon transponders and provides traffic advisories and resolution advisories in the vertical and horizontal planes to the pilot.

Time in service, with respect to maintenance time records, means the time from the moment an aircraft leaves the surface of the earth until it touches it at the next point of landing.

True airspeed means the airspeed of an aircraft relative to undisturbed air. True airspeed is equal to equivalent airspeed multiplied by $(\rho 0/\rho)^{\frac{1}{2}}$.

Traffic pattern means the traffic flow that is prescribed for aircraft landing at, taxiing on, or taking off from, an airport.

Type:

(1) As used with respect to the certification, ratings, privileges, and limitations of airmen, means a specific make and basic model of aircraft, including modifications thereto that do not change its handling or flight characteristics. Examples include: DC-7, 1049, and F-27; and

(2) As used with respect to the certification of aircraft, means those aircraft which are similar in design. Examples include: DC-7 and DC-7C; 1049G and 1049H; and F-27 and F-27F.

(3) As used with respect to the certification of aircraft engines means those engines which are similar in design. For example, JT8D and JT8D-7 are engines of the same type, and JT9D-3A and JT9D-7 are engines of the same type.

United States, in a geographical sense, means (1) the States, the District of Columbia, Puerto Rico, and the possessions, including the territorial waters, and (2) the airspace of those areas.

United States air carrier means a citizen of the United States who undertakes directly by lease, or other arrangement, to engage in air transportation.

Unmanned aircraft means an aircraft operated without the possibility of direct human intervention from within or on the aircraft.

Unmanned aircraft system means an unmanned aircraft and its associated elements (including communication links and the components that control the unmanned aircraft) that are required for the safe and efficient operation of the unmanned aircraft in the airspace of the United States.

VFR over-the-top, with respect to the operation of aircraft, means the operation of an aircraft over-the-top under VFR when it is not being operated on an IFR flight plan.

Warning area. A warning area is airspace of defined dimensions, extending from 3 nautical miles outward from the coast of the United States, that contains activity that may be hazardous to nonparticipating aircraft. The purpose of such warning areas is to warn nonparticipating pilots of the potential danger. A warning area may be located over domestic or international waters or both.

Weight-shift-control aircraft means a powered aircraft with a framed pivoting wing and a fuselage controllable only in pitch and roll by the pilot's ability to change the aircraft's center of gravity with respect to the wing. Flight control of the aircraft depends on the wing's ability to flexibly deform rather than the use of control surfaces.

Winglet or tip fin means an out-of-plane surface extending from a lifting surface. The surface may or may not have control surfaces.

[Doc. No. 1150, 27 FR 4588, May 15, 1962]

EDITORIAL NOTE: For FEDERAL REGISTER citations affecting §1.1, see the List of CFR Sections Affected, which appears in the Finding Aids section of the printed volume and at www.govinfo.gov.

§1.2 Abbreviations and symbols.

In Subchapters A through K of this chapter:

AFM means airplane flight manual.

AGL means above ground level.

ALS means approach light system.

APU means auxiliary power unit.

ASR means airport surveillance radar.

ATC means air traffic control.

ATS means Air Traffic Service.

CAMP means continuous airworthiness maintenance program.

CAS means calibrated airspeed.

CAT II means Category II.

CMP means configuration, maintenance, and procedures.

DH means decision height.

DME means distance measuring equipment compatible with TACAN.

EAS means equivalent airspeed.

EFVS means enhanced flight vision system.

Equi-Time Point means a point on the route of flight where the flight time, considering wind, to each of two selected airports is equal.

ETOPS means extended operations.

EWIS, as defined by §25.1701 of this chapter, means electrical wiring interconnection system.

FAA means Federal Aviation Administration.

FFS means full flight simulator.

FM means fan marker.

FSTD means flight simulation training device.

FTD means flight training device.

GS means glide slope.

HIRL means high-intensity runway light system.

IAS means indicated airspeed.

ICAO means International Civil Aviation Organization.

IFR means instrument flight rules.

IFSD means in-flight shutdown.

ILS means instrument landing system.

IM means ILS inner marker.

INT means intersection.

LDA means localizer-type directional aid.

LFR means low-frequency radio range.

LMM means compass locator at middle marker.

LOC means ILS localizer.

LOM means compass locator at outer marker.

M means mach number.

MAA means maximum authorized IFR altitude.

MALS means medium intensity approach light system.

MALSR means medium intensity approach light system with runway alignment indicator lights.

MCA means minimum crossing altitude.

MDA means minimum descent altitude.

MEA means minimum en route IFR altitude.

MEL means minimum equipment list.

MM means ILS middle marker.

MOCA means minimum obstruction clearance altitude.

MRA means minimum reception altitude.

MSL means mean sea level.

NDB (ADF) means nondirectional beacon (automatic direction finder).

NM means nautical mile.

NOPAC means North Pacific area of operation.

NOPT means no procedure turn required.

OEI means one engine inoperative.

OM means ILS outer marker.

OPSPECS means operations specifications.

PACOTS means Pacific Organized Track System.

PAR means precision approach radar.

PMA means parts manufacturer approval.

POC means portable oxygen concentrator.

PTRS means Performance Tracking and Reporting System.

RAIL means runway alignment indicator light system.

RBN means radio beacon.

RCLM means runway centerline marking.

RCLS means runway centerline light system.

REIL means runway end identification lights.

RFFS means rescue and firefighting services.

RNAV means area navigation.

RR means low or medium frequency radio range station.

RVR means runway visual range as measured in the touchdown zone area.

SALS means short approach light system.

SATCOM means satellite communications.

SSALS means simplified short approach light system.

SSALSR means simplified short approach light system with runway alignment indicator lights.

TACAN means ultra-high frequency tactical air navigational aid.

TAS means true airspeed.

TCAS means a traffic alert and collision avoidance system.

TDZL means touchdown zone lights.

TSO means technical standard order.

TVOR means very high frequency terminal omnirange station.

V_A means design maneuvering speed.

V_B means design speed for maximum gust intensity.

V_C means design cruising speed.

V_D means design diving speed.

V_{DF}/M_{DF} means demonstrated flight diving speed.

V_{EF} means the speed at which the critical engine is assumed to fail during takeoff.

V_F means design flap speed.

V_{FC}/M_{FC} means maximum speed for stability characteristics.

V_{FE} means maximum flap extended speed.

V_{FTO} means final takeoff speed.

V_H means maximum speed in level flight with maximum continuous power.

V_{LE} means maximum landing gear extended speed.

V_{LO} means maximum landing gear operating speed.

V_{LOF} means lift-off speed.

V_{MC} means minimum control speed with the critical engine inoperative.

V_{MO}/M_{MO} means maximum operating limit speed.

V_{MU} means minimum unstick speed.

V_{NE} means never-exceed speed.

V_{NO} means maximum structural cruising speed.

V_R means rotation speed.

V_{REF} means reference landing speed.

V_S means the stalling speed or the minimum steady flight speed at which the airplane is controllable.

V_{S0} means the stalling speed or the minimum steady flight speed in the landing configuration.

V_{S1} means the stalling speed or the minimum steady flight speed obtained in a specific configuration.

V_{SR} means reference stall speed.

V_{SR0} means reference stall speed in the landing configuration.

V_{SR1} means reference stall speed in a specific configuration.

V_{SW} means speed at which onset of natural or artificial stall warning occurs.

V_{TOSS} means takeoff safety speed for Category A rotorcraft.

V_X means speed for best angle of climb.

V_Y means speed for best rate of climb.

V_1 means the maximum speed in the takeoff at which the pilot must take the first action (e.g., apply brakes, reduce thrust, deploy speed brakes) to stop the airplane within the accelerate-stop distance. V_1 also means the minimum speed in the takeoff, following a failure of the critical engine at V_{EF}, at which the pilot can continue the takeoff and achieve the required height above the takeoff surface within the takeoff distance.

V_2 means takeoff safety speed.

V_{2min} means minimum takeoff safety speed.

VFR means visual flight rules.

VGSI means visual glide slope indicator.

VHF means very high frequency.

VOR means very high frequency omnirange station.

VORTAC means collocated VOR and TACAN.

[Doc. No. 1150, 27 FR 4590, May 15, 1962]

EDITORIAL NOTE: For FEDERAL REGISTER citations affecting §1.2, see the List of CFR Sections Affected, which appears in the Finding Aids section of the printed volume and at www.govinfo.gov.

§1.3 Rules of construction.

(a) In Subchapters A through K of this chapter, unless the context requires otherwise:

(1) Words importing the singular include the plural;

(2) Words importing the plural include the singular; and

(3) Words importing the masculine gender include the feminine.

(b) In Subchapters A through K of this chapter, the word:

(1) "Shall" is used in an imperative sense;

(2) "May" is used in a permissive sense to state authority or permission to do the act prescribed, and the words "no person may * * *" or "a person may not * * *" mean that no person is required, authorized, or permitted to do the act prescribed; and

(3) "Includes" means "includes but is not limited to".

[Docket No. 1150, 27 FR 4590, May 15, 1962; as amended by Amdt. 1–10, 31 FR 5055, March 29, 1966]

PART 5

SAFETY MANAGEMENT SYSTEMS

Authority: 49 U.S.C. 106(f), 106(g), 40101, 40113, 40119, 41706, 44101, 44701–44702, 44705, 44709–44711, 44713, 44716–44717, 44722, 46105; Sec. 102, Pub. L. 116-260, 134 Stat. 2309; Sec 215, Pub. L. 111–216, 124 Stat. 2366.

Source: Docket No. FAA–2009–0671, 80 FR 1326, Jan. 8, 2015, unless otherwise noted.

Subpart A—General

§5.1 Applicability.

This part applies to all of the following:

(a) Any person that holds or applies for a certificate issued under part 119 of this chapter authorizing the person to conduct operations under part 121 of this chapter.

(b) Any person that holds or applies for a certificate issued under part 119 of this chapter authorizing the person to conduct operations under part 135 of this chapter.

(c) Any person that holds or applies for a Letter of Authorization issued under §91.147 of this chapter.

(d) Any person that holds both a type certificate and a production certificate issued under part 21 of this chapter for the same product.

(e) Any person that holds a production certificate issued under part 21 of this chapter for a product for which the person is a licensee of the type certificate for the same product.

(f) Any person that applies for a production certificate under part 21 of this chapter for a product for which the person is the holder or licensee of the type certificate for the same product.

(g) Any person that holds a type certificate issued under part 21 of this chapter for a product, except for persons that hold only type certificates issued under §21.29 of this chapter, that allows another person to use the type certificate to manufacture the same product under a production certificate.

[Docket No. FAA–2021–0419, Amdt. 5–2, 89 FR 33104, April 26, 2024]

§5.3 Definitions.

Hazard means a condition or an object that could foreseeably cause or contribute to an incident or aircraft accident, as defined in 49 CFR 830.2.

Risk means the composite of predicted severity and likelihood of the potential effect of a hazard.

Risk control means a means to reduce or eliminate the effects of hazards.

Safety assurance means processes within the SMS that function systematically to ensure the performance and effectiveness of safety risk controls and that the organization meets or exceeds its safety objectives through the collection, analysis, and assessment of information.

Safety Management System (SMS) means the formal, top-down, organization-wide approach to managing safety risk and assuring the effectiveness of safety risk controls. It includes systematic procedures, practices, and policies for the management of safety risk.

Safety objective means a measurable goal or desirable outcome related to safety.

Safety performance means realized or actual safety accomplishment relative to the organization's safety objectives.

Safety policy means the person's documented commitment to safety, which defines its safety objectives and the accountabilities and responsibilities of its employees in regards to safety.

Safety promotion means a combination of training and communication of safety information to support the implementation and operation of an SMS in an organization.

Safety Risk Management means a process within the SMS composed of describing the system, identifying the hazards, and analyzing, assessing, and controlling risk.

[Docket No. FAA–2021–0419, Amdt. 5–2, 89 FR 33105, April 26, 2024]

§5.5 General requirements.

(a) *SMS components.* An SMS under this part must be appropriate to the size, scope, and complexity of the person's organization and include, at a minimum, all of the following components:

(1) Safety policy that meets the requirements of subpart B of this part.

(2) Safety risk management that meets the requirements of subpart C of this part.

(3) Safety assurance that meets the requirements of subpart D of this part.

(4) Safety promotion that meets the requirements of subpart E of this part.

(b) *Continuing requirements.* Any person required to develop and implement an SMS under this part must maintain the SMS in accordance with this part.

[Docket No. FAA–2021–0419, Amdt. 5–2, 89 FR 33105, April 26, 2024]

§5.7 Requirements for domestic, flag, and supplemental operations.

(a) Any person authorized to conduct operations under part 121 of this chapter that has an SMS acceptable to the FAA on or before May 28, 2024, must revise its SMS to meet the requirements of this part no later than May 28, 2025.

(b) Any person applying for authorization to conduct operations under part 121 of this chapter or with such application pending on or after May 28, 2024, must develop and implement an SMS that meets the requirements of this part.

(c) Any person required to develop and implement an SMS under this section must maintain the SMS as long as the person is authorized to conduct operations under part 121 of this chapter.

(d) Any person required to develop and implement an SMS under this section must make available to the Administrator, upon request, all necessary information and data that demonstrates that the person has an SMS that meets the requirements set forth in this part.

[Docket No. FAA–2021–0419, Amdt. 5–2, 89 FR 33105, April 26, 2024]

§5.9 Requirements for commuter and on-demand operations or passenger-carrying flights for compensation or hire.

(a) Any person authorized to conduct operations under part 135 of this chapter or that holds a Letter of Authorization issued under §91.147 of this chapter before May 28, 2024, must:

(1) Develop and implement an SMS that meets the requirements of this part no later than May 28, 2027.

(2) Submit to the FAA, a declaration of compliance with this part in a form and manner acceptable to the Administrator no later than May 28, 2027.

(b) Any person applying for authorization to conduct operations under part 135 of this chapter or a Letter of Authorization under §91.147 of this chapter, or with such application pending on or after May 28, 2024, must develop and implement an SMS that meets the requirements of this part.

(c) Any person required to develop and implement an SMS under this section must maintain the SMS as long as the person is authorized to conduct operations under either part 135 or §91.147 of this chapter.

(d) Any person required to develop and implement an SMS under this section must make available to the Administrator, upon request, all necessary information and data that demonstrates that the person has an SMS that meets the requirements set forth in this part.

(e) The following requirements do not apply to those organizations with a single pilot who is the sole individual performing all necessary functions in the conduct and execution related to, or in direct support of, the safe operation of the aircraft: §§5.21(a)(4), 5.21(a)(5), 5.21(c), 5.23(a)(2), 5.23(a)(3), 5.23(b), 5.25(b)(3), 5.25(c), 5.27(a), 5.27(b), 5.71(a)(7), 5.93, and 5.97(d) of this part.

[Docket No. FAA–2021–0419, Amdt. 5–2, 89 FR 33105, April 26, 2024]

§5.11 Requirements for production certificate holders that are holders or licensees of a type certificate for the same product.

Any person that holds a production certificate issued under part 21 of this chapter for a product for which the person is the holder or licensee of the type certificate for the same product on or before May 28, 2024, must:

(a) Develop and maintain an organizational system description in accordance with §5.17 of this subpart.

(b) Submit an implementation plan in accordance with §5.19 of this subpart for FAA approval in a form and manner acceptable to the Administrator no later than November 28, 2024.

(c) Develop an SMS that meets the requirements of this part.

(d) Implement the SMS in accordance with this part no later than May 28, 2027.

(e) Make available to the Administrator, upon request, all necessary information and data that demonstrates that the person has an SMS that meets the requirements set forth in this part.

(f) Maintain the SMS as long as the person is both a holder of a production certificate and a holder or licensee of a type certificate for the same product.

[Docket No. FAA–2021–0419, Amdt. 5–2, 89 FR 33105, April 26, 2024]

§5.13 Requirements for type certificate holders or licensees applying for a production certificate for the same product.

(a) This section applies to any holder or licensee of a type certificate for a product who either:

(1) Applies for a production certificate for that same product under part 21 of this chapter on or after May 28, 2024, or

(2) Has an application for a production certificate for that same product under part 21 of this chapter pending on May 28, 2024.

(b) Any person that meets paragraph (a) of this section must:

(1) Develop and maintain an organizational system description in accordance with §5.17 of this subpart.

(2) Submit an implementation plan in accordance with §5.19 of this subpart for FAA approval in a form and manner acceptable to the Administrator during the certification process.

(3) Develop an SMS that meets the requirements of this part.

(4) Implement the SMS in accordance with this part no later than 36 months after submission of the implementation plan.

(5) Make available to the Administrator, upon request, all necessary information and data that demonstrates that the person has an SMS that meets the requirements set forth in this part.

(6) Maintain the SMS as long as the person is both a holder of a production certificate and a holder or licensee of a type certificate for the same product.

[Docket No. FAA–2021–0419, Amdt. 5–2, 89 FR 33106, April 26, 2024]

§5.15 Requirements for type certificate holders that allow another person to use the type certificate to obtain a production certificate for the same product.

(a) This section applies to any person that holds a type certificate issued under part 21 of this chapter for a product, except for persons that hold only type certificates issued under §21.29 of this chapter, that allows another person to use the type certificate to manufacture the same product under a production certificate.

(b) Any person that meets paragraph (a) of this section and has a licensing agreement in accordance with §21.55 of this chapter on May 28, 2024, must:

(1) Develop and maintain an organizational system description in accordance with §5.17 of this subpart.

(2) Submit an implementation plan in accordance with §5.19 of this subpart for FAA approval in a form and manner acceptable to the Administrator no later than November 28, 2024.

(3) Develop an SMS that meets the requirements of this part.

(4) Implement the SMS in accordance with this part no later than May 28, 2027.

(5) Make available to the Administrator, upon request, all necessary information and data that demonstrates that the person has an SMS that meets the requirements set forth in this part.

(6) Maintain the SMS as long as the person continues to meet paragraph (a) of this section.

(c) Any person that meets paragraph (a) of this section and enters into a licensing agreement in

accordance with §21.55 of this chapter after May 28, 2024, must:

(1) Develop and maintain an organizational system description in accordance with §5.17 of this subpart.

(2) Submit an implementation plan in accordance with §5.19 of this subpart for FAA approval in a form and manner acceptable to the Administrator when providing written licensing agreements in accordance with §21.55 of this chapter.

(3) Develop an SMS that meets the requirements of this part.

(4) Implement the SMS in accordance with this part no later than 36 months after submission of the person's implementation plan.

(5) Make available to the Administrator, upon request, all necessary information and data that demonstrates that the person has an SMS that meets the requirements set forth in this part.

(6) Maintain the SMS as long as the person continues to meet paragraph (a) of this section.

[Docket No. FAA–2021–0419, Amdt. 5–2, 89 FR 33106, April 26, 2024]

§5.17 Organizational system description.

An organizational system description developed and maintained under this part must include a summary of the following information about the safety of the aviation products or services provided by the person:

(a) The person's aviation-related processes, procedures, and activities.

(b) The function and purpose of the aviation products or services.

(c) The operating environment.

(d) The personnel, equipment, and facilities necessary for operation.

[Docket No. FAA–2021–0419, Amdt. 5–2, 89 FR 33106, April 26, 2024]

§5.19 Implementation plan.

(a) An implementation plan filed under this part must be based on the organizational system description as defined in §5.17 and describe the means of compliance (including, but not limited to, new or existing policies, processes, or procedures) used to meet the requirements of this part.

(b) A person required to submit an implementation plan under this part must make available to the Administrator, upon request, all necessary information and data that demonstrates that the SMS has been or will be implemented in accordance with the implementation plan.

[Docket No. FAA–2021–0419, Amdt. 5–2, 89 FR 33106, April 26, 2024]

Subpart B—Safety Policy

§5.21 Safety policy.

(a) Any person required to have an SMS under this part must have a safety policy that includes at least the following:

(1) The person's safety objectives.

(2) The person's commitment to fulfill the safety objectives.

(3) A clear statement about the provision of the necessary resources for the implementation of the SMS.

(4) A safety reporting policy that defines requirements for employee reporting of safety hazards or issues.

(5) A policy that defines unacceptable behavior and conditions for disciplinary action.

(6) An emergency response plan that provides for the safe transition from normal to emergency operations in accordance with the requirements of §5.27.

(7) A code of ethics that is applicable to all employees, including management personnel and officers, which clarifies that safety is the organization's highest priority.

(b) The safety policy must be signed by the accountable executive described in §5.25.

(c) The safety policy must be documented and communicated throughout the person's organization.

(d) The safety policy must be regularly reviewed by the accountable executive to ensure it remains relevant and appropriate to the person.

[Docket No. FAA–2021–0419, Amdt. 5–2, 89 FR 33106, April 26, 2024]

§5.23 Safety accountability and authority.

(a) Any person required to have an SMS under this part must define in its safety policy the accountability for safety of the following individuals:

(1) Accountable executive, as described in §5.25.

(2) All members of management in regard to developing, implementing, and maintaining SMS processes within their area of responsibility, including, but not limited to:

(i) Hazard identification and safety risk assessment.

(ii) Assuring the effectiveness of safety risk controls.

(iii) Promoting safety as required in subpart E of this part.

(iv) Advising the accountable executive on the performance of the SMS and on any need for improvement.

(3) Employees relative to the person's safety performance.

(b) The person must identify the levels of management with the authority to make decisions regarding safety risk acceptance.

[Docket No. FAA–2021–0419, Amdt. 5–2, 89 FR 33106, April 26, 2024]

§5.25 Designation and responsibilities of required safety management personnel.

(a) *Designation of the accountable executive.* Any person required to have an SMS under this part must identify an accountable executive who, irrespective of other functions, satisfies the following:

(1) Is the final authority over operations authorized to be conducted under the person's certificate(s) or Letter(s) of Authorization.

(2) Controls the financial resources required for the operations to be conducted under the person's certificate(s) or Letter(s) of Authorization.

(3) Controls the human resources required for the operations authorized to be conducted under the person's certificate(s) or Letter(s) of Authorization.

(4) Retains ultimate responsibility for the safety performance of the operations conducted under the person's certificate(s) or Letter(s) of Authorization.

(b) *Responsibilities of the accountable executive.* The accountable executive must accomplish the following:

(1) Ensure that the SMS is properly implemented and is performing across all pertinent areas.

(2) Develop and sign the safety policy.

(3) Communicate the safety policy throughout the person's organization.

(4) Regularly review the safety policy to ensure it remains relevant and appropriate to the person.

(5) Regularly review the safety performance and direct actions necessary to address substandard safety performance in accordance with §5.75.

(c) *Designation of management personnel.* The accountable executive must designate sufficient management personnel who, on behalf of the accountable executive, are responsible for the following:

(1) Coordinate implementation, maintenance, and integration of the SMS throughout the person's organization.

(2) Facilitate hazard identification and safety risk analysis.

(3) Monitor the effectiveness of safety risk controls.

(4) Ensure safety promotion throughout the person's organization as required in subpart E of this part.

(5) Regularly report to the accountable executive on the performance of the SMS and on any need for improvement.

[Docket No. FAA–2021–0419, Amdt. 5–2, 89 FR 33106, April 26, 2024]

§5.27 Coordination of emergency response planning.

Where emergency response procedures are necessary, any person required to have an SMS under this part must develop, and the accountable executive must approve as part of the safety policy, an emergency response plan that addresses at least the following:

(a) Delegation of emergency authority throughout the person's organization.

(b) Assignment of employee responsibilities during the emergency.

(c) Coordination of the emergency response plans with the emergency response plans of other organizations it must interface with during the provision of its services.

[Docket No. FAA–2021–0419, Amdt. 5–2, 89 FR 33107, April 26, 2024]

Subpart C— Safety Risk Management

§5.51 Applicability.

Any person required to have an SMS under this part must apply safety risk management to the following:

(a) Implementation of new systems.

(b) Revision of existing systems.

(c) Development of operational procedures.

(d) Identification of hazards or ineffective risk controls through the safety assurance processes in subpart D of this part.

[Docket No. FAA–2021–0419, Amdt. 5–2, 89 FR 33107, April 26, 2024]

§5.53 System analysis and hazard identification.

(a) When applying safety risk management, any person required to have an SMS under this part must analyze the systems identified in §5.51. Those system analyses must be used to identify hazards under paragraph (c) of this section and in developing and implementing risk controls related to the system under §5.55(c).

(b) In conducting the system analysis, the following information must be considered:

(1) Function and purpose of the system.

(2) The system's operating environment.

(3) An outline of the system's processes and procedures.

(4) The personnel, equipment, and facilities necessary for operation of the system.

(5) The interfaces of the system.

(c) Any person required to have an SMS under this part must develop and maintain processes to identify hazards within the context of the system analysis.

[Docket No. FAA–2021–0419, Amdt. 5–2, 89 FR 33107, April 26, 2024]

§5.55 Safety risk assessment and control.

Any person required to have an SMS under this part must:

(a) Develop and maintain processes to analyze safety risk associated with the hazards identified in §5.53(c).

(b) Define a process for conducting risk assessment that allows for the determination of acceptable safety risk.

(c) Develop and maintain processes to develop safety risk controls that are necessary as a result of the safety risk assessment process under paragraph (b) of this section.

(d) Evaluate whether the risk will be acceptable with the proposed safety risk control applied before the safety risk control is implemented.

[Docket No. FAA–2021–0419, Amdt. 5–2, 89 FR 33107, April 26, 2024]

§5.57 Notification of hazards to interfacing persons.

If a person required to have an SMS under this part identifies a hazard in the operating environment, the person must provide notice of the hazard to any interfacing person that, to the best of the person's knowledge, could address the hazard or mitigate the risk. For the purpose of this section, interfacing persons are those that contribute to the safety of the certificate or Letter of Authorization holder's aviation-related products and services.

[Docket No. FAA–2021–0419, Amdt. 5–2, 89 FR 33107, April 26, 2024]

Subpart D—Safety Assurance

§5.71 Safety performance monitoring and measurement.

(a) Any person required to have an SMS under this part must develop and maintain processes and systems to acquire data with respect to its operations, products, and services to monitor the safety performance of the organization. These processes and systems must include, at a minimum, the following:

(1) Monitoring of operational processes.

(2) Monitoring of the operational environment to detect changes.

(3) Auditing of operational processes and systems.

(4) Evaluations of the SMS and operational processes and systems.

(5) Investigations of incidents and accidents.

(6) Investigations of reports regarding potential non-compliance with regulatory standards or other safety risk controls established by the person through the safety risk management process established in subpart C of this part.

(7) A confidential employee reporting system in which employees can report hazards, issues, concerns, occurrences, incidents, as well as propose solutions and safety improvements, without concern of reprisal for reporting.

(8) Investigations of hazard notifications that have been received from external sources.

(b) Any person required to have an SMS under this part must develop and maintain processes that analyze the data acquired through the processes and systems identified under paragraph (a) of this section and any other relevant data with respect to its operations, products, and services.

(c) Any person that holds both a type certificate and a production certificate issued under part 21 of this chapter for the same product must submit a summary of the confidential employee reports received under paragraph (a)(7) of this section to the Administrator once every 6 months.

[80 FR 1326, Jan. 8, 2015, as amended at 82 FR 24010, May 25, 2017; Amdt. 5–2, 89 FR 33107, April 26, 2024]

§5.73 Safety performance assessment.

(a) Any person required to have an SMS under this part must conduct assessments of its safety performance against its safety objectives, which include reviews by the accountable executive, to:

(1) Ensure compliance with the safety risk controls established by the person.

(2) Evaluate the performance of the SMS.

(3) Evaluate the effectiveness of the safety risk controls established under §5.55(c) and identify any ineffective controls.

(4) Identify changes in the operational environment that may introduce new hazards.

(5) Identify new hazards.

(b) Upon completion of the assessment, if ineffective controls or new hazards are identified under paragraphs (a)(2) through (5) of this section, the person must use the safety risk management process described in subpart C of this part.

[Docket No. FAA–2021–0419, Amdt. 5–2, 89 FR 33108, April 26, 2024]

§5.75 Continuous improvement.

Any person required to have an SMS under this part must establish and implement processes to correct safety performance deficiencies identified in the assessments conducted under §5.73.

[Docket No. FAA–2021–0419, Amdt. 5–2, 89 FR 33108, April 26, 2024]

Subpart E—Safety Promotion

§5.91 Competencies and training.

Any person required to have an SMS under this part must provide training to each individual identified in §5.23 of this part to ensure the individuals attain and maintain the competencies necessary to perform their duties relevant to the operation and performance of the SMS.

[Docket No. FAA–2021–0419, Amdt. 5–2, 89 FR 33108, April 26, 2024]

§5.93 Safety communication.

Any person required to have an SMS under this part must develop and maintain means for communicating safety information that, at a minimum:

(a) Ensures that employees are aware of the SMS policies, processes, and tools that are relevant to their responsibilities.

(b) Conveys hazard information relevant to the employee's responsibilities.

(c) Explains why safety actions have been taken.

(d) Explains why safety procedures are introduced or changed.

[Docket No. FAA–2021–0419, Amdt. 5–2, 89 FR 33108, April 26, 2024]

Subpart F—SMS Documentation and Recordkeeping

§5.95 SMS documentation.

Any person required to have an SMS under this part must develop and maintain the following SMS documentation:

(a) Safety policy.

(b) SMS processes and procedures.

[Docket No. FAA–2021–0419, Amdt. 5–2, 89 FR 33108, April 26, 2024]

§5.97 SMS records.

Any person required to have an SMS under this part must:

(a) Maintain records of outputs of safety risk management processes as described in subpart C of this part. Such records must be retained for as long as the control remains relevant to the operation.

(b) Maintain records of outputs of safety assurance processes as described in subpart D of this part. Such records must be retained for a minimum of 5 years.

(c) Maintain a record of all training provided under §5.91 for each individual. Such records must be retained for as long as the individual is employed by the person.

(d) Retain records of all communications provided under §5.93 or §5.57 for a minimum of 24 consecutive calendar months.

[Docket No. FAA–2021–0419, Amdt. 5–2, 89 FR 33108, April 26, 2024]

PART 43

MAINTENANCE, PREVENTIVE MAINTENANCE, REBUILDING, AND ALTERATION

Authority: 42 U.S.C. 7572; 49 U.S.C. 106(f), 106(g), 40105, 40113, 44701–44702, 44704, 44707, 44709, 44711, 44713, 44715, 45303.

Source: Docket No. 1993, 29 FR 5451, April 23, 1964, unless otherwise noted.

Editorial Note: For miscellaneous technical amendments to this Part 43, see Amdt. 43–3, 31 FR 3336, March 3, 1966, and Amdt. 43–6, 31 FR 9211, July 6, 1966.

§43.1 Applicability.

(a) Except as provided in paragraphs (b) and (d) of this section, this part prescribes rules governing the maintenance, preventive maintenance, rebuilding, and alteration of any—

(1) Aircraft having a U.S. airworthiness certificate;

(2) Foreign-registered civil aircraft used in common carriage or carriage of mail under the provisions of part 121 or 135 of this chapter; and

(3) Airframe, aircraft engines, propellers, appliances, and component parts of such aircraft.

(b) This part does not apply to—

(1) Any aircraft for which the FAA has issued an experimental certificate, unless the FAA has previously issued a different kind of airworthiness certificate for that aircraft;

(2) Any aircraft for which the FAA has issued an experimental certificate under the provisions of §21.191(i)(3) of this chapter, and the aircraft was previously issued a special airworthiness certificate in the light-sport category under the provisions of §21.190 of this chapter; or

(3) Any aircraft that is operated under part 107 of this chapter, except as described in §107.140(d).

(c) This part applies to all life-limited parts that are removed from a type certificated product, segregated, or controlled as provided in §43.10.

(d) This part applies to any aircraft issued a special airworthiness certificate in the light-sport category except:

(1) The repair or alteration form specified in §§43.5(b) and 43.9(d) is not required to be completed for products not produced under an FAA approval;

(2) Major repairs and major alterations for products not produced under an FAA approval are not required to be recorded in accordance with appendix B of this part; and

(3) The listing of major alterations and major repairs specified in paragraphs (a) and (b) of appendix A of this part is not applicable to products not produced under an FAA approval.

[Docket No. 1993, 29 FR 5451, April 23, 1964, as amended by Amdt. 43–23, 47 FR 41084, Sept. 16, 1982; Amdt. 43–37, 66 FR 21066, April 27, 2001; Amdt. 43–38, 67 FR 2109, Jan. 15, 2002; Amdt. 43–39, 69 FR 44863, July 27, 2004; Amdt. 43–44, 75 FR 5219, Feb. 1, 2010; Docket FAA–2015–0150, Amdt. 43–48, 81 FR 42208, June 28, 2016; Docket FAA–2018–1087, Amdt. 43–51, 86 FR 4381, Jan. 15, 2021]

§43.2 Records of overhaul and rebuilding.

(a) No person may describe in any required maintenance entry or form an aircraft, airframe, aircraft engine, propeller, appliance, or component part as being overhauled unless—

(1) Using methods, techniques, and practices acceptable to the Administrator, it has been disassembled, cleaned, inspected, repaired as necessary, and reassembled; and

(2) It has been tested in accordance with approved standards and technical data, or in accordance with current standards and technical data acceptable to the Administrator, which have been developed and documented by the holder of the type certificate, supplemental type certificate, or a material, part, process, or appliance approval under part 21 of this chapter.

(b) No person may describe in any required maintenance entry or form an aircraft, airframe, aircraft engine, propeller, appliance, or component part as being rebuilt unless it has been disassembled, cleaned, inspected, repaired as necessary, reassembled, and tested to the same tolerances and limits as a new item, using either new parts or used parts that either conform to new part tolerances and limits or to approved oversized or undersized dimensions.

[Amdt. 43–23, 47 FR 41084, Sept. 16, 1982, as amended by Amdt. 43–43, 74 FR 53394, Oct. 16, 2009]

§43.3 Persons authorized to perform maintenance, preventive maintenance, rebuilding, and alterations.

(a) Except as provided in this section and §43.17, no person may maintain, rebuild, alter, or perform preventive maintenance on an aircraft, airframe, aircraft engine, propeller, appliance, or component part to which this part applies. Those items, the performance of which is a major alteration, a major repair, or preventive maintenance, are listed in Appendix A.

(b) The holder of a mechanic certificate may perform maintenance, preventive maintenance, and alterations as provided in Part 65 of this chapter.

(c) The holder of a repairman certificate may perform maintenance, preventive maintenance, and alterations as provided in Part 65 of this chapter.

(d) A person working under the supervision of a holder of a mechanic or repairman certificate may perform the maintenance, preventive maintenance, and alterations that his supervisor is authorized to perform, if the supervisor personally observes the work being done to the extent necessary to ensure that it is being done properly and if the supervisor is readily available, in person, for consultation. However, this paragraph does not authorize the performance of any inspection required by Part 91 or Part 125 of this chapter or any inspection performed after a major repair or alteration.

(e) The holder of a repair station certificate may perform maintenance, preventive maintenance, and alterations as provided in Part 145 of this chapter.

(f) The holder of an air carrier operating certificate or an operating certificate issued under Part 121 or 135, may perform maintenance, preventive maintenance, and alterations as provided in Part 121 or 135.

(g) Except for holders of a sport pilot certificate, the holder of a pilot certificate issued under part 61 may perform preventive maintenance on any aircraft owned or operated by that pilot which is not used under Part 121, 129, or 135 of this chapter. The holder of a sport pilot certificate may perform preventive maintenance on an aircraft owned or operated by that pilot and issued a special airworthiness certificate in the light-sport category.

(h) Notwithstanding the provisions of paragraph (g) of this section, the Administrator may approve a certificate holder under Part 135 of this chapter, operating rotorcraft in a remote area, to allow a pilot to perform specific preventive maintenance items provided—

(1) The items of preventive maintenance are a result of a known or suspected mechanical difficulty or malfunction that occurred en route to or in a remote area;

(2) The pilot has satisfactorily completed an approved training program and is authorized in writing by the certificate holder for each item of preventive maintenance that the pilot is authorized to perform;

(3) There is no certificated mechanic available to perform preventive maintenance;

(4) The certificate holder has procedures to evaluate the accomplishment of a preventive maintenance item that requires a decision concerning the airworthiness of the rotorcraft; and

(5) The items of preventive maintenance authorized by this section are those listed in paragraph (c) of Appendix A of this part.

(i) Notwithstanding the provisions of paragraph (g) of this section, in accordance with an approval issued to the holder of a certificate issued under

Part 135 of this chapter, a pilot of an aircraft type-certificated for 9 or fewer passenger seats, excluding any pilot seat, may perform the removal and reinstallation of approved aircraft cabin seats, approved cabin-mounted stretchers, and when no tools are required, approved cabin-mounted medical oxygen bottles, provided—

(1) The pilot has satisfactorily completed an approved training program and is authorized in writing by the certificate holder to perform each task; and

(2) The certificate holder has written procedures available to the pilot to evaluate the accomplishment of the task.

(j) A manufacturer may—

(1) Rebuild or alter any aircraft, aircraft engine, propeller, or appliance manufactured by him under a type or production certificate;

(2) Rebuild or alter any appliance or part of aircraft, aircraft engines, propellers, or appliances manufactured by him under a Technical Standard Order Authorization, an FAA-Parts Manufacturer Approval, or Product and Process Specification issued by the Administrator; and

(3) Perform any inspection required by part 91 or Part 125 of this chapter on aircraft it manufactured under a type certificate, or currently manufactures under a production certificate.

(k) Updates of databases in installed avionics meeting the conditions of this paragraph are not considered maintenance and may be performed by pilots provided:

(1) The database upload is:

(i) Initiated from the flight deck;

(ii) Performed without disassembling the avionics unit; and

(iii) Performed without the use of tools and/or special equipment.

(2) The pilot must comply with the certificate holder's procedures or the manufacturer's instructions.

(3) The holder of operating certificates must make available written procedures consistent with manufacturer's instructions to the pilot that describe how to:

(i) Perform the database update; and

(ii) Determine the status of the data upload.

[Docket No. 1993, 29 FR 5451, Apr. 23, 1964; as amended by Amdt. 43–4, 31 FR 5249, April 1, 1966; Amdt. 43–23, 47 FR 41084, Sept. 16, 1982; Amdt. 43–25, 51 FR 40702, Nov. 7, 1986; Amdt. 43–36, 61 FR 19501, May 1, 1996; Amdt. 43–37, 66 FR 21066, April 27, 2001; Amdt. 43–39, 69 FR 44863, July 27, 2004; Amdt. 43–43, 74 FR 53394, Oct. 16, 2009; Amdt. 43–45, 77 FR 71096, Nov. 29, 2012]

§43.5 Approval for return to service after maintenance, preventive maintenance, rebuilding, or alteration.

No person may approve for return to service any aircraft, airframe, aircraft engine, propeller, or appliance, that has undergone maintenance, preventive maintenance, rebuilding, or alteration unless—

(a) The maintenance record entry required by §43.9 or §43.11, as appropriate, has been made;

(b) The repair or alteration form authorized by or furnished by the Administrator has been executed in a manner prescribed by the Administrator; and

(c) If a repair or an alteration results in any change in the aircraft operating limitations or flight data contained in the approved aircraft flight manual, those operating limitations or flight data are appropriately revised and set forth as prescribed in §91.9 of this chapter.

[Docket No. 1993, 29 FR 5451, April 23, 1964; as amended by Amdt. 43–23, 47 FR 41084, Sept. 16, 1982; Amdt. 43–31, 54 FR 34330, Aug. 18, 1989]

§43.7 Persons authorized to approve aircraft, airframes, aircraft engines, propellers, appliances, or component parts for return to service after maintenance, preventive maintenance, rebuilding, or alteration.

(a) Except as provided in this section and §43.17, no person, other than the Administrator, may approve an aircraft, airframe, aircraft engine, propeller, appliance, or component part for return to service after it has undergone maintenance, preventive maintenance, rebuilding, or alteration.

(b) The holder of a mechanic certificate or an inspection authorization may approve an aircraft, airframe, aircraft engine, propeller, appliance, or component part for return to service as provided in Part 65 of this chapter.

(c) The holder of a repair station certificate may approve an aircraft, airframe, aircraft engine, propeller, appliance, or component part for return to service as provided in Part 145 of this chapter.

(d) A manufacturer may approve for return to service any aircraft, airframe, aircraft engine, propeller, appliance, or component part which that manufacturer has worked on under §43.3(j). However, except for minor alterations, the work must have been done in accordance with technical data approved by the Administrator.

(e) The holder of an air carrier operating certificate or an operating certificate issued under Part 121 or 135, may approve an aircraft, airframe, aircraft engine, propeller, appliance, or component part for return to service as provided in Part 121 or 135 of this chapter, as applicable.

(f) A person holding at least a private pilot certificate may approve an aircraft for return to service after performing preventive maintenance under the provisions of §43.3(g).

(g) The holder of a repairman certificate (light-sport aircraft) with a maintenance rating may approve an aircraft issued a special airworthiness certificate in light-sport category for return to service, as provided in Part 65 of this chapter.

(h) The holder of at least a sport pilot certificate may approve an aircraft owned or operated by that pilot and issued a special airworthiness certificate in the light-sport category for return to service after performing preventive maintenance under the provisions of §43.3(g).

[Amdt. 43–23, 47 FR 41084, Sept. 16, 1982, as amended by Amdt. 43–36, 61 FR 19501, May 1, 1996; Amdt. 43–37, 66 FR 21066, April 27, 2001; Amdt. 43–39, 69 FR 44863, July 27, 2004]

§43.9 Content, form, and disposition of maintenance, preventive maintenance, rebuilding, and alteration records (except inspections performed in accordance with Part 91, Part 125, §135.411(a)(1), and §135.419 of this chapter).

(a) *Maintenance record entries.* Except as provided in paragraphs (b) and (c) of this section, each person who maintains, performs preventive maintenance, rebuilds, or alters an aircraft, airframe, aircraft engine, propeller, appliance, or component part shall make an entry in the maintenance record of that equipment containing the following information:

(1) A description (or reference to data acceptable to the Administrator) of work performed.

(2) The date of completion of the work performed.

(3) The name of the person performing the work if other than the person specified in paragraph (a)(4) of this section.

(4) If the work performed on the aircraft, airframe, aircraft engine, propeller, appliance, or component part has been performed satisfactorily, the signature, certificate number, and kind of certificate held by the person approving the work. The signature constitutes the approval for return to service only for the work performed.

(b) Each holder of an air carrier operating certificate or an operating certificate issued under Part 121 or 135, that is required by its approved operations specifications to provide for a continuous airworthiness maintenance program, shall make a record of the maintenance, preventive maintenance, rebuilding, and alteration, on aircraft, airframes, aircraft engines, propellers, appliances, or component parts which it operates in accordance with the applicable provisions of part 121 or 135 of this chapter, as appropriate.

(c) This section does not apply to persons performing inspections in accordance with Part 91, 125, §135.411(a)(1), or §135.419 of this chapter.

(d) In addition to the entry required by paragraph (a) of this section, major repairs and major alterations shall be entered on a form, and the form disposed of, in the manner prescribed in appendix B, by the person performing the work.

[Amdt. 43–23, 47 FR 41085, Sept. 16, 1982, as amended by Amdt. 43–37, 66 FR 21066, April 27, 2001; Amdt. 43–39, 69 FR 44863, July 27, 2004]

§43.10 Disposition of life-limited aircraft parts.

(a) *Definitions used in this section.* For the purposes of this section the following definitions apply.

Life-limited part means any part for which a mandatory replacement limit is specified in the type design, the Instructions for Continued Airworthiness, or the maintenance manual.

Life status means the accumulated cycles, hours, or any other mandatory replacement limit of a life-limited part.

(b) *Temporary removal of parts from type-certificated products.* When a life-limited part is temporarily removed and reinstalled for the purpose of performing maintenance, no disposition under paragraph (c) of this section is required if—

(1) The life status of the part has not changed;

(2) The removal and reinstallation is performed on the same serial numbered product; and

(3) That product does not accumulate time in service while the part is removed.

(c) *Disposition of parts removed from type-certificated products.* Except as provided in paragraph (b) of this section, after April 15, 2002 each person who removes a life-limited part from a type-certificated product must ensure that the part is controlled using one of the methods in this paragraph. The method must deter the installation of the part after it has reached its life limit. Acceptable methods include:

(1) *Record keeping system.* The part may be controlled using a record keeping system that substantiates the part number, serial number, and current life status of the part. Each time the part is removed from a type certificated product, the record must be updated with the current life status. This system may include electronic, paper, or other means of record keeping.

(2) *Tag or record attached to part.* A tag or other record may be attached to the part. The tag or record must include the part number, serial number, and current life status of the part. Each time the part is removed from a type certificated product, either a new tag or record must be created, or the

existing tag or record must be updated with the current life status.

(3) *Non-permanent marking.* The part may be legibly marked using a non-permanent method showing its current life status. The life status must be updated each time the part is removed from a type certificated product, or if the mark is removed, another method in this section may be used. The mark must be accomplished in accordance with the instructions under §45.16 of this chapter in order to maintain the integrity of the part.

(4) *Permanent marking.* The part may be legibly marked using a permanent method showing its current life status. The life status must be updated each time the part is removed from a type certificated product. Unless the part is permanently removed from use on type certificated products, this permanent mark must be accomplished in accordance with the instructions under §45.16 of this chapter in order to maintain the integrity of the part.

(5) *Segregation.* The part may be segregated using methods that deter its installation on a type-certificated product. These methods must include, at least—

(i) Maintaining a record of the part number, serial number, and current life status, and

(ii) Ensuring the part is physically stored separately from parts that are currently eligible for installation.

(6) *Mutilation.* The part may be mutilated to deter its installation in a type certificated product. The mutilation must render the part beyond repair and incapable of being reworked to appear to be airworthy.

(7) *Other methods.* Any other method approved or accepted by the FAA.

(d) *Transfer of life-limited parts.* Each person who removes a life-limited part from a type certificated product and later sells or otherwise transfers that part must transfer with the part the mark, tag, or other record used to comply with this section, unless the part is mutilated before it is sold or transferred.

[Docket No. FAA–2000–8017, 67 FR 2110, Jan. 15, 2002; as amended by Amdt. 43–38A, 79 FR 67055, Nov. 12, 2014]

§43.11 Content, form, and disposition of records for inspections conducted under Parts 91 and 125 and §§135.411(a)(1) and 135.419 of this chapter.

(a) *Maintenance record entries.* The person approving or disapproving for return to service an aircraft, airframe, aircraft engine, propeller, appliance, or component part after any inspection performed in accordance with part 91, 125, §135.411(a)(1), or §135.419 shall make an entry in the maintenance record of that equipment containing the following information:

(1) The type of inspection and a brief description of the extent of the inspection.

(2) The date of the inspection and aircraft total time in service.

(3) The signature, the certificate number, and kind of certificate held by the person approving or disapproving for return to service the aircraft, airframe, aircraft engine, propeller, appliance, component part, or portions thereof.

(4) Except for progressive inspections, if the aircraft is found to be airworthy and approved for return to service, the following or a similarly worded statement—"I certify that this aircraft has been inspected in accordance with (insert type) inspection and was determined to be in airworthy condition."

(5) Except for progressive inspections, if the aircraft is not approved for return to service because of needed maintenance, noncompliance with applicable specifications, airworthiness directives, or other approved data, the following or a similarly worded statement—"I certify that this aircraft has been inspected in accordance with (insert type) inspection and a list of discrepancies and unairworthy items dated (date) has been provided for the aircraft owner or operator."

(6) For progressive inspections, the following or a similarly worded statement—"I certify that in accordance with a progressive inspection program, a routine inspection of (identify whether aircraft or components) and a detailed inspection of (identify components) were performed and the (aircraft or components) are (approved or disapproved) for return to service." If disapproved, the entry will further state "and a list of discrepancies and unairworthy items dated (date) has been provided to the aircraft owner or operator."

(7) If an inspection is conducted under an inspection program provided for in part 91, 125, or §135.411(a)(1), the entry must identify the inspection program, that part of the inspection program accomplished, and contain a statement that the inspection was performed in accordance with the inspections and procedures for that particular program.

(b) *Listing of discrepancies and placards.* If the person performing any inspection required by part 91 or 125 or §135.411(a)(1) of this chapter finds that the aircraft is unairworthy or does not meet the applicable type certificate data, airworthiness directives, or other approved data upon which its airworthiness depends, that persons must give the owner or lessee a signed and dated list of those discrepancies. For those items permitted to be inoperative under §91.213(d)(2)

of this chapter, that person shall place a placard, that meets the aircraft's airworthiness certification regulations, on each inoperative instrument and the cockpit control of each item of inoperative equipment, marking it "Inoperative," and shall add the items to the signed and dated list of discrepancies given to the owner or lessee.

[Amdt. 43–23, 47 FR 41085, Sept. 16, 1982, as amended by Amdt. 43–30, 53 FR 50195, Dec. 13, 1988; Amdt. 43–36, 61 FR 19501, May 1, 1996; 71 FR 44188, Aug. 4, 2006]

§43.12 Maintenance records: Falsification, reproduction, or alteration.

(a) No person may make or cause to be made:
(1) Any fraudulent or intentionally false entry in any record or report that is required to be made, kept, or used to show compliance with any requirement under this part;
(2) Any reproduction, for fraudulent purpose, of any record or report under this part; or
(3) Any alteration, for fraudulent purpose, of any record or report under this part.

(b) The commission by any person of an act prohibited under paragraph (a) of this section is a basis for suspending or revoking the applicable airman, operator, or production certificate, Technical Standard Order Authorization, FAA-Parts Manufacturer Approval, or Product and Process Specification issued by the Administrator and held by that person.

[Amdt. 43–19, 43 FR 22639, May 25, 1978, as amended by Amdt. 43–23, 47 FR 41085, Sept. 16, 1982]

§43.13 Performance rules (general).

(a) Each person performing maintenance, alteration, or preventive maintenance on an aircraft, engine, propeller, or appliance shall use the methods, techniques, and practices prescribed in the current manufacturer's maintenance manual or Instructions for Continued Airworthiness prepared by its manufacturer, or other methods, techniques, and practices acceptable to the Administrator, except as noted in §43.16. He shall use the tools, equipment, and test apparatus necessary to assure completion of the work in accordance with accepted industry practices. If special equipment or test apparatus is recommended by the manufacturer involved, he must use that equipment or apparatus or its equivalent acceptable to the Administrator.

(b) Each person maintaining or altering, or performing preventive maintenance, shall do that work in such a manner and use materials of such a quality, that the condition of the aircraft, airframe, aircraft engine, propeller, or appliance worked on will be at least equal to its original or properly altered condition (with regard

to aerodynamic function, structural strength, resistance to vibration and deterioration, and other qualities affecting airworthiness).

(c) *Special provisions for holders of air carrier operating certificates and operating certificates issued under the provisions of Part 121 or 135 and Part 129 operators holding operations specifications.* Unless otherwise notified by the administrator, the methods, techniques, and practices contained in the maintenance manual or the maintenance part of the manual of the holder of an air carrier operating certificate or an operating certificate under Part 121 or 135 and Part 129 operators holding operations specifications (that is required by its operating specifications to provide a continuous airworthiness maintenance and inspection program) constitute acceptable means of compliance with this section.

[Docket No. 1993, 29 FR 5451, April 23, 1964; as amended by Amdt. 43–20, 45 FR 60182, Sept. 11, 1980; Amdt. 43–23, 47 FR 41085, Sept. 16, 1982; Amdt. 43–28, 52 FR 20028, June 16, 1987; Amdt. 43–37, 66 FR 21066, April 27, 2001]

§43.15 Additional performance rules for inspections.

(a) *General.* Each person performing an inspection required by part 91, 125, or 135 of this chapter, shall—
(1) Perform the inspection so as to determine whether the aircraft, or portion(s) thereof under inspection, meets all applicable airworthiness requirements; and
(2) If the inspection is one provided for in Part 125, 135, or §91.409(e) of this chapter, perform the inspection in accordance with the instructions and procedures set forth in the inspection program for the aircraft being inspected.

(b) *Rotorcraft.* Each person performing an inspection required by Part 91 on a rotorcraft shall inspect the following systems in accordance with the maintenance manual or Instructions for Continued Airworthiness of the manufacturer concerned:
(1) The drive shafts or similar systems.
(2) The main rotor transmission gear box for obvious defects.
(3) The main rotor and center section (or the equivalent area).
(4) The auxiliary rotor on helicopters.

(c) *Annual and 100-hour inspections.*
(1) Each person performing an annual or 100-hour inspection shall use a checklist while performing the inspection. The checklist may be of the person's own design, one provided by the manufacturer of the equipment being inspected or one obtained from another source. This checklist must include the scope and detail of the items contained in Appendix D to this part and paragraph (b) of this section.

(2) Each person approving a reciprocating-engine-powered aircraft for return to service after an annual or 100-hour inspection shall, before that approval, run the aircraft engine or engines to determine satisfactory performance in accordance with the manufacturer's recommendations of—
(i) Power output (static and idle r.p.m.);
(ii) Magnetos;
(iii) Fuel and oil pressure; and
(iv) Cylinder and oil temperature.
(3) Each person approving a turbine-engine-powered aircraft for return to service after an annual, 100-hour, or progressive inspection shall, before that approval, run the aircraft engine or engines to determine satisfactory performance in accordance with the manufacturer's recommendations.

(d) Progressive inspection.
(1) Each person performing a progressive inspection shall, at the start of a progressive inspection system, inspect the aircraft completely. After this initial inspection, routine and detailed inspections must be conducted as prescribed in the progressive inspection schedule. Routine inspections consist of visual examination or check of the appliances, the aircraft, and its components and systems, insofar as practicable without disassembly. Detailed inspections consist of a thorough examination of the appliances, the aircraft, and its components and systems, with such disassembly as is necessary. For the purposes of this subparagraph, the overhaul of a component or system is considered to be a detailed inspection.
(2) If the aircraft is away from the station where inspections are normally conducted, an appropriately rated mechanic, a certificated repair station, or the manufacturer of the aircraft may perform inspections in accordance with the procedures and using the forms of the person who would otherwise perform the inspection.

[Docket No. 1993, 29 FR 5451, April 23, 1964; as amended by Amdt. 43–23, 47 FR 41086, Sept. 16, 1982; Amdt. 43–25, 51 FR 40702, Nov. 7, 1986; Amdt. 43–31, 54 FR 34330, Aug. 18, 1989; 71 FR 44188, Aug. 4, 2006]

§43.16 Airworthiness Limitations.

Each person performing an inspection or other maintenance specified in an Airworthiness Limitations section of a manufacturer's maintenance manual or Instructions for Continued Airworthiness shall perform the inspection or other maintenance in accordance with that section, or in accordance with operations specifications approved by the Administrator under Part 121 or 135, or an inspection program approved under §91.409(e).

[71 FR 44188, Aug. 4, 2006]

§43.17 Maintenance, preventive maintenance, and alterations performed on U.S. aeronautical products by certain Canadian persons.

(a) Definitions. For purposes of this section:
Aeronautical product means any civil aircraft or airframe, aircraft engine, propeller, appliance, component, or part to be installed thereon.
Canadian aeronautical product means any aeronautical product under airworthiness regulation by Transport Canada Civil Aviation.
U.S. aeronautical product means any aeronautical product under airworthiness regulation by the FAA.
(b) Applicability. This section does not apply to any U.S. aeronautical products maintained or altered under any bilateral agreement made between Canada and any country other than the United States.
(c) Authorized persons.
(1) A person holding a valid Transport Canada Civil Aviation Maintenance Engineer license and appropriate ratings may, with respect to a U.S.-registered aircraft located in Canada, perform maintenance, preventive maintenance, and alterations in accordance with the requirements of paragraph (d) of this section and approve the affected aircraft for return to service in accordance with the requirements of paragraph (e) of this section.
(2) A Transport Canada Civil Aviation Approved Maintenance Organization (AMO) holding appropriate ratings may, with respect to a U.S.-registered aircraft or other U.S. aeronautical products located in Canada, perform maintenance, preventive maintenance, and alterations in accordance with the requirements of paragraph (d) of this section and approve the affected products for return to service in accordance with the requirements of paragraph (e) of this section.
(d) Performance requirements. A person authorized in paragraph (c) of this section may perform maintenance (including any inspection required by §91.409 of this chapter, except an annual inspection), preventive maintenance, and alterations, provided—
(1) The person performing the work is authorized by Transport Canada Civil Aviation to perform the same type of work with respect to Canadian aeronautical products;
(2) The maintenance, preventive maintenance, or alteration is performed in accordance with a Bilateral Aviation Safety Agreement between the United States and Canada and associated Maintenance Implementation Procedures that provide a level of safety equivalent to that provided by the provisions of this chapter;

(3) The maintenance, preventive maintenance, or alteration is performed such that the affected product complies with the applicable requirements of part 36 of this chapter; and

(4) The maintenance, preventive maintenance, or alteration is recorded in accordance with a Bilateral Aviation Safety Agreement between the United States and Canada and associated Maintenance Implementation Procedures that provide a level of safety equivalent to that provided by the provisions of this chapter.

(e) *Approval requirements.*

(1) To return an affected product to service, a person authorized in paragraph (c) of this section must approve (certify) maintenance, preventive maintenance, and alterations performed under this section, except that an Aircraft Maintenance Engineer may not approve a major repair or major alteration.

(2) An AMO whose system of quality control for the maintenance, preventive maintenance, alteration, and inspection of aeronautical products has been approved by Transport Canada Civil Aviation, or an authorized employee performing work for such an AMO, may approve (certify) a major repair or major alteration performed under this section if the work was performed in accordance with technical data approved by the FAA.

(f) No person may operate in air commerce an aircraft, airframe, aircraft engine, propeller, or appliance on which maintenance, preventive maintenance, or alteration has been performed under this section unless it has been approved for return to service by a person authorized in this section.

[Amdt. 43–33, 56 FR 57571, Nov. 12, 1991, as amended by Amdt. 43–40, 71 FR 40877, July 14, 2005]

APPENDIX A TO PART 43

MAJOR ALTERATIONS, MAJOR REPAIRS, AND PREVENTIVE MAINTENANCE

(a) *Major alterations—*

(1) *Airframe major alterations.* Alterations of the following parts and alterations of the following types, when not listed in the aircraft specifications issued by the FAA, are airframe major alterations:

(i) Wings.
(ii) Tail surfaces.
(iii) Fuselage.
(iv) Engine mounts.
(v) Control system.
(vi) Landing gear.
(vii) Hull or floats.
(viii) Elements of an airframe including spars, ribs, fittings, shock absorbers, bracing, cowling, fairings, and balance weights.
(ix) Hydraulic and electrical actuating system of components.
(x) Rotor blades.

(xi) Changes to the empty weight or empty balance which result in an increase in the maximum certificated weight or center of gravity limits of the aircraft.

(xii) Changes to the basic design of the fuel, oil, cooling, heating, cabin pressurization, electrical, hydraulic, de-icing, or exhaust systems.

(xiii) Changes to the wing or to fixed or movable control surfaces which affect flutter and vibration characteristics.

(2) *Powerplant major alterations.* The following alterations of a powerplant when not listed in the engine specifications issued by the FAA, are powerplant major alterations.

(i) Conversion of an aircraft engine from one approved model to another, involving any changes in compression ratio, propeller reduction gear, impeller gear ratios or the substitution of major engine parts which requires extensive rework and testing of the engine.

(ii) Changes to the engine by replacing aircraft engine structural parts with parts not supplied by the original manufacturer or parts not specifically approved by the Administrator.

(iii) Installation of an accessory which is not approved for the engine.

(iv) Removal of accessories that are listed as required equipment on the aircraft or engine specification.

(v) Installation of structural parts other than the type of parts approved for the installation.

(vi) Conversions of any sort for the purpose of using fuel of a rating or grade other than that listed in the engine specifications.

(3) *Propeller major alterations.* The following alterations of a propeller when not authorized in the propeller specifications issued by the FAA are propeller major alterations:

(i) Changes in blade design.
(ii) Changes in hub design.
(iii) Changes in the governor or control design.
(iv) Installation of a propeller governor or feathering system.
(v) Installation of propeller de-icing system.
(vi) Installation of parts not approved for the propeller.

(4) *Appliance major alterations.* Alterations of the basic design not made in accordance with recommendations of the appliance manufacturer or in accordance with an FAA Airworthiness Directive are appliance major alterations. In addition, changes in the basic design of radio communication and navigation equipment approved under type certification or a Technical Standard Order that have an effect on frequency stability, noise level, sensitivity, selectivity, distortion, spurious radiation, AVC characteristics, or ability to meet environmental test conditions and other changes that have an effect on the performance of the equipment are also major alterations.

(b) *Major repairs*—

(1) *Airframe major repairs.* Repairs to the following parts of an airframe and repairs of the following types, involving the strengthening, reinforcing, splicing, and manufacturing of primary structural members or their replacement, when replacement is by fabrication such as riveting or welding, are airframe major repairs.

(i) Box beams.

(ii) Monocoque or semimonocoque wings or control surfaces.

(iii) Wing stringers or chord members.

(iv) Spars.

(v) Spar flanges.

(vi) Members of truss-type beams.

(vii) Thin sheet webs of beams.

(viii) Keel and chine members of boat hulls or floats.

(ix) Corrugated sheet compression members which act as flange material of wings or tail surfaces.

(x) Wing main ribs and compression members.

(xi) Wing or tail surface brace struts.

(xii) Engine mounts.

(xiii) Fuselage longerons.

(xiv) Members of the side truss, horizontal truss, or bulkheads.

(xv) Main seat support braces and brackets.

(xvi) Landing gear brace struts.

(xvii) Axles.

(xviii) Wheels.

(xix) Skis, and ski pedestals.

(xx) Parts of the control system such as control columns, pedals, shafts, brackets, or horns.

(xxi) Repairs involving the substitution of material.

(xxii) The repair of damaged areas in metal or plywood stressed covering exceeding six inches in any direction.

(xxiii) The repair of portions of skin sheets by making additional seams.

(xxiv) The splicing of skin sheets.

(xxv) The repair of three or more adjacent wing or control surface ribs or the leading edge of wings and control surfaces, between such adjacent ribs.

(xxvi) Repair of fabric covering involving an area greater than that required to repair two adjacent ribs.

(xxvii) Replacement of fabric on fabric covered parts such as wings, fuselages, stabilizers, and control surfaces.

(xxviii) Repairing, including rebottoming, of removable or integral fuel tanks and oil tanks.

(2) *Powerplant major repairs.* Repairs of the following parts of an engine and repairs of the following types, are powerplant major repairs:

(i) Separation or disassembly of a crankcase or crankshaft of a reciprocating engine equipped with an integral supercharger.

(ii) Separation or disassembly of a crankcase or crankshaft of a reciprocating engine equipped with other than spur-type propeller reduction gearing.

(iii) Special repairs to structural engine parts by welding, plating, metalizing, or other methods.

(3) *Propeller major repairs.* Repairs of the following types to a propeller are propeller major repairs:

(i) Any repairs to, or straightening of steel blades.

(ii) Repairing or machining of steel hubs.

(iii) Shortening of blades.

(iv) Retipping of wood propellers.

(v) Replacement of outer laminations on fixed pitch wood propellers.

(vi) Repairing elongated bolt holes in the hub of fixed pitch wood propellers.

(vii) Inlay work on wood blades.

(viii) Repairs to composition blades.

(ix) Replacement of tip fabric.

(x) Replacement of plastic covering.

(xi) Repair of propeller governors.

(xii) Overhaul of controllable pitch propellers.

(xiii) Repairs to deep dents, cuts, scars, nicks, etc., and straightening of aluminum blades.

(xiv) The repair or replacement of internal elements of blades.

(4) *Appliance major repairs.* Repairs of the following types to appliances are appliance major repairs:

(i) Calibration and repair of instruments.

(ii) Calibration of radio equipment.

(iii) Rewinding the field coil of an electrical accessory.

(iv) Complete disassembly of complex hydraulic power valves.

(v) Overhaul of pressure type carburetors, and pressure type fuel, oil and hydraulic pumps.

(c) *Preventive maintenance.* Preventive maintenance is limited to the following work, provided it does not involve complex assembly operations:

(1) Removal, installation, and repair of landing gear tires.

(2) Replacing elastic shock absorber cords on landing gear.

(3) Servicing landing gear shock struts by adding oil, air, or both.

(4) Servicing landing gear wheel bearings, such as cleaning and greasing.

(5) Replacing defective safety wiring or cotter keys.

(6) Lubrication not requiring disassembly other than removal of nonstructural items such as cover plates, cowlings, and fairings.

(7) Making simple fabric patches not requiring rib stitching or the removal of structural parts or control surfaces. In the case of balloons, the making of small fabric repairs to envelopes (as defined in, and in accordance with, the balloon

manufacturers' instructions) not requiring load tape repair or replacement.

(8) Replenishing hydraulic fluid in the hydraulic reservoir.

(9) Refinishing decorative coating of fuselage, balloon baskets, wings tail group surfaces (excluding balanced control surfaces), fairings, cowlings, landing gear, cabin, or cockpit interior when removal or disassembly of any primary structure or operating system is not required.

(10) Applying preservative or protective material.to components where no disassembly of any primary structure or operating system is involved and where such coating is not prohibited or is not contrary to good practices.

(11) Repairing upholstery and decorative furnishings of the cabin, cockpit, or balloon basket interior when the repairing does not require disassembly of any primary structure or operating system or interfere with an operating system or affect the primary structure of the aircraft.

(12) Making small simple repairs to fairings, nonstructural cover plates, cowlings, and small patches and reinforcements not changing the contour so as to interfere with proper air flow.

(13) Replacing side windows where that work does not interfere with the structure or any operating system such as controls, electrical equipment, etc.

(14) Replacing safety belts.

(15) Replacing seats or seat parts with replacement parts approved for the aircraft, not involving disassembly of any primary structure or operating system.

(16) Trouble shooting and repairing broken circuits in landing light wiring circuits.

(17) Replacing bulbs, reflectors, and lenses of position and landing lights.

(18) Replacing wheels and skis where no weight and balance computation is involved.

(19) Replacing any cowling not requiring removal of the propeller or disconnection of flight controls.

(20) Replacing or cleaning spark plugs and setting of spark plug gap clearance.

(21) Replacing any hose connection except hydraulic connections.

(22) Replacing prefabricated fuel lines.

(23) Cleaning or replacing fuel and oil strainers or filter elements.

(24) Replacing and servicing batteries.

(25) Cleaning of balloon burner pilot and main nozzles in accordance with the balloon manufacturer's instructions.

(26) Replacement or adjustment of nonstructural standard fasteners incidental to operations.

(27) The interchange of balloon baskets and burners on envelopes when the basket or burner is designated as interchangeable in the balloon type certificate data and the baskets and burners

are specifically designed for quick removal and installation.

(28) The installations of anti-misfueling devices to reduce the diameter of fuel tank filler openings provided the specific device has been made a part of the aircraft type certificate data by the aircraft manufacturer, the aircraft manufacturer has provided FAA-approved instructions for installation of the specific device, and installation does not involve the disassembly of the existing tank filler opening.

(29) Removing, checking, and replacing magnetic chip detectors.

(30) The inspection and maintenance tasks prescribed and specifically identified as preventive maintenance in a primary category aircraft type certificate or supplemental type certificate holder's approved special inspection and preventive maintenance program when accomplished on a primary category aircraft provided:

(i) They are performed by the holder of at least a private pilot certificate issued under part 61 of this chapter who is the registered owner (including co-owners) of the affected aircraft and who holds a certificate of competency for the affected aircraft (1) issued by the holder of the production certificate for that primary category aircraft that has a special training program approved under §21.24 of this subchapter; or (2) issued by another entity that has a course approved by the Administrator; and

(ii) The inspections and maintenance tasks are performed in accordance with instructions contained by the special inspection and preventive maintenance program approved as part of the aircraft's type design or supplemental type design.

(31) Removing and replacing self-contained, front instrument panel-mounted navigation and communication devices that employ tray-mounted connectors that connect the unit when the unit is installed into the instrument panel, (excluding automatic flight control systems, transponders, and microwave frequency distance measuring equipment (DME)). The approved unit must be designed to be readily and repeatedly removed and replaced, and pertinent instructions must be provided. Prior to the unit's intended use, an operational check must be performed in accordance with the applicable sections of part 91 of this chapter.

(Secs. 313, 601 through 610, and 1102, Federal Aviation Act of 1958 as amended (49 U.S.C. 1354, 1421 through 1430 and 1502); (49 U.S.C. 106(g) (Revised Pub. L. 97–449, Jan. 21, 1983); and 14 CFR 11.45)

[Docket No. 1993, 29 FR 5451, April 23, 1964, as amended by Amdt. 43–14, 37 FR 14291, June 19, 1972; Amdt. 43–23, 47 FR 41086, Sept. 16, 1982; Amdt. 43–24, 49 FR 44602, Nov. 7, 1984; Amdt. 43–25, 51 FR 40703, Nov. 7, 1986; Amdt. 43–27, 52 FR 17277, May 6, 1987; Amdt. 43–34, 57 FR 41369, Sept. 9, 1992; Amdt.

43–36, 61 FR 19501, May 1, 1996; Amdt. 43–45, 77 FR 71096, Nov. 29, 2012; Docket No. FAA–2021–0237, Amdt. No. 43–52, 87 FR 31414, May 24, 2022]

Appendix B to Part 43
Recording of Major Repairs and Major Alterations

(a) Except as provided in paragraphs (b), (c), and (d) of this appendix, each person performing a major repair or major alteration shall—

(1) Execute FAA Form 337 at least in duplicate;

(2) Give a signed copy of that form to the aircraft owner; and

(3) Forward a copy of that form to the FAA Aircraft Registration Branch in Oklahoma City, Oklahoma, within 48 hours after the aircraft, airframe, aircraft engine, propeller, or appliance is approved for return to service.

(b) For major repairs made in accordance with a manual or specifications acceptable to the Administrator, a certificated repair station may, in place of the requirements of paragraph (a)—

(1) Use the customer's work order upon which the repair is recorded;

(2) Give the aircraft owner a signed copy of the work order and retain a duplicate copy for at least two years from the date of approval for return to service of the aircraft, airframe, aircraft engine, propeller, or appliance;

(3) Give the aircraft owner a maintenance release signed by an authorized representative of the repair station and incorporating the following information:

(i) Identity of the aircraft, airframe, aircraft engine, propeller or appliance.

(ii) If an aircraft, the make, model, serial number, nationality and registration marks, and location of the repaired area.

(iii) If an airframe, aircraft engine, propeller, or appliance, give the manufacturer's name, name of the part, model, and serial numbers (if any); and

(4) Include the following or a similarly worded statement—

"The aircraft, airframe, aircraft engine, propeller, or appliance identified above was repaired and inspected in accordance with current Regulations of the Federal Aviation Agency and is approved for return to service.

Pertinent details of the repair are on file at this repair station under Order No. _____
Date _____
Signed _____
(For signature of authorized representative)

(Repair station name)
(Certificate No.) _____ ."
(Address)

(c) Except as provided in paragraph (d) of this appendix, for a major repair or major alteration made by a person authorized in §43.17, the person who performs the major repair or major alteration and the person authorized by §43.17 to approve that work shall execute an FAA Form 337 at least in duplicate. A completed copy of that form shall be—

(1) Given to the aircraft owner; and

(2) Forwarded to the Federal Aviation Administration, Aircraft Registration Branch, Post Office Box 25504, Oklahoma City, OK 73125, within 48 hours after the work is inspected.

(d) For extended-range fuel tanks installed within the passenger compartment or a baggage compartment, the person who performs the work and the person authorized to approve the work by §43.7 shall execute an FAA Form 337 in at least triplicate. A completed copy of that form shall be—

(1) Placed on board the aircraft as specified in §91.417 of this chapter;

(2) Given to the aircraft owner; and

(3) Forwarded to the Federal Aviation Administration, Aircraft Registration Branch, Post Office Box 25724, Oklahoma City, OK 73125, within 48 hours after the work is inspected.

(Secs. 101, 610, 72 Stat. 737, 780, 49 U.S.C. 1301, 1430)

[Docket No. 1993, 29 FR 5451, April 23, 1964; as amended by Amdt. 43–10, 33 FR 15989, Oct. 31, 1968; Amdt. 43–29, 52 FR 34101, Sept. 9, 1987; Amdt. 43–31, 54 FR 34330, Aug. 18, 1989; 71 FR 58495, Oct. 4, 2006; Amdt. 43–41, 72 FR 53680, Sept. 20, 2007; Docket No. FAA–2018–0119, Amdt. 43–50, 83 FR 9170, March 5, 2018]

Appendix C to Part 43—[Reserved]

APPENDIX D TO PART 43

SCOPE AND DETAIL OF ITEMS (AS
APPLICABLE TO THE PARTICULAR AIRCRAFT)
TO BE INCLUDED IN ANNUAL AND
100-HOUR INSPECTIONS

(a) Each person performing an annual or 100-hour inspection shall, before that inspection, remove or open all necessary inspection plates, access doors, fairing, and cowling. He shall thoroughly clean the aircraft and aircraft engine.

(b) Each person performing an annual or 100-hour inspection shall inspect (where applicable) the following components of the fuselage and hull group:

(1) Fabric and skin—for deterioration, distortion, other evidence of failure, and defective or insecure attachment of fittings.

(2) Systems and components—for improper installation, apparent defects, and unsatisfactory operation.

(3) Envelope, gas bags, ballast tanks, and related parts—for poor condition.

(c) Each person performing an annual or 100-hour inspection shall inspect (where applicable) the following components of the cabin and cockpit group:

(1) Generally—for uncleanliness and loose equipment that might foul the controls.

(2) Seats and safety belts—for poor condition and apparent defects.

(3) Windows and windshields—for deterioration and breakage.

(4) Instruments—for poor condition, mounting, marking, and (where practicable) improper operation.

(5) Flight and engine controls—for improper installation and improper operation.

(6) Batteries—for improper installation and improper charge.

(7) All systems—for improper installation, poor general condition, apparent and obvious defects, and insecurity of attachment.

(d) Each person performing an annual or 100-hour inspection shall inspect (where applicable) components of the engine and nacelle group as follows:

(1) Engine section—for visual evidence of excessive oil, fuel, or hydraulic leaks, and sources of such leaks.

(2) Studs and nuts—for improper torquing and obvious defects.

(3) Internal engine—for cylinder compression and for metal particles or foreign matter on screens and sump drain plugs. If there is weak cylinder compression, for improper internal condition and improper internal tolerances.

(4) Engine mount—for cracks, looseness of mounting, and looseness of engine to mount.

(5) Flexible vibration dampeners—for poor condition and deterioration.

(6) Engine controls—for defects, improper travel, and improper safetying.

(7) Lines, hoses, and clamps—for leaks, improper condition and looseness.

(8) Exhaust stacks—for cracks, defects, and improper attachment.

(9) Accessories—for apparent defects in security of mounting.

(10) All systems—for improper installation, poor general condition, defects, and insecure attachment.

(11) Cowling—for cracks, and defects.

(e) Each person performing an annual or 100-hour inspection shall inspect (where applicable) the following components of the landing gear group:

(1) All units—for poor condition and insecurity of attachment.

(2) Shock absorbing devices—for improper oleo fluid level.

(3) Linkages, trusses, and members—for undue or excessive wear fatigue, and distortion.

(4) Retracting and locking mechanism—for improper operation.

(5) Hydraulic lines—for leakage.

(6) Electrical system—for chafing and improper operation of switches.

(7) Wheels—for cracks, defects, and condition of bearings.

(8) Tires—for wear and cuts.

(9) Brakes—for improper adjustment.

(10) Floats and skis—for insecure attachment and obvious or apparent defects.

(f) Each person performing an annual or 100-hour inspection shall inspect (where applicable) all components of the wing and center section assembly for poor general condition, fabric or skin deterioration, distortion, evidence of failure, and insecurity of attachment.

(g) Each person performing an annual or 100-hour inspection shall inspect (where applicable) all components and systems that make up the complete empennage assembly for poor general condition, fabric or skin deterioration, distortion, evidence of failure, insecure attachment, improper component installation, and improper component operation.

(h) Each person performing an annual or 100-hour inspection shall inspect (where applicable) the following components of the propeller group:

(1) Propeller assembly—for cracks, nicks, binds, and oil leakage.

(2) Bolts—for improper torquing and lack of safetying.

(3) Anti-icing devices—for improper operations and obvious defects.

(4) Control mechanisms—for improper operation, insecure mounting, and restricted travel.

(i) Each person performing an annual or 100-hour inspection shall inspect (where applicable) the following components of the radio group:

(1) Radio and electronic equipment—for improper installation and insecure mounting.

(2) Wiring and conduits—for improper routing, insecure mounting, and obvious defects.

(3) Bonding and shielding—for improper installation and poor condition.

(4) Antenna including trailing antenna—for poor condition, insecure mounting, and improper operation.

(j) Each person performing an annual or 100-hour inspection shall inspect (where applicable) each installed miscellaneous item that is not otherwise covered by this listing for improper installation and improper operation.

APPENDIX E TO PART 43
ALTIMETER SYSTEM TEST AND INSPECTION

Each person performing the altimeter system tests and inspections required by §91.411 of this chapter must comply with the following:

(a) Static pressure system:

(1) Ensure freedom from entrapped moisture and restrictions.

(2) Perform a proof test to demonstrate the integrity of the static pressure system in a manner acceptable to the Administrator. For airplanes certificated under part 25 of this chapter, determine that leakage is within the tolerances established by §25.1325.

(3) Determine that the static port heater, if installed, is operative.

(4) Ensure that no alterations or deformations of the airframe surface have been made that would affect the relationship between air pressure in the static pressure system and true ambient static air pressure for any flight condition.

(b) Altimeter:

(1) Test by an appropriately rated repair facility in accordance with the following subparagraphs. Unless otherwise specified, each test for performance may be conducted with the instrument subjected to vibration. When tests are conducted with the temperature substantially different from ambient temperature of approximately 25 degrees C., allowance shall be made for the variation from the specified condition.

(i) *Scale error.* With the barometric pressure scale at 29.92 inches of mercury, the altimeter shall be subjected successively to pressures corresponding to the altitude specified in Table I up to the maximum normally expected operating altitude of the airplane in which the altimeter is to be installed. The reduction in pressure shall be made at a rate not in excess of 20,000 feet per minute to within approximately 2,000 feet of the

test point. The test point shall be approached at a rate compatible with the test equipment. The altimeter shall be kept at the pressure corresponding to each test point for at least 1 minute, but not more than 10 minutes, before a reading is taken. The error at all test points must not exceed the tolerances specified in Table I.

(ii) *Hysteresis.* The hysteresis test shall begin not more than 15 minutes after the altimeter's initial exposure to the pressure corresponding to the upper limit of the scale error test prescribed in subparagraph (i); and while the altimeter is at this pressure, the hysteresis test shall commence. Pressure shall be increased at a rate simulating a descent in altitude at the rate of 5,000 to 20,000 feet per minute until within 3,000 feet of the first test point (50 percent of maximum altitude). The test point shall then be approached at a rate of approximately 3,000 feet per minute. The altimeter shall be kept at this pressure for at least 5 minutes, but not more than 15 minutes, before the test reading is taken. After the reading has been taken, the pressure shall be increased further, in the same manner as before, until the pressure corresponding to the second test point (40 percent of maximum altitude) is reached. The altimeter shall be kept at this pressure for at least 1 minute, but not more than 10 minutes, before the test reading is taken. After the reading has been taken, the pressure shall be increased further, in the same manner as before, until atmospheric pressure is reached. The reading of the altimeter at either of the two test points shall not differ by more than the tolerance specified in Table II from the reading of the altimeter for the corresponding altitude recorded during the scale error test prescribed in paragraph (b)(i).

(iii) *After effect.* Not more than 5 minutes after the completion of the hysteresis test prescribed in paragraph (b)(ii), the reading of the altimeter (corrected for any change in atmospheric pressure) shall not differ from the original atmospheric pressure reading by more than the tolerance specified in Table II.

(iv) *Friction.* The altimeter shall be subjected to a steady rate of decrease of pressure approximating 750 feet per minute. At each altitude listed in Table III, the change in reading of the pointers after vibration shall not exceed the corresponding tolerance listed in Table III.

(v) *Case leak.* The leakage of the altimeter case, when the pressure within it corresponds to an altitude of 18,000 feet, shall not change the altimeter reading by more than the tolerance shown in Table II during an interval of 1 minute.

(vi) *Barometric scale error.* At constant atmospheric pressure, the barometric pressure scale shall be set at each of the pressures (falling within its range of adjustment) that are listed in Table IV, and shall cause the pointer to indicate the

equivalent altitude difference shown in Table IV with a tolerance of 25 feet.

(2) Altimeters which are the air data computer type with associated computing systems, or which incorporate air data correction internally, may be tested in a manner and to specifications developed by the manufacturer which are acceptable to the Administrator.

(c) Automatic Pressure Altitude Reporting Equipment and ATC Transponder System Integration Test. The test must be conducted by an appropriately rated person under the conditions specified in paragraph (a). Measure the automatic pressure altitude at the output of the installed ATC transponder when interrogated on Mode C at a sufficient number of test points to ensure that the altitude reporting equipment, altimeters, and ATC transponders perform their intended functions as installed in the aircraft. The difference between the automatic reporting output and the altitude displayed at the altimeter shall not exceed 125 feet.

(d) Records: Comply with the provisions of §43.9 of this chapter as to content, form, and disposition of the records. The person performing the altimeter tests shall record on the altimeter the date and maximum altitude to which the altimeter has been tested and the persons approving the airplane for return to service shall enter that data in the airplane log or other permanent record.

Table I

Altitude	Equivalent pressure (inches of mercury)	Tolerance ± (feet)
-1,000	31.018	20
0	29.921	20
500	29.385	20
1,000	28.856	20
1,500	28.335	25
2,000	27.821	30
3,000	26.817	30
4,000	25.842	35
6,000	23.978	40
8,000	22.225	60
10,000	20.577	80
12,000	19.029	90
14,000	17.577	100
16,000	16.216	110
18,000	14.942	120
20,000	13.750	130
22,000	12.636	140
25,000	11.104	155
30,000	8.885	180
35,000	7.041	205
40,000	5.538	230
45,000	4.355	255
50,000	3.425	280

Table II — Test Tolerances

Test	Tolerance (feet)
Case Leak Test	±100
Hysteresis Test:	
First Test Point (50 percent of maximum altitude)	75
Second Test Point (40 percent of maximum altitude)	75
After Effect Test	30

Table III — Friction

Altitude (feet)	Tolerance (feet)
1,000	±70
2,000	70
3,000	70
5,000	70
10,000	80
15,000	90
20,000	100
25,000	120
30,000	140
35,000	160
40,000	180
50,000	250

Table IV — Pressure-Altitude Difference

Pressure (inches of Hg)	Altitude difference (feet)
28.10	-1,727
28.50	-1,340
29.00	- 863
29.50	-392
29.92	0
30.50	+531
30.90	+893
30.99	+974

(Secs. 313, 314, and 601 through 610 of the Federal Aviation Act of 1958 (49 U.S.C. 1354, 1355, and 1421 through 1430) and sec. 6(c), Dept. of Transportation Act (49 U.S.C. 1655(c)))

[Amdt. 43–2, 30 FR 8262, June 29, 1965, as amended by Amdt. 43–7, 32 FR 7587, May 24, 1967; Amdt. 43–19, 43 FR 22639, May 25, 1978; Amdt. 43–23, 47 FR 41086, Sept. 16, 1982; Amdt. 43–31, 54 FR 34330, Aug. 18, 1989; Doc. No. FAA–2015–1621, Amdt. 43–49, 81 FR 96700, Dec. 30, 2016]

APPENDIX F TO PART 43

ATC TRANSPONDER TESTS AND INSPECTIONS

The ATC transponder tests required by §91.413 of this chapter may be conducted using a bench check or portable test equipment and must meet the requirements prescribed in paragraphs (a) through (j) of this appendix. If portable test equipment with appropriate coupling to the aircraft antenna system is used, operate the test equipment for ATCRBS transponders at a nominal rate of 235 interrogations per second to avoid possible ATCRBS interference. Operate the test equipment at a nominal rate of 50 Mode S interrogations per second for Mode S. An additional 3 dB loss is allowed to compensate for antenna coupling errors during receiver sensitivity measurements conducted in accordance with paragraph (c)(1) when using portable test equipment.

(a) Radio Reply Frequency:

(1) For all classes of ATCRBS transponders, interrogate the transponder and verify that the reply frequency is 1090±3 Megahertz (MHz).

(2) For classes 1B, 2B, and 3B Mode S transponders, interrogate the transponder and verify that the reply frequency is 1090±3 MHz.

(3) For classes 1B, 2B, and 3B Mode S transponders that incorporate the optional 1090±1 MHz reply frequency, interrogate the transponder and verify that the reply frequency is correct.

(4) For classes 1A, 2A, 3A, and 4 Mode S transponders, interrogate the transponder and verify that the reply frequency is 1090±1 MHz.

(b) Suppression: When Classes 1B and 2B ATCRBS Transponders, or Classes 1B, 2B, and 3B Mode S transponders are interrogated Mode 3/A at an interrogation rate between 230 and 1,000 interrogations per second; or when Classes 1A and 2A ATCRBS Transponders, or Classes 1B, 2A, 3A, and 4 Mode S transponders are interrogated at a rate between 230 and 1,200 Mode 3/A interrogations per second:

(1) Verify that the transponder does not respond to more than 1 percent of ATCRBS interrogations when the amplitude of P_2 pulse is equal to the P_1 pulse.

(2) Verify that the transponder replies to at least 90 percent of ATCRBS interrogations when the amplitude of the P_2 pulse is 9 dB less than the P_1 pulse. If the test is conducted with a radiated test signal, the interrogation rate shall be 235±5 interrogations per second unless a higher rate has been approved for the test equipment used at that location.

(c) Receiver Sensitivity:

(1) Verify that for any class of ATCRBS Transponder, the receiver minimum triggering level (MTL) of the system is −73 ±4 dbm, or that for any class of Mode S transponder the receiver MTL for Mode S format (P6 type) interrogations is −74 ±3 dbm by use of a test set either:

(i) Connected to the antenna end of the transmission line;

(ii) Connected to the antenna terminal of the transponder with a correction for transmission line loss; or

(iii) Utilized radiated signal.

(2) Verify that the difference in Mode 3/A and Mode C receiver sensitivity does not exceed 1 db for either any class of ATCRBS transponder or any class of Mode S transponder.

(d) Radio Frequency (RF) Peak Output Power:

(1) Verify that the transponder RF output power is within specifications for the class of transponder. Use the same conditions as described in (c)(1) (i), (ii), and (iii) above.

(i) For Class 1A and 2A ATCRBS transponders, verify that the minimum RF peak output power is at least 21.0 dbw (125 watts).

(ii) For Class 1B and 2B ATCRBS Transponders, verify that the minimum RF peak output power is at least 18.5 dbw (70 watts).

(iii) For Class 1A, 2A, 3A, and 4 and those Class 1B, 2B, and 3B Mode S transponders that include the optional high RF peak output power, verify that the minimum RF peak output power is at least 21.0 dbw (125 watts).

(iv) For Classes 1B, 2B, and 3B Mode S transponders, verify that the minimum RF peak output power is at least 18.5 dbw (70 watts).

(v) For any class of ATCRBS or any class of Mode S transponders, verify that the maximum RF peak output power does not exceed 27.0 dbw (500 watts).

Note: The tests in (e) through (j) apply only to Mode S transponders.

(e) Mode S Diversity Transmission Channel Isolation: For any class of Mode S transponder that incorporates diversity operation, verify that the RF peak output power transmitted from the selected antenna exceeds the power transmitted from the nonselected antenna by at least 20 db.

(f) Mode S Address: Interrogate the Mode S transponder and verify that it replies only to its assigned address. Use the correct address and at least two incorrect addresses. The interrogations should be made at a nominal rate of 50 interrogations per second.

(g) Mode S Formats: Interrogate the Mode S transponder with uplink formats (UF) for which it is equipped and verify that the replies are made in the correct format. Use the surveillance formats UF=4 and 5. Verify that the altitude reported in the replies to UF=4 are the same as that reported in a valid ATCRBS Mode C reply. Verify that the

identity reported in the replies to UF=5 are the same as that reported in a valid ATCRBS Mode 3/A reply. If the transponder is so equipped, use the communication formats UF=20, 21, and 24.

(h) Mode S All-Call Interrogations: Interrogate the Mode S transponder with the Mode S-only all-call format UF = 11 and verify that the correct address and capability are reported in the replies (downlink format DF = 11).

(i) ATCRBS-Only All-Call Interrogation: Interrogate the Mode S transponder with the ATCRBS-only all-call interrogation (0.8 microsecond P_4 pulse) and verify that no reply is generated.

(j) Squitter: Verify that the Mode S transponder generates a correct acquisition squitter approximately once per second.

(k) Records: Comply with the provisions of §43.9 of this chapter as to content, form, and disposition of the records.

[Amdt. 43–26, 52 FR 3390, Feb. 3, 1987; 52 FR 6651, March 4, 1987, as amended by Amdt. 43–31, 54 FR 34330, Aug. 18, 1989; Amdt. 43–53, 88 FR 71476, Oct. 17, 2023]

PART 48

REGISTRATION AND MARKING REQUIREMENTS FOR SMALL UNMANNED AIRCRAFT

Authority: 49 U.S.C. 106(f), 106(g), 40101, 40103, 40113–40114, 41703, 44101–44103, 44105–44106, 44110–44113, 44809(f), 45302, 45305, 46104, 46301, 46306.

Source: Docket No. FAA–2015–7396, 80 FR 78645, December 16, 2015, unless otherwise noted.

Subpart A—General

§48.1 Applicability.

(a) This part provides registration and identification requirements for small unmanned aircraft that are part of a small unmanned aircraft system as defined in §1.1 of this chapter.

(b) Small unmanned aircraft eligible for registration in the United States must be registered and identified in accordance with either:

(1) The registration and identification requirements in this part; or

(2) The registration requirements in part 47 and the identification and registration marking requirements in subparts A and C of part 45.

(c) Small unmanned aircraft intended to be operated outside of the territorial airspace of the United States, or registered through a trust or voting trust, must be registered in accordance with subparts A and B of part 47 and satisfy the identification and registration marking requirements of subparts A and C of part 45.

§48.5 [Reserved]

§48.10 Definitions.

For purposes of this part, the following definitions apply:

Citizen of the United States or U.S. citizen means one of the following:

(1) An individual who is a citizen of the United States or one of its possessions.

(2) A partnership each of whose partners is an individual who is a citizen of the United States.

(3) A corporation or association organized under the laws of the United States or a State, the District of Columbia, or a territory or possession of the United States, of which the president and at least two-thirds of the board of directors and other managing officers are citizens of the United States, which is under the actual control of citizens of the United States, and in which at least 75 percent of the voting interest is owned or controlled by persons that are citizens of the United States.

Registry means the FAA, Civil Aviation Registry, Aircraft Registration Branch.

Resident alien means an individual citizen of a foreign country lawfully admitted for permanent residence in the United States as an immigrant in conformity with the regulations of the Department of Homeland Security (8 CFR Chapter 1).

§48.15 Requirement to register.

No person may operate a small unmanned aircraft that is eligible for registration under 49 U.S.C. 44101-44103 unless one of the following criteria has been satisfied:

(a) The owner has registered and marked the aircraft in accordance with this part;

(b) The aircraft is operated exclusively in compliance with 49 U.S.C. 44809 and weighs 0.55 pounds or less on takeoff, including everything that is on board or otherwise attached to the aircraft; or

(c) The aircraft is an aircraft of the Armed Forces of the United States.

[Docket No. FAA–2015–7396; Amdt. No. 48–1; 80 FR 78645, Dec. 16, 2015, as amended by Doc. No. FAA–2019–1100; Amdt. No. 48–3; 86 FR 4504, Jan. 15, 2021]

§48.20 Eligibility for registration.

A small unmanned aircraft may be registered under 49 U.S.C. 44103 and under this part only when the aircraft is not registered under the laws of a foreign country and is—

(a) Owned by a U.S. citizen;

(b) Owned by an individual citizen of a foreign country lawfully admitted for permanent residence in the United States;

(c) Owned by a corporation not a citizen of the United States when the corporation is organized and doing business under the laws of the United States or a State within the United States, and the aircraft is based and primarily used in the United States; or

(d) An aircraft of—

(1) The United States Government; or

(2) A State, the District of Columbia, a territory or possession of the United States, or a political subdivision of a State, territory, or possession.

§48.25 Applicants.

(a) To register a small unmanned aircraft in the United States under this part, a person must provide the information required by §48.110 to the Registry in a form and manner prescribed by the Administrator. Upon submission of this information, the FAA issues a Certificate of Aircraft Registration to that person.

(b) A small unmanned aircraft must be registered by its owner using the legal name of its owner, unless the owner is less than 13 years of age. If the owner is less than 13 years of age, then the small unmanned aircraft must be registered by a person who is at least 13 years of age.

(c) In accordance with 49 U.S.C. 44103(c), registration is not evidence of aircraft ownership in any proceeding in which ownership of an unmanned aircraft by a particular person is in issue.

(d) In this part, "owner" includes a buyer in possession, a bailee, a lessee of a small unmanned aircraft under a contract of conditional sale, and the assignee of that person.

[Docket No. FAA–2015–7396; Amdt. No. 48–1; 80 FR 78645, Dec. 16, 2015, as amended by Doc. No. FAA–2019–1100; Amdt. No. 48–3; 86 FR 4504, Jan. 15, 2021]

§48.30 Fees.

(a) The fee for issuing or renewing a Certificate of Aircraft Registration as described in §48.100 is $5.00 per aircraft.

(b) The fee for issuing or renewing a Certificate of Aircraft Registration as described in §48.105 is $5.00 per certificate.

(c) Each application for and renewal of a Certificate of Aircraft Registration must be accompanied by the fee described in paragraphs (a) and (b), as applicable, paid to the Federal Aviation Administration through the web-based aircraft registration system, or in another manner if prescribed by the Administrator.

[Docket No. FAA–2015–7396; Amdt. No. 48–1; 80 FR 78645, Dec. 16, 2015, as amended by Doc. No. FAA–2019–1100; Amdt. No. 48–3; 86 FR 4504, Jan. 15, 20211]

Subpart B—Certificates of Aircraft Registration for Small Unmanned Aircraft

§48.100 Registration: Small unmanned aircraft operated for any purpose other than exclusively limited recreational operations.

(a) *Certificate of Aircraft Registration.* A Certificate of Aircraft Registration issued in accordance with §48.110 to a small unmanned aircraft used for any purpose other than operating exclusively in compliance with 49 U.S.C. 44809 constitutes registration for the small unmanned aircraft identified on the application.

(b) *Effective date of registration.* An aircraft is registered when the applicant receives a Certificate of Aircraft Registration for the specific aircraft. The effective date of registration is shown by the date of issue on the Certificate of Aircraft Registration issued for the aircraft.

(c) *Registration renewal.* A Certificate of Aircraft registration issued under this part expires 3 years after the date of issue unless it is renewed.

(1) The holder of a Certificate of Aircraft Registration must renew the Certificate by verifying, in a form and manner prescribed by the Administrator, that the information provided in accordance with §48.110 is accurate and if it is not, provide updated information. The verification may take place at any time within the six months preceding the month in which the Certificate of Aircraft registration expires.

(2) A certificate issued under this paragraph expires three years from the expiration date of the previous certificate.

(d) *Other events affecting effectiveness of Certificate.* Each Certificate of Aircraft Registration issued by the FAA under this subpart is effective, unless registration has ended by reason of having been revoked, canceled, expired, or the ownership is transferred, until the date upon which one of the following events occurs:

(1) Subject to the Convention on the International Recognition of Rights in Aircraft when applicable, the aircraft is registered under the laws of a foreign country.

(2) The small unmanned aircraft is totally destroyed or scrapped.

(3) The holder of the Certificate of Aircraft Registration loses U.S. citizenship.

(4) Thirty days have elapsed since the death of the holder of the Certificate of Aircraft Registration.

(5) The owner, if an individual who is not a citizen of the United States, loses status as a resident alien, unless that person becomes a citizen of the United States at the same time.

(6) The owner is a corporation other than a corporation which is a citizen of the United States and one of the following events occurs:

(i) The corporation ceases to be lawfully organized and doing business under the laws of the United States or any State thereof; or

(ii) The aircraft was not operated exclusively within the United States during the period of registration under this part.

[Docket No. FAA–2015–7396; Amdt. No. 48–1; 80 FR 78645, Dec. 16, 2015. Redesignated and amended by Doc. No. FAA–2019–1100; Amdt. No. 48–3, 86 FR 4504, Jan. 15, 2021]

§48.105 Registration: Small unmanned aircraft intended exclusively for limited recreational operations.

(a) *Certificate of Aircraft Registration.* A Certificate of Aircraft Registration issued in accordance with §48.110 for small unmanned aircraft to be operated exclusively in compliance with 49 U.S.C. 44809 constitutes registration for all the small unmanned aircraft used exclusively for operations in compliance with 49 U.S.C. 44809 owned by the individual identified on the application.

(b) *Effective date of registration.* An aircraft is registered when the applicant receives a Certificate of Aircraft Registration. The effective date of registration is shown by the date of issue on the Certificate of Aircraft Registration issued under this part.

(c) *Registration renewal.* A Certificate of Aircraft Registration issued under this part expires 3 years after the date of issue unless it is renewed.

(1) The holder of a Certificate of Aircraft Registration must renew the Certificate by verifying, in a form and manner prescribed by the Administrator, that the information provided in accordance with §48.110 is accurate and if it is not, provide updated information. The verification may take place at any time within the six months preceding the month in which the Certificate of Aircraft registration expires.

(2) A certificate issued under this paragraph expires three years from the expiration date of the previous certificate.

(d) *Other events affecting effectiveness of Certificate.* Each Certificate of Aircraft Registration issued by the FAA under this part is effective, unless registration has ended by reason of having been revoked, canceled or expired, or until the date upon which one of the following events occurs:

(1) The holder of the Certificate of Aircraft Registration loses U.S. citizenship.

(2) Thirty days have elapsed since the death of the holder of the Certificate of Aircraft Registration.

(3) The owner, if an individual who is not a citizen of the United States, loses status as a resident alien, unless that person becomes a citizen of the United States at the same time.

[Docket No. FAA–2015–7396; Amdt. No. 48–1; 80 FR 78645, Dec. 16, 2015. Redesignated and amended by Doc. No. FAA–2019–1100; Amdt. No. 48–3, 86 FR 4504, Jan. 15, 2021]

§48.110 Application.

(a) *Required information.* Each applicant for a Certificate of Aircraft Registration issued under this part must submit all of the following information to the Registry:

(1) Applicant's name and, for an applicant other than an individual, the name of the authorized representative applying for a Certificate of Aircraft Registration.

(2) Applicant's physical address and, for an applicant other than an individual, the physical address of the authorized representative. If the applicant or authorized representative cannot receive mail at a physical address, then provide a mailing address.

(3) Applicant's email address or, for applicants other than individuals, the email address of the authorized representative.

(4) Applicant's telephone number(s) and, for an applicant other than an individual, the telephone number(s) of the authorized representative.

(5) The aircraft manufacturer and model name.

(6) For any standard remote identification unmanned aircraft, the serial number issued by the manufacturer of the unmanned aircraft in accordance with the design and production requirements of part 89 of this chapter. The serial number provided in this application must not be listed on more than one Certificate of Aircraft Registration at the same time.

(7) For any unmanned aircraft equipped with a remote identification broadcast module, the serial number issued by the manufacturer of the remote identification broadcast module in accordance with the design and production requirements of part 89 of this chapter. An applicant may submit the serial number of more than one remote identification broadcast module as part of the application for aircraft registration under §48.105. The

serial number of a remote identification broadcast module provided in this application must not be listed on more than one Certificate of Aircraft Registration at the same time.

(8) Other information as required by the Administrator.

(b) *Provision of information.* The information identified in paragraph (a) of this section must be submitted to the Registry through the web-based small unmanned aircraft registration system in a form and manner prescribed by the Administrator.

(c) *Issuance of Certificate of Aircraft Registration.* The FAA will issue a Certificate of Aircraft Registration upon completion of the application requirements provided in paragraph (a) of this section.

[Docket No. FAA–2015–7396; Amdt. No. 48–1; 80 FR 78645, Dec. 16, 2015. Redesignated and amended by Doc. No. FAA–2019–1100; Amdt. No. 48–3, 86 FR 4504, Jan. 15, 2021]

§48.115 Requirement to maintain current information.

(a) The holder of a Certificate of Aircraft Registration must ensure that the information provided under §48.110 remains accurate.

(b) The holder of a Certificate of Aircraft Registration must update the information using the web-based small unmanned aircraft registration system within 14 calendar days of the following:

(1) A change in the information provided under §48.110.

(2) When aircraft registration requires cancellation for any reason including sale or transfer, destruction, or export.

[Docket No. FAA–2015–7396; Amdt. No. 48–1; 80 FR 78645, Dec. 16, 2015. Redesignated and amended by Doc. No. FAA–2019–1100; Amdt. No. 48–3, 86 FR 4504, Jan. 15, 2021]

§48.120 Invalid registration.

The registration of a small unmanned aircraft is invalid if, at the time it is made—

(a) The aircraft is registered in a foreign country;

(b) The applicant is not the owner, except when the applicant registers on behalf of an owner who is under 13 years of age;

(c) The applicant is not eligible to submit an application under this part; or

(d) The interest of the applicant in the aircraft was created by a transaction that was not entered into in good faith, but rather was made to avoid (with or without the owner's knowledge) compliance with 49 U.S.C. 44101-44103.

§48.125 Foreign civil aircraft.

Except for corporations eligible to register under §48.20(c), the FAA will issue a recognition of ownership to persons required to comply with the provisions of this part pursuant to an authorization to operate issued under part 375 of this title. The recognition of ownership does not have the effect of U.S. aircraft registration.

Subpart C— Aircraft Marking

§48.200 General.

(a) No person may operate a small unmanned aircraft registered in accordance with this part unless the aircraft displays a unique identifier in accordance with the requirements of §48.205 of this subpart.

(b) A unique identifier is one of the following:

(1) The registration number issued to an individual or the registration number issued to the aircraft by the Registry upon completion of the registration process provided by this part; or

(2) If authorized by the Administrator, the small unmanned aircraft serial number provided with the application for Certificate of Aircraft Registration under §48.110(a).

[Docket No. FAA–2015–7396; Amdt. No. 48–1; 80 FR 78645, Dec. 16, 2015. Redesignated and amended by Doc. No. FAA–2019–1100; Amdt. No. 48–3, 86 FR 4504, Jan. 15, 2021]

§48.205 Display and location of unique identifier.

(a) The unique identifier must be maintained in a condition that is legible.

(b) The unique identifier must be affixed to the small unmanned aircraft by any means necessary to ensure that it will remain affixed for the duration of each operation.

(c) The unique identifier must be legibly displayed on an external surface of the small unmanned aircraft.

[Docket No. FAA–2015–7396; Amdt. No. 48–1; 80 FR 78645, Dec. 16, 2015, as amended by Doc. No. FAA–2018–1084, 84 FR 3673, Feb. 13, 2019]

PART 61

CERTIFICATION: PILOTS, FLIGHT INSTRUCTORS, AND GROUND INSTRUCTORS

61

Subpart C—Student Pilots

61.81 Applicability.
61.83 Eligibility requirements for student pilots.
61.85 Application.
61.87 Solo requirements for student pilots.
61.89 General limitations.
61.91 [Reserved]
61.93 Solo cross-country flight requirements.
61.94 Student pilot seeking a sport pilot certificate or a recreational pilot certificate: Operations at airports within, and in airspace located within, Class B, C, and D airspace, or at airports with an operational control tower in other airspace.
61.95 Operations in Class B airspace and at airports located within Class B airspace.

Subpart D—Recreational Pilots

61.96 Applicability and eligibility requirements: General.
61.97 Aeronautical knowledge.
61.98 Flight proficiency.
61.99 Aeronautical experience.
61.100 Pilots based on small islands.
61.101 Recreational pilot privileges and limitations.

Subpart E—Private Pilots

61.102 Applicability.
61.103 Eligibility requirements: General.
61.105 Aeronautical knowledge.
61.107 Flight proficiency.
61.109 Aeronautical experience.
61.110 Night flying exceptions.
61.111 Cross-country flights: Pilots based on small islands.
61.113 Private pilot privileges and limitations: Pilot in command.
61.115 Balloon rating: Limitations.
61.117 Private pilot privileges and limitations: Second in command of aircraft requiring more than one pilot.
61.118 – 61.120 [Reserved]

Subpart F—Commercial Pilots

61.121 Applicability.
61.123 Eligibility requirements: General.
61.125 Aeronautical knowledge.
61.127 Flight proficiency.
61.129 Aeronautical experience.
61.131 Exceptions to the night flying requirements.
61.133 Commercial pilot privileges and limitations.
61.135 – 61.141 [Reserved]

Subpart G—Airline Transport Pilots

61.151 Applicability.
61.153 Eligibility requirements: General.
61.155 Aeronautical knowledge.
61.156 Training requirements: Airplane category—multiengine class or multiengine airplane type rating concurrently with an airline transport pilot certificate.
*61.157 **Flight proficiency.**
61.158 [Reserved]
61.159 Aeronautical experience: Airplane category rating.
61.160 Aeronautical experience—airplane category restricted privileges.
61.161 Aeronautical experience: Rotorcraft category and helicopter class rating.
61.163 Aeronautical experience: Powered-lift category rating.
61.165 Additional aircraft category and class ratings.
61.167 Airline transport pilot privileges and limitations.
61.169 Letters of authorization for institutions of higher education.
61.170 – 61.171 [Reserved]

Subpart H—Flight Instructors Other than Flight Instructors With a Sport Pilot Rating

61.181 Applicability.
61.183 Eligibility requirements.
61.185 Aeronautical knowledge.
61.187 Flight proficiency.
61.189 Flight instructor records.
61.191 Additional flight instructor ratings.
61.193 Flight instructor privileges.
61.195 Flight instructor limitations and qualifications.
61.197 Renewal requirements for flight instructor certification.
61.199 Reinstatement requirements of an expired flight instructor certificate.
61.201 [Reserved]

Subpart I—Ground Instructors

61.211 Applicability.
61.213 Eligibility requirements.
61.215 Ground instructor privileges.
61.217 Recent experience requirements.

Subpart J—Sport Pilots

61.301 What is the purpose of this subpart and to whom does it apply?
61.303 If I want to operate a light-sport aircraft, what operating limits and endorsement requirements in this subpart must I comply with?

61.305 What are the age and language requirements for a sport pilot certificate?

61.307 What tests do I have to take to obtain a sport pilot certificate?

61.309 What aeronautical knowledge must I have to apply for a sport pilot certificate?

61.311 What flight proficiency requirements must I meet to apply for a sport pilot certificate?

61.313 What aeronautical experience must I have to apply for a sport pilot certificate?

61.315 What are the privileges and limits of my sport pilot certificate?

61.317 Is my sport pilot certificate issued with aircraft category and class ratings?

61.319 [Reserved]

***61.321 How do I obtain privileges to operate an additional category or class of light-sport aircraft?**

61.323 [Reserved]

61.325 How do I obtain privileges to operate a light-sport aircraft at an airport within, or in airspace within, Class B, C, and D airspace, or in other airspace with an airport having an operational control tower?

61.327 Are there specific endorsement requirements to operate a light-sport aircraft based on V_H?

Subpart K—
Flight Instructors With a Sport Pilot Rating

61.401 What is the purpose of this subpart?

61.403 What are the age, language, and pilot certificate requirements for a flight instructor certificate with a sport pilot rating?

61.405 What tests do I have to take to obtain a flight instructor certificate with a sport pilot rating?

61.407 What aeronautical knowledge must I have to apply for a flight instructor certificate with a sport pilot rating?

61.409 What flight proficiency requirements must I meet to apply for a flight instructor certificate with a sport pilot rating?

61.411 What aeronautical experience must I have to apply for a flight instructor certificate with a sport pilot rating?

61.412 Do I need additional training to provide instruction on control and maneuvering an airplane solely by reference to the instruments in a light-sport aircraft based on V_H?

61.413 What are the privileges of my flight instructor certificate with a sport pilot rating?

61.415 What are the limits of a flight instructor certificate with a sport pilot rating?

61.417 Will my flight instructor certificate with a sport pilot rating list aircraft category and class ratings?

***61.419 How do I obtain privileges to provide training in an additional category or class of light-sport aircraft?**

61.421 May I give myself an endorsement?

61.423 What are the recordkeeping requirements for a flight instructor with a sport pilot rating?

61.425 How do I renew my flight instructor certificate?

61.427 What must I do if my flight instructor certificate with a sport pilot rating expires?

61.429 May I exercise the privileges of a flight instructor certificate with a sport pilot rating if I hold a flight instructor certificate with another rating?

APPENDICES TO PART 61

***Appendix A—Airman Certification Standards and Practical Test Standards**

Authority: 49 U.S.C. 106(f), 106(g), 40113, 44701–44703, 44707, 44709–44711, 44729, 44903, 45102–45103, 45301–45302; Sec. 2307 Pub. L. 114–190, 130 Stat. 615 (49 U.S.C. 44703 note); and sec. 318, Pub. L. 115–254, 132 Stat. 3186 (49 U.S.C. 44703 note).

Source: Docket No. 25910, 62 FR 16298, April 4, 1997, unless otherwise noted.

SPECIAL FEDERAL AVIATION REGULATIONS

SFAR No. 73

ROBINSON R-22 / R-44 SPECIAL TRAINING AND EXPERIENCE REQUIREMENTS

Sections

1. *Applicability.*

2. *Required training, aeronautical experience, endorsements, and flight review.*

3. *Expiration date.*

1. **Applicability.** Under the procedures prescribed herein, this SFAR applies to all persons who seek to manipulate the controls or act as pilot in command of a Robinson model R-22 or R-44 helicopter. The requirements stated in this SFAR are in addition to the current requirements of part 61.

2. *Required training, aeronautical experience, endorsements, and flight review.*

(a) Awareness Training:

(1) Except as provided in paragraph (a)(2) of this section, no person may manipulate the controls of a Robinson model R-22 or R-44 helicopter after March 27, 1995, for the purpose of flight unless the awareness training specified in paragraph (a)(3) of this section is completed and the person's logbook has been endorsed by a certified flight instructor authorized under paragraph (b)(5) of this section.

(2) A person who holds a rotorcraft category and helicopter class rating on that person's pilot certificate and meets the experience requirements of paragraph (b)(1) or paragraph (b)(2) of this section may not manipulate the controls of a Robinson model R-22 or R-44 helicopter for the purpose of flight after April 26, 1995, unless the awareness training specified in paragraph (a)(3) of this section is completed and the person's logbook has been endorsed by a certified flight instructor authorized under paragraph (b)(5) of this section.

(3) Awareness training must be conducted by a certified flight instructor who has been endorsed under paragraph (b)(5) of this section and consists of instruction in the following general subject areas:

(i) Energy management;

(ii) Mast bumping;

(iii) Low rotor RPM (blade stall);

(iv) Low G hazards; and

(v) Rotor RPM decay.

(4) A person who can show satisfactory completion of the manufacturer's safety course after January 1, 1994, may obtain an endorsement from an FAA aviation safety inspector in lieu of completing the awareness training required in paragraphs (a)(1) and (a)(2) of this section.

(b) Aeronautical Experience:

(1) No person may act as pilot in command of a Robinson model R-22 unless that person:

(i) Has had at least 200 flight hours in helicopters, at least 50 flight hours of which were in the Robinson R-22; or

(ii) Has had at least 10 hours dual instruction in the Robinson R-22 and has received an endorsement from a certified flight instructor authorized under paragraph (b)(5) of this section that the individual has been given the training required by this paragraph and is proficient to act as pilot in command of an R-22. Beginning 12 calendar months after the date of the endorsement, the individual may not act as pilot in command unless the individual has completed a flight review in an R-22 within the preceding 12 calendar months and obtained an endorsement for that flight review. The dual instruction must include at least

the following abnormal and emergency procedures flight training:

(A) Enhanced training in autorotation procedures,

(B) Engine rotor RPM control without the use of the governor,

(C) Low rotor RPM recognition and recovery, and

(D) Effects of low G maneuvers and proper recovery procedures.

(2) No person may act as pilot in command of a Robinson R-44 unless that person—

(i) Has had at least 200 flight hours in helicopters, at least 50 flight hours of which were in the Robinson R-44. The pilot in command may credit up to 25 flight hours in the Robinson R-22 toward the 50 hour requirement in the Robinson R-44; or

(ii) Has had at least 10 hours dual instruction in a Robinson helicopter, at least 5 hours of which must have been accomplished in the Robinson R-44 helicopter and has received an endorsement from a certified flight instructor authorized under paragraph (b)(5) of this section that the individual has been given the training required by this paragraph and is proficient to act as pilot in command of an R-44. Beginning 12 calendar months after the date of the endorsement, the individual may not act as pilot in command unless the individual has completed a flight review in a Robinson R-44 within the preceding 12 calendar months and obtained an endorsement for that flight review. The dual instruction must include at least the following abnormal and emergency procedures flight training—

(A) Enhanced training in autorotation procedures;

(B) Engine rotor RPM control without the use of the governor;

(C) Low rotor RPM recognition and recovery; and

(D) Effects of low G maneuvers and proper recovery procedures.

(3) A person who does not hold a rotorcraft category and helicopter class rating must have had at least 20 hours of dual instruction in a Robinson R-22 helicopter prior to operating it in solo flight. In addition, the person must obtain an endorsement from a certified flight instructor authorized under paragraph (b)(5) of this section that instruction has been given in those maneuvers and procedures, and the instructor has found the applicant proficient to solo a Robinson R-22. This endorsement is valid for a period of 90 days. The dual instruction must include at least the following abnormal and emergency procedures flight training:

(i) Enhanced training in autorotation procedures,

(ii) Engine rotor RPM control without the use of the governor,

(iii) Low rotor RPM recognition and recovery, and

(iv) Effects of low G maneuvers and proper recovery procedures.

(4) A person who does not hold a rotorcraft category and helicopter class rating must have had at least 20 hours of dual instruction in a Robinson R-44 helicopter prior to operating it in solo flight. In addition, the person must obtain an endorsement from a certified flight instructor authorized under paragraph (b)(5) of this section that instruction has been given in those maneuvers and procedures, and the instructor has found the applicant proficient to solo a Robinson R-44. This endorsement is valid for a period of 90 days. The dual instruction must include at least the following abnormal and emergency procedures flight training:

(i) Enhanced training in autorotation procedures,

(ii) Engine rotor RPM control without the use of the governor,

(iii) Low rotor RPM recognition and recovery, and

(iv) Effects of low G maneuvers and proper recovery procedures.

(5) No certificated flight instructor may provide instruction or conduct a flight review in a Robinson R-22 or R-44 unless that instructor—

(i) Completes the awareness training in paragraph (2)(a) of this SFAR.

(ii) For the Robinson R-22, has had at least 200 flight hours in helicopters, at least 50 flight hours of which were in the Robinson R-22, or for the Robinson R-44, has had at least 200 flight hours in helicopters, 50 flight hours of which were in Robinson helicopters. Up to 25 flight hours of Robinson R-22 flight time may be credited toward the 50 hour requirement.

(iii) Has completed flight training in a Robinson R-22, R-44, or both, on the following abnormal and emergency procedures—

(A) Enhanced training in autorotation procedures;

(B) Engine rotor RPM control without the use of the governor;

(C) Low rotor RPM recognition and recovery; and

(D) Effects of low G maneuvers and proper recovery procedures.

(iv) Has been authorized by endorsement from an FAA aviation safety inspector or authorized designated examiner that the instructor has completed the appropriate training, meets the experience requirements and has satisfactorily demonstrated an ability to provide instruction on the general subject areas of paragraph 2(a)(3) of this SFAR, and the flight training identified in paragraph 2(b)(5)(iii) of this SFAR.

(c) Flight Review:

(1) No flight review completed to satisfy §61.56 by an individual after becoming eligible to function as pilot in command in a Robinson R-22 helicopter shall be valid for the operation of R-22 helicopter unless that flight review was taken in an R-22.

(2) No flight review completed to satisfy §61.56 by an individual after becoming eligible to function as pilot in command in a Robinson R-44 helicopter shall be valid for the operation of R-44 helicopter unless that flight review was taken in the R-44.

(3) The flight review will include a review of the awareness training subject areas of paragraph 2(a)(3) of this SFAR and the flight training identified in paragraph 2(b) of this SFAR.

(d) Currency Requirements: No person may act as pilot in command of a Robinson model R-22 or R-44 helicopter carrying passengers unless the pilot in command has met the recency of flight experience requirements of §61.57 in an R-22 or R-44, as appropriate.

3. *Expiration date*. This SFAR No. 73 shall remain in effect until it is revised or rescinded.

[Docket No. 25910, 62 FR 16298, April 4, 1997, as amended by SFAR 73–1, 63 FR 666, Jan. 7, 1998; 68 FR 43, Jan. 2, 2003; Amdt. 61–120, 73 FR 17246, April 1, 2008; Amdt. SFAR 73–2, 74 FR 25650, May 29, 2009]

SFAR No. 100–2

RELIEF FOR U.S. MILITARY AND CIVILIAN PERSONNEL WHO ARE ASSIGNED OUTSIDE THE UNITED STATES IN SUPPORT OF U.S. ARMED FORCES OPERATIONS

1. *Applicability*. Flight Standards offices are authorized to accept from an eligible person, as described in paragraph 2 of this SFAR, the following:

(a) An expired flight instructor certificate to show eligibility for renewal of a flight instructor certificate under §61.197, or an expired written test report to show eligibility under part 61 to take a practical test;

(b) An expired written test report to show eligibility under §§63.33 and 63.57 to take a practical test; and

(c) An expired written test report to show eligibility to take a practical test required under part 65 or an expired inspection authorization to show eligibility for renewal under §65.93.

2. *Eligibility*. A person is eligible for the relief described in paragraph 1 of this SFAR if:

(a) The person served in a U.S. military or civilian capacity outside the United States in support of the U.S. Armed Forces' operation during some period of time from September 11, 2001, to termination of SFAR 100–2;

(b) The person's flight instructor certificate, airman written test report, or inspection authorization expired some time between September 11,

2001, and 6 calendar months after returning to the United States or termination of SFAR 100–2, whichever is earlier; and

(c) The person complies with §61.197 or §65.93 of this chapter, as appropriate, or completes the appropriate practical test within 6 calendar months after returning to the United States, or upon termination of SFAR 100–2, whichever is earlier.

3. *Required documents.* The person must send the Airman Certificate and/or Rating Application (FAA Form 8710–1) to the appropriate Flight Standards office. The person must include with the application one of the following documents, which must show the date of assignment outside the United States and the date of return to the United States:

(a) An official U.S. Government notification of personnel action, or equivalent document, showing the person was a civilian on official duty for the U.S. Government outside the United States and was assigned to a U.S. Armed Forces' operation some time between September 11, 2001, to termination of SFAR 100–2;

(b) Military orders showing the person was assigned to duty outside the United States and was assigned to a U.S. Armed Forces' operation some time between September 11, 2001, to termination of SFAR 100–2; or

(c) A letter from the person's military commander or civilian supervisor providing the dates during which the person served outside the United States and was assigned to a U.S. Armed Forces' operation some time between September 11, 2001, to termination of SFAR 100–2.

4. *Expiration date.* This Special Federal Aviation Regulation No. 100–2 is effective until further notice.

[Docket No. FAA–2009–0923, 75 FR 9766, March 4, 2010, as amended by Docket FAA–2018–0119, Amdt. 61–141, 83 FR 9170, March 5, 2018]

Subpart A—General

§61.1 Applicability and definitions.

(a) Except as provided in part 107 of this chapter, this part prescribes:

(1) The requirements for issuing pilot, flight instructor, and ground instructor certificates and ratings; the conditions under which those certificates and ratings are necessary; and the privileges and limitations of those certificates and ratings.

(2) The requirements for issuing pilot, flight instructor, and ground instructor authorizations; the conditions under which those authorizations are necessary; and the privileges and limitations of those authorizations.

(3) The requirements for issuing pilot, flight instructor, and ground instructor certificates and

ratings for persons who have taken courses approved by the Administrator under other parts of this chapter.

(b) For the purpose of this part:

Accredited has the same meaning as defined by the Department of Education in 34 CFR 600.2.

Aeronautical experience means pilot time obtained in an aircraft, flight simulator, or flight training device for meeting the appropriate training and flight time requirements for an airman certificate, rating, flight review, or recency of flight experience requirements of this part.

Authorized instructor means—

(i) A person who holds a ground instructor certificate issued under part 61 of this chapter and is in compliance with §61.217, when conducting ground training in accordance with the privileges and limitations of his or her ground instructor certificate;

(ii) A person who holds a flight instructor certificate issued under part 61 of this chapter and is in compliance with §61.197, when conducting ground training or flight training in accordance with the privileges and limitations of his or her flight instructor certificate; or

(iii) A person authorized by the Administrator to provide ground training or flight training under part 61, 121, 135, or 142 of this chapter when conducting ground training or flight training in accordance with that authority.

Aviation training device means a training device, other than a full flight simulator or flight training device, that has been evaluated, qualified, and approved by the Administrator.

Complex airplane means an airplane that has a retractable landing gear, flaps, and a controllable pitch propeller, including airplanes equipped with an engine control system consisting of a digital computer and associated accessories for controlling the engine and propeller, such as a full authority digital engine control; or, in the case of a seaplane, flaps and a controllable pitch propeller, including seaplanes equipped with an engine control system consisting of a digital computer and associated accessories for controlling the engine and propeller, such as a full authority digital engine control.

Cross-country time means—

(i) Except as provided in paragraphs (ii) through (vi) of this definition, time acquired during flight—

(A) Conducted by a person who holds a pilot certificate;

(B) Conducted in an aircraft;

(C) That includes a landing at a point other than the point of departure; and

(D) That involves the use of dead reckoning, pilotage, electronic navigation aids, radio aids, or other navigation systems to navigate to the landing point.

(ii) For the purpose of meeting the aeronautical experience requirements (except for a rotorcraft category rating), for a private pilot certificate (except for a powered parachute category rating), a commercial pilot certificate, or an instrument rating, or for the purpose of exercising recreational pilot privileges (except in a rotorcraft) under §61.101(c), time acquired during a flight—

(A) Conducted in an appropriate aircraft;

(B) That includes a point of landing that was at least a straight-line distance of more than 50 nautical miles from the original point of departure; and

(C) That involves the use of dead reckoning, pilotage, electronic navigation aids, radio aids, or other navigation systems to navigate to the landing point.

(iii) For the purpose of meeting the aeronautical experience requirements for a sport pilot certificate (except for powered parachute privileges), time acquired during a flight conducted in an appropriate aircraft that—

(A) Includes a point of landing at least a straight line distance of more than 25 nautical miles from the original point of departure; and

(B) Involves, as applicable, the use of dead reckoning; pilotage; electronic navigation aids; radio aids; or other navigation systems to navigate to the landing point.

(iv) For the purpose of meeting the aeronautical experience requirements for a sport pilot certificate with powered parachute privileges or a private pilot certificate with a powered parachute category rating, time acquired during a flight conducted in an appropriate aircraft that—

(A) Includes a point of landing at least a straight line distance of more than 15 nautical miles from the original point of departure; and

(B) Involves, as applicable, the use of dead reckoning; pilotage; electronic navigation aids; radio aids; or other navigation systems to navigate to the landing point.

(v) For the purpose of meeting the aeronautical experience requirements for any pilot certificate with a rotorcraft category rating or an instrument-helicopter rating, or for the purpose of exercising recreational pilot privileges, in a rotorcraft, under §61.101(c), time acquired during a flight—

(A) Conducted in an appropriate aircraft;

(B) That includes a point of landing that was at least a straight-line distance of more than 25 nautical miles from the original point of departure; and

(C) That involves the use of dead reckoning, pilotage, electronic navigation aids, radio aids, or other navigation systems to navigate to the landing point.

(vi) For the purpose of meeting the aeronautical experience requirements for an airline transport pilot certificate (except with a rotorcraft category rating), time acquired during a flight—

(A) Conducted in an appropriate aircraft;

(B) That is at least a straight-line distance of more than 50 nautical miles from the original point of departure; and

(C) That involves the use of dead reckoning, pilotage, electronic navigation aids, radio aids, or other navigation systems.

(vii) For a military pilot who qualifies for a commercial pilot certificate (except with a rotorcraft category rating) under §61.73 of this part, time acquired during a flight—

(A) Conducted in an appropriate aircraft;

(B) That is at least a straight-line distance of more than 50 nautical miles from the original point of departure; and

(C) That involves the use of dead reckoning, pilotage, electronic navigation aids, radio aids, or other navigation systems.

Examiner means any person who is authorized by the Administrator to conduct a pilot proficiency test or a practical test for an airman certificate or rating issued under this part, or a person who is authorized to conduct a knowledge test under this part.

Flight training means that training, other than ground training, received from an authorized instructor in flight in an aircraft.

Ground training means that training, other than flight training, received from an authorized instructor.

Institution of higher education has the same meaning as defined by the Department of Education in 34 CFR 600.4.

Instrument approach means an approach procedure defined in part 97 of this chapter.

Instrument training means that time in which instrument training is received from an authorized instructor under actual or simulated instrument conditions.

Knowledge test means a test on the aeronautical knowledge areas required for an airman certificate or rating that can be administered in written form or by a computer.

Nationally recognized accrediting agency has the same meaning as defined by the Department of Education in 34 CFR 600.2.

Night vision goggles means an appliance worn by a pilot that enhances the pilot's ability to maintain visual surface reference at night.

Night vision goggle operation means the portion of a flight that occurs during the time period from 1 hour after sunset to 1 hour before sunrise where the pilot maintains visual surface reference using night vision goggles in an aircraft that is approved for such an operation.

Pilot time means that time in which a person—

(i) Serves as a required pilot flight crewmember;

(ii) Receives training from an authorized instructor in an aircraft, full flight simulator, flight training device, or aviation training device;

61

(iii) Gives training as an authorized instructor in an aircraft, full flight simulator, flight training device, or aviation training device; or

(iv) Serves as second in command in operations conducted in accordance with §135.99(c) of this chapter when a second pilot is not required under the type certification of the aircraft or the regulations under which the flight is being conducted, provided the requirements in §61.159(c) are satisfied.

Practical test means a test on the areas of operations for an airman certificate, rating, or authorization that is conducted by having the applicant respond to questions and demonstrate maneuvers in flight, in a flight simulator, or in a flight training device.

Set of aircraft means aircraft that share similar performance characteristics, such as similar airspeed and altitude operating envelopes, similar handling characteristics, and the same number and type of propulsion systems.

Student pilot seeking a sport pilot certificate means a person who has received an endorsement—

(i) To exercise student pilot privileges from a certificated flight instructor with a sport pilot rating; or

(ii) That includes a limitation for the operation of a light-sport aircraft specified in §61.89(c) issued by a certificated flight instructor with other than a sport pilot rating.

Technically advanced airplane (TAA) means an airplane equipped with an electronically advanced avionics system.

Training time means training received—

(i) In flight from an authorized instructor;

(ii) On the ground from an authorized instructor; or

(iii) In a flight simulator or flight training device from an authorized instructor.

[Docket No. 25910, 62 FR 16298, April 4, 1997; Amdt. 61–103, 62 FR 40893, July 30, 1997 as amended by Amdt. 61–110, 69 FR 44864, July 27, 2004; Amdt. 61–124, 74 FR 42546, Aug. 21, 2009; Amdt. 61–128, 76 FR 54105, Aug. 31, 2011; Amdt. 61–130, 78 FR 42372, July 15, 2013; Amdt. 61–137, 81 FR 42208, June 28, 2016; Amdt. 61–142, 83 FR 30276, June 27, 2018]

§61.2 Exercise of Privilege.

(a) *Validity.* No person may:

(1) Exercise privileges of a certificate, rating, endorsement, or authorization issued under this part if the certificate, rating or authorization is surrendered, suspended, revoked or expired.

(2) Exercise privileges of a flight instructor certificate if that flight instructor certificate is surrendered, suspended, revoked or expired.

(3) Exercise privileges of a foreign pilot certificate to operate an aircraft of foreign registry under §61.3(b) if the certificate is surrendered, suspended, revoked or expired.

(4) Exercise privileges of a pilot certificate issued under §61.75, or an authorization issued under §61.77, if the foreign pilot certificate relied upon for the issuance of the U.S. pilot certificate or authorization is surrendered, suspended, revoked or expired.

(5) Exercise privileges of a medical certificate issued under part 67 to meet any requirements of part 61 if the medical certificate is surrendered, suspended, revoked or expired according to the duration standards set forth in §61.23(d).

(6) Use an official government issued driver's license to meet any requirements of part 61 related to holding that driver's license, if the driver's license is surrendered, suspended, revoked or expired.

(b) *Currency.* No person may:

(1) Exercise privileges of an airman certificate, rating, endorsement, or authorization issued under this part unless that person meets the appropriate airman and medical recency requirements of this part, specific to the operation or activity.

(2) Exercise privileges of a foreign pilot license within the United States to conduct an operation described in §61.3(b), unless that person meets the appropriate airman and medical recency requirements of the country that issued the license, specific to the operation.

[Docket No. FAA–2006–26661, 74 FR 42546, Aug. 21, 2009]

§61.3 Requirement for certificates, ratings, and authorizations.

(a) *Required pilot certificate for operating a civil aircraft of the United States.* No person may serve as a required pilot flight crewmember of a civil aircraft of the United States, unless that person:

(1) Has in the person's physical possession or readily accessible in the aircraft when exercising the privileges of that pilot certificate or authorization—

(i) A pilot certificate issued under this part and in accordance with §61.19;

(ii) A special purpose pilot authorization issued under §61.77;

(iii) A temporary certificate issued under §61.17;

(iv) A document conveying temporary authority to exercise certificate privileges issued by the Airmen Certification Branch under §61.29(e);

(v) When engaged in a flight operation within the United States for a part 119 certificate holder authorized to conduct operations under part 121 or 135 of this chapter, a temporary document provided by that certificate holder under an approved certificate verification plan;

(vi) When engaged in a flight operation within the United States for a fractional ownership program manager authorized to conduct operations under part 91, subpart K, of this chapter, a temporary document provided by that program manager under an approved certificate verification plan; or

(vii) When operating an aircraft within a foreign country, a pilot license issued by that country may be used.

(2) Has a photo identification that is in that person's physical possession or readily accessible in the aircraft when exercising the privileges of that pilot certificate or authorization. The photo identification must be a:

(i) Driver's license issued by a State, the District of Columbia, or territory or possession of the United States;

(ii) Government identification card issued by the Federal government, a State, the District of Columbia, or a territory or possession of the United States;

(iii) U.S. Armed Forces' identification card;

(iv) Official passport;

(v) Credential that authorizes unescorted access to a security identification display area at an airport regulated under 49 CFR part 1542; or

(vi) Other form of identification that the Administrator finds acceptable.

(b) *Required pilot certificate for operating a foreign-registered aircraft within the United States.* No person may serve as a required pilot flight crewmember of a civil aircraft of foreign registry within the United States, unless—

(1) That person's pilot certificate or document issued under §61.29(e) is in that person's physical possession or readily accessible in the aircraft when exercising the privileges of that pilot certificate; and

(2) Has been issued in accordance with this part, or has been issued or validated by the country in which the aircraft is registered.

(c) *Medical certificate.*

(1) A person may serve as a required pilot flight crewmember of an aircraft only if that person holds the appropriate medical certificate issued under part 67 of this chapter, or other documentation acceptable to the FAA, that is in that person's physical possession or readily accessible in the aircraft. Paragraph (c)(2) of this section provides certain exceptions to the requirement to hold a medical certificate.

(2) A person is not required to meet the requirements of paragraph (c)(1) of this section if that person—

(i) Is exercising the privileges of a student pilot certificate while seeking a pilot certificate with a glider category rating, a balloon class rating, or glider or balloon privileges;

(ii) Is exercising the privileges of a student pilot certificate while seeking a sport pilot certificate with other than glider or balloon privileges and holds a U.S. driver's license;

(iii) Is exercising the privileges of a student pilot certificate while seeking a pilot certificate with a weight-shift-control aircraft category rating or a powered parachute category rating and holds a U.S. driver's license;

(iv) Is exercising the privileges of a sport pilot certificate with glider or balloon privileges;

(v) Is exercising the privileges of a sport pilot certificate with other than glider or balloon privileges and holds a U.S. driver's license. A person who has applied for or held a medical certificate may exercise the privileges of a sport pilot certificate using a U.S. driver's license only if that person—

(A) Has been found eligible for the issuance of at least a third-class airman medical certificate at the time of his or her most recent application; and

(B) Has not had his or her most recently issued medical certificate suspended or revoked or most recent Authorization for a Special Issuance of a Medical Certificate withdrawn.

(vi) Is holding a pilot certificate with a balloon class rating and that person—

(A) Is exercising the privileges of a private pilot certificate in a balloon; or

(B) Is providing flight training in a balloon in accordance with §61.133(a)(2)(ii);

(vii) Is holding a pilot certificate or a flight instructor certificate with a glider category rating, and is piloting or providing training in a glider, as appropriate;

(viii) Is exercising the privileges of a flight instructor certificate, provided the person is not acting as pilot in command or as a required pilot flight crewmember;

(ix) Is exercising the privileges of a ground instructor certificate;

(x) Is operating an aircraft within a foreign country using a pilot license issued by that country and possesses evidence of current medical qualification for that license;

(xi) Is operating an aircraft with a U.S. pilot certificate, issued on the basis of a foreign pilot license, issued under §61.75, and holds a medical certificate issued by the foreign country that issued the foreign pilot license, which is in that person's physical possession or readily accessible in the aircraft when exercising the privileges of that airman certificate;

(xii) Is a pilot of the U.S. Armed Forces, has an up-to-date U.S. military medical examination, and holds military pilot flight status;

(xiii) Is exercising the privileges of a student, recreational or private pilot certificate for operations conducted under the conditions and limitations set forth in §61.113(i) and holds a U.S. driver's license;

61

(xiv) Is exercising the privileges of a flight instructor certificate and acting as pilot in command or a required flightcrew member for operations conducted under the conditions and limitations set forth in §61.113(i) and holds a U.S. driver's license; or

(xv) Is exercising the privileges of a student pilot certificate or higher while acting as pilot in command on a special medical flight test authorized under part 67 of this chapter.

(d) *Flight instructor certificate.*

(1) A person who holds a flight instructor certificate issued under this part must have that certificate, or other documentation acceptable to the Administrator, in that person's physical possession or readily accessible in the aircraft when exercising the privileges of that flight instructor certificate.

(2) Except as provided in paragraph (d)(3) of this section, no person other than the holder of a flight instructor certificate issued under this part with the appropriate rating on that certificate may—

(i) Give training required to qualify a person for solo flight and solo cross-country flight;

(ii) Endorse an applicant for a—

(A) Pilot certificate or rating issued under this part;

(B) Flight instructor certificate or rating issued under this part; or

(C) Ground instructor certificate or rating issued under this part;

(iii) Endorse a pilot logbook to show training given; or

(iv) Endorse a logbook for solo operating privileges.

(3) A flight instructor certificate issued under this part is not necessary—

(i) Under paragraph (d)(2) of this section, if the training is given by the holder of a commercial pilot certificate with a lighter-than-air rating, provided the training is given in accordance with the privileges of the certificate in a lighter-than-air aircraft;

(ii) Under paragraph (d)(2) of this section, if the training is given by the holder of an airline transport pilot certificate with a rating appropriate to the aircraft in which the training is given, provided the training is given in accordance with the privileges of the certificate and conducted in accordance with an approved air carrier training program approved under part 121 or part 135 of this chapter;

(iii) Under paragraph (d)(2) of this section, if the training is given by a person who is qualified in accordance with subpart C of part 142 of this chapter, provided the training is conducted in accordance with an approved part 142 training program;

(iv) Under paragraphs (d)(2)(i), (d)(2)(ii)(C), and (d)(2)(iii) of this section, if the training is given by the holder of a ground instructor certificate in accordance with the privileges of the certificate; or

(v) Under paragraph (d)(2)(iii) of this section, if the training is given by an authorized flight instructor under §61.41 of this part.

(e) *Instrument rating.* No person may act as pilot in command of a civil aircraft under IFR or in weather conditions less than the minimums prescribed for VFR flight unless that person holds:

(1) The appropriate aircraft category, class, type (if required), and instrument rating on that person's pilot certificate for any airplane, helicopter, or powered-lift being flown;

(2) An airline transport pilot certificate with the appropriate aircraft category, class, and type rating (if required) for the aircraft being flown;

(3) For a glider, a pilot certificate with a glider category rating and an airplane instrument rating; or

(4) For an airship, a commercial pilot certificate with a lighter-than-air category rating and airship class rating.

(f) *Category II pilot authorization.* Except for a pilot conducting Category II operations under part 121 or part 135, a person may not:

(1) Act as pilot in command of a civil aircraft during Category II operations unless that person—

(i) Holds a Category II pilot authorization for that category or class of aircraft, and the type of aircraft, if applicable; or

(ii) In the case of a civil aircraft of foreign registry, is authorized by the country of registry to act as pilot in command of that aircraft in Category II operations.

(2) Act as second in command of a civil aircraft during Category II operations unless that person—

(i) Holds a pilot certificate with category and class ratings for that aircraft and an instrument rating for that category aircraft;

(ii) Holds an airline transport pilot certificate with category and class ratings for that aircraft; or

(iii) In the case of a civil aircraft of foreign registry, is authorized by the country of registry to act as second in command of that aircraft during Category II operations.

(g) *Category III pilot authorization.* Except for a pilot conducting Category III operations under part 121 or part 135, a person may not:

(1) Act as pilot in command of a civil aircraft during Category III operations unless that person—

(i) Holds a Category III pilot authorization for that category or class of aircraft, and the type of aircraft, if applicable; or

(ii) In the case of a civil aircraft of foreign registry, is authorized by the country of registry to act

as pilot in command of that aircraft in Category III operations.

(2) Act as second in command of a civil aircraft during Category III operations unless that person—

(i) Holds a pilot certificate with category and class ratings for that aircraft and an instrument rating for that category aircraft;

(ii) Holds an airline transport pilot certificate with category and class ratings for that aircraft; or

(iii) In the case of a civil aircraft of foreign registry, is authorized by the country of registry to act as second in command of that aircraft during Category III operations.

(h) *Category A aircraft pilot authorization.* The Administrator may issue a certificate of authorization for a Category II or Category III operation to the pilot of a small aircraft that is a Category A aircraft, as identified in §97.3(b)(1) of this chapter if:

(1) The Administrator determines that the Category II or Category III operation can be performed safely by that pilot under the terms of the certificate of authorization; and

(2) The Category II or Category III operation does not involve the carriage of persons or property for compensation or hire.

(i) *Ground instructor certificate.*

(1) Each person who holds a ground instructor certificate issued under this part must have that certificate or a temporary document issued under §61.29(e) in that person's physical possession or immediately accessible when exercising the privileges of that certificate.

(2) Except as provided in paragraph (i)(3) of this section, no person other than the holder of a ground instructor certificate, issued under this part or part 143, with the appropriate rating on that certificate may—

(i) Give ground training required to qualify a person for solo flight and solo cross-country flight;

(ii) Endorse an applicant for a knowledge test required for a pilot, flight instructor, or ground instructor certificate or rating issued under this part; or

(iii) Endorse a pilot logbook to show ground training given.

(3) A ground instructor certificate issued under this part is not necessary—

(i) Under paragraph (i)(2) of this section, if the training is given by the holder of a flight instructor certificate issued under this part in accordance with the privileges of that certificate;

(ii) Under paragraph (i)(2) of this section, if the training is given by the holder of a commercial pilot certificate with a lighter-than-air rating, provided the training is given in accordance with the privileges of the certificate in a lighter-than-air aircraft;

(iii) Under paragraph (i)(2) of this section, if the training is given by the holder of an airline transport pilot certificate with a rating appropriate to the aircraft in which the training is given, provided the training is given in accordance with the privileges of the certificate and conducted in accordance with an approved air carrier training program approved under part 121 or part 135 of this chapter;

(iv) Under paragraph (i)(2) of this section, if the training is given by a person who is qualified in accordance with subpart C of part 142 of this chapter, provided the training is conducted in accordance with an approved part 142 training program; or

(v) Under paragraph (i)(2)(iii) of this section, if the training is given by an authorized flight instructor under §61.41 of this part.

(j) *Age limitation for certain operations.*

(1) *Age limitation.* No person who holds a pilot certificate issued under this part may serve as a pilot on a civil airplane of U.S. registry in the following operations if the person has reached his or her 60th birthday or, in the case of operations with more than one pilot, his or her 65th birthday:

(i) Scheduled international air services carrying passengers in turbojet-powered airplanes;

(ii) Scheduled international air services carrying passengers in airplanes having a passenger-seat configuration of more than nine passenger seats, excluding each crewmember seat;

(iii) Nonscheduled international air transportation for compensation or hire in airplanes having a passenger-seat configuration of more than 30 passenger seats, excluding each crewmember seat; or

(iv) Scheduled international air services, or nonscheduled international air transportation for compensation or hire, in airplanes having a payload capacity of more than 7,500 pounds.

(2) *Definitions.*

(i) "International air service," as used in this paragraph (j), means scheduled air service performed in airplanes for the public transport of passengers, mail, or cargo, in which the service passes through the airspace over the territory of more than one country.

(ii) "International air transportation," as used in this paragraph (j), means air transportation performed in airplanes for the public transport of passengers, mail, or cargo, in which the service passes through the airspace over the territory of more than one country.

(k) *Special purpose pilot authorization.* Any person that is required to hold a special purpose pilot authorization, issued in accordance with §61.77 of this part, must have that authorization and the person's foreign pilot license in that person's physical possession or have it readily

61

accessible in the aircraft when exercising the privileges of that authorization.

(l) *Inspection of certificate.* Each person who holds an airman certificate, temporary document in accordance with paragraph (a)(1)(v) or (vi) of this section, medical certificate, documents establishing alternative medical qualification under part 68 of this chapter, authorization, or license required by this part must present it and their photo identification as described in paragraph (a)(2) of this section for inspection upon a request from:

(1) The Administrator;

(2) An authorized representative of the National Transportation Safety Board;

(3) Any Federal, State, or local law enforcement officer; or

(4) An authorized representative of the Transportation Security Administration.

[Docket No. 25910, 62 FR 16298, April 4, 1997; Amdt. 61–103, 62 FR 40894, July 30, 1997; Amdt. 61–111, 67 FR 65861, Oct. 28, 2002; Amdt. 61–110, 69 FR 44864, July 27, 2004; Amdt. 61–123, 74 FR 34234, July 15, 2009; Amdt. 61–124, 74 FR 42546, Aug. 21, 2009; Amdt. 61–124A, 74 FR 53644, Oct. 20, 2009; Amdt. 61–131, 78 FR 56828, Sept. 16, 2013; Amdt. 61–134, 80 FR 33400, June 12, 2015; Docket FAA–2010–1127, Amdt. 61–135, 81 FR 1306, Jan. 12, 2016; Doc. No. FAA–2016–9157, Amdt. 61–140, 82 FR 3164, Jan. 11, 2017; Amdt. 60–6, 83 FR 30276, June 27, 2018; Docket No. FAA–2021–1040, Amdt. No. 61–152, 87 FR 71236, Nov. 22, 2022; Docket No. FAA–2021–1040; Amdt. No. 61–152, 87 FR 71236, Nov. 22, 2022]

§61.4 Qualification and approval of flight simulators and flight training devices.

(a) Except as specified in paragraph (b) or (c) of this section, each flight simulator and flight training device used for training, and for which an airman is to receive credit to satisfy any training, testing, or checking requirement under this chapter, must be qualified and approved by the Administrator for—

(1) The training, testing, and checking for which it is used;

(2) Each particular maneuver, procedure, or crewmember function performed; and

(3) The representation of the specific category and class of aircraft, type of aircraft, particular variation within the type of aircraft, or set of aircraft for certain flight training devices.

(b) Any device used for flight training, testing, or checking that has been determined to be acceptable to or approved by the Administrator prior to August 1, 1996, which can be shown to function as originally designed, is considered to be a flight training device, provided it is used for the same purposes for which it was originally accepted or approved and only to the extent of such acceptance or approval.

(c) The Administrator may approve a device other than a flight simulator or flight training device for specific purposes.

[Docket No. 25910, 62 FR 16298, April 4, 1997; Amdt. 61–103, 62 FR 40895, July 30, 1997]

§61.5 Certificates and ratings issued under this part.

(a) The following certificates are issued under this part to an applicant who satisfactorily accomplishes the training and certification requirements for the certificate sought:

(1) Pilot certificates—

(i) Student pilot.

(ii) Sport pilot.

(iii) Recreational pilot.

(iv) Private pilot.

(v) Commercial pilot.

(vi) Airline transport pilot.

(2) Flight instructor certificates.

(3) Ground instructor certificates.

(b) The following ratings are placed on a pilot certificate (other than student pilot) when an applicant satisfactorily accomplishes the training and certification requirements for the rating sought:

(1) Aircraft category ratings—

(i) Airplane.

(ii) Rotorcraft.

(iii) Glider.

(iv) Lighter-than-air.

(v) Powered-lift.

(vi) Powered parachute.

(vii) Weight-shift-control aircraft.

(2) Airplane class ratings—

(i) Single-engine land.

(ii) Multiengine land.

(iii) Single-engine sea.

(iv) Multiengine sea.

(3) Rotorcraft class ratings—

(i) Helicopter.

(ii) Gyroplane.

(4) Lighter-than-air class ratings—

(i) Airship.

(ii) Balloon.

(5) Weight-shift-control aircraft class ratings—

(i) Weight-shift-control aircraft land.

(ii) Weight-shift-control aircraft sea.

(6) Powered parachute class ratings—

(i) Powered parachute land.

(ii) Powered parachute sea.

(7) Aircraft type ratings—

(i) Large aircraft other than lighter-than-air.

(ii) Turbojet-powered airplanes.

(iii) Other aircraft type ratings specified by the Administrator through the aircraft type certification procedures.

(iv) Second-in-command pilot type rating for aircraft that is certificated for operations with a minimum crew of at least two pilots.

(8) Instrument ratings (on private and commercial pilot certificates only)—
(i) Instrument—Airplane.
(ii) Instrument—Helicopter.
(iii) Instrument—Powered-lift.

(c) The following ratings are placed on a flight instructor certificate when an applicant satisfactorily accomplishes the training and certification requirements for the rating sought:
(1) Aircraft category ratings—
(i) Airplane.
(ii) Rotorcraft.
(iii) Glider.
(iv) Powered-lift.

(2) Airplane class ratings—
(i) Single-engine.
(ii) Multiengine.

(3) Rotorcraft class ratings—
(i) Helicopter.
(ii) Gyroplane.

(4) Instrument ratings—
(i) Instrument—Airplane.
(ii) Instrument—Helicopter.
(iii) Instrument—Powered-lift.

(5) Sport pilot rating.

(d) The following ratings are placed on a ground instructor certificate when an applicant satisfactorily accomplishes the training and certification requirements for the rating sought:
(1) Basic.
(2) Advanced.
(3) Instrument.

[Docket No. 25910, 62 FR 16298, April 4, 1997; as amended by Amdt. 61–110, 69 FR 44864, July 27, 2004; Amdt. 61–113, 70 FR 45271, Aug. 4, 2005]

§61.7 Obsolete certificates and ratings.

(a) The holder of a free-balloon pilot certificate issued before November 1, 1973, may not exercise the privileges of that certificate.

(b) The holder of a pilot certificate that bears any of the following category ratings without an associated class rating may not exercise the privileges of that category rating:
(1) Rotorcraft.
(2) Lighter-than-air.
(3) Helicopter.
(4) Autogyro.

§61.8 Inapplicability of unmanned aircraft operations.

Any action conducted pursuant to part 107 of this chapter cannot be used to meet the requirements of this part.

[FAA–2020–1067, Amdt. No. 61-148, 85 FR 79825, Dec. 11, 2020]

§61.9 [Reserved]

§61.11 Expired pilot certificates and reissuance.

(a) No person who holds an expired pilot certificate or rating may act as pilot in command or as a required pilot flight crewmember of an aircraft of the same category or class that is listed on that expired pilot certificate or rating.

(b) The following pilot certificates and ratings have expired and will not be reissued:
(1) An airline transport pilot certificate issued before May 1, 1949, or an airline transport pilot certificate that contains a horsepower limitation.
(2) A private or commercial pilot certificate issued before July 1, 1945.
(3) A pilot certificate with a lighter-than-air or free-balloon rating issued before July 1, 1945.

(c) An airline transport pilot certificate that was issued after April 30, 1949, and that bears an expiration date but does not contain a horsepower limitation, may have that airline transport pilot certificate re-issued without an expiration date.

(d) A private or commercial pilot certificate that was issued after June 30, 1945, and that bears an expiration date, may have that pilot certificate reissued without an expiration date.

(e) A pilot certificate with a lighter-than-air or free-balloon rating that was issued after June 30, 1945, and that bears an expiration date, may have that pilot certificate reissued without an expiration date.

[Docket No. FAA–2006–26661, 74 FR 42547, Aug. 21, 2009]

§61.13 Issuance of airman certificates, ratings, and authorizations.

(a) *Application.*
(1) An applicant for an airman certificate, rating, or authorization under this part must make that application on a form and in a manner acceptable to the Administrator.
(2) An applicant must show evidence that the appropriate fee prescribed in appendix A to part 187 of this chapter has been paid when that person applies for airmen certification services administered outside the United States.
(3) An applicant who is neither a citizen of the United States nor a resident alien of the United States may be refused issuance of any U.S. airman certificate, rating or authorization by the Administrator.
(4) Except as provided in paragraph (a)(3) of this section, an applicant who satisfactorily accomplishes the training and certification requirements for the certificate, rating, or authorization

sought is entitled to receive that airman certificate, rating, or authorization.

(b) Limitations.

(1) An applicant who cannot comply with certain areas of operation required on the practical test because of physical limitations may be issued an airman certificate, rating, or authorization with the appropriate limitation placed on the applicant's airman certificate provided the—

(i) Applicant is able to meet all other certification requirements for the airman certificate, rating, or authorization sought;

(ii) Physical limitation has been recorded with the FAA on the applicant's medical records; and

(iii) Administrator determines that the applicant's inability to perform the particular area of operation will not adversely affect safety.

(2) A limitation placed on a person's airman certificate may be removed, provided that person demonstrates for an examiner satisfactory proficiency in the area of operation appropriate to the airman certificate, rating, or authorization sought.

(c) Additional requirements for Category II and Category III pilot authorizations.

(1) A Category II or Category III pilot authorization is issued by a letter of authorization as part of an applicant's instrument rating or airline transport pilot certificate.

(2) Upon original issue, the authorization contains the following limitations:

(i) For Category II operations, the limitation is 1,600 feet RVR and a 150-foot decision height; and

(ii) For Category III operations, each initial limitation is specified in the authorization document.

(3) The limitations on a Category II or Category III pilot authorization may be removed as follows:

(i) In the case of Category II limitations, a limitation is removed when the holder shows that, since the beginning of the sixth preceding month, the holder has made three Category II ILS approaches with a 150-foot decision height to a landing under actual or simulated instrument conditions.

(ii) In the case of Category III limitations, a limitation is removed as specified in the authorization.

(4) To meet the experience requirements of paragraph (c)(3) of this section, and for the practical test required by this part for a Category II or a Category III pilot authorization, a flight simulator or flight training device may be used if it is approved by the Administrator for such use.

(d) Application during suspension or revocation.

(1) Unless otherwise authorized by the Administrator, a person whose pilot, flight instructor, or ground instructor certificate has been suspended may not apply for any certificate, rating, or authorization during the period of suspension.

(2) Unless otherwise authorized by the Administrator, a person whose pilot, flight instructor, or ground instructor certificate has been revoked may not apply for any certificate, rating, or authorization for 1 year after the date of revocation.

[Docket No. 25910, 62 FR 40895, July 30, 1997; as amended by Amdt. 61–116, 72 FR 18558, April 12, 2007; Amdt. 61–132, 78 FR 77572, Dec. 24, 2013]

§61.14 Incorporation by Reference.

Certain material is incorporated by reference into this part with the approval of the Director of the Federal Register under 5 U.S.C. 552(a) and 1 CFR Part 51. All approved incorporation by reference (IBR) material is available for inspection at the Federal Aviation Administration (FAA) and at the National Archives and Records Administration (NARA). Contact FAA, Training and Certification Group, 202-267-1100, *ACSPTSinquiries @faa.gov*. For information on the availability of this material at NARA, visit *www.archives.gov /federal-register/cfr/ibr-locations* or email *fr.inspection@nara.gov*. The material may be obtained from the Federal Aviation Administration, 800 Independence Avenue SW, Washington DC 20591, 866-835-5322, *www.faa.gov/ training_testing*.

(a) Practical Test Standards.

(1) FAA-S-8081-3B, Recreational Pilot Practical Test Standards for Airplane Category and Rotorcraft Category, November 2023; IBR approved for §61.43 and appendix A to this part.

(2) FAA-S-8081-7C, Flight Instructor Practical Test Standards for Rotorcraft Category Gyroplane Rating, November 2023; IBR approved for §61.43 and appendix A to this part.

(3) FAA-S-8081-8C, Flight Instructor Practical Test Standards for Glider Category, November 2023; IBR approved for §61.43 and appendix A to this part.

(4) FAA-S-8081-9E, Flight Instructor Instrument Practical Test Standards for Airplane Rating and Helicopter Rating, November 2023; IBR approved for §61.43 and appendix A to this part.

(5) FAA-S-8081-15B, Private Pilot Practical Test Standards for Rotorcraft Category Gyroplane Rating, November 2023; IBR approved for §61.43 and appendix A to this part.

(6) FAA-S-8081-16C, Commercial Pilot Practical Test Standards for Rotorcraft Category Gyroplane Rating, November 2023; IBR approved for §61.43 and appendix A to this part.

(7) FAA-S-8081-17A, Private Pilot Practical Test Standards for Lighter-Than-Air Category, November 2023; IBR approved for §61.43 and appendix A to this part.

(8) FAA-S-8081-18A, Commercial Pilot Practical Test Standards for Lighter-Than-Air Category, November 2023; IBR approved for §61.43 and appendix A to this part.

(9) FAA-S-8081-20A, Airline Transport Pilot and Aircraft Type Rating Practical Test Standards for

Rotorcraft Category Helicopter Rating, November 2023; IBR approved for §§61.43 and 61.58, and appendix A to this part.

(10) FAA-S-8081-22A, Private Pilot Practical Test Standards for Glider Category, November 2023; IBR approved for §61.43 and appendix A to this part.

(11) FAA-S-8081-23B, Commercial Pilot Practical Test Standards for Glider Category, November 2023; IBR approved for §61.43 and appendix A to this part.

(12) FAA-S-8081-29A, Sport Pilot and Sport Pilot Flight Instructor Rating Practical Test Standards for Airplane Category, Rotorcraft Category, and Glider Category, November 2023; IBR approved for §§61.43, 61.321, and 61.419, and appendix A to this part.

(13) FAA-S-8081-30A, Sport Pilot and Sport Pilot Flight Instructor Rating Practical Test Standards for Lighter-Than-Air Category, November 2023; IBR approved for §§61.43, 61.321, and 61.419, and appendix A to this part.

(14) FAA-S-8081-31A, Sport Pilot and Sport Pilot Flight Instructor Practical Test Standards for Powered Parachute Category and Weight-Shift-Control Aircraft Category, November 2023; IBR approved for §§61.43, 61.321, and 61.419, and appendix A to this part.

(15) FAA-S-8081-32A Private Pilot Practical Test Standards for Powered Parachute Category and Weight-Shift-Control Aircraft Category, November 2023; IBR approved for §61.43 and appendix A to this part.

(b) Airman Certification Standards.

(1) FAA-S-ACS-2, Commercial Pilot for Powered-Lift Category Airman Certification Standards, November 2023; IBR approved for §61.43 and appendix A to this part.

(2) FAA-S-ACS-3, Instrument Rating—Powered-Lift Airman Certification Standards, November 2023; IBR approved for §§61.43 and 61.57, and appendix A to this part.

(3) FAA-S-ACS-6C, Private Pilot for Airplane Category Airman Certification Standards, November 2023; IBR approved for §61.43 and appendix A to this part.

(4) FAA-S-ACS-7B, Commercial Pilot for Airplane Category Airman Certification Standards, November 2023; IBR approved for §61.43 and appendix A to this part.

(5) FAA-S-ACS-8C, Instrument Rating—Airplane Airman Certification Standards, November 2023; IBR approved for §§61.43 and 61.57, and appendix A to this part.

(6) FAA-S-ACS-11A, Airline Transport Pilot and Type Rating for Airplane Category Airman Certification Standards, November 2023; IBR approved for §§61.43 and 61.58, and appendix A to this part.

(7) FAA-S-ACS-13, Private Pilot for Powered-Lift Category Airman Certification Standards, November 2023; IBR approved for §61.43 and appendix A to this part.

(8) FAA-S-ACS-14, Instrument Rating—Helicopter Airman Certification Standards, November 2023; IBR approved for §§61.43 and 61.57, and appendix A to this part.

(9) FAA-S-ACS-15, Private Pilot for Rotorcraft Category Helicopter Rating Airman Certification Standards, November 2023; IBR approved for §61.43 and appendix A to this part.

(10) FAA-S-ACS-16, Commercial Pilot for Rotorcraft Category Helicopter Rating Airman Certification Standards, November 2023; IBR approved for §61.43 and appendix A to this part.

(11) FAA-S-ACS-17, Airline Transport Pilot and Type Rating for Powered-Lift Category Airman Certification Standards, November 2023; IBR approved for §§61.43 and 61.58, and appendix A to this part.

(12) FAA-S-ACS-25, Flight Instructor for Airplane Category Airman Certification Standards, November 2023; IBR approved for §61.43 and appendix A to this part.

(13) FAA-S-ACS-27, Flight Instructor for Powered-Lift Category Airman Certification Standards, November 2023; IBR approved for §61.43 and appendix A to this part.

(14) FAA-S-ACS-28, Flight Instructor—Instrument Rating Powered-Lift Airman Certification Standards, November 2023; IBR approved for §61.43 and appendix A to this part.

(15) FAA-S-ACS-29, Flight Instructor for Rotorcraft Category Helicopter Rating Airman Certification Standards, November 2023; IBR approved for §61.43 and appendix A to this part.

[Docket No. FAA–2022–1463, Amdt. 61–153, 89 FR 22516, April 1, 2024]

§61.15 Offenses involving alcohol or drugs.

(a) A conviction for the violation of any Federal or State statute relating to the growing, processing, manufacture, sale, disposition, possession, transportation, or importation of narcotic drugs, marijuana, or depressant or stimulant drugs or substances is grounds for:

(1) Denial of an application for any certificate, rating, or authorization issued under this part for a period of up to 1 year after the date of final conviction; or

(2) Suspension or revocation of any certificate, rating, or authorization issued under this part.

(b) Committing an act prohibited by §91.17(a) or §91.19(a) of this chapter is grounds for:

(1) Denial of an application for a certificate, rating, or authorization issued under this part for a period of up to 1 year after the date of that act; or

(2) Suspension or revocation of any certificate, rating, or authorization issued under this part.

(c) For the purposes of paragraphs (d), (e), and (f) of this section, a motor vehicle action means:

(1) A conviction after November 29, 1990, for the violation of any Federal or State statute relating to the operation of a motor vehicle while intoxicated by alcohol or a drug, while impaired by alcohol or a drug, or while under the influence of alcohol or a drug;

(2) The cancellation, suspension, or revocation of a license to operate a motor vehicle after November 29, 1990, for a cause related to the operation of a motor vehicle while intoxicated by alcohol or a drug, while impaired by alcohol or a drug, or while under the influence of alcohol or a drug; or

(3) The denial after November 29, 1990, of an application for a license to operate a motor vehicle for a cause related to the operation of a motor vehicle while intoxicated by alcohol or a drug, while impaired by alcohol or a drug, or while under the influence of alcohol or a drug.

(d) Except for a motor vehicle action that results from the same incident or arises out of the same factual circumstances, a motor vehicle action occurring within 3 years of a previous motor vehicle action is grounds for:

(1) Denial of an application for any certificate, rating, or authorization issued under this part for a period of up to 1 year after the date of the last motor vehicle action; or

(2) Suspension or revocation of any certificate, rating, or authorization issued under this part.

(e) Each person holding a certificate issued under this part shall provide a written report of each motor vehicle action to the FAA, Civil Aviation Security Division (AMC–700), P.O. Box 25810, Oklahoma City, OK 73125, not later than 60 days after the motor vehicle action. The report must include:

(1) The person's name, address, date of birth, and airman certificate number;

(2) The type of violation that resulted in the conviction or the administrative action;

(3) The date of the conviction or administrative action;

(4) The State that holds the record of conviction or administrative action; and

(5) A statement of whether the motor vehicle action resulted from the same incident or arose out of the same factual circumstances related to a previously reported motor vehicle action.

(f) Failure to comply with paragraph (e) of this section is grounds for:

(1) Denial of an application for any certificate, rating, or authorization issued under this part for a period of up to 1 year after the date of the motor vehicle action; or

(2) Suspension or revocation of any certificate, rating, or authorization issued under this part.

§61.16 Refusal to submit to an alcohol test or to furnish test results.

A refusal to submit to a test to indicate the percentage by weight of alcohol in the blood, when requested by a law enforcement officer in accordance with §91.17(c) of this chapter, or a refusal to furnish or authorize the release of the test results requested by the Administrator in accordance with§91.17(c) or (d) of this chapter, is grounds for:

(a) Denial of an application for any certificate, rating, or authorization issued under this part for a period of up to 1 year after the date of that refusal; or

(b) Suspension or revocation of any certificate, rating, or authorization issued under this part.

§61.17 Temporary certificate.

(a) A temporary pilot, flight instructor, or ground instructor certificate or rating is issued for up to 120 days, at which time a permanent certificate will be issued to a person whom the Administrator finds qualified under this part.

(b) A temporary pilot, flight instructor, or ground instructor certificate or rating expires:

(1) On the expiration date shown on the certificate;

(2) Upon receipt of the permanent certificate; or

(3) Upon receipt of a notice that the certificate or rating sought is denied or revoked.

§61.18 [Reserved]

§61.19 Duration of pilot and instructor certificates and privileges.

(a) *General.*

(1) The holder of a certificate with an expiration date may not, after that date, exercise the privileges of that certificate.

(2) Except for a certificate issued with an expiration date, a pilot certificate is valid unless it is surrendered, suspended, or revoked.

(b) *Paper student pilot certificate.* A student pilot certificate issued under this part prior to April 1, 2016 expires:

(1) For student pilots who have not reached their 40th birthday, 60 calendar months after the month of the date of examination shown on the medical certificate.

(2) For student pilots who have reached their 40th birthday, 24 calendar months after the month of the date of examination shown on the medical certificate.

(3) For student pilots seeking a glider rating, balloon rating, or a sport pilot certificate, 60 calendar months after the month of the date issued, regardless of the person's age.

(c) *Pilot certificates.*

(1) A pilot certificate (including a student pilot certificate issued after April 1, 2016) issued under

this part is issued without a specific expiration date.

(2) The holder of a pilot certificate issued on the basis of a foreign pilot license may exercise the privileges of that certificate only while that person's foreign pilot license is effective.

(d) *Flight instructor certificate.* Except as specified in §61.197(b), a flight instructor certificate expires 24 calendar months from the month in which it was issued, renewed, or reinstated, as appropriate.

(e) *Ground instructor certificate.* A ground instructor certificate is issued without a specific expiration date.

(f) *Return of certificates.* The holder of any airman certificate that is issued under this part, and that has been suspended or revoked, must return that certificate to the FAA when requested to do so by the Administrator.

(g) *Duration of pilot certificates.* Except for a temporary certificate issued under §61.17 or a student pilot certificate issued under paragraph (b) of this section, the holder of a paper pilot certificate issued under this part may not exercise the privileges of that certificate after March 31, 2010.

[Docket No. 25910, 62 FR 16298, April 4, 1997, as amended by Amdt. 61–118, 73 FR 10668, Feb. 28, 2008; Amdt. 61–124, 74 FR 42547, Aug. 21, 2009; Amdt. 61–124A, 74 FR 53644, Oct. 20, 2009; Docket FAA–2010–1127, Amdt. 61–135, 81 FR 1306, Jan. 12, 2016]

§61.21 Duration of a Category II and a Category III pilot authorization (for other than Part 121 and Part 135 use).

(a) A Category II pilot authorization or a Category III pilot authorization expires at the end of the sixth calendar month after the month in which it was issued or renewed.

(b) Upon passing a practical test for a Category II or Category III pilot authorization, the authorization may be renewed for each type of aircraft for which the authorization is held.

(c) A Category II or Category III pilot authorization for a specific type aircraft for which an authorization is held will not be renewed beyond 12 calendar months from the month the practical test was accomplished in that type aircraft.

(d) If the holder of a Category II or Category III pilot authorization passes the practical test for a renewal in the month before the authorization expires, the holder is considered to have passed it during the month the authorization expired.

§61.23 Medical certificates: Requirement and duration.

(a) *Operations requiring a medical certificate.* Except as provided in paragraphs (b) and (c) of this section, a person—

(1) Must hold a first-class medical certificate:

(i) When exercising the pilot-in-command privileges of an airline transport pilot certificate;

(ii) When exercising the second-in-command privileges of an airline transport pilot certificate in a flag or supplemental operation in part 121 of this chapter that requires three or more pilots; or

(iii) When serving as a required pilot flightcrew member in an operation conducted under part 121 of this chapter if the pilot has reached his or her 60th birthday.

(2) Must hold at least a second-class medical certificate when exercising:

(i) Second-in-command privileges of an airline transport pilot certificate in part 121 of this chapter (other than operations specified in paragraph (a)(1)(ii) of this section);

(ii) Privileges of a commercial pilot certificate in an aircraft other than a balloon or glider; or

(iii) Except as provided in paragraph (b)(5) of this section, privileges of a commercial pilot certificate with a balloon class rating for compensation or hire; or

(3) Must hold at least a third-class medical certificate—

(i) When exercising the privileges of a private pilot certificate, recreational pilot certificate, or student pilot certificate, except when operating under the conditions and limitations set forth in §61.113(i);

(ii) When exercising the privileges of a flight instructor certificate and acting as the pilot in command or as a required flightcrew member, except when operating under the conditions and limitations set forth in §61.113(i);

(iii) When taking a practical test in an aircraft for a recreational pilot, private pilot, commercial pilot, or airline transport pilot certificate, or for a flight instructor certificate, except when operating under the conditions and limitations set forth in §61.113(i); or

(iv) When performing the duties as an Examiner in an aircraft when administering a practical test or proficiency check for an airman certificate, rating, or authorization

(b) *Operations not requiring a medical certificate.* A person is not required to hold a medical certificate—

(1) When exercising the privileges of a student pilot certificate while seeking—

(i) A sport pilot certificate with glider or balloon privileges; or

(ii) A pilot certificate with a glider category rating or balloon class rating;

(2) When exercising the privileges of a sport pilot certificate with privileges in a glider or balloon;

(3) When exercising the privileges of a pilot certificate with a glider category rating in a glider;

(4) When exercising the privileges of a private pilot certificate with a balloon class rating in a balloon;

61

(5) When exercising the privileges of a commercial pilot certificate with a balloon class rating in a balloon if the person is providing flight training in accordance with § 61.133(a)(2)(ii);

(6) When exercising the privileges of a flight instructor certificate with—

(i) A sport pilot rating in a glider or balloon; or

(ii) A glider category rating;

(7) When exercising the privileges of a flight instructor certificate if the person is not acting as pilot in command or serving as a required pilot flight crewmember;

(8) When exercising the privileges of a ground instructor certificate;

(9) When serving as an Examiner or check airman and administering a practical test or proficiency check for an airman certificate, rating, or authorization conducted in a glider, balloon, flight simulator, or flight training device;

(10) When taking a practical test or a proficiency check for a certificate, rating, authorization or operating privilege conducted in a glider, balloon, flight simulator, or flight training device;

(11) When a military pilot of the U.S. Armed Forces can show evidence of an up-to-date medical examination authorizing pilot flight status issued by the U.S. Armed Forces and—

(i) The flight does not require higher than a third-class medical certificate; and

(ii) The flight conducted is a domestic flight operation within U.S. airspace; or

(12) When exercising the privileges of a student pilot certificate or higher while acting as pilot in command on a special medical flight test authorized under part 67 of this chapter.

(c) Operations requiring either a medical certificate or U.S. driver's license.

(1) A person must hold and possess either a medical certificate issued under part 67 of this chapter or a U.S. driver's license when—

(i) Exercising the privileges of a student pilot certificate while seeking sport pilot privileges in a light-sport aircraft other than a glider or balloon;

(ii) Exercising the privileges of a sport pilot certificate in a light-sport aircraft other than a glider or balloon;

(iii) Exercising the privileges of a flight instructor certificate with a sport pilot rating while acting as pilot in command or serving as a required flight crewmember of a light-sport aircraft other than a glider or balloon;

(iv) Serving as an Examiner and administering a practical test for the issuance of a sport pilot certificate in a light-sport aircraft other than a glider or balloon;

(v) Exercising the privileges of a student, recreational or private pilot certificate if the flight is conducted under the conditions and limitations set forth in §61.113(i); or

(vi) Exercising the privileges of a flight instructor certificate and acting as the pilot in command or as a required flight crewmember if the flight is conducted under the conditions and limitations set forth in §61.113(i).

(2) A person using a U.S. driver's license to meet the requirements of paragraph (c) while exercising sport pilot privileges must—

(i) Comply with each restriction and limitation imposed by that person's U.S. driver's license and any judicial or administrative order applying to the operation of a motor vehicle;

(ii) Have been found eligible for the issuance of at least a third-class airman medical certificate at the time of his or her most recent application (if the person has applied for a medical certificate);

(iii) Not have had his or her most recently issued medical certificate (if the person has held a medical certificate) suspended or revoked or most recent Authorization for a Special Issuance of a Medical Certificate withdrawn; and

(iv) Not know or have reason to know of any medical condition that would make that person unable to operate a light-sport aircraft in a safe manner.

(3) A person using a U.S. driver's license to meet the requirements of paragraph (c) while operating under the conditions and limitations of §61.113(i) must meet the following requirements—

(i) The person must—

(A) Comply with all medical requirements or restrictions associated with his or her U.S. driver's license;

(B) At any point after July 14, 2006, have held a medical certificate issued under part 67 of this chapter;

(C) Complete the medical education course set forth in §68.3 of this chapter during the 24 calendar months before acting as pilot in command or serving as a required flightcrew member in an operation conducted under §61.113(i) and retain a certification of course completion in accordance with §68.3(b)(1) of this chapter;

(D) Receive a comprehensive medical examination from a State-licensed physician during the 48 months before acting as pilot in command or serving as a required flightcrew member of an operation conducted under §61.113(i) and that medical examination is conducted in accordance with the requirements in part 68 of this chapter; and

(E) If the individual has been diagnosed with any medical condition that may impact the ability of the individual to fly, be under the care and treatment of a State-licensed physician when acting as pilot in command or serving as a required flightcrew member of an operation conducted under §61.113(i).

(ii) The most recently issued medical certificate—

(A) May include an authorization for special issuance;

(B) May be expired; and

(C) Cannot have been suspended or revoked.

(iii) The most recently issued Authorization for a Special Issuance of a Medical Certificate cannot have been withdrawn; and

(iv) The most recent application for an airman medical certificate submitted to the FAA cannot have been completed and denied.

(d) Duration of a medical certificate. Use the following table to determine duration for each class of medical certificate:

Medical Certificates: Requirement and Duration

If you hold	And on the date of examination for your most recent medical certificate you were	And you are conducting an operation requiring	Then your medical certificate expires, for that operation, at the end of the last day of the
(1) A first-class medical certificate	(i) Under age 40	an airline transport pilot certificate for pilot-in-command privileges, or for second-in-command privileges in a flag or supplemental operation in part 121 requiring three or more pilots	12th month after the month of the date of examination shown on the medical certificate.
	(ii) Age 40 or older	an airline transport pilot certificate for pilot-in-command privileges, for second-in-command privileges in a flag or supplemental operation in part 121 requiring three or more pilots, or for a pilot flightcrew member in part 121 operations who has reached his or her 60th birthday.	6th month after the month of the date of examination shown on the medical certificate.
	(iii) Any age	a commercial pilot certificate (other than a commercial pilot certificate with a balloon rating when conducting flight training), a flight engineer certificate, or an air traffic control tower operator certificate.	12th month after the month of the date of examination shown on the medical certificate.
	(iv) Under age 40	a recreational pilot certificate, a private pilot certificate, a flight instructor certificate (when acting as pilot in command or a required pilot flight crewmember in operations other than glider or balloon), a student pilot certificate, or a sport pilot certificate (when not using a U.S. driver's license as medical qualification)	60th month after the month of the date of examination shown on the medical certificate.
	(v) Age 40 or older	a recreational pilot certificate, a private pilot certificate, a flight instructor certificate (when acting as pilot in command or a required pilot flight crewmember in operations other than glider or balloon), a student pilot certificate, or a sport pilot certificate (when not using a U.S. driver's license as medical qualification)	24th month after the month of the date of examination shown on the medical certificate.
(2) A second-class medical certificate	(i) Any age	an airline transport pilot certificate for second-in-command privileges (other than the operations specified in paragraph (d)(1) of this section), a commercial pilot certificate (other than a commercial pilot certificate with a balloon rating when conducting flight training), a flight engineer certificate, or an air traffic control tower operator certificate.	12th month after the month of the date of examination shown on the medical certificate
	(ii) Under age 40	a recreational pilot certificate, a private pilot certificate, a flight instructor certificate (when acting as pilot in command or a required pilot flight crewmember in operations other than glider or balloon), a student pilot certificate, or a sport pilot certificate (when not using a U.S. driver's license as medical qualification)	60th month after the month of the date of examination shown on the medical certificate
	(iii) Age 40 or older	a recreational pilot certificate, a private pilot certificate, a flight instructor certificate (when acting as pilot in command or a required pilot flight crewmember in operations other than glider or balloon), a student pilot certificate, or a sport pilot certificate (when not using a U.S. driver's license as medical qualification)	24th month after the month of the date of examination shown on the medical certificate

(continued)

Medical Certificates: Requirement and Duration

If you hold	And on the date of examination for your most recent medical certificate you were	And you are conducting an operation requiring	Then your medical certificate expires, for that operation, at the end of the last day of the
(3) A third-class medical certificate	(i) Under age 40	a recreational pilot certificate, a private pilot certificate, a flight instructor certificate (when acting as pilot in command or a required pilot flight crewmember in operations other than glider or balloon), a student pilot certificate, or a sport pilot certificate (when not using a U.S. driver's license as medical qualification)	60th month after the month of the date of examination shown on the medical certificate
	(ii) Age 40 or older	a recreational pilot certificate, a private pilot certificate, a flight instructor certificate (when acting as pilot in command or a required pilot flight crewmember in operations other than glider or balloon), a student pilot certificate, or a sport pilot certificate (when not using a U.S. driver's license as medical qualification)	24th month after the month of the date of examination shown on the medical certificate

[Docket No. 25910, 62 FR 16298, April 4, 1997; Amdt. 61–103, 62 FR 40895, July 30, 1997; Amdt. 61–110, 69 FR 44864, July 27, 2004, as amended by Amdt. 61–121, 73 FR 43064, July 24, 2008; Amdt. 61–121, 73 FR 48125, Aug. 18, 2008; Amdt. 61–123, 74 FR 34234, July 15, 2009; Amdt. 61–124, 74 FR 42547, Aug. 21, 2009; Amdt. 61–129, 76 FR 78143, Dec. 16, 2011; Amdt. 61–129A,77 FR 61721, Oct. 11, 2012; Amdt. 61–130, 78 FR 42372, July 15, 2013; Docket FAA–2016–9157, Amdt. 61–140, 82 FR 3164, Jan. 11, 2017; Docket No. FAA–2021–1040, Amdt. 61–152, 87 FR 71236, Nov. 22, 2022; Docket No. FAA–2021–1040; Amdt. Nos. 61–152, 87 FR 71237, Nov. 22, 2022]

§61.25 Change of name.

(a) An application to change the name on a certificate issued under this part must be accompanied by the applicant's:

(1) Airman certificate; and

(2) A copy of the marriage license, court order, or other document verifying the name change.

(b) The documents in paragraph (a) of this section will be returned to the applicant after inspection.

[Docket No. 25910, 62 FR 16298, April 4, 1997; as amended by Amdt. 61–124, 74 FR 42548, Aug. 21, 2009]

§61.27 Voluntary surrender or exchange of certificate.

(a) The holder of a certificate issued under this part may voluntarily surrender it for:

(1) Cancellation;

(2) Issuance of a lower grade certificate; or

(3) Another certificate with specific ratings deleted.

(b) Any request made under paragraph (a) of this section must include the following signed statement or its equivalent: "This request is made for my own reasons, with full knowledge that my (insert name of certificate or rating, as appropriate) may not be reissued to me unless I again pass the tests prescribed for its issuance."

§61.29 Replacement of a lost or destroyed airman or medical certificate or knowledge test report.

(a) A request for the replacement of a lost or destroyed airman certificate issued under this part must be made:

(1) By letter to the Department of Transportation, FAA, Airmen Certification Branch, P.O. Box 25082, Oklahoma City, OK 73125, and must be accompanied by a check or money order for the appropriate fee payable to the FAA; or

(2) In any other manner and form approved by the Administrator including a request online to Airmen Services at *http://www.faa.gov*, and must be accompanied by acceptable form of payment for the appropriate fee.

(b) A request for the replacement of a lost or destroyed medical certificate must be made:

(1) By letter to the Department of Transportation, FAA, Aerospace Medical Certification Division, P.O. Box 26200, Oklahoma City, OK 73125, and must be accompanied by a check or money order for the appropriate fee payable to the FAA; or

(2) In any other manner and form approved by the Administrator and must be accompanied by acceptable form of payment for the appropriate fee.

(c) A request for the replacement of a lost or destroyed knowledge test report must be made:

(1) By letter to the Department of Transportation, FAA, Airmen Certification Branch, P.O. Box 25082, Oklahoma City, OK 73125, and must be accompanied by a check or money order for the appropriate fee payable to the FAA; or

(2) In any other manner and form approved by the Administrator and must be accompanied by acceptable form of payment for the appropriate fee.

(d) The letter requesting replacement of a lost or destroyed airman certificate, medical certificate, or knowledge test report must state:

(1) The name of the person;

(2) The permanent mailing address (including ZIP code), or if the permanent mailing address includes a post office box number, then the person's current residential address;

(3) The certificate holder's date and place of birth; and

(4) Any information regarding the—

(i) Grade, number, and date of issuance of the airman certificate and ratings, if appropriate;

(ii) Class of medical certificate, the place and date of the medical exam, name of the Airman Medical Examiner (AME), and the circumstances concerning the loss of the original medical certificate, as appropriate; and

(iii) Date the knowledge test was taken, if appropriate.

(e) A person who has lost an airman certificate, medical certificate, or knowledge test report may obtain, in a form or manner approved by the Administrator, a document conveying temporary authority to exercise certificate privileges from the FAA Aeromedical Certification Branch or the Airman Certification Branch, as appropriate, and the:

(1) Document may be carried as an airman certificate, medical certificate, or knowledge test report, as appropriate, for up to 60 days pending the person's receipt of a duplicate under paragraph (a), (b), or (c) of this section, unless the person has been notified that the certificate has been suspended or revoked.

(2) Request for such a document must include the date on which a duplicate certificate or knowledge test report was previously requested.

[Docket No. 25910, 62 FR 16298, April 4, 1997; Amdt. 61–103, 62 FR 40896, July 30, 1997; Amdt. 61–121, 73 FR 43065, July 24, 2008; Amdt. 61–124, 74 FR 42548, Aug. 21, 2009; Amdt. 61–131, 78 FR 56828, Sept. 16, 2013]

§61.31 Type rating requirements, additional training, and authorization requirements.

(a) *Type ratings required.* A person who acts as a pilot in command of any of the following aircraft must hold a type rating for that aircraft:

(1) Large aircraft (except lighter-than-air).

(2) Turbojet-powered airplanes.

(3) Other aircraft specified by the Administrator through aircraft type certificate procedures.

(b) *Authorization in lieu of a type rating.* A person may be authorized to operate without a type rating for up to 60 days an aircraft requiring a type rating, provided—

(1) The Administrator has authorized the flight or series of flights;

(2) The Administrator has determined that an equivalent level of safety can be achieved through the operating limitations on the authorization;

(3) The person shows that compliance with paragraph (a) of this section is impracticable for the flight or series of flights; and

(4) The flight—

(i) Involves only a ferry flight, training flight, test flight, or practical test for a pilot certificate or rating;

(ii) Is within the United States;

(iii) Does not involve operations for compensation or hire unless the compensation or hire involves payment for the use of the aircraft for training or taking a practical test; and

(iv) Involves only the carriage of flight crewmembers considered essential for the flight.

(5) If the flight or series of flights cannot be accomplished within the time limit of the authorization, the Administrator may authorize an additional period of up to 60 days to accomplish the flight or series of flights.

(c) *Aircraft category, class, and type ratings:* Limitations on the carriage of persons, or operating for compensation or hire. Unless a person holds a category, class, and type rating (if a class and type rating is required) that applies to the aircraft, that person may not act as pilot in command of an aircraft that is carrying another person, or is operated for compensation or hire. That person also may not act as pilot in command of that aircraft for compensation or hire.

(d) *Aircraft category, class, and type ratings:* Limitations on operating an aircraft as the pilot in command. To serve as the pilot in command of an aircraft, a person must—

(1) Hold the appropriate category, class, and type rating (if a class or type rating is required) for the aircraft to be flown; or

(2) Have received training required by this part that is appropriate to the pilot certification level, aircraft category, class, and type rating (if a class or type rating is required) for the aircraft to be flown, and have received an endorsement for solo flight in that aircraft from an authorized instructor.

(e) *Additional training required for operating complex airplanes.*

(1) Except as provided in paragraph (e)(2) of this section, no person may act as pilot in command of a complex airplane, unless the person has—

(i) Received and logged ground and flight training from an authorized instructor in a complex airplane, or in a full flight simulator or flight training device that is representative of a complex airplane, and has been found proficient in the operation and systems of the airplane; and

(ii) Received a one-time endorsement in the pilot's logbook from an authorized instructor who certifies the person is proficient to operate a complex airplane.

(2) The training and endorsement required by paragraph (e)(1) of this section is not required if—

(i) The person has logged flight time as pilot in command of a complex airplane, or in a full flight simulator or flight training device that is representative of a complex airplane prior to August 4, 1997; or

(ii) The person has received ground and flight training under an approved training program and has satisfactorily completed a competency check under §135.293 of this chapter in a complex airplane, or in a full flight simulator or flight training device that is representative of a complex airplane which must be documented in the pilot's logbook or training record.

(f) *Additional training required for operating high-performance airplanes.*

(1) Except as provided in paragraph (f)(2) of this section, no person may act as pilot in command of a high-performance airplane (an airplane with an engine of more than 200 horsepower), unless the person has—

(i) Received and logged ground and flight training from an authorized instructor in a high-performance airplane, or in a full flight simulator or flight training device that is representative of a high-performance airplane, and has been found proficient in the operation and systems of the airplane; and

(ii) Received a one-time endorsement in the pilot's logbook from an authorized instructor who certifies the person is proficient to operate a high-performance airplane.

(2) The training and endorsement required by paragraph (f)(1) of this section is not required if—

(i) The person has logged flight time as pilot in command of a high-performance airplane, or in a full flight simulator or flight training device that is representative of a high-performance airplane prior to August 4, 1997; or

(ii) The person has received ground and flight training under an approved training program and has satisfactorily completed a competency check under §135.293 of this chapter in a high performance airplane, or in a full flight simulator or flight training device that is representative of a high performance airplane which must be documented in the pilot's logbook or training record.

(g) *Additional training required for operating pressurized aircraft capable of operating at high altitudes.*

(1) Except as provided in paragraph (g)(3) of this section, no person may act as pilot in command of a pressurized aircraft (an aircraft that has a service ceiling or maximum operating altitude, whichever is lower, above 25,000 feet MSL), unless that person has received and logged ground training from an authorized instructor and obtained an endorsement in the person's logbook or training record from an authorized instructor who certifies the person has satisfactorily accomplished the ground training. The ground training must include at least the following subjects:

(i) High-altitude aerodynamics and meteorology;

(ii) Respiration;

(iii) Effects, symptoms, and causes of hypoxia and any other high-altitude sickness;

(iv) Duration of consciousness without supplemental oxygen;

(v) Effects of prolonged usage of supplemental oxygen;

(vi) Causes and effects of gas expansion and gas bubble formation;

(vii) Preventive measures for eliminating gas expansion, gas bubble formation, and high-altitude sickness;

(viii) Physical phenomena and incidents of decompression; and

(ix) Any other physiological aspects of high-altitude flight.

(2) Except as provided in paragraph (g)(3) of this section, no person may act as pilot in command of a pressurized aircraft unless that person has received and logged training from an authorized instructor in a pressurized aircraft, or in a full flight simulator or flight training device that is representative of a pressurized aircraft, and obtained an endorsement in the person's logbook or training record from an authorized instructor who found the person proficient in the operation of a pressurized aircraft. The flight training must include at least the following subjects:

(i) Normal cruise flight operations while operating above 25,000 feet MSL;

(ii) Proper emergency procedures for simulated rapid decompression without actually depressurizing the aircraft; and

(iii) Emergency descent procedures.

(3) The training and endorsement required by paragraphs (g)(1) and (g)(2) of this section are not required if that person can document satisfactory accomplishment of any of the following in a pressurized aircraft, or in a full flight simulator or flight training device that is representative of a pressurized aircraft:

(i) Serving as pilot in command before April 15, 1991;

(ii) Completing a pilot proficiency check for a pilot certificate or rating before April 15, 1991;

(iii) Completing an official pilot-in-command check conducted by the military services of the United States; or

(iv) Completing a pilot-in-command proficiency check under part 121, 125, or 135 of this chapter conducted by the Administrator or by an approved pilot check airman.

(h) *Additional aircraft type-specific training.* No person may serve as pilot in command of an aircraft that the Administrator has determined

requires aircraft type-specific training unless that person has—

(1) Received and logged type-specific training in the aircraft, or in a full flight simulator or flight training device that is representative of that type of aircraft; and

(2) Received a logbook endorsement from an authorized instructor who has found the person proficient in the operation of the aircraft and its systems.

(i) *Additional training required for operating tailwheel airplanes.*

(1) Except as provided in paragraph (i)(2) of this section, no person may act as pilot in command of a tailwheel airplane unless that person has received and logged flight training from an authorized instructor in a tailwheel airplane and received an endorsement in the person's logbook from an authorized instructor who found the person proficient in the operation of a tailwheel airplane. The flight training must include at least the following maneuvers and procedures:

(i) Normal and crosswind takeoffs and landings;

(ii) Wheel landings (unless the manufacturer has recommended against such landings); and

(iii) Go-around procedures.

(2) The training and endorsement required by paragraph (i)(1) of this section is not required if the person logged pilot-in-command time in a tailwheel airplane before April 15, 1991.

(j) *Additional training required for operating a glider.*

(1) No person may act as pilot in command of a glider—

(i) Using ground-tow procedures, unless that person has satisfactorily accomplished ground and flight training on ground-tow procedures and operations, and has received an endorsement from an authorized instructor who certifies in that pilot's logbook that the pilot has been found proficient in ground-tow procedures and operations;

(ii) Using aerotow procedures, unless that person has satisfactorily accomplished ground and flight training on aerotow procedures and operations, and has received an endorsement from an authorized instructor who certifies in that pilot's logbook that the pilot has been found proficient in aerotow procedures and operations; or

(iii) Using self-launch procedures, unless that person has satisfactorily accomplished ground and flight training on self-launch procedures and operations, and has received an endorsement from an authorized instructor who certifies in that pilot's logbook that the pilot has been found proficient in self-launch procedures and operations.

(2) The holder of a glider rating issued prior to August 4, 1997, is considered to be in compliance with the training and logbook endorsement requirements of this paragraph for the specific operating privilege for which the holder is already qualified.

(k) *Additional training required for night vision goggle operations.*

(1) Except as provided under paragraph (k)(3) of this section, a person may act as pilot in command of an aircraft using night vision goggles only if that person receives and logs ground training from an authorized instructor and obtains a logbook or training record endorsement from an authorized instructor who certifies the person completed the ground training. The ground training must include the following subjects:

(i) Applicable portions of this chapter that relate to night vision goggle limitations and flight operations;

(ii) Aeromedical factors related to the use of night vision goggles, including how to protect night vision, how the eyes adapt to night, self-imposed stresses that affect night vision, effects of lighting on night vision, cues used to estimate distance and depth perception at night, and visual illusions;

(iii) Normal, abnormal, and emergency operations of night vision goggle equipment;

(iv) Night vision goggle performance and scene interpretation; and

(v) Night vision goggle operation flight planning, including night terrain interpretation and factors affecting terrain interpretation.

(2) Except as provided under paragraph (k)(3) of this section, a person may act as pilot in command of an aircraft using night vision goggles only if that person receives and logs flight training from an authorized instructor and obtains a logbook or training record endorsement from an authorized instructor who found the person proficient in the use of night vision goggles. The flight training must include the following tasks:

(i) Preflight and use of internal and external aircraft lighting systems for night vision goggle operations;

(ii) Preflight preparation of night vision goggles for night vision goggle operations;

(iii) Proper piloting techniques when using night vision goggles during the takeoff, climb, enroute, descent, and landing phases of flight; and

(iv) Normal, abnormal, and emergency flight operations using night vision goggles.

(3) The requirements under paragraphs (k)(1) and (2) of this section do not apply if a person can document satisfactory completion of any of the following pilot proficiency checks using night vision goggles in an aircraft:

(i) A pilot proficiency check on night vision goggle operations conducted by the U.S. Armed Forces.

(ii) A pilot proficiency check on night vision goggle operations under part 135 of this chapter conducted by an Examiner or Check Airman.

(iii) A pilot proficiency check on night vision goggle operations conducted by a night vision

goggle manufacturer or authorized instructor, when the pilot—

(A) Is employed by a Federal, State, county, or municipal law enforcement agency; and

(B) Has logged at least 20 hours as pilot in command in night vision goggle operations.

(l) Exceptions.

(1) This section does not require a category and class rating for aircraft not type-certificated as airplanes, rotorcraft, gliders, lighter-than-air aircraft, powered-lifts, powered parachutes, or weight-shift-control aircraft.

(2) The rating limitations of this section do not apply to—

(i) An applicant when taking a practical test given by an examiner;

(ii) The holder of a student pilot certificate;

(iii) The holder of a pilot certificate when operating an aircraft under the authority of—

(A) A provisional type certificate; or

(B) An experimental certificate, unless the operation involves carrying a passenger;

(iv) The holder of a pilot certificate with a lighter-than-air category rating when operating a balloon;

(v) The holder of a recreational pilot certificate operating under the provisions of §61.101(h); or

(vi) The holder of a sport pilot certificate when operating a light-sport aircraft.

[Docket No. 25910, 62 FR 40896, July 30, 1997; as amended by Amdt. 61–104, 63 FR 20286, April 23, 1998; Amdt. 61–110, 69 FR 44865, July 27, 2004; Amdt. 61–124, 74 FR 42548, Aug. 21, 2009; Amdt. 61–128, 76 FR 54105, Aug. 31, 2011; Amdt. 61–142, 83 FR 30276, June 27, 2018]

§61.33 Tests: General procedure.

Tests prescribed by or under this part are given at times and places, and by persons designated by the Administrator.

§61.35 Knowledge test: Prerequisites and passing grades.

(a) An applicant for a knowledge test must have:

(1) Received an endorsement, if required by this part, from an authorized instructor certifying that the applicant accomplished the appropriate ground-training or a home-study course required by this part for the certificate or rating sought and is prepared for the knowledge test;

(2) For the knowledge test for an airline transport pilot certificate with an airplane category multiengine class rating, a graduation certificate for the airline transport pilot certification training program specified in §61.156; and

(3) Proper identification at the time of application that contains the applicant's—

(i) Photograph;

(ii) Signature;

(iii) Date of birth, which shows:

(A) For issuance of certificates other than the ATP certificate with an airplane category multiengine class rating, the applicant meets or will meet the age requirements of this part for the certificate sought before the expiration date of the airman knowledge test report; and

(B) For issuance of an ATP certificate with an airplane category multiengine class rating obtained under the aeronautical experience requirements of §61.159 or §61.160, the applicant is at least 18 years of age at the time of the knowledge test;

(iv) If the permanent mailing address is a post office box number, then the applicant must provide a current residential address.

(b) The Administrator shall specify the minimum passing grade for the knowledge test.

[Docket No. 25910, 62 FR 16298, April 4, 1997, as amended by Amdt. 61–104, 63 FR 20286, Apr. 23, 1998; Amdt. 61–124, 74 FR 42548, Aug. 21, 2009; Amdt. 61–130, 78 FR 42373, July 15, 2013; Amdt. 61–130B, 78 FR 77573, Dec. 24, 2013; Amdt. 61–149, 86 FR 62087, Nov. 9, 2021]

§61.37 Knowledge tests: Cheating or other unauthorized conduct.

(a) An applicant for a knowledge test may not:

(1) Copy or intentionally remove any knowledge test;

(2) Give to another applicant or receive from another applicant any part or copy of a knowledge test;

(3) Give assistance on, or receive assistance on, a knowledge test during the period that test is being given;

(4) Take any part of a knowledge test on behalf of another person;

(5) Be represented by, or represent, another person for a knowledge test;

(6) Use any material or aid during the period that the test is being given, unless specifically authorized to do so by the Administrator; and

(7) Intentionally cause, assist, or participate in any act prohibited by this paragraph.

(b) An applicant who the Administrator finds has committed an act prohibited by paragraph (a) of this section is prohibited, for 1 year after the date of committing that act, from:

(1) Applying for any certificate, rating, or authorization issued under this chapter; and

(2) Applying for and taking any test under this chapter.

(c) Any certificate or rating held by an applicant may be suspended or revoked if the Administrator finds that person has committed an act prohibited by paragraph (a) of this section.

§61.39 Prerequisites for practical tests.

(a) Except as provided in paragraphs (b), (c), and (e) of this section, to be eligible for a practical test for a certificate or rating issued under this part, an applicant must:

(1) Pass the required knowledge test:

(i) Within the 24-calendar-month period preceding the month the applicant completes the practical test, if a knowledge test is required; or

(ii) Within the 60-calendar month period preceding the month the applicant completes the practical test for those applicants who complete the airline transport pilot certification training program in §61.156 and pass the knowledge test for an airline transport pilot certificate with a multiengine class rating after July 31, 2014;

(2) Present the knowledge test report at the time of application for the practical test, if a knowledge test is required;

(3) Have satisfactorily accomplished the required training and obtained the aeronautical experience prescribed by this part for the certificate or rating sought, and if applying for the practical test with flight time accomplished under §61.159(c), present a copy of the records required by §135.63(a)(4)(vi) and (x) of this chapter;

(4) Hold at least a third-class medical certificate, if a medical certificate is required;

(5) Meet the prescribed age requirement of this part for the issuance of the certificate or rating sought;

(6) Have an endorsement, if required by this part, in the applicant's logbook or training record that has been signed by an authorized instructor who certifies that the applicant—

(i) Has received and logged training time within 2 calendar months preceding the month of application in preparation for the practical test;

(ii) Is prepared for the required practical test; and

(iii) Has demonstrated satisfactory knowledge of the subject areas in which the applicant was deficient on the airman knowledge test; and

(7) Have a completed and signed application form.

(b) An applicant for an airline transport pilot certificate with an airplane category multiengine class rating or an airline transport pilot certificate obtained concurrently with a multiengine airplane type rating may take the practical test with an expired knowledge test only if the applicant passed the knowledge test after July 31, 2014, and is employed:

(1) As a flightcrew member by a part 119 certificate holder conducting operations under parts 125 or 135 of this chapter at the time of the practical test and has satisfactorily accomplished that operator's approved pilot-in-command training or checking program; or

(2) As a flightcrew member by a part 119 certificate holder conducting operations under part 121 of this chapter at the time of the practical test and has satisfactorily accomplished that operator's approved initial training program; or

(3) By the U.S. Armed Forces as a flight crewmember in U.S. military air transport operations at the time of the practical test and has completed the pilot in command aircraft qualification training program that is appropriate to the pilot certificate and rating sought.

(c) An applicant for an airline transport pilot certificate with a rating other than those ratings set forth in paragraph (b) of this section may take the practical test for that certificate or rating with an expired knowledge test report, provided that the applicant is employed:

(1) As a flightcrew member by a part 119 certificate holder conducting operations under parts 125 or 135 of this chapter at the time of the practical test and has satisfactorily accomplished that operator's approved pilot-in-command training or checking program; or

(2) By the U.S. Armed Forces as a flight crewmember in U.S. military air transport operations at the time of the practical test and has completed the pilot in command aircraft qualification training program that is appropriate to the pilot certificate and rating sought.

(d) In addition to the requirements in paragraph (a) of this section, to be eligible for a practical test for an airline transport pilot certificate with an airplane category multiengine class rating or airline transport pilot certificate obtained concurrently with a multiengine airplane type rating, an applicant must:

(1) If the applicant passed the knowledge test after July 31, 2014, present the graduation certificate for the airline transport pilot certification training program in §61.156, at the time of application for the practical test;

(2) If applying for the practical test under the aeronautical experience requirements of §61.160(a), the applicant must present the documents required by that section to substantiate eligibility; and

(3) If applying for the practical test under the aeronautical experience requirements of §61.160(b), (c), or (d), the applicant must present an official transcript and certifying document from an institution of higher education that holds a letter of authorization from the Administrator under §61.169.

(e) A person is not required to comply with the provisions of paragraph (a)(6) of this section if that person:

(1) Holds a foreign pilot license issued by a contracting State to the Convention on International Civil Aviation that authorizes at least the privileges of the pilot certificate sought;

(2) Is only applying for a type rating; or

(3) Is applying for an airline transport pilot certificate or an additional rating to an airline transport pilot certificate in an aircraft that does not require an aircraft type rating practical test.

(f) If all increments of the practical test for a certificate or rating are not completed on the same date, then all the remaining increments of the test must be completed within 2 calendar months after the month the applicant began the test.

(g) If all increments of the practical test for a certificate or rating are not completed within 2 calendar months after the month the applicant began the test, the applicant must retake the entire practical test.

[Docket No. 25910, 62 FR 16298, April 4, 1997; Amdt. 61–103, 62 FR 40897, July 30, 1997, as amended by Amdt. 61–104, 63 FR 20286, April 23, 1998; Amdt. 61–124, 74 FR 42548, Aug. 21, 2009; Amdt. 61–130, 78 FR 42373, July 15, 2013; Amdt. 61–130B, 78 FR 77573, Dec. 24, 2013; Amdt. 61–142, 83 FR 30726, June 27, 2018; Amdt. 61–149, 86 FR 62087, Nov. 9, 2021]

§61.41 Flight training received from flight instructors not certificated by the FAA.

(a) A person may credit flight training toward the requirements of a pilot certificate or rating issued under this part, if that person received the training from:

(1) A flight instructor of an Armed Force in a program for training military pilots of either—

(i) The United States; or

(ii) A foreign contracting State to the Convention on International Civil Aviation.

(2) A flight instructor who is authorized to give such training by the licensing authority of a foreign contracting State to the Convention on International Civil Aviation, and the flight training is given outside the United States.

(b) A flight instructor described in paragraph (a) of this section is only authorized to give endorsements to show training given.

§61.43 Practical tests: General procedures.

(a) Completion of the practical test for a certificate or rating consists of—

(1) Performing the tasks specified in the areas of operation contained in the applicable Airman Certification Standards or Practical Test Standards (incorporated by reference, see §61.14) as listed in appendix A of this part for the airman certificate or rating sought;

(2) Demonstrating mastery of the aircraft by performing each task required by paragraph (a)(1) of this section successfully;

(3) Demonstrating proficiency and competency of the tasks required by paragraph (a)(1) of this section within the approved standards; and

(4) Demonstrating sound judgment.

(b) The pilot flight crew complement required during the practical test is based on one of the following requirements that applies to the aircraft being used on the practical test:

(1) If the aircraft's FAA-approved flight manual requires the pilot flight crew complement be a single pilot, then the applicant must demonstrate single pilot proficiency on the practical test.

(2) If the aircraft's type certification data sheet requires the pilot flight crew complement be a single pilot, then the applicant must demonstrate single pilot proficiency on the practical test.

(3) If the FAA Flight Standardization Board report, FAA-approved aircraft flight manual, or aircraft type certification data sheet allows the pilot flight crew complement to be either a single pilot, or a pilot and a copilot, then the applicant may demonstrate single pilot proficiency or have a copilot on the practical test. If the applicant performs the practical test with a copilot, the limitation of "Second in Command Required" will be placed on the applicant's pilot certificate. The limitation may be removed if the applicant passes the practical test by demonstrating single-pilot proficiency in the aircraft in which single-pilot privileges are sought.

(c) If an applicant fails any area of operation, that applicant fails the practical test.

(d) An applicant is not eligible for a certificate or rating sought until all the areas of operation are passed.

(e) The examiner or the applicant may discontinue a practical test at any time:

(1) When the applicant fails one or more of the areas of operation; or

(2) Due to inclement weather conditions, aircraft airworthiness, or any other safety-of-flight concern.

(f) If a practical test is discontinued, the applicant is entitled credit for those areas of operation that were passed, but only if the applicant:

(1) Passes the remainder of the practical test within the 60-day period after the date the practical test was discontinued;

(2) Presents to the examiner for the retest the original notice of disapproval form or the letter of discontinuance form, as appropriate;

(3) Satisfactorily accomplishes any additional training needed and obtains the appropriate instructor endorsements, if additional training is required; and

(4) Presents to the examiner for the retest a properly completed and signed application.

[Docket No. 25910, 62 FR 16298, April 4, 1997; as amended by Amdt. 61–124, 74 FR 42549, Aug. 21, 2009; Amdt. 61–142, 83 FR 30276, June 27, 2018; Docket No. FAA–2022–1463, Amdt. 61–153, 89 FR 22517, April 1, 2024]

§61.45 Practical tests: Required aircraft and equipment.

(a) *General.* Except as provided in paragraph (a)(2) of this section or when permitted to accomplish the entire flight increment of the practical test in a flight simulator or a flight training device, an applicant for a certificate or rating issued under this part must furnish:

(1) An aircraft of U.S. registry for each required test that—

(i) Is of the category, class, and type, if applicable, for which the applicant is applying for a certificate or rating; and

(ii) Has a standard airworthiness certificate or special airworthiness certificate in the limited, primary, or light-sport category.

(2) At the discretion of the examiner who administers the practical test, the applicant may furnish—

(i) An aircraft that has an airworthiness certificate other than a standard airworthiness certificate or special airworthiness certificate in the limited, primary, or light-sport category, but that otherwise meets the requirements of paragraph (a)(1) of this section;

(ii) An aircraft of the same category, class, and type, if applicable, of foreign registry that is properly certificated by the country of registry; or

(iii) A military aircraft of the same category, class, and type, if aircraft class and type are appropriate, for which the applicant is applying for a certificate or rating, and provided—

(A) The aircraft is under the direct operational control of the U.S. Armed Forces;

(B) The aircraft is airworthy under the maintenance standards of the U.S. Armed Forces; and

(C) The applicant has a letter from his or her commanding officer authorizing the use of the aircraft for the practical test.

(b) *Required equipment (other than controls).*

(1) Except as provided in paragraph (b)(2) of this section, an aircraft used for a practical test must have—

(i) The equipment for each area of operation required for the practical test;

(ii) No prescribed operating limitations that prohibit its use in any of the areas of operation required for the practical test;

(iii) Except as provided in paragraphs (e) and (f) of this section, at least two pilot stations with adequate visibility for each person to operate the aircraft safely; and

(iv) Cockpit and outside visibility adequate to evaluate the performance of the applicant when an additional jump seat is provided for the examiner.

(2) An applicant for a certificate or rating may use an aircraft with operating characteristics that preclude the applicant from performing all of the tasks required for the practical test. However, the applicant's certificate or rating, as appropriate, will be issued with an appropriate limitation.

(c) *Required controls.* Except for lighter-than-air aircraft, and a glider without an engine, an aircraft used for a practical test must have engine power controls and flight controls that are easily reached and operable in a conventional manner by both pilots, unless the Examiner determines that the practical test can be conducted safely in the aircraft without the controls easily reached by the Examiner.

(d) *Simulated instrument flight equipment.* An applicant for a practical test that involves maneuvering an aircraft solely by reference to instruments must furnish:

(1) Equipment on board the aircraft that permits the applicant to pass the areas of operation that apply to the rating sought; and

(2) A device that prevents the applicant from having visual reference outside the aircraft, but does not prevent the examiner from having visual reference outside the aircraft, and is otherwise acceptable to the Administrator.

(e) *Aircraft with single controls.* A practical test may be conducted in an aircraft having a single set of controls, provided the:

(1) Examiner agrees to conduct the test;

(2) Test does not involve a demonstration of instrument skills; and

(3) Proficiency of the applicant can be observed by an examiner who is in a position to observe the applicant.

(f) *Light-sport aircraft with a single seat.* A practical test for a sport pilot certificate may be conducted in a light-sport aircraft having a single seat provided that the—

(1) Examiner agrees to conduct the test;

(2) Examiner is in a position to observe the operation of the aircraft and evaluate the proficiency of the applicant; and

(3) Pilot certificate of an applicant successfully passing the test is issued a pilot certificate with a limitation "No passenger carriage and flight in a single-seat light-sport aircraft only."

[Docket No. 25910, 62 FR 16298, April 4, 1997; Amdt. 61–103, 62 FR 40897, July 30, 1997; Amdt. 61–104, 63 FR 20286, April 23, 1998; Amdt. 61–110, 69 FR 44865, July 27, 2004; Amdt. 61–124, 74 FR 42549, Aug. 21, 2009]

§61.47 Status of an examiner who is authorized by the Administrator to conduct practical tests.

(a) An examiner represents the Administrator for the purpose of conducting practical tests for certificates and ratings issued under this part and to observe an applicant's ability to perform the areas of operation on the practical test.

(b) The examiner is not the pilot in command of the aircraft during the practical test unless the examiner agrees to act in that capacity for the flight or for a portion of the flight by prior arrangement with:

(1) The applicant; or

(2) A person who would otherwise act as pilot in command of the flight or for a portion of the flight.

(c) Notwithstanding the type of aircraft used during the practical test, the applicant and the examiner (and any other occupants authorized to be on board by the examiner) are not subject to the requirements or limitations for the carriage of passengers that are specified in this chapter.

[Docket No. 25910, 62 FR 16298, April 4, 1997; Amdt. 61–103, 62 FR 40897, July 30, 1997]

§61.49 Retesting after failure.

(a) An applicant for a knowledge or practical test who fails that test may reapply for the test only after the applicant has received:

(1) The necessary training from an authorized instructor who has determined that the applicant is proficient to pass the test; and

(2) An endorsement from an authorized instructor who gave the applicant the additional training.

(b) An applicant for a flight instructor certificate with an airplane category rating or, for a flight instructor certificate with a glider category rating, who has failed the practical test due to deficiencies in instructional proficiency on stall awareness, spin entry, spins, or spin recovery must:

(1) Comply with the requirements of paragraph (a) of this section before being retested;

(2) Bring an aircraft to the retest that is of the appropriate aircraft category for the rating sought and is certificated for spins; and

(3) Demonstrate satisfactory instructional proficiency on stall awareness, spin entry, spins, and spin recovery to an examiner during the retest.

§61.51 Pilot logbooks.

(a) *Training time and aeronautical experience.* Each person must document and record the following time in a manner acceptable to the Administrator:

(1) Training and aeronautical experience used to meet the requirements for a certificate, rating, or flight review of this part.

(2) The aeronautical experience required for meeting the recent flight experience requirements of this part.

(b) *Logbook entries.* For the purposes of meeting the requirements of paragraph (a) of this section, each person must enter the following information for each flight or lesson logged:

(1) General—

(i) Date.

(ii) Total flight time or lesson time.

(iii) Location where the aircraft departed and arrived, or for lessons in a full flight simulator or flight training device, the location where the lesson occurred.

(iv) Type and identification of aircraft, full flight simulator, flight training device, or aviation training device, as appropriate.

(v) The name of a safety pilot, if required by §91.109 of this chapter.

(2) Type of pilot experience or training—

(i) Solo.

(ii) Pilot in command.

(iii) Second in command.

(iv) Flight and ground training received from an authorized instructor.

(v) Training received in a full flight simulator, flight training device, or aviation training device from an authorized instructor.

(3) Conditions of flight—

(i) Day or night.

(ii) Actual instrument.

(iii) Simulated instrument conditions in flight, a full flight simulator, flight training device, or aviation training device.

(iv) Use of night vision goggles in an aircraft in flight, in a full flight simulator, or in a flight training device.

(c) *Logging of pilot time.* The pilot time described in this section may be used to:

(1) Apply for a certificate or rating issued under this part or a privilege authorized under this part; or

(2) Satisfy the recent flight experience requirements of this part.

(d) *Logging of solo flight time.* Except for a student pilot performing the duties of pilot in command of an airship requiring more than one pilot flight crewmember, a pilot may log as solo flight time only that flight time when the pilot is the sole occupant of the aircraft.

(e) *Logging pilot-in-command flight time.*

(1) A sport, recreational, private, commercial, or airline transport pilot may log pilot in command flight time for flights—

(i) Except when logging flight time under §61.159(c), when the pilot is the sole manipulator of the controls of an aircraft for which the pilot is rated, or has sport pilot privileges for that category and class of aircraft, if the aircraft class rating is appropriate;

(ii) When the pilot is the sole occupant in the aircraft;

(iii) When the pilot, except for a holder of a sport or recreational pilot certificate, acts as pilot in command of an aircraft for which more than one pilot is required under the type certification of the aircraft or the regulations under which the flight is conducted; or

(iv) When the pilot performs the duties of pilot in command while under the supervision of a qualified pilot in command provided—

(A) The pilot performing the duties of pilot in command holds a commercial or airline transport pilot certificate and aircraft rating that is appropriate to the category and class of aircraft being flown, if a class rating is appropriate;

(B) The pilot performing the duties of pilot in command is undergoing an approved pilot in command training program that includes ground and flight training on the following areas of operation—

(1) Preflight preparation;
(2) Preflight procedures;
(3) Takeoff and departure;
(4) In-flight maneuvers;
(5) Instrument procedures;
(6) Landings and approaches to landings;
(7) Normal and abnormal procedures;
(8) Emergency procedures; and
(9) Postflight procedures;

(C) The supervising pilot in command holds—

(1) A commercial pilot certificate and flight instructor certificate, and aircraft rating that is appropriate to the category, class, and type of aircraft being flown, if a class or type rating is required; or

(2) An airline transport pilot certificate and aircraft rating that is appropriate to the category, class, and type of aircraft being flown, if a class or type rating is required; and

(D) The supervising pilot in command logs the pilot in command training in the pilot's logbook, certifies the pilot in command training in the pilot's logbook and attests to that certification with his or her signature, and flight instructor certificate number.

(2) If rated to act as pilot in command of the aircraft, an airline transport pilot may log all flight time while acting as pilot in command of an operation requiring an airline transport pilot certificate.

(3) A certificated flight instructor may log pilot in command flight time for all flight time while serving as the authorized instructor in an operation if the instructor is rated to act as pilot in command of that aircraft.

(4) A student pilot may log pilot-in-command time only when the student pilot—

(i) Is the sole occupant of the aircraft or is performing the duties of pilot in command of an airship requiring more than one pilot flight crewmember;

(ii) Has a solo flight endorsement as required under §61.87 of this part; and

(iii) Is undergoing training for a pilot certificate or rating.

(5) A commercial pilot or airline transport pilot may log all flight time while acting as pilot in command of an operation in accordance with §135.99(c) of this chapter if the flight is conducted in accordance with an approved second-in-command professional development program that meets the requirements of §135.99(c) of this chapter.

(f) *Logging second-in-command flight time.* A person may log second-in-command time only for that flight time during which that person:

(1) Is qualified in accordance with the second-in-command requirements of §61.55, and occupies a crewmember station in an aircraft that requires more than one pilot by the aircraft's type certificate;

(2) Holds the appropriate category, class, and instrument rating (if an instrument rating is required for the flight) for the aircraft being flown, and more than one pilot is required under the type certification of the aircraft or the regulations under which the flight is being conducted; or

(3) Serves as second in command in operations conducted in accordance with §135.99(c) of this chapter when a second pilot is not required under the type certification of the aircraft or the regulations under which the flight is being conducted, provided the requirements in §61.159(c) are satisfied.

(g) *Logging instrument time.*

(1) A person may log instrument time only for that flight time when the person operates the aircraft solely by reference to instruments under actual or simulated instrument flight conditions.

(2) An authorized instructor may log instrument time when conducting instrument flight instruction in actual instrument flight conditions.

(3) For the purposes of logging instrument time to meet the recent instrument experience requirements of §61.57(c) of this part, the following information must be recorded in the person's logbook—

(i) The location and type of each instrument approach accomplished; and

(ii) The name of the safety pilot, if required.

(4) A person may use time in a full flight simulator, flight training device, or aviation training device for acquiring instrument aeronautical experience for a pilot certificate or rating provided an authorized instructor is present to observe that time and signs the person's logbook or training record to verify the time and the content of the training session.

(5) A person may use time in a full flight simulator, flight training device, or aviation training device for satisfying instrument recency experience requirements provided a logbook or training record is maintained to specify the training device, time, and the content.

(h) *Logging training time.*

(1) A person may log training time when that person receives training from an authorized instructor in an aircraft, full flight simulator, flight training device, or aviation training device.

61

(2) The training time must be logged in a logbook and must:

(i) Be endorsed in a legible manner by the authorized instructor; and

(ii) Include a description of the training given, the length of the training lesson, and the authorized instructor's signature, certificate number, and certificate expiration date.

(i) Presentation of required documents.

(1) Persons must present their pilot certificate, medical certificate, logbook, or any other record required by this part for inspection upon a reasonable request by—

(i) The Administrator;

(ii) An authorized representative from the National Transportation Safety Board; or

(iii) Any Federal, State, or local law enforcement officer.

(2) A student pilot must carry the following items in the aircraft on all solo cross-country flights as evidence of the required authorized instructor clearances and endorsements—

(i) Pilot logbook;

(ii) Student pilot certificate; and

(iii) Any other record required by this section.

(3) A sport pilot must carry his or her logbook or other evidence of required authorized instructor endorsements on all flights.

(4) A recreational pilot must carry his or her logbook with the required authorized instructor endorsements on all solo flights—

(i) That exceed 50 nautical miles from the airport at which training was received;

(ii) Within airspace that requires communication with air traffic control;

(iii) Conducted between sunset and sunrise; or

(iv) In an aircraft for which the pilot does not hold an appropriate category or class rating.

(5) A flight instructor with a sport pilot rating must carry his or her logbook or other evidence of required authorized instructor endorsements on all flights when providing flight training.

(j) Aircraft requirements for logging flight time. For a person to log flight time, the time must be acquired in an aircraft that is identified as an aircraft under §61.5(b), and is—

(1) An aircraft of U.S. registry with either a standard or special airworthiness certificate;

(2) An aircraft of foreign registry with an airworthiness certificate that is approved by the aviation authority of a foreign country that is a Member State to the Convention on International Civil Aviation Organization;

(3) A military aircraft under the direct operational control of the U.S. Armed Forces; or

(4) A public aircraft under the direct operational control of a Federal, State, county, or municipal law enforcement agency, if the flight time was acquired by the pilot while engaged on an official law enforcement flight for a Federal, State, County, or Municipal law enforcement agency.

(k) Logging night vision goggle time.

(1) A person may log night vision goggle time only for the time the person uses night vision goggles as the primary visual reference of the surface and operates:

(i) An aircraft during a night vision goggle operation; or

(ii) A full flight simulator or flight training device with the lighting system adjusted to represent the period beginning 1 hour after sunset and ending 1 hour before sunrise.

(2) An authorized instructor may log night vision goggle time when that person conducts training using night vision goggles as the primary visual reference of the surface and operates:

(i) An aircraft during a night goggle operation; or

(ii) A full flight simulator or flight training device with the lighting system adjusted to represent the period beginning 1 hour after sunset and ending 1 hour before sunrise.

(3) To log night vision goggle time to meet the recent night vision goggle experience requirements under §61.57(f), a person must log the information required under §61.51(b).

[Docket No. 25910, 62 FR 16298, April 4, 1997; Amdt. 61–103, 62 FR 40897, July 30, 1997; Amdt. 61–104, 63 FR 20286, April 23, 1998; Amdt. 61–110, 69 FR 44865, July 27, 2004; Amdt. 61–124, 74 FR 42549, Aug. 21, 2009; Amdt. 61–128, 76 FR 54105, Aug. 31, 2011; Amdt. 61–142, 83 FR 30277, June 27, 2018]

§61.52 Use of aeronautical experience obtained in ultralight vehicles.

(a) Before January 31, 2012, a person may use aeronautical experience obtained in an ultralight vehicle to meet the requirements for the following certificates and ratings issued under this part:

(1) A sport pilot certificate.

(2) A flight instructor certificate with a sport pilot rating;

(3) A private pilot certificate with a weight-shift-control or powered parachute category rating.

(b) Before January 31, 2012, a person may use aeronautical experience obtained in an ultralight vehicle to meet the provisions of §61.69.

(c) A person using aeronautical experience obtained in an ultralight vehicle to meet the requirements for a certificate or rating specified in paragraph (a) of this section or the requirements of paragraph (b) of this section must—

(1) Have been a registered ultralight pilot with an FAA-recognized ultralight organization when that aeronautical experience was obtained;

(2) Document and log that aeronautical experience in accordance with the provisions for logging aeronautical experience specified by an

FAA-recognized ultralight organization and in accordance with the provisions for logging pilot time in aircraft as specified in §61.51;

(3) Obtain the aeronautical experience in a category and class of vehicle corresponding to the rating or privileges sought; and

(4) Provide the FAA with a certified copy of his or her ultralight pilot records from an FAA-recognized ultralight organization, that—

(i) Document that he or she is a registered ultralight pilot with that FAA-recognized ultralight organization; and

(ii) Indicate that he or she is recognized to operate the category and class of aircraft for which sport pilot privileges are sought.

[Docket No. FAA–2001–11133, 69 FR 44865, July 27, 2004; as amended by Amdt. 61–125, 75 FR 5220, Feb. 1, 2010]

§61.53 Prohibition on operations during medical deficiency.

(a) *Operations that require a medical certificate.* Except as provided for in paragraph (b) of this section, no person who holds a medical certificate issued under part 67 of this chapter may act as pilot in command, or in any other capacity as a required pilot flight crewmember, while that person:

(1) Knows or has reason to know of any medical condition that would make the person unable to meet the requirements for the medical certificate necessary for the pilot operation; or

(2) Is taking medication or receiving other treatment for a medical condition that results in the person being unable to meet the requirements for the medical certificate necessary for the pilot operation.

(b) *Operations that do not require a medical certificate.* For operations provided for in §61.23(b) of this part, a person shall not act as pilot in command, or in any other capacity as a required pilot flight crewmember, while that person knows or has reason to know of any medical condition that would make the person unable to operate the aircraft in a safe manner.

(c) *Operations requiring a medical certificate or a U.S. driver's license.* For operations provided for in §61.23(c), a person must meet the provisions of—

(1) Paragraph (a) of this section if that person holds a medical certificate issued under part 67 of this chapter and does not hold a U.S. driver's license.

(2) Paragraph (b) of this section if that person holds a U.S. driver's license.

[Docket No. 25910, 62 FR 16298, April 4, 1997; as amended by Amdt. 61–110, 69 FR 44866, July 27, 2004; Amdt. 61–124, 74 FR 42550, Aug. 21, 2009]

§61.55 Second-in-command qualifications.

(a) A person may serve as a second-in-command of an aircraft type certificated for more than one required pilot flight crewmember or in operations requiring a second-in-command pilot flight crewmember only if that person holds:

(1) At least a private pilot certificate with the appropriate category and class rating; and

(2) An instrument rating or privilege that applies to the aircraft being flown if the flight is under IFR; and

(3) At least a pilot type rating for the aircraft being flown unless the flight will be conducted as domestic flight operations within the United States airspace.

(b) Except as provided in paragraph (e) of this section, no person may serve as a second-in-command of an aircraft type certificated for more than one required pilot flight crewmember or in operations requiring a second-in-command unless that person has within the previous 12 calendar months:

(1) Become familiar with the following information for the specific type aircraft for which second-in-command privileges are requested—

(i) Operational procedures applicable to the powerplant, equipment, and systems.

(ii) Performance specifications and limitations.

(iii) Normal, abnormal, and emergency operating procedures.

(iv) Flight manual.

(v) Placards and markings.

(2) Except as provided in paragraph (g) of this section, performed and logged pilot time in the type of aircraft or in a flight simulator that represents the type of aircraft for which second-in-command privileges are requested, which includes—

(i) Three takeoffs and three landings to a full stop as the sole manipulator of the flight controls;

(ii) Engine-out procedures and maneuvering with an engine out while executing the duties of pilot in command; and

(iii) Crew resource management training.

(c) If a person complies with the requirements in paragraph (b) of this section in the calendar month before or the calendar month after the month in which compliance with this section is required, then that person is considered to have accomplished the training and practice in the month it is due.

(d) A person may receive a second-in-command pilot type rating for an aircraft after satisfactorily completing the second-in-command familiarization training requirements under paragraph (b) of this section in that type of aircraft provided the training was completed within the 12 calendar months before the month of application for

the SIC pilot type rating. The person must comply with the following application and pilot certification procedures:

(1) The person who provided the training must sign the applicant's logbook or training record after each lesson in accordance with §61.51(h)(2) of this part. In lieu of the trainer, it is permissible for a qualified management official within the organization to sign the applicant's training records or logbook and make the required endorsement. The qualified management official must hold the position of Chief Pilot, Director of Training, Director of Operations, or another comparable management position within the organization that provided the training and must be in a position to verify the applicant's training records and that the training was given.

(2) The trainer or qualified management official must make an endorsement in the applicant's logbook that states "[Applicant's Name and Pilot Certificate Number] has demonstrated the skill and knowledge required for the safe operation of the [Type of Aircraft], relevant to the duties and responsibilities of a second in command."

(3) If the applicant's flight experience and/or training records are in an electronic form, the applicant must present a paper copy of those records containing the signature of the trainer or qualified management official to a Flight Standards office or Examiner.

(4) The applicant must complete and sign an Airman Certificate and/or Rating Application, FAA Form 8710-1, and present the application to a Flight Standards office or to an Examiner.

(5) The person who provided the ground and flight training to the applicant must sign the "Instructor's Recommendation" section of the Airman Certificate and/or Rating Application, FAA Form 8710-1. In lieu of the trainer, it is permissible for a qualified management official within the organization to sign the applicant's FAA Form 8710-1.

(6) The applicant must appear in person at a Flight Standards office or to an Examiner with his or her logbook/training records and with the completed and signed FAA Form 8710-1.

(7) There is no practical test required for the issuance of the "SIC Privileges Only" pilot type rating.

(e) A person may receive a second-in-command pilot type rating for the type of aircraft after satisfactorily completing an approved second-in-command training program, proficiency check, or competency check under subpart K of part 91, part 125, or part 135, as appropriate, in that type of aircraft provided the training was completed within the 12 calendar months before the month of application for the SIC pilot type rating. The person must comply with the following application and pilot certification procedures:

(1) The person who provided the training must sign the applicant's logbook or training record after each lesson in accordance with §61.51(h)(2) of this part. In lieu of the trainer, it is permissible for a qualified management official within the organization to sign the applicant's training records or logbook and make the required endorsement. The qualified management official must hold the position of Chief Pilot, Director of Training, Director of Operations, or another comparable management position within the organization that provided the training and must be in a position to verify the applicant's training records and that the training was given.

(2) The trainer or qualified management official must make an endorsement in the applicant's logbook that states "[Applicant's Name and Pilot Certificate Number] has demonstrated the skill and knowledge required for the safe operation of the [Type of Aircraft], relevant to the duties and responsibilities of a second in command."

(3) If the applicant's flight experience and/or training records are in an electronic form, the applicant must provide a paper copy of those records containing the signature of the trainer or qualified management official to a Flight Standards office, an Examiner, or an Aircrew Program Designee.

(4) The applicant must complete and sign an Airman Certificate and/or Rating Application, FAA Form 8710-1, and present the application to a Flight Standards office or to an Examiner or to an authorized Aircrew Program Designee.

(5) The person who provided the ground and flight training to the applicant must sign the "Instructor's Recommendation" section of the Airman Certificate and/or Rating Application, FAA Form 8710-1. In lieu of the trainer, it is permissible for a qualified management official within the organization to sign the applicant's FAA Form 8710-1.

(6) The applicant must appear in person at a Flight Standards office or to an Examiner or to an authorized Aircrew Program Designee with his or her logbook/training records and with the completed and signed FAA Form 8710-1.

(7) There is no practical test required for the issuance of the "SIC Privileges Only" pilot type rating.

(f) The familiarization training requirements of paragraph (b) of this section do not apply to a person who is:

(1) Designated and qualified as pilot in command under subpart K of part 91, part 121, 125, or 135 of this chapter in that specific type of aircraft;

(2) Designated as the second in command under subpart K of part 91, part 121, 125, or 135 of this chapter in that specific type of aircraft;

(3) Designated as the second in command in that specific type of aircraft for the purpose of

receiving flight training required by this section, and no passengers or cargo are carried on the aircraft; or

(4) Designated as a safety pilot for purposes required by §91.109 of this chapter.

(g) The holder of a commercial or airline transport pilot certificate with the appropriate category and class rating is not required to meet the requirements of paragraph (b)(2) of this section, provided the pilot:

(1) Is conducting a ferry flight, aircraft flight test, or evaluation flight of an aircraft's equipment; and

(2) Is not carrying any person or property on board the aircraft, other than necessary for conduct of the flight.

(h) For the purpose of meeting the requirements of paragraph (b) of this section, a person may serve as second in command in that specific type aircraft, provided:

(1) The flight is conducted under day VFR or day IFR; and

(2) No person or property is carried on board the aircraft, other than necessary for conduct of the flight.

(i) The training under paragraphs (b) and (d) of this section and the training, proficiency check, and competency check under paragraph (e) of this section may be accomplished in a flight simulator that is used in accordance with an approved training course conducted by a training center certificated under part 142 of this chapter or under subpart K of part 91, part 121 or part 135 of this chapter.

(j) When an applicant for an initial second-in-command qualification for a particular type of aircraft receives all the training in a flight simulator, that applicant must satisfactorily complete one takeoff and one landing in an aircraft of the same type for which the qualification is sought. This requirement does not apply to an applicant who completes a proficiency check under part 121 or competency check under subpart K, part 91, part 125, or part 135 for the particular type of aircraft.

[Docket No. 25910, 62 FR 16298, April 4, 1997; Amdt. 61–103, 62 FR 40898, July 30, 1997; Amdt. 61–109, 68 FR 54559, Sept. 17, 2003; Amdt. 61–113, 70 FR 45271, Aug. 4, 2005; Amdt. 61–109, 70 FR 61890, Oct. 27, 2005; Amdt. 61–124, 74 FR 42550, Aug. 21, 2009; Amdt. 61–128, 76 FR 54105, Aug. 31, 2011; Amdt. 61–130, 78 FR 42374, July 15, 2013; Docket FAA–2018–0119, Amdt. 61–141, 83 FR 9170, March 5, 2018]

§61.56 Flight review.

(a) Except as provided in paragraphs (b) and (f) of this section, a flight review consists of a minimum of 1 hour of flight training and 1 hour of ground training. The review must include:

(1) A review of the current general operating and flight rules of part 91 of this chapter; and

(2) A review of those maneuvers and procedures that, at the discretion of the person giving the review, are necessary for the pilot to demonstrate the safe exercise of the privileges of the pilot certificate.

(b) Glider pilots may substitute a minimum of three instructional flights in a glider, each of which includes a flight to traffic pattern altitude, in lieu of the 1 hour of flight training required in paragraph (a) of this section.

(c) Except as provided in paragraphs (d), (e), and (g) of this section, no person may act as pilot in command of an aircraft unless, since the beginning of the 24th calendar month before the month in which that pilot acts as pilot in command, that person has—

(1) Accomplished a flight review given in an aircraft for which that pilot is rated by an authorized instructor; and

(2) A logbook endorsed from an authorized instructor who gave the review certifying that the person has satisfactorily completed the review.

(d) A person who has, within the period specified in paragraph (c) of this section, passed any of the following need not accomplish the flight review required by this section:

(1) A pilot proficiency check or practical test conducted by an examiner, an approved pilot check airman, or a U.S. Armed Force, for a pilot certificate, rating, or operating privilege.

(2) A practical test conducted by an examiner for the issuance of a flight instructor certificate, an additional rating on a flight instructor certificate, renewal of a flight instructor certificate, or reinstatement of a flight instructor certificate.

(e) A person who has, within the period specified in paragraph (c) of this section, satisfactorily accomplished one or more phases of an FAA-sponsored pilot proficiency award program need not accomplish the flight review required by this section.

(f) A person who holds a flight instructor certificate and who has, within the period specified in paragraph (c) of this section, satisfactorily completed a renewal of a flight instructor certificate under the provisions in §61.197 need not accomplish the one hour of ground training specified in paragraph (a) of this section.

(g) A student pilot need not accomplish the flight review required by this section provided the student pilot is undergoing training for a certificate and has a current solo flight endorsement as required under §61.87 of this part.

(h) The requirements of this section may be accomplished in combination with the requirements of §61.57 and other applicable recent experience requirements at the discretion of the authorized instructor conducting the flight review.

61

(i) A flight simulator or flight training device may be used to meet the flight review requirements of this section subject to the following conditions:

(1) The flight simulator or flight training device must be used in accordance with an approved course conducted by a training center certificated under part 142 of this chapter.

(2) Unless the flight review is undertaken in a flight simulator that is approved for landings, the applicant must meet the takeoff and landing requirements of §61.57(a) or §61.57(b) of this part.

(3) The flight simulator or flight training device used must represent an aircraft or set of aircraft for which the pilot is rated.

[Docket No. 25910, 62 FR 16298, April 4, 1997; Amdt. 61–103, 62 FR 40898, July 30, 1997; Amdt. 61–104, 63 FR 20287, April 23, 1998; Amdt. 61–124, 74 FR 42550, Aug. 21, 2009; Amdt. 61–131, 78 FR 56828, Sept. 16, 2013]

§61.57 Recent flight experience: Pilot in command.

(a) General experience.

(1) Except as provided in paragraph (e) of this section, no person may act as a pilot in command of an aircraft carrying passengers or of an aircraft certificated for more than one pilot flight crewmember unless that person has made at least three takeoffs and three landings within the preceding 90 days, and—

(i) The person acted as the sole manipulator of the flight controls; and

(ii) The required takeoffs and landings were performed in an aircraft of the same category, class, and type (if a type rating is required), and, if the aircraft to be flown is an airplane with a tailwheel, the takeoffs and landings must have been made to a full stop in an airplane with a tailwheel.

(2) For the purpose of meeting the requirements of paragraph (a)(1) of this section, a person may act as a pilot in command of an aircraft under day VFR or day IFR, provided no persons or property are carried on board the aircraft, other than those necessary for the conduct of the flight.

(3) The takeoffs and landings required by paragraph (a)(1) of this section may be accomplished in a full flight simulator or flight training device that is—

(i) Approved by the Administrator for landings; and

(ii) Used in accordance with an approved course conducted by a training center certificated under part 142 of this chapter.

(b) Night takeoff and landing experience.

(1) Except as provided in paragraph (e) of this section, no person may act as pilot in command of an aircraft carrying passengers during the period beginning 1 hour after sunset and ending 1 hour before sunrise, unless within the preceding 90 days that person has made at least three takeoffs and three landings to a full stop during the period beginning 1 hour after sunset and ending 1 hour before sunrise, and—

(i) That person acted as sole manipulator of the flight controls; and

(ii) The required takeoffs and landings were performed in an aircraft of the same category, class, and type (if a type rating is required).

(2) The takeoffs and landings required by paragraph (b)(1) of this section may be accomplished in a full flight simulator that is—

(i) Approved by the Administrator for takeoffs and landings, if the visual system is adjusted to represent the period described in paragraph (b)(1) of this section; and

(ii) Used in accordance with an approved course conducted by a training center certificated under part 142 of this chapter.

(c) Instrument experience. Except as provided in paragraph (e) of this section, a person may act as pilot in command under IFR or weather conditions less than the minimums prescribed for VFR only if:

(1) *Use of an airplane, powered-lift, helicopter, or airship for maintaining instrument experience.* Within the 6 calendar months preceding the month of the flight, that person performed and logged at least the following tasks and iterations in an airplane, powered-lift, helicopter, or airship, as appropriate, for the instrument rating privileges to be maintained in actual weather conditions, or under simulated conditions using a view-limiting device that involves having performed the following—

(i) Six instrument approaches.

(ii) Holding procedures and tasks.

(iii) Intercepting and tracking courses through the use of navigational electronic systems.

(2) *Use of a full flight simulator, flight training device, or aviation training device for maintaining instrument experience.* A pilot may accomplish the requirements in paragraph (c)(1) of this section in a full flight simulator, flight training device, or aviation training device provided the device represents the category of aircraft for the instrument rating privileges to be maintained and the pilot performs the tasks and iterations in simulated instrument conditions. A person may complete the instrument experience in any combination of an aircraft, full flight simulator, flight training device, or aviation training device.

(3) *Maintaining instrument recent experience in a glider.*

(i) Within the 6 calendar months preceding the month of the flight, that person must have performed and logged at least the following instrument currency tasks, iterations, and flight time, and the instrument currency must have been performed in actual weather conditions or under simulated weather conditions—

(A) One hour of instrument flight time in a glider or in a single engine airplane using a view-limiting device while performing interception and tracking courses through the use of navigation electronic systems.

(B) Two hours of instrument flight time in a glider or a single engine airplane with the use of a view-limiting device while performing straight glides, turns to specific headings, steep turns, flight at various airspeeds, navigation, and slow flight and stalls.

(ii) Before a pilot is allowed to carry a passenger in a glider under IFR or in weather conditions less than the minimums prescribed for VFR, that pilot must—

(A) Have logged and performed 2 hours of instrument flight time in a glider within the 6 calendar months preceding the month of the flight.

(B) Use a view-limiting-device while practicing performance maneuvers, performance airspeeds, navigation, slow flight, and stalls.

(d) Instrument proficiency check.

(1) Except as provided in paragraph (e) of this section, a person who has failed to meet the instrument experience requirements of paragraph (c) of this section for more than six calendar months may reestablish instrument currency only by completing an instrument proficiency check. The instrument proficiency check must include the areas of operation contained in the applicable Airman Certification Standards (incorporated by reference, see §61.14) as listed in appendix A of this part as appropriate to the rating held.

(i) Air traffic control clearances and procedures;

(ii) Flight by reference to instruments;

(iii) Navigation systems;

(iv) Instrument approach procedures;

(v) Emergency operations; and

(vi) Postflight procedures.

(2) The instrument proficiency check must be—

(i) In an aircraft that is appropriate to the aircraft category;

(ii) For other than a glider, in a full flight simulator or flight training device that is representative of the aircraft category; or

(iii) For a glider, in a single-engine airplane or a glider.

(3) The instrument proficiency check must be given by—

(i) An examiner;

(ii) A person authorized by the U.S. Armed Forces to conduct instrument flight tests, provided the person being tested is a member of the U.S. Armed Forces;

(iii) A company check pilot who is authorized to conduct instrument flight tests under part 121, 125, or 135 of this chapter or subpart K of part 91 of this chapter, and provided that both the check pilot and the pilot being tested are employees of

that operator or fractional ownership program manager, as applicable;

(iv) An authorized instructor; or

(v) A person approved by the Administrator to conduct instrument practical tests.

(e) Exceptions.

(1) Paragraphs (a) and (b) of this section do not apply to a pilot in command who is employed by a part 119 certificate holder authorized to conduct operations under part 125 when the pilot is engaged in a flight operation for that certificate holder if the pilot in command is in compliance with §§125.281 and 125.285 of this chapter.

(2) This section does not apply to a pilot in command who is employed by a part 119 certificate holder authorized to conduct operations under part 121 when the pilot is engaged in a flight operation under part 91 or 121 for that certificate holder if the pilot in command complies with §§121.436 and 121.439 of this chapter.

(3) This section does not apply to a pilot in command who is employed by a part 119 certificate holder authorized to conduct operations under part 135 when the pilot is engaged in a flight operation under parts 91 or 135 for that certificate holder if the pilot in command is in compliance with §§135.243 and 135.247 of this chapter.

(4) Paragraph (b) of this section does not apply to a pilot in command of a turbine-powered airplane that is type certificated for more than one pilot crewmember, provided that pilot has complied with the requirements of paragraph (e)(4)(i) or (ii) of this section:

(i) The pilot in command must hold at least a commercial pilot certificate with the appropriate category, class, and type rating for each airplane that is type certificated for more than one pilot crewmember that the pilot seeks to operate under this alternative, and:

(A) That pilot must have logged at least 1,500 hours of aeronautical experience as a pilot;

(B) In each airplane that is type certificated for more than one pilot crewmember that the pilot seeks to operate under this alternative, that pilot must have accomplished and logged the daytime takeoff and landing recent flight experience of paragraph (a) of this section, as the sole manipulator of the flight controls;

(C) Within the preceding 90 days prior to the operation of that airplane that is type certificated for more than one pilot crewmember, the pilot must have accomplished and logged at least 15 hours of flight time in the type of airplane that the pilot seeks to operate under this alternative; and

(D) That pilot has accomplished and logged at least 3 takeoffs and 3 landings to a full stop, as the sole manipulator of the flight controls, in a turbine-powered airplane that requires more than one pilot crewmember. The pilot must have

61

performed the takeoffs and landings during the period beginning 1 hour after sunset and ending 1 hour before sunrise within the preceding 6 months prior to the month of the flight.

(ii) The pilot in command must hold at least a commercial pilot certificate with the appropriate category, class, and type rating for each airplane that is type certificated for more than one pilot crewmember that the pilot seeks to operate under this alternative, and:

(A) That pilot must have logged at least 1,500 hours of aeronautical experience as a pilot;

(B) In each airplane that is type certificated for more than one pilot crewmember that the pilot seeks to operate under this alternative, that pilot must have accomplished and logged the daytime takeoff and landing recent flight experience of paragraph (a) of this section, as the sole manipulator of the flight controls;

(C) Within the preceding 90 days prior to the operation of that airplane that is type certificated for more than one pilot crewmember, the pilot must have accomplished and logged at least 15 hours of flight time in the type of airplane that the pilot seeks to operate under this alternative; and

(D) Within the preceding 12 months prior to the month of the flight, the pilot must have completed a training program that is approved under part 142 of this chapter. The approved training program must have required and the pilot must have performed, at least 6 takeoffs and 6 landings to a full stop as the sole manipulator of the controls in a full flight simulator that is representative of a turbine-powered airplane that requires more than one pilot crewmember. The full flight simulator's visual system must have been adjusted to represent the period beginning 1 hour after sunset and ending 1 hour before sunrise.

(f) Night vision goggle operating experience.

(1) A person may act as pilot in command in a night vision goggle operation with passengers on board only if, within 2 calendar months preceding the month of the flight, that person performs and logs the following tasks as the sole manipulator of the controls on a flight during a night vision goggle operation—

(i) Three takeoffs and three landings, with each takeoff and landing including a climbout, cruise, descent, and approach phase of flight (only required if the pilot wants to use night vision goggles during the takeoff and landing phases of the flight).

(ii) Three hovering tasks (only required if the pilot wants to use night vision goggles when operating helicopters or powered-lifts during the hovering phase of flight).

(iii) Three area departure and area arrival tasks.

(iv) Three tasks of transitioning from aided night flight (*aided night flight* means that the pilot uses night vision goggles to maintain visual surface reference) to unaided night flight (*unaided night flight* means that the pilot does not use night vision goggles) and back to aided night flight.

(v) Three night vision goggle operations, or when operating helicopters or powered-lifts, six night vision goggle operations.

(2) A person may act as pilot in command using night vision goggles only if, within the 4 calendar months preceding the month of the flight, that person performs and logs the tasks listed in paragraph (f)(1)(i) through (v) of this section as the sole manipulator of the controls during a night vision goggle operation.

(g) Night vision goggle proficiency check. A person must either meet the night vision goggle experience requirements of paragraphs (f)(1) or (f)(2) of this section or pass a night vision goggle proficiency check to act as pilot in command using night vision goggles. The proficiency check must be performed in the category of aircraft that is appropriate to the night vision goggle operation for which the person is seeking the night vision goggle privilege or in a full flight simulator or flight training device that is representative of that category of aircraft. The check must consist of the tasks listed in §61.31(k), and the check must be performed by:

(1) An Examiner who is qualified to perform night vision goggle operations in that same aircraft category and class;

(2) A person who is authorized by the U.S. Armed Forces to perform night vision goggle proficiency checks, provided the person being administered the check is also a member of the U.S. Armed Forces;

(3) A company check pilot who is authorized to perform night vision goggle proficiency checks under parts 121, 125, or 135 of this chapter, provided that both the check pilot and the pilot being tested are employees of that operator;

(4) An authorized flight instructor who is qualified to perform night vision goggle operations in that same aircraft category and class;

(5) A person who is qualified as pilot in command for night vision goggle operations in accordance with paragraph (f) of this section; or

(6) A person approved by the FAA to perform night vision goggle proficiency checks.

[Docket No. 25910, 62 FR 16298, April 4, 1997; Amdt. 61–103, 62 FR 40898, July 30, 1997; Docket No. FAA-2022–1463, Amdt. 61–153, 89 FR 22517, April 1, 2024]

§61.58 Pilot-in-command proficiency check: Operation of an aircraft that requires more than one pilot flight crewmember or is turbojet-powered.

(a) Except as otherwise provided in this section, to serve as pilot in command of an aircraft that is type certificated for more than one required pilot flight crewmember or is turbojet-powered, a person must—

(1) Within the preceding 12 calendar months, complete a pilot-in-command proficiency check in an aircraft that is type certificated for more than one required pilot flight crewmember or is turbojet-powered; and

(2) Within the preceding 24 calendar months, complete a pilot-in-command proficiency check in the particular type of aircraft in which that person will serve as pilot in command, that is type certificated for more than one required pilot flight crewmember or is turbojet-powered.

(b) This section does not apply to persons conducting operations under subpart K of part 91, part 121, 125, 133, 135, or 137 of this chapter, or persons maintaining continuing qualification under an Advanced Qualification program approved under Subpart Y of Part 121 of this chapter.

(c) The pilot-in-command proficiency check given in accordance with the provisions of subpart K of part 91, part 121, 125, or 135 of this chapter may be used to satisfy the requirements of this section.

(d) The pilot-in-command proficiency check required by paragraph (a) of this section may be accomplished by satisfactory completion of one of the following:

(1) A pilot-in-command proficiency check conducted by a person authorized by the Administrator, consisting of the areas of operation contained in the applicable Airman Certification Standards or Practical Test Standards (incorporated by reference, see §61.14); as listed in appendix A of this part appropriate to the rating held, in an aircraft that is type certificated for more than one pilot flight crewmember or is turbojet powered;

(2) The practical test required for a type rating, in an aircraft that is type certificated for more than one required pilot flight crewmember or is turbojet-powered;

(3) The initial or periodic practical test required for the issuance of a pilot examiner or check airman designation, in an aircraft that is type certificated for more than one required pilot flight crewmember or is turbojet-powered;

(4) A pilot proficiency check administered by a U.S. Armed Force that qualifies the military pilot for pilot-in-command designation with instrument privileges, and was performed in a military aircraft that the military requires to be operated by more than one pilot flight crewmember or is turbojet-powered;

(5) For a pilot authorized by the Administrator to operate an experimental turbojet-powered aircraft that possesses, by original design or through modification, more than a single seat, the required proficiency check for all of the experimental turbojet-powered aircraft for which the pilot holds an authorization may be accomplished by completing any one of the following:

(i) A single proficiency check, conducted by an examiner authorized by the Administrator, in any one of the experimental turbojet-powered aircraft for which the airman holds an authorization to operate if conducted within the prior 12 months;

(ii) A single proficiency check, conducted by an examiner authorized by the Administrator, in any experimental turbojet-powered aircraft (e.g., if a pilot acquires a new authorization to operate an additional experimental turbojet-powered aircraft, the check for that new authorization will meet the intent), if conducted within the prior 12 months;

(iii) Current qualification under an Advanced Qualification Program (AQP) under subpart Y of part 121 of this chapter;

(iv) Any proficiency check conducted under subpart K of part 91, part 121, or part 135 of this chapter within the prior 12 months if conducted in a turbojet-powered aircraft; or

(v) Any other §61.58 proficiency check conducted within the prior 12 months if conducted in a turbojet-powered aircraft.

(e) The pilot of a multi-seat experimental turbojet-powered aircraft who has not received a proficiency check within the prior 12 months in accordance with this section may continue to operate such aircraft in accordance with the pilot's authorizations. However, the pilot is prohibited from carriage of any persons in any experimental turbojet-powered aircraft with the exception of those individuals authorized by the Administrator to conduct training, conduct flight checks, or perform pilot certification functions in such aircraft, and only during flights specifically related to training, flight checks, or certification in such aircraft.

(f) This section will not apply to a pilot authorized by the Administrator to serve as pilot in command in experimental turbojet-powered aircraft that possesses, by original design, a single seat, when operating such single-seat aircraft.

(g) A check or test described in paragraphs (d)(1) through (5) of this section may be accomplished in a flight simulator under part 142 of this chapter, subject to the following:

(1) Except as provided for in paragraphs (g)(2) and (3) of this section, if an otherwise qualified and approved flight simulator used for a pilot-in-command proficiency check is not qualified and approved for a specific required maneuver—

(i) The training center must annotate, in the applicant's training record, the maneuver or maneuvers omitted; and

(ii) Prior to acting as pilot in command, the pilot must demonstrate proficiency in each omitted maneuver in an aircraft or flight simulator qualified and approved for each omitted maneuver.

(2) If the flight simulator used pursuant to paragraph (g) of this section is not qualified and approved for circling approaches—

(i) The applicant's record must include the statement, "Proficiency in circling approaches not demonstrated"; and

(ii) The applicant may not perform circling approaches as pilot in command when weather conditions are less than the basic VFR conditions described in §91.155 of this chapter, until proficiency in circling approaches has been successfully demonstrated in a flight simulator qualified and approved for circling approaches or in an aircraft to a person authorized by the Administrator to conduct the check required by this section.

(3) If the flight simulator used pursuant to paragraph (g) of this section is not qualified and approved for landings, the applicant must—

(i) Hold a type rating in the airplane represented by the simulator; and

(ii) Have completed within the preceding 90 days at least three takeoffs and three landings (one to a full stop) as the sole manipulator of the flight controls in the type airplane for which the pilot-in-command proficiency check is sought.

(h) For the purpose of meeting the pilot-in-command proficiency check requirements of paragraph (a) of this section, a person may act as pilot in command of a flight under day VFR conditions or day IFR conditions if no person or property is carried, other than as necessary to demonstrate compliance with this part.

(i) If a pilot takes the pilot-in-command proficiency check required by this section in the calendar month before or the calendar month after the month in which it is due, the pilot is considered to have taken it in the month in which it was due for the purpose of computing when the next pilot-in-command proficiency check is due.

[Docket No. 25910, 62 FR 40899, July 30, 1997, as amended by Amdt. 61–109, 68 FR 54559, Sept. 17, 2003; Amdt. 61–112, 70 FR 54814, Sept. 16, 2005; Amdt. 61–128, 76 FR 54106, Aug. 31, 2011; 76 FR 63184, Oct. 12, 2011; Docket No. FAA–2022–1355, Amdt. No. 61–151, 87 FR 75845, Dec. 9, 2022; Docket No. FAA–2022–1463, Amdt. 61–153, 89 FR 22517, April 1, 2024]

§61.59 Falsification, reproduction, or alteration of applications, certificates, logbooks, reports, or records.

(a) No person may make or cause to be made:

(1) Any fraudulent or intentionally false statement on any application for a certificate, rating, authorization, or duplicate thereof, issued under this part;

(2) Any fraudulent or intentionally false entry in any logbook, record, or report that is required to be kept, made, or used to show compliance with any requirement for the issuance or exercise of the privileges of any certificate, rating, or authorization under this part;

(3) Any reproduction for fraudulent purpose of any certificate, rating, or authorization, under this part; or

(4) Any alteration of any certificate, rating, or authorization under this part.

(b) The commission of an act prohibited under paragraph (a) of this section is a basis for suspending or revoking any airman certificate, rating, or authorization held by that person.

§61.60 Change of address.

The holder of a pilot, flight instructor, or ground instructor certificate who has made a change in permanent mailing address may not, after 30 days from that date, exercise the privileges of the certificate unless the holder has notified in writing the FAA, Airman Certification Branch, P.O. Box 25082, Oklahoma City, OK 73125, of the new permanent mailing address, or if the permanent mailing address includes a post office box number, then the holder's current residential address.

Subpart B—
Aircraft Ratings and
Pilot Authorizations

§61.61 Applicability.

This subpart prescribes the requirements for the issuance of additional aircraft ratings after a pilot certificate is issued, issuance of a type rating concurrently with a pilot certificate, and the requirements for and limitations of pilot authorizations issued by the Administrator.

[Docket No. FAA–2006–26661, 76 FR 78143, Dec. 16, 2011]

§61.63 Additional aircraft ratings (other than for ratings at the airline transport pilot certification level).

(a) *General.* For an additional aircraft rating on a pilot certificate, other than for an airline transport pilot certificate, a person must meet the requirements of this section appropriate to the additional aircraft rating sought.

(b) *Additional aircraft category rating.* A person who applies to add a category rating to a pilot certificate:

(1) Must complete the training and have the applicable aeronautical experience.

(2) Must have a logbook or training record endorsement from an authorized instructor attesting that the person was found competent in the appropriate aeronautical knowledge areas and proficient in the appropriate areas of operation.

(3) Must pass the practical test.

(4) Need not take an additional knowledge test, provided the applicant holds an airplane, rotorcraft, powered-lift, weight-shift-control aircraft, powered parachute, or airship rating at that pilot certificate level.

(c) Additional aircraft class rating. A person who applies for an additional class rating on a pilot certificate:

(1) Must have a logbook or training record endorsement from an authorized instructor attesting that the person was found competent in the appropriate aeronautical knowledge areas and proficient in the appropriate areas of operation.

(2) Must pass the practical test.

(3) Need not meet the specified training time requirements prescribed by this part that apply to the pilot certificate for the aircraft class rating sought; unless, the person only holds a lighter-than-air category rating with a balloon class rating and is seeking an airship class rating, then that person must receive the specified training time requirements and possess the appropriate aeronautical experience.

(4) Need not take an additional knowledge test, provided the applicant holds an airplane, rotorcraft, powered-lift, weight-shift-control aircraft, powered parachute, or airship rating at that pilot certificate level.

(d) Additional aircraft type rating. Except as provided under paragraph (d)(6) of this section, a person who applies for an aircraft type rating or an aircraft type rating to be completed concurrently with an aircraft category or class rating—

(1) Must hold or concurrently obtain an appropriate instrument rating, except as provided in paragraph (e) of this section.

(2) Must have a logbook or training record endorsement from an authorized instructor attesting that the person is competent in the appropriate aeronautical knowledge areas and proficient in the appropriate areas of operation at the airline transport pilot certification level.

(3) Must pass the practical test at the airline transport pilot certification level.

(4) Must perform the practical test in actual or simulated instrument conditions, except as provided in paragraph (e) of this section.

(5) Need not take an additional knowledge test if the applicant holds an airplane, rotorcraft, powered-lift, or airship rating on the pilot certificate.

(6) In the case of a pilot employee of a part 121 or part 135 certificate holder or of a fractional ownership program manager under subpart K of part 91 of this chapter, the pilot must—

(i) Meet the appropriate requirements under paragraphs (d)(1), (d)(3), and (d)(4) of this section; and

(ii) Receive a flight training record endorsement from the certificate holder attesting that the person completed the certificate holder's approved ground and flight training program.

(e) Aircraft not capable of instrument maneuvers and procedures.

(1) An applicant for a type rating or a type rating in addition to an aircraft category and/or class rating who provides an aircraft that is not capable of the instrument maneuvers and procedures required on the practical test:

(i) May apply for the type rating, but the rating will be limited to "VFR only."

(ii) May have the "VFR only" limitation removed for that aircraft type after the applicant:

(A) Passes a practical test in that type of aircraft in actual or simulated instrument conditions;

(B) Passes a practical test in that type of aircraft on the appropriate instrument maneuvers and procedures in §61.157; or

(C) Becomes qualified under §61.73(d) for that type of aircraft.

(2) When an instrument rating is issued to a person who holds one or more type ratings, the amended pilot certificate must bear the "VFR only" limitation for each aircraft type rating that the person did not demonstrate instrument competency.

(f) Multiengine airplane with a single-pilot station. An applicant for a type rating, at other than the ATP certification level, in a multiengine airplane with a single-pilot station must perform the practical test in the multi-seat version of that airplane, or the practical test may be performed in the single-seat version of that airplane if the Examiner is in a position to observe the applicant during the practical test and there is no multi-seat version of that multiengine airplane.

(g) Single engine airplane with a single-pilot station. An applicant for a type rating, at other than the ATP certification level, in a single engine airplane with a single-pilot station must perform the practical test in the multi-seat version of that single engine airplane, or the practical test may be performed in the single-seat version of that airplane if the Examiner is in a position to observe the applicant during the practical test and there is no multi-seat version of that single engine airplane.

(h) Aircraft category and class rating for the operation of aircraft with an experimental certificate. A person holding a recreational, private, or commercial pilot certificate may apply for a category and class rating limited to a specific make and model of experimental aircraft, provided—

(1) The person logged 5 hours flight time while acting as pilot in command in the same category, class, make, and model of aircraft.

(2) The person received a logbook endorsement from an authorized instructor who determined the pilot's proficiency to act as pilot in command of the same category, class, make, and model of aircraft.

(3) The flight time specified under paragraph (h)(1) of this section was logged between September 1, 2004 and August 31, 2005.

(i) *Waiver authority.* An Examiner who conducts a practical test may waive any task for which the FAA has provided waiver authority.

[Docket No. FAA–2006–26661, 74 FR 42552, Aug. 21, 2009; as amended by Amdt. 61–125, 75 FR 5220, Feb. 1, 2010]

§61.65 Use of a flight simulator and flight training device.

(a) *Use of a flight simulator or flight training device.* If an applicant for a certificate or rating uses a flight simulator or flight training device for training or any portion of the practical test, the flight simulator and flight training device—

(1) Must represent the category, class, and type (if a type rating is applicable) for the rating sought; and

(2) Must be qualified and approved by the Administrator and used in accordance with an approved course of training under part 141 or part 142 of this chapter; or under part 121 or part 135 of this chapter, provided the applicant is a pilot employee of that air carrier operator.

(b) Except as provided in paragraph (f) of this section, if an airplane is not used during the practical test for a type rating for a turbojet airplane (except for preflight inspection), an applicant must accomplish the entire practical test in a Level C or higher flight simulator and the applicant must—

(1) Hold a type rating in a turbojet airplane of the same class of airplane for which the type rating is sought, and that type rating may not contain a supervised operating experience limitation;

(2) Have 1,000 hours of flight time in two different turbojet airplanes of the same class of airplane for which the type rating is sought;

(3) Have been appointed by the U.S. Armed Forces as pilot in command in a turbojet airplane of the same class of airplane for which the type rating is sought;

(4) Have 500 hours of flight time in the same type of airplane for which the type rating is sought; or

(5) Have logged at least 2,000 hours of flight time, of which 500 hours were in turbine-powered airplanes of the same class of airplane for which the type rating is sought.

(c) Except as provided in paragraph (f) of this section, if an airplane is not used during the practical test for a type rating for a turbo-propeller airplane (except for preflight inspection), an applicant must accomplish the entire practical test in a Level C or higher flight simulator and the applicant must—

(1) Hold a type rating in a turbo-propeller airplane of the same class of airplane for which the type rating is sought, and that type rating may not contain a supervised operating experience limitation;

(2) Have 1,000 hours of flight time in two different turbo-propeller airplanes of the same class of airplane for which the type rating is sought;

(3) Have been appointed by the U.S. Armed Forces as pilot in command in a turbo-propeller airplane of the same class of airplane for which the type rating is sought;

(4) Have 500 hours of flight time in the same type of airplane for which the type rating is sought; or

(5) Have logged at least 2,000 hours of flight time, of which 500 hours were in turbine-powered airplanes of the same class of airplane for which the type rating is sought.

(d) Except as provided in paragraph (f) of this section, if a helicopter is not used during the practical test for a type rating in a helicopter (except for preflight inspection), an applicant must accomplish the entire practical test in a Level C or higher flight simulator and the applicant must meet one of the following requirements—

(1) Hold a type rating in a helicopter and that type rating may not contain the supervised operating experience limitation;

(2) Have been appointed by the U.S. Armed Forces as pilot in command of a helicopter;

(3) Have 500 hours of flight time in the type of helicopter; or

(4) Have 1,000 hours of flight time in two different types of helicopters.

(e) Except as provided in paragraph (f) of this section, if a powered-lift is not used during the practical test for a type rating in a powered-lift (except for preflight inspection), an applicant must accomplish the entire practical test in a Level C or higher flight simulator and the applicant must meet one of the following requirements—

(1) Hold a type rating in a powered-lift without a supervised operating experience limitation;

(2) Have been appointed by the U.S. Armed Forces as pilot in command of a powered-lift;

(3) Have 500 hours of flight time in the type of powered-lift for which the rating is sought; or

(4) Have 1,000 hours of flight time in two different types of powered-lifts.

(f) If the applicant does not meet one of the experience requirements of paragraphs (b)(1) through (5), (c)(1) through (5), (d)(1) through (4) or (e)(1) through (4) of this section, as appropriate to the type rating sought, then—

(1) The applicant must complete the following tasks on the practical test in an aircraft appropriate to category, class, and type for the rating sought: Preflight inspection, normal takeoff, normal instrument landing system approach, missed approach, and normal landing; or

(2) The applicant's pilot certificate will be issued with a limitation that states: "The [name of the additional type rating] is subject to pilot in command limitations," and the applicant is restricted from serving as pilot in command in an aircraft of that type.

(g) The limitation described under paragraph (f)(2) of this section may be removed from the pilot certificate if the applicant complies with the following—

(1) Performs 25 hours of flight time in an aircraft of the category, class, and type for which the limitation applies under the direct observation of the pilot in command who holds a category, class, and type rating, without limitations, for the aircraft;

(2) Logs each flight and the pilot in command who observed the flight attests in writing to each flight;

(3) Obtains the flight time while performing the duties of pilot in command; and

(4) Presents evidence of the supervised operating experience to any Examiner or Flight Standards office to have the limitation removed.

[Docket No. FAA–2006–26661, 76 FR 78143, Dec. 16, 2011, as amended by Docket FAA–2018–0119, Amdt. 61–141, 83 FR 9170, March 5, 2018]

§61.65 Instrument rating requirements.

(a) *General.* A person who applies for an instrument rating must:

(1) Hold at least a current private pilot certificate, or be concurrently applying for a private pilot certificate, with an airplane, helicopter, or powered-lift rating appropriate to the instrument rating sought;

(2) Be able to read, speak, write, and understand the English language. If the applicant is unable to meet any of these requirements due to a medical condition, the Administrator may place such operating limitations on the applicant's pilot certificate as are necessary for the safe operation of the aircraft;

(3) Receive and log ground training from an authorized instructor or accomplish a home-study course of training on the aeronautical knowledge areas of paragraph (b) of this section that apply to the instrument rating sought;

(4) Receive a logbook or training record endorsement from an authorized instructor certifying that the person is prepared to take the required knowledge test;

(5) Receive and log training on the areas of operation of paragraph (c) of this section from an authorized instructor in an aircraft, full flight simulator, or flight training device that represents an airplane, helicopter, or powered-lift appropriate to the instrument rating sought;

(6) Receive a logbook or training record endorsement from an authorized instructor certifying that the person is prepared to take the required practical test;

(7) Pass the required knowledge test on the aeronautical knowledge areas of paragraph (b) of this section; however, an applicant is not required to take another knowledge test when that person already holds an instrument rating; and

(8) Pass the required practical test on the areas of operation in paragraph (c) of this section in—

(i) An airplane, helicopter, or powered-lift appropriate to the rating sought; or

(ii) A full flight simulator or a flight training device appropriate to the rating sought and for the specific maneuver or instrument approach procedure performed. If an approved flight training device is used for the practical test, the instrument approach procedures conducted in that flight training device are limited to one precision and one nonprecision approach, provided the flight training device is approved for the procedure performed.

(b) *Aeronautical knowledge.* A person who applies for an instrument rating must have received and logged ground training from an authorized instructor or accomplished a home-study course on the following aeronautical knowledge areas that apply to the instrument rating sought:

(1) Federal Aviation Regulations of this chapter that apply to flight operations under IFR;

(2) Appropriate information that applies to flight operations under IFR in the "Aeronautical Information Manual;"

(3) Air traffic control system and procedures for instrument flight operations;

(4) IFR navigation and approaches by use of navigation systems;

(5) Use of IFR en route and instrument approach procedure charts;

(6) Procurement and use of aviation weather reports and forecasts and the elements of forecasting weather trends based on that information and personal observation of weather conditions;

(7) Safe and efficient operation of aircraft under instrument flight rules and conditions;

(8) Recognition of critical weather situations and windshear avoidance;

(9) Aeronautical decision making and judgment; and

(10) Crew resource management, including crew communication and coordination.

(c) *Flight proficiency.* A person who applies for an instrument rating must receive and log training from an authorized instructor in an aircraft, or in a full flight simulator or flight training device, in accordance with paragraph (g) of this section, that includes the following areas of operation:

(1) Preflight preparation;

(2) Preflight procedures;

(3) Air traffic control clearances and procedures;

(4) Flight by reference to instruments;

(5) Navigation systems;

(6) Instrument approach procedures;

(7) Emergency operations; and

(8) Postflight procedures.

(d) Aeronautical experience for the instrument–airplane rating. A person who applies for an instrument–airplane rating must have logged:

(1) Except as provided in paragraph (g) of this section, 50 hours of cross-country flight time as pilot in command, of which 10 hours must have been in an airplane; and

(2) Forty hours of actual or simulated instrument time in the areas of operation listed in paragraph (c) of this section, of which 15 hours must have been received from an authorized instructor who holds an instrument–airplane rating, and the instrument time includes:

(i) Three hours of instrument flight training from an authorized instructor in an airplane that is appropriate to the instrument–airplane rating within 2 calendar months before the date of the practical test; and

(ii) Instrument flight training on cross country flight procedures, including one cross country flight in an airplane with an authorized instructor, that is performed under instrument flight rules, when a flight plan has been filed with an air traffic control facility, and that involves—

(A) A flight of 250 nautical miles along airways or by directed routing from an air traffic control facility;

(B) An instrument approach at each airport; and

(C) Three different kinds of approaches with the use of navigation systems.

(e) Aeronautical experience for the instrument–helicopter rating. A person who applies for an instrument–helicopter rating must have logged:

(1) Except as provided in paragraph (g) of this section, 50 hours of cross-country flight time as pilot in command, of which 10 hours must have been in a helicopter; and

(2) Forty hours of actual or simulated instrument time in the areas of operation listed under paragraph (c) of this section, of which 15 hours must have been with an authorized instructor who holds an instrument–helicopter rating, and the instrument time includes:

(i) Three hours of instrument flight training from an authorized instructor in a helicopter that is appropriate to the instrument–helicopter rating within 2 calendar months before the date of the practical test; and

(ii) Instrument flight training on cross country flight procedures, including one cross country flight in a helicopter with an authorized instructor that is performed under instrument flight rules and a flight plan has been filed with an air traffic control facility, and involves—

(A) A flight of 100 nautical miles along airways or by directed routing from an air traffic control facility;

(B) An instrument approach at each airport; and

(C) Three different kinds of approaches with the use of navigation systems.

(f) Aeronautical experience for the instrument–powered-lift rating. A person who applies for an instrument–powered-lift rating must have logged:

(1) Except as provided in paragraph (g) of this section, 50 hours of cross-country flight time as pilot in command, of which 10 hours must have been in a powered-lift; and

(2) Forty hours of actual or simulated instrument time in the areas of operation listed under paragraph (c) of this section, of which 15 hours must have been received from an authorized instructor who holds an instrument–powered-lift rating, and the instrument time includes:

(i) Three hours of instrument flight training from an authorized instructor in a powered-lift that is appropriate to the instrument–powered-lift rating within 2 calendar months before the date of the practical test; and

(ii) Instrument flight training on cross country flight procedures, including one cross country flight in a powered-lift with an authorized instructor that is performed under instrument flight rules, when a flight plan has been filed with an air traffic control facility, that involves—

(A) A flight of 250 nautical miles along airways or by directed routing from an air traffic control facility;

(B) An instrument approach at each airport; and

(C) Three different kinds of approaches with the use of navigation systems.

(g) An applicant for a combined private pilot certificate with an instrument rating may satisfy the cross-country flight time requirements of this section by crediting:

(1) For an instrument-airplane rating or an instrument-powered-lift rating, up to 45 hours of cross-country flight time performing the duties of pilot in command with an authorized instructor; or

(2) For an instrument-helicopter rating, up to 47 hours of cross-country flight time performing the duties of pilot in command with an authorized instructor.

(h) Use of full flight simulators or flight training devices. If the instrument time was provided by an authorized instructor in a full flight simulator or flight training device—

(1) A maximum of 30 hours may be performed in that full flight simulator or flight training device if the instrument time was completed in accordance with part 142 of this chapter; or

(2) A maximum of 20 hours may be performed in that full flight simulator or flight training device if the instrument time was not completed in accordance with part 142 of this chapter.

(i) *Use of an aviation training device.* A maximum of 10 hours of instrument time received in a basic aviation training device or a maximum of 20 hours of instrument time received in an advanced aviation training device may be credited for the instrument time requirements of this section if—

(1) The device is approved and authorized by the FAA;

(2) An authorized instructor provides the instrument time in the device; and

(3) The FAA approved the instrument training and instrument tasks performed in the device.

(j) Except as provided in paragraph (h)(1) of this section, a person may not credit more than 20 total hours of instrument time in a full flight simulator, flight training device, aviation training device, or a combination towards the instrument time requirements of this section.

[Docket No. 25910, 62 FR 16298, April 4, 1997; Amdt. 61–103, 62 FR 40900, July 30, 1997; Amdt. 61–124, 74 FR 42554, Aug. 21, 2009; Amdt. 61–127, 76 FR 19267, April 7, 2011; Amdt. 61–128, 76 FR 54106, Aug. 31, 2011; Docket FAA–2015–1846, Amdt. 61–136, 81 FR 21460, April 12, 2016]

§61.66 Enhanced Flight Vision System Pilot Requirements

(a) *Ground training.*

(1) Except as provided under paragraphs (f) and (h) of this section, no person may manipulate the controls of an aircraft or act as pilot in command of an aircraft during an EFVS operation conducted under §91.176(a) or (b) of this chapter, or serve as a required pilot flightcrew member during an EFVS operation conducted under §91.176(a) of this chapter, unless that person—

(i) Receives and logs ground training under a training program approved by the Administrator; and

(ii) Obtains a logbook or training record endorsement from an authorized training provider certifying the person satisfactorily completed the ground training appropriate to the category of aircraft for which the person is seeking the EFVS privilege.

(2) The ground training must include the following subjects:

(i) Those portions of this chapter that relate to EFVS flight operations and limitations, including the Airplane Flight Manual or Rotorcraft Flight Manual limitations;

(ii) EFVS sensor imagery, required aircraft flight information, and flight symbology;

(iii) EFVS display, controls, modes, features, symbology, annunciations, and associated systems and components;

(iv) EFVS sensor performance, sensor limitations, scene interpretation, visual anomalies, and other visual effects;

(v) Preflight planning and operational considerations associated with using EFVS during taxi, takeoff, climb, cruise, descent and landing phases of flight, including the use of EFVS for instrument approaches, operating below DA/DH or MDA, executing missed approaches, landing, rollout, and balked landings;

(vi) Weather associated with low visibility conditions and its effect on EFVS performance;

(vii) Normal, abnormal, emergency, and crew coordination procedures when using EFVS; and

(viii) Interpretation of approach and runway lighting systems and their display characteristics when using an EFVS.

(b) *Flight training.*

(1) Except as provided under paragraph (h) of this section, no person may manipulate the controls of an aircraft or act as pilot in command of an aircraft during an EFVS operation under §91.176(a) or (b) of this chapter unless that person—

(i) Receives and logs flight training for the EFVS operation under a training program approved by the Administrator; and

(ii) Obtains a logbook or training record endorsement from an authorized training provider certifying the person is proficient in the use of EFVS in the category of aircraft in which the training was provided for the EFVS operation to be conducted.

(2) Flight training must include the following tasks:

(i) Preflight and inflight preparation of EFVS equipment for EFVS operations, including EFVS setup and use of display, controls, modes and associated systems, and adjustments for brightness and contrast under day and night conditions;

(ii) Proper piloting techniques associated with using EFVS during taxi, takeoff, climb, cruise, descent, landing, and rollout, including missed approaches and balked landings;

(iii) Proper piloting techniques for the use of EFVS during instrument approaches, to include operations below DA/DH or MDA as applicable to the EFVS operations to be conducted, under both day and night conditions;

(iv) Determining enhanced flight visibility;

(v) Identifying required visual references appropriate to EFVS operations;

(vi) Transitioning from EFVS sensor imagery to natural vision acquisition of required visual references and the runway environment;

(vii) Using EFVS sensor imagery, required aircraft flight information, and flight symbology to touchdown and rollout, if the person receiving training will conduct EFVS operations under §91.176(a) of this chapter; and

(viii) Normal, abnormal, emergency, and crew coordination procedures when using an EFVS.

(c) *Supplementary EFVS training.* A person qualified to conduct an EFVS operation under §91.176(a) or (b) of this chapter who seeks to conduct an additional EFVS operation for which that person has not received training must—

(1) Receive and log the ground and flight training required by paragraphs (a) and (b) of this section, under a training program approved by the Administrator, appropriate to the additional EFVS operation to be conducted; and

(2) Obtain a logbook or training record endorsement from the authorized training provider certifying the person is proficient in the use of EFVS in the category of aircraft in which the training was provided for the EFVS operation to be conducted.

(d) *Recent flight experience: EFVS.* Except as provided in paragraphs (f) and (h) of this section, no person may manipulate the controls of an aircraft during an EFVS operation or act as pilot in command of an aircraft during an EFVS operation unless, within 6 calendar months preceding the month of the flight, that person performs and logs six instrument approaches as the sole manipulator of the controls using an EFVS under any weather conditions in the category of aircraft for which the person seeks the EFVS privilege. The instrument approaches may be performed in day or night conditions; and

(1) One approach must terminate in a full stop landing; and

(2) For persons authorized to exercise the privileges of §91.176(a), the full stop landing must be conducted using the EFVS.

(e) *EFVS refresher training.*

(1) Except as provided in paragraph (h) of this section, a person who has failed to meet the recent flight experience requirements of paragraph (d) of this section for more than six calendar months may reestablish EFVS currency only by satisfactorily completing an approved EFVS refresher course in the category of aircraft for which the person seeks the EFVS privilege. The EFVS refresher course must consist of the subjects and tasks listed in paragraphs (a)(2) and (b)(2) of this section applicable to the EFVS operations to be conducted.

(2) The EFVS refresher course must be conducted by an authorized training provider whose instructor meets the training requirements of this section and, if conducting EFVS operations in an aircraft, the recent flight experience requirements of this section.

(f) *Military pilots and former military pilots in the U.S. Armed Forces.*

(1) The training requirements of paragraphs (a) and (b) of this section applicable to EFVS operations conducted under §91.176(a) of this chapter do not apply to a military pilot or former military pilot in the U.S. Armed Forces if that person documents satisfactory completion of ground and flight training in EFVS operations to touchdown and rollout by the U.S. Armed Forces.

(2) The training requirements in paragraphs (a) and (b) of this section applicable to EFVS operations conducted under §91.176(b) of this chapter do not apply to a military pilot or former military pilot in the U.S. Armed Forces if that person documents satisfactory completion of ground and flight training in EFVS operations to 100 feet above the touchdown zone elevation by the U.S. Armed Forces.

(3) A military pilot or former military pilot in the U.S. Armed Forces may satisfy the recent flight experience requirements of paragraph (d) of this section if he or she documents satisfactory completion of an EFVS proficiency check in the U.S. Armed Forces within 6 calendar months preceding the month of the flight, the check was conducted by a person authorized by the U.S. Armed Forces to administer the check, and the person receiving the check was a member of the U.S. Armed Forces at the time the check was administered.

(g) *Use of full flight simulators.* A level C or higher full flight simulator (FFS) equipped with an EFVS may be used to meet the flight training, recent flight experience, and refresher training requirements of this section. The FFS must be evaluated and qualified for EFVS operations by the Administrator, and must be:

(1) Qualified and maintained in accordance with part 60 of this chapter, or a previously qualified device, as permitted in accordance with §60.17 of this chapter;

(2) Approved by the Administrator for the tasks and maneuvers to be conducted; and

(3) Equipped with a daylight visual display if being used to meet the flight training requirements of this section.

(h) *Exceptions.*

(1) A person may manipulate the controls of an aircraft during an EFVS operation without meeting the requirements of this section in the following circumstances:

(i) When receiving flight training to meet the requirements of this section under an approved training program, provided the instructor meets the requirements in this section to perform the EFVS operation in the category of aircraft for which the training is being conducted.

(ii) During an EFVS operation performed in the course of satisfying the recent flight experience

requirements of paragraph (d) of this section, provided another individual is serving as pilot in command of the aircraft during the EFVS operation and that individual meets the requirements in this section to perform the EFVS operation in the category of aircraft in which the flight is being conducted.

(iii) During an EFVS operation performed in the course of completing EFVS refresher training in accordance with paragraph (e) of this section, provided the instructor providing the refresher training meets the requirements in this section to perform the EFVS operation in the category of aircraft for which the training is being conducted.

(2) The requirements of paragraphs (a) and (b) of this section do not apply if a person is conducting a flight or series of flights in an aircraft issued an experimental airworthiness certificate under §21.191 of this chapter for the purpose of research and development or showing compliance with regulations, provided the person has knowledge of the subjects specified in paragraph (a)(2) of this section and has experience with the tasks specified in paragraph (b)(2) of this section applicable to the EFVS operations to be conducted.

(3) The requirements specified in paragraphs (d) and (e) of this section do not apply to a pilot who:

(i) Is employed by a part 119 certificate holder authorized to conduct operations under part 121, 125, or 135 when the pilot is conducting an EFVS operation for that certificate holder under part 91, 121, 125, or 135, as applicable, provided the pilot conducts the operation in accordance with the certificate holder's operations specifications for EFVS operations;

(ii) Is employed by a person who holds a letter of deviation authority issued under §125.3 of this chapter when the pilot is conducting an EFVS operation for that person under part 125, provided the pilot is conducting the operation in accordance with that person's letter of authorization for EFVS operations; or

(iii) Is employed by a fractional ownership program manager to conduct operations under part 91 subpart K when the pilot is conducting an EFVS operation for that program manager under part 91, provided the pilot is conducting the operation in accordance with the program manager's management specifications for EFVS operations.

(4) The requirements of paragraphs (a) and (b) of this section do not apply if a person is conducting EFVS operations under §91.176(b) of this chapter and that person documents that prior to March 13, 2018, that person satisfactorily completed ground and flight training on EFVS operations to 100 feet above the touchdown zone elevation.

[Docket FAA–2013–0485, Amdt. 61–139, 81 FR 90170, Dec. 13, 2016, as amended by Docket FAA–2013–0485, Amdt. 61–139, 81 FR 90172, Dec. 13, 2016]

§61.67 Category II pilot authorization requirements.

(a) *General.* A person who applies for a Category II pilot authorization must hold:

(1) At least a private or commercial pilot certificate with an instrument rating or an airline transport pilot certificate;

(2) A type rating for the aircraft for which the authorization is sought if that aircraft requires a type rating; and

(3) A category and class rating for the aircraft for which the authorization is sought.

(b) *Experience requirements.* An applicant for a Category II pilot authorization must have at least—

(1) 50 hours of night flight time as pilot in command.

(2) 75 hours of instrument time under actual or simulated instrument conditions that may include not more than—

(i) A combination of 25 hours of simulated instrument flight time in a flight simulator or flight training device; or

(ii) 40 hours of simulated instrument flight time if accomplished in an approved course conducted by an appropriately rated training center certificated under part 142 of this chapter.

(3) 250 hours of cross-country flight time as pilot in command.

(c) *Practical test requirements.*

(1) A practical test must be passed by a person who applies for—

(i) Issuance or renewal of a Category II pilot authorization; and

(ii) The addition of another type aircraft to the applicant's Category II pilot authorization.

(2) To be eligible for the practical test for an authorization under this section, an applicant must—

(i) Meet the requirements of paragraphs (a) and (b) of this section; and

(ii) If the applicant has not passed a practical test for this authorization during the 12 calendar months preceding the month of the test, then that person must—

(A) Meet the requirements of §61.57(c); and

(B) Have performed at least six ILS approaches during the 6 calendar months preceding the month of the test, of which at least three of the approaches must have been conducted without the use of an approach coupler.

(3) The approaches specified in paragraph (c)(2)(ii)(B) of this section—

(i) Must be conducted under actual or simulated instrument flight conditions;

(ii) Must be conducted to the decision height for the ILS approach in the type aircraft in which the practical test is to be conducted;

(iii) Need not be conducted to the decision height authorized for Category II operations;

(iv) Must be conducted to the decision height authorized for Category II operations only if conducted in a flight simulator or flight training device; and

(v) Must be accomplished in an aircraft of the same category and class, and type, as applicable, as the aircraft in which the practical test is to be conducted or in a flight simulator that—

(A) Represents an aircraft of the same category and class, and type, as applicable, as the aircraft in which the authorization is sought; and

(B) Is used in accordance with an approved course conducted by a training center certificated under part 142 of this chapter.

(4) The flight time acquired in meeting the requirements of paragraph (c)(2)(ii)(B) of this section may be used to meet the requirements of paragraph (c)(2)(ii)(A) of this section.

(d) *Practical test procedures.* The practical test consists of an oral increment and a flight increment.

(1) Oral increment. In the oral increment of the practical test an applicant must demonstrate knowledge of the following:

(i) Required landing distance;

(ii) Recognition of the decision height;

(iii) Missed approach procedures and techniques using computed or fixed attitude guidance displays;

(iv) Use and limitations of RVR;

(v) Use of visual clues, their availability or limitations, and altitude at which they are normally discernible at reduced RVR readings;

(vi) Procedures and techniques related to transition from nonvisual to visual flight during a final approach under reduced RVR;

(vii) Effects of vertical and horizontal windshear;

(viii) Characteristics and limitations of the ILS and runway lighting system;

(ix) Characteristics and limitations of the flight director system, auto approach coupler (including split axis type if equipped), auto throttle system (if equipped), and other required Category II equipment;

(x) Assigned duties of the second in command during Category II approaches, unless the aircraft for which authorization is sought does not require a second in command; and

(xi) Instrument and equipment failure warning systems.

(2) Flight increment. The following requirements apply to the flight increment of the practical test:

(i) The flight increment must be conducted in an aircraft of the same category, class, and type, as applicable, as the aircraft in which the authorization is sought or in a flight simulator that—

(A) Represents an aircraft of the same category and class, and type, as applicable, as the aircraft in which the authorization is sought; and

(B) Is used in accordance with an approved course conducted by a training center certificated under part 142 of this chapter.

(ii) The flight increment must consist of at least two ILS approaches to 100 feet AGL including at least one landing and one missed approach.

(iii) All approaches performed during the flight increment must be made with the use of an approved flight control guidance system, except if an approved auto approach coupler is installed, at least one approach must be hand flown using flight director commands.

(iv) If a multiengine airplane with the performance capability to execute a missed approach with one engine inoperative is used for the practical test, the flight increment must include the performance of one missed approach with an engine, which shall be the most critical engine, if applicable, set at idle or zero thrust before reaching the middle marker.

(v) If a multiengine flight simulator or multiengine flight training device is used for the practical test, the applicant must execute a missed approach with the most critical engine, if applicable, failed.

(vi) For an authorization for an aircraft that requires a type rating, the practical test must be performed in coordination with a second in command who holds a type rating in the aircraft in which the authorization is sought.

(vii) Oral questioning may be conducted at any time during a practical test.

[Docket No. 25910, 62 FR 16298, April 4, 1997; Amdt. 61–103, 62 FR 40900, July 30, 1997]

§61.68 Category III pilot authorization requirements.

(a) *General.* A person who applies for a Category III pilot authorization must hold:

(1) At least a private pilot certificate or commercial pilot certificate with an instrument rating or an airline transport pilot certificate;

(2) A type rating for the aircraft for which the authorization is sought if that aircraft requires a type rating; and

(3) A category and class rating for the aircraft for which the authorization is sought.

(b) *Experience requirements.* An applicant for a Category III pilot authorization must have at least—

(1) 50 hours of night flight time as pilot in command.

(2) 75 hours of instrument flight time during actual or simulated instrument conditions that may include not more than—

(i) A combination of 25 hours of simulated instrument flight time in a flight simulator or flight training device; or

(ii) 40 hours of simulated instrument flight time if accomplished in an approved course conducted by an appropriately rated training center certificated under part 142 of this chapter.

(3) 250 hours of cross-country flight time as pilot in command.

(c) Practical test requirements.

(1) A practical test must be passed by a person who applies for—

(i) Issuance or renewal of a Category III pilot authorization; and

(ii) The addition of another type of aircraft to the applicant's Category III pilot authorization.

(2) To be eligible for the practical test for an authorization under this section, an applicant must—

(i) Meet the requirements of paragraphs (a) and (b) of this section; and

(ii) If the applicant has not passed a practical test for this authorization during the 12 calendar months preceding the month of the test, then that person must—

(A) Meet the requirements of §61.57(c); and

(B) Have performed at least six ILS approaches during the 6 calendar months preceding the month of the test, of which at least three of the approaches must have been conducted without the use of an approach coupler.

(3) The approaches specified in paragraph (c)(2)(ii)(B) of this section—

(i) Must be conducted under actual or simulated instrument flight conditions;

(ii) Must be conducted to the alert height or decision height for the ILS approach in the type aircraft in which the practical test is to be conducted;

(iii) Need not be conducted to the decision height authorized for Category III operations;

(iv) Must be conducted to the alert height or decision height, as applicable, authorized for Category III operations only if conducted in a flight simulator or flight training device; and

(v) Must be accomplished in an aircraft of the same category and class, and type, as applicable, as the aircraft in which the practical test is to be conducted or in a flight simulator that—

(A) Represents an aircraft of the same category and class, and type, as applicable, as the aircraft for which the authorization is sought; and

(B) Is used in accordance with an approved course conducted by a training center certificated under part 142 of this chapter.

(4) The flight time acquired in meeting the requirements of paragraph (c)(2)(ii)(B) of this section may be used to meet the requirements of paragraph (c)(2)(ii)(A) of this section.

(d) Practical test procedures. The practical test consists of an oral increment and a flight increment.

(1) *Oral increment.* In the oral increment of the practical test an applicant must demonstrate knowledge of the following:

(i) Required landing distance;

(ii) Determination and recognition of the alert height or decision height, as applicable, including use of a radar altimeter;

(iii) Recognition of and proper reaction to significant failures encountered prior to and after reaching the alert height or decision height, as applicable;

(iv) Missed approach procedures and techniques using computed or fixed attitude guidance displays and expected height loss as they relate to manual go-around or automatic go-around, and initiation altitude, as applicable;

(v) Use and limitations of RVR, including determination of controlling RVR and required transmissometers;

(vi) Use, availability, or limitations of visual cues and the altitude at which they are normally discernible at reduced RVR readings including—

(A) Unexpected deterioration of conditions to less than minimum RVR during approach, flare, and rollout;

(B) Demonstration of expected visual references with weather at minimum conditions;

(C) The expected sequence of visual cues during an approach in which visibility is at or above landing minima; and

(D) Procedures and techniques for making a transition from instrument reference flight to visual flight during a final approach under reduced RVR.

(vii) Effects of vertical and horizontal wind-shear;

(viii) Characteristics and limitations of the ILS and runway lighting system;

(ix) Characteristics and limitations of the flight director system auto approach coupler (including split axis type if equipped), auto throttle system (if equipped), and other Category III equipment;

(x) Assigned duties of the second in command during Category III operations, unless the aircraft for which authorization is sought does not require a second in command;

(xi) Recognition of the limits of acceptable aircraft position and flight path tracking during approach, flare, and, if applicable, rollout; and

(xii) Recognition of, and reaction to, airborne or ground system faults or abnormalities, particularly after passing alert height or decision height, as applicable.

(2) *Flight increment.* The following requirements apply to the flight increment of the practical test—

(i) The flight increment may be conducted in an aircraft of the same category and class, and type, as applicable, as the aircraft for which the authorization is sought, or in a flight simulator that—

(A) Represents an aircraft of the same category and class, and type, as applicable, as the aircraft in which the authorization is sought; and

(B) Is used in accordance with an approved course conducted by a training center certificated under part 142 of this chapter.

(ii) The flight increment must consist of at least two ILS approaches to 100 feet AGL, including one landing and one missed approach initiated from a very low altitude that may result in a touchdown during the go-around maneuver;

(iii) All approaches performed during the flight increment must be made with the approved automatic landing system or an equivalent landing system approved by the Administrator;

(iv) If a multiengine aircraft with the performance capability to execute a missed approach with one engine inoperative is used for the practical test, the flight increment must include the performance of one missed approach with the most critical engine, if applicable, set at idle or zero thrust before reaching the middle or outer marker;

(v) If a multiengine flight simulator or multiengine flight training device is used, a missed approach must be executed with an engine, which shall be the most critical engine, if applicable, failed;

(vi) For an authorization for an aircraft that requires a type rating, the practical test must be performed in coordination with a second in command who holds a type rating in the aircraft in which the authorization is sought;

(vii) Oral questioning may be conducted at any time during the practical test;

(viii) Subject to the limitations of this paragraph, for Category IIIb operations predicated on the use of a fail-passive rollout control system, at least one manual rollout using visual reference or a combination of visual and instrument references must be executed. The maneuver required by this paragraph shall be initiated by a fail-passive disconnect of the rollout control system—

(A) After main gear touchdown;

(B) Prior to nose gear touchdown;

(C) In conditions representative of the most adverse lateral touchdown displacement allowing a safe landing on the runway; and

(D) In weather conditions anticipated in Category IIIb operations.

[Docket No. 25910, 62 FR 16298, April 4, 1997; Amdt. 61–103, 62 FR 40900, July 30, 1997]

§61.69 Glider and unpowered ultralight vehicle towing: Experience and training requirements.

(a) No person may act as pilot in command for towing a glider or unpowered ultralight vehicle unless that person—

(1) Holds a private, commercial or airline transport pilot certificate with a category rating for powered aircraft;

(2) Has logged at least 100 hours of pilot-in-command time in the aircraft category, class and type, if required, that the pilot is using to tow a glider or unpowered ultralight vehicle;

(3) Has a logbook endorsement from an authorized instructor who certifies that the person has received ground and flight training in gliders or unpowered ultralight vehicles and is proficient in—

(i) The techniques and procedures essential to the safe towing of gliders or unpowered ultralight vehicles, including airspeed limitations;

(ii) Emergency procedures;

(iii) Signals used; and

(iv) Maximum angles of bank.

(4) Except as provided in paragraph (b) of this section, has logged at least three flights as the sole manipulator of the controls of an aircraft while towing a glider or unpowered ultralight vehicle, or has simulated towing flight procedures in an aircraft while accompanied by a pilot who meets the requirements of paragraphs (c) and (d) of this section.

(5) Except as provided in paragraph (b) of this section, has received a logbook endorsement from the pilot, described in paragraph (a)(4) of this section, certifying that the person has accomplished at least 3 flights in an aircraft while towing a glider or unpowered ultralight vehicle, or while simulating towing flight procedures; and

(6) Within 24 calendar months before the flight has—

(i) Made at least three actual or simulated tows of a glider or unpowered ultralight vehicle while accompanied by a qualified pilot who meets the requirements of this section; or

(ii) Made at least three flights as pilot in command of a glider or unpowered ultralight vehicle towed by an aircraft.

(b) Any person who, before May 17, 1967, has made and logged 10 or more flights as pilot in command of an aircraft towing a glider or unpowered ultralight vehicle in accordance with a certificate of waiver need not comply with paragraphs (a)(4) and (a)(5) of this section.

(c) The pilot, described in paragraph (a)(4) of this section, who endorses the logbook of a person seeking towing privileges must have—

(1) Met the requirements of this section prior to endorsing the logbook of the person seeking towing privileges; and

(2) Logged at least 10 flights as pilot in command of an aircraft while towing a glider or unpowered ultralight vehicle.

(d) If the pilot described in paragraph (a)(4) of this section holds only a private pilot certificate, then that pilot must have—

(1) Logged at least 100 hours of pilot-in-command time in airplanes, or 200 hours of pilot-in-command time in a combination of powered and other-than-powered aircraft; and

(2) Performed and logged at least three flights within the 12 calendar months preceding the month that pilot accompanies or endorses the logbook of a person seeking towing privileges—

(i) In an aircraft while towing a glider or unpowered ultralight vehicle accompanied by another pilot who meets the requirements of this section; or

(ii) As pilot in command of a glider or unpowered ultralight vehicle being towed by another aircraft.

[Docket No. FAA–2001–11133, 69 FR 44866, July 27, 2004; as amended by Amdt. 61–124, 74 FR 42555, Aug. 21, 2009]

§61.71 Graduates of an approved training program other than under this part: Special rules.

(a) A person who graduates from an approved training program under part 141 or part 142 of this chapter is considered to have met the applicable aeronautical experience, aeronautical knowledge, and areas of operation requirements of this part if that person presents the graduation certificate and passes the required practical test within the 60-day period after the date of graduation.

(b) A person may apply for an airline transport pilot certificate, type rating, or both under this part, and will be considered to have met the applicable requirements under §61.157, except for the airline transport pilot certification training program required by §61.156, for that certificate and rating, if that person has:

(1) Satisfactorily accomplished an approved training curriculum and a proficiency check for that airplane type that includes all the tasks and maneuvers required by §§121.424 and 121.441 of this chapter to serve as pilot in command in operations conducted under part 121 of this chapter; and

(2) Applied for an airline transport pilot certificate, type rating, or both within the 60-day period from the date the person satisfactorily accomplished the requirements of paragraph (b)(1) for that airplane type.

(c) A person who holds a foreign pilot license and is applying for an equivalent U.S. pilot certificate on the basis of a Bilateral Aviation Safety Agreement and associated Implementation Procedures for Licensing may be considered to have met the applicable aeronautical experience, aeronautical knowledge, and areas of operation requirements of this part.

[Docket No. 25910, 62 FR 16298, April 4, 1997; Amdt. 61–103, 62 FR 40901, July 30, 1997; Amdt. 61–128, 76 FR 54107, Aug. 31, 2011; Amdt. 61–130, 78 FR 42374, July 15, 2013; Amdt. 61–144, 85 FR 10920, Feb. 25, 2020]

§61.73 Military pilots or former military pilots: Special rules.

(a) *General.* Except for a person who has been removed from flying status for lack of proficiency or because of a disciplinary action involving aircraft operations, a U.S. military pilot or former military pilot who meets the requirements of this section may apply, on the basis of his or her military pilot qualifications, for:

(1) A commercial pilot certificate with the appropriate aircraft category and class rating.

(2) An instrument rating with the appropriate aircraft rating.

(3) A type rating.

(b) *Military pilots and former military pilots in the U.S. Armed Forces.* A person who qualifies as a military pilot or former military pilot in the U.S. Armed Forces may apply for a pilot certificate and ratings under paragraph (a) of this section if that person—

(1) Presents evidentiary documents described under paragraphs (h)(1), (2), and (3) of this section that show the person's status in the U.S. Armed Forces.

(2) Has passed the military competency aeronautical knowledge test on the appropriate parts of this chapter for commercial pilot privileges and limitations, air traffic and general operating rules, and accident reporting rules.

(3) Presents official U.S. military records that show compliance with one of the following requirements—

(i) Before the date of the application, passing an official U.S. military pilot and instrument proficiency check in a military aircraft of the kind of aircraft category, class, and type, if class or type of aircraft is applicable, for the ratings sought; or

(ii) Before the date of application, logging 10 hours of pilot time as a military pilot in a U.S. military aircraft in the kind of aircraft category, class, and type, if a class rating or type rating is applicable, for the aircraft rating sought.

(c) *A military pilot in the Armed Forces of a foreign contracting State to the Convention on International Civil Aviation.* A person who is a military pilot in the Armed Forces of a foreign contracting State to the Convention on International Civil Aviation and is assigned to pilot duties in the U.S. Armed Forces, for purposes other than receiving flight training, may apply for a commercial pilot certificate and ratings under paragraph (a) of this section, provided that person—

(1) Presents evidentiary documents described under paragraph (h)(4) of this section that show the person is a military pilot in the Armed Forces of a foreign contracting State to the Convention on International Civil Aviation, and is assigned

to pilot duties in the U.S. Armed Forces, for purposes other than receiving flight training.

(2) Has passed the military competency aeronautical knowledge test on the appropriate parts of this chapter for commercial pilot privileges and limitations, air traffic and general operating rules, and accident reporting rules.

(3) Presents official U.S. military records that show compliance with one of the following requirements:

(i) Before the date of the application, passed an official U.S. military pilot and instrument proficiency check in a military aircraft of the kind of aircraft category, class, or type, if class or type of aircraft is applicable, for the ratings; or

(ii) Before the date of the application, logged 10 hours of pilot time as a military pilot in a U.S. military aircraft of the kind of category, class, and type of aircraft, if a class rating or type rating is applicable, for the aircraft rating.

(d) *Instrument rating.* A person who is qualified as a U.S. military pilot or former military pilot may apply for an instrument rating to be added to a pilot certificate if that person—

(1) Has passed an instrument proficiency check in the U.S. Armed Forces in the aircraft category for the instrument rating sought; and

(2) Has an official U.S. Armed Forces record that shows the person is instrument pilot qualified by the U.S. Armed Forces to conduct instrument flying on Federal airways in that aircraft category and class for the instrument rating sought.

(e) *Aircraft type rating.* An aircraft type rating may only be issued for a type of aircraft that has a comparable civilian type designation by the Administrator.

(f) *Aircraft type rating placed on an airline transport pilot certificate.* A person who is a military pilot or former military pilot of the U.S. Armed Forces and requests an aircraft type rating to be placed on an existing U.S. airline transport pilot certificate may be issued the rating at the airline transport pilot certification level, provided that person:

(1) Holds a category and class rating for that type of aircraft at the airline transport pilot certification level; and

(2) Has passed an official U.S. military pilot check and instrument proficiency check in that type of aircraft.

(g) *Flight instructor certificate and ratings.* A person who can show official U.S. military documentation of being a U.S. military instructor pilot or U.S. military pilot examiner, or a former instructor pilot or pilot examiner may apply for and be issued a flight instructor certificate with the appropriate ratings if that person:

(1) Holds a commercial or airline transport pilot certificate with the appropriate aircraft category

and class rating, if a class rating is appropriate, for the flight instructor rating sought;

(2) Holds an instrument rating, or has instrument privileges, on the pilot certificate that is appropriate to the flight instructor rating sought; and

(3) Presents the following documents:

(i) A knowledge test report that shows the person passed a knowledge test on the aeronautical knowledge areas listed under §61.185(a) appropriate to the flight instructor rating sought and the knowledge test was passed within the preceding 24 calendar months prior to the month of application. If the U.S. military instructor pilot or pilot examiner already holds a flight instructor certificate, holding of a flight instructor certificate suffices for the knowledge test report.

(ii) An official U.S. Armed Forces record or order that shows the person is or was qualified as a U.S. Armed Forces military instructor pilot or pilot examiner for the flight instructor rating sought.

(iii) An official U.S. Armed Forces record or order that shows the person completed a U.S. Armed Forces' instructor pilot or pilot examiner training course and received an aircraft rating qualification as a military instructor pilot or pilot examiner that is appropriate to the flight instructor rating sought.

(iv) An official U.S. Armed Forces record or order that shows the person passed a U.S. Armed Forces instructor pilot or pilot examiner proficiency check in an aircraft as a military instructor pilot or pilot examiner that is appropriate to the flight instructor rating sought.

(h) *Documents for qualifying for a pilot certificate and rating.* The following documents are required for a person to apply for a pilot certificate and rating:

(1) An official U.S. Armed Forces record that shows the person is or was a military pilot.

(2) An official U.S. Armed Forces record that shows the person graduated from a U.S. Armed Forces undergraduate pilot training school and received a rating qualification as a military pilot.

(3) An official U.S. Armed Forces record that shows the pilot passed a pilot proficiency check and instrument proficiency check in an aircraft as a military pilot.

(4) If a person is a military pilot in the Armed Forces from a foreign contracting State to the Convention on International Civil Aviation and is applying for a pilot certificate and rating, that person must present the following:

(i) An official U.S. Armed Forces record that shows the person is a military pilot in the U.S. Armed Forces;

(ii) An official U.S. Armed Forces record that shows the person is assigned as a military pilot in the U.S. Armed Forces for purposes other than receiving flight training;

(iii) An official record that shows the person graduated from a military undergraduate pilot training school from the Armed Forces from a foreign contracting State to the Convention on International Civil Aviation or from the U.S. Armed Forces, and received a qualification as a military pilot; and

(iv) An official U.S. Armed Forces record that shows that the person passed a pilot proficiency check and instrument proficiency check in an aircraft as a military pilot in the U.S. Armed Forces.

[Docket No. FAA–2006–26661, 74 FR 42555, Aug. 21, 2009]

§61.75 Private pilot certificate issued on the basis of a foreign pilot license.

(a) *General.* A person who holds a foreign pilot license at the private pilot level or higher that was issued by a contracting State to the Convention on International Civil Aviation may apply for and be issued a U.S. private pilot certificate with the appropriate ratings if the foreign pilot license meets the requirements of this section.

(b) *Certificate issued.* A U.S. private pilot certificate issued under this section must specify the person's foreign license number and country of issuance. A person who holds a foreign pilot license issued by a contracting State to the Convention on International Civil Aviation may be issued a U.S. private pilot certificate based on the foreign pilot license without any further showing of proficiency, provided the applicant:

(1) Meets the requirements of this section;

(2) Holds a foreign pilot license, at the private pilot license level or higher, that does not contain a limitation stating that the applicant has not met all of the standards of ICAO for that license;

(3) Does not hold a U.S. pilot certificate other than a U.S. student pilot certificate;

(4) Holds a medical certificate issued under part 67 of this chapter or a medical license issued by the country that issued the person's foreign pilot license; and

(5) Is able to read, speak, write, and understand the English language. If the applicant is unable to meet one of these requirements due to medical reasons, then the Administrator may place such operating limitations on that applicant's pilot certificate as are necessary for the safe operation of the aircraft.

(c) *Aircraft ratings issued.* Aircraft ratings listed on a person's foreign pilot license, in addition to any issued after testing under the provisions of this part, may be placed on that person's U.S. pilot certificate for private pilot privileges only.

(d) *Instrument ratings issued.* A person who holds an instrument rating on the foreign pilot license issued by a contracting State to the Convention on International Civil Aviation may be issued an instrument rating on a U.S. pilot certificate provided:

(1) The person's foreign pilot license authorizes instrument privileges;

(2) Within 24 months preceding the month in which the person applies for the instrument rating, the person passes the appropriate knowledge test; and

(3) The person is able to read, speak, write, and understand the English language. If the applicant is unable to meet one of these requirements due to medical reasons, then the Administrator may place such operating limitations on that applicant's pilot certificate as are necessary for the safe operation of the aircraft.

(e) *Operating privileges and limitations.* A person who receives a U.S. private pilot certificate that has been issued under the provisions of this section:

(1) May act as pilot in command of a civil aircraft of the United States in accordance with the pilot privileges authorized by this part and the limitations placed on that U.S. pilot certificate;

(2) Is limited to the privileges placed on the certificate by the Administrator;

(3) Is subject to the limitations and restrictions on the person's U.S. certificate and foreign pilot license when exercising the privileges of that U.S. pilot certificate in an aircraft of U.S. registry operating within or outside the United States; and

(f) *Limitation on licenses used as the basis for a U.S. certificate.* A person may use only one foreign pilot license as a basis for the issuance of a U.S. pilot certificate. The foreign pilot license and medical certification used as a basis for issuing a U.S. pilot certificate under this section must be written in English or accompanied by an English transcription that has been signed by an official or representative of the foreign aviation authority that issued the foreign pilot license.

(g) *Limitation placed on a U.S. pilot certificate.* A U.S. pilot certificate issued under this section can only be exercised when the pilot has the foreign pilot license, upon which the issuance of the U.S. pilot certificate was based, in the holder's possession or readily accessible in the aircraft.

[Docket No. 25910, 62 FR 16298, April 4, 1997; as amended by Amdt. 61–124, 74 FR 42556, Aug. 21, 2009]

§61.77 Special purpose pilot authorization: Operation of a civil aircraft of the United States and leased by a non-U.S. citizen.

(a) *General.* The holder of a foreign pilot license issued by a contracting State to the Convention on International Civil Aviation who meets the requirements of this section may be issued a special purpose pilot authorization by the

Administrator for the purpose of performing pilot duties.

(1) On a civil aircraft of U.S. registry that is leased to a person who is not a citizen of the United States, and

(2) For carrying persons or property for compensation or hire for operations in—

(i) Scheduled international air services in turbojet-powered airplanes of U.S. registry;

(ii) Scheduled international air services in airplanes of U.S. registry having a configuration of more than nine passenger seats, excluding crewmember seats;

(iii) Nonscheduled international air transportation in airplanes of U.S. registry having a configuration of more than 30 passenger seats, excluding crewmember seats; or

(iv) Scheduled international air services, or nonscheduled international air transportation, in airplanes of U.S. registry having a payload capacity of more than 7,500 pounds.

(b) *Eligibility.* To be eligible for the issuance or renewal of a special purpose pilot authorization, an applicant must present the following to a Flight Standards office:

(1) A foreign pilot license issued by the aeronautical authority of a contracting State to the Convention on International Civil Aviation that contains the appropriate aircraft category, class, type rating, if appropriate, and instrument rating for the aircraft to be flown;

(2) A certification by the lessee of the aircraft—

(i) Stating that the applicant is employed by the lessee;

(ii) Specifying the aircraft type on which the applicant will perform pilot duties; and

(iii) Stating that the applicant has received ground and flight instruction that qualifies the applicant to perform the duties to be assigned on the aircraft.

(3) Documentation showing when the applicant will reach the age of 65 years (an official copy of the applicant's birth certificate or other official documentation);

(4) Documentation the applicant meets the medical standards for the issuance of the foreign pilot license from the aeronautical authority of that contracting State to the Convention on International Civil Aviation; and

(5) A statement that the applicant does not already hold a special purpose pilot authorization; however, if the applicant already holds a special purpose pilot authorization, then that special purpose pilot authorization must be surrendered to either the Flight Standards office that issued it, or the Flight Standards office processing the application for the authorization, prior to being issued another special purpose pilot authorization.

(c) *Privileges.* A person issued a special purpose pilot authorization under this section—

(1) May exercise the privileges prescribed on the special purpose pilot authorization; and

(2) Must comply with the limitations specified in this section and any additional limitations specified on the special purpose pilot authorization.

(d) *General limitations.* A special purpose pilot authorization may be used only—

(1) For flights between foreign countries or for flights in foreign air commerce within the time period allotted on the authorization.

(2) If the foreign pilot license required by paragraph (b)(1) of this section, the medical documentation required by paragraph (b)(4) of this section, and the special purpose pilot authorization issued under this section are in the holder's physical possession or immediately accessible in the aircraft.

(3) While the holder is employed by the person to whom the aircraft described in the certification required by paragraph (b)(2) of this section is leased.

(4) While the holder is performing pilot duties on the U.S.-registered aircraft described in the certification required by paragraph (b)(2) of this section.

(5) If the holder has only one special purpose pilot authorization as provided in paragraph (b)(5) of this section.

(e) *Age limitation.* No person who holds a special purpose pilot authorization issued under this part may serve as a pilot on a civil airplane of U.S. registry in the following operations if the person has reached his or her 60th birthday or, in the case of operations with more than one pilot, his or her 65th birthday:

(1) Scheduled international air services carrying passengers in turbojet-powered airplanes;

(2) Scheduled international air services carrying passengers in airplanes having a passenger-seat configuration of more than nine passenger seats, excluding each crewmember seat;

(3) Nonscheduled international air transportation for compensation or hire in airplanes having a passenger-seat configuration of more than 30 passenger seats, excluding each crewmember seat; or

(4) Scheduled international air services, or nonscheduled international air transportation for compensation or hire, in airplanes having a payload capacity of more than 7,500 pounds.

(f) *Definitions.*

(1) International air service, as used in paragraph (e) of this section, means scheduled air service performed in airplanes for the public transport of passengers, mail, or cargo, in which the service passes through the air space over the territory of more than one country.

(2) International air transportation, as used in paragraph (e) of this section, means air transportation performed in airplanes for the public transport of passengers, mail, or cargo, in which service passes through the air space over the territory of more than one country.

(g) *Expiration date.* Each special purpose pilot authorization issued under this section expires—

(1) 60 calendar months from the month it was issued, unless sooner suspended or revoked;

(2) When the lease agreement for the aircraft expires or the lessee terminates the employment of the person who holds the special purpose pilot authorization;

(3) Whenever the person's foreign pilot license has been suspended, revoked, or is no longer valid; or

(4) When the person no longer meets the medical standards for the issuance of the foreign pilot license.

(h) *Renewal.* A person exercising the privileges of a special purpose pilot authorization may apply for a 60-calendar-month extension of that authorization, provided the person—

(1) Continues to meet the requirements of this section; and

(2) Surrenders the expired special purpose pilot authorization upon receipt of the new authorization.

(i) *Surrender.* The holder of a special purpose pilot authorization must surrender the authorization to the Administrator within 7 days after the date the authorization terminates.

[Docket No. 25910, 62 FR 40901, July 30, 1997, as amended by Amdt. 61–123, 74 FR 34234, July 15, 2009; Amdt. 61–124, 74 FR 42557, Aug. 21, 2009; Amdt. 61–134, 80 FR 33401, June 12, 2015; Docket FAA–2018–0119, Amdt. 61–141, 83 FR 9170, March 5, 2018]

Subpart C—Student Pilots

§61.81 Applicability.

This subpart prescribes the requirements for the issuance of student pilot certificates, the conditions under which those certificates are necessary, and the general operating rules and limitations for the holders of those certificates.

§61.83 Eligibility requirements for student pilots.

To be eligible for a student pilot certificate, an applicant must:

(a) Be at least 16 years of age for other than the operation of a glider or balloon.

(b) Be at least 14 years of age for the operation of a glider or balloon.

(c) Be able to read, speak, write, and understand the English language. If the applicant is

unable to meet one of these requirements due to medical reasons, then the Administrator may place such operating limitations on that applicant's pilot certificate as are necessary for the safe operation of the aircraft.

§61.85 Application.

An applicant for a student pilot certificate:

(a) Must make that application in a form acceptable to the Administrator; and

(b) Must submit the application to a Flight Standards office, a designated pilot examiner, an airman certification representative associated with a pilot school, a flight instructor, or other person authorized by the Administrator.

[Docket FAA–2010–1127, Amdt. 61–135, 81 FR 1306, Jan. 12, 2016, as amended by Docket FAA–2018–0119, Amdt. 61–141, 83 FR 9170, March 5, 2018]

§61.87 Solo requirements for student pilots.

(a) *General.* A student pilot may not operate an aircraft in solo flight unless that student has met the requirements of this section. The term "solo flight" as used in this subpart means that flight time during which a student pilot is the sole occupant of the aircraft or that flight time during which the student performs the duties of a pilot in command of a gas balloon or an airship requiring more than one pilot flight crewmember.

(b) *Aeronautical knowledge.* A student pilot must demonstrate satisfactory aeronautical knowledge on a knowledge test that meets the requirements of this paragraph:

(1) The test must address the student pilot's knowledge of—

(i) Applicable sections of parts 61 and 91 of this chapter;

(ii) Airspace rules and procedures for the airport where the solo flight will be performed; and

(iii) Flight characteristics and operational limitations for the make and model of aircraft to be flown.

(2) The student's authorized instructor must—

(i) Administer the test; and

(ii) At the conclusion of the test, review all incorrect answers with the student before authorizing that student to conduct a solo flight.

(c) *Pre-solo flight training.* Prior to conducting a solo flight, a student pilot must have:

(1) Received and logged flight training for the maneuvers and procedures of this section that are appropriate to the make and model of aircraft to be flown; and

(2) Demonstrated satisfactory proficiency and safety, as judged by an authorized instructor, on the maneuvers and procedures required by this section in the make and model of aircraft or similar make and model of aircraft to be flown.

(d) Maneuvers and procedures for pre-solo flight training in a single-engine airplane. A student pilot who is receiving training for a single-engine airplane rating or privileges must receive and log flight training for the following maneuvers and procedures:

(1) Proper flight preparation procedures, including preflight planning and preparation, powerplant operation, and aircraft systems;

(2) Taxiing or surface operations, including runups;

(3) Takeoffs and landings, including normal and crosswind;

(4) Straight and level flight, and turns in both directions;

(5) Climbs and climbing turns;

(6) Airport traffic patterns, including entry and departure procedures;

(7) Collision avoidance, windshear avoidance, and wake turbulence avoidance;

(8) Descents, with and without turns, using high and low drag configurations;

(9) Flight at various airspeeds from cruise to slow flight;

(10) Stall entries from various flight attitudes and power combinations with recovery initiated at the first indication of a stall, and recovery from a full stall;

(11) Emergency procedures and equipment malfunctions;

(12) Ground reference maneuvers;

(13) Approaches to a landing area with simulated engine malfunctions;

(14) Slips to a landing; and

(15) Go-arounds.

(e) Maneuvers and procedures for pre-solo flight training in a multiengine airplane. A student pilot who is receiving training for a multiengine airplane rating must receive and log flight training for the following maneuvers and procedures:

(1) Proper flight preparation procedures, including preflight planning and preparation, powerplant operation, and aircraft systems;

(2) Taxiing or surface operations, including runups;

(3) Takeoffs and landings, including normal and crosswind;

(4) Straight and level flight, and turns in both directions;

(5) Climbs and climbing turns;

(6) Airport traffic patterns, including entry and departure procedures;

(7) Collision avoidance, windshear avoidance, and wake turbulence avoidance;

(8) Descents, with and without turns, using high and low drag configurations;

(9) Flight at various airspeeds from cruise to slow flight;

(10) Stall entries from various flight attitudes and power combinations with recovery initiated at the first indication of a stall, and recovery from a full stall;

(11) Emergency procedures and equipment malfunctions;

(12) Ground reference maneuvers;

(13) Approaches to a landing area with simulated engine malfunctions; and

(14) Go-arounds.

(f) Maneuvers and procedures for pre-solo flight training in a helicopter. A student pilot who is receiving training for a helicopter rating must receive and log flight training for the following maneuvers and procedures:

(1) Proper flight preparation procedures, including preflight planning and preparation, powerplant operation, and aircraft systems;

(2) Taxiing or surface operations, including runups;

(3) Takeoffs and landings, including normal and crosswind;

(4) Straight and level flight, and turns in both directions;

(5) Climbs and climbing turns;

(6) Airport traffic patterns, including entry and departure procedures;

(7) Collision avoidance, windshear avoidance, and wake turbulence avoidance;

(8) Descents with and without turns;

(9) Flight at various airspeeds;

(10) Emergency procedures and equipment malfunctions;

(11) Ground reference maneuvers;

(12) Approaches to the landing area;

(13) Hovering and hovering turns;

(14) Go-arounds;

(15) Simulated emergency procedures, including autorotational descents with a power recovery and power recovery to a hover;

(16) Rapid decelerations; and

(17) Simulated one-engine-inoperative approaches and landings for multiengine helicopters.

(g) Maneuvers and procedures for pre-solo flight training in a gyroplane. A student pilot who is receiving training for a gyroplane rating or privileges must receive and log flight training for the following maneuvers and procedures:

(1) Proper flight preparation procedures, including preflight planning and preparation, powerplant operation, and aircraft systems;

(2) Taxiing or surface operations, including runups;

(3) Takeoffs and landings, including normal and crosswind;

(4) Straight and level flight, and turns in both directions;

(5) Climbs and climbing turns;

(6) Airport traffic patterns, including entry and departure procedures;

(7) Collision avoidance, windshear avoidance, and wake turbulence avoidance;

(8) Descents with and without turns;

(9) Flight at various airspeeds;

(10) Emergency procedures and equipment malfunctions;

(11) Ground reference maneuvers;

(12) Approaches to the landing area;

(13) High rates of descent with power on and with simulated power off, and recovery from those flight configurations;

(14) Go-arounds; and

(15) Simulated emergency procedures, including simulated power-off landings and simulated power failure during departures.

(h) Maneuvers and procedures for pre-solo flight training in a powered-lift. A student pilot who is receiving training for a powered-lift rating must receive and log flight training in the following maneuvers and procedures:

(1) Proper flight preparation procedures, including preflight planning and preparation, powerplant operation, and aircraft systems;

(2) Taxiing or surface operations, including runups;

(3) Takeoffs and landings, including normal and crosswind;

(4) Straight and level flight, and turns in both directions;

(5) Climbs and climbing turns;

(6) Airport traffic patterns, including entry and departure procedures;

(7) Collision avoidance, windshear avoidance, and wake turbulence avoidance;

(8) Descents with and without turns;

(9) Flight at various airspeeds from cruise to slow flight;

(10) Stall entries from various flight attitudes and power combinations with recovery initiated at the first indication of a stall, and recovery from a full stall;

(11) Emergency procedures and equipment malfunctions;

(12) Ground reference maneuvers;

(13) Approaches to a landing with simulated engine malfunctions;

(14) Go-arounds;

(15) Approaches to the landing area;

(16) Hovering and hovering turns; and

(17) For multiengine powered-lifts, simulated one-engine-inoperative approaches and landings.

(i) Maneuvers and procedures for pre-solo flight training in a glider. A student pilot who is receiving training for a glider rating or privileges must receive and log flight training for the following maneuvers and procedures:

(1) Proper flight preparation procedures, including preflight planning, preparation, aircraft systems, and, if appropriate, powerplant operations;

(2) Taxiing or surface operations, including runups, if applicable;

(3) Launches, including normal and crosswind;

(4) Straight and level flight, and turns in both directions, if applicable;

(5) Airport traffic patterns, including entry procedures;

(6) Collision avoidance, windshear avoidance, and wake turbulence avoidance;

(7) Descents with and without turns using high and low drag configurations;

(8) Flight at various airspeeds;

(9) Emergency procedures and equipment malfunctions;

(10) Ground reference maneuvers, if applicable;

(11) Inspection of towline rigging and review of signals and release procedures, if applicable;

(12) Aerotow, ground tow, or self-launch procedures;

(13) Procedures for disassembly and assembly of the glider;

(14) Stall entry, stall, and stall recovery;

(15) Straight glides, turns, and spirals;

(16) Landings, including normal and crosswind;

(17) Slips to a landing;

(18) Procedures and techniques for thermalling; and

(19) Emergency operations, including towline break procedures.

(j) Maneuvers and procedures for pre-solo flight training in an airship. A student pilot who is receiving training for an airship rating or privileges must receive and log flight training for the following maneuvers and procedures:

(1) Proper flight preparation procedures, including preflight planning and preparation, powerplant operation, and aircraft systems;

(2) Taxiing or surface operations, including runups;

(3) Takeoffs and landings, including normal and crosswind;

(4) Straight and level flight, and turns in both directions;

(5) Climbs and climbing turns;

(6) Airport traffic patterns, including entry and departure procedures;

(7) Collision avoidance, windshear avoidance, and wake turbulence avoidance;

(8) Descents with and without turns;

(9) Flight at various airspeeds from cruise to slow flight;

(10) Emergency procedures and equipment malfunctions;

(11) Ground reference maneuvers;

(12) Rigging, ballasting, and controlling pressure in the ballonets, and superheating; and

(13) Landings with positive and with negative static trim.

(k) *Maneuvers and procedures for pre-solo flight training in a balloon.* A student pilot who is receiving training in a balloon must receive and log flight training for the following maneuvers and procedures:

(1) Layout and assembly procedures;

(2) Proper flight preparation procedures, including preflight planning and preparation, and aircraft systems;

(3) Ascents and descents;

(4) Landing and recovery procedures;

(5) Emergency procedures and equipment malfunctions;

(6) Operation of hot air or gas source, ballast, valves, vents, and rip panels, as appropriate;

(7) Use of deflation valves or rip panels for simulating an emergency;

(8) The effects of wind on climb and approach angles; and

(9) Obstruction detection and avoidance techniques.

(l) *Maneuvers and procedures for pre-solo flight training in a powered parachute.* A student pilot who is receiving training for a powered parachute rating or privileges must receive and log flight training for the following maneuvers and procedures:

(1) Proper flight preparation procedures, including preflight planning and preparation, preflight assembly and rigging, aircraft systems, and powerplant operations.

(2) Taxiing or surface operations, including run-ups.

(3) Takeoffs and landings, including normal and crosswind.

(4) Straight and level flight, and turns in both directions.

(5) Climbs, and climbing turns in both directions.

(6) Airport traffic patterns, including entry and departure procedures.

(7) Collision avoidance, windshear avoidance, and wake turbulence avoidance.

(8) Descents, and descending turns in both directions.

(9) Emergency procedures and equipment malfunctions.

(10) Ground reference maneuvers.

(11) Straight glides, and gliding turns in both directions.

(12) Go-arounds.

(13) Approaches to landing areas with a simulated engine malfunction.

(14) Procedures for canopy packing and aircraft disassembly.

(m) *Maneuvers and procedures for pre-solo flight training in a weight-shift-control aircraft.* A student pilot who is receiving training for a weight-shift-control aircraft rating or privileges must receive and log flight training for the following maneuvers and procedures:

(1) Proper flight preparation procedures, including preflight planning and preparation, preflight assembly and rigging, aircraft systems, and powerplant operations.

(2) Taxiing or surface operations, including run-ups.

(3) Takeoffs and landings, including normal and crosswind.

(4) Straight and level flight, and turns in both directions.

(5) Climbs, and climbing turns in both directions.

(6) Airport traffic patterns, including entry and departure procedures.

(7) Collision avoidance, windshear avoidance, and wake turbulence avoidance.

(8) Descents, and descending turns in both directions.

(9) Flight at various airspeeds from maximum cruise to slow flight.

(10) Emergency procedures and equipment malfunctions.

(11) Ground reference maneuvers.

(12) Stall entry, stall, and stall recovery.

(13) Straight glides, and gliding turns in both directions.

(14) Go-arounds.

(15) Approaches to landing areas with a simulated engine malfunction.

(16) Procedures for disassembly.

(n) *Limitations on student pilots operating an aircraft in solo flight.* A student pilot may not operate an aircraft in solo flight unless that student pilot has received an endorsement in the student's logbook for the specific make and model aircraft to be flown by an authorized instructor who gave the training within the 90 days preceding the date of the flight.

(o) *Limitations on student pilots operating an aircraft in solo flight at night.* A student pilot may not operate an aircraft in solo flight at night unless that student pilot has received:

(1) Flight training at night on night flying procedures that includes takeoffs, approaches, landings, and go-arounds at night at the airport where the solo flight will be conducted;

(2) Navigation training at night in the vicinity of the airport where the solo flight will be conducted; and

(3) An endorsement in the student's logbook for the specific make and model aircraft to be flown for night solo flight by an authorized instructor who gave the training within the 90-day period preceding the date of the flight.

(p) *Limitations on flight instructors authorizing solo flight.* No instructor may authorize a student pilot to perform a solo flight unless that instructor has—

(1) Given that student pilot training in the make and model of aircraft or a similar make and model of aircraft in which the solo flight is to be flown;

(2) Determined the student pilot is proficient in the maneuvers and procedures prescribed in this section;

(3) Determined the student pilot is proficient in the make and model of aircraft to be flown; and

(4) Endorsed the student pilot's logbook for the specific make and model aircraft to be flown, and that endorsement remains current for solo flight privileges, provided an authorized instructor updates the student's logbook every 90 days thereafter.

[Docket No. 25910, 62 FR 16298, April 4, 1997; Amdt. 61–103, 62 FR 40902, July 30, 1997; Amdt. 61–104, 63 FR 20287, April 23, 1998; Amdt. 61–110, 69 FR 44866, July 27, 2004; Amdt. 61–124, 74 FR 42557, Aug. 21, 2009; Docket FAA–2010–1127, Amdt. 61–135, 81 FR 1306, Jan. 12, 2016]

§61.89 General limitations.

(a) A student pilot may not act as pilot in command of an aircraft:

(1) That is carrying a passenger;

(2) That is carrying property for compensation or hire;

(3) For compensation or hire;

(4) In furtherance of a business;

(5) On an international flight, except that a student pilot may make solo training flights from Haines, Gustavus, or Juneau, Alaska, to White Horse, Yukon, Canada, and return over the province of British Columbia;

(6) With a flight or surface visibility of less than 3 statute miles during daylight hours or 5 statute miles at night;

(7) When the flight cannot be made with visual reference to the surface; or

(8) In a manner contrary to any limitations placed in the pilot's logbook by an authorized instructor.

(b) A student pilot may not act as a required pilot flight crewmember on any aircraft for which more than one pilot is required by the type certificate of the aircraft or regulations under which the flight is conducted, except when receiving flight training from an authorized instructor on board an airship, and no person other than a required flight crewmember is carried on the aircraft.

(c) A student pilot seeking a sport pilot certificate must comply with the provisions of paragraphs (a) and (b) of this section and may not act as pilot in command—

(1) Of an aircraft other than a light-sport aircraft;

(2) At night;

(3) At an altitude of more than 10,000 feet MSL or 2,000 feet AGL, whichever is higher;

(4) In Class B, C, and D airspace, at an airport located in Class B, C, or D airspace, and to, from, through, or on an airport having an operational control tower without having received the ground

and flight training specified in §61.94 and an endorsement from an authorized instructor;

(5) Of a light-sport aircraft without having received the applicable ground training, flight training, and instructor endorsements specified in §61.327 (a) and (b).

(d) The holder of a student pilot certificate may act as pilot in command of an aircraft without holding a medical certificate issued under part 67 of this chapter provided the student pilot holds a valid U.S. driver's license, meets the requirements of §61.23(c)(3), and the operation is conducted consistent with the requirements of paragraphs (a) and (b) of this section and the conditions of §61.113(i). Where the requirements of paragraphs (a) and (b) of this section conflict with §61.113(i), a student pilot must comply with paragraphs (a) and (b) of this section.

[Docket No. 25910, 62 FR 16298, April 4, 1997, as amended by Amdt. 61–110, 69 FR 44867, July 27, 2004; Amdt. 61–125, 75 FR 5220, Feb. 1, 2010; Docket FAA–2016–9157, Amdt. 61–140, 82 FR 3165, Jan. 11, 2017]

§61.91 [Reserved]

§61.93 Solo cross-country flight requirements.

(a) General.

(1) Except as provided in paragraph (b) of this section, a student pilot must meet the requirements of this section before—

(i) Conducting a solo cross-country flight, or any flight greater than 25 nautical miles from the airport from where the flight originated.

(ii) Making a solo flight and landing at any location other than the airport of origination.

(2) Except as provided in paragraph (b) of this section, a student pilot who seeks solo cross-country flight privileges must:

(i) Have received flight training from an instructor authorized to provide flight training on the maneuvers and procedures of this section that are appropriate to the make and model of aircraft for which solo cross-country privileges are sought;

(ii) Have demonstrated cross-country proficiency on the appropriate maneuvers and procedures of this section to an authorized instructor;

(iii) Have satisfactorily accomplished the pre-solo flight maneuvers and procedures required by §61.87 of this part in the make and model of aircraft or similar make and model of aircraft for which solo cross-country privileges are sought; and

(iv) Comply with any limitations included in the authorized instructor's endorsement that are required by paragraph (c) of this section.

(3) A student pilot who seeks solo cross-country flight privileges must have received ground and flight training from an authorized instructor

on the cross-country maneuvers and procedures listed in this section that are appropriate to the aircraft to be flown.

(b) *Authorization to perform certain solo flights and cross-country flights.* A student pilot must obtain an endorsement from an authorized instructor to make solo flights from the airport where the student pilot normally receives training to another location. A student pilot who receives this endorsement must comply with the requirements of this paragraph.

(1) Solo flights may be made to another airport that is within 25 nautical miles from the airport where the student pilot normally receives training, provided—

(i) An authorized instructor has given the student pilot flight training at the other airport, and that training includes flight in both directions over the route, entering and exiting the traffic pattern, and takeoffs and landings at the other airport;

(ii) The authorized instructor who gave the training endorses the student pilot's logbook authorizing the flight;

(iii) The student pilot has a solo flight endorsement in accordance with §61.87 of this part;

(iv) The authorized instructor has determined that the student pilot is proficient to make the flight; and

(v) The purpose of the flight is to practice takeoffs and landings at that other airport.

(2) Repeated specific solo cross-country flights may be made to another airport that is within 50 nautical miles of the airport from which the flight originated, provided—

(i) The authorized instructor has given the student flight training in both directions over the route, including entering and exiting the traffic patterns, takeoffs, and landings at the airports to be used;

(ii) The authorized instructor who gave the training has endorsed the student's logbook certifying that the student is proficient to make such flights;

(iii) The student has a solo flight endorsement in accordance with §61.87 of this part; and

(iv) The student has a solo cross country flight endorsement in accordance with paragraph (c) of this section; however, for repeated solo cross country flights to another airport within 50 nautical miles from which the flight originated, separate endorsements are not required to be made for each flight.

(c) *Endorsements for solo cross-country flights.* Except as specified in paragraph (b)(2) of this section, a student pilot must have the endorsements prescribed in this paragraph for each cross-country flight:

(1) A student pilot must have a solo cross-country endorsement from the authorized instructor who conducted the training that is placed in that person's logbook for the specific category of aircraft to be flown.

(2) A student pilot must have a solo cross-country endorsement from an authorized instructor that is placed in that person's logbook for the specific make and model of aircraft to be flown.

(3) For each cross-country flight, the authorized instructor who reviews the cross-country planning must make an endorsement in the person's logbook after reviewing that person's cross-country planning, as specified in paragraph (d) of this section. The endorsement must—

(i) Specify the make and model of aircraft to be flown;

(ii) State that the student's preflight planning and preparation is correct and that the student is prepared to make the flight safely under the known conditions; and

(iii) State that any limitations required by the student's authorized instructor are met.

(d) *Limitations on authorized instructors to permit solo cross-country flights.* An authorized instructor may not permit a student pilot to conduct a solo cross-country flight unless that instructor has:

(1) Determined that the student's cross-country planning is correct for the flight;

(2) Reviewed the current and forecast weather conditions and has determined that the flight can be completed under VFR;

(3) Determined that the student is proficient to conduct the flight safely;

(4) Determined that the student has the appropriate solo cross-country endorsement for the make and model of aircraft to be flown; and

(5) Determined that the student's solo flight endorsement is current for the make and model aircraft to be flown.

(e) *Maneuvers and procedures for cross-country flight training in a single-engine airplane.* A student pilot who is receiving training for cross-country flight in a single-engine airplane must receive and log flight training in the following maneuvers and procedures:

(1) Use of aeronautical charts for VFR navigation using pilotage and dead reckoning with the aid of a magnetic compass;

(2) Use of aircraft performance charts pertaining to cross-country flight;

(3) Procurement and analysis of aeronautical weather reports and forecasts, including recognition of critical weather situations and estimating visibility while in flight;

(4) Emergency procedures;

(5) Traffic pattern procedures that include area departure, area arrival, entry into the traffic pattern, and approach;

(6) Procedures and operating practices for collision avoidance, wake turbulence precautions, and windshear avoidance;

(7) Recognition, avoidance, and operational restrictions of hazardous terrain features in the geographical area where the cross-country flight will be flown;

(8) Procedures for operating the instruments and equipment installed in the aircraft to be flown, including recognition and use of the proper operational procedures and indications;

(9) Use of radios for VFR navigation and two-way communication, except that a student pilot seeking a sport pilot certificate must only receive and log flight training on the use of radios installed in the aircraft to be flown;

(10) Takeoff, approach, and landing procedures, including short-field, soft-field, and crosswind takeoffs, approaches, and landings;

(11) Climbs at best angle and best rate; and

(12) Control and maneuvering solely by reference to flight instruments, including straight and level flight, turns, descents, climbs, use of radio aids, and ATC directives. For student pilots seeking a sport pilot certificate, the provisions of this paragraph only apply when receiving training for cross-country flight in an airplane that has a V_H greater than 87 knots CAS.

(f) *Maneuvers and procedures for cross-country flight training in a multiengine airplane.* A student pilot who is receiving training for cross-country flight in a multiengine airplane must receive and log flight training in the following maneuvers and procedures:

(1) Use of aeronautical charts for VFR navigation using pilotage and dead reckoning with the aid of a magnetic compass;

(2) Use of aircraft performance charts pertaining to cross-country flight;

(3) Procurement and analysis of aeronautical weather reports and forecasts, including recognition of critical weather situations and estimating visibility while in flight;

(4) Emergency procedures;

(5) Traffic pattern procedures that include area departure, area arrival, entry into the traffic pattern, and approach;

(6) Procedures and operating practices for collision avoidance, wake turbulence precautions, and windshear avoidance;

(7) Recognition, avoidance, and operational restrictions of hazardous terrain features in the geographical area where the cross-country flight will be flown;

(8) Procedures for operating the instruments and equipment installed in the aircraft to be flown, including recognition and use of the proper operational procedures and indications;

(9) Use of radios for VFR navigation and two-way communications;

(10) Takeoff, approach, and landing procedures, including short-field, soft-field, and crosswind takeoffs, approaches, and landings;

(11) Climbs at best angle and best rate; and

(12) Control and maneuvering solely by reference to flight instruments, including straight and level flight, turns, descents, climbs, use of radio aids, and ATC directives.

(g) *Maneuvers and procedures for cross-country flight training in a helicopter.* A student pilot who is receiving training for cross-country flight in a helicopter must receive and log flight training for the following maneuvers and procedures:

(1) Use of aeronautical charts for VFR navigation using pilotage and dead reckoning with the aid of a magnetic compass;

(2) Use of aircraft performance charts pertaining to cross-country flight;

(3) Procurement and analysis of aeronautical weather reports and forecasts, including recognition of critical weather situations and estimating visibility while in flight;

(4) Emergency procedures;

(5) Traffic pattern procedures that include area departure, area arrival, entry into the traffic pattern, and approach;

(6) Procedures and operating practices for collision avoidance, wake turbulence precautions, and windshear avoidance;

(7) Recognition, avoidance, and operational restrictions of hazardous terrain features in the geographical area where the cross-country flight will be flown;

(8) Procedures for operating the instruments and equipment installed in the aircraft to be flown, including recognition and use of the proper operational procedures and indications;

(9) Use of radios for VFR navigation and two-way communications; and

(10) Takeoff, approach, and landing procedures.

(h) *Maneuvers and procedures for cross-country flight training in a gyroplane.* A student pilot who is receiving training for cross-country flight in a gyroplane must receive and log flight training in the following maneuvers and procedures:

(1) Use of aeronautical charts for VFR navigation using pilotage and dead reckoning with the aid of a magnetic compass;

(2) Use of aircraft performance charts pertaining to cross-country flight;

(3) Procurement and analysis of aeronautical weather reports and forecasts, including recognition of critical weather situations and estimating visibility while in flight;

(4) Emergency procedures;

(5) Traffic pattern procedures that include area departure, area arrival, entry into the traffic pattern, and approach;

(6) Procedures and operating practices for collision avoidance, wake turbulence precautions, and windshear avoidance;

61

(7) Recognition, avoidance, and operational restrictions of hazardous terrain features in the geographical area where the cross-country flight will be flown;

(8) Procedures for operating the instruments and equipment installed in the aircraft to be flown, including recognition and use of the proper operational procedures and indications;

(9) Use of radios for VFR navigation and two-way communication, except that a student pilot seeking a sport pilot certificate must only receive and log flight training on the use of radios installed in the aircraft to be flown; and

(10) Takeoff, approach, and landing procedures, including short-field and soft-field takeoffs, approaches, and landings.

(i) *Maneuvers and procedures for cross-country flight training in a powered-lift.* A student pilot who is receiving training for cross-country flight training in a powered-lift must receive and log flight training in the following maneuvers and procedures:

(1) Use of aeronautical charts for VFR navigation using pilotage and dead reckoning with the aid of a magnetic compass;

(2) Use of aircraft performance charts pertaining to cross-country flight;

(3) Procurement and analysis of aeronautical weather reports and forecasts, including recognition of critical weather situations and estimating visibility while in flight;

(4) Emergency procedures;

(5) Traffic pattern procedures that include area departure, area arrival, entry into the traffic pattern, and approach;

(6) Procedures and operating practices for collision avoidance, wake turbulence precautions, and windshear avoidance;

(7) Recognition, avoidance, and operational restrictions of hazardous terrain features in the geographical area where the cross-country flight will be flown;

(8) Procedures for operating the instruments and equipment installed in the aircraft to be flown, including recognition and use of the proper operational procedures and indications;

(9) Use of radios for VFR navigation and two-way communications;

(10) Takeoff, approach, and landing procedures that include high-altitude, steep, and shallow take-offs, approaches, and landings; and

(11) Control and maneuvering solely by reference to flight instruments, including straight and level flight, turns, descents, climbs, use of radio aids, and ATC directives.

(j) *Maneuvers and procedures for cross-country flight training in a glider.* A student pilot who is receiving training for cross-country flight in a glider must receive and log flight training in the following maneuvers and procedures:

(1) Use of aeronautical charts for VFR navigation using pilotage and dead reckoning with the aid of a magnetic compass;

(2) Use of aircraft performance charts pertaining to cross-country flight;

(3) Procurement and analysis of aeronautical weather reports and forecasts, including recognition of critical weather situations and estimating visibility while in flight;

(4) Emergency procedures;

(5) Traffic pattern procedures that include area departure, area arrival, entry into the traffic pattern, and approach;

(6) Procedures and operating practices for collision avoidance, wake turbulence precautions, and windshear avoidance;

(7) Recognition, avoidance, and operational restrictions of hazardous terrain features in the geographical area where the cross-country flight will be flown;

(8) Procedures for operating the instruments and equipment installed in the aircraft to be flown, including recognition and use of the proper operational procedures and indications;

(9) Landings accomplished without the use of the altimeter from at least 2,000 feet above the surface; and

(10) Recognition of weather and upper air conditions favorable for cross-country soaring, ascending and descending flight, and altitude control.

(k) *Maneuvers and procedures for cross-country flight training in an airship.* A student pilot who is receiving training for cross-country flight in an airship must receive and log flight training for the following maneuvers and procedures:

(1) Use of aeronautical charts for VFR navigation using pilotage and dead reckoning with the aid of a magnetic compass;

(2) Use of aircraft performance charts pertaining to cross-country flight;

(3) Procurement and analysis of aeronautical weather reports and forecasts, including recognition of critical weather situations and estimating visibility while in flight;

(4) Emergency procedures;

(5) Traffic pattern procedures that include area departure, area arrival, entry into the traffic pattern, and approach;

(6) Procedures and operating practices for collision avoidance, wake turbulence precautions, and windshear avoidance;

(7) Recognition, avoidance, and operational restrictions of hazardous terrain features in the geographical area where the cross-country flight will be flown;

(8) Procedures for operating the instruments and equipment installed in the aircraft to be flown, including recognition and use of the proper operational procedures and indications;

(9) Use of radios for VFR navigation and two-way communication, except that a student pilot seeking a sport pilot certificate must only receive and log flight training on the use of radios installed in the aircraft to be flown;

(10) Control of air pressure with regard to ascending and descending flight and altitude control;

(11) Control of the airship solely by reference to flight instruments, except for a student pilot seeking a sport pilot certificate; and

(12) Recognition of weather and upper air conditions conducive for the direction of cross-country flight.

(l) Maneuvers and procedures for cross-country flight training in a powered parachute. A student pilot who is receiving training for cross-country flight in a powered parachute must receive and log flight training in the following maneuvers and procedures:

(1) Use of aeronautical charts for VFR navigation using pilotage and dead reckoning with the aid of a magnetic compass, as appropriate.

(2) Use of aircraft performance charts pertaining to cross-country flight.

(3) Procurement and analysis of aeronautical weather reports and forecasts, including recognizing critical weather situations and estimating visibility while in flight.

(4) Emergency procedures.

(5) Traffic pattern procedures that include area departure, area arrival, entry into the traffic pattern, and approach.

(6) Procedures and operating practices for collision avoidance, wake turbulence precautions, and windshear avoidance.

(7) Recognition, avoidance, and operational restrictions of hazardous terrain features in the geographical area where the cross-country flight will be flown.

(8) Procedures for operating the instruments and equipment installed in the aircraft to be flown, including recognition and use of the proper operational procedures and indications.

(9) If equipped for flight with navigation radios, the use of radios for VFR navigation.

(10) Recognition of weather and upper air conditions favorable for the cross-country flight.

(11) Takeoff, approach and landing procedures.

(m) Maneuvers and procedures for cross-country flight training in a weight-shift-control aircraft. A student pilot who is receiving training for cross-country flight in a weight-shift-control aircraft must receive and log flight training for the following maneuvers and procedures:

(1) Use of aeronautical charts for VFR navigation using pilotage and dead reckoning with the aid of a magnetic compass, as appropriate.

(2) Use of aircraft performance charts pertaining to cross-country flight.

(3) Procurement and analysis of aeronautical weather reports and forecasts, including recognizing critical weather situations and estimating visibility while in flight.

(4) Emergency procedures.

(5) Traffic pattern procedures that include area departure, area arrival, entry into the traffic pattern, and approach.

(6) Procedures and operating practices for collision avoidance, wake turbulence precautions, and windshear avoidance.

(7) Recognition, avoidance, and operational restrictions of hazardous terrain features in the geographical area where the cross-country flight will be flown.

(8) Procedures for operating the instruments and equipment installed in the aircraft to be flown, including recognition and use of the proper operational procedures and indications.

(9) If equipped for flight using navigation radios, the use of radios for VFR navigation.

(10) Recognition of weather and upper air conditions favorable for the cross-country flight.

(11) Takeoff, approach and landing procedures, including crosswind approaches and landings.

[Docket No. 25910, 62 FR 16298, April 4, 1997; Amdt. 61–103, 62 FR 40902, July 30, 1997; Amdt. 61–110, 69 FR 44867, July 27, 2004; Amdt. 61–124, 74 FR 42557, Aug. 21, 2009; Amdt. 61–125, 75 FR 5220, Feb. 1, 2010; Docket FAA–2010–1127, Amdt. 61–135, 81 FR 1306, Jan. 12, 2016]

§61.94 Student pilot seeking a sport pilot certificate or a recreational pilot certificate: Operations at airports within, and in airspace located within, Class B, C, and D airspace, or at airports with an operational control tower in other airspace.

(a) A student pilot seeking a sport pilot certificate or a recreational pilot certificate who wants to obtain privileges to operate in Class B, C, and D airspace, at an airport located in Class B, C, or D airspace, and to, from, through, or at an airport having an operational control tower, must receive and log ground and flight training from an authorized instructor in the following aeronautical knowledge areas and areas of operation:

(1) The use of radios, communications, navigation systems and facilities, and radar services.

(2) Operations at airports with an operating control tower, to include three takeoffs and landings to a full stop, with each landing involving a flight in the traffic pattern, at an airport with an operating control tower.

(3) Applicable flight rules of part 91 of this chapter for operations in Class B, C, and D airspace and air traffic control clearances.

(4) Ground and flight training for the specific Class B, C, or D airspace for which the solo flight is authorized, if applicable, within the 90-day period preceding the date of the flight in that airspace. The flight training must be received in the specific airspace area for which solo flight is authorized.

(5) Ground and flight training for the specific airport located in Class B, C, or D airspace for which the solo flight is authorized, if applicable, within the 90-day period preceding the date of the flight at that airport. The flight and ground training must be received at the specific airport for which solo flight is authorized.

(b) The authorized instructor who provides the training specified in paragraph (a) of this section must provide a logbook endorsement that certifies the student has received that training and is proficient to conduct solo flight in that specific airspace or at that specific airport and in those aeronautical knowledge areas and areas of operation specified in this section.

[Docket No. FAA–2001–11133, 69 FR 44867, July 27, 2004]

§61.95 Operations in Class B airspace and at airports located within Class B airspace.

(a) A student pilot may not operate an aircraft on a solo flight in Class B airspace unless:

(1) The student pilot has received both ground and flight training from an authorized instructor on that Class B airspace area, and the flight training was received in the specific Class B airspace area for which solo flight is authorized;

(2) The logbook of that student pilot has been endorsed by the authorized instructor who gave the student pilot flight training, and the endorsement is dated within the 90-day period preceding the date of the flight in that Class B airspace area; and

(3) The logbook endorsement specifies that the student pilot has received the required ground and flight training, and has been found proficient to conduct solo flight in that specific Class B airspace area.

(b) A student pilot may not operate an aircraft on a solo flight to, from, or at an airport located within Class B airspace pursuant to §91.131(b) of this chapter unless:

(1) The student pilot has received both ground and flight training from an instructor authorized to provide training to operate at that airport, and the flight and ground training has been received at the specific airport for which the solo flight is authorized;

(2) The logbook of that student pilot has been endorsed by an authorized instructor who gave the student pilot flight training, and the

endorsement is dated within the 90-day period preceding the date of the flight at that airport; and

(3) The logbook endorsement specifies that the student pilot has received the required ground and flight training, and has been found proficient to conduct solo flight operations at that specific airport.

(c) This section does not apply to a student pilot seeking a sport pilot certificate or a recreational pilot certificate.

[Docket No. 25910, 62 FR 16298, April 4, 1997; Amdt. 61–103, 62 FR 40902, July 30, 1997; Amdt. 61–110, 69 FR 44868, July 27, 2004]

Subpart D— Recreational Pilots

§61.96 Applicability and eligibility requirements: General.

(a) This subpart prescribes the requirement for the issuance of recreational pilot certificates and ratings, the conditions under which those certificates and ratings are necessary, and the general operating rules for persons who hold those certificates and ratings.

(b) To be eligible for a recreational pilot certificate, a person who applies for that certificate must:

(1) Be at least 17 years of age;

(2) Be able to read, speak, write, and understand the English language. If the applicant is unable to meet one of these requirements due to medical reasons, then the Administrator may place such operating limitations on that applicant's pilot certificate as are necessary for the safe operation of the aircraft;

(3) Receive a logbook endorsement from an authorized instructor who—

(i) Conducted the training or reviewed the applicant's home study on the aeronautical knowledge areas listed in §61.97(b) of this part that apply to the aircraft category and class rating sought; and

(ii) Certified that the applicant is prepared for the required knowledge test.

(4) Pass the required knowledge test on the aeronautical knowledge areas listed in §61.97(b) of this part;

(5) Receive flight training and a logbook endorsement from an authorized instructor who—

(i) Conducted the training on the areas of operation listed in §61.98(b) of this part that apply to the aircraft category and class rating sought; and

(ii) Certified that the applicant is prepared for the required practical test.

(6) Meet the aeronautical experience requirements of §61.99 of this part that apply to the aircraft category and class rating sought before applying for the practical test;

(7) Pass the practical test on the areas of operation listed in §61.98(b) that apply to the aircraft category and class rating;

(8) Comply with the sections of this part that apply to the aircraft category and class rating; and

(9) Hold either a student pilot certificate or sport pilot certificate.

[Docket No. 25910, 62 FR 16298, April 4, 1997; Amdt. 61–103, 62 FR 40902, July 30, 1997; Amdt. 61–124, 74 FR 42558, Aug. 21, 2009]

§61.97 Aeronautical knowledge.

(a) *General.* A person who applies for a recreational pilot certificate must receive and log ground training from an authorized instructor or complete a home-study course on the aeronautical knowledge areas of paragraph (b) of this section that apply to the aircraft category and class rating sought.

(b) *Aeronautical knowledge areas.*

(1) Applicable Federal Aviation Regulations of this chapter that relate to recreational pilot privileges, limitations, and flight operations;

(2) Accident reporting requirements of the National Transportation Safety Board;

(3) Use of the applicable portions of the "Aeronautical Information Manual" and FAA advisory circulars;

(4) Use of aeronautical charts for VFR navigation using pilotage with the aid of a magnetic compass;

(5) Recognition of critical weather situations from the ground and in flight, windshear avoidance, and the procurement and use of aeronautical weather reports and forecasts;

(6) Safe and efficient operation of aircraft, including collision avoidance, and recognition and avoidance of wake turbulence;

(7) Effects of density altitude on takeoff and climb performance;

(8) Weight and balance computations;

(9) Principles of aerodynamics, powerplants, and aircraft systems;

(10) Stall awareness, spin entry, spins, and spin recovery techniques, if applying for an airplane single-engine rating;

(11) Aeronautical decision making and judgment; and

(12) Preflight action that includes—

(i) How to obtain information on runway lengths at airports of intended use, data on takeoff and landing distances, weather reports and forecasts, and fuel requirements; and

(ii) How to plan for alternatives if the planned flight cannot be completed or delays are encountered.

[Docket No. 25910, 62 FR 16298, April 4, 1997; Amdt. 61–103, 62 FR 40902, July 30, 1997]

§61.98 Flight proficiency.

(a) *General.* A person who applies for a recreational pilot certificate must receive and log ground and flight training from an authorized instructor on the areas of operation of this section that apply to the aircraft category and class rating sought.

(b) *Areas of operation.*

(1) For a single-engine airplane rating:
(i) Preflight preparation;
(ii) Preflight procedures;
(iii) Airport operations;
(iv) Takeoffs, landings, and go-arounds;
(v) Performance maneuvers;
(vi) Ground reference maneuvers;
(vii) Navigation;
(viii) Slow flight and stalls;
(ix) Emergency operations; and
(x) Postflight procedures.

(2) For a helicopter rating:
(i) Preflight preparation;
(ii) Preflight procedures;
(iii) Airport and heliport operations;
(iv) Hovering maneuvers;
(v) Takeoffs, landings, and go-arounds;
(vi) Performance maneuvers;
(vii) Ground reference maneuvers;
(viii) Navigation;
(ix) Emergency operations; and
(x) Postflight procedures.

(3) For a gyroplane rating:
(i) Preflight preparation;
(ii) Preflight procedures;
(iii) Airport operations;
(iv) Takeoffs, landings, and go-arounds;
(v) Performance maneuvers;
(vi) Ground reference maneuvers;
(vii) Navigation;
(viii) Flight at slow airspeeds;
(ix) Emergency operations; and
(x) Postflight procedures.

[Docket No. 25910, 62 FR 16298, April 4, 1997; Amdt. 61–103, 62 FR 40902, July 30, 1997]

§61.99 Aeronautical experience.

(a) A person who applies for a recreational pilot certificate must receive and log at least 30 hours of flight time that includes at least—

(1) 15 hours of flight training from an authorized instructor on the areas of operation listed in §61.98 that consists of at least:

(i) Except as provided in §61.100, 2 hours of flight training en route to an airport that is located more than 25 nautical miles from the airport where the applicant normally trains, which includes at least three takeoffs and three landings at the airport located more than 25 nautical miles from the airport where the applicant normally trains; and

(ii) Three hours of flight training with an authorized instructor in the aircraft for the rating sought in preparation for the practical test within the preceding 2 calendar months from the month of the test.

(2) Three hours of solo flying in the aircraft for the rating sought, on the areas of operation listed in §61.98 that apply to the aircraft category and class rating sought.

(b) The holder of a sport pilot certificate may credit flight training received from a flight instructor with a sport pilot rating toward the aeronautical experience requirements of this section if the following conditions are met:

(1) The flight training was accomplished in the same category and class of aircraft for which the rating is sought;

(2) The flight instructor with a sport pilot rating was authorized to provide the flight training; and

(3) The flight training included training on areas of operation that are required for both a sport pilot certificate and a recreational pilot certificate.

[Docket FAA–2016–6142, Amdt. 61–142, 83 FR 30277, June 27, 2018]

§61.100 Pilots based on small islands.

(a) An applicant located on an island from which the flight training required in §61.99(a)(1) of this part cannot be accomplished without flying over water for more than 10 nautical miles from the nearest shoreline need not comply with the requirements of that section. However, if other airports that permit civil operations are available to which a flight may be made without flying over water for more than 10 nautical miles from the nearest shoreline, the applicant must show completion of a dual flight between two airports, which must include three landings at the other airport.

(b) An applicant who complies with paragraph (a) of this section and meets all requirements for the issuance of a recreational pilot certificate, except the requirements of §61.99(a)(1) of this part, will be issued a pilot certificate with an endorsement containing the following limitation, "Passenger carrying prohibited on flights more than 10 nautical miles from (the appropriate island)." The limitation may be subsequently amended to include another island if the applicant complies with the requirements of paragraph (a) of this section for another island.

(c) Upon meeting the requirements of §61.99(a)(1) of this part, the applicant may have the limitation(s) in paragraph (b) of this section removed.

§61.101 Recreational pilot privileges and limitations.

(a) A person who holds a recreational pilot certificate may:

(1) Carry no more than one passenger; and

(2) Not pay less than the pro rata share of the operating expenses of a flight with a passenger, provided the expenses involve only fuel, oil, airport expenses, or aircraft rental fees.

(b) A person who holds a recreational pilot certificate may act as pilot in command of an aircraft on a flight within 50 nautical miles from the departure airport, provided that person has—

(1) Received ground and flight training for takeoff, departure, arrival, and landing procedures at the departure airport;

(2) Received ground and flight training for the area, terrain, and aids to navigation that are in the vicinity of the departure airport;

(3) Been found proficient to operate the aircraft at the departure airport and the area within 50 nautical miles from that airport; and

(4) Received from an authorized instructor a logbook endorsement, which is carried in the person's possession in the aircraft, that permits flight within 50 nautical miles from the departure airport.

(c) A person who holds a recreational pilot certificate may act as pilot in command of an aircraft on a flight that exceeds 50 nautical miles from the departure airport, provided that person has—

(1) Received ground and flight training from an authorized instructor on the cross-country training requirements of subpart E of this part that apply to the aircraft rating held;

(2) Been found proficient in cross-country flying; and

(3) Received from an authorized instructor a logbook endorsement, which is carried on the person's possession in the aircraft, that certifies the person has received and been found proficient in the cross-country training requirements of subpart E of this part that apply to the aircraft rating held.

(d) A person who holds a recreational pilot certificate may act as pilot in command of an aircraft in Class B, C, and D airspace, at an airport located in Class B, C, or D airspace, and to, from, through, or at an airport having an operational control tower, provided that person has—

(1) Received and logged ground and flight training from an authorized instructor on the following aeronautical knowledge areas and areas of operation, as appropriate to the aircraft rating held:

(i) The use of radios, communications, navigation system and facilities, and radar services.

(ii) Operations at airports with an operating control tower to include three takeoffs and landings to

a full stop, with each landing involving a flight in the traffic pattern at an airport with an operating control tower.

(iii) Applicable flight rules of part 91 of this chapter for operations in Class B, C, and D airspace and air traffic control clearances;

(2) Been found proficient in those aeronautical knowledge areas and areas of operation specified in paragraph (d)(1) of this section; and

(3) Received from an authorized instructor a logbook endorsement, which is carried on the person's possession or readily accessible in the aircraft, that certifies the person has received and been found proficient in those aeronautical knowledge areas and areas of operation specified in paragraph (d)(1) of this section.

(e) Except as provided in paragraphs (d) and (i) of this section, a recreational pilot may not act as pilot in command of an aircraft—

(1) That is certificated—

(i) For more than four occupants;

(ii) With more than one powerplant;

(iii) With a powerplant of more than 180 horsepower, except aircraft certificated in the rotorcraft category; or

(iv) With retractable landing gear;

(2) That is classified as a multiengine airplane, powered-lift, glider, airship, balloon, powered parachute, or weight-shift-control aircraft;

(3) That is carrying a passenger or property for compensation or hire;

(4) For compensation or hire;

(5) In furtherance of a business;

(6) Between sunset and sunrise;

(7) In Class A, B, C, and D airspace, at an airport located in Class B, C, or D airspace, or to, from, through, or at an airport having an operational control tower;

(8) At an altitude of more than 10,000 feet MSL or 2,000 feet AGL, whichever is higher;

(9) When the flight or surface visibility is less than 3 statute miles;

(10) Without visual reference to the surface;

(11) On a flight outside the United States, unless authorized by the country in which the flight is conducted;

(12) To demonstrate that aircraft in flight as an aircraft salesperson to a prospective buyer;

(13) That is used in a passenger-carrying airlift and sponsored by a charitable organization; and

(14) That is towing any object.

(f) A recreational pilot may not act as a pilot flight crewmember on any aircraft for which more than one pilot is required by the type certificate of the aircraft or the regulations under which the flight is conducted, except when:

(1) Receiving flight training from a person authorized to provide flight training on board an airship; and

(2) No person other than a required flight crewmember is carried on the aircraft.

(g) A person who holds a recreational pilot certificate, has logged fewer than 400 flight hours, and has not logged pilot-in-command time in an aircraft within the 180 days preceding the flight shall not act as pilot in command of an aircraft until the pilot receives flight training and a logbook endorsement from an authorized instructor, and the instructor certifies that the person is proficient to act as pilot in command of the aircraft. This requirement can be met in combination with the requirements of §§61.56 and 61.57 of this part, at the discretion of the authorized instructor.

(h) A recreational pilot certificate issued under this subpart carries the notation, "Holder does not meet ICAO requirements."

(i) For the purpose of obtaining additional certificates or ratings while under the supervision of an authorized instructor, a recreational pilot may fly as the sole occupant of an aircraft:

(1) For which the pilot does not hold an appropriate category or class rating;

(2) Within airspace that requires communication with air traffic control; or

(3) Between sunset and sunrise, provided the flight or surface visibility is at least 5 statute miles.

(j) In order to fly solo as provided in paragraph (i) of this section, the recreational pilot must meet the appropriate aeronautical knowledge and flight training requirements of §61.87 for that aircraft. When operating an aircraft under the conditions specified in paragraph (i) of this section, the recreational pilot shall carry the logbook that has been endorsed for each flight by an authorized instructor who:

(1) Has given the recreational pilot training in the make and model of aircraft in which the solo flight is to be made;

(2) Has found that the recreational pilot has met the applicable requirements of §61.87; and

(3) Has found that the recreational pilot is competent to make solo flights in accordance with the logbook endorsement.

(k) A recreational pilot may act as pilot in command of an aircraft without holding a medical certificate issued under part 67 of this chapter provided the pilot holds a valid U.S. driver's license, meets the requirements of §61.23(c)(3), and the operation is conducted consistent with this section and the conditions of §61.113(i). Where the requirements of this section conflict with §61.113(i), a recreational pilot must comply with this section.

[Docket No. 25910, 62 FR 16298, April 4, 1997, as amended by Amdt. 61–110, 69 FR 44868, July 27, 2004; Amdt. 61–124, 74 FR 42558, Aug. 21, 2009; Docket FAA–2016–9157, Amdt. 61–140, 82 FR 3165, Jan. 11, 2017]

Subpart E—Private Pilots

§61.102 Applicability.

This subpart prescribes the requirements for the issuance of private pilot certificates and ratings, the conditions under which those certificates and ratings are necessary, and the general operating rules for persons who hold those certificates and ratings.

§61.103 Eligibility requirements: General.

To be eligible for a private pilot certificate, a person must:

(a) Be at least 17 years of age for a rating in other than a glider or balloon.

(b) Be at least 16 years of age for a rating in a glider or balloon.

(c) Be able to read, speak, write, and understand the English language. If the applicant is unable to meet one of these requirements due to medical reasons, then the Administrator may place such operating limitations on that applicant's pilot certificate as are necessary for the safe operation of the aircraft.

(d) Receive a logbook endorsement from an authorized instructor who:

(1) Conducted the training or reviewed the person's home study on the aeronautical knowledge areas listed in §61.105(b) of this part that apply to the aircraft rating sought; and

(2) Certified that the person is prepared for the required knowledge test.

(e) Pass the required knowledge test on the aeronautical knowledge areas listed in §61.105(b) of this part.

(f) Receive flight training and a logbook endorsement from an authorized instructor who:

(1) Conducted the training in the areas of operation listed in §61.107(b) of this part that apply to the aircraft rating sought; and

(2) Certified that the person is prepared for the required practical test.

(g) Meet the aeronautical experience requirements of this part that apply to the aircraft rating sought before applying for the practical test.

(h) Pass a practical test on the areas of operation listed in §61.107(b) of this part that apply to the aircraft rating sought.

(i) Comply with the appropriate sections of this part that apply to the aircraft category and class rating sought.

(j) Hold a U.S. student pilot certificate, sport pilot certificate, or recreational pilot certificate.

[Docket No. 25910, 62 FR 16298, April 4, 1997; as amended by Amdt. 61–124, 74 FR 42558, Aug. 21, 2009]

§61.105 Aeronautical knowledge.

(a) *General.* A person who is applying for a private pilot certificate must receive and log ground training from an authorized instructor or complete a home-study course on the aeronautical knowledge areas of paragraph (b) of this section that apply to the aircraft category and class rating sought.

(b) *Aeronautical knowledge areas.*

(1) Applicable Federal Aviation Regulations of this chapter that relate to private pilot privileges, limitations, and flight operations;

(2) Accident reporting requirements of the National Transportation Safety Board;

(3) Use of the applicable portions of the "Aeronautical Information Manual" and FAA advisory circulars;

(4) Use of aeronautical charts for VFR navigation using pilotage, dead reckoning, and navigation systems;

(5) Radio communication procedures;

(6) Recognition of critical weather situations from the ground and in flight, windshear avoidance, and the procurement and use of aeronautical weather reports and forecasts;

(7) Safe and efficient operation of aircraft, including collision avoidance, and recognition and avoidance of wake turbulence;

(8) Effects of density altitude on takeoff and climb performance;

(9) Weight and balance computations;

(10) Principles of aerodynamics, powerplants, and aircraft systems;

(11) Stall awareness, spin entry, spins, and spin recovery techniques for the airplane and glider category ratings;

(12) Aeronautical decision making and judgment; and

(13) Preflight action that includes—

(i) How to obtain information on runway lengths at airports of intended use, data on takeoff and landing distances, weather reports and forecasts, and fuel requirements; and

(ii) How to plan for alternatives if the planned flight cannot be completed or delays are encountered.

[Docket No. 25910, 62 FR 16298, April 4, 1997; Amdt. 61–103, 62 FR 40902, July 30, 1997]

§61.107 Flight proficiency.

(a) *General.* A person who applies for a private pilot certificate must receive and log ground and flight training from an authorized instructor on the areas of operation of this section that apply to the aircraft category and class rating sought.

(b) *Areas of operation.*

(1) For an airplane category rating with a single-engine class rating:

(i) Preflight preparation;

(ii) Preflight procedures;
(iii) Airport and seaplane base operations;
(iv) Takeoffs, landings, and go-arounds;
(v) Performance maneuvers;
(vi) Ground reference maneuvers;
(vii) Navigation;
(viii) Slow flight and stalls;
(ix) Basic instrument maneuvers;
(x) Emergency operations;
(xi) Night operations, except as provided in §61.110 of this part; and
(xii) Postflight procedures.

(2) For an airplane category rating with a multiengine class rating:
(i) Preflight preparation;
(ii) Preflight procedures;
(iii) Airport and seaplane base operations;
(iv) Takeoffs, landings, and go-arounds;
(v) Performance maneuvers;
(vi) Ground reference maneuvers;
(vii) Navigation;
(viii) Slow flight and stalls;
(ix) Basic instrument maneuvers;
(x) Emergency operations;
(xi) Multiengine operations;
(xii) Night operations, except as provided in §61.110 of this part; and
(xiii) Postflight procedures.

(3) For a rotorcraft category rating with a helicopter class rating:
(i) Preflight preparation;
(ii) Preflight procedures;
(iii) Airport and heliport operations;
(iv) Hovering maneuvers;
(v) Takeoffs, landings, and go-arounds;
(vi) Performance maneuvers;
(vii) Navigation;
(viii) Emergency operations;
(ix) Night operations, except as provided in §61.110 of this part; and
(x) Postflight procedures.

(4) For a rotorcraft category rating with a gyroplane class rating:
(i) Preflight preparation;
(ii) Preflight procedures;
(iii) Airport operations;
(iv) Takeoffs, landings, and go-arounds;
(v) Performance maneuvers;
(vi) Ground reference maneuvers;
(vii) Navigation;
(viii) Flight at slow airspeeds;
(ix) Emergency operations;
(x) Night operations, except as provided in §61.110 of this part; and
(xi) Postflight procedures.

(5) For a powered-lift category rating:
(i) Preflight preparation;
(ii) Preflight procedures;
(iii) Airport and heliport operations;

(iv) Hovering maneuvers;
(v) Takeoffs, landings, and go-arounds;
(vi) Performance maneuvers;
(vii) Ground reference maneuvers;
(viii) Navigation;
(ix) Slow flight and stalls;
(x) Basic instrument maneuvers;
(xi) Emergency operations;
(xii) Night operations, except as provided in §61.110 of this part; and
(xiii) Postflight procedures.

(6) For a glider category rating:
(i) Preflight preparation;
(ii) Preflight procedures;
(iii) Airport and gliderport operations;
(iv) Launches and landings;
(v) Performance speeds;
(vi) Soaring techniques;
(vii) Performance maneuvers;
(viii) Navigation;
(ix) Slow flight and stalls;
(x) Emergency operations; and
(xi) Postflight procedures.

(7) For a lighter-than-air category rating with an airship class rating:
(i) Preflight preparation;
(ii) Preflight procedures;
(iii) Airport operations;
(iv) Takeoffs, landings, and go-arounds;
(v) Performance maneuvers;
(vi) Ground reference maneuvers;
(vii) Navigation;
(viii) Emergency operations; and
(ix) Postflight procedures.

(8) For a lighter-than-air category rating with a balloon class rating:
(i) Preflight preparation;
(ii) Preflight procedures;
(iii) Airport operations;
(iv) Launches and landings;
(v) Performance maneuvers;
(vi) Navigation;
(vii) Emergency operations; and
(viii) Postflight procedures.

(9) For a powered parachute category rating—
(i) Preflight preparation;
(ii) Preflight procedures;
(iii) Airport and seaplane base operations, as applicable;
(iv) Takeoffs, landings, and go-arounds;
(v) Performance maneuvers;
(vi) Ground reference maneuvers;
(vii) Navigation;
(viii) Night operations, except as provided in §61.110;
(ix) Emergency operations; and
(x) Post-flight procedures.

(10) For a weight-shift-control aircraft category rating—

(i) Preflight preparation;

(ii) Preflight procedures;

(iii) Airport and seaplane base operations, as applicable;

(iv) Takeoffs, landings, and go-arounds;

(v) Performance maneuvers;

(vi) Ground reference maneuvers;

(vii) Navigation;

(viii) Slow flight and stalls;

(ix) Night operations, except as provided in §61.110;

(x) Emergency operations; and

(xi) Post-flight procedures.

[Docket No. 25910, 62 FR 16298, April 4, 1997; as amended by Amdt. 61–110, 69 FR 44868, July 27, 2004]

§61.109 Aeronautical experience.

(a) *For an airplane single-engine rating.* Except as provided in paragraph (k) of this section, a person who applies for a private pilot certificate with an airplane category and single-engine class rating must log at least 40 hours of flight time that includes at least 20 hours of flight training from an authorized instructor and 10 hours of solo flight training in the areas of operation listed in §61.107(b)(1) of this part, and the training must include at least—

(1) 3 hours of cross-country flight training in a single-engine airplane;

(2) Except as provided in §61.110 of this part, 3 hours of night flight training in a single-engine airplane that includes—

(i) One cross-country flight of over 100 nautical miles total distance; and

(ii) 10 takeoffs and 10 landings to a full stop (with each landing involving a flight in the traffic pattern) at an airport.

(3) 3 hours of flight training in a single-engine airplane on the control and maneuvering of an airplane solely by reference to instruments, including straight and level flight, constant airspeed climbs and descents, turns to a heading, recovery from unusual flight attitudes, radio communications, and the use of navigation systems/facilities and radar services appropriate to instrument flight;

(4) 3 hours of flight training with an authorized instructor in a single-engine airplane in preparation for the practical test, which must have been performed within the preceding 2 calendar months from the month of the test; and

(5) 10 hours of solo flight time in a single-engine airplane, consisting of at least—

(i) 5 hours of solo cross-country time;

(ii) One solo cross country flight of 150 nautical miles total distance, with full-stop landings at three points, and one segment of the flight consisting of a straight-line distance of more than 50 nautical miles between the takeoff and landing locations; and

(iii) Three takeoffs and three landings to a full stop (with each landing involving a flight in the traffic pattern) at an airport with an operating control tower.

(b) *For an airplane multiengine rating.* Except as provided in paragraph (k) of this section, a person who applies for a private pilot certificate with an airplane category and multiengine class rating must log at least 40 hours of flight time that includes at least 20 hours of flight training from an authorized instructor and 10 hours of solo flight training in the areas of operation listed in §61.107(b)(2) of this part, and the training must include at least—

(1) 3 hours of cross-country flight training in a multiengine airplane;

(2) Except as provided in §61.110 of this part, 3 hours of night flight training in a multiengine airplane that includes—

(i) One cross-country flight of over 100 nautical miles total distance; and

(ii) 10 takeoffs and 10 landings to a full stop (with each landing involving a flight in the traffic pattern) at an airport.

(3) 3 hours of flight training in a multiengine airplane on the control and maneuvering of an airplane solely by reference to instruments, including straight and level flight, constant airspeed climbs and descents, turns to a heading, recovery from unusual flight attitudes, radio communications, and the use of navigation systems/facilities and radar services appropriate to instrument flight;

(4) 3 hours of flight training with an authorized instructor in a multiengine airplane in preparation for the practical test, which must have been performed within the preceding 2 calendar months from the month of the test; and

(5) 10 hours of solo flight time in an airplane consisting of at least—

(i) 5 hours of solo cross-country time;

(ii) One solo cross country flight of 150 nautical miles total distance, with full-stop landings at three points, and one segment of the flight consisting of a straight-line distance of more than 50 nautical miles between the takeoff and landing locations; and

(iii) Three takeoffs and three landings to a full stop (with each landing involving a flight in the traffic pattern) at an airport with an operating control tower.

(c) *For a helicopter rating.* Except as provided in paragraph (k) of this section, a person who applies for a private pilot certificate with rotorcraft category and helicopter class rating must log at least 40 hours of flight time that includes at least 20 hours of flight training from an authorized instructor and 10 hours of solo flight training in the areas of operation listed in §61.107(b)(3) of this part, and the training must include at least—

(1) 3 hours of cross-country flight training in a helicopter;

(2) Except as provided in §61.110 of this part, 3 hours of night flight training in a helicopter that includes—

(i) One cross-country flight of over 50 nautical miles total distance; and

(ii) 10 takeoffs and 10 landings to a full stop (with each landing involving a flight in the traffic pattern) at an airport.

(3) 3 hours of flight training with an authorized instructor in a helicopter in preparation for the practical test, which must have been performed within the preceding 2 calendar months from the month of the test; and

(4) 10 hours of solo flight time in a helicopter, consisting of at least—

(i) 3 hours cross-country time;

(ii) One solo cross country flight of 100 nautical miles total distance, with landings at three points, and one segment of the flight being a straight-line distance of more than 25 nautical miles between the takeoff and landing locations; and

(iii) Three takeoffs and three landings to a full stop (with each landing involving a flight in the traffic pattern) at an airport with an operating control tower.

(d) *For a gyroplane rating.* Except as provided in paragraph (k) of this section, a person who applies for a private pilot certificate with rotorcraft category and gyroplane class rating must log at least 40 hours of flight time that includes at least 20 hours of flight training from an authorized instructor and 10 hours of solo flight training in the areas of operation listed in §61.107(b)(4) of this part, and the training must include at least—

(1) 3 hours of cross-country flight training in a gyroplane;

(2) Except as provided in §61.110 of this part, 3 hours of night flight training in a gyroplane that includes—

(i) One cross-country flight of over 50 nautical miles total distance; and

(ii) 10 takeoffs and 10 landings to a full stop (with each landing involving a flight in the traffic pattern) at an airport.

(3) 3 hours of flight training with an authorized instructor in a gyroplane in preparation for the practical test, which must have been performed within the preceding 2 calendar months from the month of the test; and

(4) 10 hours of solo flight time in a gyroplane, consisting of at least—

(i) 3 hours of cross-country time;

(ii) One solo cross country flight of 100 nautical miles total distance, with landings at three points, and one segment of the flight being a straight-line distance of more than 25 nautical miles between the takeoff and landing locations; and

(iii) Three takeoffs and three landings to a full stop (with each landing involving a flight in the traffic pattern) at an airport with an operating control tower.

(e) *For a powered-lift rating.* Except as provided in paragraph (k) of this section, a person who applies for a private pilot certificate with a powered-lift category rating must log at least 40 hours of flight time that includes at least 20 hours of flight training from an authorized instructor and 10 hours of solo flight training in the areas of operation listed in §61.107(b)(5) of this part, and the training must include at least—

(1) 3 hours of cross-country flight training in a powered-lift;

(2) Except as provided in §61.110 of this part, 3 hours of night flight training in a powered-lift that includes—

(i) One cross-country flight of over 100 nautical miles total distance; and

(ii) 10 takeoffs and 10 landings to a full stop (with each landing involving a flight in the traffic pattern) at an airport.

(3) 3 hours of flight training in a powered-lift on the control and maneuvering of a powered-lift solely by reference to instruments, including straight and level flight, constant airspeed climbs and descents, turns to a heading, recovery from unusual flight attitudes, radio communications, and the use of navigation systems/facilities and radar services appropriate to instrument flight;

(4) 3 hours of flight training with an authorized instructor in a powered-lift in preparation for the practical test, which must have been performed within the preceding 2 calendar months from the month of the test; and

(5) 10 hours of solo flight time in an airplane or powered-lift consisting of at least—

(i) 5 hours cross-country time;

(ii) One solo cross country flight of 150 nautical miles total distance, with full-stop landings at three points, and one segment of the flight consisting of a straight-line distance of more than 50 nautical miles between the takeoff and landing locations; and

(iii) Three takeoffs and three landings to a full stop (with each landing involving a flight in the traffic pattern) at an airport with an operating control tower.

(f) *For a glider category rating.*

(1) If the applicant for a private pilot certificate with a glider category rating has not logged at least 40 hours of flight time as a pilot in a heavier-than-air aircraft, the applicant must log at least 10 hours of flight time in a glider in the areas of operation listed in §61.107(b)(6) of this part, and that flight time must include at least—

(i) 20 flights in a glider in the areas of operations listed in §61.107(b)(6) of this part, including

at least 3 training flights with an authorized instructor in a glider in preparation for the practical test that must have been performed within the preceding 2 calendar months from the month of the test; and

(ii) 2 hours of solo flight time in a glider in the areas of operation listed in §61.107(b)(6) of this part, with not less than 10 launches and landings being performed.

(2) If the applicant has logged at least 40 hours of flight time in a heavier-than-air aircraft, the applicant must log at least 3 hours of flight time in a glider in the areas of operation listed in §61.107(b)(6) of this part, and that flight time must include at least—

(i) 10 solo flights in a glider in the areas of operation listed in §61.107(b)(6) of this part; and

(ii) 3 training flights with an authorized instructor in a glider in preparation for the practical test that must have been performed within the preceding 2 calendar months from the month of the test.

(g) For an airship rating. A person who applies for a private pilot certificate with a lighter-than-air category and airship class rating must log at least:

(1) 25 hours of flight training in airships on the areas of operation listed in §61.107(b)(7) of this part, which consists of at least:

(i) 3 hours of cross-country flight training in an airship;

(ii) Except as provided in §61.110 of this part, 3 hours of night flight training in an airship that includes:

(A) A cross-country flight of over 25 nautical miles total distance; and

(B) Five takeoffs and five landings to a full stop (with each landing involving a flight in the traffic pattern) at an airport.

(2) 3 hours of flight training in an airship on the control and maneuvering of an airship solely by reference to instruments, including straight and level flight, constant airspeed climbs and descents, turns to a heading, recovery from unusual flight attitudes, radio communications, and the use of navigation systems/facilities and radar services appropriate to instrument flight;

(3) Three hours of flight training with an authorized instructor in an airship in preparation for the practical test within the preceding 2 calendar months from the month of the test; and

(4) 5 hours performing the duties of pilot in command in an airship with an authorized instructor.

(h) For a balloon rating. A person who applies for a private pilot certificate with a lighter-than-air category and balloon class rating must log at least 10 hours of flight training that includes at least six training flights with an authorized instructor in the areas of operation listed in §61.107(b)(8) of this part, that includes—

(1) *Gas balloon.* If the training is being performed in a gas balloon, at least two flights of 2 hours each that consists of—

(i) At least one training flight with an authorized instructor in a gas balloon in preparation for the practical test within the preceding 2 calendar months from the month of the test;

(ii) At least one flight performing the duties of pilot in command in a gas balloon with an authorized instructor; and

(iii) At least one flight involving a controlled ascent to 3,000 feet above the launch site.

(2) *Balloon with an airborne heater.* If the training is being performed in a balloon with an airborne heater, at least—

(i) At least two training flights of 1 hour each with an authorized instructor in a balloon with an airborne heater in preparation for the practical test within the preceding 2 calendar months from the month of the test;

(ii) One solo flight in a balloon with an airborne heater; and

(iii) At least one flight involving a controlled ascent to 2,000 feet above the launch site.

(i) For a powered parachute rating. A person who applies for a private pilot certificate with a powered parachute category rating must log at least 25 hours of flight time in a powered parachute that includes at least 10 hours of flight training with an authorized instructor, including 30 takeoffs and landings, and 10 hours of solo flight training in the areas of operation listed in §61.107(b)(9) and the training must include at least—

(1) One hour of cross-country flight training in a powered parachute that includes a 1-hour cross-country flight with a landing at an airport at least 25 nautical miles from the airport of departure;

(2) Except as provided in §61.110, 3 hours of night flight training in a powered parachute that includes 10 takeoffs and landings (with each landing involving a flight in the traffic pattern) at an airport;

(3) Three hours of flight training with an authorized instructor in a powered parachute in preparation for the practical test, which must have been performed within the preceding 2 calendar months from the month of the test;

(4) Three hours of solo flight time in a powered parachute, consisting of at least—

(i) One solo cross-country flight with a landing at an airport at least 25 nautical miles from the departure airport; and

(ii) Twenty solo takeoffs and landings to a full stop (with each landing involving a flight in a traffic pattern) at an airport; and

(5) Three takeoffs and landings (with each landing involving a flight in the traffic pattern) in an aircraft at an airport with an operating control tower.

(j) *For a weight-shift-control aircraft rating.* A person who applies for a private pilot certificate with a weight-shift-control rating must log at least 40 hours of flight time that includes at least 20 hours of flight training with an authorized instructor and 10 hours of solo flight training in the areas of operation listed in §61.107(b)(10) and the training must include at least—

(1) Three hours of cross-country flight training in a weight-shift-control aircraft;

(2) Except as provided in §61.110, 3 hours of night flight training in a weight-shift-control aircraft that includes—

(i) One cross-country flight of over 75 nautical miles total distance that includes a point of landing that is a straight-line distance of more than 50 nautical miles from the original point of departure; and

(ii) Ten takeoffs and landings (with each landing involving a flight in the traffic pattern) at an airport;

(3) Three hours of flight training with an authorized instructor in a weight-shift-control aircraft in preparation for the practical test, which must have been performed within the preceding 2 calendar months from the month of the test;

(4) Ten hours of solo flight time in a weight-shift-control aircraft, consisting of at least—

(i) Five hours of solo cross-country time; and

(ii) One solo cross-country flight over 100 nautical miles total distance, with landings at a minimum of three points, and one segment of the flight being a straight line distance of at least 50 nautical miles between takeoff and landing locations; and

(5) Three takeoffs and landings (with each landing involving a flight in the traffic pattern) in an aircraft at an airport with an operating control tower.

(k) *Permitted credit for use of a full flight simulator or flight training device.*

(1) Except as provided in paragraphs (k)(2) of this section, a maximum of 2.5 hours of training in a full flight simulator or flight training device representing the category, class, and type, if applicable, of aircraft appropriate to the rating sought, may be credited toward the flight training time required by this section, if received from an authorized instructor.

(2) A maximum of 5 hours of training in a flight simulator or flight training device representing the category, class, and type, if applicable, of aircraft appropriate to the rating sought, may be credited toward the flight training time required by this section if the training is accomplished in a course conducted by a training center certificated under part 142 of this chapter.

(3) Except when fewer hours are approved by the Administrator, an applicant for a private pilot certificate with an airplane, rotorcraft, or powered-lift rating, who has satisfactorily completed an approved private pilot course conducted by a training center certificated under part 142 of this chapter, need only have a total of 35 hours of aeronautical experience to meet the requirements of this section.

(l) *Permitted credit for flight training received from a flight instructor with a sport pilot rating.* The holder of a sport pilot certificate may credit flight training received from a flight instructor with a sport pilot rating toward the aeronautical experience requirements of this section if the following conditions are met:

(1) The flight training was accomplished in the same category and class of aircraft for which the rating is sought;

(2) The flight instructor with a sport pilot rating was authorized to provide the flight training; and

(3) The flight training included either—

(i) Training on areas of operation that are required for both a sport pilot certificate and a private pilot certificate; or

(ii) For airplanes with a V_H greater than 87 knots CAS, training on the control and maneuvering of an airplane solely by reference to the flight instruments, including straight and level flight, turns, descents, climbs, use of radio aids, and ATC directives, provided the training was received from a flight instructor with a sport pilot rating who holds an endorsement required by §61.412(c).

[Docket No. 25910, 62 FR 40902, July 30, 1997, as amended by Amdt. 61–104, 63 FR 20287, April 23, 1998; Amdt. 61–110, 69 FR 44868, July 27, 2004; Amdt. 61–124, 74 FR 42558, Aug. 21, 2009; Amdt. 61–124A, 74 FR 53645, Oct. 20, 2009; Amdt. 61–125, 75 FR 5220, Feb. 1, 2010; Amdt. 61–142, 83 FR 30278, June 27, 2018]

§61.110 Night flying exceptions.

(a) Subject to the limitations of paragraph (b) of this section, a person is not required to comply with the night flight training requirements of this subpart if the person receives flight training in and resides in the State of Alaska.

(b) A person who receives flight training in and resides in the State of Alaska but does not meet the night flight training requirements of this section:

(1) May be issued a pilot certificate with a limitation "Night flying prohibited"; and

(2) Must comply with the appropriate night flight training requirements of this subpart within the 12-calendar-month period after the issuance of the pilot certificate. At the end of that period, the certificate will become invalid for use until the person complies with the appropriate night training requirements of this subpart. The person may have the "Night flying prohibited" limitation removed if the person—

(i) Accomplishes the appropriate night flight training requirements of this subpart; and

(ii) Presents to an examiner a logbook or training record endorsement from an authorized instructor that verifies accomplishment of the appropriate night flight training requirements of this subpart.

(c) A person who does not meet the night flying requirements in §61.109 (d)(2), (i)(2), or (j)(2) may be issued a private pilot certificate with the limitation "Night flying prohibited." This limitation may be removed by an examiner if the holder complies with the requirements of §61.109(d)(2), (i)(2), or (j) (2), as appropriate.

[Docket No. 25910, 62 FR 16298, April 4, 1997; Amdt. 61–103, 62 FR 40904, July 30, 1997; Amdt. 61–110, 69 FR 44869, July 27, 2004]

§61.111 Cross-country flights: Pilots based on small islands.

(a) Except as provided in paragraph (b) of this section, an applicant located on an island from which the cross-country flight training required in §61.109 of this part cannot be accomplished without flying over water for more than 10 nautical miles from the nearest shoreline need not comply with the requirements of that section.

(b) If other airports that permit civil operations are available to which a flight may be made without flying over water for more than 10 nautical miles from the nearest shoreline, the applicant must show completion of two round-trip solo flights between those two airports that are farthest apart, including a landing at each airport on both flights.

(c) An applicant who complies with paragraph (a) or paragraph (b) of this section, and meets all requirements for the issuance of a private pilot certificate, except the cross-country training requirements of §61.109 of this part, will be issued a pilot certificate with an endorsement containing the following limitation, "Passenger carrying prohibited on flights more than 10 nautical miles from (the appropriate island)." The limitation may be subsequently amended to include another island if the applicant complies with the requirements of paragraph (b) of this section for another island.

(d) Upon meeting the cross-country training requirements of §61.109 of this part, the applicant may have the limitation in paragraph (c) of this section removed.

[Docket No. 25910, 62 FR 16298, April 4, 1997; Amdt. 61–103, 62 FR 40904, July 30, 1997]

§61.113 Private pilot privileges and limitations: Pilot in command.

(a) Except as provided in paragraphs (b) through (h) of this section, no person who holds a private pilot certificate may act as pilot in command of an aircraft that is carrying passengers or property for compensation or hire; nor may that person, for compensation or hire, act as pilot in command of an aircraft.

(b) A private pilot may, for compensation or hire, act as pilot in command of an aircraft in connection with any business or employment if:

(1) The flight is only incidental to that business or employment; and

(2) The aircraft does not carry passengers or property for compensation or hire.

(c) A private pilot may not pay less than the pro rata share of the operating expenses of a flight with passengers, provided the expenses involve only fuel, oil, airport expenditures, or rental fees.

(d) A private pilot may act as pilot in command of a charitable, nonprofit, or community event flight described in §91.146, if the sponsor and pilot comply with the requirements of §91.146.

(e) A private pilot may be reimbursed for aircraft operating expenses that are directly related to search and location operations, provided the expenses involve only fuel, oil, airport expenditures, or rental fees, and the operation is sanctioned and under the direction and control of:

(1) A local, State, or Federal agency; or

(2) An organization that conducts search and location operations.

(f) A private pilot who is an aircraft salesman and who has at least 200 hours of logged flight time may demonstrate an aircraft in flight to a prospective buyer.

(g) A private pilot who meets the requirements of §61.69 may act as a pilot in command of an aircraft towing a glider or unpowered ultralight vehicle.

(h) A private pilot may act as pilot in command for the purpose of conducting a production flight test in a light-sport aircraft intended for certification in the light-sport category under §21.190 of this chapter, provided that—

(1) The aircraft is a powered parachute or a weight-shift-control aircraft;

(2) The person has at least 100 hours of pilot-in-command time in the category and class of aircraft flown; and

(3) The person is familiar with the processes and procedures applicable to the conduct of production flight testing, to include operations conducted under a special flight permit and any associated operating limitations.

(i) A private pilot may act as pilot in command or serve as a required flightcrew member of an aircraft without holding a medical certificate issued under part 67 of this chapter provided the pilot holds a valid U.S. driver's license, meets the requirements of §61.23(c)(3), and complies with this section and all of the following conditions and limitations:

(1) The aircraft is authorized to carry not more than 6 occupants, has a maximum takeoff weight

of not more than 6,000 pounds, and is operated with no more than five passengers on board; and

(2) The flight, including each portion of the flight, is not carried out—

(i) At an altitude that is more than 18,000 feet above mean sea level;

(ii) Outside the United States unless authorized by the country in which the flight is conducted; or

(iii) At an indicated airspeed exceeding 250 knots; and

(3) The pilot has available in his or her logbook—

(i) The completed medical examination checklist required under §68.7 of this chapter; and

(ii) The certificate of course completion required under §61.23(c)(3).

[Docket No. 25910, 62 FR 16298, April 4, 1997, as amended by Amdt. 61–110, 69 FR 44869, July 27, 2004; Amdt. 61–115, 72 FR 6910, Feb. 13, 2007; Amdt. 61–125, 75 FR 5220, Feb. 1, 2010; Docket FAA–2016–9157, Amdt. 61–140, 82 FR 3165, Jan. 11, 2017; Docket No. FAA–2021–1040, Amdt. Nos. 61–152, 87 FR 71237, Nov. 22, 2022]

§61.115 Balloon rating: Limitations.

(a) If a person who applies for a private pilot certificate with a balloon rating takes a practical test in a balloon with an airborne heater:

(1) The pilot certificate will contain a limitation restricting the exercise of the privileges of that certificate to a balloon with an airborne heater; and

(2) The limitation may be removed when the person obtains the required aeronautical experience in a gas balloon and receives a logbook endorsement from an authorized instructor who attests to the person's accomplishment of the required aeronautical experience and ability to satisfactorily operate a gas balloon.

(b) If a person who applies for a private pilot certificate with a balloon rating takes a practical test in a gas balloon:

(1) The pilot certificate will contain a limitation restricting the exercise of the privilege of that certificate to a gas balloon; and

(2) The limitation may be removed when the person obtains the required aeronautical experience in a balloon with an airborne heater and receives a logbook endorsement from an authorized instructor who attests to the person's accomplishment of the required aeronautical experience and ability to satisfactorily operate a balloon with an airborne heater.

§61.117 Private pilot privileges and limitations: Second in command of aircraft requiring more than one pilot.

Except as provided in §61.113 of this part, no private pilot may, for compensation or hire, act as second in command of an aircraft that is type certificated for more than one pilot, nor may that pilot act as second in command of such an aircraft that is carrying passengers or property for compensation or hire.

[Docket No. 25910, 62 FR 16298, April 4, 1997; Amdt. 61–103, 62 FR 40904, July 30, 1997]

§61.118–61.120 [Reserved]

Subpart F— Commercial Pilots

§61.121 Applicability.

This subpart prescribes the requirements for the issuance of commercial pilot certificates and ratings, the conditions under which those certificates and ratings are necessary, and the general operating rules for persons who hold those certificates and ratings.

§61.123 Eligibility requirements: General.

To be eligible for a commercial pilot certificate, a person must:

(a) Be at least 18 years of age;

(b) Be able to read, speak, write, and understand the English language. If the applicant is unable to meet one of these requirements due to medical reasons, then the Administrator may place such operating limitations on that applicant's pilot certificate as are necessary for the safe operation of the aircraft.

(c) Receive a logbook endorsement from an authorized instructor who:

(1) Conducted the required ground training or reviewed the person's home study on the aeronautical knowledge areas listed in §61.125 of this part that apply to the aircraft category and class rating sought; and

(2) Certified that the person is prepared for the required knowledge test that applies to the aircraft category and class rating sought.

(d) Pass the required knowledge test on the aeronautical knowledge areas listed in §61.125 of this part;

(e) Receive the required training and a logbook endorsement from an authorized instructor who:

(1) Conducted the training on the areas of operation listed in §61.127(b) of this part that apply to the aircraft category and class rating sought; and

(2) Certified that the person is prepared for the required practical test.

(f) Meet the aeronautical experience requirements of this subpart that apply to the aircraft category and class rating sought before applying for the practical test;

(g) Pass the required practical test on the areas of operation listed in §61.127(b) of this part

that apply to the aircraft category and class rating sought;

(h) Hold at least a private pilot certificate issued under this part or meet the requirements of §61.73; and

(i) Comply with the sections of this part that apply to the aircraft category and class rating sought.

§61.125 Aeronautical knowledge.

(a) *General.* A person who applies for a commercial pilot certificate must receive and log ground training from an authorized instructor, or complete a home-study course, on the aeronautical knowledge areas of paragraph (b) of this section that apply to the aircraft category and class rating sought.

(b) *Aeronautical knowledge areas.*

(1) Applicable Federal Aviation Regulations of this chapter that relate to commercial pilot privileges, limitations, and flight operations;

(2) Accident reporting requirements of the National Transportation Safety Board;

(3) Basic aerodynamics and the principles of flight;

(4) Meteorology to include recognition of critical weather situations, windshear recognition and avoidance, and the use of aeronautical weather reports and forecasts;

(5) Safe and efficient operation of aircraft;

(6) Weight and balance computations;

(7) Use of performance charts;

(8) Significance and effects of exceeding aircraft performance limitations;

(9) Use of aeronautical charts and a magnetic compass for pilotage and dead reckoning;

(10) Use of air navigation facilities;

(11) Aeronautical decision making and judgment;

(12) Principles and functions of aircraft systems;

(13) Maneuvers, procedures, and emergency operations appropriate to the aircraft;

(14) Night and high-altitude operations;

(15) Procedures for operating within the National Airspace System; and

(16) Procedures for flight and ground training for lighter-than-air ratings.

§61.127 Flight proficiency.

(a) *General.* A person who applies for a commercial pilot certificate must receive and log ground and flight training from an authorized instructor on the areas of operation of this section that apply to the aircraft category and class rating sought.

(b) *Areas of operation.*

(1) For an airplane category rating with a single-engine class rating:
(i) Preflight preparation;
(ii) Preflight procedures;
(iii) Airport and seaplane base operations;
(iv) Takeoffs, landings, and go-arounds;
(v) Performance maneuvers;
(vi) Ground reference maneuvers;
(vii) Navigation;
(viii) Slow flight and stalls;
(ix) Emergency operations;
(x) High-altitude operations; and
(xi) Postflight procedures.

(2) For an airplane category rating with a multiengine class rating:
(i) Preflight preparation;
(ii) Preflight procedures;
(iii) Airport and seaplane base operations;
(iv) Takeoffs, landings, and go-arounds;
(v) Performance maneuvers;
(vi) Navigation;
(vii) Slow flight and stalls;
(viii) Emergency operations;
(ix) Multiengine operations;
(x) High-altitude operations; and
(xi) Postflight procedures.

(3) For a rotorcraft category rating with a helicopter class rating:
(i) Preflight preparation;
(ii) Preflight procedures;
(iii) Airport and heliport operations;
(iv) Hovering maneuvers;
(v) Takeoffs, landings, and go-arounds;
(vi) Performance maneuvers;
(vii) Navigation;
(viii) Emergency operations;
(ix) Special operations; and
(x) Postflight procedures.

(4) For a rotorcraft category rating with a gyroplane class rating:
(i) Preflight preparation;
(ii) Preflight procedures;
(iii) Airport operations;
(iv) Takeoffs, landings, and go-arounds;
(v) Performance maneuvers;
(vi) Ground reference maneuvers;
(vii) Navigation;
(viii) Flight at slow airspeeds;
(ix) Emergency operations; and
(x) Postflight procedures.

(5) For a powered-lift category rating:
(i) Preflight preparation;
(ii) Preflight procedures;
(iii) Airport and heliport operations;
(iv) Hovering maneuvers;
(v) Takeoffs, landings, and go-arounds;
(vi) Performance maneuvers;
(vii) Navigation;
(viii) Slow flight and stalls;
(ix) Emergency operations;
(x) High-altitude operations;
(xi) Special operations; and

(xii) Postflight procedures.

(6) For a glider category rating:
(i) Preflight preparation;
(ii) Preflight procedures;
(iii) Airport and gliderport operations;
(iv) Launches and landings;
(v) Performance speeds;
(vi) Soaring techniques;
(vii) Performance maneuvers;
(viii) Navigation;
(ix) Slow flight and stalls;
(x) Emergency operations; and
(xi) Postflight procedures.

(7) For a lighter-than-air category rating with an airship class rating:
(i) Fundamentals of instructing;
(ii) Technical subjects;
(iii) Preflight preparation;
(iv) Preflight lesson on a maneuver to be performed in flight;
(v) Preflight procedures;
(vi) Airport operations;
(vii) Takeoffs, landings, and go-arounds;
(viii) Performance maneuvers;
(ix) Navigation;
(x) Emergency operations; and
(xi) Postflight procedures.

(8) For a lighter-than-air category rating with a balloon class rating:
(i) Fundamentals of instructing;
(ii) Technical subjects;
(iii) Preflight preparation;
(iv) Preflight lesson on a maneuver to be performed in flight;
(v) Preflight procedures;
(vi) Airport operations;
(vii) Launches and landings;
(viii) Performance maneuvers;
(ix) Navigation;
(x) Emergency operations; and
(xi) Postflight procedures.

[Docket No. 25910, 62 FR 16298, April 4, 1997; as amended by Amdt. 61–124, 74 FR 42558, Aug. 21, 2009]

§61.129 Aeronautical experience.

(a) *For an airplane single-engine rating.* Except as provided in paragraph (i) of this section, a person who applies for a commercial pilot certificate with an airplane category and single-engine class rating must log at least 250 hours of flight time as a pilot that consists of at least:

(1) 100 hours in powered aircraft, of which 50 hours must be in airplanes.

(2) 100 hours of pilot-in-command flight time, which includes at least—
(i) 50 hours in airplanes; and
(ii) 50 hours in cross-country flight of which at least 10 hours must be in airplanes.

(3) 20 hours of training on the areas of operation listed in §61.127(b)(1) of this part that includes at least—

(i) Ten hours of instrument training using a view-limiting device including attitude instrument flying, partial panel skills, recovery from unusual flight attitudes, and intercepting and tracking navigational systems. Five hours of the 10 hours required on instrument training must be in a single engine airplane;

(ii) 10 hours of training in a complex airplane, a turbine-powered airplane, or a technically advanced airplane (TAA) that meets the requirements of paragraph (j) of this section, or any combination thereof. The airplane must be appropriate to land or sea for the rating sought;

(iii) One 2-hour cross country flight in a single engine airplane in daytime conditions that consists of a total straight-line distance of more than 100 nautical miles from the original point of departure;

(iv) One 2-hour cross country flight in a single engine airplane in nighttime conditions that consists of a total straight-line distance of more than 100 nautical miles from the original point of departure; and

(v) Three hours in a single-engine airplane with an authorized instructor in preparation for the practical test within the preceding 2 calendar months from the month of the test.

(4) Ten hours of solo flight time in a single engine airplane or 10 hours of flight time performing the duties of pilot in command in a single engine airplane with an authorized instructor on board (either of which may be credited towards the flight time requirement under paragraph (a)(2) of this section), on the areas of operation listed under §61.127(b)(1) that include—

(i) One cross-country flight of not less than 300 nautical miles total distance, with landings at a minimum of three points, one of which is a straight-line distance of at least 250 nautical miles from the original departure point. However, if this requirement is being met in Hawaii, the longest segment need only have a straight-line distance of at least 150 nautical miles; and

(ii) 5 hours in night VFR conditions with 10 take-offs and 10 landings (with each landing involving a flight in the traffic pattern) at an airport with an operating control tower.

(b) *For an airplane multiengine rating.* Except as provided in paragraph (i) of this section, a person who applies for a commercial pilot certificate with an airplane category and multiengine class rating must log at least 250 hours of flight time as a pilot that consists of at least:

(1) 100 hours in powered aircraft, of which 50 hours must be in airplanes.

(2) 100 hours of pilot-in-command flight time, which includes at least—

61

(i) 50 hours in airplanes; and

(ii) 50 hours in cross-country flight of which at least 10 hours must be in airplanes.

(3) 20 hours of training on the areas of operation listed in §61.127(b)(2) of this part that includes at least—

(i) Ten hours of instrument training using a view-limiting device including attitude instrument flying, partial panel skills, recovery from unusual flight attitudes, and intercepting and tracking navigational systems. Five hours of the 10 hours required on instrument training must be in a multiengine airplane;

(ii) 10 hours of training in a multiengine complex or turbine-powered airplane; or for an applicant seeking a multiengine seaplane rating, 10 hours of training in a multiengine seaplane that has flaps and a controllable pitch propeller, including seaplanes equipped with an engine control system consisting of a digital computer and associated accessories for controlling the engine and propeller, such as a full authority digital engine control;

(iii) One 2-hour cross country flight in a multiengine airplane in daytime conditions that consists of a total straight-line distance of more than 100 nautical miles from the original point of departure;

(iv) One 2-hour cross country flight in a multiengine airplane in nighttime conditions that consists of a total straight-line distance of more than 100 nautical miles from the original point of departure; and

(v) Three hours in a multiengine airplane with an authorized instructor in preparation for the practical test within the preceding 2 calendar months from the month of the test.

(4) 10 hours of solo flight time in a multiengine airplane or 10 hours of flight time performing the duties of pilot in command in a multiengine airplane with an authorized instructor (either of which may be credited towards the flight time requirement in paragraph (b)(2) of this section), on the areas of operation listed in §61.127(b)(2) of this part that includes at least—

(i) One cross-country flight of not less than 300 nautical miles total distance with landings at a minimum of three points, one of which is a straight-line distance of at least 250 nautical miles from the original departure point. However, if this requirement is being met in Hawaii, the longest segment need only have a straight-line distance of at least 150 nautical miles; and

(ii) 5 hours in night VFR conditions with 10 takeoffs and 10 landings (with each landing involving a flight with a traffic pattern) at an airport with an operating control tower.

(c) *For a helicopter rating.* Except as provided in paragraph (i) of this section, a person who applies for a commercial pilot certificate with a rotorcraft category and helicopter class rating must log at least 150 hours of flight time as a pilot that consists of at least:

(1) 100 hours in powered aircraft, of which 50 hours must be in helicopters.

(2) 100 hours of pilot-in-command flight time, which includes at least—

(i) 35 hours in helicopters; and

(ii) 10 hours in cross-country flight in helicopters.

(3) 20 hours of training on the areas of operation listed in §61.127(b)(3) of this part that includes at least—

(i) Five hours on the control and maneuvering of a helicopter solely by reference to instruments using a view-limiting device including attitude instrument flying, partial panel skills, recovery from unusual flight attitudes, and intercepting and tracking navigational systems. This aeronautical experience may be performed in an aircraft, full flight simulator, flight training device, or an aviation training device;

(ii) One 2-hour cross country flight in a helicopter in daytime conditions that consists of a total straight-line distance of more than 50 nautical miles from the original point of departure;

(iii) One 2-hour cross country flight in a helicopter in nighttime conditions that consists of a total straight-line distance of more than 50 nautical miles from the original point of departure; and

(iv) Three hours in a helicopter with an authorized instructor in preparation for the practical test within the preceding 2 calendar months from the month of the test.

(4) Ten hours of solo flight time in a helicopter or 10 hours of flight time performing the duties of pilot in command in a helicopter with an authorized instructor on board (either of which may be credited towards the flight time requirement under paragraph (c)(2) of this section), on the areas of operation listed under §61.127(b)(3) that includes—

(i) One cross-country flight with landings at a minimum of three points, with one segment consisting of a straight-line distance of at least 50 nautical miles from the original point of departure; and

(ii) 5 hours in night VFR conditions with 10 takeoffs and 10 landings (with each landing involving a flight in the traffic pattern).

(d) *For a gyroplane rating.* A person who applies for a commercial pilot certificate with a rotorcraft category and gyroplane class rating must log at least 150 hours of flight time as a pilot (of which 5 hours may have been accomplished in a full flight simulator or flight training device that is representative of a gyroplane) that consists of at least:

(1) 100 hours in powered aircraft, of which 25 hours must be in gyroplanes.

(2) 100 hours of pilot-in-command flight time, which includes at least—

(i) 10 hours in gyroplanes; and

(ii) 3 hours in cross-country flight in gyroplanes.

(3) 20 hours of training on the areas of operation listed in §61.127(b)(4) of this part that includes at least—

(i) 2.5 hours on the control and maneuvering of a gyroplane solely by reference to instruments using a view-limiting device including attitude instrument flying, partial panel skills, recovery from unusual flight attitudes, and intercepting and tracking navigational systems. This aeronautical experience may be performed in an aircraft, full flight simulator, flight training device, or an aviation training device;

(ii) One 2-hour cross country flight in a gyroplane in daytime conditions that consists of a total straight-line distance of more than 50 nautical miles from the original point of departure;

(iii) Two hours of flight training during nighttime conditions in a gyroplane at an airport, that includes 10 takeoffs and 10 landings to a full stop (with each landing involving a flight in the traffic pattern); and

(iv) Three hours in a gyroplane with an authorized instructor in preparation for the practical test within the preceding 2 calendar months from the month of the test.

(4) Ten hours of solo flight time in a gyroplane or 10 hours of flight time performing the duties of pilot in command in a gyroplane with an authorized instructor on board (either of which may be credited towards the flight time requirement under paragraph (d)(2) of this section), on the areas of operation listed in §61.127(b)(4) that includes—

(i) One cross-country flight with landings at a minimum of three points, with one segment consisting of a straight-line distance of at least 50 nautical miles from the original point of departure; and

(ii) 5 hours in night VFR conditions with 10 takeoffs and 10 landings (with each landing involving a flight in the traffic pattern).

(e) *For a powered-lift rating.* Except as provided in paragraph (i) of this section, a person who applies for a commercial pilot certificate with a powered-lift category rating must log at least 250 hours of flight time as a pilot that consists of at least:

(1) 100 hours in powered aircraft, of which 50 hours must be in a powered-lift.

(2) 100 hours of pilot-in-command flight time, which includes at least—

(i) 50 hours in a powered-lift; and

(ii) 50 hours in cross-country flight of which 10 hours must be in a powered-lift.

(3) 20 hours of training on the areas of operation listed in §61.127(b)(5) of this part that includes at least—

(i) Ten hours of instrument training using a view-limiting device including attitude instrument flying, partial panel skills, recovery from unusual flight attitudes, and intercepting and tracking navigational systems. Five hours of the 10 hours required on instrument training must be in a powered-lift;

(ii) One 2-hour cross country flight in a powered-lift in daytime conditions that consists of a total straight-line distance of more than 100 nautical miles from the original point of departure;

(iii) One 2-hour cross country flight in a powered-lift in nighttime conditions that consists of a total straight-line distance of more than 100 nautical miles from the original point of departure; and

(iv) 3 hours in a powered-lift with an authorized instructor in preparation for the practical test within the preceding 2 calendar months from the month of the test.

(4) Ten hours of solo flight time in a powered-lift or 10 hours of flight time performing the duties of pilot in command in a powered-lift with an authorized instructor on board (either of which may be credited towards the flight time requirement under paragraph (e)(2) of this section, on the areas of operation listed in §61.127(b)(5) that includes—

(i) One cross-country flight of not less than 300 nautical miles total distance with landings at a minimum of three points, one of which is a straight-line distance of at least 250 nautical miles from the original departure point. However, if this requirement is being met in Hawaii the longest segment need only have a straight-line distance of at least 150 nautical miles; and

(ii) 5 hours in night VFR conditions with 10 takeoffs and 10 landings (with each landing involving a flight in the traffic pattern) at an airport with an operating control tower.

(f) *For a glider rating.* A person who applies for a commercial pilot certificate with a glider category rating must log at least—

(1) 25 hours of flight time as a pilot in a glider and that flight time must include at least 100 flights in a glider as pilot in command, including at least—

(i) Three hours of flight training in a glider with an authorized instructor or 10 training flights in a glider with an authorized instructor on the areas of operation listed in §61.127(b)(6) of this part, including at least 3 training flights in a glider with an authorized instructor in preparation for the practical test within the preceding 2 calendar months from the month of the test; and

(ii) 2 hours of solo flight that include not less than 10 solo flights in a glider on the areas of operation listed in §61.127(b)(6) of this part; or

(2) 200 hours of flight time as a pilot in heavier-than-air aircraft and at least 20 flights in a glider as pilot in command, including at least—

(i) Three hours of flight training in a glider or 10 training flights in a glider with an authorized instructor on the areas of operation listed in §61.127(b)(6) of this part including at least 3 training flights in a glider with an authorized instructor in preparation for the practical test within the preceding 2 calendar months from the month of the test; and

(ii) 5 solo flights in a glider on the areas of operation listed in §61.127(b)(6) of this part.

(g) *For an airship rating.* A person who applies for a commercial pilot certificate with a lighter-than-air category and airship class rating must log at least 200 hours of flight time as a pilot, which includes at least the following hours:

(1) 50 hours in airships.

(2) Thirty hours of pilot in command flight time in airships or performing the duties of pilot in command in an airship with an authorized instructor aboard, which consists of—

(i) 10 hours of cross-country flight time in airships; and

(ii) 10 hours of night flight time in airships.

(3) Forty hours of instrument time to include—

(i) Instrument training using a view-limiting device for attitude instrument flying, partial panel skills, recovery from unusual flight attitudes, and intercepting and tracking navigational systems; and

(ii) Twenty hours of instrument flight time, of which 10 hours must be in flight in airships.

(4) 20 hours of flight training in airships on the areas of operation listed in §61.127(b)(7) of this part, which includes at least—

(i) Three hours in an airship with an authorized instructor in preparation for the practical test within the preceding 2 calendar months from the month of the test;

(ii) One hour cross country flight in an airship in daytime conditions that consists of a total straight-line distance of more than 25 nautical miles from the point of departure; and

(iii) One hour cross country flight in an airship in nighttime conditions that consists of a total straight-line distance of more than 25 nautical miles from the point of departure.

(5) 10 hours of flight training performing the duties of pilot in command with an authorized instructor on the areas of operation listed in §61.127(b)(7) of this part, which includes at least—

(i) One cross-country flight with landings at a minimum of three points, with one segment consisting of a straight-line distance of at least 25 nautical miles from the original point of departure; and

(ii) 5 hours in night VFR conditions with 10 takeoffs and 10 landings (with each landing involving a flight in the traffic pattern).

(h) *For a balloon rating.* A person who applies for a commercial pilot certificate with a lighter-than-air category and a balloon class rating must log at least 35 hours of flight time as a pilot, which includes at least the following requirements:

(1) 20 hours in balloons;

(2) 10 flights in balloons;

(3) Two flights in balloons as the pilot in command; and

(4) 10 hours of flight training that includes at least 10 training flights with an authorized instructor in balloons on the areas of operation listed in §61.127(b)(8) of this part, which consists of at least—

(i) For a gas balloon—

(A) Two training flights of 2 hours each in a gas balloon with an authorized instructor in preparation for the practical test within the preceding 2 calendar months from the month of the test;

(B) 2 flights performing the duties of pilot in command in a gas balloon with an authorized instructor on the appropriate areas of operation; and

(C) One flight involving a controlled ascent to 5,000 feet above the launch site.

(ii) For a balloon with an airborne heater—

(A) Two training flights of 1 hour each in a balloon with an airborne heater with an authorized instructor in preparation for the practical test within the preceding 2 calendar months from the month of the test;

(B) Two solo flights in a balloon with an airborne heater on the appropriate areas of operation; and

(C) One flight involving a controlled ascent to 3,000 feet above the launch site.

(i) *Permitted credit for use of a flight simulator or flight training device.*

(1) Except as provided in paragraph (i)(2) of this section, an applicant who has not accomplished the training required by this section in a course conducted by a training center certificated under part 142 of this chapter may:

(i) Credit a maximum of 50 hours toward the total aeronautical experience requirements for an airplane or powered-lift rating, provided the aeronautical experience was obtained from an authorized instructor in a full flight simulator or flight training device that represents that class of airplane or powered-lift category and type, if applicable, appropriate to the rating sought; and

(ii) Credit a maximum of 25 hours toward the total aeronautical experience requirements of this section for a helicopter rating, provided the aeronautical experience was obtained from an authorized instructor in a full flight simulator or flight training device that represents a helicopter and type, if applicable, appropriate to the rating sought.

(2) An applicant who has accomplished the training required by this section in a course conducted by a training center certificated under part 142 of this chapter may:

(i) Credit a maximum of 100 hours toward the total aeronautical experience requirements of this section for an airplane and powered-lift rating, provided the aeronautical experience was obtained from an authorized instructor in a full flight simulator or flight training device that represents that class of airplane or powered-lift category and type, if applicable, appropriate to the rating sought; and

(ii) Credit a maximum of 50 hours toward the total aeronautical experience requirements of this section for a helicopter rating, provided the aeronautical experience was obtained from an authorized instructor in a full flight simulator or flight training device that represents a helicopter and type, if applicable, appropriate to the rating sought.

(3) Except when fewer hours are approved by the FAA, an applicant for the commercial pilot certificate with the airplane or powered-lift rating who has completed 190 hours of aeronautical experience is considered to have met the total aeronautical experience requirements of this section, provided the applicant satisfactorily completed an approved commercial pilot course under part 142 of this chapter and the approved course was appropriate to the commercial pilot certificate and aircraft rating sought.

(j) Technically advanced airplane. Unless otherwise authorized by the Administrator, a technically advanced airplane must be equipped with an electronically advanced avionics system that includes the following installed components:

(1) An electronic Primary Flight Display (PFD) that includes, at a minimum, an airspeed indicator, turn coordinator, attitude indicator, heading indicator, altimeter, and vertical speed indicator;

(2) An electronic Multifunction Display (MFD) that includes, at a minimum, a moving map using Global Positioning System (GPS) navigation with the aircraft position displayed;

(3) A two axis autopilot integrated with the navigation and heading guidance system; and

(4) The display elements described in paragraphs (j)(1) and (2) of this section must be continuously visible.

[Docket No. 25910, 62 FR 16298, April 4, 1997; Amdt. 61–101, 62 FR 16892, April 8, 1997; Amdt. 61–103, 62 FR 40904, July 30, 1997; Amdt. 61–104, 63 FR 20288, April 23, 1998; Amdt. 61–124, 74 FR 42558, Aug. 21, 2009; Amdt. 61–124A, 74 FR 53645, Oct. 20, 2009; Amdt. 61–142, 83 FR 30278, June 27, 2018]

§61.131 Exceptions to the night flying requirements.

(a) Subject to the limitations of paragraph (b) of this section, a person is not required to comply with the night flight training requirements of this subpart if the person receives flight training in and resides in the State of Alaska.

(b) A person who receives flight training in and resides in the State of Alaska but does not meet the night flight training requirements of this section:

(1) May be issued a pilot certificate with the limitation "night flying prohibited."

(2) Must comply with the appropriate night flight training requirements of this subpart within the 12-calendar-month period after the issuance of the pilot certificate. At the end of that period, the certificate will become invalid for use until the person complies with the appropriate night flight training requirements of this subpart. The person may have the "night flying prohibited" limitation removed if the person—

(i) Accomplishes the appropriate night flight training requirements of this subpart; and

(ii) Presents to an examiner a logbook or training record endorsement from an authorized instructor that verifies accomplishment of the appropriate night flight training requirements of this subpart.

[Docket No. 25910, 62 FR 16298, April 4, 1997; Amdt. 61–103, 62 FR 40905, July 30, 1997]

§61.133 Commercial pilot privileges and limitations.

(a) Privileges.

(1) General. A person who holds a commercial pilot certificate may act as pilot in command of an aircraft—

(i) Carrying persons or property for compensation or hire, provided the person is qualified in accordance with this part and with the applicable parts of this chapter that apply to the operation; and

(ii) For compensation or hire, provided the person is qualified in accordance with this part and with the applicable parts of this chapter that apply to the operation.

(2) Commercial pilots with lighter-than-air category ratings. A person with a commercial pilot certificate with a lighter-than-air category rating may—

(i) For an airship—

(A) Give flight and ground training in an airship for the issuance of a certificate or rating;

(B) Give an endorsement for a pilot certificate with an airship rating;

(C) Endorse a pilot's logbook for solo operating privileges in an airship;

(D) Act as pilot in command of an airship under IFR or in weather conditions less than the minimum prescribed for VFR flight; and

(E) Give flight and ground training and endorsements that are required for a flight review, an operating privilege, or recency-of-experience requirements of this part.

(ii) For a balloon—

(A) Give flight and ground training in a balloon for the issuance of a certificate or rating;

(B) Give an endorsement for a pilot certificate with a balloon rating;

(C) Endorse a pilot's logbook for solo operating privileges in a balloon; and

(D) Give ground and flight training and endorsements that are required for a flight review, an operating privilege, or recency-of-experience requirements of this part.

(b) Limitations.

(1) A person who applies for a commercial pilot certificate with an airplane category or powered-lift category rating and does not hold an instrument rating in the same category and class will be issued a commercial pilot certificate that contains the limitation, "The carriage of passengers for hire in (airplanes) (powered-lifts) on cross-country flights in excess of 50 nautical miles or at night is prohibited." The limitation may be removed when the person satisfactorily accomplishes the requirements listed in §61.65 of this part for an instrument rating in the same category and class of aircraft listed on the person's commercial pilot certificate.

(2) If a person who applies for a commercial pilot certificate with a balloon rating takes a practical test in a balloon with an airborne heater—

(i) The pilot certificate will contain a limitation restricting the exercise of the privileges of that certificate to a balloon with an airborne heater.

(ii) The limitation specified in paragraph (b)(2)(i) of this section may be removed when the person obtains the required aeronautical experience in a gas balloon and receives a logbook endorsement from an authorized instructor who attests to the person's accomplishment of the required aeronautical experience and ability to satisfactorily operate a gas balloon.

(3) If a person who applies for a commercial pilot certificate with a balloon rating takes a practical test in a gas balloon—

(i) The pilot certificate will contain a limitation restricting the exercise of the privileges of that certificate to a gas balloon.

(ii) The limitation specified in paragraph (b)(3)(i) of this section may be removed when the person obtains the required aeronautical experience in a balloon with an airborne heater and receives a logbook endorsement from an authorized instructor who attests to the person's accomplishment of the required aeronautical experience and ability to satisfactorily operate a balloon with an airborne heater.

[Docket No. 25910, 62 FR 16298, April 4, 1997; Amdt. 61–103, 62 FR 40905, July 30, 1997; Docket FAA–2010–1127, Amdt. 61–135, 81 FR 1306, Jan. 12, 2016]

§61.135–61.141 [Reserved]

Subpart G— Airline Transport Pilots

§61.151 Applicability.

This subpart prescribes the requirements for the issuance of airline transport pilot certificates and ratings, the conditions under which those certificates and ratings are necessary, and the general operating rules for persons who hold those certificates and ratings.

§61.153 Eligibility requirements: General.

To be eligible for an airline transport pilot certificate, a person must:

(a) Meet the following age requirements:

(1) For an airline transport pilot certificate obtained under the aeronautical experience requirements of §§61.159, 61.161, or 61.163, be at least 23 years of age; or

(2) For an airline transport pilot certificate obtained under the aeronautical experience requirements of §61.160, be at least 21 years of age.

(b) Be able to read, speak, write, and understand the English language. If the applicant is unable to meet one of these requirements due to medical reasons, then the Administrator may place such operating limitations on that applicant's pilot certificate as are necessary for the safe operation of the aircraft;

(c) Be of good moral character;

(d) Meet at least one of the following requirements:

(1) Holds a commercial pilot certificate with an instrument rating issued under this part;

(2) Meet the military experience requirements under §61.73 of this part to qualify for a commercial pilot certificate, and an instrument rating if the person is a rated military pilot or former rated military pilot of an Armed Force of the United States; or

(3) Holds either a foreign airline transport pilot license with instrument privileges, or a foreign commercial pilot license with an instrument rating, that—

(i) Was issued by a contracting State to the Convention on International Civil Aviation; and

(ii) Contains no geographical limitations.

(e) For an airline transport pilot certificate with an airplane category multiengine class rating or

an airline transport pilot certificate obtained concurrently with a multiengine airplane type rating, receive a graduation certificate from an authorized training provider certifying completion of the airline transport pilot certification training program specified in §61.156 before applying for the knowledge test required by paragraph (g) of this section;

(f) Meet the aeronautical experience requirements of this subpart that apply to the aircraft category and class rating sought before applying for the practical test;

(g) Pass a knowledge test on the aeronautical knowledge areas of §61.155(c) of this part that apply to the aircraft category and class rating sought;

(h) Pass the practical test on the areas of operation listed in §61.157(e) of this part that apply to the aircraft category and class rating sought; and

(i) Comply with the sections of this subpart that apply to the aircraft category and class rating sought.

[Docket No. 25910, 62 FR 16298, April 4, 1997; Amdt. 61–103, 62 FR 40905, July 30, 1997; Amdt. 61–124, 74 FR 42559, Aug. 21, 2009; Amdt. 61–130, 78 FR 42374, July 15, 2013; Amdt. 61–149, 86 FR 62087, Nov. 9, 2021]

§61.155 Aeronautical knowledge.

(a) *General.* The knowledge test for an airline transport pilot certificate is based on the aeronautical knowledge areas listed in paragraph (c) of this section that are appropriate to the aircraft category and class rating sought.

(b) *Aircraft type rating.* A person who is applying for an additional aircraft type rating to be added to an airline transport pilot certificate is not required to pass a knowledge test if that person's airline transport pilot certificate lists the aircraft category and class rating that is appropriate to the type rating sought.

(c) *Aeronautical knowledge areas.*

(1) Applicable Federal Aviation Regulations of this chapter that relate to airline transport pilot privileges, limitations, and flight operations;

(2) Meteorology, including knowledge of and effects of fronts, frontal characteristics, cloud formations, icing, and upper-air data;

(3) General system of weather and NOTAM collection, dissemination, interpretation, and use;

(4) Interpretation and use of weather charts, maps, forecasts, sequence reports, abbreviations, and symbols;

(5) National Weather Service functions as they pertain to operations in the National Airspace System;

(6) Windshear and microburst awareness, identification, and avoidance;

(7) Principles of air navigation under instrument meteorological conditions in the National Airspace System;

(8) Air traffic control procedures and pilot responsibilities as they relate to en route operations, terminal area and radar operations, and instrument departure and approach procedures;

(9) Aircraft loading, weight and balance, use of charts, graphs, tables, formulas, and computations, and their effect on aircraft performance;

(10) Aerodynamics relating to an aircraft's flight characteristics and performance in normal and abnormal flight regimes;

(11) Human factors;

(12) Aeronautical decision making and judgment;

(13) Crew resource management to include crew communication and coordination; and

(14) For an airline transport pilot certificate with an airplane category multiengine class rating or an airline transport pilot certificate obtained concurrently with a multiengine airplane type rating, the content of the airline transport pilot certification training program in §61.156.

[Docket No. 25910, 62 FR 16298, April 4, 1997; as amended by Amdt. 61–130, 78 FR 42374, July 15, 2013; Amdt. 61–130C, 81 FR 2, Jan. 4, 2016; Amdt. 61–149, 86 FR 62087, Nov. 9, 2021]

§61.156 Training requirements: Airplane category—multiengine class or multiengine airplane type rating concurrently with an airline transport pilot certificate.

A person who applies for the knowledge test for an airline transport pilot certificate with an airplane category multiengine class rating must present a graduation certificate from an authorized training provider under part 121, 135, 141, or 142 of this chapter certifying the applicant has completed the following training in a course approved by the Administrator.

(a) *Academic training.* The applicant for the knowledge test must receive at least 30 hours of classroom instruction that includes the following:

(1) At least 8 hours of instruction on aerodynamics including high altitude operations;

(2) At least 2 hours of instruction on meteorology, including adverse weather phenomena and weather detection systems; and

(3) At least 14 hours of instruction on air carrier operations, including the following areas:

(i) Physiology;

(ii) Communications;

(iii) Checklist philosophy;

(iv) Operational control;

(v) Minimum equipment list/configuration deviation list;

(vi) Ground operations;

(vii) Turbine engines;

(viii) Transport category aircraft performance;

(ix) Automation, navigation, and flight path warning systems.

(4) At least 6 hours of instruction on leadership, professional development, crew resource management, and safety culture.

(b) *FSTD training.* The applicant for the knowledge test must receive at least 10 hours of training in a flight simulation training device qualified under part 60 of this chapter that represents a multiengine turbine airplane. The training must include the following:

(1) At least 6 hours of training in a Level C or higher full flight simulator qualified under part 60 of this chapter that represents a multiengine turbine airplane with a maximum takeoff weight of 40,000 pounds or greater. The training must include the following areas:

(i) Low energy states/stalls;

(ii) Upset recovery techniques; and

(iii) Adverse weather conditions, including icing, thunderstorms, and crosswinds with gusts.

(2) The remaining FSTD training may be completed in a Level 4 or higher flight simulation training device. The training must include the following areas:

(i) Navigation including flight management systems; and

(ii) Automation including autoflight.

(c) *Deviation authority.* The Administrator may issue deviation authority from the weight requirement in paragraph (b)(1) of this section upon a determination that the objectives of the training can be met in an alternative device.

[Docket No. FAA–2010–0100, 78 FR 42375, July 15, 2013, as amended by Amdt. 61–149, 86 FR 62087, Nov. 9, 2021]

§61.157 Flight proficiency.

(a) *General.*

(1) The practical test for an airline transport pilot certificate is given for—

(i) An airplane category and single engine class rating.

(ii) An airplane category and multiengine class rating.

(iii) A rotorcraft category and helicopter class rating.

(iv) A powered-lift category rating.

(v) An aircraft type rating.

(2) A person who is applying for an airline transport pilot practical test must meet—

(i) The eligibility requirements of §61.153; and

(ii) The aeronautical knowledge and aeronautical experience requirements of this subpart that apply to the aircraft category and class rating sought.

(b) *Aircraft type rating.* Except as provided in paragraph (c) of this section, a person who applies for an aircraft type rating to be added to an airline transport pilot certificate or applies for a type rating to be concurrently completed with an airline transport pilot certificate:

(1) Must receive and log ground and flight training from an authorized instructor on the areas of operation under this section that apply to the aircraft type rating;

(2) Must receive a logbook endorsement from an authorized instructor that certifies the applicant completed the training on the areas of operation listed under paragraph (e) of this section that apply to the aircraft type rating; and

(3) Must perform the practical test in actual or simulated instrument conditions, except as provided under paragraph (g) of this section.

(c) *Exceptions.* A person who applies for an aircraft type rating to be added to an airline transport pilot certificate or an aircraft type rating concurrently with an airline transport pilot certificate, and who is an employee of a certificate holder operating under part 121 or part 135 of this chapter, does not need to comply with the requirements of paragraph (b) of this section if the applicant presents a training record that shows completion of that certificate holder's approved training program for the aircraft type rating.

(d) *Upgrading type ratings.* Any type rating(s) and limitations on a pilot certificate of an applicant who completes an airline transport pilot practical test will be included at the airline transport pilot certification level, provided the applicant passes the practical test in the same category and class of aircraft for which the applicant holds the type rating(s).

(e) *Areas of operation.* A practical test will include normal and abnormal procedures, as applicable, within the areas of operation for practical tests for an airplane category and powered-lift category rating.

(1) For an airplane category—single engine class rating:

(i) Preflight preparation;

(ii) Preflight procedures;

(iii) Takeoffs and Landings;

(iv) In-flight maneuvers;

(v) Stall Prevention;

(vi) Instrument procedures;

(vii) Emergency operations; and

(viii) Postflight procedures.

(2) For an airplane category—multiengine class rating:

(i) Preflight preparation;

(ii) Preflight procedures;

(iii) Takeoffs and Landings;

(iv) In-flight maneuvers;

(v) Stall Prevention.

(vi) Instrument procedures;

(vii) Emergency operations; and

(viii) Postflight procedures.

(3) For a powered-lift category rating:
(i) Preflight preparation;
(ii) Preflight procedures;
(iii) Takeoffs and Departure phase;
(iv) In-flight maneuvers;
(v) Instrument procedures;
(vi) Landings and approaches to landings;
(vii) Emergency operations; and
(viii) Postflight procedures.

(4) For a rotorcraft category—helicopter class rating:
(i) Preflight preparation;
(ii) Preflight procedures;
(iii) Takeoff and departure phase;
(iv) In-flight maneuvers;
(v) Instrument procedures;
(vi) Landings and approaches to landings;
(vii) Normal and abnormal procedures;
(viii) Emergency procedures; and
(ix) Postflight procedures.

(f) *Proficiency and competency checks conducted under part 121, part 135, or subpart K of part 91.*
(1) Successful completion of any of the following checks satisfies the flight proficiency requirements of this section for the issuance of an airline transport pilot certificate and/or the appropriate aircraft rating:
(i) A proficiency check under §121.441 of this chapter.
(ii) Both a competency check under §135.293 (a)(2) and §135.293(b) of this chapter and pilot-in-command instrument proficiency check under §135.297 of this chapter.
(iii) Both a competency check under §91.1065 of this chapter and a pilot-in-command instrument proficiency check under §91.1069 of this chapter.
(2) The checks specified in paragraph (f)(1) of this section must be conducted by one of the following:
(i) An FAA Aviation Safety Inspector.
(ii) An Aircrew Program Designee who is authorized to perform proficiency and/or competency checks for the air carrier whose approved training program has been satisfactorily completed by the pilot applicant.
(iii) A Training Center Evaluator with appropriate certification authority who is also authorized to perform the portions of the competency and/or proficiency checks required by paragraph (f)(1) of this section for the air carrier whose approved training program has been satisfactorily completed by the pilot applicant.
(g) *Aircraft not capable of instrument maneuvers and procedures.* An applicant may add a type rating to an airline transport pilot certificate with an aircraft that is not capable of the instrument maneuvers and procedures required on the practical test under the following circumstances—

(1) The rating is limited to "VFR only."
(2) The type rating is added to an airline transport pilot certificate that has instrument privileges in that category and class of aircraft.
(3) The "VFR only" limitation may be removed for that aircraft type after the applicant:
(i) Passes a practical test in that type of aircraft on the appropriate instrument maneuvers and procedures in §61.157; or
(ii) Becomes qualified in §61.73(d) for that type of aircraft.
(h) *Multiengine airplane with a single-pilot station.* An applicant for a type rating, at the ATP certification level, in a multiengine airplane with a single-pilot station must perform the practical test in the multi-seat version of that airplane. The practical test may be performed in the single-seat version of that airplane if the Examiner is in a position to observe the applicant during the practical test in the case where there is no multi-seat version of that multiengine airplane.
(i) *Single engine airplane with a single-pilot station.* An applicant for a type rating, at the ATP certification level, in a single engine airplane with a single-pilot station must perform the practical test in the multi-seat version of that single engine airplane. The practical test may be performed in the single-seat version of that airplane if the Examiner is in a position to observe the applicant during the practical test in the case where there is no multi-seat version of that single engine airplane.
(j) *Waiver authority.* An Examiner who conducts a practical test may waive any task for which the FAA has provided waiver authority.

[Docket No. FAA–2006–26661, 74 FR 42560, Aug. 21, 2009; Amdt. 61–124A, 74 FR 53647, Oct. 20, 2009; Amdt. 61–130, 78 FR 42375, July 15, 2013; Docket No. FAA–2022–1463, Amdt. 61–153, 89 FR 22517, April 1, 2024]

§61.158 [Reserved]

§61.159 Aeronautical experience: Airplane category rating.

(a) Except as provided in paragraphs (b), (c), and (d) of this section, a person who is applying for an airline transport pilot certificate with an airplane category and class rating must have at least 1,500 hours of total time as a pilot that includes at least:
(1) 500 hours of cross-country flight time.
(2) 100 hours of night flight time.
(3) 50 hours of flight time in the class of airplane for the rating sought. A maximum of 25 hours of training in a full flight simulator representing the class of airplane for the rating sought may be credited toward the flight time requirement of this paragraph if the training was accomplished as part of an approved training course in parts

121, 135, 141, or 142 of this chapter. A flight training device or aviation training device may not be used to satisfy this requirement.

(4) 75 hours of instrument flight time, in actual or simulated instrument conditions, subject to the following:

(i) Except as provided in paragraph (a)(4)(ii) of this section, an applicant may not receive credit for more than a total of 25 hours of simulated instrument time in a full flight simulator or flight training device.

(ii) A maximum of 50 hours of training in a full flight simulator or flight training device may be credited toward the instrument flight time requirements of paragraph (a)(4) of this section if the training was accomplished in a course conducted by a training center certificated under part 142 of this chapter.

(iii) Training in a full flight simulator or flight training device must be accomplished in a full flight simulator or flight training device, representing an airplane.

(5) 250 hours of flight time in an airplane as a pilot in command, or as second in command performing the duties of pilot in command while under the supervision of a pilot in command, or any combination thereof, subject to the following:

(i) The flight time requirement must include at least—

(A) 100 hours of cross-country flight time; and

(B) 25 hours of night flight time.

(ii) Except for a person who has been removed from flying status for lack of proficiency or because of a disciplinary action involving aircraft operations, a U.S. military pilot or former U.S. military pilot who meets the requirements of §61.73(b)(1), or a military pilot in the Armed Forces of a foreign contracting State to the Convention on International Civil Aviation who meets the requirements of §61.73(c)(1), may credit flight time in a powered-lift aircraft operated in horizontal flight toward the flight time requirement.

(6) Not more than 100 hours of the total aeronautical experience requirements of paragraph (a) of this section or §61.160 may be obtained in a full flight simulator or flight training device provided the device represents an airplane and the aeronautical experience was accomplished as part of an approved training course in parts 121, 135, 141, or 142 of this chapter.

(b) A person who has performed at least 20 night takeoffs and landings to a full stop may substitute each additional night takeoff and landing to a full stop for 1 hour of night flight time to satisfy the requirements of paragraph (a)(2) of this section; however, not more than 25 hours of night flight time may be credited in this manner.

(c) A commercial pilot may log second-in-command pilot time toward the aeronautical experience requirements of paragraph (a) of this section

and the aeronautical experience requirements in §61.160, provided the pilot is employed by a part 119 certificate holder authorized to conduct operations under part 135 of this chapter and the second-in-command pilot time is obtained in operations conducted for the certificate holder under part 91 or 135 of this chapter when a second pilot is not required under the type certification of the aircraft or the regulations under which the flight is being conducted, and the following requirements are met—

(1) The experience must be accomplished as part of a second-in-command professional development program approved by the Administrator under §135.99 of this chapter;

(2) The flight operation must be conducted in accordance with the certificate holder's operations specification for the second-in-command professional development program;

(3) The pilot in command of the operation must certify in the pilot's logbook that the second-in-command pilot time was accomplished under this section; and

(4) The pilot time may not be logged as pilot-in-command time even when the pilot is the sole manipulator of the controls and may not be used to meet the aeronautical experience requirements in paragraph (a)(5) of this section.

(d) A commercial pilot may log the following flight engineer flight time toward the 1,500 hours of total time as a pilot required by paragraph (a) of this section and the total time as a pilot required by §61.160:

(1) Flight-engineer time, provided the time—

(i) Is acquired in an airplane required to have a flight engineer by the airplane's flight manual or type certificate;

(ii) Is acquired while engaged in operations under part 121 of this chapter for which a flight engineer is required;

(iii) Is acquired while the person is participating in a pilot training program approved under part 121 of this chapter; and

(iv) Does not exceed more than 1 hour for each 3 hours of flight engineer flight time for a total credited time of no more than 500 hours.

(2) Flight-engineer time, provided the flight time—

(i) Is acquired as a U.S. Armed Forces' flight engineer crewmember in an airplane that requires a flight engineer crewmember by the flight manual;

(ii) Is acquired while the person is participating in a flight engineer crewmember training program for the U.S. Armed Forces; and

(iii) Does not exceed 1 hour for each 3 hours of flight engineer flight time for a total credited time of no more than 500 hours.

(e) An applicant who credits time under paragraphs (b), (c), and (d) of this section is issued

an airline transport pilot certificate with the limitation, "Holder does not meet the pilot in command aeronautical experience requirements of ICAO," as prescribed under Article 39 of the Convention on International Civil Aviation.

(f) An applicant is entitled to an airline transport pilot certificate without the ICAO limitation specified under paragraph (e) of this section when the applicant presents satisfactory evidence of having met the ICAO requirements under paragraph (e) of this section and otherwise meets the aeronautical experience requirements of this section.

[Docket No. 25910, 62 FR 16298, April 4, 1997; as amended by Amdt. 61–103, 62 FR 40906, July 30, 1997; Amdt. 61–104, 63 FR 20288, April 23, 1998; Amdt. 61–109, 68 FR 54560, Sept. 17, 2003; Amdt. 61–124, 74 FR 42561, Aug. 21, 2009; Amdt. 61–130, 78 FR 42375, July 15, 2013; Amdt. 61–130A, 78 FR 44874, July 25, 2013; Amdt. 61–130B, 78 FR 77573, Dec. 24, 2013; Amdt. 61–142, 83 FR 30278, June 27, 2018; Amdt. 61–150, 87 FR 57590, Sept. 21, 2022]

§61.160 Aeronautical experience— airplane category restricted privileges.

(a) Except for a person who has been removed from flying status for lack of proficiency or because of a disciplinary action involving aircraft operations, a U.S. military pilot or former U.S. military pilot may apply for an airline transport pilot certificate with an airplane category multiengine class rating or an airline transport pilot certificate concurrently with a multiengine airplane type rating with a minimum of 750 hours of total time as a pilot if the pilot presents:

(1) An official Form DD-214 (Certificate of Release or Discharge from Active Duty) indicating that the person was honorably discharged from the U.S. Armed Forces or an official U.S. Armed Forces record that shows the pilot is currently serving in the U.S. Armed Forces; and

(2) An official U.S. Armed Forces record that shows the person graduated from a U.S. Armed Forces undergraduate pilot training school and received a rating qualification as a military pilot.

(b) A person may apply for an airline transport pilot certificate with an airplane category multiengine class rating or an airline transport pilot certificate concurrently with a multiengine airplane type rating with a minimum of 1,000 hours of total time as a pilot if the person:

(1) Holds a Bachelor's degree with an aviation major from an institution of higher education, as defined in §61.1, that has been issued a letter of authorization by the Administrator under §61.169;

(2) Completes 60 semester credit hours of aviation and aviation-related coursework that has been recognized by the Administrator as coursework designed to improve and enhance the knowledge and skills of a person seeking a career as a professional pilot;

(3) Holds a commercial pilot certificate with an airplane category and instrument rating if:

(i) The required ground training was completed as part of an approved part 141 curriculum at the institution of higher education; and

(ii) The required flight training was completed as part of an approved part 141 curriculum at the institution of higher education or at a part 141 pilot school that has a training agreement under §141.26 of this chapter with the institution of higher education; and

(4) Presents official transcripts or other documentation acceptable to the Administrator from the institution of higher education certifying that the graduate has satisfied the requirements in paragraphs (b)(1) through (3) of this section.

(c) A person may apply for an airline transport pilot certificate with an airplane category multiengine class rating or an airline transport pilot certificate concurrently with a multiengine airplane type rating with a minimum of 1,250 hours of total time as a pilot if the person:

(1) Holds an Associate's degree with an aviation major from an institution of higher education, as defined in §61.1, that has been issued a letter of authorization by the Administrator under §61.169;

(2) Completes at least 30 semester credit hours of aviation and aviation-related coursework that has been recognized by the Administrator as coursework designed to improve and enhance the knowledge and skills of a person seeking a career as a professional pilot;

(3) Holds a commercial pilot certificate with an airplane category and instrument rating if:

(i) The required ground training was completed as part of an approved part 141 curriculum at the institution of higher education; and

(ii) The required flight training was completed as part of an approved part 141 curriculum at the institution of higher education or at a part 141 pilot school that has a written training agreement under §141.26 of this chapter with the institution of higher education; and

(4) Presents official transcripts or other documentation acceptable to the Administrator from the institution of higher education certifying that the graduate has satisfied the requirements in paragraphs (c)(1) through (3) of this section.

(d) A graduate of an institution of higher education who completes fewer than 60 semester credit hours but at least 30 credit hours and otherwise satisfies the requirements of paragraph (b) of this section may apply for an airline transport pilot certificate with an airplane category multiengine class rating or an airline transport pilot certificate concurrently with a multiengine airplane type rating with a minimum of 1,250 hours of total time as a pilot.

(e) A person who applies for an airline transport pilot certificate under the total flight times listed in paragraphs (a), (b), (c), and (d) of this section must otherwise meet the aeronautical experience requirements of §61.159, except that the person may apply for an airline transport pilot certificate with 200 hours of cross-country flight time.

(f) A person may apply for an airline transport pilot certificate with an airplane category multiengine class rating or an airline transport pilot certificate concurrently with a multiengine airplane type rating if the person has 1,500 hours total time as a pilot, 200 hours of cross-country flight time, and otherwise meets the aeronautical experience requirements of §61.159.

(g) An airline transport pilot certificate obtained under this section is subject to the pilot in command limitations set forth in §61.167(b) and must contain the following limitation, "Restricted in accordance with 14 CFR 61.167." The pilot is entitled to an airline transport pilot certificate without the limitation specified in this paragraph when the applicant presents satisfactory evidence of having met the aeronautical experience requirements of §61.159 and the age requirement of §61.153(a)(1).

(h) An applicant who meets the aeronautical experience requirements of paragraphs (a), (b), (c), and (d) of this section is issued an airline transport pilot certificate with the limitation, "Holder does not meet the pilot in command aeronautical experience requirements of ICAO," as prescribed under Article 39 of the Convention on International Civil Aviation if the applicant does not meet the ICAO requirements contained in Annex 1 "Personnel Licensing" to the Convention on International Civil Aviation. An applicant is entitled to an airline transport pilot certificate without the ICAO limitation specified under this paragraph when the applicant presents satisfactory evidence of having met the ICAO requirements and otherwise meets the aeronautical experience requirements of §61.159.

[Docket No. FAA–2010–0100, 78 FR 42375, July 15, 2013, as amended by Amdt. 61–149, 86 FR 62087, Nov. 9, 2021]

§61.161 Aeronautical experience: Rotorcraft category and helicopter class rating.

(a) A person who is applying for an airline transport pilot certificate with a rotorcraft category and helicopter class rating, must have at least 1,200 hours of total time as a pilot that includes at least:

(1) 500 hours of cross-country flight time;

(2) 100 hours of night flight time, of which 15 hours are in helicopters;

(3) 200 hours of flight time in helicopters, which includes at least 75 hours as a pilot in command,

or as second in command performing the duties of a pilot in command under the supervision of a pilot in command, or any combination thereof; and

(4) 75 hours of instrument flight time in actual or simulated instrument meteorological conditions, of which at least 50 hours are obtained in flight with at least 25 hours in helicopters as a pilot in command, or as second in command performing the duties of a pilot in command under the supervision of a pilot in command, or any combination thereof.

(b) Training in a full flight simulator or flight training device may be credited toward the instrument flight time requirements of paragraph (a)(4) of this section, subject to the following:

(1) Training in a full flight simulator or a flight training device must be accomplished in a full flight simulator or flight training device that represents a rotorcraft.

(2) Except as provided in paragraph (b)(3) of this section, an applicant may receive credit for not more than a total of 25 hours of simulated instrument time in a full flight simulator and flight training device.

(3) A maximum of 50 hours of training in a full flight simulator or flight training device may be credited toward the instrument flight time requirements of paragraph (a)(4) of this section if the aeronautical experience is accomplished in an approved course conducted by a training center certificated under part 142 of this chapter.

(c) Flight time logged under §61.159(c) may be counted toward the 1,200 hours of total time as a pilot required by paragraph (a) of this section and the flight time requirements of paragraphs (a)(1), (2), and (4) of this section, except for the specific helicopter flight time requirements.

(d) An applicant who credits time under paragraph (c) of this section is issued an airline transport pilot certificate with the limitation, "Holder does not meet the pilot in command aeronautical experience requirements of ICAO," as prescribed under Article 39 of the Convention on International Civil Aviation.

(e) An applicant is entitled to an airline transport pilot certificate without the ICAO limitation specified under paragraph (d) of this section when the applicant presents satisfactory evidence of having met the ICAO requirements under paragraph (d) of this section and otherwise meets the aeronautical experience requirements of this section.

[Docket No. 25910, 62 FR 16298, April 4, 1997; Amdt. 61–103, 62 FR 40906, July 30, 1997; Amdt. 61–104, 63 FR 20289, April 23, 1998; Docket FAA–2016–6142, Amdt. 61–142, 83 FR 30279, June 27, 2018]

§61.163 Aeronautical experience: Powered-lift category rating.

(a) A person who is applying for an airline transport pilot certificate with a powered-lift category rating must have at least 1,500 hours of total time as a pilot that includes at least:

(1) 500 hours of cross-country flight time;

(2) 100 hours of night flight time;

(3) 250 hours in a powered-lift as a pilot in command, or as a second in command performing the duties of a pilot in command under the supervision of a pilot in command, or any combination thereof, which includes at least—

(i) 100 hours of cross-country flight time; and

(ii) 25 hours of night flight time.

(4) 75 hours of instrument flight time in actual or simulated instrument conditions, subject to the following:

(i) Except as provided in paragraph (a)(4)(ii) of this section, an applicant may not receive credit for more than a total of 25 hours of simulated instrument time in a flight simulator or flight training device.

(ii) A maximum of 50 hours of training in a flight simulator or flight training device may be credited toward the instrument flight time requirements of paragraph (a)(4) of this section if the training was accomplished in a course conducted by a training center certificated under part 142 of this chapter.

(iii) Training in a flight simulator or flight training device must be accomplished in a flight simulator or flight training device that represents a powered-lift.

(b) Not more than 100 hours of the total aeronautical experience requirements of paragraph (a) of this section may be obtained in a flight simulator or flight training device that represents a powered-lift, provided the aeronautical experience was obtained in an approved course conducted by a training center certificated under part 142 of this chapter.

[Docket No. 25910, 62 FR 16298, April 4, 1997; Amdt. 61–103, 62 FR 40906, July 30, 1997; Amdt. 61–104, 63 FR 20289, April 23, 1998]

§61.165 Additional aircraft category and class ratings.

(a) *Rotorcraft category and helicopter class rating.* A person applying for an airline transport certificate with a rotorcraft category and helicopter class rating who holds an airline transport pilot certificate with another aircraft category rating must:

(1) Meet the eligibility requirements of §61.153 of this part;

(2) Pass a knowledge test on the aeronautical knowledge areas of §61.155(c) of this part;

(3) Comply with the requirements in §61.157(b) of this part, if appropriate;

(4) Meet the applicable aeronautical experience requirements of §61.161 of this part; and

(5) Pass the practical test on the areas of operation of §61.157(e)(4) of this part.

(b) *Airplane category rating with a single-engine class rating.* A person applying for an airline transport certificate with an airplane category and single-engine class rating who holds an airline transport pilot certificate with another aircraft category rating must:

(1) Meet the eligibility requirements of §61.153 of this part;

(2) Pass a knowledge test on the aeronautical knowledge areas of §61.155(c) of this part;

(3) Comply with the requirements in §61.157(b) of this part, if appropriate;

(4) Meet the applicable aeronautical experience requirements of §61.159 of this part; and

(5) Pass the practical test on the areas of operation of §61.157(e)(1) of this part.

(c) *Airplane category rating with a multiengine class rating.* A person applying for an airline transport certificate with an airplane category and multiengine class rating who holds an airline transport certificate with another aircraft category rating must:

(1) Meet the eligibility requirements of §61.153 of this part;

(2) Successfully complete the airline transport pilot certification training program specified in §61.156;

(3) Pass a knowledge test for an airplane category multiengine class rating or type rating on the aeronautical knowledge areas of §61.155(c);

(4) Comply with the requirements in §61.157(b) of this part, if appropriate;

(5) Meet the aeronautical experience requirements of §61.159 or §61.160; and

(6) Pass the practical test on the areas of operation of §61.157(e)(2) of this part.

(d) *Powered-lift category.* A person applying for an airline transport pilot certificate with a powered-lift category rating who holds an airline transport certificate with another aircraft category rating must:

(1) Meet the eligibility requirements of §61.153 of this part;

(2) Pass a required knowledge test on the aeronautical knowledge areas of §61.155(c) of this part;

(3) Comply with the requirements in §61.157(b) of this part, if appropriate;

(4) Meet the applicable aeronautical experience requirements of §61.163 of this part; and

(5) Pass the required practical test on the areas of operation of §61.157(e)(3) of this part.

(e) Additional class rating within the same aircraft category. Except as provided in paragraph (f) of this section, a person applying for an airline transport pilot certificate with an additional class rating who holds an airline transport certificate in the same aircraft category must—

(1) Meet the eligibility requirements of §61.153, except paragraph (g) of that section;

(2) Comply with the requirements in §61.157(b) of this part, if applicable;

(3) Meet the applicable aeronautical experience requirements of subpart G of this part; and

(4) Pass a practical test on the areas of operation of §61.157(e) appropriate to the aircraft rating sought.

(f) Adding a multiengine class rating to an airline transport pilot certificate with a single engine class rating. A person applying to add a multiengine class rating, or a multiengine class rating concurrently with a multiengine airplane type rating, to an airline transport pilot certificate with an airplane category single engine class rating must—

(1) Meet the eligibility requirements of §61.153;

(2) Pass a required knowledge test on the aeronautical knowledge areas of §61.155(c), as applicable to multiengine airplanes;

(3) Comply with the requirements in §61.157(b), if applicable;

(4) Meet the applicable aeronautical experience requirements of §61.159; and

(5) Pass a practical test on the areas of operation of §61.157(e)(2).

(g) Category class ratings for the operation of aircraft with experimental certificates. Notwithstanding the provisions of paragraphs (a) through (f) of this section, a person holding an airline transport certificate may apply for a category and class rating limited to a specific make and model of experimental aircraft, provided—

(1) The person has logged at least 5 hours flight time while acting as pilot in command in the same category, class, make, and model of aircraft that has been issued an experimental certificate;

(2) The person has received a logbook endorsement from an authorized instructor who has determined that he or she is proficient to act as pilot in command of the same category, class, make, and model of aircraft for which application is made; and

(3) The flight time specified in paragraph (g)(1) of this section must be logged between September 1, 2004 and August 31, 2005.

[Docket No. 25910, 62 FR 16298, April 4, 1997; Amdt. 61–103, 62 FR 40906, July 30, 1997, as amended by Amdt. 61–110, 69 FR 44869, July 27, 2004; Amdt. 61–130, 78 FR 42376, July 15, 2013; Amdt. 61–130B, 78 FR 77574, Dec. 24, 2013; Amdt. 61–130C, 81 FR 2, Jan. 4, 2016]

§61.167 Airline transport pilot privileges and limitations.

(a) Privileges.

(1) A person who holds an airline transport pilot certificate is entitled to the same privileges as a person who holds a commercial pilot certificate with an instrument rating.

(2) A person who holds an airline transport pilot certificate and has met the aeronautical experience requirements of §61.159 or §61.161, and the age requirements of §61.153(a)(1) of this part may instruct—

(i) Other pilots in air transportation service in aircraft of the category, class, and type, as applicable, for which the airline transport pilot is rated and endorse the logbook or other training record of the person to whom training has been given;

(ii) In flight simulators, and flight training devices representing the aircraft referenced in paragraph (a)(2)(i) of this section, when instructing under the provisions of this section and endorse the logbook or other training record of the person to whom training has been given;

(iii) Only as provided in this section, except that an airline transport pilot who also holds a flight instructor certificate can exercise the instructor privileges under subpart H of this part for which he or she is rated; and

(iv) In an aircraft, only if the aircraft has functioning dual controls, when instructing under the provisions of this section.

(3) Excluding briefings and debriefings, an airline transport pilot may not instruct in aircraft, flight simulators, and flight training devices under this section—

(i) For more than 8 hours in any 24-consecutive-hour period; or

(ii) For more than 36 hours in any 7-consecutive-day period.

(4) An airline transport pilot may not instruct in Category II or Category III operations unless he or she has been trained and successfully tested under Category II or Category III operations, as applicable.

(b) Limitations. A person who holds an airline transport pilot certificate and has not satisfied the age requirement of §61.153(a)(1) and the aeronautical experience requirements of §61.159 may not:

(1) Act as pilot in command in operations conducted under part 121, §91.1053(a)(2)(i), or §135.243(a)(1) of this chapter, or

(2) Serve as second in command in flag or supplemental operations in part 121 of this chapter requiring three or more pilots.

[Docket No. FAA–2010–0100, 78 FR 42376, July 15, 2013, as amended by Amdt. 61–130B, 78 FR 77574, Dec. 24, 2013; Amdt. 61–130C, 81 FR 2, Jan. 4, 2016]

§61.169 Letters of authorization for institutions of higher education.

(a) An institution of higher education that is accredited, as defined in §61.1, may apply for a letter of authorization for the purpose of certifying its graduates for an airline transport pilot certificate under the academic and aeronautical experience requirements in §61.160. The application must be in a form and manner acceptable to the Administrator.

(b) An institution of higher education must comply with the provisions of the letter of authorization and may not certify a graduate unless it determines that the graduate has satisfied the requirements of §61.160, as appropriate.

(c) The Administrator may rescind or amend a letter of authorization if the Administrator determines that the institution of higher education is not complying or is unable to comply with the provisions of the letter of authorization.

[Docket No. FAA–2010–0100, 78 FR 42377, July 15, 2013]

§61.170–61.171 [Reserved]

Subpart H— Flight Instructors Other than Flight Instructors With a Sport Pilot Rating

§61.181 Applicability.

This subpart prescribes the requirements for the issuance of flight instructor certificates and ratings (except for flight instructor certificates with a sport pilot rating), the conditions under which those certificates and ratings are necessary, and the limitations on those certificates and ratings.

[Docket No. FAA–2001–11133, 69 FR 44869, July 27, 2004]

§61.183 Eligibility requirements.

To be eligible for a flight instructor certificate or rating a person must:

(a) Be at least 18 years of age;

(b) Be able to read, speak, write, and understand the English language. If the applicant is unable to meet one of these requirements due to medical reasons, then the Administrator may place such operating limitations on that applicant's flight instructor certificate as are necessary;

(c) Hold either a commercial pilot certificate or airline transport pilot certificate with:

(1) An aircraft category and class rating that is appropriate to the flight instructor rating sought; and

(2) An instrument rating or privileges on that person's pilot certificate that are appropriate to the flight instructor rating sought, if applying for—

(i) A flight instructor certificate with an airplane category and single-engine class rating;

(ii) A flight instructor certificate with an airplane category and multiengine class rating;

(iii) A flight instructor certificate with a powered-lift rating; or

(iv) A flight instructor certificate with an instrument rating.

(d) Receive a logbook endorsement from an authorized instructor on the fundamentals of instructing listed in §61.185 of this part appropriate to the required knowledge test;

(e) Pass a knowledge test on the areas listed in §61.185(a)(1) of this part, unless the applicant:

(1) Holds a flight instructor certificate or ground instructor certificate issued under this part;

(2) Holds a teacher's certificate issued by a State, county, city, or municipality that authorizes the person to teach at an educational level of the 7th grade or higher; or

(3) Is employed as a teacher at an accredited college or university.

(f) Pass a knowledge test on the aeronautical knowledge areas listed in §61.185(a)(2) and (a)(3) of this part that are appropriate to the flight instructor rating sought;

(g) Receive a logbook endorsement from an authorized instructor on the areas of operation listed in §61.187(b) of this part, appropriate to the flight instructor rating sought;

(h) Pass the required practical test that is appropriate to the flight instructor rating sought in an:

(1) Aircraft that is representative of the category and class of aircraft for the aircraft rating sought; or

(2) Flight simulator or approved flight training device that is representative of the category and class of aircraft for the rating sought, and used in accordance with a course at a training center certificated under part 142 of this chapter.

(i) Accomplish the following for a flight instructor certificate with an airplane or a glider rating:

(1) Receive a logbook endorsement from an authorized instructor indicating that the applicant is competent and possesses instructional proficiency in stall awareness, spin entry, spins, and spin recovery procedures after providing the applicant with flight training in those training areas in an airplane or glider, as appropriate, that is certificated for spins; and

(2) Demonstrate instructional proficiency in stall awareness, spin entry, spins, and spin recovery procedures. However, upon presentation of the endorsement specified in paragraph (i)(1) of this section an examiner may accept that endorsement as satisfactory evidence of instructional

proficiency in stall awareness, spin entry, spins, and spin recovery procedures for the practical test, provided that the practical test is not a retest as a result of the applicant failing the previous test for deficiencies in the knowledge or skill of stall awareness, spin entry, spins, or spin recovery instructional procedures. If the retest is a result of deficiencies in the ability of an applicant to demonstrate knowledge or skill of stall awareness, spin entry, spins, or spin recovery instructional procedures, the examiner must test the person on stall awareness, spin entry, spins, and spin recovery instructional procedures in an airplane or glider, as appropriate, that is certificated for spins;

(j) Log at least 15 hours as pilot in command in the category and class of aircraft that is appropriate to the flight instructor rating sought; and

(k) Comply with the appropriate sections of this part that apply to the flight instructor rating sought.

[Docket No. 25910, 62 FR 16298, April 4, 1997; Amdt. 61–103, 62 FR 40907, July 30, 1997; Amdt. 61–124, 74 FR 42561, Aug. 21, 2009]

§61.185 Aeronautical knowledge.

(a) A person who is applying for a flight instructor certificate must receive and log ground training from an authorized instructor on:

(1) Except as provided in paragraph (b) of this section, the fundamentals of instructing, including:

(i) The learning process;

(ii) Elements of effective teaching;

(iii) Student evaluation and testing;

(iv) Course development;

(v) Lesson planning; and

(vi) Classroom training techniques.

(2) The aeronautical knowledge areas for a recreational, private, and commercial pilot certificate applicable to the aircraft category for which flight instructor privileges are sought; and

(3) The aeronautical knowledge areas for the instrument rating applicable to the category for which instrument flight instructor privileges are sought.

(b) The following applicants do not need to comply with paragraph (a)(1) of this section:

(1) The holder of a flight instructor certificate or ground instructor certificate issued under this part;

(2) The holder of a current teacher's certificate issued by a State, county, city, or municipality that authorizes the person to teach at an educational level of the 7th grade or higher; or

(3) A person employed as a teacher at an accredited college or university.

[Docket No. 25910, 62 FR 16298, April 4, 1997; Amdt. 61–103, 62 FR 40907, July 30, 1997]

§61.187 Flight proficiency.

(a) *General.* A person who is applying for a flight instructor certificate must receive and log flight and ground training from an authorized instructor on the areas of operation listed in this section that apply to the flight instructor rating sought. The applicant's logbook must contain an endorsement from an authorized instructor certifying that the person is proficient to pass a practical test on those areas of operation.

(b) *Areas of operation.*

(1) For an airplane category rating with a single-engine class rating:

(i) Fundamentals of instructing;

(ii) Technical subject areas;

(iii) Preflight preparation;

(iv) Preflight lesson on a maneuver to be performed in flight;

(v) Preflight procedures;

(vi) Airport and seaplane base operations;

(vii) Takeoffs, landings, and go-arounds;

(viii) Fundamentals of flight;

(ix) Performance maneuvers;

(x) Ground reference maneuvers;

(xi) Slow flight, stalls, and spins;

(xii) Basic instrument maneuvers;

(xiii) Emergency operations; and

(xiv) Postflight procedures.

(2) For an airplane category rating with a multiengine class rating:

(i) Fundamentals of instructing;

(ii) Technical subject areas;

(iii) Preflight preparation;

(iv) Preflight lesson on a maneuver to be performed in flight;

(v) Preflight procedures;

(vi) Airport and seaplane base operations;

(vii) Takeoffs, landings, and go-arounds;

(viii) Fundamentals of flight;

(ix) Performance maneuvers;

(x) Ground reference maneuvers;

(xi) Slow flight and stalls;

(xii) Basic instrument maneuvers;

(xiii) Emergency operations;

(xiv) Multiengine operations; and

(xv) Postflight procedures.

(3) For a rotorcraft category rating with a helicopter class rating:

(i) Fundamentals of instructing;

(ii) Technical subject areas;

(iii) Preflight preparation;

(iv) Preflight lesson on a maneuver to be performed in flight;

(v) Preflight procedures;

(vi) Airport and heliport operations;

(vii) Hovering maneuvers;

(viii) Takeoffs, landings, and go-arounds;

(ix) Fundamentals of flight;

(x) Performance maneuvers;

(xi) Emergency operations;
(xii) Special operations; and
(xiii) Postflight procedures.

(4) For a rotorcraft category rating with a gyro-plane class rating:
(i) Fundamentals of instructing;
(ii) Technical subject areas;
(iii) Preflight preparation;
(iv) Preflight lesson on a maneuver to be performed in flight;
(v) Preflight procedures;
(vi) Airport operations;
(vii) Takeoffs, landings, and go-arounds;
(viii) Fundamentals of flight;
(ix) Performance maneuvers;
(x) Flight at slow airspeeds;
(xi) Ground reference maneuvers;
(xii) Emergency operations; and
(xiii) Postflight procedures.

(5) For a powered-lift category rating:
(i) Fundamentals of instructing;
(ii) Technical subject areas;
(iii) Preflight preparation;
(iv) Preflight lesson on a maneuver to be performed in flight;
(v) Preflight procedures;
(vi) Airport and heliport operations;
(vii) Hovering maneuvers;
(viii) Takeoffs, landings, and go-arounds;
(ix) Fundamentals of flight;
(x) Performance maneuvers;
(xi) Ground reference maneuvers;
(xii) Slow flight and stalls;
(xiii) Basic instrument maneuvers;
(xiv) Emergency operations;
(xv) Special operations; and
(xvi) Postflight procedures.

(6) For a glider category rating:
(i) Fundamentals of instructing;
(ii) Technical subject areas;
(iii) Preflight preparation;
(iv) Preflight lesson on a maneuver to be performed in flight;
(v) Preflight procedures;
(vi) Airport and gliderport operations;
(vii) Launches and landings;
(viii) Fundamentals of flight;
(ix) Performance speeds;
(x) Soaring techniques;
(xi) Performance maneuvers;
(xii) Slow flight, stalls, and spins;
(xiii) Emergency operations; and
(xiv) Postflight procedures.

(7) For an instrument rating with the appropri-ate aircraft category and class rating:
(i) Fundamentals of instructing;
(ii) Technical subject areas;
(iii) Preflight preparation;

(iv) Preflight lesson on a maneuver to be performed in flight;
(v) Air traffic control clearances and procedures;
(vi) Flight by reference to instruments;
(vii) Navigation aids;
(viii) Instrument approach procedures;
(ix) Emergency operations; and
(x) Postflight procedures.

(c) The flight training required by this section may be accomplished:
(1) In an aircraft that is representative of the cat-egory and class of aircraft for the rating sought; or
(2) In a flight simulator or flight training device representative of the category and class of air-craft for the rating sought, and used in accor-dance with an approved course at a training cen-ter certificated under part 142 of this chapter.

[Docket No. 25910, 62 FR 16298, April 4, 1997; Amdt. 61–103, 62 FR 40907, July 30, 1997; Amdt. 61–124, 74 FR 42561, Aug. 21, 2009]

§61.189 Flight instructor records.

(a) A flight instructor must sign the logbook of each person to whom that instructor has given flight training or ground training.

(b) A flight instructor must maintain a record in a logbook or a separate document that contains the following:
(1) The name of each person whose logbook that instructor has endorsed for solo flight privi-leges, and the date of the endorsement; and
(2) The name of each person that instructor has endorsed for a knowledge test or practical test, and the record shall also indicate the kind of test, the date, and the results.

(c) Each flight instructor must retain the records required by this section for at least 3 years.

[Docket No. 25910, 62 FR 16298, April 4, 1997; as amended by Amdt. 61–135, 81 FR 1306, Jan. 12, 2016]

§61.191 Additional flight instructor ratings.

(a) A person who applies for an additional flight instructor rating on a flight instructor certificate must meet the eligibility requirements listed in §61.183 of this part that apply to the flight instruc-tor rating sought.

(b) A person who applies for an additional rat-ing on a flight instructor certificate is not required to pass the knowledge test on the areas listed in §61.185(a)(1) of this part.

[Docket No. 25910, 62 FR 16298, April 4, 1997; Amdt. 61–103, 62 FR 40907, July 30, 1997]

§61.193 Flight instructor privileges.

(a) A person who holds a flight instructor cer-tificate is authorized within the limitations of that person's flight instructor certificate and ratings to

train and issue endorsements that are required for:

(1) A student pilot certificate;

(2) A pilot certificate;

(3) A flight instructor certificate;

(4) A ground instructor certificate;

(5) An aircraft rating;

(6) An instrument rating;

(7) A flight review, operating privilege, or recency of experience requirement of this part;

(8) A practical test; and

(9) A knowledge test.

(b) A person who holds a flight instructor certificate is authorized, in a form and manner acceptable to the Administrator, to:

(1) Accept an application for a student pilot certificate or, for an applicant who holds a pilot certificate (other than a student pilot certificate) issued under part 61 of this chapter and meets the flight review requirements specified in §61.56, a remote pilot certificate with a small UAS rating;

(2) Verify the identity of the applicant; and

(3) Verify that an applicant for a student pilot certificate meets the eligibility requirements in §61.83 or an applicant for a remote pilot certificate with a small UAS rating meets the eligibility requirements in §107.61 of this chapter.

[Docket FAA–2010–1127, Amdt. 61–135, 81 FR 1306, Jan. 12, 2016, as amended by Docket FAA–2015–0150, Amdt. 61–137, 81 FR 42208, June 28, 2016]

§61.195 Flight instructor limitations and qualifications.

A person who holds a flight instructor certificate is subject to the following limitations:

(a) *Hours of training.* In any 24-consecutive-hour period, a flight instructor may not conduct more than 8 hours of flight training.

(b) *Aircraft ratings.* Except as provided in paragraph (c) of this section, a flight instructor may not conduct flight training in any aircraft unless the flight instructor:

(1) Holds a flight instructor certificate with the applicable category and class rating;

(2) Holds a pilot certificate with the applicable category and class rating; and

(3) Meets the requirements of paragraph (e) of this section, if applicable.

(c) *Instrument rating.* A flight instructor may conduct instrument training for the issuance of an instrument rating, a type rating not limited to VFR, or the instrument training required for commercial pilot and airline transport pilot certificates if the following requirements are met:

(1) Except as provided in paragraph (c)(2) of this section, the flight instructor must hold an instrument rating appropriate to the aircraft used for the instrument training on his or her flight instructor certificate, and—

(i) Meet the requirements of paragraph (b) of this section; or

(ii) Hold a commercial pilot certificate or airline transport pilot certificate with the appropriate category and class ratings for the aircraft in which the instrument training is conducted provided the pilot receiving instrument training holds a pilot certificate with category and class ratings appropriate to the aircraft in which the instrument training is being conducted.

(2) If the flight instructor is conducting the instrument training in a multiengine airplane, the flight instructor must hold an instrument rating appropriate to the aircraft used for the instrument training on his or her flight instructor certificate and meet the requirements of paragraph (b) of this section.

(d) *Limitations on endorsements.* A flight instructor may not endorse a:

(1) Student pilot's logbook for solo flight privileges, unless that flight instructor has—

(i) Given that student the flight training required for solo flight privileges required by this part; and

(ii) Determined that the student is prepared to conduct the flight safely under known circumstances, subject to any limitations listed in the student's logbook that the instructor considers necessary for the safety of the flight.

(2) Student pilot's logbook for a solo cross-country flight, unless that flight instructor has determined the student's flight preparation, planning, equipment, and proposed procedures are adequate for the proposed flight under the existing conditions and within any limitations listed in the logbook that the instructor considers necessary for the safety of the flight;

(3) Student pilot's logbook for solo flight in a Class B airspace area or at an airport within Class B airspace unless that flight instructor has—

(i) Given that student ground and flight training in that Class B airspace or at that airport; and

(ii) Determined that the student is proficient to operate the aircraft safely.

(4) Logbook of a recreational pilot, unless that flight instructor has—

(i) Given that pilot the ground and flight training required by this part; and

(ii) Determined that the recreational pilot is proficient to operate the aircraft safely.

(5) Logbook of a pilot for a flight review, unless that instructor has conducted a review of that pilot in accordance with the requirements of §61.56(a) of this part; or

(6) Logbook of a pilot for an instrument proficiency check, unless that instructor has tested that pilot in accordance with the requirements of §61.57(d) of this part.

(e) *Training in an aircraft that requires a type rating.* A flight instructor may not give flight instruction, including instrument training, in an

aircraft that requires the pilot in command to hold a type rating unless the flight instructor holds a type rating for that aircraft on his or her pilot certificate.

(f) *Training received in a multiengine airplane, a helicopter, or a powered-lift.* A flight instructor may not give training required for the issuance of a certificate or rating in a multiengine airplane, a helicopter, or a powered-lift unless that flight instructor has at least 5 flight hours of pilot-in-command time in the specific make and model of multiengine airplane, helicopter, or powered-lift, as appropriate.

(g) *Position in aircraft and required pilot stations for providing flight training.*

(1) A flight instructor must perform all training from in an aircraft that complies with the requirements of §91.109 of this chapter.

(2) A flight instructor who provides flight training for a pilot certificate or rating issued under this part must provide that flight training in an aircraft that meets the following requirements—

(i) The aircraft must have at least two pilot stations and be of the same category, class, and type, if appropriate, that applies to the pilot certificate or rating sought.

(ii) For single-place aircraft, the pre-solo flight training must have been provided in an aircraft that has two pilot stations and is of the same category, class, and type, if appropriate.

(h) *Qualifications of the flight instructor for training first-time flight instructor applicants.*

(1) The ground training provided to an initial applicant for a flight instructor certificate must be given by an authorized instructor who—

(i) Holds a ground or flight instructor certificate with the appropriate rating, has held that certificate for at least 24 calendar months, and has given at least 40 hours of ground training; or

(ii) Holds a ground or flight instructor certificate with the appropriate rating, and has given at least 100 hours of ground training in an FAA-approved course.

(2) Except for an instructor who meets the requirements of paragraph (h)(3)(ii) of this section, a flight instructor who provides training to an initial applicant for a flight instructor certificate must—

(i) Meet the eligibility requirements prescribed in §61.183 of this part;

(ii) Hold the appropriate flight instructor certificate and rating;

(iii) Have held a flight instructor certificate for at least 24 months;

(iv) For training in preparation for an airplane, rotorcraft, or powered-lift rating, have given at least 200 hours of flight training as a flight instructor; and

(v) For training in preparation for a glider rating, have given at least 80 hours of flight training as a flight instructor.

(3) A flight instructor who serves as a flight instructor in an FAA-approved course for the issuance of a flight instructor rating must hold a flight instructor certificate with the appropriate rating and pass the required initial and recurrent flight instructor proficiency tests, in accordance with the requirements of the part under which the FAA-approved course is conducted, and must—

(i) Meet the requirements of paragraph (h)(2) of this section; or

(ii) Have trained and endorsed at least five applicants for a practical test for a pilot certificate, flight instructor certificate, ground instructor certificate, or an additional rating, and at least 80 percent of those applicants passed that test on their first attempt; and

(A) Given at least 400 hours of flight training as a flight instructor for training in an airplane, a rotorcraft, or for a powered-lift rating; or

(B) Given at least 100 hours of flight training as a flight instructor, for training in a glider rating.

(i) *Prohibition against self-endorsements.* A flight instructor shall not make any self-endorsement for a certificate, rating, flight review, authorization, operating privilege, practical test, or knowledge test that is required by this part.

(j) *Additional qualifications required to give training in Category II or Category III operations.* A flight instructor may not give training in Category II or Category III operations unless the flight instructor has been trained and tested in Category II or Category III operations, pursuant to §61.67 or §61.68 of this part, as applicable.

(k) *Training for night vision goggle operations.* A flight instructor may not conduct training for night vision goggle operations unless the flight instructor:

(1) Has a pilot and flight instructor certificate with the applicable category and class rating for the training;

(2) If appropriate, has a type rating on his or her pilot certificate for the aircraft;

(3) Is pilot in command qualified for night vision goggle operations, in accordance with §61.31(k);

(4) Has logged 100 night vision goggle operations as the sole manipulator of the controls;

(5) Has logged 20 night vision goggle operations as the sole manipulator of the controls in the category and class, and type of aircraft, if aircraft class and type is appropriate, that the training will be given in;

(6) Is qualified to act as pilot in command in night vision goggle operations under §61.57(f) or (g); and

(7) Has a logbook endorsement from an FAA Aviation Safety Inspector or a person who is authorized by the FAA to provide that logbook endorsement that states the flight instructor is authorized to perform the night vision goggle pilot in command qualification and recent flight

experience requirements under §61.31(k) and §61.57(f) and (g).

(l) *Training on control and maneuvering an aircraft solely by reference to the instruments.* A flight instructor may conduct flight training on control and maneuvering an airplane solely by reference to the flight instruments, provided the flight instructor—

(1) Holds a flight instructor certificate with the applicable category and class rating; or

(2) Holds an instrument rating appropriate to the aircraft used for the training on his or her flight instructor certificate, and holds a commercial pilot certificate or airline transport pilot certificate with the appropriate category and class ratings for the aircraft in which the training is conducted provided the pilot receiving the training holds a pilot certificate with category and class ratings appropriate to the aircraft in which the training is being conducted.

[Docket No. 25910, 62 FR 16298, April 4, 1997; Amdt. 61–103, 62 FR 40907, July 30, 1997; Amdt. 61–124, 74 FR 42561, Aug. 21, 2009; Docket FAA–2010–1127, Amdt. 61–135, 81 FR 1307, Jan. 12, 2016; Docket FAA–2016–6142, Amdt. 61–142, 83 FR 30729, June 27, 2018]

§61.197 Renewal requirements for flight instructor certification.

(a) A person who holds a flight instructor certificate that has not expired may renew that flight instructor certificate by—

(1) Passing a practical test for—

(i) One of the ratings listed on the current flight instructor certificate; or

(ii) An additional flight instructor rating; or

(2) Submitting a completed and signed application with the FAA and satisfactorily completing one of the following renewal requirements—

(i) A record of training students showing that, during the preceding 24 calendar months, the flight instructor has endorsed at least 5 students for a practical test for a certificate or rating and at least 80 percent of those students passed that test on the first attempt.

(ii) A record showing that, within the preceding 24 calendar months, the flight instructor has served as a company check pilot, chief flight instructor, company check airman, or flight instructor in a part 121 or in a part 135 operation, or in a position involving the regular evaluation of pilots.

(iii) A graduation certificate showing that, within the preceding 3 calendar months, the person has successfully completed an approved flight instructor refresher course consisting of ground training or flight training, or a combination of both.

(iv) A record showing that, within the preceding 24 months from the month of application, the flight instructor passed an official U.S. Armed Forces military instructor pilot or pilot examiner proficiency check in an aircraft for which the military

instructor already holds a rating or in an aircraft for an additional rating.

(b) The expiration month of a renewed flight instructor certificate shall be 24 calendar months from—

(1) The month the renewal requirements of paragraph (a) of this section are accomplished; or

(2) The month of expiration of the current flight instructor certificate provided—

(i) The renewal requirements of paragraph (a) of this section are accomplished within the 3 calendar months preceding the expiration month of the current flight instructor certificate, and

(ii) If the renewal is accomplished under paragraph (a)(2)(iii) of this section, the approved flight instructor refresher course must be completed within the 3 calendar months preceding the expiration month of the current flight instructor certificate.

(c) The practical test required by paragraph (a)(1) of this section may be accomplished in a full flight simulator or flight training device if the test is accomplished pursuant to an approved course conducted by a training center certificated under part 142 of this chapter.

[Docket No. 25910, 63 FR 20289, April 23, 1998, as amended by Amdt. 61–124, 74 FR 42562, Aug. 21, 2009; Amdt. 61–142, 83 FR 30279, June 27, 2018]

§61.199 Reinstatement requirements of an expired flight instructor certificate.

(a) *Flight instructor certificates.* The holder of an expired flight instructor certificate who has not complied with the flight instructor renewal requirements of §61.197 may reinstate that flight instructor certificate and ratings by filing a completed and signed application with the FAA and satisfactorily completing one of the following reinstatement requirements:

(1) A flight instructor certification practical test, as prescribed by §61.183(h), for one of the ratings held on the expired flight instructor certificate.

(2) A flight instructor certification practical test for an additional rating.

(3) For military instructor pilots, provide a record showing that, within the preceding 6 calendar months from the date of application for reinstatement, the person—

(i) Passed a U.S. Armed Forces instructor pilot or pilot examiner proficiency check; or

(ii) Completed a U.S. Armed Forces' instructor pilot or pilot examiner training course and received an additional aircraft rating qualification as a military instructor pilot or pilot examiner that is appropriate to the flight instructor rating sought.

(b) *Flight instructor ratings.*

(1) A flight instructor rating or a limited flight instructor rating on a pilot certificate is no longer valid and may not be exchanged for a similar rating or a flight instructor certificate.

(2) The holder of a flight instructor rating or a limited flight instructor rating on a pilot certificate may be issued a flight instructor certificate with the current ratings, but only if the person passes the required knowledge and practical test prescribed in this subpart for the issuance of the current flight instructor certificate and rating.

(c) *Certain military instructors and examiners.* The holder of an expired flight instructor certificate issued prior to October 20, 2009, may apply for reinstatement of that certificate by presenting the following:

(1) A record showing that, since the date the flight instructor certificate was issued, the person passed a U.S. Armed Forces instructor pilot or pilot examiner proficiency check for an additional military rating; and

(2) A knowledge test report that shows the person passed a knowledge test on the aeronautical knowledge areas listed under §61.185(a) appropriate to the flight instructor rating sought and the knowledge test was passed within the preceding 24 calendar months prior to the month of application.

(d) *Expiration date.* The requirements of paragraph (c) of this section will expire on August 26, 2019.

[Docket No. 25910, 62 FR 16298, April 4, 1997; as amended by Amdt. 61–104, 63 FR 20289, April 23, 1998; Amdt. 61–124, 74 FR 42562, Aug. 21, 2009; Amdt. 61– 142, 83 FR 30279, June 27, 2018]

§61.201 [Reserved]

Subpart I— Ground Instructors

§61.211 Applicability.

This subpart prescribes the requirements for the issuance of ground instructor certificates and ratings, the conditions under which those certificates and ratings are necessary, and the limitations upon those certificates and ratings.

§61.213 Eligibility requirements.

(a) To be eligible for a ground instructor certificate or rating a person must:

(1) Be at least 18 years of age;

(2) Be able to read, write, speak, and understand the English language. If the applicant is unable to meet one of these requirements due to medical reasons, then the Administrator may place such operating limitations on that applicant's ground instructor certificate as are necessary;

(3) Except as provided in paragraph (b) of this section, pass a knowledge test on the fundamentals of instructing to include—

(i) The learning process;

(ii) Elements of effective teaching;

(iii) Student evaluation and testing;

(iv) Course development;

(v) Lesson planning; and

(vi) Classroom training techniques.

(4) Pass a knowledge test on the aeronautical knowledge areas in—

(i) For a basic ground instructor rating §§61.97, 61.105, and 61.309;

(ii) For an advanced ground instructor rating §§61.97, 61.105, 61.125, 61.155, and 61.309; and

(iii) For an instrument ground instructor rating, §61.65.

(b) The knowledge test specified in paragraph (a)(3) of this section is not required if the applicant:

(1) Holds a ground instructor certificate or flight instructor certificate issued under this part;

(2) Holds a teacher's certificate issued by a State, county, city, or municipality that authorizes the person to teach at an educational level of the 7th grade or higher; or

(3) Is employed as a teacher at an accredited college or university.

[Docket No. 25910, 62 FR 16298, April 4, 1997; as amended by Amdt. 61–110, 69 FR 44869, July 27, 2004; Amdt. 61–124, 74 FR 42562, Aug. 21, 2009]

§61.215 Ground instructor privileges.

(a) A person who holds a basic ground instructor rating is authorized to provide—

(1) Ground training in the aeronautical knowledge areas required for the issuance of a sport pilot certificate, recreational pilot certificate, private pilot certificate, or associated ratings under this part;

(2) Ground training required for a sport pilot, recreational pilot, and private pilot flight review; and

(3) A recommendation for a knowledge test required for the issuance of a sport pilot certificate, recreational pilot certificate, or private pilot certificate under this part.

(b) A person who holds an advanced ground instructor rating is authorized to provide:

(1) Ground training on the aeronautical knowledge areas required for the issuance of any certificate or rating under this part except for the aeronautical knowledge areas required for an instrument rating.

(2) The ground training required for any flight review except for the training required for an instrument rating.

(3) A recommendation for a knowledge test required for the issuance of any certificate or rating under this part except for an instrument rating.

(c) A person who holds an instrument ground instructor rating is authorized to provide:

(1) Ground training in the aeronautical knowledge areas required for the issuance of an instrument rating under this part;

(2) Ground training required for an instrument proficiency check; and

(3) A recommendation for a knowledge test required for the issuance of an instrument rating under this part.

(d) A person who holds a ground instructor certificate is authorized, within the limitations of the ratings on the ground instructor certificate, to endorse the logbook or other training record of a person to whom the holder has provided the training or recommendation specified in paragraphs (a) through (c) of this section.

[Docket No. 25910, 62 FR 16298, April 4, 1997; as amended by Amdt. 61–110, 69 FR 44869, July 27, 2004; Amdt. 61–124, 74 FR 42562, Aug. 21, 2009]

§61.217 Recent experience requirements.

The holder of a ground instructor certificate may not perform the duties of a ground instructor unless the person can show that one of the following occurred during the preceding 12 calendar months:

(a) Employment or activity as a ground instructor giving pilot, flight instructor, or ground instructor training;

(b) Employment or activity as a flight instructor giving pilot, flight instructor, or ground instructor ground or flight training;

(c) Completion of an approved flight instructor refresher course and receipt of a graduation certificate for that course; or

(d) An endorsement from an authorized instructor certifying that the person has demonstrated knowledge in the subject areas prescribed under §61.213(a)(3) and (a)(4), as appropriate.

[Docket No. FAA–2006–26661, 74 FR 42562, Aug. 21, 2009]

Subpart J—Sport Pilots

Source: Docket No. FAA–2001–11133, 69 FR 44869, July 27, 2004, unless otherwise noted.

§61.301 What is the purpose of this subpart and to whom does it apply?

(a) This subpart prescribes the following requirements that apply to a sport pilot certificate:

(1) Eligibility.
(2) Aeronautical knowledge.
(3) Flight proficiency.
(4) Aeronautical experience.
(5) Endorsements.
(6) Privileges and limits.

(b) Other provisions of this part apply to the logging of flight time and testing.

(c) This subpart applies to applicants for, and holders of, sport pilot certificates. It also applies to holders of recreational pilot certificates and higher, as provided in §61.303.

[Docket No. FAA–2001–11133, 69 FR 44869, July 27, 2004; as amended by Amdt. 61–125, 75 FR 5221, Feb. 1, 2010]

§61.303 If I want to operate a light-sport aircraft, what operating limits and endorsement requirements in this subpart must I comply with?

(a) Use the following table to determine what operating limits and endorsement requirements in this subpart, if any, apply to you when you operate a light-sport aircraft. The medical certificate specified in this table must be in compliance with §61.2 in regards to currency and validity. If you hold a recreational pilot certificate, but not a medical certificate, you must comply with cross country requirements in §61.101(c), even if your flight does not exceed 50 nautical miles from your departure airport. You must also comply with requirements in other subparts of this part that apply to your certificate and the operation you conduct.

If you hold	And you hold	Then you may operate	And
(1) A medical certificate,	(i) A sport pilot certificate,	(A) Any light-sport aircraft for which you hold the endorsements required for its category and class,	(1) You must hold any other endorsements required by this subpart, and comply with the limitations in §61.315.
	(ii) At least a recreational pilot certificate with a category and class rating,	(A) Any light-sport aircraft in that category and class,	(1) You do not have to hold any of the endorsements required by this subpart, nor do you have to comply with the limitations in §61.315.
	(iii) At least a recreational pilot certificate but not a rating for the category and class of light-sport aircraft you operate,	(A) That light-sport aircraft, only if you hold the endorsements required in §61.321 for its category and class,	(1) You must comply with the limitations in §61.315, except §61.315 (c)(14) and, if a private pilot or higher, §61.315(c)(7).

(continued)

If you hold	And you hold	Then you may operate	And
(2) Only a U.S. driver's license,	(i) A sport pilot certificate,	(A) Any light-sport aircraft for which you hold the endorsements required for its category and class,	(1) You must hold any other endorsements required by this subpart, and comply with the limitations in §61.315.
	(ii) At least a recreational pilot certificate with a category and class rating,	(A) Any light-sport aircraft in that category and class,	(1) You do not have to hold any of the endorsements required by this subpart, but you must comply with the limitations in §61.315.
	(iii) At least a recreational pilot certificate but not a rating for the category and class of light-sport aircraft you operate,	(A) That light-sport aircraft, only if you hold the endorsements required in §61.321 for its category and class,	(1) You must comply with the limitations in §61.315, except §61.315(c)(14) and, if a private pilot or higher, §61.315(c)(7).
(3) Neither a medical certificate nor a U.S. driver's license,	(i) A sport pilot certificate,	(A) Any light-sport glider or balloon for which you hold the endorsements required for its category and class,	(1) You must hold any other endorsements required by this subpart, and comply with the limitations in §61.315.
	(ii) At least a private pilot certificate with a category and class rating for glider or balloon,	(A) Any light-sport glider or balloon in that category and class,	(1) You do not have to hold any of the endorsements required by this subpart, nor do you have to comply with the limitations in §61.315.
	(iii) At least a private pilot certificate but not a rating for glider or balloon,	(A) Any light-sport glider or balloon, only if you hold the endorsements required in §61.321 for its category and class,	(1) You must comply with the limitations in §61.315, except §61.315(c)(14) and, if a private pilot or higher, §61.315(c)(7).

(b) A person using a U.S. driver's license to meet the requirements of this paragraph must—

(1) Comply with each restriction and limitation imposed by that person's U.S. driver's license and any judicial or administrative order applying to the operation of a motor vehicle;

(2) Have been found eligible for the issuance of at least a third-class airman medical certificate at the time of his or her most recent application (if the person has applied for a medical certificate);

(3) Not have had his or her most recently issued medical certificate (if the person has held a medical certificate) suspended or revoked or most recent Authorization for a Special Issuance of a Medical Certificate withdrawn; and

(4) Not know or have reason to know of any medical condition that would make that person unable to operate a light-sport aircraft in a safe manner.

[Docket No. FAA–2001–11133, 69 FR 44869, July 27, 2004; as amended by Amdt. 61–124, 74 FR 42562, Aug. 21, 2009; Amdt. 61–125, 75 FR 5221, Feb. 1, 2010]

§61.305 What are the age and language requirements for a sport pilot certificate?

(a) To be eligible for a sport pilot certificate you must:

(1) Be at least 17 years old (or 16 years old if you are applying to operate a glider or balloon).

(2) Be able to read, speak, write, and understand English. If you cannot read, speak, write, and understand English because of medical reasons, the FAA may place limits on your certificate as are necessary for the safe operation of light-sport aircraft.

§61.307 What tests do I have to take to obtain a sport pilot certificate?

To obtain a sport pilot certificate, you must pass the following tests:

(a) *Knowledge test.* You must pass a knowledge test on the applicable aeronautical knowledge areas listed in §61.309. Before you may take the knowledge test for a sport pilot certificate, you must receive a logbook endorsement from the authorized instructor who trained you or reviewed and evaluated your home-study course on the aeronautical knowledge areas listed in §61.309 certifying you are prepared for the test.

(b) *Practical test.* You must pass a practical test on the applicable areas of operation listed in §§61.309 and 61.311. Before you may take the practical test for a sport pilot certificate, you must receive a logbook endorsement from the authorized instructor who provided you with flight training on the areas of operation specified in §§61.309 and 61.311 in preparation for the practical test. This endorsement certifies that you meet the applicable aeronautical knowledge and experience requirements and are prepared for the practical test.

§61.309　What aeronautical knowledge must I have to apply for a sport pilot certificate?

To apply for a sport pilot certificate you must receive and log ground training from an authorized instructor or complete a home-study course on the following aeronautical knowledge areas:

(a) Applicable regulations of this chapter that relate to sport pilot privileges, limits, and flight operations.

(b) Accident reporting requirements of the National Transportation Safety Board.

(c) Use of the applicable portions of the aeronautical information manual and FAA advisory circulars.

(d) Use of aeronautical charts for VFR navigation using pilotage, dead reckoning, and navigation systems, as appropriate.

(e) Recognition of critical weather situations from the ground and in flight, windshear avoidance, and the procurement and use of aeronautical weather reports and forecasts.

(f) Safe and efficient operation of aircraft, including collision avoidance, and recognition and avoidance of wake turbulence.

(g) Effects of density altitude on takeoff and climb performance.

(h) Weight and balance computations.

(i) Principles of aerodynamics, powerplants, and aircraft systems.

(j) Stall awareness, spin entry, spins, and spin recovery techniques, as applicable.

(k) Aeronautical decision making and risk management.

(l) Preflight actions that include—

(1) How to get information on runway lengths at airports of intended use, data on takeoff and landing distances, weather reports and forecasts, and fuel requirements; and

(2) How to plan for alternatives if the planned flight cannot be completed or if you encounter delays.

[Docket No. FAA–2001–11133, 69 FR 44869, July 27, 2004; as amended by Amdt. 61–125, 75 FR 5221, Feb. 1, 2010]

§61.311　What flight proficiency requirements must I meet to apply for a sport pilot certificate?

To apply for a sport pilot certificate you must receive and log ground and flight training from an authorized instructor on the following areas of operation, as appropriate, for airplane single-engine land or sea, glider, gyroplane, airship, balloon, powered parachute land or sea, and weight-shift-control aircraft land or sea privileges:

(a) Preflight preparation.

(b) Preflight procedures.

(c) Airport, seaplane base, and gliderport operations, as applicable.

(d) Takeoffs (or launches), landings, and go-arounds.

(e) Performance maneuvers, and for gliders, performance speeds.

(f) Ground reference maneuvers (not applicable to gliders and balloons).

(g) Soaring techniques (applicable only to gliders).

(h) Navigation.

(i) Slow flight (not applicable to lighter-than-air aircraft and powered parachutes).

(j) Stalls (not applicable to lighter-than-air aircraft, gyroplanes, and powered parachutes).

(k) Emergency operations.

(l) Post-flight procedures.

[Docket No. FAA–2001–11133, 69 FR 44869, July 27, 2004; as amended by Amdt. 61–125, 75 FR 5221, Feb. 1, 2010]

§61.313　What aeronautical experience must I have to apply for a sport pilot certificate?

Use the following table to determine the aeronautical experience you must have to apply for a sport pilot certificate:

If you are applying for a sport pilot certificate with...	Then you must log at least...	Which must include at least...
(a) Airplane category and single-engine land or sea class privileges,	(1) 20 hours of flight time, including at least 15 hours of flight training from an authorized instructor in a single-engine airplane and at least 5 hours of solo flight training in the areas of operation listed in §61.311,	(i) 2 hours of cross-country flight training, (ii) 10 takeoffs and landings to a full stop (with each landing involving a flight in the traffic pattern) at an airport; (iii) One solo cross-country flight of at least 75 nautical miles total distance, with a full-stop landing at a minimum of two points and one segment of the flight consisting of a straight-line distance of at least 25 nautical miles between the takeoff and landing locations, and (iv) 2 hours of flight training with an authorized instructor on those areas of operation specified in §61.311 in preparation for the practical test within the preceding 2 calendar months from the month of the test.
(b) Glider category privileges, and you have not logged at least 20 hours of flight time in a heavier-than-air aircraft,	(1) 10 hours of flight time in a glider, including 10 flights in a glider receiving flight training from an authorized instructor and at least 2 hours of solo flight training in the areas of operation listed in §61.311,	(i) Five solo launches and landings, and (ii) at least 3 training flights with an authorized instructor on those areas of operation specified in §61.311 in preparation for the practical test within the preceding 2 calendar months from the month of the test.
(c) Glider category privileges, and you have logged 20 hours flight time in a heavier-than-air aircraft,	(1) 3 hours of flight time in a glider, including five flights in a glider while receiving flight training from an authorized instructor and at least 1 hour of solo flight training in the areas of operation listed in §61.311,	(i) Three solo launches and landings, and (ii) at least 3 training flights with an authorized instructor on those areas of operation specified in §61.311 in preparation for the practical test within the preceding 2 calendar months from the month of the test.
(d) Rotorcraft category and gyroplane class privileges,	(1) 20 hours of flight time, including 15 hours of flight training from an authorized instructor in a gyroplane and at least 5 hours of solo flight training in the areas of operation listed in §61.311,	(i) 2 hours of cross-country flight training, (ii) 10 takeoffs and landings to a full stop (with each landing involving a flight in the traffic pattern) at an airport, (iii) One solo cross-country flight of at least 50 nautical miles total distance, with a full-stop landing at a minimum of two points, and one segment of the flight consisting of a straight-line distance of at least 25 nautical miles between the takeoff and landing locations, and (iv) 2 hours of flight training with an authorized instructor on those areas of operation specified in §61.311 in preparation for the practical test within the preceding 2 calendar months from the month of the test.
(e) Lighter-than-air category and airship class privileges,	(1) 20 hours of flight time, including 15 hours of flight training from an authorized instructor in an airship and at least 3 hours performing the duties of pilot in command in an airship with an authorized instructor in the areas of operation listed in §61.311,	(i) 2 hours of cross-country flight training, (ii) Three takeoffs and landings to a full stop (with each landing involving a flight in the traffic pattern) at an airport, (iii) One cross-country flight of at least 25 nautical miles between the takeoff and landing locations, and (iv) 2 hours of flight training with an authorized instructor on those areas of operation specified in §61.311 in preparation for the practical test within the preceding 2 calendar months from the month of the test.

61

(continued)

If you are applying for a sport pilot certificate with...	Then you must log at least...	Which must include at least...
(f) Lighter-than-air category and balloon class privileges,	(1) 7 hours of flight time in a balloon, including three flights with an authorized instructor and one flight performing the duties of pilot in command in a balloon with an authorized instructor in the areas of operation listed in §61.311,	(i) 2 hours of cross-country flight training and (ii) 1 hour of flight training with an authorized instructor on those areas of operation specified in §61.311 in preparation for the practical test within the preceding 2 calendar months from the month of the test.
(g) Powered parachute category land or sea class privileges,	(1) 12 hours of flight time in a powered parachute, including 10 hours of flight training from an authorized instructor in a powered parachute, and at least 2 hours of solo flight training in the areas of operation listed in §61.311,	(i) 1 hour of cross-country flight training, (ii) 20 takeoffs and landings to a full stop in a powered parachute with each landing involving flight in the traffic pattern at an airport; (iii) 10 solo takeoffs and landings to a full stop (with each landing involving a flight in the traffic pattern) at an airport, (iv) One solo flight with a landing at a different airport and one segment of the flight consisting of a straight-line distance of at least 10 nautical miles between takeoff and landing locations, and (v) 1 hour of flight training with an authorized instructor on those areas of operation specified in §61.311 in preparation for the practical test within the preceding 2 calendar months from the month of the test.
(h) Weight-shift-control aircraft category land or sea class privileges,	(1) 20 hours of flight time, including 15 hours of flight training from an authorized instructor in a weight-shift-control aircraft and at least 5 hours of solo flight training in the areas of operation listed in §61.311,	(i) 2 hours of cross-country flight training; (ii) 10 takeoffs and landings to a full stop (with each landing involving a flight in the traffic pattern) at an airport, (iii) One solo cross-country flight of at least 50 nautical miles total distance, with a full-stop landing at a minimum of two points, and one segment of the flight consisting of a straight-line distance of at least 25 nautical miles between takeoff and landing locations, and (iv) 2 hours of flight training with an authorized instructor on those areas of operation specified in §61.311 in preparation for the practical test within the preceding 2 calendar months from the month of the test.

[Docket No. FAA–2001–11133, 69 FR 44869, July 27, 2004; Amdt. 61–124A, 74 FR 53647, Oct. 20, 2009; Amdt. 61–125, 75 FR 5221, Feb. 1, 2010; Docket No. FAA–2022–1355, Amdt. No. 61–151, 87 FR 75845, Dec. 9, 2022]

§61.315 What are the privileges and limits of my sport pilot certificate?

(a) If you hold a sport pilot certificate you may act as pilot in command of a light-sport aircraft, except as specified in paragraph (c) of this section.

(b) You may share the operating expenses of a flight with a passenger, provided the expenses involve only fuel, oil, airport expenses, or aircraft rental fees. You must pay at least half the operating expenses of the flight.

(c) You may not act as pilot in command of a light-sport aircraft:

(1) That is carrying a passenger or property for compensation or hire.
(2) For compensation or hire.
(3) In furtherance of a business.
(4) While carrying more than one passenger.
(5) At night.
(6) In Class A airspace.
(7) In Class B, C, and D airspace, at an airport located in Class B, C, or D airspace, and to, from, through, or at an airport having an operational control tower unless you have met the requirements specified in §61.325.

(8) Outside the United States, unless you have prior authorization from the country in which you seek to operate. Your sport pilot certificate carries the limit "Holder does not meet ICAO requirements."

(9) To demonstrate the aircraft in flight to a prospective buyer if you are an aircraft salesperson.

(10) In a passenger-carrying airlift sponsored by a charitable organization.

(11) At an altitude of more than 10,000 feet MSL or 2,000 feet AGL, whichever is higher.

(12) When the flight or surface visibility is less than 3 statute miles.

(13) Without visual reference to the surface.

(14) If the aircraft:

(i) Has a V_H greater than 87 knots CAS, unless you have met the requirements of §61.327(b).

(ii) Has a V_H less than or equal to 87 knots CAS, unless you have met the requirements of §61.327(a) or have logged flight time as pilot in command of an airplane with a V_H less than or equal to 87 knots CAS before April 2, 2010.

(15) Contrary to any operating limitation placed on the airworthiness certificate of the aircraft being flown.

(16) Contrary to any limit on your pilot certificate or airman medical certificate, or any other limit or endorsement from an authorized instructor.

(17) Contrary to any restriction or limitation on your U.S. driver's license or any restriction or limitation imposed by judicial or administrative order when using your driver's license to satisfy a requirement of this part.

(18) While towing any object.

(19) As a pilot flight crewmember on any aircraft for which more than one pilot is required by the type certificate of the aircraft or the regulations under which the flight is conducted.

[Docket No. FAA–2001–11133, 69 FR 44869, July 27, 2004; as amended by Amdt. 61–125, 75 FR 5221, Feb. 1, 2010; Amdt. 61–125A, 75 FR 15610, March 30, 2010]

§61.317 Is my sport pilot certificate issued with aircraft category and class ratings?

Your sport pilot certificate does not list aircraft category and class ratings. When you successfully pass the practical test for a sport pilot certificate, regardless of the light-sport aircraft privileges you seek, the FAA will issue you a sport pilot certificate without any category and class ratings. The FAA will provide you with a logbook endorsement for the category and class of aircraft in which you are authorized to act as pilot in command.

[Docket No. FAA–2001–11133, 69 FR 44869, July 27, 2004; as amended by Amdt. 61–125A, 75 FR 15610, March 30, 2010]

§61.319 [Reserved]

§61.321 How do I obtain privileges to operate an additional category or class of light-sport aircraft?

If you hold a sport pilot certificate and seek to operate an additional category or class of light-sport aircraft, you must—

(a) Receive a logbook endorsement from the authorized instructor who trained you on the applicable aeronautical knowledge areas specified in §61.309 and areas of operation specified in §61.311. The endorsement certifies you have met the aeronautical knowledge and flight proficiency requirements for the additional light-sport aircraft privilege you seek;

(b) Successfully complete a proficiency check from an authorized instructor, other than the instructor who trained you, consisting of the tasks in the appropriate areas of operation contained in the applicable Practical Test Standards (incorporated by reference, see §61.14) as listed in appendix A of this part for the additional light-sport aircraft privilege you seek;

(c) Complete an application for those privileges on a form and in a manner acceptable to the FAA and present this application to the authorized instructor who conducted the proficiency check specified in paragraph (b) of this section; and

(d) Receive a logbook endorsement from the instructor who conducted the proficiency check specified in paragraph (b) of this section certifying you are proficient in the applicable areas of operation and aeronautical knowledge areas, and that you are authorized for the additional category and class light-sport aircraft privilege.

[Docket No. FAA–2022–1463, Amdt. 61–153, 89 FR 22518, April 1, 2024]

§61.323 [Reserved]

§61.325 How do I obtain privileges to operate a light-sport aircraft at an airport within, or in airspace within, Class B, C, and D airspace, or in other airspace with an airport having an operational control tower?

If you hold a sport pilot certificate and seek privileges to operate a light-sport aircraft in Class B, C, or D airspace, at an airport located in Class B, C, or D airspace, or to, from, through, or at an airport having an operational control tower, you must receive and log ground and flight training. The authorized instructor who provides this training must provide a logbook endorsement that certifies you are proficient in the following aeronautical knowledge areas and areas of operation:

(a) The use of radios, communications, navigation system/facilities, and radar services.

(b) Operations at airports with an operating control tower to include three takeoffs and landings to a full stop, with each landing involving a flight in the traffic pattern, at an airport with an operating control tower.

(c) Applicable flight rules of part 91 of this chapter for operations in Class B, C, and D airspace and air traffic control clearances.

§61.327 Are there specific endorsement requirements to operate a light-sport aircraft based on V_H?

(a) Except as specified in paragraph (c) of this section, if you hold a sport pilot certificate and you seek to operate a light-sport aircraft that is an airplane with a V_H less than or equal to 87 knots CAS you must—

(1) Receive and log ground and flight training from an authorized instructor in an airplane that has a V_H less than or equal to 87 knots CAS; and

(2) Receive a logbook endorsement from the authorized instructor who provided the training specified in paragraph (a)(1) of this section certifying that you are proficient in the operation of light-sport aircraft that is an airplane with a V_H less than or equal to 87 knots CAS.

(b) If you hold a sport pilot certificate and you seek to operate a light-sport aircraft that has a V_H greater than 87 knots CAS you must—

(1) Receive and log ground and flight training from an authorized instructor in an aircraft that has a V_H greater than 87 knots CAS; and

(2) Receive a logbook endorsement from the authorized instructor who provided the training specified in paragraph (b)(1) of this section certifying that you are proficient in the operation of light-sport aircraft with a V_H greater than 87 knots CAS.

(c) The training and endorsements required by paragraph (a) of this section are not required if you have logged flight time as pilot in command of an airplane with a V_H less than or equal to 87 knots CAS prior to April 2, 2010.

[Docket No. FAA–2007–29015, 75 FR 5222, Feb. 1, 2010; Amdt. 61–125A, 75 FR 15610, March 30, 2010]

Subpart K—Flight Instructors With a Sport Pilot Rating

Source: Docket No. FAA–2001–11133, 69 FR 44875, July 27, 2004 unless otherwise noted.

§61.401 What is the purpose of this subpart?

(a) This part prescribes the following requirements that apply to a flight instructor certificate with a sport pilot rating:

(1) Eligibility.

(2) Aeronautical knowledge.

(3) Flight proficiency.

(4) Endorsements.

(5) Privileges and limits.

(b) Other provisions of this part apply to the logging of flight time and testing.

[Docket No. FAA–2001–11133, 69 FR 44875, July 27, 2004; as amended by Amdt. 61–125, 75 FR 5222, Feb. 1, 2010]

§61.403 What are the age, language, and pilot certificate requirements for a flight instructor certificate with a sport pilot rating?

To be eligible for a flight instructor certificate with a sport pilot rating you must:

(a) Be at least 18 years old.

(b) Be able to read, speak, write, and understand English. If you cannot read, speak, write, and understand English because of medical reasons, the FAA may place limits on your certificate as are necessary for the safe operation of light-sport aircraft.

(c) Hold at least a sport pilot certificate with category and class ratings or privileges, as applicable, that are appropriate to the flight instructor privileges sought.

[Docket No. FAA–2001–11133, 69 FR 44875, July 27, 2004; as amended by Amdt. 61–124, 74 FR 42562, Aug. 21, 2009]

§61.405 What tests do I have to take to obtain a flight instructor certificate with a sport pilot rating?

To obtain a flight instructor certificate with a sport pilot rating you must pass the following tests:

(a) *Knowledge test.* Before you take a knowledge test, you must receive a logbook endorsement certifying you are prepared for the test from an authorized instructor who trained you or evaluated your home-study course on the aeronautical knowledge areas listed in §61.407. You must pass knowledge tests on—

(1) The fundamentals of instructing listed in §61.407(a), unless you meet the requirements of §61.407(c); and

(2) The aeronautical knowledge areas for a sport pilot certificate applicable to the aircraft category and class for which flight instructor privileges are sought.

(b) *Practical test.*

(1) Before you take the practical test, you must—

(i) Receive a logbook endorsement from the authorized instructor who provided you with flight training on the areas of operation specified in §61.409 that apply to the category and class of aircraft privileges you seek. This endorsement certifies you meet the applicable aeronautical knowledge and experience requirements and are prepared for the practical test;

(ii) If you are seeking privileges to provide instruction in an airplane or glider, receive a logbook endorsement from an authorized instructor indicating that you are competent and possess instructional proficiency in stall awareness, spin entry, spins, and spin recovery procedures after you have received flight training in those training areas in an airplane or glider, as appropriate, that is certificated for spins;

(2) You must pass a practical test—

(i) On the areas of operation listed in §61.409 that are appropriate to the category and class of aircraft privileges you seek;

(ii) In an aircraft representative of the category and class of aircraft for the privileges you seek;

(iii) In which you demonstrate that you are able to teach stall awareness, spin entry, spins, and spin recovery procedures if you are seeking privileges to provide instruction in an airplane or glider. If you have not failed a practical test based on deficiencies in your ability to demonstrate knowledge or skill in these areas and you provide the endorsement required by paragraph (b)(1)(ii) of this section, an examiner may accept the endorsement instead of the demonstration required by this paragraph. If you are taking a test because you previously failed a test based on not meeting the requirements of this paragraph, you must pass a practical test on stall awareness, spin entry, spins, and spin recovery instructional competency and proficiency in the applicable category and class of aircraft that is certificated for spins.

§61.407 What aeronautical knowledge must I have to apply for a flight instructor certificate with a sport pilot rating?

(a) Except as specified in paragraph (c) of this section you must receive and log ground training from an authorized instructor on the fundamentals of instruction that includes:

(1) The learning process.
(2) Elements of effective teaching.
(3) Student evaluation and testing.
(4) Course development.
(5) Lesson planning.
(6) Classroom training techniques.

(b) You must receive and log ground training from an authorized instructor on the aeronautical knowledge areas applicable to a sport pilot certificate for the aircraft category and class in which you seek flight instructor privileges.

(c) You do not have to meet the requirements of paragraph (a) of this section if you—

(1) Hold a flight instructor certificate or ground instructor certificate issued under this part;

(2) Hold a teacher's certificate issued by a State, county, city, or municipality; or

(3) Are employed as a teacher at an accredited college or university.

[Docket No. FAA–2001–11133, 69 FR 44875, July 27, 2004; as amended by Amdt. 61–124, 74 FR 42562, Aug. 21, 2009]

§61.409 What flight proficiency requirements must I meet to apply for a flight instructor certificate with a sport pilot rating?

You must receive and log ground and flight training from an authorized instructor on the following areas of operation for the aircraft category and class in which you seek flight instructor privileges:

(a) Technical subject areas.
(b) Preflight preparation.
(c) Preflight lesson on a maneuver to be performed in flight.
(d) Preflight procedures.
(e) Airport, seaplane base, and gliderport operations, as applicable.
(f) Takeoffs (or launches), landings, and go-arounds.
(g) Fundamentals of flight.
(h) Performance maneuvers and for gliders, performance speeds.
(i) Ground reference maneuvers (except for gliders and lighter-than-air).
(j) Soaring techniques.
(k) Slow flight (not applicable to lighter-than-air and powered parachutes).
(l) Stalls (not applicable to lighter-than-air, powered parachutes, and gyroplanes).
(m) Spins (applicable to airplanes and gliders).
(n) Emergency operations.
(o) Tumble entry and avoidance techniques (applicable to weight-shift-control aircraft).
(p) Post-flight procedures.

§61.411 What aeronautical experience must I have to apply for a flight instructor certificate with a sport pilot rating?

Use the following table to determine the experience you must have for each aircraft category and class:

If you are applying for a flight instructor certificate with a sport pilot rating for...	Then you must log at least...	Which must include at least...
(a) Airplane category and single-engine class privileges,	(1) 150 hours of flight time as a pilot,	(i) 100 hours of flight time as pilot in command in powered aircraft, (ii) 50 hours of flight time in a single-engine airplane, (iii) 25 hours of cross-country flight time, (iv) 10 hours of cross-country flight time in a single-engine airplane, and (v) 15 hours of flight time as pilot in command in a single-engine airplane that is a light-sport aircraft.
(b) Glider category privileges,	(1) 25 hours of flight time as pilot in command in a glider, 100 flights in a glider, and 15 flights as pilot in command in a glider that is a light-sport aircraft, or (2) 100 hours in heavier-than-air aircraft, 20 flights in a glider, and 15 flights as pilot in command in a glider that is a light-sport aircraft.	
(c) Rotorcraft category and gyroplane class privileges,	(1) 125 hours of flight time as a pilot,	(i) 100 hours of flight time as pilot in command in powered aircraft, (ii) 50 hours of flight time in a gyroplane, (iii) 10 hours of cross-country flight time, (iv) 3 hours of cross-country flight time in a gyroplane, and (v) 15 hours of flight time as pilot in command in a gyroplane that is a light-sport aircraft.
(d) Lighter-than-air category and airship class privileges,	(1) 100 hours of flight time as a pilot,	(i) 40 hours of flight time in an airship, (ii) 20 hours of pilot in command time in an airship, (iii) 10 hours of cross-country flight time, (iv) 5 hours of cross-country flight time in an airship, and (v) 15 hours of flight time as pilot in command in an airship that is a light-sport aircraft.
(e) Lighter-than-air category and balloon class privileges,	(1) 35 hours of flight time as pilot-in-command,	(i) 20 hours of flight time in a balloon, (ii) 10 flights in a balloon, and (iii) 5 flights as pilot in command in a balloon that is a light-sport aircraft.
(f) Weight-shift-control aircraft category privileges,	(1) 150 hours of flight time as a pilot,	(i) 100 hours of flight time as pilot in command in powered aircraft, (ii) 50 hours of flight time in a weight-shift-control aircraft, (iii) 25 hours of cross-country flight time, (iv) 10 hours of cross-country flight time in a weight-shift-control aircraft, and (v) 15 hours of flight time as pilot in command in a weight-shift-control aircraft that is a light-sport aircraft.

(continued)

If you are applying for a flight instructor certificate with a sport pilot rating for...	Then you must log at least...	Which must include at least...
(g) Powered-parachute category privileges,	(1) 100 hours of flight time as a pilot,	(i) 75 hours of flight time as pilot in command in powered aircraft, (ii) 50 hours of flight time in a powered parachute, (iii) 15 hours of cross-country flight time, (iv) 5 hours of cross-country flight time in a powered parachute, and (v) 15 hours of flight time as pilot in command in a powered parachute that is a light-sport aircraft.

§61.412 Do I need additional training to provide instruction on control and maneuvering an airplane solely by reference to the instruments in a light-sport aircraft based on V_H?

To provide flight training under §61.93(e)(12) on control and maneuvering an airplane solely by reference to the flight instruments for the purpose of issuing a solo cross-country endorsement under §61.93(c)(1) to a student pilot seeking a sport pilot certificate, a flight instructor with a sport pilot rating must:

(a) Hold an endorsement required by §61.327(b);

(b) Receive and log a minimum of 1 hour of ground training and 3 hours of flight training from an authorized instructor in an airplane with a V_H greater than 87 knots CAS or in a full flight simulator, flight training device, or aviation training device that replicates an airplane with a V_H greater than 87 knots CAS; and

(c) Receive a one-time endorsement in his or her logbook from an instructor authorized under subpart H of this part who certifies that the person is proficient in providing training on control and maneuvering solely by reference to the flight instruments in an airplane with a V_H greater than 87 knots CAS. This flight training must include straight and level flight, turns, descents, climbs, use of radio navigation aids, and ATC directives.

[Amdt. 61–142, 83 FR 30280, June 27, 2018]

§61.413 What are the privileges of my flight instructor certificate with a sport pilot rating?

(a) If you hold a flight instructor certificate with a sport pilot rating, you are authorized, within the limits of your certificate and rating, to provide training and endorsements that are required for, and relate to—

(1) A student pilot seeking a sport pilot certificate;

(2) A sport pilot certificate;

(3) A flight instructor certificate with a sport pilot rating;

(4) A powered parachute or weight-shift-control aircraft rating;

(5) Sport pilot privileges;

(6) A flight review or operating privilege for a sport pilot;

(7) A practical test for a sport pilot certificate, a private pilot certificate with a powered parachute or weight-shift-control aircraft rating or a flight instructor certificate with a sport pilot rating;

(8) A knowledge test for a sport pilot certificate, a private pilot certificate with a powered parachute or weight-shift-control aircraft rating or a flight instructor certificate with a sport pilot rating; and

(9) A proficiency check for an additional category or class privilege for a sport pilot certificate or a flight instructor certificate with a sport pilot rating.

(b) A person who holds a flight instructor certificate with a sport pilot rating is authorized, in a form and manner acceptable to the Administrator, to:

(1) Accept an application for a student pilot certificate or, for an applicant who holds a pilot certificate (other than a student pilot certificate) issued under part 61 of this chapter and meets the flight review requirements specified in §61.56, a remote pilot certificate with a small UAS rating;

(2) Verify the identity of the applicant; and

(3) Verify that an applicant for a student pilot certificate meets the eligibility requirements in §61.83.

[Docket FAA–2010–1127, Amdt. 61–135, 81 FR 1307, Jan. 12, 2016, as amended by Docket FAA–2015–0150, Amdt. 61–137, 81 FR 42208, June 28, 2016]

§61.415 What are the limits of a flight instructor certificate with a sport pilot rating?

If you hold a flight instructor certificate with a sport pilot rating, you may only provide flight training in a light-sport aircraft and are subject to the following limits:

(a) You may not provide ground or flight training in any aircraft for which you do not hold:

(1) A sport pilot certificate with applicable category and class privileges or a pilot certificate with the applicable category and class rating; and

(2) Applicable category and class privileges for your flight instructor certificate with a sport pilot rating.

(b) You may not provide ground or flight training for a private pilot certificate with a powered parachute or weight-shift-control aircraft rating unless you hold:

(1) At least a private pilot certificate with the applicable category and class rating; and

(2) Applicable category and class privileges for your flight instructor certificate with a sport pilot rating.

(c) You may not conduct more than 8 hours of flight training in any 24-consecutive-hour period.

(d) You may not endorse a:

(1) Student pilot's logbook for solo flight privileges, unless you have—

(i) Given that student the flight training required for solo flight privileges required by this part; and

(ii) Determined that the student is prepared to conduct the flight safely under known circumstances, subject to any limitations listed in the student's logbook that you consider necessary for the safety of the flight.

(2) Student pilot's logbook for a solo cross-country flight, unless you have determined the student's flight preparation, planning, equipment, and proposed procedures are adequate for the proposed flight under the existing conditions and within any limitations listed in the logbook that you consider necessary for the safety of the flight.

(3) Student pilot's logbook for solo flight in Class B, C and D airspace areas, at an airport within Class B, C, or D airspace and to from, through or on an airport having an operational control tower, unless you have—

(i) Given that student ground and flight training in that airspace or at that airport; and

(ii) Determined that the student is proficient to operate the aircraft safely.

(4) Logbook of a pilot for a flight review, unless you have conducted a review of that pilot in accordance with the requirements of §61.56.

(e) You may not provide training to operate a light-sport aircraft in Class B, C, and D airspace, at an airport located in Class B, C, or D airspace, and to, from, through, or at an airport having an operational control tower, unless you have the endorsement specified in § 61.325, or are otherwise authorized to conduct operations in this airspace and at these airports.

(f) You may not provide training in a light-sport aircraft that is an airplane with a V_H less than or equal to 87 knots CAS unless you have the endorsement specified in §61.327(a), or are otherwise authorized to operate that light-sport aircraft.

(g) You may not provide training in a light-sport aircraft with a V_H greater than 87 knots CAS unless you have the endorsement specified in §61.327(b), or are otherwise authorized to operate that light-sport aircraft.

(h) You may not provide training on the control and maneuvering of an aircraft solely by reference to the instruments in a light sport airplane with a V_H greater than 87 knots CAS unless you meet the requirements in §61.412.

(i) You must perform all training in an aircraft that complies with the requirements of §91.109 of this chapter.

(j) If you provide flight training for a certificate, rating or privilege, you must provide that flight training in an aircraft that meets the following:

(1) The aircraft must have at least two pilot stations and be of the same category and class appropriate to the certificate, rating or privilege sought.

(2) For single place aircraft, pre-solo flight training must be provided in an aircraft that has two pilot stations and is of the same category and class appropriate to the certificate, rating, or privilege sought.

[Docket No. FAA–2001–11133, 69 FR 44875, July 27, 2004, as amended by Amdt. 61–125, 75 FR 5222, Feb. 1, 2010; Amdt. 61–125A, 75 FR 15610, March 30, 2010; Docket FAA–2010–1127, Amdt. 61–135, 81 FR 1307, Jan. 12, 2016; Amdt. 61–142, 83 FR 30280, June 27, 2018]

§61.417 Will my flight instructor certificate with a sport pilot rating list aircraft category and class ratings?

Your flight instructor certificate does not list aircraft category and class ratings. When you successfully pass the practical test for a flight instructor certificate with a sport pilot rating, regardless of the light-sport aircraft privileges you seek, the FAA will issue you a flight instructor certificate with a sport pilot rating without any category and class ratings. The FAA will provide you with a logbook endorsement for the category and class of light-sport aircraft you are authorized to provide training in.

§61.419 How do I obtain privileges to provide training in an additional category or class of light-sport aircraft?

If you hold a flight instructor certificate with a sport pilot rating and seek to provide training in an additional category or class of light-sport aircraft you must—

(a) Receive a logbook endorsement from the authorized instructor who trained you on the applicable areas of operation specified in §61.409 certifying you have met the aeronautical knowledge and flight proficiency requirements for the additional category and class flight instructor privilege you seek;

(b) Successfully complete a proficiency check from an authorized instructor, other than the instructor who trained you, consisting of the tasks in the appropriate areas of operation contained in the applicable Practical Test Standards (incorporated by reference, see §61.14) as listed in appendix A of this part for the additional category and class flight instructor privilege you seek;

(c) Complete an application for those privileges on a form and in a manner acceptable to the FAA and present this application to the authorized instructor who conducted the proficiency check specified in paragraph (b) of this section; and

(d) Receive a logbook endorsement from the instructor who conducted the proficiency check specified in paragraph (b) of this section certifying you are proficient in the areas of operation and authorized for the additional category and class flight instructor privilege.

[Docket No. FAA–2022–1463, Amdt. 61–153, 89 FR 22518, April 1, 2024]

§61.421 May I give myself an endorsement?

No. If you hold a flight instructor certificate with a sport pilot rating, you may not give yourself an endorsement for any certificate, privilege, rating, flight review, authorization, practical test, knowledge test, or proficiency check required by this part.

§61.423 What are the recordkeeping requirements for a flight instructor with a sport pilot rating?

(a) As a flight instructor with a sport pilot rating you must:

(1) Sign the logbook of each person to whom you have given flight training or ground training.

(2) Keep a record of the name, date, and type of endorsement for:

(i) Each person whose logbook you have endorsed for solo flight privileges.

(ii) Each person for whom you have provided an endorsement for a knowledge test, practical test, or proficiency check, and the record must indicate the kind of test or check, and the results.

(iii) Each person whose logbook you have endorsed as proficient to operate—

(A) An additional category or class of light-sport aircraft;

(B) In Class B, C, and D airspace; at an airport located in Class B, C, or D airspace; and to, from,

through, or at an airport having an operational control tower;

(C) A light-sport aircraft that is an airplane with a V_H less than or equal to 87 knots CAS; and

(D) A light-sport aircraft with a V_H greater than 87 knots CAS.

(iv) Each person whose logbook you have endorsed as proficient to provide flight training in an additional category or class of light-sport aircraft.

(b) Within 10 days after providing an endorsement for a person to operate or provide training in an additional category and class of light-sport aircraft you must—

(1) Complete, sign, and submit to the FAA the application presented to you to obtain those privileges; and

(2) Retain a copy of the form.

(c) You must keep the records listed in this section for 3 years. You may keep these records in a logbook or a separate document.

[Docket No. FAA–2001–11133, 69 FR 44875, July 27, 2004, as amended by Amdt. 61–125, 75 FR 5222, Feb. 1, 2010; Amdt. 61–125A, 75 FR 15610, March 30, 2010; Docket FAA–2010–1127, Amdt. 61–135, 81 FR 1307, Jan. 12, 2016]

§61.425 How do I renew my flight instructor certificate?

If you hold a flight instructor certificate with a sport pilot rating you may renew your certificate in accordance with the provisions of §61.197.

§61.427 What must I do if my flight instructor certificate with a sport pilot rating expires?

You may exchange your expired flight instructor certificate with a sport pilot rating for a new certificate with a sport pilot rating and any other rating on that certificate by passing a practical test as prescribed in §61.405(b) or §61.183(h) for one of the ratings listed on the expired flight instructor certificate. The FAA will reinstate any privilege authorized by the expired certificate.

§61.429 May I exercise the privileges of a flight instructor certificate with a sport pilot rating if I hold a flight instructor certificate with another rating?

If you hold a flight instructor certificate, a commercial pilot certificate with an airship rating, or a commercial pilot certificate with a balloon rating issued under this part, and you seek to exercise the privileges of a flight instructor certificate with a sport pilot rating, you may do so without any further showing of proficiency, subject to the following limits:

(a) You are limited to the aircraft category and class ratings listed on your flight instructor certificate, commercial pilot certificate with an airship rating, or commercial pilot certificate with a balloon rating, as appropriate, when exercising your flight instructor privileges and the privileges specified in §61.413.

(b) You must comply with the limits specified in §61.415 and the recordkeeping requirements of §61.423.

(c) If you want to exercise the privileges of your flight instructor certificate in a category or class of light-sport aircraft for which you are not currently rated, you must meet all applicable requirements to provide training in an additional category or class of light-sport aircraft specified in §61.419.

[Docket No. FAA–2001–11133, 69 FR 44875, July 27, 2004; as amended by Amdt. 61–124, 74 FR 42562, Aug. 21, 2009; Amdt. 61–125, 75 FR 5222, Feb. 1, 2010]

APPENDIX A TO PART 61
AIRMAN CERTIFICATION STANDARDS AND PRACTICAL TEST STANDARDS

If you are seeking this certificate, rating, and/or privilege...	Then this ACS/PTS (incorporated by reference, see §61.14) is applicable:
Airline Transport Pilot Certificate; Airplane Category—Single-Engine Land Rating, Airplane Category—Single-Engine Sea Rating, Airplane Category—Multiengine Land Rating, Airplane Category—Multiengine Sea Rating.	FAA-S-ACS-11A, Airline Transport Pilot and Type Rating for Airplane Category Airman Certification Standards, November 2023.
Airline Transport Pilot Certificate; Rotorcraft Category—Helicopter Rating.	FAA-S-8081-20A, Airline Transport Pilot and Aircraft Type Rating Practical Test Standards for Rotorcraft Category Helicopter Rating, November 2023.
Airline Transport Pilot Certificate; Powered-Lift Category	FAA-S-ACS-17, Airline Transport Pilot and Type Rating for Powered-Lift Category Airman Certification Standards, November 2023.
Commercial Pilot Certificate; Airplane Category—Single-Engine Land Rating, Airplane Category—Single-Engine Sea Rating, Airplane Category—Multiengine Land Rating, Airplane Category—Multiengine Sea Rating.	FAA-S-ACS-7B, Commercial Pilot for Airplane Category Airman Certification Standards, November 2023.
Commercial Pilot Certificate; Rotorcraft Category—Helicopter Rating	FAA-S-ACS-16, Commercial Pilot for Rotorcraft Category Helicopter Rating Airman Certification Standards, November 2023.
Commercial Pilot Certificate; Rotorcraft Category—Gyroplane Rating	FAA-S-8081-16C, Commercial Pilot Practical Test Standards for Rotorcraft Category Gyroplane Rating, November 2023.
Commercial Pilot Certificate; Powered-Lift Category	FAA-S-ACS-2, Commercial Pilot for Powered-Lift Category Airman Certification Standards, November 2023.
Commercial Pilot Certificate; Glider Category	FAA-S-8081-23B, Commercial Pilot Practical Test Standards for Glider Category, November 2023.
Commercial Pilot Certificate; Lighter-Than-Air Category—Airship Rating, Lighter-Than-Air Category—Balloon Rating.	FAA-S-8081-18A, Commercial Pilot Practical Test Standards for Lighter-Than-Air Category, November 2023.
Private Pilot Certificate; Airplane Category—Single-Engine Land Rating, Airplane Category—Single-Engine Sea Rating, Airplane Category— Multiengine Land Rating, Airplane Category—Multiengine Sea Rating.	FAA-S-ACS-6C, Private Pilot for Airplane Category Airman Certification Standards, November 2023.
Private Pilot Certificate; Rotorcraft Category—Helicopter Rating	FAA-S-ACS-15, Private Pilot for Rotorcraft Category Helicopter Rating Airman Certification Standards, November 2023.

(continued)

If you are seeking this certificate, rating, and/or privilege...	Then this ACS/PTS (incorporated by reference, see §61.14) is applicable:
Private Pilot Certificate; Rotorcraft Category—Gyroplane Rating	FAA-S-8081-15B, Private Pilot Practical Test Standards for Rotorcraft Category Gyroplane Rating, November 2023.
Private Pilot Certificate; Powered-Lift Category	FAA-S-ACS-13, Private Pilot for Powered-Lift Category Airman Certification Standards, November 2023.
Private Pilot Certificate; Glider Category	FAA-S-8081-22A, Private Pilot Practical Test Standards for Glider Category, November 2023.
Private Pilot Certificate; Lighter-Than-Air Category—Airship Rating, Lighter-Than-Air Category—Balloon Rating.	FAA-S-8081-17A, Private Pilot Practical Test Standards for Lighter-Than-Air Category, November 2023.
Private Pilot Certificate; Powered Parachute Category—Land Rating, Powered Parachute Category—Sea Rating, Weight-Shift-Control Aircraft Category—Land Rating, Weight-Shift-Control Aircraft Category—Sea Rating.	FAA-S-8081-32A, Private Pilot Practical Test Standards for Powered Parachute Category and Weight-Shift-Control Category, November 2023.
Recreational Pilot Certificate; Airplane Category—Single-Engine Land Rating, Airplane Category—Single-Engine Sea Rating, Rotorcraft Category—Helicopter Rating, Rotorcraft Category—Gyroplane Rating.	FAA-S-8081-3B, Recreational Pilot Practical Test Standards for Airplane Category and Rotorcraft Category, November 2023.
Sport Pilot Certificate; Airplane Category—Single-Engine Land Privileges, Airplane Category—Single-Engine Sea Privileges, Rotorcraft Category—Gyroplane Privileges, Glider Category.	FAA-S-8081-29A, Sport Pilot and Sport Pilot Flight Instructor Rating Practical Test Standards for Airplane Category, Rotorcraft Category, and Glider Category, November 2023.
Flight Instructor Certificate with a Sport Pilot Rating; Airplane Category—Single-Engine Privileges, Rotorcraft Category—Gyroplane Privileges, Glider Category.	
Sport Pilot Certificate; Lighter-Than-Air Category—Airship Privileges, Lighter-Than-Air Category—Balloon Privileges.	FAA-S-8081-30A, Sport Pilot and Sport Pilot Flight Instructor Rating Practical Test Standards for Lighter-Than-Air Category, November 2023.
Flight Instructor Certificate with a Sport Pilot Rating; Lighter-Than-Air Category—Airship Privileges, Lighter-Than-Air Category—Balloon Privileges.	
Sport Pilot Certificate; Powered Parachute Category—Land Privileges, Powered Parachute Category—Sea Privileges, Weight-Shift-Control Aircraft Category—Land Privileges, Weight-Shift-Control Aircraft Category—Sea Privileges.	FAA-S-8081-31A, Sport Pilot and Sport Pilot Flight Instructor Rating Practical Test Standards for Powered Parachute Category and Weight-Shift-Control Category, November 2023.
Flight Instructor Certificate with a Sport Pilot Rating; Powered Parachute Category Privileges, Weight-Shift-Control Aircraft Category Privileges.	
Instrument Rating—Airplane, Instrument Proficiency Check—Airplane	FAA-S-ACS-8C, Instrument Rating—Airplane Airman Certification Standards, November 2023.
Instrument Rating—Helicopter, Instrument Proficiency Check—Helicopter.	FAA-S-ACS-14, Instrument Rating—Helicopter Airman Certification Standards, November 2023.
Instrument Rating—Powered-Lift, Instrument Proficiency Check—Powered-Lift.	FAA-S-ACS-3, Instrument Rating—Powered-Lift Airman Certification Standards, November 2023.

(continued)

If you are seeking this certificate, rating, and/or privilege...	Then this ACS/PTS (incorporated by reference, see §61.14) is applicable:
Flight Instructor Certificate; Airplane Category—Single Engine Rating, Airplane Category—Multiengine Rating.	FAA-S-ACS-25, Flight Instructor for Airplane Category Airman Certification Standards, November 2023.
Flight Instructor Certificate; Rotorcraft Category—Helicopter Rating	FAA-S-ACS-29, Flight Instructor for Rotorcraft Category Helicopter Rating Airman Certification Standards, November 2023.
Flight Instructor Certificate; Rotorcraft Category—Gyroplane Rating	FAA-S-8081-7C, Flight Instructor Practical Test Standards for Rotorcraft Category Gyroplane Rating, November 2023.
Flight Instructor Certificate; Powered-lift Category	FAA-S-ACS-27, Flight Instructor for Powered-Lift Category Airman Certification Standards, November 2023.
Flight Instructor Certificate; Glider Category	FAA-S-8081-8C, Flight Instructor Practical Test Standards for Glider Category, November 2023.
Flight Instructor Certificate; Instrument—Airplane Rating, Instrument—Helicopter Rating.	FAA-S-8081-9E, Flight Instructor Instrument Practical Test Standards for Airplane Rating and Helicopter Rating, November 2023.
Flight Instructor Certificate; Instrument—Powered-Lift Rating	FAA-S-ACS-28, Flight Instructor—Instrument Rating Powered-Lift Airman Certification Standards, November 2023.
Aircraft Type Rating—Airplane	FAA-S-ACS-11A, Airline Transport Pilot and Type Rating for Airplane Category Airman Certification Standards, November 2023.
Aircraft Type Rating—Helicopter	FAA-S-8081-20A, Airline Transport Pilot and Aircraft Type Rating Practical Test Standards for Rotorcraft Category Helicopter Rating, November 2023.
Aircraft Type Rating—Powered-Lift	FAA-S-ACS-17, Airline Transport Pilot and Type Rating for Powered-Lift Category Airman Certification Standards, November 2023.
Pilot-in-Command Proficiency Check—Airplane	FAA-S-ACS-11A, Airline Transport Pilot and Type Rating for Airplane Category Airman Certification Standards; November 2023
Pilot-in-Command Proficiency Check—Helicopter	FAA-S-8081-20A, Airline Transport Pilot and Aircraft Type Rating Practical Test Standards for Rotorcraft Category Helicopter Rating, November 2023.
Pilot-in-Command Proficiency Check—Powered-Lift	FAA-S-ACS-17, Airline Transport Pilot and Type Rating for Powered-Lift Category Airman Certification Standards, November 2023.

[Docket No. FAA–2022–1463, Amdt. 61–153, 89 FR 22518, April 1, 2024]

PART 67
MEDICAL STANDARDS AND CERTIFICATION

Authority: 49 U.S.C. 106(g), 40113, 44701–44703, 44707, 44709–44711, 45102–45103, 45301–45303.

Source: Docket No. 27940, 61 FR 11256, March 19, 1996, unless otherwise noted.

Subpart A—General

§67.1 Applicability.
This part prescribes the medical standards and certification procedures for issuing medical certificates for airmen and for remaining eligible for a medical certificate.

§67.3 Issue.
A person who meets the medical standards prescribed in this part, based on medical examination and evaluation of the person's history and condition, is entitled to an appropriate medical certificate.

[Docket No. FAA–2007–27812, 73 FR 43065, July 24, 2008]

§67.4 Application.
An applicant for first-, second- and third-class medical certification must:

(a) Apply on a form and in a manner prescribed by the Administrator;

(b) Be examined by an aviation medical examiner designated in accordance with part 183 of this chapter. An applicant may obtain a list of aviation medical examiners from the FAA Office of Aerospace Medicine homepage on the FAA Web site, from any FAA Regional Flight Surgeon, or by contacting the Manager of the Aerospace Medical Education Division, P.O. Box 25082, Oklahoma City, Oklahoma 73125.

(c) Show proof of age and identity by presenting a government-issued photo identification (such as a valid U.S. driver's license, identification card issued by a driver's license authority, military identification, or passport). If an applicant does not have government-issued identification, he or she may use non-photo, government-issued identification (such as a birth certificate or voter registration card) in conjunction with photo identification (such as a work identification card or a student identification card).

[Docket No. FAA–2007–27812, 73 FR 43065, July 24, 2008, as amended by Docket No. FAA–2022–1355, Amdt. No. 67–22, 87 FR 75845, Dec. 9, 2022]

§67.7 Access to the National Driver Register.

At the time of application for a certificate issued under this part, each person who applies for a medical certificate shall execute an express consent form authorizing the Administrator to request the chief driver licensing official of any state designated by the Administrator to transmit information contained in the National Driver Register about the person to the Administrator. The Administrator shall make information received from the National Driver Register, if any, available on request to the person for review and written comment.

Subpart B— First-Class Airman Medical Certificate

§67.101 Eligibility.

To be eligible for a first-class airman medical certificate, and to remain eligible for a first-class airman medical certificate, a person must meet the requirements of this subpart.

§67.103 Eye.

Eye standards for a first-class airman medical certificate are:

(a) Distant visual acuity of 20/20 or better in each eye separately, with or without corrective lenses. If corrective lenses (spectacles or contact lenses) are necessary for 20/20 vision, the person may be eligible only on the condition that corrective lenses are worn while exercising the privileges of an airman certificate.

(b) Near vision of 20/40 or better, Snellen equivalent, at 16 inches in each eye separately, with or without corrective lenses. If age 50 or older, near vision of 20/40 or better, Snellen equivalent, at both 16 inches and 32 inches in each eye separately, with or without corrective lenses.

(c) Ability to perceive those colors necessary for the safe performance of airman duties.

(d) Normal fields of vision.

(e) No acute or chronic pathological condition of either eye or adnexa that interferes with the proper function of an eye, that may reasonably be expected to progress to that degree, or that may reasonably be expected to be aggravated by flying.

(f) Bifoveal fixation and vergence-phoria relationship sufficient to prevent a break in fusion under conditions that may reasonably be expected to occur in performing airman duties. Tests for the factors named in this paragraph are not required except for persons found to have more than 1 prism diopter of hyperphoria, 6 prism diopters

of esophoria, or 6 prism diopters of exophoria. If any of these values are exceeded, the Federal Air Surgeon may require the person to be examined by a qualified eye specialist to determine if there is bifoveal fixation and an adequate vergence-phoria relationship. However, if otherwise eligible, the person is issued a medical certificate pending the results of the examination.

§67.105 Ear, nose, throat, and equilibrium.

Ear, nose, throat, and equilibrium standards for a first-class airman medical certificate are:

(a) The person shall demonstrate acceptable hearing by at least one of the following tests:

(1) Demonstrate an ability to hear an average conversational voice in a quiet room, using both ears, at a distance of 6 feet from the examiner, with the back turned to the examiner.

(2) Demonstrate an acceptable understanding of speech as determined by audiometric speech discrimination testing to a score of at least 70 percent obtained in one ear or in a sound field environment.

(3) Provide acceptable results of pure tone audiometric testing of unaided hearing acuity according to the following table of worst acceptable thresholds, using the calibration standards of the American National Standards Institute, 1969 (11 West 42d Street, New York, NY 10036):

Frequency (Hz)	500 Hz	1000 Hz	2000 Hz	3000 Hz
Better ear (Db)	35	30	30	40
Poorer ear (Db)	35	50	50	60

(b) No disease or condition of the middle or internal ear, nose, oral cavity, pharynx, or larynx that—

(1) Interferes with, or is aggravated by, flying or may reasonably be expected to do so; or

(2) Interferes with, or may reasonably be expected to interfere with, clear and effective speech communication.

(c) No disease or condition manifested by, or that may reasonably be expected to be manifested by, vertigo or a disturbance of equilibrium.

§67.107 Mental.

Mental standards for a first-class airman medical certificate are:

(a) No established medical history or clinical diagnosis of any of the following:

(1) A personality disorder that is severe enough to have repeatedly manifested itself by overt acts.

(2) A psychosis. As used in this section, "psychosis" refers to a mental disorder in which:

(i) The individual has manifested delusions, hallucinations, grossly bizarre or disorganized

behavior, or other commonly accepted symptoms of this condition; or

(ii) The individual may reasonably be expected to manifest delusions, hallucinations, grossly bizarre or disorganized behavior, or other commonly accepted symptoms of this condition.

(3) A bipolar disorder.

(4) Substance dependence, except where there is established clinical evidence, satisfactory to the Federal Air Surgeon, of recovery, including sustained total abstinence from the substance(s) for not less than the preceding 2 years. As used in this section—

(i) "Substance" includes: Alcohol; other sedatives and hypnotics; anxiolytics; opioids; central nervous system stimulants such as cocaine, amphetamines, and similarly acting sympathomimetics; hallucinogens; phencyclidine or similarly acting arylcyclohexylamines; cannabis; inhalants; and other psychoactive drugs and chemicals; and

(ii) "Substance dependence" means a condition in which a person is dependent on a substance, other than tobacco or ordinary xanthine-containing (e.g., caffeine) beverages, as evidenced by—

(A) Increased tolerance;

(B) Manifestation of withdrawal symptoms;

(C) Impaired control of use; or

(D) Continued use despite damage to physical health or impairment of social, personal, or occupational functioning.

(b) No substance abuse within the preceding 2 years defined as:

(1) Use of a substance in a situation in which that use was physically hazardous, if there has been at any other time an instance of the use of a substance also in a situation in which that use was physically hazardous;

(2) A verified positive drug test result, an alcohol test result of 0.04 or greater alcohol concentration, or a refusal to submit to a drug or alcohol test required by the U.S. Department of Transportation or an agency of the U.S. Department of Transportation; or

(3) Misuse of a substance that the Federal Air Surgeon, based on case history and appropriate, qualified medical judgment relating to the substance involved, finds—

(i) Makes the person unable to safely perform the duties or exercise the privileges of the airman certificate applied for or held; or

(ii) May reasonably be expected, for the maximum duration of the airman medical certificate applied for or held, to make the person unable to perform those duties or exercise those privileges.

(c) No other personality disorder, neurosis, or other mental condition that the Federal Air Surgeon, based on the case history and appropriate, qualified medical judgment relating to the condition involved, finds—

(1) Makes the person unable to safely perform the duties or exercise the privileges of the airman certificate applied for or held; or

(2) May reasonably be expected, for the maximum duration of the airman medical certificate applied for or held, to make the person unable to perform those duties or exercise those privileges.

[Docket No. 27940, 61 FR 11256, March 19, 1996; as amended by Amdt. 67–19, 71 FR 35764, June 21, 2006]

§67.109 Neurologic.

Neurologic standards for a first-class airman medical certificate are:

(a) No established medical history or clinical diagnosis of any of the following:

(1) Epilepsy;

(2) A disturbance of consciousness without satisfactory medical explanation of the cause; or

(3) A transient loss of control of nervous system function(s) without satisfactory medical explanation of the cause.

(b) No other seizure disorder, disturbance of consciousness, or neurologic condition that the Federal Air Surgeon, based on the case history and appropriate, qualified medical judgment relating to the condition involved, finds—

(1) Makes the person unable to safely perform the duties or exercise the privileges of the airman certificate applied for or held; or

(2) May reasonably be expected, for the maximum duration of the airman medical certificate applied for or held, to make the person unable to perform those duties or exercise those privileges.

§67.111 Cardiovascular.

Cardiovascular standards for a first-class airman medical certificate are:

(a) No established medical history or clinical diagnosis of any of the following:

(1) Myocardial infarction;

(2) Angina pectoris;

(3) Coronary heart disease that has required treatment or, if untreated, that has been symptomatic or clinically significant;

(4) Cardiac valve replacement;

(5) Permanent cardiac pacemaker implantation; or

(6) Heart replacement;

(b) A person applying for first-class medical certification must demonstrate an absence of myocardial infarction and other clinically significant abnormality on electrocardiographic examination:

(1) At the first application after reaching the 35th birthday; and

(2) On an annual basis after reaching the 40th birthday.

(c) An electrocardiogram will satisfy a requirement of paragraph (b) of this section if it is dated no earlier than 60 days before the date of the application it is to accompany and was performed and transmitted according to acceptable standards and techniques.

§67.113 General medical condition.

The general medical standards for a first-class airman medical certificate are:

(a) No established medical history or clinical diagnosis of diabetes mellitus that requires insulin or any other hypoglycemic drug for control.

(b) No other organic, functional, or structural disease, defect, or limitation that the Federal Air Surgeon, based on the case history and appropriate, qualified medical judgment relating to the condition involved, finds—

(1) Makes the person unable to safely perform the duties or exercise the privileges of the airman certificate applied for or held; or

(2) May reasonably be expected, for the maximum duration of the airman medical certificate applied for or held, to make the person unable to perform those duties or exercise those privileges.

(c) No medication or other treatment that the Federal Air Surgeon, based on the case history and appropriate, qualified medical judgment relating to the medication or other treatment involved, finds—

(1) Makes the person unable to safely perform the duties or exercise the privileges of the airman certificate applied for or held; or

(2) May reasonably be expected, for the maximum duration of the airman medical certificate applied for or held, to make the person unable to perform those duties or exercise those privileges.

§67.115 Discretionary issuance.

A person who does not meet the provisions of §§67.103 through 67.113 may apply for the discretionary issuance of a certificate under §67.401.

Subpart C—
Second-Class Airman
Medical Certificate

§67.201 Eligibility.

To be eligible for a second-class airman medical certificate, and to remain eligible for a second-class airman medical certificate, a person must meet the requirements of this subpart.

§67.203 Eye.

Eye standards for a second-class airman medical certificate are:

(a) Distant visual acuity of 20/20 or better in each eye separately, with or without corrective lenses. If corrective lenses (spectacles or contact lenses) are necessary for 20/20 vision, the person may be eligible only on the condition that corrective lenses are worn while exercising the privileges of an airman certificate.

(b) Near vision of 20/40 or better, Snellen equivalent, at 16 inches in each eye separately, with or without corrective lenses. If age 50 or older, near vision of 20/40 or better, Snellen equivalent, at both 16 inches and 32 inches in each eye separately, with or without corrective lenses.

(c) Ability to perceive those colors necessary for the safe performance of airman duties.

(d) Normal fields of vision.

(e) No acute or chronic pathological condition of either eye or adnexa that interferes with the proper function of an eye, that may reasonably be expected to progress to that degree, or that may reasonably be expected to be aggravated by flying.

(f) Bifoveal fixation and vergence-phoria relationship sufficient to prevent a break in fusion under conditions that may reasonably be expected to occur in performing airman duties. Tests for the factors named in this paragraph are not required except for persons found to have more than 1 prism diopter of hyperphoria, 6 prism diopters of esophoria, or 6 prism diopters of exophoria. If any of these values are exceeded, the Federal Air Surgeon may require the person to be examined by a qualified eye specialist to determine if there is bifoveal fixation and an adequate vergence-phoria relationship. However, if otherwise eligible, the person is issued a medical certificate pending the results of the examination.

§67.205 Ear, nose, throat, and equilibrium.

Ear, nose, throat, and equilibrium standards for a second-class airman medical certificate are:

(a) The person shall demonstrate acceptable hearing by at least one of the following tests:

(1) Demonstrate an ability to hear an average conversational voice in a quiet room, using both ears, at a distance of 6 feet from the examiner, with the back turned to the examiner.

(2) Demonstrate an acceptable understanding of speech as determined by audiometric speech discrimination testing to a score of at least 70 percent obtained in one ear or in a sound field environment.

(3) Provide acceptable results of pure tone audiometric testing of unaided hearing acuity according to the following table of worst acceptable thresholds, using the calibration standards of the American National Standards Institute, 1969:

Frequency (Hz)	500 Hz	1000 Hz	2000 Hz	3000 Hz
Better ear (Db)	35	30	30	40
Poorer ear (Db)	35	50	50	60

(b) No disease or condition of the middle or internal ear, nose, oral cavity, pharynx, or larynx that—

(1) Interferes with, or is aggravated by, flying or may reasonably be expected to do so; or

(2) Interferes with, or may reasonably be expected to interfere with, clear and effective speech communication.

(c) No disease or condition manifested by, or that may reasonably be expected to be manifested by, vertigo or a disturbance of equilibrium.

§67.207 Mental.

Mental standards for a second-class airman medical certificate are:

(a) No established medical history or clinical diagnosis of any of the following:

(1) A personality disorder that is severe enough to have repeatedly manifested itself by overt acts.

(2) A psychosis. As used in this section, "psychosis" refers to a mental disorder in which:

(i) The individual has manifested delusions, hallucinations, grossly bizarre or disorganized behavior, or other commonly accepted symptoms of this condition; or

(ii) The individual may reasonably be expected to manifest delusions, hallucinations, grossly bizarre or disorganized behavior, or other commonly accepted symptoms of this condition.

(3) A bipolar disorder.

(4) Substance dependence, except where there is established clinical evidence, satisfactory to the Federal Air Surgeon, of recovery, including sustained total abstinence from the substance(s) for not less than the preceding 2 years. As used in this section—

(i) "Substance" includes: Alcohol; other sedatives and hypnotics; anxiolytics; opioids; central nervous system stimulants such as cocaine, amphetamines, and similarly acting sympathomimetics; hallucinogens; phencyclidine or similarly acting arylcyclohexylamines; cannabis; inhalants; and other psychoactive drugs and chemicals; and

(ii) "Substance dependence" means a condition in which a person is dependent on a substance, other than tobacco or ordinary xanthine-containing (e.g., caffeine) beverages, as evidenced by—

(A) Increased tolerance;

(B) Manifestation of withdrawal symptoms;

(C) Impaired control of use; or

(D) Continued use despite damage to physical health or impairment of social, personal, or occupational functioning.

(b) No substance abuse within the preceding 2 years defined as:

(1) Use of a substance in a situation in which that use was physically hazardous, if there has been at any other time an instance of the use of a substance also in a situation in which that use was physically hazardous;

(2) A verified positive drug test result, an alcohol test result of 0.04 or greater alcohol concentration, or a refusal to submit to a drug or alcohol test required by the U.S. Department of Transportation or an agency of the U.S. Department of Transportation; or

(3) Misuse of a substance that the Federal Air Surgeon, based on case history and appropriate, qualified medical judgment relating to the substance involved, finds—

(i) Makes the person unable to safely perform the duties or exercise the privileges of the airman certificate applied for or held; or

(ii) May reasonably be expected, for the maximum duration of the airman medical certificate applied for or held, to make the person unable to perform those duties or exercise those privileges.

(c) No other personality disorder, neurosis, or other mental condition that the Federal Air Surgeon, based on the case history and appropriate, qualified medical judgment relating to the condition involved, finds—

(1) Makes the person unable to safely perform the duties or exercise the privileges of the airman certificate applied for or held; or

(2) May reasonably be expected, for the maximum duration of the airman medical certificate applied for or held, to make the person unable to perform those duties or exercise those privileges.

[Docket No. 27940, 61 FR 11256, March 19, 1996; as amended by Amdt. 67–19, 71 FR 35764, June 21, 2006]

§67.209 Neurologic.

Neurologic standards for a second-class airman medical certificate are:

(a) No established medical history or clinical diagnosis of any of the following:

(1) Epilepsy;

(2) A disturbance of consciousness without satisfactory medical explanation of the cause; or

(3) A transient loss of control of nervous system function(s) without satisfactory medical explanation of the cause;

(b) No other seizure disorder, disturbance of consciousness, or neurologic condition that the Federal Air Surgeon, based on the case history and appropriate, qualified medical judgment relating to the condition involved, finds—

(1) Makes the person unable to safely perform the duties or exercise the privileges of the airman certificate applied for or held; or

(2) May reasonably be expected, for the maximum duration of the airman medical certificate applied for or held, to make the person unable to perform those duties or exercise those privileges.

§67.211 Cardiovascular.

Cardiovascular standards for a second-class medical certificate are no established medical history or clinical diagnosis of any of the following:

(a) Myocardial infarction;

(b) Angina pectoris;

(c) Coronary heart disease that has required treatment or, if untreated, that has been symptomatic or clinically significant;

(d) Cardiac valve replacement;

(e) Permanent cardiac pacemaker implantation; or

(f) Heart replacement.

§67.213 General medical condition.

The general medical standards for a second-class airman medical certificate are:

(a) No established medical history or clinical diagnosis of diabetes mellitus that requires insulin or any other hypoglycemic drug for control.

(b) No other organic, functional, or structural disease, defect, or limitation that the Federal Air Surgeon, based on the case history and appropriate, qualified medical judgment relating to the condition involved, finds—

(1) Makes the person unable to safely perform the duties or exercise the privileges of the airman certificate applied for or held; or

(2) May reasonably be expected, for the maximum duration of the airman medical certificate applied for or held, to make the person unable to perform those duties or exercise those privileges.

(c) No medication or other treatment that the Federal Air Surgeon, based on the case history and appropriate, qualified medical judgment relating to the medication or other treatment involved, finds—

(1) Makes the person unable to safely perform the duties or exercise the privileges of the airman certificate applied for or held; or

(2) May reasonably be expected, for the maximum duration of the airman medical certificate applied for or held, to make the person unable to perform those duties or exercise those privileges.

§67.215 Discretionary issuance.

A person who does not meet the provisions of §§67.203 through 67.213 may apply for the discretionary issuance of a certificate under §67.401.

Subpart D— Third-Class Airman Medical Certificate

§67.301 Eligibility.

To be eligible for a third-class airman medical certificate, or to remain eligible for a third-class airman medical certificate, a person must meet the requirements of this subpart.

§67.303 Eye.

Eye standards for a third-class airman medical certificate are:

(a) Distant visual acuity of 20/40 or better in each eye separately, with or without corrective lenses. If corrective lenses (spectacles or contact lenses) are necessary for 20/40 vision, the person may be eligible only on the condition that corrective lenses are worn while exercising the privileges of an airman certificate.

(b) Near vision of 20/40 or better, Snellen equivalent, at 16 inches in each eye separately, with or without corrective lenses.

(c) Ability to perceive those colors necessary for the safe performance of airman duties.

(d) No acute or chronic pathological condition of either eye or adnexa that interferes with the proper function of an eye, that may reasonably be expected to progress to that degree, or that may reasonably be expected to be aggravated by flying.

§67.305 Ear, nose, throat, and equilibrium.

Ear, nose, throat, and equilibrium standards for a third-class airman medical certificate are:

(a) The person shall demonstrate acceptable hearing by at least one of the following tests:

(1) Demonstrate an ability to hear an average conversational voice in a quiet room, using both ears, at a distance of 6 feet from the examiner, with the back turned to the examiner.

(2) Demonstrate an acceptable understanding of speech as determined by audiometric speech discrimination testing to a score of at least 70 percent obtained in one ear or in a sound field environment.

(3) Provide acceptable results of pure tone audiometric testing of unaided hearing acuity according to the following table of worst acceptable thresholds, using the calibration standards of the American National Standards Institute, 1969:

Frequency (Hz)	500 Hz	1000 Hz	2000 Hz	3000 Hz
Better ear (Db)	35	30	30	40
Poorer ear (Db)	35	50	50	60

(b) No disease or condition of the middle or internal ear, nose, oral cavity, pharynx, or larynx that—

(1) Interferes with, or is aggravated by, flying or may reasonably be expected to do so; or

(2) Interferes with clear and effective speech communication.

(c) No disease or condition manifested by, or that may reasonably be expected to be manifested by, vertigo or a disturbance of equilibrium.

§67.307 Mental.

Mental standards for a third-class airman medical certificate are:

(a) No established medical history or clinical diagnosis of any of the following:

(1) A personality disorder that is severe enough to have repeatedly manifested itself by overt acts.

(2) A psychosis. As used in this section, "psychosis" refers to a mental disorder in which—

(i) The individual has manifested delusions, hallucinations, grossly bizarre or disorganized behavior, or other commonly accepted symptoms of this condition; or

(ii) The individual may reasonably be expected to manifest delusions, hallucinations, grossly bizarre or disorganized behavior, or other commonly accepted symptoms of this condition.

(3) A bipolar disorder.

(4) Substance dependence, except where there is established clinical evidence, satisfactory to the Federal Air Surgeon, of recovery, including sustained total abstinence from the substance(s) for not less than the preceding 2 years. As used in this section—

(i) "Substance" includes: alcohol; other sedatives and hypnotics; anxiolytics; opioids; central nervous system stimulants such as cocaine, amphetamines, and similarly acting sympathomimetics; hallucinogens; phencyclidine or similarly acting arylcyclohexylamines; cannabis; inhalants; and other psychoactive drugs and chemicals; and

(ii) "Substance dependence" means a condition in which a person is dependent on a substance, other than tobacco or ordinary xanthine-containing (e.g., caffeine) beverages, as evidenced by—

(A) Increased tolerance;

(B) Manifestation of withdrawal symptoms;

(C) Impaired control of use; or

(D) Continued use despite damage to physical health or impairment of social, personal, or occupational functioning.

(b) No substance abuse within the preceding 2 years defined as:

(1) Use of a substance in a situation in which that use was physically hazardous, if there has been at any other time an instance of the use of a substance also in a situation in which that use was physically hazardous;

(2) A verified positive drug test result, an alcohol test result of 0.04 or greater alcohol concentration, or a refusal to submit to a drug or alcohol test required by the U.S. Department of Transportation or an agency of the U.S. Department of Transportation; or

(3) Misuse of a substance that the Federal Air Surgeon, based on case history and appropriate, qualified medical judgment relating to the substance involved, finds—

(i) Makes the person unable to safely perform the duties or exercise the privileges of the airman certificate applied for or held; or

(ii) May reasonably be expected, for the maximum duration of the airman medical certificate applied for or held, to make the person unable to perform those duties or exercise those privileges.

(c) No other personality disorder, neurosis, or other mental condition that the Federal Air Surgeon, based on the case history and appropriate, qualified medical judgment relating to the condition involved, finds—

(1) Makes the person unable to safely perform the duties or exercise the privileges of the airman certificate applied for or held; or

(2) May reasonably be expected, for the maximum duration of the airman medical certificate applied for or held, to make the person unable to perform those duties or exercise those privileges.

[Docket No. 27940, 61 FR 11256, March 19, 1996; as amended by Amdt. 67–19, 71 FR 35764, June 21, 2006]

§67.309 Neurologic.

Neurologic standards for a third-class airman medical certificate are:

(a) No established medical history or clinical diagnosis of any of the following:

(1) Epilepsy;

(2) A disturbance of consciousness without satisfactory medical explanation of the cause; or

(3) A transient loss of control of nervous system function(s) without satisfactory medical explanation of the cause.

(b) No other seizure disorder, disturbance of consciousness, or neurologic condition that the Federal Air Surgeon, based on the case history and appropriate, qualified medical judgment relating to the condition involved, finds—

(1) Makes the person unable to safely perform the duties or exercise the privileges of the airman certificate applied for or held; or

(2) May reasonably be expected, for the maximum duration of the airman medical certificate applied for or held, to make the person unable to perform those duties or exercise those privileges.

§67.311 Cardiovascular.

Cardiovascular standards for a third-class airman medical certificate are no established medical history or clinical diagnosis of any of the following:

(a) Myocardial infarction;

(b) Angina pectoris;

(c) Coronary heart disease that has required treatment or, if untreated, that has been symptomatic or clinically significant;

(d) Cardiac valve replacement;

(e) Permanent cardiac pacemaker implantation; or

(f) Heart replacement.

§67.313 General medical condition.

The general medical standards for a third-class airman medical certificate are:

(a) No established medical history or clinical diagnosis of diabetes mellitus that requires insulin or any other hypoglycemic drug for control.

(b) No other organic, functional, or structural disease, defect, or limitation that the Federal Air Surgeon, based on the case history and appropriate, qualified medical judgment relating to the condition involved, finds—

(1) Makes the person unable to safely perform the duties or exercise the privileges of the airman certificate applied for or held; or

(2) May reasonably be expected, for the maximum duration of the airman medical certificate applied for or held, to make the person unable to perform those duties or exercise those privileges.

(c) No medication or other treatment that the Federal Air Surgeon, based on the case history and appropriate, qualified medical judgment relating to the medication or other treatment involved, finds—

(1) Makes the person unable to safely perform the duties or exercise the privileges of the airman certificate applied for or held; or

(2) May reasonably be expected, for the maximum duration of the airman medical certificate applied for or held, to make the person unable to perform those duties or exercise those privileges.

§67.315 Discretionary issuance.

A person who does not meet the provisions of §§67.303 through 67.313 may apply for the discretionary issuance of a certificate under §67.401.

Subpart E— Certification Procedures

§67.401 Special issuance of medical certificates.

(a) At the discretion of the Federal Air Surgeon, an Authorization for Special Issuance of a Medical Certificate (Authorization), valid for a specified period, may be granted to a person who does not meet the provisions of subparts B, C, or D of this part if the person shows to the satisfaction of the Federal Air Surgeon that the duties authorized by the class of medical certificate applied for can be performed without endangering public safety during the period in which the Authorization would be in force. The Federal Air Surgeon may authorize a special medical flight test, practical test, or medical evaluation for this purpose. A medical certificate of the appropriate class may be issued to a person who does not meet the provisions of subparts B, C, or D of this part if that person possesses a valid Authorization and is otherwise eligible. An airman medical certificate issued in accordance with this section shall expire no later than the end of the validity period or upon the withdrawal of the Authorization upon which it is based. At the end of its specified validity period, for grant of a new Authorization, the person must again show to the satisfaction of the Federal Air Surgeon that the duties authorized by the class of medical certificate applied for can be performed without endangering public safety during the period in which the Authorization would be in force.

(b) At the discretion of the Federal Air Surgeon, a Statement of Demonstrated Ability (SODA) may be granted, instead of an Authorization, to a person whose disqualifying condition is static or nonprogressive and who has been found capable of performing airman duties without endangering public safety. A SODA does not expire and authorizes a designated aviation medical examiner

to issue a medical certificate of a specified class if the examiner finds that the condition described on its face has not adversely changed.

(c) In granting an Authorization or SODA, the Federal Air Surgeon may consider the person's operational experience and any medical facts that may affect the ability of the person to perform airman duties including—

(1) The combined effect on the person of failure to meet more than one requirement of this part; and

(2) The prognosis derived from professional consideration of all available information regarding the person.

(d) In granting an Authorization or SODA under this section, the Federal Air Surgeon specifies the class of medical certificate authorized to be issued and may do any or all of the following:

(1) Limit the duration of an Authorization;

(2) Condition the granting of a new Authorization on the results of subsequent medical tests, examinations, or evaluations;

(3) State on the Authorization or SODA, and any medical certificate based upon it, any operational limitation needed for safety; or

(4) Condition the continued effect of an Authorization or SODA, and any second- or third-class medical certificate based upon it, on compliance with a statement of functional limitations issued to the person in coordination with the Director of Flight Standards or the Director's designee.

(e) In determining whether an Authorization or SODA should be granted to an applicant for a third-class medical certificate, the Federal Air Surgeon considers the freedom of an airman, exercising the privileges of a private pilot certificate, to accept reasonable risks to his or her person and property that are not acceptable in the exercise of commercial or airline transport pilot privileges, and, at the same time, considers the need to protect the safety of persons and property in other aircraft and on the ground.

(f) An Authorization or SODA granted under the provisions of this section to a person who does not meet the applicable provisions of subparts B, C, or D of this part may be withdrawn, at the discretion of the Federal Air Surgeon, at any time if—

(1) There is adverse change in the holder's medical condition;

(2) The holder fails to comply with a statement of functional limitations or operational limitations issued as a condition of certification under this section;

(3) Public safety would be endangered by the holder's exercise of airman privileges;

(4) The holder fails to provide medical information reasonably needed by the Federal Air Surgeon for certification under this section; or

(5) The holder makes or causes to be made a statement or entry that is the basis for withdrawal of an Authorization or SODA under §67.403.

(g) A person who has been granted an Authorization or SODA under this section based on a special medical flight or practical test need not take the test again during later physical examinations unless the Federal Air Surgeon determines or has reason to believe that the physical deficiency has or may have degraded to a degree to require another special medical flight test or practical test.

(h) The authority of the Federal Air Surgeon under this section is also exercised by the Manager, Aeromedical Certification Division, and each Regional Flight Surgeon.

(i) If an Authorization or SODA is withdrawn under paragraph (f) of this section the following procedures apply:

(1) The holder of the Authorization or SODA will be served a letter of withdrawal, stating the reason for the action;

(2) By not later than 60 days after the service of the letter of withdrawal, the holder of the Authorization or SODA may request, in writing, that the Federal Air Surgeon provide for review of the decision to withdraw. The request for review may be accompanied by supporting medical evidence;

(3) Within 60 days of receipt of a request for review, a written final decision either affirming or reversing the decision to withdraw will be issued; and

(4) A medical certificate rendered invalid pursuant to a withdrawal, in accordance with paragraph (a) of this section, shall be surrendered to the Administrator upon request.

[Docket No. 27940, 61 FR 11256, March 19, 1996; as amended by Amdt. 67–20, 73 FR 43066, July 24, 2008; Amdt. 67–21, 77 FR 16668, March 22, 2012]

§67.403 Applications, certificates, logbooks, reports, and records: Falsification, reproduction, or alteration; incorrect statements.

(a) No person may make or cause to be made—

(1) A fraudulent or intentionally false statement on any application for a medical certificate or on a request for any Authorization for Special Issuance of a Medical Certificate (Authorization) or Statement of Demonstrated Ability (SODA) under this part;

(2) A fraudulent or intentionally false entry in any logbook, record, or report that is kept, made, or used, to show compliance with any requirement for any medical certificate or for any Authorization or SODA under this part;

(3) A reproduction, for fraudulent purposes, of any medical certificate under this part; or

(4) An alteration of any medical certificate under this part.

(b) The commission by any person of an act prohibited under paragraph (a) of this section is a basis for—

(1) Suspending or revoking all airman, ground instructor, and medical certificates and ratings held by that person;

(2) Withdrawing all Authorizations or SODA's held by that person; and

(3) Denying all applications for medical certification and requests for Authorizations or SODA's.

(c) The following may serve as a basis for suspending or revoking a medical certificate; withdrawing an Authorization or SODA; or denying an application for a medical certificate or request for an authorization or SODA:

(1) An incorrect statement, upon which the FAA relied, made in support of an application for a medical certificate or request for an Authorization or SODA.

(2) An incorrect entry, upon which the FAA relied, made in any logbook, record, or report that is kept, made, or used to show compliance with any requirement for a medical certificate or an Authorization or SODA.

§67.405 Medical examinations: Who may perform?

(a) *First-class.* Any aviation medical examiner who is specifically designated for the purpose may perform examinations for the first-class medical certificate.

(b) *Second- and third-class.* Any aviation medical examiner may perform examinations for the second-or third-class medical certificate.

[Docket No. FAA–2007–27812, 73 FR 43066, July 24, 2008]

§67.407 Delegation of authority.

(a) The authority of the Administrator under 49 U.S.C. 44703 to issue or deny medical certificates is delegated to the Federal Air Surgeon to the extent necessary to—

(1) Examine applicants for and holders of medical certificates to determine whether they meet applicable medical standards; and

(2) Issue, renew, and deny medical certificates, and issue, renew, deny, and withdraw Authorizations for Special Issuance of a Medical Certificate and Statements of Demonstrated Ability to a person based upon meeting or failing to meet applicable medical standards.

(b) Subject to limitations in this chapter, the delegated functions of the Federal Air Surgeon to examine applicants for and holders of medical certificates for compliance with applicable medical standards and to issue, renew, and deny medical certificates are also delegated to aviation medical examiners and to authorized representatives of the Federal Air Surgeon within the FAA.

(c) The authority of the Administrator under 49 U.S.C. 44702, to reconsider the action of an aviation medical examiner is delegated to the Federal Air Surgeon; the Manager, Aeromedical Certification Division; and each Regional Flight Surgeon. Where the person does not meet the standards of §§67.107(b)(3) and (c), 67.109(b), 67.113(b) and (c), 67.207(b)(3) and (c), 67.209(b), 67.213(b) and (c), 67.307(b)(3) and (c), 67.309(b), or 67.313(b) and (c), any action taken under this paragraph other than by the Federal Air Surgeon is subject to reconsideration by the Federal Air Surgeon. A certificate issued by an aviation medical examiner is considered to be affirmed as issued unless an FAA official named in this paragraph (authorized official) reverses that issuance within 60 days after the date of issuance. However, if within 60 days after the date of issuance an authorized official requests the certificate holder to submit additional medical information, an authorized official may reverse the issuance within 60 days after receipt of the requested information.

(d) The authority of the Administrator under 49 U.S.C. 44709 to re-examine any civil airman to the extent necessary to determine an airman's qualification to continue to hold an airman medical certificate, is delegated to the Federal Air Surgeon and his or her authorized representatives within the FAA.

§67.409 Denial of medical certificate.

(a) Any person who is denied a medical certificate by an aviation medical examiner may, within 30 days after the date of the denial, apply in writing to the Federal Air Surgeon, Attention: Manager, Aeromedical Certification Division, AAM-300, Federal Aviation Administration, P.O. Box 25082, Oklahoma City, Oklahoma 73126, for reconsideration of that denial. If the person does not ask for reconsideration during the 30-day period after the date of the denial, he or she is considered to have withdrawn the application for a medical certificate.

(b) The denial of a medical certificate—

(1) By an aviation medical examiner is not a denial by the Administrator under 49 U.S.C. 44703.

(2) By the Federal Air Surgeon is considered to be a denial by the Administrator under 49 U.S.C. 44703.

(3) By the Manager, Aeromedical Certification Division, or a Regional Flight Surgeon is considered to be a denial by the Administrator under 49 U.S.C. 44703 except where the person does not meet the standards of §§67.107(b)(3) and (c), 67.109(b), or 67.113(b) and (c); 67.207(b)(3) and (c), 67.209(b), or 67.213(b) and (c); or 67.307(b)(3) and (c), 67.309(b), or 67.313(b) and (c).

(c) Any action taken under §67.407(c) that wholly or partly reverses the issue of a medical certificate by an aviation medical examiner is the denial of a medical certificate under paragraph (b) of this section.

(d) If the issue of a medical certificate is wholly or partly reversed by the Federal Air Surgeon; the Manager, Aeromedical Certification Division; or a Regional Flight Surgeon, the person holding that certificate shall surrender it, upon request of the FAA.

[Docket No. 27940, 61 FR 11256, March 19, 1996, as amended by Docket No. FAA–2022–1355, Amdt. No. 67–22, 87 FR 75845, Dec. 9, 2022]

§67.411 [Reserved]

§67.413 Medical records.

(a) Whenever the Administrator finds that additional medical information or history is necessary to determine whether you meet the medical standards required to hold a medical certificate, you must:

(1) Furnish that information to the FAA; or

(2) Authorize any clinic, hospital, physician, or other person to release to the FAA all available information or records concerning that history.

(b) If you fail to provide the requested medical information or history or to authorize its release, the FAA may suspend, modify, or revoke your medical certificate or, in the case of an applicant, deny the application for a medical certificate.

(c) If your medical certificate is suspended, modified, or revoked under paragraph (b) of this section, that suspension or modification remains in effect until you provide the requested information, history, or authorization to the FAA and until the FAA determines that you meet the medical standards set forth in this part.

[Docket No. FAA–2007–27812, 73 FR 43066, July 24, 2008]

§67.415 Return of medical certificate after suspension or revocation.

The holder of any medical certificate issued under this part that is suspended or revoked shall, upon the Administrator's request, return it to the Administrator.

PART 68

REQUIREMENTS FOR OPERATING CERTAIN SMALL AIRCRAFT WITHOUT A MEDICAL CERTIFICATE

Authority: 49 U.S.C. 106(f), 44701–44703, sec. 2307 of Pub. L. 114–190, 130 Stat. 615 (49 U.S.C. 44703 note).

Source: Docket FAA–2016–9157, Amdt. 68–1, 82 FR 3165, Jan. 11, 2017, unless otherwise noted.

§68.1 Applicability.

This part prescribes the medical education and examination requirements for operating an aircraft under §61.113(i) of this chapter without holding a medical certificate issued under part 67 of this chapter.

§68.3 Medical education course requirements.

(a) The medical education course required to act as pilot in command or serve as a required flightcrew member in an operation under §61.113(i) of this chapter must—

(1) Educate pilots on conducting medical self-assessments;

(2) Advise pilots on identifying warning signs of potential serious medical conditions;

(3) Identify risk mitigation strategies for medical conditions;

(4) Increase awareness of the impacts of potentially impairing over-the-counter and prescription drug medications;

(5) Encourage regular medical examinations and consultations with primary care physicians;

(6) Inform pilots of the regulations pertaining to the prohibition on operations during medical deficiency and medically disqualifying conditions; and

(7) Provide the checklist developed by the FAA in accordance with §68.7.

(b) Upon successful completion of the medical education course, the following items must be electronically provided to the individual seeking to act as pilot in command or serve as a required flightcrew member under the conditions and limitations of §61.113(i) of this chapter and transmitted to the FAA—

(1) A certification of completion of the medical education course, which shall be retained in the individual's logbook and made available upon request, and shall contain the individual's name, address, and airman certificate number;

(2) A release authorizing single access to the National Driver Register through a designated State Department of Motor Vehicles to furnish to the FAA information pertaining to the individual's driving record;

(3) A certification by the individual that the individual is under the care and treatment of a physician if the individual has been diagnosed with any medical condition that may impact the ability of the individual to fly, as required under §61.23(c)(3) of this chapter;

(4) A form that includes—

(i) The name, address, telephone number, and airman certificate number of the individual;

(ii) The name, address, telephone number, and State medical license number of the physician performing the comprehensive medical examination;

(iii) The date of the comprehensive medical examination; and

(iv) A certification by the individual that the checklist described in §68.7 was followed and signed by the physician during the medical examination required by this section; and

(5) A statement, which shall be signed by the individual certifying that the individual understands the existing prohibition on operations during medical deficiency by stating: "I understand that I cannot act as pilot in command, or any other capacity as a required flight crew member, if I know or have reason to know of any medical condition that would make me unable to operate the aircraft in a safe manner."

[Amdt. 68–2, 87 FR 71238, Nov. 22, 2022]

§68.5 Comprehensive medical examination.

(a) Prior to the medical examination required by §61.23(c)(3) of this chapter, an individual must—

(1) Complete the individual's section of the checklist described in §68.7; and

(2) Provide the completed checklist to the State-licensed physician performing the medical examination.

(b) The physician must—

(1) Conduct the medical examination in accordance with the checklist set forth in §68.7;

68

(2) Check each item specified during the examination; and

(3) Address, as medically appropriate, every medical condition listed and any medications the individual is taking.

§68.7 Comprehensive medical examination checklist.

The comprehensive medical examination required to conduct operations under §61.113(i) must include a checklist containing the following:

(a) A section, for the individual to complete that contains—

(1) Boxes 3 through 13 and boxes 16 through 19 of the FAA Form 8500-8 (3-99); and

(2) A signature line for the individual to affirm that—

(i) The answers provided by the individual on that checklist, including the individual's answers regarding medical history, are true and complete;

(ii) The individual understands that he or she is prohibited under FAA regulations from acting as pilot in command, or any other capacity as a required flight crew member, if he or she knows or has reason to know of any medical deficiency or medically disqualifying condition that would make the individual unable to operate the aircraft in a safe manner; and

(iii) The individual is aware of the regulations pertaining to the prohibition on operations during medical deficiency and has no medically disqualifying conditions in accordance with applicable law;

(b) A section with instructions for the individual to provide the completed checklist to the State-licensed physician performing the comprehensive medical examination required under §68.5; and

(c) A section, for the physician to complete, that instructs the physician—

(1) To perform a clinical examination of—

(i) Head, face, neck, and scalp;

(ii) Nose, sinuses, mouth, and throat;

(iii) Ears, general (internal and external canals), and eardrums (perforation);

(iv) Eyes (general), ophthalmoscopic, pupils (equality and reaction), and ocular motility (associated parallel movement, nystagmus);

(v) Lungs and chest (not including breast examination);

(vi) Heart (precordial activity, rhythm, sounds, and murmurs);

(vii) Vascular system (pulse, amplitude, and character, and arms, legs, and others);

(viii) Abdomen and viscera (including hernia);

(ix) Anus (not including digital examination);

(x) Skin;

(xi) G-U system (not including pelvic examination);

(xii) Upper and lower extremities (strength and range of motion);

(xiii) Spine and other musculoskeletal;

(xiv) Identifying body marks, scars, and tattoos (size and location);

(xv) Lymphatics;

(xvi) Neurologic (tendon reflexes, equilibrium, senses, cranial nerves, and coordination, etc.);

(xvii) Psychiatric (appearance, behavior, mood, communication, and memory);

(xviii) General systemic;

(xix) Hearing;

(xx) Vision (distant, near, and intermediate vision, field of vision, color vision, and ocular alignment);

(xxi) Blood pressure and pulse; and

(xxii) Anything else the physician, in his or her medical judgment, considers necessary;

(2) To exercise medical discretion to address, as medically appropriate, any medical conditions identified, and to exercise medical discretion in determining whether any medical tests are warranted as part of the comprehensive medical examination;

(3) To discuss all drugs the individual reports taking (prescription and nonprescription) and their potential to interfere with the safe operation of an aircraft or motor vehicle;

(4) To sign the checklist, stating: "I certify that I discussed all items on this checklist with the individual during my examination, discussed any medications the individual is taking that could interfere with his or her ability to safely operate an aircraft or motor vehicle, and performed an examination that included all of the items on this checklist. I certify that I am not aware of any medical condition that, as presently treated, could interfere with the individual's ability to safely operate an aircraft."; and

(5) To provide the date the comprehensive medical examination was completed, and the physician's full name, address, telephone number, and State medical license number.

§68.9 Special Issuance process.

(a) *General.* An individual who has met the qualifications to operate an aircraft under §61.113(i) of this chapter and is seeking to act as a pilot in command or serve as a required flight-crew member under that section must have completed the process for obtaining an Authorization for Special Issuance of a Medical Certificate for each of the following:

(1) A mental health disorder, limited to an established medical history or clinical diagnosis of—

(i) A personality disorder that is severe enough to have repeatedly manifested itself by overt acts;

(ii) A psychosis, defined as a case in which an individual—

(A) Has manifested delusions, hallucinations, grossly bizarre or disorganized behavior, or other commonly accepted symptoms of psychosis; or

(B) May reasonably be expected to manifest delusions, hallucinations, grossly bizarre or disorganized behavior, or other commonly accepted symptoms of psychosis;

(iii) A bipolar disorder; or

(iv) A substance dependence within the previous 2 years, as defined in §67.307(a)(4) of this chapter.

(2) A neurological disorder, limited to an established medical history or clinical diagnosis of any of the following:

(i) Epilepsy;

(ii) Disturbance of consciousness without satisfactory medical explanation of the cause; or

(iii) A transient loss of control of nervous system functions without satisfactory medical explanation of the cause.

(3) A cardiovascular condition, limited to a one-time special issuance for each diagnosis of the following:

(i) Myocardial infarction;

(ii) Coronary heart disease that has required treatment;

(iii) Cardiac valve replacement; or

(iv) Heart replacement.

(b) *Special rule for cardiovascular conditions.* In the case of an individual with a cardiovascular condition, the process for obtaining an Authorization for Special Issuance of a Medical Certificate shall be satisfied with the successful completion of an appropriate clinical evaluation without a mandatory wait period.

(c) *Special rule for mental health conditions.* (1) In the case of an individual with a clinically diagnosed mental health condition, the ability to operate an aircraft under §61.113(i) of this chapter shall not apply if—

(i) In the judgment of the individual's State-licensed medical specialist, the condition—

(A) Renders the individual unable to safely perform the duties or exercise the airman privileges required to operate an aircraft under §61.113(i) of this chapter; or

(B) May reasonably be expected to make the individual unable to perform the duties or exercise the privileges required to operate an aircraft under §61.113(i) of this chapter; or

(ii) The individual's driver's license is revoked by the issuing agency as a result of a clinically diagnosed mental health condition.

(2) Subject to paragraph (c)(1) of this section, an individual clinically diagnosed with a mental health condition shall certify every 2 years, in conjunction with the certification under §68.3(b)(3), that the individual is under the care of a State-licensed medical specialist for that mental health condition.

(d) *Special rule for neurological conditions.* (1) In the case of an individual with a clinically diagnosed neurological condition, the ability to operate an aircraft under §61.113(i) of this chapter shall not apply if—

(i) In the judgment of the individual's State-licensed medical specialist, the condition—

(A) Renders the individual unable to safely perform the duties or exercise the airman privileges required to operate an aircraft under §61.113(i) of this chapter; or

(B) May reasonably be expected to make the individual unable to perform the duties or exercise the privileges required to operate an aircraft under §61.113(i) of this chapter; or

(ii) The individual's driver's license is revoked by the issuing agency as a result of a clinically diagnosed neurological condition.

(2) Subject to paragraph (d)(1) of this section, an individual clinically diagnosed with a neurological condition shall certify every 2 years, in conjunction with the certification under §68.3(b)(3), that the individual is under the care of a State-licensed medical specialist for that neurological condition.

[Docket FAA–2016–9157, Amdt. 68–1, 82 FR 3165, Jan. 11, 2017, as amended by Docket No. FAA–2021–1040, Amdt. Nos. 61–152, 87 FR 71238, Nov. 22, 2022]

§68.11 Authority to require additional information.

(a) If the Administrator receives credible or urgent information, including from the National Driver Register or the Administrator's Safety Hotline, that reflects on an individual's ability to safely operate an aircraft under §61.113(i) of this chapter, the Administrator may require the individual to provide additional information or history so that the Administrator may determine whether the individual is safe to continue operating under that section.

(b) The Administrator may use credible or urgent information received under paragraph (a) to request an individual to provide additional information or to take actions under 49 U.S.C. 44709(b).

PART 71

DESIGNATION OF CLASS A, B, C, D, AND E AIRSPACE AREAS; AIR TRAFFIC SERVICE ROUTES; AND REPORTING POINTS

SFAR No. 97 [Note]

Authority: 49 U.S.C. 106(f), 106(g), 40103, 40113, 40120; E.O. 10854, 24 FR 9565, 3 CFR, 1959–1963 Comp., p. 389.

Source: Amdt. 71–14, 56 FR 65654, Dec. 17, 1991, unless otherwise noted.

SFAR No. 97

SPECIAL OPERATING RULES FOR THE CONDUCT OF INSTRUMENT FLIGHT RULES (IFR) AREA NAVIGATION (RNAV) OPERATIONS USING GLOBAL POSITIONING SYSTEMS (GPS) IN ALASKA

Editorial Note: For the text of SFAR No. 97, see Part 91 of this chapter.

§71.1 Applicability.

A listing for Class A, B, C, D, and E airspace areas; air traffic service routes; and reporting points can be found in FAA Order JO 7400.11H, Airspace Designations and Reporting Points, dated August 11, 2023. This incorporation by reference was approved by the Director of the Federal Register in accordance with 5 U.S.C. 552(a) and 1 CFR part 51. The approval to incorporate by reference FAA Order JO 7400.11H is effective September 15, 2023, through September 15, 2024. During the incorporation by reference period, proposed changes to the listings of Class A, B, C, D, and E airspace areas; air traffic service routes; and reporting points will be published in full text as proposed rule documents in the **Federal Register**, unless there is good cause to forego notice and comment. Amendments to the listings of Class A, B, C, D, and E airspace areas; air traffic service routes; and reporting points will be published in full text as final rules in the **Federal Register**. Periodically, the final rule amendments will be integrated into a revised edition of the Order and submitted to the Director of the Federal Register for approval for incorporation by reference in this section. This incorporation by reference (IBR) material is available for inspection at the Federal Aviation Administration (FAA) and at the National Archives and Records Administration (NARA). Contact the FAA at: Rules and Regulations Group, Federal Aviation Administration, 800 Independence Avenue SW, Washington, DC 20591, (202) 267-8783. An electronic version of FAA Order JO 7400.11H is available on the FAA website at *www.faa.gov/air_traffic/publications*. Copies of FAA Order JO 7400.11H may be inspected in Docket No. FAA-2023-1785; Amendment No. 71–55, on *www.regulations.gov*. For information on the availability of this material at NARA, visit *www.archives.gov/federal-register/cfr/ibr-locations.html* or email *fr.inspection@nara.gov*.

[Docket No. FAA–2023–1785; Amendment No. 71–55, 88 FR 58072, Aug. 25, 2023]

§71.3 [Reserved]

§71.5 Reporting points.

The reporting points listed in Subpart H of FAA Order JO 7400.11H (incorporated by reference, see §71.1) consist of geographic locations at which the position of an aircraft must be reported in accordance with part 91 of this chapter.

[Docket No. 29334, 73 FR 54495, Sept. 22, 2008, as amended by Amdt. 71–40, 73 FR 60940, Oct. 15, 2008; Amdt. 71–41, 74 FR 46490, Sept. 10, 2009; Amdt. 71–42, 75 FR 55268, Sept. 10, 2010; Amdt. 71–43, 76 FR 53329, Aug. 26, 2011; Amdt. 71–44, 77 FR 50908, Aug. 23, 2012; Amdt. 71–45, 78 FR 52848, Aug. 27, 2013; Amdt. 71–46, 79 FR 51888, Sept. 2, 2014; Amdt. 71–47, 80 FR 51937, Aug. 27, 2015; Amdt. 71–48, 81 FR 55372, Aug. 19, 2016; Amdt. 71–49, 82 FR 40068, Aug. 24, 2017; Amdt. 71–50, 83 FR 43757, Aug. 28, 2018; Amdt. 71–51, 84 FR 45652, Aug. 30, 2019; Amdt. 71–52, 85 FR 50780, Aug. 18, 2020; Amdt. No. 71–53, 86 FR 46963, Aug. 23, 2021; Docket No. FAA–2022–1022, Amdt. No. 71–54, 87 FR 54878, Sept. 8, 2022; Docket No. FAA–2023–1785; Amendment No. 71–55, 88 FR 58072, Aug. 25, 2023]

§71.7 Bearings, radials, and mileages.

All bearings and radials in this part are true and are applied from point of origin and all mileages in this part are stated as nautical miles.

§71.9 Overlapping airspace designations.

(a) When overlapping airspace designations apply to the same airspace, the operating rules associated with the more restrictive airspace designation apply.

(b) For the purpose of this section—

(1) Class A airspace is more restrictive than Class B, Class C, Class D, Class E, or Class G airspace;

(2) Class B airspace is more restrictive than Class C, Class D, Class E, or Class G airspace;

(3) Class C airspace is more restrictive than Class D, Class E, or Class G airspace;

(4) Class D airspace is more restrictive than Class E or Class G airspace; and

(5) Class E is more restrictive than Class G airspace.

§71.11 Air Traffic Service (ATS) routes.

Unless otherwise specified, the following apply:

(a) An Air Traffic Service (ATS) route is based on a centerline that extends from one navigation aid, fix, or intersection, to another navigation aid, fix, or intersection (or through several navigation aids, fixes, or intersections) specified for that route.

(b) An ATS route does not include the airspace of a prohibited area.

[Docket No. FAA–2003–14698, 68 FR 16947, April 8, 2003; as amended by Amdt. 71–33, 70 FR 23004, May 3, 2005]

§71.13 Classification of Air Traffic Service (ATS) routes.

Unless otherwise specified, ATS routes are classified as follows:

(a) In subpart A of this part:

(1) Jet routes.

(2) Area navigation (RNAV) routes.

(b) In subpart E of this part:

(1) VOR Federal airways.

(2) Colored Federal airways.

(i) Green Federal airways.

(ii) Amber Federal airways.

(iii) Red Federal airways.

(iv) Blue Federal airways.

(3) Area navigation (RNAV) routes.

[Docket No. FAA–2003–14698, 68 FR 16947, April 8, 2003]

§71.15 Designation of jet routes and VOR Federal airways.

Unless otherwise specified, the place names appearing in the descriptions of airspace areas designated as jet routes in Subpart A of FAA Order JO 7400.11H, and as VOR Federal airways in Subpart E of FAA Order JO 7400.11H, are the names of VOR or VORTAC navigation aids. FAA Order JO 7400.11H is incorporated by reference in §71.1.

[Docket No. 29334, 73 FR 54495, Sept. 22, 2008, as amended by Amdt. 71–40, 73 FR 60940, Oct. 15, 2008; Amdt. 71–41, 74 FR 46490, Sept. 10, 2009; Amdt. 71–42, 75 FR 55268, Sept. 10, 2010; Amdt. 71–43, 76 FR 53329, Aug. 26, 2011; Amdt. 71–44, 77 FR 50908, Aug. 23, 2012; Amdt. 71–45, 78 FR 52848, Aug. 27, 2013; Amdt. 71–46, 79 FR 51888, Sept. 2, 2014; Amdt. 71–47, 80 FR 51937, Aug. 27, 2015; Amdt. 71–48, 81 FR 55372, Aug. 19, 2016; Amdt. 71–49, 82 FR 40068, Aug. 24, 2017; Amdt. 71–50, 83 FR 43757, Aug. 28, 2018; Docket FAA–2019–0627, Amdt. 71–51, 84 FR 45652, Aug. 30, 2019; Amdt. 71–52, 85 FR 50780, Aug. 18, 2020; Amdt. No. 71–53, 86 FR 46963, Aug. 23, 2021; Docket No. FAA–2022–1022, Amdt. No. 71–54, 87 FR 54878, Sept. 8, 2022; Docket No. FAA–2023–1785; Amendment No. 71–55, 88 FR 58072, Aug. 25, 2023]

Subpart A— Class A Airspace

§71.31 Class A airspace.

The airspace descriptions contained in §71.33 and the routes contained in Subpart A of FAA Order JO 7400.11H (incorporated by reference, see §71.1) are designated as Class A airspace within which all pilots and aircraft are subject to the rating requirements, operating rules, and equipment requirements of part 91 of this chapter.

[Docket No. 29334, 73 FR 54495, Sept. 22, 2008, as amended by Amdt. 71–40, 73 FR 60940, Oct. 15, 2008; Amdt. 71–41, 74 FR 46490, Sept. 10, 2009; Amdt. 71–42, 75 FR 55268, Sept. 10, 2010; Amdt. 71–43, 76 FR 53329, Aug. 26, 2011; Amdt. 71–44, 77 FR 50908, Aug. 23, 2012; Amdt. 71–45, 78 FR 52848, Aug. 27, 2013; Amdt. 71–46, 79 FR 51888, Sept. 2, 2014; Amdt. 71–47, 80 FR 51937, Aug. 27, 2015; Amdt. 71–48, 81 FR 55372, Aug. 19, 2016; Amdt. 71–49, 82 FR 40068, Aug. 24, 2017; Amdt. 71–50, 83 FR 43757, Aug. 28, 2018; Amdt. 71–51, 84 FR 45652, Aug. 30, 2019; Amdt. 71–52,

85 FR 50780, Aug. 18, 2020; Amdt. No. 71–53, 86 FR 46963, Aug. 23, 2021; Docket No. FAA–2022–1022, Amdt. No. 71–54, 87 FR 54878, Sept. 8, 2022; Docket No. FAA–2023–1785; Amendment No. 71–55, 88 FR 58072, Aug. 25, 2023]

§71.33 Class A airspace areas.

(a) That airspace of the United States, including that airspace overlying the waters within 12 nautical miles of the coast of the 48 contiguous States, from 18,000 feet MSL to and including FL600 excluding the states of Alaska and Hawaii.

(b) That airspace of the State of Alaska, including that airspace overlying the waters within 12 nautical miles of the coast, from 18,000 feet MSL to and including FL600 but not including the airspace less than 1,500 feet above the surface of the earth and the Alaska Peninsula west of longitude 160°00'00" West.

(c) The airspace areas listed as offshore airspace areas in Subpart A of FAA Order JO 7400.11H (incorporated by reference, see §71.1) that are designated in international airspace within areas of domestic radio navigational signal or ATC radar coverage, and within which domestic ATC procedures are applied.

[Amdt. 71–14, 56 FR 65654, Dec. 17, 1991]

Editorial Note: For Federal Register citations affecting §71.33, see the List of CFR Sections Affected, which appears in the Finding Aids section of the printed volume and at www.govinfo.gov.

Subpart B—
Class B Airspace

§71.41 Class B airspace.

The Class B airspace areas listed in Subpart B of FAA Order JO 7400.11H (incorporated by reference, see §71.1) consist of specified airspace within which all aircraft operators are subject to the minimum pilot qualification requirements, operating rules, and aircraft equipment requirements of part 91 of this chapter. Each Class B airspace area designated for an airport in Subpart B of FAA Order JO 7400.11H (incorporated by reference, see §71.1) contains at least one primary airport around which the airspace is designated.

[Docket No. 29334, 73 FR 54495, Sept. 22, 2008, as amended by Amdt. 71–40, 73 FR 60940, Oct. 15, 2008; Amdt. 71–41, 74 FR 46490, Sept. 10, 2009; Amdt. 71–42, 75 FR 55268, Sept. 10, 2010; Amdt. 71–43, 76 FR 53329, Aug. 26, 2011; Amdt. 71–44, 77 FR 50908, Aug. 23, 2012; Amdt. 71–45, 78 FR 52848, Aug. 27, 2013; Amdt. 71–46, 79 FR 51888, Sept. 2, 2014; Amdt. 71–47, 80 FR 51937, Aug. 27, 2015; Amdt. 71–48, 81 FR 55372, Aug. 19, 2016; Amdt. 71–49, 82 FR 40068, Aug. 24, 2017; Amdt. 71–50, 83 FR 43757, Aug. 28, 2018; Amdt. 71–51, 84 FR 45652, Aug. 30, 2019; Amdt. 71–52, 85 FR 50780, Aug. 18, 2020; Amdt. No. 71–53, 86 FR 46963, Aug. 23, 2021; Docket No. FAA–2022–1022,

Subpart C—
Class C Airspace

§71.51 Class C airspace.

The Class C airspace areas listed in Subpart C of FAA Order JO 7400.11H (incorporated by reference, see §71.1) consist of specified airspace within which all aircraft operators are subject to operating rules and equipment requirements specified in part 91 of this chapter. Each Class C airspace area designated for an airport in Subpart C of FAA Order JO 7400.11H (incorporated by reference, see §71.1) contains at least one primary airport around which the airspace is designated.

[Docket No. 29334, 73 FR 54495, Sept. 22, 2008, as amended by Amdt. 71–40, 73 FR 60940, Oct. 15, 2008; Amdt. 71–41, 74 FR 46490, Sept. 10, 2009; Amdt. 71–42, 75 FR 55269, Sept. 10, 2010; Amdt. 71–43, 76 FR 53329, Aug. 26, 2011; Amdt. 71–44, 77 FR 50908, Aug. 23, 2012; Amdt. 71–45, 78 FR 52848, Aug. 27, 2013; Amdt. 71–46, 79 FR 51888, Sept. 2, 2014; Amdt. 71–47, 80 FR 51937, Aug. 27, 2015; Amdt. 71–48, 81 FR 55372, Aug. 19, 2016; Amdt. 71–49, 82 FR 40068, Aug. 24, 2017; Amdt. 71–50, 83 FR 43757, Aug. 28, 2018; Amdt. 71–51, 84 FR 45652, Aug. 30, 2019; Amdt. 71–52, 85 FR 50780, Aug. 18, 2020; Amdt. No. 71–53, 86 FR 46963, Aug. 23, 2021; Docket No. FAA–2022–1022, Amdt. No. 71–54, 87 FR 54878, Sept. 8, 2022; Docket No. FAA–2023–1785; Amendment No. 71–55, 88 FR 58072, Aug. 25, 2023]

Subpart D—
Class D Airspace

§71.61 Class D airspace.

The Class D airspace areas listed in Subpart D of FAA Order JO 7400.11H (incorporated by reference, see §71.1) consist of specified airspace within which all aircraft operators are subject to operating rules and equipment requirements specified in part 91 of this chapter. Each Class D airspace area designated for an airport in Subpart D of FAA Order JO 7400.11H (incorporated by reference, see §71.1) contains at least one primary airport around which the airspace is designated.

[Docket No. 29334, 73 FR 54495, Sept. 22, 2008, as amended by Amdt. 71–40, 73 FR 60940, Oct. 15, 2008; Amdt. 71–41, 74 FR 46490, Sept. 10, 2009; Amdt. 71–42, 75 FR 55269, Sept. 10, 2010; Amdt. 71–43, 76 FR 53329, Aug. 26, 2011; Amdt. 71–44, 77 FR 50908, Aug. 23, 2012; Amdt. 71–45, 78 FR 52848, Aug. 27, 2013; Amdt. 71–46, 79 FR 51888, Sept. 2, 2014; Amdt. 71–47, 80 FR 51937, Aug. 27, 2015; Amdt. 71–48, 81 FR 55372, Aug. 19, 2016; Amdt. 71–49, 82 FR 40069, Aug. 24, 2017; Amdt. 71–50, 83 FR 43757, Aug. 28, 2018; Amdt. 71–51, 84 FR 45652, Aug. 30, 2019; Amdt. 71–52,

71

85 FR 50780, Aug. 18, 2020; Amdt. No. 71–53, 86 FR 46963, Aug. 23, 2021; Docket No. FAA–2022–1022, Amdt. No. 71–54, 87 FR 54878, Sept. 8, 2022; Docket No. FAA–2023–1785; Amendment No. 71–55, 88 FR 58072, Aug. 25, 2023]

Subpart E—
Class E Airspace

§71.71 Class E airspace.

Class E Airspace consists of:

(a) The airspace of the United States, including that airspace overlying the waters within 12 nautical miles of the coast of the 48 contiguous states and Alaska, extending upward from 14,500 feet MSL up to, but not including 18,000 feet MSL, and the airspace above FL600, excluding—

(1) The Alaska peninsula west of longitude 160°00'00" W.; and

(2) The airspace below 1,500 feet above the surface of the earth.

(b) The airspace areas designated for an airport in Subpart E of FAA Order JO 7400.11H (incorporated by reference, see §71.1) within which all aircraft operators are subject to the operating rules specified in part 91 of this chapter.

(c) The airspace areas listed as domestic airspace areas in Subpart E of FAA Order JO 7400.11H (incorporated by reference, see §71.1) which extend upward from 700 feet or more above the surface of the earth when designated in conjunction with an airport for which an approved instrument approach procedure has been prescribed, or from 1,200 feet or more above the surface of the earth for the purpose of transitioning to or from the terminal or en route environment. When such areas are designated in conjunction with airways or routes, the extent of such designation has the lateral extent identical to that of a Federal airway and extends upward from 1,200 feet or higher. Unless otherwise specified, the airspace areas in the paragraph extend upward from 1,200 feet or higher above the surface to, but not including, 14,500 feet MSL.

(d) The Federal airways described in Subpart E of FAA Order JO 7400.11H (incorporated by reference, see §71.1).

(e) The airspace areas listed as en route domestic airspace areas in Subpart E of FAA Order JO 7400.11H (incorporated by reference, see §71.1). Unless otherwise specified, each airspace area has a lateral extent identical to that of a Federal airway and extends upward from 1,200 feet above the surface of the earth to the overlying or adjacent controlled airspace.

(f) The airspace areas listed as offshore airspace areas in Subpart E of FAA Order JO 7400.11H (incorporated by reference, see §71.1) that are designated in international airspace within areas of domestic radio navigational signal or ATC radar coverage, and within which domestic ATC procedures are applied. Unless otherwise specified, each airspace area extends upward from a specified altitude up to, but not including, 18,000 feet MSL.

[Docket No. 29334, 73 FR 54495, Sept. 22, 2008, as amended by Amdt. 71–40, 73 FR 60940, Oct. 15, 2008; Amdt. 71–41, 74 FR 46490, Sept. 10, 2009; Amdt. 71–42, 75 FR 55269, Sept. 10, 2010; Amdt. 71–43, 76 FR 53329, Aug. 26, 2011; Amdt. 71–44, 77 FR 50908, Aug. 23, 2012; Amdt. 71–45, 78 FR 52848, Aug. 27, 2013; Amdt. 71–46, 79 FR 51888, Sept. 2, 2014; Amdt. 71–47, 80 FR 51937, Aug. 27, 2015; Amdt. 71–48, 81 FR 55372, Aug. 19, 2016; Amdt. 71–49, 82 FR 40069, Aug. 24, 2017; Amdt. 71–50, 83 FR 43757, Aug. 28, 2018; Amdt. 71–51, 84 FR 45652, Aug. 30, 2019; Amdt. 71–52, 85 FR 50780, Aug. 18, 2020; Amdt. No. 71–53, 86 FR 46963, Aug. 23, 2021; Docket No. FAA–2022–1022, Amdt. No. 71–54, 87 FR 54878, Sept. 8, 2022; Docket No. FAA–2023–1785; Amendment No. 71–55, 88 FR 58072, Aug. 25, 2023]

Subparts F–G—[Reserved]

Subpart H—
Reporting Points

§71.901 Applicability.

Unless otherwise designated:

(a) Each reporting point listed in Subpart H of FAA Order JO 7400.11H (incorporated by reference, see §71.1) applies to all directions of flight. In any case where a geographic location is designated as a reporting point for less than all airways passing through that point, or for a particular direction of flight along an airway only, it is so indicated by including the airways or direction of flight in the designation of geographical location.

(b) Place names appearing in the reporting point descriptions indicate VOR or VORTAC facilities identified by those names.

[Docket No. 29334, 73 FR 54495, Sept. 22, 2008, as amended by Amdt. 71–40, 73 FR 60940, Oct. 15, 2008; Amdt. 71–41, 74 FR 46490, Sept. 10, 2009; Amdt. 71–42, 75 FR 55269, Sept. 10, 2010; Amdt. 71–43, 76 FR 53329, Aug. 26, 2011; Amdt. 71–44, 77 FR 50908, Aug. 23, 2012; Amdt. 71–45, 78 FR 52848, Aug. 27, 2013; Amdt. 71–46, 79 FR 51888, Sept. 2, 2014; Amdt. 71–47, 80 FR 51937, Aug. 27, 2015; Amdt. 71–48, 81 FR 55372, Aug. 19, 2016; Amdt. 71–49, 82 FR 40069, Aug. 24, 2017; Amdt. 71–50, 83 FR 43757, Aug. 28, 2018; Amdt. 71–51, 84 FR 45652, Aug. 30, 2019; Amdt. 71–52, 85 FR 50780, Aug. 18, 2020; Amdt. No. 71–53, 86 FR 46963, Aug. 23, 2021; Docket No. FAA–2022–1022, Amdt. No. 71–54, 87 FR 54878, Sept. 8, 2022; Docket No. FAA–2023–1785; Amendment No. 71–55, 88 FR 58072, Aug. 25, 2023]

PART 73
SPECIAL USE AIRSPACE

Authority: 49 U.S.C. 106(f), 106(g), 40103, 40113, 40120; E.O. 10854, 24 FR 9565, 3 CFR, 1959–1963 Comp., p. 389.

Source: 46 FR 779, January 2, 1981, unless otherwise noted.

Subpart A—General

§73.1 Applicability.
The airspace that is described in subpart B and subpart C of this part is designated as special use airspace. These parts prescribe the requirements for the use of that airspace.

§73.3 Special use airspace.
(a) Special use airspace consists of airspace of defined dimensions identified by an area on the surface of the earth wherein activities must be confined because of their nature, or wherein limitations are imposed upon aircraft operations that are not a part of those activities, or both.

(b) The vertical limits of special use airspace are measured by designated altitude floors and ceilings expressed as flight levels or as feet above mean sea level. Unless otherwise specified, the word "to" (an altitude or flight level) means "to and including" (that altitude or flight level).

(c) The horizontal limits of special use airspace are measured by boundaries described by geographic coordinates or other appropriate references that clearly define their perimeter.

(d) The period of time during which a designation of special use airspace is in effect is stated in the designation.

§73.5 Bearings; radials; miles.
(a) All bearings and radials in this part are true from point of origin.

(b) Unless otherwise specified, all mileages in this part are stated as statute miles.

Subpart B— Restricted Areas

§73.11 Applicability.
This subpart designates restricted areas and prescribes limitations on the operation of aircraft within them.

§73.13 Restrictions.
No person may operate an aircraft within a restricted area between the designated altitudes and during the time of designation, unless he has the advance permission of

(a) The using agency described in §73.15; or

(b) The controlling agency described in §73.17.

§73.15 Using agency.
(a) For the purposes of this subpart, the following are using agencies;

(1) The agency, organization, or military command whose activity within a restricted area necessitated the area being so designated.

(b) Upon the request of the FAA, the using agency shall execute a letter establishing procedures for joint use of a restricted area by the using agency and the controlling agency, under which the using agency would notify the controlling agency whenever the controlling agency may grant permission for transit through the restricted area in accordance with the terms of the letter.

(c) The using agency shall—

(1) Schedule activities within the restricted area;

(2) Authorize transit through, or flight within, the restricted area as feasible; and

(3) Contain within the restricted area all activities conducted therein in accordance with the purpose for which it was designated.

§73.17 Controlling agency.
For the purposes of this part, the controlling agency is the FAA facility that may authorize transit through or flight within a restricted area in accordance with a joint-use letter issued under §73.15.

§73.19 Reports by using agency.

(a) Each using agency must prepare a report on the use of each restricted area assigned thereto during any part of the preceding 12-month period ended September 30, and transmit it by the following January 31 of each year to the Manager, Operations Support Group in the ATO Service Center office of the Federal Aviation Administration having jurisdiction over the area in which the restricted area is located, with a copy to the Manager, Airspace Policy Group, Federal Aviation Administration, 800 Independence Avenue SW, Washington, DC 20591.

(b) In the report under this section the using agency must:

(1) State the name and number of the restricted area as published in this part, and the period covered by the report.

(2) State the activities (including average daily number of operations if appropriate) conducted in the area, and any other pertinent information concerning current and future electronic monitoring devices.

(3) State the number of hours daily, the days of the week, and the number of weeks during the year that the area was used.

(4) For restricted areas having a joint-use designation, also state the number of hours daily, the days of the week, and the number of weeks during the year that the restricted area was released to the controlling agency for public use.

(5) State the mean sea level altitudes or flight levels (whichever is appropriate) used in aircraft operations and the maximum and average ordinate of surface firing (expressed in feet, mean sea level altitude) used on a daily, weekly, and yearly basis.

(6) Include a chart of the area (of optional scale and design) depicting, if used, aircraft operating areas, flight patterns, ordnance delivery areas, surface firing points, and target, fan, and impact areas. After once submitting an appropriate chart, subsequent annual charts are not required unless there is a change in the area, activity or altitude (or flight levels) used, which might alter the depiction of the activities originally reported. If no change is to be submitted, a statement indicating "no change" shall be included in the report.

(7) Include any other information not otherwise required under this part which is considered pertinent to activities carried on in the restricted area.

(c) If it is determined that the information submitted under paragraph (b) of this section is not sufficient to evaluate the nature and extent of the use of a restricted area, the FAA may request the using agency to submit supplementary reports. Within 60 days after receiving a request for additional information, the using agency must submit such information as the FAA Service Center Operations Support Group Manager considers appropriate. Supplementary reports must be sent to the FAA officials designated in paragraph (a) of this section.

(Secs. 307 and 313(a), Federal Aviation Act of 1958 (49 U.S.C. 1348 and 1354(a)))

[Docket No. 15379, 42 FR 54798, Oct. 11, 1977; as amended by Amdt. 73–5, 54 FR 39292, Sept. 25, 1989; Amdt. 73–6, 58 FR 42001, Aug. 6, 1993; Amdt. 73–8, 61 FR 26435, May 28, 1996; Amdt. 73–8, 63 FR 16890, April 7, 1998; Docket No. FAA-2022-1355, Amdt. No. 73-9, 87 FR 75845, Dec. 9, 2022; 88 FR 2813, Jan. 18, 2023]

Editorial Note: The restricted areas formerly carried as §§608.21 to 608.72 of this title were transferred to Part 73 as §§73.21 to 73.72 under Subpart B but are not carried in the Code of Federal Regulations. For Federal Register citations affecting these restricted areas, see the List of CFR Sections Affected, which appears in the Finding Aids section of the printed volume and at www.govinfo.gov.

Subpart C— Prohibited Areas

§73.81 Applicability.

This subpart designates prohibited areas and prescribes limitations on the operation of aircraft therein.

§73.83 Restrictions.

No person may operate an aircraft within a prohibited area unless authorization has been granted by the using agency.

§73.85 Using agency.

For the purpose of this subpart, the using agency is the agency, organization or military command that established the requirements for the prohibited area.

Editorial Note: Sections 73.87 through 73.99 are reserved for descriptions of designated prohibited areas. For Federal Register citations affecting these prohibited areas, see the List of CFR Sections Affected, which appears in the Finding Aids section of the printed volume and at www.govinfo.gov.

PART 89
REMOTE IDENTIFICATION OF UNMANNED AIRCRAFT

Authority: 49 U.S.C. 106(f), 106(g), 40101(d), 40103(b), 44701, 44805, 44809(f); Section 2202 of Pub. L. 114-190, 130 Stat. 629.

Source: Amdt. No. 89–1, 86 FR 4505, Jan. 15, 2021, unless otherwise noted.

Subpart A—General

§89.1 Definitions.
The following definitions apply to this part.

Declaration of compliance means a record submitted to the FAA by the producer of a standard remote identification unmanned aircraft or remote identification broadcast module to attest that all the requirements of subpart F of this part have been met.

Home-built unmanned aircraft means an unmanned aircraft that an individual built solely for education or recreation.

§89.5 Falsification, reproduction, alteration, or omission.

(a) No person may make or cause to be made any of the following:

(1) Any fraudulent or intentionally false statement in any document related to any acceptance, application, approval, authorization, certificate, declaration, designation, qualification, record, report, request for reconsideration, or similar, submitted under this part.

(2) Any fraudulent or intentionally false statement in any document required to be developed, provided, kept, or used to show compliance with any requirement under this part.

(3) Any reproduction or alteration, for fraudulent purpose, of any document related to any acceptance, application, approval, authorization, certificate, declaration, designation, qualification, record, report, request for reconsideration, or similar, submitted or granted under this part.

(b) No person may, by omission, knowingly conceal or cause to be concealed, a material fact in—

(1) Any document related to any acceptance, application, approval, authorization, certificate, declaration, designation, qualification, record, report, request for reconsideration, or similar, submitted under this part; or

(2) Any document required to be developed, provided, kept, or used to show compliance with any requirement under this part.

(c) The commission by any person of an act prohibited under paragraph (a) or (b) of this section is a basis for—

(1) Denial, suspension, rescission, or revocation of any acceptance, application, approval, authorization, certificate, declaration, declaration of compliance, designation, document, filing, qualification, means of compliance, record, report, request for reconsideration, or similar instrument issued or granted by the Administrator and held by that person; or

(2) A civil penalty.

Subpart B—Operating Requirement

§89.101 Applicability.

(a) Except as provided in paragraph (b) of this section, this subpart applies to the following:

(1) Persons operating unmanned aircraft registered or required to be registered under part 47 or 48 of this chapter.

(2) Persons operating foreign civil unmanned aircraft in the United States.

(b) This subpart does not apply to unmanned aircraft operations under part 91 of this chapter that are transmitting ADS-B Out pursuant to §91.225.

§89.105 Remote identification requirement.

Except as otherwise authorized by the Administrator or as provided in §89.120, after September 16, 2023, no person may operate an unmanned aircraft within the airspace of the United States unless the operation meets the requirements of §89.110 or §89.115.

§89.110 Operation of standard remote identification unmanned aircraft.

Unless otherwise authorized by the Administrator, a person may comply with the remote identification requirement of §89.105 by operating a standard remote identification unmanned aircraft under the following conditions:

(a) *Operational requirements.* A person may operate a standard remote identification unmanned aircraft only if the person operating the standard remote identification unmanned aircraft ensures that all of the following conditions are met:

(1) From takeoff to shutdown, the standard remote identification unmanned aircraft must broadcast the message elements of §89.305.

(2) The person manipulating the flight controls of the unmanned aircraft system must land the unmanned aircraft as soon as practicable if the standard remote identification unmanned aircraft is no longer broadcasting the message elements of §89.305.

(b) *Standard remote identification unmanned aircraft requirements.* A person may operate a standard remote identification unmanned aircraft only if the unmanned aircraft meets all of the following requirements:

(1) Its serial number is listed on an FAA-accepted declaration of compliance, or the standard remote identification unmanned aircraft is covered by a design approval or production approval issued under part 21 of this chapter and meets the requirements of subpart F of this part.

(2) Its remote identification equipment is functional and complies with the requirements of this part from takeoff to shutdown.

(3) Its remote identification equipment and functionality have not been disabled.

(4) The Certificate of Aircraft Registration of the unmanned aircraft used in the operation must include the serial number of the unmanned aircraft, as per applicable requirements of parts 47 and 48 of this chapter, or the serial number of the unmanned aircraft must be provided to the FAA in a notice of identification pursuant to §89.130 prior to the operation.

§89.115 Alternative remote identification.

A person operating an unmanned aircraft that is not a standard remote identification unmanned aircraft may comply with the remote identification requirement of §89.105 by meeting all of the requirements of either paragraph (a) or (b) of this section.

(a) *Remote identification broadcast modules.* Unless otherwise authorized by the Administrator, a person may operate an unmanned aircraft that is not a standard remote identification unmanned aircraft if all of the following conditions are met:

(1) *Equipage.*

(i) The unmanned aircraft used in the operation must be equipped with a remote identification broadcast module that meets the requirements of §89.320 and the serial number of the remote identification broadcast module must be listed on an FAA-accepted declaration of compliance.

(ii) The Certificate of Aircraft Registration of the unmanned aircraft used in the operation must include the serial number of the remote identification broadcast module, as per applicable requirements of parts 47 and 48 of this chapter, or the serial number of the unmanned aircraft must be provided to the FAA in a notice of identification pursuant to §89.130 prior to the operation.

(2) *Remote identification operating requirements.* Unless otherwise authorized by the Administrator, a person may operate an unmanned aircraft under this paragraph (a) only if all of the following conditions are met:

(i) From takeoff to shutdown, the person operating the unmanned aircraft must ensure that the remote identification broadcast module broadcasts the remote identification message elements of §89.315 directly from the unmanned aircraft.

(ii) The person manipulating the flight controls of the unmanned aircraft system must be able to see the unmanned aircraft at all times throughout the operation.

(3) *Pre-flight requirement.* Prior to takeoff, the person manipulating the flight controls of the unmanned aircraft system must ensure the remote identification broadcast module is functioning in accordance with this subpart.

(4) *In-flight loss of remote identification broadcast.* The person manipulating the flight controls of the unmanned aircraft system must land the unmanned aircraft as soon as practicable if the unmanned aircraft is no longer broadcasting the message elements of §89.315.

(b) *Operations at FAA-recognized identification areas.* Unless otherwise authorized by the Administrator, a person may operate an unmanned aircraft without remote identification equipment only if all of the following conditions are met:

(1) The unmanned aircraft and the person manipulating the flight controls of the unmanned aircraft system remain within the boundaries of an FAA-recognized identification area throughout the operation; and

(2) The person manipulating the flight controls of the unmanned aircraft system must be able to see the unmanned aircraft at all times throughout the operation.

§89.120 Operations for aeronautical research or to show compliance with regulations.

The Administrator may authorize operations without remote identification where the operation is solely for the purpose of aeronautical research or to show compliance with regulations.

§89.125 Automatic Dependent Surveillance–Broadcast (ADS-B) Out prohibition.

Automatic Dependent Surveillance–Broadcast (ADS-B) Out equipment cannot be used to comply with the remote identification requirements of this part.

§89.130 Confirmation of identification.

(a) *Notification requirement.* No person may operate a foreign registered civil unmanned aircraft with remote identification in the airspace of the United States unless, prior to the operation, the person submits a notice of identification in a form and manner acceptable to the Administrator. The notice of identification must include all of the following:

(1) The name of the person operating the foreign registered civil unmanned aircraft in the United States, and, if applicable, the person's authorized representative.

(2) The physical address of the person operating the foreign registered civil unmanned aircraft in the United States, and, if applicable, the physical address for the person's authorized representative. If the operator or authorized representative does not receive mail at the physical address, a mailing address must also be provided.

(3) The telephone number(s) where the person operating the foreign registered civil unmanned aircraft in the United States, and, if applicable, the person's authorized representative can be reached while in the United States.

(4) The email address of the person operating the foreign registered civil unmanned aircraft in the United States, and, if applicable, the email address of the person's authorized representative.

(5) The unmanned aircraft manufacturer and model name.

(6) The serial number of the unmanned aircraft or remote identification broadcast module.

(7) The country of registration of the unmanned aircraft.

(8) The registration number.

(b) *Issuance of a Confirmation of Identification.*

(1) The FAA will issue a Confirmation of Identification upon completion of the notification requirements provided in paragraph (a) of this section.

(2) The filing of a notification under paragraph (a) of this section and the Confirmation of Identification issued under paragraph (b)(1) of this section do not have the effect of United States aircraft registration.

(c) *Proof of notification.* No person may operate a foreign registered civil unmanned aircraft with remote identification in the United States unless the person obtains a Confirmation of Identification under paragraph (b)(1) of this section, maintains such Confirmation of Identification at the unmanned aircraft's control station, and produces the Confirmation of Identification when requested by the FAA or a law enforcement officer.

(d) *Requirement to maintain current information.* The holder of a Confirmation of Identification must ensure that the information provided under paragraph (a) of this section remains accurate and must update the information prior to operating a foreign registered civil unmanned aircraft in the United States.

Subpart C— FAA-Recognized Identification Areas

§89.201 Applicability.

This subpart prescribes procedural requirements to establish an FAA-recognized identification area.

§89.205 Eligibility.

Only the following persons are eligible to apply for the establishment of an FAA-recognized identification area under this subpart:

(a) A community-based organization recognized by the Administrator.

(b) An educational institution, including primary and secondary educational institutions, trade schools, colleges, and universities.

§89.210 Requests for establishment of an FAA-recognized identification area.

(a) *Application.* An eligible person requesting the establishment of an FAA-recognized identification area under this subpart may submit an application in a form and manner acceptable to the Administrator.

(b) *Required documentation.* A request under this subpart must contain all of the following information:

(1) The name of the eligible person under §89.205.

(2) The name of the individual making the request on behalf of the eligible person.

(3) A declaration that the individual making the request has the authority to act on behalf of the community-based organization or educational institution.

(4) The name and contact information of the primary point of contact for communications with the FAA.

(5) The physical address of the proposed FAA-recognized identification area.

(6) The location of the proposed FAA-recognized identification area in a form and manner prescribed by the Administrator.

(7) If applicable, a copy of any existing letter of agreement regarding the flying site.

(8) Description of the intended purpose of the FAA-recognized identification area and why the proposed FAA-recognized identification area is necessary for that purpose.

(9) Any other information required by the Administrator.

§89.215 Approval of FAA-recognized identification areas.

The Administrator will assess applications for FAA-recognized identification areas and may require additional information or documentation, as needed, to supplement an application. The Administrator will approve or deny an application, and may take into consideration matters such as, but not limited to:

(a) The existence of any FAA established flight or airspace restriction limiting the operation of unmanned aircraft systems, such as special use airspace designations under part 73 of this chapter, temporary flight restrictions issued under part 91 of this chapter, or any other special flight rule, restriction or regulation in this chapter limiting the operation of unmanned aircraft systems in the interest of safety, efficiency, national security and/or homeland security, which overlaps with the proposed FAA-recognized identification area.

(b) The safe and efficient use of airspace by other aircraft.

(c) The safety and security of persons or property on the ground.

(d) The need for an FAA-recognized identification area in the proposed location and proximity of other FAA-recognized identification areas.

§89.220 Amendment.

(a) From the time of application until expiration or termination of an FAA-recognized identification area, any change to the information submitted in the application including but not limited to a change to the point of contact for the FAA-recognized identification area or a change to the FAA-recognized identification area's organizational affiliation must be submitted to the FAA within 10 calendar days of the change.

(b) If the person who has been granted an FAA-recognized identification area wishes to change the geographic boundaries of the FAA-recognized identification area, the person must submit a request describing the change to the FAA for review. The geographic boundaries of the FAA-recognized identification area will not change unless the requested change is approved in accordance with §89.215.

(c) The establishment of an FAA-recognized identification area is subject to ongoing review in accordance with §89.215 by the Administrator that may result in the termination of the FAA-recognized identification area pursuant to §89.230 or modification of the FAA-recognized identification area.

§89.225 Duration of an FAA-recognized identification area.

(a) *Duration.* Except as otherwise provided in this subpart, an FAA-recognized identification area will be in effect for 48 calendar months after the date the FAA approves the request for establishment of an FAA-recognized identification area.

(b) *Renewal.* A person wishing to renew an FAA-recognized identification area must submit a request for renewal no later than 120 days prior to the expiration of the FAA-recognized identification area in a form and manner acceptable to the Administrator. The Administrator may deny requests submitted after that deadline or requests submitted after the expiration.

§89.230 Expiration and termination.

(a) *Expiration.* Unless renewed, an FAA-recognized identification area issued under this subpart will expire automatically and will have no further force or effect as of the day that immediately follows the date of expiration.

(b) *Termination prior to expiration—*
(1) Termination by request. An individual identified as the point of contact for an approved FAA-recognized identification area may submit a request to the Administrator to terminate that FAA-recognized identification area.

(2) Termination by FAA.
(i) The FAA may terminate an FAA-recognized identification area upon a finding that—
(A) The FAA-recognized identification area may pose a risk to aviation safety, public safety, homeland security, or national security;
(B) The FAA-recognized identification area is no longer associated with a person eligible for an FAA-recognized identification area; or
(C) The person who submitted a request for establishment of an FAA-recognized identification area provided false or misleading information during the submission, amendment, or renewal process.

(ii) The Administrator will notify the primary point of contact of the decision to terminate the FAA-recognized identification area and the reasons for the termination. Except as provided in paragraph (c) of this section, if the FAA terminates an FAA-recognized identification area based upon a finding that the FAA-recognized identification area may pose a risk to aviation safety, public safety, homeland security, or national security, that area will no longer be eligible to be an FAA-recognized identification area for as long as those conditions remain in effect.

(c) *Petition to reconsider the FAA's decision to terminate an FAA-recognized identification area.* No later than 30 calendar days after the termination of an FAA-recognized identification area, a person may petition the Administrator for reconsideration of the decision. The petition must state the reasons justifying the request for reconsideration and include any supporting documentation. Upon consideration of the information submitted by the petitioner, the Administrator will notify the petitioner of the decision on the request for reconsideration.

(d) *Inapplicability of part 13, subpart D, of this chapter.* Part 13, subpart D, of this chapter does not apply to the procedures of paragraphs (b) and (c) of this section.

89

Subpart D—Requirements for Standard Remote Identification Unmanned Aircraft and Remote Identification Broadcast Modules

§89.301 Applicability.

This subpart prescribes the minimum message element set and minimum performance requirements for standard remote identification unmanned aircraft and remote identification broadcast modules.

§89.305 Minimum message elements broadcast by standard remote identification unmanned aircraft.

A standard remote identification unmanned aircraft must be capable of broadcasting the following remote identification message elements:

(a) The identity of the unmanned aircraft, consisting of:

(1) A serial number assigned to the unmanned aircraft by the person responsible for the production of the standard remote identification unmanned aircraft; or

(2) A session ID.

(b) An indication of the latitude and longitude of the control station.

(c) An indication of the geometric altitude of the control station.

(d) An indication of the latitude and longitude of the unmanned aircraft.

(e) An indication of the geometric altitude of the unmanned aircraft.

(f) An indication of the velocity of the unmanned aircraft.

(g) A time mark identifying the Coordinated Universal Time (UTC) time of applicability of a position source output.

(h) An indication of the emergency status of the unmanned aircraft.

§89.310 Minimum performance requirements for standard remote identification unmanned aircraft.

A standard remote identification unmanned aircraft must meet the following minimum performance requirements:

(a) *Control station location.* The location of the control station of the unmanned aircraft must be generated and encoded into the message elements and must correspond to the location of the person manipulating the flight controls of the unmanned aircraft system.

(b) *Time mark.* The time mark message element must be synchronized with all other remote identification message elements.

(c) *Self-testing and monitoring.*

(1) Prior to takeoff, the unmanned aircraft must automatically test the remote identification functionality and notify the person manipulating the flight controls of the unmanned aircraft system of the result of the test.

(2) The unmanned aircraft must not be able to take off if the remote identification equipment is not functional.

(3) The unmanned aircraft must continuously monitor the remote identification functionality from takeoff to shutdown and must provide notification of malfunction or failure to the person manipulating the flight controls of the unmanned aircraft system.

(d) *Tamper resistance.* The unmanned aircraft must be designed and produced in a way that reduces the ability of a person to tamper with the remote identification functionality.

(e) *Error correction.* The remote identification equipment must incorporate error correction in the broadcast of the message elements in §89.305.

(f) *Interference considerations.* The remote identification equipment must not interfere with other systems or equipment installed on the unmanned aircraft, and other systems or equipment installed on the unmanned aircraft must not interfere with the remote identification equipment.

(g) *Message broadcast.*

(1) The unmanned aircraft must be capable of broadcasting the message elements in §89.305 using a non-proprietary broadcast specification and using radio frequency spectrum compatible with personal wireless devices in accordance with 47 CFR part 15, where operations may occur without an FCC individual license.

(2) Any broadcasting device used to meet the requirements of this section must be integrated into the unmanned aircraft without modification to its authorized radio frequency parameters and designed to maximize the range at which the broadcast can be received, while complying with 47 CFR part 15 and any other applicable laws in effect as of the date the declaration of compliance is submitted to the FAA for acceptance.

(h) *Message elements performance requirements.*

(1) The reported geometric position of the unmanned aircraft and the control station must be accurate to within 100 feet of the true position, with 95 percent probability.

(2) The reported geometric altitude of the control station must be accurate to within 15 feet of the true geometric altitude, with 95 percent probability.

(3) The reported geometric altitude of the unmanned aircraft must be accurate to within 150 feet of the true geometric altitude, with 95 percent probability.

(4) The unmanned aircraft must broadcast the latitude, longitude, and geometric altitude of the unmanned aircraft and its control station no later than 1.0 seconds from the time of measurement to the time of broadcast.

(5) The unmanned aircraft must broadcast the message elements at a rate of at least 1 message per second.

(i) *Take-off limitation.* The unmanned aircraft must not be able to take off unless it is broadcasting the message elements in §89.305.

§89.315 Minimum message elements broadcast by remote identification broadcast modules.

Remote identification broadcast modules must be capable of broadcasting the following remote identification message elements:

(a) The identity of the unmanned aircraft, consisting of the serial number assigned to the remote identification broadcast module by the person responsible for the production of the remote identification broadcast module.

(b) An indication of the latitude and longitude of the unmanned aircraft.

(c) An indication of the geometric altitude of the unmanned aircraft.

(d) An indication of the velocity of the unmanned aircraft.

(e) An indication of the latitude and longitude of the take-off location of the unmanned aircraft.

(f) An indication of the geometric altitude of the take-off location of the unmanned aircraft.

(g) A time mark identifying the Coordinated Universal Time (UTC) time of applicability of a position source output.

§89.320 Minimum performance requirements for remote identification broadcast modules.

Remote identification broadcast modules must meet the following minimum performance requirements:

(a) *Take-off location.* The remote identification broadcast module must be capable of determining the take-off location of the unmanned aircraft.

(b) *Time mark.* The time mark message element must be synchronized with all other remote identification message elements.

(c) *Self-testing and monitoring.*

(1) Prior to take-off, the remote identification broadcast module must automatically test the remote identification functionality and notify the

person manipulating the flight controls of the unmanned aircraft system of the result of the test.

(2) The remote identification broadcast module must continuously monitor the remote identification functionality from takeoff to shutdown and must provide notification of malfunction or failure to the person manipulating the flight controls of the unmanned aircraft system.

(d) *Tamper resistance.* The remote identification broadcast module must be designed and produced in a way that reduces the ability of a person to tamper with the remote identification functionality.

(e) *Error correction.* The remote identification broadcast module must incorporate error correction in the broadcast of the message elements in §89.315.

(f) *Interference considerations.* The remote identification broadcast module must not interfere with other systems or equipment installed on compatible unmanned aircraft, and other systems or equipment installed on compatible unmanned aircraft must not interfere with the remote identification equipment.

(g) *Message broadcast.*

(1) The remote identification broadcast module must be capable of broadcasting the message elements in §89.315 using a non-proprietary broadcast specification and using radio frequency spectrum compatible with personal wireless devices in accordance with 47 CFR part 15, where operations may occur without an FCC individual license.

(2) The remote identification broadcast module must be designed to maximize the range at which the broadcast can be received, while complying with 47 CFR part 15 and any other applicable laws in effect as of the date the declaration of compliance is submitted to the FAA for acceptance.

(h) *Message elements performance requirements.*

(1) The reported geometric position of the unmanned aircraft must be accurate to within 100 feet of the true position, with 95 percent probability.

(2) The reported geometric altitude of the unmanned aircraft must be accurate to within 150 feet of the true geometric altitude, with 95 percent probability.

(3) The reported geometric position of the take-off location must be accurate to within 100 feet of the true geometric position, with 95 percent probability.

(4) The reported geometric altitude of the take-off location must be accurate to within 150 feet of the true geometric altitude, with 95 percent probability.

(5) The remote identification broadcast module must broadcast the latitude, longitude, and geometric altitude of the unmanned aircraft no later

than 1.0 seconds from the time of measurement to the time of broadcast.

(6) The remote identification broadcast module must broadcast the message elements at a rate of at least 1 message per second.

Subpart E—Means of Compliance

§89.401 Applicability.

This subpart prescribes—

(a) Requirements for means of compliance with subpart D of this part.

(b) Procedural requirements for the submission and acceptance of means of compliance used in the design and production of standard remote identification unmanned aircraft or remote identification broadcast modules to ensure they meet the minimum performance requirements of this part.

(c) Rules governing persons submitting means of compliance for FAA acceptance.

§89.405 Submission of a means of compliance for FAA acceptance.

(a) *Eligibility.* Any person may submit a means of compliance for acceptance by the FAA.

(b) *Required information.* A person requesting acceptance of a means of compliance must submit the following information to the FAA in a form and manner acceptable to the Administrator:

(1) The name of the person or entity submitting the means of compliance, the name of the main point of contact for communications with the FAA, the physical address, email address, and other contact information.

(2) A detailed description of the means of compliance.

(3) An explanation of how the means of compliance addresses all of the minimum performance requirements established in subpart D of this part so that any standard remote identification unmanned aircraft or remote identification broadcast module designed and produced in accordance with such means of compliance meets the remote identification requirements of this part.

(4) Any substantiating material the person wishes the FAA to consider as part of the request.

(c) *Testing and validation.* A means of compliance submitted for acceptance by the FAA must include testing and validation procedures for persons responsible for the production of standard remote identification unmanned aircraft or remote identification broadcast modules to demonstrate through analysis, ground test, or flight test, as appropriate, how the standard remote identification unmanned aircraft or the remote identification broadcast module performs its intended functions and meets the requirements in subpart D of this

part, including any applicable FAA performance requirements for radio station operation.

§89.410 Acceptance of a means of compliance.

(a) A person requesting acceptance of a means of compliance must demonstrate to the Administrator that the means of compliance addresses all of the requirements of subparts D and E of this part, and that any standard remote identification unmanned aircraft or remote identification broadcast module designed and produced in accordance with such means of compliance would meet the performance requirements of subpart D of this part.

(b) The Administrator will evaluate a means of compliance that is submitted to the FAA and may request additional information or documentation, as needed, to supplement the submission.

(c) If the Administrator determines the person has demonstrated that the means of compliance meets the requirements of subparts D and E of this part, the FAA will notify the person that the Administrator has accepted the means of compliance.

§89.415 Rescission.

(a) *Rescission of an FAA-accepted means of compliance.*

(1) A means of compliance is subject to ongoing review by the Administrator. The Administrator may rescind acceptance of a means of compliance if the Administrator determines that a means of compliance does not meet any or all of the requirements of subpart D or E of this part.

(2) The Administrator will publish a notice of rescission in the Federal Register.

(b) *Inapplicability of part 13, subpart D, of this chapter.* Part 13, subpart D, of this chapter does not apply to the procedures of paragraph (a) of this section.

§89.420 Record retention.

A person who submits a means of compliance that is accepted by the Administrator under this subpart must retain the following information for as long as the means of compliance is accepted plus an additional 24 calendar months, and must make available for inspection by the Administrator the following:

(a) All documentation and substantiating data submitted to the FAA for acceptance of the means of compliance.

(b) Records of all test procedures, methodology, and other procedures, as applicable.

(c) Any other information necessary to justify and substantiate how the means of compliance enables compliance with the remote identification requirements of this part.

Subpart F—Remote Identification Design and Production

§89.501 Applicability.

(a) This subpart prescribes—

(1) Requirements for the design and production of unmanned aircraft with remote identification produced for operation in the airspace of the United States.

(2) Requirements for the design and production of remote identification broadcast modules.

(3) Procedural requirements for the submission, acceptance, and rescission of declarations of compliance.

(4) Rules governing persons submitting declarations of compliance for FAA acceptance under this part.

(b) Except as provided in paragraph (c) of this section, this subpart applies to the design and production of all unmanned aircraft operated in the airspace of the United States.

(c) Except for unmanned aircraft designed and produced to be standard remote identification unmanned aircraft, this subpart does not apply to the design or production of:

(1) Home-built unmanned aircraft.

(2) Unmanned aircraft of the United States Government.

(3) Unmanned aircraft that weigh 0.55 pounds or less on takeoff, including everything that is on board or otherwise attached to the aircraft.

(4) Unmanned aircraft designed or produced exclusively for the purpose of aeronautical research or to show compliance with regulations.

§89.505 Serial numbers.

No person may produce a standard remote identification unmanned aircraft under §89.510 or §89.515 or a remote identification broadcast module under §89.520, unless the producer assigns to the unmanned aircraft or remote identification broadcast module a serial number that complies with ANSI/CTA-2063-A. ANSI/CTA-2063-A, *Small Unmanned Aerial Systems Serial Numbers* (September 2019) is incorporated by reference into this section with the approval of the Director of the Office of the Federal Register under 5 U.S.C. 552(a) and 1 CFR part 51. All approved material is available for inspection at the FAA's Office of Rulemaking (ARM-1), 800 Independence Avenue SW, Washington, DC 20590 (telephone 202-267-9677) and is available from Consumer Technology Association (CTA), 1919 South Eads Street, Arlington, VA 22202, CTA@CTA.tech, 703-907-7600 or at *https://www.cta.tech*. It is also available for inspection at the National Archives and Records Administration (NARA). For information on the availability of this material at NARA, email *fedreg.legal@nara.gov*, or go to *www.archives.gov/federal-register/cfr/ibr-locations.html*.

§89.510 Production requirements for unmanned aircraft produced under a design approval or production approval issued under part 21 of this chapter.

After September 16, 2022, no person may produce an unmanned aircraft for operation in the airspace of the United States under a design approval or production approval issued under part 21 of this chapter unless:

(a) All applicable requirements of part 21 of this chapter are met; and

(b) The unmanned aircraft is—

(1) Designed and produced to meet the minimum performance requirements for standard remote identification unmanned aircraft established in §89.310 in accordance with an FAA-accepted means of compliance; or

(2) Equipped with Automatic Dependent Surveillance–Broadcast (ADS-B) Out equipment that meets the requirements of §91.225 of this chapter.

§89.515 Production requirements for unmanned aircraft without design approval or production approval issued under part 21 of this chapter.

Except as provided in §89.510, after September 16, 2022, no person may produce an unmanned aircraft for operation in the airspace of the United States unless—

(a) The unmanned aircraft is designed and produced to meet the minimum performance requirements for standard remote identification unmanned aircraft established in §89.310 in accordance with an FAA-accepted means of compliance; and

(b) All of the following conditions are met:

(1) *Inspection requirements for production of standard unmanned aircraft.* A person responsible for the production of standard remote identification unmanned aircraft must, upon request, allow the Administrator to inspect the person's facilities, technical data, and any standard remote identification unmanned aircraft the person produces, and to witness any tests necessary to determine compliance with this subpart.

(2) *Audit requirements.* A person responsible for the production of standard remote identification unmanned aircraft must cause independent audits to be performed on a recurring basis, and additionally whenever the FAA provides notice of noncompliance or potential noncompliance, to demonstrate the unmanned aircraft listed under a declaration of compliance meet the requirements

89

of this subpart. The person responsible for the production of standard remote identification unmanned aircraft must provide the results of all such audits to the FAA upon request.

(3) *Product support and notification.* A person responsible for the production of standard remote identification unmanned aircraft must maintain product support and notification procedures to notify the public and the FAA of any defect or condition that causes an unmanned aircraft to no longer meet the requirements of this subpart, within 15 calendar days of the date the person becomes aware of the defect or condition.

§89.520 Production requirements for remote identification broadcast modules.

After April 21, 2021, no person may produce remote identification broadcast modules unless:

(a) The remote identification broadcast module is designed and produced to meet the minimum performance requirements for remote identification broadcast modules established in §89.320 in accordance with an FAA-accepted means of compliance; and

(b) All of the following conditions are met:

(1) *Inspection requirements for production of remote identification broadcast modules.* A person responsible for the production of remote identification broadcast modules must, upon request, allow the Administrator to inspect the person's facilities, technical data, and any remote identification broadcast modules the person produces, and to witness any tests necessary to determine compliance with this subpart.

(2) *Audit requirements.* A person responsible for the production of remote identification broadcast modules must cause independent audits to be performed on a recurring basis, and additionally whenever the FAA provides notice of noncompliance or potential noncompliance, to demonstrate the remote identification broadcast modules listed under a declaration of compliance meet the requirements of this subpart. The person responsible for the production of remote identification broadcast modules must provide the results of all such audits to the FAA upon request.

(3) *Product support and notification.* A person responsible for the production of remote identification broadcast modules must maintain product support and notification procedures to notify the public and the FAA of any defect or condition that causes the remote identification broadcast module to no longer meet the requirements of this subpart, within 15 calendar days of the date the person becomes aware of the defect or condition.

(4) *Instructions.* A person responsible for the production of a remote identification broadcast module must make available instructions for

installing and operating the remote identification broadcast module to any person operating an unmanned aircraft with the remote identification broadcast module.

[Amdt. No. 89–1, 86 FR 4505, Jan. 15, 2021; 86 FR 13630, March 10, 2021]

§89.525 Labeling.

(a) No person may produce a standard remote identification unmanned aircraft under §89.515 unless it displays a label indicating that the unmanned aircraft meets the requirements of this part. The label must be in English and be legible, prominent, and permanently affixed to the unmanned aircraft.

(b) No person may produce a remote identification broadcast module under §89.520 unless it displays a label indicating that the equipment meets the requirements of this part. The label must be in English and be legible, prominent, and permanently affixed to the broadcast module.

§89.530 Submission of a declaration of compliance for FAA acceptance.

(a) *Eligibility.* A person responsible for the production of a standard remote identification unmanned aircraft under §89.515 or a remote identification broadcast module under §89.520 must submit a declaration of compliance for acceptance by the FAA.

(b) *Required information for standard remote identification unmanned aircraft.* The person responsible for the production of a standard remote identification unmanned aircraft requesting acceptance of a declaration of compliance must declare that the unmanned aircraft complies with the requirements of this subpart by submitting a declaration of compliance to the FAA in a form and manner acceptable to the Administrator. The declaration must include at a minimum the following information:

(1) The name, physical address, telephone number, and email address of the person responsible for production of the unmanned aircraft.

(2) The unmanned aircraft's make and model.

(3) The unmanned aircraft's serial number, or the range of serial numbers for which the person responsible for production is declaring compliance.

(4) The FCC Identifier of the 47 CFR part 15-compliant radio frequency equipment used and integrated into the unmanned aircraft.

(5) The means of compliance used in the design and production of the unmanned aircraft.

(6) Whether the declaration of compliance is an initial declaration or an amended declaration, and if the declaration of compliance is an amended declaration, the reason for the amendment.

(7) A declaration that the person responsible for the production of the unmanned aircraft:

(i) Can demonstrate that the unmanned aircraft was designed and produced to meet the minimum performance requirements of §89.310 by using an FAA-accepted means of compliance.

(ii) Complies with the requirements of §89.515(b).

(8) A statement that 47 CFR part 15-compliant radio frequency equipment is used and is integrated into the unmanned aircraft without modification to its authorized radio frequency parameters.

(c) *Required information for remote identification broadcast modules.* The person responsible for the production of a remote identification broadcast module under §89.520 that is requesting acceptance of a declaration of compliance must declare that the remote identification broadcast module complies with the requirements of this subpart by submitting a declaration of compliance to the FAA in a form and manner acceptable to the Administrator. The declaration must include at a minimum the following information:

(1) The name, physical address, telephone number, and email address of the person responsible for production of the remote identification broadcast module.

(2) The remote identification broadcast module's make and model.

(3) The remote identification broadcast module's serial number, or the range of serial numbers for which the person responsible for production is declaring compliance.

(4) The FCC Identifier of the 47 CFR part 15-compliant radio frequency equipment used and integrated into the remote identification broadcast module.

(5) The means of compliance used in the design and production of the remote identification broadcast module.

(6) Whether the declaration of compliance is an initial declaration or an amended declaration, and if the declaration of compliance is an amended declaration, the reason for the amendment.

(7) A declaration that the person responsible for the production of the remote identification broadcast module:

(i) Can demonstrate that the remote identification broadcast module was designed and produced to meet the minimum performance requirements of §89.320 by using an FAA-accepted means of compliance.

(ii) Complies with the requirements of §89.520(b).

(8) A statement that 47 CFR part 15-compliant radio frequency equipment is used and is integrated into the remote identification broadcast module without modification to its authorized radio frequency parameters, and a statement that instructions have been provided for installation of 47 CFR part 15-compliant remote identification broadcast module without modification to the broadcast module's authorized radio frequency parameters.

§89.535 Acceptance of a declaration of compliance.

(a) The Administrator will evaluate a declaration of compliance that is submitted to the FAA and may request additional information or documentation, as needed, to supplement the declaration of compliance.

(b) If the Administrator determines that the submitter has demonstrated compliance with the requirements of this subpart, the FAA will notify the submitter that the Administrator has accepted the declaration of compliance.

§89.540 Rescission and reconsideration.

(a) *Rescission of the FAA's acceptance of a declaration of compliance.*

(1) A declaration of compliance is subject to ongoing review by the Administrator. The Administrator may rescind acceptance of a declaration of compliance under circumstances including but not limited to the following:

(i) A standard remote identification unmanned aircraft or remote identification broadcast module listed under an accepted declaration of compliance does not meet the minimum performance requirements of §89.310 or §89.320.

(ii) A previously FAA-accepted declaration of compliance does not meet a requirement of this subpart; or

(iii) The FAA rescinds acceptance of the means of compliance listed in an FAA-accepted declaration of compliance.

(2) The Administrator will notify the person who submitted the FAA-accepted declaration of compliance of any issue of noncompliance.

(3) If the Administrator determines that it is in the public interest, prior to rescinding acceptance of a declaration of compliance, the Administrator may provide a reasonable period of time for the person who submitted the declaration of compliance to remediate the noncompliance. A failure to remediate the noncompliance constitutes cause for rescission of the FAA's acceptance of the declaration of compliance.

(4) The Administrator will notify the person who submitted the declaration of compliance of the decision to rescind acceptance of the declaration of compliance by publishing a notice of rescission in the Federal Register.

(b) *Petition to reconsider the FAA's decision to rescind acceptance of a declaration of compliance.*

(1) The person who submitted the FAA-accepted declaration of compliance or any person adversely affected by the rescission of the Administrator's acceptance of a declaration of compliance may petition for a reconsideration of the decision by submitting a request to the FAA in a form and manner acceptable to the Administrator within 60 calendar days of the date of publication in the Federal Register of notification of rescission.

(2) A petition to reconsider the rescission of the Administrator's acceptance of a declaration of compliance must show that the petitioner is an interested party and has been adversely affected by the decision of the FAA. The petition must also demonstrate at least one of the following:

(i) The petitioner adduces a significant additional fact not previously presented to the FAA.

(ii) The Administrator made a material error of fact in the decision to rescind acceptance of the declaration of compliance.

(iii) The Administrator did not correctly interpret a law, regulation, or precedent.

(3) Upon consideration of the information submitted by the petitioner, the Administrator will notify the petitioner and the person who submitted the declaration of compliance (if different) of the decision on whether to reinstate the Administrator's acceptance of the declaration of compliance.

(c) *Inapplicability of part 13, subpart D, of this chapter.* Part 13, subpart D, of this chapter does not apply to the procedures of paragraphs (a) and (b) of this section.

§89.545 Record retention.

A person who submits a declaration of compliance under this subpart that is accepted by the Administrator must retain the following information for as long as the standard remote identification unmanned aircraft or remote identification broadcast module listed on that declaration of compliance is produced plus an additional 24 calendar months, and must make available for inspection by the Administrator the following:

(a) The means of compliance, all documentation, and substantiating data related to the means of compliance used.

(b) Records of all test results.

(c) Any other information necessary to demonstrate compliance with the means of compliance so that the standard remote identification unmanned aircraft or remote identification broadcast module meets the remote identification requirements and the design and production requirements of this part.

PART 91

GENERAL OPERATING AND FLIGHT RULES

91

91

Authority: 49 U.S.C. 106(f), 106(g), 40101, 40103, 40105, 40113, 40120, 44101, 44111; 44701, 44704, 44709, 44711, 44712, 44715, 44716, 44717, 44722, 46306, 46315, 46316, 46504, 46506–46507, 47122, 47508, 47528–47531, 47534, Pub. L. 114-190, 130 Stat. 615 (49 U.S.C. 44703 note); articles 12 and 29 of the Convention on International Civil Aviation (61 Stat. 1180), (126 Stat. 11).

Special Federal Aviation Regulations

SFAR No. 50–2

Special Flight Rules in the Vicinity of
the Grand Canyon National Park, AZ

1. Applicability. This rule prescribes special operating rules for all persons operating aircraft in the following airspace, designated as the Grand Canyon National Park Special Flight Rules Area:

That airspace extending upward from the surface up to but not including 14,500 feet MSL within an area bounded by a line beginning at lat. 36°09'30" N., long. 114°03'00" W.; northeast to lat. 36°14'00" N., long. 113°09'50" W.; thence northeast along the boundary of the Grand Canyon National Park to lat. 36°24'47" N., long. 112°52'00" W.; to lat. 36°30'30" N., long. 112°36'15" W. to lat. 36°21'30" N., long. 112°00'00" W. to lat. 36°35'30" N., long. 111°53'10" W., to lat. 36°53'00" N., long. 111°36'45" W. to lat. 36°53'00" N., long. 111°33'00" W.; to lat. 36°19'00" N., long. 111°50'50" W.; to lat. 36°17'00" N., long. 111°42'00" W.; to lat. 35°59'30" N., long. 111°42'00" W.; to lat. 35°57'30" N., long. 112°03'55" W.; thence counterclockwise via the 5 statute mile radius of the Grand Canyon Airport airport reference point (lat. 35°57'09" N., long. 112°08'47" W.) to lat. 35°57'30" N., long. 112°14'00" W.; to lat. 35°57'30" N., long. 113°11'00" W.; to lat. 35°42'30" N., long. 113°11'00" W.; to 35°38'30" N.; long. 113°27'30" W.; thence counterclockwise via the 5 statute mile radius of the Peach Springs VORTAC to lat. 35°41'20" N., long. 113°36'00" W.; to lat. 35°55'25" N., long. 113°49'10" W.; to lat. 35°57'45" N., 113°45'20" W.; thence northwest along the park boundary to lat. 36°02'20" N., long. 113°50'15" W.; to 36°00'10" N., long. 113°53'45" W.; thence to the point of beginning.

[Editorial Note: Section 2 is intentionally omitted by the FAA]

3. Aircraft operations: general. Except in an emergency, no person may operate an aircraft in the Special Flight Rules, Area under VFR on or after September 22, 1988, or under IFR on or after April 6, 1989, unless the operation—

(a) Is conducted in accordance with the following procedures:

Note: The following procedures do not relieve the pilot from see-and-avoid responsibility or compliance with FAR 91.119.

(1) Unless necessary to maintain a safe distance from other aircraft or terrain—
(i) Remain clear of the areas described in Section 4; and
(ii) Remain at or above the following altitudes in each sector of the canyon:
Eastern section from Lees Ferry to North Canyon and North Canyon to Boundary Ridge: as prescribed in Section 5.

Boundary Ridge to Supai Point (Yumtheska Point): 10,000 feet MSL.

Western section from Diamond Creek to the Grant Wash Cliffs: 8,000 feet MSL.

(2) Proceed through the four flight corridors described in Section 4 at the following altitudes unless otherwise authorized in writing by the responsible Flight Standards office:
Northbound
11,500 or
13,500 feet MSL
Southbound
>10,500 or
>12,500 feet MSL

(b) Is authorized in writing by the responsible Flight Standards office and is conducted in compliance with the conditions contained in that authorization. Normally authorization will be granted for operation in the areas described in Section 4 or below the altitudes listed in Section 5 only for operations of aircraft necessary for law enforcement, firefighting, emergency medical treatment/evacuation of persons in the vicinity of the Park; for support of Park maintenance or activities; or for aerial access to and maintenance of other property located within the Special Flight Rules Area. Authorization may be issued on a continuing basis.

(c)(1) Prior to November 1, 1988, is conducted in accordance with a specific authorization to operate in that airspace incorporated in the operator's part 135 operations specifications in accordance with the provisions of SFAR 50–1, notwithstanding the provisions of Sections 4 and 5; and

(2) On or after November 1, 1988, is conducted in accordance with a specific authorization to operate in that airspace incorporated in the operated in the operator's operations specifications and approved by the responsible Flight Standards office in accordance with the provisions of SFAR 50–2.

(d) Is a search and rescue mission directed by the U.S. Air Force Rescue Coordination Center.

(e) Is conducted within 3 nautical miles of Whitmore Airstrip, Pearce Ferry Airstrip, North Rim Airstrip, Cliff Dwellers Airstrip, or Marble Canyon Airstrip at an altitudes less than 3,000 feet above airport elevation, for the purpose of landing at or taking off from that facility. Or

(f) Is conducted under an IFR clearance and the pilot is acting in accordance with ATC instructions. An IFR flight plan may not be filed on a route or at an altitude that would require operation in an area described in Section 4.

4. Flight-free zones. Except in an emergency or if otherwise necessary for safety of flight, or unless otherwise authorized by the responsible Flight Standards office for a purpose listed in Section 3(b), no person may operate an aircraft

in the Special Flight Rules Area within the following areas:

(a) Desert View Flight-Free Zone. Within an area bounded by a line beginning at Lat. 35°59'30" N., Long. 111°46'20" W. to 35°59'30" N., Long. 111°52'45" W.; to Lat. 36°04'50" N., Long. 111°52'00" W.; to Lat. 36°06'00" N., Long. 111°46'20" W.; to the point of origin; but not including the airspace at and above 10,500 feet MSL within 1 mile of the western boundary of the zone. The area between the Desert View and Bright Angel Flight-Free Zones is designated the "Zuni Point Corridor."

(b) Bright Angel Flight-Free Zone. Within an area bounded by a line beginning at Lat. 35°59'30" N., Long. 111°55'30" W.; to Lat. 35°59'30" N., Long. 112°04'00" W.; thence counterclockwise via the 5 statute mile radius of the Grand Canyon Airport point (Lat. 35°57'09" N., Long. 112°08'47" W.) to Lat. 36°01'30" N., Long. 112°11'00" W.; to Lat. 36°06'15" N., Long. 112°12'50" W.; to Lat. 36°14'40" N., Long. 112°08'50" W.; to Lat. 36°14'40" N., Long. 111°57'30" W.; to Lat. 36°12'30" N., Long. 111°53'50" W.; to the point of origin; but not including the airspace at and above 10,500 feet MSL within 1 mile of the eastern boundary between the southern boundary and Lat. 36°04'50" N. or the airspace at and above 10,500 feet MSL within 2 miles of the northwest boundary. The area bounded by the Bright Angel and Shinumo Flight-Free Zones is designated the "Dragon Corridor."

(c) Shinumo Flight-Free Zone. Within an area bounded by a line beginning at Lat. 36°04'00" N., Long. 112°16'40" W.; northwest along the park boundary to a point at Lat. 36°12'47" N., Long. 112°30'53" W.; to Lat. 36°21'15" N., Long. 112°20'20" W.; east along the park boundary to Lat. 36°21'15" N., Long. 112°13'55" W.; to Lat. 36°14'40" N., Long. 112°11'25" W.; to the point of origin. The area between the Thunder River/Toroweap and Shinumo Flight Free Zones is designated the "Fossil Canyon Corridor."

(d) Toroweap/Thunder River Flight-Free Zone. Within an area bounded by a line beginning at Lat. 36°22'45" N., Long. 112°20'35" W.; thence northwest along the boundary of the Grand Canyon National Park to Lat. 36°17'48" N., Long. 113°03'15" W.; to Lat. 36°15'00" N., Long. 113°07'10" W.; to Lat. 36°10'30" N., Long. 113°07'10" W.; thence east along the Colorado River to the confluence of Havasu Canyon (Lat. 36°18'40" N., Long. 112°45'45" W.;) including that area within a 1.5 nautical mile radius of Toroweap Overlook (Lat. 36°12'45" N., Long. 113°03'30" W.); to the point of origin; but not including the following airspace designated as the "Tuckup Corridor": at or above 10,500 feet MSL within 2 nautical miles either side of a line extending between Lat. 36°24'47" N.,

Long. 112°48'50" W. and Lat. 36°17'10" N., Long. 112°48'50" W.; to the point of origin.

5. Minimum flight altitudes. Except in an emergency or if otherwise necessary for safety of flight, or unless otherwise authorized by the responsible Flight Standards office for a purpose listed in Section 3(b), no person may operate an aircraft in the Special Flight Rules Area at an altitude lower than the following:

(a) Eastern section from Lees Ferry to North Canyon: 5,000 feet MSL.

(b) Eastern section from North Canyon to Boundary Ridge: 6,000 feet MSL.

(c) Boundary Ridge to Supai (Yumtheska) Point: 7,500 feet MSL.

(d) Supai Point to Diamond Creek: 6,500 feet MSL.

(e) Western section from Diamond Creek to the Grand Wash Cliffs: 5,000 feet MSL.

[Editorial Note: Sections 6, 7, and 8 are intentionally omitted by the FAA]

9. Termination date. Section 1. Applicability, Section 4, Flight-free zones, and Section 5. Minimum flight altitudes, expire on April 19, 2001.

[66 FR 1003, Jan. 4, 2001, as amended by 66 FR 16584, March 26, 2001; 72 FR 9846, March 6, 2007; Docket FAA–2018–0119, Amdt. 91–350, 83 FR 9171, March 5, 2018]

SFAR No. 60
AIR TRAFFIC CONTROL SYSTEM
EMERGENCY OPERATION

1. Each person shall, before conducting any operation under the Federal Aviation Regulations (14 CFR chapter I), be familiar with all available information concerning that operation, including Notices to Airmen issued under §91.139 and, when activated, the provisions of the National Air Traffic Reduced Complement Operations Plan available for inspection at operating air traffic facilities and Regional air traffic division offices, and the General Aviation Reservation Program. No operator may change the designated airport of intended operation for any flight contained in the October 1, 1990, OAG.

2. Notwithstanding any provision of the Federal Aviation Regulations to the contrary, no person may operate an aircraft in the Air Traffic Control System:

(a) Contrary to any restriction, prohibition, procedure or other action taken by the Director of the Office of Air Traffic Systems Management (Director) pursuant to paragraph 3 of this regulation and announced in a Notice to Airmen pursuant to §91.139 of the Federal Aviation Regulations.

(b) When the National Air Traffic Reduced Complement Operations Plan is activated

pursuant to paragraph 4 of this regulation, except in accordance with the pertinent provisions of the National Air Traffic Reduced Complement Operations Plan.

3. Prior to or in connection with the implementation of the RCOP, and as conditions warrant, the Director is authorized to:

(a) Restrict, prohibit, or permit VFR and/or IFR operations at any airport, Class B airspace area, Class C airspace area, or other class of controlled airspace.

(b) Give priority at any airport to flights that are of military necessity, or are medical emergency flights, Presidential flights, and flights transporting critical Government employees.

(c) Implement, at any airport, traffic management procedures, that may include reduction of flight operations. Reduction of flight operations will be accomplished, to the extent practical, on a pro rata basis among and between air carrier, commercial operator, and general aviation operations. Flights canceled under this SFAR at a high density traffic airport will be considered to have been operated for purposes of part 93 of the Federal Aviation Regulations.

4. The Director may activate the National Air Traffic Reduced Complement Operations Plan at any time he finds that it is necessary for the safety and efficiency of the National Airspace System. Upon activation of the RCOP and notwithstanding any provision of the FAR to the contrary, the Director is authorized to suspend or modify any airspace designation.

5. Notice of restrictions, prohibitions, procedures and other actions taken by the Director under this regulation with respect to the operation of the Air Traffic Control system will be announced in Notices to Airmen issued pursuant to §91.139 of the Federal Aviation Regulations.

6. The Director may delegate his authority under this regulation to the extent he considers necessary for the safe and efficient operation of the National Air Traffic Control System.

Authority: 49 U.S.C. app. 1301(7), 1303, 1344, 1348, 1352 through 1355, 1401, 1421 through 1431, 1471, 1472, 1502, 1510, 1522, and 2121 through 2125; articles 12, 29, 31, and 32(a) of the Convention on International Civil Aviation (61 stat. 1180); 42 U.S.C. 4321 et seq.; E.O. 11514, 35 FR 4247, 3 CFR, 1966–1970 Comp., p. 902; 49 U.S.C. 106(g).

[Docket No. 26351, 55 FR 40760, Oct. 4, 1990; as amended by Amdt. 91–227, 56 FR 65652, Dec. 17, 1991]

SFAR No. 97
SPECIAL OPERATING RULES FOR THE CONDUCT OF INSTRUMENT FLIGHT RULES (IFR) AREA NAVIGATION (RNAV) OPERATIONS USING GLOBAL POSITIONING SYSTEMS (GPS) IN ALASKA

Those persons identified in Section 1 may conduct IFR en route RNAV operations in the State of Alaska and its airspace on published air traffic routes using TSO C145a/C146a navigation systems as the only means of IFR navigation. Despite contrary provisions of parts 71, 91, 95, 121, 125, and 135 of this chapter, a person may operate aircraft in accordance with this SFAR if the following requirements are met.

1. Purpose, use, and limitations

(a) This SFAR permits TSO C145a/C146a GPS (RNAV) systems to be used for IFR en route operations in the United States airspace over and near Alaska (as set forth in paragraph c of this section) at Special Minimum En Route Altitudes (MEA) that are outside the operational service volume of ground-based navigation aids, if the aircraft operation also meets the requirements of sections 3 and 4 of this SFAR.

(b) Certificate holders and part 91 operators may operate aircraft under this SFAR provided that they comply with the requirements of this SFAR.

(c) Operations conducted under this SFAR are limited to United States Airspace within and near the State of Alaska as defined in the following area description:

From 62°00'00.000"N, Long. 141°00'00.00"W.;
to Lat. 59°47'54.11"N., Long. 135°28'38.34"W.;
to Lat. 56°00'04.11"N., Long. 130°00'07.80"W.;
to Lat. 54°43'00.00"N., Long. 130°37'00.00"W.;
to Lat. 51°24'00.00"N., Long. 167°49'00.00"W.;
to Lat. 50°08'00.00"N., Long. 176°34'00.00"W.;
to Lat. 45°42'00.00"N., Long. -162°55'00.00"E.;
to Lat. 50°05'00.00"N., Long. -159°00'00.00"E.;
to Lat. 54°00'00.00"N., Long. -169°00'00.00"E.;
to Lat. 60°00'00.00"N., Long. -180°00'00.00"E;
to Lat. 65°00'00.00"N., Long. 168°58'23.00"W.;
to Lat. 90°00'00.00"N., Long. 00°00'0.00"W.;
to Lat. 62°00'00.000"N, Long. 141°00'00.00"W.

(d) No person may operate an aircraft under IFR during the en route portion of flight below the standard MEA or at the special MEA unless the operation is conducted in accordance with sections 3 and 4 of this SFAR.

2. Definitions and abbreviations

For the purposes of this SFAR, the following definitions and abbreviations apply.

Area navigation (RNAV). RNAV is a method of navigation that permits aircraft operations on any desired flight path.

Area navigation (RNAV) route. RNAV route is a published route based on RNAV that can be used by suitably equipped aircraft.

Certificate holder. A certificate holder means a person holding a certificate issued under part 119 or part 125 of this chapter or holding operations specifications issued under part 129 of this chapter.

Global Navigation Satellite System (GNSS). GNSS is a world-wide position and time determination system that uses satellite ranging signals to determine user location. It encompasses all satellite ranging technologies, including GPS and additional satellites. Components of the GNSS include GPS, the Global Orbiting Navigation Satellite System, and WAAS satellites.

Global Positioning System (GPS). GPS is a satellite-based radio navigational, positioning, and time transfer system. The system provides highly accurate position and velocity information and precise time on a continuous global basis to properly equipped users.

Minimum crossing altitude (MCA). The minimum crossing altitude (MCA) applies to the operation of an aircraft proceeding to a higher minimum en route altitude when crossing specified fixes.

Required navigation system. Required navigation system means navigation equipment that meets the performance requirements of TSO C145a / C146a navigation systems certified for IFR en route operations.

Route segment. Route segment is a portion of a route bounded on each end by a fix or NAVAID.

Special MEA. Special MEA refers to the minimum en route altitudes, using required navigation systems, on published routes outside the operational service volume of ground-based navigation aids and are depicted on the published Low Altitude and High Altitude En Route Charts using the color blue and with the suffix "G." For example, a GPS MEA of 4000 feet MSL would be depicted using the color blue, as 4000G.

Standard MEA. Standard MEA refers to the minimum en route IFR altitude on published routes that uses ground-based navigation aids and are depicted on the published Low Altitude and High Altitude En Route Charts using the color black.

Station referenced. Station referenced refers to radio navigational aids or fixes that are referenced by ground based navigation facilities such as VOR facilities.

Wide Area Augmentation System (WAAS). WAAS is an augmentation to GPS that calculates GPS integrity and correction data on the ground and uses geo-stationary satellites to broadcast GPS integrity and correction data to GPS/WAAS users and to provide ranging signals. It is a safety critical system consisting of a ground network of reference and integrity monitor data processing sites to assess current GPS performance, as well as a space segment that broadcasts that assessment to GNSS users to support en route through precision approach navigation. Users of the system include all aircraft applying the WAAS data and ranging signal.

3. Operational Requirements

To operate an aircraft under this SFAR, the following requirements must be met:

(a) Training and qualification for operations and maintenance personnel on required navigation equipment used under this SFAR.

(b) Use authorized procedures for normal, abnormal, and emergency situations unique to these operations, including degraded navigation capabilities, and satellite system outages.

(c) For certificate holders, training of flight crewmembers and other personnel authorized to exercise operational control on the use of those procedures specified in paragraph b of this section.

(d) Part 129 operators must have approval from the State of the operator to conduct operations in accordance with this SFAR.

(e) In order to operate under this SFAR, a certificate holder must be authorized in operations specifications.

4. Equipment Requirements

(a) The certificate holder must have properly installed, certificated, and functional dual required navigation systems as defined in section 2 of this SFAR for the en route operations covered under this SFAR.

(b) When the aircraft is being operated under part 91, the aircraft must be equipped with at least one properly installed, certificated, and functional required navigation system as defined in section 2 of this SFAR for the en route operations covered under this SFAR.

5. Expiration date

This Special Federal Aviation Regulation will remain in effect until rescinded.

[Docket FAA–2003–14305, 68 FR 14077, March 21, 2003]

SFAR No. 104
PROHIBITION AGAINST CERTAIN FLIGHTS BY SYRIAN AIR CARRIERS TO THE UNITED STATES

1. Applicability. This Special Federal Aviation Regulation (SFAR) No. 104 applies to any air carrier owned or controlled by Syria that is engaged in scheduled international air services.

2. Special flight restrictions. Except as provided in paragraphs 3 and 4 of this SFAR No. 104, no air carrier described in paragraph 1 may take off from or land in the territory of the United States.

3. *Permitted operations.* This SFAR does not prohibit overflights of the territory of the United States by any air carrier described in paragraph 1.

4. *Emergency situations.* In an emergency that requires immediate decision and action for the safety of the flight, the pilot in command of an aircraft of any air carrier described in paragraph 1 may deviate from this SFAR to the extent required by that emergency. Each person who deviates from this rule must, within 10 days of the deviation, excluding Saturdays, Sundays, and Federal holidays, submit to the responsible Flight Standards office a complete report of the operations or the aircraft involved in the deviation, including a description of the deviation and the reasons therefor.

5. *Duration.* This SFAR No. 104 will remain in effect until further notice.

[Docket No. FAA–2004–17763, 69 FR 31719, June 4, 2004, as amended by Docket FAA–2018–0119, Amdt. 91–350, 83 FR 9171, March 5, 2018]

Subpart A—General

Source: Docket No. 18334, 54 FR 34292, Aug. 18, 1989, unless otherwise noted.

§91.1 Applicability.

(a) Except as provided in paragraphs (b), (c), (e), and (f) of this section and §§ 91.701 and 91.703, this part prescribes rules governing the operation of aircraft within the United States, including the waters within 3 nautical miles of the U.S. coast.

(b) Each person operating an aircraft in the airspace overlying the waters between 3 and 12 nautical miles from the coast of the United States must comply with §§91.1 through 91.21; §§91.101 through 91.143; §§91.151 through 91.159; §§91.167 through 91.193; §91.203; §91.205; §§91.209 through 91.217; §91.221, §91.225; §§91.303 through 91.319; §§91.323 through 91.327; §91.605; §91.609; §§91.703 through 91.715; and §91.903.

(c) This part applies to each person on board an aircraft being operated under this part, unless otherwise specified.

(d) This part also establishes requirements for operators to take actions to support the continued airworthiness of each airplane.

(e) This part does not apply to any aircraft or vehicle governed by part 103 of this chapter, or subparts B, C, or D of part 101 of this chapter.

(f) Except as provided in §§107.13, 107.27, 107.47, 107.57, and 107.59 of this chapter, this part does not apply to any aircraft governed by part 107 of this chapter.

[Docket No. 18334, 54 FR 34292, Aug. 18, 1989; as amended by Amdt. 91–257, 64 FR 1079, Jan. 7, 1999; Amdt. 91–282, 69 FR 44880, July 27, 2004; Amdt. 91–297, 72 FR 63410, Nov. 8, 2007; Amdt. 91–314, 75 FR 30193, May 28, 2010; Amdt. 91–343, 81 FR 42208, June 28, 2016]

§91.3 Responsibility and authority of the pilot in command.

(a) The pilot in command of an aircraft is directly responsible for, and is the final authority as to, the operation of that aircraft.

(b) In an in-flight emergency requiring immediate action, the pilot in command may deviate from any rule of this part to the extent required to meet that emergency.

(c) Each pilot in command who deviates from a rule under paragraph (b) of this section shall, upon the request of the Administrator, send a written report of that deviation to the Administrator.

(Approved by the Office of Management and Budget under control number 2120–0005)

§91.5 Pilot in command of aircraft requiring more than one required pilot.

No person may operate an aircraft that is type certificated for more than one required pilot flight crewmember unless the pilot in command meets the requirements of §61.58 of this chapter.

§91.7 Civil aircraft airworthiness.

(a) No person may operate a civil aircraft unless it is in an airworthy condition.

(b) The pilot in command of a civil aircraft is responsible for determining whether that aircraft is in condition for safe flight. The pilot in command shall discontinue the flight when unairworthy mechanical, electrical, or structural conditions occur.

§91.9 Civil aircraft flight manual, marking, and placard requirements.

(a) Except as provided in paragraph (d) of this section, no person may operate a civil aircraft without complying with the operating limitations specified in the approved Airplane or Rotorcraft Flight Manual, markings, and placards, or as otherwise prescribed by the certificating authority of the country of registry.

(b) No person may operate a U.S.-registered civil aircraft—

(1) For which an Airplane or Rotorcraft Flight Manual is required by §21.5 of this chapter unless there is available in the aircraft a current, approved Airplane or Rotorcraft Flight Manual or the manual provided for in §121.141(b); and

(2) For which an Airplane or Rotorcraft Flight Manual is not required by §21.5 of this chapter, unless there is available in the aircraft a current approved Airplane or Rotorcraft Flight Manual, approved manual material, markings, and placards, or any combination thereof.

(c) No person may operate a U.S.-registered civil aircraft unless that aircraft is identified in accordance with part 45 or 48 of this chapter.

(d) Any person taking off or landing a helicopter certificated under part 29 of this chapter at a heliport constructed over water may make such momentary flight as is necessary for takeoff or landing through the prohibited range of the limiting height-speed envelope established for the helicopter if that flight through the prohibited range takes place over water on which a safe ditching can be accomplished and if the helicopter is amphibious or is equipped with floats or other emergency flotation gear adequate to accomplish a safe emergency ditching on open water.

[Amdt. 91–366, 87 FR 75846, Dec. 9, 2022]

§91.11 Prohibition on interference with crewmembers.

No person may assault, threaten, intimidate, or interfere with a crewmember in the performance of the crewmember's duties aboard an aircraft being operated.

§91.13 Careless or reckless operation.

(a) Aircraft operations for the purpose of air navigation. No person may operate an aircraft in a careless or reckless manner so as to endanger the life or property of another.

(b) Aircraft operations other than for the purpose of air navigation. No person may operate an aircraft, other than for the purpose of air navigation, on any part of the surface of an airport used by aircraft for air commerce (including areas used by those aircraft for receiving or discharging persons or cargo), in a careless or reckless manner so as to endanger the life or property of another.

§91.15 Dropping objects.

No pilot in command of a civil aircraft may allow any object to be dropped from that aircraft in flight that creates a hazard to persons or property. However, this section does not prohibit the dropping of any object if reasonable precautions are taken to avoid injury or damage to persons or property.

§91.17 Alcohol or drugs.

(a) No person may act or attempt to act as a crewmember of a civil aircraft—

(1) Within 8 hours after the consumption of any alcoholic beverage;

(2) While under the influence of alcohol;

(3) While using any drug that affects the person's faculties in any way contrary to safety; or

(4) While having an alcohol concentration of 0.04 or greater in a blood or breath specimen. Alcohol concentration means grams of alcohol per deciliter of blood or grams of alcohol per 210 liters of breath.

(b) Except in an emergency, no pilot of a civil aircraft may allow a person who appears to be intoxicated or who demonstrates by manner or physical indications that the individual is under the influence of drugs (except a medical patient under proper care) to be carried in that aircraft.

(c) A crewmember shall do the following:

(1) On request of a law enforcement officer, submit to a test to indicate the alcohol concentration in the blood or breath, when—

(i) The law enforcement officer is authorized under State or local law to conduct the test or to have the test conducted; and

(ii) The law enforcement officer is requesting submission to the test to investigate a suspected violation of State or local law governing the same or substantially similar conduct prohibited by paragraph (a)(1), (a)(2), or (a)(4) of this section.

(2) Whenever the FAA has a reasonable basis to believe that a person may have violated paragraph (a)(1), (a)(2), or (a)(4) of this section, on request of the FAA, that person must furnish to the FAA the results, or authorize any clinic, hospital, or doctor, or other person to release to the FAA, the results of each test taken within 4 hours after acting or attempting to act as a crewmember that indicates an alcohol concentration in the blood or breath specimen.

(d) Whenever the Administrator has a reasonable basis to believe that a person may have violated paragraph (a)(3) of this section, that person shall, upon request by the Administrator, furnish the Administrator, or authorize any clinic, hospital, doctor, or other person to release to the Administrator, the results of each test taken within 4 hours after acting or attempting to act as a crewmember that indicates the presence of any drugs in the body.

(e) Any test information obtained by the Administrator under paragraph (c) or (d) of this section may be evaluated in determining a person's qualifications for any airman certificate or possible violations of this chapter and may be used as evidence in any legal proceeding under section 602, 609, or 901 of the Federal Aviation Act of 1958.

[Docket No. 18334, 54 FR 34292, Aug. 18, 1989; as amended by Amdt. 91–291, 71 FR 35764, June 21, 2006]

91

§91.19 Carriage of narcotic drugs, marihuana, and depressant or stimulant drugs or substances.

(a) Except as provided in paragraph (b) of this section, no person may operate a civil aircraft within the United States with knowledge that narcotic drugs, marihuana, and depressant or stimulant drugs or substances as defined in Federal or State statutes are carried in the aircraft.

(b) Paragraph (a) of this section does not apply to any carriage of narcotic drugs, marihuana, and depressant or stimulant drugs or substances authorized by or under any Federal or State statute or by any Federal or State agency.

§91.21 Portable electronic devices.

(a) Except as provided in paragraph (b) of this section, no person may operate, nor may any operator or pilot in command of an aircraft allow the operation of, any portable electronic device on any of the following U.S.-registered civil aircraft:

(1) Aircraft operated by a holder of an air carrier operating certificate or an operating certificate; or

(2) Any other aircraft while it is operated under IFR.

(b) Paragraph (a) of this section does not apply to—

(1) Portable voice recorders;

(2) Hearing aids;

(3) Heart pacemakers;

(4) Electric shavers; or

(5) Any other portable electronic device that the operator of the aircraft has determined will not cause interference with the navigation or communication system of the aircraft on which it is to be used.

(c) In the case of an aircraft operated by a holder of an air carrier operating certificate or an operating certificate, the determination required by paragraph (b)(5) of this section shall be made by that operator of the aircraft on which the particular device is to be used. In the case of other aircraft, the determination may be made by the pilot in command or other operator of the aircraft.

§91.23 Truth-in-leasing clause requirement in leases and conditional sales contracts.

(a) Except as provided in paragraph (b) of this section, the parties to a lease or contract of conditional sale involving a U.S.-registered large civil aircraft and entered into after January 2, 1973, shall execute a written lease or contract and include therein a written truth-in-leasing clause as a concluding paragraph in large print, immediately preceding the space for the signature of the parties, which contains the following with respect to each such aircraft:

(1) Identification of the Federal Aviation Regulations under which the aircraft has been maintained and inspected during the 12 months preceding the execution of the lease or contract of conditional sale, and certification by the parties thereto regarding the aircraft's status of compliance with applicable maintenance and inspection requirements in this part for the operation to be conducted under the lease or contract of conditional sale.

(2) The name and address (printed or typed) and the signature of the person responsible for operational control of the aircraft under the lease or contract of conditional sale, and certification that each person understands that person's responsibilities for compliance with applicable Federal Aviation Regulations.

(3) A statement that an explanation of factors bearing on operational control and pertinent Federal Aviation Regulations can be obtained from the responsible Flight Standards office.

(b) The requirements of paragraph (a) of this section do not apply—

(1) To a lease or contract of conditional sale when—

(i) The party to whom the aircraft is furnished is a foreign air carrier or certificate holder under part 121, 125, 135, or 141 of this chapter, or

(ii) The party furnishing the aircraft is a foreign air carrier or a person operating under part 121, 125, and 141 of this chapter, or a person operating under part 135 of this chapter having authority to engage in on-demand operations with large aircraft.

(2) To a contract of conditional sale, when the aircraft involved has not been registered anywhere prior to the execution of the contract, except as a new aircraft under a dealer's aircraft registration certificate issued in accordance with §47.61 of this chapter.

(c) No person may operate a large civil aircraft of U.S. registry that is subject to a lease or contract of conditional sale to which paragraph (a) of this section applies, unless—

(1) The lessee or conditional buyer, or the registered owner if the lessee is not a citizen of the United States, has mailed a copy of the lease or contract that complies with the requirements of paragraph (a) of this section, within 24 hours of its execution, to the Aircraft Registration Branch, Attn: Technical Section, P.O. Box 25724, Oklahoma City, OK 73125;

(2) A copy of the lease or contract that complies with the requirements of paragraph (a) of this section is carried in the aircraft. The copy of the lease or contract shall be made available for review upon request by the Administrator, and

(3) The lessee or conditional buyer, or the registered owner if the lessee is not a citizen of the United States, has notified by telephone or in person the responsible Flight Standards office. Unless otherwise authorized by that office, the notification shall be given at least 48 hours before takeoff in the case of the first flight of that aircraft under that lease or contract and inform the FAA of—

(i) The location of the airport of departure;

(ii) The departure time; and

(iii) The registration number of the aircraft involved.

(d) The copy of the lease or contract furnished to the FAA under paragraph (c) of this section is commercial or financial information obtained from a person. It is, therefore, privileged and confidential and will not be made available by the FAA for public inspection or copying under 5 U.S.C. 552(b)(4) unless recorded with the FAA under part 49 of this chapter.

(e) For the purpose of this section, a lease means any agreement by a person to furnish an aircraft to another person for compensation or hire, whether with or without flight crewmembers, other than an agreement for the sale of an aircraft and a contract of conditional sale under section 101 of the Federal Aviation Act of 1958. The person furnishing the aircraft is referred to as the lessor, and the person to whom it is furnished the lessee.

(Approved by the Office of Management and Budget under control number 2120–0005)

[Docket No. 18334, 54 FR 34292, Aug. 18, 1989, as amended by Amdt. 91–212, 54 FR 39293, Sept. 25, 1989; Amdt. 91–253, 62 FR 13253, March 19, 1997; Amdt. 91–267, 66 FR 21066, April 27, 2001; Docket FAA–2018–0119, Amdt. 91–350, 83 FR 9171, March 5, 2018]

§91.25 Aviation Safety Reporting Program: Prohibition against use of reports for enforcement purposes.

The Administrator of the FAA will not use reports submitted to the National Aeronautics and Space Administration under the Aviation Safety Reporting Program (or information derived therefrom) in any enforcement action except information concerning accidents or criminal offenses which are wholly excluded from the Program.

§91.27–91.99 [Reserved]

Subpart B—Flight Rules

Source: Docket No. 18334, 54 FR 34294, Aug. 18, 1989, unless otherwise noted.

GENERAL

§91.101 Applicability.

This subpart prescribes flight rules governing the operation of aircraft within the United States and within 12 nautical miles from the coast of the United States.

§91.103 Preflight action.

Each pilot in command shall, before beginning a flight, become familiar with all available information concerning that flight. This information must include—

(a) For a flight under IFR or a flight not in the vicinity of an airport, weather reports and forecasts, fuel requirements, alternatives available if the planned flight cannot be completed, and any known traffic delays of which the pilot in command has been advised by ATC;

(b) For any flight, runway lengths at airports of intended use, and the following takeoff and landing distance information:

(1) For civil aircraft for which an approved Airplane or Rotorcraft Flight Manual containing takeoff and landing distance data is required, the takeoff and landing distance data contained therein; and

(2) For civil aircraft other than those specified in paragraph (b)(1) of this section, other reliable information appropriate to the aircraft, relating to aircraft performance under expected values of airport elevation and runway slope, aircraft gross weight, and wind and temperature.

§91.105 Flight crewmembers at stations.

(a) During takeoff and landing, and while en route, each required flight crewmember shall—

(1) Be at the crewmember station unless the absence is necessary to perform duties in connection with the operation of the aircraft or in connection with physiological needs; and

(2) Keep the safety belt fastened while at the crewmember station.

(b) Each required flight crewmember of a U.S.-registered civil aircraft shall, during takeoff and landing, keep his or her shoulder harness fastened while at his or her assigned duty station. This paragraph does not apply if—

(1) The seat at the crewmember's station is not equipped with a shoulder harness; or

(2) The crewmember would be unable to perform required duties with the shoulder harness fastened.

[Docket No. 18334, 54 FR 34294, Aug. 18, 1989; as amended by Amdt. 91–231, 57 FR 42671, Sept. 15, 1992]

§91.107 Use of safety belts, shoulder harnesses, and child restraint systems.

(a) Unless otherwise authorized by the Administrator—

(1) No pilot may take off a U.S.-registered civil aircraft (except a free balloon that incorporates a basket or gondola, or an airship type certificated before November 2, 1987) unless the pilot in command of that aircraft ensures that each person on board is briefed on how to fasten and unfasten that person's safety belt and, if installed, shoulder harness.

(2) No pilot may cause to be moved on the surface, take off, or land a U.S.-registered civil aircraft (except a free balloon that incorporates a basket or gondola, or an airship type certificated before November 2, 1987) unless the pilot in command of that aircraft ensures that each person on board has been notified to fasten his or her safety belt and, if installed, his or her shoulder harness.

(3) Except as provided in this paragraph, each person on board a U.S.-registered civil aircraft (except a free balloon that incorporates a basket or gondola or an airship type certificated before November 2, 1987) must occupy an approved seat or berth with a safety belt and, if installed, shoulder harness, properly secured about him or her during movement on the surface, takeoff and landing. For seaplane and float equipped rotorcraft operations during movement on the surface, the person pushing off the seaplane or rotorcraft from the dock and the person mooring the seaplane or rotor craft at the dock are excepted from the preceding seating and safety belt requirements. Notwithstanding the preceding requirements of this paragraph, a person may:

(i) Be held by an adult who is occupying an approved seat or berth, provided that the person being held has not reached his or her second birthday and does not occupy or use any restraining device;

(ii) Use the floor of the aircraft as a seat, provided that the person is on board for the purpose of engaging in sport parachuting; or

(iii) Notwithstanding any other requirement of this chapter, occupy an approved child restraint system furnished by the operator or one of the persons described in paragraph (a)(3)(iii)(A) of this section provided that:

(A) The child is accompanied by a parent, guardian, or attendant designated by the child's parent or guardian to attend to the safety of the child during the flight;

(B) Except as provided in paragraph (a)(3)(iii) (B)(4) of this action, the approved child restraint system bears one or more labels as follows:

(1) Seats manufactured to U.S. standards between January 1, 1981, and February 25, 1985, must bear the label: "This child restraint system conforms to all applicable Federal motor vehicle safety standards.";

(2) Seats manufactured to U.S. standards on or after February 26, 1985, must bear two labels:

(i) "This child restraint system conforms to all applicable Federal motor vehicle safety standards;" and

(ii) "THIS RESTRAINT IS CERTIFIED FOR USE IN MOTOR VEHICLES AND AIRCRAFT" in red lettering;

(3) Seats that do not qualify under paragraphs (a)(3)(iii)(B)(1) and (a)(3)(iii)(B)(2) of this section must bear a label or markings showing:

(i) That the seat was manufactured under the standards of the United Nations;

(ii) That the seat was manufactured under the standards of the United Nations;

(iii) That the seat or child restraint device furnished by the operator was approved by the FAA through Type Certificate or Supplemental Type Certificate; or

(iv) That the seat or child restraint device furnished by the operator, or one of the persons described in paragraph (a)(3)(iii)(A) of this section, was approved by the FAA in accordance with §21.8(d) of this chapter or Technical Standard Order C-100b or a later version. The child restraint device manufactured by AmSafe, Inc. (CARES, Part No. 4082) and approved by the FAA in accordance with §21.305(d) (2010 ed.) of this chapter may continue to bear a label or markings showing FAA approval in accordance with §21.305(d) (2010 ed.) of this chapter.

(4) Except as provided in §91.107 (a)(3)(iii)(B) (3)(iii) and §91.107(a)(3)(iii)(B)(3)(iv), booster-type child restraint systems (as defined in Federal Motor Vehicle Safety Standard No. 213 (49 CFR 571.213)), vest- and harness-type child restraint systems, and lap held child restraints are not approved for use in aircraft; and

(C) The operator complies with the following requirements:

(1) The restraint system must be properly secured to an approved forward-facing seat or berth:

(2) The child must be properly secured in the restraint system and must not exceed the specified weight limit for the restraint system; and

(3) The restraint system must bear the appropriate label(s).

(b) Unless otherwise stated, this section does not apply to operations conducted under part 121, 125, or 135 of this chapter. Paragraph (a)(3) of this section does not apply to person subject to §91.105.

[Docket No. 26142, 57 FR 42671, Sept. 15, 1992; as amended by Amdt. 91–250, 61 FR 28421, June 4, 1996; Amdt. 91–289, 70 FR 50906, Aug. 26, 2005; Amdt. 91–292, 71 FR 40009, July 14, 2006; Amdt. 91–317, 75 FR 48857, Aug. 12, 2010; Amdt. 91–332, 79 FR 28812, May 20, 2014]

§91.109 Flight instruction; Simulated instrument flight and certain flight tests.

(a) No person may operate a civil aircraft (except a manned free balloon) that is being used for flight instruction unless that aircraft has fully functioning dual controls. However, instrument flight instruction may be given in an airplane that is equipped with a single, functioning throwover control wheel that controls the elevator and ailerons, in place of fixed, dual controls, when—

(1) The instructor has determined that the flight can be conducted safely; and

(2) The person manipulating the controls has at least a private pilot certificate with appropriate category and class ratings.

(b) An airplane equipped with a single, functioning throwover control wheel that controls the elevator and ailerons, in place of fixed, dual controls may be used for flight instruction to conduct a flight review required by §61.56 of this chapter, or to obtain recent flight experience or an instrument proficiency check required by §61.57 when—

(1) The airplane is equipped with operable rudder pedals at both pilot stations;

(2) The pilot manipulating the controls is qualified to serve and serves as pilot in command during the entire flight;

(3) The instructor is current and qualified to serve as pilot in command of the airplane, meets the requirements of §61.195(b), and has logged at least 25 hours of pilot-in-command flight time in the make and model of airplane; and

(4) The pilot in command and the instructor have determined the flight can be conducted safely.

(c) No person may operate a civil aircraft in simulated instrument flight unless—

(1) The other control seat is occupied by a safety pilot who possesses at least:

(i) A private pilot certificate with category and class ratings appropriate to the aircraft being flown; or

(ii) For purposes of providing training for a solo cross-country endorsement under §61.93 of this chapter, a flight instructor certificate with an appropriate sport pilot rating and meets the requirements of §61.412 of this chapter.

(2) The safety pilot has adequate vision forward and to each side of the aircraft, or a competent observer in the aircraft adequately supplements the vision of the safety pilot; and

(3) Except in the case of lighter-than-air aircraft, that aircraft is equipped with fully functioning dual controls. However, simulated instrument flight may be conducted in a single-engine airplane, equipped with a single, functioning, throwover control wheel, in place of fixed, dual controls of the elevator and ailerons, when—

(i) The safety pilot has determined that the flight can be conducted safely; and

(ii) The person manipulating the controls has at least a private pilot certificate with appropriate category and class ratings.

(d) No person may operate a civil aircraft that is being used for a flight test for an airline transport pilot certificate or a class or type rating on that certificate, or for a part 121 proficiency flight test, unless the pilot seated at the controls, other than the pilot being checked, is fully qualified to act as pilot in command of the aircraft.

[Docket No. 18334, 54 FR 34294, Aug. 18, 1989; as amended by Amdt. 91–324, 76 FR 54107, Aug. 31, 2011; Amdt. 91–351, 83 FR 30281, June 27, 2018]

§91.111 Operating near other aircraft.

(a) No person may operate an aircraft so close to another aircraft as to create a collision hazard.

(b) No person may operate an aircraft in formation flight except by arrangement with the pilot in command of each aircraft in the formation.

(c) No person may operate an aircraft, carrying passengers for hire, in formation flight.

§91.113 Right-of-way rules: Except water operations.

(a) *Inapplicability.* This section does not apply to the operation of an aircraft on water.

(b) *General.* When weather conditions permit, regardless of whether an operation is conducted under instrument flight rules or visual flight rules, vigilance shall be maintained by each person operating an aircraft so as to see and avoid other aircraft. When a rule of this section gives another aircraft the right-of-way, the pilot shall give way to that aircraft and may not pass over, under, or ahead of it unless well clear.

(c) *In distress.* An aircraft in distress has the right-of-way over all other air traffic.

(d) *Converging.* When aircraft of the same category are converging at approximately the same altitude (except head-on, or nearly so), the aircraft to the other's right has the right-of-way. If the aircraft are of different categories—

(1) A balloon has the right-of-way over any other category of aircraft;

(2) A glider has the right-of-way over an airship, powered parachute, weight-shift-control aircraft, airplane, or rotorcraft.

(3) An airship has the right-of-way over a powered parachute, weight-shift-control aircraft, airplane, or rotorcraft.

However, an aircraft towing or refueling other aircraft has the right-of-way over all other engine-driven aircraft.

(e) *Approaching head-on.* When aircraft are approaching each other head-on, or nearly so, each pilot of each aircraft shall alter course to the right.

(f) *Overtaking.* Each aircraft that is being overtaken has the right-of-way and each pilot of an overtaking aircraft shall alter course to the right to pass well clear.

(g) *Landing.* Aircraft, while on final approach to land or while landing, have the right-of-way over other aircraft in flight or operating on the surface, except that they shall not take advantage of this rule to force an aircraft off the runway surface which has already landed and is attempting to make way for an aircraft on final approach. When two or more aircraft are approaching an airport for the purpose of landing, the aircraft at the lower altitude has the right-of-way, but it shall not take advantage of this rule to cut in front of another which is on final approach to land or to overtake that aircraft.

[Docket No. 18334, 54 FR 34294, Aug. 18, 1989; as amended by Amdt. 91–282, 69 FR 44880, July 27, 2004]

§91.115 Right-of-way rules: Water operations.

(a) *General.* Each person operating an aircraft on the water shall, insofar as possible, keep clear of all vessels and avoid impeding their navigation, and shall give way to any vessel or other aircraft that is given the right-of-way by any rule of this section.

(b) *Crossing.* When aircraft, or an aircraft and a vessel, are on crossing courses, the aircraft or vessel to the other's right has the right-of-way.

(c) *Approaching head-on.* When aircraft, or an aircraft and a vessel, are approaching head-on, or nearly so, each shall alter its course to the right to keep well clear.

(d) *Overtaking.* Each aircraft or vessel that is being overtaken has the right-of-way, and the one overtaking shall alter course to keep well clear.

(e) *Special circumstances.* When aircraft, or an aircraft and a vessel, approach so as to involve risk of collision, each aircraft or vessel shall proceed with careful regard to existing circumstances, including the limitations of the respective craft.

§91.117 Aircraft speed.

(a) Unless otherwise authorized by the Administrator, no person may operate an aircraft below 10,000 feet MSL at an indicated airspeed of more than 250 knots (288 m.p.h.).

(b) Unless otherwise authorized or required by ATC, no person may operate an aircraft at or below 2,500 feet above the surface within 4 nautical miles of the primary airport of a Class C or Class D airspace area at an indicated airspeed of more than 200 knots (230 m.p.h.). This paragraph (b) does not apply to any operations within a Class B airspace area. Such operations shall comply with paragraph (a) of this section.

(c) No person may operate an aircraft in the airspace underlying a Class B airspace area designated for an airport or in a VFR corridor designated through such a Class B airspace area, at an indicated airspeed of more than 200 knots (230 mph).

(d) If the minimum safe airspeed for any particular operation is greater than the maximum speed prescribed in this section, the aircraft may be operated at that minimum speed.

[Docket No. 18334, 54 FR 34292, Aug. 18, 1989; as amended by Amdt. 91–219, 55 FR 34708, Aug. 24, 1990; Amdt. 91–227, 56 FR 65657, Dec. 17, 1991; Amdt. 91–233, 58 FR 43554, Aug. 17, 1993]

§91.119 Minimum safe altitudes: General.

Except when necessary for takeoff or landing, no person may operate an aircraft below the following altitudes:

(a) *Anywhere.* An altitude allowing, if a power unit fails, an emergency landing without undue hazard to persons or property on the surface.

(b) *Over congested areas.* Over any congested area of a city, town, or settlement, or over any open air assembly of persons, an altitude of 1,000 feet above the highest obstacle within a horizontal radius of 2,000 feet of the aircraft.

(c) *Over other than congested areas.* An altitude of 500 feet above the surface, except over open water or sparsely populated areas. In those cases, the aircraft may not be operated closer than 500 feet to any person, vessel, vehicle, or structure.

(d) *Helicopters, powered parachutes, and weight-shift-control aircraft.* If the operation is conducted without hazard to persons or property on the surface—

(1) A helicopter may be operated at less than the minimums prescribed in paragraph (b) or (c) of this section, provided each person operating the helicopter complies with any routes or altitudes specifically prescribed for helicopters by the FAA; and

(2) A powered parachute or weight-shift-control aircraft may be operated at less than the minimums prescribed in paragraph (c) of this section.

[Docket No. 18334, 54 FR 34294, Aug. 18, 1989; as amended by Amdt. 91–311, 75 FR 5223, Feb. 1, 2010]

§91.121 Altimeter settings.

(a) Each person operating an aircraft shall maintain the cruising altitude or flight level of that aircraft, as the case may be, by reference to an altimeter that is set, when operating—

(1) Below 18,000 feet MSL, to—

(i) The current reported altimeter setting of a station along the route and within 100 nautical miles of the aircraft;

(ii) If there is no station within the area prescribed in paragraph (a)(1)(i) of this section, the current reported altimeter setting of an appropriate available station; or

(iii) In the case of an aircraft not equipped with a radio, the elevation of the departure airport or an appropriate altimeter setting available before departure; or

(2) At or above 18,000 feet MSL, to 29.92" Hg.

(b) The lowest usable flight level is determined by the atmospheric pressure in the area of operation as shown in the following table:

Current altimeter setting	Lowest usable flight level
29.92 (or higher)	180
29.91 through 29.42	185
29.41 through 28.92	190
28.91 through 28.42	195
28.41 through 27.92	200
27.91 through 27.42	205
27.41 through 26.92	210

(c) To convert minimum altitude prescribed under §§91.119 and 91.177 to the minimum flight level, the pilot shall take the flight level equivalent of the minimum altitude in feet and add the appropriate number of feet specified below, according to the current reported altimeter setting:

Current altimeter setting	Adjustment factor
29.92 (or higher)	None
29.91 through 29.42	500
29.41 through 28.92	1,000
28.91 through 28.42	1,500
28.41 through 27.92	2,000
27.91 through 27.42	2,500
27.41 through 26.92	3,000

§91.123 Compliance with ATC clearances and instructions.

(a) When an ATC clearance has been obtained, no pilot in command may deviate from that clearance unless an amended clearance is obtained, an emergency exists, or the deviation is in response to a traffic alert and collision avoidance system resolution advisory. However, except in Class A airspace, a pilot may cancel an IFR flight plan if the operation is being conducted in VFR weather conditions. When a pilot is uncertain of an ATC clearance, that pilot shall immediately request clarification from ATC.

(b) Except in an emergency, no person may operate an aircraft contrary to an ATC instruction in an area in which air traffic control is exercised.

(c) Each pilot in command who, in an emergency, or in response to a traffic alert and collision avoidance system resolution advisory, deviates from an ATC clearance or instruction shall notify ATC of that deviation as soon as possible.

(d) Each pilot in command who (though not deviating from a rule of this subpart) is given priority by ATC in an emergency, shall submit a detailed report of that emergency within 48 hours to the manager of that ATC facility, if requested by ATC.

(e) Unless otherwise authorized by ATC, no person operating an aircraft may operate that aircraft according to any clearance or instruction that has been issued to the pilot of another aircraft for radar air traffic control purposes.

(Approved by the Office of Management and Budget under control number 2120–0005)

[Docket No. 18834, 54 FR 34294, Aug. 18, 1989; as amended by Amdt. 91–227, 56 FR 65658, Dec. 17, 1991; Amdt. 91–244, 60 FR 50679, Sept. 29, 1995]

§91.125 ATC light signals.

ATC light signals have the meaning shown in the following table:

Color and type of signal	Meaning with respect to aircraft on the surface	Meaning with respect to aircraft in flight
Steady green	Cleared for takeoff	Cleared to land
Flashing green	Cleared to taxi	Return for landing (to be followed by steady green at proper time)
Steady red	Stop	Give way to other aircraft and continue circling
Flashing red	Taxi clear of runway in use	Airport unsafe—do not land
Flashing white	Return to starting point on airport	Not applicable
Alternating red and green	Exercise extreme caution	Exercise extreme caution

§91.126 Operating on or in the vicinity of an airport in Class G airspace.

(a) *General.* Unless otherwise authorized or required, each person operating an aircraft on or in the vicinity of an airport in a Class G airspace area must comply with the requirements of this section.

(b) *Direction of turns.* When approaching to land at an airport without an operating control tower in Class G airspace—

(1) Each pilot of an airplane must make all turns of that airplane to the left unless the airport displays approved light signals or visual markings indicating that turns should be made to the right, in which case the pilot must make all turns to the right; and

(2) Each pilot of a helicopter or a powered parachute must avoid the flow of fixed-wing aircraft.

(c) *Flap settings.* Except when necessary for training or certification, the pilot in command of a civil turbojet-powered aircraft must use, as a final flap setting, the minimum certificated landing flap setting set forth in the approved performance information in the Airplane Flight Manual for the applicable conditions. However, each pilot in command has the final authority and responsibility for the safe operation of the pilot's airplane, and may use a different flap setting for that airplane if the pilot determines that it is necessary in the interest of safety.

(d) *Communications with control towers.* Unless otherwise authorized or required by ATC, no person may operate an aircraft to, from, through, or on an airport having an operational control tower unless two-way radio communications are maintained between that aircraft and the control tower. Communications must be established prior to 4 nautical miles from the airport, up to and including 2,500 feet AGL. However, if the aircraft radio fails in flight, the pilot in command may operate that aircraft and land if weather conditions are at or above basic VFR weather minimums, visual contact with the tower is maintained, and a clearance to land is received. If the aircraft radio fails while in flight under IFR, the pilot must comply with §91.185.

[Docket No. 24458, 56 FR 65658, Dec. 17, 1991; as amended by Amdt. 91–239, 59 FR 11693, March 11, 1994; Amdt. 91–282, 69 FR 44880, July 27, 2004]

§91.127 Operating on or in the vicinity of an airport in Class E airspace.

(a) Unless otherwise required by part 93 of this chapter or unless otherwise authorized or required by the ATC facility having jurisdiction over the Class E airspace area, each person operating an aircraft on or in the vicinity of an airport in a Class E airspace area must comply with the requirements of §91.126.

(b) *Departures.* Each pilot of an aircraft must comply with any traffic patterns established for that airport in part 93 of this chapter.

(c) *Communications with control towers.* Unless otherwise authorized or required by ATC, no person may operate an aircraft to, from, through, or on an airport having an operational control tower unless two-way radio communications are maintained between that aircraft and the control tower. Communications must be established prior to 4 nautical miles from the airport, up to and including 2,500 feet AGL. However, if the aircraft radio fails in flight, the pilot in command may operate that aircraft and land if weather conditions are at or above basic VFR weather minimums, visual contact with the tower is maintained, and a clearance to land is received. If the aircraft radio fails while in flight under IFR, the pilot must comply with §91.185.

[Docket No. 24458, 56 FR 65658, Dec. 17, 1991; as amended by Amdt. 91–239, 59 FR 11693, March 11, 1994]

§91.129 Operations in Class D airspace.

(a) *General.* Unless otherwise authorized or required by the ATC facility having jurisdiction over the Class D airspace area, each person operating an aircraft in Class D airspace must comply with the applicable provisions of this section. In addition, each person must comply with §§91.126 and 91.127. For the purpose of this section, the primary airport is the airport for which the Class D airspace area is designated. A satellite airport is any other airport within the Class D airspace area.

(b) *Deviations.* An operator may deviate from any provision of this section under the provisions of an ATC authorization issued by the ATC facility having jurisdiction over the airspace concerned. ATC may authorize a deviation on a continuing basis or for an individual flight, as appropriate.

(c) *Communications.* Each person operating an aircraft in Class D airspace must meet the following two-way radio communications requirements:

(1) *Arrival or through flight.* Each person must establish two-way radio communications with the ATC facility (including foreign ATC in the case of foreign airspace designated in the United States) providing air traffic services prior to entering that airspace and thereafter maintain those communications while within that airspace.

(2) *Departing flight.* Each person—

(i) From the primary airport or satellite airport with an operating control tower must establish and maintain two-way radio communications with the control tower, and thereafter as instructed by ATC while operating in the Class D airspace area; or

(ii) From a satellite airport without an operating control tower, must establish and maintain two-way radio communications with the ATC facility having jurisdiction over the Class D airspace area as soon as practicable after departing.

(d) Communications failure. Each person who operates an aircraft in a Class D airspace area must maintain two-way radio communications with the ATC facility having jurisdiction over that area.

(1) If the aircraft radio fails in flight under IFR, the pilot must comply with §91.185 of the part.

(2) If the aircraft radio fails in flight under VFR, the pilot in command may operate that aircraft and land if—

(i) Weather conditions are at or above basic VFR weather minimums;

(ii) Visual contact with the tower is maintained; and

(iii) A clearance to land is received.

(e) Minimum altitudes when operating to an airport in Class D airspace.

(1) Unless required by the applicable distance-from-cloud criteria, each pilot operating a large or turbine-powered airplane must enter the traffic pattern at an altitude of at least 1,500 feet above the elevation of the airport and maintain at least 1,500 feet until further descent is required for a safe landing.

(2) Each pilot operating a large or turbine-powered airplane approaching to land on a runway served by an instrument approach procedure with vertical guidance, if the airplane is so equipped, must:

(i) Operate that airplane at an altitude at or above the glide path between the published final approach fix and the decision altitude (DA), or decision height (DH), as applicable; or

(ii) If compliance with the applicable distance-from-cloud criteria requires glide path interception closer in, operate that airplane at or above the glide path, between the point of interception of glide path and the DA or the DH.

(3) Each pilot operating an airplane approaching to land on a runway served by a visual approach slope indicator must maintain an altitude at or above the glide path until a lower altitude is necessary for a safe landing.

(4) Paragraphs (e)(2) and (e)(3) of this section do not prohibit normal bracketing maneuvers above or below the glide path that are conducted for the purpose of remaining on the glide path.

(f) Approaches. Except when conducting a circling approach under Part 97 of this chapter or unless otherwise required by ATC, each pilot must—

(1) Circle the airport to the left, if operating an airplane; or

(2) Avoid the flow of fixed-wing aircraft, if operating a helicopter.

(g) Departures. No person may operate an aircraft departing from an airport except in compliance with the following:

(1) Each pilot must comply with any departure procedures established for that airport by the FAA.

(2) Unless otherwise required by the prescribed departure procedure for that airport or the applicable distance from clouds criteria, each pilot of a turbine-powered airplane and each pilot of a large airplane must climb to an altitude of 1,500 feet above the surface as rapidly as practicable.

(h) Noise abatement. Where a formal runway use program has been established by the FAA, each pilot of a large or turbine-powered airplane assigned a noise abatement runway by ATC must use that runway. However, consistent with the final authority of the pilot in command concerning the safe operation of the aircraft as prescribed in §91.3(a), ATC may assign a different runway if requested by the pilot in the interest of safety.

(i) Takeoff, landing, taxi clearance. No person may, at any airport with an operating control tower, operate an aircraft on a runway or taxiway, or take off or land an aircraft, unless an appropriate clearance is received from ATC.

[Docket No. 24458, 56 FR 65658, Dec. 17, 1991; as amended by Amdt. 91–234, 58 FR 48793, Sept. 20, 1993; Amdt. 91–296, 72 FR 31678, June 7, 2007; Docket No. FAA–2011–1396, 77 FR 28250, May 14, 2012]

§91.130 Operations in Class C airspace.

(a) General. Unless otherwise authorized by ATC each aircraft operation in Class C airspace must be conducted in compliance with this section and §91.129. For the purpose of this section, the primary airport is the airport for which the Class C airspace area is designated. A satellite airport is any other airport within the Class C airspace area.

(b) Traffic patterns. No person may take off or land an aircraft at a satellite airport within a Class C airspace area except in compliance with FAA arrival and departure traffic patterns.

(c) Communications. Each person operating an aircraft in Class C airspace must meet the following two-way radio communications requirements:

(1) Arrival or through flight. Each person must establish two-way radio communications with the ATC facility (including foreign ATC in the case of foreign airspace designated in the United States) providing air traffic services prior to entering that airspace and thereafter maintain those communications while within that airspace.

(2) Departing flight. Each person—

(i) From the primary airport or satellite airport with an operating control tower must establish and maintain two-way radio communications with

the control tower, and thereafter as instructed by ATC while operating in the Class C airspace area; or

(ii) From a satellite airport without an operating control tower, must establish and maintain two-way radio communications with the ATC facility having jurisdiction over the Class C airspace area as soon as practicable after departing.

(d) *Equipment requirements.* Unless otherwise authorized by the ATC having jurisdiction over the Class C airspace area, no person may operate an aircraft within a Class C airspace area designated for an airport unless that aircraft is equipped with the applicable equipment specified in §91.215, and after January 1, 2020, §91.225.

(e) *Deviations.* An operator may deviate from any provision of this section under the provisions of an ATC authorization issued by the ATC facility having jurisdiction over the airspace concerned. ATC may authorize a deviation on a continuing basis or for an individual flight, as appropriate.

[Docket No. 24458, 56 FR 65659, Dec. 17, 1991; as amended by Amdt. 91–232, 58 FR 40736, July 30, 1993; Amdt. 91–239, 59 FR 11693, March 11, 1994; Amdt. 91–314, 75 FR 30193, May 28, 2010]

§91.131 Operations in Class B airspace.

(a) *Operating rules.* No person may operate an aircraft within a Class B airspace area except in compliance with §91.129 and the following rules:

(1) The operator must receive an ATC clearance from the ATC facility having jurisdiction for that area before operating an aircraft in that area.

(2) Unless otherwise authorized by ATC, each person operating a large turbine engine-powered airplane to or from a primary airport for which a Class B airspace area is designated must operate at or above the designated floors of the Class B airspace area while within the lateral limits of that area.

(3) Any person conducting pilot training operations at an airport within a Class B airspace area must comply with any procedures established by ATC for such operations in that area.

(b) *Pilot requirements.*

(1) No person may take off or land a civil aircraft at an airport within a Class B airspace area or operate a civil aircraft within a Class B airspace area unless—

(i) The pilot in command holds at least a private pilot certificate;

(ii) The pilot in command holds a recreational pilot certificate and has met—

(A) The requirements of §61.101(d) of this chapter; or

(B) The requirements for a student pilot seeking a recreational pilot certificate in §61.94 of this chapter;

(iii) The pilot in command holds a sport pilot certificate and has met—

(A) The requirements of §61.325 of this chapter; or

(B) The requirements for a student pilot seeking a recreational pilot certificate in §61.94 of this chapter; or

(iv) The aircraft is operated by a student pilot who has met the requirements of §61.94 or §61.95 of this chapter, as applicable.

(2) Notwithstanding the provisions of paragraphs (b)(1)(ii), (b)(1)(iii) and (b)(1)(iv) of this section, no person may take off or land a civil aircraft at those airports listed in section 4 of appendix D to this part unless the pilot in command holds at least a private pilot certificate.

(c) *Communications and navigation equipment requirements.* Unless otherwise authorized by ATC, no person may operate an aircraft within a Class B airspace area unless that aircraft is equipped with—

(1) For IFR operation. An operable VOR or TACAN receiver or an operable and suitable RNAV system; and

(2) For all operations. An operable two-way radio capable of communications with ATC on appropriate frequencies for that Class B airspace area.

(d) *Other equipment requirements.* No person may operate an aircraft in a Class B airspace area unless the aircraft is equipped with—

(1) The applicable operating transponder and automatic altitude reporting equipment specified in §91.215(a), except as provided in §91.215(e), and

(2) After January 1, 2020, the applicable Automatic Dependent Surveillance–Broadcast Out equipment specified in §91.225.

[Docket No. 24458, 56 FR 65658, Dec. 17, 1991; as amended by Amdt. 91–282, 69 FR 44880, July 27, 2004; Amdt. 91–296, 72 FR 31678, June 7, 2007; Amdt. 91–314, 75 FR 30193, May 28, 2010]

§91.133 Restricted and prohibited areas.

(a) No person may operate an aircraft within a restricted area (designated in part 73) contrary to the restrictions imposed, or within a prohibited area, unless that person has the permission of the using or controlling agency, as appropriate.

(b) Each person conducting, within a restricted area, an aircraft operation (approved by the using agency) that creates the same hazards as the operations for which the restricted area was designated may deviate from the rules of this subpart that are not compatible with the operation of the aircraft.

§91.135 Operations in Class A airspace.

Except as provided in paragraph (d) of this section, each person operating an aircraft in Class A airspace must conduct that operation under instrument flight rules (IFR) and in compliance with the following:

(a) *Clearance.* Operations may be conducted only under an ATC clearance received prior to entering the airspace.

(b) *Communications.* Unless otherwise authorized by ATC, each aircraft operating in Class A airspace must be equipped with a two-way radio capable of communicating with ATC on a frequency assigned by ATC. Each pilot must maintain two-way radio communications with ATC while operating in Class A airspace.

(c) *Equipment requirements.* Unless otherwise authorized by ATC, no person may operate an aircraft within Class A airspace unless that aircraft is equipped with the applicable equipment specified in §91.215, and after January 1, 2020, §91.225.

(d) *ATC authorizations.* An operator may deviate from any provision of this section under the provisions of an ATC authorization issued by the ATC facility having jurisdiction of the airspace concerned. In the case of an inoperative transponder, ATC may immediately approve an operation within a Class A airspace area allowing flight to continue, if desired, to the airport of ultimate destination, including any intermediate stops, or to proceed to a place where suitable repairs can be made, or both. Requests for deviation from any provision of this section must be submitted in writing, at least 4 days before the proposed operation. ATC may authorize a deviation on a continuing basis or for an individual flight.

[Docket No. 24458, 56 FR 65659, Dec. 17, 1991; as amended by Amdt. 91–314, 75 FR 30193, May 28, 2010]

§91.137 Temporary flight restrictions in the vicinity of disaster/hazard areas.

(a) The Administrator will issue a Notice to Airmen (NOTAM) designating an area within which temporary flight restrictions apply and specifying the hazard or condition requiring their imposition, whenever he determines it is necessary in order to—

(1) Protect persons and property on the surface or in the air from a hazard associated with an incident on the surface;

(2) Provide a safe environment for the operation of disaster relief aircraft; or

(3) Prevent an unsafe congestion of sightseeing and other aircraft above an incident or event which may generate a high degree of public interest.

The Notice to Airmen will specify the hazard or condition that requires the imposition of temporary flight restrictions.

(b) When a NOTAM has been issued under paragraph (a)(1) of this section, no person may operate an aircraft within the designated area unless that aircraft is participating in the hazard relief activities and is being operated under the direction of the official in charge of on scene emergency response activities.

(c) When a NOTAM has been issued under paragraph (a)(2) of this section, no person may operate an aircraft within the designated area unless at least one of the following conditions are met:

(1) The aircraft is participating in hazard relief activities and is being operated under the direction of the official in charge of on scene emergency response activities.

(2) The aircraft is carrying law enforcement officials.

(3) The aircraft is operating under the ATC approved IFR flight plan.

(4) The operation is conducted directly to or from an airport within the area, or is necessitated by the impracticability of VFR flight above or around the area due to weather, or terrain; notification is given to the Flight Service Station (FSS) or ATC facility specified in the NOTAM to receive advisories concerning disaster relief aircraft operations; and the operation does not hamper or endanger relief activities and is not conducted for the purpose of observing the disaster.

(5) The aircraft is carrying properly accredited news representatives, and, prior to entering the area, a flight plan is filed with the appropriate FAA or ATC facility specified in the Notice to Airmen and the operation is conducted above the altitude used by the disaster relief aircraft, unless otherwise authorized by the official in charge of on scene emergency response activities.

(d) When a NOTAM has been issued under paragraph (a)(3) of this section, no person may operate an aircraft within the designated area unless at least one of the following conditions is met:

(1) The operation is conducted directly to or from an airport within the area, or is necessitated by the impracticability of VFR flight above or around the area due to weather or terrain, and the operation is not conducted for the purpose of observing the incident or event.

(2) The aircraft is operating under an ATC approved IFR flight plan.

(3) The aircraft is carrying incident or event personnel, or law enforcement officials.

(4) The aircraft is carrying properly accredited news representatives and, prior to entering that area, a flight plan is filed with the appropriate FSS or ATC facility specified in the NOTAM.

91

(e) Flight plans filed and notifications made with an FSS or ATC facility under this section shall include the following information:

(1) Aircraft identification, type and color.

(2) Radio communications frequencies to be used.

(3) Proposed times of entry of, and exit from, the designated area.

(4) Name of news media or organization and purpose of flight.

(5) Any other information requested by ATC.

§91.138 Temporary flight restrictions in national disaster areas in the State of Hawaii.

(a) When the Administrator has determined, pursuant to a request and justification provided by the Governor of the State of Hawaii, or the Governor's designee, that an inhabited area within a declared national disaster area in the State of Hawaii is in need of protection for humanitarian reasons, the Administrator will issue a Notice to Airmen (NOTAM) designating an area within which temporary flight restrictions apply. The Administrator will designate the extent and duration of the temporary flight restrictions necessary to provide for the protection of persons and property on the surface.

(b) When a NOTAM has been issued in accordance with this section, no person may operate an aircraft within the designated area unless at least one of the following conditions is met:

(1) That person has obtained authorization from the official in charge of associated emergency or disaster relief response activities, and is operating the aircraft under the conditions of that authorization.

(2) The aircraft is carrying law enforcement officials.

(3) The aircraft is carrying persons involved in an emergency or a legitimate scientific purpose.

(4) The aircraft is carrying properly accredited newspersons, and that prior to entering the area, a flight plan is filed with the appropriate FAA or ATC facility specified in the NOTAM and the operation is conducted in compliance with the conditions and restrictions established by the official in charge of on-scene emergency response activities.

(5) The aircraft is operating in accordance with an ATC clearance or instruction.

(c) A NOTAM issued under this section is effective for 90 days or until the national disaster area designation is terminated, whichever comes first, unless terminated by notice or extended by the Administrator at the request of the Governor of the State of Hawaii or the Governor's designee.

[Docket No. 26476, 56 FR 23178, May 20, 1991; as amended by Amdt. 91–270, 66 FR 47377, Sept. 11, 2001]

§91.139 Emergency air traffic rules.

(a) This section prescribes a process for utilizing Notices to Airmen (NOTAMs) to advise of the issuance and operations under emergency air traffic rules and regulations and designates the official who is authorized to issue NOTAMs on behalf of the Administrator in certain matters under this section.

(b) Whenever the Administrator determines that an emergency condition exists, or will exist, relating to the FAA's ability to operate the air traffic control system and during which normal flight operations under this chapter cannot be conducted consistent with the required levels of safety and efficiency—

(1) The Administrator issues an immediately effective air traffic rule or regulation in response to that emergency condition; and

(2) The Administrator or the Associate Administrator for Air Traffic may utilize the NOTAM system to provide notification of the issuance of the rule or regulation.

Those NOTAMs communicate information concerning the rules and regulations that govern flight operations, the use of navigation facilities, and designation of that airspace in which the rules and regulations apply.

(c) When a NOTAM has been issued under this section, no person may operate an aircraft, or other device governed by the regulation concerned, within the designated airspace except in accordance with the authorizations, terms, and conditions prescribed in the regulation covered by the NOTAM.

§91.141 Flight restrictions in the proximity of the Presidential and other parties.

No person may operate an aircraft over or in the vicinity of any area to be visited or traveled by the President, the Vice President, or other public figures contrary to the restrictions established by the Administrator and published in a Notice to Airmen (NOTAM).

§91.143 Flight limitation in the proximity of space flight operations.

When a Notice to Airmen (NOTAM) is issued in accordance with this section, no person may operate any aircraft of U.S. registry, or pilot any aircraft under the authority of an airman certificate issued by the Federal Aviation Administration, within areas designated in a NOTAM for space flight operation except when authorized by ATC.

[Docket No. FAA–2004–19246, 69 FR 59753, Oct. 5, 2004]

§91.144 Temporary restriction on flight operations during abnormally high barometric pressure conditions.

(a) *Special flight restrictions.* When any information indicates that barometric pressure on the route of flight currently exceeds or will exceed 31 inches of mercury, no person may operate an aircraft or initiate a flight contrary to the requirements established by the Administrator and published in a Notice to Airmen issued under this section.

(b) *Waivers.* The administrator is authorized to waive any restriction issued under paragraph (a) of this section to permit emergency supply, transport, or medical services to be delivered to isolated communities, where the operation can be conducted with an acceptable level of safety.

[Amdt. 91–240, 59 FR 17452, April 12, 1994; 59 FR 37669, July 25, 1994]

§91.145 Management of aircraft operations in the vicinity of aerial demonstrations and major sporting events.

(a) The FAA will issue a Notice to Airmen (NOTAM) designating an area of airspace in which a temporary flight restriction applies when it determines that a temporary flight restriction is necessary to protect persons or property on the surface or in the air, to maintain air safety and efficiency, or to prevent the unsafe congestion of aircraft in the vicinity of an aerial demonstration or major sporting event. These demonstrations and events may include:

(1) United States Naval Flight Demonstration Team (Blue Angels);

(2) United States Air Force Air Demonstration Squadron (Thunderbirds);

(3) United States Army Parachute Team (Golden Knights);

(4) Summer/Winter Olympic Games;

(5) Annual Tournament of Roses Football Game;

(6) World Cup Soccer;

(7) Major League Baseball All-Star Game;

(8) World Series;

(9) Kodak Albuquerque International Balloon Fiesta;

(10) Sandia Classic Hang Gliding Competition;

(11) Indianapolis 500 Mile Race;

(12) Any other aerial demonstration or sporting event the FAA determines to need a temporary flight restriction in accordance with paragraph (b) of this section.

(b) In deciding whether a temporary flight restriction is necessary for an aerial demonstration or major sporting event not listed in paragraph (a) of this section, the FAA considers the following factors:

(1) Area where the event will be held.

(2) Effect flight restrictions will have on known aircraft operations.

(3) Any existing ATC airspace traffic management restrictions.

(4) Estimated duration of the event.

(5) Degree of public interest.

(6) Number of spectators.

(7) Provisions for spectator safety.

(8) Number and types of participating aircraft.

(9) Use of mixed high and low performance aircraft.

(10) Impact on non-participating aircraft.

(11) Weather minimums.

(12) Emergency procedures that will be in effect.

(c) A NOTAM issued under this section will state the name of the aerial demonstration or sporting event and specify the effective dates and times, the geographic features or coordinates, and any other restrictions or procedures governing flight operations in the designated airspace.

(d) When a NOTAM has been issued in accordance with this section, no person may operate an aircraft or device, or engage in any activity within the designated airspace area, except in accordance with the authorizations, terms, and conditions of the temporary flight restriction published in the NOTAM, unless otherwise authorized by:

(1) Air traffic control; or

(2) A Flight Standards Certificate of Waiver or Authorization issued for the demonstration or event.

(e) For the purpose of this section:

(1) Flight restricted airspace area for an aerial demonstration—

The amount of airspace needed to protect persons and property on the surface or in the air, to maintain air safety and efficiency, or to prevent the unsafe congestion of aircraft will vary depending on the aerial demonstration and the factors listed in paragraph (b) of this section. The restricted airspace area will normally be limited to a 5 nautical mile radius from the center of the demonstration and an altitude 17,000 mean sea level (for high performance aircraft) or 13,000 feet above the surface (for certain parachute operations), but will be no greater than the minimum airspace necessary for the management of aircraft operations in the vicinity of the specified area.

(2) Flight restricted area for a major sporting event—

The amount of airspace needed to protect persons and property on the surface or in the air, to maintain air safety and efficiency, or to prevent the unsafe congestion of aircraft will vary depending on the size of the event and the factors listed in paragraph (b) of this section. The restricted

airspace will normally be limited to a 3 nautical mile radius from the center of the event and 2,500 feet above the surface but will not be greater than the minimum airspace necessary for the management of aircraft operations in the vicinity of the specified area.

(f) A NOTAM issued under this section will be issued at least 30 days in advance of an aerial demonstration or a major sporting event, unless the FAA finds good cause for a shorter period and explains this in the NOTAM.

(g) When warranted, the FAA Administrator may exclude the following flights from the provisions of this section:

(1) Essential military.

(2) Medical and rescue.

(3) Presidential and Vice Presidential.

(4) Visiting heads of state.

(5) Law enforcement and security.

(6) Public health and welfare.

[Docket No. FAA–2000–8274, 66 FR 47378, Sept. 11, 2001]

§91.146 Passenger-carrying flights for the benefit of a charitable, nonprofit, or community event.

(a) *Definitions.* For purposes of this section, the following definitions apply:

Charitable event means an event that raises funds for the benefit of a charitable organization recognized by the Department of the Treasury whose donors may deduct contributions under section 170 of the Internal Revenue Code (26 U.S.C. Section 170).

Community event means an event that raises funds for the benefit of any local or community cause that is not a charitable event or non-profit event.

Nonprofit event means an event that raises funds for the benefit of a non-profit organization recognized under State or Federal law, as long as one of the organization's purposes is the promotion of aviation safety.

(b) Passenger-carrying flights in airplanes, powered-lift, or rotorcraft for the benefit of a charitable, nonprofit, or community event identified in paragraph (c) of this section are not subject to the certification requirements of part 119 of this chapter or the drug and alcohol testing requirements in part 120 of this chapter, provided the following conditions are satisfied and the limitations in paragraphs (c) and (d) of this section are not exceeded:

(1) The flight is nonstop and begins and ends at the same airport and is conducted within a 25-statute mile radius of that airport;

(2) The flight is conducted from a public airport that is adequate for the aircraft used, or from another location the FAA approves for the operation;

(3) The aircraft has a maximum of 30 seats, excluding each crewmember seat, and a maximum payload capacity of 7,500 pounds;

(4) The flight is not an aerobatic or a formation flight;

(5) Each aircraft holds a standard airworthiness certificate, is airworthy, and is operated in compliance with the applicable requirements of subpart E of this part;

(6) Each flight is made during day VFR conditions;

(7) Reimbursement of the operator of the aircraft is limited to that portion of the passenger payment for the flight that does not exceed the pro rata cost of owning, operating, and maintaining the aircraft for that flight, which may include fuel, oil, airport expenditures, and rental fees;

(8) The beneficiary of the funds raised is not in the business of transportation by air;

(9) A private pilot acting as pilot in command has at least 500 hours of flight time;

(10) Each flight is conducted in accordance with the safety provisions of part 136, subpart A of this chapter; and

(11) Flights are not conducted over a national park, unit of a national park, or abutting tribal lands, unless the operator has secured a letter of agreement from the FAA, as specified under subpart B of part 136 of this chapter, and is operating in accordance with that agreement during the flights.

(c) (1) Passenger-carrying flights or series of flights are limited to a total of four charitable events or non-profit events per year, with no event lasting more than three consecutive days.

(2) Passenger-carrying flights or series of flights are limited to one community event per year, with no event lasting more than three consecutive days.

(d) Pilots and sponsors of events described in this section are limited to no more than 4 events per calendar year.

(e) At least seven days before the event, each sponsor of an event described in this section must furnish to the responsible Flight Standards office for the area where the event is scheduled:

(1) A signed letter detailing the name of the sponsor, the purpose of the event, the date and time of the event, the location of the event, all prior events under this section participated in by the sponsor in the current calendar year;

(2) A photocopy of each pilot in command's pilot certificate, medical certificate, and logbook entries that show the pilot is current in accordance with §§61.56 and 61.57 of this chapter and that any private pilot has at least 500 hours of flight time; and

(3) A signed statement from each pilot that lists all prior events under this section in which the pilot has participated during the current calendar year.

[Docket No. FAA–1998–4521, 72 FR 6911, Feb. 13, 2007; as amended by Amdt. 91–308, 74 FR 32804, July 9, 2009; Amdt. 91–350, 83 FR 9171, March 5, 2018; Docket No. FAA–2022–1563, Amdt. 91–370, 88 FR 48087, July 26, 2023]

§91.147 Passenger-carrying flights for compensation or hire.

(a) *Definitions.* For the purposes of this section, *Operator* means any person conducting non-stop passenger-carrying flights in an airplane, powered-lift, or rotorcraft for compensation or hire in accordance with §§119.1(e)(2), 135.1(a)(5), or 121.1(d) of this chapter that begin and end at the same airport and are conducted within a 25-statute mile radius of that airport.

(b) *General requirements.* An Operator conducting passenger-carrying flights for compensation or hire must meet the following requirements unless all flights are conducted under §91.146. The Operator must:

(1) Comply with the safety provisions of part 136, subpart A of this chapter.

(2) Register and implement its drug and alcohol testing programs in accordance with part 120 of this chapter.

(3) Comply with the applicable requirements of part 5 of this chapter.

(4) Apply for and receive a Letter of Authorization from the responsible Flight Standards office.

(c) *Letter of Authorization.* Each application for a Letter of Authorization must include the following information:

(1) Name of Operator, agent, and any d/b/a (doing-business-as) under which that Operator does business.

(2) Principal business address and mailing address.

(3) Principal place of business (if different from business address).

(4) Name of person responsible for management of the business.

(5) Name of person responsible for aircraft maintenance.

(6) Type of aircraft, registration number(s), and make/model/series.

(7) Antidrug and Alcohol Misuse Prevention Program registration.

(d) *Compliance.* The Operator must comply with the provisions of the Letter of Authorization received.

[Docket No. FAA–1998–4521, 72 FR 6910, Feb. 13, 2007; as amended by Amdt. 91–307, 74 FR 22652, May 14, 2009; Amdt. 91–320, 76 FR 8893, Feb. 16, 2011; Docket FAA–2018–0119, Amdt. 91–350, 83 FR 9171, March 5, 2018; Docket No. FAA–2022–1563, Amdt. 91–370, 88 FR 48087, July 26, 2023; Amdt. 91–374, 89 FR 33108, April 26, 2024]

§91.148–91.149 [Reserved]

VISUAL FLIGHT RULES

§91.151 Fuel requirements for flight in VFR conditions.

(a) No person may begin a flight in an airplane under VFR conditions unless (considering wind and forecast weather conditions) there is enough fuel to fly to the first point of intended landing and, assuming normal cruising speed—

(1) During the day, to fly after that for at least 30 minutes; or

(2) At night, to fly after that for at least 45 minutes.

(b) No person may begin a flight in a rotorcraft under VFR conditions unless (considering wind and forecast weather conditions) there is enough fuel to fly to the first point of intended landing and, assuming normal cruising speed, to fly after that for at least 20 minutes.

§91.153 VFR flight plan: Information required.

(a) *Information required.* Unless otherwise authorized by ATC, each person filing a VFR flight plan shall include in it the following information:

(1) The aircraft identification number and, if necessary, its radio call sign.

(2) The type of the aircraft or, in the case of a formation flight, the type of each aircraft and the number of aircraft in the formation.

(3) The full name and address of the pilot in command or, in the case of a formation flight, the formation commander.

(4) The point and proposed time of departure.

(5) The proposed route, cruising altitude (or flight level), and true airspeed at that altitude.

(6) The point of first intended landing and the estimated elapsed time until over that point.

(7) The amount of fuel on board (in hours).

(8) The number of persons in the aircraft, except where that information is otherwise readily available to the FAA.

(9) Any other information the pilot in command or ATC believes is necessary for ATC purposes.

(b) *Cancellation.* When a flight plan has been activated, the pilot in command, upon canceling or completing the flight under the flight plan, shall notify an FAA Flight Service Station or ATC facility.

§91.155 Basic VFR weather minimums.

(a) Except as provided in paragraph (b) of this section and §91.157, no person may operate an aircraft under VFR when the flight visibility is less, or at a distance from clouds that is less, than that prescribed for the corresponding altitude and class of airspace in the following table:

Airspace	Flight visibility	Distance from clouds
Class A	Not applicable	Not applicable.
Class B	3 statute miles	Clear of clouds.
Class C	3 statute miles	500 feet below. 1,000 feet above. 2,000 feet horizontal.
Class D	3 statute miles	500 feet below. 1,000 feet above. 2,000 feet horizontal.
Class E:		
Less than 10,000 feet MSL	3 statute miles	500 feet below. 1,000 feet above. 2,000 feet horizontal.
At or above 10,000 feet MSL	5 statute miles	1,000 feet below. 1,000 feet above. 1 statute mile horizontal.
Class G:		
1,200 feet or less above the surface (regardless of MSL altitude)		
For aircraft other than helicopters:		
Day, except as provided in §91.155(b)	1 statute mile	Clear of clouds.
Night, except as provided in §91.155(b)	3 statute miles	500 feet below. 1,000 feet above. 2,000 feet horizontal.
For helicopters:		
Day	½ statute mile	Clear of clouds.
Night, except as provided in §91.155(b)	1 statute mile	Clear of clouds.
More than 1,200 feet above the surface but less than 10,000 feet MSL		
Day	1 statute mile	500 feet below. 1,000 feet above. 2,000 feet horizontal.
Night	3 statute miles	500 feet below. 1,000 feet above. 2,000 feet horizontal.
More than 1,200 feet above the surface and at or above 10,000 feet MSL	5 statute miles	1,000 feet below. 1,000 feet above. 1 statute mile horizontal.

(b) *Class G Airspace.* Notwithstanding the provisions of paragraph (a) of this section, the following operations may be conducted in Class G airspace below 1,200 feet above the surface:

(1) *Helicopter.* A helicopter may be operated clear of clouds in an airport traffic pattern within 1/2 mile of the runway or helipad of intended landing if the flight visibility is not less than 1/2 statute mile.

(2) *Airplane, powered parachute, or weight-shift-control aircraft.* If the visibility is less than 3 statute miles but not less than 1 statute mile during night hours and you are operating in an airport traffic pattern within 1/2 mile of the runway, you may operate an airplane, powered parachute, or weight-shift-control aircraft clear of clouds.

(c) Except as provided in §91.157, no person may operate an aircraft beneath the ceiling under VFR within the lateral boundaries of controlled airspace designated to the surface for an airport when the ceiling is less than 1,000 feet.

(d) Except as provided in §91.157 of this part, no person may take off or land an aircraft, or enter the traffic pattern of an airport, under VFR, within the lateral boundaries of the surface areas of Class B, Class C, Class D, or Class E airspace designated for an airport—

(1) Unless ground visibility at that airport is at least 3 statute miles; or

(2) If ground visibility is not reported at that airport, unless flight visibility during landing or takeoff, or while operating in the traffic pattern is at least 3 statute miles.

(e) For the purpose of this section, an aircraft operating at the base altitude of a Class E airspace area is considered to be within the airspace directly below that area.

[Docket No. 24458, 56 FR 65660, Dec. 17, 1991; as amended by Amdt. 91–235, 58 FR 51968, Oct. 5, 1993; Amdt. 91–282, 69 FR 44880, July 27, 2004; Amdt. 91–330, 79 FR 9972, Feb. 21, 2014; Amdt. 91–330A, 79 FR 41125, July 15, 2014]

§91.157 Special VFR weather minimums.

(a) Except as provided in Appendix D, section 3, of this part, special VFR operations may be conducted under the weather minimums and requirements of this section, instead of those contained in §91.155, below 10,000 feet MSL within the airspace contained by the upward extension of the lateral boundaries of the controlled airspace designated to the surface for an airport.

(b) Special VFR operations may only be conducted—

(1) With an ATC clearance;

(2) Clear of clouds;

(3) Except for helicopters, when flight visibility is at least 1 statute mile; and

(4) Except for helicopters, between sunrise and sunset (or in Alaska, when the sun is 6 degrees or less below the horizon) unless—

(i) The person being granted the ATC clearance meets the applicable requirements for instrument flight under part 61 of this chapter;

(ii) The aircraft is equipped as required in §91.205(d).

(c) No person may take off or land an aircraft (other than a helicopter) under special VFR—

(1) Unless ground visibility is at least 1 statute mile; or

(2) If ground visibility is not reported, unless flight visibility is at least 1 statute mile. For the purposes of this paragraph, the term flight visibility includes the visibility from the cockpit of an aircraft in takeoff position if:

(i) The flight is conducted under this Part 91; and

(ii) The airport at which the aircraft is located is a satellite airport that does not have weather reporting capabilities.

(d) The determination of visibility by a pilot in accordance with paragraph (c)(2) of this section is not an official weather report or an official ground visibility report.

[Amdt. 91–235, 58 FR 51968, Oct. 5, 1993, as amended by Amdt. 91–247, 60 FR 66874, Dec. 27, 1995; Amdt. 91–262, 65 FR 16116, March 24, 2000; Docket No. FAA-2022–1355, Amdt. No. 91–366, 87 FR 75846, Dec. 9, 2022]

§91.159 VFR cruising altitude or flight level.

Except while holding in a holding pattern of 2 minutes or less, or while turning, each person operating an aircraft under VFR in level cruising flight more than 3,000 feet above the surface shall maintain the appropriate altitude or flight level prescribed below, unless otherwise authorized by ATC:

(a) When operating below 18,000 feet MSL and—

(1) On a magnetic course of zero degrees through 179 degrees, any odd thousand foot MSL altitude +500 feet (such as 3,500, 5,500, or 7,500); or

(2) On a magnetic course of 180 degrees through 359 degrees, any even thousand foot MSL altitude +500 feet (such as 4,500, 6,500, or 8,500).

(b) When operating above 18,000 feet MSL, maintain the altitude or flight level assigned by ATC.

[Amdt. 91–235, 58 FR 51968, Oct. 5, 1993, as amended by Amdt. 91–247, 60 FR 66874, Dec. 27, 1995; Amdt. 91–262, 65 FR 16116, March 24, 2000; Docket No. FAA-2022–1355, Amdt. No. 91–366, 87 FR 75846, Dec. 9, 2022]

§91.161 Special awareness training required for pilots flying under visual flight rules within a 60-nautical mile radius of the Washington, DC VOR/DME.

(a) *Operations within a 60-nautical mile radius of the Washington, DC VOR/DME under visual flight rules (VFR).* Except as provided under paragraph (e) of this section, no person may serve as a pilot in command or as second in command of an aircraft while flying within a 60-nautical mile radius of the DCA VOR/DME, under VFR, unless that pilot has completed Special Awareness Training and holds a certificate of training completion.

(b) *Special Awareness Training.* The Special Awareness Training consists of information to educate pilots about the procedures for flying in the Washington, DC area and, more generally, in other types of special use airspace. This free training is available on the FAA's Web site. Upon completion of the training, each person will need to print out a copy of the certificate of training completion.

(c) *Inspection of certificate of training completion.* Each person who holds a certificate for completing the Special Awareness Training must present it for inspection upon request from:

(1) An authorized representative of the FAA;

(2) An authorized representative of the National Transportation Safety Board;

(3) Any Federal, State, or local law enforcement officer; or

(4) An authorized representative of the Transportation Security Administration.

(d) *Emergency declared.* The failure to complete the Special Awareness Training course on flying in and around the Washington, DC Metropolitan Area is not a violation of this section if an emergency is declared by the pilot, as described under §91.3(b), or there was a failure of two-way radio communications when operating under IFR as described under §91.185.

(e) *Exceptions.* The requirements of this section do not apply if the flight is being performed in an aircraft of an air ambulance operator certificated to conduct part 135 operations under this chapter, the U.S. Armed Forces, or a law enforcement agency.

[Docket No. FAA–2006–25250, 73 FR 46803, Aug. 12, 2008]

§91.162–91.165 [Reserved]

INSTRUMENT FLIGHT RULES

§91.167 Fuel requirements for flight in IFR conditions.

(a) No person may operate a civil aircraft in IFR conditions unless it carries enough fuel (considering weather reports and forecasts and weather conditions) to—

(1) Complete the flight to the first airport of intended landing;

(2) Except as provided in paragraph (b) of this section, fly from that airport to the alternate airport; and

(3) Fly after that for 45 minutes at normal cruising speed or, for helicopters, fly after that for 30 minutes at normal cruising speed.

(b) Paragraph (a)(2) of this section does not apply if:

(1) Part 97 of this chapter prescribes a standard instrument approach procedure to, or a special instrument approach procedure has been issued by the Administrator to the operator for, the first airport of intended landing; and

(2) Appropriate weather reports or weather forecasts, or a combination of them, indicate the following:

(i) For aircraft other than helicopters. For at least 1 hour before and for 1 hour after the estimated time of arrival, the ceiling will be at least 2,000 feet above the airport elevation and the visibility will be at least 3 statute miles.

(ii) For helicopters. At the estimated time of arrival and for 1 hour after the estimated time of arrival, the ceiling will be at least 1,000 feet above the airport elevation, or at least 400 feet above the lowest applicable approach minima, whichever is higher, and the visibility will be at least 2 statute miles.

[Docket No. 98–4390, 65 FR 3546, Jan. 21, 2000]

§91.169 IFR flight plan: Information required.

(a) *Information required.* Unless otherwise authorized by ATC, each person filing an IFR flight plan must include in it the following information:

(1) Information required under §91.153(a) of this part;

(2) Except as provided in paragraph (b) of this section, an alternate airport.

(b) Paragraph (a)(2) of this section does not apply if:

(1) Part 97 of this chapter prescribes a standard instrument approach procedure to, or a special instrument approach procedure has been issued by the Administrator to the operator for, the first airport of intended landing; and

(2) Appropriate weather reports or weather forecasts, or a combination of them, indicate the following:

(i) For aircraft other than helicopters. For at least 1 hour before and for 1 hour after the estimated time of arrival, the ceiling will be at least 2,000 feet above the airport elevation and the visibility will be at least 3 statute miles.

(ii) For helicopters. At the estimated time of arrival and for 1 hour after the estimated time of arrival, the ceiling will be at least 1,000 feet above the airport elevation, or at least 400 feet above the lowest applicable approach minima, whichever is higher, and the visibility will be at least 2 statute miles.

(c) *IFR alternate airport weather minima.* Unless otherwise authorized by the Administrator, no person may include an alternate airport in an IFR flight plan unless appropriate weather reports or weather forecasts, or a combination of them, indicate that, at the estimated time of arrival at the alternate airport, the ceiling and visibility at that airport will be at or above the following weather minima:

(1) If an instrument approach procedure has been published in part 97 of this chapter, or a special instrument approach procedure has been issued by the Administrator to the operator, for that airport, the following minima:

(i) For aircraft other than helicopters: The alternate airport minima specified in that procedure, or if none are specified the following standard approach minima:

(A) For a precision approach procedure. Ceiling 600 feet and visibility 2 statute miles.

(B) For a nonprecision approach procedure. Ceiling 800 feet and visibility 2 statute miles.

(ii) For helicopters: Ceiling 200 feet above the minimum for the approach to be flown, and

visibility at least 1 statute mile but never less than the minimum visibility for the approach to be flown, and

(2) If no instrument approach procedure has been published in part 97 of this chapter and no special instrument approach procedure has been issued by the Administrator to the operator, for the alternate airport, the ceiling and visibility minima are those allowing descent from the MEA, approach, and landing under basic VFR.

(d) *Cancellation.* When a flight plan has been activated, the pilot in command, upon canceling or completing the flight under the flight plan, shall notify an FAA Flight Service Station or ATC facility.

[Docket No. 18334, 54 FR 34294, Aug. 18, 1989; as amended by Amdt. 91–259, 65 FR 3546, Jan. 21, 2000]

§91.171 VOR equipment check for IFR operations.

(a) No person may operate a civil aircraft under IFR using the VOR system of radio navigation unless the VOR equipment of that aircraft—

(1) Is maintained, checked, and inspected under an approved procedure; or

(2) Has been operationally checked within the preceding 30 days, and was found to be within the limits of the permissible indicated bearing error set forth in paragraph (b) or (c) of this section.

(b) Except as provided in paragraph (c) of this section, each person conducting a VOR check under paragraph (a)(2) of this section shall—

(1) Use, at the airport of intended departure, an FAA-operated or approved test signal or a test signal radiated by a certificated and appropriately rated radio repair station or, outside the United States, a test signal operated or approved by an appropriate authority to check the VOR equipment (the maximum permissible indicated bearing error is plus or minus 4 degrees); or

(2) Use, at the airport of intended departure, a point on the airport surface designated as a VOR system checkpoint by the Administrator, or, outside the United States, by an appropriate authority (the maximum permissible bearing error is plus or minus 4 degrees);

(3) If neither a test signal nor a designated checkpoint on the surface is available, use an airborne checkpoint designated by the Administrator or, outside the United States, by an appropriate authority (the maximum permissible bearing error is plus or minus 6 degrees); or

(4) If no check signal or point is available, while in flight—

(i) Select a VOR radial that lies along the centerline of an established VOR airway;

(ii) Select a prominent ground point along the selected radial preferably more than 20 nautical miles from the VOR ground facility and maneuver the aircraft directly over the point at a reasonably low altitude; and

(iii) Note the VOR bearing indicated by the receiver when over the ground point (the maximum permissible variation between the published radial and the indicated bearing is 6 degrees).

(c) If dual system VOR (units independent of each other except for the antenna) is installed in the aircraft, the person checking the equipment may check one system against the other in place of the check procedures specified in paragraph (b) of this section. Both systems shall be tuned to the same VOR ground facility and note the indicated bearings to that station. The maximum permissible variation between the two indicated bearings is 4 degrees.

(d) Each person making the VOR operational check, as specified in paragraph (b) or (c) of this section, shall enter the date, place, bearing error, and sign the aircraft log or other record. In addition, if a test signal radiated by a repair station, as specified in paragraph (b)(1) of this section, is used, an entry must be made in the aircraft log or other record by the repair station certificate holder or the certificate holder's representative certifying to the bearing transmitted by the repair station for the check and the date of transmission.

(Approved by the Office of Management and Budget under control number 2120–0005)

§91.173 ATC clearance and flight plan required.

No person may operate an aircraft in controlled airspace under IFR unless that person has—

(a) Filed an IFR flight plan; and

(b) Received an appropriate ATC clearance.

§91.175 Takeoff and landing under IFR.

(a) *Instrument approaches to civil airports.* Unless otherwise authorized by the FAA, when it is necessary to use an instrument approach to a civil airport, each person operating an aircraft must use a standard instrument approach procedure prescribed in part 97 of this chapter for that airport. This paragraph does not apply to United States military aircraft.

(b) *Authorized DA/DH or MDA.* For the purpose of this section, when the approach procedure being used provides for and requires the use of a DA/DH or MDA, the authorized DA/DH or MDA is the highest of the following:

(1) The DA/DH or MDA prescribed by the approach procedure.

(2) The DA/DH or MDA prescribed for the pilot in command.

(3) The DA/DH or MDA appropriate for the aircraft equipment available and used during the approach.

(c) *Operation below DA/DH or MDA.* Except as provided in §91.176 of this chapter, where a DA/DH or MDA is applicable, no pilot may operate an aircraft, except a military aircraft of the United States, below the authorized MDA or continue an approach below the authorized DA/DH unless—

(1) The aircraft is continuously in a position from which a descent to a landing on the intended runway can be made at a normal rate of descent using normal maneuvers, and for operations conducted under part 121 or part 135 unless that descent rate will allow touchdown to occur within the touchdown zone of the runway of intended landing;

(2) The flight visibility is not less than the visibility prescribed in the standard instrument approach being used; and

(3) Except for a Category II or Category III approach where any necessary visual reference requirements are specified by the Administrator, at least one of the following visual references for the intended runway is distinctly visible and identifiable to the pilot:

(i) The approach light system, except that the pilot may not descend below 100 feet above the touchdown zone elevation using the approach lights as a reference unless the red terminating bars or the red side row bars are also distinctly visible and identifiable.

(ii) The threshold.

(iii) The threshold markings.

(iv) The threshold lights.

(v) The runway end identifier lights.

(vi) The visual glideslope indicator.

(vii) The touchdown zone or touchdown zone markings.

(viii) The touchdown zone lights.

(ix) The runway or runway markings.

(x) The runway lights.

(d) *Landing.* No pilot operating an aircraft, except a military aircraft of the United States, may land that aircraft when—

(1) For operations conducted under §91.176 of this part, the requirements of paragraphs (a)(3)(iii) or (b)(3)(iii), as applicable, of that section are not met; or

(2) For all other operations under this part and parts 121, 125, 129, and 135, the flight visibility is less than the visibility prescribed in the standard instrument approach procedure being used.

(e) *Missed approach procedures.* Each pilot operating an aircraft, except a military aircraft of the United States, shall immediately execute an appropriate missed approach procedure when either of the following conditions exist:

(1) Whenever operating an aircraft pursuant to paragraph (c) of this section or §91.176 of this part, and the requirements of that paragraph or section are not met at either of the following times:

(i) When the aircraft is being operated below MDA; or

(ii) Upon arrival at the missed approach point, including a DA/DH where a DA/DH is specified and its use is required, and at any time after that until touchdown.

(2) Whenever an identifiable part of the airport is not distinctly visible to the pilot during a circling maneuver at or above MDA, unless the inability to see an identifiable part of the airport results only from a normal bank of the aircraft during the circling approach.

(f) *Civil airport takeoff minimums.* This paragraph applies to persons operating an aircraft under part 121, 125, 129, or 135 of this chapter.

(1) Unless otherwise authorized by the FAA, no pilot may takeoff from a civil airport under IFR unless the weather conditions at time of takeoff are at or above the weather minimums for IFR takeoff prescribed for that airport under part 97 of this chapter.

(2) If takeoff weather minimums are not prescribed under part 97 of this chapter for a particular airport, the following weather minimums apply to takeoffs under IFR:

(i) For aircraft, other than helicopters, having two engines or less—1 statute mile visibility.

(ii) For aircraft having more than two engines—1/2 statute mile visibility.

(iii) For helicopters—1/2 statute mile visibility.

(3) Except as provided in paragraph (f)(4) of this section, no pilot may takeoff under IFR from a civil airport having published obstacle departure procedures (ODPs) under part 97 of this chapter for the takeoff runway to be used, unless the pilot uses such ODPs or an alternative procedure or route assigned by air traffic control.

(4) Notwithstanding the requirements of paragraph (f)(3) of this section, no pilot may takeoff from an airport under IFR unless:

(i) For part 121 and part 135 operators, the pilot uses a takeoff obstacle clearance or avoidance procedure that ensures compliance with the applicable airplane performance operating limitations requirements under part 121, subpart I or part 135, subpart I for takeoff at that airport; or

(ii) For part 129 operators, the pilot uses a takeoff obstacle clearance or avoidance procedure that ensures compliance with the airplane performance operating limitations prescribed by the State of the operator for takeoff at that airport.

(g) *Military airports.* Unless otherwise prescribed by the Administrator, each person operating a civil aircraft under IFR into or out of a military airport shall comply with the instrument approach procedures and the takeoff and landing minimum prescribed by the military authority having jurisdiction of that airport.

(h) Comparable values of RVR and ground visibility.

(1) Except for Category II or Category III minimums, if RVR minimums for takeoff or landing are prescribed in an instrument approach procedure, but RVR is not reported for the runway of intended operation, the RVR minimum shall be converted to ground visibility in accordance with the table in paragraph (h)(2) of this section and shall be the visibility minimum for takeoff or landing on that runway.

(2)

RVR (feet)	Visibility (statute miles)
1,600	1/4
2,400	1/2
3,200	5/8
4,000	3/4
4,500	7/8
5,000	1
6,000	1-1/4

(i) Operations on unpublished routes and use of radar in instrument approach procedures. When radar is approved at certain locations for ATC purposes, it may be used not only for surveillance and precision radar approaches, as applicable, but also may be used in conjunction with instrument approach procedures predicated on other types of radio navigational aids. Radar vectors may be authorized to provide course guidance through the segments of an approach to the final course or fix. When operating on an unpublished route or while being radar vectored, the pilot, when an approach clearance is received, shall, in addition to complying with §91.177, maintain the last altitude assigned to that pilot until the aircraft is established on a segment of a published route or instrument approach procedure unless a different altitude is assigned by ATC. After the aircraft is so established, published altitudes apply to descent within each succeeding route or approach segment unless a different altitude is assigned by ATC. Upon reaching the final approach course or fix, the pilot may either complete the instrument approach in accordance with a procedure approved for the facility or continue a surveillance or precision radar approach to a landing.

(j) Limitation on procedure turns. In the case of a radar vector to a final approach course or fix, a timed approach from a holding fix, or an approach for which the procedure specifies "No PT," no pilot may make a procedure turn unless cleared to do so by ATC.

(k) ILS components. The basic components of an ILS are the localizer, glide slope, and outer marker, and, when installed for use with Category II or Category III instrument approach procedures, an inner marker. The following means may be used to substitute for the outer marker: Compass locator; precision approach radar (PAR) or airport surveillance radar (ASR); DME, VOR, or nondirectional beacon fixes authorized in the standard instrument approach procedure; or a suitable RNAV system in conjunction with a fix identified in the standard instrument approach procedure. Applicability of, and substitution for, the inner marker for a Category II or III approach is determined by the appropriate 14 CFR part 97 approach procedure, letter of authorization, or operations specifications issued to an operator.

[Docket No. 18334, 54 FR 34294, Aug. 18, 1989, as amended by Amdt. 91–267, 66 FR 21066, April 27, 2001; Amdt. 91–281, 69 FR 1640, Jan. 9, 2004; Amdt. 91–296, 72 FR 31678, June 7, 2007; Amdt. 91–306, 74 FR 20205, May 1, 2009; Docket FAA–2013–0485, Amdt. 91–345, 81 FR 90172, Dec. 13, 2016; Amdt. 91–345B, 83 FR 10568, March 12, 2018]

§91.176 Straight-in landing operations below DA/DH or MDA using an enhanced flight vision system (EFVS) under IFR.

(a) EFVS operations to touchdown and rollout. Unless otherwise authorized by the Administrator to use an MDA as a DA/DH with vertical navigation on an instrument approach procedure, or unless paragraph (d) of this section applies, no person may conduct an EFVS operation in an aircraft, except a military aircraft of the United States, at any airport below the authorized DA/DH to touchdown and rollout unless the minimums used for the particular approach procedure being flown include a DA or DH, and the following requirements are met:

(1) Equipment.

(i) The aircraft must be equipped with an operable EFVS that meets the applicable airworthiness requirements. The EFVS must:

(A) Have an electronic means to provide a display of the forward external scene topography (the applicable natural or manmade features of a place or region especially in a way to show their relative positions and elevation) through the use of imaging sensors, including but not limited to forward-looking infrared, millimeter wave radiometry, millimeter wave radar, or low-light level image intensification.

(B) Present EFVS sensor imagery, aircraft flight information, and flight symbology on a head up display, or an equivalent display, so that the imagery, information and symbology are clearly visible to the pilot flying in his or her normal position with the line of vision looking forward along the flight path. Aircraft flight information and flight symbology must consist of at least airspeed, vertical speed, aircraft attitude, heading, altitude, height above ground level such as that provided

by a radio altimeter or other device capable of providing equivalent performance, command guidance as appropriate for the approach to be flown, path deviation indications, flight path vector, and flight path angle reference cue. Additionally, for aircraft other than rotorcraft, the EFVS must display flare prompt or flare guidance.

(C) Present the displayed EFVS sensor imagery, attitude symbology, flight path vector, and flight path angle reference cue, and other cues, which are referenced to the EFVS sensor imagery and external scene topography, so that they are aligned with, and scaled to, the external view.

(D) Display the flight path angle reference cue with a pitch scale. The flight path angle reference cue must be selectable by the pilot to the desired descent angle for the approach and be sufficient to monitor the vertical flight path of the aircraft.

(E) Display the EFVS sensor imagery, aircraft flight information, and flight symbology such that they do not adversely obscure the pilot's outside view or field of view through the cockpit window.

(F) Have display characteristics, dynamics, and cues that are suitable for manual control of the aircraft to touchdown in the touchdown zone of the runway of intended landing and during rollout.

(ii) When a minimum flightcrew of more than one pilot is required, the aircraft must be equipped with a display that provides the pilot monitoring with EFVS sensor imagery. Any symbology displayed may not adversely obscure the sensor imagery of the runway environment.

(2) *Operations.*

(i) The pilot conducting the EFVS operation may not use circling minimums.

(ii) Each required pilot flightcrew member must have adequate knowledge of, and familiarity with, the aircraft, the EFVS, and the procedures to be used.

(iii) The aircraft must be equipped with, and the pilot flying must use, an operable EFVS that meets the equipment requirements of paragraph (a)(1) of this section.

(iv) When a minimum flightcrew of more than one pilot is required, the pilot monitoring must use the display specified in paragraph (a)(1)(ii) to monitor and assess the safe conduct of the approach, landing, and rollout.

(v) The aircraft must continuously be in a position from which a descent to a landing on the intended runway can be made at a normal rate of descent using normal maneuvers.

(vi) The descent rate must allow touchdown to occur within the touchdown zone of the runway of intended landing.

(vii) Each required pilot flightcrew member must meet the following requirements—

(A) A person exercising the privileges of a pilot certificate issued under this chapter, any person serving as a required pilot flightcrew member of a U.S.-registered aircraft, or any person serving as a required pilot flightcrew member for a part 121, 125, or 135 operator, must be qualified in accordance with part 61 and, as applicable, the training, testing, and qualification provisions of subpart K of this part, part 121, 125, or 135 of this chapter that apply to the operation; or

(B) Each person acting as a required pilot flightcrew member for a foreign air carrier subject to part 129, or any person serving as a required pilot flightcrew member of a foreign registered aircraft, must be qualified in accordance with the training requirements of the civil aviation authority of the State of the operator for the EFVS operation to be conducted.

(viii) A person conducting operations under this part must conduct the operation in accordance with a letter of authorization for the use of EFVS unless the operation is conducted in an aircraft that has been issued an experimental certificate under §21.191 of this chapter for the purpose of research and development or showing compliance with regulations, or the operation is being conducted by a person otherwise authorized to conduct EFVS operations under paragraphs (a)(2)(ix) through (xii) of this section. A person applying to the FAA for a letter of authorization must submit an application in a form and manner prescribed by the Administrator.

(ix) A person conducting operations under subpart K of this part must conduct the operation in accordance with management specifications authorizing the use of EFVS.

(x) A person conducting operations under part 121, 129, or 135 of this chapter must conduct the operation in accordance with operations specifications authorizing the use of EFVS.

(xi) A person conducting operations under part 125 of this chapter must conduct the operation in accordance with operations specifications authorizing the use of EFVS or, for a holder of a part 125 letter of deviation authority, a letter of authorization for the use of EFVS.

(xii) A person conducting an EFVS operation during an authorized Category II or Category III operation must conduct the operation in accordance with operations specifications, management specifications, or a letter of authorization authorizing EFVS operations during authorized Category II or Category III operations.

(3) *Visibility and visual reference requirements.* No pilot operating under this section or §§121.651, 125.381, or 135.225 of this chapter may continue an approach below the authorized DA/DH and land unless:

(i) The pilot determines that the enhanced flight visibility observed by use of an EFVS is not less than the visibility prescribed in the instrument approach procedure being used.

(ii) From the authorized DA/DH to 100 feet above the touchdown zone elevation of the runway of intended landing, any approach light system or both the runway threshold and the touchdown zone are distinctly visible and identifiable to the pilot using an EFVS.

(A) The pilot must identify the runway threshold using at least one of the following visual references—

(1) The beginning of the runway landing surface;

(2) The threshold lights; or

(3) The runway end identifier lights.

(B) The pilot must identify the touchdown zone using at least one of the following visual references—

(1) The runway touchdown zone landing surface;

(2) The touchdown zone lights;

(3) The touchdown zone markings; or

(4) The runway lights.

(iii) At 100 feet above the touchdown zone elevation of the runway of intended landing and below that altitude, the enhanced flight visibility using EFVS must be sufficient for one of the following visual references to be distinctly visible and identifiable to the pilot—

(A) The runway threshold;

(B) The lights or markings of the threshold;

(C) The runway touchdown zone landing surface; or

(D) The lights or markings of the touchdown zone.

(4) *Additional requirements.* The Administrator may prescribe additional equipment, operational, and visibility and visual reference requirements to account for specific equipment characteristics, operational procedures, or approach characteristics. These requirements will be specified in an operator's operations specifications, management specifications, or letter of authorization authorizing the use of EFVS.

(b) *EFVS operations to 100 feet above the touchdown zone elevation.* Except as specified in paragraph (d) of this section, no person may conduct an EFVS operation in an aircraft, except a military aircraft of the United States, at any airport below the authorized DA/DH or MDA to 100 feet above the touchdown zone elevation unless the following requirements are met:

(1) *Equipment.*

(i) The aircraft must be equipped with an operable EFVS that meets the applicable airworthiness requirements.

(ii) The EFVS must meet the requirements of paragraph (a)(1)(i)(A) through (F) of this section, but need not present flare prompt, flare guidance, or height above ground level.

(2) *Operations.*

(i) The pilot conducting the EFVS operation may not use circling minimums.

(ii) Each required pilot flightcrew member must have adequate knowledge of, and familiarity with, the aircraft, the EFVS, and the procedures to be used.

(iii) The aircraft must be equipped with, and the pilot flying must use, an operable EFVS that meets the equipment requirements of paragraph (b)(1) of this section.

(iv) The aircraft must continuously be in a position from which a descent to a landing on the intended runway can be made at a normal rate of descent using normal maneuvers.

(v) For operations conducted under part 121 or part 135 of this chapter, the descent rate must allow touchdown to occur within the touchdown zone of the runway of intended landing.

(vi) Each required pilot flightcrew member must meet the following requirements—

(A) A person exercising the privileges of a pilot certificate issued under this chapter, any person serving as a required pilot flightcrew member of a U.S.-registered aircraft, or any person serving as a required pilot flightcrew member for a part 121, 125, or 135 operator, must be qualified in accordance with part 61 and, as applicable, the training, testing, and qualification provisions of subpart K of this part, part 121, 125, or 135 of this chapter that apply to the operation; or

(B) Each person acting as a required pilot flightcrew member for a foreign air carrier subject to part 129, or any person serving as a required pilot flightcrew member of a foreign registered aircraft, must be qualified in accordance with the training requirements of the civil aviation authority of the State of the operator for the EFVS operation to be conducted.

(vii) A person conducting operations under subpart K of this part must conduct the operation in accordance with management specifications authorizing the use of EFVS.

(viii) A person conducting operations under part 121, 129, or 135 of this chapter must conduct the operation in accordance with operations specifications authorizing the use of EFVS.

(ix) A person conducting operations under part 125 of this chapter must conduct the operation in accordance with operations specifications authorizing the use of EFVS or, for a holder of a part 125 letter of deviation authority, a letter of authorization for the use of EFVS.

(x) A person conducting an EFVS operation during an authorized Category II or Category III operation must conduct the operation in accordance with operations specifications, management specifications, or a letter of authorization authorizing EFVS operations during authorized Category II or Category III operations.

(3) *Visibility and Visual Reference Requirements.* No pilot operating under this section or §121.651, §125.381, or §135.225 of this chapter may continue an approach below the authorized MDA or continue an approach below the authorized DA/DH and land unless:

(i) The pilot determines that the enhanced flight visibility observed by use of an EFVS is not less than the visibility prescribed in the instrument approach procedure being used.

(ii) From the authorized MDA or DA/DH to 100 feet above the touchdown zone elevation of the runway of intended landing, any approach light system or both the runway threshold and the touchdown zone are distinctly visible and identifiable to the pilot using an EFVS.

(A) The pilot must identify the runway threshold using at least one of the following visual references—

(1) The beginning of the runway landing surface;

(2) The threshold lights; or

(3) The runway end identifier lights.

(B) The pilot must identify the touchdown zone using at least one of the following visual references—

(1) The runway touchdown zone landing surface;

(2) The touchdown zone lights;

(3) The touchdown zone markings; or

(4) The runway lights.

(iii) At 100 feet above the touchdown zone elevation of the runway of intended landing and below that altitude, the flight visibility must be sufficient for one of the following visual references to be distinctly visible and identifiable to the pilot without reliance on the EFVS—

(A) The runway threshold;

(B) The lights or markings of the threshold;

(C) The runway touchdown zone landing surface; or

(D) The lights or markings of the touchdown zone.

(4) *Compliance Date.* Beginning on March 13, 2018, a person conducting an EFVS operation to 100 feet above the touchdown zone elevation must comply with the requirements of paragraph (b) of this section.

(c) *Public aircraft certification and training requirements.* A public aircraft operator, other than the U.S. military, may conduct an EFVS operation under paragraph (a) or (b) of this section only if:

(1) The aircraft meets all of the civil certification and airworthiness requirements of paragraph (a)(1) or (b)(1) of this section, as applicable to the EFVS operation to be conducted; and

(2) The pilot flightcrew member, or any other person who manipulates the controls of an aircraft during an EFVS operation, meets the training, recent flight experience and refresher training requirements of §61.66 of this chapter applicable to EFVS operations.

(d) *Exception for Experimental Aircraft.* The requirement to use an EFVS that meets the applicable airworthiness requirements specified in paragraphs (a)(1)(i), (a)(2)(iii), (b)(1)(i), and (b)(2)(iii) of this section does not apply to operations conducted in an aircraft issued an experimental certificate under §21.191 of this chapter for the purpose of research and development or showing compliance with regulations, provided the Administrator has determined that the operations can be conducted safely in accordance with operating limitations issued for that purpose.

[Docket FAA–2013–0485, Amdt. 91–345, 81 FR 90172, Dec. 13, 2016; 82 FR 2193, Jan. 9, 2017]

§91.177 Minimum altitudes for IFR operations.

(a) *Operation of aircraft at minimum altitudes.* Except when necessary for takeoff or landing, or unless otherwise authorized by the FAA, no person may operate an aircraft under IFR below—

(1) The applicable minimum altitudes prescribed in parts 95 and 97 of this chapter. However, if both a MEA and a MOCA are prescribed for a particular route or route segment, a person may operate an aircraft below the MEA down to, but not below, the MOCA, provided the applicable navigation signals are available. For aircraft using VOR for navigation, this applies only when the aircraft is within 22 nautical miles of that VOR (based on the reasonable estimate by the pilot operating the aircraft of that distance); or

(2) If no applicable minimum altitude is prescribed in parts 95 and 97 of this chapter, then—

(i) In the case of operations over an area designated as a mountainous area in part 95 of this chapter, an altitude of 2,000 feet above the highest obstacle within a horizontal distance of 4 nautical miles from the course to be flown; or

(ii) In any other case, an altitude of 1,000 feet above the highest obstacle within a horizontal distance of 4 nautical miles from the course to be flown.

(b) *Climb.* Climb to a higher minimum IFR altitude shall begin immediately after passing the point beyond which that minimum altitude applies, except that when ground obstructions intervene, the point beyond which that higher minimum altitude applies shall be crossed at or above the applicable MCA.

[Docket No. 18334, 54 FR 34294, Aug. 18, 1989, as amended by Amdt. 91–296, 72 FR 31678, June 7, 2007; Amdt. 91–315, 75 FR 30690, June 2, 2010]

§91.179 IFR cruising altitude or flight level.

Unless otherwise authorized by ATC, the following rules apply—

(a) *In controlled airspace.* Each person operating an aircraft under IFR in level cruising flight in controlled airspace shall maintain the altitude or flight level assigned that aircraft by ATC. However, if the ATC clearance assigns "VFR conditions on-top," that person shall maintain an altitude or flight level as prescribed by §91.159.

(b) *In uncontrolled airspace.* Except while in a holding pattern of 2 minutes or less or while turning, each person operating an aircraft under IFR in level cruising flight in uncontrolled airspace shall maintain an appropriate altitude as follows:

(1) When operating below 18,000 feet MSL and—

(i) On a magnetic course of zero degrees through 179 degrees, any odd thousand foot MSL altitude (such as 3,000, 5,000, or 7,000); or

(ii) On a magnetic course of 180 degrees through 359 degrees, any even thousand foot MSL altitude (such as 2,000, 4,000, or 6,000).

(2) When operating at or above 18,000 feet MSL but below flight level 290, and—

(i) On a magnetic course of zero degrees through 179 degrees, any odd flight level (such as 190, 210, or 230); or

(ii) On a magnetic course of 180 degrees through 359 degrees, any even flight level (such as 180, 200, or 220).

(3) When operating at flight level 290 and above in non-RVSM airspace, and—

(i) On a magnetic course of zero degrees through 179 degrees, any flight level, at 4,000-foot intervals, beginning at and including flight level 290 (such as flight level 290, 330, or 370); or

(ii) On a magnetic course of 180 degrees through 359 degrees, any flight level, at 4,000-foot intervals, beginning at and including flight level 310 (such as flight level 310, 350, or 390).

(4) When operating at flight level 290 and above in airspace designated as Reduced Vertical Separation Minimum (RVSM) airspace and—

(i) On a magnetic course of zero degrees through 179 degrees, any odd flight level, at 2,000-foot intervals beginning at and including flight level 290 (such as flight level 290, 310, 330, 350, 370, 390, 410); or

(ii) On a magnetic course of 180 degrees through 359 degrees, any even flight level, at 2000-foot intervals beginning at and including flight level 300 (such as 300, 320, 340, 360, 380, 400).

[Docket No. 18334, 54 FR 34294, Aug. 18, 1989; as amended by Amdt. 91–276, 68 FR 61321, Oct. 27, 2003; Amdt. 91–276, 68 FR 70133, Dec. 17, 2003; Amdt. 91–296, 72 FR 31679, June 7, 2007]

§91.180 Operations within airspace designated as Reduced Vertical Separation Minimum airspace.

(a) Except as provided in paragraph (b) of this section, no person may operate a civil aircraft in airspace designated as Reduced Vertical Separation Minimum (RVSM) airspace unless:

(1) The operator and the operator's aircraft comply with the minimum standards of appendix G of this part; and

(2) The operator is authorized by the Administrator or the country of registry to conduct such operations.

(b) The Administrator may authorize a deviation from the requirements of this section.

[Amdt. 91–276, 68 FR 70133, Dec. 17, 2003]

§91.181 Course to be flown.

Unless otherwise authorized by ATC, no person may operate an aircraft within controlled airspace under IFR except as follows:

(a) On an ATS route, along the centerline of that airway.

(b) On any other route, along the direct course between the navigational aids or fixes defining that route. However, this section does not prohibit maneuvering the aircraft to pass well clear of other air traffic or the maneuvering of the aircraft in VFR conditions to clear the intended flight path both before and during climb or descent.

[Docket No. 18334, 54 FR 34294, Aug. 18, 1989; as amended by Amdt. 91–296, 72 FR 31679, June 7, 2007]

§91.183 IFR communications.

Unless otherwise authorized by ATC, the pilot in command of each aircraft operated under IFR in controlled airspace must ensure that a continuous watch is maintained on the appropriate frequency and must report the following as soon as possible—

(a) The time and altitude of passing each designated reporting point, or the reporting points specified by ATC, except that while the aircraft is under radar control, only the passing of those reporting points specifically requested by ATC need be reported;

(b) Any unforecast weather conditions encountered; and

(c) Any other information relating to the safety of flight.

[Docket No. 18334, 54 FR 34294, Aug. 18, 1989; as amended by Amdt. 91–296, 72 FR 31679, June 7, 2007]

91

§91.185 IFR operations: Two-way radio communications failure.

(a) *General.* Unless otherwise authorized by ATC, each pilot who has two-way radio communications failure when operating under IFR shall comply with the rules of this section.

(b) *VFR conditions.* If the failure occurs in VFR conditions, or if VFR conditions are encountered after the failure, each pilot shall continue the flight under VFR and land as soon as practicable.

(c) *IFR conditions.* If the failure occurs in IFR conditions, or if paragraph (b) of this section cannot be complied with, each pilot shall continue the flight according to the following:

(1) *Route.*

(i) By the route assigned in the last ATC clearance received;

(ii) If being radar vectored, by the direct route from the point of radio failure to the fix, route, or airway specified in the vector clearance;

(iii) In the absence of an assigned route, by the route that ATC has advised may be expected in a further clearance; or

(iv) In the absence of an assigned route or a route that ATC has advised may be expected in a further clearance, by the route filed in the flight plan.

(2) *Altitude.* At the highest of the following altitudes or flight levels for the route segment being flown:

(i) The altitude or flight level assigned in the last ATC clearance received;

(ii) The minimum altitude (converted, if appropriate, to minimum flight level as prescribed in §91.121(c)) for IFR operations; or

(iii) The altitude or flight level ATC has advised may be expected in a further clearance.

(3) *Leave clearance limit.*

(i) When the clearance limit is a fix from which an approach begins, commence descent or descent and approach as close as possible to the expect-further-clearance time if one has been received, or if one has not been received, as close as possible to the estimated time of arrival as calculated from the filed or amended (with ATC) estimated time en route.

(ii) If the clearance limit is not a fix from which an approach begins, leave the clearance limit at the expect-further-clearance time if one has been received, or if none has been received, upon arrival over the clearance limit, and proceed to a fix from which an approach begins and commence descent or descent and approach as close as possible to the estimated time of arrival as calculated from the filed or amended (with ATC) estimated time en route.

[Docket No. 18334, 54 FR 34294, Aug. 18, 1989; as amended by Amdt. 91–211, 54 FR 41211, Oct. 5, 1989]

§91.187 Operation under IFR in controlled airspace: Malfunction reports.

(a) The pilot in command of each aircraft operated in controlled airspace under IFR shall report as soon as practical to ATC any malfunctions of navigational, approach, or communication equipment occurring in flight.

(b) In each report required by paragraph (a) of this section, the pilot in command shall include the—

(1) Aircraft identification;

(2) Equipment affected;

(3) Degree to which the capability of the pilot to operate under IFR in the ATC system is impaired; and

(4) Nature and extent of assistance desired from ATC.

§91.189 Category II and III operations: General operating rules.

(a) No person may operate a civil aircraft in a Category II or III operation unless—

(1) The flight crew of the aircraft consists of a pilot in command and a second in command who hold the appropriate authorizations and ratings prescribed in §61.3 of this chapter;

(2) Each flight crewmember has adequate knowledge of, and familiarity with, the aircraft and the procedures to be used; and

(3) The instrument panel in front of the pilot who is controlling the aircraft has appropriate instrumentation for the type of flight control guidance system that is being used.

(b) Unless otherwise authorized by the Administrator, no person may operate a civil aircraft in a Category II or Category III operation unless each ground component required for that operation and the related airborne equipment is installed and operating.

(c) *Authorized DA/DH.* For the purpose of this section, when the approach procedure being used provides for and requires the use of a DA/DH, the authorized DA/DH is the highest of the following:

(1) The DA/DH prescribed by the approach procedure.

(2) The DA/DH prescribed for the pilot in command.

(3) The DA/DH for which the aircraft is equipped.

(d) Except as provided in §91.176 of this part or unless otherwise authorized by the Administrator, no pilot operating an aircraft in a Category II or Category III approach that provides and requires the use of a DA/DH may continue the approach below the authorized decision height unless the following conditions are met:

(1) The aircraft is in a position from which a descent to a landing on the intended runway can be made at a normal rate of descent using normal maneuvers, and where that descent rate will allow touchdown to occur within the touchdown zone of the runway of intended landing.

(2) At least one of the following visual references for the intended runway is distinctly visible and identifiable to the pilot:

(i) The approach light system, except that the pilot may not descend below 100 feet above the touchdown zone elevation using the approach lights as a reference unless the red terminating bars or the red side row bars are also distinctly visible and identifiable.

(ii) The threshold.

(iii) The threshold markings.

(iv) The threshold lights.

(v) The touchdown zone or touchdown zone markings.

(vi) The touchdown zone lights.

(e) Except as provided in §91.176 of this part or unless otherwise authorized by the Administrator, each pilot operating an aircraft shall immediately execute an appropriate missed approach whenever, prior to touchdown, the requirements of paragraph (d) of this section are not met.

(f) No person operating an aircraft using a Category III approach without decision height may land that aircraft except in accordance with the provisions of the letter of authorization issued by the Administrator.

(g) Paragraphs (a) through (f) of this section do not apply to operations conducted by certificate holders operating under part 121, 125, 129, or 135 of this chapter, or holders of management specifications issued in accordance with subpart K of this part. Holders of operations specifications or management specifications may operate a civil aircraft in a Category II or Category III operation only in accordance with their operations specifications or management specifications, as applicable.

[Docket No. 18334, 54 FR 34294, Aug. 18, 1989, as amended by Amdt. 91–280, 68 FR 54560, Sept. 17, 2003; Amdt. 91–296, 72 FR 31679, June 7, 2007; Docket FAA–2013–0485, Amdt. 91–345, 81 FR 90175, Dec. 13, 2016]

§91.191 Category II and Category III manual.

(a) Except as provided in paragraph (c) of this section, after August 4, 1997, no person may operate a U.S.-registered civil aircraft in a Category II or a Category III operation unless—

(1) There is available in the aircraft a current and approved Category II or Category III manual, as appropriate, for that aircraft;

(2) The operation is conducted in accordance with the procedures, instructions, and limitations in the appropriate manual; and

(3) The instruments and equipment listed in the manual that are required for a particular Category II or Category III operation have been inspected and maintained in accordance with the maintenance program contained in the manual.

(b) Each operator must keep a current copy of each approved manual at its principal base of operations and must make each manual available for inspection upon request by the Administrator.

(c) This section does not apply to operations conducted by a certificate holder operating under part 121 or part 135 of this chapter or a holder of management specifications issued in accordance with subpart K of this part.

[Docket No. 26933, 61 FR 34560, July 2, 1996, as amended by Amdt. 91–280, 68 FR 54560, Sept. 17, 2003]

§91.193 Certificate of authorization for certain Category II operations.

The Administrator may issue a certificate of authorization authorizing deviations from the requirements of §§91.189, 91.191, and 91.205(f) for the operation of small aircraft identified as Category A aircraft in §97.3 of this chapter in Category II operations if the Administrator finds that the proposed operation can be safely conducted under the terms of the certificate. Such authorization does not permit operation of the aircraft carrying persons or property for compensation or hire.

§91.195–91.199 [Reserved]

Subpart C—Equipment, Instrument, and Certificate Requirements

Source: Docket No. 18334, 54 FR 34304, Aug. 18, 1989, unless otherwise noted.

§91.201 [Reserved]

§91.203 Civil aircraft: Certifications required.

(a) Except as provided in §91.715, no person may operate a civil aircraft unless it has within it the following:

(1) An appropriate and current airworthiness certificate. Each U.S. airworthiness certificate used to comply with this subparagraph (except a special flight permit, a copy of the applicable operations specifications issued under §21.197(c) of this chapter, appropriate sections of the air carrier manual required by parts 121 and 135 of this

chapter containing that portion of the operations specifications issued under §21.197(c), or an authorization under §91.611) must have on it the registration number assigned to the aircraft under part 47 or 48 of this chapter. However, the airworthiness certificate need not have on it an assigned special identification number before 10 days after that number is first affixed to the aircraft. A revised airworthiness certificate having on it an assigned special identification number, that has been affixed to an aircraft, may only be obtained upon application to the responsible Flight Standards office.

(2) An effective U.S. registration certificate issued to its owner or, for operation within the United States, the second copy of the Aircraft registration Application as provided for in §47.31(c), a Certificate of Aircraft registration as provided in part 48, or a registration certification issued under the laws of a foreign country.

(b) No person may operate a civil aircraft unless the airworthiness certificate required by paragraph (a) of this section or a special flight authorization issued under §91.715 is displayed at the cabin or cockpit entrance so that it is legible to passengers or crew.

(c) No person may operate an aircraft with a fuel tank installed within the passenger compartment or a baggage compartment unless the installation was accomplished pursuant to part 43 of this chapter, and a copy of FAA Form 337 authorizing that installation is on board the aircraft.

(d) No person may operate a civil airplane (domestic or foreign) into or out of an airport in the United States unless it complies with the fuel venting and exhaust emissions requirements of part 34 of this chapter.

[Docket No. 18334, 54 FR 34292, Aug. 18, 1989, as amended by Amdt. 91–218, 55 FR 32861, Aug. 10, 1990; Amdt. 91–318, 75 FR 41983, July 20, 2010; Amdt. 91–338, 80 FR 78648, Dec. 16, 2015; Docket FAA–2018–0119, Amdt. 91–350, 83 FR 9171, March 5, 2018; Docket No. FAA–2022–1355, Amdt. No. 91–366, 87 FR 75846, Dec. 9, 2022]

§91.205 Powered civil aircraft with standard category U.S. airworthiness certificates: Instrument and equipment requirements.

(a) *General.* Except as provided in paragraphs (c)(3) and (e) of this section, no person may operate a powered civil aircraft with a standard category U.S. airworthiness certificate in any operation described in paragraphs (b) through (f) of this section unless that aircraft contains the instruments and equipment specified in those paragraphs (or FAA-approved equivalents) for that type of operation, and those instruments and items of equipment are in operable condition.

(b) *Visual-flight rules (day).* For VFR flight during the day, the following instruments and equipment are required:
(1) Airspeed indicator.
(2) Altimeter.
(3) Magnetic direction indicator.
(4) Tachometer for each engine.
(5) Oil pressure gauge for each engine using pressure system.
(6) Temperature gauge for each liquid-cooled engine.
(7) Oil temperature gauge for each air-cooled engine.
(8) Manifold pressure gauge for each altitude engine.
(9) Fuel gauge indicating the quantity of fuel in each tank.
(10) Landing gear position indicator, if the aircraft has a retractable landing gear.
(11) For small civil airplanes certificated after March 11, 1996, in accordance with part 23 of this chapter, an approved aviation red or aviation white anticollision light system. In the event of failure of any light of the anticollision light system, operation of the aircraft may continue to a location where repairs or replacement can be made.
(12) If the aircraft is operated for hire over water and beyond power-off gliding distance from shore, approved flotation gear readily available to each occupant and, unless the aircraft is operating under part 121 of this subchapter, at least one pyrotechnic signaling device. As used in this section, "shore" means that area of the land adjacent to the water which is above the high water mark and excludes land areas which are intermittently under water.
(13) An approved safety belt with an approved metal-to-metal latching device, or other approved restraint system for each occupant 2 years of age or older.
(14) For small civil airplanes manufactured after July 18, 1978, an approved shoulder harness or restraint system for each front seat. For small civil airplanes manufactured after December 12, 1986, an approved shoulder harness or restraint system for all seats. Shoulder harnesses installed at flightcrew stations must permit the flightcrew member, when seated and with the safety belt and shoulder harness fastened, to perform all functions necessary for flight operations. For purposes of this paragraph—
(i) The date of manufacture of an airplane is the date the inspection acceptance records reflect that the airplane is complete and meets the FAA-approved type design data; and
(ii) A front seat is a seat located at a flightcrew member station or any seat located alongside such a seat.

(15) An emergency locator transmitter, if required by §91.207.

(16) [Reserved].

(17) For rotorcraft manufactured after September 16, 1992, a shoulder harness for each seat that meets the requirements of §27.2 or §29.2 of this chapter in effect on September 16, 1991.

(c) *Visual flight rules (night).* For VFR flight at night, the following instruments and equipment are required:

(1) Instruments and equipment specified in paragraph (b) of this section.

(2) Approved position lights.

(3) An approved aviation red or aviation white anticollision light system on all U.S.-registered civil aircraft. Anticollision light systems initially installed after August 11, 1971, on aircraft for which a type certificate was issued or applied for before August 11, 1971, must at least meet the anticollision light standards of part 23, 25, 27, or 29 of this chapter, as applicable, that were in effect on August 10, 1971, except that the color may be either aviation red or aviation white. In the event of failure of any light of the anticollision light system, operations with the aircraft may be continued to a stop where repairs or replacement can be made.

(4) If the aircraft is operated for hire, one electric landing light.

(5) An adequate source of electrical energy for all installed electrical and radio equipment.

(6) One spare set of fuses, or three spare fuses of each kind required, that are accessible to the pilot in flight.

(d) *Instrument flight rules.* For IFR flight, the following instruments and equipment are required:

(1) Instruments and equipment specified in paragraph (b) of this section, and, for night flight, instruments and equipment specified in paragraph (c) of this section.

(2) Two-way radio communication and navigation equipment suitable for the route to be flown.

(3) Gyroscopic rate-of-turn indicator, except on the following aircraft:

(i) Airplanes with a third attitude instrument system usable through flight attitudes of 360 degrees of pitch and roll and installed in accordance with the instrument requirements prescribed in §121.305(j) of this chapter; and

(ii) Rotorcraft with a third attitude instrument system usable through flight attitudes of ±80 degrees of pitch and ±120 degrees of roll and installed in accordance with §29.1303(g) of this chapter.

(4) Slip-skid indicator.

(5) Sensitive altimeter adjustable for barometric pressure.

(6) A clock displaying hours, minutes, and seconds with a sweep-second pointer or digital presentation.

(7) Generator or alternator of adequate capacity.

(8) Gyroscopic pitch and bank indicator (artificial horizon).

(9) Gyroscopic direction indicator (directional gyro or equivalent).

(e) *Flight at and above 24,000 feet MSL (FL 240).* If VOR navigation equipment is required under paragraph (d)(2) of this section, no person may operate a U.S.-registered civil aircraft within the 50 states and the District of Columbia at or above FL 240 unless that aircraft is equipped with approved DME or a suitable RNAV system. When the DME or RNAV system required by this paragraph fails at and above FL 240, the pilot in command of the aircraft must notify ATC immediately, and then may continue operations at and above FL 240 to the next airport of intended landing where repairs or replacement of the equipment can be made.

(f) *Category II operations.* The requirements for Category II operations are the instruments and equipment specified in—

(1) Paragraph (d) of this section; and

(2) Appendix A to this part.

(g) *Category III operations.* The instruments and equipment required for Category III operations are specified in paragraph (d) of this section.

(h) *Night vision goggle operations.* For night vision goggle operations, the following instruments and equipment must be installed in the aircraft, functioning in a normal manner, and approved for use by the FAA:

(1) Instruments and equipment specified in paragraph (b) of this section, instruments and equipment specified in paragraph (c) of this section;

(2) Night vision goggles;

(3) Interior and exterior aircraft lighting system required for night vision goggle operations;

(4) Two-way radio communications system;

(5) Gyroscopic pitch and bank indicator (artificial horizon);

(6) Generator or alternator of adequate capacity for the required instruments and equipment; and

(7) Radar altimeter.

(i) *Exclusions.* Paragraphs (f) and (g) of this section do not apply to operations conducted by a holder of a certificate issued under part 121 or part 135 of this chapter.

[Docket No. 18334, 54 FR 34292, Aug. 18, 1989; as amended by Amdt. 91–220, 55 FR 43310, Oct. 26, 1990; Amdt. 91–223, 56 FR 41052, Aug. 16, 1991; Amdt. 91–231, 57 FR 42672, Sept. 15, 1992; Amdt. 91–247, 61 FR 5171, Feb. 9, 1996; Amdt. 91–251, 61 FR 34560, July 2, 1996; Amdt. 91–285, 69 FR 77599, Dec. 27, 2004; Amdt. 91–296, 72 FR 31679, June 7, 2007; Amdt. 91–309, 74 FR 42563, Aug. 21, 2009; Amdt. 91–346, 81 FR 96700, Dec. 30, 2016]

§91.207 Emergency locator transmitters.

(a) Except as provided in paragraphs (e) and (f) of this section, no person may operate a U.S. registered civil airplane unless—

(1) There is attached to the airplane an approved automatic type emergency locator transmitter that is in operable condition for the following operations, except that after June 21, 1995, an emergency locator transmitter that meets the requirements of TSO-C91 may not be used for new installations:

(i) Those operations governed by the supplemental air carrier and commercial operator rules of parts 121 and 125;

(ii) Charter flights governed by the domestic and flag air carrier rules of part 121 of this chapter; and

(iii) Operations governed by part 135 of this chapter; or

(2) For operations other than those specified in paragraph (a)(1) of this section, there must be attached to the airplane an approved personal type or an approved automatic type emergency locator transmitter that is in operable condition, except that after June 21, 1995, an emergency locator transmitter that meets the requirements of TSO-C91 may not be used for new installations.

(b) Each emergency locator transmitter required by paragraph (a) of this section must be attached to the airplane in such a manner that the probability of damage to the transmitter in the event of crash impact is minimized. Fixed and deployable automatic type transmitters must be attached to the airplane as far aft as practicable.

(c) Batteries used in the emergency locator transmitters required by paragraphs (a) and (b) of this section must be replaced (or recharged, if the batteries are rechargeable)—

(1) When the transmitter has been in use for more than 1 cumulative hour; or

(2) When 50 percent of their useful life (or, for rechargeable batteries, 50 percent of their useful life of charge) has expired, as established by the transmitter manufacturer under its approval. The new expiration date for replacing (or recharging) the battery must be legibly marked on the outside of the transmitter and entered in the aircraft maintenance record. Paragraph (c)(2) of this section does not apply to batteries (such as water-activated batteries) that are essentially unaffected during probable storage intervals.

(d) Each emergency locator transmitter required by paragraph (a) of this section must be inspected within 12 calendar months after the last inspection for—

(1) Proper installation;

(2) Battery corrosion;

(3) Operation of the controls and crash sensor; and

(4) The presence of a sufficient signal radiated from its antenna.

(e) Notwithstanding paragraph (a) of this section, a person may—

(1) Ferry a newly acquired airplane from the place where possession of it was taken to a place where the emergency locator transmitter is to be installed; and

(2) Ferry an airplane with an inoperative emergency locator transmitter from a place where repairs or replacements cannot be made to a place where they can be made.

No person other than required crewmembers may be carried aboard an airplane being ferried under paragraph (e) of this section.

(f) Paragraph (a) of this section does not apply to—

(1) Before January 1, 2004, turbojet-powered aircraft;

(2) Aircraft while engaged in scheduled flights by scheduled air carriers;

(3) Aircraft while engaged in training operations conducted entirely within a 50-nautical mile radius of the airport from which such local flight operations began;

(4) Aircraft while engaged in flight operations incident to design and testing;

(5) New aircraft while engaged in flight operations incident to their manufacture, preparation, and delivery;

(6) Aircraft while engaged in flight operations incident to the aerial application of chemicals and other substances for agricultural purposes;

(7) Aircraft certificated by the Administrator for research and development purposes;

(8) Aircraft while used for showing compliance with regulations, crew training, exhibition, air racing, or market surveys;

(9) Aircraft equipped to carry not more than one person.

(10) An aircraft during any period for which the transmitter has been temporarily removed for inspection, repair, modification, or replacement, subject to the following:

(i) No person may operate the aircraft unless the aircraft records contain an entry which includes the date of initial removal, the make, model, serial number, and reason for removing the transmitter, and a placard located in view of the pilot to show "ELT not installed."

(ii) No person may operate the aircraft more than 90 days after the ELT is initially removed from the aircraft; and

(11) On and after January 1, 2004, aircraft with a maximum payload capacity of more than 18,000 pounds when used in air transportation.

[Docket No. 18334, 54 FR 34304, Aug. 18, 1989, as amended by Amdt. 91–242, 59 FR 32057, June 21, 1994; 59 FR 34578, July 6, 1994; Amdt. 91–265, 65 FR 81319, Dec. 22, 2000; 66 FR 16316, March 23, 2001]

§91.209 Aircraft lights.

No person may:

(a) During the period from sunset to sunrise (or, in Alaska, during the period a prominent unlighted object cannot be seen from a distance of 3 statute miles or the sun is more than 6 degrees below the horizon)—

(1) Operate an aircraft unless it has lighted position lights;

(2) Park or move an aircraft in, or in dangerous proximity to, a night flight operations area of an airport unless the aircraft—

(i) Is clearly illuminated;

(ii) Has lighted position lights; or

(iii) is in an area that is marked by obstruction lights;

(3) Anchor an aircraft unless the aircraft—

(i) Has lighted anchor lights; or

(ii) Is in an area where anchor lights are not required on vessels; or

(b) Operate an aircraft that is equipped with an anticollision light system, unless it has lighted anticollision lights. However, the anticollision lights need not be lighted when the pilot-in-command determines that, because of operating conditions, it would be in the interest of safety to turn the lights off.

[Docket No. 27806, 61 FR 5171, Feb. 9, 1996]

§91.211 Supplemental oxygen.

(a) *General.* No person may operate a civil aircraft of U.S. registry—

(1) At cabin pressure altitudes above 12,500 feet (MSL) up to and including 14,000 feet (MSL) unless the required minimum flight crew is provided with and uses supplemental oxygen for that part of the flight at those altitudes that is of more than 30 minutes duration;

(2) At cabin pressure altitudes above 14,000 feet (MSL) unless the required minimum flight crew is provided with and uses supplemental oxygen during the entire flight time at those altitudes; and

(3) At cabin pressure altitudes above 15,000 feet (MSL) unless each occupant of the aircraft is provided with supplemental oxygen.

(b) *Pressurized cabin aircraft.*

(1) No person may operate a civil aircraft of U.S. registry with a pressurized cabin—

(i) At flight altitudes above flight level 250 unless at least a 10-minute supply of supplemental oxygen, in addition to any oxygen required to satisfy paragraph (a) of this section, is available for each occupant of the aircraft for use in the event that a descent is necessitated by loss of cabin pressurization; and

(ii) At flight altitudes above flight level 350 unless one pilot at the controls of the airplane is wearing and using an oxygen mask that is secured and sealed and that either supplies oxygen at all times or automatically supplies oxygen whenever the cabin pressure altitude of the airplane exceeds 14,000 feet (MSL), except that the one pilot need not wear and use an oxygen mask while at or below flight level 410 if there are two pilots at the controls and each pilot has a quick-donning type of oxygen mask that can be placed on the face with one hand from the ready position within 5 seconds, supplying oxygen and properly secured and sealed.

(2) Notwithstanding paragraph (b)(1)(ii) of this section, if for any reason at any time it is necessary for one pilot to leave the controls of the aircraft when operating at flight altitudes above flight level 350, the remaining pilot at the controls shall put on and use an oxygen mask until the other pilot has returned to that crewmember's station.

§91.213 Inoperative instruments and equipment.

(a) Except as provided in paragraph (d) of this section, no person may take off an aircraft with inoperative instruments or equipment installed unless the following conditions are met:

(1) An approved Minimum Equipment List exists for that aircraft.

(2) The aircraft has within it a letter of authorization, issued by the responsible Flight Standards office authorizing operation of the aircraft under the Minimum Equipment List. The letter of authorization may be obtained by written request of the airworthiness certificate holder. The Minimum Equipment List and the letter of authorization constitute a supplemental type certificate for the aircraft.

(3) The approved Minimum Equipment List must—

(i) Be prepared in accordance with the limitations specified in paragraph (b) of this section; and

(ii) Provide for the operation of the aircraft with the instruments and equipment in an inoperable condition.

(4) The aircraft records available to the pilot must include an entry describing the inoperable instruments and equipment.

(5) The aircraft is operated under all applicable conditions and limitations contained in the Minimum Equipment List and the letter authorizing use of the list.

(b) The following instruments and equipment may not be included in a Minimum Equipment List:

(1) Instruments and equipment that are either specifically or otherwise required by the airworthiness requirements under which the aircraft is type certificated and which are essential for safe operations under all operating conditions.

91

(2) Instruments and equipment required by an airworthiness directive to be in operable condition unless the airworthiness directive provides otherwise.

(3) Instruments and equipment required for specific operations by this part.

(c) A person authorized to use an approved Minimum Equipment List issued for a specific aircraft under subpart K of this part, part 121, 125, or 135 of this chapter must use that Minimum Equipment List to comply with the requirements in this section.

(d) Except for operations conducted in accordance with paragraph (a) or (c) of this section, a person may takeoff an aircraft in operations conducted under this part with inoperative instruments and equipment without an approved Minimum Equipment List provided—

(1) The flight operation is conducted in a—

(i) Rotorcraft, non-turbine-powered airplane, glider, lighter-than-air aircraft, powered parachute, or weight-shift-control aircraft, for which a master minimum equipment list has not been developed; or

(ii) Small rotorcraft, nonturbine-powered small airplane, glider, or lighter-than-air aircraft for which a Master Minimum Equipment List has been developed; and

(2) The inoperative instruments and equipment are not—

(i) Part of the VFR-day type certification instruments and equipment prescribed in the applicable airworthiness regulations under which the aircraft was type certificated;

(ii) Indicated as required on the aircraft's equipment list, or on the Kinds of Operations Equipment List for the kind of flight operation being conducted;

(iii) Required by §91.205 or any other rule of this part for the specific kind of flight operation being conducted; or

(iv) Required to be operational by an airworthiness directive; and

(3) The inoperative instruments and equipment are—

(i) Removed from the aircraft, the cockpit control placarded, and the maintenance recorded in accordance with §43.9 of this chapter; or

(ii) Deactivated and placarded "Inoperative." If deactivation of the inoperative instrument or equipment involves maintenance, it must be accomplished and recorded in accordance with part 43 of this chapter; and

(4) A determination is made by a pilot, who is certificated and appropriately rated under part 61 of this chapter, or by a person, who is certificated and appropriately rated to perform maintenance on the aircraft, that the inoperative instrument or equipment does not constitute a hazard to the aircraft.

An aircraft with inoperative instruments or equipment as provided in paragraph (d) of this section is considered to be in a properly altered condition acceptable to the Administrator.

(e) Notwithstanding any other provision of this section, an aircraft with inoperative instruments or equipment may be operated under a special flight permit issued in accordance with §§21.197 and 21.199 of this chapter.

[Docket No. 18334, 54 FR 34304, Aug. 18, 1989, as amended by Amdt. 91–280, 68 FR 54560, Sept. 17, 2003; Amdt. 91–282, 69 FR 44880, July 27, 2004; Docket FAA–2018–0119, Amdt. 91–350, 83 FR 9171, March 5, 2018]

§91.215 ATC transponder and altitude reporting equipment and use.

(a) *All airspace: U.S.-registered civil aircraft.* For operations not conducted under part 121 or 135 of this chapter, ATC transponder equipment installed must meet the performance and environmental requirements of any class of TSO-C74b (Mode A) or any class of TSO-C74c (Mode A with altitude reporting capability) as appropriate, or the appropriate class of TSO-C112 (Mode S).

(b) *All airspace.* Unless otherwise authorized or directed by ATC, and except as provided in paragraph (e)(1) of this section, no person may operate an aircraft in the airspace described in paragraphs (b)(1) through (5) of this section, unless that aircraft is equipped with an operable coded radar beacon transponder having either Mode A 4096 code capability, replying to Mode A interrogations with the code specified by ATC, or a Mode S capability, replying to Mode A interrogations with the code specified by ATC and Mode S interrogations in accordance with the applicable provisions specified in TSO-C112, and that aircraft is equipped with automatic pressure altitude reporting equipment having a Mode C capability that automatically replies to Mode C interrogations by transmitting pressure altitude information in 100-foot increments. The requirements of this paragraph (b) apply to—

(1) *All aircraft.* In Class A, Class B, and Class C airspace areas;

(2) *All aircraft.* In all airspace within 30 nautical miles of an airport listed in Appendix D, section 1 of this part from the surface upward to 10,000 feet MSL;

(3) Notwithstanding paragraph (b)(2) of this section, any aircraft which was not originally certificated with an engine-driven electrical system or which has not subsequently been certified with such a system installed, balloon or glider may conduct operations in the airspace within 30 nautical miles of an airport listed in Appendix D, section 1 of this part provided such operations are conducted—

(i) Outside any Class A, Class B, or Class C airspace area; and

(ii) Below the altitude of the ceiling of a Class B or Class C airspace area designated for an airport or 10,000 feet MSL, whichever is lower; and

(4) All aircraft in all airspace above the ceiling and within the lateral boundaries of a Class B or Class C airspace area designated for an airport upward to 10,000 feet MSL; and

(5) All aircraft except any aircraft which was not originally certificated with an engine-driven electrical system or which has not subsequently been certified with such a system installed, balloon, or glider—

(i) In all airspace of the 48 contiguous states and the District of Columbia at and above 10,000 feet MSL, excluding the airspace at and below 2,500 feet above the surface; and

(ii) In the airspace from the surface to 10,000 feet MSL within a 10-nautical-mile radius of any airport listed in Appendix D, section 2 of this part, excluding the airspace below 1,200 feet outside of the lateral boundaries of the surface area of the airspace designated for that airport.

(c) Transponder-on operation. Except as provided in paragraph (e)(2) of this section, while in the airspace as specified in paragraph (b) of this section or in all controlled airspace, each person operating an aircraft equipped with an operable ATC transponder maintained in accordance with §91.413 shall operate the transponder, including Mode C equipment if installed, and shall reply on the appropriate code or as assigned by ATC, unless otherwise directed by ATC when transmitting would jeopardize the safe execution of air traffic control functions.

(d) ATC authorized deviations. Requests for ATC authorized deviations must be made to the ATC facility having jurisdiction over the concerned airspace within the time periods specified as follows:

(1) For operation of an aircraft with an operating transponder but without operating automatic pressure altitude reporting equipment having a Mode C capability, the request may be made at any time.

(2) For operation of an aircraft with an inoperative transponder to the airport of ultimate destination, including any intermediate stops, or to proceed to a place where suitable repairs can be made or both, the request may be made at any time.

(3) For operation of an aircraft that is not equipped with a transponder, the request must be made at least one hour before the proposed operation.

(e) Unmanned aircraft. (1) The requirements of paragraph (b) of this section do not apply to a person operating an unmanned aircraft under this part unless the operation is conducted under a flight plan and the person operating the unmanned aircraft maintains two-way communication with ATC.

(2) No person may operate an unmanned aircraft under this part with a transponder on unless:

(i) The operation is conducted under a flight plan and the person operating the unmanned aircraft maintains two-way communication with ATC; or

(ii) The use of a transponder is otherwise authorized by the Administrator.

(Approved by the Office of Management and Budget under control number 2120–0005)

[Docket No. 18334, 54 FR 34304, Aug. 18, 1989; as amended by Amdt. 91–221, 56 FR 469, Jan. 4, 1991; Amdt. 91–227, 56 FR 65660, Dec. 17, 1991; Amdt. 91–227, 7 FR 328, Jan. 3, 1992; Amdt. 91–229, 57 FR 34618, Aug. 5, 1992; Amdt. 91–267, 66 FR 21066, April 27, 2001; Amdt. 91–355, 84 FR 34287, July 18, 2019; Amdt. 91–361, 86 FR 4512, Jan. 15, 2021; Amdt. 91–371, 88 FR 71476, Oct. 17, 2023]

§91.217 Data correspondence between automatically reported pressure altitude data and the pilot's altitude reference.

(a) No person may operate any automatic pressure altitude reporting equipment associated with a radar beacon transponder—

(1) When deactivation of that equipment is directed by ATC;

(2) Unless, as installed, that equipment was tested and calibrated to transmit altitude data corresponding within 125 feet (on a 95 percent probability basis) of the indicated or calibrated datum of the altimeter normally used to maintain flight altitude, with that altimeter referenced to 29.92 inches of mercury for altitudes from sea level to the maximum operating altitude of the aircraft; or

(3) Unless the altimeters and digitizers in that equipment meet the standards of TSO-C10b and TSO-C88, respectively.

(b) No person may operate any automatic pressure altitude reporting equipment associated with a radar beacon transponder or with ADS-B Out equipment unless the pressure altitude reported for ADS-B Out and Mode C/S is derived from the same source for aircraft equipped with both a transponder and ADS-B Out.

[Docket No. 18334, 54 FR 34304, Aug. 18, 1989; as amended by Amdt. 91–314, 75 FR 30193, May 28, 2010]

§91.219 Altitude alerting system or device: Turbojet-powered civil airplanes.

(a) Except as provided in paragraph (d) of this section, no person may operate a turbojet-powered U.S.-registered civil airplane unless

that airplane is equipped with an approved altitude alerting system or device that is in operable condition and meets the requirements of paragraph (b) of this section.

(b) Each altitude alerting system or device required by paragraph (a) of this section must be able to—

(1) Alert the pilot—

(i) Upon approaching a preselected altitude in either ascent or descent, by a sequence of both aural and visual signals in sufficient time to establish level flight at that preselected altitude; or

(ii) Upon approaching a preselected altitude in either ascent or descent, by a sequence of visual signals in sufficient time to establish level flight at that preselected altitude, and when deviating above and below that preselected altitude, by an aural signal;

(2) Provide the required signals from sea level to the highest operating altitude approved for the airplane in which it is installed;

(3) Preselect altitudes in increments that are commensurate with the altitudes at which the aircraft is operated;

(4) Be tested without special equipment to determine proper operation of the alerting signals; and

(5) Accept necessary barometric pressure settings if the system or device operates on barometric pressure. However, for operation below 3,000 feet AGL, the system or device need only provide one signal, either visual or aural, to comply with this paragraph. A radio altimeter may be included to provide the signal if the operator has an approved procedure for its use to determine DA/DH or MDA, as appropriate.

(c) Each operator to which this section applies must establish and assign procedures for the use of the altitude alerting system or device and each flight crewmember must comply with those procedures assigned to him.

(d) Paragraph (a) of this section does not apply to any operation of an airplane that has an experimental certificate or to the operation of any airplane for the following purposes:

(1) Ferrying a newly acquired airplane from the place where possession of it was taken to a place where the altitude alerting system or device is to be installed.

(2) Continuing a flight as originally planned, if the altitude alerting system or device becomes inoperative after the airplane has taken off; however, the flight may not depart from a place where repair or replacement can be made.

(3) Ferrying an airplane with any inoperative altitude alerting system or device from a place where repairs or replacements cannot be made to a place where it can be made.

(4) Conducting an airworthiness flight test of the airplane.

(5) Ferrying an airplane to a place outside the United States for the purpose of registering it in a foreign country.

(6) Conducting a sales demonstration of the operation of the airplane.

(7) Training foreign flight crews in the operation of the airplane before ferrying it to a place outside the United States for the purpose of registering it in a foreign country.

[Docket No. 18334, 54 FR 34304, Aug. 18, 1989; as amended by Amdt. 91–296, 72 FR 31679, June 7, 2007]

§91.221 Traffic alert and collision avoidance system equipment and use.

(a) *All airspace: U.S.-registered civil aircraft.* Any traffic alert and collision avoidance system installed in a U.S.-registered civil aircraft must be approved by the Administrator.

(b) *Traffic alert and collision avoidance system, operation required.* Each person operating an aircraft equipped with an operable traffic alert and collision avoidance system shall have that system on and operating.

§91.223 Terrain awareness and warning system.

(a) *Airplanes manufactured after March 29, 2002.* Except as provided in paragraph (d) of this section, no person may operate a turbine-powered U.S.-registered airplane configured with six or more passenger seats, excluding any pilot seat, unless that airplane is equipped with an approved terrain awareness and warning system that as a minimum meets the requirements for Class B equipment in Technical Standard Order (TSO)-C151.

(b) *Airplanes manufactured on or before March 29, 2002.* Except as provided in paragraph (d) of this section, no person may operate a turbine-powered U.S.-registered airplane configured with six or more passenger seats, excluding any pilot seat, after March 29, 2005, unless that airplane is equipped with an approved terrain awareness and warning system that as a minimum meets the requirements for Class B equipment in Technical Standard Order (TSO)-C151.

(Approved by the Office of Management and Budget under control number 2120-0631)

(c) *Airplane Flight Manual.* The Airplane Flight Manual shall contain appropriate procedures for—

(1) The use of the terrain awareness and warning system; and

(2) Proper flight crew reaction in response to the terrain awareness and warning system audio and visual warnings.

(d) *Exceptions.* Paragraphs (a) and (b) of this section do not apply to—

(1) Parachuting operations when conducted entirely within a 50 nautical mile radius of the airport from which such local flight operations began.

(2) Firefighting operations.

(3) Flight operations when incident to the aerial application of chemicals and other substances.

[Docket No. 29312, 65 FR 16755, March 29, 2000]

§91.225 Automatic Dependent Surveillance–Broadcast (ADS-B) Out equipment and use.

(a) After January 1, 2020, unless otherwise authorized by ATC, no person may operate an aircraft in Class A airspace unless the aircraft has equipment installed that—

(1) Meets the performance requirements in—

(i) TSO-C166b and Section 2 of RTCA DO-260B (as referenced in TSO-C166b); or

(ii) TSO-C166c and Section 2 of RTCA DO-260C as modified by DO-260C—Change 1 (as referenced in TSO-C166c); and

(2) Meets the requirements of §91.227.

(b) After January 1, 2020, except as prohibited in paragraph (h)(2) of this section or unless otherwise authorized by ATC, no person may operate an aircraft below 18,000 feet MSL and in airspace described in paragraph (d) of this section unless the aircraft has equipment installed that—

(1) Meets the performance requirements in—

(i) TSO-C166b and Section 2 of RTCA DO-260B (as referenced in TSO-C166b);

(ii) TSO-C166c and Section 2 of RTCA DO-260C as modified by DO-260C—Change 1 (as referenced in TSO-C166c);

(iii) TSO-C154c and Section 2 of RTCA DO-282B (as referenced in TSO-C154c); or

(iv) TSO-C154d and Section 2 of RTCA DO-282C (as referenced in TSO-C154d);

(2) Meets the requirements of §91.227.

(c) Operators with equipment installed with an approved deviation under §21.618 of this chapter also are in compliance with this section.

(d) After January 1, 2020, except as prohibited in paragraph (h)(2) of this section or unless otherwise authorized by ATC, no person may operate an aircraft in the following airspace unless the aircraft has equipment installed that meets the requirements in paragraph (b) of this section:

(1) Class B and Class C airspace areas;

(2) Except as provided for in paragraph (e) of this section, within 30 nautical miles of an airport listed in appendix D, section 1 to this part from the surface upward to 10,000 feet MSL;

(3) Above the ceiling and within the lateral boundaries of a Class B or Class C airspace area designated for an airport upward to 10,000 feet MSL;

(4) Except as provided in paragraph (e) of this section, Class E airspace within the 48 contiguous states and the District of Columbia at and above 10,000 feet MSL, excluding the airspace at and below 2,500 feet above the surface; and

(5) Class E airspace at and above 3,000 feet MSL over the Gulf of Mexico from the coastline of the United States out to 12 nautical miles.

(e) The requirements of paragraph (b) of this section do not apply to any aircraft that was not originally certificated with an engine-driven electrical system, or that has not subsequently been certified with such a system installed, including balloons and gliders. These aircraft may conduct operations without ADS-B Out in the airspace specified in paragraph (d)(4) of this section. These aircraft may also conduct operations in the airspace specified in paragraph (d)(2) of this section if those operations are conducted—

(1) Outside any Class B or Class C airspace area; and

(2) Below the altitude of the ceiling of a Class B or Class C airspace area designated for an airport, or 10,000 feet MSL, whichever is lower.

(f) Except as prohibited in paragraph (h)(2) of this section, each person operating an aircraft equipped with ADS-B Out must operate this equipment in the transmit mode at all times unless—

(1) Otherwise authorized by the FAA when the aircraft is performing a sensitive government mission for national defense, homeland security, intelligence or law enforcement purposes and transmitting would compromise the operations security of the mission or pose a safety risk to the aircraft, crew, or people and property in the air or on the ground; or

(2) Otherwise directed by ATC when transmitting would jeopardize the safe execution of air traffic control functions.

(g) Requests for ATC authorized deviations from the requirements of this section must be made to the ATC facility having jurisdiction over the concerned airspace within the time periods specified as follows:

(1) For operation of an aircraft with an inoperative ADS-B Out, to the airport of ultimate destination, including any intermediate stops, or to proceed to a place where suitable repairs can be made or both, the request may be made at any time.

(2) For operation of an aircraft that is not equipped with ADS-B Out, the request must be made at least 1 hour before the proposed operation.

(h) For unmanned aircraft:

(1) No person may operate an unmanned aircraft under a flight plan and in two way communication with ATC unless:

(i) That aircraft has equipment installed that meets the performance requirements in TSO-C166b (including Section 2 of RTCA DO-260B, as referenced in TSO-C166b), TSO-C166c (including Section 2 of RTCA DO-260C as modified by DO-260C—Change 1, as referenced in TSO-C166c), TSO-C154c (including Section 2 of RTCA DO-282B, as referenced in TSO-C154c), or TSO-C154d (including Section 2 of RTCA DO-282C, as referenced in TSO-C154d); and

(ii) The equipment meets the requirements of §91.227.

(2) No person may operate an unmanned aircraft under this part with Automatic Dependent Surveillance–Broadcast Out equipment in transmit mode unless:

(i) The operation is conducted under a flight plan and the person operating that unmanned aircraft maintains two-way communication with ATC; or

(ii) The use of ADS-B Out is otherwise authorized by the Administrator.

(i) The standards required in this section are incorporated by reference with the approval of the Director of the Office of the Federal Register under 5 U.S.C. 552(a) and 1 CFR part 51. This incorporation by reference (IBR) material is available for inspection at the FAA and the National Archives and Records Administration (NARA). Contact the FAA at: Office of Rulemaking (ARM-1), 800 Independence Avenue SW, Washington, DC 20590 (telephone 202-267-9677). For information on the availability of this material at NARA, visit *https://www.archives.gov/federal-register/cfr/ibr-locations.html* or email *fr.inspection@nara.gov*. This material is also available from the following sources in this paragraph (i).

(1) U.S. Department of Transportation, Subsequent Distribution Office, DOT Warehouse M30, Ardmore East Business Center, 3341 Q 75th Avenue, Landover, MD 20785; telephone (301) 322-5377; website: *www.faa.gov/aircraft/air_cert/design_approvals/tso/* (select the link "Search Technical Standard Orders").

(i) TSO-C166b, Extended Squitter Automatic Dependent Surveillance–Broadcast (ADS-B) and Traffic Information Service–Broadcast (TIS-B) Equipment Operating on the Radio Frequency of 1090 Megahertz (MHz), December 2, 2009.

(ii) TSO-C166c, Extended Squitter Automatic Dependent Surveillance–Broadcast (ADS-B) and Traffic Information Service–Broadcast (TIS-B) Equipment Operating on the Radio Frequency of 1090 Megahertz (MHz), March 10, 2023.

(iii) TSO-C154c, Universal Access Transceiver (UAT) Automatic Dependent Surveillance–Broadcast (ADS-B) Equipment Operating on the Frequency of 978 MHz, December 2, 2009.

(iv) TSO-C154d, Universal Access Transceiver (UAT) Automatic Dependent Surveillance–Broadcast (ADS-B) Equipment Operating on the Radio Frequency of 978 Megahertz (MHz), March 10, 2023.

(2) RTCA, Inc., 1150 18th St. NW, Suite 910, Washington, DC 20036; telephone (202) 833-9339; website: *www.rtca.org/products*.

(i) RTCA DO-260B, Minimum Operational Performance Standards for 1090 MHz Extended Squitter Automatic Dependent Surveillance–Broadcast (ADS-B) and Traffic Information Services–Broadcast (TIS-B), Section 2, Equipment Performance Requirements and Test Procedures, December 2, 2009.

(ii) RTCA DO-260C, Minimum Operational Performance Standards for 1090 MHz Extended Squitter Automatic Dependent Surveillance–Broadcast (ADS-B) and Traffic Information Services–Broadcast (TIS-B), Section 2, Equipment Performance Requirements and Test Procedures, December 17, 2020.

(iii) RTCA DO-260C, Minimum Operational Performance Standards for 1090 MHz Extended Squitter Automatic Dependent Surveillance–Broadcast (ADS-B) and Traffic Information Services–Broadcast (TIS-B), Change 1, January 25, 2022.

(iv) RTCA DO-282B, Minimum Operational Performance Standards for Universal Access Transceiver (UAT) Automatic Dependent Surveillance–Broadcast (ADS-B), Section 2, Equipment Performance Requirements and Test Procedures, December 2, 2009.

(v) RTCA DO-282C, Minimum Operational Performance Standards (MOPS) for Universal Access Transceiver (UAT) Automatic Dependent Surveillance–Broadcast (ADS-B), Section 2, Equipment Performance Requirements and Test Procedures, June 23, 2022.

[Docket No. FAA–2007–29305, 75 FR 30193, May 28, 2010; Amdt. 91–314–A, 75 FR 37712, June 30, 2010; Amdt. 91–316, 75 FR 37712, June 30, 2010; Amdt. 91–336, 80 FR 6900, Feb. 9, 2015; Amdt. 91–336A, 80 FR 11537, March 4, 2015; Amdt. 91–355, 84 FR 34287, July 18, 2019; Amdt. No. 91–361, 86 FR 4513, Jan. 15, 2021; Amdt. 91–371, 88 FR 71476, Oct. 17, 2023 Amdt. 91–371B, 89 FR 33224, April 29, 2024]

§91.227 Automatic Dependent Surveillance–Broadcast (ADS-B) Out equipment performance requirements.

(a) *Definitions.* For the purposes of this section:

ADS-B Out is a function of an aircraft's onboard avionics that periodically broadcasts the aircraft's state vector (3-dimensional position and 3-dimensional velocity) and other required information as described in this section.

Navigation Accuracy Category for Position (NAC$_P$) specifies the accuracy of a reported aircraft's position.

Navigation Accuracy Category for Velocity (NAC$_V$) specifies the accuracy of a reported aircraft's velocity.

Navigation Integrity Category (NIC) specifies an integrity containment radius around an aircraft's reported position.

Position Source refers to the equipment installed onboard an aircraft used to process and provide aircraft position (for example, latitude, longitude, and velocity) information.

Source Integrity Level (SIL) indicates the probability of the reported horizontal position exceeding the containment radius defined by the NIC on a per sample or per hour basis.

System Design Assurance (SDA) indicates the probability of an aircraft malfunction causing false or misleading information to be transmitted.

Total latency is the total time between when the position is measured and when the position is transmitted by the aircraft.

Uncompensated latency is the time for which the aircraft does not compensate for latency.

(b) *1090 MHz ES and UAT Broadcast Links and Power Requirements—*

(1) Aircraft operating in Class A airspace must have equipment installed that meets the antenna and power output requirements of Class A1S, A1, A2, A3, B1S, or B1 equipment as defined in TSO-C166b and Section 2 of RTCA DO-260B (as referenced in TSO-C166b), or TSO-C166c and Section 2 of RTCA DO-260C as modified by DO-260C—Change 1 (as referenced in TSO-C166c).

(2) Aircraft operating in airspace designated for ADS-B Out, but outside of Class A airspace, must have equipment installed that meets the antenna and output power requirements of either:

(i) Class A1S, A1, A2, A3, B1S, or B1 as defined in TSO-C166b and Section 2 of RTCA DO-260B (as referenced in TSO-C166b) or TSO-C166c and Section 2 of RTCA DO-260C as modified by DO-260C—Change 1 (as referenced in TSO-C166c); or

(ii) Class A1S, A1H, A2, A3, B1S, or B1 equipment as defined in TSO-C154c and Section 2 of RTCA DO-282B (as referenced in TSO-C154c), or TSO-C154d and Section 2 of RTCA DO-282C (as referenced in TSO-C154d).

(c) *ADS-B Out Performance Requirements for NAC$_P$, NAC$_V$, NIC, SDA, and SIL—*

(1) For aircraft broadcasting ADS-B Out as required under §91.225 (a) and (b)—

(i) The aircraft's NAC$_P$ must be less than 0.05 nautical miles;

(ii) The aircraft's NAC$_V$ must be less than 10 meters per second;

(iii) The aircraft's NIC must be less than 0.2 nautical miles;

(iv) The aircraft's SDA must be less than or equal to 10^{-5} per flight hour; and

(v) The aircraft's SIL must be less than or equal to 10^{-7} per flight hour or per sample.

(2) Changes in NAC$_P$, NAC$_V$, SDA, and SIL must be broadcast within 10 seconds.

(3) Changes in NIC must be broadcast within 12 seconds.

(d) *Minimum Broadcast Message Element Set for ADS-B Out.* Each aircraft must broadcast the following information, as defined in TSO-C166b (including Section 2 of RTCA DO-260B, as referenced in TSO-C166b), TSO-C166c (including Section 2 of RTCA DO-260C as modified by DO-260C—Change 1, as referenced in TSO-C166c), TSO-C154c (including Section 2 of RTCA DO-282B, as referenced in TSO-C154c), or TSO-C154d (including Section 2 of RTCA DO-282C, as referenced in TSO-C154d). The pilot must enter information for message elements listed in paragraphs (d)(7) through (10) of this section during the appropriate phase of flight.

(1) The length and width of the aircraft;

(2) An indication of the aircraft's latitude and longitude;

(3) An indication of the aircraft's barometric pressure altitude;

(4) An indication of the aircraft's velocity;

(5) An indication if a collision avoidance system is installed and operating in a mode that can generate resolution advisory alerts;

(6) If an operable collision avoidance system is installed, an indication if a resolution advisory is in effect;

(7) An indication of the Mode A transponder code specified by ATC;

(8) An indication of the aircraft identification that is submitted on the flight plan or used for communicating with ATC, except when the pilot has not filed a flight plan, has not requested ATC services, and is using a TSO-C154c or TSO-C154d self-assigned temporary 24-bit address;

(9) An indication if the flightcrew has identified an emergency, radio communication failure, or unlawful interference;

(10) An indication of the aircraft's "IDENT" to ATC;

(11) An indication of the aircraft assigned ICAO 24-bit address, except when the pilot has not filed a flight plan, has not requested ATC services, and is using a TSO-C154c or TSO-C154d self-assigned temporary 24-bit address;

(12) An indication of the aircraft's emitter category;

(13) An indication of whether an ADS-B In capability is available;

(14) An indication of the aircraft's geometric altitude;

(15) An indication of the Navigation Accuracy Category for Position (NAC$_P$);

(16) An indication of the Navigation Accuracy Category for Velocity (NAC$_V$);

(17) An indication of the Navigation Integrity Category (NIC);

(18) An indication of the System Design Assurance (SDA); and

(19) An indication of the Source Integrity Level (SIL).

(e) ADS-B Latency Requirements—

(1) The aircraft must transmit its geometric position no later than 2.0 seconds from the time of measurement of the position to the time of transmission.

(2) Within the 2.0 total latency allocation, a maximum of 0.6 seconds can be uncompensated latency. The aircraft must compensate for any latency above 0.6 seconds up to the maximum 2.0 seconds total by extrapolating the geometric position to the time of message transmission.

(3) The aircraft must transmit its position and velocity at least once per second while airborne or while moving on the airport surface.

(4) The aircraft must transmit its position at least once every 5 seconds while stationary on the airport surface.

(f) Equipment with an approved deviation. Operators with equipment installed with an approved deviation under §21.618 of this chapter also are in compliance with this section.

(g) Incorporation by reference. The standards required in this section are incorporated by reference with the approval of the Director of the Office of the Federal Register under 5 U.S.C. 552(a) and 1 CFR part 51. This incorporation by reference (IBR) material is available for inspection at the FAA and the National Archives and Records Administration (NARA). Contact the FAA at: Office of Rulemaking (ARM-1), 800 Independence Avenue SW, Washington, DC 20590 (telephone 202-267-9677). For information on the availability of this material at NARA, visit *www.archives.gov /federal-register/cfr/ibr-locations.html* or email *fr.inspection@nara.gov.* This material is also available from the following sources indicated in this paragraph (g).

(1) U.S. Department of Transportation, Subsequent Distribution Office, DOT Warehouse M30, Ardmore East Business Center, 3341 Q 75th Avenue, Landover, MD 20785; telephone (301) 322-5377; website: *www.faa.gov/aircraft/air_cert /design_approvals/tso/* (select the link "Search Technical Standard Orders").

(i) TSO-C166b, Extended Squitter Automatic Dependent Surveillance–Broadcast (ADS-B) and Traffic Information Service–Broadcast (TIS-B) Equipment Operating on the Radio Frequency of 1090 Megahertz (MHz), December 2, 2009.

(ii) TSO-C166c, Extended Squitter Automatic Dependent Surveillance–Broadcast (ADS-B) and Traffic Information Service–Broadcast (TIS-B) Equipment Operating on the Radio Frequency of 1090 Megahertz (MHz), March 10, 2023.

(iii) TSO-C154c, Universal Access Transceiver (UAT) Automatic Dependent Surveillance–Broadcast (ADS-B) Equipment Operating on the Frequency of 978 MHz, December 2, 2009.

(iv) TSO-C154d, Universal Access Transceiver (UAT) Automatic Dependent Surveillance–Broadcast (ADS-B) Equipment Operating on the Radio Frequency of 978 Megahertz (MHz), March 10, 2023.

(2) RTCA, Inc., 1150 18th St. NW, Suite 910, Washington, DC 20036; telephone (202) 833-9339; website: *www.rtca.org/products.*

(i) RTCA DO-260B, Minimum Operational Performance Standards for 1090 MHz Extended Squitter Automatic Dependent Surveillance–Broadcast (ADS-B) and Traffic Information Services–Broadcast (TIS-B), Section 2, Equipment Performance Requirements and Test Procedures, December 2, 2009.

(ii) RTCA DO-260C, Minimum Operational Performance Standards for 1090 MHz Extended Squitter Automatic Dependent Surveillance–Broadcast (ADS-B) and Traffic Information Services–Broadcast (TIS-B), Section 2, Equipment Performance Requirements and Test Procedures, December 17, 2020.

(iii) RTCA DO-260C, Minimum Operational Performance Standards for 1090 MHz Extended Squitter Automatic Dependent Surveillance–Broadcast (ADS-B) and Traffic Information Services–Broadcast (TIS-B), Change 1, January 25, 2022.

(iv) RTCA DO-282B, Minimum Operational Performance Standards for Universal Access Transceiver (UAT) Automatic Dependent Surveillance–Broadcast (ADS-B), Section 2, Equipment Performance Requirements and Test Procedures, December 2, 2009.

(v) RTCA DO-282C, Minimum Operational Performance Standards (MOPS) for Universal Access Transceiver (UAT) Automatic Dependent Surveillance–Broadcast (ADS-B), Section 2, Equipment Performance Requirements and Test Procedures, June 23, 2022.

[Docket No. FAA–2007–29305, 75 FR 30194, May 28, 2010; Amdt. 91–314–A, 75 FR 37712, June 30, 2010; Amdt. 91–316, 75 FR 37712, June 30, 2010; Amdt. 91–371, 88 FR 71477, Oct. 17, 2023]

§91.228–91.299 [Reserved]

Subpart D—
Special Flight Operations

Source: Docket No. 18334, 54 FR 34308, Aug. 18, 1989, unless otherwise noted.

§91.301 [Reserved]

§91.303 Aerobatic flight.

No person may operate an aircraft in aerobatic flight—

(a) Over any congested area of a city, town, or settlement;

(b) Over an open air assembly of persons;

(c) Within the lateral boundaries of the surface areas of Class B, Class C, Class D, or Class E airspace designated for an airport;

(d) Within 4 nautical miles of the center line of any Federal airway;

(e) Below an altitude of 1,500 feet above the surface; or

(f) When flight visibility is less than 3 statute miles.

For the purposes of this section, aerobatic flight means an intentional maneuver involving an abrupt change in an aircraft's attitude, an abnormal attitude, or abnormal acceleration, not necessary for normal flight.

[Docket No. 18834, 54 FR 34308, Aug. 18, 1989; as amended by Amdt. 91–227, 56 FR 65661, Dec. 17, 1991]

§91.305 Flight test areas.

No person may flight test an aircraft except over open water, or sparsely populated areas, having light air traffic.

§91.307 Parachutes and parachuting.

(a) No pilot of a civil aircraft may allow a parachute that is available for emergency use to be carried in that aircraft unless it is an approved type and has been packed by a certificated and appropriately rated parachute rigger—

(1) Within the preceding 180 days, if its canopy, shrouds, and harness are composed exclusively of nylon, rayon, or other similar synthetic fiber or materials that are substantially resistant to damage from mold, mildew, or other fungi and other rotting agents propagated in a moist environment; or

(2) Within the preceding 60 days, if any part of the parachute is composed of silk, pongee, or other natural fiber or materials not specified in paragraph (a)(1) of this section.

(b) Except in an emergency, no pilot in command may allow, and no person may conduct, a parachute operation from an aircraft within the United States except in accordance with part 105 of this chapter.

(c) Unless each occupant of the aircraft is wearing an approved parachute, no pilot of a civil aircraft carrying any person (other than a crewmember) may execute any intentional maneuver that exceeds—

(1) A bank of 60 degrees relative to the horizon; or

(2) A nose-up or nose-down attitude of 30 degrees relative to the horizon.

(d) Paragraph (c) of this section does not apply to—

(1) Flight tests for pilot certification or rating; or

(2) Spins and other flight maneuvers required by the regulations for any certificate or rating when given by—

(i) A certificated flight instructor; or

(ii) An airline transport pilot instructing in accordance with §61.67 of this chapter.

(e) For the purposes of this section, approved parachute means—

(1) A parachute manufactured under a type certificate or a technical standard order (C-23 series); or

(2) A personnel-carrying military parachute identified by an NAF, AAF, or AN drawing number, an AAF order number, or any other military designation or specification number.

[Docket No. 18334, 54 FR 34308, Aug. 18, 1989; as amended by Amdt. 91–255, 62 FR 68137, Dec. 30, 1997; Amdt. 91–268, 66 FR 23553, May 9, 2001; Amdt. 91–305, 73 FR 69530, Nov. 19, 2008]

§91.309 Towing: Gliders and unpowered ultralight vehicles.

(a) No person may operate a civil aircraft towing a glider or unpowered ultralight vehicle unless—

(1) The pilot in command of the towing aircraft is qualified under §61.69 of this chapter;

(2) The towing aircraft is equipped with a tow-hitch of a kind, and installed in a manner, that is approved by the Administrator;

(3) The towline used has breaking strength not less than 80 percent of the maximum certificated operating weight of the glider or unpowered ultralight vehicle and not more than twice this operating weight. However, the towline used may have a breaking strength more than twice the maximum certificated operating weight of the glider or unpowered ultralight vehicle if—

(i) A safety link is installed at the point of attachment of the towline to the glider or unpowered ultralight vehicle with a breaking strength not less than 80 percent of the maximum certificated operating weight of the glider or unpowered ultralight vehicle and not greater than twice this operating weight;

(ii) A safety link is installed at the point of attachment of the towline to the towing aircraft with a breaking strength greater, but not more than 25

percent greater, than that of the safety link at the towed glider or unpowered ultralight vehicle end of the towline and not greater than twice the maximum certificated operating weight of the glider or unpowered ultralight vehicle;

(4) Before conducting any towing operation within the lateral boundaries of the surface areas of Class B, Class C, Class D, or Class E airspace designated for an airport, or before making each towing flight within such controlled airspace if required by ATC, the pilot in command notifies the control tower. If a control tower does not exist or is not in operation, the pilot in command must notify the FAA flight service station serving that controlled airspace before conducting any towing operations in that airspace; and

(5) The pilots of the towing aircraft and the glider or unpowered ultralight vehicle have agreed upon a general course of action, including takeoff and release signals, airspeeds, and emergency procedures for each pilot.

(b) No pilot of a civil aircraft may intentionally release a towline, after release of a glider or unpowered ultralight vehicle, in a manner that endangers the life or property of another.

[Docket No. 18834, 54 FR 34308, Aug. 18, 1989; as amended by Amdt. 91–227, 56 FR 65661, Dec. 17, 1991; Amdt. 91–282, 69 FR 44880, July 27, 2004]

§91.311 Towing: Other than under §91.309.

No pilot of a civil aircraft may tow anything with that aircraft (other than under §91.309) except in accordance with the terms of a certificate of waiver issued by the Administrator.

§91.313 Restricted category civil aircraft: Operating limitations.

(a) No person may operate a restricted category civil aircraft—

(1) For other than the special purpose for which it is certificated; or

(2) In an operation other than one necessary to accomplish the work activity directly associated with that special purpose.

(b) For the purpose of paragraph (a) of this section, the following operations are considered necessary to accomplish the work activity directly associated with a special purpose operation:

(1) Flights conducted for flight crewmember training in a special purpose operation for which the aircraft is certificated.

(2) Flights conducted to satisfy proficiency check and recent flight experience requirements under part 61 of this chapter provided the flight crewmember holds the appropriate category, class, and type ratings and is employed by the operator to perform the appropriate special purpose operation.

(3) Flights conducted to relocate the aircraft for delivery, repositioning, or maintenance.

(c) No person may operate a restricted category civil aircraft carrying persons or property for compensation or hire. For the purposes of this paragraph (c), a special purpose operation involving the carriage of persons or material necessary to accomplish that operation, such as crop dusting, seeding, spraying, and banner towing (including the carrying of required persons or material to the location of that operation), an operation for the purpose of providing flight crewmember training in a special purpose operation, and an operation conducted under the authority provided in paragraph (h) of this section are not considered to be the carriage of persons or property for compensation or hire.

(d) No person may be carried on a restricted category civil aircraft unless that person—

(1) Is a flight crewmember;

(2) Is a flight crewmember trainee;

(3) Performs an essential function in connection with a special purpose operation for which the aircraft is certificated;

(4) Is necessary to accomplish the work activity directly associated with that special purpose; or

(5) Is necessary to accomplish an operation under paragraph (h) of this section.

(e) Except when operating in accordance with the terms and conditions of a certificate of waiver or special operating limitations issued by the Administrator, no person may operate a restricted category civil aircraft within the United States—

(1) Over a densely populated area;

(2) In a congested airway; or

(3) Near a busy airport where passenger transport operations are conducted.

(f) This section does not apply to nonpassenger-carrying civil rotorcraft external-load operations conducted under part 133 of this chapter.

(g) No person may operate a small restricted-category civil airplane manufactured after July 18, 1978, unless an approved shoulder harness or restraint system is installed for each front seat. The shoulder harness or restraint system installation at each flightcrew station must permit the flightcrew member, when seated and with the safety belt and shoulder harness fastened or the restraint system engaged, to perform all functions necessary for flight operation. For purposes of this paragraph—

(1) The date of manufacture of an airplane is the date the inspection acceptance records reflect that the airplane is complete and meets the FAA-approved type design data; and

(2) A front seat is a seat located at a flight crewmember station or any seat located alongside such a seat.

(h)(1) An operator may apply for deviation authority from the provisions of paragraph (a) of this

section to conduct operations for the following purposes:

(i) Flight training and the practical test for issuance of a type rating provided—

(A) The pilot being trained and tested holds at least a commercial pilot certificate with the appropriate category and class ratings for the aircraft type;

(B) The pilot receiving flight training is employed by the operator to perform a special purpose operation; and

(C) The flight training is conducted by the operator who employs the pilot to perform a special purpose operation.

(ii) Flights to designate an examiner or qualify an FAA inspector in the aircraft type and flights necessary to provide continuing oversight and evaluation of an examiner.

(2) The FAA will issue this deviation authority as a letter of deviation authority.

(3) The FAA may cancel or amend a letter of deviation authority at any time.

(4) An applicant must submit a request for deviation authority in a form and manner acceptable to the Administrator at least 60 days before the date of intended operations. A request for deviation authority must contain a complete description of the proposed operation and justification that establishes a level of safety equivalent to that provided under the regulations for the deviation requested.

[Docket No. 18334, 54 FR 34308, Aug. 18, 1989, as amended by Docket FAA–2015–1621, Amdt. 91–346, 81 FR 96700, Dec. 30, 2016; Amdt. 60–6, 83 FR 30281, June 27, 2018]

§91.315 Limited category civil aircraft: Operating limitations.

No person may operate a limited category civil aircraft carrying persons or property for compensation or hire.

§91.317 Provisionally certificated civil aircraft: Operating limitations.

(a) No person may operate a provisionally certificated civil aircraft unless that person is eligible for a provisional airworthiness certificate under §21.213 of this chapter.

(b) No person may operate a provisionally certificated civil aircraft outside the United States unless that person has specific authority to do so from the Administrator and each foreign country involved.

(c) Unless otherwise authorized by the Executive Director, Flight Standards Service, no person may operate a provisionally certificated civil aircraft in air transportation.

(d) Unless otherwise authorized by the Administrator, no person may operate a provisionally certificated civil aircraft except—

(1) In direct conjunction with the type or supplemental type certification of that aircraft;

(2) For training flight crews, including simulated air carrier operations;

(3) Demonstration flight by the manufacturer for prospective purchasers;

(4) Market surveys by the manufacturer;

(5) Flight checking of instruments, accessories, and equipment that do not affect the basic airworthiness of the aircraft; or

(6) Service testing of the aircraft.

(e) Each person operating a provisionally certificated civil aircraft shall operate within the prescribed limitations displayed in the aircraft or set forth in the provisional aircraft flight manual or other appropriate document. However, when operating in direct conjunction with the type or supplemental type certification of the aircraft, that person shall operate under the experimental aircraft limitations of §21.191 of this chapter and when flight testing, shall operate under the requirements of §91.305 of this part.

(f) Each person operating a provisionally certificated civil aircraft shall establish approved procedures for—

(1) The use and guidance of flight and ground personnel in operating under this section; and

(2) Operating in and out of airports where takeoffs or approaches over populated areas are necessary. No person may operate that aircraft except in compliance with the approved procedures.

(g) Each person operating a provisionally certificated civil aircraft shall ensure that each flight crewmember is properly certificated and has adequate knowledge of, and familiarity with, the aircraft and procedures to be used by that crewmember.

(h) Each person operating a provisionally certificated civil aircraft shall maintain it as required by applicable regulations and as may be specially prescribed by the Administrator.

(i) Whenever the manufacturer, or the Administrator, determines that a change in design, construction, or operation is necessary to ensure safe operation, no person may operate a provisionally certificated civil aircraft until that change has been made and approved. Section 21.99 of this chapter applies to operations under this section.

(j) Each person operating a provisionally certificated civil aircraft—

(1) May carry in that aircraft only persons who have a proper interest in the operations allowed by this section or who are specifically authorized by both the manufacturer and the Administrator; and

(2) Shall advise each person carried that the aircraft is provisionally certificated.

(k) The Administrator may prescribe additional limitations or procedures that the Administrator considers necessary, including limitations on the

91

number of persons who may be carried in the aircraft.

(Approved by the Office of Management and Budget under control number 2120–0005)

[Docket No. 18334, 54 FR 34308, Aug. 18, 1989; as amended by Amdt. 91–212, 54 FR 39293, Sept. 25, 1989; Docket FAA–2018–0119, Amdt. 91–350, 83 FR 9171, March 5, 2018]

§91.319 Aircraft having experimental certificates: Operating limitations.

(a) No person may operate an aircraft that has an experimental certificate—

(1) For other than the purpose for which the certificate was issued; or

(2) Carrying persons or property for compensation or hire.

(b) No person may operate an aircraft that has an experimental certificate outside of an area assigned by the Administrator until it is shown that—

(1) The aircraft is controllable throughout its normal range of speeds and throughout all the maneuvers to be executed; and

(2) The aircraft has no hazardous operating characteristics or design features.

(c) Unless otherwise authorized by the Administrator in special operating limitations, no person may operate an aircraft that has an experimental certificate over a densely populated area or in a congested airway. The Administrator may issue special operating limitations for particular aircraft to permit takeoffs and landings to be conducted over a densely populated area or in a congested airway, in accordance with terms and conditions specified in the authorization in the interest of safety in air commerce.

(d) Each person operating an aircraft that has an experimental certificate shall—

(1) Advise each person carried of the experimental nature of the aircraft;

(2) Operate under VFR, day only, unless otherwise specifically authorized by the Administrator; and

(3) Notify the control tower of the experimental nature of the aircraft when operating the aircraft into or out of airports with operating control towers.

(e) No person may operate an aircraft that is issued an experimental certificate under §21.191(i) of this chapter for compensation or hire, except a person may operate an aircraft issued an experimental certificate under §21.191(i)(1) for compensation or hire to—

(1) Tow a glider that is a light-sport aircraft or unpowered ultralight vehicle in accordance with §91.309; or

(2) Conduct flight training in an aircraft which that person provides prior to January 31, 2010.

(f) No person may lease an aircraft that is issued an experimental certificate under §21.191(i) of this chapter, except in accordance with paragraph (e)(1) of this section.

(g) No person may operate an aircraft issued an experimental certificate under §21.191(i)(1) of this chapter to tow a glider that is a light-sport aircraft or unpowered ultralight vehicle for compensation or hire or to conduct flight training for compensation or hire in an aircraft which that persons provides unless within the preceding 100 hours of time in service the aircraft has—

(1) Been inspected by a certificated repairman (light-sport aircraft) with a maintenance rating, an appropriately rated mechanic, or an appropriately rated repair station in accordance with inspection procedures developed by the aircraft manufacturer or a person acceptable to the FAA; or

(2) Received an inspection for the issuance of an airworthiness certificate in accordance with part 21 of this chapter.

(h) The FAA may issue deviation authority providing relief from the provisions of paragraph (a) of this section for the purpose of conducting flight training. The FAA will issue this deviation authority as a letter of deviation authority.

(1) The FAA may cancel or amend a letter of deviation authority at any time.

(2) An applicant must submit a request for deviation authority to the FAA at least 60 days before the date of intended operations. A request for deviation authority must contain a complete description of the proposed operation and justification that establishes a level of safety equivalent to that provided under the regulations for the deviation requested.

(i) The Administrator may prescribe additional limitations that the Administrator considers necessary, including limitations on the persons that may be carried in the aircraft.

(j) No person may operate an aircraft that has an experimental certificate under §61.113(i) of this chapter unless the aircraft is carrying not more than 6 occupants.

[Docket No. 18334, 54 FR 34308, Aug. 18, 1989, as amended by Amdt. 91–282, 69 FR 44881, July 27, 2004; Docket FAA–2016–9157, Amdt. 91–347, 82 FR 3167, Jan. 11, 2017]

§91.321 Carriage of candidates in elections.

(a) As an aircraft operator, you may receive payment for carrying a candidate, agent of a candidate, or person traveling on behalf of a candidate, running for Federal, State, or local election, without having to comply with the rules in parts 121, 125 or 135 of this chapter, under the following conditions:

(1) Your primary business is not as an air carrier or commercial operator;

(2) You carry the candidate, agent, or person traveling on behalf of a candidate, under the rules of part 91; and

(3) By Federal, state or local law, you are required to receive payment for carrying the candidate, agent, or person traveling on behalf of a candidate. For federal elections, the payment may not exceed the amount required by the Federal Election Commission. For a state or local election, the payment may not exceed the amount required under the applicable state or local law.

(b) For the purposes of this section, for Federal elections, the terms candidate and election have the same meaning as set forth in the regulations of the Federal Election Commission. For State or local elections, the terms candidate and election have the same meaning as provided by the applicable State or local law and those terms relate to candidates for election to public office in State and local government elections.

[Docket No. FAA–2005–20168, 70 FR 4982, Jan. 31, 2005]

§91.323 Increased maximum certificated weights for certain airplanes operated in Alaska.

(a) Notwithstanding any other provision of the Federal Aviation Regulations, the Administrator will approve, as provided in this section, an increase in the maximum certificated weight of an airplane type certificated under Aeronautics Bulletin No. 7–A of the U.S. Department of Commerce dated January 1, 1931, as amended, or under the normal category of part 4a of the former Civil Air Regulations (14 CFR part 4a, 1964 ed.) if that airplane is operated in the State of Alaska by—

(1) A certificate holder conducting operations under part 121 or part 135 of this chapter; or

(2) The U.S. Department of Interior in conducting its game and fish law enforcement activities or its management, fire detection, and fire suppression activities concerning public lands.

(b) The maximum certificated weight approved under this section may not exceed—

(1) 12,500 pounds;

(2) 115 percent of the maximum weight listed in the FAA aircraft specifications;

(3) The weight at which the airplane meets the positive maneuvering load factor n, where $n = 2.1 + (24,000/(W+10,000))$ and W = design maximum takeoff weight, except that n need not be more than 3.8; or

(4) The weight at which the airplane meets the climb performance requirements under which it was type certificated.

(c) In determining the maximum certificated weight, the Administrator considers the structural soundness of the airplane and the terrain to be traversed.

(d) The maximum certificated weight determined under this section is added to the airplane's operation limitations and is identified as the maximum weight authorized for operations within the State of Alaska.

[Docket No. 18334, 54 FR 34308, Aug. 18, 1989; Amdt. 91–211, 54 FR 41211, Oct. 5, 1989, as amended by Amdt. 91–253, 62 FR 13253, March 19, 1997; Docket FAA–2015–1621, Amdt. 91–346, 81 FR 96700, Dec. 30, 2016]

§91.325 Primary category aircraft: Operating limitations.

(a) No person may operate a primary category aircraft carrying persons or property for compensation or hire.

(b) No person may operate a primary category aircraft that is maintained by the pilot-owner under an approved special inspection and maintenance program except—

(1) The pilot-owner; or

(2) A designee of the pilot-owner, provided that the pilot-owner does not receive compensation for the use of the aircraft.

[Docket No. 23345, 57 FR 41370, Sept. 9, 1992]

§91.327 Aircraft having a special airworthiness certificate in the light-sport category: Operating limitations.

(a) No person may operate an aircraft that has a special airworthiness certificate in the light-sport category for compensation or hire except—

(1) To tow a glider or an unpowered ultralight vehicle in accordance with §91.309 of this chapter; or

(2) To conduct flight training.

(b) No person may operate an aircraft that has a special airworthiness certificate in the light-sport category unless—

(1) The aircraft is maintained by a certificated repairman with a light-sport aircraft maintenance rating, an appropriately rated mechanic, or an appropriately rated repair station in accordance with the applicable provisions of part 43 of this chapter and maintenance and inspection procedures developed by the aircraft manufacturer or a person acceptable to the FAA;

(2) A condition inspection is performed once every 12 calendar months by a certificated repairman (light-sport aircraft) with a maintenance rating, an appropriately rated mechanic, or an appropriately rated repair station in accordance with inspection procedures developed by the aircraft manufacturer or a person acceptable to the FAA;

(3) The owner or operator complies with all applicable airworthiness directives;

(4) The owner or operator complies with each safety directive applicable to the aircraft that corrects an existing unsafe condition. In lieu of

91

complying with a safety directive an owner or operator may—

(i) Correct the unsafe condition in a manner different from that specified in the safety directive provided the person issuing the directive concurs with the action; or

(ii) Obtain an FAA waiver from the provisions of the safety directive based on a conclusion that the safety directive was issued without adhering to the applicable consensus standard;

(5) Each alteration accomplished after the aircraft's date of manufacture meets the applicable and current consensus standard and has been authorized by either the manufacturer or a person acceptable to the FAA;

(6) Each major alteration to an aircraft product produced under a consensus standard is authorized, performed and inspected in accordance with maintenance and inspection procedures developed by the manufacturer or a person acceptable to the FAA; and

(7) The owner or operator complies with the requirements for the recording of major repairs and major alterations performed on type-certificated products in accordance with §43.9(d) of this chapter, and with the retention requirements in §91.417.

(c) No person may operate an aircraft issued a special airworthiness certificate in the light-sport category to tow a glider or unpowered ultralight vehicle for compensation or hire or conduct flight training for compensation or hire in an aircraft which that persons provides unless within the preceding 100 hours of time in service the aircraft has—

(1) Been inspected by a certificated repairman with a light-sport aircraft maintenance rating, an appropriately rated mechanic, or an appropriately rated repair station in accordance with inspection procedures developed by the aircraft manufacturer or a person acceptable to the FAA and been approved for return to service in accordance with part 43 of this chapter; or

(2) Received an inspection for the issuance of an airworthiness certificate in accordance with part 21 of this chapter.

(d) Each person operating an aircraft issued a special airworthiness certificate in the light-sport category must operate the aircraft in accordance with the aircraft's operating instructions, including any provisions for necessary operating equipment specified in the aircraft's equipment list.

(e) Each person operating an aircraft issued a special airworthiness certificate in the light-sport category must advise each person carried of the special nature of the aircraft and that the aircraft does not meet the airworthiness requirements for an aircraft issued a standard airworthiness certificate.

(f) The FAA may prescribe additional limitations that it considers necessary.

[Docket No. FAA–2001–11133, 69 FR 44881, July 27, 2004]

§91.328–91.399 [Reserved]

Subpart E—Maintenance, Preventive Maintenance, and Alterations

Source: Docket No. 18334, 54 FR 34311, Aug. 18, 1989, unless otherwise noted.

§91.401 Applicability.

(a) This subpart prescribes rules governing the maintenance, preventive maintenance, and alterations of U.S.-registered civil aircraft operating within or outside of the United States.

(b) Sections 91.405, 91.409, 91.411, 91.417, and 91.419 of this subpart do not apply to an aircraft maintained in accordance with a continuous airworthiness maintenance program as provided in part 121, 129, or §§91.1411 or 135.411(a)(2) of this chapter.

(c) Sections 91.405 and 91.409 of this part do not apply to an airplane inspected in accordance with part 125 of this chapter.

[Docket No. 18334, 54 FR 34311, Aug. 18, 1989; as amended by Amdt. 91–267, 66 FR 21066, April 27, 2001; Amdt. 91–280, 68 FR 54560, Sept. 17, 2003]

§91.403 General.

(a) The owner or operator of an aircraft is primarily responsible for maintaining that aircraft in an airworthy condition, including compliance with part 39 of this chapter.

(b) No person may perform maintenance, preventive maintenance, or alterations on an aircraft other than as prescribed in this subpart and other applicable regulations, including part 43 of this chapter.

(c) No person may operate an aircraft for which a manufacturer's maintenance manual or instructions for continued airworthiness has been issued that contains an airworthiness limitations section unless the mandatory replacement times, inspection intervals, and related procedures specified in that section or alternative inspection intervals and related procedures set forth in an operations specification approved by the Administrator under part 121 or 135 of this chapter or in accordance with an inspection program approved under §91.409(e) have been complied with.

(d) A person must not alter an aircraft based on a supplemental type certificate unless the owner or operator of the aircraft is the holder of

the supplemental type certificate, or has written permission from the holder.

[Docket No. 18334, 54 FR 34311, Aug. 18, 1989, as amended by Amdt. 91–267, 66 FR 21066, April 27, 2001; Amdt. 91–293, 71 FR 56005, Sept. 26, 2006]

§91.405 Maintenance required.

Each owner or operator of an aircraft—

(a) Shall have that aircraft inspected as prescribed in subpart E of this part and shall between required inspections, except as provided in paragraph (c) of this section, have discrepancies repaired as prescribed in part 43 of this chapter;

(b) Shall ensure that maintenance personnel make appropriate entries in the aircraft maintenance records indicating the aircraft has been approved for return to service;

(c) Shall have any inoperative instrument or item of equipment, permitted to be inoperative by §91.213(d)(2) of this part, repaired, replaced, removed, or inspected at the next required inspection; and

(d) When listed discrepancies include inoperative instruments or equipment, shall ensure that a placard has been installed as required by §43.11 of this chapter.

§91.407 Operation after maintenance, preventive maintenance, rebuilding, or alteration.

(a) No person may operate any aircraft that has undergone maintenance, preventive maintenance, rebuilding, or alteration unless—

(1) It has been approved for return to service by a person authorized under §43.7 of this chapter; and

(2) The maintenance record entry required by §43.9 or §43.11, as applicable, of this chapter has been made.

(b) No person may carry any person (other than crewmembers) in an aircraft that has been maintained, rebuilt, or altered in a manner that may have appreciably changed its flight characteristics or substantially affected its operation in flight until an appropriately rated pilot with at least a private pilot certificate flies the aircraft, makes an operational check of the maintenance performed or alteration made, and logs the flight in the aircraft records.

(c) The aircraft does not have to be flown as required by paragraph (b) of this section if, prior to flight, ground tests, inspection, or both show conclusively that the maintenance, preventive maintenance, rebuilding, or alteration has not appreciably changed the flight characteristics or substantially affected the flight operation of the aircraft.

(Approved by the Office of Management and Budget under control number 2120–0005)

§91.409 Inspections.

(a) Except as provided in paragraph (c) of this section, no person may operate an aircraft unless, within the preceding 12 calendar months, it has had—

(1) An annual inspection in accordance with part 43 of this chapter and has been approved for return to service by a person authorized by §43.7 of this chapter; or

(2) An inspection for the issuance of an airworthiness certificate in accordance with part 21 of this chapter.

No inspection performed under paragraph (b) of this section may be substituted for any inspection required by this paragraph unless it is performed by a person authorized to perform annual inspections and is entered as an "annual" inspection in the required maintenance records.

(b) Except as provided in paragraph (c) of this section, no person may operate an aircraft carrying any person (other than a crewmember) for hire, and no person may give flight instruction for hire in an aircraft which that person provides, unless within the preceding 100 hours of time in service the aircraft has received an annual or 100-hour inspection and been approved for return to service in accordance with part 43 of this chapter or has received an inspection for the issuance of an airworthiness certificate in accordance with part 21 of this chapter. The 100-hour limitation may be exceeded by not more than 10 hours while en route to reach a place where the inspection can be done. The excess time used to reach a place where the inspection can be done must be included in computing the next 100 hours of time in service.

(c) Paragraphs (a) and (b) of this section do not apply to—

(1) An aircraft that carries a special flight permit, a current experimental certificate, or a light-sport or provisional airworthiness certificate;

(2) An aircraft inspected in accordance with an approved aircraft inspection program under part 125 or 135 of this chapter and so identified by the registration number in the operations specifications of the certificate holder having the approved inspection program;

(3) An aircraft subject to the requirements of paragraph (d) or (e) of this section; or

(4) Turbine-powered rotorcraft when the operator elects to inspect that rotorcraft in accordance with paragraph (e) of this section.

(d) *Progressive inspection.* Each registered owner or operator of an aircraft desiring to use a progressive inspection program must submit a written request to the responsible Flight Standards office, and shall provide—

(1) A certificated mechanic holding an inspection authorization, a certificated airframe repair

station, or the manufacturer of the aircraft to supervise or conduct the progressive inspection;

(2) A current inspection procedures manual available and readily understandable to pilot and maintenance personnel containing, in detail—

(i) An explanation of the progressive inspection, including the continuity of inspection responsibility, the making of reports, and the keeping of records and technical reference material;

(ii) An inspection schedule, specifying the intervals in hours or days when routine and detailed inspections will be performed and including instructions for exceeding an inspection interval by not more than 10 hours while en route and for changing an inspection interval because of service experience;

(iii) Sample routine and detailed inspection forms and instructions for their use; and

(iv) Sample reports and records and instructions for their use;

(3) Enough housing and equipment for necessary disassembly and proper inspection of the aircraft; and

(4) Appropriate current technical information for the aircraft.

The frequency and detail of the progressive inspection shall provide for the complete inspection of the aircraft within each 12 calendar months and be consistent with the manufacturer's recommendations, field service experience, and the kind of operation in which the aircraft is engaged. The progressive inspection schedule must ensure that the aircraft, at all times, will be airworthy and will conform to all applicable FAA aircraft specifications, type certificate data sheets, airworthiness directives, and other approved data. If the progressive inspection is discontinued, the owner or operator shall immediately notify the responsible Flight Standards office, in writing, of the discontinuance. After the discontinuance, the first annual inspection under §91.409(a)(1) is due within 12 calendar months after the last complete inspection of the aircraft under the progressive inspection. The 100-hour inspection under §91.409(b) is due within 100 hours after that complete inspection. A complete inspection of the aircraft, for the purpose of determining when the annual and 100-hour inspections are due, requires a detailed inspection of the aircraft and all its components in accordance with the progressive inspection. A routine inspection of the aircraft and a detailed inspection of several components is not considered to be a complete inspection.

(e) *Large airplanes (to which part 125 is not applicable), turbojet multiengine airplanes, turbopropeller-powered multiengine airplanes, and turbine-powered rotorcraft.* No person may operate a large airplane, turbojet multiengine airplane, turbopropeller-powered

multiengine airplane, or turbine-powered rotorcraft unless the replacement times for life-limited parts specified in the aircraft specifications, type data sheets, or other documents approved by the Administrator are complied with and the airplane or turbine-powered rotorcraft, including the airframe, engines, propellers, rotors, appliances, survival equipment, and emergency equipment, is inspected in accordance with an inspection program selected under the provisions of paragraph (f) of this section, except that, the owner or operator of a turbine-powered rotorcraft may elect to use the inspection provisions of §91.409(a), (b), (c), or (d) in lieu of an inspection option of §91.409(f).

(f) *Selection of inspection program under paragraph (e) of this section.* The registered owner or operator of each airplane or turbine-powered rotorcraft described in paragraph (e) of this section must select, identify in the aircraft maintenance records, and use one of the following programs for the inspection of the aircraft:

(1) A continuous airworthiness inspection program that is part of a continuous airworthiness maintenance program currently in use by a person holding an air carrier operating certificate or an operating certificate issued under part 121 or 135 of this chapter and operating that make and model aircraft under part 121 of this chapter or operating that make and model under part 135 of this chapter and maintaining it under §135.411(a)(2) of this chapter.

(2) An approved aircraft inspection program approved under §135.419 of this chapter and currently in use by a person holding an operating certificate issued under part 135 of this chapter.

(3) A current inspection program recommended by the manufacturer.

(4) Any other inspection program established by the registered owner or operator of that airplane or turbine-powered rotorcraft and approved by the Administrator under paragraph (g) of this section. However, the Administrator may require revision of this inspection program in accordance with the provisions of §91.415.

Each operator shall include in the selected program the name and address of the person responsible for scheduling the inspections required by the program and make a copy of that program available to the person performing inspections on the aircraft and, upon request, to the Administrator.

(g) *Inspection program approved under paragraph (e) of this section.* Each operator of an airplane or turbine-powered rotorcraft desiring to establish or change an approved inspection program under paragraph (f)(4) of this section must submit the program for approval to the responsible Flight Standards office. The program

must be in writing and include at least the following information:

(1) Instructions and procedures for the conduct of inspections for the particular make and model airplane or turbine-powered rotorcraft, including necessary tests and checks. The instructions and procedures must set forth in detail the parts and areas of the airframe, engines, propellers, rotors, and appliances, including survival and emergency equipment required to be inspected.

(2) A schedule for performing the inspections that must be performed under the program expressed in terms of the time in service, calendar time, number of system operations, or any combination of these.

(h) Changes from one inspection program to another. When an operator changes from one inspection program under paragraph (f) of this section to another, the time in service, calendar times, or cycles of operation accumulated under the previous program must be applied in determining inspection due times under the new program.

(Approved by the Office of Management and Budget under control number 2120–0005)

[Docket No. 18334, 54 FR 34311, Aug. 18, 1989; Amdt. 91–211, 54 FR 41211, Oct. 5, 1989; Amdt. 91–267, 66 FR 21066, April 27, 2001; Amdt. 91–282, 69 FR 44882, July 27, 2004; Docket FAA–2018–0119, Amdt. 91–350, 83 FR 9171, March 5, 2018]

§91.410 [Reserved]

§91.411 Altimeter system and altitude reporting equipment tests and inspections.

(a) No person may operate an airplane, or helicopter, in controlled airspace under IFR unless—

(1) Within the preceding 24 calendar months, each static pressure system, each altimeter instrument, and each automatic pressure altitude reporting system has been tested and inspected and found to comply with appendices E and F of part 43 of this chapter;

(2) Except for the use of system drain and alternate static pressure valves, following any opening and closing of the static pressure system, that system has been tested and inspected and found to comply with paragraph (a), appendix E, of part 43 of this chapter; and

(3) Following installation or maintenance on the automatic pressure altitude reporting system of the ATC transponder where data correspondence error could be introduced, the integrated system has been tested, inspected, and found to comply with paragraph (c), Appendix E, of part 43 of this chapter.

(b) The tests required by paragraph (a) of this section must be conducted by—

(1) The manufacturer of the airplane, or helicopter, on which the tests and inspections are to be performed;

(2) A certificated repair station properly equipped to perform those functions and holding—

(i) An instrument rating, Class I;

(ii) A limited instrument rating appropriate to the make and model of appliance to be tested;

(iii) A limited rating appropriate to the test to be performed;

(iv) An airframe rating appropriate to the airplane, or helicopter, to be tested; or

(3) A certificated mechanic with an airframe rating (static pressure system tests and inspections only).

(c) Altimeter and altitude reporting equipment approved under Technical Standard Orders are considered to be tested and inspected as of the date of their manufacture.

(d) No person may operate an airplane, or helicopter, in controlled airspace under IFR at an altitude above the maximum altitude at which all altimeters and the automatic altitude reporting system of that airplane, or helicopter, have been tested.

[Docket No. 18334, 54 FR 34311, Aug. 18, 1989; as amended by Amdt. 91–269, 66 FR 41116, Aug. 6, 2001; 72 FR 7739, Feb. 20, 2007]

§91.413 ATC transponder tests and inspections.

(a) No persons may use an ATC transponder that is specified in §91.215(a), §121.345(c), or §135.143(c) of this chapter unless, within the preceding 24 calendar months, the ATC transponder has been tested and inspected and found to comply with Appendix F of part 43 of this chapter; and

(b) Following any installation or maintenance on an ATC transponder where data correspondence error could be introduced, the integrated system has been tested, inspected, and found to comply with paragraph (c), Appendix E, of part 43 of this chapter.

(c) The tests and inspections specified in this section must be conducted by—

(1) A certificated repair station properly equipped to perform those functions and holding—

(i) A radio rating, Class III;

(ii) A limited radio rating appropriate to the make and model transponder to be tested;

(iii) A limited rating appropriate to the test to be performed;

(2) A holder of a continuous airworthiness maintenance program as provided in part 121 or §135.411(a)(2) of this chapter; or

(3) The manufacturer of the aircraft on which the transponder to be tested is installed, if the transponder was installed by that manufacturer.

[Docket No. 18334, 54 FR 34311, Aug. 18, 1989; as amended by Amdt. 91–267, 66 FR 21066, April 27, 2001; Amdt. 91–269, 66 FR 41116, Aug. 6, 2001]

§91.415 Changes to aircraft inspection programs.

(a) Whenever the Administrator finds that revisions to an approved aircraft inspection program under §91.409(f)(4) or §91.1109 are necessary for the continued adequacy of the program, the owner or operator must, after notification by the Administrator, make any changes in the program found to be necessary by the Administrator.

(b) The owner or operator may petition the Administrator to reconsider the notice to make any changes in a program in accordance with paragraph (a) of this section.

(c) The petition must be filed with the Executive Director, Flight Standards Service within 30 days after the certificate holder or fractional ownership program manager receives the notice.

(d) Except in the case of an emergency requiring immediate action in the interest of safety, the filing of the petition stays the notice pending a decision by the Administrator.

[Docket No. 18334, 54 FR 34311, Aug. 18, 1989; as amended by Amdt. 91–280, 68 FR 54560, Sept. 17, 2003; Docket FAA–2018–0119, Amdt. 91–350, 83 FR 9171, March 5, 2018]

§91.417 Maintenance records.

(a) Except for work performed in accordance with §91.411 and 91.413, each registered owner or operator shall keep the following records for the periods specified in paragraph (b) of this section:

(1) Records of the maintenance, preventive maintenance, and alteration and records of the 100-hour, annual, progressive, and other required or approved inspections, as appropriate, for each aircraft (including the airframe) and each engine, propeller, rotor, and appliance of an aircraft. The records must include—

(i) A description (or reference to data acceptable to the Administrator) of the work performed; and

(ii) The date of completion of the work performed; and

(iii) The signature, and certificate number of the person approving the aircraft for return to service.

(2) Records containing the following information:

(i) The total time in service of the airframe, each engine, each propeller, and each rotor.

(ii) The current status of life-limited parts of each airframe, engine, propeller, rotor, and appliance.

(iii) The time since last overhaul of all items installed on the aircraft which are required to be overhauled on a specified time basis.

(iv) The current inspection status of the aircraft, including the time since the last inspection required by the inspection program under which the aircraft and its appliances are maintained.

(v) The current status of applicable airworthiness directives (AD) and safety directives including, for each, the method of compliance, the AD or safety directive number and revision date. If the AD or safety directive involves recurring action, the time and date when the next action is required.

(vi) Copies of the forms prescribed by §43.9(d) of this chapter for each major alteration to the airframe and currently installed engines, rotors, propellers, and appliances.

(b) The owner or operator shall retain the following records for the periods prescribed:

(1) The records specified in paragraph (a)(1) of this section shall be retained until the work is repeated or superseded by other work or for 1 year after the work is performed.

(2) The records specified in paragraph (a)(2) of this section shall be retained and transferred with the aircraft at the time the aircraft is sold.

(3) A list of defects furnished to a registered owner or operator under §43.11 of this chapter shall be retained until the defects are repaired and the aircraft is approved for return to service.

(c) The owner or operator shall make all maintenance records required to be kept by this section available for inspection by the Administrator or any authorized representative of the National Transportation Safety Board (NTSB). In addition, the owner or operator shall present Form 337 described in paragraph (d) of this section for inspection upon request of any law enforcement officer.

(d) When a fuel tank is installed within the passenger compartment or a baggage compartment pursuant to part 43 of this chapter, a copy of FAA Form 337 shall be kept on board the modified aircraft by the owner or operator.

(Approved by the Office of Management and Budget under control number 2120–0005)

[Docket No. 18334, 54 FR 34311, Aug. 18, 1989, as amended by Amdt. 91–311, 75 FR 5223, Feb. 1, 2010; Amdt. 91–323, 76 FR 39260, July 6, 2011]

§91.419 Transfer of maintenance records.

Any owner or operator who sells a U.S.-registered aircraft shall transfer to the purchaser, at the time of sale, the following records of that aircraft, in plain language form or in coded form at the election of the purchaser, if the coded form provides for the preservation and retrieval of information in a manner acceptable to the Administrator:

(a) The records specified in §91.417(a)(2).

(b) The records specified in §91.417(a)(1) which are not included in the records covered by paragraph (a) of this section, except that the purchaser may permit the seller to keep physical custody of such records. However, custody of records by the seller does not relieve the purchaser of the responsibility under §91.417(c) to make the records available for inspection by the Administrator or any authorized representative of the National Transportation Safety Board (NTSB).

§91.421 Rebuilt engine maintenance records.

(a) The owner or operator may use a new maintenance record, without previous operating history, for an aircraft engine rebuilt by the manufacturer or by an agency approved by the manufacturer.

(b) Each manufacturer or agency that grants zero time to an engine rebuilt by it shall enter in the new record—

(1) A signed statement of the date the engine was rebuilt;

(2) Each change made as required by airworthiness directives; and

(3) Each change made in compliance with manufacturer's service bulletins, if the entry is specifically requested in that bulletin.

(c) For the purposes of this section, a rebuilt engine is a used engine that has been completely disassembled, inspected, repaired as necessary, reassembled, tested, and approved in the same manner and to the same tolerances and limits as a new engine with either new or used parts. However, all parts used in it must conform to the production drawing tolerances and limits for new parts or be of approved oversized or undersized dimensions for a new engine.

§91.423–91.499 [Reserved]

Subpart F—Large and Turbine-Powered Multiengine Airplanes and Fractional Ownership Program Aircraft

Source: Docket No. 18334, 54 FR 34314, Aug. 18, 1989, unless otherwise noted.

§91.501 Applicability.

(a) This subpart prescribes operating rules, in addition to those prescribed in other subparts of this part, governing the operation of large airplanes of U.S. registry, turbojet-powered multiengine civil airplanes of U.S. registry, and fractional ownership program aircraft of U.S. registry that are operating under subpart K of this part in operations not involving common carriage. The operating rules in this subpart do not apply to those aircraft when they are required to be operated under parts 121, 125, 129, 135, and 137 of this chapter. (Section 91.409 prescribes an inspection program for large and for turbine-powered (turbojet and turboprop) multiengine airplanes and turbine-powered rotorcraft of U.S. registry when they are operated under this part or part 129 or 137.)

(b) Operations that may be conducted under the rules in this subpart instead of those in parts 121, 129, 135, and 137 of this chapter when common carriage is not involved, include—

(1) Ferry or training flights;

(2) Aerial work operations such as aerial photography or survey, or pipeline patrol, but not including fire fighting operations;

(3) Flights for the demonstration of an airplane to prospective customers when no charge is made except for those specified in paragraph (d) of this section;

(4) Flights conducted by the operator of an airplane for his personal transportation, or the transportation of his guests when no charge, assessment, or fee is made for the transportation;

(5) Carriage of officials, employees, guests, and property of a company on an airplane operated by that company, or the parent or a subsidiary of the company or a subsidiary of the parent, when the carriage is within the scope of, and incidental to, the business of the company (other than transportation by air) and no charge, assessment or fee is made for the carriage in excess of the cost of owning, operating, and maintaining the airplane, except that no charge of any kind may be made for the carriage of a guest of a company, when the carriage is not within the scope of, and incidental to, the business of that company;

(6) The carriage of company officials, employees, and guests of the company on an airplane operated under a time sharing, interchange, or joint ownership agreement as defined in paragraph (c) of this section;

(7) The carriage of property (other than mail) on an airplane operated by a person in the furtherance of a business or employment (other than transportation by air) when the carriage is within the scope of, and incidental to, that business or employment and no charge, assessment, or fee is made for the carriage other than those specified in paragraph (d) of this section;

(8) The carriage on an airplane of an athletic team, sports group, choral group, or similar group having a common purpose or objective when there is no charge, assessment, or fee of any kind made by any person for that carriage; and

(9) The carriage of persons on an airplane operated by a person in the furtherance of a

business other than transportation by air for the purpose of selling them land, goods, or property, including franchises or distributorships, when the carriage is within the scope of, and incidental to, that business and no charge, assessment, or fee is made for that carriage.

(10) Any operation identified in paragraphs (b)(1) through (b)(9) of this section when conducted—

(i) By a fractional ownership program manager, or

(ii) By a fractional owner in a fractional ownership program aircraft operated under subpart K of this part, except that a flight under a joint ownership arrangement under paragraph (b)(6) of this section may not be conducted. For a flight under an interchange agreement under paragraph (b)(6) of this section, the exchange of equal time for the operation must be properly accounted for as part of the total hours associated with the fractional owner's share of ownership.

(c) As used in this section—

(1) *A time sharing agreement* means an arrangement whereby a person leases his airplane with flight crew to another person, and no charge is made for the flights conducted under that arrangement other than those specified in paragraph (d) of this section;

(2) *An interchange agreement* means an arrangement whereby a person leases his airplane to another person in exchange for equal time, when needed, on the other person's airplane, and no charge, assessment, or fee is made, except that a charge may be made not to exceed the difference between the cost of owning, operating, and maintaining the two airplanes;

(3) *A joint ownership agreement* means an arrangement whereby one of the registered joint owners of an airplane employs and furnishes the flight crew for that airplane and each of the registered joint owners pays a share of the charge specified in the agreement.

(d) The following may be charged, as expenses of a specific flight, for transportation as authorized by paragraphs (b)(3) and (7) and (c)(1) of this section:

(1) Fuel, oil, lubricants, and other additives.

(2) Travel expenses of the crew, including food, lodging, and ground transportation.

(3) Hangar and tie-down costs away from the aircraft's base of operation.

(4) Insurance obtained for the specific flight.

(5) Landing fees, airport taxes, and similar assessments.

(6) Customs, foreign permit, and similar fees directly related to the flight.

(7) In flight food and beverages.

(8) Passenger ground transportation.

(9) Flight planning and weather contract services.

(10) An additional charge equal to 100 percent of the expenses listed in paragraph (d)(1) of this section.

[Docket No. 18334, 54 FR 34314, Aug. 18, 1989; as amended by Amdt. 91–280, 68 FR 54560, Sept. 17, 2003]

§91.503 Flying equipment and operating information.

(a) The pilot in command of an airplane shall ensure that the following flying equipment and aeronautical charts and data, in current and appropriate form, are accessible for each flight at the pilot station of the airplane:

(1) A flashlight having at least two size "D" cells, or the equivalent, that is in good working order.

(2) A cockpit checklist containing the procedures required by paragraph (b) of this section.

(3) Pertinent aeronautical charts.

(4) For IFR, VFR over-the-top, or night operations, each pertinent navigational en route, terminal area, and approach and letdown chart.

(5) In the case of multiengine airplanes, one-engine inoperative climb performance data.

(b) Each cockpit checklist must contain the following procedures and shall be used by the flight crewmembers when operating the airplane:

(1) Before starting engines.

(2) Before takeoff.

(3) Cruise.

(4) Before landing.

(5) After landing.

(6) Stopping engines.

(7) Emergencies.

(c) Each emergency cockpit checklist procedure required by paragraph (b)(7) of this section must contain the following procedures, as appropriate:

(1) Emergency operation of fuel, hydraulic, electrical, and mechanical systems.

(2) Emergency operation of instruments and controls.

(3) Engine inoperative procedures.

(4) Any other procedures necessary for safety.

(d) The equipment, charts, and data prescribed in this section shall be used by the pilot in command and other members of the flight crew, when pertinent.

§91.505 Familiarity with operating limitations and emergency equipment.

(a) Each pilot in command of an airplane shall, before beginning a flight, become familiar with the Airplane Flight Manual for that airplane, if one is required, and with any placards, listings, instrument markings, or any combination thereof, containing each operating limitation prescribed for

that airplane by the Administrator, including those specified in §91.9(b).

(b) Each required member of the crew shall, before beginning a flight, become familiar with the emergency equipment installed on the airplane to which that crewmember is assigned and with the procedures to be followed for the use of that equipment in an emergency situation.

§91.507 Equipment requirements: Over-the-top or night VFR operations.

No person may operate an airplane over-the-top or at night under VFR unless that airplane is equipped with the instruments and equipment required for IFR operations under §91.205(d) and one electric landing light for night operations. Each required instrument and item of equipment must be in operable condition.

§91.509 Survival equipment for overwater operations.

(a) No person may take off an airplane for a flight over water more than 50 nautical miles from the nearest shore unless that airplane is equipped with a life preserver or an approved flotation means for each occupant of the airplane.

(b) Except as provided in paragraph (c) of this section, no person may take off an airplane for flight over water more than 30 minutes flying time or 100 nautical miles from the nearest shore, whichever is less, unless it has on board the following survival equipment:

(1) A life preserver, equipped with an approved survivor locator light, for each occupant of the airplane.

(2) Enough liferafts (each equipped with an approved survival locator light) of a rated capacity and buoyancy to accommodate the occupants of the airplane.

(3) At least one pyrotechnic signaling device for each liferaft.

(4) One self-buoyant, water-resistant, portable emergency radio signaling device that is capable of transmission on the appropriate emergency frequency or frequencies and not dependent upon the airplane power supply.

(5) A lifeline stored in accordance with §25.1411(g) of this chapter.

(c) A fractional ownership program manager under subpart K of this part may apply for a deviation from paragraphs (b)(2) through (5) of this section for a particular over water operation or the Administrator may amend the management specifications to require the carriage of all or any specific items of the equipment listed in paragraphs (b)(2) through (5) of this section.

(d) The required life rafts, life preservers, and signaling devices must be installed in conspicuously marked locations and easily accessible in the event of a ditching without appreciable time for preparatory procedures.

(e) A survival kit, appropriately equipped for the route to be flown, must be attached to each required life raft.

(f) As used in this section, the term shore means that area of the land adjacent to the water that is above the high water mark and excludes land areas that are intermittently under water.

[Docket No. 18334, 54 FR 34314, Aug. 18, 1989; as amended by Amdt. 91–280, 68 FR 54560, Sept. 17, 2003]

§91.511 Communication and navigation equipment for overwater operations.

(a) Except as provided in paragraphs (c), (d), and (f) of this section, no person operating under this subpart may take off an airplane for a flight over water more than 30 minutes flying time or 100 nautical miles from the nearest shore unless it has at least the following operable equipment:

(1) Radio communication equipment appropriate to the facilities to be used and able to transmit to, and receive from, at least one communication facility from any place along the route:

(i) Two transmitters.

(ii) Two microphones.

(iii) Two headsets or one headset and one speaker.

(iv) Two independent receivers.

(2) Appropriate electronic navigational equipment consisting of at least two independent electronic navigation units capable of providing the pilot with the information necessary to navigate the airplane within the airspace assigned by air traffic control. However, a receiver that can receive both communications and required navigational signals may be used in place of a separate communications receiver and a separate navigational signal receiver or unit.

(b) For the purposes of paragraphs (a)(1)(iv) and (a)(2) of this section, a receiver or electronic navigation unit is independent if the function of any part of it does not depend on the functioning of any part of another receiver or electronic navigation unit.

(c) Notwithstanding the provisions of paragraph (a) of this section, a person may operate an airplane on which no passengers are carried from a place where repairs or replacement cannot be made to a place where they can be made, if not more than one of each of the dual items of radio communication and navigational equipment specified in paragraphs (a)(1)(i) through (iv) and (a)(2) of this section malfunctions or becomes inoperative.

(d) Notwithstanding the provisions of paragraph (a) of this section, when both VHF and HF communications equipment are required for the route and the airplane has two VHF transmitters

and two VHF receivers for communications, only one HF transmitter and one HF receiver is required for communications.

(e) As used in this section, the term shore means that area of the land adjacent to the water which is above the high-water mark and excludes land areas which are intermittently under water.

(f) Notwithstanding the requirements in paragraph (a)(2) of this section, a person may operate in the Gulf of Mexico, the Caribbean Sea, and the Atlantic Ocean west of a line which extends from 44° 47'00" N / 67° 00'00" W to 39° 00'00" N / 67° 00'00" W to 38° 30'00" N / 60° 00'00" W south along the 60° 00'00" W longitude line to the point where the line intersects with the northern coast of South America, when:

(1) A single long-range navigation system is installed, operational, and appropriate for the route; and

(2) Flight conditions and the aircraft's capabilities are such that no more than a 30-minute gap in two-way radio very high frequency communications is expected to exist.

[Docket No. 18334, 54 FR 334314, Aug. 18, 1989; as amended by Amdt. 91–249, 61 FR 7190, Feb. 26, 1996; Amdt. 91–296, 72 FR 31679, June 7, 2007; Docket No. FAA–2022–1355, Amdt. No. 91–366, 87 FR 75846, Dec. 9, 2022]

§91.513 Emergency equipment.

(a) No person may operate an airplane unless it is equipped with the emergency equipment listed in this section.

(b) Each item of equipment—

(1) Must be inspected in accordance with §91.409 to ensure its continued serviceability and immediate readiness for its intended purposes;

(2) Must be readily accessible to the crew;

(3) Must clearly indicate its method of operation; and

(4) When carried in a compartment or container, must have that compartment or container marked as to contents and date of last inspection.

(c) Hand fire extinguishers must be provided for use in crew, passenger, and cargo compartments in accordance with the following:

(1) The type and quantity of extinguishing agent must be suitable for the kinds of fires likely to occur in the compartment where the extinguisher is intended to be used.

(2) At least one hand fire extinguisher must be provided and located on or near the flight deck in a place that is readily accessible to the flight crew.

(3) At least one hand fire extinguisher must be conveniently located in the passenger compartment of each airplane accommodating more than six but less than 31 passengers, and at least two hand fire extinguishers must be conveniently located in the passenger compartment of each airplane accommodating more than 30 passengers.

(4) Hand fire extinguishers must be installed and secured in such a manner that they will not interfere with the safe operation of the airplane or adversely affect the safety of the crew and passengers. They must be readily accessible and, unless the locations of the fire extinguishers are obvious, their stowage provisions must be properly identified.

(d) First aid kits for treatment of injuries likely to occur in flight or in minor accidents must be provided.

(e) Each airplane accommodating more than 19 passengers must be equipped with a crash axe.

(f) Each passenger-carrying airplane must have a portable battery-powered megaphone or megaphones readily accessible to the crewmembers assigned to direct emergency evacuation, installed as follows:

(1) One megaphone on each airplane with a seating capacity of more than 60 but less than 100 passengers, at the most rearward location in the passenger cabin where it would be readily accessible to a normal flight attendant seat. However, the Administrator may grant a deviation from the requirements of this subparagraph if the Administrator finds that a different location would be more useful for evacuation of persons during an emergency.

(2) On each airplane with a seating capacity of 100 or more passengers, one megaphone installed at the forward end and one installed at the most rearward location where it would be readily accessible to a normal flight attendant seat.

§91.515 Flight altitude rules.

(a) Notwithstanding §91.119, and except as provided in paragraph (b) of this section, no person may operate an airplane under VFR at less than—

(1) One thousand feet above the surface, or 1,000 feet from any mountain, hill, or other obstruction to flight, for day operations; and

(2) The altitudes prescribed in §91.177, for night operations.

(b) This section does not apply—

(1) During takeoff or landing;

(2) When a different altitude is authorized by a waiver to this section under subpart J of this part; or

(3) When a flight is conducted under the special VFR weather minimums of §91.157 with an appropriate clearance from ATC.

§91.517 Passenger information.

(a) Except as provided in paragraph (b) of this section, no person may operate an airplane carrying passengers unless it is equipped with signs that are visible to passengers and flight attendants to notify them when smoking is prohibited

and when safety belts must be fastened. The signs must be so constructed that the crew can turn them on and off. They must be turned on during airplane movement on the surface, for each takeoff, for each landing, and when otherwise considered to be necessary by the pilot in command.

(b) The pilot in command of an airplane that is not required, in accordance with applicable aircraft and equipment requirements of this chapter, to be equipped as provided in paragraph (a) of this section shall ensure that the passengers are notified orally each time that it is necessary to fasten their safety belts and when smoking is prohibited.

(c) If passenger information signs are installed, no passenger or crewmember may smoke while any "no smoking" sign is lighted nor may any passenger or crewmember smoke in any lavatory.

(d) Each passenger required by §91.107 (a)(3) to occupy a seat or berth shall fasten his or her safety belt about him or her and keep it fastened while any "fasten seat belt" sign is lighted.

(e) Each passenger shall comply with instructions given him or her by crewmembers regarding compliance with paragraphs (b), (c), and (d) of this section.

[Docket No. 26142, 57 FR 42672, Sept. 15, 1992]

§91.519 Passenger briefing.

(a) Before each takeoff the pilot in command of an airplane carrying passengers shall ensure that all passengers have been orally briefed on—

(1) *Smoking.* Each passenger shall be briefed on when, where, and under what conditions smoking is prohibited. This briefing shall include a statement, as appropriate, that the Federal Aviation Regulations require passenger compliance with lighted passenger information signs and no smoking placards, prohibit smoking in lavatories, and require compliance with crewmember instructions with regard to these items;

(2) *Use of safety belts and shoulder harnesses.* Each passenger shall be briefed on when, where, and under what conditions it is necessary to have his or her safety belt and, if installed, his or her shoulder harness fastened about him or her. This briefing shall include a statement, as appropriate, that Federal Aviation Regulations require passenger compliance with the lighted passenger sign and/or crewmember instructions with regard to these items;

(3) Location and means for opening the passenger entry door and emergency exits;

(4) Location of survival equipment;

(5) Ditching procedures and the use of flotation equipment required under §91.509 for a flight over water; and

(6) The normal and emergency use of oxygen equipment installed on the airplane.

(b) The oral briefing required by paragraph (a) of this section shall be given by the pilot in command or a member of the crew, but need not be given when the pilot in command determines that the passengers are familiar with the contents of the briefing. It may be supplemented by printed cards for the use of each passenger containing—

(1) A diagram of, and methods of operating, the emergency exits; and

(2) Other instructions necessary for use of emergency equipment.

(c) Each card used under paragraph (b) must be carried in convenient locations on the airplane for the use of each passenger and must contain information that is pertinent only to the type and model airplane on which it is used.

(d) For operations under subpart K of this part, the passenger briefing requirements of §91.1035 apply, instead of the requirements of paragraphs (a) through (c) of this section.

[Docket No. 18334, 54 FR 34314, Aug. 18, 1989; as amended by Amdt. 91–231, 57 FR 42672, Sept. 15, 1992; Amdt. 91–280, 68 FR 54561, Sept. 17, 2003]

§91.521 Shoulder harness.

(a) No person may operate a transport category airplane that was type certificated after January 1, 1958, unless it is equipped at each seat at a flight deck station with a combined safety belt and shoulder harness that meets the applicable requirements specified in §25.785 of this chapter, except that—

(1) Shoulder harnesses and combined safety belt and shoulder harnesses that were approved and installed before March 6, 1980, may continue to be used; and

(2) Safety belt and shoulder harness restraint systems may be designed to the inertia load factors established under the certification basis of the airplane.

(b) No person may operate a transport category airplane unless it is equipped at each required flight attendant seat in the passenger compartment with a combined safety belt and shoulder harness that meets the applicable requirements specified in §25.785 of this chapter, except that—

(1) Shoulder harnesses and combined safety belt and shoulder harnesses that were approved and installed before March 6, 1980, may continue to be used; and

(2) Safety belt and shoulder harness restraint systems may be designed to the inertia load factors established under the certification basis of the airplane.

§91.523 Carry-on baggage.

No pilot in command of an airplane having a seating capacity of more than 19 passengers may permit a passenger to stow baggage aboard that airplane except—

(a) In a suitable baggage or cargo storage compartment, or as provided in §91.525; or

(b) Under a passenger seat in such a way that it will not slide forward under crash impacts severe enough to induce the ultimate inertia forces specified in §25.561(b)(3) of this chapter, or the requirements of the regulations under which the airplane was type certificated. Restraining devices must also limit sideward motion of under-seat baggage and be designed to withstand crash impacts severe enough to induce sideward forces specified in §25.561(b)(3) of this chapter.

§91.525 Carriage of cargo.

(a) No pilot in command may permit cargo to be carried in any airplane unless—

(1) It is carried in an approved cargo rack, bin, or compartment installed in the airplane;

(2) It is secured by means approved by the Administrator; or

(3) It is carried in accordance with each of the following:

(i) It is properly secured by a safety belt or other tiedown having enough strength to eliminate the possibility of shifting under all normally anticipated flight and ground conditions.

(ii) It is packaged or covered to avoid possible injury to passengers.

(iii) It does not impose any load on seats or on the floor structure that exceeds the load limitation for those components.

(iv) It is not located in a position that restricts the access to or use of any required emergency or regular exit, or the use of the aisle between the crew and the passenger compartment.

(v) It is not carried directly above seated passengers.

(b) When cargo is carried in cargo compartments that are designed to require the physical entry of a crewmember to extinguish any fire that may occur during flight, the cargo must be loaded so as to allow a crewmember to effectively reach all parts of the compartment with the contents of a hand fire extinguisher.

§91.527 Operating in icing conditions.

(a) No pilot may take off an airplane that has frost, ice, or snow adhering to any propeller, windshield, stabilizing or control surface; to a powerplant installation; or to an airspeed, altimeter, rate of climb, or flight attitude instrument system or wing, except that takeoffs may be made with frost under the wing in the area of the fuel tanks if authorized by the FAA.

(b) No pilot may fly under IFR into known or forecast light or moderate icing conditions, or under VFR into known light or moderate icing conditions, unless—

(1) The aircraft has functioning deicing or anti-icing equipment protecting each rotor blade, propeller, windshield, wing, stabilizing or control surface, and each airspeed, altimeter, rate of climb, or flight attitude instrument system;

(2) The airplane has ice protection provisions that meet section 34 of Special Federal Aviation Regulation No. 23; or

(3) The airplane meets transport category airplane type certification provisions, including the requirements for certification for flight in icing conditions.

(c) Except for an airplane that has ice protection provisions that meet the requirements in section 34 of Special Federal Aviation Regulation No. 23, or those for transport category airplane type certification, no pilot may fly an airplane into known or forecast severe icing conditions.

(d) If current weather reports and briefing information relied upon by the pilot in command indicate that the forecast icing conditions that would otherwise prohibit the flight will not be encountered during the flight because of changed weather conditions since the forecast, the restrictions in paragraphs (b) and (c) of this section based on forecast conditions do not apply.

[Docket No. 18334, 54 FR 34314, Aug. 18, 1989; as amended by Amdt. 91–310, 74 FR 62696, Dec. 1, 2009]

§91.529 Flight engineer requirements.

(a) No person may operate the following airplanes without a flight crewmember holding a current flight engineer certificate:

(1) An airplane for which a type certificate was issued before January 2, 1964, having a maximum certificated takeoff weight of more than 80,000 pounds.

(2) An airplane type certificated after January 1, 1964, for which a flight engineer is required by the type certification requirements.

(b) No person may serve as a required flight engineer on an airplane unless, within the preceding 6 calendar months, that person has had at least 50 hours of flight time as a flight engineer on that type airplane or has been checked by the Administrator on that type airplane and is found to be familiar and competent with all essential current information and operating procedures.

§91.531 Second-in-command requirements.

(a) Except as provided in paragraph (b) of this section, no person may operate the following airplanes without a pilot designated as second-in-command:

(1) Any airplane that is type certificated for more than one required pilot.

(2) Any large airplane.

(3) Any commuter category airplane.

(b) A person may operate the following airplanes without a pilot designated as second-in-command:

(1) Any airplane certificated for operation with one pilot.

(2) A large airplane or turbojet-powered multi-engine airplane that holds a special airworthiness certificate, if:

(i) The airplane was originally designed with only one pilot station; or

(ii) The airplane was originally designed with more than one pilot station, but single pilot operations were permitted by the airplane flight manual or were otherwise permitted by a branch of the United States Armed Forces or the armed forces of a foreign contracting State to the Convention on International Civil Aviation.

(c) No person may designate a pilot to serve as second-in-command, nor may any pilot serve as second-in-command, of an airplane required under this section to have two pilots unless that pilot meets the qualifications for second-in-command prescribed in §61.55 of this chapter.

[Docket FAA–2016–6142, Amdt. 91–351, 83 FR 30282, June 27, 2018]

§91.533 Flight attendant requirements.

(a) No person may operate an airplane unless at least the following number of flight attendants are on board the airplane:

(1) For airplanes having more than 19 but less than 51 passengers on board, one flight attendant.

(2) For airplanes having more than 50 but less than 101 passengers on board, two flight attendants.

(3) For airplanes having more than 100 passengers on board, two flight attendants plus one additional flight attendant for each unit (or part of a unit) of 50 passengers above 100.

(b) No person may serve as a flight attendant on an airplane when required by paragraph (a) of this section unless that person has demonstrated to the pilot in command familiarity with the necessary functions to be performed in an emergency or a situation requiring emergency evacuation and is capable of using the emergency equipment installed on that airplane.

§91.535 Stowage of food, beverage, and passenger service equipment during aircraft movement on the surface, takeoff, and landing.

(a) No operator may move an aircraft on the surface, takeoff or land when any food, beverage, or tableware furnished by the operator is located at any passenger seat.

(b) No operator may move an aircraft on the surface, takeoff, or land unless each food and beverage tray and seat back tray is secured in its stowed position.

(c) No operator may permit an aircraft to move on the surface, takeoff, or land unless each passenger serving cart is secured in its stowed position.

(d) No operator may permit an aircraft to move on the surface, takeoff, or land unless each movie screen that extends into the aisle is stowed.

(e) Each passenger shall comply with instructions given by a crewmember with regard to compliance with this section.

[Docket No. 26142, 57 FR 42672, Sept. 15, 1992]

§91.536–91.599 [Reserved]

Subpart G—
Additional Equipment and Operating Requirements for Large and Transport Category Aircraft

Source: Docket No. 18334, 54 FR 34318, Aug. 18, 1989, unless otherwise noted.

§91.601 Applicability.

This subpart applies to operation of large and transport category U.S.-registered civil aircraft.

§91.603 Aural speed warning device.

No person may operate a transport category airplane in air commerce unless that airplane is equipped with an aural speed warning device that complies with §25.1303(c)(1).

§91.605 Transport category civil airplane weight limitations.

(a) No person may take off any transport category airplane (other than a turbine-engine-powered airplane certificated after September 30, 1958) unless—

(1) The takeoff weight does not exceed the authorized maximum takeoff weight for the elevation of the airport of takeoff;

(2) The elevation of the airport of takeoff is within the altitude range for which maximum takeoff weights have been determined;

(3) Normal consumption of fuel and oil in flight to the airport of intended landing will leave a weight on arrival not in excess of the authorized maximum landing weight for the elevation of that airport; and

91

(4) The elevations of the airport of intended landing and of all specified alternate airports are within the altitude range for which the maximum landing weights have been determined.

(b) No person may operate a turbine-engine-powered transport category airplane certificated after September 30, 1958, contrary to the Airplane Flight Manual, or take off that airplane unless—

(1) The takeoff weight does not exceed the takeoff weight specified in the Airplane Flight Manual for the elevation of the airport and for the ambient temperature existing at the time of takeoff;

(2) Normal consumption of fuel and oil in flight to the airport of intended landing and to the alternate airports will leave a weight on arrival not in excess of the landing weight specified in the Airplane Flight Manual for the elevation of each of the airports involved and for the ambient temperatures expected at the time of landing;

(3) The takeoff weight does not exceed the weight shown in the Airplane Flight Manual to correspond with the minimum distances required for takeoff, considering the elevation of the airport, the runway to be used, the effective runway gradient, the ambient temperature and wind component at the time of takeoff, and, if operating limitations exist for the minimum distances required for takeoff from wet runways, the runway surface condition (dry or wet). Wet runway distances associated with grooved or porous friction course runways, if provided in the Airplane Flight Manual, may be used only for runways that are grooved or treated with a porous friction course (PFC) overlay, and that the operator determines are designed, constructed, and maintained in a manner acceptable to the Administrator.

(4) Where the takeoff distance includes a clearway, the clearway distance is not greater than one-half of—

(i) The takeoff run, in the case of airplanes certificated after September 30, 1958, and before August 30, 1959; or

(ii) The runway length, in the case of airplanes certificated after August 29, 1959.

(c) No person may take off a turbine-engine-powered transport category airplane certificated after August 29, 1959, unless, in addition to the requirements of paragraph (b) of this section—

(1) The accelerate-stop distance is no greater than the length of the runway plus the length of the stopway (if present); and

(2) The takeoff distance is no greater than the length of the runway plus the length of the clearway (if present); and

(3) The takeoff run is no greater than the length of the runway.

[Docket No. 18334, 54 FR 34318, Aug. 18, 1989; as amended by Amdt. 91–256, 63 FR 8321, Feb. 18, 1998]

§91.607 Emergency exits for airplanes carrying passengers for hire.

(a) Notwithstanding any other provision of this chapter, no person may operate a large airplane (type certificated under the Civil Air Regulations effective before April 9, 1957) in passenger-carrying operations for hire, with more than the number of occupants—

(1) Allowed under Civil Air Regulations §4b.362 (a), (b), and (c) as in effect on December 20, 1951; or

(2) Approved under Special Civil Air Regulations SR–387, SR–389, SR–389A, or SR–389B, or under this section as in effect.

However, an airplane type listed in the following table may be operated with up to the listed number of occupants (including crewmembers) and the corresponding number of exits (including emergency exits and doors) approved for the emergency exit of passengers or with an occupant-exit configuration approved under paragraph (b) or (c) of this section.

Airplane type	Maximum number of occupants including all crewmembers	Corresponding number of exits authorized for passenger use
B-307	61	4
B-377	96	9
C-46	67	4
CV-240	53	6
CV-340 and CV-440	53	6
DC-3	35	4
DC-3 (Super)	39	5
DC-4	86	5
DC-6	87	7
DC-6B	112	11
L-18	17	3
L-049, L-649, L-749	87	7
L-1049 series	96	9
M-202	53	6
M-404	53	7
Viscount 700 series	53	7

(b) Occupants in addition to those authorized under paragraph (a) of this section may be carried as follows:

(1) For each additional floor-level exit at least 24 inches wide by 48 inches high, with an unobstructed 20-inch-wide access aisleway between the exit and the main passenger aisle, 12 additional occupants.

(2) For each additional window exit located over a wing that meets the requirements of the airworthiness standards under which the airplane was type certificated or that is large enough to

inscribe an ellipse 19 x 26 inches, eight additional occupants.

(3) For each additional window exit that is not located over a wing but that otherwise complies with paragraph (b)(2) of this section, five additional occupants.

(4) For each airplane having a ratio (as computed from the table in paragraph (a) of this section) of maximum number of occupants to number of exits greater than 14:1, and for each airplane that does not have at least one full-size, door-type exit in the side of the fuselage in the rear part of the cabin, the first additional exit must be a floor-level exit that complies with paragraph (b)(1) of this section and must be located in the rear part of the cabin on the opposite side of the fuselage from the main entrance door. However, no person may operate an airplane under this section carrying more than 115 occupants unless there is such an exit on each side of the fuselage in the rear part of the cabin.

(c) No person may eliminate any approved exit except in accordance with the following:

(1) The previously authorized maximum number of occupants must be reduced by the same number of additional occupants authorized for that exit under this section.

(2) Exits must be eliminated in accordance with the following priority schedule: First, non-over-wing window exits; second, over-wing window exits; third, floor-level exits located in the forward part of the cabin; and fourth, floor-level exits located in the rear of the cabin.

(3) At least one exit must be retained on each side of the fuselage regardless of the number of occupants.

(4) No person may remove any exit that would result in a ratio of maximum number of occupants to approved exits greater than 14:1.

(d) This section does not relieve any person operating under part 121 of this chapter from complying with §121.291.

§91.609 Flight data recorders and cockpit voice recorders.

(a) No holder of an air carrier operating certificate or an operating certificate may conduct any operation under this part with an aircraft listed in the holder's operations specifications or current list of aircraft used in air transportation unless that aircraft complies with any applicable flight recorder and cockpit voice recorder requirements of the part under which its certificate is issued except that the operator may—

(1) Ferry an aircraft with an inoperative flight recorder or cockpit voice recorder from a place where repair or replacement cannot be made to a place where they can be made;

(2) Continue a flight as originally planned, if the flight recorder or cockpit voice recorder becomes inoperative after the aircraft has taken off;

(3) Conduct an airworthiness flight test during which the flight recorder or cockpit voice recorder is turned off to test it or to test any communications or electrical equipment installed in the aircraft; or

(4) Ferry a newly acquired aircraft from the place where possession of it is taken to a place where the flight recorder or cockpit voice recorder is to be installed.

(b) Notwithstanding paragraphs (c) and (e) of this section, an operator other than the holder of an air carrier or a commercial operator certificate may—

(1) Ferry an aircraft with an inoperative flight recorder or cockpit voice recorder from a place where repair or replacement cannot be made to a place where they can be made;

(2) Continue a flight as originally planned if the flight recorder or cockpit voice recorder becomes inoperative after the aircraft has taken off;

(3) Conduct an airworthiness flight test during which the flight recorder or cockpit voice recorder is turned off to test it or to test any communications or electrical equipment installed in the aircraft;

(4) Ferry a newly acquired aircraft from a place where possession of it was taken to a place where the flight recorder or cockpit voice recorder is to be installed; or

(5) Operate an aircraft:

(i) For not more than 15 days while the flight recorder and/or cockpit voice recorder is inoperative and/or removed for repair provided that the aircraft maintenance records contain an entry that indicates the date of failure, and a placard is located in view of the pilot to show that the flight recorder or cockpit voice recorder is inoperative.

(ii) For not more than an additional 15 days, provided that the requirements in paragraph (b)(5)(i) are met and that a certified pilot, or a certified person authorized to return an aircraft to service under §43.7 of this chapter certifies in the aircraft maintenance records that additional time is required to complete repairs or obtain a replacement unit.

(c)(1) No person may operate a U.S. civil registered, multiengine, turbine-powered airplane or rotorcraft having a passenger seating configuration, excluding any pilot seats of 10 or more that has been manufactured after October 11, 1991, unless it is equipped with one or more approved flight recorders that utilize a digital method of recording and storing data and a method of readily retrieving that data from the storage medium, that are capable of recording the data specified in Appendix E to this part, for an airplane, or Appendix F to this part, for a rotorcraft, of this part within the

range, accuracy, and recording interval specified, and that are capable of retaining no less than 8 hours of aircraft operation.

(2) All airplanes subject to paragraph (c)(1) of this section that are manufactured before April 7, 2010, by April 7, 2012, must meet the requirements of §23.1459(a)(7) or §25.1459(a)(8) of this chapter, as applicable.

(3) All airplanes and rotorcraft subject to paragraph (c)(1) of this section that are manufactured on or after April 7, 2010, must meet the flight data recorder requirements of §23.1459, §25.1459, §27.1459, or §29.1459 of this chapter, as applicable, and retain at least the last 25 hours of recorded information using a recorder that meets the standards of TSO-C124a, or later revision.

(d) Whenever a flight recorder, required by this section, is installed, it must be operated continuously from the instant the airplane begins the takeoff roll or the rotorcraft begins lift-off until the airplane has completed the landing roll or the rotorcraft has landed at its destination.

(e) Unless otherwise authorized by the Administrator, after October 11, 1991, no person may operate a U.S. civil registered multiengine, turbine-powered airplane or rotorcraft having a passenger seating configuration of six passengers or more and for which two pilots are required by type certification or operating rule unless it is equipped with an approved cockpit voice recorder that:

(1) Is installed in compliance with §23.1457(a)(1) and (2), (b), (c), (d)(1)(i), (2) and (3), (e), (f), and (g); §25.1457(a)(1) and (2), (b), (c), (d)(1)(i), (2) and (3), (e), (f), and (g); §27.1457(a)(1) and (2), (b), (c), (d)(1)(i), (2) and (3), (e), (f), and (g); or §29.1457(a)(1) and (2), (b), (c), (d)(1)(i), (2) and (3), (e), (f), and (g) of this chapter, as applicable; and

(2) Is operated continuously from the use of the checklist before the flight to completion of the final checklist at the end of the flight.

(f) In complying with this section, an approved cockpit voice recorder having an erasure feature may be used, so that at any time during the operation of the recorder, information recorded more than 15 minutes earlier may be erased or otherwise obliterated.

(g) In the event of an accident or occurrence requiring immediate notification to the National Transportation Safety Board under 49 CFR part 830 of its regulations that results in the termination of the flight, any operator who has installed approved flight recorders and approved cockpit voice recorders shall keep the recorded information for at least 60 days or, if requested by the Administrator or the Board, for a longer period. Information obtained from the record is used to assist in determining the cause of accidents or occurrences in connection with the investigation under 49 CFR part 830. The Administrator does

not use the cockpit voice recorder record in any civil penalty or certificate action.

(h) All airplanes required by this section to have a cockpit voice recorder and a flight data recorder, that are manufactured before April 7, 2010, must by April 7, 2012, have a cockpit voice recorder that also—

(1) Meets the requirements of §23.1457(d)(6) or §25.1457(d)(6) of this chapter, as applicable; and

(2) If transport category, meets the requirements of §25.1457(a)(3), (a)(4), and (a)(5) of this chapter.

(i) All airplanes or rotorcraft required by this section to have a cockpit voice recorder and flight data recorder, that are manufactured on or after April 7, 2010, must have a cockpit voice recorder installed that also—

(1) Is installed in accordance with the requirements of §23.1457 (except for paragraphs (a)(6) and (d)(5)); §25.1457 (except for paragraphs (a)(6) and (d)(5)); §27.1457 (except for paragraphs (a)(6) and (d)(5)); or §29.1457 (except for paragraphs (a) (6) and (d)(5)) of this chapter, as applicable; and

(2) Retains at least the last 2 hours of recorded information using a recorder that meets the standards of TSO-C123a, or later revision.

(3) For all airplanes or rotorcraft manufactured on or after April 6, 2012, also meets the requirements of §23.1457(a)(6) and (d)(5); §25.1457 (a)(6) and (d)(5); §27.1457(a)(6) and (d)(5); or §29.1457(a) (6) and (d)(5) of this chapter, as applicable.

(j) All airplanes or rotorcraft required by this section to have a cockpit voice recorder and a flight data recorder, that install datalink communication equipment on or after April 6, 2012, must record all datalink messages as required by the certification rule applicable to the aircraft.

(k) An aircraft operated under this part under deviation authority from part 125 of this chapter must comply with all of the applicable flight data recorder requirements of part 125 applicable to the aircraft, notwithstanding such deviation authority.

[Docket No. 18334, 54 FR 34318, Aug. 18, 1989; as amended by Amdt. 91–226, 56 FR 51621, Oct. 11, 1991; Amdt. 91–228, 57 FR 19353, May 5, 1992; Amdt. 91–300, 73 FR 12564, March 7, 2008; Amdt. 91–304, 73 FR 73178, Dec. 2, 2008; Amdt. 91–300, 74 FR 32800, July 9, 2009; Amdt. 91–313, 75 FR 17045, April 5, 2010; Docket No. FAA–2022–1355, Amdt. 91–366, 87 FR 75846, Dec. 9, 2022]

§91.611 Authorization for ferry flight with one engine inoperative.

(a) *General.* The holder of an air carrier operating certificate or an operating certificate issued under part 125 may conduct a ferry flight of a four-engine airplane or a turbine-engine-powered airplane equipped with three engines, with one

engine inoperative, to a base for the purpose of repairing that engine subject to the following:

(1) The airplane model has been test flown and found satisfactory for safe flight in accordance with paragraph (b) or (c) of this section, as appropriate. However, each operator who before November 19, 1966, has shown that a model of airplane with an engine inoperative is satisfactory for safe flight by a test flight conducted in accordance with performance data contained in the applicable Airplane Flight Manual under paragraph (a)(2) of this section need not repeat the test flight for that model.

(2) The approved Airplane Flight Manual contains the following performance data and the flight is conducted in accordance with that data:

(i) Maximum weight.

(ii) Center of gravity limits.

(iii) Configuration of the inoperative propeller (if applicable).

(iv) Runway length for takeoff (including temperature accountability).

(v) Altitude range.

(vi) Certificate limitations.

(vii) Ranges of operational limits.

(viii) Performance information.

(ix) Operating procedures.

(3) The operator has FAA approved procedures for the safe operation of the airplane, including specific requirements for—

(i) Limiting the operating weight on any ferry flight to the minimum necessary for the flight plus the necessary reserve fuel load;

(ii) A limitation that takeoffs must be made from dry runways unless, based on a showing of actual operating takeoff techniques on wet runways with one engine inoperative, takeoffs with full controllability from wet runways have been approved for the specific model aircraft and included in the Airplane Flight Manual;

(iii) Operations from airports where the runways may require a takeoff or approach over populated areas; and

(iv) Inspection procedures for determining the operating condition of the operative engines.

(4) No person may take off an airplane under this section if—

(i) The initial climb is over thickly populated areas; or

(ii) Weather conditions at the takeoff or destination airport are less than those required for VFR flight.

(5) Persons other than required flight crewmembers shall not be carried during the flight.

(6) No person may use a flight crewmember for flight under this section unless that crewmember is thoroughly familiar with the operating procedures for one-engine inoperative ferry flight contained in the certificate holder's manual and the

limitations and performance information in the Airplane Flight Manual.

(b) *Flight tests: reciprocating-engine-powered airplanes.* The airplane performance of a reciprocating-engine-powered airplane with one engine inoperative must be determined by flight test as follows:

(1) A speed not less than 1.3 V_{S1} must be chosen at which the airplane may be controlled satisfactorily in a climb with the critical engine inoperative (with its propeller removed or in a configuration desired by the operator and with all other engines operating at the maximum power determined in paragraph (b)(3) of this section.

(2) The distance required to accelerate to the speed listed in paragraph (b)(1) of this section and to climb to 50 feet must be determined with—

(i) The landing gear extended;

(ii) The critical engine inoperative and its propeller removed or in a configuration desired by the operator; and

(iii) The other engines operating at not more than maximum power established under paragraph (b)(3) of this section.

(3) The takeoff, flight and landing procedures, such as the approximate trim settings, method of power application, maximum power, and speed must be established.

(4) The performance must be determined at a maximum weight not greater than the weight that allows a rate of climb of at least 400 feet per minute in the en route configuration set forth in §25.67(d) of this chapter in effect on January 31, 1977, at an altitude of 5,000 feet.

(5) The performance must be determined using temperature accountability for the takeoff field length, computed in accordance with §25.61 of this chapter in effect on January 31, 1977.

(c) *Flight tests: Turbine-engine-powered airplanes.* The airplane performance of a turbine-engine-powered airplane with one engine inoperative must be determined by flight tests, including at least three takeoff tests, in accordance with the following:

(1) Takeoff speeds V_R and V_2, not less than the corresponding speeds under which the airplane was type certificated under §25.107 of this chapter, must be chosen at which the airplane may be controlled satisfactorily with the critical engine inoperative (with its propeller removed or in a configuration desired by the operator, if applicable) and with all other engines operating at not more than the power selected for type certification as set forth in §25.101 of this chapter.

(2) The minimum takeoff field length must be the horizontal distance required to accelerate and climb to the 35-foot height at V_2 speed (including any additional speed increment obtained in the tests) multiplied by 115 percent and determined with—

91

(i) The landing gear extended;

(ii) The critical engine inoperative and its propeller removed or in a configuration desired by the operator (if applicable); and

(iii) The other engine operating at not more than the power selected for type certification as set forth in §25.101 of this chapter.

(3) The takeoff, flight, and landing procedures such as the approximate trim setting, method of power application, maximum power, and speed must be established. The airplane must be satisfactorily controllable during the entire takeoff run when operated according to these procedures.

(4) The performance must be determined at a maximum weight not greater than the weight determined under §25.121(c) of this chapter but with—

(i) The actual steady gradient of the final takeoff climb requirement not less than 1.2 percent at the end of the takeoff path with two critical engines inoperative; and

(ii) The climb speed not less than the two-engine inoperative trim speed for the actual steady gradient of the final takeoff climb prescribed by paragraph (c)(4)(i) of this section.

(5) The airplane must be satisfactorily controllable in a climb with two critical engines inoperative. Climb performance may be shown by calculations based on, and equal in accuracy to, the results of testing.

(6) The performance must be determined using temperature accountability for takeoff distance and final takeoff climb computed in accordance with §25.101 of this chapter.

For the purpose of paragraphs (c)(4) and (5) of this section, *two critical engines* means two adjacent engines on one side of an airplane with four engines, and the center engine and one outboard engine on an airplane with three engines.

§91.613 Materials for compartment interiors.

(a) No person may operate an airplane that conforms to an amended or supplemental type certificate issued in accordance with SFAR No. 41 for a maximum certificated takeoff weight in excess of 12,500 pounds unless within 1 year after issuance of the initial airworthiness certificate under that SFAR the airplane meets the compartment interior requirements set forth in §25.853 (a), (b), (b-1), (b-2), and (b-3) of this chapter in effect on September 26, 1978.

(b) *Thermal/acoustic insulation materials.* For transport category airplanes type certificated after January 1, 1958:

(1) For airplanes manufactured before September 2, 2005, when thermal/acoustic insulation is installed in the fuselage as replacements after September 2, 2005, the insulation must meet the flame propagation requirements of §25.856 of this chapter, effective September 2, 2003, if it is:

(i) Of a blanket construction or

(ii) Installed around air ducting.

(2) For airplanes manufactured after September 2, 2005, thermal/acoustic insulation materials installed in the fuselage must meet the flame propagation requirements of §25.856 of this chapter, effective September 2, 2003.

[Docket No. 18334, 54 FR 34318, Aug. 18, 1989, as amended by Amdt. 91–279, 68 FR 45083, July 31, 2003; Amdt. 91–290, 70 FR 77752, Dec. 30, 2005]

§91.615–91.699 [Reserved]

Subpart H—Foreign Aircraft Operations and Operations of U.S.-Registered Civil Aircraft Outside of the United States; and Rules Governing Persons on Board Such Aircraft

Source: Docket No. 18334, 54 FR 34320, Aug. 18, 1989, unless otherwise noted.

§91.701 Applicability.

(a) This subpart applies to the operations of civil aircraft of U.S. registry outside of the United States and the operations of foreign civil aircraft within the United States.

(b) Section 91.702 of this subpart also applies to each person on board an aircraft operated as follows:

(1) A U.S. registered civil aircraft operated outside the United States;

(2) Any aircraft operated outside the United States—

(i) That has its next scheduled destination or last place of departure in the United States if the aircraft next lands in the United States; or

(ii) If the aircraft lands in the United States with the individual still on the aircraft regardless of whether it was a scheduled or otherwise planned landing site.

[Docket No. FAA–1998–4954, 64 FR 1079, Jan. 7, 1999]

§91.702 Persons on board.

Section 91.11 of this part (Prohibitions on interference with crewmembers) applies to each person on board an aircraft.

[Docket No. FAA–1998–4954, 64 FR 1079, Jan. 7, 1999]

§91.703 Operations of civil aircraft of U.S. registry outside of the United States.

(a) Each person operating a civil aircraft of U.S. registry outside of the United States shall—

(1) When over the high seas, comply with Annex 2 (Rules of the Air) to the Convention on International Civil Aviation and with §§91.117(c), 91.127, 91.129, and 91.131;

(2) When within a foreign country, comply with the regulations relating to the flight and maneuver of aircraft there in force;

(3) Except for §§91.117(a), 91.307(b), 91.309, 91.323, and 91.711, comply with this part so far as it is not inconsistent with applicable regulations of the foreign country where the aircraft is operated or Annex 2 of the Convention on International Civil Aviation; and

(4) When operating within airspace designated as Reduced Vertical Separation Minimum (RVSM) airspace, comply with §91.706.

(5) For aircraft subject to ICAO Annex 16, carry on board the aircraft documents that summarize the noise operating characteristics and certifications of the aircraft that demonstrate compliance with this part and part 36 of this chapter.

(b) Annex 2 to the Convention on International Civil Aviation, Rules of the Air, Tenth Edition—July 2005, with Amendments through Amendment 45, applicable November 10, 2016, is incorporated by reference into this section with the approval of the Director of the Federal Register under 5 U.S.C. 552(a) and 1 CFR part 51. To enforce any edition other than that specified in this section, the FAA must publish a document in the Federal Register and the material must be available to the public. All approved material is available for inspection at U.S. Department of Transportation, Docket Operations, West Building Ground Floor, Room W12-140, 1200 New Jersey Avenue SE., Washington, DC 20590 and is available from the International Civil Aviation Organization (ICAO), Marketing and Customer Relations Unit, 999 Robert Bourassa Boulevard, Montreal, Quebec H3C 5H7, Canada; *http://store1.icao.int/*; or by contacting the ICAO Marketing and Customer Relations Unit by telephone at (514) 954-8022 or by email at *sales@ icao.int*. For questions about ICAO Annex 2, contact the FAA's Office of International Affairs at (202) 267-1000. It is also available for inspection at the National Archives and Records Administration (NARA). For information on the availability of this material at NARA, call (202) 741-6030, or go to *http://www.archives.gov/federal_register/code_ of_federal_regulations/ibr_locations.html.*

[Docket No. 18834, 54 FR 34320, Aug. 18, 1989, as amended by Amdt. 91–227, 56 FR 65661, Dec. 17, 1991; Amdt. 91–254, 62 FR 17487, April 9, 1997; 69 FR 18803, April 9, 2004; Amdt. 91–299, 73 FR 10143, Feb. 26, 2008; Amdt. 91–312, 75 FR 9333, March 2, 2010; Docket FAA–2016–9154, Amdt. 91–348, 82 FR 39664, Aug. 22, 2017]]

§91.705 [Reserved]

§91.706 Operations within airspace designated as Reduced Vertical Separation Minimum Airspace.

(a) Except as provided in paragraph (b) of this section, no person may operate a civil aircraft of U.S. registry in airspace designated as Reduced Vertical Separation Minimum (RVSM) airspace unless:

(1) The operator and the operator's aircraft comply with the requirements of Appendix G of this part; and

(2) The operator is authorized by the Administrator to conduct such operations.

(b) The Administrator may authorize a deviation from the requirements of this section in accordance with Section 5 of Appendix G to this part.

[Docket No. 28870, 62 FR 17487, April 9, 1997]

§91.707 Flights between Mexico or Canada and the United States.

Unless otherwise authorized by ATC, no person may operate a civil aircraft between Mexico or Canada and the United States without filing an IFR or VFR flight plan, as appropriate.

§91.709 Operations to Cuba.

No person may operate a civil aircraft from the United States to Cuba unless—

(a) Departure is from an international airport of entry designated in §6.13 of the Air Commerce Regulations of the Bureau of Customs (19 CFR 6.13); and

(b) In the case of departure from any of the 48 contiguous States or the District of Columbia, the pilot in command of the aircraft has filed—

(1) A DVFR or IFR flight plan as prescribed in §99.11 or §99.13 of this chapter; and

(2) A written statement, within 1 hour before departure, with the Office of Immigration and Naturalization Service at the airport of departure, containing—

(i) All information in the flight plan;

(ii) The name of each occupant of the aircraft;

(iii) The number of occupants of the aircraft; and

(iv) A description of the cargo, if any.

This section does not apply to the operation of aircraft by a scheduled air carrier over routes authorized in operations specifications issued by the Administrator.

(Approved by the Office of Management and Budget under control number 2120–0005)

§91.711 Special rules for foreign civil aircraft.

(a) *General.* In addition to the other applicable regulations of this part, each person operating a foreign civil aircraft within the United States shall comply with this section.

(b) *VFR.* No person may conduct VFR operations which require two-way radio communications under this part unless at least one crewmember of that aircraft is able to conduct two-way radio communications in the English language and is on duty during that operation.

(c) *IFR.* No person may operate a foreign civil aircraft under IFR unless—

(1) That aircraft is equipped with—

(i) Radio equipment allowing two-way radio communication with ATC when it is operated in controlled airspace; and

(ii) Navigation equipment suitable for the route to be flown.

(2) Each person piloting the aircraft—

(i) Holds a current United States instrument rating or is authorized by his foreign airman certificate to pilot under IFR; and

(ii) Is thoroughly familiar with the United States en route, holding, and letdown procedures; and

(3) At least one crewmember of that aircraft is able to conduct two-way radiotelephone communications in the English language and that crewmember is on duty while the aircraft is approaching, operating within, or leaving the United States.

(d) *Over water.* Each person operating a foreign civil aircraft over water off the shores of the United States shall give flight notification or file a flight plan in accordance with the Supplementary Procedures for the ICAO region concerned.

(e) *Flight at and above FL 240.* If VOR navigation equipment is required under paragraph (c)(1) (ii) of this section, no person may operate a foreign civil aircraft within the 50 States and the District of Columbia at or above FL 240, unless the aircraft is equipped with approved DME or a suitable RNAV system. When the DME or RNAV system required by this paragraph fails at and above FL 240, the pilot in command of the aircraft must notify ATC immediately and may then continue operations at and above FL 240 to the next airport of intended landing where repairs or replacement of the equipment can be made. A foreign civil aircraft may be operated within the 50 States and the District of Columbia at or above FL 240 without DME or an RNAV system when operated for the following purposes, and ATC is notified before each takeoff:

(1) Ferry flights to and from a place in the United States where repairs or alterations are to be made.

(2) Ferry flights to a new country of registry.

(3) Flight of a new aircraft of U.S. manufacture for the purpose of—

(i) Flight testing the aircraft;

(ii) Training foreign flight crews in the operation of the aircraft; or

(iii) Ferrying the aircraft for export delivery outside the United States.

(4) Ferry, demonstration, and test flight of an aircraft brought to the United States for the purpose of demonstration or testing the whole or any part thereof.

[Docket No. 18834, 54 FR 34320, Aug. 18, 1989; as amended by Amdt. 91–227, 56 FR 65661, Dec. 17, 1991; Amdt. 91–296, 72 FR 31679, June 7, 2007]

§91.713 Operation of civil aircraft of Cuban registry.

No person may operate a civil aircraft of Cuban registry except in controlled airspace and in accordance with air traffic clearance or air traffic control instructions that may require use of specific airways or routes and landings at specific airports.

§91.715 Special flight authorizations for foreign civil aircraft.

(a) Foreign civil aircraft may be operated without airworthiness certificates required under §91.203 if a special flight authorization for that operation is issued under this section. Application for a special flight authorization must be made to the appropriate Flight Standards Division Manager, or Aircraft Certification Service Division Director. However, in the case of an aircraft to be operated in the U.S. for the purpose of demonstration at an airshow, the application may be made to the appropriate Flight Standards Division Manager or Aircraft Certification Service Division Director responsible for the airshow location.

(b) The Administrator may issue a special flight authorization for a foreign civil aircraft subject to any conditions and limitations that the Administrator considers necessary for safe operation in the U.S. airspace.

(c) No person may operate a foreign civil aircraft under a special flight authorization unless that operation also complies with part 375 of the Special Regulations of the Department of Transportation (14 CFR part 375).

(Approved by the Office of Management and Budget under control number 2120–0005)

[Docket No. 18334, 54 FR 34320, Aug. 18, 1989; as amended by Amdt. 91–212, 54 FR 39293, Sept. 25, 1989; Amdt. 91–350, 83 FR 9171, March 5, 2018]

§91.717–91.799 [Reserved]

Subpart I—
Operating Noise Limits

Source: Docket No. 18334, 54 FR 34321, Aug. 18, 1989, unless otherwise noted.

§91.801 Applicability: Relation to Part 36.

(a) This subpart prescribes operating noise limits and related requirements that apply, as follows, to the operation of civil aircraft in the United States.

(1) Sections 91.803, 91.805, 91.807, 91.809, and 91.811 apply to civil subsonic jet (turbojet) airplanes with maximum weights of more than 75,000 pounds and—

(i) If U.S. registered, that have standard airworthiness certificates; or

(ii) If foreign registered, that would be required by this chapter to have a U.S. standard airworthiness certificate in order to conduct the operations intended for the airplane were it registered in the United States. Those sections apply to operations to or from airports in the United States under this part and parts 121, 125, 129, and 135 of this chapter.

(2) Section 91.813 applies to U.S. operators of civil subsonic jet (turbojet) airplanes covered by this subpart. This section applies to operators operating to or from airports in the United States under this part and parts 121, 125, and 135, but not to those operating under part 129 of this chapter.

(3) Sections 91.803, 91.819, and 91.821 apply to U.S.-registered civil supersonic airplanes having standard airworthiness certificates and to foreign-registered civil supersonic airplanes that, if registered in the United States, would be required by this chapter to have U.S. standard airworthiness certificates in order to conduct the operations intended for the airplane. Those sections apply to operations under this part and under parts 121, 125, 129, and 135 of this chapter.

(b) Unless otherwise specified, as used in this subpart "part 36" refers to 14 CFR part 36, including the noise levels under Appendix C of that part, notwithstanding the provisions of that part excepting certain airplanes from the specified noise requirements. For purposes of this subpart, the various stages of noise levels, the terms used to describe airplanes with respect to those levels, and the terms "subsonic airplane" and "supersonic airplane" have the meanings specified under part 36 of this chapter. For purposes of this subpart, for subsonic airplanes operated in foreign air commerce in the United States, the Administrator may accept compliance with the noise requirements under annex 16 of the International Civil Aviation Organization when those requirements have been shown to be substantially compatible with, and achieve results equivalent to

those achievable under, part 36 for that airplane. Determinations made under these provisions are subject to the limitations of §36.5 of this chapter as if those noise levels were part 36 noise levels.

(c) Sections 91.851 through 91.877 of this subpart prescribe operating noise limits and related requirements that apply to any civil subsonic turbojet airplane (for which an airworthiness certificate other than an experimental certificate has been issued by the Administrator) with a maximum certificated takeoff weight of more than 75,000 pounds operating to or from an airport in the 48 contiguous United States and the District of Columbia under this part, parts 121, 125, 129, or 135 of this chapter on and after September 25, 1991.

(d) Section 91.877 prescribes reporting requirements that apply to any civil subsonic jet (turbojet) airplane with a maximum weight of more than 75,000 pounds operated by an air carrier or foreign air carrier between the contiguous United States and the State of Hawaii, between the State of Hawaii and any point outside of the 48 contiguous United States, or between the islands of Hawaii in turnaround service, under part 121 or 129 of this chapter on or after November 5, 1990.

(e) Sections 91.881 through 91.883 of this subpart prescribe operating noise limits and related requirements that apply to any civil subsonic jet airplane with a maximum takeoff weight of 75,000 pounds or less and for which an airworthiness certificate (other than an experimental certificate) has been issued, operating to or from an airport in the contiguous United States under this part, part 121, 125, 129, or 135 of this chapter on and after December 31, 2015.

[Docket No. 18334, 54 FR 34321, Aug. 18, 1989; Amdt. 91–211, 54 FR 41211, Oct. 5, 1989, as amended by Amdt. 91–225, 56 FR 48658, Sept. 25, 1991; Amdt. 91–252, 61 FR 66185, Dec. 16, 1996; Amdt. 91–275, 67 FR 45237, July 8, 2002; Amdt. 91–276, 67 FR 46571, July 15, 2002; Amdt. 91–328, 78 FR 39583, July 2, 2013]

§91.803 Part 125 operators: Designation of applicable regulations.

For airplanes covered by this subpart and operated under part 125 of this chapter, the following regulations apply as specified:

(a) For each airplane operation to which requirements prescribed under this subpart applied before November 29, 1980, those requirements of this subpart continue to apply.

(b) For each subsonic airplane operation to which requirements prescribed under this subpart did not apply before November 29, 1980, because the airplane was not operated in the United States under this part or part 121, 129, or 135 of this chapter, the requirements prescribed under §91.805 of this subpart apply.

(c) For each supersonic airplane operation to which requirements prescribed under this subpart did not apply before November 29, 1980, because the airplane was not operated in the United States under this part or part 121, 129, or 135 of this chapter, the requirements of §§91.819 and 91.821 of this subpart apply.

(d) For each airplane required to operate under part 125 for which a deviation under that part is approved to operate, in whole or in part, under this part or part 121, 129, or 135 of this chapter, notwithstanding the approval, the requirements prescribed under paragraphs (a), (b), and (c) of this section continue to apply.

[Docket No. 18334, 54 FR 34321, Aug. 18, 1989; as amended by Amdt. 91–276, 67 FR 46571, July 15, 2002]

§91.805 Final compliance: Subsonic airplanes.

Except as provided in §§91.809 and 91.811, on and after January 1, 1985, no person may operate to or from an airport in the United States any subsonic airplane covered by this subpart unless that airplane has been shown to comply with Stage 2 or Stage 3 noise levels under part 36 of this chapter.

§91.807–91.813 [Reserved]

§91.815 Agricultural and fire fighting airplanes: Noise operating limitations.

(a) This section applies to propeller-driven, small airplanes having standard airworthiness certificates that are designed for "agricultural aircraft operations" (as defined in §137.3 of this chapter, as effective on January 1, 1966) or for dispensing fire fighting materials.

(b) If the Airplane Flight Manual, or other approved manual material information, markings, or placards for the airplane indicate that the airplane has not been shown to comply with the noise limits under part 36 of this chapter, no person may operate that airplane, except—

(1) To the extent necessary to accomplish the work activity directly associated with the purpose for which it is designed;

(2) To provide flight crewmember training in the special purpose operation for which the airplane is designed; and

(3) To conduct "nondispensing aerial work operations" in accordance with the requirements under §137.29(c) of this chapter.

§91.817 Civil aircraft sonic boom.

(a) No person may operate a civil aircraft in the United States at a true flight Mach number greater than 1 except in compliance with conditions and limitations in an authorization to exceed

Mach 1 issued to the operator in accordance with §91.818.

(b) In addition, no person may operate a civil aircraft for which the maximum operating limit speed M_{MO} exceeds a Mach number of 1, to or from an airport in the United States, unless—

(1) Information available to the flight crew includes flight limitations that ensure that flights entering or leaving the United States will not cause a sonic boom to reach the surface within the United States; and

(2) The operator complies with the flight limitations prescribed in paragraph (b)(1) of this section or complies with conditions and limitations in an authorization to exceed Mach 1 issued in accordance with §91.818.

(Approved by the Office of Management and Budget under control number 2120–0005)

[Docket No. 2019–0451, Amdt. 91–362, 86 FR 3792, Jan. 15, 2021]

§91.818 Special flight authorization to exceed Mach 1.

For all civil aircraft, any operation that exceeds Mach 1 may be conducted only in accordance with a special flight authorization issued to an operator in accordance with the requirements of this section.

(a) *Application.* Application for a special flight authorization to exceed Mach 1 must be made to the FAA Office of Environment and Energy for consideration by the Administrator. Each application must include:

(1) The name of the operator;

(2) The number and model(s) of the aircraft to be operated;

(3) The number of proposed flights;

(4) The date range during which the flight(s) would be conducted;

(5) The time of day the flight(s) would be conducted. Proposed night operations may require further justification for their necessity;

(6) A description of the flight area requested by the applicant, including any environmental information required to be submitted pursuant to paragraph (c) of this section;

(7) All conditions and limitations on the flight(s) that will ensure that no measurable sonic boom overpressure will reach the surface outside of the proposed flight area; and

(8) The reason(s) that operation at a speed greater than Mach 1 is necessary. A special flight authorization to exceed Mach 1 may be granted only for operations that are intended to:

(i) Show compliance with airworthiness requirements;

(ii) Determine the sonic boom characteristics of an aircraft;

(iii) Establish a means of reducing or eliminating the effects of sonic boom, including flight profiles and special features of an aircraft;

(iv) Demonstrate the conditions and limitations under which speeds in excess of Mach 1 will not cause a measurable sonic boom overpressure to reach the surface; or

(v) Measure the noise characteristics of an aircraft to demonstrate compliance with noise requirements imposed under this chapter, or to determine the limits for operation in accordance with §91.817(b).

(9) For any purpose listed in paragraph (a)(8) of this section, each applicant must indicate why its intended operation cannot be safely or properly accomplished over the ocean at a distance ensuring that no sonic boom overpressure reaches any land surface in the United States.

(b) *Operation outside a test area.* An applicant may apply for an authorization to conduct flights outside a test area under certain conditions and limitations upon a conservative showing that:

(1) Flight(s) within a test area have been conducted in accordance with an authorization issued for the purpose specified in paragraph (a)(8)(iv) of this section;

(2) The results of the flight test(s) required by paragraph (b)(1) of this section demonstrate that a speed in excess of Mach 1 does not cause a measurable sonic boom overpressure to reach the surface; and

(3) The conditions and limitations determined by the test(s) represent all foreseeable operating conditions and are effective on all flights conducted under an authorization.

(c) *Environmental findings.* (1) No special flight authorization will be granted if the Administrator finds that such action is necessary to protect or enhance the environment.

(2) The Administrator is required to consider the potential environmental impacts resulting from the issuance of an authorization for a particular flight area pursuant to the National Environmental Policy Act of 1969 (NEPA) (42 U.S.C 4321 et seq.), all applicable regulations implementing NEPA, and related Executive orders and guidance. Accordingly, each applicant must provide information that sufficiently describes the potential environmental impact of any flight in excess of Mach 1, including the effect of a sonic boom reaching the surface in the proposed flight area, to enable the FAA to determine whether such impacts are significant within the meaning of NEPA.

(d) *Issuance.* An authorization to operate a civil aircraft in excess of Mach 1 may be issued only after an applicant has submitted the information described in this section and the Administrator has taken the required action regarding the environmental findings described in paragraph (c) of this section.

(e) *Duration.* (1) An authorization to exceed Mach 1 will be granted for the time the Administrator determines necessary to conduct the flights for the described purposes.

(2) An authorization to exceed Mach 1 is effective until it expires or is surrendered.

(3) An authorization to exceed Mach 1 may be terminated, suspended, or amended by the Administrator at any time the Administrator finds that such action is necessary to protect the environment.

(4) The holder of an authorization to exceed Mach 1 may request reconsideration of a termination, amendment, or suspension issued under paragraph (e)(3) of this section within 30 days of notice of the action. Failure to request reconsideration and provide information why the Administrator's action is not appropriate will result in permanent termination of the authorization.

(5) Findings made by and actions taken by the Administrator under this section do not affect any certificate issued under chapter 447 of Title 49 of the United States Code.

[No. 18334, 54 FR 34321, Aug. 18, 1989, as amended by Amdt. No. 91–362, 86 FR 3792, Jan. 15, 2021]

§91.819 Civil supersonic airplanes that do not comply with part 36.

(a) *Applicability.* This section applies to civil supersonic airplanes that have not been shown to comply with the Stage 2 noise limits of part 36 in effect on October 13, 1977, using applicable trade-off provisions, and that are operated in the United States, after July 31, 1978.

(b) *Airport use.* Except in an emergency, the following apply to each person who operates a civil supersonic airplane to or from an airport in the United States:

(1) Regardless of whether a type design change approval is applied for under part 21 of this chapter, no person may land or take off an airplane covered by this section for which the type design is changed, after July 31, 1978, in a manner constituting an "acoustical change" under §21.93 unless the acoustical change requirements of part 36 are complied with.

(2) No flight may be scheduled, or otherwise planned, for takeoff or landing after 10 p.m. and before 7 a.m. local time.

§91.821 Civil supersonic airplanes: Noise limits.

Except for Concorde airplanes having flight time before January 1, 1980, no person may operate in the United States, a civil supersonic airplane that does not comply with Stage 2 noise limits of part 36 in effect on October 13, 1977, using applicable trade-off provisions.

§91.823–91.849 [Reserved]

§91.851 Definitions.

For the purposes of §§91.851 through 91.877 of this subpart:

Chapter 4 noise level means a noise level at or below the maximum noise level prescribed in Chapter 4, Paragraph 4.4, Maximum Noise Levels, of the International Civil Aviation Organization (ICAO) Annex 16, Volume I, Amendment 7, effective March 21, 2002. The Director of the Federal Register in accordance with 5 U.S.C. 552(a) and 1 CFR part 51 approved the incorporation by reference of this document, which can be obtained from the International Civil Aviation Organization (ICAO), Document Sales Unit, 999 University Street, Montreal, Quebec H3C 5H7, Canada. Also, you may obtain documents on the Internet at *http://www.ICAO.int/eshop/index .cfm*. Copies may be reviewed at the U.S. Department of Transportation, Docket Operations, West Building Ground Floor, Room W12-140, 1200 New Jersey Avenue SE, Washington, DC 20590 or at the National Archives and Records Administration (NARA). For information on the availability of this material at NARA, call 202-741-6030, or go to: *http://www.archives.gov/federal_register /code_of_federal_regulations/ibr_locations.html*.

Contiguous United States means the area encompassed by the 48 contiguous United States and the District of Columbia.

Fleet means those civil subsonic jet (turbojet) airplanes with a maximum certificated weight of more than 75,000 pounds that are listed on an operator's operations specifications as eligible for operation in the contiguous United States.

Import means a change in ownership of an airplane from a non-U.S. person to a U.S. person when the airplane is brought into the United States for operation.

Operations specifications means an enumeration of airplanes by type, model, series, and serial number operated by the operator or foreign air carrier on a given day, regardless of how or whether such airplanes are formally listed or designated by the operator.

Owner means any person that has indicia of ownership sufficient to register the airplane in the United States pursuant to part 47 of this chapter.

New entrant means an air carrier or foreign air carrier that, on or before November 5, 1990, did not conduct operations under part 121 or 129 of this chapter using an airplane covered by this subpart to or from any airport in the contiguous United States, but that initiates such operation after that date.

Stage 2 noise levels mean the requirements for Stage 2 noise levels as defined in part 36 of this chapter in effect on November 5, 1990.

Stage 3 noise levels mean the requirements for Stage 3 noise levels as defined in part 36 of this chapter in effect on November 5, 1990.

Stage 4 noise level means a noise level at or below the Stage 4 noise limit prescribed in part 36 of this chapter.

Stage 2 airplane means a civil subsonic jet (turbojet) airplane with a maximum certificated weight of 75,000 pounds or more that complies with Stage 2 noise levels as defined in part 36 of this chapter.

Stage 3 airplane means a civil subsonic jet (turbojet) airplane with a maximum certificated weight of 75,000 pounds or more that complies with Stage 3 noise levels as defined in part 36 of this chapter.

Stage 4 airplane means an airplane that has been shown not to exceed the Stage 4 noise limit prescribed in part 36 of this chapter. A Stage 4 airplane complies with all of the noise operating rules of this part.

Stage 5 airplane means an airplane that has been shown not to exceed the Stage 5 noise limit prescribed in part 36 of this chapter. A Stage 5 airplane complies with all of the noise operating rules of this part.

Stage 5 noise level means a noise level at or below the Stage 5 noise limit prescribed in part 36 of this chapter.

[No. 26433, 56 FR 48658, Sept. 25, 1991, as amended by Amdt. 91–252, 61 FR 66185, Dec. 16, 1996; Amdt. 91–275, 67 FR 45237, July 8, 2002; Amdt. 91–288, 70 FR 38749, July 5, 2005; 72 FR 68475, Dec. 5, 2007; Docket FAA–2015–3782, Amdt. 91–349, 82 FR 46132, Oct. 4, 2017]

§91.853 Final compliance: Civil subsonic airplanes.

Except as provided in §91.873, after December 31, 1999, no person shall operate to or from any airport in the contiguous United States any airplane subject to §91.801(c), unless that airplane has been shown to comply with Stage 3, Stage 4, or Stage 5 noise levels.

[Docket FAA–2015–3782, Amdt. 91–349, 82 FR 46132, Oct. 4, 2017]

§91.855 Entry and nonaddition rule.

No person may operate any airplane subject to §91.801(c) of this subpart to or from an airport in the contiguous United States unless one or more of the following apply:

(a) The airplane complies with Stage 3, Stage 4, or Stage 5 noise levels.

(b) The airplane complies with Stage 2 noise levels and was owned by a U.S. person on and since November 5, 1990. Stage 2 airplanes that meet these criteria and are leased to foreign

airlines are also subject to the return provisions of paragraph (e) of this section.

(c) The airplane complies with Stage 2 noise levels, is owned by a non-U.S. person, and is the subject of a binding lease to a U.S. person effective before and on September 25, 1991. Any such airplane may be operated for the term of the lease in effect on that date, and any extensions thereof provided for in that lease.

(d) The airplane complies with Stage 2 noise levels and is operated by a foreign air carrier.

(e) The airplane complies with Stage 2 noise levels and is operated by a foreign operator other than for the purpose of foreign air commerce.

(f) The airplane complies with Stage 2 noise levels and—

(1) On November 5, 1990, was owned by:

(i) A corporation, trust, or partnership organized under the laws of the United States or any State (including individual States, territories, possessions, and the District of Columbia);

(ii) An individual who is a citizen of the United States; or

(iii) An entity owned or controlled by a corporation, trust, partnership, or individual described in paragraph (f)(1)(i) or (ii) of this section; and

(2) Enters into the United States not later than 6 months after the expiration of a lease agreement (including any extensions thereof) between an owner described in paragraph (f)(1) of this section and a foreign airline.

(g) The airplane complies with Stage 2 noise levels and was purchased by the importer under a written contract executed before November 5, 1990.

(h) Any Stage 2 airplane described in this section is eligible for operation in the contiguous United States only as provided under §§91.865 or 91.867.

[Docket No. 26433, 56 FR 48658, Sept. 25, 1991; 56 FR 51167, Oct. 10, 1991; as amended by Amdt. 91–288, 70 FR 38750, July 5, 2005; Docket FAA–2015–3782, Amdt. 91–349, 82 FR 46132, Oct. 4, 2017]

§91.857 Stage 2 operations outside of the 48 contiguous United States.

An operator of a Stage 2 airplane that is operating only between points outside the contiguous United States on or after November 5, 1990, must include in its operations specifications a statement that such airplane may not be used to provide air transportation to or from any airport in the contiguous United States.

[Docket No. FAA–2002–12771, 67 FR 46571, July 15, 2002]

§91.858 Special flight authorizations for non-revenue Stage 2 operations.

(a) After December 31, 1999, any operator of a Stage 2 airplane over 75,000 pounds may operate that airplane in nonrevenue service in the contiguous United States only for the following purposes:

(1) Sell, lease, or scrap the airplane;

(2) Obtain modifications to meet Stage 3, Stage 4, or Stage 5 noise levels;

(3) Obtain scheduled heavy maintenance or significant modifications;

(4) Deliver the airplane to a lessee or return it to a lessor;

(5) Park or store the airplane; and

(6) Prepare the airplane for any of the purposes listed in paragraph (a)(1) through (a)(5) of this section.

(b) An operator of a Stage 2 airplane that needs to operate in the contiguous United States for any of the purposes listed above may apply to FAA's Office of Environment and Energy for a special flight authorization. The applicant must file in advance. Applications are due 30 days in advance of the planned flight and must provide the information necessary for the FAA to determine that the planned flight is within the limits prescribed in the law.

[Docket No. FAA–2002–12771, 67 FR 46571, July 15, 2002; as amended by Docket FAA–2015–3782, Amdt. 91–349, 82 FR 46132, Oct. 4, 2017]

§91.859 Modification to meet Stage 3, Stage 4, or Stage 5 noise levels.

For an airplane subject to §91.801(c) of this subpart and otherwise prohibited from operation to or from an airport in the contiguous United States by §91.855, any person may apply for a special flight authorization for that airplane to operate in the contiguous United States for the purpose of obtaining modifications to meet Stage 3, Stage 4, or Stage 5 noise levels.

[Docket FAA–2015–3782, Amdt. 91–349, 82 FR 46132, Oct. 4, 2017]

§91.861 Base level.

(a) *U.S. Operators.* The base level of a U.S. operator is equal to the number of owned or leased Stage 2 airplanes subject to §91.801(c) of this subpart that were listed on that operator's operations specifications for operations to or from airports in the contiguous United States on any one day selected by the operator during the period January 1, 1990, through July 1, 1991, plus or minus adjustments made pursuant to paragraphs (a)(1) and (2).

(1) The base level of a U.S. operator shall be increased by a number equal to the total of the following—

(i) The number of Stage 2 airplanes returned to service in the United States pursuant to §91.855(f);

(ii) The number of Stage 2 airplanes purchased pursuant to §91.855(g); and

(iii) Any U.S. operator base level acquired with a Stage 2 airplane transferred from another person under §91.863.

(2) The base level of a U.S. operator shall be decreased by the amount of U.S. operator base level transferred with the corresponding number of Stage 2 airplanes to another person under §91.863.

(b) *Foreign air carriers.* The base level of a foreign air carrier is equal to the number of owned or leased Stage 2 airplanes that were listed on that carrier's U.S. operations specifications on any one day during the period January 1, 1990, through July 1, 1991, plus or minus any adjustments to the base levels made pursuant to paragraphs (b)(1) and (2).

(1) The base level of a foreign air carrier shall be increased by the amount of foreign air carrier base level acquired with a Stage 2 airplane from another person under §91.863.

(2) The base level of a foreign air carrier shall be decreased by the amount of foreign air carrier base level transferred with a Stage 2 airplane to another person under §91.863.

(c) *New entrants* do not have a base level.

[Docket No. 26433, 56 FR 48659, Sept. 25, 1991; 56 FR 51167, Oct. 10, 1991]

§91.863 Transfers of Stage 2 airplanes with base level.

(a) Stage 2 airplanes may be transferred with or without the corresponding amount of base level. Base level may not be transferred without the corresponding number of Stage 2 airplanes.

(b) No portion of a U.S. operator's base level established under §91.861(a) may be used for operations by a foreign air carrier. No portion of a foreign air carrier's base level established under §91.861(b) may be used for operations by a U.S. operator.

(c) Whenever a transfer of Stage 2 airplanes with base level occurs, the transferring and acquiring parties shall, within 10 days, jointly submit written notification of the transfer to the FAA, Office of Environment and Energy. Such notification shall state:

(1) The names of the transferring and acquiring parties;

(2) The name, address, and telephone number of the individual responsible for submitting the notification on behalf of the transferring and acquiring parties;

(3) The total number of Stage 2 airplanes transferred, listed by airplane type, model, series, and serial number;

(4) The corresponding amount of base level transferred and whether it is U.S. operator or foreign air carrier base level; and

(5) The effective date of the transaction.

(d) If, taken as a whole, a transaction or series of transactions made pursuant to this section does not produce an increase or decrease in the number of Stage 2 airplanes for either the acquiring or transferring operator, such transaction or series of transactions may not be used to establish compliance with the requirements of §91.865.

[Docket No. 26433, 56 FR 48659, Sept. 25, 1991]

§91.865 Phased compliance for operators with base level.

Except as provided in paragraph (a) of this section, each operator that operates an airplane under part 91, 121, 125, 129, or 135 of this chapter, regardless of the national registry of the airplane, shall comply with paragraph (b) or (d) of this section at each interim compliance date with regard to its subsonic airplane fleet covered by §91.801(c) of this subpart.

(a) This section does not apply to new entrants covered by §91.867 or to foreign operators not engaged in foreign air commerce.

(b) Each operator that chooses to comply with this paragraph pursuant to any interim compliance requirement shall reduce the number of Stage 2 airplanes it operates that are eligible for operation in the contiguous United States to a maximum of:

(1) After December 31, 1994, 75 percent of the base level held by the operator;

(2) After December 31, 1996, 50 percent of the base level held by the operator;

(3) After December 31, 1998, 25 percent of the base level held by the operator.

(c) Except as provided under §91.871, the number of Stage 2 airplanes that must be reduced at each compliance date contained in paragraph (b) of this section shall be determined by reference to the amount of base level held by the operator on that compliance date, as calculated under §91.861.

(d) Each operator that chooses to comply with this paragraph pursuant to any interim compliance requirement shall operate a fleet that consists of:

(1) After December 31, 1994, not less than 55 percent Stage 3 airplanes;

(2) After December 31, 1996, not less than 65 percent Stage 3 airplanes;

(3) After December 31, 1998, not less than 75 percent Stage 3 airplanes.

(e) Calculations resulting in fractions may be rounded to permit the continued operation of the next whole number of Stage 2 airplanes.

[Docket No. 26433, 56 FR 48659, Sept. 25, 1991]

§91.867 Phased compliance for new entrants.

(a) *New entrant U.S. air carriers.*

(1) A new entrant initiating operations under part 121 of this chapter on or before December 31, 1994, may initiate service without regard to the percentage of its fleet composed of Stage 3 airplanes.

(2) After December 31, 1994, at least 25 percent of the fleet of a new entrant must comply with Stage 3 noise levels.

(3) After December 31, 1996, at least 50 percent of the fleet of a new entrant must comply with Stage 3 noise levels.

(4) After December 31, 1998, at least 75 percent of the fleet of a new entrant must comply with Stage 3 noise levels.

(b) *New entrant foreign air carriers.*

(1) A new entrant foreign air carrier initiating part 129 operations on or before December 31, 1994, may initiate service without regard to the percentage of its fleet composed of Stage 3 airplanes.

(2) After December 31, 1994, at least 25 percent of the fleet on U.S. operations specifications of a new entrant foreign air carrier must comply with Stage 3 noise levels.

(3) After December 31, 1996, at least 50 percent of the fleet on U.S. operations specifications of a new entrant foreign air carrier must comply with Stage 3 noise levels.

(4) After December 31, 1998, at least 75 percent of the fleet on U.S. operations specifications of a new entrant foreign air carrier must comply with Stage 3 noise levels.

(c) Calculations resulting in fractions may be rounded to permit the continued operation of the next whole number of Stage 2 airplanes.

[Docket No. 26433, 56 FR 48659, Sept. 25, 1991; as amended by Amdt. 91–252, 61 FR 66185, Dec. 16, 1996]

§91.869 Carry-forward compliance.

(a) Any operator that exceeds the requirements of paragraph (b) of §91.865 of this part on or before December 31, 1994, or on or before December 31, 1996, may claim a credit that may be applied at a subsequent interim compliance date.

(b) Any operator that eliminates or modifies more Stage 2 airplanes pursuant to §91.865(b) than required as of December 31, 1994, or December 31, 1996, may count the number of additional Stage 2 airplanes reduced as a credit toward—

(1) The number of Stage 2 airplanes it would otherwise be required to reduce following a subsequent interim compliance date specified in §91.865(b); or

(2) The number of Stage 3 airplanes it would otherwise be required to operate in its fleet following a subsequent interim compliance date to meet the percentage requirements specified in §91.865(d).

[Docket No. 26433, 56 FR 48659, Sept. 25, 1991; 56 FR 65783, Dec. 18, 1991]

§91.871 Waivers from interim compliance requirements.

(a) Any U.S. operator or foreign air carrier subject to the requirements of §§91.865 or 91.867 of this subpart may request a waiver from any individual compliance requirement.

(b) Applications must be filed with the Secretary of Transportation at least 120 days prior to the compliance date from which the waiver is requested.

(c) Applicants must show that a grant of waiver would be in the public interest, and must include in its application its plans and activities for modifying its fleet, including evidence of good faith efforts to comply with the requirements of §§91.865 or 91.867. The application should contain all information the applicant considers relevant, including, as appropriate, the following:

(1) The applicant's balance sheet and cash flow positions;

(2) The composition of the applicant's current fleet; and

(3) The applicant's delivery position with respect to new airplanes or noise-abatement equipment.

(d) Waivers will be granted only upon a showing by the applicant that compliance with the requirements of §91.865 or 91.867 at a particular interim compliance date is financially onerous, physically impossible, or technologically infeasible, or that it would have an adverse effect on competition or on service to small communities.

(e) The conditions of any waiver granted under this section shall be determined by the circumstances presented in the application, but in no case may the term extend beyond the next interim compliance date.

(f) A summary of any request for a waiver under this section will be published in the Federal Register, and public comment will be invited. Unless the Secretary finds that circumstances require otherwise, the public comment period will be at least 14 days.

[Docket No. 26433, 56 FR 48660, Sept. 25, 1991]

§91.873 Waivers from final compliance.

(a) A U.S. air carrier or a foreign air carrier may apply for a waiver from the prohibition contained in §91.853 of this part for its remaining Stage 2 airplanes, provided that, by July 1, 1999, at least 85 percent of the airplanes used by the carrier to provide service to or from an airport in the contiguous United States will comply with the Stage 3 noise levels.

(b) An application for the waiver described in paragraph (a) of this section must be filed with the Secretary of Transportation no later than January 1, 1999, or, in the case of a foreign air carrier, no later than April 20, 2000. Such application must include a plan with firm orders for replacing or modifying all airplanes to comply with Stage 3 noise levels at the earliest practicable time.

(c) To be eligible to apply for the waiver under this section, a new entrant U.S. air carrier must initiate service no later than January 1, 1999, and must comply fully with all provisions of this section.

(d) The Secretary may grant a waiver under this section if the Secretary finds that granting such waiver is in the public interest. In making such a finding, the Secretary shall include consideration of the effect of granting such waiver on competition in the air carrier industry and the effect on small community air service, and any other information submitted by the applicant that the Secretary considers relevant.

(e) The term of any waiver granted under this section shall be determined by the circumstances presented in the application, but in no case will the waiver permit the operation of any Stage 2 airplane covered by this subchapter in the contiguous United States after December 31, 2003.

(f) A summary of any request for a waiver under this section will be published in the Federal Register, and public comment will be invited. Unless the secretary finds that circumstances require otherwise, the public comment period will be at least 14 days.

[Docket No. 26433, 56 FR 48660, Sept. 25, 1991; 56 FR 51167 Oct. 10, 1991; Amdt. 91–276, 67 FR 46571, July 15, 2002]

§91.875 Annual progress reports.

(a) Each operator subject to §91.865 or §91.867 of this chapter shall submit an annual report to the FAA, Office of Environment and Energy, on the progress it has made toward complying with the requirements of that section. Such reports shall be submitted no later than 45 days after the end of a calendar year. All progress reports must provide the information through the end of the calendar year, be certified by the operator as true and complete (under penalty of 18 U.S.C. 1001), and include the following information:

(1) The name and address of the operator;

(2) The name, title, and telephone number of the person designated by the operator to be responsible for ensuring the accuracy of the information in the report;

(3) The operator's progress during the reporting period toward compliance with the requirements of §91.853, §91.865 or §91.867. For airplanes on U.S. operations specifications, each operator shall identify the airplanes by type, model, series, and serial number.

(i) Each Stage 2 airplane added or removed from operation or U.S. operations specifications (grouped separately by those airplanes acquired with and without base level);

(ii) Each Stage 2 airplane modified to Stage 3 noise levels (identifying the manufacturer and model of noise abatement retrofit equipment;

(iii) Each Stage 3 airplane on U.S. operations specifications as of the last day of the reporting period; and

(iv) For each Stage 2 airplane transferred or acquired, the name and address of the recipient or transferor; and, if base level was transferred, the person to or from whom base level was transferred or acquired pursuant to Section 91.863 along with the effective date of each base level transaction, and the type of base level transferred or acquired.

(b) Each operator subject to §91.865 or §91.867 of this chapter shall submit an initial progress report covering the period from January 1, 1990, through December 31, 1991, and provide:

(1) For each operator subject to §91.865:

(i) The date used to establish its base level pursuant to §91.861(a); and

(ii) A list of those Stage 2 airplanes (by type, model, series and serial number) in its base level, including adjustments made pursuant to §91.861 after the date its base level was established.

(2) For each U.S. operator:

(i) A plan to meet the compliance schedules in §91.865 or §91.867 and the final compliance date of §91.853, including the schedule for delivery of replacement Stage 3 airplanes or the installation of noise abatement retrofit equipment; and

(ii) A separate list (by type, model, series, and serial number) of those airplanes included in the operator's base level, pursuant to §91.861(a)(1)(i) and (ii), under the categories "returned" or "purchased," along with the date each was added to its operations specifications.

(c) Each operator subject to §91.865 or §91.867 of this chapter shall submit subsequent annual progress reports covering the calendar year preceding the report and including any changes in the information provided in paragraphs (a) and (b) of this section; including the use of any carry-forward credits pursuant to §91.869.

(d) An operator may request, in any report, that specific planning data be considered proprietary.

(e) If an operator's actions during any reporting period cause it to achieve compliance with §91.853, the report should include a statement to that effect. Further progress reports are not required unless there is any change in the information reported pursuant to paragraph (a) of this section.

(f) For each U.S. operator subject to §91.865, progress reports submitted for calendar years 1994, 1996, and 1998, shall also state how the operator achieved compliance with the requirements of that section, i.e.—

(1) By reducing the number of Stage 2 airplanes in its fleet to no more than the maximum permitted percentage of its base level under §91.865(b), or

(2) By operating a fleet that consists of at least the minimum required percentage of Stage 3 airplanes under §91.865(d).

(Approved by the Office of Management and Budget under control number 2120–0553)

[Docket No. 26433, 56 FR 48660, Sept. 25, 1991; 56 FR 51168, Oct. 10, 1991; as amended by 57 FR 5977, Feb. 19, 1992]

§91.877 Annual reporting of Hawaiian operations.

(a) Each air carrier or foreign air carrier subject to §91.865 or §91.867 of this part that conducts operations between the contiguous United States and the State of Hawaii, between the State of Hawaii and any point outside of the contiguous United States, or between the islands of Hawaii in turnaround service, on or since November 5, 1990, shall include in its annual report the information described in paragraph (c) of this section.

(b) Each air carrier or foreign air carrier not subject to §91.865 or §91.867 of this part that conducts operations between the contiguous U.S. and the State of Hawaii, between the State of Hawaii and any point outside of the contiguous United States, or between the islands of Hawaii in turnaround service, on or since November 5, 1990, shall submit an annual report to the FAA, Office of Environment and Energy, on its compliance with the Hawaiian operations provisions of 49 U.S.C. 47528. Such reports shall be submitted no later than 45 days after the end of a calendar year. All progress reports must provide the information through the end of the calendar year, be certified by the operator as true and complete (under penalty of 18 U.S.C. 1001), and include the following information—

(1) The name and address of the air carrier or foreign air carrier;

(2) The name, title, and telephone number of the person designated by the air carrier or foreign air carrier to be responsible for ensuring the accuracy of the information in the report; and

(3) The information specified in paragraph (c) of this section.

(c) The following information must be included in reports filed pursuant to this section—

(1) For operations conducted between the contiguous United States and the State of Hawaii—

(i) The number of Stage 2 airplanes used to conduct such operations as of November 5, 1990;

(ii) Any change to that number during the calendar year being reported, including the date of such change;

(2) For air carriers that conduct inter-island turnaround service in the State of Hawaii—

(i) The number of Stage 2 airplanes used to conduct such operations as of November 5, 1990;

(ii) Any change to that number during the calendar year being reported, including the date of such change;

(iii) For an air carrier that provided inter-island turnaround service within the state of Hawaii on November 5, 1990, the number reported under paragraph (c)(2)(i) of this section may include all Stage 2 airplanes with a maximum certificated takeoff weight of more than 75,000 pounds that were owned or leased by the air carrier on November 5, 1990, regardless of whether such airplanes were operated by that air carrier or foreign air carrier on that date.

(3) For operations conducted between the State of Hawaii and a point outside the contiguous United States—

(i) The number of Stage 2 airplanes used to conduct such operations as of November 5, 1990; and

(ii) Any change to that number during the calendar year being reported, including the date of such change.

(d) Reports or amended reports for years predating this regulation are required to be filed concurrently with the next annual report.

[Docket No. 28213, 61 FR 66185, Dec. 16, 1996]

§91.879–91.880 [Reserved]

§91.881 Final compliance: Civil subsonic jet airplanes weighing 75,000 pounds or less.

Except as provided in §91.883, after December 31, 2015, a person may not operate to or from an airport in the contiguous United States a civil subsonic jet airplane subject to §91.801(e) of this subpart that weighs less than 75,000 pounds unless that airplane has been shown to comply with Stage 3, Stage 4, or Stage 5 noise levels.

[Docket FAA–2015–3782, Amdt. 91–349, 82 FR 46132, Oct. 4, 2017]

§91.883 Special flight authorizations for jet airplanes weighing 75,000 pounds or less.

(a) After December 31, 2015, an operator of a jet airplane weighing 75,000 pounds or less that does not comply with Stage 3 noise levels may, when granted a special flight authorization by the FAA, operate that airplane in the contiguous United States only for one of the following purposes:

(1) To sell, lease, or use the airplane outside the 48 contiguous States;

(2) To scrap the airplane;

(3) To obtain modifications to the airplane to meet Stage 3, Stage 4, or Stage 5 noise levels;

(4) To perform scheduled heavy maintenance or significant modifications on the airplane at a maintenance facility located in the contiguous 48 States;

(5) To deliver the airplane to an operator leasing the airplane from the owner or return the airplane to the lessor;

(6) To prepare, park, or store the airplane in anticipation of any of the activities described in paragraphs (a)(1) through (a)(5) of this section;

(7) To provide transport of persons and goods in the relief of an emergency situation; or

(8) To divert the airplane to an alternative airport in the 48 contiguous States on account of weather, mechanical, fuel, air traffic control, or other safety reasons while conducting a flight in order to perform any of the activities described in paragraphs (a)(1) through (a)(7) of this section.

(b) An operator of an affected airplane may apply for a special flight authorization for one of the purposes listed in paragraph (a) of this section by filing an application with the FAA's Office of Environment and Energy. Except for emergency relief authorizations sought under paragraph (a)(7) of this section, applications must be filed at least 30 days in advance of the planned flight. All applications must provide the information necessary for the FAA to determine that the planned flight is within the limits prescribed in the law.

[Docket No. FAA–2013–0503, 78 FR 39583, July 2, 2013; as amended by Amdt. 91–349, 82 FR 46132, Oct. 4, 2017]

§91.884–91.899 [Reserved]

Subpart J—Waivers

§91.901 [Reserved]

§91.903 Policy and procedures.

(a) The Administrator may issue a certificate of waiver authorizing the operation of aircraft in deviation from any rule listed in this subpart if the Administrator finds that the proposed operation can be safely conducted under the terms of that certificate of waiver.

(b) An application for a certificate of waiver under this part is made on a form and in a manner prescribed by the Administrator and may be submitted to any FAA office.

(c) A certificate of waiver is effective as specified in that certificate of waiver.

[Docket No. 18334, 54 FR 34325, Aug. 18, 1989]

§91.905 List of rules subject to waivers.

Sec.
91.107 Use of safety belts.
91.111 Operating near other aircraft.
91.113 Right-of-way rules: Except water operations.
91.115 Right-of-way rules: Water operations.
91.117 Aircraft speed.
91.119 Minimum safe altitudes: General.
91.121 Altimeter settings.
91.123 Compliance with ATC clearances and instructions.
91.125 ATC light signals.
91.126 Operating on or in the vicinity of an airport in Class G airspace.
91.127 Operating on or in the vicinity of an airport in Class E airspace.
91.129 Operations in Class D airspace.
91.130 Operations in Class C airspace.
91.131 Operations in Class B airspace.
91.133 Restricted and prohibited areas.
91.135 Operations in Class A airspace.
91.137 Temporary flight restrictions.
91.141 Flight restrictions in the proximity of the Presidential and other parties.
91.143 Flight limitation in the proximity of space flight operations.
91.153 VFR flight plan: Information required.
91.155 Basic VFR weather minimums.
91.157 Special VFR weather minimums.
91.159 VFR cruising altitude or flight level.
91.169 IFR flight plan: Information required.
91.173 ATC clearance and flight plan required.
91.175 Takeoff and landing under IFR.
91.176 Operations below DA/DH or MDA using an enhanced flight vision system (EFVS) under I(FR.
91.177 Minimum altitudes for IFR operations.
91.179 IFR cruising altitude or flight level.
91.181 Course to be flown.

91.183 IFR radio communications.
91.185 IFR operations: Two-way radio
 communications failure.
91.187 Operation under IFR in controlled
 airspace: Malfunction reports.
91.209 Aircraft lights.
91.303 Aerobatic flights.
91.305 Flight test areas.
91.311 Towing: Other than under §91.309.
91.313(e) Restricted category civil aircraft:
 Operating limitations.
91.515 Flight altitude rules.
91.707 Flights between Mexico or Canada and
 the United States.
91.713 Operation of civil aircraft of Cuban
 registry.

[Docket No. 18334, 54 FR 34325, Aug. 18, 1989, as amended by Amdt. 91–227, 56 FR 65661, Dec. 17, 1991; Docket FAA–2013–0485, Amdt. 91–345, 81 FR 90175, Dec. 13, 2016; Docket FAA–2016–9154, Amdt. 91–348, 82 FR 39664, Aug. 22, 20177]

§91.907–91.999 [Reserved]

Subpart K—Fractional Ownership Operations

Source: Docket No. FAA–2001–10047, 68 FR 54561, Sept. 17, 2003 unless otherwise noted.

§91.1001 Applicability.

(a) This subpart prescribes rules, in addition to those prescribed in other subparts of this part, that apply to fractional owners and fractional ownership program managers governing—

(1) The provision of program management services in a fractional ownership program;

(2) The operation of a fractional ownership program aircraft in a fractional ownership program; and

(3) The operation of a program aircraft included in a fractional ownership program managed by an affiliate of the manager of the program to which the owner belongs.

(b) As used in this part—

(1) **Affiliate of a program manager** means a manager that, directly, or indirectly, through one or more intermediaries, controls, is controlled by, or is under common control with, another program manager. The holding of at least forty percent (40 percent) of the equity and forty percent (40 percent) of the voting power of an entity will be presumed to constitute control for purposes of determining an affiliation under this subpart.

(2) A *dry-lease aircraft exchange* means an arrangement, documented by the written program agreements, under which the program aircraft are available, on an as needed basis without crew, to each fractional owner.

(3) A *fractional owner or owner* means an individual or entity that possesses a minimum fractional ownership interest in a program aircraft and that has entered into the applicable program agreements; provided, however, that in the case of the flight operations described in paragraph (b)(6)(ii) of this section, and solely for purposes of requirements pertaining to those flight operations, the fractional owner operating the aircraft will be deemed to be a fractional owner in the program managed by the affiliate.

(4) A *fractional ownership interest* means the ownership of an interest or holding of a multi-year leasehold interest and/or a multi-year leasehold interest that is convertible into an ownership interest in a program aircraft.

(5) A *fractional ownership program or program* means any system of aircraft ownership and exchange that consists of all of the following elements:

(i) The provision for fractional ownership program management services by a single fractional ownership program manager on behalf of the fractional owners.

(ii) Two or more airworthy aircraft.

(iii) One or more fractional owners per program aircraft, with at least one program aircraft having more than one owner.

(iv) Possession of at least a minimum fractional ownership interest in one or more program aircraft by each fractional owner.

(v) A dry-lease aircraft exchange arrangement among all of the fractional owners.

(vi) Multi-year program agreements covering the fractional ownership, fractional ownership program management services, and dry-lease aircraft exchange aspects of the program.

(6) A *fractional ownership program aircraft or program aircraft* means:

(i) An aircraft in which a fractional owner has a minimal fractional ownership interest and that has been included in the dry-lease aircraft exchange pursuant to the program agreements, or

(ii) In the case of a fractional owner from one program operating an aircraft in a different fractional ownership program managed by an affiliate of the operating owner's program manager, the aircraft being operated by the fractional owner, so long as the aircraft is:

(A) Included in the fractional ownership program managed by the affiliate of the operating owner's program manager, and

(B) Included in the operating owner's program's dry-lease aircraft exchange pursuant to the program agreements of the operating owner's program.

(iii) An aircraft owned in whole or in part by the program manager that has been included in the dry-lease aircraft exchange and is used to supplement program operations.

(7) A *Fractional Ownership Program Flight or Program Flight* means a flight under this subpart when one or more passengers or property designated by a fractional owner are on board the aircraft.

(8) **Fractional ownership program management services or program management services** mean administrative and aviation support services furnished in accordance with the applicable requirements of this subpart or provided by the program manager on behalf of the fractional owners, including, but not limited to, the—

(i) Establishment and implementation of program safety guidelines;

(ii) Employment, furnishing, or contracting of pilots and other crewmembers;

(iii) Training and qualification of pilots and other crewmembers and personnel;

(iv) Scheduling and coordination of the program aircraft and crews;

(v) Maintenance of program aircraft;

(vi) Satisfaction of recordkeeping requirements;

(vii) Development and use of a program operations manual and procedures; and

(viii) Application for and maintenance of management specifications and other authorizations and approvals.

(9) A *fractional ownership program manager or program manager* means the entity that offers fractional ownership program management services to fractional owners, and is designated in the multi-year program agreements referenced in paragraph (b)(5)(vi) of this section to fulfill the requirements of this chapter applicable to the manager of the program containing the aircraft being flown. When a fractional owner is operating an aircraft in a fractional ownership program managed by an affiliate of the owner's program manager, the references in this subpart to the flight-related responsibilities of the program manager apply, with respect to that particular flight, to the affiliate of the owner's program manager rather than to the owner's program manager.

(10) A *minimum fractional ownership interest* means—

(i) A fractional ownership interest equal to, or greater than, one-sixteenth (1/16) of at least one subsonic, fixed-wing or powered-lift program aircraft; or

(ii) A fractional ownership interest equal to, or greater than, one-thirty-second (1/32) of at least one rotorcraft program aircraft.

(c) The rules in this subpart that refer to a fractional owner or a fractional ownership program manager also apply to any person who engages in an operation governed by this subpart without the management specifications required by this subpart.

[Docket No. FAA–2001–10047, 68 FR 54561, Sept. 17, 2003,, as amended by Docket No. FAA–2022–1355, Amdt. No. 91–366, 87 FR 75846, Dec. 9, 2022]

§91.1002 Compliance date.

No person that conducted flights before November 17, 2003 under a program that meets the definition of fractional ownership program in §91.1001 may conduct such flights after February 17, 2005 unless it has obtained management specifications under this subpart.

[Docket No. FAA–2001–10047, 68 FR 54561, Sept. 17, 2003; 69 FR 74413, Dec. 14, 2004]

§91.1003 Management contract between owner and program manager.

Each owner must have a contract with the program manager that—

(a) Requires the program manager to ensure that the program conforms to all applicable requirements of this chapter.

(b) Provides the owner the right to inspect and to audit, or have a designee of the owner inspect and audit, the records of the program manager pertaining to the operational safety of the program and those records required to show compliance with the management specifications and all applicable regulations. These records include, but are not limited to, the management specifications, authorizations, approvals, manuals, log books, and maintenance records maintained by the program manager.

(c) Designates the program manager as the owner's agent to receive service of notices pertaining to the program that the FAA seeks to provide to owners and authorizes the FAA to send such notices to the program manager in its capacity as the agent of the owner for such service.

(d) Acknowledges the FAA's right to contact the owner directly if the Administrator determines that direct contact is necessary.

§91.1005 Prohibitions and limitations.

(a) Except as provided in §91.321 or §91.501, no owner may carry persons or property for compensation or hire on a program flight.

(b) During the term of the multi-year program agreements under which a fractional owner has obtained a minimum fractional ownership interest in a program aircraft, the flight hours used during that term by the owner on program aircraft must not exceed the total hours associated with the fractional owner's share of ownership.

(c) No person may sell or lease an aircraft interest in a fractional ownership program that is smaller than that prescribed in the definition of "minimum fractional ownership interest" in §91.1001(b)(10) unless flights associated with that interest are operated under part 121 or 135 of this chapter and are conducted by an air carrier or commercial operator certificated under part 119 of this chapter.

§91.1007 Flights conducted under part 121 or part 135 of this chapter.

(a) Except as provided in §91.501(b), when a nonprogram aircraft is used to substitute for a program flight, the flight must be operated in compliance with part 121 or part 135 of this chapter, as applicable.

(b) A program manager who holds a certificate under part 119 of this chapter may conduct a flight for the use of a fractional owner under part 121 or part 135 of this chapter if the aircraft is listed on that certificate holder's operations specifications for part 121 or part 135, as applicable.

(c) The fractional owner must be informed when a flight is being conducted as a program flight or is being conducted under part 121 or part 135 of this chapter.

OPERATIONAL CONTROL

§91.1009 Clarification of operational control.

(a) An owner is in operational control of a program flight when the owner—

(1) Has the rights and is subject to the limitations set forth in §§91.1003 through 91.1013;

(2) Has directed that a program aircraft carry passengers or property designated by that owner; and

(3) The aircraft is carrying those passengers or property.

(b) An owner is not in operational control of a flight in the following circumstances:

(1) A program aircraft is used for a flight for administrative purposes such as demonstration, positioning, ferrying, maintenance, or crew training, and no passengers or property designated by such owner are being carried; or

(2) The aircraft being used for the flight is being operated under part 121 or 135 of this chapter.

§91.1011 Operational control responsibilities and delegation.

(a) Each owner in operational control of a program flight is ultimately responsible for safe operations and for complying with all applicable requirements of this chapter, including those related to airworthiness and operations in connection with the flight. Each owner may delegate some or all of the performance of the tasks associated with carrying out this responsibility to the program manager, and may rely on the program manager for aviation expertise and program management services. When the owner delegates performance of tasks to the program manager or relies on the program manager's expertise, the owner and the program manager are jointly and individually responsible for compliance.

(b) The management specifications, authorizations, and approvals required by this subpart are issued to, and in the sole name of, the program manager on behalf of the fractional owners collectively. The management specifications, authorizations, and approvals will not be affected by any change in ownership of a program aircraft, as long as the aircraft remains a program aircraft in the identified program.

§91.1013 Operational control briefing and acknowledgment.

(a) Upon the signing of an initial program management services contract, or a renewal or extension of a program management services contract, the program manager must brief the fractional owner on the owner's operational control responsibilities, and the owner must review and sign an acknowledgment of these operational control responsibilities. The acknowledgment must be included with the program management services contract. The acknowledgment must define when a fractional owner is in operational control and the owner's responsibilities and liabilities under the program. These include:

(1) Responsibility for compliance with the management specifications and all applicable regulations.

(2) Enforcement actions for any noncompliance.

(3) Liability risk in the event of a flight-related occurrence that causes personal injury or property damage.

(b) The fractional owner's signature on the acknowledgment will serve as the owner's affirmation that the owner has read, understands, and accepts the operational control responsibilities described in the acknowledgment.

(c) Each program manager must ensure that the fractional owner or owner's representatives have access to the acknowledgments for such owner's program aircraft. Each program manager must ensure that the FAA has access to the acknowledgments for all program aircraft.

PROGRAM MANAGEMENT

§91.1014 Issuing or denying management specifications.

(a) A person applying to the Administrator for management specifications under this subpart must submit an application—

(1) In a form and manner prescribed by the Administrator; and

(2) Containing any information the Administrator requires the applicant to submit.

(b) Management specifications will be issued to the program manager on behalf of the fractional owners if, after investigation, the Administrator finds that the applicant:

(1) Meets the applicable requirements of this subpart; and

(2) Is properly and adequately equipped in accordance with the requirements of this chapter and is able to conduct safe operations under appropriate provisions of part 91 of this chapter and management specifications issued under this subpart.

(c) An application for management specifications will be denied if the Administrator finds that the applicant is not properly or adequately equipped or is not able to conduct safe operations under this part.

§91.1015 Management specifications.

(a) Each person conducting operations under this subpart or furnishing fractional ownership program management services to fractional owners must do so in accordance with management specifications issued by the Administrator to the fractional ownership program manager under this subpart. Management specifications must include:

(1) The current list of all fractional owners and types of aircraft, registration markings and serial numbers;

(2) The authorizations, limitations, and certain procedures under which these operations are to be conducted,

(3) Certain other procedures under which each class and size of aircraft is to be operated;

(4) Authorization for an inspection program approved under §91.1109, including the type of aircraft, the registration markings and serial numbers of each aircraft to be operated under the program. No person may conduct any program flight using any aircraft not listed.

(5) Time limitations, or standards for determining time limitations, for overhauls, inspections, and checks for airframes, engines, propellers, rotors, appliances, and emergency equipment of aircraft.

(6) The specific location of the program manager's principal base of operations and, if different, the address that will serve as the primary point of contact for correspondence between the FAA and the program manager and the name and mailing address of the program manager's agent for service;

(7) Other business names the program manager may use;

(8) Authorization for the method of controlling weight and balance of aircraft;

(9) Any authorized deviation and exemption that applies to the person conducting operations under this subpart; and

(10) Any other information the Administrator determines is necessary.

(b) The program manager may keep the current list of all fractional owners required by paragraph (a)(1) of this section at its principal base of operation or other location approved by the Administrator and referenced in its management specifications. Each program manager shall make this list of owners available for inspection by the Administrator.

(c) Management specifications issued under this subpart are effective unless—

(1) The management specifications are amended as provided in §91.1017; or

(2) The Administrator suspends or revokes the management specifications.

(d) At least 30 days before it proposes to establish or change the location of its principal base of operations, its main operations base, or its main maintenance base, a program manager must provide written notification to the Flight Standards office that issued the program manager's management specifications.

(e) Each program manager must maintain a complete and separate set of its management specifications at its principal base of operations, or at a place approved by the Administrator, and must make its management specifications available for inspection by the Administrator and the fractional owner(s) to whom the program manager furnishes its services for review and audit.

(f) Each program manager must insert pertinent excerpts of its management specifications, or references thereto, in its program manual and must—

(1) Clearly identify each such excerpt as a part of its management specifications; and

(2) State that compliance with each management specifications requirement is mandatory.

(g) Each program manager must keep each of its employees and other persons who perform duties material to its operations informed of the provisions of its management specifications that apply to that employee's or person's duties and responsibilities.

(h) A program manager may obtain approval to provide a temporary document verifying a flightcrew member's airman certificate and medical certificate privileges under an approved certificate verification plan set forth in the program manager's management specifications. A document provided by the program manager may be carried as an airman certificate or medical certificate on flights within the United States for up to 72 hours.

[Docket No. FAA–2001–10047, 68 FR 54561, Sept. 17, 2003; as amended by Amdt. 91–350, 83 FR 9171, March 5, 2018; Amdt. 91–351, 83 FR 30281, June 27, 2018; Docket No. FAA–2022–1563, Amdt. 91–370, 88 FR 48087, July 26, 2023]

§91.1017 Amending program manager's management specifications.

(a) The Administrator may amend any management specifications issued under this subpart if—

(1) The Administrator determines that safety and the public interest require the amendment of any management specifications; or

(2) The program manager applies for the amendment of any management specifications, and the Administrator determines that safety and the public interest allows the amendment.

(b) Except as provided in paragraph (e) of this section, when the Administrator initiates an amendment of a program manager's management specifications, the following procedure applies:

(1) The Flight Standards office that issued the program manager's management specifications will notify the program manager in writing of the proposed amendment.

(2) The Flight Standards office that issued the program manager's management specifications will set a reasonable period (but not less than 7 days) within which the program manager may submit written information, views, and arguments on the amendment.

(3) After considering all material presented, the Flight Standards office that issued the program manager's management specifications will notify the program manager of—

(i) The adoption of the proposed amendment,

(ii) The partial adoption of the proposed amendment, or

(iii) The withdrawal of the proposed amendment.

(4) If the Flight Standards office that issued the program manager's management specifications issues an amendment of the management specifications, it becomes effective not less than 30 days after the program manager receives notice of it unless—

(i) The Flight Standards office that issued the program manager's management specifications finds under paragraph (e) of this section that there is an emergency requiring immediate action with respect to safety; or

(ii) The program manager petitions for reconsideration of the amendment under paragraph (d) of this section.

(c) When the program manager applies for an amendment to its management specifications, the following procedure applies:

(1) The program manager must file an application to amend its management specifications—

(i) At least 90 days before the date proposed by the applicant for the amendment to become effective, unless a shorter time is approved, in cases such as mergers, acquisitions of operational assets that require an additional showing of safety (for example, proving tests or validation tests), and resumption of operations following a suspension of operations as a result of bankruptcy actions.

(ii) At least 15 days before the date proposed by the applicant for the amendment to become effective in all other cases.

(2) The application must be submitted to the Flight Standards office that issued the program manager's management specifications in a form and manner prescribed by the Administrator.

(3) After considering all material presented, the Flight Standards office that issued the program manager's management specifications will notify the program manager of—

(i) The adoption of the applied for amendment;

(ii) The partial adoption of the applied for amendment; or

(iii) The denial of the applied for amendment. The program manager may petition for reconsideration of a denial under paragraph (d) of this section.

(4) If the Flight Standards office that issued the program manager's management specifications approves the amendment, following coordination with the program manager regarding its implementation, the amendment is effective on the date the Administrator approves it.

(d) When a program manager seeks reconsideration of a decision of the Flight Standards office that issued the program manager's management specifications concerning the amendment of management specifications, the following procedure applies:

(1) The program manager must petition for reconsideration of that decision within 30 days of the date that the program manager receives a notice of denial of the amendment of its management specifications, or of the date it receives notice of an FAA-initiated amendment of its management specifications, whichever circumstance applies.

(2) The program manager must address its petition to the Executive Director, Flight Standards Service.

(3) A petition for reconsideration, if filed within the 30-day period, suspends the effectiveness of any amendment issued by the Flight Standards office that issued the program manager's management specifications unless that office has found, under paragraph (e) of this section, that an emergency exists requiring immediate action with respect to safety.

(4) If a petition for reconsideration is not filed within 30 days, the procedures of paragraph (c) of this section apply.

(e) If the Flight Standards office that issued the program manager's management specifications finds that an emergency exists

91

requiring immediate action with respect to safety that makes the procedures set out in this section impracticable or contrary to the public interest—

(1) The Flight Standards office amends the management specifications and makes the amendment effective on the day the program manager receives notice of it; and

(2) In the notice to the program manager, the Flight Standards office will articulate the reasons for its finding that an emergency exists requiring immediate action with respect to safety or that makes it impracticable or contrary to the public interest to stay the effectiveness of the amendment.

[Docket No. FAA–2001–10047, 68 FR 54561, Sept. 17, 2003; as amended by Docket FAA–2018–0119, Amdt. 91–350, 83 FR 9171, March 5, 2018]

§91.1019 Conducting tests and inspections.

(a) At any time or place, the Administrator may conduct an inspection or test, other than an en route inspection, to determine whether a program manager under this subpart is complying with title 49 of the United States Code, applicable regulations, and the program manager's management specifications.

(b) The program manager must—

(1) Make available to the Administrator at the program manager's principal base of operations, or at a place approved by the Administrator, the program manager's management specifications; and

(2) Allow the Administrator to make any test or inspection, other than an en route inspection, to determine compliance respecting any matter stated in paragraph (a) of this section.

(c) Each employee of, or person used by, the program manager who is responsible for maintaining the program manager's records required by or necessary to demonstrate compliance with this subpart must make those records available to the Administrator.

(d) The Administrator may determine a program manager's continued eligibility to hold its management specifications on any grounds listed in paragraph (a) of this section, or any other appropriate grounds.

(e) Failure by any program manager to make available to the Administrator upon request, the management specifications, or any required record, document, or report is grounds for suspension of all or any part of the program manager's management specifications.

§91.1021 Internal safety reporting and incident/accident response.

(a) Each program manager must establish an internal anonymous safety reporting procedure that fosters an environment of safety without any potential for retribution for filing the report.

(b) Each program manager must establish procedures to respond to an aviation incident/accident.

§91.1023 Program operating manual requirements.

(a) Each program manager must prepare and keep current a program operating manual setting forth procedures and policies acceptable to the Administrator. The program manager's management, flight, ground, and maintenance personnel must use this manual to conduct operations under this subpart. However, the Administrator may authorize a deviation from this paragraph if the Administrator finds that, because of the limited size of the operation, part of the manual is not necessary for guidance of management, flight, ground, or maintenance personnel.

(b) Each program manager must maintain at least one copy of the manual at its principal base of operations.

(c) No manual may be contrary to any applicable U.S. regulations, foreign regulations applicable to the program flights in foreign countries, or the program manager's management specifications.

(d) The program manager must make a copy of the manual, or appropriate portions of the manual (and changes and additions), available to its maintenance and ground operations personnel and must furnish the manual to—

(1) Its crewmembers; and

(2) Representatives of the Administrator assigned to the program manager.

(e) Each employee of the program manager to whom a manual or appropriate portions of it are furnished under paragraph (d)(1) of this section must keep it up-to-date with the changes and additions furnished to them.

(f) The program manager must ensure the appropriate parts of the manual are accessible to flight, ground, and maintenance personnel at all times when such personnel are performing their assigned duties.

(g) The information and instructions contained in the manual must be displayed clearly and be retrievable in the English language.

(h) Program managers that are also certificated to operate under part 121 or 135 of this chapter may be authorized to use the operating manual required by those parts to meet the manual requirements of subpart K, provided:

(1) The policies and procedures are consistent for both operations, or

(2) When policies and procedures are different, the applicable policies and procedures are identified and used.

[Docket No. FAA–2001–10047, 68 FR 54561, Sept. 17, 2003, as amended by Docket No. FAA–2022–0912, Amdt. No. 91–368, 88 FR 34443, May 30, 2023]

§91.1025 Program operating manual contents.

Each program operating manual accessed in paper format must display the date of last revision on each page. Each program operating manual accessed in electronic format must display the date of last revision in a manner in which a person can immediately ascertain it. Unless otherwise authorized by the Administrator, the manual must include the following:

(a) Procedures for ensuring compliance with aircraft weight and balance limitations;

(b) Copies of the program manager's management specifications or appropriate extracted information, including area of operations authorized, category and class of aircraft authorized, crew complements, and types of operations authorized;

(c) Procedures for complying with accident notification requirements;

(d) Procedures for ensuring that the pilot in command knows that required airworthiness inspections have been made and that the aircraft has been approved for return to service in compliance with applicable maintenance requirements;

(e) Procedures for reporting and recording mechanical irregularities that come to the attention of the pilot in command before, during, and after completion of a flight;

(f) Procedures to be followed by the pilot in command for determining that mechanical irregularities or defects reported for previous flights have been corrected or that correction of certain mechanical irregularities or defects have been deferred;

(g) Procedures to be followed by the pilot in command to obtain maintenance, preventive maintenance, and servicing of the aircraft at a place where previous arrangements have not been made by the program manager or owner, when the pilot is authorized to so act for the operator;

(h) Procedures under §91.213 for the release of, and continuation of flight if any item of equipment required for the particular type of operation becomes inoperative or unserviceable en route;

(i) Procedures for refueling aircraft, eliminating fuel contamination, protecting from fire (including electrostatic protection), and supervising and protecting passengers during refueling;

(j) Procedures to be followed by the pilot in command in the briefing under §91.1035.

(k) Procedures for ensuring compliance with emergency procedures, including a list of the functions assigned each category of required crewmembers in connection with an emergency and emergency evacuation duties;

(l) The approved aircraft inspection program, when applicable;

(m) Procedures for the evacuation of persons who may need the assistance of another person to move expeditiously to an exit if an emergency occurs;

(n) Procedures for performance planning that take into account take off, landing and en route conditions;

(o) An approved Destination Airport Analysis, when required by §91.1037(c), that includes the following elements, supported by aircraft performance data supplied by the aircraft manufacturer for the appropriate runway conditions—

(1) Pilot qualifications and experience;

(2) Aircraft performance data to include normal, abnormal and emergency procedures as supplied by the aircraft manufacturer;

(3) Airport facilities and topography;

(4) Runway conditions (including contamination);

(5) Airport or area weather reporting;

(6) Appropriate additional runway safety margins, if required;

(7) Airplane inoperative equipment;

(8) Environmental conditions; and

(9) Other criteria that affect aircraft performance.

(p) A suitable system (which may include a coded or electronic system) that provides for preservation and retrieval of maintenance recordkeeping information required by §91.1113 in a manner acceptable to the Administrator that provides—

(1) A description (or reference to date acceptable to the Administrator) of the work performed;

(2) The name of the person performing the work if the work is performed by a person outside the organization of the program manager; and

(3) The name or other positive identification of the individual approving the work.

(q) Flight locating and scheduling procedures; and

(r) Other procedures and policy instructions regarding program operations that are issued by the program manager or required by the Administrator.

[Docket No. FAA–2022–0912, Amdt. 91–368, 88 FR 34443, May 30, 2023]

§91.1027 Recordkeeping.

(a) Each program manager must keep at its principal base of operations or at other places approved by the Administrator, and must make available for inspection by the Administrator all of the following:

(1) The program manager's management specifications.

(2) A current list of the aircraft used or available for use in operations under this subpart, the operations for which each is equipped (for example, RNP5/10, RVSM).

(3) An individual record of each pilot used in operations under this subpart, including the following information:

(i) The full name of the pilot.

(ii) The pilot certificate (by type and number) and ratings that the pilot holds.

(iii) The pilot's aeronautical experience in sufficient detail to determine the pilot's qualifications to pilot aircraft in operations under this subpart.

(iv) The pilot's current duties and the date of the pilot's assignment to those duties.

(v) The effective date and class of the medical certificate that the pilot holds.

(vi) The date and result of each of the initial and recurrent competency tests and proficiency checks required by this subpart and the type of aircraft flown during that test or check.

(vii) The pilot's flight time in sufficient detail to determine compliance with the flight time limitations of this subpart.

(viii) The pilot's check pilot authorization, if any.

(ix) Any action taken concerning the pilot's release from employment for physical or professional disqualification; and

(x) The date of the satisfactory completion of initial, transition, upgrade, and differences training and each recurrent training phase required by this subpart.

(4) An individual record for each flight attendant used in operations under this subpart, including the following information:

(i) The full name of the flight attendant, and

(ii) The date and result of training required by §91.1063, as applicable.

(5) A current list of all fractional owners and associated aircraft. This list or a reference to its location must be included in the management specifications and should be of sufficient detail to determine the minimum fractional ownership interest of each aircraft.

(b) Each program manager must keep each record required by paragraph (a)(2) of this section for at least 6 months, and must keep each record required by paragraphs (a)(3) and (a)(4) of this section for at least 12 months. When an employee is no longer employed or affiliated with the program manager or fractional owner, each

record required by paragraphs (a)(3) and (a)(4) of this section must be retained for at least 12 months.

(c) Each program manager is responsible for the preparation and accuracy of a load manifest in duplicate containing information concerning the loading of the aircraft. The manifest must be prepared before each takeoff and must include—

(1) The number of passengers;

(2) The total weight of the loaded aircraft;

(3) The maximum allowable takeoff weight for that flight;

(4) The center of gravity limits;

(5) The center of gravity of the loaded aircraft, except that the actual center of gravity need not be computed if the aircraft is loaded according to a loading schedule or other approved method that ensures that the center of gravity of the loaded aircraft is within approved limits. In those cases, an entry must be made on the manifest indicating that the center of gravity is within limits according to a loading schedule or other approved method;

(6) The registration number of the aircraft or flight number;

(7) The origin and destination; and

(8) Identification of crewmembers and their crew position assignments.

(d) The pilot in command of the aircraft for which a load manifest must be prepared must carry a copy of the completed load manifest in the aircraft to its destination. The program manager must keep copies of completed load manifest for at least 30 days at its principal operations base, or at another location used by it and approved by the Administrator.

(e) Each program manager is responsible for providing a written document that states the name of the entity having operational control on that flight and the part of this chapter under which the flight is operated. The pilot in command of the aircraft must carry a copy of the document in the aircraft to its destination. The program manager must keep a copy of the document for at least 30 days at its principal operations base, or at another location used by it and approved by the Administrator.

(f) Records may be kept either in paper or other form acceptable to the Administrator.

(g) Program managers that are also certificated to operate under part 121 or 135 of this chapter may satisfy the recordkeeping requirements of this section and of §91.1113 with records maintained to fulfill equivalent obligations under part 121 or 135 of this chapter.

[Docket No. FAA–2001–10047, 68 FR 54561, Sept. 17, 2003; as amended by Docket FAA–2016–9154, Amdt. 91–348, 82 FR 39664, Aug. 22, 2017]

§91.1029 Flight scheduling and locating requirements.

(a) Each program manager must establish and use an adequate system to schedule and release program aircraft.

(b) Except as provided in paragraph (d) of this section, each program manager must have adequate procedures established for locating each flight, for which a flight plan is not filed, that—

(1) Provide the program manager with at least the information required to be included in a VFR flight plan;

(2) Provide for timely notification of an FAA facility or search and rescue facility, if an aircraft is overdue or missing; and

(3) Provide the program manager with the location, date, and estimated time for reestablishing radio or telephone communications, if the flight will operate in an area where communications cannot be maintained.

(c) Flight locating information must be retained at the program manager's principal base of operations, or at other places designated by the program manager in the flight locating procedures, until the completion of the flight.

(d) The flight locating requirements of paragraph (b) of this section do not apply to a flight for which an FAA flight plan has been filed and the flight plan is canceled within 25 nautical miles of the destination airport.

§91.1031 Pilot in command or second in command: Designation required.

(a) Each program manager must designate a—
(1) Pilot in command for each program flight; and
(2) Second in command for each program flight requiring two pilots.

(b) The pilot in command, as designated by the program manager, must remain the pilot in command at all times during that flight.

§91.1033 Operating information required.

(a) Each program manager must, for all program operations, provide the following materials, in current and appropriate form, accessible to the pilot at the pilot station, and the pilot must use them—

(1) A cockpit checklist;

(2) For multiengine aircraft or for aircraft with retractable landing gear, an emergency cockpit checklist containing the procedures required by paragraph (c) of this section, as appropriate;

(3) At least one set of pertinent aeronautical charts; and

(4) For IFR operations, at least one set of pertinent navigational en route, terminal area, and instrument approach procedure charts.

(b) Each cockpit checklist required by paragraph (a)(1) of this section must contain the following procedures:
(1) Before starting engines;
(2) Before takeoff;
(3) Cruise;
(4) Before landing;
(5) After landing; and
(6) Stopping engines.

(c) Each emergency cockpit checklist required by paragraph (a)(2) of this section must contain the following procedures, as appropriate:
(1) Emergency operation of fuel, hydraulic, electrical, and mechanical systems.
(2) Emergency operation of instruments and controls.
(3) Engine inoperative procedures.
(4) Any other emergency procedures necessary for safety.

§91.1035 Passenger awareness.

(a) Prior to each takeoff, the pilot in command of an aircraft carrying passengers on a program flight must ensure that all passengers have been orally briefed on—

(1) *Smoking:* Each passenger must be briefed on when, where, and under what conditions smoking is prohibited. This briefing must include a statement, as appropriate, that the regulations require passenger compliance with lighted passenger information signs and no smoking placards, prohibit smoking in lavatories, and require compliance with crewmember instructions with regard to these items;

(2) *Use of safety belts, shoulder harnesses, and child restraint systems:* Each passenger must be briefed on when, where and under what conditions it is necessary to have his or her safety belt and, if installed, his or her shoulder harness fastened about him or her, and if a child is being transported, the appropriate use of child restraint systems, if available. This briefing must include a statement, as appropriate, that the regulations require passenger compliance with the lighted passenger information sign and/or crewmember instructions with regard to these items;

(3) The placement of seat backs in an upright position before takeoff and landing;

(4) Location and means for opening the passenger entry door and emergency exits;

(5) Location of survival equipment;

(6) Ditching procedures and the use of flotation equipment required under §91.509 for a flight over water;

(7) The normal and emergency use of oxygen installed in the aircraft; and

(8) Location and operation of fire extinguishers.

(b) Prior to each takeoff, the pilot in command of an aircraft carrying passengers on a program flight must ensure that each person who may

need the assistance of another person to move expeditiously to an exit if an emergency occurs and that person's attendant, if any, has received a briefing as to the procedures to be followed if an evacuation occurs. This paragraph does not apply to a person who has been given a briefing before a previous leg of that flight in the same aircraft.

(c) Prior to each takeoff, the pilot in command must advise the passengers of the name of the entity in operational control of the flight.

(d) The oral briefings required by paragraphs (a), (b), and (c) of this section must be given by the pilot in command or another crewmember.

(e) The oral briefing required by paragraph (a) of this section may be delivered by means of an approved recording playback device that is audible to each passenger under normal noise levels.

(f) The oral briefing required by paragraph (a) of this section must be supplemented by printed cards that must be carried in the aircraft in locations convenient for the use of each passenger. The cards must—

(1) Be appropriate for the aircraft on which they are to be used;

(2) Contain a diagram of, and method of operating, the emergency exits; and

(3) Contain other instructions necessary for the use of emergency equipment on board the aircraft.

§91.1037 Large transport category airplanes: Turbine engine powered; Limitations; Destination and alternate airports.

(a) No program manager or any other person may permit a turbine engine powered large transport category airplane on a program flight to take off that airplane at a weight that (allowing for normal consumption of fuel and oil in flight to the destination or alternate airport) the weight of the airplane on arrival would exceed the landing weight in the Airplane Flight Manual for the elevation of the destination or alternate airport and the ambient temperature expected at the time of landing.

(b) Except as provided in paragraph (c) of this section, no program manager or any other person may permit a turbine engine powered large transport category airplane on a program flight to take off that airplane unless its weight on arrival, allowing for normal consumption of fuel and oil in flight (in accordance with the landing distance in the Airplane Flight Manual for the elevation of the destination airport and the wind conditions expected there at the time of landing), would allow a full stop landing at the intended destination airport within 60 percent of the effective length of each runway described below from a point 50 feet above the intersection of the obstruction clearance plane and the runway. For the purpose of

determining the allowable landing weight at the destination airport, the following is assumed:

(1) The airplane is landed on the most favorable runway and in the most favorable direction, in still air.

(2) The airplane is landed on the most suitable runway considering the probable wind velocity and direction and the ground handling characteristics of that airplane, and considering other conditions such as landing aids and terrain.

(c) A program manager or other person flying a turbine engine powered large transport category airplane on a program flight may permit that airplane to take off at a weight in excess of that allowed by paragraph (b) of this section if all of the following conditions exist:

(1) The operation is conducted in accordance with an approved Destination Airport Analysis in that person's program operating manual that contains the elements listed in §91.1025(o).

(2) The airplane's weight on arrival, allowing for normal consumption of fuel and oil in flight (in accordance with the landing distance in the Airplane Flight Manual for the elevation of the destination airport and the wind conditions expected there at the time of landing), would allow a full stop landing at the intended destination airport within 80 percent of the effective length of each runway described below from a point 50 feet above the intersection of the obstruction clearance plane and the runway. For the purpose of determining the allowable landing weight at the destination airport, the following is assumed:

(i) The airplane is landed on the most favorable runway and in the most favorable direction, in still air.

(ii) The airplane is landed on the most suitable runway considering the probable wind velocity and direction and the ground handling characteristics of that airplane, and considering other conditions such as landing aids and terrain.

(3) The operation is authorized by management specifications.

(d) No program manager or other person may select an airport as an alternate airport for a turbine engine powered large transport category airplane unless (based on the assumptions in paragraph (b) of this section) that airplane, at the weight expected at the time of arrival, can be brought to a full stop landing within 80 percent of the effective length of the runway from a point 50 feet above the intersection of the obstruction clearance plane and the runway.

(e) Unless, based on a showing of actual operating landing techniques on wet runways, a shorter landing distance (but never less than that required by paragraph (b) or (c) of this section) has been approved for a specific type and model airplane and included in the Airplane Flight Manual, no person may take off a turbojet airplane

when the appropriate weather reports or forecasts, or any combination of them, indicate that the runways at the destination or alternate airport may be wet or slippery at the estimated time of arrival unless the effective runway length at the destination airport is at least 115 percent of the runway length required under paragraph (b) or (c) of this section.

§91.1039 IFR takeoff, approach and landing minimums.

(a) No pilot on a program aircraft operating a program flight may begin an instrument approach procedure to an airport unless—

(1) Either that airport or the alternate airport has a weather reporting facility operated by the U.S. National Weather Service, a source approved by the U.S. National Weather Service, or a source approved by the Administrator; and

(2) The latest weather report issued by the weather reporting facility includes a current local altimeter setting for the destination airport. If no local altimeter setting is available at the destination airport, the pilot must obtain the current local altimeter setting from a source provided by the facility designated on the approach chart for the destination airport.

(b) For flight planning purposes, if the destination airport does not have a weather reporting facility described in paragraph (a)(1) of this section, the pilot must designate as an alternate an airport that has a weather reporting facility meeting that criteria.

(c) The MDA or Decision Altitude and visibility landing minimums prescribed in part 97 of this chapter or in the program manager's management specifications are increased by 100 feet and 1/2 mile respectively, but not to exceed the ceiling and visibility minimums for that airport when used as an alternate airport, for each pilot in command of a turbine-powered aircraft who has not served at least 100 hours as pilot in command in that type of aircraft.

(d) No person may take off an aircraft under IFR from an airport where weather conditions are at or above takeoff minimums but are below authorized IFR landing minimums unless there is an alternate airport within one hour's flying time (at normal cruising speed, in still air) of the airport of departure.

(e) Except as provided in §91.176 of this chapter, each pilot making an IFR takeoff or approach and landing at an airport must comply with applicable instrument approach procedures and takeoff and landing weather minimums prescribed by the authority having jurisdiction over the airport. In addition, no pilot may take off at that airport when the visibility is less than 600 feet, unless otherwise authorized in the program manager's management specifications for EFVS operations.

[Docket No. FAA–2001–10047, 68 FR 54561, Sept. 17, 2003; as amended by Docket FAA–2013–0485, Amdt. 91–345, 81 FR 90175, Dec. 13, 2016]

§91.1041 Aircraft proving and validation tests.

(a) No program manager may permit the operation of an aircraft, other than a turbojet aircraft, for which two pilots are required by the type certification requirements of this chapter for operations under VFR, if it has not previously proved such an aircraft in operations under this part in at least 25 hours of proving tests acceptable to the Administrator including—

(1) Five hours of night time, if night flights are to be authorized;

(2) Five instrument approach procedures under simulated or actual conditions, if IFR flights are to be authorized; and

(3) Entry into a representative number of en route airports as determined by the Administrator.

(b) No program manager may permit the operation of a turbojet airplane if it has not previously proved a turbojet airplane in operations under this part in at least 25 hours of proving tests acceptable to the Administrator including—

(1) Five hours of night time, if night flights are to be authorized;

(2) Five instrument approach procedures under simulated or actual conditions, if IFR flights are to be authorized; and

(3) Entry into a representative number of en route airports as determined by the Administrator.

(c) No program manager may carry passengers in an aircraft during proving tests, except those needed to make the tests and those designated by the Administrator to observe the tests. However, pilot flight training may be conducted during the proving tests.

(d) Validation testing is required to determine that a program manager is capable of conducting operations safely and in compliance with applicable regulatory standards. Validation tests are required for the following authorizations:

(1) The addition of an aircraft for which two pilots are required for operations under VFR or a turbojet airplane, if that aircraft or an aircraft of the same make or similar design has not been previously proved or validated in operations under this part.

(2) Operations outside U.S. airspace.

(3) Class II navigation authorizations.

(4) Special performance or operational authorizations.

(e) Validation tests must be accomplished by test methods acceptable to the Administrator. Actual flights may not be required when an applicant can demonstrate competence and compliance with appropriate regulations without conducting a flight.

(f) Proving tests and validation tests may be conducted simultaneously when appropriate.

(g) The Administrator may authorize deviations from this section if the Administrator finds that special circumstances make full compliance with this section unnecessary.

§91.1043 [Reserved]

§91.1045 Additional equipment requirements.

No person may operate a program aircraft on a program flight unless the aircraft is equipped with the following—

(a) Airplanes having a passenger-seat configuration of more than 30 seats or a payload capacity of more than 7,500 pounds:

(1) A cockpit voice recorder as required by §121.359 of this chapter as applicable to the aircraft specified in that section.

(2) A flight recorder as required by §121.343 or §121.344 of this chapter as applicable to the aircraft specified in that section.

(3) A terrain awareness and warning system as required by §121.354 of this chapter as applicable to the aircraft specified in that section.

(4) A traffic alert and collision avoidance system as required by §121.356 of this chapter as applicable to the aircraft specified in that section.

(5) Airborne weather radar as required by §121.357 of this chapter, as applicable to the aircraft specified in that section.

(b) Airplanes having a passenger-seat configuration of 30 seats or fewer, excluding each crewmember, and a payload capacity of 7,500 pounds or less, and any rotorcraft (as applicable):

(1) A cockpit voice recorder as required by §135.151 of this chapter as applicable to the aircraft specified in that section.

(2) A flight recorder as required by §135.152 of this chapter as applicable to the aircraft specified in that section.

(3) A terrain awareness and warning system as required by §135.154 of this chapter as applicable to the aircraft specified in that section.

(4) A traffic alert and collision avoidance system as required by §135.180 of this chapter as applicable to the aircraft specified in that section.

(5) As applicable to the aircraft specified in that section, either:

(i) Airborne thunderstorm detection equipment as required by §135.173 of this chapter; or

(ii) Airborne weather radar as required by §135.175 of this chapter.

§91.1047 Drug and alcohol misuse education program.

(a) Each program manager must provide each direct employee performing flight crewmember,

flight attendant, flight instructor, or aircraft maintenance duties with drug and alcohol misuse education.

(b) No program manager may use any contract employee to perform flight crewmember, flight attendant, flight instructor, or aircraft maintenance duties for the program manager unless that contract employee has been provided with drug and alcohol misuse education.

(c) Program managers must disclose to their owners and prospective owners the existence of a company drug and alcohol misuse testing program. If the program manager has implemented a company testing program, the program manager's disclosure must include the following:

(1) Information on the substances that they test for, for example, alcohol and a list of the drugs;

(2) The categories of employees tested, the types of tests, for example, pre-employment, random, reasonable cause/suspicion, post accident, return to duty and follow-up; and

(3) The degree to which the program manager's company testing program is comparable to the federally mandated drug and alcohol testing program required under part 120 of this chapter regarding the information in paragraphs (c)(1) and (c)(2) of this section.

(d) If a program aircraft is operated on a program flight into an airport at which no maintenance personnel are available that are subject to the requirements of paragraphs (a) or (b) of this section and emergency maintenance is required, the program manager may use persons not meeting the requirements of paragraphs (a) or (b) of this section to provide such emergency maintenance under both of the following conditions:

(1) The program manager must notify the Drug Abatement Program Division, AAM-800, 800 Independence Avenue, SW, Washington, DC 20591 in writing within 10 days after being provided emergency maintenance in accordance with this paragraph. The program manager must retain copies of all such written notifications for two years.

(2) The aircraft must be reinspected by maintenance personnel who meet the requirements of paragraph (a) or (b) of this section when the aircraft is next at an airport where such maintenance personnel are available.

(e) For purposes of this section, emergency maintenance means maintenance that—

(1) Is not scheduled, and

(2) Is made necessary by an aircraft condition not discovered prior to the departure for that location.

(f) Notwithstanding paragraphs (a) and (b) of this section, drug and alcohol misuse education conducted under an FAA-approved drug and alcohol misuse prevention program may be used to satisfy these requirements.

[Docket No. FAA–2001–10047, 68 FR 54561, Sept. 17, 2003; as amended by Amdt. 91–307, 74 FR 22653, May 14, 2009]

§91.1049 Personnel.

(a) Each program manager and each fractional owner must use in program operations on program aircraft flight crews meeting §91.1053 criteria and qualified under the appropriate regulations. The program manager must provide oversight of those crews.

(b) Each program manager must employ (either directly or by contract) an adequate number of pilots per program aircraft. Flight crew staffing must be determined based on the following factors, at a minimum:

(1) Number of program aircraft.

(2) Program manager flight, duty, and rest time considerations, and in all cases within the limits set forth in §§91.1057 through 91.1061.

(3) Vacations.

(4) Operational efficiencies.

(5) Training.

(6) Single pilot operations, if authorized by deviation under paragraph (d) of this section.

(c) Each program manager must publish pilot and flight attendant duty schedules sufficiently in advance to follow the flight, duty, and rest time limits in §§91.1057 through 91.1061 in program operations.

(d) Unless otherwise authorized by the Administrator, when any program aircraft is flown in program operations with passengers onboard, the crew must consist of at least two qualified pilots employed or contracted by the program manager or the fractional owner.

(e) The program manager must ensure that trained and qualified scheduling or flight release personnel are on duty to schedule and release program aircraft during all hours that such aircraft are available for program operations.

§91.1050 Employment of former FAA employees.

(a) Except as specified in paragraph (c) of this section, no fractional owner or fractional ownership program manager may knowingly employ or make a contractual arrangement which permits an individual to act as an agent or representative of the fractional owner or fractional ownership program manager in any matter before the Federal Aviation Administration if the individual, in the preceding 2 years—

(1) Served as, or was directly responsible for the oversight of, a Flight Standards Service aviation safety inspector; and

(2) Had direct responsibility to inspect, or oversee the inspection of, the operations of the fractional owner or fractional ownership program manager.

(b) For the purpose of this section, an individual shall be considered to be acting as an agent or representative of a fractional owner or fractional ownership program manager in a matter before the agency if the individual makes any written or oral communication on behalf of the fractional owner or fractional ownership program manager to the agency (or any of its officers or employees) in connection with a particular matter, whether or not involving a specific party and without regard to whether the individual has participated in, or had responsibility for, the particular matter while serving as a Flight Standards Service aviation safety inspector.

(c) The provisions of this section do not prohibit a fractional owner or fractional ownership program manager from knowingly employing or making a contractual arrangement which permits an individual to act as an agent or representative of the fractional owner or fractional ownership program manager in any matter before the Federal Aviation Administration if the individual was employed by the fractional owner or fractional ownership program manager before October 21, 2011.

[Docket No. FAA–2008–1154, 76 FR 52235, Aug. 22, 2011]

§91.1051 Pilot safety background check.

Within 90 days of an individual beginning service as a pilot, the program manager must request the following information:

(a) FAA records pertaining to—

(1) Current pilot certificates and associated type ratings.

(2) Current medical certificates.

(3) Summaries of legal enforcement actions resulting in a finding by the Administrator of a violation.

(b) Records from all previous employers during the five years preceding the date of the employment application where the applicant worked as a pilot. If any of these firms are in bankruptcy, the records must be requested from the trustees in bankruptcy for those employees. If the previous employer is no longer in business, a documented good faith effort must be made to obtain the records. Records from previous employers must include, as applicable—

(1) Crew member records.

(2) Drug testing—collection, testing, and rehabilitation records pertaining to the individual.

(3) Alcohol misuse prevention program records pertaining to the individual.

(4) The applicant's individual record that includes certifications, ratings, aeronautical experience, effective date and class of the medical certificate.

§91.1053 Crewmember experience.

(a) No program manager or owner may use any person, nor may any person serve, as a pilot in command or second in command of a program aircraft, or as a flight attendant on a program aircraft, in program operations under this subpart unless that person has met the applicable requirements of part 61 of this chapter and has the following experience and ratings:

(1) Total flight time for all pilots:

(i) Pilot in command—A minimum of 1,500 hours.

(ii) Second in command—A minimum of 500 hours.

(2) For multi-engine turbine-powered fixed-wing and powered-lift aircraft, the following FAA certification and ratings requirements:

(i) Pilot in command—Airline transport pilot and applicable type ratings.

(ii) Second in command—Commercial pilot and instrument ratings.

(iii) Flight attendant (if required or used)—Appropriately trained personnel.

(3) For all other aircraft, the following FAA certification and rating requirements:

(i) Pilot in command—Commercial pilot and instrument ratings.

(ii) Second in command—Commercial pilot and instrument ratings.

(iii) Flight attendant (if required or used)—Appropriately trained personnel.

(b) The Administrator may authorize deviations from paragraph (a)(1) of this section if the Flight Standards office that issued the program manager's management specifications finds that the crewmember has comparable experience, and can effectively perform the functions associated with the position in accordance with the requirements of this chapter. Grants of deviation under this paragraph may be granted after consideration of the size and scope of the operation, the qualifications of the intended personnel and the circumstances set forth in §91.1055(b)(1) through (3). The Administrator may, at any time, terminate any grant of deviation authority issued under this paragraph.

[Docket No. FAA–2001–10047, 68 FR 54561, Sept. 17, 2003; as amended by Docket FAA–2018–0119, Amdt. 91–350, 83 FR 9171, March 5, 2018]

§91.1055 Pilot operating limitations and pairing requirement.

(a) If the second in command of a fixed-wing program aircraft has fewer than 100 hours of flight time as second in command flying in the aircraft make and model and, if a type rating is required, in the type aircraft being flown, and the pilot in command is not an appropriately qualified check

pilot, the pilot in command shall make all takeoffs and landings in any of the following situations:

(1) Landings at the destination airport when a Destination Airport Analysis is required by §91.1037(c); and

(2) In any of the following conditions:

(i) The prevailing visibility for the airport is at or below 3/4 mile.

(ii) The runway visual range for the runway to be used is at or below 4,000 feet.

(iii) The runway to be used has water, snow, slush, ice or similar contamination that may adversely affect aircraft performance.

(iv) The braking action on the runway to be used is reported to be less than "good."

(v) The crosswind component for the runway to be used is in excess of 15 knots.

(vi) Windshear is reported in the vicinity of the airport.

(vii) Any other condition in which the pilot in command determines it to be prudent to exercise the pilot in command's authority.

(b) No program manager may release a program flight under this subpart unless, for that aircraft make or model and, if a type rating is required, for that type aircraft, either the pilot in command or the second in command has at least 75 hours of flight time, either as pilot in command or second in command. The Administrator may, upon application by the program manager, authorize deviations from the requirements of this paragraph by an appropriate amendment to the management specifications in any of the following circumstances:

(1) A newly authorized program manager does not employ any pilots who meet the minimum requirements of this paragraph.

(2) An existing program manager adds to its fleet a new category and class aircraft not used before in its operation.

(3) An existing program manager establishes a new base to which it assigns pilots who will be required to become qualified on the aircraft operated from that base.

(c) No person may be assigned in the capacity of pilot in command in a program operation to more than two aircraft types that require a separate type rating.

§91.1057 Flight, duty and rest time requirements: All crewmembers.

(a) For purposes of this subpart—

Augmented flight crew means at least three pilots.

Calendar day means the period of elapsed time, using Coordinated Universal Time or local time that begins at midnight and ends 24 hours later at the next midnight.

Duty period means the period of elapsed time between reporting for an assignment involving flight time and release from that assignment by the program manager. All time between these two points is part of the duty period, even if flight time is interrupted by nonflight-related duties. The time is calculated using either Coordinated Universal Time or local time to reflect the total elapsed time.

Extension of flight time means an increase in the flight time because of circumstances beyond the control of the program manager or flight crewmember (such as adverse weather) that are not known at the time of departure and that prevent the flightcrew from reaching the destination within the planned flight time.

Flight attendant means an individual, other than a flight crewmember, who is assigned by the program manager, in accordance with the required minimum crew complement under the program manager's management specifications or in addition to that minimum complement, to duty in an aircraft during flight time and whose duties include but are not necessarily limited to cabin-safety-related responsibilities.

Multi-time zone flight means an easterly or westerly flight or multiple flights in one direction in the same duty period that results in a time zone difference of 5 or more hours and is conducted in a geographic area that is south of 60 degrees north latitude and north of 60 degrees south latitude.

Reserve status means that status in which a flight crewmember, by arrangement with the program manager: Holds himself or herself fit to fly to the extent that this is within the control of the flight crewmember; remains within a reasonable response time of the aircraft as agreed between the flight crewmember and the program manager; and maintains a ready means whereby the flight crewmember may be contacted by the program manager. Reserve status is not part of any duty period or rest period.

Rest period means a period of time required pursuant to this subpart that is free of all responsibility for work or duty prior to the commencement of, or following completion of, a duty period, and during which the flight crewmember or flight attendant cannot be required to receive contact from the program manager. A rest period does not include any time during which the program manager imposes on a flight crewmember or flight attendant any duty or restraint, including any actual work or present responsibility for work should the occasion arise.

Standby means that portion of a duty period during which a flight crewmember is subject to the control of the program manager and holds himself or herself in a condition of readiness to undertake a flight. Standby is not part of any rest period.

(b) A program manager may assign a crewmember and a crewmember may accept an assignment for flight time only when the applicable requirements of this section and §§91.1059–91.1062 are met.

(c) No program manager may assign any crewmember to any duty during any required rest period.

(d) Time spent in transportation, not local in character, that a program manager requires of a crewmember and provides to transport the crewmember to an airport at which he or she is to serve on a flight as a crewmember, or from an airport at which he or she was relieved from duty to return to his or her home station, is not considered part of a rest period.

(e) A flight crewmember may continue a flight assignment if the flight to which he or she is assigned would normally terminate within the flight time limitations, but because of circumstances beyond the control of the program manager or flight crewmember (such as adverse weather conditions), is not at the time of departure expected to reach its destination within the planned flight time. The extension of flight time under this paragraph may not exceed the maximum time limits set forth in §91.1059.

(f) Each flight assignment must provide for at least 10 consecutive hours of rest during the 24-hour period that precedes the completion time of the assignment.

(g) The program manager must provide each crewmember at least 13 rest periods of at least 24 consecutive hours each in each calendar quarter.

(h) A flight crewmember may decline a flight assignment if, in the flight crewmember's determination, to do so would not be consistent with the standard of safe operation required under this subpart, this part, and applicable provisions of this title.

(i) Any rest period required by this subpart may occur concurrently with any other rest period.

(j) If authorized by the Administrator, a program manager may use the applicable unscheduled flight time limitations, duty period limitations, and rest requirements of part 121 or part 135 of this chapter instead of the flight time limitations, duty period limitations, and rest requirements of this subpart.

§91.1059 Flight time limitations and rest requirements: One or two pilot crews.

(a) No program manager may assign any flight crewmember, and no flight crewmember may accept an assignment, for flight time as a member of a one- or two-pilot crew if that crewmember's total flight time in all commercial flying will exceed—

(1) 500 hours in any calendar quarter;

(2) 800 hours in any two consecutive calendar quarters;

(3) 1,400 hours in any calendar year.

(b) Except as provided in paragraph (c) of this section, during any 24 consecutive hours the total flight time of the assigned flight, when added to any commercial flying by that flight crewmember, may not exceed—

(1) 8 hours for a flight crew consisting of one pilot; or

(2) 10 hours for a flight crew consisting of two pilots qualified under this subpart for the operation being conducted.

(c) No program manager may assign any flight crewmember, and no flight crewmember may accept an assignment, if that crewmember's flight time or duty period will exceed, or rest time will be less than—

	Normal duty	Extension of flight time
(1) Minimum Rest Immediately Before Duty	10 hours	10 hours
(2) Duty Period	Up to 14 hours	Up to 14 hours
(3) Flight Time For 1 Pilot	Up to 8 hours	Exceeding 8 hours up to 9 hours
(4) Flight Time For 2 Pilots	Up to 10 hours	Exceeding 10 hours up to 12 hours
(5) Minimum After Duty Rest	10 hours	12 hours
(6) Minimum After Duty Rest Period for Multi-Time Zone Flights	14 hours	18 hours

§91.1061 Augmented flight crews.

(a) No program manager may assign any flight crewmember, and no flight crewmember may accept an assignment, for flight time as a member of an augmented crew if that crewmember's total flight time in all commercial flying will exceed—

(1) 500 hours in any calendar quarter;

(2) 800 hours in any two consecutive calendar quarters;

(3) 1,400 hours in any calendar year.

(b) No program manager may assign any pilot to an augmented crew, unless the program manager ensures:

(1) Adequate sleeping facilities are installed on the aircraft for the pilots.

(2) No more than 8 hours of flight deck duty is accrued in any 24 consecutive hours.

(3) For a three-pilot crew, the crew must consist of at least the following:

(i) A pilot in command (PIC) who meets the applicable flight crewmember requirements of this subpart and §61.57 of this chapter.

(ii) A PIC qualified pilot who meets the applicable flight crewmember requirements of this subpart and §61.57(c) and (d) of this chapter.

(iii) A second in command (SIC) who meets the SIC qualifications of this subpart. For flight under IFR, that person must also meet the recent instrument experience requirements of part 61 of this chapter.

(4) For a four-pilot crew, at least three pilots who meet the conditions of paragraph (b)(3) of this section, plus a fourth pilot who meets the SIC qualifications of this subpart. For flight under IFR, that person must also meet the recent instrument experience requirements of part 61 of this chapter.

(c) No program manager may assign any flight crewmember, and no flight crewmember may accept an assignment, if that crewmember's flight time or duty period will exceed, or rest time will be less than—

	3-Pilot Crew	4-Pilot Crew
(1) Minimum Rest Immediately Before Duty	10 hours	10 hours
(2) Duty Period	Up to 16 hours	Up to 18 hours
(3) Flight Time	Up to 12 hours	Up to 16 hours
(4) Minimum After Duty Rest	12 hours	18 hours
(5) Minimum After Duty Rest Period for Multi-Time Zone Flights	18 hours	24 hours

§91.1062 Duty periods and rest requirements: Flight attendants.

(a) Except as provided in paragraph (b) of this section, a program manager may assign a duty period to a flight attendant only when the assignment meets the applicable duty period limitations and rest requirements of this paragraph.

(1) Except as provided in paragraphs (a)(4), (a)(5), and (a)(6) of this section, no program manager may assign a flight attendant to a scheduled duty period of more than 14 hours.

(2) Except as provided in paragraph (a)(3) of this section, a flight attendant scheduled to a duty period of 14 hours or less as provided under paragraph (a)(1) of this section must be given a scheduled rest period of at least 9 consecutive hours. This rest period must occur between the completion of the scheduled duty period and the commencement of the subsequent duty period.

(3) The rest period required under paragraph (a)(2) of this section may be scheduled or reduced to 8 consecutive hours if the flight attendant is provided a subsequent rest period of at least 10 consecutive hours; this subsequent rest period

must be scheduled to begin no later than 24 hours after the beginning of the reduced rest period and must occur between the completion of the scheduled duty period and the commencement of the subsequent duty period.

(4) A program manager may assign a flight attendant to a scheduled duty period of more than 14 hours, but no more than 16 hours, if the program manager has assigned to the flight or flights in that duty period at least one flight attendant in addition to the minimum flight attendant complement required for the flight or flights in that duty period under the program manager's management specifications.

(5) A program manager may assign a flight attendant to a scheduled duty period of more than 16 hours, but no more than 18 hours, if the program manager has assigned to the flight or flights in that duty period at least two flight attendants in addition to the minimum flight attendant complement required for the flight or flights in that duty period under the program manager's management specifications.

(6) A program manager may assign a flight attendant to a scheduled duty period of more than 18 hours, but no more than 20 hours, if the scheduled duty period includes one or more flights that land or take off outside the 48 contiguous states and the District of Columbia, and if the program manager has assigned to the flight or flights in that duty period at least three flight attendants in addition to the minimum flight attendant complement required for the flight or flights in that duty period under the program manager's management specifications.

(7) Except as provided in paragraph (a)(8) of this section, a flight attendant scheduled to a duty period of more than 14 hours but no more than 20 hours, as provided in paragraphs (a)(4), (a)(5), and (a)(6) of this section, must be given a scheduled rest period of at least 12 consecutive hours. This rest period must occur between the completion of the scheduled duty period and the commencement of the subsequent duty period.

(8) The rest period required under paragraph (a)(7) of this section may be scheduled or reduced to 10 consecutive hours if the flight attendant is provided a subsequent rest period of at least 14 consecutive hours; this subsequent rest period must be scheduled to begin no later than 24 hours after the beginning of the reduced rest period and must occur between the completion of the scheduled duty period and the commencement of the subsequent duty period.

(9) Notwithstanding paragraphs (a)(4), (a)(5), and (a)(6) of this section, if a program manager elects to reduce the rest period to 10 hours as authorized by paragraph (a)(8) of this section, the program manager may not schedule a flight attendant for a duty period of more than 14 hours

during the 24-hour period commencing after the beginning of the reduced rest period.

(b) Notwithstanding paragraph (a) of this section, a program manager may apply the flight crewmember flight time and duty limitations and rest requirements of this part to flight attendants for all operations conducted under this part provided that the program manager establishes written procedures that—

(1) Apply to all flight attendants used in the program manager's operation;

(2) Include the flight crewmember rest and duty requirements of §§91.1057, 91.1059, and 91.1061, as appropriate to the operation being conducted, except that rest facilities on board the aircraft are not required;

(3) Include provisions to add one flight attendant to the minimum flight attendant complement for each flight crewmember who is in excess of the minimum number required in the aircraft type certificate data sheet and who is assigned to the aircraft under the provisions of §91.1061; and

(4) Are approved by the Administrator and described or referenced in the program manager's management specifications.

§91.1063 Testing and training: Applicability and terms used.

(a) Sections 91.1065 through 91.1107:

(1) Prescribe the tests and checks required for pilots and flight attendant crewmembers and for the approval of check pilots in operations under this subpart;

(2) Prescribe the requirements for establishing and maintaining an approved training program for crewmembers, check pilots and instructors, and other operations personnel employed or used by the program manager in program operations;

(3) Prescribe the requirements for the qualification, approval and use of aircraft simulators and flight training devices in the conduct of an approved training program; and

(4) Permits training center personnel authorized under part 142 of this chapter who meet the requirements of §91.1075 to conduct training, testing and checking under contract or other arrangements to those persons subject to the requirements of this subpart.

(b) If authorized by the Administrator, a program manager may comply with the applicable training and testing sections of part 121, subparts N and O of this chapter instead of §§91.1065 through 91.1107, provided that the following additional limitations and allowances apply to program managers so authorized:

(1) *Operating experience and operations familiarization.* Program managers are not required to comply with the operating experience requirements of §121.434 or the operations familiarization requirements of §121.435 of this chapter.

(2) *Upgrade training.* (i) Each program manager must include in upgrade ground training for pilots, instruction in at least the subjects identified in §121.419(a) of this chapter, as applicable to their assigned duties; and, for pilots serving in crews of two or more pilots, beginning on April 27, 2022, instruction and facilitated discussion in the subjects identified in §121.419(c) of this chapter.

(ii) Each program manager must include in upgrade flight training for pilots, flight training for the maneuvers and procedures required in §121.424(a), (c), (e), and (f) of this chapter; and, for pilots serving in crews of two or more pilots, beginning on April 27, 2022, the flight training required in §121.424(b) of this chapter.

(3) *Initial and recurrent leadership and command and mentoring training.* Program managers are not required to include leadership and command training in §§121.409(b)(2)(ii)(B)*(6)*, 121.419(c)(1), 121.424(b) and 121.427(d)(1) of this chapter, and mentoring training in §§121.419(c)(2) and 121.427(d)(1) of this chapter in initial and recurrent training for pilots in command who serve in operations that use only one pilot.

(4) *One-time leadership and command and mentoring training.* §121.429 of this chapter does not apply to program managers conducting operations under this subpart when those operations use only one pilot.

(c) If authorized by the Administrator, a program manager may comply with the applicable training and testing sections of subparts G and H of part 135 of this chapter instead of §§91.1065 through 91.1107, except for the operating experience requirements of §135.244 of this chapter.

(d) For the purposes of this subpart, the following terms and definitions apply:

(1) *Initial training.* The training required for crewmembers who have not qualified and served in the same capacity on an aircraft.

(2) *Transition training.* The training required for crewmembers who have qualified and served in the same capacity on another aircraft.

(3) *Upgrade training.* The training required for crewmembers who have qualified and served as second in command on a particular aircraft type, before they serve as pilot in command on that aircraft.

(4) *Differences training.* The training required for crewmembers who have qualified and served on a particular type aircraft, when the Administrator finds differences training is necessary before a crewmember serves in the same capacity on a particular variation of that aircraft.

(5) *Recurrent training.* The training required for crewmembers to remain adequately trained and currently proficient for each aircraft crewmember position, and type of operation in which the crewmember serves.

(6) *In flight.* The maneuvers, procedures, or functions that will be conducted in the aircraft.

(7) *Training center.* An organization governed by the applicable requirements of part 142 of this chapter that conducts training, testing, and checking under contract or other arrangement to program managers subject to the requirements of this subpart.

(8) *Requalification training.* The training required for crewmembers previously trained and qualified, but who have become unqualified because of not having met within the required period any of the following:

(i) Recurrent crewmember training requirements of §91.1107.

(ii) Instrument proficiency check requirements of §91.1069.

(iii) Testing requirements of §91.1065.

(iv) Recurrent flight attendant testing requirements of §91.1067.

[Docket No. FAA–2001–10047, 68 FR 54561, Sept. 17, 2003; as amended by Amdt. 91–356, 85 FR 10921, Feb. 25, 2020]

§91.1065 Initial and recurrent pilot testing requirements.

(a) No program manager or owner may use a pilot, nor may any person serve as a pilot, unless, since the beginning of the 12th month before that service, that pilot has passed either a written or oral test (or a combination), given by the Administrator or an authorized check pilot, on that pilot's knowledge in the following areas—

(1) The appropriate provisions of parts 61 and 91 of this chapter and the management specifications and the operating manual of the program manager;

(2) For each type of aircraft to be flown by the pilot, the aircraft powerplant, major components and systems, major appliances, performance and operating limitations, standard and emergency operating procedures, and the contents of the accepted operating manual or equivalent, as applicable;

(3) For each type of aircraft to be flown by the pilot, the method of determining compliance with weight and balance limitations for takeoff, landing and en route operations;

(4) Navigation and use of air navigation aids appropriate to the operation or pilot authorization, including, when applicable, instrument approach facilities and procedures;

(5) Air traffic control procedures, including IFR procedures when applicable;

(6) Meteorology in general, including the principles of frontal systems, icing, fog, thunderstorms, and windshear, and, if appropriate for the operation of the program manager, high altitude weather;

(7) Procedures for—

(i) Recognizing and avoiding severe weather situations;

(ii) Escaping from severe weather situations, in case of inadvertent encounters, including low-altitude windshear (except that rotorcraft aircraft pilots are not required to be tested on escaping from low-altitude windshear); and

(iii) Operating in or near thunderstorms (including best penetration altitudes), turbulent air (including clear air turbulence), icing, hail, and other potentially hazardous meteorological conditions; and

(8) New equipment, procedures, or techniques, as appropriate.

(b) No program manager or owner may use a pilot, nor may any person serve as a pilot, in any aircraft unless, since the beginning of the 12th month before that service, that pilot has passed a competency check given by the Administrator or an authorized check pilot in that class of aircraft, if single-engine aircraft other than turbojet, or that type of aircraft, if rotorcraft, multiengine aircraft, or turbojet airplane, to determine the pilot's competence in practical skills and techniques in that aircraft or class of aircraft. The extent of the competency check will be determined by the Administrator or authorized check pilot conducting the competency check. The competency check may include any of the maneuvers and procedures currently required for the original issuance of the particular pilot certificate required for the operations authorized and appropriate to the category, class and type of aircraft involved. For the purposes of this paragraph, type, as to an airplane, means any one of a group of airplanes determined by the Administrator to have a similar means of propulsion, the same manufacturer, and no significantly different handling or flight characteristics. For the purposes of this paragraph, type, as to a rotorcraft, means a basic make and model.

(c) The instrument proficiency check required by §91.1069 may be substituted for the competency check required by this section for the type of aircraft used in the check.

(d) For the purpose of this subpart, competent performance of a procedure or maneuver by a person to be used as a pilot requires that the pilot be the obvious master of the aircraft, with the successful outcome of the maneuver never in doubt.

(e) The Administrator or authorized check pilot certifies the competency of each pilot who passes the knowledge or flight check in the program manager's pilot records.

(f) All or portions of a required competency check may be given in an aircraft simulator or other appropriate training device, if approved by the Administrator.

(g) If the program manager is authorized to conduct EFVS operations, the competency check

in paragraph (b) of this section must include tasks appropriate to the EFVS operations the certificate holder is authorized to conduct.

[Docket No. FAA–2001–10047, 68 FR 54561, Sept. 17, 2003; as amended by Docket FAA–2013–0485, Amdt. 91–345, 81 FR 90175, Dec. 13, 2016]

§91.1067 Initial and recurrent flight attendant crewmember testing requirements.

No program manager or owner may use a flight attendant crewmember, nor may any person serve as a flight attendant crewmember unless, since the beginning of the 12th month before that service, the program manager has determined by appropriate initial and recurrent testing that the person is knowledgeable and competent in the following areas as appropriate to assigned duties and responsibilities—

(a) Authority of the pilot in command;

(b) Passenger handling, including procedures to be followed in handling deranged persons or other persons whose conduct might jeopardize safety;

(c) Crewmember assignments, functions, and responsibilities during ditching and evacuation of persons who may need the assistance of another person to move expeditiously to an exit in an emergency;

(d) Briefing of passengers;

(e) Location and operation of portable fire extinguishers and other items of emergency equipment;

(f) Proper use of cabin equipment and controls;

(g) Location and operation of passenger oxygen equipment;

(h) Location and operation of all normal and emergency exits, including evacuation slides and escape ropes; and

(i) Seating of persons who may need assistance of another person to move rapidly to an exit in an emergency as prescribed by the program manager's operations manual.

§91.1069 Flight crew: Instrument proficiency check requirements.

(a) No program manager or owner may use a pilot, nor may any person serve, as a pilot in command of an aircraft under IFR unless, since the beginning of the 6th month before that service, that pilot has passed an instrument proficiency check under this section administered by the Administrator or an authorized check pilot.

(b) No program manager or owner may use a pilot, nor may any person serve, as a second command pilot of an aircraft under IFR unless, since the beginning of the 12th month before that service, that pilot has passed an instrument

proficiency check under this section administered by the Administrator or an authorized check pilot.

(c) No pilot may use any type of precision instrument approach procedure under IFR unless, since the beginning of the 6th month before that use, the pilot satisfactorily demonstrated that type of approach procedure. No pilot may use any type of nonprecision approach procedure under IFR unless, since the beginning of the 6th month before that use, the pilot has satisfactorily demonstrated either that type of approach procedure or any other two different types of nonprecision approach procedures. The instrument approach procedure or procedures must include at least one straight-in approach, one circling approach, and one missed approach. Each type of approach procedure demonstrated must be conducted to published minimums for that procedure.

(d) The instrument proficiency checks required by paragraphs (a) and (b) of this section consists of either an oral or written equipment test (or a combination) and a flight check under simulated or actual IFR conditions. The equipment test includes questions on emergency procedures, engine operation, fuel and lubrication systems, power settings, stall speeds, best engine-out speed, propeller and supercharger operations, and hydraulic, mechanical, and electrical systems, as appropriate. The flight check includes navigation by instruments, recovery from simulated emergencies, and standard instrument approaches involving navigational facilities which that pilot is to be authorized to use.

(e) Each pilot taking the instrument proficiency check must show that standard of competence required by §91.1065(d).

(1) The instrument proficiency check must—

(i) For a pilot in command of an aircraft requiring that the PIC hold an airline transport pilot certificate, include the procedures and maneuvers for an airline transport pilot certificate in the particular type of aircraft, if appropriate; and

(ii) For a pilot in command of a rotorcraft or a second in command of any aircraft requiring that the SIC hold a commercial pilot certificate include the procedures and maneuvers for a commercial pilot certificate with an instrument rating and, if required, for the appropriate type rating.

(2) The instrument proficiency check must be given by an authorized check pilot or by the Administrator.

(f) If the pilot is assigned to pilot only one type of aircraft, that pilot must take the instrument proficiency check required by paragraph (a) of this section in that type of aircraft.

(g) If the pilot in command is assigned to pilot more than one type of aircraft, that pilot must take the instrument proficiency check required by paragraph (a) of this section in each type of

aircraft to which that pilot is assigned, in rotation, but not more than one flight check during each period described in paragraph (a) of this section.

(h) If the pilot in command is assigned to pilot both single-engine and multiengine aircraft, that pilot must initially take the instrument proficiency check required by paragraph (a) of this section in a multiengine aircraft, and each succeeding check alternately in single-engine and multiengine aircraft, but not more than one flight check during each period described in paragraph (a) of this section.

(i) All or portions of a required flight check may be given in an aircraft simulator or other appropriate training device, if approved by the Administrator.

§91.1071 Crewmember: Tests and checks, grace provisions, training to accepted standards.

(a) If a crewmember who is required to take a test or a flight check under this subpart, completes the test or flight check in the month before or after the month in which it is required, that crewmember is considered to have completed the test or check in the month in which it is required.

(b) If a pilot being checked under this subpart fails any of the required maneuvers, the person giving the check may give additional training to the pilot during the course of the check. In addition to repeating the maneuvers failed, the person giving the check may require the pilot being checked to repeat any other maneuvers that are necessary to determine the pilot's proficiency. If the pilot being checked is unable to demonstrate satisfactory performance to the person conducting the check, the program manager may not use the pilot, nor may the pilot serve, as a flight crewmember in operations under this subpart until the pilot has satisfactorily completed the check. If a pilot who demonstrates unsatisfactory performance is employed as a pilot for a certificate holder operating under part 121, 125, or 135 of this chapter, he or she must notify that certificate holder of the unsatisfactory performance.

§91.1073 Training program: General.

(a) Each program manager must have a training program and must:

(1) Establish, obtain the appropriate initial and final approval of, and provide a training program that meets this subpart and that ensures that each crewmember, including each flight attendant if the program manager uses a flight attendant crewmember, flight instructor, check pilot, and each person assigned duties for the carriage and handling of hazardous materials (as defined in 49 CFR 171.8) is adequately trained to perform these assigned duties.

(2) Provide adequate ground and flight training facilities and properly qualified ground instructors for the training required by this subpart.

(3) Provide and keep current for each aircraft type used and, if applicable, the particular variations within the aircraft type, appropriate training material, examinations, forms, instructions, and procedures for use in conducting the training and checks required by this subpart.

(4) Provide enough flight instructors, check pilots, and simulator instructors to conduct required flight training and flight checks, and simulator training courses allowed under this subpart.

(b) Whenever a crewmember who is required to take recurrent training under this subpart completes the training in the month before, or the month after, the month in which that training is required, the crewmember is considered to have completed it in the month in which it was required.

(c) Each instructor, supervisor, or check pilot who is responsible for a particular ground training subject, segment of flight training, course of training, flight check, or competence check under this subpart must certify as to the proficiency and knowledge of the crewmember, flight instructor, or check pilot concerned upon completion of that training or check. That certification must be made a part of the crewmember's record. When the certification required by this paragraph is made by an entry in a computerized recordkeeping system, the certifying instructor, supervisor, or check pilot, must be identified with that entry. However, the signature of the certifying instructor, supervisor, or check pilot is not required for computerized entries.

(d) Training subjects that apply to more than one aircraft or crewmember position and that have been satisfactorily completed during previous training while employed by the program manager for another aircraft or another crewmember position, need not be repeated during subsequent training other than recurrent training.

(e) Aircraft simulators and other training devices may be used in the program manager's training program if approved by the Administrator.

(f) Each program manager is responsible for establishing safe and efficient crew management practices for all phases of flight in program operations including crew resource management training for all crewmembers used in program operations.

(g) If an aircraft simulator has been approved by the Administrator for use in the program manager's training program, the program manager must ensure that each pilot annually completes at least one flight training session in an approved simulator for at least one program aircraft. The training session may be the flight training portion of any of the pilot training or check requirements of this subpart, including the initial, transition,

upgrade, requalification, differences, or recurrent training, or the accomplishment of a competency check or instrument proficiency check. If there is no approved simulator for that aircraft type in operation, then all flight training and checking must be accomplished in the aircraft.

§91.1075 Training program: Special rules.

Other than the program manager, only the following are eligible under this subpart to conduct training, testing, and checking under contract or other arrangement to those persons subject to the requirements of this subpart.

(a) Another program manager operating under this subpart:

(b) A training center certificated under part 142 of this chapter to conduct training, testing, and checking required by this subpart if the training center—

(1) Holds applicable training specifications issued under part 142 of this chapter;

(2) Has facilities, training equipment, and courseware meeting the applicable requirements of part 142 of this chapter;

(3) Has approved curriculums, curriculum segments, and portions of curriculum segments applicable for use in training courses required by this subpart; and

(4) Has sufficient instructors and check pilots qualified under the applicable requirements of §§91.1089 through 91.1095 to conduct training, testing, and checking to persons subject to the requirements of this subpart.

(c) A part 119 certificate holder operating under part 121 or part 135 of this chapter.

(d) As authorized by the Administrator, a training center that is not certificated under part 142 of this chapter.

§91.1077 Training program and revision: Initial and final approval.

(a) To obtain initial and final approval of a training program, or a revision to an approved training program, each program manager must submit to the Administrator—

(1) An outline of the proposed or revised curriculum, that provides enough information for a preliminary evaluation of the proposed training program or revision; and

(2) Additional relevant information that may be requested by the Administrator.

(b) If the proposed training program or revision complies with this subpart, the Administrator grants initial approval in writing after which the program manager may conduct the training under that program. The Administrator then evaluates the effectiveness of the training program and

91

advises the program manager of deficiencies, if any, that must be corrected.

(c) The Administrator grants final approval of the proposed training program or revision if the program manager shows that the training conducted under the initial approval in paragraph (b) of this section ensures that each person who successfully completes the training is adequately trained to perform that person's assigned duties.

(d) Whenever the Administrator finds that revisions are necessary for the continued adequacy of a training program that has been granted final approval, the program manager must, after notification by the Administrator, make any changes in the program that are found necessary by the Administrator. Within 30 days after the program manager receives the notice, it may file a petition to reconsider the notice with the Administrator. The filing of a petition to reconsider stays the notice pending a decision by the Administrator. However, if the Administrator finds that there is an emergency that requires immediate action in the interest of safety, the Administrator may, upon a statement of the reasons, require a change effective without stay.

§91.1079 Training program: Curriculum.

(a) Each program manager must prepare and keep current a written training program curriculum for each type of aircraft for each crewmember required for that type aircraft. The curriculum must include ground and flight training required by this subpart.

(b) Each training program curriculum must include the following:

(1) A list of principal ground training subjects, including emergency training subjects, that are provided.

(2) A list of all the training devices, mock-ups, systems trainers, procedures trainers, or other training aids that the program manager will use.

(3) Detailed descriptions or pictorial displays of the approved normal, abnormal, and emergency maneuvers, procedures and functions that will be performed during each flight training phase or flight check, indicating those maneuvers, procedures and functions that are to be performed during the inflight portions of flight training and flight checks.

§91.1081 Crewmember training requirements.

(a) Each program manager must include in its training program the following initial and transition ground training as appropriate to the particular assignment of the crewmember:

(1) Basic indoctrination ground training for newly hired crewmembers including instruction in at least the—

(i) Duties and responsibilities of crewmembers as applicable;

(ii) Appropriate provisions of this chapter;

(iii) Contents of the program manager's management specifications (not required for flight attendants); and

(iv) Appropriate portions of the program manager's operating manual.

(2) The initial and transition ground training in §§91.1101 and 91.1105, as applicable.

(3) Emergency training in §91.1083.

(b) Each training program must provide the initial and transition flight training in §91.1103, as applicable.

(c) Each training program must provide recurrent ground and flight training as provided in §91.1107.

(d) Upgrade training in §§91.1101 and 91.1103 for a particular type aircraft may be included in the training program for crewmembers who have qualified and served as second in command on that aircraft.

(e) In addition to initial, transition, upgrade and recurrent training, each training program must provide ground and flight training, instruction, and practice necessary to ensure that each crewmember—

(1) Remains adequately trained and currently proficient for each aircraft, crewmember position, and type of operation in which the crewmember serves; and

(2) Qualifies in new equipment, facilities, procedures, and techniques, including modifications to aircraft.

§91.1083 Crewmember emergency training.

(a) Each training program must provide emergency training under this section for each aircraft type, model, and configuration, each crewmember, and each kind of operation conducted, as appropriate for each crewmember and the program manager.

(b) Emergency training must provide the following:

(1) Instruction in emergency assignments and procedures, including coordination among crewmembers.

(2) Individual instruction in the location, function, and operation of emergency equipment including—

(i) Equipment used in ditching and evacuation;

(ii) First aid equipment and its proper use; and

(iii) Portable fire extinguishers, with emphasis on the type of extinguisher to be used on different classes of fires.

(3) Instruction in the handling of emergency situations including—

(i) Rapid decompression;

(ii) Fire in flight or on the surface and smoke control procedures with emphasis on electrical equipment and related circuit breakers found in cabin areas;

(iii) Ditching and evacuation;

(iv) Illness, injury, or other abnormal situations involving passengers or crewmembers; and

(v) Hijacking and other unusual situations.

(4) Review and discussion of previous aircraft accidents and incidents involving actual emergency situations.

(c) Each crewmember must perform at least the following emergency drills, using the proper emergency equipment and procedures, unless the Administrator finds that, for a particular drill, the crewmember can be adequately trained by demonstration:

(1) Ditching, if applicable.

(2) Emergency evacuation.

(3) Fire extinguishing and smoke control.

(4) Operation and use of emergency exits, including deployment and use of evacuation slides, if applicable.

(5) Use of crew and passenger oxygen.

(6) Removal of life rafts from the aircraft, inflation of the life rafts, use of lifelines, and boarding of passengers and crew, if applicable.

(7) Donning and inflation of life vests and the use of other individual flotation devices, if applicable.

(d) Crewmembers who serve in operations above 25,000 feet must receive instruction in the following:

(1) Respiration.

(2) Hypoxia.

(3) Duration of consciousness without supplemental oxygen at altitude.

(4) Gas expansion.

(5) Gas bubble formation.

(6) Physical phenomena and incidents of decompression.

§91.1085 Hazardous materials recognition training.

No program manager may use any person to perform, and no person may perform, any assigned duties and responsibilities for the handling or carriage of hazardous materials (as defined in 49 CFR 171.8), unless that person has received training in the recognition of hazardous materials.

§91.1087 Approval of aircraft simulators and other training devices.

(a) Training courses using aircraft simulators and other training devices may be included in the program manager's training program if approved by the Administrator.

(b) Each aircraft simulator and other training device that is used in a training course or in

checks required under this subpart must meet the following requirements:

(1) It must be specifically approved for—

(i) The program manager; and

(ii) The particular maneuver, procedure, or crewmember function involved.

(2) It must maintain the performance, functional, and other characteristics that are required for approval.

(3) Additionally, for aircraft simulators, it must be—

(i) Approved for the type aircraft and, if applicable, the particular variation within type for which the training or check is being conducted; and

(ii) Modified to conform with any modification to the aircraft being simulated that changes the performance, functional, or other characteristics required for approval.

(c) A particular aircraft simulator or other training device may be used by more than one program manager.

(d) In granting initial and final approval of training programs or revisions to them, the Administrator considers the training devices, methods, and procedures listed in the program manager's curriculum under §91.1079.

§91.1089 Qualifications: Check pilots (aircraft) and check pilots (simulator).

(a) For the purposes of this section and §91.1093:

(1) A check pilot (aircraft) is a person who is qualified to conduct flight checks in an aircraft, in a flight simulator, or in a flight training device for a particular type aircraft.

(2) A check pilot (simulator) is a person who is qualified to conduct flight checks, but only in a flight simulator, in a flight training device, or both, for a particular type aircraft.

(3) Check pilots (aircraft) and check pilots (simulator) are those check pilots who perform the functions described in §91.1073(a)(4) and (c).

(b) No program manager may use a person, nor may any person serve as a check pilot (aircraft) in a training program established under this subpart unless, with respect to the aircraft type involved, that person—

(1) Holds the pilot certificates and ratings required to serve as a pilot in command in operations under this subpart;

(2) Has satisfactorily completed the training phases for the aircraft, including recurrent training, that are required to serve as a pilot in command in operations under this subpart;

(3) Has satisfactorily completed the proficiency or competency checks that are required to serve as a pilot in command in operations under this subpart;

(4) Has satisfactorily completed the applicable training requirements of §91.1093;

(5) Holds at least a Class III medical certificate unless serving as a required crewmember, in which case holds a Class I or Class II medical certificate as appropriate; and

(6) Has been approved by the Administrator for the check pilot duties involved.

(c) No program manager may use a person, nor may any person serve as a check pilot (simulator) in a training program established under this subpart unless, with respect to the aircraft type involved, that person meets the provisions of paragraph (b) of this section, or—

(1) Holds the applicable pilot certificates and ratings, except medical certificate, required to serve as a pilot in command in operations under this subpart;

(2) Has satisfactorily completed the appropriate training phases for the aircraft, including recurrent training, that are required to serve as a pilot in command in operations under this subpart;

(3) Has satisfactorily completed the appropriate proficiency or competency checks that are required to serve as a pilot in command in operations under this subpart;

(4) Has satisfactorily completed the applicable training requirements of §91.1093; and

(5) Has been approved by the Administrator for the check pilot (simulator) duties involved.

(d) Completion of the requirements in paragraphs (b)(2), (3), and (4) or (c)(2), (3), and (4) of this section, as applicable, must be entered in the individual's training record maintained by the program manager.

(e) A check pilot who does not hold an appropriate medical certificate may function as a check pilot (simulator), but may not serve as a flightcrew member in operations under this subpart.

(f) A check pilot (simulator) must accomplish the following—

(1) Fly at least two flight segments as a required crewmember for the type, class, or category aircraft involved within the 12-month period preceding the performance of any check pilot duty in a flight simulator; or

(2) Before performing any check pilot duty in a flight simulator, satisfactorily complete an approved line-observation program within the period prescribed by that program.

(g) The flight segments or line-observation program required in paragraph (f) of this section are considered to be completed in the month required if completed in the month before or the month after the month in which they are due.

§91.1091 Qualifications: Flight instructors (aircraft) and flight instructors (simulator).

(a) For the purposes of this section and §91.1095:

(1) A flight instructor (aircraft) is a person who is qualified to instruct in an aircraft, in a flight simulator, or in a flight training device for a particular type, class, or category aircraft.

(2) A flight instructor (simulator) is a person who is qualified to instruct in a flight simulator, in a flight training device, or in both, for a particular type, class, or category aircraft.

(3) Flight instructors (aircraft) and flight instructors (simulator) are those instructors who perform the functions described in §91.1073(a)(4) and (c).

(b) No program manager may use a person, nor may any person serve as a flight instructor (aircraft) in a training program established under this subpart unless, with respect to the type, class, or category aircraft involved, that person—

(1) Holds the pilot certificates and ratings required to serve as a pilot in command in operations under this subpart or part 121 or 135 of this chapter;

(2) Has satisfactorily completed the training phases for the aircraft, including recurrent training, that are required to serve as a pilot in command in operations under this subpart;

(3) Has satisfactorily completed the proficiency or competency checks that are required to serve as a pilot in command in operations under this subpart;

(4) Has satisfactorily completed the applicable training requirements of §91.1095; and

(5) Holds at least a Class III medical certificate.

(c) No program manager may use a person, nor may any person serve as a flight instructor (simulator) in a training program established under this subpart, unless, with respect to the type, class, or category aircraft involved, that person meets the provisions of paragraph (b) of this section, or—

(1) Holds the pilot certificates and ratings, except medical certificate, required to serve as a pilot in command in operations under this subpart or part 121 or 135 of this chapter;

(2) Has satisfactorily completed the appropriate training phases for the aircraft, including recurrent training, that are required to serve as a pilot in command in operations under this subpart;

(3) Has satisfactorily completed the appropriate proficiency or competency checks that are required to serve as a pilot in command in operations under this subpart; and

(4) Has satisfactorily completed the applicable training requirements of §91.1095.

(d) Completion of the requirements in paragraphs (b)(2), (3), and (4) or (c)(2), (3), and (4) of this section, as applicable, must be entered in the

individual's training record maintained by the program manager.

(e) A pilot who does not hold a medical certificate may function as a flight instructor in an aircraft if functioning as a non-required crewmember, but may not serve as a flightcrew member in operations under this subpart.

(f) A flight instructor (simulator) must accomplish the following—

(1) Fly at least two flight segments as a required crewmember for the type, class, or category aircraft involved within the 12-month period preceding the performance of any flight instructor duty in a flight simulator; or

(2) Satisfactorily complete an approved line-observation program within the period prescribed by that program preceding the performance of any flight instructor duty in a flight simulator.

(g) The flight segments or line-observation program required in paragraph (f) of this section are considered completed in the month required if completed in the month before, or in the month after, the month in which they are due.

[Docket No. FAA–2001–10047, 68 FR 54561, Sept. 17, 2003; as amended by Amdt. 91–322, 76 FR 31823, June 2, 2011]

§91.1093 Initial and transition training and checking: Check pilots (aircraft), check pilots (simulator).

(a) No program manager may use a person nor may any person serve as a check pilot unless—

(1) That person has satisfactorily completed initial or transition check pilot training; and

(2) Within the preceding 24 months, that person satisfactorily conducts a proficiency or competency check under the observation of an FAA inspector or an aircrew designated examiner employed by the program manager. The observation check may be accomplished in part or in full in an aircraft, in a flight simulator, or in a flight training device.

(b) The observation check required by paragraph (a)(2) of this section is considered to have been completed in the month required if completed in the month before or the month after the month in which it is due.

(c) The initial ground training for check pilots must include the following:

(1) Check pilot duties, functions, and responsibilities.

(2) The applicable provisions of the Code of Federal Regulations and the program manager's policies and procedures.

(3) The applicable methods, procedures, and techniques for conducting the required checks.

(4) Proper evaluation of student performance including the detection of—

(i) Improper and insufficient training; and

(ii) Personal characteristics of an applicant that could adversely affect safety.

(5) The corrective action in the case of unsatisfactory checks.

(6) The approved methods, procedures, and limitations for performing the required normal, abnormal, and emergency procedures in the aircraft.

(d) The transition ground training for a check pilot must include the approved methods, procedures, and limitations for performing the required normal, abnormal, and emergency procedures applicable to the aircraft to which the check pilot is in transition.

(e) The initial and transition flight training for a check pilot (aircraft) must include the following—

(1) The safety measures for emergency situations that are likely to develop during a check;

(2) The potential results of improper, untimely, or nonexecution of safety measures during a check;

(3) Training and practice in conducting flight checks from the left and right pilot seats in the required normal, abnormal, and emergency procedures to ensure competence to conduct the pilot flight checks required by this subpart; and

(4) The safety measures to be taken from either pilot seat for emergency situations that are likely to develop during checking.

(f) The requirements of paragraph (e) of this section may be accomplished in full or in part in flight, in a flight simulator, or in a flight training device, as appropriate.

(g) The initial and transition flight training for a check pilot (simulator) must include the following:

(1) Training and practice in conducting flight checks in the required normal, abnormal, and emergency procedures to ensure competence to conduct the flight checks required by this subpart. This training and practice must be accomplished in a flight simulator or in a flight training device.

(2) Training in the operation of flight simulators, flight training devices, or both, to ensure competence to conduct the flight checks required by this subpart.

§91.1095 Initial and transition training and checking: Flight instructors (aircraft), flight instructors (simulator).

(a) No program manager may use a person nor may any person serve as a flight instructor unless—

(1) That person has satisfactorily completed initial or transition flight instructor training; and

(2) Within the preceding 24 months, that person satisfactorily conducts instruction under the observation of an FAA inspector, a program manager check pilot, or an aircrew designated examiner employed by the program manager. The

observation check may be accomplished in part or in full in an aircraft, in a flight simulator, or in a flight training device.

(b) The observation check required by paragraph (a)(2) of this section is considered to have been completed in the month required if completed in the month before, or the month after, the month in which it is due.

(c) The initial ground training for flight instructors must include the following:

(1) Flight instructor duties, functions, and responsibilities.

(2) The applicable Code of Federal Regulations and the program manager's policies and procedures.

(3) The applicable methods, procedures, and techniques for conducting flight instruction.

(4) Proper evaluation of student performance including the detection of—

(i) Improper and insufficient training; and

(ii) Personal characteristics of an applicant that could adversely affect safety.

(5) The corrective action in the case of unsatisfactory training progress.

(6) The approved methods, procedures, and limitations for performing the required normal, abnormal, and emergency procedures in the aircraft.

(7) Except for holders of a flight instructor certificate—

(i) The fundamental principles of the teaching-learning process;

(ii) Teaching methods and procedures; and

(iii) The instructor-student relationship.

(d) The transition ground training for flight instructors must include the approved methods, procedures, and limitations for performing the required normal, abnormal, and emergency procedures applicable to the type, class, or category aircraft to which the flight instructor is in transition.

(e) The initial and transition flight training for flight instructors (aircraft) must include the following—

(1) The safety measures for emergency situations that are likely to develop during instruction;

(2) The potential results of improper or untimely safety measures during instruction;

(3) Training and practice from the left and right pilot seats in the required normal, abnormal, and emergency maneuvers to ensure competence to conduct the flight instruction required by this subpart; and

(4) The safety measures to be taken from either the left or right pilot seat for emergency situations that are likely to develop during instruction.

(f) The requirements of paragraph (e) of this section may be accomplished in full or in part in flight, in a flight simulator, or in a flight training device, as appropriate.

(g) The initial and transition flight training for a flight instructor (simulator) must include the following:

(1) Training and practice in the required normal, abnormal, and emergency procedures to ensure competence to conduct the flight instruction required by this subpart. These maneuvers and procedures must be accomplished in full or in part in a flight simulator or in a flight training device.

(2) Training in the operation of flight simulators, flight training devices, or both, to ensure competence to conduct the flight instruction required by this subpart.

§91.1097 Pilot and flight attendant crewmember training programs.

(a) Each program manager must establish and maintain an approved pilot training program, and each program manager who uses a flight attendant crewmember must establish and maintain an approved flight attendant training program, that is appropriate to the operations to which each pilot and flight attendant is to be assigned, and will ensure that they are adequately trained to meet the applicable knowledge and practical testing requirements of §§91.1065 through 91.1071.

(b) Each program manager required to have a training program by paragraph (a) of this section must include in that program ground and flight training curriculums for—

(1) Initial training;

(2) Transition training;

(3) Upgrade training;

(4) Differences training;

(5) Recurrent training; and

(6) Requalification training.

(c) Each program manager must provide current and appropriate study materials for use by each required pilot and flight attendant.

(d) The program manager must furnish copies of the pilot and flight attendant crewmember training program, and all changes and additions, to the assigned representative of the Administrator. If the program manager uses training facilities of other persons, a copy of those training programs or appropriate portions used for those facilities must also be furnished. Curricula that follow FAA published curricula may be cited by reference in the copy of the training program furnished to the representative of the Administrator and need not be furnished with the program.

§91.1099 Crewmember initial and recurrent training requirements.

No program manager may use a person, nor may any person serve, as a crewmember in operations under this subpart unless that crewmember has completed the appropriate initial or recurrent

training phase of the training program appropriate to the type of operation in which the crewmember is to serve since the beginning of the 12th month before that service.

§91.1101 Pilots: Initial, transition, and upgrade ground training.

Initial, transition, and upgrade ground training for pilots must include instruction in at least the following, as applicable to their duties:

(a) General subjects—

(1) The program manager's flight locating procedures;

(2) Principles and methods for determining weight and balance, and runway limitations for takeoff and landing;

(3) Enough meteorology to ensure a practical knowledge of weather phenomena, including the principles of frontal systems, icing, fog, thunderstorms, windshear and, if appropriate, high altitude weather situations;

(4) Air traffic control systems, procedures, and phraseology;

(5) Navigation and the use of navigational aids, including instrument approach procedures;

(6) Normal and emergency communication procedures;

(7) Visual cues before and during descent below Decision Altitude or MDA; and

(8) Other instructions necessary to ensure the pilot's competence.

(b) For each aircraft type—

(1) A general description;

(2) Performance characteristics;

(3) Engines and propellers;

(4) Major components;

(5) Major aircraft systems (that is, flight controls, electrical, and hydraulic), other systems, as appropriate, principles of normal, abnormal, and emergency operations, appropriate procedures and limitations;

(6) Knowledge and procedures for—

(i) Recognizing and avoiding severe weather situations;

(ii) Escaping from severe weather situations, in case of inadvertent encounters, including low-altitude windshear (except that rotorcraft pilots are not required to be trained in escaping from low-altitude windshear);

(iii) Operating in or near thunderstorms (including best penetration altitudes), turbulent air (including clear air turbulence), inflight icing, hail, and other potentially hazardous meteorological conditions; and

(iv) Operating airplanes during ground icing conditions, (that is, any time conditions are such that frost, ice, or snow may reasonably be expected to adhere to the aircraft), if the program

manager expects to authorize takeoffs in ground icing conditions, including:

(A) The use of holdover times when using deicing/anti-icing fluids;

(B) Airplane deicing/anti-icing procedures, including inspection and check procedures and responsibilities;

(C) Communications;

(D) Airplane surface contamination (that is, adherence of frost, ice, or snow) and critical area identification, and knowledge of how contamination adversely affects airplane performance and flight characteristics;

(E) Types and characteristics of deicing/anti-icing fluids, if used by the program manager;

(F) Cold weather preflight inspection procedures;

(G) Techniques for recognizing contamination on the airplane;

(7) Operating limitations;

(8) Fuel consumption and cruise control;

(9) Flight planning;

(10) Each normal and emergency procedure; and

(11) The approved Aircraft Flight Manual or equivalent.

§91.1103 Pilots: Initial, transition, upgrade, requalification, and differences flight training.

(a) Initial, transition, upgrade, requalification, and differences training for pilots must include flight and practice in each of the maneuvers and procedures contained in each of the curriculums that are a part of the approved training program.

(b) The maneuvers and procedures required by paragraph (a) of this section must be performed in flight, except to the extent that certain maneuvers and procedures may be performed in an aircraft simulator, or an appropriate training device, as allowed by this subpart.

(c) If the program manager's approved training program includes a course of training using an aircraft simulator or other training device, each pilot must successfully complete—

(1) Training and practice in the simulator or training device in at least the maneuvers and procedures in this subpart that are capable of being performed in the aircraft simulator or training device; and

(2) A flight check in the aircraft or a check in the simulator or training device to the level of proficiency of a pilot in command or second in command, as applicable, in at least the maneuvers and procedures that are capable of being performed in an aircraft simulator or training device.

§91.1105 Flight attendants: Initial and transition ground training.

Initial and transition ground training for flight attendants must include instruction in at least the following—

(a) General subjects—

(1) The authority of the pilot in command; and

(2) Passenger handling, including procedures to be followed in handling deranged persons or other persons whose conduct might jeopardize safety.

(b) For each aircraft type—

(1) A general description of the aircraft emphasizing physical characteristics that may have a bearing on ditching, evacuation, and inflight emergency procedures and on other related duties;

(2) The use of both the public address system and the means of communicating with other flight crewmembers, including emergency means in the case of attempted hijacking or other unusual situations; and

(3) Proper use of electrical galley equipment and the controls for cabin heat and ventilation.

§91.1107 Recurrent training.

(a) Each program manager must ensure that each crewmember receives recurrent training and is adequately trained and currently proficient for the type aircraft and crewmember position involved.

(b) Recurrent ground training for crewmembers must include at least the following:

(1) A quiz or other review to determine the crewmember's knowledge of the aircraft and crewmember position involved.

(2) Instruction as necessary in the subjects required for initial ground training by this subpart, as appropriate, including low-altitude windshear training and training on operating during ground icing conditions, as prescribed in §91.1097 and described in §91.1101, and emergency training.

(c) Recurrent flight training for pilots must include, at least, flight training in the maneuvers or procedures in this subpart, except that satisfactory completion of the check required by §91.1065 within the preceding 12 months may be substituted for recurrent flight training.

§91.1109 Aircraft maintenance: Inspection program.

Each program manager must establish an aircraft inspection program for each make and model program aircraft and ensure each aircraft is inspected in accordance with that inspection program.

(a) The inspection program must be in writing and include at least the following information:

(1) Instructions and procedures for the conduct of inspections for the particular make and model aircraft, including necessary tests and checks. The instructions and procedures must set forth in detail the parts and areas of the airframe, engines, propellers, rotors, and appliances, including survival and emergency equipment required to be inspected.

(2) A schedule for performing the inspections that must be accomplished under the inspection program expressed in terms of the time in service, calendar time, number of system operations, or any combination thereof.

(3) The name and address of the person responsible for scheduling the inspections required by the inspection program. A copy of the inspection program must be made available to the person performing inspections on the aircraft and, upon request, to the Administrator.

(b) Each person desiring to establish or change an approved inspection program under this section must submit the inspection program for approval to the Flight Standards office that issued the program manager's management specifications. The inspection program must be derived from one of the following programs:

(1) An inspection program currently recommended by the manufacturer of the aircraft, aircraft engines, propellers, appliances, and survival and emergency equipment;

(2) An inspection program that is part of a continuous airworthiness maintenance program currently in use by a person holding an air carrier or operating certificate issued under part 119 of this chapter and operating that make and model aircraft under part 121 or 135 of this chapter;

(3) An aircraft inspection program approved under §135.419 of this chapter and currently in use under part 135 of this chapter by a person holding a certificate issued under part 119 of this chapter; or

(4) An airplane inspection program approved under §125.247 of this chapter and currently in use under part 125 of this chapter.

(5) An inspection program that is part of the program manager's continuous airworthiness maintenance program under §§91.1411 through 91.1443.

(c) The Administrator may require revision of the inspection program approved under this section in accordance with the provisions of §91.415.

[Docket No. FAA–2001–10047, 68 FR 54561, Sept. 17, 2003; as amended by Docket FAA–2018–0119, Amdt. 91–350, 83 FR 9171, March 5, 2018]

§91.1111 Maintenance training.

The program manager must ensure that all employees who are responsible for maintenance related to program aircraft undergo appropriate initial and annual recurrent training and are competent to perform those duties.

§91.1113 Maintenance recordkeeping.

Each fractional ownership program manager must keep (using the system specified in the manual required in §91.1025) the records specified in §91.417(a) for the periods specified in §91.417(b).

§91.1115 Inoperable instruments and equipment.

(a) No person may take off an aircraft with inoperable instruments or equipment installed unless the following conditions are met:

(1) An approved Minimum Equipment List exists for that aircraft.

(2) The program manager has been issued management specifications authorizing operations in accordance with an approved Minimum Equipment List. The flight crew must have direct access at all times prior to flight to all of the information contained in the approved Minimum Equipment List through printed or other means approved by the Administrator in the program manager's management specifications. An approved Minimum Equipment List, as authorized by the management specifications, constitutes an approved change to the type design without requiring recertification.

(3) The approved Minimum Equipment List must:

(i) Be prepared in accordance with the limitations specified in paragraph (b) of this section.

(ii) Provide for the operation of the aircraft with certain instruments and equipment in an inoperable condition.

(4) Records identifying the inoperable instruments and equipment and the information required by (a)(3)(ii) of this section must be available to the pilot.

(5) The aircraft is operated under all applicable conditions and limitations contained in the Minimum Equipment List and the management specifications authorizing use of the Minimum Equipment List.

(b) The following instruments and equipment may not be included in the Minimum Equipment List:

(1) Instruments and equipment that are either specifically or otherwise required by the airworthiness requirements under which the airplane is type certificated and that are essential for safe operations under all operating conditions.

(2) Instruments and equipment required by an airworthiness directive to be in operable condition unless the airworthiness directive provides otherwise.

(3) Instruments and equipment required for specific operations by this part.

(c) Notwithstanding paragraphs (b)(1) and (b)(3) of this section, an aircraft with inoperable instruments or equipment may be operated under a special flight permit under §§21.197 and 21.199 of this chapter.

(d) A person authorized to use an approved Minimum Equipment List issued for a specific aircraft under part 121, 125, or 135 of this chapter must use that Minimum Equipment List to comply with this section.

§91.1411 Continuous airworthiness maintenance program use by fractional ownership program manager.

Fractional ownership program aircraft may be maintained under a continuous airworthiness maintenance program (CAMP) under §§91.1413 through 91.1443. Any program manager who elects to maintain the program aircraft using a continuous airworthiness maintenance program must comply with §§91.1413 through 91.1443.

§91.1413 CAMP: Responsibility for airworthiness.

(a) For aircraft maintained in accordance with a Continuous Airworthiness Maintenance Program, each program manager is primarily responsible for the following:

(1) Maintaining the airworthiness of the program aircraft, including airframes, aircraft engines, propellers, rotors, appliances, and parts.

(2) Maintaining its aircraft in accordance with the requirements of this chapter.

(3) Repairing defects that occur between regularly scheduled maintenance required under part 43 of this chapter.

(b) Each program manager who maintains program aircraft under a CAMP must—

(1) Employ a Director of Maintenance or equivalent position. The Director of Maintenance must be a certificated mechanic with airframe and powerplant ratings who has responsibility for the maintenance program on all program aircraft maintained under a continuous airworthiness maintenance program. This person cannot also act as Chief Inspector.

(2) Employ a Chief Inspector or equivalent position. The Chief Inspector must be a certificated mechanic with airframe and powerplant ratings who has overall responsibility for inspection aspects of the CAMP. This person cannot also act as Director of Maintenance.

(3) Have the personnel to perform the maintenance of program aircraft, including airframes, aircraft engines, propellers, rotors, appliances, emergency equipment and parts, under its manual and this chapter; or make arrangements with another person for the performance of maintenance. However, the program manager must ensure that any maintenance, preventive maintenance, or alteration that is performed by another person is performed under the program manager's operating manual and this chapter.

§91.1415 CAMP: Mechanical reliability reports.

(a) Each program manager who maintains program aircraft under a CAMP must report the occurrence or detection of each failure, malfunction, or defect in an aircraft concerning—

(1) Fires during flight and whether the related fire-warning system functioned properly;

(2) Fires during flight not protected by related fire-warning system;

(3) False fire-warning during flight;

(4) An exhaust system that causes damage during flight to the engine, adjacent structure, equipment, or components;

(5) An aircraft component that causes accumulation or circulation of smoke, vapor, or toxic or noxious fumes in the crew compartment or passenger cabin during flight;

(6) Engine shutdown during flight because of flameout;

(7) Engine shutdown during flight when external damage to the engine or aircraft structure occurs;

(8) Engine shutdown during flight because of foreign object ingestion or icing;

(9) Shutdown of more than one engine during flight;

(10) A propeller feathering system or ability of the system to control overspeed during flight;

(11) A fuel or fuel-dumping system that affects fuel flow or causes hazardous leakage during flight;

(12) An unwanted landing gear extension or retraction or opening or closing of landing gear doors during flight;

(13) Brake system components that result in loss of brake actuating force when the aircraft is in motion on the ground;

(14) Aircraft structure that requires major repair;

(15) Cracks, permanent deformation, or corrosion of aircraft structures, if more than the maximum acceptable to the manufacturer or the FAA; and

(16) Aircraft components or systems that result in taking emergency actions during flight (except action to shut down an engine).

(b) For the purpose of this section, *during flight* means the period from the moment the aircraft leaves the surface of the earth on takeoff until it touches down on landing.

(c) In addition to the reports required by paragraph (a) of this section, each program manager must report any other failure, malfunction, or defect in an aircraft that occurs or is detected at any time if, in the manager's opinion, the failure, malfunction, or defect has endangered or may endanger the safe operation of the aircraft.

(d) Each program manager must send each report required by this section, in writing, covering each 24-hour period beginning at 0900 hours local time of each day and ending at 0900 hours local time on the next day to the Flight Standards office that issued the program manager's management specifications. Each report of occurrences during a 24-hour period must be mailed or transmitted to that office within the next 72 hours. However, a report that is due on Saturday or Sunday may be mailed or transmitted on the following Monday and one that is due on a holiday may be mailed or transmitted on the next workday. For aircraft operated in areas where mail is not collected, reports may be mailed or transmitted within 72 hours after the aircraft returns to a point where the mail is collected.

(e) The program manager must transmit the reports required by this section on a form and in a manner prescribed by the Administrator, and must include as much of the following as is available:

(1) The type and identification number of the aircraft.

(2) The name of the program manager.

(3) The date.

(4) The nature of the failure, malfunction, or defect.

(5) Identification of the part and system involved, including available information pertaining to type designation of the major component and time since last overhaul, if known.

(6) Apparent cause of the failure, malfunction or defect (for example, wear, crack, design deficiency, or personnel error).

(7) Other pertinent information necessary for more complete identification, determination of seriousness, or corrective action.

(f) A program manager that is also the holder of a type certificate (including a supplemental type certificate), a Parts Manufacturer Approval, or a Technical Standard Order Authorization, or that is the licensee of a type certificate need not report a failure, malfunction, or defect under this section if the failure, malfunction, or defect has been reported by it under §21.3 of this chapter or under the accident reporting provisions of part 830 of the regulations of the National Transportation Safety Board.

(g) No person may withhold a report required by this section even when not all information required by this section is available.

(h) When the program manager receives additional information, including information from the manufacturer or other agency, concerning a report required by this section, the program manager must expeditiously submit it as a supplement to the first report and reference the date and place of submission of the first report.

[Docket No. FAA–2001–10047, 68 FR 54561, Sept. 17, 2003; as amended by Docket FAA–2018–0119, Amdt. 91–350, 83 FR 9171, March 5, 2018]

§91.1417 CAMP: Mechanical interruption summary report.

Each program manager who maintains program aircraft under a CAMP must mail or deliver, before the end of the 10th day of the following month, a summary report of the following occurrences in multiengine aircraft for the preceding month to the Flight Standards office that issued the management specifications:

(a) Each interruption to a flight, unscheduled change of aircraft en route, or unscheduled stop or diversion from a route, caused by known or suspected mechanical difficulties or malfunctions that are not required to be reported under §91.1415.

(b) The number of propeller featherings in flight, listed by type of propeller and engine and aircraft on which it was installed. Propeller featherings for training, demonstration, or flight check purposes need not be reported.

[Docket No. FAA–2001–10047, 68 FR 54561, Sept. 17, 2003; as amended by Amdt. 91–350, 83 FR 9171, March 5, 2018]

§91.1423 CAMP: Maintenance organization.

(a) Each program manager who maintains program aircraft under a CAMP that has its personnel perform any of its maintenance (other than required inspections), preventive maintenance, or alterations, and each person with whom it arranges for the performance of that work, must have an organization adequate to perform the work.

(b) Each program manager who has personnel perform any inspections required by the program manager's manual under §91.1427(b)(2) or (3), (in this subpart referred to as required inspections), and each person with whom the program manager arranges for the performance of that work, must have an organization adequate to perform that work.

(c) Each person performing required inspections in addition to other maintenance, preventive maintenance, or alterations, must organize the performance of those functions so as to separate the required inspection functions from the other maintenance, preventive maintenance, or alteration functions. The separation must be below the level of administrative control at which overall responsibility for the required inspection functions and other maintenance, preventive maintenance, or alterations is exercised.

§91.1425 CAMP: Maintenance, preventive maintenance, and alteration programs.

Each program manager who maintains program aircraft under a CAMP must have an inspection program and a program covering other maintenance, preventive maintenance, or alterations that ensures that—

(a) Maintenance, preventive maintenance, or alterations performed by its personnel, or by other persons, are performed under the program manager's manual;

(b) Competent personnel and adequate facilities and equipment are provided for the proper performance of maintenance, preventive maintenance, or alterations; and

(c) Each aircraft released to service is airworthy and has been properly maintained for operation under this part.

§91.1427 CAMP: Manual requirements.

(a) Each program manager who maintains program aircraft under a CAMP must put in the operating manual the chart or description of the program manager's organization required by §91.1423 and a list of persons with whom it has arranged for the performance of any of its required inspections, and other maintenance, preventive maintenance, or alterations, including a general description of that work.

(b) Each program manager must put in the operating manual the programs required by §91.1425 that must be followed in performing maintenance, preventive maintenance, or alterations of that program manager's aircraft, including airframes, aircraft engines, propellers, rotors, appliances, emergency equipment, and parts, and must include at least the following:

(1) The method of performing routine and non-routine maintenance (other than required inspections), preventive maintenance, or alterations.

(2) A designation of the items of maintenance and alteration that must be inspected (required inspections) including at least those that could result in a failure, malfunction, or defect endangering the safe operation of the aircraft, if not performed properly or if improper parts or materials are used.

(3) The method of performing required inspections and a designation by occupational title of personnel authorized to perform each required inspection.

91

(4) Procedures for the reinspection of work performed under previous required inspection findings (buy-back procedures).

(5) Procedures, standards, and limits necessary for required inspections and acceptance or rejection of the items required to be inspected and for periodic inspection and calibration of precision tools, measuring devices, and test equipment.

(6) Procedures to ensure that all required inspections are performed.

(7) Instructions to prevent any person who performs any item of work from performing any required inspection of that work.

(8) Instructions and procedures to prevent any decision of an inspector regarding any required inspection from being countermanded by persons other than supervisory personnel of the inspection unit, or a person at the level of administrative control that has overall responsibility for the management of both the required inspection functions and the other maintenance, preventive maintenance, or alterations functions.

(9) Procedures to ensure that maintenance (including required inspections), preventive maintenance, or alterations that are not completed because of work interruptions are properly completed before the aircraft is released to service.

(c) Each program manager must put in the manual a suitable system (which may include an electronic or coded system) that provides for the retention of the following information—

(1) A description (or reference to data acceptable to the Administrator) of the work performed;

(2) The name of the person performing the work if the work is performed by a person outside the organization of the program manager; and

(3) The name or other positive identification of the individual approving the work.

(d) For the purposes of this part, the program manager must prepare that part of its manual containing maintenance information and instructions, in whole or in part, in a format acceptable to the Administrator, that is retrievable in the English language.

§91.1429 CAMP: Required inspection personnel.

(a) No person who maintains an aircraft under a CAMP may use any person to perform required inspections unless the person performing the inspection is appropriately certificated, properly trained, qualified, and authorized to do so.

(b) No person may allow any person to perform a required inspection unless, at the time the work was performed, the person performing that inspection is under the supervision and control of the chief inspector.

(c) No person may perform a required inspection if that person performed the item of work required to be inspected.

(d) Each program manager must maintain, or must ensure that each person with whom it arranges to perform required inspections maintains, a current listing of persons who have been trained, qualified, and authorized to conduct required inspections. The persons must be identified by name, occupational title, and the inspections that they are authorized to perform. The program manager (or person with whom it arranges to perform its required inspections) must give written information to each person so authorized, describing the extent of that person's responsibilities, authorities, and inspectional limitations. The list must be made available for inspection by the Administrator upon request.

§91.1431 CAMP: Continuing analysis and surveillance.

(a) Each program manager who maintains program aircraft under a CAMP must establish and maintain a system for the continuing analysis and surveillance of the performance and effectiveness of its inspection program and the program covering other maintenance, preventive maintenance, and alterations and for the correction of any deficiency in those programs, regardless of whether those programs are carried out by employees of the program manager or by another person.

(b) Whenever the Administrator finds that the programs described in paragraph (a) of this section does not contain adequate procedures and standards to meet this part, the program manager must, after notification by the Administrator, make changes in those programs requested by the Administrator.

(c) A program manager may petition the Administrator to reconsider the notice to make a change in a program. The petition must be filed with the Executive Director, Flight Standards Service, within 30 days after the program manager receives the notice. Except in the case of an emergency requiring immediate action in the interest of safety, the filing of the petition stays the notice pending a decision by the Administrator.

[Docket No. FAA–2001–10047, 68 FR 54561, Sept. 17, 2003; as amended by Docket FAA–2018–0119, Amdt. 91–350, 83 FR 9171, March 5, 2018]

§91.1433 CAMP: Maintenance and preventive maintenance training program.

Each program manager who maintains program aircraft under a CAMP or a person performing maintenance or preventive maintenance functions for it must have a training program to ensure that each person (including inspection personnel) who determines the adequacy of work done is fully informed about procedures and techniques and new equipment in use and is competent to perform that person's duties.

§91.1435 CAMP: Certificate requirements.

(a) Except for maintenance, preventive maintenance, alterations, and required inspections performed by repair stations located outside the United States certificated under the provisions of part 145 of this chapter, each person who is directly in charge of maintenance, preventive maintenance, or alterations for a CAMP, and each person performing required inspections for a CAMP must hold an appropriate airman certificate.

(b) For the purpose of this section, a person "directly in charge" is each person assigned to a position in which that person is responsible for the work of a shop or station that performs maintenance, preventive maintenance, alterations, or other functions affecting airworthiness. A person who is directly in charge need not physically observe and direct each worker constantly but must be available for consultation and decision on matters requiring instruction or decision from higher authority than that of the person performing the work.

§91.1437 CAMP: Authority to perform and approve maintenance.

A program manager who maintains program aircraft under a CAMP may employ maintenance personnel, or make arrangements with other persons to perform maintenance and preventive maintenance as provided in its maintenance manual. Unless properly certificated, the program manager may not perform or approve maintenance for return to service.

§91.1439 CAMP: Maintenance recording requirements.

(a) Each program manager who maintains program aircraft under a CAMP must keep (using the system specified in the manual required in §91.1427) the following records for the periods specified in paragraph (b) of this section:

(1) All the records necessary to show that all requirements for the issuance of an airworthiness release under §91.1443 have been met.

(2) Records containing the following information:

(i) The total time in service of the airframe, engine, propeller, and rotor.

(ii) The current status of life-limited parts of each airframe, engine, propeller, rotor, and appliance.

(iii) The time since last overhaul of each item installed on the aircraft that are required to be overhauled on a specified time basis.

(iv) The identification of the current inspection status of the aircraft, including the time since the last inspections required by the inspection program under which the aircraft and its appliances are maintained.

(v) The current status of applicable airworthiness directives, including the date and methods of compliance, and, if the airworthiness directive involves recurring action, the time and date when the next action is required.

(vi) A list of current major alterations and repairs to each airframe, engine, propeller, rotor, and appliance.

(b) Each program manager must retain the records required to be kept by this section for the following periods:

(1) Except for the records of the last complete overhaul of each airframe, engine, propeller, rotor, and appliance the records specified in paragraph (a)(1) of this section must be retained until the work is repeated or superseded by other work or for one year after the work is performed.

(2) The records of the last complete overhaul of each airframe, engine, propeller, rotor, and appliance must be retained until the work is superseded by work of equivalent scope and detail.

(3) The records specified in paragraph (a)(2) of this section must be retained as specified unless transferred with the aircraft at the time the aircraft is sold.

(c) The program manager must make all maintenance records required to be kept by this section available for inspection by the Administrator or any representative of the National Transportation Safety Board.

§91.1441 CAMP: Transfer of maintenance records.

When a U.S.-registered fractional ownership program aircraft maintained under a CAMP is removed from the list of program aircraft in the management specifications, the program manager must transfer to the purchaser, at the time of the sale, the following records of that aircraft, in plain language form or in coded form that provides for the preservation and retrieval of information in a manner acceptable to the Administrator:

(a) The records specified in §91.1439(a)(2).

(b) The records specified in §91.1439(a)(1) that are not included in the records covered by paragraph (a) of this section, except that the purchaser may allow the program manager to keep physical custody of such records. However, custody of records by the program manager does not relieve the purchaser of its responsibility under §91.1439(c) to make the records available for inspection by the Administrator or any representative of the National Transportation Safety Board.

§91.1443 CAMP: Airworthiness release or aircraft maintenance log entry.

(a) No program aircraft maintained under a CAMP may be operated after maintenance, preventive maintenance, or alterations are performed unless qualified, certificated personnel employed by the program manager prepare, or cause the person with whom the program manager arranges for the performance of the maintenance, preventive maintenance, or alterations, to prepare—

(1) An airworthiness release; or

(2) An appropriate entry in the aircraft maintenance log.

(b) The airworthiness release or log entry required by paragraph (a) of this section must—

(1) Be prepared in accordance with the procedure in the program manager's manual;

(2) Include a certification that—

(i) The work was performed in accordance with the requirements of the program manager's manual;

(ii) All items required to be inspected were inspected by an authorized person who determined that the work was satisfactorily completed;

(iii) No known condition exists that would make the aircraft unairworthy;

(iv) So far as the work performed is concerned, the aircraft is in condition for safe operation; and

(3) Be signed by an authorized certificated mechanic.

(c) Notwithstanding paragraph (b)(3) of this section, after maintenance, preventive maintenance, or alterations performed by a repair station certificated under the provisions of part 145 of this chapter, the approval for return to service or log entry required by paragraph (a) of this section may be signed by a person authorized by that repair station.

(d) Instead of restating each of the conditions of the certification required by paragraph (b) of this section, the program manager may state in its manual that the signature of an authorized certificated mechanic or repairman constitutes that certification.

Subpart L— Continued Airworthiness and Safety Improvements

Source: Amdt. 91–297, 72 FR 63410, November 8, 2007, unless otherwise noted.

§91.1501 Purpose and definition.

(a) This subpart requires operators to support the continued airworthiness of each airplane. These requirements may include, but are not limited to, revising the inspection program, incorporating design changes, and incorporating revisions to Instructions for Continued Airworthiness.

(b) [Reserved]

[Docket No. FAA–2004–18379, 72 FR 63410, November 8, 2007; as amended by Docket FAA–2018–0119, Amdt. 91–350, 83 FR 9171, March 5, 2018]

§91.1503 [Reserved]

§91.1505 Repairs assessment for pressurized fuselages.

(a) No person may operate an Airbus Model A300 (excluding the –600 series), British Aerospace Model BAC 1–11, Boeing Model 707, 720, 727, 737 or 747, McDonnell Douglas Model DC–8, DC–9/MD–80 or DC–10, Fokker Model F28, or Lockheed Model L–1011 airplane beyond applicable flight cycle implementation time specified below, or May 25, 2001, whichever occurs later, unless repair assessment guidelines applicable to the fuselage pressure boundary (fuselage skin, door skin, and bulkhead webs) are incorporated within its inspection program. The repair assessment guidelines must be approved by the responsible Aircraft Certification Service office for the type certificate for the affected airplane.

(1) For the Airbus Model A300 (excluding the –600 series), the flight cycle implementation time is:

(i) Model B2: 36,000 flights.

(ii) Model B4–100 (including Model B4–2C): 30,000 flights above the window line, and 36,000 flights below the window line.

(iii) Model B4–200: 25,500 flights above the window line, and 34,000 flights below the window line.

(2) For all models of the British Aerospace BAC 1–11, the flight cycle implementation time is 60,000 flights.

(3) For all models of the Boeing 707, the flight cycle implementation time is 15,000 flights.

(4) For all models of the Boeing 720, the flight cycle implementation time is 23,000 flights.

(5) For all models of the Boeing 727, the flight cycle implementation time is 45,000 flights.

(6) For all models of the Boeing 737, the flight cycle implementation time is 60,000 flights.

(7) For all models of the Boeing 747, the flight cycle implementation time is 15,000 flights.

(8) For all models of the McDonnell Douglas DC–8, the flight cycle implementation time is 30,000 flights.

(9) For all models of the McDonnell Douglas DC–9/MD–80, the flight cycle implementation time is 60,000 flights.

(10) For all models of the McDonnell Douglas DC–10, the flight cycle implementation time is 30,000 flights.

(11) For all models of the Lockheed L–1011, the flight cycle implementation time is 27,000 flights.

(12) For the Fokker F–28 Mark 1000, 2000, 3000, and 4000, the flight cycle implementation time is 60,000 flights.

(b) [Reserved]

[Docket No. 29104, 65 FR 24125, April 25, 2000; 65 FR 35703, June 5, 2000; 65 FR 50744, Aug. 21, 2000; as amended by Amdt. 91–266, 66 FR 23130, May 7, 2001; Amdt. 91–277, 67 FR 72834, Dec. 9, 2002; Amdt. 91–283, 69 FR 45941, July 30, 2004. Redesignated and amended by Amdt. 91–297, 72 FR 63410, Nov. 8, 2007; Docket FAA–2018–0119, Amdt. 91–350, 83 FR 9171, March 5, 2018]

§91.1507 Fuel tank system inspection program.

(a) Except as provided in paragraph (g) of this section, this section applies to transport category, turbine-powered airplanes with a type certificate issued after January 1, 1958, that, as a result of original type certification or later increase in capacity, have—

(1) A maximum type-certificated passenger capacity of 30 or more, or

(2) A maximum payload capacity of 7,500 pounds or more.

(b) For each airplane on which an auxiliary fuel tank is installed under a field approval, before June 16, 2008, the operator must submit to the responsible Aircraft Certification Service office proposed maintenance instructions for the tank that meet the requirements of Special Federal Aviation Regulation No. 88 (SFAR 88) of this chapter.

(c) After December 16, 2008, no operator may operate an airplane identified in paragraph (a) of this section unless the inspection program for that airplane has been revised to include applicable inspections, procedures, and limitations for fuel tank systems.

(d) The proposed fuel tank system inspection program revisions specified in paragraph (c) of this section must be based on fuel tank system Instructions for Continued Airworthiness (ICA) that have been developed in accordance with the applicable provisions of SFAR 88 of this chapter or §25.1529 and part 25, Appendix H, of this chapter, in effect on June 6, 2001 (including those developed for auxiliary fuel tanks, if any, installed under supplemental type certificates or other design approval) and that have been approved by the responsible Aircraft Certification Service office.

(e) After December 16, 2008, before returning an airplane to service after any alterations for which fuel tank ICA are developed under SFAR 88, or under §25.1529 in effect on June 6, 2001, the operator must include in the inspection program for the airplane inspections and procedures for the fuel tank system based on those ICA.

(f) The fuel tank system inspection program changes identified in paragraphs (d) and (e) of this section and any later fuel tank system revisions must be submitted to the Flight Standards office responsible for review and approval.

(g) This section does not apply to the following airplane models:

(1) Bombardier CL-44

(2) Concorde

(3) deHavilland D.H. 106 Comet 4C

(4) VFW-Vereinigte Flugtechnische Werk VFW-614

(5) Illyushin Aviation IL 96T

(6) Bristol Aircraft Britannia 305

(7) Handley Page Herald Type 300

(8) Avions Marcel Dassault—Breguet Aviation Mercure 100C

(9) Airbus Caravelle

(10) Lockheed L-300

[Amdt. 91–297, 72 FR 63410, Nov. 8, 2007; as amended by Docket FAA–2018–0119, Amdt. 91–350, 83 FR 9172, March 5, 2018]

Subpart M—Special Federal Aviation Regulations

Source: Docket No. FAA–2011–0246, 76 FR 16238, Mar. 23, 2011 unless otherwise noted.

§91.1603 Special Federal Aviation Regulation No. 112—Prohibition Against Certain Flights in the Territory and Airspace of Libya.

(a) *Applicability.* This Special Federal Aviation Regulation (SFAR) applies to the following persons:

(1) All U.S. air carriers and U.S. commercial operators;

(2) All persons exercising the privileges of an airman certificate issued by the FAA, except when such persons are operating U.S.-registered aircraft for a foreign air carrier; and

(3) All operators of U.S.-registered civil aircraft, except when the operator of such aircraft is a foreign air carrier.

(b) *Flight prohibition.* Except as provided in paragraphs (c) and (d) of this section, no person described in paragraph (a) of this section may conduct flight operations in the territory and airspace of Libya.

(c) *Permitted operations.* This section does not prohibit persons described in paragraph (a) of this section from conducting flight operations in the territory and airspace of Libya, provided that such flight operations occur under a contract, grant, or cooperative agreement with a department, agency, or instrumentality of the U.S.

Government (or under a subcontract between the prime contractor of the department, agency, or instrumentality and the person described in paragraph (a) of this section), with the approval of the FAA, or under an exemption issued by the FAA. The FAA will consider requests for approval or exemption in a timely manner, with the order of preference being: First, for those operations in support of U.S. Government-sponsored activities; second, for those operations in support of government-sponsored activities of a foreign country with the support of a U.S. Government department, agency, or instrumentality; and third, for all other operations.

(d) *Emergency situations.* In an emergency that requires immediate decision and action for the safety of the flight, the pilot in command of an aircraft may deviate from this section to the extent required by that emergency. Except for U.S. air carriers and commercial operators that are subject to the requirements of 14 CFR part 119, 121, 125, or 135, each person who deviates from this section must, within 10 days of the deviation, excluding Saturdays, Sundays, and Federal holidays, submit to the responsible Flight Standards Office a complete report of the operations of the aircraft involved in the deviation, including a description of the deviation and the reasons for it.

(e) *Expiration.* This SFAR will remain in effect until March 20, 2025. The FAA may amend, rescind, or extend this SFAR, as necessary.

[Docket No FAA–2011–0246; Amdt. No. 91–321E, 85 FR 45091, July 27, 2020; as amended by Docket No. FAA–2011–0246; Amdt. No. 91–321F, 88 FR 16878, March 21, 2023]

§91.1605 Special Federal Aviation Regulation No. 77—Prohibition Against Certain Flights in the Baghdad Flight Information Region (FIR) (ORBB).

(a) *Applicability.* This section applies to the following persons:

(1) All U.S. air carriers and U.S. commercial operators;

(2) All persons exercising the privileges of an airman certificate issued by the FAA, except when such persons are operating U.S.-registered aircraft for a foreign air carrier; and

(3) All operators of civil aircraft registered in the United States, except when the operator of such aircraft is a foreign air carrier.

(b) *Flight prohibition.* Except as provided in paragraphs (c) and (d) of this section, no person described in paragraph (a) of this section may conduct flight operations in the Baghdad Flight Information Region (FIR) (ORBB) at altitudes below Flight Level (FL) 320.

(c) *Permitted operations.* This section does not prohibit persons described in paragraph (a) of this section from conducting flight operations in the Baghdad FIR (ORBB) at altitudes below FL320, provided that such flight operations occur under a contract, grant, or cooperative agreement with a department, agency, or instrumentality of the U.S. Government (or under a subcontract between the prime contractor of the department, agency, or instrumentality, and the person described in paragraph (a) of this section) with the approval of the FAA, or under an exemption issued by the FAA. The FAA will consider requests for approval or exemption in a timely manner, with the order of preference being: first, for those operations in support of U.S. Government-sponsored activities; second, for those operations in support of government-sponsored activities of a foreign country with the support of a U.S. Government department, agency, or instrumentality; and third, for all other operations.

(d) *Emergency situations.* In an emergency that requires immediate decision and action for the safety of the flight, the pilot in command of an aircraft may deviate from this section to the extent required by that emergency. Except for U.S. air carriers and commercial operators that are subject to the requirements of part 119, 121, 125, or 135 of this chapter, each person who deviates from this section must, within 10 days of the deviation, excluding Saturdays, Sundays, and Federal holidays, submit to the responsible Flight Standards office a complete report of the operations of the aircraft involved in the deviation, including a description of the deviation and the reasons for it.

(e) *Expiration.* This SFAR will remain in effect until October 26, 2024. The FAA may amend, rescind, or extend this SFAR, as necessary.

[Docket No. FAA–2018–0927, Amdt. No. 91–353A, 85 FR 65693, Oct. 16, 2020, as amended by Amdt. No. 91–353B, 87 FR 57390, Sept. 20, 2022]

§91.1607 [Reserved]

§91.1609 Special Federal Aviation Regulation No. 114—Prohibition Against Certain Flights in the Damascus Flight Information Region (FIR) (OSTT).

(a) *Applicability.* This section applies to the following persons:

(1) All U.S. air carriers and U.S. commercial operators;

(2) All persons exercising the privileges of an airman certificate issued by the FAA, except when such persons are operating U.S.-registered aircraft for a foreign air carrier; and

(3) All operators of U.S.-registered civil aircraft, except when the operator of such aircraft is a foreign air carrier.

(b) *Flight prohibition.* Except as provided in paragraphs (c) and (d) of this section, no person described in paragraph (a) of this section may conduct flight operations in the Damascus Flight Information Region (FIR) (OSTT).

(c) *Permitted operations.* This section does not prohibit persons described in paragraph (a) of this section from conducting flight operations in the Damascus Flight Information Region (FIR) (OSTT), provided that such flight operations are conducted under a contract, grant, or cooperative agreement with a department, agency, or instrumentality of the U.S. government (or under a subcontract between the prime contractor of the department, agency, or instrumentality and the person described in paragraph (a) of this section) with the approval of the FAA, or under an exemption issued by the FAA. The FAA will consider requests for approval or exemption in a timely manner, with the order of preference being: First, for those operations in support of U.S. government-sponsored activities; second, for those operations in support of government-sponsored activities of a foreign country with the support of a U.S. government department, agency, or instrumentality; and third, for all other operations.

(d) *Emergency situations.* In an emergency that requires immediate decision and action for the safety of the flight, the pilot in command of an aircraft may deviate from this section to the extent required by that emergency. Except for U.S. air carriers and commercial operators that are subject to the requirements of 14 CFR part 119, 121, 125, or 135, each person who deviates from this section must, within 10 days of the deviation, excluding Saturdays, Sundays, and Federal holidays, submit to the responsible Flight Standards office a complete report of the operations of the aircraft involved in the deviation, including a description of the deviation and the reasons for it.

(e) *Expiration.* This SFAR will remain in effect until December 30, 2028. The FAA may amend, rescind, or extend this SFAR, as necessary.

[Docket FAA–2017–0768, Amdt. 91–348, 82 FR 40949, Aug. 29, 2017; Amdt. 91–348A, 82 FR 42592, Sept. 11, 2017; as amended by Amdt. No. 91-348B, 83 FR 63414, Dec. 10, 2018; Amdt. No. 91–348C; 85 FR 75845, Nov. 27, 2020; Amdt. 91-348D, 88 FR 89300, Dec. 27, 2023]

§91.1611 Special Federal Aviation Regulation No. 115—Prohibition Against Certain Flights in Specified Areas of the Sanaa Flight Information Region (FIR) (OYSC).

(a) *Applicability.* This Special Federal Aviation Regulation (SFAR) applies to the following persons:

(1) All U.S. air carriers and U.S. commercial operators;

(2) All persons exercising the privileges of an airman certificate issued by the FAA, except when such persons are operating U.S.-registered aircraft for a foreign air carrier; and

(3) All operators of U.S.-registered civil aircraft, except when the operator of such aircraft is a foreign air carrier.

(b) *Flight prohibition.* Except as provided in paragraphs (c) and (d) of this section, no person described in paragraph (a) of this section may conduct flight operations in the portion of the Sanaa Flight Information Region (FIR) (OYSC) that is west of a line drawn direct from KAPET (163322N 0530614E) to NODMA (152603N 0533359E), northwest of a line drawn direct from IMPAG (140638N 0503924E) then from IMPAG to TIMAD (115500N 0463500E), north of a line drawn direct from TIMAD to PARIM (123200N 0432720E), and east of a line drawn direct from PARIM to RIBOK (154700N 0415230E). Use of jet route UN303 is not authorized.

(c) *Permitted operations.* This section does not prohibit persons described in paragraph (a) of this section from conducting flight operations in the Sanaa FIR (OYSC) under the following circumstances:

(1) *Permitted operations that do not require an approval or exemption from the FAA.* Flight operations may be conducted in the Sanaa FIR (OYSC) in that airspace east of a line drawn direct from KAPET (163322N 0530614E) to NODMA (152603N 0533359E), southeast of a line drawn direct from NODMA to IMPAG (140638N 0503924E) then from IMPAG to TIMAD (115500N 0463500E), south of a line drawn direct from TIMAD to PARIM (123200N 0432720E), and west of a line drawn direct from PARIM to RIBOK (154700N 0415230E). Use of jet routes UT702 and M999 are authorized. All flight operations conducted under this subparagraph must be conducted subject to the approval of, and in accordance with the conditions established by, the appropriate authorities of Yemen.

(2) *Operations permitted under an approval or exemption issued by the FAA.* Flight operations may be conducted in the Sanaa FIR (OYSC) in that airspace west of a line drawn direct from KAPET (163322N 0530614E) to NODMA (152603N 0533359E), northwest of a line drawn direct from

NODMA to IMPAG (140638N 0503924E) then from IMPAG to TIMAD (115500N 0463500E), north of a line drawn direct from TIMAD to PARIM (123200N 0432720E), and east of a line drawn direct from PARIM to RIBOK (154700N 0415230E) if such flight operations are conducted under a contract, grant, or cooperative agreement with a department, agency, or instrumentality of the U.S. Government (or under a subcontract between the prime contractor of the U.S. Government department, agency, or instrumentality and the person subject to paragraph (a)), with the approval of the FAA, or under an exemption issued by the FAA. The FAA will consider requests for approval or exemption in a timely manner, with the order of preference being: First, for those operations in support of U.S. Government-sponsored activities; second, for those operations in support of government-sponsored activities of a foreign country with the support of a U.S. government department, agency, or instrumentality; and third, for all other operations.

(d) *Emergency situations.* In an emergency that requires immediate decision and action for the safety of the flight, the pilot in command of an aircraft may deviate from this section to the extent required by that emergency. Except for U.S. air carriers and commercial operators that are subject to the requirements of 14 CFR part 119, 121, 125, or 135, each person who deviates from this section must, within 10 days of the deviation, excluding Saturdays, Sundays, and Federal holidays, submit to the responsible Flight Standards office a complete report of the operations of the aircraft involved in the deviation, including a description of the deviation and the reasons for it.

(e) *Expiration.* This SFAR will remain in effect until January 7, 2025. The FAA may amend, rescind, or extend this SFAR, as necessary.

Issued in Washington, DC, under the authority of 49 U.S.C. 106(f) and (g), 40101(d)(1), 40105(b)(1)(A), and 44701(a)(5), on September 15, 2023.

[Amdt. 91–340B, 84 FR 67665, Dec. 11, 2019, as amended by Amdt. 91-340C, 86 FR 69173, Dec. 7, 2021; Docket No. FAA-2015–8672, Amdt. 91–340D, 88 FR 65320, Sept. 22, 2023]

§91.1613 Special Federal Aviation Regulation No. 107—Prohibition Against Certain Flights in the Territory and Airspace of Somalia.

(a) *Applicability.* This Special Federal Aviation Regulation (SFAR) applies to the following persons:

(1) All U.S. air carriers and U.S. commercial operators;

(2) All persons exercising the privileges of an airman certificate issued by the FAA, except when such persons are operating U.S.-registered aircraft for a foreign air carrier; and

(3) All operators of U.S.-registered civil aircraft, except when the operator of such aircraft is a foreign air carrier.

(b) *Flight prohibition.* Except as provided in paragraphs (c) and (d) of this section, no person described in paragraph (a) of this section may conduct flight operations in the territory and airspace of Somalia at altitudes below Flight Level (FL) 260.

(c) *Permitted operations.* This section does not prohibit persons described in paragraph (a) of this section from conducting flight operations in the territory and airspace of Somalia under the following circumstances:

(1) Overflights of Somalia may be conducted at altitudes at or above FL260 subject to the approval of, and in accordance with the conditions established by, the appropriate authorities of Somalia.

(2) Aircraft departing from Djibouti Ambouli International Airport (International Civil Aviation Organization (ICAO) code: HDAM) may operate overwater in the territory and airspace of Somalia at altitudes below FL260 only to the extent necessary to permit a climb during takeoff if the operator of that aircraft:

(i) Receives any necessary approval from the appropriate authorities of Djibouti;

(ii) Conducts operations that comply with applicable conditions established by the appropriate authorities of Djibouti and air traffic control instructions; and

(iii) Is either on a published instrument procedure or under the direction of air traffic control.

(3) Aircraft descending into Djibouti Ambouli International Airport (HDAM) may operate overwater at altitudes below FL260 in the territory and airspace of Somalia only to the extent necessary to permit descent for landing at Djibouti Ambouli International Airport (HDAM), if the operator of that aircraft:

(i) Receives any necessary approval from the appropriate authorities of Djibouti;

(ii) Conducts operations that comply with applicable conditions established by the appropriate authorities of Djibouti and air traffic control instructions; and

(iii) Is either on a published instrument procedure or under the direction of air traffic control.

(4) Flight operations may be conducted in the territory and airspace of Somalia at altitudes below FL260 if such flight operations are conducted under a contract, grant, or cooperative agreement with a department, agency, or instrumentality of the U.S. Government (or under a subcontract between the prime contractor of the U.S. Government department, agency, or instrumentality and the person described in paragraph (a) of this

section) with the approval of the FAA or under an exemption issued by the FAA. The FAA will consider requests for approval or exemption in a timely manner, with the order of preference being: First, for those operations in support of U.S. Government-sponsored activities; second, for those operations in support of government-sponsored activities of a foreign country with the support of a U.S. Government department, agency, or instrumentality; and third, for all other operations.

(d) *Emergency situations.* In an emergency that requires immediate decision and action for the safety of the flight, the pilot in command of an aircraft may deviate from this section to the extent required by that emergency. Except for U.S. air carriers and commercial operators that are subject to the requirements of 14 CFR part 119, 121, 125, or 135, each person who deviates from this section must, within 10 days of the deviation, excluding Saturdays, Sundays, and Federal holidays, submit to the responsible Flight Standards office a complete report of the operations of the aircraft involved in the deviation, including a description of the deviation and the reasons for it.

(e) *Expiration.* This SFAR will remain in effect until January 7, 2027. The FAA may amend, rescind, or extend this SFAR, as necessary.

[Docket No. FAA–2007–27602, 81 FR 726, Jan. 7, 2016; as amended by Amdt. 91–339A, 82 FR 58550, Dec. 13, 2017; Amdt. 91–350, 83 FR 9171, March 5, 2018; Amdt. 91–339B, 84 FR 67671, Dec 11, 2019; Amdt. 91–339C, 87 FR 79245, Dec. 27, 2022]

§91.1615 Special Federal Aviation Regulation No. 79—Prohibition Against Certain Flights in the Pyongyang Flight Information Region (FIR) (ZKKP).

(a) *Applicability.* This Special Federal Aviation Regulation (SFAR) applies to the following persons:

(1) All U.S. air carriers and U.S. commercial operators;

(2) All persons exercising the privileges of an airman certificate issued by the FAA, except when such persons are operating U.S.-registered aircraft for a foreign air carrier; and

(3) All operators of U.S.-registered civil aircraft, except when the operator of such aircraft is a foreign air carrier.

(b) *Flight prohibition.* Except as provided in paragraphs (c) and (d) of this section, no person described in paragraph (a) of this section may conduct flight operations in the Pyongyang Flight Information Region (FIR) (ZKKP).

(c) *Permitted operations.* This section does not prohibit persons described in paragraph (a) of this section from conducting flight operations in the Pyongyang Flight Information Region (FIR)

(ZKKP), provided that such flight operations are conducted under a contract, grant, or cooperative agreement with a department, agency, or instrumentality of the U.S. government (or under a subcontract between the prime contractor of the department, agency, or instrumentality and the person described in paragraph (a) of this section) with the approval of the FAA, or under an exemption issued by the FAA. The FAA will consider requests for approval or exemption in a timely manner, with the order of preference being: First, for those operations in support of U.S. government-sponsored activities; second, for those operations in support of government-sponsored activities of a foreign country with the support of a U.S. Government department, agency, or instrumentality; and third, for all other operations.

(d) *Emergency situations.* In an emergency that requires immediate decision and action for the safety of the flight, the pilot in command of an aircraft may deviate from this section to the extent required by that emergency. Except for U.S. air carriers and commercial operators that are subject to the requirements of 14 CFR part 119, 121, 125, or 135, each person who deviates from this section must, within 10 days of the deviation, excluding Saturdays, Sundays, and Federal holidays, submit to the responsible Flight Standards Office a complete report of the operations of the aircraft involved in the deviation, including a description of the deviation and the reasons for it.

(e) *Expiration.* This SFAR will remain in effect until September 18, 2028. The FAA may amend, rescind, or extend this SFAR, as necessary.

Issued in Washington, DC, under the authority of 49 U.S.C. 106(f) and (g), 40101(d)(1), 40105(b)(1)(A), and 44701(a)(5).

[Docket No. FAA–2018–0838, Amdt. No. 91–352, 83 FR 47064, Sept. 18, 2018; as amended by Amdt. No. 91–352A, 85 FR 55377, Sept. 8, 2020; Amdt. 91–352B, 88 FR 63525, Sept. 15, 2023]

§91.1617 Special Federal Aviation Regulation No. 117—Prohibition Against Certain Flights in the Tehran Flight Information Region (FIR) (OIIX).

(a) *Applicability.* This Special Federal Aviation Regulation (SFAR) applies to the following persons:

(1) All U.S. air carriers and U.S. commercial operators;

(2) All persons exercising the privileges of an airman certificate issued by the FAA, except when such persons are operating U.S.-registered aircraft for a foreign air carrier; and

(3) All operators of U.S.-registered civil aircraft, except when the operator of such aircraft is a foreign air carrier.

(b) *Flight prohibition.* Except as provided in paragraphs (c) and (d) of this section, no person described in paragraph (a) of this section may conduct flight operations in the Tehran Flight Information Region (FIR) (OIIX).

(c) *Permitted operations.* This section does not prohibit persons described in paragraph (a) of this section from conducting flight operations in the Tehran FIR (OIIX), provided that such flight operations are conducted under a contract, grant, or cooperative agreement with a department, agency, or instrumentality of the U.S. Government (or under a subcontract between the prime contractor of the department, agency, or instrumentality and the person described in paragraph (a) of this section) with the approval of the FAA, or under an exemption issued by the FAA. The FAA will consider requests for approval or exemption in a timely manner, with the order of preference being: First, for those operations in support of U.S. Government-sponsored activities; second, for those operations in support of government-sponsored activities of a foreign country with the support of a U.S. Government department, agency, or instrumentality; and third, for all other operations.

(d) *Emergency situations.* In an emergency that requires immediate decision and action for the safety of the flight, the pilot in command of an aircraft may deviate from this section to the extent required by that emergency. Except for U.S. air carriers and commercial operators that are subject to the requirements of 14 CFR parts 119, 121, 125, or 135, each person who deviates from this section must, within 10 days of the deviation, excluding Saturdays, Sundays, and Federal holidays, submit to the responsible Flight Standards Office a complete report of the operations of the aircraft involved in the deviation, including a description of the deviation and the reasons for it.

(e) *Expiration.* This SFAR will remain in effect until October 31, 2024. The FAA may amend, rescind, or extend this SFAR, as necessary.

[Docket No. FAA-2020-0874, Amdt. No. 91-359, 85 FR 68440, Oct. 29, 2020; as amended by Amdt. No. 91–359A, 87 FR 57834, Sept. 20, 2022]

§91.1619 Special Federal Aviation Regulation No. 119—Prohibition Against Certain Flights in the Kabul Flight Information Region (FIR) (OAKX).

(a) *Applicability.* This Special Federal Aviation Regulation (SFAR) applies to the following persons:

(1) All U.S. air carriers and U.S. commercial operators;

(2) All persons exercising the privileges of an airman certificate issued by the FAA, except when such persons are operating U.S.-registered aircraft for a foreign air carrier; and

(3) All operators of U.S.-registered civil aircraft, except when the operator of such aircraft is a foreign air carrier.

(b) *Flight prohibition.* Except as provided in paragraphs (c) and (d) of this section, no person described in paragraph (a) of this section may conduct flight operations in the Kabul Flight Information Region (FIR) (OAKX).

(c) *Permitted operations.* This section does not prohibit persons described in paragraph (a) of this section from conducting flight operations in the Kabul Flight Information Region (FIR) (OAKX) under the following circumstances:

(1) Overflights of the Kabul Flight Information Region (FIR) (OAKX) may be conducted at altitudes at and above Flight Level (FL) 320, subject to the approval of, and in accordance with the conditions established by, the appropriate authorities of Afghanistan.

(2) Flight operations may be conducted in the Kabul Flight Information Region (FIR) (OAKX) at altitudes below FL320, provided that such flight operations occur under a contract, grant, or cooperative agreement with a department, agency, or instrumentality of the U.S. Government (or under a subcontract between the prime contractor of the U.S. Government department, agency, or instrumentality and the person described in paragraph (a) of this section) with the approval of the FAA or under an exemption issued by the FAA. The FAA will consider requests for approval or exemption in a timely manner, with the order of preference being: first, for those operations in support of U.S. Government-sponsored activities; second, for those operations in support of government-sponsored activities of a foreign country with the support of a U.S. Government department, agency, or instrumentality; and third, for all other operations.

(d) *Emergency situations.* In an emergency that requires immediate decision and action for the safety of the flight, the pilot in command of an aircraft may deviate from this section to the extent required by that emergency. Except for U.S. air carriers and commercial operators that are subject to the requirements of 14 CFR part 119, 121, 125, or 135, each person who deviates from this section must, within 10 days of the deviation, excluding Saturdays, Sundays, and Federal holidays, submit to the responsible Flight Standards Office a complete report of the operations of the aircraft involved in the deviation, including a description of the deviation and the reasons for it.

(e) *Expiration.* This SFAR will remain in effect until July 25, 2025. The FAA may amend, rescind, or extend this SFAR as necessary.

[Docket No. FAA–2023–1415, Amdt. No. 91–369, 88 FR 47771, July 25, 2023]

Subpart N—Mitsubishi MU–2B Series Special Training, Experience, and Operating Requirements

Source: Docket No. FAA–2006–24981, Amdt. 91–344, 81 FR 61591, Sept. 7, 2016, unless otherwise noted.

§91.1701 Applicability.

(a) On and after November 7, 2016, all training conducted in an MU–2B must follow an approved MU–2B training program that meets the standards of this subpart.

(b) This subpart applies to all persons who operate a Mitsubishi MU–2B series airplane, including those who act as pilot in command, act as second-in-command, or other persons who manipulate the controls while under the supervision of a pilot in command.

(c) This subpart also applies to those persons who provide pilot training for a Mitsubishi MU–2B series airplane. The requirements in this subpart are in addition to the requirements of parts 61, 91, and 135 of this chapter.

§91.1703 Compliance and eligibility.

(a) Except as provided in paragraph (b) of this section, no person may manipulate the controls, act as PIC, act as second-in-command, or provide pilot training for a Mitsubishi MU–2B series airplane unless that person meets the requirements of this subpart.

(b) A person who does not meet the requirements of this subpart may manipulate the controls of a Mitsubishi MU–2B series airplane if a pilot in command who meets the requirements of this subpart is occupying a pilot station, no passengers or cargo are carried on board the airplane, and the flight is being conducted for one of the following reasons—

(1) The pilot in command is providing pilot training to the manipulator of the controls;

(2) The pilot in command is conducting a maintenance test flight with a second pilot or certificated mechanic; or

(3) The pilot in command is conducting simulated instrument flight and is using a safety pilot other than the pilot in command who manipulates the controls for the purposes of §91.109(b).

(c) A person is required to complete *Initial/transition training* if that person has fewer than—

(1) 50 hours of documented flight time manipulating the controls while serving as pilot in command of a Mitsubishi MU–2B series airplane in the preceding 24 months; or

(2) 500 hours of documented flight time manipulating the controls while serving as pilot in command of a Mitsubishi MU–2B series airplane.

(d) A person is eligible to receive *Requalification training* in lieu of Initial/transition training if that person has at least—

(1) 50 hours of documented flight time manipulating the controls while serving as pilot in command of a Mitsubishi MU–2B series airplane in the preceding 24 months; or

(2) 500 hours of documented flight time manipulating the controls while serving as pilot in command of a Mitsubishi MU–2B series airplane.

(e) A person is required to complete *Recurrent training* within the preceding 12 months. Successful completion of Initial/transition or Requalification training within the preceding 12 months satisfies the requirement of Recurrent training. A person must successfully complete Initial/transition training or Requalification training before being eligible to receive Recurrent training.

(f) Successful completion of Initial/transition training or Requalification training is a one-time requirement. A person may elect to retake Initial/transition training or Requalification training in lieu of Recurrent training.

(g) A person is required to complete Differences training in accordance with an FAA approved MU–2B training program if that person operates more than one MU–2B model as specified in §91.1707(c).

§91.1705 Required pilot training.

(a) Except as provided in §91.1703(b), no person may manipulate the controls, act as pilot in command, or act as second-in-command of a Mitsubishi MU–2B series airplane for the purpose of flight unless—

(1) The requirements for ground and flight training on Initial/transition, Requalification, Recurrent, and Differences training have been completed in accordance with an FAA approved MU–2B training program that meets the standards of this subpart; and

(2) That person's logbook has been endorsed in accordance with paragraph (f) of this section.

(b) Except as provided in §91.1703(b), no person may manipulate the controls, act as pilot in command, or act as second-in-command, of a Mitsubishi MU–2B series airplane for the purpose of flight unless—

(1) That person satisfactorily completes, if applicable, annual Recurrent pilot training on the *Special Emphasis Items*, and all items listed in the *Training Course Final Phase Check* in accordance with an FAA approved MU–2B training program that meets the standards of this subpart; and

(2) That person's logbook has been endorsed in accordance with paragraph (f) of this section.

(c) Satisfactory completion of the competency check required by §135.293 of this chapter within the preceding 12 calendar months may not be

91

substituted for the Mitsubishi MU–2B series airplane annual recurrent flight training of this section.

(d) Satisfactory completion of a Federal Aviation Administration sponsored pilot proficiency program, as described in §61.56(e) of this chapter may not be substituted for the Mitsubishi MU–2B series airplane annual recurrent flight training of this section.

(e) If a person complies with the requirements of paragraph (a) or (b) of this section in the calendar month before or the calendar month after the month in which compliance with these paragraphs are required, that person is considered to have accomplished the training requirement in the month the training is due.

(f) The endorsement required under paragraph (a) and (b) of this section must be made by—

(1) A certificated flight instructor or a simulator instructor authorized by a Training Center certificated under part 142 of this chapter and meeting the qualifications of §91.1713; or

(2) For persons operating the Mitsubishi MU–2B series airplane for a 14 CFR part 119 certificate holder within the last 12 calendar months, the part 119 certificate holder's flight instructor if authorized by the FAA and if that flight instructor meets the requirements of §91.1713.

(g) All training conducted for a Mitsubishi MU–2B series airplane must be completed in accordance with an MU–2B series airplane checklist that has been accepted by the Federal Aviation Administration's MU–2B Flight Standardization Board or the applicable MU–2B series checklist (incorporated by reference, see §91.1721).

(h) MU–2B training programs must contain ground training and flight training sufficient to ensure pilot proficiency for the safe operation of MU–2B aircraft, including:

(1) A ground training curriculum sufficient to ensure pilot knowledge of MU–2B aircraft, aircraft systems, and procedures, necessary for safe operation; and

(2) Flight training curriculum including flight training maneuver profiles sufficient in number and detail to ensure pilot proficiency in all MU–2B operations for each MU–2B model in correlation with MU–2B limitations, procedures, aircraft performance, and MU–2B Cockpit Checklist procedures applicable to the MU–2B model being trained. A MU–2B training program must contain, at a minimum, the following flight training maneuver profiles applicable to the MU–2B model being trained:

(i) Normal takeoff with 5- and 20-degrees flaps;

(ii) Takeoff engine failure with 5- and 20-degrees flaps;

(iii) Takeoff engine failure on runway or rejected takeoff;

(iv) Takeoff engine failure after liftoff—unable to climb (may be completed in classroom or flight training device only);

(v) Steep turns;

(vi) Slow flight maneuvers;

(vii) One engine inoperative maneuvering with loss of directional control;

(viii) Approach to stall in clean configuration and with wings level;

(ix) Approach to stall in takeoff configuration with 15- to 30-degrees bank;

(x) Approach to stall in landing configuration with gear down and 40-degrees of flaps;

(xi) Accelerated stall with no flaps;

(xii) Emergency descent at low speed;

(xiii) Emergency descent at high speed;

(xiv) Unusual attitude recovery with the nose high;

(xv) Unusual attitude recovery with the nose low;

(xvi) Normal landing with 20- and 40-degrees flaps;

(xvii) Go around and rejected landing;

(xviii) No flap or 5-degrees flaps landing;

(xix) One engine inoperative landing with 5- and 20-degrees flaps;

(xx) Crosswind landing;

(xxi) Instrument landing system (ILS) and missed approach;

(xxii) Two engine missed approach;

(xxiii) One engine inoperative ILS and missed approach;

(xxiv) One engine inoperative missed approach;

(xxv) Non-precision and missed approach;

(xxvi) Non-precision continuous descent final approach and missed approach;

(xxvii) One engine inoperative non-precision and missed approach;

(xxviii) One engine inoperative non-precision CDFA and missed approach;

(xxix) Circling approach at weather minimums;

(xxx) One engine inoperative circling approach at weather minimums.

(3) Flight training must include a final phase check sufficient to document pilot proficiency in the flight training maneuver profiles at the completion of training; and

(4) Differences training for applicable MU–2B model variants sufficient to ensure pilot proficiency in each model operated. Current MU–2B differences requirements are specified in §91.1707(c). A person must complete Differences training if a person operates more than one MU–2B model as specified in §91.1707(c). Differences training between the factory type design K and M models of the MU–2B airplane, and the factory type design J and L models of the MU–2B airplane, may be accomplished with Level A training. All other factory type design differences training must be accomplished with Level B training

unless otherwise specified in §91.1707(c). A Level A or B differences training is not a recurring annual requirement. Once a person has completed Initial Level A or B Differences training between the applicable different models, no additional differences training between those models is required.

(5) Icing training sufficient to ensure pilot knowledge and safe operation of the MU–2B aircraft in icing conditions as established by the FAA;

(6) Ground and flight training programs must include training hours identified by §91.1707(a) for ground instruction, §91.1707(b) for flight instruction, and §91.1707(c) for differences training.

(i) No training credit is given for second-in-command training and no credit is given for right seat time under this program. Only the sole manipulator of the controls of the MU–2B airplane, flight training device, or Level C or D simulator can receive training credit under this program;

(ii) An MU–2B airplane must be operated in accordance with an FAA approved MU–2B training program that meets the standards of this subpart and the training hours in §91.1707.

(7) Endorsements given for compliance with paragraph (f) of this section must be appropriate to the content of that specific MU–2B training program's compliance with standards of this subpart.

§91.1707 Training program hours.

(a) Ground instruction hours are listed in the following table:

Initial/transition	Requalificaton	Recurrent
20 hours	12 hours	8 hours

(b) Flight instruction hours are listed in the following table:

Initial/transition	Requalificaton	Recurrent
12 hours with a minimum of 6 hours at level E	8 hours level C or level E	4 hours at level E, or 6 hours at level C

(c) Differences training hours are listed in the following table:

2 factory type design models concurrently	1.5 hours required at level B
More than 2 factory type design models concurrently	3 hours at level B
Each additional factory type design model added separately	1.5 hours at level B

(d) Definitions of levels of training as used in this subpart:

(1) LEVEL A Training—Training that is conducted through self-instruction by the pilot.

(2) LEVEL B Training—Training that is conducted in the classroom environment with the aid of a qualified instructor who meets the requirements of this subpart.

(3) LEVEL C Training—Training that is accomplished in an FAA-approved Level 5 or 6 flight training device. In addition to the basic FTD requirements, the FTD must be representative of the MU–2B cockpit controls and be specifically approved by the FAA for the MU–2B airplane.

(4) LEVEL E Training—Training that must be accomplished in the MU–2B airplane, Level C simulator, or Level D simulator.

§91.1709 Training program approval.

To obtain approval for an MU–2B training program, training providers must submit a proposed training program to the Administrator.

(a) Only training programs approved by the Administrator may be used to satisfy the standards of this subpart.

(b) For part 91 training providers, training programs will be approved for 24 months, unless sooner superseded or rescinded.

(c) The Administrator may require revision of an approved MU–2B training program at any time.

(d) A training provider must present its approved training program and FAA approval documentation to any representative of the Administrator, upon request.

§91.1711 Aeronautical experience.

No person may act as a pilot in command of a Mitsubishi MU–2B series airplane for the purpose of flight unless that person holds an airplane category and multi-engine land class rating, and has logged a minimum of 100 flight hours of PIC time in multi-engine airplanes.

§91.1713 Instruction, checking, and evaluation.

(a) *Flight Instructor (Airplane).* No flight instructor may provide instruction or conduct a flight review in a Mitsubishi MU–2B series airplane unless that flight instructor

(1) Meets the pilot training and documentation requirements of §91.1705 before giving flight instruction in the Mitsubishi MU–2B series airplane;

(2) Meets the currency requirements of §§91.1715(a) and 91.1715(c)

(3) Has a minimum total pilot time of 2,000 pilot-in-command hours and 800 pilot-in-command hours in multi-engine airplanes; and

(4) Has:

(i) 300 pilot-in-command hours in the Mitsubishi MU–2B series airplane, 50 hours of which must have been within the preceding 12 months; or

(ii) 100 pilot-in-command hours in the Mitsubishi MU–2B series airplane, 25 hours of which must have been within the preceding 12 months, and 300 hours providing instruction in a FAA-approved Mitsubishi MU–2B simulator or

FAA-approved Mitsubishi MU–2B flight training device, 25 hours of which must have been within the preceding 12 months.

(b) *Flight Instructor (Simulator/Flight Training Device).* No flight instructor may provide instruction for the Mitsubishi MU–2B series airplane unless that instructor meets the requirements of this paragraph—

(1) Each flight instructor who provides flight training for the Mitsubishi MU–2B series airplane must meet the pilot training and documentation requirements of §91.1705 before giving flight instruction for the Mitsubishi MU–2B series airplane;

(2) Each flight instructor who provides flight training for the Mitsubishi MU–2B series airplane must meet the currency requirements of §91.1715(c) before giving flight instruction for the Mitsubishi MU–2B series airplane;

(3) Each flight instructor who provides flight training for the Mitsubishi MU–2B series airplane must have:

(i) A minimum total pilot time of 2,000 pilot-in-command hours and 800 pilot-in-command hours in multi-engine airplanes; and

(ii) Within the preceding 12 months, either 50 hours of Mitsubishi MU–2B series airplane pilot-in-command experience or 50 hours providing simulator or flight training device instruction for the Mitsubishi MU–2B.

(c) *Checking and evaluation.* No person may provide checking or evaluation for the Mitsubishi MU–2B series airplane unless that person meets the requirements of this paragraph—

(1) For the purpose of checking, designated pilot examiners, training center evaluators, and check airmen must have completed the appropriate training in the Mitsubishi MU–2B series airplane in accordance with §91.1705;

(2) For checking conducted in the Mitsubishi MU–2B series airplane, each designated pilot examiner and check airman must have 100 hours pilot-in-command flight time in the Mitsubishi MU–2B series airplane and maintain currency in accordance with §91.1715.

§91.1715 Currency requirements and flight review.

(a) The takeoff and landing currency requirements of §61.57 of this chapter must be maintained in the Mitsubishi MU–2B series airplane. Takeoff and landings in other multiengine airplanes do not meet the takeoff and landing currency requirements for the Mitsubishi MU–2B series plane. Takeoff and landings in either the short-body or long-body Mitsubishi MU–2B model airplane may be credited toward takeoff and landing currency for both Mitsubishi MU–2B model groups.

(b) Instrument experience obtained in other category and class of aircraft may be used to satisfy the instrument currency requirements of §61.57 of this chapter for the Mitsubishi MU–2B series airplane.

(c) Satisfactory completion of a flight review to satisfy the requirements of §61.56 of this chapter is valid for operation of a Mitsubishi MU–2B series airplane only if that flight review is conducted in a Mitsubishi MU–2B series airplane or an MU–2B Simulator approved for landings with an approved course conducted under part 142 of this chapter. The flight review for Mitsubishi MU–2B series airplanes must include the *Special Emphasis Items*, and all items listed in the *Training Course Final Phase Check* in accordance with an approved MU–2B Training Program.

(d) A person who successfully completes the Initial/transition, Requalification, or Recurrent training requirements under §91.1705 of this chapter also meet the requirements of §61.56 of this chapter and need not accomplish a separate flight review provided that at least 1 hour of the flight training was conducted in the Mitsubishi MU–2B series airplane or an MU–2B Simulator approved for landings with an approved course conducted under part 142 of this chapter.

[Docket FAA–2006–24981, Amdt. 91–344, 81 FR 61591, Sept. 7, 2016; Amdt. 91–344A, 82 FR 21472, May 9, 2017]

§91.1717 Operating requirements.

(a) Except as provided in paragraph (b) of this section, no person may operate a Mitsubishi MU–2B airplane in single pilot operations unless that airplane has a functional autopilot.

(b) A person may operate a Mitsubishi MU–2B airplane in single pilot operations without a functional autopilot when—

(1) Operating under day visual flight rule requirements; or

(2) Authorized under a FAA approved minimum equipment list for that airplane, operating under instrument flight rule requirements in daytime visual meteorological conditions.

(c) No person may operate a Mitsubishi MU–2B series airplane unless a copy of the appropriate Mitsubishi Heavy Industries MU–2B Airplane Flight Manual is carried on board the airplane and is accessible during each flight at the pilot station.

(d) No person may operate a Mitsubishi MU–2B series airplane unless an MU–2B series airplane checklist, appropriate for the model being operated and accepted by the Federal Aviation Administration MU–2B Flight Standardization Board, is accessible for each flight at the pilot station and is used by the flight crewmembers when operating the airplane.

(e) No person may operate a Mitsubishi MU–2B series airplane contrary to the standards of this subpart.

(f) If there are any differences between the training and operating requirements of this subpart and the MU–2B Airplane Flight Manual's procedures sections (Normal, Abnormal, and Emergency) and the MU–2B airplane series checklist incorporated by reference in §91.1721, the person operating the airplane must operate the airplane in accordance with the training specified in this subpart.

§91.1719 Credit for prior training.

Initial/transition, requalification, recurrent or Level B differences training conducted prior to November 7, 2016, compliant with SFAR No. 108, Section 3 of this part, is considered to be compliant with this subpart, if the student met the eligibility requirements for the applicable category of training and the student's instructor met the experience requirements of this subpart.

§91.1721 Incorporation by reference.

(a) The Mitsubishi Heavy Industries MU–2B Cockpit Checklists are incorporated by reference into this part. The Director of the Federal Register approved this incorporation by reference in accordance with 5 U.S.C. 552(a) and 1 CFR part 51. All approved material is available for inspection at U.S. Department of Transportation, Docket Management Facility, Room W 12-140, West Building Ground Floor, 1200 New Jersey Ave. SE., Washington, DC 20590-0001, or at the National Archives and Records Administration, call 202-741-6030, or go to: *http://www.archives.gov/federal_register/code_of_federal_regulations/ibr_locations.html.*

(b) Mitsubishi Heavy Industries America, Inc., 4951 Airport Parkway, Suite 530, Addison, TX 75001.

(1) Mitsubishi Heavy Industries MU–2B Checklists:

(i) Cockpit Checklist, Model MU–2B–60, Type Certificate A10SW, MHI Document No. YET06220C, accepted by FSB on February 12, 2007.

(ii) Cockpit Checklist, Model MU–2B–40, Type Certificate A10SW, MHI Document No. YET06256A, accepted by FSB on February 12, 2007.

(iii) Cockpit Checklist, Model MU–2B–36A, Type Certificate A10SW, MHI Document No. YET06257B, accepted by FSB on February 12, 2007.

(iv) Cockpit Checklist, Model MU–2B–36, Type Certificate A2PC, MHI Document No. YET06252B, accepted by FSB on February 12, 2007.

(v) Cockpit Checklist, Model MU–2B–35, Type Certificate A2PC, MHI Document No. YET06251B, accepted by FSB on February 12, 2007.

(vi) Cockpit Checklist, Model MU–2B–30, Type Certificate A2PC, MHI Document No. YET06250A, accepted by FSB on March 2, 2007.

(vii) Cockpit Checklist, Model MU–2B–26A, Type Certificate A10SW, MHI Document No. YET06255A, accepted by FSB on February 12, 2007.

(viii) Cockpit Checklist, Model MU–2B–26, Type Certificate A2PC, MHI Document No. YET06249A, accepted by FSB on March 2, 2007.

(ix) Cockpit Checklist, Model MU–2B–26, Type Certificate A10SW, MHI Document No. YET06254A, accepted by FSB on March 2, 2007.

(x) Cockpit Checklist, Model MU–2B–25, Type Certificate A10SW, MHI Document No. YET06253A, accepted by FSB on March 2, 2007.

(xi) Cockpit Checklist, Model MU–2B–25, Type Certificate A2PC, MHI Document No. YET06248A, accepted by FSB on March 2, 2007.

(xii) Cockpit Checklist, Model MU–2B–20, Type Certificate A2PC, MHI Document No. YET06247A, accepted by FSB on February 12, 2007.

(xiii)–(xiv) [Reserved]

(xv) Cockpit Checklist, Model MU–2B–15, Type Certificate A2PC, MHI Document No. YET06246A, accepted by FSB on March 2, 2007.

(xvi) Cockpit Checklist, Model MU–2B–10, Type Certificate A2PC, MHI Document No. YET06245A, accepted by FSB on March 2, 2007.

(xvii) Cockpit Checklist, Model MU–2B, Type Certificate A2PC, MHI Document No. YET06244A, accepted by FSB on March 2, 2007.

(2) [Reserved]

[Docket FAA–2006–24981, Amdt. 91–344, 81 FR 61591, Sept. 7, 2016; Amdt. 91–344A, 82 FR 21472, May 9, 2017]

APPENDIX A TO PART 91
CATEGORY II OPERATIONS: MANUAL, INSTRUMENTS, EQUIPMENT, AND MAINTENANCE

1. *Category II Manual*

(a) *Application for approval.* An applicant for approval of a Category II manual or an amendment to an approved Category II manual must submit the proposed manual or amendment to the responsible Flight Standards office. If the application requests an evaluation program, it must include the following:

(1) The location of the aircraft and the place where the demonstrations are to be conducted; and

(2) The date the demonstrations are to commence (at least 10 days after filing the application).

(b) *Contents.* Each Category II manual must contain:

(1) The registration number, make, and model of the aircraft to which it applies;

(2) A maintenance program as specified in section 4 of this appendix; and

(3) The procedures and instructions related to recognition of decision height, use of runway visual range information, approach monitoring, the decision region (the region between the middle marker and the decision height), the maximum permissible deviations of the basic ILS indicator within the decision region, a missed approach, use of airborne low approach equipment, minimum altitude for the use of the autopilot, instrument and equipment failure warning systems, instrument failure, and other procedures, instructions, and limitations that may be found necessary by the Administrator.

2. Required Instruments and Equipment

The instruments and equipment listed in this section must be installed in each aircraft operated in a Category II operation. This section does not require duplication of instruments and equipment required by §91.205 or any other provisions of this chapter.

(a) *Group I.*

(1) Two localizer and glide slope receiving systems. Each system must provide a basic ILS display and each side of the instrument panel must have a basic ILS display. However, a single localizer antenna and a single glide slope antenna may be used.

(2) A communications system that does not affect the operation of at least one of the ILS systems.

(3) A marker beacon receiver that provides distinctive aural and visual indications of the outer and the middle markers.

(4) Two gyroscopic pitch and bank indicating systems.

(5) Two gyroscopic direction indicating systems.

(6) Two airspeed indicators.

(7) Two sensitive altimeters adjustable for barometric pressure, each having a placarded correction for altimeter scale error and for the wheel height of the aircraft. After June 26, 1979, two sensitive altimeters adjustable for barometric pressure, having markings at 20-foot intervals and each having a placarded correction for altimeter scale error and for the wheel height of the aircraft.

(8) Two vertical speed indicators.

(9) A flight control guidance system that consists of either an automatic approach coupler or a flight director system. A flight director system must display computed information as steering command in relation to an ILS localizer and, on the same instrument, either computed information as pitch command in relation to an ILS glide slope or basic ILS glide slope information. An automatic approach coupler must provide at least automatic steering in relation to an ILS localizer. The flight control guidance system may be operated from one of the receiving systems required by subparagraph (1) of this paragraph.

(10) For Category II operations with decision heights below 150 feet either a marker beacon receiver providing aural and visual indications of the inner marker or a radio altimeter.

(b) *Group II.*

(1) Warning systems for immediate detection by the pilot of system faults in items (1), (4), (5), and (9) of Group I and, if installed for use in Category III operations, the radio altimeter and autothrottle system.

(2) Dual controls.

(3) An externally vented static pressure system with an alternate static pressure source.

(4) A windshield wiper or equivalent means of providing adequate cockpit visibility for a safe visual transition by either pilot to touchdown and rollout.

(5) A heat source for each airspeed system pitot tube installed or an equivalent means of preventing malfunctioning due to icing of the pitot system.

3. Instruments and Equipment Approval

(a) *General.* The instruments and equipment required by section 2 of this appendix must be approved as provided in this section before being used in Category II operations. Before presenting an aircraft for approval of the instruments and equipment, it must be shown that since the beginning of the 12th calendar month before the date of submission—

(1) The ILS localizer and glide slope equipment were bench checked according to the manufacturer's instructions and found to meet those standards specified in RTCA Paper 23–63/DO–117 dated March 14, 1963, "Standard Adjustment Criteria for Airborne Localizer and Glide Slope Receivers," which may be obtained from the RTCA Secretariat, 1425 K St. NW., Washington, DC 20005.

(2) The altimeters and the static pressure systems were tested and inspected in accordance with Appendix E to part 43 of this chapter; and

(3) All other instruments and items of equipment specified in section 2(a) of this appendix that are listed in the proposed maintenance program were bench checked and found to meet the manufacturer's specifications.

(b) *Flight control guidance system.* All components of the flight control guidance system must be approved as installed by the evaluation program specified in paragraph (e) of this section if they have not been approved for Category III

operations under applicable type or supplemental type certification procedures. In addition, subsequent changes to make, model, or design of the components must be approved under this paragraph. Related systems or devices, such as the autothrottle and computed missed approach guidance system, must be approved in the same manner if they are to be used for Category II operations.

(c) *Radio altimeter.* A radio altimeter must meet the performance criteria of this paragraph for original approval and after each subsequent alteration.

(1) It must display to the flight crew clearly and positively the wheel height of the main landing gear above the terrain.

(2) It must display wheel height above the terrain to an accuracy of plus or minus 5 feet or 5 percent, whichever is greater, under the following conditions:

(i) Pitch angles of zero to plus or minus 5 degrees about the mean approach attitude.

(ii) Roll angles of zero to 20 degrees in either direction.

(iii) Forward velocities from minimum approach speed up to 200 knots.

(iv) Sink rates from zero to 15 feet per second at altitudes from 100 to 200 feet.

(3) Over level ground, it must track the actual altitude of the aircraft without significant lag or oscillation.

(4) With the aircraft at an altitude of 200 feet or less, any abrupt change in terrain representing no more than 10 percent of the aircraft's altitude must not cause the altimeter to unlock, and indicator response to such changes must not exceed 0.1 seconds and, in addition, if the system unlocks for greater changes, it must reacquire the signal in less than 1 second.

(5) Systems that contain a push-to-test feature must test the entire system (with or without an antenna) at a simulated altitude of less than 500 feet.

(6) The system must provide to the flight crew a positive failure warning display any time there is a loss of power or an absence of ground return signals within the designed range of operating altitudes.

(d) *Other instruments and equipment.* All other instruments and items of equipment required by §2 of this appendix must be capable of performing as necessary for Category II operations. Approval is also required after each subsequent alteration to these instruments and items of equipment.

(e) *Evaluation program—*

(1) *Application.* Approval by evaluation is requested as a part of the application for approval of the Category II manual.

(2) *Demonstrations.* Unless otherwise authorized by the Administrator, the evaluation program

for each aircraft requires the demonstrations specified in this paragraph. At least 50 ILS approaches must be flown with at least five approaches on each of three different ILS facilities and no more than one half of the total approaches on any one ILS facility. All approaches shall be flown under simulated instrument conditions to a 100-foot decision height and 90 percent of the total approaches made must be successful. A successful approach is one in which—

(i) At the 100-foot decision height, the indicated airspeed and heading are satisfactory for a normal flare and landing (speed must be plus or minus 5 knots of programmed airspeed, but may not be less than computed threshold speed if autothrottles are used);

(ii) The aircraft at the 100-foot decision height, is positioned so that the cockpit is within, and tracking so as to remain within, the lateral confines of the runway extended;

(iii) Deviation from glide slope after leaving the outer marker does not exceed 50 percent of full-scale deflection as displayed on the ILS indicator;

(iv) No unusual roughness or excessive attitude changes occur after leaving the middle marker; and

(v) In the case of an aircraft equipped with an approach coupler, the aircraft is sufficiently in trim when the approach coupler is disconnected at the decision height to allow for the continuation of a normal approach and landing.

(3) *Records.* During the evaluation program the following information must be maintained by the applicant for the aircraft with respect to each approach and made available to the Administrator upon request:

(i) Each deficiency in airborne instruments and equipment that prevented the initiation of an approach.

(ii) The reasons for discontinuing an approach, including the altitude above the runway at which it was discontinued.

(iii) Speed control at the 100-foot decision height if auto throttles are used.

(iv) Trim condition of the aircraft upon disconnecting the auto coupler with respect to continuation to flare and landing.

(v) Position of the aircraft at the middle marker and at the decision height indicated both on a diagram of the basic ILS display and a diagram of the runway extended to the middle marker. Estimated touchdown point must be indicated on the runway diagram.

(vi) Compatibility of flight director with the auto coupler, if applicable.

(vii) Quality of overall system performance.

(4) *Evaluation.* A final evaluation of the flight control guidance system is made upon successful completion of the demonstrations. If no hazardous tendencies have been displayed or are

otherwise known to exist, the system is approved as installed.

4. *Maintenance program*

(a) Each maintenance program must contain the following:

(1) A list of each instrument and item of equipment specified in §2 of this appendix that is installed in the aircraft and approved for Category II operations, including the make and model of those specified in §2(a).

(2) A schedule that provides for the performance of inspections under subparagraph (5) of this paragraph within 3 calendar months after the date of the previous inspection. The inspection must be performed by a person authorized by part 43 of this chapter, except that each alternate inspection may be replaced by a functional flight check. This functional flight check must be performed by a pilot holding a Category II pilot authorization for the type aircraft checked.

(3) A schedule that provides for the performance of bench checks for each listed instrument and item of equipment that is specified in section 2(a) within 12 calendar months after the date of the previous bench check.

(4) A schedule that provides for the performance of a test and inspection of each static pressure system in accordance with Appendix E to part 43 of this chapter within 12 calendar months after the date of the previous test and inspection.

(5) The procedures for the performance of the periodic inspections and functional flight checks to determine the ability of each listed instrument and item of equipment specified in section 2(a) of this appendix to perform as approved for Category II operations including a procedure for recording functional flight checks.

(6) A procedure for assuring that the pilot is informed of all defects in listed instruments and items of equipment.

(7) A procedure for assuring that the condition of each listed instrument and item of equipment upon which maintenance is performed is at least equal to its Category II approval condition before it is returned to service for Category II operations.

(8) A procedure for an entry in the maintenance records required by §43.9 of this chapter that shows the date, airport, and reasons for each discontinued Category II operation because of a malfunction of a listed instrument or item of equipment.

(b) *Bench check.* A bench check required by this section must comply with this paragraph.

(1) It must be performed by a certificated repair station holding one of the following ratings as appropriate to the equipment checked:

(i) An instrument rating.

(ii) A radio rating.

(2) It must consist of removal of an instrument or item of equipment and performance of the following:

(i) A visual inspection for cleanliness, impending failure, and the need for lubrication, repair, or replacement of parts;

(ii) Correction of items found by that visual inspection; and

(iii) Calibration to at least the manufacturer's specifications unless otherwise specified in the approved Category II manual for the aircraft in which the instrument or item of equipment is installed.

(c) *Extensions.* After the completion of one maintenance cycle of 12 calendar months, a request to extend the period for checks, tests, and inspections is approved if it is shown that the performance of particular equipment justifies the requested extension.

[Docket No. 18334, 54 FR 34325, Aug. 18, 1989; as amended by Amdt. 91–269, 66 FR 41116, Aug. 6, 2001; Docket FAA–2018–0119, Amdt. 91–350, 83 FR 9171, March 5, 2018]

APPENDIXES B–C
[RESERVED]

APPENDIX D TO PART 91
AIRPORTS / LOCATIONS:
SPECIAL OPERATING RESTRICTIONS

1. Locations at which the requirements of §91.215(b)(2) and §91.225(d)(2) apply. The requirements of §91.215(b)(2) and §91.225(d)(2) apply below 10,000 feet MSL within a 30-nautical-mile radius of each location in the following list.

Atlanta, GA (Hartsfield-Jackson Atlanta International Airport)

Baltimore, MD (Baltimore/Washington International Thurgood Marshall Airport)

Boston, MA (General Edward Lawrence Logan International Airport)

Camp Springs, MD (Joint Base Andrews)

Chantilly, VA (Washington Dulles International Airport)

Charlotte, NC (Charlotte/Douglas International Airport)

Chicago, IL (Chicago-O'Hare International Airport)

Cleveland, OH (Cleveland Hopkins International Airport)

Covington, KY (Cincinnati/Northern Kentucky International Airport)

Dallas, TX (Dallas/Fort Worth International Airport)

Denver, CO (Denver International Airport)

Detroit, MI (Detroit Metropolitan Wayne County Airport)
Honolulu, HI (Honolulu International Airport)
Houston, TX (George Bush Intercontinental/Houston Airport)
Houston, TX (William P. Hobby Airport)
Kansas City, MO (Kansas City International Airport)
Las Vegas, NV (McCarran International Airport)
Los Angeles, CA (Los Angeles International Airport)
Memphis, TN (Memphis International Airport)
Miami, FL (Miami International Airport)
Minneapolis, MN (Minneapolis-St. Paul International/Wold-Chamberlain Airport)
Newark, NJ (Newark Liberty International Airport)
New Orleans, LA (Louis Armstrong New Orleans International Airport)
New York, NY (John F. Kennedy International Airport)
New York, NY (LaGuardia Airport)
Orlando, FL (Orlando International Airport)
Philadelphia, PA (Philadelphia International Airport)
Phoenix, AZ (Phoenix Sky Harbor International Airport)
Pittsburgh, PA (Pittsburgh International Airport)
St. Louis, MO (Lambert-St. Louis International Airport)
Salt Lake City, UT (Salt Lake City International Airport)
San Diego, CA (Miramar Marine Corps Air Station)
San Diego, CA (San Diego International Airport)
San Francisco, CA (San Francisco International Airport)
Seattle, WA (Seattle-Tacoma International Airport)
Tampa, FL (Tampa International Airport)
Washington, DC (Ronald Reagan Washington National Airport)

2. Airports at which the requirements of §91.215(b)(5)(ii) apply.
[Reserved]

3. Locations at which fixed-wing Special VFR operations are prohibited.
The Special VFR weather minimums of §91.157 do not apply to the following airports:
Atlanta, GA (Hartsfield-Jackson Atlanta International Airport)
Baltimore, MD (Baltimore/Washington International Thurgood Marshall Airport)
Boston, MA (General Edward Lawrence Logan International Airport)

Buffalo, NY (Greater Buffalo International Airport)
Camp Springs, MD (Joint Base Andrews)
Chicago, IL (Chicago-O'Hare International Airport)
Cleveland, OH (Cleveland-Hopkins International Airport)
Columbus, OH (Port Columbus International Airport)
Covington, KY (Cincinnati/Northern Kentucky International Airport)
Dallas, TX (Dallas/Fort Worth International Airport)
Dallas, TX (Dallas Love Field Airport)
Denver, CO (Denver International Airport)
Detroit, MI (Detroit Metropolitan Wayne County Airport)
Honolulu, HI (Honolulu International Airport)
Houston, TX (George Bush Intercontinental/Houston Airport)
Indianapolis, IN (Indianapolis International Airport)
Los Angeles, CA (Los Angeles International Airport)
Louisville, KY (Louisville International Airport-Standiford Field)
Memphis, TN (Memphis International Airport)
Miami, FL (Miami International Airport)
Minneapolis, MN (Minneapolis-St. Paul International/Wold-Chamberlain Airport)
Newark, NJ (Newark Liberty International Airport)
New York, NY (John F. Kennedy International Airport)
New York, NY (LaGuardia Airport)
New Orleans, LA (Louis Armstrong New Orleans International Airport)
Philadelphia, PA (Philadelphia International Airport)
Pittsburgh, PA (Pittsburgh International Airport)
Portland, OR (Portland International Airport)
San Francisco, CA (San Francisco International Airport)
Seattle, WA (Seattle-Tacoma International Airport)
St. Louis, MO (Lambert-St. Louis International Airport)
Tampa, FL (Tampa International Airport)
Washington, DC (Ronald Reagan Washington National Airport)

4. Locations at which solo student, sport, and recreational pilot activity is not permitted.
Pursuant to §91.131(b)(2), solo student, sport, and recreational pilot operations are not permitted at any of the following airports.
Atlanta, GA (Hartsfield-Jackson Atlanta International Airport)

Boston, MA (General Edward Lawrence
 Logan International Airport)
Camp Springs, MD (Joint Base Andrews)
Chicago, IL (Chicago-O'Hare International
 Airport)
Dallas, TX (Dallas/Fort Worth International
 Airport)
Los Angeles, CA (Los Angeles International
 Airport)
Miami, FL (Miami International Airport)
Newark, NJ (Newark Liberty International
 Airport)
New York, NY (John F. Kennedy International
 Airport)
New York, NY (LaGuardia Airport)
San Francisco, CA (San Francisco
 International Airport)
Washington, DC (Ronald Reagan Washington
 National Airport)

[Amdt. 91–227, 56 FR 65661, Dec. 17, 1991]

APPENDIX E TO PART 91
AIRPLANE FLIGHT RECORDER SPECIFICATIONS

Parameters	Range	Installed system[1] minimum accuracy (to recovered data)	Sampling interval (per second)	Resolution[4] read out
Relative Time (From Recorded on Prior to Takeoff)	8 hr minimum	±0.125% per hour	1	1 sec.
Indicated Airspeed	V_{S0} to V_D (KIAS)	±5% or ± 10 kts., whichever is greater. Resolution 2 kts. below 175 KIAS.	1	1%[3]
Altitude	–1,000 ft. to max cert. alt. of A/C	±100 to ± 700 ft. (see Table 1, TSO C51-a)	1	25 to 150 ft.
Magnetic Heading	360°	±5°	1	1°
Vertical Acceleration	–3g to +6g	±0.2g in addition to ± 0.3g maximum datum	4 (or 1 per second where peaks, ref. to 1g are recorded)	0.03g
Longitudinal Acceleration	±1.0g	±1.5% max. range excluding datum error of ±5%	2	0.01g
Pitch Attitude	100% of usable	±2°	1	0.8°
Roll Attitude	±60° of 100% of usable range, whichever is greater	±2°	1	0.8°
Stabilizer Trim Position, or Pitch Control Position[5]	Full Range	±3% unless higher uniquely required	1	1%[3]
Engine Power, Each Engine:	Full Range	±3% unless higher uniquely required	1	1%[3]
Fan or N1 Speed or EPR or cockpit indications used for aircraft certification OR	Maximum Range	±5%	1	1%[3]
Prop. speed and Torque (sample once/sec as close together as practicable)	—	—	1 (prop speed); 1 (torque)	1%[3]; 1%[3]
Altitude Rate[2] (need depends on altitude resolution)	±8,000 fpm	±10%. Resolution 250 fpm below 12,000 ft. indicated	1	250 fpm below 12,000
Angle of Attack[2] (need depends on altitude resolution)	–20° to 40° or 100% of usable range	±2°	1	0.8%[3]
Radio Transmitter Keying (Discrete)	On / Off	—	1	—
TE Flaps (Discrete or Analog)	Each discrete position (U.D. T/O. AAP) OR	—	1	—
LE Flaps (Discrete or Analog)	Analog 0–100% range	±3%	1	1%[3]
	Each discrete position (U.D. T/O, AAP) OR	—	1	—
Thrust Reverser, Each Engine (Discrete)	Analog 0–100% range	±3%	1	1%[3]
Spoiler / Speed brake (Discrete)	Stowed or full reverse	—	—	—
Autopilot Engaged (Discrete)	Stowed or out	—	1	—
	Engaged or Disengaged (Discrete)	—	1	—

See Appendix E footnotes on the next page.

¹ When data sources are aircraft instruments (except altimeters) of acceptable quality to fly the aircraft the recording system excluding these sensors (but including all other characteristics of the recording system) shall contribute no more than half of the values in this column.

² If data from the altitude encoding altimeter (100 ft. resolution) is used, then either one of these parameters should also be recorded. If however, altitude is recorded at a minimum resolution of 25 feet, then these two parameters can be omitted.

³ Percent of full range.

⁴ This column applies to aircraft manufactured after October 11, 1991.

⁵ For Pitch Control Position only, for all aircraft manufactured on or after April 6, 2012, the sampling interval (per second) is 8. Each input must be recorded at this rate. Alternately sampling inputs (interleaving) to meet this sampling interval is prohibited.

[Docket No. 18334, 54 FR 34327, Aug. 18, 1989, as amended by Amdt. 91–300, 73 FR 12565, Mar. 7, 2008; 73 FR 15280, March 21, 2008; Amdt. 91–313, 75 FR 17046, April 5, 2010; Amdt. 91–329, 78 FR 39971, July 3, 2013]

APPENDIX F TO PART 91
HELICOPTER FLIGHT RECORDER SPECIFICATIONS

Parameters	Range	Installed system[1] minimum accuracy (to recovered data)	Sampling interval (per second)	Resolution[3] read out
Relative Time (from recorded on prior to takeoff)	4 hr minimum	±0.125% per hour	1	1 sec.
Indicated Airspeed	V_{min} to V_D (KIAS) (minimum airspeed signal attainable with installed pilot-static system)	±5% or ±10 kts., whichever is greater	1	1 kt.
Altitude	–1,000 ft. to 20,000 ft. pressure altitude	±100 to ±700 ft. (see Table 1. TSO C51-a)	1	25 to 150 ft.
Magnetic Heading	360°	±5°	1	1°
Vertical Acceleration	–3g to +6g	±0.2g in addition to ±0.3g maximum datum	4 (or 1 per second where peaks, ref. to 1g are recorded)	0.05g
Longitudinal Acceleration	±1.0g	±1.5% max. range excluding datum error of ±5%	2	0.03g
Pitch Attitude	100% of usable range	±2°	1	0.8°
Roll Attitude	±60 or 100% of usable range, whichever is greater	±2°	1	0.8°
Altitude Rate	±8,000 fpm	±10% Resolution 250 fpm below 12,000 ft. indicated	1	250 fpm below 12,000
Engine Power, Each Engine:				
Main Rotor Speed	Maximum Range	±5%	1	1%[2]
Free or Power Turbine	Maximum Range	±5%	1	1%[2]
Engine Torque	Maximum Range	±5%	1	1%[2]
Flight Control Hydraulic Pressure:				
Primary (Discrete)	High / Low		1	
Secondary – if applicable (Discrete)	High / Low		1	
Radio Transmitter Keying (Discrete)	On / Off		1	
Autopilot Engaged (Discrete)	Engaged or Disengaged		1	
SAS Status – Engaged (Discrete)	Engaged or Disengaged		1	
SAS Fault Status (Discrete)	Fault / OK		1	
Flight Controls:				
Collective[4]	Full range	±3%	2	1%[2]
Pedal Position[4]	Full range	±3%	2	1%[2]
Lat. Cyclic[4]	Full range	±3%	2	1%[2]
Long. Cyclic[4]	Full range	±3%	2	1%[2]
Controllable Stabilator Position[4]	Full range	±3%	2	1%[2]

See Appendix F footnotes on the next page.

91

[1] When data sources are aircraft instruments (except altimeters) of acceptable quality to fly the aircraft the recording system excluding these sensors (but including all other characteristics of the recording system) shall contribute no more than half of the values in this column.

[2] Percent of full range.

[3] This column applies to aircraft manufactured after October 11, 1991.

[4] For all aircraft manufactured on or after April 6, 2012, the sampling interval per second is 4.

[Docket No. 18334, 54 FR 34328, Aug. 18, 1989; 54 FR 41211, Oct. 5, 1989; 54 FR 53036, Dec. 26, 1989; Amdt. 91–300, 73 FR 12565, March 7, 2008; 73 FR 15280, March 21, 2008; Amdt. 91–313, 75 FR 17046, April 5, 2010]

APPENDIX G TO PART 91

OPERATIONS IN REDUCED VERTICAL SEPARATION MINIMUM (RVSM) AIRSPACE

1. Definitions

Reduced Vertical Separation Minimum (RVSM) Airspace. Within RVSM airspace, air traffic control (ATC) separates aircraft by a minimum of 1,000 feet vertically between FL 290 and FL 410 inclusive. Air-traffic control notifies operators of RVSM airspace by providing route planning information.

RVSM Group Aircraft. Aircraft within a group of aircraft, approved as a group by the Administrator, in which each of the aircraft satisfy each of the following:

(a) The aircraft have been manufactured to the same design, and have been approved under the same type certificate, amended type certificate, or supplemental type certificate.

(b) The static system of each aircraft is installed in a manner and position that is the same as those of the other aircraft in the group. The same static source error correction is incorporated in each aircraft of the group.

(c) The avionics units installed in each aircraft to meet the minimum RVSM equipment requirements of this appendix are:

(1) Manufactured to the same manufacturer specification and have the same part number; or

(2) Of a different manufacturer or part number, if the applicant demonstrates that the equipment provides equivalent system performance.

RVSM Nongroup Aircraft. An aircraft that is approved for RVSM operations as an individual aircraft.

RVSM Flight envelope. An RVSM flight envelope includes the range of Mach number, weight divided by atmospheric pressure ratio, and altitudes over which an aircraft is approved to be operated in cruising flight within RVSM airspace. RVSM flight envelopes are defined as follows:

(a) The *full RVSM flight envelope* is bounded as follows:

(1) The altitude flight envelope extends from FL 290 upward to the lowest altitude of the following:

(i) FL 410 (the RVSM altitude limit);

(ii) The maximum certificated altitude for the aircraft; or

(iii) The altitude limited by cruise thrust, buffet, or other flight limitations.

(2) The airspeed flight envelopes extends:

(i) From the airspeed of the slats/flaps-up maximum endurance (holding) airspeed, or the maneuvering airspeed, whichever is lower;

(ii) To the maximum operating airspeed (V_{MO}/M_{MO}), or airspeed limited by cruise thrust buffet, or other flight limitations, whichever is lower.

(3) All permissible gross weights within the flight envelopes defined in paragraphs (1) and (2) of this definition.

(b) The *basic RVSM flight envelope* is the same as the full RVSM flight envelope except that the airspeed flight envelope extends:

(1) From the airspeed of the slats/flaps-up maximum endurance (holding) airspeed, or the maneuver airspeed, whichever is lower;

(2) To the upper Mach/airspeed boundary defined for the full RVSM flight envelope, or a specified lower value not less than the long-range cruise Mach number plus .04 Mach, unless further limited by available cruise thrust, buffet, or other flight limitations.

2. Aircraft Approval

(a) Except as specified in Section 9 of this appendix, an operator may be authorized to conduct RVSM operations if the Administrator finds that its aircraft comply with this section.

(b) The application for authorization shall submit the appropriate data package for aircraft approval. The package must consist of at least the following:

(1) An identification of the RVSM aircraft group or the nongroup aircraft;

(2) A definition of the RVSM flight envelopes applicable to the subject aircraft;

(3) Documentation that establishes compliance with the applicable RVSM aircraft requirements of this section; and

(4) The conformity tests used to ensure that aircraft approved with the data package meet the RVSM aircraft requirements.

(c) *Altitude-keeping equipment: All aircraft.* To approve an aircraft group or a nongroup aircraft, the Administrator must find that the aircraft meets the following requirements:

(1) The aircraft must be equipped with two operational independent altitude measurement systems.

(2) The aircraft must be equipped with at least one automatic altitude control system that controls the aircraft altitude—

(i) Within a tolerance band of ± 65 feet about an acquired altitude when the aircraft is operated in straight and level flight under nonturbulent, non-gust conditions; or

(ii) Within a tolerance band of ±130 feet under nonturbulent, nongust conditions for aircraft for which application for type certification occurred on or before April 9, 1997 that are equipped with an automatic altitude control system with flight management/performance system inputs.

(3) The aircraft must be equipped with an altitude alert system that signals an alert when the altitude displayed to the flight crew deviates from the selected altitude by more than:

(i) ± 300 feet for aircraft for which application for type certification was made on or before April 9, 1997; or

(ii) ± 200 feet for aircraft for which application for type certification is made after April 9, 1997.

(d) *Altimetry system error containment: Group aircraft for which application for type certification was made on or before April 9, 1997.* To approve group aircraft for which application for type certification was made on or before April 9, 1997, the Administrator must find that the altimetry system error (ASE) is contained as follows:

(1) At the point in the basic RVSM flight envelope where mean ASE reaches its largest absolute value, the absolute value may not exceed 80 feet.

(2) At the point in the basic RVSM flight envelope where mean ASE plus three standard deviations reaches its largest absolute value, the absolute value may not exceed 200 feet.

(3) At the point in the full RVSM flight envelope where mean ASE reaches its largest absolute value, the absolute value may not exceed 120 feet.

(4) At the point in the full RVSM flight envelope where mean ASE plus three standard deviations reaches its largest absolute value, the absolute value may not exceed 245 feet.

(5) *Necessary operating restrictions.* If the applicant demonstrates that its aircraft otherwise comply with the ASE containment requirements, the Administrator may establish an operating restriction on that applicant's aircraft to restrict the aircraft from operating in areas of the basic RVSM flight envelope where the absolute value of mean ASE exceeds 80 feet, and/or the absolute value of mean ASE plus three standard deviations exceeds 200 feet; or from operating in areas of the full RVSM flight envelope where the absolute value of the mean ASE exceeds 120 feet and/or the absolute value of the mean ASE plus three standard deviations exceeds 245 feet.

(e) *Altimetry system error containment: Group aircraft for which application for type certification is made after April 9, 1997.* To approve group aircraft for which application for type certification is made after April 9, 1997, the Administrator must find that the altimetry system error (ASE) is contained as follows:

(1) At the point in the full RVSM flight envelope where mean ASE reaches its largest absolute value, the absolute value may not exceed 80 feet.

(2) At the point in the full RVSM flight envelope where mean ASE plus three standard deviations reaches its largest absolute value may not exceed 200 feet.

(f) *Altimetry system error containment: Nongroup aircraft.* To approve a nongroup aircraft, the Administrator must find that the altimetry system error (ASE) is contained as follows:

(1) For each condition in the basic RVSM flight envelope, the largest combined absolute value for residual static source error plus the avionics error may not exceed 160 feet.

(2) For each condition in the full RVSM flight envelope, the largest combined absolute value for residual static source error plus the avionics error may not exceed 200 feet.

(g) Traffic Alert and Collision Avoidance System (TCAS) Compatibility With RVSM Operations: All aircraft. After March 31, 2002, unless otherwise authorized by the Administrator, if you operate an aircraft that is equipped with TCAS II in RVSM airspace, it must be a TCAS II that meets TSO C-119b (Version 7.0), or a later version.

(h) If the Administrator finds that the applicant's aircraft comply with this section, the Administrator notifies the applicant in writing.

3. *Operator Authorization*

(a) Except as specified in Section 9 of this appendix, authority for an operator to conduct flight in airspace where RVSM is applied is issued in operations specifications, a Letter of Authorization, or management specifications issued under subpart K of this part, as appropriate. To issue an RVSM authorization under this section, the Administrator must find that the operator's aircraft have been approved in accordance with Section 2 of this appendix and the operator complies with this section.

(b) Except as specified in Section 9 of this appendix, an applicant seeking authorization to operate within RVSM airspace must apply in a form and manner prescribed by the Administrator. The application must include the following:

(1) [Reserved]

(2) For an applicant who operates under part 121 or 135 of this chapter or under subpart K of this part, initial and recurring pilot training requirements.

(3) Policies and procedures: An applicant who operates under part 121 or 135 of this chapter or under subpart K of this part must submit RVSM policies and procedures that will enable it to conduct RVSM operations safely.

(c) In a manner prescribed by the Administrator, an operator seeking authorization under this section must provide evidence that:

(1) It is capable to operate and maintain each aircraft or aircraft group for which it applies for approval to operate in RVSM airspace; and

(2) Each pilot has knowledge of RVSM requirements, policies, and procedures sufficient for the conduct of operations in RVSM airspace.

4. RVSM Operations

(a) Each person requesting a clearance to operate within RVSM airspace shall correctly annotate the flight plan filed with air traffic control with the status of the operator and aircraft with regard to RVSM approval. Each operator shall verify RVSM applicability for the flight planned route through the appropriate flight planning information sources.

(b) No person may show, on the flight plan filed with air traffic control, an operator or aircraft as approved for RVSM operations, or operate on a route or in an area where RVSM approval is required, unless:

(1) The operator is authorized by the Administrator to perform such operations in accordance with Section 3 or Section 9 of this appendix, as applicable.

(2) The aircraft—

(i) Has been approved and complies with Section 2 of this appendix; or

(ii) Complies with Section 9 of this appendix.

(3) Each pilot has knowledge of RVSM requirements, policies, and procedures sufficient for the conduct of operations in RVSM airspace.

5. Deviation Authority Approval

The Administrator may authorize an aircraft operator to deviate from the requirements of §§91.180 or 91.706 for a specific flight in RVSM airspace if—

(a) The operator submits a request in a time and manner acceptable to the Administrator; and

(b) At the time of filing the flight plan for that flight, ATC determines that the aircraft may be provided appropriate separation and that the flight will not interfere with, or impose a burden on, RVSM operations.

6. Reporting altitude-Keeping Errors

Each operator shall report to the Administrator each event in which the operator's aircraft has exhibited the following altitude-keeping performance:

(a) Total vertical error of 300 feet or more;

(b) Altimetry system error of 245 feet or more; or

(c) Assigned altitude deviation of 300 feet or more.

7. Removal or Amendment of Authority

The Administrator may prohibit or restrict an operator from conducting operations in RVSM airspace, if the Administrator determines that the operator is not complying, or is unable to comply, with this appendix or subpart H of this part. Examples of reasons for amendment, revocation,

or restriction include, but are not limited to, an operator's:

(a) Committing one or more altitude-keeping errors in RVSM airspace;

(b) Failing to make an effective and timely response to identify and correct an altitude-keeping error; or

(c) Failing to report an altitude-keeping error.

8. Airspace Designation

RVSM may be applied in all ICAO Flight Information Regions (FIRs).

9. Aircraft Equipped With Automatic Dependent Surveillance—Broadcast Out

An operator is authorized to conduct flight in airspace in which RVSM is applied provided:

(a) The aircraft is equipped with the following:

(1) Two operational independent altitude measurement systems.

(2) At least one automatic altitude control system that controls the aircraft altitude—

(i) Within a tolerance band of ±65 feet about an acquired altitude when the aircraft is operated in straight and level flight under nonturbulent, nongust conditions; or

(ii) Within a tolerance band of ±130 feet under nonturbulent, nongust conditions for aircraft for which application for type certification occurred on or before April 9, 1997, that are equipped with an automatic altitude control system with flight management/performance system inputs.

(3) An altitude alert system that signals an alert when the altitude displayed to the flightcrew deviates from the selected altitude by more than—

(i) ±300 feet for aircraft for which application for type certification was made on or before April 9, 1997; or

(ii) ±200 feet for aircraft for which application for type certification is made after April 9, 1997.

(4) A TCAS II that meets TSO C-119b (Version 7.0), or a later version, if equipped with TCAS II, unless otherwise authorized by the Administrator.

(5) Unless authorized by ATC or the foreign country where the aircraft is operated, an ADS-B Out system that meets the equipment performance requirements of §91.227 of this part. The aircraft must have its height-keeping performance monitored in a form and manner acceptable to the Administrator.

(b) The altimetry system error (ASE) of the aircraft does not exceed 200 feet when operating in RVSM airspace.

[Docket No. 28870, 62 FR 17487, April 9, 1997, as amended by Amdt. 91–261, 65 FR 5942, Feb. 7, 2000; Amdt. 91–271, 66 FR 63895, Dec. 10, 2001; Amdt. 91–274, 68 FR 54584, Sept. 17, 2003; Amdt. 91–276, 68 FR 70133, Dec. 17, 2003; Docket FAA–2015–1746, Amdt. 91–342, 81 FR 47017, July 20, 2016; Docket FAA–2016–9154, Amdt. 91–348, 82 FR 39664, Aug. 22, 2017; FAA-2017-0782, Amdt. No. 91-354, 83 FR 65492, Dec. 21, 2018]

PART 97

STANDARD INSTRUMENT PROCEDURES

Subpart A—General

Sec.
97.1 Applicability.
97.3 Symbols and terms used in procedures.
97.5 Bearings, courses, tracks, headings, radials, miles.

Subpart B—Procedures

97.10 [Reserved]

Subpart C—TERPs Procedures

97.20 General.

Authority: 49 U.S.C. 106(f), 106(g), 40103, 40106, 40113, 40114, 40120, 44502, 44514, 44701, 44719, and 44721–44722.

Source: Docket No. 1580, 28 FR 6719, June 29, 1963, unless otherwise noted.

Subpart A—General

§97.1 Applicability.

(a) This part prescribes standard instrument approach procedures to civil airports in the United States and the weather minimums that apply to landings under IFR at those airports.

(b) This part also prescribes obstacle departure procedures (ODPs) for certain civil airports in the United States and the weather minimums that apply to takeoffs under IFR at civil airports in the United States.

[Docket No. FAA–2002–14002, 72 FR 31679, June 7, 2007]

§97.3 Symbols and terms used in procedures.

As used in the standard instrument procedures prescribed in this part—

Aircraft approach category means a grouping of aircraft based on a speed of V_{REF}, if specified, or if V_{REF} is not specified, 1.3 V_{S0} at the maximum certificated landing weight. V_{REF}, V_{S0}, and the maximum certificated landing weight are those values as established for the aircraft by the certification authority of the country of registry. The categories are as follows—

(1) Category A: Speed less than 91 knots.

(2) Category B: Speed 91 knots or more but less than 121 knots.

(3) Category C: Speed 121 knots or more but less than 141 knots.

(4) Category D: Speed 141 knots or more but less than 166 knots.

(5) Category E: Speed 166 knots or more.

Approach procedure segments for which altitudes (minimum altitudes, unless otherwise specified) and paths are prescribed in procedures, are as follows—

(1) Initial approach is the segment between the initial approach fix and the intermediate fix or the point where the aircraft is established on the intermediate course or final approach course.

(2) Initial approach altitude is the altitude (or altitudes, in high altitude procedure) prescribed for the initial approach segment of an instrument approach.

(3) Intermediate approach is the segment between the intermediate fix or point and the final approach fix.

(4) Final approach is the segment between the final approach fix or point and the runway, airport, or missed approach point.

(5) Missed approach is the segment between the missed approach point, or point of arrival at decision altitude or decision height (DA/DH), and the missed approach fix at the prescribed altitude.

Ceiling means the minimum ceiling, expressed in feet above the airport elevation, required for takeoff or required for designating an airport as an alternate airport.

Copter procedures means helicopter procedures, with applicable minimums as prescribed in §97.35. Helicopters may also use other procedures prescribed in subpart C of this part and may use the Category A minimum descent altitude (MDA), or decision altitude or decision height (DA/DH). For other than "copter-only" approaches, the required visibility minimum for Category I approaches may be reduced to one-half the published visibility minimum for Category A aircraft, but in no case may it be reduced to less than one-quarter mile prevailing visibility, or, if reported, 1,200 feet RVR. Reduction of visibility minima on Category II instrument approach procedures is prohibited.

FAF means final approach fix.

HAA means height above airport and is expressed in feet.

HAL means height above landing and is the height of the DA/MDA above a designated helicopter landing area elevation used for helicopter instrument approach procedures and is expressed in feet.

HAS means height above the surface and is the height of the DA/MDA above the highest terrain/surface within a 5,200-foot radius of the missed

approach point used in helicopter instrument approach procedures and is expressed in feet above ground level (AGL).

HAT means height above touchdown.

HCH means helipoint crossing height and is the computed height of the vertical guidance path above the helipoint elevation at the helipoint expressed in feet.

Helipoint means the aiming point for the final approach course. It is normally the center point of the touchdown and lift-off area (TLOF).

Hold in lieu of PT means a holding pattern established under applicable FAA criteria, and used in lieu of a procedure turn to execute a course reversal.

MAP means missed approach point.

More than 65 knots means an aircraft that has a stalling speed of more than 65 knots (as established in an approved flight manual) at maximum certificated landing weight with full flaps, landing gear extended, and power off.

MSA means minimum safe altitude, expressed in feet above mean sea level, depicted on an approach chart that provides at least 1,000 feet of obstacle clearance for emergency use within a certain distance from the specified navigation facility or fix.

NA means not authorized.

NOPT means no procedure turn required. Altitude prescribed applies only if procedure turn is not executed.

Procedure turn means the maneuver prescribed when it is necessary to reverse direction to establish the aircraft on an intermediate or final approach course. The outbound course, direction of turn, distance within which the turn must be completed, and minimum altitude are specified in the procedure. However, the point at which the turn may be begun, and the type and rate of turn, is left to the discretion of the pilot.

RA means radio altimeter setting height.

RVV means runway visibility value.

SIAP means standard instrument approach procedure.

65 knots or less means an aircraft that has a stalling speed of 65 knots or less (as established in an approved flight manual) at maximum certificated landing weight with full flaps, landing gear extended, and power off.

T means nonstandard takeoff minimums or specified departure routes/procedures or both.

TDZ means touchdown zone.

Visibility minimum means the minimum visibility specified for approach, landing, or takeoff, expressed in statute miles, or in feet where RVR is reported.

[Docket No. FAA–2002–14002, 72 FR 31679, June 7, 2007]

§97.5 Bearings, courses, tracks, headings, radials, miles.

(a) All bearings, courses, tracks, headings, and radials in this part are magnetic, unless otherwise designated.

(b) RVR values are stated in feet. Other visibility values are stated in statute miles. All other mileages are stated in nautical miles.

[Docket No. 561, 32 FR 13912, Oct. 6, 1967; as amended by Amdt. 97–1336, 72 FR 31680, June 7, 2007]

Subpart B—Procedures

Editorial Note: The procedures set forth in this subpart were formerly carried as §§609.100 through 609.500 of this title and were transferred to part 97 as §§97.11 through 97.19, respectively, but are not carried in the Code of Federal Regulations. For Federal Register citations affecting these procedures, see the List of CFR Sections Affected, which appears in the Finding Aids section of the printed volume and at www.govinfo.gov.

§97.10 [Reserved]

Subpart C— TERPs Procedures

Source: Docket No. 8130, 32 FR 13912, Oct. 6, 1967, unless otherwise noted.

§97.20 General.

(a) This subpart prescribes standard instrument approach procedures and takeoff minimums and obstacle departure procedures (ODPs) based on the criteria contained in FAA Order 8260.3, U.S. Standard for Terminal Instrument Procedures (TERPs), and other related Orders in the 8260 series that also address instrument procedure design criteria.

(b) Standard instrument approach procedures and associated supporting data adopted by the FAA are documented on FAA Forms 8260-3, 8260-4, 8260-5. Takeoff minimums and obstacle departure procedures (ODPs) are documented on FAA Form 8260-15A. These forms are incorporated by reference. The Director of the Federal Register approved this incorporation by reference pursuant to 5 U.S.C. 552(a) and 1 CFR part 51. The standard instrument approach procedures and takeoff minimums and obstacle departure procedures (ODPs) are available for examination at the U.S. Department of Transportation, Docket Operations, 1200 New Jersey Avenue SE, West Building Ground Floor, Room W12–140, Washington, DC 20590, and at Aeronautical Information Services, 1305 East-West Highway, Silver Spring, MD 20910, or at the National Archives and Records Administration (NARA). For information on

the availability of this material at NARA, email: *fedreg.legal@nara.gov*, or go to *http://www.archives.gov/federal_register/code_of_federal_regulations/ibr_locations.html*.

(c) Standard instrument approach procedures and takeoff minimums and obstacle departure procedures (ODPs) are depicted on aeronautical charts published by the FAA. These charts are available from the FAA at *https://www.faa.gov/air_traffic/flight_info/aeronav/digital_products/*.

[Docket No. FAA–2002–14002, 72 FR 31680, June 7, 2007, as amended by Docket FAA–2018–0119, Amdt. 97–1338, 83 FR 9172, March 5, 2018; Docket No. FAA–2022–1355, Amdt. No. 97–1339, 87 FR 75846, Dec. 9, 2022]

Editorial Note: The procedures for §§97.21 through 97.37, respectively, are not carried in the Code of Federal Regulations. For Federal Register citations affecting these procedures, see the List of CFR Sections Affected, which appears in the Finding Aids section of the printed volume and at www.govinfo.gov.

97

PART 103

ULTRALIGHT VEHICLES

Subpart A—General

Sec.
103.1 Applicability.
103.3 Inspection requirements.
103.5 Waivers.
103.7 Certification and registration.

Subpart B—Operating Rules

103.9 Hazardous operations.
103.11 Daylight operations.
103.13 Operation near aircraft; right-of-way rules.
103.15 Operations over congested areas.
103.17 Operations in certain airspace.
103.19 Operations in prohibited or restricted areas.
103.20 Flight restrictions in the proximity of certain areas designated by notice to airmen.
103.21 Visual reference with the surface.
103.23 Flight visibility and cloud clearance requirements.

Authority: 49 U.S.C. 106(g), 40103–40104, 40113, 44701.

Source: Docket No. 21631, 47 FR 38776, Sept. 2, 1982, unless otherwise noted.

Subpart A—General

§103.1 Applicability.

This part prescribes rules governing the operation of ultralight vehicles in the United States. For the purposes of this part, an ultralight vehicle is a vehicle that:

(a) Is used or intended to be used for manned operation in the air by a single occupant;

(b) Is used or intended to be used for recreation or sport purposes only;

(c) Does not have any U.S. or foreign airworthiness certificate; and

(d) If unpowered, weighs less than 155 pounds; or

(e) If powered:

(1) Weighs less than 254 pounds empty weight, excluding floats and safety devices which are intended for deployment in a potentially catastrophic situation;

(2) Has a fuel capacity not exceeding 5 U.S. gallons;

(3) Is not capable of more than 55 knots calibrated airspeed at full power in level flight; and

(4) Has a power-off stall speed which does not exceed 24 knots calibrated airspeed.

§103.3 Inspection requirements.

(a) Any person operating an ultralight vehicle under this part shall, upon request, allow the Administrator, or his designee, to inspect the vehicle to determine the applicability of this part.

(b) The pilot or operator of an ultralight vehicle must, upon request of the Administrator, furnish satisfactory evidence that the vehicle is subject only to the provisions of this part.

§103.5 Waivers.

No person may conduct operations that require a deviation from this part except under a written waiver issued by the Administrator.

§103.7 Certification and registration.

(a) Notwithstanding any other section pertaining to certification of aircraft or their parts or equipment, ultralight vehicles and their component parts and equipment are not required to meet the airworthiness certification standards specified for aircraft or to have certificates of airworthiness.

(b) Notwithstanding any other section pertaining to airman certification, operators of ultralight vehicles are not required to meet any aeronautical knowledge, age, or experience requirements to operate those vehicles or to have airman or medical certificates.

(c) Notwithstanding any other section pertaining to registration and marking of aircraft, ultralight vehicles are not required to be registered or to bear markings of any type.

Subpart B— Operating Rules

§103.9 Hazardous operations.

(a) No person may operate any ultralight vehicle in a manner that creates a hazard to other persons or property.

(b) No person may allow an object to be dropped from an ultralight vehicle if such action creates a hazard to other persons or property.

§103.11 Daylight operations.

(a) No person may operate an ultralight vehicle except between the hours of sunrise and sunset.

(b) Notwithstanding paragraph (a) of this section, ultralight vehicles may be operated during the twilight periods 30 minutes before official sunrise and 30 minutes after official sunset or, in Alaska, during the period of civil twilight as defined in the Air Almanac, if:

(1) The vehicle is equipped with an operating anticollision light visible for at least 3 statute miles; and

(2) All operations are conducted in uncontrolled airspace.

§103.13 Operation near aircraft; right-of-way rules.

(a) Each person operating an ultralight vehicle shall maintain vigilance so as to see and avoid aircraft and shall yield the right-of-way to all aircraft.

(b) No person may operate an ultralight vehicle in a manner that creates a collision hazard with respect to any aircraft.

(c) Powered ultralights shall yield the right-of-way to unpowered ultralights.

§103.15 Operations over congested areas.

No person may operate an ultralight vehicle over any congested area of a city, town, or settlement, or over any open air assembly of persons.

§103.17 Operations in certain airspace.

No person may operate an ultralight vehicle within Class A, Class B, Class C, or Class D airspace or within the lateral boundaries of the surface area of Class E airspace designated for an airport unless that person has prior authorization from the ATC facility having jurisdiction over that airspace.

[Amdt. 103–17, 56 FR 65662, Dec. 17, 1991]

§103.19 Operations in prohibited or restricted areas.

No person may operate an ultralight vehicle in prohibited or restricted areas unless that person has permission from the using or controlling agency, as appropriate.

§103.20 Flight restrictions in the proximity of certain areas designated by notice to airmen.

No person may operate an ultralight vehicle in areas designated in a Notice to Airmen under §91.137, §91.138, §91.141, §91.143 or §91.145 of this chapter, unless authorized by:

(a) Air Traffic Control (ATC); or

(b) A Flight Standards Certificate of Waiver or Authorization issued for the demonstration or event.

[Docket No. FAA–2000–8274, 66 FR 47378, Sept. 11, 2001]

§103.21 Visual reference with the surface.

No person may operate an ultralight vehicle except by visual reference with the surface.

§103.23 Flight visibility and cloud clearance requirements.

No person may operate an ultralight vehicle when the flight visibility or distance from clouds is less than that in the table found below. All operations in Class A, Class B, Class C, and Class D airspace or Class E airspace designated for an airport must receive prior ATC authorization as required in §103.17 of this part.

Airspace	Flight visibility	Distance from clouds
Class A	Not applicable	Not Applicable
Class B	3 statute miles	Clear of Clouds
Class C	3 statute miles	500 feet below 1,000 feet above 2,000 feet horizontal
Class D	3 statute miles	500 feet below 1,000 feet above 2,000 feet horizontal
Class E:		
Less than 10,000 feet MSL	3 statute miles	500 feet below 1,000 feet above 2,000 feet horizontal
At or above 10,000 feet MSL	5 statute miles	1,000 feet below 1,000 feet above 1 statute mile horizontal
Class G:		
1,200 feet or less above the surface (regardless of MSL altitude)	1 statute mile	Clear of clouds
More than 1,200 feet above the surface but less than 10,000 feet MSL	1 statute mile	500 feet below 1,000 feet above 2,000 feet horizontal
More than 1,200 feet above the surface and at or above 10,000 feet MSL	5 statute miles	1,000 feet below 1,000 feet above 1 statute mile horizontal.

[Amdt. 103–17, 56 FR 65662, Dec. 17, 1991]

PART 105
PARACHUTE OPERATIONS

Authority: 49 U.S.C. 106(g), 40113–40114, 44701–44702, 44721.

Source: Docket No. FAA–1999–5483, 66 FR 23553, May 9, 2001, unless otherwise noted.

Subpart A—General

§105.1 Applicability.

(a) Except as provided in paragraphs (b) and (c) of this section, this part prescribes rules governing parachute operations conducted in the United States.

(b) This part does not apply to a parachute operation conducted—

(1) In response to an in-flight emergency, or

(2) To meet an emergency on the surface when it is conducted at the direction or with the approval of an agency of the United States, or of a State, Puerto Rico, the District of Columbia, or a possession of the United States, or an agency or political subdivision thereof.

(c) Sections 105.5, 105.9, 105.13, 105.15, 105.17, 105.19 through 105.23, 105.25(a)(1) and 105.27 of this part do not apply to a parachute operation conducted by a member of an Armed Force—

(1) Over or within a restricted area when that area is under the control of an Armed Force.

(2) During military operations in uncontrolled airspace.

§105.3 Definitions.

For the purposes of this part—

Approved parachute means a parachute manufactured under a type certificate or a Technical Standard Order (C-23 series), or a personnel-carrying U.S. military parachute (other than a high altitude, high speed, or ejection type) identified by a Navy Air Facility, an Army Air Field, and Air Force-Navy drawing number, an Army Air Field order number, or any other military designation or specification number.

Automatic Activation Device means a self-contained mechanical or electro-mechanical device that is attached to the interior of the reserve parachute container, which automatically initiates parachute deployment of the reserve parachute at a pre-set altitude, time, percentage of terminal velocity, or combination thereof.

Direct Supervision means that a certificated rigger personally observes a non-certificated person packing a main parachute to the extent necessary to ensure that it is being done properly, and takes responsibility for that packing.

Drop Zone means any pre-determined area upon which parachutists or objects land after making an intentional parachute jump or drop. The center-point target of a drop zone is expressed in nautical miles from the nearest VOR facility when 30 nautical miles or less; or from the nearest airport, town, or city depicted on the appropriate Coast and Geodetic Survey World Aeronautical Chart or Sectional Aeronautical Chart, when the nearest VOR facility is more than 30 nautical miles from the drop zone.

Foreign parachutist means a parachutist who is neither a U.S. citizen or a resident alien and is participating in parachute operations within the United States using parachute equipment not manufactured in the United States.

Freefall means the portion of a parachute jump or drop between aircraft exit and parachute deployment in which the parachute is activated

105

manually by the parachutist at the parachutist's discretion or automatically, or, in the case of an object, is activated automatically.

Main parachute means a parachute worn as the primary parachute used or intended to be used in conjunction with a reserve parachute.

Object means any item other than a person that descends to the surface from an aircraft in flight when a parachute is used or is intended to be used during all or part of the descent.

Parachute drop means the descent of an object to the surface from an aircraft in flight when a parachute is used or intended to be used during all or part of that descent.

Parachute jump means a parachute operation that involves the descent of one or more persons to the surface from an aircraft in flight when an aircraft is used or intended to be used during all or part of that descent.

Parachute operation means the performance of all activity for the purpose of, or in support of, a parachute jump or a parachute drop. This parachute operation can involve, but is not limited to, the following persons: parachutist, parachutist in command and passenger in tandem parachute operations, drop zone or owner or operator, jump master, certificated parachute rigger, or pilot.

Parachutist means a person who intends to exit an aircraft while in flight using a single-harness, dual parachute system to descend to the surface.

Parachutist in command means the person responsible for the operation and safety of a tandem parachute operation.

Passenger parachutist means a person who boards an aircraft, acting as other than the parachutist in command of a tandem parachute operation, with the intent of exiting the aircraft while in-flight using the forward harness of a dual harness tandem parachute system to descend to the surface.

Pilot chute means a small parachute used to initiate and/or accelerate deployment of a main or reserve parachute.

Ram-air parachute means a parachute with a canopy consisting of an upper and lower surface that is inflated by ram air entering through specially designed openings in the front of the canopy to form a gliding airfoil.

Reserve parachute means an approved parachute worn for emergency use to be activated only upon failure of the main parachute or in any other emergency where use of the main parachute is impractical or use of the main parachute would increase risk.

Single-harness, dual parachute system means the combination of a main parachute, approved reserve parachute, and approved single person harness and dual-parachute container. This

parachute system may have an operational automatic activation device installed.

Tandem parachute operation means a parachute operation in which more than one person simultaneously uses the same tandem parachute system while descending to the surface from an aircraft in flight.

Tandem parachute system means the combination of a main parachute, approved reserve parachute, and approved harness and dual parachute container, and a separate approved forward harness for a passenger parachutist. This parachute system must have an operational automatic activation device installed.

§105.5 General.

No person may conduct a parachute operation, and no pilot in command of an aircraft may allow a parachute operation to be conducted from an aircraft, if that operation creates a hazard to air traffic or to persons or property on the surface.

§105.7 Use of alcohol and drugs.

No person may conduct a parachute operation, and no pilot in command of an aircraft may allow a person to conduct a parachute operation from that aircraft, if that person is or appears to be under the influence of—

(a) Alcohol, or

(b) Any drug that affects that person's faculties in any way contrary to safety.

§105.9 Inspections.

The Administrator may inspect any parachute operation to which this part applies (including inspections at the site where the parachute operation is being conducted) to determine compliance with the regulations of this part.

Subpart B—
Operating Rules

§105.13 Radio equipment and use requirements.

(a) Except when otherwise authorized by air traffic control—

(1) No person may conduct a parachute operation, and no pilot in command of an aircraft may allow a parachute operation to be conducted from that aircraft, in or into controlled airspace unless, during that flight—

(i) The aircraft is equipped with a functioning two-way radio communication system appropriate to the air traffic control facilities being used; and

(ii) Radio communications have been established between the aircraft and the air traffic control facility having jurisdiction over the affected

airspace of the first intended exit altitude at least 5 minutes before the parachute operation begins. The pilot in command must establish radio communications to receive information regarding air traffic activity in the vicinity of the parachute operation.

(2) The pilot in command of an aircraft used for any parachute operation in or into controlled airspace must, during each flight—

(i) Continuously monitor the appropriate frequency of the aircraft's radio communications system from the time radio communications are first established between the aircraft and air traffic control, until the pilot advises air traffic control that the parachute operation has ended for that flight.

(ii) Advise air traffic control when the last parachutist or object leaves the aircraft.

(b) Parachute operations must be aborted if, prior to receipt of a required air traffic control authorization, or during any parachute operation in or into controlled airspace, the required radio communications system is or becomes inoperative.

§105.15 Information required and notice of cancellation or postponement of a parachute operation.

(a) Each person requesting an authorization under §§105.21(b) and 105.25(a)(2) of this part and each person submitting a notification under §105.25(a)(3) of this part must provide the following information (on an individual or group basis):

(1) The date and time the parachute operation will begin.

(2) The radius of the drop zone around the target expressed in nautical miles.

(3) The location of the center of the drop zone in relation to—

(i) The nearest VOR facility in terms of the VOR radial on which it is located and its distance in nautical miles from the VOR facility when that facility is 30 nautical miles or less from the drop zone target; or

(ii) the nearest airport, town, or city depicted on the appropriate Coast and Geodetic Survey World Aeronautical Chart or Sectional Aeronautical Chart, when the nearest VOR facility is more than 30 nautical miles from the drop zone target.

(4) Each altitude above mean sea level at which the aircraft will be operated when parachutists or objects exit the aircraft.

(5) The duration of the intended parachute operation.

(6) The name, address, and telephone number of the person who requests the authorization or gives notice of the parachute operation.

(7) The registration number of the aircraft to be used.

(8) The name of the air traffic control facility with jurisdiction of the airspace at the first intended exit altitude to be used for the parachute operation.

(b) Each holder of a certificate of authorization issued under §§105.21(b) and 105.25(b) of this part must present that certificate for inspection upon the request of the Administrator or any Federal, State, or local official.

(c) Each person requesting an authorization under §§105.21(b) and 105.25(a)(2) of this part and each person submitting a notice under §105.25(a) (3) of this part must promptly notify the air traffic control facility having jurisdiction over the affected airspace if the proposed or scheduled parachute operation is canceled or postponed.

§105.17 Flight visibility and clearance from cloud requirements.

No person may conduct a parachute operation, and no pilot in command of an aircraft may allow a parachute operation to be conducted from that aircraft—

(a) Into or through a cloud, or

(b) When the flight visibility or the distance from any cloud is less than that prescribed in the following table:

Altitude	Flight visibility (statute miles)	Distance from clouds
1,200 feet or less above the surface regardless of the MSL altitude	3	500 feet below. 1,000 feet above. 2,000 feet horizontal.
More than 1,200 feet above the surface but less than 10,000 feet MSL	3	500 feet below. 1,000 feet above. 2,000 feet horizontal.
More than 1,200 feet above the surface and at or above 10,000 feet MSL	5	1,000 feet below. 1,000 feet above. 1 mile horizontal.

§105.19 Parachute operations between sunset and sunrise.

(a) No person may conduct a parachute operation, and no pilot in command of an aircraft may allow a person to conduct a parachute operation from an aircraft between sunset and sunrise, unless the person or object descending from the aircraft displays a light that is visible for at least 3 statute miles.

(b) The light required by paragraph (a) of this section must be displayed from the time that the person or object is under a properly functioning open parachute until that person or object reaches the surface.

§105.21 Parachute operations over or into a congested area or an open-air assembly of persons.

(a) No person may conduct a parachute operation, and no pilot in command of an aircraft may allow a parachute operation to be conducted from that aircraft, over or into a congested area of a city, town, or settlement, or an open-air assembly of persons unless a certificate of authorization for that parachute operation has been issued under this section. However, a parachutist may drift over a congested area or an open-air assembly of persons with a fully deployed and properly functioning parachute if that parachutist is at a sufficient altitude to avoid creating a hazard to persons or property on the surface.

(b) An application for a certificate of authorization issued under this section must—

(1) Be made in the form and manner prescribed by the Administrator, and

(2) Contain the information required in §105.15(a) of this part.

(c) Each holder of, and each person named as a participant in a certificate of authorization issued under this section must comply with all requirements contained in the certificate of authorization.

(d) Each holder of a certificate of authorization issued under this section must present that certificate for inspection upon the request of the Administrator, or any Federal, State, or local official.

§105.23 Parachute operations over or onto airports.

No person may conduct a parachute operation, and no pilot in command of an aircraft may allow a parachute operation to be conducted from that aircraft, over or onto any airport unless—

(a) For airports with an operating control tower:

(1) Prior approval has been obtained from the management of the airport to conduct parachute operations over or on that airport.

(2) Approval has been obtained from the control tower to conduct parachute operations over or onto that airport.

(3) Two-way radio communications are maintained between the pilot of the aircraft involved in the parachute operation and the control tower of the airport over or onto which the parachute operation is being conducted.

(b) For airports without an operating control tower, prior approval has been obtained from the management of the airport to conduct parachute operations over or on that airport.

(c) A parachutist may drift over that airport with a fully deployed and properly functioning parachute if the parachutist is at least 2,000 feet above that airport's traffic pattern, and avoids creating a hazard to air traffic or to persons and property on the ground.

§105.25 Parachute operations in designated airspace.

(a) No person may conduct a parachute operation, and no pilot in command of an aircraft may allow a parachute operation to be conducted from that aircraft—

(1) Over or within a restricted area or prohibited area unless the controlling agency of the area concerned has authorized that parachute operation;

(2) Within or into a Class A, B, C, D airspace area without, or in violation of the requirements of, an air traffic control authorization issued under this section;

(3) Except as provided in paragraph (c) and (d) of this section, within or into Class E or G airspace area unless the air traffic control facility having jurisdiction over the airspace at the first intended exit altitude is notified of the parachute operation no earlier than 24 hours before or no later than 1 hour before the parachute operation begins.

(b) Each request for a parachute operation authorization or notification required under this section must be submitted to the air traffic control facility having jurisdiction over the airspace at the first intended exit altitude and must include the information prescribed by §105.15(a) of this part.

(c) For the purposes of paragraph (a)(3) of this section, air traffic control facilities may accept a written notification from an organization that conducts parachute operations and lists the scheduled series of parachute operations to be conducted over a stated period of time not longer than 12 calendar months. The notification must contain the information prescribed by §105.15(a) of this part, identify the responsible persons associated with that parachute operation, and be submitted at least 15 days, but not more than 30 days, before the parachute operation begins. The FAA may revoke the acceptance of the notification for any failure of the organization conducting the parachute operations to comply with its requirements.

(d) Paragraph (a)(3) of this section does not apply to a parachute operation conducted by a member of an Armed Force within a restricted area that extends upward from the surface when that area is under the control of an Armed Force.

Subpart C—Parachute Equipment and Packing

§105.41 Applicability.

This subpart prescribed rules governing parachute equipment used in civil parachute operations.

§105.43 Use of single-harness, dual-parachute systems.

No person may conduct a parachute operation using a single-harness, dual-parachute system, and no pilot in command of an aircraft may allow any person to conduct a parachute operation from that aircraft using a single-harness, dual-parachute system, unless that system has at least one main parachute, one approved reserve parachute, and one approved single person harness and container that are packed as follows:

(a) The main parachute must have been packed within 180 days before the date of its use by a certificated parachute rigger, the person making the next jump with that parachute, or a non-certificated person under the direct supervision of a certificated parachute rigger.

(b) The reserve parachute must have been packed by a certificated parachute rigger—

(1) Within 180 days before the date of its use, if its canopy, shroud, and harness are composed exclusively of nylon, rayon, or similar synthetic fiber or material that is substantially resistant to damage from mold, mildew, and other fungi, and other rotting agents propagated in a moist environment; or

(2) Within 60 days before the date of its use, if it is composed of any amount of silk, pongee, or other natural fiber, or material not specified in paragraph (b)(1) of this section.

(c) If installed, the automatic activation device must be maintained in accordance with manufacturer instructions for that automatic activation device.

[Docket No. FAA–1999–5483, 66 FR 23553, May 9, 2001; as amended by Amdt. 105–13, 73 FR 69531, Nov. 19, 2008]

§105.45 Use of tandem parachute systems.

(a) No person may conduct a parachute operation using a tandem parachute system, and no pilot in command of an aircraft may allow any person to conduct a parachute operation from that aircraft using a tandem parachute system, unless—

(1) One of the parachutists using the tandem parachute system is the parachutist in command, and meets the following requirements:

(i) Has a minimum of 3 years of experience in parachuting, and must provide documentation that the parachutist—

(ii) Has completed a minimum of 500 freefall parachute jumps using a ram-air parachute, and

(iii) Holds a master parachute license issued by an organization recognized by the FAA, and

(iv) Has successfully completed a tandem instructor course given by the manufacturer of the tandem parachute system used in the parachute operation or a course acceptable to the Administrator.

(v) Has been certified by the appropriate parachute manufacturer or tandem course provider as being properly trained on the use of the specific tandem parachute system to be used.

(2) The person acting as parachutist in command:

(i) Has briefed the passenger parachutist before boarding the aircraft. The briefing must include the procedures to be used in case of an emergency with the aircraft or after exiting the aircraft, while preparing to exit and exiting the aircraft, freefall, operating the parachute after freefall, landing approach, and landing.

(ii) Uses the harness position prescribed by the manufacturer of the tandem parachute equipment.

(b) No person may make a parachute jump with a tandem parachute system unless—

(1) The main parachute has been packed by a certificated parachute rigger, the parachutist in command making the next jump with that parachute, or a person under the direct supervision of a certificated parachute rigger.

(2) The reserve parachute has been packed by a certificated parachute rigger in accordance with §105.43(b) of this part.

(3) The tandem parachute system contains an operational automatic activation device for the reserve parachute, approved by the manufacturer of that tandem parachute system. The device must—

(i) Have been maintained in accordance with manufacturer instructions, and

(ii) Be armed during each tandem parachute operation.

(4) The passenger parachutist is provided with a manual main parachute activation device and instructed on the use of that device, if required by the owner/operator.

(5) The main parachute is equipped with a single-point release system.

(6) The reserve parachute meets Technical Standard Order C23 specifications.

105

§105.47 Use of static lines.

(a) Except as provided in paragraph (c) of this section, no person may conduct a parachute operation using a static line attached to the aircraft and the main parachute unless an assist device, described and attached as follows, is used to aid the pilot chute in performing its function, or, if no pilot chute is used, to aid in the direct deployment of the main parachute canopy. The assist device must—

(1) Be long enough to allow the main parachute container to open before a load is placed on the device.

(2) Have a static load strength of—

(i) At least 28 pounds but not more than 160 pounds if it is used to aid the pilot chute in performing its function; or

(ii) At least 56 pounds but not more than 320 pounds if it is used to aid in the direct deployment of the main parachute canopy; and

(3) Be attached as follows:

(i) At one end, to the static line above the static-line pins or, if static-line pins are not used, above the static-line ties to the parachute cone.

(ii) At the other end, to the pilot chute apex, bridle cord, or bridle loop, or, if no pilot chute is used, to the main parachute canopy.

(b) No person may attach an assist device required by paragraph (a) of this section to any main parachute unless that person is a certificated parachute rigger or that person makes the next parachute jump with that parachute.

(c) An assist device is not required for parachute operations using direct-deployed, ram-air parachutes.

§105.49 Foreign parachutists and equipment.

(a) No person may conduct a parachute operation, and no pilot in command of an aircraft may allow a parachute operation to be conducted from that aircraft with an unapproved foreign parachute system unless—

(1) The parachute system is worn by a foreign parachutist who is the owner of that system.

(2) The parachute system is of a single-harness dual parachute type.

(3) The parachute system meets the civil aviation authority requirements of the foreign parachutist's country.

(4) All foreign non-approved parachutes deployed by a foreign parachutist during a parachute operation conducted under this section shall be packed as follows—

(i) The main parachute must be packed by the foreign parachutist making the next parachute jump with that parachute, a certificated parachute rigger, or any other person acceptable to the Administrator.

(ii) The reserve parachute must be packed in accordance with the foreign parachutist's civil aviation authority requirements, by a certificated parachute rigger, or any other person acceptable to the Administrator.

PART 107

SMALL UNMANNED AIRCRAFT SYSTEMS

Authority: 49 U.S.C. 106(f), 40101 note, 40103(b), 44701(a)(5), 46105(c), 46110, 44807.

Source: Docket FAA–2015–0150, Amdt. 107–1, 81 FR 42209, June 28, 2016, unless otherwise noted.

107

Subpart A—General

§107.1 Applicability.

(a) Except as provided in paragraph (b) of this section, this part applies to the registration, airman certification, and operation of civil small unmanned aircraft systems within the United States. This part also applies to the eligibility of civil small unmanned aircraft systems to operate over human beings in the United States.

(b) This part does not apply to the following:

(1) Air carrier operations;

(2) Any aircraft subject to the provisions of 49 U.S.C. 44809;

(3) Any operation that the holder of an exemption under section 333 of Public Law 112-95 or 49 U.S.C. 44807 elects to conduct pursuant to the exemption, unless otherwise specified in the exemption; or

(4) Any operation that a person elects to conduct under part 91 of this chapter with a small unmanned aircraft system that has been issued an airworthiness certificate.

[Amdt. No. 107–8, 86 FR 4381, Jan. 15, 2021]

§107.2 Applicability of certification procedures for products and articles.

The provisions of part 21 of this chapter do not apply to small unmanned aircraft systems operated under this part unless the small unmanned aircraft system will operate over human beings in accordance with §107.140.

[Amdt. No. 107–8, 86 FR 4381, Jan. 15, 2021]

§107.3 Definitions.

The following definitions apply to this part. If there is a conflict between the definitions of this part and definitions specified in §1.1 of this chapter, the definitions in this part control for purposes of this part:

Control station means an interface used by the remote pilot to control the flight path of the small unmanned aircraft.

Corrective lenses means spectacles or contact lenses.

Declaration of compliance means a record submitted to the FAA that certifies the small unmanned aircraft conforms to the Category 2 or Category 3 requirements under subpart D of this part.

Small unmanned aircraft means an unmanned aircraft weighing less than 55 pounds on takeoff, including everything that is on board or otherwise attached to the aircraft.

Small unmanned aircraft system (small UAS) means a small unmanned aircraft and its associated elements (including communication links and the components that control the small unmanned aircraft) that are required for the safe and efficient operation of the small unmanned aircraft in the national airspace system.

Unmanned aircraft means an aircraft operated without the possibility of direct human intervention from within or on the aircraft.

Visual observer means a person who is designated by the remote pilot in command to assist the remote pilot in command and the person manipulating the flight controls of the small UAS to see and avoid other air traffic or objects aloft or on the ground.

[Docket FAA–2015–0150, Amdt. 107–1, 81 FR 42209, June 28, 2016, as amended by Amdt. No. 107–8, 86 FR 4381, Jan. 15, 2021]

§107.5 Falsification, reproduction, or alteration.

(a) No person may make or cause to be made—

(1) Any fraudulent or intentionally false record or report that is required to be made, kept, or used to show compliance with any requirement under this part.

(2) Any reproduction or alteration, for fraudulent purpose, of any certificate, rating, authorization, record or report under this part.

(b) The commission by any person of an act prohibited under paragraph (a) of this section is a basis for any of the following:

(1) Denial of an application for a remote pilot certificate or a certificate of waiver;

(2) Denial of a declaration of compliance;

(3) Suspension or revocation of any certificate, waiver, or declaration of compliance issued or accepted by the Administrator under this part and held by that person; or

(4) A civil penalty.

[Docket FAA–2015–0150, Amdt. 107–1, 81 FR 42209, June 28, 2016, as amended by Amdt. No. 107–8, 86 FR 4381, Jan. 15, 2021]

§107.7 Inspection, testing, and demonstration of compliance.

(a) A remote pilot in command, owner, or person manipulating the flight controls of a small unmanned aircraft system must—

(1) Have in that person's physical possession and readily accessible the remote pilot certificate with a small UAS rating and identification when exercising the privileges of that remote pilot certificate.

(2) Present his or her remote pilot certificate with a small UAS rating and identification that contains the information listed at §107.67(b)(1) through (3) for inspection upon a request from—

(i) The Administrator;

(ii) An authorized representative of the National Transportation Safety Board;

(iii) Any Federal, State, or local law enforcement officer; or

(iv) An authorized representative of the Transportation Security Administration.

(3) Make available, upon request, to the Administrator any document, record, or report required to be kept under the regulations of this chapter.

(b) The remote pilot in command, visual observer, owner, operator, or person manipulating the flight controls of a small unmanned aircraft system must, upon request, allow the Administrator to make any test or inspection of the small unmanned aircraft system, the remote pilot in command, the person manipulating the flight controls of a small unmanned aircraft system, and, if applicable, the visual observer to determine compliance with this part.

(c) Any person holding an FAA-accepted declaration of compliance under subpart D of this part must, upon request, make available to the Administrator:

(1) The declaration of compliance required under subpart D of this part; and

(2) Any other document, record, or report required to be kept under the regulations of this chapter.

(d) Any person holding an FAA-accepted declaration of compliance under subpart D of this part must, upon request, allow the Administrator to inspect its facilities, technical data, and any manufactured small UAS and witness any tests necessary to determine compliance with that subpart.

[Amdt. No. 107–8, 86 FR 4381, Jan. 15, 2021]

§107.9 Safety event reporting.

No later than 10 calendar days after an operation that meets the criteria of either paragraph (a) or (b) of this section, a remote pilot in command must report to the FAA, in a manner acceptable to the Administrator, any operation of the small unmanned aircraft involving at least:

(a) Serious injury to any person or any loss of consciousness; or

(b) Damage to any property, other than the small unmanned aircraft, unless one of the following conditions is satisfied:

(1) The cost of repair (including materials and labor) does not exceed $500; or

(2) The fair market value of the property does not exceed $500 in the event of total loss.

[Amdt. 107–10, 87 FR 75846, Dec. 9, 2022]

Subpart B— Operating Rules

§107.11 Applicability.

This subpart applies to the operation of all civil small unmanned aircraft systems subject to this part.

§107.12 Requirement for a remote pilot certificate with a small UAS rating.

(a) Except as provided in paragraph (c) of this section, no person may manipulate the flight controls of a small unmanned aircraft system unless:

(1) That person has a remote pilot certificate with a small UAS rating issued pursuant to Subpart C of this part and satisfies the requirements of §107.65; or

(2) That person is under the direct supervision of a remote pilot in command and the remote pilot in command has the ability to immediately take direct control of the flight of the small unmanned aircraft.

(b) Except as provided in paragraph (c) of this section, no person may act as a remote pilot in command unless that person has a remote pilot certificate with a small UAS rating issued pursuant to Subpart C of this part and satisfies the requirements of §107.65.

(c) The Administrator may, consistent with international standards, authorize an airman to operate a civil foreign-registered small unmanned aircraft without an FAA-issued remote pilot certificate with a small UAS rating.

§107.13 Registration.

A person operating a civil small unmanned aircraft system for purposes of flight must comply with the provisions of §91.203(a)(2) of this chapter.

§107.15 Condition for safe operation.

(a) No person may operate a civil small unmanned aircraft system unless it is in a condition for safe operation. Prior to each flight, the remote pilot in command must check the small unmanned aircraft system to determine whether it is in a condition for safe operation.

(b) No person may continue flight of the small unmanned aircraft when he or she knows or has reason to know that the small unmanned aircraft system is no longer in a condition for safe operation.

§107.17 Medical condition.

No person may manipulate the flight controls of a small unmanned aircraft system or act as a remote pilot in command, visual observer, or

direct participant in the operation of the small unmanned aircraft if he or she knows or has reason to know that he or she has a physical or mental condition that would interfere with the safe operation of the small unmanned aircraft system.

§107.19 Remote pilot in command.

(a) A remote pilot in command must be designated before or during the flight of the small unmanned aircraft.

(b) The remote pilot in command is directly responsible for and is the final authority as to the operation of the small unmanned aircraft system.

(c) The remote pilot in command must ensure that the small unmanned aircraft will pose no undue hazard to other people, other aircraft, or other property in the event of a loss of control of the small unmanned aircraft for any reason.

(d) The remote pilot in command must ensure that the small UAS operation complies with all applicable regulations of this chapter.

(e) The remote pilot in command must have the ability to direct the small unmanned aircraft to ensure compliance with the applicable provisions of this chapter.

[Docket FAA–2015–0150, Amdt. 107–1, 81 FR 42209, June 28, 2016, as amended by Amdt. No. 107–8, 86 FR 4382, Jan. 15, 2021]

§107.21 In-flight emergency.

(a) In an in-flight emergency requiring immediate action, the remote pilot in command may deviate from any rule of this part to the extent necessary to meet that emergency.

(b) Each remote pilot in command who deviates from a rule under paragraph (a) of this section must, upon request of the Administrator, send a written report of that deviation to the Administrator.

§107.23 Hazardous operation.

No person may:

(a) Operate a small unmanned aircraft system in a careless or reckless manner so as to endanger the life or property of another; or

(b) Allow an object to be dropped from a small unmanned aircraft in a manner that creates an undue hazard to persons or property.

§107.25 Operation from a moving vehicle or aircraft.

No person may operate a small unmanned aircraft system—

(a) From a moving aircraft; or

(b) From a moving land or water-borne vehicle unless the small unmanned aircraft is flown over a sparsely populated area and is not transporting another person's property for compensation or hire.

§107.27 Alcohol or drugs.

A person manipulating the flight controls of a small unmanned aircraft system or acting as a remote pilot in command or visual observer must comply with the provisions of §§91.17 and 91.19 of this chapter.

§107.29 Operation at night.

(a) Except as provided in paragraph (d) of this section, no person may operate a small unmanned aircraft system at night unless—

(1) The remote pilot in command of the small unmanned aircraft has completed an initial knowledge test or training, as applicable, under §107.65 after April 6, 2021; and

(2) The small unmanned aircraft has lighted anti-collision lighting visible for at least 3 statute miles that has a flash rate sufficient to avoid a collision. The remote pilot in command may reduce the intensity of, but may not extinguish, the anti-collision lighting if he or she determines that, because of operating conditions, it would be in the interest of safety to do so.

(b) No person may operate a small unmanned aircraft system during periods of civil twilight unless the small unmanned aircraft has lighted anti-collision lighting visible for at least 3 statute miles that has a flash rate sufficient to avoid a collision. The remote pilot in command may reduce the intensity of, but may not extinguish, the anti-collision lighting if he or she determines that, because of operating conditions, it would be in the interest of safety to do so.

(c) For purposes of paragraph (b) of this section, civil twilight refers to the following:

(1) Except for Alaska, a period of time that begins 30 minutes before official sunrise and ends at official sunrise;

(2) Except for Alaska, a period of time that begins at official sunset and ends 30 minutes after official sunset; and

(3) In Alaska, the period of civil twilight as defined in the Air Almanac.

(d) After May 17, 2021, no person may operate a small unmanned aircraft system at night in accordance with a certificate of waiver issued prior to April 21, 2021 under §107.200. The certificates of waiver issued prior to March 16, 2021 under §107.200 that authorize deviation from §107.29 terminate on May 17, 2021.

[Docket FAA–2015–0150, Amdt. 107–1, 81 FR 42209, June 28, 2016, as amended by Amdt. No. 107–8, 86 FR 4382, Jan. 15, 2021; 86 FR 13631, March 10, 2020]

§107.31 Visual line of sight aircraft operation.

(a) With vision that is unaided by any device other than corrective lenses, the remote pilot in command, the visual observer (if one is used), and the person manipulating the flight control of the small unmanned aircraft system must be able to see the unmanned aircraft throughout the entire flight in order to:

(1) Know the unmanned aircraft's location;

(2) Determine the unmanned aircraft's attitude, altitude, and direction of flight;

(3) Observe the airspace for other air traffic or hazards; and

(4) Determine that the unmanned aircraft does not endanger the life or property of another.

(b) Throughout the entire flight of the small unmanned aircraft, the ability described in paragraph (a) of this section must be exercised by either:

(1) The remote pilot in command and the person manipulating the flight controls of the small unmanned aircraft system; or

(2) A visual observer.

§107.33 Visual observer.

If a visual observer is used during the aircraft operation, all of the following requirements must be met:

(a) The remote pilot in command, the person manipulating the flight controls of the small unmanned aircraft system, and the visual observer must maintain effective communication with each other at all times.

(b) The remote pilot in command must ensure that the visual observer is able to see the unmanned aircraft in the manner specified in §107.31.

(c) The remote pilot in command, the person manipulating the flight controls of the small unmanned aircraft system, and the visual observer must coordinate to do the following:

(1) Scan the airspace where the small unmanned aircraft is operating for any potential collision hazard; and

(2) Maintain awareness of the position of the small unmanned aircraft through direct visual observation.

§107.35 Operation of multiple small unmanned aircraft.

A person may not manipulate flight controls or act as a remote pilot in command or visual observer in the operation of more than one unmanned aircraft at the same time.

[Amdt. No. 107–8, 86 FR 4382, Jan. 15, 2021]

§107.36 Carriage of hazardous material.

A small unmanned aircraft may not carry hazardous material. For purposes of this section, the term hazardous material is defined in 49 CFR 171.8.

§107.37 Operation near aircraft; right-of-way rules.

(a) Each small unmanned aircraft must yield the right of way to all aircraft, airborne vehicles, and launch and reentry vehicles. Yielding the right of way means that the small unmanned aircraft must give way to the aircraft or vehicle and may not pass over, under, or ahead of it unless well clear.

(b) No person may operate a small unmanned aircraft so close to another aircraft as to create a collision hazard.

§107.39 Operation over human beings.

No person may operate a small unmanned aircraft over a human being unless—

(a) That human being is directly participating in the operation of the small unmanned aircraft;

(b) That human being is located under a covered structure or inside a stationary vehicle that can provide reasonable protection from a falling small unmanned aircraft; or

(c) The operation meets the requirements of at least one of the operational categories specified in subpart D of this part.

[Amdt. No. 107–8, 86 FR 4382, Jan. 15, 2021]

§107.41 Operation in certain airspace.

No person may operate a small unmanned aircraft in Class B, Class C, or Class D airspace or within the lateral boundaries of the surface area of Class E airspace designated for an airport unless that person has prior authorization from Air Traffic Control (ATC).

§107.43 Operation in the vicinity of airports.

No person may operate a small unmanned aircraft in a manner that interferes with operations and traffic patterns at any airport, heliport, or seaplane base.

§107.45 Operation in prohibited or restricted areas.

No person may operate a small unmanned aircraft in prohibited or restricted areas unless that person has permission from the using or controlling agency, as appropriate.

§107.47 Flight restrictions in the proximity of certain areas designated by notice to airmen.

A person acting as a remote pilot in command must comply with the provisions of §§91.137 through 91.145 and 99.7 of this chapter.

§107.49 Preflight familiarization, inspection, and actions for aircraft operation.

Prior to flight, the remote pilot in command must:

(a) Assess the operating environment, considering risks to persons and property in the immediate vicinity both on the surface and in the air. This assessment must include:

(1) Local weather conditions;

(2) Local airspace and any flight restrictions;

(3) The location of persons and property on the surface; and

(4) Other ground hazards.

(b) Ensure that all persons directly participating in the small unmanned aircraft operation are informed about the operating conditions, emergency procedures, contingency procedures, roles and responsibilities, and potential hazards;

(c) Ensure that all control links between ground control station and the small unmanned aircraft are working properly;

(d) If the small unmanned aircraft is powered, ensure that there is enough available power for the small unmanned aircraft system to operate for the intended operational time;

(e) Ensure that any object attached or carried by the small unmanned aircraft is secure and does not adversely affect the flight characteristics or controllability of the aircraft; and

(f) If the operation will be conducted over human beings under subpart D of this part, ensure that the aircraft meets the requirements of §107.110, §107.120(a), §107.130(a), or §107.140, as applicable.

[Docket FAA–2015–0150, Amdt. 107–1, 81 FR 42209, June 28, 2016, as amended by Amdt. No. 107–8, 86 FR 4382, Jan. 15, 2021]

§107.51 Operating limitations for small unmanned aircraft.

A remote pilot in command and the person manipulating the flight controls of the small unmanned aircraft system must comply with all of the following operating limitations when operating a small unmanned aircraft system:

(a) The groundspeed of the small unmanned aircraft may not exceed 87 knots (100 miles per hour).

(b) The altitude of the small unmanned aircraft cannot be higher than 400 feet above ground level, unless the small unmanned aircraft:

(1) Is flown within a 400-foot radius of a structure; and

(2) Does not fly higher than 400 feet above the structure's immediate uppermost limit.

(c) The minimum flight visibility, as observed from the location of the control station must be no less than 3 statute miles. For purposes of this section, flight visibility means the average slant distance from the control station at which prominent unlighted objects may be seen and identified by day and prominent lighted objects may be seen and identified by night.

(d) The minimum distance of the small unmanned aircraft from clouds must be no less than:

(1) 500 feet below the cloud; and

(2) 2,000 feet horizontally from the cloud.

Subpart C—Remote Pilot Certification

§107.52 ATC transponder equipment prohibition.

Unless otherwise authorized by the Administrator, no person may operate a small unmanned aircraft system under this part with a transponder on.

[Amdt. No. 107–7, 86 FR 4513, Jan. 15, 2021]

§107.53 Automatic Dependent Surveillance–Broadcast (ADS-B) Out prohibition.

Unless otherwise authorized by the Administrator, no person may operate a small unmanned aircraft system under this part with ADS-B Out equipment in transmit mode.

[Amdt. No. 107–7, 86 FR 4513, Jan. 15, 2021]

§107.56 Applicability.

This subpart prescribes the requirements for issuing a remote pilot certificate with a small UAS rating.

[Docket FAA–2015–0150, Amdt. 107–1, 81 FR 42209, June 28, 2016. Redesignated by Amdt. No. 107–7, 86 FR 4513, Jan. 15, 2021]

§107.57 Offenses involving alcohol or drugs.

(a) A conviction for the violation of any Federal or State statute relating to the growing, processing, manufacture, sale, disposition, possession, transportation, or importation of narcotic drugs, marijuana, or depressant or stimulant drugs or substances is grounds for:

(1) Denial of an application for a remote pilot certificate with a small UAS rating for a period of up to 1 year after the date of final conviction; or

(2) Suspension or revocation of a remote pilot certificate with a small UAS rating.

(b) Committing an act prohibited by §91.17(a) or §91.19(a) of this chapter is grounds for:

(1) Denial of an application for a remote pilot certificate with a small UAS rating for a period of up to 1 year after the date of that act; or

(2) Suspension or revocation of a remote pilot certificate with a small UAS rating.

§107.59 Refusal to submit to an alcohol test or to furnish test results.

A refusal to submit to a test to indicate the percentage by weight of alcohol in the blood, when requested by a law enforcement officer in accordance with §91.17(c) of this chapter, or a refusal to furnish or authorize the release of the test results requested by the Administrator in accordance with §91.17(c) or (d) of this chapter, is grounds for:

(a) Denial of an application for a remote pilot certificate with a small UAS rating for a period of up to 1 year after the date of that refusal; or

(b) Suspension or revocation of a remote pilot certificate with a small UAS rating.

§107.61 Eligibility.

Subject to the provisions of §§107.57 and 107.59, in order to be eligible for a remote pilot certificate with a small UAS rating under this subpart, a person must:

(a) Be at least 16 years of age;

(b) Be able to read, speak, write, and understand the English language. If the applicant is unable to meet one of these requirements due to medical reasons, the FAA may place such operating limitations on that applicant's certificate as are necessary for the safe operation of the small unmanned aircraft;

(c) Not know or have reason to know that he or she has a physical or mental condition that would interfere with the safe operation of a small unmanned aircraft system; and

(d) Demonstrate aeronautical knowledge by satisfying one of the following conditions, in a manner acceptable to the Administrator:

(1) Pass an initial aeronautical knowledge test covering the areas of knowledge specified in §107.73; or

(2) If a person holds a pilot certificate (other than a student pilot certificate) issued under part 61 of this chapter and meets the flight review requirements specified in §61.56, complete training covering the areas of knowledge specified in §107.74.

[Docket FAA–2015–0150, Amdt. 107–1, 81 FR 42209, June 28, 2016, as amended by Amdt. No. 107–8, 86 FR 4382, Jan. 15, 2021]

§107.63 Issuance of a remote pilot certificate with a small UAS rating.

An applicant for a remote pilot certificate with a small UAS rating under this subpart must make the application in a form and manner acceptable to the Administrator.

(a) The application must include either:

(1) Evidence showing that the applicant passed an initial aeronautical knowledge test. If applying using a paper application, this evidence must be an airman knowledge test report showing passage of the knowledge test; or

(2) If a person holds a pilot certificate (other than a student pilot certificate) issued under part 61 of this chapter and meets the flight review requirements specified in §61.56, a certificate of completion of an initial training course under this part that covers the areas of knowledge specified in §107.74.

(b) If the application is being made pursuant to paragraph (a)(2) of this section:

(1) The application must be submitted to the responsible Flight Standards office, a designated pilot examiner, an airman certification representative for a pilot school, a certificated flight instructor, or other person authorized by the Administrator;

(2) The person accepting the application submission must verify the identity of the applicant in a manner acceptable to the Administrator; and

(3) The person making the application must, by logbook endorsement or other manner acceptable to the Administrator, show the applicant meets the flight review requirements specified in §61.56 of this chapter.

[Docket FAA–2015–0150, Amdt. 107–1, 81 FR 42209, June 28, 2016, as amended by Docket FAA–2018–0119, Amdt. 107–2, 83 FR 9172, March 5, 2018; Amdt. No. 107–8, 86 FR 4382, Jan. 15, 2021]

§107.64 Temporary Certificate

(a) A temporary remote pilot certificate with a small UAS rating is issued for up to 120 calendar days, at which time a permanent certificate will be issued to a person whom the Administrator finds qualified under this part.

(b) A temporary remote pilot certificate with a small UAS rating expires:

(1) On the expiration date shown on the certificate;

(2) Upon receipt of the permanent certificate; or

(3) Upon receipt of a notice that the certificate sought is denied or revoked.

§107.65 Aeronautical knowledge recency.

A person may not exercise the privileges of a remote pilot in command with small UAS rating unless that person has accomplished one of the following in a manner acceptable to the Administrator within the previous 24 calendar months:

(a) Passed an initial aeronautical knowledge test covering the areas of knowledge specified in §107.73;

(b) Completed recurrent training covering the areas of knowledge specified in §107.73; or

(c) If a person holds a pilot certificate (other than a student pilot certificate) issued under part 61 of this chapter and meets the flight review requirements specified in §61.56, completed training covering the areas of knowledge specified in §107.74.

(d) A person who has passed a recurrent aeronautical knowledge test in a manner acceptable to the Administrator or who has satisfied the training requirement of paragraph (c) of this section prior to April 6, 2021 within the previous 24 calendar months is considered to be in compliance with the requirement of paragraph (b) or (c) of this section, as applicable.

[Amdt. No. 107–8, 86 FR 4382, Jan. 15, 2021; 86 FR 13631, March 10, 2021]

§107.67 Knowledge tests: General procedures and passing grades.

(a) Knowledge tests prescribed by or under this part are given by persons and in the manner designated by the Administrator.

(b) An applicant for a knowledge test must have proper identification at the time of application that contains the applicant's:

(1) Photograph;

(2) Signature;

(3) Date of birth, which shows the applicant meets or will meet the age requirements of this part for the certificate and rating sought before the expiration date of the airman knowledge test report; and

(4) Permanent mailing address. If the applicant's permanent mailing address is a post office box number, then the applicant must also provide a current residential address.

(c) The minimum passing grade for the knowledge test will be specified by the Administrator.

§107.69 Knowledge tests: Cheating or other unauthorized conduct.

(a) An applicant for a knowledge test may not:

(1) Copy or intentionally remove any knowledge test;

(2) Give to another applicant or receive from another applicant any part or copy of a knowledge test;

(3) Give or receive assistance on a knowledge test during the period that test is being given;

(4) Take any part of a knowledge test on behalf of another person;

(5) Be represented by, or represent, another person for a knowledge test;

(6) Use any material or aid during the period that the test is being given, unless specifically authorized to do so by the Administrator; and

(7) Intentionally cause, assist, or participate in any act prohibited by this paragraph.

(b) An applicant who the Administrator finds has committed an act prohibited by paragraph (a) of this section is prohibited, for 1 year after the date of committing that act, from:

(1) Applying for any certificate, rating, or authorization issued under this chapter; and

(2) Applying for and taking any test under this chapter.

(c) Any certificate or rating held by an applicant may be suspended or revoked if the Administrator finds that person has committed an act prohibited by paragraph (a) of this section.

§107.71 Retesting after failure.

An applicant for a knowledge test who fails that test may not reapply for the test for 14 calendar days after failing the test.

§107.73 Knowledge and training.

An initial aeronautical knowledge test and recurrent training covers the following areas of knowledge:

(a) Applicable regulations relating to small unmanned aircraft system rating privileges, limitations, and flight operation;

(b) Airspace classification, operating requirements, and flight restrictions affecting small unmanned aircraft operation;

(c) Aviation weather sources and effects of weather on small unmanned aircraft performance;

(d) Small unmanned aircraft loading;

(e) Emergency procedures;

(f) Crew resource management;

(g) Radio communication procedures;

(h) Determining the performance of the small unmanned aircraft;

(i) Physiological effects of drugs and alcohol;

(j) Aeronautical decision-making and judgment;

(k) Airport operations;

(l) Maintenance and preflight inspection procedures; and

(m) Operation at night.

[Amdt. No. 107–8, 86 FR 4383, Jan. 15, 2021]

§107.74 Small unmanned aircraft system training.

Training for pilots who hold a pilot certificate (other than a student pilot certificate) issued under part 61 of this chapter and meet the flight review requirements specified in §61.56 covers the following areas of knowledge:

(a) Applicable regulations relating to small unmanned aircraft system rating privileges, limitations, and flight operation;

(b) Effects of weather on small unmanned aircraft performance;

(c) Small unmanned aircraft loading;

(d) Emergency procedures;

(e) Crew resource management;

(f) Determining the performance of the small unmanned aircraft;

(g) Maintenance and preflight inspection procedures; and

(h) Operation at night.

[Amdt. No. 107–8, 86 FR 4383, Jan. 15, 2021]

§107.77 Change of name or address.

(a) *Change of name.* An application to change the name on a certificate issued under this subpart must be accompanied by the applicant's:

(1) Remote pilot certificate with small UAS rating; and

(2) A copy of the marriage license, court order, or other document verifying the name change.

(b) The documents in paragraph (a) of this section will be returned to the applicant after inspection.

(c) *Change of address.* The holder of a remote pilot certificate with small UAS rating issued under this subpart who has made a change in permanent mailing address may not, after 30 days from that date, exercise the privileges of the certificate unless the holder has notified the FAA of the change in address using one of the following methods:

(1) By letter to the FAA Airman Certification Branch, P.O. Box 25082, Oklahoma City, OK 73125 providing the new permanent mailing address, or if the permanent mailing address includes a post office box number, then the holder's current residential address; or

(2) By using the FAA website portal at *www.faa.gov* providing the new permanent mailing address, or if the permanent mailing address includes a post office box number, then the holder's current residential address.

§107.79 Voluntary surrender of certificate.

(a) The holder of a certificate issued under this subpart may voluntarily surrender it for cancellation.

(b) Any request made under paragraph (a) of this section must include the following signed statement or its equivalent: "I voluntarily surrender my remote pilot certificate with a small UAS rating for cancellation. This request is made for my own reasons, with full knowledge that my certificate will not be reissued to me unless I again complete the requirements specified in §§107.61 and 107.63."

Subpart D—Operations Over Human Beings

Source: Amdt. No. 107–8, 86 FR 4382, Jan. 15, 2021

§107.100 Applicability.

This subpart prescribes the eligibility and operating requirements for civil small unmanned aircraft to operate over human beings or over moving vehicles in the United States, in addition to those operations permitted by §107.39(a) and (b).

§107.105 Limitations on operations over human beings.

Except as provided in §§107.39(a) and (b) and 107.145, a remote pilot in command may conduct operations over human beings only in accordance with the following, as applicable: §107.110 for Category 1 operations; §§107.115 and 107.120 for Category 2 operations; §§107.125 and 107.130 for Category 3 operations; or §107.140 for Category 4 operations.

§107.110 Category 1 operations.

To conduct Category 1 operations—

(a) A remote pilot in command must use a small unmanned aircraft that—

(1) Weighs 0.55 pounds or less on takeoff and throughout the duration of each operation under Category 1, including everything that is on board or otherwise attached to the aircraft; and

(2) Does not contain any exposed rotating parts that would lacerate human skin upon impact with a human being.

(b) No remote pilot in command may operate a small unmanned aircraft in sustained flight over open-air assemblies of human beings unless the operation meets the requirements of either §89.110 or §89.115(a) of this chapter.

[Amdt. No. 107–8, 86 FR 4382, Jan. 15, 2021, as amended by 86 FR 62473, Nov. 10, 2021]

§107.115 Category 2 operations: Operating requirements.

To conduct Category 2 operations—

(a) A remote pilot in command must use a small unmanned aircraft that—

(1) Is eligible for Category 2 operations pursuant to §107.120(a);

(2) Is listed on an FAA-accepted declaration of compliance as eligible for Category 2 operations in accordance with §107.160; and

(3) Is labeled as eligible to conduct Category 2 operations in accordance with §107.120(b)(1).

(b) No remote pilot in command may operate a small unmanned aircraft in sustained flight over open-air assemblies of human beings unless the operation meets the requirements of either §89.110 or §89.115(a) of this chapter.

§107.120 Category 2 operations: Eligibility of small unmanned aircraft and other applicant requirements.

(a) To be eligible for use in Category 2 operations, the small unmanned aircraft must be designed, produced, or modified such that it—

(1) Will not cause injury to a human being that is equivalent to or greater than the severity of injury caused by a transfer of 11 foot-pounds of kinetic energy upon impact from a rigid object;

(2) Does not contain any exposed rotating parts that would lacerate human skin upon impact with a human being; and

(3) Does not contain any safety defects.

(b) The applicant for a declaration of compliance for a small unmanned aircraft that is eligible for use in Category 2 operations in accordance with paragraph (a) of this section, must meet all of the following requirements for the applicant's unmanned aircraft to be used in Category 2 operations:

(1) Display a label on the small unmanned aircraft indicating eligibility to conduct Category 2 operations. The label must be in English and be legible, prominent, and permanently affixed to the small unmanned aircraft.

(2) Have remote pilot operating instructions that apply to the operation of the small unmanned aircraft system. The applicant for a declaration of compliance must make available these instructions upon sale or transfer of the aircraft or use of the aircraft by someone other than the applicant who submitted a declaration of compliance pursuant to §107.160. Such instructions must address, at a minimum—

(i) A system description that includes the required small unmanned aircraft system components, any system limitations, and the declared category or categories of operation;

(ii) Modifications that will not change the ability of the small unmanned aircraft system to meet the requirements for the category or categories of operation the small unmanned aircraft system is eligible to conduct; and

(iii) Instructions for how to verify and change the mode or configuration of the small unmanned aircraft system, if they are variable.

(3) Maintain a product support and notification process. The applicant for a declaration of compliance must maintain product support and notification procedures to notify the public and the FAA of—

(i) Any defect or condition that causes the small unmanned aircraft to no longer meet the requirements of this subpart; and

(ii) Any identified safety defect that causes the small unmanned aircraft to exceed a low probability of casualty.

§107.125 Category 3 operations: Operating requirements.

To conduct Category 3 operations, a remote pilot in command—

(a) Must use a small unmanned aircraft that—

(1) Is eligible for Category 3 operations pursuant to §107.130(a);

(2) Is listed on an FAA-accepted declaration of compliance as eligible for Category 3 operations in accordance with §107.160; and

(3) Is labeled as eligible for Category 3 operations in accordance with §107.130(b)(1);

(b) Must not operate the small unmanned aircraft over open-air assemblies of human beings; and

(c) May only operate the small unmanned aircraft above any human being if operation meets one of the following conditions:

(1) The operation is within or over a closed- or restricted-access site and all human beings located within the closed- or restricted-access site must be on notice that a small unmanned aircraft may fly over them; or

(2) The small unmanned aircraft does not maintain sustained flight over any human being unless that human being is—

(i) Directly participating in the operation of the small unmanned aircraft; or

(ii) Located under a covered structure or inside a stationary vehicle that can provide reasonable protection from a falling small unmanned aircraft.

[Amdt. No. 107–8, 86 FR 4382, Jan. 15, 2021, as amended by 86 FR 62473, Nov. 10, 2021]

§107.130 Category 3 operations: Eligibility of small unmanned aircraft and other applicant requirements.

(a) To be eligible for use in Category 3 operations, the small unmanned aircraft must be designed, produced, or modified such that it—

(1) Will not cause injury to a human being that is equivalent to or greater than the severity of the injury caused by a transfer of 25 foot-pounds of kinetic energy upon impact from a rigid object;

(2) Does not contain any exposed rotating parts that would lacerate human skin upon impact with a human being; and

(3) Does not contain any safety defects.

(b) The applicant for a declaration of compliance for a small unmanned aircraft that is eligible for use in Category 3 operations in accordance with paragraph (a) of this section, must meet all of the following requirements for the applicant's small unmanned aircraft to be used in Category 3 operations:

(1) Display a label on the small unmanned aircraft indicating eligibility to conduct Category 3 operations. The label must be in English and be legible, prominent, and permanently affixed to the small unmanned aircraft.

(2) Have remote pilot operating instructions that apply to the operation of the small unmanned aircraft system. The applicant for a declaration of compliance must make available these instructions upon sale or transfer of the aircraft or use of the aircraft by someone other than the applicant who submitted a declaration of compliance pursuant to §107.160. Such instructions must address, at a minimum—

(i) A system description that includes the required small unmanned aircraft system components, any system limitations, and the declared category or categories of operation;

(ii) Modifications that will not change the ability of the small unmanned aircraft system to meet the requirements for the category or categories of operation the small unmanned aircraft system is eligible to conduct; and

(iii) Instructions for how to verify and change the mode or configuration of the small unmanned aircraft system, if they are variable.

(3) Maintain a product support and notification process. The applicant for a declaration of compliance must maintain product support and notification procedures to notify the public and the FAA of—

(i) Any defect or condition that causes the small unmanned aircraft to no longer meet the requirements of this subpart; and

(ii) Any identified safety defect that causes the small unmanned aircraft to exceed a low probability of fatality.

§107.135 Labeling by remote pilot in command for Category 2 and 3 operations.

If a Category 2 or Category 3 label affixed to a small unmanned aircraft is damaged, destroyed, or missing, a remote pilot in command must label the aircraft in English such that the label is legible, prominent, and will remain on the small unmanned aircraft for the duration of the operation before conducting operations over human beings. The label must correctly identify the category or categories of operation over human beings that the small unmanned aircraft is qualified to conduct in accordance with this subpart.

§107.140 Category 4 operations.

(a) *Remote pilot in command requirements.* To conduct Category 4 operations—

(1) A remote pilot in command—

(i) Must use a small unmanned aircraft that is eligible for Category 4 operations pursuant to paragraph (b) of this section; and

(ii) Must operate the small unmanned aircraft in accordance with all operating limitations that apply to the small unmanned aircraft, as specified by the Administrator.

(2) No remote pilot in command may operate a small unmanned aircraft in sustained flight over open-air assemblies of human beings unless the operation meets the requirements of either §89.110 or §89.115(a) of this chapter.

(b) *Small unmanned aircraft requirements for Category 4.* To be eligible to operate over human beings under this section, the small unmanned aircraft must—

(1) Have an airworthiness certificate issued under part 21 of this chapter.

(2) Be operated in accordance with the operating limitations specified in the approved Flight Manual or as otherwise specified by the Administrator. The operating limitations must not prohibit operations over human beings.

(3) Have maintenance, preventive maintenance, alterations, or inspections performed in accordance with paragraph (c)(1) of this section.

(c) *Maintenance requirements for Category 4.* The owner must (unless the owner enters into an agreement with an operator to meet the requirements of this paragraph (c), then the operator must) meet the requirements of this paragraph (c):

(1) Ensure the person performing any maintenance, preventive maintenance, alterations, or inspections:

(i) Uses the methods, techniques, and practices prescribed in the manufacturer's current maintenance manual or Instructions for Continued Airworthiness that are acceptable to the Administrator, or other methods, techniques, and practices acceptable to the Administrator;

(ii) Has the knowledge, skill, and appropriate equipment to perform the work;

(iii) Performs the maintenance, preventive maintenance, or alterations on the small unmanned aircraft in a manner using the methods, techniques, and practices prescribed in the manufacturer's current maintenance manual or

107

Instructions for Continued Airworthiness prepared by its manufacturer, or other methods, techniques, and practices acceptable to the Administrator;

(iv) Inspects the small unmanned aircraft in accordance with the manufacturer's instructions or other instructions acceptable to the Administrator; and

(v) Performs the maintenance, preventive maintenance, or alterations using parts of such a quality that the condition of the aircraft will be at least equal to its original or properly altered condition.

(2) Maintain all records of maintenance, preventive maintenance, and alterations performed on the aircraft and ensure the records are documented in a manner acceptable to the Administrator. The records must contain the description of the work performed, the date the work was completed, and the name of the person who performed the work.

(3) Maintain all records containing—

(i) The status of life-limited parts that are installed on, or part of, the small unmanned aircraft;

(ii) The inspection status of the aircraft; and

(iii) The status of applicable airworthiness directives including the method of compliance, the airworthiness directive number, and revision date. If the airworthiness directive involves recurring action, the record must contain the time and date of the next required action.

(4) Retain the records required under paragraphs (c)(2) and (3) of this section, as follows:

(i) The records documenting maintenance, preventive maintenance, or alterations performed must be retained for 1 year from when the work is completed or until the maintenance is repeated or superseded by other work.

(ii) The records documenting the status of life-limited parts, compliance with airworthiness directives, and inspection status of the small unmanned aircraft must be retained and transferred with the aircraft upon change in ownership.

(5) Ensure all records under paragraphs (c)(2) and (3) of this section are available for inspection upon request from the Administrator or any authorized representative of the National Transportation Safety Board (NTSB).

(d) *Compliance with parts 43 and 91 of this chapter.* Compliance with part 43 and part 91, subpart E, of this chapter fulfills the requirements in paragraphs (b)(3) and (c) of this section.

[Amdt. No. 107–8, 86 FR 4383, Jan. 15, 2021; 86 FR 13633, March 10, 2021]

§107.145 Operations over moving vehicles.

No person may operate a small unmanned aircraft over a human being located inside a moving vehicle unless the following conditions are met:

(a) The operation occurs in accordance with §107.110 for Category 1 operations; §107.115 for Category 2 operations; §107.125 for Category 3 operations; or §107.140 for Category 4 operations.

(b) For an operation under Category 1, Category 2, or Category 3, the small unmanned aircraft, throughout the operation—

(1) Must remain within or over a closed- or restricted-access site, and all human beings located inside a moving vehicle within the closed- or restricted-access site must be on notice that a small unmanned aircraft may fly over them; or

(2) Must not maintain sustained flight over moving vehicles.

(c) For a Category 4 operation, the small unmanned aircraft must—

(1) Have an airworthiness certificate issued under part 21 of this chapter.

(2) Be operated in accordance with the operating limitations specified in the approved Flight Manual or as otherwise specified by the Administrator. The operating limitations must not prohibit operations over human beings located inside moving vehicles.

§107.150 Variable mode and variable configuration of small unmanned aircraft systems.

A small unmanned aircraft system may be eligible for one or more categories of operation over human beings under this subpart, as long as a remote pilot in command cannot inadvertently switch between modes or configurations.

§107.155 Means of compliance.

(a) *Establishment of compliance.* To meet the requirements of §107.120(a) for operations in Category 2, or the requirements of §107.130(a) for operations in Category 3, the means of compliance must consist of test, analysis, or inspection.

(b) *Required information.* An applicant requesting FAA acceptance of a means of compliance must submit the following information to the FAA in a manner specified by the Administrator:

(1) *Procedures.* Detailed description of the means of compliance, including applicable test, analysis, or inspection procedures to demonstrate how the small unmanned aircraft meets the requirements of §107.120(a) for operations in Category 2 or the requirements of §107.130(a) for operations in Category 3. The description should include conditions, environments, and methods, as applicable.

(2) *Compliance explanation.* Explanation of how application of the means of compliance fulfills the requirements of §107.120(a) for operations in Category 2 or the requirements of §107.130(a) for operations in Category 3.

(c) *FAA acceptance.* If the FAA determines the applicant has demonstrated compliance with paragraphs (a) and (b) of this section, it will notify the applicant that it has accepted the means of compliance.

(d) *Rescission.* (1) A means of compliance is subject to ongoing review by the Administrator. The Administrator may rescind its acceptance of a means of compliance if the Administrator determines that a means of compliance does not meet any or all of the requirements of this subpart.

(2) The Administrator will publish a notice of rescission in the Federal Register.

(e) *Inapplicability of part 13, subpart D, of this chapter.* Part 13, subpart D, of this chapter does not apply to the procedures of paragraph (a) of this section.

§107.160 Declaration of compliance.

(a) *Required information.* In order for an applicant to declare a small unmanned aircraft is compliant with the requirements of this subpart for Category 2 or Category 3 operations, an applicant must submit a declaration of compliance for acceptance by the FAA, in a manner specified by the Administrator, that includes the following information:

(1) Applicant's name;

(2) Applicant's physical address;

(3) Applicant's email address;

(4) The small unmanned aircraft make and model name, and series, if applicable;

(5) The small unmanned aircraft serial number or range of serial numbers that are the subject of the declaration of compliance;

(6) Whether the declaration of compliance is an initial declaration or an amended declaration;

(7) If the declaration of compliance is an amended declaration, the reason for the re-submittal;

(8) The accepted means of compliance the applicant used to fulfill requirements of §107.120(a) or §107.130(a) or both;

(9) A declaration that the applicant—

(i) Has demonstrated that the small unmanned aircraft, or specific configurations of that aircraft, satisfies §107.120(a) or §107.130(a) or both, through the accepted means of compliance identified in paragraph (a)(8) of this section;

(ii) Has verified that the unmanned aircraft does not contain any safety defects;

(iii) Has satisfied §107.120(b)(3) or §107.130(b)(3), or both; and

(iv) Will, upon request, allow the Administrator to inspect its facilities, technical data, and any manufactured small unmanned aircraft and witness any tests necessary to determine compliance with this subpart; and

(10) Other information as required by the Administrator.

(b) *FAA acceptance.* If the FAA determines the applicant has demonstrated compliance with the requirements of this subpart, it will notify the applicant that it has accepted the declaration of compliance.

(c) *Notification of a safety issue.* Prior to initiating rescission proceedings pursuant to paragraphs (d)(1) through (3) of this section, the FAA will notify the applicant if a safety issue has been identified for the declaration of compliance.

(d) *Rescission.* (1) No person may operate a small unmanned aircraft identified on a declaration of compliance that the FAA has rescinded pursuant to this subpart while that declaration of compliance is rescinded.

(2) The FAA may rescind a declaration of compliance if any of the following conditions occur:

(i) A small unmanned aircraft for which a declaration of compliance was accepted no longer complies with §107.120(a) or §107.130(a);

(ii) The FAA finds a declaration of compliance is in violation of §107.5(a); or

(iii) The Administrator determines an emergency exists related to safety in accordance with the authority in 49 U.S.C. 46105.

(3) If a safety issue identified under paragraph (c) of this section has not been resolved, the FAA may rescind the declaration of compliance as follows:

(i) The FAA will issue a notice proposing to rescind the declaration of compliance. The notice will set forth the Agency's basis for the proposed rescission and provide the holder of the declaration of compliance with 30 calendar days from the date of issuance of the proposed notice to submit evidentiary information to refute the proposed notice.

(ii) The holder of the declaration of compliance must submit information demonstrating how the small unmanned aircraft meets the requirements of this subpart within 30 calendar days from the date of issuance of the proposed notice.

(iii) If the FAA does not receive the information required by paragraph (d)(3)(ii) of this section within 30 calendar days from the date of the issuance of the proposed notice, the FAA will issue a notice rescinding the declaration of compliance.

(4) If the Administrator determines that an emergency exists in accordance with paragraph (d)(2)(iii) of this section, the FAA will exercise its authority under 49 U.S.C. 46105(c) to issue an order rescinding a declaration of compliance without initiating the process in paragraph (d)(3) of this section.

(e) *Petition to reconsider the rescission of a declaration of compliance.* A person subject to an order of rescission under paragraph (d)(3) of this section may petition the FAA to reconsider the rescission of a declaration of compliance by submitting a request to the FAA in a manner

specified by the Administrator within 60 days of the date of issuance of the rescission.

(1) A petition to reconsider the rescission of a declaration of compliance must demonstrate at least one of the following:

(i) A material fact that was not present in the original response to the notification of the safety issue and an explanation for why it was not present in the original response;

(ii) The FAA made a material factual error in the decision to rescind the declaration of compliance; or

(iii) The FAA did not correctly interpret a law, regulation, or precedent.

(2) Upon consideration of the information submitted under paragraph (e)(1) of this section, the FAA will issue a notice either affirming the rescission or withdrawing the rescission.

(f) Inapplicability of part 13, subpart D, of this chapter. Part 13, subpart D, of this chapter does not apply to the procedures of paragraphs (d) and (e) of this section.

§107.165 Record retention.

(a) A person who submits a declaration of compliance under this subpart must retain and make available to the Administrator, upon request, the information described in paragraph (a)(1) of this section for the period of time described in paragraph (a)(2) of this section.

(1) All supporting information used to demonstrate the small unmanned aircraft meets the requirements of §§107.120(a), for operations in Category 2, and 107.130(a), for operations in Category 3.

(2) The following time periods apply:

(i) If the person who submits a declaration of compliance produces a small unmanned aircraft, that person must retain the information described in paragraph (a)(1) of this section for two years after the cessation of production of the small unmanned aircraft system for which the person declared compliance.

(ii) If the person who submits a declaration of compliance designs or modifies a small unmanned aircraft, that person must retain the information described in paragraph (a)(1) of this section for two years after the person submitted the declaration of compliance.

(b) A person who submits a means of compliance under this subpart must retain and make available to the Administrator, upon request, and for as long as the means of compliance remains accepted, the detailed description of the means of compliance and justification showing how the means of compliance meets the requirements of §§107.120(a), for operations in Category 2, and 107.130(a), for operations in Category 3.

Subpart E—Waivers

§107.200 Waiver policy and requirements.

(a) The Administrator may issue a certificate of waiver authorizing a deviation from any regulation specified in §107.205 if the Administrator finds that a proposed small UAS operation can safely be conducted under the terms of that certificate of waiver.

(b) A request for a certificate of waiver must contain a complete description of the proposed operation and justification that establishes that the operation can safely be conducted under the terms of a certificate of waiver.

(c) The Administrator may prescribe additional limitations that the Administrator considers necessary.

(d) A person who receives a certificate of waiver issued under this section:

(1) May deviate from the regulations of this part to the extent specified in the certificate of waiver; and

(2) Must comply with any conditions or limitations that are specified in the certificate of waiver.

§107.205 List of regulations subject to waiver.

A certificate of waiver issued pursuant to §107.200 may authorize a deviation from the following regulations of this part:

(a) Section 107.25—Operation from a moving vehicle or aircraft. However, no waiver of this provision will be issued to allow the carriage of property of another by aircraft for compensation or hire.

(b) Section 107.29(a)(2) and (b)—Anti-collision light required for operations at night and during periods of civil twilight.

(c) Section 107.31—Visual line of sight aircraft operation. However, no waiver of this provision will be issued to allow the carriage of property of another by aircraft for compensation or hire.

(d) Section 107.33—Visual observer.

(e) Section 107.35—Operation of multiple small unmanned aircraft systems.

(f) Section 107.37(a)—Yielding the right of way.

(g) Section 107.39—Operation over people.

(h) Section 107.41—Operation in certain airspace.

(i) Section 107.51—Operating limitations for small unmanned aircraft.

(j) Section 107.145—Operations over moving vehicles.

[Docket FAA–2015–0150, Amdt. 107–1, 81 FR 42209, June 28, 2016, as amended by Amdt. No. 107–8, 86 FR 4387, Jan. 15, 2021]

PART 110

GENERAL REQUIREMENTS

Sec.
110.1 Applicability.
***110.2 Definitions.**

Authority: 49 U.S.C. 106(f), 106(g), 40101, 40102, 40103, 40113, 44105, 44106, 44111, 44701-44717, 44722, 44901, 44903, 44904, 44906, 44912, 44914, 44936, 44938, 46103, 46105.

Source: Docket No. FAA–2009–0140, 76 FR 7486, Feb. 10, 2011, unless otherwise noted.

§110.1 Applicability.

This part governs all operations conducted under subchapter G of this chapter.

§110.2 Definitions

For the purpose of this subchapter, the term—

All-cargo operation means any operation for compensation or hire that is other than a passenger-carrying operation or, if passengers are carried, they are only those specified in §121.583(a) or §135.85 of this chapter.

Commercial air tour means a flight conducted for compensation or hire in an airplane, powered-lift, or rotorcraft where a purpose of the flight is sightseeing. The FAA may consider the following factors in determining whether a flight is a commercial air tour:

(1) Whether there was a holding out to the public of willingness to conduct a sightseeing flight for compensation or hire;

(2) Whether the person offering the flight provided a narrative that referred to areas or points of interest on the surface below the route of the flight;

(3) The area of operation;

(4) How often the person offering the flight conducts such flights;

(5) The route of flight;

(6) The inclusion of sightseeing flights as part of any travel arrangement package;

(7) Whether the flight in question would have been canceled based on poor visibility of the surface below the route of the flight; and

(8) Any other factors that the FAA considers appropriate.

Commuter operation means any scheduled operation conducted by any person operating one of the following types of aircraft with a frequency of operations of at least five round trips per week on at least one route between two or more points according to the published flight schedules:

(1) Rotorcraft; or

(2) Airplanes or powered-lift that:

(i) Are not turbojet-powered;

(ii) Have a maximum passenger-seat configuration of 9 seats or less, excluding each crewmember seat; and

(iii) Have a maximum payload capacity of 7,500 pounds or less.

Direct air carrier means a person who provides or offers to provide air transportation and who has control over the operational functions performed in providing that transportation.

DOD commercial air carrier evaluator means a qualified Air Mobility Command, Survey and Analysis Office cockpit evaluator performing the duties specified in Public Law 99-661 when the evaluator is flying on an air carrier that is contracted or pursuing a contract with the U.S. Department of Defense (DOD).

Domestic operation means any scheduled operation conducted by any person operating any aircraft described in paragraph (1) of this definition at locations described in paragraph (2) of this definition:

(1) Airplanes or powered-lift that:

(i) Are turbojet-powered;

(ii) Have a passenger-seat configuration of more than 9 passenger seats, excluding each crewmember seat; or

(iii) Have a payload capacity of more than 7,500 pounds.

(2) Locations:

(i) Between any points within the 48 contiguous States of the United States or the District of Columbia; or

(ii) Operations solely within the 48 contiguous States of the United States or the District of Columbia; or

(iii) Operations entirely within any State, territory, or possession of the United States; or

(iv) When specifically authorized by the Administrator, operations between any point within the 48 contiguous States of the United States or the District of Columbia and any specifically authorized point located outside the 48 contiguous States of the United States or the District of Columbia.

Empty weight means the weight of the airframe, engines, propellers, rotors, and fixed equipment. Empty weight excludes the weight of the crew and payload, but includes the weight of all fixed ballast, unusable fuel supply, undrainable oil, total quantity of engine coolant, and total quantity of hydraulic fluid.

Flag operation means any scheduled operation conducted by any person operating any aircraft described in paragraph (1) of this definition at locations described in paragraph (2) of this definition:

(1) Airplanes or powered-lift that:

(i) Are turbojet-powered;

(ii) Have a passenger-seat configuration of more than 9 passenger seats, excluding each crewmember seat; or

(iii) Have a payload capacity of more than 7,500 pounds.

(2) Locations:

(i) Between any point within the State of Alaska or the State of Hawaii or any territory or possession of the United States and any point outside the State of Alaska or the State of Hawaii or any territory or possession of the United States, respectively; or

(ii) Between any point within the 48 contiguous States of the United States or the District of Columbia and any point outside the 48 contiguous States of the United States and the District of Columbia.

(iii) Between any point outside the U.S. and another point outside the U.S.

Justifiable aircraft equipment means any equipment necessary for the operation of the aircraft. It does not include equipment or ballast specifically installed, permanently or otherwise, for the purpose of altering the empty weight of an aircraft to meet the maximum payload capacity.

Kind of operation means one of the various operations a certificate holder is authorized to conduct, as specified in its operations specifications, i.e., domestic, flag, supplemental, commuter, or on-demand operations.

Maximum payload capacity means:

(1) For an aircraft for which a maximum zero fuel weight is prescribed in FAA technical specifications, the maximum zero fuel weight, less empty weight, less all justifiable aircraft equipment, and less the operating load (consisting of minimum flightcrew, foods and beverages, and supplies and equipment related to foods and beverages, but not including disposable fuel or oil).

(2) For all other aircraft, the maximum certificated takeoff weight of an aircraft, less the empty weight, less all justifiable aircraft equipment, and less the operating load (consisting of minimum fuel load, oil, and flightcrew). The allowance for the weight of the crew, oil, and fuel is as follows:

(i) Crew—for each crewmember required by the Federal Aviation Regulations—

(A) For male flightcrew members—180 pounds.

(B) For female flightcrew members—140 pounds.

(C) For male flight attendants—180 pounds.

(D) For female flight attendants—130 pounds.

(E) For flight attendants not identified by gender—140 pounds.

(ii) Oil—350 pounds or the oil capacity as specified on the Type Certificate Data Sheet.

(iii) Fuel—the minimum weight of fuel required by the applicable Federal Aviation Regulations for a flight between domestic points 174 nautical miles apart under VFR weather conditions that does not involve extended overwater operations.

Maximum zero fuel weight means the maximum permissible weight of an aircraft with no disposable fuel or oil. The zero fuel weight figure may be found in either the aircraft type certificate data sheet, the approved Aircraft Flight Manual, or both.

Noncommon carriage means an aircraft operation for compensation or hire that does not involve a holding out to others.

On-demand operation means any operation for compensation or hire that is one of the following:

(1) Passenger-carrying operations conducted as a public charter under part 380 of this chapter or any operations in which the departure time, departure location, and arrival location are specifically negotiated with the customer or the customer's representative that are any of the following types of operations:

(i) Common carriage operations conducted with airplanes or powered-lift, including any that are turbojet-powered, having a passenger-seat configuration of 30 seats or fewer, excluding each crewmember seat, and a payload capacity of 7,500 pounds or less. The operations described in this paragraph do not include operations using a specific airplane or powered-lift that is also used in domestic or flag operations and that is so listed in the operations specifications as required by §119.49(a)(4) of this chapter for those operations are considered supplemental operations;

(ii) Noncommon or private carriage operations conducted with airplanes or powered-lift having a passenger-seat configuration of less than 20 seats, excluding each crewmember seat, and a payload capacity of less than 6,000 pounds; or

(iii) Any rotorcraft operation.

(2) Scheduled passenger-carrying operations conducted with one of the following types of aircraft, other than turbojet-powered aircraft, with a frequency of operations of less than five round trips per week on at least one route between two or more points according to the published flight schedules:

(i) Airplanes or powered-lift having a maximum passenger-seat configuration of 9 seats or less, excluding each crewmember seat, and a maximum payload capacity of 7,500 pounds or less; or

(ii) Rotorcraft.

(3) All-cargo operations conducted with airplanes or powered-lift having a payload capacity of 7,500 pounds or less, or with rotorcraft.

Passenger-carrying operation means any aircraft operation carrying any person, unless the only persons on the aircraft are those identified in §§121.583(a) or 135.85 of this chapter, as applicable. An aircraft used in a passenger-carrying operation may also carry cargo or mail in addition to passengers.

Principal base of operations means the primary operating location of a certificate holder as established by the certificate holder.

Provisional airport means an airport approved by the Administrator for use by a certificate holder for the purpose of providing service to a community when the regular airport used by the certificate holder is not available.

Regular airport means an airport used by a certificate holder in scheduled operations and listed in its operations specifications.

Scheduled operation means any common carriage passenger-carrying operation for compensation or hire conducted by an air carrier or commercial operator for which the certificate holder or its representative offers in advance the departure location, departure time, and arrival location. It does not include any passenger-carrying operation that is conducted as a public charter operation under part 380 of this chapter.

Supplemental operation means any common carriage operation for compensation or hire conducted with any aircraft described in paragraph (1) of this definition that is a type of operation described in paragraph (2) of this definition:

(1) Airplanes or powered-lift that:

(i) Have a passenger-seat configuration of more than 30 seats, excluding each crewmember seat.

(ii) Have a payload capacity of more than 7,500 pounds.

(iii) Are propeller-powered and:

(A) Have a passenger-seat configuration of more than 9 seats and less than 31 seats, excluding each crewmember seat; and

(B) Are used in domestic or flag operations but are so listed in the operations specifications as required by §119.49(a)(4) of this chapter for such operations.

(iv) Are turbojet-powered and:

(A) Have a passenger seat configuration of 1 or more but less than 31 seats, excluding each crewmember seat; and

(B) Are used in domestic or flag operations and are so listed in the operations specifications as required by §119.49(a)(4) of this chapter for such operations.

(2) Types of operation:

(i) Operations for which the departure time, departure location, and arrival location are specifically negotiated with the customer or the customer's representative.

(ii) All-cargo operations.

(iii) Passenger-carrying public charter operations conducted under part 380 of this chapter.

Wet lease means any leasing arrangement whereby a person agrees to provide an entire aircraft and at least one crewmember. A wet lease does not include a code-sharing arrangement.

When common carriage is not involved or operations not involving common carriage means any of the following:

(1) Noncommon carriage.

(2) Operations in which persons or cargo are transported without compensation or hire.

(3) Operations not involving the transportation of persons or cargo.

(4) Private carriage.

Years in service means the calendar time elapsed since an aircraft was issued its first U.S. or first foreign airworthiness certificate.

[Docket No. FAA–2009–0140, 76 FR 7486, Feb. 10, 2011; as amended by Amdt. 110–2, 83 FR 9172, March 5, 2018; Docket No. FAA-2022-1563, Amdt. 110–3, 88 FR 48087, July 26, 2023]

PART 119

CERTIFICATION: AIR CARRIERS AND COMMERCIAL OPERATORS

Authority: 49 U.S.C. 106(f), 106(g), 40101, 40102, 40103, 40113, 44105, 44106, 44111, 44701–44717, 44722, 44901, 44903, 44904, 44906, 44912, 44914, 44936, 44938, 46103, 46105; sec. 215, Pub. L. 111–216, 124 Stat. 2348.

Source: Docket No. 28154, 60 FR 65913, Dec. 20, 1995, unless otherwise noted.

Subpart A—General

§119.1 Applicability.

(a) This part applies to each person operating or intending to operate civil aircraft—

(1) As an air carrier or commercial operator, or both, in air commerce or

(2) When common carriage is not involved, in operations of any U.S.-registered civil airplane or powered-lift with a seat configuration of 20 or more passengers, or a maximum payload capacity of 6,000 pounds or more; or

(3) When noncommon carriage is involved, except as provided in §91.501(b) of this chapter, or in private carriage for compensation or hire, in operations of any U.S.-registered civil airplane or powered-lift with a passenger-seat configuration of less than 20 seats and a payload capacity of less than 6,000 pounds.

119

(b) This part prescribes—

(1) The types of air operator certificates issued by the Federal Aviation Administration, including air carrier certificates and operating certificates;

(2) The certification requirements an operator must meet in order to obtain and hold a certificate authorizing operations under part 121, 125, or 135 of this chapter and operations specifications for each kind of operation to be conducted and each class and size of aircraft to be operated under part 121 or 135 of this chapter;

(3) The requirements an operator must meet to conduct operations under part 121, 125, or 135 of this chapter and in operating each class and size of aircraft authorized in its operations specifications;

(4) Requirements affecting wet leasing of aircraft and other arrangements for transportation by air;

(5) Requirements for obtaining deviation authority to perform operations under a military contract and obtaining deviation authority to perform an emergency operation; and

(6) Requirements for management personnel for operations conducted under part 121 or part 135 of this chapter.

(c) Persons subject to this part must comply with the other requirements of this chapter, except where those requirements are modified by or where additional requirements are imposed by part 119, 121, 125, or 135 of this chapter.

(d) This part does not govern operations conducted under part 91, subpart K (when common carriage is not involved) nor does it govern operations conducted under part 129, 133, 137, or 139 of this chapter.

(e) Except for operations when common carriage is not involved conducted with any airplane or powered-lift having a passenger-seat configuration of 20 seats or more, excluding any required crewmember seat, or a payload capacity of 6,000 pounds or more, this part does not apply to—

(1) Student instruction;

(2) Nonstop Commercial Air Tours that occur in an airplane, powered-lift, or rotorcraft having a standard airworthiness certificate and passenger-seat configuration of 30 seats or fewer and a maximum payload capacity of 7,500 pounds or less that begin and end at the same airport, and are conducted within a 25-statute mile radius of that airport, in compliance with the Letter of Authorization issued under §91.147 of this chapter. For nonstop Commercial Air Tours conducted in accordance with part 136, subpart B, of this chapter, National Parks Air Tour Management, the requirements of this part apply unless excepted in §136.37(g)(2). For Nonstop Commercial Air Tours conducted in the vicinity of the Grand Canyon National Park, Arizona, the requirements of SFAR 50-2, part 93, subpart U, of the chapter and this part, as applicable, apply.

(3) Ferry or training flights;

(4) Aerial work operations, including—

(i) Crop dusting, seeding, spraying, and bird chasing;

(ii) Banner towing;

(iii) Aerial photography or survey;

(iv) Fire fighting;

(v) Powered-lift or rotorcraft operations in construction or repair work (but part 119 of this chapter does apply to transportation to and from the site of operations); and

(vi) Powerline or pipeline patrol;

(5) Sightseeing flights conducted in hot air balloons or gliders;

(6) Nonstop flights conducted within a 25-statute-mile radius of the airport of takeoff carrying persons or objects for the purpose of conducting intentional parachute operations.

(7) Powered-lift or rotorcraft flights conducted within a 25 statute mile radius of the airport of takeoff if—

(i) Not more than two passengers are carried in the aircraft in addition to the required flightcrew;

(ii) Each flight is made under day VFR conditions;

(iii) The aircraft used is certificated in the standard category and complies with the 100-hour inspection requirements of part 91 of this chapter;

(iv) The operator notifies the responsible Flight Standards office at least 72 hours before each flight and furnishes any essential information that the office requests;

(v) The number of flights does not exceed a total of six in any calendar year;

(vi) Each flight has been approved by the Administrator; and

(vii) Cargo is not carried in or on the aircraft;

(8) Operations conducted under part 133 of this chapter or 375 of this title;

(9) Emergency mail service conducted under 49 U.S.C. 41906;

(10) Operations conducted under the provisions of §91.321 of this chapter; or

(11) Small UAS operations conducted under part 107 of this chapter.

[Docket No. 28154, 60 FR 65913, Dec. 20, 1995; as amended by Amdt. 119–4, 66 FR 23557, May 9, 2001; Amdt. 119–5, 67 FR 9554, March 1, 2002; Amdt. 119–7, 68 FR 54584, Sept. 17, 2003; Docket No. FAA–1998–4521, 72 FR 6911, Feb. 13, 2007; Amdt. 119–18, 81 FR 42213, June 28, 2016; Amdt. 119–19, 83 FR 9172, March 5, 2018; Docket No. FAA–2022–1563, Amdt. 119–20, 88 FR 48088, July 26, 2023]

§119.3 [Reserved]

§119.5 Certifications, authorizations, and prohibitions.

(a) A person authorized by the Administrator to conduct operations as a direct air carrier will be issued an Air Carrier Certificate.

(b) A person not authorized to conduct direct air carrier operations, but authorized by the Administrator to conduct operations as a U.S. commercial operator, will be issued an Operating Certificate.

(c) A person not authorized to conduct direct air carrier operations, but authorized by the Administrator to conduct operations when common carriage is not involved as an operator of any U.S.-registered civil airplane or powered-lift with a seat configuration of 20 or more passengers, or a maximum payload capacity of 6,000 pounds or more, will be issued an Operating Certificate.

(d) A person authorized to engage in common carriage under part 121 or part 135 of this chapter, or both, shall be issued only one certificate authorizing such common carriage, regardless of the kind of operation or the class or size of aircraft to be operated.

(e) A person authorized to engage in noncommon or private carriage under part 125 or part 135 of this chapter, or both, shall be issued only one certificate authorizing such carriage, regardless of the kind of operation or the class or size of aircraft to be operated.

(f) A person conducting operations under more than one paragraph of §§119.21, 119.23, or 119.25 shall conduct those operations in compliance with—

(1) The requirements specified in each paragraph of those sections for the kind of operation conducted under that paragraph; and

(2) The appropriate authorizations, limitations, and procedures specified in the operations specifications for each kind of operation.

(g) No person may operate as a direct air carrier or as a commercial operator without, or in violation of, an appropriate certificate and appropriate operations specifications. No person may operate as a direct air carrier or as a commercial operator in violation of any deviation or exemption authority, if issued to that person or that person's representative.

(h) A person holding an Operating Certificate authorizing noncommon or private carriage operations shall not conduct any operations in common carriage. A person holding an Air Carrier Certificate or Operating Certificate authorizing common carriage operations shall not conduct any operations in noncommon carriage.

(i) No person may operate as a direct air carrier without holding appropriate economic authority from the Department of Transportation.

(j) A certificate holder under this part may not operate aircraft under part 121 or part 135 of this chapter in a geographical area unless its operations specifications specifically authorize the certificate holder to operate in that area.

(k) No person may advertise or otherwise offer to perform an operation subject to this part unless that person is authorized by the Federal Aviation Administration to conduct that operation.

(l) No person may operate an aircraft under this part, part 121 of this chapter, or part 135 of this chapter in violation of an air carrier operating certificate, operating certificate, or appropriate operations specifications issued under this part.

[Docket No. 28154, 60 FR 65913, Dec. 20, 1995; as amended by Amdt. 119–3, 62 FR 13253, March 19, 1997; Docket No. FAA–2022–1563, Amdt. 119–20, 88 FR 48089, July 26, 2023]

§119.7 Operations specifications.

(a) Each certificate holder's operations specifications must contain—

(1) The authorizations, limitations, and certain procedures under which each kind of operation, if applicable, is to be conducted; and

(2) Certain other procedures under which each class and size of aircraft is to be operated.

(b) Except for operations specifications paragraphs identifying authorized kinds of operations, operations specifications are not a part of a certificate.

§119.8 Safety Management Systems.

Certificate holders authorized to conduct operations under part 121 or 135 of this chapter must have a safety management system that meets the requirements of part 5 of this chapter.

[Docket No. FAA–2009–0671, 80 FR 1328, Jan. 8, 2015; Amdt. 119–21, 89 FR 33109, April 26, 2024]

§119.9 Use of business names.

(a) A certificate holder under this part may not operate an aircraft under part 121 or part 135 of this chapter using a business name other than a business name appearing in the certificate holder's operations specifications.

(b) No person may operate an aircraft under part 121 or part 135 of this chapter unless the name of the certificate holder who is operating the aircraft, or the air carrier or operating certificate number of the certificate holder who is operating the aircraft, is legibly displayed on the aircraft and is clearly visible and readable from the outside of the aircraft to a person standing on the ground at any time except during flight time. The means of displaying the name on the aircraft and its readability must be acceptable to the Administrator.

[Docket No. 28154, 60 FR 65913, Dec. 20, 1995; as amended by Amdt. 119–3, 62 FR 13253, March 19, 1997]

Subpart B— Applicability of Operating Requirements to Different Kinds of Operations Under Parts 121, 125, and 135 of this Chapter

§119.21 Commercial operators engaged in intrastate common carriage and direct air carriers.

(a) Each person who conducts airplane or powered-lift operations as a commercial operator engaged in intrastate common carriage of persons or property for compensation or hire in air commerce, or as a direct air carrier, shall comply with the certification and operations specifications requirements in subpart C of this part, and shall conduct its:

(1) Domestic operations in accordance with the applicable requirements of part 121 of this chapter, and shall be issued operations specifications for those operations in accordance with those requirements. However, based on a showing of safety in air commerce, the Administrator may permit persons who conduct domestic operations between any point located within any of the following Alaskan islands and any point in the State of Alaska to comply with the requirements applicable to flag operations contained in subpart U of part 121 of this chapter:

(i) The Aleutian Islands.

(ii) The Pribilof Islands.

(iii) The Shumagin Islands.

(2) Flag operations in accordance with the applicable requirements of part 121 of this chapter, and shall be issued operations specifications for those operations in accordance with those requirements.

(3) Supplemental operations in accordance with the applicable requirements of part 121 of this chapter, and shall be issued operations specifications for those operations in accordance with those requirements. However, based on a determination of safety in air commerce, the Administrator may authorize or require those operations to be conducted under paragraph (a)(1) or (a)(2) of this section.

(4) Commuter operations in accordance with the applicable requirements of part 135 of this chapter, and shall be issued operations specifications for those operations in accordance with those requirements.

(5) On-demand operations in accordance with the applicable requirements of part 135 of this chapter, and shall be issued operations specifications for those operations in accordance with those requirements.

(b) Persons who are subject to the requirements of paragraph (a)(4) of this section may conduct those operations in accordance with the requirements of paragraph (a)(1) or (a)(2) of this section, provided they obtain authorization from the Administrator.

(c) Persons who are subject to the requirements of paragraph (a)(5) of this section may conduct those operations in accordance with the requirements of paragraph (a)(3) of this section, provided they obtain authorization from the Administrator.

[Docket No. 28154, 60 FR 65913, Dec. 20, 1995; as amended by Amdt. 119–2, 61 FR 30433, June 14, 1996; Amdt. 119–3, 62 FR 13254, March 19, 1997; Amdt. 119–13, 75 FR 26645, May 12, 2010; Docket No. FAA–2022–1563, Amdt. 119–20, 88 FR 48089, July 26, 2023]

§119.23 Operators engaged in passenger-carrying operations, cargo operations, or both with airplanes or powered-lift when common carriage is not involved.

(a) Each person who conducts operations when common carriage is not involved with any airplane or powered-lift having a passenger-seat configuration of 20 seats or more, excluding each crewmember seat, or a payload capacity of 6,000 pounds or more, must, unless deviation authority is issued—

(1) Comply with the certification and operations specifications requirements of part 125 of this chapter;

(2) Conduct its operations in accordance with the requirements of part 125 of this chapter; and

(3) Be issued operations specifications in accordance with those requirements.

(b) Each person who conducts noncommon carriage (except as provided in §91.501(b) of this chapter) or private carriage operations for compensation or hire with any airplane or powered-lift having a passenger-seat configuration of less than 20 seats, excluding each crewmember seat, and a payload capacity of less than 6,000 pounds, must—

(1) Comply with the certification and operations specifications requirements in subpart C of this part;

(2) Conduct those operations in accordance with the requirements of part 135 of this chapter, except for those requirements applicable only to commuter operations; and

(3) Be issued operations specifications in accordance with those requirements.

[Docket No. 28154, 60 FR 65913, Dec. 20, 1995; as amended by Amdt. 119–2, 61 FR 30434, June 14, 1996; Docket No. FAA–2022–1563, Amdt. 119–20, 88 FR 48089, July 26, 2023]

§119.25 Rotorcraft operations: Direct air carriers and commercial operators.

Each person who conducts rotorcraft operations for compensation or hire must comply with the certification and operations specifications requirements of Subpart C of this part, and shall conduct its:

(a) Commuter operations in accordance with the applicable requirements of part 135 of this chapter, and shall be issued operations specifications for those operations in accordance with those requirements.

(b) On-demand operations in accordance with the applicable requirements of part 135 of this chapter, and shall be issued operations specifications for those operations in accordance with those requirements.

Subpart C— Certification, Operations Specifications, and Certain Other Requirements for Operations Conducted Under Part 121 or Part 135 of this Chapter

§119.31 Applicability.

This subpart sets out certification requirements and prescribes the content of operations specifications and certain other requirements for operations conducted under part 121 or part 135 of this chapter.

§119.33 General requirements.

(a) A person may not operate as a direct air carrier unless that person—

(1) Is a citizen of the United States;

(2) Obtains an Air Carrier Certificate; and

(3) Obtains operations specifications that prescribe the authorizations, limitations, and procedures under which each kind of operation must be conducted.

(b) A person other than a direct air carrier may not conduct any commercial passenger or cargo aircraft operation for compensation or hire under part 121 or part 135 of this chapter unless that person—

(1) Is a citizen of the United States;

(2) Obtains an Operating Certificate; and

(3) Obtains operations specifications that prescribe the authorizations, limitations, and procedures under which each kind of operation must be conducted.

(c) Each applicant for a certificate under this part and each applicant for operations specifications authorizing a new kind of operation that is subject to §121.163 or §135.145 of this chapter shall conduct proving tests as authorized by the Administrator during the application process for authority to conduct operations under part 121 or part 135 of this chapter. All proving tests must be conducted in a manner acceptable to the Administrator. All proving tests must be conducted under the appropriate operating and maintenance requirements of part 121 or 135 of this chapter that would apply if the applicant were fully certificated. The Administrator will issue a letter of authorization to each person stating the various authorities under which the proving tests shall be conducted.

[Docket No. 28154, 60 FR 65913, Dec. 20, 1995; as amended by Amdt. 119–2, 61 FR 30434, June 14, 1996]

§119.35 Certificate application requirements for all operators.

(a) A person applying to the Administrator for an Air Carrier Certificate or Operating Certificate under this part (applicant) must submit an application—

(1) In a form and manner prescribed by the Administrator; and

(2) Containing any information the Administrator requires the applicant to submit.

(b) Each applicant must submit the application to the Administrator at least 90 days before the date of intended operation.

[Docket No. 28154, 62 FR 13254, March 19, 1997; as amended by Amdt. 119–3, 62 FR 15570, April 1, 1997]

§119.36 Additional certificate application requirements for commercial operators.

(a) Each applicant for the original issue of an operating certificate for the purpose of conducting intrastate common carriage operations under part 121 or part 135 of this chapter must submit an application in a form and manner prescribed by the Administrator to the responsible Flight Standards office.

(b) Each application submitted under paragraph (a) of this section must contain a signed statement showing the following:

(1) For corporate applicants:

(i) The name and address of each stockholder who owns 5 percent or more of the total voting stock of the corporation, and if that stockholder is not the sole beneficial owner of the stock, the name and address of each beneficial owner. An individual is considered to own the stock owned, directly or indirectly, by or for his or her spouse, children, grandchildren, or parents.

119

(ii) The name and address of each director and each officer and each person employed or who will be employed in a management position described in §§119.65 and 119.69, as applicable.

(iii) The name and address of each person directly or indirectly controlling or controlled by the applicant and each person under direct or indirect control with the applicant.

(2) For non-corporate applicants:

(i) The name and address of each person having a financial interest therein and the nature and extent of that interest.

(ii) The name and address of each person employed or who will be employed in a management position described in §§119.65 and 119.69, as applicable.

(c) In addition, each applicant for the original issue of an operating certificate under paragraph (a) of this section must submit with the application a signed statement showing—

(1) The nature and scope of its intended operation, including the name and address of each person, if any, with whom the applicant has a contract to provide services as a commercial operator and the scope, nature, date, and duration of each of those contracts; and

(2) For applicants intending to conduct operations under part 121 of this chapter, the financial information listed in paragraph (e) of this section.

(d) Each applicant for, or holder of, a certificate issued under paragraph (a) of this section, shall notify the Administrator within 10 days after—

(1) A change in any of the persons, or the names and addresses of any of the persons, submitted to the Administrator under paragraph (b)(1) or (b)(2) of this section; or

(2) For applicants intending to conduct operations under part 121 of this chapter, a change in the financial information submitted to the Administrator under paragraph (e) of this section that occurs while the application for the issue is pending before the FAA and that would make the applicant's financial situation substantially less favorable than originally reported.

(e) Each applicant for the original issue of an operating certificate under paragraph (a) of this section who intends to conduct operations under part 121 of this chapter must submit the following financial information:

(1) A balance sheet that shows assets, liabilities, and net worth, as of a date not more than 60 days before the date of application.

(2) An itemization of liabilities more than 60 days past due on the balance sheet date, if any, showing each creditor's name and address, a description of the liability, and the amount and due date of the liability.

(3) An itemization of claims in litigation, if any, against the applicant as of the date of application

showing each claimant's name and address and a description and the amount of the claim.

(4) A detailed projection of the proposed operation covering 6 complete months after the month in which the certificate is expected to be issued including—

(i) Estimated amount and source of both operating and nonoperating revenue, including identification of its existing and anticipated income producing contracts and estimated revenue per mile or hour of operation by aircraft type;

(ii) Estimated amount of operating and nonoperating expenses by expense objective classification; and

(iii) Estimated net profit or loss for the period.

(5) An estimate of the cash that will be needed for the proposed operations during the first 6 months after the month in which the certificate is expected to be issued, including—

(i) Acquisition of property and equipment (explain);

(ii) Retirement of debt (explain);

(iii) Additional working capital (explain);

(iv) Operating losses other than depreciation and amortization (explain); and

(v) Other (explain).

(6) An estimate of the cash that will be available during the first 6 months after the month in which the certificate is expected to be issued, from—

(i) Sale of property or flight equipment (explain);

(ii) New debt (explain);

(iii) New equity (explain);

(iv) Working capital reduction (explain);

(v) Operations (profits) (explain);

(vi) Depreciation and amortization (explain); and

(vii) Other (explain).

(7) A schedule of insurance coverage in effect on the balance sheet date showing insurance companies; policy numbers; types, amounts, and period of coverage; and special conditions, exclusions, and limitations.

(8) Any other financial information that the Administrator requires to enable him or her to determine that the applicant has sufficient financial resources to conduct his or her operations with the degree of safety required in the public interest.

(f) Each financial statement containing financial information required by paragraph (e) of this section must be based on accounts prepared and maintained on an accrual basis in accordance with generally accepted accounting principles applied on a consistent basis, and must contain the name and address of the applicant's public accounting firm, if any. Information submitted must be signed by an officer, owner, or partner of the applicant or certificate holder.

[Docket No. 28154, 62 FR 133254, March 19, 1999; as amended by Amdt. 119–3, 62 FR 15570, April 1, 1997; Amdt. 119–19, 83 FR 9172, March 5, 2018]

§119.37 Contents of an Air Carrier Certificate or Operating Certificate.

The Air Carrier Certificate or Operating Certificate includes—

(a) The certificate holder's name;

(b) The location of the certificate holder's principal base of operations;

(c) The certificate number;

(d) The certificate's effective date; and

(e) The name or the designator of the responsible Flight Standards office.

[Docket No. 28154, 62 FR 133254, March 19, 1999; as amended by Amdt. 119–19, 83 FR 9172, March 5, 2018]

§119.39 Issuing or denying a certificate.

(a) An applicant may be issued an Air Carrier Certificate or Operating Certificate if, after investigation, the Administrator finds that the applicant—

(1) Meets the applicable requirements of this part;

(2) Holds the economic authority applicable to the kinds of operations to be conducted, issued by the Department of Transportation, if required; and

(3) Is properly and adequately equipped in accordance with the requirements of this chapter and is able to conduct a safe operation under appropriate provisions of part 121 or part 135 of this chapter and operations specifications issued under this part.

(b) An application for a certificate may be denied if the Administrator finds that—

(1) The applicant is not properly or adequately equipped or is not able to conduct safe operations under this subchapter;

(2) The applicant previously held an Air Carrier Certificate or Operating Certificate which was revoked;

(3) The applicant intends to or fills a key management position listed in §119.65(a) or §119.69(a), as applicable, with an individual who exercised control over or who held the same or a similar position with a certificate holder whose certificate was revoked, or is in the process of being revoked, and that individual materially contributed to the circumstances causing revocation or causing the revocation process;

(4) An individual who will have control over or have a substantial ownership interest in the applicant had the same or similar control or interest in a certificate holder whose certificate was revoked, or is in the process of being revoked, and that individual materially contributed to the circumstances causing revocation or causing the revocation process; or

(5) In the case of an applicant for an Operating Certificate for intrastate common carriage, that for financial reasons the applicant is not able to conduct a safe operation.

§119.41 Amending a certificate.

(a) The Administrator may amend any certificate issued under this part if—

(1) The Administrator determines, under 49 U.S.C. 44709 and part 13 of this chapter, that safety in air commerce and the public interest requires the amendment; or

(2) The certificate holder applies for the amendment and the responsible Flight Standards office determines that safety in air commerce and the public interest allows the amendment.

(b) When the Administrator proposes to issue an order amending, suspending, or revoking all or part of any certificate, the procedure in §13.19 of this chapter applies.

(c) When the certificate holder applies for an amendment of its certificate, the following procedure applies:

(1) The certificate holder must file an application to amend its certificate with the responsible Flight Standards office at least 15 days before the date proposed by the applicant for the amendment to become effective, unless the administrator approves filing within a shorter period; and

(2) The application must be submitted to the responsible Flight Standards office in the form and manner prescribed by the Administrator.

(d) When a certificate holder seeks reconsideration of a decision from the responsible Flight Standards office concerning amendments of a certificate, the following procedure applies:

(1) The petition for reconsideration must be made within 30 days after the certificate holder receives the notice of denial; and

(2) The certificate holder must petition for reconsideration to the Executive Director, Flight Standards Service.

[Docket No. 28154, 62 FR 133254, March 19, 1999; as amended by Amdt. 119–19, 83 FR 9172, March 5, 2018]

§119.43 Certificate holder's duty to maintain operations specifications.

(a) Each certificate holder shall maintain a complete and separate set of its operations specifications at its principal base of operations.

(b) Each certificate holder shall insert pertinent excerpts of its operations specifications, or references thereto, in its manual and shall—

(1) Clearly identify each such excerpt as a part of its operations specifications; and

(2) State that compliance with each operations specifications requirement is mandatory.

(c) Each certificate holder shall keep each of its employees and other persons used in its operations informed of the provisions of its operations specifications that apply to that employee's or person's duties and responsibilities.

§119.45 [Reserved]

§119.47 Maintaining a principal base of operations, main operations base, and main maintenance base; change of address.

(a) Each certificate holder must maintain a principal base of operations. Each certificate holder may also establish a main operations base and a main maintenance base which may be located at either the same location as the principal base of operations or at separate locations.

(b) At least 30 days before it proposes to establish or change the location of its principal base of operations, its main operations base, or its main maintenance base, a certificate holder must provide written notification to its responsible Flight Standards office.

[Docket No. 28154, 62 FR 133254, March 19, 1999; as amended by Amdt. 119–19, 83 FR 9172, March 5, 2018]

§119.49 Contents of operations specifications.

(a) Each certificate holder conducting domestic, flag, or commuter operations must obtain operations specifications containing all of the following:

(1) The specific location of the certificate holder's principal base of operations and, if different, the address that shall serve as the primary point of contact for correspondence between the FAA and the certificate holder and the name and mailing address of the certificate holder's agent for service.

(2) Other business names under which the certificate holder may operate.

(3) Reference to the economic authority issued by the Department of Transportation, if required.

(4) Type of aircraft, registration markings, and serial numbers of each aircraft authorized for use, each regular and alternate airport to be used in scheduled operations, and, except for commuter operations, each provisional and refueling airport.

(i) Subject to the approval of the Administrator with regard to form and content, the certificate holder may incorporate by reference the items listed in paragraph (a)(4) of this section into the certificate holder's operations specifications by maintaining a current listing of those items and by referring to the specific list in the applicable paragraph of the operations specifications.

(ii) The certificate holder may not conduct any operation using any aircraft or airport not listed.

(5) Kinds of operations authorized.

(6) Authorization and limitations for routes and areas of operations.

(7) Airport limitations.

(8) Time limitations, or standards for determining time limitations, for overhauling, inspecting, and checking airframes, engines, propellers, rotors, appliances, and emergency equipment.

(9) Authorization for the method of controlling weight and balance of aircraft.

(10) Interline equipment interchange requirements, if relevant.

(11) Aircraft wet lease information required by §119.21(a)(c).

(12) Any authorized deviation or exemption from any requirement of this chapter that applies to the certificate holder. |

(13) An authorization permitting, or a prohibition against, accepting, handling, and transporting materials regulated as hazardous materials in transport under 49 CFR parts 171 through 180.

(14) Any other item the Administrator determines is necessary.

(b) Each certificate holder conducting supplemental operations must obtain operations specifications containing all of the following:

(1) The specific location of the certificate holder's principal base of operations, and, if different, the address that shall serve as the primary point of contact for correspondence between the FAA and the certificate holder and the name and mailing address of the certificate holder's agent for service.

(2) Other business names under which the certificate holder may operate.

(3) Reference to the economic authority issued by the Department of Transportation, if required.

(4) Type of aircraft, registration markings, and serial number of each aircraft authorized for use.

(i) Subject to the approval of the Administrator with regard to form and content, the certificate holder may incorporate by reference the items listed in paragraph (b)(4) of this section into the certificate holder's operations specifications by maintaining a current listing of those items and by referring to the specific list in the applicable paragraph of the operations specifications.

(ii) The certificate holder may not conduct any operation using any aircraft not listed.

(5) Kinds of operations authorized.

(6) Authorization and limitations for routes and areas of operations.

(7) Special airport authorizations and limitations.

(8) Time limitations, or standards for determining time limitations, for overhauling, inspecting, and checking airframes, engines, propellers, appliances, and emergency equipment.

(9) Authorization for the method of controlling weight and balance of aircraft.

(10) Aircraft wet lease information required by §119.53(c).

(11) Any authorization or requirement to conduct supplemental operations as provided by §119.21(a)(3).

(12) Any authorized deviation or exemption from any requirement of this chapter that applies to the certificate holder. |

(13) An authorization permitting, or a prohibition against, accepting, handling, and transporting materials regulated as hazardous materials in transport under 49 CFR parts 171 through 180.

(14) Any other item the Administrator determines is necessary.

(c) Each certificate holder conducting on-demand operations must obtain operations specifications containing all of the following:

(1) The specific location of the certificate holder's principal base of operations, and if different, the address that shall serve as the primary point of contact for correspondence between the FAA and the name and mailing address of the certificate holder's agent for service.

(2) Other business names under which the certificate holder may operate.

(3) Reference to the economic authority issued by the Department of Transportation, if required.

(4) Kind and area of operations authorized.

(5) Category and class of aircraft that may be used in those operations.

(6) Type of aircraft, registration markings, and serial number of each aircraft that is subject to an airworthiness maintenance program required by §135.411(a)(2) of this chapter.

(i) Subject to the approval of the Administrator with regard to form and content, the certificate holder may incorporate by reference the items listed in paragraph (c)(6) of this section into the certificate holder's operations specifications by maintaining a current listing of those items and by referring to the specific list in the applicable paragraph of the operations specifications.

(ii) The certificate holder may not conduct any operation using any aircraft not listed.

(7) Registration markings of each aircraft that is to be inspected under an approved aircraft inspection program under §135.419 of this chapter.

(8) Time limitations or standards for determining time limitations, for overhauls, inspections, and checks for airframes, engines, propellers, rotors, appliances, and emergency equipment of aircraft that are subject to an airworthiness maintenance program required by §135.411(a)(2) of this chapter.

(9) Additional maintenance items required by the Administrator under §135.421 of this chapter.

(10) Aircraft wet lease information required by §119.53(c).

(11) Any authorized deviation or exemption from any requirement of this chapter that applies to the certificate holder.

(12) An authorization permitting, or a prohibition against, accepting, handling, and transporting materials regulated as hazardous materials in transport under 49 CFR parts 171 through 180.

(13) Any other item the Administrator determines is necessary.

[Docket No. 28154, 60 FR 65913, Dec. 20, 1995; as amended by Amdt. 119–10, 70 FR 58823, Oct. 7, 2005; Amdt. 119–13, 75 FR 26645, May 12, 2010; Docket No. FAA–2022–1563, Amdt. 119–20, 88 FR 48089, July 26, 2023]

§119.51 Amending operations specifications.

(a) The Administrator may amend any operations specifications issued under this part if—

(1) The Administrator determines that safety in air commerce and the public interest require the amendment; or

(2) The certificate holder applies for the amendment, and the Administrator determines that safety in air commerce and the public interest allows the amendment.

(b) Except as provided in paragraph (e) of this section, when the Administrator initiates an amendment to a certificate holder's operations specifications, the following procedure applies:

(1) The responsible Flight Standards office notifies the certificate holder in writing of the proposed amendment.

(2) The responsible Flight Standards office sets a reasonable period (but not less than 7 days) within which the certificate holder may submit written information, views, and arguments on the amendment.

(3) After considering all material presented, the responsible Flight Standards office notifies the certificate holder of—

(i) The adoption of the proposed amendment;

(ii) The partial adoption of the proposed amendment; or

(iii) The withdrawal of the proposed amendment.

(4) If the responsible Flight Standards office issues an amendment to the operations specifications, it becomes effective not less than 30 days after the certificate holder receives notice of it unless—

(i) The responsible Flight Standards office finds under paragraph (e) of this section that there is an emergency requiring immediate action with respect to safety in air commerce; or

(ii) The certificate holder petitions for reconsideration of the amendment under paragraph (d) of this section.

(c) When the certificate holder applies for an amendment to its operations specifications, the following procedure applies:

(1) The certificate holder must file an application to amend its operations specifications—

(i) At least 90 days before the date proposed by the applicant for the amendment to become effective, unless a shorter time is approved, in cases of mergers; acquisitions of airline operational assets that require an additional showing of safety (e.g., proving tests); changes in the kind of operation as

defined in §110.2; resumption of operations following a suspension of operations as a result of bankruptcy actions; or the initial introduction of aircraft not before proven for use in air carrier or commercial operator operations.

(ii) At least 15 days before the date proposed by the applicant for the amendment to become effective in all other cases.

(2) The application must be submitted to the responsible Flight Standards office in a form and manner prescribed by the Administrator.

(3) After considering all material presented, the responsible Flight Standards office notifies the certificate holder of—

(i) The adoption of the applied for amendment;

(ii) The partial adoption of the applied for amendment; or

(iii) The denial of the applied for amendment. The certificate holder may petition for reconsideration of a denial under paragraph (d) of this section.

(4) If the responsible Flight Standards office approves the amendment, following coordination with the certificate holder regarding its implementation, the amendment is effective on the date the Administrator approves it.

(d) When a certificate holder seeks reconsideration of a decision from the responsible Flight Standards office concerning the amendment of operations specifications, the following procedure applies:

(1) The certificate holder must petition for reconsideration of that decision within 30 days of the date that the certificate holder receives a notice of denial of the amendment to its operations specifications, or of the date it receives notice of an FAA-initiated amendment to its operations specifications, whichever circumstance applies.

(2) The certificate holder must address its petition to the Executive Director, Flight Standards Service.

(3) A petition for reconsideration, if filed within the 30-day period, suspends the effectiveness of any amendment issued by the responsible Flight Standards office unless the responsible Flight Standards office has found, under paragraph (e) of this section, that an emergency exists requiring immediate action with respect to safety in air transportation or air commerce.

(4) If a petition for reconsideration is not filed within 30 days, the procedures of paragraph (c) of this section apply.

(e) If the responsible Flight Standards office finds that an emergency exists requiring immediate action with respect to safety in air commerce or air transportation that makes the procedures set out in this section impracticable or contrary to the public interest:

(1) The responsible Flight Standards office amends the operations specifications and makes the amendment effective on the day the certificate holder receives notice of it.

(2) In the notice to the certificate holder, the responsible Flight Standards office articulates the reasons for its finding that an emergency exists requiring immediate action with respect to safety in air transportation or air commerce or that makes it impracticable or contrary to the public interest to stay the effectiveness of the amendment.

[Docket No. 28154, 62 FR 133254, March 19, 1999; as amended by Amdt. 119–19, 83 FR 9172, March 5, 2018]

§119.53 Wet leasing of aircraft and other arrangements for transportation by air.

(a) Unless otherwise authorized by the Administrator, prior to conducting operations involving a wet lease, each certificate holder under this part authorized to conduct common carriage operations under this subchapter shall provide the Administrator with a copy of the wet lease to be executed which would lease the aircraft to any other person engaged in common carriage operations under this subchapter, including foreign air carriers, or to any other foreign person engaged in common carriage wholly outside the United States.

(b) No certificate holder under this part may wet lease from a foreign air carrier or any other foreign person or any person not authorized to engage in common carriage.

(c) Upon receiving a copy of a wet lease, the Administrator determines which party to the agreement has operational control of the aircraft and issues amendments to the operations specifications of each party to the agreement, as needed. The lessor must provide the following information to be incorporated into the operations specifications of both parties, as needed.

(1) The names of the parties to the agreement and the duration thereof.

(2) The nationality and registration markings of each aircraft involved in the agreement.

(3) The kind of operation (e.g., domestic, flag, supplemental, commuter, or on-demand).

(4) The airports or areas of operation.

(5) A statement specifying the party deemed to have operational control and the times, airports, or areas under which such operational control is exercised.

(d) In making the determination of paragraph (c) of this section, the Administrator will consider the following:

(1) Crewmembers and training.

(2) Airworthiness and performance of maintenance.

(3) Dispatch.

(4) Servicing the aircraft.

(5) Scheduling.

(6) Any other factor the Administrator considers relevant.

(e) Other arrangements for transportation by air: Except as provided in paragraph (f) of this section, a certificate holder under this part operating under part 121 or 135 of this chapter may not conduct any operation for another certificate holder under this part or a foreign air carrier under part 129 of this chapter or a foreign person engaged in common carriage wholly outside the United States unless it holds applicable Department of Transportation economic authority, if required, and is authorized under its operations specifications to conduct the same kinds of operations (as defined in §110.2). The certificate holder conducting the substitute operation must conduct that operation in accordance with the same operations authority held by the certificate holder arranging for the substitute operation. These substitute operations must be conducted between airports for which the substitute certificate holder holds authority for scheduled operations or within areas of operations for which the substitute certificate holder has authority for supplemental or on-demand operations.

(f) A certificate holder under this part may, if authorized by the Department of Transportation under §380.3 of this title and the Administrator in the case of interstate commuter, interstate domestic, and flag operations, or the Administrator in the case of scheduled intrastate common carriage operations, conduct one or more flights for passengers who are stranded because of the cancellation of their scheduled flights. These flights must be conducted under the rules of part 121 or part 135 of this chapter applicable to supplemental or on-demand operations.

§119.55 Obtaining deviation authority to perform operations under a U.S. military contract.

(a) The Administrator may authorize a certificate holder that is authorized to conduct supplemental or on-demand operations to deviate from the applicable requirements of this part, part 117, part 121, or part 135 of this chapter in order to perform operations under a U.S. military contract.

(b) A certificate holder that has a contract with the U.S. Department of Defense's Air Mobility Command (AMC) must submit a request for deviation authority to AMC. AMC will review the requests, then forward the carriers' consolidated requests, along with AMC's recommendations, to the FAA for review and action.

(c) The Administrator may authorize a deviation to perform operations under a U.S. military contract under the following conditions—

(1) The Department of Defense certifies to the Administrator that the operation is essential to the national defense;

(2) The Department of Defense further certifies that the certificate holder cannot perform the operation without deviation authority;

(3) The certificate holder will perform the operation under a contract or subcontract for the benefit of a U.S. armed service; and

(4) The Administrator finds that the deviation is based on grounds other than economic advantage either to the certificate holder or to the United States.

(d) In the case where the Administrator authorizes a deviation under this section, the Administrator will issue an appropriate amendment to the certificate holder's operations specifications.

(e) The Administrator may, at any time, terminate any grant of deviation authority issued under this section.

[Docket No. 28154, 60 FR 65913, Dec. 20, 1995; as amended by Amdt. 119–16, 77 FR 402, Jan. 4, 2012]

§119.57 Obtaining deviation authority to perform an emergency operation.

(a) In emergency conditions, the Administrator may authorize deviations if—

(1) Those conditions necessitate the transportation of persons or supplies for the protection of life or property; and

(2) The Administrator finds that a deviation is necessary for the expeditious conduct of the operations.

(b) When the Administrator authorizes deviations for operations under emergency conditions—

(1) The Administrator will issue an appropriate amendment to the certificate holder's operations specifications; or

(2) If the nature of the emergency does not permit timely amendment of the operations specifications—

(i) The Administrator may authorize the deviation orally; and

(ii) The certificate holder shall provide documentation describing the nature of the emergency to the responsible Flight Standards office within 24 hours after completing the operation.

[Docket No. 28154, 62 FR 133254, March 19, 1999; as amended by Amdt. 119–19, 83 FR 9172, March 5, 2018]

§119.59 Conducting tests and inspections.

(a) At any time or place, the Administrator may conduct an inspection or test to determine whether a certificate holder under this part is complying with title 49 of the United States Code, applicable regulations, the certificate, or the certificate holder's operations specifications.

(b) The certificate holder must—

(1) Make available to the Administrator at the certificate holder's principal base of operations—

(i) The certificate holder's Air Carrier Certificate or the certificate holder's Operating Certificate and the certificate holder's operations specifications; and

(ii) A current listing that will include the location and persons responsible for each record, document, and report required to be kept by the certificate holder under title 49 of the United States Code applicable to the operation of the certificate holder.

(2) Allow the Administrator to make àny test or inspection to determine compliance respecting any matter stated in paragraph (a) of this section.

(c) Each employee of, or person used by, the certificate holder who is responsible for maintaining the certificate holder's records must make those records available to the Administrator.

(d) The Administrator may determine a certificate holder's continued eligibility to hold its certificate and/or operations specifications on any grounds listed in paragraph (a) of this section, or any other appropriate grounds.

(e) Failure by any certificate holder to make available to the Administrator upon request, the certificate, operations specifications, or any required record, document, or report is grounds for suspension of all or any part of the certificate holder's certificate and operations specifications.

(f) In the case of operators conducting intrastate common carriage operations, these inspections and tests include inspections and tests of financial books and records.

§119.61 Duration and surrender of certificate and operations specifications.

(a) An Air Carrier Certificate or Operating Certificate issued under this part is effective until—

(1) The certificate holder surrenders it to the Administrator; or

(2) The Administrator suspends, revokes, or otherwise terminates the certificate.

(b) Operations specifications issued under this part, part 121, or part 135 of this chapter are effective unless—

(1) The Administrator suspends, revokes, or otherwise terminates the certificate;

(2) The operations specifications are amended as provided in §119.51;

(3) The certificate holder does not conduct a kind of operation for more than the time specified in §119.63 and fails to follow the procedures of §119.63 upon resuming that kind of operation; or

(4) The Administrator suspends or revokes the operations specifications for a kind of operation.

(c) Within 30 days after a certificate holder terminates operations under part 135 of this chapter, the operating certificate and operations specifications must be surrendered by the certificate holder to the responsible Flight Standards office.

[Docket No. 28154, 62 FR 133254, March 19, 1999; as amended by Amdt. 119–19, 83 FR 9172, March 5, 2018]

§119.63 Recency of operation.

(a) Except as provided in paragraph (b) of this section, no certificate holder may conduct a kind of operation for which it holds authority in its operations specifications unless the certificate holder has conducted that kind of operation within the preceding number of consecutive calendar days specified in this paragraph:

(1) For domestic, flag, or commuter operations—30 days.

(2) For supplemental or on-demand operations—90 days, except that if the certificate holder has authority to conduct domestic, flag, or commuter operations, and has conducted domestic, flag or commuter operations within the previous 30 days, this paragraph does not apply.

(b) If a certificate holder does not conduct a kind of operation for which it is authorized in its operations specifications within the number of calendar days specified in paragraph (a) of this section, it shall not conduct such kind of operation unless—

(1) It advises the Administrator at least 5 consecutive calendar days before resumption of that kind of operation; and

(2) It makes itself available and accessible during the 5 consecutive calendar day period in the event that the FAA decides to conduct a full inspection reexamination to determine whether the certificate holder remains properly and adequately equipped and able to conduct a safe operation.

[Docket No. 28154, 60 FR 65913, Dec. 20, 1995; as amended by Amdt. 119–2, 61 FR 30434, June 14, 1996]

§119.65 Management personnel required for operations conducted under part 121 of this chapter.

(a) Each certificate holder must have sufficient qualified management and technical personnel to ensure the highest degree of safety in its operations. The certificate holder must have qualified personnel serving full-time in the following or equivalent positions:

(1) Director of Safety.

(2) Director of Operations.

(3) Chief Pilot for each category of aircraft the certificate holder uses, as listed in §61.5(b)(1) of this chapter.

(4) Director of Maintenance.

(5) Chief Inspector.

 ASA

(b) The Administrator may approve positions or numbers of positions other than those listed in paragraph (a) of this section for a particular operation if the certificate holder shows that it can perform the operation with the highest degree of safety under the direction of fewer or different categories of management personnel due to—

(1) The kind of operation involved;

(2) The number and type of aircraft used; and

(3) The area of operations.

(c) The title of the positions required under paragraph (a) of this section or the title and number of equivalent positions approved under paragraph (b) of this section shall be set forth in the certificate holder's operations specifications.

(d) The individuals who serve in the positions required or approved under paragraph (a) or (b) of this section and anyone in a position to exercise control over operations conducted under the operating certificate must—

(1) Be qualified through training, experience, and expertise;

(2) To the extent of their responsibilities, have a full understanding of the following materials with respect to the certificate holder's operation—

(i) Aviation safety standards and safe operating practices;

(ii) 14 CFR Chapter I (Federal Aviation Regulations);

(iii) The certificate holder's operations specifications;

(iv) All appropriate maintenance and airworthiness requirements of this chapter (e.g., parts 1, 21, 23, 25, 43, 45, 47, 65, 91, and 121 of this chapter); and

(v) The manual required by §121.133 of this chapter; and

(3) Discharge their duties to meet applicable legal requirements and to maintain safe operations.

(e) Each certificate holder must:

(1) State in the general policy provisions of the manual required by §121.133 of this chapter, the duties, responsibilities, and authority of personnel required under paragraph (a) of this section;

(2) List in the manual the names and business addresses of the individuals assigned to those positions; and

(3) Notify the responsible Flight Standards office within 10 days of any change in personnel or any vacancy in any position listed.

[Docket No. 28154, 62 FR 133254, March 19, 1999; as amended by Amdt. 119–19, 83 FR 9172, March 5, 2018; Docket No. FAA–2022–1563, Amdt. 119–20, 88 FR 48089, July 26, 2023]

§119.67 Management personnel: Qualifications for operations conducted under part 121 of this chapter.

(a) *Director of Operations.* To serve as Director of Operations under §119.65(a), a person must hold an airline transport pilot certificate and—

(1) If the certificate holder uses large aircraft, at least 3 years of supervisory or managerial experience within the last 6 years in large aircraft, in a position that exercised operational control over any operations conducted under part 121 or 135 of this chapter.

(2) If the certificate holder uses large aircraft, at least 3 years of experience as pilot in command under part 121 or 135 of this chapter in large aircraft in at least one of the categories of aircraft the certificate holder uses, as listed in §61.5(b)(1) of this chapter. In the case of a person becoming Director of Operations for the first time, he or she must have accumulated this experience as pilot in command within the past 6 years.

(3) If the certificate holder uses only small aircraft in its operations, the experience required in paragraphs (a)(1) and (2) of this section may be obtained in either large or small aircraft.

(b) *Chief Pilot.* To serve as Chief Pilot under §119.65(a), a person must:

(1) Hold an airline transport pilot certificate with appropriate ratings in the category of aircraft that the certificate holder uses in its operations under part 121 of this chapter and over which the Chief Pilot exercises responsibility; and

(2) Have at least 3 years of experience as pilot in command in the same category of aircraft that the certificate holder uses, as listed in §61.5(b) of this chapter. The experience as pilot in command described in this paragraph (b)(2) must:

(i) Have occurred within the past 6 years, in the case of a person becoming a Chief Pilot for the first time.

(ii) Have occurred in large aircraft operated under part 121 or 135 of this chapter. If the certificate holder uses only small aircraft in its operation, this experience may be obtained in either large or small aircraft.

(iii) Be in the same category of aircraft over which the Chief Pilot exercises responsibility.

(c) *Director of Maintenance.* To serve as Director of Maintenance under §119.65(a), a person must:

(1) Hold a mechanic certificate with airframe and powerplant ratings;

(2) Have 1 year of experience in a position responsible for returning aircraft to service;

(3) Have at least 1 year of experience in a supervisory capacity under either paragraph (c)(4) (i) or (ii) of this section maintaining the same category and class of aircraft as the certificate holder uses; and

(4) Have 3 years of experience within the past 6 years in one or a combination of the following—

(i) Maintaining large aircraft with 10 or more passenger seats, including, at the time of appointment as Director of Maintenance, experience in maintaining the same category and class of aircraft as the certificate holder uses; or

(ii) Repairing aircraft in a certificated airframe repair station that is rated to maintain aircraft in the same category and class of aircraft as the certificate holder uses.

(d) *Chief Inspector.* To serve as Chief Inspector under §119.65(a), a person must:

(1) Hold a mechanic certificate with both airframe and powerplant ratings, and have held these ratings for at least 3 years;

(2) Have at least 3 years of maintenance experience on different types of large aircraft with 10 or more passenger seats with an air carrier or certificated repair station, 1 year of which must have been as maintenance inspector; and

(3) Have at least 1 year of experience in a supervisory capacity maintaining the same category and class of aircraft as the certificate holder uses.

(e) *Deviation.* A certificate holder may request a deviation to employ a person who does not meet the appropriate airman experience, managerial experience, or supervisory experience requirements of this section if the Manager of the Air Transportation Division or the Manager of the Aircraft Maintenance Division, as appropriate, finds that the person has comparable experience and can effectively perform the functions associated with the position in accordance with the requirements of this chapter and the procedures outlined in the certificate holder's manual. Deviations under this paragraph (e) may be issued after consideration of the size and scope of the operation and the qualifications of the intended personnel. The Administrator may, at any time, terminate any grant of deviation authority issued under this paragraph (e).

[Docket No. 28154, 60 FR 65913, Dec. 20, 1995; as amended by Amdt. 119–2, 61 FR 30434, June 14, 1996; Amdt. 119–3, 62 FR 13255, March 19, 1997; Docket No. FAA–2022–1563, Amdt. 119–20, 88 FR 48089, July 26, 2023]

§119.69 Management personnel required for operations conducted under part 135 of this chapter.

(a) Each certificate holder must have sufficient qualified management and technical personnel to ensure the safety of its operations. Except for a certificate holder using only one pilot in its operations, the certificate holder must have qualified personnel serving in the following or equivalent positions:

(1) Director of Operations.

(2) Chief Pilot.

(3) Director of Maintenance.

(b) The Administrator may approve positions or numbers of positions other than those listed in paragraph (a) of this section for a particular operation if the certificate holder shows that it can perform the operation with the highest degree of safety under the direction of fewer or different categories of management personnel due to—

(1) The kind of operation involved;

(2) The number and type of aircraft used; and

(3) The area of operations.

(c) The title of the positions required under paragraph (a) of this section or the title and number of equivalent positions approved under paragraph (b) of this section shall be set forth in the certificate holder's operations specifications.

(d) The individuals who serve in the positions required or approved under paragraph (a) or (b) of this section and anyone in a position to exercise control over operations conducted under the operating certificate must—

(1) Be qualified through training, experience, and expertise;

(2) To the extent of their responsibilities, have a full understanding of the following material with respect to the certificate holder's operation—

(i) Aviation safety standards and safe operating practices;

(ii) 14 CFR Chapter I (Federal Aviation Regulations);

(iii) The certificate holder's operations specifications;

(iv) All appropriate maintenance and airworthiness requirements of this chapter (e.g., parts 1, 21, 23, 25, 43, 45, 47, 65, 91, and 135 of this chapter); and

(v) The manual required by §135.21 of this chapter; and

(3) Discharge their duties to meet applicable legal requirements and to maintain safe operations.

(e) Each certificate holder must—

(1) State in the general policy provisions of the manual required by §135.21 of this chapter, the duties, responsibilities, and authority of personnel required or approved under paragraph (a) or (b), respectively, of this section;

(2) List in the manual the names and business addresses of the individuals assigned to those positions; and

(3) Notify the responsible Flight Standards office within 10 days of any change in personnel or any vacancy in any position listed.

[Docket No. 28154, 62 FR 133254, March 19, 1999; as amended by Amdt. 119–19, 83 FR 9172, March 5, 2018]

§119.71 Management personnel: Qualifications for operations conducted under part 135 of this chapter.

(a) To serve as Director of Operations under §119.69(a) for a certificate holder conducting any operations for which the pilot in command is required to hold an airline transport pilot certificate a person must hold an airline transport pilot certificate and either:

(1) Have at least 3 years supervisory or managerial experience within the last 6 years in a position that exercised operational control over any operations conducted under part 121 or part 135 of this chapter; or

(2) In the case of a person becoming Director of Operations—

(i) For the first time ever, have at least 3 years experience, within the past 6 years, as pilot in command of an aircraft operated under part 121 or part 135 of this chapter.

(ii) In the case of a person with previous experience as a Director of Operations, have at least 3 years experience, as pilot in command of an aircraft operated under part 121 or part 135 of this chapter.

(b) To serve as Director of Operations under §119.69(a) for a certificate holder that only conducts operations for which the pilot in command is required to hold a commercial pilot certificate, a person must hold at least a commercial pilot certificate. If an instrument rating is required for any pilot in command for that certificate holder, the Director of Operations must also hold an instrument rating. In addition, the Director of Operations must either—

(1) Have at least 3 years supervisory or managerial experience within the last 6 years in a position that exercised operational control over any operations conducted under part 121 or part 135 of this chapter; or

(2) In the case of a person becoming Director of Operations—

(i) For the first time ever, have at least 3 years experience, within the past 6 years, as pilot in command of an aircraft operated under part 121 or part 135 of this chapter.

(ii) In the case of a person with previous experience as a Director of Operations, have at least 3 years experience as pilot in command of an aircraft operated under part 121 or part 135 of this chapter.

(c) To serve as Chief Pilot under §119.69(a) for a certificate holder conducting any operation for which the pilot in command is required to hold an airline transport pilot certificate a person must hold an airline transport pilot certificate with appropriate ratings and be qualified to serve as pilot in command in at least one aircraft used in the certificate holder's operation and:

(1) In the case of a person becoming a Chief Pilot for the first time ever, have at least 3 years experience, within the past 6 years, as pilot in command of an aircraft operated under part 121 or part 135 of this chapter.

(2) In the case of a person with previous experience as a Chief Pilot, have at least 3 years experience as pilot in command of an aircraft operated under part 121 or part 135 of this chapter.

(d) To serve as Chief Pilot under §119.69(a) for a certificate holder that only conducts operations for which the pilot in command is required to hold a commercial pilot certificate, a person must hold at least a commercial pilot certificate. If an instrument rating is required for any pilot in command for that certificate holder, the Chief Pilot must also hold an instrument rating. The Chief Pilot must be qualified to serve as pilot in command in at least one aircraft used in the certificate holder's operation. In addition, the Chief Pilot must:

(1) In the case of a person becoming a Chief Pilot for the first time ever, have at least 3 years experience, within the past 6 years, as pilot in command of an aircraft operated under part 121 or part 135 of this chapter.

(2) In the case of a person with previous experience as a Chief Pilot, have at least 3 years experience as pilot in command of an aircraft operated under part 121 or part 135 of this chapter.

(e) To serve as Director of Maintenance under §119.69(a) a person must hold a mechanic certificate with airframe and powerplant ratings and either:

(1) Have 3 years of experience within the past 6 years maintaining aircraft as a certificated mechanic, including, at the time of appointment as Director of Maintenance, experience in maintaining the same category and class of aircraft as the certificate holder uses; or

(2) Have 3 years of experience within the past 6 years repairing aircraft in a certificated airframe repair station, including 1 year in the capacity of approving aircraft for return to service.

(f) A certificate holder may request a deviation to employ a person who does not meet the appropriate airmen experience requirements, managerial experience requirements, or supervisory experience requirements of this section if the Manager of the Air Transportation Division, AFS–200, or the Manager of the Aircraft Maintenance Division, AFS–300, as appropriate, find that the person has comparable experience, and can effectively perform the functions associated with the position in accordance with the requirements of this chapter and the procedures outlined in the certificate holder's manual. Grants of deviation under this paragraph may be granted after consideration of the size and scope of the operation and the qualifications of the intended personnel. The Administrator may, at any time, terminate

119

any grant of deviation authority issued under this paragraph.

[Docket No. 28154, 60 FR 65913, Dec. 20, 1995; as amended by Amdt. 119–3, 62 FR 13255, March 19, 1997; Amdt. 119–12, 72 FR 54816, Sept. 27, 2007]

§119.73 Employment of former FAA employees.

(a) Except as specified in paragraph (c) of this section, no certificate holder conducting operations under part 121 or 135 of this chapter may knowingly employ or make a contractual arrangement which permits an individual to act as an agent or representative of the certificate holder in any matter before the Federal Aviation Administration if the individual, in the preceding 2 years—

(1) Served as, or was directly responsible for the oversight of, a Flight Standards Service aviation safety inspector; and

(2) Had direct responsibility to inspect, or oversee the inspection of, the operations of the certificate holder.

(b) For the purpose of this section, an individual shall be considered to be acting as an agent or representative of a certificate holder in a matter before the agency if the individual makes any written or oral communication on behalf of the certificate holder to the agency (or any of its officers or employees) in connection with a particular matter, whether or not involving a specific party and without regard to whether the individual has participated in, or had responsibility for, the particular matter while serving as a Flight Standards Service aviation safety inspector.

(c) The provisions of this section do not prohibit a certificate holder from knowingly employing or making a contractual arrangement which permits an individual to act as an agent or representative of the certificate holder in any matter before the Federal Aviation Administration if the individual was employed by the certificate holder before October 21, 2011.

[Docket No. 2008–1154, 76 FR 52235, Aug. 22, 2011]

PART 136

COMMERCIAL AIR TOURS AND NATIONAL PARKS AIR TOUR MANAGEMENT

Authority: 49 U.S.C. 106(f), 106(g), 40113, 40119, 44101, 44701–44702, 44705, 44709–44711, 44713, 44716–44717, 44722, 44901, 44903–44904, 44912, 46105.

Source: Docket No. FAA–2001–8690, 67 FR 65667, October 25, 2002 unless otherwise noted.

Subpart A—National Air Tour Safety Standards

Source: Docket No. FAA–1998–4521, 72 FR 6912, Feb. 13, 2007, unless otherwise noted.

§136.1 Applicability and definitions.

(a) This subpart applies to each person operating or intending to operate a commercial air tour in an airplane, powered-lift, or rotorcraft and, when applicable, to all occupants of those aircraft engaged in a commercial air tour. When any requirement of this subpart is more stringent than any other requirement of this chapter, the person operating the commercial air tour must comply with the requirement in this subpart.

(b) This subpart applies to:
(1) Part 121 or 135 operators conducting a commercial air tour and holding a part 119 certificate;
(2) Part 91 operators conducting flights as described in §119.1(e)(2); and
(3) Part 91 operators conducting flights as described in 14 CFR 91.146

(c) This subpart does not apply to operations conducted in balloons, gliders (powered and unpowered), parachutes (powered and un-powered), gyroplanes, or airships.

(d) For the purposes of this subpart the following definitions apply:

Commercial air tour means a flight conducted for compensation or hire in an airplane, powered-lift, or rotorcraft where a purpose of the flight is sightseeing. The FAA may consider the following factors in determining whether a flight is a commercial air tour for purposes of this subpart:

(i) Whether there was a holding out to the public of willingness to conduct a sightseeing flight for compensation or hire;

(ii) Whether the person offering the flight provided a narrative that referred to areas or points of interest on the surface below the route of the flight;

(iii) The area of operation;

(iv) How often the person offering the flight conducts such flights;

(v) The route of the flight;

(vi) The inclusion of sightseeing flights as part of any travel arrangement package;

(vii) Whether the flight in question would have been canceled based on poor visibility of the surface below the route of the flight; and

(viii) Any other factors that the FAA considers appropriate.

Commercial Air Tour operator means any person who conducts a commercial air tour.

Life preserver means a flotation device used by an aircraft occupant if the aircraft ditches in water. If an inflatable device, it must be un-inflated and ready for its intended use once inflated. In evaluating whether a non-inflatable life preserver is acceptable to the FAA, the operator must demonstrate to the FAA that such a preserver can be used during an evacuation and will allow all passengers to exit the aircraft without blocking the exit. Each occupant must have the physical capacity to wear and inflate the type of device used once briefed by the commercial air tour operator. Seat cushions do not meet this definition.

Raw terrain means any area on the surface, including water, devoid of any person, structure, vehicle, or vessel.

Shoreline means that area of the land adjacent to the water of an ocean, sea, lake, pond, river or tidal basin that is above the high water mark and excludes land areas unsuitable for landing such as vertical cliffs or land intermittently under water during the particular flight.

❚ *Suitable landing area for rotorcraft* means an area that provides the operator reasonable capability to land in an emergency without causing serious injury to persons. These suitable landing areas must be site specific, designated by the operator, and accepted by the FAA.

(e) In an in-flight emergency requiring immediate action, the pilot in command may deviate from any rule of this subpart to the extent required to meet that emergency.

[Docket No. FAA–2022–1563, Amdt. 136–2, 88 FR 48091, July 26, 2023]

§136.3 Letters of Authorization.

Operators subject to this subpart who have Letters of Authorization may use the procedures ❚ described in §119.51 of this chapter to amend or have the FAA reconsider those Letters of Authorization.

[Docket No. FAA–2022–1563, Amdt. 136–2, 88 FR 48091, July 26, 2023]

§136.5 Additional requirements for Hawaii.

Any operator subject to this subpart who meets the criteria of §136.71 must comply with the additional requirements and restrictions in subpart D of this part.

[Docket No. FAA–2022–1563, Amdt. 136–2, 88 FR 48091, July 26, 2023]

§136.7 Passenger briefings.

(a) Before takeoff each pilot in command shall ensure that each passenger has been briefed on the following:

(1) Procedures for fastening and unfastening seatbelts;

(2) Prohibition on smoking; and

(3) Procedures for opening exits and exiting the aircraft.

(b) For flight segments over water beyond the shoreline, briefings must also include:

(1) Procedures for water ditching;

(2) Use of required life preservers; and

(3) Procedures for emergency exit from the aircraft in the event of a water landing.

§136.9 Life preservers for operations over water. ❚

(a) Except as provided in paragraphs (b) or (c) of this section, the operator and pilot in command of commercial air tours over water beyond the shoreline must ensure that each occupant is wearing a life preserver from before takeoff until flight is no longer over water.

(b) The operator and pilot in command of a commercial air tour over water beyond the shoreline must ensure that a life preserver is readily available for its intended use and easily accessible to each occupant if:

(1) The aircraft is equipped with floats; ❚

(2) The airplane is within power-off gliding distance to the shoreline for the duration of the time that the flight is over water; or

(3) The aircraft is a multiengine that can be ❚ operated with the critical engine inoperative at a weight that will allow it to climb, at least 50 feet a minute, at an altitude of 1,000 feet above the surface, as provided in the approved aircraft flight manual for that aircraft. ❚

(c) No life preserver is required if the overwater operation is necessary only for takeoff or landing.

[Docket No. FAA–2022–1563, Amdt. 136–2, 88 FR 48091, July 26, 2023]

§136.11 Rotorcraft floats for over water.

(a) A rotorcraft used in commercial air tours ❚ over water beyond the shoreline must be equipped with fixed floats or an inflatable flotation system adequate to accomplish a safe emergency ditching, if—

(1) It is a single-engine rotorcraft; or

(2) It is a multi-engine rotorcraft that cannot be ❚ operated with the critical engine inoperative at a weight that will allow it to climb, at least 50 feet a minute, at an altitude of 1,000 feet above the surface, as provided in the approved aircraft flight manual for that aircraft. ❚

(b) Each rotorcraft that is required to be equipped with an inflatable flotation system under this section must have:

(1) The activation switch for the flotation system on one of the primary flight controls; and

(2) The flotation system armed when the rotorcraft is over water beyond the shoreline and is flying at a speed that does not exceed the maximum speed prescribed in the approved aircraft flight manual for flying with the flotation system armed.

(c) Neither fixed floats nor an inflatable flotation system is required for a rotorcraft under this section when that rotorcraft is:

(1) Over water only during the takeoff or landing portion of the flight; or

(2) Operated within power-off gliding distance to the shoreline for the duration of the flight and each occupant is wearing a life preserver from before takeoff until the aircraft is no longer over water.

[Docket No. FAA-2022–1563, Amdt. 136–2, 88 FR 48091, July 26, 2023]

§136.13 Performance plan.

(a) Each operator that uses a rotorcraft must complete a performance plan before each commercial air tour or flight operated under §91.146 or §91.147 of this chapter. The pilot in command must review for accuracy and comply with the performance plan on the day the flight occurs. The performance plan must be based on information in the approved aircraft flight manual for that aircraft taking into consideration the maximum density altitude for which the operation is planned, in order to determine:

(1) Maximum gross weight and center of gravity (CG) limitations for hovering in ground effect;

(2) Maximum gross weight and CG limitations for hovering out of ground effect; and

(3) Maximum combination of weight, altitude, and temperature for which height/velocity information in the approved aircraft flight manual is valid.

(b) Except for the approach to and transition from a hover for the purpose of takeoff and landing, or during takeoff and landing, the pilot in command must make a reasonable plan to operate the rotorcraft outside of the caution/warning/avoid area of the limiting height/velocity diagram.

(c) Except for the approach to and transition from a hover for the purpose of takeoff and landing, during takeoff and landing, or when necessary for safety of flight, the pilot in command must operate the rotorcraft in compliance with the plan described in paragraph (b) of this section.

[Docket No. FAA-2022-1563, Amdt. 136–2, 88 FR 48091, July 26, 2023]

§§136.15–136.29 [Reserved]

Subpart B— National Parks Air Tour Management

Source: Docket No. FAA–1998–4521, 72 FR 6912, Feb. 13, 2007, unless otherwise noted.

§136.31 Applicability.

(a) This subpart restates and paraphrases several sections of the National Parks Air Tour Management Act of 2000, including section 803 (codified at 49 U.S.C. 40128) and sections 806 and 809. This subpart clarifies the requirements for the development of an air tour management plan for each park in the national park system where commercial air tour operations are flown.

(b) Except as provided in paragraph (c) of this section, this subpart applies to each commercial air tour operator who conducts a commercial air tour operation over—

(1) A unit of the national park system;

(2) Tribal lands as defined in this subpart; or

(3) Any area within one-half mile outside the boundary of any unit of the national park system.

(c) This subpart does not apply to a commercial air tour operator conducting a commercial air tour operation—

(1) Over the Grand Canyon National Park;

(2) Over that portion of tribal lands within or abutting the Grand Canyon National Park;

(3) Over any land or waters located in the State of Alaska; or

(4) While flying over or near the Lake Mead Recreation Area, solely as a transportation route, to conduct a commercial air tour over the Grand Canyon National Park.

§136.33 Definitions.

For purposes of this subpart—

(a) *Commercial air tour operator* means any person who conducts a commercial air tour operation.

(b) *Existing commercial air tour operator* means a commercial air tour operator that was actively engaged in the business of providing commercial air tour operations over a national park at any time during the 12-month period ending on April 5, 2000.

(c) *New entrant commercial air tour operator* means a commercial air tour operator that—

(1) Applies for operating authority as a commercial air tour operator for a national park or tribal lands; and

(2) Has not engaged in the business of providing commercial air tour operations over the national park or tribal lands for the 12-month period preceding enactment.

(d) *Commercial air tour operation*—

(1) Means any flight, conducted for compensation or hire in a powered aircraft where a purpose of the flight is sightseeing over a national park, within 1/2 mile outside the boundary of any national park, or over tribal lands, during which the aircraft flies—

(i) Below 5,000 feet above ground level (except for the purpose of takeoff or landing, or as necessary for the safe operation of an aircraft as determined under the rules and regulations of the Federal Aviation Administration requiring the pilot-in-command to take action to ensure the safe operation of the aircraft);

(ii) Less than 1 mile laterally from any geographic feature within the park (unless more than 1/2 mile outside the boundary); or

(iii) Except as provided in §136.35.

(2) The Administrator may consider the following factors in determining whether a flight is a commercial air tour operation for purposes of this subpart—

(i) Whether there was a holding out to the public of willingness to conduct a sightseeing flight for compensation or hire;

(ii) Whether a narrative that referred to areas or points of interest on the surface below the route of the flight was provided by the person offering the flight;

(iii) The area of operation;

(iv) The frequency of flights conducted by the person offering the flight;

(v) The route of flight;

(vi) The inclusion of sightseeing flights as part of any travel arrangement package offered by the person offering the flight;

(vii) Whether the flight would have been canceled based on poor visibility of the surface below the route of the flight; and

(viii) Any other factors that the Administrator and Director consider appropriate.

(3) For purposes of §136.35, means any flight conducted for compensation or hire in a powered aircraft where a purpose of the flight is sightseeing over a national park.

(e) *National park* means any unit of the national park system. (See title 16 of the U.S. Code, section 1, et seq.)

(f) *Tribal lands* means that portion of Indian country (as that term is defined in section 1151 of title 18 of the U.S. Code) that is within or abutting a national park.

(g) *Administrator* means the Administrator of the Federal Aviation Administration.

(h) *Director* means the Director of the National Park Service.

(i) *Superintendent* means the duly appointed representative of the National Park Service for a particular unit of the national park system.

[Docket No. FAA–1998–4521, 72 FR 6912, Feb. 13, 2007; as amended by Amdt. 136–1, 72 FR 31450, June 7, 2007]

§136.35 Prohibition of commercial air tour operations over the Rocky Mountain National Park.

All commercial air tour operations in the airspace over the Rocky Mountain National Park are prohibited regardless of altitude.

§136.37 Overflights of national parks and tribal lands.

(a) *General.* A commercial air tour operator may not conduct commercial air tour operations over a national park or tribal land except—

(1) In accordance with this section;

(2) In accordance with conditions and limitations prescribed for that operator by the Administrator; and

(3) In accordance with any applicable air tour management plan for the park or tribal lands.

(b) *Application for operating authority.* Before commencing commercial air tour operations over a national park or tribal lands, a commercial air tour operator shall apply to the Administrator for authority to conduct the operations over the park or tribal lands.

(c) *Number of operations authorized.* In determining the number of authorizations to issue to provide commercial air tour operations over a national park, the Administrator, in cooperation with the Director, shall take into consideration the provisions of the air tour management plan, the number of existing commercial air tour operators and current level of service and equipment provided by any such operators, and the financial viability of each commercial air tour operation.

(d) *Cooperation with National Park Service.* Before granting an application under this subpart, the Administrator, in cooperation with the Director, shall develop an air tour management plan in accordance with §136.39 and implement such a plan.

(e) *Time limit on response to applications.* Every effort will be made to act on any application under this subpart and issue a decision on the application not later than 24 months after it is received or amended.

(f) *Priority.* In acting on applications under this paragraph to provide commercial air tour operations over a national park, the Administrator shall give priority to an application under this paragraph in any case where a new entrant commercial air tour operator is seeking operating authority with respect to that national park.

(g) *Exception.* Notwithstanding this section, commercial air tour operators may conduct commercial air tour operations over a national park under Part 91 of this chapter if—

(1) Such activity is permitted under Part 119 of this chapter;

(2) The operator secures a letter of agreement from the Administrator and the Superintendent for that park describing the conditions under which the operations will be conducted; and

(3) The number of operations under this exception is limited to not more than a total of 5 flights by all operators in any 30-day period over a particular park.

(h) *Special rule for safety requirement.* Notwithstanding §136.41, an existing commercial air tour operator shall apply, not later than January 23, 2003 for operating authority under Part 119 of this chapter, for certification under Part 121 or Part 135 of this chapter. A new entrant commercial air tour operator shall apply for such authority before conducting commercial air tour operations over a national park or tribal lands that are within or abut a national park. The Administrator shall make every effort to act on such application for a new entrant and issue a decision on the application not later than 24 months after it is received or amended.

[Docket No. FAA–1998–4521, 72 FR 6912, Feb. 13, 2007; as amended by Amdt. 136–1, 72 FR 31450, June 7, 2007]

§136.39 Air tour management plans (ATMP).

(a) *Establishment.* The Administrator, in cooperation with the Director, shall establish an air tour management plan for any national park or tribal land for which such a plan is not in effect whenever a person applies for authority to conduct a commercial air tour operation over the park. The air tour management plan shall be developed by means of a public process in accordance with paragraph (d) of this section. The objective of any air tour management plan is to develop acceptable and effective measures to mitigate or prevent the significant adverse impacts, if any, of commercial air tour operations upon the natural and cultural resources, visitor experiences, and tribal lands.

(b) *Environmental determination.* In establishing an air tour management plan under this section, the Administrator and the Director shall each sign the environmental decision document required by section 102 of the National Environmental Policy Act of 1969 (42 U.S.C. 4332) which may include a finding of no significant impact, an environmental assessment, or an environmental impact statement and the record of decision for the air tour management plan.

(c) *Contents.* An air tour management plan for a park—

(1) May prohibit commercial air tour operations in whole or in part;

(2) May establish conditions for the conduct of commercial air tour operations, including, but not limited to, commercial air tour routes, maximum number of flights per unit of time, maximum and minimum altitudes, time of day restrictions, restrictions for particular events, intrusions on privacy on tribal lands, and mitigation of noise, visual, or other impacts;

(3) Shall apply to all commercial air tour operations within 1/2 mile outside the boundary of a national park;

(4) Shall include incentives (such as preferred commercial air tour routes and altitudes, and relief from caps and curfews) for the adoption of quiet technology aircraft by commercial air tour operators conducting commercial air tour operations at the park;

(5) Shall provide for the initial allocation of opportunities to conduct commercial air tour operations if the plan includes a limitation on the number of commercial air tour operations for any time period; and

(6) Shall justify and document the need for measures taken pursuant to paragraphs (c)(1) through (c)(5) of this section and include such justification in the record of decision.

(d) *Procedure.* In establishing an ATMP for a national park or tribal lands, the Administrator and Director shall—

(1) Hold at least one public meeting with interested parties to develop the air tour management plan;

(2) Publish the proposed plan in the Federal Register for notice and comment and make copies of the proposed plan available to the public;

(3) Comply with the regulations set forth in 40 CFR 1501.3 and 1501.5 through 1501.8 (for the purposes of complying with 40 CFR 1501.3 and 1501.5 through 1501.8, the Federal Aviation Administration is the lead agency and the National Park Service is a cooperating agency); and

(4) Solicit the participation of any Indian tribe whose tribal lands are, or may be, overflown by aircraft involved in a commercial air tour operation over the park or tribal lands to which the plan applies, as a cooperating agency under the regulations referred to in paragraph (d)(3) of this section.

(e) *Amendments.* The Administrator, in cooperation with the Director, may make amendments to an air tour management plan. Any such amendments will be published in the Federal Register for notice and comment. A request for amendment of an ATMP will be made in accordance with §11.25 of this chapter as a petition for rulemaking.

§136.41 Interim operating authority.

(a) *General.* Upon application for operating authority, the Administrator shall grant interim operating authority under this section to a commercial air tour operator for commercial air tour operations over a national park or tribal land for which the operator is an existing commercial air tour operator.

(b) *Requirements and limitations.* Interim operating authority granted under this section—

(1) Shall provide annual authorization only for the greater of—

(i) The number of flights used by the operator to provide the commercial air tour operations within the 12-month period prior to April 5, 2000; or

(ii) The average number of flights per 12-month period used by the operator to provide such operations within the 36-month period prior to April 5, 2000, and for seasonal operations, the number of flights so used during the season or seasons covered by that 12-month period;

(2) May not provide for an increase in the number of commercial air tour operations conducted during any time period by the commercial air tour operator above the number the air tour operator was originally granted unless such an increase is agreed to by the Administrator and the Director;

(3) Shall be published in the Federal Register to provide notice and opportunity for comment;

(4) May be revoked by the Administrator for cause;

(5) Shall terminate 180 days after the date on which an air tour management plan is established for the park and tribal lands;

(6) Shall promote protection of national park resources, visitor experiences, and tribal lands;

(7) Shall promote safe commercial air tour operations;

(8) Shall promote the adoption of quiet technology, as appropriate, and

(9) Shall allow for modifications of the interim operating authority based on experience if the modification improves protection of national park resources and values and of tribal lands.

(c) *New entrant operators.* The Administrator, in cooperation with the Director, may grant interim operating authority under this paragraph (c) to an air tour operator for a national park or tribal lands for which that operator is a new entrant air tour operator if the Administrator determines the authority is necessary to ensure competition in the provision of commercial air tour operations over the park or tribal lands.

(1) *Limitation.* The Administrator may not grant interim operating authority under this paragraph (c) if the Administrator determines that it would create a safety problem at the park or on the tribal lands, or if the Director determines that it would create a noise problem at the park or on the tribal lands.

(2) *ATMP limitation.* The Administrator may grant interim operating authority under this paragraph (c) only if the ATMP for the park or tribal lands to which the application relates has not been developed within 24 months after April 5, 2000.

§§136.15–136.29 [Reserved]

Subpart C—Grand Canyon National Park

§136.51–136.69 [Reserved]

Subpart D—Special Operating Rules for Air Tour Operators in the State of Hawaii

Source: Docket No. FAA-2022–1563, Amdt. 136–2, 88 FR 48092, July 26, 2023, unless otherwise noted.

§136.71 Applicability.

(a) Except as provided in paragraph (b) of this section, this subpart prescribes operating rules for air tour flights conducted in airplanes, powered-lift, or rotorcraft under visual flight rules in the State of Hawaii pursuant to parts 91, 121, and 135 of this chapter.

(b) This subpart does not apply to:

(1) Operations conducted under part 121 of this chapter in airplanes with a passenger seating configuration of more than 30 seats or a payload capacity of more than 7,500 pounds.

(2) Flights conducted in gliders or hot air balloons.

§136.73 Definitions.

For the purposes of this subpart:

Air tour means any sightseeing flight conducted under visual flight rules in an airplane, powered-lift, or rotorcraft for compensation or hire.

Air tour operator means any person who conducts an air tour.

§136.75 Equipment and requirements.

(a) *Flotation equipment.* No person may conduct an air tour in Hawaii in a rotorcraft beyond the shore of any island, regardless of whether the rotorcraft is within gliding distance of the shore, unless:

(1) The rotorcraft is amphibious or is equipped with floats adequate to accomplish a safe emergency ditching and approved flotation gear is easily accessible for each occupant; or

(2) Each person on board the rotorcraft is wearing approved flotation gear.

(b) *Performance plan.* Each operator must complete a performance plan that meets the requirements of this paragraph (b) before each air tour flight conducted in a rotorcraft.

(1) The performance plan must be based on information from the current approved aircraft flight manual for that aircraft, considering the maximum density altitude for which the operation is planned to determine the following:

(i) Maximum gross weight and center of gravity (CG) limitations for hovering in ground effect;

(ii) Maximum gross weight and CG limitations for hovering out of ground effect; and

(iii) Maximum combination of weight, altitude, and temperature for which height-velocity information from the performance data is valid.

(2) The pilot in command (PIC) must comply with the performance plan.

(c) *Operating limitations.* Except for approach to and transition from a hover, and except for the purpose of takeoff and landing, the PIC of a rotorcraft may only operate such aircraft at a combination of height and forward speed (including hover) that would permit a safe landing in event of engine power loss, in accordance with the height-speed envelope for that rotorcraft under current weight and aircraft altitude.

(d) *Minimum flight altitudes.* Except when necessary for takeoff and landing, or operating in compliance with an air traffic control clearance, or as otherwise authorized by the Administrator, no person may conduct an air tour in Hawaii:

(1) Below an altitude of 1,500 feet above the surface over all areas of the State of Hawaii;

(2) Closer than 1,500 feet to any person or property; or

(3) Below any altitude prescribed by Federal statute or regulation.

(e) *Passenger briefing.* Before takeoff, each PIC of an air tour flight of Hawaii with a flight segment beyond the ocean shore of any island shall ensure that each passenger has been briefed on the following, in addition to requirements set forth in §91.107, §121.571, or §135.117 of this chapter:

(1) Water ditching procedures;

(2) Use of required flotation equipment; and

(3) Emergency egress from the aircraft in event of a water landing.

Issued in Washington, DC, under the authority of 49 U.S.C. 106(f) and (g), 40101(d)(1), 40105(b)(1)(A), and 44701(a)(5).

APPENDIX A TO PART 136—[REMOVED]

PART 137
AGRICULTURAL AIRCRAFT OPERATIONS

Authority: 49 U.S.C. 106(g), 40103, 40113, 44701–44702.

Source: Docket No. 1464, 30 FR 8106, June 24, 1965, unless otherwise noted.

Subpart A—General

§137.1 Applicability.

(a) This part prescribes rules governing—
(1) Agricultural aircraft operations within the United States; and
(2) The issue of commercial and private agricultural aircraft operator certificates for those operations.

(b) In a public emergency, a person conducting agricultural aircraft operations under this part may, to the extent necessary, deviate from the operating rules of this part for relief and welfare activities approved by an agency of the United States or of a State or local government.

(c) Each person who, under the authority of this section, deviates from a rule of this part shall, within 10 days after the deviation send to the responsible Flight Standards office a complete report of the aircraft operation involved, including a description of the operation and the reasons for it.

[Docket No. 1464, 30 FR 8106, June 24, 1965; as amended by Amdt. 137–13, 54 FR 39294, Sept. 25, 1989; Amdt. 137–17, 83 FR 9175, March 5, 2018]

§137.3 Definition of terms.

For the purposes of this part—

Agricultural aircraft operation means the operation of an aircraft for the purpose of (1) dispensing any economic poison, (2) dispensing any other substance intended for plant nourishment, soil treatment, propagation of plant life, or pest control, or (3) engaging in dispensing activities directly affecting agriculture, horticulture, or forest preservation, but not including the dispensing of live insects.

Economic poison means (1) any substance or mixture of substances intended for preventing, destroying, repelling, or mitigating any insects, rodents, nematodes, fungi, weeds, and other forms of plant or animal life or viruses, except viruses on or in living man or other animals, which the Secretary of Agriculture shall declare to be a pest, and (2) any substance or mixture of substances intended for use as a plant regulator, defoliant or desiccant.

[Docket No. 1464, 30 FR 8106, June 24, 1965; as amended by Amdt. 137–3, 33 FR 9601, July 2, 1968]

137

Subpart B— Certification Rules

§137.11 Certificate required.

(a) Except as provided in paragraphs (c) and (d) of this section, no person may conduct agricultural aircraft operations without, or in violation of, an agricultural aircraft operator certificate issued under this part.

(b) Notwithstanding part 133 of this chapter, an operator may, if he complies with this part, conduct agricultural aircraft operations with a rotorcraft with external dispensing equipment in place without a rotorcraft external-load operator certificate.

(c) A Federal, State, or local government conducting agricultural aircraft operations with public aircraft need not comply with this subpart.

(d) The holder of a rotorcraft external-load operator certificate under part 133 of this chapter conducting an agricultural aircraft operation, involving only the dispensing of water on forest fires by rotorcraft external-load means, need not comply with this subpart.

[Docket No. 1464, 30 FR 8106, June 24, 1965; as amended by Amdt. 137–3, 33 FR 9601, July 2, 1968; Amdt. 137–6, 41 FR 35060, Aug. 19, 1976]

§137.15 Application for certificate.

An application for an agricultural aircraft operator certificate is made on a form and in a manner prescribed by the Administrator, and filed with the responsible Flight Standards office for the area in which the applicant's home base of operations is located.

[Docket No. 1464, 30 FR 8106, June 24, 1965; as amended by Amdt. 137–13, 54 FR 39294, Sept. 25, 1989; Amdt. 137–17, 83 FR 9175, March 5, 2018]

§137.17 Amendment of certificate.

(a) An agricultural aircraft operator certificate may be amended—

(1) On the Administrator's own initiative, under section 609 of the Federal Aviation Act of 1958 (49 U.S.C. 1429) and part 13 of this chapter; or

(2) Upon application by the holder of that certificate.

(b) An application to amend an agricultural aircraft operator certificate is submitted on a form and in a manner prescribed by the Administrator. The applicant must file the application with the responsible Flight Standards office for the area in which the applicant's home base of operations is located at least 15 days before the date that it proposes the amendment become effective, unless a shorter filing period is approved by that office.

(c) The responsible Flight Standards office grants a request to amend a certificate if it determines that safety in air commerce and the public interest so allow.

(d) Within 30 days after receiving a refusal to amend, the holder may petition the Executive Director, Flight Standards Service, to reconsider the refusal.

[Docket No. 1464, 30 FR 8106, June 24, 1965; as amended by Amdt. 137–9, 43 FR 52206, Nov. 9, 1978; Amdt. 137–11, 45 FR 47838, July 17, 1980; Amdt. 137–13, 54 FR 39294, Sept. 25, 1989; Amdt. 137–17, 83 FR 9175, March 5, 2018]

§137.19 Certification requirements.

(a) *General.* An applicant for a private agricultural aircraft operator certificate is entitled to that certificate if he shows that he meets the requirements of paragraphs (b), (d), and (e) of this section. An applicant for a commercial agricultural aircraft operator certificate is entitled to that certificate if he shows that he meets the requirements of paragraphs (c), (d), and (e) of this section. However, if an applicant applies for an agricultural aircraft operator certificate containing a prohibition against the dispensing of economic poisons, that applicant is not required to demonstrate the knowledge required in paragraphs (e)(1) (ii) through (iv) of this section.

(b) *Private operator—pilot.* The applicant must hold a current U.S. private, commercial, or airline transport pilot certificate and be properly rated for the aircraft to be used.

(c) *Commercial operator—pilots.* The applicant must have available the services of at least one person who holds a current U.S. commercial or airline transport pilot certificate and who is properly rated for the aircraft to be used. The applicant himself may be the person available.

(d) *Aircraft.* The applicant must have at least one certificated and airworthy aircraft, equipped for agricultural operation.

(e) *Knowledge and skill tests.* The applicant must show, or have the person who is designated as the chief supervisor of agricultural aircraft operations for him show, that he has satisfactory knowledge and skill regarding agricultural aircraft operations, as described in paragraphs (e)(1) and (2) of this section.

(1) The test of knowledge consists of the following:

(i) Steps to be taken before starting operations, including survey of the area to be worked.

(ii) Safe handling of economic poisons and the proper disposal of used containers for those poisons.

(iii) The general effects of economic poisons and agricultural chemicals on plants, animals,

and persons, with emphasis on those normally used in the areas of intended operations; and the precautions to be observed in using poisons and chemicals.

(iv) Primary symptoms of poisoning of persons from economic poisons, the appropriate emergency measures to be taken, and the location of poison control centers.

(v) Performance capabilities and operating limitations of the aircraft to be used.

(vi) Safe flight and application procedures.

(2) The test of skill consists of the following maneuvers that must be shown in any of the aircraft specified in paragraph (d) of this section, and at that aircraft's maximum certificated takeoff weight, or the maximum weight established for the special purpose load, whichever is greater:

(i) Short-field and soft-field takeoffs (airplanes and gyroplanes only).

(ii) Approaches to the working area.

(iii) Flare-outs.

(iv) Swath runs.

(v) Pullups and turnarounds.

(vi) Rapid deceleration (quick stops) in helicopters only.

[Docket No. 1464, 30 FR 8106, June 24, 1965; as amended by Amdt. 137–1, 30 FR 15143, Dec. 8, 1965; Amdt. 137–7, 43 FR 22643, May 25, 1978]

§137.21 Duration of certificate.

An agricultural aircraft operator certificate is effective until it is surrendered, suspended, or revoked. The holder of an agricultural aircraft operator certificate that is suspended or revoked shall return it to the Administrator.

§137.23 Carriage of narcotic drugs, marihuana, and depressant or stimulant drugs or substances.

If the holder of a certificate issued under this part permits any aircraft owned or leased by that holder to be engaged in any operation that the certificate holder knows to be in violation of §91.19(a) of this chapter, that operation is a basis for suspending or revoking the certificate.

[Docket No. 12035, 38 FR 17493, July 2, 1973; as amended by Amdt. 137–12, 54 FR 34332, Aug. 18, 1989]

Subpart C— Operating Rules

§137.29 General.

(a) Except as provided in paragraphs (d) and (e) of this section, this subpart prescribes rules that apply to persons and aircraft used in agricultural aircraft operations conducted under this part.

(b) [Reserved]

(c) The holder of an agricultural aircraft operator certificate may deviate from the provisions of part 91 of this chapter without a certificate of waiver, as authorized in this subpart for dispensing operations, when conducting nondispensing aerial work operations related to agriculture, horticulture, or forest preservation in accordance with the operating rules of this subpart.

(d) Sections 137.31 through 137.35, §§137.41, and 137.53 through 137.59 do not apply to persons and aircraft used in agricultural aircraft operations conducted with public aircraft.

(e) Sections 137.31 through 137.35, §§137.39, 137.41, 137.51 through 137.59, and subpart D do not apply to persons and rotorcraft used in agricultural aircraft operations conducted by a person holding a certificate under part 133 of this chapter and involving only the dispensing of water on forest fires by rotorcraft external-load means. However, the operation shall be conducted in accordance with—

(1) The rules of part 133 of this chapter governing rotorcraft external-load operations; and

(2) The operating rules of this subpart contained in §§137.29, 137.37, and §§137.43 through 137.49.

[Docket No. 1464, 30 FR 8106, June 24, 1965; as amended by Amdt. 137–3, 33 FR 9601, July 2, 1968; Amdt. 137–6, 41 FR 35060, Aug. 19, 1976]

§137.31 Aircraft requirements.

No person may operate an aircraft unless that aircraft—

(a) Meets the requirements of §137.19(d); and

(b) Is equipped with a suitable and properly installed shoulder harness for use by each pilot.

§137.33 Carrying of certificate.

(a) No person may operate an aircraft unless a facsimile of the agricultural aircraft operator certificate, under which the operation is conducted, is carried on that aircraft. The facsimile shall be presented for inspection upon the request of the Administrator or any Federal, State, or local law enforcement officer.

(b) Notwithstanding part 91 of this chapter, the registration and airworthiness certificates issued for the aircraft need not be carried in the aircraft. However, when those certificates are not carried in the aircraft they shall be kept available for inspection at the base from which the dispensing operation is conducted.

[Docket No. 1464, 30 FR 8106, June 24, 1965; as amended by Amdt. 137–3, 33 FR 9601, July 2, 1968]

§137.35　Limitations on private agricultural aircraft operator.

No person may conduct an agricultural aircraft operation under the authority of a private agricultural aircraft operator certificate—

(a) For compensation or hire;

(b) Over a congested area; or

(c) Over any property unless he is the owner or lessee of the property, or has ownership or other property interest in the crop located on that property.

§137.37　Manner of dispensing.

No persons may dispense, or cause to be dispensed, from an aircraft, any material or substance in a manner that creates a hazard to persons or property on the surface.

[Docket No. 1464, 30 FR 8106, June 24, 1965; as amended by Amdt. 137–3, 33 FR 9601, July 2, 1968]

§137.39　Economic poison dispensing.

(a) Except as provided in paragraph (b) of this section, no person may dispense or cause to be dispensed from an aircraft, any economic poison that is registered with the U.S. Department of Agriculture under the Federal Insecticide, Fungicide, and Rodenticide Act (7 U.S.C. 135–135k)—

(1) For a use other than that for which it is registered;

(2) Contrary to any safety instructions or use limitations on its label; or

(3) In violation of any law or regulation of the United States.

(b) This section does not apply to any person dispensing economic poisons for experimental purposes under—

(1) The supervision of a Federal or State agency authorized by law to conduct research in the field of economic poisons; or

(2) A permit from the U.S. Department of Agriculture issued pursuant to the Federal Insecticide, Fungicide, and Rodenticide Act (7 U.S.C. 135–135k).

[Amdt. 137–2, 31 FR 6686, May 5, 1966]

§137.40　Employment of former FAA employees.

(a) Except as specified in paragraph (c) of this section, no certificate holder may knowingly employ or make a contractual arrangement which permits an individual to act as an agent or representative of the certificate holder in any matter before the Federal Aviation Administration if the individual, in the preceding 2 years—

(1) Served as, or was directly responsible for the oversight of, a Flight Standards Service aviation safety inspector; and

(2) Had direct responsibility to inspect, or oversee the inspection of, the operations of the certificate holder.

(b) For the purpose of this section, an individual shall be considered to be acting as an agent or representative of a certificate holder in a matter before the agency if the individual makes any written or oral communication on behalf of the certificate holder to the agency (or any of its officers or employees) in connection with a particular matter, whether or not involving a specific party and without regard to whether the individual has participated in, or had responsibility for, the particular matter while serving as a Flight Standards Service aviation safety inspector.

(c) The provisions of this section do not prohibit a certificate holder from knowingly employing or making a contractual arrangement which permits an individual to act as an agent or representative of the certificate holder in any matter before the Federal Aviation Administration if the individual was employed by the certificate holder before October 21, 2011.

[Docket No. FAA–2008–1154, 76 FR 52236, Aug. 22, 2011]

§137.41　Personnel.

(a) *Information.* The holder of an agricultural aircraft operator certificate shall insure that each person used in the holder's agricultural aircraft operation is informed of that person's duties and responsibilities for the operation.

(b) *Supervisors.* No person may supervise an agricultural aircraft operation unless he has met the knowledge and skill requirements of §137.19(e).

(c) *Pilot-in-command.* No person may act as pilot in command of an aircraft unless he holds a pilot certificate and rating prescribed by §137.19(b) or (c), as appropriate to the type of operation conducted. In addition, he must demonstrate to the holder of the Agricultural Aircraft Operator Certificate conducting the operation that he has met the knowledge and skill requirements of §137.19(e). If the holder of that certificate has designated a person under §137.19(e) to supervise his agricultural aircraft operations the demonstration must

be made to the person so designated. However, a demonstration of the knowledge and skill requirement is not necessary for any pilot in command who—

(1) Is, at the time of the filing of an application by an agricultural aircraft operator, working as a pilot in command for that operator; and

(2) Has a record of operation under that applicant that does not disclose any question regarding the safety of his flight operations or his competence in dispensing agricultural materials or chemicals.

§137.42 Fastening of safety belts and shoulder harnesses.

No person may operate an aircraft in operations required to be conducted under part 137 without a safety belt and shoulder harness properly secured about that person except that the shoulder harness need not be fastened if that person would be unable to perform required duties with the shoulder harness fastened.

[Amdt. 137–10, 44 FR 61325, Oct. 25, 1979]

§137.43 Operations in controlled airspace designated for an airport.

(a) Except for flights to and from a dispensing area, no person may operate an aircraft within the lateral boundaries of the surface area of Class D airspace designated for an airport unless authorization for that operation has been obtained from the ATC facility having jurisdiction over that area.

(b) No person may operate an aircraft in weather conditions below VFR minimums within the lateral boundaries of a Class E airspace area that extends upward from the surface unless authorization for that operation has been obtained from the ATC facility having jurisdiction over that area.

(c) Notwithstanding §91.157(b)(4) of this chapter, an aircraft may be operated under the special VFR weather minimums without meeting the requirements prescribed therein.

[Docket No. 24456, 56 FR 65664, Dec. 17, 1991; as amended by Amdt. 137–14, 58 FR 32840, June 14, 1993; 74 FR 13099, Mar. 26, 2009]

§137.45 Nonobservance of airport traffic pattern.

Notwithstanding part 91 of this chapter, the pilot in command of an aircraft may deviate from an airport traffic pattern when authorized by the control tower concerned. At an airport without a functioning control tower, the pilot in command may deviate from the traffic pattern if—

(a) Prior coordination is made with the airport management concerned;

(b) Deviations are limited to the agricultural aircraft operation;

(c) Except in an emergency, landing and takeoffs are not made on ramps, taxiways, or other areas of the airport not intended for such use; and

(d) The aircraft at all times remains clear of, and gives way to, aircraft conforming to the traffic pattern for the airport.

§137.47 Operation without position lights.

Notwithstanding part 91 of this chapter, an aircraft may be operated without position lights if prominent unlighted objects are visible for at least 1 mile and takeoffs and landings at—

(a) Airports with a functioning control tower are made only as authorized by the control tower operator; and

(b) Other airports are made only with the permission of the airport management and no other aircraft operations requiring position lights are in progress at that airport.

§137.49 Operations over other than congested areas.

Notwithstanding part 91 of this chapter, during the actual dispensing operation, including approaches, departures, and turnarounds reasonably necessary for the operation, an aircraft may be operated over other than congested areas below 500 feet above the surface and closer than 500 feet to persons, vessels, vehicles, and structures, if the operations are conducted without creating a hazard to persons or property on the surface.

[Amdt. 137–3, 33 FR 9601, July 2, 1968]

§137.51 Operation over congested areas: General.

(a) Notwithstanding part 91 of this chapter, an aircraft may be operated over a congested area at altitudes required for the proper accomplishment of the agricultural aircraft operation if the operation is conducted—

(1) With the maximum safety to persons and property on the surface, consistent with the operation; and

(2) In accordance with the requirements of paragraph (b) of this section.

(b) No person may operate an aircraft over a congested area except in accordance with the requirements of this paragraph.

(1) Prior written approval must be obtained from the appropriate official or governing body of the political subdivision over which the operations are conducted.

137

(2) Notice of the intended operation must be given to the public by some effective means, such as daily newspapers, radio, television, or door-to-door notice.

(3) A plan for each complete operation must be submitted to, and approved by appropriate personnel of the responsible Flight Standards office for the area where the operation is to be conducted. The plan must include consideration of obstructions to flight; the emergency landing capabilities of the aircraft to be used; and any necessary coordination with air traffic control.

(4) Single engine aircraft must be operated as follows:

(i) Except for helicopters, no person may take off a loaded aircraft, or make a turnaround over a congested area.

(ii) No person may operate an aircraft over a congested area below the altitudes prescribed in part 91 of this chapter except during the actual dispensing operation, including the approaches and departures necessary for that operation.

(iii) No person may operate an aircraft over a congested area during the actual dispensing operation, including the approaches and departures for that operation, unless it is operated in a pattern and at such an altitude that the aircraft can land, in an emergency, without endangering persons or property on the surface.

(5) Multiengine aircraft must be operated as follows:

(i) No person may take off a multiengine airplane over a congested area except under conditions that will allow the airplane to be brought to a safe stop within the effective length of the runway from any point on takeoff up to the time of attaining, with all engines operating at normal takeoff power, 105 percent of the minimum control speed with the critical engine inoperative in the takeoff configuration or 115 percent of the power-off stall speed in the takeoff configuration, whichever is greater, as shown by the accelerate stop distance data. In applying this requirement, takeoff data is based upon still-air conditions, and no correction is made for any uphill gradient of 1 percent or less when the percentage is measured as the difference between elevation at the end points of the runway divided by the total length. For uphill gradients greater than 1 percent, the effective takeoff length of the runway is reduced 20 percent for each 1-percent grade.

(ii) No person may operate a multiengine airplane at a weight greater than the weight that, with the critical engine inoperative, would permit a rate of climb of at least 50 feet per minute at an altitude of at least 1,000 feet above the elevation of the highest ground or obstruction within the area to be worked or at an altitude of 5,000 feet, whichever is higher. For the purposes of this subdivision, it is assumed that the propeller of the inoperative engine is in the minimum drag position; that the wing flaps and landing gear are in the most favorable positions; and that the remaining engine or engines are operating at the maximum continuous power available.

(iii) No person may operate any multiengine aircraft over a congested area below the altitudes prescribed in part 91 of this chapter except during the actual dispensing operation, including the approaches, departures, and turnarounds necessary for that operation.

[Docket No. 1464, 30 FR 8106, June 24, 1965; as amended by Docket No. 8084, 32 FR 5769, April 11, 1967; Amdt. 137–13, 54 FR 39294, Sept. 25, 1989; Amdt. 137–17, 83 FR 9175, March 5, 2018]

§137.53 Operation over congested areas: Pilots and aircraft.

(a) *General.* No person may operate an aircraft over a congested area except in accordance with the pilot and aircraft rules of this section.

(b) *Pilots.* Each pilot in command must have at least—

(1) 25 hours of pilot-in-command flight time in the make and basic model of the aircraft, at least 10 hours of which must have been acquired within the preceding 12 calendar months; and

(2) 100 hours of flight experience as pilot in command in dispensing agricultural materials or chemicals.

(c) *Aircraft.*

(1) Each aircraft must—

(i) If it is an aircraft not specified in paragraph (c)(1)(ii) of this section, have had within the preceding 100 hours of time in service a 100-hour or annual inspection by a person authorized by part 65 or 145 of this chapter, or have been inspected under a progressive inspection system; and

(ii) If it is a large or turbine-powered multiengine civil airplane of U.S. registry, have been inspected in accordance with the applicable inspection program requirements of §91.409 of this chapter.

(2) If other than a helicopter, it must be equipped with a device capable of jettisoning at least one-half of the aircraft's maximum authorized load of agricultural material within 45 seconds. If the aircraft is equipped with a device for releasing the tank or hopper as a unit, there must be a means to prevent inadvertent release by the pilot or other crewmember.

[Docket No. 1464, 30 FR 8106, June 24, 1965; as amended by Amdt. 137–5, 41 FR 16796, April 22, 1976; Amdt. 137–12, 54 FR 34332, Aug. 18, 1989]

§137.55 Business name: Commercial agricultural aircraft operator.

No person may operate under a business name that is not shown on his commercial agricultural aircraft operator certificate.

§137.57 Availability of certificate.

Each holder of an agricultural aircraft operator certificate shall keep that certificate at his home base of operations and shall present it for inspection on the request of the Administrator or any Federal, State, or local law enforcement officer.

§137.59 Inspection authority.

Each holder of an agricultural aircraft operator certificate shall allow the Administrator at any time and place to make inspections, including on-the-job inspections, to determine compliance with applicable regulations and his agricultural aircraft operator certificate.

Subpart D— Records and Reports

§137.71 Records: Commercial agricultural aircraft operator.

(a) Each holder of a commercial agricultural aircraft operator certificate shall maintain and keep current, at the home base of operations designated in his application, the following records:

(1) The name and address of each person for whom agricultural aircraft services were provided;

(2) The date of the service;

(3) The name and quantity of the material dispensed for each operation conducted; and

(4) The name, address, and certificate number of each pilot used in agricultural aircraft operations and the date that pilot met the knowledge and skill requirements of §137.19(e).

(b) The records required by this section must be kept at least 12 months and made available for inspection by the Administrator upon request.

§137.75 Change of address.

Each holder of an agricultural aircraft operator certificate shall notify the FAA in writing in advance of any change in the address of his home base of operations.

§137.77 Termination of operations.

Whenever a person holding an agricultural aircraft operator certificate ceases operations under this part, he shall surrender that certificate to the responsible Flight Standards office for his operation.

[Docket No. 1464, 30 FR 8106, June 24, 1965; as amended by Amdt. 137–13, 54 FR 39294, Sept. 25, 1989; 54 FR 52872, Dec. 22, 1989; Amdt. 137–17, 83 FR 9175, March 5, 2018]

137

PART 141
PILOT SCHOOLS

141

Authority: 49 U.S.C. 106(f), 106(g), 40113, 44701–44703, 44707, 44709, 44711, 45102–45103, 45301–45302.

Source: Docket No. 25910, 62 FR 16347, April 4, 1997, unless otherwise noted.

Subpart A—General

§141.1 Applicability.

This part prescribes the requirements for issuing pilot school certificates, provisional pilot school certificates, and associated ratings, and the general operating rules applicable to a holder of a certificate or rating issued under this part.

§141.3 Certificate required.

No person may operate as a certificated pilot school without, or in violation of, a pilot school certificate or provisional pilot school certificate issued under this part.

§141.5 Requirements for a pilot school certificate.

The FAA may issue a pilot school certificate with the appropriate ratings if, within the 24 calendar months before the date application is made, the applicant—

(a) Completes the application for a pilot school certificate on the form and in the manner prescribed by the FAA;

(b) Has held a provisional pilot school certificate;

(c) Meets the applicable requirements under subparts A through C of this part for the school certificate and associated ratings sought;

(d) Has established a pass rate of 80 percent or higher on the first attempt for all:

(1) Knowledge tests leading to a certificate or rating;

(2) Practical tests leading to a certificate or rating;

(3) End-of-course tests for an approved training course specified in appendix K of this part; and

(4) End-of-course tests for special curricula courses approved under §141.57.

(e) Has graduated at least 10 different people from the school's approved training courses.

[Docket No. FAA–2006–26661, 74 FR 42563, Aug. 21, 2009; Amdt. 141–14, 75 FR 56858, Sept. 17, 2010; as amended by Amdt. 141–20, 83 FR 30283, June 27, 2018]

§141.7 Provisional pilot school certificate.

An applicant that meets the applicable requirements of subparts A, B, and C of this part, but does not meet the recent training activity requirements of §141.5(d) of this part, may be issued a provisional pilot school certificate with ratings.

§141.9 Examining authority.

The FAA issues examining authority to a pilot school for a training course if the pilot school and its training course meet the requirements of subpart D of this part.

[Docket No. FAA–2006–26661, 74 FR 42563, Aug. 21, 2009]

§141.11 Pilot school ratings.

(a) The ratings listed in paragraph (b) of this section may be issued to an applicant for:

(1) A pilot school certificate, provided the applicant meets the requirements of §141.5 of this part; or

(2) A provisional pilot school certificate, provided the applicant meets the requirements of §141.7 of this part.

(b) An applicant may be authorized to conduct the following courses:

(1) *Certification and rating courses.* (Appendixes A through J).

(i) Recreational pilot course.

(ii) Private pilot course.

(iii) Commercial pilot course.

(iv) Instrument rating course.

(v) Airline transport pilot course.

(vi) Flight instructor course.

(vii) Flight instructor instrument course.

(viii) Ground instructor course.

(ix) Additional aircraft category or class rating course.

(x) Aircraft type rating course.

(2) *Special preparation courses.* (Appendix K).

(i) Pilot refresher course.

(ii) Flight instructor refresher course.

(iii) Ground instructor refresher course.

(iv) Agricultural aircraft operations course.

(v) Rotorcraft external-load operations course.

(vi) Special operations course.

(vii) Test pilot course.

(viii) Airline transport pilot certification training program.

(3) *Pilot ground school course.* (Appendix L).

[Docket No. 25910, 62 FR 16347, April 4, 1997; as amended by Amdt. 141–17, 78 FR 42379, July 15, 2013; Amdt. 141–17A, 78 FR 53026, Aug. 28, 2013]

§141.13 Application for issuance, amendment, or renewal.

(a) Application for an original certificate and rating, an additional rating, or the renewal of a certificate under this part must be made on a form and in a manner prescribed by the Administrator.

(b) Application for the issuance or amendment of a certificate or rating must be accompanied by two copies of each proposed training course curriculum for which approval is sought.

§141.17 Duration of certificate and examining authority.

(a) Unless surrendered, suspended, or revoked, a pilot school's certificate or a provisional pilot school's certificate expires:

(1) On the last day of the 24th calendar month from the month the certificate was issued;

(2) Except as provided in paragraph (b) of this section, on the date that any change in ownership of the school occurs;

(3) On the date of any change in the facilities upon which the school's certificate is based occurs; or

(4) Upon notice by the Administrator that the school has failed for more than 60 days to maintain the facilities, aircraft, or personnel required for any one of the school's approved training courses.

(b) A change in the ownership of a pilot school or provisional pilot school does not terminate that school's certificate if, within 30 days after the date that any change in ownership of the school occurs:

(1) Application is made for an appropriate amendment to the certificate; and

(2) No change in the facilities, personnel, or approved training courses is involved.

(c) An examining authority issued to the holder of a pilot school certificate expires on the date that the pilot school certificate expires, or is surrendered, suspended, or revoked.

§141.18 Carriage of narcotic drugs, marijuana, and depressant or stimulant drugs or substances.

If the holder of a certificate issued under this part permits any aircraft owned or leased by that holder to be engaged in any operation that the certificate holder knows to be in violation of §91.19(a) of this chapter, that operation is a basis for suspending or revoking the certificate.

§141.19 Display of certificate.

(a) Each holder of a pilot school certificate or a provisional pilot school certificate must display that certificate in a place in the school that is normally accessible to the public and is not obscured.

(b) A certificate must be made available for inspection upon request by:

(1) The Administrator;

(2) An authorized representative of the National Transportation Safety Board; or

(3) A Federal, State, or local law enforcement officer.

§141.21 Inspections.

Each holder of a certificate issued under this part must allow the Administrator to inspect its personnel, facilities, equipment, and records to determine the certificate holder's:

(a) Eligibility to hold its certificate;

(b) Compliance with 49 U.S.C. 40101 et seq., formerly the Federal Aviation Act of 1958, as amended; and

(c) Compliance with the Federal Aviation Regulations.

§141.23 Advertising limitations.

(a) The holder of a pilot school certificate or a provisional pilot school certificate may not make any statement relating to its certification and ratings that is false or designed to mislead any person contemplating enrollment in that school.

(b) The holder of a pilot school certificate or a provisional pilot school certificate may not advertise that the school is certificated unless it clearly differentiates between courses that have been approved under part 141 of this chapter and those that have not been approved under part 141 of this chapter.

(c) The holder of a pilot school certificate or a provisional pilot school certificate must promptly remove:

(1) From vacated premises, all signs indicating that the school was certificated by the Administrator; or

(2) All indications (including signs), wherever located, that the school is certificated by the Administrator when its certificate has expired or has been surrendered, suspended, or revoked.

§141.25 Business office and operations base.

(a) Each holder of a pilot school or a provisional pilot school certificate must maintain a principal business office with a mailing address in the name shown on its certificate.

(b) The facilities and equipment at the principal business office must be adequate to maintain the files and records required to operate the business of the school.

(c) The principal business office may not be shared with, or used by, another pilot school.

(d) Before changing the location of the principal business office or the operations base, each certificate holder must notify the responsible Flight Standards office having jurisdiction over the area of the new location, and the notice must be:

(1) Submitted in writing at least 30 days before the change of location; and

(2) Accompanied by any amendments needed for the certificate holder's approved training course outline.

(e) A certificate holder may conduct training at an operations base other than the one specified in its certificate, if:

(1) The Administrator has inspected and approved the base for use by the certificate holder; and

(2) The course of training and any needed amendments have been approved for use at that base.

[Docket No. 25910, 62 FR 16347, April 4, 1997; as amended by Amdt. 141–19, 83 FR 9175, March 5, 2018]

§141.26 Training agreements.

(a) A training center certificated under part 142 of this chapter may provide the training, testing, and checking for pilot schools certificated under this part and is considered to meet the requirements of this part, provided—

(1) There is a training agreement between the certificated training center and the pilot school;

(2) The training, testing, and checking provided by the certificated training center is approved and conducted under part 142;

(3) The pilot school certificated under this part obtains the Administrator's approval for a training course outline that includes the training, testing, and checking to be conducted under this part and the training, testing, and checking to be conducted under part 142; and

(4) Upon completion of the training, testing, and checking conducted under part 142, a copy of each student's training record is forwarded to the part 141 school and becomes part of the student's permanent training record.

(b) A pilot school that provides flight training for an institution of higher education that holds a letter of authorization under §61.169 of this chapter must have a training agreement with that institution of higher education.

[Docket No. 25910, 62 FR 16347, April 4, 1997; as amended by Amdt. 141–17, 78 FR 42379, July 15, 2013; Amdt. 141–17A, 78 FR 53026, Aug. 28, 2013]

§141.27 Renewal of certificates and ratings.

(a) *Pilot school.*

(1) A pilot school may apply for renewal of its school certificate and ratings within 30 days preceding the month the pilot school's certificate expires, provided the school meets the requirements prescribed in paragraph (a)(2) of this section for renewal of its certificate and ratings.

(2) A pilot school may have its school certificate and ratings renewed for an additional 24 calendar months if the Administrator determines the school's personnel, aircraft, facility and airport, approved training courses, training records, and

recent training ability and quality meet the requirements of this part.

(3) A pilot school that does not meet the renewal requirements in paragraph (a)(2) of this section, may apply for a provisional pilot school certificate if the school meets the requirements of §141.7 of this part.

(b) *Provisional pilot school.*

(1) Except as provided in paragraph (b)(3) of this section, a provisional pilot school may not have its provisional pilot school certificate or the ratings on that certificate renewed.

(2) A provisional pilot school may apply for a pilot school certificate and associated ratings provided that school meets the requirements of §141.5 of this part.

(3) A former provisional pilot school may apply for another provisional pilot school certificate, provided 180 days have elapsed since its last provisional pilot school certificate expired.

§141.29 [Reserved]

Subpart B— Personnel, Aircraft, and Facilities Requirements

§141.31 Applicability.

(a) This subpart prescribes:

(1) The personnel and aircraft requirements for a pilot school certificate or a provisional pilot school certificate; and

(2) The facilities that a pilot school or provisional pilot school must have available on a continuous basis.

(b) As used in this subpart, to have continuous use of a facility, including an airport, the school must have:

(1) Ownership of the facility or airport for at least 6 calendar months after the date the application for initial certification and on the date of renewal of the school's certificate is made; or

(2) A written lease agreement for the facility or airport for at least 6 calendar months after the date the application for initial certification and on the date of renewal of the school's certificate is made.

[Docket No. 25910, 62 FR 16347, April 4, 1997; as amended by Amdt. 141–9, 62 FR 40907, July 30, 1997]

§141.33 Personnel.

(a) An applicant for a pilot school certificate or for a provisional pilot school certificate must meet the following personnel requirements:

(1) Each applicant must have adequate personnel, including certificated flight instructors,

certificated ground instructors, or holders of a commercial pilot certificate with a lighter-than-air rating, and a chief instructor for each approved course of training who is qualified and competent to perform the duties to which that instructor is assigned.

(2) If the school employs dispatchers, aircraft handlers, and line and service personnel, then it must instruct those persons in the procedures and responsibilities of their employment.

(3) Each instructor to be used for ground or flight training must hold a flight instructor certificate, ground instructor certificate, or commercial pilot certificate with a lighter-than-air rating, as appropriate, with ratings for the approved course of training and any aircraft used in that course.

(4) In addition to meeting the requirements of paragraph (a)(3) of this section, each instructor used for the airline transport pilot certification training program in § 61.156 of this chapter must:

(i) Hold an airline transport pilot certificate with an airplane category multiengine class rating;

(ii) Have at least 2 years of experience as a pilot in command in operations conducted under §91.1053(a)(2)(i) or §135.243(a)(1) of this chapter, or as a pilot in command or second in command in any operation conducted under part 121 of this chapter; and

(iii) If providing training in a flight simulation training device, have received training and evaluation within the preceding 12 months from the certificate holder on—

(A) Proper operation of flight simulator and flight training device controls and systems;

(B) Proper operation of environmental and fault panels,

(C) Data and motion limitations of simulation;

(D) Minimum equipment requirements for each curriculum; and

(E) The maneuvers that will be demonstrated in the flight simulation training device.

(b) An applicant for a pilot school certificate or for a provisional pilot school certificate must designate a chief instructor for each of the school's approved training courses, who must meet the requirements of §141.35 of this part.

(c) When necessary, an applicant for a pilot school certificate or for a provisional pilot school certificate may designate a person to be an assistant chief instructor for an approved training course, provided that person meets the requirements of §141.36 of this part.

(d) A pilot school and a provisional pilot school may designate a person to be a check instructor for conducting student stage checks, end-of-course tests, and instructor proficiency checks, provided:

(1) That person meets the requirements of §141.37 of this part; and

(2) The school has an enrollment of at least 10 students at the time designation is sought.

(e) A person, as listed in this section, may serve in more than one position for a school, provided that person is qualified for each position.

[Docket No. 25910, 62 FR 16347, April 4, 1997; as amended by Amdt. 141–9, 62 FR 40907, July 30, 1997; Amdt. 141–12, 74 FR 42563, Aug. 21, 2009; Amdt. 141–17, 78 FR 42379, July 15, 2013; Amdt. 141–17A, 78 FR 53026, Aug. 28, 2013]

§141.34 Employment of former FAA employees.

(a) Except as specified in paragraph (c) of this section, no holder of a pilot school certificate or a provisional pilot school certificate may knowingly employ or make a contractual arrangement which permits an individual to act as an agent or representative of the certificate holder in any matter before the Federal Aviation Administration if the individual, in the preceding 2 years—

(1) Served as, or was directly responsible for the oversight of, a Flight Standards Service aviation safety inspector; and

(2) Had direct responsibility to inspect, or oversee the inspection of, the operations of the certificate holder.

(b) For the purpose of this section, an individual shall be considered to be acting as an agent or representative of a certificate holder in a matter before the agency if the individual makes any written or oral communication on behalf of the certificate holder to the agency (or any of its officers or employees) in connection with a particular matter, whether or not involving a specific party and without regard to whether the individual has participated in, or had responsibility for, the particular matter while serving as a Flight Standards Service aviation safety inspector.

(c) The provisions of this section do not prohibit a holder of a pilot school certificate or a provisional pilot school certificate from knowingly employing or making a contractual arrangement which permits an individual to act as an agent or representative of the certificate holder in any matter before the Federal Aviation Administration if the individual was employed by the certificate holder before October 21, 2011.

[Docket No. FAA–2008–1154, 76 FR 52236, Aug. 22, 2011]

§141.35 Chief instructor qualifications.

(a) To be eligible for designation as a chief instructor for a course of training, a person must meet the following requirements:

(1) Hold a commercial pilot certificate or an airline transport pilot certificate, and, except for a chief instructor for a course of training solely for

a lighter-than-air rating, a current flight instructor certificate. The certificates must contain the appropriate aircraft category and class ratings for the category and class of aircraft used in the course and an instrument rating, if an instrument rating is required for enrollment in the course of training;

(2) Meet the pilot-in-command recent flight experience requirements of §61.57 of this chapter;

(3) Pass a knowledge test on—

(i) Teaching methods;

(ii) Applicable provisions of the "Aeronautical Information Manual";

(iii) Applicable provisions of parts 61, 91, and 141 of this chapter; and

(iv) The objectives and approved course completion standards of the course for which the person seeks to obtain designation.

(4) Pass a proficiency test on instructional skills and ability to train students on the flight procedures and maneuvers appropriate to the course;

(5) Except for a course of training for gliders, balloons, or airships, the chief instructor must meet the applicable requirements in paragraphs (b), (c), and (d) of this section; and

(6) A chief instructor for a course of training for gliders, balloons or airships is only required to have 40 percent of the hours required in paragraphs (b) and (d) of this section.

(b) For a course of training leading to the issuance of a recreational or private pilot certificate or rating, a chief instructor must have:

(1) At least 1,000 hours as pilot in command; and

(2) Primary flight training experience, acquired as either a certificated flight instructor or an instructor in a military pilot flight training program, or a combination thereof, consisting of at least—

(i) 2 years and a total of 500 flight hours; or

(ii) 1,000 flight hours.

(c) For a course of training leading to the issuance of an instrument rating or a rating with instrument privileges, a chief instructor must have:

(1) At least 100 hours of flight time under actual or simulated instrument conditions;

(2) At least 1,000 hours as pilot in command; and

(3) Instrument flight instructor experience, acquired as either a certificated flight instructor–instrument or an instructor in a military pilot flight training program, or a combination thereof, consisting of at least—

(i) 2 years and a total of 250 flight hours; or

(ii) 400 flight hours.

(d) For a course of training other than one leading to the issuance of a recreational or private pilot certificate or rating, or an instrument rating or a rating with instrument privileges, a chief instructor must have:

(1) At least 2,000 hours as pilot in command; and

(2) Flight training experience, acquired as either a certificated flight instructor or an instructor in a military pilot flight training program, or a combination thereof, consisting of at least—

(i) 3 years and a total of 1,000 flight hours; or

(ii) 1,500 flight hours.

(e) To be eligible for designation as chief instructor for a ground school course, a person must have 1 year of experience as a ground school instructor at a certificated pilot school.

[Docket No. 25910, 62 FR 16347, April 4, 1997; as amended by Amdt. 141–9, 62 FR 40907, July 30, 1997; Amdt. No. 141–10, 63 FR 20289, April 23, 1998]

§141.36 Assistant chief instructor qualifications.

(a) To be eligible for designation as an assistant chief instructor for a course of training, a person must meet the following requirements:

(1) Hold a commercial pilot or an airline transport pilot certificate and, except for the assistant chief instructor for a course of training solely for a lighter-than-air rating, a current flight instructor certificate. The certificates must contain the appropriate aircraft category, class, and instrument ratings if an instrument rating is required by the course of training for the category and class of aircraft used in the course;

(2) Meet the pilot-in-command recent flight experience requirements of §61.57 of this chapter;

(3) Pass a knowledge test on—

(i) Teaching methods;

(ii) Applicable provisions of the "Aeronautical Information Manual";

(iii) Applicable provisions of parts 61, 91, and 141 of this chapter; and

(iv) The objectives and approved course completion standards of the course for which the person seeks to obtain designation.

(4) Pass a proficiency test on the flight procedures and maneuvers appropriate to that course; and

(5) Meet the applicable requirements in paragraphs (b), (c), and (d) of this section. However, an assistant chief instructor for a course of training for gliders, balloons, or airships is only required to have 40 percent of the hours required in paragraphs (b) and (d) of this section.

(b) For a course of training leading to the issuance of a recreational or private pilot certificate or rating, an assistant chief instructor must have:

(1) At least 500 hours as pilot in command; and

(2) Flight training experience, acquired as either a certificated flight instructor or an instructor in a military pilot flight training program, or a combination thereof, consisting of at least—

(i) 1 year and a total of 250 flight hours; or

(ii) 500 flight hours.

(c) For a course of training leading to the issuance of an instrument rating or a rating with instrument privileges, an assistant chief flight instructor must have:

(1) At least 50 hours of flight time under actual or simulated instrument conditions;

(2) At least 500 hours as pilot in command; and

(3) Instrument flight instructor experience, acquired as either a certificated flight instructor–instrument or an instructor in a military pilot flight training program, or a combination thereof, consisting of at least—

(i) 1 year and a total of 125 flight hours; or

(ii) 200 flight hours.

(d) For a course of training other than one leading to the issuance of a recreational or private pilot certificate or rating, or an instrument rating or a rating with instrument privileges, an assistant chief instructor must have:

(1) At least 1,000 hours as pilot in command; and

(2) Flight training experience, acquired as either a certificated flight instructor or an instructor in a military pilot flight training program, or a combination thereof, consisting of at least—

(i) 1½ years and a total of 500 flight hours; or

(ii) 750 flight hours.

(e) To be eligible for designation as an assistant chief instructor for a ground school course, a person must have 6 months of experience as a ground school instructor at a certificated pilot school.

[Docket No. 25910, 62 FR 16347, April 4, 1997; as amended by Amdt. 141–9, 62 FR 40907, July 30, 1997; Amdt. No. 141–10, 63 FR 20289, April 23, 1998]

§141.37 Check instructor qualifications.

(a) To be designated as a check instructor for conducting student stage checks, end-of-course tests, and instructor proficiency checks under this part, a person must meet the eligibility requirements of this section:

(1) For checks and tests that relate to either flight or ground training, the person must pass a test, given by the chief instructor, on—

(i) Teaching methods;

(ii) Applicable provisions of the "Aeronautical Information Manual";

(iii) Applicable provisions of parts 61, 91, and 141 of this chapter; and

(iv) The objectives and course completion standards of the approved training course for the designation sought.

(2) For checks and tests that relate to a flight training course, the person must—

(i) Meet the requirements in paragraph (a)(1) of this section;

(ii) Hold a commercial pilot certificate or an airline transport pilot certificate and, except for a check instructor for a course of training for a lighter-than-air rating, a current flight instructor certificate. The certificates must contain the appropriate aircraft category, class, and instrument ratings for the category and class of aircraft used in the course;

(iii) Meet the pilot-in-command recent flight experience requirements of §61.57 of this chapter; and

(iv) Pass a proficiency test, given by the chief instructor or assistant chief instructor, on the flight procedures and maneuvers of the approved training course for the designation sought.

(3) For checks and tests that relate to ground training, the person must—

(i) Meet the requirements in paragraph (a)(1) of this section;

(ii) Except for a course of training for a lighter-than-air rating, hold a current flight instructor certificate or ground instructor certificate with ratings appropriate to the category and class of aircraft used in the course; and

(iii) For a course of training for a lighter-than-air rating, hold a commercial pilot certificate with a lighter-than-air category rating and the appropriate class rating.

(b) A person who meets the eligibility requirements in paragraph (a) of this section must:

(1) Be designated, in writing, by the chief instructor to conduct student stage checks, end-of-course tests, and instructor proficiency checks; and

(2) Be approved by the responsible Flight Standards office.

(c) A check instructor may not conduct a stage check or an end-of-course test of any student for whom the check instructor has:

(1) Served as the principal instructor; or

(2) Recommended for a stage check or end-of-course test.

[Docket No. 25910, 62 FR 16347, April 4, 1997; as amended by Amdt. 141–9, 62 FR 40907, July 30, 1997; Amdt. 141–19, 83 FR 9175, March 5, 2018]

§141.38 Airports.

(a) An applicant for a pilot school certificate or a provisional pilot school certificate must show that he or she has continuous use of each airport at which training flights originate.

(b) Each airport used for airplanes and gliders must have at least one runway or takeoff area that allows training aircraft to make a normal takeoff or landing under the following conditions at the aircraft's maximum certificated takeoff gross weight:

(1) Under wind conditions of not more than 5 miles per hour;

(2) At temperatures in the operating area equal to the mean high temperature for the hottest month of the year;

(3) If applicable, with the powerplant operation, and landing gear and flap operation recommended by the manufacturer; and

(4) In the case of a takeoff—

(i) With smooth transition from liftoff to the best rate of climb speed without exceptional piloting skills or techniques; and

(ii) Clearing all obstacles in the takeoff flight path by at least 50 feet.

(c) Each airport must have a wind direction indicator that is visible from the end of each runway at ground level;

(d) Each airport must have a traffic direction indicator when:

(1) The airport does not have an operating control tower; and

(2) UNICOM advisories are not available.

(e) Except as provided in paragraph (f) of this section, each airport used for night training flights must have permanent runway lights;

(f) An airport or seaplane base used for night training flights in seaplanes is permitted to use adequate nonpermanent lighting or shoreline lighting, if approved by the Administrator.

[Docket No. 25910, 62 FR 16347, April 4, 1997; as amended by Amdt. 141–9, 62 FR 40907, July 30, 1997]

§141.39 Aircraft.

(a) When the school's training facility is located within the U.S., an applicant for a pilot school certificate or provisional pilot school certificate must show that each aircraft used by the school for flight training and solo flights:

(1) Is a civil aircraft of the United States;

(2) Is certificated with a standard airworthiness certificate, a primary airworthiness certificate, or a special airworthiness certificate in the light-sport category unless the FAA determines otherwise because of the nature of the approved course;

(3) Is maintained and inspected in accordance with the requirements for aircraft operated for hire under part 91, subpart E, of this chapter;

(4) Has two pilot stations with engine-power controls that can be easily reached and operated in a normal manner from both pilot stations (for flight training); and

(5) Is equipped and maintained for IFR operations if used in a course involving IFR en route operations and instrument approaches. For training in the control and precision maneuvering of an aircraft by reference to instruments, the aircraft may be equipped as provided in the approved course of training.

(b) When the school's training facility is located outside the U.S. and the training will be conducted outside the U.S., an applicant for a pilot school certificate or provisional pilot school certificate must show that each aircraft used by the school for flight training and solo flights:

(1) Is either a civil aircraft of the United States or a civil aircraft of foreign registry;

(2) Is certificated with a standard or primary airworthiness certificate or an equivalent certification from the foreign aviation authority;

(3) Is maintained and inspected in accordance with the requirements for aircraft operated for hire under part 91, subpart E of this chapter, or in accordance with equivalent maintenance and inspection from the foreign aviation authority's requirements;

(4) Has two pilot stations with engine-power controls that can be easily reached and operated in a normal manner from both pilot stations (for flight training); and

(5) Is equipped and maintained for IFR operations if used in a course involving IFR en route operations and instrument approaches. For training in the control and precision maneuvering of an aircraft by reference to instruments, the aircraft may be equipped as provided in the approved course of training.

[Docket No. FAA–2006–26661, 74 FR 42563, Aug. 21, 2009; as amended by Amdt. 141–13, 75 FR 5223, Feb. 1, 2010]

§141.41 Full flight simulators, flight training devices, aviation training devices, and training aids.

An applicant for a pilot school certificate or a provisional pilot school certificate must show that its full flight simulators, flight training devices, aviation training devices, training aids, and equipment meet the following requirements:

(a) *Full flight simulators and flight training devices.* Each full flight simulator and flight training device used to obtain flight training credit in an approved pilot training course curriculum must be:

(1) Qualified under part 60 of this chapter, or a previously qualified device, as permitted in accordance with §60.17 of this chapter; and

(2) Approved by the Administrator for the tasks and maneuvers.

(b) *Aviation training devices.* Each basic or advanced aviation training device used to obtain flight training credit in an approved pilot training course curriculum must be evaluated, qualified, and approved by the Administrator.

(c) *Training aids and equipment.* Each training aid, including any audiovisual aid, projector, mockup, chart, or aircraft component listed in the approved training course outline, must be accurate and relevant to the course for which it is used.

[Docket No. 25910, 62 FR 16347, April 4, 1997; as amended by Amdt. 141–9, 62 FR 40908, July 30, 1997; Amdt. 141–18, 81 FR 21460, April 12, 2016]

§141.43 Pilot briefing areas.

(a) An applicant for a pilot school certificate or provisional pilot school certificate must show that the applicant has continuous use of a briefing area located at each airport at which training flights originate that is:

(1) Adequate to shelter students waiting to engage in their training flights;

(2) Arranged and equipped for the conduct of pilot briefings; and

(3) Except as provided in paragraph (c) of this section, for a school with an instrument rating or commercial pilot course, equipped with private landline or telephone communication to the nearest FAA Flight Service Station.

(b) A briefing area required by paragraph (a) of this section may not be used by the applicant if it is available for use by any other pilot school during the period it is required for use by the applicant.

(c) The communication equipment required by paragraph (a)(3) of this section is not required if the briefing area and the flight service station are located on the same airport, and are readily accessible to each other.

§141.45 Ground training facilities.

An applicant for a pilot school or provisional pilot school certificate must show that:

(a) Except as provided in paragraph (c) of this section, each room, training booth, or other space used for instructional purposes is heated, lighted, and ventilated to conform to local building, sanitation, and health codes.

(b) Except as provided in paragraph (c) of this section, the training facility is so located that the students in that facility are not distracted by the training conducted in other rooms, or by flight and maintenance operations on the airport.

(c) If a training course is conducted through an internet-based medium, the holder of a pilot school certificate or provisional pilot school certificate that provides such training need not comply with paragraphs (a) and (b) of this section but must maintain in current status a permanent business location and business telephone number.

[Docket No. 25910, 62 FR 16347, April 4, 1997; as amended by Amdt. 141–15, 76 FR 54107, Aug. 31, 2011]

Subpart C— Training Course Outline and Curriculum

§141.51 Applicability.

This subpart prescribes the curriculum and course outline requirements for the issuance of a pilot school certificate or provisional pilot school certificate and ratings.

§141.53 Approval procedures for a training course: General.

(a) *General.* An applicant for a pilot school certificate or provisional pilot school certificate must obtain the Administrator's approval of the outline of each training course for which certification and rating is sought.

(b) *Application.*

(1) An application for the approval of an initial or amended training course must be submitted in duplicate to the responsible Flight Standards office for the area where the school is based.

(2) An application for the approval of an initial or amended training course must be submitted at least 30 days before any training under that course, or any amendment thereto, is scheduled to begin.

(3) An application for amending a training course must be accompanied by two copies of the amendment.

(c) *Training courses.* An applicant for a pilot school certificate or provisional pilot school certificate may request approval for the training courses specified under §141.11(b).

(d) *Additional rules for internet based training courses.* An application for an initial or amended training course offered through an internet based medium must comply with the following:

(1) All amendments must be identified numerically by page, date, and screen. Minor editorial and typographical changes do not require FAA approval, provided the school notifies the FAA within 30 days of their insertion.

(2) For monitoring purposes, the school must provide the FAA an acceptable means to log-in and log-off from a remote location to review all elements of the course as viewed by attendees and to by-pass the normal attendee restrictions.

(3) The school must incorporate adequate security measures into its internet-based courseware information system and into its operating and maintenance procedures to ensure the following fundamental areas of security and protection:

(i) Integrity.

(ii) Identification/Authentication.
(iii) Confidentiality.
(iv) Availability.
(v) Access control.

[Docket No. 25910, 62 FR 16347, April 4, 1997; as amended by Amdt. 141–9, 62 FR 40908, July 30, 1997; Amdt. 141–12, 74 FR 42563, Aug. 21, 2009; Amdt. 141–15, 76 FR 54107, Aug. 31, 2011; Amdt. 141–19, 83 FR 9175, March 5, 2018]

§141.55 Training course: Contents.

(a) Each training course for which approval is requested must meet the minimum curriculum requirements in accordance with the appropriate appendix of this part.

(b) Except as provided in paragraphs (d) and (e) of this section, each training course for which approval is requested must meet the minimum ground and flight training time requirements in accordance with the appropriate appendix of this part.

(c) Each training course for which approval is requested must contain:

(1) A description of each room used for ground training, including the room's size and the maximum number of students that may be trained in the room at one time, unless the course is provided via an internet-based training medium;

(2) A description of each type of audiovisual aid, projector, tape recorder, mockup, chart, aircraft component, and other special training aids used for ground training;

(3) A description of each flight simulator or flight training device used for training;

(4) A listing of the airports at which training flights originate and a description of the facilities, including pilot briefing areas that are available for use by the school's students and personnel at each of those airports;

(5) A description of the type of aircraft including any special equipment used for each phase of training;

(6) The minimum qualifications and ratings for each instructor assigned to ground or flight training; and

(7) A training syllabus that includes the following information—

(i) The prerequisites for enrolling in the ground and flight portion of the course that include the pilot certificate and rating (if required by this part), training, pilot experience, and pilot knowledge;

(ii) A detailed description of each lesson, including the lesson's objectives, standards, and planned time for completion;

(iii) A description of what the course is expected to accomplish with regard to student learning;

(iv) The expected accomplishments and the standards for each stage of training; and

(v) A description of the checks and tests to be used to measure a student's accomplishments for each stage of training.

(d) A pilot school may request and receive initial approval for a period of not more than 24 calendar months for any training course under this part that does not meet the minimum ground and flight training time requirements, provided the following provisions are met:

(1) The school holds a pilot school certificate issued under this part and has held that certificate for a period of at least 24 consecutive calendar months preceding the month of the request;

(2) In addition to the information required by paragraph (c) of this section, the training course specifies planned ground and flight training time requirements for the course;

(3) The school does not request the training course to be approved for examining authority, nor may that school hold examining authority for that course; and

(4) The practical test or knowledge test for the course is to be given by—

(i) An FAA inspector; or

(ii) An examiner who is not an employee of the school.

(e) A pilot school may request and receive final approval for any training course under this part that does not meet the minimum ground and flight training time requirements, provided the following conditions are met:

(1) The school has held initial approval for that training course for at least 24 calendar months.

(2) The school has—

(i) Trained at least 10 students in that training course within the preceding 24 calendar months and recommended those students for a pilot, flight instructor, or ground instructor certificate or rating; and

(ii) At least 80 percent of those students passed the practical or knowledge test, as appropriate, on the first attempt, and that test was given by—

(A) An FAA inspector; or

(B) An examiner who is not an employee of the school.

(3) In addition to the information required by paragraph (c) of this section, the training course specifies planned ground and flight training time requirements for the course.

(4) The school does not request that the training course be approved for examining authority nor may that school hold examining authority for that course.

[Docket No. 25910, 62 FR 16347, April 4, 1997; as amended by Amdt. 141–12, 74 FR 42563, Aug. 21, 2009; Amdt 141–15, 76 FR 54107, Aug. 31, 2011]

§141.57 Special curricula.

An applicant for a pilot school certificate or provisional pilot school certificate may apply for approval to conduct a special course of airman training for which a curriculum is not prescribed in the appendixes of this part, if the applicant shows that the training course contains features that could achieve a level of pilot proficiency equivalent to that achieved by a training course prescribed in the appendixes of this part or the requirements of part 61 of this chapter.

Subpart D— Examining Authority

§141.61 Applicability.

This subpart prescribes the requirements for the issuance of examining authority to the holder of a pilot school certificate, and the privileges and limitations of that examining authority.

§141.63 Examining authority qualification requirements.

(a) A pilot school must meet the following prerequisites to receive initial approval for examining authority:

(1) The school must complete the application for examining authority on a form and in a manner prescribed by the Administrator;

(2) The school must hold a pilot school certificate and rating issued under this part;

(3) The school must have held the rating in which examining authority is sought for at least 24 consecutive calendar months preceding the month of application for examining authority;

(4) The training course for which examining authority is requested may not be a course that is approved without meeting the minimum ground and flight training time requirements of this part; and

(5) Within 24 calendar months before the date of application for examining authority, that school must meet the following requirements—

(i) The school must have trained at least 10 students in the training course for which examining authority is sought and recommended those students for a pilot, flight instructor, or ground instructor certificate or rating; and

(ii) At least 90 percent of those students passed the required practical or knowledge test, or any combination thereof, for the pilot, flight instructor, or ground instructor certificate or rating on the first attempt, and that test was given by—

(A) An FAA inspector; or

(B) An examiner who is not an employee of the school.

(b) A pilot school must meet the following requirements to retain approval of its examining authority:

(1) The school must complete the application for renewal of its examining authority on a form and in a manner prescribed by the Administrator;

(2) The school must hold a pilot school certificate and rating issued under this part;

(3) The school must have held the rating for which continued examining authority is sought for at least 24 calendar months preceding the month of application for renewal of its examining authority; and

(4) The training course for which continued examining authority is requested may not be a course that is approved without meeting the minimum ground and flight training time requirements of this part.

[Docket No. 25910, 62 FR 16347, April 4, 1997; as amended by Amdt. 141–9, 62 FR 40908, July 30, 1997]

§141.65 Privileges.

A pilot school that holds examining authority may recommend a person who graduated from its course for the appropriate pilot, flight instructor, or ground instructor certificate or rating without taking the FAA knowledge test or practical test in accordance with the provisions of this subpart.

§141.67 Limitations and reports.

A pilot school that holds examining authority may only recommend the issuance of a pilot, flight instructor, or ground instructor certificate and rating to a person who does not take an FAA knowledge test or practical test, if the recommendation for the issuance of that certificate or rating is in accordance with the following requirements:

(a) The person graduated from a training course for which the pilot school holds examining authority.

(b) Except as provided in this paragraph, the person satisfactorily completed all the curriculum requirements of that pilot school's approved training course. A person who transfers from one part 141 approved pilot school to another part 141 approved pilot school may receive credit for that previous training, provided the following requirements are met:

(1) The maximum credited training time does not exceed one-half of the receiving school's curriculum requirements;

(2) The person completes a knowledge and proficiency test conducted by the receiving school for the purpose of determining the amount of pilot experience and knowledge to be credited;

(3) The receiving school determines (based on the person's performance on the knowledge and

proficiency test required by paragraph (b)(2) of this section) the amount of credit to be awarded, and records that credit in the person's training record;

(4) The person who requests credit for previous pilot experience and knowledge obtained the experience and knowledge from another part 141 approved pilot school and training course; and

(5) The receiving school retains a copy of the person's training record from the previous school.

(c) Tests given by a pilot school that holds examining authority must be approved by the Administrator and be at least equal in scope, depth, and difficulty to the comparable knowledge and practical tests prescribed by the Administrator under part 61 of this chapter.

(d) A pilot school that holds examining authority may not use its knowledge or practical tests if the school:

(1) Knows, or has reason to believe, the test has been compromised; or

(2) Is notified by the responsible Flight Standards office that there is reason to believe or it is known that the test has been compromised.

(e) A pilot school that holds examining authority must maintain a record of all temporary airman certificates it issues, which consist of the following information:

(1) A chronological listing that includes—

(i) The date the temporary airman certificate was issued;

(ii) The student to whom the temporary airman certificate was issued, and that student's permanent mailing address and telephone number;

(iii) The training course from which the student graduated;

(iv) The name of person who conducted the knowledge or practical test;

(v) The type of temporary airman certificate or rating issued to the student; and

(vi) The date the student's airman application file was sent to the FAA for processing for a permanent airman certificate.

(2) A copy of the record containing each student's graduation certificate, airman application, temporary airman certificate, superseded airman certificate (if applicable), and knowledge test or practical test results; and

(3) The records required by paragraph (e) of this section must be retained for 1 year and made available to the Administrator upon request. These records must be surrendered to the Administrator when the pilot school ceases to have examining authority.

(f) Except for pilot schools that have an airman certification representative, when a student passes the knowledge test or practical test, the pilot school that holds examining authority must submit that student's airman application file and training record to the FAA for processing for the issuance of a permanent airman certificate.

[Docket No. 25910, 62 FR 16347, April 4, 1997; as amended by Amdt. 141–9, 62 FR 40908, July 30, 1997; Amdt. 141–19, 83 FR 9175, March 5, 2018]

Subpart E— Operating Rules

§141.71 Applicability.

This subpart prescribes the operating rules applicable to a pilot school or provisional pilot school certificated under the provisions of this part.

§141.73 Privileges.

(a) The holder of a pilot school certificate or a provisional pilot school certificate may advertise and conduct approved pilot training courses in accordance with the certificate and any ratings that it holds.

(b) A pilot school that holds examining authority for an approved training course may recommend a graduate of that course for the issuance of an appropriate pilot, flight instructor, or ground instructor certificate and rating, without taking an FAA knowledge test or practical test, provided the training course has been approved and meets the minimum ground and flight training time requirements of this part.

§141.75 Aircraft requirements.

The following items must be carried on each aircraft used for flight training and solo flights:

(a) A pretakeoff and prelanding checklist; and

(b) The operator's handbook for the aircraft, if one is furnished by the manufacturer, or copies of the handbook if furnished to each student using the aircraft.

[Docket No. 25910, 62 FR 40908, July 30, 1997]

§141.77 Limitations.

(a) The holder of a pilot school certificate or a provisional pilot school certificate may not issue a graduation certificate to a student, or recommend a student for a pilot certificate or rating, unless the student has:

(1) Completed the training specified in the pilot school's course of training; and

(2) Passed the required final tests.

(b) Except as provided in paragraph (c) of this section, the holder of a pilot school certificate or a provisional pilot school certificate may not graduate a student from a course of training unless the student has completed all of the curriculum requirements of that course;

(c) A student may be given credit towards the curriculum requirements of a course for previous training under the following conditions:

(1) If the student completed a proficiency test and knowledge test that was conducted by the receiving pilot school and the previous training was based on a part 141- or a part 142-approved flight training course, the credit is limited to not more than 50 percent of the flight training requirements of the curriculum.

(2) If the student completed a knowledge test that was conducted by the receiving pilot school and the previous training was based on a part 141- or a part 142-approved aeronautical knowledge training course, the credit is limited to not more than 50 percent of the aeronautical knowledge training requirements of the curriculum.

(3) If the student completed a proficiency test and knowledge test that was conducted by the receiving pilot school and the training was received from other than a part 141- or a part 142-approved flight training course, the credit is limited to not more than 25 percent of the flight training requirements of the curriculum.

(4) If the student completed a knowledge test that was conducted by the receiving pilot school and the previous training was received from other than a part 141- or a part 142-approved aeronautical knowledge training course, the credit is limited to not more than 25 percent of the aeronautical knowledge training requirements of the curriculum.

(5) Completion of previous training must be certified in the student's training record by the training provider or a management official within the training provider's organization, and must contain—

(i) The kind and amount of training provided; and

(ii) The result of each stage check and end-of-course test, if appropriate.

[Docket No. 25910, 62 FR 16347, April 4, 1997; as amended by Amdt. 141–9, 62 FR 40908, July 30, 1997; Amdt. 141–12, 74 FR 42564, Aug. 21, 2009]

§141.79 Flight training.

(a) No person other than a certificated flight instructor or commercial pilot with a lighter-than-air rating who has the ratings and the minimum qualifications specified in the approved training course outline may give a student flight training under an approved course of training.

(b) No student pilot may be authorized to start a solo practice flight from an airport until the flight has been approved by a certificated flight instructor or commercial pilot with a lighter-than-air rating who is present at that airport.

(c) Each chief instructor and assistant chief instructor assigned to a training course must complete, at least once every 12 calendar months, an approved syllabus of training consisting of ground or flight training, or both, or an approved flight instructor refresher course.

(d) Each certificated flight instructor or commercial pilot with a lighter-than-air rating who is assigned to a flight training course must satisfactorily complete the following tasks, which must be administered by the school's chief instructor, assistant chief instructor, or check instructor:

(1) Prior to receiving authorization to train students in a flight training course, must—

(i) Accomplish a review of and receive a briefing on the objectives and standards of that training course; and

(ii) Accomplish an initial proficiency check in each make and model of aircraft used in that training course in which that person provides training; and

(2) Every 12 calendar months after the month in which the person last complied with the requirements of paragraph (d)(1)(ii) of this section, accomplish a recurrent proficiency check in one of the aircraft in which the person trains students.

[Docket No. 25910, 62 FR 16347, April 4, 1997; as amended by Amdt. 141–9, 62 FR 40908, July 30, 1997]

§141.81 Ground training.

(a) Except as provided in paragraph (b) of this section, each instructor who is assigned to a ground training course must hold a flight or ground instructor certificate, or a commercial pilot certificate with a lighter-than-air rating, with the appropriate rating for that course of training.

(b) A person who does not meet the requirements of paragraph (a) of this section may be assigned ground training duties in a ground training course, if:

(1) The chief instructor who is assigned to that ground training course finds the person qualified to give that training; and

(2) The training is given while under the supervision of the chief instructor or the assistant chief instructor who is present at the facility when the training is given.

(c) An instructor may not be used in a ground training course until that instructor has been briefed on the objectives and standards of that course by the chief instructor, assistant chief instructor, or check instructor.

[Docket No. 25910, 62 FR 16347, April 4, 1997; as amended by Amdt. 141–9, 62 FR 40908, July 30, 1997]

141

§141.83 Quality of training.

(a) Each pilot school or provisional pilot school must meet the following requirements:

(1) Comply with its approved training course; and

(2) Provide training of such quality that meets the requirements of §141.5(d) of this part.

(b) The failure of a pilot school or provisional pilot school to maintain the quality of training specified in paragraph (a) of this section may be the basis for suspending or revoking that school's certificate.

(c) When requested by the Administrator, a pilot school or provisional pilot school must allow the FAA to administer any knowledge test, practical test, stage check, or end-of-course test to its students.

(d) When a stage check or end-of-course test is administered by the FAA under the provisions of paragraph (c) of this section, and the student has not completed the training course, then that test will be based on the standards prescribed in the school's approved training course.

(e) When a practical test or knowledge test is administered by the FAA under the provisions of paragraph (c) of this section, to a student who has completed the school's training course, that test will be based upon the areas of operation approved by the Administrator.

[Docket No. 25910, 62 FR 16347, April 4, 1997; as amended by Amdt. 141–9, 62 FR 40908, July 30, 1997]

§141.85 Chief instructor responsibilities.

(a) A chief instructor designated for a pilot school or provisional pilot school is responsible for:

(1) Certifying each student's training record, graduation certificate, stage check and end-of-course test reports, and recommendation for course completion, unless the duties are delegated by the chief instructor to an assistant chief instructor or recommending instructor;

(2) Ensuring that each certificated flight instructor, certificated ground instructor, or commercial pilot with a lighter-than-air rating passes an initial proficiency check prior to that instructor being assigned instructing duties in the school's approved training course, and thereafter that the instructor passes a recurrent proficiency check every 12 calendar months after the month in which the initial test was accomplished;

(3) Ensuring that each student accomplishes the required stage checks and end-of-course tests in accordance with the school's approved training course; and

(4) Maintaining training techniques, procedures, and standards for the school that are acceptable to the Administrator.

(b) The chief instructor or an assistant chief instructor must be available at the pilot school or, if away from the pilot school, be available by telephone, radio, or other electronic means during the time that training is given for an approved training course.

(c) The chief instructor may delegate authority for conducting stage checks, end-of-course tests, and flight instructor proficiency checks to the assistant chief instructor or a check instructor.

[Docket No. 25910, 62 FR 16347, April 4, 1997; as amended by Amdt. 141–9, 62 FR 40908, July 30, 1997; Amdt. 141–12, 74 FR 42564, Aug. 21, 2009]

§141.87 Change of chief instructor.

Whenever a pilot school or provisional pilot school makes a change of designation of its chief instructor, that school:

(a) Must immediately provide the responsible Flight Standards office in which the school is located with written notification of the change;

(b) May conduct training without a chief instructor for that training course for a period not to exceed 60 days while awaiting the designation and approval of another chief instructor;

(c) May, for a period not to exceed 60 days, have the stage checks and end-of-course tests administered by:

(1) The training course's assistant chief instructor, if one has been designated;

(2) The training course's check instructor, if one has been designated;

(3) An FAA inspector; or

(4) An examiner.

(d) Must, after 60 days without a chief instructor, cease operations and surrender its certificate to the Administrator; and

(e) May have its certificate reinstated, upon:

(1) Designating and approving another chief instructor;

(2) Showing it meets the requirements of §141.27(a)(2) of this part; and

(3) Applying for reinstatement on a form and in a manner prescribed by the Administrator.

[Docket No. 25910, 62 FR 16347, April 4, 1997; as amended by Amdt. 141–19, 83 FR 9175, March 5, 2018]

§141.89 Maintenance of personnel, facilities, and equipment.

The holder of a pilot school certificate or provisional pilot school certificate may not provide training to a student who is enrolled in an approved course of training unless:

(a) Each airport, aircraft, and facility necessary for that training meets the standards specified in the holder's approved training course outline and the appropriate requirements of this part; and

(b) Except as provided in §141.87 of this part, each chief instructor, assistant chief instructor, check instructor, or instructor meets the qualifications specified in the holder's approved course of training and the appropriate requirements of this part.

§141.91 Satellite bases.

The holder of a pilot school certificate or provisional pilot school certificate may conduct ground training or flight training in an approved course of training at a base other than its main operations base if:

(a) An assistant chief instructor is designated for each satellite base, and that assistant chief instructor is available at that base or, if away from the premises, by telephone, radio, or other electronic means during the time that training is provided for an approved training course;

(b) The airport, facilities, and personnel used at the satellite base meet the appropriate requirements of subpart B of this part and its approved training course outline;

(c) The instructors are under the direct supervision of the chief instructor or assistant chief instructor for the appropriate training course, who is readily available for consultation in accordance with §141.85(b) of this part; and

(d) The responsible Flight Standards office for the area in which the school is located is notified in writing if training is conducted at a base other than the school's main operations base for more than 7 consecutive days.

[Docket No. 25910, 62 FR 16347, April 4, 1997; as amended by Amdt. 141–9, 62 FR 40908, July 30, 1997; Amdt. 141–19, 83 FR 9175, March 5, 2018]

§141.93 Enrollment.

(a) The holder of a pilot school certificate or a provisional pilot school certificate must, at the time a student is enrolled in an approved training course, furnish that student with a copy of the following:

(1) A certificate of enrollment containing—

(i) The name of the course in which the student is enrolled; and

(ii) The date of that enrollment.

(2) A copy of the student's training syllabus.

(3) Except for a training course offered through an internet based medium, a copy of the safety procedures and practices developed by the school that describe the use of the school's facilities and the operation of its aircraft. Those procedures and practices shall include training on at least the following information—

(i) The weather minimums required by the school for dual and solo flights;

(ii) The procedures for starting and taxiing aircraft on the ramp;

(iii) Fire precautions and procedures;

(iv) Redispatch procedures after unprogrammed landings, on and off airports;

(v) Aircraft discrepancies and approval for return-to-service determinations;

(vi) Securing of aircraft when not in use;

(vii) Fuel reserves necessary for local and cross-country flights;

(viii) Avoidance of other aircraft in flight and on the ground;

(ix) Minimum altitude limitations and simulated emergency landing instructions; and

(x) A description of and instructions regarding the use of assigned practice areas.

(b) The holder of a pilot school certificate or provisional pilot school certificate must maintain a monthly listing of persons enrolled in each training course offered by the school.

[Docket No. 25910, 62 FR 16347, April 4, 1997; as amended by Amdt. 141–9, 62 FR 40908, July 30, 1997; Amdt. 141–15, 76 FR 54107, Aug. 31, 2011]

§141.95 Graduation certificate.

(a) The holder of a pilot school certificate or provisional pilot school certificate must issue a graduation certificate to each student who completes its approved course of training.

(b) The graduation certificate must be issued to the student upon completion of the course of training and contain at least the following information:

(1) The name of the school and the certificate number of the school;

(2) The name of the graduate to whom it was issued;

(3) The course of training for which it was issued;

(4) The date of graduation;

(5) A statement that the student has satisfactorily completed each required stage of the approved course of training including the tests for those stages;

(6) A certification of the information contained on the graduation certificate by the chief instructor for that course of training; and

(7) A statement showing the cross-country training that the student received in the course of training.

(8) Certificates issued upon graduating from a course based on internet media must be uniquely identified using an alphanumeric code that is specific to the student graduating from that course.

[Docket No. 25910, 62 FR 16347, April 4, 1997; as amended by Amdt. 141–9, 62 FR 40908, July 30, 1997; Amdt. 141–15, 76 FR 54108, Aug. 31, 2011]

141

Subpart F—Records

§141.101 Training records.

(a) Each holder of a pilot school certificate or provisional pilot school certificate must establish and maintain a current and accurate record of the participation of each student enrolled in an approved course of training conducted by the school that includes the following information:

(1) The date the student was enrolled in the approved course;

(2) A chronological log of the student's course attendance, subjects, and flight operations covered in the student's training, and the names and grades of any tests taken by the student; and

(3) The date the student graduated, terminated training, or transferred to another school. In the case of graduation from a course based on internet media, the school must maintain the identifying graduation certificate code required by §141.95(b)(8).

(b) The records required to be maintained in a student's logbook will not suffice for the record required by paragraph (a) of this section.

(c) Whenever a student graduates, terminates training, or transfers to another school, the student's record must be certified to that effect by the chief instructor.

(d) The holder of a pilot school certificate or a provisional pilot school certificate must retain each student record required by this section for at least 1 year from the date that the student:

(1) Graduates from the course to which the record pertains;

(2) Terminates enrollment in the course to which the record pertains; or

(3) Transfers to another school.

(e) The holder of a pilot school certificate or a provisional pilot school certificate must make a copy of the student's training record available upon request by the student.

[Docket No. 25910, 62 FR 16347, April 4, 1997; as amended by Amdt. 141–9, 62 FR 40908, July 30, 1997; Amdt 141–15, 76 FR 54108, Aug. 31, 2011]

APPENDIX A TO PART 141
RECREATIONAL PILOT CERTIFICATION COURSE

1. *Applicability.* This appendix prescribes the minimum curriculum required for a recreational pilot certification course under this part, for the following ratings:

(a) Airplane single-engine.

(b) Rotorcraft helicopter.

(c) Rotorcraft gyroplane.

2. *Eligibility for enrollment.* A person must hold a student pilot certificate prior to enrolling in the flight portion of the recreational pilot certification course.

3. *Aeronautical knowledge training.* Each approved course must include at least 20 hours of ground training on the following aeronautical knowledge areas, appropriate to the aircraft category and class for which the course applies:

(a) Applicable Federal Aviation Regulations for recreational pilot privileges, limitations, and flight operations;

(b) Accident reporting requirements of the National Transportation Safety Board;

(c) Applicable subjects in the "Aeronautical Information Manual" and the appropriate FAA advisory circulars;

(d) Use of aeronautical charts for VFR navigation using pilotage with the aid of a magnetic compass;

(e) Recognition of critical weather situations from the ground and in flight, windshear avoidance, and the procurement and use of aeronautical weather reports and forecasts;

(f) Safe and efficient operation of aircraft, including collision avoidance, and recognition and avoidance of wake turbulence;

(g) Effects of density altitude on takeoff and climb performance;

(h) Weight and balance computations;

(i) Principles of aerodynamics, powerplants, and aircraft systems;

(j) Stall awareness, spin entry, spins, and spin recovery techniques, if applying for an airplane single-engine rating;

(k) Aeronautical decision making and judgment; and

(l) Preflight action that includes—

(1) How to obtain information on runway lengths at airports of intended use, data on takeoff and landing distances, weather reports and forecasts, and fuel requirements; and

(2) How to plan for alternatives if the planned flight cannot be completed or delays are encountered.

4. *Flight training.*

(a) Each approved course must include at least 30 hours of flight training (of which 15 hours must be with a certificated flight instructor and 3 hours must be solo flight training as provided in section No. 5 of this appendix) on the approved areas of operation listed in paragraph (c) of this section that are appropriate to the aircraft category and class rating for which the course applies, including:

(1) Except as provided in §61.100 of this chapter, 2 hours of dual flight training to and at an airport that is located more than 25 nautical miles from the airport where the applicant normally trains, with at least three takeoffs and three landings; and

(2) 3 hours of dual flight training in an aircraft that is appropriate to the aircraft category and class for which the course applies, in preparation

for the practical test within 60 days preceding the date of the test.

(b) Each training flight must include a preflight briefing and a postflight critique of the student by the flight instructor assigned to that flight.

(c) Flight training must include the following approved areas of operation appropriate to the aircraft category and class rating—

(1) *For an airplane single-engine course:*
(i) Preflight preparation;
(ii) Preflight procedures;
(iii) Airport operations;
(iv) Takeoffs, landings, and go-arounds;
(v) Performance maneuvers;
(vi) Ground reference maneuvers;
(vii) Navigation;
(viii) Slow flight and stalls;
(ix) Emergency operations; and
(x) Postflight procedures.

(2) *For a rotorcraft helicopter course:*
(i) Preflight preparation;
(ii) Preflight procedures;
(iii) Airport and heliport operations;
(iv) Hovering maneuvers;
(v) Takeoffs, landings, and go-arounds;
(vi) Performance maneuvers;
(vii) Navigation;
(viii) Emergency operations; and
(ix) Postflight procedures.

(3) *For a rotorcraft gyroplane course:*
(i) Preflight preparation;
(ii) Preflight procedures;
(iii) Airport operations;
(iv) Takeoffs, landings, and go-arounds;
(v) Performance maneuvers;
(vi) Ground reference maneuvers;
(vii) Navigation;
(viii) Flight at slow airspeeds;
(ix) Emergency operations; and
(x) Postflight procedures.

5. *Solo flight training.* Each approved course must include at least 3 hours of solo flight training on the approved areas of operation listed in paragraph (c) of section No. 4 of this appendix that are appropriate to the aircraft category and class rating for which the course applies.

6. *Stage checks and end-of-course tests.*
(a) Each student enrolled in a recreational pilot course must satisfactorily accomplish the stage checks and end-of-course tests, in accordance with the school's approved training course, consisting of the approved areas of operation listed in paragraph (c) of section No. 4 of this appendix that are appropriate to the aircraft category and class rating for which the course applies.

(b) Each student must demonstrate satisfactory proficiency prior to receiving an endorsement to operate an aircraft in solo flight.

[Docket No. 25910, 62 FR 16347, April 4, 1997; as amended by Amdt. 141–9, 62 FR 40908, July 30, 1997]

APPENDIX B TO PART 141
PRIVATE PILOT CERTIFICATION COURSE

1. *Applicability.* This appendix prescribes the minimum curriculum for a private pilot certification course required under this part, for the following ratings:
(a) Airplane single-engine.
(b) Airplane multiengine.
(c) Rotorcraft helicopter.
(d) Rotorcraft gyroplane.
(e) Powered-lift.
(f) Glider.
(g) Lighter-than-air airship.
(h) Lighter-than-air balloon.

2. *Eligibility for enrollment.* A person must hold either a recreational pilot certificate, sport pilot certificate, or student pilot certificate before enrolling in the solo flight phase of the private pilot certification course.

3. *Aeronautical knowledge training.*
(a) Each approved course must include at least the following ground training on the aeronautical knowledge areas listed in paragraph (b) of this section, appropriate to the aircraft category and class rating:
(1) 35 hours of training if the course is for an airplane, rotorcraft, or powered-lift category rating.
(2) 15 hours of training if the course is for a glider category rating.
(3) 10 hours of training if the course is for a lighter-than-air category with a balloon class rating.
(4) 35 hours of training if the course is for a lighter-than-air category with an airship class rating.
(b) Ground training must include the following aeronautical knowledge areas:
(1) Applicable Federal Aviation Regulations for private pilot privileges, limitations, and flight operations;
(2) Accident reporting requirements of the National Transportation Safety Board;
(3) Applicable subjects of the "Aeronautical Information Manual" and the appropriate FAA advisory circulars;
(4) Aeronautical charts for VFR navigation using pilotage, dead reckoning, and navigation systems;
(5) Radio communication procedures;
(6) Recognition of critical weather situations from the ground and in flight, windshear avoidance, and the procurement and use of aeronautical weather reports and forecasts;

141

(7) Safe and efficient operation of aircraft, including collision avoidance, and recognition and avoidance of wake turbulence;

(8) Effects of density altitude on takeoff and climb performance;

(9) Weight and balance computations;

(10) Principles of aerodynamics, powerplants, and aircraft systems;

(11) If the course of training is for an airplane category or glider category rating, stall awareness, spin entry, spins, and spin recovery techniques;

(12) Aeronautical decision making and judgment; and

(13) Preflight action that includes—

(i) How to obtain information on runway lengths at airports of intended use, data on takeoff and landing distances, weather reports and forecasts, and fuel requirements; and

(ii) How to plan for alternatives if the planned flight cannot be completed or delays are encountered.

4. Flight training.

(a) Each approved course must include at least the following flight training, as provided in this section and section No. 5 of this appendix, on the approved areas of operation listed in paragraph (d) of this section, appropriate to the aircraft category and class rating:

(1) 35 hours of training if the course is for an airplane, rotorcraft, powered-lift, or airship rating.

(2) 6 hours of training if the course is for a glider rating.

(3) 8 hours of training if the course is for a balloon rating.

(b) Each approved course must include at least the following flight training:

(1) *For an airplane single-engine course:* 20 hours of flight training from a certificated flight instructor on the approved areas of operation in paragraph (d)(1) of this section that includes at least—

(i) Except as provided in §61.111 of this chapter, 3 hours of cross-country flight training in a single-engine airplane;

(ii) 3 hours of night flight training in a single-engine airplane that includes—

(A) One cross-country flight of more than 100-nautical-miles total distance; and

(B) 10 takeoffs and 10 landings to a full stop (with each landing involving a flight in the traffic pattern) at an airport.

(iii) Three hours of flight training in a single engine airplane on the control and maneuvering of a single engine airplane solely by reference to instruments, including straight and level flight, constant airspeed climbs and descents, turns to a heading, recovery from unusual flight attitudes, radio communications, and the use of navigation systems/facilities and radar services appropriate to instrument flight; and

(iv) 3 hours of flight training in a single-engine airplane in preparation for the practical test within 60 days preceding the date of the test.

(2) *For an airplane multiengine course:* 20 hours of flight training from a certificated flight instructor on the approved areas of operation in paragraph (d)(2) of this section that includes at least—

(i) Except as provided in §61.111 of this chapter, 3 hours of cross-country flight training in a multi-engine airplane;

(ii) 3 hours of night flight training in a multiengine airplane that includes—

(A) One cross-country flight of more than 100-nautical-miles total distance; and

(B) 10 takeoffs and 10 landings to a full stop (with each landing involving a flight in the traffic pattern) at an airport.

(iii) Three hours of flight training in a multiengine airplane on the control and maneuvering of a multiengine airplane solely by reference to instruments, including straight and level flight, constant airspeed climbs and descents, turns to a heading, recovery from unusual flight attitudes, radio communications, and the use of navigation systems/facilities and radar services appropriate to instrument flight; and

(iv) 3 hours of flight training in a multiengine airplane in preparation for the practical test within 60 days preceding the date of the test.

(3) *For a rotorcraft helicopter course:* 20 hours of flight training from a certificated flight instructor on the approved areas of operation in paragraph (d)(3) of this section that includes at least—

(i) Except as provided in §61.111 of this chapter, 3 hours of cross-country flight training in a helicopter.

(ii) 3 hours of night flight training in a helicopter that includes—

(A) One cross-country flight of more than 50-nautical-miles total distance; and

(B) 10 takeoffs and 10 landings to a full stop (with each landing involving a flight in the traffic pattern) at an airport.

(iii) 3 hours of flight training in a helicopter in preparation for the practical test within 60 days preceding the date of the test.

(4) *For a rotorcraft gyroplane course:* 20 hours of flight training from a certificated flight instructor on the approved areas of operation in paragraph (d)(4) of this section that includes at least—

(i) Except as provided in §61.111 of this chapter, 3 hours of cross-country flight training in a gyroplane.

(ii) 3 hours of night flight training in a gyroplane that includes—

(A) One cross-country flight over 50-nautical-miles total distance; and

(B) 10 takeoffs and 10 landings to a full stop (with each landing involving a flight in the traffic pattern) at an airport.

(iii) 3 hours of flight training in a gyroplane in preparation for the practical test within 60 days preceding the date of the test.

(5) *For a powered-lift course:* 20 hours of flight training from a certificated flight instructor on the approved areas of operation in paragraph (d)(5) of this section that includes at least—

(i) Except as provided in §61.111 of this chapter, 3 hours of cross-country flight training in a powered-lift;

(ii) 3 hours of night flight training in a powered-lift that includes—

(A) One cross-country flight of more than 100-nautical-miles total distance; and

(B) 10 takeoffs and 10 landings to a full stop (with each landing involving a flight in the traffic pattern) at an airport.

(iii) Three hours of flight training in a powered-lift on the control and maneuvering of a powered-lift solely by reference to instruments, including straight and level flight, constant airspeed climbs and descents, turns to a heading, recovery from unusual flight attitudes, radio communications, and the use of navigation systems/facilities and radar services appropriate to instrument flight; and

(iv) 3 hours of flight training in a powered-lift in preparation for the practical test, within 60 days preceding the date of the test.

(6) *For a glider course:* 4 hours of flight training from a certificated flight instructor on the approved areas of operation in paragraph (d)(6) of this section that includes at least—

(i) Five training flights in a glider with a certificated flight instructor on the launch/tow procedures approved for the course and on the appropriate approved areas of operation listed in paragraph (d)(6) of this section; and

(ii) Three training flights in a glider with a certificated flight instructor in preparation for the practical test within 60 days preceding the date of the test.

(7) *For a lighter-than-air airship course:* 20 hours of flight training from a commercial pilot with an airship rating on the approved areas of operation in paragraph (d)(7) of this section that includes at least—

(i) Except as provided in §61.111 of this chapter, 3 hours of cross-country flight training in an airship;

(ii) 3 hours of night flight training in an airship that includes—

(A) One cross-country flight over 25-nautical-miles total distance; and

(B) Five takeoffs and five landings to a full stop (with each landing involving a flight in the traffic pattern) at an airport.

(iii) 3 hours of instrument training in an airship; and

(iv) 3 hours of flight training in an airship in preparation for the practical test within 60 days preceding the date of the test.

(8) *For a lighter-than-air balloon course:* 8 hours of flight training, including at least five training flights, from a commercial pilot with a balloon rating on the approved areas of operation in paragraph (d)(8) of this section, that includes—

(i) If the training is being performed in a gas balloon—

(A) Two flights of 1 hour each;

(B) One flight involving a controlled ascent to 3,000 feet above the launch site; and

(C) Two flights in preparation for the practical test within 60 days preceding the date of the test.

(ii) If the training is being performed in a balloon with an airborne heater—

(A) Two flights of 30 minutes each;

(B) One flight involving a controlled ascent to 2,000 feet above the launch site; and

(C) Two flights in preparation for the practical test within 60 days preceding the date of the test.

(c) For use of full flight simulators or flight training devices:

(1) The course may include training in a full flight simulator or flight training device, provided it is representative of the aircraft for which the course is approved, meets the requirements of this paragraph, and the training is given by an authorized instructor.

(2) Training in a full flight simulator that meets the requirements of §141.41(a) may be credited for a maximum of 20 percent of the total flight training hour requirements of the approved course, or of this section, whichever is less.

(3) Training in a flight training device that meets the requirements of §141.41(a) may be credited for a maximum of 15 percent of the total flight training hour requirements of the approved course, or of this section, whichever is less.

(4) Training in full flight simulators or flight training devices described in paragraphs (c)(2) and (3) of this section, if used in combination, may be credited for a maximum of 20 percent of the total flight training hour requirements of the approved course, or of this section, whichever is less. However, credit for training in a flight training device that meets the requirements of §141.41(a) cannot exceed the limitation provided for in paragraph (c)(3) of this section.

(d) Each approved course must include the flight training on the approved areas of operation listed in this paragraph that are appropriate to the aircraft category and class rating—

(1) *For a single-engine airplane course:*
(i) Preflight preparation;
(ii) Preflight procedures;
(iii) Airport and seaplane base operations;

(iv) Takeoffs, landings, and go-arounds;
(v) Performance maneuvers;
(vi) Ground reference maneuvers;
(vii) Navigation;
(viii) Slow flight and stalls;
(ix) Basic instrument maneuvers;
(x) Emergency operations;
(xi) Night operations, and
(xii) Postflight procedures.

(2) *For a multiengine airplane course:*
(i) Preflight preparation;
(ii) Preflight procedures;
(iii) Airport and seaplane base operations;
(iv) Takeoffs, landings, and go-arounds;
(v) Performance maneuvers;
(vi) Ground reference maneuvers;
(vii) Navigation;
(viii) Slow flight and stalls;
(ix) Basic instrument maneuvers;
(x) Emergency operations;
(xi) Multiengine operations;
(xii) Night operations; and
(xiii) Postflight procedures.

(3) *For a rotorcraft helicopter course:*
(i) Preflight preparation;
(ii) Preflight procedures;
(iii) Airport and heliport operations;
(iv) Hovering maneuvers;
(v) Takeoffs, landings, and go-arounds;
(vi) Performance maneuvers;
(vii) Navigation;
(viii) Emergency operations;
(ix) Night operations; and
(x) Postflight procedures.

(4) *For a rotorcraft gyroplane course:*
(i) Preflight preparation;
(ii) Preflight procedures;
(iii) Airport operations;
(iv) Takeoffs, landings, and go-arounds;
(v) Performance maneuvers;
(vi) Ground reference maneuvers;
(vii) Navigation;
(viii) Flight at slow airspeeds;
(ix) Emergency operations;
(x) Night operations; and
(xi) Postflight procedures.

(5) *For a powered-lift course:*
(i) Preflight preparation;
(ii) Preflight procedures;
(iii) Airport and heliport operations;
(iv) Hovering maneuvers;
(v) Takeoffs, landings, and go-arounds;
(vi) Performance maneuvers;
(vii) Ground reference maneuvers;
(viii) Navigation;
(ix) Slow flight and stalls;
(x) Basic instrument maneuvers;
(xi) Emergency operations;
(xii) Night operations; and

(xiii) Postflight procedures.

(6) *For a glider course:*
(i) Preflight preparation;
(ii) Preflight procedures;
(iii) Airport and gliderport operations;
(iv) Launches/tows, as appropriate, and landings;
(v) Performance speeds;
(vi) Soaring techniques;
(vii) Performance maneuvers;
(viii) Navigation;
(ix) Slow flight and stalls;
(x) Emergency operations; and
(xi) Postflight procedures.

(7) *For a lighter-than-air airship course:*
(i) Preflight preparation;
(ii) Preflight procedures;
(iii) Airport operations;
(iv) Takeoffs, landings, and go-arounds;
(v) Performance maneuvers;
(vi) Ground reference maneuvers;
(vii) Navigation;
(viii) Emergency operations; and
(ix) Postflight procedures.

(8) *For a lighter-than-air balloon course:*
(i) Preflight preparation;
(ii) Preflight procedures;
(iii) Airport operations;
(iv) Launches and landings;
(v) Performance maneuvers;
(vi) Navigation;
(vii) Emergency operations; and
(viii) Postflight procedures.

5. *Solo flight training.* Each approved course must include at least the following solo flight training:

(a) *For an airplane single-engine course:* 5 hours of solo flight training in a single-engine airplane on the approved areas of operation in paragraph (d)(1) of section No. 4 of this appendix that includes at least—

(1) One solo 100 nautical miles cross country flight with landings at a minimum of three points and one segment of the flight consisting of a straight-line distance of more than 50 nautical miles between the takeoff and landing locations; and

(2) Three takeoffs and three landings to a full stop (with each landing involving a flight in the traffic pattern) at an airport with an operating control tower.

(b) *For an airplane multiengine course:* 5 hours of flight training in a multiengine airplane performing the duties of a pilot in command while under the supervision of a certificated flight instructor. The training must consist of the approved areas of operation in paragraph (d)(2) of section No. 4 of this appendix, and include at least—

(1) One 100 nautical miles cross country flight with landings at a minimum of three points and one segment of the flight consisting of a straight-line distance of more than 50 nautical miles between the takeoff and landing locations; and

(2) Three takeoffs and three landings to a full stop (with each landing involving a flight in the traffic pattern) at an airport with an operating control tower.

(c) *For a rotorcraft helicopter course:* 5 hours of solo flight training in a helicopter on the approved areas of operation in paragraph (d)(3) of section No. 4 of this appendix that includes at least—

(1) One solo 100 nautical miles cross country flight with landings at a minimum of three points and one segment of the flight consisting of a straight-line distance of more than 25 nautical miles between the takeoff and landing locations; and

(2) Three takeoffs and three landings to a full stop (with each landing involving a flight in the traffic pattern) at an airport with an operating control tower.

(d) *For a rotorcraft gyroplane course:* 5 hours of solo flight training in gyroplanes on the approved areas of operation in paragraph (d)(4) of section No. 4 of this appendix that includes at least—

(1) One solo 100 nautical miles cross country flight with landings at a minimum of three points and one segment of the flight consisting of a straight-line distance of more than 25 nautical miles between the takeoff and landing locations; and

(2) Three takeoffs and three landings to a full stop (with each landing involving a flight in the traffic pattern) at an airport with an operating control tower.

(e) *For a powered-lift course:* 5 hours of solo flight training in a powered-lift on the approved areas of operation in paragraph (d)(5) of section No. 4 of this appendix that includes at least—

(1) One solo 100 nautical miles cross country flight with landings at a minimum of three points and one segment of the flight consisting of a straight-line distance of more than 50 nautical miles between the takeoff and landing locations; and

(2) Three takeoffs and three landings to a full stop (with each landing involving a flight in the traffic pattern) at an airport with an operating control tower.

(f) *For a glider course:* Two solo flights in a glider on the approved areas of operation in paragraph (d)(6) of section No. 4 of this appendix, and the launch and tow procedures appropriate for the approved course.

(g) *For a lighter-than-air airship course:* 5 hours of flight training in an airship performing the duties of pilot in command while under the supervision

of a commercial pilot with an airship rating. The training must consist of the approved areas of operation in paragraph (d)(7) of section No. 4 of this appendix.

(h) *For a lighter-than-air balloon course:* Two solo flights in a balloon with an airborne heater if the course involves a balloon with an airborne heater, or, if the course involves a gas balloon, at least two flights in a gas balloon performing the duties of pilot in command while under the supervision of a commercial pilot with a balloon rating. The training must consist of the approved areas of operation in paragraph (d)(8) of section No. 4 of this appendix, in the kind of balloon for which the course applies.

6. *Stage checks and end-of-course tests.*

(a) Each student enrolled in a private pilot course must satisfactorily accomplish the stage checks and end-of-course tests in accordance with the school's approved training course, consisting of the approved areas of operation listed in paragraph (d) of section No. 4 of this appendix that are appropriate to the aircraft category and class rating for which the course applies.

(b) Each student must demonstrate satisfactory proficiency prior to receiving an endorsement to operate an aircraft in solo flight.

[Docket No. 25910, 62 FR 16347, April 4, 1997; as amended by Amdt. 141–9, 62 FR 40908, July 30, 1997; Amdt. No. 141–10, 63 FR 20289, April 23, 1998; Amdt. 141–12, 74 FR 42564, Aug. 21, 2009; Amdt. 141–18, 81 FR 21460, April 12, 2016]

APPENDIX C TO PART 141
INSTRUMENT RATING COURSE

1. *Applicability.* This appendix prescribes the minimum curriculum for an instrument rating course and an additional instrument rating course, required under this part, for the following ratings:

(a) Instrument—airplane.

(b) Instrument—helicopter.

(c) Instrument—powered-lift.

2. *Eligibility for enrollment.* A person must hold at least a private pilot certificate with an aircraft category and class rating appropriate to the instrument rating for which the course applies prior to enrolling in the flight portion of the instrument rating course.

3. *Aeronautical knowledge training.*

(a) Each approved course must include at least the following ground training on the aeronautical knowledge areas listed in paragraph (b) of this section appropriate to the instrument rating for which the course applies:

(1) 30 hours of training if the course is for an initial instrument rating.

141

(2) 20 hours of training if the course is for an additional instrument rating.

(b) Ground training must include the following aeronautical knowledge areas:

(1) Applicable Federal Aviation Regulations for IFR flight operations;

(2) Appropriate information in the "Aeronautical Information Manual";

(3) Air traffic control system and procedures for instrument flight operations;

(4) IFR navigation and approaches by use of navigation systems;

(5) Use of IFR en route and instrument approach procedure charts;

(6) Procurement and use of aviation weather reports and forecasts, and the elements of forecasting weather trends on the basis of that information and personal observation of weather conditions;

(7) Safe and efficient operation of aircraft under instrument flight rules and conditions;

(8) Recognition of critical weather situations and windshear avoidance;

(9) Aeronautical decision making and judgment; and

(10) Crew resource management, to include crew communication and coordination.

4. *Flight training.*

(a) Each approved course must include at least the following flight training on the approved areas of operation listed in paragraph (d) of this section, appropriate to the instrument-aircraft category and class rating for which the course applies:

(1) 35 hours of instrument training if the course is for an initial instrument rating.

(2) 15 hours of instrument training if the course is for an additional instrument rating.

(b) For the use of full flight simulators, flight training devices, or aviation training devices—

(1) The course may include training in a full flight simulator, flight training device, or aviation training device, provided it is representative of the aircraft for which the course is approved, meets the requirements of this paragraph, and the training is given by an authorized instructor.

(2) Credit for training in a full flight simulator that meets the requirements of §141.41(a) cannot exceed 50 percent of the total flight training hour requirements of the course or of this section, whichever is less.

(3) Credit for training in a flight training device that meets the requirements of §141.41(a), an advanced aviation training device that meets the requirements of §141.41(b), or a combination of these devices cannot exceed 40 percent of the total flight training hour requirements of the course or of this section, whichever is less. Credit for training in a basic aviation training device that meets the requirements of §141.41(b) cannot

exceed 25 percent of the total training hour requirements permitted under this paragraph.

(4) Credit for training in full flight simulators, flight training devices, and aviation training devices if used in combination, cannot exceed 50 percent of the total flight training hour requirements of the course or of this section, whichever is less. However, credit for training in a flight training device or aviation training device cannot exceed the limitation provided for in paragraph (b)(3) of this section.

(c) Each approved course must include the following flight training—

(1) For an instrument airplane course: Instrument training time from a certificated flight instructor with an instrument rating on the approved areas of operation in paragraph (d) of this section including at least one cross-country flight that—

(i) Is in the category and class of airplane that the course is approved for, and is performed under IFR;

(ii) Is a distance of at least 250 nautical miles along airways or ATC-directed routing with one segment of the flight consisting of at least a straight-line distance of 100 nautical miles between airports;

(iii) Involves an instrument approach at each airport; and

(iv) Involves three different kinds of approaches with the use of navigation systems.

(2) For an instrument helicopter course: Instrument training time from a certificated flight instructor with an instrument rating on the approved areas of operation in paragraph (d) of this section including at least one cross-country flight that—

(i) Is in a helicopter and is performed under IFR;

(ii) Is a distance of at least 100 nautical miles along airways or ATC-directed routing with one segment of the flight consisting of at least a straight-line distance of 50 nautical miles between airports;

(iii) Involves an instrument approach at each airport; and

(iv) Involves three different kinds of approaches with the use of navigation systems.

(3) For an instrument powered-lift course: Instrument training time from a certificated flight instructor with an instrument rating on the approved areas of operation in paragraph (d) of this section including at least one cross-country flight that—

(i) Is in a powered-lift and is performed under IFR;

(ii) Is a distance of at least 250 nautical miles along airways or ATC-directed routing with one segment of the flight consisting of at least a straight-line distance of 100 nautical miles between airports;

(iii) Involves an instrument approach at each airport; and

(iv) Involves three different kinds of approaches with the use of navigation systems.

(d) Each course must include flight training on the areas of operation listed under this paragraph appropriate to the instrument aircraft category and class rating (if a class rating is appropriate) for which the course applies:

(1) Preflight preparation;

(2) Preflight procedures;

(3) Air traffic control clearances and procedures;

(4) Flight by reference to instruments;

(5) Navigation systems;

(6) Instrument approach procedures;

(7) Emergency operations; and

(8) Postflight procedures.

5. *Stage checks and end-of-course tests.*

Each student enrolled in an instrument rating course must satisfactorily accomplish the stage checks and end-of-course tests, in accordance with the school's approved training course, consisting of the approved areas of operation listed in paragraph (d) of section No. 4 of this appendix that are appropriate to the aircraft category and class rating for which the course applies.

[Docket No. 25910, 62 FR 16347, April 4, 1997; as amended by Amdt. 141–9, 62 FR 40909, July 30, 1997; Amdt. 141–12, 74 FR 42564, Aug. 21, 2009; Amdt. 141–18, 81 FR 21460, April 12, 2016]

APPENDIX D TO PART 141
COMMERCIAL PILOT CERTIFICATION COURSE

1. *Applicability.* This appendix prescribes the minimum curriculum for a commercial pilot certification course required under this part, for the following ratings:

(a) Airplane single-engine.

(b) Airplane multiengine.

(c) Rotorcraft helicopter.

(d) Rotorcraft gyroplane.

(e) Powered-lift.

(f) Glider.

(g) Lighter-than-air airship.

(h) Lighter-than-air balloon.

2. *Eligibility for enrollment.* A person must hold the following prior to enrolling in the flight portion of the commercial pilot certification course:

(a) At least a private pilot certificate; and

(b) If the course is for a rating in an airplane or a powered-lift category, then the person must:

(1) Hold an instrument rating in the aircraft that is appropriate to the aircraft category rating for which the course applies; or

(2) Be concurrently enrolled in an instrument rating course that is appropriate to the aircraft

category rating for which the course applies, and pass the required instrument rating practical test prior to completing the commercial pilot certification course.

3. *Aeronautical knowledge training.*

(a) Each approved course must include at least the following ground training on the aeronautical knowledge areas listed in paragraph (b) of this section, appropriate to the aircraft category and class rating for which the course applies:

(1) 35 hours of training if the course is for an airplane category rating or a powered-lift category rating.

(2) 65 hours of training if the course is for a lighter-than-air category with an airship class rating.

(3) 30 hours of training if the course is for a rotorcraft category rating.

(4) 20 hours of training if the course is for a glider category rating.

(5) 20 hours of training if the course is for lighter-than-air category with a balloon class rating.

(b) Ground training must include the following aeronautical knowledge areas:

(1) Federal Aviation Regulations that apply to commercial pilot privileges, limitations, and flight operations;

(2) Accident reporting requirements of the National Transportation Safety Board;

(3) Basic aerodynamics and the principles of flight;

(4) Meteorology, to include recognition of critical weather situations, windshear recognition and avoidance, and the use of aeronautical weather reports and forecasts;

(5) Safe and efficient operation of aircraft;

(6) Weight and balance computations;

(7) Use of performance charts;

(8) Significance and effects of exceeding aircraft performance limitations;

(9) Use of aeronautical charts and a magnetic compass for pilotage and dead reckoning;

(10) Use of air navigation facilities;

(11) Aeronautical decision making and judgment;

(12) Principles and functions of aircraft systems;

(13) Maneuvers, procedures, and emergency operations appropriate to the aircraft;

(14) Night and high-altitude operations;

(15) Descriptions of and procedures for operating within the National Airspace System; and

(16) Procedures for flight and ground training for lighter-than-air ratings.

4. *Flight training.*

(a) Each approved course must include at least the following flight training, as provided in this section and section No. 5 of this appendix, on the approved areas of operation listed in paragraph (d) of this section that are appropriate to

141

the aircraft category and class rating for which the course applies:

(1) 120 hours of training if the course is for an airplane or powered-lift rating.

(2) 155 hours of training if the course is for an airship rating.

(3) 115 hours of training if the course is for a rotorcraft rating.

(4) 6 hours of training if the course is for a glider rating.

(5) 10 hours of training and 8 training flights if the course is for a balloon rating.

(b) Each approved course must include at least the following flight training:

(1) *For an airplane single-engine course:* 55 hours of flight training from a certificated flight instructor on the approved areas of operation listed in paragraph (d)(1) of this section that includes at least—

(i) Ten hours of instrument training using a view-limiting device including attitude instrument flying, partial panel skills, recovery from unusual flight attitudes, and intercepting and tracking navigational systems. Five hours of the 10 hours required on instrument training must be in a single engine airplane;

(ii) Ten hours of training in a complex airplane, a turbine-powered airplane, or a technically advanced airplane that meets the requirements of §61.129(j) of this chapter, or any combination thereof. The airplane must be appropriate to land or sea for the rating sought;

(iii) One 2-hour cross country flight in daytime conditions in a single engine airplane that consists of a total straight-line distance of more than 100 nautical miles from the original point of departure;

(iv) One 2-hour cross country flight in nighttime conditions in a single engine airplane that consists of a total straight-line distance of more than 100 nautical miles from the original point of departure; and

(v) 3 hours in a single-engine airplane in preparation for the practical test within 60 days preceding the date of the test.

(2) *For an airplane multiengine course:* 55 hours of flight training from a certificated flight instructor on the approved areas of operation listed in paragraph (d)(2) of this section that includes at least—

(i) Ten hours of instrument training using a view-limiting device including attitude instrument flying, partial panel skills, recovery from unusual flight attitudes, and intercepting and tracking navigational systems. Five hours of the 10 hours required on instrument training must be in a multiengine airplane;

(ii) 10 hours of training in a multiengine complex or turbine-powered airplane, or any combination thereof;

(iii) One 2-hour cross country flight in daytime conditions in a multiengine airplane that consists of a total straight-line distance of more than 100 nautical miles from the original point of departure;

(iv) One 2-hour cross country flight in nighttime conditions in a multiengine airplane that consists of a total straight-line distance of more than 100 nautical miles from the original point of departure; and

(v) 3 hours in a multiengine airplane in preparation for the practical test within 60 days preceding the date of the test.

(3) *For a rotorcraft helicopter course:* 30 hours of flight training from a certificated flight instructor on the approved areas of operation listed in paragraph (d)(3) of this section that includes at least—

(i) Five hours on the control and maneuvering of a helicopter solely by reference to instruments, including using a view-limiting device for attitude instrument flying, partial panel skills, recovery from unusual flight attitudes, and intercepting and tracking navigational systems. This aeronautical experience may be performed in an aircraft, full flight simulator, flight training device, or an aviation training device;

(ii) One 2-hour cross country flight in daytime conditions in a helicopter that consists of a total straight-line distance of more than 50 nautical miles from the original point of departure;

(iii) One 2-hour cross country flight in nighttime conditions in a helicopter that consists of a total straight-line distance of more than 50 nautical miles from the original point of departure; and

(iv) 3 hours in a helicopter in preparation for the practical test within 60 days preceding the date of the test.

(4) *For a rotorcraft gyroplane course:* 30 hours of flight training from a certificated flight instructor on the approved areas of operation listed in paragraph (d)(4) of this section that includes at least—

(i) 2.5 hours on the control and maneuvering of a gyroplane solely by reference to instruments, including using a view-limiting device for attitude instrument flying, partial panel skills, recovery from unusual flight attitudes, and intercepting and tracking navigational systems. This aeronautical experience may be performed in an aircraft, full flight simulator, flight training device, or an aviation training device;

(ii) One 2-hour cross country flight in daytime conditions in a gyroplane that consists of a total straight-line distance of more than 50 nautical miles from the original point of departure;

(iii) Two hours of flight training in nighttime conditions in a gyroplane at an airport, that includes 10 takeoffs and 10 landings to a full stop (with each landing involving a flight in the traffic pattern); and

(iv) 3 hours in a gyroplane in preparation for the practical test within 60 days preceding the date of the test.

(5) *For a powered-lift course:* 55 hours of flight training from a certificated flight instructor on the approved areas of operation listed in paragraph (d)(5) of this section that includes at least—

(i) Ten hours of instrument training using a view-limiting device including attitude instrument flying, partial panel skills, recovery from unusual flight attitudes, and intercepting and tracking navigational systems. Five hours of the 10 hours required on instrument training must be in a powered-lift;

(ii) One 2-hour cross country flight in daytime conditions in a powered-lift that consists of a total straight-line distance of more than 100 nautical miles from the original point of departure;

(iii) One 2-hour cross country flight in nighttime conditions in a powered-lift that consists of a total straight-line distance of more than 100 nautical miles from the original point of departure; and

(iv) 3 hours in a powered-lift in preparation for the practical test within 60 days preceding the date of the test.

(6) *For a glider course:* 4 hours of flight training from a certificated flight instructor on the approved areas of operation in paragraph (d)(6) of this section, that includes at least—

(i) Five training flights in a glider with a certificated flight instructor on the launch/tow procedures approved for the course and on the appropriate approved areas of operation listed in paragraph (d)(6) of this section; and

(ii) Three training flights in a glider with a certificated flight instructor in preparation for the practical test within 60 days preceding the date of the test.

(7) *For a lighter-than-air airship course:* 55 hours of flight training in airships from a commercial pilot with an airship rating on the approved areas of operation in paragraph (d)(7) of this section that includes at least—

(i) Three hours of instrument training in an airship, including using a view-limiting device for attitude instrument flying, partial panel skills, recovery from unusual flight attitudes, and intercepting and tracking navigational systems;

(ii) One hour cross country flight in daytime conditions in an airship that consists of a total straight-line distance of more than 25 nautical miles from the original point of departure;

(iii) One hour cross country flight in nighttime conditions in an airship that consists of a total straight-line distance of more than 25 nautical miles from the original point of departure; and

(iv) 3 hours in an airship, in preparation for the practical test within 60 days preceding the date of the test.

(8) *For a lighter-than-air balloon course:* Flight training from a commercial pilot with a balloon rating on the approved areas of operation in paragraph (d)(8) of this section that includes at least—

(i) If the course involves training in a gas balloon:

(A) Two flights of 1 hour each;

(B) One flight involving a controlled ascent to at least 5,000 feet above the launch site; and

(C) Two flights in preparation for the practical test within 60 days preceding the date of the test.

(ii) If the course involves training in a balloon with an airborne heater:

(A) Two flights of 30 minutes each;

(B) One flight involving a controlled ascent to at least 3,000 feet above the launch site; and

(C) Two flights in preparation for the practical test within 60 days preceding the date of the test.

(c) For the use of full flight simulators or flight training devices:

(1) The course may include training in a full flight simulator or flight training device, provided it is representative of the aircraft for which the course is approved, meets the requirements of this paragraph, and is given by an authorized instructor.

(2) Training in a full flight simulator that meets the requirements of §141.41(a) may be credited for a maximum of 30 percent of the total flight training hour requirements of the approved course, or of this section, whichever is less.

(3) Training in a flight training device that meets the requirements of §141.41(a) may be credited for a maximum of 20 percent of the total flight training hour requirements of the approved course, or of this section, whichever is less.

(4) Training in the flight training devices described in paragraphs (c)(2) and (3) of this section, if used in combination, may be credited for a maximum of 30 percent of the total flight training hour requirements of the approved course, or of this section, whichever is less. However, credit for training in a flight training device that meets the requirements of §141.41(a) cannot exceed the limitation provided for in paragraph (c)(3) of this section.

(d) Each approved course must include the flight training on the approved areas of operation listed in this paragraph that are appropriate to the aircraft category and class rating—

(1) *For an airplane single-engine course:*
(i) Preflight preparation;
(ii) Preflight procedures;
(iii) Airport and seaplane base operations;
(iv) Takeoffs, landings, and go-arounds;
(v) Performance maneuvers;
(vi) Navigation;
(vii) Slow flight and stalls;
(viii) Emergency operations;

(ix) High-altitude operations; and
(x) Postflight procedures.

(2) *For an airplane multiengine course:*
(i) Preflight preparation;
(ii) Preflight procedures;
(iii) Airport and seaplane base operations;
(iv) Takeoffs, landings, and go-arounds;
(v) Performance maneuvers;
(vi) Navigation;
(vii) Slow flight and stalls;
(viii) Emergency operations;
(ix) Multiengine operations;
(x) High-altitude operations; and
(xi) Postflight procedures.

(3) *For a rotorcraft helicopter course:*
(i) Preflight preparation;
(ii) Preflight procedures;
(iii) Airport and heliport operations;
(iv) Hovering maneuvers;
(v) Takeoffs, landings, and go-arounds;
(vi) Performance maneuvers;
(vii) Navigation;
(viii) Emergency operations;
(ix) Special operations; and
(x) Postflight procedures.

(4) *For a rotorcraft gyroplane course:*
(i) Preflight preparation;
(ii) Preflight procedures;
(iii) Airport operations;
(iv) Takeoffs, landings, and go-arounds;
(v) Performance maneuvers;
(vi) Ground reference maneuvers;
(vii) Navigation;
(viii) Flight at slow airspeeds;
(ix) Emergency operations; and
(x) Postflight procedures.

(5) *For a powered-lift course:*
(i) Preflight preparation;
(ii) Preflight procedures;
(iii) Airport and heliport operations;
(iv) Hovering maneuvers;
(v) Takeoffs, landings, and go-arounds;
(vi) Performance maneuvers;
(vii) Navigation;
(viii) Slow flight and stalls;
(ix) Emergency operations;
(x) High altitude operations;
(xi) Special operations; and
(xii) Postflight procedures.

(6) *For a glider course:*
(i) Preflight preparation;
(ii) Preflight procedures;
(iii) Airport and gliderport operations;
(iv) Launches/tows, as appropriate, and landings;
(v) Performance speeds;
(vi) Soaring techniques;

(vii) Performance maneuvers;
(viii) Navigation;
(ix) Slow flight and stalls;
(x) Emergency operations; and
(xi) Postflight procedures.

(7) *For a lighter-than-air airship course:*
(i) Fundamentals of instructing;
(ii) Technical subjects;
(iii) Preflight preparation;
(iv) Preflight lessons on a maneuver to be performed in flight;
(v) Preflight procedures;
(vi) Airport operations;
(vii) Takeoffs, landings, and go-arounds;
(viii) Performance maneuvers;
(ix) Navigation;
(x) Emergency operations; and
(xi) Postflight procedures.

(8) *For a lighter-than-air balloon course:*
(i) Fundamentals of instructing;
(ii) Technical subjects;
(iii) Preflight preparation;
(iv) Preflight lesson on a maneuver to be performed in flight;
(v) Preflight procedures;
(vi) Airport operations;
(vii) Launches and landings;
(viii) Performance maneuvers;
(ix) Navigation;
(x) Emergency operations; and
(xi) Postflight procedures.

5. *Solo training.* Each approved course must include at least the following solo flight training:

(a) *For an airplane single engine course.* Ten hours of solo flight time in a single engine airplane, or 10 hours of flight time while performing the duties of pilot in command in a single engine airplane with an authorized instructor on board. The training must consist of the approved areas of operation under paragraph (d)(1) of section 4 of this appendix, and include—

(1) One cross-country flight, if the training is being performed in the State of Hawaii, with landings at a minimum of three points, and one of the segments consisting of a straight-line distance of at least 150 nautical miles;

(2) One cross-country flight, if the training is being performed in a State other than Hawaii, with landings at a minimum of three points, and one segment of the flight consisting of a straight-line distance of at least 250 nautical miles; and

(3) 5 hours in night VFR conditions with 10 takeoffs and 10 landings (with each landing involving a flight with a traffic pattern) at an airport with an operating control tower.

(b) *For an airplane multiengine course.* Ten hours of solo flight time in a multiengine airplane, or 10 hours of flight time while performing the

duties of pilot in command in a multiengine airplane with an authorized instructor on board. The training must consist of the approved areas of operation under paragraph (d)(2) of section 4 of this appendix, and include—

(1) One cross-country flight, if the training is being performed in the State of Hawaii, with landings at a minimum of three points, and one of the segments consisting of a straight-line distance of at least 150 nautical miles;

(2) One cross-country flight, if the training is being performed in a State other than Hawaii, with landings at a minimum of three points and one segment of the flight consisting of straight-line distance of at least 250 nautical miles; and

. (3) 5 hours in night VFR conditions with 10 takeoffs and 10 landings (with each landing involving a flight with a traffic pattern) at an airport with an operating control tower.

(c) *For a rotorcraft helicopter course.* Ten hours of solo flight time in a helicopter, or 10 hours of flight time while performing the duties of pilot in command in a helicopter with an authorized instructor on board. The training must consist of the approved areas of operation under paragraph (d) (3) of section 4 of this appendix, and include—

(1) One cross-country flight with landings at a minimum of three points and one segment of the flight consisting of a straight-line distance of at least 50 nautical miles from the original point of departure; and

(2) 5 hours in night VFR conditions with 10 takeoffs and 10 landings (with each landing involving a flight with a traffic pattern) at an airport with an operating control tower.

(d) *For a rotorcraft–gyroplane course.* Ten hours of solo flight time in a gyroplane, or 10 hours of flight time while performing the duties of pilot in command in a gyroplane with an authorized instructor on board. The training must consist of the approved areas of operation under paragraph (d)(4) of section 4 of this appendix, and include—

(1) One cross-country flight with landings at a minimum of three points, and one segment of the flight consisting of a straight-line distance of at least 50 nautical miles from the original point of departure; and

(2) 5 hours in night VFR conditions with 10 takeoffs and 10 landings (with each landing involving a flight with a traffic pattern) at an airport with an operating control tower.

(e) *For a powered-lift course.* Ten hours of solo flight time in a powered-lift, or 10 hours of flight time while performing the duties of pilot in command in a powered-lift with an authorized instructor on board. The training must consist of the approved areas of operation under paragraph (d)(5) of section No. 4 of this appendix, and include—

(1) One cross-country flight, if the training is being performed in the State of Hawaii, with landings at a minimum of three points, and one segment of the flight consisting of a straight-line distance of at least 150 nautical miles;

(2) One cross-country flight, if the training is being performed in a State other than Hawaii, with landings at a minimum of three points, and one segment of the flight consisting of a straight-line distance of at least 250 nautical miles; and

(3) 5 hours in night VFR conditions with 10 takeoffs and 10 landings (with each landing involving a flight with a traffic pattern) at an airport with an operating control tower.

(f) *For a glider course.* 5 solo flights in a glider on the approved areas of operation in paragraph (d)(6) of section No. 4 of this appendix.

(g) *For a lighter-than-air airship course.* 10 hours of flight training in an airship performing the duties of pilot in command while under the supervision of a commercial pilot with an airship rating. The training must consist of the approved areas of operation in paragraph (d)(7) of section No. 4 of this appendix and include at least—

(1) One cross-country flight with landings at a minimum of three points, and one segment of the flight consisting of a straight-line distance of at least 25 nautical miles from the original point of departure; and

(2) 5 hours in night VFR conditions with 10 takeoffs and 10 landings (with each landing involving a flight with a traffic pattern).

(h) *For a lighter-than-air balloon course.* Two solo flights if the course is for a hot air balloon rating, or, if the course is for a gas balloon rating, at least two flights in a gas balloon, while performing the duties of pilot in command under the supervision of a commercial pilot with a balloon rating. The training shall consist of the approved areas of operation in paragraph (d)(8) of section No. 4 of this appendix, in the kind of balloon for which the course applies.

6. *Stage checks and end-of-course tests.*

(a) Each student enrolled in a commercial pilot course must satisfactorily accomplish the stage checks and end-of-course tests, in accordance with the school's approved training course, consisting of the approved areas of operation listed in paragraph (d) of section No. 4 of this appendix that are appropriate to aircraft category and class rating for which the course applies.

(b) Each student must demonstrate satisfactory proficiency prior to receiving an endorsement to operate an aircraft in solo flight.

[Docket No. 25910, 62 FR 16347, April 4, 1997; as amended by Amdt. 141–9, 62 FR 40909, July 30, 1997; Amdt. No. 141–10, 63 FR 20290, April 23, 1998; Amdt. 141–12, 74 FR 42565, Aug. 21, 2009; Amdt. 141–18, 81 FR 21461, April 12, 2016; Amdt. 141–20, 83 FR 30283, June 27, 2018]

APPENDIX E TO PART 141
AIRLINE TRANSPORT PILOT
CERTIFICATION COURSE

1. Applicability. This appendix prescribes the minimum curriculum for an airline transport pilot certification course under this part, for the following ratings:

(a) Airplane single-engine.

(b) Airplane multiengine.

(c) Rotorcraft helicopter.

(d) Powered-lift.

2. Eligibility for enrollment. Before completing the flight portion of the airline transport pilot certification course, a person must meet the aeronautical experience requirements for an airline transport pilot certificate under part 61, subpart G of this chapter that is appropriate to the aircraft category and class rating for which the course applies, and:

(a) Hold a commercial pilot certificate and an instrument rating, or an airline transport pilot certificate with instrument privileges;

(b) Meet the military experience requirements under §61.73 of this chapter to qualify for a commercial pilot certificate and an instrument rating, if the person is a rated military pilot or former rated military pilot of an Armed Force of the United States; or

(c) Hold either a foreign airline transport pilot license or foreign commercial pilot license and an instrument rating, if the person holds a pilot license issued by a contracting State to the Convention on International Civil Aviation.

3. Aeronautical knowledge areas.

(a) Each approved course must include at least 40 hours of ground training on the aeronautical knowledge areas listed in paragraph (b) of this section, appropriate to the aircraft category and class rating for which the course applies.

(b) Ground training must include the following aeronautical knowledge areas:

(1) Applicable Federal Aviation Regulations of this chapter that relate to airline transport pilot privileges, limitations, and flight operations;

(2) Meteorology, including knowledge of and effects of fronts, frontal characteristics, cloud formations, icing, and upper-air data;

(3) General system of weather and NOTAM collection, dissemination, interpretation, and use;

(4) Interpretation and use of weather charts, maps, forecasts, sequence reports, abbreviations, and symbols;

(5) National Weather Service functions as they pertain to operations in the National Airspace System;

(6) Windshear and microburst awareness, identification, and avoidance;

(7) Principles of air navigation under instrument meteorological conditions in the National Airspace System;

(8) Air traffic control procedures and pilot responsibilities as they relate to en route operations, terminal area and radar operations, and instrument departure and approach procedures;

(9) Aircraft loading; weight and balance; use of charts, graphs, tables, formulas, and computations; and the effects on aircraft performance;

(10) Aerodynamics relating to an aircraft's flight characteristics and performance in normal and abnormal flight regimes;

(11) Human factors;

(12) Aeronautical decision making and judgment; and

(13) Crew resource management to include crew communication and coordination.

4. Flight training.

(a) Each approved course must include at least 25 hours of flight training on the approved areas of operation listed in paragraph (c) of this section appropriate to the aircraft category and class rating for which the course applies. At least 15 hours of this flight training must be instrument flight training.

(b) For the use of full flight simulators or flight training devices—

(1) The course may include training in a full flight simulator or flight training device, provided it is representative of the aircraft for which the course is approved, meets the requirements of this paragraph, and the training is given by an authorized instructor.

(2) Training in a full flight simulator that meets the requirements of §141.41(a) may be credited for a maximum of 50 percent of the total flight training hour requirements of the approved course, or of this section, whichever is less.

(3) Training in a flight training device that meets the requirements of §141.41(a) may be credited for a maximum of 25 percent of the total flight training hour requirements of the approved course, or of this section, whichever is less.

(4) Training in full flight simulators or flight training devices described in paragraphs (b)(2) and (3) of this section, if used in combination, may be credited for a maximum of 50 percent of the total flight training hour requirements of the approved course, or of this section, whichever is less. However, credit for training in a flight training device that meets the requirements of §141.41(a) cannot exceed the limitation provided for in paragraph (b)(3) of this section.

(c) Each approved course must include flight training on the approved areas of operation listed in this paragraph appropriate to the aircraft category and class rating for which the course applies:

(1) Preflight preparation;

(2) Preflight procedures;

(3) Takeoff and departure phase;
(4) In-flight maneuvers;
(5) Instrument procedures;
(6) Landings and approaches to landings;
(7) Normal and abnormal procedures;
(8) Emergency procedures; and
(9) Postflight procedures.

5. *Stage checks and end-of-course tests.*

(a) Each student enrolled in an airline transport pilot course must satisfactorily accomplish the stage checks and end-of-course tests, in accordance with the school's approved training course, consisting of the approved areas of operation listed in paragraph (c) of section No. 4 of this appendix that are appropriate to the aircraft category and class rating for which the course applies.

(b) Each student must demonstrate satisfactory proficiency prior to receiving an endorsement to operate an aircraft in solo flight.

[Docket No. 25910, 62 FR 16347, April 4, 1997; as amended by Amdt. 141–9, 62 FR 40909, July 30, 1997; Amdt. 141–12, 74 FR 42566, Aug. 21, 2009; Amdt. 141–18, 81 FR 21461, April 12, 2016]

APPENDIX F TO PART 141
FLIGHT INSTRUCTOR CERTIFICATION COURSE

1. *Applicability.* This appendix prescribes the minimum curriculum for a flight instructor certification course and an additional flight instructor rating course required under this part, for the following ratings:

(a) Airplane single-engine.
(b) Airplane multiengine.
(c) Rotorcraft helicopter.
(d) Rotorcraft gyroplane.
(e) Powered-lift.
(f) Glider category.

2. *Eligibility for enrollment.* A person must hold the following prior to enrolling in the flight portion of the flight instructor or additional flight instructor rating course:

(a) A commercial pilot certificate or an airline transport pilot certificate, with an aircraft category and class rating appropriate to the flight instructor rating for which the course applies; and

(b) An instrument rating or privilege in an aircraft that is appropriate to the aircraft category and class rating for which the course applies, if the course is for a flight instructor airplane or powered-lift instrument rating.

3. *Aeronautical knowledge training.*

(a) Each approved course must include at least the following ground training in the aeronautical knowledge areas listed in paragraph (b) of this section:

(1) 40 hours of training if the course is for an initial issuance of a flight instructor certificate; or

(2) 20 hours of training if the course is for an additional flight instructor rating.

(b) Ground training must include the following aeronautical knowledge areas:

(1) The fundamentals of instructing including—
(i) The learning process;
(ii) Elements of effective teaching;
(iii) Student evaluation and testing;
(iv) Course development;
(v) Lesson planning; and
(vi) Classroom training techniques.

(2) The aeronautical knowledge areas in which training is required for—

(i) A recreational, private, and commercial pilot certificate that is appropriate to the aircraft category and class rating for which the course applies; and

(ii) An instrument rating that is appropriate to the aircraft category and class rating for which the course applies, if the course is for an airplane or powered-lift aircraft rating.

(c) A student who satisfactorily completes 2 years of study on the principles of education at a college or university may be credited with no more than 20 hours of the training required in paragraph (a)(1) of this section.

4. *Flight training.*

(a) Each approved course must include at least the following flight training on the approved areas of operation of paragraph (c) of this section appropriate to the flight instructor rating for which the course applies:

(1) 25 hours, if the course is for an airplane, rotorcraft, or powered-lift rating; and

(2) 10 hours, which must include 10 flights, if the course is for a glider category rating.

(b) For the use of full flight simulators or flight training devices:

(1) The course may include training in a full flight simulator or flight training device, provided it is representative of the aircraft for which the course is approved, meets the requirements of this paragraph, and the training is given by an authorized instructor.

(2) Training in a full flight simulator that meets the requirements of §141.41(a), may be credited for a maximum of 10 percent of the total flight training hour requirements of the approved course, or of this section, whichever is less.

(3) Training in a flight training device that meets the requirements of §141.41(a), may be credited for a maximum of 5 percent of the total flight training hour requirements of the approved course, or of this section, whichever is less.

(4) Training in full flight simulators or flight training devices described in paragraphs (b)(2) and (3) of this section, if used in combination, may be credited for a maximum of 10 percent of the total flight training hour requirements of the approved course, or of this section, whichever is

less. However, credit for training in a flight training device that meets the requirements of §141.41(a) cannot exceed the limitation provided for in paragraph (b)(3) of this section.

(c) Each approved course must include flight training on the approved areas of operation listed in this paragraph that are appropriate to the aircraft category and class rating for which the course applies—

(1) *For an airplane—single-engine course:*
(i) Fundamentals of instructing;
(ii) Technical subject areas;
(iii) Preflight preparation;
(iv) Preflight lesson on a maneuver to be performed in flight;
(v) Preflight procedures;
(vi) Airport and seaplane base operations;
(vii) Takeoffs, landings, and go-arounds;
(viii) Fundamentals of flight;
(ix) Performance maneuvers;
(x) Ground reference maneuvers;
(xi) Slow flight, stalls, and spins;
(xii) Basic instrument maneuvers;
(xiii) Emergency operations; and
(xiv) Postflight procedures.

(2) *For an airplane—multiengine course:*
(i) Fundamentals of instructing;
(ii) Technical subject areas;
(iii) Preflight preparation;
(iv) Preflight lesson on a maneuver to be performed in flight;
(v) Preflight procedures;
(vi) Airport and seaplane base operations;
(vii) Takeoffs, landings, and go-arounds;
(viii) Fundamentals of flight;
(ix) Performance maneuvers;
(x) Ground reference maneuvers;
(xi) Slow flight and stalls;
(xii) Basic instrument maneuvers;
(xiii) Emergency operations;
(xiv) Multiengine operations; and
(xv) Postflight procedures.

(3) *For a rotorcraft—helicopter course:*
(i) Fundamentals of instructing;
(ii) Technical subject areas;
(iii) Preflight preparation;
(iv) Preflight lesson on a maneuver to be performed in flight;
(v) Preflight procedures;
(vi) Airport and heliport operations;
(vii) Hovering maneuvers;
(viii) Takeoffs, landings, and go-arounds;
(ix) Fundamentals of flight;
(x) Performance maneuvers;
(xi) Emergency operations;
(xii) Special operations; and
(xiii) Postflight procedures.

(4) *For a rotorcraft—gyroplane course:*
(i) Fundamentals of instructing;

(ii) Technical subject areas;
(iii) Preflight preparation;
(iv) Preflight lesson on a maneuver to be performed in flight;
(v) Preflight procedures;
(vi) Airport operations;
(vii) Takeoffs, landings, and go-arounds;
(viii) Fundamentals of flight;
(ix) Performance maneuvers;
(x) Flight at slow airspeeds;
(xi) Ground reference maneuvers;
(xii) Emergency operations; and
(xiii) Postflight procedures.

(5) *For a powered-lift course:*
(i) Fundamentals of instructing;
(ii) Technical subject areas;
(iii) Preflight preparation;
(iv) Preflight lesson on a maneuver to be performed in flight;
(v) Preflight procedures;
(vi) Airport and heliport operations;
(vii) Hovering maneuvers;
(viii) Takeoffs, landings, and go-arounds;
(ix) Fundamentals of flight;
(x) Performance maneuvers;
(xi) Ground reference maneuvers;
(xii) Slow flight and stalls;
(xiii) Basic instrument maneuvers;
(xiv) Emergency operations;
(xv) Special operations; and
(xvi) Postflight procedures.

(6) *For a glider course:*
(i) Fundamentals of instructing;
(ii) Technical subject areas;
(iii) Preflight preparation;
(iv) Preflight lesson on a maneuver to be performed in flight;
(v) Preflight procedures;
(vi) Airport and gliderport operations;
(vii) Tows or launches, landings, and go-arounds, if applicable;
(viii) Fundamentals of flight;
(ix) Performance speeds;
(x) Soaring techniques;
(xi) Performance maneuvers;
(xii) Slow flight, stalls, and spins;
(xiii) Emergency operations; and
(xiv) Postflight procedures.

5. Stage checks and end-of-course tests.
(a) Each student enrolled in a flight instructor course must satisfactorily accomplish the stage checks and end-of-course tests, in accordance with the school's approved training course, consisting of the appropriate approved areas of operation listed in paragraph (c) of section No. 4 of this appendix appropriate to the flight instructor rating for which the course applies.

(b) In the case of a student who is enrolled in a flight instructor–airplane rating or flight

instructor–glider rating course, that student must have:

(1) Received a logbook endorsement from a certificated flight instructor certifying the student received ground and flight training on stall awareness, spin entry, spins, and spin recovery procedures in an aircraft that is certificated for spins and is appropriate to the rating sought; and

(2) Demonstrated instructional proficiency in stall awareness, spin entry, spins, and spin recovery procedures.

[Docket No. 25910, 62 FR 16347, April 4, 1997; as amended by Amdt. 141–9, 62 FR 40909, July 30, 1997; Amdt. 141–18, 81 FR 21461, April 12, 2016]

APPENDIX G TO PART 141
FLIGHT INSTRUCTOR INSTRUMENT
(FOR AN AIRPLANE, HELICOPTER, OR POWERED-LIFT INSTRUMENT INSTRUCTOR RATING, AS APPROPRIATE)
CERTIFICATION COURSE

1. Applicability. This appendix prescribes the minimum curriculum for a flight instructor instrument certification course required under this part, for the following ratings:

(a) Flight Instructor Instrument—Airplane.

(b) Flight Instructor Instrument—Helicopter.

(c) Flight Instructor Instrument—Powered-lift aircraft.

2. Eligibility for enrollment. A person must hold the following prior to enrolling in the flight portion of the flight instructor instrument course:

(a) A commercial pilot certificate or airline transport pilot certificate with an aircraft category and class rating appropriate to the flight instructor category and class rating for which the course applies; and

(b) An instrument rating or privilege on that flight instructor applicant's pilot certificate that is appropriate to the flight instructor instrument rating (for an airplane-, helicopter-, or powered-lift-instrument rating, as appropriate) for which the course applies.

3. Aeronautical knowledge training.

(a) Each approved course must include at least 15 hours of ground training on the aeronautical knowledge areas listed in paragraph (b) of this section, appropriate to the flight instructor instrument rating (for an airplane-, helicopter-, or powered-lift-instrument rating, as appropriate) for which the course applies:

(b) Ground training must include the following aeronautical knowledge areas:

(1) The fundamentals of instructing including:

(i) The learning process;

(ii) Elements of effective teaching;

(iii) Student evaluation and testing;

(iv) Course development;

(v) Lesson planning; and

(vi) Classroom training techniques.

(2) The aeronautical knowledge areas in which training is required for an instrument rating that is appropriate to the aircraft category and class rating for the course which applies.

4. Flight training.

(a) Each approved course must include at least 15 hours of flight training in the approved areas of operation of paragraph (c) of this section appropriate to the flight instructor rating for which the course applies.

(b) For the use of full flight simulators or flight training devices:

(1) The course may include training in a full flight simulator or flight training device, provided it is representative of the aircraft for which the course is approved for, meets requirements of this paragraph, and the training is given by an instructor.

(2) Training in a full flight simulator that meets the requirements of §141.41(a), may be credited for a maximum of 10 percent of the total flight training hour requirements of the approved course, or of this section, whichever is less.

(3) Training in a flight training device that meets the requirements of §141.41(a), may be credited for a maximum of 5 percent of the total flight training hour requirements of the approved course, or of this section, whichever is less.

(4) Training in full flight simulators or flight training devices described in paragraphs (b)(2) and (3) of this section, if used in combination, may be credited for a maximum of 10 percent of the total flight training hour requirements of the approved course, or of this section, whichever is less. However, credit for training in a flight training device that meets the requirements of §141.41(b) cannot exceed the limitation provided for in paragraph (b)(3) of this section.

(c) An approved course for the flight instructor–instrument rating must include flight training on the following approved areas of operation that are appropriate to the instrument–aircraft category and class rating for which the course applies:

(1) Fundamentals of instructing;

(2) Technical subject areas;

(3) Preflight preparation;

(4) Preflight lesson on a maneuver to be performed in flight;

(5) Air traffic control clearances and procedures;

(6) Flight by reference to instruments;

(7) Navigation systems;

(8) Instrument approach procedures;

(9) Emergency operations; and

(10) Postflight procedures.

5. *Stage checks and end-of-course tests.*

Each student enrolled in a flight instructor instrument course must satisfactorily accomplish the stage checks and end-of-course tests, in accordance with the school's approved training course, consisting of the approved areas of operation listed in paragraph (c) of section No. 4 of this appendix that are appropriate to the flight instructor instrument rating (for an airplane-, helicopter-, or powered-lift-instrument rating, as appropriate) for which the course applies.

[Docket No. 25910, 62 FR 16347, April 4, 1997; as amended by Amdt. 141–9, 62 FR 40909, July 30, 1997; Amdt. 141–18, 81 FR 21461, April 12, 2016]

APPENDIX H TO PART 141
GROUND INSTRUCTOR
CERTIFICATION COURSE

1. *Applicability.* This appendix prescribes the minimum curriculum for a ground instructor certification course and an additional ground instructor rating course, required under this part, for the following ratings:

(a) Ground Instructor—Basic.

(b) Ground Instructor—Advanced.

(c) Ground Instructor—Instrument.

2. *Aeronautical knowledge training.*

(a) Each approved course must include at least the following ground training on the knowledge areas listed in paragraphs (b), (c), (d), and (e) of this section, appropriate to the ground instructor rating for which the course applies:

(1) 20 hours of training if the course is for an initial issuance of a ground instructor certificate; or

(2) 10 hours of training if the course is for an additional ground instructor rating.

(b) Ground training must include the following aeronautical knowledge areas:

(1) Learning process;

(2) Elements of effective teaching;

(3) Student evaluation and testing;

(4) Course development;

(5) Lesson planning; and

(6) Classroom training techniques.

(c) Ground training for a basic ground instructor certificate must include the aeronautical knowledge areas applicable to a recreational and private pilot.

(d) Ground training for an advanced ground instructor rating must include the aeronautical knowledge areas applicable to a recreational, private, commercial, and airline transport pilot.

(e) Ground training for an instrument ground instructor rating must include the aeronautical knowledge areas applicable to an instrument rating.

(f) A student who satisfactorily completed 2 years of study on the principles of education at a college or university may be credited with 10 hours of the training required in paragraph (a)(1) of this section.

3. *Stage checks and end-of-course tests.*

Each student enrolled in a ground instructor course must satisfactorily accomplish the stage checks and end-of-course tests, in accordance with the school's approved training course, consisting of the approved knowledge areas in paragraph (b), (c), (d), and (e) of section No. 2 of this appendix appropriate to the ground instructor rating for which the course applies.

APPENDIX I TO PART 141
ADDITIONAL AIRCRAFT CATEGORY AND/OR
CLASS RATING COURSE

1. *Applicability.* This appendix prescribes the minimum curriculum for an additional aircraft category rating course or an additional aircraft class rating course required under this part, for the following ratings:

(a) Airplane single-engine.

(b) Airplane multiengine.

(c) Rotorcraft helicopter.

(d) Rotorcraft gyroplane.

(e) Powered-lift.

(f) Glider.

(g) Lighter-than-air airship.

(h) Lighter-than-air balloon.

2. *Eligibility for enrollment.* A person must hold the level of pilot certificate for the additional aircraft category and class rating for which the course applies prior to enrolling in the flight portion of an additional aircraft category or additional aircraft class rating course.

3. *Aeronautical knowledge training.*

(a) For a recreational pilot certificate, the following aeronautical knowledge areas must be included in a 10-hour ground training course for an additional aircraft category and/or class rating:

(1) Applicable regulations issued by the Federal Aviation Administration for recreational pilot privileges, limitations, and flight operations;

(2) Safe and efficient operation of aircraft, including collision avoidance, and recognition and avoidance of wake turbulence;

(3) Effects of density altitude on takeoff and climb performance;

(4) Weight and balance computations;

(5) Principles of aerodynamics, powerplants, and aircraft systems;

(6) Stall awareness, spin entry, spins, and spin recovery techniques if applying for an airplane single engine rating; and

(7) Preflight action that includes how to obtain information on runway lengths at airports of

intended use, data on takeoff and landing distances, weather reports and forecasts, and fuel requirements.

(b) For a private pilot certificate, the following aeronautical knowledge areas must be included in a 10-hour ground training course for an additional class rating or a 15-hour ground training course for an additional aircraft category and class rating:

(1) Applicable regulations issued by the Federal Aviation Administration for private pilot privileges, limitations, and flight operations;

(2) Safe and efficient operation of aircraft, including collision avoidance, and recognition and avoidance of wake turbulence;

(3) Effects of density altitude on takeoff and climb performance;

(4) Weight and balance computations;

(5) Principles of aerodynamics, powerplants, and aircraft systems;

(6) Stall awareness, spin entry, spins, and spin recovery techniques if applying for an airplane single engine rating; and

(7) Preflight action that includes how to obtain information on runway lengths at airports of intended use, data on takeoff and landing distances, weather reports and forecasts, and fuel requirements.

(c) For a commercial pilot certificate, the following aeronautical knowledge areas must be included in a 15-hour ground training course for an additional class rating or a 20-hour ground training course for an additional aircraft category and class rating:

(1) Applicable regulations issued by the Federal Aviation Administration for commercial pilot privileges, limitations, and flight operations;

(2) Basic aerodynamics and the principles of flight;

(3) Safe and efficient operation of aircraft;

(4) Weight and balance computations;

(5) Use of performance charts;

(6) Significance and effects of exceeding aircraft performance limitations;

(7) Principles and functions of aircraft systems;

(8) Maneuvers, procedures, and emergency operations appropriate to the aircraft;

(9) Nighttime and high-altitude operations; and

(10) Procedures for flight and ground training for lighter-than-air ratings.

(d) For an airline transport pilot certificate, the following aeronautical knowledge areas must be included in a 25-hour ground training course for an additional aircraft category and/or class rating:

(1) Applicable regulations issued by the Federal Aviation Administration for airline transport pilot privileges, limitations, and flight operations;

(2) Meteorology, including knowledge and effects of fronts, frontal characteristics, cloud formations, icing, and upper-air data;

(3) General system of weather and NOTAM collection, dissemination, interpretation, and use;

(4) Interpretation and use of weather charts, maps, forecasts, sequence reports, abbreviations, and symbols;

(5) National Weather Service functions as they pertain to operations in the National Airspace System;

(6) Windshear and microburst awareness, identification, and avoidance;

(7) Principles of air navigation under instrument meteorological conditions in the National Airspace System;

(8) Air traffic control procedures and pilot responsibilities as they relate to en route operations, terminal area and radar operations, and instrument departure and approach procedures;

(9) Aircraft loading; weight and balance; use of charts, graphs, tables, formulas, and computations; and the effects on aircraft performance;

(10) Aerodynamics relating to an aircraft's flight characteristics and performance in normal and abnormal flight regimes;

(11) Human factors;

(12) Aeronautical decision making and judgment; and

(13) Crew resource management to include crew communication and coordination.

4. Flight training.

(a) Course for an additional airplane category and single engine class rating.

(1) For the recreational pilot certificate, the course must include 15 hours of flight training on the areas of operations under part 141, appendix A, paragraph 4(c)(1) that include—

(i) Two hours of flight training to an airport and at an airport that is located more than 25 nautical miles from the airport where the applicant normally trains, with three takeoffs and three landings, except as provided under §61.100 of this chapter; and

(ii) Three hours of flight training in an aircraft with the airplane category and single engine class within 2 calendar months before the date of the practical test.

(2) For the private pilot certificate, the course must include 20 hours of flight training on the areas of operations under part 141, appendix B, paragraph 4(d)(1). A flight simulator and flight training device cannot be used to meet more than 4 hours of the training requirements, and the use of the flight training device is limited to 3 hours of the 4 hours permitted. The course must include—

(i) Three hours of cross country training in a single engine airplane, except as provided under §61.111 of this chapter;

(ii) Three hours of nighttime flight training in a single engine airplane that includes one cross country flight of more than 100 nautical miles total distance, and 10 takeoffs and 10 landings to a

full stop (with each landing involving a flight in the traffic pattern) at an airport;

(iii) Three hours of flight training in a single engine airplane on the control and maneuvering of the airplane solely by reference to instruments, including straight and level flight, constant airspeed climbs and descents, turns to a heading, recovery from unusual flight attitudes, radio communications, and the use of navigation systems/facilities and radar services appropriate to instrument flight; and

(iv) Three hours of flight training in a single engine airplane within 2 calendar months before the date of the practical test.

(3) For the commercial pilot certificate, the course must include 55 hours of flight training on the areas of operations under part 141, appendix D, paragraph 4(d)(1). A flight simulator and flight training device cannot be used to meet more than 16.5 hours of the training requirements, and the use of the flight training device is limited to 11 hours of the 16.5 hours permitted. The course must include—

(i) Five hours of instrument training in a single engine airplane that includes training using a view-limiting device on attitude instrument flying, partial panel skills, recovery from unusual flight attitudes, and intercepting and tracking navigational systems;

(ii) Ten hours of training in a complex airplane, a turbine-powered airplane, or a technically advanced airplane that meets the requirements of §61.129(j), or any combination thereof. The airplane must be appropriate to land or sea for the rating sought;

(iii) One 2-hour cross country flight during daytime conditions in a single engine airplane, a total straight-line distance of more than 100 nautical miles from the original point of departure;

(iv) One 2-hour cross country flight during nighttime conditions in a single engine airplane, a total straight-line distance of more than 100 nautical miles from the original point of departure; and

(v) Three hours in a single engine airplane within 2 calendar months before the date of the practical test.

(4) For the airline transport pilot certificate, the course must include 25 hours flight training, including 15 hours of instrument training, in a single engine airplane on the areas of operation under part 141, appendix E, paragraph 4.(c). A flight simulator and flight training device cannot be used to meet more than 12.5 hours of the training requirements; and the use of the flight training device is limited to 6.25 hours of the 12.5 hours permitted.

(b) Course for an additional airplane category and multiengine class rating.

(1) For the private pilot certificate, the course requires 20 hours flight training on the areas of operations under part 141, appendix B, paragraph

4.(d)(2). A flight simulator and flight training device cannot be used more than 4 hours to meet the training requirements, and use of the flight training device is limited to 3 hours of the 4 hours permitted. The course must include—

(i) Three hours of cross country training in a multiengine airplane, except as provided under §61.111 of this chapter;

(ii) Three hours of nighttime flight training in a multiengine airplane that includes one cross country flight of more than 100 nautical miles total distance, and 10 takeoffs and 10 landings to a full stop (with each landing involving a flight in the traffic pattern) at an airport;

(iii) Three hours of flight training in a multiengine airplane on the control and maneuvering of a multiengine airplane solely by reference to instruments, including straight and level flight, constant airspeed climbs and descents, turns to a heading, recovery from unusual flight attitudes, radio communications, and the use of navigation systems/facilities and radar services appropriate to instrument flight; and

(iv) Three hours of flight training in a multiengine airplane in preparation for the practical test within 2 calendar months before the date of the test.

(2) For the commercial pilot certificate, the course requires 55 hours flight training on the areas of operations under part 141, appendix D, paragraph 4.(d)(2). A flight simulator and flight training device cannot be used more than 16.5 hours to meet the training requirements, and use of the flight training device is limited to 11 hours of the 16.5 hours permitted. The course must include—

(i) Five hours of instrument training in a multiengine airplane including training using a view-limiting device for attitude instrument flying, partial panel skills, recovery from unusual flight attitudes, and intercepting and tracking navigational systems;

(ii) Ten hours of training in a multiengine airplane that has retractable landing gear, flaps, and a controllable pitch propeller, or is turbine-powered;

(iii) One 2-hour cross country flight during daytime conditions in a multiengine airplane, and a total straight-line distance of more than 100 nautical miles from the original point of departure;

(iv) One 2-hour cross country flight during nighttime conditions in a multiengine airplane, and a total straight-line distance of more than 100 nautical miles from the original point of departure; and

(v) Three hours in a multiengine airplane within 2 calendar months before the date of the practical test.

(3) For the airline transport pilot certificate, the course requires 25 hours of flight training in

a multiengine airplane on the areas of operation under part 141, appendix E, paragraph 4.(c) that includes 15 hours of instrument training. A flight simulator and flight training device cannot be used more than 12.5 hours to meet the training requirements, and use of the flight training device is limited to 6.25 hours of the 12.5 hours permitted.

(c) Course for an additional rotorcraft category and helicopter class rating.

(1) For the recreational pilot certificate, the course requires 15 hours of flight training on the areas of operations under part 141, appendix A, paragraph 4.(c)(2) that includes—

(i) Two hours of flight training to and at an airport that is located more than 25 nautical miles from the airport where the applicant normally trains, with three takeoffs and three landings, except as provided under §61.100 of this chapter; and

(ii) Three hours of flight training in a rotorcraft category and a helicopter class aircraft within 2 calendar months before the date of the practical test.

(2) For the private pilot certificate, the course requires 20 hours flight training on the areas of operations under part 141, appendix B, paragraph 4.(d)(3). A flight simulator and flight training device cannot be used more than 4 hours to meet the training requirements, and use of the flight training device is limited to 3 hours of the 4 hours permitted. The course must include—

(i) Except as provided under §61.111 of this chapter, 3 hours of cross country flight training in a helicopter;

(ii) Three hours of nighttime flight training in a helicopter that includes one cross country flight of more than 50 nautical miles total distance, and 10 takeoffs and 10 landings to a full stop (with each landing involving a flight in the traffic pattern) at an airport; and

(iii) Three hours of flight training in a helicopter within 2 calendar months before the date of the practical test.

(3) The commercial pilot certificate level requires 30 hours flight training on the areas of operations under appendix D of part 141, paragraph 4.(d)(3). A flight simulator and flight training device cannot be used more than 9 hours to meet the training requirements, and use of the flight training device is limited to 6 hours of the 9 hours permitted. The course must include—

(i) Five hours on the control and maneuvering of a helicopter solely by reference to instruments, and must include training using a view-limiting device for attitude instrument flying, partial panel skills, recovery from unusual flight attitudes, and intercepting and tracking navigational systems. This aeronautical experience may be performed in an aircraft, flight simulator, flight training device, or an aviation training device;

(ii) One 2-hour cross country flight during daytime conditions in a helicopter, a total straight-line distance of more than 50 nautical miles from the original point of departure;

(iii) One 2-hour cross country flight during nighttime conditions in a helicopter, a total straight-line distance of more than 50 nautical miles from the original point of departure; and

(iv) Three hours in a helicopter within 2 calendar months before the date of the practical test.

(4) For the airline transport pilot certificate, the course requires 25 hours of flight training, including 15 hours of instrument training, in a helicopter on the areas of operation under part 141, appendix E, paragraph 4.(c). A flight simulator and flight training device cannot be used more than 12.5 hours to meet the training requirements, and use of the flight training device is limited to 6.25 hours of the 12.5 hours permitted.

(d) Course for an additional rotorcraft category and a gyroplane class rating.

(1) For the recreational pilot certificate, the course requires 15 hours flight training on the areas of operations under part 141, appendix A, paragraph 4.(c)(3) that includes—

(i) Two hours of flight training to and at an airport that is located more than 25 nautical miles from the airport where the applicant normally trains, with three takeoffs and three landings, except as provided under §61.100 of this chapter; and

(ii) Three hours of flight training in a gyroplane class within 2 calendar months before the date of the practical test.

(2) For the private pilot certificate, the course requires 20 hours flight training on the areas of operations under part 141, appendix B, paragraph 4.(d)(4). A flight simulator and flight training device cannot be used more than 4 hours to meet the training requirements, and use of the flight training device is limited to 3 hours of the 4 hours permitted. The course must include—

(i) Three hours of cross country flight training in a gyroplane, except as provided under §61.111 of this chapter;

(ii) Three hours of nighttime flight training in a gyroplane that includes one cross country flight of more than 50 nautical miles total distance, and 10 takeoffs and 10 landings to a full stop (with each landing involving a flight in the traffic pattern) at an airport; and

(iii) Three hours of flight training in a gyroplane within 2 calendar months before the date of the practical test.

(3) For the commercial pilot certificate, the course requires 30 hours flight training on the areas of operations of appendix D to part 141, paragraph 4.(d)(4). A flight simulator and flight training device cannot be used more than 6 hours to meet the training requirements, and use of the

flight training device is limited to 6 hours of the 9 hours permitted. The course must include—

(i) 2.5 hours on the control and maneuvering of a gyroplane solely by reference to instruments, and must include training using a view-limiting device for attitude instrument flying, partial panel skills, recovery from unusual flight attitudes, and intercepting and tracking navigational systems. This aeronautical experience may be performed in an aircraft, flight simulator, flight training device, or an aviation training device.

(ii) One 2-hour cross country flight during daytime conditions in a gyroplane, a total straight-line distance of more than 50 nautical miles from the original point of departure;

(iii) Two hours of flight training during nighttime conditions in a gyroplane at an airport, that includes 10 takeoffs and 10 landings to a full stop (with each landing involving a flight in the traffic pattern); and

(iv) Three hours in a gyroplane within 2 calendar months before the date of the practical test.

(e) Course for an additional lighter-than-air category and airship class rating.

(1) For the private pilot certificate, the course requires 20 hours of flight training on the areas of operation under part 141, appendix B, paragraph 4.(d)(7). A flight simulator and flight training device cannot be used more than 4 hours to meet the training requirements, and use of the flight training device is limited to 3 hours of the 4 hours permitted. The course must include—

(i) Three hours of cross country flight training in an airship, except as provided under §61.111 of this chapter;

(ii) Three hours of nighttime flight training in an airship that includes one cross country flight of more than 25 nautical miles total distance and 5 takeoffs and 5 landings to a full stop (with each landing involving a flight in the traffic pattern) at an airport;

(iii) Three hours of flight training in an airship on the control and maneuvering of an airship solely by reference to instruments, including straight and level flight, constant airspeed climbs and descents, turns to a heading, recovery from unusual flight attitudes, radio communications, and the use of navigation systems/facilities and radar services appropriate to instrument flight; and

(iv) Three hours of flight training in an airship within 2 calendar months before the date of the practical test.

(2) For the commercial pilot certificate, the course requires 55 hours of flight training on the areas of operation under part 141, appendix D, paragraph 4.(d)(7). A flight simulator and flight training device cannot be used more than 16.5 hours to meet the training requirements, and use of the flight training device is limited to 11 hours

of the 16.5 hours permitted. The course must include—

(i) Three hours of instrument training in an airship that must include training using a view-limiting device for attitude instrument flying, partial panel skills, recovery from unusual flight attitudes, and intercepting and tracking navigational systems;

(ii) One hour cross country flight during daytime conditions in an airship that consists of, a total straight-line distance of more than 25 nautical miles from the original point of departure;

(iii) One hour cross country flight during nighttime conditions in an airship that consists of a total straight-line distance of more than 25 nautical miles from the original point of departure; and

(iv) Three hours of flight training in an airship within 2 calendar months before the date of the practical test.

(f) Course for an additional lighter-than-air category and a gas balloon class rating.

(1) For the private pilot certificate, the course requires eight hours of flight training that includes 5 training flights on the areas of operations under part 141, appendix B, paragraph 4(d)(8). A flight simulator and flight training device cannot be used more than 1.6 hours to meet the training requirements, and use of the flight training device is limited to 1.2 hours of the 1.6 hours permitted. The course must include—

(i) Two flights of 1 hour each;

(ii) One flight involving a controlled ascent to 3,000 feet above the launch site; and

(iii) Two flights within 2 calendar months before the date of the practical test.

(2) For the commercial pilot certificate, the course requires 10 hours of flight training that includes eight training flights on the areas of operations under part 141, appendix D, paragraph 4(d)(8). A flight simulator and flight training device cannot be used more than 3 hours to meet the training requirements, and use of the flight training device is limited to 2 hours of the 3 hours permitted. The course must include—

(i) Two flights of 1 hour each;

(ii) One flight involving a controlled ascent to 5,000 feet above the launch site; and

(iii) Two flights within 2 calendar months before the date of the practical test.

(g) Course for an additional lighter-than-air category and a hot air balloon class rating.

(1) For the private pilot certificate, the course requires eight hours of flight training that includes 5 training flights on the areas of operations under part 141, appendix B, paragraph 4(d)(8). A flight simulator and flight training device cannot be used more than 1.6 hours to meet the training requirements, and use of the flight training device is limited to 1.2 hours of the 1.6 hours permitted. The course must include—

(i) Two flights of 30 minutes each;

(ii) One flight involving a controlled ascent to 2,000 feet above the launch site; and

(iii) Two flights within 2 calendar months before the date of the practical test.

(2) For the commercial pilot certificate, the course requires 10 hours of flight training that includes eight training flights on the areas of operation under part 141, appendix D, paragraph 4(d)(8). A flight simulator and flight training device cannot be used more than 3 hours to meet the training requirements, and use of the flight training device is limited to 2 hours of the 3 hours permitted. The course must include—

(i) Two flights of 30 minutes each;

(ii) One flight involving a controlled ascent to 3,000 feet above the launch site; and

(iii) Two flights within 2 calendar months before the date of the practical test.

(h) Course for an additional powered-lift category rating.

(1) For the private pilot certificate, the course requires 20 hours flight training on the areas of operations under part 141, appendix B, paragraph 4(d)(5). A flight simulator and flight training device cannot be used more than 4 hours to meet the training requirements, and use of the flight training device is limited to 3 hours of the 4 hours permitted. The course must include—

(i) Three hours of cross country flight training in a powered-lift except as provided under §61.111 of this chapter;

(ii) Three hours of nighttime flight training in a powered-lift that includes one cross-country flight of more than 100 nautical miles total distance, and 10 takeoffs and 10 landings to a full stop (with each landing involving a flight in the traffic pattern) at an airport;

(iii) Three hours of flight training in a powered-lift on the control and maneuvering of a powered-lift solely by reference to instruments, including straight and level flight, constant airspeed climbs and descents, turns to a heading, recovery from unusual flight attitudes, radio communications, and the use of navigation systems/facilities and radar services appropriate to instrument flight;

(iv) Three hours of flight training in a powered-lift within 2 calendar months before the date of the practical test.

(2) For the commercial pilot certificate, the course requires 55 hours flight training on the areas of operations under part 141, appendix D, paragraph 4(d)(5). A flight simulator and flight training device cannot be used more than 16.5 hours to meet the training requirements, and use of the flight training device is limited to 11 hours of the 16.5 hours permitted. The course includes—

(i) Five hours of instrument training in a powered-lift that must include training using a view-limiting device for attitude instrument flying,

partial panel skills, recovery from unusual flight attitudes, and intercepting and tracking navigational systems;

(ii) One 2-hour cross country flight during daytime conditions in a powered-lift, a total straight-line distance of more than 100 nautical miles from the original point of departure;

(iii) One 2-hour cross country flight during nighttime conditions in a powered-lift, a total straight-line distance of more than 100 nautical miles from the original point of departure; and

(iv) Three hours of flight training in a powered-lift within 2 calendar months before the date of the practical test.

(3) For the airline transport pilot certificate, the course requires 25 hours flight training in a powered-lift on the areas of operation under part 141, appendix E, paragraph 4(c) that includes 15 hours of instrument training. A flight simulator and flight training device cannot be used more than 12.5 hours to meet the training requirements, and use of the flight training device is limited to 6.25 hours of the 12.5 hours permitted.

(i) Course for an additional glider category rating.

(1) For the private pilot certificate, the course requires 4 hours of flight training in a glider on the areas of operations under part 141, appendix B, paragraph 4(d)(6). A flight simulator and flight training device cannot be used more than 0.8 hours to meet the training requirements, and use of the flight training device is limited to 0.6 hours of the 0.8 hours permitted. The course must include—

(i) Five training flights in a glider with a certificated flight instructor on the launch/tow procedures approved for the course and on the appropriate approved areas of operation listed under appendix B, paragraph 4(d)(6) of this part; and

(ii) Three training flights in a glider with a certificated flight instructor within 2 calendar months before the date of the practical test.

(2) The commercial pilot certificate level requires 4 hours of flight training in a glider on the areas of operation under part 141, appendix D, paragraph 4.(d)(6). A flight simulator and flight training device cannot be used more than 0.8 hours to meet the training requirements, and use of the flight training device is limited to 0.6 hours of the 0.8 hours permitted. The course must include—

(i) Five training flights in a glider with a certificated flight instructor on the launch/tow procedures approved for the course and on the appropriate approved areas of operation listed in appendix D of part 141, paragraph 4.(d)(6); and

(ii) Three training flights in a glider with a certificated flight instructor in preparation for the practical test within 2 calendar months preceding the date of the test.

(j) Course for an airplane additional single engine class rating.

(1) For the private pilot certificate, the course requires 3 hours of flight training in the areas of operations under part 141, appendix B, paragraph 4.(d)(1). A flight simulator and flight training device cannot be used more than 0.6 hours to meet the training requirements, and use of the flight training device is limited to 0.4 hours of the 0.6 hours permitted. The course must include—

(i) Three hours of cross country training in a single engine airplane, except as provided under §61.111 of this chapter;

(ii) Three hours of nighttime flight training in a single engine airplane that includes one cross country flight of more than 100 nautical miles total distance in a single engine airplane and 10 takeoffs and 10 landings to a full stop (with each landing involving a flight in the traffic pattern) at an airport;

(iii) Three hours of flight training in a single engine airplane on the control and maneuvering of a single engine airplane solely by reference to instruments, including straight and level flight, constant airspeed climbs and descents, turns to a heading, recovery from unusual flight attitudes, radio communications, and the use of navigation systems/facilities and radar services appropriate to instrument flight; and

(iv) Three hours of flight training in a single engine airplane within 2 calendar months before the date of the practical test.

(2) For the commercial pilot certificate, the course requires 10 hours of flight training on the areas of operations under part 141, appendix D, paragraph 4.(d)(1).

(i) Five hours of instrument training in a single engine airplane that must include training using a view-limiting device for attitude instrument flying, partial panel skills, recovery from unusual flight attitudes, and intercepting and tracking navigational systems.

(ii) Ten hours of flight training in an airplane that has retractable landing gear, flaps, and a controllable pitch propeller, or is turbine-powered.

(iii) One 2-hour cross country flight during daytime conditions in a single engine airplane and a total straight-line distance of more than 100 nautical miles from the original point of departure;

(iv) One 2-hour cross country flight during nighttime conditions in a single engine airplane and a total straight-line distance of more than 100 nautical miles from the original point of departure; and

(iv) Three hours of flight training in a single engine airplane within 2 calendar months before the date of the practical test.

(3) For the airline transport pilot certificate, the course requires 25 hours flight training in a single engine airplane on the areas of operation under appendix E to part 141, paragraph 4.(c), that includes 15 hours of instrument training. A flight simulator and flight training device cannot be used more than 12.5 hours to meet the training requirements, and use of the flight training device is limited to 6.25 hours of the 12.5 hours permitted.

(k) Course for an airplane additional multiengine class rating.

(1) For the private pilot certificate, the course requires 3 hours of flight training on the areas of operations of appendix B to part 141, paragraph 4(d)(2). A flight simulator and flight training device cannot be used more than 0.6 hours to meet the training requirements, and use of the flight training device is limited to 0.4 hours of the 0.6 hours permitted. The course must include—

(i) Three hours of cross country training in a multiengine airplane, except as provided under §61.111 of this chapter;

(ii) Three hours of nighttime flight training in a multiengine airplane that includes one cross country flight of more than 100 nautical miles total distance in a multiengine airplane, and 10 takeoffs and 10 landings to a full stop (with each landing involving a flight in the traffic pattern) at an airport;

(iii) Three hours of flight training in a multiengine airplane on the control and maneuvering of a multiengine airplane solely by reference to instruments, including straight and level flight, constant airspeed climbs and descents, turns to a heading, recovery from unusual flight attitudes, radio communications, and the use of navigation systems/facilities and radar services appropriate to instrument flight; and

(iv) Three hours of flight training in a multiengine airplane within 2 calendar months before the date of the practical test.

(2) For the commercial pilot certificate, the course requires 10 hours of training on the areas of operations under appendix D of part 141, paragraph 4(d)(2). A flight simulator and flight training device cannot be used more than 3 hours to meet the training requirements, and use of the flight training device is limited to 2 hours of the 3 hours permitted. The course must include—

(i) Five hours of instrument training in a multiengine airplane that must include training using a view-limiting device on for attitude instrument flying, partial panel skills, recovery from unusual flight attitudes, and intercepting and tracking navigational systems;

(ii) Ten hours of training in a multiengine airplane that has retractable landing gear, flaps, and a controllable pitch propeller, or is turbine-powered;

(iii) One 2-hour cross country flight during daytime conditions in a multiengine airplane and, a total straight-line distance of more than 100 nautical miles from the original point of departure;

(iv) One 2-hour cross country flight during nighttime conditions in a multiengine airplane and, a total straight-line distance of more than 100 nautical miles from the original point of departure; and

(v) Three hours of flight training in a multiengine airplane within 2 calendar months before the date of the practical test.

(3) For the airline transport pilot certificate, the course requires 25 hours of training in a multiengine airplane on the areas of operation of appendix E to part 141, paragraph 4.(c) that includes 15 hours of instrument training. A flight simulator and flight training device cannot be used more than 12.5 hours to meet the training requirements, and use of the flight training device is limited to 6.25 hours of the 12.5 hours permitted.

(l) Course for a rotorcraft additional helicopter class rating.

(1) For the recreational pilot certificate, the course requires 3 hours of flight training on the areas of operations under appendix A of part 141, paragraph 4.(c)(2) that includes—

(i) Two hours of flight training to and at an airport that is located more than 25 nautical miles from the airport where the applicant normally trains, with three takeoffs and three landings, except as provided under §61.100 of this chapter; and

(ii) Three hours of flight training in a helicopter within 2 calendar months before the date of the practical test.

(2) For the private pilot certificate, the course requires 3 hours flight training on the areas of operations under appendix B of part 141, paragraph 4.(d)(3). A flight simulator and flight training device cannot be used more than 0.6 hours to meet the training requirements, and use of the flight training device is limited to 0.4 hours of the 0.6 hours permitted. The course must include—

(i) Three hours of cross country training in a helicopter, except as provided under §61.111 of this chapter;

(ii) Three hours of nighttime flight training in a helicopter that includes one cross country flight of more than 50 nautical miles total distance, and 10 takeoffs and 10 landings to a full stop (with each landing involving a flight in the traffic pattern) at an airport; and

(iii) Three hours of flight training in a helicopter within 2 calendar months before the date of the practical test.

(3) For the commercial pilot certificate, the course requires 5 hours flight training on the areas of operations under appendix D of part 141, paragraph 4.(d)(3). Use of a flight simulator and flight training device in the approved training course cannot exceed 1 hour; however, use of the flight training device cannot exceed 0.7 of the one hour. The course must include—

(i) Five hours on the control and maneuvering of a helicopter solely by reference to instruments, and must include training using a view-limiting device for attitude instrument flying, partial panel skills, recovery from unusual flight attitudes, and intercepting and tracking navigational systems. This aeronautical experience may be performed in an aircraft, flight simulator, flight training device, or an aviation training device;

(ii) One 2-hour cross country flight during daytime conditions in a helicopter and, a total straight-line distance of more than 50 nautical miles from the original point of departure;

(iii) One 2-hour cross country flight during nighttime conditions in a helicopter and a total straight-line distance of more than 50 nautical miles from the original point of departure; and

(iv) Three hours of flight training in a helicopter within 2 calendar months before the date of the practical test.

(4) For the airline transport pilot certificate, the course requires 25 hours of flight training in a helicopter on the areas of operation under appendix E of part 141, paragraph 4.(c) that includes 15 hours of instrument training. A flight simulator and flight training device cannot be used more than 12.5 hours to meet the training requirements, and use of the flight training device is limited to 6.25 hours of the 12.5 hours permitted.

(m) Course for a rotorcraft additional gyroplane class rating.

(1) For the recreational pilot certificate, the course requires 3 hours flight training on the areas of operations of appendix A to part 141, paragraph 4.(c)(3) that includes—

(i) Except as provided under §61.100 of this chapter, 2 hours of flight training to and at an airport that is located more than 25 nautical miles from the airport where the applicant normally trains, with three takeoffs and three landings; and

(ii) Within 2 calendar months before the date of the practical test, 3 hours of flight training in a gyroplane.

(2) For the private pilot certificate, the course requires 3 hours flight training on the areas of operations of appendix B to part 141, paragraph 4.(d)(4). A flight simulator and flight training device cannot be used more than 0.6 hours to meet the training requirements, and use of the flight training device is limited to 0.4 hours of the 0.6 hours permitted. The course must include—

(i) Three hours of cross country training in a gyroplane;

(ii) Three hours of nighttime flight training in a gyroplane that includes one cross country flight of more than 50 nautical miles total distance, and 10 takeoffs and 10 landings to a full stop (with each landing involving a flight in the traffic pattern) at an airport; and

(iii) Three hours of flight training in a gyroplane within 2 calendar months before the date of the practical test.

(3) For the commercial pilot certificate, the course requires 5 hours flight training on the areas of operations of appendix D to part 141, paragraph 4.(d)(4). A flight simulator and flight training device cannot be used more than 1 hour to meet the training requirements, and use of the flight training device is limited to 0.7 hours of the 1 hour permitted. The course must include—

(i) 2.5 hours on the control and maneuvering of a gyroplane solely by reference to instruments, and must include training using a view-limiting device for attitude instrument flying, partial panel skills, recovery from unusual flight attitudes, and intercepting and tracking navigational systems. This aeronautical experience may be performed in an aircraft, flight simulator, flight training device, or an aviation training device.

(ii) Three hours of cross country flight training in a gyroplane, except as provided under §61.111 of this chapter;

(iii) Two hours of flight training during night-time conditions in a gyroplane at an airport that includes 10 takeoffs and 10 landings to a full stop (with each landing involving a flight in the traffic pattern); and

(iv) Three hours of flight training in a gyroplane within 2 calendar months before the date of the practical test.

(n) Course for a lighter-than-air additional airship class rating.

(1) For the private pilot certificate, the course requires 20 hours of flight training on the areas of operation under appendix B of part 141, paragraph 4.(d)(7). A flight simulator and flight training device cannot be used more than 4 hours to meet the training requirements, and use of the flight training device is limited to 3 hours of the 4 hours permitted. The course must include—

(i) Three hours of cross country training in an airship, except as provided under §61.111 of this chapter;

(ii) Three hours of nighttime flight training in an airship that includes one cross country flight of more than 25 nautical miles total distance, and 5 takeoffs and 5 landings to a full stop (with each landing involving a flight in the traffic pattern) at an airport;

(iii) Three hours of flight training in an airship on the control and maneuvering of an airship solely by reference to instruments, including straight and level flight, constant airspeed climbs and descents, turns to a heading, recovery from unusual flight attitudes, radio communications, and the use of navigation systems/facilities and radar services appropriate to instrument flight; and

(iv) Three hours of flight training in an airship within 2 calendar months before the date of the practical test.

(2) For the commercial pilot certificate, the course requires 55 hours of flight training on the areas of operation under appendix D of part 141, paragraph 4.(d)(7). A flight simulator and flight training device cannot be used more than 16.5 hours to meet the training requirements, and use of the flight training device is limited to 11 hours of the 16.5 hours permitted. The course must include—

(i) Three hours of instrument training in an airship that must include training using a view-limiting device for attitude instrument flying, partial panel skills, recovery from unusual flight attitudes, and intercepting and tracking navigational systems;

(ii) One hour cross country flight during daytime conditions in an airship that consists of a total straight-line distance of more than 25 nautical miles from the original point of departure;

(iii) One hour cross country flight during nighttime conditions in an airship that consists of a total straight-line distance of more than 25 nautical miles from the original point of departure; and

(iv) Three hours of flight training in an airship within 2 calendar months before the date of the practical test.

(o) Course for a lighter-than-air additional gas balloon class rating.

(1) For the private pilot certificate, the course requires eight hours of flight training that includes 5 training flights on the areas of operations under appendix B of part 141, paragraph 4.(d)(8). A flight simulator and flight training device cannot be used more than 1.6 hours to meet the training requirements, and use of the flight training device is limited to 1.2 hours of the 1.6 hours permitted. The course must include—

(i) Two flights of 1 hour each;

(ii) One flight involving a controlled ascent to 3,000 feet above the launch site; and

(iii) Two flights within 2 calendar months before the date of the practical test.

(2) For the commercial pilot certificate, the course requires 10 hours of flight training that includes eight training flights on the areas of operations of appendix D to part 141, paragraph 4.(d)(8). A flight simulator and flight training device cannot be used more than 3 hours to meet the training requirements, and use of the flight training device is limited to 2 hours of the 3 hours permitted. The course must include—

(i) Two flights of 1 hour each;

(ii) One flight involving a controlled ascent to 5,000 feet above the launch site; and

(iii) Two flights within 2 calendar months before the date of the practical test.

(p) Course for a lighter-than-air additional hot air balloon class rating.

(1) For the private pilot certificate, the course requires 8 hours of flight training that includes 5 training flights on the areas of operations of appendix B to part 141, paragraph 4.(d)(8). A flight simulator and flight training device cannot be used more than 1.6 hours to meet the training requirements, and use of the flight training device is limited to 1.2 hours of the 1.6 hours permitted. The course must include—

(i) Two flights of 30 minutes each;

(ii) One flight involving a controlled ascent to 2,000 feet above the launch site; and

(iii) Two flights within 2 calendar months before the date of the practical test.

(2) For the commercial pilot certificate, the course requires 10 hours of flight training that includes eight training flight on the areas of operation of appendix D to part 141, paragraph 4.(d)(8). A flight simulator and flight training device cannot be used more than 3 hours to meet the training requirements, and use of the flight training device is limited to 2 hours of the 3 hours permitted. The course must include—

(i) Two flights of 30 minutes each.

(ii) One flight involving a controlled ascent to 3,000 feet above the launch site; and

(iii) Two flights within 2 calendar months before the date of the practical test.

5. Stage checks and end-of-course tests.

(a) Each student enrolled in an additional aircraft category rating course or an additional aircraft class rating course must satisfactorily accomplish the stage checks and end-of-course tests, in accordance with the school's approved training course, consisting of the approved areas of operation in section No. 4 of this appendix that are appropriate to the aircraft category and class rating for which the course applies at the appropriate pilot certificate level.

(b) Each student must demonstrate satisfactory proficiency prior to receiving an endorsement to operate an aircraft in solo flight.

[Docket No. 25910, 62 FR 16347, April 4, 1997; as amended by Amdt. 141–9, 62 FR 40909, July 30, 1997; Amdt. 141–12, 74 FR 42566, Aug. 21, 2009; Amdt. 141–24, 87 FR 75848, Dec. 9, 2022]

APPENDIX J TO PART 141

AIRCRAFT TYPE RATING COURSE,
FOR OTHER THAN AN
AIRLINE TRANSPORT PILOT CERTIFICATE

1. Applicability. This appendix prescribes the minimum curriculum for an aircraft type rating course other than an airline transport pilot certificate, for:

(a) A type rating in an airplane category—single-engine class.

(b) A type rating in an airplane category—multi-engine class.

(c) A type rating in a rotorcraft category—helicopter class.

(d) A type rating in a powered-lift category.

(e) Other aircraft type ratings specified by the Administrator through the aircraft type certificate procedures.

2. Eligibility for enrollment. Prior to enrolling in the flight portion of an aircraft type rating course, a person must hold at least a private pilot certificate and:

(a) An instrument rating in the category and class of aircraft that is appropriate to the aircraft type rating for which the course applies, provided the aircraft's type certificate does not have a VFR limitation; or

(b) Be concurrently enrolled in an instrument rating course in the category and class of aircraft that is appropriate to the aircraft type rating for which the course applies, and pass the required instrument rating practical test concurrently with the aircraft type rating practical test.

3. Aeronautical knowledge training.

(a) Each approved course must include at least 10 hours of ground training on the aeronautical knowledge areas listed in paragraph (b) of this section, appropriate to the aircraft type rating for which the course applies.

(b) Ground training must include the following aeronautical areas:

(1) Proper control of airspeed, configuration, direction, altitude, and attitude in accordance with procedures and limitations contained in the aircraft's flight manual, checklists, or other approved material appropriate to the aircraft type;

(2) Compliance with approved en route, instrument approach, missed approach, ATC, or other applicable procedures that apply to the aircraft type;

(3) Subjects requiring a practical knowledge of the aircraft type and its powerplant, systems, components, operational, and performance factors;

(4) The aircraft's normal, abnormal, and emergency procedures, and the operations and limitations relating thereto;

(5) Appropriate provisions of the approved aircraft's flight manual;

(6) Location of and purpose for inspecting each item on the aircraft's checklist that relates to the exterior and interior preflight; and

(7) Use of the aircraft's prestart checklist, appropriate control system checks, starting procedures, radio and electronic equipment checks, and the selection of proper navigation and communication radio facilities and frequencies.

4. *Flight training.*

(a) Each approved course must include at least:

(1) Flight training on the approved areas of operation of paragraph (c) of this section in the aircraft type for which the course applies; and

(2) 10 hours of training of which at least 5 hours must be instrument training in the aircraft for which the course applies.

(b) For the use of full flight simulators or flight training devices:

(1) The course may include training in a full flight simulator or flight training device, provided it is representative of the aircraft for which the course is approved, meets requirements of this paragraph, and the training is given by an authorized instructor.

(2) Training in a full flight simulator that meets the requirements of §141.41(a), may be credited for a maximum of 50 percent of the total flight training hour requirements of the approved course, or of this section, whichever is less.

(3) Training in a flight training device that meets the requirements of §141.41(a), may be credited for a maximum of 25 percent of the total flight training hour requirements of the approved course, or of this section, whichever is less.

(4) Training in the full flight simulators or flight training devices described in paragraphs (b)(2) and (3) of this section, if used in combination, may be credited for a maximum of 50 percent of the total flight training hour requirements of the approved course, or of this section, whichever is less. However, credit training in a flight training device that meets the requirements of §141.41(a) cannot exceed the limitation provided for in paragraph (b)(3) of this section.

(c) Each approved course must include the flight training on the areas of operation listed in this paragraph, that are appropriate to the aircraft category and class rating for which the course applies:

(1) *A type rating for an airplane—single-engine course:*
(i) Preflight preparation;
(ii) Preflight procedures;
(iii) Takeoff and departure phase;
(iv) In-flight maneuvers;
(v) Instrument procedures;
(vi) Landings and approaches to landings;
(vii) Normal and abnormal procedures;
(viii) Emergency procedures; and
(ix) Postflight procedures.

(2) *A type rating for an airplane—multiengine course:*
(i) Preflight preparation;
(ii) Preflight procedures;
(iii) Takeoff and departure phase;

(iv) In-flight maneuvers;
(v) Instrument procedures;
(vi) Landings and approaches to landings;
(vii) Normal and abnormal procedures;
(viii) Emergency procedures; and
(ix) Postflight procedures.

(3) *A type rating for a powered-lift course:*
(i) Preflight preparation;
(ii) Preflight procedures;
(iii) Takeoff and departure phase;
(iv) In-flight maneuvers;
(v) Instrument procedures;
(vi) Landings and approaches to landings;
(vii) Normal and abnormal procedures;
(viii) Emergency procedures; and
(ix) Postflight procedures.

(4) *A type rating for a rotorcraft—helicopter course:*
(i) Preflight preparation;
(ii) Preflight procedures;
(iii) Takeoff and departure phase;
(iv) In-flight maneuvers;
(v) Instrument procedures;
(vi) Landings and approaches to landings;
(vii) Normal and abnormal procedures;
(viii) Emergency procedures; and
(ix) Postflight procedures.

(5) *Other aircraft type ratings specified by the Administrator through aircraft type certificate procedures:*
(i) Preflight preparation;
(ii) Preflight procedures;
(iii) Takeoff and departure phase;
(iv) In-flight maneuvers;
(v) Instrument procedures;
(vi) Landings and approaches to landings;
(vii) Normal and abnormal procedures;
(viii) Emergency procedures; and
(ix) Postflight procedures.

5. *Stage checks and end-of-course tests.*

(a) Each student enrolled in an aircraft type rating course must satisfactorily accomplish the stage checks and end-of-course tests, in accordance with the school's approved training course, consisting of the approved areas of operation that are appropriate to the aircraft type rating for which the course applies at the airline transport pilot certificate level; and

(b) Each student must demonstrate satisfactory proficiency prior to receiving an endorsement to operate an aircraft in solo flight.

[Docket No. 25910, 62 FR 16347, April 4, 1997; as amended by Amdt. 141–9, 62 FR 40910, July 30, 1997; Amdt. 141–18, 81 FR 21461, April 12, 2016]

APPENDIX K TO PART 141
SPECIAL PREPARATION COURSES

1. Applicability. This appendix prescribes the minimum curriculum for the special preparation courses that are listed in §141.11 of this part.

2. Eligibility for enrollment. Prior to enrolling in the flight portion of a special preparation course, a person must hold a pilot certificate, flight instructor certificate, or ground instructor certificate that is appropriate for the exercise of the operating privileges or authorizations sought.

3. General requirements.

(a) To be approved, a special preparation course must:

(1) Meet the appropriate requirements of this appendix; and

(2) Prepare the graduate with the necessary skills, competency, and proficiency to exercise safely the privileges of the certificate, rating, or authorization for which the course is established.

(b) An approved special preparation course must include ground and flight training on the operating privileges or authorization sought, for developing competency, proficiency, resourcefulness, self-confidence, and self-reliance in the student.

4. Use of full flight simulators or flight training devices.

(a) The approved special preparation course may include training in a full flight simulator or flight training device, provided it is representative of the aircraft for which the course is approved, meets requirements of this paragraph, and the training is given by an authorized instructor.

(b) Except for the airline transport pilot certification program in section 13 of this appendix, training in a full flight simulator that meets the requirements of §141.41(a), may be credited for a maximum of 10 percent of the total flight training hour requirements of the approved course, or of this section, whichever is less.

(c) Except for the airline transport pilot certification program in section 13 of this appendix, training in a flight training device that meets the requirements of §141.41(a), may be credited for a maximum of 5 percent of the total flight training hour requirements of the approved course, or of this section, whichever is less.

(d) Training in the full flight simulators or flight training devices described in paragraphs (b) and (c) of this section, if used in combination, may be credited for a maximum of 10 percent of the total flight training hour requirements of the approved course, or of this section, whichever is less. However, credit for training in a flight training device that meets the requirements of §141.41(a) cannot exceed the limitation provided for in paragraph (c) of this section.

5. Stage check and end-of-course tests.

Each person enrolled in a special preparation course must satisfactorily accomplish the stage checks and end-of-course tests, in accordance with the school's approved training course, consisting of the approved areas of operation that are appropriate to the operating privileges or authorization sought, and for which the course applies.

6. Agricultural aircraft operations course.

An approved special preparation course for pilots in agricultural aircraft operations must include at least the following—

(a) 25 hours of training on:

(1) Agricultural aircraft operations;

(2) Safe piloting and operating practices and procedures for handling, dispensing, and disposing agricultural and industrial chemicals, including operating in and around congested areas; and

(3) Applicable provisions of part 137 of this chapter.

(b) 15 hours of flight training on agricultural aircraft operations.

7. Rotorcraft external-load operations course. An approved special preparation course for pilots of external-load operations must include at least the following—

(a) 10 hours of training on:

(1) Rotorcraft external-load operations;

(2) Safe piloting and operating practices and procedures for external-load operations, including operating in and around congested areas; and

(3) Applicable provisions of part 133 of this chapter.

(b) 15 hours of flight training on external-load operations.

8. Test pilot course. An approved special preparation course for pilots in test pilot duties must include at least the following—

(a) Aeronautical knowledge training on:

(1) Performing aircraft maintenance, quality assurance, and certification test flight operations;

(2) Safe piloting and operating practices and procedures for performing aircraft maintenance, quality assurance, and certification test flight operations;

(3) Applicable parts of this chapter that pertain to aircraft maintenance, quality assurance, and certification tests; and

(4) Test pilot duties and responsibilities.

(b) 15 hours of flight training on test pilot duties and responsibilities.

9. Special operations course. An approved special preparation course for pilots in special operations that are mission-specific for certain aircraft must include at least the following—

(a) Aeronautical knowledge training on:

(1) Performing that special flight operation;

(2) Safe piloting operating practices and procedures for performing that special flight operation;

141

(3) Applicable parts of this chapter that pertain to that special flight operation; and

(4) Pilot in command duties and responsibilities for performing that special flight operation.

(b) Flight training:

(1) On that special flight operation; and

(2) To develop skills, competency, proficiency, resourcefulness, self-confidence, and self-reliance in the student for performing that special flight operation in a safe manner.

10. Pilot refresher course. An approved special preparation pilot refresher course for a pilot certificate, aircraft category and class rating, or an instrument rating must include at least the following—

(a) 4 hours of aeronautical knowledge training on:

(1) The aeronautical knowledge areas that are applicable to the level of pilot certificate, aircraft category and class rating, or instrument rating, as appropriate, that pertain to that course;

(2) Safe piloting operating practices and procedures; and

(3) Applicable provisions of parts 61 and 91 of this chapter for pilots.

(b) 6 hours of flight training on the approved areas of operation that are applicable to the level of pilot certificate, aircraft category and class rating, or instrument rating, as appropriate, for performing pilot-in-command duties and responsibilities.

11. Flight instructor refresher course. An approved special preparation flight instructor refresher course must include at least a combined total of 16 hours of aeronautical knowledge training, flight training, or any combination of ground and flight training on the following—

(a) Aeronautical knowledge training on:

(1) The aeronautical knowledge areas of part 61 of this chapter that apply to student, recreational, private, and commercial pilot certificates and instrument ratings;

(2) The aeronautical knowledge areas of part 61 of this chapter that apply to flight instructor certificates;

(3) Safe piloting operating practices and procedures, including airport operations and operating in the National Airspace System; and

(4) Applicable provisions of parts 61 and 91 of this chapter that apply to pilots and flight instructors.

(b) Flight training to review:

(1) The approved areas of operations applicable to student, recreational, private, and commercial pilot certificates and instrument ratings; and

(2) The skills, competency, and proficiency for performing flight instructor duties and responsibilities.

12. Ground instructor refresher course. An approved special preparation ground instructor refresher course must include at least 16 hours of aeronautical knowledge training on:

(a) The aeronautical knowledge areas of part 61 of this chapter that apply to student, private, and commercial pilots and instrument rated pilots;

(b) The aeronautical knowledge areas of part 61 of this chapter that apply to ground instructors;

(c) Safe piloting operating practices and procedures, including airport operations and operating in the National Airspace System; and

(d) Applicable provisions of parts 61 and 91 of this chapter that apply to pilots and ground instructors.

13. Airline transport pilot certification training program. An approved airline transport pilot certification training program must include the academic and FSTD training set forth in §61.156 of this chapter. The FAA will not approve a course with fewer hours than those prescribed in §61.156 of this chapter.

[Docket No. 25910, 62 FR 16347, April 4, 1997; as amended by Amdt. 141–9, 62 FR 40910, July 30, 1997; Amdt. 141–17, 78 FR 42380, July 15, 2013; Amdt. 141–17A, 78 FR 53026, Aug. 28, 2013; Amdt. 141–18, 81 FR 21462, April 12, 2016]

APPENDIX L TO PART 141
PILOT GROUND SCHOOL COURSE

1. Applicability. This appendix prescribes the minimum curriculum for a pilot ground school course required under this part.

2. General requirements. An approved course of training for a pilot ground school must include training on the aeronautical knowledge areas that are:

(a) Needed to safely exercise the privileges of the certificate, rating, or authority for which the course is established; and

(b) Conducted to develop competency, proficiency, resourcefulness, self-confidence, and self-reliance in each student.

3. Aeronautical knowledge training requirements. Each approved pilot ground school course must include:

(a) The aeronautical knowledge training that is appropriate to the aircraft rating and pilot certificate level for which the course applies; and

(b) An adequate number of total aeronautical knowledge training hours appropriate to the aircraft rating and pilot certificate level for which the course applies.

4. Stage checks and end-of-course tests. Each person enrolled in a pilot ground school course must satisfactorily accomplish the stage checks and end-of-course tests, in accordance with the school's approved training course, consisting of the approved areas of operation that are

appropriate to the operating privileges or authorization that graduation from the course will permit and for which the course applies.

APPENDIX M TO PART 141
COMBINED PRIVATE PILOT CERTIFICATION AND INSTRUMENT RATING COURSE

1. Applicability. This appendix prescribes the minimum curriculum for a combined private pilot certification and instrument rating course required under this part, for the following ratings:

(a) Airplane.

(1) Airplane single-engine.

(2) Airplane multiengine.

(b) Rotorcraft helicopter.

(c) Powered-lift.

2. Eligibility for enrollment. A person must hold a sport pilot, recreational, or student pilot certificate prior to enrolling in the flight portion of a combined private pilot certification and instrument rating course.

3. Aeronautical knowledge training.

(a) Each approved course must include at least 65 hours of ground training on the aeronautical knowledge areas listed in paragraph (b) of this section that are appropriate to the aircraft category and class rating of the course:

(b) Ground training must include the following aeronautical knowledge areas:

(1) Applicable Federal Aviation Regulations for private pilot privileges, limitations, flight operations, and instrument flight rules (IFR) flight operations.

(2) Accident reporting requirements of the National Transportation Safety Board.

(3) Applicable subjects of the "Aeronautical Information Manual" and the appropriate FAA advisory circulars.

(4) Aeronautical charts for visual flight rules (VFR) navigation using pilotage, dead reckoning, and navigation systems.

(5) Radio communication procedures.

(6) Recognition of critical weather situations from the ground and in flight, windshear avoidance, and the procurement and use of aeronautical weather reports and forecasts.

(7) Safe and efficient operation of aircraft under instrument flight rules and conditions.

(8) Collision avoidance and recognition and avoidance of wake turbulence.

(9) Effects of density altitude on takeoff and climb performance.

(10) Weight and balance computations.

(11) Principles of aerodynamics, powerplants, and aircraft systems.

(12) If the course of training is for an airplane category, stall awareness, spin entry, spins, and spin recovery techniques.

(13) Air traffic control system and procedures for instrument flight operations.

(14) IFR navigation and approaches by use of navigation systems.

(15) Use of IFR en route and instrument approach procedure charts.

(16) Aeronautical decision making and judgment.

(17) Preflight action that includes—

(i) How to obtain information on runway lengths at airports of intended use, data on takeoff and landing distances, weather reports and forecasts, and fuel requirements.

(ii) How to plan for alternatives if the planned flight cannot be completed or delays are encountered.

(iii) Procurement and use of aviation weather reports and forecasts, and the elements of forecasting weather trends on the basis of that information and personal observation of weather conditions.

4. Flight training.

(a) Each approved course must include at least 70 hours of training, as described in section 4 and section 5 of this appendix, on the approved areas of operation listed in paragraph (d) of section 4 of this appendix that are appropriate to the aircraft category and class rating of the course:

(b) Each approved course must include at least the following flight training:

(1) *For an airplane single engine course:* 70 hours of flight training from an authorized instructor on the approved areas of operation in paragraph (d)(1) of this section that includes at least—

(i) Except as provided in §61.111 of this chapter, 3 hours of cross-country flight training in a single engine airplane.

(ii) 3 hours of night flight training in a single-engine airplane that includes—

(A) One cross-country flight of more than 100 nautical miles total distance.

(B) 10 takeoffs and 10 landings to a full stop (with each landing involving a flight in the traffic pattern) at an airport.

(iii) 35 hours of instrument flight training in a single-engine airplane that includes at least one cross-country flight that is performed under IFR and—

(A) Is a distance of at least 250 nautical miles along airways or air traffic control-directed (ATC-directed) routing with one segment of the flight consisting of at least a straight-line distance of 100 nautical miles between airports.

(B) Involves an instrument approach at each airport.

(C) Involves three different kinds of approaches with the use of navigation systems.

(iv) 3 hours of flight training in a single-engine airplane in preparation for the practical test within 60 days preceding the date of the test.

(2) *For an airplane multiengine course:* 70 hours of training from an authorized instructor on the approved areas of operation in paragraph (d)(2) of this section that includes at least—

(i) Except as provided in §61.111 of this chapter, 3 hours of cross-country flight training in a multiengine airplane.

(ii) 3 hours of night flight training in a multiengine airplane that includes—

(A) One cross-country flight of more than 100 nautical miles total distance.

(B) 10 takeoffs and 10 landings to a full stop (with each landing involving a flight in the traffic pattern) at an airport.

(iii) 35 hours of instrument flight training in a multiengine airplane that includes at least one cross-country flight that is performed under IFR and—

(A) Is a distance of at least 250 nautical miles along airways or ATC-directed routing with one segment of the flight consisting of at least a straight-line distance of 100 nautical miles between airports.

(B) Involves an instrument approach at each airport.

(C) Involves three different kinds of approaches with the use of navigation systems.

(iv) 3 hours of flight training in a multiengine airplane in preparation for the practical test within 60 days preceding the date of the test.

(3) *For a rotorcraft helicopter course:* 70 hours of training from an authorized instructor on the approved areas of operation in paragraph (d)(3) of this section that includes at least—

(i) Except as provided in §61.111 of this chapter, 3 hours of cross-country flight training in a helicopter.

(ii) 3 hours of night flight training in a helicopter that includes—

(A) One cross-country flight of more than 50 nautical miles total distance.

(B) 10 takeoffs and 10 landings to a full stop (with each landing involving a flight in the traffic pattern) at an airport.

(iii) 35 hours of instrument flight training in a helicopter that includes at least one cross-country flight that is performed under IFR and—

(A) Is a distance of at least 100 nautical miles along airways or ATC-directed routing with one segment of the flight consisting of at least a straight-line distance of 50 nautical miles between airports.

(B) Involves an instrument approach at each airport.

(C) Involves three different kinds of approaches with the use of navigation systems.

(iv) 3 hours of flight training in a helicopter in preparation for the practical test within 60 days preceding the date of the test.

(4) *For a powered-lift course:* 70 hours of training from an authorized instructor on the approved areas of operation in paragraph (d)(4) of this section that includes at least—

(i) Except as provided in §61.111 of this chapter, 3 hours of cross-country flight training in a powered-lift.

(ii) 3 hours of night flight training in a powered-lift that includes—

(A) One cross-country flight of more than 100 nautical miles total distance.

(B) 10 takeoffs and 10 landings to a full stop (with each landing involving a flight in the traffic pattern) at an airport.

(iii) 35 hours of instrument flight training in a powered-lift that includes at least one cross-country flight that is performed under IFR and—

(A) Is a distance of at least 250 nautical miles along airways or ATC directed routing with one segment of the flight consisting of at least a straight-line distance of 100 nautical miles between airports.

(B) Involves an instrument approach at each airport.

(C) Involves three different kinds of approaches with the use of navigation systems.

(iv) 3 hours of flight training in a powered-lift in preparation for the practical test, within 60 days preceding the date of the test.

(c) For use of full flight simulators or flight training devices:

(1) The course may include training in a combination of full flight simulators, flight training devices, and aviation training devices, provided it is representative of the aircraft for which the course is approved, meets the requirements of this section, and the training is given by an authorized instructor.

(2) Training in a full flight simulator that meets the requirements of §141.41(a) may be credited for a maximum of 35 percent of the total flight training hour requirements of the approved course, or of this section, whichever is less.

(3) Training in a flight training device that meets the requirements of §141.41(a) or an aviation training device that meets the requirements of §141.41(b) may be credited for a maximum of 25 percent of the total flight training hour requirements of the approved course, or of this section, whichever is less.

(4) Training in a combination of flight simulators, flight training devices, or aviation training devices, described in paragraphs (c)(2) and (3) of this section, may be credited for a maximum of 35 percent of the total flight training hour requirements of the approved course, or of this section, whichever is less. However, credit for training in a flight training device and aviation training device, that meets the requirements of §141.41(b), cannot

exceed the limitation provided for in paragraph (c)(3) of this section.

(d) Each approved course must include the flight training on the approved areas of operation listed in this section that are appropriate to the aircraft category and class rating course—

(1) *For a combined private pilot certification and instrument rating course involving a single-engine airplane:*

(i) Preflight preparation.

(ii) Preflight procedures.

(iii) Airport and seaplane base operations.

(iv) Takeoffs, landings, and go-arounds.

(v) Performance maneuvers.

(vi) Ground reference maneuvers.

(vii) Navigation and navigation systems.

(viii) Slow flight and stalls.

(ix) Basic instrument maneuvers and flight by reference to instruments.

(x) Instrument approach procedures.

(xi) Air traffic control clearances and procedures.

(xii) Emergency operations.

(xiii) Night operations.

(xiv) Postflight procedures.

(2) *For a combined private pilot certification and instrument rating course involving a multiengine airplane:*

(i) Preflight preparation.

(ii) Preflight procedures.

(iii) Airport and seaplane base operations.

(iv) Takeoffs, landings, and go-arounds.

(v) Performance maneuvers.

(vi) Ground reference maneuvers.

(vii) Navigation and navigation systems.

(viii) Slow flight and stalls.

(ix) Basic instrument maneuvers and flight by reference to instruments.

(x) Instrument approach procedures.

(xi) Air traffic control clearances and procedures.

(xii) Emergency operations.

(xiii) Multiengine operations.

(xiv) Night operations.

(xv) Postflight procedures.

(3) *For a combined private pilot certification and instrument rating course involving a rotorcraft helicopter:*

(i) Preflight preparation.

(ii) Preflight procedures.

(iii) Airport and heliport operations.

(iv) Hovering maneuvers.

(v) Takeoffs, landings, and go-arounds.

(vi) Performance maneuvers.

(vii) Navigation and navigation systems.

(viii) Basic instrument maneuvers and flight by reference to instruments.

(ix) Instrument approach procedures.

(x) Air traffic control clearances and procedures.

(xi) Emergency operations.

(xii) Night operations.

(xiii) Postflight procedures.

(4) *For a combined private pilot certification and instrument rating course involving a powered-lift:*

(i) Preflight preparation.

(ii) Preflight procedures.

(iii) Airport and heliport operations.

(iv) Hovering maneuvers.

(v) Takeoffs, landings, and go-arounds.

(vi) Performance maneuvers.

(vii) Ground reference maneuvers.

(viii) Navigation and navigation systems.

(ix) Slow flight and stalls.

(x) Basic instrument maneuvers and flight by reference to instruments.

(xi) Instrument approach procedures.

(xii) Air traffic control clearances and procedures.

(xiii) Emergency operations.

(xiv) Night operations.

(xv) Postflight procedures.

5. *Solo flight training.* Each approved course must include at least the following solo flight training:

(a) *For a combined private pilot certification and instrument rating course involving an airplane single engine:* Five hours of flying solo in a single-engine airplane on the appropriate areas of operation in paragraph (d)(1) of section 4 of this appendix that includes at least—

(1) One solo cross-country flight of at least 100 nautical miles with landings at a minimum of three points, and one segment of the flight consisting of a straight-line distance of at least 50 nautical miles between the takeoff and landing locations.

(2) Three takeoffs and three landings to a full stop (with each landing involving a flight in the traffic pattern) at an airport with an operating control tower.

(b) *For a combined private pilot certification and instrument rating course involving an airplane multiengine:* Five hours of flying solo in a multiengine airplane or 5 hours of performing the duties of a pilot in command while under the supervision of an authorized instructor. The training must consist of the appropriate areas of operation in paragraph (d)(2) of section 4 of this appendix, and include at least—

(1) One cross-country flight of at least 100 nautical miles with landings at a minimum of three points, and one segment of the flight consisting of a straight-line distance of at least 50 nautical miles between the takeoff and landing locations.

(2) Three takeoffs and three landings to a full stop (with each landing involving a flight in the traffic pattern) at an airport with an operating control tower.

141

(c) *For a combined private pilot certification and instrument rating course involving a helicopter:* Five hours of flying solo in a helicopter on the appropriate areas of operation in paragraph (d)(3) of section 4 of this appendix that includes at least—

(1) One solo cross-country flight of more than 50 nautical miles with landings at a minimum of three points, and one segment of the flight consisting of a straight-line distance of at least 25 nautical miles between the takeoff and landing locations.

(2) Three takeoffs and three landings to a full stop (with each landing involving a flight in the traffic pattern) at an airport with an operating control tower.

(d) *For a combined private pilot certification and instrument rating course involving a powered-lift:* Five hours of flying solo in a powered-lift on the appropriate areas of operation in paragraph (d)(4) of section 4 of this appendix that includes at least—

(1) One solo cross-country flight of at least 100 nautical miles with landings at a minimum of three points, and one segment of the flight consisting of a straight-line distance of at least 50 nautical miles between the takeoff and landing locations.

(2) Three takeoffs and three landings to a full stop (with each landing involving a flight in the traffic pattern) at an airport with an operating control tower.

6. *Stage checks and end-of-course tests.*

(a) Each student enrolled in a private pilot course must satisfactorily accomplish the stage checks and end-of-course tests in accordance with the school's approved training course that consists of the approved areas of operation listed in paragraph (d) of section 4 of this appendix that are appropriate to the aircraft category and class rating for which the course applies.

(b) Each student must demonstrate satisfactory proficiency prior to receiving an endorsement to operate an aircraft in solo flight.

[Docket No. FAA–2008–0938, 76 FR 54108, Aug. 31, 2011; as amended by Amdt. 141–18, 81 FR 21462, April 12, 2016]

PART 142
TRAINING CENTERS

Authority: 49 U.S.C. 106(f), 106(g), 40113, 40119, 44101, 44701–44703, 44705, 44707, 44709–44711, 45102–45103, 45301–45302.

Source: Docket No. 26933, 61 FR 34562, July 2, 1996, unless otherwise noted.

Subpart A—General

§142.1 Applicability.

(a) This subpart prescribes the requirements governing the certification and operation of training centers. Except as provided in paragraph (b) of this section, this part provides an alternative means to accomplish training required by parts 61, 63, 65, 91, 121, 125, 135, or 137 of this chapter.

(b) Certification under this part is not required for training that is—

(1) Approved under the provisions of parts 63, 91, 121, 127, 135, or 137 of this chapter;

(2) Approved under subpart Y of part 121 of this chapter, Advanced Qualification Programs, for the authorization holder's own employees;

(3) Conducted under part 61 unless that part requires certification under this part;

(4) Conducted by a part 121 certificate holder for another part 121 certificate holder;

(5) Conducted by a part 135 certificate holder for another part 135 certificate holder; or

(6) Conducted by a part 91 fractional ownership program manager for another part 91 fractional ownership program manager.

(c) Except as provided in paragraph (b) of this section, after August 3, 1998, no person may conduct training, testing, or checking in advanced flight training devices or flight simulators without, or in violation of, the certificate and training specifications required by this part.

[Docket No. 26933, 61 FR 34562, July 2, 1996; as amended by Amdt. 142–4, 66 FR 21066, April 27, 2001; Amdt. 142–5, 68 FR 54588, Sept. 17, 2003; Amdt. 142–9, 78 FR 42380, July 15, 2013]

142

§142.3 Definitions.

As used in this part:

Advanced Flight Training Device as used in this part, means a flight training device as defined in part 61 of this chapter that has a cockpit that accurately replicates a specific make, model, and type aircraft cockpit, and handling characteristics that accurately model the aircraft handling characteristics.

Core Curriculum means a set of courses approved by the Administrator, for use by a training center and its satellite training centers. The core curriculum consists of training which is required for certification. It does not include training for tasks and circumstances unique to a particular user.

Course means—

(1) A program of instruction to obtain pilot certification, qualification, authorization, or currency;

(2) A program of instruction to meet a specified number of requirements of a program for pilot training, certification, qualification, authorization, or currency; or

(3) A curriculum, or curriculum segment, as defined in subpart Y of part 121 of this chapter.

Courseware means instructional material developed for each course or curriculum, including lesson plans, flight event descriptions, computer software programs, audiovisual programs, workbooks, and handouts.

Evaluator means a person employed by a training center certificate holder who performs tests for certification, added ratings, authorizations, and proficiency checks that are authorized by the certificate holder's training specification, and who is authorized by the Administrator to administer such checks and tests.

Flight training equipment means full flight simulators, as defined in §1.1 of this chapter, flight training devices, as defined in §1.1 of this chapter, and aircraft.

Instructor means a person employed by a training center and designated to provide instruction in accordance with subpart C of this part.

Line-Operational Simulation means simulation conducted using operational-oriented flight scenarios that accurately replicate interaction among flightcrew members and between flightcrew members and dispatch facilities, other crewmembers, air traffic control, and ground operations. Line operational simulation simulations are conducted for training and evaluation purposes and include random, abnormal, and emergency occurrences. Line operational simulation specifically includes line-oriented flight training, special purpose operational training, and line operational evaluation.

Specialty Curriculum means a set of courses that is designed to satisfy a requirement of the Federal Aviation Regulations and that is approved by the Administrator for use by a particular training center or satellite training center. The specialty curriculum includes training requirements unique to one or more training center clients.

Training center means an organization governed by the applicable requirements of this part that provides training, testing, and checking under contract or other arrangement to airmen subject to the requirements of this chapter.

Training program consists of courses, courseware, facilities, flight training equipment, and personnel necessary to accomplish a specific training objective. It may include a core curriculum and a specialty curriculum.

Training specifications means a document issued to a training center certificate holder by the Administrator that prescribes that center's training, checking, and testing authorizations and limitations, and specifies training program requirements.

[Docket No. 26933, 61 FR 34562, July 2, 1996; as amended by Amdt. 142–2, 62 FR 68137, Dec. 30, 1997; Amdt. 142–9, 78 FR 42380, July 15, 2013]

§142.5 Certificate and training specifications required.

(a) No person may operate a certificated training center without, or in violation of, a training center certificate and training specifications issued under this part.

(b) An applicant will be issued a training center certificate and training specifications with appropriate limitations if the applicant shows that it has adequate facilities, equipment, personnel, and courseware required by §142.11 to conduct training approved under §142.37.

§142.7 Duration of a certificate.

(a) Except as provided in paragraph (b) of this section, a training center certificate issued under this part is effective until the certificate is surrendered or until the Administrator suspends, revokes, or terminates it.

(b) Unless sooner surrendered, suspended, or revoked, a certificate issued under this part for a training center located outside the United States expires at the end of the twelfth month after the month in which it is issued or renewed.

(c) If the Administrator suspends, revokes, or terminates a training center certificate, the holder of that certificate shall return the certificate to the Administrator within 5 working days after being notified that the certificate is suspended, revoked, or terminated.

§142.9 Deviations or waivers.

(a) The Administrator may issue deviations or waivers from any of the requirements of this part.

(b) A training center applicant requesting a deviation or waiver under this section must provide the Administrator with information acceptable to the Administrator that shows—

(1) Justification for the deviation or waiver; and

(2) That the deviation or waiver will not adversely affect the quality of instruction or evaluation.

§142.11 Application for issuance or amendment.

(a) An application for a training center certificate and training specifications shall—

(1) Be made on a form and in a manner prescribed by the Administrator;

(2) Be filed with the responsible Flight Standards office for the area in which the applicant's principal business office is located; and

(3) Be made at least 120 calendar days before the beginning of any proposed training or 60 calendar days before effecting an amendment to any approved training, unless a shorter filing period is approved by the Administrator.

(b) Each application for a training center certificate and training specification shall provide—

(1) A statement showing that the minimum qualification requirements for each management position are met or exceeded;

(2) A statement acknowledging that the applicant shall notify the Administrator within 10 working days of any change made in the assignment of persons in the required management positions;

(3) The proposed training authorizations and training specifications requested by the applicant;

(4) The proposed evaluation authorization;

(5) A description of the flight training equipment that the applicant proposes to use;

(6) A description of the applicant's training facilities, equipment, qualifications of personnel to be used, and proposed evaluation plans;

(7) A training program curriculum, including syllabi, outlines, courseware, procedures, and documentation to support the items required in subpart B of this part, upon request by the Administrator;

(8) A description of a recordkeeping system that will identify and document the details of training, qualification, and certification of students, instructors, and evaluators;

(9) A description of quality control measures proposed; and

(10) A method of demonstrating the applicant's qualification and ability to provide training for a certificate or rating in fewer than the minimum hours prescribed in part 61 of this chapter if the applicant proposes to do so.

(c) The facilities and equipment described in paragraph (b)(6) of this section shall—

(1) Be available for inspection and evaluation prior to approval; and

(2) Be in place and operational at the location of the proposed training center prior to issuance of a certificate under this part.

(d) An applicant who meets the requirements of this part and is approved by the Administrator is entitled to—

(1) A training center certificate containing all business names included on the application under which the certificate holder may conduct operations and the address of each business office used by the certificate holder; and

(2) Training specifications, issued by the Administrator to the certificate holder, containing—

(i) The type of training authorized, including approved courses;

(ii) The category, class, and type of aircraft that may be used for training, testing, and checking;

(iii) For each flight simulator or flight training device, the make, model, and series of airplane or the set of airplanes being simulated and the qualification level assigned, or the make, model, and series of rotorcraft, or set of rotorcraft being simulated and the qualification level assigned;

(iv) For each flight simulator and flight training device subject to qualification evaluation by the Administrator, the identification number assigned by the FAA;

(v) The name and address of all satellite training centers, and the approved courses offered at each satellite training center;

(vi) Authorized deviations or waivers from this part; and

(vii) Any other items the Administrator may require or allow.

(e) The Administrator may deny, suspend, revoke, or terminate a certificate under this part if the Administrator finds that the applicant or the certificate holder—

(1) Held a training center certificate that was revoked, suspended, or terminated within the previous 5 years; or

(2) Employs or proposes to employ a person who—

(i) Was previously employed in a management or supervisory position by the holder of a training center certificate that was revoked, suspended, or terminated within the previous 5 years;

(ii) Exercised control over any certificate holder whose certificate has been revoked, suspended, or terminated within the last 5 years; and

(iii) Contributed materially to the revocation, suspension, or termination of that certificate and who will be employed in a management or supervisory position, or who will be in control of or have a substantial ownership interest in the training center.

(3) Has provided incomplete, inaccurate, fraudulent, or false information for a training center certificate;

(4) Should not be granted a certificate if the grant would not foster aviation safety.

(f) At any time, the Administrator may amend a training center certificate—

(1) On the Administrator's own initiative, under section 609 of the Federal Aviation Act of 1958 (49 U.S.C. 1429), as amended, and part 13 of this chapter; or

(2) Upon timely application by the certificate holder.

(g) The certificate holder must file an application to amend a training center certificate at least 60 calendar days prior to the applicant's proposed effective amendment date unless a different filing period is approved by the Administrator.

[Docket No. 26933, 61 FR 34562, July 2, 1996; as amended by Amdt. No. 142–1, 62 FR 13791, March 21, 1997; Amdt. 142–10, 83 FR 9176, March 5, 2018]

§142.13 Management and personnel requirements.

An applicant for a training center certificate must show that—

(a) For each proposed curriculum, the training center has, and shall maintain, a sufficient number of instructors who are qualified in accordance with subpart C of this part to perform the duties to which they are assigned;

(b) The training center has designated, and shall maintain, a sufficient number of approved evaluators to provide required checks and tests to graduation candidates within 7 calendar days of training completion for any curriculum leading to airman certificates or ratings, or both;

(c) The training center has, and shall maintain, a sufficient number of management personnel who are qualified and competent to perform required duties; and

(d) A management representative, and all personnel who are designated by the training center to conduct direct student training, are able to understand, read, write, and fluently speak the English language.

§142.14 Employment of former FAA employees.

(a) Except as specified in paragraph (c) of this section, no holder of a training center certificate may knowingly employ or make a contractual arrangement which permits an individual to act as an agent or representative of the certificate holder in any matter before the Federal Aviation Administration if the individual, in the preceding 2 years—

(1) Served as, or was directly responsible for the oversight of, a Flight Standards Service aviation safety inspector; and

(2) Had direct responsibility to inspect, or oversee the inspection of, the operations of the certificate holder.

(b) For the purpose of this section, an individual shall be considered to be acting as an agent or representative of a certificate holder in a matter before the agency if the individual makes any written or oral communication on behalf of the certificate holder to the agency (or any of its officers or employees) in connection with a particular matter, whether or not involving a specific party and without regard to whether the individual has participated in, or had responsibility for, the particular matter while serving as a Flight Standards Service aviation safety inspector.

(c) The provisions of this section do not prohibit a holder of a training center certificate from knowingly employing or making a contractual arrangement which permits an individual to act as an agent or representative of the certificate holder in any matter before the Federal Aviation Administration if the individual was employed by the certificate holder before October 21, 2011.

[Docket No. FAA–2008–1154, 76 FR 52236, Aug. 22, 2011]

§142.15 Facilities.

(a) An applicant for, or holder of, a training center certificate shall ensure that—

(1) Each room, training booth, or other space used for instructional purposes is heated, lighted, and ventilated to conform to local building, sanitation, and health codes; and

(2) The facilities used for instruction are not routinely subject to significant distractions caused by flight operations and maintenance operations at the airport.

(b) An applicant for, or holder of, a training center certificate shall establish and maintain a principal business office that is physically located at the address shown on its training center certificate.

(c) The records required to be maintained by this part must be located in facilities adequate for that purpose.

(d) An applicant for, or holder of, a training center certificate must have available exclusively, for adequate periods of time and at a location approved by the Administrator, adequate flight training equipment and courseware, including at least one flight simulator or advanced flight training device.

[Docket No. 26933, 61 FR 34562, July 2, 1996; as amended by Amdt. 142–3, 63 FR 53536, Oct. 5, 1998]

§142.17 Satellite training centers.

(a) The holder of a training center certificate may conduct training in accordance with an approved training program at a satellite training center if—

(1) The facilities, equipment, personnel, and course content of the satellite training center meet the applicable requirements of this part;

(2) The instructors and evaluators at the satellite training center are under the direct supervision of management personnel of the principal training center;

(3) The Administrator is notified in writing that a particular satellite is to begin operations at least 60 days prior to proposed commencement of operations at the satellite training center; and

(4) The certificate holder's training specifications reflect the name and address of the satellite training center and the approved courses offered at the satellite training center.

(b) The certificate holder's training specifications shall prescribe the operations required and authorized at each satellite training center.

[Docket No. 26933, 61 FR 34562, July 2, 1996; as amended by Amdt. 142–3, 63 FR 53536, Oct. 5, 1998]

§142.21–142.25 [Reserved]

§142.27 Display of certificate.

(a) Each holder of a training center certificate must prominently display that certificate in a place accessible to the public in the principal business office of the training center.

(b) A training center certificate and training specifications must be made available for inspection upon request by—

(1) The Administrator;

(2) An authorized representative of the National Transportation Safety Board; or

(3) Any Federal, State, or local law enforcement agency.

§142.29 Inspections.

Each certificate holder must allow the Administrator to inspect training center facilities, equipment, and records at any reasonable time and in any reasonable place in order to determine compliance with or to determine initial or continuing eligibility under 49 U.S.C. 44701, 44707, formerly the Federal Aviation Act of 1958, as amended, and the training center's certificate and training specifications.

§142.31 Advertising limitations.

(a) A certificate holder may not conduct, and may not advertise to conduct, any training, testing, and checking that is not approved by the Administrator if that training is designed to satisfy any requirement of this chapter.

(b) A certificate holder whose certificate has been surrendered, suspended, revoked, or terminated must—

(1) Promptly remove all indications, including signs, wherever located, that the training center was certificated by the Administrator; and

(2) Promptly notify all advertising agents, or advertising media, or both, employed by the certificate holder to cease all advertising indicating that the training center is certificated by the Administrator.

§142.33 Training agreements.

A pilot school certificated under part 141 of this chapter may provide training, testing, and checking for a training center certificated under this part if—

(a) There is a training, testing, and checking agreement between the certificated training center and the pilot school;

(b) The training, testing, and checking provided by the certificated pilot school is approved and conducted in accordance with this part;

(c) The pilot school certificated under part 141 obtains the Administrator's approval for a training course outline that includes the portion of the training, testing, and checking to be conducted under part 141; and

(d) Upon completion of training, testing, and checking conducted under part 141, a copy of each student's training record is forwarded to the part 142 training center and becomes part of the student's permanent training record.

142

Subpart B—
Aircrew Curriculum and
Syllabus Requirements

§142.35 Applicability.

This subpart prescribes the curriculum and syllabus requirements for the issuance of a training center certificate and training specifications for training, testing, and checking conducted to meet the requirements of part 61 of this chapter.

§142.37 Approval of flight aircrew training program.

(a) Except as provided in paragraph (b) of this section, each applicant for, or holder of, a training center certificate must apply to the Administrator for training program approval.

(b) A curriculum approved under SFAR 58 of part 121 of this chapter is approved under this part without modifications.

(c) Application for training program approval shall be made in a form and in a manner acceptable to the Administrator.

(d) Each application for training program approval must indicate—

(1) Which courses are part of the core curriculum and which courses are part of the specialty curriculum;

(2) Which requirements of part 61 of this chapter would be satisfied by the curriculum or curriculums; and

(3) Which requirements of part 61 of this chapter would not be satisfied by the curriculum or curriculums.

(e) If, after a certificate holder begins operations under an approved training program, the Administrator finds that the certificate holder is not meeting the provisions of its approved training program, the Administrator may require the certificate holder to make revisions to that training program.

(f) If the Administrator requires a certificate holder to make revisions to an approved training program and the certificate holder does not make those required revisions, within 30 calendar days, the Administrator may suspend, revoke, or terminate the training center certificate under the provisions of §142.11(e).

§142.39 Training program curriculum requirements.

Each training program curriculum submitted to the Administrator for approval must meet the applicable requirements of this part and must contain—

(a) A syllabus for each proposed curriculum;

(b) Minimum aircraft and flight training equipment requirements for each proposed curriculum;

(c) Minimum instructor and evaluator qualifications for each proposed curriculum;

(d) A curriculum for initial training and continuing training of each instructor or evaluator employed to instruct in a proposed curriculum; and

(e) For each curriculum that provides for the issuance of a certificate or rating in fewer than the minimum hours prescribed by part 61 of this chapter—

(1) A means of demonstrating the ability to accomplish such training in the reduced number of hours; and

(2) A means of tracking student performance.

Subpart C—
Personnel and Flight
Training Equipment
Requirements

§142.45 Applicability.

This subpart prescribes the personnel and flight training equipment requirements for a certificate holder that is training to meet the requirements of part 61 of this chapter.

§142.47 Training center instructor eligibility requirements.

(a) A certificate holder may not employ a person as an instructor in a flight training course that is subject to approval by the Administrator unless that person—

(1) Is at least 18 years of age;

(2) Is able to read, write, and speak and understand in the English language;

(3) If instructing in an aircraft in flight, is qualified in accordance with subpart H of part 61 of this chapter;

(4) Satisfies the requirements of paragraph (c) of this section; and

(5) Meets at least one of the following requirements—

(i) Except as allowed by paragraph (a)(5)(ii) of this section, meets the aeronautical experience requirements of §61.129(a), (b), (c), or (e) of this chapter, as applicable, excluding the required hours of instruction in preparation for the commercial pilot practical test;

(ii) If instructing in flight simulator or flight training device that represents an airplane requiring a type rating or if instructing in a curriculum leading to the issuance of an airline transport pilot certificate or an added rating to an airline transport pilot certificate, meets the aeronautical experience requirements of §61.159, §61.161, or §61.163 of this chapter, as applicable; or

(iii) Is employed as a flight simulator instructor or a flight training device instructor for a training center providing instruction and testing to meet the requirements of part 61 of this chapter on August 1, 1996.

(b) A training center must designate each instructor in writing to instruct in each approved course, prior to that person functioning as an instructor in that course.

(c) Prior to initial designation, each instructor shall:

(1) Complete at least 8 hours of ground training on the following subject matter:

(i) Instruction methods and techniques.

(ii) Training policies and procedures.

(iii) The fundamental principles of the learning process.

(iv) Instructor duties, privileges, responsibilities, and limitations.

(v) Proper operation of simulation controls and systems.

(vi) Proper operation of environmental control and warning or caution panels.

(vii) Limitations of simulation.

(viii) Minimum equipment requirements for each curriculum.

(ix) Revisions to the training courses.

(x) Cockpit resource management and crew coordination.

(2) Satisfactorily complete a written test—

(i) On the subjects specified in paragraph (c)(1) of this section; and

(ii) That is accepted by the Administrator as being of equivalent difficulty, complexity, and scope as the tests provided by the Administrator for the flight instructor airplane and instrument flight instructor knowledge tests.

[Docket No. 26933, 61 FR 34562, July 2, 1996; as amended by Amdt. 142–2, 62 FR 68137, Dec. 30, 1997]

§142.49 Training center instructor and evaluator privileges and limitations.

(a) A certificate holder may allow an instructor to provide:

(1) Instruction for each curriculum for which that instructor is qualified.

(2) Testing and checking for which that instructor is qualified.

(3) Instruction, testing, and checking intended to satisfy the requirements of any part of this chapter.

(b) A training center whose instructor or evaluator is designated in accordance with the requirements of this subpart to conduct training, testing, or checking in qualified and approved flight training equipment, may allow its instructor or evaluator to give endorsements required by part 61 of this chapter if that instructor or evaluator is authorized by the Administrator to instruct or evaluate in a part 142 curriculum that requires such endorsements.

(c) A training center may not allow an instructor to—

(1) Excluding briefings and debriefings, conduct more than 8 hours of instruction in any 24-consecutive-hour period;

(2) Provide flight training equipment instruction unless that instructor meets the requirements of §142.53(a)(1) through (a)(4), and §142.53(b), as applicable; or

(3) Provide flight instruction in an aircraft unless that instructor—

(i) Meets the requirements of §142.53(a)(1), (a)(2), and (a)(5);

(ii) Is qualified and authorized in accordance with subpart H of part 61 of this chapter;

(iii) Holds certificates and ratings specified by part 61 of this chapter appropriate to the category, class, and type aircraft in which instructing;

(iv) If instructing or evaluating in an aircraft in flight while serving as a required crewmember, holds at least a valid second class medical certificate; and

(v) Meets the recency of experience requirements of part 61 of this chapter.

[Docket No. 26933, 61 FR 34562, July 2, 1996; as amended by Amdt. 142–2, 62 FR 68137, Dec. 30, 1997; Amdt. 142–9, 78 FR 42380, July 15, 2013]

§142.51 [Reserved]

§142.53 Training center instructor training and testing requirements.

(a) Except as provided in paragraph (c) of this section, prior to designation and every 12 calendar months beginning the first day of the month following an instructor's initial designation, a certificate holder must ensure that each of its instructors meets the following requirements:

(1) Each instructor must satisfactorily demonstrate to an authorized evaluator knowledge of, and proficiency in, instructing in a representative segment of each curriculum for which that instructor is designated to instruct under this part.

(2) Each instructor must satisfactorily complete an approved course of ground instruction in at least—

(i) The fundamental principles of the learning process;

(ii) Elements of effective teaching, instruction methods, and techniques;

(iii) Instructor duties, privileges, responsibilities, and limitations;

(iv) Training policies and procedures;

(v) Cockpit resource management and crew coordination; and

(vi) Evaluation.

142

(3) Each instructor who instructs in a qualified and approved flight simulator or flight training device must satisfactorily complete an approved course of training in the operation of the flight simulator, and an approved course of ground instruction, applicable to the training courses the instructor is designated to instruct.

(4) The flight simulator training course required by paragraph (a)(3) of this section which must include—

(i) Proper operation of flight simulator and flight training device controls and systems;

(ii) Proper operation of environmental and fault panels;

(iii) Limitations of simulation; and

(iv) Minimum equipment requirements for each curriculum.

(5) Each flight instructor who provides training in an aircraft must satisfactorily complete an approved course of ground instruction and flight training in an aircraft, flight simulator, or flight training device.

(6) The approved course of ground instruction and flight training required by paragraph (a)(5) of this section which must include instruction in—

(i) Performance and analysis of flight training procedures and maneuvers applicable to the training courses that the instructor is designated to instruct;

(ii) Technical subjects covering aircraft subsystems and operating rules applicable to the training courses that the instructor is designated to instruct;

(iii) Emergency operations;

(iv) Emergency situations likely to develop during training; and

(v) Appropriate safety measures.

(7) Each instructor who instructs in qualified and approved flight training equipment must pass a written test and annual proficiency check—

(i) In the flight training equipment in which the instructor will be instructing; and

(ii) On the subject matter and maneuvers of a representative segment of each curriculum for which the instructor will be instructing.

(b) In addition to the requirements of paragraphs (a)(1) through (a)(7) of this section, each certificate holder must ensure that each instructor who instructs in a flight simulator that the Administrator has approved for all training and all testing for the airline transport pilot certification test, aircraft type rating test, or both, has met at least one of the following three requirements:

(1) Each instructor must have performed 2 hours in flight, including three takeoffs and three landings as the sole manipulator of the controls of an aircraft of the same category and class, and, if a type rating is required, of the same type replicated by the approved flight simulator in which that instructor is designated to instruct;

(2) Each instructor must have participated in an approved line-observation program under part 121 or part 135 of this chapter, and that—

(i) Was accomplished in the same airplane type as the airplane represented by the flight simulator in which that instructor is designated to instruct; and

(ii) Included line-oriented flight training of at least 1 hour of flight during which the instructor was the sole manipulator of the controls in a flight simulator that replicated the same type aircraft for which that instructor is designated to instruct; or

(3) Each instructor must have participated in an approved in-flight observation training course that—

(i) Consisted of at least 2 hours of flight time in an airplane of the same type as the airplane replicated by the flight simulator in which the instructor is designated to instruct; and

(ii) Included line-oriented flight training of at least 1 hour of flight during which the instructor was the sole manipulator of the controls in a flight simulator that replicated the same type aircraft for which that instructor is designated to instruct.

(c) An instructor who satisfactorily completes a curriculum required by paragraph (a) or (b) of this section in the calendar month before or after the month in which it is due is considered to have taken it in the month in which it was due for the purpose of computing when the next training is due.

(d) The Administrator may give credit for the requirements of paragraph (a) or (b) of this section to an instructor who has satisfactorily completed an instructor training course for a part 121 or part 135 certificate holder if the Administrator finds such a course equivalent to the requirements of paragraph (a) or (b) of this section.

[Docket No. 26933, 61 FR 34562, July 2, 1996; as amended by Amdt. 142–1, 62 FR 13791, March 21, 1997]

§142.54 Airline transport pilot certification training program.

No certificate holder may use a person nor may any person serve as an instructor in a training program approved to meet the requirements of §61.156 of this chapter unless the instructor:

(a) Holds an airline transport pilot certificate with an airplane category multiengine class rating;

(b) Has at least 2 years of experience as a pilot in command in operations conducted under §91.1053(a)(2)(i) or §135.243(a)(1) of this chapter, or as a pilot in command or second in command in any operation conducted under part 121 of this chapter;

(c) Except for the holder of a flight instructor certificate, receives initial training on the following topics:

(1) The fundamental principles of the learning process;

(2) Elements of effective teaching, instruction methods, and techniques;

(3) Instructor duties, privileges, responsibilities, and limitations;

(4) Training policies and procedures; and

(5) Evaluation.

(d) If providing training in a flight simulation training device—

(1) Holds an aircraft type rating for the aircraft represented by the flight simulation training device utilized in the training program and have received training and evaluation within the preceding 12 months from the certificate holder on the maneuvers that will be demonstrated in the flight simulation training device; and

(2) Satisfies the requirements of §142.53(a)(4).

(e) A certificate holder may not issue a graduation certificate to a student unless that student has completed all the curriculum requirements of the course.

(f) A certificate holder must conduct evaluations to ensure that training techniques, procedures, and standards are acceptable to the Administrator.

[Docket No. FAA–2010–0100, 78 FR 42380, July 15, 2013]

§142.55 Training center evaluator requirements.

(a) Except as provided by paragraph (d) of this section, a training center must ensure that each person authorized as an evaluator—

(1) Is approved by the Administrator;

(2) Is in compliance with §§142.47, 142.49, and 142.53 and applicable sections of part 183 of this chapter; and

(3) Prior to designation, and except as provided in paragraph (b) of this section, every 12-calendar-month period following initial designation, the certificate holder must ensure that the evaluator satisfactorily completes a curriculum that includes the following:

(i) Evaluator duties, functions, and responsibilities;

(ii) Methods, procedures, and techniques for conducting required tests and checks;

(iii) Evaluation of pilot performance; and

(iv) Management of unsatisfactory tests and subsequent corrective action; and

(4) If evaluating in qualified and approved flight training equipment must satisfactorily pass a written test and annual proficiency check in a flight simulator or aircraft in which the evaluator will be evaluating.

(b) An evaluator who satisfactorily completes a curriculum required by paragraph (a) of this section in the calendar month before or the calendar month after the month in which it is due is considered to have taken it in the month is which it was due for the purpose of computing when the next training is due.

(c) The Administrator may give credit for the requirements of paragraph (a)(3) of this section to an evaluator who has satisfactorily completed an evaluator training course for a part 121 or part 135 certificate holder if the Administrator finds such a course equivalent to the requirements of paragraph (a)(3) of this section.

(d) An evaluator who is qualified under subpart Y of part 121 of this chapter shall be authorized to conduct evaluations under the Advanced Qualification Program without complying with the requirements of this section.

[Docket No. 26933, 61 FR 34562, July 2, 1996; as amended by Amdt. 142–9, 78 FR 42380, July 15, 2013]

§142.57 Aircraft requirements.

(a) An applicant for, or holder of, a training center certificate must ensure that each aircraft used for flight instruction and solo flights meets the following requirements:

(1) Except for flight instruction and solo flights in a curriculum for agricultural aircraft operations, external load operations, and similar aerial work operations, the aircraft must have an FAA standard airworthiness certificate or a foreign equivalent of an FAA standard airworthiness certificate, acceptable to the Administrator.

(2) The aircraft must be maintained and inspected in accordance with—

(i) The requirements of part 91, subpart E, of this chapter; and

(ii) An approved program for maintenance and inspection.

(3) The aircraft must be equipped as provided in the training specifications for the approved course for which it is used.

(b) Except as provided in paragraph (c) of this section, an applicant for, or holder of, a training center certificate must ensure that each aircraft used for flight instruction is at least a two-place aircraft with engine power controls and flight controls that are easily reached and that operate in a conventional manner from both pilot stations.

(c) Airplanes with controls such as nose-wheel steering, switches, fuel selectors, and engine air flow controls that are not easily reached and operated in a conventional manner by both pilots may be used for flight instruction if the certificate holder determines that the flight instruction can be conducted in a safe manner considering the location of controls and their nonconventional operation, or both.

142

§142.59 Flight simulators and flight training devices.

(a) An applicant for, or holder of, a training center certificate must show that each flight simulator and flight training device used for training, testing, and checking (except AQP) will be or is specifically qualified and approved by the Administrator for—

(1) Each maneuver and procedure for the make, model, and series of aircraft, set of aircraft, or aircraft type simulated, as applicable; and

(2) Each curriculum or training course in which the flight simulator or flight training device is used, if that curriculum or course is used to satisfy any requirement of 14 CFR chapter I.

(b) The approval required by paragraph (a)(2) of this section must include—

(1) The set of aircraft, or type aircraft;

(2) If applicable, the particular variation within type, for which the training, testing, or checking is being conducted; and

(3) The particular maneuver, procedure, or crewmember function to be performed.

(c) Each qualified and approved flight simulator or flight training device used by a training center must—

(1) Be maintained to ensure the reliability of the performances, functions, and all other characteristics that were required for qualification;

(2) Be modified to conform with any modification to the aircraft being simulated if the modification results in changes to performance, function, or other characteristics required for qualification;

(3) Be given a functional preflight check each day before being used; and

(4) Have a discrepancy log in which the instructor or evaluator, at the end of each training session, enters each discrepancy.

(d) Unless otherwise authorized by the Administrator, each component on a qualified and approved flight simulator or flight training device used by a training center must be operative if the component is essential to, or involved in, the training, testing, or checking of airmen.

(e) Training centers shall not be restricted to specific—

(1) Route segments during line-oriented flight training scenarios; and

(2) Visual data bases replicating a specific customer's bases of operation.

(f) Training centers may request evaluation, qualification, and continuing evaluation for qualification of flight simulators and flight training devices without—

(1) Holding an air carrier certificate; or

(2) Having a specific relationship to an air carrier certificate holder.

Subpart D— Operating Rules

§142.61 Applicability.

This subpart prescribes the operating rules applicable to a training center certificated under this part and operating a course or training program curriculum approved in accordance with subpart B of this part.

§142.63 Privileges.

A certificate holder may allow flight simulator instructors and evaluators to meet recency of experience requirements through the use of a qualified and approved flight simulator or qualified and approved flight training device if that flight simulator or flight training device is—

(a) Used in a course approved in accordance with subpart B of this part; or

(b) Approved under the Advanced Qualification Program for meeting recency of experience requirements.

§142.65 Limitations.

(a) A certificate holder shall—

(1) Ensure that a flight simulator or flight training device freeze, slow motion, or repositioning feature is not used during testing or checking; and

(2) Ensure that a repositioning feature is used during line operational simulation for evaluation and line-oriented flight training only to advance along a flight route to the point where the descent and approach phase of the flight begins.

(b) When flight testing, flight checking, or line operational simulation is being conducted, the certificate holder must ensure that one of the following occupies each crewmember position:

(1) A crewmember qualified in the aircraft category, class, and type, if a type rating is required, provided that no flight instructor who is giving instruction may occupy a crewmember position.

(2) A student, provided that no student may be used in a crewmember position with any other student not in the same specific course.

(c) The holder of a training center certificate may not recommend a trainee for a certificate or rating, unless the trainee—

(1) Has satisfactorily completed the training specified in the course approved under §142.37; and

(2) Has passed the final tests required by §142.37.

(d) The holder of a training center certificate may not graduate a student from a course unless the student has satisfactorily completed the curriculum requirements of that course.

Subpart E—
Recordkeeping

§142.71 Applicability.

This subpart prescribes the training center recordkeeping requirements for trainees enrolled in a course, and instructors and evaluators designated to instruct a course, approved in accordance with subpart B of this part.

§142.73 Recordkeeping requirements.

(a) A certificate holder must maintain a record for each trainee that contains—

(1) The name of the trainee;

(2) A copy of the trainee's pilot certificate, if any, and medical certificate;

(3) The name of the course and the make and model of flight training equipment used;

(4) The trainee's prerequisite experience and course time completed;

(5) The trainee's performance on each lesson and the name of the instructor providing instruction;

(6) The date and result of each end-of-course practical test and the name of the evaluator conducting the test; and

(7) The number of hours of additional training that was accomplished after any unsatisfactory practical test.

(b) A certificate holder shall maintain a record for each instructor or evaluator designated to instruct a course approved in accordance with subpart B of this part that indicates that the instructor or evaluator has complied with the requirements of §§142.13, 142.45, 142.47, 142.49, and 142.53, as applicable.

(c) The certificate holder shall—

(1) Maintain the records required by paragraphs (a) of this section for at least 1 year following the completion of training, testing, or checking;

(2) Maintain the qualification records required by paragraph (b) of this section while the instructor or evaluator is in the employ of the certificate holder and for 1 year thereafter; and

(3) Maintain the recurrent demonstration of proficiency records required by paragraph (b) of this section for at least 1 year.

(d) The certificate holder must provide the records required by this section to the Administrator, upon request and at a reasonable time, and shall keep the records required by—

(1) Paragraph (a) of this section at the training center, or satellite training center where the training, testing, or checking, if appropriate, occurred; and

(2) Paragraph (b) of this section at the training center or satellite training center where the instructor or evaluator is primarily employed.

(e) The certificate holder shall provide to a trainee, upon request and at a reasonable time, a copy of his or her training records.

Subpart F—
Other Approved Courses

§142.81 Conduct of other approved courses.

(a) An applicant for, or holder of, a training center certificate may apply for approval to conduct a course for which a curriculum is not prescribed by this part.

(b) The course for which application is made under paragraph (a) of this section may be for flight crewmembers other than pilots, airmen other than flight crewmembers, material handlers, ground servicing personnel, and security personnel, and others approved by the Administrator.

(c) An applicant for course approval under this subpart must comply with the applicable requirements of subpart A through subpart F of this part.

(d) The Administrator approves the course for which the application is made if the training center or training center applicant shows that the course contains a curriculum that will achieve a level of competency equal to, or greater than, that required by the appropriate part of this chapter.

[Docket No. 26933, 61 FR 34562, July 2, 1996]

142

49 CFR PART 830

NOTIFICATION AND REPORTING OF AIRCRAFT ACCIDENTS OR INCIDENTS AND OVERDUE AIRCRAFT, AND PRESERVATION OF AIRCRAFT WRECKAGE, MAIL, CARGO, AND RECORDS

Subpart A—General

Sec.
830.1 Applicability.
830.2 Definitions.

Subpart B—
Initial Notification of Aircraft Accidents, Incidents, and Overdue Aircraft

830.5 Immediate notification.
830.6 Information to be given in notification.

Subpart C—
Preservation of Aircraft Wreckage, Mail, Cargo, and Records

830.10 Preservation of aircraft wreckage, mail, cargo, and records.

Subpart D—
Reporting of Aircraft Accidents, Incidents, and Overdue Aircraft

830.15 Reports and statements to be filed.

Authority: 49 U.S.C. 1101-1155; Pub. L. 85-726, 72 Stat. 731 (codified as amended at 49 U.S.C. 40101).

Source: 53 FR 36982, Sept. 23, 1988, unless otherwise noted.

Subpart A—General

§830.1 Applicability.

This part contains rules pertaining to:

(a) Initial notification and later reporting of aircraft incidents and accidents and certain other occurrences in the operation of aircraft, wherever they occur, when they involve civil aircraft of the United States; when they involve certain public aircraft, as specified in this part, wherever they occur; and when they involve foreign civil aircraft where the events occur in the United States, its territories, or its possessions.

(b) Preservation of aircraft wreckage, mail, cargo, and records involving all civil and certain public aircraft accidents, as specified in this part, in the United States and its territories or possessions.

[53 FR 36982, Sept. 23, 1988; as amended by 60 FR 40112, Aug. 7, 1995]

§830.2 Definitions.

As used in this part the following words or phrases are defined as follows:

Aircraft accident means an occurrence associated with the operation of an aircraft which takes place between the time any person boards the aircraft with the intention of flight and all such persons have disembarked, and in which any person suffers death or serious injury, or in which the aircraft receives substantial damage. For purposes of this part, the definition of "aircraft accident" includes "unmanned aircraft accident," as defined herein.

Civil aircraft means any aircraft other than a public aircraft.

Fatal injury means any injury which results in death within 30 days of the accident.

Incident means an occurrence other than an accident, associated with the operation of an aircraft, which affects or could affect the safety of operations.

Operator means any person who causes or authorizes the operation of an aircraft, such as the owner, lessee, or bailee of an aircraft.

Public aircraft means an aircraft used only for the United States Government, or an aircraft owned and operated (except for commercial purposes) or exclusively leased for at least 90 continuous days by a government other than the United States Government, including a State, the District of Columbia, a territory or possession of the United States, or a political subdivision of that government. "Public aircraft" does not include a government-owned aircraft transporting property for commercial purposes and does not include a government-owned aircraft transporting passengers other than: transporting (for other than commercial purposes) crewmembers or other persons aboard the aircraft whose presence is required to perform, or is associated with the performance of, a governmental function such as firefighting, search and rescue, law enforcement, aeronautical research, or biological or geological resource management; or transporting (for other than commercial purposes) persons aboard the aircraft if the aircraft is operated by the Armed Forces or an intelligence agency of the United States. Notwithstanding any limitation relating to use of the aircraft for commercial purposes, an aircraft shall be considered to be a public aircraft without regard to whether it is operated by a unit of government on behalf of another unit of government pursuant to a cost reimbursement agreement, if the unit of government on whose behalf the operation is conducted certifies to the Administrator of the Federal Aviation Administration that the operation

was necessary to respond to a significant and imminent threat to life or property (including natural resources) and that no service by a private operator was reasonably available to meet the threat.

Serious injury means any injury which: (1) Requires hospitalization for more than 48 hours, commencing within 7 days from the date of the injury was received; (2) results in a fracture of any bone (except simple fractures of fingers, toes, or nose); (3) causes severe hemorrhages, nerve, muscle, or tendon damage; (4) involves any internal organ; or (5) involves second- or third-degree burns, or any burns affecting more than 5 percent of the body surface.

Substantial damage means damage or failure which adversely affects the structural strength, performance, or flight characteristics of the aircraft, and which would normally require major repair or replacement of the affected component. Engine failure or damage limited to an engine if only one engine fails or is damaged, bent fairings or cowling, dented skin, small punctured holes in the skin or fabric, ground damage to rotor or propeller blades, and damage to landing gear, wheels, tires, flaps, engine accessories, brakes, or wingtips are not considered "substantial damage" for the purpose of this part.

Unmanned aircraft accident means an occurrence associated with the operation of any public or civil unmanned aircraft system that takes place between the time that the system is activated with the purpose of flight and the time that the system is deactivated at the conclusion of its mission, in which:

(1) Any person suffers death or serious injury; or

(2) The aircraft holds an airworthiness certificate and sustains substantial damage.

[53 FR 36982, Sept. 23, 1988; as amended by 60 FR 40112, Aug. 7, 1995; Docket No. 2010–20864, 75 FR 51955, August 24, 2010; Doc. No. NTSB–2021-0004, 87 FR 42104, Jul. 14, 2022]

Subpart B— Initial Notification of Aircraft Accidents, Incidents, and Overdue Aircraft

§830.5 Immediate notification.

The operator of any civil aircraft, or any public aircraft not operated by the Armed Forces or an intelligence agency of the United States, or any foreign aircraft shall immediately, and by the most expeditious means available, notify the nearest

National Transportation Safety Board (NTSB) office[1] when:

(a) An aircraft accident or any of the following listed serious incidents occur:

(1) Flight control system malfunction or failure;

(2) Inability of any required flight crewmember to perform normal flight duties as a result of injury or illness;

(3) Failure of any internal turbine engine component that results in the escape of debris other than out the exhaust path;

(4) In-flight fire;

(5) Aircraft collision in flight;

(6) Damage to property, other than the aircraft, estimated to exceed $25,000 for repair (including materials and labor) or fair market value in the event of total loss, whichever is less.

(7) For large multiengine aircraft (more than 12,500 pounds maximum certificated takeoff weight):

(i) In-flight failure of electrical systems which requires the sustained use of an emergency bus powered by a back-up source such as a battery, auxiliary power unit, or air-driven generator to retain flight control or essential instruments;

(ii) In-flight failure of hydraulic systems that results in sustained reliance on the sole remaining hydraulic or mechanical system for movement of flight control surfaces;

(iii) Sustained loss of the power or thrust produced by two or more engines; and

(iv) An evacuation of an aircraft in which an emergency egress system is utilized.

(8) Release of all or a portion of a propeller blade from an aircraft, excluding release caused solely by ground contact;

(9) A complete loss of information, excluding flickering, from more than 50 percent of an aircraft's cockpit displays known as:

(i) Electronic Flight Instrument System (EFIS) displays;

(ii) Engine Indication and Crew Alerting System (EICAS) displays;

(iii) Electronic Centralized Aircraft Monitor (ECAM) displays; or

(iv) Other displays of this type, which generally include a primary flight display (PFD), primary navigation display (PND), and other integrated displays;

(10) Airborne Collision and Avoidance System (ACAS) resolution advisories issued when an aircraft is being operated on an instrument flight

[1] NTSB headquarters is located at 490 L'Enfant Plaza SW., Washington, DC 20594. Contact information for the NTSB's regional offices is available at *http://www.ntsb.gov*. To report an accident or incident, you may call the NTSB Response Operations Center, at 844-373-9922 or 202-314-6290

rules flight plan and compliance with the advisory is necessary to avert a substantial risk of collision between two or more aircraft.

(11) Damage to helicopter tail or main rotor blades, including ground damage, that requires major repair or replacement of the blade(s);

(12) Any event in which an operator, when operating an airplane as an air carrier at a public-use airport on land:

(i) Lands or departs on a taxiway, incorrect runway, or other area not designed as a runway; or

(ii) Experiences a runway incursion that requires the operator or the crew of another aircraft or vehicle to take immediate corrective action to avoid a collision.

(b) An aircraft is overdue and is believed to have been involved in an accident.

[53 FR 36982, Sept. 23, 1988; as amended by 60 FR 40113, Aug. 7, 1995; 75 FR 927, Jan. 7, 2010; 75 FR 35330, June 22, 2010; 80 FR 77587, Dec. 15, 2015]

§830.6 Information to be given in notification.

The notification required in §830.5 shall contain the following information, if available:

(a) Type, nationality, and registration marks of the aircraft;

(b) Name of owner, and operator of the aircraft;

(c) Name of the pilot-in-command;

(d) Date and time of the accident;

(e) Last point of departure and point of intended landing of the aircraft;

(f) Position of the aircraft with reference to some easily defined geographical point;

(g) Number of persons aboard, number killed, and number seriously injured;

(h) Nature of the accident, the weather and the extent of damage to the aircraft, so far as is known; and

(i) A description of any explosives, radioactive materials, or other dangerous articles carried.

Subpart C— Preservation of Aircraft Wreckage, Mail, Cargo, and Records

§830.10 Preservation of aircraft wreckage, mail, cargo, and records.

(a) The operator of an aircraft involved in an accident or incident for which notification must be given is responsible for preserving to the extent possible any aircraft wreckage, cargo, and mail aboard the aircraft, and all records, including all recording mediums of flight, maintenance, and voice recorders, pertaining to the operation and maintenance of the aircraft and to the airmen until the Board takes custody thereof or a release is granted pursuant to §831.12(b) of this chapter.

(b) Prior to the time the Board or its authorized representative takes custody of aircraft wreckage, mail, or cargo, such wreckage, mail, or cargo may not be disturbed or moved except to the extent necessary:

(1) To remove persons injured or trapped;

(2) To protect the wreckage from further damage; or

(3) To protect the public from injury.

(c) Where it is necessary to move aircraft wreckage, mail or cargo, sketches, descriptive notes, and photographs shall be made, if possible, of the original positions and condition of the wreckage and any significant impact marks.

(d) The operator of an aircraft involved in an accident or incident shall retain all records, reports, internal documents, and memoranda dealing with the accident or incident, until authorized by the Board to the contrary.

Subpart D— Reporting of Aircraft Accidents, Incidents, and Overdue Aircraft

§830.15 Reports and statements to be filed.

(a) *Reports.* The operator of a civil, public (as specified in §830.5), or foreign aircraft shall file a report on Board Form 6120.1/2 (OMB No. 3147–0001)[2] within 10 days after an accident, or after 7 days if an overdue aircraft is still missing. A report on an incident for which immediate notification is required by §830.5(a) shall be filed only as requested by an authorized representative of the Board.

(b) *Crewmember statement.* Each crewmember, if physically able at the time the report is submitted, shall attach a statement setting forth the facts, conditions, and circumstances relating to the accident or incident as they appear to him. If the crewmember is incapacitated, he shall submit the statement as soon as he is physically able.

(c) *Where to file the reports.* The operator of an aircraft shall file any report with the field office of the Board nearest the accident or incident.

[53 FR 36982, Sept. 23, 1988; as amended by 60 FR 40113, Aug. 7, 1995]

[2] Forms are available from the Board field offices (see footnote 1), from Board headquarters in Washington, DC, and from the Federal Aviation Administration, Flight Standards District Offices.

49 CFR PART 1552
FLIGHT TRAINING SECURITY PROGRAM

Editorial Note: The changes shown below to this Part are effective July 30, 2024.

Authority: 49 U.S.C. 114, 44939, and 6 U.S.C. 469.

Source: Docket No. TSA–2004–19147; 69 FR 56340, Sept. 20, 2004, unless otherwise noted.

Subpart A—Definitions and General Requirements

§1552.1 Scope.

This part includes requirements for the following persons:

(a) Persons who provide flight training or flight training equipment governed by 49 U.S.C. subtitle VII, part A, to any individual.

(b) Persons who lease flight training equipment.

(c) Non-U.S. citizens who apply for or participate in flight training.

(d) U.S. citizens and U.S. nationals who participate in flight training.

[Amdt. 1552–1, 89 FR 35626, May 1, 2024]

§1552.3 Terms used in this part.

In addition to the terms in §§1500.3 and 1540.5 of this chapter, the following terms apply to this part:

Aircraft simulator means a flight simulator or flight training device, as those terms are defined under 14 CFR part 61. Simulated flights for entertainment purposes or personal computer, video game, or mobile device software programs involving aircraft flight are not aircraft simulators for purposes of the requirements in this part.

Candidate means a non-U.S. citizen who applies for flight training or recurrent training from a flight training provider. The term does not include foreign military personnel who are endorsed for flight training by the U.S. Department of Defense (DoD), as described in §1552.7(a)(2); and does not include a non-U.S. citizen providing in-aircraft or in-simulator services or support to another candidate's training event (commonly referred to as "side-seat support") if the individual providing this support holds a type rating or other set of pilot certificates required to operate the aircraft or simulator in which the supported individual is receiving instruction.

Demonstration flight for marketing purposes means a flight for the purpose of demonstrating aircraft capabilities or characteristics to a potential purchaser; an orientation, familiarization, discovery flight for the purpose of demonstrating a flight training provider's training program to a potential candidate; or an acceptance flight after an aircraft manufacturer delivers an aircraft to a purchaser.

DoD means the Department of Defense.

DoD endorsee means a non-U.S. citizen who is or will be employed as a pilot by a foreign military, endorsed by the DoD or one of its component services, and validated by a DoD attaché for flight training as required by §1552.7(a)(2).

Determination of Eligibility means a finding by TSA, upon completion of a security threat assessment, that an individual meets the standards of a security threat assessment, and is eligible for a program, benefit, or credential administered by TSA.

Determination of Ineligibility means a finding by TSA, upon completion of a security threat assessment, that an individual does not meet the standards of a security threat assessment, and is not eligible for a program, benefit, or credential administered by TSA.

Flight training means instruction in a fixed-wing or rotary-wing aircraft or aircraft simulator that is consistent with the requirements to obtain a new

skill, certificate, or type rating, or to maintain a pilot certificate or rating. For the purposes of this rule, flight training does not include instruction in a balloon, glider, ultralight, or unmanned aircraft; ground training; demonstration flights for marketing purposes; simulated flights for entertainment purposes; or any flight training provided by the DoD, the U.S. Coast Guard, or any entity providing flight training under a contract with the DoD or the Coast Guard.

Flight training provider means—

(1) Any person that provides instruction under 49 U.S.C. subtitle VII, part A, in the operation of any aircraft or aircraft simulator in the United States or outside the United States, including any pilot school, flight training center, air carrier flight training facility, or individual flight instructor certificated under 14 CFR parts 61, 121, 135, 141, or 142;

(2) Similar persons certificated by foreign aviation authorities recognized by the Federal Aviation Administration (FAA), who provide flight training services in the United States; and

(3) Any lessor of an aircraft or aircraft simulator for flight training, if the person leasing their equipment is not covered by paragraph (1) or (2) of this definition.

Flight training provider employee means an individual who provides services to a flight training provider in return for financial or other compensation, or a volunteer, and who has direct contact with flight training students and candidates. A flight training provider employee may be an instructor, other authorized representative, or independent contractor.

Flight Training Security Program (FTSP) means the TSA program that provides regulatory oversight of the requirements in this part and provides related resources for individuals within the scope of this part.

FTSP Portal means a website that must be used to submit and receive certain information and notices as required by this part.

FTSP Portal account means an account created to access the FTSP Portal.

Recurrent training means

(1) Periodic flight training—

(i) Required for certificated pilots under 14 CFR parts 61, 121, 125, 135, or subpart K of part 91 to maintain a certificate or type rating; or

(ii) Similar training required by a civil aviation authority recognized by the FAA and conducted within the United States and its territories.

(2) Recurrent training does not include—

(i) Training that may be credited toward a new certificate or a new type rating; or

(ii) Checks or tests that do not affect the validity of the certificate(s) or the qualifications of a type rating.

Security threat means an individual determined by TSA to pose or to be suspected of posing a threat to national security, to transportation security, or of terrorism.

Security threat assessment means both a product and process of evaluating information regarding an individual seeking or holding approval for a program administered by TSA, including criminal, immigration, intelligence, law enforcement, and other security-related records, to verify the individual's identity and to determine whether the individual meets the eligibility criteria for the program. An individual who TSA determines is a security threat, or who does not otherwise meet the eligibility criteria for the program, is ineligible for that program.

Simulated flight for entertainment purposes means a ground-based aviation experience offered exclusively for the purpose of entertainment by a person that is not a flight training provider. Any simulated aviation experience that could be applied or credited toward an airman certification is not a simulated flight for entertainment purposes.

Type rating means an endorsement on a pilot certificate that the holder of the certificate has completed the appropriate training and testing required by a civil or military aviation authority to operate a certain make and type of aircraft.

[Amdt. 1552–1, 89 FR 35626, May 1, 2024]

§1552.5 Applicability.

Each of the following persons must comply with the requirements in this part:

(a) Any individual applying for flight training or recurrent flight training from a flight training provider;

(b) Flight training providers;

(c) Flight training provider employees; and

(d) Persons using a leased aircraft simulator to provide flight training as follows:

(1) If one or more persons using the leased aircraft simulator to provide flight training is certificated by the FAA as a flight instructor, then at least one of those certificated persons must register with TSA as a flight training provider and comply with the requirements of this part; or

(2) If one or more persons using a leased aircraft simulator to provide flight training are neither registered with TSA as a flight training provider nor certificated by the FAA as an instructor, then the lessor of the aircraft simulator must register with TSA as a flight training provider and comply with the requirements of this part.

[Amdt. 1552–1, 89 FR 35627, May 1, 2024]

§1552.7 Verification of eligibility.

(a) No flight training provider may provide flight training or access to flight training equipment to any individual before establishing that the individual is a U.S. citizen, U.S. national, DoD endorsee, or candidate with a valid Determination of Eligibility resulting from a TSA-accepted security threat assessment completed in accordance with subpart B of this part.

(1) To establish that an individual is a U.S. citizen or a U.S. national, each flight training provider must examine the individual's government-issued documentation as proof of U.S. citizenship or U.S. nationality. A student who claims to be a U.S. citizen or a U.S. national and who fails to provide valid, acceptable identification documents must be denied flight training. A list of acceptable identification documents may be found on the FTSP Portal.

(2) To establish that an individual has been endorsed by the DoD to receive U.S. Government-sponsored flight training in the United States, each flight training provider must use the FTSP Portal to confirm that the endorsee's government-issued photo identification matches the information provided in the U.S. DoD endorsement available on the FTSP Portal. A DoD endorsee is exempt from the requirement to undergo the security threat assessment required by this part if the DoD attaché with jurisdiction for the foreign military pilot's country of citizenship has notified TSA through the FTSP Portal that the pilot may participate in U.S. Government-sponsored flight training.

(3) To establish that a candidate has undergone a TSA-accepted security threat assessment, each flight training provider must use the FTSP Portal to confirm that TSA has issued a Determination of Eligibility to that candidate and that the determination is valid.

(b) Each flight training provider must immediately terminate a candidate's participation in all ongoing or planned flight training events when TSA either sends a Determination of Ineligibility for that candidate or notifies the flight training provider that the candidate presents a security threat.

(c) Each flight training provider must acknowledge through the FTSP Portal receipt of any of the following TSA notifications: Determination of Ineligibility; Candidate Security Threat; and Deny Candidate Flight Training.

(d) Each flight training provider must notify TSA if the provider becomes aware that a candidate is involved in any alleged criminal disqualifying offenses, as described under §1544.229(d) of this subchapter; is no longer permitted to remain in the United States, as described in §1552.35; or has reason to believe the individual otherwise poses a security threat.

[Amdt. 1552–1, 89 FR 35627, May 1, 2024]

§1552.9 Security Coordinator.

(a) *Designation of a Security Coordinator.* Each flight training provider must designate and use a primary Security Coordinator. The Security Coordinator must be designated at the corporate level.

(b) *Notification to TSA.* Each flight training provider must provide to TSA the names, title(s), phone number(s), and email address(es) of the Security Coordinator and the alternate Security Coordinator(s), as applicable, no later than November 1, 2024. Once a flight training provider has notified TSA of the contact information for the designated Security Coordinator and the alternate Security Coordinator(s), as applicable, the provider must notify TSA within 5 days of any changes in any of the information required by this section. This information must be provided through the FTSP Portal.

(c) *Role of Security Coordinator.* Each flight training provider must ensure that at least one Security Coordinator—

(1) Serves as the primary contact for intelligence information and security-related activities and communications with TSA. Any individual designated as a Security Coordinator may perform other duties in addition to those described in this section.

(2) Is accessible to TSA on a 24-hours a day, 7 days a week basis.

(3) Coordinates security practices and procedures internally, and with appropriate law enforcement and emergency response agencies.

(d) *Training for Security Coordinator.* Security Coordinator must satisfactorily complete the security awareness training required by §1552.13, and have the resources and knowledge necessary to quickly contact the following, as applicable:

(1) Their local TSA office;

(2) The local Federal Bureau of Investigation (FBI) office; and

(3) Local law enforcement, if a situation or an individual's behavior could pose an immediate threat.

[Amdt. 1552–1, 89 FR 35628, May 1, 2024]

§1552.11 [Reserved]

§1552.13 Security awareness training.

(a) Each flight training provider must ensure that each flight training provider employee who has direct contact with flight students completes a security awareness training program that meets the requirements of this section.

(b) Each flight training provider must ensure that each flight training provider employee who has direct contact with flight students receives initial security awareness training within 60 days of

hiring. At a minimum, initial security awareness training must—

(1) Require direct participation by the flight training provider employee receiving the training, either in person or through an online training module;

(2) Provide situational scenarios requiring the flight training provider employee receiving the training to assess specific situations and determine appropriate courses of action; and

(3) Contain information that enables a flight training provider employee to identify the following:

(i) Any restricted areas of the flight training provider or airport where the flight training provider operates and individuals authorized to be in these areas or in or on equipment, including designations such as uniforms or badges unique to the flight training provider and required to be worn by employees or other authorized persons.

(ii) Behavior that may be considered suspicious, including, but not limited to—

(A) Excessive or unusual interest in restricted airspace or restricted ground structures by unauthorized individuals;

(B) Unusual questions or interest regarding aircraft capabilities;

(C) Aeronautical knowledge inconsistent with the individual's existing airman credentialing; and

(D) Sudden termination of instruction by a candidate or other student.

(iii) Indications that candidates are being trained without a Determination of Eligibility or validation of exempt status.

(iv) Behavior by other persons on site that may be considered suspicious, including, but not limited to—

(A) Loitering on or around the operations of a flight training provider for extended periods of time; and

(B) Entering "authorized access only" areas without permission.

(v) Circumstances regarding aircraft that may be considered suspicious, including, but not limited to—

(A) Unusual modifications to aircraft, such as the strengthening of landing gear, changes to the tail number, or stripping of the aircraft of seating or equipment;

(B) Damage to propeller locks or other parts of an aircraft that is inconsistent with the pilot training or aircraft flight log; and

(C) Dangerous or hazardous cargo loaded into an aircraft.

(vi) Appropriate flight training provider employee responses to specific situations and scenarios, including—

(A) Identifying suspicious behavior requiring action, such as identifying anomalies within the operational environment considering the totality of the circumstances, and appropriate actions to take;

(B) When and how to safely question an individual if the individual's behavior is suspicious; and

(C) Informing a supervisor and the flight training provider's Security Coordinator, if a situation or an individual's behavior warrants further investigation.

(vii) Any other information relevant to security measures or procedures unique to the flight training provider's business, such as threats, past security incidents, or a site-specific TSA requirement.

(c) All flight training providers must ensure that each employee receives refresher security awareness training at least every 2 years. At a minimum, a refresher security awareness training program must—

(1) Include all the elements from the initial security awareness training;

(2) Provide instruction on any new security measures or procedures implemented by the flight training provider since the last security awareness training program;

(3) Relay information about recent security incidents at the flight training provider's business, if any, and any lessons learned as a result of such incidents;

(4) Cover any new threats posed by, or incidents involving, general or commercial aviation aircraft; and

(5) Provide instruction on any new TSA requirements concerning the security of general or commercial aviation aircraft, airports, or flight training operations.

(d) Flight training providers who must conduct security awareness training under part 1544 or 1546 of this subchapter may deliver that training in lieu of compliance with paragraphs (a) through (c) of this section.

[Amdt. 1552–1, 89 FR 35628, May 1, 2024]

§1552.15 Recordkeeping.

(a) *Retention.* Except as provided in paragraph (e) of this section, each flight training provider subject to the requirements in this part must, at a minimum, retain the records described in this section to demonstrate compliance with TSA's requirements and make these records available to TSA upon request for inspection and copying.

(b) *Employee records.* Each flight training provider required to provide security awareness training under §1552.13 must—

(1) Retain security awareness training records for each employee required to receive training that includes, at a minimum—

(i) The employee's name;

(ii) The dates the employee received security awareness training;

49 CFR

(iii) The name of the instructor or manager for training; and

(iv) The curricula or syllabus used for the most recently provided training that establishes the training meets the criteria specified in §1552.13.

(2) Retain records of security training for no less than 1 year after the individual is no longer an employee.

(3) Provide records to current and former employees upon request and at no charge as necessary to provide proof of training. At a minimum, the information provided must include—

(i) The information in paragraph (b)(1) of this section, except that, in lieu of providing the curriculum or syllabus, the flight training provider may provide a statement certifying that the training program used by the flight training provider met the criteria specified in §1552.13; and

(ii) The signature or e-signature of an authorized official of the provider.

(4) A flight training provider that conducts security awareness training under parts 1544 or 1546 of this subchapter may retain that documentation in lieu of compliance with this section.

(c) *Records demonstrating eligibility for flight training for U.S. citizens and U.S. nationals.*

(1) Each flight training provider must maintain records that document the provider's verification of U.S. citizenship or U.S. nationality as described in §1552.7(a)(1).

(2) Each flight training provider may certify that verification of U.S. citizenship or U.S. nationality occurred by making the following endorsement in both the instructor's and the student's logbooks: "I certify that [insert student's full name] has presented to me a [insert type of document presented, such as U.S. birth certificate or U.S. passport, and the relevant control or sequential number on the document, if any] establishing that [the student] is a U.S. citizen or U.S. national in accordance with 49 CFR 1552.7(a). [Insert date and the instructor's signature and certificate number.]"

(3) In lieu of paragraph (c)(1) or (2) of this section, the flight training provider may make and retain copies of the documentation establishing an individual as a U.S. citizen or U.S. national.

(d) *Leasing agreements.* Each flight training provider must retain all lease agreement records for aircraft simulators leased from another person, as identified under this section, as necessary to demonstrate compliance with the requirements of this part.

(e) *Records maintenance.*

(1) With the exception of the retention schedule for training records required under paragraph (b)(2) of this section, all records required by this part must be maintained electronically using methods approved by TSA or as paper records for at least 5 years after expiration or discontinuance of use.

(2) A flight training provider that uses its FTSP Portal account to confirm or manage the following records is not required to maintain separate electronic or paper copies of the following records:

(i) Security awareness training records;

(ii) Security Coordinator training records;

(iii) Verification of U.S. citizenship or U.S. nationality;

(iv) Verification of DoD Endorsee identity; or

(v) Aircraft or aircraft simulator lease agreements.

[Amdt. 1552–1, 89 FR 35629, May 1, 2024]

§1552.17 FTSP Portal.

(a) Candidates must obtain an FTSP Portal account and use the FTSP Portal to submit the information and fees necessary to initiate a security threat assessment under subpart B of this part.

(b) Flight training providers who provide flight training to candidates must obtain an FTSP Portal account and use the FTSP Portal to notify TSA of all candidate flight training events and confirm that a candidate is eligible for flight training. The flight training provider also may use the FTSP Portal for other recordkeeping purposes related to the requirements in §1552.15.

(c) The FTSP Portal account administrator for flight training providers who operate under 14 CFR part 61, either as an individual certified flight instructor, or for a group of certified flight instructors, must be an FAA certificate holder. The FTSP Portal account administrator for flight training providers who operate under 14 CFR parts 121, 135, 141, and 142 is not required to be an FAA certificate holder.

(d) TSA may suspend a flight training provider's access to the FTSP Portal at any time, without advance notice.

[Amdt. 1552–1, 89 FR 35629, May 1, 2024]

§1552.19 Fraud, falsification, misrepresentation, or omission.

If an individual covered by this part commits fraud, makes a false statement or misrepresentation, or omits a material fact when submitting any information required under this part, the individual may be—

(a) Subject to fine or imprisonment or both under Federal law, including, but not limited to, 18 U.S.C. 1001 and 49 U.S.C. 46301;

(b) Denied a security threat assessment under this chapter; and/or

(c) Subject to other enforcement or administrative action, as appropriate, including, but not limited to, proceedings under §1540.103 of this subchapter.

[Amdt. 1552–1, 89 FR 35629, May 1, 2024]

Subpart B—Security Threat Assessments

§1552.31 Security threat assessment required for flight training candidates.

(a) *Scope of security threat assessment.* Each candidate must complete a security threat assessment and receive a Determination of Eligibility from TSA prior to initiating flight training.

(b) *Information required.* To apply for a security threat assessment, each candidate must submit the following, in a form and manner acceptable to TSA—

(1) Biographic and biometric information determined by TSA to be necessary for conducting a security threat assessment;

(2) Identity verification documents; and

(3) The applicable security threat assessment fee identified in §1552.39.

(c) *TSA Determination of Eligibility.* TSA may issue a Determination of Eligibility to the flight training provider after conducting a security threat assessment of the candidate that includes, at a minimum—

(1) Confirmation of the candidate's identity;

(2) A check of relevant databases and other information to determine whether the candidate may pose or poses a security threat and to confirm the individual's identity;

(3) An immigration check; and

(4) An FBI fingerprint-based criminal history records check to determine whether the individual has a disqualifying criminal offense in accordance with the requirements of §1544.229 of this subchapter.

(d) *Term of TSA Determination of Eligibility.*

(1) The TSA Determination of Eligibility expires 5 years after the date it was issued, unless—

(i) The candidate commits a disqualifying criminal offense described in §1544.229(d) of this subchapter and, in such case, the Determination of Eligibility expires on the date the candidate was convicted or found not guilty by reason of insanity;

(ii) TSA determines that the candidate poses a security threat; or

(iii) The candidate's authorization to remain in the United States expires earlier than 5 years and, in such case, the Determination of Eligibility expires on the date that the candidate's authorization to remain in the United States expires. Candidates may extend the term of their Determination of Eligibility up to a total of 5 years by submitting updated documentation of authorization to remain in the United States.

(2) No candidate may engage in flight training after the expiration of the candidate's Determination of Eligibility.

(e) *Processing time.* TSA will process complete security threat assessment applications within 30 days.

(f) *Correction of the record.* A Determination of Ineligibility made by TSA on the basis of a candidate's complete and accurate record is final. If the Determination of Ineligibility was based on a record that the candidate believes is erroneous, the candidate may correct the record by submitting all missing or corrected documents, plus all additional documents or information that TSA may request, within 180 days of TSA's initial determination.

[Amdt. 1552–1, 89 FR 35629, May 1, 2024]

§1552.33 [Reserved]

§1552.35 Presence in the United States.

(a) A candidate may be eligible to participate in flight training if the candidate—

(1) Is lawfully admitted to the United States, or entered the United States and has been granted permission to stay by the U.S. Government, or is otherwise authorized to be employed in the United States; and

(2) Is within their period of authorized stay in the United States.

(b) A candidate who has yet to obtain a valid document issued by the United States evidencing eligibility to take flight training may be issued a preliminary Determination of Eligibility pending the individual's ability to provide proof of eligibility.

(c) A candidate who engages in a flight training event that takes place entirely outside the United States is not required to provide eligibility for flight training in the United States, but must provide any United States visas held by the candidate.

(d) Any history of denial of a United States visa may be a factor in determining whether a candidate is eligible to participate in flight training, regardless of training location.

[Amdt. 1552–1, 89 FR 35630, May 1, 2024]

§1552.37 Comparable security threat assessments.

(a) TSA may accept the results of a comparable, valid, and unexpired security threat assessment, background check, or investigation conducted by TSA or by another U.S. Government agency, which TSA generally describes as a Determination of Eligibility. A candidate seeking to rely on a comparable security threat assessment must submit documents confirming their Determination of Eligibility through the FTSP Portal, including the biographic and biometric information required under §1552.31. TSA will post a list of acceptable comparable security threat assessments on the FTSP Portal.

49 CFR

(b) TSA will charge a fee to cover the costs of confirming a comparable security threat assessment, but this fee may be a reduced fee.

(c) An FTSP reduced-fee security threat assessment based on a comparable security threat assessment will be valid in accordance with §1552.31.

[Amdt. 1552–1, 89 FR 35630, May 1, 2024]

§1552.39 Fees.

(a) *Imposition of fees.*

(1) A candidate must remit the fees required by this part, as determined by TSA, which will be published through notice in the **Federal Register** and posted on the FTSP Portal.

(2) Changes to the fee amounts will be published through notice in the **Federal Register** and posted on the FTSP Portal.

(3) TSA will publish the details of the fee methodology in the rulemaking docket.

(b) *Refunding fees.* TSA will not issue fee refunds unless the fee is paid in error.

[Amdt. 1552–1, 89 FR 35630, May 1, 2024]

Subpart C—Flight Training Event Management

§1552.51 Notification and processing of flight training events.

(a) *Notification of flight training events.* Each flight training provider must notify TSA through the FTSP Portal of all proposed and actual flight training events scheduled by a candidate, without regard to whether that training is intended to result in certification.

(b) *Training event details.* Each flight training provider must include the following information with each flight training event notification:

(1) Candidate name;

(2) The rating(s) that the candidate could receive upon completion of the flight training, if any;

(3) For recurrent flight training, the type rating for which the recurrent training is required;

(4) Estimated start and end dates of the flight training; and

(5) Location(s) where the flight training is anticipated to occur.

(c) *Acknowledgement.* TSA will acknowledge receipt of the information required by paragraphs (a) and (b) of this section.

(d) *Candidate photograph.* When the candidate arrives for training, each flight training provider must take a photograph of the candidate and must upload it to the FTSP Portal within 5 business days of the date that the candidate arrived for flight training.

(e) *Waiting period.* Each flight training provider may initiate flight training if more than 30 days have elapsed since TSA acknowledged receipt of the information required by paragraphs (a) and (b) of this section.

(f) *Waiting period for expedited processing.* A flight training provider may initiate flight training if:

(1) More than 5 business days have elapsed since TSA acknowledged receipt of the information required by paragraphs (a) and (b) of this section; and

(2) TSA has provided confirmation in its acknowledgement to the flight training provider that the candidate is eligible for expedited processing. A candidate is eligible for expedited processing if the candidate has provided proof to TSA that the candidate—

(i) Holds an FAA airman certificate with a type rating;

(ii) Holds an airman certificate, with a type rating, from a foreign country that is recognized by an agency of the United States, including a military agency;

(iii) Is employed by a domestic or foreign air carrier that has an approved security program under parts 1544 or 1546 of this subchapter, respectively;

(iv) Is an individual that has unescorted access to a secured area of an airport as determined under part 1542 of this subchapter; or

(v) Is a lawful permanent resident.

(g) *Update training event details.* Each flight training provider must update on the FTSP Portal the following information for each reported flight training event:

(1) Actual start and end dates.

(2) Actual training location(s).

(3) Notification if training was not completed, to include a brief description of why the training was not completed, e.g., cancellation by the provider or the candidate, failure of the candidate to meet the required standard, or abandonment of training by the candidate.

[Amdt. 1552–1, 89 FR 35630, May 1, 2024]

AIM Contents

Aeronautical Information Manual
Official Guide to Basic Flight Information and ATC Procedures
U.S. Department of Transportation • Federal Aviation Administration

Ch 1
Ch 2
Ch 3
Ch 4
Ch 5
Ch 6
Ch 7
Ch 8
Ch 9
Ch 10
Ch 11
APP
P/C

Federal Aviation Administration (FAA)

The Federal Aviation Administration is responsible for ensuring the safe, efficient, and secure use of the Nation's airspace, by military as well as civil aviation, for promoting safety in air commerce, for encouraging and developing civil aeronautics, including new aviation technology, and for supporting the requirements of national defense.

The activities required to carry out these responsibilities include: safety regulations; airspace management and the establishment, operation, and maintenance of a civil–military common system of air traffic control (ATC) and navigation facilities; research and development in support of the fostering of a national system of airports, promulgation of standards and specifications for civil airports, and administration of Federal grants-in-aid for developing public airports; various joint and cooperative activities with the Department of Defense; and technical assistance (under State Department auspices) to other countries.

Aeronautical Information Manual (AIM)

Basic Flight Information and ATC Procedures

This manual is designed to provide the aviation community with basic flight information and ATC procedures for use in the National Airspace System (NAS) of the United States. An international version called the Aeronautical Information Publication contains parallel information, as well as specific information on the international airports for use by the international community.

This manual contains the fundamentals required in order to fly in the United States NAS. It also contains items of interest to pilots concerning health and medical facts, factors affecting flight safety, a pilot/controller glossary of terms used in the ATC System, and information on safety, accident, and hazard reporting.

This manual is complemented by other operational publications which are available via separate subscriptions. These publications are:

The Chart Supplement U.S., the Chart Supplement Alaska, and the Chart Supplement Pacific—These publications contain information on airports, communications, navigation aids, instrument landing systems, VOR receiver check points, preferred routes, Flight Service Station/Weather Service telephone numbers, Air Route Traffic Control Center (ARTCC) frequencies, part-time surface areas, and various other pertinent special notices essential to air navigation. These publications are available through a network of FAA approved print providers. A listing of products, dates of latest editions, and print providers is available on the Aeronautical Information Services (AIS) website at: http://www.faa.gov/air_traffic/flight_info/aeronav/print_providers/.

Publication Schedule		
Basic or Change	Cutoff Date for Completion	Effective Date of Publication
Basic Manual	11/3/22	4/20/23
Change 1	4/20/23	10/5/23
Change 2	10/5/23	3/21/24
Change 3	3/21/24	9/5/24
Basic Manual	9/5/24	2/20/25
Change 1	2/20/25	8/7/25
Change 2	8/7/25	1/22/26
Change 3	1/22/26	7/9/26

Flight Information Publication Policy

The following is in essence, the statement issued by the FAA Administrator and published in the December 10, 1964, issue of the Federal Register, concerning the FAA policy as pertaining to the type of information that will be published as NOTAMs and in the *Aeronautical Information Manual.*

a. It is a pilot's inherent responsibility to be alert at all times for and in anticipation of all circumstances, situations, and conditions affecting the safe operation of the aircraft. For example, a pilot should expect to find air traffic at any time or place. At or near both civil and military airports and in the vicinity of known training areas, a pilot should expect concentrated air traffic and realize concentrations of air traffic are not limited to these places.

b. It is the general practice of the agency to advertise by NOTAM or other flight information publications such information it may deem appropriate; information which the agency may from time to time make available to pilots is solely for the purpose of assisting them in executing their regulatory responsibilities. Such information serves the aviation community as a whole and not pilots individually.

c. The fact that the agency under one particular situation or another may or may not furnish information does not serve as a precedent of the agency's responsibility to the aviation community; neither does it give assurance that other information of the same or similar nature will be advertised, nor, does it guarantee that any and all information known to the agency will be advertised.

d. This publication, while not regulatory, provides information which reflects examples of operating techniques and procedures which may be requirements in other federal publications or regulations. It is made available solely to assist pilots in executing their responsibilities required by other publications.

Consistent with the foregoing, it is the policy of the Federal Aviation Administration to furnish information only when, in the opinion of the agency, a unique situation should be advertised and not to furnish routine information such as concentrations of air traffic, either civil or military. The *Aeronautical Information Manual* will not contain informative items concerning everyday circumstances that pilots should, either by good practices or regulation, expect to encounter or avoid.

Aeronautical Information Manual (AIM)

Code of Federal Regulations and Advisory Circulars

Code of Federal Regulations—The FAA publishes the Code of Federal Regulations (CFRs) to make readily available to the aviation community the regulatory requirements placed upon them. These regulations are sold as individual parts by the Superintendent of Documents.

The more frequently amended parts are sold on subscription service with subscribers receiving changes automatically as issued. Less active parts are sold on a single-sale basis. Changes to single-sale parts will be sold separately as issued. Information concerning these changes will be furnished by the FAA through its Status of Federal Aviation Regulations, AC 00-44.

Advisory Circulars—The FAA issues Advisory Circulars (ACs) to inform the aviation public in a systematic way of nonregulatory material. Unless incorporated into a regulation by reference, the contents of an advisory circular are not binding on the public. Advisory Circulars are issued in a numbered subject system corresponding to the subject areas of the Code of Federal Regulations (CFRs) (Title 14, Chapter 1, FAA).

Note: *Current AC information can be found at: https://www.faa.gov/regulations_policies/advisory_circulars/.*

External References—All references to Advisory Circulars and other FAA publications in the *Aeronautical Information Manual* include the FAA Advisory Circular or Order identification numbers (when available). However, due to varied publication dates, the basic publication letter is not included.

Example

FAA Order JO 7110.65X, Air Traffic Control, is referenced as FAA Order JO 7110.65.

Comments/Corrections

The office of primary responsibility (OPR) for this manual is:

FAA Headquarters, Mission Support Services
Policy Directorate (AJV-P)
600 Independence Avenue SW
Washington, DC 20597

Proposed changes must be submitted electronically, using the following format, to the Policy Directorate Correspondence Mailbox at 9-AJV-P-HQ-Correspondence@faa.gov.

Notice to Editor

The following comments/corrections are submitted concerning the information contained in:

Paragraph number _____

Title _____

Page _____

Dated _____

Name_____

Street_____

City _____

State _____

Zip _____

Subscription Information

This manual is available by its effective date on the FAA's Air Traffic Plans and Publications website at https://www.faa.gov/air_traffic/publications/.

This manual is distributed electronically to all who subscribe to receive email notifications through the FAA's website. All organizations are responsible for viewing, downloading, and subscribing to receive email notifications when changes occur to this manual. Subscriptions to air traffic directives can be made through the Air Traffic Plans and Publications website at https://www.faa.gov/air_traffic/publications/ or directly via the following link: https://public.govdelivery.com/accounts/USAFAA/subscriber/new?topic_id=USAFAA_39.

Explanation of Major Changes

Change 1 effective October 5, 2023, and Change 2 effective March 21, 2024 (to Basic Manual effective April 20, 2023).

1–1–9. Instrument Landing System (ILS)
This change reflects the FAA Order JO 7110.65 guidance that allows a preceding arrival or departure in or over the ILS critical area when the weather is above 200' ceiling and 2000 RVR. The new guidance warns pilots of signal disturbances that may be encountered in any weather at or above standard CAT I minima.

1–1–17. Global Positioning System
This change aligns the AIM with Flight Standards B036 issuance policy that two GPS receivers are considered independent systems for extended overwater operations.

1–1–20. Precision Approach Systems Other Than ILS and GPS
Appendix 3. Abbreviations/Acronyms
This change will result in the removal of references to SCAT–I DGPS from the AIM.

2–3–8. Mandatory Instruction Signs
This change addresses a change to the mandatory instruction sign to include the departure runway information in the sign legend. The sign for holding positions protecting both the approach area of a runway end and the departure area for the opposite runway end will now display "DEP" in addition to "APCH" (e.g., 15 APCH–33 DEP). Holding positions signs on taxiways that traverse the approach area but not the departure area (e.g., displaced threshold) will continue to display just the APCH legend. This change does not address changes to the hold line marking or implement conditional holding for protection of approach/departure areas.

3–5–2. Military Training Routes
This change adds language to paragraph 3-5-2 that defines what the Department of Defense Flight Information Publications (DoD FLIP) represent and describes instrument/visual routes (IR/VR) that can be found in charts and narratives. It also describes FAA's responsibility for providing information about them on IFR and VFR routes. Additionally, a note was added for users who require copies of the FLIP.

3–5–8. Washington DC Special Flight Rules Area (SFRA) Including the Flight Restricted Zone (FRZ)
This change adds a new paragraph 3-5-8, Washington DC Special Flight Rules Area (SFRA) including the Flight Restricted Zone (FRZ), to the AIM to better inform pilots and reduce violations reference the requirements of 14 CFR Part 93.339 and Part 91.161, and 14 CFR 99.7 Special Security Instruction NOTAMs. The current paragraphs 3-5-8 and 3-5-9 are being renumbered 3-5-9 and 3-5-10, respectively.

4–1–21. Airport Reservation Operations and Special Traffic Management Programs
Dual-tone multi-frequency (telephone touch-tone signaling) interfaces are no longer available for use to receive an Electronic Special Traffic Management Program or Enhanced Computer Voice Reservation System reservation. Procedures for coordination processing are updated and some content has been revised for clarification.

4–3–20. Standard Taxi Routes
This change adds a paragraph to Chapter 4, Air Traffic Control, Section 3, Airport Operations, of the AIM, to provide guidance to pilots about Standard Taxi Routes (STRs). This new paragraph will support the implementation of a new directive, FAA Order JO 7110.664, Standard Taxi Routes. All subsequent paragraphs will be renumbered.

7–1–3. Use of Aviation Products
7–1–4. Graphical Forecasts for Aviation Weather (GFA)
7–1–11. Weather Radar Services
7–1–18. Pilot Weather Reports (PIREPS)
This change updates the references to AC 00-45 to the *Aviation Weather Handbook*, FAA-H-8083-28.

7–1–5. Preflight Briefing
This change updates the subparagraph to use true north rather than magnetic north.

7–3–5. Cold Temperature Airport Procedures
This change adds an additional segment to Figure 7-3-1, Example Cold Temperature Restricted Airport List—Required Segments, along with guidance on how to apply a temperature correction to this segment. The change also rearranges the section for better flow, swapping the positions of updated subparagraphs e and f.

7–6–4. Obstructions to Flight
This change provides pilots guidance on the distinctive hazards when flying near wind turbines and their unique marking and lighting. Additionally, other updates were made to improve the readability of the paragraphs addressing other obstruction types.

9–1–4. General Description of Each Chart Series
As a result of the Chart Supplement Modernization Initiative, the Chart Supplement U.S. descriptions were revised and expanded creating Chart Supplement, Chart Supplement Alaska, and Chart Supplement Pacific. Figure 9-1-14 was

(continued)

repositioned and renumbered to immediately follow subparagraph d2 for better readability.

Appendix 4. FAA Form 7233-4—International Flight Plan

This change modifies codes used in field 18 of the ICAO flight plan for indication of ADS-B equipage in compliance with international agreements.

Appendix 4. FAA Form 7233-4—International Flight Plan

This change modifies an existing note to identify three Item 18 NAV and PBN codes that require all civil operators to obtain specific operational approval prior to including on their flight plan. Additionally, an identical comment was added to Appendix 2 of the U.S. AIP.

Editorial Changes

Editorial changes include updated and corrected references and typos; rewording subparagraph 8-1-2d to eliminate confusion between high altitude of aircraft vs. low cabin altitude pressure; clarifying language in subparagraph 11-2-2c2 to say that UAS that are flown exclusively for recreational purposes must be registered if they weigh more than 0.55 pounds (250 grams); updating the subscription information for this publication; a hyperlink fix and hyperlink update for Helicopter Association International in subparagraph 10-2-1a; updates to the term Chart Supplement and Chart Supplement U.S.; the addition of RX Receive/Receiver and edit of REDL to Runway Edge Light in 5-1-3, Table 5-1-2; a change reconciling the discrepancy between FAA Order JO 7210.3 and the *Aeronautical Information Manual* by changing the time for requesting Remote Airport Information Service (RAIS) support from 60 days to 30 days; correcting the spelling of "Juliet" to "Juliett" in paragraph 4-1-16; a couple of simple editorial changes in paragraphs 3-2-3 and 5-4-1; correcting non-radar to nonradar in 5-3-2c4; and a simple editorial correcting "four" to "these" in 7-1-10d1(a).

Entire Publication

Additional editorial/format changes were made where necessary. Revision bars were not used because of the insignificant nature of these changes.

Chapter 1 Air Navigation

Chapter 2 Aeronautical Lighting
and Other Airport Visual Aids

Chapter 3 Airspace

Chapter 4 Air Traffic Control

Chapter 5 Air Traffic Procedures

Chapter 6 Emergency Procedures

Chapter 7 Safety of Flight

Chapter 8 Medical Facts for Pilots

Chapter 9 Aeronautical Charts and Related Publications

Chapter 10 Helicopter Operations

Chapter 11 Unmanned Aircraft Systems (UAS)

Chapter 1
Air Navigation

Section 1 Navigation Aids

1–1–1 General

a. Various types of air navigation aids are in use today, each serving a special purpose. These aids have varied owners and operators, namely: the Federal Aviation Administration (FAA), the military services, private organizations, individual states and foreign governments. The FAA has the statutory authority to establish, operate, maintain air navigation facilities and to prescribe standards for the operation of any of these aids which are used for instrument flight in federally controlled airspace. These aids are tabulated in the Chart Supplement.

b. Pilots should be aware of the possibility of momentary erroneous indications on cockpit displays when the primary signal generator for a ground-based navigational transmitter (for example, a glideslope, VOR, or nondirectional beacon) is inoperative. Pilots should disregard any navigation indication, regardless of its apparent validity, if the particular transmitter was identified by NOTAM or otherwise as unusable or inoperative.

1–1–2 Nondirectional Radio Beacon (NDB)

a. A low or medium frequency radio beacon transmits nondirectional signals whereby the pilot of an aircraft properly equipped can determine bearings and "home" on the station. These facilities normally operate in a frequency band of 190 to 535 kilohertz (kHz), according to ICAO Annex 10 the frequency range for NDBs is between 190 and 1750 kHz, and transmit a continuous carrier with either 400 or 1020 hertz (Hz) modulation. All radio beacons except the compass locators transmit a continuous three-letter identification in code except during voice transmissions.

b. When a radio beacon is used in conjunction with the Instrument Landing System markers, it is called a Compass Locator.

c. Voice transmissions are made on radio beacons unless the letter "W" (without voice) is included in the class designator (HW).

d. Radio beacons are subject to disturbances that may result in erroneous bearing information. Such disturbances result from such factors as lightning, precipitation static, etc. At night, radio beacons are vulnerable to interference from distant stations. Nearly all disturbances which affect the Automatic Direction Finder (ADF) bearing also affect the facility's identification. Noisy identification usually occurs when the ADF needle is erratic. Voice, music or erroneous identification may be heard when a steady false bearing is being displayed. Since ADF receivers do not have a "flag" to warn the pilot when erroneous bearing information is being displayed, the pilot should continuously monitor the NDB's identification.

1–1–3 VHF Omni-Directional Range (VOR)

a. VORs operate within the 108.0 to 117.95 MHz frequency band and have a power output necessary to provide coverage within their assigned operational service volume. They are subject to line-of-sight restrictions, and the range varies proportionally to the altitude of the receiving equipment.

Note: Normal service ranges for the various classes of VORs are given in Navigational Aid (NAVAID) Service Volumes, paragraph 1-1-8.

b. Most VORs are equipped for voice transmission on the VOR frequency. VORs without voice capability are indicated by the letter "W" (without voice) included in the class designator (VORW).

c. The only positive method of identifying a VOR is by its Morse Code identification or by the recorded automatic voice identification which is always indicated by use of the word "VOR" following the range's name. Reliance on determining the identification of an omnirange should never be placed on listening to voice transmissions by the Flight Service Station (FSS) (or approach control facility) involved. Many FSSs remotely operate several omniranges with different names. In some cases, none of the VORs have the name of the "parent" FSS. During periods of maintenance, the facility may radiate a T-E-S-T code (– • •••–) or the code may be removed. Some VOR equipment decodes the identifier and displays it to the pilot for verification to charts, while other equipment simply displays the expected identifier from a database to aid in verification to the audio tones. You should be familiar with your equipment and use it appropriately. If your equipment automatically decodes the identifier, it is not necessary to listen to the audio identification.

d. Voice identification has been added to numerous VORs. The transmission consists of a voice announcement, "AIRVILLE VOR" alternating with the usual Morse Code identification.

e. The effectiveness of the VOR depends upon proper use and adjustment of both ground and airborne equipment.

1. Accuracy. The accuracy of course alignment of the VOR is excellent, being generally plus or minus 1 degree.

2. Roughness. On some VORs, minor course roughness may be observed, evidenced by course needle or brief flag alarm activity (some receivers are more susceptible to these irregularities than others). At a few stations, usually in mountainous terrain, the pilot may occasionally observe a brief course needle oscillation, similar to the indication of "approaching station." Pilots flying over unfamiliar routes are cautioned to be on the alert for these vagaries, and in particular, to use the "to/from" indicator to determine positive station passage.

(a) Certain propeller revolutions per minute (RPM) settings or helicopter rotor speeds can cause the VOR Course Deviation Indicator to fluctuate as much as plus or minus six degrees. Slight changes to the RPM setting will normally smooth out this roughness. Pilots are urged to check for this modulation phenomenon prior to reporting a VOR station or aircraft equipment for unsatisfactory operation.

f. The VOR Minimum Operational Network (MON). As flight procedures and route structure based on VORs are gradually being replaced with Performance-Based Navigation (PBN) procedures, the FAA is removing selected VORs from service. PBN procedures are primarily enabled by GPS and its augmentation systems, collectively referred to as Global Navigation Satellite System (GNSS). Aircraft that carry DME/DME equipment can also use RNAV which provides a backup to continue flying PBN during a GNSS disruption. For those aircraft that do not carry DME/DME, the FAA is retaining a limited network of VORs, called the VOR MON, to provide a basic conventional navigation service for operators to use if GNSS becomes unavailable. During a GNSS disruption, the MON will enable aircraft to navigate through the affected area or to a safe landing at a MON airport without reliance on GNSS. Navigation using the MON will not be as efficient as the new PBN route structure, but use of the MON will provide nearly continuous VOR signal coverage at 5,000 feet AGL across the NAS, outside of the Western U.S. Mountainous Area (WUSMA).

Note: There is no plan to change the NAVAID and route structure in the WUSMA.

The VOR MON has been retained principally for IFR aircraft that are not equipped with DME/DME avionics. However, VFR aircraft may use the MON as desired. Aircraft equipped with DME/DME navigation systems would, in most cases, use DME/DME to continue flight using RNAV to their destination. However, these aircraft may, of course, use the MON.

1. Distance to a MON airport. The VOR MON will ensure that regardless of an aircraft's position in the contiguous United States (CONUS), a MON airport (equipped with legacy ILS or VOR approaches) will be within 100 nautical miles. These airports are referred to as "MON airports" and will have an ILS approach or a VOR approach if an ILS is not available. VORs to support these approaches will be retained in the VOR MON. MON airports are charted on low-altitude en route charts and are contained in the Chart Supplement U.S. and other appropriate publications.

Note: Any suitable airport can be used to land in the event of a VOR outage. For example, an airport with a DME-required ILS approach may be available and could be used by aircraft that are equipped with DME. The intent of the MON airport is to provide an approach that can be used by aircraft without ADF or DME when radar may not be available.

2. Navigating to an airport. The VOR MON will retain sufficient VORs and increase VOR service volume to ensure that pilots will have nearly continuous signal reception of a VOR when flying at 5,000 feet AGL. A key concept of the MON is to ensure that an aircraft will always be within 100 NM of an airport with an instrument approach that is not dependent on GPS. (See paragraph 1-1-8.) If the pilot encounters a GPS outage, the pilot will be able to proceed via VOR-to-VOR navigation at 5,000 feet AGL through the GPS outage area or to a safe landing at a MON airport or another suitable airport, as appropriate. Nearly all VORs inside of the WUSMA and outside the CONUS are being retained. In these areas, pilots use the existing (Victor and Jet) route structure and VORs to proceed through a GPS outage or to a landing.

3. Using the VOR MON.

(a) In the case of a planned GPS outage (for example, one that is in a published NOTAM), pilots may plan to fly through the outage using the MON as appropriate and as cleared by ATC. Similarly, aircraft not equipped with GPS may plan to fly and land using the MON, as appropriate and as cleared by ATC.

Note: In many cases, flying using the MON may involve a more circuitous route than flying GPS-enabled RNAV.

(b) In the case of an unscheduled GPS outage, pilots and ATC will need to coordinate the best outcome for all aircraft. It is possible that a GPS outage could be disruptive, causing high workload and demand for ATC service. Generally, the VOR MON concept will enable pilots to navigate through the GPS outage or land at a MON airport or at another airport that may have an appropriate approach or may be in visual conditions.

(1) The VOR MON is a reversionary service provided by the FAA for use by aircraft that are unable to continue RNAV during a GPS disruption. The FAA has not mandated that preflight or inflight planning include provisions for GPS- or WAAS-equipped aircraft to carry sufficient fuel to proceed to a MON airport in case of an unforeseen GPS outage. Specifically, flying to a MON airport as a filed alternate will not be explicitly required. Of course, consideration for the possibility of a GPS outage is prudent during flight planning as is maintaining proficiency with VOR navigation.

(2) Also, in case of a GPS outage, pilots may coordinate with ATC and elect to continue through the outage or land. The VOR MON is designed to ensure that an aircraft is within 100 NM of an airport, but pilots may decide to proceed to any appropriate airport where a landing can be made. WAAS users flying under Part 91 are not required to carry VOR avionics. These users do not have the ability or requirement to use the VOR MON. Prudent flight planning, by these WAAS-only aircraft, should consider the possibility of a GPS outage.

Note: The FAA recognizes that non-GPS-based approaches will be reduced when VORs are eliminated, and that most airports with an instrument approach may only have GPS- or WAAS-based approaches. Pilots flying GPS- or WAAS-equipped aircraft that also have VOR/ILS avionics should be diligent to maintain proficiency in VOR and ILS approaches in the event of a GPS outage.

1–1–4 VOR Receiver Check

a. The FAA VOR test facility (VOT) transmits a test signal which provides users a convenient means to determine the operational status and accuracy of a VOR receiver while on the ground where a VOT is located. The airborne use of VOT is permitted; however, its use is strictly limited to those areas/altitudes specifically authorized in the Chart Supplement or appropriate supplement.

b. To use the VOT service, tune in the VOT frequency on your VOR receiver. With the Course Deviation Indicator (CDI) centered, the omnibearing selector should read 0 degrees with the to/from indication showing "from" or the omnibearing selector should read 180 degrees with the to/from indication showing "to." Should the VOR receiver operate an RMI (Radio Magnetic Indicator), it will indicate 180 degrees on any omni-bearing selector (OBS) setting. Two means of identification are used. One is a series of dots and the other is a continuous tone. Information concerning an individual test signal can be obtained from the local FSS.

c. Periodic VOR receiver calibration is most important. If a receiver's Automatic Gain Control or modulation circuit deteriorates, it is possible for it to display acceptable accuracy and sensitivity close into the VOR or VOT and display out-of-tolerance readings when located at greater distances where weaker signal areas exist. The likelihood of this deterioration varies between receivers, and is generally considered a function of time. The best assurance of having an accurate receiver is periodic calibration. Yearly intervals are recommended at which time an authorized repair facility should recalibrate the receiver to the manufacturer's specifications.

d. Federal Aviation Regulations (14 CFR Section 91.171) provides for certain VOR equipment accuracy checks prior to flight under instrument flight rules. To comply with this requirement and to ensure satisfactory operation of the airborne system, the FAA has provided pilots with the following means of checking VOR receiver accuracy:

1. VOT or a radiated test signal from an appropriately rated radio repair station.

2. Certified airborne checkpoints and airways.

3. Certified checkpoints on the airport surface.

4. If an airborne checkpoint is not available, select an established VOR airway. Select a prominent ground point, preferably more than 20 NM from the VOR ground facility and maneuver the aircraft directly over the point at a reasonably low altitude above terrain and obstructions.

e. A radiated VOT from an appropriately rated radio repair station serves the same purpose as an FAA VOR signal and the check is made in much the same manner as a VOT with the following differences:

1. The frequency normally approved by the Federal Communications Commission is 108.0 MHz.

2. Repair stations are not permitted to radiate the VOR test signal continuously; consequently, the owner or operator must make arrangements with the repair station to have the test signal transmitted. This service is not provided by all radio repair stations. The aircraft owner or operator must determine which repair station in the local area provides this service. A representative of the repair station must make an entry into the aircraft logbook or other permanent record certifying to the radial accuracy and the date of transmission. The owner, operator or representative of the repair station may accomplish the necessary checks in the aircraft and make a logbook entry stating the results. It is necessary to verify which test radial is being transmitted and whether you should get a "to" or "from" indication.

f. Airborne and ground check points consist of certified radials that should be received at specific points on the airport surface or over specific landmarks while airborne in the immediate vicinity of the airport.

1. Should an error in excess of plus or minus 4 degrees be indicated through use of a ground check, or plus or minus 6 degrees using the airborne check, Instrument Flight Rules (IFR) flight must not be attempted without first correcting the source of the error.

Caution: No correction other than the correction card figures supplied by the manufacturer should be applied in making these VOR receiver checks.

2. Locations of airborne check points, ground check points and VOTs are published in the Chart Supplement.

3. If a dual system VOR (units independent of each other except for the antenna) is installed in the aircraft, one system may be checked against the other. Turn both systems to the same VOR ground facility and note the indicated bearing to that station. The maximum permissible variations between the two indicated bearings is 4 degrees.

1-1-5 Tactical Air Navigation (TACAN)

a. For reasons peculiar to military or naval operations (unusual siting conditions, the pitching and rolling of a naval vessel, etc.) the civil VOR/ Distance Measuring Equipment (DME) system of air navigation was considered unsuitable for military or naval use. A new navigational system, TACAN, was therefore developed by the military and naval forces to more readily lend itself to military and naval requirements. As a result, the FAA has integrated TACAN facilities with the civil VOR/ DME program. Although the theoretical, or technical principles of operation of TACAN equipment are quite different from those of VOR/DME facilities, the end result, as far as the navigating pilot is concerned, is the same. These integrated facilities are called VORTACs.

b. TACAN ground equipment consists of either a fixed or mobile transmitting unit. The airborne unit in conjunction with the ground unit reduces the transmitted signal to a visual presentation of both azimuth and distance information. TACAN is a pulse system and operates in the Ultrahigh Frequency (UHF) band of frequencies. Its use requires TACAN airborne equipment and does not operate through conventional VOR equipment.

1-1-6 VHF Omni-Directional Range/ Tactical Air Navigation (VORTAC)

a. A VORTAC is a facility consisting of two components, VOR and TACAN, which provides three individual services: VOR azimuth, TACAN azimuth and TACAN distance (DME) at one site. Although consisting of more than one component, incorporating more than one operating frequency, and using more than one antenna system, a VORTAC is considered to be a unified navigational aid. Both components of a VORTAC are envisioned as operating simultaneously and providing the three services at all times.

b. Transmitted signals of VOR and TACAN are each identified by three-letter code transmission and are interlocked so that pilots using VOR azimuth with TACAN distance can be assured that both signals being received are definitely from the same ground station. The frequency channels of the VOR and the TACAN at each VORTAC facility are "paired" in accordance with a national plan to simplify airborne operation.

1-1-7 Distance Measuring Equipment (DME)

a. In the operation of DME, paired pulses at a specific spacing are sent out from the aircraft (this is the interrogation) and are received at the ground station. The ground station (transponder) then transmits paired pulses back to the aircraft at the same pulse spacing but on a different frequency. The time required for the round trip of this signal exchange is measured in the airborne DME unit and is translated into distance (nautical miles) from the aircraft to the ground station.

b. Operating on the line-of-sight principle, DME furnishes distance information with a very high degree of accuracy. Reliable signals may be received at distances up to 199 NM at line-of-sight altitude with an accuracy of better than 1/2 mile or 3 percent of the distance, whichever is greater. Distance information received from DME equipment is SLANT RANGE distance and not actual horizontal distance.

c. Operating frequency range of a DME according to ICAO Annex 10 is from 960 MHz to 1215 MHz. Aircraft equipped with TACAN equipment will receive distance information from a VORTAC automatically, while aircraft equipped with VOR must have a separate DME airborne unit.

d. VOR/DME, VORTAC, Instrument Landing System (ILS)/DME, and localizer (LOC)/DME navigation facilities established by the FAA provide course and distance information from collocated components under a frequency pairing plan. Aircraft receiving equipment which provides for automatic DME selection assures reception of azimuth and distance information from a common source when designated VOR/DME, VORTAC, ILS/DME, and LOC/DME are selected.

e. Due to the limited number of available frequencies, assignment of paired frequencies is required for certain military noncollocated VOR and TACAN facilities which serve the same area but which may be separated by distances up to a few miles.

f. VOR/DME, VORTAC, ILS/DME, and LOC/ DME facilities are identified by synchronized identifications which are transmitted on a time share basis. The VOR or localizer portion of the facility is identified by a coded tone modulated at 1020 Hz

or a combination of code and voice. The TACAN or DME is identified by a coded tone modulated at 1350 Hz. The DME or TACAN coded identification is transmitted one time for each three or four times that the VOR or localizer coded identification is transmitted. When either the VOR or the DME is inoperative, it is important to recognize which identifier is retained for the operative facility. A single coded identification with a repetition interval of approximately 30 seconds indicates that the DME is operative.

g. Aircraft equipment which provides for automatic DME selection assures reception of azimuth and distance information from a common source when designated VOR/DME, VORTAC and ILS/DME navigation facilities are selected. Pilots are cautioned to disregard any distance displays from automatically selected DME equipment when VOR or ILS facilities, which do not have the DME feature installed, are being used for position determination.

1–1–8 NAVAID Service Volumes

a. The FAA publishes Standard Service Volumes (SSVs) for most NAVAIDs. The SSV is a three-dimensional volume within which the FAA ensures that a signal can be received with adequate signal strength and course quality, and is free from interference from other NAVAIDs on similar frequencies (e.g., co-channel or adjacent-channel interference). However, the SSV signal protection does not include potential blockage from terrain or obstructions. The SSV is principally intended for off-route navigation, such as proceeding direct to or from a VOR when not on a published instrument procedure or route. Navigation on published instrument procedures (e.g., approaches or departures) or routes (e.g., Victor routes) may use NAVAIDs outside of the SSV, when Extended Service Volume (ESV) is approved, since adequate signal strength, course quality, and freedom from interference are verified by the FAA prior to the publishing of the instrument procedure or route.

Note: A conical area directly above the NAVAID is generally not usable for navigation.

b. A NAVAID will have service volume restrictions if it does not conform to signal strength and course quality standards throughout the published SSV. Service volume restrictions are first published in Notices to Air Missions (NOTAMs) and then with the alphabetical listing of the NAVAIDs in the Chart Supplement. Service volume restrictions do not generally apply to published instrument procedures or routes unless published in NOTAMs for the affected instrument procedure or route.

c. VOR/DME/TACAN Standard Service Volumes (SSV).

1. The three original SSVs are shown in Figure 1-1-1 and are designated with three classes of NAVAIDs: Terminal (T), Low (L), and High (H). The usable distance of the NAVAID depends on the altitude Above the Transmitter Height (ATH) for each class. The lower edge of the usable distance when below 1,000 feet ATH is shown in Figure 1-1-2 for Terminal NAVAIDs and in Figure 1-1-3 for Low and High NAVAIDs.

Figure 1–1–1
Original Standard Service Volumes

Figure 1–1–2
Lower Edge of the Terminal Service Volume (in altitude ATH)

FIGURE 1–1–3
Lower Edge of Low and High Service Volumes (in altitude ATH)

2. With the progression of navigation capabilities to Performance Based Navigation (PBN), additional capabilities for off-route navigation are necessary. For example, the VOR MON (See paragraph 1-1-3f.) requires the use of VORs at 5,000 feet AGL, which is beyond the original SSV ranges. Additionally, PBN procedures using DME require extended ranges. As a result, the FAA created four additional SSVs. Two of the new SSVs are associated with VORs: VOR Low (VL) and VOR High (VH), as shown in Figure 1-1-4. The other two new SSVs are associated with DME: DME Low (DL) and DME High (DH), as shown in Figure 1-1-5. The SSV at altitudes below 1,000 feet for the VL and VH are the same as Figure 1-1-3. The SSVs at altitudes below 12,900 feet for the DL and DH SSVs correspond to a conservative estimate of the DME radio line of sight (RLOS) coverage at each altitude (not including possible terrain blockage).

FIGURE 1–1–4
New VOR Service Volumes

FIGURE 1–1–5
New DME Service Volumes

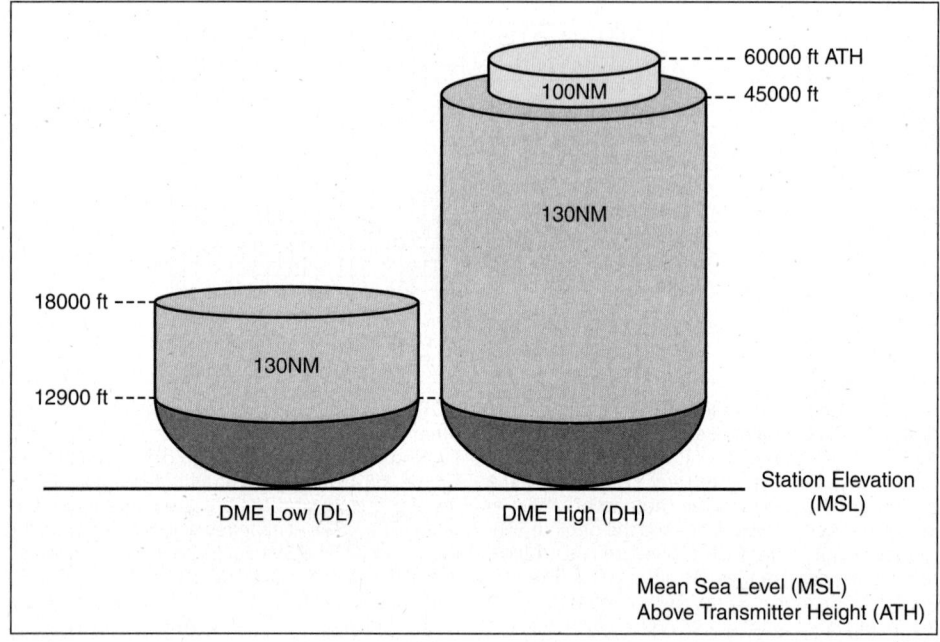

Note 1: In the past, NAVAIDs at one location typi-cally all had the same SSV. For example, a VOR-TAC typically had a High (H) SSV for the VOR, the TACAN azimuth, and the TACAN DME, or a Low (L) or Terminal (T) SSV for all three. A VOR/DME typically had a High (H), Low (L), or Termi-nal (T) for both the VOR and the DME. A common SSV may no longer be the case at all locations. A VOR/DME, for example, could have an SSV of VL for the VOR and DH for the DME, or other combinations.

Note 2: The TACAN azimuth will only be classi-fied as T, L, or H.

3. Table 1-1-1 is a tabular summary of the VOR, DME, and TACAN NAVAID SSVs, not in-cluding altitudes below 1,000 feet ATH for VOR and TACAN Azimuth, and not including ranges for altitudes below 12,900 feet for TACAN and DME.

TABLE 1–1–1
VOR/DME/TACAN STANDARD SERVICE VOLUMES

SSV Designator	Altitude and Range Boundaries
T (Terminal)	From 1,000 feet ATH up to and including 12,000 feet ATH at radial distances out to 25 NM.
L (Low Altitude)	From 1,000 feet ATH up to and including 18,000 feet ATH at radial distances out to 40 NM.
H (High Altitude)	From 1,000 feet ATH up to and including 14,500 feet ATH at radial distances out to 40 NM. From 14,500 ATH up to and including 60,000 feet at radial distances out to 100 NM. From 18,000 feet ATH up to and including 45,000 feet ATH at radial distances out to 130 NM.
VL (VOR Low)	From 1,000 feet ATH up to but not including 5,000 feet ATH at radial distances out to 40 NM. From 5,000 feet ATH up to but not including 18,000 feet ATH at radial distances out to 70 NM.

(continued)

SSV Designator	Altitude and Range Boundaries
VH (VOR High)	From 1,000 feet ATH up to but not including 5,000 feet ATH at radial distances out to 40 NM. From 5,000 feet ATH up to but not including 14,500 feet ATH at radial distances out to 70 NM. From 14,500 ATH up to and including 60,000 feet at radial distances out to 100 NM. From 18,000 feet ATH up to and including 45,000 feet ATH at radial distances out to 130 NM.
DL (DME Low)	For altitudes up to 12,900 feet ATH at a radial distance corresponding to the LOS to the NAVAID. From 12,900 feet ATH up to but not including 18,000 feet ATH at radial distances out to 130 NM
DH (DME High)	For altitudes up to 12,900 feet ATH at a radial distance corresponding to the LOS to the NAVAID. From 12,900 ATH up to and including 60,000 feet at radial distances out to 100 NM. From 12,900 feet ATH up to and including 45,000 feet ATH at radial distances out to 130 NM.

d. Nondirectional Radio Beacon (NDB) SSVs. NDBs are classified according to their intended use. The ranges of NDB service volumes are shown in Table 1-1-2. The distance (radius) is the same at all altitudes for each class.

TABLE 1–1–2
NDB SERVICE VOLUMES

Class	Distance (Radius) (NM)
Compass Locator	15
MH	25
H	50*
HH	75

Service ranges of individual facilities may be less than 50 nautical miles (NM). Restrictions to service volumes are first published as a Notice to Air Missions and then with the alphabetical listing of the NAVAID in the Chart Supplement.

1-1-9 Instrument Landing System (ILS)

a. General

1. The ILS is designed to provide an approach path for exact alignment and descent of an aircraft on final approach to a runway.

2. The basic components of an ILS are the localizer, glide slope, and Outer Marker (OM) and, when installed for use with Category II or Category III instrument approach procedures, an Inner Marker (IM).

3. The system may be divided functionally into three parts:

(a) Guidance information: localizer, glide slope.

(b) Range information: marker beacon, DME.

(c) Visual information: approach lights, touchdown and centerline lights, runway lights.

4. The following means may be used to substitute for the OM:

(a) Compass locator; or

(b) Precision Approach Radar (PAR); or

(c) Airport Surveillance Radar (ASR); or

(d) Distance Measuring Equipment (DME), Very High Frequency Omni-directional Range (VOR), or Nondirectional beacon fixes authorized in the Standard Instrument Approach Procedure; or

(e) Very High Frequency Omni-directional Radio Range (VOR); or

(f) Nondirectional beacon fixes authorized in the Standard Instrument Approach Procedure; or

(g) A suitable RNAV system with Global Positioning System (GPS), capable of fix identification on a Standard Instrument Approach Procedure.

5. Where a complete ILS system is installed on each end of a runway; (i.e., the approach end of Runway 4 and the approach end of Runway 22) the ILS systems are not in service simultaneously.

b. Localizer

1. The localizer transmitter operates on one of 40 ILS channels within the frequency range of 108.10 to 111.95 MHz. Signals provide the pilot with course guidance to the runway centerline.

2. The approach course of the localizer is called the front course and is used with other functional parts, e.g., glide slope, marker beacons, etc. The localizer signal is transmitted at the far end of the runway. It is adjusted for a course width of (full scale fly-left to a full scale fly-right) of 700 feet at the runway threshold.

3. The course line along the extended centerline of a runway, in the opposite direction to the front course is called the back course.

Caution: Unless the aircraft's ILS equipment includes reverse sensing capability, when flying inbound on the back course it is necessary to steer the aircraft in the direction opposite the needle deflection when making corrections from off-course to on-course. This "flying away from the needle" is also required when flying outbound on the front course of the localizer. Do not use back course signals for approach unless a back course approach procedure is published for that particular runway and the approach is authorized by ATC.

4. Identification is in International Morse Code and consists of a three-letter identifier preceded by the letter I (••) transmitted on the localizer frequency.

Example: *I-DIA*

5. The localizer provides course guidance throughout the descent path to the runway threshold from a distance of 18 NM from the antenna between an altitude of 1,000 feet above the highest terrain along the course line and 4,500 feet above the elevation of the antenna site. Proper off-course indications are provided throughout the following angular areas of the operational service volume:

(a) To 10 degrees either side of the course along a radius of 18 NM from the antenna; and

(b) From 10 to 35 degrees either side of the course along a radius of 10 NM. (See Figure 1-1-6.)

6. Unreliable signals may be received outside of these areas. ATC may clear aircraft on procedures beyond the service volume when the controller initiates the action or when the pilot requests, and radar monitoring is provided.

7. The areas described in paragraph 1-1-9 b5 and depicted in Figure 1-1-6 represent a Standard Service Volume (SSV) localizer. All charted procedures with localizer coverage beyond the 18 NM SSV have been through the approval process for Expanded Service Volume (ESV), and have been validated by flight inspection. (See Figure 1-1-7.)

FIGURE 1–1–6
Limits of Localizer Coverage

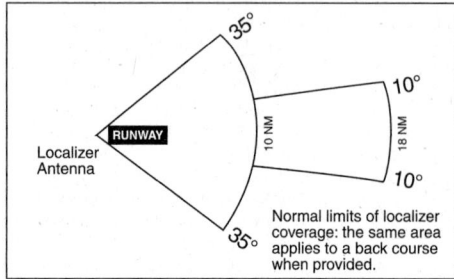

FIGURE 1–1–7
ILS Expanded Service Volume

CHICAGO, ILLINOIS		AL-166 (FAA)	21112

LOC/DME I-IAC **110.5** Chan **42**	APP CRS **273°**	Rwy ldg **7782** TDZE **654** Apt Elev **680**	**ILS RWY 27L** (SA CAT I) CHICAGO O'HARE INTL (ORD)

From VOGLR: RNAV 1-GPS required. Aircraft not GPS equipped - RADAR required for procedure entry. DME or RADAR required.

▼ Simultaneous approach authorized. Requires specific OPSPEC, MSPEC, or LOA approval and use of HUD to DH. For inop ALS, increase S-LOC 27L Cat C/D visibility to 1⅜ SM.

ALSF-2 ⒶⅢ

MISSED APPROACH: Climb to 1200 then climb to 4000 on heading 265° and on CGT VORTAC R-307 to WASCO/CGT 45.8 DME/RADAR and hold.

D-ATIS 135.4 282.225	CHICAGO APP CON 119.0 292.125	O'HARE TOWERS 128.15 348.0 (Rwy 9L/27R) 133.0 348.0 (10R/28L) 120.75 121.15 126.9 132.7 348.0 (CENTER)		GND CON 124.125 (TWR NORTH) 118.05 (TWR SOUTH) 226.675 (ALL TWRS)	(TWR CENTER) 121.75 (OBND) 121.9 (IBND)

CLNC DEL 121.6 CPDLC

Example: The ORD ILS 27L contains the fix NRMAH (093 degrees at 26.2 DME). Since NRMAH is published on the charted procedure, the LOC (I-IAC) signal has been certified by FAA flight inspection beyond the standard 18NM service volume out to 26.2 DME.

LOCALIZER 110.5 I-IAC Chan 42

c. Localizer Type Directional Aid (LDA)

1. The LDA is of comparable use and accuracy to a localizer but is not part of a complete ILS. The LDA course usually provides a more precise approach course than the similar Simplified Directional Facility (SDF) installation, which may have a course width of 6 or 12 degrees.

2. The LDA is not aligned with the runway. Straight-in minimums may be published where alignment does not exceed 30 degrees between the course and runway. Circling minimums only are published where this alignment exceeds 30 degrees.

3. A very limited number of LDA approaches also incorporate a glideslope. These are annotated in the plan view of the instrument approach chart with a note, "LDA/Glideslope." These procedures fall under a newly defined category of approaches called Approach with Vertical Guidance (APV) described in paragraph 5-4-5, Instrument Approach Procedure Charts, subparagraph a7(b), Approach with Vertical Guidance (APV). LDA minima for with and without glideslope is provided and annotated on the minima lines of the approach chart as S-LDA/GS and S-LDA. Because the final approach course is not aligned with the runway centerline, additional maneuvering will be required compared to an ILS approach.

d. Glide Slope/Glide Path

1. The UHF glide slope transmitter, operating on one of the 40 ILS channels within the frequency range 329.15 MHz, to 335.00 MHz radiates its signals in the direction of the localizer front course. The term "glide path" means that portion of the glide slope that intersects the localizer.

Caution: False glide slope signals may exist in the area of the localizer back course approach which can cause the glide slope flag alarm to disappear and present unreliable glide slope information. Disregard all glide slope signal indications when making a localizer back course approach unless a glide slope is specified on the approach and landing chart.

2. The glide slope transmitter is located between 750 feet and 1,250 feet from the approach end of the runway (down the runway) and offset 250 to 650 feet from the runway centerline. It transmits a glide path beam 1.4 degrees wide (vertically). The signal provides descent information for navigation down to the lowest authorized decision height (DH) specified in the approved ILS approach procedure. The glidepath may not be suitable for navigation below the lowest authorized DH and any reference to glidepath indications below that height must be supplemented by visual reference to the runway environment. Glidepaths with no published DH are usable to runway threshold.

3. The glide path projection angle is normally adjusted to 3 degrees above horizontal so that it intersects the MM at about 200 feet and the OM at about 1,400 feet above the runway elevation. The glide slope is normally usable to the distance of 10 NM. However, at some locations, the glide slope has been certified for an extended service volume which exceeds 10 NM.

4. Pilots must be alert when approaching the glidepath interception. False courses and reverse sensing will occur at angles considerably greater than the published path.

5. Make every effort to remain on the indicated glide path.

Caution: Avoid flying below the glide path to assure obstacle/terrain clearance is maintained.

6. The published glide slope threshold crossing height (TCH) DOES NOT represent the height of the actual glide path on-course indication above the runway threshold. It is used as a reference for planning purposes which represents the height above the runway threshold that an aircraft's glide slope antenna should be, if that aircraft remains on a trajectory formed by the four-mile-to-middle marker glidepath segment.

7. Pilots must be aware of the vertical height between the aircraft's glide slope antenna and the main gear in the landing configuration and, at the DH, plan to adjust the descent angle accordingly if the published TCH indicates the wheel crossing height over the runway threshold may not be satisfactory. Tests indicate a comfortable wheel crossing height is approximately 20 to 30 feet, depending on the type of aircraft.

Note: The TCH for a runway is established based on several factors including the largest aircraft category that normally uses the runway, how airport layout affects the glide slope antenna placement, and terrain. A higher than optimum TCH, with the same glide path angle, may cause the aircraft to touch down further from the threshold if the trajectory of the approach is maintained until the flare. Pilots should consider the effect of a high TCH on the runway available for stopping the aircraft.

e. Distance Measuring Equipment (DME)

1. When installed with the ILS and specified in the approach procedure, DME may be used:

(a) In lieu of the OM;

(b) As a back course (BC) final approach fix (FAF); and

(c) To establish other fixes on the localizer course.

2. In some cases, DME from a separate facility may be used within Terminal Instrument Procedures (TERPS) limitations:

(a) To provide ARC initial approach segments;

(b) As a FAF for BC approaches; and

(c) As a substitute for the OM.

f. Marker Beacon

1. ILS marker beacons have a rated power output of 3 watts or less and an antenna array designed to produce an elliptical pattern with dimensions, at 1,000 feet above the antenna, of approximately 2,400 feet in width and 4,200 feet in length. Airborne marker beacon receivers with a selective sensitivity feature should always be operated in the "low" sensitivity position for proper reception of ILS marker beacons.

2. ILS systems may have an associated OM. An MM is no longer required. Locations with a Category II ILS also have an Inner Marker (IM). Due to advances in both ground navigation equipment and airborne avionics, as well as the numerous means that may be used as a substitute for a marker beacon, the current requirements for the use of marker beacons are:

(a) An OM or suitable substitute identifies the Final Approach Fix (FAF) for nonprecision approach (NPA) operations (for example, localizer only); and

(b) The MM indicates a position approximately 3,500 feet from the landing threshold. This is also the position where an aircraft on the glide path will be at an altitude of approximately 200 feet above the elevation of the touchdown zone. An MM is no longer operationally required. There are some MMs still in use, but there are no MMs being installed at new ILS sites by the FAA; and

(c) An IM, where installed, indicates the point at which an aircraft is at decision height on the glide path during a Category II ILS approach. An IM is only required for CAT II operations that do not have a published radio altitude (RA) minimum.

TABLE 1-1-3
MARKER PASSAGE INDICATIONS

Marker	Code	Light
OM	– – –	Blue
MM	• – • –	Amber
IM	• • • •	White
BC	• • • •	White

3. A back course marker normally indicates the ILS back course final approach fix where approach descent is commenced.

g. Compass Locator

1. Compass locator transmitters are often situated at the MM and OM sites. The transmitters have a power of less than 25 watts, a range of at least 15 miles and operate between 190 and 535 kHz. At some locations, higher powered radio beacons, up to 400 watts, are used as OM compass locators.

2. Compass locators transmit two letter identification groups. The outer locator transmits the first two letters of the localizer identification group,

and the middle locator transmits the last two letters of the localizer identification group.

h. ILS Frequency (See Table 1-1-4.)

TABLE 1-1-4
FREQUENCY PAIRS ALLOCATED FOR ILS

Localizer MHz	Glide Slope
108.10	334.70
108.15	334.55
108.3	334.10
108.35	333.95
108.5	329.90
108.55	329.75
108.7	330.50
108.75	330.35
108.9	329.30
108.95	329.15
109.1	331.40
109.15	331.25
109.3	332.00
109.35	331.85
109.50	332.60
109.55	332.45
109.70	333.20
109.75	333.05
109.90	333.80
109.95	333.65
110.1	334.40
110.15	334.25
110.3	335.00
110.35	334.85
110.5	329.60
110.55	329.45
110.70	330.20
110.75	330.05
110.90	330.80
110.95	330.65
111.10	331.70
111.15	331.55
111.30	332.30
111.35	332.15
111.50	332.9
111.55	332.75
111.70	333.5
111.75	333.35
111.90	331.1
111.95	330.95

i. ILS Minimums

1. The lowest authorized ILS minimums, with all required ground and airborne systems components operative, are:

(a) Category I. Decision Height (DH) 200 feet and Runway Visual Range (RVR) 2,400 feet (with touchdown zone and centerline lighting, RVR 1,800 feet), or (with Autopilot or FD or HUD, RVR 1,800 feet);

(b) Special Authorization Category I. DH 150 feet and Runway Visual Range (RVR) 1,400 feet, HUD to DH;

(c) Category II. DH 100 feet and RVR 1,200 feet (with autoland or HUD to touchdown and noted on authorization, RVR 1,000 feet);

(d) Special Authorization Category II with Reduced Lighting. DH 100 feet and RVR 1,200 feet with autoland or HUD to touchdown and noted on authorization, (touchdown zone, centerline lighting and ALSF–2 are not required);

(e) Category IIIa. No DH or DH below 100 feet and RVR not less than 700 feet;

(f) Category IIIb. No DH or DH below 50 feet and RVR less than 700 feet but not less than 150 feet; and

(g) Category IIIc. No DH and no RVR limitation.

Note: Special authorization and equipment required for Categories II and III.

j. Inoperative ILS Components
1. Inoperative localizer. When the localizer fails, an ILS approach is not authorized.
2. Inoperative glide slope. When the glide slope fails, the ILS reverts to a nonprecision localizer approach.

Reference: See the inoperative component table in the U.S. Government Terminal Procedures Publication (TPP), for adjustments to minimums due to inoperative airborne or ground system equipment.

k. ILS Course and Glideslope Distortion
1. All pilots should be aware that ILS installations are subject to signal interference by surface vehicles and aircraft (either on the ground or airborne). ILS CRITICAL AREAS are established near each localizer and glide slope antenna. Pilots should be aware of the level of critical area protection they can expect in various weather conditions and understand that signal disturbances may occur as a result of normal airport operations irrespective of the official weather observation.
2. ATC is not always required to issue control instructions to avoid interfering operations within ILS critical areas at controlled airports during the hours the Airport Traffic Control Tower (ATCT) is in operation. ATC responsibilities vary depending on the official weather observation and are described as follows:

(a) Weather Conditions. Official weather observation indicates a ceiling of 800 feet or higher and visibility 2 miles or greater, no localizer or glideslope critical area protection is provided by ATC unless specifically requested by the flight crew.

(b) Weather Conditions. Official weather observation indicates a ceiling of less than 800 feet or visibility less than 2 miles.

(1) Holding. Aircraft holding below 5,000 feet between the outer marker and the airport may cause localizer signal variations for aircraft conducting the ILS approach. Accordingly, such holding will not be authorized by ATC.

(2) Localizer Critical Area. When an arriving aircraft is inside the outer marker (OM) or the fix used in lieu of the OM, vehicles and aircraft will not be authorized in or over the precision approach critical area except:

[a] A preceding arriving aircraft on the same or another runway may pass over or through the localizer critical area, and;

[b] A preceding departing aircraft or missed approach on the same or another runway may pass through or over the localizer critical area.

(3) Glide Slope Critical Area. ATC will not authorize vehicles or aircraft operations in or over the glideslope critical area when an arriving aircraft is inside the outer marker (OM), or the fix used in lieu of the OM, unless the arriving aircraft has reported the runway in sight and is circling or side-stepping to land on another runway.

(c) Weather Conditions. Official weather observation indicates a ceiling less than 200 feet or runway visual range (RVR) less than 2000 feet.

(1) Localizer Critical Area. In addition to the critical area protection described in 1-1-9k2(b) above, when an arriving aircraft is inside the middle marker (MM), or in the absence of a MM, ½ mile final, ATC will not authorize:

[a] A preceding arriving aircraft on the same or another runway to pass over or through the localizer critical area, or;

[b] A preceding departing aircraft or missed approach on the same or another runway to pass through or over the localizer critical area.

3. In order to ensure that pilot and controller expectations match with respect to critical area protection for a given approach and landing operation, a flight crew should advise the tower any time it intends to conduct any autoland operation or use an SA CAT I, any CAT II, or any CAT III line of minima anytime the official weather observation is at or above a ceiling of 800 feet and 2 miles visibility. If ATC is unable to protect the critical area, they will advise the flight crew.

Example: Denver Tower, United 1153, Request Autoland (runway) ATC replies with: United 1153, Denver Tower, Roger, Critical Areas not protected.

4. Pilots are cautioned that even when the critical areas are considered to be protected, unless the official weather observation including controller observations indicates a ceiling less than 200 feet or RVR less than 2000 feet, ATC may still authorize a preceding arriving, departing, or missed approach aircraft to pass through or over the localizer critical area and that this may

cause signal disturbances that could result in an undesired aircraft state during the final stages of the approach, landing, and rollout.

5. Pilots are cautioned that vehicular traffic not subject to ATC may cause momentary deviation to ILS course or glide slope signals. Also, critical areas are not protected at uncontrolled airports or at airports with an operating control tower when weather or visibility conditions are above those requiring protective measures. Aircraft conducting coupled or autoland operations should be especially alert in monitoring automatic flight control systems and be prepared to intervene as necessary. (See Figure 1-1-8.)

Note: Unless otherwise coordinated through Flight Standards, ILS signals to Category I runways are not flight inspected below the point that is 100 feet less than the decision altitude (DA). Guidance signal anomalies may be encountered below this altitude.

1-1-10 Simplified Directional Facility (SDF)

a. The SDF provides a final approach course similar to that of the ILS localizer. It does not provide glide slope information. A clear understanding of the ILS localizer and the additional factors listed below completely describe the operational characteristics and use of the SDF.

b. The SDF transmits signals within the range of 108.10 to 111.95 MHz.

c. The approach techniques and procedures used in an SDF instrument approach are essentially the same as those employed in executing a standard localizer approach except the SDF course may not be aligned with the runway and the course may be wider, resulting in less precision.

d. Usable off-course indications are limited to 35 degrees either side of the course centerline. Instrument indications received beyond 35 degrees should be disregarded.

e. The SDF antenna may be offset from the runway centerline. Because of this, the angle of convergence between the final approach course and the runway bearing should be determined by reference to the instrument approach procedure chart. This angle is generally not more than 3 degrees. However, it should be noted that inasmuch as the approach course originates at the antenna site, an approach which is continued beyond the runway threshold will lead the aircraft to the SDF offset position rather than along the runway centerline.

f. The SDF signal is fixed at either 6 degrees or 12 degrees as necessary to provide maximum flyability and optimum course quality.

g. Identification consists of a three-letter identifier transmitted in Morse Code on the SDF

frequency. The appropriate instrument approach chart will indicate the identifier used at a particular airport.

1-1-11 NAVAID Identifier Removal During Maintenance

During periods of routine or emergency maintenance, coded identification (or code and voice, where applicable) is removed from certain FAA NAVAIDs. Removal of identification serves as a warning to pilots that the facility is officially off the air for tune-up or repair and may be unreliable even though intermittent or constant signals are received.

Note: During periods of maintenance VHF ranges may radiate a T-E-S-T code (– • ••• –).

Note: DO NOT attempt to fly a procedure that is NOTAMed out of service even if the identification is present. In certain cases, the identification may be transmitted for short periods as part of the testing.

1-1-12 NAVAIDs with Voice

a. Voice equipped en route radio navigational aids are under the operational control of either a Flight Service Station (FSS) or an approach control facility. Facilities with two-way voice communication available are indicated in the Chart Supplement and aeronautical charts.

b. Unless otherwise noted on the chart, all radio navigation aids operate continuously except during shutdowns for maintenance. Hours of operation of facilities not operating continuously are annotated on charts and in the Chart Supplement.

1-1-13 User Reports Requested on NAVAID Outages

a. Users of the National Airspace System (NAS) can render valuable assistance in the early correction of NAVAID malfunctions or GNSS problems and are encouraged to report their observations of undesirable avionics performance. Although NAVAIDs are monitored by electronic detectors, adverse effects of electronic interference, new obstructions or changes in terrain near the NAVAID can exist without detection by the ground monitors. Some of the characteristics of malfunction or deteriorating performance which should be reported are: erratic course or bearing indications; intermittent, or full, flag alarm; garbled, missing or obviously improper coded identification; poor quality communications reception; or, in the case of frequency interference, an audible hum or tone accompanying radio communications or NAVAID identification. GNSS problems are often characterized by navigation degradation or service loss indications. For instance, pilots conducting operations in areas where there

FIGURE 1–1–8
FAA Instrument Landing Systems

Ch 1

is GNSS interference may be unable to use GPS for navigation, and ADS-B may be unavailable for surveillance. Radio frequency interference may affect both navigation for the pilot and surveillance by the air traffic controller. Depending on the equipment and integration, either an advisory light or message may alert the pilot. Air traffic controllers monitoring ADS-B reports may stop receiving ADS-B position messages and associated aircraft tracks.

b. Malfunctioning, faulty, inappropriately installed, operated, or modified GPS re-radiator systems, intended to be used for aircraft maintenance activities, have resulted in unintentional disruption of aviation GPS receivers. This type of disruption could result in unflagged, erroneous position-information output to primary flight displays/indicators and to other aircraft and air traffic control systems. Since Receiver Autonomous Integrity Monitoring (RAIM) is only partially effective against this type of disruption (effectively a "signal spoofing"), the pilot may not be aware of any erroneous navigation indications; ATC may be the only means available to identify these disruptions and detect unexpected aircraft positions while monitoring aircraft for IFR separation.

c. Pilots encountering navigation error events should transition to another source of navigation and request amended clearances from ATC as necessary.

d. Pilots are encouraged to submit detailed reports of NAVAID or GPS anomaly as soon as practical. Pilot reports of navigation error events should contain the following information:

1. Date and time the anomaly was observed, and NAVAID ID (or GPS).

2. Location of the aircraft at the time the anomaly started and ended (e.g., latitude/longitude or bearing/distance from a reference point),

3. Heading, altitude, type of aircraft (make/model/call sign),

4. Type of avionics/receivers in use (e.g., make/model/software series or version),

5. Number of satellites being tracked, if applicable,

6. Description of the position/navigation/timing anomaly observed, and duration of the event,

7. Consequences/operational impact(s) of the NAVAID or GPS anomaly,

8. Actions taken to mitigate the anomaly and/or remedy provided by the ATC facility,

9. Post flight pilot/maintenance actions taken.

e. Pilots operating an aircraft in controlled airspace under IFR shall comply with CFR § 91.187 and promptly report as soon as practical to ATC any malfunctions of navigational equipment occurring in flight; pilots should submit initial reports:

1. Immediately, by radio to the controlling ATC facility or FSS.

2. By telephone to the nearest ATC facility controlling the airspace where the disruption was experienced.

3. Additionally, GPS problems should be reported, post flight, by Internet via the GPS Anomaly Reporting Form at http://www.faa.gov/air_traffic/nas/gps_reports/.

f. To minimize ATC workload, GPS anomalies associated with known testing NOTAMs should NOT be reported in-flight to ATC in detail; EXCEPT when:

1. GPS degradation is experienced outside the NOTAMed area,

2. Pilot observes any unexpected consequences (e.g., equipment failure, suspected spoofing, failure of unexpected aircraft systems, such as TAWS).

1-1-14 LORAN

Note: In accordance with the 2010 DHS Appropriations Act, the U.S. Coast Guard (USCG) terminated the transmission of all U.S. LORAN-C signals on 08 Feb 2010. The USCG also terminated the transmission of the Russian American signals on 01 Aug 2010, and the Canadian LORAN-C signals on 03 Aug 2010. For more information, visit http://www.navcen.uscg.gov. Operators should also note that TSO-C60b, AIRBORNE AREA NAVIGATION EQUIPMENT USING LORAN-C INPUTS, has been canceled by the FAA.

1-1-15 Inertial Reference Unit (IRU), Inertial Navigation System (INS), and Attitude Heading Reference System (AHRS)

a. IRUs are self-contained systems comprised of gyros and accelerometers that provide aircraft attitude (pitch, roll, and heading), position, and velocity information in response to signals resulting from inertial effects on system components. Once aligned with a known position, IRUs continuously calculate position and velocity. IRU position accuracy decays with time. This degradation is known as "drift."

b. INSs combine the components of an IRU with an internal navigation computer. By programming a series of waypoints, these systems will navigate along a predetermined track.

c. AHRSs are electronic devices that provide attitude information to aircraft systems such as weather radar and autopilot, but do not directly compute position information.

d. Aircraft equipped with slaved compass systems may be susceptible to heading errors caused by exposure to magnetic field disturbances (flux fields) found in materials that are commonly located on the surface or buried under taxiways and ramps. These materials generate a magnetic flux

field that can be sensed by the aircraft's compass system flux detector or "gate," which can cause the aircraft's system to align with the material's magnetic field rather than the earth's natural magnetic field. The system's erroneous heading may not self-correct. Prior to take off pilots should be aware that a heading misalignment may have occurred during taxi. Pilots are encouraged to follow the manufacturer's or other appropriate procedures to correct possible heading misalignment before take off is commenced.

1-1-16 Doppler Radar

Doppler Radar is a semiautomatic self-contained dead reckoning navigation system (radar sensor plus computer) which is not continuously dependent on information derived from ground based or external aids. The system employs radar signals to detect and measure ground speed and drift angle, using the aircraft compass system as its directional reference. Doppler is less accurate than INS, however, and the use of an external reference is required for periodic updates if acceptable position accuracy is to be achieved on long range flights.

1-1-17 Global Positioning System (GPS)

a. System Overview

1. System Description. The Global Positioning System is a space-based radio navigation system used to determine precise position anywhere in the world. The 24 satellite constellation is designed to ensure at least five satellites are always visible to a user worldwide. A minimum of four satellites is necessary for receivers to establish an accurate three-dimensional position. The receiver uses data from satellites above the mask angle (the lowest angle above the horizon at which a receiver can use a satellite). The Department of Defense (DOD) is responsible for operating the GPS satellite constellation and monitors the GPS satellites to ensure proper operation. Each satellite's orbital parameters (ephemeris data) are sent to each satellite for broadcast as part of the data message embedded in the GPS signal. The GPS coordinate system is the Cartesian earth-centered, earth-fixed coordinates as specified in the World Geodetic System 1984 (WGS-84).

2. System Availability and Reliability.

(a) The status of GPS satellites is broadcast as part of the data message transmitted by the GPS satellites. GPS status information is also available by means of the U.S. Coast Guard navigation information service: (703) 313-5907, Internet: http://www.navcen.uscg.gov/. Additionally, satellite status is available through the Notice to Air Missions (NOTAM) system.

(b) GNSS operational status depends on the type of equipment being used. For GPS-only equipment TSO-C129 or TSO-C196(), the operational status of non-precision approach capability for flight planning purposes is provided through a prediction program that is embedded in the receiver or provided separately.

3. Receiver Autonomous Integrity Monitoring (RAIM). RAIM is the capability of a GPS receiver to perform integrity monitoring on itself by ensuring available satellite signals meet the integrity requirements for a given phase of flight. Without RAIM, the pilot has no assurance of the GPS position integrity. RAIM provides immediate feedback to the pilot. This fault detection is critical for performance-based navigation (PBN) (see Paragraph 1-2-1, Performance-Based Navigation (PBN) and Area Navigation (RNAV), for an introduction to PBN), because delays of up to two hours can occur before an erroneous satellite transmission is detected and corrected by the satellite control segment.

(a) In order for RAIM to determine if a satellite is providing corrupted information, at least one satellite, in addition to those required for navigation, must be in view for the receiver to perform the RAIM function. RAIM requires a minimum of 5 satellites, or 4 satellites and barometric altimeter input (baro-aiding), to detect an integrity anomaly. Baro-aiding is a method of augmenting the GPS integrity solution by using a non-satellite input source in lieu of the fifth satellite. Some GPS receivers also have a RAIM capability, called fault detection and exclusion (FDE), that excludes a failed satellite from the position solution; GPS receivers capable of FDE require 6 satellites or 5 satellites with baro-aiding. This allows the GPS receiver to isolate the corrupt satellite signal, remove it from the position solution, and still provide an integrity-assured position. To ensure that baro-aiding is available, enter the current altimeter setting into the receiver as described in the operating manual. Do not use the GPS derived altitude due to the large GPS vertical errors that will make the integrity monitoring function invalid.

(b) There are generally two types of RAIM fault messages. The first type of message indicates that there are not enough satellites available to provide RAIM integrity monitoring. The GPS navigation solution may be acceptable, but the integrity of the solution cannot be determined. The second type indicates that the RAIM integrity monitor has detected a potential error and that there is an inconsistency in the navigation solution for the given phase of flight. Without RAIM capability, the pilot has no assurance of the accuracy of the GPS position.

4. Selective Availability. Selective Availability (SA) is a method by which the accuracy of GPS is intentionally degraded. This feature was designed

Ch 1

to deny hostile use of precise GPS positioning data. SA was discontinued on May 1, 2000, but many GPS receivers are designed to assume that SA is still active. New receivers may take advantage of the discontinuance of SA based on the performance values in ICAO Annex 10.

b. Operational Use of GPS. U.S. civil operators may use approved GPS equipment in oceanic airspace, certain remote areas, the National Airspace System and other States as authorized (please consult the applicable Aeronautical Information Publication). Equipage other than GPS may be required for the desired operation. GPS navigation is used for both Visual Flight Rules (VFR) and Instrument Flight Rules (IFR) operations.

1. VFR Operations

(a) GPS navigation has become an asset to VFR pilots by providing increased navigational capabilities and enhanced situational awareness. Although GPS has provided many benefits to the VFR pilot, care must be exercised to ensure that system capabilities are not exceeded. VFR pilots should integrate GPS navigation with electronic navigation (when possible), as well as pilotage and dead reckoning.

(b) GPS receivers used for VFR navigation vary from fully integrated IFR/VFR installation used to support VFR operations to hand-held devices. Pilots must understand the limitations of the receivers prior to using in flight to avoid misusing navigation information. (See Table 1-1-6.) Most receivers are not intuitive. The pilot must learn the various keystrokes, knob functions, and displays that are used in the operation of the receiver. Some manufacturers provide computer-based tutorials or simulations of their receivers that pilots can use to become familiar with operating the equipment.

(c) When using GPS for VFR operations, RAIM capability, database currency, and antenna location are critical areas of concern.

(1) RAIM Capability. VFR GPS panel mount receivers and hand-held units have no RAIM alerting capability. This prevents the pilot from being alerted to the loss of the required number of satellites in view, or the detection of a position error. Pilots should use a systematic cross-check with other navigation techniques to verify position. Be suspicious of the GPS position if a disagreement exists between the two positions.

(2) Database Currency. Check the currency of the database. Databases must be updated for IFR operations and should be updated for all other operations. However, there is no requirement for databases to be updated for VFR navigation. It is not recommended to use a moving map with an outdated database in and around critical airspace. Pilots using an outdated database should verify waypoints using current

aeronautical products; for example, Chart Supplement, Sectional Chart, or En Route Chart.

(3) Antenna Location. The antenna location for GPS receivers used for IFR and VFR operations may differ. VFR antennae are typically placed for convenience more than performance, while IFR installations ensure a clear view is provided with the satellites. Antennae not providing a clear view have a greater opportunity to lose the satellite navigational signal. This is especially true in the case of hand-held GPS receivers. Typically, suction cups are used to place the GPS antennas on the inside of cockpit windows. While this method has great utility, the antenna location is limited to the cockpit or cabin which rarely provides a clear view of all available satellites. Consequently, signal losses may occur due to aircraft structure blocking satellite signals, causing a loss of navigation capability. These losses, coupled with a lack of RAIM capability, could present erroneous position and navigation information with no warning to the pilot. While the use of a hand-held GPS for VFR operations is not limited by regulation, modification of the aircraft, such as installing a panel- or yoke-mounted holder, is governed by 14 CFR Part 43. Consult with your mechanic to ensure compliance with the regulation and safe installation.

(d) Do not solely rely on GPS for VFR navigation. No design standard of accuracy or integrity is used for a VFR GPS receiver. VFR GPS receivers should be used in conjunction with other forms of navigation during VFR operations to ensure a correct route of flight is maintained. Minimize head-down time in the aircraft by being familiar with your GPS receiver's operation and by keeping eyes outside scanning for traffic, terrain, and obstacles.

(e) VFR Waypoints

(1) VFR waypoints provide VFR pilots with a supplementary tool to assist with position awareness while navigating visually in aircraft equipped with area navigation receivers. VFR waypoints should be used as a tool to supplement current navigation procedures. The uses of VFR waypoints include providing navigational aids for pilots unfamiliar with an area, waypoint definition of existing reporting points, enhanced navigation in and around Class B and Class C airspace, enhanced navigation around Special Use Airspace, and entry points for commonly flown mountain passes. VFR pilots should rely on appropriate and current aeronautical charts published specifically for visual navigation. If operating in a terminal area, pilots should take advantage of the Terminal Area Chart available for that area, if published. The use of VFR waypoints does not relieve the pilot of any responsibility to comply with the operational requirements of 14 CFR Part 91.

(2) VFR waypoint names (for computer-entry and flight plans) consist of five letters beginning with the letters "VP" and are retrievable from navigation databases. The VFR waypoint names are not intended to be pronounceable, and they are not for use in ATC communications. On VFR charts, stand-alone VFR waypoints will be portrayed using the same four-point star symbol used for IFR waypoints. VFR waypoints collocated with visual check-points on the chart will be identified by small magenta flag symbols. VFR waypoints collocated with visual check-points will be pronounceable based on the name of the visual check-point and may be used for ATC communications. Each VFR waypoint name will appear in parentheses adjacent to the geographic location on the chart. Latitude/longitude data for all established VFR waypoints may be found in FAA Order JO 7350.9, Location Identifiers.

(3) VFR waypoints may not be used on IFR flight plans. VFR waypoints are not recognized by the IFR system and will be rejected for IFR routing purposes.

(4) Pilots may use the five-letter identifier as a waypoint in the route of flight section on a VFR flight plan. Pilots may use the VFR waypoints only when operating under VFR conditions. The point may represent an intended course change or describe the planned route of flight. This VFR filing would be similar to how a VOR would be used in a route of flight.

(5) VFR waypoints intended for use during flight should be loaded into the receiver while on the ground. Once airborne, pilots should avoid programming routes or VFR waypoint chains into their receivers.

(6) Pilots should be vigilant to see and avoid other traffic when near VFR waypoints. With the increased use of GPS navigation and accuracy, expect increased traffic near VFR waypoints. Regardless of the class of airspace, monitor the available ATC frequency for traffic information on other aircraft operating in the vicinity. See paragraph 7-6-3, VFR in Congested Areas, for more information.

(7) Mountain pass entry points are marked for convenience to assist pilots with flight planning and visual navigation. Do not attempt to fly a mountain pass directly from VFR waypoint to VFR waypoint—they do not create a path through the mountain pass. Alternative routes are always available. It is the pilot in command's responsibility to choose a suitable route for the intended flight and known conditions.

Reference: AIM, ¶7-6-7, Mountain Flying.

2. IFR Use of GPS
(a) **General Requirements.** Authorization to conduct any GPS operation under IFR requires:

(1) GPS navigation equipment used for IFR operations must be approved in accordance with the requirements specified in Technical Standard Order (TSO) TSO-C129(), TSO-C196(), TSO-C145(), or TSO-C146(), and the installation must be done in accordance with Advisory Circular AC 20-138, *Airworthiness Approval of Positioning and Navigation Systems*. Equipment approved in accordance with TSO-C115a does not meet the requirements of TSO-C129. Visual flight rules (VFR) and hand-held GPS systems are not authorized for IFR navigation, instrument approaches, or as a principal instrument flight reference.

(2) Aircraft using un-augmented GPS (TSO-C129() or TSO-C196()) for navigation under IFR must be equipped with an alternate approved and operational means of navigation suitable for navigating the proposed route of flight. (Examples of alternate navigation equipment include VOR or DME/DME/IRU capability). Active monitoring of alternative navigation equipment is not required when RAIM is available for integrity monitoring. Active monitoring of an alternate means of navigation is required when the GPS RAIM capability is lost.

(3) Procedures must be established for use in the event that the loss of RAIM capability is predicted to occur. In situations where RAIM is predicted to be unavailable, the flight must rely on other approved navigation equipment, re-route to where RAIM is available, delay departure, or cancel the flight.

(4) The GPS operation must be conducted in accordance with the FAA-approved aircraft flight manual (AFM) or flight manual supplement. Flight crew members must be thoroughly familiar with the particular GPS equipment installed in the aircraft, the receiver operation manual, and the AFM or flight manual supplement. Operation, receiver presentation and capabilities of GPS equipment vary. Due to these differences, operation of GPS receivers of different brands, or even models of the same brand, under IFR should not be attempted without thorough operational knowledge. Most receivers have a built-in simulator mode, which allows the pilot to become familiar with operation prior to attempting operation in the aircraft.

(5) Aircraft navigating by IFR-approved GPS are considered to be performance-based navigation (PBN) aircraft and have special equipment suffixes. File the appropriate equipment suffix in accordance with Appendix 4, Table 4-2, on the ATC flight plan. If GPS avionics become inoperative, the pilot should advise ATC and amend the equipment suffix.

(6) Prior to any GPS IFR operation, the pilot must review appropriate NOTAMs and aeronautical information. (See GPS NOTAMs/Aeronautical Information).

(b) Database Requirements. The onboard navigation data must be current and appropriate for the region of intended operation and should include the navigation aids, waypoints, and relevant coded terminal airspace procedures for the departure, arrival, and alternate airfields.

(1) Further database guidance for terminal and en route requirements may be found in AC 90-100, *U.S. Terminal and En Route Area Navigation (RNAV) Operations.*

(2) Further database guidance on Required Navigation Performance (RNP) instrument approach operations, RNP terminal, and RNP en route requirements may be found in AC 90-105, *Approval Guidance for RNP Operations and Barometric Vertical Navigation in the U.S. National Airspace System.*

(3) All approach procedures to be flown must be retrievable from the current airborne navigation database supplied by the equipment manufacturer or other FAA-approved source. The system must be able to retrieve the procedure by name from the aircraft navigation database, not just as a manually entered series of waypoints. Manual entry of waypoints using latitude/longitude or place/bearing is not permitted for approach procedures.

(4) Prior to using a procedure or waypoint retrieved from the airborne navigation database, the pilot should verify the validity of the database. This verification should include the following preflight and inflight steps:

[a] Preflight:

[1] Determine the date of database issuance, and verify that the date/time of proposed use is before the expiration date/time.

[2] Verify that the database provider has not published a notice limiting the use of the specific waypoint or procedure.

[b] Inflight:

[1] Determine that the waypoints and transition names coincide with names found on the procedure chart. Do not use waypoints which do not exactly match the spelling shown on published procedure charts.

[2] Determine that the waypoints are logical in location, in the correct order, and their orientation to each other is as found on the procedure chart, both laterally and vertically.

Note: There is no specific requirement to check each waypoint latitude and longitude, type of waypoint and/or altitude constraint, only the general relationship of waypoints in the procedure, or the logic of an individual waypoint's location.

[3] If the cursory check of procedure logic or individual waypoint location, specified in [b] above, indicates a potential error, do not use the retrieved procedure or waypoint until a verification of latitude and longitude, waypoint type, and altitude constraints indicate full conformity with the published data.

(5) Air carrier and commercial operators must meet the appropriate provisions of their approved operations specifications.

[a] During domestic operations for commerce or for hire, operators must have a second navigation system capable of reversion or contingency operations.

[b] Operators must have two independent navigation systems appropriate to the route to be flown or one system that is suitable and a second, independent backup system that allows the operator to proceed safely to a suitable airport, complete an instrument approach; and the aircraft must have sufficient fuel (reference 14 CFR 121.349, 125.203, 129.17, and 135.165). These rules ensure the safety of the operation by preventing a single point of failure.

Note: An aircraft approved for multi-sensor navigation and equipped with a single navigation system must maintain an ability to navigate or proceed safely in the event that any one component of the navigation system fails, including the flight management system (FMS). Retaining an FMS-independent VOR capability would satisfy this requirement.

[c] The requirements for a second system apply to the entire set of equipment needed to achieve the navigation capability, not just the individual components of the system such as the radio navigation receiver. For example, to use two RNAV systems (e.g., GPS and DME/DME/IRU) to comply with the requirements, the aircraft must be equipped with two independent radio navigation receivers and two independent navigation computers (e.g., flight management systems (FMS)). Alternatively, to comply with the requirements using a single RNAV system with an installed and operable VOR capability, the VOR capability must be independent of the FMS.

[d] Due to low risk of disruption or manipulation of GPS signals beyond 50 NM offshore, FAA differentiates between extended and non-extended over-water operations. To satisfy the requirement for two independent navigation systems:

[1] For all extended over-water operations (defined in 14 CFR Part 1 as greater than 50 NM from the nearest shoreline), operators may consider dual GPS-based systems to meet the "independent" criteria stipulated by regulation, e.g., §121.349, §135.165.

[2] For all "non-extended overwater" operations, if the primary navigation system is GPS-based, the second system must be independent of GPS (for example, VOR or DME/DME/IRU). This allows continued navigation in case of failure of the GPS or WAAS services. Recognizing that GPS interference and test events resulting in the loss of GPS services have become more common, the FAA requires operators conducting IFR operations under 14 CFR 121.349, 125.203, 129.17, and 135.65 to retain a non-GPS navigation capability, for example, either DME/DME, IRU, or VOR for en route and terminal operations and VOR and ILS for final approach. Since this system is to be used as a reversionary capability, single equipage is sufficient.

3. Oceanic, Domestic, En Route, and Terminal Area Operations

(a) Conduct GPS IFR operations in oceanic areas only when approved avionics systems are installed. TSO-C196() users and TSO-C129() GPS users authorized for Class A1, A2, B1, B2, C1, or C2 operations may use GPS in place of another approved means of long-range navigation, such as dual INS. (See Table 1-1-5 and Table 1-1-6.) Aircraft with a single installation GPS, meeting the above specifications, are authorized to operate on short oceanic routes requiring one means of long-range navigation (reference AC 20-138, Appendix 1).

(b) Conduct GPS domestic, en route, and terminal IFR operations only when approved avionics systems are installed. Pilots may use GPS via TSO-C129() authorized for Class A1, B1, B3, C1, or C3 operations GPS via TSO-C196(); or GPS/WAAS with either TSO-C145() or TSO-C146(). When using TSO-C129() or TSO-C196() receivers, the avionics necessary to receive all of the ground-based facilities appropriate for the route to the destination airport and any required alternate airport must be installed and operational. Ground-based facilities necessary for these routes must be operational.

(1) GPS en route IFR operations may be conducted in Alaska outside the operational service volume of ground-based navigation aids when a TSO-C145() or TSO-C146() GPS/wide area augmentation system (WAAS) system is installed and operating. WAAS is the U.S. version of a satellite-based augmentation system (SBAS).

[a] In Alaska, aircraft may operate on GNSS Q-routes with GPS (TSO-C129() or TSO-C196()) equipment while the aircraft remains in Air Traffic Control (ATC) radar surveillance or with GPS/WAAS (TSO-C145() or TSO-C146()) which does not require ATC radar surveillance.

[b] In Alaska, aircraft may only operate on GNSS T-routes with GPS/WAAS (TSO-C145() or TSO-C146()) equipment.

(2) Ground-based navigation equipment is not required to be installed and operating for en route IFR operations when using GPS/WAAS navigation systems. All operators should ensure that an alternate means of navigation is available in the unlikely event the GPS/WAAS navigation system becomes inoperative.

(3) Q-routes and T-routes outside Alaska. Q-routes require system performance currently met by GPS, GPS/WAAS, or DME/DME/IRU RNAV systems that satisfy the criteria discussed in AC 90-100(), *U.S. Terminal and En Route Area Navigation (RNAV) Operations.* T-routes require GPS or GPS/WAAS equipment.

Reference: *AIM, ¶5-3-4, Airways and Route Systems*

(c) GPS IFR approach/departure operations can be conducted when approved avionics systems are installed and the following requirements are met:

(1) The aircraft is TSO-C145() or TSO-C146() or TSO-C196() or TSO-C129() in Class A1, B1, B3, C1, or C3; and

(2) The approach/departure must be retrievable from the current airborne navigation database in the navigation computer. The system must be able to retrieve the procedure by name from the aircraft navigation database. Manual entry of waypoints using latitude/longitude or place/bearing is not permitted for approach procedures.

(3) The authorization to fly instrument approaches/departures with GPS is limited to U.S. airspace.

(4) The use of GPS in any other airspace must be expressly authorized by the FAA Administrator.

(5) GPS instrument approach/departure operations outside the U.S. must be authorized by the appropriate sovereign authority.

TABLE 1–1–5
GPS IFR EQUIPMENT CLASSES/CATEGORIES

Equipment Class	RAIM	Int. Nav Sys. to Prov. RAIM Equiv.	Oceanic	En Route	Terminal	Nonprecision Approach Capable
Class A—GPS sensor and navigation capability.						
A1	yes		yes	yes	yes	yes
A2	yes		yes	yes	yes	no
Class B—GPS sensor data to an integrated navigation system (i.e. FMS, multi-sensor navigation system, etc.)						
B1	yes		yes	yes	yes	yes
B2	yes		yes	yes	yes	no
B3		yes	yes	yes	yes	yes
B4		yes	yes	yes	yes	no
Class C—GPS sensor data to an integrated navigation system (as in Class B) which provides enhanced guidance to an autopilot, or flight director, to reduce flight tech. errors. Limited to 14 CFR Part 121 or equivalent criteria.						
C1	yes		yes	yes	yes	yes
C2	yes		yes	yes	yes	no
C3		yes	yes	yes	yes	yes
C4		yes	yes	yes	yes	no

TABLE 1–1–6
GPS APPROVAL REQUIRED/AUTHORIZED USE

Equipment Type[1]	Installation Approval Required	Operational Approval Required	IFR En Route[2]	IFR Terminal[2]	IFR Approach[3]	Oceanic Remote	In Lieu of ADF and/or DME[3]
Hand held[4]	X[5]						
VFR Panel Mount[4]	X						
IFR En Route and Terminal	X	X	X	X			X
IFR Oceanic/ Remote	X	X	X	X		X	X
IFR En Route, Terminal, and Approach	X	X	X	X	X		X

[1] To determine equipment approvals and limitations, refer to the AFM, AFM supplements, or pilot guides.
[2] Requires verification of data for correctness if database is expired.
[3] Requires current database or verification that the procedure has not been amended since the expiration of the database.
[4] VFR and hand-held GPS systems are not authorized for IFR navigation, instrument approaches, or as a primary instrument flight reference. During IFR operations they may be considered only an aid to situational awareness.
[5] Hand-held receivers require no approval. However, any aircraft modification to support the hand-held receiver; i.e., installation of an external antenna or a permanent mounting bracket, does require approval.

4. Departures and Instrument Departure Procedures (DPs)

The GPS receiver must be set to terminal (±1 NM) CDI sensitivity and the navigation routes contained in the database in order to fly published IFR charted departures and DPs. Terminal RAIM should be automatically provided by the receiver. (Terminal RAIM for departure may not be available unless the waypoints are part of the active flight plan rather than proceeding direct to the first destination.) Certain segments of a DP may require some manual intervention by the pilot, especially when radar vectored to a course or required to intercept a specific course to a waypoint. The database may not contain all of the transitions or departures from all runways and some GPS receivers do not contain DPs in the database. It is necessary that helicopter procedures be flown at 70 knots or less since helicopter departure procedures and missed approaches use a 20:1 obstacle clearance surface (OCS), which is double the fixed-wing OCS, and turning areas are based on this speed as well.

5. GPS Instrument Approach Procedures

(a) GPS overlay approaches are designated non-precision instrument approach procedures that pilots are authorized to fly using GPS avionics. Localizer (LOC), localizer type directional aid (LDA), and simplified directional facility (SDF) procedures are not authorized. Overlay procedures are identified by the "name of the procedure" and "or GPS" (e.g., VOR/DME or GPS

RWY 15) in the title. Authorized procedures must be retrievable from a current onboard navigation database. The navigation database may also enhance position orientation by displaying a map containing information on conventional NAVAID approaches. This approach information should not be confused with a GPS overlay approach (see the receiver operating manual, AFM, or AFM Supplement for details on how to identify these approaches in the navigation database).

Note: Overlay approaches do not adhere to the design criteria described in Paragraph 5-4-5m, Area Navigation (RNAV) Instrument Approach Charts, for stand-alone GPS approaches. Overlay approach criteria is based on the design criteria used for ground-based NAVAID approaches.

(b) Stand-alone approach procedures specifically designed for GPS systems have replaced many of the original overlay approaches. All approaches that contain "GPS" in the title (e.g., "VOR or GPS RWY 24," "GPS RWY 24 ," or "RNAV (GPS) RWY 24") can be flown using GPS. GPS-equipped aircraft do not need underlying ground-based NAVAIDs or associated aircraft avionics to fly the approach. Monitoring the underlying approach with ground-based NAVAIDs is suggested when able. Existing overlay approaches may be requested using the GPS title; for example, the VOR or GPS RWY 24 may be requested as "GPS RWY 24." Some GPS procedures have a Terminal Arrival Area (TAA) with an underlining RNAV approach.

(c) For flight planning purposes, TSO-C129() and TSO-C196()-equipped users (GPS users) whose navigation systems have fault detection and exclusion (FDE) capability, who perform a preflight RAIM prediction for the approach integrity at the airport where the RNAV (GPS) approach will be flown, and have proper knowledge and any required training and/or approval to conduct a GPS-based IAP, may file based on a GPS-based IAP at either the destination or the alternate airport, but not at both locations. At the alternate airport, pilots may plan for:

(1) Lateral navigation (LNAV) or circling minimum descent altitude (MDA);

(2) LNAV/vertical navigation (LNAV/VNAV) DA, if equipped with and using approved barometric vertical navigation (baro-VNAV) equipment;

(3) RNP 0.3 DA on an RNAV (RNP) IAP, if they are specifically authorized users using approved baro-VNAV equipment and the pilot has verified required navigation performance (RNP) availability through an approved prediction program.

(d) If the above conditions cannot be met, any required alternate airport must have an approved instrument approach procedure other than

GPS-based that is anticipated to be operational and available at the estimated time of arrival, and which the aircraft is equipped to fly.

(e) Procedures for Accomplishing GPS Approaches

(1) An RNAV (GPS) procedure may be associated with a Terminal Arrival Area (TAA). The basic design of the RNAV procedure is the "T" design or a modification of the "T" (See Paragraph 5-4-5d, Terminal Arrival Area (TAA), for complete information).

(2) Pilots cleared by ATC for an RNAV (GPS) approach should fly the full approach from an Initial Approach Waypoint (IAWP) or feeder fix. Randomly joining an approach at an intermediate fix does not assure terrain clearance.

(3) When an approach has been loaded in the navigation system, GPS receivers will give an "arm" annunciation 30 NM straight line distance from the airport/heliport reference point. Pilots should arm the approach mode at this time if not already armed (some receivers arm automatically). Without arming, the receiver will not change from en route CDI and RAIM sensitivity of ±5 NM either side of centerline to ±1 NM terminal sensitivity. Where the IAWP is inside this 30 mile point, a CDI sensitivity change will occur once the approach mode is armed and the aircraft is inside 30 NM. Where the IAWP is beyond 30 NM from the airport/heliport reference point and the approach is armed, the CDI sensitivity will not change until the aircraft is within 30 miles of the airport/heliport reference point. Feeder route obstacle clearance is predicated on the receiver being in terminal (±1 NM) CDI sensitivity and RAIM within 30 NM of the airport/heliport reference point; therefore, the receiver should always be armed (if required) not later than the 30 NM annunciation.

(4) The pilot must be aware of what bank angle/turn rate the particular receiver uses to compute turn anticipation, and whether wind and airspeed are included in the receiver's calculations. This information should be in the receiver operating manual. Over or under banking the turn onto the final approach course may significantly delay getting on course and may result in high descent rates to achieve the next segment altitude.

(5) When within 2 NM of the Final Approach Waypoint (FAWP) with the approach mode armed, the approach mode will switch to active, which results in RAIM and CDI changing to approach sensitivity. Beginning 2 NM prior to the FAWP, the full scale CDI sensitivity will smoothly change from ±1 NM to ±0.3 NM at the FAWP. As sensitivity changes from ±1 NM to ±0.3 NM approaching the FAWP, with the CDI not centered, the corresponding increase in CDI displacement may give the impression that the aircraft is moving further away from the intended course even

though it is on an acceptable intercept heading. Referencing the digital track displacement information (cross track error), if it is available in the approach mode, may help the pilot remain position oriented in this situation. Being established on the final approach course prior to the beginning of the sensitivity change at 2 NM will help prevent problems in interpreting the CDI display during ramp down. Therefore, requesting or accepting vectors which will cause the aircraft to intercept the final approach course within 2 NM of the FAWP is not recommended.

(6) When receiving vectors to final, most receiver operating manuals suggest placing the receiver in the non-sequencing mode on the FAWP and manually setting the course. This provides an extended final approach course in cases where the aircraft is vectored onto the final approach course outside of any existing segment which is aligned with the runway. Assigned altitudes must be maintained until established on a published segment of the approach. Required altitudes at waypoints outside the FAWP or stepdown fixes must be considered. Calculating the distance to the FAWP may be required in order to descend at the proper location.

(7) Overriding an automatically selected sensitivity during an approach will cancel the approach mode annunciation. If the approach mode is not armed by 2 NM prior to the FAWP, the approach mode will not become active at 2 NM prior to the FAWP, and the equipment will flag. In these conditions, the RAIM and CDI sensitivity will not ramp down, and the pilot should not descend to MDA, but fly to the MAWP and execute a missed approach. The approach active annunciator and/or the receiver should be checked to ensure the approach mode is active prior to the FAWP.

(8) Do not attempt to fly an approach unless the procedure in the onboard database is current and identified as "GPS" on the approach chart. The navigation database may contain information about non-overlay approach procedures that enhances position orientation generally by providing a map, while flying these approaches using conventional NAVAIDs. This approach information should not be confused with a GPS overlay approach (see the receiver operating manual, AFM, or AFM Supplement for details on how to identify these procedures in the navigation database). Flying point to point on the approach does not assure compliance with the published approach procedure. The proper RAIM sensitivity will not be available and the CDI sensitivity will not automatically change to ±0.3 NM. Manually setting CDI sensitivity does not automatically change the RAIM sensitivity on some receivers. Some existing non-precision approach procedures cannot be coded for use with GPS and will not be available as overlays.

(9) Pilots should pay particular attention to the exact operation of their GPS receivers for performing holding patterns and in the case of overlay approaches, operations such as procedure turns. These procedures may require manual intervention by the pilot to stop the sequencing of waypoints by the receiver and to resume automatic GPS navigation sequencing once the maneuver is complete. The same waypoint may appear in the route of flight more than once consecutively (for example, IAWP, FAWP, MAHWP on a procedure turn). Care must be exercised to ensure that the receiver is sequenced to the appropriate waypoint for the segment of the procedure being flown, especially if one or more fly-overs are skipped (for example, FAWP rather than IAWP if the procedure turn is not flown). The pilot may have to sequence past one or more fly-overs of the same waypoint in order to start GPS automatic sequencing at the proper place in the sequence of waypoints.

(10) Incorrect inputs into the GPS receiver are especially critical during approaches. In some cases, an incorrect entry can cause the receiver to leave the approach mode.

(11) A fix on an overlay approach identified by a DME fix will not be in the waypoint sequence on the GPS receiver unless there is a published name assigned to it. When a name is assigned, the along track distance (ATD) to the waypoint may be zero rather than the DME stated on the approach chart. The pilot should be alert for this on any overlay procedure where the original approach used DME.

(12) If a visual descent point (VDP) is published, it will not be included in the sequence of waypoints. Pilots are expected to use normal piloting techniques for beginning the visual descent, such as ATD.

(13) Unnamed stepdown fixes in the final approach segment may or may not be coded in the waypoint sequence of the aircraft's navigation database and must be identified using ATD. Stepdown fixes in the final approach segment of RNAV (GPS) approaches are being named, in addition to being identified by ATD. However, GPS avionics may or may not accommodate waypoints between the FAF and MAP. Pilots must know the capabilities of their GPS equipment and continue to identify stepdown fixes using ATD when necessary.

(f) Missed Approach

(1) A GPS missed approach requires pilot action to sequence the receiver past the MAWP to the missed approach portion of the procedure. The pilot must be thoroughly familiar with the activation procedure for the particular GPS receiver installed in the aircraft and must initiate appropriate action after the MAWP. Activating the missed approach prior to the MAWP will cause CDI sensitivity to immediately change to terminal

(±1 NM) sensitivity and the receiver will continue to navigate to the MAWP. The receiver will not sequence past the MAWP. Turns should not begin prior to the MAWP. If the missed approach is not activated, the GPS receiver will display an extension of the inbound final approach course and the ATD will increase from the MAWP until it is manually sequenced after crossing the MAWP.

(2) Missed approach routings in which the first track is via a course rather than direct to the next waypoint require additional action by the pilot to set the course. Being familiar with all of the inputs required is especially critical during this phase of flight.

(g) Receiver Autonomous Integrity Monitoring (RAIM)

(1) RAIM outages may occur due to an insufficient number of satellites or due to unsuitable satellite geometry which causes the error in the position solution to become too large. Loss of satellite reception and RAIM warnings may occur due to aircraft dynamics (changes in pitch or bank angle). Antenna location on the aircraft, satellite position relative to the horizon, and aircraft attitude may affect reception of one or more satellites. Since the relative positions of the satellites are constantly changing, prior experience with the airport does not guarantee reception at all times, and RAIM availability should always be checked.

(2) Civilian pilots may obtain GPS RAIM availability information for nonprecision approach procedures by using a manufacturer-supplied RAIM prediction tool, or using the Service Availability Prediction Tool (SAPT) on the FAA en route and terminal RAIM prediction website. Pilots can also request GPS RAIM aeronautical information from a flight service station during preflight briefings. GPS RAIM aeronautical information can be obtained for a period of 3 hours (for example, if you are scheduled to arrive at 1215 hours, then the GPS RAIM information is available from 1100 to 1400 hours) or a 24-hour timeframe at a particular airport. FAA briefers will provide RAIM information for a period of 1 hour before to 1 hour after the ETA hour, unless a specific timeframe is requested by the pilot. If flying a published GPS departure, a RAIM prediction should also be requested for the departure airport.

(3) The military provides airfield specific GPS RAIM NOTAMs for nonprecision approach procedures at military airfields. The RAIM outages are issued as M-series NOTAMs and may be obtained for up to 24 hours from the time of request.

(4) Receiver manufacturers and/or database suppliers may supply "NOTAM" type information concerning database errors. Pilots should check these sources when available, to ensure that they have the most current information concerning their electronic database.

(5) If RAIM is not available, use another type of navigation and approach system; select another route or destination; or delay the trip until RAIM is predicted to be available on arrival. On longer flights, pilots should consider rechecking the RAIM prediction for the destination during the flight. This may provide an early indication that an unscheduled satellite outage has occurred since takeoff.

(6) If a RAIM failure/status annunciation occurs prior to the final approach waypoint (FAWP), the approach should not be completed since GPS no longer provides the required integrity. The receiver performs a RAIM prediction by 2 NM prior to the FAWP to ensure that RAIM is available as a condition for entering the approach mode. The pilot should ensure the receiver has sequenced from "Armed" to "Approach" prior to the FAWP (normally occurs 2 NM prior). Failure to sequence may be an indication of the detection of a satellite anomaly, failure to arm the receiver (if required), or other problems which preclude flying the approach.

(7) If the receiver does not sequence into the approach mode or a RAIM failure/status annunciation occurs prior to the FAWP, the pilot must not initiate the approach nor descend, but instead, proceed to the missed approach waypoint (MAWP) via the FAWP, perform a missed approach, and contact ATC as soon as practical. The GPS receiver may continue to operate after a RAIM flag/status annunciation appears, but the navigation information should be considered advisory only. Refer to the receiver operating manual for specific indications and instructions associated with loss of RAIM prior to the FAF.

(8) If the RAIM flag/status annunciation appears after the FAWP, the pilot should initiate a climb and execute the missed approach. The GPS receiver may continue to operate after a RAIM flag/status annunciation appears, but the navigation information should be considered advisory only. Refer to the receiver operating manual for operating mode information during a RAIM annunciation.

(h) Waypoints

(1) GPS receivers navigate from one defined point to another retrieved from the aircraft's onboard navigational database. These points are waypoints (5-letter pronounceable name), existing VHF intersections, DME fixes with 5-letter pronounceable names and 3-letter NAVAID IDs. Each waypoint is a geographical location defined by a latitude/longitude geographic coordinate. These 5-letter waypoints, VHF intersections, 5-letter pronounceable DME fixes and 3-letter NAVAID IDs are published on various FAA aeronautical navigation products (IFR Enroute Charts, VFR Charts, Terminal Procedures Publications, etc.).

(2) A Computer Navigation Fix (CNF) is also a point defined by a latitude/longitude coordinate and is required to support Performance-Based Navigation (PBN) operations. The GPS receiver uses CNFs in conjunction with waypoints to navigate from point to point. However, CNFs are not recognized by ATC. ATC does not maintain CNFs in their database and they do not use CNFs for any air traffic control purpose. CNFs may or may not be charted on FAA aeronautical navigation products, are listed in the chart legends, and are for advisory purposes only. Pilots are not to use CNFs for point to point navigation (proceed direct), filing a flight plan, or in aircraft/ATC communications. CNFs that do appear on aeronautical charts allow pilots increased situational awareness by identifying points in the aircraft database route of flight with points on the aeronautical chart. CNFs are random five-letter identifiers, not pronounceable like waypoints and placed in parenthesis. Eventually, all CNFs will begin with the letters "CF" followed by three consonants (for example, CFWBG). This five-letter identifier will be found next to an "x" on enroute charts and possibly on an approach chart. On instrument approach procedures (charts) in the terminal procedures publication, CNFs may represent unnamed DME fixes, beginning and ending points of DME arcs, and sensor (ground-based signal i.e., VOR, NDB, ILS) final approach fixes on GPS overlay approaches. These CNFs provide the GPS with points on the procedure that allow the overlay approach to mirror the ground-based sensor approach. These points should only be used by the GPS system for navigation and should not be used by pilots for any other purpose on the approach. The CNF concept has not been adopted or recognized by the International Civil Aviation Organization (ICAO).

(3) GPS approaches use fly-over and fly-by waypoints to join route segments on an approach. Fly-by waypoints connect the two segments by allowing the aircraft to turn prior to the current waypoint in order to roll out on course to the next waypoint. This is known as turn anticipation and is compensated for in the airspace and terrain clearances. The missed approach waypoint (MAWP) will always be a fly-over waypoint. A holding waypoint will always be designed as a fly-over waypoint in the navigational database but may be charted as a fly-by event unless the holding waypoint is used for another purpose in the procedure and both events require the waypoint to be a fly-over event. Some waypoints may have dual use; for example, as a fly-by waypoint when used as an IF for a NoPT route and as a fly-over waypoint when the same waypoint is also used as an IAF/IF hold-in-lieu of PT. Since the waypoint can only be charted one way, when this situation occurs, the fly-by waypoint symbol will be charted in all uses of the waypoint.

(4) Unnamed waypoints for each airport will be uniquely identified in the database. Although the identifier may be used at different airports (for example, RW36 will be the identifier at each airport with a runway 36), the actual point, at each airport, is defined by a specific latitude/longitude coordinate.

(5) The runway threshold waypoint, normally the MAWP, may have a five-letter identifier (for example, SNEEZ) or be coded as RW## (for example, RW36, RW36L). MAWPs located at the runway threshold are being changed to the RW## identifier, while MAWPs not located at the threshold will have a five-letter identifier. This may cause the approach chart to differ from the aircraft database until all changes are complete. The runway threshold waypoint is also used as the center of the Minimum Safe Altitude (MSA) on most GPS approaches.

(i) Position Orientation

Pilots should pay particular attention to position orientation while using GPS. Distance and track information are provided to the next active waypoint, not to a fixed navigation aid. Receivers may sequence when the pilot is not flying along an active route, such as when being vectored or deviating for weather, due to the proximity to another waypoint in the route. This can be prevented by placing the receiver in the non-sequencing mode. When the receiver is in the non-sequencing mode, bearing and distance are provided to the selected waypoint and the receiver will not sequence to the next waypoint in the route until placed back in the auto sequence mode or the pilot selects a different waypoint. The pilot may have to compute the ATD to stepdown fixes and other points on overlay approaches, due to the receiver showing ATD to the next waypoint rather than DME to the VOR or ILS ground station.

(j) Impact of Magnetic Variation on PBN Systems

(1) Differences may exist between PBN systems and the charted magnetic courses on ground-based NAVAID instrument flight procedures (IFP), enroute charts, approach charts, and Standard Instrument Departure/Standard Terminal Arrival (SID/STAR) charts. These differences are due to the magnetic variance used to calculate the magnetic course. Every leg of an instrument procedure is first computed along a desired ground track with reference to true north. A magnetic variation correction is then applied to the true course in order to calculate a magnetic course for publication. The type of procedure will determine what magnetic variation value is added to the true course. A ground-based NAVAID IFP applies the facility magnetic variation of record to the true course to get the charted magnetic

course. Magnetic courses on PBN procedures are calculated two different ways. SID/STAR procedures use the airport magnetic variation of record, while IFR enroute charts use magnetic reference bearing. PBN systems make a correction to true north by adding a magnetic variation calculated with an algorithm based on aircraft position, or by adding the magnetic variation coded in their navigational database. This may result in the PBN system and the procedure designer using a different magnetic variation, which causes the magnetic course *displayed* by the PBN system and the magnetic course *charted* on the IFP plate to be different. It is important to understand, however, that PBN systems, (with the exception of VOR/DME RNAV equipment) navigate by reference to true north and display magnetic course only for pilot reference. As such, a *properly functioning* PBN system, containing a *current and accurate navigational database*, should fly the correct ground track for any loaded instrument procedure, despite differences in displayed magnetic course that may be attributed to magnetic variation application. Should significant differences between the approach chart and the PBN system avionics' application of the navigation database arise, the published approach chart, supplemented by NOTAMs, holds precedence.

(2) The course into a waypoint may not always be 180 degrees different from the course leaving the previous waypoint, due to the PBN system avionics' computation of geodesic paths, distance between waypoints, and differences in magnetic variation application. Variations in distances may also occur since PBN system distance-to-waypoint values are ATDs computed to the next waypoint and the DME values published on underlying procedures are slant-range distances measured to the station. This difference increases with aircraft altitude and proximity to the NAVAID.

(k) GPS Familiarization
Pilots should practice GPS approaches in visual meteorological conditions (VMC) until thoroughly proficient with all aspects of their equipment (receiver and installation) prior to attempting flight in instrument meteorological conditions (IMC). Pilots should be proficient in the following areas:

(1) Using the receiver autonomous integrity monitoring (RAIM) prediction function;

(2) Inserting a DP into the flight plan, including setting terminal CDI sensitivity, if required, and the conditions under which terminal RAIM is available for departure;

(3) Programming the destination airport;

(4) Programming and flying the approaches (especially procedure turns and arcs);

(5) Changing to another approach after selecting an approach;

(6) Programming and flying "direct" missed approaches;

(7) Programming and flying "routed" missed approaches;

(8) Entering, flying, and exiting holding patterns, particularly on approaches with a second waypoint in the holding pattern;

(9) Programming and flying a "route" from a holding pattern;

(10) Programming and flying an approach with radar vectors to the intermediate segment;

(11) Indication of the actions required for RAIM failure both before and after the FAWP; and

(12) Programming a radial and distance from a VOR (often used in departure instructions).

1-1-18 Wide Area Augmentation System (WAAS)

a. General
1. The FAA developed the WAAS to improve the accuracy, integrity and availability of GPS signals. WAAS will allow GPS to be used, as the aviation navigation system, from takeoff through approach when it is complete. WAAS is a critical component of the FAA's strategic objective for a seamless satellite navigation system for civil aviation, improving capacity and safety.

2. The International Civil Aviation Organization (ICAO) has defined Standards and Recommended Practices (SARPs) for satellite-based augmentation systems (SBAS) such as WAAS. India and Europe are building similar systems: EGNOS, the European Geostationary Navigation Overlay System; and India's GPS and Geo-Augmented Navigation (GAGAN) system. The merging of these systems will create an expansive navigation capability similar to GPS, but with greater accuracy, availability, and integrity.

3. Unlike traditional ground-based navigation aids, WAAS will cover a more extensive service area. Precisely surveyed wide-area reference stations (WRS) are linked to form the U.S. WAAS network. Signals from the GPS satellites are monitored by these WRSs to determine satellite clock and ephemeris corrections and to model the propagation effects of the ionosphere. Each station in the network relays the data to a wide-area master station (WMS) where the correction information is computed. A correction message is prepared and uplinked to a geostationary earth orbit satellite (GEO) via a GEO uplink subsystem (GUS) which is located at the ground earth station (GES). The message is then broadcast on the same frequency as GPS (L1, 1575.42 MHz) to WAAS receivers within the broadcast coverage area of the WAAS GEO.

4. In addition to providing the correction signal, the WAAS GEO provides an additional

pseudorange measurement to the aircraft receiver, improving the availability of GPS by providing, in effect, an additional GPS satellite in view. The integrity of GPS is improved through real-time monitoring, and the accuracy is improved by providing differential corrections to reduce errors. The performance improvement is sufficient to enable approach procedures with GPS/WAAS glide paths (vertical guidance).

5. The FAA has completed installation of 3 GEO satellite links, 38 WRSs, 3 WMSs, 6 GES, and the required terrestrial communications to support the WAAS network including 2 operational control centers. Prior to the commissioning of the WAAS for public use, the FAA conducted a series of test and validation activities. Future dual frequency operations are planned.

6. GNSS navigation, including GPS and WAAS, is referenced to the WGS-84 coordinate system. It should only be used where the Aeronautical Information Publications (including electronic data and aeronautical charts) conform to WGS-84 or equivalent. Other countries' civil aviation authorities may impose additional limitations on the use of their SBAS systems.

b. Instrument Approach Capabilities

1. A class of approach procedures which provide vertical guidance, but which do not meet the ICAO Annex 10 requirements for precision approaches has been developed to support satellite navigation use for aviation applications worldwide. These procedures are not precision and are referred to as Approach with Vertical Guidance (APV), are defined in ICAO Annex 6, and include approaches such as the LNAV/VNAV and localizer performance with vertical guidance (LPV). These approaches provide vertical guidance, but do not meet the more stringent standards of a precision approach. Properly certified WAAS receivers will be able to fly to LPV minima and LNAV/VNAV minima, using a WAAS electronic glide path, which eliminates the errors that can be introduced by using Barometric altimetry.

2. LPV minima takes advantage of the high accuracy guidance and increased integrity provided by WAAS. This WAAS generated angular guidance allows the use of the same TERPS approach criteria used for ILS approaches. LPV minima may have a decision altitude as low as 200 feet height above touchdown with visibility minimums as low as 1/2 mile, when the terrain and airport infrastructure support the lowest minima. LPV minima is published on the RNAV (GPS) approach charts (see paragraph 5-4-5, Instrument Approach Procedure Charts).

3. A different WAAS-based line of minima, called Localizer Performance (LP) is being added in locations where the terrain or obstructions do not allow publication of vertically guided LPV minima. LP takes advantage of the angular lateral guidance and smaller position errors provided by WAAS to provide a lateral only procedure similar to an ILS Localizer. LP procedures may provide lower minima than a LNAV procedure due to the narrower obstacle clearance surface.

Note: WAAS receivers certified prior to TSO-C145b and TSO-C146b, even if they have LPV capability, do not contain LP capability unless the receiver has been upgraded. Receivers capable of flying LP procedures must contain a statement in the Aircraft Flight Manual (AFM), AFM Supplement, or Approved Supplemental Flight Manual stating that the receiver has LP capability, as well as the capability for the other WAAS and GPS approach procedure types.

4. WAAS provides a level of service that supports all phases of flight, including RNAV (GPS) approaches to LNAV, LP, LNAV/VNAV and LPV lines of minima, within system coverage. Some locations close to the edge of the coverage may have a lower availability of vertical guidance.

c. General Requirements

1. WAAS avionics must be certified in accordance with Technical Standard Order (TSO) TSO-C145(), Airborne Navigation Sensors Using the (GPS) Augmented by the Wide Area Augmentation System (WAAS); or TSO-C146, Stand-Alone Airborne Navigation Equipment Using the Global Positioning System (GPS) Augmented by the Wide Area Augmentation System (WAAS), and installed in accordance with AC 20-138, *Airworthiness Approval of Positioning and Navigation Systems.*

2. GPS/WAAS operation must be conducted in accordance with the FAA-approved aircraft flight manual (AFM) and flight manual supplements. Flight manual supplements will state the level of approach procedure that the receiver supports. IFR approved WAAS receivers support all GPS only operations as long as lateral capability at the appropriate level is functional. WAAS monitors both GPS and WAAS satellites and provides integrity.

3. GPS/WAAS equipment is inherently capable of supporting oceanic and remote operations if the operator obtains a fault detection and exclusion (FDE) prediction program.

4. Air carrier and commercial operators must meet the appropriate provisions of their approved operations specifications.

5. Prior to GPS/WAAS IFR operation, the pilot must review appropriate Notices to Air Missions (NOTAMs) and aeronautical information. This information is available on request from a Flight Service Station. The FAA will provide NOTAMs to advise pilots of the status of the WAAS and level of service available.

(a) The term MAY NOT BE AVBL is used in conjunction with WAAS NOTAMs and indicates

that due to ionospheric conditions, lateral guidance may still be available when vertical guidance is unavailable. Under certain conditions, both lateral and vertical guidance may be unavailable. This NOTAM language is an advisory to pilots indicating the expected level of WAAS service (LNAV/VNAV, LPV, LP) may not be available.

Example:
!FDC FDC NAV WAAS VNAV/LPV/LP MINIMA MAY NOT BE AVBL 1306111330-1306141930EST
or
!FDC FDC NAV WAAS VNAV/LPV MINIMA NOT AVBL, WAAS LP MINIMA MAY NOT BE AVBL 1306021200-1306031200EST

WAAS MAY NOT BE AVBL NOTAMs are predictive in nature and published for flight planning purposes. Upon commencing an approach at locations NOTAMed WAAS MAY NOT BE AVBL, if the WAAS avionics indicate LNAV/VNAV or LPV service is available, then vertical guidance may be used to complete the approach using the displayed level of service. Should an outage occur during the approach, reversion to LNAV minima or an alternate instrument approach procedure may be required. When GPS testing NOTAMs are published and testing is actually occurring, Air Traffic Control will advise pilots requesting or cleared for a GPS or RNAV (GPS) approach that GPS may not be available and request intentions. If pilots have reported GPS anomalies, Air Traffic Control will request the pilot's intentions and/or clear the pilot for an alternate approach, if available and operational.

(b) WAAS area-wide NOTAMs are originated when WAAS assets are out of service and impact the service area. Area-wide WAAS NOT AVAILABLE (AVBL) NOTAMs indicate loss or malfunction of the WAAS system. In flight, Air Traffic Control will advise pilots requesting a GPS or RNAV (GPS) approach of WAAS NOT AVBL NOTAMs if not contained in the ATIS broadcast.

Example:
For unscheduled loss of signal or service, an example NOTAM is: !FDC FDC NAV WAAS NOT AVBL 1311160600-1311191200EST.
For scheduled loss of signal or service, an example NOTAM is: !FDC FDC NAV WAAS NOT AVBL 1312041015-1312082000EST.

(c) Site-specific WAAS MAY NOT BE AVBL NOTAMs indicate an expected level of service; for example, LNAV/VNAV, LP, or LPV may not be available. Pilots must request site-specific WAAS NOTAMs during flight planning. In flight, Air Traffic Control will not advise pilots of WAAS MAY NOT BE AVBL NOTAMs.

Note: Though currently unavailable, the FAA is updating its prediction tool software to provide this site-service in the future.

(d) Most of North America has redundant coverage by two or more geostationary satellites. One exception is the northern slope of Alaska. If there is a problem with the satellite providing coverage to this area, a NOTAM similar to the following example will be issued:

Example:
!FDC 4/3406 (PAZA A0173/14) ZAN NAV WAAS SIGNAL MAY NOT BE AVBL NORTH OF LINE FROM 7000N150000W TO 6400N16400W. RMK WAAS USERS SHOULD CONFIRM RAIM AVAILABILITY FOR IFR OPERATIONS IN THIS AREA. T-ROUTES IN THIS SECTOR NOT AVBL. ANY REQUIRED ALTERNATE AIRPORT IN THIS AREA MUST HAVE AN APPROVED INSTRUMENT APPROACH PROCEDURE OTHER THAN GPS THAT IS ANTICIPATED TO BE OPERATIONAL AND AVAILABLE AT THE ESTIMATED TIME OF ARRIVAL AND WHICH THE AIRCRAFT IS EQUIPPED TO FLY. 1406030812-1406050812EST.

6. When GPS-testing NOTAMs are published and testing is actually occurring, Air Traffic Control will advise pilots requesting or cleared for a GPS or RNAV (GPS) approach that GPS may not be available and request intentions. If pilots have reported GPS anomalies, Air Traffic Control will request the pilot's intentions and/or clear the pilot for an alternate approach, if available and operational.

Example:
Here is an example of a GPS testing NOTAM:
!GPS 06/001 ZAB NAV GPS (INCLUDING WAAS, GBAS, AND ADS-B) MAY NOT BE AVAILABLE WITHIN A 468NM RADIUS CENTERED AT 330702N1062540W (TCS 093044) FL400-UNL DECREASING IN AREA WITH A DECREASE IN ALTITUDE DEFINED AS: 425NM RADIUS AT FL250, 360NM RADIUS AT 10000FT, 354NM RADIUS AT 4000FT AGL, 327NM RADIUS AT 50FT AGL. 1406070300-1406071200.

7. When the approach chart is annotated with the W symbol, site-specific WAAS MAY NOT BE AVBL NOTAMs or Air Traffic advisories are not provided for outages in WAAS LNAV/VNAV and LPV vertical service. Vertical outages may occur daily at these locations due to being close to the edge of WAAS system coverage. Use LNAV or circling minima for flight planning at these locations, whether as a destination or alternate. For flight operations at these locations, when the WAAS avionics indicate that LNAV/VNAV or LPV service is available, then the vertical guidance may be used to complete the approach using the displayed level of service. Should an outage occur during the procedure, reversion to LNAV minima may be required.

Note: Area-wide WAAS NOT AVBL NOTAMs apply to all airports in the WAAS NOT AVBL area designated in the NOTAM, including approaches at airports where an approach chart is annotated with the ⓦ symbol.

8. GPS/WAAS was developed to be used within GEO coverage over North America without the need for other radio navigation equipment appropriate to the route of flight to be flown. Outside the WAAS coverage or in the event of a WAAS failure, GPS/WAAS equipment reverts to GPS-only operation and satisfies the requirements for basic GPS equipment. (See paragraph 1-1-17 for these requirements).

9. Unlike TSO-C129 avionics, which were certified as a supplement to other means of navigation, WAAS avionics are evaluated without reliance on other navigation systems. As such, installation of WAAS avionics does not require the aircraft to have other equipment appropriate to the route to be flown. (See paragraph 1-1-17d for more information on equipment requirements.)

(a) Pilots with WAAS receivers may flight plan to use any instrument approach procedure authorized for use with their WAAS avionics as the planned approach at a required alternate, with the following restrictions. When using WAAS at an alternate airport, flight planning must be based on flying the RNAV (GPS) LNAV or circling minima line, or minima on a GPS approach procedure, or conventional approach procedure with "or GPS" in the title. Code of Federal Regulation (CFR) Part 91 nonprecision weather requirements must be used for planning. Upon arrival at an alternate, when the WAAS navigation system indicates that LNAV/VNAV or LPV service is available, then vertical guidance may be used to complete the approach using the displayed level of service. The FAA has begun removing the △ NA (Alternate Minimums Not Authorized) symbol from select RNAV (GPS) and GPS approach procedures so they may be used by approach approved WAAS receivers at alternate airports. Some approach procedures will still require the △ NA for other reasons, such as no weather reporting, so it cannot be removed from all procedures. Since every procedure must be individually evaluated, removal of the △ NA from RNAV (GPS) and GPS procedures will take some time.

Note: Properly trained and approved, as required, TSO-C145() and TSO-C146() equipped users (WAAS users) with and using approved baro-VNAV equipment may plan for LNAV/VNAV DA at an alternate airport. Specifically authorized WAAS users with and using approved baro-VNAV equipment may also plan for RNP 0.3 DA at the alternate airport as long as the pilot has verified RNP availability through an approved prediction program.

d. Flying Procedures with WAAS

1. WAAS receivers support all basic GPS approach functions and provide additional capabilities. One of the major improvements is the ability to generate glide path guidance, independent of ground equipment or barometric aiding. This eliminates several problems such as hot and cold temperature effects, incorrect altimeter setting or lack of a local altimeter source. It also allows approach procedures to be built without the cost of installing ground stations at each airport or runway. Some approach certified receivers may only generate a glide path with performance similar to Baro–VNAV and are only approved to fly the LNAV/VNAV line of minima on the RNAV (GPS) approach charts. Receivers with additional capability (including faster update rates and smaller integrity limits) are approved to fly the LPV line of minima. The lateral integrity changes dramatically from the 0.3 NM (556 meter) limit for GPS, LNAV and LNAV/VNAV approach mode, to 40 meters for LPV. It also provides vertical integrity monitoring, which bounds the vertical error to 50 meters for LNAV/VNAV and LPVs with minima of 250' or above, and bounds the vertical error to 35 meters for LPVs with minima below 250'.

2. When an approach procedure is selected and active, the receiver will notify the pilot of the most accurate level of service supported by the combination of the WAAS signal, the receiver, and the selected approach, using the naming conventions on the minima lines of the selected approach procedure. For example, if an approach is published with LPV minima and the receiver is only certified for LNAV/VNAV, the equipment would indicate "LNAV/VNAV available," even though the WAAS signal would support LPV. If flying an existing LNAV/VNAV procedure with no LPV minima, the receiver will notify the pilot "LNAV/VNAV available," even if the receiver is certified for LPV and the signal supports LPV. If the signal does not support vertical guidance on procedures with LPV and/or LNAV/VNAV minima, the receiver annunciation will read "LNAV available." On lateral only procedures with LP and LNAV minima the receiver will indicate "LP available" or "LNAV available" based on the level of lateral service available. Once the level of service notification has been given, the receiver will operate in this mode for the duration of the approach procedure, unless that level of service becomes unavailable. The receiver cannot change back to a more accurate level of service until the next time an approach is activated.

Note: Receivers do not "fail down" to lower levels of service once the approach has been activated. If only the vertical off flag appears, the pilot may elect to use the LNAV minima if the rules under which the flight is operating allow changing the

type of approach being flown after commencing the procedure. If the lateral integrity limit is exceeded on an LP approach, a missed approach will be necessary since there is no way to reset the lateral alarm limit while the approach is active.

3. Another additional feature of WAAS receivers is the ability to exclude a bad GPS signal and continue operating normally. This is normally accomplished by the WAAS correction information. Outside WAAS coverage or when WAAS is not available, it is accomplished through a receiver algorithm called FDE. In most cases this operation will be invisible to the pilot since the receiver will continue to operate with other available satellites after excluding the "bad" signal. This capability increases the reliability of navigation.

4. Both lateral and vertical scaling for the LNAV/VNAV and LPV approach procedures are different than the linear scaling of basic GPS. When the complete published procedure is flown, ±1 NM linear scaling is provided until two (2) NM prior to the FAF, where the sensitivity increases to be similar to the angular scaling of an ILS. There are two differences in the WAAS scaling and ILS: 1) on long final approach segments, the initial scaling will be ±0.3 NM to achieve equivalent performance to GPS (and better than ILS, which is less sensitive far from the runway); 2) close to the runway threshold, the scaling changes to linear instead of continuing to become more sensitive. The width of the final approach course is tailored so that the total width is usually 700 feet at the runway threshold. Since the origin point of the lateral splay for the angular portion of the final is not fixed due to antenna placement like localizer, the splay angle can remain fixed, making a consistent width of final for aircraft being vectored onto the final approach course on different length runways. When the complete published procedure is not flown, and instead the aircraft needs to capture the extended final approach course similar to ILS, the vector to final (VTF) mode is used. Under VTF, the scaling is linear at ±1 NM until the point where the ILS angular splay reaches a width of ±1 NM regardless of the distance from the FAWP.

5. The WAAS scaling is also different than GPS TSO-C129() in the initial portion of the missed approach. Two differences occur here. First, the scaling abruptly changes from the approach scaling to the missed approach scaling, at approximately the departure end of the runway or when the pilot selects missed approach guidance rather than ramping as GPS does. Second, when the first leg of the missed approach is a Track to Fix (TF) leg aligned within 3 degrees of the inbound course, the receiver will change to 0.3 NM linear sensitivity until the turn initiation point for the first waypoint in the missed approach procedure, at which time it will abruptly change to

terminal (±1 NM) sensitivity. This allows the elimination of close in obstacles in the early part of the missed approach that may otherwise cause the DA to be raised.

6. There are two ways to select the final approach segment of an instrument approach. Most receivers use menus where the pilot selects the airport, the runway, the specific approach procedure and finally the IAF, there is also a channel number selection method. The pilot enters a unique 5-digit number provided on the approach chart, and the receiver recalls the matching final approach segment from the aircraft database. A list of information including the available IAFs is displayed and the pilot selects the appropriate IAF. The pilot should confirm that the correct final approach segment was loaded by cross checking the Approach ID, which is also provided on the approach chart.

7. The Along-Track Distance (ATD) during the final approach segment of an LNAV procedure (with a minimum descent altitude) will be to the MAWP. On LNAV/VNAV and LPV approaches to a decision altitude, there is no missed approach waypoint so the along-track distance is displayed to a point normally located at the runway threshold. In most cases the MAWP for the LNAV approach is located on the runway threshold at the centerline, so these distances will be the same. This distance will always vary slightly from any ILS DME that may be present, since the ILS DME is located further down the runway. Initiation of the missed approach on the LNAV/VNAV and LPV approaches is still based on reaching the decision altitude without any of the items listed in 14 CFR Section 91.175 being visible, and must not be delayed while waiting for the ATD to reach zero. The WAAS receiver, unlike a GPS receiver, will automatically sequence past the MAWP if the missed approach procedure has been designed for RNAV. The pilot may also select missed approach prior to the MAWP, however, navigation will continue to the MAWP prior to waypoint sequencing taking place.

1–1–19 Ground Based Augmentation System (GBAS) Landing System (GLS)

a. A GBAS ground installation at an airport can provide localized, differential augmentation to the Global Positioning System (GPS) signal-in-space enabling an aircraft's GLS precision approach capability. Through the GBAS service and the aircraft's GLS installation a pilot may complete an instrument approach offering three-dimensional angular, lateral, and vertical guidance for exact alignment and descent to a runway. The operational benefits of a GLS approach are similar to the benefits of an ILS or LPV approach operation.

Note: To remain consistent with international terminology, the FAA will use the term GBAS in place of the former term Local Area Augmentation System (LAAS).

b. An aircraft's GLS approach capability relies on the broadcast from a GBAS Ground Facility (GGF) installation. The GGF installation includes at least four ground reference stations near the airport's runway(s), a corrections processor, and a VHF Data Broadcast (VDB) uplink antenna. To use the GBAS GGF output and be eligible to conduct a GLS approach, the aircraft requires eligibility to conduct RNP approach (RNP APCH) operations and must meet the additional, specific airworthiness requirements for installation of a GBAS receiver intended to support GLS approach operations. When the aircraft achieves GLS approach eligibility, the aircraft's onboard navigation database may then contain published GLS instrument approach procedures.

c. During a GLS instrument approach procedure, the installation of an aircraft's GLS capability provides the pilot three-dimensional (3D) lateral and vertical navigation guidance much like an ILS instrument approach. GBAS corrections augment the GPS signal-in-space by offering position corrections, ensures the availability of enhanced integrity parameters, and then transmits the actual approach path definition over the VDB uplink antenna. A single GBAS ground station can support multiple GLS approaches to one or more runways.

d. Through the GBAS ground station, a GLS approach offers a unique operational service volume distinct from the traditional ILS approach service volume (see Figure 1-1-9). However, despite the unique service volume, in the final approach segment, a GLS approach provides precise 3D angular lateral and vertical guidance mimicking the precision guidance of an ILS approach.

e. Transitions to and segments of the published GLS instrument approach procedures may rely on use of RNAV 1 or RNP 1 prior to an IAF. Then, during the approach procedure, prior to the aircraft entering the GLS approach mode, a GLS approach procedure design uses the RNP APCH procedure design criteria to construct the procedural path (the criteria used to publish procedures titled "RNAV (GPS)" in the US). Thus, a GLS approach procedure may include paths requiring turns after the aircraft crosses the IAF, prior to the aircraft's flight guidance entering the GLS approach flight guidance mode. Likewise, the missed approach procedure for a GLS approach procedure relies exclusively on the same missed approach criteria supporting an RNP APCH.

f. When maneuvering the aircraft in compliance with an ATC clearance to intercept a GLS approach prior to the final approach segment (e.g. "being vectored"), the pilot should adhere to the clearance and ensure the aircraft intercepts the extended GLS final approach course within the specified service volume. Once on the GLS final approach course, the pilot should ensure the aircraft is in the GLS approach mode prior to reaching the procedure's glidepath intercept point. Once the aircraft is in the GLS flight guidance mode and captures the GLS glidepath, the pilot should fly the GLS final approach segment using the same pilot techniques they use to fly an ILS final approach or the final approach of an RNAV (GPS) approach flown to LPV minimums. See also the Instrument Procedures Handbook for more information on how to conduct a GLS instrument approach procedure.

1-1-20 Precision Approach Systems other than ILS and GLS

a. General

Approval and use of precision approach systems other than ILS and GLS require the issuance of special instrument approach procedures.

b. Special Instrument Approach Procedure

1. Special instrument approach procedures must be issued to the aircraft operator if pilot training, aircraft equipment, and/or aircraft performance is different than published procedures. Special instrument approach procedures are not distributed for general public use. These procedures are issued to an aircraft operator when the conditions for operations approval are satisfied.

2. General aviation operators requesting approval for special procedures should contact the local Flight Standards District Office to obtain a letter of authorization. Air carrier operators requesting approval for use of special procedures should contact their Certificate Holding District Office for authorization through their Operations Specification.

Reference: AIM, ¶5-4-7j, Instrument Approach Procedures.

Figure 1–1–9
GLS Standard Approach Service Volume

Section 2 Performance-Based Navigation (PBN) and Area Navigation (RNAV)

1-2-1 General

a. Introduction to PBN. As air travel has evolved, methods of navigation have improved to give operators more flexibility. PBN exists under the umbrella of area navigation (RNAV). The term RNAV in this context, as in procedure titles, just means "area navigation," regardless of the equipment capability of the aircraft. (See Figure 1-2-1.) Many operators have upgraded their systems to obtain the benefits of PBN. Within PBN there are two main categories of navigation methods or specifications: area navigation (RNAV) and required navigation performance (RNP). In this context, the term RNAV *x* means a specific navigation specification with a specified lateral accuracy value. For an aircraft to meet the requirements of PBN, a specified RNAV or RNP accuracy must be met 95 percent of the flight time. RNP is a PBN system that includes onboard performance monitoring and alerting capability (for example, Receiver Autonomous Integrity Monitoring (RAIM)). PBN also introduces the concept of navigation specifications (NavSpecs) which are a set of aircraft and aircrew requirements needed to support a navigation application within a defined airspace concept. For both RNP and RNAV NavSpecs, the numerical designation refers to the lateral navigation accuracy in nautical miles which is expected to be achieved at least 95 percent of the flight time by the population of aircraft operating within the airspace, route, or procedure. This information is detailed in International Civil Aviation Organization's (ICAO) Doc 9613, *Performance-based Navigation (PBN) Manual* and the latest FAA AC 90-105, *Approval Guidance for RNP Operations and Barometric Vertical Navigation in the U.S. National Airspace System and in Remote and Oceanic Airspace.*

FIGURE 1–2–1
Navigation Specifications

b. Area Navigation (RNAV)

1. General. RNAV is a method of navigation that permits aircraft operation on any desired flight path within the coverage of ground- or space-based navigation aids or within the limits of the capability of self-contained aids, or a combination of these. In the future, there will be an increased dependence on the use of RNAV in lieu of routes defined by ground-based navigation aids. RNAV routes and terminal procedures, including departure procedures (DPs) and standard terminal arrivals (STARs), are designed with RNAV systems in mind. There are several potential advantages of RNAV routes and procedures:

(a) Time and fuel savings;

(b) Reduced dependence on radar vectoring, altitude, and speed assignments allowing a reduction in required ATC radio transmissions; and

(c) More efficient use of airspace.

In addition to information found in this manual, guidance for domestic RNAV DPs, STARs, and

routes may also be found in AC 90-100, *U.S. Terminal and En Route Area Navigation (RNAV) Operations.*

2. RNAV Operations. RNAV procedures, such as DPs and STARs, demand strict pilot awareness and maintenance of the procedure centerline. Pilots should possess a working knowledge of their aircraft navigation system to ensure RNAV procedures are flown in an appropriate manner. In addition, pilots should have an understanding of the various waypoint and leg types used in RNAV procedures; these are discussed in more detail below.

(a) Waypoints. A waypoint is a predetermined geographical position that is defined in terms of latitude/longitude coordinates. Waypoints may be a simple named point in space or associated with existing NAVAIDs, intersections, or fixes. A waypoint is most often used to indicate a change in direction, speed, or altitude along the desired path. RNAV procedures make use of both fly-over and fly-by waypoints.

(1) Fly-by waypoints. Fly-by waypoints are used when an aircraft should begin a turn to the next course prior to reaching the waypoint separating the two route segments. This is known as turn anticipation.

(2) Fly-over waypoints. Fly-over waypoints are used when the aircraft must fly over the point prior to starting a turn.

Note: *Figure 1-2-2 illustrates several differences between a fly-by and a fly-over waypoint.*

**FIGURE 1–2–2
Fly-by and Fly-over Waypoints**

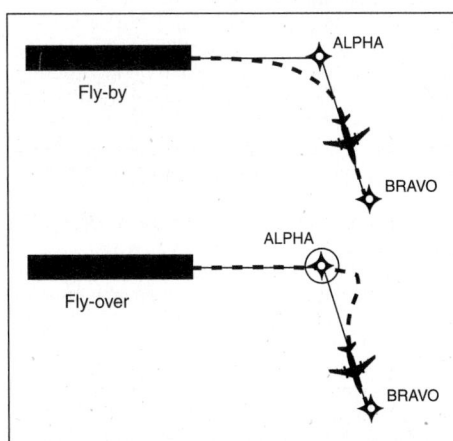

(b) RNAV Leg Types. A leg type describes the desired path proceeding, following, or between waypoints on an RNAV procedure. Leg types are identified by a two-letter code that describes the path (e.g., heading, course, track, etc.) and the termination point (e.g., the path terminates at an altitude, distance, fix, etc.). Leg types used for procedure design are included in the aircraft navigation database, but not normally provided on the procedure chart. The narrative depiction of the RNAV chart describes how a procedure is flown. The "path and terminator concept" defines that every leg of a procedure has a termination point and some kind of path into that termination point. Some of the available leg types are described below.

(1) Track to Fix. A Track to Fix (TF) leg is intercepted and acquired as the flight track to the following waypoint. Track to a Fix legs are sometimes called point-to-point legs for this reason. **Narrative:** *"direct ALPHA, then on course to BRAVO WP."* See Figure 1-2-3.

(2) Direct to Fix. A Direct to Fix (DF) leg is a path described by an aircraft's track from an initial area direct to the next waypoint. **Narrative:** *"turn right direct BRAVO WP."* See Figure 1-2-4.

**FIGURE 1–2–3
Track to Fix Leg Type**

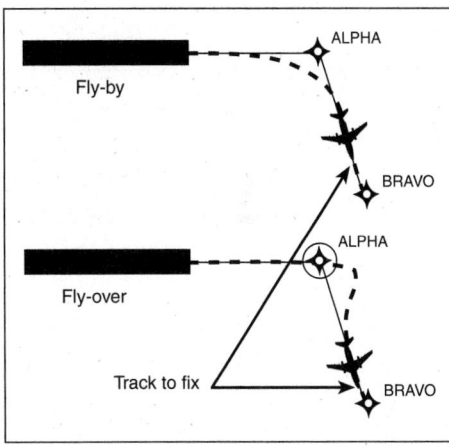

**FIGURE 1–2–4
Direct to Fix Leg Type**

(3) Course to Fix. A Course to Fix (CF) leg is a path that terminates at a fix with a specified course at that fix. ***Narrative:*** *"on course 150 to ALPHA WP."* See Figure 1-2-5.

(4) Radius to Fix. A Radius to Fix (RF) leg is defined as a constant radius circular path around a defined turn center that terminates at a fix. See Figure 1-2-6.

FIGURE 1–2–5
Course to Fix Leg Type

FIGURE 1–2–6
Radius to Fix Leg Type

(5) Heading. A Heading leg may be defined as, but not limited to, a Heading to Altitude (VA), Heading to DME range (VD), and Heading to Manual Termination, i.e., Vector (VM). ***Narrative:*** *"climb heading 350 to 1500," "heading 265, at 9 DME west of PXR VORTAC, right turn heading 360," "fly heading 090, expect radar vectors to DRYHT INT."*

(c) Navigation Issues. Pilots should be aware of their navigation system inputs, alerts, and annunciations in order to make better-informed decisions. In addition, the availability and suitability of particular sensors/systems should be considered.

(1) GPS/WAAS. Operators using TSO-C129(), TSO-C196(), TSO-C145() or TSO-C146() systems should ensure departure and arrival airports are entered to ensure proper RAIM availability and CDI sensitivity.

(2) DME/DME. Operators should be aware that DME/DME position updating is dependent on navigation system logic and DME facility proximity, availability, geometry, and signal masking.

(3) VOR/DME. Unique VOR characteristics may result in less accurate values from VOR/DME position updating than from GPS or DME/DME position updating.

(4) Inertial Navigation. Inertial reference units and inertial navigation systems are often coupled with other types of navigation inputs, e.g., DME/DME or GPS, to improve overall navigation system performance.

Note: *Specific inertial position updating requirements may apply.*

(d) Flight Management System (FMS). An FMS is an integrated suite of sensors, receivers, and computers, coupled with a navigation database. These systems generally provide performance and RNAV guidance to displays and automatic flight control systems.

Inputs can be accepted from multiple sources such as GPS, DME, VOR, LOC and IRU. These inputs may be applied to a navigation solution one at a time or in combination. Some FMSs provide for the detection and isolation of faulty navigation information.

When appropriate navigation signals are available, FMSs will normally rely on GPS and/or DME/DME (that is, the use of distance information from two or more DME stations) for position updates. Other inputs may also be incorporated based on FMS system architecture and navigation source geometry.

Note: *DME/DME inputs coupled with one or more IRU(s) are often abbreviated as DME/DME/IRU or D/D/I.*

(e) RNAV Navigation Specifications (Nav Specs)
Nav Specs are a set of aircraft and aircrew requirements needed to support a navigation application within a defined airspace concept. For both RNP and RNAV designations, the numerical designation refers to the lateral navigation accuracy in nautical miles which is expected to be achieved at least 95 percent of the flight time by the population of aircraft operating within the airspace, route, or procedure. (See Figure 1-2-1.)

(1) RNAV 1. Typically RNAV 1 is used for DPs and STARs and appears on the charts. Aircraft must maintain a total system error of not more than 1 NM for 95 percent of the total flight time.

(2) RNAV 2. Typically RNAV 2 is used for en route operations unless otherwise specified. T-routes and Q-routes are examples of this Nav Spec. Aircraft must maintain a total system error of not more than 2 NM for 95 percent of the total flight time.

(3) RNAV 10. Typically RNAV 10 is used in oceanic operations. See paragraph 4-7-1 for specifics and explanation of the relationship between RNP 10 and RNAV 10 terminology.

1–2–2 Required Navigation Performance (RNP)

a. General. While both RNAV navigation specifications (NavSpecs) and RNP NavSpecs contain specific performance requirements, RNP is RNAV with the added requirement for onboard performance monitoring and alerting (OBPMA). RNP is also a statement of navigation performance necessary for operation within a defined airspace. A critical component of RNP is the *ability of the aircraft navigation system to monitor its achieved navigation performance, and to identify for the pilot whether the operational requirement is, or is not, being met during an operation.* OBPMA capability therefore allows a lessened reliance on air traffic control intervention and/or procedural separation to achieve the overall safety of the operation. RNP capability of the aircraft is a major component in determining the separation criteria to ensure that the overall containment of the operation is met. The RNP capability of an aircraft will vary depending upon the aircraft equipment and the navigation infrastructure. For example, an aircraft may be eligible for RNP 1, but may not be capable of RNP 1 operations due to limited NAVAID coverage or avionics failure. The Aircraft Flight Manual (AFM) or avionics documents for your aircraft should specifically state the aircraft's RNP eligibilities. Contact the manufacturer of the avionics or the aircraft if this information is missing or incomplete. NavSpecs should be considered different from one another, not "better" or "worse" based on the described lateral navigation accuracy. It is this concept that requires each NavSpec eligibility to be listed separately in the avionics documents or AFM. For example, RNP 1 is different from RNAV 1, and an RNP 1 eligibility does *not* mean automatic RNP 2 or RNAV 1 eligibility. As a safeguard, the FAA requires that aircraft navigation databases hold only those procedures that the aircraft maintains eligibility for. If you look for a specific instrument procedure in your aircraft's navigation database and cannot find it, it's likely that procedure contains PBN elements your aircraft is ineligible for or cannot compute and fly. Further, optional capabilities such as Radius-to-fix (RF) turns or scalability should be described in the AFM or avionics documents. Use the capabilities of your avionics suite to verify the

appropriate waypoint and track data after loading the procedure from your database.

b. PBN Operations

1. Lateral Accuracy Values. Lateral Accuracy values are applicable to a selected airspace, route, or procedure. The lateral accuracy value is a value typically expressed as a distance in nautical miles from the intended centerline of a procedure, route, or path. RNP applications also account for potential errors at some multiple of lateral accuracy value (for example, twice the RNP lateral accuracy values).

(a) RNP NavSpecs. U.S. standard NavSpecs supporting typical RNP airspace uses are as specified below. Other NavSpecs may include different lateral accuracy values as identified by ICAO or other states. (See Figure 1-2-1.)

(1) RNP Approach (RNP APCH). In the U.S., RNP APCH procedures are titled RNAV (GPS) and offer several lines of minima to accommodate varying levels of aircraft equipage: either lateral navigation (LNAV), LNAV/vertical navigation (LNAV/VNAV), Localizer Performance with Vertical Guidance (LPV), and Localizer Performance with Vertical Guidance (LPV), and Localizer Performance (LP). GPS with or without Space-Based Augmentation System (SBAS) (for example, WAAS) can provide the lateral information to support LNAV minima. LNAV/VNAV incorporates LNAV lateral with vertical path guidance for systems and operators capable of either barometric or SBAS vertical. Pilots are required to use SBAS to fly to the LPV or LP minima. RF turn capability is optional in RNP APCH eligibility. This means that your aircraft may be eligible for RNP APCH operations, but you may not fly an RF turn unless RF turns are also specifically listed as a feature of your avionics suite. GBAS Landing System (GLS) procedures are also constructed using RNP APCH NavSpecs and provide precision approach capability. RNP APCH has a lateral accuracy value of 1 in the terminal and missed approach segments and essentially scales to RNP 0.3 (or 40 meters with SBAS) in the final approach. (See paragraph 5-4-18, RNP AR (Authorization Required) Instrument Procedures.)

(2) RNP Authorization Required Approach (RNP AR APCH). In the U.S., RNP AR APCH procedures are titled RNAV (RNP). These approaches have stringent equipage and pilot training standards and require special FAA authorization to fly. Scalability and RF turn capabilities are mandatory in RNP AR APCH eligibility. RNP AR APCH vertical navigation performance is based upon barometric VNAV or SBAS. RNP AR is intended to provide specific benefits at specific locations. It is not intended for every operator or aircraft. RNP AR capability requires specific aircraft performance, design, operational processes, training, and specific procedure design criteria to achieve the required target level of safety. RNP

AR APCH has lateral accuracy values that can range below 1 in the terminal and missed approach segments and essentially scale to RNP 0.3 or lower in the final approach. Before conducting these procedures, operators should refer to the latest AC 90-101, *Approval Guidance for RNP Procedures with AR*. (See paragraph 5-4-18.)

(3) RNP Authorization Required Departure (RNP AR DP). Similar to RNP AR approaches, RNP AR departure procedures have stringent equipage and pilot training standards and require special FAA authorization to fly. Scalability and RF turn capabilities is mandatory in RNP AR DP eligibility. RNP AR DP is intended to provide specific benefits at specific locations. It is not intended for every operator or aircraft. RNP AR DP capability requires specific aircraft performance, design, operational processes, training, and specific procedure design criteria to achieve the required target level of safety. RNP AR DP has lateral accuracy values that can scale to no lower than RNP 0.3 in the initial departure flight path. Before conducting these procedures, operators should refer to the latest AC 90-101, *Approval Guidance for RNP Procedures with AR*. (See paragraph 5-4-18.)

(4) Advanced RNP (A-RNP). Advanced RNP is a NavSpec with a minimum set of mandatory functions enabled in the aircraft's avionics suite. In the U.S., these minimum functions include capability to calculate and perform RF turns, scalable RNP, and parallel offset flight path generation. Higher continuity (such as dual systems) may be required for certain oceanic and remote continental airspace. Other "advanced" options for use in the en route environment (such as fixed radius transitions and Time of Arrival Control) are optional in the U.S. Typically, an aircraft eligible for A-RNP will also be eligible for operations comprising: RNP APCH, RNP/RNAV 1, RNP/RNAV 2, RNP 4, and RNP/RNAV 10. A-RNP allows for scalable RNP lateral navigation values (either 1.0 or 0.3) in the terminal environment. Use of these reduced lateral accuracies will normally require use of the aircraft's autopilot and/or flight director. See the latest AC 90-105 for more information on A-RNP, including NavSpec bundling options, eligibility determinations, and operations approvals.

Note: A-RNP eligible aircraft are NOT automatically eligible for RNP AR APCH or RNP AR DP operations, as RNP AR eligibility requires a separate determination process and special FAA authorization.

(5) RNP 1. RNP 1 requires a lateral accuracy value of 1 for arrival and departure in the terminal area, and the initial and intermediate approach phase when used on conventional procedures with PBN segments (for example, an ILS with a PBN feeder, IAF, or missed approach). RF turn capability is optional in RNP 1 eligibility. This means that your aircraft may be eligible for RNP 1 operations, but you may not fly an RF turn unless RF turns are also specifically listed as a feature of your avionics suite.

(6) RNP 2. RNP 2 will apply to both domestic and oceanic/remote operations with a lateral accuracy value of 2.

(7) RNP 4. RNP 4 will apply to oceanic and remote operations only with a lateral accuracy value of 4. RNP 4 eligibility will automatically confer RNP 10 eligibility.

(8) RNP 10. The RNP 10 NavSpec applies to certain oceanic and remote operations with a lateral accuracy of 10. In such airspace, the RNAV 10 NavSpec will be applied, so any aircraft eligible for RNP 10 will be deemed eligible for RNAV 10 operations. Further, any aircraft eligible for RNP 4 operations is automatically qualified for RNP 10/RNAV 10 operations. (See also the latest AC 91-70, *Oceanic and Remote Continental Airspace Operations*, for more information on oceanic RNP/RNAV operations.)

(9) RNP 0.3. The RNP 0.3 NavSpec requires a lateral accuracy value of 0.3 for all authorized phases of flight. RNP 0.3 is not authorized for oceanic, remote, or the final approach segment. Use of RNP 0.3 by slow-flying fixed-wing aircraft is under consideration, but the RNP 0.3 NavSpec initially will apply only to rotorcraft operations. RF turn capability is optional in RNP 0.3 eligibility. This means that your aircraft may be eligible for RNP 0.3 operations, but you may not fly an RF turn unless RF turns are also specifically listed as a feature of your avionics suite.

Note: On terminal procedures or en route charts, do not confuse a charted RNP value of 0.30, or any standard final approach course segment width of 0.30, with the NavSpec title "RNP 0.3." Charted RNP values of 0.30 or below should contain two decimal places (for example, RNP 0.15, or 0.10, or 0.30) whereas the NavSpec title will only state "RNP 0.3."

(b) Application of Standard Lateral Accuracy Values. U.S. standard lateral accuracy values typically used for various routes and procedures supporting RNAV operations may be based on use of a specific navigational system or sensor such as GPS, or on multi-sensor RNAV systems having suitable performance.

(c) Depiction of PBN Requirements. In the U.S., PBN requirements like Lateral Accuracy Values or NavSpecs applicable to a procedure will be depicted on affected charts and procedures. In the U.S., a specific procedure's Performance-Based Navigation (PBN) requirements will be prominently displayed in separate, standardized notes boxes. For procedures with PBN elements, the "PBN box" will contain the procedure's NavSpec(s); and, if required: specific sensors or

infrastructure needed for the navigation solution, any additional or advanced functional requirements, the minimum RNP value, and any amplifying remarks. Items listed in this PBN box are *required* to fly the procedure's PBN elements. For example, an ILS with an RNAV missed approach would require a specific capability to fly the missed approach portion of the procedure. That required capability will be listed in the PBN box. The separate Equipment Requirements box will list ground-based equipment and/or airport specific requirements. On procedures with both PBN elements and ground-based equipment requirements, the PBN requirements box will be listed first. (See Figure 5-4-1.)

c. Other RNP Applications Outside the U.S. The FAA and ICAO member states have led initiatives in implementing the RNP concept to oceanic operations. For example, RNP-10 routes have been established in the northern Pacific (NOPAC) which has increased capacity and efficiency by reducing the distance between tracks to 50 NM. (See paragraph 4-7-1.)

d. Aircraft and Airborne Equipment Eligibility for RNP Operations. Aircraft eligible for RNP operations will have an appropriate entry including special conditions and limitations in its AFM, avionics manual, or a supplement. Operators of aircraft not having specific RNP eligibility statements in the AFM or avionics documents may be issued operational approval including special conditions and limitations for specific RNP eligibilities.

Note: Some airborne systems use Estimated Position Uncertainty (EPU) as a measure of the current estimated navigational performance. EPU may also be referred to as Actual Navigation Performance (ANP) or Estimated Position Error (EPE).

TABLE 1–2–1
U.S. STANDARD RNP LEVELS

RNP Level	Typical Application	Primary Route Width (NM)—Centerline to Boundary
0.1 to 1.0	RNP AR Approach Segments	0.1 to 1.0
0.3 to 1.0	RNP Approach Segments	0.3 to 1.0
1	Terminal and En Route	1.0
2	En Route	2.0
4	Oceanic/remote areas where performance-based horizontal separation is applied.	4.0
10	Oceanic/remote areas where performance-based horizontal separation is applied.	10.0

1-2-3 Use of Suitable Area Navigation (RNAV) Systems on Conventional Procedures and Routes

a. Discussion. This paragraph sets forth policy, while providing operational and airworthiness guidance regarding the suitability and use of RNAV systems when operating on, or transitioning to, conventional, non-RNAV routes and procedures within the U.S. National Airspace System (NAS):

1. Use of a suitable RNAV system as a Substitute Means of Navigation when a Very-High Frequency (VHF) Omni-directional Range (VOR), Distance Measuring Equipment (DME), Tactical Air Navigation (TACAN), VOR/TACAN (VORTAC), VOR/DME, Non-directional Beacon (NDB), or compass locator facility including locator outer marker and locator middle marker is out-of-service (that is, the navigation aid (NAVAID) information is not available); an aircraft is not equipped with an Automatic Direction Finder (ADF) or DME; or the installed ADF or DME on an aircraft is not operational. For example, if equipped with a suitable RNAV system, a pilot may hold over an out-of-service NDB.

2. Use of a suitable RNAV system as an Alternate Means of Navigation when a VOR, DME, VORTAC, VOR/DME, TACAN, NDB, or compass locator facility including locator outer marker and locator middle marker is operational and the respective aircraft is equipped with operational navigation equipment that is compatible with conventional NAVAIDs. For example, if equipped with a suitable RNAV system, a pilot may fly a procedure or route based on operational VOR using that RNAV system without monitoring the VOR.

Note 1: Additional information and associated requirements are available in Advisory Circular 90-108 titled "Use of Suitable RNAV Systems on Conventional Routes and Procedures."

Note 2: Good planning and knowledge of your RNAV system are critical for safe and successful operations.

Note 3: Pilots planning to use their RNAV system as a substitute means of navigation guidance in lieu of an out-of-service NAVAID may need to advise ATC of this intent and capability.

Note 4: The navigation database should be current for the duration of the flight. If the AIRAC cycle will change during flight, operators and pilots should establish procedures to ensure the accuracy of navigation data, including suitability of navigation facilities used to define the routes and procedures for flight. To facilitate validating database currency, the FAA has developed procedures for publishing the amendment date that instrument approach procedures were last

revised. *The amendment date follows the amend-ment number, e.g., Amdt 4 14Jan10. Currency of graphic departure procedures and STARs may be ascertained by the numerical designation in the procedure title. If an amended chart is published for the procedure, or the procedure amendment date shown on the chart is on or after the expira-tion date of the database, the operator must not use the database to conduct the operation.*

b. Types of RNAV Systems that Qualify as a Suitable RNAV System. When installed in ac-cordance with appropriate airworthiness instal-lation requirements and operated in accordance with applicable operational guidance (for exam-ple, aircraft flight manual and Advisory Circular material), the following systems qualify as a suit-able RNAV system:

1. An RNAV system with TSO-C129/-C145/-C146 equipment, installed in accordance with AC 20-138, Airworthiness Approval of Global Posi-tioning System (GPS) Navigation Equipment for Use as a VFR and IFR Supplemental Navigation System, and authorized for instrument flight rules (IFR) en route and terminal operations (including those systems previously qualified for "GPS in lieu of ADF or DME" operations), or

2. An RNAV system with DME/DME/IRU in-puts that is compliant with the equipment provi-sions of AC 90-100A, U.S. Terminal and En Route Area Navigation (RNAV) Operations, for RNAV routes. A table of compliant equipment is avail-able at the following website:

https://www.faa.gov/about/office_org/
headquarters_offices/avs/offices/afx/afs/afs400
/afs410/media/AC90-100compliance.pdf

Note: *Approved RNAV systems using DME/DME/IRU, without GPS/WAAS position input, may only be used as a substitute means of naviga-tion when specifically authorized by a Notice to Air Missions (NOTAM) or other FAA guidance for a specific procedure. The NOTAM or other FAA guidance authorizing the use of DME/DME/IRU systems will also identify any required DME fa-cilities based on an FAA assessment of the DME navigation infrastructure.*

c. Uses of Suitable RNAV Systems. Subject to the operating requirements, operators may use a suitable RNAV system in the following ways.

1. Determine aircraft position relative to, or distance from a VOR (see Note 6 below), TACAN, NDB, compass locator, DME fix; or a named fix defined by a VOR radial, TACAN course, NDB bearing, or compass locator bearing intersecting a VOR or localizer course.

2. Navigate to or from a VOR, TACAN, NDB, or compass locator.

3. Hold over a VOR, TACAN, NDB, compass locator, or DME fix.

4. Fly an arc based upon DME.

Note 1: *The allowances described in this sec-tion apply even when a facility is identified as re-quired on a procedure (for example, "Note ADF required").*

Note 2: *These operations do not include lateral navigation on localizer-based courses (including localizer back-course guidance) without reference to raw localizer data.*

Note 3: *Unless otherwise specified, a suitable RNAV system cannot be used for navigation on procedures that are identified as not authorized ("NA") without exception by a NOTAM. For exam-ple, an operator may not use a RNAV system to navigate on a procedure affected by an expired or unsatisfactory flight inspection, or a procedure that is based upon a recently decommissioned NAVAID.*

Note 4: *Pilots may not substitute for the NAVAID (for example, a VOR or NDB) providing lateral guidance for the final approach segment. This restriction does not refer to instrument approach procedures with "or GPS" in the title when using GPS or WAAS. These allowances do not apply to procedures that are identified as not authorized (NA) without exception by a NOTAM, as other con-ditions may still exist and result in a procedure not being available. For example, these allowances do not apply to a procedure associated with an expired or unsatisfactory flight inspection, or is based upon a recently decommissioned NAVAID.*

Note 5: *Use of a suitable RNAV system as a means to navigate on the final approach seg-ment of an instrument approach procedure based on a VOR, TACAN or NDB signal, is allowable. The underlying NAVAID must be operational and the NAVAID monitored for final segment course alignment.*

Note 6: *For the purpose of paragraph c, "VOR" includes VOR, VOR/DME, and VORTAC facili-ties and "compass locator" includes locator outer marker and locator middle marker.*

d. Alternate Airport Considerations. For the purposes of flight planning, any required al-ternate airport must have an available instrument approach procedure that does not require the use of GPS. This restriction includes conduct-ing a conventional approach at the alternate air-port using a substitute means of navigation that is based upon the use of GPS. For example, these restrictions would apply when planning to use GPS equipment as a substitute means of naviga-tion for an out-of-service VOR that supports an ILS missed approach procedure at an alternate airport. In this case, some other approach not re-liant upon the use of GPS must be available. This restriction does not apply to RNAV systems using

TSO-C145/-C146 WAAS equipment. For further WAAS guidance, see paragraph 1-1-18.

1. For flight planning purposes, TSO-C129() and TSO-C196() equipped users (GPS users) whose navigation systems have fault detection and exclusion (FDE) capability, who perform a preflight RAIM prediction at the airport where the RNAV (GPS) approach will be flown, and have proper knowledge and any required training and/or approval to conduct a GPS-based IAP, may file based on a GPS-based IAP at either the destination or the alternate airport, but not at both locations. At the alternate airport, pilots may plan for applicable alternate airport weather minimums using:

(a) Lateral navigation (LNAV) or circling minimum descent altitude (MDA);

(b) LNAV/vertical navigation (LNAV/VNAV) DA, if equipped with and using approved barometric vertical navigation (baro-VNAV) equipment;

(c) RNP 0.3 DA on an RNAV (RNP) IAP, if they are specifically authorized users using approved baro-VNAV equipment and the pilot has verified required navigation performance (RNP) availability through an approved prediction program.

2. If the above conditions cannot be met, any required alternate airport must have an approved instrument approach procedure other than GPS that is anticipated to be operational and available at the estimated time of arrival, and which the aircraft is equipped to fly.

3. This restriction does not apply to TSO-C145() and TSO-C146() equipped users (WAAS users). For further WAAS guidance see paragraph 1-1-18.

1–2–4 Recognizing, Mitigating and Adapting to GPS Interference (Jamming or Spoofing)

a. The low-strength data transmission signals from GPS satellites are vulnerable to various anomalies that can significantly reduce the reliability of the navigation signal. Because of the many uses of GPS in aviation (e.g., navigation, ADS-B, terrain awareness/warning systems), operators of aircraft using GPS need to be aware of these vulnerabilities, and be able to recognize and adjust to degraded signals. Aircraft should have additional navigation equipment for their intended route.

b. GPS signals are vulnerable to intentional and unintentional interference from a wide variety of sources, including radars, microwave links, iono-sphere effects, solar activity, multi-path error, satellite communications, GPS repeaters, and even some systems onboard the aircraft. In general, these types of unintentional interference are localized and intermittent. Of greater and growing concern is the intentional and unauthorized interference of GPS signals by persons using "jammers" or "spoofers" to disrupt air navigation by interfering with the reception of valid satellite signals.

Note: The U.S. government regularly conducts GPS tests, training activities, and exercises that interfere with GPS signals. These events are geographically limited, coordinated, scheduled, and advertised via GPS and/or WAAS NOTAMs. Operators of GPS aircraft should always check for GPS and/or WAAS NOTAMs for their route of flight.

c. GPS is a critical component of essential communication, navigation, and surveillance (CNS) in the NAS; and flight safety/control systems. Additionally, some satellite communications avionics use GPS signals for operations in oceanic and remote airspaces. It is the sole aircraft position-reporting source for Automatic Dependent Surveillance–Broadcast (ADS-B). Some business aircraft are using GPS as a reference source for aircraft flight control and stability systems. GPS is also a necessary component of the Aircraft Terrain Awareness and Warning System (TAWS)—an aircraft safety system that alerts pilots of upcoming terrain. There are examples of false "terrain-pull up" warnings during GPS anomalies.

d. When flying IFR, pilots should have additional navigation equipment for their intended route to crosscheck their position. Routine checks of position against VOR or DME information, for example, could help detect a compromised GPS signal. Pilots transitioning to VOR navigation in response to GPS anomalies should refer to the Chart Supplement U.S. to identify airports with available conventional approaches associated with the VOR Minimum Operational Network (MON) program. (Reference 1-3f.)

e. When flying GPS approaches, particularly in IMC, pilots should have a backup plan in the event of GPS anomalies. Although the appropriate response will vary with the situation, in general pilots should:

1. Maintain control of the aircraft,

2. Use the last reliable navigation information as the basis for initial headings, and climb above terrain,

3. Change to another source of navigation, if available (i.e., VOR, DME radar vectors).

4. Contact ATC as soon as practical.

f. Pilots should promptly notify ATC if they experience GPS anomalies. Pilots should not normally inform ATC of GPS interference or outages when flying through a known NOTAMed testing area, unless they require ATC assistance. (See 1-1-13.)

Chapter 2
Aeronautical Lighting and Other Airport Visual Aids

Section 1 Airport Lighting Aids

2–1–1 Approach Light Systems (ALS)

a. ALS provide the basic means to transition from instrument flight to visual flight for landing. Operational requirements dictate the sophistication and configuration of the approach light system for a particular runway.

b. ALS are a configuration of signal lights starting at the landing threshold and extending into the approach area a distance of 2,400–3,000 feet for precision instrument runways and 1,400–1,500 feet for nonprecision instrument runways. Some systems include sequenced flashing lights which appear to the pilot as a ball of light traveling towards the runway at high speed (twice a second). (See Figure 2-1-1.)

FIGURE 2–1–1
Precision and Nonprecision Configurations

2–1–2 Visual Glideslope Indicators

a. Visual Approach Slope Indicator (VASI)

1. VASI installations may consist of either 2, 4, 6, 12, or 16 light units arranged in bars referred to as near, middle, and far bars. Most VASI installations consist of 2 bars, near and far, and may consist of 2, 4, or 12 light units. Some VASIs consist of three bars, near, middle, and far, which provide an additional visual glide path to accommodate high cockpit aircraft. This installation may consist of either 6 or 16 light units. VASI installations consisting of 2, 4, or 6 light units are located on one side of the runway, usually the left. Where the installation consists of 12 or 16 light units, the units are located on both sides of the runway.

2. Two-bar VASI installations provide one visual glide path which is normally set at 3 degrees. Three-bar VASI installations provide two visual glide paths. The lower glide path is provided by the near and middle bars and is normally set at 3 degrees while the upper glide path, provided by the middle and far bars, is normally 1/4 degree higher. This higher glide path is intended for use only by high cockpit aircraft to provide a sufficient threshold crossing height. Although normal glide path angles are three degrees, angles at some locations may be as high as 4.5 degrees to give proper obstacle clearance. Pilots of high performance aircraft are cautioned that use of VASI angles in excess of 3.5 degrees may cause an increase in runway length required for landing and rollout.

3. The basic principle of the VASI is that of color differentiation between red and white. Each light unit projects a beam of light having a white segment in the upper part of the beam and red segment in the lower part of the beam. The light units are arranged so that the pilot using the VASIs during an approach will see the combination of lights shown below.

4. The VASI is a system of lights so arranged to provide visual descent guidance information during the approach to a runway. These lights are visible from 3–5 miles during the day and up to 20 miles or more at night. The visual glide path of the VASI provides safe obstruction clearance within plus or minus 10 degrees of the extended runway centerline and to 4 NM from the runway threshold. Descent, using the VASI, should not be initiated until the aircraft is visually aligned with the runway. Lateral course guidance is provided by the runway or runway lights. In certain circumstances, the safe obstruction clearance area may be reduced by narrowing the beam width or shortening the usable distance due to local limitations, or the VASI may be offset from the extended runway centerline. This will be noted in the Chart Supplement and/or applicable Notices to Air Missions (NOTAMs).

5. For 2-bar VASI (4 light units) see Figure 2-1-2.

6. For 3-bar VASI (6 light units) see Figure 2-1-3.

7. For other VASI configurations see Figure 2-1-4.

b. Precision Approach Path Indicator (PAPI).

The precision approach path indicator (PAPI) uses light units similar to the VASI but are installed in a single row of either two or four light units. These lights are visible from about 5 miles during the day and up to 20 miles at night. The visual glide path of the PAPI typically provides safe obstruction clearance within plus or minus 10 degrees of the extended runway centerline and to 3.4 NM from the runway threshold. Descent, using the PAPI, should not be initiated until the aircraft is visually aligned with the runway. The row of light units is normally installed on the left side of the runway and the glide path indications are as depicted. Lateral course guidance is provided by the runway or runway lights. In certain circumstances, the safe obstruction clearance area may be reduced by narrowing the beam width or shortening the usable distance due to local limitations, or the PAPI may be offset from the extended runway centerline. This will be noted in the Chart Supplement and/or applicable NOTAMs. (See Figure 2-1-5.)

c. Tri-color Systems.

Tri-color visual approach slope indicators normally consist of a single light unit projecting a three-color visual approach path into the final approach area of the runway upon which the indicator is installed. The below glide path indication is red, the above glide path indication is amber, and the on glide path indication is green. These types of indicators have a useful range of approximately one-half to one mile during the day and up to five miles at night depending upon the visibility conditions. (See Figure 2-1-6.)

d. Pulsating Systems.

Pulsating visual approach slope indicators normally consist of a single light unit projecting a two-color visual approach path into the final approach area of the runway upon which the indicator is installed. The on glide path indication may be a steady white light or alternating RED and WHITE light. The slightly below glide path indication is a steady red light. If the aircraft descends further below the glide path, the red light starts to pulsate. The above glide path indication is a pulsating white light. The pulsating rate increases as the aircraft gets further above or below the desired glide slope. The useful range of the system is about four miles during the day and up to ten miles at night. (See Figure 2-1-7.)

e. Alignment of Elements Systems.

Alignment of elements systems are installed on some small general aviation airports and are a low-cost system consisting of painted plywood panels, normally black and white or fluorescent orange. Some

of these systems are lighted for night use. The useful range of these systems is approximately three-quarter miles. To use the system the pilot positions the aircraft so the elements are in alignment. The glide path indications are shown in Figure 2-1-8.

FIGURE 2–1–2
2-Bar VASI

FIGURE 2–1–3
3-Bar VASI

FIGURE 2–1–4
VASI Variations

FIGURE 2–1–5
Precision Approach Path Indicator (PAPI)

FIGURE 2–1–6
Tri-Color Visual Approach Slope Indicator

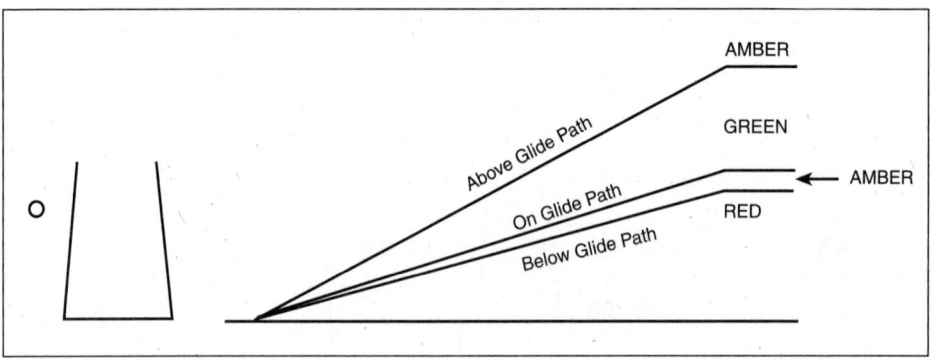

Notes:

1. Since the tri-color VASI consists of a single light source which could possibly be confused with other light sources, pilots should exercise care to properly locate and identify the light signal.

2. When the aircraft descends from green to red, the pilot may see a dark amber color during the transition from green to red.

FIGURE 2–1–7
Pulsating Visual Approach Slope Indicator

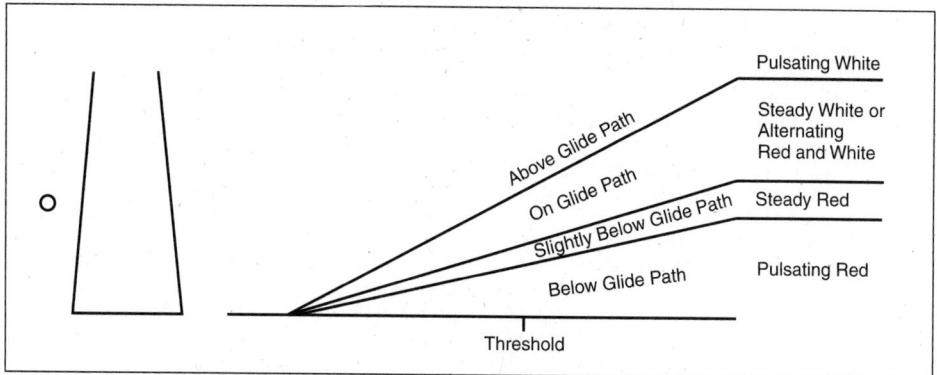

Note: *Since the PVASI consists of a single light source which could possibly be confused with other light sources, pilots should exercise care to properly locate and identify the light signal.*

FIGURE 2–1–8
Alignment of Elements

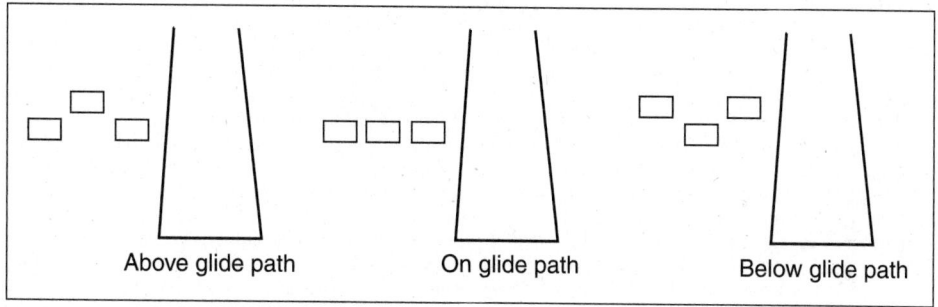

2-1-3 Runway End Identifier Lights (REIL)

REILs are installed at many airfields to provide rapid and positive identification of the approach end of a particular runway. The system consists of a pair of synchronized flashing lights located laterally on each side of the runway threshold. REILs may be either omnidirectional or unidirectional facing the approach area. They are effective for:

a. Identification of a runway surrounded by a preponderance of other lighting.

b. Identification of a runway which lacks contrast with surrounding terrain.

c. Identification of a runway during reduced visibility.

2-1-4 Runway Edge Light Systems

a. Runway edge lights are used to outline the edges of runways during periods of darkness or restricted visibility conditions. These light systems are classified according to the intensity or brightness they are capable of producing: they are the High Intensity Runway Lights (HIRL), Medium Intensity Runway Lights (MIRL), and the Low Intensity Runway Lights (LIRL). The HIRL and MIRL systems have variable intensity controls, whereas the LIRLs normally have one intensity setting.

b. The runway edge lights are white, except on instrument runways yellow replaces white on the last 2,000 feet or half the runway length, whichever is less, to form a caution zone for landings.

c. The lights marking the ends of the runway emit red light toward the runway to indicate the end of runway to a departing aircraft and emit green outward from the runway end to indicate the threshold to landing aircraft.

2–1–5 In-Runway Lighting

a. Runway Centerline Lighting System (RCLS). Runway centerline lights are installed on some precision approach runways to facilitate landing under adverse visibility conditions. They are located along the runway centerline and are spaced at 50-foot intervals. When viewed from the landing threshold, the runway centerline lights are white until the last 3,000 feet of the runway. The white lights begin to alternate with red for the next 2,000 feet, and for the last 1,000 feet of the runway, all centerline lights are red.

b. Touchdown Zone Lights (TDZL). Touchdown zone lights are installed on some precision approach runways to indicate the touchdown zone when landing under adverse visibility conditions. They consist of two rows of transverse light bars disposed symmetrically about the runway centerline. The system consists of steady-burning white lights which start 100 feet beyond the landing threshold and extend to 3,000 feet beyond the landing threshold or to the midpoint of the runway, whichever is less.

c. Taxiway Centerline Lead-Off Lights. Taxiway centerline lead-off lights provide visual guidance to persons exiting the runway. They are color-coded to warn pilots and vehicle drivers that they are within the runway environment or instrument landing system (ILS) critical area, whichever is more restrictive. Alternate green and yellow lights are installed, beginning with green, from the runway centerline to one centerline light position beyond the runway holding position or ILS critical area holding position.

d. Taxiway Centerline Lead-On Lights. Taxiway centerline lead-on lights provide visual guidance to persons entering the runway. These "lead-on" lights are also color-coded with the same color pattern as lead-off lights to warn pilots and vehicle drivers that they are within the runway environment or instrument landing system (ILS) critical area, whichever is more conservative. The fixtures used for lead-on lights are bidirectional, i.e., one side emits light for the lead-on function while the other side emits light for the lead-off function. Any fixture that emits yellow light for the lead-off function must also emit yellow light for the lead-on function. (See Figure 2-1-12.)

e. Land and Hold Short Lights. Land and hold short lights are used to indicate the hold short point on certain runways which are approved for Land and Hold Short Operations (LAHSO). Land and hold short lights consist of a row of pulsing white lights installed across the runway at the hold short point. Where installed, the lights will be on anytime LAHSO is in effect. These lights will be off when LAHSO is not in effect.

Reference: AIM, ¶4-3-11, Pilot Responsibilities When Conducting Land and Hold Short Operations (LAHSO).

2–1–6 Runway Status Light (RWSL) System

a. Introduction.
RWSL is a fully automated system that provides runway status information to pilots and surface vehicle operators to clearly indicate when it is unsafe to enter, cross, takeoff from, or land on a runway. The RWSL system processes information from surveillance systems and activates Runway Entrance Lights (REL) and Takeoff Hold Lights (THL), in accordance with the position and velocity of the detected surface traffic and approach traffic. REL and THL are in-pavement light fixtures that are directly visible to pilots and surface vehicle operators. RWSL is an independent safety enhancement that does not substitute for or convey an ATC clearance. Clearance to enter, cross, takeoff from, land on, or operate on a runway must still be received from ATC. Although ATC has limited control over the system, personnel do not directly use and may not be able to view light fixture activations and deactivations during the conduct of daily ATC operations.

b. Runway Entrance Lights (REL): The REL system is composed of flush mounted, in-pavement, unidirectional light fixtures that are parallel to and focused along the taxiway centerline and directed toward the pilot at the hold line. An array of REL lights include the first light at the hold line followed by a series of evenly spaced lights to the runway edge; one additional light at the runway centerline is in line with the last two lights before the runway edge (see Figure 2-1-9 and Figure 2-1-10). When activated, the red lights indicate that there is high speed traffic on the runway or there is an aircraft on final approach within the activation area.

1. REL Operating Characteristics—Departing Aircraft:
When a departing aircraft reaches a site adaptable speed of approximately 30 knots, all taxiway intersections with REL arrays along the runway ahead of the aircraft will illuminate (see Figure 2-1-9). As the aircraft approaches an REL equipped taxiway intersection, the lights at that intersection extinguish approximately 3 to 4 seconds before the aircraft reaches it. This allows controllers to apply "anticipated separation" to permit ATC to move traffic more expeditiously without compromising safety. After the aircraft is declared "airborne" by the system, all REL lights associated with this runway will extinguish.

2. REL Operating Characteristics—Arriving Aircraft:
When an aircraft on final approach is approximately 1 mile from the runway threshold, all sets of taxiway REL light arrays that intersect the runway illuminate. The distance is adjustable and can be configured for specific operations at particular

FIGURE 2–1–9
Runway Status Light System

RWSL OPERATIONAL CONCEPT

Airport Surface Detection Equipment (ASDE)

THLs

RELs

RELs

RELs

RELs

RELs

RELs

RELs

RELs

THLs — Transponder Multilateration

RELs: Runway Entrance Lights
THLs: Takeoff Hold Lights

Airport Surveillance Radar (ASR)

airports. Lights extinguish at each equipped taxiway intersection approximately 3 to 4 seconds before the aircraft reaches it to apply anticipated separation until the aircraft has slowed to approximately 80 knots (site adjustable parameter). Below 80 knots, all arrays that are not within 30 seconds of the aircraft's forward path are extinguished. Once the arriving aircraft slows to approximately 34 knots (site adjustable parameter), it is declared to be in a taxi state, and all lights extinguish.

3. What a pilot would observe: A pilot at or approaching the hold line to a runway will observe RELs illuminate and extinguish in reaction to an aircraft or vehicle operating on the runway, or an arriving aircraft operating less than 1 mile from the runway threshold.

4. When a pilot observes the red lights of the REL, that pilot will stop at the hold line or remain stopped. The pilot will then contact ATC for resolution if the clearance is in conflict with the lights. Should pilots note illuminated lights under circumstances when remaining clear of the runway is impractical for safety reasons (for example, aircraft is already on the runway), the crew should proceed according to their best judgment while understanding the illuminated lights indicate the runway is unsafe to enter or cross. Contact ATC at the earliest possible opportunity.

c. Takeoff Hold Lights (THL): The THL system is composed of flush mounted, in-pavement, unidirectional light fixtures in a double longitudinal row aligned either side of the runway centerline lighting. Fixtures are focused toward the arrival end of the runway at the "line up and wait" point. THLs extend for 1,500 feet in front of the holding aircraft starting at a point 375 feet from the departure threshold (see Figure 2-1-11). Illuminated red lights provide a signal, to an aircraft in position for takeoff or rolling, that it is unsafe to takeoff because the runway is occupied or about to be occupied by another aircraft or ground vehicle. Two aircraft, or a surface vehicle and an aircraft, are required for the lights to illuminate. The departing aircraft must be in position for takeoff or beginning takeoff roll. Another aircraft or a surface vehicle must be on or about to cross the runway.

1. THL Operating Characteristics—Departing Aircraft:

THLs will illuminate for an aircraft in position for departure or departing when there is another aircraft or vehicle on the runway or about to enter the runway (see Figure 2-1-9). Once that aircraft or vehicle exits the runway, the THLs extinguish. A pilot may notice lights extinguish prior to the downfield aircraft or vehicle being completely clear of the runway but still moving. Like RELs, THLs have an "anticipated separation" feature.

FIGURE 2–1–10
Runway Entrance Lights

Note: *When the THLs extinguish, this is not clearance to begin a takeoff roll. All takeoff clearances will be issued by ATC.*

2. What a pilot would observe: A pilot in position to depart from a runway, or has begun takeoff roll, will observe THLs illuminate in reaction to an aircraft or vehicle on the runway or entering or crossing it. Lights will extinguish when the runway is clear. A pilot may observe several cycles of illumination and extinguishing depending on the amount of crossing traffic.

3. When a pilot observes the red light of the THLs, the pilot should safely stop if it's feasible or remain stopped. The pilot must contact ATC for resolution if any clearance is in conflict with the lights. Should pilots note illuminated lights while in takeoff roll and under circumstances when stopping is impractical for safety reasons, the crew should proceed according to their best judgment while understanding the illuminated lights indicate that continuing the takeoff is unsafe. Contact ATC at the earliest possible opportunity.

d. Pilot Actions:

1. When operating at airports with RWSL, pilots will operate with the transponder/ADS-B "On" when departing the gate or parking area until it is shut down upon arrival at the gate or parking area. This ensures interaction with the FAA surveillance systems such as ASDE-X/Airport Surface Surveillance Capability (ASSC) which provide information to the RWSL system.

2. Pilots must always inform the ATCT when they have stopped due to an RWSL indication that is in conflict with ATC instructions. Pilots must request clarification of the taxi or takeoff clearance.

3. Never cross over illuminated red lights. Under normal circumstances, RWSL will confirm the pilot's taxi or takeoff clearance previously issued by ATC. If RWSL indicates that it is unsafe to takeoff from, land on, cross, or enter a runway, immediately notify ATC of the conflict and re-confirm the clearance.

4. Do not proceed when lights have extinguished without an ATC clearance. RWSL verifies an ATC clearance; it does not substitute for an ATC clearance.

e. ATC Control of RWSL System:

1. Controllers can set in-pavement lights to one of five (5) brightness levels to assure maximum conspicuity under all visibility and lighting conditions. REL and THL subsystems may be independently set.

2. System lights can be disabled should RWSL operations impact the efficient movement of air traffic or contribute, in the opinion of the assigned ATC Manager, to unsafe operations. REL and THL light fixtures may be disabled separately. Whenever the system or a component is disabled, a NOTAM must be issued, and the Automatic Terminal Information System (ATIS) must be updated.

2-1-7 Control of Lighting Systems

a. Operation of approach light systems and runway lighting is controlled by the control tower (ATCT). At some locations the FSS may control the lights where there is no control tower in operation.

b. Pilots may request that lights be turned on or off. Runway edge lights, in-pavement lights and approach lights also have intensity controls which may be varied to meet the pilots request. Sequenced flashing lights (SFL) may be turned on and off. Some sequenced flashing light systems also have intensity control.

2-1-8 Pilot Control of Airport Lighting

Radio control of lighting is available at selected airports to provide airborne control of lights by keying the aircraft's microphone. Control of lighting systems is often available at locations without specified hours for lighting and where there is no control tower or FSS or when the tower or FSS is closed (locations with a part-time tower or FSS) or specified hours. All lighting systems which are radio controlled at an airport, whether on a single runway or multiple runways, operate on the same radio frequency. (See Tables 2-1-1 and 2-1-2.)

Ch 2

FIGURE 2–1–11
Takeoff Hold Lights

FIGURE 2–1–12
Taxiway Lead-On Light Configuration

TABLE 2–1–1
RUNWAYS WITH APPROACH LIGHTS

Lighting System	No. of Int. Steps	Status During Nonuse Period	Intensity Step Selected Per No. of Mike Clicks		
			3 Clicks	5 Clicks	7 Clicks
Approach Lights (Med. Int.)	2	Off	Low	Low	High
Approach Lights (Med. Int.)	3	Off	Low	Med	High
MIRL	3	Off or Low	◆		◆
HIRL	5	Off or Low	◆	◆	◆
VASI	2	Off	☆	☆	☆

Notes: ◆ Predetermined intensity step.
 ☆ Low intensity for night use. High intensity for day use as determined by photocell control.

TABLE 2–1–2
RUNWAYS WITHOUT APPROACH LIGHTS

Lighting System	No. of Int. Steps	Status During Nonuse Period	Intensity Step Selected Per No. of Mike Clicks		
			3 Clicks	5 Clicks	7 Clicks
MIRL	3	Off or Low	Low	Med	High
HIRL	5	Off or Low	Step 1 or 2	Step 3	Step 5
LIRL	1	Off	On	On	On
VASI ☆	2	Off	◆	◆	◆
REIL ☆	1	Off	Off	On/Off	On
REIL ☆	3	Off	Low	Med	High

Notes: ◆ Low intensity for night use. High intensity for day use as determined by photocell control.
 ☆ The control of VASI and/or REIL may be independent of other lighting systems.

a. With FAA approved systems, various combinations of medium intensity approach lights, runway lights, taxiway lights, VASI and/or REIL may be activated by radio control. On runways with both approach lighting and runway lighting (runway edge lights, taxiway lights, etc.) systems, the approach lighting system takes precedence for air-to-ground radio control over the runway lighting system which is set at a predetermined intensity step, based on expected visibility conditions. Runways without approach lighting may provide radio controlled intensity adjustments of runway edge lights. Other lighting systems, including VASI, REIL, and taxiway lights may be either controlled with the runway edge lights or controlled independently of the runway edge lights.

b. The control system consists of a 3-step control responsive to 7, 5, and/or 3 microphone clicks. This 3-step control will turn on lighting facilities capable of either 3-step, 2-step or 1-step operation. The 3-step and 2-step lighting facilities can be altered in intensity, while the 1-step cannot. All lighting is illuminated for a period of 15 minutes from the most recent time of activation and may not be extinguished prior to end of the 15 minute period (except for 1-step and 2-step REILs which may be turned off when desired by keying the mike 5 or 3 times respectively).

c. Suggested use is to always initially key the mike 7 times; this assures that all controlled lights are turned on to the maximum available intensity. If desired, adjustment can then be made, where the capability is provided, to a lower intensity (or the REIL turned off) by keying 5 and/or 3 times. Due to the close proximity of airports using the same frequency, radio controlled lighting receivers may be set at a low sensitivity requiring the aircraft to be relatively close to activate the system. Consequently, even when lights are on, always key mike as directed when overflying an airport of intended landing or just prior to entering the final segment of an approach. This will assure the aircraft is close enough to activate the system and a full 15 minutes lighting duration is available. Approved lighting systems may be activated by keying the mike (within 5 seconds) as indicated in Table 2-1-3.

TABLE 2-1-3
RADIO CONTROL SYSTEM

Key Mike	Function
7 times within 5 seconds	Highest intensity available
5 times within 5 seconds	Medium or lower intensity (Lower REIL or REIL-off)
3 times within 5 seconds	Lowest intensity available (Lower REIL or REIL-off)

d. For all public use airports with FAA standard systems the Chart Supplement contains the types of lighting, runway and the frequency that is used to activate the system. Airports with IAPs include data on the approach chart identifying the light system, the runway on which they are installed, and the frequency that is used to activate the system.

Note: Although the CTAF is used to activate the lights at many airports, other frequencies may also be used. The appropriate frequency for activating the lights on the airport is provided in the Chart Supplement and the standard instrument approach procedures publications. It is not identified on the sectional charts.

e. Where the airport is not served by an IAP, it may have either the standard FAA approved control system or an independent type system of different specification installed by the airport sponsor. The Chart Supplement contains descriptions of pilot controlled lighting systems for each airport having other than FAA approved systems, and explains the type lights, method of control, and operating frequency in clear text.

2-1-9 Airport/Heliport Beacons

a. Airport and heliport beacons have a vertical light distribution to make them most effective from one to ten degrees above the horizon; however, they can be seen well above and below this peak spread. The beacon may be an omnidirectional capacitor-discharge device, or it may rotate at a constant speed which produces the visual effect of flashes at regular intervals. Flashes may be one or two colors alternately. The total number of flashes are:

1. 24 to 30 per minute for beacons marking airports, landmarks, and points on Federal airways.

2. 30 to 45 per minute for beacons marking heliports.

b. The colors and color combinations of beacons are:

1. White and Green—Lighted land airport.

2. *Green alone—Lighted land airport.

3. White and Yellow—Lighted water airport.

4. *Yellow alone—Lighted water airport.

5. Green, Yellow, and White—Lighted heliport.

*Note: *Green alone or yellow alone is used only in connection with a white-and-green or white-and-yellow beacon display, respectively.*

c. Military airport beacons flash alternately white and green, but are differentiated from civil beacons by dualpeaked (two quick) white flashes between the green flashes.

d. In Class B, Class C, Class D and Class E surface areas, operation of the airport beacon during the hours of daylight often indicates that the ground visibility is less than 3 miles and/or the ceiling is less than 1,000 feet. ATC clearance in accordance with 14 CFR Part 91 is required for landing, takeoff and flight in the traffic pattern. Pilots should not rely solely on the operation of the airport beacon to indicate if weather conditions are IFR or VFR. At some locations with operating control towers, ATC personnel turn the beacon on or off when controls are in the tower. At many airports the airport beacon is turned on by a photoelectric cell or time clocks and ATC personnel cannot control them. There is no regulatory requirement for daylight operation and it is the pilot's responsibility to comply with proper preflight planning as required by 14 CFR Section 91.103.

2-1-10 Taxiway Lights

a. Taxiway Edge Lights. Taxiway edge lights are used to outline the edges of taxiways during periods of darkness or restricted visibility conditions. These fixtures emit blue light.

Note: At most major airports these lights have variable intensity settings and may be adjusted at pilot request or when deemed necessary by the controller.

b. Taxiway Centerline Lights. Taxiway centerline lights are used to facilitate ground traffic under low visibility conditions. They are located along the taxiway centerline in a straight line on straight portions, on the centerline of curved portions, and along designated taxiing paths in portions of runways, ramp, and apron areas. Taxiway centerline lights are steady burning and emit green light.

c. Clearance Bar Lights. Clearance bar lights are installed at holding positions on taxiways in order to increase the conspicuity of the holding position in low visibility conditions. They may also be installed to indicate the location of an intersecting taxiway during periods of darkness. Clearance bars consist of three in-pavement steady-burning yellow lights.

d. Runway Guard Lights. Runway guard lights are installed at taxiway/runway intersections. They are primarily used to enhance the conspicuity of taxiway/runway intersections during low visibility conditions, but may be used in all weather conditions. Runway guard lights consist of either a pair of elevated flashing yellow lights installed on either side of the taxiway, or a row of in-pavement yellow lights installed across the entire taxiway, at the runway holding position marking.

Note: Some airports may have a row of three or five in-pavement yellow lights installed at taxiway/runway intersections. They should not be confused with clearance bar lights described in paragraph 2-1-10c, Clearance Bar Lights.

e. Stop Bar Lights. Stop bar lights, when installed, are used to confirm the ATC clearance to enter or cross the active runway in low visibility conditions (below 1,200 ft Runway Visual Range). A stop bar consists of a row of red, unidirectional, steady-burning in-pavement lights installed across the entire taxiway at the runway holding position, and elevated steady-burning red lights on each side. A controlled stop bar is operated in conjunction with the taxiway centerline lead-on lights which extend from the stop bar toward the runway. Following the ATC clearance to proceed, the stop bar is turned off and the lead-on lights are turned on. The stop bar and lead-on lights are automatically reset by a sensor or backup timer.

Caution: Pilots should never cross a red illuminated stop bar, even if an ATC clearance has been given to proceed onto or across the runway.

Note: If after crossing a stop bar, the taxiway centerline lead-on lights inadvertently extinguish, pilots should hold their position and contact ATC for further instructions.

Section 2 Air Navigation and Obstruction Lighting

2-2-1 Aeronautical Light Beacons

a. An aeronautical light beacon is a visual NAVAID displaying flashes of white and/or colored light to indicate the location of an airport, a heliport, a landmark, a certain point of a Federal airway in mountainous terrain, or an obstruction. The light used may be a rotating beacon or one or more flashing lights. The flashing lights may be supplemented by steady burning lights of lesser intensity.

b. The color or color combination displayed by a particular beacon and/or its auxiliary lights tell whether the beacon is indicating a landing place, landmark, point of the Federal airways, or an obstruction. Coded flashes of the auxiliary lights, if employed, further identify the beacon site.

2-2-2 Code Beacons and Course Lights

a. Code Beacons. The code beacon, which can be seen from all directions, is used to identify airports and landmarks. The code beacon flashes the three or four character airport identifier in International Morse Code six to eight times per minute. Green flashes are displayed for land airports while yellow flashes indicate water airports.

b. Course Lights. The course light, which can be seen clearly from only one direction, is used only with rotating beacons of the Federal Airway System: two course lights, back to back, direct coded flashing beams of light in either direction along the course of airway.

Note: Airway beacons are remnants of the "lighted" airways which antedated the present electronically equipped federal airways system. Only a few of these beacons exist today to mark airway segments in remote mountain areas. Flashes in Morse code identify the beacon site.

2-2-3 Obstruction Lights

a. Obstructions are marked/lighted to warn airmen of their presence during daytime and nighttime conditions. They may be marked/lighted in any of the following combinations:

1. Aviation Red Obstruction Lights. Flashing aviation red beacons (20 to 40 flashes per minute) and steady burning aviation red lights during nighttime operation. Aviation orange and white paint is used for daytime marking.

2. Medium Intensity Flashing White Obstruction Lights. Medium intensity flashing white obstruction lights may be used during daytime and twilight with automatically selected reduced intensity for nighttime operation. When this system is used on structures 500 feet (153m) AGL or less in height, other methods of marking and lighting the structure may be omitted. Aviation orange and white paint is always required for daytime marking on structures exceeding 500 feet (153m) AGL. This system is not normally installed on structures less than 200 feet (61m) AGL.

3. High Intensity White Obstruction Lights. Flashing high intensity white lights during daytime with reduced intensity for twilight and nighttime operation. When this type system is used, the marking of structures with red obstruction lights and aviation orange and white paint may be omitted.

4. Dual Lighting. A combination of flashing aviation red beacons and steady burning aviation red lights for nighttime operation and flashing high intensity white lights for daytime operation. Aviation orange and white paint may be omitted.

5. Catenary Lighting. Lighted markers are available for increased night conspicuity of high-voltage (69KV or higher) transmission line catenary wires. Lighted markers provide conspicuity both day and night.

b. Medium intensity omnidirectional flashing white lighting system provides conspicuity both day and night on catenary support structures. The unique sequential/simultaneous flashing light system alerts pilots of the associated catenary wires.

c. High intensity flashing white lights are being used to identify some supporting structures of overhead transmission lines located across rivers, chasms, gorges, etc. These lights flash in a middle, top, lower light sequence at approximately 60 flashes per minute. The top light is normally installed near the top of the supporting structure, while the lower light indicates the approximate lower portion of the wire span. The lights are beamed towards the companion structure and identify the area of the wire span.

d. High intensity flashing white lights are also employed to identify tall structures, such as chimneys and towers, as obstructions to air navigation. The lights provide a 360 degree coverage about the structure at 40 flashes per minute and consist of from one to seven levels of lights depending upon the height of the structure. Where more than one level is used the vertical banks flash simultaneously.

Ch 2

2–2–4 LED Lighting Systems

Certain light-emitting diode (LED) lighting systems fall outside the combined visible and near-infrared spectrum of night vision goggles (NVGs) and thus will not be visible to a flightcrew using NVGs.

The FAA changed specifications for LED-based red obstruction lights to make them visible to pilots using certain NVG systems, however, other colors may not be visible.

It is recommended that air carriers/operators—including Part 91 operators—who use NVGs incorporate procedures into manuals and/or standard operating procedures (SOPs) requiring periodic, unaided scanning when operating at low altitudes and when performing a reconnaissance of landing areas.

Section 3 Airport Marking Aids and Signs

2-3-1 General

a. Airport pavement markings and signs provide information that is useful to a pilot during takeoff, landing, and taxiing.

b. Uniformity in airport markings and signs from one airport to another enhances safety and improves efficiency. Pilots are encouraged to work with the operators of the airports they use to achieve the marking and sign standards described in this section.

c. Pilots who encounter ineffective, incorrect, or confusing markings or signs on an airport should make the operator of the airport aware of the problem. These situations may also be reported under the Aviation Safety Reporting Program as described in paragraph 7-7-1, Aviation Safety Reporting Program. Pilots may also report these situations to the FAA regional airports division.

d. The markings and signs described in this section of the AIM reflect the current FAA recommended standards.

Reference
AC 150/5340-1, Standards for Airport Markings.
AC 150/5340-18, Standards for Airport Sign Systems.

2-3-2 Airport Pavement Markings

a. General. For the purpose of this section, the airport pavement markings have been grouped into four areas:

1. **Runway Markings.**
2. **Taxiway Markings.**
3. **Holding Position Markings.**
4. **Other Markings.**

b. Marking Colors. Markings for runways are white. Markings defining the landing area on a heliport are also white except for hospital heliports which use a red "H" on a white cross. Markings for taxiways, areas not intended for use by aircraft (closed and hazardous areas), and holding positions (even if they are on a runway) are yellow.

2-3-3 Runway Markings

a. General. There are three types of markings for runways: visual, nonprecision instrument, and precision instrument. Table 2-3-1 identifies the marking elements for each type of runway and Table 2-3-2 identifies runway threshold markings.

b. Runway Designators. Runway numbers and letters are determined from the approach direction. The runway number is the whole number nearest one-tenth the magnetic azimuth of the centerline of the runway, measured clockwise from the magnetic north. The letters, differentiate between left (L), right (R), or center (C) parallel runways, as applicable:

1. For two parallel runways "L" "R."
2. For three parallel runways "L" "C" "R."

c. Runway Centerline Marking. The runway centerline identifies the center of the runway and provides alignment guidance during takeoff and landings. The centerline consists of a line of uniformly spaced stripes and gaps.

d. Runway Aiming Point Marking. The aiming point marking serves as a visual aiming point for a landing aircraft. These two rectangular markings consist of a broad white stripe located on each side of the runway centerline and approximately 1,000 feet from the landing threshold, as shown in Figure 2-3-1, Precision Instrument Runway Markings.

e. Runway Touchdown Zone Markers. The touchdown zone markings identify the touchdown zone for landing operations and are coded to provide distance information in 500 feet (150m) increments. These markings consist of groups of one, two, and three rectangular bars symmetrically arranged in pairs about the runway centerline, as shown in Figure 2-3-1. For runways having touchdown zone markings on both ends, those pairs of markings which extend to within 900 feet (270m) of the midpoint between the thresholds are eliminated.

f. Runway Side Stripe Marking. Runway side stripes delineate the edges of the runway. They provide a visual contrast between runway and the abutting terrain or shoulders. Side stripes consist of continuous white stripes located on each side of the runway as shown in Figure 2-3-4.

g. Runway Shoulder Markings. Runway shoulder stripes may be used to supplement runway side stripes to identify pavement areas contiguous to the runway sides that are not intended for use by aircraft. Runway shoulder stripes are yellow. (See Figure 2-3-5.)

h. Runway Threshold Markings. Runway threshold markings come in two configurations. They either consist of eight longitudinal stripes of uniform dimensions disposed symmetrically about the runway centerline (as shown in Figure 2-3-1), or the number of stripes is related to the runway width as indicated in Table 2-3-2. A threshold marking helps identify the beginning of the runway that is available for landing. In some instances the landing threshold may be relocated or displaced.

TABLE 2–3–1
RUNWAY MARKING ELEMENTS

Marking Element	Visual Runway	Nonprecision Instrument Runway	Precision Instrument Runway
Designation	X	X	X
Centerline	X	X	X
Threshold	X[1]	X	X
Aiming Point	X[2]	X	X
Touchdown Zone			X
Side Stripes			X

[1] On runways used, or intended to be used, by international commercial transports.
[2] On runways 4,000 feet (1200 m) or longer used by jet aircraft.

TABLE 2–3–2
NUMBER OF RUNWAY THRESHOLD STRIPES

Runway Width	Number of Stripes
60 feet (18 m)	4
75 feet (23 m)	6
100 feet (30 m)	8
150 feet (45 m)	12
200 feet (60 m)	16

1. Relocation of a Threshold. Sometimes construction, maintenance, or other activities require the threshold to be relocated towards the rollout end of the runway. (See Figure 2-3-3.) When a threshold is relocated, it closes not only a set portion of the approach end of a runway, but also shortens the length of the opposite direction runway. In these cases, a NOTAM should be issued by the airport operator identifying the portion of the runway that is closed (for example, 10/28 W 900 CLSD). Because the duration of the relocation can vary from a few hours to several months, methods identifying the new threshold may vary. One common practice is to use a ten feet wide white threshold bar across the width of the runway. Although the runway lights in the area between the old threshold and new threshold will not be illuminated, the runway markings in this area may or may not be obliterated, removed, or covered.

2. Displaced Threshold. A displaced threshold is a threshold located at a point on the runway other than the designated beginning of the runway. Displacement of a threshold reduces the length of runway available for landings. The portion of runway behind a displaced threshold is available for takeoffs in either direction and landings from the opposite direction. A ten feet wide white threshold bar is located across the width of the runway at the displaced threshold. White arrows are located along the centerline in the area between the beginning of the runway and displaced threshold. White arrow heads are located across the width of the runway just prior to the threshold bar, as shown in Figure 2-3-4.

Note: Airport operator. When reporting the relocation or displacement of a threshold, the airport operator should avoid language which confuses the two.

i. Demarcation Bar. A demarcation bar delineates a runway with a displaced threshold from a blast pad, stopway or taxiway that precedes the runway. A demarcation bar is 3 feet (1m) wide and yellow, since it is not located on the runway as shown in Figure 2-3-6.

1. Chevrons. These markings are used to show pavement areas aligned with the runway that are unusable for landing, takeoff, and taxiing. Chevrons are yellow. (See Figure 2-3-7.)

j. Runway Threshold Bar. A threshold bar delineates the beginning of the runway that is available for landing when the threshold has been relocated or displaced. A threshold bar is 10 feet (3m) in width and extends across the width of the runway, as shown in Figure 2-3-4.

FIGURE 2–3–1
Precision Instrument Runway Markings

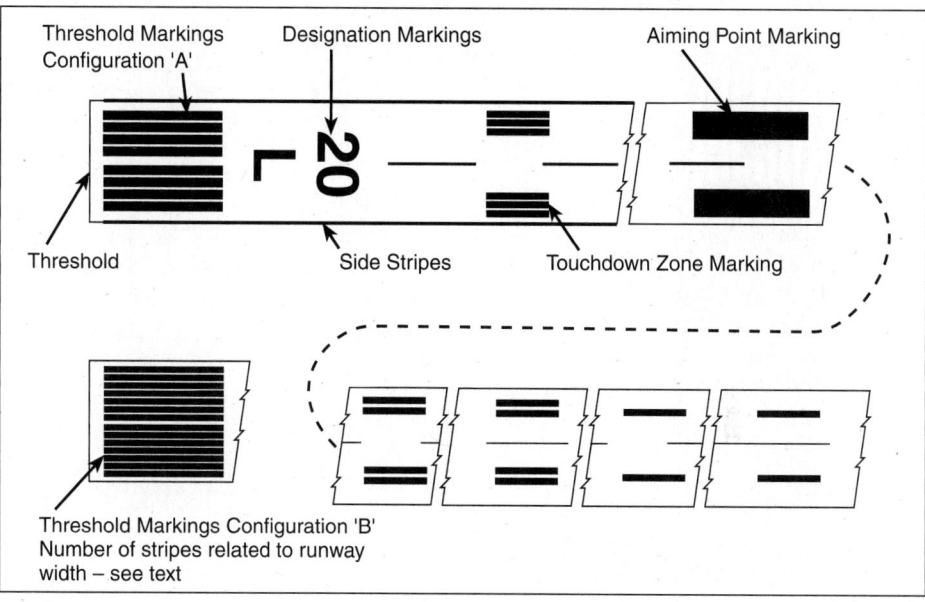

FIGURE 2–3–2
Nonprecision Instrument Runway and Visual Runway Markings

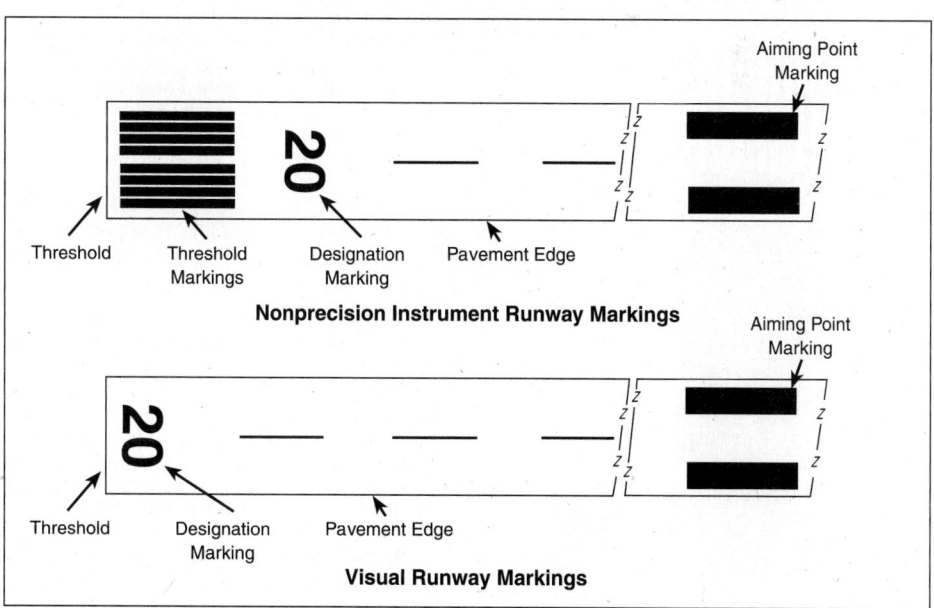

FIGURE 2–3–3
Relocation of a Threshold with Markings for Taxiway Aligned with Runway

FIGURE 2–3–5
Runway Shoulder Markings

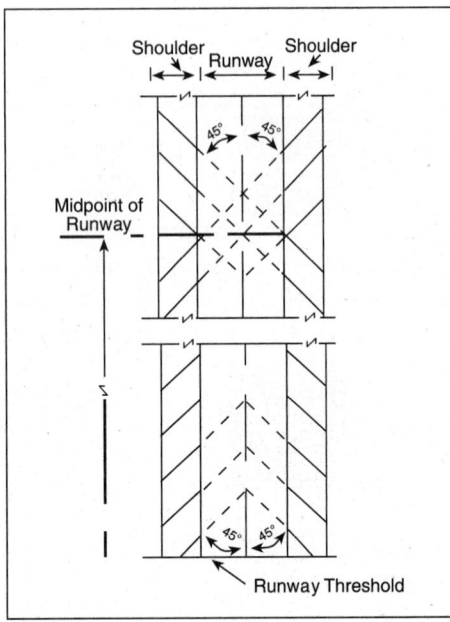

FIGURE 2–3–4
Displaced Threshold Markings

2-3-4 Taxiway Markings

a. General. All taxiways should have centerline markings and runway holding position markings whenever they intersect a runway. Taxiway edge markings are present whenever there is a need to separate the taxiway from a pavement that is not intended for aircraft use or to delineate the edge of the taxiway. Taxiways may also have shoulder markings and holding position markings for Instrument Landing System (ILS) critical areas, and taxiway/taxiway intersection markings.

Reference: AIM, ¶2-3-5, Holding Position Markings.

b. Taxiway Centerline.

1. Normal Centerline. The taxiway centerline is a single continuous yellow line, 6 inches (15 cm) to 12 inches (30 cm) in width. This provides a visual cue to permit taxiing along a designated path. Ideally the aircraft should be kept centered over this line during taxi. However, being centered on the taxiway centerline does not guarantee wingtip clearance with other aircraft or other objects.

2. Enhanced Centerline. At some airports, mostly the larger commercial service airports, an enhanced taxiway centerline will be used. The enhanced taxiway centerline marking consists of

a parallel line of yellow dashes on either side of the normal taxiway centerline. The taxiway centerlines are enhanced for a maximum of 150 feet prior to a runway holding position marking. The purpose of this enhancement is to warn the pilot that he/she is approaching a runway holding position marking and should prepare to stop unless he/she has been cleared onto or across the runway by ATC. (See Figure 2-3-8.)

c. Taxiway Edge Markings. Taxiway edge markings are used to define the edge of the taxiway. They are primarily used when the taxiway edge does not correspond with the edge of the pavement. There are two types of markings depending upon whether the aircraft is supposed to cross the taxiway edge:

1. Continuous Markings. These consist of a continuous double yellow line, with each line being at least 6 inches (15 cm) in width spaced 6 inches (15 cm) apart. They are used to define the taxiway edge from the shoulder or some other abutting paved surface not intended for use by aircraft.

2. Dashed Markings. These markings are used when there is an operational need to define the edge of a taxiway or taxilane on a paved surface where the adjoining pavement is intended for use by aircraft (for example, an apron). Dashed taxiway edge markings consist of a broken double yellow line, with each line being at least 6 inches (15 cm) in width, spaced 6 inches (15 cm) apart (edge to edge). These lines are 15 feet (4.5 m) in length with 25 foot (7.5 m) gaps. (See Figure 2-3-9.)

d. Taxi Shoulder Markings. Taxiways, holding bays, and aprons are sometimes provided with paved shoulders to prevent blast and water erosion. Although shoulders may have the appearance of full strength pavement they are not intended for use by aircraft, and may be unable to support an aircraft. Usually the taxiway edge marking will define this area. Where conditions exist such as islands or taxiway curves that may cause confusion as to which side of the edge stripe is for use by aircraft, taxiway shoulder markings may be used to indicate the pavement is unusable. Taxiway shoulder markings are yellow. (See Figure 2-3-10.)

e. Surface Painted Taxiway Direction Signs. Surface painted taxiway direction signs have a yellow background with a black inscription, and are provided when it is not possible to provide taxiway direction signs at intersections, or when necessary to supplement such signs. These markings are located adjacent to the centerline with signs indicating turns to the left being on the left side of the taxiway centerline and signs indicating turns to the right being on the right side of the centerline. (See Figure 2-3-11.)

f. Surface Painted Location Signs. Surface painted location signs have a black background with a yellow inscription. When necessary, these markings are used to supplement location signs located along side the taxiway and assist the pilot in confirming the designation of the taxiway on which the aircraft is located. These markings are located on the right side of the centerline. (See Figure 2-3-11.)

g. Geographic Position Markings. These markings are located at points along low visibility taxi routes designated in the airport's Surface Movement Guidance Control System (SMGCS) plan. They are used to identify the location of taxiing aircraft during low visibility operations. Low visibility operations are those that occur when the runway visible range (RVR) is below 1200 feet (360m). They are positioned to the left of the taxiway centerline in the direction of taxiing. (See Figure 2-3-12.) The geographic position marking is a circle comprised of an outer black ring contiguous to a white ring with a pink circle in the middle. When installed on asphalt or other dark-colored pavements, the white ring and the black ring are reversed (i.e., the white ring becomes the outer ring and the black ring becomes the inner ring). It is designated with either a number or a number and letter. The number corresponds to the consecutive position of the marking on the route.

Ch 2

FIGURE 2-3-6
Markings for Blast Pad or Stopway or Taxiway Preceding a Displaced Threshold

FIGURE 2-3-6
Markings for Blast Pad or Stopway or Taxiway Preceding a Displaced Threshold

Demarcation bar, yellow, 3' (1 m) wide, painted on blast pad or stopway

Demarcation bar, yellow, 3' (1 m) wide, painted on taxiway

FIGURE 2–3–7
Markings for Blast Pads and Stopways

FIGURE 2–3–8
Enhanced Taxiway Centerline

FIGURE 2–3–9
Dashed Markings

FIGURE 2–3–10
Taxi Shoulder Markings

FIGURE 2–3–11
Surface Painted Signs

FIGURE 2–3–12
Geographic Position Markings

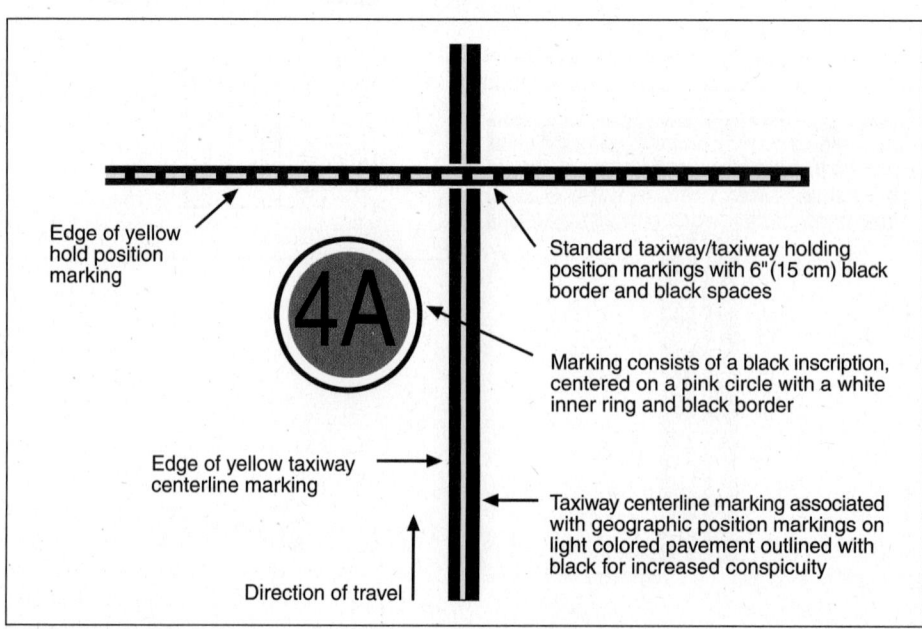

2-3-5 Holding Position Markings

a. Runway Holding Position Markings. For runways, these markings indicate where aircraft MUST STOP when approaching a runway. They consist of four yellow lines, two solid and two dashed, spaced six or twelve inches apart, and extending across the width of the taxiway or runway. The solid lines are always on the side where the aircraft must hold. There are three locations where runway holding position markings are encountered.

1. Runway Holding Position Markings on Taxiways. These markings identify the locations on a taxiway where aircraft MUST STOP when a clearance has not been issued to proceed onto the runway. Generally, runway holding position markings also identify the boundary of the runway safety area (RSA) for aircraft exiting the runway. Runway holding position markings are shown in Figure 2-3-13 and Figure 2-3-16. When instructed by ATC, "*Hold short of Runway XX*," the pilot MUST STOP so that no part of the aircraft extends beyond the runway holding position marking. When approaching runways at airports with an operating control tower, pilots must not cross the runway holding position marking without ATC clearance. Pilots approaching runways at airports without an operating control tower must ensure adequate separation from other aircraft, vehicles, and pedestrians prior to crossing the holding position markings. An aircraft exiting a runway is not clear of the runway until all parts of the aircraft have crossed the applicable holding position marking.

Note: *Runway holding position markings identify the beginning of an RSA, and a pilot MUST STOP to get clearance before crossing (at airports with operating control towers).*

Reference: *AIM, ¶4-3-21, Exiting the Runway After Landing.*

2. Runway Holding Position Markings on Runways. These markings identify the locations on runways where aircraft MUST STOP. These markings are located on runways used by ATC for Land And Hold Short Operations (for example, see Figure 4-3-8) and Taxiing operations. For taxiing operations, the pilot MUST STOP prior to the holding position markings unless explicitly authorized to cross by ATC. A sign with a white inscription on a red background is located adjacent to these holding position markings. (See Figure 2-3-14.) The holding position markings are placed on runways prior to the intersection with another runway, or some designated point. Pilots receiving and accepting instructions "*Cleared to land Runway XX, hold short of Runway YY*" from ATC must either exit Runway XX prior to the holding position markings, or stop at the holding position markings prior to Runway YY. Otherwise, pilots are authorized to use the entire landing length of the runway and disregard the holding position markings.

3. Holding Position Markings on Taxiways Located in Runway Approach Areas. These markings are used at some airports where it is necessary to hold an aircraft on a taxiway located in the approach or departure area of a runway so that the aircraft does not interfere with the operations on that runway. This marking is collocated with the runway approach/departure area holding position sign. When specifically instructed by ATC, "*Hold short of Runway XX approach or Runway XX departure area*," the pilot MUST STOP so that no part of the aircraft extends beyond the holding position marking. (See subparagraph 2-3-8b2, Runway Approach Area Holding Position Sign, and Figure 2-3-15.)

b. Holding Position Markings for Instrument Landing System (ILS). Holding position markings for ILS critical areas consist of two yellow solid lines spaced two feet apart connected by pairs of solid lines spaced ten feet apart extending across the width of the taxiway as shown. (See Figure 2-3-16.) A sign with an inscription in white on a red background is located adjacent to these hold position markings. When instructed by ATC to hold short of the ILS critical area, pilots MUST STOP so that no part of the aircraft extends beyond the holding position marking. When approaching the holding position marking, pilots must not cross the marking without ATC clearance. The ILS critical area is not clear until all parts of the aircraft have crossed the applicable holding position marking.

Reference: *AIM, ¶1-1-9, Instrument Landing System (ILS).*

c. Holding Position Markings for Intersecting Taxiways. Holding position markings for intersecting taxiways consist of a single dashed line extending across the width of the taxiway as shown. (See Figure 2-3-17.) They are located on taxiways where ATC holds aircraft short of a taxiway intersection. When instructed by ATC "*Hold short of Taxiway XX*," the pilot MUST STOP so that no part of the aircraft extends beyond the holding position marking. When the marking is not present, the pilot MUST STOP the aircraft at a point which provides adequate clearance from an aircraft on the intersecting taxiway.

d. Surface Painted Holding Position Signs. Surface painted holding position signs have a red background with a white inscription and supplement the signs located at the holding position. This type of marking is normally used where the width of the holding position on the taxiway is greater than 200 feet (60 m). It is located to the left side of the taxiway centerline on the holding side and prior to the holding position marking. (See Figure 2-3-11.)

FIGURE 2–3–13
Runway Holding Position Markings on Taxiway

Example of holding position markings
extended across holding bay

FIGURE 2–3–14
Runway Holding Position Markings on Runways

Runways 9/27 are used
for land and hold short
operations or used as taxiways.
Note the holdline markings
across the runways.

FIGURE 2–3–15
Taxiways Located in Runway Approach and Departure Areas

Note 1: *Refer to Advisory Circular 150/5300-13 for additional information on obstruction surfaces.*

Note 2: *Because Taxiway C does not enter the departure area of Runway 33, the sign on Taxiway C does not include the "33 DEP" legend.*

Note 3: *The location of a holding position is relative to the point on the aircraft that infringes the surface; for inclining surfaces such as an approach surface, the location of the holdline position may differ from the location of the infringement point.*

FIGURE 2–3–16
Holding Position Markings: ILS Critical Area

FIGURE 2–3–17
Holding Position Markings: Taxiway/Taxiway Intersections

2-3-6 Other Markings

a. Vehicle Roadway Markings. The vehicle roadway markings are used when necessary to define a pathway for vehicle operations on or crossing areas that are also intended for aircraft. These markings consist of a white solid line to delineate each edge of the roadway and a dashed line to separate lanes within the edges of the roadway. In lieu of the solid lines, zipper markings may be used to delineate the edges of the vehicle roadway. (See Figure 2-3-18.) Details of the zipper markings are shown in Figure 2-3-19.

b. VOR Receiver Checkpoint Markings. The VOR receiver checkpoint marking allows the pilot to check aircraft instruments with navigational aid signals. It consists of a painted circle with an arrow in the middle; the arrow is aligned in the direction of the checkpoint azimuth. This marking, and an associated sign, is located on the airport apron or taxiway at a point selected for easy access by aircraft but where other airport traffic is not to be unduly obstructed. (See Figure 2-3-20.)

Note: The associated sign contains the VOR station identification letter and course selected (published) for the check, the words "VOR check course," and DME data (when applicable). The color of the letters and numerals are black on a yellow background.

Example:
DCA 176-356
VOR check course
DME XXX

c. Nonmovement Area Boundary Markings. These markings delineate the movement area (i.e., area under ATC). These markings are yellow and located on the boundary between the movement and nonmovement area. The nonmovement area boundary markings consist of two yellow lines (one solid and one dashed) 6 inches (15cm) in width. The solid line is located on the nonmovement area side while the dashed yellow line is located on the movement area side. The nonmovement boundary marking area is shown in Figure 2-3-21.

FIGURE 2–3–18
Vehicle Roadway Markings

FIGURE 2–3–19
Roadway Edge Stripes, White, Zipper Style

FIGURE 2–3–19
Roadway Edge Stripes, White, Zipper Style

FIGURE 2–3–20
Ground Receiver Checkpoint Markings

1. White
2. Yellow
3. Yellow arrow aligned toward the facility
4. Interior of circle black (concrete surface only)
5. Circle may be bordered on inside and outside with
 6" black band if necessary for contrast

FIGURE 2–3–21
Nonmovement Area Boundary Markings

d. Marking and Lighting of Permanently Closed Runways and Taxiways. For runways and taxiways which are permanently closed, the lighting circuits will be disconnected. The runway threshold, runway designation, and touchdown markings are obliterated and yellow crosses are placed at each end of the runway and at 1,000 foot intervals. (See Figure 2-3-22.)

FIGURE 2–3–22
Closed or Temporarily Closed Runway and Taxiway Markings

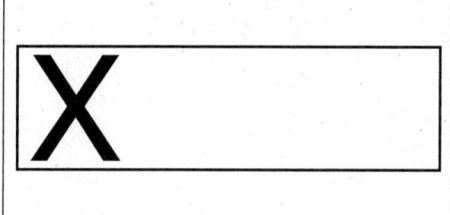

e. Temporarily Closed Runways and Taxiways. To provide a visual indication to pilots that a runway is temporarily closed, crosses are placed on the runway only at each end of the runway. The crosses are yellow in color. (See Figure 2-3-22.)

1. A raised lighted yellow cross may be placed on each runway end in lieu of the markings described in subparagraph e, Temporarily Closed Runways and Taxiways, to indicate the runway is closed.

2. A visual indication may not be present depending on the reason for the closure, duration of the closure, airfield configuration, and the existence and the hours of operation of an airport traffic control tower. Pilots should check NOTAMs and the Automated Terminal Information System (ATIS) for local runway and taxiway closure information.

3. Temporarily closed taxiways are usually treated as hazardous areas, in which no part of an aircraft may enter, and are blocked with barricades. However, as an alternative, a yellow cross may be installed at each entrance to the taxiway.

f. Helicopter Landing Areas. The markings illustrated in Figure 2-3-23 are used to identify the landing and takeoff area at a public use heliport and hospital heliport. The letter "H" in the markings is oriented to align with the intended direction of approach. Figure 2-3-23 also depicts the markings for a closed airport.

FIGURE 2-3-23
Helicopter Landing Areas

Recommended Marking for Civil Heliports | Recommended Marking for Hospital Heliports | Recommended Marking for Closed Heliports

2-3-7 Airport Signs

There are six types of signs installed on airfields: mandatory instruction signs, location signs, direction signs, destination signs, information signs, and runway distance remaining signs. The characteristics and use of these signs are discussed in paragraph 2-3-8, Mandatory Instruction Signs, through paragraph 2-3-13, Runway Distance Remaining Signs.

Reference: AC150/5340-18, Standards for Airport Sign Systems for Detailed Information on Airport Signs.

2-3-8 Mandatory Instruction Signs

a. These signs have a red background with a white inscription and are used to denote:

1. An entrance to a runway or critical area; and

2. Areas where an aircraft is prohibited from entering.

b. Typical mandatory signs and applications are:

1. Runway Holding Position Sign. This sign is located at the holding position on taxiways that intersect a runway or on runways that intersect other runways. The inscription on the sign contains the designation of the intersecting runway as shown in Figure 2-3-24. The runway numbers on the sign are arranged to correspond to the respective runway threshold. For example, "15-33" indicates that the threshold for Runway 15 is to the left and the threshold for Runway 33 is to the right.

(a) On taxiways that intersect the beginning of the takeoff runway, only the designation of the takeoff runway may appear on the sign (as shown in Figure 2-3-25), while all other signs will have the designation of both runway directions.

(b) If the sign is located on a taxiway that intersects the intersection of two runways, the designations for both runways will be shown on the sign along with arrows showing the approximate alignment of each runway, as shown in Figure 2-3-26. In addition to showing the approximate runway alignment, the arrow indicates the direction to the threshold of the runway whose designation is immediately next to the arrow.

(c) A runway holding position sign on a taxiway will be installed adjacent to holding position markings on the taxiway pavement. On runways, holding position markings will be located only on the runway pavement adjacent to the sign, if the runway is normally used by ATC for "Land, Hold Short" operations or as a taxiway. The holding position markings are described in paragraph 2-3-5, Holding Position Markings.

FIGURE 2–3–24
Runway Holding Position Sign

FIGURE 2–3–25
**Holding Position Sign at
Beginning of Takeoff Runway**

FIGURE 2–3–26
**Holding Position Sign for a Taxiway that Intersects
the Intersection of Two Runways**

2. Runway Approach Area Holding Position Sign. At some airports, it is necessary to hold an aircraft on a taxiway located in the approach or departure area for a runway so that the aircraft does not interfere with operations on that runway. Figure 2-3-15 depicts common situations. A sign with the runway designation(s) and the protected area(s) will be located at applicable holding positions on the taxiway. For locations protecting only the approach area, the holding position on the taxiway includes a sign identifying the approach end runway designation (e.g., 15) followed by a dash (–) and the letters "APCH". For locations protecting both the approach and departure areas, the holding position on the taxiway includes a sign with the approach end runway designation and letters "APCH" followed by a dash (–), the departure end runway designation and the letters "DEP". The arrangement of the runway designations and protected areas legend on the sign reflects the orientation of the runway as viewed from the holding position. Holding position markings in accordance with paragraph 2-3-5, Holding Position Markings, are co-located on the taxiway pavement in line with the sign. Examples of these signs are shown in Figure 2-3-27.

3. ILS Critical Area Holding Position Sign. At some airports, when the instrument landing system is being used, it is necessary to hold an aircraft on a taxiway at a location other than the holding position described in paragraph 2-3-5, Holding Position Markings. In these situations, the holding position sign for these operations will have the inscription "ILS" and be located adjacent to the holding position marking on the taxiway described in paragraph 2-3-5. An example of this sign is shown in Figure 2-3-28.

4. No Entry Sign. This sign, shown in Figure 2-3-29, prohibits an aircraft from entering an area. Typically, this sign would be located on a taxiway intended to be used in only one direction or at the intersection of vehicle roadways with runways, taxiways or aprons where the roadway may be mistaken as a taxiway or other aircraft movement surface.

Note: Holding position signs provide the pilot with a visual cue as to the location of the holding position marking.

Reference: AIM, ¶2-3-5, Holding Position Markings.

FIGURE 2–3–27
Holding Position Sign for Runway Approach and Departure Areas

FIGURE 2–3–28
Holding Position Sign for ILS Critical Area

FIGURE 2–3–29
Sign Prohibiting Aircraft Entry into an Area

2–3–9 Location Signs

a. Location signs are used to identify either a taxiway or runway on which the aircraft is located. Other location signs provide a visual cue to pilots to assist them in determining when they have exited an area. The various location signs are described below.

1. Taxiway Location Sign. This sign has a black background with a yellow inscription and yellow border, as shown in Figure 2-3-30. The inscription is the designation of the taxiway on which the aircraft is located. These signs are installed along taxiways either by themselves or in conjunction with direction signs or runway holding position signs. (See Figure 2-3-35 and Figure 2-3-31.)

2. Runway Location Sign. This sign has a black background with a yellow inscription and yellow border, as shown in Figure 2-3-32. The inscription is the designation of the runway on which the aircraft is located. These signs are intended to complement the information available to pilots through their magnetic compass and typically are installed where the proximity of two or more runways to one another could cause pilots to be confused as to which runway they are on.

3. Runway Boundary Sign. This sign has a yellow background with a black inscription with a graphic depicting the pavement holding position marking, as shown in Figure 2-3-33. This sign, which faces the runway and is visible to the pilot exiting the runway, is located adjacent to the holding position marking on the pavement. The sign is intended to provide pilots with another visual cue which they can use as a guide in deciding when they are "clear of the runway."

4. ILS Critical Area Boundary Sign. This sign has a yellow background with a black inscription with a graphic depicting the ILS pavement holding position marking as shown in Figure 2-3-34. This sign is located adjacent to the ILS holding position marking on the pavement and can be seen by pilots leaving the critical area. The sign is intended to provide pilots with another visual cue which they can use as a guide in deciding when they are "clear of the ILS critical area."

FIGURE 2–3–30
Taxiway Location Sign

FIGURE 2–3–32
Runway Location Sign

FIGURE 2–3–31
Taxiway Location Sign Collocated with Runway Holding Position Sign

FIGURE 2–3–33
Runway Boundary Sign

FIGURE 2–3–34
ILS Critical Area Boundary Sign

2–3–10 Direction Signs

a. Direction signs have a yellow background with a black inscription. The inscription identifies the designation(s) of the intersecting taxiway(s) leading out of the intersection that a pilot would normally be expected to turn onto or hold short of. Each designation is accompanied by an arrow indicating the direction of the turn.

b. Except as noted in subparagraph e, each taxiway designation shown on the sign is accompanied by only one arrow. When more than one taxiway designation is shown on the sign each designation and its associated arrow is separated from the other taxiway designations by either a

Ch 2

FIGURE 2–3–35
Direction Sign Array with Location Sign on Far Side of Intersection

NOTE: Orientation of signs are from left to right in a clockwise manner. Left turn signs are on the left of the location sign and right turn signs are on the right side of the location sign.

Alternate array of signs shown to illustrate sign orientation when location sign not installed.

vertical message divider or a taxiway location sign as shown in Figure 2-3-35.

c. Direction signs are normally located on the left prior to the intersection. When used on a runway to indicate an exit, the sign is located on the same side of the runway as the exit. Figure 2-3-36 shows a direction sign used to indicate a runway exit.

d. The taxiway designations and their associated arrows on the sign are arranged clockwise starting from the first taxiway on the pilot's left. (See Figure 2-3-35.)

e. If a location sign is located with the direction signs, it is placed so that the designations for all turns to the left will be to the left of the location sign; the designations for continuing straight ahead or for all turns to the right would be located to the right of the location sign. (See Figure 2-3-35.)

f. When the intersection is comprised of only one crossing taxiway, it is permissible to have two arrows associated with the crossing taxiway as shown in Figure 2-3-37. In this case, the location sign is located to the left of the direction sign.

FIGURE 2–3–36
Direction Sign for Runway Exit

FIGURE 2–3–37
Direction Sign Array for Simple Intersection

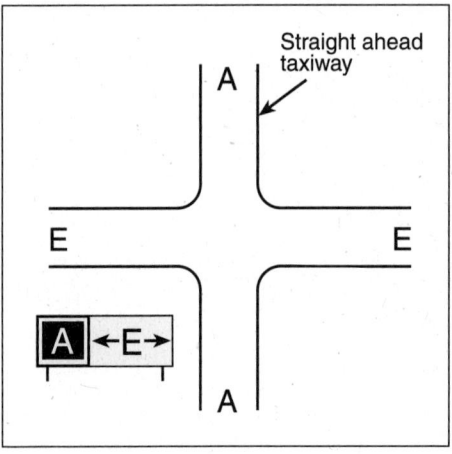

FIGURE 2–3–37
Direction Sign Array for Simple Intersection

on a sign, the destinations are separated by a "dot" (•) and one arrow would be used as shown in Figure 2-3-39. When the inscription on a sign contains two or more destinations having different taxiing routes, each destination will be accompanied by an arrow and will be separated from the other destinations on the sign with a vertical black message divider, as shown in Figure 2-3-40.

FIGURE 2–3–38
Destination Sign for Military Area

2–3–11 Destination Signs

a. Destination signs also have a yellow background with a black inscription indicating a destination on the airport. These signs always have an arrow showing the direction of the taxiing route to that destination. Figure 2-3-38 is an example of a typical destination sign. When the arrow on the destination sign indicates a turn, the sign is located prior to the intersection.

b. Destinations commonly shown on these types of signs include runways, aprons, terminals, military areas, civil aviation areas, cargo areas, international areas, and fixed base operators. An abbreviation may be used as the inscription on the sign for some of these destinations.

c. When the inscription for two or more destinations having a common taxiing route are placed

FIGURE 2–3–39
Destination Sign for Common Taxiing Route to Two Runways

FIGURE 2–3–40
Destination Sign for Different Taxiing Routes to Two Runways

2-3-12 Information Signs

Information signs have a yellow background with a black inscription. They are used to provide the pilot with information on such things as areas that cannot be seen from the control tower, applicable radio frequencies, and noise abatement procedures. The airport operator determines the need, size, and location for these signs.

2-3-13 Runway Distance Remaining Signs

Runway distance remaining signs have a black background with a white numeral inscription and may be installed along one or both side(s) of the runway. The number on the signs indicates the distance (in thousands of feet) of landing runway remaining. The last sign (i.e., the sign with the numeral "1") will be located at least 950 feet from the runway end. Figure 2-3-41 shows an example of a runway distance remaining sign.

FIGURE 2–3–41
Runway Distance Remaining Sign
Indicating 3,000 feet of Runway Remaining

2-3-14 Aircraft Arresting Systems

a. Certain airports are equipped with a means of rapidly stopping military aircraft on a runway. This equipment, normally referred to as EMERGENCY ARRESTING GEAR, generally consists of pendant cables supported over the runway surface by rubber "donuts." Although most devices are located in the overrun areas, a few of these arresting systems have cables stretched over the operational areas near the ends of a runway.

b. Arresting cables which cross over a runway require special markings on the runway to identify the cable location. These markings consist of 10 feet diameter solid circles painted "identification yellow," 30 feet on center, perpendicular to the runway centerline across the entire runway width. Additional details are contained in AC 150/5220-9, Aircraft Arresting Systems for Joint Civil/Military Airports.

Note: Aircraft operations on the runway are not restricted by the installation of aircraft arresting devices.

c. Engineered Materials Arresting Systems (EMAS). EMAS, which is constructed of high energy-absorbing materials of selected strength, is located in the safety area beyond the end of the runway. EMAS will be marked with yellow chevrons. EMAS is designed to crush under the weight of commercial aircraft and will exert deceleration forces on the landing gear. These systems do not affect the normal landing and takeoff of airplanes. More information concerning EMAS is in AC 150/5220-22, Engineered Materials Arresting Systems (EMAS) for Aircraft Overruns.

Note: EMAS may be located as close as 35 feet beyond the end of the runway. Aircraft and ground vehicles should never taxi or drive across the EMAS or beyond the end of the runway if EMAS is present.

Ch 2

FIGURE 2–3–42
Engineered Materials Arresting System (EMAS)

2–3–15 Security Identification Display Area (SIDA)

a. Security Identification Display Areas (SIDA) are limited access areas that require a badge issued in accordance with procedures in 49 CFR Part 1542. A SIDA can include the Air Operations Area (AOA), e.g., aircraft movement area or parking area, or a Secured Area, such as where commercial passengers enplane. The AOA may not be a SIDA, but a Secured Area is always a SIDA. Movement through or into a SIDA is prohibited without authorization and proper identification being displayed. If you are unsure of the location of a SIDA, contact the airport authority for additional information. Airports that have a SIDA will have a description and map detailing boundaries and pertinent features available.

b. Pilots or passengers without proper identification that are observed entering a SIDA may be reported to the Transportation Security Administration (TSA) or airport security and may be subject to civil and criminal fines and prosecution. Pilots are advised to brief passengers accordingly. Report suspicious activity to the TSA by calling

AOPA's Airport Watch Program, 866-427-3287. 49 CFR 1540 requires each individual who holds an airman certificate, medical certificate, authorization, or license issued by the FAA to present it for inspection upon a request from TSA.

FIGURE 2–3–43
Sample SIDA Warning Sign

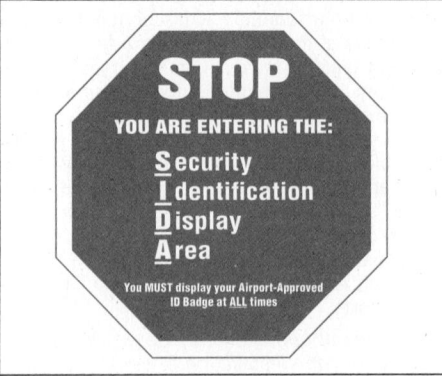

Chapter 3
Airspace

Section 1 General

3–1–1 General

a. There are two categories of airspace or airspace areas:

1. Regulatory (Class A, B, C, D and E airspace areas, restricted and prohibited areas); and

2. Nonregulatory (military operations areas [MOA], warning areas, alert areas, controlled firing areas [CFA], and national security areas [NSA]).

Note: Additional information on special use airspace (prohibited areas, restricted areas [permanent or temporary], warning areas, MOAs [permanent or temporary], alert areas, CFAs, and NSAs) may be found in Chapter 3, Airspace, Section 4, Special Use Airspace, paragraphs 3-4-1 through 3-4-8.

b. Within these two categories, there are four types:

1. Controlled,

2. Uncontrolled,

3. Special use, and

4. Other airspace.

c. The categories and types of airspace are dictated by:

1. The complexity or density of aircraft movements,

2. The nature of the operations conducted within the airspace,

3. The level of safety required, and

4. The national and public interest.

d. It is important that pilots be familiar with the operational requirements for each of the various types or classes of airspace. Subsequent sections will cover each class in sufficient detail to facilitate understanding.

3–1–2 General Dimensions of Airspace Segments

Refer to Title 14 of the U.S. Code of Federal Regulations (CFR) for specific dimensions, exceptions, geographical areas covered, exclusions, specific transponder/ADS-B or other equipment requirements, and flight operations.

3–1–3 Hierarchy of Overlapping Airspace Designations

a. When overlapping airspace designations apply to the same airspace, the operating rules associated with the more restrictive airspace designation apply.

b. For the purpose of clarification:

1. Class A airspace is more restrictive than Class B, Class C, Class D, Class E, or Class G airspace;

2. Class B airspace is more restrictive than Class C, Class D, Class E, or Class G airspace;

3. Class C airspace is more restrictive than Class D, Class E, or Class G airspace;

4. Class D airspace is more restrictive than Class E or Class G airspace; and

5. Class E is more restrictive than Class G airspace.

3–1–4 Basic VFR Weather Minimums

a. No person may operate an aircraft under basic VFR when the flight visibility is less, or at a distance from clouds that is less, than that prescribed for the corresponding altitude and class of airspace. (See Table 3-1-1.)

Note: Student pilots must comply with 14 CFR Section 61.89(a) (6) and (7).

b. Except as provided in 14 CFR Section 91.157, Special VFR Weather Minimums, no person may operate an aircraft beneath the ceiling under VFR within the lateral boundaries of controlled airspace designated to the surface for an airport when the ceiling is less than 1,000 feet. (See 14 CFR Section 91.155(c).)

TABLE 3–1–1
BASIC VFR WEATHER MINIMUMS

Airspace	Flight Visibility	Distance from Clouds
Class A	Not Applicable	Not Applicable
Class B	3 statute miles	Clear of Clouds
Class C	3 statute miles	500 feet below; 1,000 feet above; 2,000 feet horizontal
Class D	3 statute miles	500 feet below; 1,000 feet above; 2,000 feet horizontal
Class E Less than 10,000 feet MSL	3 statute miles	500 feet below; 1,000 feet above; 2,000 feet horizontal
At or above 10,000 feet MSL	5 statute miles	1,000 feet below; 1,000 feet above; 1 statute mile horizontal
Class G 1,200 feet or less above the surface (regardless of MSL altitude) For aircraft other than helicopters:		
Day, except as provided in §91.155(b)	1 statute mile	Clear of clouds
Night, except as provided in §91.155(b)	3 statute miles	500 feet below; 1,000 feet above; 2,000 feet horizontal
For helicopters:		
Day	½ statute mile	Clear of clouds
Night, except as provided in §91.155(b)	1 statute mile	Clear of clouds
More than 1,200 feet above the surface but less than 10,000 feet MSL		
Day	1 statute mile	500 feet below; 1,000 feet above; 2,000 feet horizontal
Night	3 statute miles	500 feet below; 1,000 feet above; 2,000 feet horizontal
More than 1,200 feet above the surface and at or above 10,000 feet MSL	5 statute miles	1,000 feet below; 1,000 feet above; 1 statute mile horizontal

3–1–5 VFR Cruising Altitudes and Flight Levels

(See Table 3-1-2.)

TABLE 3–1–2
VFR CRUISING ALTITUDES AND FLIGHT LEVELS

If your magnetic course (ground track) is:	And you are more than 3,000 feet above the surface but below 18,000 feet MSL, fly:	And you are above 18,000 feet MSL to FL290, fly:
0° to 179°	Odd thousands MSL, plus 500 feet (3,500; 5,500; 7,500, etc.)	Odd Flight Levels plus 500 feet (FL195; FL215; FL235, etc.)
180° to 359°	Even thousands MSL, plus 500 feet (4,500; 6,500; 8,500, etc.)	Even Flight Levels plus 500 feet (FL185; FL205; FL225, etc.)

Section 2 Controlled Airspace

3-2-1 General

a. Controlled Airspace. A generic term that covers the different classification of airspace (Class A, Class B, Class C, Class D, and Class E airspace) and defined dimensions within which air traffic control service is provided to IFR flights and to VFR flights in accordance with the airspace classification. (See Figure 3-2-1.)

b. IFR Requirements. IFR operations in any class of controlled airspace requires that a pilot must file an IFR flight plan and receive an appropriate ATC clearance.

c. IFR Separation. Standard IFR separation is provided to all aircraft operating under IFR in controlled airspace.

d. VFR Requirements. It is the responsibility of the pilot to ensure that ATC clearance or radio communication requirements are met prior to entry into Class B, Class C, or Class D airspace. The pilot retains this responsibility when receiving ATC radar advisories. (See 14 CFR Part 91.)

e. Traffic Advisories. Traffic advisories will be provided to all aircraft as the controller's work situation permits.

f. Safety Alerts. Safety Alerts are mandatory services and are provided to ALL aircraft. There are two types of Safety Alerts:

1. Terrain/Obstruction Alert. A Terrain/Obstruction Alert is issued when, in the controller's judgment, an aircraft's altitude places it in unsafe proximity to terrain and/or obstructions; and

2. Aircraft Conflict/Mode C Intruder Alert. An Aircraft Conflict/Mode C Intruder Alert is issued if the controller observes another aircraft which places it in an unsafe proximity. When feasible, the controller will offer the pilot an alternative course of action.

g. Ultralight Vehicles. No person may operate an ultralight vehicle within Class A, Class B, Class C, or Class D airspace or within the lateral boundaries of the surface area of Class E airspace designated for an airport unless that person has prior authorization from the ATC facility having jurisdiction over that airspace. (See 14 CFR Part 103.)

h. Unmanned Free Balloons. Unless otherwise authorized by ATC, no person may operate an unmanned free balloon below 2,000 feet above the surface within the lateral boundaries of Class B, Class C, Class D, or Class E airspace designated for an airport. (See 14 CFR Part 101.)

i. Parachute Jumps. No person may make a parachute jump, and no pilot-in-command may allow a parachute jump to be made from that aircraft, in or into Class A, Class B, Class C, or Class D airspace without, or in violation of, the terms of an ATC authorization issued by the ATC facility having jurisdiction over the airspace. (See 14 CFR Part 105.)

FIGURE 3-2-1
Airspace Classes

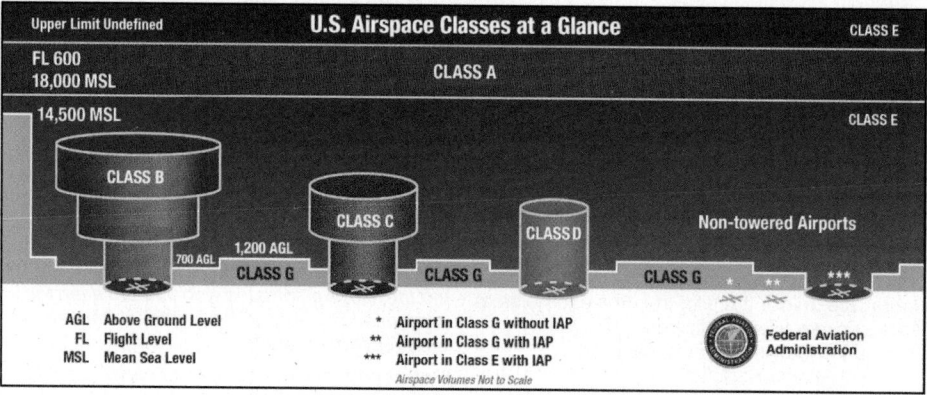

3-2-2 Class A Airspace

a. Definition. Generally, that airspace from 18,000 feet MSL up to and including FL600, including the airspace overlying the waters within 12 nautical miles off the coast of the 48 contiguous States and Alaska; and designated international airspace beyond 12 nautical miles off the coast of the 48 contiguous States and Alaska within areas of domestic radio navigational signal or ATC radar coverage, and within which domestic procedures are applied.

b. Operating Rules and Pilot/Equipment Requirements. Unless otherwise authorized, all persons must operate their aircraft under IFR. (See 14 CFR Section 71.33, Sections 91.167 through 91.193, Sections 91.215 through 91.217, and Sections 91.225 through 91.227.)

c. Charts. Class A airspace is not specifically charted.

3-2-3 Class B Airspace

a. Definition. Generally, that airspace from the surface to 10,000 feet MSL surrounding the nation's busiest airports in terms of IFR operations or passenger enplanements. The configuration of each Class B airspace area is individually tailored and consists of a surface area and two or more layers (some Class B airspace areas resemble upside-down wedding cakes), and is designed to contain all published instrument procedures once an aircraft enters the airspace. An ATC clearance is required for all aircraft to operate in the area, and all aircraft that are so cleared receive separation services within the airspace. The cloud clearance requirement for VFR operations is "clear of clouds."

b. Operating Rules and Pilot/Equipment Requirements. Regardless of weather conditions, an ATC clearance is required prior to operating within Class B airspace. Pilots should not request a clearance to operate within Class B airspace unless the requirements of 14 CFR Sections 91.131, 91.215, and 91.225 are met. Included among these requirements are:

1. Unless otherwise authorized by ATC, aircraft must be equipped with an operable two-way radio capable of communicating with ATC on appropriate frequencies for that Class B airspace.

2. No person may take off or land a civil aircraft at the following primary airports within Class B airspace unless the pilot-in-command holds at least a private pilot certificate:

 (a) Andrews Air Force Base, MD

 (b) Atlanta Hartsfield Airport, GA

 (c) Boston Logan Airport, MA

 (d) Chicago O'Hare Intl. Airport, IL

 (e) Dallas/Fort Worth Intl. Airport, TX

 (f) Los Angeles Intl. Airport, CA

 (g) Miami Intl. Airport, FL

 (h) Newark Intl. Airport, NJ

 (i) New York Kennedy Airport, NY

 (j) New York La Guardia Airport, NY

 (k) Ronald Reagan Washington National Airport, DC

 (l) San Francisco Intl. Airport, CA

3. No person may take off or land a civil aircraft at an airport within Class B airspace or operate a civil aircraft within Class B airspace unless:

 (a) The pilot-in-command holds at least a private pilot certificate; or

 (b) The pilot-in-command holds a recreational pilot certificate and has met the requirements of 14 CFR Section 61.101; or

 (c) The pilot-in-command holds a sport pilot certificate and has met the requirements of 14 CFR Section 61.325; or

 (d) The aircraft is operated by a student pilot:

 (1) Who seeks a private pilot certificate and has met the requirements of 14 CFR Section 61.95.

 (2) Who seeks a recreational pilot or sport pilot certificate and has met the requirements of 14 CFR Section 61.94.

4. Unless otherwise authorized by ATC, each person operating a large turbine engine-powered airplane to or from a primary airport must operate at or above the designated floors while within the lateral limits of Class B airspace.

5. Unless otherwise authorized by ATC, each aircraft must be equipped as follows:

 (a) For IFR operations, an operable VOR or TACAN receiver or an operable and suitable RNAV system; and

 (b) For all operations, a two-way radio capable of communications with ATC on appropriate frequencies for that area; and

 (c) Unless otherwise authorized by ATC, an operable radar beacon transponder with automatic altitude reporting capability and operable ADS-B Out equipment.

Note: ATC may, upon notification, immediately authorize a deviation from the altitude reporting equipment requirement; however, a request for a deviation from the 4096 transponder equipment requirement must be submitted to the controlling ATC facility at least one hour before the proposed operation. A request for a deviation from the ADS-B equipage requirement must be submitted using the FAA's automated web authorization tool at least one hour but not more than 24 hours before the proposed operation.

Reference: AIM, ¶4-1-20, Transponder and ADS-B Out Operation; AC 90-114, Automatic Dependent Surveillance–Broadcast Operations.

6. Mode C Veil. The airspace within 30 nautical miles of an airport listed in Appendix D, Section 1 of 14 CFR Part 91 (generally primary

airports within Class B airspace areas), from the surface upward to 10,000 feet MSL. Unless otherwise authorized by ATC, aircraft operating within this airspace must be equipped with an operable radar beacon transponder with automatic altitude reporting capability and operable ADS-B Out equipment.

However, aircraft that were not originally certificated with an engine-driven electrical system or that have not subsequently been certified with a system installed may conduct operations within a Mode C veil provided the aircraft remains outside Class A, B or C airspace; and below the altitude of the ceiling of a Class B or Class C airspace area designated for an airport or 10,000 feet MSL, whichever is lower.

c. Charts. Class B airspace is charted on Sectional Charts, IFR En Route Low Altitude, and Terminal Area Charts.

d. Flight Procedures.

1. Flights. Aircraft within Class B airspace are required to operate in accordance with current IFR procedures. A clearance for a visual approach to a primary airport is not authorization for turbine-powered airplanes to operate below the designated floors of the Class B airspace.

2. VFR Flights.

(a) Arriving aircraft must obtain an ATC clearance prior to entering Class B airspace and must contact ATC on the appropriate frequency, and in relation to geographical fixes shown on local charts. Although a pilot may be operating beneath the floor of the Class B airspace on initial contact, communications with ATC should be established in relation to the points indicated for spacing and sequencing purposes.

(b) Departing aircraft require a clearance to depart Class B airspace and should advise the clearance delivery position of their intended altitude and route of flight. ATC will normally advise VFR aircraft when leaving the geographical limits of the Class B airspace. Radar service is not automatically terminated with this advisory unless specifically stated by the controller.

(c) Aircraft not landing or departing the primary airport may obtain an ATC clearance to transit the Class B airspace when traffic conditions permit and provided the requirements of 14 CFR Section 91.131 are met. Such VFR aircraft are encouraged, to the extent possible, to operate at altitudes above or below the Class B airspace or transit through established VFR corridors. Pilots operating in VFR corridors are urged to use frequency 122.750 MHz for the exchange of aircraft position information.

e. ATC Clearances and Separation. An ATC clearance is required to enter and operate within Class B airspace. VFR pilots are provided sequencing and separation from other aircraft while operating within Class B airspace.

Reference: AIM, ¶4-1-18, Terminal Radar Services for VFR Aircraft.

Note: *Separation and sequencing of VFR aircraft will be suspended in the event of a radar outage as this service is dependent on radar. The pilot will be advised that the service is not available and issued wind, runway information and the time or place to contact the tower.*

1. VFR aircraft are separated from all VFR/IFR aircraft which weigh 19,000 pounds or less by a minimum of:

(a) Target resolution, or

(b) 500 feet vertical separation, or

(c) Visual separation.

2. VFR aircraft are separated from all VFR/IFR aircraft which weigh more than 19,000 and turbojets by no less than:

(a) 1-1/2 miles lateral separation, or

(b) 500 feet vertical separation, or

(c) Visual separation.

3. This program is not to be interpreted as relieving pilots of their responsibilities to see and avoid other traffic operating in basic VFR weather conditions, to adjust their operations and flight path as necessary to preclude serious wake encounters, to maintain appropriate terrain and obstruction clearance or to remain in weather conditions equal to or better than the minimums required by 14 CFR Section 91.155. Approach control should be advised and a revised clearance or instruction obtained when compliance with an assigned route, heading and/or altitude is likely to compromise pilot responsibility with respect to terrain and obstruction clearance, vortex exposure, and weather minimums.

4. ATC may assign altitudes to VFR aircraft that do not conform to 14 CFR Section 91.159. **"RESUME APPROPRIATE VFR ALTITUDES"** will be broadcast when the altitude assignment is no longer needed for separation or when leaving Class B airspace. Pilots must return to an altitude that conforms to 14 CFR Section 91.159.

f. Proximity Operations. VFR aircraft operating in proximity to Class B airspace are cautioned against operating too closely to the boundaries, especially where the floor of the Class B airspace is 3,000 feet or less above the surface or where VFR cruise altitudes are at or near the floor of higher levels. Observance of this precaution will reduce the potential for encountering an aircraft operating at the altitudes of Class B floors. Additionally, VFR aircraft are encouraged to utilize the VFR Planning Chart as a tool for planning flight in proximity to Class B airspace. Charted VFR Flyway Planning Charts are published on the back of the existing VFR Terminal Area Charts.

Ch 3

3-2-4 Class C Airspace

a. Definition. Generally, that airspace from the surface to 4,000 feet above the airport elevation (charted in MSL) surrounding those airports that have an operational control tower, are serviced by a radar approach control, and that have a certain number of IFR operations or passenger enplanements. Although the configuration of each Class C airspace area is individually tailored, the airspace usually consists of a 5 NM radius core surface area that extends from the surface up to 4,000 feet above the airport elevation, and a 10 NM radius shelf area that extends no lower than 1,200 feet up to 4,000 feet above the airport elevation.

b. Charts. Class C airspace is charted on Sectional Charts, IFR En Route Low Altitude, and Terminal Area Charts where appropriate.

c. Operating Rules and Pilot/Equipment Requirements:

1. Pilot Certification. No specific certification required.

2. Equipment.

(a) Two-way radio; and

(b) Unless otherwise authorized by ATC, an operable radar beacon transponder with automatic altitude reporting capability and operable ADS-B Out equipment.

Note: See Paragraph 4-1-20, Transponder and ADS-B Out Operation, subparagraph f for Mode C transponder/ADS-B requirements for operating above Class C airspace.

3. Arrival or Through Flight Entry Requirements. Two-way radio communication must be established with the ATC facility providing ATC services prior to entry and thereafter maintain those communications while in Class C airspace. Pilots of arriving aircraft should contact the Class C airspace ATC facility on the publicized frequency and give their position, altitude, radar beacon code, destination, and request Class C service. Radio contact should be initiated far enough from the Class C airspace boundary to preclude entering Class C airspace before two-way radio communications are established.

Note 1: If the controller responds to a radio call with, "(aircraft callsign) standby," radio communications have been established and the pilot can enter the Class C airspace.

Note 2: If workload or traffic conditions prevent immediate provision of Class C services, the controller will inform the pilot to remain outside the Class C airspace until conditions permit the services to be provided.

Note 3: It is important to understand that if the controller responds to the initial radio call without using the aircraft identification, radio communications have not been established and the pilot may not enter the Class C airspace.

Note 4: Class C airspace areas have a procedural Outer Area. Normally this area is 20 NM from the primary Class C airport. Its vertical limit extends from the lower limits of radio/radar coverage up to the ceiling of the approach control's delegated airspace, excluding the Class C airspace itself, and other airspace as appropriate. (This outer area is not charted.)

Note 5: Pilots approaching an airport with Class C service should be aware that if they descend below the base altitude of the 5 to 10 mile shelf during an instrument or visual approach, they may encounter non-transponder/non-ADS-B VFR aircraft.

Example:

1. [Aircraft callsign] "remain outside the Class Charlie airspace and standby."

2. "Aircraft calling Dulles approach control, standby."

4. Departures from:

(a) A primary or satellite airport with an operating control tower. Two-way radio communications must be established and maintained with the control tower, and thereafter as instructed by ATC while operating in Class C airspace.

(b) A satellite airport without an operating control tower. Two-way radio communications must be established as soon as practicable after departing with the ATC facility having jurisdiction over the Class C airspace.

5. Aircraft Speed. Unless otherwise authorized or required by ATC, no person may operate an aircraft at or below 2,500 feet above the surface within 4 nautical miles of the primary airport of a Class C airspace area at an indicated airspeed of more than 200 knots (230 mph).

d. Air Traffic Services. When two-way radio communications and radar contact are established, all VFR aircraft are:

1. Sequenced to the primary airport.

2. Provided Class C services within the Class C airspace and the outer area.

3. Provided basic radar services beyond the outer area on a workload permitting basis. This can be terminated by the controller if workload dictates.

e. Aircraft Separation. Separation is provided within the Class C airspace and the outer area after two-way radio communications and radar contact are established. VFR aircraft are separated from IFR aircraft within the Class C airspace by any of the following:

1. Visual separation.
2. 500 feet vertical separation.
3. Target resolution.
4. Wake turbulence separation will be provided to all aircraft operating:

 (a) Behind and less than 1,000 feet below super or heavy aircraft,

 (b) To small aircraft operating behind and less than 500 feet below B757 aircraft, and

 (c) To small aircraft following a large aircraft on final approach.

Note 1: Separation and sequencing of VFR aircraft will be suspended in the event of a radar outage as this service is dependent on radar. The pilot will be advised that the service is not available and issued wind, runway information and the time or place to contact the tower.

Note 2: Pilot participation is voluntary within the outer area and can be discontinued, within the outer area, at the pilot's request. Class C services will be provided in the outer area unless the pilot requests termination of the service.

Note 3: Some facilities provide Class C services only during published hours. At other times, terminal IFR radar service will be provided. It is important to note that the communications and transponder/ADS-B requirements are dependent on the class of airspace established outside of the published hours.

f. Secondary Airports

1. In some locations Class C airspace may overlie the Class D surface area of a secondary airport. In order to allow that control tower to provide service to aircraft, portions of the overlapping Class C airspace may be procedurally excluded when the secondary airport tower is in operation. Aircraft operating in these procedurally excluded areas will only be provided airport traffic control services when in communication with the secondary airport tower.

2. Aircraft proceeding inbound to a satellite airport will be terminated at a sufficient distance to allow time to change to the appropriate tower or advisory frequency. Class C services to these aircraft will be discontinued when the aircraft is instructed to contact the tower or change to advisory frequency.

3. Aircraft departing secondary controlled airports will not receive Class C services until they have been radar identified and two-way communications have been established with the Class C airspace facility.

4. This program is not to be interpreted as relieving pilots of their responsibilities to see and avoid other traffic operating in basic VFR weather conditions, to adjust their operations

and flight path as necessary to preclude serious wake encounters, to maintain appropriate terrain and obstruction clearance or to remain in weather conditions equal to or better than the minimums required by 14 CFR Section 91.155. Approach control should be advised and a revised clearance or instruction obtained when compliance with an assigned route, heading and/or altitude is likely to compromise pilot responsibility with respect to terrain and obstruction clearance, vortex exposure, and weather minimums.

g. Class C Airspace Areas by State
These states currently have designated Class C airspace areas that are depicted on sectional charts. Pilots should consult current sectional charts and NOTAMs for the latest information on services available. Pilots should be aware that some Class C airspace underlies or is adjacent to Class B airspace (See Table 3-2-1).

TABLE 3–2–1

CLASS C AIRSPACE AREAS BY STATE	
State/City	**Airport**
Alabama	
Birmingham	Birmingham–Shuttlesworth International
Huntsville	International – Carl T. Jones Field
Mobile	Regional
Alaska	
Anchorage	Ted Stevens International
Arizona	
Davis-Monthan	AFB
Tucson	International
Arkansas	
Fayetteville (Springdale)	Northwest Arkansas Regional
Little Rock	Adams Field
California	
Beale	AFB
Burbank	Bob Hope
Fresno	Yosemite International
Monterey	Peninsula
Oakland	Metropolitan Oakland Int'l
Ontario	International
Riverside	March AFB
Sacramento	International
San Jose	Norman Y. Mineta International
Santa Ana	John Wayne / Orange County
Santa Barbara	Municipal
Colorado	
Colorado Springs	Municipal
Connecticut	
Windsor Locks	Bradley International

(continued)

CLASS C AIRSPACE AREAS BY STATE	
State/City	Airport
Florida	
Daytona Beach	International
Fort Lauderdale	Hollywood International
Fort Myers	SW Florida Regional
Jacksonville	International
Orlando	Sanford International
Palm Beach	International
Pensacola	NAS
Pensacola	Regional
Sarasota	Bradenton International
Tallahassee	Regional
Whiting	NAS
Georgia	
Savannah	Hilton Head International
Hawaii	
Kahului	Kahului
Idaho	
Boise	Air Terminal
Illinois	
Champaign	Urbana U of Illinois–Willard
Chicago	Midway International
Moline	Quad City International
Peoria	Greater Peoria Regional
Springfield	Abraham Lincoln Capital
Indiana	
Evansville	Regional
Fort Wayne	International
Indianapolis	International
South Bend	Regional
Iowa	
Cedar Rapids	The Eastern Iowa
Des Moines	International
Kansas	
Wichita	Mid-Continent
Kentucky	
Lexington	Blue Grass
Louisville	International–Standiford Field
Louisiana	
Baton Rouge	Metropolitan, Ryan Field
Lafayette	Regional
Shreveport	Barksdale AFB
Shreveport	Regional
Maine	
Bangor	International
Portland	International Jetport
Michigan	
Flint	Bishop International
Grand Rapids	Gerald R. Ford International
Lansing	Capital City
Mississippi	
Columbus	AFB
Jackson	Jackson–Evers International
Missouri	
Springfield	Springfield–Branson National

CLASS C AIRSPACE AREAS BY STATE	
State/City	Airport
Montana	
Billings	Logan International
Nebraska	
Lincoln	Lincoln
Omaha	Eppley Airfield
Offutt	AFB
Nevada	
Reno	Reno/Tahoe International
New Hampshire	
Manchester	Manchester
New Jersey	
Atlantic City	International
New Mexico	
Albuquerque	International Sunport
New York	
Albany	International
Buffalo	Niagra International
Islip	Long Island MacArthur
Rochester	Greater Rochester Int'l
Syracuse	Hancock International
North Carolina	
Asheville	Regional
Fayetteville	Regional/Grannis Field
Greensboro	Piedmont Triad International
Pope	AFB
Raleigh	Raleigh-Durham International
Ohio	
Akron	Akron-Canton Regional
Columbus	Port Columbus International
Dayton	James M. Cox International
Toledo	Express
Oklahoma	
Oklahoma City	Will Rogers World
Tinker	AFB
Tulsa	International
Oregon	
Portland	International
Pennsylvania	
Allentown	Lehigh Valley International
Puerto Rico	
San Juan	Luis Munoz Marin Int'l
Rhode Island	
Providence	Theodore Francis Green State
South Carolina	
Charleston	AFB/International
Columbia	Metropolitan
Greer	Greenville-Spartanburg International
Myrtle Beach	Myrtle Beach International
Shaw	AFB
Tennessee	
Chattanooga	Lovell Field
Knoxville	McGhee Tyson
Nashville	International

CLASS C AIRSPACE AREAS BY STATE	
State/City	**Airport**
Texas	
Abilene	Regional
Amarillo	Rick Husband International
Austin	Austin–Bergstrom Int'l
Corpus Christi	International
Dyess	AFB
El Paso	International
Harlingen	Valley International
Laughlin	AFB
Lubbock	Preston Smith International
Midland	International
San Antonio	International
Vermont	
Burlington	International
Virgin Islands	
St. Thomas	Charlotte Amalie Cyril E. King
Virginia	
Richmond	International
Norfolk	International
Roanoke	Regional/Woodrum Field
Washington	
Point Roberts	Vancouver International
Spokane	Fairchild AFB
Spokane	International
Whidbey Island	NAS, Ault Field
West Virginia	
Charleston	Yeager
Wisconsin	
Green Bay	Austin Straubel International
Madison	Dane County Regional–Traux Field
Milwaukee	General Mitchell International

3–2–5 Class D Airspace

a. Definition. Generally, Class D airspace extends upward from the surface to 2,500 feet above the airport elevation (charted in MSL) surrounding those airports that have an operational control tower. The configuration of each Class D airspace area is individually tailored and when instrument procedures are published, the airspace will normally be designed to contain the procedures.

1. Class D surface areas may be designated as full-time (24 hour tower operations) or part-time. Part-time Class D effective times are published in the Chart Supplement.

2. Where a Class D surface area is part-time, the airspace may revert to either a Class E surface area (see paragraph 3-2-6e1) or Class G airspace. When a part-time Class D surface area changes to Class G, the surface area becomes Class G airspace up to, but not including, the overlying controlled airspace.

Note 1. The airport listing in the Chart Supplement will state the part-time surface area status (for example, "other times CLASS E" or "other times CLASS G").

Note 2. Normally, the overlying controlled airspace is the Class E transition area airspace that begins at either 700 feet AGL (charted as magenta vignette) or 1200 feet AGL (charted as blue vignette). This may be determined by consulting the applicable VFR Sectional or Terminal Area Charts.

b. Operating Rules and Pilot/Equipment Requirements:

1. Pilot Certification. No specific certification required.

2. Equipment. Unless otherwise authorized by ATC, an operable two-way radio is required.

3. Arrival or Through Flight Entry Requirements. Two-way radio communication must be established with the ATC facility providing ATC services prior to entry and thereafter maintain those communications while in the Class D airspace. Pilots of arriving aircraft should contact the control tower on the publicized frequency and give their position, altitude, destination, and any request(s). Radio contact should be initiated far enough from the Class D airspace boundary to preclude entering the Class D airspace before two-way radio communications are established.

Note 1: If the controller responds to a radio call with, "[aircraft callsign] standby," radio communications have been established and the pilot can enter the Class D airspace.

Note 2: If workload or traffic conditions prevent immediate entry into Class D airspace, the controller will inform the pilot to remain outside the Class D airspace until conditions permit entry.

Example 1: "[Aircraft callsign] remain outside the Class Delta airspace and standby."

It is important to understand that if the controller responds to the initial radio call without using the aircraft callsign, radio communications have not been established and the pilot may not enter the Class D airspace.

Example 2: "Aircraft calling Manassas tower standby."

At those airports where the control tower does not operate 24 hours a day, the operating hours of the tower will be listed on the appropriate charts and in the Chart Supplement. During the hours the tower is not in operation, the Class E surface area rules or a combination of Class E rules to 700 feet above ground level and Class G rules to the surface will become applicable. Check the Chart Supplement for specifics.

4. Departures from:

(a) A primary or satellite airport with an operating control tower. Two-way radio communications must be established and maintained with the control tower, and thereafter as instructed by ATC while operating in the Class D airspace.

(b) A satellite airport without an operating control tower. Two-way radio communications must be established as soon as practicable after departing with the ATC facility having jurisdiction over the Class D airspace as soon as practicable after departing.

5. Aircraft Speed. Unless otherwise authorized or required by ATC, no person may operate an aircraft at or below 2,500 feet above the surface within 4 nautical miles of the primary airport of a Class D airspace area at an indicated airspeed of more than 200 knots (230 mph).

c. Class D airspace areas are depicted on Sectional and Terminal charts with blue segmented lines, and on IFR En Route Lows with a boxed [D].

d. Surface area arrival extensions:

1. Class D surface area arrival extensions for instrument approach procedures may be Class D or Class E airspace. As a general rule, if all extensions are 2 miles or less, they remain part of the Class D surface area. However, if any one extension is greater than 2 miles, then all extensions will be Class E airspace.

2. Surface area arrival extensions are effective during the published times of the surface area. For part-time Class D surface areas that revert to Class E airspace, the arrival extensions will remain in effect as Class E airspace. For part-time Class D surface areas that change to Class G airspace, the arrival extensions will become Class G at the same time.

e. Separation for VFR Aircraft. No separation services are provided to VFR aircraft.

3-2-6 Class E Airspace

a. Definition. Class E airspace is controlled airspace that is designated to serve a variety of terminal or en route purposes as described in this paragraph.

b. Operating Rules and Pilot/Equipment Requirements:

1. Pilot Certification. No specific certification required.

2. Equipment. Unless otherwise authorized by ATC:

(a) An operable radar beacon transponder with automatic altitude reporting capability and operable ADS-B Out equipment are required at and above 10,000 feet MSL within the 48 contiguous states and the District of Columbia, excluding the airspace at and below 2,500 feet above the surface, and

(b) Operable ADS-B Out equipment at and above 3,000 feet MSL over the Gulf of Mexico from the coastline of the United States out to 12 nautical miles.

Note: The airspace described in (b) is specified in 14 CFR §91.225 for ADS-B Out requirements. However, 14 CFR §91.215 does not include this airspace for transponder requirements.

3. Arrival or Through Flight Entry Requirements. No specific requirements.

c. Charts. Class E airspace below 14,500 feet MSL is charted on Sectional, Terminal, and IFR Enroute Low Altitude charts.

d. Vertical limits. Except where designated at a lower altitude (see paragraph 3-2-6e, below, for specifics), Class E airspace in the United States consists of:

1. The airspace extending upward from 14,500 feet MSL to, but not including, 18,000 feet MSL overlying the 48 contiguous states, the District of Columbia and Alaska, including the waters within nautical 12 miles from the coast of the 48 contiguous states and Alaska; excluding:

(a) The Alaska peninsula west of longitude 160°00'00"W.; and

(b) The airspace below 1,500 feet above the surface of the earth unless specifically designated lower (for example, in mountainous terrain higher than 13,000 feet MSL).

2. The airspace above FL 600 is Class E airspace.

e. Functions of Class E Airspace. Class E airspace may be designated for the following purposes:

1. Surface area designated for an airport where a control tower is not in operation. Class E surface areas extend upward from the surface to a designated altitude, or to the adjacent or overlying controlled airspace. The airspace will be configured to contain all instrument procedures.

(a) To qualify for a Class E surface area, the airport must have weather observation and reporting capability, and communications capability must exist with aircraft down to the runway surface.

(b) A Class E surface area may also be designated to accommodate part-time operations at a Class C or Class D airspace location (for example, those periods when the control tower is not in operation).

(c) Pilots should refer to the airport page in the applicable Chart Supplement for surface area status information.

2. Extension to a surface area. Class E airspace may be designated as extensions to Class B, Class C, Class D, and Class E surface areas. Class E airspace extensions begin at the

surface and extend up to the overlying controlled airspace. The extensions provide controlled airspace to contain standard instrument approach procedures without imposing a communications requirement on pilots operating under VFR. Surface area arrival extensions become part of the surface area and are in effect during the same times as the surface area.

Note: When a Class C or Class D surface area is not in effect continuously (for example, where a control tower only operates part-time), the surface area airspace will change to either a Class E surface area or Class G airspace. In such cases, the "Airspace" entry for the airport in the Chart Supplement will state "other times Class E" or "other times Class G." When a part-time surface area changes to Class E airspace, the Class E arrival extensions will remain in effect as Class E airspace. If a part-time Class C, Class D, or Class E surface area becomes Class G airspace, the arrival extensions will change to Class G at the same time.

3. Airspace used for transition. Class E airspace areas may be designated for transitioning aircraft to/from the terminal or en route environment.

(a) Class E transition areas extend upward from either 700 feet AGL (shown as magenta vignette on sectional charts) or 1,200 feet AGL (blue vignette) and are designated for airports with an approved instrument procedure.

(b) The 700-foot/1200-foot AGL Class E airspace transition areas remain in effect continuously, regardless of airport operating hours or surface area status.

Note: Do not confuse the 700-foot and 1200-foot Class E transition areas with surface areas or surface area extensions.

4. En Route Domestic Areas. There are Class E airspace areas that extend upward from a specified altitude and are en route domestic airspace areas that provide controlled airspace in those areas where there is a requirement to provide IFR en route ATC services but the Federal airway system is inadequate.

5. Federal Airways and Low-Altitude RNAV Routes. Federal airways and low-altitude RNAV routes are Class E airspace areas and, unless otherwise specified, extend upward from 1,200 feet AGL to, but not including, 18,000 feet MSL.

(a) Federal airways consist of Low/Medium Frequency (L/MF) airways (colored Federal airways) and VOR Federal airways.

(1) L/MF airways are based on non-directional beacons (NDB) and are identified as green, red, amber, or blue.

(2) VOR Federal airways are based on VOR/VORTAC facilities and are identified by a "V" prefix.

(b) Low-altitude RNAV routes consist of T-routes and helicopter RNAV routes (TK-routes).

Note: See AIM Paragraph 5-3-4, Airways and Route Systems, for more details and charting information.

6. Offshore Airspace Areas. There are Class E airspace areas that extend upward from a specified altitude to, but not including, 18,000 feet MSL and are designated as offshore airspace areas. These areas provide controlled airspace beyond 12 miles from the coast of the U.S. in those areas where there is a requirement to provide IFR en route ATC services and within which the U.S. is applying domestic procedures.

f. Separation for VFR Aircraft. No separation services are provided to VFR aircraft.

Section 3 Class G Airspace

3-3-1 General

Class G airspace (uncontrolled) is that portion of airspace that has not been designated as Class A, Class B, Class C, Class D, or Class E airspace.

3-3-2 VFR Requirements

Rules governing VFR flight have been adopted to assist the pilot in meeting the responsibility to see and avoid other aircraft. Minimum flight visibility and distance from clouds required for VFR flight are contained in 14 CFR Section 91.155. (See Table 3-1-1.)

3-3-3 IFR Requirements

a. Title 14 CFR specifies the pilot and aircraft equipment requirements for IFR flight. Pilots are reminded that in addition to altitude or flight level requirements, 14 CFR Section 91.177 includes a requirement to remain at least 1,000 feet (2,000 feet in designated mountainous terrain) above the highest obstacle within a horizontal distance of 4 nautical miles from the course to be flown.

b. IFR Altitudes. (See Table 3-3-1.)

TABLE 3-3-1
IFR ALTITUDES
CLASS G AIRSPACE

If your magnetic course (ground track) is:	And you are below 18,000 feet MSL, fly:
0° to 179°	Odd thousands MSL, (3,000; 5,000; 7,000, etc.)
180° to 359°	Even thousands MSL, (2,000; 4,000; 6,000, etc.)

Section 4 Special Use Airspace

3–4–1 General

a. Special use airspace (SUA) consists of that airspace wherein activities must be confined because of their nature, or wherein limitations are imposed upon aircraft operations that are not a part of those activities, or both. SUA areas are depicted on aeronautical charts, except for controlled firing areas (CFA), temporary military operations areas (MOA), and temporary restricted areas.

b. Prohibited and restricted areas are regulatory special use airspace and are established in 14 CFR Part 73 through the rulemaking process.

c. Warning areas, MOAs, alert areas, CFAs, and national security areas (NSA) are nonregulatory special use airspace.

d. Special use airspace descriptions (except CFAs) are contained in FAA Order JO 7400.10, Special Use Airspace.

e. Permanent SUA (except CFAs) is charted on Sectional Aeronautical, VFR Terminal Area, and applicable En Route charts, and include the hours of operation, altitudes, and the controlling agency.

Note: For temporary restricted areas and temporary MOAs, pilots should review the Domestic Notices found on the Federal NOTAM System (FNS) NOTAM Search website under External Links or the Air Traffic Plans and Publications website, the FAA SUA website, and/or contact the appropriate overlying ATC facility to determine the effect of non-depicted SUA areas along their routes of flight.

3–4–2 Prohibited Areas

Prohibited areas contain airspace of defined dimensions identified by an area on the surface of the earth within which the flight of aircraft is prohibited. Such areas are established for security or other reasons associated with the national welfare. These areas are published in the Federal Register and are depicted on aeronautical charts.

3–4–3 Restricted Areas

a. Restricted areas contain airspace identified by an area on the surface of the earth within which the flight of aircraft, while not wholly prohibited, is subject to restrictions. Activities within these areas must be confined because of their nature or limitations imposed upon aircraft operations that are not a part of those activities or both. Restricted areas denote the existence of unusual, often invisible, hazards to aircraft such as artillery firing, aerial gunnery, or guided missiles. Penetration of restricted areas without authorization from the using or controlling agency may be extremely hazardous to the aircraft and its occupants. Restricted areas are published in the Federal Register and constitute 14 CFR Part 73.

b. ATC facilities apply the following procedures when aircraft are operating on an IFR clearance (including those cleared by ATC to maintain VFR-on-top) via a route which lies within joint-use restricted airspace.

1. If the restricted area is not active and has been released to the controlling agency (FAA), the ATC facility will allow the aircraft to operate in the restricted airspace without issuing specific clearance for it to do so.

2. If the restricted area is active and has not been released to the controlling agency (FAA), the ATC facility will issue a clearance which will ensure the aircraft avoids the restricted airspace unless it is on an approved altitude reservation mission or has obtained its own permission to operate in the airspace and so informs the controlling facility.

Note: The above apply only to joint-use restricted airspace and not to prohibited and nonjoint-use airspace. For the latter categories, the ATC facility will issue a clearance so the aircraft will avoid the restricted airspace unless it is on an approved altitude reservation mission or has obtained its own permission to operate in the airspace and so informs the controlling facility.

c. Permanent restricted areas are charted on Sectional Aeronautical, VFR Terminal Area, and the appropriate En Route charts.

Note: Temporary restricted areas are not charted.

3–4–4 Warning Areas

A warning area is airspace of defined dimensions, extending from three nautical miles outward from the coast of the U.S., that contains activity that may be hazardous to nonparticipating aircraft. The purpose of such warning areas is to warn nonparticipating pilots of the potential danger. A warning area may be located over domestic or international waters or both.

3–4–5 Military Operations Areas

a. MOAs consist of airspace of defined vertical and lateral limits established for the purpose of separating certain military training activities from IFR traffic. Whenever a MOA is being used, nonparticipating IFR traffic may be cleared through a MOA if IFR separation can be provided by ATC. Otherwise, ATC will reroute or restrict nonparticipating IFR traffic.

b. Examples of activities conducted in MOAs include, but are not limited to: air combat tactics, air intercepts, aerobatics, formation training, and low-altitude tactics. Military pilots flying in an

active MOA are exempted from the provisions of 14 CFR Section 91.303(c) and (d) which prohibits aerobatic flight within Class D and Class E surface areas, and within Federal airways. Additionally, the Department of Defense has been issued an authorization to operate aircraft at indicated airspeeds in excess of 250 knots below 10,000 feet MSL within active MOAs.

c. Pilots operating under VFR should exercise extreme caution while flying within a MOA when military activity is being conducted. The activity status (active/inactive) of MOAs may change frequently. Therefore, pilots should contact any FSS within 100 miles of the area to obtain accurate real-time information concerning the MOA hours of operation. Prior to entering an active MOA, pilots should contact the controlling agency for traffic advisories.

d. Permanent MOAs are charted on Sectional Aeronautical, VFR Terminal Area, and the appropriate En Route Low Altitude charts.

Note: Temporary MOAs are not charted.

3–4–6 Alert Areas

Alert areas are depicted on aeronautical charts to inform nonparticipating pilots of areas that may contain a high volume of pilot training or an unusual type of aerial activity. Pilots should be particularly alert when flying in these areas. All activity within an alert area must be conducted in accordance with CFRs, without waiver, and pilots of participating aircraft as well as pilots transiting the area must be equally responsible for collision avoidance.

3–4–7 Controlled Firing Areas

CFAs contain activities which, if not conducted in a controlled environment, could be hazardous to nonparticipating aircraft. The distinguishing feature of the CFA, as compared to other special use airspace, is that its activities are suspended immediately when spotter aircraft, radar, or ground lookout positions indicate an aircraft might be approaching the area. There is no need to chart CFAs since they do not cause a nonparticipating aircraft to change its flight path.

3–4–8 National Security Areas

NSAs consist of airspace of defined vertical and lateral dimensions established at locations where there is a requirement for increased security and safety of ground facilities. Pilots are requested to voluntarily avoid flying through the depicted NSA. When it is necessary to provide a greater level of security and safety, flight in NSAs may be temporarily prohibited by regulation under the provisions of 14 CFR Section 99.7. Regulatory prohibitions will be issued by System Operations Security and disseminated via NOTAM. Inquiries about NSAs should be directed to System Operations Security.

Reference: AIM, ¶5-6-1, National Security.

3–4–9 Obtaining Special Use Airspace Status

a. Pilots can request the status of SUA by contacting the using or controlling agency. The frequency for the controlling agency is tabulated in the margins of the applicable IFR and VFR charts.

b. An airspace NOTAM will be issued for SUA when the SUA airspace (permanent and/or temporary) requires a NOTAM for activation. Pilots should check ARTCC NOTAMs for airspace activation.

c. Special Use Airspace Information Service (SUAIS) (Alaska Only). The SUAIS is a 24-hour service operated by the military that provides civilian pilots, flying VFR, with information regarding military flight operations in certain MOAs and restricted airspace within central Alaska. The service provides "near real time" information on military flight activity in the interior Alaska MOA and Restricted Area complex. SUAIS also provides information on artillery firing, known helicopter operations, and unmanned aerial vehicle operations. Pilots flying VFR are encouraged to use SUAIS. See the Alaska Chart Supplement for hours of operation, phone numbers, and radio frequencies.

d. Special use airspace scheduling data for preflight planning is available via the FAA SUA website.

Section 5 Other Airspace Areas

3-5-1 Airport Advisory/Information Services

a. There are two advisory type services available at selected airports.

1. Local Airport Advisory (LAA) service is available only in Alaska and is operated within 10 statute miles of an airport where a control tower is not operating but where a FSS is located on the airport. At such locations, the FSS provides a complete local airport advisory service to arriving and departing aircraft. During periods of fast changing weather the FSS will automatically provide Final Guard as part of the service from the time the aircraft reports "on-final" or "taking-the-active-runway" until the aircraft reports "on-the-ground" or "airborne."

Note: Current policy, when requesting remote ATC services, requires that a pilot monitor the automated weather broadcast at the landing airport prior to requesting ATC services. The FSS automatically provides Final Guard, when appropriate, during LAA/Remote Airport Advisory (RAA) operations. Final Guard is a value added wind/altimeter monitoring service, which provides an automatic wind and altimeter check during active weather situations when the pilot reports on-final or taking the active runway. During the landing or take-off operation when the winds or altimeter are actively changing the FSS will blind broadcast significant changes when the specialist believes the change might affect the operation. Pilots should acknowledge the first wind/altimeter check but due to cockpit activity no acknowledgement is expected for the blind broadcasts. It is prudent for a pilot to report on-the-ground or airborne to end the service.

2. Remote Airport Information Service (RAIS) is provided in support of short term special events like small to medium fly-ins. The service is advertised by NOTAM D only. The FSS will not have access to a continuous readout of the current winds and altimeter; therefore, RAIS does not include weather and/or Final Guard service. However, known traffic, special event instructions, and all other services are provided.

Note: The airport authority and/or manager should request RAIS support on official letterhead directly with the manager of the FSS that will provide the service at least 30 days in advance. Approval authority rests with the FSS manager and is based on workload and resource availability.

Reference: AIM, ¶4-1-9, Traffic Advisory Practices at Airports Without Operating Control Towers.

b. It is not mandatory that pilots participate in the Airport Advisory programs. Participation enhances safety for everyone operating around busy GA airports; therefore, everyone is encouraged to participate and provide feedback that will help improve the program.

3-5-2 Military Training Routes

a. National security depends largely on the deterrent effect of our airborne military forces. To be proficient, the military services must train in a wide range of airborne tactics. One phase of this training involves "low level" combat tactics. The required maneuvers and high speeds are such that they may occasionally make the see-and-avoid aspect of VFR flight more difficult without increased vigilance in areas containing such operations. In an effort to ensure the greatest practical level of safety for all flight operations, the Military Training Route (MTR) program was conceived.

b. The MTR program is a joint venture by the FAA and the Department of Defense (DOD). MTRs are mutually developed for use by the military for the purpose of conducting low-altitude, high-speed training. The routes above 1,500 feet AGL are developed to be flown, to the maximum extent possible, under IFR. The routes at 1,500 feet AGL and below are generally developed to be flown under VFR.

c. Generally, MTRs are established below 10,000 feet MSL for operations at speeds in excess of 250 knots. However, route segments may be defined at higher altitudes for purposes of route continuity. For example, route segments may be defined for descent, climbout, and mountainous terrain. There are IFR and VFR routes as follows:

1. IFR Military Training Routes—(IR). Operations on these routes are conducted in accordance with IFR regardless of weather conditions.

2. VFR Military Training Routes—(VR). Operations on these routes are conducted in accordance with VFR except flight visibility must be 5 miles or more; and flights must not be conducted below a ceiling of less than 3,000 feet AGL.

d. Military training routes will be identified and charted as follows:

1. Route identification.

(a) MTRs with no segment above 1,500 feet AGL must be identified by four number characters; e.g., IR1206, VR1207.

(b) MTRs that include one or more segments above 1,500 feet AGL must be identified by three number characters; e.g., IR206, VR207.

(c) Alternate IR/VR routes or route segments are identified by using the basic/principal route designation followed by a letter suffix, e.g., IR008A, VR1007B, etc.

2. Route charting.

(a) IFR Enroute Low Altitude Chart. This chart will depict all IR routes and all VR routes that accommodate operations above 1,500 feet AGL.

(b) VFR Sectional Aeronautical Charts. These charts will depict military training activities such as IR and VR information.

(c) Area Planning (AP/1B) Chart (DOD Flight Information Publication—FLIP). This chart is published by the National Geospatial-Intelligence Agency (NGA) primarily for military users and contains detailed information on both IR and VR routes.

Reference: AIM, ¶9-1-5, Subparagraph a, National Geospatial-Intelligence Agency (NGA) Products.

e. DoD FLIP—Department of Defense Flight Information Publications describe IR/VR routes through charts and narratives, and the FAA provides information regarding these routes to all users via IFR and VFR charts.

Note: DoD users that require copies of FLIP should contact:

Defense Logistics Agency for Aviation
Mapping Customer Operations (DLA AVN/QAM)
8000 Jefferson Davis Highway
Richmond, VA 23297-5339
Toll free phone: 1-800-826-0342
Commercial: 804-279-6500

MTR information from the FLIP is available for pilot briefings through Flight Service. (See subparagraph f below.)

f. Availability of MTR information.

1. Pilots may obtain preflight MTR information through Flight Service (see paragraph 5-1-1, Preflight Preparation).

2. MTR routes are depicted on IFR En Route Low Altitude Charts and VFR Sectional Charts, which are available for free download on the FAA website at https://www.faa.gov/air_traffic /flight_info/aeronav/digital_products/.

g. Nonparticipating aircraft are not prohibited from flying within an MTR; however, extreme vigilance should be exercised when conducting flight through or near these routes. Pilots, while inflight, should contact the FSS within 100 NM of a particular MTR to obtain current information or route usage in their vicinity. Information available includes times of scheduled activity, altitudes in use on each route segment, and actual route width. Route width varies for each MTR and can extend several miles on either side of the charted MTR centerline. Route width information for IFR Military Training Route (IR) and VFR Military Training Route (VR) MTRs is also available in the FLIP AP/1B along with additional MTR (slow routes/air refueling routes) information. When requesting

MTR information, pilots should give the FSS their position, route of flight, and destination in order to reduce frequency congestion and permit the FSS specialist to identify the MTR which could be a factor.

3–5–3 Temporary Flight Restrictions

a. General. This paragraph describes the types of conditions under which the FAA may impose temporary flight restrictions. It also explains which FAA elements have been delegated authority to issue a temporary flight restrictions NOTAM and lists the types of responsible agencies/offices from which the FAA will accept requests to establish temporary flight restrictions. The 14 CFR is explicit as to what operations are prohibited, restricted, or allowed in a temporary flight restrictions area. Pilots are responsible to comply with 14 CFR Sections 91.137, 91.138, 91.141 and 91.143 when conducting flight in an area where a temporary flight restrictions area is in effect, and should check appropriate NOTAMs during flight planning.

b. The purpose for establishing a temporary flight restrictions area is to:

1. Protect persons and property in the air or on the surface from an existing or imminent hazard associated with an incident on the surface when the presence of low flying aircraft would magnify, alter, spread, or compound that hazard (14 CFR Section 91.137(a)(1));

2. Provide a safe environment for the operation of disaster relief aircraft (14 CFR Section 91.137(a)(2)); or

3. Prevent an unsafe congestion of sightseeing aircraft above an incident or event which may generate a high degree of public interest (14 CFR Section 91.137(a)(3)).

4. Protect declared national disasters for humanitarian reasons in the State of Hawaii (14 CFR Section 91.138).

5. Protect the President, Vice President, or other public figures (14 CFR Section 91.141).

6. Provide a safe environment for space agency operations (14 CFR Section 91.143).

c. Except for hijacking situations, when the provisions of 14 CFR Section 91.137(a)(1) or (a)(2) are necessary, a temporary flight restrictions area will only be established by or through the area manager at the Air Route Traffic Control Center (ARTCC) having jurisdiction over the area concerned. A temporary flight restrictions NOTAM involving the conditions of 14 CFR Section 91.137(a)(3) will be issued at the direction of the service area office director having oversight of the airspace concerned. When hijacking situations are involved, a temporary flight restrictions area will be implemented through the TSA Aviation Command Center. The appropriate FAA air traffic element, upon receipt of such a request,

will establish a temporary flight restrictions area under 14 CFR Section 91.137(a)(1).

d. The FAA accepts recommendations for the establishment of a temporary flight restrictions area under 14 CFR Section 91.137(a)(1) from military major command headquarters, regional directors of the Office of Emergency Planning, Civil Defense State Directors, State Governors, or other similar authority. For the situations involving 14 CFR Section 91.137(a)(2), the FAA accepts recommendations from military commanders serving as regional, subregional, or Search and Rescue (SAR) coordinators; by military commanders directing or coordinating air operations associated with disaster relief; or by civil authorities directing or coordinating organized relief air operations (includes representatives of the Office of Emergency Planning, U.S. Forest Service, and State aeronautical agencies). Appropriate authorities for a temporary flight restrictions establishment under 14 CFR Section 91.137(a)(3) are any of those listed above or by State, county, or city government entities.

e. The type of restrictions issued will be kept to a minimum by the FAA consistent with achievement of the necessary objective. Situations which warrant the extreme restrictions of 14 CFR Section 91.137(a)(1) include, but are not limited to: toxic gas leaks or spills, flammable agents, or fumes which if fanned by rotor or propeller wash could endanger persons or property on the surface, or if entered by an aircraft could endanger persons or property in the air; imminent volcano eruptions which could endanger airborne aircraft and occupants; nuclear accident or incident; and hijackings. Situations which warrant the restrictions associated with 14 CFR Section 91.137(a)(2) include: forest fires which are being fought by releasing fire retardants from aircraft; and aircraft relief activities following a disaster (earthquake, tidal wave, flood, etc.). 14 CFR Section 91.137(a)(3) restrictions are established for events and incidents that would attract an unsafe congestion of sightseeing aircraft.

f. The amount of airspace needed to protect persons and property or provide a safe environment for rescue/relief aircraft operations is normally limited to within 2,000 feet above the surface and within a 3-nautical-mile radius. Incidents occurring within Class B, Class C, or Class D airspace will normally be handled through existing procedures and should not require the issuance of a temporary flight restrictions NOTAM. Temporary flight restrictions affecting airspace outside of the U.S. and its territories and possessions are issued with verbiage excluding that airspace outside of the 12-mile coastal limits.

g. The FSS nearest the incident site is normally the "coordination facility." When FAA communications assistance is required, the designated FSS will function as the primary communications facility for coordination between emergency control authorities and affected aircraft. The ARTCC may act as liaison for the emergency control authorities if adequate communications cannot be established between the designated FSS and the relief organization. For example, the coordination facility may relay authorizations from the on-scene emergency response official in cases where news media aircraft operations are approved at the altitudes used by relief aircraft.

h. ATC may authorize operations in a temporary flight restrictions area under its own authority only when flight restrictions are established under 14 CFR Section 91.137(a)(2) and (a)(3). The appropriate ARTCC/airport traffic control tower manager will, however, ensure that such authorized flights do not hamper activities or interfere with the event for which restrictions were implemented. However, ATC will not authorize local IFR flights into the temporary flight restrictions area.

i. To preclude misunderstanding, the implementing NOTAM will contain specific and formatted information. The facility establishing a temporary flight restrictions area will format a NOTAM beginning with the phrase "FLIGHT RESTRICTIONS" followed by: the location of the temporary flight restrictions area; the effective period; the area defined in statute miles; the altitudes affected; the FAA coordination facility and commercial telephone number; the reason for the temporary flight restrictions; the agency directing any relief activities and its commercial telephone number; and other information considered appropriate by the issuing authority.

Example 1: 14 CFR Section 91.137(a)(1)

The following NOTAM prohibits all aircraft operations except those specified in the NOTAM.

Flight restrictions Matthews, Virginia, effective immediately until 9610211200. Pursuant to 14 CFR Section 91.137(a)(1) temporary flight restrictions are in effect. Rescue operations in progress. Only relief aircraft operations under the direction of the Department of Defense are authorized in the airspace at and below 5,000 feet MSL within a 2-nautical-mile radius of Laser AFB, Matthews, Virginia. Commander, Laser AFB, in charge (897) 946-5543 (122.4). Steenson FSS (792) 555-6141 (123.1) is the FAA coordination facility.

Example 2: 14 CFR Section 91.137(a)(2)

The following NOTAM permits flight operations in accordance with 14 CFR Section 91.137(a)(2). The on-site emergency response official to authorize media aircraft operations below the altitudes used by the relief aircraft.

Flight restrictions 25 miles east of Bransome, Idaho, effective immediately until 9601202359 UTC. Pursuant to 14 CFR Section 91.137(a)(2)

temporary flight restrictions are in effect within a 4-nautical-mile radius of the intersection of county roads 564 and 315 at and below 3,500 feet MSL to provide a safe environment for fire fighting aircraft operations. Davis County sheriff's department (792) 555-8122 (122.9) is in charge of on-scene emergency response activities. Glivings FSS (792) 555-1618 (122.2) is the FAA coordination facility.

Example 3: 14 CFR Section 91.137(a)(3)

The following NOTAM prohibits sightseeing aircraft operations.

Flight restrictions Brown, Tennessee, due to Olympic activity. Effective 9606181100 UTC until 9607190200 UTC. Pursuant to 14 CFR Section 91.137(a)(3) temporary flight restrictions are in effect within a 3-nautical-mile radius of N355783/W835242 and Volunteer VORTAC 019 degree radial 3.7 DME fix at and below 2,500 feet MSL. Norton FSS (423) 555-6742 (126.6) is the FAA coordination facility.

Example 4: 14 CFR Section 91.138

The following NOTAM prohibits all aircraft except those operating under the authorization of the official in charge of associated emergency or disaster relief response activities, aircraft carrying law enforcement officials, aircraft carrying personnel involved in an emergency or legitimate scientific purposes, carrying properly accredited news media, and aircraft operating in accordance with an ATC clearance or instruction.

Flight restrictions Kapalua, Hawaii, effective 9605101200 UTC until 9605151500 UTC. Pursuant to 14 CFR Section 91.138 temporary flight restrictions are in effect within a 3-nautical-mile radius of N205778/W1564038 and Maui/OGG/VORTAC 275 degree radial at 14.1 nautical miles. John Doe 808-757-4469 or 122.4 is in charge of the operation. Honolulu/HNL 808-757-4470 (123.6) FSS is the FAA coordination facility.

Example 5: 14 CFR Section 91.141

The following NOTAM prohibits all aircraft.

Flight restrictions Stillwater, Oklahoma, June 21, 1996. Pursuant to 14 CFR Section 91.141 aircraft flight operations are prohibited within a 3-nautical-mile radius, below 2000 feet AGL of N360962/W970515 and the Stillwater/SWO/VOR/DME 176 degree radial 3.8- nautical-mile fix from 1400 local time to 1700 local time June 21, 1996, unless otherwise authorized by ATC.

Example 6: 14 CFR Section 91.143

The following NOTAM prohibits any aircraft of U.S. registry, or pilot any aircraft under the authority of an airman certificate issued by the FAA.

Kennedy space center space operations area effective immediately until 9610152100 UTC. Pursuant to 14 CFR Section 91.143, flight operations conducted by FAA certificated pilots or conducted in aircraft of U.S. registry are prohibited at any altitude from surface to unlimited, within the following area 30-nautical-mile radius of the Melbourne/MLB/VORTAC 010 degree radial 21-nautical-mile fix. St. Petersburg, Florida/PIE/FSS 813-545-1645 (122.2) is the FAA coordination facility and should be contacted for the current status of any airspace associated with the space shuttle operations. This airspace encompasses R2933, R2932, R2931, R2934, R2935, W497A and W158A. Additional warning and restricted areas will be active in conjunction with the operations. Pilots must consult all NOTAMs regarding this operation.

3–5–4 Parachute Jump Aircraft Operations

a. Procedures relating to parachute jump areas are contained in 14 CFR Part 105. Tabulations of parachute jump areas in the U.S. are contained in the Chart Supplement.

b. Pilots of aircraft engaged in parachute jump operations are reminded that all reported altitudes must be with reference to mean sea level, or flight level, as appropriate, to enable ATC to provide meaningful traffic information.

c. Parachute operations in the vicinity of an airport without an operating control tower—there is no substitute for alertness while in the vicinity of an airport. It is essential that pilots conducting parachute operations be alert, look for other traffic, and exchange traffic information as recommended in paragraph 4-1-9, Traffic Advisory Practices at Airports Without Operating Control Towers. In addition, pilots should avoid releasing parachutes while in an airport traffic pattern when there are other aircraft in that pattern. Pilots should make appropriate broadcasts on the designated Common Traffic Advisory Frequency (CTAF), and monitor that CTAF until all parachute activity has terminated or the aircraft has left the area. Prior to commencing a jump operation, the pilot should broadcast the aircraft's altitude and position in relation to the airport, the approximate relative time when the jump will commence and terminate, and listen to the position reports of other aircraft in the area.

3–5–5 Published VFR Routes

Published VFR routes for transitioning around, under and through complex airspace such as Class B airspace were developed through a number of FAA and industry initiatives. All of the following terms, i.e., "VFR Flyway" "VFR Corridor" and "Class B Airspace VFR Transition Route" have been used when referring to the same or different types of routes or airspace. The following paragraphs identify and clarify the functionality of each type of route, and specify where and when an ATC clearance is required.

a. VFR Flyways.

1. VFR Flyways and their associated Flyway Planning Charts were developed from the recommendations of a National Airspace Review Task Group. A VFR Flyway is defined as a general flight path not defined as a specific course, for use by pilots in planning flights into, out of, through or near complex terminal airspace to avoid Class B airspace. An ATC clearance is NOT required to fly these routes.

2. VFR Flyways are depicted on the reverse side of some of the VFR Terminal Area Charts (TAC), commonly referred to as Class B airspace charts. (See Figure 3-5-1.) Eventually all TACs will include a VFR Flyway Planning Chart. These charts identify VFR flyways designed to help VFR pilots avoid major controlled traffic flows. They may further depict multiple VFR routings throughout the area which may be used as an alternative to flight within Class B airspace. The ground references provide a guide for improved visual navigation. These routes are not intended to discourage requests for VFR operations within Class B airspace but are designed solely to assist pilots in planning for flights under and around busy Class B airspace without actually entering Class B airspace.

3. It is very important to remember that these suggested routes are not sterile of other traffic. The entire Class B airspace, and the airspace underneath it, may be heavily congested with many different types of aircraft. Pilot adherence to VFR rules must be exercised at all times. Further, when operating beneath Class B airspace, communications must be established and maintained between your aircraft and any control tower while transiting the Class B, Class C, and Class D surface areas of those airports under Class B airspace.

Ch 3

FIGURE 3–5–1
VFR Flyway Planning Chart

b. VFR Corridors.

1. The design of a few of the first Class B airspace areas provided a corridor for the passage of uncontrolled traffic. A VFR corridor is defined as airspace through Class B airspace, with defined vertical and lateral boundaries, in which aircraft may operate without an ATC clearance or communication with air traffic control.

2. These corridors are, in effect, a "hole" through Class B airspace. (See Figure 3-5-2.) A classic example would be the corridor through the Los Angeles Class B airspace, which has been subsequently changed to Special Flight Rules airspace (SFR). A corridor is surrounded on all sides by Class B airspace and does not extend down to the surface like a VFR Flyway. Because of their finite lateral and vertical limits, and the volume of VFR traffic using a corridor, extreme caution and vigilance must be exercised.

FIGURE 3–5–2
Class B Airspace

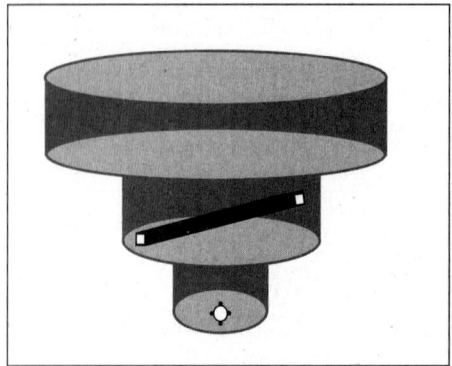

3. Because of the heavy traffic volume and the procedures necessary to efficiently manage the flow of traffic, it has not been possible to incorporate VFR corridors in the development or modifications of Class B airspace in recent years.

c. Class B Airspace VFR Transition Routes.

1. To accommodate VFR traffic through certain Class B airspace, such as Seattle, Phoenix and Los Angeles, Class B Airspace VFR Transition Routes were developed. A Class B Airspace VFR Transition Route is defined as a specific flight course depicted on a TAC for transiting a specific Class B airspace. These routes include specific ATC-assigned altitudes, and pilots must obtain an ATC clearance prior to entering Class B airspace on the route.

2. These routes, as depicted in Figure 3-5-3, are designed to show the pilot where to position the aircraft outside of, or clear of, the Class B airspace where an ATC clearance can normally be expected with minimal or no delay. Until ATC authorization is received, pilots must remain clear of Class B airspace. On initial contact, pilots should advise ATC of their position, altitude, route name desired, and direction of flight. After a clearance is received, pilots must fly the route as depicted and, most importantly, adhere to ATC instructions.

3-5-6 Terminal Radar Service Area (TRSA)

a. Background. TRSAs were originally established as part of the Terminal Radar Program at selected airports. TRSAs were never controlled airspace from a regulatory standpoint because the establishment of TRSAs was never subject to the rulemaking process; consequently, TRSAs are not contained in 14 CFR Part 71 nor are there any TRSA operating rules in 14 CFR Part 91. Part of the Airport Radar Service Area (ARSA) program was to eventually replace all TRSAs. However, the ARSA requirements became relatively stringent and it was subsequently decided that TRSAs would have to meet ARSA criteria before they would be converted. TRSAs do not fit into any of the U.S. airspace classes; therefore, they will continue to be non-Part 71 airspace areas where participating pilots can receive additional radar services which have been redefined as TRSA Service.

b. TRSAs. The primary airport(s) within the TRSA become(s) Class D airspace. The remaining portion of the TRSA overlies other controlled airspace which is normally Class E airspace beginning at 700 or 1,200 feet and established to transition to/from the en route/terminal environment.

c. Participation. Pilots operating under VFR are encouraged to contact the radar approach control and avail themselves of the TRSA Services. However, participation is voluntary on the part of the pilot. See Chapter 4, Air Traffic Control, for details and procedures.

d. Charts. TRSAs are depicted on VFR sectional and terminal area charts with a solid black line and altitudes for each segment. The Class D portion is charted with a blue segmented line.

3-5-7 Special Air Traffic Rules (SATR) and Special Flight Rules Area (SFRA)

a. Background. The Code of Federal Regulations (CFR) prescribes special air traffic rules for aircraft operating within the boundaries of certain designated airspace. These areas are listed in 14 CFR Part 93 and can be found throughout the NAS. Procedures, nature of operations, configuration, size, and density of traffic vary among the identified areas.

FIGURE 3–5–3
VFR Transition Route

Phoenix
VFR Transition Route
(ATC clearance required)
⟺ ⟺
Altitude assigned by ATC

This chart also identifies VFR transition routes in the Phoenix Class B airspace. Operation on these routes requires ATC authorization from Phoenix Approach Control. Until authorization is received, remain outside Class B airspace. Depiction of these routes is to assist pilots in positioning the aircraft in an area outside the Class B airspace where ATC clearance can normally be expected with minimal or no delay. On initial contact, advise ATC of position altitude, route name desired and direction of flight. Refer to current Phoenix VFR Terminal Area Chart for user requirements.

(Not to be used for navigation)

b. SFRAs. Airspace of defined dimensions, above land areas or territorial waters, within which the flight of aircraft is subject to the rules set forth in 14 CFR Part 93, unless otherwise authorized by air traffic control. Not all areas listed in 14 CFR Part 93 are designated SFRA, but special air traffic rules apply to all areas described in 14 CFR Part 93.

Reference: 14 CFR Part 93, Special Air Traffic Rules; FAA Order JO 7110.65, ¶9-2-10, Special Air Traffic Rules (SATR) and Special Flight Rules

Area (SFRA); Pilot/Controller Glossary—Special Air Traffic Rules (SATR)

c. Participation. Each person operating an aircraft to, from, or within airspace designated as a SATR area or SFRA must adhere to the special air traffic rules set forth in 14 CFR Part 93, as applicable, unless otherwise authorized or required by ATC.

d. Charts. SFRAs are depicted on VFR sectional, terminal area, and helicopter route charts. (See Figure 3-5-4.)

FIGURE 3–5–4
SFRA Boundary

FIGURE 3–5–4
SFRA Boundary

e. Additional information and resources regarding SFRA, including procedures for flight in individual areas, may be found on the FAA Safety website at www.faasafety.gov.

3-5-8 Washington, DC, Special Flight Rules Area (SFRA) including the Flight Restricted Zone (FRZ)

A pilot conducting any type of flight operation in the Washington, DC, SFRA/FRZ must comply with the requirements in:

a. 14 CFR Section 93.339, Washington, DC, Metropolitan Area Special Flight Rules Area including the FRZ.

b. 14 CFR Section 91.161, Special Awareness Training for the DC SFRA/FRZ, also located on the FAA website at https://www.faasafety.gov/.

c. Any 14 CFR Section 99.7 special security instructions for the DC SFRA/FRZ published via NOTAM by FAA in the interest of national security.

3-5-9 Weather Reconnaissance Area (WRA)

a. General. Hurricane Hunters from the United States Air Force Reserve 53rd Weather Reconnaissance Squadron (WRS) and the National Oceanic and Atmospheric Administration (NOAA) Aircraft Operations Center (AOC) operate weather reconnaissance/research aircraft missions, in support of the National Hurricane Operations Plan (NHOP), to gather meteorological data on hurricanes and tropical cyclones. 53rd WRS and NOAA AOC aircraft normally conduct these missions in airspace identified in a published WRA Notice to Air Missions (NOTAM).

b. WRAs. Airspace with defined dimensions and published by a NOTAM, which is established to support weather reconnaissance/research flights. ATC services are not provided within WRAs. Only participating weather reconnaissance/research aircraft from the 53rd WRS and NOAA AOC are permitted to operate within a WRA. A WRA may only be established in airspace within U.S. Flight Information Regions (FIR) outside of U.S. territorial airspace.

c. A published WRA NOTAM describes the airspace dimensions of the WRA and the expected activities within the WRA. WRAs may border adjacent foreign FIRs, but are wholly contained within U.S. FIRs. As ATC services are not provided within a WRA, non-participating aircraft should avoid WRAs, and IFR aircraft should expect to be rerouted to avoid WRAs.

3-5-10 Other Non-Charted Airspace Areas

a. Stationary or Moving Altitude Reservation (ALTRV). A Stationary or Moving ALTRV is announced via an airspace NOTAM issued by the Central Altitude Reservation Facility (CARF) or ARTCC. These announcements will appear in CARF and/or ARTCC NOTAMs. This airspace ensures non-participating IFR aircraft remain separated from special activity. Non-participating VFR aircraft are permitted to fly through the area but should exercise vigilance.

b. ATC ASSIGNED AIRSPACE. Airspace of defined vertical/lateral limits, assigned by ATC, for the purpose of providing air traffic segregation between the specified activities being conducted within the assigned airspace and other IFR air traffic. ATCAA locations and scheduled activation information can be found on the FAA SUA website; a NOTAM will not be issued to announce the activation of this airspace.

Chapter 4
Air Traffic Control

Section 1 Services Available to Pilots

4-1-1 Air Route Traffic Control Centers

Centers are established primarily to provide air traffic service to aircraft operating on IFR flight plans within controlled airspace, and principally during the en route phase of flight.

4-1-2 Control Towers

Towers have been established to provide for a safe, orderly and expeditious flow of traffic on and in the vicinity of an airport. When the responsibility has been so delegated, towers also provide for the separation of IFR aircraft in the terminal areas.

Reference: AIM, ¶5-4-3, Approach Control.

4-1-3 Flight Service Stations

Flight Service Stations (FSSs) are air traffic facilities that provide pilot briefings, flight plan processing, en route flight advisories, search and rescue services, and assistance to lost aircraft and aircraft in emergency situations. FSSs also relay ATC clearances, process Notices to Air Missions, and broadcast aviation weather and aeronautical information. In Alaska, designated FSSs also take weather observations, and provide Airport Advisory Services (AAS).

4-1-4 Recording and Monitoring

a. Calls to air traffic control (ATC) facilities (ARTCCs, Towers, FSSs, Central Flow, and Operations Centers) over radio and ATC operational telephone lines (lines used for operational purposes such as controller instructions, briefings, opening and closing flight plans, issuance of IFR clearances and amendments, counter hijacking activities, etc.) may be monitored and recorded for operational uses such as accident investigations, accident prevention, search and rescue purposes, specialist training and evaluation, and technical evaluation and repair of control and communications systems.

b. Where the public access telephone is recorded, a beeper tone is not required. In place of the "beep" tone the FCC has substituted a mandatory requirement that persons to be recorded be given notice they are to be recorded and give consent. Notice is given by this entry, consent to record is assumed by the individual placing a call to the operational facility.

4-1-5 Communications Release of IFR Aircraft Landing at an Airport Without an Operating Control Tower

Aircraft operating on an IFR flight plan, landing at an airport without an operating control tower will be advised to change to the airport advisory frequency when direct communications with ATC are no longer required. Towers and centers do not have nontower airport traffic and runway in use information. The instrument approach may not be aligned with the runway in use; therefore, if the information has not already been obtained, pilots should make an expeditious change to the airport advisory frequency when authorized.

Reference: AIM, ¶5-4-4, Advance Information on Instrument Approach.

4-1-6 Pilot Visits to Air Traffic Facilities

Pilots are encouraged to participate in local pilot/air traffic control outreach activities. However, due to security and workload concerns, requests for air traffic facility visits may not always be approved. Therefore, visit requests should be submitted through the air traffic facility as early as possible. Pilots should contact the facility and advise them of the number of persons in the group, the time and date of the proposed visit, and the primary interest of the group. The air traffic facility will provide further instructions if a request can be approved.

Reference: FAA Order 1600.69, FAA Facility Security Management Program

4-1-7 Operation Rain Check

Operation Rain Check is a program designed and managed by local air traffic control facility management. Its purpose is to familiarize pilots and aspiring pilots with the ATC system, its functions, responsibilities and benefits.

Reference: FAA Order JO 7210.3, ¶4-2-2, Pilot Education; FAA Order 1600.69, FAA Facility Security Management Program

4-1-8 Approach Control Service for VFR Arriving Aircraft

a. Numerous approach control facilities have established programs for arriving VFR aircraft to contact approach control for landing information. This information includes: wind, runway, and altimeter setting at the airport of intended landing. This information may be omitted if contained in the Automatic Terminal Information Service (ATIS) broadcast and the pilot states the appropriate ATIS code.

Note: Pilot use of "have numbers" does not indicate receipt of the ATIS broadcast. In addition, the controller will provide traffic advisories on a workload permitting basis.

b. Such information will be furnished upon initial contact with concerned approach control facility. The pilot will be requested to change to the tower frequency at a predetermined time or point, to receive further landing information.

c. Where available, use of this procedure will not hinder the operation of VFR flights by requiring excessive spacing between aircraft or devious routing.

d. Compliance with this procedure is not mandatory but pilot participation is encouraged.

Reference: AIM, ¶4-1-18, Terminal Radar Services for VFR Aircraft.

Note: Approach control services for VFR aircraft are normally dependent on ATC radar. These services are not available during periods of a radar outage.

4-1-9 Traffic Advisory Practices at Airports Without Operating Control Towers

(See Table 4-1-1.)

a. Airport Operations Without Operating Control Tower

1. There is no substitute for alertness while in the vicinity of an airport. It is essential that pilots be alert and look for other traffic and exchange traffic information when approaching or departing an airport without an operating control tower. This is of particular importance since other aircraft may not have communication capability or, in some cases, pilots may not communicate their presence or intentions when operating into or out of such airports. To achieve the greatest degree of safety, it is essential that:

(a) All radio-equipped aircraft transmit/receive on a common frequency identified for the purpose of airport advisories; and

(b) Pilots use the correct airport name, as identified in appropriate aeronautical publications, to reduce the risk of confusion when communicating their position, intentions, and/or exchanging traffic information.

2. An airport may have a full or part-time tower or FSS located on the airport, a full or part-time UNICOM station or no aeronautical station at all. There are three ways for pilots to communicate their intention and obtain airport/traffic information when operating at an airport that does not have an operating tower: by communicating with an FSS, a UNICOM operator, or by making a self-announce broadcast.

Note: FSS airport advisories are available only in Alaska.

3. Many airports are now providing completely automated weather, radio check capability and airport advisory information on an automated UNICOM system. These systems offer a variety of features, typically selectable by microphone clicks, on the UNICOM frequency. Availability of the automated UNICOM will be published in the Chart Supplement and approach charts. ∎

b. Communicating on a Common Frequency

1. The key to communicating at an airport without an operating control tower is selection of the correct common frequency. The acronym CTAF which stands for Common Traffic Advisory Frequency, is synonymous with this program. A CTAF is a frequency designated for the purpose of carrying out airport advisory practices while operating to or from an airport without an operating control tower. The CTAF may be a UNICOM, MULTICOM, FSS, or tower frequency and is identified in appropriate aeronautical publications.

Note: FSS frequencies are available only in Alaska.

2. CTAF (Alaska Only). In Alaska, a CTAF may also be designated for the purpose of carrying out advisory practices while operating in designated areas with a high volume of VFR traffic.

3. The CTAF frequency for a particular airport or area is contained in the Chart Supplement U.S., Chart Supplement Alaska, Alaska Terminal Publication, Instrument Approach Procedure Charts, and Instrument Departure Procedure (DP) Charts. Also, the CTAF frequency can be obtained by contacting any FSS. Use of the appropriate CTAF, combined with a visual alertness and application of the following recommended good operating practices, will enhance safety of flight into and out of all uncontrolled airports.

c. Recommended Traffic Advisory Practices

1. Pilots of inbound traffic should monitor and communicate as appropriate on the designated CTAF from 10 miles to landing. Pilots of departing aircraft should monitor/communicate on the appropriate frequency from start-up, during taxi, and until 10 miles from the airport unless the CFRs or local procedures require otherwise.

TABLE 4–1–1
SUMMARY OF RECOMMENDED COMMUNICATION PROCEDURES

	Facility at Airport	Frequency Use	Communication/Broadcast Procedures		
			Outbound	Inbound	Practice Instrument Approach
1.	UNICOM (No Tower or FSS)	Communicate with UNICOM station on published CTAF frequency (122.7; 122.8; 122.725; 122.975; or 123.0). If unable to contact UNICOM station, use self-announce procedures on CTAF.	Before taxiing and before taxiing on the runway for departure.	10 miles out. Entering downwind, base, and final. Leaving the runway.	
2.	No Tower, FSS, or UNICOM	Self-announce on MULTICOM frequency 122.9.	Before taxiing and before taxiing on the runway for departure.	10 miles out. Entering downwind, base, and final. Leaving the runway.	Departing final approach fix (name) or on final approach segment inbound.
3.	No Tower in operation, FSS open (Alaska only)	Communicate with FSS on CTAF frequency.	Before taxiing and before taxiing on the runway for departure.	10 miles out. Entering downwind, base, and final. Leaving the runway.	Approach completed/ terminated.
4.	FSS Closed (No Tower)	Self-announce on CTAF.	Before taxiing and before taxiing on the runway for departure.	10 miles out. Entering downwind, base, and final. Leaving the runway.	
5.	Tower or FSS not in operation	Self-announce on CTAF.	Before taxiing and before taxiing on the runway for departure.	10 miles out. Entering downwind, base, and final. Leaving the runway.	
6.	Designated CTAF Area (Alaska only)	Self-announce on CTAF designated on chart or Chart Supplement Alaska.	Before taxiing and before taxiing on the runway for departure until leaving designated area.	When entering designated CTAF area.	

Ch 4

2. Pilots of aircraft conducting other than arriving or departing operations at altitudes normally used by arriving and departing aircraft should monitor/communicate on the appropriate frequency while within 10 miles of the airport unless required to do otherwise by the CFRs or local procedures. Such operations include parachute jumping/dropping, en route, practicing maneuvers, etc.

3. In Alaska, pilots of aircraft conducting other than arriving or departing operations in designated CTAF areas should monitor/communicate on the appropriate frequency while within the designated area, unless required to do otherwise by CFRs or local procedures. Such operations include parachute jumping/dropping, en route, practicing maneuvers, etc.

Reference: AIM, ¶3-5-4, Parachute Jump Aircraft Operations.

d. Airport Advisory/Information Services Provided by a FSS

1. There are two advisory type services provided at selected airports.

(a) Local Airport Advisory (LAA) is available only in Alaska and provided at airports that have a FSS physically located on the airport, which does not have a control tower or where the tower is operated on a part-time basis. The CTAF for LAA airports is disseminated in the appropriate aeronautical publications.

(b) Remote Airport Information Service (RAIS) is provided in support of special events at nontowered airports by request from the airport authority.

2. In communicating with a CTAF FSS, check the airport's automated weather and establish two-way communications before transmitting outbound/inbound intentions or information. An inbound aircraft should initiate contact approximately 10 miles from the airport, reporting aircraft identification and type, altitude, location relative to the airport, intentions (landing or over

flight), possession of the automated weather, and request airport advisory or airport information service. A departing aircraft should initiate contact before taxiing, reporting aircraft identification and type, VFR or IFR, location on the airport, intentions, direction of take-off, possession of the automated weather, and request airport advisory or information service. Also, report intentions before taxiing onto the active runway for departure. If you must change frequencies for other service after initial report to FSS, return to FSS frequency for traffic update.

(a) Inbound

Example: Vero Beach radio, Centurion Six Niner Delta Delta is ten miles south, two thousand, landing Vero Beach. I have the automated weather, request airport advisory.

(b) Outbound

Example: Vero Beach radio, Centurion Six Niner Delta Delta, ready to taxi to runway 22, VFR, departing to the southwest. I have the automated weather, request airport advisory.

3. Airport advisory service includes wind direction and velocity, favored or designated runway, altimeter setting, known airborne and ground traffic, NOTAMs, airport taxi routes, airport traffic pattern information, and instrument approach procedures. These elements are varied so as to best serve the current traffic situation. Some airport managers have specified that under certain wind or other conditions designated runways be used. Pilots should advise the FSS of the runway they intend to use.

Caution: All aircraft in the vicinity of an airport may not be in communication with the FSS.

e. Information Provided by Aeronautical Advisory Stations (UNICOM)

1. UNICOM is a nongovernment air/ground radio communication station which may provide airport information at public use airports where there is no tower or FSS.

2. On pilot request, UNICOM stations may provide pilots with weather information, wind direction, the recommended runway, or other necessary information. If the UNICOM frequency is designated as the CTAF, it will be identified in appropriate aeronautical publications.

f. Unavailability of Information from FSS or UNICOM

Should LAA by an FSS or Aeronautical Advisory Station UNICOM be unavailable, wind and weather information may be obtainable from nearby controlled airports via Automatic Terminal Information Service (ATIS) or Automated Weather Observing System (AWOS) frequency.

g. Self-Announce Position and/or Intentions

1. **General.** Self-announce is a procedure whereby pilots broadcast their position or intended flight activity or ground operation on the designated CTAF. This procedure is used primarily at airports which do not have an FSS on the airport. The self-announce procedure should also be used if a pilot is unable to communicate with the FSS on the designated CTAF. Pilots stating, *"Traffic in the area, please advise"* is not a recognized Self-Announce Position and/or Intention phrase and should not be used under any condition.

2. If an airport has a tower and it is temporarily closed, or operated on a part-time basis and there is no FSS on the airport or the FSS is closed, use the CTAF to self-announce your position or intentions.

3. Where there is no tower, FSS, or UNICOM station on the airport, use MULTICOM frequency 122.9 for self-announce procedures. Such airports will be identified in appropriate aeronautical information publications.

4. **Straight-in Landings.** The FAA discourages VFR straight-in approaches to landings due to the increased risk of a mid-air collision. However, if a pilot chooses to execute a straight-in approach for landing without entering the airport traffic pattern, the pilot should self-announce their position on the designated CTAF approximately 8 to 10 miles from the airport and coordinate their straight-in approach and landing with other airport traffic. Pilots executing a straight-in approach (IFR or VFR) do not have priority over other aircraft in the traffic pattern, and must comply with the provisions of 14 CFR 91.113 (g), Right-of-way rules.

5. **Traffic Pattern Operations.** All traffic within a 10-mile radius of a non-towered airport or a part-time-towered airport when the control tower is not operating, should monitor and communicate on the designated CTAF when entering the traffic pattern. Pilots operating in the traffic pattern or on a straight-in approach must be alert at all times to other aircraft in the pattern, or conducting straight-in approaches, and communicate their position to avoid a possible traffic conflict. In the airport traffic pattern and while on straight-in approaches to a runway, effective communication and a pilot's responsibility to see-and-avoid are essential mitigations to avoid a possible midair collision. In addition, following established traffic pattern procedures eliminates excessive maneuvering at low altitudes, reducing the risk of loss of aircraft control.

Reference: FAA Advisory Circular (AC) 90-66, Non-Towered Airport Flight Operations.

6. Practice Approaches. Pilots conducting practice instrument approaches should be particularly alert for other aircraft that may be departing in the opposite direction. When conducting any practice approach, regardless of its direction relative to other airport operations, pilots should make announcements on the CTAF as follows:

(a) Departing the final approach fix, inbound (nonprecision approach) or departing the outer marker or fix used in lieu of the outer marker, inbound (precision approach);

(b) Established on the final approach segment or immediately upon being released by ATC;

(c) Upon completion or termination of the approach; and

(d) Upon executing the missed approach procedure.

7. Departing aircraft should always be alert for arrival aircraft coming from the opposite direction.

8. Recommended self-announce broadcasts: It should be noted that aircraft operating to or from another nearby airport may be making self-announce broadcasts on the same UNICOM or MULTICOM frequency. To help identify one airport from another, the airport name should be spoken at the beginning and end of each self-announce transmission. When referring to a specific runway, pilots should use the runway number and not use the phrase "Active Runway."

(a) Inbound

Example: Strawn traffic, Apache Two Two Five Zulu, (position), (altitude), (descending) or entering downwind/base/final (as appropriate) runway one seven full stop, touch-and-go, Strawn.

Strawn traffic Apache Two Two Five Zulu clear of runway one seven Strawn.

(b) Outbound

Example: Strawn traffic, Queen Air Seven One Five Five Bravo (location on airport) taxiing to runway two six Strawn.

Strawn traffic, Queen Air Seven One Five Five Bravo departing runway two six. Departing the pattern to the (direction), climbing to (altitude) Strawn.

(c) Practice Instrument Approach

Example: Strawn traffic, Cessna Two One Four Three Quebec (position from airport) inbound descending through (altitude) practice (name of approach) approach runway three five Strawn.

Strawn traffic, Cessna Two One Four Three Quebec practice (type) approach completed or terminated runway three five Strawn.

h. UNICOM Communications Procedures

1. In communicating with a UNICOM station, the following practices will help reduce frequency congestion, facilitate a better understanding of pilot intentions, help identify the location of aircraft in the traffic pattern, and enhance safety of flight:

(a) Select the correct UNICOM frequency.

(b) State the identification of the UNICOM station you are calling in each transmission.

(c) Speak slowly and distinctly.

(d) Report approximately 10 miles from the airport, reporting altitude, and state your aircraft type, aircraft identification, location relative to the airport, state whether landing or overflight, and request wind information and runway in use.

(e) Report on downwind, base, and final approach.

(f) Report leaving the runway.

2. Recommended UNICOM phraseologies:

(a) Inbound

Phraseology:
Frederick Unicom Cessna Eight Zero One Tango Foxtrot 10 Miles Southeast Descending Through (altitude) Landing Frederick, Request Wind And Runway Information Frederick.

Frederick Traffic Cessna Eight Zero One Tango Foxtrot Entering Downwind/Base/Final (as appropriate) For Runway One Niner (full stop/touch-and-go) Frederick.

Frederick Traffic Cessna Eight Zero One Tango Foxtrot Clear Of Runway One Niner Frederick.

(b) Outbound

Phraseology:
Frederick Unicom Cessna Eight Zero One Tango Foxtrot (location on airport) Taxiing To Runway One Niner, Request Wind And Traffic Information Frederick.

Frederick Traffic Cessna Eight Zero One Tango Foxtrot Departing Runway One Niner. "Remaining In The Pattern" Or "Departing The Pattern To The (direction) (as appropriate)" Frederick.

4–1–10 IFR Approaches/Ground Vehicle Operations

a. IFR Approaches. When operating in accordance with an IFR clearance and ATC approves a change to the advisory frequency, make an expeditious change to the CTAF and employ the recommended traffic advisory procedures.

b. Ground Vehicle Operation. Airport ground vehicles equipped with radios should monitor the CTAF frequency when operating on the airport movement area and remain clear of runways/taxiways being used by aircraft. Radio transmissions from ground vehicles should be confined to safety-related matters.

c. Radio Control of Airport Lighting Systems. Whenever possible, the CTAF will be used to control airport lighting systems at airports without operating control towers. This eliminates the

need for pilots to change frequencies to turn the lights on and allows a continuous listening watch on a single frequency. The CTAF is published on the instrument approach chart and in other appropriate aeronautical information publications.

4-1-11 Designated UNICOM/ MULTICOM Frequencies

Frequency use

a. The following listing depicts UNICOM and MULTICOM frequency uses as designated by the Federal Communications Commission (FCC). (See Table 4-1-2.)

TABLE 4–1–2
UNICOM/MULTICOM FREQUENCY USAGE

Use	Frequency
Airports without an operating control tower.	122.700 122.725 122.800 122.975 123.000 123.050 123.075
(MULTICOM FREQUENCY) Activities of a temporary, seasonal, emergency nature or search and rescue, as well as, airports with no tower, FSS, or UNICOM.	122.900
(MULTICOM FREQUENCY) Forestry management and fire suppression, fish and game management and protection, and environmental monitoring and protection.	122.925
Airports with a control tower or FSS on airport.	122.950

Note 1: *In some areas of the country, frequency interference may be encountered from nearby airports using the same UNICOM frequency. Where there is a problem, UNICOM operators are encouraged to develop a "least interference" frequency assignment plan for airports concerned using the frequencies designated for airports without operating control towers. UNICOM licensees are encouraged to apply for UNICOM 25 kHz spaced channel frequencies. Due to the extremely limited number of frequencies with 50 kHz channel spacing, 25 kHz channel spacing should be implemented. UNICOM licensees may then request FCC to assign frequencies in accordance with the plan, which FCC will review and consider for approval.*

Note 2: *Wind direction and runway information may not be available on UNICOM frequency 122.950.*

b. The following listing depicts other frequency uses as designated by the Federal Communications Commission (FCC). (See Table 4-1-3.)

TABLE 4–1–3
OTHER FREQUENCY USAGE DESIGNATED BY FCC

Use	Frequency
Air-to-air communication (private fixed wing aircraft).	122.750
Helicopter air-to-air communications; air traffic control operations.	123.025
Aviation instruction, Glider, Hot Air Balloon **(not to be used for advisory service).**	123.300 123.500
Assignment to flight test land and aircraft stations (not for air-to-air communication except for those aircraft operating in an oceanic FIR).	123.400[1] 123.450[2]

[1] This frequency is available only to itinerant stations that have a requirement to be periodically transferred to various locations.

[2] Mobile station operations on these frequencies are limited to an area within 320 km (200 mi) of an associated flight test land station.

4-1-12 Use of UNICOM for ATC Purposes

UNICOM service may be used for ATC purposes, only under the following circumstances:

a. Revision to proposed departure time.

b. Takeoff, arrival, or flight plan cancellation time.

c. ATC clearance, provided arrangements are made between the ATC facility and the UNICOM licensee to handle such messages.

4-1-13 Automatic Terminal Information Service (ATIS)

a. ATIS is the continuous broadcast of recorded noncontrol information in selected high activity terminal areas. Its purpose is to improve controller effectiveness and to relieve frequency congestion by automating the repetitive transmission of essential but routine information. The information is continuously broadcast over a discrete VHF radio frequency or the voice portion of a local NAVAID. Arrival ATIS transmissions on a discrete VHF radio frequency are engineered according to the individual facility requirements, which would normally be a protected service volume of 20 NM to 60 NM from the ATIS site and a maximum altitude of 25,000 feet AGL. In the case of a departure ATIS, the protected service volume cannot exceed 5 NM and 100 feet AGL. At most locations, ATIS signals may be received on the surface of the airport, but local conditions may limit the maximum ATIS reception distance and/or altitude. Pilots are urged to cooperate in the ATIS program as it relieves frequency congestion on approach control, ground control, and local control frequencies. The Chart Supplement indicates airports for which ATIS is provided.

b. ATIS information includes:
1. Airport/facility name
2. Phonetic letter code
3. Time of the latest weather sequence (UTC)
4. Weather information consisting of:
 (a) Wind direction and velocity
 (b) Visibility
 (c) Obstructions to vision
 (d) Present weather consisting of: sky condition, temperature, dew point, altimeter, a density altitude advisory when appropriate, and other pertinent remarks included in the official weather observation
5. Instrument approach and runway in use.

The ceiling/sky condition, visibility, and obstructions to vision may be omitted from the ATIS broadcast if the ceiling is above 5,000 feet and the visibility is more than 5 miles. The departure runway will only be given if different from the landing runway except at locations having a separate ATIS for departure. The broadcast may include the appropriate frequency and instructions for VFR arrivals to make initial contact with approach control. Pilots of aircraft arriving or departing the terminal area can receive the continuous ATIS broadcast at times when cockpit duties are least pressing and listen to as many repeats as desired. ATIS broadcast must be updated upon the receipt of any official hourly and special weather. A new recording will also be made when there is a change in other pertinent data such as runway change, instrument approach in use, etc.

Example: "Dulles International information Sierra. One four zero zero zulu. Wind three five zero at eight. Visibility one zero. Ceiling four thousand five hundred broken. Temperature three four. Dew point two eight. Altimeter three zero one zero. ILS runway one right approach in use. Departing runway three zero. Advise on initial contact you have information sierra."

c. Pilots should listen to ATIS broadcasts whenever ATIS is in operation.

d. Pilots should notify controllers on initial contact that they have received the ATIS broadcast by repeating the alphabetical code word appended to the broadcast.

Example: "Information Sierra received."

e. When a pilot acknowledges receipt of the ATIS broadcast, controllers may omit those items contained in the broadcast if they are current. Rapidly changing conditions will be issued by ATC and the ATIS will contain words as follows:

Example: "Latest ceiling/visibility/altimeter/wind/ (other conditions) will be issued by approach control/tower."

Note: The absence of a sky condition or ceiling and/or visibility on ATIS indicates a sky condition or ceiling of 5,000 feet or above and visibility of 5 miles or more. A remark may be made on the broadcast, "the weather is better than 5,000 and 5," or the existing weather may be broadcast.

f. Controllers will issue pertinent information to pilots who do not acknowledge receipt of a broadcast or who acknowledge receipt of a broadcast which is not current.

g. To serve frequency limited aircraft, FSSs are equipped to transmit on the omnirange frequency at most en route VORs used as ATIS voice outlets. Such communication interrupts the ATIS broadcast. Pilots of aircraft equipped to receive on other FSS frequencies are encouraged to do so in order that these override transmissions may be kept to an absolute minimum.

h. While it is a good operating practice for pilots to make use of the ATIS broadcast where it is available, some pilots use the phrase "have numbers" in communications with the control tower. Use of this phrase means that the pilot has received wind, runway, and altimeter information ONLY and the tower does not have to repeat this information. It does not indicate receipt of the ATIS broadcast and should never be used for this purpose.

4-1-14 Automatic Flight Information Service (AFIS)—Alaska FSSs Only

a. AFIS is the continuous broadcast of recorded non-control information at airports in Alaska where an FSS provides local airport advisory service. Its purpose is to improve FSS specialist efficiency by reducing frequency congestion on the local airport advisory frequency.

1. The AFIS broadcast will automate the repetitive transmission of essential but routine information (for example, weather, favored runway, braking action, airport NOTAMs, etc.). The information is continuously broadcast over a discrete VHF radio frequency (usually the ASOS frequency).

2. Use of AFIS is not mandatory, but pilots who choose to utilize two-way radio communications with the FSS are urged to listen to AFIS, as it relieves frequency congestion on the local airport advisory frequency. AFIS broadcasts are updated upon receipt of any official hourly and special weather, and changes in other pertinent data.

3. When a pilot acknowledges receipt of the AFIS broadcast, FSS specialists may omit those items contained in the broadcast if they are current. When rapidly changing conditions exist, the latest ceiling, visibility, altimeter, wind or other conditions may be omitted from the AFIS and will

be issued by the FSS specialist on the appropriate radio frequency.

Example: *"Kotzebue information ALPHA. One six five five zulu. Wind, two one zero at five; visibility two, fog; ceiling one hundred overcast; temperature minus one two, dew point minus one four; altimeter three one zero five. Altimeter in excess of three zero zero zero, high pressure altimeter setting procedures are in effect. Favored runway two six. Weather in Kotzebue surface area is below V-F-R minima—an ATC clearance is required. Contact Kotzebue Radio on 123.6 for traffic advisories and advise intentions. Notice to Air Missions, Hotham NDB out of service. Transcribed Weather Broadcast out of service. Advise on initial contact you have ALPHA."*

Note: *The absence of a sky condition or ceiling and/or visibility on Alaska FSS AFIS indicates a sky condition or ceiling of 5,000 feet or above and visibility of 5 miles or more. A remark may be made on the broadcast, "the weather is better than 5,000 and 5."*

b. Pilots should listen to Alaska FSSs AFIS broadcasts whenever Alaska FSSs AFIS is in operation.

Note: *Some Alaska FSSs are open part time and/or seasonally.*

c. Pilots should notify controllers on initial contact that they have received the Alaska FSSs AFIS broadcast by repeating the phonetic alphabetic letter appended to the broadcast.

Example: *"Information Alpha received."*

d. While it is a good operating practice for pilots to make use of the Alaska FSS AFIS broadcast where it is available, some pilots use the phrase "have numbers" in communications with the FSS. Use of this phrase means that the pilot has received wind, runway, and altimeter information ONLY and the Alaska FSS does not have to repeat this information. It does not indicate receipt of the AFIS broadcast and should never be used for this purpose.

4-1-15 Radar Traffic Information Service

This is a service provided by radar ATC facilities. Pilots receiving this service are advised of any radar target observed on the radar display which may be in such proximity to the position of their aircraft or its intended route of flight that it warrants their attention. This service is not intended to relieve the pilot of the responsibility for continual vigilance to see and avoid other aircraft.

a. Purpose of the Service
1. The issuance of traffic information as observed on a radar display is based on the principle of assisting and advising a pilot that a particular

radar target's position and track indicates it may intersect or pass in such proximity to that pilot's intended flight path that it warrants attention. This is to alert the pilot to the traffic, to be on the lookout for it, and thereby be in a better position to take appropriate action should the need arise.

2. Pilots are reminded that the surveillance radar used by ATC does not provide altitude information unless the aircraft is equipped with Mode C and the radar facility is capable of displaying altitude information.

b. Provisions of the Service
1. Many factors, such as limitations of the radar, volume of traffic, controller workload and communications frequency congestion, could prevent the controller from providing this service. Controllers possess complete discretion for determining whether they are able to provide or continue to provide this service in a specific case. The controller's reason against providing or continuing to provide the service in a particular case is not subject to question nor need it be communicated to the pilot. In other words, the provision of this service is entirely dependent upon whether controllers believe they are in a position to provide it. Traffic information is routinely provided to all aircraft operating on IFR flight plans except when the pilot declines the service, or the pilot is operating within Class A airspace. Traffic information may be provided to flights not operating on IFR flight plans when requested by pilots of such flights.

Note: *Radar ATC facilities normally display and monitor both primary and secondary radar as well as ADS-B, except that secondary radar or ADS-B may be used as the sole display source in Class A airspace, and under some circumstances outside of Class A airspace (beyond primary coverage and in en route areas where only secondary and/or ADS-B is available). Secondary radar and/or ADS-B may also be used outside Class A airspace as the sole display source when the primary radar is temporarily unusable or out of service. Pilots in contact with the affected ATC facility are normally advised when a temporary outage occurs; i.e., "primary radar out of service; traffic advisories available on transponder or ADS-B aircraft only." This means simply that only aircraft that have transponders and ADS-B installed and in use will be depicted on ATC displays when the primary and/or secondary radar is temporarily out of service.*

2. When receiving VFR radar advisory service, pilots should monitor the assigned frequency at all times. This is to preclude controllers' concern for radio failure or emergency assistance to aircraft under the controller's jurisdiction. VFR radar advisory service does not include vectors away from conflicting traffic unless requested by

the pilot. When advisory service is no longer desired, advise the controller before changing frequencies and then change your transponder code to 1200, if applicable. Pilots should also inform the controller when changing VFR cruising altitude. Except in programs where radar service is automatically terminated, the controller will advise the aircraft when radar is terminated.

Note: *Participation by VFR pilots in formal programs implemented at certain terminal locations constitutes pilot request. This also applies to participating pilots at those locations where arriving VFR flights are encouraged to make their first contact with the tower on the approach control frequency.*

c. Issuance of Traffic Information. Traffic information will include the following concerning a target which may constitute traffic for an aircraft that is:

1. Radar identified

(a) Azimuth from the aircraft in terms of the 12 hour clock, or

(b) When rapidly maneuvering civil test or military aircraft prevent accurate issuance of traffic as in (a) above, specify the direction from an aircraft's position in terms of the eight cardinal compass points (N, NE, E, SE, S, SW, W, NW). This method must be terminated at the pilot's request.

(c) Distance from the aircraft in nautical miles;

(d) Direction in which the target is proceeding; and

(e) Type of aircraft and altitude if known.

Example: *Traffic 10 o'clock, 3 miles, west-bound (type aircraft and altitude, if known, of the observed traffic). The altitude may be known, by means of Mode C, but not verified with the pilot for accuracy. (To be valid for separation purposes by ATC, the accuracy of Mode C readouts must be verified. This is usually accomplished upon initial entry into the radar system by a comparison of the readout to pilot stated altitude, or the field elevation in the case of continuous readout being received from an aircraft on the airport.) When necessary to issue traffic advisories containing unverified altitude information, the controller will issue the indicated altitude of the aircraft. The pilot may upon receipt of traffic information, request a vector (heading) to avoid such traffic. The vector will be provided to the extent possible as determined by the controller provided the aircraft to be vectored is within the airspace under the jurisdiction of the controller.*

2. Not radar identified

(a) Distance and direction with respect to a fix;

(b) Direction in which the target is proceeding; and

(c) Type of aircraft and altitude if known.

Example: *Traffic 8 miles south of the airport northeastbound, (type aircraft and altitude if known).*

d. The examples depicted in the following figures point out the possible error in the position of this traffic when it is necessary for a pilot to apply drift correction to maintain this track. This error could also occur in the event a change in course is made at the time radar traffic information is issued.

FIGURE 4–1–1
Induced Error in Position of Traffic

Example: *In Figure 4-1-1 traffic information would be issued to the pilot of aircraft "A" as 12 o'clock. The actual position of the traffic as seen by the pilot of aircraft "A" would be 2 o'clock. Traffic information issued to aircraft "B" would also be given as 12 o'clock, but in this case, the pilot of "B" would see the traffic at 10 o'clock.*

FIGURE 4–1–2
Induced Error in Position of Traffic

Example: *In Figure 4-1-2 traffic information would be issued to the pilot of aircraft "C" as 2 o'clock. The actual position of the traffic as seen by the pilot of aircraft "C" would be 3 o'clock. Traffic information issued to aircraft "D" would be at an 11 o'clock position. Since it is not necessary for the pilot of aircraft "D" to apply wind correction (crab) to remain on track, the actual position of the traffic issued would be correct. Since the radar controller can only observe aircraft track (course) on the radar display, traffic advisories are issued accordingly, and pilots should give due consideration to this fact when looking for reported traffic.*

4-1-16 Safety Alert

A safety alert will be issued to pilots of aircraft being controlled by ATC if the controller is aware the aircraft is at an altitude which, in the controller's judgment, places the aircraft in unsafe proximity to terrain, obstructions or other aircraft. The provision of this service is contingent upon the capability of the controller to have an awareness of a situation involving unsafe proximity to terrain, obstructions and uncontrolled aircraft. The issuance of a safety alert cannot be mandated, but it can be expected on a reasonable, though intermittent basis. Once the alert is issued, it is solely the pilot's prerogative to determine what course of action, if any, to take. This procedure is intended for use in time critical situations where aircraft safety is in question. Noncritical situations should be handled via the normal traffic alert procedures.

a. Terrain or Obstruction Alert

1. Controllers will immediately issue an alert to the pilot of an aircraft under their control when they recognize that the aircraft is at an altitude which, in their judgment, may be in an unsafe proximity to terrain/obstructions. The primary method of detecting unsafe proximity is through Mode C automatic altitude reports.

Example: *Low altitude alert Cessna Three Four Juliett, check your altitude immediately. And if the aircraft is not yet on final approach, the MVA (MEA/MIA/MOCA) in your area is six thousand.*

2. Most En Route and Terminal radar facilities have an automated function which, if operating, alerts controllers when a tracked Mode C equipped aircraft under their control is below or is predicted to be below a predetermined minimum safe altitude. This function, called Minimum Safe Altitude Warning (MSAW), is designed solely as a controller aid in detecting potentially unsafe aircraft proximity to terrain/obstructions. The radar facility will, when MSAW is operating, provide MSAW monitoring for all aircraft with an operating Mode C altitude encoding transponder that are tracked by the system and are:

(a) Operating on an IFR flight plan; or

(b) Operating VFR and have requested MSAW monitoring.

Note: *Pilots operating VFR may request MSAW monitoring if their aircraft are equipped with Mode C transponders.*

Example: *Apache Three Three Papa request MSAW monitoring.*

3. Due to the lack of terrain and obstacle clearance data, accurate automation databases may not be available for providing MSAW information to aircraft overflying Mexico and Canada. Air traffic facilities along the United States/Mexico/Canada borders may have MSAW computer processing inhibited where accurate terrain data is not available.

b. Aircraft Conflict Alert.

1. Controllers will immediately issue an alert to the pilot of an aircraft under their control if they are aware of another aircraft which is not under their control, at an altitude which, in the controller's judgment, places both aircraft in unsafe proximity to each other. With the alert, when feasible, the controller will offer the pilot the position of the traffic if time permits and an alternate course(s) of action. Any alternate course(s) of action the controller may recommend to the pilot will be predicated only on other traffic being worked by the controller.

Example: *American Three, traffic alert, (position of traffic, if time permits), advise you turn right/left heading (degrees) and/or climb/descend to (altitude) immediately.*

4-1-17 Radar Assistance to VFR Aircraft

a. Radar equipped FAA ATC facilities provide radar assistance and navigation service (vectors) to VFR aircraft provided the aircraft can communicate with the facility, are within radar coverage, and can be radar identified.

b. Pilots should clearly understand that authorization to proceed in accordance with such radar navigational assistance does not constitute authorization for the pilot to violate CFRs. In effect, assistance provided is on the basis that navigational guidance information issued is advisory in nature and the job of flying the aircraft safely, remains with the pilot.

c. In many cases, controllers will be unable to determine if flight into instrument conditions will result from their instructions. To avoid possible hazards resulting from being vectored into IFR conditions, pilots should keep controllers advised of the weather conditions in which they are operating and along the course ahead.

d. Radar navigation assistance (vectors) may be initiated by the controller when one of the following conditions exist:

1. The controller suggests the vector and the pilot concurs.

2. A special program has been established and vectoring service has been advertised.

3. In the controller's judgment the vector is necessary for air safety.

e. Radar navigation assistance (vectors) and other radar derived information may be provided in response to pilot requests. Many factors, such as limitations of radar, volume of traffic, communications frequency, congestion, and controller workload could prevent the controller from providing it. Controllers have complete discretion for

determining if they are able to provide the service in a particular case. Their decision not to provide the service in a particular case is not subject to question.

4-1-18 Terminal Radar Services for VFR Aircraft

a. Basic Radar Service:

1. In addition to the use of radar for the control of IFR aircraft, all commissioned radar facilities provide the following basic radar services for VFR aircraft:

(a) Safety alerts.

(b) Traffic advisories.

(c) Limited radar vectoring (on a workload permitting basis).

(d) Sequencing at locations where procedures have been established for this purpose and/or when covered by a Letter of Agreement.

Note: When the stage services were developed, two basic radar services (traffic advisories and limited vectoring) were identified as "Stage I." This definition became unnecessary and the term "Stage I" was eliminated from use. The term "Stage II" has been eliminated in conjunction with the airspace reclassification, and sequencing services to locations with local procedures and/or letters of agreement to provide this service have been included in basic services to VFR aircraft. These basic services will still be provided by all terminal radar facilities whether they include Class B, Class C, Class D or Class E airspace. "Stage III" services have been replaced with "Class B" and "TRSA" service where applicable.

2. Vectoring service may be provided when requested by the pilot or with pilot concurrence when suggested by ATC.

3. Pilots of arriving aircraft should contact approach control on the publicized frequency and give their position, altitude, aircraft call sign, type aircraft, radar beacon code (if transponder equipped), destination, and request traffic information.

4. Approach control will issue wind and runway, except when the pilot states "have numbers" or this information is contained in the ATIS broadcast and the pilot states that the current ATIS information has been received. Traffic information is provided on a workload permitting basis. Approach control will specify the time or place at which the pilot is to contact the tower on local control frequency for further landing information. Radar service is automatically terminated and the aircraft need not be advised of termination when an arriving VFR aircraft receiving radar services to a tower-controlled airport where basic radar service is provided has landed, or to all other airports, is instructed to change to tower or advisory frequency. (See FAA Order JO 7110.65, Air Traffic Control, paragraph 5-1-9, Radar Service Termination.)

5. Sequencing for VFR aircraft is available at certain terminal locations (see locations listed in the Chart Supplement). The purpose of the service is to adjust the flow of arriving VFR and IFR aircraft into the traffic pattern in a safe and orderly manner and to provide radar traffic information to departing VFR aircraft. Pilot participation is urged but is not mandatory. Traffic information is provided on a workload permitting basis. Standard radar separation between VFR or between VFR and IFR aircraft is not provided.

(a) Pilots of arriving VFR aircraft should initiate radio contact on the publicized frequency with approach control when approximately 25 miles from the airport at which sequencing services are being provided. On initial contact by VFR aircraft, approach control will assume that sequencing service is requested. After radar contact is established, the pilot may use pilot navigation to enter the traffic pattern or, depending on traffic conditions, approach control may provide the pilot with routings or vectors necessary for proper sequencing with other participating VFR and IFR traffic en route to the airport. When a flight is positioned behind a preceding aircraft and the pilot reports having that aircraft in sight, the pilot will be instructed to follow the preceding aircraft. THE ATC INSTRUCTION TO FOLLOW THE PRECEDING AIRCRAFT DOES NOT AUTHORIZE THE PILOT TO COMPLY WITH ANY ATC CLEARANCE OR INSTRUCTION ISSUED TO THE PRECEDING AIRCRAFT. If other "nonparticipating" or "local" aircraft are in the traffic pattern, the tower will issue a landing sequence. If an arriving aircraft does not want radar service, the pilot should state "NEGATIVE RADAR SERVICE" or make a similar comment, on initial contact with approach control.

(b) Pilots of departing VFR aircraft are encouraged to request radar traffic information by notifying ground control, or where applicable, clearance delivery, on initial contact with their request and proposed direction of flight.

Example: Xray ground control, November One Eight Six, Cessna One Seventy Two, ready to taxi, VFR southbound at 2,500, have information bravo and request radar traffic information.

Note: Following takeoff, the tower will advise when to contact departure control.

(c) Pilots of aircraft transiting the area and in radar contact/communication with approach control will receive traffic information on a controller workload permitting basis. Pilots of such aircraft should give their position, altitude, aircraft call sign, aircraft type, radar beacon code (if transponder equipped), destination, and/or route of flight.

Ch 4

b. TRSA Service (Radar Sequencing and Separation Service for VFR Aircraft in a TRSA).

1. This service has been implemented at certain terminal locations. The service is advertised in the Chart Supplement. The purpose of this service is to provide separation between all participating VFR aircraft and all IFR aircraft operating within the airspace defined as the Terminal Radar Service Area (TRSA). Pilot participation is urged but is not mandatory.

2. If any aircraft does not want the service, the pilot should state "NEGATIVE TRSA SERVICE" or make a similar comment, on initial contact with approach control or ground control, as appropriate.

3. TRSAs are depicted on sectional aeronautical charts and listed in the Chart Supplement.

4. While operating within a TRSA, pilots are provided TRSA service and separation as prescribed in this paragraph. In the event of a radar outage, separation and sequencing of VFR aircraft will be suspended as this service is dependent on radar. The pilot will be advised that the service is not available and issued wind, runway information, and the time or place to contact the tower. Traffic information will be provided on a workload permitting basis.

5. Visual separation is used when prevailing conditions permit and it will be applied as follows:

(a) When a VFR flight is positioned behind a preceding aircraft and the pilot reports having that aircraft in sight, the pilot will be instructed by ATC to follow the preceding aircraft. Radar service will be continued to the runway. THE ATC INSTRUCTION TO FOLLOW THE PRECEDING AIRCRAFT DOES NOT AUTHORIZE THE PILOT TO COMPLY WITH ANY ATC CLEARANCE OR INSTRUCTION ISSUED TO THE PRECEDING AIRCRAFT.

(b) If other "nonparticipating" or "local" aircraft are in the traffic pattern, the tower will issue a landing sequence.

(c) Departing VFR aircraft may be asked if they can visually follow a preceding departure out of the TRSA. The pilot will be instructed to follow the other aircraft provided that the pilot can maintain visual contact with that aircraft.

6. Participating VFR aircraft will be separated from IFR and other participating VFR aircraft by one of the following:

(a) 500 feet vertical separation.

(b) Visual separation.

(c) Target resolution (a process to ensure that correlated radar targets do not touch).

7. Participating pilots operating VFR in a TRSA:

(a) Must maintain an altitude when assigned by ATC unless the altitude assignment is to maintain at or below a specified altitude. ATC may assign altitudes for separation that do not conform to 14 CFR Section 91.159. When the altitude assignment is no longer needed for separation or when leaving the TRSA, the instruction will be broadcast, "RESUME APPROPRIATE VFR ALTITUDES." Pilots must then return to an altitude that conforms to 14 CFR Section 91.159 as soon as practicable.

(b) When not assigned an altitude, the pilot should coordinate with ATC prior to any altitude change.

8. Within the TRSA, traffic information on observed but unidentified targets will, to the extent possible, be provided to all IFR and participating VFR aircraft. The pilot will be vectored upon request to avoid the observed traffic, provided the aircraft to be vectored is within the airspace under the jurisdiction of the controller.

9. Departing aircraft should inform ATC of their intended destination and/or route of flight and proposed cruising altitude.

10. ATC will normally advise participating VFR aircraft when leaving the geographical limits of the TRSA. Radar service is not automatically terminated with this advisory unless specifically stated by the controller.

c. Class C Service. This service provides, in addition to basic radar service, approved separation between IFR and VFR aircraft, and sequencing of VFR arrivals to the primary airport.

d. Class B Service. This service provides, in addition to basic radar service, approved separation of aircraft based on IFR, VFR, and/or weight, and sequencing of VFR arrivals to the primary airport(s).

e. *Pilot responsibility.* THESE SERVICES ARE NOT TO BE INTERPRETED AS RELIEVING PILOTS OF THEIR RESPONSIBILITIES TO SEE AND AVOID OTHER TRAFFIC OPERATING IN BASIC VFR WEATHER CONDITIONS, TO ADJUST THEIR OPERATIONS AND FLIGHT PATH AS NECESSARY TO PRECLUDE SERIOUS WAKE ENCOUNTERS, TO MAINTAIN APPROPRIATE TERRAIN AND OBSTRUCTION CLEARANCE, OR TO REMAIN IN WEATHER CONDITIONS EQUAL TO OR BETTER THAN THE MINIMUMS REQUIRED BY 14 CFR SECTION 91.155. WHENEVER COMPLIANCE WITH AN ASSIGNED ROUTE, HEADING AND/OR ALTITUDE IS LIKELY TO COMPROMISE PILOT RESPONSIBILITY RESPECTING TERRAIN AND OBSTRUCTION CLEARANCE, VORTEX EXPOSURE, AND WEATHER MINIMUMS, APPROACH CONTROL SHOULD BE SO ADVISED AND A REVISED CLEARANCE OR INSTRUCTION OBTAINED.

f. ATC services for VFR aircraft participating in terminal radar services are dependent on ATC radar. Services for VFR aircraft are not available during periods of a radar outage. The pilot will

be advised when VFR services are limited or not available.

Note: Class B and Class C airspace are areas of regulated airspace. The absence of ATC radar does not negate the requirement of an ATC clearance to enter Class B airspace or two way radio contact with ATC to enter Class C airspace.

4-1-19 Tower En Route Control (TEC)

a. TEC is an ATC program to provide a service to aircraft proceeding to and from metropolitan areas. It links designated Approach Control Areas by a network of identified routes made up of the existing airway structure of the National Airspace System. The FAA initiated an expanded TEC program to include as many facilities as possible. The program's intent is to provide an overflow resource in the low altitude system which would enhance ATC services. A few facilities have historically allowed turbojets to proceed between certain city pairs, such as Milwaukee and Chicago, via tower en route and these locations may continue this service. However, the expanded TEC program will be applied, generally, for nonturbojet aircraft operating at and below 10,000 feet. The program is entirely within the approach control airspace of multiple terminal facilities. Essentially, it is for relatively short flights. Participating pilots are encouraged to use TEC for flights of two hours duration or less. If longer flights are planned, extensive coordination may be required within the multiple complex which could result in unanticipated delays.

b. Pilots requesting TEC are subject to the same delay factor at the destination airport as other aircraft in the ATC system. In addition, departure and en route delays may occur depending upon individual facility workload. When a major metropolitan airport is incurring significant delays, pilots in the TEC program may want to consider an alternative airport experiencing no delay.

c. There are no unique requirements upon pilots to use the TEC program. Normal flight plan filing procedures will ensure proper flight plan processing. Pilots should include the acronym "TEC" in the remarks section of the flight plan when requesting tower en route control.

d. All approach controls in the system may not operate up to the maximum TEC altitude of 10,000 feet. IFR flight may be planned to any satellite airport in proximity to the major primary airport via the same routing.

4-1-20 Transponder and ADS-B Out Operation

a. General

1. Pilots should be aware that proper application of transponder and ADS-B operating procedures will provide both VFR and IFR aircraft with a higher degree of safety while operating on the ground and airborne. Transponder/ADS-B panel designs differ; therefore, a pilot should be thoroughly familiar with the operation of their particular equipment to maximize its full potential. ADS-B Out, and transponders with altitude reporting mode turned ON (Mode C or S), substantially increase the capability of surveillance systems to see an aircraft. This provides air traffic controllers, as well as pilots of suitably equipped aircraft (TCAS and ADS-B In), increased situational awareness and the ability to identify potential traffic conflicts. Even VFR pilots who are not in contact with ATC will be afforded greater protection from IFR aircraft and VFR aircraft that are receiving traffic advisories. Nevertheless, pilots should never relax their visual scanning for other aircraft, and should include the ADS-B In display (if equipped) in their normal traffic scan.

2. Air Traffic Control Radar Beacon System (ATCRBS) is similar to and compatible with military coded radar beacon equipment. Civil Mode A is identical to military Mode 3.

3. Transponder and ADS-B operations on the ground. Civil and military aircraft should operate with the transponder in the altitude reporting mode (consult the aircraft's flight manual to determine the specific transponder position to enable altitude reporting) and ADS-B Out transmissions enabled at all airports, any time the aircraft is positioned on any portion of the airport movement area. This includes all defined taxiways and runways. Pilots must pay particular attention to ATIS and airport diagram notations, General Notes (included on airport charts), and comply with directions pertaining to transponder and ADS-B usage. Generally, these directions are:

(a) **Departures.** Select the transponder mode which allows altitude reporting and enable ADS-B during pushback or taxi-out from parking spot. Select TA or TA/RA (if equipped with TCAS) when taking the active runway.

(b) **Arrivals.** If TCAS equipped, deselect TA or TA/RA upon leaving the active runway, but continue transponder and ADS-B transmissions in the altitude reporting mode. Select STBY or OFF for transponder and ADS-B upon arriving at the aircraft's parking spot or gate.

4. Transponder and ADS-B Operations While Airborne

(a) Unless otherwise requested by ATC, aircraft equipped with an ATC transponder maintained in accordance with 14 CFR Section 91.413

MUST operate with this equipment on the appropriate Mode 3/A code, or other code as assigned by ATC, and with altitude reporting enabled whenever in controlled airspace. If practicable, aircraft SHOULD operate with the transponder enabled in uncontrolled airspace.

(b) Aircraft equipped with ADS-B Out MUST operate with this equipment in the transmit mode at all times, unless otherwise requested by ATC.

5. Transponder and ADS-B Operation Under Visual Flight Rules (VFR).

(a) Unless otherwise instructed by an ATC facility, adjust transponder/ADS-B to reply on Mode 3/A Code 1200 regardless of altitude.

(b) When required to operate their transponder/ADS-B, pilots must always operate that equipment with altitude reporting enabled unless otherwise instructed by ATC or unless the installed equipment has not been tested and calibrated as required by 14 CFR Section 91.217. If deactivation is required, turn off altitude reporting.

(c) When participating in a VFR standard formation flight that is not receiving ATC services, only the lead aircraft should operate its transponder and ADS-B Out and squawk code 1203. Once established in formation, all other aircraft should squawk standby and disable ADS-B transmissions.

Note 1: If the formation flight is receiving ATC services, pilots can expect ATC to direct all non-lead aircraft to STOP Squawk, and should not do so until instructed.

Note 2: Firefighting aircraft not in contact with ATC may squawk 1255 in lieu of 1200 while en route to, from, or within the designated firefighting area(s).

Note 3: VFR aircraft flying authorized SAR missions for the USAF or USCG may be advised to squawk 1277 in lieu of 1200 while en route to, from, or within the designated search area.

Note 4: VFR gliders should squawk 1202 in lieu of 1200.

Reference: FAA Order JO 7110.66, National Beacon Code Allocation Plan (NBCAP).

6. A pilot on an IFR flight who elects to cancel the IFR flight plan prior to reaching their destination, should adjust the transponder/ADS-B according to VFR operations.

7. If entering a U.S. OFFSHORE AIRSPACE AREA from outside the U.S., the pilot should advise on first radio contact with a U.S. radar ATC facility that such equipment is available by adding "transponder" or "ADS-B" (if equipped) to the aircraft identification.

8. It should be noted by all users of ATC transponders and ADS-B Out systems that the surveillance coverage they can expect is limited to "line of sight" with ground radar and ADS-B radio sites. Low altitude or aircraft antenna shielding by the aircraft itself may result in reduced range or loss of aircraft contact. Though ADS-B often provides superior reception at low altitudes, poor coverage from any surveillance system can be improved by climbing to a higher altitude.

Note: Pilots should refer to AIM, Paragraph 4-5-7, Automatic Dependent Surveillance–Broadcast (ADS-B) Services, for a complete description of operating limitations and procedures.

b. Transponder/ADS-B Code Designation

1. For ATC to utilize one of the 4096 discrete codes, a four-digit code designation will be used; for example, code 2102 will be expressed as "TWO ONE ZERO TWO."

Note: Circumstances may occasionally require ATC to assign a non-discrete code; i.e., a code ending in "00."

Reference: FAA Order JO 7110.66, National Beacon Code Allocation Plan (NBCAP).

c. Automatic Altitude Reporting

1. Most transponders (Modes C and S) and all ADS-B Out systems are capable of automatic altitude reporting. This system converts aircraft altitude in 100-foot increments to coded digital information that is transmitted to the appropriate surveillance facility as well as to ADS-B In and TCAS systems.

2. Adjust the transponder/ADS-B to reply on the Mode 3/A code specified by ATC and with altitude reporting enabled, unless otherwise directed by ATC or unless the altitude reporting equipment has not been tested and calibrated as required by 14 CFR Section 91.217. If deactivation is required by ATC, turn off the altitude reporting feature of your transponder/ADS-B. An instruction by ATC to "STOP ALTITUDE SQUAWK, ALTITUDE DIFFERS BY (number of feet) FEET," may be an indication that the transmitted altitude information is incorrect, or that the aircraft's altimeter setting is incorrect. While an incorrect altimeter setting has no effect on the transmitted altitude information, it will cause the aircraft to fly at a true altitude different from the assigned altitude. When a controller indicates that an altitude readout is invalid, the pilot should verify that the aircraft altimeter is set correctly.

Note: Altitude encoders are preset at standard atmospheric pressure. Local altimeter correction is applied by the surveillance facility before the altitude information is presented to ATC.

3. Pilots should report exact altitude or flight level to the nearest hundred foot increment when establishing initial contact with an ATC facility. Exact altitude or flight level reports on initial contact provide ATC with information that is required prior to using automatically reported altitude

information for separation purposes. This will significantly reduce altitude verification requests.

d. IDENT Feature
Transponder/ADS-B Out equipment must be operated only as specified by ATC. Activate the "IDENT" feature only when requested by ATC.

e. Code Changes

1. When making routine code changes, pilots should avoid inadvertent selection of Codes 7500, 7600 or 7700 thereby causing momentary false alarms at automated ground facilities. For example, when switching from Code 2700 to Code 7200, switch first to 2200 then to 7200, NOT to 7700 and then 7200. This procedure applies to nondiscrete Code 7500 and all discrete codes in the 7600 and 7700 series (i.e. 7600–7677, 7700–7777) which will trigger special indicators in automated facilities. Only nondiscrete Code 7500 will be decoded as the hijack code.

2. Under no circumstances should a pilot of a civil aircraft operate the transponder on Code 7777. This code is reserved for military interceptor operations.

3. Military pilots operating VFR or IFR within restricted/warning areas should adjust their transponders to Code 4000 unless another code has been assigned by ATC.

f. Mode C Transponder and ADS-B Out Requirements

1. Specific details concerning requirements to carry and operate Mode C transponders and ADS-B Out, as well as exceptions and ATC authorized deviations from those requirements, are found in 14 CFR Sections 91.215, 91.225, and 99.13.

2. In general, the CFRs require aircraft to be equipped with an operable Mode C transponder and ADS-B Out when operating:

(a) In Class A, Class B, or Class C airspace areas;

(b) Above the ceiling and within the lateral boundaries of Class B or Class C airspace up to 10,000 feet MSL;

(c) Class E airspace at and above 10,000 feet MSL in the 48 contiguous states and the District of Columbia, excluding the airspace at and below 2,500 feet AGL;

(d) Within 30 miles of a Class B airspace primary airport, below 10,000 feet MSL (commonly referred to as the "Mode C Veil");

(e) For ADS-B Out: Class E airspace at and above 3,000 feet MSL over the Gulf of Mexico from the coastline of the United States out to 12 nautical miles.

Note: The airspace described in (e) above is specified in 14 CFR §91.225 for ADS-B Out requirements. However, 14 CFR §91.215 does not include this airspace for ATC transponder requirements.

(f) Transponder and ADS-B Out requirements do not apply to any aircraft that was not originally certificated with an electrical system, or that has not subsequently been certified with such a system installed, including balloons and gliders. These aircraft may conduct operations without a transponder or ADS-B Out when operating:

(1) Outside any Class B or Class C airspace area; and

(2) Below the altitude of the ceiling of a Class B or Class C airspace area designated for an airport, or 10,000 feet MSL, whichever is lower.

3. 14 CFR Section 99.13 requires all aircraft flying into, within, or across the contiguous U.S. ADIZ be equipped with a Mode C or Mode S transponder. Balloons, gliders and aircraft not equipped with an engine-driven electrical system are excepted from this requirement.

Reference: AIM, Chapter 5, Section 6, National Security and Interception Procedures

4. Pilots must ensure that their aircraft transponder/ADS-B is operating on an appropriate ATC-assigned VFR/IFR code with altitude reporting enabled when operating in such airspace. If in doubt about the operational status of either feature of your transponder while airborne, contact the nearest ATC facility or FSS and they will advise you what facility you should contact for determining the status of your equipment.

5. In-flight requests for "immediate" deviation from the transponder requirements may be approved by controllers only for failed equipment, and only when the flight will continue IFR or when weather conditions prevent VFR descent and continued VFR flight in airspace not affected by the CFRs. All other requests for deviation should be made at least 1 hour before the proposed operation by contacting the nearest Flight Service or Air Traffic facility in person or by telephone. The nearest ARTCC will normally be the controlling agency and is responsible for coordinating requests involving deviations in other ARTCC areas.

6. In-flight requests for "immediate" deviation from the ADS-B Out requirements may be approved by ATC only for failed equipment, and may be accommodated based on workload, alternate surveillance availability, or other factors. All other requests for deviation must be made at least 1 hour before the proposed operation, following the procedures contained in Advisory Circular (AC) 90-114, Automatic Dependent Surveillance–Broadcast Operations.

g. Cooperative Surveillance Phraseology. Air traffic controllers, both civil and military, will use the following phraseology when referring to operation of cooperative ATC surveillance equipment. Except as noted, the following ATC instructions do not apply to military transponders operating in other than Mode 3/A/C/S.

1. SQUAWK (number). Operate radar beacon transponder/ADS-B on designated code with altitude reporting enabled.

2. IDENT. Engage the "IDENT" feature (military I/P) of the transponder/ADS-B.

3. SQUAWK (number) and IDENT. Operate transponder/ADS-B on specified code with altitude reporting enabled, and engage the "IDENT" (military I/P) feature.

4. SQUAWK STANDBY. Switch transponder /ADS-B to standby position.

5. SQUAWK NORMAL. Resume normal transponder/ADS-B operation on previously assigned code. (Used after "SQUAWK STANDBY," or by military after specific transponder tests).

6. SQUAWK ALTITUDE. Activate Mode C with automatic altitude reporting.

7. STOP ALTITUDE SQUAWK. Turn off automatic altitude reporting.

8. STOP SQUAWK (mode in use). Stop transponder and ADS-B Out transmissions, or switch off only specified mode of the aircraft transponder (military).

9. SQUAWK MAYDAY. Operate transponder/ADS-B in the emergency position (Mode A Code 7700 for civil transponder. Mode 3 Code 7700 and emergency feature for military transponder.)

10. SQUAWK VFR. Operate radar beacon transponder/ADS-B on Code 1200 in the Mode A/3, or other appropriate VFR code, with altitude reporting enabled.

4-1-21 Airport Reservation Operations and Special Traffic Management Programs

This section describes procedures for obtaining required airport reservations at airports designated by the FAA and for airports operating under Special Traffic Management Programs.

a. Slot Controlled Airports.

1. The FAA may adopt rules to require advance reservations for unscheduled operations at certain airports. In addition to the information in the rules adopted by the FAA, a listing of the airports and relevant information will be maintained on the FAA website www.fly.faa.gov/ecvrs.

2. The FAA has established an Airport Reservation Office (ARO) to receive and process reservations for unscheduled flights at the slot controlled airports. The ARO uses the Enhanced Computer Voice Reservation System (e-CVRS) to allocate reservations. Reservations will be available beginning 72 hours in advance of the operation at the slot controlled airport. Standby lists are not maintained. Flights with declared emergencies do not require reservations. Refer to the website for the current listing of slot controlled airports, limitations, and reservation procedures.

3. For more detailed information on operations and reservation procedures at a Slot Controlled Airport, please see 14 CFR Part 93, Subpart K—High Density Traffic Airports.

b. Special Traffic Management Programs (STMP).

1. Special programs may be established when a location requires special traffic handling to accommodate above normal traffic demand (for example, EAA AirVenture Oshkosh, SUN 'n FUN Aerospace Expo) or reduced airport capacity (for example, airport runway/taxiway closures for airport construction). The special programs may remain in effect until the problem has been resolved or until local traffic management procedures can handle the volume and a need for special handling no longer exists.

2. If an STMP is used to accommodate a special event, a domestic notice will be issued relaying the website address: www.fly.faa.gov /estmp. Domestic notice information includes: what airports are included in the STMP, the dates and times reservations are required, the time limits for reservation requests, the point of contact for reservations, and any other instructions.

c. Making Reservations. Detailed information and User Instruction Guides for using the Web reservation systems are available on the websites for the slot controlled airports (e-CVRS), www.fly.faa.gov/ecvrs; and STMPs (e-STMP), www.fly.faa.gov/estmp.

Note: Users may contact the ARO at (540) 422-4246 if they have a problem with their reservation.

4-1-22 Requests for Waivers and Authorizations from Title 14, Code of Federal Regulations (14 CFR)

a. Requests for a Certificate of Waiver or Authorization (FAA Form 7711-2), or requests for renewal of a waiver or authorization, may be accepted by any FAA facility and will be forwarded, if necessary, to the appropriate office having waiver authority.

b. The grant of a Certificate of Waiver or Authorization from 14 CFR constitutes relief from specific regulations, to the degree and for the period of time specified in the certificate, and does not waive any state law or local ordinance. Should the proposed operations conflict with any state law or local ordinance, or require permission of local authorities or property owners, it is the applicant's responsibility to resolve the matter. The holder of a waiver is responsible for compliance with the terms of the waiver and its provisions.

c. A waiver may be canceled at any time by the Administrator, the person authorized to grant the waiver, or the representative designated to monitor a specific operation. In such case either written notice of cancellation, or written confirmation of a verbal cancellation will be provided to the holder.

4-1-23 Weather Systems Processor

The Weather Systems Processor (WSP) was developed for use in the National Airspace System to provide weather processor enhancements to selected Airport Surveillance Radar (ASR)-9 facilities. The WSP provides Air Traffic with warnings of hazardous wind shear and microbursts. The WSP also provides users with terminal area 6-level weather, storm cell locations and movement, as well as the location and predicted future position and intensity of wind shifts that may affect airport operations.

Ch 4

Section 2 Radio Communications Phraseology and Techniques

4–2–1 General

a. Radio communications are a critical link in the ATC system. The link can be a strong bond between pilot and controller or it can be broken with surprising speed and disastrous results. Discussion herein provides basic procedures for new pilots and also highlights safe operating concepts for all pilots.

b. The single, most important thought in pilot-controller communications is understanding. It is essential, therefore, that pilots acknowledge each radio communication with ATC by using the appropriate aircraft call sign. Brevity is important, and contacts should be kept as brief as possible, but controllers must know what you want to do before they can properly carry out their control duties. And you, the pilot, must know exactly what the controller wants you to do. Since concise phraseology may not always be adequate, use whatever words are necessary to get your message across. Pilots are to maintain vigilance in monitoring air traffic control radio communications frequencies for potential traffic conflicts with their aircraft especially when operating on an active runway and/or when conducting a final approach to landing.

c. All pilots will find the Pilot/Controller Glossary very helpful in learning what certain words or phrases mean. Good phraseology enhances safety and is the mark of a professional pilot. Jargon, chatter, and "CB" slang have no place in ATC communications. The Pilot/Controller Glossary is the same glossary used in FAA Order JO 7110.65, Air Traffic Control. We recommend that it be studied and reviewed from time to time to sharpen your communication skills.

4–2–2 Radio Technique

a. Listen before you transmit. Many times you can get the information you want through ATIS or by monitoring the frequency. Except for a few situations where some frequency overlap occurs, if you hear someone else talking, the keying of your transmitter will be futile and you will probably jam their receivers causing them to repeat their call. If you have just changed frequencies, pause, listen, and make sure the frequency is clear.

b. Think before keying your transmitter. Know what you want to say and if it is lengthy; e.g., a flight plan or IFR position report, jot it down.

c. The microphone should be very close to your lips and after pressing the mike button, a slight pause may be necessary to be sure the first word is transmitted. Speak in a normal, conversational tone.

d. When you release the button, wait a few seconds before calling again. The controller or FSS specialist may be jotting down your number, looking for your flight plan, transmitting on a different frequency, or selecting the transmitter for your frequency.

e. Be alert to the sounds *or the lack of sounds* in your receiver. Check your volume, recheck your frequency, and *make sure that your microphone is not stuck* in the transmit position. Frequency blockage can, and has, occurred for extended periods of time due to unintentional transmitter operation. This type of interference is commonly referred to as a "stuck mike," and controllers may refer to it in this manner when attempting to assign an alternate frequency. If the assigned frequency is completely blocked by this type of interference, use the procedures described for en route IFR radio frequency outage to establish or reestablish communications with ATC.

f. Be sure that you are within the performance range of your radio equipment and the ground station equipment. Remote radio sites do not always transmit and receive on all of a facility's available frequencies, particularly with regard to VOR sites where you can hear but not reach a ground station's receiver. Remember that higher altitudes increase the range of VHF "line of sight" communications.

4–2–3 Contact Procedures

a. Initial Contact.

1. The terms *initial contact* or *initial callup* means the first radio call you make to a given facility or the first call to a different controller or FSS specialist within a facility. Use the following format:

(a) Name of the facility being called;

(b) Your full aircraft identification as filed in the flight plan or as discussed in paragraph 4-2-4, Aircraft Call Signs;

(c) When operating on an airport surface, state your position.

(d) The type of message to follow or your request if it is short; and

(e) The word "Over" if required.

Example 1: "New York Radio, Mooney Three One One Echo."

Example 2: "Columbia Ground, Cessna Three One Six Zero Foxtrot, south ramp, I-F-R Memphis."

Example 3: "Miami Center, Baron Five Six Three Hotel, request V-F-R traffic advisories."

2. Many FSSs are equipped with Remote Communications Outlets (RCOs) and can transmit on the same frequency at more than one location. The frequencies available at specific locations are indicated on charts above FSS communications boxes. To enable the specialist to utilize the correct transmitter, advise the location and the frequency on which you expect a reply.

Example: St. Louis FSS can transmit on frequency 122.3 at either Farmington, Missouri, or Decatur, Illinois, if you are in the vicinity of Decatur, your callup should be "Saint Louis radio, Piper Six Niner Six Yankee, receiving Decatur One Two Two Point Three."

3. If radio reception is reasonably assured, inclusion of your request, your position or altitude, and the phrase "(ATIS) Information Charlie received" in the initial contact helps decrease radio frequency congestion. Use discretion; do not overload the controller with information unneeded or superfluous. If you do not get a response from the ground station, recheck your radios or use another transmitter, but keep the next contact short.

Example: "Atlanta Center, Duke Four One Romeo, request V-F-R traffic advisories, Twenty Northwest Rome, seven thousand five hundred, over."

b. Initial Contact When Your Transmitting and Receiving Frequencies are Different.

1. If you are attempting to establish contact with a ground station and you are receiving on a different frequency than that transmitted, indicate the VOR name or the frequency on which you expect a reply. Most FSSs and control facilities can transmit on several VOR stations in the area. Use the appropriate FSS call sign as indicated on charts.

Example: New York FSS transmits on the Kennedy, the Hampton, and the Calverton VORTACs. If you are in the Calverton area, your callup should be "New York radio, Cessna Three One Six Zero Foxtrot, receiving Calverton V-O-R, over."

2. If the chart indicates FSS frequencies above the VORTAC or in the FSS communications boxes, transmit or receive on those frequencies nearest your location.

3. When unable to establish contact and you wish to call any ground station, use the phrase "ANY RADIO (TOWER) (STATION), GIVE CESSNA THREE ONE SIX ZERO FOXTROT A CALL ON (FREQUENCY) OR (V-O-R)." If an emergency exists or you need assistance, so state.

c. Subsequent Contacts and Responses to Callup from a Ground Facility.
Use the same format as used for the initial contact except you should state your message or request

with the callup in one transmission. The ground station name and the word "Over" may be omitted if the message requires an obvious reply and there is no possibility for misunderstandings. *You should acknowledge all callups or clearances* unless the controller or FSS specialist advises otherwise. There are some occasions when controllers must issue time-critical instructions to other aircraft, and they may be in a position to observe your response, either visually or on radar. If the situation demands your response, take appropriate action or immediately advise the facility of any problem. Acknowledge with your aircraft identification, either at the beginning or at the end of your transmission, and one of the words "Wilco," "Roger," "Affirmative," "Negative," or other appropriate remarks; e.g., "PIPER TWO ONE FOUR LIMA, ROGER." If you have been receiving services; e.g., VFR traffic advisories and you are leaving the area or changing frequencies, advise the ATC facility and terminate contact.

d. Acknowledgement of Frequency Changes.

1. When advised by ATC to change frequencies, acknowledge the instruction. If you select the new frequency without an acknowledgement, the controller's workload is increased because there is no way of knowing whether you received the instruction or have had radio communications failure.

2. At times, a controller/specialist may be working a sector with multiple frequency assignments. In order to eliminate unnecessary verbiage and to free the controller/specialist for higher priority transmissions, the controller/specialist may request the pilot "(Identification), change to my frequency 134.5." This phrase should alert the pilot that the controller/specialist is only changing frequencies, not controller/specialist, and that initial callup phraseology may be abbreviated.

Example: "United Two Twenty-Two on one three four point five" or "one three four point five, United Two Twenty-Two."

e. Compliance with Frequency Changes.
When instructed by ATC to change frequencies, select the new frequency as soon as possible unless instructed to make the change at a specific time, fix, or altitude. A delay in making the change could result in an untimely receipt of important information. If you are instructed to make the frequency change at a specific time, fix, or altitude, monitor the frequency you are on until reaching the specified time, fix, or altitudes unless instructed otherwise by ATC.

Reference: AIM, ¶5-3-1, ARTCC Communications.

Ch 4

4-2-4 Aircraft Call Signs

a. Precautions in the Use of Call Signs.

1. Improper use of call signs can result in pilots executing a clearance intended for another aircraft. Call signs should *never be abbreviated on an initial contact or at any time when other aircraft call signs have similar numbers/sounds or identical letters/number*, e.g., Cessna 6132F, Cessna 1622F, Baron 123F, Cherokee 7732F, etc.

Example: Assume that a controller issues an approach clearance to an aircraft at the bottom of a holding stack and an aircraft with a similar call sign (at the top of the stack) acknowledges the clearance with the last two or three numbers of the aircraft's call sign. If the aircraft at the bottom of the stack did not hear the clearance and intervene, flight safety would be affected, and there would be no reason for either the controller or pilot to suspect that anything is wrong. This kind of "human factors" error can strike swiftly and is extremely difficult to rectify.

2. Pilots, therefore, must be certain that aircraft identification is complete and clearly identified before taking action on an ATC clearance. ATC specialists will not abbreviate call signs of air carrier or other civil aircraft having authorized call signs. ATC specialists may initiate abbreviated call signs of other aircraft by using the *prefix and the last three digits/letters* of the aircraft identification after communications are established. The pilot may use the abbreviated call sign in subsequent contacts with the ATC specialist. When aware of similar/identical call signs, ATC specialists will take action to minimize errors by emphasizing certain numbers/letters, by repeating the entire call sign, by repeating the prefix, or by asking pilots to use a different call sign temporarily. Pilots should use the phrase "VERIFY CLEARANCE FOR (your complete call sign)" if doubt exists concerning proper identity.

3. Civil aircraft pilots should state the aircraft type, model or manufacturer's name, followed by the digits/letters of the registration number. When the aircraft manufacturer's name or model is stated, the prefix "N" is dropped; e.g., Aztec Two Four Six Four Alpha.

Example 1: Bonanza Six Five Five Golf.

Example 2: Breezy Six One Three Romeo Experimental (omit "Experimental" after initial contact).

4. Air Taxi or other commercial operators not having FAA authorized call signs should prefix their normal identification with the phonetic word "Tango."

Example: Tango Aztec Two Four Six Four Alpha.

5. Air carriers and commuter air carriers having FAA authorized call signs should identify themselves by stating the complete call sign (using group form for the numbers) and the word "super" or "heavy" if appropriate.

Example 1: United Twenty-Five Heavy.

Example 2: Midwest Commuter Seven Eleven.

6. Military aircraft use a variety of systems including serial numbers, word call signs, and combinations of letters/numbers. Examples include Army Copter 48931; Air Force 61782; REACH 31792; Pat 157; Air Evac 17652; Navy Golf Alfa Kilo 21; Marine 4 Charlie 36, etc.

b. Air Ambulance Flights.

Because of the priority afforded air ambulance flights in the ATC system, extreme discretion is necessary when using the term "MEDEVAC." It is only intended for those missions of an urgent medical nature and to be utilized only for that portion of the flight requiring priority handling. It is important for ATC to be aware of a flight's MEDEVAC status, and it is the pilot's responsibility to ensure that this information is provided to ATC.

1. To receive priority handling from ATC, the pilot must verbally identify the flight in radio transmissions by stating "MEDEVAC" followed by the FAA authorized call sign (ICAO 3LD, US Special, or local) or the aircraft civil "N" registration numbers/letters.

Example: If the aircraft identification of the flight indicates DAL51, the pilot states "MEDEVAC Delta Fifty One."

If the aircraft identification of the flight indicates MDSTR1, the pilot states "MEDEVAC Medstar One."

If the aircraft identification of the flight indicates N123G or LN123G, the pilot states "MEDEVAC One Two Three Golf".

2. If requested by the pilot, ATC will provide additional assistance (e.g., landline notifications) to expedite ground handling of patients, vital organs, or urgently needed medical materials. When possible make these requests to ATC via methods other than through ATC radio frequencies.

3. MEDEVAC flights may include:

(a) Civilian air ambulance flights responding to medical emergencies (e.g., first call to an accident scene, carrying patients, organ donors, organs, or other urgently needed lifesaving medical material).

(b) Air carrier and air taxi flights responding to medical emergencies. The nature of these medical emergency flights usually concerns the transportation of urgently needed lifesaving

medical materials or vital organs, but can include inflight medical emergencies. It is imperative that the company/pilot determine, by the nature/urgency of the specific medical cargo, if priority ATC assistance is required.

4. When filing a flight plan, pilots may include "L" for MEDEVAC with the aircraft registration letters/digits and/or include "MEDEVAC" in Item 11 (Remarks) of the flight plan or Item 18 (Other Information) of an international flight plan. However, ATC will only use these flight plan entries for informational purposes or as a visual indicator. ATC will only provide priority handling when the pilot verbally identifies the "MEDEVAC" status of the flight as described in subparagraph b1 above.

Note: Civilian air ambulance aircraft operating VFR and without a filed flight plan are eligible for priority handling in accordance with subparagraph b1 above.

5. ATC will also provide priority handling to HOSP and AIR EVAC flights when verbally requested. These aircraft may file "HOSP" or "AIR EVAC" in either Item 11 (Remarks) of the flight plan or Item 18 of an international flight plan. For aircraft identification in radio transmissions, civilian pilots will use normal call signs when filing "HOSP" and military pilots will use the "EVAC" call sign.

c. Student Pilots Radio Identification.

1. The FAA desires to help student pilots in acquiring sufficient practical experience in the environment in which they will be required to operate. To receive additional assistance while operating in areas of concentrated air traffic, student pilots need only identify themselves as a student pilot during their initial call to an FAA radio facility.

Example: Dayton tower, Fleetwing One Two Three Four, student pilot.

2. This special identification will alert FAA ATC personnel and enable them to provide student pilots with such extra assistance and consideration as they may need. It is recommended that student pilots identify themselves as such, on initial contact with each clearance delivery prior to taxiing, ground control, tower, approach and departure control frequency, or FSS contact.

4-2-5 Description of Interchange or Leased Aircraft

a. Controllers issue traffic information based on familiarity with airline equipment and color/markings. When an air carrier dispatches a flight using another company's equipment and the pilot does not advise the terminal ATC facility, the possible confusion in aircraft identification can compromise safety.

b. Pilots flying an "interchange" or "leased" aircraft not bearing the colors/markings of the company operating the aircraft should inform the terminal ATC facility on first contact the name of the operating company and trip number, followed by the company name as displayed on the aircraft, and aircraft type.

Example: Air Cal Three Eleven, United (interchange/lease), Boeing Seven Two Seven.

4-2-6 Ground Station Call Signs

Pilots, when calling a ground station, should begin with the name of the facility being called followed by the type of the facility being called as indicated in Table 4-2-1.

TABLE 4-2-1
CALLING A GROUND STATION

Facility	Call Sign
Airport UNICOM	"Shannon UNICOM"
FAA Flight Service Station	"Chicago Radio"
Airport Traffic Control Tower	"Augusta Tower"
Clearance Delivery Position (IFR)	"Dallas Clearance Delivery"
Ground Control Position in Tower	"Miami Ground"
Radar or Nonradar Approach Control Position	"Oklahoma City Approach"
Radar Departure Control Position	"St. Louis Departure"
FAA Air Route Traffic Control Center	"Washington Center"

4-2-7 Phonetic Alphabet

The International Civil Aviation Organization (ICAO) phonetic alphabet is used by FAA personnel when communications conditions are such that the information cannot be readily received without their use. ATC facilities may also request pilots to use phonetic letter equivalents when aircraft with similar sounding identifications are receiving communications on the same frequency. Pilots should use the phonetic alphabet when identifying their aircraft during initial contact with air traffic control facilities. Additionally, use the phonetic equivalents for single letters and to spell out groups of letters or difficult words during adverse communications conditions. (See Table 4-2-2.)

TABLE 4–2–2
PHONETIC ALPHABET/MORSE CODE

Character	Morse Code	Telephony	Phonic (Pronunciation)
A	• —	Alfa	(AL-FAH)
B	— • • •	Bravo	(BRAH-VOH)
C	— • — •	Charlie	(CHAR-LEE) or (SHAR-LEE)
D	— • •	Delta	(DELL-TAH)
E	•	Echo	(ECK-OH)
F	• • — •	Foxtrot	(FOKS-TROT)
G	— — •	Golf	(GOLF)
H	• • • •	Hotel	(HOH-TEL)
I	• •	India	(IN-DEE-AH)
J	• — — —	Juliett	(JEW-LEE-ETT)
K	— • —	Kilo	(KEY-LOH)
L	• — • •	Lima	(LEE-MAH)
M	— —	Mike	(MIKE)
N	— •	November	(NO-VEM-BER)
O	— — —	Oscar	(OSS-CAH)
P	• — — •	Papa	(PAH-PAH)
Q	— — • —	Quebec	(KEH-BECK)
R	• — •	Romeo	(ROW-ME-OH)
S	• • •	Sierra	(SEE-AIR-RAH)
T	—	Tango	(TANG-GO)
U	• • —	Uniform	(YOU-NEE-FORM) or (OO-NEE-FORM)
V	• • • —	Victor	(VIK-TAH)
W	• — —	Whiskey	(WISS-KEY)
X	— • • —	Xray	(ECKS-RAY)
Y	— • — —	Yankee	(YANG-KEY)
Z	— — • •	Zulu	(ZOO-LOO)
1	• — — — —	One	(WUN)
2	• • — — —	Two	(TOO)
3	• • • — —	Three	(TREE)
4	• • • • —	Four	(FOW-ER)
5	• • • • •	Five	(FIFE)
6	— • • • •	Six	(SIX)
7	— — • • •	Seven	(SEV-EN)
8	— — — • •	Eight	(AIT)
9	— — — — •	Nine	(NIN-ER)
0	— — — — —	Zero	(ZEE-RO)

4-2-8 Figures

a. Figures indicating hundreds and thousands in round number, as for ceiling heights, and upper wind levels up to 9,900 must be spoken in accordance with the following.

Examples:
1. 500...*five hundred*
2. 4,500 *four thousand five hundred*

b. Numbers above 9,900 must be spoken by separating the digits preceding the word "thousand."

Examples:
1. 10,000.................................*one zero thousand*
2. 13,500 *one three thousand five hundred*

c. Transmit airway or jet route numbers as follows.

Examples:
1. V12... *Victor Twelve*
2. J533................................... *J Five Thirty-Three*

d. All other numbers must be transmitted by pronouncing each digit.

Example:
10...*one zero*

e. When a radio frequency contains a decimal point, the decimal point is spoken as "**point**."

Example:
122.1 *one two two point one*

Note: *ICAO procedures require the decimal point be spoken as "**decimal**." The FAA will honor such usage by military aircraft and all other aircraft required to use ICAO procedures.*

4-2-9 Altitudes and Flight Levels

a. Up to but not including 18,000 feet MSL, state the separate digits of the thousands plus the hundreds if appropriate.

Examples:
1. 12,000..................................*one two thousand*
2. 12,500*one two thousand five hundred*

b. At and above 18,000 feet MSL (FL180), state the words "flight level" followed by the separate digits of the flight level.

Examples:
1. 190........................ *Flight Level One Niner Zero*
2. 275........................*Flight Level Two Seven Five*

4-2-10 Directions

The three digits of bearing, course, heading, or wind direction should always be magnetic. The word "true" must be added when it applies.

Examples:
1. (Magnetic course) 005 *zero zero five*
2. (True course) 050................*zero five zero true*
3. (Magnetic bearing) 360..............*three six zero*
4. (Magnetic heading) 100*heading one zero zero*
5. (Wind direction) 220............ *wind two two zero*

4–2–11 Speeds

The separate digits of the speed followed by the word "**knots**." Except, controllers may omit the word "**knots**" when using speed adjustment procedures; e.g., "**reduce/increase speed to two five zero.**"

Examples:

(Speed) 250.............................two five zero knots
(Speed) 190..........................one niner zero knots

The separate digits of the Mach Number preceded by "Mach."

Examples:

(Mach number) 1.5...............Mach one point five
(Mach number) 0.64..............Mach point six four
(Mach number) 0.7.................Mach point seven

4–2–12 Time

a. FAA uses Coordinated Universal Time (UTC) for all operations. The word "local" or the time zone equivalent must be used to denote local when local time is given during radio and telephone communications. The term "Zulu" may be used to denote UTC.

Example:

0920 UTC.............................. zero niner two zero,
zero one two zero Pacific or local,
or one twenty AM

b. To convert from Standard Time to Coordinated Universal Time:

TABLE 4–2–3
STANDARD TIME TO COORDINATED UNIVERSAL TIME

Eastern Standard Time	Add 5 hours
Central Standard Time	Add 6 hours
Mountain Standard Time	Add 7 hours
Pacific Standard Time	Add 8 hours
Alaska Standard Time	Add 9 hours
Hawaii Standard Time	Add 10 hours

Note: For daylight time, subtract 1 hour.

c. A reference may be made to local daylight or standard time utilizing the 24-hour clock system. The hour is indicated by the first two figures and the minutes by the last two figures.

Examples:

0000zero zero zero zero
0920zero niner two zero

d. Time may be stated in minutes only (two figures) in radiotelephone communications when no misunderstanding is likely to occur.

e. Current time in use at a station is stated in the nearest quarter minute in order that pilots may use this information for time checks. Fractions of a quarter minute less than 8 seconds are stated as the preceding quarter minute; fractions of a quarter minute of 8 seconds or more are stated as the succeeding quarter minute.

Examples:

0929:05time, zero niner two niner
0929:10 time, zero niner two niner
and one-quarter

4–2–13 Communications with Tower when Aircraft Transmitter or Receiver or Both are Inoperative

a. Arriving Aircraft.

1. Receiver inoperative.

(a) If you have reason to believe your receiver is inoperative, remain outside or above the Class D surface area until the direction and flow of traffic has been determined; then, advise the tower of your type aircraft, position, altitude, intention to land, and request that you be controlled with light signals.

Reference: *AIM, ¶4-3-13, Traffic Control Light Signals.*

(b) When you are approximately 3 to 5 miles from the airport, advise the tower of your position and join the airport traffic pattern. From this point on, watch the tower for light signals. Thereafter, if a complete pattern is made, transmit your position downwind and/or turning base leg.

2. Transmitter inoperative. Remain outside or above the Class D surface area until the direction and flow of traffic has been determined; then, join the airport traffic pattern. Monitor the primary local control frequency as depicted on Sectional Charts for landing or traffic information, and look for a light signal which may be addressed to your aircraft. During hours of daylight, acknowledge tower transmissions or light signals by rocking your wings. At night, acknowledge by blinking the landing or navigation lights. To acknowledge tower transmissions during daylight hours, hovering helicopters will turn in the direction of the controlling facility and flash the landing light. While in flight, helicopters should show their acknowledgment of receiving a transmission by making shallow banks in opposite directions. At night, helicopters will acknowledge receipt of transmissions by flashing either the landing or the search light.

3. Transmitter and receiver inoperative. Remain outside or above the Class D surface area until the direction and flow of traffic has been determined; then, join the airport traffic pattern and maintain visual contact with the tower to receive light signals. Acknowledge light signals as noted above.

b. Departing Aircraft. If you experience radio failure prior to leaving the parking area, make every effort to have the equipment repaired. If you are unable to have the malfunction repaired, call the tower by telephone and request authorization to depart without two-way radio communications. If tower authorization is granted, you will be given departure information and requested to monitor the tower frequency or watch for light signals as appropriate. During daylight hours, acknowledge tower transmissions or light signals by moving the ailerons or rudder. At night, acknowledge by blinking the landing or navigation lights. If radio malfunction occurs after departing the parking area, watch the tower for light signals or monitor tower frequency.

Reference: *14 CFR §§91.125 and 91.129.*

4–2–14 Communications for VFR Flights

a. FSSs and Supplemental Weather Service Locations (SWSL) are allocated frequencies for different functions; for example, in Alaska, certain FSSs provide Local Airport Advisory on 123.6 MHz or other frequencies which can be found in the Chart Supplement. If you are in doubt as to what frequency to use, 122.2 MHz is assigned to the majority of FSSs as a common en route simplex frequency.

Note: In order to expedite communications, state the frequency being used and the aircraft location during initial callup.

Example: *Dayton radio, November One Two Three Four Five on one two two point two, over Springfield V-O-R, over.*

b. Certain VOR voice channels are being utilized for recorded broadcasts; for example, ATIS. These services and appropriate frequencies are listed in the Chart Supplement. On VFR flights, pilots are urged to monitor these frequencies. When in contact with a control facility, notify the controller if you plan to leave the frequency to monitor these broadcasts.

Section 3 Airport Operations

4–3–1 General

Increased traffic congestion, aircraft in climb and descent attitudes, and pilot preoccupation with cockpit duties are some factors that increase the hazardous accident potential near the airport. The situation is further compounded when the weather is marginal, that is, just meeting VFR requirements. Pilots must be particularly alert when operating in the vicinity of an airport. This section defines some rules, practices, and procedures that pilots should be familiar with and adhere to for safe airport operations.

4–3–2 Airports with an Operating Control Tower

a. When operating at an airport where traffic control is being exercised by a control tower, pilots are required to maintain two-way radio contact with the tower while operating within the Class B, Class C, and Class D surface area unless the tower authorizes otherwise. Initial callup should be made about 15 miles from the airport. Unless there is a good reason to leave the tower frequency before exiting the Class B, Class C, and Class D surface areas, it is a good operating practice to remain on the tower frequency for the purpose of receiving traffic information. In the interest of reducing tower frequency congestion, pilots are reminded that it is not necessary to request permission to leave the tower frequency once outside of Class B, Class C, and Class D surface areas. Not all airports with an operating control tower will have Class D airspace. These airports do not have weather reporting which is a requirement for surface based controlled airspace, previously known as a control zone. The controlled airspace over these airports will normally begin at 700 feet or 1,200 feet above ground level and can be determined from the visual aeronautical charts. Pilots are expected to use good operating practices and communicate with the control tower as described in this section.

b. When necessary, the tower controller will issue clearances or other information for aircraft to generally follow the desired flight path (traffic patterns) when flying in Class B, Class C, and Class D surface areas and the proper taxi routes when operating on the ground. If not otherwise authorized or directed by the tower, pilots of fixed-wing aircraft approaching to land must circle the airport to the left. Pilots approaching to land in a helicopter must avoid the flow of fixed-wing traffic. However, in all instances, an appropriate clearance must be received from the tower before landing.

FIGURE 4–3–1
Components of a Traffic Pattern

Note: This diagram is intended only to illustrate terminology used in identifying various components of a traffic pattern. It should not be used as a reference or guide on how to enter a traffic pattern.

c. The following terminology for the various components of a traffic pattern has been adopted as standard for use by control towers and pilots (See Figure 4-3-1):

1. Upwind leg. A flight path parallel to the landing runway in the direction of landing.

2. Crosswind leg. A flight path at right angles to the landing runway off its takeoff end.

3. Downwind leg. A flight path parallel to the landing runway in the opposite direction of landing.

4. Base leg. A flight path at right angles to the landing runway off its approach end and extending from the downwind leg to the intersection of the extended runway centerline.

5. Final approach. A flight path in the direction of landing along the extended runway centerline from the base leg to the runway.

6. Departure. The flight path which begins after takeoff and continues straight ahead along the extended runway centerline. The departure climb continues until reaching a point at least 1/2 mile beyond the departure end of the runway and within 300 feet of the traffic pattern altitude.

d. Many towers are equipped with a tower radar display. The radar uses are intended to enhance the effectiveness and efficiency of the local control, or tower, position. They are not intended to provide radar services or benefits to pilots except as they may accrue through a more efficient tower operation. The four basic uses are:

1. To determine an aircraft's exact location. This is accomplished by radar identifying the VFR aircraft through any of the techniques available to a radar position, such as having the aircraft *squawk ident.* Once identified, the aircraft's

position and spatial relationship to other aircraft can be quickly determined, and standard instructions regarding VFR operation in Class B, Class C, and Class D surface areas will be issued. Once initial radar identification of a VFR aircraft has been established and the appropriate instructions have been issued, radar monitoring may be discontinued; the reason being that the local controller's primary means of surveillance in VFR conditions is visually scanning the airport and local area.

2. To provide radar traffic advisories. Radar traffic advisories may be provided to the extent that the local controller is able to monitor the radar display. Local control has primary control responsibilities to the aircraft operating on the runways, which will normally supersede radar monitoring duties.

3. To provide a direction or suggested heading. The local controller may provide pilots flying VFR with generalized instructions which will facilitate operations; e.g., "PROCEED SOUTHWEST-BOUND, ENTER A RIGHT DOWNWIND RUNWAY THREE ZERO," or provide a suggested heading to establish radar identification or as an advisory aid to navigation; e.g., "SUGGESTED HEADING TWO TWO ZERO, FOR RADAR IDENTIFICATION." In both cases, the instructions are advisory aids to the pilot flying VFR and are not radar vectors.

Note: *Pilots have complete discretion regarding acceptance of the suggested headings or directions and have sole responsibility for seeing and avoiding other aircraft.*

4. To provide information and instructions to aircraft operating within Class B, Class C, and Class D surface areas. In an example of this situation, the local controller would use the radar to advise a pilot on an extended downwind when to turn base leg.

Note: *The above tower radar applications are intended to augment the standard functions of the local control position. There is no controller requirement to maintain constant radar identification. In fact, such a requirement could compromise the local controller's ability to visually scan the airport and local area to meet FAA responsibilities to the aircraft operating on the runways and within the Class B, Class C, and Class D surface areas. Normally, pilots will not be advised of being in radar contact since that continued status cannot be guaranteed and since the purpose of the radar identification is not to establish a link for the provision of radar services.*

e. A few of the radar equipped towers are authorized to use the radar to ensure separation between aircraft in specific situations, while still others may function as limited radar approach

controls. The various radar uses are strictly a function of FAA operational need. The facilities may be indistinguishable to pilots since they are all referred to as tower and no publication lists the degree of radar use. Therefore, when in communication with a tower controller who may have radar available, do not assume that constant radar monitoring and complete ATC radar services are being provided.

4–3–3 Traffic Patterns

a. It is recommended that aircraft enter the airport traffic pattern at one of the following altitudes listed below. These altitudes should be maintained unless another traffic pattern altitude is published in the Chart Supplement or unless ❚ otherwise required by the applicable distance from cloud criteria (14 CFR Section 91.155). (See Figure 4-3-2 and Figure 4-3-3):

1. Propeller-driven aircraft enter the traffic pattern at 1,000 feet above ground level (AGL).

2. Large and turbine-powered aircraft enter the traffic pattern at an altitude of not less than 1,500 feet AGL or 500 feet above the established pattern altitude.

3. Helicopters operating in the traffic pattern may fly a pattern similar to the fixed-wing aircraft pattern, but at a lower altitude (500 AGL) and closer to the runway. This pattern may be on the opposite side of the runway from fixed-wing traffic when airspeed requires or for practice power-off landings (autorotation) and if local policy permits. Landings not to the runway must avoid the flow of fixed wing traffic.

b. A pilot may vary the size of the traffic pattern depending on the aircraft's performance characteristics. Pilots of en route aircraft should be constantly alert for aircraft in traffic patterns and avoid these areas whenever possible.

c. Unless otherwise indicated, all turns in the traffic pattern must be made to the left, except for helicopters, as applicable.

d. On Sectional, Aeronautical, and VFR Terminal Area Charts, right traffic patterns are indicated at public-use and joint-use airports with the abbreviation "RP" (for Right Pattern), followed by the appropriate runway number(s) at the bottom of the airport data block.

Example:

RP 9, 18, 22R

Note 1: *Pilots are encouraged to use the standard traffic pattern. However, those pilots who choose to execute a straight-in approach, maneuvering for and execution of the approach should not disrupt the flow of arriving and departing traffic. Likewise, pilots operating in the traffic pattern should*

be alert at all times for aircraft executing straight-in approaches.

Reference: AC 90-66B, *Non-Towered Airport Flight Operations.*

Note 2: *RP indicates special conditions exist and refers pilots to the Chart Supplement.

Note 3: Right traffic patterns are not shown at airports with full-time control towers.

e. Wind conditions affect all airplanes in varying degrees. Figure 4-3-4 is an example of a chart used to determine the headwind, crosswind, and tailwind components based on wind direction and velocity relative to the runway. Pilots should refer to similar information provided by the aircraft manufacturer when determining these wind components.

FIGURE 4–3–2
Traffic Pattern Operations – Single Runway

Examples:

Key to traffic pattern operations

1. Enter pattern in level flight, abeam the midpoint of the runway, at pattern altitude.

2. Maintain pattern altitude until abeam approach end of the landing runway on downwind leg.

3. Complete turn to final at least 1/4 mile from the runway.

4. Continue straight ahead until beyond departure end of runway.

5. If remaining in the traffic pattern, commence turn to crosswind leg beyond the departure end of the runway within 300 feet of pattern altitude.

6. If departing the traffic pattern, continue straight out, or exit with a 45 degree turn (to the left when in a left-hand traffic pattern; to the right when in a right-hand traffic pattern) beyond the departure end of the runway, after reaching pattern altitude.

FIGURE 4–3–3
Traffic Pattern Operations – Parallel Runways

Examples:

Key to traffic pattern operations

1. Enter pattern in level flight, abeam the midpoint of the runway, at pattern altitude.

2. Maintain pattern altitude until abeam approach end of the landing runway on downwind leg.

3. Complete turn to final at least 1/4 mile from the runway.

4. Continue straight ahead until beyond departure end of runway.

5. If remaining in the traffic pattern, commence turn to crosswind leg beyond the departure end of the runway within 300 feet of pattern altitude.

6. If departing the traffic pattern, continue straight out, or exit with a 45 degree turn (to the left when in a left-hand traffic pattern; to the right when in a right-hand traffic pattern) beyond the departure end of the runway, after reaching pattern altitude.

7. Do not overshoot final or continue on a track which will penetrate the final approach of the parallel runway.

8. Do not continue on a track which will penetrate the departure path of the parallel runway.

FIGURE 4–3–4
Headwind/Tailwind/Crosswind Component Calculator

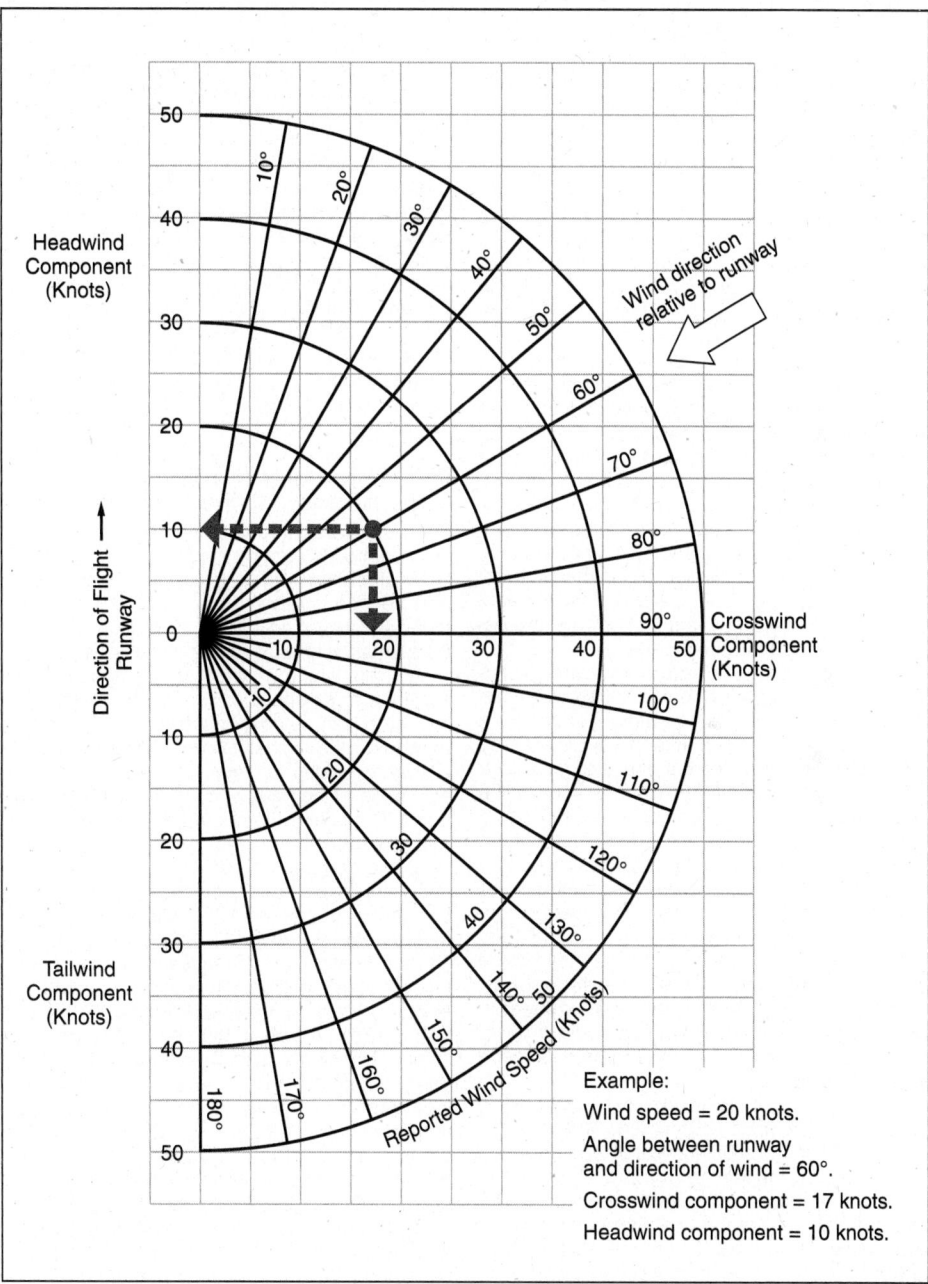

Ch 4

4–3–4 Visual Indicators at Airports Without an Operating Control Tower

a. At those airports **without an operating control tower**, a segmented circle visual indicator system, if installed, is designed to provide traffic pattern information.

Reference: AIM, ¶4-1-9, Traffic Advisory Practices at Airports Without Operating Control Towers.

b. The segmented circle system consists of the following components:

1. The segmented circle. Located in a position affording maximum visibility to pilots in the air and on the ground and providing a centralized location for other elements of the system.

2. The wind direction indicator. A wind cone, wind sock, or wind tee installed near the operational runway to indicate wind direction. The large end of the wind cone/wind sock points into the wind as does the large end (cross bar) of the wind tee. In lieu of a tetrahedron and where a wind sock or wind cone is collocated with a wind tee, the wind tee may be manually aligned with the runway in use to indicate landing direction. These signaling devices may be located in the center of the segmented circle and may be lighted for night use. Pilots are cautioned against using a tetrahedron to indicate wind direction.

3. The landing direction indicator. A tetrahedron is installed when conditions at the airport warrant its use. It may be used to indicate the direction of landings and takeoffs. A tetrahedron may be located at the center of a segmented circle and may be lighted for night operations. The small end of the tetrahedron points in the direction of landing. Pilots are cautioned against using a tetrahedron for any purpose other than as an indicator of landing direction. Further, pilots should use extreme caution when making runway selection by use of a tetrahedron in very light or calm wind conditions as the tetrahedron may not be aligned with the designated calm-wind runway. At airports with control towers, the tetrahedron should only be referenced when the control tower is not in operation. Tower instructions supersede tetrahedron indications.

4. Landing strip indicators. Installed in pairs as shown in the segmented circle diagram and used to show the alignment of landing strips.

5. Traffic pattern indicators. Arranged in pairs in conjunction with landing strip indicators and used to indicate the direction of turns when there is a variation from the normal left traffic pattern. (If there is no segmented circle installed at the airport, traffic pattern indicators may be installed on or near the end of the runway.)

c. Preparatory to landing at an airport without a control tower, or when the control tower is not in operation, pilots should concern themselves with the indicator for the approach end of the runway to be used. When approaching for landing, all turns must be made to the left unless a traffic pattern indicator indicates that turns should be made to the right. If the pilot will mentally enlarge the indicator for the runway to be used, the base and final approach legs of the traffic pattern to be flown immediately become apparent. Similar treatment of the indicator at the departure end of the runway will clearly indicate the direction of turn after takeoff.

d. When two or more aircraft are approaching an airport for the purpose of landing, the pilot of the aircraft at the lower altitude has the right-of-way over the pilot of the aircraft at the higher altitude. However, the pilot operating at the lower altitude should not take advantage of another aircraft, which is on final approach to land, by cutting in front of, or overtaking that aircraft.

4–3–5 Unexpected Maneuvers in the Airport Traffic Pattern

There have been several incidents in the vicinity of controlled airports that were caused primarily by aircraft executing unexpected maneuvers. ATC service is based upon observed or known traffic and airport conditions. Controllers establish the sequence of arriving and departing aircraft by requiring them to adjust flight as necessary to achieve proper spacing. These adjustments can only be based on observed traffic, accurate pilot reports, and anticipated aircraft maneuvers. Pilots are expected to cooperate so as to preclude disrupting traffic flows or creating conflicting patterns. The pilot-in-command of an aircraft is directly responsible for and is the final authority as to the operation of the aircraft. On occasion it may be necessary for pilots to maneuver their aircraft to maintain spacing with the traffic they have been sequenced to follow. The controller can anticipate minor maneuvering such as shallow "S" turns. The controller cannot, however, anticipate a major maneuver such as a 360 degree turn. If a pilot makes a 360 degree turn after obtaining a landing sequence, the result is usually a gap in the landing interval and, more importantly, it causes a chain reaction which may result in a conflict with following traffic and an interruption of the sequence established by the tower or approach controller. Should a pilot decide to make maneuvering turns to maintain spacing behind a preceding aircraft, the pilot should always advise the controller if at all possible. Except when requested by the controller or in emergency situations, a 360 degree turn should never be executed in the traffic pattern or when receiving radar service without first advising the controller.

4–3–6 Use of Runways/Declared Distances

a. Runways are identified by numbers that indicate the nearest 10-degree increment of the azimuth of the runway centerline. For example, where the magnetic azimuth is 183 degrees, the runway designation would be 18; for a magnetic azimuth of 87 degrees, the runway designation would be 9. For a magnetic azimuth ending in the number 5, such as 185, the runway designation could be either 18 or 19. Wind direction issued by the tower is also magnetic and wind velocity is in knots.

Note 1: At airports with multiple parallel runways whose magnetic azimuths are identical, each runway number will be supplemented by a letter and shown from left to right when viewed from the direction of approach.

Note 2: When multiple parallel runways at the same airport are separated by a large distance, such as by a central terminal or several terminals, the runways may be designated as non-parallel runways to avoid pilot confusion.

Reference: AC 150/5340-1, Standards for Airport Markings, Paragraph 2.3.5, Characteristics.

b. Airport proprietors are responsible for taking the lead in local aviation noise control. Accordingly, they may propose specific noise abatement plans to the FAA. If approved, these plans are applied in the form of Formal or Informal Runway Use Programs for noise abatement purposes.

Reference: Pilot/Controller Glossary—Runway Use Program.

1. ATC will assign the runway/s most nearly aligned with the wind when 5 knots or more, or the "calm wind" runway when less than 5 knots unless:

(a) Use of another runway is operationally advantageous, or

(b) A Runway Use Program is in effect.

Note: Tailwind and crosswind considerations take precedence over delay/capacity considerations, and noise abatement operations/procedures.

Reference: FAA Order JO 7110.65, Paragraph 3-5-1, Selection.

c. If a pilot prefers to use a runway different from that specified, the pilot is expected to advise ATC. ATC may honor such requests as soon as is operationally practicable. ATC will advise pilots when the requested runway is noise sensitive. When use of a runway other than the one assigned is requested, pilot cooperation is encouraged to preclude disruption of traffic flows or the creation of conflicting patterns.

Reference: FAA Order JO 7110.65, Paragraph 3-5-1, Selection.

d. Declared Distances.

1. Declared distances for a runway represent the maximum distances available and suitable for meeting takeoff and landing distance performance requirements. These distances are determined in accordance with FAA runway design standards by adding to the physical length of paved runway any clearway or stopway and subtracting from that sum any lengths necessary to obtain the standard runway safety areas, runway object free areas, or runway protection zones. As a result of these additions and subtractions, the declared distances for a runway may be more or less than the physical length of the runway as depicted on aeronautical charts and related publications, or available in electronic navigation databases provided by either the U.S. Government or commercial companies.

2. All 14 CFR Part 139 airports report declared distances for each runway. Other airports may also report declared distances for a runway if necessary to meet runway design standards or to indicate the presence of a clearway or stopway. Where reported, declared distances for each runway end are published in the Chart Supplement. For runways without published declared distances, the declared distances may be assumed to be equal to the physical length of the runway unless there is a displaced landing threshold, in which case the Landing Distance Available (LDA) is shortened by the amount of the threshold displacement.

Note: A symbol D is shown on U.S. Government charts to indicate that runway declared distance information is available (See appropriate Chart Supplement, Chart Supplement Alaska or Pacific).

(a) The FAA uses the following definitions for runway declared distances (See Figure 4-3-5):

Reference: Pilot/Controller Glossary—Accelerate-Stop Distance Available, Landing Distance Available, Takeoff Distance Available, Takeoff Run Available, Stopway, and Clearway.

(1) Takeoff Run Available (TORA)— The runway length declared available and suitable for the ground run of an airplane taking off. The TORA is typically the physical length of the runway, but it may be shorter than the runway length if necessary to satisfy runway design standards. For example, the TORA may be shorter than the runway length if a portion of the runway must be used to satisfy runway protection zone requirements.

(2) Takeoff Distance Available (TODA)— The takeoff run available plus the length of any remaining runway or clearway beyond the far end of the takeoff run available. The TODA is the distance declared available for satisfying takeoff

distance requirements for airplanes where the certification and operating rules and available performance data allow for the consideration of a clearway in takeoff performance computations.

Note: The length of any available clearway will be included in the TODA published in the entry for that runway end within the Chart Supplement.

(3) Accelerate-Stop Distance Available (ASDA)—The runway plus stopway length declared available and suitable for the acceleration and deceleration of an airplane aborting a takeoff. The ASDA may be longer than the physical length of the runway when a stopway has been designated available by the airport operator, or it may be shorter than the physical length of the runway if necessary to use a portion of the runway to satisfy runway design standards; for example, where the airport operator uses a portion of the runway to achieve the runway safety area requirement. ASDA is the distance used to satisfy the airplane accelerate-stop distance performance requirements where the certification and operating rules require accelerate-stop distance computations.

Note: The length of any available stopway will be included in the ASDA published in the entry for that runway end within the Chart Supplement.

(4) Landing Distance Available (LDA)— The runway length declared available and suitable for a landing airplane. The LDA may be less than the physical length of the runway or the length of the runway remaining beyond a displaced threshold if necessary to satisfy runway design standards; for example, where the airport operator uses a portion of the runway to achieve the runway safety area requirement. Although some runway elements (such as stopway length and clearway length) may be available information, pilots must use the declared distances determined by the airport operator and not attempt to independently calculate declared distances by adding those elements to the reported physical length of the runway.

(b) The airplane operating rules and/or airplane operating limitations establish minimum distance requirements for takeoff and landing and are based on performance data supplied in the *Airplane Flight Manual* or *Pilot's Operating Handbook*. The minimum distances required for takeoff and landing obtained either in planning prior to takeoff or in performance assessments conducted at the time of landing must fall within the applicable declared distances before the pilot can accept that runway for takeoff or landing.

(c) Runway design standards may impose restrictions on the amount of runway available for use in takeoff and landing that are not apparent from the reported physical length of the runway or from runway markings and lighting. The runway elements of Runway Safety Area (RSA), Runway Object Free Area (ROFA), and Runway Protection Zone (RPZ) may reduce a runway's declared distances to less than the physical length of the runway at geographically constrained airports (See Figure 4-3-6). When considering the amount of runway available for use in takeoff or landing performance calculations, the declared distances published for a runway must always be used in lieu of the runway's physical length.

Reference: AC 150/5300-13, Airport Design.

(d) While some runway elements associated with declared distances may be identifiable through runway markings or lighting (for example, a displaced threshold or a stopway), the individual declared distance limits are not marked or otherwise identified on the runway. An aircraft is **not prohibited** from operating beyond a declared distance limit during the takeoff, landing, or taxi operation provided the runway surface is appropriately marked as usable runway (See Figure 4-3-6). The following examples clarify the intent of this paragraph.

Reference: AIM, ¶2-3-3, Runway Markings; AC 150/5340-1, Standards for Airport Markings.

Example 1: The declared LDA for runway 9 must be used when showing compliance with the landing distance requirements of the applicable airplane operating rules and/or airplane operating limitations or when making a before landing performance assessment. The LDA is less than the physical runway length, not only because of the displaced threshold, but also because of the subtractions necessary to meet the RSA beyond the far end of the runway. However, during the actual landing operation, it is permissible for the airplane to roll beyond the unmarked end of the LDA.

Example 2: The declared ASDA for runway 9 must be used when showing compliance with the accelerate-stop distance requirements of the applicable airplane operating rules and/or airplane operating limitations. The ASDA is less than the physical length of the runway due to subtractions necessary to achieve the full RSA requirement. However, in the event of an aborted takeoff, it is permissible for the airplane to roll beyond the unmarked end of the ASDA as it is brought to a full-stop on the remaining usable runway.

FIGURE 4–3–5
Declared Distances with Full-Standard Runway Safety Areas, Runway Object Free Areas, and Runway Protection Zones

Runway	Length (feet)	TORA	ASDA	TODA	LDA
9	8000	8000	8500	8700	7700
27		8000	8600	8600	8000

FIGURE 4–3–6
Effects of a Geographical Constraint on a Runway's Declared Distances

Runway 27 operations: Runway 27 threshold displaced to provide the required RSA at the approach end of the runway. As a result, the LDA is reduced 200 feet.

Runway 9 operations: The ASDA is reduced by 600 feet to achieve the required RSA at the roll-out end of the runway. The LDA is reduced by 900 feet because, 1) the 300-foot displaced threshold located at the approach end of the runway (due to an approach obstacle), and 2) as result of the 600 feet of runway needed to achieve the required RSA at the roll-out end of the runway.

Runway	Length (feet)	TORA	TODA	ASDA	LDA
9	8000	8000	8000	7400	7100
27		8000	8000	8000	7800

Note: *A runway's RSA begins a set distance prior to the threshold and will extend a set distance beyond the end of the runway depending on the runway's design criteria. If these required lengths cannot be achieved, the ASDA and/or LDA will be reduced as necessary to obtain the required lengths to the extent practicable.*

4-3-7 Low Level Wind Shear/ Microburst Detection Systems

Low Level Wind Shear Alert System (LLWAS), Terminal Doppler Weather Radar (TDWR), Weather Systems Processor (WSP), and Integrated Terminal Weather System (ITWS) display information on hazardous wind shear and microburst activity in the vicinity of an airport to air traffic controllers who relay this information to pilots.

a. LLWAS provides wind shear alert and gust front information but does not provide microburst alerts. The LLWAS is designed to detect low level wind shear conditions around the periphery of an airport. It does not detect wind shear beyond that

limitation. Controllers will provide this information to pilots by giving the pilot the airport wind followed by the boundary wind.

Example: *Wind shear alert, airport wind 230 at 8, south boundary wind 170 at 20.*

b. LLWAS "network expansion," (LLWAS NE) and LLWAS Relocation/Sustainment (LLWAS-RS) are systems integrated with TDWR. These systems provide the capability of detecting microburst alerts and wind shear alerts. Controllers will issue the appropriate wind shear alerts or microburst alerts. In some of these systems controllers also have the ability to issue wind information

oriented to the threshold or departure end of the runway.

Example: *Runway 17 arrival microburst alert, 40 knot loss 3 mile final.*

Reference: *AIM, ¶7-1-24, Microbursts.*

c. More advanced systems are in the field or being developed such as ITWS. ITWS provides alerts for microbursts, wind shear, and significant thunderstorm activity. ITWS displays wind information oriented to the threshold or departure end of the runway.

d. The WSP provides weather processor enhancements to selected Airport Surveillance Radar (ASR)-9 facilities. The WSP provides Air Traffic with detection and alerting of hazardous weather such as wind shear, microbursts, and significant thunderstorm activity. The WSP displays terminal area 6 level weather, storm cell locations and movement, as well as the location and predicted future position and intensity of wind shifts that may affect airport operations. Controllers will receive and issue alerts based on Areas Noted for Attention (ARENA). An ARENA extends on the runway center line from a 3 mile final to the runway to a 2 mile departure.

e. An airport equipped with the LLWAS, ITWS, or WSP is so indicated in the Chart Supplement under Weather Data Sources for that particular airport.

4-3-8 Braking Action Reports and Advisories

a. When available, ATC furnishes pilots the quality of braking action received from pilots. The quality of braking action is described by the terms "good," "good to medium," "medium," "medium to poor," "poor," and "nil." When pilots report the quality of braking action by using the terms noted above, they should use descriptive terms that are easily understood, such as, "braking action poor the first/last half of the runway," together with the particular type of aircraft.

b. FICON NOTAMs will provide contaminant measurements for paved runways; however, a FICON NOTAM for braking action will only be used for non-paved runway surfaces, taxiways, and aprons. These NOTAMs are classified according to the most critical term ("good to medium," "medium," "medium to poor," and "poor").

1. FICON NOTAM reporting of a braking condition for paved runway surfaces is not permissible by Federally Obligated Airports or those airports certificated under 14 CFR Part 139.

2. A "NIL" braking condition at these airports must be mitigated by closure of the affected surface. Do not include the type of vehicle in the FICON NOTAM.

c. When tower controllers receive runway braking action reports which include the terms *medium, poor* or *nil*, or whenever weather conditions are conducive to deteriorating or rapidly changing runway braking conditions, the tower will include on the ATIS broadcast the statement, "BRAKING ACTION ADVISORIES ARE IN EFFECT."

d. During the time that braking action advisories are in effect, ATC will issue the most recent braking action report for the runway in use to each arriving and departing aircraft. Pilots should be prepared for deteriorating braking conditions and should request current runway condition information if not issued by controllers. Pilots should also be prepared to provide a descriptive runway condition report to controllers after landing.

4-3-9 Runway Condition Reports

a. Aircraft braking coefficient is dependent upon the surface friction between the tires on the aircraft wheels and the pavement surface. Less friction means less aircraft braking coefficient and less aircraft braking response.

b. Runway condition code (RwyCC) values range from 1 (poor) to 6 (dry). For frozen contaminants on runway surfaces, a runway condition code reading of 4 indicates the level when braking deceleration or directional control is between good and medium.

Note: *A RwyCC of "0" is used to delineate a braking action report of NIL and is prohibited from being reported in a FICON NOTAM.*

c. Airport management should conduct runway condition assessments on wet runways or runways covered with compacted snow and/or ice.

1. Numerical readings may be obtained by using the Runway Condition Assessment Matrix (RCAM). The RCAM provides the airport operator with data to complete the report that includes the following:

(a) Runway(s) in use

(b) Time of the assessment

(c) Runway condition codes for each zone (touchdown, mid-point, roll-out)

(d) Pilot-reported braking action report (if available)

(e) The contaminant (for example, wet snow, dry snow, slush, ice, etc.)

2. Assessments for each zone (see 4-3-9c1(c)) will be issued in the direction of takeoff and landing on the runway, ranging from "1" to "6" to describe contaminated surfaces.

Note: *A RwyCC of "0" is used to delineate a braking action report of NIL and is prohibited from being reported in a FICON NOTAM.*

3. When any 1 or more runway condition codes are reported as less than 6, airport management must notify ATC for dissemination to pilots.

4. Controllers will not issue runway condition codes when all 3 segments of a runway are reporting values of 6.

d. When runway condition code reports are provided by airport management, the ATC facility providing approach control or local airport advisory must provide the report to all pilots.

e. Pilots should use runway condition code information with other knowledge including aircraft performance characteristics, type, and weight, previous experience, wind conditions, and aircraft tire type (such as bias ply vs. radial constructed) to determine runway suitability.

f. The Runway Condition Assessment Matrix identifies the descriptive terms "good," "good to medium," "medium," "medium to poor," "poor," and "nil" used in braking action reports.

Reference: Advisory Circular AC 91-79A (Revision 1), Mitigating the Risks of a Runway Overrun Upon Landing, Appendix 1

FIGURE 4–3–7
Runway Condition Assessment Matrix (RCAM)

Assessment Criteria			Control/Braking Assessment Criteria	
Runway Condition Description		**RwyCC**	**Deceleration or Directional Control Observation**	**Pilot Reported Braking Action**
• Dry		6	—	—
• Frost • Wet (Includes damp and 1/8 inch depth or less of water) 1/8 inch (3 mm) depth or less of: • Slush • Dry Snow • Wet Snow		5	Braking deceleration is normal for the wheel braking effort applied AND directional control is normal.	Good
-15°C and Colder outside air temperature: • Compacted Snow		4	Braking deceleration OR directional control is between Good and Medium.	Good to Medium
• Slippery When Wet (wet runway) • Dry Snow or Wet Snow (any depth) over Compacted Snow Greater than 1/8 inch (3 mm) depth of: • Dry Snow • Wet Snow Warmer than -15°C outside air temperature: • Compacted Snow		3	Braking deceleration is noticeably reduced for the wheel braking effort applied OR directional control is noticeably reduced.	Medium
Greater than 1/8 inch (3 mm) depth of: • Water • Slush		2	Braking deceleration OR directional control is between Medium and Poor.	Medium to Poor
• Ice		1	Braking deceleration is significantly reduced for the wheel braking effort applied OR directional control is significantly reduced.	Poor
• Wet Ice • Slush over Ice • Water over Compacted Snow • Dry Snow or Wet Snow over Ice		0	Braking deceleration is minimal to non-existent for the wheel braking effort applied OR directional control is uncertain.	Nil

4–3–10 Intersection Takeoffs

a. In order to enhance airport capacities, reduce taxiing distances, minimize departure delays, and provide for more efficient movement of air traffic, controllers may initiate intersection takeoffs as well as approve them when the pilot requests. If for **any** reason a pilot prefers to use a different intersection or the full length of the runway or desires to obtain the distance between the intersection and the runway end, **the pilot is expected to inform ATC accordingly**.

b. Pilots are expected to assess the suitability of an intersection for use at takeoff during their preflight planning. They must consider the resultant length reduction to the published runway length and to the published declared distances from the intersection intended to be used for takeoff. The minimum runway required for takeoff must fall within the reduced runway length and the reduced declared distances before the intersection can be accepted for takeoff.

Reference: AIM, ¶4-3-6, Use of Runways/Declared Distances.

c. Controllers will issue the measured distance from the intersection to the runway end rounded "down" to the nearest 50 feet to any pilot who requests and to all military aircraft, unless use of the intersection is covered in appropriate directives. Controllers, however, will not be able to inform pilots of the distance from the intersection to the end of any of the published declared distances.

Reference: FAA Order JO 7110.65, ¶3-7-1, Ground Traffic Movement.

d. An aircraft is expected to taxi to (but not onto) the end of the assigned runway unless prior approval for an intersection departure is received from ground control.

e. Pilots should state their position on the airport when calling the tower for takeoff from a runway intersection.

Example: Cleveland Tower, Apache Three Seven Two Two Papa, at the intersection of taxiway Oscar and runway two three right, ready for departure.

f. Controllers are required to separate small aircraft that are departing from an intersection on the same runway (same or opposite direction) behind a large nonheavy aircraft (except B757) by ensuring that at least a 3-minute interval exists between the time the preceding large aircraft has taken off and the succeeding small aircraft begins takeoff roll. The 3-minute separation requirement will also be applied to small aircraft with a maximum certificated takeoff weight of 12,500 pounds or less departing behind a small aircraft with a maximum certificated takeoff weight of more than 12,500 pounds. To inform the pilot of the required 3-minute hold, the controller will state, "Hold for wake turbulence." If after considering wake turbulence hazards, the pilot feels that a lesser time interval is appropriate, the pilot may request a waiver to the 3-minute interval. To initiate such a request, simply say "Request waiver to 3-minute interval," or a similar statement. Controllers may then issue a takeoff clearance if other traffic permits, since the pilot has accepted the responsibility for wake turbulence separation.

g. The 3-minute interval is not required when the intersection is 500 feet or less from the departure point of the preceding aircraft and both aircraft are taking off in the same direction. Controllers may permit the small aircraft to alter course after takeoff to avoid the flight path of the preceding departure.

h. A 4-minute interval is mandatory for small, large, and heavy aircraft behind a super aircraft. The 3-minute interval is mandatory behind a heavy aircraft in all cases, and for small aircraft behind a B757.

4–3–11 Pilot Responsibilities When Conducting Land and Hold Short Operations (LAHSO)

a. LAHSO is an acronym for "Land and Hold Short Operations." These operations include landing and holding short of an intersecting runway, an intersecting taxiway, or some other designated point on a runway other than an intersecting runway or taxiway. (See Figure 4-3-8, Figure 4-3-9, Figure 4-3-10.)

b. Pilot Responsibilities and Basic Procedures.

1. LAHSO is an air traffic control procedure that requires pilot participation to balance the needs for increased airport capacity and system efficiency, consistent with safety. This procedure can be done safely provided pilots and controllers are knowledgeable and understand their responsibilities. The following paragraphs outline specific pilot/operator responsibilities when conducting LAHSO.

2. At controlled airports, air traffic may clear a pilot to land and hold short. Pilots may accept such a clearance provided that the pilot-in-command determines that the aircraft can safely land and stop within the Available Landing Distance (ALD). ALD data are published in the Chart Supplement and in the U.S. Terminal Procedures Publications. Controllers will also provide ALD data upon request. Student pilots or pilots not familiar with LAHSO should not participate in the program.

3. The pilot-in-command has the final authority to accept or decline any land and hold short clearance. The safety and operation of the aircraft remain the responsibility of the pilot. Pilots

are expected to decline a LAHSO clearance if they determine it will compromise safety.

4. To conduct LAHSO, pilots should become familiar with all available information concerning LAHSO at their destination airport. Pilots should have, *readily available,* the published ALD and runway slope information for all LAHSO runway combinations at each airport of intended landing. Additionally, knowledge about landing performance data permits the pilot to *readily* determine that the ALD for the assigned runway is sufficient for safe LAHSO. As part of a pilot's preflight planning process, pilots should determine if their destination airport has LAHSO. If so, their preflight planning process should include an assessment of which LAHSO combinations would work for them given their aircraft's required landing distance. Good pilot decision making is knowing in advance whether one can accept a LAHSO clearance if offered.

FIGURE 4–3–8
Land and Hold Short of an Intersecting Runway

Aircraft cleared to land using the full length of the runway

Aircraft cleared to land and hold short

FIGURE 4–3–9
Land and Hold Short of an Intersecting Taxiway

Taxiing aircraft

Aircraft cleared to land and hold short

FIGURE 4–3–10
Land and Hold Short of a Designated Point on a Runway Other Than an Intersecting Runway or Taxiway

Departing aircraft

Aircraft cleared to land and hold short

Example: *Figure 4-3-10—holding short at a designated point may be required to avoid conflicts with the runway safety area/flight path of a nearby runway.*

Note: *Each figure shows the approximate location of LAHSO markings, signage, and in-pavement lighting when installed.*

Reference: *AIM, Chapter 2, Aeronautical Lighting and Other Airport Visual Aids.*

5. If, for any reason, such as difficulty in discerning the location of a LAHSO intersection, wind conditions, aircraft condition, etc., the pilot elects to request to land on the full length of the runway, to land on another runway, or to decline LAHSO, a pilot is expected to promptly inform air traffic, ideally even before the clearance is issued. A LAHSO clearance, once accepted, must be adhered to, just as any other ATC clearance, unless an amended clearance is obtained or an emergency occurs. A LAHSO clearance does not preclude a rejected landing.

6. A pilot who accepts a LAHSO clearance should land and exit the runway at the first convenient taxiway (unless directed otherwise) before reaching the hold short point. Otherwise, the pilot must stop and hold at the hold short point. If a rejected landing becomes necessary after accepting a LAHSO clearance, the pilot should maintain safe separation from other aircraft or vehicles, and should promptly notify the controller.

7. Controllers need a full read back of all LAHSO clearances. Pilots should read back their LAHSO clearance and include the words, "HOLD SHORT OF (RUNWAY/TAXIWAY/OR POINT)" in their acknowledgment of all LAHSO clearances. In order to reduce frequency congestion, pilots are

encouraged to read back the LAHSO clearance without prompting. Don't make the controller have to ask for a read back!

c. LAHSO Situational Awareness

1. Situational awareness is **vital** to the success of LAHSO. Situational awareness starts with having current airport information in the cockpit, readily accessible to the pilot. (An airport diagram assists pilots in identifying their location on the airport, thus reducing requests for "progressive taxi instructions" from controllers.)

2. Situational awareness includes effective pilot-controller radio communication. ATC expects pilots to specifically acknowledge and read back all LAHSO clearances as follows:

Example:

ATC: *"(Aircraft ID) cleared to land runway six right, hold short of taxiway bravo for crossing traffic (type aircraft)."*

Aircraft: *"(Aircraft ID), Wilco, cleared to land runway six right to hold short of taxiway bravo."*

ATC: *"(Aircraft ID) cross runway six right at taxiway bravo, landing aircraft will hold short."*

Aircraft: *"(Aircraft ID), Wilco, cross runway six right at bravo, landing traffic (type aircraft) to hold."*

3. For those airplanes flown with two crewmembers, effective **intra-cockpit** communication between cockpit crewmembers is also critical. There have been several instances where the pilot working the radios accepted a LAHSO clearance but then simply forgot to tell the pilot flying the aircraft.

4. Situational awareness also includes a thorough understanding of the airport markings, signage, and lighting associated with LAHSO. These visual aids consist of a three-part system of yellow hold-short markings, red and white signage and, in certain cases, in-pavement lighting. Visual aids assist the pilot in determining where to hold short. Figure 4-3-8, Figure 4-3-9, Figure 4-3-10 depict how these markings, signage, and lighting combinations will appear once installed. Pilots are cautioned that not all airports conducting LAHSO have installed any or all of the above markings, signage, or lighting.

5. Pilots should only receive a LAHSO clearance when there is a minimum ceiling of 1,000 feet and 3 statute miles visibility. The intent of having "basic" VFR weather conditions is to allow pilots to maintain visual contact with other aircraft and ground vehicle operations. Pilots should consider the effects of prevailing inflight visibility (such as landing into the sun) and how it may affect overall situational awareness. Additionally, surface vehicles and aircraft being taxied by maintenance personnel may also be participating in LAHSO, especially in those operations that involve crossing an active runway.

4-3-12 Low Approach

a. A low approach (sometimes referred to as a low pass) is the go-around maneuver following an approach. Instead of landing or making a touch-and-go, a pilot may wish to go around (low approach) in order to expedite a particular operation (a series of practice instrument approaches is an example of such an operation). Unless otherwise authorized by ATC, the low approach should be made straight ahead, with no turns or climb made until the pilot has made a thorough visual check for other aircraft in the area.

b. When operating within a Class B, Class C, and Class D surface area, a pilot intending to make a low approach should contact the tower for approval. This request should be made prior to starting the final approach.

c. When operating to an airport, not within a Class B, Class C, and Class D surface area, a pilot intending to make a low approach should, prior to leaving the final approach fix inbound (nonprecision approach) or the outer marker or fix used in lieu of the outer marker inbound (precision approach), so advise the FSS, UNICOM, or make a broadcast as appropriate.

Reference: AIM, ¶4-1-9, Traffic Advisory Practices at Airports Without Operating Control Towers.

4-3-13 Traffic Control Light Signals

a. The following procedures are used by ATCTs in the control of aircraft, ground vehicles, equipment, and personnel not equipped with radio. These same procedures will be used to control aircraft, ground vehicles, equipment, and personnel equipped with radio if radio contact cannot be established. ATC personnel use a directive traffic control signal which emits an intense narrow light beam of a selected color (either red, white, or green) when controlling traffic by light signals.

b. Although the traffic signal light offers the advantage that some control may be exercised over nonradio equipped aircraft, pilots should be cognizant of the disadvantages which are:

1. Pilots may not be looking at the control tower at the time a signal is directed toward their aircraft.

2. The directions transmitted by a light signal are very limited since only approval or disapproval of a pilot's anticipated actions may be transmitted. No supplement or explanatory information may be transmitted except by the use of the "General Warning Signal" which advises the pilot to be on the alert.

c. Between sunset and sunrise, a pilot wishing to attract the attention of the control tower should turn on a landing light and taxi the aircraft into a position, clear of the active runway, so that light is visible to the tower. The landing light should remain on until appropriate signals are received from the tower.

d. Airport Traffic Control Tower Light Gun Signals. (See Table 4-3-1.)

e. During daylight hours, acknowledge tower transmissions or light signals by moving the ailerons or rudder. At night, acknowledge by blinking the landing or navigation lights. If radio malfunction occurs after departing the parking area, watch the tower for light signals or monitor tower frequency.

TABLE 4–3–1
AIRPORT TRAFFIC CONTROL TOWER LIGHT GUN SIGNALS

Color and Type of Signal	Movement of Vehicles, Equipment and Personnel	Aircraft on the Ground	Aircraft in Flight
Steady green	Cleared to cross, proceed or go	Cleared for takeoff	Cleared to land
Flashing green	Not applicable	Cleared for taxi	Return for landing (to be followed by steady green at the proper time)
Steady red	STOP	STOP	Give way to other aircraft and continue circling
Flashing red	Clear the taxiway/runway	Taxi clear of the runway in use	Airport unsafe, do not land
Flashing white	Return to starting point on airport	Return to starting point on airport	Not applicable
Alternating red and green	Exercise extreme caution	Exercise extreme caution	Exercise extreme caution

4-3-14 Communications

a. Pilots of departing aircraft should communicate with the control tower on the appropriate ground control/clearance delivery frequency prior to starting engines to receive engine start time, taxi and/or clearance information. Unless otherwise advised by the tower, remain on that frequency during taxiing and runup, then change to local control frequency when ready to request takeoff clearance.

Note: Pilots are encouraged to monitor the local tower frequency as soon as practical consistent with other ATC requirements.

Reference: AIM, ¶4-1-13, Automatic Terminal Information Service (ATIS).

b. The tower controller will consider that pilots of turbine-powered aircraft are ready for takeoff when they reach the runway or warm-up block unless they advised otherwise.

c. The majority of ground control frequencies are in the 121.6–121.9 MHz bandwidth. Ground control frequencies are provided to eliminate frequency congestion on the tower (local control) frequency and are limited to communications between the tower and aircraft on the ground and between the tower and utility vehicles on the airport, provide a clear VHF channel for arriving and departing aircraft. They are used for issuance of taxi information, clearances, and other necessary contacts between the tower and aircraft or other vehicles operated on the airport. A pilot who has just landed should not change from the tower frequency to the ground control frequency until directed to do so by the controller. Normally, only one ground control frequency is assigned at an airport; however, at locations where the amount of traffic so warrants, a second ground control frequency and/or another frequency designated as a clearance delivery frequency, may be assigned.

d. A controller may omit the ground or local control frequency if the controller believes the pilot knows which frequency is in use. If the ground control frequency is in the 121 MHz bandwidth the controller may omit the numbers preceding the decimal point; e.g., 121.7, "CONTACT GROUND POINT SEVEN." However, if any doubt exists as to what frequency is in use, the pilot should promptly request the controller to provide that information.

e. Controllers will normally avoid issuing a radio frequency change to helicopters, known to be single-piloted, which are hovering, air taxiing, or flying near the ground. At times, it may be necessary for pilots to alert ATC regarding single pilot operations to minimize delay of essential ATC communications. Whenever possible, ATC instructions will be relayed through the frequency being monitored until a frequency change

can be accomplished. You must promptly advise ATC if you are unable to comply with a frequency change. Also, you should advise ATC if you must land to accomplish the frequency change unless it is clear the landing will have no impact on other air traffic; e.g., on a taxiway or in a helicopter operating area.

4–3–15 Gate Holding Due to Departure Delays

a. Pilots should contact ground control or clearance delivery prior to starting engines as gate hold procedures will be in effect whenever departure delays exceed or are anticipated to exceed 15 minutes. The sequence for departure will be maintained in accordance with initial call up unless modified by flow control restrictions. Pilots should monitor the ground control or clearance delivery frequency for engine startup advisories or new proposed start time if the delay changes.

b. The tower controller will consider that pilots of turbine-powered aircraft are ready for takeoff when they reach the runway or warm-up block unless advised otherwise.

4–3–16 VFR Flights in Terminal Areas

Use reasonable restraint in exercising the prerogative of VFR flight, especially in terminal areas. The weather minimums and distances from clouds are minimums. Giving yourself a greater margin in specific instances is just good judgment.

a. Approach Area. Conducting a VFR operation in a Class B, Class C, Class D, and Class E surface area when the official visibility is 3 or 4 miles is not prohibited, but good judgment would dictate that you keep out of the approach area.

b. Reduced Visibility. It has always been recognized that precipitation reduces forward visibility. Consequently, although again it may be perfectly legal to cancel your IFR flight plan at any time you can proceed VFR, it is good practice, when precipitation is occurring, to continue IFR operation into a terminal area until you are reasonably close to your destination.

c. Simulated Instrument Flights. In conducting simulated instrument flights, be sure that the weather is good enough to compensate for the restricted visibility of the safety pilot and your greater concentration on your flight instruments. Give yourself a little greater margin when your flight plan lies in or near a busy airway or close to an airport.

4–3–17 VFR Helicopter Operations at Controlled Airports

a. General.

1. The following ATC procedures and phraseologies recognize the unique capabilities of helicopters and were developed to improve service to all users. Helicopter design characteristics and user needs often require operations from movement areas and nonmovement areas within the airport boundary. In order for ATC to properly apply these procedures, it is essential that pilots familiarize themselves with the local operations and make it known to controllers when additional instructions are necessary.

2. Insofar as possible, helicopter operations will be instructed to avoid the flow of fixed-wing aircraft to minimize overall delays; however, there will be many situations where faster/larger helicopters may be integrated with fixed-wing aircraft for the benefit of all concerned. Examples would include IFR flights, avoidance of noise sensitive areas, or use of runways/taxiways to minimize the hazardous effects of rotor downwash in congested areas.

3. Because helicopter pilots are intimately familiar with the effects of rotor downwash, they are best qualified to determine if a given operation can be conducted safely. Accordingly, the pilot has the final authority with respect to the specific airspeed/altitude combinations. ATC clearances are in no way intended to place the helicopter in a hazardous position. It is expected that pilots will advise ATC if a specific clearance will cause undue hazards to persons or property.

b. Controllers normally limit ATC ground service and instruction to *movement* areas; therefore, operations from *nonmovement* areas are conducted at pilot discretion and should be based on local policies, procedures, or letters of agreement. In order to maximize the flexibility of helicopter operations, it is necessary to rely heavily on sound pilot judgment. For example, hazards such as debris, obstructions, vehicles, or personnel must be recognized by the pilot, and action should be taken as necessary to avoid such hazards. Taxi, hover taxi, and air taxi operations are considered to be ground movements. Helicopters conducting such operations are expected to adhere to the same conditions, requirements, and practices as apply to other ground taxiing and ATC procedures in the AIM.

1. The phraseology *taxi* is used when it is intended or expected that the helicopter will taxi on the airport surface, either via taxiways or other prescribed routes. *Taxi* is used primarily for helicopters equipped with wheels or in response to a pilot request. Preference should be given to this procedure whenever it is necessary to minimize effects of rotor downwash.

Ch 4

2. Pilots may request a *hover taxi* when slow forward movement is desired or when it may be appropriate to move very short distances. Pilots should avoid this procedure if rotor downwash is likely to cause damage to parked aircraft or if blowing dust/snow could obscure visibility. If it is necessary to operate above 25 feet AGL when hover taxiing, the pilot should initiate a request to ATC.

3. *Air taxi* is the preferred method for helicopter ground movements on airports provided ground operations and conditions permit. Unless otherwise requested or instructed, pilots are expected to remain below 100 feet AGL. However, if a higher than normal airspeed or altitude is desired, the request should be made prior to liftoff. The pilot is solely responsible for selecting a safe airspeed for the altitude/operation being conducted. Use of *air taxi* enables the pilot to proceed at an optimum airspeed/altitude, minimize downwash effect, conserve fuel, and expedite movement from one point to another. Helicopters should avoid overflight of other aircraft, vehicles, and personnel during air-taxi operations. Caution must be exercised concerning active runways and pilots must be certain that air taxi instructions are understood. Special precautions may be necessary at unfamiliar airports or airports with multiple/intersecting active runways. The taxi procedures given in paragraph 4-3-18, Taxiing, paragraph 4-3-19, Taxi During Low Visibility, and paragraph 4-3-21, Exiting the Runway After Landing, also apply.

Reference
Pilot/Controller Glossary—Taxi.
Pilot/Controller Glossary—Hover Taxi.
Pilot/Controller Glossary—Air Taxi.

c. Takeoff and Landing Procedures.

1. Helicopter operations may be conducted from a runway, taxiway, portion of a landing strip, or any clear area which could be used as a landing site such as the scene of an accident, a construction site, or the roof of a building. The terms used to describe designated areas from which helicopters operate are: movement area, landing/takeoff area, apron/ramp, heliport and helipad (See Pilot/Controller Glossary). These areas may be improved or unimproved and may be separate from or located on an airport/heliport. ATC will issue takeoff clearances from *movement* areas other than active runways, or in diverse directions from active runways, with additional instructions as necessary. Whenever possible, takeoff clearance will be issued in lieu of extended hover/air taxi operations. Phraseology will be "CLEARED FOR TAKEOFF FROM (TAXIWAY, HELIPAD, RUNWAY NUMBER, ETC.), MAKE RIGHT/LEFT TURN FOR (DIRECTION, HEADING, NAVAID RADIAL) DEPARTURE/DEPARTURE ROUTE (NUMBER, NAME, ETC.)." Unless requested by the pilot, downwind takeoffs will not be issued if the tailwind exceeds 5 knots.

2. Pilots should be alert to wind information as well as to wind indications in the vicinity of the helicopter. ATC should be advised of the intended method of departing. A pilot request to takeoff in a given direction indicates that the pilot is willing to accept the wind condition and controllers will honor the request if traffic permits. Departure points could be a significant distance from the control tower and it may be difficult or impossible for the controller to determine the helicopter's relative position to the wind.

3. If takeoff is requested from *nonmovement* areas, an area not authorized for helicopter use, an area not visible from the tower, an unlighted area at night, or an area off the airport, the phraseology "DEPARTURE FROM (requested location) WILL BE AT YOUR OWN RISK (additional instructions, as necessary). USE CAUTION (if applicable)." The pilot is responsible for operating in a safe manner and should exercise due caution.

4. Similar phraseology is used for helicopter landing operations. Every effort will be made to permit helicopters to proceed direct and land as near as possible to their final destination on the airport. Traffic density, the need for detailed taxiing instructions, frequency congestion, or other factors may affect the extent to which service can be expedited. As with ground movement operations, a high degree of pilot/controller cooperation and communication is necessary to achieve safe and efficient operations.

4–3–18 Taxiing

a. General. Approval must be obtained prior to moving an aircraft or vehicle onto the movement area during the hours an Airport Traffic Control Tower is in operation.

1. Always state your position on the airport when calling the tower for taxi instructions.

2. The movement area is normally described in local bulletins issued by the airport manager or control tower. These bulletins may be found in FSSs, fixed base operators offices, air carrier offices, and operations offices.

3. The control tower also issues bulletins describing areas where they cannot provide ATC service due to nonvisibility or other reasons.

4. A clearance must be obtained prior to taxiing on a runway, taking off, or landing during the hours an Airport Traffic Control Tower is in operation.

5. A clearance must be obtained prior to crossing any runway. ATC will issue an explicit clearance for all runway crossings.

6. When assigned a takeoff runway, ATC will first specify the runway, issue taxi instructions, and state any hold short instructions or runway crossing clearances if the taxi route will cross a

runway. This does not authorize the aircraft to "enter" or "cross" the assigned departure runway at any point. In order to preclude misunderstandings in radio communications, ATC will not use the word "cleared" in conjunction with authorization for aircraft to taxi.

7. When issuing taxi instructions to any point other than an assigned takeoff runway, ATC will specify the point to taxi to, issue taxi instructions, and state any hold short instructions or runway crossing clearances if the taxi route will cross a runway.

Note: ATC is required to obtain a readback from the pilot of all runway hold short instructions.

8. If a pilot is expected to hold short of a runway approach/departure (*Runway XX* APPCH/*Runway XX* DEP) hold area or ILS holding position (see Figure 2-3-15, Taxiways Located in Runway Approach Area), ATC will issue instructions.

9. When taxi instructions are received from the controller, pilots should always read back:

(a) The runway assignment.

(b) Any clearance to enter a specific runway.

(c) Any instruction to hold short of a specific runway or line up and wait.

10. Controllers are required to request a readback of runway hold short assignment when it is not received from the pilot/vehicle.

b. ATC clearances or instructions pertaining to taxiing are predicated on known traffic and known physical airport conditions. Therefore, it is important that pilots clearly understand the clearance or instruction. Although an ATC clearance is issued for taxiing purposes, when operating in accordance with the CFRs, it is the responsibility of the pilot to avoid collision with other aircraft. Since "the pilot-in-command of an aircraft is directly responsible for, and is the final authority as to, the operation of that aircraft" the pilot should obtain clarification of any clearance or instruction which is not understood.

1. Good operating practice dictates that pilots acknowledge all runway crossing, hold short, or takeoff clearances unless there is some misunderstanding, at which time the pilot should query the controller until the clearance is understood.

Note: Air traffic controllers are required to obtain from the pilot a readback of all runway hold short instructions.

2. Pilots operating a single pilot aircraft should monitor only assigned ATC communications after being cleared onto the active runway for departure. Single pilot aircraft should not monitor other than ATC communications until flight from Class B, Class C, or Class D surface area is completed. This same procedure should be practiced from after receipt of the clearance for landing until the landing and taxi activities are complete. Proper effective scanning for other aircraft, surface vehicles, or other objects should be continuously exercised in all cases.

3. If the pilot is unfamiliar with the airport or for any reason confusion exists as to the correct taxi routing, a request may be made for progressive taxi instructions which include step-by-step routing directions. Progressive instructions may also be issued if the controller deems it necessary due to traffic or field conditions (for example, construction or closed taxiways).

c. At those airports where the U.S. Government operates the control tower and ATC has authorized noncompliance with the requirement for two-way radio communications while operating within the Class B, Class C, or Class D surface area, or at those airports where the U.S. Government does not operate the control tower and radio communications cannot be established, pilots must obtain a clearance by visual light signal prior to taxiing on a runway and prior to takeoff and landing.

d. The following phraseologies and procedures are used in radiotelephone communications with aeronautical ground stations.

1. Request for taxi instructions prior to departure. State your aircraft identification, location, type of operation planned (VFR or IFR), and the point of first intended landing.

Example:

Aircraft: *"Washington ground, Beechcraft One Three One Five Niner at hangar eight, ready to taxi, I-F-R to Chicago."*

Tower: *"Beechcraft one three one five niner, Washington ground, runway two seven, taxi via taxiways Charlie and Delta, hold short of runway three three left."*

Aircraft: *"Beechcraft One Three One Five Niner, runway two seven, hold short of runway three three left."*

2. Receipt of ATC clearance. ARTCC clearances are relayed to pilots by airport traffic controllers in the following manner.

Example:

Tower: *"Beechcraft One Three One Five Niner, cleared to the Chicago Midway Airport via Victor Eight, maintain eight thousand."*

Aircraft: *"Beechcraft One Three One Five Niner, cleared to the Chicago Midway Airport via Victor Eight, maintain eight thousand."*

Note: Normally, an ATC IFR clearance is relayed to a pilot by the ground controller. At busy locations, however, pilots may be instructed by the ground controller to "contact clearance delivery" on a frequency designated for this purpose. No

surveillance or control over the movement of traffic is exercised by this position of operation.

3. Request for taxi instructions after landing. State your aircraft identification, location, and that you request taxi instructions.

Example:

Aircraft: "Dulles ground, Beechcraft One Four Two Six One clearing runway one right on taxiway echo three, request clearance to Page."

Tower: "Beechcraft One Four Two Six One, Dulles ground, taxi to Page via taxiways echo three, echo one, and echo niner."

or

Aircraft: "Orlando ground, Beechcraft One Four Two Six One clearing runway one eight left at taxiway bravo three, request clearance to Page."

Tower: "Beechcraft One Four Two Six One, Orlando ground, hold short of runway one eight right."

Aircraft: "Beechcraft One Four Two Six One, hold short of runway one eight right."

e. During ground operations, jet blast, prop wash, and rotor wash can cause damage and upsets if encountered at close range. Pilots should consider the effects of jet blast, prop wash, and rotor wash on aircraft, vehicles, and maintenance equipment during ground operations.

4–3–19 Taxi During Low Visibility

a. Pilots and aircraft operators should be constantly aware that during certain low visibility conditions the movement of aircraft and vehicles on airports may not be visible to the tower controller. This may prevent visual confirmation of an aircraft's adherence to taxi instructions.

b. Of vital importance is the need for pilots to notify the controller when difficulties are encountered or at the first indication of becoming disoriented. Pilots should proceed with extreme caution when taxiing toward the sun. When vision difficulties are encountered pilots should immediately inform the controller.

c. Advisory Circular 120-57, Low Visibility Operations Surface Movement Guidance and Control System, commonly known as LVOSMGCS (pronounced "LVO SMIGS") describes an adequate example of a low visibility taxi plan for any airport which has takeoff or landing operations in less than 1,200 feet runway visual range (RVR) visibility conditions. These plans, which affect aircrew and vehicle operators, may incorporate additional lighting, markings, and procedures to control airport surface traffic. They will be addressed at two levels; operations less than 1,200 feet RVR to 500 feet RVR and operations less than 500 feet RVR.

Note: Specific lighting systems and surface markings may be found in ¶2-1-10, Taxiway Lights, and ¶2-3-4, Taxiway Markings.

d. When low visibility conditions exist, pilots should focus their entire attention on the safe operation of the aircraft while it is moving. Checklists and nonessential communication should be withheld until the aircraft is stopped and the brakes set.

4–3–20 Standard Taxi Routes

a. Standard Taxi Routes (STRs) provide a standard, predictable taxi route from an origination point to a termination point on the airport movement area. The use of STRs helps reduce frequency congestion and streamline taxi procedures. STRs may be available at certain airports. Absent an STR Letter of Agreement (LOA), issuance of an STR will be at the request of the pilot and discretion of ATC. STRs used under an LOA are issued by ATC and are not required to be requested by the pilot.

b. STRs are available via two methods, (LOA) or publicly-available via the Domestic Notices website: https://www.faa.gov/air_traffic /publications/domesticnotices/.

c. An LOA for STRs will be revised for updates and changes, including cancellation on an as-needed basis with the operator. It is the responsibility of the operator to distribute changes to their flight crews.

d. An STR may be requested by a pilot or assigned at the discretion of ATC to the pilot of an operator with an LOA STR. It is the responsibility of the pilot to request a full taxi clearance if not fully familiar with the STR.

e. A Letter to Airmen (LTA) will be issued by airport traffic control towers to announce availability, updates, cancelation, or changes of publicly-available STRs with appropriate updates to the Domestic Notices website. An LTA may include an airport diagram. The airport diagram will be labeled "not for navigation" and is not an acceptable substitute for the most up-to-date airport diagrams. LTAs are available via the FAA NOTAM Search website: https://notams.aim.faa .gov/notamSearch/.

f. Pilots request publicly-available STRs by stating the desired STR name (e.g., ATC facility, flight or aircraft identification, location, request STR name). By requesting an STR, a pilot acknowledges full familiarity with the STR. The issuance of a pilot-requested STR is at the discretion of ATC.

g. STRs contain the same characteristics and responsibilities:

1. Pilots should not request, and ATC may not issue STR instructions during low visibility Surface Movement Guidance and Control System (SMGCS) operations.

2. It is the pilot's responsibility to maintain familiarity and awareness of the most current versions of STRs, as well as airport diagrams and charts prior to accepting an STR assignment.

3. If a pilot is unsure about the assigned STR procedure, the pilot is encouraged to either seek clarification from ATC or decline the STR assignment.

4. Pilots who become disoriented during taxi should advise ATC immediately and request detailed taxi instructions or other assistance.

5. An STR instruction does not constitute nor imply a clearance to cross a runway.

6. Unless otherwise stated by ATC, the issuance of an STR does not give an aircraft the right of way over another taxiing aircraft.

7. Unless otherwise instructed by ATC, originating from, and terminating to a non-movement area as part of an STR is at the discretion of the pilot in coordination with ramp control, if required.

8. If ATC instructs the pilot to deviate from an STR, ATC must issue detailed taxi instructions for the remainder of the taxi.

9. Pilots are urged to exercise caution when accepting STR assignments, especially when STRs are used or available at more than one airport in the same terminal area.

h. ATC may cancel, amend, or revise an STR as necessary. Any updates to publicly-available STRs will be communicated via LTA with appropriate updates to the Domestic Notices website.

4–3–21 Exiting the Runway After Landing

The following procedures must be followed after landing and reaching taxi speed.

a. Exit the runway without delay at the first available taxiway or on a taxiway as instructed by ATC. Pilots must not exit the landing runway onto another runway unless authorized by ATC. At airports with an operating control tower, pilots should not stop or reverse course on the runway without first obtaining ATC approval.

b. Taxi clear of the runway unless otherwise directed by ATC. An aircraft is considered clear of the runway when all parts of the aircraft are past the runway edge and there are no restrictions to its continued movement beyond the runway holding position markings. In the absence of ATC instructions, the pilot is expected to taxi clear of the landing runway by taxiing beyond the runway holding position markings associated with the landing runway, even if that requires the aircraft to protrude into or cross another taxiway or ramp area. Once all parts of the aircraft have crossed the runway holding position markings, the pilot must hold unless further instructions have been issued by ATC.

Note 1: The tower will issue the pilot instructions which will permit the aircraft to enter another taxiway, runway, or ramp area when required.

Note 2: Guidance contained in subparagraphs a and b above is considered an integral part of the landing clearance and satisfies the requirement of 14 CFR Section 91.129.

c. Immediately change to ground control frequency when advised by the tower and obtain a taxi clearance.

Note 1: The tower will issue instructions required to resolve any potential conflictions with other ground traffic prior to advising the pilot to contact ground control.

Note 2: Ground control will issue taxi clearance to parking. That clearance does not authorize the aircraft to "enter" or "cross" any runways. Pilots not familiar with the taxi route should request specific taxi instructions from ATC.

4–3–22 Practice Instrument Approaches

a. Various air traffic incidents have indicated the necessity for adoption of measures to achieve more organized and controlled operations where practice instrument approaches are conducted. Practice instrument approaches are considered to be instrument approaches made by either a VFR aircraft not on an IFR flight plan or an aircraft on an IFR flight plan. To achieve this and thereby enhance air safety, it is Air Traffic's policy to provide for separation of such operations at locations where approach control facilities are located and, as resources permit, at certain other locations served by ARTCCs or parent approach control facilities. Pilot requests to practice instrument approaches may be approved by ATC subject to traffic and workload conditions. Pilots should anticipate that in some instances the controller may find it necessary to deny approval or withdraw previous approval when traffic conditions warrant. It must be clearly understood, however, that even though the controller may be providing separation, pilots on VFR flight plans are required to comply with basic VFR weather minimums (14 CFR Section 91.155). Application of ATC procedures or any action taken by the controller to avoid traffic conflictions does not relieve IFR and VFR pilots of their responsibility to see-and-avoid other traffic while operating in VFR conditions (14 CFR Section 91.113). In addition to the normal IFR separation minimums (which includes visual separation) during VFR conditions, 500 feet vertical separation may be applied between VFR aircraft and between a VFR aircraft and the IFR aircraft. Pilots not on IFR flight plans desiring practice instrument approaches should

Ch 4

always state "practice" when making requests to ATC. Controllers will instruct VFR aircraft requesting an instrument approach to maintain VFR. This is to preclude misunderstandings between the pilot and controller as to the status of the aircraft. If pilots wish to proceed in accordance with instrument flight rules, they must specifically request and obtain, an IFR clearance.

b. Before practicing an instrument approach, pilots should inform the approach control facility or the tower of the type of practice approach they desire to make and how they intend to terminate it, i.e., full-stop landing, touch-and-go, or missed or low approach maneuver. This information may be furnished progressively when conducting a series of approaches. Pilots on an IFR flight plan, who have made a series of instrument approaches to full stop landings should inform ATC when they make their final landing. The controller will control flights practicing instrument approaches so as to ensure that they do not disrupt the flow of arriving and departing itinerant IFR or VFR aircraft. The priority afforded itinerant aircraft over practice instrument approaches is not intended to be so rigidly applied that it causes grossly inefficient application of services. A minimum delay to itinerant traffic may be appropriate to allow an aircraft practicing an approach to complete that approach.

Note: *A clearance to land means that appropriate separation on the landing runway will be ensured. A landing clearance does not relieve the pilot from compliance with any previously issued restriction.*

c. At airports without a tower, pilots wishing to make practice instrument approaches should notify the facility having control jurisdiction of the desired approach as indicated on the approach chart. All approach control facilities and ARTCCs are required to publish a Letter to Airmen depicting those airports where they provide standard separation to both VFR and IFR aircraft conducting practice instrument approaches.

d. The controller will provide approved separation between both VFR and IFR aircraft when authorization is granted to make practice approaches to airports where an approach control facility is located and to certain other airports served by approach control or an ARTCC. Controller responsibility for separation of VFR aircraft begins at the point where the approach clearance becomes effective, or when the aircraft enters Class B or Class C airspace, or a TRSA, whichever comes first.

e. VFR aircraft practicing instrument approaches are not automatically authorized to execute the missed approach procedure. This authorization must be specifically requested by the pilot and approved by the controller. Where ATC procedures require application of IFR separation to VFR aircraft practicing instrument approaches, separation will be provided throughout the procedure including the missed approach. Where no separation services are provided during the practice approach, no separation services will be provided during the missed approach.

f. Except in an emergency, aircraft cleared to practice instrument approaches must not deviate from the approved procedure until cleared to do so by the controller.

g. At radar approach control locations when a full approach procedure (procedure turn, etc.,) cannot be approved, pilots should expect to be vectored to a final approach course for a practice instrument approach which is compatible with the general direction of traffic at that airport.

h. When granting approval for a practice instrument approach, the controller will usually ask the pilot to report to the tower prior to or over the final approach fix inbound (nonprecision approaches) or over the outer marker or fix used in lieu of the outer marker inbound (precision approaches).

i. When authorization is granted to conduct practice instrument approaches to an airport with a tower, but where approved standard separation is not provided to aircraft conducting practice instrument approaches, the tower will approve the practice approach, instruct the aircraft to maintain VFR and issue traffic information, as required.

j. When an aircraft notifies a FSS providing Local Airport Advisory to the airport concerned of the intent to conduct a practice instrument approach and whether or not separation is to be provided, the pilot will be instructed to contact the appropriate facility on a specified frequency prior to initiating the approach. At airports where separation is not provided, the FSS will acknowledge the message and issue known traffic information but will neither approve or disapprove the approach.

k. Pilots conducting practice instrument approaches should be particularly alert for other aircraft operating in the local traffic pattern or in proximity to the airport.

4–3–23 Option Approach

The "Cleared for the Option" procedure will permit an instructor, flight examiner or pilot the option to make a touch-and-go, low approach, missed approach, stop-and-go, or full stop landing. This procedure can be very beneficial in a training situation in that neither the student pilot nor examinee would know what maneuver would be accomplished. The pilot should make a request for this procedure passing the final approach fix inbound on an instrument approach or entering downwind for a VFR traffic pattern. After ATC approval of the option, the pilot should inform ATC as soon as possible of any delay on the runway during their stop-and-go or full stop landing. The advantages

of this procedure as a training aid are that it enables an instructor or examiner to obtain the reaction of a trainee or examinee under changing conditions, the pilot would not have to discontinue an approach in the middle of the procedure due to student error or pilot proficiency requirements, and finally it allows more flexibility and economy in training programs. This procedure will only be used at those locations with an operational control tower and will be subject to ATC approval.

4-3-24 Use of Aircraft Lights

a. Aircraft position lights are required to be lighted on aircraft operated on the surface and in flight from sunset to sunrise. In addition, aircraft equipped with an anti-collision light system are required to operate that light system during all types of operations (day and night). However, during any adverse meteorological conditions, the pilot-in-command may determine that the anti-collision lights should be turned off when their light output would constitute a hazard to safety (14 CFR Section 91.209). Supplementary strobe lights should be turned off on the ground when they adversely affect ground personnel or other pilots, and in flight when there are adverse reflection from clouds.

b. An aircraft anti-collision light system can use one or more rotating beacons and/or strobe lights, be colored either red or white, and have different (higher than minimum) intensities when compared to other aircraft. Many aircraft have both a rotating beacon and a strobe light system.

c. The FAA has a voluntary pilot safety program, Operation Lights On, to enhance the *see-and-avoid* concept. Pilots are encouraged to turn on their landing lights during takeoff; i.e., either after takeoff clearance has been received or when beginning takeoff roll. Pilots are further encouraged to turn on their landing lights when operating below 10,000 feet, day or night, especially when operating within 10 miles of any airport, or in conditions of reduced visibility and in areas where flocks of birds may be expected, i.e., coastal areas, lake areas, around refuse dumps, etc. Although turning on aircraft lights does enhance the *see-and-avoid* concept, pilots should not become complacent about keeping a sharp lookout for other aircraft. Not all aircraft are equipped with lights and some pilots may not have their lights turned on. Aircraft manufacturer's recommendations for operation of landing lights and electrical systems should be observed.

d. Prop and jet blast forces generated by large aircraft have overturned or damaged several smaller aircraft taxiing behind them. To avoid similar results, and in the interest of preventing upsets and injuries to ground personnel from such forces, the FAA recommends that air carriers and commercial operators turn on their rotating beacons anytime their aircraft engines are in operation. General aviation pilots using rotating beacon equipped aircraft are also encouraged to participate in this program which is designed to alert others to the potential hazard. Since this is a voluntary program, exercise caution and do not rely solely on the rotating beacon as an indication that aircraft engines are in operation.

e. Prior to commencing taxi, it is recommended to turn on navigation, position, anti-collision, and logo lights (if equipped). To signal intent to other pilots, consider turning on the taxi light when the aircraft is moving or intending to move on the ground, and turning it off when stopped or yielding to other ground traffic. Strobe lights should not be illuminated during taxi if they will adversely affect the vision of other pilots or ground personnel.

f. At the discretion of the pilot-in-command, all exterior lights should be illuminated when taxiing on or across any runway. This increases the conspicuousness of the aircraft to controllers and other pilots approaching to land, taxiing, or crossing the runway. Pilots should comply with any equipment operating limitations and consider the effects of landing and strobe lights on other aircraft in their vicinity.

g. When entering the departure runway for takeoff or to "line up and wait," all lights, except for landing lights, should be illuminated to make the aircraft conspicuous to ATC and other aircraft on approach. Landing lights should be turned on when takeoff clearance is received or when commencing takeoff roll at an airport without an operating control tower.

4-3-25 Flight Inspection/"Flight Check" Aircraft in Terminal Areas

a. Flight check is a call sign used to alert pilots and air traffic controllers when a FAA aircraft is engaged in flight inspection/certification of NAVAIDs and flight procedures. Flight check aircraft fly preplanned high/low altitude flight patterns such as grids, orbits, DME arcs, and tracks, including low passes along the full length of the runway to verify NAVAID performance.

b. Pilots should be especially watchful and avoid the flight paths of any aircraft using the call sign "Flight Check." These flights will normally receive special handling from ATC. Pilot patience and cooperation in allowing uninterrupted recordings can significantly help expedite flight inspections, minimize costly, repetitive runs, and reduce the burden on the U.S. taxpayer.

Ch 4

4-3-26 Hand Signals

FIGURE 4-3-11
Signalman Directs Towing

Signalman

FIGURE 4-3-12
Signalman's Position

Signalman

FIGURE 4-3-13
All Clear (O.K.)

FIGURE 4-3-14
Start Engine

Point to engine to be started

FIGURE 4–3–15
Pull Chocks

FIGURE 4–3–17
Left Turn

FIGURE 4–3–16
Proceed Straight Ahead

FIGURE 4–3–18
Right Turn

Ch 4

FIGURE 4–3–19
Slow Down

FIGURE 4–3–21
Insert Chocks

FIGURE 4–3–20
Flagman Directs Pilot

FIGURE 4–3–22
Cut Engines

FIGURE 4-3-23
Night Operation

Use same hand
movements as
day operation

FIGURE 4-3-24
Stop

Ch 4

4-3-27 Operations at Uncontrolled Airports With Automated Surface Observing System (ASOS)/ Automated Weather Observing System (AWOS)

a. Many airports throughout the National Airspace System are equipped with either ASOS or AWOS. At most airports with an operating control tower or human observer, the weather will be available to you in an Aviation Routine Weather Report (METAR) hourly or special observation format on the Automatic Terminal Information Service (ATIS) or directly transmitted from the controller/observer.

b. At uncontrolled airports that are equipped with ASOS/AWOS with ground-to-air broadcast capability, the one-minute updated airport weather should be available to you within approximately 25 NM of the airport below 10,000 feet. The frequency for the weather broadcast will be published on sectional charts and in the Chart Supplement. Some part-time towered airports may also broadcast the automated weather on their ATIS frequency during the hours that the tower is closed.

c. Controllers issue SVFR or IFR clearances based on pilot request, known traffic and reported weather, i.e., METAR/Nonroutine (Special) Aviation Weather Report (SPECI) observations, when they are available. Pilots have access to more current weather at uncontrolled ASOS/AWOS airports than do the controllers who may be located several miles away. Controllers will rely on the pilot to determine the current airport weather from the ASOS/AWOS. All aircraft arriving or departing an ASOS/AWOS equipped uncontrolled airport should monitor the airport weather frequency to ascertain the status of the airspace. Pilots in Class E airspace must be alert for changing weather conditions which may affect the status of the airspace from IFR/VFR. If ATC service is required for IFR/SVFR approach/departure or requested for VFR service, the pilot should advise the controller that he/she has received the one-minute weather and state his/her intentions.

Example: "I have the (airport) one-minute weather, request an ILS Runway 14 approach."

Reference: AIM, ¶7-1-10, Weather Observing Programs.

Section 4 ATC Clearances and Aircraft Separation

4-4-1 Clearance

a. A clearance issued by ATC is predicated on known traffic and known physical airport conditions. An ATC clearance means an authorization by ATC, for the purpose of preventing collision between known aircraft, for an aircraft to proceed under specified conditions within controlled airspace. IT IS NOT AUTHORIZATION FOR A PILOT TO DEVIATE FROM ANY RULE, REGULATION, OR MINIMUM ALTITUDE NOR TO CONDUCT UNSAFE OPERATION OF THE AIRCRAFT.

b. 14 CFR Section 91.3(a) states: "The pilot-in-command of an aircraft is directly responsible for, and is the final authority as to, the operation of that aircraft." If ATC issues a clearance that would cause a pilot to deviate from a rule or regulation, or in the pilot's opinion, would place the aircraft in jeopardy, IT IS THE PILOT'S RESPONSIBILITY TO REQUEST AN AMENDED CLEARANCE. Similarly, if a pilot prefers to follow a different course of action, such as make a 360 degree turn for spacing to follow traffic when established in a landing or approach sequence, land on a different runway, takeoff from a different intersection, takeoff from the threshold instead of an intersection, or delay operation, THE PILOT IS EXPECTED TO INFORM ATC ACCORDINGLY. When the pilot requests a different course of action, however, the pilot is expected to cooperate so as to preclude disruption of traffic flow or creation of conflicting patterns. The pilot is also expected to use the appropriate aircraft call sign to acknowledge all ATC clearances, frequency changes, or advisory information.

c. Each pilot who deviates from an ATC clearance in response to a Traffic Alert and Collision Avoidance System resolution advisory must notify ATC of that deviation as soon as possible.

Reference: Pilot/Controller Glossary Term—Traffic Alert and Collision Avoidance System.

d. When weather conditions permit, during the time an IFR flight is operating, it is the direct responsibility of the pilot to avoid other aircraft since VFR flights may be operating in the same area without the knowledge of ATC. Traffic clearances provide standard separation only between IFR flights.

4-4-2 Clearance Prefix

A clearance, control information, or a response to a request for information originated by an ATC facility and relayed to the pilot through an air-to-ground communication station will be prefixed by "ATC clears," "ATC advises," or "ATC requests."

4-4-3 Clearance Items

ATC clearances normally contain the following:

a. **Clearance Limit.** The traffic clearance issued prior to departure will normally authorize flight to the airport of intended landing. Many airports and associated NAVAIDs are collocated with the same name and/or identifier, so care should be exercised to ensure a clear understanding of the clearance limit. When the clearance limit is the airport of intended landing, the clearance should contain the airport name followed by the word "airport." Under certain conditions, a clearance limit may be a NAVAID or other fix. When the clearance limit is a NAVAID, intersection, or waypoint and the type is known, the clearance should contain type. Under certain conditions, at some locations a short-range clearance procedure is utilized whereby a clearance is issued to a fix within or just outside of the terminal area and pilots are advised of the frequency on which they will receive the long-range clearance direct from the center controller.

b. **Departure Procedure.** Headings to fly and altitude restrictions may be issued to separate a departure from other air traffic in the terminal area. Where the volume of traffic warrants, DPs have been developed.

Reference: AIM, ¶5-2-6, Abbreviated IFR Departure Clearance (Cleared...as Filed) Procedures; AIM, ¶5-2-9, Instrument Departure Procedures (DP)—Obstacle Departure Procedures (ODP) and Standard Instrument Departures (SID).

c. **Route of Flight.**

1. Clearances are normally issued for the altitude or flight level and route filed by the pilot. However, due to traffic conditions, it is frequently necessary for ATC to specify an altitude or flight level or route different from that requested by the pilot. In addition, flow patterns have been established in certain congested areas or between congested areas whereby traffic capacity is increased by routing all traffic on preferred routes. Information on these flow patterns is available in offices where preflight briefing is furnished or where flight plans are accepted.

2. When required, air traffic clearances include data to assist pilots in identifying radio reporting points. It is the responsibility of pilots to notify ATC immediately if their radio equipment cannot receive the type of signals they must utilize to comply with their clearance.

d. **Altitude Data.**

1. The altitude or flight level instructions in an ATC clearance normally require that a pilot "MAINTAIN" the altitude or flight level at which the flight will operate when in controlled airspace.

Altitude or flight level changes while en route should be requested prior to the time the change is desired.

2. When possible, if the altitude assigned is different from the altitude requested by the pilot, ATC will inform the pilot when to expect climb or descent clearance or to request altitude change from another facility. If this has not been received prior to crossing the boundary of the ATC facility's area and assignment at a different altitude is still desired, the pilot should reinitiate the request with the next facility.

3. The term "cruise" may be used instead of "MAINTAIN" to assign a block of airspace to a pilot from the minimum IFR altitude up to and including the altitude specified in the cruise clearance. The pilot may level off at any intermediate altitude within this block of airspace. Climb/descent within the block is to be made at the discretion of the pilot. However, once the pilot starts descent and verbally reports leaving an altitude in the block, the pilot may not return to that altitude without additional ATC clearance.

Reference: Pilot/Controller Glossary Term—Cruise.

e. Holding Instructions.

1. Whenever an aircraft has been cleared to a fix other than the destination airport and delay is expected, it is the responsibility of the ATC controller to issue complete holding instructions (unless the pattern is charted), an EFC time, and a best estimate of any additional en route/terminal delay.

2. If the holding pattern is charted and the controller doesn't issue complete holding instructions, the pilot is expected to hold as depicted on the appropriate chart. When the pattern is charted, the controller may omit all holding instructions except the charted holding direction and the statement *AS PUBLISHED*, e.g., "*HOLD EAST AS PUBLISHED.*" Controllers must always issue complete holding instructions when pilots request them.

Note: Only those holding patterns depicted on U.S. government or commercially produced charts which meet FAA requirements should be used.

3. If no holding pattern is charted and holding instructions have not been issued, the pilot should ask ATC for holding instructions prior to reaching the fix. This procedure will eliminate the possibility of an aircraft entering a holding pattern other than that desired by ATC. If unable to obtain holding instructions prior to reaching the fix (due to frequency congestion, stuck microphone, etc.), hold in a standard pattern on the course on which you approached the fix and request further clearance as soon as possible. In this event, the

altitude/flight level of the aircraft at the clearance limit will be protected so that separation will be provided as required.

4. When an aircraft is 3 minutes or less from a clearance limit and a clearance beyond the fix has not been received, the pilot is expected to start a speed reduction so that the aircraft will cross the fix, initially, at or below the maximum holding airspeed.

5. When no delay is expected, the controller should issue a clearance beyond the fix as soon as possible and, whenever possible, at least 5 minutes before the aircraft reaches the clearance limit.

6. Pilots should report to ATC the time and altitude/flight level at which the aircraft reaches the clearance limit and report leaving the clearance limit.

Note: In the event of two-way communications failure, pilots are required to comply with 14 CFR Section 91.185.

4-4-4 Amended Clearances

a. Amendments to the initial clearance will be issued at any time an air traffic controller deems such action necessary to avoid possible confliction between aircraft. Clearances will require that a flight "hold" or change altitude prior to reaching the point where standard separation from other IFR traffic would no longer exist.

Note: Some pilots have questioned this action and requested "traffic information" and were at a loss when the reply indicated "no traffic report." In such cases the controller has taken action to prevent a traffic confliction which would have occurred at a distant point.

b. A pilot may wish an explanation of the handling of the flight at the time of occurrence; however, controllers are not able to take time from their immediate control duties nor can they afford to overload the ATC communications channels to furnish explanations. Pilots may obtain an explanation by directing a letter or telephone call to the chief controller of the facility involved.

c. Pilots have the privilege of requesting a different clearance from that which has been issued by ATC if they feel that they have information which would make another course of action more practicable or if aircraft equipment limitations or company procedures forbid compliance with the clearance issued.

4-4-5 Coded Departure Route (CDR)

a. CDRs provide air traffic control a rapid means to reroute departing aircraft when the filed route is constrained by either weather or congestion.

b. CDRs consist of an eight-character designator that represents a route of flight. The first three alphanumeric characters represent the departure airport, characters four through six represent the arrival airport, and the last two characters are chosen by the overlying ARTCC. For example, PITORDN1 is an alternate route from Pittsburgh to Chicago. Participating aircrews may then be re-cleared by air traffic control via the CDR abbreviated clearance, PITORDN1.

c. CDRs are updated on the 56 day charting cycle. Participating aircrews must ensure that their CDR is current.

d. Traditionally, CDRs have been used by air transport companies that have signed a Memorandum of Agreement with the local air traffic control facility. General aviation customers who wish to participate in the program may now enter "CDR Capable" in the remarks section of their flight plan.

e. When "CDR Capable" is entered into the remarks section of the flight plan, the general aviation customer communicates to ATC the ability to decode the current CDR into a flight plan route and the willingness to fly a different route than that which was filed.

4-4-6 Special VFR Clearances

a. An ATC clearance must be obtained prior to operating within a Class B, Class C, Class D, or Class E surface area when the weather is less than that required for VFR flight. A VFR pilot may request and be given a clearance to enter, leave, or operate within most Class D and Class E surface areas and some Class B and Class C surface areas in special VFR conditions, traffic permitting, and providing such flight will not delay IFR operations. All special VFR flights must remain clear of clouds. The visibility requirements for special VFR aircraft (other than helicopters) are:

1. At least 1 statute mile flight visibility for operations within Class B, Class C, Class D, and Class E surface areas.

2. At least 1 statute mile ground visibility if taking off or landing. If ground visibility is not reported at that airport, the flight visibility must be at least 1 statute mile.

3. The restrictions in subparagraphs 1 and 2 do not apply to helicopters. Helicopters must remain clear of clouds and may operate in Class B, Class C, Class D, and Class E surface areas with less than 1 statute mile visibility.

b. When a control tower is located within the Class B, Class C, or Class D surface area, requests for clearances should be to the tower. In a Class E surface area, a clearance may be obtained from the nearest tower, FSS, or center.

c. It is not necessary to file a complete flight plan with the request for clearance, but pilots should state their intentions in sufficient detail to permit ATC to fit their flight into the traffic flow. The clearance will not contain a specific altitude as the pilot must remain clear of clouds. The controller may require the pilot to fly at or below a certain altitude due to other traffic, but the altitude specified will permit flight at or above the minimum safe altitude. In addition, at radar locations, flights may be vectored if necessary for control purposes or on pilot request.

Note: *The pilot is responsible for obstacle or terrain clearance.*

Reference: *14 CFR Section 91.119, Minimum safe altitudes: General.*

d. Special VFR clearances are effective within Class B, Class C, Class D, and Class E surface areas only. ATC does not provide separation after an aircraft leaves the Class B, Class C, Class D, or Class E surface area on a special VFR clearance.

e. Special VFR operations by fixed-wing aircraft are prohibited in some Class B and Class C surface areas due to the volume of IFR traffic. A list of these Class B and Class C surface areas is contained in 14 CFR Part 91, Appendix D, Section 3. They are also depicted on sectional aeronautical charts.

f. ATC provides separation between Special VFR flights and between these flights and other IFR flights.

g. Special VFR operations by fixed-wing aircraft are prohibited between sunset and sunrise unless the pilot is instrument rated and the aircraft is equipped for IFR flight.

h. Pilots arriving or departing an uncontrolled airport that has automated weather broadcast capability (ASOS/AWOS) should monitor the broadcast frequency, advise the controller that they have the "one-minute weather" and state intentions prior to operating within the Class B, Class C, Class D, or Class E surface areas.

Reference: *Pilot/Controller Glossary Term—One-minute Weather.*

4-4-7 Pilot Responsibility upon Clearance Issuance

a. Record ATC clearance. When conducting an IFR operation, make a written record of your clearance. The specified conditions which are a part of your air traffic clearance may be somewhat different from those included in your flight plan. Additionally, ATC may find it necessary to ADD conditions, such as particular departure route. The very fact that ATC specifies different or additional conditions means that other aircraft are involved in the traffic situation.

b. ATC Clearance/Instruction Readback. Pilots of airborne aircraft should read back *those parts* of ATC clearances and instructions

containing altitude assignments, vectors, or runway assignments as a means of mutual verification. The read back of the "numbers" serves as a double check between pilots and controllers and reduces the kinds of communications errors that occur when a number is either "misheard" or is incorrect.

1. Include the aircraft identification in all readbacks and acknowledgments. This aids controllers in determining that the correct aircraft received the clearance or instruction. The requirement to include aircraft identification in all readbacks and acknowledgements becomes more important as frequency congestion increases and when aircraft with similar call signs are on the same frequency.

Example: "Climbing to Flight Level three three zero, United Twelve" or "November Five Charlie Tango, roger, cleared to land runway nine left."

2. Read back altitudes, altitude restrictions, and vectors in the same sequence as they are given in the clearance or instruction.

3. Altitudes contained in charted procedures, such as DPs, instrument approaches, etc., should not be read back unless they are specifically stated by the controller.

4. Initial read back of a taxi, departure or landing clearance should include the runway assignment, including left, right, center, etc. if applicable.

c. It is the responsibility of the pilot to accept or refuse the clearance issued.

4–4–8 IFR Clearance VFR-On-Top

a. A pilot on an IFR flight plan operating in VFR weather conditions, may request VFR-on-top in lieu of an assigned altitude. This permits a pilot to select an altitude or flight level of their choice (subject to any ATC restrictions.)

b. Pilots desiring to climb through a cloud, haze, smoke, or other meteorological formation and then either cancel their IFR flight plan or operate VFR-on-top may request a climb to VFR-on-top. The ATC authorization must contain either a top report or a statement that no top report is available, and a request to report reaching VFR-on-top. Additionally, the ATC authorization may contain a clearance limit, routing and an alternative clearance if VFR-on-top is not reached by a specified altitude.

c. A pilot on an IFR flight plan, operating in VFR conditions, may request to climb/descend in VFR conditions.

d. ATC may not authorize VFR-on-top/VFR conditions operations unless the pilot requests the VFR operation or a clearance to operate in VFR conditions will result in noise abatement benefits where part of the IFR departure route does not conform to an FAA approved noise abatement route or altitude.

e. When operating in VFR conditions with an ATC authorization to "maintain VFR-on-top/maintain VFR conditions" pilots on IFR flight plans must:

1. Fly at the appropriate VFR altitude as prescribed in 14 CFR Section 91.159.

2. Comply with the VFR visibility and distance from cloud criteria in 14 CFR Section 91.155 (Basic VFR Weather Minimums).

3. Comply with instrument flight rules that are applicable to this flight; i.e., minimum IFR altitudes, position reporting, radio communications, course to be flown, adherence to ATC clearance, etc.

Note: Pilots should advise ATC prior to any altitude change to ensure the exchange of accurate traffic information.

f. ATC authorization to "maintain VFR-on-top" is not intended to restrict pilots so that they must operate only **above** an obscuring meteorological formation (layer). Instead, it permits operation above, below, between layers, or in areas where there is no meteorological obscuration. It is imperative, however, that pilots understand that clearance to operate "VFR-on-top/VFR conditions" does not imply cancellation of the IFR flight plan.

g. Pilots operating VFR-on-top/VFR conditions may receive traffic information from ATC on other pertinent IFR or VFR aircraft. However, aircraft operating in Class B airspace/TRSAs must be separated as required by FAA Order JO 7110.65, Air Traffic Control.

Note: When operating in VFR weather conditions, it is the pilot's responsibility to be vigilant so as to see-and-avoid other aircraft.

h. ATC will not authorize VFR or VFR-on-top operations in Class A airspace.

Reference: AIM, ¶3-2-2, Class A Airspace.

4–4–9 VFR/IFR Flights

A pilot departing VFR, either intending to or needing to obtain an IFR clearance en route, must be aware of the position of the aircraft and the relative terrain/obstructions. When accepting a clearance below the MEA/MIA/MVA/OROCA, pilots are responsible for their own terrain/obstruction clearance until reaching the MEA/MIA/MVA/OROCA. If pilots are unable to maintain terrain/obstruction clearance, the controller should be advised and pilots should state their intentions.

Note: OROCA is a published altitude which provides 1,000 feet of terrain and obstruction clearance in the US (2,000 feet of clearance in designated mountainous areas). These altitudes are not assessed for NAVAID signal coverage, air traffic control surveillance, or communications coverage, and are published for general situational awareness, flight planning and in-flight contingency use.

Ch 4

4-4-10 Adherence to Clearance

a. When air traffic clearance has been obtained under either visual or instrument flight rules, the pilot-in-command of the aircraft must not deviate from the provisions thereof unless an amended clearance is obtained. When ATC issues a clearance or instruction, pilots are expected to execute its provisions upon receipt. ATC, in certain situations, will include the word "IMMEDIATELY" in a clearance or instruction to impress urgency of an imminent situation and expeditious compliance by the pilot is expected and necessary for safety. The addition of a VFR or other restriction; i.e., climb or descent point or time, crossing altitude, etc., does not authorize a pilot to deviate from the route of flight or any other provision of the ATC clearance.

b. When a heading is assigned or a turn is requested by ATC, pilots are expected to promptly initiate the turn, to complete the turn, and maintain the new heading unless issued additional instructions.

c. The term "AT PILOT'S DISCRETION" included in the altitude information of an ATC clearance means that ATC has offered the pilot the option to start climb or descent when the pilot wishes, is authorized to conduct the climb or descent at any rate, and to temporarily level off at any intermediate altitude as desired. However, once the aircraft has vacated an altitude, it may not return to that altitude.

d. When ATC has not used the term "AT PILOT'S DISCRETION" nor imposed any climb or descent restrictions, pilots should initiate climb or descent promptly on acknowledgement of the clearance. Descend or climb at an optimum rate consistent with the operating characteristics of the aircraft to 1,000 feet above or below the assigned altitude, and then attempt to descend or climb at a rate of between 500 and 1,500 fpm until the assigned altitude is reached. If at anytime the pilot is unable to climb or descend at a rate of at least 500 feet a minute, advise ATC. If it is necessary to level off at an intermediate altitude during climb or descent, advise ATC, except when leveling off at 10,000 feet MSL on descent, or 2,500 feet above airport elevation (prior to entering a Class C or Class D surface area), when required for speed reduction.

Reference: 14 CFR Section 91.117.

Note: Leveling off at 10,000 feet MSL on descent or 2,500 feet above airport elevation (prior to entering a Class C or Class D surface area) to comply with 14 CFR Section 91.117 airspeed restrictions is commonplace. Controllers anticipate this action and plan accordingly. Leveling off at any other time on climb or descent may seriously affect air traffic handling by ATC. Consequently, it is imperative that pilots make every effort to fulfill the above expected actions to aid ATC in safely handling and expediting traffic.

e. If the altitude information of an ATC DESCENT clearance includes a provision to "CROSS (fix) AT" or "AT OR ABOVE/BELOW (altitude)," the manner in which the descent is executed to comply with the crossing altitude is at the pilot's discretion. This authorization to descend at pilot's discretion is only applicable to that portion of flight to which the crossing altitude restriction applies, and the pilot is expected to comply with the crossing altitude as a provision of the clearance. Any other clearance in which pilot execution is optional will so state "AT PILOT'S DISCRETION."

Example 1: *"United Four Seventeen, descend and maintain six thousand."*

Note 1: *The pilot is expected to commence descent upon receipt of the clearance and to descend at the suggested rates until reaching the assigned altitude of 6,000 feet.*

Example 2: *"United Four Seventeen, descend at pilot's discretion, maintain six thousand."*

Note 2: *The pilot is authorized to conduct descent within the context of the term at pilot's discretion as described above.*

Example 3: *"United Four Seventeen, cross Lakeview V-O-R at or above Flight Level two zero zero, descend and maintain six thousand."*

Note 3: *The pilot is authorized to conduct descent at pilot's discretion until reaching Lakeview VOR and must comply with the clearance provision to cross the Lakeview VOR at or above FL200. After passing Lakeview VOR, the pilot is expected to descend at the suggested rates until reaching the assigned altitude of 6,000 feet.*

Example 4: *"United Four Seventeen, cross Lakeview V-O-R at six thousand, maintain six thousand."*

Note 4: *The pilot is authorized to conduct descent at pilot's discretion, however, must comply with the clearance provision to cross the Lakeview VOR at 6,000 feet.*

Example 5: *"United Four Seventeen, descend now to Flight Level two seven zero, cross Lakeview V-O-R at or below one zero thousand, descend and maintain six thousand."*

Note 5: *The pilot is expected to promptly execute and complete descent to FL270 upon receipt of the clearance. After reaching FL270 the pilot is authorized to descend "at pilot's discretion" until reaching Lakeview VOR. The pilot must comply with the clearance provision to cross Lakeview VOR at or below 10,000 feet. After Lakeview VOR the pilot is expected to descend at the suggested rates until reaching 6,000 feet.*

Example 6: *"United Three Ten, descend now and maintain Flight Level two four zero, pilot's discretion after reaching Flight Level two eight zero."*

Note 6: *The pilot is expected to commence descent upon receipt of the clearance and to descend at the suggested rates until reaching FL280. At that point, the pilot is authorized to continue descent to FL240 within the context of the term "at pilot's discretion" as described above.*

f. In case emergency authority is used to deviate from provisions of an ATC clearance, the pilot-in-command must notify ATC as soon as possible and obtain an amended clearance. In an emergency situation which does not result in a deviation from the rules prescribed in 14 CFR Part 91 but which requires ATC to give priority to an aircraft, the pilot of such aircraft must, when requested by ATC, make a report within 48 hours of such emergency situation to the manager of that ATC facility.

g. The guiding principle is that the last ATC clearance has precedence over the previous ATC clearance. When the route or altitude in a previously issued clearance is amended, the controller will restate applicable altitude restrictions. If altitude to maintain is changed or restated, whether prior to departure or while airborne, and previously issued altitude restrictions are omitted, those altitude restrictions are canceled, including departure procedures and STAR altitude restrictions.

Example 1: *A departure flight receives a clearance to destination airport to maintain FL290. The clearance incorporates a DP which has certain altitude crossing restrictions. Shortly after takeoff, the flight receives a new clearance changing the maintaining FL from 290 to 250. If the altitude restrictions are still applicable, the controller restates them.*

Example 2: *A departing aircraft is cleared to cross Fluky Intersection at or above 3,000 feet, Gordonville VOR at or above 12,000 feet, maintain FL200. Shortly after departure, the altitude to be maintained is changed to FL240. If the altitude restrictions are still applicable, the controller issues an amended clearance as follows: "cross Fluky Intersection at or above three thousand, cross Gordonville V-O-R at or above one two thousand, maintain Flight Level two four zero."*

Example 3: *An arriving aircraft is cleared to the destination airport via V45 Delta VOR direct; the aircraft is cleared to cross Delta VOR at 10,000 feet, and then to maintain 6,000 feet. Prior to Delta VOR, the controller issues an amended clearance as follows: "turn right heading one eight zero for vector to runway three six I-L-S approach, maintain six thousand."*

Note: *Because the altitude restriction "cross Delta V-O-R at 10,000 feet" was omitted from the amended clearance, it is no longer in effect.*

h. Pilots of turbojet aircraft equipped with afterburner engines should advise ATC prior to takeoff if they intend to use afterburning during their climb to the en route altitude. Often, the controller may be able to plan traffic to accommodate a high performance climb and allow the aircraft to climb to the planned altitude without restriction.

i. If an "expedite" climb or descent clearance is issued by ATC, and the altitude to maintain is subsequently changed or restated without an expedite instruction, the expedite instruction is canceled. Expedite climb/descent normally indicates to the pilot that the approximate best rate of climb/descent should be used without requiring an exceptional change in aircraft handling characteristics. Normally controllers will inform pilots of the reason for an instruction to expedite.

4–4–11 IFR Separation Standards

a. ATC effects separation of aircraft vertically by assigning different altitudes; longitudinally by providing an interval expressed in time or distance between aircraft on the same, converging, or crossing courses, and laterally by assigning different flight paths.

b. Separation will be provided between all aircraft operating on IFR flight plans except during that part of the flight (outside Class B airspace or a TRSA) being conducted on a VFR-on-top/VFR conditions clearance. Under these conditions, ATC may issue traffic advisories, but it is the sole responsibility of the pilot to be vigilant so as to see and avoid other aircraft.

c. When radar is employed in the separation of aircraft at the same altitude, a minimum of 3 miles separation is provided between aircraft operating within 40 miles of the radar antenna site, and 5 miles between aircraft operating beyond 40 miles from the antenna site. These minima may be increased or decreased in certain specific situations.

Note: *Certain separation standards may be increased in the terminal environment due to radar outages or other technical reasons.*

4–4–12 Speed Adjustments

a. ATC will issue speed adjustments to pilots of radar-controlled aircraft to achieve or maintain appropriate spacing. If necessary, ATC will assign a speed when approving deviations or radar vectoring off procedures that include published speed restrictions. If no speed is assigned, speed becomes pilot's discretion. However, when the aircraft reaches the end of the STAR, the last published speed on the STAR must be maintained until ATC deletes it, assigns a new speed, issues

a vector, assigns a direct route, or issues an approach clearance.

b. ATC will express all speed adjustments in terms of knots based on indicated airspeed (IAS) in 5 or 10 knot increments except that at or above FL240 speeds may be expressed in terms of Mach numbers in 0.01 increments. The use of Mach numbers is restricted to turbojet aircraft with Mach meters.

c. Pilots complying with speed adjustments (published or assigned) are expected to maintain a speed within plus or minus 10 knots or 0.02 Mach number of the specified speed.

d. When ATC assigns speed adjustments, it will be in accordance with the following recommended minimums:

1. To aircraft operating between FL280 and 10,000 feet, a speed not less than 250 knots or the equivalent Mach number.

Note 1: On a standard day the Mach numbers equivalent to 250 knots CAS (subject to minor variations) are:

FL 240–0.6

FL 250–0.61

FL 260–0.62

FL 270–0.64

FL 280–0.65

FL 290–0.66.

Note 2: When an operational advantage will be realized, speeds lower than the recommended minima may be applied.

2. To arriving turbojet aircraft operating below 10,000 feet:

(a) A speed not less than 210 knots, except;

(b) Within 20 flying miles of the airport of intended landing, a speed not less than 170 knots.

3. To arriving reciprocating engine or turboprop aircraft within 20 flying miles of the runway threshold of the airport of intended landing, a speed not less than 150 knots.

4. To departing aircraft:

(a) Turbojet aircraft, a speed not less than 230 knots.

(b) Reciprocating engine aircraft, a speed not less than 150 knots.

e. When ATC combines a speed adjustment with a descent clearance, the sequence of delivery, with the word "then" between, indicates the expected order of execution.

Example 1: Descend and maintain (altitude); then, reduce speed to (speed).

Example 2: Reduce speed to (speed); then, descend and maintain (altitude).

Note: The maximum speeds below 10,000 feet as established in 14 CFR Section 91.117 still apply. If there is any doubt concerning the manner in

which such a clearance is to be executed, request clarification from ATC.

f. If ATC determines (before an approach clearance is issued) that it is no longer necessary to apply speed adjustment procedures, they will:

1. Advise the pilot to "resume normal speed." Normal speed is used to terminate ATC assigned speed adjustments on segments where no published speed restrictions apply. It does not cancel published restrictions on upcoming procedures. This does not relieve the pilot of those speed restrictions which are applicable to 14 CFR Section 91.117.

Example: (An aircraft is flying a SID with no published speed restrictions. ATC issues a speed adjustment and instructs the aircraft where the adjustment ends): "Maintain two two zero knots until BALTR then resume normal speed."

Note: The ATC assigned speed assignment of two two zero knots would apply until BALTR. The aircraft would then resume a normal operating speed while remaining in compliance with 14 CFR Section 91.117.

2. Instruct pilots to "comply with speed restrictions" when the aircraft is joining or resuming a charted procedure or route with published speed restrictions.

Example: (ATC vectors an aircraft off of a SID to rejoin the procedure at a subsequent waypoint. When instructing the aircraft to resume the procedure, ATC also wants the aircraft to comply with the published procedure speed restrictions): "Resume the SALTY ONE departure. Comply with speed restrictions."

Caution: The phraseology "Descend via/Climb via SID" requires compliance with all altitude and/or speed restrictions depicted on the procedure.

3. Instruct the pilot to "resume published speed." Resume published speed is issued to terminate a speed adjustment where speed restrictions are published on a charted procedure.

Note: When instructed to "comply with speed restrictions" or to "resume published speed," ATC anticipates pilots will begin adjusting speed the minimum distance necessary prior to a published speed restriction so as to cross the waypoint/fix at the published speed. Once at the published speed, ATC expects pilots will maintain the published speed until additional adjustment is required to comply with further published or ATC assigned speed restrictions or as required to ensure compliance with 14 CFR Section 91.117.

Example: (An aircraft is flying a SID/STAR with published speed restrictions. ATC issues a speed adjustment and instructs the aircraft where the adjustment ends): "Maintain two two zero knots until BALTR then resume published speed."

Note: The ATC assigned speed assignment of two two zero knots would apply until BALTR. The aircraft would then comply with the published speed restrictions.

4. Advise the pilot to "delete speed restrictions" when either ATC assigned or published speed restrictions on a charted procedure are no longer required.

Example: (An aircraft is flying a SID with published speed restrictions designed to prevent aircraft overtake on departure. ATC determines there is no conflicting traffic and deletes the speed restriction): "Delete speed restrictions."

Note: When deleting published restrictions, ATC must ensure obstacle clearance until aircraft are established on a route where no published restrictions apply. This does not relieve the pilot of those speed restrictions which are applicable to 14 CFR Section 91.117.

5. Instruct the pilot to "climb via" or "descend via." A climb via or descend via clearance cancels any previously issued speed restrictions and, once established on the depicted departure or arrival, to climb or descend, and to meet all published or assigned altitude and/or speed restrictions.

Example 1: (An aircraft is flying a SID with published speed restrictions. ATC has issued a speed restriction of 250 knots for spacing. ATC determines that spacing between aircraft is adequate and desires the aircraft to comply with published restrictions): "United 436, Climb via SID."

Example 2: (An aircraft is established on a STAR. ATC must slow an aircraft for the purposes of spacing and assigns it a speed of 280 knots. When spacing is adequate, ATC deletes the speed restriction and desires that the aircraft comply with all published restrictions on the STAR): "Gulfstream two three papa echo, descend via the TYLER One arrival."

Note 1: In example 1, when ATC issues a "Climb via SID" clearance, it deletes any previously issued speed and/or altitude restrictions. The pilot should then vertically navigate to comply with all speed and/or altitude restrictions published on the SID.

Note 2: In example 2, when ATC issues a "Descend via <STAR name> arrival," ATC has canceled any previously issued speed and/or altitude restrictions. The pilot should vertically navigate to comply with all speed and/or altitude restrictions published on the STAR.

Caution: When descending on a STAR, pilots should not speed up excessively beyond the previously issued speed. Otherwise, adequate spacing between aircraft descending on the STAR that

was established by ATC with the previous restriction may be lost.

g. Approach clearances supersede any prior speed adjustment assignments, and pilots are expected to make their own speed adjustments as necessary to complete the approach. However, under certain circumstances, it may be necessary for ATC to issue further speed adjustments after approach clearance is issued to maintain separation between successive arrivals. Under such circumstances, previously issued speed adjustments will be restated if that speed is to be maintained or additional speed adjustments are requested. Speed adjustments should not be assigned inside the final approach fix on final or a point 5 miles from the runway, whichever is closer to the runway.

h. The pilots retain the prerogative of rejecting the application of speed adjustment by ATC if the minimum safe airspeed for any particular operation is greater than the speed adjustment.

Note: In such cases, pilots are expected to advise ATC of the speed that will be used.

i. Pilots are reminded that they are responsible for rejecting the application of speed adjustment by ATC if, in their opinion, it will cause them to exceed the maximum indicated airspeed prescribed by 14 CFR §91.117(a),(c) and (d). IN SUCH CASES, THE PILOT IS EXPECTED TO SO INFORM ATC. Pilots operating at or above 10,000 feet MSL who are issued speed adjustments which exceed 250 knots IAS and are subsequently cleared below 10,000 feet MSL are expected to comply with 14 CFR §91.117(a).

j. Speed restrictions of 250 knots do not apply to U.S. registered aircraft operating beyond 12 nautical miles from the coastline within the U.S. Flight Information Region, in Class E airspace below 10,000 feet MSL. However, in airspace underlying a Class B airspace area designated for an airport, or in a VFR corridor designated through such as a Class B airspace area, pilots are expected to comply with the 200 knot speed limit specified in 14 CFR Section 91.117(c).

k. For operations in a Class C and Class D surface area, ATC is authorized to request or approve a speed greater than the maximum indicated airspeeds prescribed for operation within that airspace (14 CFR Section 91.117(b)).

Note: Pilots are expected to comply with the maximum speed of 200 knots when operating beneath Class B airspace or in a Class B VFR corridor (14 CFR Section 91.117(c) and (d)).

l. When in communications with the ARTCC or approach control facility, pilots should, as a good operating practice, state any ATC assigned speed restriction on initial radio contact associated with an ATC communications frequency change.

4–4–13 Runway Separation

Tower controllers establish the sequence of arriving and departing aircraft by requiring them to adjust flight or ground operation as necessary to achieve proper spacing. They may "HOLD" an aircraft short of the runway to achieve spacing between it and an arriving aircraft; the controller may instruct a pilot to "EXTEND DOWNWIND" in order to establish spacing from an arriving or departing aircraft. At times a clearance may include the word "IMMEDIATE." For example: "CLEARED FOR IMMEDIATE TAKEOFF." In such cases "IMMEDIATE" is used for purposes of *air traffic separation*. It is up to the pilot to refuse the clearance if, in the pilot's opinion, compliance would adversely affect the operation.

Reference: AIM, ¶4-3-15, Gate Holding due to Departure Delays.

4–4–14 Visual Separation

a. Visual separation is a means employed by ATC to separate aircraft in terminal areas and en route airspace in the NAS. There are two methods employed to effect this separation:

1. The tower controller sees the aircraft involved and issues instructions, as necessary, to ensure that the aircraft avoid each other.

2. A pilot sees the other aircraft involved and upon instructions from the controller provides separation by maneuvering the aircraft to avoid it. When pilots accept responsibility to maintain visual separation, they must maintain constant visual surveillance and not pass the other aircraft until it is no longer a factor.

Note: Traffic is no longer a factor when during approach phase the other aircraft is in the landing phase of flight or executes a missed approach; and during departure or en route, when the other aircraft turns away or is on a diverging course.

b. A pilot's acceptance of instructions to follow another aircraft or provide visual separation from it is an acknowledgment that the pilot will maneuver the aircraft as necessary to avoid the other aircraft or to maintain in-trail separation. In operations conducted behind heavy aircraft, or a small aircraft behind a B757 or other large aircraft, it is also an acknowledgment that the pilot accepts the responsibility for wake turbulence separation. Visual separation is prohibited behind super aircraft.

Note: When a pilot has been told to follow another aircraft or to provide visual separation from it, the pilot should promptly notify the controller if visual contact with the other aircraft is lost or cannot be maintained or if the pilot cannot accept the responsibility for the separation for any reason.

c. Scanning the sky for other aircraft is a key factor in collision avoidance. Pilots and copilots (or the right seat passenger) should continuously scan to cover all areas of the sky visible from the cockpit. Pilots must develop an effective scanning technique which maximizes one's visual capabilities. Spotting a potential collision threat increases directly as more time is spent looking outside the aircraft. One must use timesharing techniques to effectively scan the surrounding airspace while monitoring instruments as well.

d. Since the eye can focus only on a narrow viewing area, effective scanning is accomplished with a series of short, regularly spaced eye movements that bring successive areas of the sky into the central visual field. Each movement should not exceed ten degrees, and each area should be observed for at least one second to enable collision detection. Although many pilots seem to prefer the method of horizontal back-and-forth scanning every pilot should develop a scanning pattern that is not only comfortable but assures optimum effectiveness. Pilots should remember, however, that they have a regulatory responsibility (14 CFR Section 91.113(a)) to see and avoid other aircraft when weather conditions permit.

4–4–15 Use of Visual Clearing Procedures and Scanning Techniques

a. **Before Takeoff.** Prior to taxiing onto a runway or landing area in preparation for takeoff, pilots should scan the approach areas for possible landing traffic and execute the appropriate clearing maneuvers to provide them a clear view of the approach areas.

b. **Climbs and Descents.** During climbs and descents in flight conditions which permit visual detection of other traffic, pilots should execute gentle banks, left and right at a frequency which permits continuous visual scanning of the airspace about them.

c. **Straight and Level.** Sustained periods of straight and level flight in conditions which permit visual detection of other traffic should be broken at intervals with appropriate clearing procedures to provide effective visual scanning.

d. **Traffic Pattern.** Entries into traffic patterns while descending create specific collision hazards and should be avoided.

e. **Traffic at VOR Sites.** All operators should emphasize the need for sustained vigilance in the vicinity of VORs and airway intersections due to the convergence of traffic.

f. **Training Operations.** Operators of pilot training programs are urged to adopt the following practices:

1. Pilots undergoing flight instruction at all levels should be requested to verbalize clearing

procedures (call out "clear" left, right, above, or below) to instill and sustain the habit of vigilance during maneuvering.

2. High-wing airplane. Momentarily raise the wing in the direction of the intended turn and look.

3. Low-wing airplane. Momentarily lower the wing in the direction of the intended turn and look.

4. Appropriate clearing procedures should precede the execution of all turns including chandelles, lazy eights, stalls, slow flight, climbs, straight and level, spins, and other combination maneuvers.

g. Scanning Techniques for Traffic Avoidance.

1. Pilots must be aware of the limitations inherent in the visual scanning process. These limitations may include:

(a) Reduced scan frequency due to concentration on flight instruments or tablets and distraction with passengers.

(b) Blind spots related to high-wing and low-wing aircraft in addition to windshield posts and sun visors.

(c) Prevailing weather conditions including reduced visibility and the position of the sun.

(d) The attitude of the aircraft will create additional blind spots.

(e) The physical limitations of the human eye, including the time required to (re)focus on near and far objects, from the instruments to the horizon for example; empty field myopia, narrow field of vision and atmospheric lighting all affect our ability to detect another aircraft.

2. Best practices to see and avoid:

(a) ADS-B In is an effective system to help pilots see and avoid other aircraft. If your aircraft is equipped with ADS-B In, it is important to understand its features and how to use it properly. Many units provide visual and/or audio alerts to supplement the system's traffic display. Pilots should incorporate the traffic display in their normal traffic scan to provide awareness of nearby aircraft. Prior to entering or crossing any runway, ADS-B In can provide advance indication of arriving aircraft and aircraft in the traffic pattern. Systems that incorporate a traffic-alerting feature can help minimize the pilot's inclination to fixate on the display. Refer to 4-5-7e, ADS-B Limitations.

(b) Understand the limitations of ADS-B In. In certain airspace, not all aircraft will be equipped with ADS-B Out or transponders and will not be visible on your ADS-B In display.

(c) Limit the amount of time that you focus on flight instruments or tablets.

(d) Develop a strategic approach to scanning for traffic. Scan the entire sky and try not to focus straight ahead.

4–4–16 Traffic Alert and Collision Avoidance System (TCAS I & II)

a. TCAS I provides proximity warning only, to assist the pilot in the visual acquisition of intruder aircraft. No recommended avoidance maneuvers are provided nor authorized as a direct result of a TCAS I warning. It is intended for use by smaller commuter aircraft holding 10 to 30 passenger seats, and general aviation aircraft.

b. TCAS II provides traffic advisories (TA) and resolution advisories (RA). Resolution advisories provide recommended maneuvers in a vertical direction (climb or descend only) to avoid conflicting traffic. Transport category aircraft, and larger commuter and business aircraft holding 31 passenger seats or more, are required to be TCAS II equipped.

1. When a TA occurs, attempt to establish visual contact with the traffic but do not deviate from an assigned clearance based only on TA information.

2. When an RA occurs, pilots should respond immediately to the RA displays and maneuver as indicated unless doing so would jeopardize the safe operation of the flight, or the flight crew can ensure separation with the help of definitive visual acquisition of the aircraft causing the RA.

3. Each pilot who deviates from an ATC clearance in response to an RA must notify ATC of that deviation as soon as practicable, and notify ATC when clear of conflict and returning to their previously assigned clearance.

c. Deviations from rules, policies, or clearances should be kept to the minimum necessary to satisfy an RA. Most RA maneuvering requires minimum excursion from assigned altitude.

d. The serving IFR air traffic facility is not responsible to provide approved standard IFR separation to an IFR aircraft, from other aircraft, terrain, or obstructions after an RA maneuver until one of the following conditions exists:

1. The aircraft has returned to its assigned altitude and course.

2. Alternate ATC instructions have been issued.

3. A crew member informs ATC that the TCAS maneuver has been completed.

Note: TCAS does not alter or diminish the pilot's basic authority and responsibility to ensure safe flight. Since TCAS does not respond to aircraft which are not transponder equipped or aircraft with a transponder failure, TCAS alone does not ensure safe separation in every case. At this time, no air traffic service nor handling is predicated on the availability of TCAS equipment in the aircraft.

Ch 4

4–4–17 Traffic Information Service (TIS)

a. TIS provides proximity warning only, to assist the pilot in the visual acquisition of intruder aircraft. No recommended avoidance maneuvers are provided nor authorized as a direct result of a TIS intruder display or TIS alert. It is intended for use by aircraft in which TCAS is not required.

b. TIS does not alter or diminish the pilot's basic authority and responsibility to ensure safe flight. Since TIS does not respond to aircraft which are not transponder equipped, aircraft with a transponder failure, or aircraft out of radar coverage, TIS alone does not ensure safe separation in every case.

c. At this time, no air traffic service nor handling is predicated on the availability of TIS equipment in the aircraft.

d. Presently, no air traffic services or handling is predicated on the availability of an ADS-B cockpit display. A "traffic-in-sight" reply to ATC must be based on seeing an aircraft out-the-window, NOT on the cockpit display.

Section 5 Surveillance Systems

4-5-1 Radar

a. Capabilities

1. Radar is a method whereby radio waves are transmitted into the air and are then received when they have been reflected by an object in the path of the beam. Range is determined by measuring the time it takes (at the speed of light) for the radio wave to go out to the object and then return to the receiving antenna. The direction of a detected object from a radar site is determined by the position of the rotating antenna when the reflected portion of the radio wave is received.

2. More reliable maintenance and improved equipment have reduced radar system failures to a negligible factor. Most facilities actually have some components duplicated, one operating and another which immediately takes over when a malfunction occurs to the primary component.

b. Limitations

1. It is very important for the aviation community to recognize the fact that there are limitations to radar service and that ATC controllers may not always be able to issue traffic advisories concerning aircraft which are not under ATC control and cannot be seen on radar. (See Figure 4-5-1.)

FIGURE 4–5–1
Limitations to Radar Service

Precipitation Attenuation

AREA BLACKED OUT BY ATTENUATION

NOT OBSERVED

OBSERVED ECHO

The nearby target absorbs and scatters so much of the out-going and returning energy that the radar does not detect the distant target.

(a) The characteristics of radio waves are such that they normally travel in a continuous straight line unless they are:

(1) "Bent" by abnormal atmospheric phenomena such as temperature inversions;

(2) Reflected or attenuated by dense objects such as heavy clouds, precipitation, ground obstacles, mountains, etc.; or

(3) Screened by high terrain features.

(b) The bending of radar pulses, often called anomalous propagation or ducting, may cause many extraneous blips to appear on the radar operator's display if the beam has been bent toward the ground or may decrease the detection range if the wave is bent upward. It is difficult to solve the effects of anomalous propagation, but using beacon radar and electronically eliminating stationary and slow moving targets by a method called moving target indicator (MTI) usually negate the problem.

(c) Radar energy that strikes dense objects will be reflected and displayed on the operator's scope thereby blocking out aircraft at the same range and greatly weakening or completely eliminating the display of targets at a greater range. Again, radar beacon and MTI are very effectively used to combat ground clutter and weather phenomena, and a method of circularly polarizing the radar beam will eliminate some weather returns. A negative characteristic of MTI is that an aircraft flying a speed that coincides with the canceling signal of the MTI (tangential or "blind" speed) may not be displayed to the radar controller.

(d) Relatively low altitude aircraft will not be seen if they are screened by mountains or are below the radar beam due to earth curvature. The historical solution to screening has been the installation of strategically placed multiple radars, which has been done in some areas, but ADS-B now provides ATC surveillance in some areas with challenging terrain where multiple radar installations would be impractical.

(e) There are several other factors which affect radar control. The amount of reflective surface of an aircraft will determine the size of the radar return. Therefore, a small light airplane or a sleek jet fighter will be more difficult to see on primary radar than a large commercial jet or military bomber. Here again, the use of transponder or ADS-B equipment is invaluable. In addition, all FAA ATC facilities display automatically reported altitude information to the controller from appropriately equipped aircraft.

(f) At some locations within the ATC en route environment, secondary-radar-only (no primary radar) gap filler radar systems are used to give lower altitude radar coverage between two larger radar systems, each of which provides both primary and secondary radar coverage. ADS-B serves this same role, supplementing both primary and secondary radar. In those geographical areas served by secondary radar only or ADS-B, aircraft without either transponders or ADS-B equipment cannot be provided with radar service. Additionally, transponder or ADS-B equipped aircraft cannot be provided with radar advisories concerning primary targets and ATC radar-derived weather.

Reference: *Pilot/Controller Glossary Term— Radar.*

Ch 4

(g) With regard to air traffic radar reception, wind turbines generally do not affect the quality of air traffic surveillance radar returns for transponder and ADS-B Out equipped aircraft. Air traffic interference issues apply to the search radar and Non-Transponder/Non-ADS-B Out equipped aircraft.

Note: Generally, one or two wind turbines don't present a significant radar reception loss. A rule of thumb is three (3) or more turbines constitute a wind turbine farm and thus negatively affect the search radar product.

(1) Detection loss in the area of a wind turbine farm is substantial. In extreme circumstances, this can extend for more than 1.0 nautical mile (NM) horizontally around the nearest turbine and at all altitudes above the wind turbine farm. (See Figure 4-5-2.)

FIGURE 4–5–2
Wind Turbine Farm Area of Potential Interference

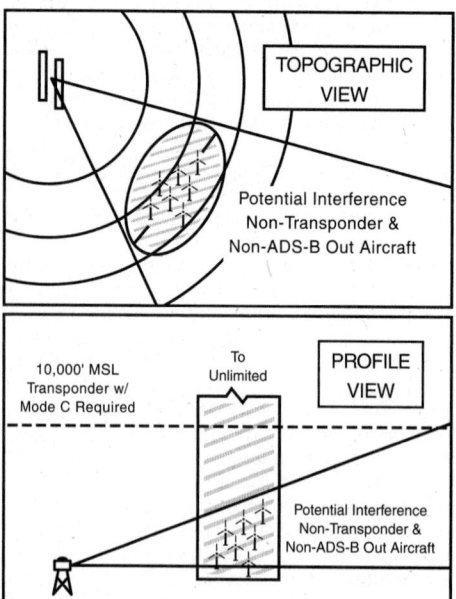

Note: All aircraft should comply with 14 CFR §91.119(c) "…aircraft may not be operated closer than 500 feet to any person, vessel, vehicle, or structure."

(2) To avoid interference Non-Transponder/Non-ADS-B Out equipped aircraft should avoid flight within 1.0 NM horizontally, at all altitudes, from the wind turbine farms.

(3) Because detection loss near and above wind turbine farms for search-only targets causes dropped tracks, erroneous tracks, and can result in loss of separation, it is imperative that Non-Transponder/Non-ADS-B Out equipped aircraft operate at the proper VFR altitudes per hemispheric rule and utilize see-and-avoid techniques.

(4) Pilots should be aware that air traffic controllers cannot provide separation from Non-Transponder/Non-ADS-B Out equipped aircraft in the vicinity of wind turbine farms. See-and-avoid is the pilot's responsibility, as these non-equipped aircraft may not appear on radar and will not appear on the Traffic Information Services–Broadcast (TIS-B).

(h) The controller's ability to advise a pilot flying on instruments or in visual conditions of the aircraft's proximity to another aircraft will be limited if the unknown aircraft is not observed on radar, if no flight plan information is available, or if the volume of traffic and workload prevent issuing traffic information. The controller's first priority is given to establishing vertical, lateral, or longitudinal separation between aircraft flying IFR under the control of ATC.

c. FAA radar units operate continuously at the locations shown in the Chart Supplement, and their services are available to all pilots, both civil and military. Contact the associated FAA control tower or ARTCC on any frequency guarded for initial instructions, or in an emergency, any FAA facility for information on the nearest radar service.

4-5-2 Air Traffic Control Radar Beacon System (ATCRBS)

a. The ATCRBS, sometimes referred to as secondary surveillance radar, consists of three main components:

1. Interrogator. Primary radar relies on a signal being transmitted from the radar antenna site and for this signal to be reflected or "bounced back" from an object (such as an aircraft). This reflected signal is then displayed as a "target" on the controller's radarscope. In the ATCRBS, the Interrogator, a ground based radar beacon transmitter-receiver, scans in synchronism with the primary radar and transmits discrete radio signals which repetitively request all transponders, on the mode being used, to reply. The replies received are then mixed with the primary returns and both are displayed on the same radarscope.

2. Transponder. This airborne radar beacon transmitter-receiver automatically receives the signals from the interrogator and selectively replies with a specific pulse group (code) only to those interrogations being received on the mode to which it is set. These replies are independent of, and much stronger than a primary radar return.

3. Radarscope. The radarscope used by the controller displays returns from both the primary radar system and the ATCRBS. These returns, called targets, are what the controller refers to in the control and separation of traffic.

b. The job of identifying and maintaining identification of primary radar targets is a long and tedious task for the controller. Some of the advantages of ATCRBS over primary radar are:

1. Reinforcement of radar targets.

2. Rapid target identification.

3. Unique display of selected codes.

c. A part of the ATCRBS ground equipment is the decoder. This equipment enables a controller to assign discrete transponder codes to each aircraft under his/her control. Normally only one code will be assigned for the entire flight. Assignments are made by the ARTCC computer on the basis of the National Beacon Code Allocation Plan. The equipment is also designed to receive Mode C altitude information from the aircraft.

Note: *Refer to figures with explanatory legends for an illustration of the target symbology depicted on radar scopes in the NAS Stage A (en route), the ARTS III (terminal) Systems, and other nonautomated (broadband) radar systems. (See Figures 4-5-3 and 4-5-4.)*

d. It should be emphasized that aircraft transponders greatly improve the effectiveness of radar systems.

Reference: *AIM, ¶4-1-20, Transponder and ADS-B Out Operation.*

Ch 4

FIGURE 4–5–3
ARTS III Radar Scope With Alphanumeric Data

NOTE: "ARTS" radar scope continue "broadband" (primary/secondary) radar targets with alphanumeric data. Lower right hand subset displays "broadband" (primary/secondary) radar and ARTS III when operating without automation.

Nonautomated "Broadband" Radar Scope in use at many terminals and certain ARTCCs. This also depicts ARTS/NAS Stage A (ARTCC) scopes when operating in the nonautomation mode. (Videomaps are not shown but there are no alphanumerics.)

Ident fills in between select code control slashes (Primary and Secondary Target)
Code 7700
Select code, e.g. 2100
Other nonselect code
Other nonselect code (beacon target only)
Primary target

Note: *A number of radar terminals do not have ARTS equipment. Those facilities and certain ARTCCs outside the contiguous U.S. would have radar displays similar to the lower right hand subset. ARTS facilities and NAS Stage A ARTCCs, when operating in the nonautomation mode, would also have similar displays and certain services based on automation may not be available.*

Example:

1. Areas of precipitation (can be reduced by CP)
2. Arrival/departure tabular list
3. Trackball (control) position symbol (A)
4. Airway (lines are sometimes deleted in part)
5. Radar limit line for control
6. Obstruction (video map)
7. Primary radar returns of obstacles or terrain (can be removed by MTI)
8. Satellite airports
9. Runway centerlines (marks and spaces indicate miles)
10. Primary airport with parallel runways
11. Approach gates
12. Tracked target (primary and beacon target)
13. Control position symbol
14. Untracked target select code (monitored) with Mode C readout of 6,000'
15. Untracked target without Mode C
16. Primary target
17. Beacon target only (secondary radar) (transponder)
18. Primary and beacon target
19. Leader line
20. Altitude Mode C readout is 6,000'

(*Note:* readouts may not be displayed because of nonreceipt of beacon information, garbled beacon signals, and flight plan data which is displayed alternately with the altitude readout)

21. Ground speed readout is 240 knots

(*Note:* readouts may not be displayed because of a loss of beacon signal, a controller alert that a pilot was squawking emergency, radio failure, etc.)

22. Aircraft ID
23. Asterisk indicates a controller entry in Mode C block. In this case 5,000' is entered and "05" would alternate with Mode C readout.
24. Indicates heavy
25. "Low ALT" flashes to indicate when an aircraft's predicted descent places the aircraft in an unsafe proximity to terrain.

(*Note:* This feature does not function if the aircraft is not squawking Mode C. When a helicopter or aircraft is known to be operating below the lower safe limit, the "low ALT" can be changed to "inhibit" and flashing ceases.)

26. NAVAIDs
27. Airways
28. Primary target only
29. Nonmonitored. No Mode C (an asterisk would indicate nonmonitored with Mode C)
30. Beacon target only (secondary radar based on aircraft transponder)
31. Tracked target (primary and beacon target) control position A
32. Aircraft is squawking emergency Code 7700 and is nonmonitored, untracked, Mode C

33. Controller assigned runway 36 right alternates with Mode C readout

(*Note:* a three letter identifier could also indicate the arrival is at specific airport)

34. Ident flashes
35. Identing target blossoms
36. Untracked target identing on a selected code
37. Range marks (10 and 15 miles) (can be changed/offset)
38. Aircraft controlled by center
39. Targets in suspend status
40. Coast/suspend list (aircraft holding, temporary loss of beacon/target, etc.)
41. Radio failure (emergency information)
42. Select beacon codes (being monitored)
43. General information (ATIS, runway, approach in use)
44. Altimeter setting
45. Time
46. System data area

Ch 4

FIGURE 4–5–4

FIGURE 4–5–4
NAS Stage A Controllers View Plan Display
This figure illustrates the controller's radar scope (PVD) when operating in the full
automation (RDP) mode, which is normally 20 hours per day.
*(When not in automation mode, the display is similar to the broadband mode shown in the ARTS III
radar scope figure. Certain ARTCCs outside the contiguous U.S. also operate in "broadband" mode.)*

Radar Services and Procedures

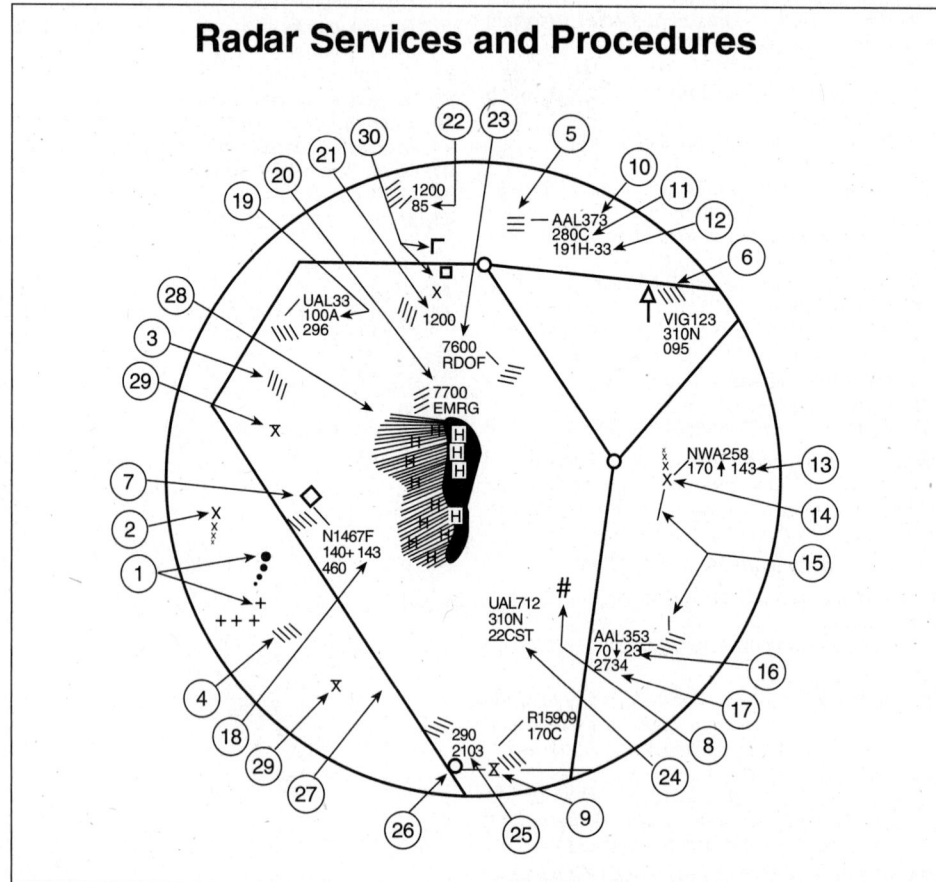

Example:

Target symbols:

1. Uncorrelated primary radar target [o] [+]
2. Correlated primary radar target [×]
 *See note below.
3. Uncorrelated beacon target [/]
4. Correlated beacon target [\]
5. Identing beacon target [≡]

***Note:** in Number 2 correlated means the asso-
ciation of radar data with the computer projected
track of an identified aircraft.

Position symbols:

6. Free track (no flight plan tracking) [Δ]
7. Flat track (flight plan tracking) [◊]

8. Coast (beacon target lost) [#]
9. Present position hold [⊠]

Data block information:

10. Aircraft ident
 *See note below.
11. Assigned altitude FL280, Mode C altitude
 same or within ± 200' of assigned altitude.
 *See note below.
12. Computer ID #191, handoff is to sector
 33 (0-33 would mean handoff accepted)
 *See note below.
13. Assigned altitude 17,000', aircraft is climbing,
 Mode C readout was 14,300 when last bea-
 con interrogation was received.

14. Leader line connecting target symbol and data block
15. Track velocity and direction vector line (projected ahead of target)
16. Assigned altitude 7,000, aircraft is descending, last Mode C readout (or last reported altitude) was 100' above FL230
17. Transponder code shows in full data block only when different than assigned code
18. Aircraft is 300' above assigned altitude
19. Reported altitude (no Mode C readout) same as assigned. (An "n" would indicate no reported altitude.)
20. Transponder set on emergency Code 7700 (EMRG flashes to attract attention)
21. Transponder Code 1200 (VFR) with no Mode C
22. Code 1200 (VFR) with Mode C and last altitude readout
23. Transponder set on radio failure Code 7600 (RDOF flashes)
24. Computer ID #228, CST indicates target is in coast status
25. Assigned altitude FL290, transponder code (these two items constitute a "limited data block")

*Note: numbers 10, 11, and 12 constitute a "full data block"

Other symbols:

26. Navigational aid
27. Airway or jet route
28. Outline of weather returns based on primary radar. "H" represents areas of high density precipitation which might be thunderstorms. Radial lines indicated lower density precipitation.
29. Obstruction
30. Airports

 Major: ☐
 Small: ⌐

4–5–3 Surveillance Radar

a. Surveillance radars are divided into two general categories: Airport Surveillance Radar (ASR) and Air Route Surveillance Radar (ARSR).

1. ASR is designed to provide relatively short-range coverage in the general vicinity of an airport and to serve as an expeditious means of handling terminal area traffic through observation of precise aircraft locations on a radarscope. The ASR can also be used as an instrument approach aid.

2. ARSR is a long-range radar system designed primarily to provide a display of aircraft locations over large areas.

b. Surveillance radars scan through 360 degrees of azimuth and present target information on a radar display located in a tower or center. This information is used independently or in conjunction with other navigational aids in the control of air traffic.

4–5–4 Precision Approach Radar (PAR)

a. PAR is designed for use as a landing aid rather than an aid for sequencing and spacing aircraft. PAR equipment may be used as a primary landing aid (See Chapter 5, Air Traffic Procedures, for additional information), or it may be used to monitor other types of approaches. It is designed to display range, azimuth and elevation information.

b. Two antennas are used in the PAR array, one scanning a vertical plane, and the other scanning horizontally. Since the range is limited to 10 miles, azimuth to 20 degrees, and elevation to 7 degrees, only the final approach area is covered. Each scope is divided into two parts. The upper half presents altitude and distance information, and the lower half presents azimuth and distance.

4–5–5 Airport Surface Detection Equipment (ASDE-X)/Airport Surface Surveillance Capability (ASSC)

a. ASDE-X/ASSC is a multi-sensor surface surveillance system the FAA is acquiring for airports in the United States. This system provides high resolution, short-range, clutter free surveillance information about aircraft and vehicles, both moving and fixed, located on or near the surface of the airport's runways and taxiways under all weather and visibility conditions. The system consists of:

1. A Primary Radar System. ASDE-X/ASSC system coverage includes the airport surface and the airspace up to 200 feet above the surface. Typically located on the control tower or other strategic location on the airport, the Primary Radar antenna is able to detect and display aircraft that are not equipped with or have malfunctioning transponders or ADS-B.

2. Interfaces. ASDE-X/ASSC contains an automation interface for flight identification via all automation platforms and interfaces with the terminal radar for position information.

3. Automation. A Multi-sensor Data Processor (MSDP) combines all sensor reports into a single target which is displayed to the air traffic controller.

4. Air Traffic Control Tower Display. A high resolution, color monitor in the control tower cab provides controllers with a seamless picture of airport operations on the airport surface.

b. The combination of data collected from the multiple sensors ensures that the most accurate information about aircraft location is received in the tower, thereby increasing surface safety and efficiency.

c. The following facilities are operational with ASDE-X:

TABLE 4–5–1

BWI	Baltimore Washington International
BOS	Boston Logan International
BDL	Bradley International
MDW	Chicago Midway
ORD	Chicago O'Hare International
CLT	Charlotte Douglas International
DFW	Dallas/Fort Worth International
DEN	Denver International
DTW	Detroit Metro Wayne County
FLL	Fort Lauderdale/Hollywood Intl
MKE	General Mitchell International
IAH	George Bush International
ATL	Hartsfield–Jackson Atlanta Intl
HNL	Honolulu International
JFK	John F. Kennedy International
SNA	John Wayne–Orange County
LGA	LaGuardia
STL	Lambert St. Louis International
LAS	Las Vegas Harry Reid International
LAX	Los Angeles International
SDF	Louisville International
MEM	Memphis International
MIA	Miami International
MSP	Minneapolis St. Paul International
EWR	Newark International
MCO	Orlando International
PHL	Philadelphia International
PHX	Phoenix Sky Harbor International
DCA	Ronald Reagan Washington National
SAN	San Diego International
SLC	Salt Lake City International
SEA	Seattle–Tacoma International
PVD	Theodore Francis Green State
IAD	Washington Dulles International
HOU	William P. Hobby International

d. The following facilities have been projected to receive ASSC:

TABLE 4–5–2

SFO	San Francisco International
CLE	Cleveland–Hopkins International
MCI	Kansas City International
CVG	Cincinnati/Northern Kentucky Intl
PDX	Portland International
MSY	Louis Armstrong New Orleans Intl
PIT	Pittsburgh International
ANC	Ted Stevens Anchorage International
ADW	Joint Base Andrews AFB

4–5–6 Traffic Information Service (TIS)

a. Introduction. The Traffic Information Service (TIS) provides information to the cockpit via data link, that is similar to VFR radar traffic advisories normally received over voice radio. Among the first FAA-provided data services, TIS is intended to improve the safety and efficiency of "see and avoid" flight through an automatic display that informs the pilot of nearby traffic and potential conflict situations. This traffic display is intended to assist the pilot in visual acquisition of these aircraft. TIS employs an enhanced capability of the terminal Mode S radar system, which contains the surveillance data, as well as the data link required to "uplink" this information to suitably-equipped aircraft (known as a TIS "client"). TIS provides estimated position, altitude, altitude trend, and ground track information for up to 8 intruder aircraft within 7 NM horizontally, +3,500 and -3,000 feet vertically of the client aircraft (see Figure 4-5-5, TIS Proximity Coverage Volume). The range of a target reported at a distance greater than 7 NM only indicates that this target will be a threat within 34 seconds and does not display a precise distance. TIS will alert the pilot to aircraft (under surveillance of the Mode S radar) that are estimated to be within 34 seconds of potential collision, regardless of distance or altitude. TIS surveillance data is derived from the same radar used by ATC; this data is uplinked to the client aircraft on each radar scan (nominally every 5 seconds).

FIGURE 4–5–5
TIS Proximity Coverage Volume

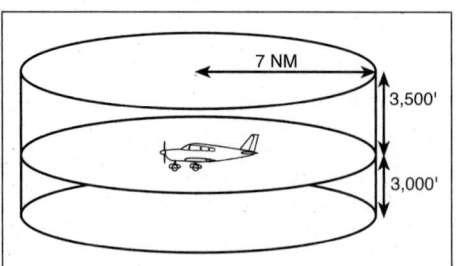

b. Requirements
1. In order to use TIS, the client and any intruder aircraft must be equipped with the appropriate cockpit equipment and fly within the radar coverage of a Mode S radar capable of providing TIS. Typically, this will be within 55 NM of the sites depicted in Figure 4-5-6, Terminal Mode S Radar Sites. ATC communication is not a requirement to receive TIS, although it may be required by the particular airspace or flight operations in which TIS is being used.

FIGURE 4–5–6
Terminal Mode S Radar Sites

ASR-9 Mode S Sites
ASR-7/8 Mode S Sites

Terminal Mode S Radar Sites
(Approximate Locations)

2. The cockpit equipment functionality required by a TIS client aircraft to receive the service consists of the following (refer to Figure 4-5-7):

 (a) Mode S data link transponder with altitude encoder.

 (b) Data link applications processor with TIS software installed.

 (c) Control-display unit.

 (d) Optional equipment includes a digital heading source to correct display errors caused by "crab angle" and turning maneuvers.

Note: Some of the above functions will likely be combined into single pieces of avionics, such as (a) and (b).

3. To be visible to the TIS client, the intruder aircraft must, at a minimum, have an operating transponder (Mode A, C or S). All altitude information provided by TIS from intruder aircraft is derived from Mode C reports, if appropriately equipped.

4. TIS will initially be provided by the terminal Mode S systems that are paired with ASR-9 digital primary radars. These systems are in locations with the greatest traffic densities, thus will provide the greatest initial benefit. The remaining terminal Mode S sensors, which are paired with ASR-7 or ASR-8 analog primary radars, will provide TIS pending modification or relocation of these sites. See Figure 4-5-6, Terminal Mode S Radar Sites, for site locations. There is no mechanism in place, such as NOTAMs, to provide status update on individual radar sites since TIS is a nonessential, supplemental information service.

The FAA also operates en route Mode S radars (not illustrated) that rotate once every 12 seconds. These sites will require additional development of TIS before any possible implementation. There are no plans to implement TIS in the en route Mode S radars at the present time.

FIGURE 4–5–7
Traffic Information Service (TIS) Avionics Block Diagram

c. Capabilities

1. TIS provides ground-based surveillance information over the Mode S data link to properly equipped client aircraft to aid in visual acquisition of proximate air traffic. The actual avionics capability of each installation will vary and the supplemental handbook material must be consulted prior to using TIS. A maximum of eight (8) intruder aircraft may be displayed; if more than eight aircraft match intruder parameters, the eight "most significant" intruders are uplinked. These "most significant" intruders are usually the ones in closest proximity and/or the greatest threat to the TIS client.

2. TIS, through the Mode S ground sensor, provides the following data on each intruder aircraft:

 (a) Relative bearing information in 6-degree increments.

 (b) Relative range information in 1/8 NM to 1 NM increments (depending on range).

 (c) Relative altitude in 100-foot increments (within 1,000 feet) or 500-foot increments (from

1,000–3,500 feet) if the intruder aircraft has operating altitude reporting capability.

(d) Estimated intruder ground track in 45-degree increments.

(e) Altitude trend data (level within 500 fpm or climbing/descending >500 fpm) if the intruder aircraft has operating altitude reporting capability.

(f) Intruder priority as either a "traffic advisory" or "proximate" intruder.

3. When flying from surveillance coverage of one Mode S sensor to another, the transfer of TIS is an automatic function of the avionics system and requires no action from the pilot.

4. There are a variety of status messages that are provided by either the airborne system or ground equipment to alert the pilot of high priority intruders and data link system status. These messages include the following:

(a) **Alert.** Identifies a potential collision hazard within 34 seconds. This alert may be visual and/or audible, such as a flashing display symbol or a headset tone. A target is a threat if the time to the closest approach in vertical and horizontal coordinates is less than 30 seconds and the closest approach is expected to be within 500 feet vertically and 0.5 nautical miles laterally.

(b) **TIS Traffic.** TIS traffic data is displayed.

(c) **Coasting.** The TIS display is more than 6 seconds old. This indicates a missing uplink from the ground system. When the TIS display information is more than 12 seconds old, the "No Traffic" status will be indicated.

(d) **No Traffic.** No intruders meet proximate or alert criteria. This condition may exist when the TIS system is fully functional or may indicate "coasting" between 12 and 59 seconds old (see (c) above).

(e) **TIS Unavailable.** The pilot has requested TIS, but no ground system is available. This condition will also be displayed when TIS uplinks are missing for 60 seconds or more.

(f) **TIS Disabled.** The pilot has not requested TIS or has disconnected from TIS.

(g) **Good-bye.** The client aircraft has flown outside of TIS coverage.

Note: Depending on the avionics manufacturer implementation, it is possible that some of these messages will not be directly available to the pilot.

5. Depending on avionics system design, TIS may be presented to the pilot in a variety of different displays, including text and/or graphics. Voice annunciation may also be used, either alone or in combination with a visual display. Figure 4-5-7, Traffic Information Service (TIS), Avionics Block Diagram, shows an example of a TIS display using symbology similar to the Traffic Alert and Collision Avoidance System (TCAS) installed on most passenger air carrier/commuter aircraft in the U.S. The small symbol in the center represents the client aircraft and the display is oriented "track up," with the 12 o'clock position at the top. The range rings indicate 2 and 5 NM. Each intruder is depicted by a symbol positioned at the approximate relative bearing and range from the client aircraft. The circular symbol near the center indicates an "alert" intruder and the diamond symbols indicate "proximate" intruders.

6. The inset in the lower right corner of Figure 4-5-7, Traffic Information Service (TIS), Avionics Block Diagram, shows a possible TIS data block display. The following information is contained in this data block:

(a) The intruder, located approximately four o'clock, three miles, is a "proximate" aircraft and currently not a collision threat to the client aircraft. This is indicated by the diamond symbol used in this example.

(b) The intruder ground track diverges to the right of the client aircraft, indicated by the small arrow.

(c) The intruder altitude is 700 feet less than or below the client aircraft, indicated by the "-07" located under the symbol.

(d) The intruder is descending >500 fpm, indicated by the downward arrow next to the "-07" relative altitude information. The absence of this arrow when an altitude tag is present indicates level flight or a climb/descent rate less than 500 fpm.

Note: If the intruder did not have an operating altitude encoder (Mode C), the altitude and altitude trend "tags" would have been omitted.

d. Limitations

1. TIS is **NOT** intended to be used as a collision avoidance system and does not relieve the pilot's responsibility to "see and avoid" other aircraft (see Paragraph 5-5-8, See and Avoid). TIS must not be used for avoidance maneuvers during IMC or other times when there is no visual contact with the intruder aircraft. TIS is intended only to assist in visual acquisition of other aircraft in VMC. Avoidance maneuvers are neither provided nor authorized as a direct result of a TIS intruder display or TIS alert.

2. While TIS is a useful aid to visual traffic avoidance, it has some system limitations that must be fully understood to ensure proper use. Many of these limitations are inherent in secondary radar surveillance. In other words, the information provided by TIS will be no better than that provided by ATC. Other limitations and anomalies are associated with the TIS predictive algorithm.

(a) **Intruder Display Limitations.** TIS will only display aircraft with operating transponders installed. TIS relies on surveillance of the Mode S radar, which is a "secondary surveillance" radar similar to the ATCRBS described in paragraph 4-5-2.

(b) TIS Client Altitude Reporting Requirement. Altitude reporting is required by the TIS client aircraft in order to receive TIS. If the altitude encoder is inoperative or disabled, TIS will be unavailable, as TIS requests will not be honored by the ground system. As such, TIS requires altitude reporting to determine the Proximity Coverage Volume as indicated in Figure 4-5-5. TIS users must be alert to altitude encoder malfunctions, as TIS has no mechanism to determine if client altitude reporting is correct. A failure of this nature will cause erroneous and possibly unpredictable TIS operation. If this malfunction is suspected, confirmation of altitude reporting with ATC is suggested.

(c) Intruder Altitude Reporting. Intruders without altitude reporting capability will be displayed without the accompanying altitude tag. Additionally, nonaltitude reporting intruders are assumed to be at the same altitude as the TIS client for alert computations. This helps to ensure that the pilot will be alerted to all traffic under radar coverage, but the actual altitude difference may be substantial. Therefore, visual acquisition may be difficult in this instance.

(d) Coverage Limitations. Since TIS is provided by ground-based, secondary surveillance radar, it is subject to all limitations of that radar. If an aircraft is not detected by the radar, it cannot be displayed on TIS. Examples of these limitations are as follows:

(1) TIS will typically be provided within 55 NM of the radars depicted in Figure 4-5-6, Terminal Mode S Radar Sites. This maximum range can vary by radar site and is always subject to "line of sight" limitations; the radar and data link signals will be blocked by obstructions, terrain, and curvature of the earth.

(2) TIS will be unavailable at low altitudes in many areas of the country, particularly in mountainous regions. Also, when flying near the "floor" of radar coverage in a particular area, intruders below the client aircraft may not be detected by TIS.

(3) TIS will be temporarily disrupted when flying directly over the radar site providing coverage if no adjacent site assumes the service. A ground-based radar, similar to a VOR or NDB, has a zenith cone, sometimes referred to as the cone of confusion or cone of silence. This is the area of ambiguity directly above the station where bearing information is unreliable. The zenith cone setting for TIS is 34 degrees: Any aircraft above that angle with respect to the radar horizon will lose TIS coverage from that radar until it is below this 34 degree angle. The aircraft may not actually lose service in areas of multiple radar coverage since an adjacent radar will provide TIS. If no other TIS-capable radar is available, the

"Goodbye" message will be received and TIS terminated until coverage is resumed.

(e) Intermittent Operations. TIS operation may be intermittent during turns or other maneuvering, particularly if the transponder system does not include antenna diversity (antenna mounted on the top and bottom of the aircraft). As in (d) above, TIS is dependent on two-way, "line of sight" communications between the aircraft and the Mode S radar. Whenever the structure of the client aircraft comes between the transponder antenna (usually located on the underside of the aircraft) and the ground-based radar antenna, the signal may be temporarily interrupted.

(f) TIS Predictive Algorithm. TIS information is collected one radar scan prior to the scan during which the uplink occurs. Therefore, the surveillance information is approximately 5 seconds old. In order to present the intruders in a "real time" position, TIS uses a "predictive algorithm" in its tracking software. This algorithm uses track history data to extrapolate intruders to their expected positions consistent with the time of display in the cockpit. Occasionally, aircraft maneuvering will cause this algorithm to induce errors in the TIS display. These errors primarily affect relative bearing information; intruder distance and altitude will remain relatively accurate and may be used to assist in "see and avoid." Some of the more common examples of these errors are as follows:

(1) When client or intruder aircraft maneuver excessively or abruptly, the tracking algorithm will report incorrect horizontal position until the maneuvering aircraft stabilizes.

(2) When a rapidly closing intruder is on a course that crosses the client at a shallow angle (either overtaking or head on) and either aircraft abruptly changes course within 1/4 NM, TIS will display the intruder on the opposite side of the client than it actually is.

These are relatively rare occurrences and will be corrected in a few radar scans once the course has stabilized.

(g) Heading/Course Reference. Not all TIS aircraft installations will have onboard heading reference information. In these installations, aircraft course reference to the TIS display is provided by the Mode S radar. The radar only determines ground track information and has no indication of the client aircraft heading. In these installations, all intruder bearing information is referenced to ground track and does not account for wind correction. Additionally, since ground-based radar will require several scans to determine aircraft course following a course change, a lag in TIS display orientation (intruder aircraft bearing) will occur. As in (f) above, intruder distance and altitude are still usable.

(h) Closely-Spaced Intruder Errors. When operating more than 30 NM from the Mode S sensor, TIS forces any intruder within 3/8 NM of the TIS client to appear at the same horizontal position as the client aircraft. Without this feature, TIS could display intruders in a manner confusing to the pilot in critical situations (for example, a closely-spaced intruder that is actually to the right of the client may appear on the TIS display to the left). At longer distances from the radar, TIS cannot accurately determine relative bearing/distance information on intruder aircraft that are in close proximity to the client.

Because TIS uses a ground-based, rotating radar for surveillance information, the accuracy of TIS data is dependent on the distance from the sensor (radar) providing the service. This is much the same phenomenon as experienced with ground-based navigational aids, such as a VOR. As distance from the radar increases, the accuracy of surveillance decreases. Since TIS does not inform the pilot of distance from the Mode S radar, the pilot must assume that any intruder appearing at the same position as the client aircraft may actually be up to 3/8 NM away in any direction. Consistent with the operation of TIS, an alert on the display (regardless of distance from the radar) should stimulate an outside visual scan, intruder acquisition, and traffic avoidance based on outside reference.

e. Reports of TIS Malfunctions

1. Users of TIS can render valuable assistance in the early correction of malfunctions by reporting their observations of undesirable performance. Reporters should identify the time of observation, location, type and identity of aircraft, and describe the condition observed; the type of transponder processor, and software in use can also be useful information. Since TIS performance is monitored by maintenance personnel rather than ATC, it is suggested that malfunctions be reported by radio or telephone to the nearest Flight Service Station (FSS) facility.

Note: TIS operates at only those terminal Mode S radar sites depicted in Figure 4-5-6. Though similar in some ways, TIS is not related to TIS-B (Traffic Information Service–Broadcast).

4–5–7 Automatic Dependent Surveillance–Broadcast (ADS-B) Services

a. Introduction

1. Automatic Dependent Surveillance–Broadcast (ADS-B) is a surveillance technology deployed throughout the NAS (see Figure 4-5-8). The ADS-B system is composed of aircraft avionics and a ground infrastructure. Onboard avionics determine the position of the aircraft by using the GNSS and transmit its position along with additional information about the aircraft to ground stations for use by ATC and other ADS-B services. This information is transmitted at a rate of approximately once per second. (See Figure 4-5-9 and Figure 4-5-10.)

2. In the United States, ADS-B equipped aircraft exchange information on one of two frequencies: 978 or 1090 MHz. The 1090 MHz frequency is also associated with Mode A, C, and S transponder operations. 1090 MHz transponders with integrated ADS-B functionality extend the transponder message sets with additional ADS-B information. This additional information is known as an "extended squitter" message and is referred to as 1090ES. ADS-B equipment operating on 978 MHz is known as the Universal Access Transceiver (UAT).

3. ADS-B avionics can have the ability to both transmit and receive information. The transmission of ADS-B information from an aircraft is known as ADS-B Out. The receipt of ADS-B information by an aircraft is known as ADS-B In. All aircraft operating within the airspace defined in 14 CFR §91.225 are required to transmit the information defined in §91.227 using ADS-B Out avionics.

4. In general, operators flying at 18,000 feet and above (Class A airspace) are required to have 1090ES equipment. Those that do not fly above 18,000 may use either UAT or 1090ES equipment. (Refer to 14 CFR §§91.225 and 91.227.) While the regulations do not require it, operators equipped with ADS-B In will realize additional benefits from ADS-B broadcast services: Traffic Information Service–Broadcast (TIS-B) (Paragraph 4-5-8) and Flight Information Service–Broadcast (FIS-B) (Paragraph 4-5-9).

Ch 4

FIGURE 4–5–8
ADS-B, TIS-B, and FIS-B: Broadcast Services Architecture

FIGURE 4–5–9
En Route – ADS-B/ADS-R/ TIS-B/FIS-B Service Ceilings/Floors

FIGURE 4–5–10
Terminal – ADS-B/ADS-R/TIS-B/FIS-B Service Ceilings/Floors

b. **ADS-B Certification and Performance Requirements**

ADS-B equipment may be certified as a surveillance source for air traffic separation services using ADS-B Out. ADS-B equipment may also be certified for use with ADS-B In advisory services that enable appropriately equipped aircraft to display traffic and flight information. Refer to the aircraft's flight manual supplement or *Pilot Operating Handbook* for the capabilities of a specific aircraft installation.

c. **ADS-B Capabilities and Procedures**

1. ADS-B enables improved surveillance services, both air-to-air and air-to-ground, especially in areas where radar is ineffective due to terrain or where it is impractical or cost prohibitive. Initial NAS applications of air-to-air ADS-B are for "advisory" use only, enhancing a pilot's visual acquisition of other nearby equipped aircraft either when airborne or on the airport surface. Additionally, ADS-B will enable ATC and fleet operators to monitor aircraft throughout the available ground station coverage area.

2. One of the data elements transmitted by ADS-B is the aircraft's Flight Identification (FLT ID). The FLT ID is comprised of a maximum of seven alphanumeric characters and must correspond to the aircraft identification filed in the flight plan. For airline and commuter aircraft, the FLT ID is usually the company name and flight number (for example, AAL3432), and is typically entered into the avionics by the flight crew during preflight. For general aviation (GA), if aircraft avionics allow dynamic modification of the FLT ID, the pilot can enter it prior to flight. However, some ADS-B avionics require the FLT ID to be set to the aircraft registration number (for example, N1234Q) by the installer and cannot be changed by the pilot

from the cockpit. In both cases, the FLT ID must correspond to the aircraft identification filed in its flight plan.

ATC automation systems use the transmitted ADS-B FLT ID to uniquely identify each aircraft within a given airspace, and to correlate it to its filed flight plan for the purpose of providing surveillance and separation services. If the FLT ID and the filed aircraft identification are not identical, a Call Sign Mis-Match (CSMM) is generated and ATC automation systems may not associate the aircraft with its filed flight plan. In this case, air traffic services may be delayed or unavailable until the CSMM is corrected. Consequently, it is imperative that flight crews and GA pilots ensure the FLT ID entry correctly matches the aircraft identification filed in their flight plan.

3. Each ADS-B aircraft is assigned a unique ICAO address (also known as a 24-bit address) that is broadcast by the ADS-B transmitter. This ICAO address is programmed at installation. Should multiple aircraft broadcast the same ICAO address while transiting the same ADS-B Only Service Volume, the ADS-B network may be unable to track the targets correctly. If radar reinforcement is available, tracking will continue. If radar is unavailable, the controller may lose target tracking entirely on one or both targets. Consequently, it is imperative that the ICAO address entry is correct.

4. Aircraft that are equipped with ADS-B avionics on the UAT datalink have a feature that allows them to broadcast an anonymous 24-bit ICAO address. In this mode, the UAT system creates a randomized address that does not match the actual ICAO address assigned to the aircraft. The UAT anonymous 24-bit address feature may

only be used when the operator has not filed an IFR flight plan and is not requesting ATC services. In the anonymity mode, the aircraft's beacon code must be set to 1200 and, depending on the manufacturer's implementation, the aircraft FLT ID might not be transmitted. Pilots should be aware that while in UAT anonymity mode, they will not be eligible to receive ATC separation and flight following services, and may not benefit from enhanced ADS-B search and rescue capabilities.

5. ADS-B systems integrated with the transponder will automatically set the applicable emergency status when 7500, 7600, or 7700 are entered into the transponder. ADS-B systems not integrated with the transponder, or systems with optional emergency codes, will require that the appropriate emergency code is entered through a pilot interface. ADS-B is intended for inflight and airport surface use. Unless otherwise directed by ATC, transponder/ADS-B systems should be turned "on" and remain "on" whenever operating in the air or on the airport surface movement area.

d. ATC Surveillance Services using ADS-B— Procedures and Recommended Phraseology Radar procedures, with the exceptions found in this paragraph, are identical to those procedures prescribed for radar in AIM Chapter 4 and Chapter 5.

1. Preflight:
If ATC services are anticipated when either a VFR or IFR flight plan is filed, the aircraft identification (as entered in the flight plan) must be entered as the FLT ID in the ADS-B avionics.

2. Inflight:
When requesting surveillance services while airborne, pilots must disable the anonymous feature, if so equipped, prior to contacting ATC. Pilots must also ensure that their transmitted ADS-B FLT ID matches the aircraft identification as entered in their flight plan.

3. Aircraft with an Inoperative/Malfunctioning ADS-B Transmitter:

(a) ATC will inform the flight crew when the aircraft's ADS-B transmitter appears to be inoperative or malfunctioning:

Phraseology:
Your ADS-B transmitter appears to be inoperative/malfunctioning. Stop ADS-B transmissions.

(b) ATC will inform the flight crew if it becomes necessary to turn off the aircraft's ADS-B transmitter.

Phraseology:
Stop ADS-B transmissions.

(c) Other malfunctions and considerations: Loss of automatic altitude reporting capabilities (encoder failure) will result in loss of ATC altitude advisory services.

4. Procedures for Accommodation of Non-ADS-B Equipped Aircraft:

(a) Pilots of aircraft not equipped with ADS-B may only operate outside airspace designated as ADS-B airspace in 14 CFR §91.225. Pilots of unequipped aircraft wishing to fly any portion of a flight in ADS-B airspace may seek a deviation from the regulation to conduct operations without the required equipment. Direction for obtaining this deviation are available in Advisory Circular 90-114.

(b) While air traffic controllers can identify which aircraft are ADS-B equipped and which are not, there is no indication if a non-equipped pilot has obtained a preflight authorization to enter ADS-B airspace. Situations may occur when the pilot of a non-equipped aircraft, without an authorization to operate in ADS-B airspace receives an ATC-initiated in-flight clearance to fly a heading, route, or altitude that would penetrate ADS-B airspace. Such clearances may be for traffic, weather, or simply to shorten the aircraft's route of flight. When this occurs, the pilot should acknowledge and execute the clearance, but must advise the controller that they are not ADS-B equipped and have not received prior authorization to operate in ADS-B airspace. The controller, at their discretion, will either acknowledge and proceed with the new clearance, or modify the clearance to avoid ADS-B airspace. In either case, the FAA will normally not take enforcement action for non-equipage in these circumstances.

Note: Pilots operating without ADS-B equipment must not request route or altitude changes that will result in an incursion into ADS-B airspace except for safety of flight; for example, weather avoidance. Unequipped aircraft that have not received a pre-flight deviation authorization will only be considered in compliance with regulation if the amendment to flight is initiated by ATC.

Example 1: ATC: "November Two Three Quebec, turn fifteen degrees left, proceed direct Bradford when able, rest of route unchanged."

Aircraft: "November Two Three Quebec, turning fifteen degrees left, direct Bradford when able, rest of route unchanged. Be advised, we are negative ADS-B equipment and have not received authorization to operate in ADS-B airspace."

ATC: "November Two Three Quebec, roger"

or

"November Two Three Quebec, roger, turn twenty degrees right, rejoin Victor Ten, rest of route unchanged."

Example 2: ATC: "November Four Alpha Tango, climb and maintain one zero thousand for traffic."

Aircraft: "November Four Alpha Tango, leaving eight thousand for one zero thousand. Be advised, we are negative ADS-B equipment and

have not received authorization to operate in ADS-B airspace."

ATC: *"November Four Alpha Tango, roger"*

or

"November Four Alpha Tango, roger, cancel climb clearance, maintain eight thousand."

Reference: *Federal Register Notice, Volume 84, Number 62, dated April 1, 2019*

e. ADS-B Limitations

1. The ADS-B cockpit display of traffic is *not* intended to be used as a collision avoidance system and does not relieve the pilot's responsibility to "see and avoid" other aircraft. (See Paragraph 5-5-8, See and Avoid). ADS-B must not be used for avoidance maneuvers during IMC or other times when there is no visual contact with the intruder aircraft. ADS-B is intended only to assist in visual acquisition of other aircraft. No avoidance maneuvers are provided or authorized, as a direct result of an ADS-B target being displayed in the cockpit.

f. Reports of ADS-B Malfunctions

Users of ADS-B can provide valuable assistance in the correction of malfunctions by reporting instances of undesirable system performance. Since ADS-B performance is monitored by maintenance personnel rather than ATC, report malfunctions to the nearest Flight Service Station (FSS) facility by radio or telephone, or by sending an email to the ADS-B help desk at adsb@faa. gov. Reports should include:

1. Condition observed;
2. Date and time of observation;
3. Altitude and location of observation;
4. Type and call sign of the aircraft; and
5. Type and software version of avionics system.

4–5–8 Traffic Information Service–Broadcast (TIS-B)

a. Introduction.

TIS-B is the broadcast of ATC derived traffic information to ADS-B equipped (1090ES or UAT) aircraft from ground radio stations. The source of this traffic information is derived from ground-based air traffic surveillance sensors. TIS-B service will be available throughout the NAS where there are both adequate surveillance coverage from ground sensors and adequate broadcast coverage from ADS-B ground radio stations. The quality level of traffic information provided by TIS-B is dependent upon the number and type of ground sensors available as TIS-B sources and the timeliness of the reported data. (See Figure 4-5-9 and Figure 4-5-10.)

b. TIS-B Requirements.

In order to receive TIS-B service, the following conditions must exist:

1. Aircraft must be equipped with an ADS-B transmitter/receiver or transceiver, and a cockpit display of traffic information (CDTI).

2. Aircraft must fly within the coverage volume of a compatible ground radio station that is configured for TIS-B uplinks. (Not all ground radio stations provide TIS-B due to a lack of radar coverage or because a radar feed is not available).

3. Aircraft must be within the coverage of and detected by at least one ATC radar serving the ground radio station in use.

c. TIS-B Capabilities.

1. TIS-B is intended to provide ADS-B equipped aircraft with a more complete traffic picture in situations where not all nearby aircraft are equipped with ADS-B Out. This advisory-only application is intended to enhance a pilot's visual acquisition of other traffic.

2. Only transponder-equipped targets (i.e., Mode A/C or Mode S transponders) are transmitted through the ATC ground system architecture. Current radar siting may result in limited radar surveillance coverage at lower altitudes near some airports, with subsequently limited TIS-B service volume coverage. If there is no radar coverage in a given area, then there will be no TIS-B coverage in that area.

d. TIS-B Limitations.

1. TIS-B is *not* intended to be used as a collision avoidance system and does not relieve the pilot's responsibility to "see and avoid" other aircraft, in accordance with 14 CFR §91.113b. TIS-B must not be used for avoidance maneuvers during times when there is no visual contact with the intruder aircraft. TIS-B is intended only to assist in the visual acquisition of other aircraft.

Note: *No aircraft avoidance maneuvers are authorized as a direct result of a TIS-B target being displayed in the cockpit.*

2. While TIS-B is a useful aid to visual traffic avoidance, its inherent system limitations must be understood to ensure proper use.

(a) A pilot may receive an intermittent TIS-B target of themselves, typically when maneuvering (e.g., climbing turns) due to the radar not tracking the aircraft as quickly as ADS-B.

(b) The ADS-B-to-radar association process within the ground system may at times have difficulty correlating an ADS-B report with corresponding radar returns from the same aircraft. When this happens the pilot may see duplicate traffic symbols (i.e., "TIS-B shadows") on the cockpit display.

(c) Updates of TIS-B traffic reports will occur less often than ADS-B traffic updates. TIS-B position updates will occur approximately once every 3–13 seconds depending on the type of radar system in use within the coverage area. In

comparison, the update rate for ADS-B is nominally once per second.

(d) The TIS-B system only uplinks data pertaining to transponder-equipped aircraft. Aircraft without a transponder will not be displayed as TIS-B traffic.

(e) There is no indication provided when any aircraft is operating inside or outside the TIS-B service volume, therefore it is difficult to know if one is receiving uplinked TIS-B traffic information.

3. Pilots and operators are reminded that the airborne equipment that displays TIS-B targets is for pilot situational awareness only and is not approved as a collision avoidance tool. Unless there is an imminent emergency requiring immediate action, any deviation from an air traffic control clearance in response to perceived converging traffic appearing on a TIS-B display must be approved by the controlling ATC facility before commencing the maneuver, except as permitted under certain conditions in 14 CFR §91.123. Uncoordinated deviations may place an aircraft in close proximity to other aircraft under ATC control not seen on the airborne equipment and may result in a pilot deviation or other incident.

e. Reports of TIS-B Malfunctions

Users of TIS-B can provide valuable assistance in the correction of malfunctions by reporting instances of undesirable system performance. Since TIS-B performance is monitored by maintenance personnel rather than ATC, report malfunctions to the nearest Flight Service Station (FSS) facility by radio or telephone, or by sending an email to the ADS-B help desk at adsb@faa.gov. Reports should include:

1. Condition observed;

2. Date and time of observation;

3. Altitude and location of observation;

4. Type and call sign of the aircraft; and

5. Type and software version of avionics system.

4-5-9 Flight Information Service–Broadcast (FIS-B)

a. Introduction.

FIS-B is a ground broadcast service provided through the ADS-B Services network over the 978 MHz UAT data link. The FAA FIS-B system provides pilots and flight crews of properly equipped aircraft with a cockpit display of certain aviation weather and aeronautical information. FIS-B reception is line-of-sight within the service volume of the ground infrastructure. (See Figure 4-5-9 and Figure 4-5-10.)

b. Weather Products.

FIS-B does not replace a preflight weather briefing from a source listed in Paragraph 7-1-2, FAA Weather Services, or inflight updates from an FSS or ATC. FIS-B information may be used by the pilot for the safe conduct of flight and aircraft movement; however, the information should not be the only source of weather or aeronautical information. A pilot should be particularly alert and understand the limitations and quality assurance issues associated with individual products. This includes graphical representation of next generation weather radar (NEXRAD) imagery and Notices to Air Missions (NOTAM)/temporary flight restrictions (TFRs).

Reference: AIM, ¶7-1-9, Flight Information Services (FIS); Advisory Circular AC 00-63, Use of Cockpit Displays of Digital Weather and Aeronautical Information

c. Reports of FIS-B Malfunctions.

Users of FIS-B can provide valuable assistance in the correction of malfunctions by reporting instances of undesirable system performance. Since FIS-B performance is monitored by maintenance personnel rather than ATC, report malfunctions to the nearest Flight Service Station (FSS) facility by radio or telephone, or by sending an email to the ADS-B help desk at adsb@faa.gov. Reports should include:

1. Condition observed;

2. Date and time of observation;

3. Altitude and location of observation;

4. Type and call sign of the aircraft; and

5. Type and software version of avionics system.

TABLE 4-5-3
FIS-B OVER UAT PRODUCT UPDATE AND TRANSMISSION INTERVAL

Product	Update Interval[1]	Transmission Interval (95%)[2]	Basic Product
AIRMET	As Available	5 minutes	Yes
AWW/WW	As Available, then at 15 minute intervals for 1 hour	5 minutes	No
Ceiling	As Available	10 minutes	No
Convective SIGMET	As Available, then at 15 minute intervals for 1 hour	5 minutes	Yes
D-ATIS	As Available	1 minute	No
Echo Top	5 minutes	5 minutes	No
METAR/SPECI	1 minute (where available), As Available otherwise	5 minutes	Yes
MRMS NEXRAD (CONUS)	2 minutes	15 minutes	Yes
MRMS NEXRAD (Regional)	2 minutes	2.5 minutes	Yes
NOTAMs-D/FDC	As Available	10 minutes	Yes
NOTAMs-TFR	As Available	10 minutes	Yes
PIREP	As Available	10 minutes	Yes
SIGMET	As Available, then at 15 minute intervals for 1 hour	5 minutes	Yes
SUA Status	As Available	10 minutes	Yes
TAF/AMEND	6 Hours (±15 minutes)	10 minutes	Yes
Temperature Aloft	12 Hours (±15 minutes)	10 minutes	Yes
TWIP	As Available	1 minute	No
Winds aloft	12 Hours (±15 minutes)	10 minutes	Yes
Lightning strikes[3]	5 minutes	5 minutes	Yes
Turbulence[3]	1 minute	15 minutes	Yes
Icing, Forecast Potential (FIP)[3]	60 minutes	15 minutes	Yes
Cloud tops[3]	30 minutes	15 minutes	Yes
1 Minute AWOS[3]	1 minute	10 minutes	No
Graphical-AIRMET[3]	As Available	5 minutes	Yes
Center Weather Advisory (CWA)[3]	As Available	10 minutes	Yes
Temporary Restricted Areas (TRA)	As Available	10 minutes	Yes
Temporary Military Operations Areas (TMOA)	As Available	10 minutes	Yes

[1] The Update Interval is the rate at which the product data is available from the source.
[2] The Transmission Interval is the amount of time within which a new or updated product transmission must be completed (95%) and the rate or repetition interval at which the product is rebroadcast (95%).
[3] The transmission and update intervals for the expanded set of basic meteorological products may be adjusted based on FAA and vendor agreement on the final product formats and performance requirements.

Note 1: *Details concerning the content, format, and symbols of the various data link products provided should be obtained from the specific avionics manufacturer.*

Note 2: *NOTAM-D and NOTAM-FDC products broadcast via FIS-B are limited to those issued or effective within the past 30 days.*

Ch 4

4–5–10 Automatic Dependent Surveillance–Rebroadcast (ADS-R)

a. Introduction

ADS-R is a datalink translation function of the ADS-B ground system required to accommodate the two separate operating frequencies (978 MHz and 1090 ES). The ADS-B system receives the ADS-B messages transmitted on one frequency and ADS-R translates and reformats the information for rebroadcast and use on the other frequency. This allows ADS-B In equipped aircraft to see nearby ADS-B Out traffic regardless of the operating link of the other aircraft. Aircraft operating on the same ADS-B frequency exchange information directly and do not require the ADS-R translation function. (See Figure 4-5-9 and Figure 4-5-10.)

b. Reports of ADS-R Malfunctions.

Users of ADS-R can provide valuable assistance in the correction of malfunctions by reporting instances of undesirable system performance. Since ADS-R performance is monitored by maintenance personnel rather than ATC, report malfunctions to the nearest Flight Service Station (FSS) facility by radio or telephone, or by sending an email to the ADS-B help desk at adsb@faa.gov. Reports should include:

1. Condition observed;

2. Date and time of observation;

3. Altitude and location of observation;

4. Type and call sign of the aircraft and;

5. Type and software version of avionics system.

Section 6 Operational Policy/Procedures for Reduced Vertical Separation Minimum (RVSM) in the Domestic U.S., Alaska, Offshore Airspace and the San Juan FIR

4–6–1 Applicability and RVSM Mandate (Date/Time and Area)

a. Applicability. The policies, guidance and direction in this section apply to RVSM operations in the airspace over the lower 48 states, Alaska, Atlantic and Gulf of Mexico High Offshore Airspace and airspace in the San Juan FIR where VHF or UHF voice direct controller-pilot communication (DCPC) is normally available. Policies, guidance and direction for RVSM operations in oceanic airspace where VHF or UHF voice DCPC is not available and the airspace of other countries can be found in the Aeronautical Information Publication (AIP), Part II–En Route, ENR 1. General Rules and Procedures, and ENR 7. Oceanic Operations

b. Requirement. The FAA implemented RVSM between flight level (FL) 290–410 (inclusive) in the following airspace: the airspace of the lower 48 states of the United States, Alaska, Atlantic and Gulf of Mexico High Offshore Airspace and the San Juan FIR. RVSM has been implemented worldwide and may be applied in all ICAO Flight Information Regions (FIR)

c. RVSM Authorization. In accordance with 14 CFR Section 91.180, with only limited exceptions, prior to operating in RVSM airspace, operators must comply with the standards of Part 91, Appendix G, and be authorized by the Administrator. If either the operator or the operator's aircraft have not met the applicable RVSM standards, the aircraft will be referred to as a "non-RVSM" aircraft. Paragraph 4-6-10 discusses ATC policies for accommodation of non-RVSM aircraft flown by the Department of Defense, Air Ambulance (MEDEVAC) operators, foreign State governments and aircraft flown for certification and development. Paragraph 4-6-11, Non-RVSM Aircraft Requesting Climb to and Descent from Flight Levels Above RVSM Airspace Without Intermediate Level Off, contains policies for non-RVSM aircraft climbing and descending through RVSM airspace to/from flight levels above RVSM airspace.

d. Benefits. RVSM enhances ATC flexibility, mitigates conflict points, enhances sector throughput, reduces controller workload and enables crossing traffic. Operators gain fuel savings and operating efficiency benefits by flying at more fuel efficient flight levels and on more user preferred routings.

4–6–2 Flight Level Orientation Scheme

Altitude assignments for direction of flight follow a scheme of odd altitude assignment for magnetic courses 000–179 degrees and even altitudes for magnetic courses 180–359 degrees for flights up to and including FL410, as indicated in Figure 4-6-1.

FIGURE 4–6–1
Flight Level Orientation Scheme

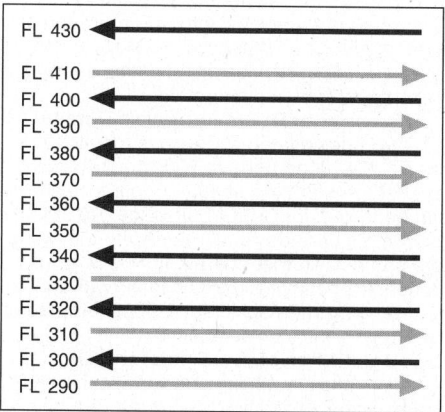

Note:
Odd Flight Levels:
Magnetic Course 000–179 Degrees

Even Flight Levels:
Magnetic Course 180–359 Degrees

4–6–3 Aircraft and Operator Approval Policy/Procedures, RVSM Monitoring and Databases for Aircraft and Operator Approval

a. RVSM Authority. 14 CFR Section 91.180 applies to RVSM operations within the U.S. 14 CFR Section 91.706 applies to RVSM operations outside the U.S. Both sections require that the operator be authorized prior to operating in RVSM airspace. For Domestic RVSM operations, an operator may choose to operate under the provisions of Part 91, Appendix G, Section 9; or if intending to operate outside U.S. airspace, hold a specific approval (OpSpec/MSpec/LOA) under the provisions of Section 3 of Part 91, Appendix G.

b. Sources of Information. Advisory Circular (AC) 91-85, *Authorization of Aircraft and Operators for Flight in Reduced Vertical Separation Minimum (RVSM) Airspace*, and the FAA RVSM website.

c. TCAS Equipage. TCAS equipage requirements are contained in 14 CFR Sections 121.356, 125.224, 129.18 and 135.189. Part 91 Appendix G does not contain TCAS equipage requirements specific to RVSM, however, Appendix G does require that aircraft equipped with TCAS II and flown in RVSM airspace be modified to incorporate TCAS II Version 7.0 or a later version.

d. Aircraft Monitoring. Operators are required to participate in the RVSM altitude-keeping performance monitoring program that is appropriate for the type of operation being conducted. The monitoring programs are described in AC 91-85. Monitoring is a quality control program that enables the FAA and other civil aviation authorities to assess the in-service altitude-keeping performance of aircraft and operators.

e. Purpose of RVSM Approvals Databases. All RVSM designated airspace is monitored airspace. ATC does not use RVSM approvals databases to determine whether or not a clearance can be issued into RVSM airspace. RVSM program managers do regularly review the operators and aircraft that operate in RVSM airspace to identify and investigate those aircraft and operators flying in RVSM airspace, but not listed on the RVSM approvals databases.

f. Registration of U.S. Operators. When U.S. operators and aircraft are granted specific RVSM authority, the Separation Standards Group at the FAA Technical Center obtains PTRS operator and aircraft information to update the FAA maintained U.S. Operator/Aircraft RVSM Approvals database. Basic database operator and aircraft information can be viewed on the RVSM Documentation Webpage in the "RVSM Approvals" section.

4-6-4 Flight Planning into RVSM Airspace

a. Operators that do not file the correct aircraft equipment suffix on the FAA or ICAO Flight Plan may be denied clearance into RVSM airspace. Policies for the FAA Flight Plan are detailed in subparagraph c below. Policies for the ICAO Flight Plan are detailed in subparagraph d.

b. The operator will annotate the equipment block of the FAA or ICAO Flight Plan with an aircraft equipment suffix indicating RVSM capability only after determining that both the operator is authorized and its aircraft are RVSM-compliant.

1. An operator may operate in RVSM airspace under the provisions of Part 91, Appendix G, Section 9, without specific authorization and should file "/w" in accordance with paragraph d.

2. An operator must get an OpSpec/MSpec/LOA when intending to operate RVSM outside U.S. airspace. Once issued, that operator can file "/w" in accordance with paragraph d.

3. An operator should not file "/w" when intending to operate in RVSM airspace outside of the U.S., if they do not hold a valid OpSpec/MSpec/LOA.

c. General Policies for FAA Flight Plan Equipment Suffix. Appendix 4, Table 4-2, allows operators to indicate that the aircraft has both RVSM and Advanced Area Navigation (RNAV) capabilities or has only RVSM capability.

1. The operator will annotate the equipment block of the FAA Flight Plan with the appropriate aircraft equipment suffix from Appendix 4, Table 4-2 and/or Table 4-3.

2. Operators can only file one equipment suffix in block 3 of the FAA Flight Plan. Only this equipment suffix is displayed directly to the controller.

3. Aircraft with RNAV Capability. For flight in RVSM airspace, aircraft with RNAV capability, but not Advanced RNAV capability, will file "/W". Filing "/W" will not preclude such aircraft from filing and flying direct routes in en route airspace.

d. Policy for ICAO Flight Plan Equipment Suffixes.

1. Operators/aircraft that are RVSM-compliant and that file ICAO flight plans will file "/W" in block 10 (Equipment) to indicate RVSM authorization and will also file the appropriate ICAO Flight Plan suffixes to indicate navigation and communication capabilities.

2. Operators/aircraft that file ICAO flight plans that include flight in Domestic U.S. RVSM airspace must file "/W" in block 10 to indicate RVSM authorization.

e. Importance of Flight Plan Equipment Suffixes. Military users, and civilians who file stereo route flight plans, must file the appropriate equipment suffix in the equipment block of the FAA Form 7233-1, Flight Plan, or DD Form 175, Military Flight Plan, or FAA Form 7233-4, International Flight Plan, or DD Form 1801, DOD International Flight Plan. All other users must file the appropriate equipment suffix in the equipment block of FAA Form 7233-4, International Flight Plan. The equipment suffix informs ATC:

1. Whether or not the operator and aircraft are authorized to fly in RVSM airspace.

2. The navigation and/or transponder capability of the aircraft (e.g., advanced RNAV, transponder with Mode C).

f. Significant ATC uses of the flight plan equipment suffix information are:

1. To issue or deny clearance into RVSM airspace.

2. To apply a 2,000 foot vertical separation minimum in RVSM airspace to aircraft that are

not authorized for RVSM, but are in one of the limited categories that the FAA has agreed to accommodate. (See paragraphs 4-6-10, Procedures for Accommodation of Non-RVSM Aircraft, and 4-6-11, Non-RVSM Aircraft Requesting Climb to and Descent from Flight Levels Above RVSM Airspace Without Intermediate Level Off, for policy on limited operation of unapproved aircraft in RVSM airspace).

3. To determine if the aircraft has "Advanced RNAV" capabilities and can be cleared to fly procedures for which that capability is required.

g. Improperly changing an aircraft equipment suffix and/or adding "NON-RVSM" in the NOTES or REMARKS section (Field 18) while not removing the "W" from Field 10, will not provide air traffic control with the proper visual indicator necessary to detect Non-RVSM aircraft. To ensure information processes correctly for Non-RVSM aircraft, the "W" in Field 10 must be removed. Entry of information in the NOTES or REMARKS section (Field 18) will not affect the determination of RVSM capability and must not be used to indicate a flight is Non-RVSM.

4-6-5 Pilot RVSM Operating Practices and Procedures

a. RVSM Mandate. If either the operator is not authorized for RVSM operations or the aircraft is not RVSM-compliant, the pilot will neither request nor accept a clearance into RVSM airspace unless:

1. The flight is conducted by a non-RVSM DOD, MEDEVAC, certification/development or foreign State (government) aircraft in accordance with paragraph 4-6-10, Procedures for Accommodation of Non-RVSM Aircraft.

2. The pilot intends to climb to or descend from FL430 or above in accordance with paragraph 4-6-11, Non-RVSM Aircraft Requesting Climb to and Descent from Flight Levels Above RVSM Airspace Without Intermediate Level Off.

3. An emergency situation exists.

b. Basic RVSM Operating Practices and Procedures. AC 91-85 contains pilot practices and procedures for RVSM. Operators must incorporate applicable practices and procedures, as supplemented by the applicable paragraphs of this section, into operator training or pilot knowledge programs and operator documents containing RVSM operational policies.

c. AC 91-85 contains practices and procedures for flight planning, preflight procedures at the aircraft, procedures prior to RVSM airspace entry, inflight (en route) procedures, contingency procedures and post flight.

d. The following paragraphs either clarify or supplement AC 91-85 practices and procedures.

4-6-6 Guidance on Severe Turbulence and Mountain Wave Activity (MWA)

a. Introduction/Explanation

1. The information and practices in this paragraph are provided to emphasize to pilots and controllers the importance of taking appropriate action in RVSM airspace when aircraft experience severe turbulence and/or MWA that is of sufficient magnitude to significantly affect altitude-keeping.

2. Severe Turbulence. Severe turbulence causes large, abrupt changes in altitude and/or attitude usually accompanied by large variations in indicated airspeed. Aircraft may be momentarily out of control. Encounters with severe turbulence must be remedied immediately in any phase of flight. Severe turbulence may be associated with MWA.

3. Mountain Wave Activity (MWA)

(a) Significant MWA occurs both below and above the floor of RVSM airspace, FL290. MWA often occurs in western states in the vicinity of mountain ranges. It may occur when strong winds blow perpendicular to mountain ranges resulting in up and down or wave motions in the atmosphere. Wave action can produce altitude excursions and airspeed fluctuations accompanied by only light turbulence. With sufficient amplitude, however, wave action can induce altitude and airspeed fluctuations accompanied by severe turbulence. MWA is difficult to forecast and can be highly localized and short lived.

(b) Wave activity is not necessarily limited to the vicinity of mountain ranges. Pilots experiencing wave activity anywhere that significantly affects altitude-keeping can follow the guidance provided below.

(c) Inflight MWA Indicators (Including Turbulence). Indicators that the aircraft is being subjected to MWA are:

(1) Altitude excursions and/or airspeed fluctuations with or without associated turbulence.

(2) Pitch and trim changes required to maintain altitude with accompanying airspeed fluctuations.

(3) Light to severe turbulence depending on the magnitude of the MWA.

4. Priority for Controller Application of Merging Target Procedures

(a) Explanation of Merging Target Procedures. As described in subparagraph c3 below, ATC will use "merging target procedures" to mitigate the effects of both severe turbulence and MWA. The procedures in subparagraph c3 have been adapted from existing procedures published in FAA Order JO 7110.65, Air Traffic Control, paragraph 5-1-4, Merging Target Procedures. Paragraph 5-1-4 calls for en route controllers to advise pilots of potential traffic that they perceive may fly

Ch 4

directly above or below his/her aircraft at minimum vertical separation. In response, pilots are given the option of requesting a radar vector to ensure their radar target will not merge or overlap with the traffic's radar target.

(b) The provision of "merging target procedures" to mitigate the effects of severe turbulence and/or MWA is not optional for the controller, but rather is a priority responsibility. Pilot requests for vectors for traffic avoidance when encountering MWA or pilot reports of "Unable RVSM due turbulence or MWA" are considered first priority aircraft separation and sequencing responsibilities. (FAA Order JO 7110.65, paragraph 2-1-2, Duty Priority, states that the controller's first priority is to separate aircraft and issue safety alerts).

(c) Explanation of the term "traffic permitting." The contingency actions for MWA and severe turbulence detailed in paragraph 4-6-9, Contingency Actions: Weather Encounters and Aircraft System Failures that Occur After Entry into RVSM Airspace, state that the controller will "vector aircraft to avoid merging targets with traffic at adjacent flight levels, traffic permitting." The term "traffic permitting" is not intended to imply that merging target procedures are not a priority duty. The term is intended to recognize that, as stated in FAA Order JO 7110.65, paragraph 2-1-2, Duty Priority, there are circumstances when the controller is required to perform more than one action and must "exercise their best judgment based on the facts and circumstances known to them" to prioritize their actions. Further direction given is: "That action which is most critical from a safety standpoint is performed first."

5. TCAS Sensitivity. For both MWA and severe turbulence encounters in RVSM airspace, an additional concern is the sensitivity of collision avoidance systems when one or both aircraft operating in close proximity receive TCAS advisories in response to disruptions in altitude hold capability.

b. Pre-flight tools. Sources of observed and forecast information that can help the pilot ascertain the possibility of MWA or severe turbulence are: Forecast Winds and Temperatures Aloft (FD), Area Forecast (FA), Graphical Turbulence Guidance (GTG), SIGMETs and PIREPs.

c. Pilot Actions When Encountering Weather (e.g., Severe Turbulence or MWA)

1. Weather Encounters Inducing Altitude Deviations of Approximately 200 feet. When the pilot experiences weather induced altitude deviations of approximately 200 feet, the pilot will contact ATC and state "Unable RVSM Due (state reason)" (e.g., turbulence, mountain wave). See contingency actions in paragraph 4-6-9.

2. Severe Turbulence (including that associated with MWA). When pilots encounter severe turbulence, they should contact ATC and

report the situation. Until the pilot reports clear of severe turbulence, the controller will apply merging target vectors to one or both passing aircraft to prevent their targets from merging:

Example:

"Yankee 123, FL310, unable RVSM due severe turbulence."

"Yankee 123, fly heading 290; traffic twelve o'clock, 10 miles, opposite direction; eastbound MD-80 at FL320" (or the controller may issue a vector to the MD-80 traffic to avoid Yankee 123).

3. MWA. When pilots encounter MWA, they should contact ATC and report the magnitude and location of the wave activity. When a controller makes a merging targets traffic call, the pilot may request a vector to avoid flying directly over or under the traffic. In situations where the pilot is experiencing altitude deviations of 200 feet or greater, the pilot will request a vector to avoid traffic. Until the pilot reports clear of MWA, the controller will apply merging target vectors to one or both passing aircraft to prevent their targets from merging:

Example:

"Yankee 123, FL310, unable RVSM due mountain wave."

"Yankee 123, fly heading 290; traffic twelve o'clock, 10 miles, opposite direction; eastbound MD-80 at FL320" (or the controller may issue a vector to the MD-80 traffic to avoid Yankee 123).

4. FL Change or Re-route. To leave airspace where MWA or severe turbulence is being encountered, the pilot may request a FL change and/or re-route, if necessary.

4-6-7 Guidance on Wake Turbulence

a. Pilots should be aware of the potential for wake turbulence encounters in RVSM airspace. Experience gained since 1997 has shown that such encounters in RVSM airspace are generally moderate or less in magnitude.

b. Prior to DRVSM implementation, the FAA established provisions for pilots to report wake turbulence events in RVSM airspace using the NASA Aviation Safety Reporting System (ASRS). A "Safety Reporting" section established on the FAA RVSM Documentation webpage provides contacts, forms, and reporting procedures.

c. To date, wake turbulence has not been reported as a significant factor in DRVSM operations. European authorities also found that reports of wake turbulence encounters did not increase significantly after RVSM implementation (eight versus seven reports in a ten-month period). In addition, they found that reported wake turbulence was generally similar to moderate clear air turbulence.

d. Pilot Action to Mitigate Wake Turbulence Encounters

 1. Pilots should be alert for wake turbulence when operating:

 (a) In the vicinity of aircraft climbing or descending through their altitude.

 (b) Approximately 10–30 miles after passing 1,000 feet below opposite-direction traffic.

 (c) Approximately 10–30 miles behind and 1,000 feet below same-direction traffic.

 2. Pilots encountering or anticipating wake turbulence in DRVSM airspace have the option of requesting a vector, FL change or if capable, a lateral offset.

Note 1: Offsets of approximately a wing span upwind generally can move the aircraft out of the immediate vicinity of another aircraft's wake vortex.

Note 2: In domestic U.S. airspace, pilots must request clearance to fly a lateral offset. Strategic lateral offsets flown in oceanic airspace do not apply.

4-6-8 Pilot/Controller Phraseology

Table 4-6-1 shows standard phraseology that pilots and controllers will use to communicate in DRVSM operations.

TABLE 4–6–1
PILOT/CONTROLLER PHRASEOLOGY

Message	Phraseology
For a controller to ascertain the RVSM approval status of an aircraft:	(call sign) confirm RVSM approved
Pilot indication that flight is RVSM approved	Affirm RVSM
Pilot report of lack of RVSM approval (non-RVSM status). Pilot will report non-RVSM status, as follows: **a.** On the initial call on any frequency in the RVSM airspace and… **b.** In all requests for flight level changes pertaining to flight levels within the RVSM airspace and… **c.** In all read backs to flight level clearances pertaining to flight levels within the RVSM airspace and… **d.** In read back of flight level clearances involving climb and descent through RVSM airspace (FL 290–410)	Negative RVSM (supplementary information, e.g., "Certification flight")
Pilot report of one of the following after entry into RVSM airspace: all primary altimeters, automatic altitude control systems or altitude alerters have failed. (See paragraph 4-6-9, Contingency Actions: Weather Encounters and Aircraft System Failures that Occur After Entry into RVSM Airspace.) **Note:** *This phrase is to be used to convey both the initial indication of RVSM aircraft system failure and on initial contact on all frequencies in RVSM airspace until the problem ceases to exist or the aircraft has exited RVSM airspace.*	Unable RVSM Due Equipment
ATC denial of clearance into RVSM airspace	Unable issue clearance into RVSM airspace, maintain FL
*Pilot reporting inability to maintain cleared flight level due to weather encounter. (See paragraph 4-6-9, Contingency Actions: Weather Encounters and Aircraft System Failures that Occur After Entry into RVSM Airspace).	*Unable RVSM due (state reason) (e.g., turbulence, mountain wave)
ATC requesting pilot to confirm that an aircraft has regained RVSM-approved status or a pilot is ready to resume RVSM	Confirm able to resume RVSM
Pilot ready to resume RVSM after aircraft system or weather contingency	Ready to resume RVSM

4-6-9 Contingency Actions: Weather Encounters and Aircraft System Failures that Occur After Entry into RVSM Airspace

Table 4-6-2 provides pilot guidance on actions to take under certain conditions of aircraft system failure that occur after entry into RVSM airspace and weather encounters. It also describes the expected ATC controller actions in these situations. It is recognized that the pilot and controller will use judgment to determine the action most appropriate to any given situation.

TABLE 4–6–2
CONTINGENCY ACTIONS: WEATHER ENCOUNTERS AND AIRCRAFT SYSTEM FAILURES
THAT OCCUR AFTER ENTRY INTO RVSM AIRSPACE

Initial Pilot Actions in Contingency Situations
Initial pilot actions when unable to maintain flight level (FL) or unsure of aircraft altitude-keeping capability: • Notify ATC and request assistance as detailed below. • Maintain cleared flight level, to the extent possible, while evaluating the situation. • Watch for conflicting traffic both visually and by reference to TCAS, if equipped. • Alert nearby aircraft by illuminating exterior lights (commensurate with aircraft limitations).

Severe Turbulence and/or Mountain Wave Activity (MWA) Induced Altitude Deviations of Approximately 200 feet	
Pilot will: • When experiencing severe turbulence and/or MWA induced altitude deviations of approximately 200 feet or greater, pilot will contact ATC and state "Unable RVSM Due (state reason)" (e.g., turbulence, mountain wave) • If not issued by the controller, request vector clear of traffic at adjacent FLs • If desired, request FL change or re-route • Report location and magnitude of turbulence or MWA to ATC	**Controller will:** • Vector aircraft to avoid merging target with traffic at adjacent flight levels, traffic permitting • Advise pilot of conflicting traffic • Issue FL change or re-route, traffic permitting • Issue PIREP to other aircraft
See paragraph 4-6-6, Guidance on Severe Turbulence and Mountain Wave Activity (MWA) for detailed guidance.	Paragraph 4-6-6 explains "traffic permitting."

Mountain Wave Activity (MWA) Encounters—General	
Pilot actions: • Contact ATC and report experiencing MWA • If so desired, pilot may request a FL change or re-route • Report location and magnitude of MWA to ATC	**Controller actions:** • Advise pilot of conflicting traffic at adjacent FL • If pilot requests, vector aircraft to avoid merging target with traffic at adjacent RVSM flight levels, traffic permitting • Issue FL change or re-route, traffic permitting • Issue PIREP to other aircraft
See paragraph 4-6-6 for guidance on MWA.	Paragraph 4-6-6 explains "traffic permitting."

Note: MWA encounters do not necessarily result in altitude deviations on the order of 200 feet. The guidance below is intended to address less significant MWA encounters.

Wake Turbulence Encounters	
Pilot should: • Contact ATC and request vector, FL change or, if capable, a lateral offset	**Controller should:** • Issue vector, FL change or lateral offset clearance, traffic permitting
See paragraph 4-6-7, Guidance on Wake Turbulence.	Paragraph 4-6-6 explains "traffic permitting."

"Unable RVSM Due Equipment" Failure of Automatic Altitude Control System, Altitude Alerter or All Primary Altimeters	
Pilot will: • Contact ATC and state "Unable RVSM Due Equipment" • Request clearance out of RVSM airspace unless operational situation dictates otherwise	**Controller will:** • Provide 2,000 feet vertical separation or appropriate horizontal separation • Clear aircraft out of RVSM airspace unless operational situation dictates otherwise

(continued)

CONTINGENCY ACTIONS: WEATHER ENCOUNTERS AND AIRCRAFT SYSTEM FAILURES
THAT OCCUR AFTER ENTRY INTO RVSM AIRSPACE *(continued)*

One Primary Altimeter Remains Operational	
Pilot will:	**Controller will:**
• Cross check stand-by altimeter • Notify ATC of operation with single primary altimeter • If unable to confirm primary altimeter accuracy, follow actions for failure of all primary altimeters	• Acknowledge operation with single primary altimeter

Transponder Failure	
Pilot will:	**Controller will:**
• Contact ATC and request authority to continue to operate at cleared flight level • Comply with revised ATC clearance, if issued *Note: 14 CFR Section 91.215 (ATC transponder and altitude reporting equipment and use) regulates operation with the transponder inoperative.*	• Consider request to continue to operate at cleared flight level • Issue revised clearance, if necessary

4–6–10 Procedures for Accommodation of Non-RVSM Aircraft

a. General Policies for Accommodation of Non-RVSM Aircraft

1. The RVSM mandate calls for only RVSM authorized aircraft/operators to fly in designated RVSM airspace with limited exceptions. The policies detailed below are intended exclusively for use by aircraft that the FAA has agreed to accommodate. They are not intended to provide other operators a means to circumvent the normal RVSM approval process.

2. If the operator is not authorized or the aircraft is not RVSM-compliant, the aircraft will be referred to as a "non-RVSM" aircraft. 14 CFR Section 91.180 and Part 91, Appendix G, enable the FAA to authorize a deviation to operate a non-RVSM aircraft in RVSM airspace.

3. Non-RVSM aircraft flights will be handled on a workload permitting basis. The vertical separation standard applied between aircraft not approved for RVSM and all other aircraft must be 2,000 feet.

4. Required Pilot Calls. The pilot of non-RVSM aircraft will inform the controller of the lack of RVSM approval in accordance with the direction provided in paragraph 4-6-8, Pilot/Controller Phraseology.

b. Categories of Non-RVSM Aircraft that may be Accommodated

Subject to FAA approval and clearance, the following categories of non-RVSM aircraft may operate in domestic U.S. RVSM airspace provided they have an operational transponder.

1. Department of Defense (DOD) aircraft.

2. Flights conducted for aircraft certification and development purposes.

3. Active air ambulance flights utilizing a "MEDEVAC" call sign.

4. Aircraft climbing/descending through RVSM flight levels (without intermediate level off) to/from FLs above RVSM airspace (Policies for these flights are detailed in paragraph 4-6-11, Non-RVSM Aircraft Requesting Climb to and Descent from Flight Levels Above RVSM Airspace Without Intermediate Level Off.)

5. Foreign State (government) aircraft.

c. Methods for operators of non-RVSM aircraft to request access to RVSM Airspace. Operators may:

1. LOA/MOU. Enter into a Letter of Agreement (LOA)/Memorandum of Understanding (MOU) with the RVSM facility (the Air Traffic facility that provides air traffic services in RVSM airspace). Operators must comply with LOA/MOU.

2. File-and-Fly. File a flight plan to notify the FAA of their intention to request access to RVSM airspace.

Note: Priority for access to RVSM airspace will be afforded to RVSM compliant aircraft, then File-and-Fly flights.

4–6–11 Non-RVSM Aircraft Requesting Climb to and Descent from Flight Levels Above RVSM Airspace Without Intermediate Level Off

a. File-and-Fly. Operators of Non-RVSM aircraft climbing to and descending from RVSM flight levels should just file a flight plan.

b. Non-RVSM aircraft climbing to and descending from flight levels above RVSM airspace will be handled on a workload permitting basis. The vertical separation standard applied in RVSM airspace between non-RVSM aircraft and all other aircraft must be 2,000 feet.

c. Non-RVSM aircraft climbing to/descending from RVSM airspace can only be considered for accommodation provided:

1. Aircraft is capable of a continuous climb/descent and does not need to level off at an intermediate altitude for any operational considerations and

2. Aircraft is capable of climb/descent at the normal rate for the aircraft.

d. Required Pilot Calls. The pilot of non-RVSM aircraft will inform the controller of the lack of RVSM approval in accordance with the direction provided in paragraph 4-6-8, Pilot/Controller Phraseology.

Section 7 Operational Policy/Procedures for the Gulf of Mexico 50 NM Lateral Separation Initiative

4-7-1 Introduction and General Policies

a. Air traffic control (ATC) may apply 50 nautical mile (NM) lateral separation (i.e., lateral spacing) between airplanes authorized for Required Navigation Performance (RNP) 10 or RNP 4 operating in the Gulf of Mexico. 50 NM lateral separation may be applied in the following airspace:

1. Houston Oceanic Control Area (CTA)/ Flight Information Region (FIR).

2. Gulf of Mexico portion of the Miami Oceanic CTA/FIR.

3. Monterrey CTA.

4. Merida High CTA within the Mexico FIR/ UTA.

b. Within the Gulf of Mexico airspace described above, pairs of airplanes whose flight plans indicate approval for PBN and either RNP 10 or RNP 4 may be spaced by ATC at lateral intervals of 50 NM. ATC will space any airplane without RNP 10 or RNP 4 capability such that at least 90 NM lateral separation is maintained with other airplanes in the Miami Oceanic CTA, and at least 100 NM separation is maintained in the Houston, Monterrey, and Merida CTAs.

c. The reduced lateral separation allows more airplanes to fly on optimum routes/altitudes over the Gulf of Mexico.

d. 50 NM lateral separation is not applied on routes defined by ground navigation aids or on Gulf RNAV Routes Q100, Q102, or Q105.

e. Useful information for flight planning and operations over the Gulf of Mexico, under this 50 NM lateral separation policy, as well as information on how to obtain RNP 10 or RNP 4 authorization, can be found in the West Atlantic, Gulf of Mexico, and Caribbean Resource Guide for U.S. Operators located at: https://www.faa.gov/headquartersoffices/avs /wat-gomex-and-caribbean-resource-guide

f. Pilots should use Strategic Lateral Offset Procedures (SLOP) in the course of regular operations within the Gulf of Mexico CTAs. SLOP procedures and limitations are published in the U.S. Aeronautical Information Publication (AIP), ENR Section 7.1, General Procedures; Advisory Circular (AC) 91-70, Oceanic and Remote Continental Airspace Operations; and ICAO Document 4444, Procedures for Air Navigation Services – Air Traffic Management.

4-7-2 Accommodating Non-RNP 10 Aircraft

a. Operators not authorized for RNP 10 or RNP 4 may still file for any route and altitude within the Gulf of Mexico CTAs. However, clearance on the operator's preferred route and/or altitude will be provided as traffic allows for 90 or 100 NM lateral separation between the non-RNP 10 aircraft and any others. Priority will be given to RNP 10 or RNP 4 aircraft.

b. Operators of aircraft not authorized RNP 10 or RNP 4 must include the annotation "RMK/ NONRNP10" in Item 18 of their ATC flight plan.

c. Pilots of non-RNP 10 aircraft are to remind ATC of their RNP status; i.e., report "negative RNP 10" upon initial contact with ATC in each Gulf CTA.

d. Operators will likely benefit from the effort they invest to obtain RNP 10 or RNP 4 authorization, provided they are flying aircraft equipped to meet RNP 10 or RNP 4 standards.

4-7-3 Obtaining RNP 10 or RNP 4 Operational Authorization

a. For U.S. operators, AC 90-105, Approval Guidance for RNP Operations and Barometric Vertical Navigation in the U.S. National Airspace System and in Oceanic and Remote Continental Airspace, provides the aircraft and operator qualification criteria for RNP 10 or RNP 4 authorizations. FAA personnel at flight standards district offices (FSDO) and certificate management offices (CMO) will use the guidance contained in AC 90-105 to evaluate an operator's application for RNP 10 or RNP 4 authorization. Authorization to conduct RNP operations in oceanic airspace is provided to all U.S. operators through issuance of Operations Specification (OpSpec), Management Specification (MSpec), or Letter of Authorization (LOA) B036, as applicable to the nature of the operation; for example, Part 121, Part 91, etc. Operators may wish to review FAA Order 8900.1, Flight Standards Information Management System, volume 3, chapter 18, section 4, to understand the specific criteria for issuing OpSpec, MSpec, and/ or LOA B036.

b. The operator's RNP 10 or RNP 4 authorization should include any equipment requirements and RNP 10 time limits (if operating solely inertial-based navigation systems), which must be observed when conducting RNP operations. RNP 4 requires tighter navigation and track maintenance accuracy than RNP 10.

Ch 4

4-7-4 Authority for Operations with a Single Long-Range Navigation System

Operators may be authorized to take advantage of 50 NM lateral separation in the Gulf of Mexico CTAs when equipped with only a single long-range navigation system. RNP 10 with a single long-range navigation system is authorized via OpSpec, MSpec, or LOA B054. Operators should contact their FSDO or CMO to obtain information on the specific requirements for obtaining B054. Volume 3, chapter 18, section 4 of FAA Order 8900.1 provides the qualification criteria to be used by FAA aviation safety inspectors in issuing B054.

4-7-5 Flight Plan Requirements

a. In order for an operator with RNP 10 or RNP 4 authorization to obtain 50 NM lateral separation in the Gulf of Mexico CTAs, and therefore obtain preferred routing available to RNP authorized aircraft, the international flight plan form (FAA 7233-4) must be annotated as follows:

1. Item 10a (Equipment) must include the letter "R."

2. Item 18 must include either "PBN/A1" for RNP 10 authorization or "PBN/L1" for RNP 4 authorization.

b. Indication of RNP 4 authorization implies the aircraft and pilots are also authorized RNP 10.

c. Chapter 5, section 1, of this manual includes information on all flight plan codes. RNP 10 has the same meaning and application as RNAV 10. They share the same code.

4-7-6 Contingency Procedures

Pilots operating under reduced lateral separation must be particularly familiar with, and prepared to rapidly implement, the standard contingency procedures specifically written for operations when outside ATC surveillance and direct VHF communications (for example, the oceanic environment). Specific procedures have been developed for weather deviations. Operators should ensure all flight crews operating in this type of environment have been provided the standard contingency procedures in a readily accessible format. The margin for error when operating at reduced separation mandates correct and expeditious application of the standard contingency procedures. These internationally accepted procedures are published in ICAO Document 4444, chapter 15. The procedures are also reprinted in the U.S. Aeronautical Information Publication (AIP), En Route (ENR) Section 7.3, Special Procedures for In-flight Contingencies in Oceanic Airspace; and AC 91-70.

Chapter 5
Air Traffic Procedures

Section 1 Preflight

5-1-1 Preflight Preparation

a. Prior to every flight, pilots should gather all information vital to the nature of the flight, assess whether the flight would be safe, and then file a flight plan. Pilots can receive a regulatory compliant briefing without contacting Flight Service. Pilots are encouraged to use automated resources and review Advisory Circular AC 91-92, Pilot's Guide to a Preflight Briefing, for more information. Pilots who prefer to contact Flight Service are encouraged to conduct a self-brief prior to calling. Conducting a self-brief before contacting Flight Service provides familiarity of meteorological and aeronautical conditions applicable to the route of flight and promotes a better understanding of weather information. Pilots may access Flight Service through www.1800wxbrief.com or by calling 1-800-WX-BRIEF. Flight planning applications are also available for conducting a self-briefing and filing flight plans.

Note: Alaska only: Pilots filing flight plans via "fast file" who desire to have their briefing recorded, should include a statement at the end of the recording as to the source of their weather briefing.

b. The information required by the FAA to process flight plans is obtained from FAA Form 7233-4, International Flight Plan. Only DOD users, and civilians who file stereo route flight plans, may use FAA Form 7233-1, Flight Plan.

Note: FAA and DOD Flight Plan Forms are equivalent. Where the FAA specifies Form 7233-1, Flight Plan and FAA Form 7233-4, International Flight Plan, the DOD may substitute their Form DD 175, Military Flight Plan and Form DD-1801, DOD International Flight Plan as necessary. NAS automation systems process and convert data in the same manner, although for computer acceptance, input fields may be adjusted to follow FAA format.

c. FSSs are required to advise of pertinent NOTAMs if a *standard* briefing is requested, but if they are overlooked, do not hesitate to remind the specialist that you have not received NOTAM information. Additionally, FSS briefers do not provide FDC NOTAM information for special instrument approach procedures unless specifically asked. Pilots authorized by the FAA to use special instrument approach procedures must specifically request FDC NOTAM information for these procedures. Pilots who receive the information electronically will receive NOTAMs for special IAPs automatically.

Note: Domestic Notices and International Notices are not provided during a briefing unless specifically requested by the pilot since the FSS specialist has no way of knowing whether the pilot has already checked the Federal NOTAM System (FNS) NOTAM Search website external links prior to calling. Airway NOTAMs, procedural NOTAMs, and NOTAMs that are general in nature and not tied to a specific airport/facility (for example, flight advisories and restrictions, open duration special security instructions, and special flight rules areas) are briefed solely by pilot request. Remember to ask for these notices if you have not already reviewed this information, and to request all pertinent NOTAMs specific to your flight.

Reference: AIM, ¶5-1-3, Notice to Air Missions (NOTAM) System.

d. Pilots are urged to use only the latest issue of aeronautical charts in planning and conducting flight operations. Aeronautical charts are revised and reissued on a regular scheduled basis to ensure that depicted data are current and reliable. In the conterminous U.S., Sectional Charts are updated every 6 months, IFR En Route Charts every 56 days, and amendments to civil IFR Approach Charts are accomplished on a 56-day cycle with a change notice volume issued on the 28-day midcycle. Charts that have been superseded by those of a more recent date may contain obsolete or incomplete flight information.

Reference: AIM, ¶9-1-4, General Description of Each Chart Series.

e. When requesting a preflight briefing, identify yourself as a pilot and provide the following:

1. Type of flight planned; e.g., VFR or IFR.
2. Aircraft's number or pilot's name.
3. Aircraft type.
4. Departure Airport.
5. Route of flight.
6. Destination.
7. Flight altitude(s).
8. ETD and ETE.

f. Prior to conducting a briefing, briefers are required to have the background information listed above so that they may tailor the briefing to the needs of the proposed flight. The objective is to communicate a "picture" of meteorological and aeronautical information necessary for the conduct of a safe and efficient flight. Briefers use all available weather and aeronautical information to summarize data applicable to the proposed flight.

Ch 5

Pilots who have briefed themselves before calling Flight Service should advise the briefer what information has been obtained from other sources.

Reference: AIM, ¶7-1-5, Preflight Briefings, contains those items of a weather briefing that should be expected or requested.

g. FAA by 14 CFR Part 93, Subpart K, has designated High Density Traffic Airports (HDTAs) and has prescribed air traffic rules and requirements for operating aircraft (excluding helicopter operations) to and from these airports.

Reference: Chart Supplement, Special Notices Section; AIM, ¶4-1-21, Airport Reservation Operations and Special Traffic Management Programs.

h. In addition to the filing of a flight plan, if the flight will traverse or land in one or more foreign countries, it is particularly important that pilots leave a complete itinerary with someone directly concerned and keep that person advised of the flight's progress. If serious doubt arises as to the safety of the flight, that person should first contact the FSS.

Reference: AIM, ¶5-1-11, Flights Outside the U.S. and U.S. Territories.

i. Pilots operating under provisions of 14 CFR Part 135 on a domestic flight without having an FAA assigned 3-letter designator, must prefix the normal registration (N) number with the letter "T" on flight plan filing; for example, TN1234B.

Reference: AIM, ¶4-2-4, Aircraft Call Signs; FAA Order JO 7110.65, ¶2-3-5, Aircraft Identity, Subpara a; FAA Order JO 7110.10, Appendix B, FAA Form 7233-1, Flight Plan.

5-1-2 Follow IFR Procedures Even When Operating VFR

a. To maintain IFR proficiency, pilots are urged to practice IFR procedures whenever possible, even when operating VFR. Some suggested practices include:

1. Obtain a complete preflight briefing and check NOTAMs. Prior to every flight, pilots should gather all information vital to the nature of the flight. Pilots can receive a regulatory compliant briefing without contacting Flight Service. Pilots are encouraged to use automated resources and review AC 91-92, Pilot's Guide to a Preflight Briefing, for more information. NOTAMs are available online from the Federal NOTAM System (FNS) NOTAM Search website (https://notams.aim.faa .gov/notamSearch/), private vendors, or on request from Flight Service

2. File a flight plan. This is an excellent low cost insurance policy. The cost is the time it takes to fill it out. The insurance includes the knowledge that someone will be looking for you if you become overdue at your destination. Pilots can file flight plans either by using a website or by calling Flight Service. Flight planning applications are also available to file, activate, and close VFR flight plans.

3. Use current charts.

4. Use the navigation aids. Practice maintaining a good course—keep the needle centered.

5. Maintain a constant altitude which is appropriate for the direction of flight.

6. Estimate en route position times.

7. Make accurate and frequent position reports to the FSSs along your route of flight.

b. Simulated IFR flight is recommended (under the hood); however, pilots are cautioned to review and adhere to the requirements specified in 14 CFR Section 91.109 before and during such flight.

c. When flying VFR at night, in addition to the altitude appropriate for the direction of flight, pilots should maintain an altitude which is at or above the minimum en route altitude as shown on charts. This is especially true in mountainous terrain, where there is usually very little ground reference. Do not depend on your eyes alone to avoid rising unlighted terrain, or even lighted obstructions such as TV towers.

5-1-3 Notice to Air Missions (NOTAM) System

a. **General.** The NOTAM system provides pilots with time critical aeronautical information that is temporary, or information to be published on aeronautical charts at a later date, or information from another operational publication. The NOTAM is cancelled when the information in the NOTAM is published on the chart or when the temporary condition is returned to normal status. NOTAMs may be disseminated up to 7 days before the start of activity. Pilots can access NOTAM information online via NOTAM Search at: https://notams.aim .faa.gov/notamSearch/ or from an FSS.

b. **Preflight.** 14 CFR § 91.103, Preflight Action directs pilots to become familiar with all available information concerning a planned flight prior to departure, including NOTAMs. Pilots may change their flight plan based on available information. Current NOTAM information may affect:

1. Aerodromes.

2. Runways, taxiways, and ramp restrictions.

3. Obstructions.

4. Communications.

5. Airspace.

6. Status of navigational aids or radar service availability.

7. Other information essential to planned en route, terminal, or landing operations.

c. **ARTCC NOTAMs.** Pilots should also review NOTAMs for the ARTCC area (for example, Washington Center (ZDC), Cleveland Center (ZOB), etc.) in which the flight will be operating.

You can find the 3 letter code for each ARTCC on the FAA's NOTAM webpage. These NOTAMs may affect the planned flight. Some of the operations include Central Altitude Reservation Function (CARF), Special Use Airspace (SUA), Temporary Flight Restrictions (TFR), Global Positioning System (GPS), Flight Data Center (FDC) changes to routes, wind turbine, and Unmanned Aircraft System (UAS).

Note: NOTAM information is transmitted using ICAO contractions to reduce transmission time. See Table 5-1-2 for a listing of the most commonly used contractions, or go online to the following URL: https://www.notams.faa.gov/downloads /contractions.pdf. For a complete listing of approved NOTAM Contractions, see FAA JO Order 7340.2, Contractions.

d. Destination Update. Pilots should also contact ATC or FSS while en route to obtain updated airfield information for their destination. This is particularly important when flying to the airports without an operating control tower. Snow removal, fire and rescue activities, construction, and wildlife encroachment, may pose hazards to pilots. This information may not be available to pilots prior to arrival/departure.

e. NAVAID NOTAMs. Pilots should check NOTAMs to ensure NAVAIDs required for the flight are in service. A NOTAM is published when a NAVAID is out of service or Unserviceable (U/S). Although a NAVAID is deemed U/S and planned for removal from service, it may be a long time before that NAVAID is officially decommissioned and removed from charts. A NOTAM is the primary method of alerting pilots to its unavailability. It is recommended that pilots using VFR charts should regularly consult the Chart Update Bulletin. This bulletin identifies any updates to the chart that have not yet been accounted for.

f. GPS NOTAMs. The FAA issues information on the status of GPS through the NOTAM system. Operators may find information on GPS satellite outages, GPS testing, and GPS anomalies by specifically searching for GPS NOTAMs prior to flight.

1. The NOTAM system uses the terms UNRELIABLE (UNREL), MAY NOT BE AVAILABLE (AVBL), and NOT AVAILABLE (AVBL) when describing the status of GPS. UNREL indicates the expected level of service of the GPS and/or WAAS may not be available. Pilots must then determine the adequacy of the signal for desired use. Aircraft should have additional navigation equipment for their intended route.

Note: Unless associated with a known testing NOTAM, pilots should report GPS anomalies, including degraded operation and/or loss of service, as soon as possible via radio or telephone, and via the GPS Anomaly Reporting Form. (See 1-1-13.)

2. GPS operations may also be NOTAMed for testing. This is indicated in the NOTAM language with the name of the test in parenthesis. When GPS testing NOTAMs are published and testing is actually occurring, ATC will advise pilots requesting or cleared for a GPS or RNAV (GPS) approach, that GPS may not be available and request the pilot's intentions. Table 5-1-1 lists an example of a GPS testing NOTAM.

g. NOTAM Classification. NOTAM information is classified as Domestic NOTAMs (NOTAM D), Flight Data Center (FDC) NOTAMs, International NOTAMs, or Military NOTAMs.

1. NOTAM (D) information is disseminated for all navigational facilities that are part of the National Airspace System (NAS), all public use aerodromes, seaplane bases, and heliports listed in the Chart Supplement. NOTAM (D) information includes taxiway closures, personnel and equipment near or crossing runways, and airport lighting aids that do not affect instrument approach criteria (i.e., VGSI). All NOTAM Ds must have one of the keywords listed in Table 5-1-1, as the first part of the text after the location identifier. These keywords categorize NOTAM Ds by subject, for example, APRON (ramp), RWY (runway), SVC (Services), etc. There are several types of NOTAM Ds:

(a) Aerodrome activity and conditions, to include field conditions.

(b) Airspace to include CARF, SUA, and general airspace activity like UAS or pyrotechnics.

(c) Visual and radio navigational aids.

(d) Communication and services.

(e) Pointer NOTAMs. NOTAMs issued to point to additional aeronautical information. When pointing to another NOTAM, the keyword in the pointer NOTAM must match the keyword in the original NOTAM. Pointer NOTAMs should be issued for, but are not limited to, TFRs, Airshows, Temporary SUA, major NAS system interruptions, etc.

2. FDC NOTAMs are issued when it is necessary to disseminate regulatory information. FDC NOTAMs include:

(a) Amendments to published IAPs and other current aeronautical charts.

(b) Temporary Flight Restrictions (TFR) restrict entrance to a certain airspace at a certain time, however, some TFRs provide relief if ATC permission is given to enter the area when requested. Online preflight resources for TFRs provide graphics and plain language interpretations.

(c) High barometric pressure warning.

(d) Laser light activity.

(e) ADS-B, TIS-B, and FIS-B service availability.

(f) Satellite-based systems such as WAAS or GPS.

(g) Special Notices.

Ch 5

3. International NOTAMs are published in ICAO format per Annex 15 and distributed to multiple countries.

(a) International NOTAMs issued by the U.S. NOTAM Office use Series A followed by 4 sequential numbers, a slant "/" and a 2-digit number representing the year the NOTAM was issued. International NOTAMs basically duplicate data found in a U.S. Domestic NOTAM.

(b) Not every topic of a U.S. Domestic NOTAM is issued as an International NOTAM by the U.S. The U.S. International NOTAM will be linked to the appropriate U.S. Domestic NOTAM when possible.

(c) International NOTAMs received by the FAA from other countries are stored in the U.S. NOTAM System.

(d) The International NOTAM format includes a "Q" Line that can be easily read/parsed by a computer and allows the NOTAM to be displayed digitally.

(1) Field A: ICAO location identifier or FIR affected by the NOTAM.

(2) Field B: Start of Validity.

(3) Field C: End of Validity (both in [Year] [Month][Day][Hour][Minute] format).

(4) Field D: (when present) Schedule.

(5) Field E: Full NOTAM description.

(6) Field F: (when present) Lowest altitude, or "SFC."

(7) Field G: (when present) Highest altitude, or "UNL."

(e) For more on International format, please see Annex 15.

4. Military NOTAMs are NOTAMs originated by the U.S. Air Force, Army, Marine, or Navy, and pertaining to military or joint-use navigational aids/airports that are part of the NAS. Military NOTAMs are published in the International NOTAM format and should be reviewed by users of a military or joint-use facility.

h. Security NOTAMs:

1. U.S. Domestic Security NOTAMs are FDC NOTAMs that inform pilots of certain U.S. security activities or requirements, such as Special Security Instructions for aircraft operations to, from, within, or transitioning U.S. territorial airspace. These NOTAMs are found on the Federal NOTAM System (FNS) NOTAM Search website under the location designator KZZZ.

2. United States International Flight Prohibitions, Potential Hostile Situations, and Foreign Notices are issued by the FAA and are found on the Federal NOTAM System (FNS) NOTAM Search website under the location designator KICZ.

TABLE 5–1–1
NOTAM KEYWORDS

Keyword	Definition
RWY	Runway
Example	BNA BNA RWY 18/36 CLSD YYMMDDHHMM–YYMMDDHHMM
TWY	Taxiway
Example	!BTV BTV TWY C EDGE LGT OBSC YYMMDDHHMM–YYMMDDHHMM
APRON	Apron/Ramp
Example	!BNA BNA APRON NORTH APN E 100FT CLSD YYMMDDHHMM–YYMMDDHHMM
AD	Aerodrome
Example	!BET BET AD AP ELK NEAR MOVEMENT AREAS YYMMDDHHMM–YYMMDDHHMM
OBST	Obstruction
Example	!SJT SJT OBST MOORED BALLOON WI AN AREA DEFINED AS 1NM RADIUS OF SJT 2430FT (510FT AGL) FLAGGED YYMMDDHHMM–YYMMDDHHMM
NAV	Navigation Aids
Example	!SHV SHV NAV ILS RWY 32 110.3 COMMISSIONED YYMMDDHHMM–PERM
COM	Communications
Example	!INW INW COM REMOTE COM OUTLET 122.6 U/S YYMMDDHHMM–YYMMDDHHMM EST (Note* EST will auto cancel)
SVC	Services
Example	!ROA ROA SVC TWR COMMISSIONED YYMMDDHHMM–PERM
AIRSPACE	Airspace
Example	!MHV MHV AIRSPACE AEROBATIC ACFT WI AN AREA DEFINED AS 4.3NM RADIUS OF MHV 5500FT–10500FT AVOIDANCE ADZ CTC JOSHUA APP DLY YYMMDDHHMM–YYMMDDHHMM
ODP	Obstacle Departure Procedure
Example	!FDC 2/9700 DIK ODP DICKINSON – THEODORE ROOSEVELT RGNL, DICKINSON, ND. TAKEOFF MINIMUMS AND (OBSTACLE) DEPARTURE PROCEDURES AMDT 1... DEPARTURE PROCEDURE: RWY 25, CLIMB HEADING 250 TO 3500 BEFORE TURNING LEFT. ALL OTHER DATA REMAINS AS PUBLISHED. THIS IS TAKEOFF MINIMUMS AND (OBSTACLE) DEPARTURE PROCEDURES, AMDT 1A. YYMMDDHHMM–PERM

Keyword	Definition
SID *Example*	**Standard Instrument Departure** !FDC x/xxxx DFW SID DALLAS/FORT WORTH INTL, DALLAS, TX. PODDE THREE DEPARTURE... CHANGE NOTES TO READ: RWYS 17C/R, 18L/R: DO NOT EXCEED 240KT UNTIL LARRN. RWYS 35L/C, 36L/R: DO NOT EXCEED 240KT UNTIL KMART YYMMDDHHMM–YYMMDDHHMM
STAR *Example*	**Standard Terminal Arrival** !FDC x/xxxx DCA STAR RONALD REAGAN WASHINGTON NATIONAL,WASHINGTON, DC. WZRRD TWO ARRIVAL... SHAAR TRANSITION: ROUTE FROM DRUZZ INT TO WZRRD INT NOT AUTHORIZED. AFTER DRUZZ INT EXPECT RADAR VECTORS TO AML VORTAC YYMMDDHHMM–YYM-MDDHHMM
CHART *Example*	**Chart** !FDC 2/9997 DAL IAP DALLAS LOVE FIELD, DALLAS, TX. ILS OR LOC RWY 31R, AMDT 5... CHART NOTE: SIMULTANEOUS APPROACH AUTHORIZED WITH RWY 31L. MISSED APPROACH: CLIMB TO 1000 THEN CLIMBING RIGHT TURN TO 5000 ON HEADING 330 AND CVE R–046 TO FINGR INT/CVE 36.4 DME AND HOLD. CHART LOC RWY 31L. THIS IS ILS OR LOC RWY 31R, AMDT 5A. YYM-MDDHHMM–PERM
DATA *Example*	**Data** !FDC 2/9700 DIK ODP DICKINSON – THEODORE ROOSEVELT RGNL, DICKINSON, ND. TAKEOFF MINIMUMS AND (OBSTACLE) DEPARTURE PROCEDURES AMDT 1... DEPARTURE PROCEDURE: RWY 25, CLIMB HEADING 250 TO 3500 BEFORE TURNING LEFT. ALL OTHER DATA REMAINS AS PUBLISHED. THIS IS TAKEOFF MINIMUMS AND (OBSTACLE) DEPARTURE PROCEDURES, AMDT 1A. YYMMDDHHMM–PERM
IAP *Example*	**Instrument Approach Procedure** !FDC 2/9997 DAL IAP DALLAS LOVE FIELD, DALLAS, TX. ILS OR LOC RWY 31R, AMDT 5... CHART NOTE: SIMULTANEOUS APPROACH AUTHORIZED WITH RWY 31L. MISSED APPROACH: CLIMB TO 1000 THEN CLIMBING RIGHT TURN TO 5000 ON HEADING 330 AND CVE R–046 TO FINGR INT/CVE 36.4 DME AND HOLD. CHART LOC RWY 31L. THIS IS ILS OR LOC RWY 31R, AMDT 5A. YYM-MDDHHMM–PERM
VFP *Example*	**Visual Flight Procedures** !FDC X/XXXX JFK VFP JOHN F KENNEDY INTL, NEW YORK, NY. PARKWAY VISUAL RWY 13L/R, ORIG...WEATHER MINIMUMS 3000 FOOT CEILING AND 3 MILES VISIBILITY. YYMMDDHHMM–YYMMDDHHMM
ROUTE *Example*	**Route** !FDC x/xxxx ZFW ROUTE ZFW ZKC. V140 SAYRE (SYO) VORTAC, OK TO TULSA (TUL) VORTAC, OK MEA 4300. YYMMDDHHMM–YYMMDDHHMM EST
SPECIAL *Example*	**Special** !FDC x/xxxx JNU SPECIAL JUNEAU INTERNATIONAL, JUNEAU, AK. LDA–2 RWY 8 AMDT 9 PROCEDURE TURN NA. YYMMDDHHMM–YYMMDDHHMM
SECURITY *Example*	**Security** !FDC x/xxxx FDC ...SPECIAL NOTICE... THIS IS A RESTATEMENT OF A PREVIOUSLY ISSUED ADVISORY NOTICE. IN THE INTEREST OF NATIONAL SECURITY AND TO THE EXTENT PRACTICABLE, PILOTS ARE STRONGLY ADVISED TO AVOID THE AIRSPACE ABOVE, OR IN PROXIMITY TO SUCH SITES AS POWER PLANTS (NUCLEAR, HYDRO-ELECTRIC, OR COAL), DAMS, REFINERIES, INDUSTRIAL COMPLEXES, MILITARY FACILITIES AND OTHER SIMILAR FACILITIES. PILOTS SHOULD NOT CIRCLE AS TO LOITER IN THE VICINITY OVER THESE TYPES OF FACILITIES.
GPS TESTING *Example*	**Global Positioning System Testing** !GPS 01/028 ZAB NAV GPS (YPG_AZ GPS 21–06)(INCLUDING WAAS, GBAS, AND ADS-B) MAYNOT BE AVBL WI A276NM RADIUS CENTERED AT 332347N1142221W (BLH108023) FL400–UNL, 232NM RADIUS AT FL250, 164NM RADIUS AT 100000FT 160NM RADIUS AT 4000FT AGL 126NM RADIUS AT 50FT AGL DLY 1830–2230 2101281830–2101292230
PRN (GPS) *Example*	Pseudo-random noise code used to differentiate GPS satellites. This code allows any receiver to identify exactly which satellite(s) it is receiving. !GPS GPS NAV PRN 16 U/S 2109231600–2109242300EST

Ch 5

TABLE 5-1-2
CONTRACTIONS COMMONLY FOUND IN NOTAMS

A	
ABN	Aerodrome Beacon
ACFT	Aircraft
ACT	Active
ADJ	Adjacent
AGL	Above Ground Level
ALS	Approach Light System
AP	Airport
APN	Apron
APP	Approach control office *or* approach control or approach control service
ARST	Arresting *(specify (part of) aircraft arresting equipment)*
ASDA	Accelerate Stop Distance Available
ASPH	Asphalt
AUTH	Authorized *or* authorization
AVBL	Available *or* availability
AVGAS	Aviation gasoline
AWOS	Automatic Weather Observing System
AZM	Azimuth
B	
BA	Braking action
BCN	Beacon *(aeronautical ground light)*
BCST	Broadcast
BDRY	Boundary
BLDG	Building
BLW	Below
BTN	Between
C	
C	Center *(preceded by runway designator number to identify a parallel runway)*
CD	Clearance delivery
CIV	Civil
CL	Centerline
CLSD	Close *or* closed *or* closing
COM	Communication
CONC	Concrete
COND	Condition
CONS	Continuous
CONST	Construction *or* constructed
CPDLC	Controller Pilot Data Link Communications
CTC	Contact
CUST	Customs
D	
DA	Decision altitude
DEG	Degrees
DEP	Depart *or* Departure
DER	Departure end of the runway
DH	Decision Height
DIST	Distance

DLY	Daily
DP	Dew Point Temperature
DPT	Depth
DTHR	Displaced Runway Threshold
E	
E	East *or* eastern longitude
EB	Eastbound
EMERG	Emergency
ENE	East-northeast
EQPT	Equipment
ESE	East-southeast
EST	Estimate *or* estimated *or* estimation *(message type designator)*
EXC	Except
F	
FL	Flight level
FREQ	Frequency
FRI	Friday
FSS	Flight Service Station
FST	First
FT	Feet *(dimensional unit)*
G	
G	Green
GA	General aviation
GLD	Glider
GND	Ground
GP	Glide path
GRVL	Gravel
H	
HEL	Helicopter
HGT	Height *or* height above
HLDG	Holding
HLP	Heliport
HVY	Heavy
I	
IFR	Instrument Flight Rules
ILS	Instrument Landing System
IM	Inner Marker
INOP	Inoperative
INT	Intersection
K	
KT	Knots
L	
L	Left *(preceded by runway designator number to identify a parallel runway)*
LAT	Latitude
LDA	Landing Distance Available
LDG	Landing
LEN	Length
LGT	Light *or* lighting
LGTD	Lighted
LOC	Localizer
LONG	Longitude

M	
MAINT	Maintenance
MBST	Microburst
MIL	Military
MIN	Minutes
MNT	Monitor *or* monitoring *or* monitored
MON	Monday
MOV	Move *or* moving *or* movement

N	
N	North
NAVAID	Navigational aid
NB	Northbound
NDB	Nondirectional Radio Beacon
NE	Northeast
NEB	Northeast bound
NM	Nautical Mile/s
NNE	North–northeast
NNW	North–northwest
NOV	November
NW	Northwest
NWB	Northwest bound

O	
OBSC	Obscure *or* obscured *or* obscuring
OBST	Obstacle
OPN	Open *or* opening *or* opened
OPS	Operations

P	
PAPI	Precision Approach Path Indicator
PARL	Parallel
PAX	Passenger/s
PCL	Pilot Controlled Lighting
PCT	Percent
PERM	Permanent
PJE	Parachute Jumping Activities
PLA	Practice Low Approach
PPR	Prior Permission Required
PRN	Pseudo-random Navigation
PT	Procedure Turn

R	
R	Red
R	Right *(preceded by runway designator number to identify a parallel runway)*
RAI	Runway Alignment Indicator
RCL	Runway Centerline
RCLL	Runway Centerline Light
REDL	Runway Edge Light
RLLS	Runway Lead-in Light System
RMK	Remark
RTS	Return to Service
RTZL	Runway Touchdown Zone Light(s)
RVR	Runway Visual Range
RWY	Runway
RX	Receive/Receiver

S	
S	South *or* southern latitude
SA	Sand
SAT	Saturday
SB	Southbound
SE	Southeast
SEC	Seconds
SFC	Surface
SN	Snow
SR	Sunrise
SS	Sunset
SSR	Secondary surveillance radar
SSW	South–southwest
STD	Standard
SUN	Sunday
SW	Southwest
SWB	Southwest bound

T	
TAR	Terminal area surveillance radar
TAX	Taxing *or* taxiing
TDZ	Touchdown Zone
TEMPO	Temporary *or* temporarily
TFC	Traffic
THR	Threshold
THU	Thursday
TKOF	Takeoff
TODA	Take-off Distance Available
TORA	Take-off Run Available
TRG	Training
TUE	Tuesday
TWR	Aerodrome Control Tower
TWY	Taxiway
TX	Taxilane

U	
U/S	Unserviceable
UAS	Unmanned Aircraft System
UNL	Unlimited
UNREL	Unreliable

V	
VIS	Visibility
VOR	VHF Omni-Directional Radio Range
VORTAC	VOR and TACAN (collocated)
VOT	VOR Test Facility

W	
W	West *or* western longitude
WB	Westbound
WDI	Wind Direction Indicator
WED	Wednesday
WI	Within
WID	Width *or* wide
WIP	Work in progress
WNW	West–northwest
WS	Wind shear
WSW	West–southwest

Ch 5

5-1-4 Operational Information System (OIS)

a. The FAA's Air Traffic Control System Command Center (ATCSCC) maintains a website with near real-time National Airspace System (NAS) status information. NAS operators are encouraged to access the website at: http://www.fly.faa.gov prior to filing their flight plan.

b. The website consolidates information from advisories. An advisory is a message that is disseminated electronically by the ATCSCC that contains information pertinent to the NAS.

1. Advisories are normally issued for the following items:

(a) Ground Stops.
(b) Ground Delay Programs.
(c) Route Information.
(d) Plan of Operations.
(e) Facility Outages and Scheduled Facility Outages.
(f) Volcanic Ash Activity Bulletins.
(g) Special Traffic Management Programs.

2. This list is not all-inclusive. Any time there is information that may be beneficial to a large number of people, an advisory may be sent. Additionally, there may be times when an advisory is not sent due to workload or the short length of time of the activity.

3. Route information is available on the website and in specific advisories. Some route information, subject to the 56-day publishing cycle, is located on the "OIS" under "Products," Route Management Tool (RMT), and "What's New" Playbook. The RMT and Playbook contain routings for use by Air Traffic and NAS operators when they are coordinated "real-time" and are then published in an ATCSCC advisory.

4. Route advisories are identified by the word "Route" in the header; the associated action is required (RQD), recommended (RMD), planned (PLN), or for your information (FYI). Operators are expected to file flight plans consistent with the Route RQD advisories.

5. Electronic System Impact Reports are on the intranet at: http://www.atcscc.faa.gov /ois/ under "System Impact Reports." This page lists scheduled outages/events/projects that significantly impact the NAS; for example, runway closures, air shows, and construction projects. Information includes anticipated delays and traffic management initiatives (TMI) that may be implemented.

5-1-5 Flight Plan—VFR Flights

(See Appendix 4, FAA Form 7233-4—International Flight Plan)

a. The requirements for the filing and activation of VFR flight plans can vary depending in which airspace the flight is operating. Pilots are responsible for activating flight plans with a Flight Service Station. Control tower personnel do not automatically activate VFR flight plans.

1. Within the continental U.S., a VFR flight plan is not normally required.

2. VFR flights (except for DOD and law enforcement flights) into an Air Defense Identification Zone (ADIZ) are required to file DVFR flight plans.

Note: Detailed ADIZ procedures are found in Section 6, National Security and Interception Procedures, of this chapter. (See 14 CFR Part 99).

3. Flights within the Washington, DC Special Flight Rules Area have additional requirements that must be met. Visit http://www.faasafety.gov for the required Special Awareness Training that must be completed before flight within this area.

4. VFR flight to an international destination requires a filed and activated flight plan.

Note: ICAO flight plan guidance is published in ICAO Document 4444 PANS-ATM Appendix 2.

b. It is strongly recommended that a VFR flight plan be filed with a Flight Service Station or equivalent flight plan filing service. When filing, pilots must use FAA Form 7233-4, International Flight Plan or DD Form 1801. Only DOD users, and civilians who file stereo route flight plans, may use FAA Form 7233-1, Flight Plan. Pilots may take advantage of advances in technology by filing their flight plans using any available electronic means. Activating the flight plan will ensure that you receive VFR Search and Rescue services.

c. When a stopover flight is anticipated, it is recommended that a separate flight plan be filed for each leg of the flight.

d. Pilots are encouraged to activate their VFR flight plans with Flight Service by the most expeditious means possible. This may be via radio or other electronic means. VFR flight plan proposals are normally retained for two hours following the proposed time of departure.

e. Pilots may also activate a VFR flight plan by using an assumed departure time. This assumed departure time will cause the flight plan to become active at the designated time. This may negate the need for communication with a flight service station or flight plan filing service upon departure. It is the pilot's responsibility to revise his actual departure time, time en route, or ETA with flight service.

Note: Pilots are strongly advised to remain mindful when using an assumed departure time. If not updated, search and rescue activities will be based on the assumed departure time.

f. U.S. air traffic control towers do not routinely activate VFR flight plans. Foreign pilots especially must be mindful of the need to communicate

Chapter 5: Air Traffic Procedures

5-1-6

directly with a flight service station, or use an assumed departure time procedure clearly communicated with the flight plan filing service.

g. Although position reports are not required for VFR flight plans, periodic reports to FSSs along the route are good practice. Such contacts permit significant information to be passed to the transiting aircraft and also serve to check the progress of the flight should it be necessary for any reason to locate the aircraft.

h. Pilots flying VFR should fly an appropriate cruising altitude for their direction of flight.

i. When filing a VFR Flight plan, indicate the appropriate aircraft equipment capability as prescribed for an IFR flight plan.

Reference: AIM, ¶5-1-6, IFR Flights.

j. ATC radar history data can be useful in finding a downed or missing aircraft; therefore, surveillance equipment should be listed in Item 18. Pilots using commercial GPS tracking services are encouraged to note the specific service in Item 19 N/ (survival equip remarks) of FAA Form 7233-4 or DD Form 1801.

5-1-6 Flight Plan—IFR Flights

(See Appendix 4, FAA Form 7233-4—International Flight Plan)

a. General

1. Use of FAA Form 7233-4 or DD Form 1801 is mandatory for:

(a) Assignment of RNAV SIDs and STARs or other PBN routing,

(b) All civilian IFR flights that will depart U.S. domestic airspace, and

(c) Domestic IFR flights except military/ DOD and civilians who file stereo route flight plans.

(d) All military/DOD IFR flights that will depart U.S. controlled airspace.

2. Military/DOD flights using FAA Form 7233-1, or DD Form 175, may not be eligible for assignment of RNAV SIDs or STARs. Military flights desiring assignment of these procedures should file using FAA Form 7233-4 or DD 1801, as described in this section.

3. When filing an IFR flight plan using FAA Form 7233-4 or DD Form 1801, it is recommended that filers include all operable navigation, communication, and surveillance equipment capabilities by adding appropriate equipment qualifiers as shown in Appendix 4, FAA Form 7233-4, International Flight Plan.

4. ATC issues clearances based on aircraft capabilities filed in Items 10 and 18 of FAA Form 7233-4 or DD 1801. Operators should file all capabilities for which the aircraft and crew is certified, capable, and authorized. PBN/capability must be filed in Item 18, Other Information. When filing a capability, ATC expects filers to use that

capability; for example, answer a SATVOICE call from ATC if code M1 or M3 is filed in Item 10a.

5. Prior to departure from within, or prior to entering controlled airspace, a pilot must submit a complete flight plan and receive an air traffic clearance, if weather conditions are below VFR minimums. IFR flight plans may be submitted to an FSS or flight plan filing service.

6. Pilots should file IFR flight plans at least 30 minutes prior to estimated time of departure to preclude possible delay in receiving a departure clearance from ATC.

7. In order to provide FAA traffic management units' strategic route planning capabilities, nonscheduled operators conducting IFR operations above FL 230 are requested to voluntarily file IFR flight plans at least 4 hours prior to estimated time of departure (ETD).

8. To minimize your delay in entering Class B, Class C, Class D, and Class E surface areas at destination when IFR weather conditions exist or are forecast at that airport, an IFR flight plan should be filed before departure. Otherwise, a 30-minute delay is not unusual in receiving an ATC clearance because of time spent in processing flight plan data.

9. Traffic saturation frequently prevents control personnel from accepting flight plans by radio. In such cases, the pilot is advised to contact a flight plan filing service for the purpose of filing the flight plan.

10. When requesting an IFR clearance, it is highly recommended that the departure airport be identified by stating the city name and state and/ or the airport location identifier in order to clarify to ATC the exact location of the intended airport of departure.

11. Multiple versions of flight plans for the same flight may lead to unsafe conditions and errors within the air traffic system. Pilots must not file more than one flight plan for the same flight without ensuring that the previous flight plan has been successfully removed.

12. When a pilot is aware that the possibility for multiple flight plans on the same aircraft may exist, ensuring receipt of a full route clearance will help mitigate chances of error.

Reference: AIM, ¶5-1-12, Change in Flight Plan; AIM, ¶5-1-13, Change in Proposed Departure Time.

b. Airways and Jet Routes Depiction on Flight Plan

1. It is vitally important that the route of flight be accurately and completely described in the flight plan. To simplify definition of the proposed route, and to facilitate ATC, pilots are requested to file via airways or jet routes established for use at the altitude or flight level planned.

2. If flight is to be conducted via designated airways or jet routes, describe the route by indicating the type and number designators of the airway(s) or jet route(s) requested. If more than one airway or jet route is to be used, clearly indicate points of transition. If the transition is made at an unnamed intersection, show the next succeeding NAVAID or named intersection on the intended route and the complete route from that point. Reporting points may be identified by using authorized name/code as depicted on appropriate aeronautical charts. The following two examples illustrate the need to specify the transition point when two routes share more than one transition fix.

Example 1: ALB J37 BUMPY J14 BHM Spelled out: from Albany, New York, via Jet Route 37 transitioning to Jet Route 14 at BUMPY intersection, thence via Jet Route 14 to Birmingham, Alabama.

Example 2: ALB J37 ENO J14 BHM Spelled out: from Albany, New York, via Jet Route 37 transitioning to Jet Route 14 at Smyrna VORTAC (ENO) thence via Jet Route 14 to Birmingham, Alabama.

3. The route of flight may also be described by naming the reporting points or NAVAIDs over which the flight will pass, provided the points named are established for use at the altitude or flight level planned.

Example: BWI V44 SWANN V433 DQO Spelled out: from Baltimore–Washington International, via Victor 44 to Swann intersection, transitioning to Victor 433 at Swann, thence via Victor 433 to Dupont.

4. When the route of flight is defined by named reporting points, whether alone or in combination with airways or jet routes, and the navigational aids (VOR, VORTAC, TACAN, NDB) to be used for the flight are a combination of different types of aids, enough information should be included to clearly indicate the route requested.

Example: LAX J5 LKV J3 GEG YXC FL 330 J500 VLR J515 YWG Spelled out: from Los Angeles International via Jet Route 5 Lakeview, Jet Route 3 Spokane, direct Cranbrook, British Columbia VOR/DME, Flight Level 330 Jet Route 500 to Langruth, Manitoba VORTAC, Jet Route 515 to Winnipeg, Manitoba.

5. When filing IFR, it is to the pilot's advantage to file a preferred route.

Reference: Preferred IFR Routes are described and tabulated in the Chart Supplement. Additionally available at U.S. http://www.fly.faa.gov/Products/Coded_Departure_Routes/NFDC_Preferred_Routes_Database/nfdc_preferred_routes_database.html.

6. ATC may issue a SID or a STAR, as appropriate.

Reference: AIM, ¶5-2-9, Instrument Departure Procedures (DP)—Obstacle Departure Procedures (ODP) and Standard Instrument Departures (SID), and Diverse Vector Areas (DVA); AIM, ¶5-4-1, Standard Terminal Arrival (STAR) Procedures.

Note: *Pilots not desiring an RNAV SID or RNAV STAR should enter in Item #18, PBN code: NAV/RNV A0 and/or D0.*

c. Direct Flights

1. All or any portions of the route which will not be flown on the radials or courses of established airways or routes, such as direct route flights, must be defined by indicating the radio fixes over which the flight will pass. Fixes selected to define the route must be those over which the position of the aircraft can be accurately determined. Such fixes automatically become compulsory reporting points for the flight, unless advised otherwise by ATC. Only those navigational aids established for use in a particular structure; i.e., in the low or high structures, may be used to define the en route phase of a direct flight within that altitude structure.

2. The azimuth feature of VOR aids and the azimuth and distance (DME) features of VORTAC and TACAN aids are assigned certain frequency protected areas of airspace which are intended for application to established airway and route use, and to provide guidance for planning flights outside of established airways or routes. These areas of airspace are expressed in terms of cylindrical service volumes of specified dimensions called "class limits" or "categories."

Reference: AIM, ¶1-1-8, Navigational Aid (NAVAID) Service Volumes.

3. An operational service volume has been established for each class in which adequate signal coverage and frequency protection can be assured. To facilitate use of VOR, VORTAC, or TACAN aids, consistent with their operational service volume limits, pilot use of such aids for defining a direct route of flight in controlled airspace should not exceed the following:

(a) Operations above FL 450—Use aids not more than 200 NM apart. These aids are depicted on en route high altitude charts.

(b) Operation off established routes from 18,000 feet MSL to FL 450—Use aids not more than 260 NM apart. These aids are depicted on en route high altitude charts.

(c) Operation off established airways below 18,000 feet MSL—Use aids not more than 80 NM apart. These aids are depicted on en route low altitude charts.

(d) Operation off established airways between 14,500 feet MSL and 17,999 feet MSL in the conterminous U.S.—(H) facilities not more than 200 NM apart may be used.

4. Increasing use of self-contained airborne navigational systems which do not rely on the VOR/VORTAC/TACAN system has resulted in pilot requests for direct routes which exceed NAVAID service volume limits.

5. At times, ATC will initiate a direct route in a surveillance environment which exceeds NAVAID service volume limits. Pilots must adhere to the altitude specified in the clearance.

6. Appropriate airway or jet route numbers may also be included to describe portions of the route to be flown.

Example: MDW V262 BDF V10 BRL STJ SLN GCK Spelled out: from Chicago Midway Airport via Victor 262 to Bradford, Victor 10 to Burlington, Iowa, direct St. Joseph, Missouri, direct Salina, Kansas, direct Garden City, Kansas.

Note: When route of flight is described by radio fixes, the pilot will be expected to fly a direct course between the points named.

7. Pilots are reminded that they are responsible for adhering to obstruction clearance requirements on those segments of direct routes that are outside of controlled airspace and ATC surveillance capability. The MEAs and other altitudes shown on IFR en route charts pertain to those route segments within controlled airspace, and those altitudes may not meet obstruction clearance criteria when operating off those routes.

Note: Refer to 14 CFR 91.177 for pilot responsibility when flying random point to point routes.

d. Area Navigation (RNAV)/Global Navigation Satellite System (GNSS)

1. When not being radar monitored, GNSS-equipped RNAV aircraft on random RNAV routes must be cleared via or reported to be established on a point-to-point route.

(a) The points must be published NAVAIDs, waypoints, fixes or airports recallable from the aircraft's navigation database. The points must be displayed on controller video maps or depicted on the controller chart displayed at the control position. When applying non-radar separation the maximum distance between points must not exceed 500 miles.

(b) ATC will protect 4 miles either side of the route centerline.

(c) Assigned altitudes must be at or above the highest MIA along the projected route segment being flown, including the protected airspace of that route segment.

2. Pilots of aircraft equipped with approved area navigational equipment may file for RNAV routes throughout the National Airspace System in accordance with the following procedures:

(a) File airport-to-airport flight plans.

(b) File the appropriate indication of RNAV and/or RNP capability in the flight plan.

(c) Plan the random route portion of the flight plan to begin and end over appropriate arrival and departure transition fixes or appropriate navigation aids for the altitude stratum within which the flight will be conducted. The use of normal preferred departure and arrival routes (DP/STAR), where established, is recommended.

(d) File route structure transitions to and from the random route portion of the flight.

(e) Define the random route by waypoints. File route description waypoints by using degree distance fixes based on navigational aids which are appropriate for the altitude stratum.

(f) File a minimum of one route description waypoint for each ARTCC through whose area the random route will be flown. These waypoints must be located within 200 NM of the preceding center's boundary.

(g) File an additional route description waypoint for each turn point in the route.

(h) Plan additional route description waypoints as required to ensure accurate navigation via the filed route of flight. Navigation is the pilot's responsibility unless ATC assistance is requested.

(i) Plan the route of flight so as to avoid prohibited and restricted airspace by 3 NM unless permission has been obtained to operate in that airspace and the appropriate ATC facilities are advised.

Note: To be approved for use in the National Airspace System, RNAV equipment must meet system availability, accuracy, and airworthiness standards. For additional information and guidance on RNAV equipment requirements see Advisory Circular (AC) 20-138 Airworthiness Approval of Positioning and Navigation Systems and AC 90-100 U.S. Terminal and En Route Area Navigation (RNAV) Operations.

3. Pilots of aircraft equipped with latitude/longitude coordinate navigation capability, independent of VOR/TACAN references, may file for random RNAV using the following procedures:

(a) File airport-to-airport flight plans prior to departure.

(b) File the appropriate RNAV capability certification suffix in the flight plan.

(c) Plan the random route portion of the flight to begin and end over published departure/arrival transition fixes or appropriate navigation aids for airports without published transition procedures. The use of preferred departure and arrival routes, such as DP and STAR, where established, is recommended.

Ch 5

(d) Plan the route of flight so as to avoid prohibited and restricted airspace by 3 NM unless permission has been obtained to operate in that airspace and the appropriate ATC facility is advised.

(e) Define the route of flight after the departure fix, including each intermediate fix (turnpoint) and the arrival fix for the destination airport in terms of latitude/longitude coordinates plotted to the nearest minute or in terms of Navigation Reference System (NRS) waypoints. For latitude/longitude filing the arrival fix must be identified by both the latitude/longitude coordinates and a fix identifier.

Example:
MIA[1] SRQ[2] 3407/10615[3] 3407/11546 TNP[4] LAX[5]

[1] Departure airport.
[2] Departure fix.
[3] Intermediate fix (turning point).
[4] Arrival fix.
[5] Destination airport.

or

ORD[1] IOW[2] KP49G[3] KD34U[4] KL16O[5] OAL[6] MOD27[7] SFO[8]

[1] Departure airport.
[2] Transition fix.
[3] Minneapolis ARTCC waypoint.
[4] Denver ARTCC Waypoint.
[5] Los Angeles ARTCC waypoint.
[6] Transition fix.
[7] Arrival.
[8] Destination airport.

(f) Record latitude/longitude coordinates by two or four figures describing latitude in degrees followed by an N or S, followed by 3 or 5 digits longitude, followed by an E or W. Separate latitude and longitude with a solidus "/." Use leading zeros if necessary.

(g) File at FL 390 or above for the random RNAV portion of the flight.

(h) Fly all routes/route segments on Great Circle tracks.

(i) Make any inflight requests for random RNAV clearances or route amendments to an en route ATC facility.

5-1-7 Flight Plans For Military/DOD Use Only

(See Appendix 4, FAA Form 7233-1, Flight Plan)

Within U.S. controlled airspace, FAA Form 7233-1 or DD Form 175 may be used by DOD aircraft. However, use of the DD Form 1801 by DOD aircraft is recommended for IFR flights and is mandatory for:

a. Any flight that will depart U.S. controlled airspace.

b. Any flight requesting routing that requires Performance Based Navigation.

c. Any flight requesting services that require filing of capabilities only supported in the international flight plan.

Note 1: The order of flight plan elements in DD Form 175 is equivalent to that of FAA Form 7233-1.

Note 2: Civilians who file stereo route flight plans, may use FAA Form 7233-1, Flight Plan.

5-1-8 Flight Plan—Defense VFR (DVFR) Flights

VFR flights (except for DOD and law enforcement flights) into an ADIZ are required to file DVFR flight plans for security purposes. Detailed ADIZ procedures are found in Section 6, National Security and Interception Procedures, of this chapter.

Reference: 14 CFR Part 99, Security Control for Air Traffic.

a. DVFR flight plans must be filed using FAA Form 7233-4 or DD Form 1801.

b. Enter the letter "D" in Item 8, Type of Flight, of FAA Form 7233-4 or DD Form 1801.

c. DVFR flights where pilots decline search and rescue coverage must clearly indicate "NORIV" in Item 18 following the indicator "RMK/." This flight plan must still be activated in order to properly notify NORAD, however no flight plan cancellation will be expected.

Example: RMK/NORIV

5-1-9 Single Flights Conducted With Both VFR and IFR Flight Plans

a. Flight plans which combine VFR operation on an active VFR flight plan for one portion of a flight, and IFR for another portion, sometimes known as a composite flight plan, cannot be accepted or processed by current en route automation systems.

b. Pilots are free to operate VFR in VFR conditions prior to accepting an IFR clearance from the appropriate control facility, or may cancel an IFR clearance and proceed VFR as desired. However, if a pilot desires to be on an active VFR flight plan, with search and rescue provisions, for the portion of flight not conducted under an IFR clearance, a separate VFR flight plan must be filed, activated, and closed.

c. If a pilot desires to be on an active VFR flight plan prior to or following the IFR portion of the flight, that flight plan must be filed and processed as a distinct and separate flight plan. The VFR flight plan must be opened and closed with either a Flight Service Station or other service provider having the capability to open and close VFR flight plans. Air Traffic Control does not have the ability to determine if an aircraft is operating on an active

VFR flight plan and cannot process the activation or cancellation of a VFR flight plan.

d. Pilots may propose to commence the IFR portion of flight at a defined airborne point. This airborne point, or fix, is entered as the departure point in Item 13 of FAA Form 7233-4 or DD Form 1801.

e. Pilots may indicate in the IFR flight plan the intention to terminate the IFR portion of flight at any defined airborne point. The airborne point, or fix, is entered as the destination point in Item 16 of FAA Form 7233-4 or DD Form 1801.

f. Prior to beginning the IFR portion of flight, a pilot must receive an IFR clearance from the appropriate control facility.

g. If the pilot does not desire further clearance after reaching the clearance limit, he or she must advise ATC to cancel the IFR clearance.

5–1–10 IFR Operations to High Altitude Destinations

a. Pilots planning IFR flights to airports located in mountainous terrain are cautioned to consider the necessity for an alternate airport even when the forecast weather conditions would technically relieve them from the requirement to file one.

Reference: 14 CFR §91.167; AIM, ¶4-1-19, Tower En Route Control (TEC).

b. The FAA has identified three possible situations where the failure to plan for an alternate airport when flying IFR to such a destination airport could result in a critical situation if the weather is less than forecast and sufficient fuel is not available to proceed to a suitable airport.

1. An IFR flight to an airport where the Minimum Descent Altitudes (MDAs) or landing visibility minimums for *all instrument approaches* are higher than the forecast weather minimums specified in 14 CFR Section 91.167(b). For example, there are 3 high altitude airports in the U.S. with approved instrument approach procedures where all of the MDAs are greater than 2,000 feet and/or the landing visibility minimums are greater than 3 miles (Bishop, California; South Lake Tahoe, California; and Aspen–Pitkin Co./Sardy Field, Colorado). In the case of these airports, it is possible for a pilot to elect, on the basis of forecasts, not to carry sufficient fuel to get to an alternate when the ceiling and/or visibility is actually lower than that necessary to complete the approach.

2. A small number of other airports in mountainous terrain have MDAs which are slightly (100 to 300 feet) below 2,000 feet AGL. In situations where there is an option as to whether to plan for an alternate, pilots should bear in mind that just a slight worsening of the weather conditions from those forecast could place the airport below the published IFR landing minimums.

3. An IFR flight to an airport which requires special equipment; i.e., DME, glide slope, etc., in order to make the available approaches to the lowest minimums. Pilots should be aware that all other minimums on the approach charts may require weather conditions better than those specified in 14 CFR §91.167(b). An inflight equipment malfunction could result in the inability to comply with the published approach procedures or, again, in the position of having the airport below the published IFR landing minimums for all remaining instrument approach alternatives.

5–1–11 Flights Outside U.S. Territorial Airspace

a. When conducting flights, particularly extended flights, outside the U.S. and its territories, full account should be taken of the amount and quality of air navigation services available in the airspace to be traversed. Every effort should be made to secure information on the location and range of navigational aids, availability of communications and meteorological services, the provision of air traffic services, including alerting service, and the existence of search and rescue services.

b. Pilots should remember that there is a need to continuously guard the VHF emergency frequency 121.5 MHz when on long over-water flights, except when communications on other VHF channels, equipment limitations, or cockpit duties prevent simultaneous guarding of two channels. Guarding of 121.5 MHz is particularly critical when operating in proximity to Flight Information Region (FIR) boundaries, for example, operations on Route R220 between Anchorage and Tokyo, since it serves to facilitate communications with regard to aircraft which may experience in-flight emergencies, communications, or navigational difficulties.

Reference: ICAO Annex 10, Vol II, Paras 5.2.2.1.1.1 and 5.2.2.1.1.2.

c. The filing of a flight plan, always good practice, takes on added significance for extended flights outside U.S. airspace and is, in fact, usually required by the laws of the countries being visited or overflown. It is also particularly important in the case of such flights that pilots leave a complete itinerary and schedule of the flight with someone directly concerned and keep that person advised of the flight's progress. If serious doubt arises as to the safety of the flight, that person should first contact the appropriate FSS. Round Robin Flight Plans to Canada and Mexico are not accepted.

d. All pilots should review the foreign airspace and entry restrictions published in the appropriate Aeronautical Information Publication (AIP) during the flight planning process. Foreign airspace

penetration without official authorization can involve both danger to the aircraft and the imposition of severe penalties and inconvenience to both passengers and crew. A flight plan on file with ATC authorities does not necessarily constitute the prior permission required by certain other authorities. The possibility of fatal consequences cannot be ignored in some areas of the world.

e. Current NOTAMs for foreign locations must also be reviewed. International Notices regarding specific countries may be obtained through the Federal NOTAM System (FNS) NOTAM Search External Links or the Air Traffic Plans and Publications website. For additional flight information at foreign locations, pilots should also review the FAA's Prohibitions, Restrictions, and Notices website at https://www.faa.gov/air_traffic /publications/us_restrictions/.

f. When customs notification to foreign locations is required, it is the responsibility of the pilot to arrange for customs notification in a timely manner.

g. Aircraft arriving to locations in U.S. territorial airspace must meet the entry requirements as described in AIM Section 6, National Security and Interception Procedures.

5-1-12 Change in Flight Plan

a. In addition to altitude or flight level, destination and/or route changes, increasing or decreasing the speed of an aircraft constitutes a change in a flight plan. Therefore, at any time the average true airspeed at cruising altitude between reporting points varies or is expected to vary from that given in the flight plan by *plus or minus 5 percent, or 10 knots, whichever is greater*, ATC should be advised.

b. All changes to existing flight plans should be completed more than 46 minutes prior to the proposed departure time. Changes must be made with the initial flight plan service provider. If the initial flight plan's service provider is unavailable, filers may contact an ATC facility or FSS to make the necessary revisions. Any revision 46 minutes or less from the proposed departure time must be coordinated through an ATC facility or FSS.

5-1-13 Change in Proposed Departure Time

a. To prevent computer saturation in the en route environment, parameters have been established to delete proposed departure flight plans which have not been activated. Most centers have this parameter set so as to delete these flight plans a minimum of 2 hours after the proposed departure time or Expect Departure Clearance Time (EDCT). To ensure that a flight plan remains active, pilots whose actual departure time will be delayed 2 hours or more beyond their filed departure time, are requested to notify ATC of their new proposed departure time.

b. Due to traffic saturation, ATC personnel frequently will be unable to accept these revisions via radio. It is recommended that you forward these revisions to a flight plan service provider or FSS.

5-1-14 Closing VFR/DVFR Flight Plans

A pilot is responsible for ensuring that his/her VFR or DVFR flight plan is canceled. You should close your flight plan with the nearest FSS, or if one is not available, you may request any ATC facility to relay your cancellation to the FSS. Control towers do not automatically close VFR or DVFR flight plans since they do not know if a particular VFR aircraft is on a flight plan. If you fail to report or cancel your flight plan within 1/2 hour after your ETA, search and rescue procedures are started.

Reference: 14 CFR §91.153; 14 CFR §91.169.

5-1-15 Canceling IFR Flight Plan

a. 14 CFR §§91.153 and 91.169 include the statement "When a flight plan has been activated, the pilot-in-command, upon canceling or completing the flight under the flight plan, must notify an FAA Flight Service Station or ATC facility."

b. An IFR flight plan may be canceled at any time the flight is operating in VFR conditions outside Class A airspace by pilots stating "CANCEL MY IFR FLIGHT PLAN" to the controller or air/ground station with which they are communicating. Immediately after canceling an IFR flight plan, a pilot should take the necessary action to change to the appropriate air/ground frequency, VFR radar beacon code and VFR altitude or flight level.

c. ATC separation and information services will be discontinued, including radar services (where applicable). Consequently, if the canceling flight desires VFR radar advisory service, the pilot must specifically request it.

Note: Pilots must be aware that other procedures may be applicable to a flight that cancels an IFR flight plan within an area where a special program, such as a designated TRSA, Class C airspace, or Class B airspace, has been established.

d. If a DVFR flight plan requirement exists, the pilot is responsible for filing this flight plan to replace the canceled IFR flight plan. If a subsequent IFR operation becomes necessary, a new IFR flight plan must be filed and an ATC clearance obtained before operating in IFR conditions.

e. If operating on an IFR flight plan to an airport with a functioning control tower, the flight plan is automatically closed upon landing.

f. If operating on an IFR flight plan to an airport where there is no functioning control tower, the pilot must initiate cancellation of the IFR flight plan. This can be done after landing if there is a functioning FSS or other means of direct communications with ATC. In the event there is no FSS and/or air/ground communications with ATC is not possible below a certain altitude, the pilot should, weather conditions permitting, cancel the IFR flight plan while still airborne and able to communicate with ATC by radio. This will not only save the time and expense of canceling the flight plan by telephone but will quickly release the airspace for use by other aircraft.

5-1-16 RNAV and RNP Operations

a. During the pre-flight planning phase the availability of the navigation infrastructure required for the intended operation, including any non-RNAV contingencies, must be confirmed for the period of intended operation. Availability of the onboard navigation equipment necessary for the route to be flown must be confirmed. Pilots are reminded that on composite VFR to IFR flight plan, or on an IFR clearance, while flying unpublished departures via RNAV into uncontrolled airspace, the PIC is responsible for terrain and obstruction clearance until reaching the MEA/MIA/MVA/OROCA.

Note: OROCA is a published altitude which provides 1,000 feet of terrain and obstruction clearance in the U.S. (2,000 feet of clearance in designated mountainous areas). These altitudes are not assessed for NAVAID signal coverage, air traffic control surveillance, or communications coverage, and are published for general situational awareness, flight planning and in-flight contingency use.

b. If a pilot determines a specified RNP level cannot be achieved, revise the route or delay the operation until appropriate RNP level can be ensured.

c. The onboard navigation database must be current and appropriate for the region of intended operation and must include the navigation aids, waypoints, and coded terminal airspace procedures for the departure, arrival and alternate airfields.

d. During system initialization, pilots of aircraft equipped with a Flight Management System or other RNAV-certified system, must confirm that the navigation database is current, and verify that the aircraft position has been entered correctly. Flight crews should crosscheck the cleared flight plan against charts or other applicable resources, as well as the navigation system textual display and the aircraft map display. This process includes confirmation of the waypoints sequence, reasonableness of track angles and distances, any altitude or speed constraints, and identification of fly-by or fly-over waypoints. A procedure must not be used if validity of the navigation database is in doubt.

e. Prior to commencing takeoff, the flight crew must verify that the RNAV system is operating correctly and the correct airport and runway data have been loaded.

f. During the preflight planning phase RAIM prediction must be performed if TSO–C129() equipment is used to solely satisfy the RNAV and RNP requirement. GPS RAIM availability must be confirmed for the intended route of flight (route and time) using current GPS satellite information. In the event of a predicted, continuous loss of RAIM of more than five (5) minutes for any part of the intended flight, the flight should be delayed, canceled, or re-routed where RAIM requirements can be met. Operators may satisfy the predictive RAIM requirement through any one of the following methods:

1. Operators may monitor the status of each satellite in its plane/slot position, by accounting for the latest GPS constellation status (for example, NOTAMs or NANUs), and compute RAIM availability using model-specific RAIM prediction software;

2. Operators may use the Service Availability Prediction Tool (SAPT) on the FAA en route and terminal RAIM prediction website;

3. Operators may contact a Flight Service Station to obtain non-precision approach RAIM;

4. Operators may use a third party interface, incorporating FAA/VOLPE RAIM prediction data without altering performance values, to predict RAIM outages for the aircraft's predicted flight path and times;

5. Operators may use the receiver's installed RAIM prediction capability (for TSO–C129a/Class A1/B1/C1 equipment) to provide nonprecision approach RAIM, accounting for the latest GPS constellation status (for example, NOTAMs or NANUs). Receiver nonprecision approach RAIM should be checked at airports spaced at intervals not to exceed 60 NM along the RNAV 1 procedure's flight track. "Terminal" or "Approach" RAIM must be available at the ETA over each airport checked; or,

6. Operators not using model-specific software or FAA/VOLPE RAIM data will need FAA operational approval.

Note: If TSO–C145/C146 equipment is used to satisfy the RNAV and RNP requirement, the pilot/operator need not perform the prediction if WAAS coverage is confirmed to be available along the entire route of flight. Outside the U.S. or in areas where WAAS coverage is not available, operators using TSO–C145/C146 receivers are required to check GPS RAIM availability.

Ch 5

5-1-17 Cold Temperature Operations

a. Pilots should begin planning for cold temperature operations during the preflight planning phase. Cold temperatures produce barometric altimetry errors, which affect instrument flight procedures. Currently there are two temperature limitations that may be published in the notes box of the middle briefing strip on an instrument approach procedure (IAP). The two published temperature limitations are:

1. A temperature range limitation associated with the use of baro-VNAV that may be published on an United States PBN IAP titled RNAV (GPS) or RNAV (RNP); and/or

2. A Cold Temperature Airport (CTA) limitation designated by a snowflake ICON and temperature in Celsius (C) that is published on every IAP for the airfield.

b. Pilots should request the lowest forecast temperature +/–1 hour for arrival and departure operations. If the temperature is forecast to be outside of the baro-VNAV or at or below the CTA temperature limitation, consider the following:

1. When using baro-VNAV with an aircraft that does not have an automated temperature compensating function, pilots should plan to use the appropriate minima and/or IAP.

(a) The LNAV/VNAV line of minima on an RNAV (GPS) may not be used without an approved automated temperature compensating function if the temperature is outside of the baro-VNAV temperature range limitation. The LNAV minima may be used.

(b) The RNAV (RNP) procedure may not be accomplished without an approved automated temperature compensating function if the temperature is outside of the baro-VNAV temperature range limitation.

2. If the temperature is forecast to be at or below the published CTA temperature, pilots should calculate a correction for the appropriate segment/s or a correction for all the segments if using the "All Segments Method."

Pilots should review the operating procedures for the aircraft's temperature compensating system when planning to use the system for any cold temperature corrections. Any planned altitude correction for the intermediate and/or missed approach holding segments must be coordinated with ATC. Pilots do not have to advise ATC of a correction in the final segment.

Note: *The charted baro-VNAV temperature range limitation does not apply to pilots operating aircraft with an airworthiness approval to conduct an RNAV (GPS) approach to LNAV/VNAV minimums with the use of SBAS vertical guidance.*

Reference: *AIM, Chapter 7, Section 3, Cold Temperature Barometric Altimeter Errors, Setting Procedures, and Cold Temperature Airports (CTA).*

Section 2 Departure Procedures

5-2-1 Pre-Taxi Clearance Procedures

a. Certain airports have established pre-taxi clearance programs whereby pilots of departing instrument flight rules (IFR) aircraft may elect to receive their IFR clearances before they start taxiing for takeoff. The following provisions are included in such procedures:

1. Pilot participation is not mandatory.

2. Participating pilots call clearance delivery or ground control not more than 10 minutes before proposed taxi time.

3. IFR clearance (or delay information, if clearance cannot be obtained) is issued at the time of this initial call-up.

4. When the IFR clearance is received on clearance delivery frequency, pilots call ground control when ready to taxi.

5. Normally, pilots need not inform ground control that they have received IFR clearance on clearance delivery frequency. Certain locations may, however, require that the pilot inform ground control of a portion of the routing or that the IFR clearance has been received.

6. If a pilot cannot establish contact on clearance delivery frequency or has not received an IFR clearance before ready to taxi, the pilot should contact ground control and inform the controller accordingly.

b. Locations where these procedures are in effect are indicated in the Chart Supplement.

5-2-2 Automated Pre-Departure Clearance Procedures

a. Many airports in the National Airspace System are equipped with the Terminal Data Link System (TDLS) that includes the Pre-Departure Clearance (PDC) and Controller Pilot Data Link Communication-Departure Clearance (CPDLC-DCL) functions. Both the PDC and CPDLC-DCL functions automate the Clearance Delivery operations in the ATCT for participating users. Both functions display IFR clearances from the ARTCC to the ATCT. The Clearance Delivery controller in the ATCT can append local departure information and transmit the clearance via data link to participating airline/service provider computers for PDC. The airline/service provider will then deliver the clearance via the Aircraft Communications Addressing and Reporting System (ACARS) or a similar data link system, or for non-data link equipped aircraft, via a printer located at the departure gate. For CPDLC-DCL, the departure clearance is uplinked from the ATCT via the Future Air Navigation System (FANS) to the aircraft avionics and requires a response from the flight crew. Both PDC and CPDLC-DCL reduce frequency congestion, controller workload, and are intended to mitigate delivery/read back errors.

b. Both services are available only to participating aircraft that have subscribed to the service through an approved service provider.

c. In all situations, the pilot is encouraged to contact clearance delivery if a question or concern exists regarding an automated clearance. Due to technical reasons, the following limitations/differences exist between the two services:

1. PDC

(a) Aircraft filing multiple flight plans are limited to one PDC clearance per departure airport within an 18-hour period. Additional clearances will be delivered verbally.

(b) If the clearance is revised or modified prior to delivery, it will be rejected from PDC and the clearance will need to be delivered verbally.

(c) No acknowledgment of receipt or read back is required for a PDC.

2. CPDLC-DCL

(a) No limitation to the number of clearances received.

(b) Allows delivery of revised flight data, including revised departure clearances.

(c) A response from the flight crew is required.

(d) Requires a logon to the FAA National Single Data Authority – KUSA – utilizing the ATC FANS application.

(e) To be eligible, operators must have received CPDLC/FANS authorization from the responsible civil aviation authority, and file appropriate equipment information in ICAO field 10a and in the ICAO field 18 DAT (Other Data Applications) of the flight plan.

5-2-3 IFR Clearances Off Uncontrolled Airports

a. Pilots departing on an IFR flight plan should consult the Chart Supplement to determine the frequency or telephone number to use to contact clearance delivery. On initial contact, pilots should advise that the flight is IFR and state the departure and destination airports.

b. Air traffic facilities providing clearance delivery services via telephone will have their telephone number published in the Chart Supplement of that airport's entry. This same section may also contain a telephone number to use for cancellation of an IFR flight plan after landing.

c. Except in Alaska, pilots of MEDEVAC flights may obtain a clearance by calling 1-877-543-4733.

Ch 5

5–2–4 Taxi Clearance

Pilots on IFR flight plans should communicate with the control tower on the appropriate ground control or clearance delivery frequency, prior to starting engines, to receive engine start time, taxi and/or clearance information.

5–2–5 Line Up and Wait (LUAW)

a. Line up and wait is an air traffic control (ATC) procedure designed to position an aircraft onto the runway for an imminent departure. The ATC instruction "LINE UP AND WAIT" is used to instruct a pilot to taxi onto the departure runway and line up and wait.

Example: Tower: "N234AR Runway 24L, line up and wait."

b. This ATC instruction is not an authorization to takeoff. In instances where the pilot has been instructed to line up and wait and has been advised of a reason/condition (wake turbulence, traffic on an intersecting runway, etc.) or the reason/condition is clearly visible (another aircraft that has landed on or is taking off on the same runway), and the reason/condition is satisfied, the pilot should expect an imminent takeoff clearance, unless advised of a delay. If you are uncertain about any ATC instruction or clearance, contact ATC immediately.

c. If a takeoff clearance is not received within a reasonable amount of time after clearance to line up and wait, ATC should be contacted.

Example:
Aircraft: Cessna 234AR holding in position Runway 24L.
Aircraft: Cessna 234AR holding in position Runway 24L at Bravo.

Note: FAA analysis of accidents and incidents involving aircraft holding in position indicate that two minutes or more elapsed between the time the instruction was issued to line up and wait and the resulting event (for example, land-over or go-around). Pilots should consider the length of time that they have been holding in position whenever they have not been advised of any expected delay to determine when it is appropriate to query the controller.

Reference: Advisory Circulars 91-73A, Part 91 and Part 135 Single-Pilot Procedures during Taxi Operations, and 120-74A, Parts 91, 121, 125, and 135 Flightcrew Procedures during Taxi Operations

d. Situational awareness during line up and wait operations is enhanced by monitoring ATC instructions/clearances issued to other aircraft. Pilots should listen carefully if another aircraft is on frequency that has a similar call sign and pay close attention to communications between ATC

and other aircraft. If you are uncertain of an ATC instruction or clearance, query ATC immediately. Care should be taken to not inadvertently execute a clearance/instruction for another aircraft.

e. Pilots should be especially vigilant when conducting line up and wait operations at night or during reduced visibility conditions. They should scan the full length of the runway and look for aircraft on final approach or landing roll out when taxiing onto a runway. ATC should be contacted anytime there is a concern about a potential conflict.

f. When two or more runways are active, aircraft may be instructed to "LINE UP AND WAIT" on two or more runways. When multiple runway operations are being conducted, it is important to listen closely for your call sign and runway. Be alert for similar sounding call signs and acknowledge all instructions with your call sign. When you are holding in position and are not sure if the takeoff clearance was for you, ask ATC before you begin takeoff roll. ATC prefers that you confirm a takeoff clearance rather than mistake another aircraft's clearance for your own.

g. When ATC issues intersection "line up and wait" and takeoff clearances, the intersection designator will be used. If ATC omits the intersection designator, call ATC for clarification.

Example: Aircraft: "Cherokee 234AR, Runway 24L at November 4, line up and wait."

h. If landing traffic is a factor during line up and wait operations, ATC will inform the aircraft in position of the closest traffic within 6 flying miles requesting a full-stop, touch-and-go, stop-and-go, or an unrestricted low approach to the same runway. Pilots should take care to note the position of landing traffic. ATC will also advise the landing traffic when an aircraft is authorized to "line up and wait" on the same runway.

Example:
Tower: "Cessna 234AR, Runway 24L, line up and wait. Traffic a Boeing 737, six mile final."
Tower: "Delta 1011, continue, traffic a Cessna 210 holding in position Runway 24L."

Note: ATC will normally withhold landing clearance to arrival aircraft when another aircraft is in position and holding on the runway.

i. Never land on a runway that is occupied by another aircraft, even if a landing clearance was issued. Do not hesitate to ask the controller about the traffic on the runway and be prepared to execute a go-around.

Note: Always clarify any misunderstanding or confusion concerning ATC instructions or clearances. ATC should be advised immediately if there is any uncertainty about the ability to comply with any of their instructions.

5-2-6 Abbreviated IFR Departure Clearance (Cleared...as Filed) Procedures

a. ATC facilities will issue an abbreviated IFR departure clearance based on the ROUTE of flight filed in the IFR flight plan, provided the filed route can be approved with little or no revision. These abbreviated clearance procedures are based on the following conditions:

1. The aircraft is on the ground or it has departed visual flight rules (VFR) and the pilot is requesting IFR clearance while airborne.

2. That a pilot will not accept an abbreviated clearance if the route or destination of a flight plan filed with ATC has been changed by the pilot or the company or the operations officer before departure.

3. That it is the responsibility of the company or operations office to inform the pilot when they make a change to the filed flight plan.

4. That it is the responsibility of the pilot to inform ATC in the initial call-up (for clearance) when the filed flight plan has been either:

(a) Amended, or

(b) Canceled and replaced with a new filed flight plan.

Note: The facility issuing a clearance may not have received the revised route or the revised flight plan by the time a pilot requests clearance.

b. Controllers will issue a detailed clearance when they know that the original filed flight plan has been changed or when the pilot requests a full route clearance.

c. The clearance as issued will include the destination airport filed in the flight plan.

d. ATC procedures now require the controller to state the DP name, the current number and the DP transition name after the phrase "Cleared to (destination) airport" and prior to the phrase, "then as filed," for ALL departure clearances when the DP or DP transition is to be flown. The procedures apply whether or not the DP is filed in the flight plan.

e. STARs, when filed in a flight plan, are considered a part of the filed route of flight and will not normally be stated in an initial departure clearance. If the ARTCCs jurisdictional airspace includes both the departure airport and the fix where a STAR or STAR transition begins, the STAR name, the current number and the STAR transition name MAY be stated in the initial clearance.

f. "Cleared to (destination) airport as filed" does NOT include the en route altitude filed in a flight plan. An en route altitude will be stated in the clearance or the pilot will be advised to expect an assigned or filed altitude within a given time frame or at a certain point after departure. This may be done verbally in the departure instructions or stated in the DP.

g. In both radar and nonradar environments, the controller will state "Cleared to (destination) airport as filed" or:

1. If a DP or DP transition is to be flown, specify the DP name, the current DP number, the DP transition name, the assigned altitude/flight level, and any additional instructions (departure control frequency, beacon code assignment, etc.) necessary to clear a departing aircraft via the DP or DP transition and the route filed.

Example: National Seven Twenty cleared to Miami Airport Intercontinental one departure, Lake Charles transition then as filed, maintain Flight Level two seven zero.

2. When there is no DP or when the pilot cannot accept a DP, the controller will specify the assigned altitude or flight level, and any additional instructions necessary to clear a departing aircraft via an appropriate departure routing and the route filed.

Note: A detailed departure route description or a radar vector may be used to achieve the desired departure routing.

3. If it is necessary to make a minor revision to the filed route, the controller will specify the assigned DP or DP transition (or departure routing), the revision to the filed route, the assigned altitude or flight level and any additional instructions necessary to clear a departing aircraft.

Example: Jet Star One Four Two Four cleared to Atlanta Airport, South Boston two departure then as filed except change route to read South Boston Victor 20 Greensboro, maintain one seven thousand.

4. Additionally, in a nonradar environment, the controller will specify one or more fixes, as necessary, to identify the initial route of flight.

Example: Cessna Three One Six Zero Foxtrot cleared to Charlotte Airport as filed via Brooke, maintain seven thousand.

h. To ensure success of the program, pilots should:

1. Avoid making changes to a filed flight plan just prior to departure.

2. State the following information in the initial call-up to the facility when no change has been made to the filed flight plan: Aircraft call sign, location, type operation (IFR) and the name of the airport (or fix) to which you expect clearance.

Example: "Washington clearance delivery (or ground control if appropriate) American Seventy Six at gate one, IFR Los Angeles."

3. If the flight plan has been changed, state the change and request a full route clearance.

Example: "Washington clearance delivery, American Seventy Six at gate one. IFR San Francisco. My flight plan route has been amended (or destination changed). Request full route clearance."

4. Request verification or clarification from ATC if any portion of the clearance is not clearly understood.

5. When requesting clearance for the IFR portion of a VFR/IFR flight, request such clearance prior to the fix where IFR operation is proposed to commence in sufficient time to avoid delay. Use the following phraseology:

Example: "Los Angeles center, Apache Six One Papa, VFR estimating Paso Robles VOR at three two, one thousand five hundred, request IFR to Bakersfield."

5–2–7 Departure Restrictions, Clearance Void Times, Hold for Release, and Release Times

a. ATC may assign departure restrictions, clearance void times, hold for release, and release times, when necessary, to separate departures from other traffic or to restrict or regulate the departure flow. Departures from an airport without an operating control tower must be issued either a departure release (along with a release time and/ or void time if applicable), or a hold for release.

Reference: FAA Order JO 7110.65, ¶4-3-4, Departure Release, Hold for Release, Release Times, Departure Restrictions, and Clearance Void Times.

1. Clearance void times. A pilot may receive a clearance, when operating from an airport without a control tower, which contains a provision for the clearance to be void if not airborne by a specific time. A pilot who does not depart prior to the clearance void time must advise ATC as soon as possible of their intentions. ATC will normally advise the pilot of the time allotted to notify ATC that the aircraft did not depart prior to the clearance void time. This time cannot exceed 30 minutes. Failure of an aircraft to contact ATC within 30 minutes after the clearance void time will result in the aircraft being considered overdue and search and rescue procedures initiated.

Note 1: Other IFR traffic for the airport where the clearance is issued is suspended until the aircraft has contacted ATC or until 30 minutes after the clearance void time or 30 minutes after the clearance release time if no clearance void time is issued.

Note 2: If the clearance void time expires, it does not cancel the departure clearance or IFR flight plan. It withdraws the pilot's authority to depart IFR until a new departure release/release time

has been issued by ATC and is acknowledged by the pilot.

Note 3: Pilots who depart at or after their clearance void time are not afforded IFR separation and may be in violation of 14 CFR Section 91.173 which requires that pilots receive an appropriate ATC clearance before operating IFR in controlled airspace.

Note 4: Pilots who choose to depart VFR after their clearance void time has expired should not depart using the previously assigned IFR transponder code.

Example: Clearance void if not off by (clearance void time) and, if required, if not off by (clearance void time) advise (facility) not later than (time) of intentions.

2. Hold for release. ATC may issue "hold for release" instructions in a clearance to delay an aircraft's departure for traffic management reasons (i.e., weather, traffic volume, etc.). When ATC states in the clearance, "hold for release," the pilot may not depart utilizing that IFR clearance until a release time or additional instructions are issued by ATC. In addition, ATC will include departure delay information in conjunction with "hold for release" instructions. The ATC instruction, "hold for release," applies to the IFR clearance and does not prevent the pilot from departing under VFR. However, prior to takeoff the pilot should cancel the IFR flight plan and operate the transponder/ADS-B on the appropriate VFR code. An IFR clearance may not be available after departure.

Example: (Aircraft identification) cleared to (destination) airport as filed, maintain (altitude), and, if required (additional instructions or information), hold for release, expect (time in hours and/or minutes) departure delay.

3. Release times. A "release time" is a departure restriction issued to a pilot by ATC, specifying the earliest time an aircraft may depart. ATC will use "release times" in conjunction with traffic management procedures and/or to separate a departing aircraft from other traffic.

Example: (Aircraft identification) released for departure at (time in hours and/or minutes).

4. Expect Departure Clearance Time (EDCT). The EDCT is the runway release time assigned to an aircraft included in traffic management programs. Aircraft are expected to depart no earlier than 5 minutes before, and no later than 5 minutes after the EDCT.

b. If practical, pilots departing uncontrolled airports should obtain IFR clearances prior to becoming airborne when two-way communications with the controlling ATC facility is available.

5-2-8 Departure Control

a. Departure Control is an approach control function responsible for ensuring separation between departures. So as to expedite the handling of departures, Departure Control may suggest a takeoff direction other than that which may normally have been used under VFR handling. Many times it is preferred to offer the pilot a runway that will require the fewest turns after takeoff to place the pilot on course or selected departure route as quickly as possible. At many locations particular attention is paid to the use of preferential runways for local noise abatement programs, and route departures away from congested areas.

b. Departure Control utilizing radar will normally clear aircraft out of the terminal area using vectors, a diverse vector area (DVA), or published DPs.

1. When a departure is to be vectored immediately following takeoff using vectors, a DVA, or published DPs that begins with an ATC assigned heading off the ground, the pilot will be advised prior to takeoff of the initial heading to be flown but may not be advised of the purpose of the heading. When ATC assigns an initial heading with the takeoff clearance that will take the aircraft off an assigned procedure (for example, an RNAV SID with a published lateral path to a waypoint and crossing restrictions from the departure end of runway), the controller will assign an altitude to maintain with the initial heading and, if necessary, a speed to maintain.

2. At some airports when a departure will fly an RNAV SID that begins at the runway, ATC may advise aircraft of the initial fix/waypoint on the RNAV route. The purpose of the advisory is to remind pilots to verify the correct procedure is programmed in the FMS before takeoff. Pilots must immediately advise ATC if a different RNAV SID is entered in the aircraft's FMC. When this advisory is absent, pilots are still required to fly the assigned SID as published.

Example: Delta 345 RNAV to MPASS, Runway 26L, cleared for takeoff.

Note 1: The SID transition is not restated as it is contained in the ATC clearance.

Note 2: Aircraft cleared via RNAV SIDs designed to begin with a vector to the initial waypoint are assigned a heading before departure.

3. Pilots operating in a radar environment are expected to associate departure headings or an RNAV departure advisory with vectors or the flight path to their planned route or flight. When given a vector taking the aircraft off a previously assigned nonradar route, the pilot will be advised briefly what the vector is to achieve. Thereafter, radar service will be provided until the aircraft has been reestablished "on-course" using an appropriate navigation aid and the pilot has been advised of the aircraft's position or a handoff is made to another radar controller with further surveillance capabilities.

c. Controllers will inform pilots of the departure control frequencies and, if appropriate, the transponder code before takeoff. Pilots must ensure their transponder/ADS-B is adjusted to the "on" or normal operating position as soon as practical and remain on during all operations unless otherwise requested to change to "standby" by ATC. Pilots should not change to the departure control frequency until requested. Controllers may omit the departure control frequency if a DP has or will be assigned and the departure control frequency is published on the DP.

5-2-9 Instrument Departure Procedures (DP)—Obstacle Departure Procedures (ODP), Standard Instrument Departures (SID), and Diverse Vector Areas (DVA)

a. Instrument departure procedures are preplanned instrument flight rule (IFR) procedures which provide obstruction clearance from the terminal area to the appropriate en route structure. There are two types of DPs, Obstacle Departure Procedures (ODP), printed either textually or graphically, and Standard Instrument Departures (SID), always printed graphically. All DPs, either textual or graphic may be designed using either conventional or RNAV criteria. RNAV procedures will have RNAV printed in the title; for example, SHEAD TWO DEPARTURE (RNAV). ODPs provide obstruction clearance via the least onerous route from the terminal area to the appropriate en route structure. ODPs are recommended for obstruction clearance and may be flown without ATC clearance unless an alternate departure procedure (SID or radar vector) has been specifically assigned by ATC. Graphic ODPs will have (OBSTACLE) printed in the procedure title; for example, GEYSR THREE DEPARTURE (OBSTACLE), or, CROWN ONE DEPARTURE (RNAV) (OBSTACLE). Standard Instrument Departures are air traffic control (ATC) procedures printed for pilot/controller use in graphic form to provide obstruction clearance and a transition from the terminal area to the appropriate en route structure. SIDs are primarily designed for system enhancement and to reduce pilot/controller workload. ATC clearance must be received prior to flying a SID. All DPs provide the pilot with a way to depart the airport and transition to the en route structure safely.

b. A Diverse Vector Area (DVA) is an area in which ATC may provide random radar vectors during an uninterrupted climb from the departure

Ch 5

runway until above the MVA/MIA, established in accordance with the TERPS criteria for diverse departures. The DVA provides obstacle and terrain avoidance in lieu of taking off from the runway under IFR using an ODP or SID.

c. Pilots operating under 14 CFR Part 91 are strongly encouraged to file and fly a DP at night, during marginal Visual Meteorological Conditions (VMC) and Instrument Meteorological Conditions (IMC), when one is available. The following paragraphs will provide an overview of the DP program, why DPs are developed, what criteria are used, where to find them, how they are to be flown, and finally pilot and ATC responsibilities.

d. Why are DPs necessary? The primary reason is to provide obstacle clearance protection information to pilots. A secondary reason, at busier airports, is to increase efficiency and reduce communications and departure delays through the use of SIDs. When an instrument approach is initially developed for an airport, the need for DPs is assessed. The procedure designer conducts an obstacle analysis to support departure operations. If an aircraft may turn in any direction from a runway within the limits of the assessment area (see paragraph 5-2-9e3) and remain clear of obstacles, that runway passes what is called a diverse departure assessment and no ODP will be published. A SID may be published if needed for air traffic control purposes. However, if an obstacle penetrates what is called the 40:1 obstacle identification surface, then the procedure designer chooses whether to:

1. Establish a steeper than normal climb gradient; or

2. Establish a steeper than normal climb gradient with an alternative that increases takeoff minima to allow the pilot to visually remain clear of the obstacle(s); or

3. Design and publish a specific departure route; or

4. A combination or all of the above.

e. What criteria is used to provide obstruction clearance during departure?

1. Unless specified otherwise, required obstacle clearance for all departures, including diverse, is based on the pilot crossing the departure end of the runway at least 35 feet above the departure end of runway elevation, climbing to 400 feet above the departure end of runway elevation before making the initial turn, and maintaining a minimum climb gradient of 200 feet per nautical mile (FPNM), unless required to level off by a crossing restriction, until the minimum IFR altitude. A greater climb gradient may be specified in the DP to clear obstacles or to achieve an ATC crossing restriction. If an initial turn higher than 400 feet above the departure end of runway elevation is specified in the DP, the turn should

be commenced at the higher altitude. If a turn is specified at a fix, the turn must be made at that fix. Fixes may have minimum and/or maximum crossing altitudes that must be adhered to prior to passing the fix. In rare instances, obstacles that exist on the extended runway centerline may make an "early turn" more desirable than proceeding straight ahead. In these cases, the published departure instructions will include the language "turn left(right) as soon as practicable." These departures will also include a ceiling and visibility minimum of at least 300 and 1. Pilots encountering one of these DPs should preplan the climb out to gain altitude and begin the turn as quickly as possible within the bounds of safe operating practices and operating limitations. This type of departure procedure is being phased out.

Note: "Practical" or "feasible" may exist in some existing departure text instead of "practicable."

2. ODPs, SIDs, and DVAs assume normal aircraft performance, and that all engines are operating. Development of contingency procedures, required to cover the case of an engine failure or other emergency in flight that may occur after liftoff, is the responsibility of the operator. (More detailed information on this subject is available in Advisory Circular AC 120-91, Airport Obstacle Analysis, and in the "Departure Procedures" section of chapter 2 in the Instrument Procedures Handbook, FAA-H-8083-16.)

3. The 40:1 obstacle identification surface (OIS) begins at the departure end of runway (DER) and slopes upward at 152 FPNM until reaching the minimum IFR altitude or entering the en route structure. This assessment area is limited to 25 NM from the airport in nonmountainous areas and 46 NM in designated mountainous areas. Beyond this distance, the pilot is responsible for obstacle clearance if not operating on a published route, if below (having not reached) the MEA or MOCA of a published route, or an ATC assigned altitude. See Figure 5-2-1. (Ref 14 CFR 91.177 for further information on en route altitudes.)

Note: ODPs are normally designed to terminate within these distance limitations, however, some ODPs will contain routes that may exceed 25/46 NM; these routes will ensure obstacle protection until reaching the end of the ODP.

FIGURE 5–2–1
Diverse Departure Obstacle Assessment to 25/46 NM

4. Obstacles that are located within 1 NM of the DER and penetrate the 40:1 OCS are referred to as "low, close-in obstacles." The standard required obstacle clearance (ROC) of 48 feet per NM to clear these obstacles would require a climb gradient greater than 200 feet per NM for a very short distance, only until the aircraft was 200 feet above the DER. To eliminate publishing an excessive climb gradient, the obstacle AGL/MSL height and location relative to the DER is noted in the "Take-off Minimums and (OBSTACLE) Departure Procedures" section of a given Terminal Procedures Publication (TPP) booklet.

(a) Pilots must refer to the TPP booklet or the Graphic ODP for information on these obstacles. These obstacle notes will no longer be published on SIDs. Pilots assigned a SID for departure must refer to the airport entry in the TPP to obtain information on these obstacles.

(b) The purpose of noting obstacles in the "Take-off Minimums and (OBSTACLE) Departure Procedures" section of the TPP is to identify the obstacle(s) and alert the pilot to the height and location of the obstacle(s) so they can be avoided. This can be accomplished in a variety of ways; for example, the pilot may be able to see the obstruction and maneuver around the obstacle(s) if necessary; early liftoff/climb performance may allow the aircraft to cross well above the obstacle(s); or if the obstacle(s) cannot be visually acquired during departure, preflight planning should take into account what turns or other maneuvers may be necessary immediately after takeoff to avoid the obstruction(s).

Example: *TAKEOFF OBSTACLE NOTES: Rwy 14, trees 2011' from DER, 29' left of centerline, 100' AGL/3829' MSL. Rwy 32, trees 1009' from DER, 697' left of centerline, 100' AGL/3839' MSL.*

Tower 4448' from DER, 1036' left of centerline, 165' AGL/3886' MSL.

Note: *Compliance with 14 CFR Part 121 or 135 one-engine-inoperative (OEI) departure performance requirements, or similar ICAO/State rules, cannot be assured by the sole use of "low, close-in" obstacle data as published in the TPP. Operators should refer to precise data sources (for example, GIS database, etc.) specifically intended for OEI departure planning for those operations.*

5. Climb gradients greater than 200 FPNM are specified when required to support procedure design constraints, obstacle clearance, and/or airspace restrictions. Compliance with a climb gradient for these purposes is mandatory when the procedure is part of the ATC clearance, unless increased takeoff minimums are provided and weather conditions allow compliance with these minimums.

Note: *Climb gradients for ATC purposes are being phased out on SIDs.*

Example: *"Cross ALPHA intersection at or below 4,000; maintain 6000." The pilot climbs at least 200 FPNM to 6,000. If 4,000 is reached before ALPHA, the pilot levels off at 4,000 until passing ALPHA; then immediately resumes at least 200 FPNM climb.*

Example: *"TAKEOFF MINIMUMS: RWY 27, Standard with a minimum climb of 280' per NM to 2,500." A climb of at least 280 FPNM is required to 2,500 and is mandatory when the departure procedure is included in the ATC clearance.*

Note: *Some SIDs still retain labeled "ATC" climb gradients published or have climb gradients that are established to meet a published altitude restriction that is not required for obstacle clearance*

or procedure design criteria. These procedures will be revised in the course of the normal procedure amendment process.

6. Climb gradients may be specified only to an altitude/fix, above which the normal gradient applies.

An ATC-required altitude restriction published at a fix, will not have an associated climb gradient published with that restriction. Pilots are expected to determine if crossing altitudes can be met, based on the performance capability of the aircraft they are operating.

Example: *"Minimum climb 340 FPNM to ALPHA." The pilot climbs at least 340 FPNM to ALPHA, then at least 200 FPNM to MIA.*

7. A Visual Climb Over Airport (VCOA) procedure is a departure option for an IFR aircraft, operating in visual meteorological conditions equal to or greater than the specified visibility and ceiling, to visually conduct climbing turns over the airport to the published "at or above" altitude. At this point, the pilot may proceed in instrument meteorological conditions to the first en route fix using a diverse departure, or to proceed via a published routing to a fix from where the aircraft may join the IFR en route structure, while maintaining a climb gradient of at least 200 feet per nautical mile. VCOA procedures are developed to avoid obstacles greater than 3 statute miles from the departure end of the runway as an alternative to complying with climb gradients greater than 200 feet per nautical mile. Pilots are responsible to advise ATC as early as possible of the intent to fly the VCOA option prior to departure. Pilots are expected to remain within the distance prescribed in the published visibility minimums during the climb over the airport until reaching the "at or above" altitude for the VCOA procedure. If no additional routing is published, then the pilot may proceed in accordance with their IFR clearance. If additional routing is published after the "at-or-above" altitude, the pilot must comply with the route to a fix that may include a climb-in-holding pattern to reach the MEA/MIA for the en route portion of their IFR flight. These textual procedures are published in the Take-Off Minimums and (Obstacle) Departure Procedures section of the Terminal Procedures Publications and/or appear as an option on a Graphic ODP.

Example: *TAKEOFF MINIMUMS: Rwy 32, standard with minimum climb of 410' per NM to 3000' or 1100-3 for VCOA.*

VCOA: Rwy 32, obtain ATC approval for VCOA when requesting IFR clearance. Climb in visual conditions to cross Broken Bow Muni/Keith Glaze Field at or above 3500' before proceeding on course.

f. Who is responsible for obstacle clearance? DPs are designed so that adherence to the procedure by the pilot will ensure obstacle protection. Additionally:

1. Obstacle clearance responsibility also rests with the pilot when he/she chooses to climb in visual conditions in lieu of flying a DP and/or depart under increased takeoff minima rather than fly the climb gradient. Standard takeoff minima are one statute mile for aircraft having two engines or less and one-half statute mile for aircraft having more than two engines. Specified ceiling and visibility minima will allow visual avoidance of obstacles during the initial climb at the standard climb gradient. When departing using the VCOA, obstacle avoidance is not guaranteed if the pilot maneuvers farther from the airport than the published visibility minimum for the VCOA prior to reaching the published VCOA altitude. DPs may also contain what are called Low Close in Obstacles. These obstacles are less than 200 feet above the departure end of runway elevation and within one NM of the runway end and do not require increased takeoff minimums. These obstacles are identified on the SID chart or in the Take-off Minimums and (Obstacle) Departure Procedures section of the U. S. Terminal Procedure booklet. These obstacles are especially critical to aircraft that do not lift off until close to the departure end of the runway or which climb at the minimum rate. Pilots should also consider drift following lift-off to ensure sufficient clearance from these obstacles. That segment of the procedure that requires the pilot to see and avoid obstacles ends when the aircraft crosses the specified point at the required altitude. In all cases continued obstacle clearance is based on having climbed a minimum of 200 feet per nautical mile to the specified point and then continuing to climb at least 200 foot per nautical mile during the departure until reaching the minimum enroute altitude unless specified otherwise.

2. ATC may vector the aircraft beginning with an ATC-assigned heading issued with the initial or takeoff clearance followed by subsequent vectors, if required, until reaching the minimum vectoring altitude by using a published Diverse Vector Area (DVA).

3. The DVA may be established below the Minimum Vectoring Altitude (MVA) or Minimum IFR Altitude (MIA) in a radar environment at the request of Air Traffic. This type of DP meets the TERPS criteria for diverse departures, obstacles, and terrain avoidance in which vectors below the MVA/MIA may be issued to departing aircraft. The DVA has been assessed for departures which do not follow a specific ground track, but will remain within the specified area. Use of a DVA is valid only when aircraft are permitted to

climb uninterrupted from the departure runway to the MVA/MIA (or higher). ATC will not assign an altitude below the MVA/MIA within a DVA. At locations that have a DVA, ATC is not permitted to utilize a SID and DVA concurrently.

(a) The existence of a DVA will be noted in the Takeoff Minimums and Obstacle Departure Procedure section of the U.S. Terminal Procedures Publication (TPP). The Takeoff Departure procedure will be listed first, followed by any applicable DVA.

Example:

DIVERSE VECTOR AREA (RADAR VECTORS) AMDT 1 14289 (FAA)

Rwy 6R, headings as assigned by ATC; requires minimum climb of 290' per NM to 400.

Rwys 6L, 7L, 7R, 24R, 25R, headings as assigned by ATC.

(b) Pilots should be aware that a published climb gradient greater than the standard 200 FPNM can exist within a DVA. Pilots should note that the DVA has been assessed for departures which do not follow a specific ground track.

(c) ATC may also vector an aircraft off a previously assigned DP. If the aircraft is airborne and established on a SID or ODP and subsequently vectored off, ATC is responsible for terrain and obstruction clearance. In all cases, the minimum 200 FPNM climb gradient is assumed.

Note: As is always the case, when used by the controller during departure, the term "radar contact" should not be interpreted as relieving pilots of their responsibility to maintain appropriate terrain and obstruction clearance, which may include flying the obstacle DP.

4. Pilots must preplan to determine if the aircraft can meet the climb gradient (expressed in feet per nautical mile) required by the departure procedure or DVA, and be aware that flying at a higher than anticipated ground speed increases the climb rate requirement in feet per minute. Higher than standard climb gradients are specified by a note on the departure procedure chart for graphic DPs, or in the Take-Off Minimums and (Obstacle) Departure Procedures section of the U.S. Terminal Procedures booklet for textual ODPs. The required climb gradient, or higher, must be maintained to the specified altitude or fix, then the standard climb gradient of 200 ft/NM can be resumed. A table for the conversion of climb gradient (feet per nautical mile) to climb rate (feet per minute), at a given ground speed, is included on the inside of the back cover of the U.S. Terminal Procedures booklets.

g. Where are DPs located? DPs and DVAs will be listed by airport in the IFR Takeoff Minimums and (Obstacle) Departure Procedures Section, Section L, of the Terminal Procedures Publications (TPP). If the DP is textual, it will be described in TPP Section L. SIDs and complex ODPs will be published graphically and named. The name will be listed by airport name and runway in Section L. Graphic ODPs will also have the term "(OBSTACLE)" printed in the charted procedure title, differentiating them from SIDs.

1. An ODP that has been developed solely for obstacle avoidance will be indicated with the symbol "T" on appropriate Instrument Approach Procedure (IAP) charts and DP charts for that airport. The "T" symbol will continue to refer users to TPP Section C. In the case of a graphic ODP, the TPP Section C will only contain the name of the ODP. Since there may be both a textual and a graphic DP, Section C should still be checked for additional information. The nonstandard takeoff minimums and minimum climb gradients found in TPP Section C also apply to charted DPs and radar vector departures unless different minimums are specified on the charted DP. Takeoff minimums and departure procedures apply to all runways unless otherwise specified. New graphic DPs will have all the information printed on the graphic depiction. As a general rule, ATC will only assign an ODP from a non-towered airport when compliance with the ODP is necessary for aircraft to aircraft separation. Pilots may use the ODP to help ensure separation from terrain and obstacles.

h. Responsibilities.

1. Each pilot, prior to departing an airport on an IFR flight should:

(a) Consider the type of terrain and other obstacles on or in the vicinity of the departure airport;

(b) Determine whether an ODP is available;

(c) Determine if obstacle avoidance can be maintained visually or if the ODP should be flown; and

(d) Consider the effect of degraded climb performance and the actions to take in the event of an engine loss during the departure. Pilots should notify ATC as soon as possible of reduced climb capability in that circumstance.

Note: Guidance concerning contingency procedures that address an engine failure on takeoff after V_1 speed on a large or turbine-powered transport category airplane may be found in AC 120-91, Airport Obstacle Analysis.

(e) Determine if a DVA is published and whether the aircraft is capable of meeting the published climb gradient. Advise ATC when requesting the IFR clearance, or as soon as possible, if unable to meet the DVA climb gradient.

(f) Check for Takeoff Obstacle Notes published in the TPP for the takeoff runway.

Ch 5

2. Pilots should not exceed a published speed restriction associated with a SID waypoint until passing that waypoint.

3. After an aircraft is established on a SID and subsequently vectored or cleared to deviate off of the SID or SID transition, pilots must consider the SID canceled, unless the controller adds "expect to resume SID;" pilots should then be prepared to rejoin the SID at a subsequent fix or procedure leg. If the SID contains published altitude and/or speed restrictions, those restrictions are canceled and pilots will receive an altitude to maintain and, if necessary, a speed. ATC may also interrupt the vertical navigation of a SID and provide alternate altitude instructions while the aircraft remains established on the published lateral path. Aircraft may be vectored off of an ODP, or issued an altitude lower than a published altitude on an ODP, at which time the ODP is canceled. In these cases, ATC assumes responsibility for terrain and obstacle clearance. In all cases, the minimum 200 FPNM climb gradient is assumed.

4. Aircraft instructed to resume a SID procedure such as a DP or SID which contains speed and/or altitude restrictions, must be:

(a) Issued/reissued all applicable restrictions, or

(b) Advised to "Climb via SID" or resume published speed.

Example: "Resume the Solar One departure, Climb via SID."

"Proceed direct CIROS, resume the Solar One departure, Climb via SID."

5. A clearance for a SID which does not contain published crossing restrictions, and/or is a SID with a Radar Vector segment or a Radar Vector SID, will be issued using the phraseology "Maintain (*altitude*)."

6. A clearance for a SID which contains published altitude restrictions may be issued using the phraseology "climb via." Climb via is an abbreviated clearance that requires compliance with the procedure lateral path, associated speed and altitude restrictions along the cleared route or procedure. Clearance to "climb via" authorizes the pilot to:

(a) When used in the IFR departure clearance, in a PDC, DCL or when cleared to a waypoint depicted on a SID, to join the procedure after departure or to resume the procedure.

(b) When vertical navigation is interrupted and an altitude is assigned to maintain which is not contained on the published procedure, to climb from that previously-assigned altitude at pilot's discretion to the altitude depicted for the next waypoint.

(c) Once established on the depicted departure, to navigate laterally and climb to meet all published or assigned altitude and speed restrictions.

Note 1: When otherwise cleared along a route or procedure that contains published speed restrictions, the pilot must comply with those speed restrictions independent of a climb via clearance.

Note 2: ATC anticipates pilots will begin adjusting speed the minimum distance necessary prior to a published speed restriction so as to cross the waypoint/fix at the published speed. Once at the published speed ATC expects pilots will maintain the published speed until additional adjustment is required to comply with further published or ATC assigned speed restrictions or as required to ensure compliance with 14 CFR Section 91.117.

Note 3: If ATC interrupts lateral/vertical navigation while an aircraft is flying a SID, ATC must ensure obstacle clearance. When issuing a "climb via" clearance to join or resume a procedure ATC must ensure obstacle clearance until the aircraft is established on the lateral and vertical path of the SID.

Note 4: ATC will assign an altitude to cross if no altitude is depicted at a waypoint/fix or when otherwise necessary/ required, for an aircraft on a direct route to a waypoint/fix where the SID will be joined or resumed.

Note 5: SIDs will have a "top altitude;" the "top altitude" is the charted "maintain" altitude contained in the procedure description or assigned by ATC.

Reference: FAA Order JO 7110.65, ¶5-6-2, Methods; Pilot/Controller Glossary—Climb Via, Top Altitude

Example 1: Lateral route clearance:

"Cleared Loop Six departure."

Note: The aircraft must comply with the SID lateral path, and any published speed restrictions.

Example 2: Routing with assigned altitude:

"Cleared Loop Six departure, climb and maintain four thousand."

Note: The aircraft must comply with the SID lateral path, and any published speed restriction while climbing unrestricted to four thousand.

Example 3: (A pilot filed a flight plan to the Johnston Airport using the Scott One departure, Jonez transition, then Q-145. The pilot filed for FL350. The Scott One includes altitude restrictions, a top altitude and instructions to expect the filed altitude ten minutes after departure). Before departure ATC uses PDC, DCL or clearance delivery to issue the clearance:

"Cleared to Johnston Airport, Scott One departure, Jonez transition, Q-OneForty-five. Climb via SID."

Note: In Example 3, the aircraft must comply with the Scott One departure lateral path and any published speed and altitude restrictions while climbing to the SID top altitude.

Example 4: (Using the Example 3 flight plan, ATC determines the top altitude must be changed to FL180). The clearance will read:

"Cleared to Johnston Airport, Scott One departure, Jonez transition, Q-One Forty-five, Climb via SID except maintain flight level one eight zero."

Note: In Example 4, the aircraft must comply with the Scott One departure lateral path and any published speed and altitude restrictions while climbing to FL180. The aircraft must stop climb at FL180 until issued further clearance by ATC.

Example 5: (An aircraft was issued the Suzan Two departure, "climb via SID" in the IFR departure clearance. After departure ATC must change a waypoint crossing restriction). The clearance will be:

"Climb via SID except cross Mkala at or above seven thousand."

Note: In Example 5, the aircraft will comply with the Suzan Two departure lateral path and any published speed and altitude restrictions and climb so as to cross Mkala at or above 7,000; remainder of the departure must be flown as published.

Example 6: (An aircraft was issued the Teddd One departure, "climb via SID" in the IFR departure clearance. An interim altitude of 10,000 was issued instead of the published top altitude of FL 230). After departure ATC is able to issue the published top altitude. The clearance will be:

"Climb via SID."

Note: In Example 6, the aircraft will track laterally and vertically on the Teddd One departure and initially climb to 10,000; Once re-issued the "climb via" clearance the interim altitude is canceled aircraft will continue climb to FL230 while complying with published restrictions.

Example 7: (An aircraft was issued the Bbear Two departure, "climb via SID" in the IFR departure clearance. An interim altitude of 16,000 was issued instead of the published top altitude of FL 190). After departure, ATC is able to issue a top altitude of FL300 and still requires compliance with the published SID restrictions. The clearance will be:

"Climb via SID except maintain flight level three zero zero."

Note: In Example 7, the aircraft will track laterally and vertically on the Bbear Two departure and initially climb to 16,000; Once re-issued the "climb via" clearance the interim altitude is canceled and the aircraft will continue climb to FL300 while complying with published restrictions.

Example 8: (An aircraft was issued the Bizee Two departure, "climb via SID." After departure, ATC vectors the aircraft off of the SID, and then issues a direct routing to rejoin the SID at Rockr waypoint which does not have a published altitude restriction. ATC wants the aircraft to cross at or above 10,000). The clearance will read:

"Proceed direct Rockr, cross Rockr at or above one-zero thousand, climb via the Bizee Two departure."

Note: In Example 8, the aircraft will join the Bizee Two SID at Rockr at or above 10,000 and then comply with the published lateral path and any published speed or altitude restrictions while climbing to the SID top altitude.

Example 9: (An aircraft was issued the Suzan Two departure, "climb via SID" in the IFR departure clearance. After departure ATC vectors the aircraft off of the SID, and then clears the aircraft to rejoin the SID at Dvine waypoint, which has a published crossing restriction). The clearance will read:

"Proceed direct Dvine, Climb via the Suzan Two departure."

Note: In Example 9, the aircraft will join the Suzan Two departure at Dvine, at the published altitude, and then comply with the published lateral path and any published speed or altitude restrictions.

7. Pilots cleared for vertical navigation using the phraseology "climb via" must inform ATC, upon initial contact, of the altitude leaving and any assigned restrictions not published on the procedure.

Example 1: (Cactus 711 is cleared to climb via the Laura Two departure. The Laura Two has a top altitude of FL190):

"Cactus Seven Eleven leaving two thousand, climbing via the Laura Two departure."

Example 2: (Cactus 711 is cleared to climb via the Laura Two departure, but ATC changed the top altitude to 16,000):

"Cactus Seven Eleven leaving two thousand for one-six thousand, climbing via the Laura Two departure."

8. If prior to or after takeoff an altitude restriction is issued by ATC, all previously issued "ATC" altitude restrictions are canceled including those published on a SID. Pilots must still comply with all speed restrictions and lateral path requirements published on the SID unless canceled by ATC.

Ch 5

Example: Prior to takeoff or after departure ATC issues an altitude change clearance to an aircraft cleared to climb via a SID but ATC no longer requires compliance with published altitude restrictions:

"Climb and maintain flight level two four zero."

Note: The published SID altitude restrictions are canceled; The aircraft should comply with the SID lateral path and begin an unrestricted climb to FL240. Compliance with published speed restrictions is still required unless specifically deleted by ATC.

9. Altitude restrictions published on an ODP are necessary for obstacle clearance and/or design constraints. Crossing altitudes and speed restrictions on ODPs cannot be canceled or amended by ATC.

i. PBN Departure Procedures

1. All public PBN SIDs and graphic ODPs are normally designed using RNAV 1, RNP1, or A-RNP NavSpecs. These procedures generally start with an initial track or heading leg near the departure end of runway (DER). In addition, these procedures require system performance currently met by GPS or DME/DME/IRU PBN systems that satisfy the criteria discussed in the latest AC 90-100, U.S. Terminal and En Route Area Navigation (RNAV) Operations. RNAV 1 and RNP 1 procedures must maintain a total system error of not more than 1 NM for 95 percent of the total flight time. Minimum values for A-RNP procedures will be charted in the PBN box (for example, 1.00 or 0.30).

2. In the U.S., a specific procedure's PBN requirements will be prominently displayed in separate, standardized notes boxes. For procedures with PBN elements, the "PBN box" will contain the procedure's NavSpec(s); and, if required: specific sensors or infrastructure needed for the navigation solution, any additional or advanced functional requirements, the minimum RNP value, and any amplifying remarks. Items listed in this PBN box are REQUIRED for the procedure's PBN elements.

Section 3 En Route Procedures

5–3–1 ARTCC Communications

a. Direct Communications, Controllers and Pilots.

1. ARTCCs are capable of direct communications with IFR air traffic on certain frequencies. Maximum communications coverage is possible through the use of Remote Center Air/Ground (RCAG) sites comprised of both VHF and UHF transmitters and receivers. These sites are located throughout the U.S. Although they may be several hundred miles away from the ARTCC, they are remoted to the various ARTCCs by land lines or microwave links. Since IFR operations are expedited through the use of direct communications, pilots are requested to use these frequencies strictly for communications pertinent to the control of IFR aircraft. Flight plan filing, en route weather, weather forecasts, and similar data should be requested through FSSs, company radio, or appropriate military facilities capable of performing these services.

2. An ARTCC is divided into sectors. Each sector is handled by one or a team of controllers and has its own sector discrete frequency. As a flight progresses from one sector to another, the pilot is requested to change to the appropriate sector discrete frequency.

3. Controller Pilot Data Link Communications (CPDLC) is a system that supplements air/ground voice communications. The CPDLC's principal operating criteria are:

(a) Voice remains the primary and controlling air/ground communications means.

(b) Participating aircraft will need to have the appropriate CPDLC avionics equipment in order to receive uplink or transmit downlink messages.

(c) En Route CPDLC Initial Services offer the following services: Altimeter Setting (AS), Transfer of Communications (TOC), Initial Contact (IC), and limited route assignments, including airborne reroutes (ABRR), limited altitude assignments, and emergency messages.

(1) Altimeter settings will be uplinked automatically when appropriate after a Monitor TOC. Altimeter settings will also be uplinked automatically when an aircraft receives an uplinked altitude assignment below FL 180. A controller may also manually send an altimeter setting message.

Note: When conducting instrument approach procedures, pilots are responsible to obtain and use the appropriate altimeter setting in accordance with 14 CFR Section 97.20. CPDLC issued altimeter settings are excluded for this purpose.

(2) Initial contact is a safety validation transaction that compares a pilot's initiated altitude downlink message with an aircraft's stored altitude in the ATC automation system. When an IC mismatch or Confirm Assigned Altitude (CAA) downlink time-out indicator is displayed in the Full Data Block (FDB) and Aircraft List (ACL), the controller who has track control of the aircraft must use voice communication to verify the assigned altitude of the aircraft, and acknowledge the IC mismatch/time-out indicator.

(3) Transfer of communications automatically establishes data link contact with a succeeding sector.

(4) Menu text transmissions are scripted nontrajectory altering uplink messages.

(5) The CPDLC Message Elements for the Initial Capabilities rollout are contained in Table 5-3-1 through Table 5-3-19, CPDLC Message Elements, below.

Note: The FAA is not implementing ATN B1; the ATN B1 column in the tables is there for informational purposes only.

Ch 5

TABLE 5–3–1
ROUTE UPLINK MESSAGE ELEMENTS (RTEU)

CPDLC Message Sets			Operational Definition in PANS-ATM (Doc 4444)		
FANS 1/A	**ATN B1**	**Response**	**Message Element Identifier**	**Message Element Intended Use**	**Format for Message Element Display**
UM74 PROCEED DIRECT TO (*position*)	UM74 PROCEED DIRECT TO (*position*)	W/U	RTEU-2	Instruction to proceed directly to the specified position.	PROCEED DIRECT TO (*position*)
UM79 CLEARED TO (*position*) via (*route clearance*)	UM79 CLEARED TO (*position*) via (*route clearance*)	W/U	RTEU-6	Instruction to proceed to the specified position via the specified route.	CLEARED TO (*position*) VIA (*departure data[O]*) (*en-route data*)
UM80 CLEARED (*route clearance*)	UM80 CLEARED (*route clearance*)	W/U	RTEU-7	Instruction to proceed via the specified route.	CLEARED (*departure data[O]*) (*en-route data*) (*arrival approach data*)
UM83 AT (*position*) CLEARED (*route clearance*)	N/A	W/U	RTEU-9	Instruction to proceed from the specified position via the specified route.	AT (*position*) CLEARED (*en-route data*) (*arrival approach data*)

TABLE 5–3–2
ROUTE DOWNLINK MESSAGE ELEMENTS (RTED)

CPDLC Message Sets			Operational Definition in PANS-ATM (Doc 4444)		
FANS 1/A	**ATN B1**	**Response**	**Message Element Identifier**	**Message Element Intended Use**	**Format for Message Element Display**
DM22 REQUEST DIRECT TO (*position*)	DM22 REQUEST DIRECT TO (*position*)	Y	RTED-1	Request for a direct clearance to the specified position.	REQUEST DIRECT TO (*position*)

TABLE 5–3–3
LATERAL DOWNLINK MESSAGE ELEMENTS (LATD)

CPDLC Message Sets			Operational Definition in PANS-ATM (Doc 4444)		
FANS 1/A	**ATN B1**	**Response**	**Message Element Identifier**	**Message Element Intended Use**	**Format for Message Element Display**
DM59 DIVERTING TO (*position*) VIA (*route clearance*) *Note 1: H alert attribute* *Note 2: N response attribute*	N/A	N[1]	LATD-5	Report indicating diverting to the specified position via the specified route, which may be sent without any previous coordination done with ATC.	DIVERTING TO (*position*) VIA (*enroute data*) (*arrival approach data[O]*)
DM60 OFFSETTING (*distance offset*) (*direction*) OF ROUTE *Note 1: H alert attribute* *Note 2: N response attribute*	N/A	N[1]	LATD-6	Report indicating that the aircraft is offsetting to a parallel track at the specified distance in the specified direction off from the cleared route.	OFFSETTING (*specified distance*) (*direction*) OF ROUTE
DM80 DEVIATING (*deviation offset*) (*direction*) OF ROUTE *Note 1: H alert attribute* *Note 2: N response attribute*	N/A	N[1]	LATD-7	Report indicating deviating specified distance or degrees in the specified direction from the cleared route.	DEVIATING (*specified deviation*) (*direction*) OF ROUTE

[1] *ICAO Document 10037, Global Operational Data Link (GOLD) Manual has these values set to Y in their table.*

Ch 5

TABLE 5–3–4
LEVEL UPLINK MESSAGE ELEMENTS (LVLU)

CPDLC Message Sets			Operational Definition in PANS-ATM (Doc 4444)		
FANS 1/A	**ATN B1**	**Response**	**Message Element Identifier**	**Message Element Intended Use**	**Format for Message Element Display**
UM19 MAINTAIN *(altitude)* Note: *Used for a single level*	UM19 MAINTAIN *(level)*	W/U	LVLU-5	Instruction to maintain the specified level or vertical range.	MAINTAIN *(level)*
UM20 CLIMB TO AND MAINTAIN *(altitude)* Note: *Used for a single level*	UM20 CLIMB TO *(level)*	W/U	LVLU-6	Instruction that a climb to the specified level or vertical range is to commence and once reached is to be maintained.	CLIMB TO *(level)*
UM23 DESCEND TO AND MAINTAIN *(altitude)* Note: *Used for a single level*	UM23 DESCEND TO *(level)*	W/U	LVLU-9	Instruction that a descent to the specified level or vertical range is to commence and once reached is to be maintained.	DESCEND TO *(level)*
UM36 EXPEDITE CLIMB TO *(altitude)* Note: *This message element is equivalent to SUPU-3 plus LVLU-6 in Doc 4444.*	N/A	W/U	LVLU-6	Instruction that a climb to the specified level or vertical range is to commence and once reached is to be maintained.	CLIMB TO *(level)*
UM37 EXPEDITE DESCEND TO *(altitude)*	N/A	W/U	LVLU-9	Instruction that a descent to the specified level or vertical range is to commence and once reached is to be maintained.	DESCEND TO *(level)*
UM38 IMMEDIATELY CLIMB TO *(altitude)* Note: *This message element is equivalent to EMGU-2 plus LVLU-6 in Doc 4444*	N/A	W/U	LVLU-6	Instruction that a climb to the specified level or vertical range is to commence and once reached is to be maintained.	CLIMB TO *(level)*
UM39 IMMEDIATELY DESCEND TO *(altitude)* Note: *This message element is equivalent to EMGU-2 plus LVLU-9 in Doc 4444*	N/A	W/U	LVLU-9	Instruction that a descent to the specified level or vertical range is to commence and once reached is to be maintained.	DESCEND TO *(level)*
UM135 CONFIRM ASSIGNED ALTITUDE Note: *NE response attribute*	N/A	Y	LVLU-27	Request to confirm the assigned level.	CONFIRM ASSIGNED LEVEL
UM177 AT PILOTS DISCRETION	N/A	NE	See Note	Request to confirm the assigned level.	

Note: *ICAO Document 10037, Global Operational Data Link (GOLD) Manual does not include this in its tables.*

TABLE 5–3–5
LEVEL DOWNLINK MESSAGE ELEMENTS (LVLD)

CPDLC Message Sets			Operational Definition in PANS-ATM (Doc 4444)		
FANS 1/A	**ATN B1**	**Response**	**Message Element Identifier**	**Message Element Intended Use**	**Format for Message Element Display**
DM6 REQUEST (*altitude*) Note: Used for a single level	DM6 REQUEST (*level*)	Y	LVLD-1	Request to fly at the specified level or vertical range.	REQUEST (*level*)
DM9 REQUEST CLIMB TO (*altitude*)	DM9 REQUEST CLIMB TO (*level*)	Y	LVLD-2	Request for a climb to the specified level or vertical range.	REQUEST CLIMB TO (*level*)
DM10 REQUEST DESCENT TO (*altitude*)	DM10 REQUEST DESCENT TO (*level*)	Y	LVLD-3	Request for a descent to the specified level or vertical range.	REQUEST DESCENT TO (*level*)
DM38 ASSIGNED LEVEL (*altitude*) Note: Used for a single level	DM38 ASSIGNED LEVEL (*level*)	N	LVLD-11	Confirmation that the assigned level or vertical range is the specified level or vertical range.	ASSIGNED LEVEL (*level*)
DM61 DESCENDING TO (*altitude*) Note: Urgent alert attribute	N/A	N	LVLD-14	Report indicating descending to the specified level.	DESCENDING TO (*level single*)

TABLE 5–3–6
CROSSING CONSTRAINT MESSAGE ELEMENTS (CSTU)

CPDLC Message Sets			Operational Definition in PANS-ATM (Doc 4444)		
FANS 1/A	**ATN B1**	**Response**	**Message Element Identifier**	**Message Element Intended Use**	**Format for Message Element Display**
UM49 CROSS (*position*) AT AND MAINTAIN (*altitude*) Note 1: A vertical range cannot be provided. Note 2: This message element is equivalent to CSTU-1 plus LVLU-5 in Doc 4444	N/A	W/U	CSTU-1	Instruction that the specified position is to be crossed at the specified level or within the specified vertical range.	CROSS (*position*) AT (*level*)
UM61 CROSS (*position*) AT AND MAINTAIN (*altitude*) AT (*speed*) Note 1: A vertical range cannot be provided. Note 2: This message element is equivalent to CSTU-14 plus LVLU-5 in Doc 4444	UM61 CROSS (*position*) AT AND MAINTAIN (*level*) AT (*speed*)	W/U	CSTU-14	Instruction that the specified position is to be crossed at the level or within the vertical range, as specified, and at the specified speed.	CROSS (*position*) AT (*level*) AT (*speed*)

TABLE 5–3–7
AIR TRAFFIC ADVISORY UPLINK MESSAGE ELEMENTS

CPDLC Message Sets			Operational Definition in PANS-ATM (Doc 4444)		
FANS 1/A	**ATN B1**	**Response**	**Message Element Identifier**	**Message Element Intended Use**	**Format for Message Element Display**
UM154 RADAR SERVICES TERMINATED	N/A	R	ADVU-2	*Advisory that the ATS surveillance service is terminated.*	SURVEILLANCE SERVICE TERMINATED

TABLE 5–3–8
VOICE COMMUNICATIONS UPLINK MESSAGE ELEMENTS (COMU)

CPDLC Message Sets			Operational Definition in PANS-ATM (Doc 4444)		
FANS 1/A	**ATN B1**	**Response**	**Message Element Identifier**	**Message Element Intended Use**	**Format for Message Element Display**
UM117 CONTACT (*ICAO unit name*) (*frequency*)	UM117 CONTACT (*unit name*) (*frequency*)	W/U	COMU-1	Instruction to establish voice contact with the specified ATS unit on the specified frequency.	CONTACT (*unit name*) (*frequency*)
UM120 MONITOR (*ICAO unit name*) (*frequency*)	UM120 MONITOR (*unit name*) (*frequency*)	W/U	COMU-5	Instruction to monitor the specified ATS unit on the specified frequency. The flight crew is not required to establish voice contact on the frequency.	MONITOR (*unit name*) (*frequency*)

TABLE 5–3–9
VOICE COMMUNICATIONS DOWNLINK MESSAGE ELEMENTS (COMD)

CPDLC Message Sets			Operational Definition in PANS-ATM (Doc 4444)		
FANS 1/A	**ATN B1**	**Response**	**Message Element Identifier**	**Message Element Intended Use**	**Format for Message Element Display**
DM20 REQUEST VOICE CONTACT *Note: Used when a frequency is not required*	N/A	Y	COMD-1	Request for voice contact on the specified frequency.	REQUEST VOICE CONTACT (*frequency*)

TABLE 5–3–10
EMERGENCY/URGENCY UPLINK MESSAGE ELEMENTS (EMGU)

CPDLC Message Sets			Operational Definition in PANS-ATM (Doc 4444)		
FANS 1/A	**ATN B1**	**Response**	**Message Element Identifier**	**Message Element Intended Use**	**Format for Message Element Display**
Used in combination with LVLU-6 and LVLU-9, which is implemented in FANS 1/A as: UM38 IMMEDIATELY CLIMB TO (*altitude*) UM39 IMMEDIATELY DESCEND TO (*altitude*)	N/A	N	EMGU-2	Instruction to immediately comply with the associated instruction to avoid imminent situation.	Immediately

TABLE 5–3–11
EMERGENCY/URGENCY DOWNLINK MESSAGE ELEMENTS (EMGD)

CPDLC Message Sets			Operational Definition in PANS-ATM (Doc 4444)		
FANS 1/A	ATN B1	Response	Message Element Identifier	Message Element Intended Use	Format for Message Element Display
DM55 PAN PAN PAN Note: N response attribute	N/A	Y	EMGD-1	Indication of an urgent situation.	PAN PAN PAN
DM56 MAYDAY MAYDAY MAYDAY Note: N response attribute	N/A	Y	EMGD-2	Indication of an emergency situation.	MAYDAY MAYDAY MAYDAY
DM57 (remaining fuel) OF FUEL REMAINING AND (remaining souls) SOULS ON BOARD Note: N response attribute	N/A	Y	EMGD-3	Report indicating fuel remaining (time) and number of persons on board.	(remaining fuel) ENDURANCE AND (persons on board) PERSONS ON BOARD
DM58 CANCEL EMERGENCY Note: N response attribute	N/A	Y	EMGD-4	Indication that the emergency situation is cancelled.	CANCEL EMERGENCY

TABLE 5–3–12
STANDARD RESPONSE UPLINK MESSAGE ELEMENTS (RSPU)

CPDLC Message Sets			Operational Definition in PANS-ATM (Doc 4444)		
FANS 1/A	ATN B1	Response	Message Element Identifier	Message Element Intended Use	Format for Message Element Display
UM0 UNABLE	UM0 UNABLE	N	RSPU-1	Indication that the message cannot be complied with.	UNABLE
UM1 STANDBY	UM1 STANDBY	N	RSPU-2	Indication that the message will be responded to shortly.	STANDBY
UM3 ROGER	UM3 ROGER	N	RSPU-4	Indication that the message is received.	ROGER

TABLE 5–3–13
STANDARD RESPONSE DOWNLINK MESSAGE ELEMENTS (RSPD)

CPDLC Message Sets			Operational Definition in PANS-ATM (Doc 4444)		
FANS 1/A	ATN B1	Response	Message Element Identifier	Message Element Intended Use	Format for Message Element Display
DM0 WILCO	DM0 WILCO	N	RSPD-1	Indication that the instruction is understood and will be complied with.	WILCO
DM1 UNABLE	DM1 UNABLE	N	RSPD-2	Indication that the message cannot be complied with.	UNABLE
DM2 STANDBY	DM2 STANDBY	N	RSPU-3	Indication that the message will be responded to shortly.	STANDBY
DM3 ROGER Note: ROGER is the only correct response to an uplink free text message.	DM3 ROGER	N	RSPU-4	Indication that the message is received.	ROGER

TABLE 5–3–14
SUPPLEMENTAL UPLINK MESSAGE ELEMENTS (SUPU)

CPDLC Message Sets			Operational Definition in PANS-ATM (Doc 4444)		
FANS 1/A	**ATN B1**	**Response**	**Message Element Identifier**	**Message Element Intended Use**	**Format for Message Element Display**
UM166 DUE TO TRAFFIC	N/A	N	SUPU-2	Indication that the associated message is issued due to the specified reason.	DUE TO (*specified reason uplink*)
UM167 DUE TO AIRSPACE RESTRICTION					

TABLE 5–3–15
SUPPLEMENTAL DOWNLINK MESSAGE ELEMENTS (SUPD)

CPDLC Message Sets			Operational Definition in PANS-ATM (Doc 4444)		
FANS 1/A	**ATN B1**	**Response**	**Message Element Identifier**	**Message Element Intended Use**	**Format for Message Element Display**
DM65 DUE TO WEATHER	DM65 DUE TO WEATHER	N	SUPD-1	Indication that the associated message is issued due to the specified reason.	DUE TO (*specified reason downlink*)
DM66 DUE TO AIRCRAFT PER-FORMANCE	DM66 DUE TO AIRCRAFT PER-FORMANCE				

TABLE 5–3–16
FREE TEXT UPLINK MESSAGE ELEMENTS (TXTU)

CPDLC Message Sets			Operational Definition in PANS-ATM (Doc 4444)		
FANS 1/A	**ATN B1**	**Response**	**Message Element Identifier**	**Message Element Intended Use**	**Format for Message Element Display**
UM169 (*free text*)	UM203 (*free text*)	R	TXTU-1		(*free text*) Note: M alert attribute
UM169 (*free text*) CPDLC NOT IN USE UNTIL FURTHER NOTIFICATION	N/A	R	See Note		(*free text*)
UM169 (*free text*) "[facility designation]" LOCAL ALTIMETER (for Altimeter Reporting Station)	N/A	R	See Note		(*free text*)
UM169 (*free text*) "[facility designation]" LOCAL ALTIMETER MORE THAN ONE HOUR OLD	N/A	R	See Note		(*free text*)
UM169 (*free text*) DUE TO WEATHER	N/A	R	See Note		(*free text*)
UM169 (*free text*) REST OF ROUTE UNCHANGED	N/A	R	See Note		(*free text*)
UM169 (*free text*) TRAFFIC FLOW MANAGEMENT REROUTE	N/A	R	See Note		(*free text*)

Note: *These are FAA scripted free text messages with no GOLD equivalent.*

TABLE 5-3-17
FREE TEXT DOWNLINK MESSAGE ELEMENTS (TXTD)

CPDLC Message Sets			Operational Definition in PANS-ATM (Doc 4444)		
FANS 1/A	ATN B1	Response	Message Element Identifier	Message Element Intended Use	Format for Message Element Display
DM68 (*free text*) *Note 1: Urgency or Distress Alr (M)* *Note 2: Selecting any of the emergency message elements will result in this message element being enabled for the flight crew to include in the emergency message at their discretion.*	N/A	Y	TXTD-1		(*free text*) *Note: M alert attribute*

TABLE 5-3-18
SYSTEM MANAGEMENT UPLINK MESSAGE ELEMENTS (SYSU)

CPDLC Message Sets			Operational Definition in PANS-ATM (Doc 4444)		
FANS 1/A	ATN B1	Response	Message Element Identifier	Message Element Intended Use	Format for Message Element Display
UM159 ERROR (*error information*)	UM159 ERROR (*error information*)	N	SYSU-1	System-generated notification of an error.	ERROR (*error information*)
UM160 NEXT DATA AUTHORITY (*ICAO facility designation*) *Note: The facility designation is required*	UM160 NEXT DATA AUTHORITY (*facility*) *Note: Facility parameter can specify a facility designation or no facility*	N	SYSU-2	System-generated notification of the next data authority or the cancellation thereof.	NEXT DATA AUTHORITY (*facility designation [O]*)

TABLE 5-3-19
SYSTEM MANAGEMENT DOWNLINK MESSAGE ELEMENTS (SYSD)

CPDLC Message Sets			Operational Definition in PANS-ATM (Doc 4444)		
FANS 1/A	ATN B1	Response	Message Element Identifier	Message Element Intended Use	Format for Message Element Display
DM62 ERROR (*error information*)	DM62 ERROR (*error information*)	N	SYSD-1	System-generated notification of an error.	SYSD-1
DM63 NOT CURRENT DATA AUTHORITY	DM63 NOT CURRENT DATA AUTHORITY	N	SYSD-3	System-generated rejection of any CPDLC message sent from a ground facility that is not the current data authority.	SYSD-3
DM64 (*ICAO facility designation*) *Note: Use by FANS 1/A aircraft in B1 environments*	DM107 NOT AUTHORIZED NEXT DATA AUTHORITY *Note: CDA and NDA cannot be provided*	N	SYSD-5	System-generated notification that the ground system is not designated as the next data authority (NDA), indicating the identity of the current data authority (CDA). Identity of the NDA, if any, is also reported.	SYSD-5

Ch 5

b. ATC Frequency Change Procedures.

1. The following phraseology will be used by controllers to effect a frequency change:

Example: (Aircraft identification) contact (facility name or location name and terminal function) (frequency) at (time, fix, or altitude).

Note: Pilots are expected to maintain a listening watch on the transferring controller's frequency until the time, fix, or altitude specified. ATC will omit frequency change restrictions whenever pilot compliance is expected upon receipt.

2. The following phraseology should be utilized by pilots for establishing contact with the designated facility:

(a) When operating in a radar environment: On initial contact, the pilot should inform the controller of the aircraft's assigned altitude preceded by the words "level," or "climbing to," or "descending to," as appropriate; and the aircraft's present vacating altitude, if applicable.

Example 1: (Name) center, (aircraft identification), level (altitude or flight level).

Example 2: (Name) center, (aircraft identification), leaving (exact altitude or flight level), climbing to or descending to (altitude of flight level).

Note: Exact altitude or flight level means to the nearest 100 foot increment. Exact altitude or flight level reports on initial contact provide ATC with information required prior to using Mode C altitude information for separation purposes.

(b) When operating in a nonradar environment:

(1) On initial contact, the pilot should inform the controller of the aircraft's present position, altitude and time estimate for the next reporting point.

Example: (Name) CENTER, (aircraft identification), (position), (altitude), ESTIMATING (reporting point) AT (time).

(2) After initial contact, when a position report will be made, the pilot should give the controller a complete position report.

Example: (Name) CENTER, (aircraft identification), (position), (time), (altitude), (type of flight plan), (ETA and name of next reporting point), (the name of the next succeeding reporting point), AND (remarks).

Reference: AIM, ¶5-3-2, Position Reporting.

3. At times controllers will ask pilots to verify that they are at a particular altitude. The phraseology used will be: "VERIFY AT (altitude)." In climbing or descending situations, controllers may ask pilots to "*VERIFY ASSIGNED ALTITUDE AS (altitude)*." Pilots should confirm that they are at the altitude stated by the controller or that the assigned altitude is correct as stated. If this is not the case, they should inform the controller of the actual altitude being maintained or the different assigned altitude.

Caution: Pilots should not take action to change their actual altitude or different assigned altitude to the altitude stated in the controllers verification request unless the controller specifically authorizes a change.

c. ARTCC Radio Frequency Outage. ARTCCs normally have at least one back-up radio receiver and transmitter system for each frequency, which can usually be placed into service quickly with little or no disruption of ATC service. Occasionally, technical problems may cause a delay but switchover seldom takes more than 60 seconds. When it appears that the outage will not be quickly remedied, the ARTCC will usually request a nearby aircraft, if there is one, to switch to the affected frequency to broadcast communications instructions. It is important, therefore, that the pilot wait at least 1 minute before deciding that the ARTCC has actually experienced a radio frequency failure. When such an outage does occur, the pilot should, if workload and equipment capability permit, maintain a listening watch on the affected frequency while attempting to comply with the following recommended communications procedures:

1. If two-way communications cannot be established with the ARTCC after changing frequencies, a pilot should attempt to recontact the transferring controller for the assignment of an alternative frequency or other instructions.

2. When an ARTCC radio frequency failure occurs after two-way communications have been established, the pilot should attempt to reestablish contact with the center on any other known ARTCC frequency, preferably that of the next responsible sector when practicable, and ask for instructions. However, when the next normal frequency change along the route is known to involve another ATC facility, the pilot should contact that facility, if feasible, for instructions. If communications cannot be reestablished by either method, the pilot is expected to request communications instructions from the FSS appropriate to the route of flight.

Note: The exchange of information between an aircraft and an ARTCC through an FSS is quicker than relay via company radio because the FSS has direct interphone lines to the responsible ARTCC sector. Accordingly, when circumstances dictate a choice between the two, during an ARTCC frequency outage, relay via FSS radio is recommended.

d. Oakland Oceanic FIR. The use of CPDLC and ADS-C in the Oakland Oceanic FIR (KZAK) is only permitted by Inmarsat and Iridium customers. All other forms of data link connectivity are not authorized. Users must ensure that the proper data link code is filed in Item 10a of the ICAO FPL in order to indicate which satellite medium(s) the aircraft is equipped with. The identifier for Inmarsat is J5 and the identifier for Iridium is J7. If J5 or J7 is not included in the ICAO FPL, then the LOGON will be rejected by KZAK and the aircraft will not be able to connect.

e. New York Oceanic FIR. The use of CPDLC and ADS-C in the New York Oceanic FIR (KZWY) is only permitted by Inmarsat and Iridium customers. All other forms of data link connectivity are not authorized. Users must ensure that the proper data link code is filed in Item 10a of the ICAO FPL in order to indicate which satellite medium(s) the aircraft is equipped with. The identifier for Inmarsat is J5 and the identifier for Iridium is J7. If J5 or J7 is not included in the ICAO FPL, then the LOGON will be rejected by KZWY and the aircraft will not be able to connect.

5-3-2 Position Reporting

The safety and effectiveness of traffic control depends to a large extent on accurate position reporting. In order to provide the proper separation and expedite aircraft movements, ATC must be able to make accurate estimates of the progress of every aircraft operating on an IFR flight plan.

a. Position Identification.

1. When a position report is to be made passing a VOR radio facility, the time reported should be the time at which the first complete reversal of the "to/from" indicator is accomplished.

2. When a position report is made passing a facility by means of an airborne ADF, the time reported should be the time at which the indicator makes a complete reversal.

3. When an aural or a light panel indication is used to determine the time passing a reporting point, such as a fan marker, Z marker, cone of silence or intersection of range courses, the time should be noted when the signal is first received and again when it ceases. The mean of these two times should then be taken as the actual time over the fix.

4. If a position is given with respect to distance and direction from a reporting point, the distance and direction should be computed as accurately as possible.

5. Except for terminal area transition purposes, position reports or navigation with reference to aids not established for use in the structure in which flight is being conducted will not normally be required by ATC.

b. Position Reporting Points. CFRs require pilots to maintain a listening watch on the appropriate frequency and, unless operating under the provisions of subparagraph c, to furnish position reports passing certain reporting points. Reporting points are indicated by symbols on en route charts. The designated compulsory reporting point symbol is a solid triangle ▲ and the "on request" reporting point symbol is the open triangle △. Reports passing an "on request" reporting point are only necessary when requested by ATC.

c. Position Reporting Requirements.

1. Flights Along Airways or Routes. A position report is required by all flights regardless of altitude, including those operating in accordance with an ATC clearance specifying "*VFR-on-Top*," over each designated compulsory reporting point along the route being flown.

2. Flights Along a Direct Route. Regardless of the altitude or flight level being flown, including flights operating in accordance with an ATC clearance specifying "*VFR-on-Top*," pilots must report over each reporting point used in the flight plan to define the route of flight.

3. Flights in a Radar Environment. When informed by ATC that their aircraft are in "Radar Contact," pilots should discontinue position reports over designated reporting points. They should resume normal position reporting when ATC advises *"RADAR CONTACT LOST"* or *"RADAR SERVICE TERMINATED."*

4. Flights in an Oceanic (Nonradar) Environment. Pilots must report over each point used in the flight plan to define the route of flight, even if the point is depicted on aeronautical charts as an "on request" (non-compulsory) reporting point. For aircraft providing automatic position reporting via an Automatic Dependent Surveillance–Contract (ADS-C) logon, pilots should discontinue voice position reports.

Note: ATC will inform pilots that they are in "radar contact":

(a) when their aircraft is initially identified in the ATC system; and

(b) when radar identification is reestablished after radar service has been terminated or radar contact lost.

Subsequent to being advised that the controller has established radar contact, this fact will not be repeated to the pilot when handed off to another controller. At times, the aircraft identity will be confirmed by the receiving controller; however, this should not be construed to mean that radar contact has been lost. The identity of transponder equipped aircraft will be confirmed by asking the pilot to "ident," "squawk standby," or to change codes. Aircraft without transponders will be advised of their position to confirm identity. In

this case, the pilot is expected to advise the controller if in disagreement with the position given. Any pilot who cannot confirm the accuracy of the position given because of not being tuned to the NAVAID referenced by the controller, should ask for another radar position relative to the tuned in NAVAID.

d. Position Report Items:

1. Position reports should include the following items:

(a) Identification;

(b) Position;

(c) Time;

(d) Altitude or flight level (include actual altitude or flight level when operating on a clearance specifying VFR-on-top);

(e) Type of flight plan (not required in IFR position reports made directly to ARTCCs or approach control);

(f) ETA and name of next reporting point;

(g) The name only of the next succeeding reporting point along the route of flight; and

(h) Pertinent remarks.

5-3-3 Additional Reports

a. The following reports should be made to ATC or FSS facilities without a specific ATC request:

1. *At all times.*

(a) When vacating any previously assigned altitude or flight level for a newly assigned altitude or flight level.

(b) When an altitude change will be made if operating on a clearance specifying VFR-on-top.

(c) When unable to climb/descend at a rate of at least 500 feet per minute.

(d) When approach has been missed. (Request clearance for specific action; i.e., to alternative airport, another approach, etc.)

(e) Change in the average true airspeed (at cruising altitude) when it varies by 5 percent or 10 knots (whichever is greater) from that filed in the flight plan.

(f) The time and altitude or flight level upon reaching a holding fix or point to which cleared.

(g) When leaving any assigned holding fix or point.

Note: The reports in subparagraphs (f) and (g) may be omitted by pilots of aircraft involved in instrument training at military terminal area facilities when radar service is being provided.

(h) Any loss, in controlled airspace, of VOR, TACAN, ADF, low frequency navigation receiver capability, GPS anomalies while using installed IFR-certified GPS/GNSS receivers, complete or partial loss of ILS receiver capability or impairment of air/ground communications capability. Reports should include aircraft identification, equipment affected, degree to which the capability to operate under IFR in the ATC system is impaired, and the nature and extent of assistance desired from ATC.

Note 1: Other equipment installed in an aircraft may effectively impair safety and/or the ability to operate under IFR. If such equipment (e.g., airborne weather radar) malfunctions and in the pilot's judgment either safety or IFR capabilities are affected, reports should be made as above.

Note 2: When reporting GPS anomalies, include the location and altitude of the anomaly. Be specific when describing the location and include duration of the anomaly if necessary.

(i) Any information relating to the safety of flight.

2. When not in radar contact.

(a) When leaving final approach fix inbound on final approach (nonprecision approach) or when leaving the outer marker or fix used in lieu of the outer marker inbound on final approach (precision approach).

(b) A corrected estimate at anytime it becomes apparent that an estimate as previously submitted is in error in excess of 2 minutes. For flights in the North Atlantic (NAT), a revised estimate is required if the error is 3 minutes or more.

b. Pilots encountering weather conditions which have not been forecast, or hazardous conditions which have been forecast, are expected to forward a report of such weather to ATC.

Reference: AIM, ¶7-1-18, Pilot Weather Reports (PIREPs); 14 CFR §91.183(B) and (C).

5-3-4 Airways and Route Systems

a. Three fixed route systems are established for air navigation purposes. They are the Federal airway system (consisting of VOR and L/MF routes), the jet route system, and the RNAV route system. To the extent possible, these route systems are aligned in an overlying manner to facilitate transition between each.

1. The VOR and L/MF (nondirectional radio beacons) Airway System consists of airways designated from 1,200 feet above the surface (or in some instances higher) up to but not including 18,000 feet MSL. These airways are depicted on IFR Enroute Low Altitude Charts.

Note: The altitude limits of a victor airway should not be exceeded except to effect transition within or between route structures.

(a) Except in Alaska, the VOR airways are: predicated solely on VOR or VORTAC navigation aids; depicted in black on aeronautical charts; and identified by a "V" (Victor) followed by the airway number (for example, V12).

Note: Segments of VOR airways in Alaska are based on L/MF navigation aids and charted in brown instead of black on en route charts.

(1) A segment of an airway which is common to two or more routes carries the numbers of all the airways which coincide for that segment. When such is the case, pilots filing a flight plan need to indicate only that airway number for the route filed.

Note: A pilot who intends to make an airway flight, using VOR facilities, will simply specify the appropriate "victor" airway(s) in the flight plan. For example, if a flight is to be made from Chicago to New Orleans at 8,000 feet, using omniranges only, the route may be indicated as "departing from Chicago–Midway, cruising 8,000 feet via Victor 9 to Moisant International." If flight is to be conducted in part by means of L/MF navigation aids and in part on omniranges, specifications of the appropriate airways in the flight plan will indicate which types of facilities will be used along the described routes, and, for IFR flight, permit ATC to issue a traffic clearance accordingly. A route may also be described by specifying the station over which the flight will pass, but in this case since many VORs and L/MF aids have the same name, the pilot must be careful to indicate which aid will be used at a particular location. This will be indicated in the route of flight portion of the flight plan by specifying the type of facility to be used after the location name in the following manner: Newark L/MF, Allentown VOR.

(2) With respect to position reporting, reporting points are designated for VOR Airway Systems. Flights using Victor Airways will report over these points unless advised otherwise by ATC.

(b) The L/MF airways (colored airways) are predicated solely on L/MF navigation aids and are depicted in brown on aeronautical charts and are identified by color name and number (e.g., Amber One). Green and Red airways are plotted east and west. Amber and Blue airways are plotted north and south.

(c) The use of TSO-C145 (as revised) or TSO-C146 (as revised) GPS/WAAS navigation systems is allowed in Alaska as the only means of navigation on published air traffic service (ATS) routes, including those Victor, T-Routes, and colored airway segments designated with a second minimum en route altitude (MEA) depicted in blue and followed by the letter G at those lower altitudes. The altitudes so depicted are below the minimum reception altitude (MRA) of the land-based navigation facility defining the route segment, and guarantee standard en route obstacle clearance and two-way communications. Air carrier operators requiring operations specifications are authorized to conduct operations on those routes in accordance with FAA operations specifications.

2. The jet route system consists of jet routes established from 18,000 feet MSL to FL450 inclusive.

(a) These routes are depicted on Enroute High Altitude Charts. Jet routes are depicted in black on aeronautical charts and are identified by a "J" (Jet) followed by the airway number (e.g., J12). Jet routes, as VOR airways, are predicated solely on VOR or VORTAC navigation facilities (except in Alaska).

Note: Segments of jet routes in Alaska are based on L/MF navigation aids and are charted in brown color instead of black on en route charts.

(b) With respect to position reporting, reporting points are designated for jet route systems. Flights using jet routes will report over these points unless otherwise advised by ATC.

3. Area Navigation (RNAV) Routes.

(a) Published RNAV routes, including Q-routes, T-routes, and Y-routes, can be flight planned for use by aircraft with RNAV capability, subject to any limitations or requirements noted on en route charts, in applicable Advisory Circulars, NOTAMs, etc. RNAV routes are normally depicted in blue on aeronautical charts and are identified by the letter "Q," "T," or "Y" followed by the airway number (for example, Q13, T205, and Y280). Published RNAV routes are RNAV 2 except when specifically charted as RNAV 1. Unless otherwise specified, these routes require system performance currently met by GPS, GPS/WAAS, or DME/DME/IRU RNAV systems that satisfy the criteria discussed in AC 90-100A, U.S. Terminal and En Route Area Navigation (RNAV) Operations.

(1) Q-routes are available for use by RNAV equipped aircraft between 18,000 feet MSL and FL 450 inclusive. Q-routes are depicted on Enroute High Altitude Charts.

Note: Aircraft in Alaska may only operate on GNSS Q-routes with GPS (TSO-C129 (as revised) or TSO-C196 (as revised)) equipment while the aircraft remains in Air Traffic Control (ATC) radar surveillance or with GPS/WAAS which does not require ATC radar surveillance.

(2) T-routes are available for use by GPS or GPS/WAAS equipped aircraft from 1,200 feet above the surface (or in some instances higher) up to but not including 18,000 feet MSL. T-routes are depicted on Enroute Low Altitude Charts.

Note: Aircraft in Alaska may only operate on GNSS T-routes with GPS/WAAS (TSO-C145 (as revised) or TSO-C146 (as revised)) equipment.

(3) Y-routes generally run in U.S. off-shore airspace, however operators can find some Y-routes over southern Florida. Pilots must use GPS for navigation and meet RNAV 2 performance requirements for all flights on Y-routes. Operators can find additional Y-route requirements in the U.S. Aeronautical Information Publication (AIP), ENR 7.10, available on the FAA website.

(b) Unpublished RNAV routes are direct routes, based on area navigation capability, between waypoints defined in terms of latitude/longitude coordinates, degree–distance fixes, or offsets from established routes/airways at a specified distance and direction. Radar monitoring by ATC is required on all unpublished RNAV routes, except for GNSS-equipped aircraft cleared via filed published waypoints recallable from the aircraft's navigation database.

(c) Magnetic Reference Bearing (MRB) is the published bearing between two waypoints on an RNAV/GPS/GNSS route. The MRB is calculated by applying magnetic variation at the waypoint to the calculated true course between two waypoints. The MRB enhances situational awareness by indicating a reference bearing (no-wind heading) that a pilot should see on the compass/HSI/RMI etc., when turning prior to/over a waypoint en route to another waypoint. Pilots should use this bearing as a reference only, because their RNAV/GPS/GNSS navigation system will fly the true course between the waypoints.

b. Operation above FL450 may be conducted on a point-to-point basis. Navigational guidance is provided on an area basis utilizing those facilities depicted on the enroute high altitude charts.

c. Radar Vectors. Controllers may vector aircraft within controlled airspace for separation purposes, noise abatement considerations, when an operational advantage will be realized by the pilot or the controller, or when requested by the pilot. Vectors outside of controlled airspace will be provided only on pilot request. Pilots will be advised as to what the vector is to achieve when the vector is controller initiated and will take the aircraft off a previously assigned nonradar route. To the extent possible, aircraft operating on RNAV routes will be allowed to remain on their own navigation.

d. When flying in Canadian airspace, pilots are cautioned to review Canadian Air Regulations.

1. Special attention should be given to the parts which differ from U.S. CFRs.

(a) The Canadian Airways Class B airspace restriction is an example. Class B airspace is all controlled low level airspace above 12,500 feet MSL or the MEA, whichever is higher, within which only IFR and controlled VFR flights are permitted. (Low level airspace means an airspace designated and defined as such in the Designated Airspace Handbook.)

(b) Unless issued a VFR flight clearance by ATC, regardless of the weather conditions or the height of the terrain, no person may operate an aircraft under VMC within Class B airspace.

(c) The requirement for entry into Class B airspace is a student pilot permit (under the guidance or control of a flight instructor).

(d) VFR flight requires visual contact with the ground or water at all times.

2. Segments of VOR airways and high level routes in Canada are based on L/MF navigation aids and are charted in brown color instead of blue on en route charts.

5–3–5 Airway or Route Course Changes

a. Pilots of aircraft are required to adhere to airways or routes being flown. Special attention must be given to this requirement during course changes. Each course change consists of variables that make the technique applicable in each case a matter only the pilot can resolve. Some variables which must be considered are turn radius, wind effect, airspeed, degree of turn, and cockpit instrumentation. An early turn, as illustrated below, is one method of adhering to airways or routes. The use of any available cockpit instrumentation, such as Distance Measuring Equipment, may be used by the pilot to lead the turn when making course changes. This is consistent with the intent of 14 CFR Section 91.181, which requires pilots to operate along the centerline of an airway and along the direct course between navigational aids or fixes.

b. Turns which begin at or after fix passage may exceed airway or route boundaries. Figure 5-3-1 contains an example flight track depicting this, together with an example of an early turn.

c. Without such actions as leading a turn, aircraft operating in excess of 290 knots true air speed (TAS) can exceed the normal airway or route boundaries depending on the amount of course change required, wind direction and velocity, the character of the turn fix (DME, overhead navigation aid, or intersection), and the pilot's technique in making a course change. For example, a flight operating at 17,000 feet MSL with a TAS of 400 knots, a 25 degree bank, and a course change of more than 40 degrees would exceed the width of the airway or route; i.e., 4 nautical miles each side of centerline. However, in the airspace below 18,000 feet MSL, operations in excess of 290 knots TAS are not prevalent and the provision of additional IFR separation in all course change situations for the occasional aircraft making a turn in excess of 290 knots TAS creates an unacceptable waste of airspace and imposes a penalty upon the preponderance of traffic which operate at low speeds. Consequently, the FAA expects pilots to lead turns and take other actions

they consider necessary during course changes to adhere as closely as possible to the airways or route being flown.

FIGURE 5–3–1
Adhering to Airways or Routes

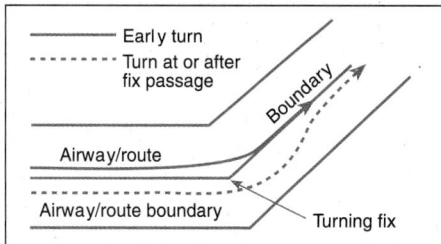

5–3–6 Changeover Points (COPs)

a. COPs are prescribed for Federal airways, jet routes, area navigation routes, or other direct routes for which an MEA is designated under 14 CFR Part 95. The COP is a point along the route or airway segment between two adjacent navigation facilities or waypoints where changeover in navigation guidance should occur. At this point, the pilot should change navigation receiver frequency from the station behind the aircraft to the station ahead.

b. The COP is normally located midway between the navigation facilities for straight route segments, or at the intersection of radials or courses forming a dogleg in the case of dogleg route segments. When the COP is **not** located at the midway point, aeronautical charts will depict the COP location and give the mileage to the radio aids.

c. COPs are established for the purpose of preventing loss of navigation guidance, to prevent frequency interference from other facilities, and to prevent use of different facilities by different aircraft in the same airspace. Pilots are urged to observe COPs to the fullest extent.

5–3–7 Minimum Turning Altitude (MTA)

Due to increased airspeeds at 10,000 ft MSL or above, the published minimum enroute altitude (MEA) may not be sufficient for obstacle clearance when a turn is required over a fix, NAVAID, or waypoint. In these instances, an expanded area in the vicinity of the turn point is examined to determine whether the published MEA is sufficient for obstacle clearance. In some locations (normally mountainous), terrain/obstacles in the expanded search area may necessitate a higher minimum altitude while conducting the turning maneuver. Turning fixes requiring a higher

minimum turning altitude (MTA) will be denoted on government charts by the minimum crossing altitude (MCA) icon ("x" flag) and an accompanying note describing the MTA restriction. An MTA restriction will normally consist of the air traffic service (ATS) route leading to the turn point, the ATS route leading from the turn point, and the required altitude; e.g., MTA V330 E TO V520 W 16000. When an MTA is applicable for the intended route of flight, pilots must ensure they are at or above the charted MTA not later than the turn point and maintain at or above the MTA until joining the centerline of the ATS route following the turn point. Once established on the centerline following the turning fix, the MEA/MOCA determines the minimum altitude available for assignment. An MTA may also preclude the use of a specific altitude or a range of altitudes during a turn. For example, the MTA may restrict the use of 10,000 through 11,000 ft MSL. In this case, any altitude greater than 11,000 ft MSL is unrestricted, as are altitudes less than 10,000 ft MSL provided MEA/MOCA requirements are satisfied.

5–3–8 Holding

a. Whenever an aircraft is cleared to a fix other than the destination airport and delay is expected, it is the responsibility of ATC to issue complete holding instructions (unless the pattern is charted), an EFC time and best estimate of any additional en route/terminal delay.

Note: *Only those holding patterns depicted on U.S. government or commercially produced (meeting FAA requirements) low/high altitude en route, and area or STAR charts should be used.*

b. If the holding pattern is charted and the controller doesn't issue complete holding instructions, the pilot is expected to hold as depicted on the appropriate chart. When the pattern is charted on the assigned procedure or route being flown, ATC may omit all holding instructions except the charted holding direction and the statement AS PUBLISHED; for example, HOLD EAST AS PUBLISHED. ATC must always issue complete holding instructions when pilots request them.

c. If no holding pattern is charted and holding instructions have not been issued, the pilot should ask ATC for holding instructions prior to reaching the fix. This procedure will eliminate the possibility of an aircraft entering a holding pattern other than that desired by ATC. If unable to obtain holding instructions prior to reaching the fix (due to frequency congestion, stuck microphone, etc.), then enter a standard pattern on the course on which the aircraft approached the fix and request further clearance as soon as possible. In this event, the altitude/flight level of the aircraft at the clearance limit will be protected so that separation will be provided as required.

Ch 5

d. When an aircraft is 3 minutes or less from a clearance limit and a clearance beyond the fix has not been received, the pilot is expected to start a speed reduction so that the aircraft will cross the fix, initially, at or below the maximum holding airspeed.

e. When no delay is expected, the controller should issue a clearance beyond the fix as soon as possible and, whenever possible, at least 5 minutes before the aircraft reaches the clearance limit.

f. Pilots should report to ATC the time and altitude/flight level at which the aircraft reaches the clearance limit and report leaving the clearance limit.

Note: In the event of two-way communications failure, pilots are required to comply with 14 CFR Section 91.185.

g. When holding at a VOR station, pilots should begin the turn to the outbound leg at the time of the first complete reversal of the to/from indicator.

h. Patterns at the most generally used holding fixes are depicted (charted) on U.S. Government or commercially produced (meeting FAA requirements) Low or High Altitude En Route, Area, Departure Procedure, and STAR Charts. Pilots are expected to hold in the pattern depicted unless specifically advised otherwise by ATC.

Note: Holding patterns that protect for a maximum holding airspeed other than the standard may be depicted by an icon, unless otherwise depicted. The icon is a standard holding pattern symbol (racetrack) with the airspeed restriction shown in the center. In other cases, the airspeed restriction will be depicted next to the standard holding pattern symbol.

Reference: AIM, ¶5-3-8j2, Holding.

i. An ATC clearance requiring an aircraft to hold at a fix where the pattern is not charted will include the following information: (See Figure 5-3-2.)

1. Direction of holding from the fix in terms of the eight cardinal compass points (i.e., N, NE, E, SE, etc.).

2. Holding fix (the fix may be omitted if included at the beginning of the transmission as the clearance limit).

3. Radial, course, bearing, airway or route on which the aircraft is to hold.

4. Leg length in miles if DME or RNAV is to be used (leg length will be specified in minutes on pilot request or if the controller considers it necessary).

5. Direction of turn if left turns are to be made, the pilot requests, or the controller considers it necessary.

6. Time to expect further clearance and any pertinent additional delay information.

FIGURE 5–3–2
Holding Patterns

Examples of Holding

Typical procedure on an ILS outer marker

Typical procedure at intersection of VOR radials

Typical procedure at DME fix

FIGURE 5–3–3
Holding Pattern Descriptive Terms

j. Holding pattern airspace protection is based on the following procedures.

1. Descriptive Terms.

(a) Standard Pattern. Right turns (See Figure 5-3-3.)

(b) Nonstandard Pattern. Left turns

2. Airspeeds.

(a) All aircraft may hold at the following altitudes and maximum holding airspeeds:

TABLE 5–3–20

Altitude (MSL)	Airspeed (KIAS)
MHA—6,000 feet	200
6,001 feet—14,000 feet	230
14,001 feet and above	265

Note: *These are the maximum indicated airspeeds applicable to all holding.*

(b) The following are exceptions to the maximum holding airspeeds:

(1) Holding patterns from 6,001' to 14,000' may be restricted to a maximum airspeed of 210 KIAS. This nonstandard pattern will be depicted by an icon.

(2) Holding patterns may be restricted to a maximum speed. The speed restriction is depicted in parenthesis inside the holding pattern on the chart: e.g., (175). The aircraft should be at or below the maximum speed prior to initially crossing the holding fix to avoid exiting the protected airspace. Pilots unable to comply with the maximum airspeed restriction should notify ATC.

(3) Holding patterns at USAF airfields only—310 KIAS maximum, unless otherwise depicted.

(4) Holding patterns at Navy fields only—230 KIAS maximum, unless otherwise depicted.

(5) All helicopter/power lift aircraft holding on a "COPTER" instrument procedure is predicated on a minimum airspeed of 90 KIAS unless charted otherwise.

(6) When a climb-in hold is specified by a published procedure (for example,

"Climb-in holding pattern to depart XYZ VORTAC at or above 10,000." or "All aircraft climb-in TRUCK holding pattern to cross TRUCK Int at or above 11,500 before proceeding on course."), additional obstacle protection area has been provided to allow for greater airspeeds in the climb for those aircraft requiring them. A maximum airspeed of 310 KIAS is permitted in Climb-in-holding, unless a maximum holding airspeed is published, in which case that maximum airspeed is applicable. The airspeed limitations in 14 CFR Section 91.117, Aircraft Speed, still apply.

(c) The following phraseology may be used by an ATCS to advise a pilot of the maximum holding airspeed for a holding pattern airspace area.

Phraseology:
(Aircraft identification) (holding instructions, when needed) maximum holding airspeed is (speed in knots).

3. Entry Procedures. Holding protected airspace is designed based in part on pilot compliance with the three recommended holding pattern entry procedures discussed below. Deviations from these recommendations, coupled with excessive airspeed crossing the holding fix, may in some cases result in the aircraft exceeding holding protected airspace. (See Figure 5-3-4.)

(a) Parallel Procedure. When approaching the holding fix from anywhere in sector (a), the parallel entry procedure would be to turn to a heading to parallel the holding course outbound on the nonholding side for one minute, turn in the direction of the holding pattern through more than 180 degrees, and return to the holding fix or intercept the holding course inbound.

(b) Teardrop Procedure. When approaching the holding fix from anywhere in sector (b), the teardrop entry procedure would be to fly to the fix, turn outbound to a heading for a 30 degree teardrop entry within the pattern (on the holding side) for a period of one minute, then turn in the direction of the holding pattern to intercept the inbound holding course.

FIGURE 5–3–4
Holding Pattern Entry Procedures

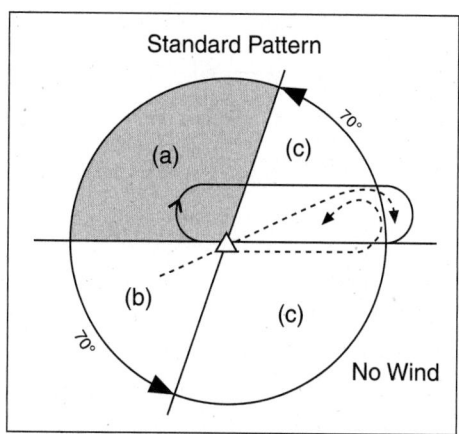

Standard Pattern

(a)

(c)

70°

(b)

(c)

70°

No Wind

(c) Direct Entry Procedure. When approaching the holding fix from anywhere in sector (c), the direct entry procedure would be to fly directly to the fix and turn to follow the holding pattern.

(d) While other entry procedures may enable the aircraft to enter the holding pattern and remain within protected airspace, the parallel, teardrop and direct entries are the procedures for entry and holding recommended by the FAA, and were derived as part of the development of the size and shape of the obstacle protection areas for holding.

(e) Nonstandard Holding Pattern. Fix end and outbound end turns are made to the left. Entry procedures to a nonstandard pattern are oriented in relation to the 70 degree line on the holding side just as in the standard pattern.

4. Timing.

 (a) Inbound Leg.

 (1) At or below 14,000 feet MSL: 1 minute.

 (2) Above 14,000 feet MSL: 1-1/2 minutes.

Note: The initial outbound leg should be flown for 1 minute or 1-1/2 minutes (appropriate to altitude). Timing for subsequent outbound legs should be adjusted, as necessary, to achieve proper inbound leg time. Pilots may use any navigational means available; i.e. DME, RNAV, etc., to ensure the appropriate inbound leg times.

 (b) Outbound leg timing begins over/abeam the fix, whichever occurs later. If the abeam position cannot be determined, start timing when turn to outbound is completed.

5. Distance Measuring Equipment (DME)/GPS Along-Track Distance (ATD). DME/GPS holding is subject to the same entry and holding procedures except that distances (nautical miles) are used in lieu of time values. The outbound course of the DME/GPS holding pattern is called the outbound leg of the pattern. The controller or the instrument approach procedure chart will specify the length of the outbound leg. The end of the outbound leg is determined by the DME or ATD readout. The holding fix on conventional procedures, or controller defined holding based on a conventional navigation aid with DME, is a specified course or radial and distances are from the DME station for both the inbound and outbound ends of the holding pattern. When flying published GPS overlay or stand alone procedures with distance specified, the holding fix will be a waypoint in the database and the end of the outbound leg will be determined by the ATD. Some GPS overlay and early stand alone procedures may have timing specified. (See Figures 5-3-5, 5-3-6 and 5-3-7.) See paragraph 1-1-18, *Global Positioning System (GPS)*, for requirements and restriction on using GPS for IFR operations.

FIGURE 5–3–5
Inbound Toward NAVAID

End outbound leg

NAVAID

15 NM

DME Fix / ATD Fix

10 NM

Note: When the inbound course is toward the NAVAID, the fix distance is 10 NM, and the leg length is 5 NM, then the end of the outbound leg will be reached when the DME reads 15 NM.

FIGURE 5–3–6
Inbound Leg Away from NAVAID

Note: *When the inbound course is away from the NAVAID and the fix distance is 28 NM, and the leg length is 8 NM, then the end of the outbound leg will be reached when the DME reads 20 NM.*

6. Use of RNAV Distance in lieu of DME Distance. Substitution of RNAV computed distance to or from a NAVAID in place of DME distance is permitted when holding. However, the actual holding location and pattern flown will be further from the NAVAID than designed due to the lack of slant range in the position solution (see Figure 5-3-7). This may result in a slight difference between RNAV distance readout in reference to the NAVAID and the DME readout, especially at higher altitudes. When used solely for DME substitution, the difference between RNAV distance to/from a fix and DME slant range distance can be considered negligible and no pilot action is required.

Reference: *AIM, ¶1-2-3, Use of Suitable Area Navigation (RNAV) Systems on Conventional Procedures and Routes.*

FIGURE 5–3–7
Difference Between DME Distance From
NAVAID & RNAV Computed Distance From NAVAID

7. Use of RNAV Guidance and Holding. RNAV systems, including multi-sensor Flight Management Systems (FMS) and stand-alone GPS receivers, may be used to furnish lateral guidance when executing a hold. The manner in which holding is implemented in an RNAV system varies widely between aircraft and RNAV system manufacturers. Holding pattern data may be extracted from the RNAV database for published holds or may be manually entered for ad-hoc ATC-assigned holds. Pilots are expected to be familiar with the capabilities and limitations of the specific RNAV system used for holding.

(a) All holding, including holding defined on an RNAV or RNP procedure, is based on the conventional NAVAID holding design criteria, including the holding protected airspace construction. There are differences between the holding entry and flight track assumed in conventional holding pattern design and the entry and track that may be flown when RNAV guidance is used to execute holding. Individually, these differences may not affect the ability of the aircraft to remain within holding pattern protected airspace. However, cumulatively, they can result in deviations sufficient to result in excursions up to limits of the holding pattern protected airspace, and in some circumstances beyond protected airspace. The following difference and considerations apply when an RNAV system furnishes the lateral guidance used to fly a holding pattern:

(1) Many systems use ground track angle instead of heading to select the entry method. While the holding pattern design allows a 5 degree tolerance, this may result in an unexpected entry when the winds induce a large drift angle.

(2) The holding protected airspace is based on the assumption that the aircraft will fly-over the holding fix upon initial entry. RNAV systems may execute a "fly-by" turn when approaching the holding fix prior to entry. A "fly-by" turn during a direct entry from the holding pattern side of holding course may result in excursions beyond protected airspace, especially as the intercept angle and ground speed increase.

(3) During holding, RNAV systems furnish lateral steering guidance using either a constant bank or constant radius to achieve the desired inbound and outbound turns. An aircraft's flight guidance system may use reduced bank angles for all turns including turns in holding, especially at higher altitudes, that may result in exceeding holding protected airspace. Use of a shallower bank angle will expand both the width and length of the aircraft track, especially as wind speed increases. If the flight guidance system's bank angle limit feature is pilot-selectable, a minimum 25 degree bank angle should be selected regardless of altitude unless aircraft operating limitations specify otherwise and the pilot advises ATC.

(4) Where a holding distance is published, the turn from the outbound leg begins at the published distance from the holding fix, thus establishing the design turn point required to remain within protected airspace. RNAV systems apply a database coded or pilot-entered leg distance as a maximum length of the *inbound* leg to the holding fix. The RNAV system then calculates a turn point from the outbound leg required to achieve this inbound leg length. This often results in an RNAV-calculated turn point on the outbound leg beyond the design turn point. (See Figure 5-3-8). With a strong headwind against the outbound leg, RNAV systems may fly up to and possibly beyond the limits of protected airspace before turning inbound. (See Figure 5-3-9.) This is especially true at higher altitudes where wind speeds are greater and ground speed results in a wider holding pattern.

FIGURE 5–3–8
RNAV Lateral Guidance and Holding—No Wind

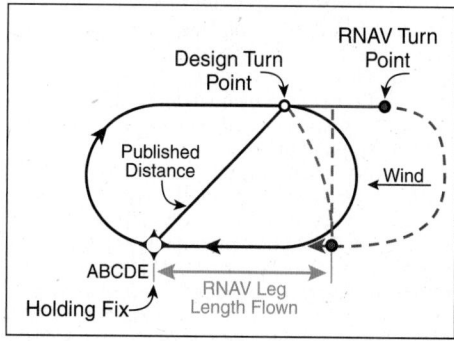

FIGURE 5–3–9
RNAV Lateral Guidance and Holding—Effect of Wind

(5) Some RNAV systems compute the holding pattern based on the aircraft's altitude and speed at a point prior to entering the hold. If the indicated airspeed is not reduced to comply with the maximum holding speed before this point, the computed pattern may exceed the protected airspace. Loading or executing a holding pattern may result in the speed and time limits applicable to the aircraft's current altitude being used to define the holding pattern for RNAV lateral guidance. This may result in an incorrect hold being flown by the RNAV system. For example, entering or executing the holding pattern above 14,000 feet when intending to hold below 14,000 feet may result in applying 1-1/2 minute timing below 14,000 feet.

Note: Some systems permit the pilot to modify leg time of holding patterns defined in the navigation database; for example, a hold-in-lieu of procedure turn. In most RNAV systems, the holding pattern time remains at the pilot-modified time and will not revert back to the coded time if the aircraft descends to a lower altitude where a shorter time interval applies.

(b) RNAV systems are not able to alert the pilot for excursions outside of holding pattern protected airspace since the dimensions of this airspace are not included in the navigation database. In addition, the dimensions of holding pattern protected airspace vary with altitude for a charted holding pattern, even when the hold is used for the same application. Close adherence to the pilot actions described in this section reduce the likelihood of exceeding the boundary of holding pattern protected airspace when using RNAV lateral guidance to conduct holding.

(c) Holding patterns may be stored in the RNAV system's navigation database and include coding with parameters defining how the RNAV system will conduct the hold. For example, coding will determine whether holding is conducted to manual termination (HM), continued holding until the aircraft reaches a specified altitude (HA), or holding is conducted until the holding fix is crossed the first time after entry (HF). Some systems do not store all holding patterns, and may only store patterns associated with missed approaches and hold-in-lieu of procedure turn (HILPT). Some store all holding as standard patterns and require pilot action to conduct non-standard holding (left turns).

(1) Pilots are cautioned that multiple holding patterns may be established at the same fix. These holding patterns may differ in respect to turn directions and leg lengths depending on their application as an en route holding pattern, a holding pattern charted on a SID or STAR, or when used on an instrument approach procedure. Many RNAV systems limit the database coding at a particular fix to a single holding pattern definition. Pilots extracting the holding pattern from the navigation database are responsible for confirming that the holding pattern conforms to the assigned charted holding pattern in terms of turn direction, speed limit, timing, and distance.

(2) If ATC assigns holding that is not charted, then the pilot is responsible for programming the RNAV system with the assigned holding course, turn direction, speed limit, leg length, or leg time.

(3) Changes made after the initial execution may not apply until the next circuit of the holding pattern if the aircraft is in close proximity to the holding fix.

8. Pilot Action. The following actions are recommended to ensure that the aircraft remains within holding protected airspace when holding is performed using either conventional NAVAID guidance or when using RNAV lateral guidance.

(a) Speed. When ATC furnishes advance notice of holding, start speed reduction to be at or below the maximum holding speed allowed at least 3 minutes prior to crossing the holding fix. If advance notice by ATC is not provided, begin speed reduction as expeditiously as practical. It is acceptable to allow RNAV systems to determine an appropriate deceleration point prior to the holding fix and to manage the speed reduction to the RNAV computed holding speed. If the pilot does not permit the RNAV system to manage the deceleration from the computed point, the actual hold pattern size at holding entry may differ from the holding pattern size computed by the RNAV system.

(1) Aircraft are expected to enter holding at or below the maximum holding speed established in paragraph 5-3-8j2(a) or the charted maximum holding speed.

[a] All fixed wing aircraft conducting holding should fly at speeds at or above 90 KIAS to minimize the influence of wind drift.

[b] When RNAV lateral guidance is used in fixed wing airplanes, it is desirable to enter and conduct holding at the lowest practical airspeed consistent with the airplane's recommended holding speed to address the cumulative errors associated with RNAV holding and increase the probability of remaining within protected airspace. It is acceptable to allow RNAV systems to determine a recommended holding speed *that is at or below the maximum holding speed.*

[c] Helicopter holding is based on a minimum airspeed of 90 KIAS.

(2) Advise ATC immediately if unable to comply with the maximum holding airspeed and request an alternate clearance.

Note: Speeds above the maximum or published holding speed may be necessary due to turbulence, icing, etc. Exceeding maximum holding airspeed may result in aircraft excursions beyond the holding pattern protected airspace. In a non-radar environment, the pilot should advise ATC that they cannot accept the assigned hold.

(3) Ensure the RNAV system applies the proper time and speed restrictions to a holding pattern. This is especially critical when climbing or descending to a holding pattern altitude where time and speed restrictions are different than at the present aircraft altitude.

(b) Bank Angle. For holding not involving the use of RNAV lateral guidance, make all turns during entry and while holding at:

(1) 3 degrees per second, or

(2) 30 degree bank angle, or

(3) 25 degree bank angle, provided a flight director system is used.

Note: Use whichever requires the least bank angle.

(4) When using RNAV lateral guidance to conduct holding, it is acceptable to permit the RNAV system to calculate the appropriate bank angle for the outbound and inbound turns. Do not use flight guidance system bank angle limiting functions of less than 25 degrees unless the feature is not pilot-selectable, required by the aircraft limitations, or its use is necessary to comply with the aircraft's minimum maneuvering speed margins. If the bank angle must be limited to less than 25 degrees, advise ATC that additional area for holding is required.

(c) Compensate for wind effect primarily by drift correction on the inbound and outbound legs. When outbound, triple the inbound drift correction to avoid major turning adjustments; for example, if correcting left by 8 degrees when inbound, correct right by 24 degrees when outbound.

(d) Determine entry turn from aircraft heading upon arrival at the holding fix; ±5 degrees in heading is considered to be within allowable good operating limits for determining entry. When using RNAV lateral guidance for holding, it is permissible to allow the system to compute the holding entry.

(e) RNAV lateral guidance may execute a fly-by turn beginning at an excessively large distance from the holding fix. Reducing speed to the maximum holding speed at least 3 minutes prior to reaching the holding fix and using the recommended 25 degree bank angle will reduce potential excursions beyond protected airspace.

(f) When RNAV guidance is used for holding, pilots should be prepared to intervene if the turn from outbound leg to the inbound leg does not begin within a reasonable distance of the charted leg length, especially when holding is used as a course reversal HILPT. Pilot intervention is not required when holding in an ATC-assigned holding pattern that is not charted. However, notify ATC when the outbound leg length becomes excessive when RNAV guidance is used for holding.

k. When holding at a fix and instructions are received specifying the time of departure from the fix, the pilot should adjust the aircraft's flight path within the limits of the established holding pattern in order to leave the fix at the exact time specified. After departing the holding fix, normal speed is to be resumed with respect to other governing speed requirements, such as terminal area speed limits, specific ATC requests, etc. Where the fix is associated with an instrument approach and timed approaches are in effect, a procedure turn must not be executed unless the pilot advises ATC, since aircraft holding are expected to proceed inbound on final approach directly from the holding pattern when approach clearance is received.

l. Radar surveillance of holding pattern airspace areas.

1. Whenever aircraft are holding, ATC will usually provide radar surveillance of the holding airspace on the controller's radar display.

2. The controller will attempt to detect any holding aircraft that stray outside the holding airspace and will assist any detected aircraft to return to the assigned airspace.

Note: Many factors could prevent ATC from providing this additional service, such as workload, number of targets, precipitation, ground clutter, and radar system capability. These circumstances may make it unfeasible to maintain radar identification of aircraft to detect aircraft straying from the holding pattern. The provision of this service depends entirely upon whether controllers believe they are in a position to provide it and does not relieve a pilot of their responsibility to adhere to an accepted ATC clearance.

3. ATC is responsible for traffic and obstruction separation when they have assigned holding that is not associated with a published (charted) holding pattern. Altitudes assigned will be at or above the minimum vectoring or minimum IFR altitude.

4. If an aircraft is established in a published holding pattern at an assigned altitude above the published minimum holding altitude and subsequently cleared for the approach, the pilot may descend to the published minimum holding altitude. The holding pattern would only be a segment of the IAP *if* it is published on the instrument procedure chart and is used in lieu of a procedure turn.

m. For those holding patterns where there are no published minimum holding altitudes, the pilot, upon receiving an approach clearance, must maintain the last assigned altitude until leaving the holding pattern and established on the inbound course. Thereafter, the published minimum altitude of the route segment being flown will apply. It is expected that the pilot will be assigned a holding altitude that will permit a normal descent on the inbound course.

Section 4 Arrival Procedures

5-4-1 Standard Terminal Arrival (STAR) Procedures

a. A STAR is an ATC coded IFR arrival route established for application to arriving IFR aircraft destined for certain airports. STARs simplify clearance delivery procedures, and also facilitate transition between en route and instrument approach procedures.

1. STAR procedures may have mandatory speeds and/or crossing altitudes published. Other STARs may have planning information depicted to inform pilots what clearances or restrictions to "expect." "Expect" altitudes/speeds are not considered STAR procedures crossing restrictions unless verbally issued by ATC. Published speed restrictions are independent of altitude restrictions and are mandatory unless modified by ATC. Pilots should plan to cross waypoints with a published speed restriction, at the published speed, and should not exceed this speed past the associated waypoint unless authorized by ATC or a published note to do so.

Note: The "expect" altitudes/speeds are published so that pilots may have the information for planning purposes. These altitudes/speeds must not be used in the event of lost communications unless ATC has specifically advised the pilot to expect these altitudes/speeds as part of a further clearance.

Reference: 14 CFR Section 91.185(c)(2)(iii).

2. Pilots navigating on, or navigating a published route inbound to, a STAR procedure must maintain last assigned altitude until receiving authorization to descend so as to comply with all published/issued restrictions. This authorization will contain the phraseology "DESCEND VIA." If vectored or cleared to deviate off a STAR, pilots must consider the STAR canceled, unless the controller adds "expect to resume STAR"; pilots should then be prepared to rejoin the STAR at a subsequent fix or procedure leg. If a descent clearance has been received that included a crossing restriction, pilots should expect the controller to issue an altitude to maintain. If the STAR contains published altitude and/or speed restrictions, those restrictions are canceled and pilots will receive an altitude to maintain and, if necessary, a speed.

(a) Clearance to "descend via" authorizes pilots to:

(1) Descend at pilot's discretion to meet published restrictions and laterally navigate on a STAR.

(2) When cleared to a waypoint depicted on a STAR, to descend from a previously assigned altitude at pilot's discretion to the altitude depicted at that waypoint.

(3) Once established on the depicted arrival, to descend and to meet all published or assigned altitude and/or speed restrictions.

Note 1: When otherwise cleared along a route or procedure that contains published speed restrictions, the pilot must comply with those speed restrictions independent of any descend via clearance.

Note 2: ATC anticipates pilots will begin adjusting speed the minimum distance necessary prior to a published speed restriction so as to cross the waypoint/fix at the published speed. Once at the published speed, ATC expects pilots will maintain the published speed until additional adjustment is required to comply with further published or ATC assigned speed restrictions or as required to ensure compliance with 14 CFR Section 91.117.

Note 3: The "descend via" is used in conjunction with STARs to reduce phraseology by not requiring the controller to restate the altitude at the next waypoint/fix to which the pilot has been cleared.

Note 4: Air traffic will assign an altitude to cross the waypoint/fix, if no altitude is depicted at the waypoint/fix, for aircraft on a direct routing to a STAR. Air traffic must ensure obstacle clearance when issuing a "descend via" instruction to the pilot.

Note 5: Minimum en route altitudes (MEA) are not considered restrictions; however, pilots must remain above all MEAs, unless receiving an ATC instruction to descend below the MEA.

Example 1: Lateral/routing clearance only.

"Cleared Tyler One arrival."

Note: In Example 1, pilots are cleared to fly the lateral path of the procedure. Compliance with any published speed restrictions is required. No descent is authorized.

Example 2: Routing with assigned altitude.

"Cleared Tyler One arrival, descend and maintain flight level two four zero."

"Cleared Tyler One arrival, descend at pilot's discretion, maintain flight level two four zero."

Note: In Example 2, the first clearance requires the pilot to descend to FL 240 as directed, comply with any published speed restrictions, and maintain FL 240 until cleared for further vertical navigation with a newly assigned altitude or a "descend via" clearance.

The second clearance authorizes the pilot to descend to FL 240 at his discretion, to comply with

Ch 5

any published speed restrictions, and then maintain FL 240 until issued further instructions.

Example 3: Lateral/routing and vertical navigation clearance.

"Descend via the Eagul Five arrival."

"Descend via the Eagul Five arrival, except, cross Vnnom at or above one two thousand."

Note: *In Example 3, the first clearance authorized the aircraft to descend at pilot's discretion on the Eagul Five arrival; the pilot must descend so as to comply with all published altitude and speed restrictions.*

The second clearance authorizes the same, but requires the pilot to descend so as to cross at Vnnom at or above 12,000.

Example 4: Lateral/routing and vertical navigation clearance when assigning altitude not published on procedure.

"Descend via the Eagul Five arrival, except after Geeno, maintain one zero thousand."

"Descend via the Eagul Five arrival, except cross Geeno at one one thousand then maintain seven thousand."

Note: *In Example 4, the first clearance authorized the aircraft to track laterally on the Eagul Five Arrival and to descend at pilot's discretion so as to comply with all altitude and speed restrictions until reaching Geeno and then maintain 10,000. Upon reaching 10,000, aircraft should maintain 10,000 until cleared by ATC to continue to descend.*

The second clearance requires the same, except the aircraft must cross Geeno at 11,000 and is then authorized to continue descent to and maintain 7,000.

Example 5: Direct routing to intercept a STAR and vertical navigation clearance.

"Proceed direct Leoni, descend via the Leoni One arrival."

"Proceed direct Denis, cross Denis at or above flight level two zero zero, then descend via the Mmell One arrival."

Note: *In Example 5, in the first clearance an altitude is published at Leoni; the aircraft proceeds to Leoni, crosses Leoni at the published altitude and then descends via the arrival. If a speed restriction is published at Leoni, the aircraft will slow to comply with the published speed.*

In the second clearance, there is no altitude published at Denis; the aircraft must cross Denis at or above FL200, and then descends via the arrival.

 (b) Pilots cleared for vertical navigation using the phraseology "descend via" must inform ATC upon initial contact with a new frequency, of

the altitude leaving, "descending via (procedure name)," the runway transition or landing direction if assigned, and any assigned restrictions not published on the procedure.

Example 1: *Delta 121 is cleared to descend via the Eagul Five arrival, runway 26 transition: "Delta One Twenty One leaving flight level one niner zero, descending via the Eagul Five arrival runway two-six transition."*

Example 2: *Delta 121 is cleared to descend via the Eagul Five arrival, but ATC has changed the bottom altitude to 12,000: "Delta One Twenty One leaving flight level one niner zero for one two thousand, descending via the Eagul Five arrival, runway two-six transition."*

Example 3: *(JetBlue 602 is cleared to descend via the Ivane Two arrival, landing south): "JetBlue six zero two leaving flight level two one zero descending via the Ivane Two arrival landing south."*

 b. Pilots of IFR aircraft destined to locations for which STARs have been published may be issued a clearance containing a STAR whenever ATC deems it appropriate.

 c. Use of STARs requires pilot possession of at least the approved chart. RNAV STARs must be retrievable by the procedure name from the aircraft database and conform to charted procedure. As with any ATC clearance or portion thereof, it is the responsibility of each pilot to accept or refuse an issued STAR. Pilots should notify ATC if they do not wish to use a STAR by placing "NO STAR" in the remarks section of the flight plan or by the less desirable method of verbally stating the same to ATC.

 d. STAR charts are published in the Terminal Procedures Publications (TPP) and are available on subscription from the National Aeronautical Charting Office.

 e. PBN STAR.

 1. Public PBN STARs are normally designed using RNAV 1, RNP 1, or A-RNP NavSpecs. These procedures require system performance currently met by GPS or DME/DME/IRU PBN systems that satisfy the criteria discussed in AC 90-100A, U.S. Terminal and En Route Area Navigation (RNAV) Operations. These procedures, using RNAV 1 and RNP 1 NavSpecs, must maintain a total system error of not more than 1 NM for 95% of the total flight time. Minimum values for A-RNP procedures will be charted in the PBN box (for example, 1.00 or 0.30).

 2. In the U.S., a specific procedure's PBN requirements will be prominently displayed in separate, standardized notes boxes. For procedures with PBN elements, the "PBN box" will contain the procedure's NavSpec(s); and, if required: specific sensors or infrastructure needed for the navigation solution, any additional or advanced

functional requirements, the minimum RNP value, and any amplifying remarks. Items listed in this PBN box are REQUIRED for the procedure's PBN elements.

5-4-2 Local Flow Traffic Management Program

a. This program is a continuing effort by the FAA to enhance safety, minimize the impact of aircraft noise and conserve aviation fuel. The enhancement of safety and reduction of noise is achieved in this program by minimizing low altitude maneuvering of arriving turbojet and turboprop aircraft weighing more than 12,500 pounds and, by permitting departure aircraft to climb to higher altitudes sooner, as arrivals are operating at higher altitudes at the points where their flight paths cross. The application of these procedures also reduces exposure time between controlled aircraft and uncontrolled aircraft at the lower altitudes in and around the terminal environment. Fuel conservation is accomplished by absorbing any necessary arrival delays for aircraft included in this program operating at the higher and more fuel efficient altitudes.

b. A fuel efficient descent is basically an uninterrupted descent (except where level flight is required for speed adjustment) from cruising altitude to the point when level flight is necessary for the pilot to stabilize the aircraft on final approach. The procedure for a fuel efficient descent is based on an altitude loss which is most efficient for the majority of aircraft being served. This will generally result in a descent gradient window of 250–350 feet per nautical mile.

c. When crossing altitudes and speed restrictions are issued verbally or are depicted on a chart, ATC will expect the pilot to descend first to the crossing altitude and then reduce speed. Verbal clearances for descent will normally permit an uninterrupted descent in accordance with the procedure as described in paragraph b above. Acceptance of a charted fuel efficient descent (Runway Profile Descent) clearance requires the pilot to adhere to the altitudes, speeds, and headings depicted on the charts unless otherwise instructed by ATC. PILOTS RECEIVING A CLEARANCE FOR A FUEL EFFICIENT DESCENT ARE EXPECTED TO ADVISE ATC IF THEY DO NOT HAVE RUNWAY PROFILE DESCENT CHARTS PUBLISHED FOR THAT AIRPORT OR ARE UNABLE TO COMPLY WITH THE CLEARANCE.

5-4-3 Approach Control

a. Approach control is responsible for controlling all instrument flight operating within its area of responsibility. Approach control may serve one or more airfields, and control is exercised primarily by direct pilot and controller communications.

Prior to arriving at the destination radio facility, instructions will be received from ARTCC to contact approach control on a specified frequency.

b. Radar Approach Control.

1. Where radar is approved for approach control service, it is used not only for radar approaches (Airport Surveillance Radar [ASR] and Precision Approach Radar [PAR]) but is also used to provide vectors in conjunction with published nonradar approaches based on radio NAVAIDs (ILS, VOR, NDB, TACAN). Radar vectors can provide course guidance and expedite traffic to the final approach course of any established IAP or to the traffic pattern for a visual approach. Approach control facilities that provide this radar service will operate in the following manner:

(a) Arriving aircraft are either cleared to an outer fix most appropriate to the route being flown with vertical separation and, if required, given holding information or, when radar handoffs are effected between the ARTCC and approach control, or between two approach control facilities, aircraft are cleared to the airport or to a fix so located that the handoff will be completed prior to the time the aircraft reaches the fix. When radar handoffs are utilized, successive arriving flights may be handed off to approach control with radar separation in lieu of vertical separation.

(b) After release to approach control, aircraft are vectored to the final approach course (ILS, RNAV, GLS, VOR, ADF, etc.). Radar vectors and altitude or flight levels will be issued as required for spacing and separating aircraft. *Therefore, pilots must not deviate from the headings issued by approach control.* Aircraft will normally be informed when it is necessary to vector across the final approach course for spacing or other reasons. If approach course crossing is imminent and the pilot has not been informed that the aircraft will be vectored across the final approach course, the pilot should query the controller.

(c) The pilot is not expected to turn inbound on the final approach course unless an approach clearance has been issued. This clearance will normally be issued with the final vector for interception of the final approach course, and the vector will be such as to enable the pilot to establish the aircraft on the final approach course prior to reaching the final approach fix.

(d) In the case of aircraft already inbound on the final approach course, approach clearance will be issued prior to the aircraft reaching the final approach fix. When established inbound on the final approach course, radar separation will be maintained and the pilot will be expected to complete the approach utilizing the approach aid designated in the clearance (ILS, RNAV, GLS, VOR, radio beacons, etc.) as the primary means of navigation. Therefore, once established on the final

Ch 5

approach course, pilots must not deviate from it unless a clearance to do so is received from ATC.

(e) After passing the final approach fix on final approach, aircraft are expected to continue inbound on the final approach course and complete the approach or effect the missed approach procedure published for that airport.

2. ARTCCs are approved for and may provide approach control services to specific airports. The radar systems used by these centers do not provide the same precision as an ASR/PAR used by approach control facilities and towers, and the update rate is not as fast. Therefore, pilots may be requested to report established on the final approach course.

3. Whether aircraft are vectored to the appropriate final approach course or provide their own navigation on published routes to it, radar service is automatically terminated when the landing is completed or when instructed to change to advisory frequency at uncontrolled airports, whichever occurs first.

5-4-4 Advance Information on Instrument Approach

a. When landing at airports with approach control services and where two or more IAPs are published, pilots will be provided in advance of their arrival with the type of approach to expect or that they may be vectored for a visual approach. This information will be broadcast either by a controller or on ATIS. It will not be furnished when the visibility is three miles or better and the ceiling is at or above the highest initial approach altitude established for any low altitude IAP for the airport.

b. The purpose of this information is to aid the pilot in planning arrival actions; however, it is not an ATC clearance or commitment and is subject to change. Pilots should bear in mind that fluctuating weather, shifting winds, blocked runway, etc., are conditions which may result in changes to approach information previously received. It is important that pilots advise ATC immediately they are unable to execute the approach ATC advised will be used, or if they prefer another type of approach.

c. Aircraft destined to uncontrolled airports, which have automated weather data with broadcast capability, should monitor the ASOS/AWOS frequency to ascertain the current weather for the airport. The pilot must advise ATC when he/she has received the broadcast weather and state his/her intentions.

Note 1: ASOS/AWOS should be set to provide one-minute broadcast weather updates at uncontrolled airports that are without weather broadcast capability by a human observer.

Note 2: Controllers will consider the long line disseminated weather from an automated weather

system at an uncontrolled airport as trend and planning information only and will rely on the pilot for current weather information for the airport. If the pilot is unable to receive the current broadcast weather, the last long line disseminated weather will be issued to the pilot. When receiving IFR services, the pilot/aircraft operator is responsible for determining if weather/visibility is adequate for approach/landing.

d. When making an IFR approach to an airport not served by a tower or FSS, after ATC advises "CHANGE TO ADVISORY FREQUENCY APPROVED," you should broadcast your intentions, including the type of approach being executed, your position, and when over the final approach fix inbound (nonprecision approach) or when over the outer marker or fix used in lieu of the outer marker inbound (precision approach). Continue to monitor the appropriate frequency (UNICOM, etc.) for reports from other pilots.

5-4-5 Instrument Approach Procedure (IAP) Charts

a. 14 CFR Section 91.175(a), Instrument approaches to civil airports, requires the use of SIAPs prescribed for the airport in 14 CFR Part 97 unless otherwise authorized by the Administrator (including ATC). If there are military procedures published at a civil airport, aircraft operating under 14 CFR Part 91 must use the civil procedure(s). Civil procedures are defined with "FAA" in parenthesis; e.g., (FAA), at the top, center of the procedure chart. DOD procedures are defined using the abbreviation of the applicable military service in parenthesis; e.g., (USAF), (USN), (USA). 14 CFR Section 91.175(g), Military airports, requires civil pilots flying into or out of military airports to comply with the IAPs and takeoff and landing minimums prescribed by the authority having jurisdiction at those airports. Unless an emergency exists, civil aircraft operating at military airports normally require advance authorization, commonly referred to as "Prior Permission Required" or "PPR." Information on obtaining a PPR for a particular military airport can be found in the Chart Supplement. ▌

Note: Civil aircraft may conduct practice VFR approaches using DOD instrument approach procedures when approved by the air traffic controller.

1. IAPs (standard and special, civil and military) are based on joint civil and military criteria contained in the U.S. Standard for TERPS. The design of IAPs based on criteria contained in TERPS, takes into account the interrelationship between airports, facilities, and the surrounding environment, terrain, obstacles, noise sensitivity, etc. Appropriate altitudes, courses, headings, distances, and other limitations are specified and, once approved, the procedures are published and

distributed by government and commercial cartographers as instrument approach charts.

2. Not all IAPs are published in chart form. Radar IAPs are established where requirements and facilities exist but they are printed in tabular form in appropriate U.S. Government Flight Information Publications.

3. The navigation equipment required to join and fly an instrument approach procedure is indicated by the title of the procedure and notes on the chart.

(a) Straight-in IAPs are identified by the navigational system providing the final approach guidance and the runway to which the approach is aligned (e.g., VOR RWY 13). Circling only approaches are identified by the navigational system providing final approach guidance and a letter (e.g., VOR A). More than one navigational system separated by a slash indicates that more than one type of equipment must be used to execute the final approach (e.g., VOR/DME RWY 31). More than one navigational system separated by the word "or" indicates either type of equipment may be used to execute the final approach (e.g., VOR or GPS RWY 15).

(b) In some cases, other types of navigation systems including radar may be required to execute other portions of the approach or to navigate to the IAF (e.g., an NDB procedure turn to an ILS, an NDB in the missed approach, or radar required to join the procedure or identify a fix). When radar or other equipment is required for procedure entry from the en route environment, a note will be charted in the planview of the approach procedure chart (e.g., RADAR REQUIRED or ADF REQUIRED). When radar or other equipment is required on portions of the procedure outside the final approach segment, including the missed approach, a note will be charted in the notes box of the pilot briefing portion of the approach chart (e.g., RADAR REQUIRED or DME REQUIRED). Notes are not charted when VOR is required outside the final approach segment. Pilots should ensure that the aircraft is equipped with the required NAVAID(s) in order to execute the approach, including the missed approach.

Note: Some military (i.e., U.S. Air Force and U.S. Navy) IAPs have these "additional equipment required" notes charted only in the planview of the approach procedure and do not conform to the same application standards used by the FAA.

(c) The FAA has initiated a program to provide a new notation for LOC approaches when charted on an ILS approach requiring other navigational aids to fly the final approach course. The LOC minimums will be annotated with the NAVAID required (e.g., "DME Required" or "RADAR Required"). During the transition period, ILS approaches will still exist without the annotation.

(d) Many ILS approaches having minima based on RVR are eligible for a landing minimum of RVR 1800. Some of these approaches are to runways that have touchdown zone and centerline lights. For many runways that do not have touchdown and centerline lights, it is still possible to allow a landing minimum of RVR 1800. For these runways, the normal ILS minimum of RVR 2400 can be annotated with a single or double asterisk or the dagger symbol "†"; for example "** 696/24 200 (200/1/2)." A note is included on the chart stating "**RVR 1800 authorized with use of FD or AP or HUD to DA." The pilot must use the flight director, or autopilot with an approved approach coupler, or head up display to decision altitude or to the initiation of a missed approach. In the interest of safety, single pilot operators should not fly approaches to 1800 RVR minimums on runways without touchdown and centerline lights using only a flight director, unless accompanied by the use of an autopilot with an approach coupler.

(e) The naming of multiple approaches of the same type to the same runway is also changing. Multiple approaches with the same guidance will be annotated with an alphabetical suffix beginning at the end of the alphabet and working backwards for subsequent procedures (e.g., ILS Z RWY 28, ILS Y RWY 28, etc.). The existing annotations such as ILS 2 RWY 28 or Silver ILS RWY 28 will be phased out and replaced with the new designation. The Cat II and Cat III designations are used to differentiate between multiple ILSs to the same runway unless there are multiples of the same type.

(f) RNAV (GPS) approaches to LNAV, LP, LNAV/VNAV and LPV lines of minima using WAAS and RNAV (GPS) approaches to LNAV and LNAV/VNAV lines of minima using GPS are charted as RNAV (GPS) RWY (Number) (e.g., RNAV (GPS) RWY 21).

(g) Performance-Based Navigation (PBN) Box. As charts are updated, a procedure's PBN requirements and conventional equipment requirements will be prominently displayed in separate, standardized notes boxes. For procedures with PBN elements, the PBN box will contain the procedure's navigation specification(s); and, if required: specific sensors or infrastructure needed for the navigation solution, any additional or advanced functional requirements, the minimum Required Navigation Performance (RNP) value, and any amplifying remarks. Items listed in this PBN box are REQUIRED for the procedure's PBN elements. For example, an ILS with an RNAV missed approach would require a specific capability to fly the missed approach portion of the procedure. That required capability will be listed in the PBN box. The separate Equipment Requirements box will list ground-based equipment requirements. On procedures with both PBN elements

and equipment requirements, the PBN requirements box will be listed first. The publication of these notes will continue incrementally until all charts have been amended to comply with the new standard.

4. Approach minimums are based on the local altimeter setting for that airport, unless annotated otherwise; e.g., Oklahoma City/Will Rogers World approaches are based on having a Will Rogers World altimeter setting. When a different altimeter source is required, or more than one source is authorized, it will be annotated on the approach chart; e.g., use Sidney altimeter setting, if not received, use Scottsbluff altimeter setting. Approach minimums may be raised when a nonlocal altimeter source is authorized. When more than one altimeter source is authorized, and the minima are different, they will be shown by separate lines in the approach minima box or a note; e.g., use Manhattan altimeter setting; when not available use Salina altimeter setting and increase all MDAs 40 feet. When the altimeter must be obtained from a source other than air traffic a note will indicate the source; e.g., Obtain local altimeter setting on CTAF. When the altimeter setting(s) on which the approach is based is not available, the approach is not authorized. Baro-VNAV must be flown using the local altimeter setting only. Where no local altimeter is available, the LNAV/VNAV line will still be published for use by WAAS receivers with a note that Baro-VNAV is not authorized. When a local and at least one other altimeter setting source is authorized and the local altimeter is not available Baro-VNAV is not authorized; however, the LNAV/VNAV minima can still be used by WAAS receivers using the alternate altimeter setting source.

Note: Barometric Vertical Navigation (baro-VNAV). An RNAV system function which uses barometric altitude information from the aircraft's altimeter to compute and present a vertical guidance path to the pilot. The specified vertical path is computed as a geometric path, typically computed between two waypoints or an angle based computation from a single waypoint. Further guidance may be found in Advisory Circular 90-105.

5. A pilot adhering to the altitudes, flight paths, and weather minimums depicted on the IAP chart or vectors and altitudes issued by the radar controller, is assured of terrain and obstruction clearance and runway or airport alignment during approach for landing.

6. IAPs are designed to provide an IFR descent from the en route environment to a point where a safe landing can be made. They are prescribed and approved by appropriate civil or military authority to ensure a safe descent during instrument flight conditions at a specific airport. It is important that pilots understand these procedures and their use prior to attempting to fly instrument approaches.

7. TERPS criteria are provided for the following types of instrument approach procedures:

(a) Precision Approach (PA). An instrument approach based on a navigation system that provides course and glidepath deviation information meeting the precision standards of ICAO Annex 10. For example, PAR, ILS, and GLS are precision approaches.

(b) Approach with Vertical Guidance (APV). An instrument approach based on a navigation system that is not required to meet the precision approach standards of ICAO Annex 10 but provides course and glidepath deviation information. For example, Baro-VNAV, LDA with glidepath, LNAV/VNAV and LPV are APV approaches.

(c) Nonprecision Approach (NPA). An instrument approach based on a navigation system which provides course deviation information, but no glidepath deviation information. For example, VOR, NDB and LNAV. As noted in subparagraph k, Vertical Descent Angle (VDA) on Nonprecision Approaches, some approach procedures may provide a Vertical Descent Angle as an aid in flying a stabilized approach, without requiring its use in order to fly the procedure. This does not make the approach an APV procedure, since it must still be flown to an MDA and has not been evaluated with a glidepath.

b. The method used to depict prescribed altitudes on instrument approach charts differs according to techniques employed by different chart publishers. Prescribed altitudes may be depicted in four different configurations: minimum, maximum, mandatory, and recommended. The U.S. Government distributes charts produced by National Geospatial–Intelligence Agency (NGA) and FAA. Altitudes are depicted on these charts in the profile view with underscore, overscore, both or none to identify them as minimum, maximum, mandatory or recommended.

1. Minimum altitude will be depicted with the altitude value underscored. Aircraft are required to maintain altitude at or above the depicted value, e.g., <u>3000</u>.

2. Maximum altitude will be depicted with the altitude value overscored. Aircraft are required to maintain altitude at or below the depicted value, e.g., 4000.

3. Mandatory altitude will be depicted with the altitude value both underscored and overscored. Aircraft are required to maintain altitude at the depicted value, e.g., <u>5000</u>.

4. Recommended altitude will be depicted with no overscore or underscore. These altitudes are depicted for descent planning, e.g., 6000.

Note 1: *Pilots are cautioned to adhere to altitudes as prescribed because, in certain instances, they may be used as the basis for vertical separation of aircraft by ATC. When a depicted altitude is specified in the ATC clearance, that altitude becomes mandatory as defined above.*

Note 2: *The ILS glide slope is intended to be intercepted at the published glide slope intercept altitude. This point marks the PFAF and is depicted by the "lightning bolt" symbol on U.S. Government charts. Intercepting the glide slope at this altitude marks the beginning of the final approach segment and ensures required obstacle clearance during descent from the glide slope intercept altitude to the lowest published decision altitude for the approach. Interception and tracking of the glide slope prior to the published glide slope interception altitude does not necessarily ensure that minimum, maximum, and/or mandatory altitudes published for any preceding fixes will be complied with during the descent. If the pilot chooses to track the glide slope prior to the glide slope interception altitude, they remain responsible for complying with published altitudes for any preceding stepdown fixes encountered during the subsequent descent.*

Note 3: *Approaches used for simultaneous (parallel) independent and simultaneous close parallel operations procedurally require descending on the glideslope from the altitude at which the approach clearance is issued (refer to 5-4-15 and 5-4-16). For simultaneous close parallel (PRM) approaches, the Attention All Users Page (AAUP) may publish a note which indicates that descending on the glideslope/glidepath meets all crossing restrictions. However, if no such note is published, and for simultaneous independent approaches (4300 and greater runway separation) where an AAUP is not published, pilots are cautioned to monitor their descent on the glideslope/path outside of the PFAF to ensure compliance with published crossing restrictions during simultaneous operations.*

Note 4: *When parallel approach courses are less than 2500 feet apart and reduced in-trail spacing is authorized for simultaneous dependent operations, a chart note will indicate that simultaneous operations require use of vertical guidance and that the pilot should maintain last assigned altitude until established on glide slope. These approaches procedurally require utilization of the ILS glide slope for wake turbulence mitigation. Pilots should not confuse these simultaneous dependent operations with (SOIA) simultaneous close parallel PRM approaches, where PRM appears in the approach title.*

5. Altitude restrictions depicted at stepdown fixes within the final approach segment are applicable only when flying a Non-Precision Approach to a straight-in or circling line of minima identified as an MDA (H). These altitude restrictions may be annotated with a note "LOC only" or "LNAV only." Stepdown fix altitude restrictions within the final approach segment do not apply to pilots using Precision Approach (ILS) or Approach with Vertical Guidance (LPV, LNAV/VNAV) lines of minima identified as a DA(H), since obstacle clearance on these approaches is based on the aircraft following the applicable vertical guidance. Pilots are responsible for adherence to stepdown fix altitude restrictions when outside the final approach segment (i.e., initial or intermediate segment), regardless of which type of procedure the pilot is flying. (See Figure 5-4-1.)

FIGURE 5–4–1
Instrument Approach Procedure Stepdown Fixes

c. The **Minimum Safe Altitudes (MSA)** is published for emergency use on IAP or departure procedure (DP) graphic charts. MSAs provide 1,000 feet of clearance over all obstacles, but do not necessarily assure acceptable navigation signal coverage. The MSA depiction on the plan view of an approach chart or on a DP graphic chart contains the identifier of the center point of the MSA, the applicable radius of the MSA, a depiction of the sector(s), and the minimum altitudes above mean sea level which provide obstacle clearance. For conventional navigation systems, the MSA is normally based on the primary omnidirectional facility on which the IAP or DP graphic chart is predicated, but may be based on the airport reference point (ARP) if no suitable facility is available. For RNAV approaches or DP graphic charts, the MSA is based on an RNAV waypoint. MSAs normally have a 25 NM radius; however, for conventional navigation systems, this radius may be expanded to 30 NM if necessary to encompass the airport landing surfaces. A single sector altitude is normally established, however when the MSA is based on a facility and it is necessary to obtain relief from obstacles, an MSA with up to four sectors may be established.

d. Terminal Arrival Area (TAA)

1. The TAA provides a transition from the en route structure to the terminal environment with little required pilot/air traffic control interface for aircraft equipped with Area Navigation (RNAV) systems. A TAA provides minimum altitudes with standard obstacle clearance when operating within the TAA boundaries. TAAs are primarily used on RNAV approaches but may be used on an ILS approach when RNAV is the sole means for navigation to the IF; however, they are not normally used in areas of heavy concentration of air traffic.

2. The basic design of the RNAV procedure underlying the TAA is normally the "T" design (also called the "Basic T"). The "T" design incorporates two IAFs plus a dual purpose IF/IAF that functions as both an intermediate fix and an initial approach fix. The T configuration continues from the IF/IAF to the final approach fix (FAF) and then to the missed approach point (MAP). The two base leg IAFs are typically aligned in a straight-line perpendicular to the intermediate course connecting at the IF/IAF. A Hold-in-Lieu-of Procedure

Turn (HILPT) is anchored at the IF/IAF and de-picted on U.S. Government publications using the "hold-in-lieu-of-PT" holding pattern symbol. When the HILPT is necessary for course alignment and/or descent, the dual purpose IF/IAF serves as an IAF during the entry into the pattern. Following entry into the HILPT pattern and when flying a route or sector labeled "NoPT," the dual-purpose fix serves as an IF, marking the beginning of the Intermediate Segment. See Figure 5-4-2 and Figure 5-4-3 for the Basic "T" TAA configuration.

FIGURE 5–4–2
Basic "T" Design

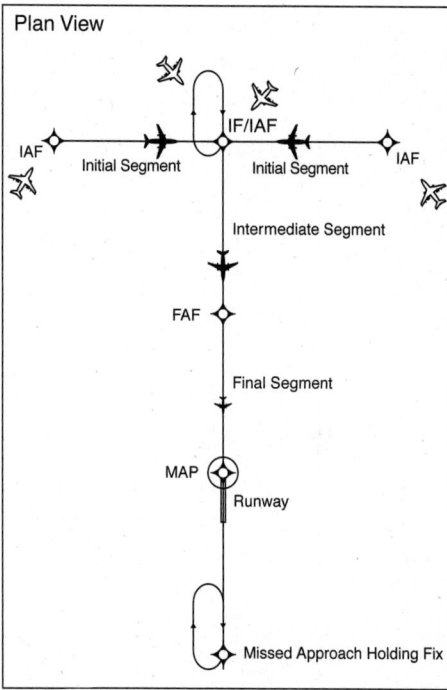

FIGURE 5–4–3
Basic "T" Design

3. The standard TAA based on the "T" design consists of three areas defined by the Initial Approach Fix (IAF) legs and the intermediate segment course beginning at the IF/IAF. These areas are called the straight-in, left-base, and right-base areas. (See Figure 5-4-4). TAA area lateral boundaries are identified by magnetic courses TO the IF/IAF. The straight-in area can be further divided into pie-shaped sectors with the boundaries identified by magnetic courses TO the (IF/ IAF), and may contain stepdown sections defined by arcs based on RNAV distances from the IF/IAF. (See Figure 5-4-5). The right/left-base areas can only be subdivided using arcs based on RNAV distances from the IAFs for those areas.

4. Entry from the terminal area onto the procedure is normally accomplished via a no procedure turn (NoPT) routing or via a course reversal maneuver. The published procedure will be annotated "NoPT" to indicate when the course reversal is not authorized when flying within a particular TAA sector. Otherwise, the pilot is expected to execute the course reversal under the provisions of 14 CFR Section 91.175. The pilot may elect to use the course reversal pattern when it is not required by the procedure, but must receive clearance from air traffic control before beginning the procedure.

(a) ATC should not clear an aircraft to the left base leg or right base leg IAF within a TAA at an intercept angle exceeding 90 degrees. Pilots must not execute the HILPT course reversal when the sector or procedure segment is labeled "NoPT."

(b) ATC may clear aircraft direct to the fix labeled IF/IAF if the course to the IF/IAF is within the straight-in sector labeled "NoPT" and the intercept angle does not exceed 90 degrees. Pilots are expected to proceed direct to the IF/IAF and accomplish a straight-in approach. Do not execute HILPT course reversal. Pilots are also expected to fly the straight-in approach when ATC provides radar vectors and monitoring to the IF/IAF and issues a "straight-in" approach clearance; otherwise, the pilot *is expected* to execute the HILPT course reversal.

Reference: AIM, ¶5-4-6, Approach Clearance

(c) On rare occasions, ATC may clear the aircraft for an approach at the airport without specifying the approach procedure by name or by a specific approach (for example, "cleared RNAV Runway 34 approach") without specifying a particular IAF. In either case, the pilot should proceed direct to the IAF or to the IF/IAF associated with the sector that the aircraft will enter the TAA and join the approach course from that point and

FIGURE 5–4–4
TAA Area

Aircraft maintain designated altitudes within each area.

if required by that sector (i.e., sector is not labeled "NoPT"), complete the HILPT course reversal.

Note: If approaching with a TO bearing that is on a sector boundary, the pilot is expected to proceed in accordance with a "NoPT" routing unless otherwise instructed by ATC.

5. Altitudes published within the TAA replace the MSA altitude. However, unlike MSA altitudes the TAA altitudes are operationally usable altitudes. These altitudes provide at least 1,000 feet of obstacle clearance, more in mountainous areas. It is important that the pilot knows which area of the TAA the aircraft will enter in order to comply with the minimum altitude requirements. The pilot can determine which area of the TAA the aircraft will enter by determining the magnetic bearing of the aircraft TO the fix labeled IF/IAF. The bearing should then be compared to the published lateral boundary bearings that define the TAA areas. Do not use magnetic bearing to the right-base or left-base IAFs to determine position.

(a) An ATC clearance direct to an IAF or to the IF/IAF without an approach clearance does not authorize a pilot to descend to a lower TAA altitude. If a pilot desires a lower altitude without

an approach clearance, request the lower TAA altitude from ATC. Pilots not sure of the clearance should confirm their clearance with ATC or request a specific clearance. Pilots entering the TAA with two-way radio communications failure (14 CFR Section 91.185, IFR Operations: Two-way Radio Communications Failure), must maintain the highest altitude prescribed by Section 91.185(c)(2) until arriving at the appropriate IAF.

(b) Once cleared for the approach, pilots may descend in the TAA sector to the minimum altitude depicted within the defined area/subdivision, unless instructed otherwise by air traffic control. Pilots should plan their descent within the TAA to permit a normal descent from the IF/IAF to the FAF. In Figure 5-4-5, pilots within the left or right-base areas are expected to maintain a minimum altitude of 6,000 feet until within 17 NM of the associated IAF. After crossing the 17 NM arc, descent is authorized to the lower charted altitudes. Pilots approaching from the northwest are expected to maintain a minimum altitude of 6,000 feet, and when within 22 NM of the IF/IAF, descend to a minimum altitude of 2,000 feet MSL until crossing the IF/IAF.

FIGURE 5–4–5
Sectored TAA Areas

6. U.S. Government charts depict TAAs using icons located in the plan view outside the depiction of the actual approach procedure. (See Figure 5-4-6). Use of icons is necessary to avoid obscuring any portion of the "T" procedure (altitudes, courses, minimum altitudes, etc.). The icon for each TAA area will be located and oriented on the plan view with respect to the direction of arrival to the approach procedure, and will show all TAA minimum altitudes and sector/radius subdivisions. The IAF for each area of the TAA is included on the icon where it appears on the approach to help the pilot orient the icon to the approach procedure. The IAF name and the distance of the TAA area boundary from the IAF are included on the outside arc of the TAA area icon.

FIGURE 5-4-6
RNAV (GPS) Approach Chart

7. TAAs may be modified from the standard size and shape to accommodate operational or ATC requirements. Some areas may be eliminated, while the other areas are expanded. The "T" design may be modified by the procedure designers where required by terrain or ATC considerations. For instance, the "T" design may appear more like a regularly or irregularly shaped "Y," upside down "L," or an "I."

(a) Figure 5-4-7 depicts a TAA without a left base leg and right base leg. In this generalized example, pilots approaching on a bearing TO the IF/IAF from 271 clockwise to 089 are expected to execute a course reversal because the amount of turn required at the IF/IAF exceeds 90 degrees. The term "NoPT" will be annotated on the boundary of the TAA icon for the other portion of the TAA.

FIGURE 5–4–7
TAA with Left and Right Base Areas Eliminated

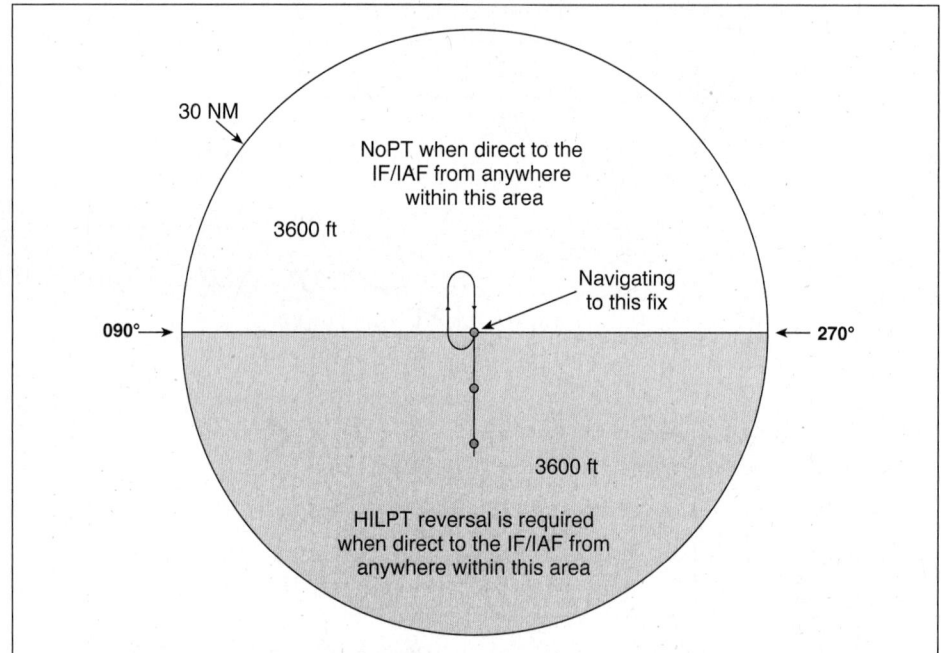

(b) Figure 5-4-8 depicts another TAA modification that pilots may encounter. In this generalized example, the left base area and part of the straight-in area have been eliminated. Pilots operating within the TAA between 210 clockwise to 360 bearing TO the IF/IAF are expected to proceed direct to the IF/IAF and then execute the course reversal in order to properly align the aircraft for entry onto the intermediate segment or to avoid an excessive descent rate. Aircraft operating in areas from 001 clockwise to 090 bearing TO the IF/IAF are expected to proceed direct to the right base IAF and not execute course reversal

maneuver. Aircraft cleared direct the IF/IAF by ATC in this sector will be expected to accomplish HILTP. Aircraft operating in areas 091 clockwise to 209 bearing TO the IF/IAF are expected to proceed direct to the IF/IAF and not execute the course reversal. These two areas are annotated "NoPT" at the TAA boundary of the icon in these areas when displayed on the approach chart's plan view.

(c) Figure 5-4-9 depicts a TAA with right base leg and part of the straight-in area eliminated.

FIGURE 5–4–8
TAA with Left Base and Part of Straight-In Area Eliminated

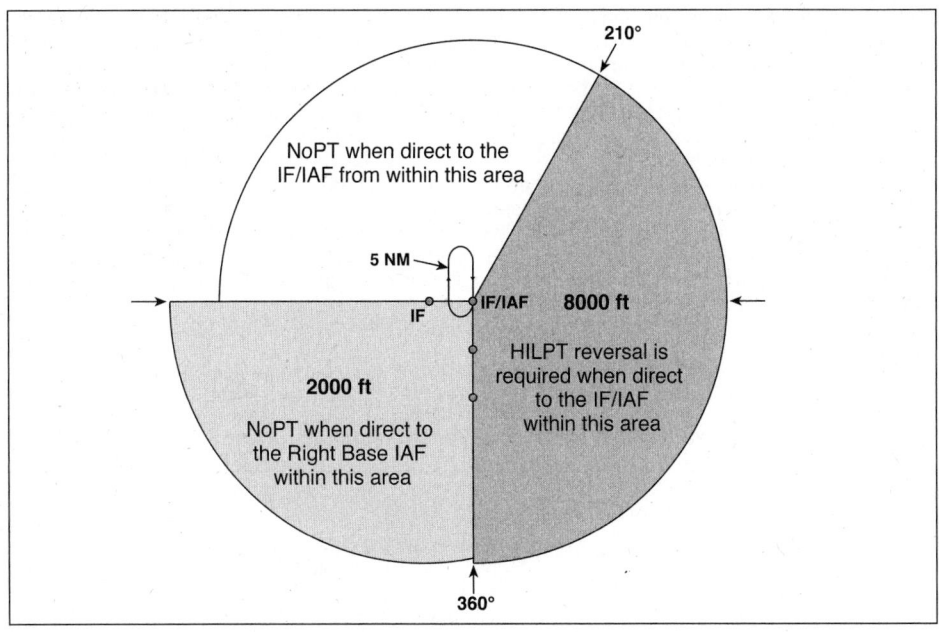

FIGURE 5–4–9
TAA with Right Base Eliminated

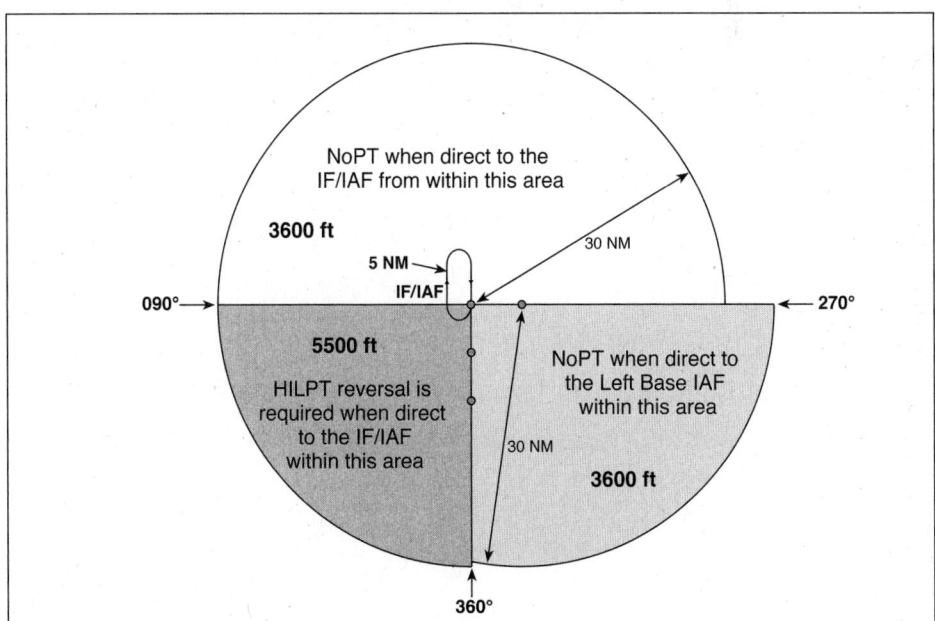

8. When an airway does not cross the lateral TAA boundaries, a feeder route will be established from an airway fix or NAVAID to the TAA boundary to provide a transition from the en route structure to the appropriate IAF. Each feeder route will terminate at the TAA boundary and will be aligned along a path pointing to the associated IAF. Pilots should descend to the TAA altitude after crossing the TAA boundary and cleared for the approach by ATC. (See Figure 5-4-10).

9. Each waypoint on the "T" is assigned a pronounceable 5-letter name, except the missed approach waypoint. These names are used for ATC communications, RNAV databases, and aeronautical navigation products. The missed approach waypoint is assigned a pronounceable name when it is not located at the runway threshold.

e. Minimum Vectoring Altitudes (MVAs) are established for use by ATC when radar ATC is exercised. MVA charts are prepared by air traffic facilities at locations where there are numerous different minimum IFR altitudes. Each MVA chart has sectors large enough to accommodate vectoring of aircraft within the sector at the MVA. Each sector boundary is at least 3 miles from the obstruction determining the MVA. To avoid a large sector with an excessively high MVA due to an isolated prominent obstruction, the obstruction may be enclosed in a buffer area whose boundaries are at least 3 miles from the obstruction. This is done to facilitate vectoring around the obstruction. (See Figure 5-4-11.)

FIGURE 5–4–10
Examples of a TAA with Feeders from an Airway

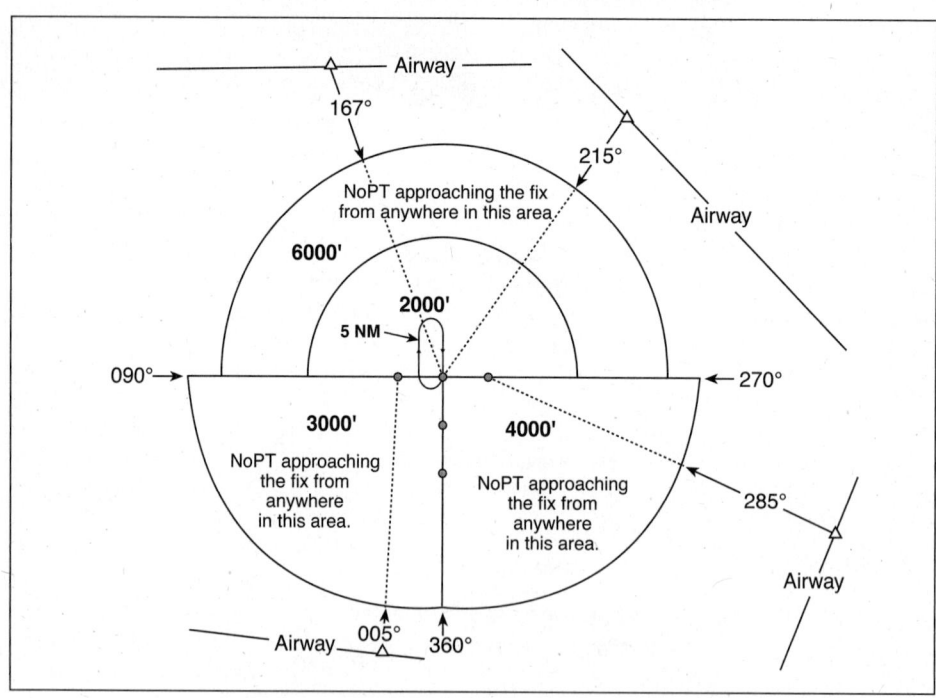

FIGURE 5–4–11
Minimum Vectoring Altitude Charts

1. The minimum vectoring altitude in each sector provides 1,000 feet above the highest obstacle in nonmountainous areas and 2,000 feet above the highest obstacle in designated mountainous areas. Where lower MVAs are required in designated mountainous areas to achieve compatibility with terminal routes or to permit vectoring to an IAP, 1,000 feet of obstacle clearance may be authorized with the use of ATC surveillance. The minimum vectoring altitude will provide at least 300 feet above the floor of controlled airspace.

Note: OROCA is a published altitude which provides 1,000 feet of terrain and obstruction clearance in the U.S. (2,000 feet of clearance in designated mountainous areas). These altitudes are not assessed for NAVAID signal coverage, air traffic control surveillance, or communications coverage, and are published for general situational awareness, flight planning and in-flight contingency use.

2. Because of differences in the areas considered for MVA, and those applied to other minimum altitudes, and the ability to isolate specific obstacles, some MVAs may be lower than the nonradar Minimum En Route Altitudes (MEAs), Minimum Obstruction Clearance Altitudes (MOCAs) or other minimum altitudes depicted on charts for a given location. While being radar vectored, IFR altitude assignments by ATC will be at or above MVA.

3. The MVA/MIA may be lower than the TAA minimum altitude. If ATC has assigned an altitude to an aircraft that is below the TAA minimum altitude, the aircraft will either be assigned an altitude to maintain until established on a segment of a published route or instrument approach procedure, or climbed to the TAA altitude.

f. Circling. Circling minimums charted on an RNAV (GPS) approach chart may be lower than the LNAV/VNAV line of minima, but never lower than the LNAV line of minima (straight-in approach). Pilots may safely perform the circling maneuver at the circling published line of minima if the approach and circling maneuver is properly performed according to aircraft category and operational limitations.

g. Figure 5-4-13 provides a visual representation of an obstacle evaluation and calculation of LNAV MDA, Circling MDA, LNAV/VNAV DA.

1. No vertical guidance (LNAV). A line is drawn horizontal at obstacle height and 250 feet added for Required Obstacle Clearance (ROC). The controlling obstacle used to determine LNAV MDA can be different than the controlling obstacle used in determining ROC for circling MDA. Other factors may force a number larger than 250 ft to be added to the LNAV OCS. The number is rounded up to the next higher 20 foot increment.

2. Circling MDA. The circling MDA will provide 300 foot obstacle clearance within the area considered for obstacle clearance and may be lower than the LNAV/VNAV DA, but never lower than the straight in LNAV MDA. This may occur when different controlling obstacles are used or when other controlling factors force the LNAV MDA to be higher than 250 feet above the LNAV OCS. In Figure 5-4-12, the required obstacle clearance for both the LNAV and Circle resulted in the same MDA, but lower than the LNAV/VNAV DA. Figure 5-4-13 provides an illustration of this type of situation.

3. Vertical guidance (LNAV/VNAV). A line is drawn horizontal at obstacle height until reaching the obstacle clearance surface (OCS). At the OCS, a vertical line is drawn until reaching the glide path. This is the DA for the approach. This method places the offending obstacle in front of the LNAV/VNAV DA so it can be seen and avoided. In some situations, this may result in the LNAV/VNAV DA being higher than the LNAV and/or Circling MDA.

Figure 5–4–12
Example of LNAV and Circling Minima Lower Than LNAV/VNAV DA.
Harrisburg International RNAV (GPS) RWY 13

CATEGORY	A	B	C	D
LPV DA	**558/24** 250 (300−½)			
LNAV/VNAV DA	**1572−5** (1264 (1300−5)			
LNAV MDA	**1180/24** 872 (900−½)	**1180/40** 872 (900−¾)	**1180/2** 870 (900−2)	**1180/2¼** 872 (900−2¼)
CIRCLING	**1180−1** 870 (900−1)	**1180−1¼** 870 (900−1¼)	**1180−2½** 870 (900−2½)	**1180−2¾** 870 (900−2¾)

Figure 5–4–13
Explanation of LNAV and/or Circling Minima Lower than LNAV/VNAV DA

h. The Visual Descent Point (VDP), identified by the symbol (V), is a defined point on the final approach course of a nonprecision straight-in approach procedure from which a stabilized visual descent from the MDA to the runway touchdown point may be commenced. The pilot should not descend below the MDA prior to reaching the VDP. The VDP will be identified by DME or RNAV along-track distance to the MAP. The VDP distance is based on the lowest MDA published on the IAP and harmonized with the angle of the visual glide slope indicator (VGSI) (if installed) or the procedure VDA (if no VGSI is installed). A VDP may not be published under certain circumstances which may result in a destabilized descent between the MDA and the runway touchdown point. Such circumstances include an obstacle penetrating the visual surface between the MDA and runway threshold, lack of distance measuring capability, or the procedure design prevents a VDP to be identified.

1. VGSI systems may be used as a visual aid to the pilot to determine if the aircraft is in a position to make a stabilized descent from the MDA.

When the visibility is close to minimums, the VGSI may not be visible at the VDP due to its location beyond the MAP.

2. Pilots not equipped to receive the VDP should fly the approach procedure as though no VDP had been provided.

3. On a straight-in nonprecision IAP, descent below the MDA between the VDP and the MAP may be inadvisable or impossible. Aircraft speed, height above the runway, descent rate, amount of turn, and runway length are some of the factors which must be considered by the pilot to determine if a safe descent and landing can be accomplished.

i. A visual segment obstruction evaluation is accomplished during procedure design on all IAPs. Obstacles (both lighted and unlighted) are allowed to penetrate the visual segment obstacle identification surfaces. Identified obstacle penetrations may cause restrictions to instrument approach operations which may include an increased approach visibility requirement, not publishing a VDP, and/or prohibiting night instrument operations to the runway. There is no implicit obstacle protection from the MDA/DA to the touchdown point. Accordingly, it is the responsibility of the pilot to visually acquire and avoid obstacles below the MDA/DA during transition to landing.

1. Unlighted obstacle penetrations may result in prohibiting night instrument operations to the runway. A chart note will be published in the pilot briefing strip "Procedure NA at Night."

2. Use of a VGSI may be approved in lieu of obstruction lighting to restore night instrument operations to the runway. A chart note will be published in the pilot briefing strip " Straight-in Rwy XX at Night, operational VGSI required, remain on or above VGSI glidepath until threshold."

j. The highest obstacle (man-made, terrain, or vegetation) will be charted on the planview of an IAP. Other obstacles may be charted in either the planview or the airport sketch based on distance from the runway and available chart space. The elevation of the charted obstacle will be shown to the nearest foot above mean sea level. Obstacles without a verified accuracy are indicated by a ± symbol following the elevation value.

k. Vertical Descent Angle (VDA). FAA policy is to publish a VDA/TCH on all nonprecision approaches except those published in conjunction with vertically guided minimums (i.e., ILS or LOC RWY XX) or no-FAF procedures without a stepdown fix (i.e., on-airport VOR or NDB). A VDA does not guarantee obstacle protection below the MDA in the visual segment. The presence of a VDA does not change any nonprecision approach requirements.

1. Obstacles may penetrate the obstacle identification surface below the MDA in the visual segment of an IAP that has a published VDA/TCH. When the VDA/TCH is not authorized due to an obstacle penetration that would require a pilot to deviate from the VDA between MDA and touchdown, the VDA/TCH will be replaced with the note "Visual Segment-Obstacles" in the profile view of the IAP (See Figure 5-4-14). Accordingly, pilots are advised to carefully review approach procedures to identify where the optimum stabilized descent to landing can be initiated. Pilots that follow the previously published descent angle, provided by the RNAV system, below the MDA on procedures with this note may encounter obstacles in the visual segment. Pilots must visually avoid any obstacles below the MDA.

(a) VDA/TCH data is furnished by FAA on the official source document for publication on IAP charts and for coding in the navigation database unless, as noted previously, replaced by the note "Visual Segment—Obstacles."

(b) Commercial chart providers and navigation systems may publish or calculate a VDA/TCH even when the FAA does not provide such data. Pilots are cautioned that they are responsible for obstacle avoidance in the visual segment regardless of the presence or absence of a VDA/TCH and associated navigation system advisory vertical guidance.

2. The threshold crossing height (TCH) used to compute the descent angle is published with the VDA. The VDA and TCH information are charted on the profile view of the IAP following the fix (FAF/stepdown) used to compute the VDA. If no PA/APV IAP is established to the same runway, the VDA will be equal to or higher than the glide path angle of the VGSI installed on the same runway provided it is within instrument procedure criteria. A chart note will indicate if the VGSI is not coincident with the VDA. Pilots must be aware that the published VDA is for advisory information only and not to be considered instrument procedure derived vertical guidance. The VDA solely offers an aid to help pilots establish a continuous, stabilized descent during final approach.

3. Pilots may use the published angle and estimated/actual groundspeed to find a target rate of descent from the rate of descent table published in the back of the U.S. Terminal Procedures Publication. This rate of descent can be flown with the Vertical Velocity Indicator (VVI) in order to use the VDA as an aid to flying a stabilized descent. No special equipment is required.

Ch 5

FIGURE 5–4–14
Example of a Chart Note

WASHINGTON, PENNSYLVANIA
Amdt 1C 21AUG14
40°08'N-80°17'W

WASHINGTON COUNTY (AFJ)
RNAV (GPS) RWY 9

4. A straight-in aligned procedure may be restricted to circling only minimums when an excessive descent gradient necessitates. The descent angle between the FAF/stepdown fix and the Circling MDA must not exceed the maximum descent angle allowed by TERPS criteria. A published VDA on these procedures does not imply that landing straight ahead is recommended or even possible. The descent rate based on the VDA may exceed the capabilities of the aircraft and the pilot must determine how to best maneuver the aircraft within the circling area in order to land safely.

l. In isolated cases, an IAP may contain a published visual flight path. These procedures are annotated "Fly Visual to Airport" or "Fly Visual." A dashed arrow indicating the visual flight path will be included in the profile and plan views with an approximate heading and distance to the end of the runway.

1. The depicted ground track associated with the "Fly Visual to Airport" segment should be flown as a "Dead Reckoning" course. When executing the "Fly Visual to Airport" segment, the flight visibility must not be less than that prescribed in the IAP; the pilot must remain clear of clouds and proceed to the airport maintaining visual contact with the ground. Altitude on the visual flight path is at the discretion of the pilot, and it is the responsibility of the pilot to visually acquire and avoid obstacles in the "Fly Visual to Airport" segment.

2. Missed approach obstacle clearance is assured only if the missed approach is commenced at the published MAP. Before initiating an IAP that contains a "Fly Visual to Airport"

segment, the pilot should have preplanned climb out options based on aircraft performance and terrain features. Obstacle clearance is the responsibility of the pilot when the approach is continued beyond the MAP.

Note: The FAA Administrator retains the authority to approve instrument approach procedures where the pilot may not necessarily have one of the visual references specified in 14 CFR §91.175 and related rules. It is not a function of procedure design to ensure compliance with §91.175. The annotation "Fly Visual to Airport" provides relief from §91.175 requirements that the pilot have distinctly visible and identifiable visual references prior to descent below MDA/DA.

m. Area Navigation (RNAV) Instrument Approach Charts. Reliance on RNAV systems for instrument operations is becoming more commonplace as new systems such as GPS and augmented GPS such as the Wide Area Augmentation System (WAAS) are developed and deployed. In order to support full integration of RNAV procedures into the National Airspace System (NAS), the FAA developed a new charting format for IAPs (See Figure 5-4-6). This format avoids unnecessary duplication and proliferation of instrument approach charts. The original stand alone GPS charts, titled simply "GPS," are being converted to the newer format as the procedures are revised. One reason for the revision is the addition of WAAS based minima to the approach chart. The reformatted approach chart is titled "RNAV (GPS) RWY XX." Up to four lines of minima are included on these charts. Ground Based Augmentation System (GBAS)

Landing System (GLS) was a placeholder for future WAAS and LAAS minima, and the minima was always listed as N/A. The GLS minima line has now been replaced by the WAAS LPV (Localizer Performance with Vertical Guidance) minima on most RNAV (GPS) charts. LNAV/VNAV (lateral navigation/vertical navigation) was added to support both WAAS electronic vertical guidance and Barometric VNAV. LPV and LNAV/VNAV are both APV procedures as described in paragraph 5-4-5a7. The original GPS minima, titled "S-XX," for straight in runway XX, is retitled LNAV (lateral navigation). Circling minima may also be published. A new type of nonprecision WAAS minima will also be published on this chart and titled LP (localizer performance). LP will be published in locations where vertically guided minima cannot be provided due to terrain and obstacles and therefore, no LPV or LNAV/VNAV minima will be published. GBAS procedures are published on a separate chart and the GLS minima line is to be used only for GBAS. ATC clearance for the RNAV procedure authorizes a properly certified pilot to utilize any minimums for which the aircraft is certified (for example, a WAAS equipped aircraft utilizes the LPV or LP minima but a GPS only aircraft may not). The RNAV chart includes information formatted for quick reference by the pilot or flight crew at the top of the chart. This portion of the chart, developed based on a study by the Department of Transportation, Volpe National Transportation System Center, is commonly referred to as the pilot briefing.

1. The minima lines are:

(a) **GLS.** "GLS" is the acronym for GBAS Landing System. The U.S. version of GBAS has traditionally been referred to as LAAS. The worldwide community has adopted GBAS as the official term for this type of navigation system. To coincide with international terminology, the FAA is also adopting the term GBAS to be consistent with the international community. This line was originally published as a placeholder for both WAAS and LAAS minima and marked as N/A since no minima was published. As the concepts for GBAS and WAAS procedure publication have evolved, GLS will now be used only for GBAS minima, which will be on a separate approach chart. Most RNAV(GPS) approach charts have had the GLS minima line replaced by a WAAS LPV line of minima.

(b) **LPV.** "LPV" is the acronym for localizer performance with vertical guidance. RNAV (GPS) approaches to LPV lines of minima take advantage of the improved accuracy of WAAS lateral and vertical guidance to provide an approach that is very similar to a Category I Instrument Landing System (ILS). The approach to LPV line of minima is designed for angular guidance with increasing sensitivity as the aircraft gets closer to the runway. The sensitivities are nearly identical to those of the ILS at similar distances. This was done intentionally to allow the skills required to proficiently fly an ILS to readily transfer to flying RNAV (GPS) approaches to the LPV line of minima. Just as with an ILS, the LPV has vertical guidance and is flown to a DA. Aircraft can fly this minima line with a statement in the Aircraft Flight Manual that the installed equipment supports LPV approaches. This includes Class 3 and 4 TSO-C146 GPS/WAAS equipment.

(c) **LNAV/VNAV.** LNAV/VNAV identifies APV minimums developed to accommodate an RNAV IAP with vertical guidance, usually provided by approach certified Baro-VNAV, but with lateral and vertical integrity limits larger than a precision approach or LPV. LNAV stands for Lateral Navigation; VNAV stands for Vertical Navigation. This minima line can be flown by aircraft with a statement in the Aircraft Flight Manual that the installed equipment supports GPS approaches and has an approach-approved barometric VNAV, or if the aircraft has been demonstrated to support LNAV/VNAV approaches. This includes Class 2, 3 and 4 TSO-C146 GPS/WAAS equipment. Aircraft using LNAV/VNAV minimums will descend to landing via an internally generated descent path based on satellite or other approach approved VNAV systems. Since electronic vertical guidance is provided, the minima will be published as a DA. Other navigation systems may be specifically authorized to use this line of minima, see Section A, Terms/Landing Minima Data, of the U.S. Terminal Procedures books.

(d) **LP.** "LP" is the acronym for localizer performance. Approaches to LP lines of minima take advantage of the improved accuracy of WAAS to provide approaches, with lateral guidance and angular guidance. Angular guidance does not refer to a glideslope angle but rather to the increased lateral sensitivity as the aircraft gets closer to the runway, similar to localizer approaches. However, the LP line of minima is a Minimum Descent Altitude (MDA) rather than a DA (H). Procedures with LP lines of minima will not be published with another approach that contains approved vertical guidance (LNAV/VNAV or LPV). It is possible to have LP and LNAV published on the same approach chart but LP will only be published if it provides lower minima than an LNAV line of minima. LP is not a fail-down mode for LPV. LP will only be published if terrain, obstructions, or some other reason prevent publishing a vertically guided procedure. WAAS avionics may provide GNSS-based advisory vertical guidance during an approach to an LP line of minima. Barometric altimeter information remains the primary altitude reference for complying with any altitude

Ch 5

restrictions. WAAS equipment may not support LP, even if it supports LPV, if it was approved before TSO C-145b and TSO C-146b. Receivers approved under previous TSOs may require an upgrade by the manufacturer in order to be used to fly to LP minima. Receivers approved for LP must have a statement in the approved Flight Manual or Supplemental Flight Manual including LP as one of the approved approach types.

(e) **LNAV.** This minima is for lateral navigation only, and the approach minimum altitude will be published as a minimum descent altitude (MDA). LNAV provides the same level of service as the present GPS stand alone approaches. LNAV minimums support the following navigation systems: WAAS, when the navigation solution will not support vertical navigation; and, GPS navigation systems which are presently authorized to conduct GPS approaches.

Note: GPS receivers approved for approach operations in accordance with: AC 20-138, Airworthiness Approval of Positioning and Navigation Systems, qualify for this minima. WAAS navigation equipment must be approved in accordance with the requirements specified in TSO-C145() or TSO-C146() and installed in accordance with Advisory Circular AC 20-138.

2. Other systems may be authorized to utilize these approaches. See the description in Section A of the U.S. Terminal Procedures books for details. Operational approval must also be obtained for Baro-VNAV systems to operate to the LNAV/VNAV minimums. Baro-VNAV may not be authorized on some approaches due to other factors, such as no local altimeter source being available. Baro-VNAV is not authorized on LPV procedures. Pilots are directed to their local Flight Standards District Office (FSDO) for additional information.

Note: RNAV and Baro-VNAV systems must have a manufacturer supplied electronic database which must include the waypoints, altitudes, and vertical data for the procedure to be flown. The system must be able to retrieve the procedure by name from the aircraft navigation database, not just as a manually entered series of waypoints.

3. ILS or RNAV (GPS) charts.

(a) Some RNAV (GPS) charts will also contain an ILS line of minima to make use of the ILS precision final in conjunction with the RNAV GPS capabilities for the portions of the procedure prior to the final approach segment and for the missed approach. Obstacle clearance for the portions of the procedure other than the final approach segment is still based on GPS criteria.

Note: Some GPS receiver installations inhibit GPS navigation whenever ANY ILS frequency is tuned. Pilots flying aircraft with receivers installed in this manner must wait until they are on the intermediate segment of the procedure prior to the PFAF (PFAF is the active waypoint) to tune the ILS frequency and must tune the ILS back to a VOR frequency in order to fly the GPS based missed approach.

(b) **Charting.** There are charting differences between ILS, RNAV (GPS), and GLS approaches.

(1) The LAAS procedure is titled "GLS RWY XX" on the approach chart.

(2) The VDB provides information to the airborne receiver where the guidance is synthesized.

(3) The LAAS procedure is identified by a four alpha-numeric character field referred to as the RPI or approach ID and is similar to the IDENT feature of the ILS.

(4) The RPI is charted.

(5) Most RNAV(GPS) approach charts have had the GLS (NA) minima line replaced by an LPV line of minima.

(6) Since the concepts for LAAS and WAAS procedure publication have evolved, GLS will now be used only for LAAS minima, which will be on a separate approach chart.

4. Required Navigation Performance (RNP)

(a) Pilots are advised to refer to the "TERMS/LANDING MINIMUMS DATA" (Section A) of the U.S. Government Terminal Procedures books for aircraft approach eligibility requirements by specific RNP level requirements.

(b) Some aircraft have RNP approval in their AFM without a GPS sensor. The lowest level of sensors that the FAA will support for RNP service is DME/DME. However, necessary DME signal may not be available at the airport of intended operations. For those locations having an RNAV chart published with LNAV/VNAV minimums, a procedure note may be provided such as "DME/DME RNP-0.3 NA." This means that RNP aircraft dependent on DME/DME to achieve RNP-0.3 are not authorized to conduct this approach. Where DME facility availability is a factor, the note may read "DME/DME RNP-0.3 Authorized; ABC and XYZ Required." This means that ABC and XYZ facilities have been determined by flight inspection to be required in the navigation solution to assure RNP-0.3. VOR/DME updating must not be used for approach procedures.

5. Chart Terminology

(a) Decision Altitude (DA) replaces the familiar term Decision Height (DH). DA conforms to the international convention where altitudes relate to MSL and heights relate to AGL. DA will eventually be published for other types of instrument approach procedures with vertical guidance, as well. DA indicates to the pilot that the published

descent profile is flown to the DA (MSL), where a missed approach will be initiated if visual references for landing are not established. Obstacle clearance is provided to allow a momentary descent below DA while transitioning from the final approach to the missed approach. The aircraft is expected to follow the missed instructions while continuing along the published final approach course to at least the published runway threshold waypoint or MAP (if not at the threshold) before executing any turns.

(b) Minimum Descent Altitude (MDA) has been in use for many years, and will continue to be used for the LNAV only and circling procedures.

(c) Threshold Crossing Height (TCH) has been traditionally used in "precision" approaches as the height of the glide slope above threshold. With publication of LNAV/VNAV minimums and RNAV descent angles, including graphically depicted descent profiles, TCH also applies to the height of the "descent angle," or glidepath, at the threshold. Unless otherwise required for larger type aircraft which may be using the IAP, the typical TCH is 30 to 50 feet.

6. The MINIMA FORMAT will also change slightly.

(a) Each line of minima on the RNAV IAP is titled to reflect the level of service available; e.g., GLS, LPV, LNAV/VNAV, LP, and LNAV. **Circling** minima will also be provided.

(b) The minima title box indicates the nature of the minimum altitude for the IAP. For example:

(1) DA will be published next to the minima line title for minimums supporting vertical guidance such as for GLS, LPV or LNAV/VNAV.

(2) MDA will be published as the minima line on approaches with lateral guidance only, LNAV, or LP. Descent below the MDA must meet the conditions stated in 14 CFR Section 91.175.

(3) Where two or more systems, such as LPV and LNAV/VNAV, share the same minima, each line of minima will be displayed separately.

7. Chart Symbology changed slightly to include:

(a) **Descent Profile.** The published descent profile and a graphical depiction of the vertical path to the runway will be shown. Graphical depiction of the RNAV vertical guidance will differ from the traditional depiction of an ILS glide slope (feather) through the use of a shorter vertical track beginning at the decision altitude.

(1) It is FAA policy to design IAPs with minimum altitudes established at fixes/waypoints to achieve optimum stabilized (constant rate) descents within each procedure segment. This design can enhance the safety of the operations and contribute toward reduction in the occurrence of controlled flight into terrain (CFIT) accidents.

Additionally, the National Transportation Safety Board (NTSB) recently emphasized that pilots could benefit from publication of the appropriate IAP descent angle for a stabilized descent on final approach. The RNAV IAP format includes the descent angle to the hundredth of a degree; e.g., 3.00 degrees. The angle will be provided in the graphically depicted descent profile.

(2) The stabilized approach may be performed by reference to vertical navigation information provided by WAAS or LNAV/VNAV systems; or for LNAV-only systems, by the pilot determining the appropriate aircraft attitude/groundspeed combination to attain a constant rate descent which best emulates the published angle. To aid the pilot, U.S. Government Terminal Procedures Publication charts publish an expanded Rate of Descent Table on the inside of the back hard cover for use in planning and executing precision descents under known or approximate groundspeed conditions.

(b) **Visual Descent Point (VDP).** A VDP will be published on most RNAV IAPs. VDPs apply only to aircraft utilizing LP or LNAV minima, not LPV or LNAV/VNAV minimums.

(c) **Missed Approach Symbology.** In order to make missed approach guidance more readily understood, a method has been developed to display missed approach guidance in the profile view through the use of quick reference icons. Due to limited space in the profile area, only four or fewer icons can be shown. However, the icons may not provide representation of the entire missed approach procedure. The entire set of textual missed approach instructions are provided at the top of the approach chart in the pilot briefing. (See Figure 5-4-6).

(d) **Waypoints.** All RNAV or GPS stand-alone IAPs are flown using data pertaining to the particular IAP obtained from an onboard database, including the sequence of all WPs used for the approach and missed approach, except that step down waypoints may not be included in some TSO-C129 receiver databases. Included in the database, in most receivers, is coding that informs the navigation system of which WPs are fly-over (FO) or fly-by (FB). The navigation system may provide guidance appropriately—including leading the turn prior to a fly-by WP; or causing overflight of a fly-over WP. Where the navigation system does not provide such guidance, the pilot must accomplish the turn lead or waypoint overflight manually. Chart symbology for the FB WP provides pilot awareness of expected actions. Refer to the legend of the U.S. Terminal Procedures books.

(e) TAAs are described in paragraph 5-4-5d, Terminal Arrival Area (TAA). When published, the RNAV chart depicts the TAA areas through

Ch 5

the use of "icons" representing each TAA area associated with the RNAV procedure (See Figure 5-4-6). These icons are depicted in the plan view of the approach chart, generally arranged on the chart in accordance with their position relative to the aircraft's arrival from the en route structure. The WP, to which navigation is appropriate and expected within each specific TAA area, will be named and depicted on the associated TAA icon. Each depicted named WP is the IAF for arrivals from within that area. TAAs may not be used on all RNAV procedures because of airspace congestion or other reasons.

 (f) Published Temperature Limitations. There are currently two temperature limitations that may be published in the notes box of the middle briefing strip on an instrument approach procedure (IAP). The two published temperature limitations are:

 (1) A temperature range limitation associated with the use of baro-VNAV that may be published on a United States PBN IAP titled RNAV (GPS) or RNAV (RNP); and/or

 (2) A Cold Temperature Airport (CTA) limitation designated by a snowflake ICON and temperature in Celsius (C) that is published on every IAP for the airfield.

Reference: AIM, Chapter 7, Section 3, Cold Temperature Barometric Altimeter Errors, Setting Procedures and Cold Temperature Airports (CTA).

 (g) WAAS Channel Number/Approach ID. The WAAS Channel Number is an optional equipment capability that allows the use of a 5-digit number to select a specific final approach segment without using the menu method. The Approach ID is an airport unique 4-character combination for verifying the selection and extraction of the correct final approach segment information from the aircraft database. It is similar to the ILS ident, but displayed visually rather than aurally. The Approach ID consists of the letter W for WAAS, the runway number, and a letter other than L, C or R, which could be confused with Left, Center and Right, e.g., W35A. Approach IDs are assigned in the order that WAAS approaches are built to that runway number at that airport. The WAAS Channel Number and Approach ID are displayed in the upper left corner of the approach procedure pilot briefing.

 (h) At locations where outages of WAAS vertical guidance may occur daily due to initial system limitations, a negative W symbol (**W**) will be placed on RNAV (GPS) approach charts. Many of these outages will be very short in duration, but may result in the disruption of the vertical portion of the approach. The **W** symbol indicates that NOTAMs or Air Traffic advisories are not provided for outages which occur in the WAAS

LNAV/VNAV or LPV vertical service. Use LNAV or circling minima for flight planning at these locations, whether as a destination or alternate. For flight operations at these locations, when the WAAS avionics indicate that LNAV/VNAV or LPV service is available, then vertical guidance may be used to complete the approach using the displayed level of service. Should an outage occur during the procedure, reversion to LNAV minima may be required. As the WAAS coverage is expanded, the **W** will be removed.

Note: Properly trained and approved, as required, TSO-C145() and TSO-C146() equipped users (WAAS users) with and using approved baro-VNAV equipment may plan for LNAV/VNAV DA at an alternate airport. Specifically authorized WAAS users with and using approved baro-VNAV equipment may also plan for RNP 0.3 DA at the alternate airport as long as the pilot has verified RNP availability through an approved prediction program.

5-4-6 Approach Clearance

 a. An aircraft which has been cleared to a holding fix and subsequently "cleared...approach" has not received new routing. Even though clearance for the approach may have been issued prior to the aircraft reaching the holding fix, ATC would expect the pilot to proceed via the holding fix (his/her last assigned route), and the feeder route associated with that fix (if a feeder route is published on the approach chart) to the initial approach fix (IAF) to commence the approach. *WHEN CLEARED FOR THE APPROACH, THE PUBLISHED OFF AIRWAY (FEEDER) ROUTES THAT LEAD FROM THE EN ROUTE STRUCTURE TO THE IAF ARE PART OF THE APPROACH CLEARANCE.*

 b. If a feeder route to an IAF begins at a fix located along the route of flight prior to reaching the holding fix, and clearance for an approach is issued, a pilot should commence the approach via the published feeder route; i.e., the aircraft would not be expected to overfly the feeder route and return to it. The pilot is expected to commence the approach in a similar manner at the IAF, if the IAF for the procedure is located along the route of flight to the holding fix.

 c. If a route of flight directly to the initial approach fix is desired, it should be so stated by the controller with phraseology to include the words "direct...," "proceed direct" or a similar phrase which the pilot can interpret without question. When uncertain of the clearance, immediately query ATC as to what route of flight is desired.

 d. The name of an instrument approach, as published, is used to identify the approach, even though a component of the approach aid, such

as the glideslope on an Instrument Landing System, is inoperative or unreliable. The controller will use the name of the approach as published, but must advise the aircraft at the time an approach clearance is issued that the inoperative or unreliable approach aid component is unusable, except when the title of the published approach procedures otherwise allows; for example, ILS Rwy 05 or LOC Rwy 05.

e. The following applies to aircraft on radar vectors and/or cleared "direct to" in conjunction with an approach clearance:

1. Maintain the last altitude assigned by ATC until the aircraft is established on a published segment of a transition route, or approach procedure segment, or other published route, for which a lower altitude is published on the chart. If already on an established route, or approach or arrival segment, you may descend to whatever minimum altitude is listed for that route or segment.

2. Continue on the vector heading until intercepting the next published ground track applicable to the approach clearance.

3. Once reaching the final approach fix via the published segments, the pilot may continue on approach to a landing.

4. If proceeding to an IAF with a published course reversal (procedure turn or hold-in-lieu of PT pattern), except when cleared for a straight in approach by ATC, the pilot must execute the procedure turn/hold-in-lieu of PT, and complete the approach.

5. If cleared to an IAF/IF via a NoPT route, or no procedure turn/hold-in-lieu of PT is published, continue with the published approach.

6. In addition to the above, RNAV aircraft may be issued a clearance direct to the IAF/IF at intercept angles not greater than 90 degrees for both conventional and RNAV instrument approaches. Controllers may issue a heading or a course direct to a fix between the IF and FAF at intercept angles not greater than 30 degrees for both conventional and RNAV instrument approaches. In all cases, controllers will assign altitudes that ensure obstacle clearance and will permit a normal descent to the FAF. When clearing aircraft direct to the IF, ATC will radar monitor the aircraft until the IF and will advise the pilot to expect clearance direct to the IF at least 5 miles from the fix. ATC must issue a straight-in approach clearance when clearing an aircraft direct to an IAF/IF with a procedure turn or hold-in-lieu of a procedure turn, and ATC does not want the aircraft to execute the course reversal.

Note: Refer to 14 CFR Section 91.175(i).

7. RNAV aircraft may be issued a clearance direct to the FAF that is also charted as an IAF, in which case the pilot is expected to execute the depicted procedure turn or hold-in-lieu of procedure turn. ATC will not issue a straight-in approach clearance. If the pilot desires a straight-in approach, they must request vectors to the final approach course outside of the FAF or fly a published "NoPT" route. When visual approaches are in use, ATC may clear an aircraft direct to the FAF.

Note 1: In anticipation of a clearance by ATC to any fix published on an instrument approach procedure, pilots of RNAV aircraft are advised to select an appropriate IAF or feeder fix when loading an instrument approach procedure into the RNAV system.

Note 2: Selection of "Vectors-to-Final" or "Vectors" option for an instrument approach may prevent approach fixes located outside of the FAF from being loaded into an RNAV system. Therefore, the selection of these options is discouraged due to increased workload for pilots to reprogram the navigation system.

8. Arrival Holding. Some approach charts have an arrival holding pattern depicted at an IAF or at a feeder fix located along an airway. The arrival hold is depicted using a "thin line" since it is not always a mandatory part of the instrument procedure.

(a) Arrival holding is charted where holding is frequently required prior to starting the approach procedure so that detailed holding instructions are not required. The arrival holding pattern is not authorized unless assigned by ATC. Holding at the same fix may also be depicted on the en route chart.

(b) Arrival holding is also charted where it is necessary to use a holding pattern to align the aircraft for procedure entry from an airway due to turn angle limitations imposed by procedure design standards. When the turn angle from an airway into the approach procedure exceeds the permissible limits, an arrival holding pattern may be published along with a note on the procedure specifying the fix, the airway, and arrival direction where use of the arrival hold is required for procedure entry. Unlike a hold-in-lieu of procedure turn, use of the arrival holding pattern is not authorized until assigned by ATC. If ATC does not assign the arrival hold before reaching the holding fix, the pilot should request the hold for procedure entry. Once established on the inbound holding course and an approach clearance has been received, the published procedure can commence. Alternatively, if using the holding pattern for procedure entry is not desired, the pilot may ask ATC for maneuvering airspace to align the aircraft with the feeder course.

Example: Planview Chart Note: "Proc NA via V343 northeast bound without holding at JOXIT. ATC CLNC REQD."

f. An RF leg is defined as a constant radius circular path around a defined turn center that starts and terminates at a fix. An RF leg may be published as part of a procedure. Since not all aircraft have the capability to fly these leg types, pilots are responsible for knowing if they can conduct an RNAV approach with an RF leg. Requirements for RF legs will be indicated on the approach chart in the notes section or at the applicable initial approach fix. Controllers will clear RNAV-equipped aircraft for instrument approach procedures containing RF legs:

 1. Via published transitions, or

 2. In accordance with paragraph e6 above, and

 3. ATC will not clear aircraft direct to any waypoint beginning or within an RF leg, and will not assign fix/waypoint crossing speeds in excess of charted speed restrictions.

Example: Controllers will not clear aircraft direct to THIRD because that waypoint begins the RF leg, and aircraft cannot be vectored or cleared to TURNN or vectored to intercept the approach segment at any point between THIRD and FORTH because this is the RF leg. (See Figure 5-4-15.)

 g. When necessary to cancel a previously issued approach clearance, the controller will advise the pilot "Cancel Approach Clearance" followed by any additional instructions when applicable.

FIGURE 5–4–15
Example of an RNAV Approach with RF Leg

5–4–7 Instrument Approach Procedures

a. Aircraft approach category means a grouping of aircraft based on a speed of V_{REF} at the maximum certified landing weight, if specified, or if V_{REF} is not specified, 1.3 V_{SO} at the maximum certified landing weight. V_{REF}, V_{SO}, and the maximum certified landing weight are those values as established for the aircraft by the certification authority of the country of registry. A pilot must maneuver the aircraft within the circling approach protected area (see Figure 5-4-27) to achieve the obstacle and terrain clearances provided by procedure design criteria.

b. In addition to pilot techniques for maneuvering, one acceptable method to reduce the risk of flying out of the circling approach protected area is to use either the minima corresponding to the category determined during certification or minima associated with a higher category. Helicopters may use Category A minima. If it is necessary to operate at a speed in excess of the upper limit of the speed range for an aircraft's category, the minimums for the higher category should be used. This may occur with certain aircraft types operating in heavy/gusty wind, icing, or non-normal conditions. For example, an airplane which fits into Category B, but is circling to land at a speed of 145 knots, should use the approach Category D minimums. As an additional example, a Category A airplane (or helicopter) which is operating at 130 knots on a straight-in approach should use the approach Category C minimums.

c. A pilot who chooses an alternative method when it is necessary to maneuver at a speed that exceeds the category speed limit (for example, where higher category minimums are not published) should consider the following factors that can significantly affect the actual ground track flown:

1. Bank angle. For example, at 165 knots groundspeed, the radius of turn increases from 4,194 feet using 30 degrees of bank to 6,654 feet when using 20 degrees of bank. When using a shallower bank angle, it may be necessary to modify the flightpath or indicated airspeed to remain within the circling approach protected area. Pilots should be aware that excessive bank angle can lead to a loss of aircraft control.

2. Indicated airspeed. Procedure design criteria typically utilize the highest speed for a particular category. If a pilot chooses to operate at a higher speed, other factors should be modified to ensure that the aircraft remains within the circling approach protected area.

3. Wind speed and direction. For example, it is not uncommon to maneuver the aircraft to a downwind leg where the groundspeed will be considerably higher than the indicated airspeed.

Pilots must carefully plan the initiation of all turns to ensure that the aircraft remains within the circling approach protected area.

4. Pilot technique. Pilots frequently have many options with regard to flightpath when conducting circling approaches. Sound planning and judgment are vital to proper execution. The lateral and vertical path to be flown should be carefully considered using current weather and terrain information to ensure that the aircraft remains within the circling approach protected area.

d. It is important to remember that 14 CFR Section 91.175(c) requires that "where a DA/DH or MDA is applicable, no pilot may operate an aircraft below the authorized MDA or continue an approach below the authorized DA/DH unless the aircraft is continuously in a position from which a descent to a landing on the intended runway can be made at a normal rate of descent using normal maneuvers, and for operations conducted under Part 121 or Part 135 unless that descent rate will allow touchdown to occur within the touchdown zone of the runway of intended landing."

e. See the following category limits:

1. *Category A:* Speed less than 91 knots.

2. *Category B:* Speed 91 knots or more but less than 121 knots.

3. *Category C:* Speed 121 knots or more but less than 141 knots.

4. *Category D:* Speed 141 knots or more but less than 166 knots.

5. *Category E:* Speed 166 knots or more.

Note: V_{REF} in the above definition refers to the speed used in establishing the approved landing distance under the airworthiness regulations constituting the type certification basis of the airplane, regardless of whether that speed for a particular airplane is 1.3 V_{SO}, 1.23 V_{SR}, or some higher speed required for airplane controllability. This speed, at the maximum certificated landing weight, determines the lowest applicable approach category for all approaches regardless of actual landing weight.

f. When operating on an unpublished route or while being radar vectored, the pilot, when an approach clearance is received, must, in addition to complying with the minimum altitudes for IFR operations (14 CFR Section 91.177), maintain the last assigned altitude unless a different altitude is assigned by ATC, or until the aircraft is established on a segment of a published route or IAP. After the aircraft is so established, published altitudes apply to descent within each succeeding route or approach segment unless a different altitude is assigned by ATC. Notwithstanding this pilot responsibility, for aircraft operating on unpublished routes or while being radar vectored, ATC will, except when conducting a radar approach, issue an IFR approach clearance only after the

aircraft is established on a segment of a published route or IAP, or assign an altitude to maintain until the aircraft is established on a segment of a published route or instrument approach procedure. For this purpose, the procedure turn of a published IAP must not be considered a segment of that IAP until the aircraft reaches the initial fix or navigation facility upon which the procedure turn is predicated.

Example:
Cross Redding VOR at or above five thousand, cleared VOR runway three four approach.
or
Five miles from outer marker, turn right heading three three zero, maintain two thousand until established on the localizer, cleared ILS runway three six approach.

Note 1: The altitude assigned will assure IFR obstruction clearance from the point at which the approach clearance is issued until established on a segment of a published route or IAP. If uncertain of the meaning of the clearance, immediately request clarification from ATC.

Note 2: An aircraft is not established on an approach while below published approach altitudes. If the MVA/MIA allows, and ATC assigns an altitude below an IF or IAF altitude, the pilot will be issued an altitude to maintain until past a point that the aircraft is established on the approach.

g. Several IAPs, using various navigation and approach aids may be authorized for an airport. ATC may advise that a particular approach procedure is being used, primarily to expedite traffic. If issued a clearance that specifies a particular approach procedure, notify ATC immediately if a different one is desired. In this event it may be necessary for ATC to withhold clearance for the different approach until such time as traffic conditions permit. However, a pilot involved in an emergency situation will be given priority. If the pilot is not familiar with the specific approach procedure, ATC should be advised and they will provide detailed information on the execution of the procedure.

Reference: AIM, ¶5-4-4, Advance Information on Instrument Approach.

h. The name of an instrument approach, as published, is used to identify the approach, even though a component of the approach aid, such as the glideslope on an Instrument Landing System, is inoperative or unreliable. The controller will use the name of the approach as published, but must advise the aircraft at the time an approach clearance is issued that the inoperative or unreliable approach aid component is unusable, except when the title of the published approach procedures otherwise allows, for example, ILS or LOC.

i. Except when being radar vectored to the final approach course, when cleared for a specifically prescribed IAP; i.e., "cleared ILS runway one niner approach" or when "cleared approach" i.e., execution of any procedure prescribed for the airport, pilots must execute the entire procedure commencing at an IAF or an associated feeder route as described on the IAP chart unless an appropriate new or revised ATC clearance is received, or the IFR flight plan is canceled.

j. Pilots planning flights to locations which are private airfields or which have instrument approach procedures based on private navigation aids should obtain approval from the owner. In addition, the pilot must be authorized by the FAA to fly special instrument approach procedures associated with private navigation aids (see paragraph 5-4-8). Owners of navigation aids that are not for public use may elect to turn off the signal for whatever reason they may have; for example, maintenance, energy conservation, etc. Air traffic controllers are not required to question pilots to determine if they have permission to land at a private airfield or to use procedures based on privately owned navigation aids, and they may not know the status of the navigation aid. Controllers presume a pilot has obtained approval from the owner and the FAA for use of special instrument approach procedures and is aware of any details of the procedure if an IFR flight plan was filed to that airport.

k. Pilots should not rely on radar to identify a fix unless the fix is indicated as "RADAR" on the IAP. Pilots may request radar identification of an OM, but the controller may not be able to provide the service due either to workload or not having the fix on the video map.

l. If a missed approach is required, advise ATC and include the reason (unless initiated by ATC). Comply with the missed approach instructions for the instrument approach procedure being executed, unless otherwise directed by ATC.

Reference: AIM, ¶5-4-21, Missed Approach; AIM, ¶5-5-5, Missed Approach.

5–4–8 Special Instrument Approach Procedures

Instrument Approach Procedure (IAP) charts reflect the criteria associated with the U.S. Standard for Terminal Instrument [Approach] Procedures (TERP), which prescribes standardized methods for use in developing IAPs. Standard IAPs are published in the Federal Register (FR) in accordance with Title 14 of the Code of Federal Regulations, Part 97, and are available for use by appropriately qualified pilots operating properly equipped and airworthy aircraft in accordance with operating rules and procedures acceptable

to the FAA. Special IAPs are also developed using TERPs but are not given public notice in the FR. The FAA authorizes only certain individual pilots and/or pilots in individual organizations to use special IAPs, and may require additional crew training and/or aircraft equipment or performance, and may also require the use of landing aids, communications, or weather services not available for public use. Additionally, IAPs that service private use airports or heliports are generally special IAPs. FDC NOTAMs for Specials, FDC T-NOTAMs, may also be used to promulgate safety-of-flight information relating to Specials provided the location has a valid landing area identifier and is serviced by the United States NOTAM system. Pilots may access NOTAMs online or through an FAA Flight Service Station (FSS). FSS specialists will not automatically provide NOTAM information to pilots for special IAPs during telephone preflight briefings. Pilots who are authorized by the FAA to use special IAPs must specifically request FDC NOTAM information for the particular special IAP they plan to use.

5–4–9 Procedure Turn and Hold-in-lieu of Procedure Turn

a. A procedure turn is the maneuver prescribed when it is necessary to reverse direction to establish the aircraft inbound on an intermediate or final approach course. The procedure turn or hold-in-lieu-of-PT is a required maneuver when it is depicted on the approach chart, unless cleared by ATC for a straight-in approach. Additionally, the procedure turn or hold-in-lieu-of-PT is not permitted when the symbol "No PT" is depicted on the initial segment being used, when a RADAR VECTOR to the final approach course is provided, or when conducting a timed approach from a holding fix. The altitude prescribed for the procedure turn is a minimum altitude until the aircraft is established on the inbound course. The maneuver must be completed within the distance specified in the profile view. For a hold-in-lieu-of-PT, the holding pattern direction must be flown as depicted and the specified leg length/timing must not be exceeded.

Note: *The pilot may elect to use the procedure turn or hold-in-lieu-of-PT when it is not required by the procedure, but must first receive an amended clearance from ATC. If the pilot is uncertain whether the ATC clearance intends for a procedure turn to be conducted or to allow for a straight-in approach, the pilot must immediately request clarification from ATC (14 CFR Section 91.123).*

1. On U.S. Government charts, a barbed arrow indicates the maneuvering side of the outbound course on which the procedure turn is made. Headings are provided for course reversal

using the 45 degree type procedure turn. However, the point at which the turn may be commenced and the type and rate of turn is left to the discretion of the pilot (limited by the charted remain within xx NM distance). Some of the options are the 45 degree procedure turn, the racetrack pattern, the tear-drop procedure turn, or the 80 degree ↔ 260 degree course reversal. Racetrack entries should be conducted on the maneuvering side where the majority of protected airspace resides. If an entry places the pilot on the non-maneuvering side of the PT, correction to intercept the outbound course ensures remaining within protected airspace. Some procedure turns are specified by procedural track. These turns must be flown exactly as depicted.

2. Descent to the procedure turn (PT) completion altitude from the PT fix altitude (when one has been published or assigned by ATC) must not begin until crossing over the PT fix or abeam and proceeding outbound. Some procedures contain a note in the chart profile view that says "Maintain (altitude) or above until established outbound for procedure turn" (See Figure 5-4-16). Newer procedures will simply depict an "at or above" altitude at the PT fix without a chart note (See Figure 5-4-17). Both are there to ensure required obstacle clearance is provided in the procedure turn entry zone (See Figure 5-4-18). Absence of a chart note or specified minimum altitude adjacent to the PT fix is an indication that descent to the procedure turn altitude can commence immediately upon crossing over the PT fix, regardless of the direction of flight. This is because the minimum altitudes in the PT entry zone and the PT maneuvering zone are the same.

3. When the approach procedure involves a procedure turn, a maximum speed of not greater than 200 knots (IAS) should be observed from first overheading the course reversal IAF through the procedure turn maneuver to ensure containment within the obstruction clearance area. Pilots should begin the outbound turn immediately after passing the procedure turn fix. The procedure turn maneuver must be executed within the distance specified in the profile view. The normal procedure turn distance is 10 miles. This may be reduced to a minimum of 5 miles where only Category A or helicopter aircraft are to be operated or increased to as much as 15 miles to accommodate high performance aircraft.

4. A teardrop procedure or penetration turn may be specified in some procedures for a required course reversal. The teardrop procedure consists of departure from an initial approach fix on an outbound course followed by a turn toward and intercepting the inbound course at or prior to the intermediate fix or point. Its purpose is to permit an aircraft to reverse direction and lose considerable altitude within reasonably limited

Ch 5

airspace. Where no fix is available to mark the beginning of the intermediate segment, it must be assumed to commence at a point 10 miles prior to the final approach fix. When the facility is located on the airport, an aircraft is considered to be on final approach upon completion of the penetration turn. However, the final approach segment begins on the final approach course 10 miles from the facility.

FIGURE 5–4–16

FIGURE 5–4–17

Figure 5-4-18

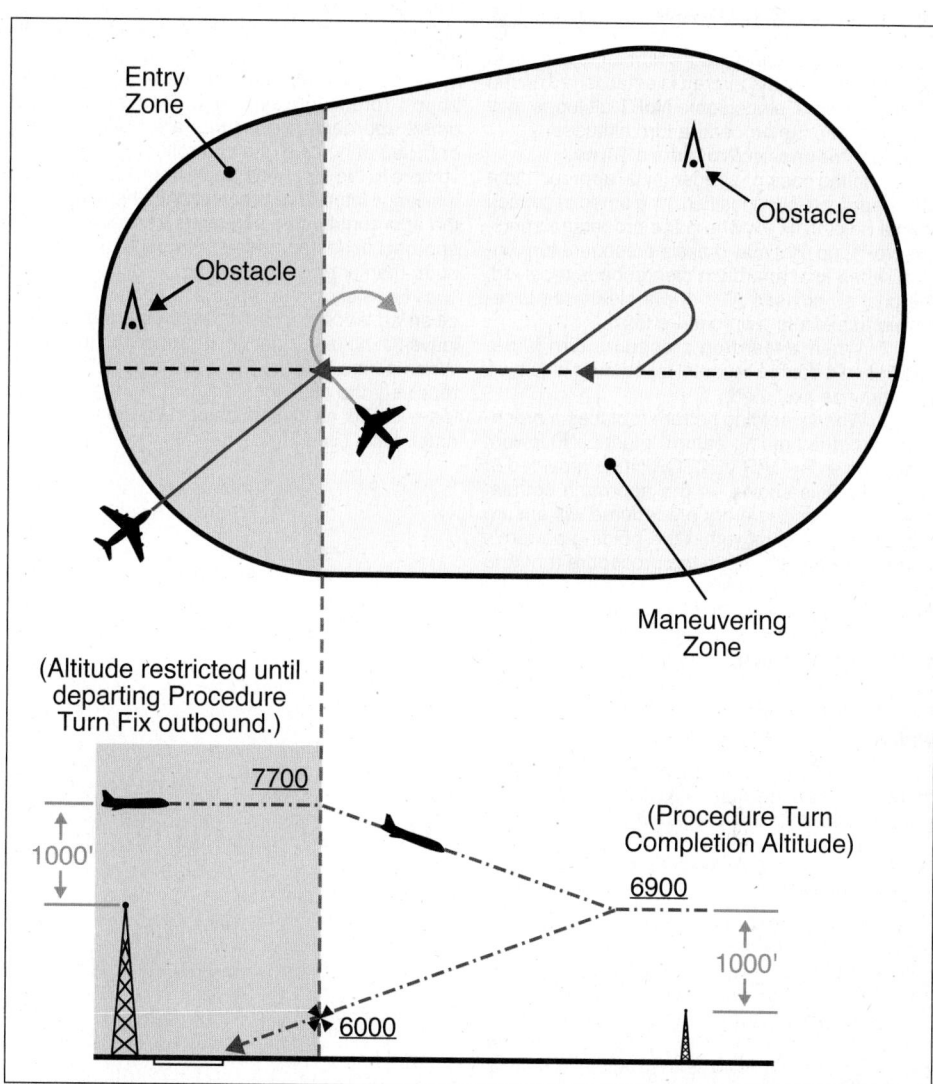

5. A holding pattern in lieu of procedure turn may be specified for course reversal in some procedures. In such cases, the holding pattern is established over an intermediate fix or a final approach fix. The holding pattern distance or time specified in the profile view must be observed. For a hold-in-lieu-of-PT, the holding pattern direction must be flown as depicted and the specified leg length/timing must not be exceeded. Maximum holding airspeed limitations as set forth for all holding patterns apply. The holding pattern maneuver is completed when the aircraft is established on the inbound course after executing the appropriate entry. If cleared for the approach prior to returning to the holding fix, and the aircraft is at the prescribed altitude, additional circuits of the holding pattern are not necessary nor expected by ATC. If pilots elect to make additional circuits to lose excessive altitude or to become better established on course, it is their responsibility to so advise ATC upon receipt of their approach clearance.

6. A procedure turn is not required when an approach can be made directly from a specified intermediate fix to the final approach fix. In such cases, the term "NoPT" is used with the

appropriate course and altitude to denote that the procedure turn is not required. If a procedure turn is desired, and when cleared to do so by ATC, descent below the procedure turn altitude should not be made until the aircraft is established on the inbound course, since some NoPT altitudes may be lower than the procedure turn altitudes.

b. Limitations on Procedure Turns.

1. In the case of a radar initial approach to a final approach fix or position, or a timed approach from a holding fix, or where the procedure specifies NoPT, no pilot may make a procedure turn unless, when final approach clearance is received, the pilot so advises ATC and a clearance is received to execute a procedure turn.

2. When a teardrop procedure turn is depicted and a course reversal is required, this type turn must be executed.

3. When a holding pattern replaces a procedure turn, the holding pattern must be followed, except when RADAR VECTORING is provided or when NoPT is shown on the approach course. The recommended entry procedures will ensure the aircraft remains within the holding pattern's protected airspace. As in the procedure turn, the descent from the minimum holding pattern altitude to the final approach fix altitude (when lower) may not commence until the aircraft is established on the inbound course. Where a holding pattern is established in-lieu-of a procedure turn, the maximum holding pattern airspeeds apply.

Reference: AIM, ¶5-3-8 j2, Holding.

4. The absence of the procedure turn barb in the plan view indicates that a procedure turn is not authorized for that procedure.

5-4-10 Timed Approaches from a Holding Fix

a. Timed approaches may be conducted when the following conditions are met:

1. A control tower is in operation at the airport where the approaches are conducted.

2. Direct communications are maintained between the pilot and the center or approach controller until the pilot is instructed to contact the tower.

3. If more than one missed approach procedure is available, none require a course reversal.

4. If only one missed approach procedure is available, the following conditions are met:

(a) Course reversal is not required; and,

(b) Reported ceiling and visibility are equal to or greater than the highest prescribed circling minimums for the IAP.

5. When cleared for the approach, pilots must not execute a procedure turn. (14 CFR Section 91.175.)

b. Although the controller will not specifically state that "timed approaches are in use," the assigning of a time to depart the final approach fix inbound (nonprecision approach) or the outer marker or fix used in lieu of the outer marker inbound (precision approach) is indicative that timed approach procedures are being utilized, or in lieu of holding, the controller may use radar vectors to the Final Approach Course to establish a mileage interval between aircraft that will ensure the appropriate time sequence between the final approach fix/outer marker or fix used in lieu of the outer marker and the airport.

c. Each pilot in an approach sequence will be given advance notice as to the time they should leave the holding point on approach to the airport. When a time to leave the holding point has been received, the pilot should adjust the flight path to leave the fix as closely as possible to the designated time. (See Figure 5-4-19.)

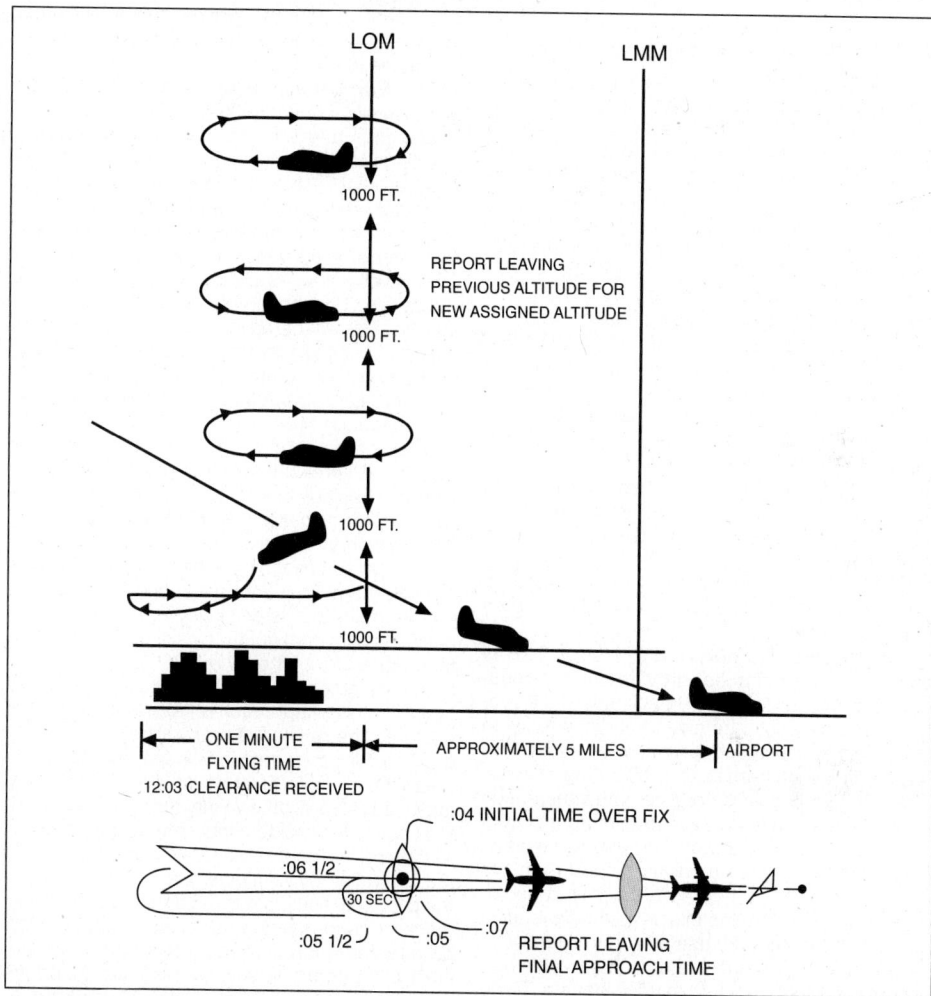

FIGURE 5–4–19
Timed Approaches from a Holding Fix

Example: *At 12:03 local time, in the example shown, a pilot holding, receives instructions to leave the fix inbound at 12:07. These instructions are received just as the pilot has completed turn at the outbound end of the holding pattern and is proceeding inbound towards the fix. Arriving back over the fix, the pilot notes that the time is 12:04 and that there are 3 minutes to lose in order to leave the fix at the assigned time. Since the time remaining is more than two minutes, the pilot plans to fly a race track pattern rather than a 360 degree turn, which would use up 2 minutes. The turns at the ends of the race track pattern will consume approximately 2 minutes. Three minutes to go, minus 2 minutes required for the turns, leaves 1 minute for level flight. Since two portions of*
level flight will be required to get back to the fix inbound, the pilot halves the 1 minute remaining and plans to fly level for 30 seconds outbound before starting the turn back to the fix on final approach. If the winds were negligible at flight altitude, this procedure would bring the pilot inbound across the fix precisely at the specified time of 12:07. However, if expecting headwind on final approach, the pilot should shorten the 30 second outbound course somewhat, knowing that the wind will carry the aircraft away from the fix faster while outbound and decrease the ground speed while returning to the fix. On the other hand, compensating for a tailwind on final approach, the pilot should lengthen the calculated 30 second outbound heading somewhat, knowing that the wind

would tend to hold the aircraft closer to the fix while outbound and increase the ground speed while returning to the fix.

5-4-11 Radar Approaches

a. The only airborne radio equipment required for radar approaches is a functioning radio transmitter and receiver. The radar controller vectors the aircraft to align it with the runway centerline. The controller continues the vectors to keep the aircraft on course until the pilot can complete the approach and landing by visual reference to the surface. There are two types of radar approaches: Precision (PAR) and Surveillance (ASR).

b. A radar approach may be given to any aircraft upon request and may be offered to pilots of aircraft in distress or to expedite traffic, however, an ASR might not be approved unless there is an ATC operational requirement, or in an unusual or emergency situation. Acceptance of a PAR or ASR by a pilot does not waive the prescribed weather minimums for the airport or for the particular aircraft operator concerned. The decision to make a radar approach when the reported weather is below the established minimums rests with the pilot.

c. PAR and ASR minimums are published on separate pages in the FAA Terminal Procedures Publication (TPP).

1. Precision Approach (PAR). A PAR is one in which a controller provides highly accurate navigational guidance in azimuth and elevation to a pilot. Pilots are given headings to fly, to direct them to, and keep their aircraft aligned with the extended centerline of the landing runway. They are told to anticipate glide path interception approximately 10 to 30 seconds before it occurs and when to start descent. The published Decision Height will be given only if the pilot requests it. If the aircraft is observed to deviate above or below the glide path, the pilot is given the relative amount of deviation by use of terms "slightly" or "well" and is expected to adjust the aircraft's rate of descent/ascent to return to the glidepath. Trend information is also issued with respect to the elevation of the aircraft and may be modified by the terms "rapidly" and "slowly"; e.g., "well above glidepath, coming down rapidly." Range from touchdown is given at least once each mile. If an aircraft is observed by the controller to proceed outside of specified safety zone limits in azimuth and/or elevation and continue to operate outside these prescribed limits, the pilot will be directed to execute a missed approach or to fly a specified course unless the pilot has the runway environment (runway, approach lights, etc.) in sight. Navigational guidance in azimuth and elevation is provided the pilot until the aircraft reaches the published Decision Height (DH). Advisory course and glidepath information is furnished by the controller until the aircraft passes over the landing threshold, at which point the pilot is advised of any deviation from the runway centerline. Radar service is automatically terminated upon completion of the approach.

2. Surveillance Approach (ASR). An ASR is one in which a controller provides navigational guidance in azimuth only. The pilot is furnished headings to fly to align the aircraft with the extended centerline of the landing runway. Since the radar information used for a surveillance approach is considerably less precise than that used for a precision approach, the accuracy of the approach will not be as great and higher minimums will apply. Guidance in elevation is not possible but the pilot will be advised when to commence descent to the Minimum Descent Altitude (MDA) or, if appropriate, to an intermediate step-down fix Minimum Crossing Altitude and subsequently to the prescribed MDA. In addition, the pilot will be advised of the location of the Missed Approach Point (MAP) prescribed for the procedure and the aircraft's position each mile on final from the runway, airport or heliport or MAP, as appropriate. If requested by the pilot, recommended altitudes will be issued at each mile, based on the descent gradient established for the procedure, down to the last mile that is at or above the MDA. Normally, navigational guidance will be provided until the aircraft reaches the MAP. Controllers will terminate guidance and instruct the pilot to execute a missed approach unless at the MAP the pilot has the runway, airport or heliport in sight or, for a helicopter point-in-space approach, the prescribed visual reference with the surface is established. Also, if, at any time during the approach the controller considers that safe guidance for the remainder of the approach cannot be provided, the controller will terminate guidance and instruct the pilot to execute a missed approach. Similarly, guidance termination and missed approach will be effected upon pilot request and, for civil aircraft only, controllers may terminate guidance when the pilot reports the runway, airport/heliport or visual surface route (point-in-space approach) in sight or otherwise indicates that continued guidance is not required. Radar service is automatically terminated at the completion of a radar approach.

Note: The published MDA for straight-in approaches will be issued to the pilot before beginning descent. When a surveillance approach will terminate in a circle-to-land maneuver, the pilot must furnish the aircraft approach category to the controller. The controller will then provide the pilot with the appropriate MDA.

3. NO-GYRO Approach. This approach is available to a pilot under radar control who experiences circumstances wherein the directional gyro or other stabilized compass is inoperative or inaccurate. When this occurs, the pilot should so advise ATC and request a No-Gyro vector or approach. Pilots of aircraft not equipped with a directional gyro or other stabilized compass who desire radar handling may also request a No-Gyro vector or approach. The pilot should make all turns at standard rate and should execute the turn immediately upon receipt of instructions. For example, "TURN RIGHT," "STOP TURN." When a surveillance or precision approach is made, the pilot will be advised after the aircraft has been turned onto final approach to make turns at half standard rate.

5-4-12 Radar Monitoring of Instrument Approaches

a. PAR facilities operated by the FAA and the military services at some joint-use (civil and military) and military installations monitor aircraft on instrument approaches and issue radar advisories to the pilot when weather is below VFR minimums (1,000 and 3), at night, or when requested by a pilot. This service is provided only when the PAR Final Approach Course coincides with the final approach of the navigational aid and only during the operational hours of the PAR. The radar advisories serve only as a secondary aid since the pilot has selected the navigational aid as the primary aid for the approach.

b. Prior to starting final approach, the pilot will be advised of the frequency on which the advisories will be transmitted. If, for any reason, radar advisories cannot be furnished, the pilot will be so advised.

c. Advisory information, derived from radar observations, includes information on:

1. Passing the final approach fix inbound (nonprecision approach) or passing the outer marker or fix used in lieu of the outer marker inbound (precision approach).

Note: At this point, the pilot may be requested to report sighting the approach lights or the runway.

2. Trend advisories with respect to elevation and/or azimuth radar position and movement will be provided.

Note: Whenever the aircraft nears the PAR safety limit, the pilot will be advised that the aircraft is well above or below the glidepath or well left or right of course. Glidepath information is given only to those aircraft executing a precision approach, such as ILS. Altitude information is not transmitted to aircraft executing other than precision approaches because the descent portions of these approaches generally do not coincide with the depicted PAR glidepath.

3. If, after repeated advisories, the aircraft proceeds outside the PAR safety limit or if a radical deviation is observed, the pilot will be advised to execute a missed approach unless the prescribed visual reference with the surface is established.

d. Radar service is automatically terminated upon completion of the approach.

5-4-13 Simultaneous Approaches to Parallel Runways

a. ATC procedures permit ILS/RNAV/GLS instrument approach operations to dual or triple parallel runway configurations. ILS/RNAV/GLS approaches to parallel runways are grouped into three classes: Simultaneous Dependent Approaches; Simultaneous Independent Approaches; and Simultaneous Close Parallel PRM Approaches. RNAV approach procedures that are approved for simultaneous operations require GPS as the sensor for position updating. VOR/DME, DME/DME and IRU RNAV updating is not authorized. The classification of a parallel runway approach procedure is dependent on adjacent parallel runway centerline separation, ATC procedures, and airport ATC final approach radar monitoring and communications capabilities. At some airports, one or more approach courses may be offset up to 3 degrees. ILS approaches with offset localizer configurations result in loss of Category II/III capabilities and an increase in decision altitude/height (50').

b. Depending on weather conditions, traffic volume, and the specific combination of runways being utilized for arrival operations, a runway may be used for different types of simultaneous operations, including closely spaced dependent or independent approaches. Pilots should ensure that they understand the type of operation that is being conducted, and ask ATC for clarification if necessary.

c. Parallel approach operations demand heightened pilot situational awareness. A thorough Approach Procedure Chart review should be conducted with, as a minimum, emphasis on the following approach chart information: name and number of the approach, localizer frequency, inbound localizer/azimuth course, glideslope/glidepath intercept altitude, glideslope crossing altitude at the final approach fix, decision height, missed approach instructions, special notes/procedures, and the assigned runway location/proximity to adjacent runways. Pilots are informed by ATC or through the ATIS that simultaneous approaches are in use.

d. The close proximity of adjacent aircraft conducting simultaneous independent approaches, especially simultaneous close parallel PRM approaches mandates strict pilot compliance with

FIGURE 5–4–20
Simultaneous Approaches
(Approach Courses Parallel and Offset between 2.5 and 3.0 degrees)

DEPENDENT

- Runway centerline spacing between 2500'* and 9000'. (*less than 2500' when specifically authorized)
- STAGGERED approaches.
- Final Monitor Controller NOT required.

WIDELY SPACED (4300' AND GREATER)

(Duals and triples)
- Runway centerlines spaced at least 4300'.
- Final Monitor Controllers and NTZ required up to 9000', 9200' above 5000' airport elevation.

PRM APPROACHES (CLOSE PARALLEL)

(Duals and triples)
- Runway centerlines spaced less than 4300' and at least 2500'.
- Final Monitor Controllers and NTZ required.
- Certain runway spacing requires one offset approach course and/or high update rate NTZ surveillance.
- Attention All Users Page (AAUP) required.

OFFSET (can also be close parallel)

STRAIGHT-IN

Rwy C/L intercept about 2800' from threshold

2.5 to 3.0° offset approach course

NO TRANSGRESSION ZONE

all ATC clearances. ATC assigned airspeeds, altitudes, and headings must be complied with in a timely manner. Autopilot coupled approaches require pilot knowledge of procedures necessary to comply with ATC instructions. Simultaneous independent approaches, particularly simultaneous close parallel PRM approaches necessitate precise approach course tracking to minimize final monitor controller intervention, and unwanted No Transgression Zone (NTZ) penetration. In the unlikely event of a breakout, ATC will not assign altitudes lower than the minimum vectoring altitude. Pilots should notify ATC immediately if there is a degradation of aircraft or navigation systems.

e. Strict radio discipline is mandatory during simultaneous independent and simultaneous close parallel PRM approach operations. This includes an alert listening watch and the avoidance of lengthy, unnecessary radio transmissions. Attention must be given to proper call sign usage to prevent the inadvertent execution of clearances intended for another aircraft. Use of abbreviated call signs must be avoided to preclude confusion of aircraft with similar sounding call signs. Pilots must be alert to unusually long periods of silence or any unusual background sounds in their radio receiver. A stuck microphone may block the issuance of ATC instructions on the tower frequency by the final monitor controller during simultaneous independent and simultaneous close parallel PRM approaches. In the case of PRM approaches, the use of a second frequency by the monitor controller mitigates the "stuck mike" or other blockage on the tower frequency.

Reference: *AIM, Chapter 4, Section 2, Radio Communications Phraseology and Techniques, gives additional communications information.*

f. Use of Traffic Collision Avoidance Systems (TCAS) provides an additional element of safety to parallel approach operations. Pilots should follow recommended TCAS operating procedures presented in approved flight manuals, original equipment manufacturer recommendations, professional newsletters, and FAA publications.

5-4-14 Simultaneous Dependent Approaches

(See Figure 5-4-21.)

FIGURE 5-4-21
Simultaneous Approaches
(Parallel Runways and Approach Courses)

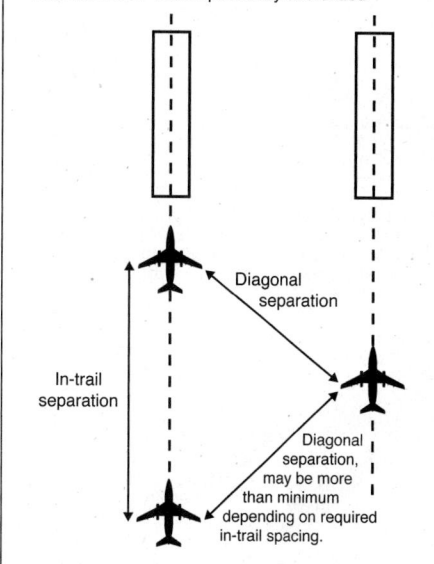

DEPENDENT APPROACHES
- Runway centerlines spaced between 2500'* and 9000'
- STAGGERED approaches
- Final monitor controllers and NTZ not required
 *less than 2500' when specifically authorized

Diagonal separation

In-trail separation

Diagonal separation, may be more than minimum depending on required in-trail spacing.

a. Simultaneous dependent approaches are an ATC procedure permitting approaches to airports having parallel runway centerlines separated by at least 2,500 feet up to 9,000 feet. Integral parts of a total system are ILS or other system providing approach navigation, radar, communications, ATC procedures, and required airborne equipment. RNAV equipment in the aircraft or GLS equipment on the ground and in the aircraft may replace the required airborne and ground based ILS equipment. Although non-precision minimums may be published, pilots must only use those procedures specifically authorized by chart note. For example, the chart note "LNAV NA during simultaneous operations," requires vertical guidance. When given a choice, pilots should always fly a precision approach whenever possible.

b. A simultaneous dependent approach differs from a simultaneous independent approach in that, the minimum distance between parallel runway centerlines may be reduced; there is no requirement for radar monitoring or advisories; and a staggered separation of aircraft on the adjacent final course is required.

c. A minimum of 1.0 NM radar separation (diagonal) is required between successive aircraft on the adjacent final approach course when runway centerlines are at least 2,500 feet but no more than 3,600 feet apart. A minimum of 1.5 NM radar separation (diagonal) is required between successive aircraft on the adjacent final approach course when runway centerlines are more than 3,600 feet but no more than 8,300 feet apart. When runway centerlines are more than 8,300 feet but no more than 9,000 feet apart a minimum of 2 NM diagonal radar separation is provided. Aircraft on the same final approach course within 10 NM of the runway end are provided a minimum of 3 NM radar separation, reduced to 2.5 NM in certain circumstances. In addition, a minimum of 1,000 feet vertical or a minimum of three miles radar separation is provided between aircraft during turn on to the parallel final approach course.

d. Whenever parallel approaches are in use, pilots are informed by ATC or via the ATIS that approaches to both runways are in use. The charted IAP also notes which runways may be used simultaneously. In addition, the radar controller will have the interphone capability of communicating with the tower controller where separation responsibility has not been delegated to the tower.

Note: *ATC will not specifically identify these operations as being dependent when advertised on the ATIS.*

Example: *Simultaneous ILS Runway 19 right and ILS Runway 19 left in use.*

e. At certain airports, simultaneous dependent approaches are permitted to runways spaced less than 2,500 feet apart. In this case, ATC will provide no less than the minimum authorized diagonal separation with the leader always arriving on the same runway. The trailing aircraft is permitted reduced diagonal separation instead of the single runway separation normally utilized for runways spaced less than 2,500 feet apart. For wake turbulence mitigation reasons:

Ch 5

1. Reduced diagonal spacing is only permitted when certain aircraft wake category pairings exist; typically when the leader is either in the large or small wake turbulence category, and

2. All aircraft must descend on the glideslope from the altitude at which they were cleared for the approach during these operations.

When reduced separation is authorized, the IAP briefing strip indicates that simultaneous operations require the use of vertical guidance and that the pilot should maintain last assigned altitude until intercepting the glideslope. No special pilot training is required to participate in these operations.

Note: Either simultaneous dependent approaches with reduced separation or SOIA PRM approaches may be conducted to Runways 28R and 28L at KSFO spaced 750 feet apart, depending on weather conditions and traffic volume. Pilots should use caution so as not to confuse these operations. Plan for SOIA procedures only when ATC assigns a PRM approach or the ATIS advertises PRM approaches are in use. KSFO is the only airport where both procedures are presently conducted.

Reference: AIM, ¶5-4-16, Simultaneous Close Parallel PRM Approaches and Simultaneous Offset Instrument Approaches (SOIA).

5-4-15 Simultaneous Independent ILS/RNAV/GLS Approaches
(See Figure 5-4-22.)

FIGURE 5–4–22
Simultaneous Independent ILS/RNAV/GLS Approaches

a. System. An approach system permitting simultaneous approaches to parallel runways with centerlines separated by at least 4,300 feet. Separation between 4,300 and 9,000 feet (9,200' for airports above 5,000') utilizing NTZ final monitor controllers. Simultaneous independent approaches require NTZ radar monitoring to ensure separation between aircraft on the adjacent parallel approach course. Aircraft position is tracked by final monitor controllers who will issue instructions to aircraft observed deviating from the assigned final approach course. Staggered radar separation procedures are not utilized. Integral parts of a total system are radar, communications, ATC procedures, and ILS or other required airborne equipment. A chart note identifies that the approach is authorized for simultaneous use.

When simultaneous operations are in use, it will be advertised on the ATIS. When advised that simultaneous approaches are in use, pilots must advise approach control immediately of malfunctioning or inoperative receivers, or if a simultaneous approach is not desired. Although non-precision minimums may be published, pilots must only use those procedures specifically authorized by chart note. For example, the chart note "LNAV NA during simultaneous operations," requires vertical guidance. When given a choice, pilots should always fly a precision approach whenever possible.

Note: ATC does not use the word independent or parallel when advertising these operations on the ATIS.

Example: Simultaneous ILS Runway 24 left and ILS Runway 24 right approaches in use.

b. Radar Services. These services are provided for each simultaneous independent approach.

1. During turn on to parallel final approach, aircraft are normally provided 3 miles radar separation or a minimum of 1,000 feet vertical separation. The assigned altitude must be maintained until intercepting the glidepath, unless cleared otherwise by ATC. Aircraft will not be vectored to intercept the final approach course at an angle greater than thirty degrees.

Note: Some simultaneous operations permit the aircraft to track an RNAV course beginning on downwind and continuing in a turn to intercept the final approach course. In this case, separation with the aircraft on the adjacent final approach course is provided by the monitor controller with reference to an NTZ.

2. The final monitor controller will have the capability of overriding the tower controller on the tower frequency.

3. Pilots will be instructed to contact the tower frequency prior to the point where NTZ monitoring begins.

4. Aircraft observed to overshoot the turn-on or to continue on a track which will penetrate the NTZ will be instructed to return to the correct final approach course immediately. The final monitor controller may cancel the approach clearance, and issue missed approach or other instructions to the deviating aircraft.

Phraseology:
"(Aircraft call sign) you have crossed the final approach course. Turn (left/right) immediately and return to the final approach course,"

or

"(Aircraft call sign) turn (left/right) and return to the final approach course."

5. If a deviating aircraft fails to respond to such instructions or is observed penetrating the NTZ, the aircraft on the adjacent final approach course (if threatened), will be issued a breakout instruction.

Phraseology:
"Traffic alert (aircraft call sign) turn (left/right) immediately heading (degrees), (climb/descend) and maintain (altitude)."

6. Radar monitoring will automatically be terminated when visual separation is applied, the aircraft reports the approach lights or runway in sight, or the aircraft is 1 NM or less from the runway threshold. Final monitor controllers will not advise pilots when radar monitoring is terminated.

Note: Simultaneous independent approaches conducted to runways spaced greater than 9,000 feet (or 9,200' at airports above 5,000') do not require an NTZ. However, from a pilot's perspective, the same alerts relative to deviating aircraft will be provided by ATC as are provided when an NTZ is being monitored. Pilots may not be aware as to whether or not an NTZ is being monitored.

Ch 5

5–4–16 Simultaneous Close Parallel PRM Approaches and Simultaneous Offset Instrument Approaches (SOIA)

(See Figure 5-4-23.)

FIGURE 5–4–23
**PRM Approaches
Simultaneous Close Parallel**

- Runway centerlines spaced less than 4300 ft but at least 2500 ft apart.
- Final monitor controllers and NTZ required.
- PRM training and procedures required.
- Certain runway spacing requires one offset approach course and/or high update rate NTZ surveillance.

3200'

2200'

Intersection or waypoint established where 3200' altitude intercepts glide slope or vertical path, NTZ begins.

Intercept glide slope at 2200'

Radar monitoring provided to ensure lateral or vertical separation between aircraft on parallel final approach courses prior to the beginning of the NTZ.

NTZ

a. System.

1. PRM is an acronym for the high update rate Precision Runway Monitor surveillance system which is required to monitor the No Transgression Zone (NTZ) for specific parallel runway separations used to conduct simultaneous close parallel approaches. PRM is also published in the title as part of the approach name for IAPs used to conduct Simultaneous Close Parallel approaches. "PRM" alerts pilots that specific airborne equipment, training, and procedures are applicable.

Because Simultaneous Close Parallel PRM approaches are independent, the NTZ and normal operating zone (NOZ) airspace between the final approach courses is monitored by two monitor controllers, one for each approach course. The NTZ monitoring system (final monitor aid) consists of a high resolution ATC radar display with automated tracking software which provides monitor controllers with aircraft identification, position, speed, and a ten-second projected position, as well as visual and aural NTZ penetration alerts. A PRM high update rate surveillance sensor is a component of this system only for specific runway spacing. Additional procedures for simultaneous independent approaches are described in paragraph 5-4-15, Simultaneous Independent ILS/RNAV/GLS Approaches.

2. Simultaneous Close Parallel PRM approaches, whether conducted utilizing a high update rate PRM surveillance sensor or not, must meet all of the following requirements: pilot training, PRM in the approach title, NTZ monitoring utilizing a final monitor aid, radar display, publication of an AAUP, and use of a secondary PRM communications frequency. PRM approaches are depicted on a separate IAP titled (Procedure type) PRM Rwy XXX (Simultaneous Close Parallel or Close Parallel).

Note: ATC does not use the word "independent" when advertising these operations on the ATIS.

Example: Simultaneous ILS PRM Runway 33 left and ILS PRM Runway 33 right approaches in use.

(a) The pilot may request to conduct a different type of PRM approach to the same runway other than the one that is presently being used; for example, RNAV instead of ILS. However, pilots must always obtain ATC approval to conduct a different type of approach. Also, in the event of the loss of ground-based NAVAIDs, the ATIS may advertise other types of PRM approaches to the affected runway or runways.

(b) The Attention All Users Page (AAUP) will address procedures for conducting PRM approaches.

b. Requirements and Procedures. Besides system requirements and pilot procedures as identified in subparagraph a1 above, all pilots must have completed special training before accepting a clearance to conduct a PRM approach.

1. Pilot Training Requirement. Pilots must complete special pilot training, as outlined below, before accepting a clearance for a simultaneous close parallel PRM approach.

(a) For operations under 14 CFR Parts 121, 129, and 135, pilots must comply with FAA-approved company training as identified in their Operations Specifications. Training includes the requirement for pilots to view the FAA training slide presentation, "Precision Runway Monitor (PRM) Pilot Procedures." Refer to https://www.faa.gov/training_testing/training/prm/ or search key words "FAA PRM" for additional information and to view or download the slide presentation.

(b) For operations under Part 91:

(1) Pilots operating transport category aircraft must be familiar with PRM operations as contained in this section of the AIM. In addition, pilots operating transport category aircraft must view the slide presentation, "Precision Runway Monitor (PRM) Pilot Procedures." Refer to https://www.faa.gov/training_testing/training/prm/ or search key words "FAA PRM" for additional information and to view or download the slide presentation.

(2) Pilots *not* operating transport category aircraft must be familiar with PRM and SOIA operations as contained in this section of the AIM. The FAA strongly recommends that pilots *not* involved in transport category aircraft operations view the FAA training slide presentation, "Precision Runway Monitor (PRM) Pilot Procedures." Refer to https://www.faa.gov/training_testing/training/prm/ or search key words "FAA PRM" for additional information and to view or download the slide presentation.

Note: Depending on weather conditions, traffic volume, and the specific combination of runways being utilized for arrival operations, a runway may be used for different types of simultaneous operations, including closely spaced dependent or independent approaches. Use PRM procedures only when the ATIS advertises their use. For other types of simultaneous approaches, see paragraphs 5-4-14 and 5-4-15.

c. ATC Directed Breakout. An ATC directed "breakout" is defined as a vector off the final approach course of a threatened aircraft in response to another aircraft penetrating the NTZ.

d. Dual Communications. The aircraft flying the PRM approach must have the capability of enabling the pilot/s to listen to two communications frequencies simultaneously. To avoid blocked transmissions, each runway will have two frequencies, a primary and a PRM monitor frequency. The tower controller will transmit on both frequencies. The monitor controller's transmissions, if needed, will override both frequencies. Pilots will ONLY transmit on the tower controller's frequency, but will listen to both frequencies. Select the PRM monitor frequency audio only when instructed by ATC to contact the tower. The volume levels should be set about the same on both radios so that the pilots will be able to hear transmissions on the PRM frequency if the tower is blocked. Site-specific procedures take precedence over the general information presented in this paragraph. Refer to the AAUP for applicable procedures at specific airports.

e. Radar Services.

1. During turn on to parallel final approach, aircraft will be provided 3 miles radar separation or a minimum of 1,000 feet vertical separation. The assigned altitude must be maintained until intercepting the glideslope/glidepath, unless cleared otherwise by ATC. Aircraft will not be vectored to intercept the final approach course at an angle greater than thirty degrees.

2. The final monitor controller will have the capability of overriding the tower controller on the tower frequency as well as transmitting on the PRM frequency.

3. Pilots will be instructed to contact the tower frequency prior to the point where NTZ monitoring begins. Pilots will begin monitoring the secondary PRM frequency at that time (see Dual VHF Communications Required below).

4. To ensure separation is maintained, and in order to avoid an imminent situation during PRM approaches, pilots must immediately comply with monitor controller instructions.

5. Aircraft observed to overshoot the turn or to continue on a track which will penetrate the NTZ will be instructed to return to the correct final approach course immediately. The final monitor controller may cancel the approach clearance, and issue missed approach or other instructions to the deviating aircraft.

Ch 5

Phraseology:

"(Aircraft call sign) YOU HAVE CROSSED THE FINAL APPROACH COURSE. TURN (left/right) IMMEDIATELY AND RETURN TO THE FINAL APPROACH COURSE,"

or

"(Aircraft call sign) TURN (left/right) AND RE-TURN TO THE FINAL APPROACH COURSE."

6. If a deviating aircraft fails to respond to such instructions or is observed penetrating the NTZ, the aircraft on the adjacent final approach course (if threatened) will be issued a breakout instruction.

Phraseology:

"TRAFFIC ALERT (aircraft call sign) TURN (left/right) IMMEDIATELY HEADING (degrees), (climb/descend) AND MAINTAIN (altitude)."

7. Radar monitoring will automatically be terminated when visual separation is applied, or the aircraft reports the approach lights or runway in sight or within 1 NM of the runway threshold. Final monitor controllers will not advise pilots when radar monitoring is terminated.

f. Attention All Users Page (AAUP). At airports that conduct PRM operations, the AAUP informs pilots under the "General" section of information relative to all the PRM approaches published at a specific airport, and this section must be briefed in its entirety. Under the "Runway Specific" section, only items relative to the runway to be used for landing need be briefed. (See Figure 5-4-24.) A single AAUP is utilized for multiple PRM approach charts at the same airport, which are listed on the AAUP. The requirement for informing ATC if the pilot is unable to accept a PRM clearance is also presented. The "General" section of AAUP addresses the following:

1. Review of the procedure for executing a climbing or descending breakout;

2. Breakout phraseology beginning with the words, "Traffic Alert;"

3. Descending on the glideslope/glidepath meets all crossing restrictions;

4. Briefing the PRM approach also satisfies the non-PRM approach briefing of the same type of approach to the same runway; and

5. Description of the dual communications procedure.

The "Runway Specific" section of the AAUP addresses those issues which only apply to certain runway ends that utilize PRM approaches. There may be no Runway Specific procedures, a single item applicable to only one runway end, or multiple items for a single or multiple runway end/s. Examples of SOIA runway specific procedures are as follows:

FIGURE 5–4–24
PRM Attention All Users Page (AAUP)

PRM APPROACH AAUP AL 155 (FAA) 15288 USA INTL (USA) USA CITY

ATTENTION ALL USERS PAGE (AAUP)
(PRM CLOSE PARALLEL)

Pilots who are unable to participate will be afforded appropriate arrival services as operational conditions permit and must notify the controlling ATC facility as soon as practical, but at least 120 miles from destination.

 ILS PRM or LOC PRM Rwys 10R, 10C, 28L, 28C
 RNAV (GPS) PRM RWYS 10R, 10C, 28L, 28C

General

- Review procedure for executing a climbing and descending PRM breakout.

- Breakout phraseology: "TRAFFIC ALERT (call sign) TURN (left/right) IMMEDIATELY HEADING (degrees) CLIMB/DESCEND AND MAINTAIN (altitude)."

- All breakouts: Hand flown, initiate immediately.

- Descending on the glideslope/glidepath ensures compliance with any charted crossing restrictions.

- Dual VHF COMM: When assigned or planning a specific PRM approach, tune a second receiver to the PRM monitor frequency or, if silent, other active frequency (i.e., ATIS), set the volume, retune the PRM frequency if necessary, then deselect the audio. When directed by ATC, immediately switch to the tower frequency and select the secondary radio audio to ON.

- If later assigned the same runway, non-PRM approach, consider it briefed provided the same minimums are utilized. PRM related chart notes and frequency no longer apply.

- TCAS during breakout: Follow TCAS climb/descend if it differs from ATC, while executing the breakout turn.

Runway Specific

- Runway 10R: Exit at taxiway Tango whenever practical.

PRM APPROACH AAUP 41°59N 87°54W USA INTL (USA) USA CITY

g. Simultaneous Offset Instrument Approach (SOIA).

1. SOIA is a procedure used to conduct simultaneous approaches to runways spaced less than 3,000 feet, but at least 750 feet apart. The SOIA procedure utilizes a straight-in PRM approach to one runway, and a PRM offset approach with glideslope/glidepath to the adjacent runway. In SOIA operations, aircraft are paired, with the aircraft conducting the straight-in PRM approach always positioned slightly ahead of the aircraft conducting the offset PRM approach.

2. The straight-in PRM approach plates used in SOIA operations are identical to other straight-in PRM approach plates, with an additional note, which provides the separation between the

two runways used for simultaneous SOIA approaches. The offset PRM approach plate displays the required notations for closely spaced approaches as well as depicts the visual segment of the approach.

3. Controllers monitor the SOIA PRM approaches in exactly the same manner as is done for other PRM approaches. The procedures and system requirements for SOIA PRM approaches are identical with those used for simultaneous close parallel PRM approaches until near the offset PRM approach missed approach point (MAP), where visual acquisition of the straight-in aircraft by the aircraft conducting the offset PRM approach occurs. Since SOIA PRM approaches are identical to other PRM approaches (except for the visual segment in the offset approach), an understanding of the procedures for conducting PRM approaches is essential before conducting a SOIA PRM operation.

4. In SOIA, the approach course separation (instead of the runway separation) meets established close parallel approach criteria. (See Figure 5-4-25 for the generic SOIA approach geometry.) A visual segment of the offset PRM approach is established between the offset MAP and the runway threshold. Aircraft transition in visual conditions from the offset course, beginning at the offset MAP, to align with the runway and can be stabilized by 500 feet above ground level (AGL) on the extended runway centerline. A cloud ceiling for the approach is established so that the aircraft conducting the offset approach has nominally at least 30 seconds or more to acquire the leading straight-in aircraft prior to reaching the offset MAP. If visual acquisition is not accomplished prior to crossing the offset MAP, a missed approach must be executed.

5. Flight Management System (FMS) coding of the offset RNAV PRM and GLS PRM approaches in a SOIA operation is different than other RNAV and GLS approach coding in that it does not match the initial missed approach procedure published on the charted IAP. In the SOIA design of the offset approach, lateral course guidance terminates at the fictitious threshold point (FTP), which is an extension of the final approach course beyond the offset MAP to a point near the runway threshold. The FTP is designated in the approach coding as the MAP so that vertical guidance is available to the pilot to the runway threshold, just as vertical guidance is provided by the offset LDA glideslope. No matter what type of offset approach is being conducted, reliance on lateral guidance is discontinued at the charted MAP and replaced by visual maneuvering to accomplish runway alignment.

(a) As a result of this approach coding, when executing a missed approach at and after passing the charted offset MAP, a heading must initially be flown (either hand-flown or using autopilot "heading mode") before engaging LNAV. If the pilot engages LNAV immediately, the aircraft may continue to track toward the FTP instead of commencing a turn toward the missed approach holding fix. Notes on the charted IAP and in the AAUP make specific reference to this procedure.

(b) Some FMSs do not code waypoints inside the FAF as part of the approach. Therefore, the depicted MAP on the charted IAP may not be included in the offset approach coding. Pilots utilizing those FMSs may identify the location of the waypoint by noting its distance from the FTP as published on the charted IAP. In those same FMSs, the straight-in SOIA approach will not display a waypoint inside the PFAF. The same procedures may be utilized to identify an uncoded waypoint. In this case, the location is determined by noting its distance from the runway waypoint or using an authorized distance as published on the charted IAP.

(c) Because the FTP is coded as the MAP, the FMS map display will depict the initial missed approach course as beginning at the FTP. This depiction does not match the charted initial missed approach procedure on the IAP. Pilots are reminded that charted IAP guidance is to be followed, not the map display. Once the aircraft completes the initial turn when commencing a missed approach, the remainder of the procedure coding is standard and can be utilized as with any other IAP.

Ch 5

FIGURE 5–4–25
SOIA Approach Geometry

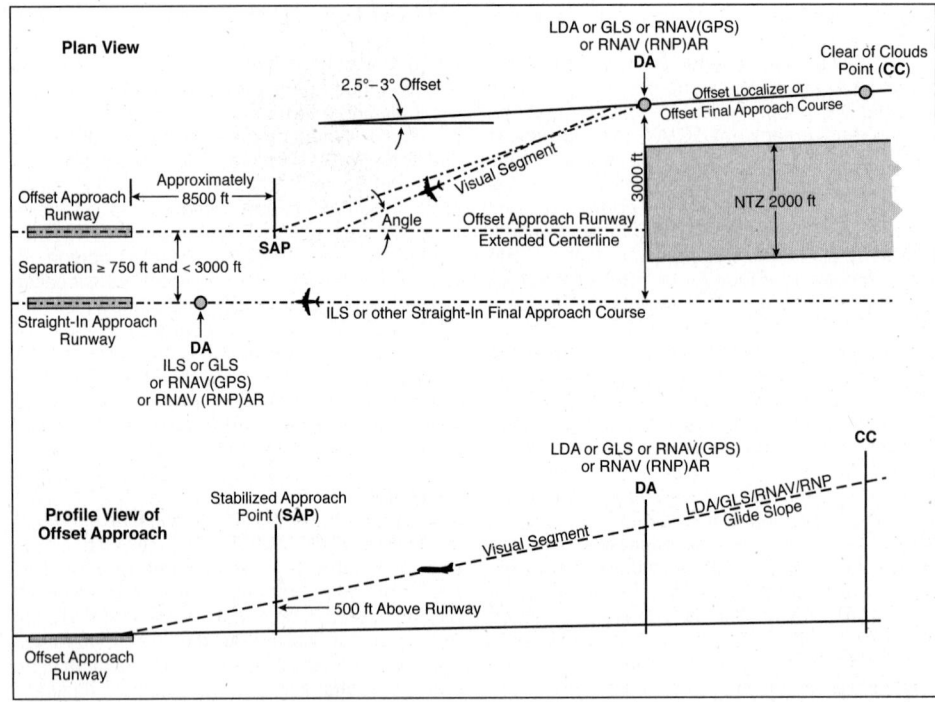

Notes:

SAP	The stabilized approach point is a design point along the extended centerline of the intended landing runway on the glide slope/glide path at 500 feet above the runway threshold elevation. It is used to verify a sufficient distance is provided for the visual maneuver after the offset course approach DA to permit the pilots to conform to approved, stabilized approach criteria. The SAP is not published on the IAP.
Offset Course DA	The point along the LDA, or other offset course, where the course separation with the adjacent ILS, or other straight-in course, reaches the minimum distance permitted to conduct closely spaced approaches. Typically that minimum distance will be 3,000 feet without the use of high update radar; with high update radar, course separation of less than 3,000 ft may be used when validated by a safety study. The altitude of the glide slope/glide path at that point determines the offset course approach decision altitude and is where the NTZ terminates. Maneuvering inside the DA is done in visual conditions.
Visual Segment Angle	Angle, as determined by the SOIA design tool, formed by the extension of the straight segment of the calculated flight track (between the offset course MAP/DA and the SAP) and the extended runway centerline. The size of the angle is dependent on the aircraft approach categories (Category D or only selected categories/speeds) that are authorized to use the offset course approach and the spacing between the runways.
Visibility	Distance from the offset course approach DA to runway threshold in statute mile.
Procedure	The aircraft on the offset course approach must see the runway-landing environment and, if ATC has advised that traffic on the straight-in approach is a factor, the offset course approach aircraft must visually acquire the straight-in approach aircraft and report it in sight to ATC prior to reaching the DA for the offset course approach.
CC	The Clear of Clouds point is the position on the offset final approach course where aircraft first operate in visual meteorological conditions below the ceiling, when the actual weather conditions are at, or near, the minimum ceiling for SOIA operations. Ceiling is defined by the Aeronautical Information Manual.

6. SOIA PRM approaches utilize the same dual communications procedures as do other PRM approaches.

Note: At KSFO, pilots conducting SOIA operations select the monitor frequency audio when communicating with the final radar controller, not the tower controller as is customary. In this special case, the monitor controller's transmissions, if required, override the final controller's frequency. This procedure is addressed on the AAUP.

(a) SOIA utilizes the same AAUP format as do other PRM approaches. The minimum weather conditions that are required are listed. Because of the more complex nature of instructions for conducting SOIA approaches, the "Runway Specific" items are more numerous and lengthy.

(b) Examples of SOIA offset runway specific notes:

(1) Aircraft must remain on the offset course until passing the offset MAP prior to maneuvering to align with the centerline of the offset approach runway.

(2) Pilots are authorized to continue past the offset MAP to align with runway centerline when:

[a] the straight-in approach traffic is in sight and is expected to remain in sight,

[b] ATC has been advised that "traffic is in sight." (ATC is not required to acknowledge this transmission),

[c] the runway environment is in sight. Otherwise, a missed approach must be executed. Between the offset MAP and the runway threshold, pilots conducting the offset PRM approach must not pass the straight-in aircraft and are responsible for separating themselves visually from traffic conducting the straight-in PRM approach to the adjacent runway, which means maneuvering the aircraft as necessary to avoid that traffic until landing, and providing wake turbulence avoidance, if applicable. Pilots maintaining visual separation should advise ATC, as soon as practical, if visual contact with the aircraft conducting the straight-in PRM approach is lost and execute a missed approach unless otherwise instructed by ATC.

(c) Examples of SOIA straight-in runway specific notes:

(1) To facilitate the offset aircraft in providing wake mitigation, pilots should descend on, not above, the glideslope/glidepath.

(2) Conducting the straight-in approach, pilots should be aware that the aircraft conducting the offset approach will be approaching from the right/left rear and will be operating in close proximity to the straight-in aircraft.

7. Recap.
The following are differences between widely spaced simultaneous approaches (at least 4,300 feet between the runway centerlines) and Simultaneous PRM close parallel approaches which are of importance to the pilot:

(a) Runway Spacing. Prior to PRM simultaneous close parallel approaches, most ATC-directed breakouts were the result of two aircraft in-trail on the same final approach course getting too close together. Two aircraft going in the same direction did not mandate quick reaction times. With PRM closely spaced approaches, two aircraft could be alongside each other, navigating on courses that are separated by less than 4,300 feet and as close as 3,000 feet. In the unlikely event that an aircraft "blunders" off its course and makes a worst case turn of 30 degrees toward the adjacent final approach course, closing speeds of 135 feet per second could occur that constitute the need for quick reaction. A blunder has to be recognized by the monitor controller, and breakout instructions issued to the endangered aircraft. The pilot will not have any warning that a breakout is imminent because the blundering aircraft will be on another frequency. It is important that, when a pilot receives breakout instructions, the assumption is made that a blundering aircraft is about to (or has penetrated the NTZ) and is heading toward his/her approach course. The pilot must initiate a breakout as soon as safety allows. While conducting PRM approaches, pilots must maintain an increased sense of awareness in order to immediately react to an ATC (breakout) instruction and maneuver (as instructed by ATC) away from a blundering aircraft.

(b) Communications. Dual VHF communications procedures should be carefully followed. One of the assumptions made that permits the safe conduct of PRM approaches is that there will be no blocked communications.

(c) Hand-flown Breakouts. The use of the autopilot is encouraged while flying a PRM approach, but the autopilot must be disengaged in the rare event that a breakout is issued. Simulation studies of breakouts have shown that a hand-flown breakout can be initiated consistently faster than a breakout performed using the autopilot.

(d) TCAS. The ATC breakout instruction is the primary means of conflict resolution. TCAS, if installed, provides another form of conflict resolution in the unlikely event other separation standards would fail. TCAS is not required to conduct a closely spaced approach.

The TCAS provides only vertical resolution of aircraft conflicts, while the ATC breakout instruction provides both vertical and horizontal guidance for conflict resolutions. Pilots should always immediately follow the TCAS Resolution Advisory (RA), whenever it is received. Should a TCAS RA be received before, during, or after an ATC breakout instruction is issued, the pilot should follow the RA, even if it conflicts with the climb/descent

portion of the breakout maneuver. If following an RA requires deviating from an ATC clearance, the pilot must advise ATC as soon as practical. While following an RA, it is extremely important that the pilot also comply with the turn portion of the ATC breakout instruction unless the pilot determines safety to be factor. Adhering to these procedures assures the pilot that acceptable "breakout" separation margins will always be provided, even in the face of a normal procedural or system failure.

5-4-17 Simultaneous Converging Instrument Approaches

a. ATC may conduct instrument approaches simultaneously to converging runways; i.e., runways having an included angle from 15 to 100 degrees, at airports where a program has been specifically approved to do so.

b. The basic concept requires that dedicated, separate standard instrument approach procedures be developed for each converging runway included. These approaches can be identified by the letter "V" in the title; for example, "ILS V Rwy 17 (CONVERGING)". Missed Approach Points must be at least 3 miles apart and missed approach procedures ensure that missed approach protected airspace does not overlap.

c. Other requirements are: radar availability, nonintersecting final approach courses, precision approach capability for each runway and, if runways intersect, controllers must be able to apply visual separation as well as intersecting runway separation criteria. Intersecting runways also require minimums of at least 700 foot ceilings and 2 miles visibility. Straight in approaches and landings must be made.

d. Whenever simultaneous converging approaches are in use, aircraft will be informed by the controller as soon as feasible after initial contact or via ATIS. Additionally, the radar controller will have direct communications capability with the tower controller where separation responsibility has not been delegated to the tower.

5-4-18 RNP AR (Authorization Required) Instrument Procedures

a. RNP AR procedures require authorization analogous to the special authorization required for Category II or III ILS procedures. All operators require specific authorization from the FAA to fly any RNP AR approach or departure procedure. The FAA issues RNP AR authorization via operations specification (OpSpec), management specification (MSpec), or letter of authorization (LOA). There are no exceptions. Operators can find comprehensive information on RNP AR aircraft eligibility, operating procedures, and training requirements in AC 90-101, Approval Guidance for RNP Procedures with AR.

b. Unique characteristics of RNP AR Operations Approach title. The FAA titles all RNP AR instrument approach procedures (IAP) as "RNAV (RNP) RWY XX." Internationally, operators may find RNP AR IAPs titled "RNP RWY XX (AR)." All RNP AR procedures will clearly state "Authorization Required" on the procedure chart.

c. RNP value. RNP AR procedures are characterized by use of a lateral Obstacle Evaluation Area (OEA) equal to two times the RNP value (2 x RNP) in nautical miles. No secondary lateral OEA or additional buffers are used. RNP AR procedures require a minimum lateral accuracy value of RNP 0.30. Each published line of minima in an RNP AR procedure has an associated RNP value that defines the procedure's lateral performance requirement in the Final Approach Segment. Each approved RNP AR operator's FAA-issued authorization will identify a minimum authorized RNP approach value. This value may vary depending on aircraft configuration or operational procedures (e.g., use of flight director or autopilot).

d. Radius-to-fix (RF) legs. Many RNP AR IFPs contain RF legs. Aircraft eligibility for RF legs is required in any authorization for RNP AR operations.

e. Missed Approach RNP value less than 1.00 NM. Some RNP AR IFPs require an RNP lateral accuracy value of less than 1.00 NM in the missed approach segment. The operator's FAA-issued RNP AR authorization will specify whether the operator may fly a missed approach procedure requiring a lateral accuracy value less than 1.00 NM. AC 90-101 identifies specific operating procedures and training requirements applicable to this aspect of RNP AR procedures.

f. Non-standard speeds or climb gradients. RNP AR approaches may require non-standard approach speeds and/or missed approach climb gradients. RNP AR approach charts will reflect any non-standard requirements and pilots must confirm they can meet those requirements before commencing the approach.

g. RNP AR Departure Procedures (RNP AR DP). RNP AR approach authorization is a mandatory prerequisite for an operator to be eligible to perform RNP AR DPs. RNP AR DPs can utilize a minimum RNP value of RNP 0.30, may include higher than standard climb gradients, and may include RF turns. Close in RF turns associated with RNP AR DPs may begin as soon as the departure end of the runway (DER). For specific eligibility guidance, operators should refer to AC 90-101.

FIGURE 5-4-26
Example of an RNP AR DP

5-4-19 Side-Step Maneuver

a. ATC may authorize a standard instrument approach procedure which serves either one of parallel runways that are separated by 1,200 feet or less followed by a straight-in landing on the adjacent runway.

b. Aircraft that will execute a side-step maneuver will be cleared for a specified approach procedure and landing on the adjacent parallel runway. Example, "cleared ILS runway 7 left approach, side-step to runway 7 right." Pilots are expected to commence the side-step maneuver as soon as possible after the runway or runway environment is in sight. Compliance with minimum altitudes associated with stepdown fixes is expected even after the side-step maneuver is initiated.

Note: Side-step minima are flown to a Minimum Descent Altitude (MDA) regardless of the approach authorized.

c. Landing minimums to the adjacent runway will be based on nonprecision criteria and therefore higher than the precision minimums to the primary runway, but will normally be lower than the published circling minimums.

5-4-20 Approach and Landing Minimums

a. Landing Minimums. The rules applicable to landing minimums are contained in 14 CFR Section 91.175. Table 5-4-1 may be used to convert RVR to ground or flight visibility. For converting RVR values that fall between listed values, use the next higher RVR value; do not interpolate. For example, when converting 1800 RVR, use 2400 RVR with the resultant visibility of 1/2 mile.

TABLE 5-4-1
RVR VALUE CONVERSIONS

RVR	Visibility (statute miles)
1600	1/4
2400	1/2
3200	5/8
4000	3/4
4500	7/8
5000	1
6000	1-1/4

b. Obstacle Clearance. Final approach obstacle clearance is provided from the start of the final segment to the runway or missed approach point, whichever occurs last. Side-step obstacle protection is provided by increasing the width of the final approach obstacle clearance area.

1. Circling approach protected areas are defined by the tangential connection of arcs drawn from each runway end (see Figure 5-4-27). Circling approach protected areas developed prior to late 2012 used fixed radius distances, dependent on aircraft approach category, as shown in the table on page B2 of the U.S. TPP. The approaches using standard circling approach areas can be identified by the absence of the "negative C" symbol on the circling line of minima. Circling approach protected areas developed after late 2012 use the radius distance shown in the table on page B2 of the U.S. TPP, dependent on aircraft approach category, and the altitude of the circling MDA, which accounts for true airspeed increase with altitude. The approaches using expanded circling approach areas can be identified by the presence of the "negative C" symbol on the circling line of minima (see Figure 5-4-28). Because of obstacles near the airport, a portion of the circling area may be restricted by a procedural note; for example, "Circling NA E of RWY 17-35." Obstacle clearance is provided at the published minimums (MDA) for the pilot who makes a straight-in approach, side-steps, or circles. Once below the MDA the pilot must see and avoid obstacles. Executing the missed approach after starting to maneuver usually places the aircraft beyond the MAP. The aircraft is clear of obstacles when at or above the MDA while inside the circling area, but simply joining the missed approach ground track

Ch 5

from the circling maneuver may not provide vertical obstacle clearance once the aircraft exits the circling area. Additional climb inside the circling area may be required before joining the missed approach track. See paragraph 5-4-21, Missed Approach, for additional considerations when starting a missed approach at other than the MAP.

See paragraph 5-4-21, Missed Approach

FIGURE 5–4–27
Final Approach Obstacle Clearance

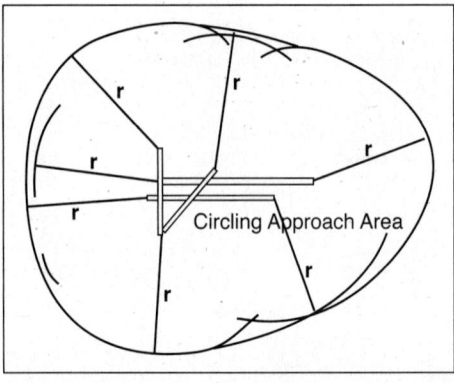

Note: *Circling approach area radii vary according to approach category and MSL circling altitude due to TAS changes—see Figure 5-4-28.*

FIGURE 5–4–28
Standard and Expanded Circling Approach Radii in the U.S. TPP

STANDARD CIRCLING APPROACH MANEUVERING RADIUS

Circling approach protected areas developed prior to late 2012 used the radius distances shown in the following table, expressed in nautical miles (NM), dependent on aircraft approach category. The approaches using standard circling approach areas can be identified by the absence of the **C** symbol on the circling line of minima.

Circling MDA in feet MSL	Approach Category and Circling Radius (NM)				
	CAT A	CAT B	CAT C	CAT D	CAT E
All Altitudes	1.3	1.5	1.7	2.3	4.5

C EXPANDED CIRCLING APPROACH MANEUVERING AIRSPACE RADIUS

Circling approach protected areas developed after late 2012 use the radius distances shown in the following table, expressed in nautical miles (NM), dependent on aircraft approach category, and the altitude of the circling MDA, which accounts for true airspeed increase with altitude. The approaches using expanded circling approach areas can be identified by the presence of the **C** symbol on the circling line of minima.

Circling MDA in feet MSL	Approach Category and Circling Radius (NM)				
	CAT A	CAT B	CAT C	CAT D	CAT E
1000 or less	1.3	1.7	2.7	3.6	4.5
1001–3000	1.3	1.8	2.8	3.7	4.6
3001–5000	1.3	1.8	2.9	3.8	4.8
5001–7000	1.3	1.9	3.0	4.0	5.0
7001–9000	1.4	2.0	3.2	4.2	5.3
9001 and above	1.4	2.1	3.3	4.4	5.5

2. Precision Obstacle Free Zone (POFZ). A volume of airspace above an area beginning at the runway threshold, at the threshold elevation, and centered on the extended runway centerline. The POFZ is 200 feet (60m) long and 800 feet (240m) wide. The POFZ must be clear when an aircraft on a vertically guided final approach is within 2 nautical miles of the runway threshold and the official weather observation is a ceiling below 250 feet or visibility less than 3/4 statute mile (SM) (or runway visual range below 4,000 feet). If the POFZ is not clear, the MINIMUM authorized height above touchdown (HAT) and visibility is 250 feet and 3/4 SM. The POFZ is considered clear even if the wing of the aircraft holding on a taxiway waiting for runway clearance penetrates the POFZ; however, neither the fuselage nor the tail may infringe on the POFZ. The POFZ is applicable at all runway ends including displaced thresholds.

FIGURE 5-4-29
Precision Obstacle Free Zone (POFZ)

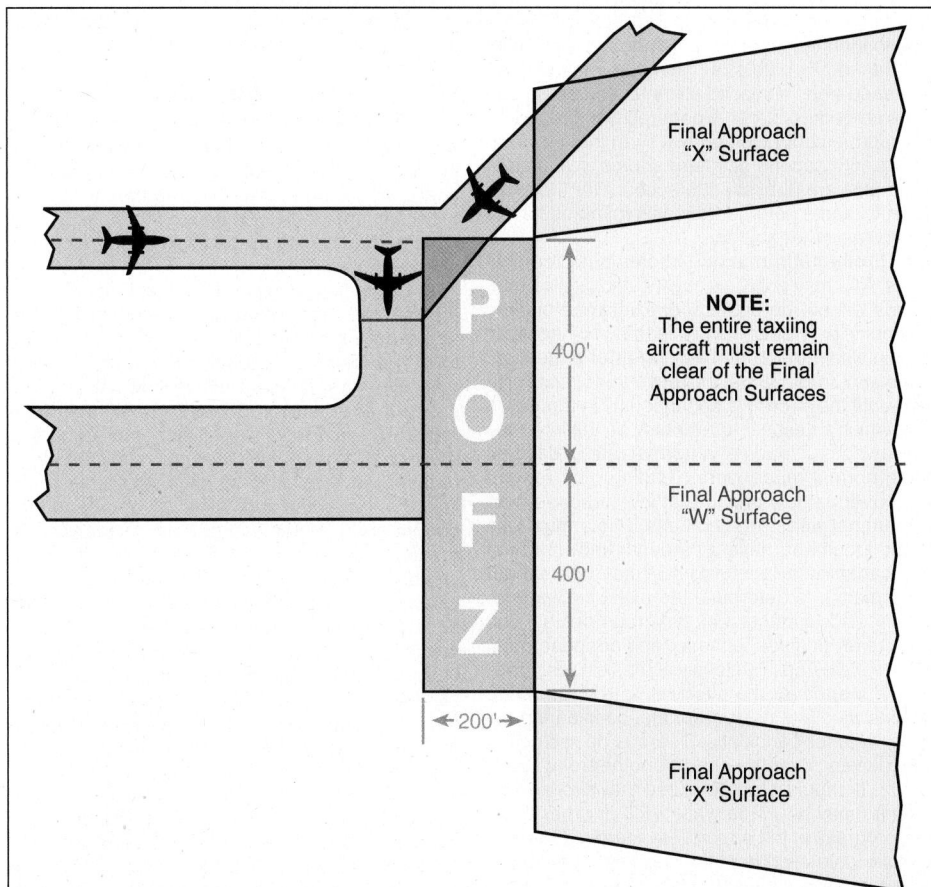

c. Straight-in Minimums are shown on the IAP when the final approach course is within 30 degrees of the runway alignment and a normal descent can be made from the IFR altitude shown on the IAP to the runway surface. When either the normal rate of descent or the runway alignment factor of 30 degrees is exceeded, a straight-in minimum is not published and a circling minimum applies. The fact that a straight-in minimum is not published does not preclude pilots from landing straight-in if they have the active runway in sight and have sufficient time to make a normal approach for landing. Under such conditions and when ATC has cleared them for landing on that

runway, pilots are not expected to circle even though only circling minimums are published. If they desire to circle, they should advise ATC.

d. Side-Step Maneuver Minimums. Landing minimums for a side-step maneuver to the adjacent runway will normally be higher than the minimums to the primary runway.

e. Published Approach Minimums. Approach minimums are published for different aircraft categories and consist of a minimum altitude (DA, DH, MDA) and required visibility. These minimums are determined by applying the appropriate TERPS criteria. When a fix is incorporated in a nonprecision final segment, two sets of minimums may be published: one for the pilot that is able to identify the fix, and a second for the pilot that cannot. Two sets of minimums may also be published when a second altimeter source is used in the procedure. When a nonprecision procedure incorporates both a stepdown fix in the final segment and a second altimeter source, two sets of minimums are published to account for the stepdown fix and a note addresses minimums for the second altimeter source.

f. Circling Minimums. In some busy terminal areas, ATC may not allow circling and circling minimums will not be published. Published circling minimums provide obstacle clearance when pilots remain within the appropriate area of protection. Pilots should remain at or above the circling altitude until the aircraft is continuously in a position from which a descent to a landing on the intended runway can be made at a normal rate of descent using normal maneuvers. Circling may require maneuvers at low altitude, at low airspeed, and in marginal weather conditions. Pilots must use sound judgment, have an indepth knowledge of their capabilities, and fully understand the aircraft performance to determine the exact circling maneuver since weather, unique airport design, and the aircraft position, altitude, and airspeed must all be considered. The following basic rules apply:

1. Maneuver the shortest path to the base or downwind leg, as appropriate, considering existing weather conditions. There is no restriction from passing over the airport or other runways.

2. It should be recognized that circling maneuvers may be made while VFR or other flying is in progress at the airport. Standard left turns or specific instruction from the controller for maneuvering must be considered when circling to land.

3. At airports without a control tower, it may be desirable to fly over the airport to observe wind and turn indicators and other traffic which may be on the runway or flying in the vicinity of the airport.

Reference: AC 90-66A, Recommended Standards Traffic patterns for Aeronautical Operations at Airports without Operating Control Towers.

4. The missed approach point (MAP) varies depending upon the approach flown. For vertically guided approaches, the MAP is at the decision altitude/decision height. Non-vertically guided and circling procedures share the same MAP and the pilot determines this MAP by timing from the final approach fix, by a fix, a NAVAID, or a waypoint. Circling from a GLS, an ILS without a localizer line of minima or an RNAV (GPS) approach without an LNAV line of minima is prohibited.

g. Instrument Approach at a Military Field. When instrument approaches are conducted by civil aircraft at military airports, they must be conducted in accordance with the procedures and minimums approved by the military agency having jurisdiction over the airport.

5-4-21 Missed Approach

a. When a landing cannot be accomplished, advise ATC and, upon reaching the missed approach point defined on the approach procedure chart, the pilot must comply with the missed approach instructions for the procedure being used or with an alternate missed approach procedure specified by ATC.

b. Obstacle protection for missed approach is predicated on the missed approach being initiated at the decision altitude/decision height (DA/DH) or at the missed approach point and not lower than minimum descent altitude (MDA). A climb gradient of at least 200 feet per nautical mile is required, (except for Copter approaches, where a climb of at least 400 feet per nautical mile is required), unless a higher climb gradient is published in the notes section of the approach procedure chart. When higher than standard climb gradients are specified, the end point of the nonstandard climb will be specified at either an altitude or a fix. Pilots must preplan to ensure that the aircraft can meet the climb gradient (expressed in feet per nautical mile) required by the procedure in the event of a missed approach, and be aware that flying at a higher than anticipated ground speed increases the climb rate requirement (feet per minute). Tables for the conversion of climb gradients (feet per nautical mile) to climb rate (feet per minute), based on ground speed, are included on page D1 of the U.S. Terminal Procedures booklets. Reasonable buffers are provided for normal maneuvers. However, no consideration is given to an abnormally early turn. Therefore, when an early missed approach is executed, pilots should, unless otherwise cleared by ATC, fly the IAP as specified on the approach plate to the missed approach point at or above the MDA or DH before executing a turning maneuver.

c. If visual reference is lost while circling-to-land from an instrument approach, the missed approach specified for that particular procedure must be followed (unless an alternate missed approach procedure is specified by ATC). To become established on the prescribed missed approach course, the pilot should make an initial climbing turn toward the landing runway and continue the turn until established on the missed approach course. Inasmuch as the circling maneuver may be accomplished in more than one direction, different patterns will be required to become established on the prescribed missed approach course, depending on the aircraft position at the time visual reference is lost. Adherence to the procedure will help assure that an aircraft will remain laterally within the circling and missed approach obstruction clearance areas. Refer to paragraph h concerning vertical obstruction clearance when starting a missed approach at other than the MAP. (See Figure 5-4-30.)

d. At locations where ATC radar service is provided, the pilot should conform to radar vectors when provided by ATC in lieu of the published missed approach procedure. (See Figure 5-4-31.)

FIGURE 5–4–30
Circling and Missed Approach Obstruction Clearance Areas

FIGURE 5–4–31
Missed Approach

e. Some locations may have a preplanned alternate missed approach procedure for use in the event the primary NAVAID used for the missed approach procedure is unavailable. To avoid confusion, the alternate missed approach instructions are not published on the chart. However, the alternate missed approach holding pattern will be depicted on the instrument approach chart for pilot situational awareness and to assist ATC by not having to issue detailed holding instructions. The alternate missed approach may be based on NAVAIDs not used in the approach procedure or the primary missed approach. When the alternate missed approach procedure is implemented by NOTAM, it becomes a mandatory part of the procedure. The NOTAM will specify both the textual instructions and any additional equipment requirements necessary to complete the procedure. Air traffic may also issue instructions for the alternate missed approach when necessary, such as when the primary missed approach NAVAID fails during the approach. Pilots may reject an ATC clearance for an alternate missed approach that requires equipment not necessary for the published approach procedure when the alternate missed approach is issued after beginning the approach. However, when the alternate missed approach is issued prior to beginning the approach the pilot must either accept the entire procedure (including the alternate missed approach), request a different approach procedure, or coordinate with ATC

Ch 5

for alternative action to be taken, i.e., proceed to an alternate airport, etc.

f. When approach has been missed, request clearance for specific action; i.e., to alternative airport, another approach, etc.

g. Pilots must ensure that they have climbed to a safe altitude prior to proceeding off the published missed approach, especially in nonradar environments. Abandoning the missed approach prior to reaching the published altitude may not provide adequate terrain clearance. Additional climb may be required after reaching the holding pattern before proceeding back to the IAF or to an alternate.

h. A clearance for an instrument approach procedure includes a clearance to fly the published missed approach procedure, unless otherwise instructed by ATC. The published missed approach procedure provides obstacle clearance only when the missed approach is conducted on the missed approach segment from or above the missed approach point, and assumes a climb rate of 200 feet/NM or higher, as published. If the aircraft initiates a missed approach at a point other than the missed approach point (see paragraph 5-4-5b), from below MDA or DA (H), or on a circling approach, obstacle clearance is not necessarily provided by following the published missed approach procedure, nor is separation assured from other air traffic in the vicinity.

In the event a balked (rejected) landing occurs at a position other than the published missed approach point, the pilot should contact ATC as soon as possible to obtain an amended clearance. If unable to contact ATC for any reason, the pilot should attempt to re-intercept a published segment of the missed approach and comply with route and altitude instructions. If unable to contact ATC, and in the pilot's judgment it is no longer appropriate to fly the published missed approach procedure, then consider either maintaining visual conditions if practicable and reattempt a landing, or a circle-climb over the airport. Should a missed approach become necessary when operating to an airport that is not served by an operating control tower, continuous contact with an air traffic facility may not be possible. In this case, the pilot should execute the appropriate go-around/missed approach procedure without delay and contact ATC when able to do so.

Prior to initiating an instrument approach procedure, the pilot should assess the actions to be taken in the event of a balked (rejected) landing beyond the missed approach point or below the MDA or DA (H) considering the anticipated weather conditions and available aircraft performance. 14 CFR 91.175(e) authorizes the pilot to fly an appropriate missed approach procedure that ensures obstruction clearance, but it does not necessarily consider separation from other air traffic. The pilot must consider other factors such as the aircraft's geographical location with respect to the prescribed missed approach point, direction of flight, and/or minimum turning altitudes in the prescribed missed approach procedure. The pilot must also consider aircraft performance, visual climb restrictions, charted obstacles, published obstacle departure procedure, takeoff visual climb requirements as expressed by nonstandard takeoff minima, other traffic expected to be in the vicinity, or other factors not specifically expressed by the approach procedures.

5-4-22 Use of Enhanced Flight Vision Systems (EFVS) on Instrument Approaches

a. Introduction. During an instrument approach, an EFVS can enable a pilot to see the approach lights, visual references associated with the runway environment, and other objects or features that might not be visible using natural vision alone. An EFVS uses a head-up display (HUD), or an equivalent display that is a head-up presentation, to combine flight information, flight symbology, navigation guidance, and a real-time image of the external scene to the pilot. Combining the flight information, navigation guidance, and sensor imagery on a HUD (or equivalent display) allows the pilot to continue looking forward along the flightpath throughout the entire approach, landing, and rollout.

An EFVS operation is an operation in which visibility conditions require an EFVS to be used in lieu of natural vision to perform an approach or landing, determine enhanced flight visibility, identify required visual references, or conduct a rollout. There are two types of EFVS operations:

1. EFVS operations to touchdown and rollout.

2. EFVS operations to 100 feet above the touchdown zone elevation (TDZE).

b. EFVS Operations to Touchdown and Rollout. An EFVS operation to touchdown and rollout is an operation in which the pilot uses the enhanced vision imagery provided by an EFVS in lieu of natural vision to descend below DA or DH to touchdown and rollout. (See Figure 5-4-32.) These operations may be conducted only on Standard Instrument Approach Procedures (SIAP) or special IAPs that have a DA or DH (for example, precision or APV approach). An EFVS operation to touchdown and rollout may not be conducted on an approach that has circling minimums. The regulations for EFVS operations to touchdown and rollout can be found in 14 CFR §91.176(a).

FIGURE 5–4–32
EFVS Operation to Touchdown and Rollout

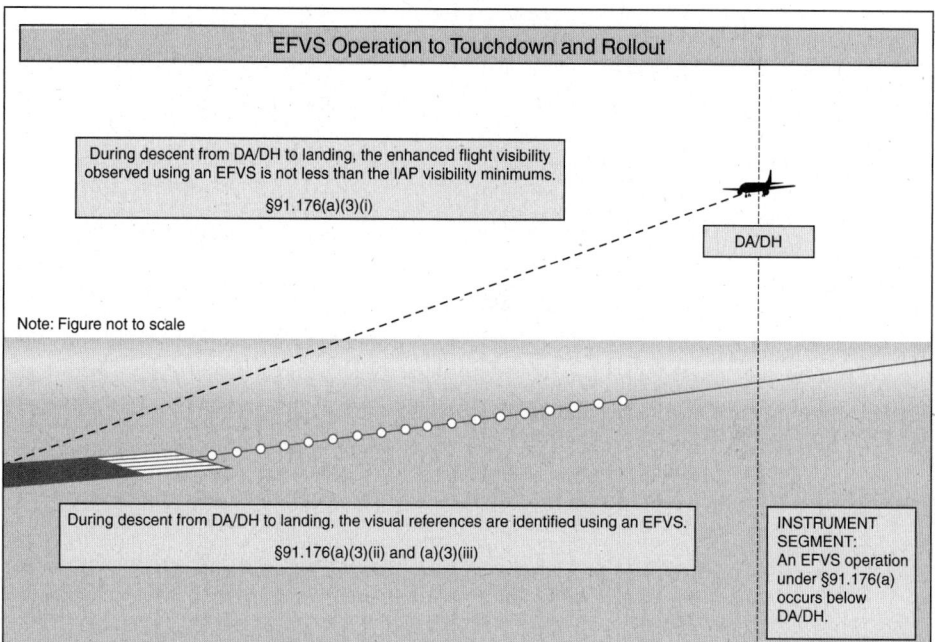

EFVS Operation to Touchdown and Rollout

During descent from DA/DH to landing, the enhanced flight visibility observed using an EFVS is not less than the IAP visibility minimums.

§91.176(a)(3)(i)

DA/DH

Note: Figure not to scale

During descent from DA/DH to landing, the visual references are identified using an EFVS.

§91.176(a)(3)(ii) and (a)(3)(iii)

INSTRUMENT SEGMENT: An EFVS operation under §91.176(a) occurs below DA/DH.

Ch 5

c. EFVS Operations to 100 Feet Above the TDZE. An EFVS operation to 100 feet above the TDZE is an operation in which the pilot uses the enhanced vision imagery provided by an EFVS in lieu of natural vision to descend below DA/DH or MDA down to 100 feet above the TDZE. (See Figure 5-4-33.) To continue the approach below 100 feet above the TDZE, a pilot must have sufficient flight visibility to identify the required visual references using natural vision and must continue to use the EFVS to ensure the enhanced flight visibility meets the visibility requirements of the IAP being flown. These operations may be conducted on SIAPs or special IAPs that have a DA/DH or MDA. An EFVS operation to 100 feet above the TDZE may not be conducted on an approach that has circling minimums. The regulations for EFVS operations to 100 feet above the TDZE can be found in 14 CFR §91.176(b).

FIGURE 5–4–33
EFVS Operation to 100 ft Above the TDZE

d. EFVS Equipment Requirements. An EFVS that is installed on a U.S.-registered aircraft and is used to conduct EFVS operations must conform to an FAA-type design approval (i.e., a type certificate (TC), amended TC, or supplemental type certificate (STC)). A foreign-registered aircraft used to conduct EFVS operations that does not have an FAA-type design approval must be equipped with an EFVS that has been approved by either the State of the Operator or the State of Registry to meet the requirements of ICAO Annex 6. Equipment requirements for an EFVS operation to touchdown and rollout can be found in 14 CFR §91.176(a)(1), and the equipment requirements for an EFVS operation to 100 feet above the TDZE can be found in 14 CFR §91.176(b)(1). An operator can determine the eligibility of their aircraft to conduct EFVS operations by referring to the Airplane Flight Manual, Airplane Flight Manual Supplement, Rotorcraft Flight Manual, or Rotorcraft Flight Manual Supplement as applicable.

e. Operating Requirements. Any operator who conducts EFVS operations to touchdown and rollout (14 CFR §91.176(a)) must have an OpSpec, MSpec, or LOA that specifically authorizes those operations. Parts 91K, 121, 125, 129, and 135 operators who conduct EFVS operations to 100 feet above the TDZE (14 CFR §91.176(b)) must have an OpSpec, MSpec, or LOA that specifically authorizes the operation. Part 91 operators (other than 91K operators) are not required to have an LOA to conduct EFVS operations to 100 feet above the TDZE in the United States. However, an optional LOA is available to facilitate operational approval from foreign Civil Aviation Authorities (CAA). To conduct an EFVS operation to touchdown and rollout during an authorized Category II or III operation, the operator must have:

1. An OpSpec, MSpec, or LOA authorizing EFVS operations to touchdown and rollout (14 CFR §91.176(a)); and

2. An OpSpec, MSpec, or LOA authorizing Category II or Category III operations.

f. EFVS Operations in Rotorcraft. Currently, EFVS operations in rotorcraft can only be conducted on IAPs that are flown to a runway. Instrument approach criteria, procedures, and appropriate visual references have not yet been developed for straight-in landing operations below DA/DH or MDA under IFR to heliports or platforms. An EFVS cannot be used in lieu of natural vision to descend below published minimums on copter approaches to a point in space (PinS) followed by a "proceed visual flight rules (VFR)" visual segment, or on approaches designed to a specific landing site using a "proceed visually" visual segment.

g. EFVS Pilot Requirements. A pilot who conducts EFVS operations must receive ground and flight training specific to the EFVS operation to be conducted. The training must be obtained from an authorized training provider under a training program approved by the FAA. Additionally, recent flight experience and proficiency or competency check requirements apply to EFVS operations. These requirements are addressed in 14 CFR §§61.66, 91.1065, 121.441, Appendix F to Part 121, 125.287, and 135.293.

h. Enhanced Flight Visibility and Visual Reference Requirements. To descend below DA/DH or MDA during EFVS operations under 14 CFR §91.176(a) or (b), a pilot must make a determination that the enhanced flight visibility observed by using an EFVS is not less than what is prescribed by the IAP being flown. In addition, the visual references required in 14 CFR §91.176(a) or (b) must be distinctly visible and identifiable to the pilot using the EFVS. The determination of enhanced flight visibility is a separate action from that of identifying required visual references, and is different from ground-reported visibility. Even though the reported visibility or the visibility observed using natural vision may be less, as long as the EFVS provides the required enhanced flight visibility and a pilot meets all of the other requirements, the pilot can continue descending below DA/DH or MDA using the EFVS. Suitable enhanced flight visibility is necessary to ensure the aircraft is in a position to continue the approach and land. It is important to understand that using an EFVS does not result in obtaining lower minima with respect to the visibility or the DA/DH or MDA specified in the IAP. An EFVS simply provides another means of operating in the visual segment of an IAP. The DA/DH or MDA and the visibility value specified in the IAP to be flown do not change.

i. Flight Planning and Beginning or Continuing an Approach Under IFR. A Part 121, 125, or 135 operator's OpSpec or LOA for EFVS operations may authorize an EFVS operational credit dispatching or releasing a flight and for beginning or continuing an instrument approach procedure. When a pilot reaches DA/DH or MDA, the pilot conducts the EFVS operation in accordance with 14 CFR §91.176(a) or (b) and their authorization to conduct EFVS operations.

j. Missed Approach Considerations. In order to conduct an EFVS operation, the EFVS must be operable. In the event of a failure of any required component of an EFVS at any point in the approach to touchdown, a missed approach is required. However, this provision does not preclude a pilot's authority to continue an approach if continuation of an approach is considered by the pilot to be a safer course of action.

k. Light Emitting Diode (LED) Airport Lighting Impact on EFVS Operations. Incandescent lamps are being replaced with LEDs at some airports in threshold lights, taxiway edge lights, taxiway centerline lights, low intensity runway edge lights, windcone lights, beacons, and some obstruction lighting. Additionally, there are plans to replace incandescent lamps with LEDs in approach lighting systems. Pilots should be aware that LED lights cannot be sensed by infrared-based EFVSs. Further, the FAA does not currently collect or disseminate information about where LED lighting is installed.

l. Other Vision Systems. Unlike an EFVS that meets the equipment requirements of 14 CFR §91.176, a Synthetic Vision System (SVS) or Synthetic Vision Guidance System (SVGS) does not provide a real-time sensor image of the outside scene and also does not meet the equipment requirements for EFVS operations. A pilot cannot use a synthetic vision image on a head-up or a head-down display in lieu of natural vision to descend below DA/DH or MDA. An EFVS can, however, be integrated with an SVS, also known as a Combined Vision System (CVS). A CVS can be used to conduct EFVS operations if all of the requirements for an EFVS are satisfied and the SVS image does not interfere with the pilot's ability to see the external scene, to identify the required visual references, or to see the sensor image.

m. Additional Information. Operational criteria for EFVS can be found in Advisory Circular (AC) 90-106, Enhanced Flight Vision System Operations, and airworthiness criteria for EFVS can be found in AC 20-167, Airworthiness Approval of Enhanced Vision System, Synthetic Vision System, Combined Vision System, and Enhanced Flight Vision System Equipment.

5-4-23 Visual Approach

a. A visual approach is conducted on an IFR flight plan and authorizes a pilot to proceed visually and clear of clouds to the airport. The pilot must have either the airport or the preceding identified aircraft in sight. This approach must be authorized and controlled by the appropriate air traffic control facility. Reported weather at the airport must have a ceiling at or above 1,000 feet and visibility 3 miles or greater. ATC may authorize this type of approach when it will be operationally beneficial. Visual approaches are an IFR procedure conducted under IFR in visual meteorological conditions. Cloud clearance requirements of 14 CFR Section 91.155 are not applicable, unless required by operation specifications. When conducting visual approaches, pilots are encouraged to use other available navigational aids to assist in positive lateral and vertical alignment with the runway.

Ch 5

b. Operating to an Airport Without Weather Reporting Service. ATC will advise the pilot when weather is not available at the destination airport. ATC may initiate a visual approach provided there is a reasonable assurance that weather at the airport is a ceiling at or above 1,000 feet and visibility 3 miles or greater (e.g., area weather reports, PIREPs, etc.).

c. Operating to an Airport With an Operating Control Tower. Aircraft may be authorized to conduct a visual approach to one runway while other aircraft are conducting IFR or VFR approaches to another parallel, intersecting, or converging runway. ATC may authorize a visual approach after advising all aircraft involved that other aircraft are conducting operations to the other runway. This may be accomplished through use of the ATIS.

1. When operating to parallel runways separated by less than 2,500 feet, ATC will ensure approved separation is provided unless the succeeding aircraft reports sighting the preceding aircraft to the adjacent parallel and visual separation is applied.

2. When operating to parallel runways separated by at least 2,500 feet but less than 4,300 feet, ATC will ensure approved separation is provided until the aircraft are issued an approach clearance and one pilot has acknowledged receipt of a visual approach clearance, and the other pilot has acknowledged receipt of a visual or instrument approach clearance, and aircraft are established on a heading or established on a direct course to a fix or cleared on an RNAV/instrument approach procedure which will intercept the extended centerline of the runway at an angle not greater than 30 degrees.

3. When operating to parallel runways separated by 4,300 feet or more, ATC will ensure approved separation is provided until one of the aircraft has been issued and the pilot has acknowledged receipt of the visual approach clearance, and each aircraft is assigned a heading, or established on a direct course to a fix, or cleared on an RNAV/instrument approach procedure which will allow the aircraft to intercept the extended centerline of the runway at an angle not greater than 30 degrees.

Note: The intent of the 30 degree intercept angle is to reduce the potential for overshoots of the final and to preclude side-by-side operations with one or both aircraft in a belly-up configuration during the turn-on.

d. Clearance for Visual Approach. At locations with an operating control tower, ATC will issue approach clearances that will include an assigned runway. At locations without an operating control tower or where a part-time tower is closed, ATC will issue a visual approach clearance to the airport only.

e. Separation Responsibilities. If the pilot has the airport in sight but cannot see the aircraft to be followed, ATC may clear the aircraft for a visual approach; however, ATC retains both separation and wake vortex separation responsibility. When visually following a preceding aircraft, acceptance of the visual approach clearance constitutes acceptance of pilot responsibility for maintaining a safe approach interval and adequate wake turbulence separation.

f. A visual approach is not an IAP and therefore has no missed approach segment. If a go-around is necessary for any reason, aircraft operating at controlled airports will be issued an appropriate clearance or instruction by the tower to enter the traffic pattern for landing or proceed as otherwise instructed. In either case, the pilot is responsible to maintain terrain and obstruction avoidance until reaching an ATC assigned altitude if issued, and ATC will provide approved separation or visual separation from other IFR aircraft. At uncontrolled airports, aircraft are expected to remain clear of clouds and complete a landing as soon as possible. If a landing cannot be accomplished, the aircraft is expected to remain clear of clouds and contact ATC as soon as possible for further clearance. Separation from other IFR aircraft will be maintained under these circumstances.

g. Visual approaches reduce pilot/controller workload and expedite traffic by shortening flight paths to the airport. It is the pilot's responsibility to advise ATC as soon as possible if a visual approach is not desired.

h. Authorization to conduct a visual approach is an IFR authorization and does not alter IFR flight plan cancellation responsibility.

Reference: AIM, ¶5-1-15, Canceling IFR Flight Plan.

i. Radar service is automatically terminated, without advising the pilot, when the aircraft is instructed to change to advisory frequency.

5-4-24 Charted Visual Flight Procedure (CVFP)

a. CVFPs are charted visual approaches established for environmental/noise considerations, and/or when necessary for the safety and efficiency of air traffic operations. The approach charts depict prominent landmarks, courses, and recommended altitudes to specific runways. CVFPs are designed to be used primarily for turbojet aircraft.

b. These procedures will be used only at airports with an operating control tower.

c. Most approach charts will depict some NAVAID information which is for supplemental navigational guidance only.

d. Unless indicating a Class B airspace floor, all depicted altitudes are for noise abatement

purposes and are recommended only. Pilots are not prohibited from flying other than recommended altitudes if operational requirements dictate.

e. When landmarks used for navigation are not visible at night, the approach will be annotated *"PROCEDURE NOT AUTHORIZED AT NIGHT."*

f. CVFPs usually begin within 20 flying miles from the airport.

g. Published weather minimums for CVFPs are based on minimum vectoring altitudes rather than the recommended altitudes depicted on charts.

h. CVFPs are not instrument approaches and do not have missed approach segments.

i. ATC will not issue clearances for CVFPs when the weather is less than the published minimum.

j. ATC will clear aircraft for a CVFP after the pilot reports siting a charted landmark or a preceding aircraft. If instructed to follow a preceding aircraft, pilots are responsible for maintaining a safe approach interval and wake turbulence separation.

k. Pilots should advise ATC if at any point they are unable to continue an approach or lose sight of a preceding aircraft. Missed approaches will be handled as a go-around.

l. When conducting visual approaches, pilots are encouraged to use other available navigational aids to assist in positive lateral and vertical alignment with the assigned runway.

5-4-25 Contact Approach

a. Pilots operating in accordance with an IFR flight plan, provided they are clear of clouds and have at least 1 mile flight visibility and can reasonably expect to continue to the destination airport in those conditions, may request ATC authorization for a contact approach.

b. Controllers may authorize a contact approach provided:

1. The contact approach is specifically requested by the pilot. ATC cannot initiate this approach.

Example: Request contact approach.

2. The reported ground visibility at the destination airport is at least 1 statute mile.

3. The contact approach will be made to an airport having a standard or special instrument approach procedure.

4. Approved separation is applied between aircraft so cleared and between these aircraft and other IFR or special VFR aircraft.

Example: Cleared contact approach (and, if required) at or below (altitude) (routing) if not possible (alternative procedures) and advise.

c. A contact approach is an approach procedure that may be used by a pilot (with prior authorization from ATC) in lieu of conducting a standard or special IAP to an airport. It is not intended for use by a pilot on an IFR flight clearance to operate to an airport not having a published and functioning IAP. Nor is it intended for an aircraft to conduct an instrument approach to one airport and then, when "in the clear," discontinue that approach and proceed to another airport. In the execution of a contact approach, the pilot assumes the responsibility for obstruction clearance. If radar service is being received, it will automatically terminate when the pilot is instructed to change to advisory frequency.

5-4-26 Landing Priority

A clearance for a specific type of approach (ILS, RNAV, GLS, ADF, VOR or Visual Approach) to an aircraft operating on an IFR flight plan does not mean that landing priority will be given over other traffic. ATCTs handle all aircraft, regardless of the type of flight plan, on a "first-come, first-served" basis. Therefore, because of local traffic or runway in use, it may be necessary for the controller in the interest of safety, to provide a different landing sequence. In any case, a landing sequence will be issued to each aircraft as soon as possible to enable the pilot to properly adjust the aircraft's flight path.

5-4-27 Overhead Approach Maneuver

a. Pilots operating in accordance with an IFR flight plan in Visual Meteorological Conditions (VMC) may request ATC authorization for an overhead maneuver. An overhead maneuver is not an instrument approach procedure. Overhead maneuver patterns are developed at airports where aircraft have an operational need to conduct the maneuver. An aircraft conducting an overhead maneuver is considered to be VFR and the IFR flight plan is cancelled when the aircraft reaches the initial point on the initial approach portion of the maneuver. (See Figure 5-4-34.) The existence of a standard overhead maneuver pattern does not eliminate the possible requirement for an aircraft to conform to conventional rectangular patterns if an overhead maneuver cannot be approved. Aircraft operating to an airport without a functioning control tower must initiate cancellation of an IFR flight plan prior to executing the overhead maneuver. Cancellation of the IFR flight plan must be accomplished after crossing the landing threshold on the initial portion of the maneuver or after landing. Controllers may authorize an overhead maneuver and issue the following to arriving aircraft:

1. Pattern altitude and direction of traffic. This information may be omitted if either is standard.

Ch 5

Phraseology:
Pattern altitude (altitude). Right turns.

 2. Request for a report on initial approach.

Phraseology:
Report initial.

 3. "Break" information and a request for the pilot to report. The "Break Point" will be specified if nonstandard. Pilots may be requested to report "break" if required for traffic or other reasons.

Phraseology:
Break at (specified point).

Report break.

FIGURE 5–4–34
Overhead Maneuver

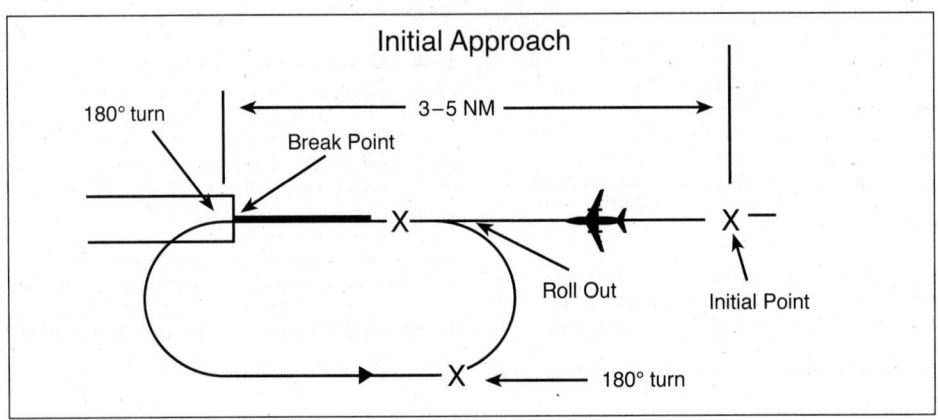

ASA

Section 5 Pilot/Controller Roles and Responsibilities

5-5-1 General

a. The roles and responsibilities of the pilot and controller for effective participation in the ATC system are contained in several documents. Pilot responsibilities are in the CFRs and the air traffic controllers' are in the FAA Order JO 7110.65, Air Traffic Control, and supplemental FAA directives. Additional and supplemental information for pilots can be found in the current Aeronautical Information Manual (AIM), Notices to Air Missions, Advisory Circulars and aeronautical charts. Since there are many other excellent publications produced by nongovernment organizations, as well as other government organizations, with various updating cycles, questions concerning the latest or most current material can be resolved by cross-checking with the above mentioned documents.

b. The pilot-in-command of an aircraft is directly responsible for, and is the final authority as to the safe operation of that aircraft. In an emergency requiring immediate action, the pilot-in-command may deviate from any rule in the General Subpart A and Flight Rules Subpart B in accordance with 14 CFR Section 91.3.

c. The air traffic controller is responsible to give first priority to the separation of aircraft and to the issuance of radar safety alerts, second priority to other services that are required, but do not involve separation of aircraft and third priority to additional services to the extent possible.

d. In order to maintain a safe and efficient air traffic system, it is necessary that each party fulfill their responsibilities to the fullest.

e. The responsibilities of the pilot and the controller intentionally overlap in many areas providing a degree of redundancy. Should one or the other fail in any manner, this overlapping responsibility is expected to compensate, in many cases, for failures that may affect safety.

f. The following, while not intended to be all inclusive, is a brief listing of pilot and controller responsibilities for some commonly used procedures or phases of flight. More detailed explanations are contained in other portions of this publication, the appropriate CFRs, ACs and similar publications. The information provided is an overview of the principles involved and is not meant as an interpretation of the rules nor is it intended to extend or diminish responsibilities.

5-5-2 Air Traffic Clearance

a. Pilot.

1. Acknowledges receipt and understanding of an ATC clearance.

2. Reads back any hold short of runway instructions issued by ATC.

3. Requests clarification or amendment, as appropriate, any time a clearance is not fully understood or considered unacceptable from a safety standpoint.

4. Promptly complies with an air traffic clearance upon receipt except as necessary to cope with an emergency. Advises ATC as soon as possible and obtains an amended clearance, if deviation is necessary.

Note: *A clearance to land means that appropriate separation on the landing runway will be ensured. A landing clearance does not relieve the pilot from compliance with any previously issued altitude crossing restriction.*

b. Controller.

1. Issues appropriate clearances for the operation to be conducted, or being conducted, in accordance with established criteria.

2. Assigns altitudes in IFR clearances that are at or above the minimum IFR altitudes in controlled airspace.

3. Ensures acknowledgement by the pilot for issued information, clearances, or instructions.

4. Ensures that readbacks by the pilot of altitude, heading, or other items are correct. If incorrect, distorted, or incomplete, makes corrections as appropriate.

5-5-3 Contact Approach

a. Pilot.

1. Must request a contact approach and makes it in lieu of a standard or special instrument approach.

2. By requesting the contact approach, indicates that the flight is operating clear of clouds, has at least one mile flight visibility, and reasonably expects to continue to the destination airport in those conditions.

3. Assumes responsibility for obstruction clearance while conducting a contact approach.

4. Advises ATC immediately if unable to continue the contact approach or if encounters less than 1 mile flight visibility.

5. Is aware that if radar service is being received, it may be automatically terminated when told to contact the tower.

Reference: *Pilot/Controller Glossary—Radar Service Terminated.*

Ch 5

b. Controller.

1. Issues clearance for a contact approach only when requested by the pilot. Does not solicit the use of this procedure.

2. Before issuing the clearance, ascertains that reported ground visibility at destination airport is at least 1 mile.

3. Provides approved separation between the aircraft cleared for a contact approach and other IFR or special VFR aircraft. When using vertical separation, does not assign a fixed altitude, but clears the aircraft at or below an altitude which is at least 1,000 feet below any IFR traffic but not below Minimum Safe Altitudes prescribed in 14 CFR Section 91.119.

4. Issues alternative instructions if, in their judgment, weather conditions may make completion of the approach impracticable.

5-5-4 Instrument Approach

a. Pilot.

1. Be aware that the controller issues clearance for approach based only on known traffic.

2. Follows the procedure as shown on the IAP, including all restrictive notations, such as:

(a) Procedure not authorized at night;

(b) Approach not authorized when local area altimeter not available;

(c) Procedure not authorized when control tower not in operation;

(d) Procedure not authorized when glide slope not used;

(e) Straight-in minimums not authorized at night; etc.

(f) Radar required; or

(g) The circling minimums published on the instrument approach chart provide adequate obstruction clearance and pilots should not descend below the circling altitude until the aircraft is in a position to make final descent for landing. Sound judgment and knowledge of the pilot's and the aircraft's capabilities are the criteria for determining the exact maneuver in each instance since airport design and the aircraft position, altitude and airspeed must all be considered.

Reference: *AIM, ¶5-4-20, Approach and Landing Minimums.*

3. Upon receipt of an approach clearance while on an unpublished route or being radar vectored:

(a) Complies with the minimum altitude for IFR; and

(b) Maintains the last assigned altitude until established on a segment of a published route or IAP, at which time published altitudes apply.

4. There are currently two temperature limitations that may be published in the notes box of the middle briefing strip on an instrument

approach procedure (IAP). The two published temperature limitations are:

(a) A temperature range limitation associated with the use of baro-VNAV that may be published on a United States PBN IAP titled RNAV (GPS) or RNAV (RNP); and/or

(b) A Cold Temperature Airport (CTA) limitation designated by a snowflake ICON and temperature in Celsius (C) that is published on every IAP for the airfield.

5. Any planned altitude correction for the intermediate and/or missed approach holding segments must be coordinated with ATC. Pilots do not have to advise ATC of a correction in the final segment.

Reference: *AIM, Chapter 7, Section 3, Cold Temperature Barometric Altimeter Errors, Setting Procedures, and Cold Temperature Airports (CTA).*

b. Controller.

1. Issues an approach clearance based on known traffic.

2. Issues an IFR approach clearance only after the aircraft is established on a segment of published route or IAP, or assigns an appropriate altitude for the aircraft to maintain until so established.

5-5-5 Missed Approach

a. Pilot.

1. Executes a missed approach when one of the following conditions exist:

(a) Arrival at the Missed Approach Point (MAP) or the Decision Height (DH) and visual reference to the runway environment is insufficient to complete the landing.

(b) Determines that a safe approach or landing is not possible (see subparagraph 5-4-21h).

(c) Instructed to do so by ATC.

2. Advises ATC that a missed approach will be made. Include the reason for the missed approach unless the missed approach is initiated by ATC.

3. Complies with the missed approach instructions for the IAP being executed from the MAP, unless other missed approach instructions are specified by ATC.

4. If executing a missed approach prior to reaching the MAP, fly the lateral navigation path of the instrument procedure to the MAP. Climb to the altitude specified in the missed approach procedure, except when a maximum altitude is specified between the final approach fix (FAF) and the MAP. In that case, comply with the maximum altitude restriction. Note, this may require a continued descent on the final approach.

5. Cold Temperature Airports (CTA) are designated by a snowflake ICON and temperature in Celsius (C) that are published in the notes box

of the middle briefing strip on an instrument approach procedure (IAP). Pilots should apply a cold temperature correction to the missed approach final holding altitude when the reported temperature is at or below the CTA temperature limitation. Pilots must inform ATC of the correction.

Reference: AIM, Chapter 7, Section 3, Cold Temperature Barometric Altimeter Errors, Setting Procedures, and Cold Temperature Airports (CTA)

6. Following a missed approach, requests clearance for specific action; i.e., another approach, hold for improved conditions, proceed to an alternate airport, etc.

b. Controller.

1. Issues an approved alternate missed approach procedure if it is desired that the pilot execute a procedure other than as depicted on the instrument approach chart.

2. May vector a radar identified aircraft executing a missed approach when operationally advantageous to the pilot or the controller.

3. In response to the pilot's stated intentions, issues a clearance to an alternate airport, to a holding fix, or for reentry into the approach sequence, as traffic conditions permit.

5-5-6 Vectors

a. Pilot.

1. Promptly complies with headings and altitudes assigned to you by the controller.

2. Questions any assigned heading or altitude believed to be incorrect.

3. If operating VFR and compliance with any radar vector or altitude would cause a violation of any CFR, advises ATC and obtains a revised clearance or instructions.

b. Controller.

1. Vectors aircraft in Class A, Class B, Class C, Class D, and Class E airspace:

(a) For separation.

(b) For noise abatement.

(c) To obtain an operational advantage for the pilot or controller.

2. Vectors aircraft in Class A, Class B, Class C, Class D, Class E, and Class G airspace when requested by the pilot.

3. Except where authorized for radar approaches, radar departures, special VFR, or when operating in accordance with vectors below minimum altitude procedures, vector IFR aircraft at or above minimum vectoring altitudes.

4. May vector aircraft off assigned procedures. When published altitude or speed restrictions are included, controllers must assign an altitude, or if necessary, a speed.

5. May vector VFR aircraft, not at an ATC assigned altitude, at any altitude. In these cases, terrain separation is the pilot's responsibility.

5-5-7 Safety Alert

a. Pilot.

1. Initiates appropriate action if a safety alert is received from ATC.

2. Be aware that this service is not always available and that many factors affect the ability of the controller to be aware of a situation in which unsafe proximity to terrain, obstructions, or another aircraft may be developing.

b. Controller.

1. Issues a safety alert if aware an aircraft under their control is at an altitude which, in the controller's judgment, places the aircraft in unsafe proximity to terrain, obstructions or another aircraft. Types of safety alerts are:

(a) **Terrain or Obstruction Alert.** Immediately issued to an aircraft under their control if aware the aircraft is at an altitude believed to place the aircraft in unsafe proximity to terrain or obstructions.

(b) **Aircraft Conflict Alert.** Immediately issued to an aircraft under their control if aware of an aircraft not under their control at an altitude believed to place the aircraft in unsafe proximity to each other. With the alert, they offer the pilot an alternative, if feasible.

2. Discontinue further alerts if informed by the pilot action is being taken to correct the situation or that the other aircraft is in sight.

5-5-8 See and Avoid

a. Pilot.

When meteorological conditions permit, regardless of type of flight plan or whether or not under control of a radar facility, the pilot is responsible to see and avoid other traffic, terrain, or obstacles.

b. Controller.

1. Provides radar traffic information to radar identified aircraft operating outside positive control airspace on a workload permitting basis.

2. Issues safety alerts to aircraft under their control if aware the aircraft is at an altitude believed to place the aircraft in unsafe proximity to terrain, obstructions, or other aircraft.

5-5-9 Speed Adjustments

a. Pilot.

1. Advises ATC any time cruising airspeed varies plus or minus 5 percent or 10 knots, whichever is greater, from that given in the flight plan.

2. Complies with speed adjustments from ATC unless:

(a) The minimum or maximum safe airspeed for any particular operation is greater or less than the requested airspeed. In such cases, advises ATC.

Note: It is the pilot's responsibility and prerogative to refuse speed adjustments considered excessive or contrary to the aircraft's operating specifications.

(b) Operating at or above 10,000 feet MSL on an ATC assigned speed adjustment of more than 250 knots IAS and subsequent clearance is received for descent below 10,000 feet MSL. In such cases, pilots are expected to comply with 14 CFR Section 91.117(a).

3. When complying with speed adjustment assignments, maintains an indicated airspeed within plus or minus 10 knots or 0.02 Mach number of the specified speed.

b. Controller.

1. Assigns speed adjustments to aircraft when necessary but not as a substitute for good vectoring technique.

2. Adheres to the restrictions published in FAA Order JO 7110.65, Air Traffic Control, as to when speed adjustment procedures may be applied.

3. Avoids speed adjustments requiring alternate decreases and increases.

4. Assigns speed adjustments to a specified IAS (Knots)/Mach number or to increase or decrease speed using increments of 5 knots or multiples thereof.

5. Terminates ATC-assigned speed adjustments when no longer required by issuing further instructions to pilots in the following manner:

(a) Advises pilots to "resume normal speed" when the aircraft is on a heading, random routing, charted procedure, or route without published speed restrictions.

(b) Instructs pilots to "comply with speed restrictions" when the aircraft is joining or resuming a charted procedure or route with published speed restrictions.

Caution: The phraseology "Climb via SID" requires compliance with all altitude and/or speed restrictions depicted on the procedure.

(c) Instructs pilots to "resume published speed" when aircraft are cleared via a charted instrument flight procedure that contains published speed restrictions.

(d) Advises aircraft to "delete speed restrictions" when ATC assigned or published speed restrictions on a charted procedure are no longer required.

(e) Clears pilots for approach without restating previously issued speed adjustments.

Reference: Pilot/Controller Glossary—Resume Normal Speed, Resume Published Speed

6. Gives due consideration to aircraft capabilities to reduce speed while descending.

7. Does not assign speed adjustments to aircraft at or above FL 390 without pilot consent.

5-5-10 Traffic Advisories (Traffic Information)

a. Pilot.

1. Acknowledges receipt of traffic advisories.

2. Informs controller if traffic in sight.

3. Advises ATC if a vector to avoid traffic is desired.

4. Does not expect to receive radar traffic advisories on all traffic. Some aircraft may not appear on the radar display. Be aware that the controller may be occupied with higher priority duties and unable to issue traffic information for a variety of reasons.

5. Advises controller if service is not desired.

b. Controller.

1. Issues radar traffic to the maximum extent consistent with higher priority duties except in Class A airspace.

2. Provides vectors to assist aircraft to avoid observed traffic when requested by the pilot.

3. Issues traffic information to aircraft in the Class B, Class C, and Class D surface areas for sequencing purposes.

4. Controllers are required to issue traffic advisories to each aircraft operating on intersecting or nonintersecting converging runways where projected flight paths will cross.

5-5-11 Visual Approach

a. Pilot.

1. If a visual approach is not desired, advises ATC.

2. Complies with controller's instructions for vectors toward the airport of intended landing or to a visual position behind a preceding aircraft.

3. The pilot must, at all times, have either the airport or the preceding aircraft in sight. After being cleared for a visual approach, proceed to the airport in a normal manner or follow the preceding aircraft. Remain clear of clouds while conducting a visual approach.

4. If the pilot accepts a visual approach clearance to visually follow a preceding aircraft, you are required to establish a safe landing interval behind the aircraft you were instructed to follow. You are responsible for wake turbulence separation.

5. Advise ATC immediately if the pilot is unable to continue following the preceding aircraft, cannot remain clear of clouds, needs to climb, or loses sight of the airport.

6. In the event of a go-around, the pilot is responsible to maintain terrain and obstruction avoidance until reaching an ATC assigned altitude if issued.

7. Be aware that radar service is automatically terminated, without being advised by ATC, when the pilot is instructed to change to advisory frequency.

8. Be aware that there may be other traffic in the traffic pattern and the landing sequence may differ from the traffic sequence assigned by approach control or ARTCC.

b. Controller.

1. Do not clear an aircraft for a visual approach unless reported weather at the airport is ceiling at or above 1,000 feet and visibility is 3 miles or greater. When weather is not available for the destination airport, inform the pilot and do not initiate a visual approach to that airport unless there is reasonable assurance that descent and flight to the airport can be made visually.

2. Issue visual approach clearance when the pilot reports sighting either the airport or a preceding aircraft which is to be followed.

3. Provide separation except when visual separation is being applied by the pilot.

4. Continue flight following and traffic information until the aircraft has landed or has been instructed to change to advisory frequency.

5. For all aircraft, inform the pilot when the preceding aircraft is a heavy. Inform the pilot of a small aircraft when the preceding aircraft is a B757. Visual separation is prohibited behind super aircraft.

6. When weather is available for the destination airport, do not initiate a vector for a visual approach unless the reported ceiling at the airport is 500 feet or more above the MVA and visibility is 3 miles or more. If vectoring weather minima are not available but weather at the airport is ceiling at or above 1,000 feet and visibility of 3 miles or greater, visual approaches may still be conducted.

5–5–12 Visual Separation

a. Pilot.

1. Acceptance of instructions to follow another aircraft or to provide visual separation from it is an acknowledgment that the pilot will maneuver the aircraft as necessary to avoid the other aircraft or to maintain in-trail separation. Pilots are responsible to maintain visual separation until flight paths (altitudes and/or courses) diverge.

2. If instructed by ATC to follow another aircraft or to provide visual separation from it, promptly notify the controller if you lose sight of that aircraft, are unable to maintain continued visual contact with it, or cannot accept the responsibility for your own separation for any reason.

3. The pilot also accepts responsibility for wake turbulence separation under these conditions.

b. Controller. Applies visual separation only:

1. Within the terminal area when a controller has both aircraft in sight or by instructing a pilot who sees the other aircraft to maintain visual separation from it.

2. Pilots are responsible to maintain visual separation until flight paths (altitudes and/or courses) diverge.

3. Within en route airspace when aircraft are on opposite courses and one pilot reports having seen the other aircraft and that the aircraft have passed each other.

5–5–13 VFR-on-Top

a. Pilot.

1. This clearance must be requested by the pilot on an IFR flight plan, and if approved, allows the pilot the choice (subject to any ATC restrictions) to select an altitude or flight level in lieu of an assigned altitude.

Note: VFR-on-top is not permitted in certain airspace areas, such as Class A airspace, certain restricted areas, etc. Consequently, IFR flights operating VFR-on-top will avoid such airspace.

References
AIM, ¶4-4-8, IFR Clearance VFR-on-top.
AIM, ¶4-4-11, IFR Separation Standards.
AIM, ¶5-3-2, Position Reporting.
AIM, ¶5-3-3, Additional Reports.

2. By requesting a VFR-on-top clearance, the pilot assumes the sole responsibility to be vigilant so as to see and avoid other aircraft and to:

(a) Fly at the appropriate VFR altitude as prescribed in 14 CFR Section 91.159.

(b) Comply with the VFR visibility and distance from clouds criteria in 14 CFR Section 91.155, Basic VFR weather minimums.

(c) Comply with instrument flight rules that are applicable to this flight; i.e., minimum IFR altitudes, position reporting, radio communications, course to be flown, adherence to ATC clearance, etc.

3. Should advise ATC prior to any altitude change to ensure the exchange of accurate traffic information.

b. Controller.

1. May clear an aircraft to maintain VFR-on-top if the pilot of an aircraft on an IFR flight plan requests the clearance.

2. Informs the pilot of an aircraft cleared to climb to VFR-on-top the reported height of the tops or that no top report is available; issues an alternate clearance if necessary; and once the aircraft reports reaching VFR-on-top, reclears the aircraft to maintain VFR-on- top.

3. Before issuing clearance, ascertain that the aircraft is not in or will not enter Class A airspace.

5-5-14 Instrument Departures

a. Pilot.

1. Prior to departure considers the type of terrain and other obstructions on or in the vicinity of the departure airport.

2. Determines if obstruction avoidance can be maintained visually or that the departure procedure should be followed.

3. Determines whether an obstacle departure procedure (ODP) and/or DP is available for obstruction avoidance. One option may be a Visual Climb Over Airport (VCOA). Pilots must advise ATC as early as possible of the intent to fly the VCOA prior to departure.

4. At airports where IAPs have not been published, hence no published departure procedure, determines what action will be necessary and takes such action that will assure a safe departure.

b. Controller.

1. At locations with airport traffic control service, when necessary, specifies direction of takeoff, turn, or initial heading to be flown after takeoff, consistent with published departure procedures (DP) or diverse vector areas (DVA), where applicable.

2. At locations without airport traffic control service but within Class E surface area when necessary to specify direction of takeoff, turn, or initial heading to be flown, obtains pilot's concurrence that the procedure will allow the pilot to comply with local traffic patterns, terrain, and obstruction avoidance.

3. When the initial heading will take the aircraft off an assigned procedure (for example, an RNAV SID with a published lateral path to a waypoint and crossing restrictions from the departure end of runway), the controller will assign an altitude to maintain with the initial heading.

4. Includes established departure procedures as part of the ATC clearance when pilot compliance is necessary to ensure separation.

5. At locations with both SIDs and DVAs, ATC will provide an amended departure clearance to cancel a previously assigned SID and subsequently utilize a DVA or vice versa. The amended clearance will be provided to the pilot in a timely manner so that the pilot may confirm adequate climb performance exists to determine if the amended clearance is acceptable, and brief the changes in advance of entering the runway.

6. At locations with a DVA, ATC is not permitted to utilize a SID and DVA concurrently.

5-5-15 Minimum Fuel Advisory

a. Pilot.

1. Advise ATC of your minimum fuel status when your fuel supply has reached a state where, upon reaching destination, you cannot accept any undue delay.

2. Be aware this is not an emergency situation, but merely an advisory that indicates an emergency situation is possible should any undue delay occur.

3. On initial contact the term "minimum fuel" should be used after stating call sign.

Example: *Salt Lake Approach, United 621, "minimum fuel."*

4. Be aware a minimum fuel advisory does not imply a need for traffic priority.

5. If the remaining usable fuel supply suggests the need for traffic priority to ensure a safe landing, you should declare an emergency due to low fuel and report fuel remaining in minutes.

Reference: *Pilot/Controller Glossary—Fuel Remaining.*

b. Controller.

1. When an aircraft declares a state of minimum fuel, relay this information to the facility to whom control jurisdiction is transferred.

2. Be alert for any occurrence which might delay the aircraft.

5-5-16 RNAV and RNP Operations

a. Pilot.

1. If unable to comply with the requirements of an RNAV or RNP procedure, pilots must advise air traffic control as soon as possible. For example, "...N1234, failure of GPS system, unable RNAV, request amended clearance."

2. Pilots are not authorized to fly a published RNAV or RNP procedure (instrument approach, departure, or arrival procedure) unless it is retrievable by the procedure name from the current aircraft navigation database and conforms to the charted procedure. The system must be able to retrieve the procedure by name from the aircraft navigation database, not just as a manually entered series of waypoints.

3. Whenever possible, RNAV routes (Q- or T-route) should be extracted from the database in their entirety, rather than loading RNAV route waypoints from the database into the flight plan individually. However, selecting and inserting individual, named fixes from the database is permitted, provided all fixes along the published route to be flown are inserted.

4. Pilots must not change any database waypoint type from a fly-by to fly-over, or vice versa. No other modification of database waypoints or the creation of user-defined waypoints

on published RNAV or RNP procedures is permitted, except to:

(a) Change altitude and/or airspeed waypoint constraints to comply with an ATC clearance/instruction.

(b) Insert a waypoint along the published route to assist in complying with ATC instruction, example, "Descend via the WILMS arrival except cross 30 north of BRUCE at/or below FL 210." This is limited only to systems that allow along-track waypoint construction.

5. Pilots of FMS-equipped aircraft, who are assigned an RNAV DP or STAR procedure and subsequently receive a change of runway, transition or procedure, must verify that the appropriate changes are loaded and available for navigation.

6. For RNAV 1 DPs and STARs, pilots must use a CDI, flight director and/or autopilot, in lateral navigation mode. Other methods providing an equivalent level of performance may also be acceptable.

7. For RNAV 1 DPs and STARs, pilots of aircraft without GPS, using DME/DME/IRU, must ensure the aircraft navigation system position is confirmed, within 1,000 feet, at the start point of take-off roll. The use of an automatic or manual runway update is an acceptable means of compliance with this requirement. Other methods providing an equivalent level of performance may also be acceptable.

8. For procedures or routes requiring the use of GPS, if the navigation system does not automatically alert the flight crew of a loss of GPS, the operator must develop procedures to verify correct GPS operation.

9. RNAV terminal procedures (DP and STAR) may be amended by ATC issuing radar vectors and/or clearances direct to a waypoint. Pilots should avoid premature manual deletion of waypoints from their active "legs" page to allow for rejoining procedures.

10. RAIM Prediction: If TSO-C129 equipment is used to solely satisfy the RNAV and RNP requirement, GPS RAIM availability must be

confirmed for the intended route of flight (route and time). If RAIM is not available, pilots need an approved alternate means of navigation.

Reference: *AIM, ¶5-1-16, RNAV and RNP Operations.*

11. Definition of "established" for RNAV and RNP operations. An aircraft is considered to be established on-course during RNAV and RNP operations anytime it is within 1 times the required accuracy for the segment being flown. For example, while operating on a Q-Route (RNAV 2), the aircraft is considered to be established on-course when it is within 2 NM of the course centerline.

Note 1: *Pilots must be aware of how their navigation system operates, along with any AFM limitations, and confirm that the aircraft's lateral deviation display (or map display if being used as an allowed alternate means) is suitable for the accuracy of the segment being flown. Automatic scaling and alerting changes are appropriate for some operations. For example, TSO-C129 systems change within 30 miles of destination and within 2 miles of FAF to support approach operations. For some navigation systems and operations, manual selection of scaling will be necessary.*

Note 2: *Pilots flying FMS equipped aircraft with barometric vertical navigation (Baro-VNAV) may descend when the aircraft is established on-course following FMS leg transition to the next segment. Leg transition normally occurs at the turn bisector for a fly-by waypoint (reference paragraph 1-2-1 for more on waypoints). When using full automation, pilots should monitor the aircraft to ensure the aircraft is turning at appropriate lead times and descending once established on-course.*

Note 3: *Pilots flying TSO-C129 navigation system equipped aircraft without full automation should use normal lead points to begin the turn. Pilots may descend when established on-course on the next segment of the approach.*

Section 6 National Security and Interception Procedures

5–6–1 National Security

National security in the control of air traffic is governed by 14 Code of Federal Regulations (CFR) Part 99, *Security Control of Air Traffic*.

5–6–2 National Security Requirements

a. Pursuant to 14 CFR 99.7, *Special Security Instructions*, each person operating an aircraft in an Air Defense Identification Zone (ADIZ) or Defense Area must, in addition to the applicable rules of Part 99, comply with special security instructions issued by the FAA Administrator in the interest of national security, pursuant to agreement between the FAA and the Department of Defense (DOD), or between the FAA and a U.S. Federal security or intelligence agency.

b. In addition to the requirements prescribed in this section, national security requirements for aircraft operations to or from, within, or transiting U.S. territorial airspace are in effect pursuant to 14 CFR 99.7; 49 United States Code (USC) 40103, *Sovereignty and Use of Airspace*; and 49 USC 41703, *Navigation of Foreign Civil Aircraft*. Aircraft operations to or from, within, or transiting U.S. territorial airspace must also comply with all other applicable regulations published in 14 CFR.

c. Due to increased security measures in place at many areas and in accordance with 14 CFR 91.103, *Preflight Action*, prior to departure, pilots must become familiar with all available information concerning that flight. Pilots are responsible to comply with 14 CFR 91.137 (*Temporary flight restrictions in the vicinity of disaster/hazard areas*), 91.138 (*Temporary flight restrictions in national disaster areas in the State of Hawaii*), 91.141 (*Flight restrictions in the proximity of the Presidential and other parties*), and 91.143 (*Flight limitation in the proximity of space flight operations*) when conducting flight in an area where a temporary flight restrictions area is in effect, and should check appropriate NOTAMs during flight planning. In addition, NOTAMs may be issued for National Security Areas (NSA) that temporarily prohibit flight operations under the provisions of 14 CFR 99.7.

Reference: AIM, ¶3-4-8, National Security Areas; AIM, ¶3-5-3, Temporary Flight Restrictions.

d. Noncompliance with the national security requirements for aircraft operations contained in this section may result in denial of flight entry into U.S. territorial airspace or ground stop of the flight at a U.S. airport.

e. Pilots of aircraft that do not adhere to the procedures in the national security requirements for aircraft operations contained in this section may be intercepted, and/or detained and interviewed by federal, state, or local law enforcement or other government personnel.

5–6–3 Definitions

a. *Air Defense Identification Zone (ADIZ)* means an area of airspace over land or water, in which the ready identification, location, and control of all aircraft (except Department of Defense and law enforcement aircraft) is required in the interest of national security.

b. *Defense Area* means any airspace of the contiguous U.S. that is not an ADIZ in which the control of aircraft is required for reasons of national security.

c. *U.S. territorial airspace*, for the purposes of this section, means the airspace over the U.S., its territories, and possessions, and the airspace over the territorial sea of the U.S., which extends 12 nautical miles from the baselines of the U.S., determined in accordance with international law.

d. *To U.S. territorial airspace* means any flight that enters U.S. territorial airspace after departure from a location outside of the U.S., its territories or possessions, for landing at a destination in the U.S., its territories or possessions.

e. *From U.S. territorial airspace* means any flight that exits U.S. territorial airspace after departure from a location in the U.S., its territories or possessions, and lands at a destination outside the U.S., its territories or possessions.

f. *Within U.S. territorial airspace* means any flight departing from a location inside of the U.S., its territories or possessions, which operates en route to a location inside the U.S., its territories or possessions.

g. *Transit or transiting U.S. territorial airspace* means any flight departing from a location outside of the U.S., its territories or possessions, which operates in U.S. territorial airspace en route to a location outside the U.S., its territories or possessions without landing at a destination in the U.S., its territories or possessions.

h. *Aeronautical facility*, for the purposes of this section, means a communications facility where flight plans or position reports are normally filed during flight operations.

5–6–4 ADIZ Requirements

a. To facilitate early identification of all aircraft in the vicinity of U.S. airspace boundaries, Air Defense Identification Zones (ADIZ) have been established. All aircraft must meet certain requirements to facilitate early identification when operating into, within, and across an ADIZ, as described in 14 CFR 99.

b. Requirements for aircraft operations are as follows:

1. Transponder Requirements. Unless otherwise authorized by ATC, each aircraft conducting operations into, within, or across the contiguous U.S. ADIZ must be equipped with an operable radar beacon transponder. The transponder must be turned on and squawking a discrete beacon code assigned by ATC or issued by FSS and displaying the aircraft altitude. Use of beacon code 1200 is not authorized. Use of the Universal Access Transceiver (UAT) anonymity mode is not authorized.

(a) For air defense purposes, aircraft equipped with an operable 1090es (DO–260b) ADS-B system operating outbound across the contiguous U.S. ADIZ may also be identified by the ICAO aircraft address (otherwise known as the aircraft Mode S code). Therefore, use of a privacy ICAO aircraft address by outbound aircraft is not authorized.

(b) Pilots of outbound VFR aircraft must squawk a discrete beacon code assigned by ATC or issued by FSS.

(c) Nothing in this section changes the ADS-B OUT requirements of 14 CFR 91.225.

Reference: 14 CFR 99.13, Transponder-On Requirements; 14 CFR 91.225, Automatic Dependent Surveillance–Broadcast (ADS-B) Out equipment and use.

2. Two-way Radio. In accordance with 14 CFR 99.9, *Radio Requirements*, any person operating in an ADIZ must maintain two-way radio communication with an appropriate aeronautical facility. For two-way radio communications failure, follow instructions contained in 14 CFR 99.9.

3. Flight Plan. In accordance with 14 CFR 99.11, *Flight Plan Requirements*, and 14 CFR 99.9, except as specified in subparagraph 5-6-4e, no person may operate an aircraft into, within, or from a departure point within an ADIZ, unless the person files, activates, and closes a flight plan with an appropriate aeronautical facility, or is otherwise authorized by air traffic control as follows:

(a) Pilots must file an Instrument Flight Rules (IFR) flight plan or file a Defense Visual Flight Rules (DVFR) flight plan containing the time and point of ADIZ penetration;

(b) The pilot must activate the DVFR flight plan with U.S. Flight Service and set the aircraft transponder to the assigned discrete beacon code prior to entering the ADIZ;

(c) The IFR or DVFR aircraft must depart within 5 minutes of the estimated departure time contained in the flight plan, except for (d) below;

(d) If the airport of departure within the Alaskan ADIZ has no facility for filing a flight plan, the flight plan must be filed immediately after takeoff or when within range of an appropriate aeronautical facility;

(e) State aircraft (U.S. or foreign) planning to operate through an ADIZ should enter ICAO Code M in Item 8 of the flight plan to assist in identification of the aircraft as a state aircraft.

c. Position Reporting Before Penetration of ADIZ.

In accordance with 14 CFR 99.15, Position Reports, before entering the ADIZ, the pilot must report to an appropriate aeronautical facility as follows:

1. IFR flights in controlled airspace. The pilot must maintain a continuous watch on the appropriate frequency and report the time and altitude of passing each designated reporting point or those reporting points specified or requested by ATC, except that while the aircraft is under radar control, only the passing of those reporting points specifically requested by ATC need be reported. (See 14 CFR 91.183(a), *IFR Communications.*)

2. DVFR flights and IFR flights in uncontrolled airspace:

(a) The time, position, and altitude at which the aircraft passed the last reporting point before penetration and the estimated time of arrival over the next appropriate reporting point along the flight route;

(b) If there is no appropriate reporting point along the flight route, the pilot reports at least 15 minutes before penetration: the estimated time, position, and altitude at which the pilot will penetrate; or

(c) If the departure airport is within an ADIZ or so close to the ADIZ boundary that it prevents the pilot from complying with (a) or (b) above, the pilot must report immediately after departure: the time of departure, the altitude, and the estimated time of arrival over the first reporting point along the flight route.

3. Foreign civil aircraft. If the pilot of a foreign civil aircraft that intends to enter the U.S. through an ADIZ cannot comply with the reporting requirements in subparagraphs c1 or c2 above, as applicable, the pilot must report the position of the aircraft to the appropriate aeronautical facility not less than 1 hour and not more than 2 hours average direct cruising distance from the U.S.

d. Land-Based ADIZ. Land-Based ADIZ are activated and deactivated over U.S. metropolitan areas as needed, with dimensions, activation dates and other relevant information disseminated via NOTAM. Pilots unable to comply with all NOTAM requirements must remain clear of Land-Based ADIZ. Pilots entering a Land-Based ADIZ without authorization or who fail to follow all requirements risk interception by military fighter aircraft.

e. Exceptions to ADIZ requirements.

1. Except for the national security requirements in paragraph 5-6-2, transponder requirements in subparagraph 5-6-4b1, and position reporting in subparagraph 5-6-4c, the ADIZ requirements in 14 CFR Part 99 described in this section do not apply to the following aircraft operations pursuant to Section 99.1(b), Applicability:

(a) Within the 48 contiguous States or within the State of Alaska, on a flight which remains within 10 NM of the point of departure;

(b) Operating at true airspeed of less than 180 knots in the Hawaii ADIZ or over any island, or within 12 NM of the coastline of any island, in the Hawaii ADIZ;

(c) Operating at true airspeed of less than 180 knots in the Alaska ADIZ while the pilot maintains a continuous listening watch on the appropriate frequency; or

(d) Operating at true airspeed of less than 180 knots in the Guam ADIZ.

2. An FAA air route traffic control center (ARTCC) may exempt certain aircraft operations on a local basis in concurrence with the DOD or pursuant to an agreement with a U.S. Federal security or intelligence agency. (See 14 CFR 99.1 for additional information.)

f. A VFR flight plan filed inflight makes an aircraft subject to interception for positive identification when entering an ADIZ. Pilots are therefore urged to file the required DVFR flight plan either in person or by telephone prior to departure when able.

5-6-5 Civil Aircraft Operations To or From U.S. Territorial Airspace

a. Civil aircraft, except as described in subparagraph 5-6-5b below, are authorized to operate to or from U.S. territorial airspace if in compliance with all of the following conditions:

1. File and are on an active flight plan (IFR, VFR, or DVFR);

2. Are equipped with an operational transponder with altitude reporting capability, and continuously squawk an ATC assigned transponder code;

3. Maintain two-way radio communications with ATC;

4. Comply with all other applicable ADIZ requirements described in paragraph 5-6-4 and any other national security requirements in paragraph 5-6-2;

5. Comply with all applicable U.S. Customs and Border Protection (CBP) requirements, including Advance Passenger Information System (APIS) requirements (see subparagraph 5-6-5c below for CBP APIS information), in accordance with 19 CFR Part 122, *Air Commerce Regulations*; and

6. Are in receipt of, and are operating in accordance with, an FAA routing authorization if the aircraft is registered in a U.S. State Department-designated special interest country or is operating with the ICAO three letter designator (3LD) of a company in a country listed as a U.S. State Department-designated special interest country, unless the operator holds valid FAA Part 129 operations specifications. VFR and DVFR flight operations are prohibited for any aircraft requiring an FAA routing authorization. (See paragraph 5-6-11 for FAA routing authorization information.)

b. Civil aircraft registered in the U.S., Canada, or Mexico with a maximum certificated takeoff gross weight of 100,309 pounds (45,500 kgs) or less that are operating without an operational transponder, and/or the ability to maintain two-way radio communications with ATC, are authorized to operate to or from U.S. territorial airspace over Alaska if in compliance with all of the following conditions:

1. Depart and land at an airport within the U.S. or Canada;

2. Enter or exit U.S. territorial airspace over Alaska north of the fifty-fourth parallel;

3. File and are on an active flight plan;

4. Comply with all other applicable ADIZ requirements described in paragraph 5-6-4 and any other national security requirements in paragraph 5-6-2;

5. Squawk 1200 if VFR and equipped with a transponder; and

6. Comply with all applicable U.S. CBP requirements, including Advance Passenger Information System (APIS) requirements (see subparagraph 5-6-5c below for CBP APIS information), in accordance with 19 CFR Part 122, *Air Commerce Regulations*.

c. CBP APIS Information. Information about U.S. CBP APIS requirements is available at http://www.cbp.gov.

5-6-6 Civil Aircraft Operations Within U.S. Territorial Airspace

a. Civil aircraft with a maximum certificated takeoff gross weight less than or equal to 100,309 pounds (45,500 kgs) are authorized to operate within U.S. territorial airspace in accordance with all applicable regulations and VFR in airport traffic pattern areas of U.S. airports near the U.S. border, except for those described in subparagraph 5-6-6b below.

b. Civil aircraft with a maximum certificated takeoff gross weight less than or equal to 100,309 pounds (45,500 kgs) and registered in a U.S. State Department-designated special interest country or operating with the ICAO 3LD of a company in a country listed as a U.S. State Department-designated special interest country, unless

the operator holds valid FAA Part 129 operations specifications, must operate within U.S. territorial airspace in accordance with the same requirements as civil aircraft with a maximum certificated takeoff gross weight greater than 100,309 pounds (45,500 kgs), as described in subparagraph 5-6-6c below.

c. Civil aircraft with a maximum certificated takeoff gross weight greater than 100,309 pounds (45,500 kgs) are authorized to operate within U.S. territorial airspace if in compliance with all of the following conditions:

1. File and are on an active flight plan (IFR or VFR);

2. Equipped with an operational transponder with altitude reporting capability, and continuously squawk an ATC assigned transponder code;

3. Equipped with an operational ADS-B Out when operating in airspace specified in 14 CFR 91.225;

4. Maintain two-way radio communications with ATC;

5. Aircraft not registered in the U.S. must operate under an approved Transportation Security Administration (TSA) aviation security program (see paragraph 5-6-10 for TSA aviation security program information) or in accordance with an FAA/TSA airspace waiver (see paragraph 5-6-9 for FAA/TSA airspace waiver information), except as authorized in 5-6-6c7 below;

6. Are in receipt of, and are operating in accordance with an FAA routing authorization and an FAA/TSA airspace waiver if the aircraft is registered in a U.S. State Department-designated special interest country or is operating with the ICAO 3LD of a company in a country listed as a U.S. State Department-designated special interest country, unless the operator holds valid FAA Part 129 operations specifications. VFR and DVFR flight operations are prohibited for any aircraft requiring an FAA routing authorization. (See paragraph 5-6-11 for FAA routing authorization information.); and

7. Aircraft not registered in the U.S., when conducting post-maintenance, manufacturer, production, or acceptance flight test operations, are exempt from the requirements in 5-6-6c5 above if all of the following requirements are met:

(a) A U.S. company must have operational control of the aircraft;

(b) An FAA-certificated pilot must serve as pilot in command;

(c) Only crewmembers are permitted onboard the aircraft; and

(d) "Maintenance Flight" is included in the remarks section of the flight plan.

5–6–7 Civil Aircraft Operations Transiting U.S. Territorial Airspace

a. Civil aircraft (except those operating in accordance with subparagraphs 5-6-7b, 5-6-7c, 5-6-7d, and 5-6-7e) are authorized to transit U.S. territorial airspace if in compliance with all of the following conditions:

1. File and are on an active flight plan (IFR, VFR, or DVFR);

2. Equipped with an operational transponder with altitude reporting capability and continuously squawk an ATC assigned transponder code;

3. Equipped with an operational ADS-B Out when operating in airspace specified in 14 CFR 91.225;

4. Maintain two-way radio communications with ATC;

5. Comply with all other applicable ADIZ requirements described in paragraph 5-6-4 and any other national security requirements in paragraph 5-6-2;

6. Are operating under an approved TSA aviation security program (see paragraph 5-6-10 for TSA aviation security program information) or are operating with and in accordance with an FAA/TSA airspace waiver (see paragraph 5-6-9 for FAA/TSA airspace waiver information), if:

(a) The aircraft is not registered in the U.S.; or

(b) The aircraft is registered in the U.S. and its maximum takeoff gross weight is greater than 100,309 pounds (45,500 kgs);

7. Are in receipt of, and are operating in accordance with, an FAA routing authorization if the aircraft is registered in a U.S. State Department-designated special interest country or is operating with the ICAO 3LD of a company in a country listed as a U.S. State Department-designated special interest country, unless the operator holds valid FAA Part 129 operations specifications. VFR and DVFR flight operations are prohibited for any aircraft requiring an FAA routing authorization. (See paragraph 5-6-11 for FAA routing authorization information.)

b. Civil aircraft registered in Canada or Mexico, and engaged in operations for the purposes of air ambulance, firefighting, law enforcement, search and rescue, or emergency evacuation are authorized to transit U.S. territorial airspace within 50 NM of their respective borders with the U.S., with or without an active flight plan, provided they have received and continuously transmit an ATC-assigned transponder code.

c. Civil aircraft registered in Canada, Mexico, Bahamas, Bermuda, Cayman Islands, or the British Virgin Islands with a maximum certificated takeoff gross weight of 100,309 pounds (45,500 kgs) or less are authorized to transit U.S. territorial

airspace if in compliance with all of the following conditions:

1. File and are on an active flight plan (IFR, VFR, or DVFR) that enters U.S. territorial airspace directly from any of the countries listed in this subparagraph 5-6-7c. Flights that include a stop in a non-listed country prior to entering U.S. territorial airspace must comply with the requirements prescribed by subparagraph 5-6-7a above, including operating under an approved TSA aviation security program (see paragraph 5-6-10 for TSA aviation program information) or operating with, and in accordance with, an FAA/TSA airspace waiver (see paragraph 5-6-9 for FAA/TSA airspace waiver information).

2. Equipped with an operational transponder with altitude reporting capability and continuously squawk an ATC assigned transponder code;

3. Equipped with an operational ADS-B Out when operating in airspace specified in 14 CFR 91.225;

4. Maintain two-way radio communications with ATC; and

5. Comply with all other applicable ADIZ requirements described in paragraph 5-6-4 and any other national security requirements in paragraph 5-6-2.

d. Civil aircraft registered in Canada, Mexico, Bahamas, Bermuda, Cayman Islands, or the British Virgin Islands with a maximum certificated takeoff gross weight greater than 100,309 pounds (45,500 kgs) must comply with the requirements subparagraph 5-6-7a, including operating under an approved TSA aviation security program (see paragraph 5-6-10 for TSA aviation program information) or operating with, and in accordance with, an FAA/TSA airspace waiver (see paragraph 5-6-9 for FAA/TSA airspace waiver information).

e. Civil aircraft registered in the U.S., Canada, or Mexico with a maximum certificated takeoff gross weight of 100,309 pounds (45,500 kgs) or less that are operating without an operational transponder and/or the ability to maintain two-way radio communications with ATC, are authorized to transit U.S. territorial airspace over Alaska if in compliance with all of the following conditions:

1. Enter and exit U.S. territorial airspace over Alaska north of the fifty-fourth parallel;

2. File and are on an active flight plan;

3. Squawk 1200 if VFR and equipped with a transponder.

4. Comply with all other applicable ADIZ requirements described in paragraph 5-6-4 and any other national security requirements in paragraph 5-6-2.

5–6–8 Foreign State Aircraft Operations

a. Foreign state aircraft are authorized to operate in U.S. territorial airspace if in compliance with all of the following conditions:

1. File and are on an active IFR flight plan;

2. Equipped with an operational transponder with altitude reporting capability and continuously squawk an ATC assigned transponder code;

3. Equipped with an operational ADS-B Out when operating in airspace specified in 14 CFR 91.225;

4. Maintain two-way radio communications with ATC; and

5. Comply with all other applicable ADIZ requirements described in paragraph 5-6-4 and any other national security requirements in paragraph 5-6-2.

b. Diplomatic Clearances. Foreign state aircraft may operate to or from, within, or in transit of U.S. territorial airspace only when authorized by the U.S. State Department by means of a diplomatic clearance, except as described in subparagraph 5-6-8i below.

1. Information about diplomatic clearances is available at the U.S. State Department website https://www.state.gov/diplomatic-aircraft -clearance-procedures-for-foreign-state-aircraft -to-operate-in-united-states-national-airspace/ (lower case only).

2. A diplomatic clearance may be initiated by contacting the U.S. State Department via email at DCAS@state.gov or via phone at (202) 453-8390.

Note: A diplomatic clearance is not required for foreign state aircraft operations that transit U.S. controlled oceanic airspace but do not enter U.S. territorial airspace. (See subparagraph 5-6-8d for flight plan information.)

c. An FAA routing authorization for state aircraft operations of special interest countries listed in subparagraph 5-6-11b. is required before the U.S. State Department will issue a diplomatic clearance for such operations. (See subparagraph 5-6-11 for FAA routing authorizations information).

d. Foreign state aircraft operating with a diplomatic clearance must navigate U.S. territorial airspace on an active IFR flight plan, unless specifically approved for VFR flight operations by the U.S. State Department in the diplomatic clearance.

Note: Foreign state aircraft operations to or from, within, or transiting U.S. territorial airspace; or transiting any U.S. controlled oceanic airspace, should enter ICAO code M in Item 8 of the flight plan to assist in identification of the aircraft as a state aircraft.

e. A foreign aircraft that operates to or from, within, or in transit of U.S. territorial airspace while conducting a state aircraft operation is not authorized to change its status as a state aircraft during any portion of the approved, diplomatically cleared itinerary.

f. A foreign aircraft described in subparagraph 5-6-8e above may operate from or within U.S. territorial airspace as a civil aircraft operation, once it has completed its approved, diplomatically cleared itinerary, if the aircraft operator is:

1. A foreign air carrier that holds valid FAA Part 129 operations specifications; and

2. Is in compliance with all other requirements applied to foreign civil aircraft operations from or within U.S. territorial airspace. (See paragraphs 5-6-5 and 5-6-6.)

g. Foreign state aircraft operations are not authorized to or from Ronald Reagan Washington National Airport (KDCA).

h. Foreign state aircraft operating with a U.S. Department of State issued Diplomatic Clearance Number in the performance of official missions are authorized to deviate from the Automatic Dependent Surveillance–Broadcast (ADS-B) Out requirements contained in 14 CFR §§91.225 and 91.227. All foreign state aircraft and/or operators associated with Department of Defense missions should contact their respective offices for further information on handling. Foreign state aircraft not associated with Department of Defense should coordinate with U.S. Department of State through the normal diplomatic clearance process.

i. Diplomatic Clearance Exceptions. State aircraft operations on behalf of the governments of Canada and Mexico conducted for the purposes of air ambulance, firefighting, law enforcement, search and rescue, or emergency evacuation are authorized to transit U.S. territorial airspace within 50 NM of their respective borders with the U.S., with or without an active flight plan, provided they have received and continuously transmit an ATC assigned transponder code. State aircraft operations on behalf of the governments of Canada and Mexico conducted under this subparagraph 5-6-8h are not required to obtain a diplomatic clearance from the U.S. State Department.

5–6–9 FAA/TSA Airspace Waivers

a. Operators may submit requests for FAA/TSA airspace waivers at https://waivers.faa.gov by selecting "international" as the waiver type.

b. Information regarding FAA/TSA airspace waivers can be found at: http://www.tsa.gov/for-industry/general-aviation or can be obtained by contacting TSA at (571) 227-2071.

c. All existing FAA/TSA waivers issued under previous FDC NOTAMs remain valid until the expiration date specified in the waiver, unless sooner superseded or rescinded.

5–6–10 TSA Aviation Security Programs

a. Applicants for U.S. air operator certificates will be provided contact information for TSA aviation security programs by the U.S. Department of Transportation during the certification process.

b. For information about applicable TSA security programs:

1. U.S. air carriers and commercial operators must contact their TSA Principal Security Specialist (PSS); and

2. Foreign air carriers must contact their International Industry Representative (IIR).

5–6–11 FAA Flight Routing Authorizations

a. Information about FAA routing authorizations for U.S. State Department-designated special interest country flight operations to or from, within, or transiting U.S. territorial airspace is available by country at:

1. FAA website http://www.faa.gov/air_traffic/publications/us_restrictions/; or

2. Phone by contacting the FAA System Operations Support Center (SOSC) at (202) 267-8115.

b. Special Interest Countries. The U.S. State Department-designated special interest countries are Cuba, Iran, The Democratic People's Republic of Korea (North Korea), The People's Republic of China, The Russian Federation, Sudan, and Syria.

Note: FAA flight routing authorizations are not required for aircraft registered in Hong Kong, Taiwan, or Macau.

c. Aircraft operating with the ICAO 3LD assigned to a company or entity from a country listed as a State Department-designated special interest country and holding valid FAA Part 129 operations specifications do not require FAA flight routing authorization.

d. FAA routing authorizations will only be granted for IFR operations. VFR and DVFR flight operations are prohibited for any aircraft requiring an FAA routing authorization.

5–6–12 Emergency Security Control of Air Traffic (ESCAT)

a. During defense emergency or air defense emergency conditions, additional special security instructions may be issued in accordance with 32 CFR Part 245, Plan for the Emergency Security Control of Air Traffic (ESCAT).

b. Under the provisions of 32 CFR Part 245, the military will direct the action to be taken in regard to landing, grounding, diversion, or dispersal of aircraft in the defense of the U.S. during emergency conditions.

Ch 5

c. At the time a portion or all of ESCAT is implemented, ATC facilities will broadcast appropriate instructions received from the Air Traffic Control System Command Center (ATCSCC) over available ATC frequencies. Depending on instructions received from the ATCSCC, VFR flights may be directed to land at the nearest available airport, and IFR flights will be expected to proceed as directed by ATC.

d. Pilots on the ground may be required to file a flight plan and obtain an approval (through FAA) prior to conducting flight operation.

5-6-13 Interception Procedures

a. General.

1. In conjunction with the FAA, Air Defense Sectors monitor air traffic and could order an intercept in the interest of national security or defense. Intercepts during peacetime operations are vastly different than those conducted under increased states of readiness. The interceptors may be fighters or rotary wing aircraft. The reasons for aircraft intercept include, but are not limited to:

 (a) Identify an aircraft;

 (b) Track an aircraft;

 (c) Inspect an aircraft;

 (d) Divert an aircraft;

 (e) Establish communications with an aircraft.

2. When specific information is required (i.e., markings, serial numbers, etc.) the interceptor pilot(s) will respond only if, in their judgment, the request can be conducted in a safe manner. Intercept procedures are described in some detail in the paragraphs below. In all situations, the interceptor pilot will consider safety of flight for all concerned throughout the intercept procedure. The interceptor pilot(s) will use caution to avoid startling the intercepted crew or passengers and understand that maneuvers considered normal for interceptor aircraft may be considered hazardous to other aircraft.

3. All aircraft operating in U.S. national airspace are highly encouraged to maintain a listening watch on VHF/UHF guard frequencies (121.5 or 243.0 MHz). If subjected to a military intercept, it is incumbent on civilian aviators to understand their responsibilities and to comply with ICAO standard signals relayed from the intercepting aircraft. Specifically, aviators are expected to contact air traffic control without delay (if able) on the local operating frequency or on VHF/UHF guard. Noncompliance may result in the use of force.

b. Fighter Intercept Phases (See Figure 5-6-1).

1. Approach Phase.

As standard procedure, intercepted aircraft are approached from behind. Typically, interceptor aircraft will be employed in pairs, however, it is not uncommon for a single aircraft to perform the intercept operation. Safe separation between interceptors and intercepted aircraft is the responsibility of the intercepting aircraft and will be maintained at all times.

2. Identification Phase.

Interceptor aircraft will initiate a controlled closure toward the aircraft of interest, holding at a distance no closer than deemed necessary to establish positive identification and to gather the necessary information. The interceptor may also fly past the intercepted aircraft while gathering data at a distance considered safe based on aircraft performance characteristics.

3. Post Intercept Phase.

An interceptor may attempt to establish communications via standard ICAO signals. In time-critical situations where the interceptor is seeking an immediate response from the intercepted aircraft or if the intercepted aircraft remains non-compliant to instruction, the interceptor pilot may initiate a divert maneuver. In this maneuver, the interceptor flies across the intercepted aircraft's flight path (minimum 500 feet separation and commencing from slightly below the intercepted aircraft altitude) in the general direction the intercepted aircraft is expected to turn. The interceptor will rock its wings (daytime) or flash external lights/select afterburners (night) while crossing the intercepted aircraft's flight path. The interceptor will roll out in the direction the intercepted aircraft is expected to turn before returning to verify the aircraft of interest is complying. The intercepted aircraft is expected to execute an immediate turn to the direction of the intercepting aircraft. If the aircraft of interest does not comply, the interceptor may conduct a second climbing turn across the intercepted aircraft's flight path (minimum 500 feet separation and commencing from slightly below the intercepted aircraft altitude) while expending flares as a warning signal to the intercepted aircraft to comply immediately and to turn in the direction indicated and to leave the area. The interceptor is responsible to maintain safe separation during these and all intercept maneuvers. Flight safety is paramount.

Note 1: NORAD interceptors will take every precaution to preclude the possibility of the intercepted aircraft experiencing jet wash/wake turbulence; however, there is a potential that this condition could be encountered.

Note 2: During Night/IMC, the intercept will be from below flight path.

FIGURE 5–6–1
Intercept Procedures

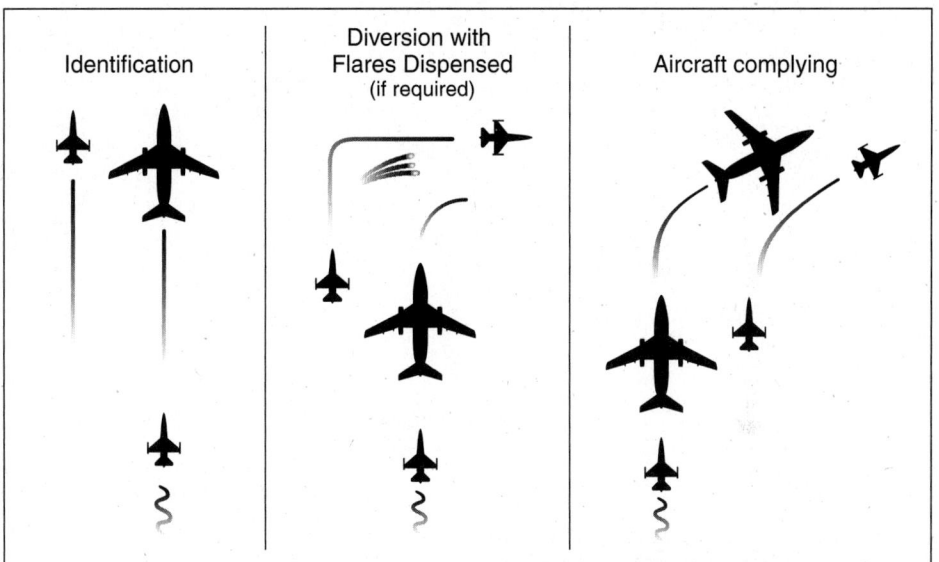

Identification	Diversion with Flares Dispensed (if required)	Aircraft complying

c. Helicopter Intercept Phases (See Figure 5-6-2).

1. Approach Phase.
Aircraft intercepted by helicopter may be approached from any direction, although the helicopter should close for identification and signaling from behind. Generally, the helicopter will approach off the left side of the intercepted aircraft. Safe separation between the helicopter and the unidentified aircraft will be maintained at all times.

2. Identification Phase.
The helicopter will initiate a controlled closure toward the aircraft of interest, holding at a distance no closer than deemed necessary to establish positive identification and gather the necessary information. The intercepted pilot should expect the interceptor helicopter to take a position off his left wing slightly forward of abeam.

3. Post Intercept Phase.
Visual signaling devices may be used in an attempt to communicate with the intercepted aircraft. Visual signaling devices may include, but are not limited to, LED scrolling signboards or blue flashing lights. If compliance is not attained through the use of radios or signaling devices, standard ICAO intercept signals (Table 5-6-1) may be employed. In order to maintain safe aircraft separation, it is incumbent upon the pilot of the intercepted aircraft not to fall into a trail position (directly behind the helicopter) if instructed to follow the helicopter. This is because the helicopter pilot may lose visual contact with the intercepted aircraft.

Note: Intercepted aircraft must not follow directly behind the helicopter thereby allowing the helicopter pilot to maintain visual contact with the intercepted aircraft and ensuring safe separation is maintained.

FIGURE 5–6–2
Helicopter Intercept Procedures

d. Summary of Intercepted Aircraft Actions.
An intercepted aircraft must, without delay:

1. Adhere to instructions relayed through the use of visual devices, visual signals, and radio communications from the intercepting aircraft.

2. Attempt to establish radio communications with the intercepting aircraft or with the appropriate air traffic control facility by making a general call on guard frequencies (121.5 or 243.0 MHz), giving the identity, position, and nature of the flight.

3. If transponder equipped, select Mode 3/A Code 7700 unless otherwise instructed by air traffic control.

Note: If instruction received from any agency conflicts with that given by the intercepting aircraft through visual or radio communications, the intercepted aircraft must seek immediate clarification.

4. The crew of the intercepted aircraft must continue to comply with interceptor aircraft signals and instructions until positively released.

5–6–14 Interception Signals

Table 5-6-1 and Table 5-6-2.

TABLE 5–6–1

INTERCEPTING SIGNALS Signals initiated by intercepting aircraft and responses by intercepted aircraft (as set forth in ICAO Annex 2—Appendix 1, 2.1)				
Series	Intercepting Aircraft Signals	Meaning	Intercepted Aircraft Responds	Meaning
1	**Day** Rocking wings from a position slightly above and ahead of, and normally to the left of, the intercepted aircraft and, after acknowledgement, a slow level turn, normally to the left, on to the desired heading. **Night** Same and, in addition, flashing navigational lights at irregular intervals. **Note 1:** Meteorological conditions or terrain may require the intercepting aircraft to take up a position slightly above and ahead of, and to the right of, the intercepted aircraft and to make the subsequent turn to the right. **Note 2:** If the intercepted aircraft is not able to keep pace with the intercepting aircraft, the latter is expected to fly a series of race-track patterns and to rock its wings each time it passes the intercepted aircraft.	You have been intercepted. Follow me.	**Aeroplanes:** **Day** Rocking wings and following. **Night** Same and, in addition, flashing navigational lights at irregular intervals. **Helicopters:** **Day** or **Night** Rocking aircraft, flashing navigational lights at irregular intervals and following.	Understood, will comply.
2	**Day** or **Night** An abrupt break-away maneuver from the intercepted aircraft consisting of a climbing turn of 90 degrees or more without crossing the line of flight of the intercepted aircraft.	You may proceed.	**Aeroplanes:** **Day** or **Night** Rocking wings. **Helicopters:** **Day** or **Night** Rocking aircraft.	Understood, will comply.
3	**Day** Circling aerodrome, lowering landing gear and overflying runway in direction of landing or, if the intercepted aircraft is a helicopter, overflying the helicopter landing area. **Night** Same and, in addition, showing steady landing lights.	Land at this aerodrome.	**Aeroplanes:** **Day** Lowering landing gear, following the intercepting aircraft and, if after overflying the runway landing is considered safe, proceeding to land. **Night** Same and, in addition, showing steady landing lights (if carried). **Helicopters:** **Day** or **Night** Following the intercepting aircraft and proceeding to land, showing a steady landing light (if carried).	Understood, will comply.

Ch 5

TABLE 5–6–2

	INTERCEPTING SIGNALS **Signals and Responses During Aircraft Intercept** **Signals initiated by intercepted aircraft and responses by intercepting aircraft** (as set forth in ICAO Annex 2—Appendix 1, 2.2)			
Series	*Intercepted* Aircraft Signals	Meaning	*Intercepting* Aircraft Responds	Meaning
4	**Day** or **Night** Raising landing gear (if fitted) and flashing landing lights while passing over runway in use or helicopter landing area at a height exceeding 300m (1,000 feet) but not exceeding 600m (2,000 feet) (in the case of a helicopter, at a height exceeding 50m (170 feet) but not exceeding 100m (330 feet) above the aerodrome level, and continuing to circle runway in use or helicopter landing area. If unable to flash landing lights, flash any other lights available.	Aerodrome you have designated is inadequate.	**Day** or **Night** If it is desired that the intercepted aircraft follow the intercepting aircraft to an alternate aerodrome, the intercepting aircraft raises its landing gear (if fitted) and uses the Series 1 signals prescribed for intercepting aircraft. If it is decided to release the intercepted aircraft, the intercepting aircraft uses the Series 2 signals prescribed for intercepting aircraft.	Understood, follow me. Understood, you may proceed.
5	**Day** or **Night** Regular switching on and off of all available lights but in such a manner as to be distinct from flashing lights.	Cannot comply.	**Day** or **Night** Use Series 2 signals prescribed for intercepting aircraft.	Understood.
6	**Day** or **Night** Irregular flashing of all available lights.	In distress.	**Day** or **Night** Use Series 2 signals prescribed for intercepting aircraft.	Understood.

5-6-15 ADIZ Boundaries and Designated Mountainous Areas

(See Figure 5-6-3.)

FIGURE 5–6–3
**Air Defense Identification Zone Boundaries
Designated Mountainous Areas**

5–6–16 Visual Warning System (VWS)

The VWS signal consists of highly-focused red and green colored laser lights designed to illuminate in an alternating red and green signal pattern. These lasers may be directed at specific aircraft suspected of making unauthorized entry into the Washington, DC Special Flight Rules Area (DC SFRA) proceeding on a heading or flight path that may be interpreted as a threat or that operate contrary to the operating rules for the DC SFRA. The beam is neither hazardous to the eyes of pilots/aircrew or passengers, regardless of altitude or distance from the source nor will the beam affect aircraft systems.

a. If you are communicating with ATC, and this signal is directed at your aircraft, you are required to contact ATC and advise that you are being illuminated by a visual warning system.

b. If this signal is directed at you, and you are not communicating with ATC, you are advised to turn to the most direct heading away from the center of the DC SFRA as soon as possible.

Immediately contact ATC on an appropriate frequency, VHF Guard 121.5 or UHF Guard 243.0, and provide your aircraft identification, position, and nature of the flight. Failure to follow these procedures may result in interception by military aircraft. Further noncompliance with interceptor aircraft or ATC may result in the use of force.

c. Pilots planning to operate aircraft in or near the DC SFRA are to familiarize themselves with aircraft intercept procedures. This information applies to all aircraft operating within the DC SFRA including DOD, Law Enforcement, and aircraft engaged in aeromedical operations and does not change procedures established for reporting unauthorized laser illumination as published in FAA Advisory Circulars and Notices.

Reference: 14 CFR §91.161

d. More details including a video demonstration of the VWS are available from the following FAA website: www.faasafety.gov/VisualWarning System/VisualWarning.htm.

Chapter 6
Emergency Procedures

Section 1 General

6-1-1 Pilot Responsibility and Authority

a. The pilot-in-command of an aircraft is directly responsible for and is the final authority as to the operation of that aircraft. In an emergency requiring immediate action, the pilot-in-command may deviate from any rule in 14 CFR Part 91, Subpart A, General, and Subpart B, Flight Rules, to the extent required to meet that emergency.

Note: In the event of a pilot incapacitation, an Emergency Autoland system or an emergency descent system may assume operation of the aircraft and deviate to meet that emergency.

Reference: 14 CFR §91.3(b).

b. If the emergency authority of 14 CFR Section 91.3(b) is used to deviate from the provisions of an ATC clearance, the pilot-in-command must notify ATC as soon as possible and obtain an amended clearance.

c. Unless deviation is necessary under the emergency authority of 14 CFR Section 91.3, pilots of IFR flights experiencing two-way radio communications failure are expected to adhere to the procedures prescribed under "IFR operations, two-way radio communications failure."

Reference: 14 CFR §91.185.

6-1-2 Emergency Condition— Request Assistance Immediately

a. An emergency can be either a *distress* or *urgency* condition as defined in the Pilot/Controller Glossary. Pilots do not hesitate to declare an emergency when they are faced with *distress* conditions such as fire, mechanical failure, or structural damage. However, some are reluctant to report an *urgency* condition when they encounter situations which may not be immediately perilous, but are potentially catastrophic. An aircraft is in at least an *urgency* condition the moment the pilot becomes doubtful about position, fuel endurance, weather, or any other condition that could adversely affect flight safety. This is the time to ask for help, not after the situation has developed into a *distress* condition.

b. Pilots who become apprehensive for their safety for any reason should *request assistance immediately*. Ready and willing help is available in the form of radio, radar, direction finding stations and other aircraft. Delay has caused accidents and cost lives. *Safety is not a luxury! Take action!*

Ch 6

Section 2 Emergency Services Available to Pilots

6-2-1 Radar Service for VFR Aircraft in Difficulty

a. Radar equipped ATC facilities can provide radar assistance and navigation service (vectors) to VFR aircraft in difficulty when the pilot can talk with the controller, and the aircraft is within radar coverage. Pilots should clearly understand that authorization to proceed in accordance with such radar navigational assistance does not constitute authorization for the pilot to violate CFRs. In effect, assistance is provided on the basis that navigational guidance information is advisory in nature, and the responsibility for flying the aircraft safely remains with the pilot.

b. Experience has shown that many pilots who are not qualified for instrument flight cannot maintain control of their aircraft when they encounter clouds or other reduced visibility conditions. In many cases, the controller will not know whether flight into instrument conditions will result from ATC instructions. To avoid possible hazards resulting from being vectored into IFR conditions, a pilot in difficulty should keep the controller advised of the current weather conditions being encountered and the weather along the course ahead and observe the following:

1. If a course of action is available which will permit flight and a safe landing in VFR weather conditions, noninstrument rated pilots should choose the VFR condition rather than requesting a vector or approach that will take them into IFR weather conditions; or

2. If continued flight in VFR conditions is not possible, the noninstrument rated pilot should so advise the controller and indicating the lack of an instrument rating, declare a *distress* condition; or

3. If the pilot is instrument rated and current, and the aircraft is instrument equipped, the pilot should so indicate by requesting an IFR flight clearance. Assistance will then be provided on the basis that the aircraft can operate safely in IFR weather conditions.

6-2-2 Transponder Emergency Operation

a. When a *distress* or *urgency* condition is encountered, the pilot of an aircraft with a coded radar beacon transponder, who desires to alert a ground radar facility, should squawk Mode 3/A, Code 7700/Emergency and Mode C altitude reporting and then immediately establish communications with the ATC facility.

b. Radar facilities are equipped so that Code 7700 normally triggers an alarm or special indicator at all control positions. Pilots should understand that they might not be within a radar coverage area. Therefore, they should continue squawking Code 7700 and establish radio communications as soon as possible.

6-2-3 Intercept and Escort

a. The concept of airborne intercept and escort is based on the Search and Rescue (SAR) aircraft establishing visual and/or electronic contact with an aircraft in difficulty, providing in-flight assistance, and escorting it to a safe landing. If bailout, crash landing or ditching becomes necessary, SAR operations can be conducted without delay. For most incidents, particularly those occurring at night and/or during instrument flight conditions, the availability of intercept and escort services will depend on the proximity of SAR units with suitable aircraft on alert for immediate dispatch. In limited circumstances, other aircraft flying in the vicinity of an aircraft in difficulty can provide these services.

b. If specifically requested by a pilot in difficulty or if a *distress* condition is declared, SAR coordinators *will* take steps to intercept and escort an aircraft. Steps may be initiated for intercept and escort if an *urgency* condition is declared and unusual circumstances make such action advisable.

c. It is the pilot's prerogative to refuse intercept and escort services. Escort services will normally be provided to the nearest adequate airport. Should the pilot receiving escort services continue onto another location after reaching a safe airport, or decide not to divert to the nearest safe airport, the escort aircraft is not obligated to continue and further escort is discretionary. The decision will depend on the circumstances of the individual incident.

6-2-4 Emergency Locator Transmitter (ELT)

a. General.

1. ELTs are required for most General Aviation airplanes.

Reference: 14 CFR §91.207.

2. ELTs of various types were developed as a means of locating downed aircraft. These electronic, battery operated transmitters operate on one of three frequencies. These operating frequencies are 121.5 MHz, 243.0 MHz, and the newer 406 MHz. ELTs operating on 121.5 MHz and 243.0 MHz are analog devices. The newer 406 MHz ELT is a digital transmitter that can be encoded with the owner's contact information or aircraft data. The latest 406 MHz ELT models can also be encoded with the aircraft's position data which can help SAR forces locate the aircraft much more quickly after a crash. The 406 MHz

from the real thing, leading to expensive and frustrating searches. A false ELT signal could also interfere with genuine emergency transmissions and hinder or prevent the timely location of crash sites. Frequent false alarms could also result in complacency and decrease the vigorous reaction that must be attached to all ELT signals.

2. Numerous cases of inadvertent activation have occurred as a result of aerobatics, hard landings, movement by ground crews and aircraft maintenance. These false alarms can be minimized by monitoring 121.5 MHz and/or 243.0 MHz as follows:

(a) In flight when a receiver is available.

(b) Before engine shut down at the end of each flight.

(c) When the ELT is handled during installation or maintenance.

(d) When maintenance is being performed near the ELT.

(e) When a ground crew moves the aircraft.

(f) If an ELT signal is heard, turn off the aircraft's ELT to determine if it is transmitting. If it has been activated, maintenance might be required before the unit is returned to the "ARMED" position. You should contact the nearest Air Traffic facility and notify it of the inadvertent activation.

d. Inflight Monitoring and Reporting.

1. Pilots are encouraged to monitor 121.5 MHz and/or 243.0 MHz while inflight to assist in identifying possible emergency ELT transmissions. On receiving a signal, report the following information to the nearest air traffic facility:

(a) Your position at the time the signal was first heard.

(b) Your position at the time the signal was last heard.

(c) Your position at maximum signal strength.

(d) Your flight altitudes and frequency on which the emergency signal was heard: 121.5 MHz or 243.0 MHz. If possible, positions should be given relative to a navigation aid. If the aircraft has homing equipment, provide the bearing to the emergency signal with each reported position.

6-2-5 FAA K-9 Explosives Detection Team Program

a. The FAA's Office of Civil Aviation Security Operations manages the FAA K-9 Explosives Detection Team Program which was established in 1972. Through a unique agreement with law enforcement agencies and airport authorities, the FAA has strategically placed FAA-certified K-9 teams (a team is one handler and one dog) at airports throughout the country. If a bomb threat is received while an aircraft is in flight, the aircraft

can be directed to an airport with this capability. The FAA provides initial and refresher training for all handlers, provides single purpose explosive detector dogs, and requires that each team is annually evaluated in five areas for FAA certification: aircraft (widebody and narrowbody), vehicles, terminal, freight (cargo), and luggage. **If you desire this service, notify your company or an FAA air traffic control facility.**

b. The following list shows the locations of current FAA K-9 teams:

TABLE 6-2-1
FAA SPONSORED EXPLOSIVES DETECTION
DOG/HANDLER TEAM LOCATIONS

Airport Symbol	Location
ATL	Atlanta, Georgia
BHM	Birmingham, Alabama
BOS	Boston, Massachusetts
BUF	Buffalo, New York
CLT	Charlotte, North Carolina
ORD	Chicago, Illinois
CVG	Cincinnati, Ohio
DFW	Dallas, Texas
DEN	Denver, Colorado
DTW	Detroit, Michigan
IAH	Houston, Texas
JAX	Jacksonville, Florida
MCI	Kansas City, Missouri
LAX	Los Angeles, California
MEM	Memphis, Tennessee
MIA	Miami, Florida
MKE	Milwaukee, Wisconsin
MSY	New Orleans, Louisiana
MCO	Orlando, Florida
PHX	Phoenix, Arizona
PIT	Pittsburgh, Pennsylvania
PDX	Portland, Oregon
SLC	Salt Lake City, Utah
SFO	San Francisco, California
SJU	San Juan, Puerto Rico
SEA	Seattle, Washington
STL	St. Louis, Missouri
TUS	Tucson, Arizona
TUL	Tulsa, Oklahoma

c. If due to weather or other considerations an aircraft with a suspected hidden explosive problem were to land or intended to land at an airport other than those listed in b above, it is recommended that they call the FAA's Washington Operations Center (telephone 202-267-3333, if appropriate) or have an air traffic facility with which you can communicate contact the above center requesting assistance.

6–2–6 Search and Rescue

a. General. SAR is a lifesaving service provided through the combined efforts of the federal agencies signatory to the National SAR Plan, and the agencies responsible for SAR within each state. Operational resources are provided by the U.S. Coast Guard, DOD components, the Civil Air Patrol, the Coast Guard Auxiliary, state, county and local law enforcement and other public safety agencies, and private volunteer organizations. Services include search for missing aircraft, survival aid, rescue, and emergency medical help for the occupants after an accident site is located.

b. National Search and Rescue Plan. By federal interagency agreement, the National Search and Rescue Plan provides for the effective use of all available facilities in all types of SAR missions. These facilities include aircraft, vessels, pararescue and ground rescue teams, and emergency radio fixing. Under the plan, the U.S. Coast Guard is responsible for the coordination of SAR in the Maritime Region, and the USAF is responsible in the Inland Region. To carry out these responsibilities, the Coast Guard and the Air Force have established Rescue Coordination Centers (RCCs) to direct SAR activities within their regions. For aircraft emergencies, distress, and urgency, information normally will be passed to the appropriate RCC through an ARTCC or FSS.

c. Coast Guard Rescue Coordination Centers. (See Table 6-2-2.)

TABLE 6–2–2
COAST GUARD RESCUE COORDINATION CENTERS

Alameda, CA 510-437-3701	Miami, FL 305-415-6800
Boston, MA 617-223-8555	New Orleans, LA 504-589-6225
Cleveland, OH 216-902-6117	Portsmouth, VA 757-398-6390
Honolulu, HI 808-541-2500	Seattle, WA 206-220-7001
Juneau, AK 907-463-2000	San Juan, PR 787-289-2042

d. Air Force Rescue Coordination Centers. (See Table 6-2-3 and Table 6-2-4.)

TABLE 6–2–3
AIR FORCE RESCUE COORDINATION CENTER
48 CONTIGUOUS STATES

Air Force Rescue Coordination Center	
Tyndall AFB, Florida	Phone
Commercial	850-283-5955
WATS	800-851-3051
DSN	523-5955

TABLE 6–2–4
AIR COMMAND RESCUE COORDINATION CENTER
ALASKA

Alaskan Air Command Rescue Coordination Center	
Elmendorf AFB, Alaska	Phone
Commercial	907-428-7230 800-420-7230 (outside Anchorage)
DSN	317-551-7230

e. Joint Rescue Coordination Center. (See Table 6-2-5.)

TABLE 6–2–5
JOINT RESCUE COORDINATION CENTER HAWAII

Honolulu Joint Rescue Coordination Center	
HQ 14th CG District Honolulu	Phone
Commercial	808-541-2500
DSN	448-0301

f. Emergency and Overdue Aircraft.

1. ARTCCs and FSSs will alert the SAR system when information is received from any source that an aircraft is in difficulty, overdue, or missing.

(a) Radar facilities providing radar flight following or advisories consider the loss of radar and radios, without service termination notice, to be a possible emergency. Pilots receiving VFR services from radar facilities should be aware that SAR may be initiated under these circumstances.

(b) A filed flight plan is the most timely and effective indicator that an aircraft is overdue. Flight plan information is invaluable to SAR forces for search planning and executing search efforts.

2. Prior to departure on every flight, local or otherwise, someone at the departure point should be advised of your destination and route of flight if other than direct. Search efforts are often wasted and rescue is often delayed because of pilots who thoughtlessly takeoff without telling anyone where they are going. File a flight plan for *your* safety.

3. According to the National Search and Rescue Plan, "The life expectancy of an injured survivor decreases as much as 80 percent during the first 24 hours, while the chances of survival of uninjured survivors rapidly diminishes after the first 3 days."

4. An Air Force Review of 325 SAR missions conducted during a 23-month period revealed that "Time works against people who experience a **distress** but are not on a flight plan, since 36 hours normally pass before family concern initiates an (alert)."

g. VFR Search and Rescue Protection.

1. To receive this valuable protection, *file a VFR or DVFR Flight Plan* with an FAA FSS. For maximum protection, file only to the point of first intended landing, and refile for each leg to final

destination. When a lengthy flight plan is filed, with several stops en route and an ETE to final destination, a mishap could occur on any leg, and unless other information is received, it is probable that no one would start looking for you until 30 minutes after your ETA at your final destination.

2. If you land at a location other than the intended destination, report the landing to the nearest FAA FSS and advise them of your original destination.

3. If you land en route and are delayed more than 30 minutes, report this information to the nearest FSS and give them your original destination.

4. If your ETE changes by 30 minutes or more, report a new ETA to the nearest FSS and give them your original destination. Remember that if you fail to respond within one-half hour after your ETA at final destination, a search will be started to locate you.

5. It is important that you *close your flight plan IMMEDIATELY AFTER ARRIVAL AT YOUR FINAL DESTINATION WITH THE FSS DESIGNATED WHEN YOUR FLIGHT PLAN WAS FILED.* The **pilot is responsible** for closure of a VFR or DVFR flight plan; they are not closed automatically. This will prevent needless search efforts.

6. The rapidity of rescue on land or water will depend on how accurately your position may be determined. If a flight plan has been followed and your position is on course, rescue will be expedited.

h. Survival Equipment.

1. For flight over uninhabited land areas, it is wise to take and know how to use survival equipment for the type of climate and terrain.

2. If a forced landing occurs at sea, chances for survival are governed by the degree of crew proficiency in emergency procedures and by the availability and effectiveness of water survival equipment.

i. Body Signal Illustrations.

1. If you are forced down and are able to attract the attention of the pilot of a rescue airplane, the body signals illustrated on these pages can be used to transmit messages to the pilot circling over your location.

2. Stand in the open when you make the signals.

3. Be sure the background, as seen from the air, is not confusing.

4. Go through the motions slowly and repeat each signal until you are positive that the pilot understands you.

j. Observance of Downed Aircraft.

1. Determine if crash is marked with a yellow cross; if so, the crash has already been reported and identified.

2. If possible, determine type and number of aircraft and whether there is evidence of survivors.

3. Fix the position of the crash as accurately as possible with reference to a navigational aid. If possible, provide geographic or physical description of the area to aid ground search parties.

4. Transmit the information to the nearest FAA or other appropriate radio facility.

5. If circumstances permit, orbit the scene to guide in other assisting units until their arrival or until you are relieved by another aircraft.

6. Immediately after landing, make a complete report to the nearest FAA facility, or Air Force or Coast Guard Rescue Coordination Center. The report can be made by a long distance collect telephone call.

FIGURE 6–2–1
Ground–Air Visual Code for Use by Survivors

No.	Message	Code Symbol
1	Require assistance	V
2	Require medical assistance	X
3	No or Negative	N
4	Yes or Affirmative	Y
5	Proceeding in this direction	↑

If In Doubt, Use International Symbol **SOS**

INSTRUCTIONS
1. Lay out symbols by using strips of fabric or parachutes, pieces of wood, stones or any available material.
2. Provide as much color contrast as possible between material used for symbols and background against which symbols are exposed.
3. Symbols should be at least 10 feet high or larger. Care should be taken to lay out symbols exactly as shown.
4. In addition to using symbols, every effort is to be made to attract attention by means of radio, flares, smoke, or other available means.
5. On snow covered ground, signals can be made by dragging, shoveling or tramping. Depressed areas forming symbols will appear black from the air.
6. Pilot should acknowledge message by rocking wings from side to side.

FIGURE 6–2–2
Ground–Air Visual Code for Use by Ground Search Parties

No.	Message	Code Symbol		
1	Operation completed.	**LLL**		
2	We have found all personnel.	**LL**		
3	We have found only some personnel.	—		—
4	We are not able to continue. Returning to base.	**XX**		
5	Have divided into two groups. Each proceeding in direction indicated.	⤢		
6	Information received that aircraft is in this direction.	→ →		
7	Nothing found. Will continue search.	**NN**		

Note: These visual signals have been accepted for international use and appear in Annex 12 to the Convention on International Civil Aviation.

FIGURE 6–2–3
Urgent Medical Assistance

NEED MEDICAL
ASSISTANCE–URGENT
Used only when life is at stake

FIGURE 6–2–4
All OK

ALL OK–DO NOT WAIT
Wave one arm overhead

FIGURE 6–2–6
Long Delay

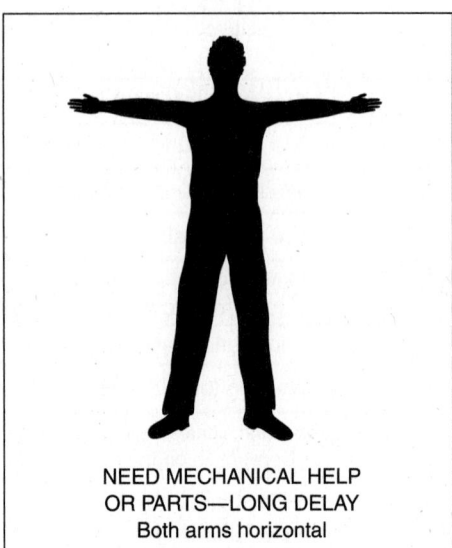

NEED MECHANICAL HELP
OR PARTS—LONG DELAY
Both arms horizontal

FIGURE 6–2–5
Short Delay

CAN PROCEED SHORTLY
WAIT IF PRACTICABLE
One arm horizontal

FIGURE 6–2–7
Drop Message

Make throwing motion

FIGURE 6–2–8
Receiver Operates

OUR RECEIVER IS OPERATING
Cup hands over ears

FIGURE 6–2–10
Land Here

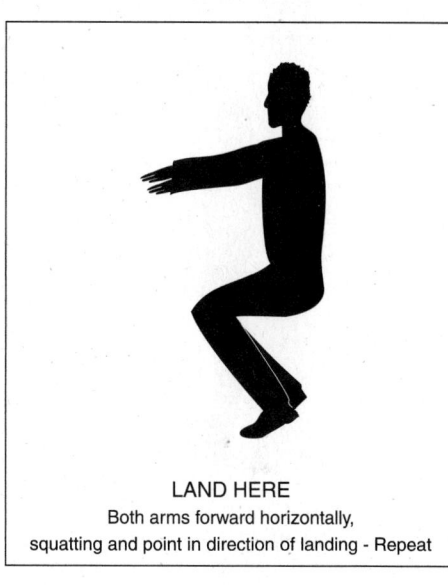

LAND HERE
Both arms forward horizontally,
squatting and point in direction of landing - Repeat

FIGURE 6–2–9
Do Not Land Here

DO NOT ATTEMPT TO LAND HERE
Both arms waved across face

FIGURE 6–2–11
Negative (Ground)

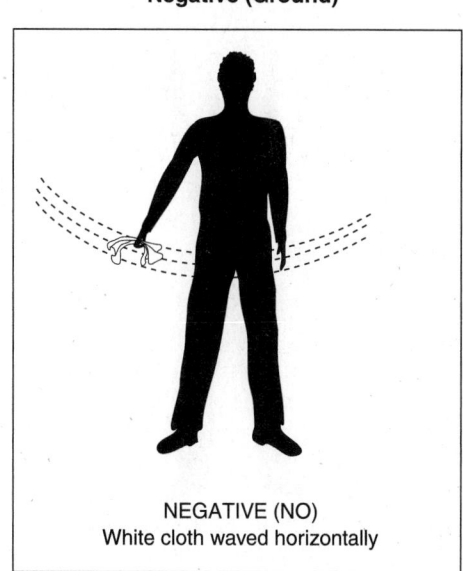

NEGATIVE (NO)
White cloth waved horizontally

Ch 6

FIGURE 6–2–12
Affirmative (Ground)

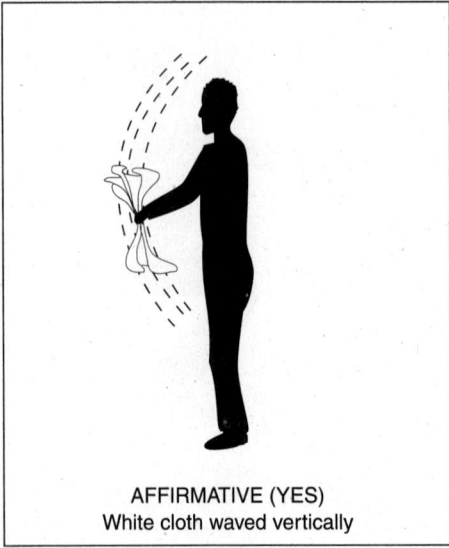

AFFIRMATIVE (YES)
White cloth waved vertically

FIGURE 6–2–13
Pick Us Up

PICK US UP—PLANE ABANDONED
Both arms vertical

FIGURE 6–2–14
Affirmative (Aircraft)

Affirmative reply from aircraft:

AFFIRMATIVE (YES)
Dip nose of plane several times

FIGURE 6–2–15
Negative (Aircraft)

Negative reply from aircraft:

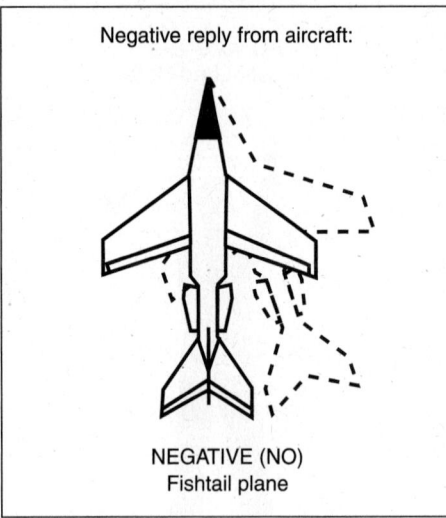

NEGATIVE (NO)
Fishtail plane

FIGURE 6–2–16
Message received and understood (Aircraft)

Message received and understood by aircraft:
Day or moonlight - Rocking wings
Night - Green flashed from signal lamp

FIGURE 6–2–17
Message received and NOT understood (Aircraft)

Message received and NOT understood by aircraft:
Day or moonlight - Making a complete right-hand circle
Night - Red flashes from signal lamp

Ch 6

Section 3 Distress and Urgency Procedures

6–3–1 Distress and Urgency Communications

a. A pilot who encounters a *distress* or *urgency* condition can obtain assistance simply by contacting the air traffic facility or other agency in whose area of responsibility the aircraft is operating, stating the nature of the difficulty, pilot's intentions and assistance desired. *Distress* and *urgency* communications procedures are prescribed by the International Civil Aviation Organization (ICAO), however, and have decided advantages over the informal procedure described above.

b. *Distress* and *urgency* communications procedures discussed in the following paragraphs relate to the use of air ground voice communications.

c. The initial communication, and if considered necessary, any subsequent transmissions by an aircraft in *distress* should begin with the signal MAYDAY, preferably repeated three times. The signal PAN-PAN should be used in the same manner for an *urgency* condition.

d. *Distress* communications have absolute priority over all other communications, and the word MAYDAY commands radio silence on the frequency in use. *Urgency* communications have priority over all other communications except *distress*, and the word PAN-PAN warns other stations not to interfere with *urgency* transmissions.

e. Normally, the station addressed will be the air traffic facility or other agency providing air traffic services, on the frequency in use at the time. If the pilot is not communicating and receiving services, the station to be called will normally be the air traffic facility or other agency in whose area of responsibility the aircraft is operating, on the appropriate assigned frequency. If the station addressed does not respond, or if time or the situation dictates, the *distress* or *urgency* message may be broadcast, or a collect call may be used, addressing "Any Station (Tower)(Radio)(Radar)."

f. The station addressed should immediately acknowledge a *distress* or *urgency* message, provide assistance, coordinate and direct the activities of assisting facilities, and alert the appropriate search and rescue coordinator if warranted. Responsibility will be transferred to another station only if better handling will result.

g. All other stations, aircraft and ground, will continue to listen until it is evident that assistance is being provided. If any station becomes aware that the station being called either has not received a *distress* or *urgency* message, or cannot communicate with the aircraft in difficulty, it will attempt to contact the aircraft and provide assistance.

h. Although the frequency in use or other frequencies assigned by ATC are preferable, the following emergency frequencies can be used for *distress* or *urgency* communications, if necessary or desirable:
121.5 MHz and 243.0 MHz. Both have a range generally limited to line of sight. 121.5 MHz is guarded by direction finding stations and some military and civil aircraft. 243.0 MHz is guarded by military aircraft. Both 121.5 MHz and 243.0 MHz are guarded by military towers, most civil towers, and radar facilities. Normally ARTCC emergency frequency capability does not extend to radar coverage limits. If an ARTCC does not respond when called on 121.5 MHz or 243.0 MHz, call the nearest tower.

6–3–2 Obtaining Emergency Assistance

a. A pilot in any *distress* or *urgency* condition should *immediately* take the following action, not necessarily in the order listed, to obtain assistance:

1. Climb, if possible, for improved communications, and better radar and direction finding detection. However, it must be understood that unauthorized climb or descent under IFR conditions within controlled airspace is prohibited, except as permitted by 14 CFR Section 91.3(b).

2. If equipped with a radar beacon transponder (civil) or IFF/SIF (military):

(a) Continue squawking assigned Mode A/3 discrete code/VFR code and Mode C altitude encoding when in radio contact with an air traffic facility or other agency providing air traffic services, unless instructed to do otherwise.

(b) If unable to immediately establish communications with an air traffic facility/agency, squawk Mode A/3, Code 7700/Emergency and Mode C.

3. Transmit a *distress* or *urgency* message consisting of as many as necessary of the following elements, preferably in the order listed:

(a) If *distress*, MAYDAY, MAYDAY, MAYDAY; if *urgency*, PAN-PAN, PAN-PAN, PAN-PAN.
(b) Name of station addressed.
(c) Aircraft identification and type.
(d) Nature of *distress* or *urgency*.
(e) Weather.
(f) Pilots intentions and request.
(g) Present position, and heading; or if lost, last known position, time, and heading since that position.

(h) Altitude or flight level.

(i) Fuel remaining in minutes.

(j) Number of people on board.

(k) Any other useful information.

Reference: Pilot/Controller Glossary—Fuel Remaining.

b. After establishing radio contact, comply with advice and instructions received. Cooperate. Do not hesitate to ask questions or clarify instructions when you do not understand or if you cannot comply with clearance. Assist the ground station to control communications on the frequency in use. Silence interfering radio stations. Do not change frequency or change to another ground station unless absolutely necessary. If you do, advise the ground station of the new frequency and station name prior to the change, transmitting in the blind if necessary. If two-way communications cannot be established on the new frequency, return immediately to the frequency or station where two-way communications last existed.

c. When in a *distress* condition with bailout, crash landing or ditching imminent, take the following additional actions to assist search and rescue units:

1. Time and circumstances permitting, transmit as many as necessary of the message elements in subparagraph a3 above, and any of the following that you think might be helpful:

 (a) ELT status.

 (b) Visible landmarks.

 (c) Aircraft color.

 (d) Number of persons on board.

 (e) Emergency equipment on board.

2. Actuate your ELT if the installation permits.

3. For bailout, and for crash landing or ditching if risk of fire is not a consideration, set your radio for continuous transmission.

4. If it becomes necessary to ditch, make every effort to ditch near a surface vessel. If time permits, an FAA facility should be able to get the position of the nearest commercial or Coast Guard vessel from a Coast Guard Rescue Coordination Center.

5. After a crash landing, unless you have good reason to believe that you will not be located by search aircraft or ground teams, it is best to remain with your aircraft and prepare means for signaling search aircraft.

6–3–3 Ditching Procedures

FIGURE 6–3–1
Single Swell (15 knot wind)

FIGURE 6–3–2
Double Swell (15 knot wind)

FIGURE 6–3–3
Double Swell (30 knot wind)

FIGURE 6–3–4
(50 knot wind)

Aircraft with low landing speeds — land into the wind.

Aircraft with high landing speeds — choose compromise heading between wind and swell.

Both — land on back side of swell.

FIGURE 6–3–5
Wind - Swell - Ditch Heading

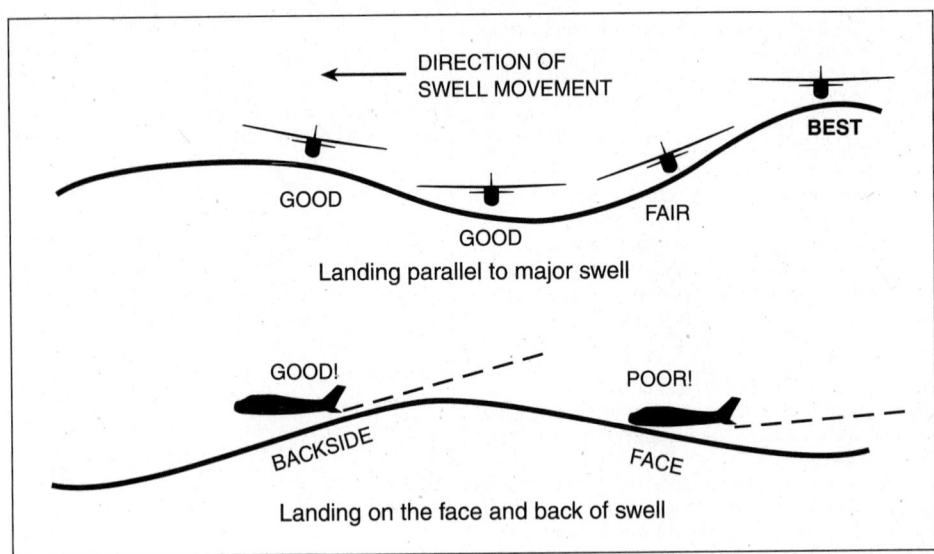

a. A successful aircraft ditching is dependent on three primary factors. In order of importance they are:

 1. Sea conditions and wind.
 2. Type of aircraft.
 3. Skill and technique of pilot.
 b. Common oceanographic terminology.
 1. Sea. The condition of the surface that is the result of both waves and swells.
 2. Wave (or Chop). The condition of the surface caused by the local winds.
 3. Swell. The condition of the surface which has been caused by a distance disturbance.
 4. Swell Face. The side of the swell toward the observer. The backside is the side away from the observer. These definitions apply regardless of the direction of swell movement.
 5. Primary Swell. The swell system having the greatest height from trough to crest.
 6. Secondary Swells. Those swell systems of less height than the primary swell.
 7. Fetch. The distance the waves have been driven by a wind blowing in a constant direction, without obstruction.
 8. Swell Period. The time interval between the passage of two successive crests at the same spot in the water, measured in seconds.
 9. Swell Velocity. The speed and direction of the swell with relation to a fixed reference point, measured in knots. There is little movement of water in the horizontal direction. Swells move primarily in a vertical motion, similar to the motion observed when shaking out a carpet.
 10. Swell Direction. The direction from which a swell is moving. This direction is not necessarily the result of the wind present at the scene. The swell may be moving into or across the local wind. Swells, once set in motion, tend to maintain their original direction for as long as they continue in deep water, regardless of changes in wind direction.
 11. Swell Height. The height between crest and trough, measured in feet. The vast majority of ocean swells are lower than 12 to 15 feet, and swells over 25 feet are not common at any spot on the oceans. Successive swells may differ considerably in height.
 c. In order to select a good heading when ditching an aircraft, a basic evaluation of the sea is required. Selection of a good ditching heading may well minimize damage and could save your life. It can be extremely dangerous to land into the wind without regard to sea conditions; the swell system, or systems, must be taken into consideration. Remember one axiom—***AVOID THE FACE OF A SWELL***.
 1. In ditching parallel to the swell, it makes little difference whether touchdown is on the top of the crest or in the trough. It is preferable, however, to land on the top or back side of the swell, if possible. After determining which heading (and its reciprocal) will parallel the swell, select the heading with the most into the wind component.
 2. If only one swell system exists, the problem is relatively simple—even with a high, fast system. Unfortunately, most cases involve two or more swell systems running in different directions. With more than one system present, the sea presents a confused appearance. One of the most difficult situations occurs when two swell systems are at right angles. For example, if one system is eight feet high, and the other three feet, plan to land parallel to the primary system, and on the down swell of the secondary system. If both systems are of equal height, a compromise may be advisable—select an intermediate heading at 45 degrees down swell to both systems. When landing down a secondary swell, attempt to touch down on the back side, not on the face of the swell.
 3. If the swell system is formidable, it is considered advisable, in landplanes, to accept more crosswind in order to avoid landing directly into the swell.
 4. The secondary swell system is often from the same direction as the wind. Here, the landing may be made parallel to the primary system, with the wind and secondary system at an angle. There is a choice to two directions paralleling primary system. One direction is downwind and down the secondary swell, and the other is into the wind and into the secondary swell, the choice will depend on the velocity of the wind versus the velocity and height of the secondary swell.
 d. The simplest method of estimating the wind direction and velocity is to examine the wind-streaks on the water. These appear as long streaks up and down wind. Some persons may have difficulty determining wind direction after seeing the streaks on the water. Whitecaps fall forward with the wind but are overrun by the waves thus producing the illusion that the foam is sliding backward. Knowing this, and by observing the direction of the streaks, the wind direction is easily determined. Wind velocity can be estimated by noting the appearance of the whitecaps, foam and wind streaks.
 1. The behavior of the aircraft on making contact with the water will vary within wide limits according to the state of the sea. If landed parallel to a single swell system, the behavior of the aircraft may approximate that to be expected on a smooth sea. If landed into a heavy swell or into a confused sea, the deceleration forces may be extremely great—resulting in breaking up of the aircraft. Within certain limits, the pilot is able to minimize these forces by proper sea evaluation and selection of ditching heading.

2. When on final approach the pilot should look ahead and observe the surface of the sea. There may be shadows and whitecaps—signs of large seas. Shadows and whitecaps close together indicate short and rough seas. Touchdown in these areas is to be avoided. Select and touchdown in any area (only about 500 feet is needed) where the shadows and whitecaps are not so numerous.

3. Touchdown should be at the *lowest* speed and rate of descent which permit safe handling and optimum nose up attitude on impact. Once first impact has been made, there is often little the pilot can do to control a landplane.

e. Once preditching preparations are completed, the pilot should turn to the ditching heading and commence let-down. The aircraft should be flown low over the water, and slowed down until ten knots or so above stall. At this point, additional power should be used to overcome the increased drag caused by the nose up attitude. When a smooth stretch of water appears ahead, cut power, and touchdown at the best recommended speed as fully stalled as possible. By cutting power when approaching a relatively smooth area, the pilot will prevent overshooting and will touchdown with less chance of planing off into a second uncontrolled landing. Most experienced seaplane pilots prefer to make contact with the water in a semi-stalled attitude, cutting power as the tail makes contact. This technique eliminates the chance of misjudging altitude with a resultant heavy drop in a fully stalled condition. Care must be taken not to drop the aircraft from too high altitude or to balloon due to excessive speed. The altitude above water depends on the aircraft. Over glassy smooth water, or at night without sufficient light, it is very easy, for even the most experienced pilots to misjudge altitude by 50 feet or more. Under such conditions, carry enough power to maintain nine to twelve degrees nose up attitude, and 10 to 20 percent over stalling speed until contact is made with the water. The proper use of power on the approach is of great importance. If power is available on one side only, a little power should be used to flatten the approach; however, the engine should not be used to such an extent that the aircraft cannot be turned against the good engines right down to the stall with a margin of rudder movement available. When near the stall, sudden application of excessive unbalanced power may result in loss of directional control. If power is available on one side only, a slightly higher than normal glide approach speed should be used. This will ensure good control and some margin of speed after leveling off without excessive use of power. The use of power in ditching is so important that when it is certain that the coast cannot be reached, the pilot

should, if possible, ditch before fuel is exhausted. The use of power in a night or instrument ditching is far more essential than under daylight contact conditions.

1. If no power is available, a greater than normal approach speed should be used down to the flare-out. This speed margin will allow the glide to be broken early and more gradually, thereby giving the pilot time and distance to feel for the surface—decreasing the possibility of stalling high or flying into the water. When landing parallel to a swell system, little difference is noted between landing on top of a crest or in the trough. If the wings of aircraft are trimmed to the surface of the sea rather than the horizon, there is little need to worry about a wing hitting a swell crest. The actual slope of a swell is very gradual. If forced to land into a swell, touchdown should be made just after passage of the crest. If contact is made on the face of the swell, the aircraft may be swamped or thrown violently into the air, dropping heavily into the next swell. If control surfaces remain intact, the pilot should attempt to maintain the proper nose above the horizon attitude by rapid and positive use of the controls.

f. After Touchdown. In most cases drift, caused by crosswind can be ignored; the forces acting on the aircraft after touchdown are of such magnitude that drift will be only a secondary consideration. If the aircraft is under good control, the "crab" may be kicked out with rudder just prior to touchdown. This is more important with high wing aircraft, for they are laterally unstable on the water in a crosswind and may roll to the side in ditching.

Reference: This information has been extracted from Appendix H of the "National Search and Rescue Manual."

6–3–4 Special Emergency (Air Piracy)

a. A special emergency is a condition of air piracy, or other hostile act by a person(s) aboard an aircraft, which threatens the safety of the aircraft or its passengers.

b. The pilot of an aircraft reporting a special emergency condition should:

1. If circumstances permit, apply distress or urgency radio-telephony procedures. Include the details of the special emergency.

Reference: AIM, ¶6-3-1, Distress and Urgency Communications.

2. If circumstances do not permit the use of prescribed *distress* or *urgency* procedures, transmit:

(a) On the air/ground frequency in use at the time.

(b) As many as possible of the following elements spoken distinctly and in the following order:

(1) Name of the station addressed (time and circumstances permitting).

(2) The identification of the aircraft and present position.

(3) The nature of the special emergency condition and pilot intentions (circumstances permitting).

(4) If unable to provide this information, use code words and/or transponder as follows:

Spoken Words
Transponder seven five zero zero
Meaning
I am being hijacked/forced to a new destination
Transponder Setting
Mode 3/A, Code 7500

Note: Code 7500 will never be assigned by ATC without prior notification from the pilot that the aircraft is being subjected to unlawful interference. The pilot should refuse the assignment of Code 7500 in any other situation and inform the controller accordingly. Code 7500 will trigger the special emergency indicator in all radar ATC facilities.

c. Air traffic controllers will acknowledge and confirm receipt of transponder Code 7500 by asking the pilot to verify it. If the aircraft is not being subjected to unlawful interference, the pilot should respond to the query by broadcasting in the clear that the aircraft is not being subjected to unlawful interference. Upon receipt of this information, the controller will request the pilot to verify the code selection depicted in the code selector windows in the transponder control panel and change the code to the appropriate setting. If the pilot replies in the affirmative or does not reply, the controller will not ask further questions but will flight follow, respond to pilot requests and notify appropriate authorities.

d. If it is possible to do so without jeopardizing the safety of the flight, the pilot of a hijacked passenger aircraft, after departing from the cleared routing over which the aircraft was operating, will attempt to do one or more of the following things, insofar as circumstances may permit:

1. Maintain a true airspeed of no more than 400 knots, and preferably an altitude of between 10,000 and 25,000 feet.

2. Fly a course toward the destination which the hijacker has announced.

e. If these procedures result in either radio contact or air intercept, the pilot will attempt to comply with any instructions received which may direct the aircraft to an appropriate landing field or alter the aircraft's flight path off its current course, away from protected airspace.

6–3–5 Fuel Dumping

a. Should it become necessary to dump fuel, the pilot should immediately advise ATC. Upon receipt of information that an aircraft will dump fuel, ATC will broadcast or cause to be broadcast immediately and every 3 minutes thereafter the following on appropriate ATC and FSS radio frequencies:

Example:
Attention all aircraft: fuel dumping in progress over (location) at (altitude) by (type aircraft) (flight direction).

b. Upon receipt of such a broadcast, pilots of aircraft affected, which are not on IFR flight plans or special VFR clearances, should clear the area specified in the advisory. Aircraft on IFR flight plans or special VFR clearances will be provided specific separation by ATC. At the termination of the fuel dumping operation, pilots should advise ATC. Upon receipt of such information, ATC will issue, on the appropriate frequencies, the following:

Example:
Attention all aircraft: Fuel dumping by (type aircraft) terminated.

Section 4 Two-Way Radio Communications Failure

6–4–1 Two-Way Radio Communications Failure

a. It is virtually impossible to provide regulations and procedures applicable to all possible situations associated with two-way radio communications failure. During two-way radio communications failure, when confronted by a situation not covered in the regulation, pilots are expected to exercise good judgment in whatever action they elect to take. Should the situation so dictate they should not be reluctant to use the emergency action contained in 14 CFR Section 91.3(b).

b. Whether two-way communications failure constitutes an emergency depends on the circumstances, and in any event, it is a determination made by the pilot. 14 CFR Section 91.3(b) authorizes a pilot to deviate from any rule in Subparts A and B to the extent required to meet an emergency.

c. In the event of two-way radio communications failure, ATC service will be provided on the basis that the pilot is operating in accordance with 14 CFR Section 91.185. A pilot experiencing two-way communications failure should (unless emergency authority is exercised) comply with 14 CFR Section 91.185 quoted below:

1. General. Unless otherwise authorized by ATC, each pilot who has two-way radio communications failure when operating under IFR must comply with the rules of this section.

2. VFR conditions. If the failure occurs in VFR conditions, or if VFR conditions are encountered after the failure, each pilot must continue the flight under VFR and land as soon as practicable.

Note: This procedure also applies when two-way radio failure occurs while operating in Class A airspace. The primary objective of this provision in 14 CFR Section 91.185 is to preclude extended IFR operation by these aircraft within the ATC system. Pilots should recognize that operation under these conditions may unnecessarily as well as adversely affect other users of the airspace, since ATC may be required to reroute or delay other users in order to protect the failure aircraft. However, it is not intended that the requirement to "land as soon as practicable" be construed to mean "as soon as possible." Pilots retain the prerogative of exercising their best judgment and are not required to land at an unauthorized airport, at an airport unsuitable for the type of aircraft flown, or to land only minutes short of their intended destination.

3. IFR conditions. If the failure occurs in IFR conditions, or if subparagraph 2 above cannot be complied with, each pilot must continue the flight according to the following:

(a) Route.

(1) By the route assigned in the last ATC clearance received;

(2) If being radar vectored, by the direct route from the point of radio failure to the fix, route, or airway specified in the vector clearance;

(3) In the absence of an assigned route, by the route that ATC has advised may be expected in a further clearance; or

(4) In the absence of an assigned route or a route that ATC has advised may be expected in a further clearance by the route filed in the flight plan.

(b) Altitude. At the *highest* of the following altitudes or flight levels *for the route segment being flown:*

(1) The altitude or flight level assigned in the last ATC clearance received;

(2) The minimum altitude (converted, if appropriate, to minimum flight level as prescribed in 14 CFR Section 91.121(c)) for IFR operations; or

(3) The altitude or flight level ATC has advised may be expected in a further clearance.

Note: The intent of the rule is that a pilot who has experienced two-way radio failure should select the appropriate altitude for the particular route segment being flown and make the necessary altitude adjustments for subsequent route segments. If the pilot received an "expect further clearance" containing a higher altitude to expect at a specified time or fix, maintain the highest of the following altitudes until that time/fix:

(1) the last assigned altitude; or

(2) the minimum altitude/flight level for IFR operations.

Upon reaching the time/fix specified, the pilot should commence climbing to the altitude advised to expect. If the radio failure occurs after the time/fix specified, the altitude to be expected is not applicable and the pilot should maintain an altitude consistent with 1 or 2 above. If the pilot receives an "expect further clearance" containing a lower altitude, the pilot should maintain the highest of 1 or 2 above until that time/fix specified in subparagraph (c) Leave clearance limit, below.

Example 1: A pilot experiencing two-way radio failure at an assigned altitude of 7,000 feet is cleared along a direct route which will require a climb to a minimum IFR altitude of 9,000 feet,

should climb to reach 9,000 feet at the time or place where it becomes necessary (see 14 CFR Section 91.177(b)). Later while proceeding along an airway with an MEA of 5,000 feet, the pilot would descend to 7,000 feet (the last assigned altitude), because that altitude is higher than the MEA.

Example 2: A pilot experiencing two-way radio failure while being progressively descended to lower altitudes to begin an approach is assigned 2,700 feet until crossing the VOR and then cleared for the approach. The MOCA along the airway is 2,700 feet and MEA is 4,000 feet. The aircraft is within 22 NM of the VOR. The pilot should remain at 2,700 feet until crossing the VOR because that altitude is the minimum IFR altitude for the route segment being flown.

Example 3: The MEA between a and b: 5,000 feet. The MEA between b and c: 5,000 feet. The MEA between c and d: 11,000 feet. The MEA between d and e: 7,000 feet. A pilot had been cleared via a, b, c, d, to e. While flying between a and b the assigned altitude was 6,000 feet and the pilot was told to expect a clearance to 8,000 feet at b. Prior to receiving the higher altitude assignment, the pilot experienced two-way failure. The pilot would maintain 6,000 to b, then climb to 8,000 feet (the altitude advised to expect). The pilot would maintain 8,000 feet, then climb to 11,000 at c, or prior to c if necessary to comply with an MCA at c. (14 CFR Section 91.177(b).) Upon reaching d, the pilot would descend to 8,000 feet (even though the MEA was 7,000 feet), as 8,000 was the highest of the altitude situations stated in the rule (14 CFR Section 91.185).

(c) Leave clearance limit.

(1) When the clearance limit is a fix from which an approach begins, commence descent or descent and approach as close as possible to the expect further clearance time if one has been received, or if one has not been received, as close as possible to the Estimated Time of Arrival (ETA) as calculated from the filed or amended (with ATC) Estimated Time En Route (ETE).

(2) If the clearance limit is not a fix from which an approach begins, leave the clearance limit at the expect further clearance time if one has been received, or if none has been received, upon arrival over the clearance limit, and proceed to a fix from which an approach begins and commence descent or descent and approach as close as possible to the estimated time of arrival as calculated from the filed or amended (with ATC) estimated time en route.

6-4-2 Transponder Operation During Two-Way Communications Failure

a. If an aircraft with a coded radar beacon transponder experiences a loss of two-way radio capability, the pilot should adjust the transponder to reply on Mode A/3, Code 7600.

b. The pilot should understand that the aircraft may not be in an area of radar coverage.

6-4-3 Reestablishing Radio Contact

a. In addition to monitoring the NAVAID voice feature, the pilot should attempt to reestablish communications by attempting contact:

1. On the previously assigned frequency; or

2. With an FSS or with New York Radio or San Francisco Radio.

b. If communications are established with an FSS or New York Radio or San Francisco Radio, the pilot should advise that radio communications on the previously assigned frequency have been lost giving the aircraft's position, altitude, last assigned frequency and then request further clearance from the controlling facility. The preceding does not preclude the use of 121.5 MHz. There is no priority on which action should be attempted first. If the capability exists, do all at the same time.

Note: New York Radio and San Francisco Radio are operated by Collins Aerospace, Incorporated (formerly ARINC) under contract with the FAA for communications services. These Radio facilities have the capability of relaying information to/from ATC facilities throughout the country.

Ch 6

Section 5 Aircraft Rescue and Fire Fighting Communications

6–5–1 Discrete Emergency Frequency

a. Direct contact between an emergency aircraft flight crew, Aircraft Rescue and Fire Fighting Incident Commander (ARFF IC), and the Airport Traffic Control Tower (ATCT), is possible on an aeronautical radio frequency (Discrete Emergency Frequency [DEF]), designated by Air Traffic Control (ATC) from the operational frequencies assigned to that facility.

b. Emergency aircraft at airports without an ATCT, (or when the ATCT is closed), may contact the ARFF IC (if ARFF service is provided), on the Common Traffic Advisory Frequency (**CTAF**) published for the airport or the civil emergency frequency **121.5 MHz**.

6–5–2 Radio Call Signs

Preferred radio call sign for the ARFF IC is "(location/facility) **Command**" when communicating with the flight crew and the FAA ATCT.

Example:
LAX Command. Washington Command.

6–5–3 ARFF Emergency Hand Signals

In the event that electronic communications cannot be maintained between the ARFF IC and the flight crew, standard emergency hand signals as depicted in Figure 6-5-1 through Figure 6-5-3 should be used. These hand signals should be known and understood by all cockpit and cabin aircrew, and all ARFF firefighters.

FIGURE 6–5–1
Recommend Evacuation

RECOMMEND EVACUATION - Evacuation recommended based on ARFF IC's assessment of external situation.

Arm extended from body, and held horizontal with hand upraised at eye level. Execute beckoning arm motion angled backward. Nonbeckoning arm held against body.

Night - Same with wands.

FIGURE 6–5–2
Recommend Stop

RECOMMEND STOP - Recommend evacuation in progress be halted. Stop aircraft movement or other activity in progress.

Arms in front of head - Crossed at wrists.

Night - Same with wands.

FIGURE 6–5–3
Emergency Contained

EMERGENCY CONTAINED - No outside evidence of dangerous condition or "all-clear."

Arms extended outward and down at a 45 degree angle. Arms moved inward below waistline simultaneously until wrists crossed, then extended outward to starting position (umpire's "safe" signal).

Night - Same with wands.

Ch 6

Chapter 7
Safety of Flight

Section 1 Meteorology

7-1-1 National Weather Service Aviation Weather Service Program

a. Weather service to aviation is a joint effort of the National Oceanic and Atmospheric Administration (NOAA), the National Weather Service (NWS), the Federal Aviation Administration (FAA), Department of Defense, and various private sector aviation weather service providers. Requirements for all aviation weather products originate from the FAA, which is the Meteorological Authority for the U.S.

b. NWS meteorologists are assigned to all air route traffic control centers (ARTCC) as part of the Center Weather Service Units (CWSU) as well as the Air Traffic Control System Command Center (ATCSCC). These meteorologists provide specialized briefings as well as tailored forecasts to support the needs of the FAA and other users of the NAS.

c. Aviation Products

1. The NWS maintains an extensive surface, upper air, and radar weather observing program; and a nationwide aviation weather forecasting service.

2. Airport observations (METAR and SPECI) supported by the NWS are provided by automated observing systems.

3. Terminal Aerodrome Forecasts (TAF) are prepared by 123 NWS Weather Forecast Offices (WFOs) for over 700 airports. These forecasts are valid for 24 or 30 hours and amended as required.

4. Inflight aviation advisories (for example, Significant Meteorological Information (SIG-METs) and Airmen's Meteorological Information (AIRMETs)) are issued by three NWS Meteorological Watch Offices (MWOs); the Aviation Weather Center (AWC) in Kansas City, MO, the Alaska Aviation Weather Unit (AAWU) in Anchorage, AK, and the Weather Service Forecast Office (WFO) in Honolulu, HI. The AWC, the AAWU, and WSFO Honolulu issue area forecasts for selected areas. In addition, NWS meteorologists assigned to most ARTCCs as part of the Center Weather Service Unit (CWSU) provide Center Weather Advisories (CWAs) and gather weather information to support the needs of the FAA and other users of the system.

5. Several NWS National Centers for Environmental Production (NCEP) provide aviation specific weather forecasts, or select public forecasts which are of interest to pilots and operators.

(a) The Aviation Weather Center (AWC) displays a variety of domestic and international aviation forecast products over the Internet at aviationweather.gov.

(b) The NCEP Central Operations (NCO) is responsible for the operation of many numerical weather prediction models, including those which produce the many wind and temperature aloft forecasts.

(c) The Storm Prediction Center (SPC) issues tornado and severe weather watches along with other guidance forecasts.

(d) The National Hurricane Center (NHC) issues forecasts on tropical weather systems (for example, hurricanes).

(e) The Space Weather Prediction Center (SWPC) provides alerts, watches, warnings and forecasts for space weather events (for example, solar storms) affecting or expected to affect Earth's environment.

(f) The Weather Prediction Center (WPC) provides analysis and forecast products on a national scale including surface pressure and frontal analyses.

6. NOAA operates two Volcanic Ash Advisory Centers (VAAC) which issue forecasts of ash clouds following a volcanic eruption in their area of responsibility.

7. Details on the products provided by the above listed offices and centers is available in FAA Advisory Circular 00-45, Aviation Weather Services.

d. Weather element values may be expressed by using different measurement systems depending on several factors, such as whether the weather products will be used by the general public, aviation interests, international services, or a combination of these users. Figure 7-1-1 provides conversion tables for the most used weather elements that will be encountered by pilots.

Ch 7

FIGURE 7–1–1
Weather Elements Conversion Tables

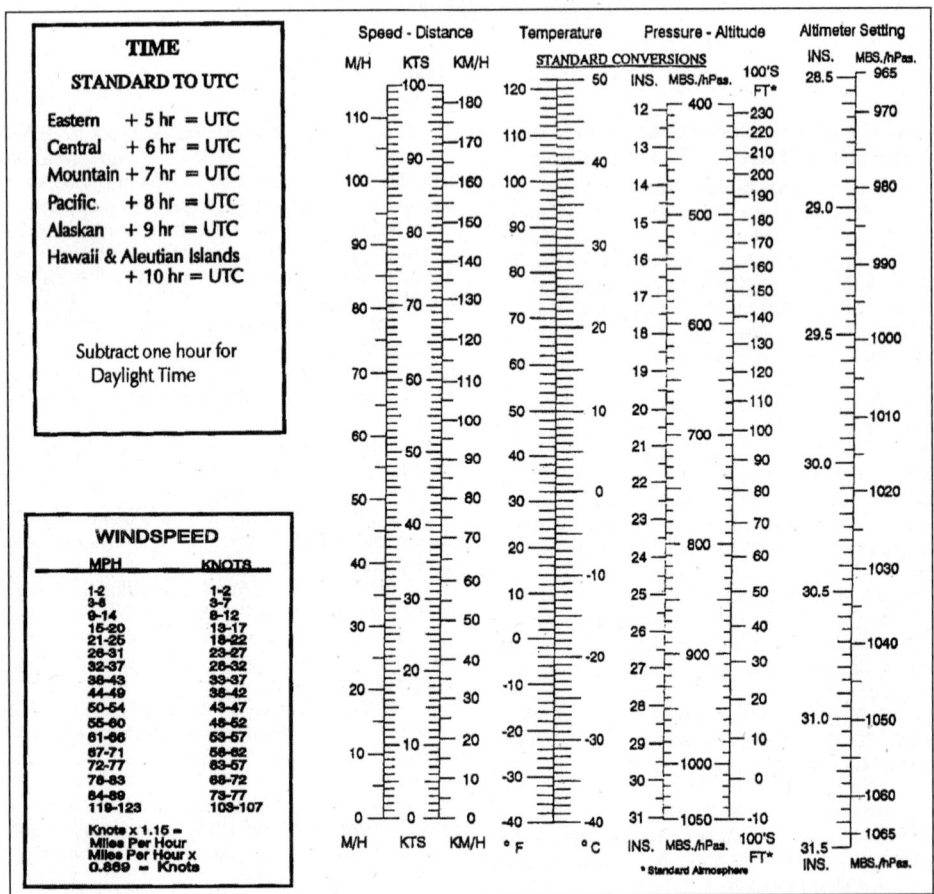

7-1-2 FAA Weather Services

a. The FAA provides the Flight Service program, which serves the weather needs of pilots through its flight service stations (FSS) (both government and contract via 1-800-WX-BRIEF) and via the Internet, through Leidos Flight Service.

b. The FAA maintains an extensive surface weather observing program. Airport observations (METAR and SPECI) in the U.S. are provided by automated observing systems. Various levels of human oversight of the METAR and SPECI reports and augmentation may be provided at select larger airports by either government or contract personnel qualified to report specified weather elements that cannot be detected by the automated observing system. The requirements to issue SPECI reports are detailed in Table 7-1-1.

TABLE 7–1–1
SPECI ISSUANCE TABLE

1	Wind Shift	Wind direction changes by 45° or more, in less than 15 minutes, and the wind speed is 10 kt or more throughout the wind shift.
2	Visibility	The surface visibility (as reported in the body of the report): • Decreases to less than 3 SM, 2 SM, 1 SM, ½ SM, ¼ SM or the lowest standard instrument approach procedure (IAP) minimum.[1] • Increases to equal to or exceed 3 SM, 2 SM, 1 SM, ½ SM, ¼ SM or the lowest standard IAP minimum.[1] [1] As published in the U.S. Terminal Procedures. If none published, use ½ SM.
3	RVR	The highest value from the designated RVR runway decreases to less than 2,400 ft during the preceding 10 minutes; or, if the RVR is below 2,400 ft, increases to equal to or exceed 2,400 ft during the preceding 10 minutes. U.S. military stations may not report a SPECI based on RVR.
4	Tornado, Funnel Cloud, or Waterspout	• Is observed. • Disappears from sight or ends.
5	Thunderstorm	• Begins (a SPECI is not required to report the beginning of a new thunderstorm if one is currently reported). • Ends.
6	Precipitation	• Hail begins or ends. • Freezing precipitation begins, ends, or changes intensity. • Ice pellets begin, end, or change intensity. • Snow begins, ends, or changes intensity.
7	Squalls	When a squall occurs. (Wind speed suddenly increases by at least 16 knots and is sustained at 22 knots or more for at least one minute.)
8	Ceiling	The ceiling changes[1] through: • 3,000 ft. • 1,500 ft. • 1,000 ft. • 500 ft. • The lowest standard IAP minimum.[2] [1] "Ceiling change" means that it forms, dissipates below, decreases to less than, or, if below, increases to equal or exceed the values listed. [2] As published in the U.S. Terminal Procedures. If none published, use 200 ft.
9	Sky Condition	A layer of clouds or obscurations aloft is present below 1,000 ft and no layer aloft was reported below 1,000 ft in the preceding METAR or SPECI.
10	Volcanic Eruption	When an eruption is first noted.
11	Aircraft Mishap	Upon notification of an aircraft mishap,[1] unless there has been an intervening observation. [1] "Aircraft mishap" is an inclusive term to denote the occurrence of an aircraft accident or incident.
12	Miscellaneous	Any other meteorological situation designated by the responsible agency of which, in the opinion of the observer, is critical.

c. Other Sources of Weather Information

1. Weather and aeronautical information are available from numerous private industry sources on an individual or contract pay basis. Prior to every flight, pilots should gather all information vital to the nature of the flight. Pilots can receive a regulatory compliant briefing without contacting Flight Service. Pilots are encouraged to use automated resources and review AC 91–92, Pilot's Guide to a Preflight Briefing, for more information.

2. Pilots can access Leidos Flight Services via the Internet at http://www.1800wxbrief.com. Pilots can receive preflight weather data and file VFR and IFR flight plans.

7-1-3 Use of Aviation Weather Products

a. Air carriers and operators certificated under the provisions of 14 CFR Part 119 are required to use the aeronautical weather information systems defined in the Operations Specifications issued to that certificate holder by the FAA. These systems may utilize basic FAA/National Weather Service (NWS) weather services, contractor- or operator-proprietary weather services and/or Enhanced Weather Information System (EWINS) when approved in the Operations Specifications. As an integral part of this system approval, the procedures for collecting, producing and disseminating aeronautical weather information, as well as the crew member and dispatcher training to support

the use of system weather products, must be accepted or approved.

b. Operators not certificated under the provisions of 14 CFR Part 119 are encouraged to use FAA/NWS products through Flight Service Stations, Leidos Flight Service, and/or Flight Information Services-Broadcast (FIS-B).

c. The suite of available aviation weather product types is expanding, with the development of new sensor systems, algorithms and forecast models. The FAA and NWS, supported by various weather research laboratories and corporations under contract to the Government, develop and implement new aviation weather product types. The FAA's NextGen Aviation Weather Research Program (AWRP) facilitates collaboration between the NWS, the FAA, and various industry and research representatives. This collaboration ensures that user needs and technical readiness requirements are met before experimental products mature to operational application.

d. The AWRP manages the transfer of aviation weather R&D to operational use through technical review panels and conducting safety assessments to ensure that newly developed aviation weather products meet regulatory requirements and enhance safety.

e. The AWRP review and decision-making process applies criteria to weather products at various stages. The stages are composed of the following:

1. Sponsorship of user needs.
2. R & D and controlled testing.
3. Experimental application.
4. Operational application.

f. Pilots and operators should be aware that weather services provided by entities other than FAA, NWS, or their contractors may not meet FAA/NWS quality control standards. Hence, operators and pilots contemplating using such services should request and/or review an appropriate description of services and provider disclosure. This should include, but is not limited to, the type of weather product (for example, current weather or forecast weather), the currency of the product (that is, product issue and valid times), and the relevance of the product. Pilots and operators should be cautious when using unfamiliar products, or products not supported by FAA/NWS technical specifications.

Note: When in doubt, consult with a FAA Flight Service Station Specialist.

g. In addition, pilots and operators should be aware there are weather services and products available from government organizations beyond the scope of the AWRP process mentioned earlier in this section. For example, governmental agencies such as the NWS and the Aviation Weather Center (AWC), or research organizations such as the National Center for Atmospheric Research (NCAR) display weather "model data" and "experimental" products which require training and/or expertise to properly interpret and use. These products are developmental prototypes that are subject to ongoing research and can change without notice. Therefore, some data on display by government organizations, or government data on display by independent organizations may be unsuitable for flight planning purposes. Operators and pilots contemplating using such services should request and/or review an appropriate description of services and provider disclosure. This should include, but is not limited to, the type of weather product (for example, current weather or forecast weather), the currency of the product (i.e., product issue and valid times), and the relevance of the product. Pilots and operators should be cautious when using unfamiliar weather products.

Note: When in doubt, consult with a FAA Flight Service Station Specialist.

h. With increased access to weather products via the public Internet, the aviation community has access to an overwhelming amount of weather information and data that support self-briefing. The *Aviation Weather Handbook*, FAA-H-8083-28 (current edition), describes the weather products distributed by the NWS. Pilots and operators using the public Internet to access weather from a third party vendor should request and/or review an appropriate description of services and provider disclosure. This should include, but is not limited to, the type of weather product (for example, current weather or forecast weather), the currency of the product (i.e., product issue and valid times), and the relevance of the product. Pilots and operators should be cautious when using unfamiliar weather products and when in doubt, consult with a Flight Service Specialist.

i. The development of new weather products, coupled with the termination of some legacy textual and graphical products may create confusion between regulatory requirements and the new products. All flight-related, aviation weather decisions must be based on all available pertinent weather products. As every flight is unique and the weather conditions for that flight vary hour by hour, day to day, multiple weather products may be necessary to meet aviation weather regulatory requirements. Many new weather products now have a Precautionary Use Statement that details the proper use or application of the specific product.

j. The FAA has identified three distinct types of weather information available to pilots and operators.

1. **Observations.** Raw weather data collected by some type of sensor suite including

surface and airborne observations, radar, lightning, satellite imagery, and profilers.

2. Analysis. Enhanced depiction and/or interpretation of observed weather data.

3. Forecasts. Predictions of the development and/or movement of weather phenomena based on meteorological observations and various mathematical models.

k. Not all sources of aviation weather information are able to provide all three types of weather information. The FAA has determined that operators and pilots may utilize the following approved sources of aviation weather information:

1. Federal Government. The FAA and NWS collect raw weather data, analyze the observations, and produce forecasts. The FAA and NWS disseminate meteorological observations, analyses, and forecasts through a variety of systems. In addition, the Federal Government is the only approval authority for sources of weather observations; for example, contract towers and airport operators may be approved by the Federal Government to provide weather observations.

2. Enhanced Weather Information System (EWINS). An EWINS is an FAA authorized, proprietary system for tracking, evaluating, reporting, and forecasting the presence or lack of adverse weather phenomena. The FAA authorizes a certificate holder to use an EWINS to produce flight movement forecasts, adverse weather phenomena forecasts, and other meteorological advisories. For more detailed information regarding EWINS, see the Aviation Weather Services Advisory Circular 00-45 and the Flight Standards Information Management System 8900.1.

3. Commercial Weather Information Providers. In general, commercial providers produce proprietary weather products based on NWS/FAA products with formatting and layout modifications but no material changes to the weather information itself. This is also referred to as "repackaging." In addition, commercial providers may produce analyses, forecasts, and other proprietary weather products that substantially alter the information contained in government-produced products. However, those proprietary weather products that substantially alter government-produced weather products or information, may only be approved for use by 14 CFR Part 121 and Part 135 certificate holders if the commercial provider is EWINS qualified.

Note: Commercial weather information providers contracted by FAA to provide weather observations, analyses, and forecasts (e.g., contract towers) are included in the Federal Government category of approved sources by virtue of maintaining required technical and quality assurance standards under Federal Government oversight.

7-1-4 Graphical Forecasts for Aviation (GFA)

a. The GFA website is intended to provide the necessary aviation weather information to give users a complete picture of the weather that may affect flight in the continental United States (CONUS). The website includes observational data, forecasts, and warnings that can be viewed from 14 hours in the past to 15 hours in the future, including thunderstorms, clouds, flight category, precipitation, icing, turbulence, and wind. Hourly model data and forecasts, including information on clouds, flight category, precipitation, icing, turbulence, wind, and graphical output from the National Weather Service's (NWS) National Digital Forecast Data (NDFD) are available. Wind, icing, and turbulence forecasts are available in 3,000 foot increments from the surface up to 30,000 feet MSL, and in 6,000 foot increments from 30,000 feet MSL to 48,000 feet MSL. Turbulence forecasts are also broken into low (below 18,000 feet MSL) and high (at or above 18,000 feet MSL) graphics. A maximum icing graphic and maximum wind velocity graphic (regardless of altitude) are also available. Built with modern geospatial information tools, users can pan and zoom to focus on areas of greatest interest. Target users are commercial and general aviation pilots, operators, briefers, and dispatchers.

b. Weather Products.

1. The Aviation Forecasts include gridded displays of various weather parameters as well as NWS textual weather observations, forecasts, and warnings. Icing, turbulence, and wind gridded products are three-dimensional. Other gridded products are two-dimensional and may represent a "composite" of a three-dimensional weather phenomenon or a surface weather variable, such as horizontal visibility. The following are examples of aviation forecasts depicted on the GFA:

 (a) Terminal Aerodrome Forecast (TAF)
 (b) Ceiling & Visibility (CIG/VIS)
 (c) Clouds
 (d) Precipitation / Weather (PCPN/WX)
 (e) Thunderstorm (TS)
 (f) Winds
 (g) Turbulence
 (h) Ice

2. Observations & Warnings (Obs/Warn). The Obs/Warn option provides an option to display weather data for the current time and the previous 14 hours (rounded to the nearest hour). Users may advance through time using the arrow buttons or by clicking on the desired hour. Provided below are the Obs/Warn product tabs available on the GFA website:

 (a) METAR
 (b) Precipitation/Weather (PCPN/WX)
 (c) Ceiling & Visibility (CIG/VIS)
 (d) Pilot Weather Report (PIREP)

Ch 7

(e) Radar & Satellite (RAD/SAT)

3. The GFA will be continuously updated and available online at http://aviationweather.gov /gfa. Upon clicking the link above, select INFO on the top right corner of the map display. The next screen presents the option of selecting Overview, Products, and Tutorial. Simply select the tab of interest to explore the enhanced digital and graphical weather products designed to replace the legacy FA. Users should also refer to the *Aviation Weather Handbook*, FAA-H-8083-28, Graphical Forecasts for Aviation (GFA) Tool, for more detailed information on the GFA.

4. GFA Static Images. Some users with limited internet connectivity may access static images via the Aviation Weather Center (AWC) at: http://www.aviationweather.gov/gfa/plot. There are two static graphical images available, titled *Aviation Cloud Forecast and Aviation Surface Forecast*. The Aviation Cloud Forecast provides cloud coverage, bases, layers, and tops with AIRMETs for mountain obscuration and AIRMETs for icing overlaid. The Aviation Surface Forecast provides visibility, weather phenomena, and winds (including wind gusts) with AIRMETs for instrument flight rules conditions and AIRMETs for sustained surface winds of 30 knots or more overlaid. These images are presented on ten separate maps providing forecast views for the entire contiguous United States (U.S.) on one and nine regional views which provide more detail for the user. They are updated every 3 hours and provide forecast snapshots for 3, 6, 9, 12, 15, and 18 hours into the future.(See Figure 7-1-2 and Figure 7-1-3.)

Note: The contiguous United States (U.S.) refers to the 48 adjoining U.S. states on the continent of North America that are south of Canada and north of Mexico, plus the District of Columbia. The term excludes the states of Alaska and Hawaii, and all off-shore U.S. territories and possessions, such as Puerto Rico.

FIGURE 7–1–2
Aviation Surface Forecast

FIGURE 7–1–3
Aviation Cloud Forecast

7–1–5 Preflight Briefing

a. Flight Service is one of the primary sources for obtaining preflight briefings and to file flight plans by phone or the Internet. Flight Service Specialists are qualified and certificated as Pilot Weather Briefers by the FAA. They are not authorized to make original forecasts, but are authorized to translate and interpret available forecasts and reports directly into terms describing the weather conditions which you can expect along your flight route and at your destination. Prior to every flight, pilots should gather all information vital to the nature of the flight. Pilots can receive a regulatory compliant briefing without contacting Flight Service. Pilots are encouraged to use automated resources and review AC 91–92, Pilot's Guide to a Preflight Briefing, for more information. Pilots who prefer to contact Flight Service are encouraged to conduct a self-brief prior to calling. Conducting a self-brief before contacting Flight Service provides familiarity of meteorological and aeronautical conditions applicable to the route of flight and promotes a better understanding of weather information. Three basic types of preflight briefings (Standard, Abbreviated, and Outlook) are available to serve the pilot's specific needs. Pilots should specify to the briefer the type of briefing they want, along with their appropriate background information. This will enable the briefer to tailor the information to the pilot's intended flight. The following paragraphs describe the types of briefings available and the information provided in each briefing.

Reference: AIM, ¶5-1-1, Preflight Preparation, for items that are required.

b. Standard Briefing. You should request a Standard Briefing any time you are planning a flight and you have not received a previous briefing or have not received preliminary information through online resources. International data may be inaccurate or incomplete. If you are planning a flight outside of U.S. controlled airspace, the briefer will advise you to check data as soon as practical after entering foreign airspace, unless you advise that you have the international cautionary advisory. The briefer will automatically provide the following information in the sequence listed, except as noted, when it is applicable to your proposed flight.

1. Adverse Conditions. Significant meteorological and/or aeronautical information that might influence the pilot to alter or cancel the

proposed flight; for example, hazardous weather conditions, airport closures, air traffic delays, etc. Pilots should be especially alert for current or forecast weather that could reduce flight minimums below VFR or IFR conditions. Pilots should also be alert for any reported or forecast icing if the aircraft is not certified for operating in icing conditions. Flying into areas of icing or weather below minimums could have disastrous results.

2. VFR Flight Not Recommended. When VFR flight is proposed and sky conditions or visibilities are present or forecast, surface or aloft, that, in the briefer's judgment, would make flight under VFR doubtful, the briefer will describe the affected locations, and use the phrase "VFR FLIGHT NOT RECOMMENDED." This recommendation is advisory in nature. The final decision as to whether the flight can be conducted safely rests solely with the pilot. Upon receiving a "VFR FLIGHT NOT RECOMMENDED" statement, the non-IFR rated pilot will need to make a "go or no go" decision. This decision should be based on weighing the current and forecast weather conditions against the pilot's experience and ratings. The aircraft's equipment, capabilities and limitations should also be considered.

Note: Pilots flying into areas of minimal VFR weather could encounter unforecasted lowering conditions that place the aircraft outside the pilot's ratings and experience level. This could result in spatial disorientation and/or loss of control of the aircraft.

3. Synopsis. A brief statement describing the type, location and movement of weather systems and/or air masses which might affect the proposed flight.

Note: These first 3 elements of a briefing may be combined in any order when the briefer believes it will help to more clearly describe conditions.

4. Current Conditions. Reported weather conditions applicable to the flight will be summarized from all available sources; e.g., METARs/SPECIs, PIREPs, RAREPs. This element will be omitted if the proposed time of departure is beyond 2 hours, unless the information is specifically requested by the pilot.

5. En Route Forecast. Forecast en route conditions for the proposed route are summarized in logical order; i.e., departure/climbout, en route, and descent. (Heights are MSL, unless the contractions "AGL" or "CIG" are denoted indicating that heights are above ground.)

6. Destination Forecast. The destination forecast for the planned ETA. Any significant changes within 1 hour before and after the planned arrival are included.

7. Winds Aloft. Forecast winds aloft will be provided in knots and degrees, referenced to true north. The briefer will interpolate wind directions and speeds between levels and stations as necessary to provide expected conditions at planned altitudes. (Heights are MSL.) Temperature information will be provided on request.

8. Notices to Air Missions (NOTAMs).

(a) Available NOTAM (D) information pertinent to the proposed flight, including special use airspace (SUA) NOTAMs for restricted areas, aerial refueling, and night vision goggles (NVG).

Note: Other SUA NOTAMs (D), such as military operations area (MOA), military training route (MTR), and warning area NOTAMs, are considered "upon request" briefing items as indicated in paragraph 7-1-4b10(a).

(b) Prohibited Areas P-40, P-49, P-56, and the special flight rules area (SFRA) for Washington, DC.

(c) FSS briefers do not provide FDC NOTAM information for special instrument approach procedures unless specifically asked. Pilots authorized by the FAA to use special instrument approach procedures must specifically request FDC NOTAM information for these procedures.

Note 1: NOTAM information may be combined with current conditions when the briefer believes it is logical to do so.

Note 2: Airway NOTAMs, procedural NOTAMs, and NOTAMs that are general in nature and not tied to a specific airport/facility (for example, flight advisories and restrictions, open duration special security instructions, and special flight rules areas) are briefed solely by pilot request. For complete flight information, pilots are urged to review the Domestic Notices and International Notices found in the External Links section of the Federal NOTAM System (FNS) NOTAM Search System and the Chart Supplement in addition to obtaining a briefing.

9. ATC Delays. Any known ATC delays and flow control advisories which might affect the proposed flight.

10. Pilots may obtain the following from flight service station briefers upon request:

(a) Information on SUA and SUA-related airspace, except those listed in paragraph 7-1-4b8.

Note 1: For the purpose of this paragraph, SUA and related airspace includes the following types of airspace: alert area, military operations area (MOA), warning area, and air traffic control assigned airspace (ATCAA). MTR data includes the following types of airspace: IFR training routes (IR), VFR training routes (VR), and slow training routes (SR).

Note 2: Pilots are encouraged to request updated information from ATC facilities while in flight.

(b) A review of airway NOTAMs, procedural NOTAMs, and NOTAMs that are general

in nature and not tied to a specific airport/facility (for example, flight advisories and restrictions, open duration special security instructions, and special flight rules areas), Domestic Notices and International Notices. Domestic Notices and International Notices are found in the External Links section of the Federal NOTAM System (FNS) NOTAM Search System.

(c) Approximate density altitude data.

(d) Information regarding such items as air traffic services and rules, customs/immigration procedures, ADIZ rules, search and rescue, etc.

(e) GPS RAIM availability for 1 hour before to 1 hour after ETA or a time specified by the pilot.

(f) Other assistance as required.

c. Abbreviated Briefing. Request an Abbreviated Briefing when you need information to supplement mass disseminated data, update a previous briefing, or when you need only one or two specific items. Provide the briefer with appropriate background information, the time you received the previous information, and/or the specific items needed. You should indicate the source of the information already received so that the briefer can limit the briefing to the information that you have not received, and/or appreciable changes in meteorological/aeronautical conditions since your previous briefing. To the extent possible, the briefer will provide the information in the sequence shown for a Standard Briefing. If you request only one or two specific items, the briefer will advise you if adverse conditions are present or forecast. (Adverse conditions contain both meteorological and/or aeronautical information.) Details on these conditions will be provided at your request. International data may be inaccurate or incomplete. If you are planning a flight outside of U.S. controlled airspace, the briefer will advise you to check data as soon as practical after entering foreign airspace, unless you advise that you have the international cautionary advisory.

d. Outlook Briefing. You should request an Outlook Briefing whenever your proposed time of departure is six or more hours from the time of the briefing. The briefer will provide available forecast data applicable to the proposed flight. This type of briefing is provided for planning purposes only. You should obtain a Standard or Abbreviated Briefing prior to departure in order to obtain such items as adverse conditions, current conditions, updated forecasts, winds aloft and NOTAMs, etc.

e. When filing a flight plan only, you will be asked if you require the latest information on adverse conditions pertinent to the route of flight.

f. Inflight Briefing. You are encouraged to conduct a self-briefing using online resources or obtain your preflight briefing by telephone or in person (Alaska only) before departure. In those cases where you need to obtain a preflight briefing or an update to a previous briefing by radio, you should contact the nearest FSS to obtain this information. After communications have been established, advise the specialist of the type briefing you require and provide appropriate background information. You will be provided information as specified in the above paragraphs, depending on the type of briefing requested. En Route advisories tailored to the phase of flight that begins after climb-out and ends with descent to land are provided upon pilot request. Besides Flight Service, there are other resources available to the pilot in flight, including:

Automatic Dependent Surveillance–Broadcast (ADS-B). Free traffic, weather, and flight information are available on ADS-B In receivers that can receive data over 978 MHz (UAT) broadcasts. These services are available across the nation to aircraft owners who equip with ADS-B In, with further advances coming from airborne and runway traffic awareness. Even search-and-rescue operations benefit from accurate ADS-B tracking.

Flight Information Services–Broadcast (FIS-B). FIS-B is a free service; but is only available to aircraft that can receive data over 978 MHz (UAT). FIS-B automatically transmits a wide range of weather products with national and regional focus to all equipped aircraft. Having current weather and aeronautical information in the cockpit helps pilots plan more safe and efficient flight paths, as well as make strategic decisions during flight to avoid potentially hazardous weather.

Pilots are encouraged to provide a continuous exchange of information on weather, winds, turbulence, flight visibility, icing, etc., between pilots and inflight specialists. Pilots should report good weather as well as bad, and confirm expected conditions as well as unexpected. Remember that weather conditions can change rapidly and that a "go or no go" decision, as mentioned in paragraph 7-1-4b2, should be assessed at all phases of flight.

g. Following any briefing, feel free to ask for any information that you or the briefer may have missed or are not understood. This way, the briefer is able to present the information in a logical sequence, and lessens the chance of important items being overlooked.

7-1-6 Inflight Aviation Weather Advisories

a. Inflight Aviation Weather Advisories are forecasts to advise en route aircraft of development of potentially hazardous weather. Inflight aviation weather advisories in the conterminous U.S. are issued by the Aviation Weather Center (AWC) in Kansas City, MO, as well as 20 Center Weather Service Units (CWSU) associated with

ARTCCs. AWC also issues advisories for portions of the Gulf of Mexico, Atlantic and Pacific Oceans, which are under the control of ARTCCs with Oceanic flight information regions (FIRs). The Weather Forecast Office (WFO) in Honolulu issues advisories for the Hawaiian Islands and a large portion of the Pacific Ocean. In Alaska, the Alaska Aviation Weather Unit (AAWU) issues inflight aviation weather advisories along with the Anchorage CWSU. All heights are referenced MSL, except in the case of ceilings (CIG) which indicate AGL.

b. There are four types of inflight aviation weather advisories: the SIGMET, the Convective SIGMET, the AIRMET, and the Center Weather Advisory (CWA). All of these advisories use VORs, airports, or well-known geographic areas to describe the hazardous weather areas.

c. The Severe Weather Watch Bulletins (WWs), (with associated Alert Messages) (AWW) supplements these Inflight Aviation Weather Advisories.

d. SIGMET. A SIGMET is a concise description of the occurrence or expected occurrence of specified en route weather phenomena which is expected to affect the safety of aircraft operations.

1. SIGMETs:

(a) Are intended for dissemination to all pilots in flight to enhance safety.

(b) Are issued by the responsible MWO as soon as it is practical to alert operators and aircrews of hazardous en route conditions.

(c) Are unscheduled products that are valid for 4 hours; except SIGMETs associated with tropical cyclones and volcanic ash clouds are valid for 6 hours. Unscheduled updates and corrections are issued as necessary.

(d) Use geographical points to describe the hazardous weather areas. These points can reference either VORs, airports, or latitude–longitude, depending on SIGMET location. If the total area to be affected during the forecast period is very large, it could be that, in actuality, only a small portion of this total area would be affected at any one time.

Example:
Example of a SIGMET:

BOSR WS 050600
SIGMET ROMEO 2 VALID UNTIL 051000
ME NH VT
FROM CAR TO YSJ TO CON TO MPV TO CAR
OCNL SEV TURB BLW 080 EXP DUE TO STG
NWLY FLOW. CONDS CONTG BYD 1000Z.

2. SIGMETs over the contiguous U.S.:

(a) Are issued corresponding to the areas described in Figure 7-1-5. and are only for non-convective weather. The U.S. issues a special category of SIGMETs for convective weather called Convective SIGMETs.

(b) Are identified by an alphabetic designator from November through Yankee, excluding Sierra and Tango. Issuance for the same phenomenon will be sequentially numbered, using the original designator until the phenomenon ends. For example, the first issuance in the Chicago (CHI) area (reference Figure 7-1-5) for phenomenon moving from the Salt Lake City (SLC) area will be SIGMET Papa 3, if the previous two issuances, Papa 1 and Papa 2, had been in the SLC area. Note that no two different phenomena across the country can have the same alphabetic designator at the same time.

(c) Use location identifiers (either VORs or airports) to describe the hazardous weather areas.

(d) Are issued when the following phenomena occur or are expected to occur:

(1) Severe icing not associated with thunderstorms.

(2) Severe or extreme turbulence or clear air turbulence (CAT) not associated with thunderstorms.

(3) Widespread dust storms or sandstorms lowering surface visibilities to below 3 miles.

(4) Volcanic ash.

3. SIGMETs over Alaska:

(a) Are issued for the Anchorage FIR including Alaska and nearby coastal waters corresponding to the areas described in Figure 7-1-4. and are only for non-convective weather. The U.S. issues a special category of SIGMETs for convective weather called Convective SIGMETs.

(b) Use location identifiers (either VORs or airports) to describe the hazardous weather areas.

(c) Use points of latitude and longitude over the ocean areas of the Alaska FIR.

(d) Are identified by an alphabetic designator from India through Mike.

(e) In addition to the phenomenon applicable to SIGMETs over the contiguous U.S., SIGMETs over Alaska are also issued for:

(1) Tornadoes.

(2) Lines of thunderstorms.

(3) Embedded thunderstorms.

(4) Hail greater than or equal to ¾ inch in diameter.

FIGURE 7-1-4
Alaska SIGMET and Area Forecast Zones

FIGURE 7-1-5
SIGMET Locations—Contiguous U.S.

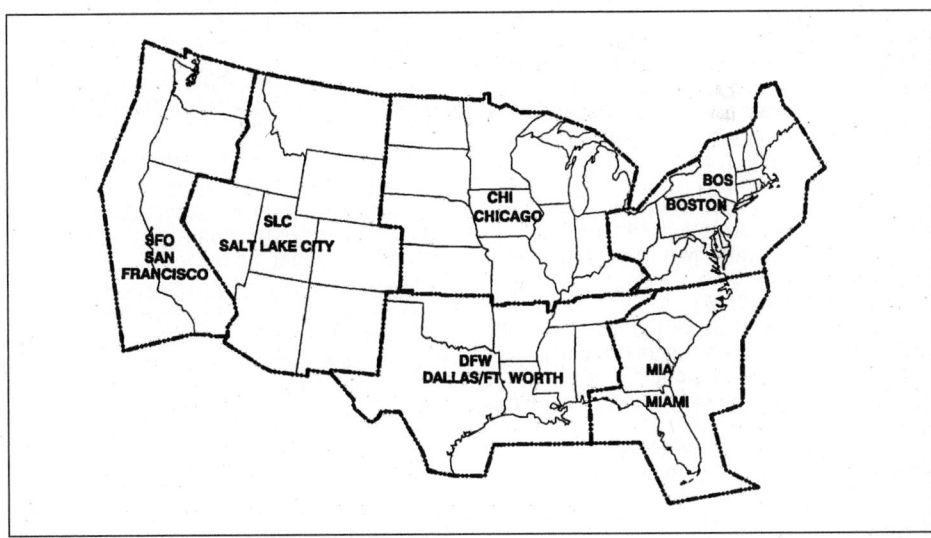

FIGURE 7–1–6
Hawaii Area Forecast Locations

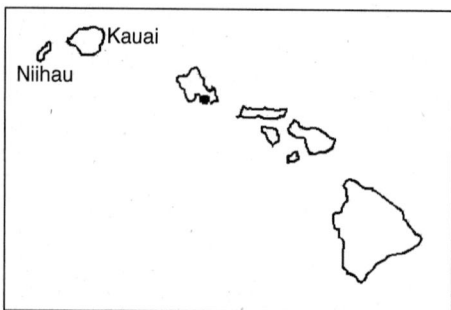

4. SIGMETs over oceanic regions (New York Oceanic FIR, Oakland Oceanic FIR including Hawaii, Houston Oceanic FIR, Miami Oceanic FIR, San Juan FIR), points of latitude and longitude are used to describe the hazard area.

(a) SIGMETs over the Oakland Oceanic FIR west of 140 west and south of 30 north (including the Hawaiian Islands) are identified by an alphabetic designator from November through Zulu.

(b) SIGMETs over the Oakland Oceanic FIR east of 140 west and north of 30 north are identified by an alphabetic designator from Alpha through Mike.

(c) SIGMETs over the New York Oceanic FIR, Houston Oceanic FIR, Miami Oceanic FIR, and San Juan FIR are identified by an alphabetic designator from Alpha through Mike.

(d) In addition to SIGMETs issued for the phenomenon for the contiguous U.S., SIGMETs in the oceanic regions are also issued for:

(1) Tornadoes.

(2) Lines of thunderstorms.

(3) Embedded thunderstorms.

(4) Hail greater than or equal to ¾ inch in diameter.

e. Convective SIGMET

1. Convective SIGMETs are issued in the conterminous U.S. for any of the following:

(a) Severe thunderstorm due to:

(1) Surface winds greater than or equal to 50 knots.

(2) Hail at the surface greater than or equal to 3/4 inches in diameter.

(3) Tornadoes.

(b) Embedded thunderstorms.

(c) A line of thunderstorms.

(d) Thunderstorms producing precipitation greater than or equal to heavy precipitation affecting 40 percent or more of an area at least 3,000 square miles.

2. Any convective SIGMET implies severe or greater turbulence, severe icing, and low-level wind shear. A convective SIGMET may be issued for any convective situation that the forecaster feels is hazardous to all categories of aircraft.

3. Convective SIGMET bulletins are issued for the western (W), central (C), and eastern (E) United States. (Convective SIGMETs are not issued for Alaska or Hawaii.) The areas are separated at 87 and 107 degrees west longitude with sufficient overlap to cover most cases when the phenomenon crosses the boundaries. Bulletins are issued hourly at H+55. Special bulletins are issued at any time as required and updated at H+55. If no criteria meeting convective SIGMET requirements are observed or forecasted, the message "CONVECTIVE SIGMET...NONE" will be issued for each area at H+55. Individual convective SIGMETs for each area (W, C, E) are numbered sequentially from number one each day, beginning at 00Z. A convective SIGMET for a continuing phenomenon will be reissued every hour at H+55 with a new number. The text of the bulletin consists of either an observation and a forecast or just a forecast. The forecast is valid for up to 2 hours.

Example:

CONVECTIVE SIGMET 44C

VALID UNTIL 1455Z

AR TX OK

FROM 40NE ADM-40ESE MLC-10W TXK-50WNW LFK-40ENE SJT-40NE ADM

AREA TS MOV FROM 26025KT. TOPS ABV FL450.

OUTLOOK VALID 061455-061855

FROM 60WSW OKC-MLC-40N TXK-40WSW IGB-VUZ-MGM-HRV-60S BTR-40N

IAH-60SW SJT-40ENE LBB-60WSW OKC

WST ISSUANCES EXPD. REFER TO MOST RECENT ACUS01 KWNS FROM STORM PREDICTION CENTER FOR SYNOPSIS AND METEOROLOGICAL DETAILS

f. AIRMET. AIRMETs are a concise description of the occurrence or expected occurrence of specified en route weather phenomena that may affect the safety of aircraft operations, but at intensities lower than those which require the issuance of a SIGMET.

1. AIRMETs contain details about IFR conditions, extensive mountain obscuration, turbulence, strong surface winds, icing, and freezing levels. Unscheduled updates and corrections are issued as necessary.

2. AIRMETs:

(a) Are intended to inform all pilots, but especially Visual Flight Rules pilots and operators of sensitive aircraft, of potentially hazardous weather phenomena.

(b) Are issued on a scheduled basis every 6 hours, except every 8 hours in Alaska. Unscheduled updates and corrections are issued as necessary.

(c) Are intended for dissemination to all pilots in the preflight and en route phase of flight to enhance safety. En route AIRMETs are available over flight service frequencies. Over the contiguous U.S., AIRMETs are also available on equipment intended to display weather and other non-air traffic control-related flight information to pilots using the Flight Information Service–Broadcast (FIS-B). In Alaska and Hawaii, AIRMETs are broadcast on air traffic frequencies.

(d) Are issued for the contiguous U.S., Alaska, and Hawaii. No AIRMETs are issued for U.S. Oceanic FIRs in the Gulf of Mexico, Caribbean, Western Atlantic, and Pacific Oceans.

TABLE 7–1–2
U. S. AIRMET ISSUANCE TIME AND FREQUENCY

Product Type	Issuance Time	Issuance Frequency
AIRMETs over the Contiguous U.S.	0245, 0845, 1445, 2045 UTC	Every 6 hours
AIRMETs over Alaska	0515, 1315, 2115 UTC (standard time)	Every 8 hours
	0415, 1215, 2015 UTC (Daylight savings time)	
AIRMETs over Hawaii	0400, 1000, 1600, 2200 UTC	Every 6 hours

3. AIRMETs over the Contiguous U.S.:

(a) Are displayed graphically on websites, such as, aviationweather.gov and 1800wxbrief.com, and equipment receiving FIS-B information.

(b) Provide a higher forecast resolution than AIRMETs issued in text format.

(c) Are valid at discrete times no more than 3 hours apart for a period of up to 12 hours into the future (for example, 00, 03, 06, 09, and 12 hours). Additional forecasts may be inserted during the first 6 hours (for example; 01, 02, 04, and 05). 00-hour represents the initial conditions, and the subsequent graphics depict the area affected by the particular hazard at that valid time. Forecasts valid at 00 through 06 hours correspond to the text AIRMET bulletin.

(d) Depict the following en route aviation weather hazards:

(1) Instrument flight rule conditions (ceiling < 1000' and/or surface visibility < 3 miles).

(2) Widespread mountain obscuration.

(3) Moderate icing.

(4) Freezing levels.

(5) Moderate turbulence.

(6) Non-convective low-level wind shear potential below 2,000 feet AGL.

(7) Sustained surface winds greater than 30 knots.

4. Interpolation of time periods between AIRMETs over the contiguous U.S. valid times: Users must keep in mind when using the AIRMET over the contiguous U.S. that if a 00-hour forecast shows no significant weather and a 03-hour forecast shows hazardous weather, they must assume a change is occurring during the period between the two forecasts. It should be taken into consideration that the hazardous weather starts immediately after the 00-hour forecast unless there is a defined initiation or ending time for the hazardous weather. The same would apply after the 03-hour forecast. The user should assume the hazardous weather condition is occurring between the snap shots unless informed otherwise. For example, if a 00-hour forecast shows no hazard, a 03-hour forecast shows the presence of hazardous weather, and a 06-hour forecast shows no hazard, the user should assume the hazard exists from the 0001 hour to the 0559 hour time period.

Ch 7

FIGURE 7-1-7
AIRMET over the Contiguous U.S.

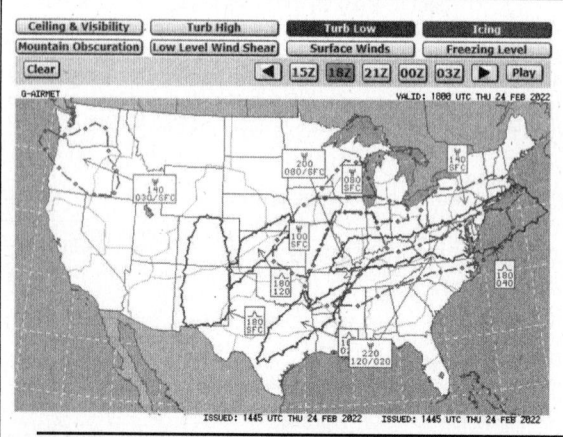

Example: G-AIRMET Valid
at 1800Z on February 24, 2022
Displaying:
 Low Level Turbulence
 and Icing

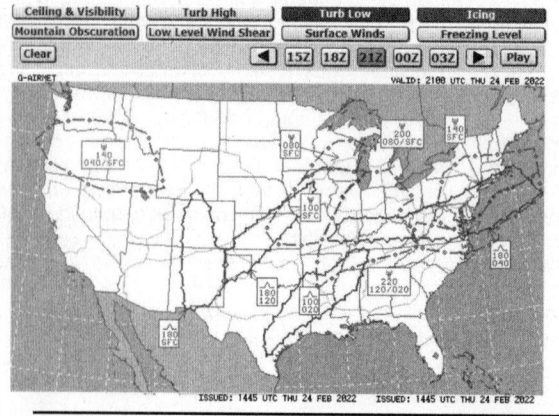

Example: G-AIRMET Valid
at 2100Z on February 24, 2022
Displaying:
 Low Level Turbulence
 and Icing

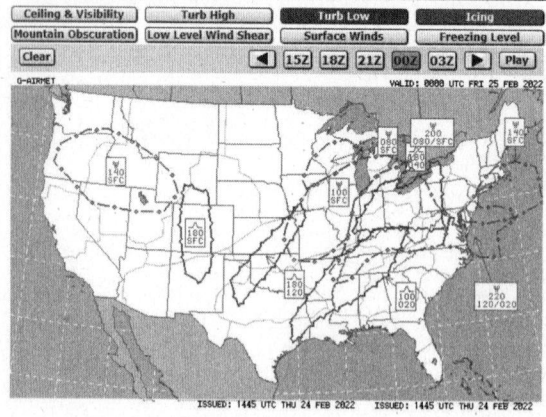

Example: G-AIRMET Valid
at 0000Z on February 25, 2022
Displaying:
 Low Level Turbulence
 and Icing

5. AIRMETs over Alaska and Hawaii:

(a) AIRMETs over Alaska and Hawaii are in text format. The hazard areas are described using well-known geographical areas. AIRMETs over Alaska are issued for three Alaskan regions corresponding to Alaska area forecasts (See Figure 7-1-4).

(b) AIRMETs over Alaska are valid up to eight hours. AIRMETs over Hawaii are valid up to six hours. Unscheduled issuances contain an update number for easier identification.

(c) AIRMET Zulu describes moderate icing and provides freezing level heights.

Example:
Example of AIRMET Sierra issued for the Southeast Alaska area:

WAAK47 PAWU 241324
WA7O
JNUS WA 241315
AIRMET SIERRA FOR IFR AND MT OBSC
VALID UNTIL 242115

LYNN CANAL AND GLACIER BAY JB
MTS OBSC BY CLDS/ISOL PCPN. NC.

CNTRL SE AK JC
MTS OCNL OBSC IN CLDS. NC.

SRN SE AK JD
PAWG–PAKT LN W OCNL CIGS BLW 010/VIS
BLW 3SM BR. IMPR.

ERN GLF CST JE
OCNL CIGS BLW 010/VIS BLW 3SM BR/–RA
BR. DTRT.

=JNUT WA 241315
AIRMET TANGO FOR TURB/STG SFC WINDS
VALID UNTIL 242115

ERN GLF CST JE
OFSHR ICY BAY W SUSTAINED SFC WND 30
KTS
OR GTR. SPRDG E. INTSF.

=JNUZ WA 241315
AIRMET ZULU FOR ICING VALID UNTIL 242115

ERN GLF CST JE
16Z TO 19Z ALG CST W ICY BAY OCNL MOD
ICEIC 080–160. FZLVL 045 EXC 015 INLAND.
WKN.

Example:
Example of AIRMET Tango issued for Hawaii FA area:

WAHW31 PHFO 241529
WA0HI

HNLS WA 241600
AIRMET SIERRA UPDATE 2 FOR IFR VALID
UNTIL 242200

NO SIGNIFICANT IFR EXP.

=HNLT WA 241600
AIRMET TANGO UPDATE 3 FOR TURB VALID
UNTIL 242200

AIRMET TURB...HI
OVER AMD IMT S THRU W OF MTN.
TEMPO MOD TURB BLW 070.
COND CONT BEYOND 2200Z.

=HNLZ WA 241600
AIRMET ZULU UPDATE 2 FOR ICE AND FZLVL
VALID UNTIL 242200
NO SIGNIFICANT ICE EXP

g. Watch Notification Messages

The Storm Prediction Center (SPC) in Norman, OK, issues Watch Notification Messages to provide an area threat alert for forecast organized severe thunderstorms that may produce tornadoes, large hail, and/or convective damaging winds within the CONUS. SPC issues three types of watch notification messages: Aviation Watch Notification Messages, Public Severe Thunderstorm Watch Notification Messages, and Public Tornado Watch Notification Messages.

It is important to note the difference between a Severe Thunderstorm (or Tornado) Watch and a Severe Thunderstorm (or Tornado) Warning. A watch means severe weather is possible during the next few hours, while a warning means that severe weather has been observed, or is expected within the hour. Only the SPC issues Severe Thunderstorm and Tornado Watches, while only NWS Weather Forecasts Offices issue Severe Thunderstorm and Tornado Warnings.

1. The Aviation Watch Notification Message. The Aviation Watch Notification Message product is an approximation of the area of the Public Severe Thunderstorm Watch or Public Tornado Watch. The area may be defined as a rectangle or parallelogram using VOR navigational aides as coordinates.

The Aviation Watch Notification Message was formerly known as the Alert Severe Weather Watch Bulletin (AWW). The NWS no longer uses that title or acronym for this product. The NWS uses the

Ch 7

acronym SAW for the Aviation Watch Notification Message, but retains AWW in the product header for processing by weather data systems.

Example of an Aviation Watch Notification Message:

WWUS30 KWNS 271559

SAW2

SPC AWW 271559

WW 568 TORNADO AR LA MS 271605Z - 280000Z

AXIS..65 STATUTE MILES EAST AND WEST OF LINE..45ESE HEZ/NATCHEZ MS/ - 50N TUP/ TUPELO MS/..AVIATION COORDS.. 55NM E/W /18WNW MCB - 60E MEM/

HAIL SURFACE AND ALOFT..3 INCHES. WIND GUSTS..70 KNOTS. MAX TOPS TO 550. MEAN STORM MOTION VECTOR 26030.

LAT...LON 31369169 34998991 34998762 31368948

THIS IS AN APPROXIMATION TO THE WATCH AREA. FOR A COMPLETE DEPICTION OF THE WATCH SEE WOUS64 KWNS FOR WOU2.

 2. Public Severe Thunderstorm Watch Notification Messages describe areas of expected severe thunderstorms. (Severe thunderstorm criteria are 1-inch hail or larger and/or wind gusts of 50 knots [58 mph] or greater.) A Public Severe Thunderstorm Watch Notification Message contains the area description and axis, the watch expiration time, a description of hail size and thunderstorm wind gusts expected, the definition of the watch, a call to action statement, a list of other valid watches, a brief discussion of meteorological reasoning and technical information for the aviation community.

 3. Public Tornado Watch Notification Messages describe areas where the threat of tornadoes exists. A Public Tornado Watch Notification Message contains the area description and axis, watch expiration time, the term "damaging tornadoes," a description of the largest hail size and strongest thunderstorm wind gusts expected, the definition of the watch, a call to action statement, a list of other valid watches, a brief discussion of meteorological reasoning and technical information for the aviation community. SPC may enhance a Public Tornado Watch Notification Message by using the words "THIS IS A PARTICULARLY DANGEROUS SITUATION" when there is a likelihood of multiple strong (damage of EF2 or EF3) or violent (damage of EF4 or EF5) tornadoes.

 4. Public severe thunderstorm and tornado watch notification messages were formerly known as the Severe Weather Watch Bulletins (WW). The NWS no longer uses that title or acronym for this product but retains WW in the product header for processing by weather data systems.

Example of a Public Tornado Watch Notification Message:

WWUS20 KWNS 050550

SEL2

SPC WW 051750

URGENT - IMMEDIATE BROADCAST REQUESTED

TORNADO WATCH NUMBER 243

NWS STORM PREDICTION CENTER NORMAN OK

1250 AM CDT MON MAY 5 2011

THE NWS STORM PREDICTION CENTER HAS ISSUED A

*TORNADO WATCH FOR PORTIONS OF WESTERN AND CENTRAL ARKANSAS

SOUTHERN MISSOURI

FAR EASTERN OKLAHOMA

*EFFECTIVE THIS MONDAY MORNING FROM 1250 AM UNTIL 600 AM CDT.

...THIS IS A PARTICULARLY DANGEROUS SITUATION...

*PRIMARY THREATS INCLUDE

NUMEROUS INTENSE TORNADOES LIKELY

NUMEROUS SIGNIFICANT DAMAGING WIND GUSTS TO 80 MPH LIKELY

NUMEROUS VERY LARGE HAIL TO 4 INCHES IN DIAMETER LIKELY

THE TORNADO WATCH AREA IS APPROXIMATELY ALONG AND 100 STATUTE MILES EAST AND WEST OF A LINE FROM 15 MILES WEST NORTHWEST OF FORT LEONARD WOOD MISSOURI TO 45 MILES SOUTHWEST OF HOT SPRINGS ARKANSAS. FOR A COMPLETE DEPICTION OF THE WATCH SEE THE ASSOCIATED WATCH OUTLINE UPDATE (WOUS64 KWNS WOU2).

REMEMBER...A TORNADO WATCH MEANS CONDITIONS ARE FAVORABLE FOR TORNADOES AND SEVERE THUNDERSTORMS IN AND CLOSE TO THE WATCH AREA. PERSONS IN THESE AREAS SHOULD BE ON THE LOOKOUT FOR THREATENING WEATHER CONDITIONS AND LISTEN FOR LATER STATEMENTS AND POSSIBLE WARNINGS.

OTHER WATCH INFORMATION...THIS TORNADO WATCH REPLACES TORNADO WATCH NUMBER 237. WATCH NUMBER 237 WILL NOT BE IN EFFECT AFTER

1250 AM CDT. CONTINUE...WW 239...WW 240... WW 241...WW 242...

DISCUSSION...SRN MO SQUALL LINE EXPECTED TO CONTINUE EWD...WHERE LONG/HOOKED HODOGRAPHS SUGGEST THREAT FOR EMBEDDED SUPERCELLS/

POSSIBLE TORNADOES. FARTHER S...MORE WIDELY SCATTERED

SUPERCELLS WITH A THREAT FOR TORNADOES WILL PERSIST IN VERY STRONGLY DEEP SHEARED/LCL ENVIRONMENT IN AR.

AVIATION...TORNADOES AND A FEW SEVERE THUNDERSTORMS WITH HAIL SURFACE AND ALOFT TO 4 INCHES. EXTREME TURBULENCE AND SURFACE WIND GUSTS TO 70 KNOTS. A FEW CUMULONIMBI WITH MAXIMUM TOPS TO 500. MEAN STORM MOTION VECTOR 26045.

5. Status reports are issued as needed to show progress of storms and to delineate areas no longer under the threat of severe storm activity. Cancellation bulletins are issued when it becomes evident that no severe weather will develop or that storms have subsided and are no longer severe.

h. Center Weather Advisories (CWAs)

1. CWAs are unscheduled inflight, flow control, air traffic, and air crew advisory. By nature of its short lead time, the CWA is not a flight planning product. It is generally a nowcast for conditions beginning within the next two hours. CWAs will be issued:

(a) As a supplement to an existing SIGMET, Convective SIGMET or AIRMET.

(b) When an Inflight Advisory has not been issued but observed or expected weather conditions meet SIGMET/AIRMET criteria based on current pilot reports and reinforced by other sources of information about existing meteorological conditions.

(c) When observed or developing weather conditions do not meet SIGMET, Convective SIGMET, or AIRMET criteria; e.g., in terms of intensity or area coverage, but current pilot reports or other weather information sources indicate that existing or anticipated meteorological phenomena will adversely affect the safe flow of air traffic within the ARTCC area of responsibility.

2. The following example is a CWA issued from the Kansas City, Missouri, ARTCC. The "3" after ZKC in the first line denotes this CWA has been issued for the third weather phenomena to occur for the day. The "301" in the second line denotes the phenomena number again (3) and the issuance number (01) for this phenomena. The CWA was issued at 2140Z and is valid until 2340Z.

Example:

ZKC3 CWA 032140

ZKC CWA 301 VALID UNTIL 032340

ISOLD SVR TSTM over KCOU MOVG SWWD 10 KTS ETC.

7-1-7 Categorical Outlooks

a. Categorical outlook terms, describing general ceiling and visibility conditions for advanced planning purposes are used only in area forecasts and are defined as follows:

1. **LIFR (Low IFR).** Ceiling less than 500 feet and/or visibility less than 1 mile.

2. **IFR.** Ceiling 500 to less than 1,000 feet and/or visibility 1 to less than 3 miles.

3. **MVFR (Marginal VFR).** Ceiling 1,000 to 3,000 feet and/or visibility 3 to 5 miles inclusive.

4. **VFR.** Ceiling greater than 3,000 feet and visibility greater than 5 miles; includes sky clear.

b. The cause of LIFR, IFR, or MVFR is indicated by either ceiling or visibility restrictions or both. The contraction "CIG" and/or weather and obstruction to vision symbols are used. If winds or gusts of 25 knots or greater are forecast for the outlook period, the word "WIND" is also included for all categories including VFR.

Example 1: LIFR CIG—low IFR due to low ceiling

Example 2: IFR FG—IFR due to visibility restricted by fog

Example 3: MVFR CIG HZ FU—marginal VFR due to both ceiling and visibility restricted by haze and smoke

Example 4: IFR CIG RA WIND—IFR due to both low ceiling and visibility restricted by rain; wind expected to be 25 knots or greater

7-1-8 Inflight Weather Advisory Broadcasts

a. ARTCCs broadcast a Convective SIGMET, SIGMET, AIRMET (except in the contiguous U.S.), Urgent Pilot Report, or CWA alert once on all frequencies, except emergency frequencies, when any part of the area described is within 150 miles of the airspace under their jurisdiction. These broadcasts advise pilots of the availability of hazardous weather advisories and to contact the nearest flight service facility for additional details.

Example 1: Attention all aircraft, SIGMET Delta Three, from Myton to Tuba City to Milford, severe turbulence and severe clear icing below one zero thousand feet. Expected to continue beyond zero three zero zero zulu.

Example 2: Attention all aircraft, convective SIGMET Two Seven Eastern. From the vicinity of Elmira to Phillipsburg. Scattered embedded thunderstorms moving east at one zero knots. A few intense level five cells, maximum tops four five zero.

Example 3: Attention all aircraft, Kansas City Center weather advisory one zero three. Numerous reports of moderate to severe icing from eight to niner thousand feet in a three zero mile radius of St. Louis. Light or negative icing reported from

Ch 7

four thousand to one two thousand feet remainder of Kansas City Center area.

Note: *Terminal control facilities have the option to limit hazardous weather information broadcast as follows: Tower cab and approach control positions may opt to broadcast hazardous weather information alerts only when any part of the area described is within 50 miles of the airspace under their jurisdiction.*

Reference: *FAA Order JO 7110.65, ¶2-6-6, Hazardous Inflight Weather Advisory.*

7-1-9 Flight Information Services (FIS)

FIS is a method of disseminating meteorological (MET) and aeronautical information (AI) to displays in the cockpit in order to enhance pilot situational awareness, provide decision support tools, and improve safety. FIS augments traditional pilot voice communication with Flight Service Stations (FSSs), ATC facilities, or Airline Operations Control Centers (AOCCs). FIS is not intended to replace traditional pilot and controller/flight service specialist/aircraft dispatcher preflight briefings or inflight voice communications. FIS, however, can provide textual and graphical information that can help abbreviate and improve the usefulness of such communications. FIS enhances pilot situational awareness and improves safety.

a. Data link Service Providers (DSPs). DSPs deploy and maintain airborne, ground-based, and, in some cases, space-based infrastructure that supports the transmission of AI/MET information over one or more physical links. A DSP may provide a free of charge or a for-fee service that permits end users to uplink and downlink AI/MET and other information. The following are examples of DSPs:

1. FAA FIS-B. A ground-based broadcast service provided through the ADS-B Universal Access Transceiver (UAT) network. The service provides users with a 978 MHz data link capability when operating within range and line-of-sight of a transmitting ground station. FIS-B enables users of properly equipped aircraft to receive and display a suite of broadcast weather and aeronautical information products.

2. Non-FAA FIS Systems. Several commercial vendors provide customers with FIS data over both the aeronautical spectrum and on other frequencies using a variety of data link protocols. Services available from these providers vary greatly and may include tier based subscriptions. Advancements in bandwidth technology permits preflight as well as inflight access to the same MET and AI information available on the ground. Pilots and operators using non-FAA FIS for MET and AI information should be knowledgeable regarding the weather services being provided as some commercial vendors may be repackaging NWS sourced weather, while other commercial vendors may alter the weather information to produce vendor-tailored or vendor-specific weather reports and forecasts.

b. Three Data Link Modes. There are three data link modes that may be used for transmitting AI and MET information to aircraft. The intended use of the AI and/or MET information will determine the most appropriate data link service.

1. Broadcast Mode: A one-way interaction in which AI and/or MET updates or changes applicable to a designated geographic area are continuously transmitted (or transmitted at repeated periodic intervals) to all aircraft capable of receiving the broadcast within the service volume defined by the system network architecture.

2. Contract/Demand Mode: A two-way interaction in which AI and/or MET information is transmitted to an aircraft in response to a specific request.

3. Contract/Update Mode: A two-way interaction that is an extension of the Demand Mode. Initial AI and/or MET report(s) are sent to an aircraft and subsequent updates or changes to the AI and/or MET information that meet the contract criteria are automatically or manually sent to an aircraft.

c. To ensure airman compliance with Federal Aviation Regulations, manufacturer's operating manuals should remind airmen to contact ATC controllers, FSS specialists, operator dispatchers, or airline operations control centers for general and mission critical aviation weather information and/or NAS status conditions (such as NOTAMs, Special Use Airspace status, and other government flight information). If FIS products are systemically modified (for example, are displayed as abbreviated plain text and/or graphical depictions), the modification process and limitations of the resultant product should be clearly described in the vendor's user guidance.

d. Operational Use of FIS. Regardless of the type of FIS system being used, several factors must be considered when using FIS:

1. Before using FIS for inflight operations, pilots and other flight crewmembers should become familiar with the operation of the FIS system to be used, the airborne equipment to be used, including its system architecture, airborne system components, coverage service volume and other limitations of the particular system, modes of operation and indications of various system failures. Users should also be familiar with the specific content and format of the services available from the FIS provider(s). Sources of information that may provide this specific guidance include manufacturer's manuals, training programs, and reference guides.

2. FIS should not serve as the sole source of aviation weather and other operational information. ATC, FSSs, and, if applicable, AOCC VHF/HF voice remain as a redundant method of communicating aviation weather, NOTAMs, and other operational information to aircraft in flight. FIS augments these traditional ATC/FSS/AOCC services and, for some products, offers the advantage of being displayed as graphical information. By using FIS for orientation, the usefulness of information received from conventional means may be enhanced. For example, FIS may alert the pilot to specific areas of concern that will more accurately focus requests made to FSS or AOCC for inflight updates or similar queries made to ATC.

3. The airspace and aeronautical environment is constantly changing. These changes occur quickly and without warning. Critical operational decisions should be based on use of the most current and appropriate data available. When differences exist between FIS and information obtained by voice communication with ATC, FSS, and/or AOCC (if applicable), pilots are cautioned to use the most recent data from the most authoritative source.

4. FIS aviation weather products (for example, graphical ground-based radar precipitation depictions) are not appropriate for tactical (typical timeframe of less than 3 minutes) avoidance of severe weather such as negotiating a path through a weather hazard area. FIS supports strategic (typical timeframe of 20 minutes or more) weather decision-making such as route selection to avoid a weather hazard area in its entirety. The misuse of information beyond its applicability may place the pilot and aircraft in jeopardy. In addition, FIS should never be used in lieu of an individual preflight weather and flight planning briefing.

5. DSPs offer numerous MET and AI products with information that can be layered on top of each other. Pilots need to be aware that too much information can have a negative effect on their cognitive work load. Pilots need to manage the amount of information to a level that offers the most pertinent information to that specific flight without creating a cockpit distraction. Pilots may need to adjust the amount of information based on numerous factors including, but not limited to, the phase of flight, single pilot operation, autopilot availability, class of airspace, and the weather conditions encountered.

6. FIS NOTAM products, including Temporary Flight Restriction (TFR) information, are advisory-use information and are intended for situational awareness purposes only. Cockpit displays of this information are not appropriate for tactical navigation—pilots should stay clear of any geographic area displayed as a TFR NOTAM. Pilots should contact FSSs and/or ATC while en route to obtain updated information and to verify the cockpit display of NOTAM information.

7. FIS supports better pilot decision-making by increasing situational awareness. Better decision-making is based on using information from a variety of sources. In addition to FIS, pilots should take advantage of other weather/NAS status sources, including, briefings from Flight Service Stations, data from other air traffic control facilities, airline operation control centers, pilot reports, as well as their own observations.

e. FAA's Flight Information Service-Broadcast (FIS-B).

1. FIS-B is a ground-based broadcast service provided through the FAA's Automatic Dependent Surveillance–Broadcast Services (ADS-B) Universal Access Transceiver (UAT) network. The service provides users with a 978 MHz data link capability when operating within range and line-of-sight of a transmitting ground station. FIS-B enables users of properly-equipped aircraft to receive and display a suite of broadcast weather and aeronautical information products.

2. Table 7-1-3 lists the text and graphical products available through FIS-B and provided free-of-charge. Detailed information concerning FIS-B meteorological products can be found in Advisory Circular 00-45, Aviation Weather Services, and AC 00-63, Use of Cockpit Displays of Digital Weather and Aeronautical Information. Information on Special Use Airspace (SUA), Temporary Flight Restriction (TFR) and Notice to Air Missions (NOTAM) products can be found in Chapters 3, 4 and 5 of this manual.

3. Users of FIS-B should familiarize themselves with the operational characteristics and limitations of the system, including: system architecture; service environment; product lifecycles; modes of operation; and indications of system failure.

Note: *The NOTAM-D and NOTAM-FDC products broadcast via FIS-B are limited to those issued or effective within the past 30 days. Except for TFRs, NOTAMs older than 30 days are not provided. The pilot in command is responsible for reviewing all necessary information prior to flight.*

4. FIS-B products are updated and transmitted at specific intervals based primarily on product issuance criteria. Update intervals are defined as the rate at which the product data is available from the source for transmission. Transmission intervals are defined as the amount of time within which a new or updated product transmission must be completed and/or the rate or repetition interval at which the product is rebroadcast. Update and transmission intervals for each product are provided in Table 7-1-3.

Ch 7

5. Where applicable, FIS-B products include a look-ahead range expressed in nautical miles (NM) for three service domains: Airport Surface; Terminal Airspace; and En Route/Gulf-of-Mexico (GOMEX). Table 7-1-4 provides service domain availability and look-ahead ranging for each FIS-B product.

6. Prior to using this capability, users should familiarize themselves with the operation of FIS-B avionics by referencing the applicable User's Guides. Guidance concerning the interpretation of information displayed should be obtained from the appropriate avionics manufacturer.

7. FIS-B malfunctions not attributed to aircraft system failures or covered by active NOTAM should be reported by radio or telephone to the nearest FSS facility, or by sending an email to the ADS-B help desk at adsb@faa.gov. Reports should include:

 (a) Condition observed;

 (b) Date and time of observation;

 (c) Altitude and location of observation;

 (d) Type and call sign of the aircraft; and

 (e) Type and software version of avionics system.

 f. Non-FAA FIS Systems. Several commercial vendors also provide customers with FIS data over both the aeronautical spectrum and on other frequencies using a variety of data link protocols. In some cases, the vendors provide only the communications system that carries customer messages, such as the Aircraft Communications Addressing and Reporting System (ACARS) used by many air carrier and other operators.

 1. Operators using non-FAA FIS data for in-flight weather and other operational information should ensure that the products used conform to FAA/NWS standards. Specifically, aviation weather and NAS status information should meet the following criteria:

 (a) The products should be either FAA/NWS "accepted" aviation weather reports or products, or based on FAA/NWS accepted aviation weather reports or products. If products are used which do not meet this criteria, they should be so identified. The operator must determine the applicability of such products to their particular flight operations.

 (b) In the case of a weather product which is the result of the application of a process which alters the form, function or content of the base FAA/NWS accepted weather product(s), that process, and any limitations to the application of the resultant product, should be described in the vendor's user guidance material. An example would be a NEXRAD radar composite/mosaic map, which has been modified by changing the scaling resolution. The methodology of assigning reflectivity values to the resultant image components should be described in the vendor's guidance material to ensure that the user can accurately interpret the displayed data.

TABLE 7-1-3

FIS-B Over UAT Product Update and Transmission Intervals

Product	Update Interval[1]	Transmission Interval (95%)[2]	Basic Product
AIRMET	As Available	5 minutes	Yes
AWW/WW	As Available, then at 15 minute intervals for 1 hour	5 minutes	No
Ceiling	As Available	10 minutes	No
Convective SIGMET	As Available, then at 15 minute intervals for 1 hour	5 minutes	Yes
D-ATIS	As Available	1 minute	No
Echo Top	5 minutes	5 minutes	No
METAR/SPECI	1 minute (where available), As Available otherwise	5 minutes	Yes
MRMS NEXRAD (CONUS)	2 minutes	15 minutes	Yes
MRMS NEXRAD (Regional)	2 minutes	2.5 minutes	Yes
NOTAMs–D/FDC	As Available	10 minutes	Yes
NOTAMs–TFR	As Available	10 minutes	Yes
PIREP	As Available	10 minutes	Yes
SIGMET	As Available, then at 15 minute intervals for 1 hour	5 minutes	Yes
SUA Status	As Available	10 minutes	Yes
TAF/AMEND	6 Hours (±15 minutes)	10 minutes	Yes
Temperature Aloft	12 Hours (±15 minutes)	10 minutes	Yes
TWIP	As Available	1 minute	No

(continued)

Product	Update Interval[1]	Transmission Interval (95%)[2]	Basic Product
Winds aloft	12 Hours (±15 minutes)	10 minutes	Yes
Lightning strikes[3]	5 minutes	5 minutes	Yes
Turbulence[3]	1 minute	15 minutes	Yes
Icing, Forecast Potential (FIP)[3]	60 minutes	15 minutes	Yes
Cloud tops[3]	30 minutes	15 minutes	Yes
1 Minute AWOS[3]	1 minute	10 minutes	No
Graphical-AIRMET[3]	As Available	5 minutes	Yes
Center Weather Advisory (CWA)[3]	As Available	10 minutes	Yes
Temporary Restricted Areas (TRA)	As Available	10 minutes	Yes
Temporary Military Operations Areas (TMOA)	As Available	10 minutes	Yes

[1] The Update Interval is the rate at which the product data is available from the source.
[2] The Transmission Interval is the amount of time within which a new or updated product transmission must be completed (95%) and the rate or repetition interval at which the product is rebroadcast (95%).
[3] The transmission and update intervals for the expanded set of basic meteorological products may be adjusted based on FAA and vendor agreement on the final product formats and performance requirements.

Note 1: *Details concerning the content, format, and symbols of the various data link products provided should be obtained from the specific avionics manufacturer.*

Note 2: *NOTAM-D and NOTAM-FDC products broadcast via FIS-B are limited to those issued or effective within the past 30 days.*

TABLE 7–1–4
PRODUCT PARAMETERS FOR LOW/MEDIUM/HIGH ALTITUDE TIER RADIOS

Product	Surface Radios	Low Altitude Tier	Medium Altitude Tier	High Altitude Tier
CONUS NEXRAD	N/A	CONUS NEXRAD not provided	CONUS NEXRAD imagery	CONUS NEXRAD imagery
Winds & Temps Aloft	500 NM look-ahead range	500 NM look-ahead range	750 NM look-ahead range	1,000 NM look-ahead range
METAR	100 NM look-ahead range	250 NM look-ahead range	375 NM look-ahead range	CONUS: CONUS Class B & C airport METARs and 500 NM look-ahead range Outside of CONUS: 500 NM look-ahead range
TAF	100 NM look-ahead range	250 NM look-ahead range	375 NM look-ahead range	CONUS: CONUS Class B & C airport TAFs and 500 NM look-ahead range Outside of CONUS: 500 NM look-ahead range
AIRMET, SIGMET, PIREP, and SUA/SAA	100 NM look-ahead range. PIREP/SUA/SAA is N/A.	250 NM look-ahead range	375 NM look-ahead range	500 NM look-ahead range
Regional NEXRAD	150 NM look-ahead range	150 NM look-ahead range	200 NM look-ahead range	250 NM look-ahead range
NOTAMs D, FDC, and TFR	100 NM look-ahead range	100 NM look-ahead range	100 NM look-ahead range	100 NM look-ahead range

Ch 7

7-1-10 Weather Observing Programs

a. Manual Observations. With only a few exceptions, these reports are from airport locations staffed by FAA personnel who manually observe, perform calculations, and enter these observations into the (WMSCR) communication system. The format and coding of these observations are contained in paragraph 7-1-28, Key to Aviation Routine Weather Report (METAR) and Aerodrome Forecasts (TAF).

b. Automated Weather Observing System (AWOS).

1. Automated weather reporting systems are increasingly being installed at airports. These systems consist of various sensors, a processor, a computer-generated voice subsystem, and a transmitter to broadcast local, minute-by-minute weather data directly to the pilot.

Note: When the barometric pressure exceeds 31.00 inches Hg., see AIM, ¶7-2-3, Altimeter Errors.

2. The AWOS observations will include the prefix "AUTO" to indicate that the data are derived from an automated system. Some AWOS locations will be augmented by certified observers who will provide weather and obstruction to vision information in the remarks of the report when the reported visibility is less than 7 miles. These sites, along with the hours of augmentation, are to be published in the Chart Supplement. Augmentation is identified in the observation as "OBSERVER WEATHER." The AWOS wind speed, direction and gusts, temperature, dew point, and altimeter setting are exactly the same as for manual observations. The AWOS will also report density altitude when it exceeds the field elevation by more than 1,000 feet. The reported visibility is derived from a sensor near the touchdown of the primary instrument runway. The visibility sensor output is converted to a visibility value using a 10-minute harmonic average. The reported sky condition/ceiling is derived from the ceilometer located next to the visibility sensor. The AWOS algorithm integrates the last 30 minutes of ceilometer data to derive cloud layers and heights. This output may also differ from the observer sky condition in that the AWOS is totally dependent upon the cloud advection over the sensor site.

3. These real-time systems are operationally classified into nine basic levels:

(a) AWOS-A only reports altimeter setting;

Note: Any other information is advisory only.

(b) AWOS-AV reports altimeter and visibility;

Note: Any other information is advisory only.

(c) AWOS-1 usually reports altimeter setting, wind data, temperature, dew point, and density altitude;

(d) AWOS-2 provides the information provided by AWOS-1 plus visibility; and

(e) AWOS-3 provides the information provided by AWOS-2 plus cloud/ceiling data.

(f) AWOS-3P provides reports the same as the AWOS-3 system, plus a precipitation identification sensor.

(g) AWOS-3PT reports the same as the AWOS-3P System, plus thunderstorm/lightning reporting capability.

(h) AWOS-3T reports the same as AWOS-3 system and includes a thunderstorm/lightning reporting capability.

(i) AWOS-4 reports the same as the AWOS-3 system, plus precipitation occurrence, type and accumulation, freezing rain, thunderstorm, and runway surface sensors.

4. The information is transmitted over a discrete VHF radio frequency or the voice portion of a local NAVAID. AWOS transmissions on a discrete VHF radio frequency are engineered to be receivable to a maximum of 25 NM from the AWOS site and a maximum altitude of 10,000 feet AGL. At many locations, AWOS signals may be received on the surface of the airport, but local conditions may limit the maximum AWOS reception distance and/or altitude. The system transmits a 20 to 30 second weather message updated each minute. Pilots should monitor the designated frequency for the automated weather broadcast. A description of the broadcast is contained in subparagraph c. There is no two-way communication capability. Most AWOS sites also have a dial-up capability so that the minute-by-minute weather messages can be accessed via telephone.

5. AWOS information (system level, frequency, phone number, etc.) concerning specific locations is published, as the systems become operational, in the Chart Supplement, and where applicable, on published Instrument Approach Procedures. Selected individual systems may be incorporated into nationwide data collection and dissemination networks in the future.

c. AWOS Broadcasts. Computer-generated voice is used in AWOS to automate the broadcast of the minute-by-minute weather observations. In addition, some systems are configured to permit the addition of an operator-generated voice message; e.g., weather remarks following the automated parameters. The phraseology used generally follows that used for other weather broadcasts. Following are explanations and examples of the exceptions.

1. Location and Time. The location/name and the phrase "AUTOMATED WEATHER OBSERVATION," followed by the time are announced.

(a) If the airport's specific location is included in the airport's name, the airport's name is announced.

Example:
"Bremerton National Airport automated weather observation, one four five six zulu;"

"Ravenswood Jackson County Airport automated weather observation, one four five six zulu."

(b) If the airport's specific location is not included in the airport's name, the location is announced followed by the airport's name.

Example:
"Sault Ste. Marie, Chippewa County International Airport automated weather observation;"

"Sandusky, Cowley Field automated weather observation."

(c) The word "TEST" is added following "OBSERVATION" when the system is not in commissioned status.

Example: "Bremerton National Airport automated weather observation test, one four five six zulu."

(d) The phrase "TEMPORARILY INOPERATIVE" is added when the system is inoperative.

Example: "Bremerton National Airport automated weather observing system temporarily inoperative."

2. Visibility.

(a) The lowest reportable visibility value in AWOS is "less than 1/4." It is announced as "VISIBILITY LESS THAN ONE QUARTER."

(b) A sensor for determining visibility is not included in some AWOS. In these systems, visibility is not announced. "VISIBILITY MISSING" is announced only if the system is configured with a visibility sensor and visibility information is not available.

3. Weather. In the future, some AWOS's are to be configured to determine the occurrence of precipitation. However, the type and intensity may not always be determined. In these systems, the word "PRECIPITATION" will be announced if precipitation is occurring, but the type and intensity are not determined.

4. Ceiling and Sky Cover.

(a) Ceiling is announced as either "CEILING" or "INDEFINITE CEILING." With the exception of indefinite ceilings, all automated ceiling heights are measured.

Example:
"Bremerton National Airport automated weather observation, one four five six zulu. Ceiling two thousand overcast;"

"Bremerton National Airport automated weather observation, one four five six zulu. Indefinite ceiling two hundred, sky obscured."

(b) The word "Clear" is not used in AWOS due to limitations in the height ranges of the sensors. No clouds detected is announced as "NO CLOUDS BELOW XXX" or, in newer systems as "CLEAR BELOW XXX" (where XXX is the range limit of the sensor).

Example:
"No clouds below one two thousand."
"Clear below one two thousand."

(c) A sensor for determining ceiling and sky cover is not included in some AWOS. In these systems, ceiling and sky cover are not announced. "SKY CONDITION MISSING" is announced only if the system is configured with a ceilometer and the ceiling and sky cover information is not available.

5. Remarks. If remarks are included in the observation, the word "REMARKS" is announced following the altimeter setting.

(a) Automated "Remarks."

(1) Density Altitude.

(2) Variable Visibility.

(3) Variable Wind Direction.

(b) Manual Input Remarks. Manual input remarks are prefaced with the phrase "OBSERVER WEATHER." As a general rule the manual remarks are limited to:

(1) Type and intensity of precipitation.

(2) Thunderstorms and direction; and

(3) Obstructions to vision when the visibility is 3 miles or less.

Example: "Remarks...density altitude, two thousand five hundred...visibility variable between one and two...wind direction variable between two four zero and three one zero...observed weather...thunderstorm moderate rain showers and fog...thunderstorm overhead."

(c) If an automated parameter is "missing" and no manual input for that parameter is available, the parameter is announced as "MISSING." For example, a report with the dew point "missing" and no manual input available, would be announced as follows:

Example: "Ceiling one thousand overcast...visibility three...precipitation...temperature three zero, dew point missing...wind calm...altimeter three zero zero one."

(d) "REMARKS" are announced in the following order of priority:

(1) Automated "REMARKS."

[a] Density Altitude.

[b] Variable Visibility.

[c] Variable Wind Direction.

(2) Manual Input "REMARKS."

[a] Sky Condition.

[b] Visibility.

[c] Weather and Obstructions to Vision.

[d] Temperature.

Ch 7

[e] Dew Point.
[f] Wind; and
[g] Altimeter Setting.

Example: *"Remarks...density altitude, two thousand five hundred...visibility variable between one and two...wind direction variable between two four zero and three one zero...observer ceiling estimated two thousand broken...observer temperature two, dew point minus five."*

d. Automated Surface Observing System (ASOS)/Automated Weather Observing System (AWOS) The ASOS/AWOS is the primary surface weather observing system of the U.S. (See Key to Decode an ASOS/AWOS (METAR) Observation, Figure 7-1-8 and Figure 7-1-9.) The program to install and operate these systems throughout the U.S. is a joint effort of the NWS, the FAA and the Department of Defense. ASOS/AWOS is designed to support aviation operations and weather forecast activities. The ASOS/AWOS will provide continuous minute-by-minute observations and perform the basic observing functions necessary to generate an aviation routine weather report (METAR) and other aviation weather information. The information may be transmitted over a discrete VHF radio frequency or the voice portion of a local NAVAID. ASOS/AWOS transmissions on a discrete VHF radio frequency are engineered to be receivable to a maximum of 25 NM from the ASOS/AWOS site and a maximum altitude of 10,000 feet AGL. At many locations, ASOS/AWOS signals may be received on the surface of the airport, but local conditions may limit the maximum reception distance and/or altitude. While the automated system and the human may differ in their methods of data collection and interpretation, both produce an observation quite similar in form and content. For the "objective" elements such as pressure, ambient temperature, dew point temperature, wind, and precipitation accumulation, both the automated system and the observer use a fixed location and time-averaging technique. The quantitative differences between the observer and the automated observation of these elements are negligible. For the "subjective" elements, however, observers use a fixed time, spatial averaging technique to describe the visual elements (sky condition, visibility and present weather), while the automated systems use a fixed location, time averaging technique. Although this is a fundamental change, the manual and automated techniques yield remarkably similar results within the limits of their respective capabilities.

1. System Description.
(a) The ASOS/AWOS at each airport location consists of these main components:
(1) Individual weather sensors.
(2) Data collection and processing units.

(3) Peripherals and displays.
(b) The ASOS/AWOS sensors perform the basic function of data acquisition. They continuously sample and measure the ambient environment, derive raw sensor data and make them available to the collection and processing units.

2. Every ASOS/AWOS will contain the following basic set of sensors:
(a) Cloud height indicator (one or possibly three).
(b) Visibility sensor (one or possibly three).
(c) Precipitation identification sensor.
(d) Freezing rain sensor (at select sites).
(e) Pressure sensors (two sensors at small airports; three sensors at large airports).
(f) Ambient temperature/Dew point temperature sensor.
(g) Anemometer (wind direction and speed sensor).
(h) Rainfall accumulation sensor.
(i) Automated Lightning Detection and Reporting System (ALDARS) (excluding Alaska and Pacific Island sites).

3. The ASOS/AWOS data outlets include:
(a) Those necessary for on-site airport users.
(b) National communications networks.
(c) Computer-generated voice (available through FAA radio broadcast to pilots, and dial-in telephone line).

Note: *Wind direction is reported relative to magnetic north in ATIS as well as ASOS and AWOS radio (voice) broadcasts.*

4. An ASOS/AWOS report without human intervention will contain only that weather data capable of being reported automatically. The modifier for this METAR report is "AUTO." When an observer augments or backs-up an ASOS/AWOS site, the "AUTO" modifier disappears.

5. There are two types of automated stations, AO1 for automated weather reporting stations without a precipitation discriminator, and AO2 for automated stations with a precipitation discriminator. As appropriate, "AO1" and "AO2" must appear in remarks. (A precipitation discriminator can determine the difference between liquid and frozen/freezing precipitation).

Note: *To decode an ASOS/AWOS report, refer to Figure 7-1-8 and Figure 7-1-9.*

Reference: *A complete explanation of METAR terminology is located in AIM, ¶7-1-28, Key to Aerodrome Forecast (TAF) and Aviation Routine Weather Report (METAR).*

FIGURE 7–1–8

Key to Decode an ASOS/AWOS (METAR) Observation (Front)

```
METAR KABC 121755Z AUTO 21016G24KT 180V240 1SM R11/P6000FT -RA BR BKN015 OVC025 06/04 A2990
RMK AO2 PK WND 20032/25 WSHFT 1715 VIS 3/4V1 1/2 VIS 3/4 RWY11 RAB07 CIG 013V017 CIG 017 RWY11 PRESFR
SLP125 P0003 6009 T00640036 10066 21012 58033 TSNO $
```

TYPE OF REPORT	METAR: hourly (scheduled) report; SPECI: special (unscheduled) report.	METAR
STATION IDENTIFIER	Four alphabetic characters; ICAO location identifier.	KABC
DATE/TIME	All dates and times in UTC using a 24-hour clock; two-digit date and four-digit time; always appended with $\underline{Z}$ to indicate UTC.	121755Z
REPORT MODIFIER	Fully automated report, no human intervention; removed when observer signed-on.	AUTO
WIND DIRECTION AND SPEED	Direction in tens of degrees from true north (first three digits); next two digits: speed in whole knots; as needed Gusts (character) followed by maximum observed speed; always appended with $\underline{KT}$ to indicate knots; 00000KT for calm; if direction varies by 60° or more a Variable wind direction group is reported.	21016G24KT 180V240
VISIBILITY	Prevailing visibility in statute miles and fractions (space between whole miles and fractions); always appended with $\underline{SM}$ to indicate statute miles; values <1/4 reported as M1/4.	1SM
RUNWAY VISUAL RANGE	10-minute RVR value in hundreds of feet; reported if prevailing visibility is ≤ one mile or RVR ≤ 6000 feet; always appended with $\underline{FT}$ to indicate feet; value prefixed with $\underline{M}$ or $\underline{P}$ to indicate value is lower or higher than the reportable RVR value .	R11/P6000FT
WEATHER PHENOMENA	RA: liquid precipitation that does not freeze; SN: frozen precipitation other than hail; UP: precipitation of unknown type; intensity prefixed to precipitation: light (-), moderate (no sign), heavy (+); FG: fog; FZFG: freezing fog (temperature below 0°C); BR: mist; HZ: haze; SQ: squall; maximum of three groups reported; augmented by observer: FC (funnel cloud/tornado/waterspout); TS (thunderstorm); GR (hail); GS (small hail; <1/4 inch); FZRA (intensity; freezing rain); VA (volcanic ash).	-RA BR
SKY CONDITION	Cloud amount and height: CLR (no clouds detected below 12000 feet); FEW (few); SCT (scattered); BKN (broken); OVC (overcast); followed by 3-digit height in hundreds of feet; or vertical visibility ($\underline{VV}$) followed by height for indefinite ceiling.	BKN015 OVC025
TEMPERATURE/DEW POINT	Each is reported in whole degrees Celsius using two digits; values are separated by a solidus; sub-zero values are prefixed with an $\underline{M}$ (minus).	06/04
ALTIMETER	Altimeter always prefixed with an $\underline{A}$ indicating inches of mercury; reported using four digits: tens, units, tenths, and hundredths.	A2990

FIGURE 7-1-9
Key to Decode an ASOS/AWOS (METAR) Observation (Back)

Description	RMK
REMARKS IDENTIFIER: RMK	RMK
TORNADIC ACTIVITY: Augmented; report should include TORNADO, FUNNEL CLOUD, or WATERSPOUT, time begin/end, location, movement; e.g., TORNADO B25 N MOV E.	
TYPE OF AUTOMATED STATION: AO2: automated station with precipitation discriminator.	AO2
PEAK WIND: PK WND dddff(f)/(hh)mm; direction in tens of degrees, speed in whole knots, and time.	PK WND 20032/25
WIND SHIFT: WSHFT (hh)mm	WSHFT 1715
TOWER OR SURFACE VISIBILITY: TWR VIS vvvvv: visibility reported by tower personnel, e.g., TWR VIS 2; SFC VIS vvvvv: visibility reported by ASOS, e.g., SFC VIS 2	
VARIABLE PREVAILING VISIBILITY: VIS $v_nv_nv_nv_nVv_xv_xv_xv_x$; reported if prevailing visibility is < 3 miles and variable.	VIS 3/4V1 1/2
VISIBILITY AT SECOND LOCATION: VIS vvvvv [LOC]; reported if different than the reported prevailing visibility in body of report.	VIS 3/4 RWY11
LIGHTNING: [FREQ] LTG [LOC]; when detected the frequency and location is reported, e.g., FRQ LTG NE.	
BEGINNING AND ENDING OF PRECIPITATION AND THUNDERSTORMS: w'w'B(hh)mmE(hh)mm; TSB(hh)mmE(hh)mm	RAB07
VIRGA: Augmented; precipitation not reaching the ground, e.g., VIRGA.	
VARIABLE CEILING HEIGHT: CIG $h_nh_nh_nVh_xh_xh_x$; reported if ceiling in body of report is < 3000 feet and variable.	CIG 013V017
CEILING HEIGHT AT SECOND LOCATION: CIG hhh [LOC]; Ceiling height reported if secondary ceilometer site is different than the ceiling height in the body of the report.	CIG 017 RWY11
PRESSURE RISING OR FALLING RAPIDLY: PRESRR or PRESFR; pressure rising or falling rapidly at time of observation.	PRESFR
SEA-LEVEL PRESSURE: SLPppp; tens, units, and tenths of SLP in hPa.	SLP125
HOURLY PRECIPITATION AMOUNT: Prrrr; in .01 inches since last METAR; a trace is P0000.	P0003
3- AND 6-HOUR PRECIPITATION AMOUNT: 6RRRR; precipitation amount in .01 inches for past 6 hours reported in 00, 06, 12, 18 UTC observations and for past 3 hours in 03, 09, 15, and 21 UTC observations; a trace is 60000.	60009
24-HOUR PRECIPITATION AMOUNT: $7R_{24}R_{24}R_{24}R_{24}$; precipitation amount in .01 inches for past 24 hours reported in 12 UTC observation, e.g., 70015.	
HOURLY TEMPERATURE AND DEW POINT: $Ts_nT_aT_aT_as_nT_aT_aT_a$: tenth of degree Celsius; s_n: 1 if temperature below 0°C and 0 if temperature 0°C or higher.	T00640036
6-HOUR MAXIMUM TEMPERATURE: $1s_nT_xT_xT_x$; tenth of degree Celsius; s_n: 1 if temperature below 0°C and 0 if temperature 0°C or higher.	10066
6-HOUR MINIMUM TEMPERATURE: $2s_nT_nT_nT_n$: tenth of degree Celsius; s_n: 1 if temperature below 0°C and 0 if temperature 0°C or higher.	21012
24-HOUR MAXIMUM AND MINIMUM TEMPERATURE: $4s_nT_xT_xT_xs_nT_nT_nT_n$: tenth of degree Celsius; reported at midnight local standard time; 1 if temperature below 0°C and 0 if temperature 0°C or higher, e.g., 400461006.	
PRESSURE TENDENCY: 5appp; the character (a) and change in pressure (ppp; tenths of hPa) the past 3 hours.	58033
SENSOR STATUS INDICATORS: RVRNO: RVR missing; PWINO: precipitation identifier information not available; PNO: precipitation amount not available; FZRANO: freezing rain information not available; TSNO: thunderstorm information not available; VISNO [LOC]: visibility at secondary location not available, e.g., VISNO RWY06; CHINO [LOC]: (cloud-height-indicator) sky condition at secondary location not available, e.g., CHINO RWY06.	TSNO
MAINTENANCE CHECK INDICATOR: Maintenance needed on the system.	$

If an element or phenomena does not occur, is missing, or cannot be observed, the corresponding group and space are omitted (body and/or remarks) from that particular report, except for Sea-Level Pressure (SLPppp). SLPNO shall be reported in a METAR when the SLP is not available.

U.S. DEPARTMENT OF TRANSPORTATION • FEDERAL AVIATION ADMINISTRATION • Aviation Weather Directorate, 400 7th Street, SW, Rooms 8200-8326, Washington, D.C. 20591

e. Table 7-1-5 contains a comparison of weather observing programs and the elements reported.

f. Service Standards. During 1995, a government/industry team worked to comprehensively reassess the requirements for surface observations at the nation's airports. That work resulted in agreement on a set of service standards, and the FAA and NWS ASOS sites to which the standards would apply. The term "Service Standards" refers to the level of detail in weather observation. The service standards consist of four different levels of service (A, B, C, and D) as described below. Specific observational elements included in each service level are listed in Table 7-1-6.

1. Service Level D defines the minimum acceptable level of service. It is a completely automated service in which the ASOS/AWOS observation will constitute the entire observation, i.e., no additional weather information is added by a human observer. This service is referred to as a stand alone D site.

2. Service Level C is a service in which the human observer, usually an air traffic controller, augments or adds information to the automated observation. Service Level C also includes backup of ASOS/AWOS elements in the event of an ASOS/AWOS malfunction or an unrepresentative ASOS/AWOS report. In backup, the human observer inserts the correct or missing value for the automated ASOS/AWOS elements. This service is provided by air traffic controllers under the Limited Aviation Weather Reporting Station (LAWRS) process, FSS and NWS observers, and, at selected sites, Non-Federal Observation Program observers.

Two categories of airports require detail beyond Service Level C in order to enhance air traffic control efficiency and increase system capacity. Services at these airports are typically provided by contract weather observers, NWS observers, and, at some locations, FSS observers.

3. Service Level B is a service in which weather observations consist of all elements provided under Service Level C, plus augmentation of additional data beyond the capability of the ASOS/AWOS. This category of airports includes smaller hubs or special airports in other ways that have worse than average bad weather operations for thunderstorms and/or freezing/frozen precipitation, and/or that are remote airports.

4. Service Level A, the highest and most demanding category, includes all the data reported in Service Standard B, plus additional requirements as specified. Service Level A covers major aviation hubs and/or high volume traffic airports with average or worse weather.

TABLE 7-1-5
WEATHER OBSERVING PROGRAMS

Type	Wind	Visibility	Temperature / Dew Point	Altimeter	Density Altimeter	Cloud/Ceiling	Precipitation Identification	Thunderstorm/ Lightning	Precipitation Occurrence	Rainfall Accumulation	Runway Surface Condition	Freezing Rain Occurrence	Remarks
ASOS	X	X	X	X	X	X	X				X	X	X
AWOS-A				X									
AWOS-A/V		X		X									
AWOS-1	X		X	X	X								
AWOS-2	X	X	X	X	X								
AWOS-3	X	X	X	X	X	X							
AWOS-3P	X	X	X	X	X	X	X						
AWOS-3T	X	X	X	X	X	X		X					
AWOS-3P/T	X	X	X	X	X	X	X	X					
AWOS-4	X	X	X	X	X	X	X	X	X	X	X	X	
Manual	X	X	X	X		X	X						X

Reference: FAA Order 7900.5, Surface Weather Observing, for element reporting.

Ch 7

TABLE 7–1–6

Service Level A	
Service Level A consists of all the elements of Service Levels B, C and D plus the elements listed to the right, if observed.	10 minute longline RVR at precedented sites or additional visibility increments of 1/8, 1/16 and 0 Sector visibility Variable sky condition Cloud layers above 12,000 feet and cloud types Widespread dust, sand and other obscurations Volcanic eruptions
Service Level B	
Service Level B consists of all the elements of Service Levels C and D plus the elements listed to the right, if observed.	Longline RVR at precedented sites (may be instantaneous readout) Freezing drizzle versus freezing rain Ice pellets Snow depth & snow increasing rapidly remarks Thunderstorm and lightning location remarks Observed significant weather not at the station remarks
Service Level C	
Service Level C consists of all the elements of Service Level D plus augmentation and backup by a human observer or an air traffic control specialist on location nearby. Backup consists of inserting the correct value if the system malfunctions or is unrepresentative. Augmentation consists of adding the elements listed to the right, if observed. During hours that the observing facility is closed, the site reverts to Service Level D.	Thunderstorms Tornadoes Hail Virga Volcanic ash Tower visibility Operationally significant remarks as deemed appropriate by the observer
Service Level D	
This level of service consists of an ASOS or AWOS continually measuring the atmosphere at a point near the runway. The ASOS or AWOS senses and measures the weather parameters listed to the right.	Wind Visibility Precipitation/Obstruction to vision Cloud height Sky cover Temperature Dew point Altimeter

7–1–11 Weather Radar Services

a. The National Weather Service operates a network of radar sites for detecting coverage, intensity, and movement of precipitation. The network is supplemented by FAA and DOD radar sites in the western sections of the country. Local warning radar sites augment the network by operating on an as needed basis to support warning and forecast programs.

b. Scheduled radar observations are taken hourly and transmitted in alpha-numeric format on weather telecommunications circuits for flight planning purposes. Under certain conditions, special radar reports are issued in addition to the hourly transmittals. Data contained in the reports are also collected by the National Center for Environmental Prediction and used to prepare national radar summary charts for dissemination on facsimile circuits.

c. A clear radar display (no echoes) does not mean that there is no significant weather within the coverage of the radar site. Clouds and fog are not detected by the radar. However, when echoes are present, turbulence can be implied by the intensity of the precipitation, and icing is implied by the presence of the precipitation at temperatures at or below zero degrees Celsius. Used in conjunction with other weather products, radar provides invaluable information for weather avoidance and flight planning.

d. All En Route Flight Advisory Service facilities and FSSs have equipment to directly access the radar displays from the individual weather radar sites. Specialists at these locations are trained to interpret the display for pilot briefing and inflight advisory services. The Center Weather Service Units located in ARTCCs also have access to weather radar displays and provide support to all air traffic facilities within their center's area.

e. For more detailed information on PIREPS, users can refer to the current version of the *Aviation Weather Handbook*, FAA-H-8083-28.

Reference: Pilot/Controller Glossary Term— Precipitation Radar Weather Descriptions; AIM, ¶7-1-26, Thunderstorms; Chart Supplement, Charts, NWS Upper Air Observing Stations and Weather Network for the location of specific radar sites.

FIGURE 7-1-10
NEXRAD Coverage

FIGURE 7-1-11
NEXRAD Coverage

FIGURE 7–1–12
NEXRAD Coverage

7-1-12 ATC Inflight Weather Avoidance Assistance

a. ATC Radar Weather Display.

1. ATC radars are able to display areas of precipitation by sending out a beam of radio energy that is reflected back to the radar antenna when it strikes an object or moisture which may be in the form of rain drops, hail, or snow. The larger the object is, or the more dense its reflective surface, the stronger the return will be presented. Radar weather processors indicate the intensity of reflective returns in terms of decibels (dBZ). ATC systems cannot detect the presence or absence of clouds. The ATC systems can often determine the intensity of a precipitation area, but the specific character of that area (snow, rain, hail, VIRGA, etc.) cannot be determined. For this reason, ATC refers to all weather areas displayed on ATC radar scopes as "precipitation."

2. All ATC facilities using radar weather processors with the ability to determine precipitation intensity, will describe the intensity to pilots as:

(a) "LIGHT" (<26 dBZ)
(b) "MODERATE" (26 to 40 dBZ)
(c) "HEAVY" (>40 to 50 dBZ)
(d) "EXTREME" (>50 dBZ)

Note: Enroute ATC radar's Weather and Radar Processor (WARP) does not display light precipitation intensity.

3. ATC facilities that, due to equipment limitations, cannot display the intensity levels of precipitation, will describe the location of the precipitation area by geographic position, or position relative to the aircraft. Since the intensity level is not available, the controller will state "INTENSITY UNKNOWN."

4. ARTCC facilities normally use a Weather and Radar Processor (WARP) to display a mosaic of data obtained from multiple NEXRAD sites. There is a time delay between actual conditions and those displayed to the controller. For example, the precipitation data on the ARTCC controller's display could be up to 6 minutes old. When the WARP is not available, a second system, the narrowband Air Route Surveillance Radar (ARSR) can display two distinct levels of precipitation intensity that will be described to pilots as "MODERATE" (30 to 40 dBZ) and "HEAVY TO EXTREME" (>40 dBZ). The WARP processor is only used in ARTCC facilities.

5. *ATC radar is not able to detect turbulence.* Generally, turbulence can be expected to occur as the rate of rainfall or intensity of precipitation increases. Turbulence associated with greater rates of rainfall/precipitation will normally be more severe than any associated with lesser rates of rainfall/precipitation. Turbulence should be expected to occur near convective activity, even in clear air. Thunderstorms are a form of convective activity that imply severe or greater turbulence. Operation within 20 miles of thunderstorms should be approached with great caution, as the severity of turbulence can be markedly greater than the precipitation intensity might indicate.

b. Weather Avoidance Assistance.

1. To the extent possible, controllers will issue pertinent information on weather or chaff areas and assist pilots in avoiding such areas when requested. Pilots should respond to a weather advisory by either acknowledging the advisory or by acknowledging the advisory and requesting an alternative course of action as follows:

(a) Request to deviate off course by stating a heading or degrees, direction of deviation, and approximate number of miles. In this case, when the requested deviation is approved, navigation is at the pilot's prerogative, but must maintain the altitude assigned, and remain within the lateral restrictions issued by ATC.

(b) An approval for lateral deviation authorizes the pilot to maneuver left or right within the lateral limits specified in the clearance.

Note 1: It is often necessary for ATC to restrict the amount of lateral deviation ("twenty degrees right," "up to fifteen degrees left," "up to ten degrees left or right of course").

Note 2: The term "when able, proceed direct," in an ATC weather deviation clearance, refers to the pilot's ability to remain clear of the weather when returning to course/route.

(c) Request a new route to avoid the affected area.

(d) Request a change of altitude.

(e) Request radar vectors around the affected areas.

2. For obvious reasons of safety, an IFR pilot must not deviate from the course or altitude or flight level without a proper ATC clearance. When weather conditions encountered are so severe that an immediate deviation is determined to be necessary and time will not permit approval by ATC, the pilot's emergency authority may be exercised.

3. When the pilot requests clearance for a route deviation or for an ATC radar vector, the controller must evaluate the air traffic picture in the affected area, and coordinate with other controllers (if ATC jurisdictional boundaries may be crossed) before replying to the request.

4. It should be remembered that the controller's primary function is to provide safe separation between aircraft. Any additional service, such as weather avoidance assistance, can only be provided to the extent that it does not derogate the primary function. It's also worth noting that the separation workload is generally greater than normal when weather disrupts the usual flow of

traffic. ATC radar limitations and frequency congestion may also be a factor in limiting the controller's capability to provide additional service.

5. It is very important, therefore, that the request for deviation or radar vector be forwarded to ATC as far in advance as possible. Delay in submitting it may delay or even preclude ATC approval or require that additional restrictions be placed on the clearance. Insofar as possible the following information should be furnished to ATC when requesting clearance to detour around weather activity:

(a) Proposed point where detour will commence.

(b) Proposed route and extent of detour (direction and distance).

(c) Point where original route will be resumed.

(d) Flight conditions (IFR or VFR).

(e) Any further deviation that may become necessary as the flight progresses.

(f) Advise if the aircraft is equipped with functioning airborne radar.

6. To a large degree, the assistance that might be rendered by ATC will depend upon the weather information available to controllers. Due to the extremely transitory nature of severe weather situations, the controller's weather information may be of only limited value if based on weather observed on radar only. Frequent updates by pilots giving specific information as to the area affected, altitudes, intensity and nature of the severe weather can be of considerable value. Such reports are relayed by radio or phone to other pilots and controllers and also receive widespread teletypewriter dissemination.

7. Obtaining IFR clearance or an ATC radar vector to circumnavigate severe weather can often be accommodated more readily in the en route areas away from terminals because there is usually less congestion and, therefore, offer greater freedom of action. In terminal areas, the problem is more acute because of traffic density, ATC coordination requirements, complex departure and arrival routes, adjacent airports, etc. As a consequence, controllers are less likely to be able to accommodate all requests for weather detours in a terminal area or be in a position to volunteer such routing to the pilot. Nevertheless, pilots should not hesitate to advise controllers of any observed severe weather and should specifically advise controllers if they desire circumnavigation of observed weather.

7-1-13 Runway Visual Range (RVR)

There are currently two configurations of RVR in the NAS commonly identified as Taskers and New Generation RVR. The Taskers are the existing configuration which uses transmissometer technology. The New Generation RVRs were

deployed in November 1994 and use forward scatter technology. The New Generation RVRs are currently being deployed in the NAS to replace the existing Taskers.

a. RVR values are measured by transmissometers mounted on 14-foot towers along the runway. A full RVR system consists of:

1. Transmissometer projector and related items.

2. Transmissometer receiver (detector) and related items.

3. Analog recorder.

4. Signal data converter and related items.

5. Remote digital or remote display programmer.

b. The transmissometer projector and receiver are mounted on towers 250 feet apart. A known intensity of light is emitted from the projector and is measured by the receiver. Any obscuring matter such as rain, snow, dust, fog, haze or smoke reduces the light intensity arriving at the receiver. The resultant intensity measurement is then converted to an RVR value by the signal data converter. These values are displayed by readout equipment in the associated air traffic facility and updated approximately once every minute for controller issuance to pilots.

c. The signal data converter receives information on the high intensity runway edge light setting in use (step 3, 4, or 5); transmission values from the transmissometer and the sensing of day or night conditions. From the three data sources, the system will compute appropriate RVR values.

d. An RVR transmissometer established on a 250 foot baseline provides digital readouts to a minimum of 600 feet, which are displayed in 200 foot increments to 3,000 feet and in 500 foot increments from 3,000 feet to a maximum value of 6,000 feet.

e. RVR values for Category IIIa operations extend down to 700 feet RVR; however, only 600 and 800 feet are reportable RVR increments. The 800 RVR reportable value covers a range of 701 feet to 900 feet and is therefore a valid minimum indication of Category IIIa operations.

f. Approach categories with the corresponding minimum RVR values. (See Table 7-1-7.)

TABLE 7-1-7
APPROACH CATEGORY/MINIMUM RVR TABLE

Category	Visibility (RVR)
Nonprecision	2,400 feet
Category I	1,800 feet*
Category II	1,000 feet
Category IIIa	700 feet
Category IIIb	150 feet
Category IIIc	0 feet

*1,400 feet with special equipment and authorization

g. Ten minute maximum and minimum RVR values for the designated RVR runway are reported in the body of the aviation weather report when the prevailing visibility is less than one mile and/or the RVR is 6,000 feet or less. ATCTs report RVR when the prevailing visibility is 1 mile or less and/or the RVR is 6,000 feet or less.

h. Details on the requirements for the operational use of RVR are contained in FAA AC 97-1, "Runway Visual Range (RVR)." Pilots are responsible for compliance with minimums prescribed for their class of operations in the appropriate CFRs and/or operations specifications.

i. RVR values are also measured by forward scatter meters mounted on 14-foot frangible fiberglass poles. A full RVR system consists of:

1. Forward scatter meter with a transmitter, receiver and associated items.

2. A runway light intensity monitor (RLIM).

3. An ambient light sensor (ALS).

4. A data processor unit (DPU).

5. Controller display (CD).

j. The forward scatter meter is mounted on a 14-foot frangible pole. Infrared light is emitted from the transmitter and received by the receiver. Any obscuring matter such as rain, snow, dust, fog, haze or smoke increases the amount of scattered light reaching the receiver. The resulting measurement along with inputs from the runway light intensity monitor and the ambient light sensor are forwarded to the DPU which calculates the proper RVR value. The RVR values are displayed locally and remotely on controller displays.

k. The runway light intensity monitors both the runway edge and centerline light step settings (steps 1 through 5). Centerline light step settings are used for CAT IIIb operations. Edge Light step settings are used for CAT I, II, and IIIa operations.

l. New Generation RVRs can measure and display RVR values down to the lowest limits of Category IIIb operations (150 feet RVR). RVR values are displayed in 100 feet increments and are reported as follows:

1. 100-feet increments for products below 800 feet.

2. 200-feet increments for products between 800 feet and 3,000 feet.

3. 500-feet increments for products between 3,000 feet and 6,500 feet.

4. 25-meter increments for products below 150 meters.

5. 50-meter increments for products between 150 meters and 800 meters.

6. 100-meter increments for products between 800 meters and 1,200 meters.

7. 200-meter increments for products between 1,200 meters and 2,000 meters.

7-1-14 Reporting of Cloud Heights

a. Ceiling, by definition in the CFRs and as used in aviation weather reports and forecasts, is the height above ground (or water) level of the lowest layer of clouds or obscuring phenomenon that is reported as "broken," "overcast," or "obscuration," e.g., an aerodrome forecast (TAF) which reads "BKN030" refers to height above ground level. An area forecast which reads "BKN030" indicates that the height is above mean sea level.

Reference: AIM, ¶7-1-28, Key to Aerodrome Forecast (TAF) and Aviation Routine Weather Report (METAR), defines "broken," "overcast," and "obscuration."

b. Pilots usually report height values above MSL, since they determine heights by the altimeter. This is taken in account when disseminating and otherwise applying information received from pilots. ("Ceiling" heights are always above ground level.) In reports disseminated as PIREPs, height references are given the same as received from pilots, that is, above MSL.

c. In area forecasts or inflight advisories, ceilings are denoted by the contraction "CIG" when used with sky cover symbols as in "LWRG TO CIG OVC005," or the contraction "AGL" after, the forecast cloud height value. When the cloud base is given in height above MSL, it is so indicated by the contraction "MSL" or "ASL" following the height value. The heights of clouds tops, freezing level, icing, and turbulence are always given in heights above ASL or MSL.

7-1-15 Reporting Prevailing Visibility

a. Surface (horizontal) visibility is reported in METAR reports in terms of statute miles and increments thereof; e.g., 1/16, 1/8, 3/16, 1/4, 5/16, 3/8, 1/2, 5/8, 3/4, 7/8, 1, 1 1/8, etc. (Visibility reported by an unaugmented automated site is reported differently than in a manual report, i.e., ASOS/AWOS: 0, 1/16, 1/8, 1/4, 1/2, 3/4, 1, 1 1/4, 1 1/2, 1 3/4, 2, 2 1/2, 3, 4, 5, etc., AWOS: M1/4, 1/4, 1/2, 3/4, 1, 1 1/4, 1 1/2, 1 3/4, 2, 2 1/2, 3, 4, 5, etc.) Visibility is determined through the ability to see and identify preselected and prominent objects at a known distance from the usual point of observation. Visibilities which are determined to be less than 7 miles, identify the obscuring atmospheric condition; e.g., fog, haze, smoke, etc., or combinations thereof.

b. Prevailing visibility is the greatest visibility equaled or exceeded throughout at least one half of the horizon circle, not necessarily contiguous. Segments of the horizon circle which may have a significantly different visibility may be reported in the remarks section of the weather report; i.e., the southeastern quadrant of the horizon circle may be determined to be 2 miles in mist while

the remaining quadrants are determined to be 3 miles in mist.

c. When the prevailing visibility at the usual point of observation, or at the tower level, is less than 4 miles, certificated tower personnel will take visibility observations in addition to those taken at the usual point of observation. The lower of these two values will be used as the prevailing visibility for aircraft operations.

7-1-16 Estimating Intensity of Rain and Ice Pellets

a. Rain

1. Light. From scattered drops that, regardless of duration, do not completely wet an exposed surface up to a condition where individual drops are easily seen.

2. Moderate. Individual drops are not clearly identifiable; spray is observable just above pavements and other hard surfaces.

3. Heavy. Rain seemingly falls in sheets; individual drops are not identifiable; heavy spray to height of several inches is observed over hard surfaces.

b. Ice Pellets

1. Light. Scattered pellets that do not completely cover an exposed surface regardless of duration. Visibility is not affected.

2. Moderate. Slow accumulation on ground. Visibility reduced by ice pellets to less than 7 statute miles.

3. Heavy. Rapid accumulation on ground. Visibility reduced by ice pellets to less than 3 statute miles.

7-1-17 Estimating Intensity of Snow or Drizzle (Based on Visibility)

a. Light. Visibility more than 1/2 statute mile.

b. Moderate. Visibility from more than 1/4 statute mile to 1/2 statute mile.

c. Heavy. Visibility 1/4 statute mile or less.

7-1-18 Pilot Weather Reports (PIREPs)

a. FAA air traffic facilities are required to solicit PIREPs when the following conditions are reported or forecast: ceilings at or below 5,000 feet; visibility at or below 5 miles (surface or aloft); thunderstorms and related phenomena; icing of light degree or greater; turbulence of moderate degree or greater; wind shear and reported or forecast volcanic ash clouds.

b. Pilots are urged to cooperate and promptly volunteer reports of these conditions and other atmospheric data such as: cloud bases, tops and layers; flight visibility; precipitation; visibility restrictions such as haze, smoke and dust; wind at altitude; and temperature aloft.

c. PIREPs should be given to the ground facility with which communications are established; i.e., FSS, ARTCC, or terminal ATC. One of the primary duties of the Inflight position is to serve as a collection point for the exchange of PIREPs with en route aircraft.

d. If pilots are not able to make PIREPs by radio, reporting upon landing of the inflight conditions encountered to the nearest FSS or Weather Forecast Office will be helpful. Some of the uses made of the reports are:

1. The ATCT uses the reports to expedite the flow of air traffic in the vicinity of the field and for hazardous weather avoidance procedures.

2. The FSS uses the reports to brief other pilots, to provide inflight advisories, and weather avoidance information to en route aircraft.

3. The ARTCC uses the reports to expedite the flow of en route traffic, to determine most favorable altitudes, and to issue hazardous weather information within the center's area.

4. The NWS uses the reports to verify or amend conditions contained in aviation forecast and advisories. In some cases, pilot reports of hazardous conditions are the triggering mechanism for the issuance of advisories. They also use the reports for pilot weather briefings.

5. The NWS, other government organizations, the military, and private industry groups use PIREPs for research activities in the study of meteorological phenomena.

6. All air traffic facilities and the NWS forward the reports received from pilots into the weather distribution system to assure the information is made available to all pilots and other interested parties.

e. The FAA, NWS, and other organizations that enter PIREPs into the weather reporting system use the format listed in Table 7-1-8. Items 1 through 6 are included in all transmitted PIREPs along with one or more of items 7 through 13. Although the PIREP should be as complete and concise as possible, pilots should not be overly concerned with strict format or phraseology. The important thing is that the information is relayed so other pilots may benefit from your observation. If a portion of the report needs clarification, the ground station will request the information. Completed PIREPs will be transmitted to weather circuits as in the following examples:

Example 1:
KCMH UA /OV APE 230010/TM 1516/FL085/TP BE20/SK BKN065/WX FV03SM HZ FU/TA 20/ TB LGT

Note 1: *One zero miles southwest of Appleton VOR; time 1516 UTC; altitude eight thousand five hundred; aircraft type BE200; bases of the broken cloud layer is six thousand five hundred; flight*

visibility 3 miles with haze and smoke; air temperature 20 degrees Celsius; light turbulence.

Example 2:
KCRW UV /OV KBKW 360015-KCRW/TM 1815/ FL120//TP BE99/SK IMC/WX RA/TA M08 /WV 290030/TB LGT-MDT/IC LGT RIME/RM MDT MXD ICG DURC KROA NWBND FL080-100 1750Z

Note 2: From 15 miles north of Beckley VOR to Charleston VOR; time 1815 UTC; altitude 12,000 feet; type aircraft, BE-99; in clouds; rain; temperature minus 8 Celsius; wind 290 degrees magnetic at 30 knots; light to moderate turbulence; light rime icing during climb northwestbound from Roanoke, VA, between 8,000 and 10,000 feet at 1750 UTC.

f. For more detailed information on PIREPs, users can refer to the current version of the *Aviation Weather Handbook*, FAA-H-8083-28.

TABLE 7-1-8
PIREP ELEMENT CODE CHART

	PIREP Element	PIREP Code	Contents
1.	3-letter station identifier	XXX	Nearest weather reporting location to the reported phenomenon
2.	Report type	UA or UUA	Routine or Urgent PIREP
3.	Location	/OV	In relation to a VOR
4.	Time	/TM	Coordinated Universal Time
5.	Altitude	/FL	Essential for turbulence and icing reports
6.	Type Aircraft	/TP	Essential for turbulence and icing reports
7.	Sky cover	/SK	Cloud height and coverage (sky clear, few, scattered, broken, or overcast)
8.	Weather	/WX	Flight visibility, precipitation, restrictions to visibility, etc.
9.	Temperature	/TA	Degrees Celsius
10.	Wind	/WV	Direction in degrees magnetic north and speed in knots
11.	Turbulence	/TB	See AIM paragraph 7-1-21
12.	Icing	/IC	See AIM paragraph 7-1-19
13.	Remarks	/RM	For reporting elements not included or to clarify previously reported items

7-1-19 PIREPs Relating to Airframe Icing

a. The effects of ice on aircraft are cumulative—thrust is reduced, drag increases, lift lessens, and weight increases. The results are an increase in stall speed and a deterioration of aircraft performance. In extreme cases, 2 to 3 inches of ice can form on the leading edge of the airfoil in less than 5 minutes. It takes but 1/2 inch of ice to reduce the lifting power of some aircraft by 50 percent and increases the frictional drag by an equal percentage.

b. A pilot can expect icing when flying in visible precipitation, such as rain or cloud droplets, and the temperature is between +02 and -10 degrees Celsius. When icing is detected, a pilot should do one of two things, particularly if the aircraft is not equipped with deicing equipment; get out of the area of precipitation; or go to an altitude where the temperature is above freezing. This "warmer" altitude may not always be a lower altitude. Proper preflight action includes obtaining information on the freezing level and the above freezing levels in precipitation areas. Report icing to ATC, and if operating IFR, request new routing or altitude if icing will be a hazard. Be sure to give the type of aircraft to ATC when reporting icing. The following describes how to report icing conditions.

1. Trace. Ice becomes noticeable. The rate of accumulation is slightly greater than the rate of sublimation. A representative accretion rate for reference purposes is less than ¼ inch (6 mm) per hour on the outer wing. The pilot should consider exiting the icing conditions before they become worse.

2. Light. The rate of ice accumulation requires occasional cycling of manual deicing systems to minimize ice accretions on the airframe. A representative accretion rate for reference purposes is ¼ inch to 1 inch (0.6 to 2.5 cm) per hour on the unprotected part of the outer wing. The pilot should consider exiting the icing condition.

3. Moderate. The rate of ice accumulation requires frequent cycling of manual deicing systems to minimize ice accretions on the airframe. A representative accretion rate for reference purposes is 1 to 3 inches (2.5 to 7.5 cm) per hour on the unprotected part of the outer wing. The pilot should consider exiting the icing condition as soon as possible.

4. Severe. The rate of ice accumulation is such that ice protection systems fail to remove the accumulation of ice and ice accumulates in

locations not normally prone to icing, such as areas aft of protected surfaces and any other areas identified by the manufacturer. A representative accretion rate for reference purposes is more than 3 inches (7.5 cm) per hour on the unprotected part of the outer wing. By regulation, immediate exit is required.

Note: Severe icing is aircraft dependent, as are the other categories of icing intensity. Severe icing may occur at any ice accumulation rate when the icing rate or ice accumulations exceed the tolerance of the aircraft.

Example: Pilot report: give aircraft identification, location, time (UTC), intensity of type, altitude/FL, aircraft type, indicated air speed (IAS), and outside air temperature (OAT).

Note 1: Rime ice. Rough, milky, opaque ice formed by the instantaneous freezing of small supercooled water droplets.

Note 2: Clear ice. A glossy, clear, or translucent ice formed by the relatively slow freezing of large supercooled water droplets.

Note 3: The OAT should be requested by the FSS or ATC if not included in the PIREP.

7–1–20 Definitions of Inflight Icing Terms

See Table 7-1-9, Icing Types, and Table 7-1-10, Icing Conditions.

TABLE 7–1–9
ICING TYPES

Clear Ice	See Glaze Ice.
Glaze Ice	Ice, sometimes clear and smooth, but usually containing some air pockets, which results in a lumpy translucent appearance. Glaze ice results from supercooled drops/droplets striking a surface but not freezing rapidly on contact. Glaze ice is denser, harder, and sometimes more transparent than rime ice. Factors, which favor glaze formation, are those that favor slow dissipation of the heat of fusion (i.e., slight supercooling and rapid accretion). With larger accretions, the ice shape typically includes "horns" protruding from unprotected leading edge surfaces. It is the ice shape, rather than the clarity or color of the ice, which is most likely to be accurately assessed from the cockpit. The terms "clear" and "glaze" have been used for essentially the same type of ice accretion, although some reserve "clear" for thinner accretions which lack horns and conform to the airfoil.
Intercycle Ice	Ice which accumulates on a protected surface between actuation cycles of a deicing system.
Known or Observed or Detected Ice Accretion	Actual ice observed visually to be on the aircraft by the flight crew or identified by on-board sensors.
Mixed Ice	Simultaneous appearance or a combination of rime and glaze ice characteristics. Since the clarity, color, and shape of the ice will be a mixture of rime and glaze characteristics, accurate identification of mixed ice from the cockpit may be difficult.
Residual Ice	Ice which remains on a protected surface immediately after the actuation of a deicing system.
Rime Ice	A rough, milky, opaque ice formed by the rapid freezing of supercooled drops/droplets after they strike the aircraft. The rapid freezing results in air being trapped, giving the ice its opaque appearance and making it porous and brittle. Rime ice typically accretes along the stagnation line of an airfoil and is more regular in shape and conformal to the airfoil than glaze ice. It is the ice shape, rather than the clarity or color of the ice, which is most likely to be accurately assessed from the cockpit.
Runback Ice	Ice which forms from the freezing or refreezing of water leaving protected surfaces and running back to unprotected surfaces.

Note: Ice types are difficult for the pilot to discern and have uncertain effects on an airplane in flight. Ice type definitions will be included in the AIM for use in the "Remarks" section of the PIREP and for use in forecasting.

Ch 7

TABLE 7–1–10
ICING CONDITIONS

Appendix C Icing Conditions	Appendix C (14 CFR, Part 25 and 29) is the certification icing condition standard for approving ice protection provisions on aircraft. The conditions are specified in terms of altitude, temperature, liquid water content (LWC), representative droplet size (mean effective drop diameter [MED]), and cloud horizontal extent.
Forecast Icing Conditions	Environmental conditions expected by a National Weather Service or an FAA-approved weather provider to be conducive to the formation of inflight icing on aircraft.
Freezing Drizzle (FZDZ)	Drizzle is precipitation at ground level or aloft in the form of liquid water drops which have diameters less than 0.5 mm and greater than 0.05 mm. Freezing drizzle is drizzle that exists at air temperatures less than 0°C (supercooled), remains in liquid form, and freezes upon contact with objects on the surface or airborne.
Freezing Precipitation	Freezing precipitation is freezing rain or freezing drizzle falling through or outside of visible cloud.
Freezing Rain (FZRA)	Rain is precipitation at ground level or aloft in the form of liquid water drops which have diameters greater than 0.5 mm. Freezing rain is rain that exists at air temperatures less than 0°C (supercooled), remains in liquid form, and freezes upon contact with objects on the ground or in the air.
Icing in Cloud	Icing occurring within visible cloud. Cloud droplets (diameter < 0.05 mm) will be present; freezing drizzle and/or freezing rain may or may not be present.
Icing in Precipitation	Icing occurring from an encounter with freezing precipitation, that is, supercooled drops with diameters exceeding 0.05 mm, within or outside of visible cloud.
Known Icing Conditions	Atmospheric conditions in which the formation of ice is observed or detected in flight. *Note: Because of the variability in space and time of atmospheric conditions, the existence of a report of observed icing does not assure the presence or intensity of icing conditions at a later time, nor can a report of no icing assure the absence of icing conditions at a later time.*
Potential Icing Conditions	Atmospheric icing conditions that are typically defined by airframe manufacturers relative to temperature and visible moisture that may result in aircraft ice accretion on the ground or in flight. The potential icing conditions are typically defined in the Airplane Flight Manual or in the Airplane Operation Manual.
Supercooled Drizzle Drops (SCDD)	Synonymous with freezing drizzle aloft.
Supercooled Drops or Droplets	Water drops/droplets which remain unfrozen at temperatures below 0°C. Supercooled drops are found in clouds, freezing drizzle, and freezing rain in the atmosphere. These drops may impinge and freeze after contact on aircraft surfaces.
Supercooled Large Drops (SLD)	Liquid droplets with diameters greater than 0.05 mm at temperatures less than 0°C, i.e., freezing rain or freezing drizzle.

7-1-21 PIREPs Relating to Turbulence

a. When encountering turbulence, pilots are urgently requested to report such conditions to ATC as soon as practicable. PIREPs relating to turbulence should state:

 1. Aircraft location.
 2. Time of occurrence in UTC.
 3. Turbulence intensity.
 4. Whether the turbulence occurred in or near clouds.
 5. Aircraft altitude or flight level.
 6. Type of aircraft.
 7. Duration of turbulence.

Example 1: Over Omaha, 1232Z, moderate turbulence in clouds at Flight Level three one zero, Boeing 707.

Example 2: From five zero miles south of Albuquerque to three zero miles north of Phoenix, 1250Z, occasional moderate chop at Flight Level three three zero, DC8.

b. Duration and classification of intensity should be made using Table 7-1-11.

TABLE 7–1–11
TURBULENCE REPORTING CRITERIA TABLE

Intensity	Aircraft Reaction	Reaction Inside Aircraft	Reporting Term: Definition
Light	Turbulence that momentarily causes slight, erratic changes in altitude and/or attitude (pitch, roll, yaw). Report as **Light Turbulence**;[1] or Turbulence that causes slight, rapid and somewhat rhythmic bumpiness without appreciable changes in altitude or attitude. Report as **Light Chop**.	Occupants may feel a slight strain against seat belts or shoulder straps. Unsecured objects may be displaced slightly. Food service may be conducted and little or no difficulty is encountered in walking.	Occasional: Less than 1/3 of the time Intermittent: 1/3 to 2/3 Continuous: More than 2/3
Moderate	Turbulence that is similar to Light Turbulence but of greater intensity. Changes in altitude and/or attitude occur but the aircraft remains in positive control at all times. It usually causes variations in indicated airspeed. Report as **Moderate Turbulence**;[1] or Turbulence that is similar to Light Chop but of greater intensity. It causes rapid bumps or jolts without appreciable changes in aircraft altitude or attitude. Report as **Moderate Chop**.[1]	Occupants feel definite strains against seat belts or shoulder straps. Unsecured objects are dislodged. Food service and walking are difficult.	**Notes** 1. Pilots should report location(s), time (UTC), intensity, whether in or near clouds, altitude, type of aircraft and, when applicable, duration of turbulence. 2. Duration may be based on time between two locations or over a single location. All locations should be readily identifiable.
Severe	Turbulence that causes large, abrupt changes in altitude and/or attitude. It usually causes large variations in indicated airspeed. Aircraft may be momentarily out of control. Report as **Severe Turbulence**.[1]	Occupants are forced violently against seat belts or shoulder straps. Unsecured objects are tossed about. Food Service and walking are impossible.	**Examples** a. Over Omaha. 1232Z, Moderate Turbulence, in cloud, Flight Level 310, B707. b. From 50 miles south of Albuquerque to 30 miles north of Phoenix, 1210Z to 1250Z, occasional Moderate Chop, Flight Level 330, DC8.
Extreme	Turbulence in which the aircraft is violently tossed about and is practically impossible to control. It may cause structural damage. Report as **Extreme Turbulence**.[1]		

[1] High level turbulence (normally above 15,000 feet ASL) not associated with cumuliform cloudiness, including thunderstorms, should be reported as CAT (clear air turbulence) preceded by the appropriate intensity, or light or moderate chop.

7-1-22 Wind Shear PIREPs

a. Because unexpected changes in wind speed and direction can be hazardous to aircraft operations at low altitudes on approach to and departing from airports, pilots are urged to promptly volunteer reports to controllers of wind shear conditions they encounter. An advance warning of this information will assist other pilots in avoiding or coping with a wind shear on approach or departure.

b. When describing conditions, use of the terms "negative" or "positive" wind shear should be avoided. PIREPs of "negative wind shear on final," intended to describe loss of airspeed and lift, have been interpreted to mean that no wind shear was encountered. The recommended method for wind shear reporting is to state the loss or gain of airspeed and the altitudes at which it was encountered.

Example 1: Denver Tower, Cessna 1234 encountered wind shear, loss of 20 knots at 400.

Example 2: Tulsa Tower, American 721 encountered wind shear on final, gained 25 knots between 600 and 400 feet followed by loss of 40 knots between 400 feet and surface.

1. Pilots who are not able to report wind shear in these specific terms are encouraged to make reports in terms of the effect upon their aircraft.

Example: Miami Tower, Gulfstream 403 Charlie encountered an abrupt wind shear at 800 feet on final, max thrust required.

2. Pilots using Inertial Navigation Systems (INSs) should report the wind and altitude both above and below the shear level.

Ch 7

c. Wind Shear Escape

1. Pilots should report to ATC when they are performing a wind shear escape maneuver. This report should be made as soon as practicable, but not until aircraft safety and control is assured, which may not be satisfied until the aircraft is clear of the wind shear or microburst. ATC should provide safety alerts and traffic advisories, as appropriate.

Example: "Denver Tower, United 1154, wind shear escape."

2. Once the pilot initiates a wind shear escape maneuver, ATC is not responsible for providing approved separation between the aircraft and any other aircraft, airspace, terrain, or obstacle until the pilot reports that the escape procedure is complete and approved separation has been re-established. Pilots should advise ATC that they are resuming the previously assigned clearance or should request an alternate clearance.

Example: "Denver Tower, United ll54, wind shear escape complete, resuming last assigned heading/(name) DP/clearance."

or

"Denver Tower, United ll54, wind shear escape complete, request further instructions."

7-1-23 Clear Air Turbulence (CAT) PIREPs

CAT has become a very serious operational factor to flight operations at all levels and especially to jet traffic flying in excess of 15,000 feet. The best available information on this phenomenon must come from pilots via the PIREP reporting procedures. All pilots encountering CAT conditions are urgently requested to report time, location, and intensity (light, moderate, severe, or extreme) of the element to the FAA facility with which they are maintaining radio contact. If time and conditions permit, elements should be reported according to the standards for other PIREPs and position reports.

Reference: AIM, ¶7-1-21, PIREPs Relating to Turbulence.

7-1-24 Microbursts

a. Relatively recent meteorological studies have confirmed the existence of microburst phenomenon. Microbursts are small scale intense downdrafts which, on reaching the surface, spread outward in all directions from the downdraft center. This causes the presence of both vertical and horizontal wind shears that can be extremely hazardous to all types and categories of aircraft, especially at low altitudes. Due to their small size, short life span, and the fact that they can occur over areas without surface precipitation, microbursts are not easily detectable using conventional weather radar or wind shear alert systems.

b. Parent clouds producing microburst activity can be any of the low or middle layer convective cloud types. Note, however, that microbursts commonly occur within the heavy rain portion of thunderstorms, and in much weaker, benign appearing convective cells that have little or no precipitation reaching the ground.

c. The life cycle of a microburst as it descends in a convective rain shaft is seen in Figure 7-1-13. An important consideration for pilots is the fact that the microburst intensifies for about 5 minutes after it strikes the ground.

d. Characteristics of microbursts include:

1. Size. The microburst downdraft is typically less than 1 mile in diameter as it descends from the cloud base to about 1,000–3,000 feet above the ground. In the transition zone near the ground, the downdraft changes to a horizontal outflow that can extend to approximately 2½ miles in diameter.

2. Intensity. The downdrafts can be as strong as 6,000 feet per minute. Horizontal winds near the surface can be as strong as 45 knots resulting in a 90 knot shear (headwind to tailwind change for a traversing aircraft) across the microburst. These strong horizontal winds occur within a few hundred feet of the ground.

3. Visual Signs. Microbursts can be found almost anywhere that there is convective activity. They may be embedded in heavy rain associated with a thunderstorm or in light rain in benign appearing virga. When there is little or no precipitation at the surface accompanying the microburst, a ring of blowing dust may be the only visual clue of its existence.

4. Duration. An individual microburst will seldom last longer than 15 minutes from the time it strikes the ground until dissipation. The horizontal winds continue to increase during the first 5 minutes with the maximum intensity winds lasting approximately 2–4 minutes. Sometimes microbursts are concentrated into a line structure, and under these conditions, activity may continue for as long as an hour. Once microburst activity starts, multiple microbursts in the same general area are not uncommon and should be expected.

e. Microburst wind shear may create a severe hazard for aircraft within 1,000 feet of the ground, particularly during the approach to landing and landing and take-off phases. The impact of a microburst on aircraft which have the unfortunate experience of penetrating one is characterized in Figure 7-1-14. The aircraft may encounter a headwind (performance increasing) followed by a downdraft and tailwind (both performance decreasing), possibly resulting in terrain impact.

FIGURE 7–1–13
Evolution of a Microburst

Vertical cross section of the evolution of a microburst wind field. T is the time of initial divegence at the surface. The shading refers to the vector wind speeds. Figure adapted from Wilson et al., 1984, Microburst Wind Structure and Evaluation of Doppler Radar for Wind Shear Detection, DOT/FAA Report No. DOT/FAA/PM-84/29, National Technical Information Service, Springfield, VA 37 pp.

FIGURE 7–1–14
Microburst Encounter During Takeoff

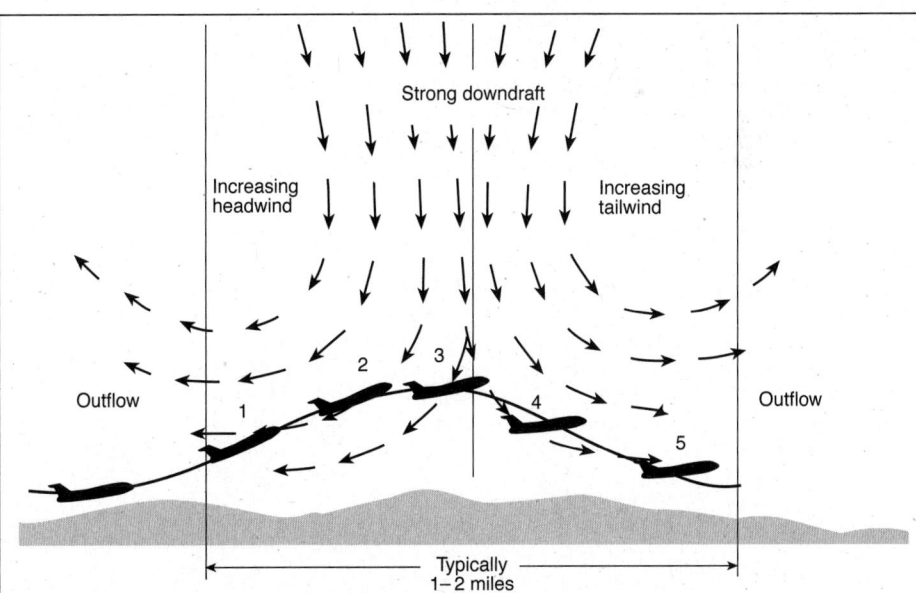

A microburst encounter during takeoff. The airplane first encounters a headwind and experiences increasing performance (1), This is followed in short succession by a decreasing headwind component (2), a downdraft (3), and finally a strong tailwind (4), where 2 through 5 all result in decreasing performance of the airplane. Position (5) represents an extreme situation just prior to impact. Figure courtesy of Walter Frost, FWG Associates, Inc., Tullahoma, Tennessee.

f. Detection of Microbursts, Wind Shear and Gust Fronts.

1. FAA's Integrated Wind Shear Detection Plan.

(a) The FAA currently employs an integrated plan for wind shear detection that will significantly improve both the safety and capacity of the majority of the airports currently served by the air carriers. This plan integrates several programs, such as the Integrated Terminal Weather System (ITWS), Terminal Doppler Weather Radar (TDWR), Weather Systems Processor (WSP), and Low Level Wind Shear Alert Systems (LLWAS) into a single strategic concept that significantly improves the aviation weather information in the terminal area. (See Figure 7-1-15.)

(b) The wind shear/microburst information and warnings are displayed on the ribbon display terminals (RBDT) located in the tower cabs. They are identical (and standardized) in the LLWAS, TDWR and WSP systems, and so designed that the controller does not need to interpret the data, but simply read the displayed information to the pilot. The RBDTs are constantly monitored by the controller to ensure the rapid and timely dissemination of any hazardous event(s) to the pilot.

(c) The early detection of a wind shear/micro-burst event, and the subsequent warning(s) issued to an aircraft on approach or departure, will alert the pilot/crew to the potential of, and to be prepared for, a situation that could become very dangerous! Without these warnings, the aircraft may NOT be able to climb out of, or safely transition, the event, resulting in a catastrophe.

The air carriers, working with the FAA, have developed specialized training programs using their simulators to train and prepare their pilots on the demanding aircraft procedures required to escape these very dangerous wind shear and/or microburst encounters.

2. Low Level Wind Shear Alert System (LLWAS).

(a) The LLWAS provides wind data and software processes to detect the presence of hazardous wind shear and microbursts in the vicinity of an airport. Wind sensors, mounted on poles sometimes as high as 150 feet, are (ideally) located 2,000–3,500 feet, but not more than 5,000 feet, from the centerline of the runway. (See Figure 7-1-16.)

(b) LLWAS was fielded in 1988 at 110 airports across the nation. Many of these systems have been replaced by new TDWR and WSP technology. While all legacy LLWAS systems will eventually be phased out, 39 airports will be upgraded to LLWAS-NE (Network Expansion) system. The new LLWAS-NE systems not only provide the controller with wind shear warnings and alerts, including wind shear/microburst detection at the airport wind sensor location, but also provide the location of the hazards relative to the airport runway(s). It also has the flexibility and capability to grow with the airport as new runways are built. As many as 32 sensors, strategically located around the airport and in relationship to its runway configuration, can be accommodated by the LLWAS-NE network.

FIGURE 7-1-15
NAS Wind Shear Product Systems

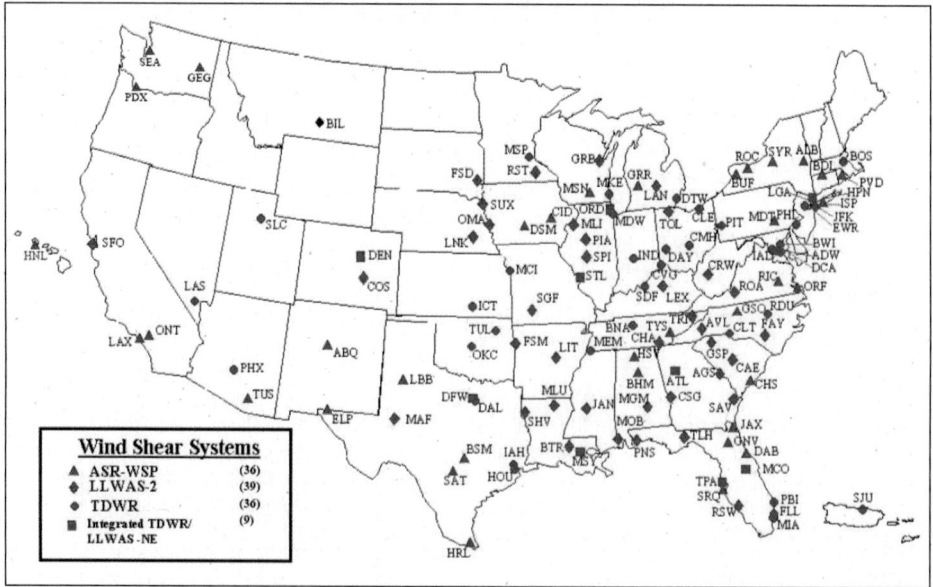

FIGURE 7-1-16
LLWAS Siting Criteria

3. Terminal Doppler Weather Radar (TDWR).

(a) TDWRs have been deployed at 45 locations across the U.S. Optimum locations for TDWRs are 8 to 12 miles off of the airport proper, and designed to look at the airspace around and over the airport to detect microbursts, gust fronts, wind shifts and precipitation intensities. TDWR products advise the controller of wind shear and microburst events impacting all runways and the areas 1/2 mile on either side of the extended centerline of the runways out to 3 miles on final approach and 2 miles out on departure. (Figure 7-1-17 is a theoretical view of the warning boxes, including the runway, that the software uses in determining the location(s) of wind shear or microbursts). These warnings are displayed (as depicted in the examples in subparagraph 5) on the RBDT.

(b) It is very important to understand what TDWR does **not do**:

(1) It **does not** warn of wind shear outside of the alert boxes (on the arrival and departure ends of the runways);

(2) It **does not** detect wind shear that is **not** a microburst or a gust front;

(3) It **does not** detect gusty or cross wind conditions; and

(4) It **does not** detect turbulence.

However, research and development is continuing on these systems. Future improvements may include such areas as storm motion (movement), improved gust front detection, storm growth and decay, microburst prediction, and turbulence detection.

(c) TDWR also provides a geographical situation display (GSD) for supervisors and traffic management specialists for planning purposes. The GSD displays (in color) 6 levels of weather (precipitation), gust fronts and predicted storm movement(s). This data is used by the tower supervisor(s), traffic management specialists and controllers to plan for runway changes and arrival/departure route changes in order to both reduce aircraft delays and increase airport capacity.

FIGURE 7-1-17
Warning Boxes

4. Weather Systems Processor (WSP).

(a) The WSP provides the controller, supervisor, traffic management specialist, and ultimately the pilot, with the same products as the

terminal Doppler weather radar (TDWR) at a fraction of the cost of a TDWR. This is accomplished by utilizing new technologies to access the weather channel capabilities of the existing ASR-9 radar located on or near the airport, thus eliminating the requirements for a separate radar location, land acquisition, support facilities and the associated communication landlines and expenses.

(b) The WSP utilizes the same RBDT display as the TDWR and LLWAS, and, just like TDWR, also has a GSD for planning purposes by supervisors, traffic management specialists and controllers. The WSP GSD emulates the TDWR display, i.e., it also depicts 6 levels of precipitation, gust fronts and predicted storm movement, and like the TDWR GSD, is used to plan for runway changes and arrival/departure route changes in order to reduce aircraft delays and to increase airport capacity.

(c) This system is installed at 34 airports across the nation, substantially increasing the safety of flying.

5. Operational aspects of LLWAS, TDWR and WSP.
To demonstrate how this data is used by both the controller and the pilot, 3 ribbon display examples and their explanations are presented:

(a) Microburst Alerts

Example: This is what the controller sees on his/her ribbon display in the tower cab.

```
27A MBA 35K- 2MF 250 20
```

Note: (See Figure 7-1-18 to see how the TDWR/WSP determines the microburst location).

This is what the controller will say when issuing the alert.

Phraseology:
Runway 27 arrival, microburst alert, 35 kt loss 2 mile final, threshold wind 250 at 20.

In plain language, the controller is telling the pilot that on approach to runway 27, there is a microburst alert on the approach lane to the runway, and to anticipate or expect a 35 knot loss of airspeed at approximately 2 miles out on final approach (where it will first encounter the phenomena). With that information, the aircrew is forewarned, and should be prepared to apply wind shear/microburst escape procedures should they decide to continue the approach. Additionally, the surface winds at the airport for landing runway 27 are reported as 250 degrees at 20 knots.

Note: Threshold wind is at pilot's request or as deemed appropriate by the controller.

Reference: FAA Order JO 7110.65, ¶3-1-8b2(a), Air Traffic Control, Low Level Wind Shear/Microburst Advisories.

(b) Wind Shear Alerts

Example: This is what the controller sees on his/her ribbon display in the tower cab.

```
27A WSA 20K- 3MF 200 15
```

Note: (See Figure 7-1-19 to see how the TDWR/WSP determines the wind shear location).

This is what the controller will say when issuing the alert.

Phraseology:
Runway 27 arrival, wind shear alert, 20 kt loss 3 mile final, threshold wind 200 at 15.

In plain language, the controller is advising the aircraft arriving on runway 27 that at about 3 miles out they can expect to encounter a wind shear condition that will decrease their airspeed by 20 knots and possibly encounter turbulence. Additionally, the airport surface winds for landing runway 27 are reported as 200 degrees at 15 knots.

Note: Threshold wind is at pilot's request or as deemed appropriate by the controller.

Reference: FAA Order JO 7110.65, ¶3-1-8, Low Level Wind Shear/Microburst Advisories, Subpara b2(a).

(c) Multiple Wind Shear Alerts

Example: This is what the controller sees on his/her ribbon display in the tower cab.

```
27A WSA 20K+ RWY 250 20
27D WSA 20K+ RWY 250 20
```

Note: (See Figure 7-1-20 to see how the TDWR/WSP determines the gust front/wind shear location.)

This is what the controller will say when issuing the alert.

Phraseology:
Multiple wind shear alerts. Runway 27 arrival, wind shear alert, 20 kt gain on runway; Runway 27 departure, wind shear alert, 20 kt gain on runway, wind 250 at 20.

Example: In this example, the controller is advising arriving and departing aircraft that they could encounter a wind shear condition right on the runway due to a gust front (significant change of wind direction) with the possibility of a 20 knot gain in airspeed associated with the gust front. Additionally, the airport surface winds (for the runway in use) are reported as 250 degrees at 20 knots.

Reference: FAA Order 7110.65, ¶3-1-8, Low Level Wind Shear/Microburst Advisories, Subpara b2(d).

FIGURE 7–1–18
Microburst Alert

FIGURE 7–1–19
Weak Microburst Alert

FIGURE 7-1-20
Gust Front Alert

6. The Terminal Weather Information for Pilots System (TWIP).

(a) With the increase in the quantity and quality of terminal weather information available through TDWR, the next step is to provide this information directly to pilots rather than relying on voice communications from ATC. The NAS has long been in need of a means of delivering terminal weather information to the cockpit more efficiently in terms of both speed and accuracy to enhance pilot awareness of weather hazards and reduce air traffic controller workload. With the TWIP capability, terminal weather information, both alphanumerically and graphically, is now available directly to the cockpit for 46 airports in the U.S. NAS. (See Figure 7-1-21.)

FIGURE 7-1-21
TWIP Image of Convective Weather at MCO International

WEATHER SITUATION	TWIP TEXT MESSAGE
HEAVY PRECIP · MODERATE PRECIP	MCO 1800 TERMINAL WEATHER -STORM(S) 3NM N-E MOD PRECIP 4NM NE HVY PRECIP MOVG W AT 15KT .EXPECTED MOD PRECIP BEGIN 1805
20 · MICRO BURST	MCO 1810 TERMINAL WEATHER *MODERATE PRECIP BEGAN 1805 -STORM(S) ARPT ALQDS MOD PRECIP 1NM N-E HVY PRECIP MOVG W AT 15KT .EXPECTED HVY PRECIP BEGIN 1815

(b) TWIP products are generated using weather data from the TDWR or the Integrated Terminal Weather System (ITWS). These products can then be accessed by pilots using the Aircraft Communications Addressing and Reporting System (ACARS) data link services. Airline dispatchers can also access this database and send messages to specific aircraft whenever wind shear activity begins or ends at an airport.

(c) TWIP products include descriptions and character graphics of microburst alerts, wind shear alerts, significant precipitation, convective activity within 30 NM surrounding the terminal area, and expected weather that will impact airport operations. During inclement weather, i.e., whenever a predetermined level of precipitation or wind shear is detected within 15 miles of the terminal area, TWIP products are updated once each minute for text messages and once every five minutes for character graphic messages. During good weather (below the predetermined precipitation or wind shear parameters) each message is updated every 10 minutes. These products are intended to improve the situational awareness of the pilot/flight crew, and to aid in flight planning prior to arriving or departing the terminal area. It is important to understand that, in the context of TWIP, the predetermined levels for inclement versus good weather has nothing to do with the criteria for VFR/MVFR/IFR/LIFR; it only deals with precipitation, wind shears and microbursts.

TABLE 7-1-12
TWIP-EQUIPPED AIRPORTS

Airport	Identifier
Andrews AFB, MD	KADW
Hartsfield-Jackson Atlanta Intl Airport	KATL
Nashville Intl Airport	KBNA
Logan Intl Airport	KBOS
Baltimore/Washington Intl Airport	KBWI
Hopkins Intl Airport	KCLE
Charlotte/Douglas Intl Airport	KCLT
Port Columbus Intl Airport	KCMH
Cincinnati/Northern Kentucky Intl Airport	KCVG
Dallas Love Field Airport	KDAL
James M. Cox Intl Airport	KDAY
Ronald Reagan Washington National Airport	KDCA
Denver Intl Airport	KDEN
Dallas-Fort Worth Intl Airport	KDFW
Detroit Metro Wayne County Airport	KDTW
Newark Liberty Intl Airport	KEWR
Fort Lauderdale-Hollywood Intl Airport	KFLL
William P. Hobby Airport	KHOU
Washington Dulles Intl Airport	KIAD
George Bush Intercontinental Airport	KIAH
Wichita Mid-Continent Airport	KICT
Indianapolis Intl Airport	KIND
John F. Kennedy Intl Airport	KJFK
Harry Reid Intl Airport	KLAS
LaGuardia Airport	KLGA
Kansas City Intl Airport	KMCI
Orlando Intl Airport	KMCO
Midway Intl Airport	KMDW
Memphis Intl Airport	KMEM
Miami Intl Airport	KMIA
General Mitchell Intl Airport	KMKE
Minneapolis St. Paul Intl Airport	KMSP
Louis Armstrong New Orleans Intl Airport	KMSY
Will Rogers World Airport	KOKC
O'Hare Intl Airport	KORD
Palm Beach Intl Airport	KPBI
Philadelphia Intl Airport	KPHL
Phoenix Sky Harbor Intl Airport	KPHX
Pittsburgh Intl Airport	KPIT
Raleigh-Durham Intl Airport	KRDU
Louisville Intl Airport	KSDF
Salt Lake City Intl Airport	KSLC
Lambert-St. Louis Intl Airport	KSTL
Tampa Intl Airport	KTPA
Tulsa Intl Airport	KTUL
Luis Munoz Marin Intl Airport	TJSJ

7-1-25 PIREPs Relating to Volcanic Ash Activity

a. Volcanic eruptions which send ash into the upper atmosphere occur somewhere around the world several times each year. Flying into a volcanic ash cloud can be extremely dangerous. At least two B747s have lost all power in all four engines after such an encounter. Regardless of the type aircraft, some damage is almost certain to ensue after an encounter with a volcanic ash cloud. Additionally, studies have shown that volcanic eruptions are the only significant source of large quantities of sulphur dioxide (SO_2) gas at jet-cruising altitudes. Therefore, the detection and subsequent reporting of SO_2 is of significant importance. Although SO_2 is colorless, its presence in the atmosphere should be suspected when a sulphur-like or rotten egg odor is present throughout the cabin.

b. While some volcanoes in the U.S. are monitored, many in remote areas are not. These unmonitored volcanoes may erupt without prior warning to the aviation community. A pilot observing a volcanic eruption who has not had previous notification of it may be the only witness to the eruption. Pilots are strongly encouraged to transmit a PIREP regarding volcanic eruptions and any observed volcanic ash clouds or detection of sulphur dioxide (SO_2) gas associated with volcanic activity.

c. Pilots should submit PIREPs regarding volcanic activity using the Volcanic Activity Reporting (VAR) form as illustrated in Appendix 2. If a VAR form is not immediately available, relay enough information to identify the position and type of volcanic activity.

d. Pilots should verbally transmit the data required in items 1 through 8 of the VAR as soon as possible. The data required in items 9 through 16 of the VAR should be relayed after landing if possible.

7-1-26 Thunderstorms

a. Turbulence, hail, rain, snow, lightning, sustained updrafts and downdrafts, icing conditions—all are present in thunderstorms. While there is some evidence that maximum turbulence exists at the middle level of a thunderstorm, recent studies show little variation of turbulence intensity with altitude.

b. There is no useful correlation between the external visual appearance of thunderstorms and the severity or amount of turbulence or hail within them. The visible thunderstorm cloud is only a portion of a turbulent system whose updrafts and downdrafts often extend far beyond the visible storm cloud. Severe turbulence can be expected up to 20 miles from severe thunderstorms. This distance decreases to about 10 miles in less severe storms.

c. Weather radar, airborne or ground based, will normally reflect the areas of moderate to heavy precipitation (radar does not detect turbulence). The frequency and severity of turbulence generally increases with the radar reflectivity which is closely associated with the areas of highest liquid water content of the storm. NO FLIGHT PATH THROUGH AN AREA OF STRONG OR VERY STRONG RADAR ECHOES SEPARATED BY 20–30 MILES OR LESS MAY BE CONSIDERED FREE OF SEVERE TURBULENCE.

d. Turbulence beneath a thunderstorm should not be minimized. This is especially true when the relative humidity is low in any layer between the surface and 15,000 feet. Then the lower altitudes may be characterized by strong out flowing winds and severe turbulence.

e. The probability of lightning strikes occurring to aircraft is greatest when operating at altitudes where temperatures are between minus 5 degrees Celsius and plus 5 degrees Celsius. Lightning can strike aircraft flying in the clear in the vicinity of a thunderstorm.

f. METAR reports do not include a descriptor for severe thunderstorms. However, by understanding severe thunderstorm criteria, i.e., 50 knot winds or 3/4 inch hail, the information is available in the report to know that one is occurring.

g. Current weather radar systems are able to objectively determine precipitation intensity. These precipitation intensity areas are described as "light," "moderate," "heavy," and "extreme."

Reference: *Pilot/Controller Glossary— Precipitation Radar Weather Descriptions.*

Example 1: *Alert provided by an ATC facility to an aircraft:*
(aircraft identification) EXTREME precipitation between ten o'clock and two o'clock, one five miles. Precipitation area is two five miles in diameter.

Example 2: *Alert provided by an FSS:*
(aircraft identification) EXTREME precipitation two zero miles west of Atlanta V-O-R, two five miles wide, moving east at two zero knots, tops flight level three niner zero.

7-1-27 Thunderstorm Flying

a. Thunderstorm Avoidance. Never regard any thunderstorm lightly, even when radar echoes are of light intensity. Avoiding thunderstorms is the best policy. Following are some Do's and Don'ts of thunderstorm avoidance:

1. Don't land or takeoff in the face of an approaching thunderstorm. A sudden gust front of low level turbulence could cause loss of control.

2. Don't attempt to fly under a thunderstorm even if you can see through to the other side.

Turbulence and wind shear under the storm could be hazardous.

3. Don't attempt to fly under the anvil of a thunderstorm. There is a potential for severe and extreme clear air turbulence.

4. Don't fly without airborne radar into a cloud mass containing scattered embedded thunderstorms. Scattered thunderstorms not embedded usually can be visually circumnavigated.

5. Don't trust the visual appearance to be a reliable indicator of the turbulence inside a thunderstorm.

6. Don't assume that ATC will offer radar navigation guidance or deviations around thunderstorms.

7. Don't use data-linked weather next generation weather radar (NEXRAD) mosaic imagery as the sole means for negotiating a path through a thunderstorm area (tactical maneuvering).

8. Do remember that the data-linked NEXRAD mosaic imagery shows where the weather was, not where the weather is. The weather conditions depicted may be 15 to 20 minutes older than indicated on the display.

9. Do listen to chatter on the ATC frequency for Pilot Weather Reports (PIREP) and other aircraft requesting to deviate or divert.

10. Do ask ATC for radar navigation guidance or to approve deviations around thunderstorms, if needed.

11. Do use data-linked weather NEXRAD mosaic imagery (for example, Flight Information Service-Broadcast (FIS-B)) for route selection to avoid thunderstorms entirely (strategic maneuvering).

12. Do advise ATC, when switched to another controller, that you are deviating for thunderstorms before accepting to rejoin the original route.

13. Do ensure that after an authorized weather deviation, before accepting to rejoin the original route, that the route of flight is clear of thunderstorms.

14. Do avoid by at least 20 miles any thunderstorm identified as severe or giving an intense radar echo. This is especially true under the anvil of a large cumulonimbus.

15. Do circumnavigate the entire area if the area has 6/10 thunderstorm coverage.

16. Do remember that vivid and frequent lightning indicates the probability of a severe thunderstorm.

17. Do regard as extremely hazardous any thunderstorm with tops 35,000 feet or higher whether the top is visually sighted or determined by radar.

18. Do give a PIREP for the flight conditions.

19. Do divert and wait out the thunderstorms on the ground if unable to navigate around an area of thunderstorms.

20. Do contact Flight Service for assistance in avoiding thunderstorms. Flight Service specialists have NEXRAD mosaic radar imagery and NEXRAD single site radar with unique features such as base and composite reflectivity, echo tops, and VAD wind profiles.

b. If you cannot avoid penetrating a thunderstorm, following are some Do's before entering the storm:

1. Tighten your safety belt, put on your shoulder harness (if installed), and secure all loose objects.

2. Plan and hold the course to take the aircraft through the storm in a minimum time.

3. To avoid the most critical icing, establish a penetration altitude below the freezing level or above the level of $-15°C$.

4. Verify that pitot heat is on and turn on carburetor heat or jet engine anti-ice. Icing can be rapid at any altitude and cause almost instantaneous power failure and/or loss of airspeed indication.

5. Establish power settings for turbulence penetration airspeed recommended in the aircraft manual.

6. Turn up cockpit lights to highest intensity to lessen temporary blindness from lightning.

7. If using automatic pilot, disengage Altitude Hold Mode and Speed Hold Mode. The automatic altitude and speed controls will increase maneuvers of the aircraft thus increasing structural stress.

8. If using airborne radar, tilt the antenna up and down occasionally. This will permit the detection of other thunderstorm activity at altitudes other than the one being flown.

c. Following are some Do's and Don'ts during the thunderstorm penetration:

1. Do keep your eyes on your instruments. Looking outside the cockpit can increase danger of temporary blindness from lightning.

2. Don't change power settings; maintain settings for the recommended turbulence penetration airspeed.

3. Do maintain constant attitude. Allow the altitude and airspeed to fluctuate.

4. Don't turn back once you are in the thunderstorm. A straight course through the storm most likely will get the aircraft out of the hazards most quickly. In addition, turning maneuvers increase stress on the aircraft.

Ch 7

7-1-28 Key to Aerodrome Forecast (TAF) and Aviation Routine Weather Report (METAR)

FIGURE 7-1-22

Key to Aerodrome Forecast (TAF) and Aviation Routine Weather Report (METAR) *Front*

TAF	KPIT 091730Z 0918/1024 15005KT 5SM HZ FEW020 WS010/31022KT
	FM01930 30015G25KT 3SM SHRA OVC015
	TEMPO 0920/0922 1/2SM +TSRA OVC008CB
	FM100100 27008KT 5SM SHRA BKN020 OVC040
	PROB30 1004/1007 1SM -RA BR
	FM101015 18005KT 6SM -SHRA OVC020
	BECMG 1013/1015 P6SM NSW SKC

Note: Users are cautioned to confirm **DATE** and **TIME** of the TAF. For example FM**100000** is 0000Z on the **10th**. Do not confuse with **1000Z!**

METAR KPIT 091955Z COR 22015G25KT 3/4SM R28L/2600FT TSRA OVC010CB 18/16 A2992 RMK SLP045 T01820159

Forecast	Explanation	Report
TAF	Message type: <u>TAF</u>: routine or <u>TAF AMD</u>: amended forecast; <u>METAR</u>: hourly; <u>SPECI</u>: special or <u>TESTM</u>: noncommissioned ASOS report	**METAR**
KPIT	ICAO location indicator	**KPIT**
091730Z	Issuance time: ALL times in UTC "<u>Z</u>", 2-digit date, 4-digit time	**091955Z**
0918/1024	Valid period: Either 24 hours or 30 hours. The first two digits of EACH four-digit number indicate the date of the valid period, the final two digits indicate the time (valid from 18Z on the 9th to 24Z on the 10th).	
	In U.S. **METAR**: <u>COR</u>rected ob; or <u>AUTO</u>mated ob for automated report with no human intervention; omitted when observer logs on.	**COR**
15005KT	Wind: 3-digit true-north direction, nearest 10 degrees (or <u>VaRiaBle</u>); next 2–3 digits for speed and unit, <u>KT</u> (KMH or MPS); as needed, <u>G</u>ust and maximum speed; 00000KT for calm; for **METAR**, if direction varies 60 degrees or more, <u>V</u>ariability appended, e.g., 180<u>V</u>260	**22015G25KT**
5SM	Prevailing visibility: In U.S., <u>S</u>tatute <u>M</u>iles and fractions; above 6 miles in **TAF** <u>P</u>lus6<u>SM</u>. (Or, 4-digit minimum visibility in meters and as required, lowest value with direction.)	**3/4SM**
	Runway Visual Range: <u>R</u>; 2-digit runway designator <u>L</u>eft, <u>C</u>enter, or <u>R</u>ight as needed; " <u>/</u>"; <u>M</u>inus or <u>P</u>lus in U.S., 4-digit value, <u>Fee</u>T in U.S. (usually meters elsewhere); 4-digit value <u>V</u>ariability, 4-digit value (and tendency <u>D</u>own, <u>U</u>p, or <u>N</u>o change)	**R28L/2600FT**
HZ	Significant present, forecast and recent weather: See table (Fig 7-1-22)	**TSRA**
FEW020	Cloud amount, height and type: <u>SK</u>y <u>C</u>lear 0/8, <u>FEW</u> >0/8-2/8, <u>SC</u>a<u>T</u>tered 3/8-4/8, <u>B</u>ro<u>KeN</u> 5/8-7/8, <u>O</u>er<u>C</u>ast 8/8; 3-digit height in hundreds of feet; <u>T</u>owering <u>CU</u>mulus or <u>C</u>umulonim<u>B</u>us in **METAR**; in **TAF**, only <u>CB</u>. <u>V</u>ertical <u>V</u>isibility for obscured sky and height "VV004". More than 1 layer may be reported or forecast. In automated **METAR** reports only, <u>CL</u>ea<u>R</u> for "clear below 12,000 feet."	**OVC010CB**
	Temperature: Degrees Celsius; first 2 digits, temperature " <u>/</u>" last 2 digits, dewpoint temperature; <u>M</u>inus for below zero, e.g., M06	**18/16**
	Altimeter setting: Indicator and 4 digits; in U.S., <u>A</u>: inches and hundredths; (<u>Q</u>: hectoPascals, e.g., Q1013)	**A2992**
WS010/ 31022KT	In U.S. **TAF**, nonconvective low-level (<u><</u>2,000 feet) <u>W</u>ind <u>S</u>hear; 3-digit height (hundreds of feet); " <u>/</u>"; 3-digit wind direction and 2–3 digit wind speed above the indicated height, and unit, <u>KT</u>	

FIGURE 7–1–23
**Key to Aerodrome Forecast (TAF) and
Aviation Routine Weather Report (METAR)** *Back*

Forecast	Explanation	Report
	In **METAR**, ReMarK indicator and remarks. For example: Sea-Level Pressure in hectoPascals and tenths, as shown: 1004.5 hPa; Temp/dewpoint in tenths °C, as shown: temp. 18.2°C, dewpoint 15.9°C	RMK SLP045 T01820159
FM091930	FroM: Changes are expected at: 2-digit date, 2-digit hour, and 2-digit minute **beginning** time: indicates significant change. Each FM starts on a new line, indented 5 spaces	
TEMPO 0920/0922	TEMPOrary: Changes expected for <1 hour and in total, < half of the period between the 2-digit date and 2-digit hour **beginning**, and 2-digit date and 2-digit hour **ending** time	
PROB30 1004/1007	PROBability and 2-digit percent (30 or 40): Probable condition in the period between the 2-digit date and 2-digit hour **beginning** time, and the 2-digit date and 2-digit hour **ending** time	
BECMG 1013/1015	BECoMinG: Change expected in the period between the 2-digit date and 2-digit hour **beginning** time, and the 2-digit date and 2-digit hour **ending** time	

Table of Significant Present, Forecast and Recent Weather – Grouped in categories and used in the order listed below; or as needed in TAF, No Significant Weather

QUALIFIERS
Intensity or Proximity
"–" = Light **No sign** = Moderate "+" = Heavy

"**VC**" = Vicinity, but not at aerodrome. In the U.S. **METAR**, 5 to 10 SM from the point of observation.
 In the U.S. **TAF**, 5 to 10 SM from the center of the runway complex. Elsewhere, within 8000m.
Descriptor

BC Patches	**BL** Blowing	**DR** Drifting	**FZ** Freezing
MI Shallow	**PR** Partial	**SH** Showers	**TS** Thunderstorm

WEATHER PHENOMENA
Precipitation

DZ Drizzle	**GR** Hail	**GS** Small hail or snow pellets	
IC Ice crystals	**PL** Ice pellets	**RA** Rain	**SG** Snow grains
SN Snow	**UP** Unknown precipitation in automated observations		

Obscuration

BR Mist (≥5/8SM)	**DU** Widespread dust	**FG** Fog (<5/8SM)	**FU** Smoke
HZ Haze	**PY** Spray	**SA** Sand	**VA** Volcanic ash

Other

DS Dust storm	**FC** Funnel cloud	**+FC** Tornado or waterspout	
PO Well-developed dust or sand whirls	**SQ** Squall	**SS** Sandstorm	

• Explanations in parentheses "()" indicate different worldwide practices.
• Ceiling is not specified; defined as the lowest broken or overcast layer, or the vertical visibility.
• NWS **TAF**s exclude BECMG groups and temperature forecasts, NWS **TAF**s do not use PROB in the first 9 hours of a TAF; NWS **METAR**s exclude trend forecasts. U.S. Military **TAF**s include Turbulence and Icing groups.

August 2009

7-1-29 International Civil Aviation Organization (ICAO) Weather Formats

The U.S. uses the ICAO world standard for aviation weather reporting and forecasting. The World Meteorological Organization's (WMO) publication No. 782 "Aerodrome Reports and Forecasts" contains the base METAR and TAF code as adopted by the WMO member countries.

a. Although the METAR code is adopted worldwide, each country is allowed to make modifications or exceptions to the code for use in their particular country, e.g., the U.S. will continue to use statute miles for visibility, feet for RVR values, knots for wind speed, and inches of mercury for altimetry. However, temperature and dew point will be reported in degrees Celsius. The U.S. reports prevailing visibility rather than lowest sector visibility. The elements in the body of a METAR report are separated with a space. The only exceptions are RVR, temperature and dew point, which are separated with a solidus (/). When an element does not occur, or cannot be observed, the preceding space and that element are omitted from that particular report. A METAR report contains the following sequence of elements in the following order:

1. Type of report.
2. ICAO Station Identifier.
3. Date and time of report.
4. Modifier (as required).
5. Wind.
6. Visibility.
7. Runway Visual Range (RVR).
8. Weather phenomena.
9. Sky conditions.
10. Temperature/dew point group.
11. Altimeter.
12. Remarks (RMK).

b. The following paragraphs describe the elements in a METAR report.

1. Type of report. There are two types of report:

(a) Aviation Routine Weather Report (METAR); and

(b) Nonroutine (Special) Aviation Weather Report (SPECI).

The type of report (METAR or SPECI) will always appear as the lead element of the report.

2. ICAO Station Identifier. The METAR code uses ICAO 4-letter station identifiers. In the contiguous 48 States, the 3-letter domestic station identifier is prefixed with a "K;" i.e., the domestic identifier for Seattle is SEA while the ICAO identifier is KSEA. Elsewhere, the first two letters of the ICAO identifier indicate what region of the world and country (or state) the station is in. For Alaska, all station identifiers start with "PA;" for Hawaii, all station identifiers start with "PH."

Canadian station identifiers start with "CU," "CW," "CY," and "CZ." Mexican station identifiers start with "MM." The identifier for the western Caribbean is "M" followed by the individual country's letter; i.e., Cuba is "MU;" Dominican Republic "MD;" the Bahamas "MY." The identifier for the eastern Caribbean is "T" followed by the individual country's letter; i.e., Puerto Rico is "TJ." For a complete worldwide listing see ICAO Document 7910, Location Indicators.

3. Date and Time of Report. The date and time the observation is taken are transmitted as a six-digit date/time group appended with Z to denote Coordinated Universal Time (UTC). The first two digits are the date followed with two digits for hour and two digits for minutes.

Example: 172345Z (the 17th day of the month at 2345Z)

4. Modifier (As Required). "AUTO" identifies a METAR/SPECI report as an automated weather report with no human intervention. If "AUTO" is shown in the body of the report, the type of sensor equipment used at the station will be encoded in the remarks section of the report. The absence of "AUTO" indicates that a report was made manually by an observer or that an automated report had human augmentation/backup. The modifier "COR" indicates a corrected report that is sent out to replace an earlier report with an error.

Note: There are two types of automated stations, AO1 for automated weather reporting stations without a precipitation discriminator, and AO2 for automated stations with a precipitation discriminator. (A precipitation discriminator can determine the difference between liquid and frozen/freezing precipitation). This information appears in the remarks section of an automated report.

5. Wind. The wind is reported as a five digit group (six digits if speed is over 99 knots). The first three digits are the direction the wind is blowing from, in tens of degrees referenced to true north, or "VRB" if the direction is variable. The next two digits is the wind speed in knots, or if over 99 knots, the next three digits. If the wind is gusty, it is reported as a "G" after the speed followed by the highest gust reported. The abbreviation "KT" is appended to denote the use of knots for wind speed.

Example:

13008KT—wind from 130 degrees at 8 knots

08032G45KT—wind from 080 degrees at 32 knots with gusts to 45 knots

VRB04KT—wind variable in direction at 4 knots

00000KT—wind calm

210103G130KT—wind from 210 degrees at 103 knots with gusts to 130 knots

If the wind direction is variable by 60 degrees or more and the speed is greater than 6 knots, a variable group consisting of the extremes of the wind direction separated by a "v" will follow the prevailing wind group.

32012G22KT 280V350

(a) Peak Wind. Whenever the peak wind exceeds 25 knots "PK WND" will be included in Remarks, e.g., PK WND 28045/1955 "Peak wind two eight zero at four five occurred at one niner five five." If the hour can be inferred from the report time, only the minutes will be appended, e.g., PK WND 34050/38 "Peak wind three four zero at five zero occurred at three eight past the hour."

(b) Wind shift. Whenever a wind shift occurs, "WSHFT" will be included in remarks followed by the time the wind shift began, e.g., WSHFT 30 FROPA "Wind shift at three zero due to frontal passage."

6. Visibility. Prevailing visibility is reported in statute miles with "SM" appended to it.

Example:
7SM—seven statute miles
15SM—fifteen statute miles
1/2SM—one-half statute mile

(a) Tower/surface visibility. If either visibility (tower or surface) is below four statute miles, the lesser of the two will be reported in the body of the report; the greater will be reported in remarks.

(b) Automated visibility. ASOS/AWOS visibility stations will show visibility 10 or greater than 10 miles as "10SM." AWOS visibility stations will show visibility less than 1/4 statute mile as "M1/4SM" and visibility 10 or greater than 10 miles as "10SM."

Note: Automated sites that are augmented by human observer to meet service level requirements can report 0, 1/16 SM, and 1/8 SM visibility increments.

(c) Variable visibility. Variable visibility is shown in remarks (when rapid increase or decrease by 1/2 statute mile or more and the average prevailing visibility is less than three miles) e.g., VIS 1V2 "visibility variable between one and two."

(d) Sector visibility. Sector visibility is shown in remarks when it differs from the prevailing visibility, and either the prevailing or sector visibility is less than three miles.

Example: VIS N2—visibility north two

7. Runway Visual Range (When Reported). "R" identifies the group followed by the runway heading (and parallel runway designator, if needed) "/" and the visual range in feet (meters in other countries) followed with "FT" (feet is not spoken).

(a) Variability Values. When RVR varies (by more than on reportable value), the lowest and highest values are shown with "V" between them.

(b) Maximum/Minimum Range. "P" indicates an observed RVR is above the maximum value for this system (spoken as "more than"). "M" indicates an observed RVR is below the minimum value which can be determined by the system (spoken as "less than").

Example:
R32L/1200FT—runway three two left R-V-R one thousand two hundred.

R27R/M1000V4000FT—runway two seven right R-V-R variable from less than one thousand to four thousand.

8. Weather Phenomena. The weather as reported in the METAR code represents a significant change in the way weather is currently reported. In METAR, weather is reported in the format:

Intensity/Proximity/Descriptor/Precipitation/Obstruction to visibility/Other

Note: The "/" above and in the following descriptions (except as the separator between the temperature and dew point) are for separation purposes in this publication and do not appear in the actual METARs.

(a) Intensity applies only to the first type of precipitation reported. A "–" denotes light, no symbol denotes moderate, and a "+" denotes heavy.

(b) Proximity applies to and reported only for weather occurring in the vicinity of the airport (between 5 and 10 miles of the point(s) of observation). It is denoted by the letters "VC." (Intensity and "VC" will not appear together in the weather group).

(c) Descriptor. These eight descriptors apply to the precipitation or obstructions to visibility:

TS ... thunderstorm
DR .. low drifting
SH .. showers
MI ..shallow
FZ ..freezing
BC ..patches
BL .. blowing
PR ..partial

Note: Although "TS" and "SH" are used with precipitation and may be preceded with an intensity symbol, the intensity still applies to the precipitation, not the descriptor.

(d) Precipitation. There are nine types of precipitation in the METAR code:

RA ..rain
DZ.. drizzle
SN.. snow
GR hail (1/4" or greater)
GS small hail/snow pellets
PL .. ice pellets
SG .. snow grains
IC ice crystals (diamond dust)
UP....................................unknown precipitation
(automated stations only)

(e) Obstructions to visibility. There are eight types of obscuration phenomena in the METAR code (obscurations are any phenomena in the atmosphere, other than precipitation, that reduce horizontal visibility):

FG......................fog (vsby less than 5/8 mile)
HZ..haze
FU ..smoke
PY ..spray
BR mist (vsby 5/8–6 miles)
SA..sand
DU ..dust
VA..volcanic ash

Note: *Fog (FG) is observed or forecast only when the visibility is less than five-eighths of mile, otherwise mist (BR) is observed or forecast.*

(f) Other. There are five categories of other weather phenomena which are reported when they occur:

SQ .. squall
SS..sandstorm
DS..duststorm
PO .. dust/sand whirls
FC..funnel cloud
+FC.................................... tornado/waterspout

Examples:

TSRA *thunderstorm with moderate rain*
+SN... *heavy snow*
-RA FG*light rain and fog*
BRHZ....................................*mist and haze*
(visibility ⅝ mile or greater)
FZDZ ... *freezing drizzle*
VCSH.......................*rain shower in the vicinity*
+SHRASNPL*heavy rain showers, snow, ice pellets*
(intensity indicator refers to the predominant rain)

9. Sky Condition. The sky condition as reported in METAR represents a significant change from the way sky condition is currently reported. In METAR, sky condition is reported in the format:

Amount/Height/(Type) or Indefinite Ceiling/Height

(a) Amount. The amount of sky cover is reported in eighths of sky cover, using the contractions:

SKC ..clear (no clouds)
FEW... >0 to 2/8
SCTscattered (3/8s to 4/8s of clouds)
BKN.................. broken (5/8s to 7/8s of clouds)
OVCovercast (8/8s clouds)
CB Cumulonimbus when present
TCUTowering cumulus when present

Note 1: *"SKC" will be reported at manual stations. "CLR" will be used at automated stations when no clouds below 12,000 feet are reported.*

Note 2: *A ceiling layer is not designated in the METAR code. For aviation purposes, the ceiling is the lowest broken or overcast layer, or vertical visibility into an obscuration. Also there is no provision for reporting thin layers in the METAR code. When clouds are thin, that layer must be reported as if it were opaque.*

(b) Height. Cloud bases are reported with three digits in hundreds of feet above ground level (AGL). (Clouds above 12,000 feet cannot be reported by an automated station).

(c) (Type). If Towering Cumulus Clouds (TCU) or Cumulonimbus Clouds (CB) are present, they are reported after the height which represents their base.

Example:
(Reported as) SCT025TCU BKN080 BKN250 (spoken as) "Two thousand five hundred scattered towering cumulus, ceiling eight thousand broken, two five thousand broken."

(Reported as) SCT008 OVC012CB (spoken as) "Eight hundred scattered ceiling one thousand two hundred overcast cumulonimbus clouds."

(d) Vertical Visibility (indefinite ceiling height). The height into an indefinite ceiling is preceded by "VV" and followed by three digits indicating the vertical visibility in hundreds of feet. This layer indicates <u>total obscuration</u>.

Example:
1/8SM FG VV006—visibility one eighth, fog, indefinite ceiling six hundred.

(e) Obscurations are reported when the sky is <u>partially obscured</u> by a ground-based phenomena by indicating the amount of obscuration as FEW, SCT, BKN followed by three zeros (000). In remarks, the obscuring phenomenon precedes the amount of obscuration and three zeros.

Example:

BKN000 (in body)........... *"sky partially obscured"*

FU BKN000 (in remarks)......... *"smoke obscuring five- to seven-eighths of the sky"*

(f) When sky conditions include a layer aloft, other than clouds, such as smoke or haze the type of phenomena, sky cover and height are shown in remarks.

Example:

BKN020 (in body). *"ceiling two thousand broken"*

RMK FU BKN020... *"broken layer of smoke aloft, based at two thousand"*

(g) Variable ceiling. When a ceiling is below three thousand and is variable, the remark "CIG" will be shown followed with the lowest and highest ceiling heights separated by a "V."

Example:

CIG 005V010......... *"ceiling variable between five hundred and one thousand"*

(h) Second site sensor. When an automated station uses meteorological discontinuity sensors, remarks will be shown to identify site specific sky conditions which differ and are lower than conditions reported in the body.

Example:

CIG 020 RY11.... *"ceiling two thousand at runway one one"*

(i) Variable cloud layer. When a layer is varying in sky cover, remarks will show the variability range. If there is more than one cloud layer, the variable layer will be identified by including the layer height.

Example:

SCT V BKN .. *"scattered layer variable to broken"*

BKN025 V OVC.... *"broken layer at two thousand five hundred variable to overcast"*

(j) Significant clouds. When significant clouds are observed, they are shown in remarks, along with the specified information as shown below:

(1) Cumulonimbus (CB), or Cumulonimbus Mammatus (CBMAM), distance (if known), direction from the station, and direction of movement, if known. If the clouds are beyond 10 miles from the airport, DSNT will indicate distance.

Example:

CB W MOV E.................... *"cumulonimbus west moving east"*

CBMAM DSNT S...... *"cumulonimbus mammatus distant south"*

(2) Towering Cumulus (TCU), location, (if known), or direction from the station.

Example:

TCU OHD.............. *"towering cumulus overhead"*

TCU W......................... *"towering cumulus west"*

(3) Altocumulus Castellanus (ACC), Stratocumulus Standing Lenticular (SCSL), Altocumulus Standing Lenticular (ACSL), Cirrocumulus Standing Lenticular (CCSL) or rotor clouds, describing the clouds (if needed) and the direction from the station.

Example:

ACC W................ *"altocumulus castellanus west"*

ACSL SW-S....... *"standing lenticular altocumulus southwest through south"*

APRNT ROTOR CLD S...... *"apparent rotor cloud south"*

CCSL OVR MT E................... *"standing lenticular cirrocumulus over the mountains east"*

10. Temperature/Dew Point. Temperature and dew point are reported in two, two-digit groups in degrees Celsius, separated by a solidus ("/"). Temperatures below zero are prefixed with an "M." If the temperature is available but the dew point is missing, the temperature is shown followed by a solidus. If the temperature is missing, the group is omitted from the report.

Example:

15/08............ *"temperature one five, dew point 8"*

00/M02 ... *"temperature zero, dew point minus 2"*

M05/ *"temperature minus five, dew point missing"*

11. Altimeter. Altimeter settings are reported in a four-digit format in inches of mercury prefixed with an "A" to denote the units of pressure.

Example:

A2995................... *"Altimeter two niner niner five"*

12. Remarks. Remarks will be included in all observations, when appropriate. The contraction "RMK" denotes the start of the remarks section of a METAR report.

Except for precipitation, phenomena located within 5 statute miles of the point of observation will be reported as at the station. Phenomena between 5 and 10 statute miles will be reported in the vicinity, "VC." Precipitation not occurring at the point of observation but within 10 statute miles is also reported as in the vicinity, "VC." Phenomena beyond 10 statute miles will be shown as distant, "DSNT." Distances are in statute miles except for automated lightning remarks which are in nautical miles. Movement of clouds or weather will be indicated by the direction toward which the phenomena is moving.

(a) There are two categories of remarks:

(1) Automated, manual, and plain language.

(2) Additive and automated maintenance data.

(b) Automated, Manual, and Plain Language.

This group of remarks may be generated from either manual or automated weather reporting

stations and generally elaborate on parameters reported in the body of the report. (Plain language remarks are only provided by manual stations).

 (1) Volcanic eruptions.
 (2) Tornado, Funnel Cloud, Waterspout.
 (3) Station Type (AO1 or AO2).
 (4) PK WND.
 (5) WSHFT (FROPA).
 (6) TWR VIS or SFC VIS.
 (7) VRB VIS.
 (8) Sector VIS.
 (9) VIS @ 2nd Site.
 (10) Lightning. When lightning is observed at a manual location, the frequency and location is reported.

When cloud-to-ground lightning is detected by an automated lightning detection system, such as ALDARS:

 [a] Within 5 nautical miles (NM) of the Airport Reference Point (ARP), it will be reported as "TS" in the body of the report with no remark;

 [b] Between 5 and 10 NM of the ARP, it will be reported as "VCTS" in the body of the report with no remark;

 [c] Beyond 10 but less than 30 NM of the ARP, it will be reported in remarks as "DSNT" followed by the direction from the ARP.

Example: LTG DSNT W or LTG DSNT ALQDS

 (11) Beginning/Ending of Precipitation/TSTMS.
 (12) TSTM Location MVMT.
 (13) Hailstone Size (GR).
 (14) Virga.
 (15) VRB CIG (height).
 (16) Obscuration.
 (17) VRB Sky Condition.
 (18) Significant Cloud Types.
 (19) Ceiling Height 2nd Location.
 (20) PRESFR PRESRR.
 (21) Sea-Level Pressure.
 (22) ACFT Mishap (not transmitted).
 (23) NOSPECI.
 (24) SNINCR.
 (25) Other SIG Info.

 (c) Additive and Automated Maintenance Data.
 (1) Hourly Precipitation.
 (2) 3- and 6-Hour Precipitation Amount.
 (3) 24-Hour Precipitation.
 (4) Snow Depth on Ground.
 (5) Water Equivalent of Snow.
 (6) Cloud Type.
 (7) Duration of Sunshine.
 (8) Hourly Temperature/Dew Point (Tenths).
 (9) 6-Hour Maximum Temperature.
 (10) 6-Hour Minimum Temperature.
 (11) 24-Hour Maximum/Minimum Temperature.

 (12) Pressure Tendency.
 (13) Sensor Status.
 PWINO
 FZRANO
 TSNO
 RVRNO
 PNO
 VISNO

Examples of METAR reports and explanation:
METAR KBNA 281250Z 33018KT 290V360 1/2SM
R31/2700FT SN BLSN FG VV008 00/M03 A2991
RMK RAE42SNB42

METAR................aviation routine weather report
KBNA...Nashville, TN
281250Z......................date 28th, time 1250 UTC
(no modifier).........This is a manually generated report, due to the absence of "AUTO" and "AO1 or AO2" in remarks
33018KT........wind three three zero at one eight
290V360...........................wind variable between two nine zero and three six zero
1/2SM..................................... visibility one half
R31/2700FT...................Runway three one RVR two thousand seven hundred
SN.. moderate snow
BLSN FG........................... visibility obscured by blowing snow and fog
VV008.................indefinite ceiling eight hundred
00/M03.....................................temperature zero, dew point minus three
A2991.....................altimeter two niner niner one
RMK..remarks
RAE42...............................rain ended at four two
SNB42..............................snow began at four two

METAR KSFO 041453Z AUTO VRB02KT 3SM
BR CLR 15/12 A3012 RMK AO2

METAR................aviation routine weather report
KSFO....................................San Francisco, CA
041453Z........................date 4th, time 1453 UTC
AUTO.... fully automated; no human intervention
VRB02KT............................. wind variable at two
3SM.. visibility three
BR.............................visibility obscured by mist
CLR..............no clouds below one two thousand
15/12.... temperature one five, dew point one two
A3012.....................altimeter three zero one two
RMK..remarks
AO2...........this automated station has a weather discriminator (for precipitation)

SPECI KCVG 152224Z 28024G36KT 3/4SM
+TSRA BKN008 OVC020CB 28/23 A3000 RMK
TSRAB24 TS W MOV E

SPECI(nonroutine) aviation special weather report

KCVG ..Cincinnati, OH

152228Zdate 15th, time 2228 UTC

(no modifier)This is a manually generated report due to the absence of "AUTO" and "AO1 or AO2" in remarks

28024G36KTwind two eight zero at two four gusts three six

3/4SMvisibility three fourths

+TSRAthunderstorms, heavy rain

BKN008 ceiling eight hundred broken

OVC020CBtwo thousand overcast cumulonimbus clouds

28/23temperature two eight, dew point two three

A3000altimeter three zero zero zero

RMK ..remarks

TSRAB24 thunderstorm and rain began at two four

TS W MOV E thunderstorm west moving east

c. Aerodrome Forecast (TAF). A concise statement of the expected meteorological conditions at an airport during a specified period. At most locations, TAFs have a 24 hour forecast period. However, TAFs for some locations have a 30 hour forecast period. These forecast periods may be shorter in the case of an amended TAF. TAFs use the same codes as METAR weather reports. They are scheduled four times daily for 24-hour periods beginning at 0000Z, 0600Z, 1200Z, and 1800Z.

Forecast times in the TAF are depicted in two ways. The first is a 6-digit number to indicate a specific point in time, consisting of a two-digit date, two-digit hour, and two-digit minute (such as issuance time or FM). The second is a pair of four-digit numbers separated by a "/" to indicate a beginning and end for a period of time. In this case, each four-digit pair consists of a two-digit date and a two-digit hour.

TAFs are issued in the following format:
TYPE OF REPORT/ICAO STATION IDENTIFIER/DATE AND TIME OF ORIGIN/ VALID PERIOD DATE AND TIME/FORECAST METEOROLOGICAL CONDITIONS

Note: The "/" above and in the following descriptions are for separation purposes in this publication and do not appear in the actual TAFs.

TAF KORD 051130Z 0512/0618 14008KT 5SM BR BKN030

TEMPO 0513/0516 1 1/2SM BR
FM051600 16010KT P6SM SKC
FM052300 20013G20KT 4SM SHRA OVC020
PROB40 0600/0606 2SM TSRA OVC008CB
BECMG 0606/0608 21015KT P6SM NSW
SCT040

TAF format observed in the above example:

TAF = type of report

KORD = ICAO station identifier

051130Z = date and time of origin (issuance time)

0512/0618 = valid period date and times

14008KT 5SM BR BKN030 = forecast meteorological conditions

Explanation of TAF elements

1. Type of Report. There are two types of TAF issuances, a routine forecast issuance (TAF) and an amended forecast (TAF AMD). An amended TAF is issued when the current TAF no longer adequately describes the on-going weather or the forecaster feels the TAF is not representative of the current or expected weather. Corrected (COR) or delayed (RTD) TAFs are identified only in the communications header which precedes the actual forecasts.

2. ICAO Station Identifier. The TAF code uses ICAO 4-letter location identifiers as described in the METAR section.

3. Date and Time of Origin. This element is the date and time the forecast is actually prepared. The format is a two-digit date and four-digit time followed, without a space, by the letter "Z."

4. Valid Period Date and Time. The UTC valid period of the forecast consists of two four-digit sets, separated by a "/". The first four-digit set is a two-digit date followed by the two-digit beginning hour, and the second four-digit set is a two-digit date followed by the two-digit ending hour. Although most airports have a 24-hour TAF, a select number of airports have a 30-hour TAF. In the case of an amended forecast, or a forecast which is corrected or delayed, the valid period may be for less than 24 hours. Where an airport or terminal operates on a part-time basis (less than 24 hours/day), the TAFs issued for those locations will have the abbreviated statement "AMD NOT SKED" added to the end of the forecasts. The time observations are scheduled to end and/or resume will be indicated by expanding the AMD NOT SKED statement. Expanded statements will include:

(a) Observation ending time (AFT DDHHmm; for example, AFT 120200)

(b) Scheduled observations resumption time (TIL DDHHmm; for example, TIL 171200Z) or

(c) Period of observation unavailability (DDHH/DDHH); for example, 2502/2512).

Ch 7

5. Forecast Meteorological Conditions. This is the body of the TAF. The basic format is:

WIND/VISIBILITY/WEATHER/SKY CONDITION/ OPTIONAL DATA (WIND SHEAR)

The wind, visibility, and sky condition elements are always included in the initial time group of the forecast. Weather is included only if significant to aviation. If a significant, lasting change in any of the elements is expected during the valid period, a new time period with the changes is included. It should be noted that with the exception of a "FM" group the new time period will include only those elements which are expected to change, i.e., if a lowering of the visibility is expected but the wind is expected to remain the same, the new time period reflecting the lower visibility would not include a forecast wind. The forecast wind would remain the same as in the previous time period.

Any temporary conditions expected during a specific time period are included with that time period. The following describes the elements in the above format.

(a) Wind. This five (or six) digit group includes the expected wind direction (first 3 digits) and speed (last 2 digits or 3 digits if 100 knots or greater). The contraction "KT" follows to denote the units of wind speed. Wind gusts are noted by the letter "G" appended to the wind speed followed by the highest expected gust.

A variable wind direction is noted by "VRB" where the three digit direction usually appears. A calm wind (3 knots or less) is forecast as "00000KT."

Example:
18010KT............ wind one eight zero at one zero
(wind is blowing from 180)

35012G20KT....... wind three five zero at one two gust two zero

(b) Visibility. The expected prevailing visibility up to and including 6 miles is forecast in statute miles, including fractions of miles, followed by "SM" to note the units of measure. Expected visibilities greater than 6 miles are forecast as P6SM (plus six statute miles).

Example:
1/2SM—visibility one-half
4SM—visibility four
P6SM—visibility more than six

(c) Weather Phenomena. The expected weather phenomena is coded in TAF reports using the same format, qualifiers, and phenomena contractions as METAR reports (except UP).

Obscurations to vision will be forecast whenever the prevailing visibility is forecast to be 6 statute miles or less.

If no significant weather is expected to occur during a specific time period in the forecast, the weather phenomena group is omitted for that time period. If, after a time period in which significant weather phenomena has been forecast, a change to a forecast of no significant weather phenomena occurs, the contraction NSW (No Significant Weather) will appear as the weather group in the new time period. (NSW is included only in TEMPO groups).

Note: It is very important that pilots understand that NSW only refers to weather phenomena, i.e., rain, snow, drizzle, etc. Omitted conditions, such as sky conditions, visibility, winds, etc., are carried over from the previous time group.

(d) Sky Condition. TAF sky condition forecasts use the METAR format described in the METAR section. Cumulonimbus clouds (CB) are the only cloud type forecast in TAFs.

When clear skies are forecast, the contraction "SKC" will always be used. The contraction "CLR" is never used in the TAF.

When the sky is obscured due to a surface-based phenomenon, vertical visibility (VV) into the obscuration is forecast. The format for vertical visibility is "VV" followed by a three-digit height in hundreds of feet.

Note: As in METAR, ceiling layers are not designated in the TAF code. For aviation purposes, the ceiling is the lowest broken or overcast layer or vertical visibility into a complete obscuration.

SKC .. "sky clear"

SCT005 BKN025CB "five hundred scattered, ceiling two thousand five hundred broken cumulonimbus clouds"

VV008 "indefinite ceiling eight hundred"

(e) Optional Data (Wind Shear). Wind shear is the forecast of nonconvective low level winds (up to 2,000 feet). The forecast includes the letters "WS" followed by the height of the wind shear, the wind direction and wind speed at the indicated height and the ending letters "KT" (knots). Height is given in hundreds of feet (AGL) up to and including 2,000 feet. Wind shear is encoded with the contraction "WS," followed by a three-digit height, slant character "/," and winds at the height indicated in the same format as surface winds. The wind shear element is omitted if not expected to occur.

WS010/18040KT—"LOW LEVEL WIND SHEAR AT ONE THOUSAND, WIND ONE EIGHT ZERO AT FOUR ZERO"

d. Probability Forecast. The probability or chance of thunderstorms or other precipitation events occurring, along with associated weather conditions (wind, visibility, and sky conditions).

The PROB30 group is used when the occurrence of thunderstorms or precipitation is 30–39% and the PROB40 group is used when the occurrence of thunderstorms or precipitation is 40–49%. This is followed by two-digit groups separated by a "/", giving the beginning date and hour, and the ending date and hour of the time period during which the thunderstorms or precipitation are expected.

Note: NWS does not use PROB 40 in the TAF. However U.S. Military generated TAFS may include PROB40. PROB30 will not be shown during the first nine hours of a NWS forecast.

Example:

PROB40 2221/2302 1/2SM +TSRA "chance between 2100Z and 0200Z of visibility one-half statute mile in thunderstorms and heavy rain."

PROB30 3010/3014 1SM RASN "chance between 1000Z and 1400Z of visibility one statute mile in mixed rain and snow."

e. Forecast Change Indicators. The following change indicators are used when either a rapid, gradual, or temporary change is expected in some or all of the forecast meteorological conditions. Each change indicator marks a time group within the TAF report.

1. From (FM) group. The FM group is used when a rapid change, usually occurring in less than one hour, in prevailing conditions is expected. Typically, a rapid change of prevailing conditions to more or less a completely new set of prevailing conditions is associated with a synoptic feature passing through the terminal area (cold or warm frontal passage). Appended to the "FM" indicator is the six-digit date, hour, and minute the change is expected to begin and continues until the next change group or until the end of the current forecast. A "FM" group will mark the beginning of a new line in a TAF report (indented 5 spaces). Each "FM" group contains all the required elements—wind, visibility, weather, and sky condition. Weather will be omitted in "FM" groups when it is not significant to aviation. FM groups will not include the contraction NSW.

Example:

FM210100 14010KT P6SM SKC—"after 0100Z on the 21st, wind one four zero at one zero, visibility more than six, sky clear."

2. Becoming (BECMG) group. The BECMG group is used when a gradual change in conditions is expected over a longer time period, usually two hours. The time period when the change is expected is two four-digit groups separated by a "/", with the beginning date and hour, and ending date and hour of the change period which follows the BECMG indicator. The gradual change will occur at an unspecified time within this time period. Only the changing forecast meteorological conditions are included in BECMG groups. The omitted conditions are carried over from the previous time group.

Note: The NWS does not use BECMG in the TAF.

Example:

OVC012 BECMG 0114/0116 BKN020—"ceiling one thousand two hundred overcast. Then a gradual change to ceiling two thousand broken between 1400Z on the 1st and 1600Z on the 1st."

3. Temporary (TEMPO) group. The TEMPO group is used for any conditions in wind, visibility, weather, or sky condition which are expected to last for generally less than an hour at a time (occasional), and are expected to occur during less than half the time period. The TEMPO indicator is followed by two four-digit groups separated by a "/". The first four digit group gives the beginning date and hour, and the second four digit group gives the ending date and hour of the time period during which the temporary conditions are expected. Only the changing forecast meteorological conditions are included in TEMPO groups. The omitted conditions are carried over from the previous time group.

Example 1:

SCT030 TEMPO 0519/0523 BKN030—"three thousand scattered with occasional ceilings three thousand broken between 1900Z on the 5th and 2300Z on the 5th."

Example 2:

4SM HZ TEMPO 1900/1906 2SM BR HZ—"visibility four in haze with occasional visibility two in mist and haze between 0000Z on the 19th and 0600Z on the 19th."

Ch 7

Section 2 Barometric Altimeter Errors and Setting Procedures

7-2-1 General

a. Aircraft altimeters are subject to the following errors and weather factors:

1. Instrument error.

2. Position error from aircraft static pressure systems.

3. Nonstandard atmospheric pressure.

4. Nonstandard temperatures.

b. The standard altimeter 29.92 inches Mercury ("Hg.) setting at the higher altitudes eliminates station barometer errors, some altimeter instrument errors, and errors caused by altimeter settings derived from different geographical sources.

7-2-2 Barometric Pressure Altimeter Errors

a. High Barometric Pressure: Cold, dry air masses may produce barometric pressures in excess of 31.00 "Hg. Many aircraft altimeters cannot be adjusted above 31.00 "Hg. When an aircraft's altimeter cannot be set to pressure settings above 31.00 "Hg, the aircraft's true altitude will be higher than the indicated altitude on the barometric altimeter.

b. Low Barometric Pressure: An abnormal low-pressure condition exists when the barometric pressure is less than 28.00 "Hg. Flight operations are not recommended when an aircraft's altimeter is unable to be set below 28.00 "Hg. In this situation, the aircraft's true altitude is lower than the indicated altitude. This situation may be exacerbated when operating in extremely cold temperatures, which may result in the aircraft's true altitude being significantly lower than the indicated altitude.

Note: EXTREME CAUTION SHOULD BE EXERCISED WHEN FLYING IN PROXIMITY TO OBSTRUCTIONS OR TERRAIN IN LOW PRESSURES AND/OR LOW TEMPERATURES.

7-2-3 Altimeter Errors

a. Manufacturing and installation specifications, along with 14 CFR Part 43, Appendix E requirement for periodic tests and inspections, helps reduce mechanical, elastic, temperature, and installation errors. (See Instrument Flying Handbook.) Scale error may be observed while performing a ground altimeter check using the following procedure:

1. Set the current reported airfield altimeter setting on the altimeter setting scale.

2. Read the altitude on the altimeter. The altitude should read the known field elevation if you

are located on the same reference level used to establish the altimeter setting.

3. If the difference from the known field elevation and the altitude read from the altimeter is plus or minus 75 feet or greater, the accuracy of the altimeter is questionable and the problem should be referred to an appropriately rated repair station for evaluation and possible correction.

b. It is important to set the current altimeter settings for the area of operation when flying at an enroute altitude that does not require a standard altimeter setting of 29.92 "Hg. If the altimeter is not set to the current altimeter setting when flying from an area of high pressure into an area of low pressure, the aircraft will be closer to the surface than the altimeter indicates. An inch Hg. error in the altimeter setting equals 1,000 feet of altitude. For example, setting 29.90 "Hg instead of 30.90 "Hg. To quote an old saying: "GOING FROM A HIGH TO A LOW, LOOK OUT BELOW."

c. The aircraft cruising altitude or flight level is maintained by referencing the barometric altimeter. Procedures for setting altimeters during high and low barometric pressure events must be set using the following procedures:

1. Below 18,000 feet mean sea level (MSL).

(a) Barometric pressure is 31.00 "Hg or less.

(1) Set the altimeter to a current reported altimeter setting from a station along the route and within 100 NM of the aircraft, or;

(2) If there is no station within this area, use the current reported altimeter setting of an appropriate available station, or;

Note: Air traffic controllers will furnish this information at least once when en route or on an instrument flight plan within their controlled airspace.

(3) If the aircraft is not equipped with a radio, set the altimeter to the elevation of the departure airport or use an available appropriate altimeter setting prior to departure.

(b) When the barometric pressure exceeds 31.00 "Hg., a NOTAM will be published to define the affected geographic area. The NOTAM will also institute the following procedures:

(1) All aircraft: All aircraft will set 31.00 "Hg. for en route operations below 18,000 feet MSL. Maintain this setting until out of the affected area or until reaching the beginning of the final approach segment on an instrument approach. Set the current altimeter setting (above 31.00 "Hg.) approaching the final segment, if possible. If no current altimeter setting is available, or if a setting

above 31.00 "Hg. cannot be made on the aircraft's altimeter, leave 31.00 "Hg. set in the altimeter and continue the approach.

(2) Set 31.00 "Hg. in the altimeter prior to reaching the lowest of any mandatory/crossing altitudes or 1,500 feet above ground level (AGL) when on a departure or missed approach.

Note: Air traffic control will issue actual altimeter settings and advise pilots to set 31.00 "Hg. in their altimeters for en route operations below 18,000 feet MSL in affected areas.

(3) No additional restrictions apply for aircraft operating into an airport that are able to set and measure altimeter settings above 31.00 "Hg.

(4) Flight operations are restricted to VFR weather conditions to and from an airport that is unable to accurately measure barometric pressures above 31.00 "Hg. These airports will report the barometric pressure as "missing" or "in excess of 31.00 "Hg.".

(5) VFR aircraft. VFR operating aircraft have no additional restrictions. Pilots must use caution when flight planning and operating in these conditions.

(6) IFR aircraft: IFR aircraft unable to set an altimeter setting above 31.00 "Hg. should apply the following:

[a] The suitability of departure alternate airports, destination airports, and destination alternate airports will be determined by increasing the published ceiling and visibility requirements when unable to set the aircraft altimeter above 31.00 "Hg. Any reported or forecast altimeter setting over 31.00 "Hg. will be rounded up to the next tenth to calculate the required increases. The ceiling will be increased by 100 feet and the visibility by 1/4 statute mile for each 1/10 "Hg. over 31.00 "Hg. Use these adjusted values in accordance with operating regulations and operations specifications.

Example: Destination airport altimeter is 31.21 "Hg. The planned approach is an instrument landing system (ILS) with a decision altitude (DA) 200 feet and visibility 1/2 mile (200–1/2). Subtract 31.00 "Hg. from 31.21 "Hg. to get .21 "Hg. .21 "Hg rounds up to .30 "Hg. Calculate the increased requirement: 100 feet per 1/10 equates to a 300 feet increase for .30 "Hg. 1/4 statute mile per 1/10 equates to a 3/4 statute mile increase for .30 "Hg. The destination weather requirement is determined by adding the 300–3/4 increase to 200–1/2. The destination weather requirement is now 500-1-1/4.

[b] 31.00 "Hg. will remain set during the complete instrument approach. The aircraft has arrived at the DA or minimum descent altitude (MDA) when the published DA or MDA is displayed on the barometric altimeter.

Note: The aircraft will be approximately 300 feet higher than the indicated barometric altitude using this method.

[c] These restrictions do not apply to authorized Category II/III ILS operations and certificate holders using approved atmospheric pressure at aerodrome elevation (QFE) altimetry systems.

(7) The FAA Flight Procedures & Airspace Group, Flight Technologies and Procedures Division may authorize temporary waivers to permit emergency resupply or emergency medical service operation.

2. At or above 18,000 feet MSL. All operators will set 29.92 "Hg. (standard setting) in the barometric altimeter. The lowest usable flight level is determined by the atmospheric pressure in the area of operation as shown in Table 7-2-1. Air Traffic Control (ATC) will assign this flight level.

TABLE 7–2–1
LOWEST USABLE FLIGHT LEVEL

Altimeter Setting (Current Reported)	Lowest Usable Flight Level
29.92 or higher	180
29.91 to 28.92	190
28.91 to 27.92	200

3. When the minimum altitude per 14 CFR Section 91.159 and 14 CFR Section 91.177 is above 18,000 feet MSL, the lowest usable flight level must be the flight level equivalent of the minimum altitude plus the number of feet specified in Table 7-2-2. ATC will accomplish this calculation.

TABLE 7–2–2
LOWEST FLIGHT LEVEL CORRECTION FACTOR

Altimeter Setting	Correction Factor
29.92 or higher	none
29.91 to 29.42	500 feet
29.41 to 28.92	1,000 feet
28.91 to 28.42	1,500 feet
28.41 to 27.92	2,000 feet
27.91 to 27.42	2,500 feet

Example: The minimum safe altitude of a route is 19,000 feet MSL and the altimeter setting is reported between 29.92 and 29.43 "Hg, the lowest usable flight level will be 195, which is the flight level equivalent of 19,500 feet MSL (minimum altitude (Table 7-2-1) plus 500 feet).

Section 3 Cold Temperature Barometric Altimeter Errors, Setting Procedures and Cold Temperature Airports (CTA)

7-3-1 Effect of Cold Temperature on Barometric Altimeters

a. Temperature has an effect on the accuracy of barometric altimeters, indicated altitude, and true altitude. The standard temperature at sea level is 15 degrees Celsius (59 degrees Fahrenheit). The temperature gradient from sea level is minus 2 degrees Celsius (3.6 degrees Fahrenheit) per 1,000 feet. For example, at 5000 feet above sea level, the ambient temperature on a standard day would be 5 degrees Celsius. When the ambient (at altitude) temperature is colder than standard, the aircraft's true altitude is lower than the indicated barometric altitude. When the ambient temperature is warmer than the standard day, the aircraft's true altitude is higher than the indicated barometric altitude.

b. Table 7-3-1 indicates how much error may exist when operating in non-standard cold temperatures. To use the table, find the reported temperature in the left column, and read across the top row to locate the height above the airport (subtract the airport elevation from the flight altitude). Find the intersection of the temperature row and height above airport column. This number represents how far the aircraft may be below the indicated altitude due to possible cold temperature induced error.

TABLE 7-3-1
ICAO COLD TEMPERATURE ERROR TABLE

Height Above Airport in Feet

Reported Temp °C	200	300	400	500	600	700	800	900	1000	1500	2000	3000	4000	5000
+10	10	10	10	10	20	20	20	20	20	30	40	60	80	90
0	20	20	30	30	40	40	50	50	60	90	120	170	230	280
-10	20	30	40	50	60	70	80	90	100	150	200	290	390	490
-20	30	50	60	70	90	100	120	130	140	210	280	420	570	710
-30	40	60	80	100	120	140	150	170	190	280	380	570	760	950
-40	50	80	100	120	150	170	190	220	240	360	480	720	970	1210
-50	60	90	120	150	180	210	240	270	300	450	590	890	1190	1500

7-3-2 Pre-Flight Planning for Cold Temperature Altimeter Errors

Flight planning into a CTA may be accomplished prior to flight. Use the predicted coldest temperature for plus or minus 1 hour of the estimated time of arrival and compare against the CTA published temperature. If the predicted temperature is at or below CTA temperature, calculate an altitude correction using Table 7-3-1. This correction may be used at the CTA if the actual arrival temperature is the same as the temperature used to calculate the altitude correction during preflight planning.

7-3-3 Effects of Cold Temperature on Baro-Vertical Navigation (VNAV) Vertical Guidance

Non-standard temperatures can result in a change to effective vertical paths and actual descent rates when using aircraft baro-VNAV equipment for vertical guidance on final approach segments. A lower than standard temperature will result in a shallower descent angle and reduced descent rate. Conversely, a higher than standard temperature will result in a steeper angle and increased descent rate. Pilots should consider potential consequences of these effects on approach minima, power settings, sight picture, visual cues, etc., especially for high-altitude or terrain-challenged locations and during low-visibility conditions.

Reference: AIM ¶5-4-5. Instrument Approach Procedure (IAP) Charts.

a. Uncompensated Baro-VNAV note on 14 CFR Part 97 IAPs. The area navigation (RNAV) global positioning system (GPS) and RNAV required navigation performance (RNP) notes, "For uncompensated Baro-VNAV systems, lateral navigation (LNAV)/VNAV NA below –XX°C (–XX°F) or above XX°C (XXX°F)" and "For uncompensated Baro-VNAV systems, procedure NA below –XX°C (–XX°F) or above XX°C (XXX°F)" apply to baro-VNAV equipped aircraft. These temperatures and how they are used are independent of the temperature and procedures applied for a Cold Temperature Airport.

1. The uncompensated baro-VNAV chart note and temperature range on an RNAV (GPS) approach is applicable to the LNAV/VNAV line of minima. Baro-VNAV equipped aircraft without a temperature compensating system may not use

the RNAV (GPS) approach LNAV/VNAV line of minima when the actual temperature is above or below the charted temperature range.

2. The uncompensated baro-VNAV chart note and temperature range on an RNAV (RNP) approach applies to the entire procedure. For aircraft without a baro-VNAV and temperature compensating system, the RNAV (RNP) approach is not authorized when the actual temperature is above or below the charted uncompensated baro-VNAV temperature range.

b. Baro-VNAV temperature range versus CTA temperature: The baro-VNAV and CTA temperatures are independent and do not follow the same correction or reporting procedures. However, there are times when both procedures, each according to its associated temperature, should be accomplished on the approach.

c. Operating and ATC reporting procedures.

1. Do not use the CTA operating or reporting procedure found in this section, 7-3-4 a. thru 7-3-5 e. when complying with the baro-VNAV temperature note on an RNAV (GPS) approach. Correction is not required nor expected to be applied to procedure altitudes or VNAV paths outside of the final approach segment.

2. Operators must advise ATC when making temperature corrections on RNP authorization required (AR) approaches while adhering to baro-VNAV temperature note.

3. Reporting altitude corrections is required when complying with CTAs in conjunction with the baro-VNAV temperature note. The CTA altitude corrections will be reported in this situation. No altitude correction reporting is required in the final segment.

Note: When executing an approach with vertical guidance at a CTA (i.e., ILS, localizer performance with vertical guidance (LPV), LNAV/VNAV), pilots are reminded to intersect the glideslope/glidepath at the corrected intermediate altitude (if applicable) and follow the published glideslope/glidepath to the corrected minima. The ILS glideslope and WAAS generated glidepath are unaffected by cold temperatures and provide vertical guidance to the corrected DA. Begin descent on the ILS glideslope or WAAS generated glidepath when directed by aircraft instrumentation. Temperature affects the precise final approach fix (PFAF) true altitude where a baro-VNAV generated glidepath begins. The PFAF altitude must be corrected when below the CTA temperature restriction for the intermediate segment or outside of the baro-VNAV temperature restriction when using the LNAV/VNAV line of minima to the corrected DA.

7–3–4 Cold Temperature Airports (CTA)

a. General: The FAA has determined that operating in cold temperatures has placed some 14 CFR Part 97 instrument approach procedures in the United States National Airspace System at risk for loss of required obstacle clearance (ROC). An airport that is determined to be at risk will have an ICON and temperature published on the instrument approach procedure (IAP) in the terminal procedures publication (TPP).

b. CTA identification in TPP: A CTA is identified by a "snowflake" icon (❄) and temperature limit, in Celsius, on U.S. Government approach charts.

c. A current list of CTAs is located at: https://www.faa.gov/air_traffic/flight_info/aeronav/digital_products/dtpp/search/. Airports are listed by ICAO code, Airport Name, Temperature in Celsius, and affected segment(s).

d. Airport Criteria. The CTA risk analysis is performed on airports that have at least one runway of 2500 ft. Pilots operating into an airport with a runway length less than 2500 ft may make a cold temperature altitude correction in cold temperature conditions, if desired. Comply with operating and reporting procedures for CTAs.

e. ATC Reporting Requirements. Pilots must advise ATC with the corrected altitude when applying an altitude correction on any approach segment with the exception of the final segment.

f. Methods to apply correction: The FAA recommends operators/pilots use either the All Segments Method or the Individual Segments Method when making corrections at CTAs.

7–3–5 Cold Temperature Airport Procedures

a. PILOTS MUST NOT MAKE AN ALTIMETER CHANGE to accomplish an altitude correction. Pilots must ensure that the altimeter is set to the current altimeter setting provided by ATC in accordance with 14 CFR §91.121.

b. Actions on when and where to make corrections: Pilots will make an altitude correction to the published, "at", "at or above", and "at or below" altitudes on all designated segment(s) to all runways for all published instrument approach procedures when the reported airport temperature is at or below the published CTA temperature on the approach plate. A pilot may request an altitude correction (if desired) on any approach at any United States airport when extreme cold temperature is encountered. Pilots making a correction must comply with ATC reporting requirements.

c. Correctable altitudes: ATC does not apply a cold temperature correction to their Minimum Vectoring Altitude (MVA) or Minimum IFR Altitude (MIA) charts. Pilots must request approval from ATC to apply a cold temperature correction to any

ATC assigned altitude. Pilots must not correct altitudes published on Standard Instrument Departures (SIDs), Obstacle Departure Procedures (ODPs), and Standard Terminal Arrivals (STARs).

d. Use of corrected MDA/DA: Pilots will use the corrected MDA or DA as the minimum altitude for an approach. Pilots must meet the requirements in 14 CFR Part 91.175 in order to operate below the corrected MDA or DA. Pilots must see and avoid obstacles when descending below the minimum altitude on the approach.

Note: The corrected DA or MDA does not affect the visibility minima published for the approach. With the application of a cold temperature correction to the DA or MDA, the airplane should be in a position on the glideslope/glidepath or at the published missed approach point to identify the runway environment.

e. Acceptable use of the table for manual CTA altitude correction (see Table 7-3-1): Pilots may calculate a correction with a visual interpolation of the chart when using reported temperature and height above airport. This calculated altitude correction may then be rounded to the nearest whole hundred or rounded up. For example, a correction of 130 ft from the chart may be rounded to 100 ft or 200 ft. A correction of 280 ft will be rounded up to 300 ft. This rounded correction will be added to the appropriate altitudes for the "Individual" or "All" segment method. The correction calculated from the table for the MDA or DA may be used as is or rounded up, but never rounded down. This number will be added to the MDA, DA, and all step-down fix altitudes inside of the FAF/PFAF.

1. No extrapolation above the 5000 ft column is required. Pilots may use the 5000 ft "height above airport in feet" column for calculating corrections when the calculated altitude is greater than 5000 ft above reporting station elevation. Pilots must add the correction(s) from the table to the affected segment altitude(s) and fly at the new corrected altitude. Do not round down when using the 5000 ft column for calculated height above airport values greater than 5000 ft. Pilots may extrapolate above the 5000 ft column to apply a correction if desired.

2. These techniques have been adopted to minimize pilot distraction by limiting the number of entries into the table when making corrections. Although not all altitudes on the approach will be corrected back to standard day values, a safe distance above the terrain/obstacle will be maintained on the corrected approach segment(s). Pilots may calculate a correction for each fix based on the fix altitude if desired.

Note: Pilots may use Real Time Mesoscale Analysis (RTMA): Alternate Report of Surface Temperature, for computing altitude corrections, when

airport temperatures are not available via normal reporting.

f. How to apply Cold Temperature Altitude Corrections on an Approach.

1. All Segments Method: Pilots may correct all segment altitudes from the IAF altitude to the MA final holding altitude. Pilots familiar with the information in this section and the procedures for accomplishing the all segments method, only need to use the published "snowflake" icon, ❄/CTA temperature limit on the approach chart for making corrections. Pilots are not required to reference the CTA list. The altitude correction is calculated as follows:

(a) Manual correction: Pilots will make a manual correction when the aircraft is not equipped with a temperature compensating system or when a compensating system is not used to make the correction. Use Table 7-3-1, ICAO Cold Temperature Error Table, to calculate the correction needed for the approach segment(s).

(1) Correct all altitudes from the FAF/PFAF up to and including the IAF altitude: Calculate the correction by taking the FAF/PFAF altitude and subtracting the airport elevation. Use this number to enter the height above airport column in Table 7-3-1 until reaching the reported temperature from the "Reported Temperature" row. Round this number as applicable and then add to all altitudes from the FAF altitude through the IAF altitude.

(2) Correct all altitudes in the final segment: Calculate the correction by taking the MDA or DA for the approach being flown and subtract the airport elevation. Use this number to enter the height above airport column in Table 7-3-1 until reaching the reported temperature from the "Reported Temperature" row. Use this number or round up to next nearest 100 ft. Add this number to MDA or DA, and any step-down fix altitudes in the final segment.

(3) Correct final holding altitude in the MA Segment: Calculate the correction by taking the MA holding altitude and subtract the airport elevation. Use this number to enter the height above airport column in Table 7-3-1 until reaching the reported temperature from the "Reported Temperature" row. Round this number as applicable and then add to the final MA altitude only.

(b) Aircraft with temperature compensating systems: If flying an aircraft equipped with a system capable of temperature compensation, follow the instructions for applying temperature compensation provided in the airplane flight manual (AFM), AFM supplement, or system operating manual. Ensure that temperature compensation system is on and active prior to the IAF and remains active throughout the entire approach and missed approach.

(1) Pilots that have a system that is able to calculate a temperature-corrected DA or MDA may use the system for this purpose.

(2) Pilots that have a system unable to calculate a temperature corrected DA or MDA will manually calculate an altitude correction for the MDA or DA.

Note: Some systems apply temperature compensation only to those altitudes associated with an instrument approach procedure loaded into the active flight plan, while other systems apply temperature compensation to all procedure altitudes or user entered altitudes in the active flight plan, including altitudes associated with a Standard Terminal Arrival (STAR). For those systems that apply temperature compensation to all altitudes in the active flight plan, delay activating temperature compensation until the aircraft has passed the last altitude constraint associated with the active STAR.

2. Individual Segment(s) Method: Pilots are allowed to correct only the marked segment(s) indicated in the CTA list (https://www.faa.gov/air_traffic/flight_info/aeronav/digital_products/dtpp/search/). Pilots using the Individual Segment(s) Method will reference the CTA list to determine which segment(s) need a correction. (See Figure 7-3-1.)

FIGURE 7–3–1
EXAMPLE COLD TEMPERATURE RESTRICTED AIRPORT LIST – REQUIRED SEGMENTS

Identifier	Airport Name	Temperature	Initial	Intermediate	Final	Missed
Montana						
KBTM	Bert Mooney	–25C	X	X	X	
KBZN	Bozeman Yellowstone Intl	–31C		X		
KEKS	Ennis Big Sky	–25C			X	
KGPI	Glacier Park Intl	–15C		X		
KHLN	Helena Rgnl	–17C	X	X	X	

(a) Manual Correction: Pilots will make a manual correction when the aircraft is not equipped with a temperature compensating system or when a compensating system is not used to make the correction. Use Table 7-3-1, ICAO Cold Temperature Error Table, to calculate the correction needed for the approach segment(s).

(1) Initial Segment: All altitudes from the intermediate fix (IF) altitude up to and including the IAF altitude. The correction may be accomplished by using the IF altitude or by using the All Segments Method (a) Manual correction (1). To correct the initial segment by using the IF altitude, subtract the airport elevation from the IF altitude. Use this number to enter the height above airport column in Table 7-3-1 until reaching the reported temperature from the "Reported Temperature" row. Round this number as applicable and then add to the IF, IAF, and any step-down fix altitudes.

(2) Intermediate Segment: All altitudes from the FAF/PFAF up to but not including the IF altitude. Calculate the correction by taking FAF/PFAF altitude and subtracting the airport elevation. Use this number to enter the height above airport column in Table 7-3-1 until reaching the reported temperature from the "Reported Temperature" row. Round this number as applicable and then add to FAF altitude and all step-down fix altitudes within the intermediate segment (inside of the waypoint labeled "IF").

(3) Final segment: Calculate the correction by taking the MDA or DA for the approach flown and subtract the airport elevation. Use this number to enter the height above airport column in Table 7-3-1 until reaching the reported temperature from the "Reported Temperature" row. Use this number or round up to next nearest 100 ft. Add this number to MDA or DA and any applicable step-down fix altitudes in the final segment.

(4) Missed Approach Segment: Calculate the correction by taking the final MA holding altitude and subtract the airport elevation. Use this number to enter the height above airport column in Table 7-3-1 until reaching the reported temperature from the "Reported Temperature" row. Round this number as applicable and then add to the final MA altitude only.

(b) Aircraft with temperature compensating system: If flying an aircraft equipped with a system capable of temperature compensation, follow the instructions for applying temperature compensation provided in the AFM, AFM supplement, or system operating manual. Ensure the temperature compensation system is on and active prior to the segment(s) being corrected. Manually calculate an altimetry correction for the MDA or DA. Determine an altimetry correction from the ICAO table based on the reported airport temperature and the height difference between the MDA or DA, as applicable, and the airport elevation, or use the compensating system to calculate a temperature corrected altitude for the published MDA or DA if able.

g. Communication: Pilots must request approval from ATC whenever applying a cold temperature altitude correction. Pilots do not need to

inform ATC of the final approach segment correction (i.e., new MDA or DA). This request should be made on initial radio contact with the ATC facility issuing the approach clearance. ATC requires this information in order to ensure appropriate vertical separation between known traffic. Pilots should query ATC when vectored altitudes to a segment are lower than the requested corrected altitude. Pilots are encouraged to self-announce corrected altitude when flying into a non-towered airfield.

1. The following are examples of appropriate pilot-to-ATC communication when applying cold-temperature altitude corrections.

(a) On initial check-in with ATC providing approach clearance: Missoula, MT (example below).

• Vectors to final approach course: Outside of IAFs: *"Request 9700 ft for cold temperature operations."*

• Vectors to final approach course: Inside of ODIRE: *"Request 7300 ft for cold temperature operations."*

• Missed Approach segment: *"Require final holding altitude, 12500 ft on missed approach for cold temperature operations."*

(b) Pilots cleared by ATC for an instrument approach procedure; "Cleared the RNAV (GPS) Y RWY 12 approach (from any IAF)". Missoula, MT (example below).

• IAF: *"Request 9700 ft for cold temperature operations at LANNY, CHARL, or ODIRE."*

7–3–6 Examples for Calculating Altitude Corrections on CTAs

All 14 CFR Part 97 IAPs must be corrected at an airport. The following example provides the steps for correcting the different segments of an approach and will be applied to all 14 CFR Part 97 IAPs:

a. Missoula Intl (KMSO). Reported Temperature –12°C: RNAV (GPS) Y RWY 12.

1. All Segments Method: All segments corrected from IAF through MA holding altitude.

(a) Manual Calculation:

(1) Cold Temperature Restricted Airport Temperature Limit: –12°C.

(2) Altitude at the Final Approach Fix (FAF) (SUPPY) = 6200 ft.

(3) Airport elevation = 3206 ft.

(4) Difference: 6200 ft – 3206 ft = 2994 ft.

(5) Use Table 7-3-1, ICAO Cold Temperature Error Table, a height above airport of 2994 ft and –12°C. Visual interpolation is approximately 300 ft. Actual interpolation is 300 ft.

(6) Add 300 ft to the FAF and all procedure altitudes outside of the FAF up to and including IAF altitude(s):

[a] LANNY (IAF), CHARL (IAF), and ODIRE (IAF Holding-in-Lieu): 9400 + 300 = 9700 ft.

[b] CALIP (stepdown fix): 7000 + 300 = 7300 ft.

[c] SUPPY (FAF): 6200 + 300 = 6500 ft.

(7) Correct altitudes within the final segment altitude based on the minima used. LP MDA = 4520 ft.

(8) Difference: 4520 ft – 3206 ft = 1314 ft.

(9) AIM 7-3-1 Table: 1314 ft at –12°C is approximately 150 ft. Use 150 ft or round up to 200 ft.

(10) Add corrections to altitudes up to but not including the FAF:

[a] BEGPE (stepdown fix): 4840 + 150 = 4990 ft.

[b] LNAV MDA: 4520 + 150 = 4670 ft.

(11) Correct JENKI/Missed Approach Holding Altitude: MA altitude is 12000:

[a] JENKI: 12000 – 3206 = 8794 ft.

(12) Table 7-3-1: 8794 ft at –12°C. Enter table at –12°C and intersect the 5000 ft height above airport column. The approximate value is 500 ft.

(13) Add correction to holding fix final altitude:

[a] JENKI: 12000 + 500 = 12500 ft.

b. Temperature Compensating System: Operators using a temperature compensating RNAV system to make altitude corrections will be set to the current airport temperature (–12°C) and activated prior to passing the IAF. A manual calculation of the cold temperature altitude correction is required for the MDA/DA.

1. Individual Segments Method: Missoula requires correction in the intermediate and final segments. However, in this example, the missed approach is also shown.

(a) Manual Calculation: Use the appropriate steps in the All Segments Method above to apply a correction to the required segment.

(1) Intermediate. Use steps 7-3-6a1(a)(1) thru (6). Do not correct the IAF or IF when using individual segments method.

(2) Final. Use steps 7-3-6a1(a)(7) thru (10).

(3) Missed Approach. Use steps 7-3-6a1(a)(11) thru (13).

(b) Temperature Compensating System: Operators using a temperature compensating RNAV system to make altitude corrections will be set to the current airport temperature (–12°C) and activated at a point needed to correct the altitude for the segment. A manual calculation of the cold temperature altitude correction is required for the MDA/DA.

FIGURE 7–3–2
Missoula Intl RNAV (GPS) Y RWY 12

Section 4 Wake Turbulence

7–4–1 General

a. Every aircraft generates wake turbulence while in flight. Wake turbulence is a function of an aircraft producing lift, resulting in the formation of two counter-rotating vortices trailing behind the aircraft.

b. Wake turbulence from the generating aircraft can affect encountering aircraft due to the strength, duration, and direction of the vortices. Wake turbulence can impose rolling moments exceeding the roll-control authority of encountering aircraft, causing possible injury to occupants and damage to aircraft. Pilots should always be aware of the possibility of a wake turbulence encounter when flying through the wake of another aircraft, and adjust the flight path accordingly.

7–4–2 Vortex Generation

a. The creation of a pressure differential over the wing surface generates lift. The lowest pressure occurs over the upper wing surface and the highest pressure under the wing. This pressure differential triggers the roll up of the airflow at the rear of the wing resulting in swirling air masses trailing downstream of the wing tips. After the roll up is completed, the wake consists of two counter-rotating cylindrical vortices. (See Figure 7-4-1.) The wake vortex is formed with most of the energy concentrated within a few feet of the vortex core.

b. More aircraft are being manufactured or retrofitted with winglets. There are several types of winglets, but their primary function is to increase fuel efficiency by improving the lift-to-drag ratio. Studies have shown that winglets have a negligible effect on wake turbulence generation, particularly with the slower speeds involved during departures and arrivals.

7–4–3 Vortex Strength

a. Weight, speed, wingspan, and shape of the generating aircraft's wing all govern the strength of the vortex. The vortex characteristics of any given aircraft can also be changed by extension of flaps or other wing configuring devices. However, the vortex strength from an aircraft increases proportionately to an increase in operating weight or a decrease in aircraft speed. Since the turbulence from a "dirty" aircraft configuration hastens wake decay, the greatest vortex strength occurs when the generating aircraft is HEAVY, CLEAN, and SLOW.

b. Induced Roll

1. In rare instances, a wake encounter could cause catastrophic inflight structural damage to an aircraft. However, the usual hazard is associated with induced rolling moments that can exceed the roll-control authority of the encountering aircraft. During inflight testing, aircraft intentionally flew directly up trailing vortex cores of larger aircraft. These tests demonstrated that the ability of aircraft to counteract the roll imposed by wake vortex depends primarily on the wingspan and counter-control responsiveness of the encountering aircraft. These tests also demonstrated the difficulty of an aircraft to remain within a wake vortex. The natural tendency is for the circulation to eject aircraft from the vortex.

2. Counter control is usually effective and induced roll minimal in cases where the wingspan and ailerons of the encountering aircraft extend beyond the rotational flow field of the vortex. It is more difficult for aircraft with short wingspan (relative to the generating aircraft) to counter the imposed roll induced by vortex flow. Pilots of short span aircraft, even of the high performance type, must be especially alert to vortex encounters. (See Figure 7-4-2.)

FIGURE 7–4–1
Wake Vortex Generation

FIGURE 7–4–2
Wake Encounter Counter Control

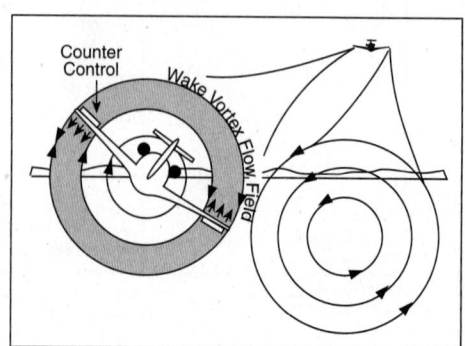

7–4–4 Vortex Behavior

a. Trailing vortices have certain behavioral characteristics which can help a pilot visualize the wake location and thereby take avoidance precautions.

1. An aircraft generates vortices from the moment it rotates on takeoff to touchdown, since trailing vortices are a by-product of wing lift. Prior to takeoff or touchdown pilots should note the rotation or touchdown point of the preceding aircraft. (See Figure 7-4-3.)

2. The vortex circulation is outward, upward and around the wing tips when viewed from either ahead or behind the aircraft. Tests with larger aircraft have shown that the vortices remain spaced a bit less than a wingspan apart, drifting with the wind, at altitudes greater than a wingspan from the ground. In view of this, if persistent vortex turbulence is encountered, a slight change of altitude (upward) and lateral position (upwind) should provide a flight path clear of the turbulence.

3. Flight tests have shown that the vortices from larger aircraft sink at a rate of several hundred feet per minute, slowing their descent and diminishing in strength with time and distance behind the generating aircraft. Pilots should fly at or above the preceding aircraft's flight path, altering course as necessary to avoid the area directly behind and below the generating aircraft. (See Figure 7-4-4.) Pilots, in all phases of flight, must remain vigilant of possible wake effects created by other aircraft. Studies have shown that atmospheric turbulence hastens wake breakup, while other atmospheric conditions can transport wake horizontally and vertically.

4. When the vortices of larger aircraft sink close to the ground (within 100 to 200 feet), they tend to move laterally over the ground at a speed of 2 or 3 knots. (See Figure 7-4-5.)

5. Pilots should be alert at all times for possible wake vortex encounters when conducting approach and landing operations. The pilot is ultimately responsible for maintaining an appropriate interval, and should consider all available information in positioning the aircraft in the terminal area, to avoid the wake turbulence created by a preceding aircraft. Test data shows that vortices can rise with the air mass in which they are embedded. The effects of wind shear can cause vortex flow field "tilting." In addition, ambient thermal lifting and orographic effects (rising terrain or tree lines) can cause a vortex flow field to rise and possibly bounce.

b. A crosswind will decrease the lateral movement of the upwind vortex and increase the movement of the downwind vortex. Thus, a light wind with a cross-runway component of 1 to 5 knots could result in the upwind vortex remaining in the touchdown zone for a period of time and hasten the drift of the downwind vortex toward another runway. (See Figure 7-4-6.) Similarly, a tailwind condition can move the vortices of the preceding aircraft forward into the touchdown zone. THE LIGHT QUARTERING TAILWIND REQUIRES MAXIMUM CAUTION. Pilots should be alert to large aircraft upwind from their approach and takeoff flight paths. (See Figure 7-4-7.)

FIGURE 7–4–3
Wake Ends/Wake Begins

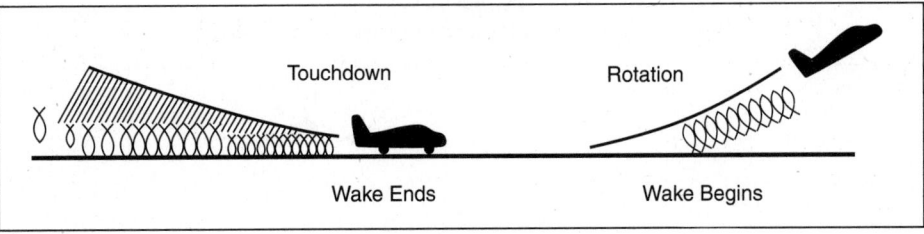

FIGURE 7–4–4
Vortex Flow Field

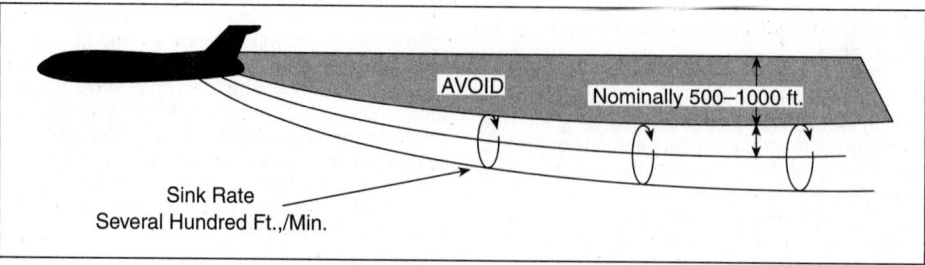

FIGURE 7–4–5
Vortex Movement Near Ground – No Wind

FIGURE 7–4–6
Vortex Movement Near Ground – with Cross Winds

FIGURE 7–4–7
Vortex Movement in Ground Effect – Tailwind

7–4–5 Operations Problem Areas

a. A wake turbulence encounter can range from negligible to catastrophic. The impact of the encounter depends on the weight, wingspan, size of the generating aircraft, distance from the generating aircraft, and point of vortex encounter. The probability of induced roll increases when the encountering aircraft's heading is generally aligned with the flight path of the generating aircraft.

b. AVOID THE AREA BELOW AND BEHIND THE WAKE GENERATING AIRCRAFT, ESPECIALLY AT LOW ALTITUDE WHERE EVEN A MOMENTARY WAKE ENCOUNTER COULD BE CATASTROPHIC.

Note: A common scenario for a wake encounter is in terminal airspace after accepting clearance for a visual approach behind landing traffic. Pilots must be cognizant of their position relative to the traffic and use all means of vertical guidance to ensure they do not fly below the flight path of the wake generating aircraft.

c. Pilots should be particularly alert in calm wind conditions and situations where the vortices could:

1. Remain in the touchdown area.

2. Drift from aircraft operating on a nearby runway.

3. Sink into the takeoff or landing path from a crossing runway.

4. Sink into the traffic pattern from other airport operations.

5. Sink into the flight path of VFR aircraft operating on the hemispheric altitude 500 feet below.

d. Pilots should attempt to visualize the vortex trail of aircraft whose projected flight path they may encounter. When possible, pilots of larger aircraft should adjust their flight paths to minimize vortex exposure to other aircraft.

7–4–6 Vortex Avoidance Procedures

a. Under certain conditions, airport traffic controllers apply procedures for separating IFR aircraft. If a pilot accepts a clearance to visually follow a preceding aircraft, the pilot accepts responsibility for separation and wake turbulence avoidance. The controllers will also provide to VFR aircraft, with whom they are in communication and which in the tower's opinion may be adversely affected by wake turbulence from a larger aircraft, the position, altitude and direction of flight of larger aircraft followed by the phrase "CAUTION – WAKE TURBULENCE." After issuing the caution for wake turbulence, the airport traffic controllers generally do not provide additional information to the following aircraft unless the airport traffic controllers know the following aircraft is overtaking the preceding aircraft. WHETHER OR NOT A WARNING OR INFORMATION HAS BEEN GIVEN, HOWEVER, THE PILOT IS EXPECTED TO ADJUST AIRCRAFT OPERATIONS AND FLIGHT PATH AS NECESSARY TO PRECLUDE SERIOUS WAKE ENCOUNTERS. When any doubt exists about maintaining safe separation distances between aircraft during approaches, pilots should ask the control tower for updates on separation distance and aircraft groundspeed.

Ch 7

b. The following vortex avoidance procedures are recommended for the various situations:

1. Landing behind a larger aircraft—same runway. Stay at or above the larger aircraft's final approach flight path-note its touchdown point-land beyond it.

2. Landing behind a larger aircraft—when parallel runway is closer than 2,500 feet. Consider possible drift to your runway. Stay at or above the larger aircraft's final approach flight path—note its touchdown point.

3. Landing behind a larger aircraft—crossing runway. Cross above the larger aircraft's flight path.

4. Landing behind a departing larger aircraft—same runway. Note the larger aircraft's rotation point—land well prior to rotation point.

5. Landing behind a departing larger aircraft—crossing runway. Note the larger aircraft's rotation point—if past the intersection—continue the approach—land prior to the intersection. If larger aircraft rotates prior to the intersection, avoid flight below the larger aircraft's flight path. Abandon the approach unless a landing is ensured well before reaching the intersection.

6. Departing behind a larger aircraft. Note the larger aircraft's rotation point and rotate prior to the larger aircraft's rotation point. Continue climbing above the larger aircraft's climb path until turning clear of the larger aircraft's wake. Avoid subsequent headings which will cross below and behind a larger aircraft. Be alert for any critical takeoff situation which could lead to a vortex encounter.

7. Intersection takeoffs—same runway. Be alert to adjacent larger aircraft operations, particularly upwind of your runway. If intersection takeoff clearance is received, avoid subsequent heading which will cross below a larger aircraft's path.

8. Departing or landing after a larger aircraft executing a low approach, missed approach, or touch-and-go landing. Because vortices settle and move laterally near the ground, the vortex hazard may exist along the runway and in your flight path after a larger aircraft has executed a low approach, missed approach, or a touch-and-go landing, particular in light quartering wind conditions. You should ensure that an interval of at least 2 minutes has elapsed before your takeoff or landing.

9. En route VFR (thousand-foot altitude plus 500 feet). Avoid flight below and behind a large aircraft's path. If a larger aircraft is observed above on the same track (meeting or overtaking) adjust your position laterally, preferably upwind.

7–4–7 Helicopters

In a slow hover taxi or stationary hover near the surface, helicopter main rotor(s) generate downwash producing high velocity outwash vortices to a distance approximately three times the diameter of the rotor. When rotor downwash hits the surface, the resulting outwash vortices have behavioral characteristics similar to wing tip vortices produced by fixed wing aircraft. However, the vortex circulation is outward, upward, around, and away from the main rotor(s) in all directions. Pilots of small aircraft should avoid operating within three rotor diameters of any helicopter in a slow hover taxi or stationary hover. In forward flight, departing or landing helicopters produce a pair of strong, high-speed trailing vortices similar to wing tip vortices of larger fixed wing aircraft. Pilots of small aircraft should use caution when operating behind or crossing behind landing and departing helicopters.

7–4–8 Pilot Responsibility

a. Research and testing have been conducted, in addition to ongoing wake initiatives, in an attempt to mitigate the effects of wake turbulence. Pilots must exercise vigilance in situations where they are responsible for avoiding wake turbulence.

b. Pilots are reminded that in operations conducted behind all aircraft, acceptance of instructions from ATC in the following situations is an acknowledgment that the pilot will ensure safe takeoff and landing intervals and accepts the responsibility for providing wake turbulence separation.

1. Traffic information.

2. Instructions to follow an aircraft; and

3. The acceptance of a visual approach clearance.

c. For operations conducted behind **super** or **heavy** aircraft, ATC will specify the word "**super**" or "**heavy**" as appropriate, when this information is known. Pilots of **super** or **heavy** aircraft should always use the word "**super**" or "**heavy**" in radio communications.

d. Super, heavy, and large jet aircraft operators should use the following procedures during an approach to landing. These procedures establish a dependable baseline from which pilots of in-trail, lighter aircraft may reasonably expect to make effective flight path adjustments to avoid serious wake vortex turbulence.

1. Pilots of aircraft that produce strong wake vortices should make every attempt to fly on the established glidepath, not above it; or, if glidepath guidance is not available, to fly as closely as possible to a "3-1" glidepath, not above it.

Example: *Fly 3,000 feet at 10 miles from touchdown, 1,500 feet at 5 miles, 1,200 feet at 4 miles, and so on to touchdown.*

2. Pilots of aircraft that produce strong wake vortices should fly as closely as possible to the approach course centerline or to the extended centerline of the runway of intended landing as appropriate to conditions.

e. Pilots operating lighter aircraft on visual approaches in-trail to aircraft producing strong wake vortices should use the following procedures to assist in avoiding wake turbulence. These procedures apply only to those aircraft that are on visual approaches.

1. Pilots of lighter aircraft should fly on or above the glidepath. Glidepath reference may be furnished by an ILS, by a visual approach slope system, by other ground-based approach slope guidance systems, or by other means. In the absence of visible glidepath guidance, pilots may very nearly duplicate a 3-degree glideslope by adhering to the "3 to 1" glidepath principle.

Example: Fly 3,000 feet at 10 miles from touchdown, 1,500 feet at 5 miles, 1,200 feet at 4 miles, and so on to touchdown.

2. If the pilot of the lighter following aircraft has visual contact with the preceding heavier aircraft and also with the runway, the pilot may further adjust for possible wake vortex turbulence by the following practices:

(a) Pick a point of landing no less than 1,000 feet from the arrival end of the runway.

(b) Establish a line-of-sight to that landing point that is above and in front of the heavier preceding aircraft.

(c) When possible, note the point of landing of the heavier preceding aircraft and adjust point of intended landing as necessary.

Example: A puff of smoke may appear at the 1,000-foot markings of the runway, showing that touchdown was that point; therefore, adjust point of intended landing to the 1,500-foot markings.

(d) Maintain the line-of-sight to the point of intended landing above and ahead of the heavier preceding aircraft; maintain it to touchdown.

(e) Land beyond the point of landing of the preceding heavier aircraft. Ensure you have adequate runway remaining, if conducting a touch-and-go landing, or adequate stopping distance available for a full stop landing.

f. During visual approaches pilots may ask ATC for updates on separation and groundspeed with respect to heavier preceding aircraft, especially when there is any question of safe separation from wake turbulence.

g. Pilots should notify ATC when a wake event is encountered. Be as descriptive as possible (i.e., bank angle, altitude deviations, intensity and duration of event, etc.) when reporting the event. ATC will record the event through their reporting system. You are also encouraged to use the Aviation Safety Reporting System (ASRS) to report wake events.

7–4–9 Air Traffic Wake Turbulence Separations

a. Because of the possible effects of wake turbulence, controllers are required to apply no less than minimum required separation to all aircraft operating behind a Super or Heavy, and to Small aircraft operating behind a B757, when aircraft are IFR; VFR and receiving Class B, Class C, or TRSA airspace services; or VFR and being radar sequenced.

1. Separation is applied to aircraft operating directly behind a super or heavy at the same altitude or less than 1,000 feet below, and to small aircraft operating directly behind a B757 at the same altitude or less than 500 feet below:

(a) Heavy behind **super**—6 miles.

(b) Large behind **super**—7 miles.

(c) Small behind **super**—8 miles.

(d) Heavy behind **heavy**—4 miles.

(e) Small/large behind **heavy**—5 miles.

(f) Small behind **B757**—4 miles.

2. Also, separation, measured at the time the preceding aircraft is over the landing threshold, is provided to small aircraft:

(a) Small landing behind **heavy**—6 miles.

(b) Small landing behind **large, non-B757** —4 miles.

Reference: Pilot/Controller Glossary—Aircraft Classes

b. Additionally, appropriate time or distance intervals are provided to departing aircraft when the departure will be from the same threshold, a parallel runway separated by less than 2,500 feet with less than 500 feet threshold stagger, or on a crossing runway and projected flight paths will cross:

1. Three minutes or the appropriate radar separation when takeoff will be behind a super aircraft;

2. Two minutes or the appropriate radar separation when takeoff will be behind a heavy aircraft.

3. Two minutes or the appropriate radar separation when a small aircraft will takeoff behind a B757.

Note: Controllers may not reduce or waive these intervals.

c. A 3-minute interval will be provided when a **small** aircraft will takeoff:

1. From an intersection on the same runway (same or opposite direction) behind a departing **large** aircraft (except B757), or

2. In the opposite direction on the same runway behind a large aircraft (except B757) takeoff or low/missed approach.

Ch 7

Note: This 3-minute interval may be waived upon specific pilot request.

d. A 3-minute interval will be provided when a small aircraft will takeoff:

1. From an intersection on the same runway (same or opposite direction) behind a departing B757, or

2. In the opposite direction on the same runway behind a B757 takeoff or low/missed approach.

Note: This 3-minute interval may not be waived.

e. A 4-minute interval will be provided for all aircraft taking off behind a super aircraft, and a 3-minute interval will be provided for all aircraft taking off behind a heavy aircraft when the operations are as described in subparagraphs c1 and c2 above, and are conducted on either the same runway or parallel runways separated by less than 2,500 feet. Controllers may not reduce or waive this interval.

f. Pilots may request additional separation (i.e., 2 minutes instead of 4 or 5 miles) for wake turbulence avoidance. This request should be made as soon as practical on ground control and at least before taxiing onto the runway.

Note: 14 CFR Section 91.3(a) states: "The pilot-in-command of an aircraft is directly responsible for and is the final authority as to the operation of that aircraft."

g. Controllers may anticipate separation and need not withhold a takeoff clearance for an aircraft departing behind a **large**, **heavy** or **super** aircraft if there is reasonable assurance the required separation will exist when the departing aircraft starts takeoff roll.

Note: With the advent of new wake turbulence separation methodologies known as Wake Turbulence Recategorization, some of the requirements listed above may vary at facilities authorized to operate in accordance with Wake Turbulence Recategorization directives.

Reference: FAA Order JO 7110.659, Wake Turbulence Recategorization; FAA Order JO 7110.123, Wake Turbulence Recategorization— Phase II; FAA Order JO 7110.126, Consolidated Wake Turbulence

7–4–10 Development and New Capabilities

a. The suite of available wake turbulence tools, rules, and procedures is expanding, with the development of new methodologies. Based on extensive analysis of wake vortex behavior, new procedures and separation standards are being developed and implemented in the U.S. and throughout the world. Wake research involves the wake generating aircraft as well as the wake toleration of the trailing aircraft.

b. The FAA and ICAO are leading initiatives, in terminal environments, to implement next-generation wake turbulence procedures and separation standards. The FAA has undertaken an effort to recategorize the existing fleet of aircraft and modify associated wake turbulence separation minima. This initiative is termed Wake Turbulence Recategorization (RECAT), and changes the current weight-based classes (Super, Heavy, B757, Large, Small+, and Small) to a wake-based categorical system that utilizes the aircraft matrices of weight, wingspan, and approach speed. RECAT is currently in use at a limited number of airports in the National Airspace System.

Section 5 Bird Hazards and Flight Over National Refuges, Parks, and Forests

7-5-1 Migratory Bird Activity

a. Bird strike risk increases because of bird migration during the months of March through April, and August through November.

b. The altitudes of migrating birds vary with winds aloft, weather fronts, terrain elevations, cloud conditions, and other environmental variables. While over 90 percent of the reported bird strikes occur at or below 3,000 feet AGL, strikes at higher altitudes are common during migration. Ducks and geese are frequently observed up to 7,000 feet AGL and pilots are cautioned to minimize en route flying at lower altitudes during migration.

c. Considered the greatest potential hazard to aircraft because of their size, abundance, or habit of flying in dense flocks are gulls, waterfowl, vultures, hawks, owls, egrets, blackbirds, and starlings. Four major migratory flyways exist in the U.S. The Atlantic flyway parallels the Atlantic Coast. The Mississippi Flyway stretches from Canada through the Great Lakes and follows the Mississippi River. The Central Flyway represents a broad area east of the Rockies, stretching from Canada through Central America. The Pacific Flyway follows the west coast and overflies major parts of Washington, Oregon, and California. There are also numerous smaller flyways which cross these major north-south migratory routes.

7-5-2 Reducing Bird Strike Risks

a. The most serious strikes are those involving ingestion into an engine (turboprops and turbine jet engines) or windshield strikes. These strikes can result in emergency situations requiring prompt action by the pilot.

b. Engine ingestions may result in sudden loss of power or engine failure. Review engine out procedures, especially when operating from airports with known bird hazards or when operating near high bird concentrations.

c. Windshield strikes have resulted in pilots experiencing confusion, disorientation, loss of communications, and aircraft control problems. Pilots are encouraged to review their emergency procedures before flying in these areas.

d. When encountering birds en route, climb to avoid collision, because birds in flocks generally distribute themselves downward, with lead birds being at the highest altitude.

e. Avoid overflight of known areas of bird concentration and flying at low altitudes during bird migration. Charted wildlife refuges and other natural areas contain unusually high local concentration of birds which may create a hazard to aircraft.

7-5-3 Reporting Bird Strikes

Pilots are urged to report any bird or other wildlife strike using FAA Form 5200-7, Bird/Other Wildlife Strike Report (Appendix 1). Additional forms are available at any FSS; at any FAA Regional Office or at https://www.faa.gov/airports/airport_safety/wildlife/. The data derived from these reports are used to develop standards to cope with this potential hazard to aircraft and for documentation of necessary habitat control on airports.

7-5-4 Reporting Bird and Other Wildlife Activities

If you observe birds or other animals on or near the runway, request airport management to disperse the wildlife before taking off. Also contact the nearest FAA ARTCC, FSS, or tower (including non-Federal towers) regarding large flocks of birds and report the:

a. Geographic location.

b. Bird type (geese, ducks, gulls, etc.).

c. Approximate numbers.

d. Altitude.

e. Direction of bird flight path.

7-5-5 Pilot Advisories on Bird and Other Wildlife Hazards

Many airports advise pilots of other wildlife hazards caused by large animals on the runway through the Chart Supplement and the NOTAM system. Collisions of landing and departing aircraft and animals on the runway are increasing and are not limited to rural airports. These accidents have also occurred at several major airports. Pilots should exercise extreme caution when warned of the presence of wildlife on and in the vicinity of airports. If you observe deer or other large animals in close proximity to movement areas, advise the FSS, tower, or airport management.

7-5-6 Flights Over Charted U.S. Wildlife Refuges, Parks, and Forest Service Areas

a. The landing of aircraft is prohibited on lands or waters administered by the National Park Service, U.S. Fish and Wildlife Service, or U.S. Forest Service without authorization from the respective agency. Exceptions include:

1. When forced to land due to an emergency beyond the control of the operator;

2. At officially designated landing sites; or

3. An approved official business of the Federal Government.

Ch 7

b. Pilots are requested to maintain a minimum altitude of 2,000 feet above the surface of the following: National Parks, Monuments, Seashores, Lakeshores, Recreation Areas and Scenic Riverways administered by the National Park Service, National Wildlife Refuges, Big Game Refuges, Game Ranges and Wildlife Ranges administered by the U.S. Fish and Wildlife Service, and Wilderness and Primitive areas administered by the U.S. Forest Service.

Note: FAA Advisory Circular AC 91-36, Visual Flight Rules (VFR) Flight Near Noise-Sensitive Areas, defines the surface of a national park area (including parks, forests, primitive areas, wilderness areas, recreational areas, national seashores, national monuments, national lakeshores, and national wildlife refuge and range areas) as: the highest terrain within 2,000 feet laterally of the route of flight, or the upper-most rim of a canyon or valley.

c. Federal statutes prohibit certain types of flight activity and/or provide altitude restrictions over designated U.S. Wildlife Refuges, Parks, and Forest Service Areas. These designated areas, for example: Boundary Waters Canoe Wilderness Areas, Minnesota; Haleakala National Park, Hawaii; Yosemite National Park, California; and Grand Canyon National Park, Arizona, are charted on Sectional Charts.

d. Federal regulations also prohibit airdrops by parachute or other means of persons, cargo, or objects from aircraft on lands administered by the three agencies without authorization from the respective agency. Exceptions include:

1. Emergencies involving the safety of human life; or

2. Threat of serious property loss.

Section 6 Potential Flight Hazards

7–6–1 Accident Cause Factors

a. The 10 most frequent cause factors for general aviation accidents that involve the pilot-in-command are:

1. Inadequate preflight preparation and/or planning.
2. Failure to obtain and/or maintain flying speed.
3. Failure to maintain direction control.
4. Improper level off.
5. Failure to see and avoid objects or obstructions.
6. Mismanagement of fuel.
7. Improper inflight decisions or planning.
8. Misjudgment of distance and speed.
9. Selection of unsuitable terrain.
10. Improper operation of flight controls.

b. This list remains relatively stable and points out the need for continued refresher training to establish a higher level of flight proficiency for all pilots. A part of the FAA's continuing effort to promote increased aviation safety is the Aviation Safety Program. For information on Aviation Safety Program activities contact your nearest Flight Standards District Office.

c. Alertness. Be alert at all times, especially when the weather is good. Most pilots pay attention to business when they are operating in full IFR weather conditions, but strangely, air collisions almost invariably have occurred under ideal weather conditions. Unlimited visibility appears to encourage a sense of security which is not at all justified. Considerable information of value may be obtained by listening to advisories being issued in the terminal area, even though controller workload may prevent a pilot from obtaining individual service.

d. Giving Way. If you think another aircraft is too close to you, give way instead of waiting for the other pilot to respect the right-of-way to which you may be entitled. It is a lot safer to pursue the right-of-way angle after you have completed your flight.

7–6–2 Reporting Radio/Radar Altimeter Anomalies

a. Background.

1. The radio altimeter (also known as radar altimeter or RADALT) is a safety-critical aircraft system used to determine an aircraft's height above terrain. It is the only sensor onboard the aircraft capable of providing a direct measurement of the clearance height above the terrain and obstacles. Information from radio altimeters is essential for flight operations as a main enabler of several safety-critical functions and systems on the aircraft. The receiver on the radio altimeter is highly accurate because it is extremely sensitive, making it susceptible to radio frequency interference (RFI). RFI in the C-band portion of the spectrum could impact the functions of the radio altimeter during any phase of flight—most critically during takeoff, approach, and landing phases. This could pose a serious risk to flight safety.

2. Installed radio altimeters normally supply critical height data to a wide range of automated safety systems, navigation systems, and cockpit displays. Harmful RFI affecting the radio altimeter can cause these safety and navigation systems to operate in unexpected ways and display erroneous information to the pilot. RFI can interrupt, or significantly degrade, radio altimeter functions—precluding radio altimeter-based terrain alerts and low-visibility approach and landing operations. Systems of concern include Terrain Awareness Warning Systems (TAWS), Enhanced Ground Proximity Warning Systems (EGPWS), and Traffic Collision Avoidance Systems (TCAS), to name a few. Pilots of radio altimeter equipped aircraft should become familiar with the radio altimeter's interdependence with the other aircraft systems and expected failure modes and indications that may be associated with harmful interference.

b. Actions. Recognizing interference/anomalies in the radio altimeter can be difficult, as it may present as inoperative or erroneous data. Pilots need to monitor their automation, as well as their radio altimeters for discrepancies, and be prepared to take action. Pilots encountering radio altimeter interference/anomalies should transition to procedures that do not require the radio altimeter, and inform Air Traffic Control (ATC).

c. Inflight Reporting. Pilots should report any radio altimeter anomaly to ATC as soon as practical.

d. Post Flight Reporting.

1. Pilots are encouraged to submit detailed reports of radio altimeter interference/anomalies post flight as soon as practical, by internet via the Radio Altimeter Anomaly Reporting Form at https://www.faa.gov/air_traffic/nas/RADALT_reports/.

2. The post flight pilot reports of radio altimeter anomalies should contain as much of the following information as applicable:

(a) Date and time the anomaly was observed;

(b) Location of the aircraft at the time the anomaly started and ended (e.g., latitude, longitude or bearing/distance from a reference point or navigational aid);

(c) Magnetic heading;

(d) Altitude (MSL/AGL);

Ch 7

(e) Aircraft Type (make/model);

(f) Flight Number or Aircraft Registration Number;

(g) Meteorological conditions;

(h) Type of radio altimeter in use (e.g., make/model/software series or version), if known;

(i) Event overview;

(j) Consequences/operational impact (e.g., impacted equipment, actions taken to mitigate the disruption and/or remedy provided by ATC, required post flight pilot and maintenance actions).

7–6–3 VFR in Congested Areas

A high percentage of near midair collisions occur below 8,000 feet AGL and within 30 miles of an airport. When operating VFR in these highly congested areas, whether you intend to land at an airport within the area or are just flying through, it is recommended that extra vigilance be maintained and that you monitor an appropriate control frequency. Normally the appropriate frequency is an approach control frequency. By such monitoring action you can "get the picture" of the traffic in your area. When the approach controller has radar, radar traffic advisories may be given to VFR pilots upon request.

Reference: AIM, ¶4-1-15, Radar Traffic Information Service.

7–6–4 Obstructions To Flight

a. General. Many structures exist that could significantly affect the safety of your flight when operating below 500 feet above ground level (AGL), and particularly below 200 feet AGL. While 14 CFR Part 91.119 allows flight below 500 feet AGL when over sparsely populated areas or open water, such operations involve increased safety risks. At and below 200 feet AGL there are numerous power lines, antenna towers, etc., that are not marked and lighted and/or charted as obstructions and, therefore, may not be seen in time to avoid a collision. Notices to Air Missions NOTAM are issued on those lighted structures experiencing temporary light outages. However, some time may pass before the FAA is notified of these outages, and the NOTAM issued, thus pilot vigilance is imperative. Additionally, new obstructions may not be on current charts because the information was not received prior to the FAA publishing the chart.

b. Antenna Towers. Extreme caution should be exercised when flying less than 2,000 feet AGL because of numerous skeletal structures, such as radio and television antenna towers, that exceed 1,000 feet AGL with some extending higher than 2,000 feet AGL. Most skeletal structures are supported by guy wires which are very difficult to see in good weather and can be invisible at dusk or during periods of reduced visibility. These wires can extend about 1,500 feet horizontally from a structure; therefore, all skeletal structures should be avoided horizontally by at least 2,000 feet.

c. Overhead Wires. Overhead transmission and utility lines often span approaches to runways, natural flyways such as lakes, rivers, gorges, and canyons, and cross other landmarks pilots frequently follow such as highways, railroad tracks, etc. As with antenna towers, these power transmission and/or utility lines and the supporting structures of these lines may not always be readily visible. The wires may be virtually impossible to see under certain conditions. Spherical markers may be used to identify overhead wires and catenary transmission lines and may be lighted. In some locations, the supporting structures of overhead transmission lines are equipped with unique sequence flashing white strobe light systems to indicate that there are wires between the structures. The flash sequence for the wire support structures will be middle, top, and bottom with all lights on the same level flashing simultaneously. However, not all power transmission and/or utility lines require notice to the FAA as they do not exceed 200 feet AGL or meet the obstruction standard of 14 CFR Part 77 and, therefore, are not marked and/or lighted. All pilots are cautioned to remain extremely vigilant for power transmission and/or utility lines and their supporting structures when following natural flyways or during the approach and landing phase. This is particularly important for seaplane and/or float equipped aircraft when landing on, or departing from, unfamiliar lakes or rivers.

d. Wind Turbines. The number, size, and height of individual wind turbines and wind turbine farms have increased over time. The locations of wind turbine farms have also expanded to areas more commonly flown by VFR pilots and to all regions of the United States. VFR pilots should be aware that many wind turbines are exceeding 499 feet AGL in height, which may affect minimum safe VFR altitudes in uncontrolled airspace. In addition, many wind turbines are encroaching on the 700 foot AGL floor of controlled airspace (Class E). Pilots are cautioned to maintain appropriate safe distance (laterally, vertically, or both). Wind turbines are typically charted on Visual Flight Rules (VFR) Sectional Charts and/or Terminal Area Charts. For a description of how wind turbines and wind turbine farms are charted, refer to the FAA Aeronautical Chart User's Guide. Wind turbines are normally painted white or light gray to improve daytime conspicuity. They are typically lit with medium-intensity, flashing red lights, placed as high as possible on the turbine nacelle (not the blade tips), that should be synchronized to flash together; however, not all wind turbine units within

a farm need to be lighted, depending on their location and height. Sometimes, only the perimeter of the wind turbine farm and an arrangement of interior wind turbines are lit. Some wind turbine farms use Aircraft Detection Lighting Systems (ADLS), which are proximity sensor-based systems designed to detect aircraft as they approach the obstruction. This system automatically activates the appropriate obstruction lights until they are no longer needed based on the position of the transiting aircraft. This technology reduces the impact of nighttime lighting on nearby communities and migratory birds and extends the life expectancy of the obstruction lights. For more information on how obstructions such as wind turbines are marked and lighted, refer to Advisory Circular 70/7460-1, Obstruction Marking and Lighting. Pilots should be aware that wind turbines in motion could result in limitations of air traffic services in the vicinity of the wind turbine farms.

Reference: AIM, ¶4-5-1, Radar.

e. Meteorological (MET) Evaluation Towers. MET towers are used by wind energy companies to determine feasible sites for wind turbines. Some of these towers are less than 200 feet AGL. These structures are portable, erected in a matter of hours, installed with guyed wires, and constructed from a galvanized material often making them difficult to see in certain atmospheric conditions. Markings for these towers include alternating bands of aviation orange and white paint, and high-visibility sleeves installed on the outer guy wires. However, not all MET towers follow these guidelines, and pilots should be vigilant when flying at low altitude in remote or rural areas.

f. Other Objects/Structures. There are other objects or structures that could adversely affect your flight such as temporary construction cranes near an airport, newly constructed buildings, new towers, etc. Many of these structures do not meet charting requirements or may not yet be charted because of the charting cycle. Some structures do not require obstruction marking and/or lighting, and some may not be marked and lighted even though the FAA recommended it. VFR pilots should carefully review NOTAMs for temporary or permanent obstructions along the planned route of flight during their preflight preparations. Particular emphasis should be given to obstructions in the vicinity of the approach and departure ends of the runway complex or any other areas where flight below 500 feet AGL is planned or likely to occur.

7–6–5 Avoid Flight Beneath Unmanned Balloons

a. The majority of unmanned free balloons currently being operated have, extending below them, either a suspension device to which the payload or instrument package is attached, or a trailing wire antenna, or both. In many instances these balloon subsystems may be invisible to the pilot until the aircraft is close to the balloon, thereby creating a potentially dangerous situation. Therefore, good judgment on the part of the pilot dictates that aircraft should remain well clear of all unmanned free balloons and flight below them should be avoided at all times.

b. Pilots are urged to report any unmanned free balloons sighted to the nearest FAA ground facility with which communication is established. Such information will assist FAA ATC facilities to identify and flight follow unmanned free balloons operating in the airspace.

7–6–6 Unmanned Aircraft Systems

a. Unmanned Aircraft Systems (UAS), formerly referred to as "Unmanned Aerial Vehicles" (UAVs) or "drones," are having an increasing operational presence in the NAS. Once the exclusive domain of the military, UAS are now being operated by various entities. Although these aircraft are "unmanned," UAS are flown by a remotely located pilot and crew. Physical and performance characteristics of unmanned aircraft (UA) vary greatly and unlike model aircraft that typically operate lower than 400 feet AGL, UA may be found operating at virtually any altitude and any speed. Sizes of UA can be as small as several pounds to as large as a commercial transport aircraft. UAS come in various categories including airplane, rotorcraft, powered-lift (tilt-rotor), and lighter-than-air. Propulsion systems of UAS include a broad range of alternatives from piston powered and turbojet engines to battery and solar-powered electric motors.

b. To ensure segregation of UAS operations from other aircraft, the military typically conducts UAS operations within restricted or other special use airspace. However, UAS operations are now being approved in the NAS outside of special use airspace through the use of FAA-issued Certificates of Waiver or Authorization (COA) or through the issuance of a special airworthiness certificate. COA and special airworthiness approvals authorize UAS flight operations to be contained within specific geographic boundaries and altitudes, usually require coordination with an ATC facility, and typically require the issuance of a NOTAM describing the operation to be conducted. UAS approvals also require observers to provide "see-and-avoid" capability to the UAS crew and to provide the necessary compliance with 14 CFR Section 91.113. For UAS operations approved at or above FL180, UAS operate under the same requirements as that of manned aircraft (i.e., flights are operated under instrument flight rules, are in communication with ATC, and are appropriately equipped).

Ch 7

c. UAS operations may be approved at either controlled or uncontrolled airports and are typically disseminated by NOTAM. In all cases, approved UAS operations must comply with all applicable regulations and/or special provisions specified in the COA or in the operating limitations of the special airworthiness certificate. At uncontrolled airports, UAS operations are advised to operate well clear of all known manned aircraft operations. Pilots of manned aircraft are advised to follow normal operating procedures and are urged to monitor the CTAF for any potential UAS activity. At controlled airports, local ATC procedures may be in place to handle UAS operations and should not require any special procedures from manned aircraft entering or departing the traffic pattern or operating in the vicinity of the airport.

d. In addition to approved UAS operations described above, a recently approved agreement between the FAA and the Department of Defense authorizes small UAS operations wholly contained within Class G airspace, and in no instance, greater than 1200 feet AGL over military owned or leased property. These operations do not require any special authorization as long as the UA remains within the lateral boundaries of the military installation as well as other provisions including the issuance of a NOTAM. Unlike special use airspace, these areas may not be depicted on an aeronautical chart.

e. There are several factors a pilot should consider regarding UAS activity in an effort to reduce potential flight hazards. Pilots are urged to exercise increased vigilance when operating in the vicinity of restricted or other special use airspace, military operations areas, and any military installation. Areas with a preponderance of UAS activity are typically noted on sectional charts advising pilots of this activity. Since the size of a UA can be very small, they may be difficult to see and track. If a UA is encountered during flight, as with manned aircraft, never assume that the pilot or crew of the UAS can see you, maintain increased vigilance with the UA and always be prepared for evasive action if necessary. Always check NOTAMs for potential UAS activity along the intended route of flight and exercise increased vigilance in areas specified in the NOTAM.

7–6–7 Mountain Flying

a. Your first experience of flying over mountainous terrain (particularly if most of your flight time has been over the flatlands of the Midwest) could be a *never-to-be-forgotten nightmare* if proper planning is not done and if you are not aware of the potential hazards awaiting. Those familiar section lines are not present in the mountains; those flat, level fields for forced landings are practically nonexistent; abrupt changes in wind direction and velocity occur; severe updrafts and downdrafts are common, particularly near or above abrupt changes of terrain such as cliffs or rugged areas; even the clouds look different and can build up with startling rapidity. Mountain flying need not be hazardous if you follow the recommendations below.

b. **File a Flight Plan.** Plan your route to avoid topography which would prevent a safe forced landing. The route should be over populated areas and well known mountain passes. Sufficient altitude should be maintained to permit gliding to a safe landing in the event of engine failure.

c. Don't fly a light aircraft when the winds aloft, at your proposed altitude, exceed 35 miles per hour. Expect the winds to be of much greater velocity over mountain passes than reported a few miles from them. Approach mountain passes with as much altitude as possible. Downdrafts of from 1,500 to 2,000 feet per minute are not uncommon on the leeward side.

d. Don't fly near or above abrupt changes in terrain. Severe turbulence can be expected, especially in high wind conditions.

e. **Understand Mountain Obscuration.** The term Mountain Obscuration (MTOS) is used to describe a visibility condition that is distinguished from IFR because ceilings, by definition, are described as "above ground level" (AGL). In mountainous terrain clouds can form at altitudes significantly higher than the weather reporting station and at the same time nearby mountaintops may be obscured by low visibility. In these areas the ground level can also vary greatly over a small area. Beware if operating VFR-on-top. You could be operating closer to the terrain than you think because the tops of mountains are hidden in a cloud deck below. MTOS areas are identified daily on The Aviation Weather Center located at: http://www.aviationweather.gov.

f. Navigating in confined terrain when flying through mountain passes can be challenging. For high-traffic mountain passes, VFR checkpoints may be provided on VFR navigation charts to increase situational awareness by indicating key landmarks inside confined terrain. A collocated VFR waypoint and checkpoint may be provided to assist with identifying natural entry points for commonly flown mountain passes. Pilots should reference the name of the charted VFR checkpoint, wherever possible, when making position reports on CTAF frequencies to reduce the risk of midair collisions. Pilots should evaluate the terrain along the route they intend to fly with respect to their aircraft type and performance capabilities, local weather, and their experience level to avoid flying into confined areas without adequate room to execute a 180 degree turn, should conditions require. Always fly with a planned escape route in mind.

Reference: AIM, ¶1-1-17, Global Positioning System (GPS).

g. VFR flight operations may be conducted at night in mountainous terrain with the application of sound judgment and common sense. Proper pre-flight planning, giving ample consideration to winds and weather, knowledge of the terrain and pilot experience in mountain flying are prerequisites for safety of flight. Continuous visual contact with the surface and obstructions is a major concern and flight operations under an overcast or in the vicinity of clouds should be approached with extreme caution.

h. When landing at a high altitude field, the same indicated airspeed should be used as at low elevation fields. *Remember:* that due to the less dense air at altitude, this same indicated airspeed actually results in higher true airspeed, a faster landing speed, and more important, a longer landing distance. During gusty wind conditions which often prevail at high altitude fields, a power approach and power landing is recommended. Additionally, due to the faster groundspeed, your takeoff distance will increase considerably over that required at low altitudes.

i. Effects of Density Altitude. Performance figures in the aircraft owner's handbook for length of takeoff run, horsepower, rate of climb, etc., are generally based on standard atmosphere conditions (59 degrees Fahrenheit (15 degrees Celsius), pressure 29.92 inches of mercury) at sea level. However, inexperienced pilots, as well as experienced pilots, may run into trouble when they encounter an altogether different set of conditions. This is particularly true in hot weather and at higher elevations. Aircraft operations at altitudes above sea level and at higher than standard temperatures are commonplace in mountainous areas. Such operations quite often result in a drastic reduction of aircraft performance capabilities because of the changing air density. Density altitude is a measure of air density. It is not to be confused with pressure altitude, true altitude or absolute altitude. It is not to be used as a height reference, but as a determining criteria in the performance capability of an aircraft. Air density decreases with altitude. As air density decreases, density altitude increases. The further effects of high temperature and high humidity are cumulative, resulting in an increasing high density altitude condition. High density altitude reduces all aircraft performance parameters. To the pilot, this means that the normal horsepower output is reduced, propeller efficiency is reduced and a higher true airspeed is required to sustain the aircraft throughout its operating parameters. It means an increase in runway length requirements for takeoff and landings, and decreased rate of climb. An average small airplane, for example, requiring 1,000 feet for takeoff at sea level under standard atmospheric conditions will require a takeoff run of approximately 2,000 feet at an operational altitude of 5,000 feet.

Note: A turbo-charged aircraft engine provides a slight advantage in that it provides sea level horsepower up to a specified altitude above sea level.

1. Density Altitude Advisories. At airports with elevations of 2,000 feet and higher, control towers and FSSs will broadcast the advisory "Check Density Altitude" when the temperature reaches a predetermined level. These advisories will be broadcast on appropriate tower frequencies or, where available, ATIS. FSSs will broadcast these advisories as a part of Local Airport Advisory.

2. These advisories are provided by air traffic facilities, as a reminder to pilots that high temperatures and high field elevations will cause significant changes in aircraft characteristics. The pilot retains the responsibility to compute density altitude, when appropriate, as a part of preflight duties.

Note: All FSSs will compute the current density altitude upon request.

j. Mountain Wave. Many pilots go all their lives without understanding what a mountain wave is. Quite a few have lost their lives because of this lack of understanding. One need not be a licensed meteorologist to understand the mountain wave phenomenon.

1. Mountain waves occur when air is being blown over a mountain range or even the ridge of a sharp bluff area. As the air hits the upwind side of the range, it starts to climb, thus creating what is generally a smooth updraft which turns into a turbulent downdraft as the air passes the crest of the ridge. From this point, for many miles downwind, there will be a series of downdrafts and updrafts. Satellite photos of the Rockies have shown mountain waves extending as far as 700 miles downwind of the range. Along the east coast area, such photos of the Appalachian chain have picked up the mountain wave phenomenon over a hundred miles eastward. All it takes to form a mountain wave is wind blowing across the range at 15 knots or better at an intersection angle of not less than 30 degrees.

2. Pilots from flatland areas should understand a few things about mountain waves in order to stay out of trouble. When approaching a mountain range from the upwind side (generally the west), there will usually be a smooth updraft; therefore, it is not quite as dangerous an area as the lee of the range. From the leeward side, it is always a good idea to add an extra thousand feet or so of altitude because downdrafts can exceed the climb capability of the aircraft. Never expect an updraft when approaching a mountain chain

Ch 7

from the leeward. Always be prepared to cope with a downdraft and turbulence.

3. When approaching a mountain ridge from the downwind side, it is recommended that the ridge be approached at approximately a 45 degree angle to the horizontal direction of the ridge. This permits a safer retreat from the ridge with less stress on the aircraft should severe turbulence and downdraft be experienced. If severe turbulence is encountered, simultaneously reduce power and adjust pitch until aircraft approaches maneuvering speed, then adjust power and trim to maintain maneuvering speed and fly away from the turbulent area.

7-6-8 Use of Runway Half-Way Signs at Unimproved Airports

When installed, runway half-way signs provide the pilot with a reference point to judge takeoff acceleration trends. Assuming that the runway length is appropriate for takeoff (considering runway condition and slope, elevation, aircraft weight, wind, and temperature), typical takeoff acceleration should allow the airplane to reach 70 percent of lift-off airspeed by the midpoint of the runway. The "rule of thumb" is that should airplane acceleration not allow the airspeed to reach this value by the midpoint, the takeoff should be aborted, as it may not be possible to liftoff in the remaining runway.

Several points are important when considering using this "rule of thumb":

a. Airspeed indicators in small airplanes are not required to be evaluated at speeds below stalling, and may not be usable at 70 percent of liftoff airspeed.

b. This "rule of thumb" is based on a uniform surface condition. Puddles, soft spots, areas of tall and/or wet grass, loose gravel, etc., may impede acceleration or even cause deceleration. Even if the airplane achieves 70 percent of liftoff airspeed by the midpoint, the condition of the remainder of the runway may not allow further acceleration. The entire length of the runway should be inspected prior to takeoff to ensure a usable surface.

c. This "rule of thumb" applies only to runway required for actual liftoff. In the event that obstacles affect the takeoff climb path, appropriate distance must be available after liftoff to accelerate to best angle of climb speed and to clear the obstacles. This will, in effect, require the airplane to accelerate to a higher speed by midpoint, particularly if the obstacles are close to the end of the runway. In addition, this technique does not take into account the effects of upslope or tailwinds on takeoff performance. These factors will also require greater acceleration than normal and, under some circumstances, prevent takeoff entirely.

d. Use of this "rule of thumb" does not alleviate the pilot's responsibility to comply with applicable Federal Aviation Regulations, the limitations and performance data provided in the FAA approved Airplane Flight Manual (AFM), or, in the absence of an FAA approved AFM, other data provided by the aircraft manufacturer.

In addition to their use during takeoff, runway half-way signs offer the pilot increased awareness of his or her position along the runway during landing operations.

Note: No FAA standard exists for the appearance of the runway half-way sign. Figure 7-6-1 shows a graphical depiction of a typical runway half-way sign.

FIGURE 7-6-1
Typical Runway Half-way Sign

7-6-9 Seaplane Safety

a. Acquiring a seaplane class rating affords access to many areas not available to landplane pilots. Adding a seaplane class rating to your pilot certificate can be relatively uncomplicated and inexpensive. However, more effort is required to become a safe, efficient, competent "bush" pilot. The natural hazards of the backwoods have given way to modern man-made hazards. Except for the far north, the available bodies of water are no longer the exclusive domain of the airman. Seaplane pilots must be vigilant for hazards such as electric power lines, power, sail and rowboats, rafts, mooring lines, water skiers, swimmers, etc.

b. Seaplane pilots must have a thorough understanding of the right-of-way rules as they apply to aircraft versus other vessels. Seaplane pilots

are expected to know and adhere to both the U.S. Coast Guard's (USCG) Navigation Rules, International—Inland, and 14 CFR §91.115, Right-of-Way Rules; Water Operations. The navigation rules of the road are a set of collision avoidance rules as they apply to aircraft on the water. A seaplane is considered a vessel when on the water for the purposes of these collision avoidance rules. In general, a seaplane on the water must keep well clear of all vessels and avoid impeding their navigation. The CFR requires, in part, that aircraft operating on the water "...shall, insofar as possible, keep clear of all vessels and avoid impeding their navigation, and shall give way to any vessel or other aircraft that is given the right-of-way..." This means that a seaplane should avoid boats and commercial shipping when on the water. If on a collision course, the seaplane should slow, stop, or maneuver to the right, away from the bow of the oncoming vessel. Also, while on the surface with an engine running, an aircraft must give way to all nonpowered vessels. Since a seaplane in the water may not be as maneuverable as one in the air, the aircraft on the water has right-of-way over one in the air, and one taking off has right-of-way over one landing. A seaplane is exempt from the USCG safety equipment requirements, including the requirements for Personal Flotation Devices (PFD). Requiring seaplanes on the water to comply with USCG equipment requirements in addition to the FAA equipment requirements would be an unnecessary burden on seaplane owners and operators.

c. Unless they are under Federal jurisdiction, navigable bodies of water are under the jurisdiction of the state, or in a few cases, privately owned. Unless they are specifically restricted, aircraft have as much right to operate on these bodies of water as other vessels. To avoid problems, check with Federal or local officials in advance of operating on unfamiliar waters. In addition to the agencies listed in Table 7-6-1, the nearest Flight Standards District Office can usually offer some practical suggestions as well as regulatory information. If you land on a restricted body of water because of an inflight emergency, or in ignorance of the restrictions you have violated, report as quickly as practical to the nearest local official having jurisdiction and explain your situation.

d. When operating a seaplane over or into remote areas, appropriate attention should be given to survival gear. Minimum kits are recommended for summer and winter, and are required by law for flight into sparsely settled areas of Canada and Alaska. Alaska State Department of Transportation and Canadian Ministry of Transport officials can provide specific information on survival gear requirements. The kit should be assembled in one container and be easily reachable and preferably floatable.

e. The FAA recommends that each seaplane owner or operator provide flotation gear for occupants any time a seaplane operates on or near water. 14 CFR Section 91.205(b)(12) requires approved flotation gear for aircraft operated for hire over water and beyond power-off gliding distance from shore. FAA-approved gear differs from that required for navigable waterways under USCG rules. FAA-approved life vests are inflatable designs as compared to the USCG's noninflatable PFDs that may consist of solid, bulky material. Such USCG PFDs are impractical for seaplanes and other aircraft because they may block passage through the relatively narrow exits available to pilots and passengers. Life vests approved under Technical Standard Order (TSO) TSO–C13E contain fully inflatable compartments. The wearer inflates the compartments (AFTER exiting the aircraft) primarily by independent CO_2 cartridges, with an oral inflation tube as a backup. The flotation gear also contains a water-activated, self-illuminating signal light. The fact that pilots and passengers can easily don and wear inflatable life vests (when not inflated) provides maximum effectiveness and allows for unrestricted movement. It is imperative that passengers are briefed on the location and proper use of available PFDs prior to leaving the dock.

f. The FAA recommends that seaplane owners and operators obtain Advisory Circular (AC) 91-69, Seaplane Safety for 14 CFR Part 91 Operations, free from the U.S. Department of Transportation, Subsequent Distribution Office, SVC-121.23, Ardmore East Business Center, 3341 Q 75th Avenue, Landover, MD 20785; fax: (301) 386-5394. The USCG Navigation Rules International-Inland (COMDTINSTM 16672.2B) is available for a fee from the Government Publishing Office by facsimile request to (202) 512-2250, and can be ordered using Mastercard or Visa.

Ch 7

TABLE 7–6–1
JURISDICTIONS CONTROLLING NAVIGABLE BODIES OF WATER

Authority to Consult For Use of a Body of Water		
Location	Authority	Contact
Wilderness Area	U.S. Department of Agriculture, Forest Service	Local forest ranger
National Forest	USDA Forest Service	Local forest ranger
National Park	U.S. Department of the Interior, National Park Service	Local park ranger
Indian Reservation	USDI, Bureau of Indian Affairs	Local Bureau office
State Park	State government or state forestry or park service	Local state aviation office for further information
Canadian National and Provincial Parks	Supervised and restricted on an individual basis from province to province and by different departments of the Canadian government; consult Canadian Flight Information Manual and/or Water Aerodrome Supplement	Park Superintendent in an emergency

7–6–10 Flight Operations in Volcanic Ash

a. Severe volcanic eruptions which send ash and sulphur dioxide (SO_2) gas into the upper atmosphere occur somewhere around the world several times each year. Flying into a volcanic ash cloud can be exceedingly dangerous. A B747-200 lost all four engines after such an encounter and a B747-400 had the same nearly catastrophic experience. Piston-powered aircraft are less likely to lose power but severe damage is almost certain to ensue after an encounter with a volcanic ash cloud which is only a few hours old.

b. Most important is to avoid any encounter with volcanic ash. The ash plume may not be visible, especially in instrument conditions or at night; and even if visible, it is difficult to distinguish visually between an ash cloud and an ordinary weather cloud. Volcanic ash clouds are not displayed on airborne or ATC radar. The pilot must rely on reports from air traffic controllers and other pilots to determine the location of the ash cloud and use that information to remain well clear of the area. Additionally, the presence of a sulphur-like odor throughout the cabin may indicate the presence of SO_2 emitted by volcanic activity, but may or may not indicate the presence of volcanic ash. Every attempt should be made to remain on the upwind side of the volcano.

c. It is recommended that pilots encountering an ash cloud should immediately reduce thrust to idle (altitude permitting), and reverse course in order to escape from the cloud. Ash clouds may extend for hundreds of miles and pilots should not attempt to fly through or climb out of the cloud. In addition, the following procedures are recommended:

1. Disengage the autothrottle if engaged. This will prevent the autothrottle from increasing engine thrust;

2. Turn on continuous ignition;

3. Turn on all accessory airbleeds including all air conditioning packs, nacelles, and wing anti-ice. This will provide an additional engine stall margin by reducing engine pressure.

d. The following has been reported by flightcrews who have experienced encounters with volcanic dust clouds:

1. Smoke or dust appearing in the cockpit.

2. An acrid odor similar to electrical smoke.

3. Multiple engine malfunctions, such as compressor stalls, increasing EGT, torching from tailpipe, and flameouts.

4. At night, St. Elmo's fire or other static discharges accompanied by a bright orange glow in the engine inlets.

5. A fire warning in the forward cargo area.

e. It may become necessary to shut down and then restart engines to prevent exceeding EGT limits. Volcanic ash may block the pitot system and result in unreliable airspeed indications.

f. If you see a volcanic eruption and have not been previously notified of it, you may have been the first person to observe it. In this case, immediately contact ATC and alert them to the existence of the eruption. If possible, use the Volcanic Activity Reporting form (VAR) depicted in Appendix 2 of this manual. Items 1 through 8 of the VAR should be transmitted immediately. The information requested in items 9 through 16 should be passed after landing. If a VAR form is not immediately available, relay enough information to identify the position and nature of the volcanic activity. Do not become unnecessarily alarmed if there is merely steam or very low-level eruptions of ash.

g. When landing at airports where volcanic ash has been deposited on the runway, be aware that even a thin layer of dry ash can be detrimental to braking action. Wet ash on the runway may also reduce effectiveness of braking. It is recommended that reverse thrust be limited to minimum practical to reduce the possibility of reduced visibility and engine ingestion of airborne ash.

h. When departing from airports where volcanic ash has been deposited, it is recommended that pilots avoid operating in visible airborne ash. Allow ash to settle before initiating takeoff roll. It is also recommended that flap extension be delayed until initiating the before takeoff checklist and that a rolling takeoff be executed to avoid blowing ash back into the air.

7–6–11 Emergency Airborne Inspection of Other Aircraft

a. Providing airborne assistance to another aircraft may involve flying in very close proximity to that aircraft. Most pilots receive little, if any, formal training or instruction in this type of flying activity. Close proximity flying without sufficient time to plan (i.e., in an emergency situation), coupled with the stress involved in a perceived emergency can be hazardous.

b. The pilot in the best position to assess the situation should take the responsibility of coordinating the airborne intercept and inspection, and take into account the unique flight characteristics and differences of the category(s) of aircraft involved.

c. Some of the safety considerations are:

1. Area, direction and speed of the intercept;

2. Aerodynamic effects (i.e., rotorcraft downwash);

3. Minimum safe separation distances;

4. Communications requirements, lost communications procedures, coordination with ATC;

5. Suitability of diverting the distressed aircraft to the nearest safe airport; and

6. Emergency actions to terminate the intercept.

d. Close proximity, inflight inspection of another aircraft is uniquely hazardous. The pilot-in-command of the aircraft experiencing the problem/emergency must not relinquish control of the situation and/or jeopardize the safety of their aircraft. The maneuver must be accomplished with minimum risk to both aircraft.

7–6–12 Precipitation Static

a. Precipitation static is caused by aircraft in flight coming in contact with uncharged particles. These particles can be rain, snow, fog, sleet, hail, volcanic ash, dust; any solid or liquid particles. When the aircraft strikes these neutral particles the positive element of the particle is reflected away from the aircraft and the negative particle adheres to the skin of the aircraft. In a very short period of time a substantial negative charge will develop on the skin of the aircraft. If the aircraft is not equipped with static dischargers, or has an ineffective static discharger system, when a sufficient negative voltage level is reached, the aircraft may go into "CORONA." That is, it will discharge the static electricity from the extremities of the aircraft, such as the wing tips, horizontal stabilizer, vertical stabilizer, antenna, propeller tips, etc. This discharge of static electricity is what you will hear in your headphones and is what we call P-static.

b. A review of pilot reports often shows different symptoms with each problem that is encountered. The following list of problems is a summary of many pilot reports from many different aircraft. Each problem was caused by P-static:

1. Complete loss of VHF communications.

2. Erroneous magnetic compass readings (30 percent in error).

3. High pitched squeal on audio.

4. Motor boat sound on audio.

5. Loss of all avionics in clouds.

6. VLF navigation system inoperative most of the time.

7. Erratic instrument readouts.

8. Weak transmissions and poor receptivity of radios.

9. "St. Elmo's Fire" on windshield.

c. Each of these symptoms is caused by one general problem on the airframe. This problem is the inability of the accumulated charge to flow easily to the wing tips and tail of the airframe, and properly discharge to the airstream.

d. Static dischargers work on the principal of creating a relatively easy path for discharging negative charges that develop on the aircraft by using a discharger with fine metal points, carbon coated rods, or carbon wicks rather than wait until a large charge is developed and discharged off the trailing edges of the aircraft that will interfere with avionics equipment. This process offers approximately 50 decibels (dB) static noise reduction which is adequate in most cases to be below the threshold of noise that would cause interference in avionics equipment.

e. It is important to remember that precipitation static problems can only be corrected with the proper number of quality static dischargers, properly installed on a properly bonded aircraft. P-static is indeed a problem in the all weather operation of the aircraft, but there are effective ways to combat it. All possible methods of reducing the effects of P-static should be considered so as to provide the best possible performance in the flight environment.

f. A wide variety of discharger designs is available on the commercial market. The inclusion of well-designed dischargers may be expected to improve airframe noise in P-static conditions by as much as 50 dB. Essentially, the discharger provides a path by which accumulated charge may leave the airframe quietly. This is generally accomplished by providing a group of tiny corona points to permit onset of corona-current flow at a low aircraft potential. Additionally, aerodynamic

Ch 7

design of dischargers to permit corona to occur at the lowest possible atmospheric pressure also lowers the corona threshold. In addition to permitting a low-potential discharge, the discharger will minimize the radiation of radio frequency (RF) energy which accompanies the corona discharge, in order to minimize effects of RF components at communications and navigation frequencies on avionics performance. These effects are reduced through resistive attachment of the corona point(s) to the airframe, preserving direct current connection but attenuating the higher-frequency components of the discharge.

g. Each manufacturer of static dischargers offers information concerning appropriate discharger location on specific airframes. Such locations emphasize the trailing outboard surfaces of wings and horizontal tail surfaces, plus the tip of the vertical stabilizer, where charge tends to accumulate on the airframe. Sufficient dischargers must be provided to allow for current-carrying capacity which will maintain airframe potential below the corona threshold of the trailing edges.

h. In order to achieve full performance of avionic equipment, the static discharge system will require periodic maintenance. A pilot knowledgeable of P-static causes and effects is an important element in assuring optimum performance by early recognition of these types of problems.

7–6–13 Light Amplification by Stimulated Emission of Radiation (Laser) Operations and Reporting Illumination of Aircraft

a. Lasers have many applications. Of concern to users of the National Airspace System are those laser events that may affect pilots, e.g., outdoor laser light shows or demonstrations for entertainment and advertisements at special events and theme parks. Generally, the beams from these events appear as bright blue-green in color; however, they may be red, yellow, or white. However, some laser systems produce light which is invisible to the human eye.

b. FAA regulations prohibit the disruption of aviation activity by any person on the ground or in the air. The FAA and the Food and Drug Administration (the Federal agency that has the responsibility to enforce compliance with Federal requirements for laser systems and laser light show products) are working together to ensure that operators of these devices do not pose a hazard to aircraft operators.

c. Pilots should be aware that illumination from these laser operations are able to create temporary vision impairment miles from the actual location. In addition, these operations can produce permanent eye damage. Pilots should

make themselves aware of where these activities are being conducted and avoid these areas if possible.

d. Recent and increasing incidents of unauthorized illumination of aircraft by lasers, as well as the proliferation and increasing sophistication of laser devices available to the general public, dictates that the FAA, in coordination with other government agencies, take action to safeguard flights from these unauthorized illuminations.

e. Pilots should report laser illumination activity to the controlling Air Traffic Control facilities, Federal Contract Towers or Flight Service Stations as soon as possible after the event. The following information should be included:

1. UTC Date and Time of Event.

2. Call Sign or Aircraft Registration Number.

3. Type Aircraft.

4. Nearest Major City.

5. Altitude.

6. Location of Event (Latitude/Longitude and/or Fixed Radial Distance (FRD)).

7. Brief Description of the Event and any other Pertinent Information.

f. Pilots are also encouraged to complete the Laser Beam Exposure Questionnaire located on the FAA Laser Safety Initiative website at http://www.faa.gov/about/initiatives/lasers/ and submit electronically per the directions on the questionnaire, as soon as possible after landing.

g. When a laser event is reported to an air traffic facility, a general caution warning will be broadcasted on all appropriate frequencies every five minutes for 20 minutes and broadcasted on the ATIS for one hour following the report.

Phraseology:
Unauthorized laser illumination event, (UTC time), (location), (altitude), (color), (direction).

Example: *"Unauthorized laser illumination event, at 0100z, 8 mile final runway 18R at 3,000 feet, green laser from the southwest."*

Reference: *FAA Order JO 7110.65, ¶10-2-14, Unauthorized Laser Illumination of Aircraft; FAA Order JO 7210.3, ¶2-1-27, Reporting Unauthorized Laser Illumination of Aircraft.*

h. When these activities become known to the FAA, Notices to Air Missions (NOTAMs) are issued to inform the aviation community of the events. Pilots should consult NOTAMs or the Chart Supplement for information regarding these activities.

7–6–14 Flying in Flat Light, Brown Out Conditions, and White Out Conditions

a. Flat Light. Flat light is an optical illusion, also known as **"sector or partial white out."** It is not as severe as "white out" but the condition causes pilots to lose their depth-of-field and contrast in vision. Flat light conditions are usually accompanied by overcast skies inhibiting any visual clues. Such conditions can occur anywhere in the world, primarily in snow covered areas but can occur in dust, sand, mud flats, or on glassy water. Flat light can completely obscure features of the terrain, creating an inability to distinguish distances and closure rates. As a result of this reflected light, it can give pilots the illusion that they are ascending or descending when they may actually be flying level. However, with good judgment and proper training and planning, it is possible to safely operate an aircraft in flat light conditions.

b. Brown Out. A brownout (or *brown-out*) is an in-flight visibility restriction due to dust or sand in the air. In a brownout, the pilot cannot see nearby objects which provide the outside visual references necessary to control the aircraft near the ground. This can cause spatial disorientation and loss of situational awareness leading to an accident.

1. The following factors will affect the probability and severity of brownout: rotor disk loading, rotor configuration, soil composition, wind, approach speed, and approach angle.

2. The brownout phenomenon causes accidents during helicopter landing and take-off operations in dust, fine dirt, sand, or arid desert terrain. Intense, blinding dust clouds stirred up by the helicopter rotor downwash during near-ground flight causes significant flight safety risks from aircraft and ground obstacle collisions, and dynamic rollover due to sloped and uneven terrain.

3. This is a dangerous phenomenon experienced by many helicopters when making landing approaches in dusty environments, whereby sand or dust particles become swept up in the rotor outwash and obscure the pilot's vision of the terrain. This is particularly dangerous because the pilot needs those visual cues from their surroundings in order to make a safe landing.

4. Blowing sand and dust can cause an illusion of a tilted horizon. A pilot not using the flight instruments for reference may instinctively try to level the aircraft with respect to the false horizon, resulting in an accident. Helicopter rotor wash also causes sand to blow around outside the cockpit windows, possibly leading the pilot to experience an illusion where the helicopter appears to be turning when it is actually in a level hover. This can also cause the pilot to make incorrect control inputs which can quickly lead to disaster when hovering near the ground. In night landings, aircraft lighting can enhance the visual illusions by illuminating the brownout cloud.

c. White Out. As defined in meteorological terms, white out occurs when a person becomes engulfed in a uniformly white glow. The glow is a result of being surrounded by blowing snow, dust, sand, mud or water. There are no shadows, no horizon or clouds and all depth-of-field and orientation are lost. A white out situation is severe in that there are no visual references. Flying is not recommended in any white out situation. Flat light conditions can lead to a white out environment quite rapidly, and both atmospheric conditions are insidious; they sneak up on you as your visual references slowly begin to disappear. White out has been the cause of several aviation accidents.

d. Self Induced White Out. This effect typically occurs when a helicopter takes off or lands on a snow-covered area. The rotor down wash picks up particles and re-circulates them through the rotor down wash. The effect can vary in intensity depending upon the amount of light on the surface. This can happen on the sunniest, brightest day with good contrast everywhere. However, when it happens, there can be a complete loss of visual clues. If the pilot has not prepared for this immediate loss of visibility, the results can be disastrous. Good planning does not prevent one from encountering flat light or white out conditions.

e. Never take off in a white out situation.

1. Realize that in flat light conditions it may be possible to depart but not to return to that site. During takeoff, make sure you have a reference point. Do not lose sight of it until you have a departure reference point in view. Be prepared to return to the takeoff reference if the departure reference does not come into view.

2. Flat light is common to snow skiers. One way to compensate for the lack of visual contrast and depth-of-field loss is by wearing amber tinted lenses (also known as blue blockers). Special note of caution: Eyewear is not ideal for every pilot. Take into consideration personal factors—age, light sensitivity, and ambient lighting conditions.

3. So what should a pilot do when all visual references are lost?

(a) Trust the cockpit instruments.

(b) Execute a 180 degree turnaround and start looking for outside references.

(c) Above all—fly the aircraft.

f. Landing in Low Light Conditions. When landing in a low light condition—use extreme caution. Look for intermediate reference points, in addition to checkpoints along each leg of the route for course confirmation and timing. The

Ch 7

lower the ambient light becomes, the more reference points a pilot should use.

g. Airport Landings.

1. Look for features around the airport or approach path that can be used in determining depth perception. Buildings, towers, vehicles or other aircraft serve well for this measurement. Use something that will provide you with a sense of height above the ground, in addition to orienting you to the runway.

2. Be cautious of snowdrifts and snow banks—anything that can distinguish the edge of the runway. Look for subtle changes in snow texture or shading to identify ridges or changes in snow depth.

h. Off-Airport Landings.

1. In the event of an off-airport landing, pilots have used a number of different visual cues to gain reference. Use whatever you must to create the contrast you need. Natural references seem to work best (trees, rocks, snow ribs, etc.)

 (a) Over flight.

 (b) Use of markers.

 (c) Weighted flags.

 (d) Smoke bombs.

 (e) Any colored rags.

 (f) Dye markers.

 (g) Kool-Aid.

 (h) Trees or tree branches.

2. It is difficult to determine the depth of snow in areas that are level. Dropping items from the aircraft to use as reference points should be used as a visual aid only and not as a primary landing reference. Unless your marker is biodegradable, be sure to retrieve it after landing. Never put yourself in a position where no visual references exist.

3. Abort landing if blowing snow obscures your reference. Make your decisions early. Don't assume you can pick up a lost reference point when you get closer.

4. Exercise extreme caution when flying from sunlight into shade. Physical awareness may tell you that you are flying straight but you may actually be in a spiral dive with centrifugal force pressing against you. Having no visual references enhances this illusion. Just because you have a good visual reference does not mean that it's safe to continue. There may be snow-covered terrain not visible in the direction that you are traveling. Getting caught in a no visual reference situation can be fatal.

i. Flying Around a Lake.

1. When flying along lakeshores, use them as a reference point. Even if you can see the other side, realize that your depth perception may be poor. It is easy to fly into the surface. If you must cross the lake, check the altimeter frequently and maintain a safe altitude while you still have a good reference. Don't descend below that altitude.

2. The same rules apply to seemingly flat areas of snow. If you don't have good references, avoid going there.

j. Other Traffic. Be on the look out for other traffic in the area. Other aircraft may be using your same reference point. Chances are greater of colliding with someone traveling in the same direction as you, than someone flying in the opposite direction.

k. Ceilings. Low ceilings have caught many pilots off guard. Clouds do not always form parallel to the surface, or at the same altitude. Pilots may try to compensate for this by flying with a slight bank and thus creating a descending turn.

l. Glaciers. Be conscious of your altitude when flying over glaciers. The glaciers may be rising faster than you are climbing.

7-6-15 Operations in Ground Icing Conditions

a. The presence of aircraft airframe icing during takeoff, typically caused by improper or no deicing of the aircraft being accomplished prior to flight has contributed to many recent accidents in turbine aircraft. The General Aviation Joint Steering Committee (GAJSC) is the primary vehicle for government-industry cooperation, communication, and coordination on GA accident mitigation. The Turbine Aircraft Operations Subgroup (TAOS) works to mitigate accidents in turbine accident aviation. While there is sufficient information and guidance currently available regarding the effects of icing on aircraft and methods for deicing, the TAOS has developed a list of recommended actions to further assist pilots and operators in this area.

While the efforts of the TAOS specifically focus on turbine aircraft, it is recognized that their recommendations are applicable to and can be adapted for the pilot of a small, piston powered aircraft too.

b. The following recommendations are offered:

1. Ensure that your aircraft's lift-generating surfaces are COMPLETELY free of contamination before flight through a tactile (hands on) check of the critical surfaces when feasible. Even when otherwise permitted, operators should avoid smooth or polished frost on lift-generating surfaces as an acceptable preflight condition.

2. Review and refresh your cold weather standard operating procedures.

3. Review and be familiar with the Airplane Flight Manual (AFM) limitations and procedures necessary to deal with icing conditions prior to flight, as well as in flight.

4. Protect your aircraft while on the ground, if possible, from sleet and freezing rain by taking advantage of aircraft hangars.

5. Take full advantage of the opportunities available at airports for deicing. Do not refuse deicing services simply because of cost.

6. Always consider canceling or delaying a flight if weather conditions do not support a safe operation.

c. If you haven't already developed a set of Standard Operating Procedures for cold weather operations, they should include:

1. Procedures based on information that is applicable to the aircraft operated, such as AFM limitations and procedures;

2. Concise and easy to understand guidance that outlines best operational practices;

3. A systematic procedure for recognizing, evaluating and addressing the associated icing risk, and offer clear guidance to mitigate this risk;

4. An aid (such as a checklist or reference cards) that is readily available during normal day-to-day aircraft operations.

d. There are several sources for guidance relating to airframe icing, including:

1. http://aircrafticing.grc.nasa.gov/index.html

2. Advisory Circular (AC) 91-74, Pilot Guide, Flight in Icing Conditions.

3. AC 135-17, Pilot Guide Small Aircraft Ground Deicing.

4. AC 135-9, FAR Part 135 Icing Limitations.

5. AC 120-60, Ground Deicing and Anti-icing Program.

6. AC 135-16, Ground Deicing and Anti-icing Training and Checking. The FAA Approved Deicing Program Updates is published annually as a Flight Standards Information Bulletin for Air Transportation and contains detailed information on deicing and anti-icing procedures and holdover times. It may be accessed at the following website by selecting the current year's information bulletins: https://www.faa.gov/other_visit/aviation_industry/airline_operators/airline_safety/deicing/.

7–6–16 Avoid Flight in the Vicinity of Exhaust Plumes (Smoke Stacks and Cooling Towers)

a. Flight Hazards Exist Around Exhaust Plumes. Exhaust plumes are defined as visible or invisible emissions from power plants, industrial production facilities, or other industrial systems that release large amounts of vertically directed unstable gases (effluent). High temperature exhaust plumes can cause significant air disturbances such as turbulence and vertical shear. Other identified potential hazards include, but are not necessarily limited to: reduced visibility, oxygen depletion, engine particulate contamination, exposure to gaseous oxides, and/or icing. Results of encountering a plume may include airframe damage, aircraft upset, and/or engine damage/failure. These hazards are most critical during low altitude flight in calm and cold air, especially in

and around approach and departure corridors or airport traffic areas.

Whether plumes are visible or invisible, the total extent of their turbulent affect is difficult to predict. Some studies do predict that the significant turbulent effects of an exhaust plume can extend to heights of over 1,000 feet above the height of the top of the stack or cooling tower. Any effects will be more pronounced in calm stable air where the plume is very hot and the surrounding area is still and cold. Fortunately, studies also predict that any amount of crosswind will help to dissipate the effects. However, the size of the tower or stack is not a good indicator of the predicted effect the plume may produce. The major effects are related to the heat or size of the plume effluent, the ambient air temperature, and the wind speed affecting the plume. Smaller aircraft can expect to feel an effect at a higher altitude than heavier aircraft.

b. When able, a pilot should steer clear of exhaust plumes by flying on the upwind side of smokestacks or cooling towers. When a plume is visible via smoke or a condensation cloud, remain clear and realize a plume may have both visible and invisible characteristics. Exhaust stacks without visible plumes may still be in full operation, and airspace in the vicinity should be treated with caution. As with mountain wave turbulence or clear air turbulence, an invisible plume may be encountered unexpectedly. Cooling towers, power plant stacks, exhaust fans, and other similar structures are depicted in Figure 7-6-2.

Pilots are encouraged to exercise caution when flying in the vicinity of exhaust plumes. Pilots are also encouraged to reference the Chart Supplement where amplifying notes may caution pilots and identify the location of structure(s) emitting exhaust plumes.

The best available information on this phenomenon must come from pilots via the PIREP reporting procedures. All pilots encountering hazardous plume conditions are urgently requested to report time, location, and intensity (light, moderate, severe, or extreme) of the element to the FAA facility with which they are maintaining radio contact. If time and conditions permit, elements should be reported according to the standards for other PIREPs and position reports (AIM Paragraph 7-1-21, PIREPS Relating to Turbulence).

FIGURE 7–6–2
Plumes

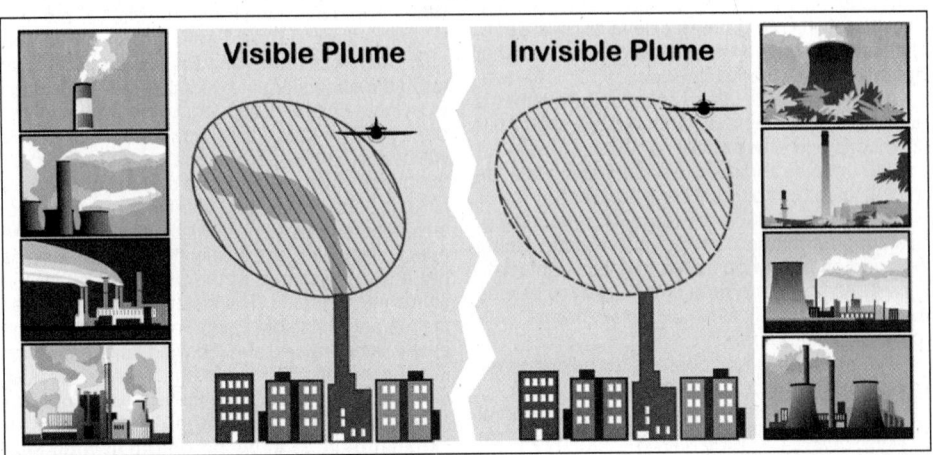

7–6–17 Space Launch and Reentry Area

Locations where commercial space launch and/or reentry operations occur. Hazardous operations occur in space launch and reentry areas, and for pilot awareness, a rocket-shaped symbol is used to depict them on sectional aeronautical charts. These locations may have vertical launches from launch pads, horizontal launches from runways, and/or reentering vehicles coming back to land. Because of the wide range of hazards associated with space launch and reentry areas, pilots are expected to check NOTAMs for the specific area prior to flight to determine the location and lateral boundaries of the associated hazard area, and the active time. NOTAMs may include terms such as "rocket launch activity," "space launch," or "space reentry," depending upon the type of operation. Space launch and reentry areas are not established for amateur rocket operations conducted per 14 CFR Part 101.

FIGURE 7–6–3
Space Launch and Reentry Area Depicted on a Sectional Chart

Section 7 Safety, Accident, and Hazard Reports

7–7–1 Aviation Safety Reporting Program

a. The FAA has established a voluntary Aviation Safety Reporting Program designed to stimulate the free and unrestricted flow of information concerning deficiencies and discrepancies in the aviation system. This is a positive program intended to ensure the safest possible system by identifying and correcting unsafe conditions before they lead to accidents. The primary objective of the program is to obtain information to evaluate and enhance the safety and efficiency of the present system.

b. This cooperative safety reporting program invites pilots, controllers, flight attendants, maintenance personnel and other users of the airspace system, or any other person, to file written reports of actual or potential discrepancies and deficiencies involving the safety of aviation operations. The operations covered by the program include departure, en route, approach, and landing operations and procedures, air traffic control procedures and equipment, crew and air traffic control communications, aircraft cabin operations, aircraft movement on the airport, near midair collisions, aircraft maintenance and record keeping and airport conditions or services.

c. The report should give the date, time, location, persons and aircraft involved (if applicable), nature of the event, and all pertinent details.

d. To ensure receipt of this information, the program provides for the waiver of certain disciplinary actions against persons, including pilots and air traffic controllers, who file timely written reports concerning potentially unsafe incidents. To be considered timely, reports must be delivered or postmarked within 10 days of the incident unless that period is extended for good cause. Reports should be submitted on NASA ARC Forms 277, which are available free of charge, postage prepaid, at FAA Flight Standards District Offices and Flight Service Stations, and from NASA, ASRS, PO Box 189, Moffet Field, CA 94035.

e. The FAA utilizes the National Aeronautics and Space Administration (NASA) to act as an independent third party to receive and analyze reports submitted under the program. This program is described in AC 00-46, Aviation Safety Reporting Program.

7–7–2 Aircraft Accident and Incident Reporting

a. Occurrences Requiring Notification. The operator of an aircraft must immediately, and by the most expeditious means available, notify the nearest National Transportation Safety Board (NTSB) Field Office when:

1. An aircraft accident or any of the following listed incidents occur:

(a) Flight control system malfunction or failure.

(b) Inability of any required flight crew member to perform their normal flight duties as a result of injury or illness.

(c) Failure of structural components of a turbine engine excluding compressor and turbine blades and vanes.

(d) Inflight fire.

(e) Aircraft collide in flight.

(f) Damage to property, other than the aircraft, estimated to exceed $25,000 for repair (including materials and labor) or fair market value in the event of total loss, whichever is less.

(g) For large multi-engine aircraft (more than 12,500 pounds maximum certificated takeoff weight):

(1) Inflight failure of electrical systems which requires the sustained use of an emergency bus powered by a back-up source such as a battery, auxiliary power unit, or air-driven generator to retain flight control or essential instruments;

(2) Inflight failure of hydraulic systems that results in sustained reliance on the sole remaining hydraulic or mechanical system for movement of flight control surfaces;

(3) Sustained loss of the power or thrust produced by two or more engines; and

(4) An evacuation of aircraft in which an emergency egress system is utilized.

2. An aircraft is overdue and is believed to have been involved in an accident.

b. Manner of Notification.

1. The most expeditious method of notification to the NTSB by the operator will be determined by the circumstances existing at that time. The NTSB has advised that any of the following would be considered examples of the type of notification that would be acceptable:

(a) Direct telephone notification.

(b) Telegraphic notification.

(c) Notification to the FAA who would in turn notify the NTSB by direct communication; i.e., dispatch or telephone.

c. Items to be Included in Notification. The notification required above must contain the following information, if available:

1. Type, nationality, and registration marks of the aircraft.

2. Name of owner and operator of the aircraft.

3. Name of the pilot-in-command.

4. Date and time of the accident, or incident.

5. Last point of departure, and point of intended landing of the aircraft.

6. Position of the aircraft with reference to some easily defined geographical point.

7. Number of persons aboard, number killed, and number seriously injured.

8. Nature of the accident, or incident, the weather, and the extent of damage to the aircraft so far as is known; and

9. A description of any explosives, radioactive materials, or other dangerous articles carried.

d. Follow-up Reports.

1. The operator must file a report on NTSB Form 6120.1 or 6120.2, available from NTSB Field Offices or from the NTSB, Washington, DC, 20594:

(a) Within 10 days after an accident;

(b) When, after 7 days, an overdue aircraft is still missing;

(c) A report on an incident for which notification is required as described in subparagraph a(1) must be filed only as requested by an authorized representative of the NTSB.

2. Each crewmember, if physically able at the time the report is submitted, must attach a statement setting forth the facts, conditions, and circumstances relating to the accident or incident as they appeared. If the crewmember is incapacitated, a statement must be submitted as soon as physically possible.

e. Where to File the Reports.

1. The operator of an aircraft must file with the NTSB Field Office nearest the accident or incident any report required by this section.

2. The NTSB Field Offices are listed under U.S. Government in the telephone directories in the following cities: Anchorage, AK; Atlanta, GA; Chicago, IL; Denver, CO; Fort Worth, TX; Los Angeles, CA; Miami, FL; Parsippany, NJ; Seattle, WA.

7–7–3 Near Midair Collision Reporting

a. Purpose and Data Uses. The primary purpose of the Near Midair Collision (NMAC) Reporting Program is to provide information for use in enhancing the safety and efficiency of the National Airspace System. Data obtained from NMAC reports are used by the FAA to improve the quality of FAA services to users and to develop programs, policies, and procedures aimed at the reduction of NMAC occurrences. All NMAC reports are thoroughly investigated by Flight Standards Facilities in coordination with Air Traffic Facilities. Data from these investigations are transmitted to FAA Headquarters in Washington, DC, where they are compiled and analyzed, and where safety programs and recommendations are developed.

b. Definition. A near midair collision is defined as an incident associated with the operation of an aircraft in which a possibility of collision occurs as a result of proximity of less than 500 feet to another aircraft, or a report is received from a pilot or a flight crew member stating that a collision hazard existed between two or more aircraft.

c. Reporting Responsibility. It is the responsibility of the pilot and/or flight crew to determine whether a near midair collision did actually occur and, if so, to initiate a NMAC report. Be specific, as ATC will not interpret a casual remark to mean that a NMAC is being reported. The pilot should state "I wish to report a near midair collision."

d. Where to File Reports. Pilots and/or flight crew members involved in NMAC occurrences are urged to report each incident immediately:

1. By radio or telephone to the nearest FAA ATC facility or FSS.

2. In writing, in lieu of the above, to the nearest Flight Standards District Office (FSDO).

e. Items to be Reported.

1. Date and time (UTC) of incident.

2. Location of incident and altitude.

3. Identification and type of reporting aircraft, aircrew destination, name and home base of pilot.

4. Identification and type of other aircraft, aircrew destination, name and home base of pilot.

5. Type of flight plans; station altimeter setting used.

6. Detailed weather conditions at altitude or flight level.

7. Approximate courses of both aircraft: indicate if one or both aircraft were climbing or descending.

8. Reported separation in distance at first sighting, proximity at closest point horizontally and vertically, and length of time in sight prior to evasive action.

9. Degree of evasive action taken, if any (from both aircraft, if possible).

10. Injuries, if any.

f. Investigation. The FSDO in whose area the incident occurred is responsible for the investigation and reporting of NMACs.

g. Existing radar, communication, and weather data will be examined in the conduct of the investigation. When possible, all cockpit crew members will be interviewed regarding factors involving the NMAC incident. Air traffic controllers will be interviewed in cases where one or more of the involved aircraft was provided ATC service.

Both flight and ATC procedures will be evaluated. When the investigation reveals a violation of an FAA regulation, enforcement action will be pursued.

7-7-4 Unidentified Flying Object (UFO) Reports

a. Persons wanting to report UFO/unexplained phenomena activity should contact a UFO/unexplained phenomena reporting data collection center, such as the National UFO Reporting Center, etc.

b. If concern is expressed that life or property might be endangered, report the activity to the local law enforcement department.

7-7-5 Safety Alerts For Operators (SAFO) and Information For Operators (InFO)

a. SAFOs contain important safety information that is often time-critical. A SAFO may contain information and/or recommended (non-regulatory) action to be taken by the respective operators or parties identified in the SAFO. The audience for SAFOs varies with each subject and may include: Air carrier certificate holders, air operator certificate holders, general aviation operators, directors of safety, directors of operations, directors of maintenance, fractional ownership program managers, training center managers, accountable managers at repair stations, and other parties as applicable.

b. InFOs are similar to SAFOs, but contain valuable information for operators that should help them meet administrative requirements or certain regulatory requirements with relatively low urgency or impact in safety.

c. The SAFO and InFO system provides a means to rapidly distribute this information to operators and can be found at the following website: http://www.faa.gov/other_visit/aviation_industry/airline_operators/airline_safety/safo and http://www.faa.gov/other_visit/aviation_industry/airline_operators/airline_safety/info or search keyword FAA SAFO or FAA INFO. Free electronic subscription is available on the "ALL SAFOs" or "ALL InFOs" page of the website.

Ch 7

Chapter 8
Medical Facts for Pilots

Section 1 Fitness for Flight

8–1–1 Fitness For Flight

a. Medical Certification.

1. All pilots except those flying gliders and free air balloons must possess valid medical certificates in order to exercise the privileges of their airman certificates. The periodic medical examinations required for medical certification are conducted by designated Aviation Medical Examiners, who are physicians with a special interest in aviation safety and training in aviation medicine.

2. The standards for medical certification are contained in 14 CFR Part 67. Pilots who have a history of certain medical conditions described in these standards are mandatorily disqualified from flying. These medical conditions include a personality disorder manifested by overt acts, a psychosis, alcoholism, drug dependence, epilepsy, an unexplained disturbance of consciousness, myocardial infarction, angina pectoris and diabetes requiring medication for its control. Other medical conditions may be temporarily disqualifying, such as acute infections, anemia, and peptic ulcer. Pilots who do not meet medical standards may still be qualified under special issuance provisions or the exemption process. This may require that either additional medical information be provided or practical flight tests be conducted.

3. Student pilots should visit an Aviation Medical Examiner as soon as possible in their flight training in order to avoid unnecessary training expenses should they not meet the medical standards. For the same reason, the student pilot who plans to enter commercial aviation should apply for the highest class of medical certificate that might be necessary in the pilot's career.

Caution: The CFRs prohibit a pilot who possesses a current medical certificate from performing crewmember duties while the pilot has a known medical condition or increase of a known medical condition that would make the pilot unable to meet the standards for the medical certificate.

b. Illness.

1. Even a minor illness suffered in day-to-day living can seriously degrade performance of many piloting tasks vital to safe flight. Illness can produce fever and distracting symptoms that can impair judgment, memory, alertness, and the ability to make calculations. Although symptoms from an illness may be under adequate control with a medication, the medication itself may decrease pilot performance.

2. The safest rule is not to fly while suffering from any illness. If this rule is considered too stringent for a particular illness, the pilot should contact an Aviation Medical Examiner for advice.

c. Medication.

1. Pilot performance can be seriously degraded by both prescribed and over-the-counter medications, as well as by the medical conditions for which they are taken. Many medications, such as tranquilizers, sedatives, strong pain relievers, and cough-suppressant preparations, have primary effects that may impair judgment, memory, alertness, coordination, vision, and the ability to make calculations. Others, such as antihistamines, blood pressure drugs, muscle relaxants, and agents to control diarrhea and motion sickness, have side effects that may impair the same critical functions. Any medication that depresses the nervous system, such as a sedative, tranquilizer or antihistamine, can make a pilot much more susceptible to hypoxia.

2. The CFRs prohibit pilots from performing crewmember duties while using any medication that affects the faculties in any way contrary to safety. The safest rule is not to fly as a crewmember while taking any medication, unless approved to do so by the FAA.

d. Alcohol.

1. Extensive research has provided a number of facts about the hazards of alcohol consumption and flying. As little as one ounce of liquor, one bottle of beer or four ounces of wine can impair flying skills, with the alcohol consumed in these drinks being detectable in the breath and blood for at least 3 hours. Even after the body completely destroys a moderate amount of alcohol, a pilot can still be severely impaired for many hours by hangover. There is simply no way of increasing the destruction of alcohol or alleviating a hangover. Alcohol also renders a pilot much more susceptible to disorientation and hypoxia.

2. A consistently high alcohol related fatal aircraft accident rate serves to emphasize that alcohol and flying are a potentially lethal combination. The CFRs prohibit pilots from performing crewmember duties within 8 hours after drinking any alcoholic beverage or while under the influence of alcohol. However, due to the slow destruction of alcohol, a pilot may still be under influence 8 hours after drinking a moderate amount

of alcohol. Therefore, an excellent rule is to allow at least 12 to 24 hours between "bottle and throttle," depending on the amount of alcoholic beverage consumed.

e. Fatigue.

1. Fatigue continues to be one of the most treacherous hazards to flight safety, as it may not be apparent to a pilot until serious errors are made. Fatigue is best described as either acute (short-term) or chronic (long-term).

2. A normal occurrence of everyday living, acute fatigue is the tiredness felt after long periods of physical and mental strain, including strenuous muscular effort, immobility, heavy mental workload, strong emotional pressure, monotony, and lack of sleep. Consequently, coordination and alertness, so vital to safe pilot performance, can be reduced. Acute fatigue is prevented by adequate rest and sleep, as well as by regular exercise and proper nutrition.

3. Chronic fatigue occurs when there is not enough time for full recovery between episodes of acute fatigue. Performance continues to fall off, and judgment becomes impaired so that unwarranted risks may be taken. Recovery from chronic fatigue requires a prolonged period of rest.

4. Obstructive Sleep Apnea (OSA). OSA is now recognized as an important preventable factor identified in transportation accidents. OSA interrupts the normal restorative sleep necessary for normal functioning and is associated with chronic illnesses such as hypertension, heart attack, stroke, obesity, and diabetes. Symptoms include snoring, excessive daytime sleepiness, intermittent prolonged breathing pauses while sleeping, memory impairment and lack of concentration. There are many available treatments which can reverse the day time symptoms and reduce the chance of an accident. OSA can be easily treated. Most treatments are acceptable for medical certification upon demonstrating effective treatment. If you have any symptoms described above, or neck size over 17 inches in men or 16 inches in women, or a body mass index greater than 30 you should be evaluated for sleep apnea by a sleep medicine specialist. (https://www.cdc.gov/healthyweight/assessing/bmi/adult_bmi/english_bmi_calculator/bmi_calculator.html) With treatment you can avoid or delay the onset of these chronic illnesses and prolong a quality life.

f. Stress.

1. Stress from the pressures of everyday living can impair pilot performance, often in very subtle ways. Difficulties, particularly at work, can occupy thought processes enough to markedly decrease alertness. Distraction can so interfere with judgment that unwarranted risks are taken, such as flying into deteriorating weather conditions to keep on schedule. Stress and fatigue (see above) can be an extremely hazardous combination.

2. Most pilots do not leave stress "on the ground." Therefore, when more than usual difficulties are being experienced, a pilot should consider delaying flight until these difficulties are satisfactorily resolved.

g. Emotion. Certain emotionally upsetting events, including a serious argument, death of a family member, separation or divorce, loss of job, and financial catastrophe, can render a pilot unable to fly an aircraft safely. The emotions of anger, depression, and anxiety from such events not only decrease alertness but also may lead to taking risks that border on self-destruction. Any pilot who experiences an emotionally upsetting event should not fly until satisfactorily recovered from it.

h. Personal Checklist. Aircraft accident statistics show that pilots should be conducting preflight checklists on themselves as well as their aircraft for pilot impairment contributes to many more accidents than failures of aircraft systems. A personal checklist, which includes all of the categories of pilot impairment as discussed in this section, that can be easily committed to memory is being distributed by the FAA in the form of a wallet-sized card.

i. Personal Checklist. *I'm physically and mentally safe to fly; not being impaired by:*

I llness
M edication
S tress
A lcohol
F atigue
E motion

8-1-2 Effects of Altitude

a. Hypoxia.

1. Hypoxia is a state of oxygen deficiency in the body sufficient to impair functions of the brain and other organs. Hypoxia from exposure to altitude is due only to the reduced barometric pressures encountered at altitude, for the concentration of oxygen in the atmosphere remains about 21 percent from the ground out to space.

2. Although a deterioration in night vision occurs at a cabin pressure altitude as low as 5,000 feet, other significant effects of altitude hypoxia usually do not occur in the normal healthy pilot below 12,000 feet. From 12,000 to 15,000 feet of altitude, judgment, memory, alertness, coordination and ability to make calculations are impaired, and headache, drowsiness, dizziness and either a sense of well-being (euphoria) or belligerence occur. The effects appear following increasingly shorter periods of exposure to increasing altitude. In fact, pilot performance can seriously deteriorate within 15 minutes at 15,000 feet.

3. At cabin pressure altitudes above 15,000 feet, the periphery of the visual field grays out to

a point where only central vision remains (tunnel vision). A blue coloration (cyanosis) of the fingernails and lips develops. The ability to take corrective and protective action is lost in 20 to 30 minutes at 18,000 feet and 5 to 12 minutes at 20,000 feet, followed soon thereafter by unconsciousness.

4. The altitude at which significant effects of hypoxia occur can be lowered by a number of factors. Carbon monoxide inhaled in smoking or from exhaust fumes, lowered hemoglobin (anemia), and certain medications can reduce the oxygen-carrying capacity of the blood to the degree that the amount of oxygen provided to body tissues will already be equivalent to the oxygen provided to the tissues when exposed to a cabin pressure altitude of several thousand feet. Small amounts of alcohol and low doses of certain drugs, such as antihistamines, tranquilizers, sedatives and analgesics can, through their depressant action, render the brain much more susceptible to hypoxia. Extreme heat and cold, fever, and anxiety increase the body's demand for oxygen, and hence its susceptibility to hypoxia.

5. The effects of hypoxia are usually quite difficult to recognize, especially when they occur gradually. Since symptoms of hypoxia do not vary in an individual, the ability to recognize hypoxia can be greatly improved by experiencing and witnessing the effects of hypoxia during an altitude chamber "flight." The FAA provides this opportunity through aviation physiology training, which is conducted at the FAA Civil Aeromedical Institute and at many military facilities across the U.S. To attend the Physiological Training Program at the Civil Aeromedical Institute, Mike Monroney Aeronautical Center, Oklahoma City, OK, contact by telephone (405) 954-6212, or by writing Aerospace Medical Education Division, AAM–400, CAMI, Mike Monroney Aeronautical Center, P.O. Box 25082, Oklahoma City, OK 73125.

Note: To attend the physiological training program at one of the military installations having the training capability, an application form and a fee must be submitted. Full particulars about location, fees, scheduling procedures, course content, individual requirements, etc., are contained in the Physiological Training Application, Form Number AC 3150-7, which is obtained by contacting the accident prevention specialist or the office forms manager in the nearest FAA office.

6. Hypoxia is prevented by heeding factors that reduce tolerance to altitude, by enriching the inspired air with oxygen from an appropriate oxygen system, and by maintaining a comfortable, safe cabin pressure altitude. For optimum protection, pilots are encouraged to use supplemental oxygen above 10,000 feet during the day, and above 5,000 feet at night. The CFRs require

that at the minimum, flight crew be provided with and use supplemental oxygen after 30 minutes of exposure to cabin pressure altitudes between 12,500 and 14,000 feet and immediately on exposure to cabin pressure altitudes above 14,000 feet. Every occupant of the aircraft must be provided with supplemental oxygen at cabin pressure altitudes above 15,000 feet.

b. Ear Block.

1. As the aircraft cabin pressure decreases during ascent, the expanding air in the middle ear pushes the eustachian tube open, and by escaping down it to the nasal passages, equalizes in pressure with the cabin pressure. But during descent, the pilot must periodically open the eustachian tube to equalize pressure. This can be accomplished by swallowing, yawning, tensing muscles in the throat, or if these do not work, by a combination of closing the mouth, pinching the nose closed, and attempting to blow through the nostrils (Valsalva maneuver).

2. Either an upper respiratory infection, such as a cold or sore throat, or a nasal allergic condition can produce enough congestion around the eustachian tube to make equalization difficult. Consequently, the difference in pressure between the middle ear and aircraft cabin can build up to a level that will hold the eustachian tube closed, making equalization difficult if not impossible. The problem is commonly referred to as an "ear block."

3. An ear block produces severe ear pain and loss of hearing that can last from several hours to several days. Rupture of the ear drum can occur in flight or after landing. Fluid can accumulate in the middle ear and become infected.

4. An ear block is prevented by not flying with an upper respiratory infection or nasal allergic condition. Adequate protection is usually not provided by decongestant sprays or drops to reduce congestion around the eustachian tubes. Oral decongestants have side effects that can significantly impair pilot performance.

5. If an ear block does not clear shortly after landing, a physician should be consulted.

c. Sinus Block.

1. During ascent and descent, air pressure in the sinuses equalizes with the aircraft cabin pressure through small openings that connect the sinuses to the nasal passages. Either an upper respiratory infection, such as a cold or sinusitis, or a nasal allergic condition can produce enough congestion around an opening to slow equalization, and as the difference in pressure between the sinus and cabin mounts, eventually plug the opening. This "sinus block" occurs most frequently during descent.

2. A sinus block can occur in the frontal sinuses, located above each eyebrow, or in the maxillary sinuses, located in each upper cheek.

Ch 8

It will usually produce excruciating pain over the sinus area. A maxillary sinus block can also make the upper teeth ache. Bloody mucus may discharge from the nasal passages.

3. A sinus block is prevented by not flying with an upper respiratory infection or nasal allergic condition. Adequate protection is usually not provided by decongestant sprays or drops to reduce congestion around the sinus openings. Oral decongestants have side effects that can impair pilot performance.

4. If a sinus block does not clear shortly after landing, a physician should be consulted.

d. Decompression Sickness After Scuba Diving.

1. A pilot or passenger who intends to fly after scuba diving should allow the body sufficient time to rid itself of excess nitrogen absorbed during diving. If not, altitude decompression sickness due to evolved nitrogen gas can occur during exposure to reduced barometric pressure (i.e., low cabin pressure) associated with increased altitude and may lead to a serious inflight emergency.

2. The recommended wait time before going to flight altitudes up to 8,000 feet is at least 12 hours after diving that did not require a controlled ascent (i.e., non-decompression stop diving), and at least 24 hours after diving that required a controlled ascent (i.e., decompression stop diving). The recommended wait time before going to flight altitudes above 8,000 feet is at least 24 hours after any SCUBA dive. These recommended altitudes are actual flight altitudes above mean sea level (AMSL) and not pressurized cabin altitudes. This takes into consideration the risk of aircraft decompression during flight.

8–1–3 Hyperventilation in Flight

a. Hyperventilation, or an abnormal increase in the volume of air breathed in and out of the lungs, can occur subconsciously when a stressful situation is encountered in flight. As hyperventilation "blows off" excessive carbon dioxide from the body, a pilot can experience symptoms of lightheadedness, suffocation, drowsiness, tingling in the extremities, and coolness and react to them with even greater hyperventilation. Incapacitation can eventually result from incoordination, disorientation, and painful muscle spasms. Finally, unconsciousness can occur.

b. The symptoms of hyperventilation subside within a few minutes after the rate and depth of breathing are consciously brought back under control. The buildup of carbon dioxide in the body can be hastened by controlled breathing in and out of a paper bag held over the nose and mouth.

c. Early symptoms of hyperventilation and hypoxia are similar. Moreover, hyperventilation and hypoxia can occur at the same time. Therefore, if a pilot is using an oxygen system when symptoms are experienced, the oxygen regulator should immediately be set to deliver 100 percent oxygen, and then the system checked to assure that it has been functioning effectively before giving attention to rate and depth of breathing.

8–1–4 Carbon Monoxide Poisoning in Flight

a. Carbon monoxide is a colorless, odorless, and tasteless gas contained in exhaust fumes. When breathed even in minute quantities over a period of time, it can significantly reduce the ability of the blood to carry oxygen. Consequently, effects of hypoxia occur.

b. Most heaters in light aircraft work by air flowing over the manifold. Use of these heaters while exhaust fumes are escaping through manifold cracks and seals is responsible every year for several nonfatal and fatal aircraft accidents from carbon monoxide poisoning.

c. A pilot who detects the odor of exhaust or experiences symptoms of headache, drowsiness, or dizziness while using the heater should suspect carbon monoxide poisoning, and immediately shut off the heater and open air vents. If symptoms are severe or continue after landing, medical treatment should be sought.

8–1–5 Illusions in Flight

a. **Introduction.** Many different illusions can be experienced in flight. Some can lead to spatial disorientation. Others can lead to landing errors. Illusions rank among the most common factors cited as contributing to fatal aircraft accidents.

b. **Illusions Leading to Spatial Disorientation.**

1. Various complex motions and forces and certain visual scenes encountered in flight can create illusions of motion and position. Spatial disorientation from these illusions can be prevented only by visual reference to reliable, fixed points on the ground or to flight instruments.

2. **The leans.** An abrupt correction of a banked attitude, which has been entered too slowly to stimulate the motion sensing system in the inner ear, can create the illusion of banking in the opposite direction. The disoriented pilot will roll the aircraft back into its original dangerous attitude, or if level flight is maintained, will feel compelled to lean in the perceived vertical plane until this illusion subsides.

(a) **Coriolis illusion.** An abrupt head movement in a prolonged constant-rate turn that has ceased stimulating the motion sensing system can create the illusion of rotation or movement in an entirely different axis. The disoriented pilot will maneuver the aircraft into a dangerous attitude in an attempt to stop rotation. This most overwhelming of all illusions in flight may be

prevented by not making sudden, extreme head movements, particularly while making prolonged constant-rate turns under IFR conditions.

(b) Graveyard spin. A proper recovery from a spin that has ceased stimulating the motion sensing system can create the illusion of spinning in the opposite direction. The disoriented pilot will return the aircraft to its original spin.

(c) Graveyard spiral. An observed loss of altitude during a coordinated constant-rate turn that has ceased stimulating the motion sensing system can create the illusion of being in a descent with the wings level. The disoriented pilot will pull back on the controls, tightening the spiral and increasing the loss of altitude.

(d) Somatogravic illusion. A rapid acceleration during takeoff can create the illusion of being in a nose up attitude. The disoriented pilot will push the aircraft into a nose low, or dive attitude. A rapid deceleration by a quick reduction of the throttles can have the opposite effect, with the disoriented pilot pulling the aircraft into a nose up, or stall attitude.

(e) Inversion illusion. An abrupt change from climb to straight and level flight can create the illusion of tumbling backwards. The disoriented pilot will push the aircraft abruptly into a nose low attitude, possibly intensifying this illusion.

(f) Elevator illusion. An abrupt upward vertical acceleration, usually by an updraft, can create the illusion of being in a climb. The disoriented pilot will push the aircraft into a nose low attitude. An abrupt downward vertical acceleration, usually by a downdraft, has the opposite effect, with the disoriented pilot pulling the aircraft into a nose up attitude.

(g) False horizon. Sloping cloud formations, an obscured horizon, a dark scene spread with ground lights and stars, and certain geometric patterns of ground light can create illusions of not being aligned correctly with the actual horizon. The disoriented pilot will place the aircraft in a dangerous attitude.

(h) Autokinesis. In the dark, a static light will appear to move about when stared at for many seconds. The disoriented pilot will lose control of the aircraft in attempting to align it with the light.

3. Illusions Leading to Landing Errors.

(a) Various surface features and atmospheric conditions encountered in landing can create illusions of incorrect height above and distance from the runway threshold. Landing errors from these illusions can be prevented by anticipating them during approaches, aerial visual inspection of unfamiliar airports before landing, using electronic glide slope or VASI systems when available, and maintaining optimum proficiency in landing procedures.

(b) Runway width illusion. A narrower-than-usual runway can create the illusion that the aircraft is at a higher altitude than it actually is. The pilot who does not recognize this illusion will fly a lower approach, with the risk of striking objects along the approach path or landing short. A wider-than-usual runway can have the opposite effect, with the risk of leveling out high and landing hard or overshooting the runway.

(c) Runway and terrain slopes illusion. An upsloping runway, upsloping terrain, or both, can create the illusion that the aircraft is at a higher altitude than it actually is. The pilot who does not recognize this illusion will fly a lower approach. A downsloping runway, downsloping approach terrain, or both, can have the opposite effect.

(d) Featureless terrain illusion. An absence of ground features, as when landing over water, darkened areas, and terrain made featureless by snow, can create the illusion that the aircraft is at a higher altitude than it actually is. The pilot who does not recognize this illusion will fly a lower approach.

(e) Atmospheric illusions. Rain on the windscreen can create the illusion of greater height, and atmospheric haze the illusion of being at a greater distance from the runway. The pilot who does not recognize these illusions will fly a lower approach. Penetration of fog can create the illusion of pitching up. The pilot who does not recognize this illusion will steepen the approach, often quite abruptly.

(f) Ground lighting illusions. Lights along a straight path, such as a road, and even lights on moving trains can be mistaken for runway and approach lights. Bright runway and approach lighting systems, especially where few lights illuminate the surrounding terrain, may create the illusion of less distance to the runway. The pilot who does not recognize this illusion will fly a higher approach. Conversely, the pilot overflying terrain which has few lights to provide height cues may make a lower than normal approach.

8-1-6 Vision in Flight

a. Introduction. Of the body senses, vision is the most important for safe flight. Major factors that determine how effectively vision can be used are the level of illumination and the technique of scanning the sky for other aircraft.

b. Vision Under Dim and Bright Illumination.

1. Under conditions of dim illumination, small print and colors on aeronautical charts and aircraft instruments become unreadable unless adequate cockpit lighting is available. Moreover, another aircraft must be much closer to be seen unless its navigation lights are on.

2. In darkness, vision becomes more sensitive to light, a process called dark adaptation. Although exposure to total darkness for at least

Ch 8

30 minutes is required for complete dark adaptation, a pilot can achieve a moderate degree of dark adaptation within 20 minutes under dim red cockpit lighting. Since red light severely distorts colors, especially on aeronautical charts, and can cause serious difficulty in focusing the eyes on objects inside the aircraft, its use is advisable only where optimum outside night vision capability is necessary. Even so, white cockpit lighting must be available when needed for map and instrument reading, especially under IFR conditions. Dark adaptation is impaired by exposure to cabin pressure altitudes above 5,000 feet, carbon monoxide inhaled in smoking and from exhaust fumes, deficiency of Vitamin A in the diet, and by prolonged exposure to bright sunlight. Since any degree of dark adaptation is lost within a few seconds of viewing a bright light, a pilot should close one eye when using a light to preserve some degree of night vision.

3. Excessive illumination, especially from light reflected off the canopy, surfaces inside the aircraft, clouds, water, snow, and desert terrain, can produce glare, with uncomfortable squinting, watering of the eyes, and even temporary blindness. Sunglasses for protection from glare should absorb at least 85 percent of visible light (15 percent transmittance) and all colors equally (neutral transmittance), with negligible image distortion from refractive and prismatic errors.

c. Scanning for Other Aircraft.

1. Scanning the sky for other aircraft is a key factor in collision avoidance. It should be used continuously by the pilot and copilot (or right seat passenger) to cover all areas of the sky visible from the cockpit. Although pilots must meet specific visual acuity requirements, the ability to read an eye chart does not ensure that one will be able to efficiently spot other aircraft. Pilots must develop an effective scanning technique which maximizes one's visual capabilities. The probability of spotting a potential collision threat obviously increases with the time spent looking outside the cockpit. Thus, one must use timesharing techniques to efficiently scan the surrounding airspace while monitoring instruments as well.

2. While the eyes can observe an approximate 200 degree arc of the horizon at one glance, only a very small center area called the fovea, in the rear of the eye, has the ability to send clear, sharply focused messages to the brain. All other visual information that is not processed directly through the fovea will be of less detail. An aircraft at a distance of 7 miles which appears in sharp focus within the foveal center of vision would have to be as close as 7/10 of a mile in order to be recognized if it were outside of foveal vision. Because the eyes can focus only on this narrow viewing area, effective scanning is accomplished with a series of short, regularly spaced eye movements that bring successive areas of the sky into the central visual field. Each movement should not exceed 10 degrees, and each area should be observed for at least 1 second to enable detection. Although horizontal back-and-forth eye movements seem preferred by most pilots, each pilot should develop a scanning pattern that is most comfortable and then adhere to it to assure optimum scanning.

3. Studies show that the time a pilot spends on visual tasks inside the cabin should represent no more that 1/4 to 1/3 of the scan time outside, or no more than 4 to 5 seconds on the instrument panel for every 16 seconds outside. Since the brain is already trained to process sight information that is presented from left to right, one may find it easier to start scanning over the left shoulder and proceed across the windshield to the right.

4. Pilots should realize that their eyes may require several seconds to refocus when switching views between items in the cockpit and distant objects. The eyes will also tire more quickly when forced to adjust to distances immediately after close-up focus, as required for scanning the instrument panel. Eye fatigue can be reduced by looking from the instrument panel to the left wing past the wing tip to the center of the first scan quadrant when beginning the exterior scan. After having scanned from left to right, allow the eyes to return to the cabin along the right wing from its tip inward. Once back inside, one should automatically commence the panel scan.

5. Effective scanning also helps avoid "empty-field myopia." This condition usually occurs when flying above the clouds or in a haze layer that provides nothing specific to focus on outside the aircraft. This causes the eyes to relax and seek a comfortable focal distance which may range from 10 to 30 feet. For the pilot, this means looking without seeing, which is dangerous.

8–1–7 Aerobatic Flight

a. Pilots planning to engage in aerobatics should be aware of the physiological stresses associated with accelerative forces during aerobatic maneuvers. Many prospective aerobatic trainees enthusiastically enter aerobatic instruction but find their first experiences with G forces to be unanticipated and very uncomfortable. To minimize or avoid potential adverse effects, the aerobatic instructor and trainee must have a basic understanding of the physiology of G force adaptation.

b. Forces experienced with a rapid push-over maneuver result in the blood and body organs being displaced toward the head. Depending on forces involved and individual tolerance, a pilot may experience discomfort, headache, "red-out," and even unconsciousness.

c. Forces experienced with a rapid pull-up maneuver result in the blood and body organ displacement toward the lower part of the body away from the head. Since the brain requires continuous blood circulation for an adequate oxygen supply, there is a physiologic limit to the time the pilot can tolerate higher forces before losing consciousness. As the blood circulation to the brain decreases as a result of forces involved, a pilot will experience "narrowing" of visual fields, "grayout," "black-out," and unconsciousness. Even a brief loss of consciousness in a maneuver can lead to improper control movement causing structural failure of the aircraft or collision with another object or terrain.

d. In steep turns, the centrifugal forces tend to push the pilot into the seat, thereby resulting in blood and body organ displacement toward the lower part of the body as in the case of rapid pull-up maneuvers and with the same physiologic effects and symptoms.

e. Physiologically, humans progressively adapt to imposed strains and stress, and with practice, any maneuver will have decreasing effect. Tolerance to G forces is dependent on human physiology and the individual pilot. These factors include the skeletal anatomy, the cardiovascular architecture, the nervous system, the quality of the blood, the general physical state, and experience and recency of exposure. The pilot should consult an Aviation Medical Examiner prior to aerobatic training and be aware that poor physical condition can reduce tolerance to accelerative forces.

f. The above information provides pilots with a brief summary of the physiologic effects of G forces. It does not address methods of "counteracting" these effects. There are numerous references on the subject of G forces during aerobatics available to pilots. Among these are "G Effects on the Pilot During Aerobatics," FAA-AM-72-28, and "G Incapacitation in Aerobatic Pilots: A Flight Hazard" FAA-AM-82-13. These are available from the National Technical Information Service, Springfield, Virginia 22161.

Reference: FAA AC 91-61, A Hazard in Aerobatics: Effects of G-forces on Pilots.

8-1-8 Judgment Aspects of Collision Avoidance

a. Introduction. The most important aspects of vision and the techniques to scan for other aircraft are described in paragraph 8-1-6, Vision in Flight. Pilots should also be familiar with the following information to reduce the possibility of mid-air collisions.

b. Determining Relative Altitude. Use the horizon as a reference point. If the other aircraft is above the horizon, it is probably on a higher flight path. If the aircraft appears to be below the horizon, it is probably flying at a lower altitude.

c. Taking Appropriate Action. Pilots should be familiar with rules on right-of-way, so if an aircraft is on an obvious collision course, one can take immediate evasive action, preferably in compliance with applicable Federal Aviation Regulations.

d. Consider Multiple Threats. The decision to climb, descend, or turn is a matter of personal judgment, but one should anticipate that the other pilot may also be making a quick maneuver. Watch the other aircraft during the maneuver and begin your scanning again immediately since there may be other aircraft in the area.

e. Collision Course Targets. Any aircraft that appears to have no relative motion and stays in one scan quadrant is likely to be on a collision course. Also, if a target shows no lateral or vertical motion, but increases in size, take evasive action.

f. Recognize High Hazard Areas.
1. Airways, especially near VORs, and Class B, Class C, Class D, and Class E surface areas are places where aircraft tend to cluster.
2. Remember, most collisions occur during days when the weather is good. Being in a "radar environment" still requires vigilance to avoid collisions.

g. Cockpit Management. Studying maps, checklists, and manuals before flight, with other proper preflight planning; e.g., noting necessary radio frequencies and organizing cockpit materials, can reduce the amount of time required to look at these items during flight, permitting more scan time.

h. Windshield Conditions. Dirty or bug-smeared windshields can greatly reduce the ability of pilots to see other aircraft. Keep a clean windshield.

i. Visibility Conditions. Smoke, haze, dust, rain, and flying towards the sun can also greatly reduce the ability to detect targets.

j. Visual Obstructions in the Cockpit.
1. Pilots need to move their heads to see around blind spots caused by fixed aircraft structures, such as door posts, wings, etc. It will be necessary at times to maneuver the aircraft; e.g., lift a wing, to facilitate seeing.
2. Pilots must ensure curtains and other cockpit objects; e.g., maps on glare shield, are removed and stowed during flight.

k. Lights On.
1. Day or night, use of exterior lights can greatly increase the conspicuity of any aircraft.
2. Keep interior lights low at night.

l. ATC Support. ATC facilities often provide radar traffic advisories on a workload-permitting basis. Flight through Class C and Class D airspace requires communication with ATC. Use this support whenever possible or when required.

Chapter 9
Aeronautical Charts and Related Publications
Section 1 Types of Charts Available

9-1-1 General

Civil aeronautical charts for the U.S. and its territories, and possessions are produced by Aeronautical Information Services (AIS), http://www.faa.gov/air_traffic/flight_info/aeronav which is part of FAA's Air Traffic Organization, Mission Support Services.

9-1-2 Obtaining Aeronautical Charts

Public sales of charts and publications are available through a network of FAA approved print providers. A listing of products, dates of latest editions and agents is available on the AIS website at: http://www.faa.gov/air_traffic/flight_info/aeronav.

9-1-3 Selected Charts and Products Available

VFR Navigation Charts

IFR Navigation Charts

Planning Charts

Supplementary Charts and Publications

Digital Products

9-1-4 General Description of Each Chart Series

a. VFR Navigation Charts.

1. Sectional Aeronautical Charts. Sectional Charts are designed for visual navigation of slow to medium speed aircraft. The topographic information consists of contour lines, shaded relief, drainage patterns, and an extensive selection of visual checkpoints and landmarks used for flight under VFR. Cultural features include cities and towns, roads, railroads, and other distinct landmarks. The aeronautical information includes visual and radio aids to navigation, airports, controlled airspace, special-use airspace, obstructions, and related data. Scale 1 inch = 6.86 NM/1:500,000. 60 x 20 inches folded to 5 x 10 inches. Revised every 56 days. (See Figure 9-1-1 and Figure 9-1-2.)

2. VFR Terminal Area Charts (TAC). TACs depict the airspace designated as Class B airspace. While similar to sectional charts, TACs have more detail because the scale is larger. The TAC should be used by pilots intending to operate to or from airfields within or near Class B or Class C airspace. Areas with TAC coverage are indicated by a • on the Sectional Chart indexes. Scale 1 inch = 3.43 NM/1:250,000. Revised every 56 days. (See Figure 9-1-1 and Figure 9-1-2.)

3. U.S. Gulf Coast VFR Aeronautical Chart. The Gulf Coast Chart is designed primarily for helicopter operation in the Gulf of Mexico area. Information depicted includes offshore mineral leasing areas and blocks, oil drilling platforms, and high density helicopter activity areas. Scale 1 inch = 13.7 NM/1:1,000,000. 55 x 27 inches folded to 5 x 10 inches. Revised every 56 days.

4. Grand Canyon VFR Aeronautical Chart. Covers the Grand Canyon National Park area and is designed to promote aviation safety, flight free zones, and facilitate VFR navigation in this popular area. The chart contains aeronautical information for general aviation VFR pilots on one side and commercial VFR air tour operators on the other side. Revised every 56 days.

5. Caribbean VFR Aeronautical Charts. Caribbean 1 and 2 (CAC-1 and CAC-2) are designed for visual navigation to assist familiarization of foreign aeronautical and topographic information. The aeronautical information includes visual and radio aids to navigation, airports, controlled airspace, special-use airspace, obstructions, and related data. The topographic information consists of contour lines, shaded relief, drainage patterns, and a selection of landmarks used for flight under VFR. Cultural features include cities and towns, roads, railroads, and other distinct landmarks. Scale 1 inch = 13.7 NM/1:1,000,000. CAC-1 consists of two sides measuring 30" x 60" each. CAC-2 consists of two sides measuring 20" x 60" each. Revised every 56 days. (See Figure 9-1-3.)

6. Helicopter Route Charts. A three-color chart series which shows current aeronautical information useful to helicopter pilots navigating in areas with high concentrations of helicopter activity. Information depicted includes helicopter routes, four classes of heliports with associated frequency and lighting capabilities, NAVAIDs, and obstructions. In addition, pictorial symbols, roads, and easily identified geographical features are portrayed. Scale 1 inch = 1.71 NM/1:125,000. 34 x 30 inches folded to 5 x 10 inches. Revised every 56 days. (See Figure 9-1-4.)

Ch 9

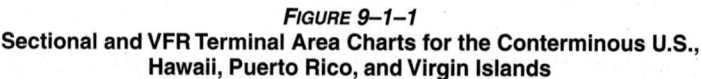

FIGURE 9–1–1
Sectional and VFR Terminal Area Charts for the Conterminous U.S.,
Hawaii, Puerto Rico, and Virgin Islands

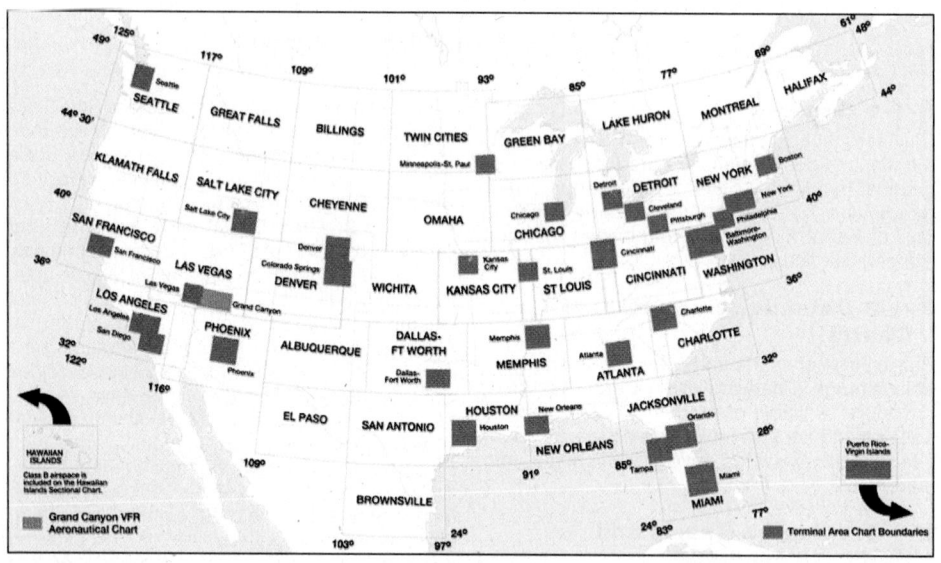

FIGURE 9–1–2
Sectional and VFR Terminal Area Charts for Alaska

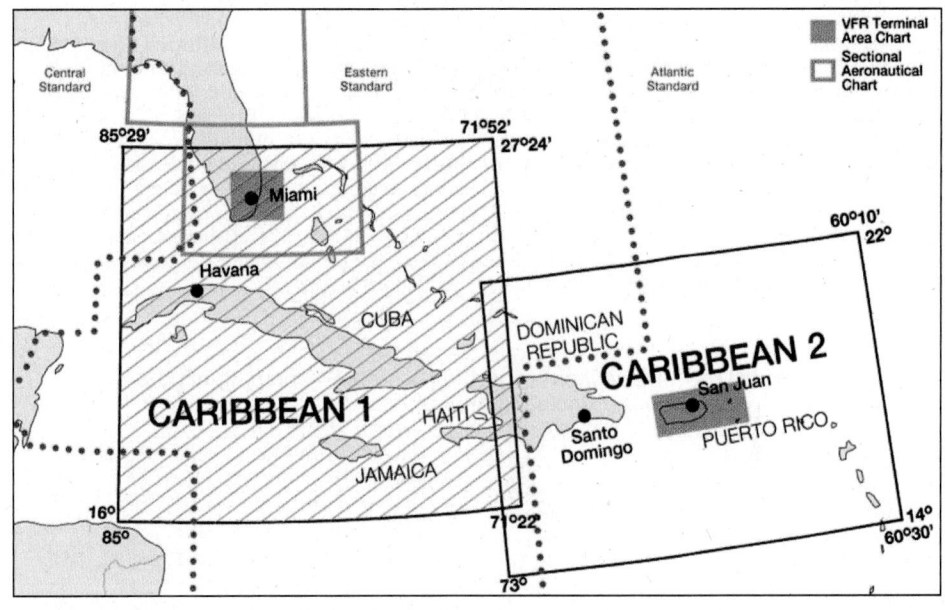

FIGURE 9–1–3
Caribbean VFR Aeronautical Charts

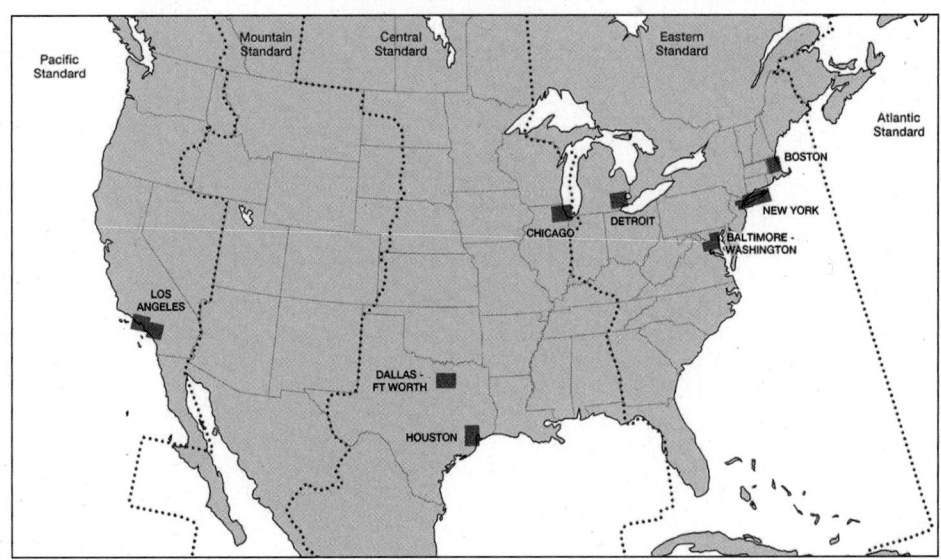

FIGURE 9–1–4
Helicopter Route Charts

b. IFR Navigation Charts.

1. IFR Enroute Low Altitude Charts (Conterminous U.S. and Alaska). Enroute low altitude charts provide aeronautical information for navigation under IFR conditions below 18,000 feet MSL. This four-color chart series includes airways; limits of controlled airspace; VHF NAVAIDs with frequency, identification, channel, geographic coordinates; airports with terminal air/ground communications; minimum en route and obstruction clearance altitudes; airway distances; reporting points; special use airspace; and military training routes. Scales vary from 1 inch = 5 NM to 1 inch = 20 NM. 50 x 20 inches folded to 5 x 10 inches. Charts revised every 56 days. *Area*

charts show congested terminal areas at a large scale. They are included with subscriptions to any conterminous U.S. Set Low (Full set, East or West sets). (See Figure 9-1-5 and Figure 9-1-6.)

2. IFR Enroute High Altitude Charts (Conterminous U.S. and Alaska). Enroute high altitude charts are designed for navigation at or above 18,000 feet MSL. This four-color chart series includes the jet route structure; VHF NAVAIDs with frequency, identification, channel, geographic coordinates; selected airports; reporting points. Scales vary from 1 inch = 45 NM to 1 inch = 18 NM. 55 x 20 inches folded to 5 x 10 inches. Revised every 56 days. (See Figure 9-1-7 and Figure 9-1-8.)

FIGURE 9–1–5
**Enroute Low Altitude Instrument Charts for the Conterminous U.S.
(Includes Area Charts)**

FIGURE 9–1–6
Alaska Enroute Low Altitude Chart

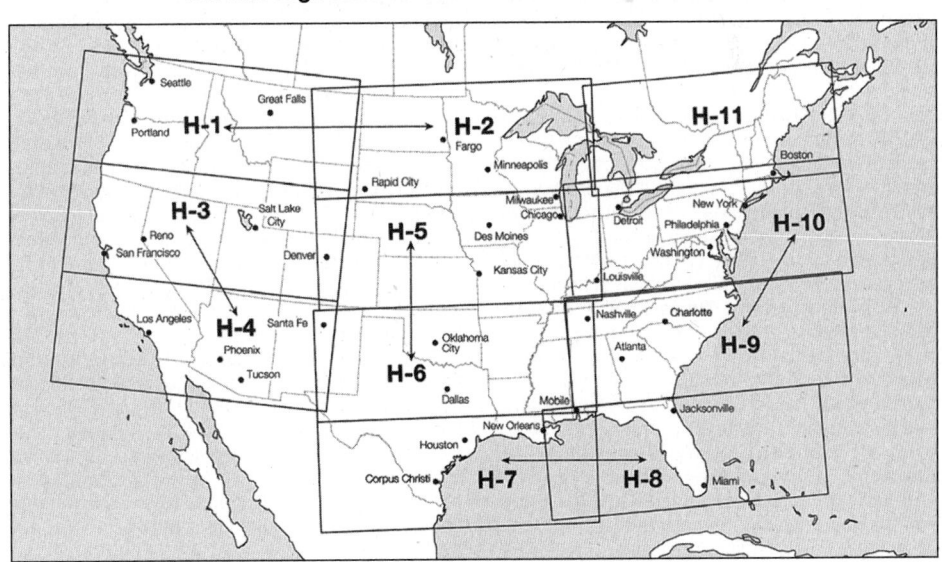

FIGURE 9–1–7
Enroute High Altitude Charts for the Conterminous U.S.

FIGURE 9–1–8
Alaska Enroute High Altitude Chart

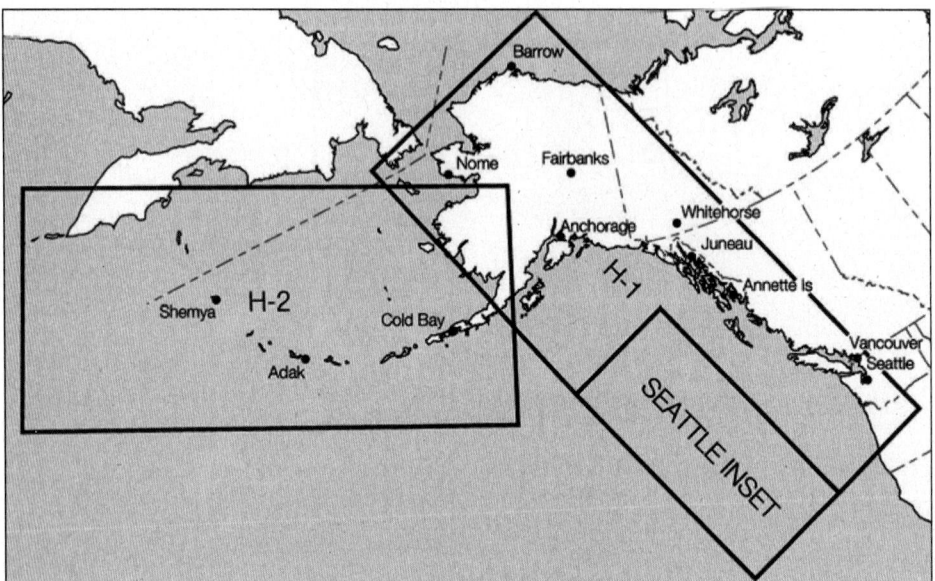

3. U.S. Terminal Procedures Publication (TPP). TPPs are published in 24 loose-leaf or perfect bound volumes covering the contermi- nous U.S., Puerto Rico and the Virgin Islands. A Change Notice is published at the midpoint between revisions in bound volume format and is available on the internet for free download at the AIS website. (See Figure 9-1-15.) The TPPs include:

(a) Instrument Approach Procedure (IAP) Charts. IAP charts portray the aeronauti- cal data that is required to execute instrument ap- proaches to airports. Each chart depicts the IAP, all related navigation data, communications infor- mation, and an airport sketch. Each procedure is designated for use with a specific electronic navi- gational aid, such as ILS, VOR, NDB, RNAV, etc.

(b) Instrument Departure Procedure (DP) Charts. DP charts are designed to expe- dite clearance delivery and to facilitate transition between takeoff and en route operations. They furnish pilots' departure routing clearance infor- mation in graphic and textual form.

(c) Standard Terminal Arrival (STAR) Charts. STAR charts are designed to expedite ATC arrival procedures and to facilitate transi- tion between en route and instrument approach operations. They depict preplanned IFR ATC ar- rival procedures in graphic and textual form. Each STAR procedure is presented as a separate chart and may serve either a single airport or more than one airport in a given geographic area.

(d) Airport Diagrams. Full page airport di- agrams are designed to assist in the movement of ground traffic at locations with complex runway/ taxiway configurations and provide information for updating geodetic position navigational systems aboard aircraft. Airport diagrams are available for free download at the AIS website.

4. Alaska Terminal Procedures Publica- tion. This publication contains all terminal flight procedures for civil and military aviation in Alaska. Included are IAP charts, DP charts, STAR charts, airport diagrams, radar minimums, and supple- mentary support data such as IFR alternate mini- mums, take-off minimums, rate of descent tables, rate of climb tables and inoperative components tables. Volume is 5-3/8 x 8-1/4 inch top bound. Publication revised every 56 days with provisions for a Terminal Change Notice, as required.

c. Planning Charts.

1. U.S. IFR/VFR Low Altitude Planning Chart. This chart is designed for preflight and en route flight planning for IFR/VFR flights. Depiction includes low altitude airways and mileage, NA- VAIDs, airports, special use airspace, cities, times zones, major drainage, a directory of airports with their airspace classification, and a mileage table showing great circle distances between major air- ports. Scale 1 inch = 47 NM/1:3,400,000. Chart revised annually, and is available either folded or unfolded for wall mounting. (See Figure 9-1-10.)

2. Gulf of Mexico and Caribbean Planning Chart. This is a VFR planning chart on the reverse side of the *Puerto Rico–Virgin Islands VFR Terminal Area Chart*. Information shown includes mileage between airports of entry, a selection of special use airspace and a directory of airports with their available services. Scale 1 inch = 85 NM/1:6,192,178. 60 x 20 inches folded to 5 x 10 inches. Revised every 56 days (See Figure 9-1-10.)

3. Alaska VFR Wall Planning Chart. This chart is designed for VFR preflight planning and chart selection. It includes aeronautical and topographic information of the state of Alaska. The aeronautical information includes public and military airports; radio aids to navigation; and Class B, Class C, TRSA and special-use airspace. The topographic information includes city tint,

populated places, principal roads, and shaded relief. Scale 1 inch = 27.4 NM/1:2,000,000. The one sided chart is 58.5 x 40.75 inches and is designed for wall mounting. Revised annually. (See Figure 9-1-9.)

4. U.S. VFR Wall Planning Chart. This chart is designed for VFR preflight planning and chart selection. It includes aeronautical and topographic information of the conterminous U.S. The aeronautical information includes airports, radio aids to navigation, Class B airspace and special use airspace. The topographic information includes city tint, populated places, principal roads, drainage patterns, and shaded relief. Scale 1 inch = 43 NM/1:3,100,000. The one-sided chart is 59 x 36 inches and ships unfolded for wall mounting. Revised annually. (See Figure 9-1-11.)

FIGURE 9–1–9
Alaska VFR Wall Planning Chart

FIGURE 9–1–10
Planning Charts

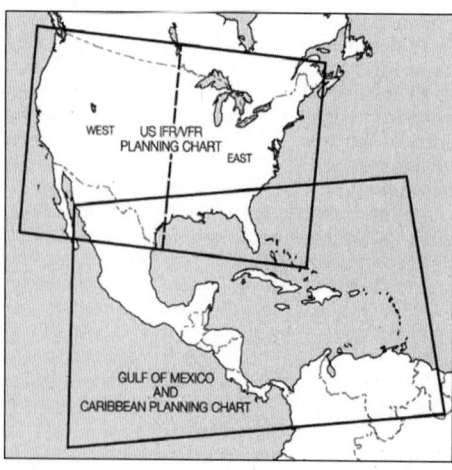

FIGURE 9–1–11
U.S. VFR Wall Planning Chart

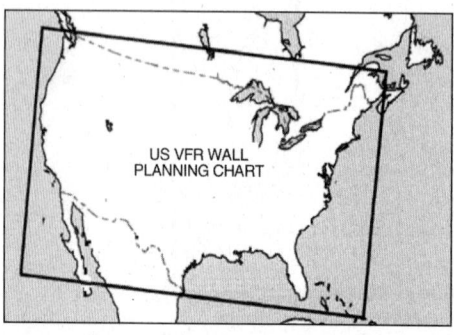

5. Charted VFR Flyway Planning Charts.
This chart is printed on the reverse side of selected TAC charts. The coverage is the same as the associated TAC. Flyway planning charts depict flight paths and altitudes recommended for use to bypass high traffic areas. Ground references are provided as a guide for visual orientation. Flyway planning charts are designed for use in conjunction with TACs and sectional charts and are not to be used for navigation. Chart scale 1 inch = 3.43 NM/1:250,000.

d. Supplementary Charts and Publications.
1. Chart Supplement refers to a series of civil/military flight information publications issued by FAA every 56 days consisting of the Chart Supplement U.S., Chart Supplement Alaska, and Chart Supplement Pacific.
2. Chart Supplement U.S. This is a civil/military flight information publication. This 7-volume book series is designed for use with appropriate IFR or VFR charts and contains data including, but not limited to, airports, NAVAIDs, communications data, weather data sources, special notices, non-regulatory operational procedures, and airport diagrams. Coverage includes the conterminous U.S., Puerto Rico, and the Virgin Islands. The Chart Supplement U.S. shows data that cannot be readily depicted in graphic form; for example, airport hours of operations, types of fuel available, run widths, and lighting codes. (See Figure 9-1-12.)
3. Chart Supplement Alaska. This is a civil/military flight information publication. This single-volume book is designed for use with appropriate IFR or VFR charts. The Chart Supplement Alaska contains data including, but not limited to, airports, NAVAIDs, communications data, weather data sources, special notices, non-regulatory operational procedures, and airport diagrams. The publication also includes uniquely geographical operational requirements as area notices and emergency procedures.
4. Chart Supplement Pacific. This is a civil/military flight information publication. This single volume book is designed for use with appropriate IFR or VFR charts. The Chart Supplement Pacific contains data including, but not limited to, airports, NAVAIDs, communications data, weather data sources, special notices, non-regulatory operational procedures, and airport diagrams. The publication also includes airspace, navigational facilities, non-regulatory Pacific area procedures, Instrument Approach Procedures (IAP), Departure Procedures (DP), Standard Terminal Arrival (STAR) charts, radar minimums, supporting data for the Hawaiian and Pacific Islands, and uniquely geographical operational requirements as area notices and emergency procedures.
5. North Atlantic Route Chart. Designed for FAA controllers to monitor transatlantic flights, this 5-color chart shows oceanic control areas, coastal navigation aids, oceanic reporting points, and NAVAID geographic coordinates. Full Size Chart: Scale 1 inch = 113.1 NM/1:8,250,000. Chart is shipped flat only. Half Size Chart: Scale 1 inch = 150.8 NM/1:11,000,000. Chart is 29-3/4 x 20-1/2 inches, shipped folded to 5 x 10 inches only. Chart revised every 56 days. (See Figure 9-1-13.)

FIGURE 9–1–12
Chart Supplement U.S. Geographic Areas

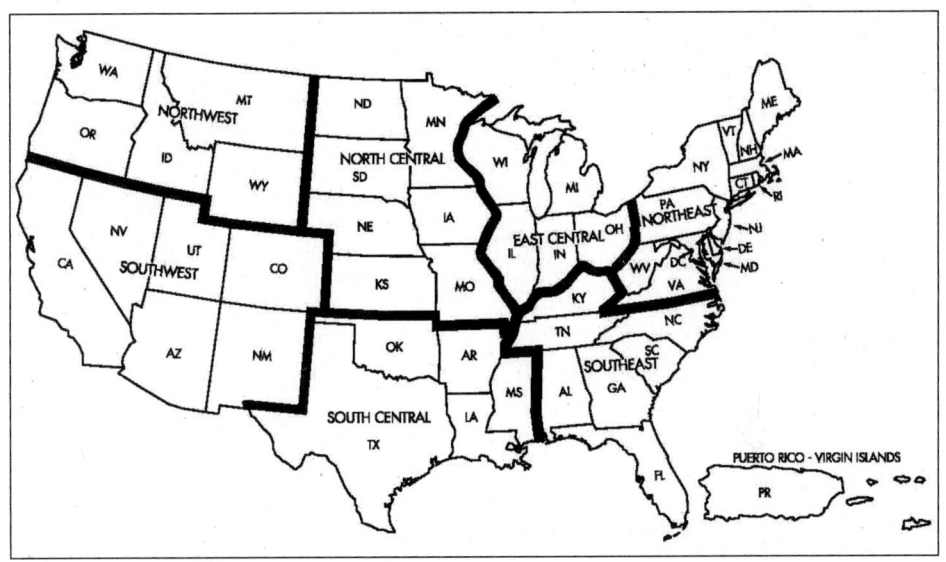

FIGURE 9–1–13
North Atlantic Route Charts

FIGURE 9–1–14
North Pacific Oceanic Route Charts

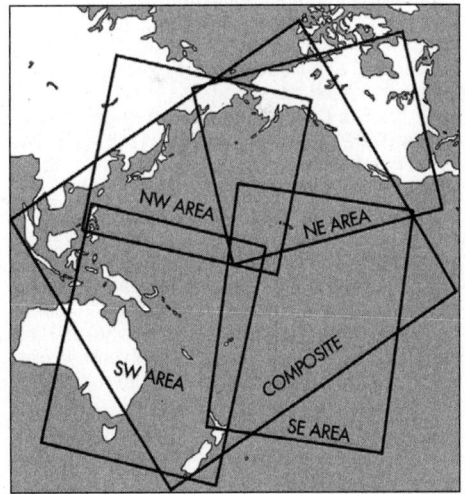

6. North Pacific Route Charts. These charts are designed for FAA controllers to monitor transoceanic flights. They show established intercontinental air routes, including reporting points with geographic positions. Composite Chart: Scale 1 inch = 164 NM/1:12,000,000. 48 x 41-1/2 inches. Area Charts: Scale 1 inch = 95.9 NM/1:7,000,000. 52 x 40-1/2 inches. All charts shipped unfolded. Charts revised every 56 days. (See Figure 9-1-14.)

7. Airport Obstruction Charts (OC). The OC is a 1:12,000 scale graphic depicting 14 CFR Part 77, Objects Affecting Navigable Airspace, surfaces, a representation of objects that penetrate these surfaces, aircraft movement and apron areas, navigational aids, prominent airport buildings, and a selection of roads and other

planimetric detail in the airport vicinity. Also included are tabulations of runway and other operational data.

8. FAA Aeronautical Chart User's Guide. A booklet designed to be used as a teaching aid and reference document. It describes the substantial amount of information provided on FAA's aeronautical charts and publications. It includes explanations and illustrations of chart terms and symbols organized by chart type. The users guide is available for free download at the AIS website.

e. Digital Products.

1. The Digital Aeronautical Information CD (DAICD). The DAICD is a combination of the NAVAID Digital Data File, the Digital Chart Supplement, and the Digital Obstacle File on one Compact Disk. These three digital products are no longer sold separately. The files are updated every 56 days and are available by subscription only.

(a) The NAVAID Digital Data File. This file contains a current listing of NAVAIDs that are compatible with the National Airspace System. This file contains all NAVAIDs including ILS and its components, in the U.S., Puerto Rico, and the Virgin Islands plus bordering facilities in Canada, Mexico, and the Atlantic and Pacific areas.

(b) The Digital Obstacle File. This file describes all obstacles of interest to aviation users in the U.S., with limited coverage of the Pacific, Caribbean, Canada, and Mexico. The obstacles are assigned unique numerical identifiers, accuracy codes, and listed in order of ascending latitude within each state or area.

2. The Coded Instrument Flight Procedures (CIFP) (ARINC 424 [Ver 13 & 15]). The CIFP is a basic digital dataset, modeled to an international standard, which can be used as a basis to support GPS navigation. Initial data elements included are: Airport and Helicopter Records, VHF and NDB Navigation aids, en route waypoints and airways. Additional data elements will be added in subsequent releases to include: departure procedures, standard terminal arrivals, and GPS/RNAV instrument approach procedures. The database is updated every 28 days. The data is available by subscription only and is distributed on CD-ROM or by ftp download.

3. digital-Visual Charts (d-VC). These digital VFR charts are geo-referenced images of FAA Sectional Aeronautical, TAC, and Helicopter Route charts. Additional digital data may easily be overlaid on the raster image using commonly available Geographic Information System software. Data such as weather, temporary flight restrictions, obstacles, or other geospatial data can be combined with d-VC data to support a variety of needs. The file resolution is 300 dots per inch and the data is 8-bit color. The data is provided as a GeoTIFF and distributed on DVD-R media and on the AIS website. The root mean square error of the transformation will not exceed two pixels. Digital-VCs are updated every 56 days and are available by subscription only.

9–1–5 Where and How to Get Charts of Foreign Areas

a. National Geospatial-Intelligence Agency (NGA) Products. For the latest information regarding publication availability visit the NGA website: **https://www.nga.mil/ProductsServices /Pages/default.aspx**

1. Flight Information Publication (FLIP) Planning Documents.

General Planning (GP)

Area Planning

Area Planning—Special Use Airspace— Planning Charts

2. FLIP Enroute Charts and Chart Supplements.

Pacific, Australasia, and Antarctica

U.S.—IFR and VFR Supplements

Flight Information Handbook

Caribbean and South America—Low Altitude

Caribbean and South America—High Altitude

Europe, North Africa, and Middle East— Low Altitude

Europe, North Africa, and Middle East— High Altitude

Africa

Eastern Europe and Asia

Area Arrival Charts

3. FLIP Instrument Approach Procedures (IAPs).

Africa

Canada and North Atlantic

Caribbean and South America

Eastern Europe and Asia

Europe, North Africa, and Middle East

Pacific, Australasia, and Antarctica

VFR Arrival/Departure Routes— Europe and Korea

U.S.

4. Miscellaneous DoD Charts and Products.

Aeronautical Chart Updating Manual (CHUM)

DoD Weather Plotting Charts (WPC)

Tactical Pilotage Charts (TPC)

Operational Navigation Charts (ONC)

Global Navigation and Planning Charts (GNC)

Jet Navigation Charts (JNC) and Universal Jet Navigation Charts (JNU)

FIGURE 9–1–15
U.S. Terminal Procedures Publication Volumes

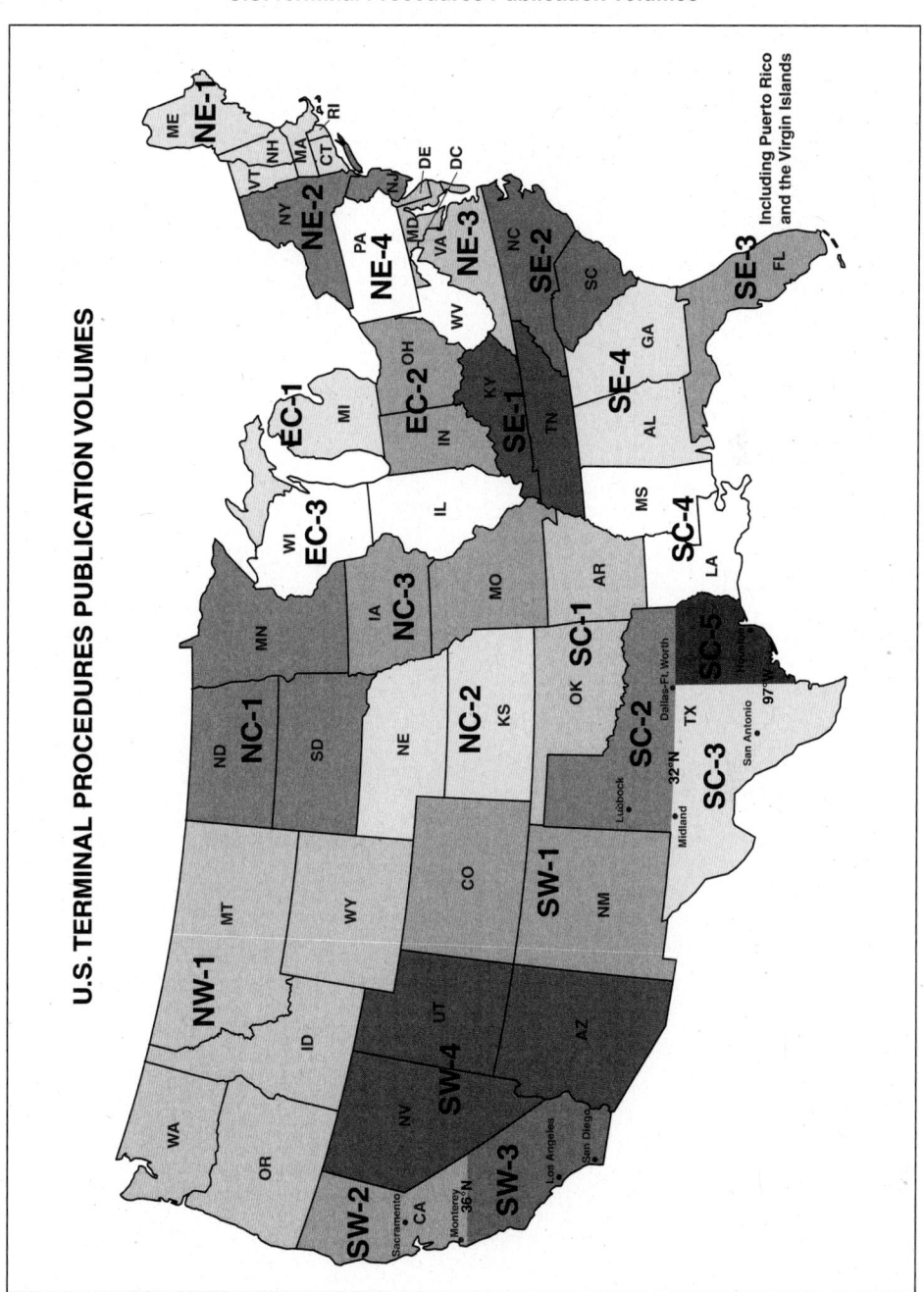

Jet Navigation Charts (JNCA)
Aerospace Planning Charts (ASC)
Oceanic Planning Charts (OPC)
Joint Operations Graphics—Air (JOG-A)
Standard Index Charts (SIC)
Universal Plotting Sheet (VP-OS)
Sight Reduction Tables for Air Navigation
 (PUB249)
Plotting Sheets (VP-30)
Dial-Up Electronic CHUM

b. Canadian Charts. Information on available Canadian charts and publications may be obtained by contacting the:

NAV CANADA
Aeronautical Publications
Sales and Distribution Unit
P.O. Box 9840, Station T
Ottawa, Ontario K1G 6S8 Canada
Telephone: 613-744-6393 or 1-866-731-7827
Fax: 613-744-7120 or 1-866-740-9992

c. Mexican Charts. Information on available Mexican charts and publications may be obtained by contacting:

Dirección de Navigacion Aereo
Blvd. Puerto Aereo 485
Zona Federal Del Aeropuerto Int'l
15620 Mexico D.F.
Mexico

d. International Civil Aviation Organization (ICAO). A list of free ICAO publications and catalogs is available at the following website: https://www.icao.int/publications/Pages/default.aspx.

Chapter 10
Helicopter Operations

Section 1 Helicopter IFR Operations

10–1–1 Helicopter Flight Control Systems

a. The certification requirements for helicopters to operate under Instrument Flight Rules (IFR) are contained in 14 CFR Part 27, Airworthiness Standards: Normal Category Rotorcraft, and 14 CFR Part 29, Airworthiness Standards: Transport Category Rotorcraft. To meet these requirements, helicopter manufacturers usually utilize a set of stabilization and/or Automatic Flight Control Systems (AFCSs).

b. Typically, these systems fall into the following categories:

1. Aerodynamic surfaces, which impart some stability or control capability not found in the basic VFR configuration.

2. Trim systems, which provide a cyclic centering effect. These systems typically involve a magnetic brake/spring device, and may also be controlled by a four-way switch on the cyclic. This is a system that supports "hands on" flying of the helicopter by the pilot.

3. Stability Augmentation Systems (SASs), which provide short-term rate damping control inputs to increase helicopter stability. Like trim systems, SAS supports "hands on" flying.

4. Attitude Retention Systems (ATTs), which return the helicopter to a selected attitude after a disturbance. Changes in desired attitude can be accomplished usually through a four-way "beep" switch, or by actuating a "force trim" switch on the cyclic, setting the attitude manually, and releasing. Attitude retention may be a SAS function, or may be the basic "hands off" autopilot function.

5. Autopilot Systems (APs), which provide for "hands off" flight along specified lateral and vertical paths, including heading, altitude, vertical speed, navigation tracking, and approach. These systems typically have a control panel for mode selection, and system for indication of mode status. Autopilots may or may not be installed with an associated Flight Director System (FD). Autopilots typically control the helicopter about the roll and pitch axes (cyclic control) but may also include yaw axis (pedal control) and collective control servos.

6. FDs, which provide visual guidance to the pilot to fly specific selected lateral and vertical modes of operation. The visual guidance is typically provided as either a "dual cue" (commonly known as a "cross-pointer") or "single cue" (commonly known as a "vee-bar") presentation superimposed over the attitude indicator. Some FDs also include a collective cue. The pilot manipulates the helicopter's controls to satisfy these commands, yielding the desired flight path, or may couple the flight director to the autopilot to perform automatic flight along the desired flight path. Typically, flight director mode control and indication is shared with the autopilot.

c. In order to be certificated for IFR operation, a specific helicopter may require the use of one or more of these systems, in any combination.

d. In many cases, helicopters are certificated for IFR operations with either one or two pilots. Certain equipment is required to be installed and functional for two pilot operations, and typically, additional equipment is required for single pilot operation. These requirements are usually described in the limitations section of the Rotorcraft Flight Manual (RFM).

e. In addition, the RFM also typically defines systems and functions that are required to be in operation or engaged for IFR flight in either the single or two pilot configuration. Often, particularly in two pilot operation, this level of augmentation is less than the full capability of the installed systems. Likewise, single pilot operation may require a higher level of augmentation.

f. The RFM also identifies other specific limitations associated with IFR flight. Typically, these limitations include, but are not limited to:

1. Minimum equipment required for IFR flight (in some cases, for both single pilot and two pilot operations).

2. V_{MINI} (minimum speed—IFR).

Note: *The manufacturer may also recommend a minimum IFR airspeed during instrument approach.*

3. V_{NEI} (never exceed speed—IFR).

4. Maximum approach angle.

5. Weight and center of gravity limits.

6. Aircraft configuration limitations (such as aircraft door positions and external loads).

7. Aircraft system limitations (generators, inverters, etc.).

8. System testing requirements (many avionics and AFCS/AP/FD systems incorporate a self-test feature).

9. Pilot action requirements (such as the pilot must have his/her hands and feet on the controls during certain operations, such as during instrument approach below certain altitudes).

Ch 10

g. It is very important that pilots be familiar with the IFR requirements for their particular helicopter. Within the same make, model and series of helicopter, variations in the installed avionics may change the required equipment or the level of augmentation for a particular operation.

h. During flight operations, pilots must be aware of the mode of operation of the augmentation systems, and the control logic and functions employed. For example, during an ILS approach using a particular system in the three-cue mode (lateral, vertical and collective cues), the flight director *collective cue* responds to glideslope deviation, while the horizontal bar of the "crosspointer" responds to airspeed deviations. The same system, while flying an ILS in the two-cue mode, provides for the *horizontal bar* to respond to glideslope deviations. This concern is particularly significant when operating using two pilots. Pilots should have an established set of procedures and responsibilities for the control of flight director/autopilot modes for the various phases of flight. Not only does a full understanding of the system modes provide for a higher degree of accuracy in control of the helicopter, it is the basis for crew identification of a faulty system.

i. Relief from the prohibition to takeoff with any inoperative instruments or equipment may be provided through a Minimum Equipment List (see 14 CFR §91.213 and 14 CFR §135.179, Inoperative Instruments and Equipment). In many cases, a helicopter configured for single pilot IFR may depart IFR with certain equipment inoperative, provided a crew of two pilots is used. Pilots are cautioned to ensure the pilot-in-command and second-in-command meet the requirements of 14 CFR §61.58, Pilot-in-Command Proficiency Check: Operation of Aircraft Requiring More Than One Pilot Flight Crewmember, and 14 CFR §61.55, Second-in-Command Qualifications, or 14 CFR Part 135, Operating Requirements: Commuter and On-Demand Operations, Subpart E, Flight Crewmember Requirements, and Subpart G, Crewmember Testing Requirements, as appropriate.

j. Experience has shown that modern AFCS/AP/FD equipment installed in IFR helicopters can, in some cases, be very complex. This complexity requires the pilot(s) to obtain and maintain a high level of knowledge of system operation, limitations, failure indications and reversionary modes. In some cases, this may only be reliably accomplished through formal training.

10–1–2 Helicopter Instrument Approaches

a. Instrument flight procedures (IFPs) permit helicopter operations to heliports and runways during periods of low ceilings and reduced visibility (e.g. approach/SID/STAR/en route). IFPs can be designed for both public and private heliports using FAA instrument criteria. The FAA does recognize there are non-FAA service providers with proprietary special criteria. Special IFPs are reviewed and approved by Flight Technologies and Procedures Division and may have specified aircraft performance or equipment requirements, special crew training, airport facility equipment, waivers from published standards, proprietary criteria and restricted access. Special IFPs are not published in the Federal Register or printed in government Flight Information Publications.

b. Helicopters are capable of flying any published IFPs, for which they are properly equipped, subject to the following limitations and conditions:

1. Helicopters flying conventional (i.e. non-Copter) IAPs may reduce the visibility minima to not less than one-half the published Category A landing visibility minima, or 1/4 statute mile visibility/1200 RVR, whichever is greater, unless the procedure is annotated with "**Visibility Reduction by Helicopters NA.**" This annotation means that there are penetrations of the final approach obstacle identification surface (OIS) and that the 14 CFR Section 97.3 visibility reduction rule does not apply and you must take precaution to avoid any obstacles in the visual segment. No reduction in MDA/DA is permitted at any time. The helicopter may initiate the final approach segment at speeds up to the upper limit of the highest approach category authorized by the procedure, but must be slowed to no more than 90 KIAS at the missed approach point (MAP) in order to apply the visibility reduction. Pilots are cautioned that such a decelerating approach may make early identification of wind shear on the approach path difficult or impossible. If required, use the Inoperative Components and Visual Aids Table provided inside the front cover of the U.S. Terminal Procedures Publication to derive the Category A minima before applying the 14 CFR Section 97.3 rule.

2. Helicopters flying Copter IAPs should use the published minima, with no reductions allowed. Unless otherwise specified on the instrument procedure chart, 90 KIAS is the maximum speed on the approach.

3. Pilots flying Area Navigation (RNAV) Copter IAPs should also limit their speed to 90 KIAS unless otherwise specified on the instrument procedure chart. The final and missed approach segment speeds must be limited to no more than 70

KIAS unless otherwise charted. Military RNAV Copter IAPs are limited to no more than 90 KIAS throughout the procedure. Use the published minima; no reductions allowed.

Note: Obstruction clearance surfaces are based on the aircraft speed identified on the approach chart and have been designed on RNAV approaches for 70 knots unless otherwise indicated. If the helicopter is flown at higher speeds, it may fly outside of protected airspace. Some helicopters have a V_{MINI} greater than 70 knots; therefore, they cannot meet the 70 knot limitation to conduct these RNAV approaches. Some helicopter autopilots, when used in the "go-around" mode, are programmed with a V_{YI} greater than 70 knots. Therefore, those helicopters when using the autopilot "go-around" mode, cannot meet the 70 knot limitation for the RNAV approach. It may be possible to use the autopilot for the missed approach in other than the "go-around" mode and meet the 70 knot limitation. When operating at speeds other than V_{YI} or V_Y, performance data may not be available in the RFM to predict compliance with climb gradient requirements. Pilots may use observed performance in similar weight/altitude/ temperature/speed conditions to evaluate the suitability of performance. Pilots are cautioned to monitor climb performance to ensure compliance with procedure requirements.

Note: V_{MINI}—Instrument flight minimum speed, utilized in complying with minimum limit speed requirements for instrument flight

V_{YI}—Instrument climb speed, utilized instead of V_Y for compliance with the climb requirements for instrument flight

V_Y—Speed for best rate of climb

4. Table 10-1-1 summarizes these requirements.

5. Even with weather conditions reported at or above minimums, under some combinations of reduced cockpit cutoff angle, approach/runway lighting, and high MDA/DH (coupled with a low visibility minima), the pilot may not be able to identify the required visual reference(s), or those references may only be visible in a very small portion of the available field of view. Even if identified by the pilot, the visual references may not support normal maneuvering and normal rates of descent to landing. The effect of such a combination may be exacerbated by other conditions such as rain on the windshield, or incomplete windshield defogging coverage.

6. Pilots should always be prepared to execute a missed approach even though weather conditions may be reported at or above minimums.

Note: See paragraph 5-4-21, Missed Approach, for additional information on missed approach procedures.

TABLE 10–1–1
HELICOPTER USE OF STANDARD INSTRUMENT APPROACH PROCEDURES

Procedure	Helicopter Visibility Minima	Helicopter MDA/DA	Maximum Speed Limitations
Conventional (non-Copter)	The greater of: one half the Category A visibility minima, 1/4 statute mile visibility, or 1200 RVR	As published for Category A	The helicopter may initiate the final approach segment at speeds up to the upper limit of the highest approach category authorized by the procedure, but must be slowed to no more than 90 KIAS at the MAP in order to apply the visibility reduction.
Copter Procedure	As published	As published	90 KIAS maximum when on a published route/track.
RNAV (GPS) Copter Procedure	As published	As published	The maximum speed for a Copter approach will be 90 KIAS or as published on the chart. Note: Higher approach angles may require a lower approach speed and aircraft V_{MINI}. Military procedures are limited to 90 KIAS for all segments.

Ch 10

Note: Several factors affect the ability of the pilot to acquire and maintain the visual references specified in 14 CFR §91.175(c), even in cases where the flight visibility may be at the minimum derived from the criteria in Table 10-1-1. These factors include, but are not limited to:

1. Cockpit cutoff angle (the angle at which the cockpit or other airframe structure limits downward visibility below the horizon).

2. Combinations of high MDA/DH and low visibility minimum, such as approaches with reduced helicopter visibility minima (per 14 CFR Section 97.3).

3. Type, configuration, and intensity of approach and runway/heliport lighting systems.

4. Type of obscuring phenomenon and/or windshield contamination.

10-1-3 Helicopter Approach Procedures to VFR Heliports

a. The FAA may develop helicopter instrument approaches for heliports that do not meet the design standards for an IFR heliport. The majority of IFR approaches to VFR heliports are developed in support of Helicopter Air Ambulance (HAA) operators. These approaches may require use of conventional NAVAIDS or a RNAV system (e.g., GPS). They may be developed either as a special approach (pilot training is required for special procedures due to their unique characteristics) or a public approach (no special training required). These instrument procedures may be designed to guide the helicopter to a specific landing area (Proceed Visually) or to a point-in-space with a "Proceed VFR" segment.

1. **An approach to a specific landing area.** This type of approach is aligned to a missed approach point from which a landing can be accomplished with a maximum course change of 30 degrees. The visual segment from the MAP to the landing area is evaluated for obstacle hazards. These procedures are annotated: "PROCEED VISUALLY FROM (named MAP) OR CONDUCT THE SPECIFIED MISSED APPROACH."

(a) "Proceed Visually" requires the pilot to acquire and maintain visual contact with the landing area at or prior to the MAP, or execute a missed approach. The visibility minimum is based on the distance from the MAP to the landing area, among other factors.

(b) The pilot is required to have the published minimum visibility throughout the visual segment flying the path described on the approach chart.

(c) Similar to an approach to a runway, the pilot is responsible for obstacle or terrain avoidance from the MAP to the landing area.

(d) Upon reaching the published MAP, or as soon as practicable thereafter, the pilot should advise ATC whether proceeding visually and canceling IFR or complying with the missed approach instructions. See paragraph 5-1-15, Canceling IFR Flight Plan.

(e) Where any necessary visual reference requirements are specified by the FAA, at least one of the following visual references for the intended heliport is visible and identifiable before the pilot may proceed visually:

(1) FATO or FATO lights.

(2) TLOF or TLOF lights.

(3) Heliport Instrument Lighting System (HILS).

(4) Heliport Approach Lighting System (HALS).

(5) Visual Glideslope Indicator (VGSI).

(6) Windsock or windsock light.

(7) Heliport beacon.

(8) Other facilities or systems approved by the Flight Technologies and Procedures Division (AFS-400).

2. **Approach to a Point-in-Space (PinS).** At locations where the MAP is located more than 2 SM from the landing area, or the path from the MAP to the landing area is populated with obstructions which require avoidance actions or requires turn greater than 30 degrees, a PinS Proceed VFR procedure may be developed. These approaches are annotated "PROCEED VFR FROM (named MAP) OR CONDUCT THE SPECIFIED MISSED APPROACH."

(a) These procedures require the pilot, at or prior to the MAP, to determine if the published minimum visibility, or the weather minimums required by the operating rule (e.g., Part 91, Part 135, etc.), or operations specifications (whichever is higher) is available to safely transition from IFR to VFR flight. If not, the pilot must execute a missed approach. For Part 135 operations, pilots may not begin the instrument approach unless the latest weather report indicates that the weather conditions are at or above the authorized IFR minimums or the VFR weather minimums (as required by the class of airspace, operating rule and/or Operations Specifications) whichever is higher.

(b) Visual contact with the landing site is not required; however, the pilot must have the appropriate VFR weather minimums throughout the visual segment. The visibility is limited to no lower than that published in the procedure, until canceling IFR.

(c) IFR obstruction clearance areas are not applied to the VFR segment between the MAP and the landing site. Pilots are responsible for obstacle or terrain avoidance from the MAP to the landing area.

(d) Upon reaching the MAP defined on the approach procedure, or as soon as practicable thereafter, the pilot should advise ATC whether proceeding VFR and canceling IFR, or complying with the missed approach instructions. See paragraph 5-1-15, Canceling IFR Flight Plan.

(e) If the visual segment penetrates Class B, C, or D airspace, pilots are responsible for obtaining a Special VFR clearance, when required.

10-1-4 The Gulf of Mexico Grid System

a. On October 8, 1998, the Southwest Regional Office of the FAA, with assistance from the Helicopter Safety Advisory Conference (HSAC), implemented the world's first Instrument Flight Rules (IFR) Grid System in the Gulf of Mexico. This navigational route structure is completely independent of ground-based navigation aids (NAVAIDs) and was designed to facilitate helicopter IFR operations to offshore destinations. The Grid System is defined by over 300 offshore waypoints located 20 minutes apart (latitude and longitude). Flight plan routes are routinely defined by just 4 segments; departure point (lat/long), first en route grid waypoint, last en route grid waypoint prior to approach procedure, and destination point (lat/long). There are over 4,000 possible offshore landing sites. Upon reaching the waypoint prior to the destination, the pilot may execute an Offshore Standard Approach Procedure (OSAP), a Helicopter En Route Descent Areas (HEDA) approach, or an Airborne Radar Approach (ARA). For more information on these helicopter instrument procedures, refer to FAA AC 90-80B, Approval of Offshore Standard Approach Procedures, Airborne Radar Approaches, and Helicopter En Route Descent Areas, on the FAA website http://www.faa.gov. under Advisory Circulars. The return flight plan is just the reverse with the requested stand-alone GPS approach contained in the remarks section.

1. The large number (over 300) of waypoints in the grid system makes it difficult to assign phonetically pronounceable names to the waypoints that would be meaningful to pilots and controllers. A unique naming system was adopted that enables pilots and controllers to derive the fix position from the name. The five-letter names are derived as follows:

(a) The waypoints are divided into sets of 3 columns each. A three-letter identifier, identifying a geographical area or a NAVAID to the north, represents each set.

(b) Each column in a set is named after its position, i.e., left (L), center (C), and right (R).

(c) The rows of the grid are named alphabetically from north to south, starting with A for the northern most row.

Example: *LCHRC would be pronounced "Lake Charles Romeo Charlie." The waypoint is in the right-hand column of the Lake Charles VOR set, in row C (third south from the northern most row).*

2. In December 2009, significant improvements to the Gulf of Mexico grid system were realized with the introduction of ATC separation services using ADS-B. In cooperation with the oil and gas services industry, HSAC and Helicopter Association International (HAI), the FAA installed an infrastructure of ADS-B ground stations, weather stations (AWOS) and VHF remote communication outlets (RCO) throughout a large area of the Gulf of Mexico. This infrastructure allows the FAA's Houston ARTCC to provide "domestic-like" air traffic control service in the offshore area beyond 12nm from the coastline to hundreds of miles offshore to aircraft equipped with ADS-B. Properly equipped aircraft can now be authorized to receive more direct routing, domestic en route separation minima and real time flight following. Operators who do not have authorization to receive ATC separation services using ADS-B, will continue to use the low altitude grid system and receive procedural separation from Houston ARTCC. Non-ADS-B equipped aircraft also benefit from improved VHF communication and expanded weather information coverage.

3. Three requirements must be met for operators to file IFR flight plans utilizing the grid:

(a) The helicopter must be equipped for IFR operations and equipped with IFR approved GPS navigational units.

(b) The operator must obtain prior written approval from the appropriate Flight Standards District Office through a Letter of Authorization or Operations Specification, as appropriate.

(c) The operator must be a signatory to the Houston ARTCC Letter of Agreement.

4. Operators who wish to benefit from ADS-B based ATC separation services must meet the following additional requirements:

(a) The Operator's installed ADS-B Out equipment must meet the performance requirements of one of the following FAA Technical Standard Orders (TSO), or later revisions: TSO-C154c, Universal Access Transceiver (UAT) Automatic Dependent Surveillance–Broadcast (ADS-B) Equipment, or TSO-C166b, Extended Squitter Automatic Dependent Surveillance–Broadcast (ADS-B) and Traffic Information.

(b) Flight crews must comply with the procedures prescribed in the Houston ARTCC Letter of Agreement dated December 17, 2009, or later.

Note: The unique ADS-B architecture in the Gulf of Mexico depends upon reception of an aircraft's Mode C in addition to the other message elements described in 14 CFR 91.227. Flight crews must be made aware that loss of Mode C also means that ATC will not receive the aircraft's ADS-B signal.

5. FAA/AIS publishes the grid system waypoints on the IFR Gulf of Mexico Vertical Flight Reference Chart. A commercial equivalent is also available. The chart is updated annually and is available from an FAA approved print provider or FAA directly, website address: http://www.faa.gov/air_traffic/flight_info/aeronav.

Ch 10

10–1–5 Departure Procedures

a. When departing from a location on a point-in-space (PinS) SID with a visual segment indicated and the departure instruction describes the visual segment the aircraft must cross the initial departure fix (IDF) outbound at-or-above the altitude depicted on the chart. The helicopter will initially establish a hover at or above the heliport crossing height (HCH) specified on the chart. The HCH specifies a minimum hover height to begin the climb to assist in avoiding obstacles. The helicopter will leave the departure location on the published outbound heading/course specified, climbing at least 400 ft/per NM (or as depicted on the chart), remaining clear of clouds, crossing at or above the IDF altitude specified, prior to proceeding outbound on the procedure. For example the chart may include these instructions: "Hover at 15 ft AGL, then climb on track 005, remaining clear of clouds, to cross PAWLY at or above 700."

b. When flying a PinS SID procedure containing a segment with instructions to "proceed VFR," the pilot must keep the aircraft clear of the clouds and cross the IDF outbound at or above the altitude depicted. Departure procedures that support multiple departure locations will have a Proceed VFR segment leading to the IDF. The chart will provide a bearing and distance to the IDF from the heliport. That bearing and distance are for pilot orientation purposes only and are not a required procedure track. The helicopter will leave the departure location via pilot navigation in order to align with the departure route and comply with the altitude specified at the IDF. For example, the chart may include these instructions: "VFR Climb to WEBBB, Cross WEBBB at or above 800."

c. Once the aircraft reaches the IDF, the aircraft should proceed out the described route as specified on the chart, crossing each consecutive fix at or above the indicated altitude(s) until reaching the end of the departure or as directed by ATC.

FIGURE 10–1–1
Departure Charts

Section 2 Special Operations

10–2–1 Offshore Helicopter Operations

a. Introduction

The offshore environment offers unique applications and challenges for helicopter pilots. The mission demands, the nature of oil and gas exploration and production facilities, and the flight environment (weather, terrain, obstacles, traffic), demand special practices, techniques and procedures not found in other flight operations. Several industry organizations have risen to the task of reducing risks in offshore operations, including the Helicopter Safety Advisory Conference (HSAC) (http://www.hsac.org), and the Offshore Committee of the Helicopter Association International (HAI) (https://www.rotor.org). The following recommended practices for offshore helicopter operations are based on guidance developed by HSAC for use in the Gulf of Mexico, and provided here with their permission. While not regulatory, these recommended practices provide aviation and oil and gas industry operators with useful information in developing procedures to avoid certain hazards of offshore helicopter operations.

Note: Like all aviation practices, these recommended practices are under constant review. In addition to normal procedures for comments, suggested changes, or corrections to the AIM (contained in the Preface), any questions or feedback concerning these recommended procedures may also be directed to the HSAC through the feedback feature of the HSAC website (http://www.hsac.org).

b. Passenger Management on and about Heliport Facilities

1. Background. Several incidents involving offshore helicopter passengers have highlighted the potential for incidents and accidents on and about the heliport area. The following practices will minimize risks to passengers and others involved in heliport operations.

2. Recommended Practices

(a) Heliport facilities should have a designated and posted passenger waiting area which is clear of the heliport, heliport access points, and stairways.

(b) Arriving passengers and cargo should be unloaded and cleared from the heliport and access route prior to loading departing passengers and cargo.

(c) Where a flight crew consists of more than one pilot, one crewmember should supervise the unloading/loading process from outside the aircraft.

(d) Where practical, a designated facility employee should assist with loading/unloading, etc.

c. Crane-Helicopter Operational Procedures

1. Background. Historical experience has shown that catastrophic consequences can occur when industry safe practices for crane/helicopter operations are not observed. The following recommended practices are designed to minimize risks during crane and helicopter operations.

2. Recommended Practices

(a) Personnel awareness

(1) Crane operators and pilots should develop a mutual understanding and respect of the others' operational limitations and cooperate in the spirit of safety;

(2) Pilots need to be aware that crane operators sometimes cannot release the load to cradle the crane boom, such as when attached to wire line lubricators or supporting diving bells; and

(3) Crane operators need to be aware that helicopters require warm up before takeoff, a two-minute cool down before shutdown, and cannot circle for extended lengths of time because of fuel consumption.

(b) It is recommended that when helicopters are approaching, maneuvering, taking off, or running on the heliport, cranes be shutdown and the operator leave the cab. Cranes not in use must have their booms cradled, if feasible. If in use, the crane's boom(s) are to be pointed away from the heliport and the crane shutdown for helicopter operations.

(c) Pilots will not approach, land on, take-off, or have rotor blades turning on heliports of structures not complying with the above practice.

(d) It is recommended that cranes on offshore platforms, rigs, vessels, or any other facility, which could interfere with helicopter operations (including approach/departure paths):

(1) Be equipped with a red rotating beacon or red high intensity strobe light connected to the system powering the crane, indicating the crane is under power;

(2) Be designed to allow the operator a maximum view of the helideck area and should be equipped with wide-angle mirrors to eliminate blind spots; and

(3) Have their boom tips, headache balls, and hooks painted with high visibility international orange.

d. Helicopter/Tanker Operations

1. Background. The interface of helicopters and tankers during shipboard helicopter operations is complex and may be hazardous unless appropriate procedures are coordinated among all parties. The following recommended practices are designed to minimize risks during helicopter/tanker operations:

Ch 10

2. Recommended Practices

(a) Management, flight operations personnel, and pilots should be familiar with and apply the operating safety standards set forth in "Guide to Helicopter/Ship Operations," International Chamber of Shipping, Third Edition, 5-89 (as amended), establishing operational guidelines/ standards and safe practices sufficient to safeguard helicopter/tanker operations.

(b) Appropriate plans, approvals, and communications must be accomplished prior to reaching the vessel, allowing tanker crews sufficient time to perform required safety preparations and position crew members to receive or dispatch a helicopter safely.

(c) Appropriate approvals and direct communications with the bridge of the tanker must be maintained throughout all helicopter/tanker operations.

(d) Helicopter/tanker operations, including landings/departures, must not be conducted until the helicopter pilot-in-command has received and acknowledged permission from the bridge of the tanker.

(e) Helicopter/tanker operations must not be conducted during product/cargo transfer.

(f) Generally, permission will not be granted to land on tankers during mooring operations or while maneuvering alongside another tanker.

e. Helideck/Heliport Operational Hazard Warning(s) Procedures
1. Background

(a) A number of operational hazards can develop on or near offshore helidecks or onshore heliports that can be minimized through procedures for proper notification or visual warning to pilots. Examples of hazards include but are not limited to:

(1) Perforating operations: subparagraph f.

(2) H_2S gas presence: subparagraph g.

(3) Gas venting: subparagraph h; or,

(4) Closed helidecks or heliports: subparagraph i (unspecified cause).

(b) These and other operational hazards are currently minimized through timely dissemination of a written Notice to Air Missions (NOTAM) for pilots by helicopter companies and operators. A NOTAM provides a written description of the hazard, time and duration of occurrence, and other pertinent information. ANY POTENTIAL HAZARD should be communicated to helicopter operators or company aviation departments as early as possible to allow the NOTAM to be activated.

(c) To supplement the existing NOTAM procedure and further assist in reducing these hazards, a standardized visual signal(s) on the helideck/heliport will provide a positive indication to an approaching helicopter of the status of the landing area. Recommended Practice(s) have been developed to reinforce the NOTAM procedures and standardize visual signals.

f. Drilling Rig Perforating Operations: Helideck/Heliport Operational Hazard Warning(s)/Procedure(s)

1. Background. A critical step in the oil well completion process is perforation, which involves the use of explosive charges in the drill pipe to open the pipe to oil or gas deposits. Explosive charges used in conjunction with perforation operations offshore can potentially be prematurely detonated by radio transmissions, including those from helicopters. The following practices are recommended.

2. Recommended Practices

(a) Personnel Conducting Perforating Operations. Whenever perforating operations are scheduled and operators are concerned that radio transmissions from helicopters in the vicinity may jeopardize the operation, personnel conducting perforating operations should take the following precautionary measures:

(1) Notify company aviation departments, helicopter operators or bases, and nearby manned platforms of the pending perforation operation so the Notice to Air Missions (NOTAM) system can be activated for the perforation operation and the temporary helideck closure.

(2) Close the deck and make the radio warning clearly visible to passing pilots, install a temporary marking (described in subparagraph 10-2-1i1(b)) with the words "NO RADIO" stenciled in red on the legs of the diagonals. The letters should be 24 inches high and 12 inches wide. (See Figure 10-2-1.)

(3) The marker should be installed during the time that charges may be affected by radio transmissions.

(b) Pilots

(1) When operating within 1,000 feet of a known perforation operation or observing the white X with red "NO RADIO" warning indicating perforation operations are underway, pilots will avoid radio transmissions from or near the helideck (within 1,000 feet) and will not land on the deck if the X is present. In addition to communications radios, radio transmissions are also emitted by aircraft radar, transponders, ADS-B equipment, radar altimeters, and DME equipment, and ELTs.

(2) Whenever possible, make radio calls to the platform being approached or to the Flight Following Communications Center at least one mile out on approach. Ensure all communications are complete outside the 1,000 foot hazard distance. If no response is received, or if the platform is not radio equipped, further radio transmissions

should not be made until visual contact with the deck indicates it is open for operation (no white "X").

g. Hydrogen Sulfide Gas Helideck/Heliport Operational Hazard Warning(s)/Procedures

1. Background. Hydrogen sulfide (H2S) gas: Hydrogen sulfide gas in higher concentrations (300–500 ppm) can cause loss of consciousness within a few seconds and presents a hazard to pilots on/near offshore helidecks. When operating in offshore areas that have been identified to have concentrations of hydrogen sulfide gas, the following practices are recommended.

2. Recommended Practices

(a) Pilots

(1) Ensure approved protective air packs are available for emergency use by the crew on the helicopter.

(2) If shutdown on a helideck, request the supervisor in charge provide a briefing on location of protective equipment and safety procedures.

(3) If while flying near a helideck and the visual red beacon alarm is observed or an unusually strong odor of "rotten eggs" is detected, immediately don the protective air pack, exit to an area upwind, and notify the suspected source field of the hazard.

FIGURE 10–2–1
Closed Helideck Marking–No Radio

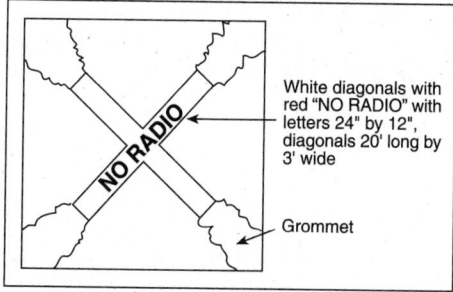

White diagonals with red "NO RADIO" with letters 24" by 12", diagonals 20' long by 3' wide

Grommet

(b) Oil Field Supervisors

(1) If presence of hydrogen sulfide is detected, a red rotating beacon or red high intensity strobe light adjacent to the primary helideck stairwell or wind indicator on the structure should be turned on to provide visual warning of hazard. If the beacon is to be located near the stairwell, the State of Louisiana "Offshore Heliport Design Guide" and FAA Advisory Circular (AC) 150/5390-2A, "Heliport Design Guide," should be reviewed to ensure proper clearance on the helideck.

(2) Notify nearby helicopter operators and bases of the hazard and advise when hazard is cleared.

(3) Provide a safety briefing to include location of protective equipment to all arriving personnel.

(4) Wind socks or indicator should be clearly visible to provide upwind indication for the pilot.

h. Gas Venting Helideck/Heliport Operational Hazard Warning(s)/Procedures— Operations Near Gas Vent Booms

1. Background. Ignited flare booms can release a large volume of natural gas and create a hot fire and intense heat with little time for the pilot to react. Likewise, unignited gas vents can release reasonably large volumes of methane gas under certain conditions. Thus, operations conducted very near unignited gas vents require precautions to prevent inadvertent ingestion of combustible gases by the helicopter engine(s). The following practices are recommended.

2. Pilots

(a) Gas will drift upwards and downwind of the vent. Plan the approach and takeoff to observe and avoid the area downwind of the vent, remaining as far away as practicable from the open end of the vent boom.

(b) Do not attempt to start or land on an offshore helideck when the deck is downwind of a gas vent unless properly trained personnel verify conditions are safe.

3. Oil Field Supervisors

(a) During venting of large amounts of unignited raw gas, a red rotating beacon or red high intensity strobe light adjacent to the primary helideck stairwell or wind indicator should be turned on to provide visible warning of hazard. If the beacon is to be located near the stairwell, the State of Louisiana "Offshore Heliport Design Guide" and FAA AC 150/5390-2A, Heliport Design Guide, should be reviewed to ensure proper clearance from the helideck.

(b) Notify nearby helicopter operators and bases of the hazard for planned operations.

(c) Wind socks or indicator should be clearly visible to provide upward indication for the pilot.

i. Helideck/Heliport Operational Warning(s)/ Procedure(s)—Closed Helidecks or Heliports

1. Background. A white "X" marked diagonally from corner to corner across a helideck or heliport touchdown area is the universally accepted visual indicator that the landing area is closed for safety of other reasons and that helicopter operations are not permitted. The following practices are recommended.

(a) Permanent Closing. If a helideck or heliport is to be permanently closed, X diagonals of the same size and location as indicated above should be used, but the markings should be painted on the landing area.

Ch 10

Note: White Decks: If a helideck is painted white, then international orange or yellow markings can be used for the temporary or permanent diagonals.

(b) Temporary Closing. A temporary marker can be used for hazards of an interim nature. This marker could be made from vinyl or other durable material in the shape of a diagonal "X." The marker should be white with legs at least 20 feet long and 3 feet in width. This marker is designed to be quickly secured and removed from the deck using grommets and rope ties. The duration, time, location, and nature of these temporary closings should be provided to and coordinated with company aviation departments, nearby helicopter bases, and helicopter operators supporting the area. These markers MUST be removed when the hazard no longer exists. (See Figure 10-2-2.)

FIGURE 10–2–2
Closed Helideck Marking

White diagonals 3 feet wide and 20 feet long

Rope ties

j. Offshore (VFR) Operating Altitudes for Helicopters
1. Background. Mid-air collisions constitute a significant percentage of total fatal offshore helicopter accidents. A method of reducing this risk is the use of coordinated VFR cruising altitudes. To enhance safety through standardized vertical separation of helicopters when flying in the offshore environment, it is recommended that helicopter operators flying in a particular area establish a cooperatively developed Standard Operating Procedure (SOP) for VFR operating altitudes. An example of such an SOP is contained in this example.
2. Recommended Practice Example
(a) Field Operations. Without compromising minimum safe operating altitudes, helicopters working within an offshore field "constituting a cluster" should use altitudes not to exceed 500 feet.
(b) En Route Operations
(1) Helicopters operating below 750' AGL should avoid transitioning through offshore fields.

(2) Helicopters en route to and from offshore locations, below 3,000 feet, weather permitting, should use en route altitudes as outlined in Table 10-2-1.

TABLE 10–2–1

Magnetic Heading	Altitude
0° to 179°	750'
	1750'
	2750'
180° to 359°	1250'
	2250'

(c) Area Agreements. See HSAC Area Agreement Maps for operating procedures for onshore high density traffic locations.

Note: Pilots of helicopters operating VFR above 3,000 feet above the surface should refer to the current Federal Aviation Regulations (14 CFR Part 91), and Paragraph 3-1-4, Basic VFR Weather Minimums, of the AIM.

(d) Landing Lights. Aircraft landing lights should be on to enhance aircraft identification:
(1) During takeoff and landings;
(2) In congested helicopter or fixed wing traffic areas;
(3) During reduced visibility; or,
(4) Anytime safety could be enhanced.
k. Offshore Helidecks/Landing Communications
1. Background. To enhance safety, and provide appropriate time to prepare for helicopter operations, the following is recommended when anticipating a landing on an offshore helideck.
2. Recommended Practices
(a) Before landing on an offshore helideck, pilots are encouraged to establish communications with the company owning or operating the helideck if frequencies exist for that purpose.
(b) When impracticable, or if frequencies do not exist, pilots or operations personnel should attempt to contact the company owning or operating the helideck by telephone. Contact should be made before the pilot departs home base/point of departure to advise of intentions and obtain landing permission if necessary.

Note: It is recommended that communications be established a minimum of 10 minutes prior to planned arrival time. This practice may be a requirement of some offshore owner/operators.

Note 1: See subparagraph 10-2-1d for Tanker Operations.

Note 2: Private use Heliport. Offshore heliports are privately owned/operated facilities and their use is limited to persons having prior authorization to utilize the facility.

l. Two (2) Helicopter Operations on Offshore Helidecks

1. Background. Standardized procedures can enhance the safety of operating a second helicopter on an offshore helideck, enabling pilots to determine/maintain minimum operational parameters. Orientation of the parked helicopter on the helideck, wind and other factors may prohibit multi-helicopter operations. More conservative Rotor Diameter (RD) clearances may be required under differing condition, i.e. temperature, wet deck, wind (velocity/direction/gusts), obstacles, approach/departure angles, etc. Operations are at the pilot's discretion.

2. Recommended Practice. Helideck size, structural weight capability, and type of main rotor on the parked and operating helicopter will aid in determining accessibility by a second helicopter. Pilots should determine that multi-helicopter deck operations are permitted by the helideck owner/operator.

3. Recommended Criteria

(a) Minimum one-third rotor diameter clearance (1/3 RD). The landing helicopter maintains a minimum 1/3 RD clearance between the tips of its turning rotor and the closest part of a parked and secured helicopter (rotors stopped and tied down).

(b) Three foot parking distance from deck edge (3'). Helicopters operating on an offshore helideck land or park the helicopter with a skid/wheel assembly no closer than 3 feet from helideck edge.

(c) Tiedowns. Main rotors on all helicopters that are shut down be properly secured (tied down) to prevent the rotor blades from turning.

(d) Medium (transport) and larger helicopters should not land on any offshore helideck where a light helicopter is parked unless the light helicopter is property secured to the helideck and has main rotor tied down.

(e) Helideck owners/operators should ensure that the helideck has a serviceable anti-skid surface.

4. Weight and limitations markings on helideck. The helideck weight limitations should be displayed by markings visible to the pilot (see State of Louisiana "Offshore Heliport Design Guide" and FAA AC 150/5390-2A, Heliport Design Guide).

Note: Some offshore helideck owners/operators have restrictions on the number of helicopters allowed on a helideck. When helideck size permits, multiple (more than two) helicopter operations are permitted by some operators.

m. Helicopter Rapid Refueling Procedures (HRR)

1. Background. Helicopter Rapid Refueling (HRR), engine(s)/rotors operating, can be conducted safely when utilizing trained personnel and observing safe practices. This recommended practice provides minimum guidance for HRR as outlined in National Fire Protection Association (NFPA) and industry practices. For detailed guidance, please refer to National Fire Protection Association (NFPA) Document 407, "Standard for Aircraft Fuel Servicing," 1990 edition, including 1993 HRR Amendment.

Note: Certain operators prohibit HRR, or "hot refueling," or may have specific procedures for certain aircraft or refueling locations. See the General Operations Manual and/or Operations Specifications to determine the applicable procedures or limitations.

2. Recommended Practices

(a) Only turbine-engine helicopters fueled with JET A or JET A-1 with fueling ports located below any engine exhausts may be fueled while an onboard engine(s) is (are) operating.

(b) Helicopter fueling while an onboard engine(s) is (are) operating should only be conducted under the following conditions:

(1) A properly certificated and current pilot is at the controls and a trained refueler attending the fuel nozzle during the entire fuel servicing process. The pilot monitors the fuel quantity and signals the refueler when quantity is reached.

(2) No electrical storms (thunderstorms) are present within 10 nautical miles. Lightning can travel great distances beyond the actual thunderstorm.

(3) Passengers disembark the helicopter and move to a safe location prior to HRR operations. When the pilot-in-command deems it necessary for passenger safety that they remain onboard, passengers should be briefed on the evacuation route to follow to clear the area.

(4) Passengers not board or disembark during HRR operations nor should cargo be loaded or unloaded.

(5) Only designated personnel, trained in HRR operations should conduct HRR written authorization to include safe handling of the fuel and equipment. (See your Company Operations/Safety Manual for detailed instructions.)

(6) All doors, windows, and access points allowing entry to the interior of the helicopter that are adjacent to or in the immediate vicinity of the fuel inlet ports kept closed during HRR operations.

Ch 10

(7) Pilots ensure that appropriate electrical/electronic equipment is placed in standby-off position, to preclude the possibility of electrical discharge or other fire hazard, such as [i.e., weather radar is on standby and no radio transmissions are made (keying of the microphone/transmitter)]. Remember, in addition to communications radios, radio transmissions are also emitted by aircraft radar, transponders, ADS-B equipment, radar altimeters, DME equipment, and ELTs.

(8) Smoking be prohibited in and around the helicopter during all HRR operations.

The HRR procedures are critical and present associated hazards requiring attention to detail regarding quality control, weather conditions, static electricity, bonding, and spill/fires potential.

Any activity associated with rotors turning (i.e.; refueling embarking/disembarking, loading/unloading baggage/freight; etc.) personnel should **only** approach the aircraft when authorized to do so. Approach should be made via safe approach path/walkway or "arc"—**remain clear of all rotors**.

Note 1: *Marine vessels, barges etc.: Vessel motion presents additional potential hazards to helicopter operations (blade flex, aircraft movement).*

Note 2: *See National Fire Protection Association (NFPA) Document 407, "Standard for Aircraft Fuel Servicing" for specifics regarding non-HRR (routine refueling operations).*

10-2-2 Helicopter Night VFR Operations

a. Effect of Lighting on Seeing Conditions in Night VFR Helicopter Operations

Note: *This guidance was developed to support safe night VFR helicopter emergency medical services (HEMS) operations. The principles of lighting and seeing conditions are useful in any night VFR operation.*

While ceiling and visibility significantly affect safety in night VFR operations, lighting conditions also have a profound effect on safety. Even in conditions in which visibility and ceiling are determined to be visual meteorological conditions, the ability to discern unlighted or low contrast objects and terrain at night may be compromised. The ability to discern these objects and terrain is the seeing condition, and is related to the amount of natural and man made lighting available, and the contrast, reflectivity, and texture of surface terrain and obstruction features. In order to conduct operations safely, seeing conditions must be accounted for in the planning and execution of night VFR operations.

Night VFR seeing conditions can be described by identifying "high lighting conditions" and "low lighting conditions."

1. High lighting conditions exist when one of two sets of conditions are present:

(a) The sky cover is less than broken (less than 5/8 cloud cover), the time is between the local Moon rise and Moon set, and the lunar disk is at least 50% illuminated; or

(b) The aircraft is operated over surface lighting which, at least, provides for the lighting of prominent obstacles, the identification of terrain features (shorelines, valleys, hills, mountains, slopes) and a horizontal reference by which the pilot may control the helicopter. For example, this surface lighting may be the result of:

(1) Extensive cultural lighting (man-made, such as a built-up area of a city),

(2) Significant reflected cultural lighting (such as the illumination caused by the reflection of a major metropolitan area's lighting reflecting off a cloud ceiling), or

(3) Limited cultural lighting combined with a high level of natural reflectivity of celestial illumination, such as that provided by a surface covered by snow or a desert surface.

2. Low lighting conditions are those that do not meet the high lighting conditions requirements.

3. Some areas may be considered a high lighting environment only in specific circumstances. For example, some surfaces, such as a forest with limited cultural lighting, normally have little reflectivity, requiring dependence on significant moonlight to achieve a high lighting condition. However, when that same forest is covered with snow, its reflectivity may support a high lighting condition based only on starlight. Similarly, a desolate area, with little cultural lighting, such as a desert, may have such inherent natural reflectivity that it may be considered a high lighting conditions area regardless of season, provided the cloud cover does not prevent starlight from being reflected from the surface. Other surfaces, such as areas of open water, may never have enough reflectivity or cultural lighting to ever be characterized as a high lighting area.

4. Through the accumulation of night flying experience in a particular area, the operator will develop the ability to determine, prior to departure, which areas can be considered supporting high or low lighting conditions. Without that operational experience, low lighting considerations should be applied by operators for both pre-flight planning and operations until high lighting conditions are observed or determined to be regularly available.

b. Astronomical Definitions and Background Information for Night Operations

1. Definitions

(a) Horizon. Wherever one is located on or near the Earth's surface, the Earth is perceived as essentially flat and, therefore, as a plane. If there are no visual obstructions, the apparent intersection of the sky with the Earth's (plane) surface is the horizon, which appears as a circle centered at the observer. For rise/set computations, the observer's eye is considered to be on the surface of the Earth, so that the horizon is geometrically exactly 90 degrees from the local vertical direction.

(b) Rise, Set. During the course of a day the Earth rotates once on its axis causing the phenomena of rising and setting. All celestial bodies, the Sun, Moon, stars and planets, seem to appear in the sky at the horizon to the East of any particular place, then to cross the sky and again disappear at the horizon to the West. Because the Sun and Moon appear as circular disks and not as points of light, a definition of rise or set must be very specific, because not all of either body is seen to rise or set at once.

(c) Sunrise and sunset refer to the times when the upper edge of the disk of the Sun is on the horizon, considered unobstructed relative to the location of interest. Atmospheric conditions are assumed to be average, and the location is in a level region on the Earth's surface.

(d) Moonrise and moonset times are computed for exactly the same circumstances as for sunrise and sunset. However, moonrise and moonset may occur at any time during a 24 hour period and, consequently, it is often possible for the Moon to be seen during daylight, and to have moonless nights. It is also possible that a moonrise or moonset does not occur relative to a specific place on a given date.

(e) Transit. The transit time of a celestial body refers to the instant that its center crosses an imaginary line in the sky—the observer's meridian—running from north to south.

(f) Twilight. Before sunrise and again after sunset there are intervals of time, known as "twilight," during which there is natural light provided by the upper atmosphere, which does receive direct sunlight and reflects part of it toward the Earth's surface.

(g) Civil twilight is defined to begin in the morning, and to end in the evening when the center of the Sun is geometrically 6 degrees below the horizon. This is the limit at which twilight illumination is sufficient, under good weather conditions, for terrestrial objects to be clearly distinguished.

2. Title 14 of the Code of Federal Regulations applies these concepts and definitions in addressing the definition of night (Section 1.1), the requirement for aircraft lighting (Section 91.209) and pilot recency of night experience (Section 61.67).

c. Information on Moon Phases and Changes in the Percentage of the Moon Illuminated

From any location on the Earth, the Moon appears to be a circular disk which, at any specific time, is illuminated to some degree by direct sunlight. During each lunar orbit (a lunar month), we see the Moon's appearance change from not visibly illuminated through partially illuminated to fully illuminated, then back through partially illuminated to not illuminated again. There are eight distinct, traditionally recognized stages, called phases. The phases designate both the degree to which the Moon is illuminated and the geometric appearance of the illuminated part. These phases of the Moon, in the sequence of their occurrence (starting from New Moon), are listed in Figure 10-2-3.

1. The percent of the Moon's surface illuminated is a more refined, quantitative description of the Moon's appearance than is the phase. Considering the Moon as a circular disk, at New Moon the percent illuminated is 0; at First and Last Quarters it is 50%; and at Full Moon it is 100%. During the crescent phases the percent illuminated is between 0 and 50% and during gibbous phases it is between 50% and 100%.

2. For practical purposes, phases of the Moon and the percent of the Moon illuminated are independent of the location on the Earth from where the Moon is observed. That is, all the phases occur at the same time regardless of the observer's position.

3. For more detailed information, refer to the United States Naval Observatory site referenced below.

d. Access to Astronomical Data for Determination of Moon Rise, Moon Set, and Percentage of Lunar Disk Illuminated

1. Astronomical data for the determination of Moon rise and set and Moon phase may be obtained from the United States Naval Observatory using an interactive query available at: **http://aa.usno.navy.mil/**

2. Click on "Data Services," and then on "Complete Sun and Moon Data for One Day."

3. You can obtain the times of sunrise, sunset, moonrise, moonset, transits of the Sun and Moon, and the beginning and end of civil twilight, along with information on the Moon's phase by specifying the date and location in one of the two forms on this web page and clicking on the "Get data" button at the end of the form. Form "A" is used for cities or towns in the U.S. or its territories. Form "B" for all other locations. An example of the data available from this site is shown in Table 10-2-2.

Ch 10

TABLE 10-2-2
SAMPLE OF ASTRONOMICAL DATA AVAILABLE FROM
THE NAVAL OBSERVATORY

The following information is provided for New Orleans, Orleans Parish, Louisiana (longitude W90.1, latitude N30.0)	
Tuesday 29 May 2007	Central Daylight Time
SUN	
Begin civil twilight	5:34 a.m.
Sunrise	6:01 a.m.
Sun transit	12:58 p.m.
Sunset	7:55 p.m.
End civil twilight	8:22 p.m.
MOON	
Moonrise	5:10 p.m. on preceding day
Moonset	4:07 a.m.
Moonrise	6:06 p.m.
Moon transit	11:26 p.m.
Moonset	4:41 a.m. on following day
Phase of the Moon on 29 May: waxing gibbous with 95% of the Moon's visible disk illuminated.	
Full Moon on 31 May 2007 at 8:04 p.m. Central Daylight Time.	

4. Additionally, a yearly table may be constructed for a particular location by using the "Table of Sunrise/Sunset, Moonrise/Moonset, or Twilight Times for an Entire Year" selection.

FIGURE 10–2–3
Phases of the Moon

New Moon: The Moon's unilluminated side is facing the Earth. The Moon is not visible (except during a solar eclipse).

Waxing Crescent: The Moon appears to be partly but less than one-half illuminated by direct sunlight. The fraction of the Moon's disk that is illuminated is increasing.

First Quarter: One-half of the Moon appears to be illuminated by direct sunlight. The fraction of the Moon's disk that is illuminated is increasing.

Waxing Gibbous: The Moon appears to be more than one-half but not fully illuminated by direct sunlight. The fraction of the Moon's disk that is illuminated is increasing.

Full Moon: The Moon's illuminated side is facing the Earth. The Moon appears to be completely illuminated by direct sunlight.

Waning Gibbous: The Moon appears to be more than one-half but not fully illuminated by direct sunlight. The fraction of the Moon's disk that is illuminated is decreasing.

Last Quarter: One-half of the Moon appears to be illuminated by direct sunlight. The fraction of the Moon's disk that is illuminated is decreasing.

Waning Crescent: The Moon appears to be partly but less than one-half illuminated by direct sunlight. The fraction of the Moon's disk that is illuminated is decreasing.

Ch 10

10–2–3 Landing Zone Safety

a. This information is provided for use by helicopter emergency medical services (HEMS) pilots, program managers, medical personnel, law enforcement, fire, and rescue personnel to further their understanding of the safety issues concerning Landing Zones (LZs). It is recommended that HEMS operators establish working relationships with the ground responder organizations they may come in contact with in their flight operations and share this information in order to establish a common frame of reference for LZ selection, operations, and safety.

b. The information provided is largely based on the booklet, LZ—Preparing the Landing Zone, issued by National Emergency Medical Services Pilots Association (NEMSPA), and the guidance developed by the University of Tennessee Medical Center's LIFESTAR program, and is used with their permission. For additional information, go to: **http://www.nemspa.org/**

c. Information concerning the estimation of wind velocity is based on the Beaufort Scale. See **http://www.spc.noaa.gov/faq/tornado /beaufort.html** for more information.

d. Selecting a Scene LZ

1. If the situation requires the use of a helicopter, first check to see if there is an area large enough to land a helicopter safely.

FIGURE 10–2–4
Recommended Minimum Landing Zone Dimensions

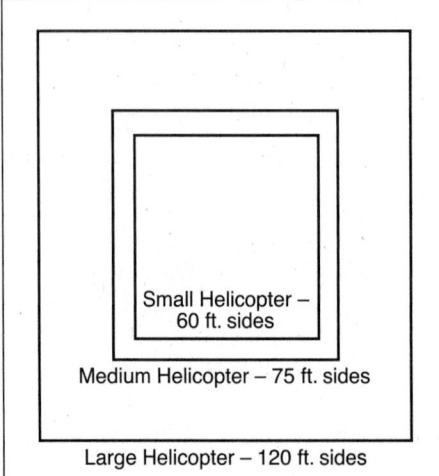

Small Helicopter – 60 ft. sides

Medium Helicopter – 75 ft. sides

Large Helicopter – 120 ft. sides

2. For the purposes of Figure 10-2-4 the following are provided as examples of relative helicopter size:

(a) Small Helicopter: Bell 206/407, Eurocopter AS-350/355, BO-105, BK-117.

(b) Medium Helicopter: Bell UH-1 (Huey) and derivatives (Bell 212/412), Bell 222/230/430 Sikorsky S-76, Eurocopter SA-365.

(c) Large Helicopter: Boeing Chinook, Eurocopter Puma, Sikorsky H-60 series (Blackhawk), SK-92.

3. The LZ should be level, firm and free of loose debris that could possibly blow up into the rotor system.

4. The LZ should be clear of people, vehicles and obstructions such as trees, poles and wires. Remember that wires are difficult to see from the air. The LZ must also be free of stumps, brush, post and large rocks. See Figure 10-2-5.

FIGURE 10–2–5
Landing Zone Hazards

5. Keep spectators back at least 200 feet. Keep emergency vehicles 100 feet away and have fire equipment (if available) standing by. Ground personnel should wear eye protection, if available, during landing and takeoff operations. To avoid loose objects being blown around in the LZ, hats should be removed; if helmets are worn, chin straps must be securely fastened.

6. Fire fighters (if available) should wet down the LZ if it is extremely dusty.

e. Helping the Flightcrew Locate the Scene

1. If the LZ coordinator has access to a GPS unit, the exact latitude and longitude of the LZ should be relayed to the HEMS pilot. If unable to contact the pilot directly, relay the information to the HEMS ground communications specialist for relaying to the pilot, so that they may locate your scene more efficiently. Recognize that the aircraft may approach from a direction different than the direct path from the takeoff point to the scene, as the pilot may have to detour around terrain, obstructions or weather en route.

2. Especially in daylight hours, mountainous and densely populated areas can make sighting a scene from the air difficult. Often, the LZ coordinator on the ground will be asked if she or he can see or hear the helicopter.

3. Flightcrews use a clock reference method for directing one another's attention to a certain direction from the aircraft. The nose of the aircraft is always 12 o'clock, the right side is 3 o'clock, etc. When the LZ coordinator sees the aircraft, he/she should use this method to assist the flightcrew by indicating the scene's clock reference position from the nose of the aircraft. For example, "Accident scene is located at your 2 o'clock position." See Figure 10-2-6.

FIGURE 10–2–6
"Clock" System for Identifying Positions Relative to the Nose of the Aircraft

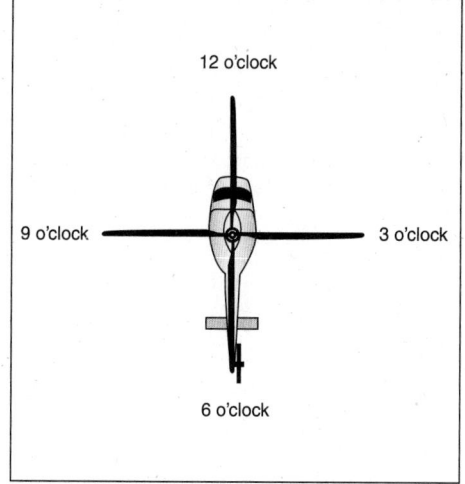

4. When the helicopter approaches the scene, it will normally orbit at least one time as the flight crew observes the wind direction and obstacles that could interfere with the landing. This is often referred to as the "high reconnaissance" maneuver.

f. Wind Direction and Touchdown Area

1. Determine from which direction the wind is blowing. Helicopters normally land and takeoff into the wind.

2. If contact can be established with the pilot, either directly or indirectly through the HEMS ground communications specialist, describe the wind in terms of the direction the wind is from and the speed.

3. Common natural sources of wind direction information are smoke, dust, vegetation movement, water streaks and waves. Flags, pennants, streamers can also be used. When describing the direction, use the compass direction from which the wind is blowing (example: from the North–West).

4. Wind speed can be measured by small hand-held measurement devices, or an observer's estimate can be used to provide velocity information. The wind value should be reported in knots (nautical miles per hour). If unable to numerically measure wind speed, use Table 10-2-3 to estimate velocity. Also, report if the wind conditions are gusty, or if the wind direction or velocity is variable or has changed recently.

5. If any obstacle(s) exist, ensure their description, position and approximate height are communicated to the pilot on the initial radio call.

Ch 10

TABLE 10–2–3
TABLE OF COMMON REFERENCES FOR ESTIMATING WIND VELOCITY

Wind (Knots)	Wind Classification	Appearance of Wind Effects	
		On the Water	On Land
Less than 1	Calm	Sea surface smooth and mirror-like	Calm, smoke rises vertically
1–3	Light Air	Scaly ripples, no foam crests	Smoke drift indicates wind direction, wind vanes are still
4–6	Light Breeze	Small wavelets, crests glassy, no breaking	Wind felt on face, leaves rustle, vanes begin to move
7–10	Gentle Breeze	Large wavelets, crests begin to break, scattered whitecaps	Leaves and small twigs constantly moving, light flags extended
11–16	Moderate Breeze	Small waves 1–4 feet becoming longer, numerous whitecaps	Dust, leaves, and loose paper lifted, small tree branches move
17–21	Fresh Breeze	Moderate waves 4–8 feet taking longer form, many whitecaps, some spray	Small trees in leaf begin to sway
22–27	Strong Breeze	Larger waves 8–13 feet, whitecaps common, more spray	Larger tree branches moving, whistling in wires
28–33	Near Gale	Sea heaps up, waves 13–20 feet, white foam streaks off breakers	Whole trees moving, resistance felt walking against wind
34–40	Gale	Moderately high (13–20 feet) waves of greater length, edges of crests begin to break into spindrift, foam blown in streaks	Whole trees in motion, resistance felt walking against wind
41–47	Strong Gale	High waves (20 feet), sea begins to roll, dense streaks of foam, spray may reduce visibility	Slight structural damage occurs, slate blows off roofs
48–55	Storm	Very high waves (20–30 feet) with overhanging crests, sea white with densely blown foam, heavy rolling, lowered visibility	Seldom experienced on land, trees broken or uprooted, "considerable structural damage"
56–63	Violent Storm	Exceptionally high (30–45 feet) waves, foam patches cover sea, visibility more reduced	—
64+	Hurricane	Air filled with foam, waves over 45 feet, sea completely white with driving spray, visibility greatly reduced	—

Example: *Wind from the South-East, estimated speed 15 knots. Wind shifted from North-East about fifteen minutes ago, and is gusty.*

g. Night LZs

1. There are several ways to light a night LZ:

(a) Mark the touchdown area with five lights or road flares, one in each corner and one indicating the direction of the wind. See Figure 10-2-7.

FIGURE 10–2–7
Recommended Lighting for Landing Zone Operations at Night

Direction of wind ———►

Light or road flare

Note: Road flares are an intense source of ignition and may be unsuitable or dangerous in certain conditions. In any case, they must be closely managed and firefighting equipment should be present when used. Other light sources are preferred, if available.

(b) If chemical light sticks may be used, care should be taken to assure they are adequately secured against being dislodged by the helicopter's rotor wash.

(c) Another method of marking a LZ uses four emergency vehicles with their low beam headlights aimed toward the intended landing area.

(d) A third method for marking a LZ uses two vehicles. Have the vehicles direct their headlight beams into the wind, crossing at the center of the LZ. (If fire/rescue personnel are available, the reflective stripes on their bunker gear will assist the pilot greatly.)

2. At night, spotlights, flood lights and hand lights used to define the LZ are not to be pointed at the helicopter. However, they are helpful when pointed toward utility poles, trees or other hazards to the landing aircraft. White lights such as spotlights, flashbulbs and hi-beam headlights ruin the pilot's night vision and temporarily blind him. Red lights, however, are very helpful in finding

accident locations and do not affect the pilot's night vision as significantly.

3. As in Day LZ operations, ensure radio contact is accomplished between ground and air, if possible.

h. Ground Guide

1. When the helicopter is in sight, one person should assist the LZ Coordinator by guiding the helicopter into a safe landing area. In selecting an LZ Coordinator, recognize that medical personnel usually are very busy with the patient at this time. It is recommended that the LZ Coordinator be someone other than a medical responder, if possible. Eye protection should be worn. The ground guide should stand with his/her back to the wind and his/her arms raised over his/her head (flashlights in each hand for night operations.)

2. The pilot will confirm the LZ sighting by radio. If possible, once the pilot has identified the LZ, the ground guide should move out of the LZ.

3. As the helicopter turns into the wind and begins a descent, the LZ coordinator should provide assistance by means of radio contact, or utilize the "unsafe signal" to wave off the helicopter if the LZ is not safe (see Figure 10-2-8). The LZ Coordinator should be far enough from the touchdown area that he/she can still maintain visual contact with the pilot.

i. Assisting the Crew

1. After the helicopter has landed, do not approach the helicopter. The crew will approach you.

2. Be prepared to assist the crew by providing security for the helicopter. If asked to provide security, allow no one but the crew to approach the aircraft.

3. Once the patient is prepared and ready to load, allow the crew to open the doors to the helicopter and guide the loading of the patient.

4. When approaching or departing the helicopter, always be aware of the tail rotor and always follow the directions of the crew. Working around a running helicopter can be potentially dangerous. The environment is very noisy and, with exhaust gases and rotor wash, often windy. In scene operations, the surface may be uneven, soft, or slippery which can lead to tripping. Be very careful of your footing in this environment.

5. The tail rotor poses a special threat to working around a running helicopter. The tail rotor turns many times faster than the main rotor, and is often invisible even at idle engine power. Avoid walking towards the tail of a helicopter beyond the end of the cabin, unless specifically directed by the crew.

Note: Helicopters typically have doors on the sides of the cabin, but many use aft mounted "clamshell" type doors for loading and unloading patients on litters or stretchers. When using these

Ch 10

doors, it is important to avoid moving any further aft than necessary to operate the doors and load/unload the patient. Again, always comply with the crew's instructions.

j. General Rules

1. When working around helicopters, always approach and depart from the front, never from the rear. Approaching from the rear can increase your risk of being struck by the tail rotor, which, when at operating engine speed, is nearly invisible.

2. To prevent injury or damage from the main rotor, never raise anything over your head.

3. If the helicopter landed on a slope, approach and depart from the down slope side only.

4. When the helicopter is loaded and ready for take off, keep the departure path free of vehicles and spectators. In an emergency, this area is needed to execute a landing.

k. Hazardous Chemicals and Gases

1. Responding to accidents involving hazardous materials requires special handling by fire/rescue units on the ground. Equally important are the preparations and considerations for helicopter operations in these areas.

2. Hazardous materials of concern are those which are toxic, poisonous, flammable, explosive, irritating, or radioactive in nature. Helicopter ambulance crews normally don't carry protective suits or breathing apparatuses to protect them from hazardous materials.

3. The helicopter ambulance crew must be told of hazardous materials on the scene in order to avoid the contamination of the crew. Patients/victims contaminated by hazardous materials may require special precautions in packaging before loading on the aircraft for the medical crew's protection, or may be transported by other means.

4. Hazardous chemicals and gases may be fatal to the unprotected person if inhaled or absorbed through the skin.

5. Upon initial radio contact, the helicopter crew must be made aware of any hazardous gases in the area. Never assume that the crew has already been informed. If the aircraft were to fly through the hazardous gases, the crew could be poisoned and/or the engines could develop mechanical problems.

6. Poisonous or irritating gases may cling to a victim's clothing and go unnoticed until the patient is loaded and the doors of the helicopter are closed. To avoid possible compromise of the crew, all of these patients must be decontaminated prior to loading.

l. Hand Signals

1. If unable to make radio contact with the HEMS pilot, use the following signals:

FIGURE 10–2–8
Recommended Landing Zone Ground Signals

Land Here (Day) LZ Unsafe (Day) Land Here (Night) LZ Unsafe (Night)

m. Emergency Situations

1. In the event of a helicopter accident in the vicinity of the LZ, consider the following:

(a) Emergency Exits:

(1) Doors and emergency exits are typically prominently marked. If possible, operators should familiarize ground responders with the door system on their helicopter in preparation for an emergency event.

(2) In the event of an accident during the LZ operation, be cautious of hazards such as sharp and jagged metal, plastic windows, glass, any rotating components, such as the rotors, and fire sources, such as the fuel tank(s) and the engine.

(b) Fire Suppression: Helicopters used in HEMS operations are usually powered by turboshaft engines, which use jet fuel. Civil HEMS aircraft typically carry between 50 and 250 gallons of fuel, depending upon the size of the helicopter, and planned flight duration, and the fuel remaining after flying to the scene. Use water to control heat and use foam over fuel to keep vapors from ignition sources.

10–2–4 Emergency Medical Service (EMS) Multiple Helicopter Operations

a. Background. EMS helicopter operators often overlap other EMS operator areas. Standardized procedures can enhance the safety of operating multiple helicopters to landing zones (LZs) and to hospital heliports. Communication is the key to successful operations and in maintaining organization between helicopters, ground units and communication centers. EMS helicopter operators which operate in the same areas should establish joint operating procedures and provide them to related agencies.

b. Recommended Procedures.

1. Landing Zone Operations. The first helicopter to arrive on-scene should establish communications with the ground unit at least 10 NMs from the LZ to receive a LZ briefing and to provide ground control the number of helicopters that can be expected. An attempt should be made to contact other helicopters on 123.025 to pass on to them pertinent LZ information and the ground unit's frequency. Subsequent helicopters arriving on scene should establish communications on 123.025 at least 10 NMs from the LZ. After establishing contact on 123.025, they should contact the ground unit for additional information. All helicopters should monitor 123.025 at all times.

(a) If the landing zone is not established by the ground unit when the first helicopter arrives, then the first helicopter should establish altitude and orbit location requirements for the other arriving helicopters. Recommended altitude separation between helicopters is 500 feet (weather and airspace permitting). Helicopters can orbit on cardinal headings from the scene coordinates. (See Figure 10-2-9.)

(b) Upon landing in the LZ, the first helicopter should update the other helicopters on the LZ conditions, i.e., space, hazards and terrain.

(c) Before initiating any helicopter movement to leave the LZ, all operators should attempt to contact other helicopters on 123.025, and state their position and route of flight intentions for departing the LZ.

2. Hospital Operations. Because many hospitals require landing permission and have established procedures (frequencies to monitor, primary and secondary routes for approaches and departures, and orbiting areas if the heliport is occupied) pilots should always receive a briefing from the appropriate facility (communication center, flight following, etc.) before proceeding to the hospital.

(a) In the event of multiple helicopters coming into the hospital heliport, the helicopter nearest to the heliport should contact other inbound helicopters on 123.025 and establish intentions. Follow the guidelines established in the LZ operations.

(b) To facilitate approach times, the pilot-in-command of the helicopter occupying the hospital heliport should advise any other operators whether the patient will be off loaded with the rotor blades turning or stopped, and the approximate time to do so.

(c) Before making any helicopter movement to leave the hospital heliport, all operators should attempt to contact other helicopters on 123.025 and state their position and route of flight intentions for departing the heliport.

Ch 10

FIGURE 10–2–9
EMS Multiple Helicopter LZ/Heliport Operation

First helicopter on-scene
500 ft AGL, $\frac{1}{2}$ NM N of LZ

Landing Zone

N

Helicopter 2
1000 ft AGL, $\frac{1}{2}$ NM W of LZ

Helicopter 3
1500 ft AGL, $\frac{1}{2}$ NM E of LZ

Helicopter 4
2000 ft AGL, $\frac{1}{2}$ NM S of LZ

Note: *If the LZ/hospital heliport weather conditions or airspace altitude restrictions prohibit the recommended vertical separation, 1 NM separations should be kept between helicopter orbit areas.*

Chapter 11
Unmanned Aircraft Systems (UAS)

Section 1 General

11-1-1 General

a. UAS operations are governed by the Code of Federal Regulations (CFR) and the United States Code (USC). The type of operation, purpose of the flight, and weight of the UAS all factor into the specific rule that governs UAS operations.

b. 14 CFR Part 107, Small Unmanned Aircraft Systems. Examples of 14 CFR Part 107 operations include commercial aerial photography, commercial aerial survey, other operations for hire, and operations that are not conducted purely for pleasure/recreation. These operations will be referred to as Part 107 operations. Part 107 operations are limited to small UAS (sUAS) weighing less than 55 pounds.

c. 49 USC 44809, Exception for Limited Recreational Operations of Unmanned Aircraft Operations. Recreational flyers operate unmanned or model aircraft for pleasure or recreation. These operations are to be referred to as Recreational Flyer operations. Recreational flyers typically operate small UAS or model also called radio-controlled (RC) aircraft. Recreational flyers operating UAS weighing more than 55 pounds may operate in compliance with standards and limitations developed by a CBO and from fixed sites, which are described in subparagraph 11-4-1c1, Fixed Sites.

d. 14 CFR Part 91, UAS Operations. 14 CFR Part 91 operations include public UAS, and civil UAS 55 pounds or more Maximum Gross Operating Weight (MGOW). These operations will be referred to as Part 91 UAS operations in Chapter 11. For more information on public UAS operations, the requirements for qualification as a public operator, and how aircraft and pilots are certified, refer to AC 00-1.1, Public Aircraft Operations—Manned and Unmanned.

Note: 14 CFR Part 91 operations can include UAS weighing less than 55 lbs.

Reference: 14 CFR Part 107, Small Unmanned Aircraft Systems; 49 USC 44809, Exception for Limited Recreational Operations of Unmanned Aircraft; FAA Order JO 7210.3, Chapter 5, Section 5, 14 CFR Part 91, UAS Operations; AC 00-1.1, Public Aircraft Operations—Manned and Unmanned.

11-1-2 Access to the National Airspace System (NAS) for UAS Operators

a. UAS operations must be integrated into the NAS while maintaining existing operational capacity and safety without introducing an unacceptable level of risk to airspace users or persons and property on the ground. The FAA is committed to striking the appropriate regulatory and oversight balance to ensure that American innovation is able to thrive without compromising the safest, most efficient aerospace system in the world.

b. UAS operators can access the NAS in multiple ways. Generally, UAS weighing less than 55 pounds MGOW are permitted to operate within Visual Line of Sight (VLOS) up to 400 feet Above Ground Level (AGL) in uncontrolled (Class G) airspace. Operations within controlled airspace require specific authorization from Air Traffic Control (ATC).

1. Part 107 sUAS operators can request airspace authorizations via Low Altitude Authorization and Notification Capability (LAANC) or DroneZone to fly within Class B, Class C, Class D or within the lateral boundaries of the surface area of Class E airspace designated for an airport. Operations within controlled airspace can be readily approved in accordance with the altitude values indicated on the corresponding UAS Facility Map (UASFM). The UASFM values indicate the maximum altitude at which a UAS operation can be approved without any further coordination with the respective ATC facility. Part 107 remote pilots and operators may request "further coordination" for an airspace authorization to operate above UASFM values, up to 400 feet AGL. (See paragraph 11-4-2 for further information regarding Part 107 operations.)

Note: Emergency airspace authorizations for Special Government Interest (SGI) UAS operations will be addressed in paragraph 11-8-5.

2. Recreational flyer operations. Recreational flyers may operate in certain controlled and uncontrolled airspace under specific conditions. In Class B, C, D or the surface area of Class E airspace designated for an airport. The operator must obtain authorization prior to operating. In Class G airspace, the aircraft must be flying not more than 400 feet AGL and comply with all airspace restrictions and prohibitions. Recreational flyers may operate at an FAA-recognized

fixed flying site above 400 feet AGL with a FAA-approved letter of agreement from the appropriate ATC authority or up to UASFM altitudes in controlled airspace with an airspace authorization obtained through LAANC.

3. Part 91 UAS Operations. Public UAS, and civil UAS 55 pounds or more MGOW operate under 14 CFR Part 91, UAS operations. Public UAS operators and civil, non-recreational UAS weighing 55 pounds or more MGOW are provided NAS access by compliance with certain parts of 14 CFR Part 21, experimental certificates, and 14 CFR Part 91, UAS Operations. Part 91 UAS operators require a COA to operate within the NAS. Specific geographic/altitude limitations are prescribed in the COA. Additional pilot and aircraft requirements are applicable to Part 91 UAS operations. See Chapter 11, Section 3, Large UAS (MGOW 55 Pounds or More), and paragraph 11-4-3, Airspace Access for PAO, for further information on Part 91 UAS operations.

Reference: 14 CFR Section 21.191, Experimental Certificates; FAA Order JO 7210.3, Chapter 5, Section 5, 14 CFR Part 91, UAS Operations.

Section 2 Small Unmanned Aircraft System (sUAS)

11–2–1 Part 107 sUAS and Recreational Flyers

a. Part 107 sUAS. A regulatory first step for civil non-recreational UAS operations. To fly under 14 CFR Part 107, the UAS must weigh less than 55 pounds and the operator (called a remote pilot) must pass a knowledge test. Also, the UAS must be registered. Part 107 enabled the vast majority of routine sUAS operations, allowing flight within VLOS while maintaining flexibility to accommodate future technological innovations. Part 107 allows sUAS operations for many different purposes without requiring airworthiness certification, exemptions, or a COA for Class G airspace access. Part 107 includes the opportunity for individuals to request waivers for certain provisions of the rules, for example, Beyond Visual Line-Of-Sight (BVLOS). Part 107 also has specific restrictions which are not subject to waiver, such as the prohibition of the carriage or transport of Hazardous Materials (HAZMAT).

b. Recreational flyer UAS:

1. The FAA considers recreational UAS to be aircraft that fall within the statutory and regulatory definitions of an aircraft, in that they are devices that are used or intended to be used for flight in the air. As aircraft, these devices generally are subject to FAA oversight and enforcement.

Reference: 49 USC 40102, Definitions; 14 CFR Part 1, Definitions and Abbreviations.

2. Recreational aircraft may operate in Class G airspace where the aircraft is flown from the surface to not more than 400 feet AGL, and the operator must comply with all airspace restrictions and prohibitions. The only exception to this altitude restriction in Class G airspace is at FAA-recognized fixed sites and sanctioned events, with specifically approved procedures for flights above 400 feet AGL.

Note: Higher altitude airspace authorizations for Recreational Flyers are obtained through the FAA's DroneZone website at: https://faadronezone.faa.gov/#/.

3. The Recreational UAS Safety Test (TRUST) module was developed in consultation with multiple UAS stakeholders and through interested party feedback. TRUST is available electronically, has no minimum age limit, and is provided by volunteer test administrators, vetted by the FAA. See AIM, paragraph 11-5-1, UAS Pilot Certification and Requirements for Part 107 and Recreational Flyers, for further information on TRUST. Also, additional information regarding TRUST is available at the FAA's The Recreational UAS Safety Test website.

Note: The FAA's The Recreational UAS Safety Test website may be viewed at: https://www.faa.gov/uas/recreational_fliers/knowledge_test_updates/.

4. Recreational UAS weighing more than .55 lbs must be registered. This can be done electronically through the FAA's DroneZone website. Owners must then label all model aircraft with their assigned registration number on the exterior of their aircraft so that the registration can be clearly seen and read from a reasonable distance. See paragraph 11-2-2, Registration Requirements, for more information on registering UAS.

Note: The FAA's DroneZone website may be viewed at: https://faadronezone.faa.gov/#/.

11–2–2 Registration Requirements

a. Nearly all UAS flown in the NAS are required to be registered in the FAA aircraft registration database. UAS weighing 55 pounds MGOW or more must be registered under 14 CFR Part 47, Aircraft Registration, while UAS less than 55 pounds may be registered under the FAA's newer 14 CFR Part 48 online system.

Note: The FAA's Aircraft Registration Unmanned Aircraft (UA) website may be viewed at: https://www.faa.gov/licenses_certificates/aircraft_certification/aircraft_registry/UA/.

Reference: 14 CFR Part 47, Aircraft Registration.

b. Registering UAS under 14 CFR Part 47. For those UAS, which do not meet the weight stipulations for registration under 14 CFR Part 48, registration is accomplished under 14 CFR Part 47. 14 CFR Part 47 registration will result in an "N"-number like those assigned to manned aircraft. To learn more about the process and to register a UAS under Part 47, see the FAA's Aircraft Registration Unmanned Aircraft (UA) website. If desired by the owner, any UAS may be registered under 14 CFR Part 47.

Note: The FAA's Aircraft Registration Unmanned Aircraft (UA) website may be viewed at: https://www.faa.gov/licenses_certificates/aircraft_certification/aircraft_registry/UA/.

c. Registering UAS under 14 CFR Part 48. For most operators of sUAS (those UAS weighing less than 55 pounds MGOW), registration under 14 CFR Part 48, Registration and Marking Requirements for Small UA, will be most expedient and the least expensive. 14 CFR Part 48 registrants are those UAS flyers operating under either of the following statutes:

Ch 11

1. Part 107. Under the provisions of Part 107, all UAS must be registered regardless of weight. Operations under Part 107 are generally those involving commerce, but can be for recreation as well.

2. Recreational Flyers. UAS that are flown exclusively for recreational purposes must be registered if they weigh more than 0.55 pounds (250 grams).

Note 1: If you are not sure what kind of a drone flyer you are, refer to the FAA's User Identification Tool at: https://www.faa.gov/uas/getting_started /user_identification_tool/, or visit the FAA Getting Started webpage at: https://www.faa.gov/uas /getting_started/.

Note 2: Registrations cannot be transferred between 14 CFR Part 107 UAS and 49 USC 44809 UAS.

Reference: 14 CFR Part 48, Registration and Marking Requirements for Small Unmanned Aircraft.

d. How to register a UAS under 14 CFR Part 48:

1. To register a UAS online under Part 48, refer to the FAA's DroneZone website. When registering a UAS online under Part 48, you will need to select registration in either Part 107 or the exception for recreational flyers.

2. Registration fees for Part 107 registration are per sUAS, and the registration is valid for three years. Each Part 107 registered sUAS will receive a different number. Recreational flyer registration fees are per UAS and valid for three years, but the same registration number can be applied to any UAS in the registrant's ownership. The recreational flyer will receive one registration number that can be used for all UAS flown by that person. In order to register, a person must be 13 years of age or older and be a U.S. citizen or legal permanent resident. If the owner is less than 13 years of age, another person 13 years of age or older must register the UAS and that person must be a U.S. citizen or legal permanent resident.

3. An FAA registration certificate will be issued after UAS registration. The registration certificate (either paper copy or digital copy) must be available for inspection during all flight operations. If an individual other than the registered owner operates a UAS, the registration certificate (either paper copy or digital copy) must also be available for inspection during all flight operations. Federal law requires registered UAS operators, if asked, to show their certificate of registration to any federal, state, or local law enforcement officer. Failure to register a UAS that requires registration may result in regulatory and criminal penalties. The FAA may assess civil penalties up to $27,500.

Note: The FAA's DroneZone website may be viewed at: https://faadronezone.faa.gov/#/.

e. Labeling a UAS with a registration number. All UAS requiring registration must be marked with a registration number before being flown. The UAS registration number can be applied to the aircraft by engraving, a permanent label, or written on with a permanent marker. The registration number must be visible on the outside surface of the UAS.

Section 3 Large UAS (MGOW 55 Pounds or More)

11-3-1 Large Public UAS Operations

a. Large public UAS may have wingspans as large as commercial airliners, and may operate in and out of public/military dual-use airfields. Due to the high altitudes at which these UAS routinely operate, and the means through which they reach and vacate operating altitudes, encounters with manned or low-altitude unmanned traffic are rare.

b. Public users operating as "public aircraft" retain the responsibility to determine airworthiness and pilot qualifications. Aircraft certification and operating rules apply to the entire UAS, including the aircraft itself, the flight crew with their associated qualifications, the control station, and command and control links.

Note: Large UAS operating in controlled airspace generally communicate on radio frequencies or through an ATC-to-PIC ground communications link assigned to that sector, terminal area, or control tower. The UAS PIC is required to comply with all ATC instructions and uses standard phraseology per FAA Order JO 7110.65, Air Traffic Control, and this manual.

Reference: 49 USC 40102, Definitions; 49 USC 40125, Qualifications for Public Aircraft Status; FAA Order JO 7110.65, Air Traffic Control; AIM, ¶11-4-3, Airspace Access for Public Aircraft Operations PAO.

c. Operating characteristics of large public UAS. To illustrate the sizes and performance of large public UAS, consider the DoD UAS classification system. The categories (see Figure 11-3-1) are separated based on MGOW, normal operating altitude, and flying speed. These classifications do not apply to non-DoD civil aircraft. Generally, Groups 1 through 3 UAS will operate on and above military bases, in restricted or prohibited airspace. For this reason, these smaller tactical public aircraft will rarely be encountered by civil pilots. Groups 4 and 5 are the largest of DoD UAS, weighing over 1,320 pounds, and operating at all speeds and altitudes. Group 4 aircraft operate at all altitudes, usually below 18,000 feet MSL. Group 5 aircraft typically operate well above 18,000 feet MSL. UAS in Groups 4 and 5 require airfields with specially approved surfaces to safely operate. For specifications and descriptions of the aircraft models that the DoD operates, refer to military service fact sheets.

Note 1: The category chart does not specify the actual high gross weights at which some DoD UAS actually operate. For instance, the RQ-4 Global Hawk regularly operates at approximately 32,000 pounds.)

Note 2: JP 3-30, III 31, Joint Publication 3-30, provides the UAS Categorization Chart and may be reviewed at: https://www.jcs.mil/Portals/36/Documents/Doctrine/pubs/jp3_30.pdf?ver=2019-09-04-142255-657.

Note 3: These websites provide unclassified descriptions, performance, and specifications of the varied UAS in the DoD's large category fleet: USAF Fact Sheets at https://www.af.mil/About-Us/Fact-Sheets/ and USN Fact Files at https://www.navy.mil/Resources/Fact-Files/.

d. Large Public UAS Engineering Characteristics and Operating Areas:

1. Large public UAS may be sharing airspace with civil aircraft in the NAS. A wide variety of aircraft performance, voice radio communications, command and control link architecture, and operating procedures exists throughout the DoD and other large public UAS enterprises. For example, Group 4 DoD aircraft, such as the MQ-1 Predator and MQ-9 Reaper, are typically propeller-driven with propulsion units that are internal combustion piston- or turbine-powered. The largest public UAS include single-engine jet aircraft such as the RQ-4 Global Hawk and MQ-4C Triton.

2. VLOS and BVLOS link systems provide command and control for these large UAS operations. Voice communication capability in the largest public UAS is far more extensive than in the smaller aircraft. Many models are limited to a single voice radio transmitter and receiver system for control inside airspace managed by and/or delegated to the DoD.

3. Many of the larger public UAS are equipped with transponders to assist ATC with position and tracking information. These UAS usually operate under IFR under positive ATC control and will tend to be found at very high altitudes; not likely to be encountered by civil aircraft operators. Launch and recovery operations will be likewise under positive ATC control and these UAS will be separated from any other known aircraft traffic. Encounters with low-altitude small UAS, being flown in uncontrolled airspace or under low-altitude controlled airspace authorizations, are therefore unlikely. In accordance with 14 CFR Section 91.215(e)(2), ATC Transponder and Altitude Reporting Equipment and Use, no person may operate an unmanned aircraft under Part 91 with a transponder on unless: (1) the operation is conducted under a flight plan and the person operating the unmanned aircraft maintains two-way communications with ATC; or (2) the use of a transponder is otherwise authorized by the Administrator.

FIGURE 11–3–1
DoD UAS Categories

Unmanned Aircraft Systems Categorization Chart

UA Category	Maximum Gross Takeoff Weight (lbs)	Normal Operating Altitude (ft)	Speed (KIAS)	Representative UAS
Group 1	0-20	< 1200 AGL	100 kts	WASP III, TACMAV RQ-14A/B, Buster, Nighthawk, RQ-11B, FPASS, RQ16A, Pointer, Aqua/Terra Puma
Group 2	21-55	< 3500 AGL	< 250	ScanEagle, Silver Fox, Aerosonde
Group 3	< 1320	< 18,000 MSL	< 250	RQ-7B Shadow, RQ-15 Neptune, XPV-1 Tern, XPV-2 Mako
Group 4	> 1320		Any Airspeed	MQ-5B Hunter, MQ-8B Fire Scout, MQ-1C Gray Eagle, MQ-1A/B/C Predator
Group 5	> 1320	> 18,000 MSL	Any Airspeed	MQ-9 Reaper, RQ-4 Global Hawk, RQ-4N Triton

Legend

AGL	above ground level		lbs	pounds
FPASS	force protection aerial surveillance system		MSL	mean sea level
ft	feet		TACMAV	tactical micro air vehicle
KIAS	knots indicated airspeed		UA	unmanned aircraft
kts	knots		UAS	unmanned aircraft system

Note: *In accordance with 14 CFR Section 107.52, ATC Transponder Equipment Prohibition, unless otherwise authorized by the Administrator, no person may operate a sUAS under Part 107 with a transponder on.*

Reference: *14 CFR Section 91.215, ATC Transponder and Altitude Reporting Equipment and Use; 14 CFR Section 107.52, ATC Transponder Equipment Prohibition.*

e. Large Public UAS Launch, Recovery, and Operating Areas:

1. Large public UAS operations are widespread, they are also carefully managed to ensure enhanced safety for other NAS users. For this reason, DoD UAS operate in many types of special use airspace. See Figure 11-3-2 for examples of Special Use Airspace (SUA) used by DoD UAS.

2. Temporary Flight Restrictions (TFRs) are issued for the surrounding UAS operating locations and allow for the launch and recovery of larger UAS. Once outside of the terminal environment, DoD UAS utilize the full range of SUA, including Military Operating Areas (MOA), restricted areas, warning areas, and alert areas to conduct their missions.

FIGURE 11–3–2
DoD Special Use Airspace

11-3-2 Exemptions Under 49 USC 44807, Special Authority for Certain Unmanned Systems

a. Exemptions are granted to UAS operations which are permitted in accordance with Public Law 115–254, 49 USC 44807, Special Authority for Certain Unmanned Aircraft Systems. The Secretary of Transportation has determined that certain UAS are eligible to operate in the NAS without possessing the airworthiness certification normally required under 49 USC 44807. 49 USC 44807 permits the FAA to use a risk-based approach to determine whether an airworthiness certificate is required for a UAS to operate. Exemptions are generally requested by civil (non-public) UAS operators who fly UAS weighing 55 pounds or more, and thus cannot fly under 14 CFR Part 107. For civil UAS operations conducted under 49 USC 44807 of PL 115–254, the Secretary has determined that specific requirements necessary for safe operation can often be addressed in the form of grants of exemption(s). Operators who desire this regulatory relief must petition the FAA for exemption in accordance with 14 CFR Part 11

and the guidance provided on the FAA's Section 44807, Special Authority for Certain Unmanned Systems website. Examples of petitions that have been granted to conduct civil UAS operations include the following activities:

1. Closed-set motion picture and television filming.

2. Agricultural survey and spraying.

3. Aerial photography.

4. Land survey and inspection.

5. Inspection of structures.

6. Search and Rescue (SAR) operations.

Note: Civil agricultural spraying operations will also require a 14 CFR Part 137 certificate; see paragraph 11-4-5, Airspace Access for 14 CFR Part 135 and 14 CFR Part 137.

b. Exemption Application. Petitioners seeking a grant of exemption should fill out an online application on the public docket located on the FAA's regulations.gov website.

Reference: 49 USC 44807, Special Authority for Certain Unmanned Aircraft Systems.

Note: The FAA's Section 44807: Special Authority for Certain Unmanned Systems website may be

Ch 11

reviewed at: https://www.faa.gov/uas/advanced_operations/certification/section_44807/. The FAA's Regulations.gov website may be reviewed at: https://www.faa.gov/regulations_policies/faa_regulations.

11–3–3 Emerging Large UAS Civil Operations

a. Large civil UAS operations in the NAS are presently considered those UAS weighing 55 pounds or more with or without aircraft airworthiness certification, along with their control stations and radio links operating under 14 CFR Part 91. These operations may or may not receive ATC separation services, but will not be operating under UAS Traffic Management (UTM) structures. Examples of current large UAS civil operators include agricultural spraying and operation as radio/telephone airborne relays. Future large UAS operations will include carriage of cargo and passengers, and very long-endurance aircraft, staying aloft for extended periods of time.

Note: Large is only used as a term to differentiate from those UAS weighing less than 55 pounds.

Large UAS is not an FAA-recognized category of aircraft.

1. Large UAS must meet performance, equipage requirements, and adhere to relevant procedures commensurate with the airspace in which the UAS is operating.

2. Absent an onboard pilot, large UAS are unable to "see and avoid" other aircraft, as required by regulations governing the general operation of aircraft in the NAS under Title 14 CFR Section 91.111, Operating Near other Aircraft, and 14 CFR Section 91.113, Right of Way Rules: Except Water Operations. As a result, they cannot use visual observation to remain "well clear" of other aircraft and avoid collisions. Therefore, an alternate means of compliance is required to remain well clear of other aircraft and surface obstacles, and avoid collisions.

3. Figure 11-3-3, A Layered Approach for Collision Avoidance, illustrates the different layers used to keep aircraft safely separated, beginning with airspace classification and design, then ending with the responsibility of the pilot to prevent collisions.

FIGURE 11–3–3
A Layered Approach for Collision Avoidance

b. Transition to full integration into the NAS. Over time, full integration of large UAS operations in the NAS will be achieved. Current large UAS operations will continue to be dependent on COAs, the issuance of NOTAMs, and possibly other measures (e.g., chase plane, segregated airspace) as currently used for accommodated operations. This integration is evolving with UAS technology advances, FAA regulatory changes, NAS automation, communications improvements, and evolving use cases and demand.

Note: Transponder equipped UAS, during lost link events, if capable, will squawk secondary surveillance radar (SSR)/Transponder code 7400. If the UAS is not programmed for use of SSR code 7400, then code 7600 may be used.

c. Large Civil Operations. The following are examples of test and evaluation operations being conducted with large civil and commercial UAS: cargo delivery, infrastructure inspection, surveillance, firefighting, environmental observation, signal relay, and atmospheric sampling.

Section 4 Airspace Access for UAS

11–4–1 Recreational Flyers

a. Advisory Circular 91-57, Exception for Limited Recreational Operations of Unmanned Aircraft, provides guidance for recreational flyers. Failure of a recreational flyer to adhere to any of the requirements for recreational status under 14 USC 44809 will result in the flight being considered 14 CFR Part 107 by the FAA, which may result in greater penalties if the operator is found operating in an unsafe manner. Recreational flyers may only operate under the statutory exception if they adhere to all of the conditions listed in the statute.

Reference: *AC 91-57, Exception for Limited Recreational Operations of Unmanned Aircraft; 49 USC 44809, Exception for Limited Recreational Operations of Unmanned Aircraft; 14 CFR Part 107, Small Unmanned Aircraft Systems.*

b. Operations in Class G airspace. Flights in Class G airspace will be the most common environment for many recreational flyers. The upper limit of recreational UAS operations in Class G airspace is 400 feet AGL. When operating in Class G airspace, the recreational flyer must follow the set of safety guidelines outlined and developed by a recognized Community-Based Organization (CBO).

c. Operations in controlled airspace or uncontrolled airspace above 400 feet AGL. If a recreational flyer desires to operate in class B, C, or D airspace, or within the lateral boundaries of the surface area of class E airspace designated for an airport, or in class G airspace above 400 feet, the operator must obtain prior authorization from the Administrator or designee before operating. For the recreational flyer wishing to enter controlled airspace, there are two basic routes:

1. Fixed sites are locations specifically authorized by the FAA, which are posted at the FAA's interactive map on the UAS Data Delivery System (UDDS). On the map, small blue circles depict the location of these sites in controlled airspace and the altitude limits imposed on those sites. The altitude restrictions are derived from the UASFM which form the basic structure of LAANC and its operating procedures. Recreational flyers can access site-specific information by clicking on the blue circle.

Note: These sites have existing letters of agreement or authorization (LOA) with the FAA. For the CBO to operate in controlled airspace, an airspace authorization agreement between the CBO and the FAA must be in place. Certain sites may have access restrictions or other operating limitations, which are available from the site sponsor.

2. By request, through the LAANC Application. LAANC provides the recreational pilot with access, when permissible, to controlled airspace at or below posted UASFM altitudes in near-real time. LAANC also gives the recreational flyer the ability to stay notified of airspace restrictions and prohibitions. See paragraph 11-8-7 of this chapter for information on downloading the LAANC application.

d. CBO Sanctioned Events. Sanctioned events, also called sponsored events are generally of short duration and take place at an existing fixed site or temporary fixed site established specifically for the event.

1. CBO's requesting a sanctioned or sponsored event authorization within Class B, C, D, or within the lateral boundaries of the surface area of Class E airspace designated for an airport are obligated to make the location known to the FAA Administrator. Mutually agreed-upon operating procedures must be established with the event organizer. This is accomplished through a fixed site application in DroneZone.

2. CBO operations and events occurring at 400 feet AGL and below in Class G airspace do not require FAA review, approval or authorization. CBO's intending to conduct events in Class G airspace that may exceed 400 feet AGL must contact the FAA for further information.

11–4–2 14 CFR Part 107 and Waivers to 14 CFR Part 107

a. 14 CFR Part 107 was the first new rule dedicated to UAS operations. It was designed to provide a path for integration into the NAS for sUAS, flown under VLOS, and operated for non-recreational purposes. Part 107 allows remote pilots to fly for recreation. Part 107 grants certain flight permissions and altitudes in excess of those provided under 49 USC 44809, The Exception for Limited Recreational Operations of UAS, in view of the greater vetting required for 14 CFR Part 107 certification. Eligibility requirements to fly under 14 CFR Part 107, are listed in 14 CFR Section 107.61, Eligibility.

Note: The Administrator may issue a certificate of waiver authorizing a deviation from 14 CFR Section 107.31, Visual Line of Sight Aircraft Operation, if the operation can safely be conducted under the terms of a certificate of waiver.

Reference: 14 CFR Part 107, sUAS; 14 CFR Section 107.61, Eligibility; 14 CFR Section 107.31, Visual Line of Sight Aircraft Operation.

b. Operations in Class G airspace. Part 107 remote pilots may fly in Class G airspace up to 400 feet AGL, and within 400 feet of a structure

Ch 11

without prior coordination with ATC. Other limitations for Part 107 operators are described in 14 CFR Part 107.51, Operating Limitations for sUAS.

Reference: 14 CFR Section 107.51, Operating Imitations for Small Unmanned Aircraft.

c. Operations in controlled airspace through LAANC. LAANC gives the remote pilot the ability to obtain near real-time airspace authorization within UASFM altitudes and stay notified of airspace restrictions and prohibitions. See paragraph 11-8-7, Resources for UAS Operators, for information on downloading LAANC.

d. Waivers to 14 CFR Part 107:

1. A waiver is an official document issued by the FAA which approves certain operations of UAS outside the limitations of a regulation. These waivers allow drone pilots to deviate from certain rules under 14 CFR Part 107 by demonstrating they can still fly safely using alternative methods or safety mitigations. 14 CFR Part 107 rules which can be waived are listed in 14 CFR Section 107.205, List of Regulations Subject to Waiver. Any subpart of 14 CFR Part 107 rule which is not specifically listed in 14 CFR Section 107.205, such as the §107.36 prohibition on the carriage or transport of HAZMAT, is not subject to waiver, and would require an exemption under 14 CFR Part 11, General Rulemaking Procedures. See paragraph 11-3-2, Exemptions Under 49 USC 44807, Special Authority for Certain Unmanned Systems, for guidance on requesting exemptions.

2. To request a 14 CFR Part 107 waiver, refer to the FAA's Part 107 Waiver website.

Note: The FAA's Part 107 waiver website may be viewed at: https://www.faa.gov/uas/commercial _operators/part_107_waivers/.

Reference: 14 CFR Section 107.205, List of Regulations Subject to Waiver; 14 CFR Part 11, General Rulemaking Procedures.

11–4–3 Airspace Access for Public Aircraft Operations (PAOs)

a. General requirements for PAO status. Governmental entities, as defined by federal law 49 USC 40102(a)(41), Definitions, can fly as a public aircraft operation as long as the flight meets the definition of a governmental function 49 USC 40125, Qualifications for Public Aircraft Status. Public aircraft are aircraft owned and operated by the government of a state, the District of Columbia, or a territory or possession of the United States, or a political subdivision of one of these governments, except as provided in 49 USC 40125(b), Qualifications for Public Aircraft Status. Public aircraft can also be aircraft exclusively leased for at least 90 continuous days by the government of a state, the District of Columbia, or a territory or possession of the United States or a political subdivision of one of these governments, except as provided in 49 USC 40125(b), Qualifications for Public Aircraft Status.

Note 1: The term "government function" refers to one of several activities undertaken by a government, such as national defense, intelligence missions, firefighting, search and rescue, law enforcement (including transportation of prisoners, detainees, and illegal aliens), aeronautical research, or biological or geopolitical resource management.

Note 2: An operation "for the public good" does not necessarily meet the qualifications for a public operation; for example, most volunteer fire departments in the United States will not qualify as PAOs.

Note 3: Public safety organizations often conduct operations under 14 CFR Part 107, as well as public aircraft operations.

Reference: 49 USC 40102, Definitions; 49 USC 40125, Qualifications for Pubic Aircraft Status.

b. A PAO is conducted under certain 14 CFR Part 91, UAS Operations Rules, with a COA granted to allow access to the NAS. A PAO COA allows blanket UAS operations in Class G airspace throughout the entire continental United States, including operations at night with appropriate lighting and training, for the duration of the COA. Waivers and/or authorizations to the COA can permit operations beyond the basic COA. Operating as a PAO requires adherence to specific conditions as directed in the COA. Operations under the public aircraft statute cannot include purposes that are not governmental functions. For example, a police UAS flying without remuneration to obtain footage for a department promotional video would not be a governmental function.

c. COA Application Process:

1. Public Declaration Letter (PDL). The first step in getting a PAO COA is to be recognized as an authorized government agency by submitting a PDL that shows the organization is indeed a governmental entity as defined by federal law. FAA general counsel reviews this letter, which is usually issued by a city, county, or state attorney Federal agencies are deemed to be governmental entities without submitting a PDL.

2. COA Request. If formally recognized as a governmental entity under federal law, entities are given access to the COA Application Process System (CAPS) or DroneZone, where a request for a PAO COA may be submitted. Operating as a PAO requires you to adhere to specific conditions as directed in your COA. Remember that an aircraft described in subparagraph (a), (b), (c), or (d) of 49 USC 40102(a)(41), Definitions, does

not qualify as a public aircraft under such section when the aircraft is used for commercial purposes (e.g., performing a non-governmental function).

Reference: AC 00-1.1, Public Aircraft Operations—Manned and Unmanned; 49 USC 40102, Definitions.

11–4–4 14 CFR Part 89 Remote Identification and FAA-Recognized Identification Areas (FRIAs)

a. Background:

1. Remote identification (RID) of UAS is crucial to UAS integration.

2. RID is the ability of a UAS in flight to provide identification and location information that can be received by other parties.

3. RID allows the FAA, national security agencies, law enforcement, and others to distinguish compliant airspace users from those potentially posing a safety or security risk. It helps these agencies find the control station when a UAS appears to be flying unsafely or where it is prohibited.

b. Remote ID Rule:

1. 14 CFR Part 89, Remote Identification (RID) of Unmanned Aircraft, will require most drones operating in U.S. airspace to have RID capability. UAS not equipped with RID capability will be limited to operating in specific FAA-approved geographic locations, such as FRIA.

Reference: 14 CFR Part 89, Remote Identification of Unmanned Aircraft.

2. There are three ways drone pilots will be able to meet the identification requirements of the RID rule: Standard RID, RID Broadcast Module, and FRIAs.

(a) Standard RID. Only standard RID drones may be manufactured after the September 16, 2022, rule effective date. Unmanned aircraft broadcast the RID message elements directly from the unmanned aircraft from takeoff to shutdown. Message elements include: (1) A unique identifier to establish the identity of the unmanned aircraft; (2) an indication of the unmanned aircraft latitude, longitude, geometric altitude, and velocity; (3) an indication of the control station latitude, longitude, and geometric altitude; (4) a time mark; and (5) an emergency status indication. Operators may choose whether to use the serial number of the unmanned aircraft or a session ID (e.g., an alternative form of identification that provides additional privacy to the operator) as the unique identifier.

(b) RID Broadcast Modules. An unmanned aircraft can be equipped with a Remote ID broadcast module that broadcasts message elements from takeoff to shutdown. Message elements include: (1) The serial number of the broadcast module assigned by the producer; (2) an indication of the latitude, longitude, geometric altitude, and velocity of the unmanned aircraft; (3) an indication of the latitude, longitude, and geometric altitude of the unmanned aircraft takeoff location; and (4) a time mark.

(c) FAA-Recognized Identification Area:

(1) An FAA-recognized identification area (FRIA) is a defined geographic area where persons can operate UAS without remote identification, provided they maintain visual line of sight. Organizations eligible to request establishment of a FRIA include CBOs recognized by the FAA and educational institutions. The latter group includes primary and secondary educational institutions, trade schools, colleges, and universities.

(2) To operate in a FRIA according to the 14 CFR Part 89, RID of unmanned aircraft, operators must be physically located within the boundaries of the FRIA, must only operate drones within those boundaries, and must operate within VLOS at all times. UAS equipped with RID broadcast capability must broadcast continuously even while operating within or transiting a FRIA.

Reference: 14 CFR Part 89, Remote Identification of Unmanned Aircraft.

(3) Figure 11-4-1 illustrates the three ways UAS operators can comply with the new RID rule.

Ch 11

FIGURE 11-4-1
RID Paths to Compliance

3 WAYS DRONE PILOTS CAN MEET REMOTE ID RULE

DRONE REMOTE IDENTIFICATION

STANDARD REMOTE ID DRONES

Drone Broadcasts Remote ID
Information Via Radio Frequency,
e.g. Wifi & Bluetooth

• Remote ID capability is built into the drone
• From takeoff to shutdown, drone broadcasts:
 • Drone ID
 • Drone location and altitude
 • Drone velocity
 • Control station location and elevation
 • Time mark
 • Emergency status

DRONE REMOTE IDENTIFICATION

**DRONES WITH REMOTE ID
BROADCAST MODULE**

Drone Broadcasts Remote ID
Information Via Radio Frequency,
e.g. Wifi & Bluetooth

• Remote ID capability through module
 attached to drone
• Limited to visual line of sight operations
• From takeoff to shutdown, drone broadcasts:
 • Drone ID
 • Drone location and altitude
 • Drone velocity
 • Takeoff location and elevation
 • Time mark

FAA-RECOGNIZED IDENTIFICATION AREA [FRIA]

DRONES WITHOUT REMOTE ID

• Drones without Remote ID can operate without
 broadcasting
• Drones without Remote ID must operate within
 visual line of sight and within the FRIA
• Anyone can fly there, but FRIAs can only be
 requested by community-based organizations
 and educational institutions

11-4-5 Airspace Access for 14 CFR Part 135 and 14 CFR Part 137

a. 14 CFR Part 135, Operating Requirements: Commuter and on Demand Operations and Rules Governing Persons on Board Such Aircraft:

1. Civil operators of UAS may conduct commercial package delivery BVLOS, or may transport HAZMAT on an interstate basis (crossing state boundaries), only under 14 CFR Part 135. These types of operations are prohibited for UAS operating under 14 CFR Part 107, sUAS. Legally, these operations must be conducted under 14 CFR Part 91, UAS operations, in accordance with an air carrier certificate issued under 14 CFR Part 135, and an exemption from certain federal aviation regulations granted under 14 CFR Part 11, general rulemaking procedures.

Reference: 14 CFR Part 135, Operating Requirements: Commuter and on Demand Operations and Rules Governing Persons on Board Such Aircraft; 14 CFR Part 107, Small Unmanned Aircraft Systems; 14 CFR Part 11, General Rulemaking Procedures; FAA Order JO 7210.3, Chapter 5, Section 5, 14 CFR Part 91, UAS Operations.

2. Generally, UAS cannot comply with certain 14 CFR regulations originally written for a manned aircraft environment and therefore require relief. UAS operators obtain relief from the requirements of these regulations through exemptions, waivers, and deviations. The relief document lists conditions and limitations which provide a level of safety at least equal to that provided by the rule from which relief is needed. Additionally, UAS operators must obtain a Certificate of Waiver or Authorization (COA) from the FAA Air Traffic Organization (ATO). Applicants for 14 CFR Part 135 certification should begin the process by contacting their local FAA Flight Standards District Office (FSDO).

Note: Examples of such regulations include requirements for the provision of seat belts for aircrew and passengers, on-board carriage of an aircraft manual, etc.

(a) Application for a 14 CFR Part 135 certificate. Application for a 14 CFR Part 135 air carrier certificate for UAS operations uses the same process as that for manned 14 CFR Part 135 applicants. For information on how to apply for an air carrier certificate issued under 14 CFR Part 135, see the FAA 14 CFR Part 135 Air Carrier and Operator Certification website.

Note: The FAA 14 CFR Part 135 Air Carrier and Operator Certification website may be reviewed at: https://www.faa.gov/licenses_certificates /airline_certification/135_certification/.

(b) Advisory Circular 120-49A, Parts 121 and 135 Certification is available to aid an applicant in Part 135 certification.

Reference: AC 120-49, Parts 121 and 135 Certification.

(c) Exemptions and COAs. Additional information on how to petition for an exemption and obtain a COA is available on the FAA Advanced Operations website.

Note: The FAA's Advanced Operations website may be reviewed at: https://www.faa.gov/uas /advanced_operations/.

b. 14 CFR Part 137, Agricultural Aircraft Operations:

1. Civil and public operators of UAS may conduct agricultural aircraft operations, as defined in 14 CFR Part 137.3, Definition of Terms. These operations must be conducted in accordance with an agricultural aircraft operator certificate issued under 14 CFR Part 137, and an exemption from certain federal aviation regulations granted under 14 CFR Part 11, General Rulemaking Procedures. Operators of sUAS, weighing less than 55 pounds MGOW may conduct agricultural aircraft operations under 14 CFR Part 107, sUAS, and 14 CFR Part 137. Operators of large UAS, weighing 55 pounds MGOW or more may conduct agricultural aircraft operations under 14 CFR Parts 91, UAS operations, and 14 CFR Part 137.

Reference: 14 CFR Part 137, Agricultural Aircraft Operations; 14 CFR Part 11, General Rulemaking Procedures; 14 CFR Part 107, Small Unmanned Aircraft Systems; FAA Order JO 7210.3, Chapter 5, Section 5, 14 CFR Part 91, UAS Operations.

2. Generally, as is the case with 14 CFR Part 135 standard cargo operations, UAS cannot comply with certain 14 CFR regulations, and therefore require relief. For example, sUAS require relief from carriage of hazardous material (§107.36), aircraft certification (§137.19(d)), carriage of agricultural aircraft operator certificate (§137.33(a)), and, for large UAS, certain aircraft airworthiness requirements (14 CFR Parts 21 and 91). UAS operators obtain relief from the requirements of these regulations through an exemption. The exemption lists conditions and limitations which provide a level of safety at least equal to that provided by the rule. Additionally, large UAS operators must obtain a COA from the FAA ATO.

(a) Obtaining an exemption for 14 CFR Part 137 operations. For additional information on how to petition for an exemption and obtain a COA, go to the FAA's Advanced Operations website.

Note: The FAA's Advanced Operations website may be viewed at: https://www.faa.gov/uas /advanced_operations/.

(b) Advisory Circular 137-1, Certification Process for Agricultural Aircraft Operators, provides additional information on how to apply for an agricultural aircraft operator certificate issued under 14 CFR Part 137.

Reference: AC 137-1, Certification Process for Agricultural Aircraft Operators.

c. Hazardous Materials (HAZMAT):

1. A hazardous material also known as HAZMAT, or dangerous goods is any substance or material that is capable of posing an unreasonable risk to health, safety, and property when transported in commerce. For example, lithium batteries, dry ice, and aerosol whipped cream are considered dangerous goods. These products may seem harmless, but when transported by air they can be very dangerous. Vibrations, static electricity, temperature and pressure variations can cause items to leak, generate toxic fumes, start a fire, or even explode if these products are not packaged and handled properly. More detailed information is located on the FAA's What are Dangerous Goods website.

Note: The FAA's What are Dangerous Goods website may be viewed at: https://www.faa.gov /hazmat/what_is_hazmat/.

2. The carriage/transportation of hazardous materials under 14 CFR Part 107, sUAS, is strictly prohibited at all times, and is not subject to waiver. In order to transport hazardous materials, UAS operators must follow the 14 CFR Part 135 certification regulatory path and must develop dangerous goods training programs and manuals as part of the 14 CFR Part 135 Air Carrier and Operator Certificates process, described on the FAA website and subparagraph 11-4-5a, and 14 CFR Part 135, Operating Requirements. A brief description of applicable regulations as they apply to UAS can be found on the FAA's UAS website.

Note: The FAA's Unmanned Aircraft System (UAS) website may be viewed at: https://www .faa.gov/hazmat/air_carriers/operations/drones/.

Reference: 14 CFR Part 107, Small Unmanned Aircraft Systems; 14 CFR Part 135, Operating Requirements: Commuter and on Demand Operations and Rules Governing Persons on Board Such Aircraft.

11-4-6 Airspace Restrictions To Flight

a. General. The NAS extends from the ground to above 60,000 feet MSL and includes various classifications of airspace, both uncontrolled and controlled. sUAS remote pilots and recreational flyers are generally permitted access to uncontrolled airspace without special permission. However, this changes when access to controlled airspace is desired. All access to controlled airspace whether by manned or unmanned aircraft must be granted by ATC.

Note 1: While the NAS is divided into controlled and uncontrolled airspace, users must remember that all airspace is regulated, and certain rules apply throughout the NAS.

Note 2: Recreational flyers are limited to 400 feet AGL in Class G airspace, without special authorization.

b. Controlled airspace is a generic term that covers the different classification of airspace (Class A, Class B, Class C, Class D, and Class E airspace) and defined dimensions within which air traffic control services can be provided to Instrument Flight Rules (IFR) flights and to Visual Flight Rules (VFR) flights, in accordance with the airspace classification.

c. Special Use Airspace (SUA). SUA consists of that airspace wherein flight activities must be confined because of their nature, or wherein limitations are imposed upon aircraft operations that are not a part of those activities, or both. These areas are generally depicted on aeronautical charts and will be indicated on the B4UFly and LAANC applications for UAS.

d. Temporary Flight Restrictions:

1. Temporary Flight Restrictions (TFRs) are non-permanent airspace restrictions created to protect persons and property in the air or on the surface from an existing or imminent hazard associated with an incident on the surface, when the presence of low flying aircraft would magnify, alter, spread, or compound that hazard (14 CFR Section 91.137(a)(1)). TFRs can exist to protect aircraft from hazards, and also to protect people/objects on the ground from aircraft hazards. Examples of TFRs include natural disaster areas especially forest fires, floods, congested flight areas, the area around spacecraft launches and recoveries, certain stadium sporting events, and the security of national public figures.

2. UAS operators should be aware that substantial fines and penalties can be levied on UAS remote pilots or recreational flyers violating a TFR.

e. Special Restrictions over Critical Infrastructure:

1. Operating a UAS over our nation's critical infrastructure such as power grids, nuclear reactors, transportation centers, political or military sites, etc., can potentially create risk to people on the ground and also to fixed site facilities and associated infrastructure. To address security concerns, Public Law 114–190 and 115–254 mandated a process that would allow applicants to petition the FAA for restrictions from unmanned aircraft overflying their property.

2. Special Security Instructions under 14 CFR Section 99.7 of the public laws allow the FAA to prohibit the operation of aircraft in certain airspace, in the interest of national security. The 14 CFR Section 99.7 interim solution prohibits UAS over approved fixed site facilities and limits the fixed site facilities to Federal owned sites UAS operations may be approved under the SGI process.

3. UAS remote pilots and recreational flyers must carefully consider the need to fly over critical infrastructure and determine the legality of doing so, infractions may result in significant fines and legal actions.

Note: For a list of critical infrastructure sites, see https://www.cisa.gov/critical-infrastructure-sectors.

Reference: Public Law 114–190, FAA Extension, Safety, and Security Act of 2016; Public Law 115–254, FAA Reauthorization Act of 2018; 14 CFR Section 99.7, Special Security Instructions.

f. Special Flight Rules Area (SFRA). SFRAs are airspaces of defined dimensions, above land areas or territorial waters, within which the flight of aircraft is subject to special rules, established after the September 11, 2001, attacks. Examples include the Washington, DC, Los Angeles, and Hudson River SFRAs. All aircraft are highly regulated within SFRAs. The inner area of some SFRAs, the Flight Restricted Zone (FRZ) is very highly restricted and prohibits all but previously vetted aircrew and aircraft from entering. Refer to VFR Sectional Charts or the FAA's Restricted Airspace website for information on specific airspace limitations and instructions for requesting entry.

Note: The FAA's Restricted Airspace website may be viewed at: https://www.faa.gov/newsroom/restricted-airspace-0.

g. There can be certain local restrictions to airspace. While the FAA is designated by federal law to be the regulator of the NAS, some state and local authorities may also restrict access to local airspace. UAS pilots should be aware of these local rules.

h. Other Restrictions & Provisions:

1. Flight over or near natural habitat or nature preserves. See paragraph 11-8-6, Environmental Best Practices, for a discussion of UAS flight restrictions over or near wildlife.

2. No Drone Zones is an FAA concept and outreach to promote safe and responsible use of UAS. The effort assists landowners (private and public) with designating their land off-limits for UAS take-offs and landings. The idea behind the outreach is to allow landowners who wish to avoid interactions on their property with UAS to state this preference in advance of UAS take-offs or landings. No Drone Zones do not apply to airspace. Generally speaking, for a No Drone Zone in a public place to be legally enforceable, there must exist underlying authority (ordinance, law, etc.). If the property in question is privately owned, the landowner's right to designate no UAS use is enforceable through trespass law.

3. Flight over or near people and manned aircraft. In general, UAS remote pilots and recreational flyers should avoid flying over or near people or manned aircraft operations, and in any manner that could be construed as reckless or dangerous. See paragraph 11-8-3, Precautions: Flight Over or Near People, Manned Aircraft, and Night Flight, for specific information on flight over or near people.

4. Correctional Institutions. Flight over some federal prisons is restricted under 14 CFR Section 99.7, Special Security Instructions. Flight near other correctional institutions may be prohibited by other federal, state or local statutes. Subparagraph 11-4-6e, Special Restrictions over Critical Infrastructure, contains additional information regarding restrictions over critical infrastructure.

Reference: 14 CFR Section 99.7, Special Security Instructions.

11-4-7 UAS Traffic Management (UTM)

a. UTM Operations. UTM is predicated on layers of information sharing and data exchange amongst a range of stakeholders including UAS operators, service providers, and the FAA to achieve safe operations. Operators share their flight intent with each other and coordinate to deconflict and safely separate trajectories. The primary means of communication and coordination between operators, the FAA, and other stakeholders is through a distributed information network, rather than between pilots and air traffic controllers via traditional voice communications. The FAA makes real-time airspace constraints available to UAS operators, who are responsible for managing their own operations safely within these constraints without receiving ATC services from the FAA. However, the FAA does have access to applicable UTM operational information as necessary.

b. UAS operators not receiving ATC separation services are required to participate in UTM at some level using applicable services to meet the performance requirements of their operations. See Figure 11-4-2 for UTM in the context of Air Traffic Management operations. The number and type of services required varies based on the type and location of the intended operation and the associated communication, navigation, surveillance (CNS), and other operational needs.

FIGURE 11-4-2
UTM Operations in Context of Airspace Classes

c. Stakeholders in UTM:

1. FAA, the federal authority over aircraft operations in all airspace, and the regulator and oversight authority for civil aircraft operations in the NAS.

2. Operator, the person or entity responsible for the overall management of their operation. The operator meets regulatory responsibilities, plans flight/operations, shares operation intent information, and safely conducts operations using all available information.

3. Remote pilot-in-command (RPIC), the person responsible for the safe conduct of each UAS flight. An individual may serve as both the operator and the RPIC.

4. Other stakeholders (e.g., public safety and general public), can access information and/or utilize UTM services via the USS Network.

Section 5 UAS Pilot Testing, Certification and Responsibilities

11-5-1 UAS Pilot Certification and Requirements for Part 107 and Recreational Flyers

a. General:

1. Part 107 Operations. Any person who operates a civil sUAS in the NAS, for any operation that is not for recreational/pleasure purposes, must have a UAS pilot's certificate (also called the "Part 107 Certificate") with a Small Unmanned Aircraft System Rating.

2. Recreational Flyer Operations. A person who is flying a UAS for recreational/pleasure purposes in the NAS must have taken and passed TRUST, as required by 14 USC 44809.

b. Eligibility for Testing:

1. Part 107 operations. Applicants must be at least 16 years of age and be able to speak and understand English. For further information on Part 107 testing see the FAA's website, Become a Drone Pilot.

2. Recreational Flyer Operations. There are no minimum age or other eligibility requirements for a recreational UAS pilot to take TRUST.

c. Initial Testing for Certification:

1. Part 107 Operations:

(a) Current 14 CFR Part 61 certificate holder (Online Training). A person who holds a Part 61 manned pilot certificate (other than a Student pilot certificate), and who has a current flight review, as per 14 CFR Section 61.56, may complete Online Training that is offered by the FAA to obtain their 14 CFR Part 107, in lieu of taking the Initial Knowledge Test. However, a Part 61 certificate holder may also take the sUAS Initial Aeronautical Knowledge Test for certification.

(b) Non 14 CFR Part 61 certificate holder, or 14 CFR Part 61 certificate holder lacking currency (Initial Aeronautical Knowledge Test). A person who does not hold a 14 CFR Part 61 manned pilot certificate and/or they do not have a current flight review must take the Initial Aeronautical Knowledge Test at an FAA designated Knowledge Testing Center to obtain their sUAS Certificate.

2. Recreational Flyer Operations. Any person who flies a UAS for recreational use under 49 USC 44809 must take and pass TRUST. See the FAA website, The Recreational UAS Safety Test (TRUST).

Note: A current 14 CFR Part 107 sUAS certificate holder may fly recreationally under that part, but must adhere entirely to 14 CFR Part 107 rules and requirements. If a Part 107 sUAS certificate holder wishes to fly under 49 USC 44809, they must take and pass TRUST.

Note: The FAA's website, The Recreational UAS Safety Test (TRUST), may be viewed at: https://www.faa.gov/uas/recreational_flyers/knowledge_test_updates.

d. Recurrent Training (Testing) Requirements:

1. Part 107 operations:

(a) To exercise the privileges of a sUAS certificate that was issued under 14 CFR Part 107, a person must maintain currency. Therefore, the FAA requires that a person take a recurrent course within 24 months from the month the Initial Aeronautical Knowledge Test was passed, or the Online Training was completed.

(b) Recurrent training (online training) is found at the FAA's Become a Drone Pilot website.

Note: The FAA's Become a Drone Pilot website may be viewed at: https://www.faa.gov/uas/commercial_operators/become_a_drone_pilot/.

2. Recreational Operations. TRUST is taken on a once-and-done basis; no recurrent testing is required.

e. Pre-test Training Requirements:

1. Part 107 Operations:

(a) No documented pre-test training is required under Part 107 to take the Initial Aeronautical Knowledge Test. However, the FAA Remote Pilot Small Unmanned Aircraft Systems Study Guide is an excellent resource.

Note: To view the FAA Remote Pilot—Small Unmanned Aircraft Systems Study Guide see: https://www.faa.gov/regulations_policies/handbooks_manuals/aviation/media/remote_pilot_study_guide.pdf.

(b) Initial Aeronautical Knowledge Test subject areas. The testing topics for the sUAS Knowledge Test can be found in 14 CFR Section 107.73, Knowledge and Training.

Reference: 14 CFR Section 107.73, Knowledge and Training.

(c) Part 107 online training. This online training may be used by those who hold a 14 CFR Part 61 pilot certificate (not including a student pilot certificate) seeking 14 CFR Part 107 remote pilot certification. A person who holds a 14 CFR Part 61 pilot certificate must also show, at the time of certification, a current Flight Review as per 14 CFR Section 61.56.

2. Recreational Flyer Operations. No pre-test training is necessary to complete TRUST.

f. Endorsements and re-testing. Neither the Part 107 Initial Aeronautical Knowledge Test nor the Recreational TRUST have any requirements for flight instructor endorsements prior to testing.

Ch 11

A person who fails the Initial Aeronautical Knowledge Test must wait 14 calendar days before they may retake the test. TRUST may be retaken at any time.

g. Registering to take the Part 107 sUAS Initial Aeronautical Knowledge Test:

1. Before a person can take the sUAS Initial Aeronautical Knowledge Test at an FAA recognized testing center, that person must obtain an FAA Tracking Number (FTN). To obtain an FTN a person must create an account in the Integrated Airman Certification and Rating Application (IACRA) system. For detailed instructions on how to obtain an FTN, see the FAA Airman Certificate Testing Service (ACTS) Contract Briefing.

Note: Any person who has any FAA Airman Certificate will already have an FTN.

Note: The FAA's Airman Certificate Testing Service (ACTS) Contract Briefing, may be viewed at: https://www.youtube.com/watch?v=ETLsH8BruBM.

2. Once an applicant has their FTN, they will go to the testing vendor's website and register for the test. The FAA testing vendor is PSI Services LLC.

Note: The PSI Services LLC website may be viewed at: https://candidate.psiexams.com/.

h. Applying for a 14 CFR Part 107 sUAS Certificate. The Become a Drone Pilot website has instructions on how to obtain the 14 CFR Part 107 Pilot Certificate, following testing or online training completion.

Note: The Become a Drone Pilot website may be viewed at: https://www.faa.gov/uas/commercial_operators/become_a_drone_pilot/.

i. Night Operations and Operations over People:

1. A person who holds a sUAS Certificate is afforded all of the privileges of the certificate. This includes the ability to operate at night and over people without a waiver, under certain conditions. See paragraph 11-8-3, Precautions: Flight Over or Near People, Vehicles, Manned Aircraft, and Night Flight, for further information on these operations.

2. Any remote pilot who holds a 14 CFR Part 107 sUAS certificate issued prior to April 6, 2021, must take the updated recurrent training (the online training) to operate at night or over people.

11–5–2 Pilot Certification and Requirements for Public Aircraft Operations (PAOs)

a. When operating as a PAO, the operator is required to train and the agency will self-certify pilots as competent to safely operate in the NAS.

b. For more information and best practices on pilot certification and training within the framework of a PAO, refer to AC 00-1.1, Public Aircraft Operations—Manned and Unmanned.

Reference: AC 00-1.1, Public Aircraft Operations—Manned and Unmanned.

11–5–3 Pilot Certification for 14 CFR Part 135, Part 137, and Large Civil UAS

a. Currently, FAA regulations require a commercial pilot certificate for 14 CFR Part 135 Remote PICs.

b. Pilot certification for 14 CFR Part 137. For civil UAS agricultural aircraft operations, the 14 CFR Section 137.19(b) and (c) requirement (that the pilot hold a private or commercial pilot certificate) is exempted; only a 14 CFR Part 107 pilot certificate is required. This policy pertains to all UAS regardless of weight. However, all civil pilots conducting agricultural aircraft operations must satisfactorily pass the knowledge and skill test of 14 CFR Section 137.19(e) and 14 CFR Section 137.41(b) or (c).

c. Pilot certification for other large civil UAS. Requirements for future large civil UAS operations will be addressed in future rulemaking.

11–5–4 Foreign Pilot Certification

a. Part 107 Operations:

1. Foreign national holding a U.S. issued 14 CFR Part 61 certificate. Foreign nationals are eligible for a sUAS certificate in the same way that a U.S. citizen is eligible.

2. Foreign national not holding a U.S. issued 14 CFR Part 61 certificate. A foreign national who does not hold a U.S.-issued 14 CFR Part 61 certificate, must take and pass the Initial Aeronautical Knowledge Test to obtain a sUAS Pilot Certificate in order to operate in the NAS.

b. Recreational Flyer Operations. A foreign national is required to have passed TRUST to fly a UAS recreationally under 49 USC 44809 in the United States.

c. Security vetting. All applicants, regardless of nationality, must pass a Transportation Security Administration (TSA) Security Threat Analysis (STA) before the FAA will issue a temporary or permanent Pilot's Certificate under Part 107.

d. Bi-lateral agreements. Currently, the United States does not have any bi-lateral agreements with any other countries that would allow the issuance of a U.S. sUAS certificate that is based on a foreign UAS Pilot's Certificate.

Section 6 Advanced Air Mobility

11-6-1 General

a. Advanced Air Mobility (AAM) is a rapidly-emerging, new sector of the aerospace industry which aims to safely and efficiently integrate highly automated aircraft into the NAS. AAM is not a single technology, but rather a collection of new and emerging technologies being applied to the aviation transportation system, particularly in new aircraft types. Notional AAM use-cases include Urban Air Mobility (UAM), Regional Air Mobility (RAM), public services, large cargo delivery, and private or recreational vehicles.

b. UAM and RAM are subsets of AAM activities occurring in urban environments.

Section 7 UAS Operations on Airports

11-7-1 UAS Operations on Airports

a. Larger public and civil UAS operate from military, civilian and dual-use airports with set protocols and agreements with local ATC, often operate under IFR.

b. sUAS operations on airports require coordination with the airport operator and respective air traffic control facility, Spectrum, the FAA Regional Airport District Office, or the State Department of Aviation, where applicable. Due to the complex nature of these operations, requests for on-airport operations within controlled airspace must be submitted via DroneZone for coordination with the air traffic control facility. On-airport operation requests are evaluated on a case-by-case basis due to the inherent risks associated with operating in close proximity to areas frequented by manned aircraft.

Note: The FAA's DroneZone website may be viewed at: https://faadronezone.faa.gov/#/.

Section 8 Other Information and Best Practices

11–8–1 Best Practices for UAS Operations

Responsibility of the UAS pilot. Just as is the case with a manned aircraft, the UAS remote pilot or recreational flyer is responsible for the safe operation of their unmanned aircraft. The remote pilot or recreational flyer must ensure that they are physically ready to fly and knowledgeable of the flight to be performed to include operational parameters, UAS limitations, local weather, and applicable flight rules; that the UAS itself is mechanically ready.

11–8–2 UAS Operations and Air Traffic Control (ATC)

Coordination and/or communication of airspace authorizations, between UAS pilots or operators and ATC, are handled within the airspace access processes (e.g., LAANC, DroneZone, CAPS). They are not coordinated extemporaneously and verbally between the UAS operator and ATC. Any requirements for coordination and/or communication between UAS operator and ATC will be contained in individual COAs, which may include operational waivers, development of LOAs, and through other application processes which allow access to controlled airspace. Any air traffic services provided to sUAS operations shall be based upon the type of airspace authorization issued, along with the mitigations and limitations included in that authorization.

Note 1: Small UAS operators should not contact ATC directly by radio or telephone for purposes of airspace access. Also, the use of an aviation radio frequency by the RPIC of a sUAS may constitute a violation of Federal Communications Commission rules. Remote pilots of larger UAS—which are usually under positive control by ATC and flying under Instrument Flight Rules—are an exception to this guideline.

Note 2: Small UAS operators are encouraged to monitor local CTAF radio traffic when operating on or near an airport, for situational awareness.

11–8–3 Precautions: Flight Over or Near People, Vehicles, Manned Aircraft, and Night Operations

a. Flight over or near people and vehicles:

1. Remote pilots and recreational flyers should carefully consider the hazards of flight operations over or near people. 14 CFR Part 107, subpart D, Operations Over Human Beings, allows certain Operations Over People (OOP) and vehicles, based upon four different operational categories of UA weight and construction, and the

likely severity of injury to people on the ground, in the case of contact. Part 107 operators may request a waiver to these restrictions.

2. Part 91 remote pilots may refer to restrictions and permissions, regarding flight over people, in their respective COAs.

3. Recreational flyers should consider the safety of other persons when flying. 49 USC 44809(a)(2), Exception for Limited Recreational Operations of Unmanned Aircraft, requires recreational flyers to operate in accordance with the safety guidelines of an accepted CBO; these guidelines will usually include safety precautions for flight near people.

4. For further information on the rules for flying over people or vehicles, see paragraph 11–4–6, Airspace Restrictions to Flight.

Reference: 14 CFR Part 107, Subpart D, Operations Over Human Beings; 49 USC 44809(a)(2), Exception for Limited Recreational Operations of Unmanned Aircraft.

b. Flight in the Vicinity of Manned Aircraft:

1. The pilot of any unmanned aircraft operation retains the ultimate responsibility to avoid manned aircraft traffic. UAS operators should remember that manned aircraft may fly below 400 feet AGL; examples include helicopters, agricultural aircraft, light civil aircraft, and military aircraft. UAS pilots must ensure they have unblocked visual access to both their UAS and the airspace around it; not seeing a manned aircraft due to blocked line of sight does not absolve the UAS pilot from responsibility for avoidance.

2. Should public safety or emergency responder aircraft (e.g., police, fire suppression, helicopter emergency medical services) operations be interfered with by UAS, substantial fines can be levied on the UAS operators involved. Enforcement actions can include revocation or suspension of a pilot certificate, and up to a $20,000 civil penalty per violation.

c. Night Operations.

1. Night operations are permitted under 14 CFR Parts 91, 14 CFR Part 107, and Section 44809. However, requirements for meteorological visibility, and for the operator or visual observer (VO) to maintain VLOS with the UAS at all times, should be considered; see subparagraph 11–5–1i.

2. 14 CFR Section 107.29, Operation at Night, requirements include initial pilot training and equipment such as an anti-collision light which is visible for at least three statute miles, with a flash rate sufficient to avoid a collision.

3. Part 91 operators civil and PAO should refer to their specific COAs for any further instructions or limitations on night flight.

Ch 11

Reference: 14 CFR Section 107.29, Operation at Night.

11–8–4 Accidents and Incidents: UAS Operator Responsibilities

a. Reporting responsibility. A drone crash or malfunction, irrespective of which flight rules govern the flight, may trigger a reporting requirement to either the FAA, the NTSB, or both. The NTSB reporting requirements listed in 49 CFR 830.5, Immediate Notification, are separate and distinct from the FAA reporting requirements. All UAS flyers operating in the NAS recreational, civil, and public are encouraged to read and follow NTSB reporting requirements should they experience a crash or malfunction that meets NTSB criteria and triggers NTSB reporting. See NTSB Reporting Requirements and subparagraph 11-8-4b. COAs issued to Part 91 civil and public operators will contain specific incident/accident reporting requirements for the operator.

1. Part 107 Operations. Part 107 operators have a reporting requirement described in 14 CFR Section 107.9, Accident Reporting. A remote pilot-in-command is required to report any sUAS crash that causes serious injury or loss of consciousness, or property damage other than to the UAS of over $500. Property damage refers to any property that is not part of the UA System or attached to the UAS.

2. Recreational Flyer Operations. Recreational flyers fully complying with the exception listed in 49 USC 44809 are not required to report crashes to the FAA. However, this does not alleviate the recreational flyer from the requirement to report the crash to the NTSB if the crash meets the NTSB reporting requirements.

3. Part 91 Operations. Part 91 operators typically flown by public aircraft operators, civil aircraft operators, or civil operators flying FAA type certificated UAS have unique reporting requirements delineated in the terms and conditions of their certificate of waiver/authorization and must comply with those specific requirements.

b. NTSB Reporting Requirements. The NTSB defines a UAS accident as an occurrence associated with the operations of any public or civil UAS that takes place between the time that the system is activated with the purpose of flight and the time that the system is deactivated at the conclusion of its mission, in which any person suffers death or serious injury, or the UAS holds an airworthiness certificate and sustains substantial damage. In the case of a midair collision involving a UAS, any midair collision must be reported.

Reference: 14 CFR Section 830.5, Immediate Notification; 14 CFR Section 107.9, Accident Reporting.

11–8–5 Emergency UAS Authorizations Through Special Government Interest (SGI) Airspace Waivers

a. Background. UAS are used by public safety agencies to respond to emergencies. The SGI process is for any Part 107 or Part 91 operator that either due to time limitations, airspace restrictions or emergency situations that requires expedited authorization by contacting the system operations support center (SOSC) at 9-ATOR-HQ-SOSC@faa.gov.

b. The SGI process, depending on the nature of the operation, can be completed in a matter of minutes. This process enables response to an emergency with UAS in an expeditious manner.

c. Public Safety organizations may apply for expedited airspace authorizations through the SGI process. The SGI process is defined in FAA Order JO 7210.3, Facility Operation and Administration.

Reference: FAA Order JO 7210.3, Facility Operation and Administration.

d. Additional information regarding SGI authorizations can be located at the FAA's Emergency Situations webpage.

Note: The FAA's Emergency Situations website may be reviewed at: https://www.faa.gov/uas/advanced_operations/emergency_situations/.

11–8–6 Environmental Best Practices

a. Unmanned aircraft operate in a similar environment to manned aircraft. Since most UAS operations are conducted at low altitude, hazards, risks and potential environment factors may be encountered on a more frequent basis. In addition to the Bird Hazards, Flight over National Refuges, Parks, and Forests, the following factors must also be considered:

1. Flight Near Protected Conservation Areas. UAS, if misused, can have devastating impacts on protected wildlife. UAS operators may check for conservation area airspace restrictions on the B4UFLY mobile app.

2. Flight(s) Near Noise Sensitive Areas. Consider the following:

(a) UAS operations and flight paths should be planned to avoid prolonged or repetitive flight at low altitude near noise sensitive areas.

(b) As described in FAA Order 1050.1, Environmental Impact: Policies and Procedures, an area is "noise sensitive" if noise interferes with any normal activities associated with the area's use.

Reference: FAA Order 1050.1, Environmental Impact: Policies and Procedures.

(c) To the extent consistent with FAA safety requirements, operators should observe best practices developed by the National Park Service, U.S. Fish and Wildlife Service, U.S. Forest Service, and National Oceanic and Atmospheric Administration when operating above areas administered by those agencies. The National Park Service provides additional guidance at their Unmanned Aircraft Systems website.

Note: The National Park Service, Unmanned Aircraft Systems website may be viewed at: https://www.nps.gov/subjects/sound/uas.htm.

b. Some bird species have shown the potential to attack UAS that approach their nesting and hunting areas too closely. The type of birds that are most likely to attack sUAS are raptors such as hawks, eagles, and falcons. However, gulls, geese, and crows have also been known to attack UAS. Aggressive bird attacks may damage UAS propellers or other critical equipment, and may result in sudden loss of power or engine failure. Remote pilots and recreational flyers should consider reviewing engine-out procedures, especially when operating near high bird concentrations.

11-8-7 Resources for UAS Operators

a. FAA.GOV/UAS. The FAA UAS website, www.faa.gov/uas, is the central point for information about FAA UAS rules, regulations, and safety best practices.

b. FAA DroneZone. The FAA DroneZone is the Agency's portal for registering drones, requesting Part 107 airspace authorizations and waivers, registering as a CBO, requesting fixed flying sites, and other tasks.

c. Local FAA offices (Flight Standards District Offices/FSDOs). FSDOs can be the best in-person source for UAS information. A list of FSDOs in the United States is at https://www.faa.gov/about/office_org/field_offices/fsdo/all_fsdos/.

d. Aeronautical Information. The FAA provides aeronautical information to NAS users, including UAS pilots, through a variety of methods, including publications like this manual, other publications, Advisory Circulars (ACs), charts, website and mobile applications, etc. Check https://www.faa.gov/air_traffic/flight_info/aeronav/ for these items.

e. The UAS Support Center. For general question or comment about UAS or drones, the FAA's Support Center is available at 844-FLY-MY-UA or UASHelp@faa.gov.

f. Clubs and Associations. Local UAS recreational clubs, CBO organizations, and business associations are excellent resources for information and updates on flying in the local region.

g. LAANC. LAANC is the Low Altitude Authorization and Notification Capability, a collaboration between FAA and industry. It automates the application and approval process for airspace authorizations. Using applications developed by an FAA-approved UAS service supplier (USS) you can apply for an airspace authorization at over 600 airports. Download the free LAANC app at https://www.faa.gov/uas/programs_partnerships/data_exchange/.

h. B4UFLY. The B4UFLY mobile application is a partnership between the FAA and Kittyhawk. The app helps recreational flyers know whether it is safe to fly their drone, as well as increases their situational awareness. Download the free B4UFLY app at https://www.faa.gov/uas/recreational_fliers/where_can_i_fly/b4ufly/.

i. Weather Sources. Aviation weather services (such as https://www.aviationweather.gov/) are generally targeted towards manned aviation, the FAA is currently working on UAS-specific weather applications.

j. NOTAMs. The Notice to Air Missions (NOTAM) system, like aviation weather sources, remains primarily predicated on manned aviation needs. However, the system provides continual updates on all aviation activity (to include UAS flight activities which have been input to the FAA), as well as airport status. The NOTAM system will be of greatest use to larger UAS activities, UAS en route operations in controlled airspace, and those flying to or from airports. NOTAMs, temporary flight restrictions (TFRs), and aircraft safety alerts can be accessed at https://www.faa.gov/pilots/safety/notams_tfr/.

Ch 11

Appendix 1
Bird/Other Wildlife Strike Report

Form Approved OMB NO. 2120-0018

Bird/Other Wildlife Strike Report

U.S. Department of Transportation
Federal Aviation Administration

1. Name of Operator	2. Aircraft Make/Model	3. Engine Make/Model

4. Aircraft Registration	5. Date of Incident ___/___/___ Month Day Year	6. Local Time of Incident ☐ Dawn ☐ Dusk ___HR ___MIN ☐ Day ☐ Night ☐ AM ☐ PM

7. Airport Name	8. Runway Used	9. Location if En Route Nearest Town/Reference & State

10. Height (AGL)	11. Speed (IAS)	

12. Phase of Flight

- ☐ A. Parked
- ☐ B. Taxi
- ☐ C. Take-off Run
- ☐ D. Climb
- ☐ E. En Route
- ☐ F. Descent
- ☐ G. Approach
- ☐ H. Landing Roll

13. Part(s) of Aircraft Struck or Damaged

	Struck	Damaged		Struck	Damaged
A. Radome	☐	☐	H. Propeller	☐	☐
B. Windshield	☐	☐	I. Wing/Rotor	☐	☐
C. Nose	☐	☐	J. Fuselage	☐	☐
D. Engine No. 1	☐	☐	K. Landing Gear	☐	☐
E. Engine No. 2	☐	☐	L. Tail	☐	☐
F. Engine No. 3	☐	☐	M. Lights	☐	☐
G. Engine No. 4	☐	☐	N. Other:	☐	☐

(Specify, if "N. Other" is checked)

14. Effect on Flight
- ☐ None
- ☐ Aborted Take-Off
- ☐ Precautionary Landing
- ☐ Engines Shut Down
- ☐ Other: (Specify)

15. Sky Condition
- ☐ No Cloud
- ☐ Some Cloud
- ☐ Overcast

16. Precipitation
- ☐ Fog
- ☐ Rain
- ☐ Snow
- ☐ None

17. Bird/Other Wildlife Species

18. Number of Birds seen and/or struck

Number of Birds	Seen	Struck
1	☐	☐
2–10	☐	☐
11–100	☐	☐
More than 100	☐	☐

19. Size of Bird(s)
- ☐ Small
- ☐ Medium
- ☐ Large

20. Pilot Warned of Birds ☐ Yes ☐ No

21. Remarks (Describe damage, injuries and other pertinent information)

DAMAGE/COST INFORMATION

22. Aircraft time out service: ___ Hours	23. Estimated cost of repairs or replacement (U.S. $): $	24. Estimated other cost (U.S. $)(e.g. Loss of revenue, fuel, hotels): $

Reported by (Optional)	Title	Date

Paperwork Reduction Act Statement: The information collected on this form is necessary to allow the Federal Aviation Administration to assess the magnitude and severity of the wildlife-aircraft strike problem in the U.S. The information is used in determining the best management practices for reducing the hazard to aviation safety caused by wildlife-aircraft strikes. We estimate that it will take approximately **5 minutes** to complete the form. If you wish to make any comments concerning the accuracy of this burden estimate and any suggestions for reducing this burden, send those comments to the Federal Aviation Administration. Management Staff, ARP-10, 800 Independence Avenue, SW, Washington, DC 20591. The information collected is voluntary. Please note that an agency may not conduct or sponsor, and a person is not required to respond to, a collection of information unless it displays a currently valid OMB control number. The OMB control number associated with this collection is 2120-0045.

FAA Form 5200-7 (3-97) Supersedes Previous Edition

☆ U.S. GPO: 1997-418-084/64203 NSN: 0052-00-651-9005

APP

Completed FAA Form 5200-7 should be mailed to:
Federal Aviation Administration
Office of Airport Safety and Standards, AAS-310
800 Independence Avenue SW
Washington, DC 20591

Appendix 2
Volcanic Activity Reporting Form (VAR)

VOLCANIC ACTIVITY REPORT

Air-reports are critically important in assessing the hazards which volcanic ash cloud presents to aircraft operations.

OPERATOR:	A/C IDENTIFICATION: (as indicated on flight plan)		
PILOT-IN-COMMAND:			
DEP FROM: DATE: TIME; UTC:	ARR AT:	DATE:	TIME; UTC:
ADDRESSEE	AIREP SPECIAL		

Items 1–8 are to be reported immediately to the ATS unit that you are in contact with.

1) AIRCRAFT IDENTIFICATION	2) POSITION
3) TIME	4) FLIGHT LEVEL OR ALTITUDE

5) VOLCANIC ACTIVITY OBSERVED AT
(position or bearing, estimated level of ash cloud and distance from aircraft)

6) AIR TEMPERATURE	7) SPOT WIND

Other _____

8) SUPPLEMENTARY INFORMATION

SO_2 detected Yes ☐ No ☐

Ash encountered Yes ☐ No ☐

(Brief description of activity especially vertical and lateral extent of ash cloud and, where possible, horizontal movement, rate of growth, etc.)

After landing complete items 9–16 then fax form to: (Fax number to be provided by the meteorological authority based on local arrangements between the meteorological authority and the operator concerned.)

9) DENSITY OF ASH CLOUD	☐ (a) Wispy	☐ (b) Moderate dense	☐ (c) Very dense
10) COLOUR OF ASH CLOUD	☐ (a) White ☐ (d) Black	☐ (b) Light grey ☐ (e) Other _____	☐ (c) Dark grey
11) ERUPTION	☐ (a) Continuous	☐ (b) Intermittent	☐ (c) Not visible
12) POSITION OF ACTIVITY	☐ (a) Summit ☐ (d) Multiple	☐ (b) Side ☐ (e) Not observed	☐ (c) Single
13) OTHER OBSERVED FEATURES OF ERUPTION	☐ (a) Lightning ☐ (d) Ash fallout	☐ (b) Glow ☐ (e) Mushroom cloud	☐ (c) Large rocks ☐ (f) All
14) EFFECT ON AIRCRAFT	☐ (a) Communication ☐ (d) Pitot static	☐ (b) Navigation systems ☐ (e) Windscreen	☐ (c) Engines ☐ (f) Windows
15) OTHER EFFECTS	☐ (a) Turbulence	☐ (b) St. Elmo's Fire	☐ (c) Other fumes

16) OTHER INFORMATION
(Any information considered useful.)

Date: 07/19/2010

Appendix 3
Abbreviations/Acronyms

As used in this manual, the following abbreviations/acronyms have the meanings indicated.

Abbreviation/ Acronym	Meaning
AAWU	Alaskan Aviation Weather Unit
AAS	Airport Advisory Service
AAM	Advanced Air Mobility
AC	Advisory Circular
ACAR	Aircraft Communications Addressing and Reporting System
ADCUS	Advise Customs
ADDS	Aviation Digital Data Service
ADF	Automatic Direction Finder
ADIZ	Air Defense Identification Zone
ADS-B	Automatic Dependent Surveillance–Broadcast
AFB	Air Force Base
AFCS	Automatic Flight Control System
AFIS	Automatic Flight Information Service
AFM	Aircraft Flight Manual
AGL	Above Ground Level
AHRS	Attitude Heading Reference System
AIM	Aeronautical Information Manual
AIRMET	Airmen's Meteorological Information
AIS	Aeronautical Information Services
ALD	Available Landing Distance
ALDARS	Automated Lightning Detection and Reporting System
ALS	Approach Light Systems
AMSL	Above Mean Sea Level
ANP	Actual Navigation Performance
AOCC	Airline Operations Control Center
AP	Autopilot System
APV	Approach with Vertical Guidance
AR	Authorization Required
ARENA	Areas Noted for Attention
ARFF IC	Aircraft Rescue and Fire Fighting Incident Commander
ARINC	Aeronautical Radio Incorporated
ARO	Airport Reservations Office
ARSA	Airport Radar Service Area
ARSR	Air Route Surveillance Radar
ARTCC	Air Route Traffic Control Center
ARTS	Automated Radar Terminal System
ASDE-X	Airport Surface Detection Equipment–Model X
ASOS	Automated Surface Observing System
ASR	Airport Surveillance Radar
ASRS	Aviation Safety Reporting System

Abbreviation/ Acronym	Meaning
ASSC	Airport Surface Surveillance Capability
ATC	Air Traffic Control
ATCRBS	Air Traffic Control Radar Beacon System
ATCSCC	Air Traffic Control System Command Center
ATCT	Airport Traffic Control Tower
ATD	Along-Track Distance
ATIS	Automatic Terminal Information Service
ATO	Air Traffic Organization
ATT	Attitude Retention System
AWC	Aviation Weather Center
AWOS	Automated Weather Observing System
AWTT	Aviation Weather Technology Transfer
AWW	Severe Weather Forecast Alert
BAASS	Bigelow Aerospace Advanced Space Studies
BBS	Bulletin Board System
BC	Back Course
BECMG	Becoming Group
BVLOS	Beyond Visual Line of Sight
C/A	Coarse Acquisition
CARTS	Common Automated Radar Terminal System (ARTS) (to include ARTS IIIE and ARTS IIE)
CAT	Clear Air Turbulence
CBO	Community-Based Organization
CD	Controller Display
CDI	Course Deviation Indicator
CDR	Coded Departure Route
CERAP	Combined Center/RAPCON
CFA	Controlled Firing Area
CFIT	Controlled Flight into Terrain
CFR	Code of Federal Regulations
COA	Certificate of Waiver or Authorization
CPDLC	Controller Pilot Data Link Communications
CTAF	Common Traffic Advisory Frequency
CVFP	Charted Visual Flight Procedure
CVRS	Computerized Voice Reservation System
CWA	Center Weather Advisory
CWSU	Center Weather Service Unit
DA	Decision Altitude

Abbreviation/ Acronym	Meaning
DCA	Ronald Reagan Washington National Airport
DCP	Data Collection Package
DER	Departure End of Runway
DH	Decision Height
DME	Distance Measuring Equipment
DME/N	Standard DME
DME/P	Precision DME
DOD	Department of Defense
DP	Instrument Departure Procedure
DPU	Data Processor Unit
DRT	Diversion Recovery Tool
DRVSM	Domestic Reduced Vertical Separation Minimum
DVA	Diverse Vector Area
DVFR	Defense Visual Flight Rules
DVRSN	Diversion
EDCT	Expect Departure Clearance Time
EFAS	En Route Flight Advisory Service
EFV	Enhanced Flight Visibility
EFVS	Enhanced Flight Vision System
ELT	Emergency Locator Transmitter
EMAS	Engineered Materials Arresting System
EPE	Estimate of Position Error
ESV	Expanded Service Volume
ETA	Estimated Time of Arrival
ETD	Estimated Time of Departure
ETE	Estimated Time En Route
EWINS	Enhanced Weather Information System
EWR	Newark International Airport
FA	Area Forecast
FAA	Federal Aviation Administration
FAF	Final Approach Fix
FAWP	Final Approach Waypoint
FB	Fly-by
FCC	Federal Communications Commission
FD	Flight Director System
FDC	Flight Data Center
FDE	Fault Detection and Exclusion
FIR	Flight Information Region
FIS	Flight Information Service
FISDL	Flight Information Services Data Link
FLIP	Flight Information Publication
FMS	Flight Management System
FO	Fly-over
FPA	Flight Path Angle
FPNM	Feet Per Nautical Mile
FPV	Flight Path Vector
FRIA	FAA-Recognized Identification Area

Abbreviation/ Acronym	Meaning
FSDO	Flight Standards District Office
FSS	Flight Service Station
GBAS	Ground Based Augmentation System
GEO	Geostationary Satellite
GLS	GBAS Landing System
GNSS	Global Navigation Satellite System
GNSSP	Global Navigation Satellite System Panel
GPS	Global Positioning System
GRI	Group Repetition Interval
GSD	Geographical Situation Display
GUS	Ground Uplink Station
HAT	Height Above Touchdown
HAZMAT	Hazardous Material
HDTA	High Density Traffic Airports
HEMS	Helicopter Emergency Medical Services
HIRL	High Intensity Runway Lights
HRR	Helicopter Rapid Refueling Procedures
HUD	Head-Up Display
Hz	Hertz
IAF	Initial Approach Fix
IAP	Instrument Approach Procedure
IAS	Indicated Air Speed
IAWP	Initial Approach Waypoint
ICAO	International Civil Aviation Organization
IF	Intermediate Fix
IFR	Instrument Flight Rules
ILS	Instrument Landing System
ILS/PRM	Instrument Landing System/ Precision Runway Monitor
IM	Inner Marker
IMC	Instrument Meteorological Conditions
InFO	Information For Operators
INS	Inertial Navigation System
IOC	Initial Operational Capability
IR	IFR Military Training Route
IRU	Inertial Reference Unit
ITWS	Integrated Terminal Weather System
JFK	John F. Kennedy International Airport
kHz	Kilohertz
LAA	Local Airport Advisory
LAANC	Low Altitude Authorization and Notification Capability
LAAS	Local Area Augmentation System
LAHSO	Land and Hold Short Operations
LAWRS	Limited Aviation Weather Reporting Station
LDA	Localizer Type Directional Aid

Abbreviation/ Acronym	Meaning
LDA/PRM	Localizer Type Directional Aid/ Precision Runway Monitor
LGA	LaGuardia Airport
LIRL	Low Intensity Runway Lights
LLWAS	Low Level Wind Shear Alert System
LLWAS NE	Low Level Wind Shear Alert System Network Expansion
LLWAS-RS	Low Level Wind Shear Alert System Relocation/Sustainment
LNAV	Lateral Navigation
LOC	Localizer
LOP	Line-Of-Position
LORAN	Long Range Navigation System
LP	Localizer Performance
LPV	Localizer Performance with Vertical Guidance
LUAW	Line Up and Wait
LZ	Landing Zone
MAHWP	Missed Approach Holding Waypoint
MAP	Missed Approach Point
MAWP	Missed Approach Waypoint
MDA	Minimum Descent Altitude
MEA	Minimum En Route Altitude
MEARTS	Micro En Route Automated Radar Tracking System
METAR	Aviation Routine Weather Report
MGOW	Maximum Gross Operating Weight
MHz	Megahertz
MIRL	Medium Intensity Runway Lights
MM	Middle Marker
MOA	Military Operations Area
MOCA	Minimum Obstruction Clearance Altitude
MRA	Minimum Reception Altitude
MRB	Magnetic Reference Bearing
MSA	Minimum Safe Altitude
MSAW	Minimum Safe Altitude Warning
MSL	Mean Sea Level
MTI	Moving Target Indicator
MTOS	Mountain Obscuration
MTR	Military Training Route
MVA	Minimum Vectoring Altitude
MWA	Mountain Wave Activity
MWO	Meteorological Watch Office
NAS	National Airspace System
NASA	National Aeronautics and Space Administration
NAVAID	Navigational Aid
NAVCEN	Coast Guard Navigation Center
NCWF	National Convective Weather Forecast
NDB	Nondirectional Radio Beacon

Abbreviation/ Acronym	Meaning
NEXRAD	Next Generation Weather Radar
NGA	National Geospatial–Intelligence Agency
NM	Nautical Mile
NMAC	Near Midair Collision
NOAA	National Oceanic and Atmospheric Administration
NOPAC	North Pacific
NoPT	No Procedure Turn Required
NPA	Nonprecision Approach
NRS	Navigation Reference System
NSA	National Security Area
NSW	No Significant Weather
NTSB	National Transportation Safety Board
NTZ	No Transgression Zone
NWS	National Weather Service
OAT	Outside Air Temperature
OBS	Omni-Bearing Selector
ODP	Obstacle Departure Procedure
OIS	Operational Information System
OIS	Obstacle Identification Surface
OM	Outer Marker
OOP	Operations Over People
ORD	Chicago O'Hare International Airport
PA	Precision Approach
PAO	Public Aircraft Operation
PAPI	Precision Approach Path Indicator
PAR	Precision Approach Radar
PAR	Preferred Arrival Route
PC	Personal Computer
P/CG	Pilot/Controller Glossary
PDC	Pre-Departure Clearance
PFD	Personal Flotation Device
PIC	Pilot-in-Command
PinS	Point-in-Space
PIREP	Pilot Weather Report
POB	Persons on Board
POFZ	Precision Obstacle Free Zone
POI	Principal Operations Inspector
PPS	Precise Positioning Service
PRM	Precision Runway Monitor
PT	Procedure Turn
QICP	Qualified Internet Communications Provider
RA	Resolution Advisory
RAA	Remote Advisory Airport
RAIM	Receiver Autonomous Integrity Monitoring
RAIS	Remote Airport Information Service
RBDT	Ribbon Display Terminals
RC	Radio-Controlled

APP

Abbreviation/ Acronym	Meaning
RCAG	Remote Center Air/Ground
RCC	Rescue Coordination Center
RCLS	Runway Centerline Lighting System
RCO	Remote Communications Outlet
RD	Rotor Diameter
REIL	Runway End Identifier Lights
REL	Runway Entrance Lights
RFM	Rotorcraft Flight Manual
RID	Remote Identification
RLIM	Runway Light Intensity Monitor
RMI	Radio Magnetic Indicator
RNAV	Area Navigation
RNP	Required Navigation Performance
ROC	Required Obstacle Clearance
RPAT	RNP Parallel Approach Runway Transitions
RPIC	Remote Pilot-in-Command
RVR	Runway Visual Range
RVSM	Reduced Vertical Separation Minimum
RWSL	Runway Status Light
SAA	Sense and Avoid
SAFO	Safety Alerts For Operators
SAM	System Area Monitor
SAR	Search and Rescue
SAS	Stability Augmentation System
SATR	Special Air Traffic Rules
SBAS	Satellite-Based Augmentation System
SDF	Simplified Directional Facility
SFL	Sequenced Flashing Lights
SFR	Special Flight Rules
SFRA	Special Flight Rules Area
SGI	Special Government Interest
SIAP	Standard Instrument Approach Procedure
SID	Standard Instrument Departure
SIGMET	Significant Meteorological Information
SM	Statute Mile
SMGCS	Surface Movement Guidance Control System
SNR	Signal-to-Noise Ratio
SOIA	Simultaneous Offset Instrument Approaches
SOP	Standard Operating Procedure
SPC	Storm Prediction Center
SPS	Standard Positioning Service
STAR	Standard Terminal Arrival
STARS	Standard Terminal Automation Replacement System
STMP	Special Traffic Management Program
sUAS	Small UAS

Abbreviation/ Acronym	Meaning
TA	Traffic Advisory
TAA	Terminal Arrival Area
TAC	Terminal Area Chart
TACAN	Tactical Air Navigation
TAF	Aerodrome Forecast
TAS	True Air Speed
TCAS	Traffic Alert and Collision Avoidance System
TCH	Threshold Crossing Height
TD	Time Difference
TDLS	Tower Data Link System
TDWR	Terminal Doppler Weather Radar
TDZ	Touchdown Zone
TDZE	Touchdown Zone Elevation
TDZL	Touchdown Zone Lights
TEC	Tower En Route Control
THL	Takeoff Hold Lights
TIS	Traffic Information Service
TIS-B	Traffic Information Service-Broadcast
TLS	Transponder Landing System
TPP	Terminal Procedures Publications
TRSA	Terminal Radar Service Area
TRUST	The Recreational UAS Safety Test
TSO	Technical Standard Order
TWIB	Terminal Weather Information for Pilots System
UA	Unmanned Aircraft
UAM	Urban Air Mobility
UAS	Unmanned Aircraft System
UASFM	UAS Facility Map
UAV	Unmanned Aerial Vehicle
UFO	Unidentified Flying Object
UHF	Ultrahigh Frequency
U.S.	United States
USCG	United States Coast Guard
UTC	Coordinated Universal Time
UTM	UAS Traffic Management
UWS	Urgent Weather SIGMET
VAR	Volcanic Activity Reporting
VASI	Visual Approach Slope Indicator
VCOA	Visual Climb Over the Airport
VDA	Vertical Descent Angle
VDP	Visual Descent Point
VFR	Visual Flight Rules
VGSI	Visual Glide Slope Indicator
VHF	Very High Frequency
VIP	Video Integrator Processor
VLOS	Visual Line of Sight
VMC	Visual Meteorological Conditions

Abbreviation/ Acronym	Meaning
V_{MINI}	Instrument flight minimum speed, utilized in complying with minimum limit speed requirements for instrument flight
VNAV	Vertical Navigation
V_{NE}	Never exceed speed
V_{NEI}	Instrument flight never exceed speed, utilized instead of V_{NE} for compliance with maximum limit speed requirements for instrument flight
VO	Visual Observer
VOR	Very High Frequency Omni-directional Range
VORTAC	VHF Omni-directional Range/Tactical Air Navigation
VOT	VOR Test Facility
VR	VFR Military Training Route
V_{REF}	The reference landing approach speed, usually about 1.3 times V_{SO} plus 50 percent of the wind gust speed in excess of the mean wind speed.
V_{SO}	The stalling speed or the minimum steady flight speed in the landing configuration at maximum weight.
VTF	Vector to Final
VV	Vertical Visibility

Abbreviation/ Acronym	Meaning
VVI	Vertical Velocity Indicator
V_Y	Speed for best rate of climb
V_{YI}	Instrument climb speed, utilized instead of V_Y for compliance with the climb requirements for instrument flight
WA	AIRMET
WAAS	Wide Area Augmentation System
WFO	Weather Forecast Office
WGS-84	World Geodetic System of 1984
WMO	World Meteorological Organization
WMS	Wide-Area Master Station
WMSC	Weather Message Switching Center
WMSCR	Weather Message Switching Center Replacement
WP	Waypoint
WRA	Weather Reconnaissance Area
WRS	Wide-Area Ground Reference Station
WS	SIGMET
WSO	Weather Service Office
WSP	Weather Systems Processor
WST	Convective Significant Meteorological Information
WW	Severe Weather Watch Bulletin

APP

Appendix 4
FAA Form 7233-4—International Flight Plan

a. The FAA will accept a flight plan in international format for IFR, VFR, SFRA, and DVFR flights. File the flight plan electronically via a Flight Service Station (FSS), FAA contracted flight plan filing service, or other commercial flight plan filing service. Depending on the filing service chosen, the method of entering data may be different but the information required is generally the same.

b. The international flight plan format is mandatory for:

1. Any flight plan filed through a FSS or FAA contracted flight plan filing service; with the exception of Department of Defense flight plans and civilian stereo route flight plans, which can still be filed using the format prescribed in FAA Form 7233-1.

Note: DOD Form DD-175 and FAA Form 7233-1 are considered to follow the same format.

2. Any flight that will depart U.S. domestic airspace. For DOD flight plan purposes, offshore Warning Areas may use FAA Form 7233-1 or military equivalent.

3. Any flight requesting routing that requires Performance Based Navigation.

4. Any flight requesting services that require filing of capabilities only supported in the international flight plan format.

c. Flight Plan Contents

1. A flight plan will include information shown below:

(a) Flight Specific Information (Table 4-1)
(b) Aircraft Specific Information (Table 4-19)
(c) Flight Routing Information (Table 4-20)
(d) Flight Specific Supplementary Information (Item 19)

2. The tables indicate where the information is located in the international flight plan format, the information required for U.S. domestic flights, and the location of equivalent information in the domestic flight plan format.

3. International flights, including those that temporarily leave domestic U.S. airspace and return, require all applicable information in the international flight plan. Additional information can be found in ICAO Doc. 4444 (Procedures for Air Navigation Services, Air Traffic Management), and ICAO Doc. 7030 (Regional Supplemental Procedures) as well as the Aeronautical Information Publications (AIPs), Aeronautical Information Circulars (AICs), and NOTAMs of applicable other countries.

TABLE 4–1
FLIGHT SPECIFIC INFORMATION

Item	International Flight Plan (FAA Form 7233-4)	Domestic U.S. Requirements	Equivalent Item on Domestic Flight Plan (FAA Form 7233-1)
Aircraft Identification	Item 7	Required	Item 2
Flight Rules	Item 8	Required	Item 1
Type of Flight	Item 8	No need to file for domestic U.S. flight	N/A
Equipment and Capabilities	Item 10 Item 18 PBN/; NAV/; COM/; DAT/; SUR/	Required	Item 3
Date of Flight	Item 18 DOF/	Include when date of flight is not today	N/A
Reasons for Special Handling	Item 18 STS/; RMK/	Include when special category is applicable	Item 11
Remarks	Item 18 RMK/	Include when necessary	Item 11
Operator	Item 18 OPR/	No need to file for domestic U.S. flight	N/A
Flight Plan Originator	Item 18 ORGN/	No need to file for domestic U.S. flight	N/A

APP

d. Instructions for Flight-Specific Information Items

1. Aircraft Identification (Item 7) Aircraft Identification is always required. Aircraft identification must not exceed seven alphanumeric characters and be either:

(a) The ICAO designator for the aircraft operating agency, followed by the flight identification (for example, KLM511, NGA213, JTR25). When in radiotelephony the call sign to be used by the aircraft will consist of the ICAO telephony designator for the operating agency followed by the flight identification (for example, KLM511, NIGERIA213, JESTER25);

(b) The nationality or common mark and registration of the aircraft (for example, EIAKO, 4XBCD, N2567GA), when:

(1) In radiotelephony, the call sign to be used by the aircraft will consist of this identification alone (for example, CGAJS) or preceded by the ICAO telephony designator for the aircraft operating agency (for example, BLIZZARD CGAJS); or

(2) The aircraft is not equipped with radio.

Note 1: Standards for nationality, common and registration marks to be used are contained in Annex 7, Chapter 2.

Note 2: Provisions for using radiotelephony call signs are contained in Annex 10, Volume II, Chapter 5. ICAO designators and telephony designators for aircraft operating agencies are contained in Doc 8585—Designators for Aircraft Operating Agencies, Aeronautical Authorities and Services.

Note: Some countries' aircraft identifications begin with a number, which cannot be processed by U.S. ATC automation. The FAA will add a leading letter temporarily to gain automation acceptance for aircraft identifications that begin with a numeral. For flight-processing systems (e.g., ERAM or STARS) which will not accept a call sign that begins with a number, if the call sign is 6 characters or less, add a Q at the beginning of the call sign. If the call sign is 7 characters, delete the first character and replace it with a Q. Put the original call sign in the remarks section of the flight plan.

Example:
9HRA becomes Q9HRA
5744233 becomes Q744233

2. Flight Rules (Item 8a)
(a) Flight rules are always required.
(b) Flight rules must indicate IFR (I) or VFR (V).
(c) For composite flight plans, submit separate flight plans for the IFR and VFR portions of the flight. Specify in Item 15 the point or points where change of flight rules is planned. The IFR plan will be routed to ATC, and the VFR plan will be routed to a Flight Service for Search and Rescue services.

Note: The pilot is responsible for opening and closing the VFR flight plan. ATC does not have knowledge of a VFR flight plan's status.

3. Type of Flight (Item 8b)
(a) The type of flight is optional for flights remaining wholly within U.S. domestic airspace.
(b) Indicate the type of flight as follows:
- G – General Aviation
- S – Scheduled Air Service
- N – Non-Scheduled Air Transport Operation
- M – Military
- X – other than any of the defined categories above

4. Equipment and Capabilities (Item 10, Item 18 NAV/, COM/, DAT/, SUR/)
(a) Equipment and capabilities that can be filed in a flight plan include:
- Navigation capabilities in Item 10a, Item 18 PBN/, and Item 18 NAV/
- Voice communication capabilities in Item 10a and Item 18 COM/
- Data communication capabilities in Item 10a and Item 18 DAT/
- Approach capabilities in Item 10a and Item 18 NAV/
- Surveillance capabilities in Item 10b and Item 18 SUR/

(b) Codes allowed in Item 10a are shown in Table 4-2. Codes allowed in Item 10b are shown in Table 4-3. Codes recognized in Item 18 NAV/, COM/, DAT/, and SUR/ are shown in Table 4-4. Note that other service providers may define additional allowable (and required) codes for use in Item 18 NAV/, COM/, DAT/, or SUR/. Codes to designate PBN capability are described in Table 4-5.

Radio communication, navigation and approach aid equipment and capabilities

ENTER one letter as follows:

N if no COM/NAV/approach aid equipment for the route to be flown is carried, or the equipment is unserviceable,

OR

S if standard COM/NAV/approach aid equipment for the route to be flown is carried and serviceable (see Note 1),

AND/OR

ENTER one or more of the following letters from Table 4-2 to indicate the serviceable COM/NAV/ approach aid equipment and capabilities available.

TABLE 4–2
ITEM 10A NAVIGATION, COMMUNICATION, AND
APPROACH AID CAPABILITIES

A	GBAS Landing System
B	LPV (APV with SBAS)
C	LORAN C
D	DME
E1	FMC WPR ACARS
E2	D-FIS ACARS
E3	PDC ACARS
F	ADF
G	GNSS (See Note 2)
H	HF RTF
I	Inertial Navigation
J1	CPDLC ATN VDL Mode 2 (See Note 3)
J2	CPDLC FANS 1/A HFDL
J3	CPDLC FANS 1/A VDL Mode A
J4	CPDLC FANS 1/A Mode 2
J5	CPDLC FANS 1/A SATCOM (INMARSAT)
J6	Reserved
J7	CPDLC FANS 1/A SATCOM (Iridium)
K	MLS
L	ILS
M1	ATC SATVOICE (INMARSAT)
M2	Reserved
M3	ATC RTF (Iridium)
O	VOR
P1	CPDLC RCP 400 (See Note 7)
P2	CPDLC RCP 240 (See Note 7)
P3	SATVOICE RCP 400 (See Note 7)
P4–P9	Reserved for RCP
R	PBN Approved (See Note 4)
T	TACAN
U	UHF RTF
V	VHF RTF
W	RVSM Approved
X	MNPS Approved /North Atlantic (NAT) High Level Airspace (HLA) approved
Y	VHF with 8.33 kHz Channel Spacing Capability
Z	Other equipment carried or other capabilities (See Note 5)

Any alphanumeric characters not indicated above are reserved.

Note 1: If the letter "S" is used, standard equipment is considered to be VHF RTF, VOR, and ILS, unless another combination is prescribed by the appropriate ATS authority.

Note 2: If the letter "G" is used, the types of external GNSS augmentation, if any, are specified in Item 18 following the indicator NAV/ and separated by a space.

Example: NAV/SBAS

Note 3: See RTCA/EUROCAE Interoperability Requirements Standard for ATN Baseline 1 (ATN B1 INTEROP Standard – DO-280B/ED-110B) for data link services air traffic control clearance and information/air traffic control communications management/air traffic control microphone check.

Note 4: If the letter "R" is used, the performance-based navigation levels that can be met are specific in Item 18 following the indicator PBN/. Guidance material on the application of performance-based navigation to a specific route segment, route, or area is contained in the Performance-based Navigation (PBN) Manual (Doc 9613)

Note 5: If the letter "Z" is used, specify in Item 18 the other equipment carried or other capabilities, preceded by COM/, NAV/, and/or DAT, as appropriate.

Note 6: Information on navigation capability is provided to ATC for clearance and routing purposes.

Note 7: Guidance on the application of performance-based communication, which prescribes RCP to an air traffic service in a specific area, is contained in the Performance-based Communication and Surveillance (PBCS) Manual (Doc 9869).

APP

TABLE 4–3
ITEM 10B SURVEILLANCE CAPABILITIES

ENTER "N" if no surveillance equipment for the route to be flown is carried, or the equipment is unserviceable,

or

ENTER One or more of the following descriptors, to a maximum of 20 characters, to describe the serviceable surveillance equipment and/or capabilities on board.

ENTER no more than one transponder code (Modes A, C, or S)

SSR Modes A and C:

A	Transponder	Mode A (4 digits – 4096 codes)
C	Transponder	Mode A (4 digits – 4096 codes) and Mode C

SSR Mode S:

E	Transponder	Mode S, including aircraft identification, pressure-altitude, and extended squitter (ADS-B) capability
H	Transponder	Mode S, including aircraft identification, pressure-altitude, and enhanced surveillance capability
I	Transponder	Mode S, including aircraft identification, but no pressure-altitude capability
L	Transponder	Mode S, including aircraft identification, pressure-altitude, extended squitter (ADS-B), and enhanced surveillance capability
P	Transponder	Mode S, including pressure-altitude, but no aircraft identification capability
S	Transponder	Mode S, including both pressure-altitude and aircraft identification capability
X	Transponder	Mode S, with neither aircraft identification nor pressure-altitude

Note: Enhanced surveillance capability is the ability of the aircraft to down-link aircraft derived data via Mode S transponder.

ADS-B:

B1	ADS-B with dedicated 1090 MHz ADS-B "out" capability
B2	ADS-B with dedicated 1090 MHz ADS-B "out" and "in" capability
U1	ADS-B with "out" capability using UAT
U2	ADS-B with "out" and "in" capability using UAT
V1	ADS-B with "out" capability using VDL Mode 4
V2	ADS-B with "out" and "in" capability using VDL Mode 4

Note: File no more than one code for each type of capability, e.g., file B1 or B2 and not both

ADS-C:

D1	ADS-C with FANS 1/A capabilities
G1	ADS-C with ATN capabilities

Alphanumeric characters not included above are reserved.

Example: *ADE3RV/HB2U2V2G1*

Note 1: The RSP specification(s), if applicable, will be listed in Item 18 following the indicator SUR/, using the characters "RSP" followed by the specifications value. Currently RSP180 and RSP400 are in use.

Note 2: List additional surveillance equipment or capabilities in Item 18 following the indicator SUR/.

TABLE 4–4
ITEM 18 NAV/, COM/, DAT/, AND SUR/ CAPABILITIES USED BY FAA

Item	Purpose	Entry	Explanation
NAV/ entries used by FAA	Radius to Fix (RF) capability	Z1	RNP-capable flight is authorized for Radius to Fix operations.
	Fixed Radius Transitions (FRT)	Z2	RNP-capable flight is authorized for Fixed Radius Transitions.
	Time of Arrival Control (TOAC)	Z5	RNP-capable flight is authorized for Time of Arrival Control.
	Advanced RNP (A-RNP)	P1	Flight is authorized for A-RNP operations.
	Helicopter RNP 0.3	R1	Flight is authorized for RNP 0.3 operations (pertains to helicopters only).
	RNP 2 Continental	M1	Flight is authorized for RNP 2 continental operations.
	RNP 2 Oceanic/ Remote	M2	Flight is authorized for RNP 2 oceanic/remote operations.
COM/ entries used by FAA	N/A	N/A	The FAA currently does not use any entries in COM/.
DAT/ entries used by FAA	Capability and preference for delivery of pre-departure clearance	Priority number followed by: • FANS • FANSP • PDC • VOICE	Entries are combined with a priority number, for example; 1FANS2PDC means a preference for departure clearance delivered via FANS 1/A; with capability to also receive the clearance via ACARS PDC. FANS = FANS 1/A DCL FANSP = FANS 1/A+ DCL PDC = ACARS PDC VOICE = PDC via voice (no automated delivery)
SUR/ entries used by FAA	Req. Surveillance Performance	RSP180	Aircraft is authorized for Required Surveillance Performance RSP180
		RSP400	Aircraft is authorized for Required Surveillance Performance RSP400
	ADS-B	A2	Aircraft has 1090 MHz Extended Squitter ADS-B compliant with RTCA DO-260B (complies with FAA requirements)
		A2	Aircraft has 978 MHz UAT ADS-B compliant with RTCA DO-282B (complies with FAA requirements)

Note 1: *Other entries in NAV/, COM/, DAT/, and SUR/ are permitted for international flights when instructed by other service providers. Direction on use of these capabilities by the FAA is detailed in the following sections.*

Note 2: *In NAV/, descriptors for advanced capabilities (Z1, P1, R1, M1, and M2) should be entered as a single character string with no intervening spaces, and separated from any other entries in NAV/ by a space.*

Example: *NAV/Z1P1M2 SBAS*

APP

TABLE 4–5
ITEM 18. PBN/ SPECIFICATIONS
(Include as many of the applicable descriptors, up to a maximum of 8 entries (not more than 16 characters).

PBN/	RNAV SPECIFICATIONS
A1	RNAV 10 (RNP 10)
B1	RNAV 5 all permitted sensors
B2	RNAV 5 GNSS
B3	RNAV 5 DME/DME
B4	RNAV 5 VOR/DME
B5	RNAV 5 INS or IRS
B6	RNAV 5 LORAN C
C1	RNAV 2 all permitted sensors
C2	RNAV 2 GNSS
C3	RNAV 2 DME/DME
C4	RNAV 2 DME/DME/IRU
D1	RNAV 1 all permitted sensors
D2	RNAV 1 GNSS
D3	RNAV 1 DME/DME
D4	RNAV 1 DME/DME/IRU
PBN/	**RNP SPECIFICATIONS**
L1	RNP 4
O1	Basic RNP 1 all permitted sensors
O2	Basic RNP 1 GNSS
O3	Basic RNP 1 DME/DME
O4	Basic RNP 1 DME/DME/IRU
S1	RNP APCH
S2	RNP APCH with BARO-VNAV
T1	RNP AR APCH with RF (special authorization required)
T2	RNP AR APCH without RF (special authorization required)

Note 1: PBN Codes B1–B6 indicates RNAV 5 capability. The FAA considers these B codes to be synonymous and qualifying for point-to-point routing but not for assignment to the PBN routes shown in the table.

Note 2: Combinations of alphanumeric characters not included above are reserved.

Note 3: The PBN/ specifications are allowed per ICAO Doc. 4444. The FAA makes use of a subset of these codes as described in the section on filing navigation capability.

(c) The following sections detail what capabilities need to be provided to obtain services from the FAA for:
• IFR flights (general).
• Assignment of Performance-Based Navigation (PBN) routes.
• Automated Departure clearance (via Datacom DCL or PDC).
• Reduced Vertical Separation Minima (if requesting FL 290 or above).
• Reduced Separation in Oceanic Airspace.

(d) Capabilities such as voice communications, required communications performance, approach aids, and ADS-C, are not required in a flight plan that remains entirely within domestic airspace.

(e) Flights that leave domestic United States airspace may be required to include additional capabilities, per requirements for the FIRs being overflown. Consult the appropriate State Aeronautical Information Publications for requirements.

(f) Include the capability only if:
• The requisite equipment is installed and operational;
• The crew is trained as required; and
• Any required Operations Specification, Letter of Authorization, or other approvals are in hand.

Note: Do not include a capability solely based on the installed equipment if an operational approval is required. For example, all U.S. civil operators require either Operations Specification, Management Specification, or Letter of Authorization B036, as applicable, in order to include NAV/ M2 (RNP 2 (oceanic/remote)), PBN/A1 (RNAV 10 (RNP 10)), or PBN/L1 (RNP 4) in Item 18.

5. Filing equipment and capability in an IFR Flight Plan. This section details the minimum requirements to identify capabilities in an IFR flight plan for flights in the domestic United States. Other requirements to file a capability are associated with obtaining specific services as described in subsequent sections. The basic capabilities that must be addressed include Navigation, Transponder, Voice, and ADS-B Out as described below. A designator for "Standard" capability is also allowed to cover a suite of commonly carried voice, navigation, and approach equipment with one code.

(a) Standard Capability and No Capability (Item 10a)
• Use "S" if VHF radio, VOR, and ILS equipment for the route to be flown are carried and serviceable. Use of the "S" removes the need to list these three capabilities separately.
• Use "N" if no communications, navigation, or approach aid equipment for the route to be flown are carried or the equipment is unserviceable.
• When there is no transponder, ADS-B, or ADS-C capability then file only the letter "W" in Item 10b.

(b) Navigation Capabilities (Item 10a, Item 18 NAV/)
• Indicate radio navigation capability by filing one or more of the codes in Table 4-6.

• Indicate Area Navigation (RNAV) capability by filing one or more of the codes in Table 4-7.

TABLE 4–6
RADIO NAVIGATION CAPABILITIES

Capability	Item 10a	Item 18 NAV/
VOR	O	
DME	D	
TACAN	T	

TABLE 4–7
AREA NAVIGATION CAPABILITIES

Capability	Item 10a	Item 18 NAV/
GNSS	G	SBAS (if WAAS equipped) GBAS (if LAAS equipped)
INS	I	
DME / DME	DR	
VOR / DME	DOR	

Note 1:
SBAS—Space-Based Augmentation System
GBAS—Ground-Based Augmentation System

Note 2: No PBN/ code needs to be filed to indicate the ability to fly point-to-point routes using GNSS or INS.

Note 3: Filing one of these four area navigation capabilities as shown does not indicate performance based navigation sufficient for flying Q-Routes, T-Routes, or RNAV SIDs or STARs. To qualify for these routes, see the section on Performance Based Navigation Routes.

(c) Transponder Capabilities (Item 10b)
• For domestic flights, it is not necessary to indicate Mode S capability. It is acceptable to simply file one of the following codes in Table 4-8.

TABLE 4–8
MODE C

Capability	Item 10b
Transponder with no Mode C	A
Transponder with Mode C	C

• International flights must file in accordance with relevant AIPs and regional supplements. Include one of the Mode S codes in Table 4-9, if appropriate.

Note: File only one transponder code.

TABLE 4–9
MODE S

Capability	Aircraft ID	Altitude Encoding	Item 10b
Mode S Transponder	No	No	X
Mode S Transponder	No	Yes	P
Mode S Transponder	Yes	No	I
Mode S Transponder	Yes	Yes	S
Mode S Transponder with Extended Squitter	Yes	Yes	E
Enhanced Mode S Transponder	Yes	Yes	H
Enhanced Mode S Transponder with Extended Squitter	Yes	Yes	L

(d) ADS-B Capabilities (Item 10b, Item 18 SUR/ and Item 18 CODE/)
• Indicate ADS-B capability as shown in Table 4-10. The accompanying entry in Item 18 indicates that the equipment is compliant with 14 CFR §91.227. Some ADS-B equipment used in other countries is based on an earlier standard and does not meet U.S. requirements.
• Do not file an ADS-B code for "in" capability only. There is currently no way to indicate that an aircraft has "in" capability but no "out" capability.
• For aircraft with ADS-B "out" on one frequency and "in" on another, include only the ADS-B "out" code. For example, B1 or U1, (See Table 4-10).

TABLE 4–10
ADS-B CAPABILITIES

Capability	Item 10b	Item 18 SUR/
1090 ES Out Capability	B1	A2
1090 ES Out and In Capability	B2	A2
UAT Out Capability	U1	A2
UAT Out and In Capability	U2	A2

(e) Voice Communication Capabilities (Item 10a)
The FAA does not require indication of voice communication capabilities in a flight plan for domestic flights, but it is permissible. For flights outside the domestic United States, all relevant capabilities must be indicated as follows (See Table 4-11)

APP

TABLE 4–11
VOICE COMMUNICATION CAPABILITIES

Capability	Item 10a
VHF Radio	V
UHF Radio	U
HF Radio	H
VHF Radio (8.33 kHZ Spacing)	Y
ATC SATVOICE (INMARSAT)	M1
ATC SATVOICE (Iridium)	M3

(f) Approach Aid Capabilities (Item 10a). The FAA does not require filing of approach aid capability in order to request a specific type of approach, however any of the codes indicated in Table 4-12 in 10a are permissible.

• International flights may be required to indicate approach capability, based on instructions from relevant service providers.

TABLE 4–12
APPROACH AID CAPABILITIES

Capability	Item 10a
ILS	L
MLS	K
LPV Approach (APV with SBAS) (WAAS)	B
GBAS Landing System (LAAS)	A

6. Performance-Based Navigation Routes (Item 10a, Item 18 PBN/, Item 18 NAV/)—When planning to fly routes that require PBN capability, file the appropriate capability as shown in Table 4-13.

TABLE 4–13
FILING FOR PERFORMANCE BASED NAVIGATION (PBN) ROUTES

Type of Routing	Capability Required	Item 10a	Item 18 PBN/ See NOTE 2	Item 18 NAV/ See NOTE 3	Notes
RNAV SID or STAR (See NOTE 1)	RNAV 1	GR	D2		If GNSS
		DIR	D4		If DME/DME/IRU
RNP SID or STAR (See NOTE 2)	RNP 1 GNSS	GR	O2		If GNSS only
	RNP 1 GNSS	DGIR	O1		If GNSS primary and DME/DME/IRU backup
RNP SID or STAR with RF required (See NOTE 2)	RNP 1 GNSS	GRZ	O2	Z1	If GNSS only
	RNP 1 GNSS	DGIRZ	O1	Z1	If GNSS primary and DME/DME/IRU backup
Domestic Q-Route (see separate requirements for Gulf of Mexico Q-Routes)	RNAV 2	GR	C2		If GNSS
		DIR	C4		If DME/DME/IRU
T–Route	RNAV 2	GR	C2		GNSS is required for T-Routes
RNAV (GPS) Approach	RNP Approach, GPS	GR	S1		Domestic arrivals do not need to file PBN approach capabilities to request the approach.
RNAV (GPS) Approach	RNP Approach, GPS Baro–VNAV	GR	S2		
RNAV (GPS) Approach with RF required	RNP Approach, GPS RF Capability	GRZ	S2	Z1	
RNP AR Approach with RF	RNP (Special Authorization Required) RF Leg Capability	GR	T1		
RNP AR Approach without RF	RNP (Special Authorization Required)	GR	T2		

Note 1: If the flight is requesting an RNAV SID only (no RNAV STAR) or RNAV STAR only (no RNAV SID) then consult guidance on the FAA website at https://www.faa.gov/about/office_org/headquarters _offices/ato/service_units/air_traffic_services/flight_plan_filing.
Note 2: PBN descriptor D1 includes the capabilities of D2, D3, and D4. PBN descriptor B1 includes the capabilities of B2, B3, B4, and B5. PBN descriptor C1 includes the capabilities of C2, C3, and C4.

Note 3: In NAV/, descriptors for advanced capabilities (Z1, P1, R1, M1, and M2) should be entered as a single character string with no intervening spaces, and separated from any other entries in NAV/ by a space.

Example: NAV/Z1P1M2 SBAS

7. Automated Departure Clearance Delivery (DCL or PDC). When planning to use automated pre-departure clearance delivery capability, file as indicated below.

(a) PDC provides pre-departure clearances from the FAA to the operator's designated flight operations center, which then delivers the clearance to the pilot by various means. Use of PDC does not require any special flight plan entry.

(b) DCL provides pre-departure clearances from the FAA directly to the cockpit/FMS via Controller Pilot Datalink Communications (CPDLC). Use of DCL requires flight plan entries as follows:

• Include CPDLC codes in Item 10a only if the flight is capable of en route/oceanic CPDLC, the codes are not required for DCL.

• Include Z in Item 10a to indicate there is information provided in Item 18 DAT/.

• Include the clearance delivery methods of which the flight is capable, and order of preference in Item 18 DAT/. (See AIM 5-2-2)

 ○ VOICE—deliver clearance via Voice

 ○ PDC—deliver clearance via PDC

 ○ FANS—deliver clearance via FANS 1/A

 ○ FANSP—deliver clearance via FANS 1/A+

Example:
DAT/1FANS2PDC
DAT/1FANSP2VOICE

8. Operating in Reduced Vertical Separation Minima (RVSM) Airspace (Item 10a). When planning to fly in RVSM airspace (FL 290 up to and including FL 410) then file as indicated below.

(a) If capable and approved for RVSM operations, per AIM 4-6-1, Applicability and RVSM Mandate (Date/Time and Area), file a W in Item 10a. Include the aircraft registration mark in Item 18 REG/, which is used to post-operationally monitor the safety of RVSM operations.

• Do not file a "W" in Item 10a if the aircraft is capable of RVSM operations, but is not approved to operate in RVSM airspace.

• If RVSM capability is lost after the flight plan is filed, request that ATC remove the "W" from Item 10a.

(b) When requesting to operate non-RVSM in RVSM airspace, using one of the exceptions identified in AIM 4-6-10, do not include a "W" in Item 10a. Include STS/NONRVSM in Item 18. STS/NONRVSM is used only as part of a request to operate non-RVSM in RVSM airspace.

9. Eligibility for Reduced Oceanic Separation. Indicate eligibility for the listed reduced separation minima as indicated in the tables below. Full Operational Requirements for these services are found in the U.S. Aeronautical Information Publication (AIP) ENR 7, Oceanic Operations, available at http://www.faa.gov/air_traffic/publications/atpubs/aip_html/index.html.

TABLE 4–14
FILING FOR GULF OF MEXICO CTA

Dimension of Separation	Separation Minima	ADS-C Surveillance Requirements	Comm. Requirement	PBN Requirement	Flight Plan Entries			
					ADS-C in Item 10b	CPDLC in Item 10a	PBN in Item 18 PBN/ (also File "R" in Item 10a)	PBN in Item 18 NAV/
Lateral	50 NM	N/A (ADS-C not required)	Voice comm—HF or VHF as required to maintain contact over the entire route to be flown.	RNP10 or RNP4	N/A	N/A	A1 or L1	N/A

Note: If not RNAV10/RNP10 capable and planning to operate in the Gulf of Mexico CTA, then put the notation NONRNP10 in Item 18 RMK/, preferably first.

APP

TABLE 4–15
FILING FOR 50 NM LATERAL SEPARATION IN ANCHORAGE ARCTIC FIR

Dimension of Separation	Separation Minima	ADS-C Surveillance Requirements	Comm. Requirement	PBN Requirement	Flight Plan Entries			
					ADS-C in Item 10b	CPDLC in Item 10a	PBN in Item 18 PBN/ (also File "R" in Item 10a)	PBN in Item 18 NAV/
Lateral	50 NM	N/A (ADS-C not required)	None beyond normal requirements for the airspace	RNP10 or RNP4	N/A	N/A	A1 or L1	N/A

TABLE 4–16
FILING FOR 30 NM LATERAL, 30 NM LONGITUDINAL, AND 50 NM LONGITUDINAL OCEANIC SEPARATION IN
ANCHORAGE, OAKLAND, AND NEW YORK OCEANIC CTAS

Dimension of Separation	Separation Minima	ADS-C Surveillance Requirements	Comm. Requirement	PBN Requirement	Flight Plan Entries			
					ADS-C in Item 10b	CPDLC in Item 10a	PBN in Item 18 PBN/ (also File "R" in Item 10a)	PBN in Item 18 NAV/
Longitudinal	50 NM	Position report at least every 27 minutes (at least every 32 minutes if both aircraft are approved for RNP-4 operations)	CPDLC	RNP10	D1	J5 and/or J7	A1	N/A
Longitudinal	30 NM	ADS-C position report at least every 10 minutes	CPDLC	RNP4	D1	J5 and/or J7	L1	N/A
Lateral	30 NM	ADS-C-based lateral deviation event contract with 5NM lateral deviation from planned routing set as threshold for triggering ADS report of lateral deviation event	CPDLC	RNP4	D1	J5 and/or J7	L1	N/A

TABLE 4–17
FILING FOR REDUCED OCEANIC SEPARATION WHEN RSP/RCP REQUIRED ON MARCH 29, 2018

Dimension of Separation	Separation Minima	RSP Requirement	RCP Requirement	PBN Requirement	Flight Plan Entries				
					RSP in Item 18 SUR/	RCP in Item 10a	CDPLC in Item 10a	PBN in Item 18 PBN/ (also File "R" in Item 10a)	PBN in Item 18 NAV/
Lateral	55.5 km 30 NM	180	240	RNP 2 or RNP 4	RSP180	P2	J5, and/or J6, and/or J7	L1	
Performance-based Longitudinal	5 Minutes	180	240	RNAV 10 (RNP 10) RNP 4, or RNP 2 oceanic/ remote	RSP180	P2	J5, and/or J6, and/or J7	A1 or L1	M2
Performance-based Longitudinal	55.5 km 30 NM	180	240	RNP 4 or RNP 2 oceanic/ remote	RSP180	P2	J5, and/or J6, and/or J7	L1	M2
Performance-based Longitudinal	93 km 50 NM	180	240	RNAV 10 (RNP 10) or RNP 4	RSP180	P2	J5, and/or J6, and/or J7	A1 or L1	

Note 1: *Filing of RNP 2 alone is not supported in FAA controlled airspace; PBN/L1 (for RNP 4) or PBN/A1 (for RNP 10) must be filed to obtain the indicated separation.*

Note 2: *Use of "RNP 2" in NAV/ signifies continental RNP 2 (and means the same as M1). Continental RNP 2 is not adequate for reduced oceanic separation. Descriptor M2 indicates RNP 2 global/oceanic RNP 2 capability.*

10. Date of Flight (Item 18 DOF/)
Flights planned more than 23 hours after the time the flight plan is filed, must include the date of flight in DOF/ expressed in a six-digit format YYMMDD, where YY equals the year (Y), MM equals the month, and DD equals the day.

Note: *FAA ATC systems will not accept flight plans more than 23 hours prior to their proposed departure time. FAA Flight Service and commercial flight planning services generally accept flight plans earlier and forward to ATC at an appropriate time, typically 2 to 4 hours before the flight.*

Example: *DOF/171130*

11. Reasons for Special Handling (Item 18 STS/)
(a) Indicate the applicable Special Handling in Item 18 STS/ as shown in Table 4-18.

Note: *Priority for a flight is not automatically granted based on filing one of these codes but is based on documented procedures. In some cases, additional information may also be required in remarks; follow all such instructions as well.*

TABLE 4–18
SPECIAL HANDLING

Special Handling	Item 18 STS/
Flight operating in accordance with an altitude reservation	ALTRV
Flight approved for exemption from ATFM measures by the appropriate ATS authority	ATFMX
Fire Fighting	FFR
Flight check for calibration of NAVAIDS	FLTCK
Flight carrying hazardous material(s)	HAZMAT
Flight with Head of State status	HEAD
Medical flight declared by medical authorities	HOSP
Flight operating on a humanitarian mission	HUM
Flight for which a military entity assumes responsibility for separation of military aircraft	MARSA
Life critical medical emergency evacuation	MEDEVAC
Non-RVSM capable flight intending to operate in RVSM airspace	NONRVSM
Flight engaged in a search and rescue mission	SAR
Flight engaged in military, customs, or police services	STATE

APP

(b) Any other requests for special handling must be made in Item 18 RMK/.

(c) Include plain-language remarks when required by ATC or deemed necessary. Do not use special characters, for example; / * - = +.

Example:
RMK/NRP
RMK/DVRSN

12. Remarks
Include when necessary.

13. Operator (Item 18 OPR/)
When the operator is not obvious from the aircraft identification, the operator may be indicated.

Example: OPR/NETJETS

14. Flight Plan Originator (Item 18 ORGN/)
(a) VFR flight plans originating outside of FAA FSS or FAA contracted flight plan filing services must enter the 8-letter AFTN address of the service where the flight plan was originally filed. Alternately, enter the name of the service where the FPL was originally filed. This information is critical to locating the FPL originator in the event additional information is needed.

(b) For IFR flight plans, the original filers AFTN address may be indicated, which is helpful in cases where a flight plan has been forwarded.

Example:
ORGN/Acme Flight Plans
ORGN/KDENXLDS

TABLE 4–19
AIRCRAFT SPECIFIC INFORMATION

Item	International Flight Plan (FAA Form 7233-4)	Domestic U.S. Requirements	Equivalent Item on Domestic Flight Plan (FAA Form 7233-1)
Number of Aircraft	Item 9	Included when more than one a/c in flight	Item 3
Type of Aircraft	Item 9	Required	Item 3
Wake Turbulence Category	Item 9	Required	N/A
Aircraft Registration	Item 18 REG/	Include when planning to operate in RVSM airspace	N/A
Mode S Address	Item 18 CODE/	Not required within U.S. controlled airspace	N/A
SELCAL Codes	Item 18 SEL/	Include when SELCAL equipped	N/A
Performance Category	Item 18 PER/	Not required for domestic flights	N/A

e. Instructions for Aircraft-Specific Information.

1. Number of Aircraft (Item 9) when there is more than one aircraft in the flight; indicate the number of aircraft up to 99.

2. Type of Aircraft (Item 9)
(a) Provide the appropriate 2–4 character aircraft type designator listed in FAA Order JO 7360.1, Aircraft Type Designators. FAA Order JO 7360.1 may be located at: Orders & Notices (faa .gov), then enter 7360.1 in the Search box.

(b) When there is no designator for the aircraft type use "ZZZZ", and provide a description in Item 18 TYP/.

3. Wake Turbulence Category (Item 9)
A Wake Turbulence Category is required for all aircraft types. Provide the appropriate wake turbulence category for the aircraft type as listed in FAA Order 7360.1. The categories include:

(a) J – SUPER, aircraft types specified as such in FAA Order JO 7360.1, Aircraft Type Designators.

(b) H – HEAVY, to indicate an aircraft type with a maximum certificated take-off mass of 300,000 lbs. or more, with the exception of aircraft types listed in FAA Order JO 7360.1 in the SUPER (J) category.

(c) M – MEDIUM, to indicate an aircraft type with a maximum certificated take-off mass of less than 300,000 lbs. but more than 15,500 lbs.

(d) L – LIGHT, to indicate an aircraft type with a maximum certificated take-off mass of 15,500 lbs. or less.

4. Aircraft Registration (Item 18 REG/)
The aircraft registration must be provided here if different from the Item 7 entry. The registration mark must not include any spaces or hyphens. Additionally, the actual aircraft registration must also be included if Item 7 would have contained a leading numeric and was modified to be prefixed with the appropriate alphabetic character for U.S. ATC acceptance.

Example:
U.S. aircraft with registration N789AK
REG/N789AK
Belgian aircraft with registration OO-FAH
REG/OOFAH

5. Mode S Address (Item 18 CODE/)
There is no U.S. requirement to file the aircraft Mode S Code in Item 18.

6. SELCAL code (Item 18 SEL/)
(a) Flights with HF radio and Selective Calling capability should include their 4-letter SELCAL code. Per the U.S. AIP, GEN 3.4, Paragraph 9, Selective Calling System (SELCAL) Facilities Available.

(b) The SELCAL is a communication system that permits the selective calling of individual aircraft over radio-telephone channels from the ground station to properly equipped aircraft, to eliminate the need for the flight crew to constantly monitor the frequency in use.

Example: SEL/CLEF

7. Performance Category (Item 18 PER/)
Include the appropriate single-letter Aircraft Approach Category as defined in the Pilot/Controller Glossary.

Example: PER/A

TABLE 4–20
FLIGHT ROUTING INFORMATION

Item	International Flight Plan (FAA Form 7233-4)	Domestic U.S. Requirements	Equivalent Item on Domestic Flight Plan (FAA Form 7233-1)
Departure Airport	Item 13	Required	Item 2
Departure Time	Item 13	Required	Item 1
Cruise Speed	Item 15	Required	N/A
Requested Altitude	Item 15	Required	Item 3
Route	Item 15	Required	N/A
Delay En Route	Item 15, Item 18 DLE/	Required	N/A
Destination Airport	Item 16	Required	Item 11
Total Estimated Elapsed Time	Item 16	Required	Item
Alternate Airport	Item 16 Item 18 ALTN/ (Destination Alternate).	If necessary	N/A
	RALT/ (En route Alternate); TALT/ (Take-off Alternate)	No need to file for domestic U.S. flight	
Estimated Elapsed Times	Item 18 EET/	Include when filing flight plan with center other than departure center	N/A

f. Instructions for Flight Routing Items
1. Departure Airport (Item 13, Item 18 DEP/)
(a) Enter the departure airport. The airport should be identified using the four-letter location identifier from FAA Order JO 7350.9, Location Identifiers, or from ICAO Document 7910. FSS and FAA contracted flight plan filing services will allow up to 11 characters in the departure field. This will permit entry of non-ICAO identifier airports, and other fixes such as an intersection, fix/radial/distance, and latitude/longitude coordinates. Other electronic filing services may require a different format.

Note: While user interfaces for flight plan filing are not specified, all flight plan filing services must adhere to the appropriate Interface Control Document upon transmission of the flight plan to the control facility.

(b) When the intended departure airport (Item 13) is outside of domestic U.S. airspace, or if using the paper version of FAA Form 7233-4, or DOD equivalent, if the chosen flight plan filing service does not allow non-ICAO airport identifiers in Item 13 or Item 16, use the following ICAO procedure. Enter four Z's (ZZZZ) in Item 13 and include the non-ICAO airport location identifier, fix, or waypoint location in Item 18 DEP/. A text description following the location identifier is permissible in Item 18 DEP/.

Note: Use of non-ICAO identifiers in Item 13 and Item 16 is only permissible when flight destination is within U.S. airspace. If the destination is outside of the U.S., then both Item 13 and Item 16 must contain either a valid ICAO airport identifier or ZZZZ. Use of non-ICAO departure point is not permitted in Item 13 if destination in Item 16 is outside of U.S.

APP

Example:
DEP/MD21
DEP/W29 BAY BRIDGE AIRPORT
DEP/EMI211017
DEP/3925N07722W

2. Departure Time (Item 13)
Indicate the expected departure time using 4 digits, 2 digits for hours and 2 digits for minutes. Time is to be entered as Coordinated Universal Time (UTC).

3. Requested Cruising Speed (Item 15)
(a) Include the requested cruising speed as True Airspeed in knots using an N followed by four digits.

Example: N0450

(b) Indicate the requested cruising speed in Mach using an M followed by three digits.

Example: M081

4. Requested Cruising Altitude or Flight Level (Item 15)
(a) Indicate a Requested Flight Level using the letter F followed by 3 digits.

Example: F350

(b) Indicate a Requested Altitude in hundreds of feet using the letter A followed by 3 digits.

Example: A080

5. Route (Item 15)
Provide the requested route of flight using a combination of published routes, latitude/longitude, and/or fixes in the following formats.

(a) Consecutive fixes, lat/long points, NAVAIDs, and waypoints should be separated by the characters "DCT", meaning direct.

Example:
FLACK DCT IRW DCT IRW12503
4020N07205W DCT MONEY

(b) A published route should be preceded by a fix that is published on the route, indicating where the route will be joined. The published route should be followed by a fix that is published as part of the route, indicating where the route will be exited.

Example: DALL3 EIC V18 MEI LGC4

(c) It is acceptable to specify intended speed and altitude changes along the route by appending an oblique stroke followed by the next speed and altitude. However, note that FAA ATC systems will neither process this information nor display it to ATC personnel. Pilots are expected to maintain the last assigned altitude and request revised altitude clearances from ATC.

Example: DCT APN J177 LEXOR/N0467F380 J177 TAM/N0464F390 J177

6. Delay En Route (Item 15, Item 18 DLE/)

(a) ICAO defines Item 18 DLE/ to provide information about a delay en route. International flights with a delay outside U.S. domestic airspace should indicate the place and duration of the delay in Item 18 DLE/. The delay is expressed by a fix identifier followed by the duration in hours (H) and minutes (M), HHMM.

Example: DLE/EMI0140

(b) U.S. ATC systems will accept but not process information in DLE/. Therefore, for flights in the lower 48 states, it is preferable to include the delay as part of the route (Item 15). Delay in this format is specified by an oblique stroke (/) followed by the letter D, followed by 2 digits for hours (H) of delay, followed by a plus sign (+), followed by 2 digits for minutes (M) of delay: /DHH+MM.

Example: DCT EMI/D01+40 DCT MAPEL/D00+30 V143 DELRO DCT

7. Destination Airport (Item 16, Item 18 DEST/)
(a) Enter the destination airport. The airport should be identified using the four-letter location identifier from FAA Order JO 7350.9, Location Identifiers, or from ICAO Document 7910. FSS and FAA contracted flight plan filing services will allow up to 11 characters in the destination field. This will permit entry of non-ICAO identifier airports, and other fixes such as an intersection, fix/radial/distance, and latitude/longitude coordinates. Other electronic filing services may require a different format.

Note: While user interfaces for flight plan filing are not specified, all flight plan filing services must adhere to the appropriate Interface Control Document upon transmission of the flight plan to the control facility.

(b) When the intended destination (Item 16) is outside of domestic U.S. airspace, or if using the paper version of FAA Form 7233-4, or if the chosen flight plan filing service does not allow non-ICAO airport identifiers in Item 13 or Item 16, use the following ICAO procedure. Enter four Z's (ZZZZ) in Item 13 and include the non-ICAO airport location identifier, fix, or waypoint location in Item 18 DEP/. A text description following the location identifier is permissible in Item 18 DEP/.

Example:
DEST/06A MOTON FIELD
DEST/4AK6
DEST/MONTK
DEST /3925N07722W

8. Total Estimated Elapsed Time (Item 16)
All flight plans must include the total estimated elapsed time from departure to destination in hours (H) and minutes (M), format HHMM.

9. Alternate Airport (Item 16, Item 18 ALTN/)

(a) When necessary, specify an alternate airport in Item 16 using the four-letter location identifier from FAA Order 7350.9 or ICAO Document 7910. When the airport does not have a four-letter location identifier, include ZZZZ in Item 16c and file the non-standard identifier in Item 18 ALTN/.

(b) While the FAA does not require filing of alternate airports in the flight plan provided to ATC, rules for establishing alternate airports must be followed.

(c) Adding an alternate may assist during Search and Rescue by identifying additional areas to search.

(d) Although alternate airport information filed in a flight plan will be accepted by air traffic computer systems, it will not be presented to controllers. If diversion to an alternate airport becomes necessary, pilots are expected to notify ATC and request an amended clearance.

Example: ALTN/W50 2W2

10. Estimated Elapsed Times (EET) at boundaries or reporting points (Item 18 EET/)
EETs are required for international or oceanic flights when crossing a Flight Information Region (FIR) boundary. The EET will include the ICAO four-letter location identifier for the FIR followed by the elapsed time to the FIR boundary (e.g., KZNY0245 indicates 2 hours, 45 minutes from departure until the New York FIR boundary).

Example: EET/MMFR0011 MMTY0039 KZAB0105

11. Remarks (Item 18 RMK/)
Enter only those remarks pertinent to ATC or to the clarification of other flight plan information. Items of a personal nature are not accepted.

Note 1: "DVRSN" should be placed in Item 11 only if the pilot/company is requesting priority handling to their original destination from ATC as a result of a diversion as defined in the Pilot/Controller Glossary.

Note 2: Do not assume that remarks will be automatically transmitted to every controller. Specific ATC or en route requests should be made directly to the appropriate controller.

g. Flight Specific Supplemental Information (Item 19)

1. Item 19 data must be included when completing FAA Form 7233-4. This information will be retained by the facility/organization that transmits the flight plan to Air Traffic Control (ATC), for Search and Rescue purposes, but it will not be transmitted to ATC as part of the flight plan.

2. Do not include Supplemental Information as part of Item 18. The information in Item 19 is retained with the flight plan filing service for retrieval only if necessary.

Note: Supplemental Information within Item 19 will be transmitted as a separate message to the destination FSS for VFR flight plans filed with a FSS or FAA contracted flight plan filing service. This will reduce the time necessary to conduct SAR actions should the flight become overdue, as this information will be readily available to the destination Flight Service Station.

3. Minimum required Item 19 entries for a domestic flight are Endurance, Persons on Board, Pilot Name and Contact Information, and Color of Aircraft. Additional entries may be required by foreign air traffic services, or at pilot discretion.

(a) After E/ Enter fuel endurance time in hours and minutes.

(b) After P/ Enter total number of persons on board using up to 30 alphanumeric characters. Enter TBN (to be notified) if the total number of persons is not known at the time of filing.

Example:
P/005
P/TBN
P/ON FILE CAPEAIR OPERATIONS

(c) R/ (Radio) Cross out items not carried
(d) S/ (Survival Equipment) Cross out items not carried.

(e) J/ (Jackets) Cross out items not carried.
(f) D/ (Life Raft/Dinghies) Enter number carried and total capacity. Indicate if covered and color.

(g) A/ (Aircraft Color and Markings) Enter aircraft color(s).

Example: White Yellow Blue

4. N/ (Remarks. Not for ATC) select N if no remarks. Enter comments concerning survival equipment and information concerning personal GPS locating service, if utilized. Enter name and contact information for responsible party to verify VFR arrival/closure, if desired. Ensure party will be available for contact at ETA. (for example; FBO is open at ETA)

5. C/ (Pilot) Enter name and contact information, including telephone number, of pilot-in-command. Ensure contact information will be valid at ETA in case SAR is necessary.

APP

FIGURE 4–1
FAA Form 7233-4, Pre-Flight Pilot Checklist and International Flight Plan

PRIVACY ACT STATEMENT: This statement is provided pursuant to the Privacy Act of 1974, 5 USC § 552a: The authority for collecting this information is contained in 49 U.S.C. §§ 40113, 44702, 44703, 44709, and 14 C.F.R. Part 6 - [Part 61, 63, 65, or 67. The principal purpose for which the information is intended to be used is to allow you to submit your flight plan. Submission of the data is voluntary. Failure to provide all required information may result in you not being able to submit your flight plan. The information collected on this form will be included in a Privacy Act System of Records known as DOT/FAA 847, titled "Aviation Records on Individuals" and will be subject to the routine uses published in the System of Records Notice (SORN) for DOT/FAA 847 (see www.dot.gov/privacy/privacyactnotices).

Paperwork Reduction Act Statement: A federal agency may not conduct or sponsor, and a person is not required to respond to, nor shall a person be subject to a penalty for failure to comply with a collection of information subject to the requirements of the Paperwork Reduction Act unless that collection of information displays a currently valid OMB Control Number. The OMB Control Number for this information collection is 2120-0026. Public reporting for this collection of information is estimated to be approximately 2.5 minutes per response, including the time for reviewing instructions, searching existing data sources, gathering and maintaining the data needed, completing and reviewing the collection of information. All responses to this collection of information are required to obtain or retain a benefit per 14 CFR Part 91. Send comments regarding this burden estimate or any other aspect of this collection of information, including suggestions for reducing this burden to the FAA at: 800 Independence Ave. SW, Washington, DC 20591, Attn: Information Collection Clearance Officer, ASP-110.

Pre-Flight Pilot Checklist

Aircraft Identification			Time of Briefing				
Weather *(Destination) (Alternate)*	☐ Present	Remarks	**Report Weather Conditions Aloft**				
	☐ Forecast		*Report immediately weather conditions encountered---particularly cloud tops, upper cloud layers, thunderstorms, ice, turbulence, winds and temperature*				
			Position	Altitude	Time	Weather Conditions	
Weather *(En Route)*	☐ Present						
	☐ Forecast						
	☐ Pireps						
Winds Aloft	Best Crzg. Alt.						
Nav. Aid & Comm. Status.	☐ Destination						
	☐ En Route						
Airport Conditions	☐ Destination						
	☐ Alternate						
ADIZ	☐ Airspace Restrictions						

Civil Aircraft Pilots

FAR Part 91 states that each person operating a civil aircraft of U.S. registry over the high seas shall comply with Annex 2 to the Convention of International Civil Aviation, International Standards - Rules of the Air. Annex 2 requires the submission of a flight plan containing items 1-1 9 prior to operating any flight across international waters. Failure to file could result in a civil penalty not to exceed $1,000 for each violation (Section 901 of the Federal Aviation Act of 1958, as amended).

International briefing information may not be current or complete. Data should be secured, at the first opportunity, from the country in whose airspace the flight will be conducted.

International Flight Plan

U S Department of Transportation
Federal Aviation Administration

PRIORITY　　ADDRESSEE(S)

<=FF

FILING TIME　　　　ORIGINATOR

<=

SPECIFIC IDENTIFICATION OF ADDRESSEE(S) AND / OR ORIGINATOR

3 MESSAGE TYPE　　7 AIRCRAFT IDENTIFICATION　　　8 FLIGHT RULES　　TYPE OF FLIGHT

<=(FPL　　　　　　　　　　　　　　　　　　　　　　　　　　　　　　　<=

9 NUMBER　　TYPE OF AIRCRAFT　　WAKE TURBULENCE CAT.　　10 EQUIPMENT

/　　　　　　　　　　/　　<=

13 DEPARTURE AERODROME　　　TIME

<=

15 CRUISING SPEED　　LEVEL　　ROUTE

<=

TOTAL EET

16 DESTINATION AERODROME　　HR　MIN　　ALTN AERODROME　　2ND ALTN AERODROME

<=

18 OTHER INFORMATION

<=

SUPPLEMENTARY INFORMATION (NOT TO BE TRANSMITTED IN FPL MESSAGES)

19 ENDURANCE　　　　　　　　　　　　　　　　　EMERGENCY RADIO

HR　MIN　　PERSONS ON BOARD　　　　　　UHF　VHF　ELT

—E/　　　　　　P/　　　　　　　　　　　R/ [U] [V] [E]

SURVIVAL EQUIPMENT　　　　　　JACKETS

POLAR DESERT MARITIME JUNGLE　　　LIGHT FLUORES UHF　VHF

[] / [P] [D] [M] [J]　　　[] / [L] [F] [U] [V]

DINGHIES

NUMBER CAPACITY COVER　　COLOR

[D] / [] [] [C] []　　<=

AIRCRAFT COLOR AND MARKINGS

A/

REMARKS

[N] /　　　　　　　　　　　　　　　　　<=

PILOT-IN-COMMAND

C/　　　　　　　　　　　)<=

FILED BY　　　　ACCEPTED BY　　　ADDITIONAL INFORMATION

FAA Form 7233-4 (7/15)

APP

Note: *Current FAA Form 7233-4 available at https://www.faa.gov/forms/.*

Appendix 5
FAA Form 7233-1—Flight Plan

Throughout this document where references are made to FAA Form 7233-1, Flight Plan, and FAA Form 7233-4, International Flight Plan, DOD use of the equivalent DOD Forms 175 and 1801 respectively, are implied and acceptable. Within U.S. controlled air space, FAA Form 7233-1, Flight Plan, may be used by filers of DOD/military flight plans and civilian stereo route flight plans. Use of the international format flight plan format is mandatory for:

a. Any flight plan filed through a FSS or FAA contracted flight plan filing service; with the exception of Department of Defense flight plans and civilian stereo route flight plans, which can still be filed using the format prescribed in FAA Form 7233-1.

Note: DOD Form DD-175 and FAA Form 7233-1 are considered to follow the same format.

b. Any flight that will depart U.S. domestic airspace. For DOD flight plan purposes, offshore Warning Areas may use FAA Form 7233-1 or military equivalent.

c. Any flight requesting routing that requires Performance Based Navigation.

d. Any flight requesting services that require filing of capabilities only supported in the international flight plan format.

Note: The order of flight plan elements in FAA Form 7233-1 is equivalent to the DD-175.

e. Explanation of IFR/VFR Flight Plan Items.
 (1) Block 1. Check the type of flight plan.
 (2) Block 2. Enter your complete aircraft identification.
 (3) Block 3. Enter the aircraft type.
 (4) Block 4. Enter the true airspeed (TAS).
 (5) Block 5. Enter the departure airport identifier.
 (6) Block 6. Enter the proposed departure time in Zulu (Z). If airborne, specify the actual or proposed departure time as appropriate.
 (7) Block 7. Enter the appropriate altitude.
 (8) Block 8. Define the route of flight by using NAVAID identifier codes and airways.
 (9) Block 9. Enter the destination airport identifier code.
 (10) Block 10. Enter the estimated time en route in hours and minutes.
 (11) Block 11. Enter remarks, if necessary.
 (12) Block 12. Specify the fuel on board in hours and minutes.
 (13) Block 13. Specify an alternate airport if desired.
 (14) Block 14. Enter name and contact information for pilot in command.

Note: This information is essential in the event of search and rescue operations.

 (15) Block 15. Enter total number of persons on board (POB) including crew.
 (16) Block 16. Enter the aircraft color.

FIGURE 5–1
FAA Form 7233-1—Flight Plan
For Military/DoD, Civilian Stereo Route Flight Plan Use Only

Note: Current FAA Form 7233-1 available at https://www.faa.gov/forms/.

Pilot/Controller Glossary

PURPOSE

a. This Glossary was compiled to promote a common understanding of the terms used in the Air Traffic Control system. It includes those terms which are intended for pilot/controller communications. Those terms most frequently used in pilot/controller communications are printed in **bold italics**. The definitions are primarily defined in an operational sense applicable to both users and operators of the National Airspace System. Use of the Glossary will preclude any misunderstandings concerning the system's design, function, and purpose.

b. Because of the international nature of flying, terms used in the Lexicon, published by the International Civil Aviation Organization (ICAO), are included when they differ from FAA definitions. These terms are followed by "[ICAO]." For the reader's convenience, there are also cross references to related terms in other parts of the Glossary and to other documents, such as the Code of Federal Regulations (CFR) and the Aeronautical Information Manual (AIM).

c. Terms used in this glossary that apply to flight service station (FSS) roles are included when they differ from air traffic control functions. These terms are followed by "[FSS]."

d. This Glossary will be revised, as necessary, to maintain a common understanding of the system.

EXPLANATION OF CHANGES

e. Terms Added:
AUTOMATED SERVICES
CHART SUPPLEMENT
CHART SUPPLEMENT ALASKA
CHART SUPPLEMENT PACIFIC
ENHANCED SPECIAL REPORTING SERVICE
FLIGHT DATA
INFLIGHT SERVICES
SE SAR
SPECIALIST-PROVIDED SERVICES
SURVEILLANCE ENHANCED SEARCH AND RESCUE

f. Terms Modified:
AERONAUTICAL INFORMATION PUBLICATION (AIP)
AIR TRAFFIC CONTROL SYSTEM COMMAND CENTER (ATCSCC)
ALPHANUMERIC DISPLAY
ALTITUDE READOUT
AUTOMATED UNICOM
CHART SUPPLEMENT U.S.
NAVAID CLASSES
PILOT BRIEFING
PRECIPITATION RADAR WEATHER DESCRIPTIONS
ROUTE ACTION NOTIFICATION
SAFETY LOGIC SYSTEM ALERTS
TERMINAL VFR RADAR SERVICE
TIE-IN FACILITY
TRAFFIC PATTERN
UNICOM
VOT

g. Editorial/format changes were made where necessary. Revision bars were not used due to the insignificant nature of the changes.

P/C

A

AAM. (See ADVANCED AIR MOBILITY.)

AAR. (See AIRPORT ARRIVAL RATE.)
(See ADAPTED ROUTES.)

ABBREVIATED IFR FLIGHT PLANS. An authorization by ATC requiring pilots to submit only that information needed for the purpose of ATC. It includes only a small portion of the usual IFR flight plan information. In certain instances, this may be only aircraft identification, location, and pilot request. Other information may be requested if needed by ATC for separation/control purposes. It is frequently used by aircraft which are airborne and desire an instrument approach or by aircraft which are on the ground and desire a climb to VFR-on-top. (See VFR-ON-TOP.) (Refer to AIM.)

ABEAM. An aircraft is "abeam" a fix, point, or object when that fix, point, or object is approximately 90 degrees to the right or left of the aircraft track. Abeam indicates a general position rather than a precise point.

ABORT. To terminate a preplanned aircraft maneuver; e.g., an aborted takeoff.

ABRR. (See AIRBORNE REROUTE)

AC. (See ADVISORY CIRCULAR.)

ACC [ICAO]. (See ICAO term AREA CONTROL CENTER.)

ACCELERATE-STOP DISTANCE AVAILABLE. The runway plus stopway length declared available and suitable for the acceleration and deceleration of an airplane aborting a takeoff.

ACCELERATE-STOP DISTANCE AVAILABLE [ICAO]. The length of the take-off run available plus the length of the stopway if provided.

ACDO. (See AIR CARRIER DISTRICT OFFICE.)

ACKNOWLEDGE. Let me know that you have received and understood this message.

ACL. (See AIRCRAFT LIST.)

ACLS. (See AUTOMATIC CARRIER LANDING SYSTEM.)

ACROBATIC FLIGHT. An intentional maneuver involving an abrupt change in an aircraft's attitude, an abnormal attitude, or abnormal acceleration not necessary for normal flight. (See ICAO term ACROBATIC FLIGHT.) (Refer to 14 CFR Part 91.)

ACROBATIC FLIGHT [ICAO]. Maneuvers intentionally performed by an aircraft involving an abrupt change in its attitude, an abnormal attitude, or an abnormal variation in speed.

ACTIVE RUNWAY. (See RUNWAY IN USE/ACTIVE RUNWAY/DUTY RUNWAY.)

ACTUAL NAVIGATION PERFORMANCE (ANP). (See REQUIRED NAVIGATION PERFORMANCE.)

ADAPTED ROUTES. Departure and/or arrival routes that are adapted in ARTCC ERAM computers to accomplish inter/intrafacility controller coordination and to ensure that flight data is posted at the proper control positions. Adapted routes are automatically applied to flight plans where appropriate. When the workload or traffic situation permits, controllers may provide radar vectors or assign requested routes to minimize circuitous routing. Adapted routes are usually confined to one ARTCC's area and are referred to by the following names or abbreviations:

a. Adapted Arrival Route (AAR). A specific arrival route from an appropriate en route point to an airport or terminal area. It may be included in a Standard Terminal Arrival (STAR) or a Preferred IFR Route.

b. Adapted Departure Route (ADR). A specific departure route from an airport or terminal area to an en route point where there is no further need for flow control. It may be included in an Instrument Departure Procedure (DP) or a Preferred IFR Route.

c. Adapted Departure and Arrival Route (ADAR). A route between two terminals which are within or immediately adjacent to one ARTCC's area. ADARs are similar to Preferred IFR Routes and may share components, but they are not synonymous.
(See PREFFERED IFR ROUTES.)

ADAR. (See ADAPTED ROUTES.)

ADDITIONAL SERVICES. Advisory information provided by ATC which includes but is not limited to the following:

a. Traffic advisories.

b. Vectors, when requested by the pilot, to assist aircraft receiving traffic advisories to avoid observed traffic.

c. Altitude deviation information of 300 feet or more from an assigned altitude as observed on a verified (reading correctly) automatic altitude readout (Mode C).

d. Advisories that traffic is no longer a factor.

e. Weather and chaff information.

f. Weather assistance.

g. Bird activity information.

h. Holding pattern surveillance. Additional services are provided to the extent possible contingent only upon the controller's capability to fit them into the performance of higher priority duties and on the basis of limitations of the radar, volume of traffic, frequency congestion, and controller workload. The controller has complete discretion for determining if he/she is able to provide or continue to provide a service in a particular case. The controller's reason not to provide or continue to provide a service in a particular case is not subject to question by the pilot and need not be made known to him/her.
(See TRAFFIC ADVISORIES.) (Refer to AIM.)

ADF. (See AUTOMATIC DIRECTION FINDER.)

ADIZ. (See AIR DEFENSE IDENTIFICATION ZONE.)

ADLY. (See ARRIVAL DELAY.)

ADMINISTRATOR. The Federal Aviation Administrator or any person to whom he/she has delegated his/her authority in the matter concerned.

ADR. (See ADAPTED ROUTES.) (See AIRPORT DEPARTURE RATE.)

ADS [ICAO]. (See ICAO term AUTOMATIC DEPENDENT SURVEILLANCE.)

ADS-B. (See AUTOMATIC DEPENDENT SURVEILLANCE–BROADCAST.)

ADS-C. (See AUTOMATIC DEPENDENT SURVEILLANCE–CONTRACT.)

ADVANCED AIR MOBILITY (AAM). A transportation system that transports people and property by air between two points in the NAS using aircraft with advanced technologies, including electric aircraft or electric vertical takeoff and landing aircraft, in both controlled and uncontrolled airspace.

ADVISE INTENTIONS. Tell me what you plan to do.

ADVISORY. Advice and information provided to assist pilots in the safe conduct of flight and aircraft movement. (See ADVISORY SERVICE.)

ADVISORY CIRCULAR (AC). An FAA publication, advisory and descriptive in nature, which is not regulatory.

ADVISORY FREQUENCY. The appropriate frequency to be used for Airport Advisory Service. (See LOCAL AIRPORT ADVISORY.) (See UNICOM.) (Refer to ADVISORY CIRCULAR NO. 90-66.) (Refer to AIM.)

ADVISORY SERVICE. Advice and information provided by a facility to assist pilots in the safe conduct of flight and aircraft movement. (See ADDITIONAL SERVICES.) (See LOCAL AIRPORT ADVISORY.) (See RADAR ADVISORY.) (See SAFETY ALERT.) (See TRAFFIC ADVISORIES.) (Refer to AIM.)

ADW. (See ARRIVAL DEPARTURE WINDOW)

AERIAL REFUELING. A procedure used by the military to transfer fuel from one aircraft to another during flight. (Refer to VFR/IFR Wall Planning Charts.)

AERODROME. A defined area on land or water (including any buildings, installations and equipment) intended to be used either wholly or in part for the arrival, departure, and movement of aircraft.

AERODROME BEACON [ICAO]. Aeronautical beacon used to indicate the location of an aerodrome from the air.

AERODROME CONTROL SERVICE [ICAO]. Air traffic control service for aerodrome traffic.

AERODROME CONTROL TOWER [ICAO]. A unit established to provide air traffic control service to aerodrome traffic.

AERODROME ELEVATION [ICAO]. The elevation of the highest point of the landing area.

AERODROME TRAFFIC CIRCUIT [ICAO]. The specified path to be flown by aircraft operating in the vicinity of an aerodrome.

AERONAUTICAL BEACON. A visual NAVAID displaying flashes of white and/or colored light to indicate the location of an airport, a heliport, a landmark, a certain point of a Federal airway in mountainous terrain, or an obstruction. (See AIRPORT ROTATING BEACON.) (Refer to AIM.)

AERONAUTICAL CHART. A map used in air navigation containing all or part of the following: topographic features, hazards and obstructions, navigation aids, navigation routes, designated airspace, and airports. Commonly used aeronautical charts are:

a. Sectional Aeronautical Charts (1:500,000). Designed for visual navigation of slow or medium speed aircraft. Topographic information on these charts features the portrayal of relief and a judicious selection of visual check points for VFR flight. Aeronautical information includes visual and radio aids to navigation, airports, controlled airspace, permanent special use airspace (SUA), obstructions, and related data.

b. VFR Terminal Area Charts (1:250,000). Depict Class B airspace which provides for the control or segregation of all the aircraft within Class B airspace. The chart depicts topographic information and aeronautical information which includes visual and radio aids to navigation, airports, controlled airspace, permanent SUA, obstructions, and related data.

c. En Route Low Altitude Charts. Provide aeronautical information for en route instrument navigation (IFR) in the low altitude stratum. Information includes the portrayal of airways, limits of controlled airspace, position identification and frequencies of radio aids, selected airports, minimum en route and minimum obstruction clearance altitudes, airway distances, reporting points, permanent SUA, and related data. Area charts, which are a part of this series, furnish terminal data at a larger scale in congested areas.

d. En Route High Altitude Charts. Provide aeronautical information for en route instrument navigation (IFR) in the high altitude stratum. Information includes the portrayal of jet routes, identification and frequencies of radio aids, selected airports, distances, time zones, special use airspace, and related information.

e. Instrument Approach Procedure (IAP) Charts. Portray the aeronautical data which is required to execute an instrument approach to an airport. These charts depict the procedures, including all related data, and the airport diagram. Each procedure is designated for use with a specific type of electronic navigation system including NDB, TACAN, VOR, ILS RNAV and GLS. These charts are identified by the type of navigational aid(s)/equipment required to provide final approach guidance.

f. Instrument Departure Procedure (DP) Charts. Designed to expedite clearance delivery and to facilitate transition between takeoff and en route operations. Each DP is presented as a separate chart and may serve a single airport or more than one airport in a given geographical location.

(continued)

P/C

g. Standard Terminal Arrival (STAR) Charts. Designed to expedite air traffic control arrival procedures and to facilitate transition between en route and instrument approach operations. Each STAR procedure is presented as a separate chart and may serve a single airport or more than one airport in a given geographical location.

h. Airport Taxi Charts. Designed to expedite the efficient and safe flow of ground traffic at an airport. These charts are identified by the official airport name; e.g., Ronald Reagan Washington National Airport. (See ICAO term AERONAUTICAL CHART.)

AERONAUTICAL CHART [ICAO]. A representation of a portion of the earth, its culture and relief, specifically designated to meet the requirements of air navigation.

AERONAUTICAL INFORMATION MANUAL (AIM). A primary FAA publication whose purpose is to instruct airmen about operating in the National Airspace System of the U.S. It provides basic flight information, ATC Procedures and general instructional information concerning health, medical facts, factors affecting flight safety, accident and hazard reporting, and types of aeronautical charts and their use.

AERONAUTICAL INFORMATION PUBLICATION (AIP) [ICAO]. A publication issued by or with the authority of a State and containing aeronautical information of a lasting character essential to air navigation. (See CHART SUPPLEMENT.)

AERONAUTICAL INFORMATION SERVICES (AIS). A facility in Silver Spring, MD, established by FAA to operate a central aeronautical information service for the collection, validation, and dissemination of aeronautical data in support of the activities of government, industry, and the aviation community. The information is published in the National Flight Data Digest. (See NATIONAL FLIGHT DATA DIGEST.)

AFFIRMATIVE. Yes.

AFIS. (See AUTOMATIC FLIGHT INFORMATION SERVICE—ALASKA FSSs ONLY.)

AFP. (See AIRSPACE FLOW PROGRAM.)

AHA. (See AIRCRAFT HAZARD AREA.)

AIM. (See AERONAUTICAL INFORMATION MANUAL.)

AIP [ICAO]. (See ICAO term AERONAUTICAL INFORMATION PUBLICATION.)

AIR CARRIER DISTRICT OFFICE. An FAA field office serving an assigned geographical area, staffed with Flight Standards personnel serving the aviation industry and the general public on matters related to the certification and operation of scheduled air carriers and other large aircraft operations.

AIR DEFENSE EMERGENCY. A military emergency condition declared by a designated authority. This condition exists when an attack upon the continental U.S., Alaska, Canada, or U.S. installations in Greenland by hostile aircraft or missiles is considered probable, is imminent, or is taking place. (Refer to AIM.)

AIR DEFENSE IDENTIFICATION ZONE (ADIZ). An area of airspace over land or water in which the ready identification, location, and control of all aircraft (except for Department of Defense and law enforcement aircraft) is required in the interest of national security.

Note: ADIZ locations and operating and flight plan requirements for civil aircraft operations are specified in 14 CFR Part 99.
(Refer to AIM.)

AIR NAVIGATION FACILITY. Any facility used in, available for use in, or designed for use in, aid of air navigation, including landing areas, lights, any apparatus or equipment for disseminating weather information, for signaling, for radio-directional finding, or for radio or other electrical communication, and any other structure or mechanism having a similar purpose for guiding or controlling flight in the air or the landing and takeoff of aircraft. (See NAVIGATIONAL AID.)

AIR ROUTE SURVEILLANCE RADAR. Air route traffic control center (ARTCC) radar used primarily to detect and display an aircraft's position while en route between terminal areas. The ARSR enables controllers to provide radar air traffic control service when aircraft are within the ARSR coverage. In some instances, ARSR may enable an ARTCC to provide terminal radar services similar to but usually more limited than those provided by a radar approach control.

AIR ROUTE TRAFFIC CONTROL CENTER (ARTCC). A facility established to provide air traffic control service to aircraft operating on IFR flight plans within controlled airspace and principally during the en route phase of flight. When equipment capabilities and controller workload permit, certain advisory/assistance services may be provided to VFR aircraft. (See EN ROUTE AIR TRAFFIC CONTROL SERVICES.) (Refer to AIM.)

AIR TAXI. Used to describe a helicopter/VTOL aircraft movement conducted above the surface but normally not above 100 feet AGL. The aircraft may proceed either via hover taxi or flight at speeds more than 20 knots. The pilot is solely responsible for selecting a safe airspeed/altitude for the operation being conducted. (See HOVER TAXI.) (Refer to AIM.)

AIR TRAFFIC. Aircraft operating in the air or on an airport surface, exclusive of loading ramps and parking areas. (See ICAO term AIR TRAFFIC.)

AIR TRAFFIC [ICAO]. All aircraft in flight or operating on the maneuvering area of an aerodrome.

AIR TRAFFIC CLEARANCE. An authorization by air traffic control for the purpose of preventing collision between known aircraft, for an aircraft to proceed under specified traffic conditions within controlled airspace. The pilot-in-command of an aircraft may not deviate from the provisions of a visual flight rules (VFR) or instrument flight rules (IFR) air traffic clearance except in an emergency or unless an amended clearance has been obtained. Additionally, the pilot may request a different clearance from that which has

been issued by air traffic control (ATC) if information available to the pilot makes another course of action more practicable or if aircraft equipment limitations or company procedures forbid compliance with the clearance issued. Pilots may also request clarification or amendment, as appropriate, any time a clearance is not fully understood, or considered unacceptable because of safety of flight. Controllers should, in such instances and to the extent of operational practicality and safety, honor the pilot's request. 14 CFR Part 91.3(a) states: "The pilot in command of an aircraft is directly responsible for, and is the final authority as to, the operation of that aircraft." THE PILOT IS RESPONSIBLE TO REQUEST AN AMENDED CLEARANCE if ATC issues a clearance that would cause a pilot to deviate from a rule or regulation, or in the pilot's opinion, would place the aircraft in jeopardy. (See ATC INSTRUCTIONS.) (See ICAO term AIR TRAFFIC CONTROL CLEARANCE.)

AIR TRAFFIC CONTROL. A service operated by appropriate authority to promote the safe, orderly and expeditious flow of air traffic. (See ICAO term AIR TRAFFIC CONTROL SERVICE.)

AIR TRAFFIC CONTROL CLEARANCE [ICAO]. Authorization for an aircraft to proceed under conditions specified by an air traffic control unit.

Note 1: For convenience, the term air traffic control clearance is frequently abbreviated to clearance when used in appropriate contexts.

Note 2: The abbreviated term clearance may be prefixed by the words taxi, takeoff, departure, en route, approach or landing to indicate the particular portion of flight to which the air traffic control clearance relates.

AIR TRAFFIC CONTROL SERVICE.
(See AIR TRAFFIC CONTROL.)

AIR TRAFFIC CONTROL SERVICE [ICAO]. A service provided for the purpose of:
a. Preventing collisions:
1. Between aircraft; and
2. On the maneuvering area between aircraft and obstructions.
b. Expediting and maintaining an orderly flow of air traffic.

AIR TRAFFIC CONTROL SPECIALIST. A person authorized to provide air traffic control service. (See AIR TRAFFIC CONTROL.) (See FLIGHT SERVICE STATION.) (See ICAO term CONTROLLER.)

AIR TRAFFIC CONTROL SYSTEM COMMAND CENTER (ATCSCC). An Air Traffic Tactical Operations facility responsible for monitoring and managing the flow of air traffic throughout the NAS, producing a safe, orderly, and expeditious flow of traffic while minimizing delays. The following functions are located at the ATCSCC.
a. Central Altitude Reservation Function (CARF). Responsible for coordinating, planning, and approving special user requirements under the Altitude Reservation (ALTRV) concept. (See ALTITUDE RESERVATION)

b. Airport Reservation Office (ARO). Monitors the operation and allocation of reservations for unscheduled operations at airports designated by the Administrator as High Density Airports. These airports are generally known as slot controlled airports. The ARO allocates reservations on a first come, first served basis determined by the time the request is received at the ARO. (Refer to 14 CFR Part 93.) (See CHART SUPPLEMENT.)

c. U.S. Notice to Air Missions (NOTAM) Office. Responsible for collecting, maintaining, and distributing NOTAMs for the U.S. civilian and military, as well as international aviation communities. (See NOTICE TO AIR MISSIONS)

d. Weather Unit. Monitor all aspects of weather for the U.S. that might affect aviation including cloud cover, visibility, winds, precipitation, thunderstorms, icing, turbulence, and more. Provide forecasts based on observations and on discussions with meteorologists from various National Weather Service offices, FAA facilities, airlines, and private weather services.

e. Air Traffic Organization (ATO) Space Operations and Unmanned Aircraft System (UAS); the Office of Primary Responsibility (OPR) for all space and upper class E tactical operations in the National Airspace System (NAS).

AIR TRAFFIC SERVICE. A generic term meaning:
a. Flight Information Service.
b. Alerting Service.
c. Air Traffic Advisory Service.
d. Air Traffic Control Service:
1. Area Control Service,
2. Approach Control Service, or
3. Airport Control Service.

AIR TRAFFIC ORGANIZATION (ATO). The FAA line of business responsible for providing safe and efficient air navigation services in the national airspace system.

AIR TRAFFIC SERVICE (ATS) ROUTES. The term "ATS Route" is a generic term that includes "VOR Federal airways," "colored Federal airways," "jet routes," and "RNAV routes." The term "ATS route" does not replace these more familiar route names, but serves only as an overall title when listing the types of routes that comprise the United States route structure.

AIRBORNE. An aircraft is considered airborne when all parts of the aircraft are off the ground.

AIRBORNE DELAY. Amount of delay to be encountered in airborne holding.

AIRBORNE REROUTE (ABRR). A capability within the Traffic Flow Management System used for the timely development and implementation of tactical reroutes for airborne aircraft. This capability defines a set of aircraft-specific reroutes that address a certain traffic flow problem and then electronically transmits them to En Route Automation Modernization (ERAM) for execution by the appropriate sector controllers.

AIRCRAFT. Device(s) that are used or intended to be used for flight in the air, and when used in air traffic control terminology, may include the flight crew. (See ICAO term AIRCRAFT.)

P/C

AIRCRAFT [ICAO]. Any machine that can derive support in the atmosphere from the reactions of the air other than the reactions of the air against the earth's surface.

AIRCRAFT APPROACH CATEGORY. A grouping of aircraft based on a speed of 1.3 times the stall speed in the landing configuration at maximum gross landing weight. An aircraft must fit in only one category. If it is necessary to maneuver at speeds in excess of the upper limit of a speed range for a category, the minimums for the category for that speed must be used. For example, an aircraft which falls in Category A, but is circling to land at a speed in excess of 91 knots, must use the approach Category B minimums when circling to land. The categories are as follows:

a. Category A. Speed less than 91 knots.

b. Category B. Speed 91 knots or more but less than 121 knots.

c. Category C. Speed 121 knots or more but less than 141 knots.

d. Category D. Speed 141 knots or more but less than 166 knots.

e. Category E. Speed 166 knots or more. (Refer to 14 CFR Part 97.)

AIRCRAFT CLASSES. For the purposes of Wake Turbulence Separation Minima, ATC classifies aircraft as Super, Heavy, Large, and Small as follows:

a. Super. The Airbus A-380-800 (A388) and the Antonov An-225 (A225) are classified as super.

b. Heavy. Aircraft capable of takeoff weights of 300,000 pounds or more whether or not they are operating at this weight during a particular phase of flight.

c. Large. Aircraft of more than 41,000 pounds, maximum certificated takeoff weight, up to but not including 300,000 pounds.

d. Small. Aircraft of 41,000 pounds or less maximum certificated takeoff weight.
(Refer to AIM.)

AIRCRAFT CONFLICT. Predicted conflict, within EDST of two aircraft, or between aircraft and airspace. A Red alert is used for conflicts when the predicted minimum separation is 5 nautical miles or less. A Yellow alert is used when the predicted minimum separation is between 5 and approximately 12 nautical miles. A Blue alert is used for conflicts between an aircraft and predefined airspace.
(See EN ROUTE DECISION SUPPORT TOOL.)

AIRCRAFT HAZARD AREA (AHA). Used by ATC to segregate air traffic from a launch vehicle, reentry vehicle, amateur rocket, jettisoned stages, hardware, or falling debris generated by failures associated with any of these activities. An AHA is designated via NOTAM as either a TFR or stationary ALTRV. Unless otherwise specified, the vertical limits of an AHA are from the surface to unlimited.
(See CONTINGENCY HAZARD AREA.) (See REFINED HAZARD AREA.) (See TRANSITIONAL HAZARD AREA.)

AIRCRAFT LIST (ACL). A view available with EDST that lists aircraft currently in or predicted to be in a particular sector's airspace. The view contains textual flight data information in line format and may be sorted into various orders based on the specific needs of the sector team.
(See EN ROUTE DECISION SUPPORT TOOL.)

AIRCRAFT SURGE LAUNCH AND RECOVERY. Procedures used at USAF bases to provide increased launch and recovery rates in instrument flight rules conditions. ASLAR is based on:

a. Reduced separation between aircraft which is based on time or distance. Standard arrival separation applies between participants including multiple flights until the DRAG point. The DRAG point is a published location on an ASLAR approach where aircraft landing second in a formation slows to a predetermined airspeed. The DRAG point is the reference point at which MARSA applies as expanding elements effect separation within a flight or between subsequent participating flights.

b. ASLAR procedures shall be covered in a Letter of Agreement between the responsible USAF military ATC facility and the concerned Federal Aviation Administration facility. Initial Approach Fix spacing requirements are normally addressed as a minimum.

AIRCRAFT WAKE TURBULENCE CATEGORIES. For the purpose of Wake Turbulence Recategorization (RECAT) Separation Minima, ATC groups aircraft into categories ranging from Category A through Category I, dependent upon the version of RECAT that is applied. Specific category assignments vary and are listed in the RECAT Orders.

AIRMEN'S METEOROLOGICAL INFORMATION (AIRMET). A concise description of an occurrence or expected occurrence of specified en route weather phenomena that may affect the safety of aircraft operations, but at intensities lower than those that require the issuance of a SIGMET. An AIRMET may be issued when any of the following weather phenomena are occurring or expected to occur:

a. Moderate turbulence

b. Low-level windshear

c. Strong surface winds greater than 30 knots

d. Moderate icing

e. Freezing level

f. Mountain obscuration

g. IFR
(See CONVECTIVE SIGMET.)(See CWA.)(See GRAPHICAL AIRMEN'S METEOROLOGICAL INFORMATION.)(See SAW.)(See SIGMET.)(Refer to AIM.)

AIRPORT. An area on land or water that is used or intended to be used for the landing and takeoff of aircraft and includes its buildings and facilities, if any.

AIRPORT ADVISORY AREA. The area within ten miles of an airport without a control tower or where the tower is not in operation, and on which a Flight Service Station is located. (See LOCAL AIRPORT ADVISORY.) (Refer to AIM.)

AIRPORT ARRIVAL RATE (AAR). A dynamic input parameter specifying the number of arriving aircraft which an airport or airspace can accept from the ARTCC per hour. The AAR is used to calculate the desired interval between successive arrival aircraft.

AIRPORT DEPARTURE RATE (ADR). A dynamic parameter specifying the number of aircraft which can depart an airport and the airspace can accept per hour.

AIRPORT ELEVATION. The highest point of an airport's usable runways measured in feet from mean sea level. (See TOUCHDOWN ZONE ELEVATION.) (See ICAO term AERODROME ELEVATION.)

AIRPORT LIGHTING. Various lighting aids that may be installed on an airport. Types of airport lighting include:

a. Approach Light System (ALS). An airport lighting facility which provides visual guidance to landing aircraft by radiating light beams in a directional pattern by which the pilot aligns the aircraft with the extended centerline of the runway on his/her final approach for landing. Condenser-Discharge Sequential Flashing Lights/Sequenced Flashing Lights may be installed in conjunction with the ALS at some airports. Types of Approach Light Systems are:

1. ALSF-1. Approach Light System with Sequenced Flashing Lights in ILS Cat-I configuration.

2. ALSF-2. Approach Light System with Sequenced Flashing Lights in ILS Cat-II configuration. The ALSF-2 may operate as an SSALR when weather conditions permit.

3. SSALF. Simplified Short Approach Light System with Sequenced Flashing Lights.

4. SSALR. Simplified Short Approach Light System with Runway Alignment Indicator Lights.

5. MALSF. Medium Intensity Approach Light System with Sequenced Flashing Lights.

6. MALSR. Medium Intensity Approach Light System with Runway Alignment Indicator Lights.

7. RLLS. Runway Lead-in Light System. Consists of one or more series of flashing lights installed at or near ground level that provides positive visual guidance along an approach path, either curving or straight, where special problems exist with hazardous terrain, obstructions, or noise abatement procedures.

8. RAIL. Runway Alignment Indicator Lights. Sequenced Flashing Lights which are installed only in combination with other light systems.

9. ODALS. Omnidirectional Approach Lighting System consists of seven omnidirectional flashing lights located in the approach area of a nonprecision runway. Five lights are located on the runway centerline extended with the first light located 300 feet from the threshold and extending at equal intervals up to 1,500 feet from the threshold. The other two lights are located, one on each side of the runway threshold, at a lateral distance of 40 feet from the runway edge, or 75 feet from the runway edge when installed on a runway equipped with a VASI. (Refer to FAA Order JO 6850.2, VISUAL GUIDANCE LIGHTING SYSTEMS.)

b. Runway Lights/Runway Edge Lights- Lights having a prescribed angle of emission used to define the lateral limits of a runway. Runway lights are uniformly spaced at intervals of approximately 200 feet, and the intensity may be controlled or preset.

c. Touchdown Zone Lighting. Two rows of transverse light bars located symmetrically about the runway centerline normally at 100 foot intervals. The basic system extends 3,000 feet along the runway.

d. Runway Centerline Lighting. Flush centerline lights spaced at 50-foot intervals beginning 75 feet from the landing threshold and extending to within 75 feet of the opposite end of the runway.

e. Threshold Lights- Fixed green lights arranged symmetrically left and right of the runway centerline, identifying the runway threshold.

f. Runway End Identifier Lights (REIL). Two synchronized flashing lights, one on each side of the runway threshold, which provide rapid and positive identification of the approach end of a particular runway.

g. Visual Approach Slope Indicator (VASI). An airport lighting facility providing vertical visual approach slope guidance to aircraft during approach to landing by radiating a directional pattern of high intensity red and white focused light beams which indicate to the pilot that he/she is "on path" if he/she sees red/white, "above path" if white/white, and "below path" if red/red. Some airports serving large aircraft have three-bar VASIs which provide two visual glide paths to the same runway.

h. Precision Approach Path Indicator (PAPI). An airport lighting facility, similar to VASI, providing vertical approach slope guidance to aircraft during approach to landing. PAPIs consist of a single row of either two or four lights, normally installed on the left side of the runway, and have an effective visual range of about 5 miles during the day and up to 20 miles at night. PAPIs radiate a directional pattern of high intensity red and white focused light beams which indicate that the pilot is "on path" if the pilot sees an equal number of white lights and red lights, with white to the left of the red; "above path" if the pilot sees more white than red lights; and "below path" if the pilot sees more red than white lights.

i. Boundary Lights. Lights defining the perimeter of an airport or landing area. (Refer to AIM.)

AIRPORT MARKING AIDS. Markings used on runway and taxiway surfaces to identify a specific runway, a runway threshold, a centerline, a hold line, etc. A runway should be marked in accordance with its present usage such as:

a. Visual.

b. Nonprecision instrument.

c. Precision instrument.

(Refer to AIM.)

AIRPORT REFERENCE POINT (ARP). The approximate geometric center of all usable runway surfaces.

AIRPORT RESERVATION OFFICE. Office responsible for monitoring the operation of slot controlled airports. It receives and processes requests for unscheduled operations at slot controlled airports.

P/C

AIRPORT ROTATING BEACON. A visual NAVAID operated at many airports. At civil airports, alternating white and green flashes indicate the location of the airport. At military airports, the beacons flash alternately white and green, but are differentiated from civil beacons by dualpeaked (two quick) white flashes between the green flashes. (See INSTRUMENT FLIGHT RULES.) (See SPECIAL VFR OPERATIONS.) (See ICAO term AERODROME BEACON.) (Refer to AIM.)

AIRPORT SURFACE DETECTION EQUIPMENT (ASDE). Surveillance equipment specifically designed to detect aircraft, vehicular traffic, and other objects, on the surface of an airport, and to present the image on a tower display. Used to augment visual observation by tower personnel of aircraft and/or vehicular movements on runways and taxiways. There are three ASDE systems deployed in the NAS:
 a. ASDE–3: A Surface Movement Radar.
 b. ASDE–X: A system that uses an X-band Surface Movement Radar, multilateration, and ADS-B.
 c. Airport Surface Surveillance Capability (ASSC): A system that uses Surface Movement Radar, multilateration, and ADS-B.

AIRPORT SURVEILLANCE RADAR. Approach control radar used to detect and display an aircraft's position in the terminal area. ASR provides range and azimuth information but does not provide elevation data. Coverage of the ASR can extend up to 60 miles.

AIRPORT TAXI CHARTS. (See AERONAUTICAL CHART.)

AIRPORT TRAFFIC CONTROL SERVICE. A service provided by a control tower for aircraft operating on the movement area and in the vicinity of an airport. (See MOVEMENT AREA.) (See TOWER.) (See ICAO term AERODROME CONTROL SERVICE.)

AIRPORT TRAFFIC CONTROL TOWER. (See TOWER.)

AIRSPACE CONFLICT. Predicted conflict of an aircraft and active Special Activity Airspace (SAA).

AIRSPACE FLOW PROGRAM (AFP). AFP is a Traffic Management (TM) process administered by the Air Traffic Control System Command Center (ATC-SCC) where aircraft are assigned an Expect Departure Clearance Time (EDCT) in order to manage capacity and demand for a specific area of the National Airspace System (NAS). The purpose of the program is to mitigate the effects of en route constraints. It is a flexible program and may be implemented in various forms depending upon the needs of the air traffic system.

AIRSPACE HIERARCHY. Within the airspace classes, there is a hierarchy and, in the event of an overlap of airspace: Class A preempts Class B, Class B preempts Class C, Class C preempts Class D, Class D preempts Class E, and Class E preempts Class G.

AIRSPEED. The speed of an aircraft relative to its surrounding air mass. The unqualified term "airspeed" means one of the following:

 a. Indicated Airspeed. The speed shown on the aircraft airspeed indicator. This is the speed used in pilot/controller communications under the general term "airspeed." (Refer to 14 CFR Part 1.)
 b. True Airspeed. The airspeed of an aircraft relative to undisturbed air. Used primarily in flight planning and en route portion of flight. When used in pilot/controller communications, it is referred to as "true airspeed" and not shortened to "airspeed."

AIRSPACE RESERVATION. The term used in oceanic ATC for airspace utilization under prescribed conditions normally employed for the mass movement of aircraft or other special user requirements which cannot otherwise be accomplished. Airspace reservations must be classified as either "moving" or "stationary." (See MOVING AIRSPACE RESERVATION.) (See STATIONARY AIRSPACE RESERVATION.) (See ALTITUDE RESERVATION.)

AIRSTART. The starting of an aircraft engine while the aircraft is airborne, preceded by engine shutdown during training flights or by actual engine failure.

AIRWAY. A Class E airspace area established in the form of a corridor, the centerline of which is defined by radio navigational aids. (See FEDERAL AIRWAYS.) (See ICAO term AIRWAY.) (Refer to 14 CFR Part 71.) (Refer to AIM.)

AIRWAY [ICAO]. A control area or portion thereof established in the form of corridor equipped with radio navigational aids.

AIRWAY BEACON. Used to mark airway segments in remote mountain areas. The light flashes Morse Code to identify the beacon site. (Refer to AIM.)

AIS. (See AERONAUTICAL INFORMATION SERVICES.)

AIT. (See AUTOMATED INFORMATION TRANSFER.)

ALERFA (Alert Phase) [ICAO]. A situation wherein apprehension exists as to the safety of an aircraft and its occupants.

ALERT. A notification to a position that there is an aircraft-to-aircraft or aircraft-to-airspace conflict, as detected by Automated Problem Detection (APD).

ALERT AREA. (See SPECIAL USE AIRSPACE.)

ALERT NOTICE (ALNOT). A request originated by a flight service station (FSS) or an air route traffic control center (ARTCC) for an extensive communication search for overdue, unreported, or missing aircraft.

ALERTING SERVICE. A service provided to notify appropriate organizations regarding aircraft in need of search and rescue aid and assist such organizations as required.

ALNOT. (See ALERT NOTICE.)

ALONG-TRACK DISTANCE (ATD). The horizontal distance between the aircraft's current position and a fix measured by an area navigation system that is not subject to slant range errors.

ALPHANUMERIC DISPLAY. Letters and numerals used to show identification, altitude, beacon code, and other information concerning a target on a radar display.

ALTERNATE AERODROME [ICAO]. An aerodrome to which an aircraft may proceed when it becomes either impossible or inadvisable to proceed to or to land at the aerodrome of intended landing.

Note: The aerodrome from which a flight departs may also be an en-route or a destination alternate aerodrome for the flight.

ALTERNATE AIRPORT. An airport at which an aircraft may land if a landing at the intended airport becomes inadvisable. (See ICAO term ALTERNATE AERODROME.)

ALTIMETER SETTING. The barometric pressure reading used to adjust a pressure altimeter for variations in existing atmospheric pressure or to the standard altimeter setting (29.92). (Refer to 14 CFR Part 91.) (Refer to AIM.)

ALTITUDE. The height of a level, point, or object measured in feet Above Ground Level (AGL) or from Mean Sea Level (MSL). (See FLIGHT LEVEL.)
 a. MSL Altitude. Altitude expressed in feet measured from mean sea level.
 b. AGL Altitude. Altitude expressed in feet measured above ground level.
 c. Indicated Altitude. The altitude as shown by an altimeter. On a pressure or barometric altimeter it is altitude as shown uncorrected for instrument error and uncompensated for variation from standard atmospheric conditions. (See ICAO term ALTITUDE.)

ALTITUDE [ICAO]. The vertical distance of a level, a point or an object considered as a point, measured from mean sea level (MSL).

ALTITUDE READOUT. An aircraft's altitude, transmitted via the Mode C transponder feature, that is visually displayed in 100-foot increments on a radar scope having readout capability. (See ALPHANUMERIC DISPLAY.) (Refer to AIM.)

ALTITUDE RESERVATION (ALTRV). Airspace utilization under prescribed conditions normally employed for the mass movement of aircraft or other special user requirements which cannot otherwise be accomplished. ALTRVs are approved by the appropriate FAA facility. ALTRVs must be classified as either "moving" or "stationary." (See MOVING ALTITUDE RESERVATION.) (See STATIONARY ALTITUDE RESERVATION.) (See AIR TRAFFIC CONTROL SYSTEM COMMAND CENTER.)

ALTITUDE RESTRICTION. An altitude or altitudes, stated in the order flown, which are to be maintained until reaching a specific point or time. Altitude restrictions may be issued by ATC due to traffic, terrain, or other airspace considerations.

ALTITUDE RESTRICTIONS ARE CANCELED. Adherence to previously imposed altitude restrictions is no longer required during a climb or descent.

ALTRV. (See ALTITUDE RESERVATION.)

AMVER. (See AUTOMATED MUTUAL-ASSISTANCE VESSEL RESCUE SYSTEM.)

APB. (See AUTOMATED PROBLEM DETECTION BOUNDARY.)

APD. (See AUTOMATED PROBLEM DETECTION.)

APDIA. (See AUTOMATED PROBLEM DETECTION INHIBITED AREA.)

APPROACH CLEARANCE. Authorization by ATC for a pilot to conduct an instrument approach. The type of instrument approach for which a clearance and other pertinent information is provided in the approach clearance when required. (See CLEARED APPROACH.) (See INSTRUMENT APPROACH PROCEDURE.) (Refer to AIM.) (Refer to 14 CFR Part 91.)

APPROACH CONTROL FACILITY. A terminal ATC facility that provides approach control service in a terminal area. (See APPROACH CONTROL SERVICE.) (See RADAR APPROACH CONTROL FACILITY.)

APPROACH CONTROL SERVICE. Air traffic control service provided by an approach control facility for arriving and departing VFR/IFR aircraft and, on occasion, en route aircraft. At some airports not served by an approach control facility, the ARTCC provides limited approach control service. (See ICAO term APPROACH CONTROL SERVICE.) (Refer to AIM.)

APPROACH CONTROL SERVICE [ICAO]. Air traffic control service for arriving or departing controlled flights.

APPROACH GATE. An imaginary point used within ATC as a basis for vectoring aircraft to the final approach course. The gate will be established along the final approach course 1 mile from the final approach fix on the side away from the airport and will be no closer than 5 miles from the landing threshold.

APPROACH/DEPARTURE HOLD AREA. The locations on taxiways in the approach or departure areas of a runway designated to protect landing or departing aircraft. These locations are identified by signs and markings.

APPROACH LIGHT SYSTEM. (See AIRPORT LIGHTING.)

APPROACH SEQUENCE. The order in which aircraft are positioned while on approach or awaiting approach clearance. (See LANDING SEQUENCE.) (See ICAO term APPROACH SEQUENCE.)

APPROACH SEQUENCE [ICAO]. The order in which two or more aircraft are cleared to approach to land at the aerodrome.

P/C

APPROACH SPEED. The recommended speed contained in aircraft manuals used by pilots when making an approach to landing. This speed will vary for different segments of an approach as well as for aircraft weight and configuration.

APPROACH WITH VERTICAL GUIDANCE (APV). A term used to describe RNAV approach procedures that provide lateral and vertical guidance but do not meet the requirements to be considered a precision approach.

APPROPRIATE ATS AUTHORITY [ICAO]. The relevant authority designated by the State responsible for providing air traffic services in the airspace concerned. In the United States, the "appropriate ATS authority" is the Program Director for Air Traffic Planning and Procedures, ATP-1.

APPROPRIATE AUTHORITY.
 a. Regarding flight over the high seas: the relevant authority is the State of Registry.
 b. Regarding flight over other than the high seas: the relevant authority is the State having sovereignty over the territory being overflown.

APPROPRIATE OBSTACLE CLEARANCE MINIMUM ALTITUDE. Any of the following: (See MINIMUM EN ROUTE IFR ALTITUDE.) (See MINIMUM IFR ALTITUDE.) (See MINIMUM OBSTRUCTION CLEARANCE ALTITUDE.) (See MINIMUM VECTORING ALTITUDE.)

APPROPRIATE TERRAIN CLEARANCE MINIMUM ALTITUDE. Any of the following: (See MINIMUM EN ROUTE IFR ALTITUDE.) (See MINIMUM IFR ALTITUDE.) (See MINIMUM OBSTRUCTION CLEARANCE ALTITUDE.) (See MINIMUM VECTORING ALTITUDE.)

APRON. A defined area on an airport or heliport intended to accommodate aircraft for purposes of loading or unloading passengers or cargo, refueling, parking, or maintenance. With regard to seaplanes, a ramp is used for access to the apron from the water. (See ICAO term APRON.)

APRON [ICAO]. A defined area, on a land aerodrome, intended to accommodate aircraft for purposes of loading or unloading passengers, mail or cargo, refueling, parking or maintenance.

ARC. The track over the ground of an aircraft flying at a constant distance from a navigational aid by reference to distance measuring equipment (DME).

AREA CONTROL CENTER [ICAO]. An air traffic control facility primarily responsible for ATC services being provided IFR aircraft during the en route phase of flight. The U.S. equivalent facility is an air route traffic control center (ARTCC).

AREA NAVIGATION (RNAV). A method of navigation which permits aircraft operation on any desired flight path within the coverage of ground- or space-based navigation aids or within the limits of the capability of self-contained aids, or a combination of these.

Note: Area navigation includes performance-based navigation as well as other operations that do not meet the definition of performance-based navigation.

AREA NAVIGATION (RNAV) APPROACH CONFIGURATION:
 a. STANDARD T. An RNAV approach whose design allows direct flight to any one of three initial approach fixes (IAF) and eliminates the need for procedure turns. The standard design is to align the procedure on the extended centerline with the missed approach point (MAP) at the runway threshold, the final approach fix (FAF), and the initial approach/intermediate fix (IAF/IF). The other two IAFs will be established perpendicular to the IF.
 b. MODIFIED T. An RNAV approach design for single or multiple runways where terrain or operational constraints do not allow for the standard T. The "T" may be modified by increasing or decreasing the angle from the corner IAF(s) to the IF or by eliminating one or both corner IAFs.
 c. STANDARD I. An RNAV approach design for a single runway with both corner IAFs eliminated. Course reversal or radar vectoring may be required at busy terminals with multiple runways.
 d. TERMINAL ARRIVAL AREA (TAA). The TAA is controlled airspace established in conjunction with the Standard or Modified T and I RNAV approach configurations. In the standard TAA, there are three areas: straight-in, left base, and right base. The arc boundaries of the three areas of the TAA are published portions of the approach and allow aircraft to transition from the en route structure direct to the nearest IAF. TAAs will also eliminate or reduce feeder routes, departure extensions, and procedure turns or course reversal.
 1. STRAIGHT-IN AREA. A 30NM arc centered on the IF bounded by a straight line extending through the IF perpendicular to the intermediate course.
 2. LEFT BASE AREA. A 30NM arc centered on the right corner IAF. The area shares a boundary with the straight-in area except that it extends out for 30NM from the IAF and is bounded on the other side by a line extending from the IF through the FAF to the arc.
 3. RIGHT BASE AREA. A 30NM arc centered on the left corner IAF. The area shares a boundary with the straight-in area except that it extends out for 30NM from the IAF and is bounded on the other side by a line extending from the IF through the FAF to the arc.

AREA NAVIGATION (RNAV) GLOBAL POSITIONING SYSTEM (GPS) PRECISION RUNWAY MONITORING (PRM) APPROACH. A GPS approach, which requires vertical guidance, used in lieu of another type of PRM approach to conduct approaches to parallel runways whose extended centerlines are separated by less than 4,300 feet and at least 3,000 feet, where simultaneous close parallel approaches are permitted. Also used in lieu of an ILS PRM and/or LDA PRM approach to conduct Simultaneous Offset Instrument Approach (SOIA) operations.

ARMY AVIATION FLIGHT INFORMATION BULLE-TIN. A bulletin that provides air operation data covering Army, National Guard, and Army Reserve aviation activities.

ARO. (See AIRPORT RESERVATION OFFICE.)

ARRESTING SYSTEM. A safety device consisting of two major components, namely, engaging or catching devices and energy absorption devices for the purpose of arresting both tailhook and/or nontail-hook-equipped aircraft. It is used to prevent aircraft from overrunning runways when the aircraft cannot be stopped after landing or during aborted takeoff. Arresting systems have various names; e.g., arresting gear, hook device, wire barrier cable. (See ABORT.) (Refer to AIM.)

ARRIVAL CENTER. The ARTCC having jurisdiction for the impacted airport.

ARRIVAL DELAY. A parameter which specifies a period of time in which no aircraft will be metered for arrival at the specified airport.

ARRIVAL/DEPARTURE WINDOW (ADW). A depiction presented on an air traffic control display, used by the controller to prevent possible conflicts between arrivals to, and departures from, a runway. The ADW identifies that point on the final approach course by which a departing aircraft must have begun takeoff.

ARRIVAL SECTOR (En Route). An operational control sector containing one or more meter fixes on or near the TRACON boundary.

ARRIVAL TIME. The time an aircraft touches down on arrival.

ARSR. (See AIR ROUTE SURVEILLANCE RADAR.)

ARTCC. (See AIR ROUTE TRAFFIC CONTROL CENTER.)

ASDA. (See ACCELERATE-STOP DISTANCE AVAILABLE.)

ASDA [ICAO]. (See ICAO Term ACCELERATE-STOP DISTANCE AVAILABLE.)

ASDE. (See AIRPORT SURFACE DETECTION EQUIPMENT.)

ASLAR. (See AIRCRAFT SURGE LAUNCH AND RECOVERY.)

ASR. (See AIRPORT SURVEILLANCE RADAR.)

ASR APPROACH. (See SURVEILLANCE APPROACH.)

ASSOCIATED. A radar target displaying a data block with flight identification and altitude information. (See UNASSOCIATED.)

ATC. (See AIR TRAFFIC CONTROL.)

ATC ADVISES. Used to prefix a message of noncontrol information when it is relayed to an aircraft by other than an air traffic controller. (See ADVISORY.)

ATC ASSIGNED AIRSPACE. Airspace of defined vertical/lateral limits, assigned by ATC, for the purpose of providing air traffic segregation between the specified activities being conducted within the assigned airspace and other IFR air traffic. (See SPECIAL USE AIRSPACE.)

ATC CLEARANCE. (See AIR TRAFFIC CLEARANCE.)

ATC CLEARS. Used to prefix an ATC clearance when it is relayed to an aircraft by other than an air traffic controller.

ATC INSTRUCTIONS. Directives issued by air traffic control for the purpose of requiring a pilot to take specific actions; e.g., "Turn left heading two five zero," "Go around," "Clear the runway." (Refer to 14 CFR Part 91.)

ATC PREFERRED ROUTE NOTIFICATION. EDST notification to the appropriate controller of the need to determine if an ATC preferred route needs to be applied, based on destination airport. (See ROUTE ACTION NOTIFICATION.) (See EN ROUTE DECISION SUPPORT TOOL.)

ATC PREFERRED ROUTES. Preferred routes that are not automatically applied by Host.

ATC REQUESTS. Used to prefix an ATC request when it is relayed to an aircraft by other than an air traffic controller.

ATC SECURITY SERVICES. Communications and security tracking provided by an ATC facility in support of the DHS, the DOD, or other Federal security elements in the interest of national security. Such security services are only applicable within designated areas. ATC security services do not include ATC basic radar services or flight following.

ATC SECURITY SERVICES POSITION. The position responsible for providing ATC security services as defined. This position does not provide ATC, IFR separation, or VFR flight following services, but is responsible for providing security services in an area comprising airspace assigned to one or more ATC operating sectors. This position may be combined with control positions.

ATC SECURITY TRACKING. The continuous tracking of aircraft movement by an ATC facility in support of the DHS, the DOD, or other security elements for national security using radar (i.e., radar tracking) or other means (e.g., manual tracking) without providing basic radar services (including traffic advisories) or other ATC services not defined in this section.

ATC SURVEILLANCE SOURCE. Used by ATC for establishing identification, control and separation using a target depicted on an air traffic control facility's video display that has met the relevant safety standards for operational use and received from one, or a combination, of the following surveillance sources:

 a. Radar (See RADAR)

 b. ADS-B (See AUTOMATIC DEPENDENT SURVEILLANCE–BROADCAST.)

 c. WAM (See WIDE AREA MULTILATERATION) (See INTERROGATOR.) (See TRANSPONDER.) (See ICAO term RADAR.) (Refer to AIM.)

ATCAA. (See ATC ASSIGNED AIRSPACE.)

P/C

ATCRBS. (See RADAR.)

ATCSCC. (See AIR TRAFFIC CONTROL SYSTEM COMMAND CENTER.)

ATCT. (See TOWER.)

ATD. (See ALONG-TRACK DISTANCE.)

ATIS. (See AUTOMATIC TERMINAL INFORMATION SERVICE.)

ATIS [ICAO]. (See ICAO Term AUTOMATIC TERMINAL INFORMATION SERVICE.)

ATO. (See AIR TRAFFIC ORGANIZATION.)

ATPA. (See AUTOMATED TERMINAL PROXIMITY ALERT.)

ATS ROUTE [ICAO]. A specified route designed for channeling the flow of traffic as necessary for the provision of air traffic services.

Note: The term "ATS Route" is used to mean variously, airway, advisory route, controlled or uncontrolled route, arrival or departure, etc.

ATS SURVEILLANCE SERVICE [ICAO]. A term used to indicate a service provided directly by means of an ATS surveillance system.

ATS SURVEILLANCE SYSTEM [ICAO]. A generic term meaning variously, ADS-B, PSR, SSR or any comparable ground-based system that enables the identification of aircraft.

Note: A comparable ground-based system is one that has been demonstrated, by comparative assessment or other methodology, to have a level of safety and performance equal to or better than monopulse SSR.

ATTENTION ALL USERS PAGE (AAUP). The AAUP provides the pilot with additional information relative to conducting a specific operation, for example, PRM approaches and RNAV departures.

AUTOLAND APPROACH. An autoland system aids by providing control of aircraft systems during a precision instrument approach to at least decision altitude and possibly all the way to touchdown, as well as in some cases, through the landing rollout. The autoland system is a sub-system of the autopilot system from which control surface management occurs. The aircraft autopilot sends instructions to the autoland system and monitors the autoland system performance and integrity during its execution.

AUTOMATED EMERGENCY DESCENT. (See EMERGENCY DESCENT MODE.)

AUTOMATED INFORMATION TRANSFER (AIT). A precoordinated process, specifically defined in facility directives, during which a transfer of altitude control and/or radar identification is accomplished without verbal coordination between controllers using information communicated in a full data block.

AUTOMATED MUTUAL-ASSISTANCE VESSEL RESCUE SYSTEM. A facility which can deliver, in a matter of minutes, a surface picture (SURPIC) of vessels in the area of a potential or actual search and rescue

incident, including their predicted positions and their characteristics. (See FAA Order JO 7110.65, Para 10-6-4, INFLIGHT CONTINGENCIES.)

AUTOMATED PROBLEM DETECTION (APD). An Automation Processing capability that compares trajectories in order to predict conflicts.

AUTOMATED PROBLEM DETECTION BOUNDARY (APB). The adapted distance beyond a facilities boundary defining the airspace within which EDST performs conflict detection. (See EN ROUTE DECISION SUPPORT TOOL.)

AUTOMATED PROBLEM DETECTION INHIBITED AREA (APDIA). Airspace surrounding a terminal area within which APD is inhibited for all flights within that airspace.

AUTOMATED SERVICES. Services delivered via an automated system (that is, without human interaction). For example, flight plans, Notices to Air Missions (NOTAM), interactive maps, computer-generated text-to-speech messages, short message service, or email.

AUTOMATED TERMINAL PROXIMITY ALERT (ATPA). Monitors the separation of aircraft on the Final Approach Course (FAC), displaying a graphical notification (cone and/or mileage) when a potential loss of separation is detected. The warning cone (Yellow) will display at 45 seconds and the alert cone (Red) will display at 24 seconds prior to predicted loss of separation. Current distance between two aircraft on final will be displayed in line 3 of the full data block of the trailing aircraft in corresponding colors.

AUTOMATED UNICOM. Provides completely automated weather, radio check capability and airport advisory information on an Automated UNICOM system. These systems offer a variety of features, typically selectable by microphone clicks, on the UNICOM frequency. Availability will be published in the Chart Supplement and approach charts.

AUTOMATED WEATHER SYSTEM. Any of the automated weather sensor platforms that collect weather data at airports and disseminate the weather information via radio and/or landline. The systems currently consist of the Automated Surface Observing System (ASOS) and Automated Weather Observation System (AWOS).

AUTOMATIC ALTITUDE REPORT. (See ALTITUDE READOUT.)

AUTOMATIC ALTITUDE REPORTING. That function of a transponder which responds to Mode C interrogations by transmitting the aircraft's altitude in 100-foot increments.

AUTOMATIC CARRIER LANDING SYSTEM. U.S. Navy final approach equipment consisting of precision tracking radar coupled to a computer data link to provide continuous information to the aircraft, monitoring capability to the pilot, and a backup approach system.

AUTOMATIC DEPENDENT SURVEILLANCE (ADS) [ICAO]. A surveillance technique in which aircraft automatically provide, via a data link, data derived from onboard navigation and position fixing systems, including aircraft identification, four dimensional position and additional data as appropriate.

AUTOMATIC DEPENDENT SURVEILLANCE–BROADCAST (ADS-B). A surveillance system in which an aircraft or vehicle to be detected is fitted with cooperative equipment in the form of a data link transmitter. The aircraft or vehicle periodically broadcasts its GNSS-derived position and other required information such as identity and velocity, which is then received by a ground-based or space-based receiver for processing and display at an air traffic control facility, as well as by suitably equipped aircraft. (See AUTOMATIC DEPENDENT SURVEILLANCE–BROADCAST IN.) (See AUTOMATIC DEPENDENT SURVEILLANCE–BROADCAST OUT.) (See COOPERATIVE SURVEILLANCE.) (See GLOBAL POSITIONING SYSTEM.) (See SPACE-BASED ADS-B.)

AUTOMATIC DEPENDENT SURVEILLANCE–BROADCAST IN (ADS-B In). Aircraft avionics capable of receiving ADS-B Out transmissions directly from other aircraft, as well as traffic or weather information transmitted from ground stations. (See AUTOMATIC DEPENDENT SURVEILLANCE–BROADCAST OUT.) (See AUTOMATIC DEPENDENT SURVEILLANCE–REBROADCAST.) (See FLIGHT INFORMATION SERVICE–BROADCAST.) (See TRAFFIC INFORMATION SERVICE–BROADCAST.)

AUTOMATIC DEPENDENT SURVEILLANCE–BROADCAST OUT (ADS-B Out). The transmitter onboard an aircraft or ground vehicle that periodically broadcasts its GNSS-derived position along with other required information, such as identity, altitude, and velocity. (See AUTOMATIC DEPENDENT SURVEILLANCE–BROADCAST.) (See AUTOMATIC DEPENDENT SURVEILLANCE–BROADCAST IN.)

AUTOMATIC DEPENDENT SURVEILLANCE–CONTRACT (ADS-C). A data link position reporting system, controlled by a ground station, that establishes contracts with an aircraft's avionics that occur automatically whenever specific events occur, or specific time intervals are reached.

AUTOMATIC DEPENDENT SURVEILLANCE–REBROADCAST (ADS-R). A datalink translation function of the ADS-B ground system required to accommodate the two separate operating frequencies (978 MHz and 1090 MHz). The ADS-B system receives the ADS-B messages transmitted on one frequency and ADS-R translates and reformats the information for rebroadcast and use on the other frequency. This allows ADS-B In equipped aircraft to see nearby ADS-B Out traffic regardless of the operating link of the other aircraft. Aircraft operating on the same ADS-B frequency exchange information directly and do not require the ADS-R translation function.

AUTOMATIC DIRECTION FINDER. An aircraft radio navigation system which senses and indicates the direction to a L/MF nondirectional radio beacon (NDB) ground transmitter. Direction is indicated to the pilot as a magnetic bearing or as a relative bearing to the longitudinal axis of the aircraft depending on the type of indicator installed in the aircraft. In certain applications, such as military, ADF operations may be based on airborne and ground transmitters in the VHF/UHF frequency spectrum. (See BEARING.) (See NONDIRECTIONAL BEACON.)

AUTOMATIC FLIGHT INFORMATION SERVICE (AFIS)—ALASKA FSSs ONLY. The continuous broadcast of recorded non-control information at airports in Alaska where a FSS provides local airport advisory service. The AFIS broadcast automates the repetitive transmission of essential but routine information such as weather, wind, altimeter, favored runway, braking action, airport NOTAMs, and other applicable information. The information is continuously broadcast over a discrete VHF radio frequency (usually the ASOS/AWOS frequency.)

AUTOMATIC TERMINAL INFORMATION SERVICE. The continuous broadcast of recorded noncontrol information in selected terminal areas. Its purpose is to improve controller effectiveness and to relieve frequency congestion by automating the repetitive transmission of essential but routine information; e.g., "Los Angeles information Alfa. One three zero zero Coordinated Universal Time. Weather, measured ceiling two thousand overcast, visibility three, haze, smoke, temperature seven one, dew point five seven, wind two five zero at five, altimeter two niner niner six. I-L-S Runway Two Five Left approach in use, Runway Two Five Right closed, advise you have Alfa. (See ICAO term AUTOMATIC TERMINAL INFORMATION SERVICE.) (Refer to AIM.)

AUTOMATIC TERMINAL INFORMATION SERVICE [ICAO]. The provision of current, routine information to arriving and departing aircraft by means of continuous and repetitive broadcasts throughout the day or a specified portion of the day.

AUTOROTATION. A rotorcraft flight condition in which the lifting rotor is driven entirely by action of the air when the rotorcraft is in motion.

a. Autorotative Landing/Touchdown Autorotation. Used by a pilot to indicate that the landing will be made without applying power to the rotor.

b. Low Level Autorotation. Commences at an altitude well below the traffic pattern, usually below 100 feet AGL and is used primarily for tactical military training.

c. 180 degrees Autorotation. Initiated from a downwind heading and is commenced well inside the normal traffic pattern. "Go around" may not be possible during the latter part of this maneuver.

AVAILABLE LANDING DISTANCE (ALD). The portion of a runway available for landing and roll-out for aircraft cleared for LAHSO. This distance is measured from the landing threshold to the hold-short point.

P/C

AVIATION WATCH NOTIFICATION MESSAGE. The Storm Prediction Center (SPC) issues Aviation Watch Notification Messages (SAW) to provide an area threat alert for the aviation meteorology community to forecast organized severe thunderstorms that may produce tornadoes, large hail, and/or convective damaging winds as indicated in Public Watch Notification Messages within the Continental U.S. A SAW message provides a description of the type of watch issued by SPC, a valid time, an approximation of the area in a watch, and primary hazard(s).

AVIATION WEATHER SERVICE. A service provided by the National Weather Service (NWS) and FAA which collects and disseminates pertinent weather information for pilots, aircraft operators, and ATC. Available aviation weather reports and forecasts are displayed at each NWS office and FAA FSS. (See TRANSCRIBED WEATHER BROADCAST.) (See WEATHER ADVISORY.) (Refer to AIM.)

B

B4UFLY. A free downloadable application, which allows operators to check airspace and local advisories before flying.

BACK-TAXI. A term used by air traffic controllers to taxi an aircraft on the runway opposite to the traffic flow. The aircraft may be instructed to back-taxi to the beginning of the runway or at some point before reaching the runway end for the purpose of departure or to exit the runway.

BASE LEG. (See TRAFFIC PATTERN.)

BEACON. (See AERONAUTICAL BEACON.) (See AIRPORT ROTATING BEACON.) (See AIRWAY BEACON.) (See MARKER BEACON.) (See NONDIRECTIONAL BEACON.) (See RADAR.)

BEARING. The horizontal direction to or from any point, usually measured clockwise from true north, magnetic north, or some other reference point through 360 degrees. (See NONDIRECTIONAL BEACON.)

BELOW MINIMUMS. Weather conditions below the minimums prescribed by regulation for the particular action involved; e.g., landing minimums, takeoff minimums.

BEYOND VISUAL LINE OF SIGHT (BVLOS). The operation of a UAS beyond the visual capability of the flight crew members (i.e., remote pilot in command [RPIC], the person manipulating the controls, and visual observer [VO]), if used to see the aircraft with vision unaided by any device other than corrective lenses, spectacles, and contact lenses.

BLAST FENCE. A barrier that is used to divert or dissipate jet or propeller blast.

BLAST PAD. A surface adjacent to the ends of a runway provided to reduce the erosive effect of jet blast and propeller wash.

BLIND SPEED. The rate of departure or closing of a target relative to the radar antenna at which cancellation of the primary radar target by moving target indicator (MTI) circuits in the radar equipment causes a reduction or complete loss of signal. (See ICAO term BLIND VELOCITY.)

BLIND SPOT. An area from which radio transmissions and/or radar echoes cannot be received. The term is also used to describe portions of the airport not visible from the control tower.

BLIND TRANSMISSION. (See TRANSMITTING IN THE BLIND.)

BLIND VELOCITY [ICAO]. The radial velocity of a moving target such that the target is not seen on primary radars fitted with certain forms of fixed echo suppression.

BLIND ZONE. (See BLIND SPOT.)

BLOCKED. Phraseology used to indicate that a radio transmission has been distorted or interrupted due to multiple simultaneous radio transmissions.

BOTTOM ALTITUDE. In reference to published altitude restrictions on a STAR or STAR runway transition, the lowest altitude authorized.

BOUNDARY LIGHTS. (See AIRPORT LIGHTING.)

BRAKING ACTION (GOOD, GOOD TO MEDIUM, MEDIUM, MEDIUM TO POOR, POOR, OR NIL). A report of conditions on the airport movement area providing a pilot with a degree/quality of braking to expect. Braking action is reported in terms of good, good to medium, medium, medium to poor, poor, or nil. (See RUNWAY CONDITION READING.) (See RUNWAY CONDITION REPORT.) (See RUNWAY CONDITION CODES.)

BRAKING ACTION ADVISORIES. When tower controllers receive runway braking action reports which include the terms "medium," "poor," or "nil," or whenever weather conditions are conducive to deteriorating or rapidly changing runway braking conditions, the tower will include on the ATIS broadcast the statement, "Braking Action Advisories are in Effect." During the time braking action advisories are in effect, ATC will issue the most current braking action report for the runway in use to each arriving and departing aircraft. Pilots should be prepared for deteriorating braking conditions and should request current runway condition information if not issued by controllers. Pilots should also be prepared to provide a descriptive runway condition report to controllers after landing.

BREAKOUT. A technique to direct aircraft out of the approach stream. In the context of simultaneous (independent) parallel operations, a breakout is used to direct threatened aircraft away from a deviating aircraft.

BROADCAST. Transmission of information for which an acknowledgement is not expected. (See ICAO term BROADCAST.)

BROADCAST [ICAO]. A transmission of information relating to air navigation that is not addressed to a specific station or stations.

BUFFER AREA. As applied to an MVA or MIA chart, a depicted 3 NM or 5 NM radius MVA/MIA sector isolating a displayed obstacle for which the sector is established. A portion of a buffer area can also be inclusive of a MVA/MIA sector polygon boundary.

BVLOS. (See BEYOND VISUAL LINE OF SIGHT.)

C

CALCULATED LANDING TIME. A term that may be used in place of tentative or actual calculated landing time, whichever applies.

CALIBRATED AIRSPEED (CAS). The indicated airspeed of an aircraft, corrected for position and instrument error. Calibrated airspeed is equal to true airspeed in standard atmosphere at sea level.

CALL FOR RELEASE. Wherein the overlying ARTCC requires a terminal facility to initiate verbal coordination to secure ARTCC approval for release of a departure into the en route environment.

CALL UP. Initial voice contact between a facility and an aircraft, using the identification of the unit being called and the unit initiating the call. (Refer to AIM.)

CANADIAN MINIMUM NAVIGATION PERFORMANCE SPECIFICATION AIRSPACE. That portion of Canadian domestic airspace within which MNPS separation may be applied.

CARDINAL ALTITUDES. "Odd" or "Even" thousand-foot altitudes or flight levels; e.g., 5,000, 6,000, 7,000, FL 250, FL 260, FL 270. (See ALTITUDE.) (See FLIGHT LEVEL.)

CARDINAL FLIGHT LEVELS. (See CARDINAL ALTITUDES.)

CAT. (See CLEAR-AIR TURBULENCE.)

CATCH POINT. A fix/waypoint that serves as a transition point from the high altitude waypoint navigation structure to an arrival procedure (STAR) or the low altitude ground-based navigation structure.

CBO. (See COMMUNITY-BASED ORGANIZATION.)

CEILING. The heights above the earth's surface of the lowest layer of clouds or obscuring phenomena that is reported as "broken," "overcast," or "obscuration," and not classified as "thin" or "partial." (See ICAO term CEILING.)

CEILING [ICAO]. The height above the ground or water of the base of the lowest layer of cloud below 6,000 meters (20,000 feet) covering more than half the sky.

CENTER. (See AIR ROUTE TRAFFIC CONTROL CENTER.)

CENTER'S AREA. The specified airspace within which an air route traffic control center (ARTCC) provides air traffic control and advisory service. (See

AIR ROUTE TRAFFIC CONTROL CENTER.) (Refer to AIM.)

CENTER WEATHER ADVISORY. An unscheduled weather advisory issued by Center Weather Service Unit meteorologists for ATC use to alert pilots of existing or anticipated adverse weather conditions within the next 2 hours. A CWA may modify or redefine a SIGMET. (See AIRMET.) (See CONVECTIVE SIGMET.) (See GRAPHICAL AIRMEN'S METEOROLOGICAL INFORMATION.) (See SAW.) (See SIGMET.) (Refer to AIM.)

CENTRAL EAST PACIFIC. An organized route system between the U.S. West Coast and Hawaii.

CEP. (See CENTRAL EAST PACIFIC.)

CERAP. (See COMBINED CENTER-RAPCON.)

CERTIFICATE OF WAIVER OR AUTHORIZATION (COA). An FAA grant of approval for a specific flight operation or airspace authorization or waiver.

CERTIFIED TOWER RADAR DISPLAY (CTRD). An FAA radar display certified for use in the NAS.

CFR. (See CALL FOR RELEASE.)

CHA. (See CONTINGENCY HAZARD AREA)

CHAFF. Thin, narrow metallic reflectors of various lengths and frequency responses, used to reflect radar energy. These reflectors, when dropped from aircraft and allowed to drift downward result in large targets on the radar display.

CHART SUPPLEMENT. A series of civil/military flight information publications issued by FAA every 56 days consisting of the Chart Supplement U.S., Chart Supplement Alaska, and Chart Supplement Pacific.

CHART SUPPLEMENT ALASKA. A flight information publication designed for use with appropriate IFR or VFR charts which contains data on all airports, seaplane bases, and heliports open to the public including communications data, navigational facilities, airport diagrams, certain special notices, and non-regulatory procedures. Also included in this publication are selected entries needed to support the unique geographical operational conditions of Alaska. This publication is issued in one volume for the state of Alaska.

CHART SUPPLEMENT PACIFIC. A flight information publication designed for use with appropriate IFR or VFR charts which contains data on all airports, seaplane bases, and heliports open to the public including communications data, navigational facilities, airport diagrams, certain special notices, and non-regulatory procedures. Also included in this publication are Instrument Approach Procedures (IAP), Departure Procedures (DP), and Standard Terminal Arrival (STAR) charts, along with selected entries needed to support the unique geographical operational conditions of the Pacific Oceanic region. This publication is issued in one volume for the Hawaiian Islands and other selected Pacific Islands.

P/C

CHART SUPPLEMENT U.S. A flight information publication designed for use with appropriate IFR or VFR charts which contains data on all airports, seaplane bases, and heliports open to the public including communications data, navigational facilities, airport diagrams, certain special notices, and non-regulatory procedures. This publication is issued for the conterminous U.S., Puerto Rico, and the Virgin Islands in seven volumes according to geographical area.

CHARTED VFR FLYWAYS. Charted VFR Flyways are flight paths recommended for use to bypass areas heavily traversed by large turbine-powered aircraft. Pilot compliance with recommended flyways and associated altitudes is strictly voluntary. VFR Flyway Planning charts are published on the back of existing VFR Terminal Area charts.

CHARTED VISUAL FLIGHT PROCEDURE APPROACH. An approach conducted while operating on an instrument flight rules (IFR) flight plan which authorizes the pilot of an aircraft to proceed visually and clear of clouds to the airport via visual landmarks and other information depicted on a charted visual flight procedure. This approach must be authorized and under the control of the appropriate air traffic control facility. Weather minimums required are depicted on the chart.

CHASE. An aircraft flown in proximity to another aircraft normally to observe its performance during training or testing.

CHASE AIRCRAFT. (See CHASE.)

CHOP. A form of turbulence.
 a. Light Chop. Turbulence that causes slight, rapid and somewhat rhythmic bumpiness without appreciable changes in altitude or attitude.
 b. Moderate Chop. Turbulence similar to Light Chop but of greater intensity. It causes rapid bumps or jolts without appreciable changes in aircraft altitude or attitude.
(See TURBULENCE.)

CIRCLE-TO-LAND MANEUVER. A maneuver initiated by the pilot to align the aircraft with a runway for landing when a straight-in landing from an instrument approach is not possible or is not desirable. At tower controlled airports, this maneuver is made only after ATC authorization has been obtained and the pilot has established required visual reference to the airport. (See CIRCLE TO RUNWAY.) (See LANDING MINIMUMS.) (Refer to AIM.)

CIRCLE TO RUNWAY (RUNWAY NUMBER). Used by ATC to inform the pilot that he/she must circle to land because the runway in use is other than the runway aligned with the instrument approach procedure. When the direction of the circling maneuver in relation to the airport/runway is required, the controller will state the direction (eight cardinal compass points) and specify a left or right downwind or base leg as appropriate; e.g., "Cleared VOR Runway Three Six Approach circle to Runway Two Two," or "Circle northwest of the airport for a right downwind to Runway

Two Two." (See CIRCLE-TO-LAND MANEUVER.) (See LANDING MINIMUMS.) (Refer to AIM.)

CIRCLING APPROACH. (See CIRCLE-TO-LAND MANEUVER.)

CIRCLING MANEUVER. (See CIRCLE-TO-LAND MANEUVER.)

CIRCLING MINIMA. (See CONTROLLED AIRSPACE.)

CIVIL AIRCRAFT OPERATION (CAO). Aircraft operations other than public use.

CLASS A AIRSPACE. (See CONTROLLED AIRSPACE.)

CLASS B AIRSPACE. (See CONTROLLED AIRSPACE.)

CLASS C AIRSPACE. (See CONTROLLED AIRSPACE.)

CLASS D AIRSPACE. (See CONTROLLED AIRSPACE.)

CLASS E AIRSPACE. (See CONTROLLED AIRSPACE.)

CLASS G AIRSPACE. Airspace that is not designated in 14 CFR Part 71 as Class A, Class B, Class C, Class D, or Class E controlled airspace is Class G (uncontrolled) airspace. (See UNCONTROLLED AIRSPACE.)

CLEAR AIR TURBULENCE (CAT). Turbulence encountered in air where no clouds are present. This term is commonly applied to high-level turbulence associated with wind shear. CAT is often encountered in the vicinity of the jet stream. (See WIND SHEAR.) (See JET STREAM.)

CLEAR OF THE RUNWAY.
 a. Taxiing aircraft, which is approaching a runway, is clear of the runway when all parts of the aircraft are held short of the applicable runway holding position marking.
 b. A pilot or controller may consider an aircraft, which is exiting or crossing a runway, to be clear of the runway when all parts of the aircraft are beyond the runway edge and there are no restrictions to its continued movement beyond the applicable runway holding position marking.
 c. Pilots and controllers shall exercise good judgment to ensure that adequate separation exists between all aircraft on runways and taxiways at airports with inadequate runway edge lines or holding position markings.

CLEARANCE. (See AIR TRAFFIC CLEARANCE.)

CLEARANCE LIMIT. The fix, point, or location to which an aircraft is cleared when issued an air traffic clearance. (See ICAO term CLEARANCE LIMIT.)

CLEARANCE LIMIT [ICAO]. The point to which an aircraft is granted an air traffic control clearance.

CLEARANCE VOID IF NOT OFF BY (TIME). Used by ATC to advise an aircraft that the departure release is automatically canceled if takeoff is not made prior to a specified time. The expiration of a clearance void time does not cancel the departure clearance or IFR flight plan. It withdraws the pilot's authority to depart IFR until a new departure release/release time has been issued by ATC. Pilots who choose to depart VFR after their clearance void time has expired should not depart

using the previously assigned IFR transponder code. (See ICAO term CLEARANCE VOID TIME.)

CLEARANCE VOID TIME [ICAO]. A time specified by an air traffic control unit at which a clearance ceases to be valid unless the aircraft concerned has already taken action to comply therewith.

CLEARED APPROACH. ATC authorization for an aircraft to execute any standard or special instrument approach procedure for that airport. Normally, an aircraft will be cleared for a specific instrument approach procedure. (See CLEARED (Type of) APPROACH.) (See INSTRUMENT APPROACH PROCEDURE.) (Refer to 14 CFR Part 91.) (Refer to AIM.)

CLEARED (Type of) APPROACH. ATC authorization for an aircraft to execute a specific instrument approach procedure to an airport; e.g., "Cleared ILS Runway Three Six Approach." (See APPROACH CLEARANCE.) (See INSTRUMENT APPROACH PROCEDURE.) (Refer to 14 CFR Part 91.) (Refer to AIM.)

CLEARED AS FILED. Means the aircraft is cleared to proceed in accordance with the route of flight filed in the flight plan. This clearance does not include the altitude, DP, or DP Transition. (See REQUEST FULL ROUTE CLEARANCE.) (Refer to AIM.)

CLEARED FOR TAKEOFF. ATC authorization for an aircraft to depart. It is predicated on known traffic and known physical airport conditions.

CLEARED FOR THE OPTION. ATC authorization for an aircraft to make a touch-and-go, low approach, missed approach, stop and go, or full stop landing at the discretion of the pilot. It is normally used in training so that an instructor can evaluate a student's performance under changing situations. Pilots should advise ATC if they decide to remain on the runway, of any delay in their stop and go, delay clearing the runway, or are unable to comply with the instruction(s). (See OPTION APPROACH.) (Refer to AIM.)

CLEARED THROUGH. ATC authorization for an aircraft to make intermediate stops at specified airports without refiling a flight plan while en route to the clearance limit.

CLEARED TO LAND. ATC authorization for an aircraft to land. It is predicated on known traffic and known physical airport conditions.

CLEARWAY. An area beyond the takeoff runway under the control of airport authorities within which terrain or fixed obstacles may not extend above specified limits. These areas may be required for certain turbine-powered operations and the size and upward slope of the clearway will differ depending on when the aircraft was certificated. (Refer to 14 CFR Part 1.)

CLIMB TO VFR. ATC authorization for an aircraft to climb to VFR conditions within Class B, C, D, and E surface areas when the only weather limitation is restricted visibility. The aircraft must remain clear of clouds while climbing to VFR. (See SPECIAL VFR CONDITIONS.) (Refer to AIM.)

CLIMB VIA. An abbreviated ATC clearance that requires compliance with the procedure lateral path, associated speed restrictions, and altitude restrictions along the cleared route or procedure.

CLIMBOUT. That portion of flight operation between takeoff and the initial cruising altitude.

CLOSE PARALLEL RUNWAYS. Two parallel runways whose extended centerlines are separated by less than 4,300 feet and at least 3,000 feet (750 feet for SOIA operations) for which ATC is authorized to conduct simultaneous independent approach operations. PRM and simultaneous close parallel appear in approach title. Dual communications, special pilot training, an Attention All Users Page (AAUP), NTZ monitoring by displays that have aural and visual alerting algorithms are required. A high update rate surveillance sensor is required for certain runway or approach course spacing.

CLOSED LOOP CLEARANCE. A vector or reroute clearance that includes a return to route point and updates ERAM to accurately reflect the anticipated route (e.g., a QU route pick that anticipates length of vector and includes the next fix that ties into the route of flight.)

CLOSED RUNWAY. A runway that is unusable for aircraft operations. Only the airport management/military operations office can close a runway.

CLOSED TRAFFIC. Successive operations involving takeoffs and landings or low approaches where the aircraft does not exit the traffic pattern.

CLOUD. A cloud is a visible accumulation of minute water droplets and/or ice particles in the atmosphere above the Earth's surface. Cloud differs from ground fog, fog, or ice fog only in that the latter are, by definition, in contact with the Earth's surface.

CLT. (See CALCULATED LANDING TIME.)

CLUTTER. In radar operations, clutter refers to the reception and visual display of radar returns caused by precipitation, chaff, terrain, numerous aircraft targets, or other phenomena. Such returns may limit or preclude ATC from providing services based on radar. (See CHAFF.) (See GROUND CLUTTER.) (See PRECIPITATION.) (See TARGET.) (See ICAO term RADAR CLUTTER.)

CMNPS. (See CANADIAN MINIMUM NAVIGATION PERFORMANCE SPECIFICATION AIRSPACE.)

COA. (See CERTIFICATE OF WAIVER OR AUTHORIZATION.)

COASTAL FIX. A navigation aid or intersection where an aircraft transitions between the domestic route structure and the oceanic route structure.

CODES. The number assigned to a particular multiple pulse reply signal transmitted by a transponder. (See DISCRETE CODE.)

COLD TEMPERATURE CORRECTION. A correction in feet, based on height above airport and temperature, that is added to the aircraft's indicated altitude to offset the effect of cold temperature on true altitude.

COLLABORATIVE TRAJECTORY OPTIONS PROGRAM (CTOP). CTOP is a traffic management program administered by the Air Traffic Control System Command Center (ATCSCC) that manages demand through constrained airspace, while considering operator preference with regard to both route and delay as defined in a Trajectory Options Set (TOS).

COMBINED CENTER-RAPCON. An air traffic facility which combines the functions of an ARTCC and a radar approach control facility. (See AIR ROUTE TRAFFIC CONTROL CENTER.) (See RADAR APPROACH CONTROL FACILITY.)

COMMON POINT. A significant point over which two or more aircraft will report passing or have reported passing before proceeding on the same or diverging tracks. To establish/maintain longitudinal separation, a controller may determine a common point not originally in the aircraft's flight plan and then clear the aircraft to fly over the point. (See SIGNIFICANT POINT.)

COMMON PORTION. (See COMMON ROUTE.)

COMMON ROUTE. That segment of a North American Route between the inland navigation facility and the coastal fix.

or

COMMON ROUTE. (See SEGMENTS OF A SID/STAR)

COMMON TRAFFIC ADVISORY FREQUENCY (CTAF). A frequency designed for the purpose of carrying out airport advisory practices while operating to or from an airport without an operating control tower. The CTAF may be a UNICOM, Multicom, FSS, or tower frequency and is identified in appropriate aeronautical publications. (See DESIGNATED COMMON TRAFFIC ADVISORY FREQUENCY (CTAF) AREA.) (Refer to AC 90-66, Non-Towered Airport Flight Operations.)

COMMUNITY-BASED ORGANIZATION (CBO). A membership-based entity, described under Section 501(a,c), whose mission is the furtherance of model aviation. (see also, 49 United States Code (USC) §44809(h) and Advisory Circular (AC) 91-57).

COMPASS LOCATOR. A low power, low or medium frequency (L/MF) radio beacon installed at the site of the outer or middle marker of an instrument landing system (ILS). It can be used for navigation at distances of approximately 15 miles or as authorized in the approach procedure.

　　a. Outer Compass Locator (LOM). A compass locator installed at the site of the outer marker of an instrument landing system. (See OUTER MARKER.)

　　b. Middle Compass Locator (LMM). A compass locator installed at the site of the middle marker of an instrument landing system. (See MIDDLE MARKER.)

(See ICAO term LOCATOR.)

COMPASS ROSE. A circle, graduated in degrees, printed on some charts or marked on the ground at an airport. It is used as a reference to either true or magnetic direction.

COMPLY WITH RESTRICTIONS. An ATC instruction that requires an aircraft being vectored back onto an arrival or departure procedure to comply with all altitude and/or speed restrictions depicted on the procedure. This term may be used in lieu of repeating each remaining restriction that appears on the procedure.

COMPOSITE FLIGHT PLAN. A flight plan which specifies VFR operation for one portion of flight and IFR for another portion. It is used primarily in military operations. (Refer to AIM.)

COMPULSORY REPORTING POINTS. Reporting points which must be reported to ATC. They are designated on aeronautical charts by solid triangles or filed in a flight plan as fixes selected to define direct routes. These points are geographical locations which are defined by navigation aids/fixes. Pilots should discontinue position reporting over compulsory reporting points when informed by ATC that their aircraft is in "radar contact."

COMPUTER NAVIGATION FIX (CNF). A Computer Navigation Fix is a point defined by a latitude/longitude coordinate and is required to support Performance-Based Navigation (PBN) operations. A five-letter identifier denoting a CNF can be found next to an "x" on en route charts and on some approach charts. Eventually, all CNFs will be labeled and begin with the letters "CF" followed by three consonants (e.g., "CFWBG"). CNFs are not recognized by ATC, are not contained in ATC fix or automation databases, and are not used for ATC purposes. Pilots should not use CNFs for point-to-point navigation (e.g., proceed direct), filing a flight plan, or in aircraft/ATC communications. Use of CNFs has not been adopted or recognized by the International Civil Aviation Organization (ICAO). (Refer to AIM 1-1-17b5(i)(2), Global Positioning System (GPS).)

CONDITIONS NOT MONITORED. When an airport operator cannot monitor the condition of the movement area or airfield surface area, this information is issued as a NOTAM. Usually necessitated due to staffing, operating hours or other mitigating factors associated with airport operations.

CONFIDENCE MANEUVER. A confidence maneuver consists of one or more turns, a climb or descent, or other maneuver to determine if the pilot in command (PIC) is able to receive and comply with ATC instructions.

CONFLICT ALERT. A function of certain air traffic control automated systems designed to alert radar controllers to existing or pending situations between tracked targets (known IFR or VFR aircraft) that require his/her immediate attention/action. (See MODE C INTRUDER ALERT.)

CONFLICT RESOLUTION. The resolution of potential conflictions between aircraft that are radar identified and in communication with ATC by ensuring that radar targets do not touch. Pertinent traffic advisories shall be issued when this procedure is applied.

Note: This procedure shall not be provided utilizing mosaic radar systems.

CONFORMANCE. The condition established when an aircraft's actual position is within the conformance region constructed around that aircraft at its position, according to the trajectory associated with the aircraft's Current Plan.

CONFORMANCE REGION. A volume, bounded laterally, vertically, and longitudinally, within which an aircraft must be at a given time in order to be in conformance with the Current Plan Trajectory for that aircraft. At a given time, the conformance region is determined by the simultaneous application of the lateral, vertical, and longitudinal conformance bounds for the aircraft at the position defined by time and aircraft's trajectory.

CONSOLAN. A low frequency, long-distance NAVAID used principally for transoceanic navigations.

CONSOLIDATED WAKE TURBULENCE (CWT). A version of RECAT that has nine categories, A through I, that refines the grouping of aircraft while optimizing wake turbulence separation.

CONSTRAINT SATISFACTION POINT (CSP). Meter Reference Elements (MREs) that are actively scheduled by TBFM. Constraint satisfaction occurs when the Scheduled Time of Arrival generated for each metered flight conforms to all the scheduling constraints specified at all the applicable CSPs.

CONTACT.
 a. Establish communication with (followed by the name of the facility and, if appropriate, the frequency to be used).
 b. A flight condition wherein the pilot ascertains the attitude of his/her aircraft and navigates by visual reference to the surface.
(See CONTACT APPROACH.) (See RADAR CONTACT.)

CONTACT APPROACH. An approach wherein an aircraft on an IFR flight plan, having an air traffic control authorization, operating clear of clouds with at least 1 mile flight visibility and a reasonable expectation of continuing to the destination airport in those conditions, may deviate from the instrument approach procedure and proceed to the destination airport by visual reference to the surface. This approach will only be authorized when requested by the pilot and the reported ground visibility at the destination airport is at least 1 statute mile. (Refer to AIM.)

CONTAMINATED RUNWAY. A runway is considered contaminated whenever standing water, ice, snow, slush, frost in any form, heavy rubber, or other substances are present. A runway is contaminated with respect to rubber deposits or other friction-degrading substances when the average friction value for any 500-foot segment of the runway within the ALD fails below the recommended minimum friction level and the average friction value in the adjacent 500-foot segments falls below the maintenance planning friction level.

CONTERMINOUS U.S. The 48 adjoining States and the District of Columbia.

CONTINENTAL UNITED STATES. The 49 States located on the continent of North America and the District of Columbia.

CONTINGENCY HAZARD AREA (CHA). Used by ATC. Areas of airspace that are defined and distributed in advance of a launch or reentry operation and are activated in response to a failure. (See AIRCRAFT HAZARD AREA.) (See REFINED HAZARD AREA.) (See TRANSITIONAL HAZARD AREA.)

CONTINUE. When used as a control instruction should be followed by another word or words clarifying what is expected of the pilot. Example: "continue taxi", "continue descent", "continue inbound" etc.

CONTROL AREA [ICAO]. A controlled airspace extending upwards from a specified limit above the earth.

CONTROL SECTOR. An airspace area of defined horizontal and vertical dimensions for which a controller or group of controllers has air traffic control responsibility, normally within an air route traffic control center or an approach control facility. Sectors are established based on predominant traffic flows, altitude strata, and controller workload. Pilot. communications during operations within a sector are normally maintained on discrete frequencies assigned to the sector. (See DISCRETE FREQUENCY.)

CONTROL SLASH. A radar beacon slash representing the actual position of the associated aircraft. Normally, the control slash is the one closest to the interrogating radar beacon site. When ARTCC radar is operating in narrowband (digitized) mode, the control slash is converted to a target symbol.

CONTROLLED AIRSPACE. An airspace of defined dimensions within which air traffic control service is provided to IFR flights and to VFR flights in accordance with the airspace classification.
 a. Controlled airspace is a generic term that covers Class A, Class B, Class C, Class D, and Class E airspace.
 b. Controlled airspace is also that airspace within which all aircraft operators are subject to certain pilot qualifications, operating rules, and equipment requirements in 14 CFR Part 91 (for specific operating requirements, please refer to 14 CFR Part 91). For IFR operations in any class of controlled airspace, a pilot must file an IFR flight plan and receive an appropriate ATC clearance. Each Class B, Class C, and Class D airspace area designated for an airport contains at least one primary airport around which the airspace is designated (for specific designations and descriptions of the airspace classes, please refer to 14 CFR Part 71).

(continued)

P/C

c. Controlled airspace in the United States is designated as follows:

1. CLASS A. Generally, that airspace from 18,000 feet MSL up to and including FL 600, including the airspace overlying the waters within 12 nautical miles of the coast of the 48 contiguous States and Alaska. Unless otherwise authorized, all persons must operate their aircraft under IFR.

2. CLASS B. Generally, that airspace from the surface to 10,000 feet MSL surrounding the nation's busiest airports in terms of airport operations or passenger enplanements. The configuration of each Class B airspace area is individually tailored and consists of a surface area and two or more layers (some Class B airspace areas resemble upside-down wedding cakes), and is designed to contain all published instrument procedures once an aircraft enters the airspace. An ATC clearance is required for all aircraft to operate in the area, and all aircraft that are so cleared receive separation services within the airspace. The cloud clearance requirement for VFR operations is "clear of clouds."

3. CLASS C. Generally, that airspace from the surface to 4,000 feet above the airport elevation (charted in MSL) surrounding those airports that have an operational control tower, are serviced by a radar approach control, and that have a certain number of IFR operations or passenger enplanements. Although the configuration of each Class C area is individually tailored, the airspace usually consists of a surface area with a 5 NM radius, a circle with a 10NM radius that extends no lower than 1,200 feet up to 4,000 feet above the airport elevation and an outer area that is not charted. Each person must establish two-way radio communications with the ATC facility providing air traffic services prior to entering the airspace and thereafter maintain those communications while within the airspace. VFR aircraft are only separated from IFR aircraft within the airspace. (See OUTER AREA.)

4. CLASS D. Generally, that airspace from the surface to 2,500 feet above the airport elevation (charted in MSL) surrounding those airports that have an operational control tower. The configuration of each Class D airspace area is individually tailored and when instrument procedures are published, the airspace will normally be designed to contain the procedures. Arrival extensions for instrument approach procedures may be Class D or Class E airspace. Unless otherwise authorized, each person must establish two-way radio communications with the ATC facility providing air traffic services prior to entering the airspace and thereafter maintain those communications while in the airspace. No separation services are provided to VFR aircraft.

5. CLASS E. Generally, if the airspace is not Class A, Class B, Class C, or Class D, and it is controlled airspace, it is Class E airspace. Class E airspace extends upward from either the surface or a designated altitude to the overlying or adjacent controlled airspace. When designated as a surface area, the airspace will be configured to contain all instrument procedures. Also in this class are Federal airways, airspace beginning at either 700 or 1,200 feet AGL used to transition to/from the terminal or en route environment, en route domestic, and offshore airspace areas designated below 18,000 feet MSL. Unless designated at a lower altitude, Class E airspace begins at 14,500 MSL over the United States, including that airspace overlying the waters within 12 nautical miles of the coast of the 48 contiguous States and Alaska, up to, but not including 18,000 feet MSL, and the airspace above FL 600.

CONTROLLED AIRSPACE [ICAO]. An airspace of defined dimensions within which air traffic control service is provided to IFR flights and to VFR flights in accordance with the airspace classification.

Note: Controlled airspace is a generic term which covers ATS airspace Classes A, B, C, D, and E.

CONTROLLED TIME OF ARRIVAL. Arrival time assigned during a Traffic Management Program. This time may be modified due to adjustments or user options.

CONTROLLER. (See AIR TRAFFIC CONTROL SPECIALIST.)

CONTROLLER [ICAO]. A person authorized to provide air traffic control services.

CONTROLLER PILOT DATA LINK COMMUNICATIONS (CPDLC). A two-way digital communications system that conveys textual air traffic control messages between controllers and pilots using ground or satellite-based radio relay stations.

CONVECTIVE SIGMET. A weather advisory concerning convective weather significant to the safety of all aircraft. Convective SIGMETs are issued for tornadoes, lines of thunderstorms, embedded thunderstorms of any intensity level, areas of thunderstorms greater than or equal to VIP level 4 with an area coverage of 4/10 (40%) or more, and hail 3/4 inch or greater. (See AIRMET.) (See CWA.) (See GRAPHICAL AIRMEN'S METEOROLOGICAL INFORMATION.) (See SAW.) (See SIGMET.) (Refer to AIM.)

CONVECTIVE SIGNIFICANT METEOROLOGICAL INFORMATION. (See CONVECTIVE SIGMET.)

COOPERATIVE SURVEILLANCE. Any surveillance system, such as secondary surveillance radar (SSR), wide-area multilateration (WAM), or ADS-B, that is dependent upon the presence of certain equipment onboard the aircraft or vehicle to be detected. (See AUTOMATIC DEPENDENT SURVEILLANCE–BROADCAST.) (See NON-COOPERATIVE SURVEILLANCE.)(See RADAR.) (See WIDE AREA MULTILATERATION.)

COORDINATES. The intersection of lines of reference, usually expressed in degrees/minutes/seconds of latitude and longitude, used to determine position or location.

COORDINATION FIX. The fix in relation to which facilities will handoff, transfer control of an aircraft, or coordinate flight progress data. For terminal facilities, it may also serve as a clearance for arriving aircraft.

COPTER. (See HELICOPTER.)

CORRECTION. An error has been made in the transmission and the correct version follows.

COUPLED APPROACH. An instrument approach performed by the aircraft autopilot, and/or visually depicted on the flight director, which is receiving position information and/or steering commands from onboard navigational equipment. In general, coupled non-precision approaches must be flown manually (autopilot disengaged) at altitudes lower than 50 feet AGL below the minimum descent altitude, and coupled precision approaches must be flown manually (autopilot disengaged) below 50 feet AGL unless authorized to conduct autoland operations. Coupled instrument approaches are commonly flown to the allowable IFR weather minima established by the operator or PIC, or flown VFR for training and safety.

COUPLED SCHEDULING (CS)/EXTENDED METERING (XM). Adds additional Constraint Satisfaction Points for metered aircraft along their route. This provides the ability to merge flows upstream from the meter fix and results in a more optimal distribution of delays over a greater distance from the airport, increased meter list accuracy, and more accurate delivery to the meter fix.

COURSE.
a. The intended direction of flight in the horizontal plane measured in degrees from north.
b. The ILS localizer signal pattern usually specified as the front course or the back course.
(See BEARING.) (See INSTRUMENT LANDING SYSTEM.) (See RADIAL.)

CPDLC. (See CONTROLLER PILOT DATA LINK COMMUNICATONS.)

CPL [ICAO]. (See ICAO term CURRENT FLIGHT PLAN.)

CREWMEMBER (UAS). A person assigned to perform an operational duty. A UAS crewmember includes the remote pilot in command, the person manipulating the controls, and visual observers but may also include other persons as appropriate or required to ensure the safe operation of the UAS (e.g., sensor operator, ground control station operator).

CRITICAL ENGINE. The engine which, upon failure, would most adversely affect the performance or handling qualities of an aircraft.

CROSS (FIX) AT (ALTITUDE). Used by ATC when a specific altitude restriction at a specified fix is required.

CROSS (FIX) AT OR ABOVE (ALTITUDE). Used by ATC when an altitude restriction at a specified fix is required. It does not prohibit the aircraft from crossing the fix at a higher altitude than specified; however, the higher altitude may not be one that will violate a succeeding altitude restriction or altitude assignment. (See ALTITUDE RESTRICTION.) (Refer to AIM.)

CROSS (FIX) AT OR BELOW (ALTITUDE). Used by ATC when a maximum crossing altitude at a specific fix is required. It does not prohibit the aircraft from crossing the fix at a lower altitude; however, it must be at or above the minimum IFR altitude. (See ALTITUDE RESTRICTION.) (See MINIMUM IFR ALTITUDES.) (Refer to 14 CFR Part 91.)

CROSSWIND.
a. When used concerning the traffic pattern, the word means "crosswind leg."
(See TRAFFIC PATTERN.)
b. When used concerning wind conditions, the word means a wind not parallel to the runway or the path of an aircraft.
(See CROSSWIND COMPONENT.)

CROSSWIND COMPONENT. The wind component measured in knots at 90 degrees to the longitudinal axis of the runway.

CRUISE. Used in an ATC clearance to authorize a pilot to conduct flight at any altitude from the minimum IFR altitude up to and including the altitude specified in the clearance. The pilot may level off at any intermediate altitude within this block of airspace. Climb/descent within the block is to be made at the discretion of the pilot. However, once the pilot starts descent and verbally reports leaving an altitude in the block, he/she may not return to that altitude without additional ATC clearance. Further, it is approval for the pilot to proceed to and make an approach at destination airport and can be used in conjunction with:
a. An airport clearance limit at locations with a standard/special instrument approach procedure. The CFRs require that if an instrument letdown to an airport is necessary, the pilot shall make the letdown in accordance with a standard/special instrument approach procedure for that airport, or
b. An airport clearance limit at locations that are within/below/outside controlled airspace and without a standard/special instrument approach procedure. Such a clearance is NOT AUTHORIZATION for the pilot to descend under IFR conditions below the applicable minimum IFR altitude nor does it imply that ATC is exercising control over aircraft in Class G airspace; however, it provides a means for the aircraft to proceed to destination airport, descend, and land in accordance with applicable CFRs governing VFR flight operations. Also, this provides search and rescue protection until such time as the IFR flight plan is closed.
(See INSTRUMENT APPROACH PROCEDURE.)

CRUISE CLIMB. A climb technique employed by aircraft, usually at a constant power setting, resulting in an increase of altitude as the aircraft weight decreases.

CRUISING ALTITUDE. An altitude or flight level maintained during en route level flight. This is a constant altitude and should not be confused with a cruise clearance. (See ALTITUDE.) (See ICAO term CRUISING LEVEL.)

P/C

CRUISING LEVEL. (See CRUISING ALTITUDE.)

CRUISING LEVEL [ICAO]. A level maintained during a significant portion of a flight.

CSP. (See CONSTRAINT SATISFACTION POINT)

CT MESSAGE. An EDCT time generated by the ATC-SCC to regulate traffic at arrival airports. Normally, a CT message is automatically transferred from the traffic management system computer to the NAS en route computer and appears as an EDCT. In the event of a communication failure between the traffic management system computer and the NAS, the CT message can be manually entered by the TMC at the en route facility.

CTA. (See CONTROLLED TIME OF ARRIVAL.) (See ICAO term CONTROL AREA.)

CTAF. (See COMMON TRAFFIC ADVISORY FREQUENCY.)

CTOP. (See COLLABORATIVE TRAJECTORY OPTIONS PROGRAM.)

CTRD. (See CERTIFIED TOWER RADAR DISPLAY.)

CURRENT FLIGHT PLAN [ICAO]. The flight plan, including changes, if any, brought about by subsequent clearances.

CVFP APPROACH. (See CHARTED VISUAL FLIGHT PROCEDURE APPROACH.)

CWA. (See CENTER WEATHER ADVISORY and WEATHER ADVISORY.)

CWT. (See CONSOLIDATED WAKE TURBULENCE.)

D

D–ATIS. (See DIGITAL–AUTOMATIC TERMINAL INFORMATION SERVICE.)

D–ATIS [ICAO]. (See ICAO Term DATA LINK AUTOMATIC TERMINAL INFORMATION SERVICE.)

DA [ICAO]. (See ICAO Term DECISION ALTITUDE/ DECISION HEIGHT.)

DAIR. (See DIRECT ALTITUDE AND IDENTITY READOUT.)

DANGER AREA [ICAO]. An airspace of defined dimensions within which activities dangerous to the flight of aircraft may exist at specified times.

Note: The term "Danger Area" is not used in reference to areas within the United States or any of its possessions or territories.

DAS. (See DELAY ASSIGNMENT.)

DATA BLOCK. (See ALPHANUMERIC DISPLAY.)

DATA LINK AUTOMATIC TERMINAL INFORMATION SERVICE (D–ATIS) [ICAO]. The provision of ATIS via data link.

DCT. (See DELAY COUNTDOWN TIMER.)

DEAD RECKONING. Dead reckoning, as applied to flying, is the navigation of an airplane solely by means of computations based on airspeed, course, heading, wind direction, and speed, groundspeed, and elapsed time.

DEBRIS RESPONSE AREA (DRA). Used by ATC. Areas of airspace that may be activated in response to unplanned falling debris in the NAS.

DECISION ALTITUDE/DECISION HEIGHT [ICAO Annex 6]. A specified altitude or height (A/H) in the precision approach at which a missed approach must be initiated if the required visual reference to continue the approach has not been established.
1. Decision altitude (DA) is referenced to mean sea level and decision height (DH) is referenced to the threshold elevation.
2. Category II and III minima are expressed as a DH and not a DA. Minima is assessed by reference to a radio altimeter and not a barometric altimeter, which makes the minima a DH.
3. The required visual reference means that section of the visual aids or of the approach area which should have been in view for sufficient time for the pilot to have made an assessment of the aircraft position and rate of change of position, in relation to the desired flight path.

DECISION ALTITUDE (DA). A specified altitude (mean sea level (MSL)) on an instrument approach procedure (ILS, GLS, vertically guided RNAV) at which the pilot must decide whether to continue the approach or initiate an immediate missed approach if the pilot does not see the required visual references.

DECISION HEIGHT (DH). With respect to the operation of aircraft, means the height at which a decision must be made during an ILS or PAR instrument approach to either continue the approach or to execute a missed approach. (See ICAO term DECISION ALTITUDE/DECISION HEIGHT.)

DECODER. The device used to decipher signals received from ATCRBS transponders to effect their display as select codes. (See CODES.) (See RADAR.)

DEFENSE AREA. Any airspace of the contiguous United States that is not an ADIZ in which the control of aircraft is required for reasons of national security.

DEFENSE VISUAL FLIGHT RULES. Rules applicable to flights within an ADIZ conducted under the visual flight rules in 14 CFR Part 91. (See AIR DEFENSE IDENTIFICATION ZONE.) (Refer to 14 CFR Part 91.) (Refer to 14 CFR Part 99.)

DELAY ASSIGNMENT (DAS). Delays are distributed to aircraft based on the traffic management program parameters. The delay assignment is calculated in 15-minute increments and appears as a table in Traffic Flow Management System (TFMS).

DELAY COUNTDOWN TIMER (DCT). The display of the delay that must be absorbed by a flight prior to crossing a Meter Reference Element (MRE) to meet the TBFM Scheduled Time of Arrival (STA). It is

calculated by taking the difference between the frozen STA and the Estimated Time of Arrival (ETA).

DELAY INDEFINITE (REASON IF KNOWN) EXPECT FURTHER CLEARANCE (TIME). Used by ATC to inform a pilot when an accurate estimate of the delay time and the reason for the delay cannot immediately be determined; e.g., a disabled aircraft on the runway, terminal or center area saturation, weather below landing minimums, etc. (See EXPECT FURTHER CLEARANCE (TIME).)

DEPARTURE CENTER. The ARTCC having jurisdiction for the airspace that generates a flight to the impacted airport.

DEPARTURE CONTROL. A function of an approach control facility providing air traffic control service for departing IFR and, under certain conditions, VFR aircraft. (See APPROACH CONTROL FACILITY.) (Refer to AIM.)

DEPARTURE SEQUENCING PROGRAM. A program designed to assist in achieving a specified interval over a common point for departures.

DEPARTURE TIME. The time an aircraft becomes airborne.

DEPARTURE VIEWER. A capability within the Traffic Flow Management System (TFMS) that provides combined displays for monitoring departure by fixes and departure airports. Traffic management personnel can customize the displays by selecting the departure airports and fixes of interest. The information displayed is the demand for the resource (fix or departure airport) in time bins with the flight list and a flight history for one flight at a time. From the display, flights can be selected for route amendment, one or more at a time, and the Route Amendment Dialogue (RAD) screen automatically opens for easy route selection and execution. Reroute options are based on Coded Departure Route (CDR) database and Trajectory Options Set (TOS) (when available).

DESCEND VIA. An abbreviated ATC clearance that requires compliance with a published procedure lateral path and associated speed restrictions and provides a pilot-discretion descent to comply with published altitude restrictions.

DESCENT SPEED ADJUSTMENTS. Speed deceleration calculations made to determine an accurate VTA. These calculations start at the transition point and use arrival speed segments to the vertex.

DESIGNATED COMMON TRAFFIC ADVISORY FREQUENCY (CTAF) AREA. In Alaska, in addition to being designated for the purpose of carrying out airport advisory practices while operating to or from an airport without an operating airport traffic control tower, a CTAF may also be designated for the purpose of carrying out advisory practices for operations in and through areas with a high volume of VFR traffic.

DESIRED COURSE.
 a. True. A predetermined desired course direction to be followed (measured in degrees from true north).

 b. Magnetic. A predetermined desired course direction to be followed (measured in degrees from local magnetic north).

DESIRED TRACK. The planned or intended track between two waypoints. It is measured in degrees from either magnetic or true north. The instantaneous angle may change from point to point along the great circle track between waypoints.

DETRESFA (DISTRESS PHASE) [ICAO]. The code word used to designate an emergency phase wherein there is reasonable certainty that an aircraft and its occupants are threatened by grave and imminent danger or require immediate assistance.

DEVIATIONS.
 a. A departure from a current clearance, such as an off course maneuver to avoid weather or turbulence.

 b. Where specifically authorized in the CFRs and requested by the pilot, ATC may permit pilots to deviate from certain regulations.

DH. (See DECISION HEIGHT.)

DH [ICAO]. (See ICAO Term DECISION ALTITUDE/ DECISION HEIGHT.)

DIGITAL-AUTOMATIC TERMINAL INFORMATION SERVICE (D-ATIS). The service provides text messages to aircraft, airlines, and other users outside the standard reception range of conventional ATIS via landline and data link communications to the cockpit. Also, the service provides a computer-synthesized voice message that can be transmitted to all aircraft within range of existing transmitters. The Terminal Data Link System (TDLS) D-ATIS application uses weather inputs from local automated weather sources or manually entered meteorological data together with preprogrammed menus to provide standard information to users. Airports with D-ATIS capability are listed in the Chart Supplement U.S.

DIGITAL TARGET. A computer-generated symbol representing an aircraft's position, based on a primary return or radar beacon reply, shown on a digital display.

DIGITAL TERMINAL AUTOMATION SYSTEM (DTAS). A system where digital radar and beacon data is presented on digital displays and the operational program monitors the system performance on a real-time basis.

DIGITIZED TARGET. A computer-generated indication shown on an analog radar display resulting from a primary radar return or a radar beacon reply.

DIRECT. Straight line flight between two navigational aids, fixes, points, or any combination thereof. When used by pilots in describing off-airway routes, points defining direct route segments become compulsory reporting points unless the aircraft is under radar contact.

DIRECTLY BEHIND. An aircraft is considered to be operating directly behind when it is following the actual flight path of the lead aircraft over the surface of the earth except when applying wake turbulence separation criteria.

DISCRETE BEACON CODE. (See DISCRETE CODE.)

DISCRETE CODE. As used in the Air Traffic Control Radar Beacon System (ATCRBS), any one of the 4096 selectable Mode 3/A aircraft transponder codes except those ending in zero zero; e.g., discrete codes: 0010, 1201, 2317, 7777; nondiscrete codes: 0100, 1200, 7700. Nondiscrete codes are normally reserved for radar facilities that are not equipped with discrete decoding capability and for other purposes such as emergencies (7700), VFR aircraft (1200), etc. (See RADAR.) (Refer to AIM.)

DISCRETE FREQUENCY. A separate radio frequency for use in direct pilot-controller communications in air traffic control which reduces frequency congestion by controlling the number of aircraft operating on a particular frequency at one time. Discrete frequencies are normally designated for each control sector in en route/terminal ATC facilities. Discrete frequencies are listed in the Chart Supplement U.S. and the DOD FLIP IFR En Route Supplement. (See CONTROL SECTOR.)

DISPLACED THRESHOLD. A threshold that is located at a point on the runway other than the designated beginning of the runway. (See THRESHOLD.) (Refer to AIM.)

DISTANCE MEASURING EQUIPMENT (DME). Equipment (airborne and ground) used to measure, in nautical miles, the slant range distance of an aircraft from the DME navigational aid. (See TACAN.) (See VORTAC.)

DISTRESS. A condition of being threatened by serious and/or imminent danger and of requiring immediate assistance.

DIVE BRAKES. (See SPEED BRAKES.)

DIVERSE VECTOR AREA. In a radar environment, that area in which a prescribed departure route is not required as the only suitable route to avoid obstacles. The area in which random radar vectors below the MVA/MIA, established in accordance with the TERPS criteria for diverse departures, obstacles and terrain avoidance, may be issued to departing aircraft.

DIVERSION (DVRSN). Flights that are required to land at other than their original destination for reasons beyond the control of the pilot/company, e.g. periods of significant weather.

DME. (See DISTANCE MEASURING EQUIPMENT.)

DME FIX. A geographical position determined by reference to a navigational aid which provides distance and azimuth information. It is defined by a specific distance in nautical miles and a radial, azimuth, or course (i.e., localizer) in degrees magnetic from that aid. (See DISTANCE MEASURING EQUIPMENT.) (See FIX.)

DME SEPARATION. Spacing of aircraft in terms of distances (nautical miles) determined by reference to distance measuring equipment (DME). (See DISTANCE MEASURING EQUIPMENT.)

DOD FLIP. Department of Defense Flight Information Publications used for flight planning, en route, and terminal operations. FLIP is produced by the National Geospatial-Intelligence Agency (NGA) for world-wide use. United States Government Flight Information Publications (en route charts and instrument approach procedure charts) are incorporated in DOD FLIP for use in the National Airspace System (NAS).

DOMESTIC AIRSPACE. Airspace which overlies the continental land mass of the United States plus Hawaii and U.S. possessions. Domestic airspace extends to 12 miles offshore.

DOMESTIC NOTICE. A special notice or notice containing graphics or plain language text pertaining to almost every aspect of aviation, such as military training areas, large scale sporting events, air show information, Special Traffic Management Programs (STMPs), and airport-specific information. These notices are applicable to operations within the United States and can be found on the Domestic Notices website.

DOWNBURST. A strong downdraft which induces an outburst of damaging winds on or near the ground. Damaging winds, either straight or curved, are highly divergent. The sizes of downbursts vary from 1/2 mile or less to more than 10 miles. An intense downburst often causes widespread damage. Damaging winds, lasting 5 to 30 minutes, could reach speeds as high as 120 knots.

DOWNWIND LEG. (See TRAFFIC PATTERN.)

DP. (See INSTRUMENT DEPARTURE PROCEDURE.)

DRA. (See DEBRIS RESPONSE AREA.)

DRAG CHUTE. A parachute device installed on certain aircraft which is deployed on landing roll to assist in deceleration of the aircraft.

DROP ZONE. Any pre-determined area upon which parachutists or objects land after making an intentional parachute jump or drop.
(Refer to 14 CFR §105.3, Definitions)

DSP. (See DEPARTURE SEQUENCING PROGRAM.)

DTAS. (See DIGITAL TERMINAL AUTOMATION SYSTEM.)

DUE REGARD. A phase of flight wherein an aircraft commander of a State-operated aircraft assumes responsibility to separate his/her aircraft from all other aircraft. (See also FAA Order JO 7110.65, Para 1-2-1, WORD MEANINGS.)

DUTY RUNWAY. (See RUNWAY IN USE/ACTIVE RUNWAY/DUTY RUNWAY.)

DVA. (See DIVERSE VECTOR AREA.)

DVFR. (See DEFENSE VISUAL FLIGHT RULES.)

DVFR FLIGHT PLAN. A flight plan filed for a VFR aircraft which intends to operate in airspace within which the ready identification, location, and control of aircraft are required in the interest of national security.

DVRSN. (See DIVERSION.)

DYNAMIC. Continuous review, evaluation, and change to meet demands.

DYNAMIC RESTRICTIONS. Those restrictions imposed by the local facility on an "as needed" basis to manage unpredictable fluctuations in traffic demands.

E

EAS. (See EN ROUTE AUTOMATION SYSTEM.)

EDCT. (See EXPECT DEPARTURE CLEARANCE TIME.)

EDST. (See EN ROUTE DECISION SUPPORT TOOL.)

EFC. (See EXPECT FURTHER CLEARANCE (TIME).)

ELT. (See EMERGENCY LOCATOR TRANSMITTER.)

EMBEDDED ROUTE TEXT. An EDST notification that an ADR/ADAR/AAR has been applied to the flight plan. Within the route field, sub-fields consisting of an adapted route or an embedded change in the route are color-coded in cyan with cyan brackets around the sub-field. (See EN ROUTE DECISION SUPPORT TOOL.)

EMERGENCY. A distress or an urgency condition.

EMERGENCY AUTOLAND SYSTEM. This system, if activated, will determine an optimal airport, plot a course, broadcast the aircraft's intentions, fly to the airport, land, and (depending on the model) shut down the engines. Though the system will broadcast the aircraft's intentions, the controller should assume that transmissions to the aircraft will not be acknowledged.

EMERGENCY DESCENT MODE. This automated system senses conditions conducive to hypoxia (cabin depressurization). If an aircraft is equipped and the system is activated, it is designed to turn the aircraft up to 90 degrees, then descend to a lower altitude and level off, giving the pilot(s) time to recover.

EMERGENCY LOCATOR TRANSMITTER (ELT). A radio transmitter attached to the aircraft structure which operates from its own power source on 121.5 MHz and 243.0 MHz. It aids in locating downed aircraft by radiating a downward sweeping audio tone, 2–4 times per second. It is designed to function without human action after an accident. (Refer to 14 CFR Part 91.) (Refer to AIM.)

E-MSAW. (See EN ROUTE MINIMUM SAFE ALTITUDE WARNING.)

ENHANCED FLIGHT VISION SYSTEM (EFVS). An EFVS is an installed aircraft system which uses an electronic means to provide a display of the forward external scene topography (the natural or man-made features of a place or region especially in a way to show their relative positions and elevation) through the use of imaging sensors, including but not limited to forward-looking infrared, millimeter wave radiometry, millimeter wave radar, or low-light level image intensification. An EFVS includes the display element, sensors, computers and power supplies, indications, and controls. An operator's authorization to conduct an EFVS operation may have provisions which allow pilots to conduct IAPs when the reported weather is below minimums prescribed on the IAP to be flown.

ENHANCED SPECIAL REPORTING SERVICE (eSRS). An automated service used to enhance search and rescue operations that provides flight service specialists in Alaska direct information from the aircraft's registered tracking device.

EN ROUTE AIR TRAFFIC CONTROL SERVICES. Air traffic control service provided aircraft on IFR flight plans, generally by centers, when these aircraft are operating between departure and destination terminal areas. When equipment, capabilities, and controller workload permit, certain advisory/assistance services may be provided to VFR aircraft. (See AIR ROUTE TRAFFIC CONTROL CENTER.) (Refer to AIM.)

EN ROUTE AUTOMATION SYSTEM (EAS). The complex integrated environment consisting of situation display systems, surveillance systems and flight data processing, remote devices, decision support tools, and the related communications equipment that form the heart of the automated IFR air traffic control system. It interfaces with automated terminal systems and is used in the control of en route IFR aircraft. (Refer to AIM.)

EN ROUTE CHARTS. (See AERONAUTICAL CHART.)

EN ROUTE DECISION SUPPORT TOOL (EDST). An automated tool provided at each Radar Associate position in selected En Route facilities. This tool utilizes flight and radar data to determine present and future trajectories for all active and proposal aircraft and provides enhanced automated flight data management.

EN ROUTE DESCENT. Descent from the en route cruising altitude which takes place along the route of flight.

EN ROUTE HIGH ALTITUDE CHARTS. (See AERONAUTICAL CHART.)

EN ROUTE LOW ALTITUDE CHARTS. (See AERONAUTICAL CHART.)

EN ROUTE MINIMUM SAFE ALTITUDE WARNING (E–MSAW). A function of the EAS that aids the controller by providing an alert when a tracked aircraft is below or predicted by the computer to go below a predetermined minimum IFR altitude (MIA).

EN ROUTE TRANSITION. (See SEGMENTS OF A SID/STAR.)

EN ROUTE TRANSITION WAYPOINT. (See SEGMENTS OF A SID/STAR.)

eSRS. (See ENHANCED SPECIAL REPORTING SERVICE.)

EST. (See ESTIMATED.)

ESTABLISHED. To be stable or fixed at an altitude or on a course, route, route segment, heading, instrument approach or departure procedure, etc.

P/C

ESTABLISHED ON RNP (EoR) CONCEPT. A system of authorized instrument approaches, ATC procedures, surveillance, and communication requirements that allow aircraft operations to be safely conducted with approved reduced separation criteria once aircraft are established on a PBN segment of a published instrument flight procedure.

ESTIMATED (EST). When used in NOTAMs "EST" is a contraction that is used by the issuing authority only when the condition is expected to return to service prior to the expiration time. Using "EST" lets the user know that this NOTAM has the possibility of returning to service earlier than the expiration time. Any NOTAM which includes an "EST" will be auto-expired at the designated expiration time.

ESTIMATED ELAPSED TIME [ICAO]. The estimated time required to proceed from one significant point to another. (See ICAO Term TOTAL ESTIMATED ELAPSED TIME.)

ESTIMATED OFF-BLOCK TIME [ICAO]. The estimated time at which the aircraft will commence movement associated with departure.

ESTIMATED POSITION ERROR (EPE). (See REQUIRED NAVIGATION PERFORMANCE.)

ESTIMATED TIME OF ARRIVAL. The time the flight is estimated to arrive at the gate (scheduled operators) or the actual runway on times for nonscheduled operators.

ESTIMATED TIME EN ROUTE. The estimated flying time from departure point to destination (lift-off to touchdown).

ETA. (See ESTIMATED TIME OF ARRIVAL.)

ETE. (See ESTIMATED TIME EN ROUTE.)

EXECUTE MISSED APPROACH. Instructions issued to a pilot making an instrument approach which means continue inbound to the missed approach point and execute the missed approach procedure as described on the Instrument Approach Procedure Chart or as previously assigned by ATC. The pilot may climb immediately to the altitude specified in the missed approach procedure upon making a missed approach. No turns should be initiated prior to reaching the missed approach point. When conducting an ASR or PAR approach, execute the assigned missed approach procedure immediately upon receiving instructions to "execute missed approach." (Refer to AIM.)

EXPECT (ALTITUDE) AT (TIME) or (FIX). Used under certain conditions to provide a pilot with an altitude to be used in the event of two-way communications failure. It also provides altitude information to assist the pilot in planning. (Refer to AIM.)

EXPECT DEPARTURE CLEARANCE TIME (EDCT). The runway release time assigned to an aircraft in a traffic management program and shown on the flight progress strip as an EDCT. (See GROUND DELAY PROGRAM.)

EXPECT FURTHER CLEARANCE (TIME). The time a pilot can expect to receive clearance beyond a clearance limit.

EXPECT FURTHER CLEARANCE VIA (AIRWAYS, ROUTES OR FIXES). Used to inform a pilot of the routing he/she can expect if any part of the route beyond a short range clearance limit differs from that filed.

EXPEDITE. Used by ATC when prompt compliance is required to avoid the development of an imminent situation. Expedite climb/descent normally indicates to a pilot that the approximate best rate of climb/descent should be used without requiring an exceptional change in aircraft handling characteristics.

F

FAA-RECOGNIZED IDENTIFICATION AREA (FRIA). A defined geographic area where persons can operate UAS without remote identification, provided they maintain visual line of sight.

FAF. (See FINAL APPROACH FIX.)

FALLEN HERO. Remains of fallen members of the United States military are often returned home by aircraft. These flights may be identified with the phrase "FALLEN HERO" added to the remarks section of the flight plan, or they may be transmitted via air/ground communications. If able, these flights will receive priority handling.

FAST FILE. An FSS system whereby a pilot files a flight plan via telephone that is recorded and later transcribed for transmission to the appropriate air traffic facility. (Alaska only.)

FAWP. Final Approach Waypoint

FEATHERED PROPELLER. A propeller whose blades have been rotated so that the leading and trailing edges are nearly parallel with the aircraft flight path to stop or minimize drag and engine rotation. Normally used to indicate shutdown of a reciprocating or turboprop engine due to malfunction.

FEDERAL AIRWAYS. (See LOW ALTITUDE AIRWAY STRUCTURE.)

FEEDER FIX. The fix depicted on Instrument Approach Procedure Charts which establishes the starting point of the feeder route.

FEEDER ROUTE. A route depicted on instrument approach procedure charts to designate routes for aircraft to proceed from the en route structure to the initial approach fix (IAF). (See INSTRUMENT APPROACH PROCEDURE.)

FERRY FLIGHT. A flight for the purpose of:
 a. Returning an aircraft to base.
 b. Delivering an aircraft from one location to another.
 c. Moving an aircraft to and from a maintenance base. Ferry flights, under certain conditions, may be conducted under terms of a special flight permit.

FIELD ELEVATION. (See AIRPORT ELEVATION.)

FILED. Normally used in conjunction with flight plans, meaning a flight plan has been submitted to ATC.

FILED EN ROUTE DELAY. Any of the following pre-planned delays at points/areas along the route of flight which require special flight plan filing and handling techniques.
 a. Terminal Area Delay. A delay within a terminal area for touch-and-go, low approach, or other terminal area activity.
 b. Special Use Airspace Delay. A delay within a Military Operations Area, Restricted Area, Warning Area, or ATC Assigned Airspace.
 c. Aerial Refueling Delay. A delay within an Aerial Refueling Track or Anchor.

FILED FLIGHT PLAN. The flight plan as filed with an ATS unit by the pilot or his/her designated representative without any subsequent changes or clearances.

FINAL. Commonly used to mean that an aircraft is on the final approach course or is aligned with a landing area. (See FINAL APPROACH COURSE.) (See FINAL APPROACH-IFR.) (See SEGMENTS OF AN INSTRUMENT APPROACH PROCEDURE.)

FINAL APPROACH [ICAO]. That part of an instrument approach procedure which commences at the specified final approach fix or point, or where such a fix or point is not specified.
 a. At the end of the last procedure turn, base turn or inbound turn of a racetrack procedure, if specified; or
 b. At the point of interception of the last track specified in the approach procedure; and ends at a point in the vicinity of an aerodrome from which:
 1. A landing can be made; or
 2. A missed approach procedure is initiated.

FINAL APPROACH COURSE. A bearing/radial/track of an instrument approach leading to a runway or an extended runway centerline all without regard to distance.

FINAL APPROACH FIX. The fix from which the final approach (IFR) to an airport is executed and which identifies the beginning of the final approach segment. It is designated on Government charts by the Maltese Cross symbol for nonprecision approaches and the lightning bolt symbol, designating the PFAF, for precision approaches; or when ATC directs a lower-than-published glideslope/path or vertical path intercept altitude, it is the resultant actual point of the glideslope/path or vertical path intercept. (See FINAL APPROACH POINT.) (See GLIDESLOPE INTERCEPT ALTITUDE.) (See SEGMENTS OF AN INSTRUMENT APPROACH PROCEDURE.)

FINAL APPROACH—IFR. The flight path of an aircraft which is inbound to an airport on a final instrument approach course, beginning at the final approach fix or point and extending to the airport or the point where a circle-to-land maneuver or a missed approach is executed. (See FINAL APPROACH COURSE.) (See FINAL APPROACH FIX.) (See FINAL APPROACH POINT.) (See SEGMENTS OF AN INSTRUMENT APPROACH PROCEDURE.) (See ICAO term FINAL APPROACH.)

FINAL APPROACH POINT. The point, applicable only to a nonprecision approach with no depicted FAF (such as an on airport VOR), where the aircraft is established inbound on the final approach course from the procedure turn and where the final approach descent may be commenced. The FAP serves as the FAF and identifies the beginning of the final approach segment. (See FINAL APPROACH FIX.) (See SEGMENTS OF AN INSTRUMENT APPROACH PROCEDURE.)

FINAL APPROACH SEGMENT. (See SEGMENTS OF AN INSTRUMENT APPROACH PROCEDURE.)

FINAL APPROACH SEGMENT [ICAO]. That segment of an instrument approach procedure in which alignment and descent for landing are accomplished.

FINAL CONTROLLER. The controller providing information and final approach guidance during PAR and ASR approaches utilizing radar equipment. (See RADAR APPROACH.)

FINAL GUARD SERVICE. A value added service provided in conjunction with LAA/RAA only during periods of significant and fast changing weather conditions that may affect landing and takeoff operations.

FINAL MONITOR AID. A high resolution color display that is equipped with the controller alert system hardware/software used to monitor the no transgression zone (NTZ) during simultaneous parallel approach operations. The display includes alert algorithms providing the target predictors, a color change alert when a target penetrates or is predicted to penetrate the no transgression zone (NTZ), synthesized voice alerts, and digital mapping. (See RADAR APPROACH.)

FINAL MONITOR CONTROLLER. Air Traffic Control Specialist assigned to radar monitor the flight path of aircraft during simultaneous parallel (approach courses spaced less than 9000 feet/9200 feet above 5000 feet) and simultaneous close parallel approach operations. Each runway is assigned a final monitor controller during simultaneous parallel and simultaneous close parallel ILS approaches.

FIR. (See FLIGHT INFORMATION REGION.)

FIRST PERSON VIEW. UAS operation in which imagery is transmitted to the UAS pilot by an onboard UA camera.

FIRST TIER CENTER. An ARTCC immediately adjacent to the impacted center.

FIS-B. (See FLIGHT INFORMATION SERVICE–BROADCAST)

FIX. A geographical position determined by visual reference to the surface, by reference to one or more radio NAVAIDs, by celestial plotting, or by another navigational device.

FIX BALANCING. A process whereby aircraft are evenly distributed over several available arrival fixes reducing delays and controller workload.

FLAG. A warning device incorporated in certain airborne navigation and flight instruments indicating that:

a. Instruments are inoperative or otherwise not operating satisfactorily, or

b. Signal strength or quality of the received signal falls below acceptable values.

FLAG ALARM. (See FLAG.)

FLAMEOUT. An emergency condition caused by a loss of engine power.

FLAMEOUT PATTERN. An approach normally conducted by a single-engine military aircraft experiencing loss or anticipating loss of engine power or control. The standard overhead approach starts at a relatively high altitude over a runway ("high key") followed by a continuous 180 degree turn to a high, wide position ("low key") followed by a continuous 180 degree turn final. The standard straight-in pattern starts at a point that results in a straight-in approach with a high rate of descent to the runway. Flameout approaches terminate in the type approach requested by the pilot (normally fullstop).

FLIGHT CHECK. A call-sign prefix used by FAA aircraft engaged in flight inspection/certification of navigational aids and flight procedures. The word "recorded" may be added as a suffix; e.g., "Flight Check 320 recorded" to indicate that an automated flight inspection is in progress in terminal areas. (See FLIGHT INSPECTION.) (Refer to AIM.)

FLIGHT DATA [FSS]. The primary task of the FSS flight data position is information management. Flight data services include the development, translation, processing, and coordination of aeronautical, meteorological, and aviation information.

FLIGHT FOLLOWING. (See TRAFFIC ADVISORIES.)

FLIGHT INFORMATION REGION. An airspace of defined dimensions within which Flight Information Service and Alerting Service are provided.

a. Flight Information Service. A service provided for the purpose of giving advice and information useful for the safe and efficient conduct of flights.

b. Alerting Service. A service provided to notify appropriate organizations regarding aircraft in need of search and rescue aid and to assist such organizations as required.

FLIGHT INFORMATION SERVICE. A service provided for the purpose of giving advice and information useful for the safe and efficient conduct of flights.

FLIGHT INFORMATION SERVICE–BROADCAST (FIS-B). A ground broadcast service provided through the ADS-B Broadcast Services network over the UAT data link that operates on 978 MHz. The FIS-B system provides pilots and flight crews of properly equipped aircraft with a cockpit display of certain aviation weather and aeronautical information.

FLIGHT INSPECTION. Inflight investigation and evaluation of a navigational aid to determine whether it meets established tolerances. (See FLIGHT CHECK.) (See NAVIGATIONAL AID.)

FLIGHT LEVEL. A level of constant atmospheric pressure related to a reference datum of 29.92 inches of mercury. Each is stated in three digits that represent hundreds of feet. For example, flight level (FL) 250 represents a barometric altimeter indication of 25,000 feet; FL 255, an indication of 25,500 feet. (See ICAO term FLIGHT LEVEL.)

FLIGHT LEVEL [ICAO]. A surface of constant atmospheric pressure which is related to a specific pressure datum, 1013.2 hPa (1013.2 mb), and is separated from other such surfaces by specific pressure intervals.

Note 1: A pressure type altimeter calibrated in accordance with the standard atmosphere:

a. When set to a QNH altimeter setting, will indicate altitude;

b. When set to a QFE altimeter setting, will indicate height above the QFE reference datum; and

c. When set to a pressure of 1013.2 hPa (1013.2 mb), may be used to indicate flight levels.

Note 2: The terms 'height' and 'altitude,' used in Note 1 above, indicate altimetric rather than geometric heights and altitudes.

FLIGHT LINE. A term used to describe the precise movement of a civil photogrammetric aircraft along a predetermined course(s) at a predetermined altitude during the actual photographic run.

FLIGHT MANAGEMENT SYSTEMS. A computer system that uses a large data base to allow routes to be preprogrammed and fed into the system by means of a data loader. The system is constantly updated with respect to position accuracy by reference to conventional navigation aids. The sophisticated program and its associated data base ensures that the most appropriate aids are automatically selected during the information update cycle.

FLIGHT PATH. A line, course, or track along which an aircraft is flying or intended to be flown. (See COURSE.) (See TRACK.)

FLIGHT PLAN. Specified information relating to the intended flight of an aircraft that is filed electronically, orally, or in writing with an FSS, third-party vendor, or an ATC facility. (See FAST FILE.) (See FILED.) (Refer to AIM.)

FLIGHT PLAN AREA (FPA). The geographical area assigned to a flight service station (FSS) for the purpose of establishing primary responsibility for services that may include search and rescue for VFR aircraft, issuance of NOTAMs, pilot briefings, inflight services, broadcast services, emergency services, flight data processing, international operations, and aviation weather services. Large consolidated FSS facilities may combine FPAs into larger areas of responsibility (AOR). (See FLIGHT SERVICE STATION.) (See TIE-IN FACILITY.)

FLIGHT RECORDER. A general term applied to any instrument or device that records information about the performance of an aircraft in flight or about conditions encountered in flight. Flight recorders may make records of airspeed, outside air temperature, vertical

acceleration, engine RPM, manifold pressure, and other pertinent variables for a given flight. (See ICAO term FLIGHT RECORDER.)

FLIGHT RECORDER [ICAO]. Any type of recorder installed in the aircraft for the purpose of complementing accident/incident investigation.

Note: See Annex 6 Part I, for specifications relating to flight recorders.

FLIGHT SERVICE STATION (FSS). An air traffic facility which provides pilot briefings, flight plan processing, en route flight advisories, search and rescue services, and assistance to lost aircraft and aircraft in emergency situations. FSS also relay ATC clearances, process Notices to Air Missions, and broadcast aviation weather and aeronautical information. In Alaska, FSS provide Airport Advisory Services. (See FLIGHT PLAN AREA.) (See TIE-IN FACILITY.)

FLIGHT STANDARDS DISTRICT OFFICE. An FAA field office serving an assigned geographical area and staffed with Flight Standards personnel who serve the aviation industry and the general public on matters relating to the certification and operation of air carrier and general aviation aircraft. Activities include general surveillance of operational safety, certification of airmen and aircraft, accident prevention, investigation, enforcement, etc.

FLIGHT TERMINATION. The intentional and deliberate process of terminating the flight of a UA in the event of an unrecoverable lost link, loss of control, or other failure that compromises the safety of flight.

FLIGHT TEST. A flight for the purpose of:
a. Investigating the operation/flight characteristics of an aircraft or aircraft component.
b. Evaluating an applicant for a pilot certificate or rating.

FLIGHT VISIBILITY. (See VISIBILITY.)

FLIP. (See DOD FLIP.)

FLY HEADING (DEGREES). Informs the pilot of the heading he/she should fly. The pilot may have to turn to, or continue on, a specific compass direction in order to comply with the instructions. The pilot is expected to turn in the shorter direction to the heading unless otherwise instructed by ATC.

FLY-BY WAYPOINT. A fly-by waypoint requires the use of turn anticipation to avoid overshoot of the next flight segment.

FLY-OVER WAYPOINT. A fly-over waypoint precludes any turn until the waypoint is overflown and is followed by an intercept maneuver of the next flight segment.

FLY VISUAL TO AIRPORT. (See PUBLISHED INSTRUMENT APPROACH PROCEDURE VISUAL SEGMENT.)

FLYAWAY. When the pilot is unable to effect control of the aircraft and, as a result, the UA is not operating in a predictable or planned manner.

FMA. (See FINAL MONITOR AID.)

FMS. (See FLIGHT MANAGEMENT SYSTEM.)

FORMATION FLIGHT. More than one aircraft which, by prior arrangement between the pilots, operate as a single aircraft with regard to navigation and position reporting. Separation between aircraft within the formation is the responsibility of the flight leader and the pilots of the other aircraft in the flight. This includes transition periods when aircraft within the formation are maneuvering to attain separation from each other to effect individual control and during join-up and breakaway.
a. A standard formation is one in which a proximity of no more than 1 mile laterally or longitudinally and within 100 feet vertically from the flight leader is maintained by each wingman.
b. Nonstandard formations are those operating under any of the following conditions:
1. When the flight leader has requested and ATC has approved other than standard formation dimensions.
2. When operating within an authorized altitude reservation (ALTRV) or under the provisions of a letter of agreement.
3. When the operations are conducted in airspace specifically designed for a special activity. (See ALTITUDE RESERVATION.)
(Refer to 14 CFR Part 91.)

FRC. (See REQUEST FULL ROUTE CLEARANCE.)

FREEZE/FROZEN. Terms used in referring to arrivals which have been assigned ACLTs and to the lists in which they are displayed.

FREEZE HORIZON. The time or point at which an aircraft's STA becomes fixed and no longer fluctuates with each radar update. This setting ensures a constant time for each aircraft, necessary for the metering controller to plan his/her delay technique. This setting can be either in distance from the meter fix or a prescribed flying time to the meter fix.

FREEZE SPEED PARAMETER. A speed adapted for each aircraft to determine fast and slow aircraft. Fast aircraft freeze on parameter FCLT and slow aircraft freeze on parameter MLDI.

FRIA. (See FAA-RECOGNIZED IDENTIFICATION AREA.)

FRICTION MEASUREMENT. A measurement of the friction characteristics of the runway pavement surface using continuous self-watering friction measurement equipment in accordance with the specifications, procedures and schedules contained in AC 150/5320-12, Measurement, Construction, and Maintenance of Skid Resistant Airport Pavement Surfaces.

FSDO. (See FLIGHT STANDARDS DISTRICT OFFICE.)

FSPD. (See FREEZE SPEED PARAMETER.)

FSS. (See FLIGHT SERVICE STATION.)

FUEL DUMPING. Airborne release of usable fuel. This does not include the dropping of fuel tanks. (See JETTISONING OF EXTERNAL STORES.)

P/C

FUEL REMAINING. A phrase used by either pilots or controllers when relating to the fuel remaining on board until actual fuel exhaustion. When transmitting such information in response to either a controller question or pilot initiated cautionary advisory to air traffic control, pilots will state the APPROXIMATE NUMBER OF MINUTES the flight can continue with the fuel remaining. All reserve fuel SHOULD BE INCLUDED in the time stated, as should an allowance for established fuel gauge system error.

FUEL SIPHONING. Unintentional release of fuel caused by overflow, puncture, loose cap, etc.

FUEL VENTING. (See FUEL SIPHONING.)

FUSED TARGET. (See DIGITAL TARGET)

FUSION [STARS]. The combination of all available surveillance sources (airport surveillance radar [ASR], air route surveillance radar [ARSR], ADS-B, etc.) into the display of a single tracked target for air traffic control separation services. FUSION is the equivalent of the current single-sensor radar display. FUSION performance is characteristic of a single-sensor radar display system. Terminal areas use mono-pulse secondary surveillance radar (ASR 9, Mode S or ASR 11, MSSR).

G

GATE HOLD PROCEDURES. Procedures at selected airports to hold aircraft at the gate or other ground location whenever departure delays exceed or are anticipated to exceed 15 minutes. The sequence for departure will be maintained in accordance with initial call-up unless modified by flow control restrictions. Pilots should monitor the ground control/clearance delivery frequency for engine start/taxi advisories or new proposed start/taxi time if the delay changes.

GCA. (See GROUND CONTROLLED APPROACH.)

GDP. (See GROUND DELAY PROGRAM.)

GENERAL AVIATION. That portion of civil aviation that does not include scheduled or unscheduled air carriers or commercial space operations. (See ICAO term GENERAL AVIATION.)

GENERAL AVIATION [ICAO]. All civil aviation operations other than scheduled air services and nonscheduled air transport operations for remuneration or hire.

GEO MAP. The digitized map markings associated with the ASR-9 Radar System.

GLIDEPATH. (See GLIDESLOPE.)

GLIDEPATH [ICAO]. A descent profile determined for vertical guidance during a final approach.

GLIDEPATH INTERCEPT ALTITUDE. (See GLIDESLOPE INTERCEPT ALTITUDE.)

GLIDESLOPE. Provides vertical guidance for aircraft during approach and landing. The glideslope/glidepath is based on the following:

a. Electronic components emitting signals which provide vertical guidance by reference to airborne instruments during instrument approaches such as ILS or

b. Visual ground aids, such as VASI, which provide vertical guidance for a VFR approach or for the visual portion of an instrument approach and landing.

c. PAR. Used by ATC to inform an aircraft making a PAR approach of its vertical position (elevation) relative to the descent profile.
(See ICAO term GLIDEPATH.)

GLIDESLOPE INTERCEPT ALTITUDE. The published minimum altitude to intercept the glideslope in the intermediate segment of an instrument approach. Government charts use the lightning bolt symbol to identify this intercept point. This intersection is called the Precise Final Approach fix (PFAF). When ATC directs a higher altitude, the resultant intercept becomes the PFAF. (See FINAL APPROACH FIX.) (See SEGMENTS OF AN INSTRUMENT APPROACH PROCEDURE.)

GLOBAL NAVIGATION SATELLITE SYSTEM (GNSS). GNSS refers collectively to the worldwide positioning, navigation, and timing determination capability available from one or more satellite constellations. A GNSS constellation may be augmented by ground stations and/or geostationary satellites to improve integrity and position accuracy. (See GROUND-BASED AUGMENTATION SYSTEM.) (See SATELLITE-BASED AUGMENTATION SYSTEM.)

GLOBAL NAVIGATION SATELLITE SYSTEM MINIMUM EN ROUTE IFR ALTITUDE (GNSS MEA). The minimum en route IFR altitude on a published ATS route or route segment which assures acceptable Global Navigation Satellite System reception and meets obstacle clearance requirements.
(Refer to 14 CFR Part 91.) (Refer to 14 CFR Part 95.)

GLOBAL POSITIONING SYSTEM (GPS). GPS refers to the worldwide positioning, navigation and timing determination capability available from the U.S. satellite constellation. The service provided by GPS for civil use is defined in the GPS Standard Positioning System Performance Standard. GPS is composed of space, control, and user elements.

GNSS [ICAO]. (See GLOBAL NAVIGATION SATELLITE SYSTEM.)

GNSS MEA. (See GLOBAL NAVIGATION SATELLITE SYSTEM MINIMUM EN ROUTE IFR ALTITUDE.

GO AHEAD. Proceed with your message. Not to be used for any other purpose.

GO AROUND. Instructions for a pilot to abandon his/her approach to landing. Additional instructions may follow. Unless otherwise advised by ATC, a VFR aircraft or an aircraft conducting visual approach should overfly the runway while climbing to traffic pattern altitude and enter the traffic pattern via the crosswind leg. A pilot on an IFR flight plan making an instrument approach should execute the published missed

approach procedure or proceed as instructed by ATC; e.g., "Go around" (additional instructions if required). (See LOW APPROACH.) (See MISSED APPROACH.)

GPD. (See GRAPHIC PLAN DISPLAY.)

GPS. (See GLOBAL POSITIONING SYSTEM.)

GRAPHICAL AIRMEN'S METEOROLOGICAL INFORMATION. A graphical depiction of weather that may be hazardous to aircraft, but are less severe than SIGMETs. G-AIRMETS are issued 3 hours apart for a period of up to 12 hours into the future for the lower 48 states and coastal waters. The weather hazards depicted can be:
 a. Moderate turbulence
 b. Low-level windshear
 c. Strong surface winds greater than 30 knots
 d. Moderate icing
 e. Freezing level
 f. Mountain obscuration
 g. IFR
(See AIRMET.) (See CONVECTIVE SIGMET.) (See CWA.) (See SAW.) (See SIGMET.) (Refer to AIM.)

GRAPHIC PLAN DISPLAY (GPD). A view available with EDST that provides a graphic display of aircraft, traffic, and notification of predicted conflicts. Graphic routes for Current Plans and Trial Plans are displayed upon controller request. (See EN ROUTE DECISION SUPPORT TOOL.)

GROSS NAVIGATION ERROR (GNE). A lateral deviation of 10 NM or more from the aircraft's cleared route.

GROUND BASED AUGMENTATION SYSTEM (GBAS). A ground based GNSS station which provides local differential corrections, integrity parameters and approach data via VHF data broadcast to GNSS users to meet real-time performance requirements for CAT I precision approaches. The aircraft applies the broadcast data to improve the accuracy and integrity of its GNSS signals and computes the deviations to the selected approach. A single ground station can serve multiple runway ends up to an approximate radius of 23 NM.

GROUND BASED AUGMENTATION SYSTEM (GBAS) LANDING SYSTEM (GLS). A type of precision IAP based on local augmentation of GNSS data using a single GBAS station to transmit locally corrected GNSS data, integrity parameters and approach information. This improves the accuracy of aircraft GNSS receivers' signal in space, enabling the pilot to fly a precision approach with much greater flexibility, reliability and complexity. The GLS procedure is published on standard IAP charts, features the title GLS with the designated runway and minima as low as 200 feet DA. Future plans are expected to support Cat II and CAT III operations.

GROUND-BASED INTERVAL MANAGEMENT-SPACING (GIM-S), SPEED ADVISORY. A calculated speed that will allow aircraft to meet the TBFM schedule at en route and TRACON boundary meter fixes.

GROUND CLUTTER. A pattern produced on the radar scope by ground returns which may degrade other radar returns in the affected area. The effect of ground clutter is minimized by the use of moving target indicator (MTI) circuits in the radar equipment resulting in a radar presentation which displays only targets which are in motion. (See CLUTTER.)

GROUND COMMUNICATION OUTLET (GCO). An unstaffed, remotely controlled, ground/ground communications facility. Pilots at uncontrolled airports may contact ATC and FSS via VHF radio to a telephone connection. If the connection goes to ATC, the pilot can obtain an IFR clearance or close an IFR flight plan. If the connection goes to Flight Service, the pilot can open or close a VFR flight plan; obtain an updated weather briefing prior to takeoff; close an IFR flight plan; or, for Alaska or MEDEVAC only, obtain an IFR clearance. Pilots will use four "key clicks" on the VHF radio to contact the appropriate ATC facility or six "key clicks" to contact the FSS. The GCO system is intended to be used only on the ground.

GROUND CONTROLLED APPROACH. A radar approach system operated from the ground by air traffic control personnel transmitting instructions to the pilot by radio. The approach may be conducted with surveillance radar (ASR) only or with both surveillance and precision approach radar (PAR). Usage of the term "GCA" by pilots is discouraged except when referring to a GCA facility. Pilots should specifically request a "PAR" approach when a precision radar approach is desired or request an "ASR" or "surveillance" approach when a nonprecision radar approach is desired. (See RADAR APPROACH.)

GROUND DELAY PROGRAM (GDP). A traffic management process administered by the ATCSCC; when aircraft are held on the ground. The purpose of the program is to support the TM mission and limit airborne holding. It is a flexible program and may be implemented in various forms depending upon the needs of the AT system. Ground delay programs provide for equitable assignment of delays to all system users.

GROUND SPEED. The speed of an aircraft relative to the surface of the earth.

GROUND STOP (GS). The GS is a process that requires aircraft that meet a specific criteria to remain on the ground. The criteria may be airport specific, airspace specific, or equipment specific; for example, all departures to San Francisco, or all departures entering Yorktown sector, or all Category I and II aircraft going to Charlotte. GS's normally occur with little or no warning.

GROUND VISIBILITY. (See VISIBILITY.)

GS. (See GROUND STOP.)

P/C

H

HAA. (See HEIGHT ABOVE AIRPORT.)

HAL. (See HEIGHT ABOVE LANDING.)

HANDOFF. An action taken to transfer the radar iden-
tification of an aircraft from one controller to another
if the aircraft will enter the receiving controller's air-
space and radio communications with the aircraft will
be transferred.

HAT. (See HEIGHT ABOVE TOUCHDOWN.)

HAVE NUMBERS. Used by pilots to inform ATC that
they have received runway, wind, and altimeter infor-
mation only.

HAZARDOUS MATERIALS (HAZMAT). Hazardous
materials as defined by 49 Code of Federal Regu-
lations (CFR) §171.8. (Refer to 49 CFR Part 171.8)
(Refer to AIM)

HAZARDOUS WEATHER INFORMATION. Summary
of significant meteorological information (SIGMET/
WS), convective significant meteorological informa-
tion (convective SIGMET/WST), urgent pilot weather
reports (urgent PIREP/UUA), center weather advi-
sories (CWA), airmen's meteorological information
(AIRMET/WA), graphical airmen's meteorological
information (G-AIRMET) and any other weather such
as isolated thunderstorms that are rapidly developing
and increasing in intensity, or low ceilings and vis-
ibilities that are becoming widespread which is con-
sidered significant and are not included in a current
hazardous weather advisory.

HAZMAT. (See HAZARDOUS MATERIALS.)

HEAVY (AIRCRAFT). (See AIRCRAFT CLASSES.)

HEIGHT ABOVE AIRPORT (HAA). The height of the
Minimum Descent Altitude above the published airport
elevation. This is published in conjunction with circling
minimums. (See MINIMUM DESCENT ALTITUDE.)

HEIGHT ABOVE LANDING (HAL). The height above
a designated helicopter landing area used for heli-
copter instrument approach procedures. (Refer to 14
CFR Part 97.)

HEIGHT ABOVE TOUCHDOWN (HAT). The height
of the Decision Height or Minimum Descent Altitude
above the highest runway elevation in the touchdown
zone (first 3,000 feet of the runway). HAT is published
on instrument approach charts in conjunction with all
straight-in minimums. (See DECISION HEIGHT.) (See
MINIMUM DESCENT ALTITUDE.)

HELICOPTER. A heavier-than-air aircraft supported in
flight chiefly by the reactions of the air on one or more
power-driven rotors on substantially vertical axes.

HELIPAD. A small, designated area, usually with a pre-
pared surface, on a heliport, airport, landing/takeoff
area, apron/ramp, or movement area used for takeoff,
landing, or parking of helicopters.

HELIPORT. An area of land, water, or structure used or
intended to be used for the landing and takeoff of heli-
copters and includes its buildings and facilities if any.

HELIPORT REFERENCE POINT (HRP). The geo-
graphic center of a heliport.

HERTZ. The standard radio equivalent of frequency in
cycles per second of an electromagnetic wave. Kilo-
hertz (kHz) is a frequency of one thousand cycles per
second. Megahertz (MHz) is a frequency of one million
cycles per second.

HF. (See HIGH FREQUENCY.)

HF COMMUNICATIONS. (See HIGH FREQUENCY
COMMUNICATIONS.)

HIGH FREQUENCY. The frequency band
between 3 and 30 MHz. (See HIGH FREQUENCY
COMMUNICATIONS.)

HIGH FREQUENCY COMMUNICATIONS. High
radio frequencies (HF) between 3 and 30 MHz used
for air-to-ground voice communication in overseas
operations.

HIGH SPEED EXIT. (See HIGH SPEED TAXIWAY.)

HIGH SPEED TAXIWAY. A long radius taxiway
designed and provided with lighting or marking to
define the path of aircraft, traveling at high speed (up
to 60 knots), from the runway center to a point on the
center of a taxiway. Also referred to as long radius
exit or turn-off taxiway. The high speed taxiway is
designed to expedite aircraft turning off the runway
after landing, thus reducing runway occupancy time.

HIGH SPEED TURNOFF. (See HIGH SPEED
TAXIWAY.)

HIGH UPDATE RATE SURVEILLANCE. A surveil-
lance system that provides a sensor update rate of
less than 4.8 seconds.

HOLD FOR RELEASE. Used by ATC to delay an air-
craft for traffic management reasons; i.e., weather,
traffic volume, etc. Hold for release instructions
(including departure delay information) are used to
inform a pilot or a controller (either directly or through
an authorized relay) that an IFR departure clearance
is not valid until a release time or additional instruc-
tions have been received. (See ICAO term HOLD-
ING POINT.)

HOLD-IN-LIEU OF PROCEDURE TURN. A hold-in-
lieu of procedure turn shall be established over a final
or intermediate fix when an approach can be made
from a properly aligned holding pattern. The hold-in-
lieu of procedure turn permits the pilot to align with the
final or intermediate segment of the approach and/or
descend in the holding pattern to an altitude that will
permit a normal descent to the final approach fix alti-
tude. The hold-in-lieu of procedure turn is a required
maneuver (the same as a procedure turn) unless the
aircraft is being radar vectored to the final approach
course, when "NoPT" is shown on the approach chart,
or when the pilot requests or the controller advises the
pilot to make a "straight-in" approach.

HOLD PROCEDURE. A predetermined maneuver which keeps aircraft within a specified airspace while awaiting further clearance from air traffic control. Also used during ground operations to keep aircraft within a specified area or at a specified point while awaiting further clearance from air traffic control. (See HOLD-ING FIX.) (Refer to AIM.)

HOLDING FIX. A specified fix identifiable to a pilot by NAVAIDs or visual reference to the ground used as a reference point in establishing and maintaining the position of an aircraft while holding. (See FIX.) (See VISUAL HOLDING.) (Refer to AIM.)

HOLDING POINT [ICAO]. A specified location, identified by visual or other means, in the vicinity of which the position of an aircraft in flight is maintained in accordance with air traffic control clearances.

HOLDING PROCEDURE. (See HOLD PROCEDURE.)

HOLD-SHORT POINT. A point on the runway beyond which a landing aircraft with a LAHSO clearance is not authorized to proceed. This point may be located prior to an intersecting runway, taxiway, predetermined point, or approach/departure flight path.

HOLD-SHORT POSITION LIGHTS. Flashing in-pavement white lights located at specified hold-short points.

HOLD-SHORT POSITION MARKING. The painted runway marking located at the hold-short point on all LAHSO runways.

HOLD-SHORT POSITION SIGNS. Red and white holding position signs located alongside the hold-short point.

HOMING. Flight toward a NAVAID, without correcting for wind, by adjusting the aircraft heading to maintain a relative bearing of zero degrees. (See BEARING.) (See ICAO term HOMING.)

HOMING [ICAO]. The procedure of using the direction-finding equipment of one radio station with the emission of another radio station, where at least one of the stations is mobile, and whereby the mobile station proceeds continuously towards the other station.

HOT SPOT. A location on an airport movement area with a history of potential risk of collision or runway incursion, and where heightened attention by pilots/drivers is necessary.

HOVER CHECK. Used to describe when a helicopter/VTOL aircraft requires a stabilized hover to conduct a performance/power check prior to hover taxi, air taxi, or takeoff. Altitude of the hover will vary based on the purpose of the check.

HOVER TAXI. Used to describe a helicopter/VTOL aircraft movement conducted above the surface and in ground effect at airspeeds less than approximately 20 knots. The actual height may vary, and some helicopters may require hover taxi above 25 feet AGL to reduce ground effect turbulence or provide clearance for cargo slingloads. (See AIR TAXI.) (See HOVER CHECK.) (Refer to AIM.)

HOW DO YOU HEAR ME? A question relating to the quality of the transmission or to determine how well the transmission is being received.

HZ. (See HERTZ.)

I

I SAY AGAIN. The message will be repeated.

IAF. (See INITIAL APPROACH FIX.)

IAP. (See INSTRUMENT APPROACH PROCEDURE.)

IAWP. Initial Approach Waypoint

ICAO. (See ICAO Term INTERNATIONAL CIVIL AVIATION ORGANIZATION.)

ICAO 3LD. (See ICAO Term ICAO THREE-LETTER DESIGNATOR.)

ICAO THREE-LETTER DESIGNATOR (3LD). An ICAO 3LD is an exclusive designator that, when used together with a flight number, becomes the aircraft call sign and provides distinct aircraft identification to air traffic control (ATC). ICAO approves 3LDs to enhance the safety and security of the air traffic system. An ICAO 3LD may be assigned to a company, agency, or organization and is used instead of the aircraft registration number for ATC operational and security purposes. An ICAO 3LD is also used for aircraft identification in the flight plan and associated messages and can be used for domestic and international flights. A telephony associated with an ICAO 3LD is used for radio communication.

ICING. The accumulation of airframe ice.
Types of icing are:
 a. Rime Ice. Rough, milky, opaque ice formed by the instantaneous freezing of small supercooled water droplets.
 b. Clear Ice. A glossy, clear, or translucent ice formed by the relatively slow freezing of large supercooled water droplets.
 c. Mixed. A mixture of clear ice and rime ice.
Intensity of icing:
 a. Trace. Ice becomes noticeable. The rate of accumulation is slightly greater than the rate of sublimation. A representative accretion rate for reference purposes is less than ¼ inch (6 mm) per hour on the outer wing. The pilot should consider exiting the icing conditions before they become worse.
 b. Light. The rate of ice accumulation requires occasional cycling of manual deicing systems to minimize ice accretions on the airframe. A representative accretion rate for reference purposes is ¼ inch to 1 inch (0.6 to 2.5 cm) per hour on the unprotected part of the outer wing. The pilot should consider exiting the icing condition.
 c. Moderate. The rate of ice accumulation requires frequent cycling of manual deicing systems to minimize ice accretions on the airframe. A representative accretion rate for reference purposes is 1 to 3 inches

(continued)

P/C

(2.5 to 7.5 cm) per hour on the unprotected part of the outer wing. The pilot should consider exiting the icing condition as soon as possible.

d. Severe. The rate of ice accumulation is such that ice protection systems fail to remove the accumulation of ice and ice accumulates in locations not normally prone to icing, such as areas aft of protected surfaces and any other areas identified by the manufacturer. A representative accretion rate for reference purposes is more than 3 inches (7.5 cm) per hour on the unprotected part of the outer wing. By regulation, immediate exit is required.

Note: Severe icing is aircraft dependent, as are the other categories of icing intensity. Severe icing may occur at any ice accumulation rate when the icing rate or ice accumulations exceed the tolerance of the aircraft.

IDAC. (See INTEGRATED DEPARTURE/ARRIVAL CAPABILITY.)

IDENT. A request for a pilot to activate the aircraft transponder identification feature. This will help the controller to confirm an aircraft identity or to identify an aircraft. (Refer to AIM.)

IDENT FEATURE. The special feature in the Air Traffic Control Radar Beacon System (ATCRBS) equipment. It is used to immediately distinguish one displayed beacon target from other beacon targets. (See IDENT.)

IDENTIFICATION [ICAO]. The situation which exists when the position indication of a particular aircraft is seen on a situation display and positively identified.

IF. (See INTERMEDIATE FIX.)

IF NO TRANSMISSION RECEIVED FOR (TIME). Used by ATC in radar approaches which should be followed by the pilot in event of lost communications. (See LOST COMMUNICATIONS.)

IFR. (See INSTRUMENT FLIGHT RULES.)

IFR AIRCRAFT. An aircraft conducting flight in accordance with instrument flight rules.

IFR CONDITIONS. Weather conditions below the minimum for flight under visual flight rules. (See INSTRUMENT METEOROLOGICAL CONDITIONS.)

IFR DEPARTURE PROCEDURE. (See IFR TAKEOFF MINIMUMS AND DEPARTURE PROCEDURES.) (Refer to AIM.)

IFR FLIGHT. (See IFR AIRCRAFT.)

IFR LANDING MINIMUMS. (See LANDING MINIMUMS.)

IFR MILITARY TRAINING ROUTES (IR). Routes used by the Department of Defense and associated Reserve and Air Guard units for the purpose of conducting low-altitude navigation and tactical training in both IFR and VFR weather conditions below 10,000 feet MSL at airspeeds in excess of 250 knots IAS.

IFR TAKEOFF MINIMUMS AND DEPARTURE PROCEDURES. Title 14 Code of Federal Regulations Part 91, prescribes standard takeoff rules for certain civil users. At some airports, obstructions or other factors require the establishment of nonstandard takeoff minimums, departure procedures, or both to assist pilots in avoiding obstacles during climb to the minimum en route altitude. Those airports are listed in FAA/DOD Instrument Approach Procedures (IAPs) Charts under a section entitled "IFR Takeoff Minimums and Departure Procedures." The FAA/DOD IAP chart legend illustrates the symbol used to alert the pilot to nonstandard takeoff minimums and departure procedures. When departing IFR from such airports or from any airports where there are no departure procedures, DPs, or ATC facilities available, pilots should advise ATC of any departure limitations. Controllers may query a pilot to determine acceptable departure directions, turns, or headings after takeoff. Pilots should be familiar with the departure procedures and must assure that their aircraft can meet or exceed any specified climb gradients.

IF/IAWP. Intermediate Fix/Initial Approach Waypoint. The waypoint where the final approach course of a T approach meets the crossbar of the T. When designated (in conjunction with a TAA) this waypoint will be used as an IAWP when approaching the airport from certain directions, and as an IFWP when beginning the approach from another IAWP.

IFWP. Intermediate Fix Waypoint

ILS. (See INSTRUMENT LANDING SYSTEM.)

ILS CATEGORIES.
1. Category I. An ILS approach procedure which provides for approach to a height above touchdown of not less than 200 feet and with runway visual range of not less than 1,800 feet.
2. Special Authorization Category I. An ILS approach procedure which provides for approach to a height above touchdown of not less than 150 feet and with runway visual range of not less than 1,400 feet, HUD to DH.
3. Category II. An ILS approach procedure which provides for approach to a height above touchdown of not less than 100 feet and with runway visual range of not less than 1,200 feet (with autoland or HUD to touchdown and noted on authorization, RVR 1,000 feet).
4. Special Authorization Category II with Reduced Lighting. An ILS approach procedure which provides for approach to a height above touchdown of not less than 100 feet and with runway visual range of not less than 1,200 feet with autoland or HUD to touchdown and noted on authorization (no touchdown zone and centerline lighting are required).
5. Category III:
a. IIIA. An ILS approach procedure which provides for approach without a decision height minimum and with runway visual range of not less than 700 feet.
b. IIIB. An ILS approach procedure which provides for approach without a decision height minimum and with runway visual range of not less than 150 feet.
c. IIIC. An ILS approach procedure which provides for approach without a decision height minimum and without runway visual range minimum.

IM. (See INNER MARKER.)

IMC. (See INSTRUMENT METEOROLOGICAL CONDITIONS.)

IMMEDIATELY. Used by ATC or pilots when such action compliance is required to avoid an imminent situation.

INCERFA (Uncertainty Phase) [ICAO]. A situation wherein uncertainty exists as to the safety of an aircraft and its occupants.

INCREASED SEPARATION REQUIRED (ISR). Indicates the confidence level of the track requires 5 NM separation. 3 NM separation, 1½ NM separation, and target resolution cannot be used.

INCREASE SPEED TO (SPEED). (See SPEED ADJUSTMENT.)

INERTIAL NAVIGATION SYSTEM (INS). An RNAV system which is a form of self-contained navigation. (See AREA NAVIGATION/RNAV.)

INFLIGHT REFUELING. (See AERIAL REFUELING.)

INFLIGHT SERVICES [FSS]. Services provided to or affecting aircraft inflight or otherwise operating on the airport surface. This includes services to airborne aircraft, such as the delivery of ATC clearances, advisories or requests, issuance of military flight advisory messages, NOTAM delivery, search and rescue communications searches, flight plan handling, transcribed or live broadcasts, weather observations, PIREPs, and pilot briefings.

INFLIGHT WEATHER ADVISORY. (See WEATHER ADVISORY.)

INFORMATION REQUEST (INREQ). A request originated by an FSS for information concerning an overdue VFR aircraft.

INITIAL APPROACH FIX (IAF). The fixes depicted on instrument approach procedure charts that identify the beginning of the initial approach segment(s). (See FIX.) (See SEGMENTS OF AN INSTRUMENT APPROACH PROCEDURE.)

INITIAL APPROACH SEGMENT. (See SEGMENTS OF AN INSTRUMENT APPROACH PROCEDURE.)

INITIAL APPROACH SEGMENT [ICAO]. That segment of an instrument approach procedure between the initial approach fix and the intermediate approach fix or, where applicable, the final approach fix or point.

INLAND NAVIGATION FACILITY. A navigation aid on a North American Route at which the common route and/or the noncommon route begins or ends.

INNER MARKER. A marker beacon used with an ILS (CAT II) precision approach located between the middle marker and the end of the ILS runway, transmitting a radiation pattern keyed at six dots per second and indicating to the pilot, both aurally and visually, that he/she is at the designated decision height (DH), normally 100 feet above the touchdown zone elevation, on the ILS CAT II approach. It also marks progress during

a CAT III approach. (See INSTRUMENT LANDING SYSTEM.) (Refer to AIM.)

INNER MARKER BEACON. (See INNER MARKER.)

INREQ. (See INFORMATION REQUEST.)

INS. (See INERTIAL NAVIGATION SYSTEM.)

INSTRUMENT APPROACH. (See INSTRUMENT APPROACH PROCEDURE.)

INSTRUMENT APPROACH OPERATIONS [ICAO] An approach and landing using instruments for navigation guidance based on an instrument approach procedure. There are two methods for executing instrument approach operations:
 a. A two-dimensional (2D) instrument approach operation, using lateral navigation guidance only; and
 b. A three-dimensional (3D) instrument approach operation, using both lateral and vertical navigation guidance.

Note: Lateral and vertical navigation guidance refers to the guidance provided either by:
 a) a ground-based radio navigation aid; or
 b) computer-generated navigation data from ground-based, space-based, self-contained navigation aids or a combination of these.

(See ICAO term INSTRUMENT APPROACH PROCEDURE.)

INSTRUMENT APPROACH PROCEDURE. A series of predetermined maneuvers for the orderly transfer of an aircraft under instrument flight conditions from the beginning of the initial approach to a landing or to a point from which a landing may be made visually. It is prescribed and approved for a specific airport by competent authority. (See SEGMENTS OF AN INSTRUMENT APPROACH PROCEDURE.) (Refer to 14 CFR Part 91.) (Refer to AIM.)
 a. U.S. civil standard instrument approach procedures are approved by the FAA as prescribed under 14 CFR Part 97 and are available for public use.
 b. U.S. military standard instrument approach procedures are approved and published by the Department of Defense.
 c. Special instrument approach procedures are approved by the FAA for individual operators but are not published in 14 CFR Part 97 for public use.
(See ICAO term INSTRUMENT APPROACH PROCEDURE.)

INSTRUMENT APPROACH PROCEDURE [ICAO]. A series of predetermined maneuvers by reference to flight instruments with specified protection from obstacles from the initial approach fix, or where applicable, from the beginning of a defined arrival route to a point from which a landing can be completed and thereafter, if a landing is not completed, to a position at which holding or en route obstacle clearance criteria apply. (See ICAO term INSTRUMENT APPROACH OPERATIONS)

INSTRUMENT APPROACH PROCEDURE CHARTS. (See AERONAUTICAL CHART.)

INSTRUMENT DEPARTURE PROCEDURE (DP). A preplanned instrument flight rule (IFR) departure procedure published for pilot use, in graphic or textual format, that provides obstruction clearance from the terminal area to the appropriate en route structure. There are two types of DP, Obstacle Departure Procedure (ODP), printed either textually or graphically, and, Standard Instrument Departure (SID), which is always printed graphically. (See IFR TAKEOFF MINIMUMS AND DEPARTURE PROCEDURES.) (See OBSTACLE DEPARTURE PROCEDURES.) (See STANDARD INSTRUMENT DEPARTURES.) (Refer to AIM.)

INSTRUMENT DEPARTURE PROCEDURE (DP) CHARTS. (See AERONAUTICAL CHART.)

INSTRUMENT FLIGHT RULES (IFR). Rules governing the procedures for conducting instrument flight. Also a term used by pilots and controllers to indicate type of flight plan. (See INSTRUMENT METEOROLOGICAL CONDITIONS.) (See VISUAL FLIGHT RULES.) (See VISUAL METEOROLOGICAL CONDITIONS.) (See ICAO term INSTRUMENT FLIGHT RULES.) (Refer to AIM.)

INSTRUMENT FLIGHT RULES [ICAO]. A set of rules governing the conduct of flight under instrument meteorological conditions.

INSTRUMENT LANDING SYSTEM (ILS). A precision instrument approach system which normally consists of the following electronic components and visual aids:
 a. Localizer. (See LOCALIZER.)
 b. Glideslope. (See GLIDESLOPE.)
 c. Outer Marker. (See OUTER MARKER.)
 d. Middle Marker. (See MIDDLE MARKER.)
 e. Approach Lights. (See AIRPORT LIGHTING.)
(Refer to 14 CFR Part 91.) (Refer to AIM.)

INSTRUMENT METEOROLOGICAL CONDITIONS (IMC). Meteorological conditions expressed in terms of visibility, distance from cloud, and ceiling less than the minima specified for visual meteorological conditions. (See INSTRUMENT FLIGHT RULES.) (See VISUAL FLIGHT RULES.) (See VISUAL METEOROLOGICAL CONDITIONS.)

INSTRUMENT RUNWAY. A runway equipped with electronic and visual navigation aids for which a precision or nonprecision approach procedure having straight-in landing minimums has been approved. (See ICAO term INSTRUMENT RUNWAY.)

INSTRUMENT RUNWAY [ICAO]. One of the following types of runways intended for the operation of aircraft using instrument approach procedures:
 a. Nonprecision Approach Runway—An instrument runway served by visual aids and a nonvisual aid providing at least directional guidance adequate for a straight-in approach.
 b. Precision Approach Runway, Category I—An instrument runway served by ILS and visual aids intended for operations down to 60 m (200 feet) decision height and down to an RVR of the order of 800 m.

c. Precision Approach Runway, Category II—An instrument runway served by ILS and visual aids intended for operations down to 30 m (100 feet) decision height and down to an RVR of the order of 400 m.
 d. Precision Approach Runway, Category III—An instrument runway served by ILS to and along the surface of the runway and:
 1. Intended for operations down to an RVR of the order of 200 m (no decision height being applicable) using visual aids during the final phase of landing;
 2. Intended for operations down to an RVR of the order of 50 m (no decision height being applicable) using visual aids for taxiing;
 3. Intended for operations without reliance on visual reference for landing or taxiing.

Note 1: See Annex 10 Volume I, Part I, Chapter 3, for related ILS specifications.

Note 2: Visual aids need not necessarily be matched to the scale of nonvisual aids provided. The criterion for the selection of visual aids is the conditions in which operations are intended to be conducted.

INTEGRATED DEPARTURE/ARRIVAL CAPABILITY (IDAC). A Tower/TRACON departure scheduling capability within TBFM that allows departures to be scheduled into either an arrival flow or an en route flow. IDAC provides a mechanism for electronic coordination of departure release times.

INTEGRITY. The ability of a system to provide timely warnings to users when the system should not be used for navigation.

INTERMEDIATE APPROACH SEGMENT. (See SEGMENTS OF AN INSTRUMENT APPROACH PROCEDURE.)

INTERMEDIATE APPROACH SEGMENT [ICAO]. That segment of an instrument approach procedure between either the intermediate approach fix and the final approach fix or point, or between the end of a reversal, race track or dead reckoning track procedure and the final approach fix or point, as appropriate.

INTERMEDIATE FIX. The fix that identifies the beginning of the intermediate approach segment of an instrument approach procedure. The fix is not normally identified on the instrument approach chart as an intermediate fix (IF). (See SEGMENTS OF AN INSTRUMENT APPROACH PROCEDURE.)

INTERMEDIATE LANDING. On the rare occasion that this option is requested, it should be approved. The departure center, however, must advise the ATCSCC so that the appropriate delay is carried over and assigned at the intermediate airport. An intermediate landing airport within the arrival center will not be accepted without coordination with and the approval of the ATCSCC.

INTERNATIONAL AIRPORT. Relating to international flight, it means:
 a. An airport of entry which has been designated by the Secretary of Treasury or Commissioner of Customs as an international airport for customs service.

b. A landing rights airport at which specific permission to land must be obtained from customs authorities in advance of contemplated use.

c. Airports designated under the Convention on International Civil Aviation as an airport for use by international commercial air transport and/or international general aviation.
(See ICAO term INTERNATIONAL AIRPORT.)
(Refer to Chart Supplement U.S.)

INTERNATIONAL AIRPORT [ICAO]. Any airport designated by the Contracting State in whose territory it is situated as an airport of entry and departure for international air traffic, where the formalities incident to customs, immigration, public health, animal and plant quarantine and similar procedures are carried out.

INTERNATIONAL CIVIL AVIATION ORGANIZATION [ICAO]. A specialized agency of the United Nations whose objective is to develop the principles and techniques of international air navigation and to foster planning and development of international civil air transport.

INTERNATIONAL NOTICE. A notice containing flight prohibitions, potential hostile situations, or other international/foreign oceanic airspace matters. These notices can be found on the International Notices website.

INTERROGATOR. The ground-based surveillance radar beacon transmitter-receiver, which normally scans in synchronism with a primary radar, transmitting discrete radio signals which repetitiously request all transponders on the mode being used to reply. The replies received are mixed with the primary radar returns and displayed on the same plan position indicator (radar scope). Also, applied to the airborne element of the TACAN/DME system. (See TRANSPONDER.) (Refer to AIM.)

INTERSECTING RUNWAYS. Two or more runways which cross or meet within their lengths. (See INTERSECTION.)

INTERSECTION.
a. A point defined by any combination of courses, radials, or bearings of two or more navigational aids.
b. Used to describe the point where two runways, a runway and a taxiway, or two taxiways cross or meet.

INTERSECTION DEPARTURE. A departure from any runway intersection except the end of the runway. (See INTERSECTION.)

INTERSECTION TAKEOFF. (See INTERSECTION DEPARTURE.)

IR. (See IFR MILITARY TRAINING ROUTES.)

IRREGULAR SURFACE. A surface that is open for use but not per regulations.

ISR. (See INCREASED SEPARATION REQUIRED.)

J

JAMMING. Denotes emissions that do not mimic Global Navigation Satellite System (GNSS) signals (e.g., GPS and WAAS), but rather interfere with the civil receiver's ability to acquire and track GNSS signals. Jamming can result in denial of GNSS navigation, positioning, timing and aircraft dependent functions.

JET BLAST. The rapid air movement produced by exhaust from jet engines.

JET ROUTE. A route designed to serve aircraft operations from 18,000 feet MSL up to and including flight level 450. The routes are referred to as "J" routes with numbering to identify the designated route; e.g., J105. (See Class A AIRSPACE.) (Refer to 14 CFR Part 71.)

JET STREAM. A migrating stream of high-speed winds present at high altitudes.

JETTISONING OF EXTERNAL STORES. Airborne release of external stores; e.g., tiptanks, ordnance. (See FUEL DUMPING.) (Refer to 14 CFR Part 91.)

JOINT USE RESTRICTED AREA. (See RESTRICTED AREA.)

JUMP ZONE. The airspace directly associated with a Drop Zone. Vertical and horizontal limits may be locally defined.

K

KNOWN TRAFFIC. With respect to ATC clearances, means aircraft whose altitude, position, and intentions are known to ATC.

L

LAA. (See LOCAL AIRPORT ADVISORY.)

LAANC. (See LOW ALTITUDE AUTHORIZATION AND NOTIFICATION CAPABILITY.)

LAHSO. An acronym for "Land and Hold Short Operation." These operations include landing and holding short of an intersecting runway, a taxiway, a predetermined point, or an approach/departure flightpath.

LAHSO–DRY. Land and hold short operations on runways that are dry.

LAHSO–WET. Land and hold short operations on runways that are wet (but not contaminated).

LAND AND HOLD SHORT OPERATIONS. Operations which include simultaneous takeoffs and landings and/or simultaneous landings when a landing aircraft is able and is instructed by the controller to hold-short of the intersecting runway/taxiway or designated hold-short point. Pilots are expected to promptly inform the controller if the hold short clearance cannot be accepted. (See PARALLEL RUNWAYS.) (Refer to AIM.)

LAND-BASED AIR DEFENSE IDENTIFICATION ZONE (ADIZ). An ADIZ over U.S. metropolitan areas, which is activated and deactivated as needed, with dimensions, activation dates, and other relevant information disseminated via NOTAM. (See AIR DEFENSE IDENTIFICATION ZONE.)

LANDING AREA. Any locality either on land, water, or structures, including airports/heliports and intermediate landing fields, which is used, or intended to be used, for the landing and takeoff of aircraft whether or not facilities are provided for the shelter, servicing, or for receiving or discharging passengers or cargo. (See ICAO term LANDING AREA.)

LANDING AREA [ICAO]. That part of a movement area intended for the landing or take-off of aircraft.

LANDING DIRECTION INDICATOR. A device which visually indicates the direction in which landings and takeoffs should be made. (See TETRAHEDRON.) (Refer to AIM.)

LANDING DISTANCE AVAILABLE (LDA). The runway length declared available and suitable for a landing airplane.
(See ICAO term LANDING DISTANCE AVAILABLE.)

LANDING DISTANCE AVAILABLE [ICAO]. The length of runway which is declared available and suitable for the ground run of an aeroplane landing.

LANDING MINIMUMS. The minimum visibility prescribed for landing a civil aircraft while using an instrument approach procedure. The minimum applies with other limitations set forth in 14 CFR Part 91 with respect to the Minimum Descent Altitude (MDA) or Decision Height (DH) prescribed in the instrument approach procedures as follows:
 a. Straight-in landing minimums. A statement of MDA and visibility, or DH and visibility, required for a straight-in landing on a specified runway, or
 b. Circling minimums. A statement of MDA and visibility required for the circle-to-land maneuver.
Note: Descent below the MDA or DH must meet the conditions stated in 14 CFR Section 91.175.
(See CIRCLE-TO-LAND MANEUVER.)
(See DECISION HEIGHT.)
(See INSTRUMENT APPROACH PROCEDURE.)
(See MINIMUM DESCENT ALTITUDE.)
(See STRAIGHT-IN LANDING.)
(See VISIBILITY.) (Refer to 14 CFR Part 91.)

LANDING ROLL. The distance from the point of touchdown to the point where the aircraft can be brought to a stop or exit the runway.

LANDING SEQUENCE. The order in which aircraft are positioned for landing. (See APPROACH SEQUENCE.)

LAST ASSIGNED ALTITUDE. The last altitude/flight level assigned by ATC and acknowledged by the pilot. (See MAINTAIN.) (Refer to 14 CFR Part 91.)

LATERAL NAVIGATION (LNAV). A function of area navigation (RNAV) equipment which calculates, displays, and provides lateral guidance to a profile or path.

LATERAL SEPARATION. The lateral spacing of aircraft at the same altitude by requiring operation on different routes or in different geographical locations. (See SEPARATION.)

LDA. (See LOCALIZER TYPE DIRECTIONAL AID.) (See ICAO Term LANDING DISTANCE AVAILABLE.) (See LANDING DISTANCE AVAILABLE.)

LF. (See LOW FREQUENCY.)

LIGHTED AIRPORT. An airport where runway and obstruction lighting is available. (See AIRPORT LIGHTING.) (Refer to AIM.)

LIGHT GUN. A handheld directional light signaling device which emits a brilliant narrow beam of white, green, or red light as selected by the tower controller. The color and type of light transmitted can be used to approve or disapprove anticipated pilot actions where radio communication is not available. The light gun is used for controlling traffic operating in the vicinity of the airport and on the airport movement area. (Refer to AIM.)

LIGHT-SPORT AIRCRAFT (LSA). An FAA-registered aircraft, other than a helicopter or powered-lift, that meets certain weight and performance. Principally it is a single-engine aircraft with a maximum of two seats and weighing no more than 1,430 pounds if intended for operation on water, or 1,320 pounds if not. It must be of simple design (fixed landing gear (except if intended for operations on water or a glider) piston powered, non-pressurized, with a fixed or ground adjustable propeller). Performance is also limited to a maximum airspeed in level flight of not more than 120 knots calibrated airspeed (CAS), have a maximum never-exceed speed of not more than 120 knots CAS for a glider, and have a maximum stalling speed, without the use of lift-enhancing devices of not more than 45 knots CAS. It may be certificated as either Experimental LSA or as a Special LSA aircraft. A minimum of a sport pilot certificate is required to operate light-sport aircraft. (Refer to 14 CFR Part 1, §1.1.)

LINE UP AND WAIT (LUAW). Used by ATC to inform a pilot to taxi onto the departure runway to line up and wait. It is not authorization for takeoff. It is used when takeoff clearance cannot immediately be issued because of traffic or other reasons. (See CLEARED FOR TAKEOFF.)

LOCAL AIRPORT ADVISORY (LAA). A service available only in Alaska and provided by facilities that are located on the landing airport, have a discrete ground-to-air communication frequency or the tower frequency when the tower is closed, automated weather reporting with voice broadcasting, and a continuous ASOS/AWOS data display, other continuous direct reading instruments, or manual observations available to the specialist. (See AIRPORT ADVISORY AREA.)

LOCAL TRAFFIC. Aircraft operating in the traffic pattern or within sight of the tower, or aircraft known to be departing or arriving from flight in local practice areas, or aircraft executing practice instrument approaches at the airport. (See TRAFFIC PATTERN.)

LOCALIZER. The component of an ILS which provides course guidance to the runway. (See INSTRUMENT LANDING SYSTEM.) (See ICAO term LOCALIZER COURSE.) (Refer to AIM.)

LOCALIZER COURSE [ICAO]. The locus of points, in any given horizontal plane, at which the DDM (difference in depth of modulation) is zero.

LOCALIZER OFFSET. An angular offset of the localizer aligned within 3° of the runway alignment.

LOCALIZER PERFORMANCE WITH VERTICAL GUIDANCE (LPV). A type of approach with vertical guidance (APV) based on WAAS, published on RNAV (GPS) approach charts. This procedure takes advantage of the precise lateral guidance available from WAAS. The minima is published as a decision altitude (DA).

LOCALIZER TYPE DIRECTIONAL AID (LDA). A localizer with an angular offset that exceeds 3° of the runway alignment used for nonprecision instrument approaches with utility and accuracy comparable to a localizer but which are not part of a complete ILS. (Refer to AIM.)

LOCALIZER TYPE DIRECTIONAL AID (LDA) PRECISION RUNWAY MONITOR (PRM) APPROACH. An approach, which includes a glidslope, used in conjunction with an ILS PRM, RNAV PRM or GLS PRM approach to an adjacent runway to conduct Simultaneous Offset Instrument Approaches (SOIA) to parallel runways whose centerlines are separated by less than 3,000 feet and at least 750 feet. NTZ monitoring is required to conduct these approaches. (See SIMULTANEOUS OFFSET INSTRUMENT APPROACH (SOIA).) (Refer to AIM)

LOCALIZER USABLE DISTANCE. The maximum distance from the localizer transmitter at a specified altitude, as verified by flight inspection, at which reliable course information is continuously received. (Refer to AIM.)

LOCATOR [ICAO]. An LM/MF NDB used as an aid to final approach.

Note: A locator usually has an average radius of rated coverage of between 18.5 and 46.3 km (10 and 25 NM).

LONG RANGE NAVIGATION. (See LORAN.)

LONGITUDINAL SEPARATION. The longitudinal spacing of aircraft at the same altitude by a minimum distance expressed in units of time or miles. (See SEPARATION.) (Refer to AIM.)

LORAN. An electronic navigational system by which hyperbolic lines of position are determined by measuring the difference in the time of reception of synchronized pulse signals from two fixed transmitters. Loran A operates in the 1750–1950 kHz frequency band. Loran C and D operate in the 100-110 kHz frequency band. In 2010, the U.S. Coast Guard terminated all U.S. LORAN-C transmissions. (Refer to AIM.)

LOST COMMUNICATIONS. Loss of the ability to communicate by radio. Aircraft are sometimes referred to as NORDO (No Radio). Standard pilot procedures are specified in 14 CFR Part 91. Radar controllers issue procedures for pilots to follow in the event of lost communications during a radar approach when weather reports indicate that an aircraft will likely encounter IFR weather conditions during the approach. (Refer to 14 CFR Part 91.) (Refer to AIM.)

LOST LINK (LL). An interruption or loss of the control link, or when the pilot is unable to effect control of the aircraft and, as a result, the UA will perform a predictable or planned maneuver. Loss of command and control link between the Control Station and the aircraft. There are two types of links:
 a. An uplink which transmits command instructions to the aircraft, and
 b. A downlink which transmits the status of the aircraft and provides situational awareness to the pilot.

LOST LINK PROCEDURE. Preprogrammed or predetermined mitigations to ensure the continued safe operation of the UA in the event of a lost link (LL). In the event positive link cannot be established, flight termination must be implemented.

LOW ALTITUDE AIRWAY STRUCTURE. The network of airways serving aircraft operations up to but not including 18,000 feet MSL. (See AIRWAY.) (Refer to AIM.)

LOW ALTITUDE ALERT, CHECK YOUR ALTITUDE IMMEDIATELY. (See SAFETY ALERT.)

LOW ALTITUDE AUTHORIZATION AND NOTIFICATION CAPABILITY (LAANC). FAA and industry collaboration which automates the process of obtaining a required authorization for operations in controlled airspace.

LOW APPROACH. An approach over an airport or runway following an instrument approach or a VFR approach including the go-around maneuver where the pilot intentionally does not make contact with the runway. (Refer to AIM.)

LOW FREQUENCY (LF). The frequency band between 30 and 300 kHz. (Refer to AIM.)

LUAW. (See LINE UP AND WAIT.)

P/C

M

MAA. (See MAXIMUM AUTHORIZED ALTITUDE.)

MACH NUMBER. The ratio of true airspeed to the speed of sound; e.g., MACH .82, MACH 1.6. (See AIRSPEED.)

MACH TECHNIQUE [ICAO]. Describes a control technique used by air traffic control whereby turbojet aircraft operating successively along suitable routes are cleared to maintain appropriate MACH numbers for a relevant portion of the en route phase of flight. The principal objective is to achieve improved utilization of the airspace and to ensure that separation between successive aircraft does not decrease below the established minima.

MAHWP. Missed Approach Holding Waypoint

MAINTAIN.
 a. Concerning altitude/flight level, the term means to remain at the altitude/flight level specified. The phrase "climb and" or "descend and" normally precedes "maintain" and the altitude assignment; e.g., "descend and maintain 5,000."
 b. Concerning other ATC instructions, the term is used in its literal sense; e.g., maintain VFR.

MAINTENANCE PLANNING FRICTION LEVEL. The friction level specified in AC 150/5320-12, Measurement, Construction, and Maintenance of Skid Resistant Airport Pavement Surfaces, which represents the friction value below which the runway pavement surface remains acceptable for any category or class of aircraft operations but which is beginning to show signs of deterioration. This value will vary depending on the particular friction measurement equipment used.

MAKE SHORT APPROACH. Used by ATC to inform a pilot to alter his/her traffic pattern so as to make a short final approach. (See TRAFFIC PATTERN.)

MAN PORTABLE AIR DEFENSE SYSTEMS (MANPADS). MANPADS are lightweight, shoulder-launched, missile systems used to bring down aircraft and create mass casualties. The potential for MANPADS use against airborne aircraft is real and requires familiarity with the subject. Terrorists choose MANPADS because the weapons are low cost, highly mobile, require minimal set-up time, and are easy to use and maintain. Although the weapons have limited range, and their accuracy is affected by poor visibility and adverse weather, they can be fired from anywhere on land or from boats where there is unrestricted visibility to the target.

MANDATORY ALTITUDE. An altitude depicted on an instrument Approach Procedure Chart requiring the aircraft to maintain altitude at the depicted value.

MANPADS. (See MAN PORTABLE AIR DEFENSE SYSTEMS.)

MAP. (See MISSED APPROACH POINT.)

MARKER BEACON. An electronic navigation facility transmitting a 75 MHz vertical fan or boneshaped radiation pattern. Marker beacons are identified by their modulation frequency and keying code, and when received by compatible airborne equipment, indicate to the pilot, both aurally and visually, that he/she is passing over the facility. (See INNER MARKER.) (See MIDDLE MARKER.) (See OUTER MARKER.) (Refer to AIM.)

MARSA. (See MILITARY AUTHORITY ASSUMES RESPONSIBILITY FOR SEPARATION OF AIRCRAFT.)

MAWP. Missed Approach Waypoint

MAXIMUM AUTHORIZED ALTITUDE. A published altitude representing the maximum usable altitude or flight level for an airspace structure or route segment. It is the highest altitude on a Federal airway, jet route, area navigation low or high route, or other direct route for which an MEA is designated in 14 CFR Part 95 at which adequate reception of navigation aid signals is assured.

MAXIMUM GROSS OPERATING WEIGHT (MGOW). The maximum gross weight of an aircraft, including fuel and any external objects, at any point during the flight.

MAYDAY. The international radiotelephony distress signal. When repeated three times, it indicates imminent and grave danger and that immediate assistance is requested. (See PAN-PAN.) (Refer to AIM.)

MCA. (See MINIMUM CROSSING ALTITUDE.)

MDA. (See MINIMUM DESCENT ALTITUDE.)

MEA. (See MINIMUM EN ROUTE IFR ALTITUDE.)

MEARTS. (See MICRO-EN ROUTE AUTOMATED RADAR TRACKING SYSTEM.)

METEOROLOGICAL IMPACT STATEMENT. An unscheduled planning forecast describing conditions expected to begin within 4 to 12 hours which may impact the flow of air traffic in a specific center's (ARTCC) area.

METER FIX ARC. A semicircle, equidistant from a meter fix, usually in low altitude relatively close to the meter fix, used to help TBFM/ERAM calculate a meter time, and determine appropriate sector meter list assignments for aircraft not on an established arrival route or assigned a meter fix.

METER REFERENCE ELEMENT (MRE). A constraint point through which traffic flows are managed. An MRE can be the runway threshold, a meter fix, or a meter arc.

METER REFERENCE POINT LIST (MRP). A list of TBFM delay information conveyed to the controller on the situation display via the Meter Reference Point View, commonly known as the "Meter List."

METERING. A method of time-regulating traffic flows in the en route and terminal environments.

METERING AIRPORTS. Airports adapted for metering and for which optimum flight paths are defined. A maximum of 15 airports may be adapted.

METERING FIX. A fix along an established route from over which aircraft will be metered prior to entering terminal airspace. Normally, this fix should be established at a distance from the airport which will facilitate a profile descent 10,000 feet above airport elevation (AAE) or above.

MGOW. (See MAXIMUM GROSS OPERATING WEIGHT.)

MHA. (See MINIMUM HOLDING ALTITUDE.)

MIA. (See MINIMUM IFR ALTITUDES.)

MICROBURST. A small downburst with outbursts of damaging winds extending 2.5 miles or less. In spite of its small horizontal scale, an intense microburst could induce wind speeds as high as 150 knots (Refer to AIM.)

MICRO–EN ROUTE AUTOMATED RADAR TRACKING SYSTEM (MEARTS). An automated radar and radar beacon tracking system capable of employing both short-range (ASR) and long-range (ARSR) radars. This microcomputer driven system provides improved tracking, continuous data recording, and use of full digital radar displays.

MID RVR. (See VISIBILITY.)

MIDDLE COMPASS LOCATOR. (See COMPASS LOCATOR.)

MIDDLE MARKER. A marker beacon that defines a point along the glideslope of an ILS normally located at or near the point of decision height (ILS Category I). It is keyed to transmit alternate dots and dashes, with the alternate dots and dashes keyed at the rate of 95 dot/dash combinations per minute on a 1300 Hz tone, which is received aurally and visually by compatible airborne equipment. (See INSTRUMENT LANDING SYSTEM.) (See MARKER BEACON.) (Refer to AIM.)

MILES-IN-TRAIL. A specified distance between aircraft, normally, in the same stratum associated with the same destination or route of flight.

MILITARY AUTHORITY ASSUMES RESPONSIBILITY FOR SEPARATION OF AIRCRAFT (MARSA). A condition whereby the military services involved assume responsibility for separation between participating military aircraft in the ATC system. It is used only for required IFR operations which are specified in letters of agreement or other appropriate FAA or military documents.

MILITARY LANDING ZONE. A landing strip used exclusively by the military for training. A military landing zone does not carry a runway designation.

MILITARY OPERATIONS AREA. (See SPECIAL USE AIRSPACE.)

MILITARY TRAINING ROUTES. Airspace of defined vertical and lateral dimensions established for the conduct of military flight training at airspeeds in excess of 250 knots IAS. (See IFR MILITARY TRAINING ROUTES.) (See VFR MILITARY TRAINING ROUTES.)

MINIMA. (See MINIMUMS.)

MINIMUM CROSSING ALTITUDE (MCA). The lowest altitude at certain fixes at which an aircraft must cross when proceeding in the direction of a higher minimum en route IFR altitude (MEA). (See MINIMUM EN ROUTE IFR ALTITUDE.)

MINIMUM DESCENT ALTITUDE (MDA). The lowest altitude, expressed in feet above mean sea level, to which descent is authorized on final approach or during circle-to-land maneuvering in execution of a standard instrument approach procedure where no electronic glideslope is provided. (See NONPRECISION APPROACH PROCEDURE.)

MINIMUM EN ROUTE IFR ALTITUDE (MEA). The lowest published altitude between radio fixes which assures acceptable navigational signal coverage and meets obstacle clearance requirements between those fixes. The MEA prescribed for a Federal airway or segment thereof, area navigation low or high route, or other direct route applies to the entire width of the airway, segment, or route between the radio fixes defining the airway, segment, or route. (Refer to 14 CFR Part 91.) (Refer to 14 CFR Part 95.) (Refer to AIM.)

MINIMUM FRICTION LEVEL. The friction level specified in AC 150/5320-12, Measurement, Construction, and Maintenance of Skid Resistant Airport Pavement Surfaces, that represents the minimum recommended wet pavement surface friction value for any turbojet aircraft engaged in LAHSO. This value will vary with the particular friction measurement equipment used.

MINIMUM FUEL. Indicates that an aircraft's fuel supply has reached a state where, upon reaching the destination, it can accept little or no delay. This is not an emergency situation but merely indicates an emergency situation is possible should any undue delay occur. (Refer to AIM.)

MINIMUM HOLDING ALTITUDE. The lowest altitude prescribed for a holding pattern which assures navigational signal coverage, communications, and meets obstacle clearance requirements.

MINIMUM IFR ALTITUDES (MIA). Minimum altitudes for IFR operations as prescribed in 14 CFR Part 91. These altitudes are published on aeronautical charts and prescribed in 14 CFR Part 95 for airways and routes, and in 14 CFR Part 97 for standard instrument approach procedures. If no applicable minimum altitude is prescribed in 14 CFR Part 95 or 14 CFR Part 97, the following minimum IFR altitude applies:

a. In designated mountainous areas, 2,000 feet above the highest obstacle within a horizontal distance of 4 nautical miles from the course to be flown; or

(continued)

P/C

b. Other than mountainous areas, 1,000 feet above the highest obstacle within a horizontal distance of 4 nautical miles from the course to be flown; or

c. As otherwise authorized by the Administrator or assigned by ATC.
(See MINIMUM CROSSING ALTITUDE.)
(See MINIMUM EN ROUTE IFR ALTITUDE.)
(See MINIMUM OBSTRUCTION CLEARANCE ALTITUDE.)
(See MINIMUM SAFE ALTITUDE.)
(See MINIMUM VECTORING ALTITUDE.)
(Refer to 14 CFR Part 91.)

MINIMUM OBSTRUCTION CLEARANCE ALTITUDE (MOCA). The lowest published altitude in effect between radio fixes on VOR airways, off-airway routes, or route segments which meets obstacle clearance requirements for the entire route segment and which assures acceptable navigational signal coverage only within 25 statute (22 nautical) miles of a VOR. (Refer to 14 CFR Part 91.) (Refer to 14 CFR Part 95.)

MINIMUM RECEPTION ALTITUDE (MRA). The lowest altitude at which an intersection can be determined. (Refer to 14 CFR Part 95.)

MINIMUM SAFE ALTITUDE (MSA).
a. The Minimum Safe Altitude (MSA) specified in 14 CFR Part 91 for various aircraft operations.

b. Altitudes depicted on approach charts or departure procedure (DP) graphic charts which provide at least 1,000 feet of obstacle clearance for emergency use. These altitudes will be identified as Minimum Safe Altitudes or Emergency Safe Altitudes and are established as follows:

1. Minimum Safe Altitude (MSA). Altitudes depicted on approach charts or on a DP graphic chart which provide at least 1,000 feet of obstacle clearance within a 25-mile radius of the navigation facility, waypoint, or airport reference point upon which the MSA is predicated. MSAs are for emergency use only and do not necessarily assure acceptable navigational signal coverage. (See ICAO term Minimum Sector Altitude.)

2. Emergency Safe Altitude (ESA). Altitudes depicted on approach charts which provide at least 1,000 feet of obstacle clearance in nonmountainous areas and 2,000 feet of obstacle clearance in designated mountainous areas within a 100-mile radius of the navigation facility or waypoint used as the ESA center. These altitudes are normally used only in military procedures and are identified on published procedures as "Emergency Safe Altitudes."

MINIMUM SAFE ALTITUDE WARNING (MSAW). A function of the EAS and STARS computer that aids the controller by alerting him/her when a tracked Mode C equipped aircraft is below or is predicted by the computer to go below a predetermined minimum safe altitude. (Refer to AIM.)

MINIMUM SECTOR ALTITUDE [ICAO]. The lowest altitude which may be used under emergency conditions which will provide a minimum clearance of 300 m (1,000 feet) above all obstacles located in an area contained within a sector of a circle of 46 km (25 NM) radius centered on a radio aid to navigation.

MINIMUMS. Weather condition requirements established for a particular operation or type of operation; e.g., IFR takeoff or landing, alternate airport for IFR flight plans, VFR flight, etc. (See IFR CONDITIONS.) (See IFR TAKEOFF MINIMUMS AND DEPARTURE PROCEDURES.) (See LANDING MINIMUMS.) (See VFR CONDITIONS.) (Refer to 14 CFR Part 91.) (Refer to AIM.)

MINIMUM VECTORING ALTITUDE (MVA). The lowest MSL altitude at which an IFR aircraft will be vectored by a radar controller, except as otherwise authorized for radar approaches, departures, and missed approaches. The altitude meets IFR obstacle clearance criteria. It may be lower than the published MEA along an airway or J-route segment. It may be utilized for radar vectoring only upon the controller's determination that an adequate radar return is being received from the aircraft being controlled. Charts depicting minimum vectoring altitudes are normally available only to the controllers and not to pilots. (Refer to AIM.)

MINUTES-IN-TRAIL. A specified interval between aircraft expressed in time. This method would more likely be utilized regardless of altitude.

MIS. (See METEOROLOGICAL IMPACT STATEMENT.)

MISSED APPROACH.
a. A maneuver conducted by a pilot when an instrument approach cannot be completed to a landing. The route of flight and altitude are shown on instrument approach procedure charts. A pilot executing a missed approach prior to the Missed Approach Point (MAP) must continue along the final approach to the MAP.

b. A term used by the pilot to inform ATC that he/she is executing the missed approach.

c. At locations where ATC radar service is provided, the pilot should conform to radar vectors when provided by ATC in lieu of the published missed approach procedure.
(See MISSED APPROACH POINT.) (Refer to AIM.)

MISSED APPROACH POINT (MAP). A point prescribed in each instrument approach procedure at which a missed approach procedure shall be executed if the required visual reference does not exist. (See MISSED APPROACH.) (See SEGMENTS OF AN INSTRUMENT APPROACH PROCEDURE.)

MISSED APPROACH PROCEDURE [ICAO]. The procedure to be followed if the approach cannot be continued.

MISSED APPROACH SEGMENT. (See SEGMENTS OF AN INSTRUMENT APPROACH PROCEDURE.)

MM. (See MIDDLE MARKER.)

MOA. (See MILITARY OPERATIONS AREA.)

MOCA. (See MINIMUM OBSTRUCTION CLEARANCE ALTITUDE.)

MODE. The letter or number assigned to a specific pulse spacing of radio signals transmitted or received by ground interrogator or airborne transponder components of the Air Traffic Control Radar Beacon System

(ATCRBS). Mode A (military Mode 3) and Mode C (altitude reporting) are used in air traffic control. (See INTERROGATOR.) (See RADAR.) (See TRANSPONDER.) (See ICAO term MODE.) (Refer to AIM.)

MODE (SSR MODE) [ICAO]. The letter or number assigned to a specific pulse spacing of the interrogation signals transmitted by an interrogator. There are 4 modes, A, B, C and D specified in Annex 10, corresponding to four different interrogation pulse spacings.

MODE C INTRUDER ALERT. A function of certain air traffic control automated systems designed to alert radar controllers to existing or pending situations between a tracked target (known IFR or VFR aircraft) and an untracked target (unknown IFR or VFR aircraft) that requires immediate attention/action. (See CONFLICT ALERT.)

MODEL AIRCRAFT. An unmanned aircraft that is: (1) capable of sustained flight in the atmosphere; (2) flown within visual line of sight of the person operating the aircraft; and (3) flown for hobby or recreational purposes.

MONITOR. (When used with communication transfer) listen on a specific frequency and stand by for instructions. Under normal circumstances do not establish communications.

MONITOR ALERT (MA). A function of the TFMS that provides traffic management personnel with a tool for predicting potential capacity problems in individual operational sectors. The MA is an indication that traffic management personnel need to analyze a particular sector for actual activity and to determine the required action(s), if any, needed to control the demand.

MONITOR ALERT PARAMETER (MAP). The number designated for use in monitor alert processing by the TFMS. The MAP is designated for each operational sector for increments of 15 minutes.

MOSAIC/MULTI-SENSOR MODE. Accepts positional data from multiple approved surveillance sources. Targets are displayed from a single source according to the hierarchy of the sources assigned in a given geographic area.

MOUNTAIN WAVE. Mountain waves occur when air is being blown over a mountain range or even the ridge of a sharp bluff area. As the air hits the upwind side of the range, it starts to climb, thus creating what is generally a smooth updraft which turns into a turbulent downdraft as the air passes the crest of the ridge. Mountain waves can cause significant fluctuations in airspeed and altitude with or without associated turbulence. (Refer to AIM.)

MOVEMENT AREA. The runways, taxiways, and other areas of an airport/heliport which are utilized for taxiing/hover taxiing, air taxiing, takeoff, and landing of aircraft, exclusive of loading ramps and parking areas. At those airports/heliports with a tower, specific approval for entry onto the movement area must be obtained from ATC. (See ICAO term MOVEMENT AREA.)

MOVEMENT AREA [ICAO]. That part of an aerodrome to be used for the takeoff, landing and taxiing of aircraft, consisting of the maneuvering area and the apron(s).

MOVING AIRSPACE RESERVATION. The term used in oceanic ATC for airspace that encompasses oceanic activities and advances with the mission progress; i.e., the reservation moves with the aircraft or flight. (See MOVING ALTITUDE RESERVATION.)

MOVING ALTITUDE RESERVATION. An altitude reservation which encompasses en route activities and advances with the mission progress; i.e., the reservation moves with the aircraft or flight.

MOVING TARGET INDICATOR. An electronic device which will permit radar scope presentation only from targets which are in motion. A partial remedy for ground clutter.

MRA. (See MINIMUM RECEPTION ALTITUDE.)

MRE. (See METER REFERENCE ELEMENT.)

MRP. (See METER REFERENCE POINT LIST.)

MSA. (See MINIMUM SAFE ALTITUDE.)

MSAW. (See MINIMUM SAFE ALTITUDE WARNING.)

MTI. (See MOVING TARGET INDICATOR.)

MTR. (See MILITARY TRAINING ROUTES.)

MULTICOM. A mobile service not open to public correspondence used to provide communications essential to conduct the activities being performed by or directed from private aircraft.

MULTIPLE RUNWAYS. The utilization of a dedicated arrival runway(s) for departures and a dedicated departure runway(s) for arrivals when feasible to reduce delays and enhance capacity.

MVA. (See MINIMUM VECTORING ALTITUDE.)

N

NAS. (See NATIONAL AIRSPACE SYSTEM.)

NAT HLA. (See NORTH ATLANTIC HIGH LEVEL AIRSPACE)

NATIONAL AIRSPACE SYSTEM. The common network of U.S. airspace; air navigation facilities, equipment and services, airports or landing areas; aeronautical charts, information and services; rules, regulations and procedures, technical information, and manpower and material. Included are system components shared jointly with the military.

NATIONAL BEACON CODE ALLOCATION PLAN AIRSPACE (NBCAP). Airspace over United States territory located within the North American continent between Canada and Mexico, including adjacent territorial waters outward to about boundaries of oceanic control areas (CTA)/Flight Information Regions (FIR). (See FLIGHT INFORMATION REGION.)

NATIONAL FLIGHT DATA DIGEST (NFDD). A daily (except weekends and Federal holidays) publication of flight information appropriate to aeronautical charts, aeronautical publications, Notices to Air Missions, or other media serving the purpose of providing operational flight data essential to safe and efficient aircraft operations.

NATIONAL SEARCH AND RESCUE PLAN. An interagency agreement which provides for the effective utilization of all available facilities in all types of search and rescue missions.

NATIONAL SECURITY AREA (NSA). (See SPECIAL USE AIRSPACE.)

NAVAID. (See NAVIGATIONAL AID.)

NAVAID CLASSES. VOR, VORTAC, and TACAN aids are classed according to their operational use. The three classes of NAVAIDs are:
a. T—Terminal.
b. L—Low altitude.
c. H—High altitude.

Note: The normal service range for T, L, and H class aids is found in the AIM. Certain operational requirements make it necessary to use some of these aids at greater service ranges than specified. Extended range is made possible through flight inspection determinations. Some aids also have lesser service range due to location, terrain, frequency protection, etc. Restrictions to service range are listed in Chart Supplement.

NAVIGABLE AIRSPACE. Airspace at and above the minimum flight altitudes prescribed in the CFRs including airspace needed for safe takeoff and landing. (Refer to 14 CFR Part 91.)

NAVIGATION REFERENCE SYSTEM (NRS). The NRS is a system of waypoints developed for use within the United States for flight planning and navigation without reference to ground based navigational aids. The NRS waypoints are located in a grid pattern along defined latitude and longitude lines. The initial use of the NRS will be in the high altitude environment. The NRS waypoints are intended for use by aircraft capable of point-to-point navigation.

NAVIGATION SPECIFICATION [ICAO]. A set of aircraft and flight crew requirements needed to support performance-based navigation operations within a defined airspace. There are two kinds of navigation specifications:
a. RNP specification. A navigation specification based on area navigation that includes the requirement for performance monitoring and alerting, designated by the prefix RNP; e.g., RNP 4, RNP APCH.
b. RNAV specification. A navigation specification based on area navigation that does not include the requirement for performance monitoring and alerting, designated by the prefix RNAV; e.g., RNAV 5, RNAV 1.

Note: The Performance-based Navigation Manual (Doc 9613), Volume II contains detailed guidance on navigation specifications.

NAVIGATIONAL AID. Any visual or electronic device airborne or on the surface which provides point-to-point guidance information or position data to aircraft in flight. (See AIR NAVIGATION FACILITY.)

NAVSPEC (See NAVIGATION SPECIFICATION [ICAO].)

NBCAP AIRSPACE. (See NATIONAL BEACON CODE ALLOCATION PLAN AIRSPACE.)

NDB. (See NONDIRECTIONAL BEACON.)

NEGATIVE. "No," or "permission not granted," or "that is not correct."

NEGATIVE CONTACT. Used by pilots to inform ATC that:
a. Previously issued traffic is not in sight. It may be followed by the pilot's request for the controller to provide assistance in avoiding the traffic.
b. They were unable to contact ATC on a particular frequency.

NFDD. (See NATIONAL FLIGHT DATA DIGEST.)

NIGHT. The time between the end of evening civil twilight and the beginning of morning civil twilight, as published in the Air Almanac, converted to local time. (See ICAO term NIGHT.)

NIGHT [ICAO]. The hours between the end of evening civil twilight and the beginning of morning civil twilight or such other period between sunset and sunrise as may be specified by the appropriate authority.

Note: Civil twilight ends in the evening when the center of the sun's disk is 6 degrees below the horizon and begins in the morning when the center of the sun's disk is 6 degrees below the horizon.

NO GYRO APPROACH. A radar approach/vector provided in case of a malfunctioning gyro-compass or directional gyro. Instead of providing the pilot with headings to be flown, the controller observes the radar track and issues control instructions "turn right/left" or "stop turn" as appropriate. (Refer to AIM.)

NO GYRO VECTOR. (See NO GYRO APPROACH.)

NO TRANSGRESSION ZONE (NTZ). The NTZ is a 2,000 foot wide zone, located equidistant between parallel runway or SOIA final approach courses in which flight is normally not allowed.

NONAPPROACH CONTROL TOWER. Authorizes aircraft to land or takeoff at the airport controlled by the tower or to transit the Class D airspace. The primary function of a nonapproach control tower is the sequencing of aircraft in the traffic pattern and on the landing area. Nonapproach control towers also separate aircraft operating under instrument flight rules clearances from approach controls and centers. They provide ground control services to aircraft, vehicles, personnel, and equipment on the airport movement area.

NONCOMMON ROUTE/PORTION. That segment of a North American Route between the inland navigation facility and a designated North American terminal.

NON-COOPERATIVE SURVEILLANCE. Any surveillance system, such as primary radar, that is not dependent upon the presence of any equipment on the aircraft or vehicle to be tracked. (See COOPERATIVE SURVEILLANCE.) (See RADAR.)

NONDIRECTIONAL BEACON. An L/MF or UHF radio beacon transmitting nondirectional signals whereby the pilot of an aircraft equipped with direction finding equipment can determine his/her bearing to or from the radio beacon and "home" on or track to or from the station. When the radio beacon is installed in conjunction with the Instrument Landing System marker, it is normally called a Compass Locator. (See AUTOMATIC DIRECTION FINDER.) (See COMPASS LOCATOR.)

NONMOVEMENT AREAS. Taxiways and apron (ramp) areas not under the control of air traffic.

NONPRECISION APPROACH. (See NONPRECISION APPROACH PROCEDURE.)

NONPRECISION APPROACH PROCEDURE. A standard instrument approach procedure in which no electronic glideslope is provided; e.g., VOR, TACAN, NDB, LOC, ASR, LDA, or SDF approaches.

NONRADAR. Precedes other terms and generally means without the use of radar, such as:
 a. Nonradar Approach. Used to describe instrument approaches for which course guidance on final approach is not provided by ground-based precision or surveillance radar. Radar vectors to the final approach course may or may not be provided by ATC. Examples of nonradar approaches are VOR, NDB, TACAN, ILS, RNAV, and GLS approaches. (See FINAL APPROACH COURSE.) (See FINAL APPROACH-IFR.) (See INSTRUMENT APPROACH PROCEDURE.) (See RADAR APPROACH.)
 b. Nonradar Approach Control. An ATC facility providing approach control service without the use of radar. (See APPROACH CONTROL FACILITY.) (See APPROACH CONTROL SERVICE.)
 c. Nonradar Arrival. An aircraft arriving at an airport without radar service or at an airport served by a radar facility and radar contact has not been established or has been terminated due to a lack of radar service to the airport. (See RADAR ARRIVAL.) (See RADAR SERVICE.)
 d. Nonradar Route. A flight path or route over which the pilot is performing his/her own navigation. The pilot may be receiving radar separation, radar monitoring, or other ATC services while on a nonradar route. (See RADAR ROUTE.)
 e. Nonradar Separation. The spacing of aircraft in accordance with established minima without the use of radar; e.g., vertical, lateral, or longitudinal separation. (See RADAR SEPARATION.)

NON-RESTRICTIVE ROUTING (NRR). Portions of a proposed route of flight where a user can flight plan the most advantageous flight path with no requirement to make reference to ground-based NAVAIDs.

NOPAC. (See NORTH PACIFIC.)

NORDO (No Radio). Aircraft that cannot or do not communicate by radio when radio communication is required are referred to as "NORDO." (See LOST COMMUNICATIONS.)

NORMAL OPERATING ZONE (NOZ). The NOZ is the operating zone within which aircraft flight remains during normal independent simultaneous parallel ILS approaches.

NORTH AMERICAN ROUTE. A numerically coded route preplanned over existing airway and route systems to and from specific coastal fixes serving the North Atlantic. North American Routes consist of the following:
 a. Common Route/Portion. That segment of a North American Route between the inland navigation facility and the coastal fix.
 b. Noncommon Route/Portion. That segment of a North American Route between the inland navigation facility and a designated North American terminal.
 c. Inland Navigation Facility. A navigation aid on a North American Route at which the common route and/or the noncommon route begins or ends.
 d. Coastal Fix. A navigation aid or intersection where an aircraft transitions between the domestic route structure and the oceanic route structure.

NORTH AMERICAN ROUTE PROGRAM (NRP). The NRP is a set of rules and procedures which are designed to increase the flexibility of user flight planning within published guidelines.

NORTH ATLANTIC HIGH LEVEL AIRSPACE (NAT HLA). That volume of airspace (as defined in ICAO Document 7030) between FL 285 and FL 420 within the Oceanic Control Areas of Bodo Oceanic, Gander Oceanic, New York Oceanic East, Reykjavik, Santa Maria, and Shanwick, excluding the Shannon and Brest Ocean Transition Areas. ICAO Doc 007 *North Atlantic Operations and Airspace Manual* provides detailed information on related aircraft and operational requirements.

NORTH PACIFIC. An organized route system between the Alaskan west coast and Japan.

NOT STANDARD. Varying from what is expected or published. For use in NOTAMs only.

NOT STD. (See NOT STANDARD.)

NOTAM. (See NOTICE TO AIR MISSIONS.)

NOTAM [ICAO]. A notice containing information concerning the establishment, condition or change in any aeronautical facility, service, procedure or hazard, the timely knowledge of which is essential to personnel concerned with flight operations.
 a. I Distribution. Distribution by means of telecommunication.
 b. II Distribution. Distribution by means other than telecommunications.

P/C

NOTICE TO AIR MISSIONS (NOTAM). A notice containing information (not known sufficiently in advance to publicize by other means) concerning the establishment, condition, or change in any component (facility, service, or procedure of, or hazard in the National Airspace System) the timely knowledge of which is essential to personnel concerned with flight operations.

a. NOTAM (D). A NOTAM given (in addition to local dissemination) distant dissemination beyond the area of responsibility of the Flight Service Station. These NOTAMs will be stored and available until canceled.

b. FDC NOTAM. A NOTAM regulatory in nature, transmitted by USNOF and given system wide dissemination.
(See ICAO term NOTAM.)

NRR. (See NON-RESTRICTIVE ROUTING.)

NRS. (See NAVIGATION REFERENCE SYSTEM.)

NUMEROUS TARGETS VICINITY (LOCATION). A traffic advisory issued by ATC to advise pilots that targets on the radar scope are too numerous to issue individually. (See TRAFFIC ADVISORIES.)

O

OBSTACLE. An existing object, object of natural growth, or terrain at a fixed geographical location or which may be expected at a fixed location within a prescribed area with reference to which vertical clearance is or must be provided during flight operation.

OBSTACLE DEPARTURE PROCEDURE (ODP). A preplanned instrument flight rule (IFR) departure procedure printed for pilot use in textual or graphic form to provide obstruction clearance via the least onerous route from the terminal area to the appropriate en route structure. ODPs are recommended for obstruction clearance and may be flown without ATC clearance unless an alternate departure procedure (SID or radar vector) has been specifically assigned by ATC. (See IFR TAKEOFF MINIMUMS AND DEPARTURE PROCEDURES.) (See STANDARD INSTRUMENT DEPARTURES.) (Refer to AIM.)

OBSTACLE FREE ZONE. The OFZ is a three-dimensional volume of airspace which protects the transition of aircraft to and from the runway. The OFZ clearing standard precludes taxiing and parked airplanes and object penetrations, except for frangible NAVAID locations that are fixed by function. Additionally, vehicles, equipment, and personnel may be authorized by air traffic control to enter the area using the provisions of FAA Order JO 7110.65, paragraph 3-1-5, Vehicles/Equipment/Personnel Near/On Runways. The runway OFZ and when applicable, the inner-approach OFZ, and the inner-transitional OFZ, comprise the OFZ.

a. Runway OFZ. The runway OFZ is a defined volume of airspace centered above the runway. The runway OFZ is the airspace above a surface whose elevation at any point is the same as the elevation of the nearest point on the runway centerline. The runway OFZ extends 200 feet beyond each end of the runway. The width is as follows:

1. For runways serving large airplanes, the greater of: (a) 400 feet, or (b) 180 feet, plus the wingspan of the most demanding airplane, plus 20 feet per 1,000 feet of airport elevation.

2. For runways serving only small airplanes: (a) 300 feet for precision instrument runways. (b) 250 feet for other runways serving small airplanes with approach speeds of 50 knots, or more. (c) 120 feet for other runways serving small airplanes with approach speeds of less than 50 knots.

b. Inner-approach OFZ. The inner-approach OFZ is a defined volume of airspace centered on the approach area. The inner-approach OFZ applies only to runways with an approach lighting system. The inner-approach OFZ begins 200 feet from the runway threshold at the same elevation as the runway threshold and extends 200 feet beyond the last light unit in the approach lighting system. The width of the inner-approach OFZ is the same as the runway OFZ and rises at a slope of 50 (horizontal) to 1 (vertical) from the beginning.

c. Inner-transitional OFZ. The inner transitional surface OFZ is a defined volume of airspace along the sides of the runway and inner-approach OFZ and applies only to precision instrument runways. The inner-transitional surface OFZ slopes 3 (horizontal) to 1 (vertical) out from the edges of the runway OFZ and inner-approach OFZ to a height of 150 feet above the established airport elevation.
(Refer to AC 150/5300-13, Chapter 3.)
(Refer to FAA Order JO 7110.65, Para 3-1-5, Vehicles/Equipment/Personnel Near/On Runways.)

OBSTRUCTION. Any object/obstacle exceeding the obstruction standards specified by 14 CFR Part 77, Subpart C.

OBSTRUCTION LIGHT. A light or one of a group of lights, usually red or white, frequently mounted on a surface structure or natural terrain to warn pilots of the presence of an obstruction.

OCEANIC AIRSPACE. Airspace over the oceans of the world, considered international airspace, where oceanic separation and procedures per the International Civil Aviation Organization are applied. Responsibility for the provisions of air traffic control service in this airspace is delegated to various countries, based generally upon geographic proximity and the availability of the required resources.

OCEANIC ERROR REPORT. A report filed when ATC observes an Oceanic Error as defined by FAA Order JO 7210.632, Air Traffic Organization Occurrence Reporting.

OCEANIC PUBLISHED ROUTE. A route established in international airspace and charted or described in flight information publications, such as Route Charts, DOD Enroute Charts, Chart Supplements, NOTAMs, and Track Messages.

OCEANIC TRANSITION ROUTE. An ATS route established for the purpose of transitioning aircraft to/from an organized track system.

ODP. (See OBSTACLE DEPARTURE PROCEDURE.)

OFF COURSE. A term used to describe a situation where an aircraft has reported a position fix or is observed on radar at a point not on the ATC-approved route of flight.

OFF-ROUTE OBSTRUCTION CLEARANCE ALTITUDE (OROCA). A published altitude which provides terrain and obstruction clearance with a 1,000 foot buffer in non-mountainous areas and a 2,000 foot buffer in designated mountainous areas within the United States, and a 3,000 foot buffer outside the US ADIZ. These altitudes are not assessed for NAVAID signal coverage, air traffic control surveillance, or communications coverage, and are published for general situational awareness, flight planning, and in-flight contingency use.

OFF-ROUTE VECTOR. A vector by ATC which takes an aircraft off a previously assigned route. Altitudes assigned by ATC during such vectors provide required obstacle clearance.

OFFSET PARALLEL RUNWAYS. Staggered runways having centerlines which are parallel.

OFFSHORE/CONTROL AIRSPACE AREA. That portion of airspace between the U.S. 12 NM limit and the oceanic CTA/FIR boundary within which air traffic control is exercised. These areas are established to provide air traffic control services. Offshore/Control Airspace Areas may be classified as either Class A airspace or Class E airspace.

OFT. (See OUTER FIX TIME.)

OM. (See OUTER MARKER.)

ON COURSE.
 a. Used to indicate that an aircraft is established on the route centerline.
 b. Used by ATC to advise a pilot making a radar approach that his/her aircraft is lined up on the final approach course. (See ON-COURSE INDICATION.)

ON-COURSE INDICATION. An indication on an instrument, which provides the pilot a visual means of determining that the aircraft is located on the centerline of a given navigational track, or an indication on a radar scope that an aircraft is on a given track.

ONE-MINUTE WEATHER. The most recent one minute updated weather broadcast received by a pilot from an uncontrolled airport ASOS/AWOS.

ONER. (See OCEANIC NAVIGATIONAL ERROR REPORT.)

OOP. (See OPERATIONS OVER PEOPLE.)

OPEN LOOP CLEARANCE. Provides a lateral vector solution that does not include a return to route point.

OPERATIONAL. (See DUE REGARD.)

OPERATIONS OVER PEOPLE (OOP). Operations of small unmanned aircraft over people. (Refer to 14 CFR Part 107)

OPERATIONS SPECIFICATIONS [ICAO]. The authorizations, conditions and limitations associated with the air operator certificate and subject to the conditions in the operations manual.

OPERATOR (UAS). The owner and/or remote pilot of a UAS.

OPPOSITE DIRECTION AIRCRAFT. Aircraft are operating in opposite directions when:
 a. They are following the same track in reciprocal directions; or
 b. Their tracks are parallel and the aircraft are flying in reciprocal directions; or
 c. Their tracks intersect at an angle of more than 135°.

OPTION APPROACH. An approach requested and conducted by a pilot which will result in either a touch-and-go, missed approach, low approach, stop-and-go, or full stop landing. Pilots should advise ATC if they decide to remain on the runway, of any delay in their stop and go, delay clearing the runway, or are unable to comply with the instruction(s). (See CLEARED FOR THE OPTION.) (Refer to AIM.)

ORGANIZED TRACK SYSTEM. A series of ATS routes which are fixed and charted; i.e., CEP, NOPAC, or flexible and described by NOTAM; i.e., NAT TRACK MESSAGE.

OTR. (See OCEANIC TRANSITION ROUTE.)

OTS. (See ORGANIZED TRACK SYSTEM.)

OUT. The conversation is ended and no response is expected.

OUT OF SERVICE/UNSERVICEABLE (U/S). When a piece of equipment, a NAVAID, a facility or a service is not operational, certified (if required) and immediately "available" for Air Traffic or public use.

OUTER AREA (associated with Class C airspace). Nonregulatory airspace surrounding designated Class C airspace airports wherein ATC provides radar vectoring and sequencing on a full-time basis for all IFR and participating VFR aircraft. The service provided in the outer area is called Class C service which includes: IFR/IFR-IFR separation; IFR/VFR-traffic advisories and conflict resolution; and VFR/VFR-traffic advisories and, as appropriate, safety alerts. The normal radius will be 20 nautical miles with some variations based on site-specific requirements. The outer area extends outward from the primary Class C airspace airport and extends from the lower limits of radar/radio coverage up to the ceiling of the approach control's delegated airspace excluding the Class C charted area and other airspace as appropriate. (See CONFLICT RESOLUTION.) (See CONTROLLED AIRSPACE.)

OUTER COMPASS LOCATOR. (See COMPASS LOCATOR.)

OUTER FIX. A general term used within ATC to describe fixes in the terminal area, other than the final approach fix. Aircraft are normally cleared to these fixes by an Air Route Traffic Control Center or an Approach Control Facility. Aircraft are normally cleared from these fixes to the final approach fix or final approach course.

or

OUTER FIX. An adapted fix along the converted route of flight, prior to the meter fix, for which crossing times are calculated and displayed in the metering position list.

OUTER FIX ARC. A semicircle, usually about a 50–70 mile radius from a meter fix, usually in high altitude, which is used by CTAS/ERAM to calculate outer fix times and determine appropriate sector meter list assignments for aircraft on an established arrival route that will traverse the arc.

OUTER FIX TIME. A calculated time to depart the outer fix in order to cross the vertex at the ACLT. The time reflects descent speed adjustments and any applicable delay time that must be absorbed prior to crossing the meter fix.

OUTER MARKER. A marker beacon at or near the glideslope intercept altitude of an ILS approach. It is keyed to transmit two dashes per second on a 400 Hz tone, which is received aurally and visually by compatible airborne equipment. The OM is normally located four to seven miles from the runway threshold on the extended centerline of the runway. (See INSTRUMENT LANDING SYSTEM.) (See MARKER BEACON.) (Refer to AIM.)

OVER. My transmission is ended; I expect a response.

OVERHEAD MANEUVER. A series of predetermined maneuvers prescribed for aircraft (often in formation) for entry into the visual flight rules (VFR) traffic pattern and to proceed to a landing. An overhead maneuver is not an instrument flight rules (IFR) approach procedure. An aircraft executing an overhead maneuver is considered VFR and the IFR flight plan is cancelled when the aircraft reaches the "initial point" on the initial approach portion of the maneuver. The pattern usually specifies the following:

 a. The radio contact required of the pilot.

 b. The speed to be maintained.

 c. An initial approach 3 to 5 miles in length.

 d. An elliptical pattern consisting of two 180 degree turns.

 e. A break point at which the first 180 degree turn is started.

 f. The direction of turns.

 g. Altitude (at least 500 feet above the conventional pattern).

 h. A "Roll-out" on final approach not less than 1/4 mile from the landing threshold and not less than 300 feet above the ground.

OVERLYING CENTER. The ARTCC facility that is responsible for arrival/departure operations at a specific terminal.

P

P TIME. (See PROPOSED DEPARTURE TIME.)

P-ACP. (See PREARRANGED COORDINATION PROCEDURES.)

PAN-PAN. The international radio-telephony urgency signal. When repeated three times, indicates uncertainty or alert followed by the nature of the urgency. (See MAYDAY.) (Refer to AIM.)

PAO. (See PUBLIC AIRCRAFT OPERATION.)

PAR. (See PRECISION APPROACH RADAR.)

PAR [ICAO]. (See ICAO Term PRECISION APPROACH RADAR.)

PARALLEL ILS APPROACHES. Approaches to parallel runways by IFR aircraft which, when established inbound toward the airport on the adjacent final approach courses, are radar-separated by at least 2 miles. (See FINAL APPROACH COURSE.) (See SIMULTANEOUS ILS APPROACHES.)

PARALLEL OFFSET ROUTE. A parallel track to the left or right of the designated or established airway/route. Normally associated with Area Navigation (RNAV) operations. (See AREA NAVIGATION.)

PARALLEL RUNWAYS. Two or more runways at the same airport whose centerlines are parallel. In addition to runway number, parallel runways are designated as L (left) and R (right) or, if three parallel runways exist, L (left), C (center), and R (right).

PBCT. (See PROPOSED BOUNDARY CROSSING TIME.)

PBN. (See ICAO Term PERFORMANCE-BASED NAVIGATION.)

PDC. (See PRE-DEPARTURE CLEARANCE.)

PDRR. (See PRE-DEPARTURE REROUTE.)

PERFORMANCE-BASED NAVIGATION (PBN) [ICAO]. Area navigation based on performance requirements for aircraft operating along an ATS route, on an instrument approach procedure or in a designated airspace.

Note: Performance requirements are expressed in navigation specifications (RNAV specification, RNP specification) in terms of accuracy, integrity, continuity, availability, and functionality needed for the proposed operation in the context of a particular airspace concept.

PERMANENT ECHO. Radar signals reflected from fixed objects on the earth's surface; e.g., buildings, towers, terrain. Permanent echoes are distinguished from "ground clutter" by being definable locations rather than large areas. Under certain conditions they may be used to check radar alignment.

PERTI. (See PLAN, EXECUTE, REVIEW, TRAIN, IMPROVE.)

PGUI. (See PLANVIEW GRAPHICAL USER INTERFACE.)

PHOTO RECONNAISSANCE. Military activity that requires locating individual photo targets and navigating to the targets at a preplanned angle and altitude. The activity normally requires a lateral route width of 16 NM and altitude range of 1,500 feet to 10,000 feet AGL.

PILOT BRIEFING. The gathering, translation, interpretation, and summarization of weather and aeronautical information into a form usable by the pilot or flight supervisory personnel to assist in flight planning and decision-making for the safe and efficient operation of aircraft. These briefings may include, but are not limited to, weather observations, forecasts, and aeronautical information (for example, NOTAMs, military activities, flow control information, and temporary flight restrictions [TFR]). (Refer to AIM.)

PILOT IN COMMAND. The pilot responsible for the operation and safety of an aircraft during flight time. (Refer to 14 CFR Part 91.)

PILOT WEATHER REPORT. A report of meteorological phenomena encountered by aircraft in flight. (Refer to AIM.)

PILOT'S DISCRETION. When used in conjunction with altitude assignments, means that ATC has offered the pilot the option of starting climb or descent whenever he/she wishes and conducting the climb or descent at any rate he/she wishes. He/she may temporarily level off at any intermediate altitude. However, once he/she has vacated an altitude, he/she may not return to that altitude.

PIREP. (See PILOT WEATHER REPORT.)

PITCH POINT. A fix/waypoint that serves as a transition point from a departure procedure or the low altitude ground-based navigation structure into the high altitude waypoint system.

PLAN, EXECUTE, REVIEW, TRAIN, IMPROVE (PERTI). A process that delivers a one-day detailed plan for NAS operations, and a two-day outlook, which sets NAS performance goals for high impact constraints. PLAN: Increase lead time for identifying aviation system constraint planning and goals while utilizing historical NAS performance data and constraints to derive successful and/or improved advance planning strategies. EXECUTE: Set goals and a strategy. The Air Traffic Control System Command Center (ATCSCC), FAA field facilities, and aviation stakeholders execute the strategy and work to achieve the desired/planned outcomes. REVIEW: Utilize post event analysis and lessons learned to define and implement future strategies and operational triggers based on past performance and outcomes, both positive and negative. TRAIN: Develop training that includes rapid and continuous feedback to operational personnel and provides increased data and weather knowledge and tools for analytical usage and planning. IMPROVE: Implement better information sharing processes, technologies, and procedures that improve the skills and technology needed to implement operational insights and improvements.

PLANS DISPLAY. A display available in EDST that provides detailed flight plan and predicted conflict information in textual format for requested Current Plans and all Trial Plans. (See EN ROUTE DECISION SUPPORT TOOL.)

PLANVIEW GRAPHICAL USER INTERFACE (PGUI). A TBFM display that provides a spatial display of individual aircraft track information.

POFZ. (See PRECISION OBSTACLE FREE ZONE.)

POINT OUT. (See RADAR POINT OUT.)

POINT-TO-POINT (PTP). A level of NRR service for aircraft that is based on traditional waypoints in their FMS's or RNAV equipage.

POLAR TRACK STRUCTURE. A system of organized routes between Iceland and Alaska which overlie Canadian MNPS Airspace.

POSITION REPORT. A report over a known location as transmitted by an aircraft to ATC. (Refer to AIM.)

POSITION SYMBOL. A computer-generated indication shown on a radar display to indicate the mode of tracking.

POSITIVE CONTROL. The separation of all air traffic within designated airspace by air traffic control.

PRACTICE INSTRUMENT APPROACH. An instrument approach procedure conducted by a VFR or an IFR aircraft for the purpose of pilot training or proficiency demonstrations.

PRE-DEPARTURE CLEARANCE. An application with the Terminal Data Link System (TDLS) that provides clearance information to subscribers, through a service provider, in text to the cockpit or gate printer.

PRE-DEPARTURE REROUTE (PDRR). A capability within the Traffic Flow Management System that enables ATC to quickly amend and execute revised departure clearances that mitigate en route constraints or balance en route traffic flows.

PREARRANGED COORDINATION. A standardized procedure which permits an air traffic controller to enter the airspace assigned to another air traffic controller without verbal coordination. The procedures are defined in a facility directive which ensures approved separation between aircraft.

PREARRANGED COORDINATION PROCEDURES. A facility's standardized procedure that describes the process by which one controller shall allow an aircraft to penetrate or transit another controller's airspace in a manner that assures approved separation without individual coordination for each aircraft.

PRECIPITATION. Any or all forms of water particles (rain, sleet, hail, or snow) that fall from the atmosphere and reach the surface.

P/C

PRECIPITATION RADAR WEATHER DESCRIP-TIONS. Existing radar systems cannot detect turbulence. However, there is a direct correlation between the degree of turbulence and other weather features associated with thunderstorms and the weather radar precipitation intensity. Controllers will issue (where capable) precipitation intensity as observed by radar when using weather and radar processor (WARP) or NAS ground based digital radars with weather capabilities. When precipitation intensity information is not available, the intensity will be described as UNKNOWN. When intensity levels can be determined, they shall be described as:

 a. LIGHT (<26 dBZ)
 b. MODERATE (26 to 40 dBZ)
 c. HEAVY (>40 to 50 dBZ)
 d. EXTREME (>50 dBZ)

(Refer to the Aviation Weather Handbook, FAA-H-8083-28.)

PRECISION APPROACH. (See PRECISION APPROACH PROCEDURE.)

PRECISION APPROACH PROCEDURE. A standard instrument approach procedure in which an electronic glideslope or other type of glidepath is provided; e.g., ILS, PAR, and GLS. (See INSTRUMENT LANDING SYSTEM.) (See PRECISION APPROACH RADAR.)

PRECISION APPROACH RADAR. Radar equipment in some ATC facilities operated by the FAA and/or the military services at joint-use civil/military locations and separate military installations to detect and display azimuth, elevation, and range of aircraft on the final approach course to a runway. This equipment may be used to monitor certain non-radar approaches, but is primarily used to conduct a precision instrument approach (PAR) wherein the controller issues guidance instructions to the pilot based on the aircraft's position in relation to the final approach course (azimuth), the glidepath (elevation), and the distance (range) from the touchdown point on the runway as displayed on the radar scope.
(See GLIDEPATH.) (See PAR.) (See ICAO term PRECISION APPROACH RADAR.) (Refer to AIM.)

PRECISION APPROACH RADAR [ICAO]. Primary radar equipment used to determine the position of an aircraft during final approach, in terms of lateral and vertical deviations relative to a nominal approach path, and in range relative to touchdown.

PRECISION OBSTACLE FREE ZONE (POFZ). An 800 foot wide by 200 foot long area centered on the runway centerline adjacent to the threshold designed to protect aircraft flying precision approaches from ground vehicles and other aircraft when ceiling is less than 250 feet or visibility is less than 3/4 statute mile (or runway visual range below 4,000 feet.)

PRECISION RUNWAY MONITOR (PRM) SYSTEM. Provides air traffic controllers monitoring the NTZ during simultaneous close parallel PRM approaches with precision, high update rate secondary surveillance data. The high update rate surveillance sensor component of the PRM system is only required for specific runway or approach course separation. The high resolution color monitoring display, Final Monitor Aid (FMA) of the PRM system, or other FMA with the same capability, presents NTZ surveillance track data to controllers along with detailed maps depicting approaches and no transgression zone and is required for all simultaneous close parallel PRM NTZ monitoring operations. (Refer to AIM)

PREDICTIVE WIND SHEAR ALERT SYSTEM (PWS). A self-contained system used onboard some aircraft to alert the flight crew to the presence of a potential wind shear. PWS systems typically monitor 3 miles ahead and 25 degrees left and right of the aircraft's heading at or below 1,200 feet AGL. Departing flights may receive a wind shear alert after they start the takeoff roll and may elect to abort the takeoff. Aircraft on approach receiving an alert may elect to go around or perform a wind shear escape maneuver.

PREFERRED IFR ROUTES. Routes established between busier airports to increase system efficiency and capacity. They normally extend through one or more ARTCC areas and are designed to achieve balanced traffic flows among high density terminals. IFR clearances are issued on the basis of these routes except when severe weather avoidance procedures or other factors dictate otherwise. Preferred IFR Routes are listed in the Chart Supplement U.S., and are also available at https://www.fly.faa.gov/rmt/nfdc_preferred_routes_database.jsp. If a flight is planned to or from an area having such routes but the departure or arrival point is not listed in the Chart Supplement U.S., pilots may use that part of a Preferred IFR Route which is appropriate for the departure or arrival point that is listed. Preferred IFR Routes may be defined by DPs, SIDs, or STARs; NAVAIDs, Waypoints, etc.; high or low altitude airways; or any combinations thereof. Because they often share elements with adapted routes, pilots' use of preferred IFR routes can minimize flight plan route amendments.
(See ADAPTED ROUTES.) (See CENTER'S AREA.) (See INSTRUMENT APPROACH PROCEDURE.) (See INSTRUMENT DEPARTURE PROCEDURE.) (See STANDARD TERMINAL ARRIVAL.) (Refer to CHART SUPPLEMENT U.S.)

PRE-FLIGHT PILOT BRIEFING. (See PILOT BRIEFING.)

PREVAILING VISIBILITY. (See VISIBILITY.)

PRIMARY RADAR TARGET. An analog or digital target, exclusive of a secondary radar target, presented on a radar display.

PRM. (See AREA NAVIGATION (RNAV) GLOBAL POSITIONING SYSTEM (GPS) PRECISION RUNWAY MONITORING (PRM) APPROACH.) (See PRM APPROACH.) (See PRECISION RUNWAY MONITOR SYSTEM.)

PRM APPROACH. An instrument approach procedure titled ILS PRM, RNAV PRM, LDA PRM, or GLS PRM conducted to parallel runways separated by less than 4,300 feet and at least 3,000 feet where independent

closely spaced approaches are permitted. Use of an enhanced display with alerting, a No Transgression Zone (NTZ), secondary monitor frequency, pilot PRM training, and publication of an Attention All Users Page are required for all PRM approaches. Depending on the runway spacing, the approach courses may be parallel or one approach course must be offset. PRM procedures are also used to conduct Simultaneous Offset Instrument Approach (SOIA) operations. In SOIA, one straight-in ILS PRM, RNAV PRM, GLS PRM, and one offset LDA PRM, RNAV PRM or GLS PRM approach are utilized. PRM procedures are terminated and a visual segment begins at the offset approach missed approach point where the minimum distance between the approach courses is 3000 feet. Runway spacing can be as close as 750 feet. (Refer to AIM.)

PROCEDURAL CONTROL [ICAO]. Term used to indicate that information derived from an ATS surveillance system is not required for the provision of air traffic control service.

PROCEDURAL SEPARATION [ICAO]. The separation used when providing procedural control.

PROCEDURE TURN. The maneuver prescribed when it is necessary to reverse direction to establish an aircraft on the intermediate approach segment or final approach course. The outbound course, direction of turn, distance within which the turn must be completed, and minimum altitude are specified in the procedure. However, unless otherwise restricted, the point at which the turn may be commenced and the type and rate of turn are left to the discretion of the pilot. (See ICAO term PROCEDURE TURN.)

PROCEDURE TURN [ICAO]. A maneuver in which a turn is made away from a designated track followed by a turn in the opposite direction to permit the aircraft to intercept and proceed along the reciprocal of the designated track.

Note 1: Procedure turns are designated "left" or "right" according to the direction of the initial turn.

Note 2: Procedure turns may be designated as being made either in level flight or while descending, according to the circumstances of each individual approach procedure.

PROCEDURE TURN INBOUND. That point of a procedure turn maneuver where course reversal has been completed and an aircraft is established inbound on the intermediate approach segment or final approach course. A report of "procedure turn inbound" is normally used by ATC as a position report for separation purposes. (See FINAL APPROACH COURSE.) (See PROCEDURE TURN.) (See SEGMENTS OF AN INSTRUMENT APPROACH PROCEDURE.)

PROFILE DESCENT. An uninterrupted descent (except where level flight is required for speed adjustment; e.g., 250 knots at 10,000 feet MSL) from cruising altitude/level to interception of a glideslope or to a minimum altitude specified for the initial or intermediate approach segment of a nonprecision instrument approach. The profile descent normally terminates at the approach gate or where the glideslope or other appropriate minimum altitude is intercepted.

PROGRESS REPORT. (See POSITION REPORT.)

PROGRESSIVE TAXI. Precise taxi instructions given to a pilot unfamiliar with the airport or issued in stages as the aircraft proceeds along the taxi route.

PROHIBITED AREA. (See SPECIAL USE AIRSPACE.) (See ICAO term PROHIBITED AREA.)

PROHIBITED AREA [ICAO]. An airspace of defined dimensions, above the land areas or territorial waters of a State, within which the flight of aircraft is prohibited.

PROMINENT OBSTACLE. An obstacle that meets one or more of the following conditions:

a. An obstacle which stands out beyond the adjacent surface of surrounding terrain and immediately projects a noticeable hazard to aircraft in flight.

b. An obstacle, not characterized as low and close in, whose height is no less than 300 feet above the departure end of takeoff runway (DER) elevation, is within 10NM from the DER, and that penetrates that airport/heliport's diverse departure obstacle clearance surface (OCS).

c. An obstacle beyond 10NM from an airport/heliport that requires an obstacle departure procedure (ODP) to ensure obstacle avoidance. (See OBSTACLE.) (See OBSTRUCTION.)

PROPELLER (PROP) WASH (PROP BLAST). The disturbed mass of air generated by the motion of a propeller.

PROPOSED BOUNDARY CROSSING TIME. Each center has a PBCT parameter for each internal airport. Proposed internal flight plans are transmitted to the adjacent center if the flight time along the proposed route from the departure airport to the center boundary is less than or equal to the value of PBCT or if airport adaptation specifies transmission regardless of PBCT.

PROPOSED DEPARTURE TIME. The time that the aircraft expects to become airborne.

PROTECTED AIRSPACE. The airspace on either side of an oceanic route/track that is equal to one-half the lateral separation minimum except where reduction of protected airspace has been authorized.

PROTECTED SEGMENT. The protected segment is a segment on the amended TFM route that is to be inhibited from automatic adapted route alteration by ERAM.

PT. (See PROCEDURE TURN.)

PTP. (See POINT-TO-POINT.)

PTS. (See POLAR TRACK STRUCTURE.)

PUBLIC AIRCRAFT OPERATION (PAO). A UAS operation meeting the qualifications and conditions required for the operation of a public aircraft. (See AC-1.1) (See AIM)

P/C

PUBLISHED INSTRUMENT APPROACH PROCEDURE VISUAL SEGMENT. A segment on an IAP chart annotated as "Fly Visual to Airport" or "Fly Visual." A dashed arrow will indicate the visual flight path on the profile and plan view with an associated note on the approximate heading and distance. The visual segment should be flown as a dead reckoning course while maintaining visual conditions.

PUBLISHED ROUTE. A route for which an IFR altitude has been established and published; e.g., Federal Airways, Jet Routes, Area Navigation Routes, Specified Direct Routes.

PWS. (See PREDICTIVE WIND SHEAR ALERT SYSTEM.)

Q ROUTE. "Q" is the designator assigned to published RNAV routes used by the United States.

QFE. The atmospheric pressure at aerodrome elevation (or at runway threshold).

QNE. The barometric pressure used for the standard altimeter setting (29.92 inches Hg.).

QNH. The barometric pressure as reported by a particular station.

QUADRANT. A quarter part of a circle, centered on a NAVAID, oriented clockwise from magnetic north as follows: NE quadrant 000-089, SE quadrant 090-179, SW quadrant 180-269, NW quadrant 270-359.

QUEUING. (See STAGING/QUEUING.)

QUICK LOOK. A feature of the EAS and STARS which provides the controller the capability to display full data blocks of tracked aircraft from other control positions.

RAD. (See ROUTE AMENDMENT DIALOG.)

RADAR. A device that provides information on range, azimuth, and/or elevation of objects by measuring the time interval between transmission and reception of directional radio pulses and correlating the angular orientation of the radiated antenna beam or beams in azimuth and/or elevation.
 a. Primary Radar. A radar system in which a minute portion of a radio pulse transmitted from a site is reflected by an object and then received back at that site for processing and display at an air traffic control facility.
 b. Secondary Radar/Radar Beacon (ATCRBS). A radar system in which the object to be detected is fitted with cooperative equipment in the form of a radio receiver/transmitter (transponder). Radar pulses transmitted from the searching transmitter/receiver (interrogator) site are received in the cooperative equipment and used to trigger a distinctive transmission from the transponder. This reply transmission, rather than a reflected signal, is then received back at the

transmitter/receiver site for processing and display at an air traffic control facility.
(See COOPERATIVE SURVEILLANCE.) (See INTERROGATOR.) (See NON-COOPERATIVE SURVEILLANCE.)(See TRANSPONDER.) (See ICAO term RADAR.) (Refer to AIM.)

RADAR [ICAO]. A radio detection device which provides information on range, azimuth and/or elevation of objects.
 a. Primary Radar. Radar system which uses reflected radio signals.
 b. Secondary Radar. Radar system wherein a radio signal transmitted from a radar station initiates the transmission of a radio signal from another station.

RADAR ADVISORY. The provision of advice and information based on radar observations. (See ADVISORY SERVICE.)

RADAR ALTIMETER. (See RADIO ALTIMETER.)

RADAR APPROACH. An instrument approach procedure which utilizes Precision Approach Radar (PAR) or Airport Surveillance Radar (ASR). (See AIRPORT SURVEILLANCE RADAR.) (See INSTRUMENT APPROACH PROCEDURE.) (See PRECISION APPROACH RADAR.) (See SURVEILLANCE APPROACH.) (See ICAO term RADAR APPROACH.) (Refer to AIM.)

RADAR APPROACH [ICAO]. An approach, executed by an aircraft, under the direction of a radar controller.

RADAR APPROACH CONTROL FACILITY. A terminal ATC facility that uses radar and nonradar capabilities to provide approach control services to aircraft arriving, departing, or transiting airspace controlled by the facility. (See APPROACH CONTROL SERVICE.)
 a. Provides radar ATC services to aircraft operating in the vicinity of one or more civil and/or military airports in a terminal area. The facility may provide services of a ground controlled approach (GCA); i.e., ASR and PAR approaches. A radar approach control facility may be operated by FAA, USAF, US Army, USN, USMC, or jointly by FAA and a military service. Specific facility nomenclatures are used for administrative purposes only and are related to the physical location of the facility and the operating service generally as follows:
 1. Army Radar Approach Control (ARAC) (US Army).
 2. Radar Air Traffic Control Facility (RATCF) (USN/FAA and USMC/FAA).
 3. Radar Approach Control (RAPCON) (USAF/FAA, USN/FAA, and USMC/FAA).
 4. Terminal Radar Approach Control (TRACON) (FAA).
 5. Airport Traffic Control Tower (ATCT) (FAA). (Only those towers delegated approach control authority).

RADAR ARRIVAL. An aircraft arriving at an airport served by a radar facility and in radar contact with the facility. (See NONRADAR.)

RADAR BEACON. (See RADAR.)

RADAR CLUTTER [ICAO]. The visual indication on a radar display of unwanted signals.

RADAR CONTACT.
a. Used by ATC to inform an aircraft that it is identified using an approved ATC surveillance source on an air traffic controller's display and that radar flight following will be provided until radar service is terminated. Radar service may also be provided within the limits of necessity and capability. When a pilot is informed of "radar contact," he/she automatically discontinues reporting over compulsory reporting points. (See ATC SURVEILLANCE SOURCE.) (See RADAR CONTACT LOST.) (See RADAR FLIGHT FOLLOWING.) (See RADAR SERVICE.) (See RADAR SERVICE TERMINATED.) (Refer to AIM.)
b. The term used to inform the controller that the aircraft is identified and approval is granted for the aircraft to enter the receiving controllers airspace. (See ICAO term RADAR CONTACT.)

RADAR CONTACT [ICAO]. The situation which exists when the radar blip or radar position symbol of a particular aircraft is seen and identified on a radar display.

RADAR CONTACT LOST. Used by ATC to inform a pilot that the surveillance data used to determine the aircraft's position is no longer being received, or is no longer reliable and radar service is no longer being provided. The loss may be attributed to several factors including the aircraft merging with weather or ground clutter, the aircraft operating below radar line of sight coverage, the aircraft entering an area of poor radar return, failure of the aircraft's equipment, or failure of the surveillance equipment. (See CLUTTER.) (See RADAR CONTACT.)

RADAR ENVIRONMENT. An area in which radar service may be provided. (See ADDITIONAL SERVICES.) (See RADAR CONTACT.) (See RADAR SERVICE.) (See TRAFFIC ADVISORIES.)

RADAR FLIGHT FOLLOWING. The observation of the progress of radar identified aircraft, whose primary navigation is being provided by the pilot, wherein the controller retains and correlates the aircraft identity with the appropriate target or target symbol displayed on the radar scope. (See RADAR CONTACT.) (See RADAR SERVICE.) (Refer to AIM.)

RADAR IDENTIFICATION. The process of ascertaining that an observed radar target is the radar return from a particular aircraft. (See RADAR CONTACT.) (See RADAR SERVICE.)

RADAR IDENTIFIED AIRCRAFT. An aircraft, the position of which has been correlated with an observed target or symbol on the radar display. (See RADAR CONTACT.) (See RADAR CONTACT LOST.)

RADAR MONITORING. (See RADAR SERVICE.)

RADAR NAVIGATIONAL GUIDANCE. (See RADAR SERVICE.)

RADAR POINT OUT. An action taken by a controller to transfer the radar identification of an aircraft to another controller if the aircraft will or may enter the airspace or protected airspace of another controller and radio communications will not be transferred.

RADAR REQUIRED. A term displayed on charts and approach plates and included in FDC NOTAMs to alert pilots that segments of either an instrument approach procedure or a route are not navigable because of either the absence or unusability of a NAVAID. The pilot can expect to be provided radar navigational guidance while transiting segments labeled with this term. (See RADAR ROUTE.) (See RADAR SERVICE.)

RADAR ROUTE. A flight path or route over which an aircraft is vectored. Navigational guidance and altitude assignments are provided by ATC. (See FLIGHT PATH.) (See ROUTE.)

RADAR SEPARATION. (See RADAR SERVICE.)

RADAR SERVICE. A term which encompasses one or more of the following services based on the use of radar which can be provided by a controller to a pilot of a radar identified aircraft.
a. Radar Monitoring. The radar flight-following of aircraft, whose primary navigation is being performed by the pilot, to observe and note deviations from its authorized flight path, airway, or route. When being applied specifically to radar monitoring of instrument approaches; i.e., with precision approach radar (PAR) or radar monitoring of simultaneous ILS, RNAV and GLS approaches, it includes advice and instructions whenever an aircraft nears or exceeds the prescribed PAR safety limit or simultaneous ILS RNAV and GLS no transgression zone. (See ADDITIONAL SERVICES.) (See TRAFFIC ADVISORIES.)
b. Radar Navigational Guidance. Vectoring aircraft to provide course guidance.
c. Radar Separation. Radar spacing of aircraft in accordance with established minima.
(See ICAO term RADAR SERVICE.)

RADAR SERVICE [ICAO]. Term used to indicate a service provided directly by means of radar.
a. Monitoring. The use of radar for the purpose of providing aircraft with information and advice relative to significant deviations from nominal flight path.
b. Separation. The separation used when aircraft position information is derived from radar sources.

RADAR SERVICE TERMINATED. Used by ATC to inform a pilot that he/she will no longer be provided any of the services that could be received while in radar contact. Radar service is automatically terminated, and the pilot is not advised in the following cases:
a. An aircraft cancels its IFR flight plan, except within Class B airspace, Class C airspace, a TRSA, or where Basic Radar service is provided.
b. An aircraft conducting an instrument, visual, or contact approach has landed or has been instructed to change to advisory frequency.
c. An arriving VFR aircraft, receiving radar service to a tower-controlled airport within Class B airspace, Class C airspace, a TRSA, or where sequencing service is provided, has landed; or to all other airports, is instructed to change to tower or advisory frequency.
d. An aircraft completes a radar approach.

P/C

RADAR SURVEILLANCE. The radar observation of a given geographical area for the purpose of performing some radar function.

RADAR TRAFFIC ADVISORIES. Advisories issued to alert pilots to known or observed radar traffic which may affect the intended route of flight of their aircraft. (See TRAFFIC ADVISORIES.)

RADAR TRAFFIC INFORMATION SERVICE. (See TRAFFIC ADVISORIES.)

RADAR VECTORING [ICAO]. Provision of navigational guidance to aircraft in the form of specific headings, based on the use of radar.

RADIAL. A magnetic bearing extending from a VOR/VORTAC/TACAN navigation facility.

RADIO.
 a. A device used for communication.
 b. Used to refer to a flight service station; e.g., "Seattle Radio" is used to call Seattle FSS.

RADIO ALTIMETER. Aircraft equipment which makes use of the reflection of radio waves from the ground to determine the height of the aircraft above the surface.

RADIO BEACON. (See NONDIRECTIONAL BEACON.)

RADIO-CONTROLLED (RC). The use of control signals transmitted radio to a remotely controlled device, as in radio-controlled model airplanes.

RADIO DETECTION AND RANGING. (See RADAR.)

RADIO MAGNETIC INDICATOR. An aircraft navigational instrument coupled with a gyro compass or similar compass that indicates the direction of a selected NAVAID and indicates bearing with respect to the heading of the aircraft.

RAIS. (See REMOTE AIRPORT INFORMATION SERVICE.)

RAMP. (See APRON.)

RANDOM ALTITUDE. An altitude inappropriate for direction of flight and/or not in accordance with FAA Order JO 7110.65, Paragraph 4-5-1, VERTICAL SEPARATION MINIMA.

RANDOM ROUTE. Any route not established or charted/published or not otherwise available to all users.

RC. (See RADIO-CONTROLLED.)

RC. (See ROAD RECONNAISSANCE.)

RCAG. (See REMOTE COMMUNICATIONS AIR/GROUND FACILITY.)

RCC. (See RESCUE COORDINATION CENTER.)

RCO. (See REMOTE COMMUNICATIONS OUTLET.)

RCR. (See RUNWAY CONDITION READING.)

READ BACK. Repeat my message back to me.

RECEIVER AUTONOMOUS INTEGRITY MONITORING (RAIM). A technique whereby a civil GNSS receiver/processor determines the integrity of the GNSS navigation signals without reference to sensors or non-DoD integrity systems other than the receiver itself. This determination is achieved by a consistency check among redundant pseudorange measurements.

RECEIVING CONTROLLER. A controller/facility receiving control of an aircraft from another controller/facility.

RECEIVING FACILITY. (See RECEIVING CONTROLLER.)

RECONFORMANCE. The automated process of bringing an aircraft's Current Plan Trajectory into conformance with its track.

RECREATIONAL FLYER. Pilot of a UAS who is operating under 49 USC §44809, Exception for Limited Recreational Operations of Unmanned Aircraft.

REDUCE SPEED TO (SPEED). (See SPEED ADJUSTMENT.)

REDUCED VERTICAL SEPARATION MINIMUM (RVSM) AIRSPACE. RVSM airspace is defined as any airspace between FL 290 and FL 410 inclusive, where eligible aircraft are separated vertically by 1,000 feet. Authorization guidance for operations in this airspace is provided in Advisory Circular AC 91-85.

REFINED HAZARD AREA (RHA). Used by ATC. Airspace that is defined and distributed after a failure of a launch or reentry operation to provide a more concise depiction of the hazard location than a Contingency Hazard Area. (See AIRCRAFT HAZARD AREA.) (See CONTINGENCY HAZARD AREA.) (See TRANSITIONAL HAZARD AREA.)

REIL. (See RUNWAY END IDENTIFIER LIGHTS.)

RELEASE TIME. A departure time restriction issued to a pilot by ATC (either directly or through an authorized relay) when necessary to separate a departing aircraft from other traffic. (See ICAO term RELEASE TIME.)

RELEASE TIME [ICAO]. Time prior to which an aircraft should be given further clearance or prior to which it should not proceed in case of radio failure.

REMOTE AIRPORT INFORMATION SERVICE (RAIS). A temporary service provided by facilities, which are not located on the landing airport, but have communication capability and automated weather reporting available to the pilot at the landing airport.

REMOTE COMMUNICATIONS AIR/GROUND FACILITY. An unmanned VHF/UHF transmitter/receiver facility which is used to expand ARTCC air/ground communications coverage and to facilitate direct contact between pilots and controllers. RCAG facilities are sometimes not equipped with emergency frequencies 121.5 MHz and 243.0 MHz. (Refer to AIM.)

REMOTE COMMUNICATIONS OUTLET (RCO). An unmanned communications facility remotely controlled by air traffic personnel. RCOs serve FSSs. Remote Transmitter/Receivers (RTR) serve terminal

ATC facilities. An RCO or RTR may be UHF or VHF and will extend the communication range of the air traffic facility. There are several classes of RCOs and RTRs. The class is determined by the number of transmitters or receivers. Classes A through G are used primarily for air/ground purposes. RCO and RTR class O facilities are nonprotected outlets subject to undetected and prolonged outages. RCO (O's) and RTR (O's) were established for the express purpose of providing ground-to-ground communications between air traffic control specialists and pilots located at a satellite airport for delivering en route clearances, issuing departure authorizations, and acknowledging instrument flight rules cancellations or departure/landing times. As a secondary function, they may be used for advisory purposes whenever the aircraft is below the coverage of the primary air/ground frequency.

REMOTE IDENTIFICATION (RID). A system for electronic identification and secure oversight of UAS. (See 4 CFR Part 89) (See AIM)

REMOTE PILOT. Pilot of a UAS who is not operating as a recreational flyer under 49 USC §44809, the Exception for Limited Recreational Operations of Unmanned Aircraft.

REMOTE PILOT IN COMMAND (RPIC). The RPIC is directly responsible for and is the final authority as to the operation of the unmanned aircraft system.

REMOTE TRANSMITTER/RECEIVER (RTR). (See REMOTE COMMUNICATIONS OUTLET.)

REPORT. Used to instruct pilots to advise ATC of specified information; e.g., "Report passing Hamilton VOR."

REPORTING POINT. A geographical location in relation to which the position of an aircraft is reported. (See COMPULSORY REPORTING POINTS.) (See ICAO term REPORTING POINT.) (Refer to AIM.)

REPORTING POINT [ICAO]. A specified geographical location in relation to which the position of an aircraft can be reported.

REQUEST FULL ROUTE CLEARANCE. Used by pilots to request that the entire route of flight be read verbatim in an ATC clearance. Such request should be made to preclude receiving an ATC clearance based on the original filed flight plan when a filed IFR flight plan has been revised by the pilot, company, or operations prior to departure.

REQUIRED NAVIGATION PERFORMANCE (RNP). A statement of the navigational performance necessary for operation within a defined airspace. The following terms are commonly associated with RNP:

a. Required Navigation Performance Level or Type (RNP-X). A value, in nautical miles (NM), from the intended horizontal position within which an aircraft would be at least 95-percent of the total flying time.

b. Advanced-Required Navigation Performance (A-RNP). A navigation specification based on RNP that requires advanced functions such as scalable RNP, radius-to-fix (RF) legs, and tactical parallel offsets. This sophisticated Navigation Specification (NavSpec) is designated by the abbreviation "A-RNP".

c. Required Navigation Performance (RNP) Airspace. A generic term designating airspace, route (s), leg (s), operation (s), or procedure (s) where minimum required navigational performance (RNP) have been established.

d. Actual Navigation Performance (ANP). A measure of the current estimated navigational performance. Also referred to as Estimated Position Error (EPE).

e. Estimated Position Error (EPE). A measure of the current estimated navigational performance. Also referred to as Actual Navigation Performance (ANP).

f. Lateral Navigation (LNAV). A function of area navigation (RNAV) equipment which calculates, displays, and provides lateral guidance to a profile or path.

g. Vertical Navigation (VNAV). A function of area navigation (RNAV) equipment which calculates, displays, and provides vertical guidance to a profile or path.

REROUTE IMPACT ASSESSMENT (RRIA). A capability within the Traffic Flow Management System that is used to define and evaluate a potential reroute prior to implementation, with or without miles-in-trail (MIT) restrictions. RRIA functions estimate the impact on demand (e.g., sector loads) and performance (e.g., flight delay). Using RRIA, traffic management personnel can determine whether the reroute will sufficiently reduce demand in the Flow Constraint Area and not create excessive "spill over" demand in the adjacent airspace on a specific route segment or point of interest (POI).

RESCUE COORDINATION CENTER (RCC). A search and rescue (SAR) facility equipped and manned to coordinate and control SAR operations in an area designated by the SAR plan. The U.S. Coast Guard and the U.S. Air Force have responsibility for the operation of RCCs. (See ICAO term RESCUE CO-ORDINATION CENTRE.)

RESCUE CO-ORDINATION CENTRE [ICAO]. A unit responsible for promoting efficient organization of search and rescue service and for coordinating the conduct of search and rescue operations within a search and rescue region.

RESOLUTION ADVISORY. A display indication given to the pilot by the traffic alert and collision avoidance systems (TCAS II) recommending a maneuver to increase vertical separation relative to an intruding aircraft. Positive, negative, and vertical speed limit (VSL) advisories constitute the resolution advisories. A resolution advisory is also classified as corrective or preventive.

RESTRICTED AREA. (See SPECIAL USE AIRSPACE.) (See ICAO term RESTRICTED AREA.)

RESTRICTED AREA [ICAO]. An airspace of defined dimensions, above the land areas or territorial waters of a State, within which the flight of aircraft is restricted in accordance with certain specified conditions.

P/C

RESUME NORMAL SPEED. Used by ATC to advise a pilot to resume an aircraft's normal operating speed. It is issued to terminate a speed adjustment where no published speed restrictions apply. It does not delete speed restrictions in published procedures of upcoming segments of flight. This does not relieve the pilot of those speed restrictions that are applicable to 14 CFR Section 91.117.

RESUME OWN NAVIGATION. Used by ATC to advise a pilot to resume his/her own navigational responsibility. It is issued after completion of a radar vector or when radar contact is lost while the aircraft is being radar vectored. (See RADAR CONTACT LOST.) (See RADAR SERVICE TERMINATED.)

RESUME PUBLISHED SPEED. Used by ATC to advise a pilot to resume published speed restrictions that are applicable to a SID, STAR, or other instrument procedure. It is issued to terminate a speed adjustment where speed restrictions are published on a charted procedure.

RHA. (See REFINED HAZARD AREA.)

RID. (See REMOTE IDENTIFICATION.)

RMI. (See RADIO MAGNETIC INDICATOR.)

RNAV. (See AREA NAVIGATION (RNAV).)

RNAV APPROACH. An instrument approach procedure which relies on aircraft area navigation equipment for navigational guidance.
(See AREA NAVIGATION (RNAV).)
(See INSTRUMENT APPROACH PROCEDURE.)

RNAV VISUAL FLIGHT PROCEDURE (RVFP). An RVFP is a special visual flight procedure flown on an IFR flight plan. It is flown in visual conditions and clear of clouds must be maintained. An RVFP is flown using an approved RNAV system to maintain published lateral and vertical paths to runways without an instrument approach procedure. It requires an ATC clearance and may begin at other points along the path of the charted procedure when approved by ATC. An RVFP is not published in the Federal Register for public use and the operator is required to have a specific Operations Specification approval. Required ceiling and visibility minima are published on the procedure chart. An RVFP does not have a missed approach procedure and is not evaluated for obstacle protection.

ROAD RECONNAISSANCE (RC). Military activity requiring navigation along roads, railroads, and rivers. Reconnaissance route/route segments are seldom along a straight line and normally require a lateral route width of 10 NM to 30 NM and an altitude range of 500 feet to 10,000 feet AGL.

ROGER. I have received all of your last transmission. It should not be used to answer a question requiring a yes or a no answer.
(See AFFIRMATIVE.) (See NEGATIVE.)

ROLLOUT RVR. (See VISIBILITY.)

ROTOR WASH. A phenomenon resulting from the vertical down wash of air generated by the main rotor(s) of a helicopter.

ROUND-ROBIN FLIGHT PLAN. A single flight plan filed from the departure airport to an intermediary destination(s) and then returning to the original departure airport.

ROUTE. A defined path, consisting of one or more courses in a horizontal plane, which aircraft traverse over the surface of the earth. (See AIRWAY.) (See JET ROUTE.) (See PUBLISHED ROUTE.) (See UNPUBLISHED ROUTE.)

ROUTE ACTION NOTIFICATION. EDST notification that an ADR/ADAR/AAR has been applied to the flight plan. (See ATC PREFERRED ROUTE NOTIFICATION.) (See EN ROUTE DECISION SUPPORT TOOL.)

ROUTE AMENDMENT DIALOG (RAD). A capability within the Traffic Flow Management System that allows traffic management personnel to submit or edit a route amendment for one or more flights.

ROUTE SEGMENT. As used in Air Traffic Control, a part of a route that can be defined by two navigational fixes, two NAVAIDs, or a fix and a NAVAID. (See FIX.) (See ROUTE.) (See ICAO term ROUTE SEGMENT.)

ROUTE SEGMENT [ICAO]. A portion of a route to be flown, as defined by two consecutive significant points specified in a flight plan.

RPIC. (See REMOTE PILOT IN COMMAND.)

RRIA. (See REROUTE IMPACT ASSESSMENT.)

RSA. (See RUNWAY SAFETY AREA.)

RTR. (See REMOTE TRANSMITTER/RECEIVER.)

RUNWAY. A defined rectangular area on a land airport prepared for the landing and takeoff run of aircraft along its length. Runways are normally numbered in relation to their magnetic direction rounded off to the nearest 10 degrees; e.g., Runway 1, Runway 25. (See PARALLEL RUNWAYS.) (See ICAO term RUNWAY.)

RUNWAY [ICAO]. A defined rectangular area on a land aerodrome prepared for the landing and takeoff of aircraft.

RUNWAY CENTERLINE LIGHTING. (See AIRPORT LIGHTING.)

RUNWAY CONDITION CODES (RwyCC). Numerical readings, provided by airport operators, that indicate runway surface contamination (for example, slush, ice, rain, etc.). These values range from "1" (poor) to "6" (dry) and must be included on the ATIS when the reportable condition is less than 6 in any one or more of the three runway zones (touchdown, midpoint, rollout).

RUNWAY CONDITION READING. Numerical decelerometer readings relayed by air traffic controllers at USAF and certain civil bases for use by the pilot in determining runway braking action. These readings

are routinely relayed only to USAF and Air National Guard Aircraft. (See BRAKING ACTION.)

RUNWAY CONDITION REPORT (RwyCR). A data collection worksheet used by airport operators that correlates the runway percentage of coverage along with the depth and type of contaminant for the purpose of creating a FICON NOTAM. (See RUNWAY CONDITION CODES.)

RUNWAY END IDENTIFIER LIGHTS (REIL). (See AIRPORT LIGHTING.)

RUNWAY ENTRANCE LIGHTS (REL). An array of red lights which include the first light at the hold line followed by a series of evenly spaced lights to the runway edge aligned with the taxiway centerline, and one additional light at the runway centerline in line with the last two lights before the runway edge.

RUNWAY GRADIENT. The average slope, measured in percent, between two ends or points on a runway. Runway gradient is depicted on government aerodrome sketches when total runway gradient exceeds 0.3%.

RUNWAY HEADING. The magnetic direction that corresponds with the runway centerline extended, not the painted runway number. When cleared to "fly or maintain runway heading," pilots are expected to fly or maintain the heading that corresponds with the extended centerline of the departure runway. Drift correction shall not be applied; e.g., Runway 4, actual magnetic heading of the runway centerline 044, fly 044.

RUNWAY IN USE/ACTIVE RUNWAY/DUTY RUNWAY. Any runway or runways currently being used for takeoff or landing. When multiple runways are used, they are all considered active runways. In the metering sense, a selectable adapted item which specifies the landing runway configuration or direction of traffic flow. The adapted optimum flight plan from each transition fix to the vertex is determined by the runway configuration for arrival metering processing purposes.

RUNWAY LIGHTS. (See AIRPORT LIGHTING.)

RUNWAY MARKINGS. (See AIRPORT MARKING AIDS.)

RUNWAY OVERRUN. In military aviation exclusively, a stabilized or paved area beyond the end of a runway, of the same width as the runway plus shoulders, centered on the extended runway centerline.

RUNWAY PROFILE DESCENT. An instrument flight rules (IFR) air traffic control arrival procedure to a runway published for pilot use in graphic and/or textual form and may be associated with a STAR. Runway Profile Descents provide routing and may depict crossing altitudes, speed restrictions, and headings to be flown from the en route structure to the point where the pilot will receive clearance for and execute an instrument approach procedure. A Runway Profile Descent may apply to more than one runway if so stated on the chart. (Refer to AIM.)

RUNWAY SAFETY AREA. A defined surface surrounding the runway prepared, or suitable, for reducing the risk of damage to airplanes in the event of an undershoot, overshoot, or excursion from the runway. The dimensions of the RSA vary and can be determined by using the criteria contained within AC 150/5300-13, Airport Design, Chapter 3. Figure 3-1 in AC 150/5300-13 depicts the RSA. The design standards dictate that the RSA shall be:

a. Cleared, graded, and have no potentially hazardous ruts, humps, depressions, or other surface variations;

b. Drained by grading or storm sewers to prevent water accumulation;

c. Capable, under dry conditions, of supporting snow removal equipment, aircraft rescue and firefighting equipment, and the occasional passage of aircraft without causing structural damage to the aircraft; and,

d. Free of objects, except for objects that need to be located in the runway safety area because of their function. These objects shall be constructed on low impact resistant supports (frangible mounted structures) to the lowest practical height with the frangible point no higher than 3 inches above grade.

(Refer to AC 150/5300-13, Airport Design, Chapter 3.)

RUNWAY STATUS LIGHTS (RWSL) SYSTEM. The RWSL is a system of runway and taxiway lighting to provide pilots increased situational awareness by illuminating runway entry lights (REL) when the runway is unsafe for entry or crossing, and take-off hold lights (THL) when the runway is unsafe for departure.

RUNWAY TRANSITION. (See SEGMENTS OF A SID/STAR)

RUNWAY TRANSITION WAYPOINT. (See SEGMENTS OF A SID/STAR.)

RUNWAY USE PROGRAM. A noise abatement runway selection plan designed to enhance noise abatement efforts with regard to airport communities for arriving and departing aircraft. These plans are developed into runway use programs and apply to all turbojet aircraft 12,500 pounds or heavier; turbojet aircraft less than 12,500 pounds are included only if the airport proprietor determines that the aircraft creates a noise problem. Runway use programs are coordinated with FAA offices, and safety criteria used in these programs are developed by the Office of Flight Operations. Runway use programs are administered by the Air Traffic Service as "Formal" or "Informal" programs.

a. Formal Runway Use Program. An approved noise abatement program which is defined and acknowledged in a Letter of Understanding between Flight Operations, Air Traffic Service, the airport proprietor, and the users. Once established, participation in the program is mandatory for aircraft operators and pilots as provided for in 14 CFR Section 91.129.

b. Informal Runway Use Program. An approved noise abatement program which does not require a Letter of Understanding, and participation in the program is voluntary for aircraft operators/pilots.

P/C

RUNWAY VISUAL RANGE (RVR). (See VISIBILITY.)

RVFP. (See RNAV VISUAL FLIGHT PROCEDURE.)

RwyCC. (See RUNWAY CONDITION CODES.)

RwyCR. (See RUNWAY CONDITION REPORT.)

S

SAA. (See SENSE AND AVOID.) (See SPECIAL ACTIVITY AIRSPACE.)

SAFETY ALERT. A safety alert issued by ATC to aircraft under their control if ATC is aware the aircraft is at an altitude which, in the controller's judgment, places the aircraft in unsafe proximity to terrain, obstructions, or other aircraft. The controller may discontinue the issuance of further alerts if the pilot advises he/she is taking action to correct the situation or has the other aircraft in sight.

 a. Terrain/Obstruction Alert. A safety alert issued by ATC to aircraft under their control if ATC is aware the aircraft is at an altitude which, in the controller's judgment, places the aircraft in unsafe proximity to terrain/obstructions; e.g., "Low Altitude Alert, check your altitude immediately."

 b. Aircraft Conflict Alert. A safety alert issued by ATC to aircraft under their control if ATC is aware of an aircraft that is not under their control at an altitude which, in the controller's judgment, places both aircraft in unsafe proximity to each other. With the alert, ATC will offer the pilot an alternate course of action when feasible; e.g., "Traffic Alert, advise you turn right heading zero niner zero or climb to eight thousand immediately."

Note: The issuance of a safety alert is contingent upon the capability of the controller to have an awareness of an unsafe condition. The course of action provided will be predicated on other traffic under ATC control. Once the alert is issued, it is solely the pilot's prerogative to determine what course of action, if any, he/she will take.

SAFETY LOGIC SYSTEM. A software enhancement to ASDE–3, ASDE–X, and ASSC, that predicts the path of aircraft landing and/or departing, and/or vehicular movements on runways. Visual and aural alarms are activated when the safety logic projects a potential collision. The Airport Movement Area Safety System (AMASS) is a safety logic system enhancement to the ASDE–3. The Safety Logic System for ASDE–X and ASSC is an integral part of the software program.

SAFETY LOGIC SYSTEM ALERTS.

 a. ALERT.

 1. An actual situation involving two real Safety Logic tracks (aircraft/aircraft, aircraft/vehicle, or aircraft/other tangible object) that the Safety Logic System has predicted will result in an imminent collision, based upon the Safety Logic parameters.

 2. An actual situation involving a single Safety Logic track arriving to, or departing from, a closed runway.

 3. An actual situation involving a single Safety Logic track arriving to a taxiway.

 b. FALSE ALERT.

 1. Alerts generated by one or more false surface radar or cooperative surveillance targets, that the ASDE system has interpreted as real tracks and placed into Safety Logic.

 2. Alerts in which the Safety Logic System did not perform correctly, based upon the design specifications and Safety Logic parameters.

 3. Alerts generated by surface radar targets caused by moderate or greater precipitation.

 c. NUISANCE ALERT. An alert in which one or more of the following is true:

 1. The alert is generated by a known situation that is not considered an unsafe operation, such as LAHSO or other approved operations.

 2. The alert is generated by inaccurate cooperative surveillance data received by the Safety Logic System.

 3. One or more of the aircraft involved in the alert is not intending to use a runway/taxiway (helicopter, pipeline patrol, non-Mode C overflight, etc.).

 d. VALID NON-ALERT. A situation in which the Safety Logic System correctly determines that an alert is not required, based upon the design specifications and Safety Logic parameters.

 e. INVALID NON-ALERT. A situation in which the Safety Logic System did not issue an alert when an alert was required, based upon the design specifications and Safety Logic parameters.

SAIL BACK. A maneuver during high wind conditions (usually with power off) where float plane movement is controlled by water rudders/opening and closing cabin doors.

SAME DIRECTION AIRCRAFT. Aircraft are operating in the same direction when:

 a. They are following the same track in the same direction; or

 b. Their tracks are parallel and the aircraft are flying in the same direction; or

 c. Their tracks intersect at an angle of less than 45 degrees.

SAR. (See SEARCH AND RESCUE.)

SATELLITE-BASED AUGMENTATION SYSTEM (SBAS). A wide coverage augmentation system in which the user receives augmentation information from a satellite-based transmitter. (See WIDE-AREA AUGMENTATION SYSTEM (WAAS.)

SAW. (See AVIATION WATCH NOTIFICATION MESSAGE.)

SAY AGAIN. Used to request a repeat of the last transmission. Usually specifies transmission or portion thereof not understood or received; e.g., "Say again all after ABRAM VOR."

SAY ALTITUDE. Used by ATC to ascertain an aircraft's specific altitude/flight level. When the aircraft is climbing or descending, the pilot should state the indicated altitude rounded to the nearest 100 feet.

SAY HEADING. Used by ATC to request an aircraft heading. The pilot should state the actual heading of the aircraft.

SCHEDULED TIME OF ARRIVAL (STA). A STA is the desired time that an aircraft should cross a certain point (landing or metering fix). It takes other traffic and airspace configuration into account. A STA time shows the results of the TBFM scheduler that has calculated an arrival time according to parameters such as optimized spacing, aircraft performance, and weather.

SDF. (See SIMPLIFIED DIRECTIONAL FACILITY.)

SE SAR. (See SURVEILLANCE ENHANCED SEARCH AND RESCUE.)

SEA LANE. A designated portion of water outlined by visual surface markers for and intended to be used by aircraft designed to operate on water.

SEARCH AND RESCUE. A service which seeks missing aircraft and assists those found to be in need of assistance. It is a cooperative effort using the facilities and services of available Federal, state and local agencies. The U.S. Coast Guard is responsible for coordination of search and rescue for the Maritime Region, and the U.S. Air Force is responsible for search and rescue for the Inland Region. Information pertinent to search and rescue should be passed through any air traffic facility or be transmitted directly to the Rescue Coordination Center by telephone. (See FLIGHT SERVICE STATION.) (See RESCUE COORDINATION CENTER.) (Refer to AIM.)

SEARCH AND RESCUE FACILITY. A facility responsible for maintaining and operating a search and rescue (SAR) service to render aid to persons and property in distress. It is any SAR unit, station, NET, or other operational activity which can be usefully employed during an SAR Mission; e.g., a Civil Air Patrol Wing, or a Coast Guard Station. (See SEARCH AND RESCUE.)

SECNOT. (See SECURITY NOTICE.)

SECONDARY RADAR TARGET. A target derived from a transponder return presented on a radar display.

SECTIONAL AERONAUTICAL CHARTS. (See AERONAUTICAL CHART.)

SECTOR LIST DROP INTERVAL. A parameter number of minutes after the meter fix time when arrival aircraft will be deleted from the arrival sector list.

SECURITY NOTICE (SECNOT). A SECNOT is a request originated by the Air Traffic Security Coordinator (ATSC) for an extensive communications search for aircraft involved, or suspected of being involved, in a security violation, or are considered a security risk. A SECNOT will include the aircraft identification, search area, and expiration time. The search area, as defined by the ATSC, could be a single airport, multiple airports, a radius of an airport or fix, or a route of flight. Once the expiration time has been reached, the SECNOT is considered to be cancelled.

SECURITY SERVICES AIRSPACE. Areas established through the regulatory process or by NOTAM, issued by the Administrator under Title 14 CFR sections 99.7, 91.141, and 91.139, which specify that ATC security services are required; i.e., ADIZ or temporary flight rules areas.

SEE AND AVOID. When weather conditions permit, pilots operating IFR or VFR are required to observe and maneuver to avoid other aircraft. Right-of-way rules are contained in 14 CFR Part 91.

SEGMENTED CIRCLE. A system of visual indicators designed to provide traffic pattern information at airports without operating control towers. (Refer to AIM.)

SEGMENTS OF A SID/STAR.
 a. En Route Transition—The segment(s) of a SID/STAR that connect to/from en route flight. Not all SIDs/STARs will contain an en route transition.
 b. En Route Transition Waypoint—The NAVAID/fix/waypoint that defines the beginning of the SID/STAR en route transition.
 c. Common Route—The segment(s) of a SID/STAR procedure that provides a single route serving an airport/runway or multiple airports/runways. The common route may consist of a single point. Not all conventional SIDs will contain a common route.
 d. Runway Transition—The segment(s) of a SID/STAR between the common route/point and the runway(s). Not all SIDs/STARs will contain a runway transition.
 e. Runway Transition Waypoint (RTW)—On a STAR, the NAVAID/fix/waypoint that defines the end of the common route or en route transition and the beginning of a runway transition (In the arrival route description found on the STAR chart, the last fix of the common route and the first fix of the runway transition(s)).

SEGMENTS OF AN INSTRUMENT APPROACH PROCEDURE. An instrument approach procedure may have as many as four separate segments depending on how the approach procedure is structured.
 a. Initial Approach. The segment between the initial approach fix and the intermediate fix or the point where the aircraft is established on the intermediate course or final approach course. (See ICAO term INITIAL APPROACH SEGMENT.)
 b. Intermediate Approach. The segment between the intermediate fix or point and the final approach fix. (See ICAO term INTERMEDIATE APPROACH SEGMENT.)
 c. Final Approach. The segment between the final approach fix or point and the runway, airport, or missed approach point. (See ICAO term FINAL APPROACH SEGMENT.)
 d. Missed Approach. The segment between the missed approach point or the point of arrival at decision height and the missed approach fix at the prescribed altitude. (Refer to 14 CFR Part 97.) (See ICAO term MISSED APPROACH PROCEDURE.)

SELF-BRIEFING. A self-briefing is a review, using automated tools, of all meteorological and aeronautical information that may influence the pilot in planning, altering, or canceling a proposed route of flight.

SENSE AND AVOID (SAA). The capability of an unmanned aircraft to detect (sense) and avoid collisions with other aircraft and all obstacles, whether airborne or on the ground while operating in the NAS.

P/C

SEPARATION. In air traffic control, the spacing of aircraft to achieve their safe and orderly movement in flight and while landing and taking off. (See SEPARATION MINIMA.) (See ICAO term SEPARATION.)

SEPARATION [ICAO]. Spacing between aircraft, levels or tracks.

SEPARATION MINIMA. The minimum longitudinal, lateral, or vertical distances by which aircraft are spaced through the application of air traffic control procedures. (See SEPARATION.)

SERVICE. A generic term that designates functions or assistance available from or rendered by air traffic control. For example, Class C service would denote the ATC services provided within a Class C airspace area.

SEVERE WEATHER AVOIDANCE PLAN (SWAP). An approved plan to minimize the affect of severe weather on traffic flows in impacted terminal and/or ARTCC areas. A SWAP is normally implemented to provide the least disruption to the ATC system when flight through portions of airspace is difficult or impossible due to severe weather.

SEVERE WEATHER FORECAST ALERTS. Preliminary messages issued in order to alert users that a Severe Weather Watch Bulletin (WW) is being issued. These messages define areas of possible severe thunderstorms or tornado activity. The messages are unscheduled and issued as required by the Storm Prediction Center (SPC) at Norman, Oklahoma. (See AIRMET.) (See CONVECTIVE SIGMET.) (See CWA.) (See GRAPHICAL AIRMEN'S METEOROLOGICAL INFORMATION.) (See SIGMET.)

SFA. (See SINGLE FREQUENCY APPROACH.)

SFO. (See SIMULATED FLAMEOUT.)

SGI. (See SPECIAL GOVERNMENT INTEREST.)

SHF. (See SUPER HIGH FREQUENCY.)

SHORT RANGE CLEARANCE. A clearance issued to a departing IFR flight which authorizes IFR flight to a specific fix short of the destination while air traffic control facilities are coordinating and obtaining the complete clearance.

SHORT TAKEOFF AND LANDING AIRCRAFT (STOL). An aircraft which, at some weight within its approved operating weight, is capable of operating from a runway in compliance with the applicable STOL characteristics, airworthiness, operations, noise, and pollution standards. (See VERTICAL TAKEOFF AND LANDING AIRCRAFT.)

SIAP. (See STANDARD INSTRUMENT APPROACH PROCEDURE.)

SID. (See STANDARD INSTRUMENT DEPARTURE.)

SIDESTEP MANEUVER. A visual maneuver accomplished by a pilot at the completion of an instrument approach to permit a straight-in landing on a parallel runway not more than 1,200 feet to either side of the runway to which the instrument approach was conducted. (Refer to AIM.)

SIGMET. A weather advisory issued concerning weather significant to the safety of all aircraft. SIGMET advisories cover severe and extreme turbulence, severe icing, and widespread dust or sandstorms that reduce visibility to less than 3 miles. (See AIRMET.) (See CONVECTIVE SIGMET.) (See CWA.) (See GRAPHICAL AIRMEN'S METEOROLOGICAL INFORMATION.) (See ICAO term SIGMET INFORMATION.) (See SAW.) (Refer to AIM.)

SIGMET INFORMATION [ICAO]. Information issued by a meteorological watch office concerning the occurrence or expected occurrence of specified en-route weather phenomena which may affect the safety of aircraft operations.

SIGNIFICANT METEOROLOGICAL INFORMATION. (See SIGMET.)

SIGNIFICANT POINT. A point, whether a named intersection, a NAVAID, a fix derived from a NAVAID(s), or geographical coordinate expressed in degrees of latitude and longitude, which is established for the purpose of providing separation, as a reporting point, or to delineate a route of flight.

SIMPLIFIED DIRECTIONAL FACILITY (SDF). A NAVAID used for nonprecision instrument approaches. The final approach course is similar to that of an ILS localizer except that the SDF course may be offset from the runway, generally not more than 3 degrees, and the course may be wider than the localizer, resulting in a lower degree of accuracy. (Refer to AIM.)

SIMULATED FLAMEOUT. A practice approach by a jet aircraft (normally military) at idle thrust to a runway. The approach may start at a runway (high key) and may continue on a relatively high and wide downwind leg with a continuous turn to final. It terminates in landing or low approach. The purpose of this approach is to simulate a flameout. (See FLAMEOUT.)

SIMULTANEOUS CLOSE PARALLEL APPROACHES. A simultaneous, independent approach operation permitting ILS/RNAV/GLS approaches to airports having parallel runways separated by at least 3,000 feet and less than 4300 feet between centerlines. Aircraft are permitted to pass each other during these simultaneous operations. Integral parts of a total system are radar, NTZ monitoring with enhanced FMA color displays that include aural and visual alerts and predictive aircraft position software, communications override, ATC procedures, an Attention All Users Page (AAUP), PRM in the approach name, and appropriate ground based and airborne equipment. High update rate surveillance sensor required for certain runway or approach course separations.

SIMULTANEOUS (CONVERGING) DEPENDENT APPROACHES. An approach operation permitting ILS/RNAV/GLS approaches to runways or missed approach courses that intersect where required minimum spacing between the aircraft on each final approach course is required.

SIMULTANEOUS (CONVERGING) INDEPENDENT APPROACHES. An approach operation permitting ILS/RNAV/GLS approaches to non-parallel runways where approach procedure design maintains the required aircraft spacing throughout the approach and missed approach and hence the operations may be conducted independently.

SIMULTANEOUS ILS APPROACHES. An approach system permitting simultaneous ILS approaches to airports having parallel runways separated by at least 4,300 feet between centerlines. Integral parts of a total system are ILS, radar, communications, ATC procedures, and appropriate airborne equipment. (See PARALLEL RUNWAYS.) (Refer to AIM.)

SIMULTANEOUS OFFSET INSTRUMENT APPROACH (SOIA). An instrument landing system comprised of an ILS PRM, RNAV PRM or GLS PRM approach to one runway and an offset LDA PRM with glideslope or an RNAV PRM or GLS PRM approach utilizing vertical guidance to another where parallel runway spaced less than 3,000 feet and at least 750 feet apart. The approach courses converge by 2.5 to 3 degrees. Simultaneous close parallel PRM approach procedures apply up to the point where the approach course separation becomes 3,000 feet, at the offset MAP. From the offset MAP to the runway threshold, visual separation by the aircraft conducting the offset approach is utilized. (Refer to AIM)

SIMULTANEOUS (PARALLEL) DEPENDENT APPROACHES. An approach operation permitting ILS/RNAV/GLS approaches to adjacent parallel runways where prescribed diagonal spacing must be maintained. Aircraft are not permitted to pass each other during simultaneous dependent operations. Integral parts of a total system ATC procedures, and appropriate airborne and ground based equipment.

SINGLE DIRECTION ROUTES. Preferred IFR Routes which are sometimes depicted on high altitude en route charts and which are normally flown in one direction only. (See PREFERRED IFR ROUTES.) (Refer to CHART SUPPLEMENT U.S.)

SINGLE FREQUENCY APPROACH. A service provided under a letter of agreement to military single-piloted turbojet aircraft which permits use of a single UHF frequency during approach for landing. Pilots will not normally be required to change frequency from the beginning of the approach to touchdown except that pilots conducting an en route descent are required to change frequency when control is transferred from the air route traffic control center to the terminal facility. The abbreviation "SFA" in the DOD FLIP IFR Supplement under "Communications" indicates this service is available at an aerodrome.

SINGLE-PILOTED AIRCRAFT. A military turbojet aircraft possessing one set of flight controls, tandem cockpits, or two sets of flight controls but operated by one pilot is considered single-piloted by ATC when determining the appropriate air traffic service to be applied. (See SINGLE FREQUENCY APPROACH.)

SKYSPOTTER. A pilot who has received specialized training in observing and reporting inflight weather phenomena.

SLASH. A radar beacon reply displayed as an elongated target.

SLDI. (See SECTOR LIST DROP INTERVAL.)

SLOW TAXI. To taxi a float plane at low power or low RPM.

SMALL UNMANNED AIRCRAFT SYSTEM (sUAS). An unmanned aircraft weighing less than 55 pounds on takeoff, including everything that is on board or otherwise attached to the aircraft.

SN. (See SYSTEM STRATEGIC NAVIGATION.)

SPACE-BASED ADS-B (SBA). A constellation of satellites that receives ADS-B Out broadcasts and relays that information to the appropriate surveillance facility. The currently deployed SBA system is only capable of receiving broadcasts from 1090ES-equipped aircraft, and not from those equipped with only a universal access transceiver (UAT). Also, aircraft with a top-of-fuselage-mounted transponder antenna (required for TCAS II installations) will be better received by SBA, especially at latitudes below 45 degrees. (See AUTOMATIC DEPENDENT SURVEILLANCE–BROADCAST.) (See AUTOMATIC DEPENDENT SURVEILLANCE–BROADCAST OUT.)

SPACE LAUNCH AND REENTRY AREA. Locations where commercial space launch and/or reentry operations occur. For pilot awareness, a rocket-shaped symbol is used to depict space launch and reentry areas on sectional aeronautical charts.

SPEAK SLOWER. Used in verbal communications as a request to reduce speech rate.

SPECIAL GOVERNMENT INTEREST (SGI). A near real-time airspace authorization for Part 91 or Part 107 UAS, which supports activities that answer significant and urgent governmental interests. These include: national defense, homeland security, law enforcement, and emergency operations objectives.

SPECIAL ACTIVITY AIRSPACE (SAA). Airspace with defined dimensions within the National Airspace System wherein limitations may be imposed upon operations for national defense, homeland security, public interest, or public safety. Special activity airspace includes but is not limited to the following; Air Traffic Control Assigned Airspace (ATCAA), Altitude Reservations (ALTRV), Military Training Routes (MTR), Air Refueling Tracks and Anchors, Temporary Flight Restrictions (TFR), Special Security Instructions (SSI), etc. Special Use Airspace (SUA) is a subset of Special Activity Airspace. (See SPECIAL USE AIRSPACE.)

SPECIAL AIR TRAFFIC RULES (SATR). Rules that govern procedures for conducting flights in certain areas listed in 14 CFR Part 93. The term "SATR" is used in the United States to describe the rules for operations in specific areas designated in the Code of Federal Regulations. (Refer to 14 CFR Part 93.)

P/C

SPECIAL EMERGENCY. A condition of air piracy or other hostile act by a person(s) aboard an aircraft which threatens the safety of the aircraft or its passengers.

SPECIAL FLIGHT RULES AREA (SFRA). An area in the NAS, described in 14 CFR Part 93, wherein the flight of aircraft is subject to special traffic rules, unless otherwise authorized by air traffic control. Not all areas listed in 14 CFR Part 93 are designated SFRA, but special air traffic rules apply to all areas described in 14 CFR Part 93.

SPECIAL INSTRUMENT APPROACH PROCEDURE. (See INSTRUMENT APPROACH PROCEDURE.)

SPECIAL USE AIRSPACE. Airspace of defined dimensions identified by an area on the surface of the earth wherein activities must be confined because of their nature and/or wherein limitations may be imposed upon aircraft operations that are not a part of those activities. Types of special use airspace are:

a. Alert Area. Airspace which may contain a high volume of pilot training activities or an unusual type of aerial activity, neither of which is hazardous to aircraft. Alert Areas are depicted on aeronautical charts for the information of nonparticipating pilots. All activities within an Alert Area are conducted in accordance with Federal Aviation Regulations, and pilots of participating aircraft as well as pilots transiting the area are equally responsible for collision avoidance.

b. Controlled Firing Area. Airspace wherein activities are conducted under conditions so controlled as to eliminate hazards to nonparticipating aircraft and to ensure the safety of persons and property on the ground.

c. Military Operations Area (MOA). Permanent and temporary MOAs are airspace established outside of Class A airspace area to separate or segregate certain nonhazardous military activities from IFR traffic and to identify for VFR traffic where these activities are conducted. Permanent MOAs are depicted on Sectional Aeronautical, VFR Terminal Area, and applicable En Route Low Altitude Charts.
Note: Temporary MOAs are not charted. (Refer to AIM.)

d. National Security Area (NSA). Airspace of defined vertical and lateral dimensions established at locations where there is a requirement for increased security of ground facilities. Pilots are requested to voluntarily avoid flying through the depicted NSA. When a greater level of security is required, flight through an NSA may be temporarily prohibited by establishing a TFR under the provisions of 14 CFR Section 99.7. Such prohibitions will be issued by FAA Headquarters and disseminated via the U.S. NOTAM System. (Refer to AIM)

e. Prohibited Area. Airspace designated under 14 CFR Part 73 within which no person may operate an aircraft without the permission of the using agency. (Refer to AIM.) (Refer to En Route Charts.)

f. Restricted Area. Permanent and temporary restricted areas are airspace designated under 14 CFR Part 73, within which the flight of aircraft, while not wholly prohibited, is subject to restriction. Most restricted areas are designated joint use and IFR/VFR operations in the area may be authorized by the controlling ATC facility when it is not being utilized by the using agency. Permanent restricted areas are depicted on Sectional Aeronautical, VFR Terminal Area, and applicable En Route charts. Where joint use is authorized, the name of the ATC controlling facility is also shown.
Note: Temporary restricted areas are not charted. (Refer to 14 CFR Part 73.) (Refer to AIM.)

g. Warning Area. A warning area is airspace of defined dimensions extending from 3 nautical miles outward from the coast of the United States, that contains activity that may be hazardous to nonparticipating aircraft. The purpose of such warning area is to warn nonparticipating pilots of the potential danger. A warning area may be located over domestic or international waters or both.

SPECIAL VFR CONDITIONS. Meteorological conditions that are less than those required for basic VFR flight in Class B, C, D, or E surface areas and in which some aircraft are permitted flight under visual flight rules. (See SPECIAL VFR OPERATIONS.) (Refer to 14 CFR Part 91.)

SPECIAL VFR FLIGHT [ICAO]. A VFR flight cleared by air traffic control to operate within Class B, C, D, and E surface areas in meteorological conditions below VMC.

SPECIAL VFR OPERATIONS. Aircraft operating in accordance with clearances within Class B, C, D, and E surface areas in weather conditions less than the basic VFR weather minima. Such operations must be requested by the pilot and approved by ATC. (See SPECIAL VFR CONDITIONS.) (See ICAO term SPECIAL VFR FLIGHT.)

SPECIALIST-PROVIDED SERVICES. Services delivered directly by a flight service specialist via ground/ground communication, air/ground communication, in-person, or technology (for example, speech-to-text, email, or short message service).

SPEED. (See AIRSPEED.) (See GROUND SPEED.)

SPEED ADJUSTMENT. An ATC procedure used to request pilots to adjust aircraft speed to a specific value for the purpose of providing desired spacing. Pilots are expected to maintain a speed of plus or minus 10 knots or 0.02 Mach number of the specified speed. Examples of speed adjustments are:
a. "Increase/reduce speed to Mach point (number.)"
b. "Increase/reduce speed to (speed in knots)" or "Increase/reduce speed (number of knots) knots."

SPEED ADVISORY. Speed advisories that are generated within Time-Based Flow Management to assist controllers to meet the Scheduled Time of Arrival (STA) at the meter fix/meter arc. See also Ground-Based Interval Management-Spacing (GIM-S) Speed Advisory.

SPEED BRAKES. Moveable aerodynamic devices on aircraft that reduce airspeed during descent and landing.

SPEED SEGMENTS. Portions of the arrival route between the transition point and the vertex along the optimum flight path for which speeds and altitudes are specified. There is one set of arrival speed segments adapted from each transition point to each vertex. Each set may contain up to six segments.

SPOOFING. Denotes emissions of GNSS-like signals that may be acquired and tracked in combination with or instead of the intended signals by civil receivers. The onset of spoofing effects can be instantaneous or delayed, and effects can persist after the spoofing has ended. Spoofing can result in false and potentially confusing, or hazardously misleading, position, navigation, and/or date/time information in addition to loss of GNSS use.

SQUAWK (Mode, Code, Function). Used by ATC to instruct a pilot to activate the aircraft transponder and ADS-B Out with altitude reporting enabled, or (military) to activate only specific modes, codes, or functions. Examples: "Squawk five seven zero seven;" "Squawk three/alpha, two one zero five." (See TRANSPONDER.)

STA. (See SCHEDULED TIME OF ARRIVAL.)

STAGING/QUEUING. The placement, integration, and segregation of departure aircraft in designated movement areas of an airport by departure fix, EDCT, and/or restriction.

STAND BY. Means the controller or pilot must pause for a few seconds, usually to attend to other duties of a higher priority. Also means to wait as in "stand by for clearance." The caller should reestablish contact if a delay is lengthy. "Stand by" is not an approval or denial.

STANDARD INSTRUMENT APPROACH PROCEDURE (SIAP). (See INSTRUMENT APPROACH PROCEDURE.)

STANDARD INSTRUMENT DEPARTURE (SID). A preplanned instrument flight rule (IFR) air traffic control (ATC) departure procedure printed for pilot/controller use in graphic form to provide obstacle clearance and a transition from the terminal area to the appropriate en route structure. SIDs are primarily designed for system enhancement to expedite traffic flow and to reduce pilot/controller workload. ATC clearance must always be received prior to flying a SID. (See IFR TAKEOFF MINIMUMS AND DEPARTURE PROCEDURES.) (See OBSTACLE DEPARTURE PROCEDURE.) (Refer to AIM.)

STANDARD RATE TURN. A turn of three degrees per second.

STANDARD TERMINAL ARRIVAL (STAR). A preplanned instrument flight rule (IFR) air traffic control arrival procedure published for pilot use in graphic and/or textual form. STARs provide transition from the en route structure to an outer fix or an instrument approach fix/arrival waypoint in the terminal area.

STANDARD TERMINAL ARRIVAL CHARTS. (See AERONAUTICAL CHART.)

STANDARD TERMINAL AUTOMATION REPLACEMENT SYSTEM (STARS). (See DTAS.)

STAR. (See STANDARD TERMINAL ARRIVAL.)

STATE AIRCRAFT. Aircraft used in military, customs and police service, in the exclusive service of any government, or of any political subdivision, thereof including the government of any state, territory, or possession of the United States or the District of Columbia, but not including any government-owned aircraft engaged in carrying persons or property for commercial purposes.

STATIC RESTRICTIONS. Those restrictions that are usually not subject to change, fixed, in place, and/or published.

STATIONARY AIRSPACE RESERVATION. The term used in oceanic ATC for airspace that encompasses activities in a fixed volume of airspace to be occupied for a specified time period. Stationary Airspace Reservations may include activities such as special tests of weapons systems or equipment; certain U.S. Navy carrier, fleet, and anti-submarine operations; rocket, missile, and drone operations; and certain aerial refueling or similar operations. (See STATIONARY ALTITUDE RESERVATION.)

STATIONARY ALTITUDE RESERVATION (STATIONARY ALTRV). An altitude reservation which encompasses activities in a fixed volume of airspace to be occupied for a specified time period. Stationary ALTRVs may include activities such as special tests of weapons systems or equipment; certain U.S. Navy carrier, fleet, and anti-submarine operations; rocket, missile, and drone operations; and certain aerial refueling or similar operations.

STEP TAXI. To taxi a float plane at full power or high RPM.

STEP TURN. A maneuver used to put a float plane in a planing configuration prior to entering an active sea lane for takeoff. The STEP TURN maneuver should only be used upon pilot request.

STEPDOWN FIX. A fix permitting additional descent within a segment of an instrument approach procedure by identifying a point at which a controlling obstacle has been safely overflown.

STEREO ROUTE. A routinely used route of flight established by users and ARTCCs identified by a coded name; e.g., ALPHA 2. These routes minimize flight plan handling and communications.

STNR ALT RESERVATION. An abbreviation for Stationary Altitude Reservation commonly used in NOTAMs. (See STATIONARY ALTITUDE RESERVATION.)

STOL AIRCRAFT. (See SHORT TAKEOFF AND LANDING AIRCRAFT.)

P/C

STOP ALTITUDE SQUAWK. Used by ATC to instruct a pilot to turn off the automatic altitude reporting feature of the aircraft transponder and ADS-B Out. It is issued when a verbally reported altitude varies by 300 feet or more from the automatic altitude report. (See ALTITUDE READOUT.) (See TRANSPONDER.)

STOP AND GO. A procedure wherein an aircraft will land, make a complete stop on the runway, and then commence a takeoff from that point. (See LOW APPROACH.) (See OPTION APPROACH.)

STOP BURST. (See STOP STREAM.)

STOP BUZZER. (See STOP STREAM.)

STOP SQUAWK (Mode or Code). Used by ATC to instruct a pilot to stop transponder and ADS-B transmissions, or to turn off only specified functions of the aircraft transponder (military). (See STOP ALTITUDE SQUAWK.) (See TRANSPONDER.)

STOP STREAM. Used by ATC to request a pilot to suspend electronic attack activity. (See JAMMING.)

STOPOVER FLIGHT PLAN. A flight plan format which permits in a single submission the filing of a sequence of flight plans through interim full-stop destinations to a final destination.

STOPWAY. An area beyond the takeoff runway no less wide than the runway and centered upon the extended centerline of the runway, able to support the airplane during an aborted takeoff, without causing structural damage to the airplane, and designated by the airport authorities for use in decelerating the airplane during an aborted takeoff.

STRAIGHT-IN APPROACH IFR. An instrument approach wherein final approach is begun without first having executed a procedure turn, not necessarily completed with a straight-in landing or made to straight-in landing minimums. (See LANDING MINIMUMS.) (See STRAIGHT-IN APPROACH VFR.) (See STRAIGHT-IN LANDING.)

STRAIGHT-IN APPROACH VFR. Entry into the traffic pattern by interception of the extended runway centerline (final approach course) without executing any other portion of the traffic pattern. (See TRAFFIC PATTERN.)

STRAIGHT-IN LANDING. A landing made on a runway aligned within 30° of the final approach course following completion of an instrument approach. (See STRAIGHT-IN APPROACH IFR.)

STRAIGHT-IN LANDING MINIMUMS. (See LANDING MINIMUMS.)

STRAIGHT-IN MINIMUMS. (See STRAIGHT-IN LANDING MINIMUMS.)

STRATEGIC PLANNING. Planning whereby solutions are sought to resolve potential conflicts.

sUAS. (See SMALL UNMANNED AIRCRAFT SYSTEM.)

SUBSTITUTE ROUTE. A route assigned to pilots when any part of an airway or route is unusable because of NAVAID status. These routes consist of:
 a. Substitute routes which are shown on U.S. Government charts.
 b. Routes defined by ATC as specific NAVAID radials or courses.
 c. Routes defined by ATC as direct to or between NAVAIDs.

SUNSET AND SUNRISE. The mean solar times of sunset and sunrise as published in the Nautical Almanac, converted to local standard time for the locality concerned. Within Alaska, the end of evening civil twilight and the beginning of morning civil twilight, as defined for each locality.

SUPPLEMENTAL WEATHER SERVICE LOCATION. Airport facilities staffed with contract personnel who take weather observations and provide current local weather to pilots via telephone or radio. (All other services are provided by the parent FSS.)

SUPPS. Refers to ICAO Document 7030 Regional Supplementary Procedures. SUPPS contain procedures for each ICAO Region which are unique to that Region and are not covered in the worldwide provisions identified in the ICAO Air Navigation Plan. Procedures contained in Chapter 8 are based in part on those published in SUPPS.

SURFACE AREA. The airspace contained by the lateral boundary of the Class B, C, D, or E airspace designated for an airport that begins at the surface and extends upward.

SURFACE METERING PROGRAM. A capability within Terminal Flight Data Manager that provides the user with the ability to tactically manage surface traffic flows through adjusting desired minimum and maximum departure queue lengths to balance surface demand with capacity. When a demand/capacity imbalance for a surface resource is predicted, a metering procedure is recommended.

SURFACE VIEWER. A capability within the Traffic Flow Management System that provides situational awareness for a user-selected airport. The Surface Viewer displays a top-down view of an airport depicting runways, taxiways, gate areas, ramps, and buildings. The display also includes icons representing aircraft and vehicles currently on the surface, with identifying information. In addition, the display includes current airport configuration information such as departure/arrival runways and airport departure/arrival rates.

SURPIC. A description of surface vessels in the area of a Search and Rescue incident including their predicted positions and their characteristics. (Refer to FAA Order 7110.65, Para 10-6-4, INFLIGHT CONTINGENCIES.)

SURVEILLANCE APPROACH. An instrument approach wherein the air traffic controller issues instructions, for pilot compliance, based on aircraft position in relation to the final approach course (azimuth), and the distance (range) from the end of the

runway as displayed on the controller's radar scope. The controller will provide recommended altitudes on final approach if requested by the pilot. (Refer to AIM.)

SURVEILLANCE ENHANCED SEARCH AND RES-CUE (SE SAR). An automated service used to enhance search and rescue operations that provides federal contract flight service specialists direct information from the aircraft's registered tracking device.

SUSPICIOUS UAS. Suspicious UAS operations may include operating without authorization, loitering in the vicinity of sensitive locations, (e.g., national security, law enforcement facilities, and critical infrastructure), or disrupting normal air traffic operations resulting in runway changes, ground stops, pilot evasive action, etc. The report of a UAS operation alone does not constitute suspicious activity. Development of a comprehensive list of suspicious activities is not possible due to the vast number of situations that could be considered suspicious. ATC must exercise sound judgment when identifying situations that could constitute or indicate a suspicious activity.

SWAP. (See SEVERE WEATHER AVOIDANCE PLAN.)

SWSL. (See SUPPLEMENTAL WEATHER SERVICE LOCATION.)

SYSTEM STRATEGIC NAVIGATION. Military activity accomplished by navigating along a preplanned route using internal aircraft systems to maintain a desired track. This activity normally requires a lateral route width of 10 NM and altitude range of 1,000 feet to 6,000 feet AGL with some route segments that permit terrain following.

T

TACAN. (See TACTICAL AIR NAVIGATION.)

TACAN-ONLY AIRCRAFT. An aircraft, normally military, possessing TACAN with DME but no VOR navigational system capability. Clearances must specify TACAN or VORTAC fixes and approaches.

TACTICAL AIR NAVIGATION (TACAN). An ultra-high frequency electronic rho-theta air navigation aid which provides suitably equipped aircraft a continuous indication of bearing and distance to the TACAN station. (See VORTAC.) (Refer to AIM.)

TAILWIND. Any wind more than 90 degrees to the longitudinal axis of the runway. The magnetic direction of the runway shall be used as the basis for determining the longitudinal axis.

TAKEOFF AREA. (See LANDING AREA.)

TAKEOFF DISTANCE AVAILABLE (TODA). The take-off run available plus the length of any remaining runway or clearway beyond the far end of the takeoff run available. (See ICAO term TAKEOFF DISTANCE AVAILABLE.)

TAKEOFF DISTANCE AVAILABLE [ICAO]. The length of the take-off run available plus the length of the clearway, if provided.

TAKEOFF HOLD LIGHTS (THL). The THL system is composed of in-pavement lighting in a double, longitudinal row of lights aligned either side of the runway centerline. The lights are focused toward the arrival end of the runway at the "line up and wait" point, and they extend for 1,500 feet in front of the holding aircraft. Illuminated red lights indicate to an aircraft in position for takeoff or rolling that it is unsafe to takeoff because the runway is occupied or about to be occupied by an aircraft or vehicle.

TAKEOFF ROLL. The process whereby an aircraft is aligned with the runway centerline and the aircraft is moving with the intent to take off. For helicopters, this pertains to the act of becoming airborne after departing a takeoff area.

TAKEOFF RUN AVAILABLE (TORA). The runway length declared available and suitable for the ground run of an airplane taking off. (See ICAO term TAKE-OFF RUN AVAILABLE.)

TAKEOFF RUN AVAILABLE [ICAO]. The length of runway declared available and suitable for the ground run of an aeroplane take-off.

TARGET. The indication shown on a display resulting from a primary radar return, a radar beacon reply, or an ADS-B report. The specific target symbol presented to ATC may vary based on the surveillance source and automation platform. (See ASSOCIATED.) (See DIGITAL TARGET.) (See DIGITIZED RADAR TARGET.) (See FUSED TARGET.) (See PRIMARY RADAR TARGET.) (See RADAR.) (See SECONDARY RADAR TARGET.)(See ICAO term TARGET.) (See UNASSOCIATED.)

TARGET [ICAO]. In radar:
 a. Generally, any discrete object which reflects or retransmits energy back to the radar equipment.
 b. Specifically, an object of radar search or surveillance.

TARGET RESOLUTION. A process to ensure that correlated radar targets do not touch. Target resolution must be applied as follows:
 a. Between the edges of two primary targets or the edges of the ASR-9/11 primary target symbol.
 b. Between the end of the beacon control slash and the edge of a primary target.
 c. Between the ends of two beacon control slashes.

Note 1: Mandatory traffic advisories and safety alerts must be issued when this procedure is used.

Note 2: This procedure must not be used when utilizing mosaic radar systems or multi-sensor mode.

TARGET SYMBOL. (See TARGET.) (See ICAO term TARGET.)

TARMAC DELAY. The holding of an aircraft on the ground either before departure or after landing with no opportunity for its passengers to deplane.

P/C

TARMAC DELAY AIRCRAFT. An aircraft whose pilot-in-command has requested to taxi to the ramp, gate, or alternate deplaning area to comply with the Three-hour Tarmac Rule.

TARMAC DELAY REQUEST. A request by the pilot-in-command to taxi to the ramp, gate, or alternate deplaning location to comply with the Three-hour Tarmac Rule.

TAS. (See TERMINAL AUTOMATION SYSTEMS.)

TAWS. (See TERRAIN AWARENESS WARNING SYSTEM.)

TAXI. The movement of an airplane under its own power on the surface of an airport (14 CFR Section 135.100 [Note]). Also, it describes the surface movement of helicopters equipped with wheels. (See AIR TAXI.) (See HOVER TAXI.) (Refer to 14 CFR Section 135.100.) (Refer to AIM.)

TAXI PATTERNS. Patterns established to illustrate the desired flow of ground traffic for the different runways or airport areas available for use.

TBM. (See TIME-BASED MANAGEMENT.)

TBO. (See TRAJECTORY-BASED OPERATIONS.)

TCAS. (See TRAFFIC ALERT AND COLLISION AVOIDANCE SYSTEM.)

TCH. (See THRESHOLD CROSSING HEIGHT.)

TDLS. (See TERMINAL DATA LINK SYSTEM.)

TDZE. (See TOUCHDOWN ZONE ELEVATION.)

TEMPORARY FLIGHT RESTRICTION (TFR). A TFR is a regulatory action issued by the FAA via the U.S. NOTAM System, under the authority of United States Code, Title 49. TFRs are issued within the sovereign airspace of the United States and its territories to restrict certain aircraft from operating within a defined area on a temporary basis to protect persons or property in the air or on the ground. While not all inclusive, TFRs may be issued for disaster or hazard situations such as: toxic gas leaks or spills, fumes from flammable agents, aircraft accident/incident sites, aviation or ground resources engaged in wildfire suppression, or aircraft relief activities following a disaster. TFRs may also be issued in support of VIP movements; for reasons of national security; or when determined necessary for the management of air traffic in the vicinity of aerial demonstrations or major sporting events. NAS users or other interested parties should contact a FSS for TFR information. Additionally, TFR information can be found in automated briefings, NOTAM publications, and on the internet at http://www.faa.gov. The FAA also distributes TFR information to aviation user groups for further dissemination.

TERMINAL AREA. A general term used to describe airspace in which approach control service or airport traffic control service is provided.

TERMINAL AREA FACILITY. A facility providing air traffic control service for arriving and departing IFR, VFR, Special VFR, and on occasion en route aircraft. (See APPROACH CONTROL FACILITY.) (See TOWER.)

TERMINAL AUTOMATION SYSTEMS (TAS). TAS is used to identify the numerous automated tracking systems including STARS and MEARTS.

TERMINAL DATA LINK SYSTEM (TDLS). A system that provides Digital Automatic Terminal Information Service (D–ATIS) both on a specified radio frequency and also, for subscribers, in a text message via data link to the cockpit or to a gate printer. TDLS also provides Pre-Departure Clearances (PDC), at selected airports, to subscribers, through a service provider, in text to the cockpit or to a gate printer. In addition, TDLS will emulate the Flight Data Input/Output (FDIO) information within the control tower.

TERMINAL FLIGHT DATA MANAGER (TFDM). An integrated tower flight data automation system to provide improved airport surface and terminal airspace management. TFDM enhances traffic flow management data integration with Time-Based Flow Management (TBFM) and Traffic Flow Management System (TFMS) to enable airlines, controllers, and airports to share and exchange real-time data. This improves surface traffic management and enhances capabilities of TFMS and TBFM. TFDM assists the Tower personnel with surface Traffic Flow Management (TFM) and Collaborative Decision Making (CDM) and enables a fundamental change in the Towers from a local airport-specific operation to a NAS-connected metering operation. The single platform consolidates multiple Tower automation systems, including: Departure Spacing Program (DSP), Airport Resource Management Tool (ARMT), Electronic Flight Strip Transfer System (EFSTS), and Surface Movement Advisor (SMA). TFDM data, integrated with other FAA systems such as TBFM and TFMS, allows airlines, controllers, and airports to manage the flow of aircraft more efficiently through all phases of flight from departure to arrival gate.

TERMINAL RADAR SERVICE AREA. Airspace surrounding designated airports wherein ATC provides radar vectoring, sequencing, and separation on a full-time basis for all IFR and participating VFR aircraft. The AIM contains an explanation of TRSA. TRSAs are depicted on VFR aeronautical charts. Pilot participation is urged but is not mandatory.

TERMINAL SEQUENCING AND SPACING (TSAS). Extends scheduling and metering capabilities into the terminal area and provides metering automation tools to terminal controllers and terminal traffic management personnel. Those controllers and traffic management personnel become active participants in time-based metering operations as they work to deliver aircraft accurately to Constraint Satisfaction Points within terminal airspace to include the runway in accordance with scheduled times at those points. Terminal controllers are better able to utilize efficient

flight paths, such as Standard Instrument Approach Procedures (SIAPs) that require a Navigational Specification (NavSpec) of RNP APCH with Radius-to-Fix (RF) legs, or Advanced RNP (A-RNP), through tools that support the merging of mixed-equipage traffic flows. For example, merging aircraft flying RNP APCH AR with RF, A-RNP, and non-RNP approach procedures. Additional fields in the flight plan will identify those flights capable of flying the RNP APCH with RF or A-RNP procedures, and those flights will be scheduled for those types of procedures when available. TSAS will schedule these and the non-RNP aircraft to a common merge point. Terminal traffic management personnel have improved situation awareness using displays that allow for the monitoring of terminal metering operations, similar to the displays used today by center traffic management personnel to monitor en route metering operations.

TERMINAL VFR RADAR SERVICE. A national program instituted to extend the terminal radar services provided instrument flight rules (IFR) aircraft to visual flight rules (VFR) aircraft. The program is divided into four types service referred to as basic radar service, terminal radar service area (TRSA) service, Class B service and Class C service. The type of service provided at a particular location is contained in the Chart | Supplement.

a. Basic Radar Service. These services are provided for VFR aircraft by all commissioned terminal radar facilities. Basic radar service includes safety alerts, traffic advisories, limited radar vectoring when requested by the pilot, and sequencing at locations where procedures have been established for this purpose and/or when covered by a letter of agreement. The purpose of this service is to adjust the flow of arriving IFR and VFR aircraft into the traffic pattern in a safe and orderly manner and to provide traffic advisories to departing VFR aircraft.

b. TRSA Service. This service provides, in addition to basic radar service, sequencing of all IFR and participating VFR aircraft to the primary airport and separation between all participating VFR aircraft. The purpose of this service is to provide separation between all participating VFR aircraft and all IFR aircraft operating within the area defined as a TRSA.

c. Class C Service. This service provides, in addition to basic radar service, approved separation between IFR and VFR aircraft, and sequencing of VFR aircraft, and sequencing of VFR arrivals to the primary airport.

d. Class B Service. This service provides, in addition to basic radar service, approved separation of aircraft based on IFR, VFR, and/or weight, and sequencing of VFR arrivals to the primary airport(s).
(See CONTROLLED AIRSPACE.)
(See TERMINAL RADAR SERVICE AREA.)
(Refer to AIM.)
(Refer to CHART SUPPLEMENT U.S.)

TERMINAL–VERY HIGH FREQUENCY OMNIDIRECTIONAL RANGE STATION (TVOR). A very high frequency terminal omnirange station located on or near an airport and used as an approach aid. (See NAVIGATIONAL AID.) (See VOR.)

TERRAIN AWARENESS WARNING SYSTEM (TAWS). An on-board, terrain proximity alerting system providing the aircrew "Low Altitude warnings" to allow immediate pilot action.

TERRAIN FOLLOWING. The flight of a military aircraft maintaining a constant AGL altitude above the terrain or the highest obstruction. The altitude of the aircraft will constantly change with the varying terrain and/or obstruction.

TETRAHEDRON. A device normally located on uncontrolled airports and used as a landing direction indicator. The small end of a tetrahedron points in the direction of landing. At controlled airports, the tetrahedron, if installed, should be disregarded because tower instructions supersede the indicator. (See SEGMENTED CIRCLE.) (Refer to AIM.)

TF. (See TERRAIN FOLLOWING.)

TFDM. (See TERMINAL FLIGHT DATA MANAGER.)

TGUI. (See TIMELINE GRAPHICAL USER INTERFACE.)

THAT IS CORRECT. The understanding you have is right.

THA. (See TRANSITIONAL HAZARD AREA.)

THE RECREATIONAL UAS SAFETY TEST (TRUST). The electronically administered free test required for all recreational UAS operators referred to as the aeronautical knowledge and safety test, under 49 USC §44809 (g).

THREE-HOUR TARMAC RULE. Rule that relates to Department of Transportation (DOT) requirements placed on airlines when tarmac delays are anticipated to reach 3 hours.

360 OVERHEAD. (See OVERHEAD MANEUVER.)

THRESHOLD. The beginning of that portion of the runway usable for landing. (See AIRPORT LIGHTING.) (See DISPLACED THRESHOLD.)

THRESHOLD CROSSING HEIGHT. The theoretical height above the runway threshold at which the aircraft's glideslope antenna would be if the aircraft maintains the trajectory established by the mean ILS glideslope or the altitude at which the calculated glidepath of an RNAV or GPS approaches.
(See GLIDESLOPE.) (See THRESHOLD.)

THRESHOLD LIGHTS. (See AIRPORT LIGHTING.)

TIE-IN FACILITY. The FSS primarily responsible for providing FSS services, including telecommunications services for landing facilities or navigational aids located within the boundaries of a flight plan area (FPA). Three-letter identifiers are assigned to each FSS/FPA and are annotated as tie-in facilities in the Chart Supplement and FAA Order JO 7350.9, Location | Identifiers. Large consolidated FSS facilities may have many tie-in facilities or FSS sectors within one facility. (See FLIGHT PLAN AREA.) (See FLIGHT SERVICE STATION.)

P/C

TIME-BASED FLOW MANAGEMENT (TBFM). A foundational Decision Support Tool for time-based management in the en route and terminal environments. TBFM's core function is the ability to schedule aircraft within a stream of traffic to reach a defined constraint point (e.g., meter fix/meter arc) at specified times, creating a time-ordered sequence of traffic. The scheduled times allow for merging of traffic flows, efficiently utilizing airport and airspace capacity while minimizing coordination and reducing the need for vectoring/holding. The TBFM schedule is calculated using current aircraft estimated time of arrival at key defined constraint points based on wind forecasts, aircraft flight plan, the desired separation at the constraint point and other parameters. The schedule applies spacing only when needed to maintain the desired separation at one or more constraint points. This includes, but is not limited to, Single Center Metering (SCM), Adjacent Center Metering (ACM), En Route Departure Capability (EDC), Integrated Departure/Arrival Capability (IDAC), Ground-based Interval Management-Spacing (GIM-S), Departure Scheduling, and Extended/Coupled Metering.

TIME-BASED MANAGEMENT (TBM). A methodology for managing the flow of air traffic through the assignment of time at specific points for an aircraft. TBM applies time to manage and condition air traffic flows to mitigate demand/capacity imbalances and enhance efficiency and predictability of the NAS. Where implemented, TBM tools will be used to manage traffic even during periods when demand does not exceed capacity. This will sustain operational predictability and assure the regional/national strategic plan is maintained. TBM uses capabilities within TFMS, TBFM, and TFDM. These programs are designed to achieve a specified interval between aircraft. Different types of programs accommodate different phases of flight.

TIME GROUP. Four digits representing the hour and minutes from the Coordinated Universal Time (UTC) clock. FAA uses UTC for all operations. The term "ZULU" may be used to denote UTC. The word "local" or the time zone equivalent shall be used to denote local when local time is given during radio and telephone communications. When written, a time zone designator is used to indicate local time; e.g. "0205M" (Mountain). The local time may be based on the 24-hour clock system. The day begins at 0000 and ends at 2359.

TIMELINE GRAPHICAL USER INTERFACE (TGUI). A TBFM display that uses timelines to display the Estimated Time of Arrival and Scheduled Time of Arrival of each aircraft to specified constraint points. The TGUI can also display pre-departure and scheduled aircraft.

TIS-B. (See TRAFFIC INFORMATION SERVICE—BROADCAST.)

TMI. (See TRAFFIC MANAGEMENT INITIATIVE.)

TMPA. (See TRAFFIC MANAGEMENT PROGRAM ALERT.)

TMU. (See TRAFFIC MANAGEMENT UNIT.)

TOD. (See TOP OF DESCENT.)

TODA. (See TAKE-OFF DISTANCE AVAILABLE)(See ICAO Term TAKE-OFF DISTANCE AVAILABLE.)

TOI. (See TRACK OF INTEREST.)

TOP ALTITUDE. In reference to SID published altitude restrictions the charted "maintain" altitude contained in the procedure description or assigned by ATC.

TOP OF DESCENT (TOD). The point at which an aircraft begins the initial descent.

TORA. (See TAKE-OFF RUN AVAILABLE.)
(See ICAO Term TAKE-OFF RUN AVAILABLE.)

TORCHING. The burning of fuel at the end of an exhaust pipe or stack of a reciprocating aircraft engine, the result of an excessive richness in the fuel air mixture.

TOS. (See TRAJECTORY OPTIONS SET.)

TOTAL ESTIMATED ELAPSED TIME [ICAO]. For IFR flights, the estimated time required from take-off to arrive over that designated point, defined by reference to navigation aids, from which it is intended that an instrument approach procedure will be commenced, or, if no navigation aid is associated with the destination aerodrome, to arrive over the destination aerodrome. For VFR flights, the estimated time required from take-off to arrive over the destination aerodrome. (See ICAO term ESTIMATED ELAPSED TIME.)

TOUCH-AND-GO. An operation by an aircraft that lands and departs on a runway without stopping or exiting the runway.

TOUCH-AND-GO LANDING.
(See TOUCH-AND-GO.)

TOUCHDOWN.
 a. The point at which an aircraft first makes contact with the landing surface.
 b. Concerning a precision radar approach (PAR), it is the point where the glide path intercepts the landing surface.
(See ICAO term TOUCHDOWN.)

TOUCHDOWN [ICAO]. The point where the nominal glide path intercepts the runway.

Note: Touchdown as defined above is only a datum and is not necessarily the actual point at which the aircraft will touch the runway.

TOUCHDOWN RVR. (See VISIBILITY.)

TOUCHDOWN ZONE. The first 3,000 feet of the runway beginning at the threshold. The area is used for determination of Touchdown Zone Elevation in the development of straight-in landing minimums for instrument approaches. (See ICAO term TOUCHDOWN ZONE.)

TOUCHDOWN ZONE [ICAO]. The portion of a runway, beyond the threshold, where it is intended landing aircraft first contact the runway.

TOUCHDOWN ZONE ELEVATION. The highest elevation in the first 3,000 feet of the landing surface. TDZE is indicated on the instrument approach procedure chart when straight-in landing minimums are authorized. (See TOUCHDOWN ZONE.)

TOUCHDOWN ZONE LIGHTING. (See AIRPORT LIGHTING.)

TOWER. A terminal facility that uses air/ground communications, visual signaling, and other devices to provide ATC services to aircraft operating in the vicinity of an airport or on the movement area. Authorizes aircraft to land or takeoff at the airport controlled by the tower or to transit the Class D airspace area regardless of flight plan or weather conditions (IFR or VFR). A tower may also provide approach control services (radar or nonradar). (See AIRPORT TRAFFIC CONTROL SERVICE.) (See APPROACH CONTROL FACILITY.) (See APPROACH CONTROL SERVICE.) (See MOVEMENT AREA.) (See TOWER EN ROUTE CONTROL SERVICE.) (See ICAO term AERODROME CONTROL TOWER.) (Refer to AIM.)

TOWER EN ROUTE CONTROL SERVICE. The control of IFR en route traffic within delegated airspace between two or more adjacent approach control facilities. This service is designed to expedite traffic and reduce control and pilot communication requirements.

TOWER TO TOWER. (See TOWER EN ROUTE CONTROL SERVICE.)

TRACEABLE PRESSURE STANDARD. The facility station pressure instrument, with certification/calibration traceable to the National Institute of Standards and Technology. Traceable pressure standards may be mercurial barometers, commissioned ASOS or dual transducer AWOS, or portable pressure standards or DASI.

TRACK. The actual flight path of an aircraft over the surface of the earth. (See COURSE.) (See FLIGHT PATH.) (See ROUTE.) (See ICAO term TRACK.)

TRACK [ICAO]. The projection on the earth's surface of the path of an aircraft, the direction of which path at any point is usually expressed in degrees from North (True, Magnetic, or Grid).

TRACK OF INTEREST (TOI). Displayed data representing an airborne object that threatens or has the potential to threaten North America or National Security. Indicators may include, but are not limited to: noncompliance with air traffic control instructions or aviation regulations; extended loss of communications; unusual transmissions or unusual flight behavior; unauthorized intrusion into controlled airspace or an ADIZ; noncompliance with issued flight restrictions/security procedures; or unlawful interference with airborne flight crews, up to and including hijack. In certain circumstances, an object may become a TOI based on specific and credible intelligence pertaining to that particular aircraft/object, its passengers, or its cargo.

TRACK OF INTEREST RESOLUTION. A TOI will normally be considered resolved when: the aircraft/object is no longer airborne; the aircraft complies with air traffic control instructions, aviation regulations, and/or issued flight restrictions/security procedures; radio contact is re-established and authorized control of the aircraft is verified; the aircraft is intercepted and intent is verified to be nonthreatening/nonhostile; TOI was identified based on specific and credible intelligence that was later determined to be invalid or unreliable; or displayed data is identified and characterized as invalid.

TRAFFIC.
a. A term used by a controller to transfer radar identification of an aircraft to another controller for the purpose of coordinating separation action. Traffic is normally issued:
1. In response to a handoff or point out,
2. In anticipation of a handoff or point out, or
3. In conjunction with a request for control of an aircraft.
b. A term used by ATC to refer to one or more aircraft.

TRAFFIC ADVISORIES. Advisories issued to alert pilots to other known or observed air traffic which may be in such proximity to the position or intended route of flight of their aircraft to warrant their attention. Such advisories may be based on:
a. Visual observation.
b. Observation of radar identified and nonidentified aircraft targets on an ATC radar display, or
c. Verbal reports from pilots or other facilities.

Note 1: The word "traffic" followed by additional information, if known, is used to provide such advisories; e.g., "Traffic, 2 o'clock, one zero miles, southbound, eight thousand."

Note 2: Traffic advisory service will be provided to the extent possible depending on higher priority duties of the controller or other limitations; e.g., radar limitations, volume of traffic, frequency congestion, or controller workload. Radar/nonradar traffic advisories do not relieve the pilot of his/her responsibility to see and avoid other aircraft. Pilots are cautioned that there are many times when the controller is not able to give traffic advisories concerning all traffic in the aircraft's proximity; in other words, when a pilot requests or is receiving traffic advisories, he/she should not assume that all traffic will be issued.
(Refer to AIM.)

TRAFFIC ALERT (aircraft call sign), TURN (left/right) IMMEDIATELY, (climb/descend) AND MAINTAIN (altitude). (See SAFETY ALERT.)

TRAFFIC ALERT AND COLLISION AVOIDANCE SYSTEM (TCAS). An airborne collision avoidance system based on radar beacon signals which operates independent of ground-based equipment. TCAS-I generates traffic advisories only. TCAS-II generates traffic advisories, and resolution (collision avoidance) advisories in the vertical plane.

TRAFFIC INFORMATION. (See TRAFFIC ADVISORIES.)

TRAFFIC INFORMATION SERVICE–BROADCAST (TIS-B). The broadcast of ATC derived traffic information to ADS-B equipped (1090ES or UAT) aircraft. The source of this traffic information is derived from ground-based air traffic surveillance sensors, typically from radar targets. TIS-B service will be available throughout the NAS where there are both adequate surveillance coverage (radar) and adequate broadcast coverage from ADS-B ground stations. Loss of TIS-B will occur when an aircraft enters an area not covered by the GBT network. If this occurs in an area with adequate surveillance coverage (radar), nearby aircraft that remain within the adequate broadcast coverage (ADS-B) area will view the first aircraft. TIS-B may continue when an aircraft enters an area with inadequate surveillance coverage (radar); nearby aircraft that remain within the adequate broadcast coverage (ADS-B) area will not view the first aircraft.

TRAFFIC IN SIGHT. Used by pilots to inform a controller that previously issued traffic is in sight. (See NEGATIVE CONTACT.) (See TRAFFIC ADVISORIES.)

TRAFFIC MANAGEMENT INITIATIVE (TMI). Tools used to manage demand with capacity in the National Airspace System (NAS). TMIs can be used to manage NAS resources (e.g., airports, sectors, airspace) or to increase the efficiency of the operation. TMIs can be either tactical (i.e., short term) or strategic (i.e., long term), depending on the type of TMI and the operational need.

TRAFFIC MANAGEMENT PROGRAM ALERT. A term used in a Notice to Air Missions (NOTAM) issued in conjunction with a special traffic management program to alert pilots to the existence of the program and to refer them to a special traffic management program advisory message for program details. The contraction TMPA is used in NOTAM text.

TRAFFIC MANAGEMENT UNIT. The entity in ARTCCs and designated terminals directly involved in the active management of facility traffic. Usually under the direct supervision of an assistant manager for traffic management.

TRAFFIC NO FACTOR. Indicates that the traffic described in a previously issued traffic advisory is no factor.

TRAFFIC NO LONGER OBSERVED. Indicates that the traffic described in a previously issued traffic advisory is no longer depicted on radar, but may still be a factor.

TRAFFIC PATTERN. The traffic flow that is prescribed for aircraft landing at, taxiing on, or taking off from an airport. The components of a typical traffic pattern are upwind leg, crosswind leg, downwind leg, base leg, and final approach.

a. Upwind Leg. A flight path parallel to the landing runway in the direction of landing.

b. Crosswind Leg. A flight path at right angles to the landing runway off its upwind end.

c. Downwind Leg. A flight path parallel to the landing runway in the direction opposite to landing. The downwind leg normally extends between the crosswind leg and the base leg.

d. Base Leg. A flight path at right angles to the landing runway off its approach end. The base leg normally extends from the downwind leg to the intersection of the extended runway centerline.

Note: ATC may instruct a pilot to report a "2-mile left base" to Runway 22. This instruction means that the pilot is expected to maneuver their aircraft into a left base leg that will intercept a straight-in final 2 miles from the approach end of Runway 22 and advise ATC.

Reference: Pilot's Handbook of Aeronautical Knowledge, FAA-H-8083-25, Chapter 14, Airport Operations, Traffic Patterns.

e. Final Approach. A flight path in the direction of landing along the extended runway centerline. The final approach normally extends from the base leg to the runway. An aircraft making a straight-in approach VFR is also considered to be on final approach.

Note: ATC may instruct a pilot to report "5-mile final" to Runway 22. This instruction means that the pilot should maneuver their aircraft onto a straight-in final and advise ATC when they are five miles from the approach end of Runway 22.

Reference: Pilot's Handbook of Aeronautical Knowledge, FAA-H-8083-25, Chapter 14, Airport Operations, Traffic Patterns.

(See STRAIGHT-IN APPROACH VFR.)
(See TAXI PATTERNS.)
(See ICAO term AERODROME TRAFFIC CIRCUIT.)
(Refer to 14 CFR Part 91.) (Refer to AIM.)

TRAFFIC SITUATION DISPLAY (TSD). TSD is a computer system that receives radar track data from all 20 CONUS ARTCCs, organizes this data into a mosaic display, and presents it on a computer screen. The display allows the traffic management coordinator multiple methods of selection and highlighting of individual aircraft or groups of aircraft. The user has the option of superimposing these aircraft positions over any number of background displays. These background options include ARTCC boundaries, any stratum of en route sector boundaries, fixes, airways, military and other special use airspace, airports, and geopolitical boundaries. By using the TSD, a coordinator can monitor any number of traffic situations or the entire system-wide traffic flows.

TRAJECTORY. A EDST representation of the path an aircraft is predicted to fly based upon a Current Plan or Trial Plan. (See EN ROUTE DECISION SUPPORT TOOL.)

TRAJECTORY-BASED OPERATIONS (TBO). An Air Traffic Management method for strategically planning and managing flights throughout the operation by using Time-Based Management (TBM), information exchange between air and ground systems, and the aircraft's ability to fly trajectories in time and space. Aircraft trajectory is defined in four dimensions—latitude, longitude, altitude, and time.

TRAJECTORY MODELING. The automated process of calculating a trajectory.

TRAJECTORY OPTIONS SET (TOS). A TOS is an electronic message, submitted by the operator, that is used by the Collaborative Trajectory Options Program (CTOP) to manage the airspace captured in the traffic management program. The TOS will allow the operator to express the route and delay trade-off options that they are willing to accept.

TRANSFER OF CONTROL. That action whereby the responsibility for the separation of an aircraft is transferred from one controller to another. (See ICAO term TRANSFER OF CONTROL.)

TRANSFER OF CONTROL [ICAO]. Transfer of responsibility for providing air traffic control service.

TRANSFERRING CONTROLLER. A controller/facility transferring control of an aircraft to another controller/facility. (See ICAO term TRANSFERRING UNIT/CONTROLLER.)

TRANSFERRING FACILITY. (See TRANSFERRING CONTROLLER.)

TRANSFERRING UNIT/CONTROLLER [ICAO]. Air traffic control unit/air traffic controller in the process of transferring the responsibility for providing air traffic control service to an aircraft to the next air traffic control unit/air traffic controller along the route of flight. *Note: See definition of accepting unit/controller.*

TRANSITION. The general term that describes the change from one phase of flight or flight condition to another; e.g., transition from en route flight to the approach or transition from instrument flight to visual flight.

TRANSITION POINT. A point at an adapted number of miles from the vertex at which an arrival aircraft would normally commence descent from its en route altitude. This is the first fix adapted on the arrival speed segments.

TRANSITIONAL AIRSPACE. That portion of controlled airspace wherein aircraft change from one phase of flight or flight condition to another.

TRANSITIONAL HAZARD AREA (THA). Used by ATC. Airspace normally associated with an Aircraft Hazard Area within which the flight of aircraft is subject to restrictions. (See AIRCRAFT HAZARD AREA.) (See CONTINGENCY HAZARD AREA.) (See REFINED HAZARD AREA.)

TRANSMISSOMETER. An apparatus used to determine visibility by measuring the transmission of light through the atmosphere. It is the measurement source for determining runway visual range (RVR). (See VISIBILITY.)

TRANSMITTING IN THE BLIND. A transmission from one station to other stations in circumstances where two-way communication cannot be established, but where it is believed that the called stations may be able to receive the transmission.

TRANSPONDER. The airborne radar beacon receiver/transmitter portion of the Air Traffic Control Radar Beacon System (ATCRBS) which automatically receives radio signals from interrogators on the ground, and selectively replies with a specific reply pulse or pulse group only to those interrogations being received on the mode to which it is set to respond. (See INTERROGATOR.) (See ICAO term TRANSPONDER.) (Refer to AIM.)

TRANSPONDER [ICAO]. A receiver/transmitter which will generate a reply signal upon proper interrogation; the interrogation and reply being on different frequencies.

TRANSPONDER CODES. (See CODES.)

TRANSPONDER OBSERVED. Phraseology used to inform a VFR pilot the aircraft's assigned beacon code and position have been observed. Specifically, this term conveys to a VFR pilot the transponder reply has been observed and its position correlated for transit through the designated area.

TRIAL PLAN. A proposed amendment which utilizes automation to analyze and display potential conflicts along the predicted trajectory of the selected aircraft.

TRSA. (See TERMINAL RADAR SERVICE AREA.)

TRUST. (See THE RECREATIONAL UAS SAFETY TEST.)

TSAS. (See TERMINAL SEQUENCING AND SPACING.)

TSD. (See TRAFFIC SITUATION DISPLAY.)

TURBOJET AIRCRAFT. An aircraft having a jet engine in which the energy of the jet operates a turbine which in turn operates the air compressor.

TURBOPROP AIRCRAFT. An aircraft having a jet engine in which the energy of the jet operates a turbine which drives the propeller.

TURBULENCE. An atmospheric phenomenon that causes changes in aircraft altitude, attitude, and or airspeed with aircraft reaction depending on intensity. Pilots report turbulence intensity according to aircraft's reaction as follows:

a. Light. Causes slight, erratic changes in altitude and or attitude (pitch, roll, or yaw).

b. Moderate. Similar to Light but of greater intensity. Changes in altitude and or attitude occur but the aircraft remains in positive control at all times. It usually causes variations in indicated airspeed.

c. Severe. Causes large, abrupt changes in altitude and or attitude. It usually causes large variations in indicated airspeed. Aircraft may be momentarily out of control.

d. Extreme. The aircraft is violently tossed about and is practically impossible to control. It may cause structural damage.
(See CHOP.) (Refer to AIM.)

TURN ANTICIPATION (maneuver anticipation).

TVOR. (See TERMINAL-VERY HIGH FREQUENCY OMNIDIRECTIONAL RANGE STATION.)

TWO-WAY RADIO COMMUNICATIONS FAILURE. (See LOST COMMUNICATIONS.)

U

UAM. (See URBAN AIR MOBILITY.)

UAS FACILITY MAP (UASFM). Defined grid squares showing maximum altitudes around airports where the FAA may authorize Part 107 sUAS operations without additional safety analysis. The maps should be consulted prior to conducting UAS operations (Part 91, Part 107 or Section 44809) in controlled airspace. The UASFM will aid in determining if the airspace authorization or waivers are necessary. UASFM(s) are charted on the UAS Data Delivery System (UDDS) at the following website address: https://faa.maps.arcgis .com/apps/webappviewer/index.html?id=9c2e44067 10048e19806ebf6a06754ad

UAS TEST SITE. Independently owned UAS test & research sites, recognized by the FAA.

UAS TRAFFIC MANAGEMENT (UTM). The unmanned aircraft traffic management ecosystem that will allow multiple low altitude BVLOS operations and which is separate from, but complementary to, FAA's Air Traffic Control System.

UASFM. (See UAS FACILITY MAP.)

UHF. (See ULTRAHIGH FREQUENCY.)

ULTRAHIGH FREQUENCY (UHF). The frequency band between 300 and 3,000 MHz. The bank of radio frequencies used for military air/ground voice communications. In some instances this may go as low as 225 MHz and still be referred to as UHF.

ULTRALIGHT VEHICLE. A single-occupant aeronautical vehicle operated for sport or recreational purposes which does not require FAA registration, an airworthiness certificate, nor pilot certification. Operation of an ultralight vehicle in certain airspace requires authorization from ATC. (Refer to 14 CFR Part 103.)

UNABLE. Indicates inability to comply with a specific instruction, request, or clearance.

UNASSOCIATED. A radar target that does not display a data block with flight identification and altitude information. (See ASSOCIATED.)

UNCONTROLLED AIRSPACE. Airspace in which aircraft are not subject to controlled airspace (Class A, B, C, D, or E) separation criteria.

UNDER THE HOOD. Indicates that the pilot is using a hood to restrict visibility outside the cockpit while simulating instrument flight. An appropriately rated pilot is required in the other control seat while this operation is being conducted. (Refer to 14 CFR Part 91.)

UNFROZEN. The Scheduled Time of Arrival (STA) tags, which are still being rescheduled by the time based flow management (TBFM) calculations. The aircraft will remain unfrozen until the time the corresponding estimated time of arrival (ETA) tag passes the preset freeze horizon for that aircraft's stream class. At this point the automatic rescheduling will stop, and the STA becomes "frozen."

UNICOM. A nongovernment communication facility which may provide airport information at certain airports. Locations and frequencies of UNICOMs are shown on aeronautical charts and publications. (See CHART SUPPLEMENT.) (Refer to AIM.)

UNMANNED AIRCRAFT (UA). A device used or intended to be used for flight that has no onboard pilot. This device can be any type of airplane, helicopter, airship, or powered-lift aircraft. Unmanned free balloons, moored balloons, tethered aircraft, gliders, and unmanned rockets are not considered to be a UA.

UNMANNED AIRCRAFT SYSTEM (UAS). An unmanned aircraft and its associated elements related to safe operations, which may include control stations (ground, ship, or air based), control links, support equipment, payloads, flight termination systems, and launch/recovery equipment. It consists of three elements: unmanned aircraft, control station, and data link.

UNPUBLISHED ROUTE. A route for which no minimum altitude is published or charted for pilot use. It may include a direct route between NAVAIDs, a radial, a radar vector, or a final approach course beyond the segments of an instrument approach procedure. (See PUBLISHED ROUTE.) (See ROUTE.)

UNRELIABLE (GPS/WAAS). An advisory to pilots indicating the expected level of service of the GPS and/or WAAS may not be available. Pilots must then determine the adequacy of the signal for desired use.

UNSERVICEABLE (U/S). (See OUT OF SERVICE/ UNSERVICEABLE.)

UPWIND LEG. (See TRAFFIC PATTERN.)

URBAN AIR MOBILITY (UAM). A subset of Advanced Air Mobility (AAM), referring to an air transportation system utilizing highly automated aircraft to transport passengers or cargo in urban/suburban areas.

URGENCY. A condition of being concerned about safety and of requiring timely but not immediate assistance; a potential distress condition. (See ICAO term URGENCY.)

URGENCY [ICAO]. A condition concerning the safety of an aircraft or other vehicle, or of person on board or in sight, but which does not require immediate assistance.

USAFIB. (See ARMY AVIATION FLIGHT INFORMATION BULLETIN.)

UTM. (See UAS TRAFFIC MANAGEMENT.)

V

VASI. (See VISUAL APPROACH SLOPE INDICATOR.)

VCOA. (See VISUAL CLIMB OVER AIRPORT.)

VDP. (See VISUAL DESCENT POINT.)

VECTOR. A heading issued to an aircraft to provide navigational guidance by radar. (See ICAO term RADAR VECTORING.)

VERIFY. Request confirmation of information; e.g., "verify assigned altitude."

VERIFY SPECIFIC DIRECTION OF TAKEOFF (OR TURNS AFTER TAKEOFF). Used by ATC to ascertain an aircraft's direction of takeoff and/or direction of turn after takeoff. It is normally used for IFR departures from an airport not having a control tower. When direct communication with the pilot is not possible, the request and information may be relayed through an FSS, dispatcher, or by other means. (See IFR TAKE-OFF MINIMUMS AND DEPARTURE PROCEDURES.)

VERTICAL NAVIGATION (VNAV). A function of area navigation (RNAV) equipment which calculates, displays, and provides vertical guidance to a profile or path.

VERTICAL SEPARATION. Separation between aircraft expressed in units of vertical distance. (See SEPARATION.)

VERTICAL TAKEOFF AND LANDING AIRCRAFT (VTOL). Aircraft capable of vertical climbs and/or descents and of using very short runways or small areas for takeoff and landings. These aircraft include, but are not limited to, helicopters. (See SHORT TAKE-OFF AND LANDING AIRCRAFT.)

VERY HIGH FREQUENCY (VHF). The frequency band between 30 and 300 MHz. Portions of this band, 108 to 118 MHz, are used for certain NAVAIDs; 118 to 136 MHz are used for civil air/ground voice communications. Other frequencies in this band are used for purposes not related to air traffic control.

VERY HIGH FREQUENCY OMNIDIRECTIONAL RANGE STATION. (See VOR.)

VERY LOW FREQUENCY (VLF). The frequency band between 3 and 30 kHz.

VFR. (See VISUAL FLIGHT RULES.)

VFR AIRCRAFT. An aircraft conducting flight in accordance with visual flight rules. (See VISUAL FLIGHT RULES.)

VFR CONDITIONS. Weather conditions equal to or better than the minimum for flight under visual flight rules. The term may be used as an ATC clearance/instruction only when:

 a. An IFR aircraft requests a climb/descent in VFR conditions.

 b. The clearance will result in noise abatement benefits where part of the IFR departure route does not conform to an FAA approved noise abatement route or altitude.

 c. A pilot has requested a practice instrument approach and is not on an IFR flight plan.

Note: All pilots receiving this authorization must comply with the VFR visibility and distance from cloud criteria in 14 CFR Part 91. Use of the term does not relieve controllers of their responsibility to separate aircraft in Class B and Class C airspace or TRSAs as required by FAA Order JO 7110.65. When used as an ATC clearance/instruction, the term may be

abbreviated "VFR;" e.g., "MAINTAIN VFR," "CLIMB/DESCEND VFR," etc.

VFR FLIGHT. (See VFR AIRCRAFT.)

VFR MILITARY TRAINING ROUTES (VR). Routes used by the Department of Defense and associated Reserve and Air Guard units for the purpose of conducting low-altitude navigation and tactical training under VFR below 10,000 feet MSL at airspeeds in excess of 250 knots IAS.

VFR NOT RECOMMENDED. An advisory provided by a flight service station to a pilot during a preflight or inflight weather briefing that flight under visual flight rules is not recommended. To be given when the current and/or forecast weather conditions are at or below VFR minimums. It does not abrogate the pilot's authority to make his/her own decision.

VFR-ON-TOP. ATC authorization for an IFR aircraft to operate in VFR conditions at any appropriate VFR altitude (as specified in 14 CFR and as restricted by ATC). A pilot receiving this authorization must comply with the VFR visibility, distance from cloud criteria, and the minimum IFR altitudes specified in 14 CFR Part 91. The use of this term does not relieve controllers of their responsibility to separate aircraft in Class B and Class C airspace or TRSAs as required by FAA Order JO 7110.65.

VFR TERMINAL AREA CHARTS. (See AERONAUTICAL CHART.)

VFR WAYPOINT. (See WAYPOINT.)

VHF. (See VERY HIGH FREQUENCY.)

VHF OMNIDIRECTIONAL RANGE/TACTICAL AIR NAVIGATION. (See VORTAC.)

VIDEO MAP. An electronically displayed map on the radar display that may depict data such as airports, heliports, runway centerline extensions, hospital emergency landing areas, NAVAIDs and fixes, reporting points, airway/route centerlines, boundaries, hand-off points, special use tracks, obstructions, prominent geographic features, map alignment indicators, range accuracy marks, and/or minimum vectoring altitudes.

VISIBILITY. The ability, as determined by atmospheric conditions and expressed in units of distance, to see and identify prominent unlighted objects by day and prominent lighted objects by night. Visibility is reported as statute miles, hundreds of feet or meters. (Refer to 14 CFR Part 91.) (Refer to AIM.)

 a. Flight Visibility. The average forward horizontal distance, from the cockpit of an aircraft in flight, at which prominent unlighted objects may be seen and identified by day and prominent lighted objects may be seen and identified by night.

 b. Ground Visibility. Prevailing horizontal visibility near the earth's surface as reported by the United States National Weather Service or an accredited observer.

(continued)

P/C

ASA 1079

c. Prevailing Visibility. The greatest horizontal visibility equaled or exceeded throughout at least half the horizon circle which need not necessarily be continuous.

d. Runway Visual Range (RVR). An instrumentally derived value, based on standard calibrations, that represents the horizontal distance a pilot will see down the runway from the approach end. It is based on the sighting of either high intensity runway lights or on the visual contrast of other targets whichever yields the greater visual range. RVR, in contrast to prevailing or runway visibility, is based on what a pilot in a moving aircraft should see looking down the runway. RVR is horizontal visual range, not slant visual range. It is based on the measurement of a transmissometer made near the touchdown point of the instrument runway and is reported in hundreds of feet. RVR, where available, is used in lieu of prevailing visibility in determining minimums for a particular runway.

1. Touchdown RVR. The RVR visibility readout values obtained from RVR equipment serving the runway touchdown zone.

2. Mid-RVR. The RVR readout values obtained from RVR equipment located midfield of the runway.

3. Rollout RVR. The RVR readout values obtained from RVR equipment located nearest the rollout end of the runway.
(See ICAO term FLIGHT VISIBILITY.)
(See ICAO term GROUND VISIBILITY.)
(See ICAO term RUNWAY VISUAL RANGE.)
(See ICAO term VISIBILITY.)

VISIBILITY [ICAO]. The ability, as determined by atmospheric conditions and expressed in units of distance, to see and identify prominent unlighted objects by day and prominent lighted objects by night.

a. Flight Visibility—The visibility forward from the cockpit of an aircraft in flight.

b. Ground Visibility—The visibility at an aerodrome as reported by an accredited observer.

c. Runway Visual Range [RVR]—The range over which the pilot of an aircraft on the centerline of a runway can see the runway surface markings or the lights delineating the runway or identifying its centerline.

VISUAL APPROACH. An approach conducted on an instrument flight rules (IFR) flight plan which authorizes the pilot to proceed visually and clear of clouds to the airport. The pilot must, at all times, have either the airport or the preceding aircraft in sight. This approach must be authorized and under the control of the appropriate air traffic control facility. Reported weather at the airport must be ceiling at or above 1,000 feet and visibility of 3 miles or greater. (See ICAO term VISUAL APPROACH.)

VISUAL APPROACH [ICAO]. An approach by an IFR flight when either part or all of an instrument approach procedure is not completed and the approach is executed in visual reference to terrain.

VISUAL APPROACH SLOPE INDICATOR (VASI). (See AIRPORT LIGHTING.)

VISUAL CLIMB OVER AIRPORT (VCOA). A departure option for an IFR aircraft, operating in visual meteorological conditions equal to or greater than the specified visibility and ceiling, to visually conduct climbing turns over the airport to the published "climb-to" altitude from which to proceed with the instrument portion of the departure. VCOA procedures are developed to avoid obstacles greater than 3 statute miles from the departure end of the runway as an alternative to complying with climb gradients greater than 200 feet per nautical mile. Pilots are responsible to advise ATC as early as possible of the intent to fly the VCOA option prior to departure. These textual procedures are published in the 'Take-Off Minimums and (Obstacle) Departure Procedures' section of the Terminal Procedures Publications and/or appear as an option on a Graphic ODP. (See AIM.)

VISUAL DESCENT POINT. A defined point on the final approach course of a nonprecision straight-in approach procedure from which normal descent from the MDA to the runway touchdown point may be commenced, provided the approach threshold of that runway, or approach lights, or other markings identifiable with the approach end of that runway are clearly visible to the pilot.

VISUAL FLIGHT RULES. Rules that govern the procedures for conducting flight under visual conditions. The term "VFR" is also used in the United States to indicate weather conditions that are equal to or greater than minimum VFR requirements. In addition, it is used by pilots and controllers to indicate type of flight plan. (See INSTRUMENT FLIGHT RULES.) (See INSTRUMENT METEOROLOGICAL CONDITIONS.) (See VISUAL METEOROLOGICAL CONDITIONS.) (Refer to 14 CFR Part 91.) (Refer to AIM.)

VISUAL HOLDING. The holding of aircraft at selected, prominent geographical fixes which can be easily recognized from the air. (See HOLDING FIX.)

VISUAL LINE OF SIGHT (VLOS). Condition of operations wherein the operator maintains continuous, unaided visual contact with the unmanned aircraft.

VISUAL METEOROLOGICAL CONDITIONS. Meteorological conditions expressed in terms of visibility, distance from cloud, and ceiling equal to or better than specified minima. (See INSTRUMENT FLIGHT RULES.) (See INSTRUMENT METEOROLOGICAL CONDITIONS.) (See VISUAL FLIGHT RULES.)

VISUAL OBSERVER (VO). A person who is designated by the remote pilot in command to assist the remote pilot in command and the person operating the flight controls of the small UAS (sUAS) to see and avoid other air traffic or objects aloft or on the ground.

VISUAL SEGMENT. (See PUBLISHED INSTRUMENT APPROACH PROCEDURE VISUAL SEGMENT.)

VISUAL SEPARATION. A means employed by ATC to separate aircraft in terminal areas and en route airspace in the NAS. There are two ways to effect this separation:

a. The tower controller sees the aircraft involved and issues instructions, as necessary, to ensure that the aircraft avoid each other.

b. A pilot sees the other aircraft involved and upon instructions from the controller provides his/her own separation by maneuvering his/her aircraft as necessary to avoid it. This may involve following another aircraft or keeping it in sight until it is no longer a factor. (See SEE AND AVOID.) (Refer to 14 CFR Part 91.)

VLF. (See VERY LOW FREQUENCY.)

VMC. (See VISUAL METEOROLOGICAL CONDITIONS.)

VOICE SWITCHING AND CONTROL SYSTEM (VSCS). A computer controlled switching system that provides air traffic controllers with all voice circuits (air to ground and ground to ground) necessary for air traffic control. (Refer to AIM.)

VOR. A ground-based electronic navigation aid transmitting very high frequency navigation signals, 360 degrees in azimuth, oriented from magnetic north. Used as the basis for navigation in the National Airspace System. The VOR periodically identifies itself by Morse Code and may have an additional voice identification feature. Voice features may be used by ATC or FSS for transmitting instructions/information to pilots. (See NAVIGATIONAL AID.) (Refer to AIM.)

VOR TEST SIGNAL. (See VOT.)

VORTAC. A navigation aid providing VOR azimuth, TACAN azimuth, and TACAN distance measuring equipment (DME) at one site. (See DISTANCE MEASURING EQUIPMENT.) (See NAVIGATIONAL AID.) (See TACAN.) (See VOR.) (Refer to AIM.)

VORTICES. Circular patterns of air created by the movement of an airfoil through the air when generating lift. As an airfoil moves through the atmosphere in sustained flight, an area of area of low pressure is created above it. The air flowing from the high pressure area to the low pressure area around and about the tips of the airfoil tends to roll up into two rapidly rotating vortices, cylindrical in shape. These vortices are the most predominant parts of aircraft wake turbulence and their rotational force is dependent upon the wing loading, gross weight, and speed of the generating aircraft. The vortices from medium to super aircraft can be of extremely high velocity and hazardous to smaller aircraft. (See AIRCRAFT CLASSES.) (See WAKE TURBULENCE.) (Refer to AIM.)

VOT. A ground facility which emits a test signal to check VOR receiver accuracy. Some VOTs are available to the user while airborne, and others are limited to ground use only. (See CHART SUPPLEMENT.) (Refer to 14 CFR Part 91.) (Refer to AIM.)

VR. (See VFR MILITARY TRAINING ROUTES.)

VSCS. (See VOICE SWITCHING AND CONTROL SYSTEM.)

VTOL AIRCRAFT. (See VERTICAL TAKEOFF AND LANDING AIRCRAFT.)

W

WA. (See AIRMET.) (See WEATHER ADVISORY.)

WAAS. (See WIDE-AREA AUGMENTATION SYSTEM.)

WAKE RE-CATEGORIZATION (RECAT). A set of optimized wake separation standards, featuring an increased number of aircraft wake categories, in use at select airports, which allows reduced wake intervals. (See WAKE TURBULENCE.)

WAKE TURBULENCE. A phenomenon that occurs when an aircraft develops lift and forms a pair of counter-rotating vortices. (See AIRCRAFT CLASSES.) (See VORTICES.) (Refer to AIM.)

WARNING AREA. (See SPECIAL USE AIRSPACE.)

WAYPOINT. A predetermined geographical position used for route/instrument approach definition, progress reports, published VFR routes, visual reporting points or points for transitioning and/or circumnavigating controlled and/or special use airspace, that is defined relative to a VORTAC station or in terms of latitude/longitude coordinates.

WEATHER ADVISORY. In aviation weather forecast practice, an expression of hazardous weather conditions not predicted in the Aviation Surface Forecast, Aviation Cloud Forecast, or area forecast, as they affect the operation of air traffic and as prepared by the NWS. (See AIRMET.) (See GRAPHICAL AIRMEN'S METEOROLOGICAL INFORMATION.) (See SIGMET.)

WEATHER RECONNAISSANCE AREA (WRA). A WRA is airspace with defined dimensions and published by Notice to Air Missions, which is established to support weather reconnaissance/research flights. Air traffic control services are not provided within WRAs. Only participating weather reconnaissance/research aircraft from the 53rd Weather Reconnaissance Squadron and National Oceanic and Atmospheric Administration Aircraft Operations Center are permitted to operate within a WRA. A WRA may only be established in airspace within U.S. Flight Information Regions outside of U.S. territorial airspace.

WHEN ABLE.

a. In conjunction with ATC instructions, gives the pilot the latitude to delay compliance until a condition or event has been reconciled. Unlike "pilot discretion," when instructions are prefaced "when able," the pilot is expected to seek the first opportunity to comply.

b. In conjunction with a weather deviation clearance, requires the pilot to determine when he/she is clear of weather, then execute ATC instructions.

c. Once a maneuver has been initiated, the pilot is expected to continue until the specifications of the instructions have been met. "When able," should not be used when expeditious compliance is required.

P/C

WIDE-AREA AUGMENTATION SYSTEM (WAAS). The WAAS is a satellite navigation system consisting of the equipment and software which augments the GPS Standard Positioning Service (SPS). The WAAS provides enhanced integrity, accuracy, availability, and continuity over and above GPS SPS. The differential correction function provides improved accuracy required for precision approach.

WIDE AREA MULTILATERATION (WAM). A distributed surveillance technology which may utilize any combination of signals from Air Traffic Control Radar Beacon System (ATCRBS) (Modes A and C) and Mode S transponders, and ADS-B transmissions. Multiple geographically dispersed ground sensors measure the time-of-arrival of the transponder messages. Aircraft position is determined by joint processing of the time-difference-of-arrival (TDOA) measurements computed between a reference and the ground stations' measured time-of-arrival.

WILCO. I have received your message, understand it, and will comply with it.

WIND GRID DISPLAY. A display that presents the latest forecasted wind data overlaid on a map of the ARTCC area. Wind data is automatically entered and updated periodically by transmissions from the National Weather Service. Winds at specific altitudes, along with temperatures and air pressure can be viewed.

WIND SHEAR. A change in wind speed and/or wind direction in a short distance resulting in a tearing or shearing effect. It can exist in a horizontal or vertical direction and occasionally in both.

WIND SHEAR ESCAPE. An unplanned abortive maneuver initiated by the pilot in command (PIC) as a result of onboard cockpit systems. Wind shear escapes are characterized by maximum thrust climbs in the low altitude terminal environment until wind shear conditions are no longer detected.

WING TIP VORTICES. (See VORTICES.)

WORDS TWICE.
 a. As a request: "Communication is difficult. Please say every phrase twice."
 b. As information: "Since communications are difficult, every phrase in this message will be spoken twice."

WS. (See SIGMET.) (See WEATHER ADVISORY.)

WST. (See CONVECTIVE SIGMET.) (See WEATHER ADVISORY.)

NASA Aviation Safety Reporting System

Note: Please visit the Aviation Safety Reporting System website at **http://asrs.arc.nasa.gov/** to submit this form electronically or download the most current PDF form to print and mail in.

IDENTIFICATION STRIP: *Please fill in all blanks to ensure return of strip.*
NO RECORD WILL BE KEPT OF YOUR IDENTITY. This section will be returned to you.

(SPACE BELOW RESERVED FOR ASRS DATE/TIME STAMP)

TELEPHONE NUMBERS where we may reach you for further details of this occurrence:

HOME _____ Hours _____

OTHER _____ Hours _____

NAME _____

ADDRESS/PO BOX _____

ADDRESS LINE 2 _____

CITY _____ STATE _____ ZIP _____

TYPE OF EVENT/SITUATION _____

DATE OF OCCURRENCE _____ (MM/DD/YYYY)

LOCAL TIME (24 hr. clock) _____ (HH:MM)

PLEASE FILL IN APPROPRIATE SPACES AND CHECK ALL ITEMS WHICH APPLY TO THIS EVENT OR SITUATION.

REPORTER
- O Captain
- O First Officer
- ☐ pilot flying
- ☐ pilot not flying
- ☐ relief pilot
- ☐ check airman
- O Single Pilot
- O Instructor
- O Dispatcher: _____ yrs
- O Other: _____

FLYING TIME (in hours)
- Total Time _____ hrs
- Last 90 Days _____ hrs
- Time in Type _____ hrs

CERTIFICATES & RATINGS
- O Student
- O Sport/Rec
- O Private
- O Commercial
- O ATP
- ☐ Flight Instructor
- ☐ Multiengine
- ☐ Instrument
- ☐ Flight Engineer
- ☐ Other: _____

ATC EXPERIENCE
- O FPL O Developmental
- radar _____ yrs
- non-radar _____ yrs
- supervisory _____ yrs
- military _____ yrs

AIRSPACE
- ☐ Class A
- ☐ Class B
- ☐ Class C
- ☐ Class D
- ☐ Class E
- ☐ Class G
- ☐ Special Use
- ☐ TFR

CONDITIONS / WEATHER ELEMENTS
- O VMC
- O IMC
- O Mixed
- O Marginal
- ☐ fog
- ☐ hail
- ☐ haze/smoke
- ☐ icing
- ☐ rain
- ☐ snow
- ☐ thunderstorm
- ☐ turbulence
- ☐ windshear
- ☐ other: _____

LIGHT / VISIBILITY
- O dawn
- O daylight
- O night
- O dusk
- Ceiling _____ feet
- Visibility _____ miles
- RVR _____ feet

ATC / ADVISORY SVC.
- O Ramp O Center
- O Ground O FSS
- O Tower O UNICOM
- O TRACON O CTAF
- ATC Facility Name: _____

AIRCRAFT 1

Your Aircraft Type (Make/Model) (e.g. B737) NOT "N #", Flt #, etc.: _____

Operator FAR Part: _____

Operator	☐ air carrier ☐ air taxi ☐ corporate	☐ fractional ☐ FBO ☐ government	☐ military ☐ personal ☐ other: _____
Mission	☐ passenger ☐ personal	☐ cargo/freight ☐ training	☐ ferry ☐ other: _____
Flight Plan	☐ VFR ☐ IFR	☐ SVFR ☐ DVFR	☐ none
Flight Phase	☐ taxi ☐ parked ☐ takeoff ☐ initial climb	☐ climb ☐ cruise ☐ descent ☐ initial approach	☐ final approach ☐ missed/GAR ☐ landing ☐ other: _____
Route in Use	☐ airway (ID): _____ ☐ STAR (ID): _____ ☐ SID (ID): _____	☐ direct ☐ oceanic ☐ vectors	☐ visual approach ☐ none ☐ other: _____

AIRCRAFT 2

Other Aircraft: _____

Operator FAR Part: _____

☐ air carrier ☐ air taxi ☐ corporate	☐ fractional ☐ FBO ☐ government	☐ military ☐ personal ☐ other: _____
☐ passenger ☐ personal	☐ cargo/freight ☐ training	☐ ferry ☐ other: _____
☐ VFR ☐ IFR	☐ SVFR ☐ DVFR	☐ none
☐ taxi ☐ parked ☐ takeoff ☐ initial climb	☐ climb ☐ cruise ☐ descent ☐ initial approach	☐ final approach ☐ missed/GAR ☐ landing ☐ other: _____
☐ airway (ID): _____ ☐ STAR (ID): _____ ☐ SID (ID): _____	☐ direct ☐ oceanic ☐ vectors	☐ visual approach ☐ none ☐ other: _____

If more than two aircraft were involved, please describe the additional aircraft in the "Describe Event/Situation" section.

LOCATION

Altitude: _____ (single value) O MSL O AGL

Distance: _____ and/or Radial (bearing): _____ from:

O Airport _____ O ATC Fac _____

O Intersection _____ O NAVAID _____

CONFLICTS

Estimated miss distance in feet: horiz _____ vert _____

Was evasive action taken? O Yes O No

Was TCAS a factor? O TA O RA O No

Did terrain warning system activate? O Yes O No

NASA ARC 277B (May 2009)

GENERAL FORM

Note: Please visit the Aviation Safety Reporting System website at **http://asrs.arc.nasa.gov/** to submit this form electronically or download the most current PDF form to print and mail in.

DESCRIBE EVENT/SITUATION

Keeping in mind the topics shown below, discuss those which you feel are relevant and anything else you think is important. Include what you believe really caused the problem, and what can be done to prevent a recurrence, or correct the situation. (USE ADDITIONAL PAPER IF NEEDED)

CHAIN OF EVENTS		HUMAN PERFORMANCE CONSIDERATIONS	
- How the problem arose	- How it was discovered	- Perceptions, judgments, decisions - Actions or inactions	
- Contributing factors	- Corrective actions	- Factors affecting the quality of human performance	

If you want to mail this form, please fold both pages (and additional pages if required), enclose in a sealed, stamped envelope, and mail to:

NASA AVIATION SAFETY REPORTING SYSTEM
POST OFFICE BOX 189
MOFFETT FIELD, CALIFORNIA 94035-0189

From the NASA Aviation Safety Reporting System:

NASA has established an Aviation Safety Reporting System (ASRS) to identify issues in the aviation system which need to be addressed. The program of which this system is a part is described in detail in FAA Advisory Circular 00-46F. Your assistance in informing us about such issues is essential to the success of the program. Please fill out this form as completely as possible.

The information you provide on the identity strip will be used only if NASA determines that it is necessary to contact you for further information. THIS IDENTITY STRIP WILL BE RETURNED DIRECTLY TO YOU. The return of the identity strip assures your anonymity.

Section 91.25 of the Federal Aviation Regulations (14 CFR 91.25) prohibits reports filed with NASA from being used for FAA enforcement purposes. This report will not be made available to the FAA for civil penalty or certificate actions for violations of the Federal Air Regulations. Your identity strip, stamped by NASA, is proof that you have submitted a report to the Aviation Safety Reporting System.

We can only return the strip to you if you have provided a mailing address. Equally important, we can often obtain additional useful information if our safety analysts can talk with you directly by telephone. For this reason, we have requested telephone numbers where we may reach you.

NOTE: Aircraft accidents should not be reported on this form. Such events should be filed with the National Transportation Safety Board as required by NTSB Regulation 830.5 (49CFR830.5).

Paperwork Reduction Act Statement - This information collection meets the requirements of 44 U.S.C. § 3507, as amended by section 2 of the Paperwork Reduction Act of 1995. You do not need to answer these questions unless we display a valid Office of Management and Budget control number. The OMB control number for this information collection is 2700-0172. We estimate that it will take about 30 minutes to read the instructions, gather the facts, and answer the questions. You may send comments on our time estimate above to: P.O. Box 189 Moffett Field, CA 94035-0189.

Thank you for your contribution to aviation safety.

NASA ARC 277B (May 2009)

ASA

Index

§ = FAR section
¶ = AIM paragraph

Please submit terms you think should be added to the index, including the FAR section number and/or AIM paragraph number, to: **asa@asa2fly.com** *~Thank you!*

Index

Index

Index

Index